Full Life

BIBLE COMMENTARY
TO THE NEW TESTAMENT

Full Life

BIBLE COMMENTARY
TO THE NEW TESTAMENT

AN INTERNATIONAL COMMENTARY FOR SPIRIT-FILLED CHRISTIANS

Edited by
FRENCH L. ARRINGTON
AND ROGER STRONSTAD

ZondervanPublishingHouse
Grand Rapids, Michigan

A Division of HarperCollins*Publishers*

Full Life Bible Commentary to the New Testament

Requests for information should be addressed to:

ZondervanPublishingHouse
Grand Rapids, Michigan 49530

Library of Congress Cataloging-in-Publication Data

Full life Bible commentary to the New Testament : an international commentary for spirit-filled Christians / edited by French L. Arrington and Roger Stronstad.
p. cm.
Includes bibliographical references.
ISBN: 0–310–20118-7 (hardcover : alk. paper)
1. Bible. N.T.—Commentaries. 2. Gifts, Spiritual—Biblical teaching.
I. Arrington, French L. II. Stronstad, Roger.
BS2341.2.F85 1999 225.7—dc21 98–51044
CIP

This edition printed on acid-free paper and meets the American National Standards Institute Z39.48 standard.

Printed in the United States of America

99 00 01 02 03 04 05 /❖ DC/ 10 9 8 7 6 5 4 3 2 1

CONTENTS

LIST OF CONTRIBUTORS

Matthew	James Shelton	Professor at Oral Roberts University, Tulsa, Oklahoma
Mark	Jerry Camery-Hoggatt	Professor at Southern California College, Costa Mesa, California
Luke	French Arrington	Professor at Church of God School of Theology, Cleveland, Tennessee
John	Ben Aker	Professor at Assemblies of God Theological Seminary, Springfield, Missouri
Acts	French Arrington	Professor at Church of God School of Theology, Cleveland, Tennessee
Romans	Van Johnson	Dean, Canadian Pentecostal Seminary, Toronto, Ontario
1 Corinthians	Anthony Palma	Retired professor from Assemblies of God Theological Seminary, Springfield, Missouri
2 Corinthians	James Hernando	Professor at Assemblies of God Theological Seminary, Springfield, Missouri
Galatians	William Simmons	Professor at Lee University, Cleveland, Tennessee
Ephesians	Wesley Adams	Professor and Chairman, School of the Word, at Grace Training Center, Kansas City, Missouri
	(with Donald Stamps)	Author of notes in *Full Life Study Bible* and missionary to Brazil (deceased)
Philippians	Dave Demchuk	Administrator, Broadway Pentecostal Church, Vancouver, British Columbia
Colossians, Philemon	Sven Soderlund	Professor at Regent College, Vancouver, British Columbia
1 & 2 Thessalonians	Brian Glubish	Professor at Central Pentecostal College, Saskatoon, Saskatchewan
1 & 2 Timothy, Titus	Deborah Gill	Senior pastor, Church of the Living Hope, Shoreview, Minnesota
Hebrews	Wesley Adams	Professor and Chairman, School of the Word at Grace Training Center, Kansas City, Missouri
James	Timothy Cargal	Former professor at Western Kentucky University; now pastor of Northwood Presbyterian Church, Silver Springs, Maryland
1 & 2 Peter, Jude	Roger Stronstad	Academic Dean, Western Pentecostal Bible College, Clayburn, British Columbia
1, 2, & 3 John	Robert Berg	Professor at Evangel University, Springfield, Missouri
Revelation	Timothy Jenney	Professor at North Central University, Minneapolis, Minnesota

PREFACE

What the late Donald Stamps, the writer of the notes of the *Full Life Study Bible*, stated about the study Bible holds true for this commentary:

> The major purpose . . . is to lead you, the reader, towards a deeper faith in the New Testament's apostolic message and towards a greater expectancy for a New Testament experience made possible by the fullness of Christ dwelling in the church (Eph. 4:13) and by the fullness of the Holy Spirit dwelling in the believer (Acts 2:4; 4:31).

The *Full Life Study Bible* and the *Full Life Bible Commentary* are companion volumes. This commentary has been planned and written to complement the study Bible. Of course, the study Bible deals with subjects and prominent themes in Scripture, whereas the commentary focuses on the background of the books of the New Testament and their exposition. Each volume stands alone, is complete in itself, and can be used independently. One enriches the other, and used together the study Bible and the commentary constitute a small library for Bible study.

The contributors to this commentary owe a great debt to biblical scholars of the past and the present and have learned from their labors and insights into God's Word. They accept the Bible as the inspired, authoritative Word of God and come from backgrounds that stress the importance of the presence and gifts of the Holy Spirit in the present-day church. The contributors have tried their best not to be apologetic, polemical, or overly technical. Their aim has been to use a style and vocabulary that makes the message of the New Testament accessible to all who read the commentary.

The commentary itself is based on the New International Version, but the writers in their exposition of individual books do cite other current English versions where one or more translations help to clarify the meaning. At places the Greek text is referred to. Nevertheless when the original language is cited, a transliteration is provided so that the readers may read and pronounce the words. Often an explanation stands immediately beside the transliteration. The intent is to express with precision and yet in an interesting way the meaning of the New Testament. Though it is not explicitly devotional, this commentary provides an interpretation of the text that is a sound basis for devotional use and practical application. It should be of use to Sunday School teachers and Christian workers, but also of considerable help to preachers, and in particular, to theological students.

The commentaries in this volume focus on the books of the New Testament. Each contributor provides an introduction to the book, an outline, a section-by-section interpretation of the book, and a brief bibliography. The introductions give information and orientation needed for study. The interpretation is based on the structure, language, and the background of the book. The purpose of approaching interpretation in this manner is to preserve the power and the significance that the gospel had for the first century and that which it has for today.

Except for the Gospels, the commentaries in this volume follow the canonical order reflected in our English versions of the Bible. In the *Full Life Bible Commentary* the order of the Gospels is: John, Matthew, Mark, and Luke. This commentary discusses the Gospels in this order to meet the following objectives: (1) to link Luke and Acts together, so that they can be seen as a continuous, unified account of the life of Christ and the acts of the apostles; (2) to retain Acts adjacent to the Pauline letters; and (3) to keep the Synoptic Gospels together. As we meet these objectives, John has been moved to stand first. This location is appropriate since its prologue opens with the preexistence of Christ.

With gratitude we remember Donald Stamps for his devotion to God and his Word. To him we owe an immense debt for providing a study Bible for Pentecostal and charismatic Christians. His vision and work on the *Full Life Study Bible* gave much of the impetus and inspiration for the preparation of this *Full Life Bible Commentary*.

Mention must be made of the skills and labor of the editorial staff at Zondervan Publishing House. The person deserving special mention is Dr. Verlyn D. Verbrugge, the senior editor, who has carried "the lion's share" of the burden for bringing this commentary from its initial conception to this published form. His knowledge and skills and his careful reading of all the manuscripts have been vital to the completion and quality of the work. It has been a pleasure to be associated with him. Also, in completing our task we want to thank all the contributors to this volume for their cooperation, patience, kindness, and labor.

Finally, we offer this commentary with a prayer that it will prove to be a great blessing to all those who use it, especially to those who seek God's will for their lives by being "filled with the Spirit," and with the conviction that the work of the Holy Spirit is not confined to biblical times. The Spirit still empowers Christians and does "signs and wonders" today as he did in the ministry of Jesus and continued to do in the ministry of the apostles. From the initial outpouring of the Holy Spirit on the Day of Pentecost, the ministry of the Spirit has remained the same. His work still is: to exalt Jesus Christ, to lead us into all truth, and to empower us for service and evangelism.

French L. Arrington and
Roger Stronstad, Editors

PICTURES, MAPS, AND CHARTS

All photos, unless otherwise noted, are from the photos of Neal and Joel Bierling.

ABBREVIATIONS

1QM	War Scroll
1QS	Rule of the Community
AB	Anchor Bible
ASV	American Standard Version
Ant.	Josephus, *Jewish Antiquities*
b.	Babylonian Talmud
BAGD	Bauer, W. F. Arndt, F. W. Gingrich, *A Greek-English Lexicon of the New Testament and Other Early Christian Literature*, Chicago, 1979
CBQ	*Catholic Biblical Quarterly*
CGTC	Cambridge Greek Testament Commentary
CTJ	*Calvin Theological Journal*
DPL	*Dictionary of Paul and His Letters*
DSB	Daily Study Bible
DJG	*Dictionary of Jesus and the Gospels*. Ed. J. B. Green and S. McKnight. Downers Grove, 1992
EBC	*Expositor's Bible Commentary*
Eccl. Hist.	Eusebius, *Ecclesiastical History*
EDNT	*Exegetical Dictionary of the New Testament*. Ed. H. Balz, G. Schneider. Grand Rapids, 1990–1993
EGGNT	Exegetical Guide to the Greek New Testament
EGT	*The Expositor's Greek Testament*
EvQ	*Evangelical Quarterly*
ExpTim	*Expository Times*
GNB	Good News Bible
FLSB	*Full Life Study Bible*
HNTC	Harper New Testament Commentary
ICC	International Critical Commentary
Interp	*Interpretation*
JB	Jerusalem Bible
JBL	*Journal of Biblical Literature*
JBP	J. B. Phillips translation
JETS	*Journal of the Evangelical Theological Society*
JSNT	*Journal for the Study of the New Testament*
KJV	King James Version
LXX	Septuagint
m.	Mishnah
Meg.	*Megillah*
Mek.	*Mekilta*
MNTC	Moffatt New Testament Commentary
NAB	New American Bible
NAC	New American Commentary

NASB	New American Standard Bible
NCB	New Century Bible
NCBC	New Century Bible Commentary
NEB	New English Bible
Neot	*Neotestamentica*
NIBC	New International Biblical Commentary
NICNT	New International Commentary on the New Testament
NIDNTT	*New International Dictionary of New Testament Theology*. Ed. C. Brown. 4 vols. Grand Rapids, 1975–1985
NIDOTTE	*New International Dictionary of Old Testament Theology and Exegesis*. Ed. W. A. VanGemeren. 5 vols. Grand Rapids, 1997
NIGTC	New International Greek Testament Commentary
NIV	New International Version
NJB	New Jerusalem Bible
NKJV	New King James Version
NovT	*Novum Testamentum*
NRSV	New Revised Standard Version
NTS	*New Testament Studies*
REB	Revised English Bible
RevExp	*Review and Expositor*
RSV	Revised Standard Version
RV	Revised Version
SBLDS	Society of Biblical Literature Dissertation Series
SEÅ	Svensk exegtisk Årsbok
SJLA	*Studies in Judaism in Late Antiquity*
TDNT	*Theological Dictionary of the New Testament*. Ed. G. Kittel and G. Friedrich. Grand Rapids, 1964–1976
TEV	Today's English Version
TNTC	Tyndale New Testament Commentary
TS	*Theological Studies*
WBC	Word Biblical Commentary
WTJ	*Westminster Theological Journal*

JOHN

Benny C. Aker

For why John is presented first, see Preface, p. vii.

INTRODUCTION

"But . . . John, last of all, . . . divinely moved by the Spirit, composed a spiritual Gospel."
—Clement of Alexandria

The Gospel according to John long ago achieved the hallmark of being a spiritual Gospel. Personal evangelists often have new converts read it, for it is written in simple language, speaking to the heart in a way they can relate to. Under careful scrutiny, however, the Gospel bristles with logic, argumentation, and content that antagonizes some and puzzles others. Its simple words, loaded with freight, do not pull easily. This spiritual Gospel fits well among the others, as Eusebius noted long ago, in fourth place following Matthew, Mark, and Luke (*Eccl. Hist.* 3.24.2).

1. The Kind of Writing

God inspired the author of John's Gospel to write to a particular group of people. Though he wrote to a particular audience, he also wrote for all Christians. This ancient book speaks authoritatively to people today when the interpreter enters that world and considers the context of the human writer, while giving just consideration to its divine origin.

One way to do this is to understand what kind of writing this Gospel is. Church tradition has labeled this as the "Gospel According to John." Some modern scholars also call it the Fourth Gospel to indicate that it differs in some respects from the other three canonical Gospels—called the Synoptic Gospels, because in general they present common views of Jesus' life and teaching. The term *gospel*, used for all four Gospels, pertains to Jesus, who is the "gospel" (Gk. *euangelion*, lit., good news) for all people. Though all the Gospels declare Jesus as the Good News, each one has special features, which include different human authors, times of writing, congregational and geographical destinations, and church problems. In addition, each Gospel contains smaller kinds of material, which fit together to help the writer tell his powerful story of Jesus. These smaller units include such forms as parables, prayers, sermons, and sayings.

Each Gospel writer places his account of Jesus' life and teaching in narrative form. Thus we need to know something about narrative. In narrative, the author's signature shows up in indirect and subtle ways. For example, as the custom was in antiquity, Matthew and Mark do not attach their names, nor do they state plainly their purpose for writing. The authors of Luke and John do not attach their names either, though they do show more readily observable personal touches than do Matthew and Mark. For example, in Luke 1:3 (and Acts 1:1), the author uses the first person pronoun to refer to himself, supplying his reason for writing (see Luke 1:1–4).

The author of John does not use the same vocabulary or writing style as the Synoptics do. Thus, it is difficult to know in the longer teaching material in John where Jesus stops speaking and John starts. The author's signature is everywhere—Jesus is so caught up in his mind and experience. He also provides numerous places of explanation for readers who are not familiar with Palestinian locations, Hebrew or Aramaic languages, or customs. Here are several illustrations. In 1:19, "Now this was John's testimony" is the author's way of introducing the first episode of John the Baptist. In 1:28, the author explains where John the Baptist's ministry occurred. In 1:42, the Aramaic "Cephas" becomes "Peter" for Greek readers (both mean "rock"; see also 1:38, where "rabbi" is translated "teacher"). In 20:30–31, the author alludes to himself in a roundabout way and through a passive verb: "But these are written that you may believe that Jesus is the Christ, the Son of God." In 21:24, the author refers to himself in the third person as the "disciple who testifies to these things and who wrote them down."

Discretion in narrative also comes through what authors chose to include and interpret.

For instance, Matthew includes a genealogy and key Old Testament Scriptures in the infancy of Jesus (Matt. 1–2). Likewise, in John 1:1–18, the author provides an eternal perspective of Jesus as the Word. He does not cover any of the infancy material of Jesus. What an author does not include is often as important as the way he narrates the life of Jesus. It is important, then, for understanding to allow each Gospel to tell its own life of Jesus.

It also helps to consider the Gospels as narrative sermons. As sermons speak to the needs of congregations, so do the Gospels. This perspective helps us remove some of the problems that modern readers find in the Gospels, such as order of events (this is especially true for John's Gospel). The Gospels were written as inspired answers to church problems, with Jesus as the sacred text on an equal basis with the Old Testament. That Jesus had already reached this level during the writing period is indicated in John 2:22: "Then they believed the Scripture and the words that Jesus had spoken": "Scripture" and the "words of Jesus" are parallel.

In this narrative sermon, the interpreter must be alert to the two levels of understanding. The first level is the material about what Jesus did and said, standing as sacred text. Such material is not just for historical or biographical reasons, however, though it is both. These stories respond to specific needs of the writer and reader—this is the second level of understanding. These two worlds blend, as a beautiful musical piece blends many tones, speaking guidance and encouragement. On the one level, Jesus enters into the debate with leaders of Judaism; on the other, his words through the author speak to the setting of the author's audience.

2. Purpose in Writing

Knowing why the author penned his Gospel is important for understanding. John 20:30–31 gives the purpose, though these two verses are not without debate. Verse 31 contains different manuscript readings that express two purposes. The NIV indicates these possibilities within the text and in a note.

Here is the issue: Does the book as a Gospel seek new converts, or does it offer an apology for Christians whom outsiders are attacking for their faith and who stand in need of persuasion or encouragement to continue their faith in Jesus? The point of contention is over the verb "may believe." Should it be past tense and be translated "may begin to believe," indicating initial belief? Or should the verb be present tense, emphasizing ongoing belief as a Christian?

If we simply look at the manuscript evidence, it is difficult to determine which reading is the most probable. In terms of numerical support and a wider range of evidence, the past tense gathers a slight advantage. Significant older manuscripts, however, support the present tense. The argument and the purpose of the Gospel itself gives weight to the present tense. The nature of this Gospel suggests that the believers addressed by John needed to be encouraged to keep on believing in Jesus as God's divine Son. The writer found his congregation challenged by others regarding the nature and work of Jesus. This in turn caused them to question the religious community they belonged to, even the nature of the church.

To encourage his readers, the author selectively chose certain miraculous signs, which form a basis of his work and establish a fundamental belief in Jesus as the divine Messiah. This Messiah, however, was not the same kind of messiah that Judaism expected, for Jesus exceeded that expectation. Judaism had difficulty believing that Jesus was divine. John presents Jesus as the messianic Deliverer from sin and its power and the Giver of eternal life, as heralded by the Old Testament, its feasts, and other institutions. By continuing to believe on this One, people will have eternal life.

What is the precise nature of the problem John faced in the congregation(s) to whom he wrote? Was a form of Gnosticism, an early heresy, invading it? This Gnosticism did not believe in the humanity of Jesus and thus placed in danger the Christian belief in the Incarnation. True faith was characterized by trust in the human and divine Jesus. To stop believing in Jesus in this way would remove them from the church; they would no longer have eternal life. It is not clear, however, that Gnosticism was the problem in the Gospel. The author emphasizes the divinity of Jesus; and while he does present the human nature of Jesus, he does not focus on it.

Rather, the problem faced by John seems to be a pending split with Judaism, as the result of a debate concerning the person and nature of Jesus and his resulting salvation. This scenario arises particularly at the end of John 12, when the conflict between Judaism's leaders and Jesus reaches a climax. Judaism had difficulty believing in a divine Messiah such as John describes because to do so would significantly alter its long-sanctioned life of worship and covenant. This is John's point, however: Jesus was divine (and human) and his death did bring about a new way of salvation. Ethnic and religious distinctives made no special plea since the whole world lay in the power of sin. John, then, wrote to substantiate true belief in Jesus and his work of salvation in the minds and lives of Christians and to encourage their faith.

3. The Relationship Between John and the Synoptics

a. Vocabulary and Style

Several important features mark off John from the other three canonical Gospels. John does not have Synoptic-like vocabulary or style. Words such as "abide," "light," "darkness," "truth," and "witness" play an important role in this Gospel. The expression "kingdom of God" occurs only twice in John but often in the others. John's writing style is smooth and simple. At times a Semitic style lies behind the Greek, which poses some roughness. At other places, literary seams provide rough transitions from one section to another.

b. Content

John's Gospel contains no Synoptic-like parables. In fact, the word "parable" does not appear. Instead, the author used the word *paroimia*, which has a variety of meanings (including "parable"). John substituted the parables with allegories about the good shepherd and vine. In reality, their substance is similar to that of the parables, only the form and name vary. John also has longer teaching blocks in contrast with the shorter episodic blocks in the Synoptics. In John, Jesus' ministry covers up to three years, while the others imply that it lasted only about a year.

Several aspects of teachings about Jesus also are unique in John—the "I Am" sayings and Jesus as the Lamb of God. Moreover, only a few of the Synoptic miracles and other blocks of teachings occur in John (though themes from them do). John's Gospel does not speak of demon possession or of exorcisms. Furthermore, the Lord's Supper does not appear in John the same way as it does in the Synoptics. The time of its appearance is different, and its name has changed (the Synoptics call it a "Passover," while John calls it a "dinner"). In the Synoptics, Jesus' ministry occurs mostly in Galilee, while in John Jesus is more in Jerusalem and environs.

c. The Text, Narrative, and Order of the Gospel Events

A combination of elements complicates an easy reading of John. One, for instance, is the order of events in John when compared to the other three Gospels. Another has to do with textual variants in John. Still another has to do with the rough geographical transition in the ministry of Jesus in John's Gospel.

One event, the cleansing of the temple, is worth mentioning. It is placed toward the end of the Synoptics but at the beginning of John (ch. 2). One way to resolve the issue is to hold that there were two cleansings. This is less than satisfying, however. A better explanation is that the writer placed the cleansing at the start of Jesus' ministry to give his readers some predisposition as to what Jesus was to do and who he was (see comments on ch. 2). This episode molded certain impressions on the readers, in the same way as Matthew and Luke's Sermon on the Mount/Plain did. This process in John foreshadows and anticipates the result of Jesus' work.

The most famous of the disputed portions is the woman caught in adultery in 7:53–8:11. Bibles have included this story for so long that problems arise if translators and commentators leave it out. The story more than likely comes from the first century but was lodged in John at a later time. Another textual problem involves the angel-troubled waters in 5:3b–4, which many translations omit (cf. NIV).

The movement of Jesus in John seems to take great jumps or contain gaps of information at certain places. For example, in 6:1 Jesus crossed the Sea of Galilee for Tiberias, whereas his ministry in chapter 5 occurred in Jerusalem. Furthermore, some scholars believe that chapter 21 was not a part of the original Gospel. Critical scholars of John have sought to explain these issues with various misplacement or rearrangement theories of the text of the Gospel.

It is now common, however, to focus on other interpretative methods that do not ignore these difficulties but that look at John as a whole narrative. Interpreters have moved away from attempting to reconstruct or recover the world behind the narrative and text of John to the world located in the narrative of the Gospel and to the person reading it. They distinguish between the actual world from which John came, including that of Jesus, and the world that the writer "creates" in his narrative. The author created a world by omitting some events and including others; in this case, John's events are unique since few are found in the other Gospels. He also rearranged the sequence of events. This activity is much like that of a preacher constructing a sermon today. The writer, with his audience and their needs in mind, focused on material that would speak to their needs and problems.

John's world is the world of confrontation and debate. In his Gospel, he offers solutions that produce a new way of living. He thus encourages his readers to adopt a new lifestyle worthy of the gospel of Jesus. The method of interpretation that focuses on the text itself and on the reader produces fewer problems than other methods of interpretation.

It is important to read John's Gospel as we now have it, problems notwithstanding. The problems we find in the text will help resolve problems in the world today.

d. Literary Relationship

What is the literary relationship of John to the other three Gospels? There are few literary connections between them. No doubt John knew about the other Gospels. Certainly as an eyewitness of Jesus and as a close confidant he would have been familiar with his teachings and sayings. A credible solution suggests that John's material came from an earlier common bank of oral traditions, of which he also was a part—that is, teachings of Jesus, now filtered through John's life and experience in the Spirit and directed to ministry needs.

4. Authorship

Thus far we have used the name of John when referring to the author. We now turn to discuss the issue of authorship. Two types of sources provide evidence regarding authorship: The external source includes information from church history; the internal, the Gospel itself.

(1) Regarding external evidence, early students of John's Gospel associated the apostle John son of Zebedee with this Gospel. Polycarp, who died around A.D. 156 at the age of 86, likely associated with the apostle in Asia and transmitted information about John being the author of the Fourth Gospel (see Eusebius, *Eccl. Hist.* 5.20.4). Among his associates was Papias, bishop of Hierapolis in Asia Minor and disciple of John (Irenaus, *Against Heresies* 5.33.4; Papias *Frag*. 4; Eusebius, *Eccl. Hist.* 3.39). Sources note Papias to be a "hearer" of John, who bore witness to John's teaching of Jesus.

At one place Papias wrote of two Johns: John son of Zebedee and John the elder. Though both are mentioned as disciples of Jesus, the first seems to have passed off the scene while the other was alive during the time of Papias's writing. At any rate, this dual reference has proved to be a problem for modern scholars regarding John's authorship of the Gospel.

For Eusebius, too, this was a problem. He doubts that Papias ever saw or heard John the Evangelist (*Eccl. Hist.* 3.39ff.). However, Eusebius, drawing on Clement, did not doubt that John was the author. In his *Ecclesiastical History* 3.24.7–18, he included the names of the authors of all four canonical Gospels and their reasons for writing. Regarding John, he notes that he wrote last. After preaching the gospel orally for many years, he finally wrote down his account of Jesus. John penned his Gospel because others, who were aware of the other three Gospels, said that no information about Jesus' early ministry existed. John provided this.

Irenaeus, too, believed that the author was John (see *Against Heresies* 5.33.3–4; Eusebius *Eccl. Hist.* 3.39). Another source also wrote of this matter. About mid-second century A.D., Marcion truncated the New Testament canon and thus aroused responses. One of these, an anti-Marcionite prologue to John, claimed that the Gospel of John was written by the hand of Papias while John dictated it. Sometime between the writing of John and its acceptance by the Apostolic Fathers in the second century, people did not receive well John's Gospel, perhaps because of Gnosticism. This hesitancy did not last long, however, for John's Gospel is quoted in several ancient sources (cf. the above; see also *First Apology of Justin* 61). Clement's statement in Eusebius's *Ecclesiastical History* 3.24.2 that John's Gospel was known to all the churches under heaven and that it was genuine supports this. That John the apostle wrote this Gospel is strongly attested in the early church.

(2) More problems have arisen in the minds of modern scholars over the internal evidence. For much of this century, scholars either denied that John was involved in this Gospel or they said it passed through several stages (from three to five, depending on the scholar) under the leadership of a Johannine school. This school in essence produced this Gospel.

More conservative scholars have held to the theory that the Gospel was written by "the disciple whom Jesus loved." Arguments either attach this person with John the apostle or with someone else, like Lazarus (from John 11:3, 36). Eusebius called John the apostle and evangelist as the one whom Jesus loved (*Eccl. Hist.* 3.23.1).

At no place does the author explicitly identify himself. Only in 21:24 do we read anything directly about him: "This is the disciple who testifies to these things and who wrote them down. We know that his testimony is true." We can, however, say certain things about the author from the Gospel itself. He was a Jew from Palestine, who knew well his geography and preserved some of the earliest Jesus traditions. He knew Jewish traditions about feasts, customs, and other traditions, and he used effectively several of Hillel's interpretive methods to articulate his Christology, soteriology, and ecclesiology (see Theological Themes, below). Also, the Gospel has many Semitic undertones.

I suggest that "the disciple whom Jesus loved" was John the apostle and evangelist. Most important, "John," the name attached to the Gospel and traditionally identified as the apostle, is never mentioned in the Gospel. The only "Johns" are John the Baptist and the surname of Simon ("Son of John"). If John the apostle is the author, he intended to show himself in some other manner. This manner could be through the expression, "the disciple whom Jesus loved."

The various words for "love" in the Gospel express feelings and attitudes among various members of the Godhead and between God and people. God loved the world. Jesus loved all the disciples, including Lazarus (who has a similar reference as the beloved disciple). But according to the evidence of the Gospel, a special relationship existed between Jesus and this unnamed disciple. The phrase "the disciple whom Jesus loved" occurs five times in the Gospel (13:23; 19:26; 20:2; 21:7, 20). This information is significant. Two unnamed disciples of John the Baptist, who later become followers of Jesus, appear in 1:37–42. They return with Jesus to where he is staying. In verse 40 one of them is named—he is Andrew, the brother of Simon Peter; but the other disciple remains nameless. In the Synoptic accounts, John is among the first four to be called; in John's Gospel, if this person is John, he is one of the first two. I suggest that this nameless one is John.

In the call sections of the Synoptics, two sets of brothers stand out as being the first called disciples of Jesus: Peter and Andrew, and James and John. They are always found together fishing (Matt. 4:18–22; Mark 1:16–20). According to Luke 5:10, these four are business partners. John, then, follows this well-known tradition but leaves out his own name (as well as that of his brother). This suggests a principle to be applied to the authorship question: He purposefully left out his name from a well-known tradition. All would have known who the author was.

Also significant is the fact that at the end of John's Gospel (21:24) is a reference to the disciple who testified to these things—he is the one who also wrote. By following through on this "testimony" aspect, we find supporting evidence. In 15:27, "And you [plural] also must testify, for you have been with me from the beginning." Here is a clear statement about the length of the witnessing: "from the beginning," that is, 1:37–42, where several people become disciples of Jesus. This marks out distinctly the first parameter of witness. The final parameter is in 21:24. Note also that in chapter 21, Simon Peter and the beloved disciple are together and serve as the point of discussion. They are together as associates from the beginning.

A further reference to "testifying" occurs at 19:35. Here, though nameless, the disciple whom Jesus loved (19:26) sees and testifies to Jesus' death. A few verses earlier, this same disciple is mentioned among the women at the cross. It is the specific function of the beloved disciple to testify of Jesus from beginning to end, especially to testify of his death. In 19:35, the testimony serves to authenticate faith. This fits well the purpose, given in 20:30–31, for writing the book and the selection of the "signs" to be included.

With the clause "whom Jesus loved" (lit., "whom Jesus was loving") John purposely makes himself known by some other attribute than his name. This indicates a humility on his part. The apostolic leaders in the primitive church did not elevate themselves, though they did not shirk their leadership roles. Furthermore, the phrase implies an ongoing and personal relationship with Jesus and suggests that the author had unique, inside information. These humble and personal elements increase the Gospel's aura of credibility and authenticity.

Finally, well-attested traditions say that John survived into Trajan's reign (A.D. 98–117). John 21:21–23 seems to support this tradition, that the author in fact did not die before the end of the first century. This frame allows sufficient time for John to have written his Gospel.

5. The Date of the Gospel

Scholars have not yet resolved the matter of the time of writing. One theory believes John wrote before the 70s, while another thinks that he wrote around the turn of the first century. A mid-range theory places it somewhere in between, usually around the composition and use of the *birkath ha-minim* in the synagogue (see below). Those who hold to a series of editions of this Gospel suggest that the final edition occurred late in the first century.

The date cannot be settled with certainty, yet this does not mean that an evaluation of the material is not important. Two factors regarding the date emerge to assist the reader. (1) One involves the *birkath ha-minim*. This is the name for the twelfth benediction of the *Shemoneh Esreh* ("The Eighteen Benedictions"). These benedictions served as a central prayer in synagogue worship in the first century. The twelfth benediction was created to separate the heretics from other worshipers by serving as a basis for excommunication. Scholars still debate the time of the composition of this benediction.

Nonetheless, this situation does provide a fruitful background for understanding apologetic language in the Gospel of John and for reconstructing its environment. After the war of A.D. 70, in which the Romans destroyed Jerusalem and its temple, a time of turmoil and confrontation existed between church and synagogue. Of the streams of Judaism that survived, the Pharisees dominated. They attempted to fortify Jewish faith in the land of Israel and in the Diaspora. In this context Christianity and Judaism finally broke ranks. To be sure, the Judaism that confronted John's church was not the same as later rabbinic Judaism, nor was it the same as the Judaism in the time of Jesus. Nonetheless, this was a Judaism that took its religious heritage and traditions seriously. Their expression in the background of John's Gospel bound both past and later Jewish traditions. This makes it possible to interpret this Gospel with more specific data.

(2) A second factor involves the discovery of several important manuscripts containing parts of the Gospel. While the Gospel was not quoted before the second half of the second century, allusions may exist earlier in First Clement, the Epistle of Barnabas, and Ignatius, all in the late first century and early second centuries. Of course it is impossible to know if these reflect actual contact with a written gospel or with oral traditions. But two important manuscripts have come to light—designated as p^{52} and p^{66}.

The first originated in Egypt and came to light in 1934 from among the holdings of the unpublished papyri of John Rylands Library at Manchester. This small papyrus fragment holds only a small portion of the Gospel (18:31–33, 37–38) but contributes in a large way to Johannine studies. Scholars date it in the first half of the second century, around A.D. 125. The Gospel was thus in circulation in Egypt at an early date, far removed from its place of writing. The Gospel must thus have been written sometime before. This fragment is the oldest copy of any manuscript of the New Testament.

The second papyrus manuscript, likewise one of the oldest of the New Testament, known as the Bodmer Papyrus II, was published in 1956. This manuscript is dated around A.D. 200

and contains 1:1–6:11; 6:35b–14:26, 29–30; 15:2–26; 16:2–4, 6–7; 16:10–20:23; 20:25–21:9.

6. Place of Writing and Destination

Theories regarding time and place of the writing of this Gospel abound: Egypt, places in the land of Israel, Ephesus (to name just the major ones). Furthermore, where was the author when he wrote? Ephesus is the name commonly mentioned in early church tradition and is a good starting point. John the evangelist and apostle, an eyewitness of Jesus, engaged in ministry throughout Israel and Asia Minor. According to church tradition, wherever he went, he established churches and appointed leaders.

All the while, John preached and taught about Jesus. His sermons and lessons were given in a number of different situations over the years. He may have kept in written form much of the material. Finally, when he served in a role similar to that of bishop, where he had oversight of several churches, he put together his Gospel. He wrote it from Ephesus to other house churches in Ephesus and surrounding environs. His Gospel was a defense of Christianity and a guide for confrontations between his churches and the opposition they were receiving from synagogues.

That such confrontations occurred in Asia Minor can be substantiated from the Johannine letters, Revelation, and the writings of Ignatius. This may explain the appearance of literary stages, seams, sermons, and the other characteristics referred to above, while allowing the early eyewitness aspects to come out. It also explains the well-thought and digested material about Jesus, which is now so much a part of his own world. Jesus' worldview and teachings have completely absorbed John.

7. Theological Themes

An awareness of John's major theological themes alerts us to some of the problems John faces and addresses. Three major themes emerge: Christology (a discussion of Jesus' person and nature), soteriology (a presentation of Jesus' saving work), and ecclesiology (a demonstration of the nature of the church). Theology, then as now, formed a foundation of faith and practice, a standard by which to measure religious life. The church today would not be as rich theologically without John's Gospel. His perspective offers a diversity within the unity of New Testament theology—diversity because of the New Testament believers' problems, language, thought forms, and John's unique personality.

As to methodology, John narrates his story of Jesus, allowing theology to come through in narrative form. Perhaps only in his preface and in the "*amen, amen*" sayings does he engage in a propositional method of presenting truth.

a. Christology

John provided a unique view of the person and work of Jesus. Some scholars have insisted that the New Testament emphasized the work of Jesus and that little or nothing is said about the person of Jesus (such as his two natures). True, most of the New Testament does emphasize the work of Jesus. But in John, Jesus' person and nature, because of the threats to his church, draw significant attention. Judaism simply could not believe in a divine Messiah. For John, this issue was important. Without a divine King (Messiah), salvation was impossible.

By using one of Hillel's rules, John sketched the fundamental nature of Jesus. Rule 6 in effect said this: Whatever is said of something or someone (point A), the same thing can be said of something or someone else (point B). Applied in this way, what Yahweh (God; point A) did in the Old Testament, Jesus did in the New (point B). As God gave life, so Jesus gave life. As God created, so Jesus created. Jesus had the authority and power to do what God in the Old Testament did. Jesus was divine and equal yet subordinate to God the Father. One of the purposes Jesus served was to reveal the Father on earth. He revealed the image of God (see Col. 1:15). At the same time, John did not ignore Jesus' humanity.

Closely associated with Christology is John's theology of the Spirit. As in the rest of the New Testament, the Spirit is subjugated to the Father and Son. The doctrine of the Spirit is entirely Christ-centered. Jesus is both the subject and goal of Spirit theology especially in John. The Spirit, who bears witness and speaks of the Father and the Son, reveals to people their sinful condition and draws them to the atoning sacrifice that God through Jesus has provided. The Son and the Father then send the Spirit to give life.

John focuses on the Spirit in regeneration. The baptism of the Spirit, prominent in Luke and Acts, occurs only in subtle ways in John. For example, John's baptism of Jesus, which Luke's Gospel records as an anointing of the Spirit, is not mentioned in John's Gospel, though the Spirit does give a divine testimony of Jesus by descending on him.

Eschatology is another theme attached to Christology. John does not emphasize futuristic eschatology. Instead, he focuses on the present (realized eschatology). The resurrection is the key to his eschatology. In the now time, when persons are born again by the Spirit, they have in them heavenly life. They have experienced life from God that endures forever. John did this because of the threat from Judaism. The Spirit in regeneration, the new creation, was the way people knew if they were truly members of God's people.

b. Soteriology

In the New Testament, one must speak simultaneously of Christology and soteriology (the doctrine of salvation). Without Jesus' being both divine and human, salvation would not have been possible. His sacrificial death had to be of immense value, so his deity provided this. But his humanity made it possible for him to die. If this doctrine of faith fell, so would the experience and provision of salvation.

The key to understanding this theme in John arises out of a context of confrontation between John's congregation(s) and Judaism. This confrontation began with Jesus, but in time it spread, both in depth and in breadth, so that by John's time, tensions were high. Issues had become much clearer.

Scholars today view this confrontation with Judaism in sectarian terms. Both Jews and Christians claimed the same Scriptures, the same traditions of the Old Testament. Judaism claimed the Exodus, the Passover, the covenant, and the patriarchs (especially Abraham and his merits). It had a whole system of tradition, both written and oral, that lived through its community. The Jews needed no personal salvation, for God had long ago provided such for them. At special times of the year, with ritual celebrations clustered around temple and law, God simply extended his work of promise and forgiveness among his people.

The Jews did not, of course, accept Jesus as the Son of the God of the Hebrew Scriptures and as a way of forgiveness. This is where transformation entered. Jesus, through whom God created the world initially, was the One through whom God created the second time. He created a new order called the church. John took important feasts, holy days, and rituals of the Old Testament, kept some fundamental ideas inherent in them, but added significant concepts, thus transforming them. For example, he transformed the Passover feast into the Lord's Supper; the Sabbath into Sunday (lit., "the first of the Sabbaths," 20:1), the day of the resurrection; the Feast of Booths (Tabernacles) into Jesus and the coming of the Spirit. He changed allegiance from the patriarchs Jacob (ch. 4) and Abraham (ch. 8) to Jesus and the apostles.

Through this confrontational context and through God's transforming power, John showed discontinuity between the New and Old Testaments while maintaining continuity. (1) He believed that Jesus fulfilled promises in the Scriptures. (2) He arrived at his conclusions by interpreting Scriptures to show their connection to Jesus and salvation. (3) His experience with Jesus shaped his presuppositions and influenced the way he approached Scripture. Judaism used many of the same Scripture passages, but John saw them in the light of Jesus and the Spirit. God had done a new thing in Jesus. It required a new worship, one of life and Spirit, which also brought new liturgy and ritual.

The whole system of salvation brought about by Jesus, then, transformed the old. Jesus was the end-times Passover Lamb, who took away the sin of the world. By offering him as the Lamb of God on the cross at Passover, God has removed all offense between him and his people. By placing faith in Jesus and becoming his disciples, people receive a new nature by the Spirit from both the Father and the Son. Through this experience, the new believer enters the kingdom of God—the new, true, heavenly reality. His death and resurrection are central to the creation of the church.

With the coming of this new era, the old has lost its significance. The Passover no longer holds any value for atonement. Since the world is under the influence of sin and the devil, people cannot appeal to ethnic realities, prejudices, or patriarchal connections to dispose of sin's power. Sin is inherent in human nature and in the various social, political, and religious structures of the world. Jesus in his incarnation has invaded the world, atoned for its sin, and sent the Spirit to deliver us from its power. Jesus is the divine Messiah, who delivers people and rules over all.

c. Ecclesiology

Embedded deeply within the structure of John's Gospel lies a picture of the church. In the confrontational context of this Gospel, a discussion ensued regarding the identity of the people of God. Were they Jews or Christians (i.e., believers in Jesus)? How could one know? On the one hand, Judaism appealed to its traditions, feasts, holy sites, Scripture interpretations, the temple, and its founders, the patriarchs. It especially referred to its ethnicity as the glue holding together the various traditions. But in John's view, the entire world lay under the dominion of sin, even Jewish people. The church (or people of God) is the temple, Christ's body (John 2). Jesus' body, and the believer through it, hung on the cross. Believers must eat of that body to be one with it. Having faith in him releases the Spirit to bring new life and enables one to participate in this body.

Believers, then, together have the Spirit of God dwelling in and among them. They now have become the new temple of God. Wherever they are in the world, there is God's temple. Old temple sites are no longer important. Furthermore, this is the only way one can worship God—truly in a spiritual way. The presence of the Spirit, then, characterizes the new and true people of God as temple, which stands in discontinuity with the old, since its foundation is Jesus.

OUTLINE

1. **Preface** (1:1–18)
   - **1.1.** The Word in Eternity (1:1–5)
   - **1.2.** The Light: The Word in the World (1:6–13)
   - **1.3.** The Incarnation: The Word in the Church (1:14–18)
2. **The Manifestation of the Light in the World** (1:19–12:50)
   - **2.1.** The Witness of John (1:19–42)
   - **2.2.** The Witness of Philip and Nathanael (1:43–51)
   - **2.3.** The First and Second Signs: Temple Transformation (2:1–4:54)
     - **2.3.1.** The First Sign and the Cana Wedding (2:1–11)
     - **2.3.2.** Temple Cleansing (2:12–25)
     - **2.3.3.** Jesus and Nicodemus (3:1–21)
     - **2.3.4.** Jesus and John the Baptist (3:22–35)
     - **2.3.5.** The Samaritan Woman (4:1–26)
     - **2.3.6.** Jesus, His Disciples, and the Samaritan Woman (4:27–38)
     - **2.3.7.** The Savior of the World (4:39–42)
     - **2.3.8.** A Prophet's Own Country (4:43–45)
     - **2.3.9.** The Second Sign (4:46–54)
   - **2.4.** The Other Signs: Transformation of Holy Days (5:1–12:50)
     - **2.4.1.** The Healing at the Pool (5:1–47)
       - **2.4.1.1.** The Lame Man at the Pool (5:1–5)
       - **2.4.1.2.** Healing of the Lame Man (5:6–9b)
       - **2.4.1.3.** The Challenge to Jesus' Work (5:9c–18)
       - **2.4.1.4.** The Gift of Life: Jesus' and the Father's Work (5:19–30)
       - **2.4.1.5.** Witnesses to Jesus (5:31–47)
     - **2.4.2.** The Feeding of the Five Thousand and Consequences (6:1–71)
       - **2.4.2.1.** Feeding of the Five Thousand (6:1–15)
       - **2.4.2.2.** Jesus Walks on the Water (6:16–24)
       - **2.4.2.3.** Elaboration on Jesus the Bread of Life (6:25–59)
       - **2.4.2.4.** Many Disciples Depart (6:60–71)
     - **2.4.3.** Jesus and Tabernacles (7:1–12:50)
       - **2.4.3.1.** Jesus at Tabernacles (7:1–13)
       - **2.4.3.2.** Jesus' Teaching at the Feast (7:14–24)
       - **2.4.3.3.** Jesus as Messiah? (7:25–36)
       - **2.4.3.4.** The Gift of the Life-Giving Spirit (7:37–44)
       - **2.4.3.5.** Unbelieving Jewish Leaders (7:45–52)

COMMENTARY

1. Preface (1:1–18)

Though this part of the Gospel functions as a preface, it is more than that. Written in poetic form, especially the first thirteen verses, it prepares the reader for what is to follow and, indeed, summarizes the entire Gospel. In this part, one finds rejection and conflict on the one hand, and revelation, salvation, and life on the other. Also, the author sets forth the person and work of Jesus and how he fits into God's eternal plan. Verses 6–13 provide the summary of 1:19–12:50 and verses 14–18, of chapters 13–21. These themes originated from the Old Testament, current thinking within Judaism, and noncanonical wisdom literature (see comments below).

1.1. The Word in Eternity (1:1–5)

John 1:1 begins in much the same way as Genesis 1:1 does, "In the beginning." This is intentional and in harmony with the plan of the Gospel. John intends to show that, with Jesus, God has created something new—the church. The conflict between Christianity and Judaism apparent in this Gospel concerned which one was the true heir of the Old Testament. Since Judaism appealed to sacred sites, personalities, and other Old Testament traditions, John would have argued less effectively had he appealed to the same materials. John did indeed appeal to Old Testament traditions and texts, even in similar ways as Judaism, but his belief in and experience with Jesus as his Lord made the difference. Old Testament texts, then, do not occur frequently in John in overt ways. Nonetheless, the Old Testament undergirds the Gospel at every point.

This section focuses on the Word, the Logos. Attempts to trace the source of the term *Logos* are many. More than likely, the term and its concept come from Jewish literature and thinking, although it was at home within the larger Greco-Roman world. The two themes of wisdom and agency come together in "Logos." Beginning in the Old Testament, wisdom and law (Torah, a Hebrew word for law and associated with the five books of Moses) are associated and become one. Proverbs 8 especially not only personalized wisdom but placed it at the side of God before, and involved it in, creation. Law, the epitome of wisdom, was developed further in later noncanonical Jewish literature (Sirach, Wisdom of Solomon, the Aramaic translations of the Hebrew Scriptures, rabbinic commentaries, and Philo, a Jewish writer).

Implied also in this combination of law/wisdom is the idea of agency. Wisdom was the means by which God created the world (Prov. 8:30). Particularly in the Aramaic translations called the Targums, the Aramaic word *memra*, translated "word," functioned as the agency by which God created the world. While Memra in this case helped some in Judaism to guard against profaning the name of God (it was thus a roundabout way of referring to God), it served the author of John's Gospel as a way of expressing the creative agency of the Word (cf. Ps. 33:6, where God created by means of "the word"). John took a common theme in

Jewish liturgical contexts, expanded its meaning, and used it to express the doctrine of the Son of God, the Logos.

The author also uses the theme revelation inherent in wisdom/law. In John's Gospel, the Logos is the full revelation of God, just as the law, from the writing of Hebrew Scriptures until his own time, was a revelation of God. The theme that the Word, the Son of God, revealed God *fully* completes this section at verse 18.

These ideas of wisdom, agency, and revelation set forth for the believer a Christ-centered view of creation and redemption. One cannot know the ultimate purpose of creation or redemption, nor can one understand one's day-by-day existence, God, or any spiritual revelation, without coming through the Logos, the Son of God.

Verses 1–4 set out the preexistent state of Jesus and how he functioned in God's eternal plan. "In the beginning" (v. 1a) speaks of the Word's eternal existence. The next two phrases express the divinity of Jesus and his relationship with God [the Father]. This relationship is a dynamic one, in which communication and fellowship are constantly exchanged within the Godhead. Verse 2 summarizes verse 1 and prepares for divine activity outside the Godhead's relationship in verse 3. In verse 4 he is the mediated Creator. The use of the preposition "through" accurately lets the reader know that the original Creator was God the Father, who created all things through the Word.

The verbs John uses in these verses distinguish between the uncreated Creator, the Word, and the created order. In good translation the NIV notes this distinction: the Word "was" but "all things were made."

Verse 4 tells the reader several things. (1) The divine Word, like God the Father, has unoriginated life in himself (i.e., is the source of eternal life). (2) This life revealed God's person and nature to all people. (3) "Light" here pertains to the authoritative and authentic revelation of God; it is best explained in terms of the Old Testament, perhaps connecting with "in the beginning" in Genesis 1. "Light" occurs first here in a series of concepts that oppose one another. The opposite of light is darkness (later in this Gospel, other terms will emerge as opposites). "Light" also refers to God's righteous character, opposed by the unrighteous world of darkness. This word also will take up the meaning of "glory" in the next section of the preface. This set of opposite terms was common in the ancient world.

Verse 5 expresses the response of these unrighteous people to the light: "The light shines in the darkness, but the darkness has not understood it." The translation "understood" conveys the inability of sinners to understand God. While this translation is acceptable, the translation in the NIV note is to be preferred. That is, in view of the theme of conflict with Judaism found in the Gospel, John is asserting that the darkness did not overcome the light.

1.2. The Light: The Word in the World (1:6–13)

This section expands themes from the last paragraph and adds two key elements: John (this Gospel does not call him "the Baptist"), and "witness." John, though sent by God, is inferior to the Word. One is created, the other uncreated. One is the witness to the light, the other is the true Light. This statement suggests that John played a significant role in the minds of the original readers and that his followers may have been part of the problem in John's congregation. This situation is verified by information about John the Baptist in Luke's Gospel and in the book of Acts (esp. Acts 19:1–7).

"Witness" plays a major role in John's Gospel. The word, used in connection with such ideas and persons as "sign," Abraham, the Spirit, and the Father, verifies and testifies that Jesus is truly the Son of God. John's witness also assists others to believe in the Light.

The "world" is first introduced here (v. 9) in the Gospel. This word refers to the people among whom Jesus came. They rejected him as the true Light because they were sinful. John here assumes the fall of all peoples. Furthermore, the fall means that people in this condition cannot know God. Their religious quest has gone astray, and they cannot find him without the Light. But their traditions are their security and they stumble about blindly. Thus, sinners reject the Light when he comes into the world.

Though the world rejects the Creator, he gives them a measure of light. This measure is usually expressed in our day as common grace—God's grace that draws and comes to every person. This is one of the possible interpretations of verse 9 (cf. NIV note: "This was the true light that gives light to every man who comes into the world"). Interpretation depends on which noun "who comes into the world" modifies. Does it modify "the true light" or "every man"? This clause comes after "every man" in the Greek text and thus likely modifies it.

After saying generally that the world rejected the Light, John specifically narrows his window to note the exception. In verses 12–13, he draws a sharp contrast between them and notes what made the difference. "Receive" means to "believe." "Believe" emphasizes not a one-time event, such as occurs in an altar call, but a continuous act, a lifestyle or state of being. With habitual belief comes the "right" to be God's children. Furthermore, in response to belief, God causes people to be born as his children. The verb "born" used with God contains a causative element. The imagery is this: God is the father, not the mother.

The structure of verse 13 shows a strong contrast between human effort and divine activity. Three parallel, negative elements, "children born not of natural descent, nor of human decision or a husband's will," contrast with the single positive one, "but born of God." By using these three elements, John emphasizes that no human effort can make one a child of God—it takes divine activity. This contrast challenges such things as ethnic and religious distinctives and would have made it difficult for Judaism to receive, certainly to believe.

John's Gospel reserves the word "children" as a name for believers in Jesus (cf. Paul, who uses "sons of God"). John distinguishes between Christians and Jesus' nature on the one hand, and yet speaks of similarity of relationship on the other. John uses the word "son" for Jesus but "children" for all believers who call God Father, the source of their new birth.

1.3. The Incarnation: The Word in the Church (1:14–18)

Now John tells the reader that "the Word became flesh." The word "became" is the word used earlier with creation. The One who is God has now become a human being. This is the meaning of the Incarnation; the divine Word, the Son of God, is now both divine and human. God is present everywhere, but the Incarnation has added a new dimension. God is now present in the same sphere of humanity (a great foundation for true empathy!). In the Incarnation, God comes near in a new way.

The information in this verse may be responding to Gnosticism and Judaism, for Gnosticism did not believe that a divine person could also be human, and Judaism did not believe that a human could at the same time be divine. Knowledge of the Incarnation, in the sense that John intends, comes only through revelation, and revelation comes through the divine activity of regeneration. Revelation is only such when it is comprehended and only when God provides this kind of ability to comprehend these kinds of matters.

John speaks of the Incarnation in terms of a temple. The word "made his dwelling" in verse 14 is associated with the dwelling of God in the Hebrew Scriptures and here states that the Incarnation is God's temple among his people in the last days. Like the temple of old, it has "glory," but even more—the temple is God himself, full of grace and truth. "Grace and truth" pick up two key attributes of God and further identify the Word with the God of the Old Testament.

The author also alludes to the Old Testament declaration that no one has ever seen God. In the end times, however, God has come in the flesh, seen as God only by people of faith. So this new, ultimate temple is vastly superior to the old. It has glory that does not fade away, as Paul noted of glory in 2 Corinthians 3:7–11. The reference to Moses in verse 17 indirectly elaborates on this Old Testament idea. While Moses gave a measure of grace in the law, the superior grace came through Jesus Christ. The NIV translates it this way in verse 16: "We [believers] have all received one blessing after another."

The expression "One and Only" in verse 14 of the NIV is the Greek word *monogenous* and is commonly translated "only begotten" (see NIV note). An interpreter must avoid the root fallacy when seeking the meaning of any word—that is, taking what the root meant and applying it every place the word is used. The meaning of a word must be determined by its context. In this case, *monogenous* comes from two roots: "one/only" and "begotten." The way this word is used in biblical contexts suggests that this word is to be understood as "only" or "unique"—thus the NIV's "One and Only." The creative process (i.e., "begotten") is not part of the meaning of this word. The Logos is God's only Son.

Verse 15 seems to be out of order or else is parenthetical. However, this testimony fits well with what this section teaches. The Logos is God's unique revelation of himself. The only way in which any human can see God is through the Son, the revelatory Logos. The Logos is thus divine and greater than John. The divine Logos existed in eternity before God ever sent John. John's testimony heightens this fact.

From manuscript evidence two possible readings exist at verse 18 with the repeated word *monogenous*: "Son" or "God." The 1984 edition of the NIV chooses "God" as the most probable reading. Though manuscript evidence is divided, the witness of the Gospel itself supports the reading "God." This is the most direct statement of the deity of Jesus in the New Testament.

2. The Manifestation of the Light in the World (1:19–12:50)

This major division shows that the world does not have the right answer and rejects Jesus. John 1:19–51 places before the inquiring reader of this Gospel an important question about the identity of Jesus. In the initial paragraph (1:19–28) leaders from Jerusalem send messengers to ask of John if he is the Messiah, Elijah, or the Prophet; he denied being any of these. A bit later (1:29–34), John testifies that he himself would not have known who Jesus was if it were not for God's giving him these directions: "the man on whom you see the Spirit come down and remain." John's disciples, too, inquire about Jesus (1:35–42).

Chapter 1 orients the reader to anticipate the identity of Jesus in the coming narrative by providing the answer on the lips of two people: John the Baptist declares that he is the Lamb of God, and Nathanael says of Jesus, "Rabbi, you are the Son of God; you are the King of Israel." The rest of the book enlarges on the meaning of these key titles. Jesus provides atonement for the sins of the world and is reigning as God's Son and messianic King.

2.1. The Witness of John (1:19–42)

The beginning of the story of Jesus in John 1:19–51, unlike Matthew and Luke, contains nothing about Jesus' infancy. Rather, John moves from his summary of the Logos of 1:1–18 directly to the witness of John the Baptist and the call of the early disciples. Verses 19–28 contain the dialogue between the envoy of the Jerusalem leaders and John the Baptist. John's testimony at verse 19 and the geographical note at verse 28 bracket this dialogue. The issue here focuses on John the Baptist's identity and witness that he is not the Christ (i.e., the Messiah), Elijah, or the Prophet. In the various traditions of Judaism, these figures played a role in the coming age of the Messiah. John's answer is subtle—nowhere does he say who the Messiah is. Rather, these leaders do not know, even though he stands among them (v. 26). This suggests that they do not have the nature or the ability to know (cf. comments on 1:10–11).

John's answer about the true Messiah (v. 23) does not involve a superior means of baptism (i.e., with the Spirit), as in the other Gospels. Rather, his use of Isaiah 40:3 subtly states that Jesus is "the Lord" and John the Baptist is simply his forerunner. For John's readers, the answer comes in verses 29–34. It is sufficient for the moment to know that John the Baptist is merely a witness, inferior to Jesus, and that ignorance rules the leaders from Jerusalem.

The conclusion of the paragraph (v. 28) may point to John's earliest place of baptizing and connects with Bethsaida. The author distinguishes between the leaders from Jerusalem, who are not friendly, and John the Baptist's disciples from Bethsaida, who become Jesus' disciples. Though Jesus makes Capernaum his headquarters, a significant number of his disciples originate from the area of Bethsaida. This city, in the area ruled by Herod Philip, was somewhat tolerant, open to Gentiles and even to pious Jews of differing sects.

Scholars dispute the identity and location of Bethany (v. 28). This geographical reference is ambiguous in the Greek text: "Bethany" does not have the definite article "the" with it, and the accompanying phrase, "the other side of the Jordan," is vague. Bethany here may not be a city name. Instead, it may denote the northeast

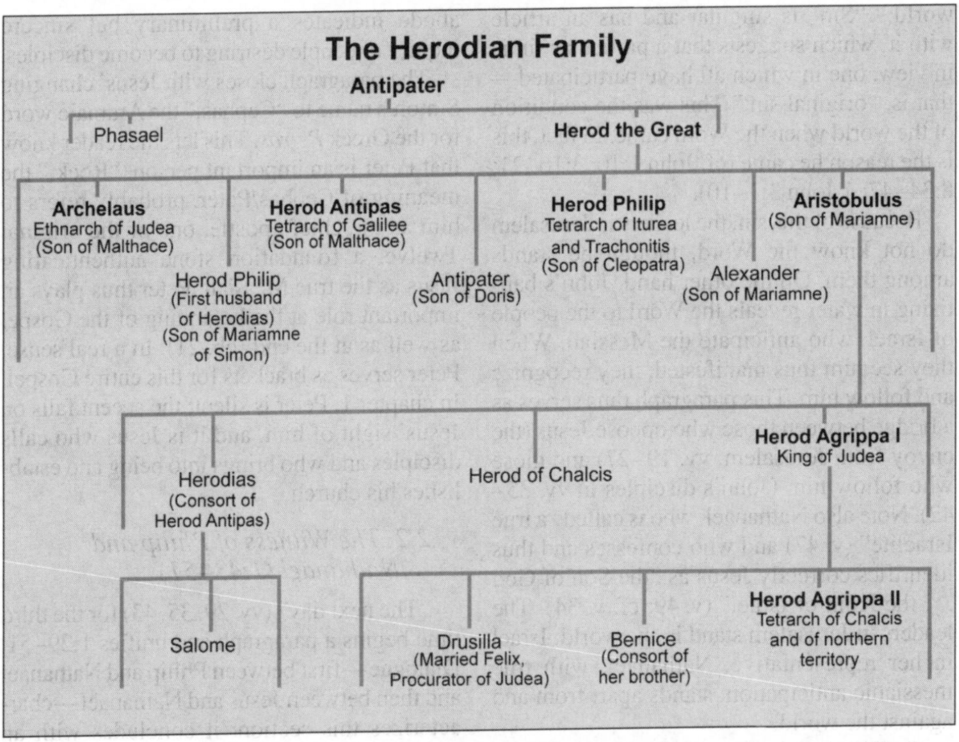

Herod the Great was king of Judea when Jesus was born. When Herod died soon after, his kingdom was divided among his remaining sons Antipas, Archelaus, and Philip.

regional name of Batanea (and thus be associated with Bethsaida). Presumably, John baptized Jesus at a different location (vv. 29–34).

Verse 30 ties this paragraph with the previous one and John's words: "This is the one I meant when I said. . . ." The author intends to answer who this greater one is and how one knows. John the Baptist's testimony culminates in this paragraph where we have no dialogue—only the words of the Baptist in testimony fashion that reflects a legal setting. The Baptist himself notes here that he does not know either: "I would not have known him, except that the one who sent me to baptize with water told me" (v. 33). The statement that he does not know occurs twice (vv. 31, 33) to emphasize his ignorance. The voice of the one who sent him said that the way John would know is that the Spirit would descend and remain on Jesus. The abiding Spirit, then, becomes the identifying characteristic of Jesus.

The Spirit's affirmation of Jesus as the greater one is important for the Gospel writer's audience in their debate with Judaism. Both Christians and Judaizers appealed to the Hebrew Scriptures, the latter to traditions as well. But it is the coming of the Spirit that denotes who the true heirs of the old covenant are. Further, this makes Jesus the legitimate dispenser of the Spirit (v. 33); it also establishes the fact that he is the one who by the Spirit regenerates those who believe and fills them with the Spirit. John intends "baptize" to refer comprehensively to all Spirit activities to and in the church, though in this Gospel, because of the nature of the problem he is facing, John emphasizes regeneration. Jesus thus stands as the focus of all Spirit doctrine.

In this paragraph the Spirit denotes regeneration, for he is connected with the opening words of verse 29, which identify Jesus: "Look, the Lamb of God, who takes away the sin of the world!" Jesus as the Lamb of God occurs only in John's Gospel and Revelation. While various theories exist about what kind of lamb to which John is referring, the Gospel itself suggests that Jesus is the end-time Passover Lamb. He replaces the lamb offered each Passover (see the comment on chs. 13 and 20). This Lamb "takes away the sin of the world." "Sin" is singular and has an article with it, which suggests that a particular sin is in view, one in which all have participated—that is, "original sin." This was the condition of the world when the Word came. In fact, this is the reason he came (cf. John 1:10; 3:16–21; 8:34–47; 1 John 3:1–10).

Because of this sin, the leaders in Jerusalem do not know the Word, though he stands among them. On the other hand, John's baptizing in water reveals the Word to the people of Israel, who anticipate the Messiah. When they see him thus manifested, they recognize and follow him. This paragraph thus serves as a bridge between those who oppose Jesus (the envoy from Jerusalem, vv. 19–27) and those who follow him (John's disciples in vv. 35–42). Note also Nathanael, who is called "a true Israelite" (v. 47) and who confesses and thus identifies correctly Jesus as "the Son of God . . . the King of Israel" (v. 49; cf. v. 34). The leaders in Jerusalem stand in the world; Israel in her representative, Nathanael, with true messianic anticipation, stands apart from and against the world.

On "the next day" (v. 35) separates the Baptist's witness regarding the identity of Jesus and his witness to two of his disciples. This phrase also connects this witness to that of the preceding paragraph, as does "Look, the Lamb of God." Only in John do we read that the first disciples initially followed the Baptist. Here we find the most information about Andrew. He is the brother of Simon Peter, the first to follow Jesus, and the one to tell his brother about finding the Messiah. We also learn that the disciples' call and responses are not spontaneous and instantaneous. Rather, they are thoughtful, protracted, and judicious.

Discipleship language fills verses 35–42. The Baptist's action and words point to his followers that they are to become disciples of Jesus. The readers of this Gospel will thus know whom they ought to follow and why. Only Jesus as the Lamb can take away the sin of the world. The two disciples of the Baptist, as yet nameless in the text, hear him say this about Jesus and begin following. "Hear" and "follow" (v. 37) are both discipleship words. The dialogue then switches to Jesus, who turns and asks, "What do you want?" This important question is still appropriate today. Their response and return with Jesus to his place of abode indicates a preliminary but sincere inquiry of people desiring to become disciples.

The paragraph closes with Jesus' changing Simon's name to "Cephas," the Aramaic word for the Greek *Petros*. This lets the reader know that Peter is an important person. "Rock," the meaning of Cephas/Peter, probably refers to him as the chief apostle, one of the original Twelve, a foundation stone authenticating Jesus as the true Messiah. Peter thus plays an important role at the beginning of the Gospel as well as at the end (ch. 21). In a real sense, Peter serves as brackets for this entire Gospel. In chapter 1, Peter is silent; the accent falls on Jesus' sight of him, and it is Jesus who calls disciples and who brings into being and establishes his church.

2.2. The Witness of Philip and Nathanael (1:43–51)

"The next day" (vv. 29, 35, 43) for the third time begins a paragraph and unifies 1:29–51. Dialogue—first between Philip and Nathanael and then between Jesus and Nathanael—characterizes this section; it concludes with an important statement identifying Jesus. Discipleship is still the theme. Jesus' circle of followers is expanding, which in itself models what disciples are to do—to tell others about the Messiah. The setting also changes, though the author notes that Philip, too, comes from Bethsaida, the same place as Andrew and Peter. Apparently, Philip knows of Nathanael and that he too is seeking the Messiah. Nathanael is a pious person, who studies Scripture under a fig tree (cf. *Mek.* Piska 12), looking for the Messiah. Philip testifies to him that he has found the Messiah; Nathanael is skeptical because Jesus comes from Nazareth, a place of ill reputation. The invitation to discipleship is extended, "Come and see" (see vv. 39, 46), and Nathanael responds.

Jesus speaks to no one in particular, and thus to everyone, about the piety of Nathanael, a model of a "true Israelite" (v .47). This leads to Nathanael's confession: "You are the Son of God . . . the King of Israel," thus repeating John's confession in verse 34 but adding an important title—"the King of Israel." Nathanael believes Jesus to be the Messiah. At this, Jesus indicates how his faith will advance: not merely because Jesus saw him under the fig tree, but because of "greater things"—his death and resurrection, which are to come. Faith, then, is based not on the study of law but on the death, resurrection, and ascension of Jesus. Those truly pious people who anticipate the Messiah must believe that Jesus is the Messiah.

The chapter concludes with an "*amen, amen*" saying (NIV, "I tell you the truth," v. 51). In this Gospel, "*amen, amen*" introduces important doctrinal statements from the lips of Jesus. This first one points to a new mode of access to heaven and replaces a Judaistic tradition, based on Jacob's vision in Genesis 28:12 and attached to the sacred stone in the Most Holy Place in the Jerusalem temple. Now Jesus, the incarnate Son of God, is the meeting place of heaven and earth. The title "Son of Man," not used as frequently as in the other Gospels, is nonetheless significant and means the same as "Son of God" (see vv. 49–50). Both refer to Jesus as Messiah.

2.3. The First and Second Signs: Temple Transformation (2:1–4:54)

Since two signs (and the word "sign") act as brackets (i.e., literary bookends) distinguishing this section and giving it focus, we must spend some time discussing this concept and related ideas. Scholars have long discussed the significance of the term *sign* (*semeion*; NIV, "miraculous sign") in the Gospel of John. A consideration of this word assists us in discovering how the Gospel should be divided and interpreted.

To begin, John intends "signs" to benefit his readers for their own sake—they signify something more than a mere miracle. A sign refers to a special outstanding event, drawing attention to the saving activity of Jesus and pointing to his death and resurrection. The word in 20:30–31 reflects both a general and special use and fuels the difficulty of settling discussion about the significance of *semeion*: "Jesus did many other miraculous signs in the presence of his disciples, which are not recorded in this book. But these are written that you may believe that Jesus is the Christ, the Son of God, and that by believing you may have life in his name."

As to these two uses in the Gospel itself, in 2:18, 23; 3:2; 4:48; 6:2, 26, 30; 7:31; 9:16; 10:41; 11:47; and 12:18, 37, *semeion* refers to "miracle" in a general sense and to a mark of authority (in 2:18). In 2:11 and 4:54, however, the only other two other places where *semeion* is used, it has a special sense (see next paragraph). These various nuances of the word make the number of signs debatable.

In 2:11 and 4:54 *semeion* has special significance. (1) These two verses are connected by the author to two specific "signs": the changing of the water into wine and the healing of the royal official's son in Cana. (2) Among all the "signs," only these two have a numerical signification attached: "first" and "second." Both signs are performed at Cana. In this way, these words bring some sort of attention to this section. After chapter 4, the narrative simply moves on to a new event in chapter 5—it contains the next "miracle" (not specified as *semeion* but referred to as a healing or as "things"[5:16] or "work" [5:17]).

The word "first" (*arche*) at 2:11 may have several possible meanings. The NIV translates this Greek word numerically as "first"; others take it to mean "beginning" or the initiation of something. But neither translation brings special attention to the meaning of the content bracketed within these signs. The meaning "beginning" suggests that "others" will follow—of the same nature or else this first one has "primary status." In either case, there is an interrelatedness among the "beginning" and those that follow.

John used the word *deuteron* (NIV, "second") with *semeion* at 4:54. Whether one can observe any special significance to the way John puts these two words together is determined in part by how one understands "second"—whether it emphasizes Cana (i.e., this is the second miracle *in Cana*) or whether it stresses the "sign." Note that Cana occurs in 4:46 but not in 4:54, with the "second sign," where only Galilee is mentioned. This strengthens the conclusion that "second" should emphasize the "sign" in Galilee and not the exact geographical location of Cana. This fact, then, draws the reader's attention to the material between these two signs.

Other factors need to be considered to support this. (1) One of these involves the use of other significant Johannine clauses or words with "sign"—for instance, the clause, "He thus revealed his glory" (2:11). "Revealed" and "glory" do not appear together in any other place in this Gospel. This initial sign, then, is special when compared to the others in that it reveals in some way Jesus' glory. John attaches "glory" to the raising of Lazarus in 11:4 and 40 but without the verb "reveal." The transformation of water into wine as the beginning of signs, then, points the reader toward and anticipates the conclusion of the Gospel.

(2) Another factor pertains to the following clause in 2:11, "and his disciples put their faith in him." These elements, "disciples" and "put their faith," do not occur again in this clear manner until chapter 20, when various people come to faith in view of the empty tomb and risen Christ. In between, especially at 9:38; 11:27; and 12:11, 42, several believe in Jesus but in a way that also points to the climax of faith in chapter 20. Thus, the first sign anticipates the climactic point of the resurrection.

One other word needs discussion with this grouping of words and clauses—the word "time" in 2:4. The Greek word for "time" is *hora* (lit., "hour," though not the same meaning as the modern Western word). This word both distinguishes and connects this first sign ("My time has not yet come," 2:4) and its fulfillment, the death of Jesus ("Father, the time has come," 17:1). "Time" thus emphasizes this beginning of signs and, therefore, is attached to the time of Jesus' death and resurrection. Jesus' hour comes in the last week of his life and especially receives its fulfillment in his death (12:23, 27; 13:1; 17:1 [where "glory" occurs in verb form]).

This conclusion that the "first" and "second" signs bracket together significant material removes any possibility of the events between as being signs. This excludes, for example, the cleansing of the temple in chapter 2 from being a sign. Another implication pertains to how chapters 2–12 ought to be structured. I suggest that the first two signs (2:1–4:54) constitute Part 1 of the Book of Signs; the Other Signs (5:1–12:50) constitute Part 2 of this Book of Signs.

The most significant factor here pertains to the temple. Since the temple was one of the most important factors in Judaism prior to the Bar Cochba war, ending in A.D. 135 (even after its destruction by the Romans in A.D. 70), it is only natural that the temple served as a major point of contention between these two religions. The temple was the center of Old Testament faith and later Judaism. It had for centuries united all the tribes of Israel and symbolized the place of God's dwelling on earth among his people. All of Israel's religious and social life revolved around it. John here addresses this situation for Christians by noting that Jesus has transformed the idea of the physical temple with the constitution of a new one from his body.

Two references in 2:1–4:54 discuss temples: 2:13–22 and 4:19–24. In the first, Jesus transforms the Jerusalem one by replacing it with his own body (the "three days" in 2:20 notes that the resurrection will be the transforming event). In chapter 4, the Jerusalem temple is legitimated in comparison to the Samaritan one, but both are replaced since they place limits on where people can meet God. God's new temple will be believers in Jesus, who can be any place on earth. The allusion to Zechariah 14:21 at John 2:16 suggests that Jesus is making the new temple into a place where all nations can come. This, then, sheds light on why John uses the Samaritan material in his Gospel, especially in this close proximity to chapter 2 and in this section: Not only will the Gentiles be included but despised Samaritans as well.

Since Jesus' body becomes the new temple, how do believers become his body? The answer is given in chapter 3—through the birth from above. When people believe in Jesus and are born by the Spirit, they have a new godly nature and become the dwelling place of the Spirit, the new temple. This is the transforming experience of the water into wine, illustrated in the healing of the sick, giving sight to the blind, raising the dead to life, and culminating in the death and resurrection of Jesus. The relationship between Jesus and his followers as "body" is explained in the vine imagery of chapter 15—he is the stock, they are its branches.

The two signs in 2:1–4:54, then, reveal in a dramatic way what Jesus has come to do. The longer dialogue and teaching blocks of material contained in this section elaborate on the signs. Thus, John provides for the reader an event of God, which he calls "signs," and a doctrinal explanation about them (sign and sign narrative).

All the signs in John's Gospel share the same character. Each one is connected with Jesus' work of salvation for a blinded and sinful world. Each one points beyond itself to the

self-revealing nature and work of God in Jesus. Each one is uniquely a revelation of Jesus' work of salvation on the cross, not to be duplicated by any human being. This work, though, can be done by his disciples by offering it through evangelism. On the one hand, without faith, people only see these signs as apparitions, attention-getters. On the other, with faith, they reveal God's work of salvation.

2.3.1. The First Sign and the Cana Wedding (2:1–11). With "on the third day," 2:1 continues in a smooth way the theme of chapter 1, picking up the three references to "the next day" there. The first sign (2:11), about Jesus' changing water into wine, anticipates the rest of the signs, summarizes them, and elaborates on the call to discipleship and the significance of Jesus' work and titles in chapter 1. This sign also anticipates the conclusion of the Gospel.

Chapter 2 has three parts: (1) the sign (vv. 1–11), (2) a transitional verse (v. 12), and (3) the account of the cleansing of the temple (vv. 13–25). The sign ends in a recapping statement (v. 11), while the last part concludes with a note about miraculous signs that Jesus performed, people's reaction to them, and Jesus' response to them. Why is the temple cleansing placed here in chapter 2 rather than toward the end of Jesus' life (as in the Synoptics)? As to a possible solution we need to look closely at the beginning of Jesus' ministry, when he calls disciples to true faith. Jesus establishes the radical nature of his work and thus graphically portrays the new nature of his people. The goal of his work is anticipated and set forth here.

Jesus performs the sign of changing water into wine in the presence of his disciples. The wine that ran out had not been associated with the six stone water jars. Rather, they were "used by the Jews for ceremonial washing." In mentioning these things in this way, attention shifts from a social to a religious setting. With this, Jesus makes an implicit statement about Judaism as a religion: Its containers hold no substance by which to effect a cleansing, which God expects and demands of adherents. This allusion likely mirrors a debate in John's time between Christians and opponents over the nature of the true religion.

Furthermore, the writer carefully mentions the size of jars. The amount they hold approx-

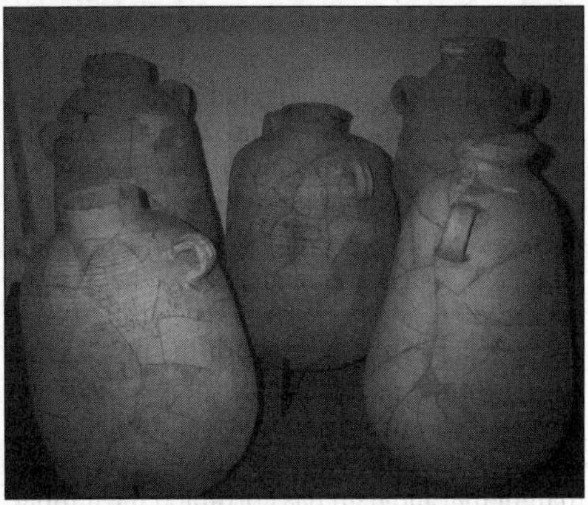

Jesus changed water into wine at a wedding in Cana in Galilee. John writes that the disciples, who witnessed that first miracle, put their faith in Jesus. The jars at Cana may have been similar to these, which date back to the Roman era and were uncovered in the Golan.

imates the amount of water a Jewish mikveh would hold. A mikveh was a ceremonial holding place for water, built into the floor of houses (and placed around the temple in Jerusalem), something like a bathtub in a modern house, and was used for religious cleansing. Guidelines for handling this water were strict. The fact that they are empty is significant.

Elsewhere, Jesus used wine as a metaphor to indicate new things. For example, in Matthew 9:17 Jesus used new wine and new skins to speak of the new thing he was doing. Similarly, here in John 2 Jesus transforms the water into the best wine in the stone jars that the servants have filled. (By saving the best until last, he changes social custom.) The salvation and community that Jesus creates is clearly superior to that of Judaism.

The dialogue between Mary and Jesus in verses 2–5 also points in this direction. She says, "They have no more wine" (v. 3). Jesus responds in a direct manner, "My time [lit., hour] has not yet come." This statement occurs in significant places in the movement and development of the Gospel (see esp. 5:25; 7:30; 8:20; 12:23, 27; 13:1; 17:1). Jesus' "time" finally arrives with his death and resurrection. In this first sign, then, the direction for true understanding is given: that which he will supply through his death and resurrection is indicated by the miraculous new wine of 2:1–11.

2.3.2. Temple Cleansing (2:12–25). After a transitional verse (v. 12), the cleansing of the temple in 2:13–25 makes sense to the reader when understood in light of the new thing that Jesus plans to do, as indicated in the first sign. Moreover, both 2:1–11 and 2:13–25 use the number three: "third day" (v. 1) and "three days" (v. 19); both of these references point to the resurrection—the day of the new creation. Note too that the cleansing of the temple occurred at Passover, the same setting of the death of Jesus, the offering of the new Lamb. As the former paragraph has shown the water jars of Judaism to be empty and thus of no effect, in a similar way this paragraph brings to light that Judaism has corrupted the temple; it no longer serves God's purpose, so that a new temple is in order.

The "Jews" (not to be taken in an ethnic sense) think that Jesus is referring to the literal temple when they ask about his authority to overturn their practice of money changing. Going far beyond their intention and comprehension, Jesus' answer in verse 19 introduces into the dialogue his bodily resurrection and links it to the new temple. Their response in verse 20 manifests their constant lack of spiritual understanding, something that also occurs in chapter 3 with Nicodemus. In contrast, after the resurrection the disciples understand Jesus' words spoken here (v. 22). His "body" thus becomes a metaphor for the church. Verse 21 explained to John's readers the meaning of Jesus' words by connecting "temple" and "body" (cf. the use of this metaphor in Eph. 2:11–22; 4:1–13). John addresses this new spiritual temple in chapter 4.

By seeing the first sign as pointing to a new thing that Jesus will do—a new creation arising from his death and resurrection, a creation of a new temple, his body—John 2:1–11 and 2:13–25 fit well together. This sign manifests his glory (v. 11), the same glory that belongs to God and glorifies the Son through the resurrection of Lazarus (11:4). This glorious sign and its fulfillment is the basis for the disciples' faith. This belief differs from the belief of others in 2:23, who believe in Jesus only because they see the many signs he performs. At least two things make this belief different. (1) The people are only impressed by his miracle-working ability, which calls for no change in lifestyle or allegiance. (2) They have not caught the significance of this sign. Jesus will do a new work by dying and rising from the dead, requiring new faith and resulting in salvation and a new people of God, his temple.

We should note briefly two other items in chapter 2. (1) The first confrontation in the Gospel between Jesus and his opponents occurs in 2:13–23. (2) Jesus' omniscience and sovereignty interfaces with his ministry. In verses 23–25, he knows the hearts of all people and refuses to be governed by their expectations.

2.3.3. Jesus and Nicodemus (3:1–21). Having finished the dialogue with the Jews and the remarks about the cleansing of the temple, John now launches into a new dialogue of Jesus with a single person. John devotes some attention to individuals throughout his Gospel. These individuals (in this case Nicodemus) are larger than life—they serve as models and represent others. Nicodemus, who comes secretly at night, relates well to secret believers in synagogues in John's day. Like Nicodemus, they should seek a public faith in Jesus.

Through the question-and-answer method, Jesus extends his teaching. The Nicodemus paragraph concludes at verse 21, although Nicodemus's last question occurs at verse 9. At verse 11b, Jesus switches from singular "you" to plural "you," so that the implied participants in the dialogue widen. It is also the place where a third "*amen, amen*" saying (NIV, "I tell you the truth") in the Nicodemus paragraph occurs. This third saying authenticates the first two.

John uses irony in the dialogue between Jesus and Nicodemus. But the irony becomes rather biting as the dialogue progresses. This progression reveals how ignorant one is of spiritual things if not spiritually reborn. Nicodemus's situation follows naturally that described in 2:23–25 of "all men." Jesus gives Nicodemus revelation about the kingdom of God, and he, a teacher in Israel, cannot understand, even though Jesus uses "natural" illustrations of the birth process and the blowing of the wind. Rebirth from above is a revelatory experience. Rebirth is the basis of a common spiritual nature in which revelation between God and his people can occur. Obviously, Nicodemus is not yet born from above.

The time of Nicodemus's coming to Jesus may be significant. "At night" in verse 2 may point to a sinister context, since the phrase indicates the kind of time: It is nighttime as opposed to daytime. On the other hand, it may simply represent a normal time for rabbis to engage in religious discussion or study of the law, since they worked during the day (Nicodemus was a ruler of the Pharisees). His opening remark to Jesus is in the form of an ambiguous statement, to which Jesus replies with an "*amen, amen*" statement (v. 3).

In 3:1–21, three such sayings exist (vv. 3, 5, 11). These sayings usually come in groups. The two sayings in verses 3 and 5 are conceptually synonymous and provide the doctrinal heart of the first sign; it is important to analyze these two together, as John surely intends. Let us lay out their structure so we may analyze them carefully in this way.

Verse 3	*Verse 5*
A: I tell you the truth	A: I tell you the truth
B: no one can see the kingdom of God	B: no one can enter the kingdom of God
C: unless he is born again.	C: unless he is born of water and the Spirit.

Part A is the same in both sayings. In Parts B and C some differences exist: "Enter" in B of verse 5 replaces "see" of B in verse 3, though one is hard-pressed to see anything distinct in these two words. Both refer to the experience of being born again by the Spirit. Furthermore, the kingdom of God refers to the new life of the Spirit that the believer enters at the point of rebirth. It is to possess eternal life (cf. Matt. 18:3; 19:17, 23–24). This fact is emphasized in this Gospel.

Part C of verse 3 has the adverb *anothen*, which the NIV translates as "again." The context of John's Gospel lends weight to translating *anothen* as "from above" (cf. NIV note; note the contrast between earth/heaven, flesh/spirit, below/above). In the immediate context, *anothen* has two meanings: For the spiritually inept Nicodemus, it means "again," but Jesus intends it in the sense of "born from above," that is, by the Spirit. This adverb, then, denotes the source of rebirth.

Part C of verse 5, however, substitutes "of water and the Spirit" for *anothen* in verse 3. Scholars debate what these words mean. Do they refer to two different aspects, such as natural and spiritual births? Or to water baptism and regeneration? Or to the sacramental nature of water in regeneration? It is natural to refer these words to the source of the rebirth. "Water" is best seen as meaning "spiritual water," thus referring to the Spirit. The following discussion provides reasons for this conclusion.

(1) This phrase forms a figure of speech called a hendiadys—a device an author uses when he wants to emphasize an idea by connecting what would otherwise be two independent nouns. One noun becomes an adjective modifying the other. Here, then, John emphasizes the means of rebirth, which throughout his Gospel is by the Spirit.

(2) Why then does he add "water"? The context of the sign supplies the answer and adds support for the interpretation given above. The author's problem is Judaism, and he has already noted that God in Jesus is doing something new. In the first sign, Judaism's method of cleansing (the empty jars) is no longer valid. Jesus replaces the jars' content with something new. In contrast, then, Jesus' followers have been cleansed through faith and rebirth of the Spirit, that is, through "Spiritual water." "Spirit," then, becomes an adjective modifying "water." Together, they serve as a metaphor for the "regenerating Spirit" as opposed to Judaism's sacramentalism.

(3) Water, especially in John's Gospel, is a symbol of the Spirit (cf. 7:37–39). Judaism had two kinds of baptism-like events, both involving water, by which defilement was removed: one for proselytes and the other for ablution of adherents. In proselyte baptism, the convert experienced an identity shift and became a new person; this is the meaning of sacramentalism. In ablution, special water was the cleansing agent to remove defilement of sin.

(4) The context of verses 6–8 and verses 12–18 support the interpretation of "spiritual water." Verses 6–8 directly refer to the Spirit as the means. Verse 6 militates against the "water" of verse 5 referring to natural birth and emphasizes regeneration by the Spirit. In verse 7, the sayings in verses 3 and 5 are recapped positively with "You must be born again." The "wind and Spirit" of verse 8 are from the same Greek word, *pneuma*. John uses this word in a subtle manner. It is possible to see a reference to the Spirit in both instances. This reflects John's style of using certain words with a double meaning. John 1:12–13 also supports this view of "spiritual water."

(5) Furthermore, 3:12–18 talks about the manner of cleansing the world from its sins—through the lifting up of God's Son. This lifting up is an atonement for its sins, resulting in forgiveness through faith. Forgiveness results in eternal life (vv. 13–16). Verse 14 draws a comparison between what Moses and God did. Verse 16 recaps and extends part B of the comparison. The "giving" of verse 16 parallels the lifting up of the serpent by Moses in verse 14a and the lifting up of the Son of Man in 14b. As Moses lifted up the serpent and those who looked upon it received life, so God lifts up his Son. In this way, John emphasizes Jesus' death on the cross (cf. 12:32). The "so" in the clause of 3:16, "For God so loved," shows the manner of God's love more than the extent of it.

(6) Finally, in 3:34 the reference to "for God gives the Spirit without limit" supports the above interpretation. The Greek expression translated "without limit" (NIV) occurs only here in the New Testament. The context of the first sign and John's elaboration of its significance assists one in understanding this phrase. Implicitly, "without limit" reflects the further shortcoming of Judaism as noted in the empty jars of 2:1–11. The jars had definite measurements and limits. By contrast, the new thing that God will do with the Spirit knows no limits. Further, "without limits" suggests that rebirth is the basis for the fullness of the Spirit.

Verses 1–16, then, focus on one's rebirth by the Spirit and how this rebirth connects to Jesus' death and resurrection. With the advent of verse 17, a new theme emerges. On the other side are those who do not believe and who lie under condemnation. God's sending his Son and lifting him up has removed this condemnation from all who believe. All people stand under this condemnation prior to the coming of the Light. The writer assumes the fall of humankind and its consequences for everyone. Those who refuse to come out of the darkness do so because they love it. Should they come out of it, they know that the Light will expose their evil deeds. Evil and righteousness are concrete and practical—both are something that people habitually practice. Belief in God's Son brings cleansing (freedom from condemnation) and a new lifestyle. On the other hand, unbelief confirms one in the state of condemnation.

2.3.4. Jesus and John the Baptist (3:22–35). In an abrupt manner, verse 22 gives another of John the Baptist's testimonies about Jesus. John has appeared in 1:6–8, 15, 19–27, 29–34, 35. Others will refer to him later (cf. 5:33, 36; 10:40–41), but in 3:22–30, the Baptist comes onstage for the sixth time. The overriding purpose that he serves in this Gospel is to witness to Jesus as the greater One. The material on John the Baptist in chapter 1 and here contain similar themes to this effect. In chapter 1, John's disciples began turning to Jesus, while here Jesus has followers (though they remain nameless). John clearly passes from the scene in this paragraph, although the author does note that this incident happened before his imprisonment. Jesus now comes to the forefront.

We learn information here about Jesus and his disciples that is not in the other Gospels: They are baptizing before his death. John 4:2 clarifies 3:22 in that Jesus himself does not baptize; rather, his disciples do. The verb tenses in verse 22 suggest that they have spent some time staying and baptizing in Judea. It is difficult to say what kind of baptism this is. More than likely, it is similar to, though not the same as, John the Baptist's. In light of Jesus' baptism in chapter 1, it may have indicated an identification and a mark of solidarity with the people of Israel in God's saving event.

This incident of the Baptist (v. 23) precipitates an argument with "a certain Jew" (v. 25). In the next verse, however, the subject is plural ("they"). Presumably the reference in verse 26 is to a group whom the Jew in verse 25 represents; this group may be the Pharisees (cf. 4:1).

The point of the argument is not given, other than "over the matter of ceremonial washing." Certainly John's baptism was different from Judaism's, although they call him "Rabbi" (v. 26), a familiar title for a Jewish teacher and cleric. The use of this title suggests that they perceive him to be similar in some way to themselves or that they attribute honor to him. The important element to note is the reason for this dialogue: They are worried that Jesus is attracting more followers than both they and the Baptist (cf. 4:1, even though the Baptist is successful [cf. v. 23b], Jesus is making more disciples than him). This Jewish group, in other words, comes to join forces with John so that both groups can together come against Jesus.

This incident serves well the purpose of the author of this Gospel. The Baptist's answer focuses on God's sovereign will: "A man can receive only what is given him from heaven" (v. 27). What he goes on to say completes what God's will is: Jesus is the Christ (the Messiah). The Baptist relates to Jesus only as a "friend" relates to the groom. A "friend" was roughly equivalent to the modern, Western tradition's best man. Like the "friend," the Baptist attends the bridegroom and is filled with joy when he hears the groom's voice. By implication, the voice says, "The wedding is over." That is, Jesus has come, the forerunner is no longer needed.

The point the dialogue makes, especially in the Baptist's elaboration on the Jewish statement, is that both he and Judaism *must* pass away. There is a divine necessity in this statement (v. 30). That is the point of verse 28, where the Baptist says, "You yourselves can testify that I said. . . ." This point serves well the significance of the first sign of 2:1–11 about the new thing that God in Jesus is doing: All ceremonial washing is nullified; it is "spiritual water" that brings eternal life (3:3, 5).

This section (vv. 22–35) implies that in the author's day, the Baptist still has followers who are at odds with Christians. As we have suggested, it also provides clues that John's church is having problems with Judaism. This material, presented in this way, indirectly encourages the Baptist's followers, some of whom may have been quasi-followers of Jesus, to turn their allegiance to Jesus. Other Jewish believers in Jesus who may be thinking about returning to Judaism will also be encouraged to remain as believers in Jesus.

The place where Jesus and his disciples are at this time is simply in "the Judean countryside" (v. 22)—likely somewhere in the Jordan valley. On the other hand, John the Baptist is baptizing at Aenon (Aramaic word for "the Place of Springs"), near Salim. The location of Salim cannot be identified with certainty, but it is north of where Jesus has been baptizing. This may indicate that John the Baptist is already submitting to the coming of Jesus.

The NIV considers verses 31–36 to continue the Baptist's comments (note the quotation marks). On the other hand, an NIV note allows for the quote to end at verse 30. Does this section continue the Baptist's words or does it bracket a larger block of material and serve as a conclusion to chapter 3 and transition to the next section? Certainly, verse 31 continues the theme of the greater One of verse 30: The One about whom the Baptist speaks is greater because he is from heaven. But this comment can easily be seen as the author's reflection on the difference between the Baptist and Jesus. The words of verses 31–33 echo 1:1–15 regarding the nature and existence of the Logos, the witness of John, the rejection of the Word by his own, and the acceptance of him by others.

Verses 34–36 pertain to the Father and Jesus. God sent the revelatory Word (cf. 1:14–18; 3:16–17), and the Word "speaks the words of God" (v. 34). The Father has placed under his Son all things, especially the gift of eternal life for all who believe (vv. 35–36).

The verb in the second half of verse 34 in Greek contains an ambiguous subject. The NIV supplies the subject "God" in the following clause: "for [God] gives the Spirit without limit" (cf. NIV note, "he"). The question is whether "God" is to be supplied from the subject of the first sentence in verse 34 or whether the subject is Jesus. It seems best to take the second part of verse 34 as explaining the first part: "For the one whom God has sent speaks the words of God" is explained by, "for God gives the Spirit without limit." That is, Jesus, in contrast to the one who "speaks as one from the earth" (v. 31b), speaks the words of God because God gives him the Spirit. The "without limit" suggests that only a superior person is so privileged. Jesus is clearly the superior Revealer, sent from heaven to explain the Father. With this status the Son has the authority to give eternal life and to pass judgment, both themes of this section.

2.3.5. The Samaritan Woman (4:1–26). Verses 1–2 connect back with John 3 by referring to the Baptist and Jesus' disciples and provide a transition to a new section. Verse 3 puts Jesus on the move from Judea to Galilee. The narrative focuses on Samaria in 4:4–42: "Now he had to go through Samaria" (v. 4). Perhaps he has to leave Galilee because of pressure from the Pharisees, insofar as he was making more disciples than they and John the Baptist were. He is not compelled to go through Samaria because of the road system, however. He chooses to go through Samaria because of divine compulsion.

This scene focuses on a time of evangelism and instruction in Samaria, highlighting a dialogue between Jesus and a woman. His disciples appear in a secondary role; they play the role of a foil in that they demonstrate a lack of an awareness of God's mission through Jesus among these Samaritans. At the end, Jesus directs them toward Samaria as a present harvest field. This evangelism connects two themes of this section: eternal life attached to the living water, and a new temple. These intertwined themes were part of the first sign at Cana (cf. comments on ch. 2). This second theme partially explains why the author includes this Samaritan account: It allows him to expand on the implication of a new temple, which consists of the resurrected Christ and his body of believers. Since they all possess eternal life through the Spirit, he thus inhabits them as his temple.

The country of Samaria lay between Judea on the south and Galilee on the north. The people of Samaria had an eight-hundred-year history of racial and religious tensions with Jews. Though the Samaritans had mixed geographical and ethnic backgrounds, they did consider themselves, like the Jews, to be the true Israel, the people of God. Samaritan distinctions emerged in the time of the Assyrians when, in the resettlement of Israel elsewhere in 722 B.C., people of other ethnic origins were brought into the land of Israel. From these settlers, religious differences between Jews and Samaritans developed. Tensions eased toward the last quarter of the first century A.D. This explains why John adds the parenthetical note in verse 9.

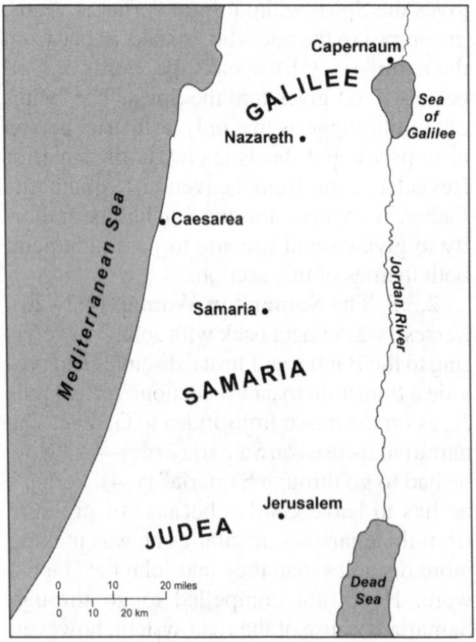

Jesus had to travel through Samaria on his return to Galilee from Judea.

The major city in Samaria was also called Samaria, which lay on a hill north and west of the twin peaks of Gerizim and Ebal. To get to this city from the south, one traveled west through a pass between these two mountains. Herod the Great had rebuilt the city and renamed it Sebaste. Early church tradition connects John the Baptist with this city.

To the south, on top of Mount Gerizim, sat the ruins of the Samaritan temple, destroyed some 150 years previously (cf. the reference to the temple in 4:19–21). Sychar (v. 5), the place of Jacob's well, lay to the east of the pass in the valley floor. It cannot be known if the author associated Sychar with the ancient city of Shechem. No one has located ancient Sychar with certainty, and Shechem was about 200–300 yards from Jacob's well. Excavated tombs in the area witness to a Christian presence there in the first century.

Jesus and his disciples arrive at Jacob's well at the sixth hour—that is, about 12:00 noon. Since women gathered water at earlier or later hours, this time was significant. Either John subtly connects this time with the crucifixion hour of 19:14 and thus with salvation/eternal life, or with the fact that the Samaritan woman, as a prostitute, was a social outcast. Both fit the context.

Regarding the later possibility (see 4:16–18), the Samaritan woman says she has no "husband" (*aner*). Jesus readily admits that to be true, for she has had five *aner* (i.e., men) and is currently living with another *aner* ("man," v. 18). There is an obvious play on the Greek word *aner*. Both Jesus and the Samaritans adhere to the authority of the Pentateuch. This woman is surely aware of what it teaches about her situation. Jesus brings her around to see that this is an adulterous (i.e., promiscuous) situation. These verses do not support the fact that these men may have died in turn and that she married a new one after each one's death. Otherwise, she could have legitimately an-

swered that the man she now lives with is her husband; she denies that ("I have no husband," v. 17). Thus these verses indicate the route Jesus takes to bring the woman under conviction. It also allows him the opportunity to reveal that he indeed is their Messiah too.

John provides a brief note about Jesus' humanity, noting that the trip has tired him and made him thirsty (vv. 6–7). This note also gives a reason why Jesus does not go to town with his disciples. He thus sits down by Jacob's well (a stone wall surrounds and covers the shaft today).

Jacob's well is particularly highlighted in this passage, a fact that is important for this Gospel's theme. Jacob was an important figure in both Jewish and Samaritan religions. He was an ancestor, a patriarch, a founding father, who therefore served as a guarantor of God's promises to the patriarchs. Because of his prominent position in both religions, Jacob was one of the mediators between God and his people in prayer, in forgiveness, and in extension of the covenant promises. Sites attached to such prominent people also anchored ownership of portions of land and made them holy sites.

Jesus' request for water, a break with social customs of the time, begins the dialogue with this Samaritan woman. Verse 9 establishes the conflict between Jews and Samaritans ("gender" is not the issue as much as it is later in v. 27). The verb "associate" in the parenthesis of verse 9 occurs only here in the New Testament, and it is difficult to know its exact nuance. We must derive its meaning from the context. Since the disciples have gone to purchase food—and this seems not to be a problem—this verb takes on special social implications apart from business dealings. It refers to an intimate social dialogue, such as in this hospitable act of giving life-sustaining substance such as water. To extend such an act of kindness meant that one accepted and welcomed the person. Indeed, such hospitality is extended and deepened in the last part of this chapter: Jesus, his disciples, and the Samaritans involve themselves in such an act.

Why then does the author even mention this conflict in verse 9? One explanation is that John's readers do not know of this tension, so that this statement helps the woman's question make more sense. Also, meaning shifts between verses 9 and 10: from the woman's literal water to Jesus' spiritual water; this parenthesis makes for a smoother transition. But it serves one further purpose: to heighten the ethnic gap, noting the differences between the Jewish religious leadership and the despised Samaritans. These leaders have rejected Jesus, but Samaritans readily receive him. John 1:10–13 is clearly illustrated here: His own people did not receive him; yet those who did, to them he gave the right to become his children, not through physical processes but through spiritual.

Jacob's Well can still be seen in this unfinished church in Shechem in Samaria. The opening to the original well, visible in these two shelters, is now 20 feet below ground level. The water in the well is more than 125 feet below ground level.

The water of the well lay some 90–100 feet below the surface and required the right equipment to secure it. This factor is a subtle reminder of the empty Jewish water pots in 2:6–10. Jesus has neither rope nor container with which to draw its water. His request for a drink sets up the woman's answer, out of which he makes his point. When Jesus says that God has for her "living water," she immediately sees the right implication: "Are you greater than our father Jacob?" This allows Jesus to extend his point by drawing out the difference between the Samaritan religion and that brought about through the new gift of life by the Spirit. "Living water" here—as in John, the Old Testament, and Jewish literature—symbolizes the Spirit. In contrast to well water or water from a cistern, it brings life to an often dry (lifeless) country; similarly, the Spirit

brings eternal life to (lifeless) people who believe in Jesus.

Significant is the fact that Jesus himself gives this water (i.e., Spirit), which will produce eternal life. Jesus, who has life in himself (cf. 1:4; 5:21) and is the source of life, gives the Spirit, who in turn gives eternal life. Both the Father and Jesus the Son give the Spirit and eternal life, a function clearly taught in chapters 14–16. In 4:14, the Spirit's giving life to the believer occurs in figurative terms as "a spring of water welling up to eternal life." In 7:37–39, where Jesus as the source of this water is emphasized, the figurative expression "rivers of living water" (NRSV) occurs.[1]

This woman has the same condition as Nicodemus had in the last chapter. Without the revelation that eternal life brings, she only misunderstands Jesus' invitation. She assumes one meaning of "water," Jesus has another. Had she been born from above, she would have had the right kind of nature to understand what Jesus as God is saying to her (v. 10). This point is made further on (see comment on vv. 21–26).

It is not until Jesus reveals to the woman her own private past and present about the many men she has known that she begins to realize that someone different stands before her. She addresses him three times (vv. 11, 15, 19) with the polite and respectful "sir." The last "sir" in verse 19 is pivotal, for she now recognizes him to be a prophet. But at verses 24–25, she enlarges her perception to include "'Messiah' (called Christ)." In response, Jesus goes even further by saying, "I who speak to you am he" (v. 26). This is the first occurrence of the expression "I am" (*ego eimi*) in John—here with the predicate *ho lalon* ("who speaks"). *Ego eimi* is one of the names for Yahweh in the Old Testament (cf. Ex. 3:14) and no doubt contains that connotation here. It also is one of the names for the Messiah in John; the connection is plain here in verse 26. Note how Jesus is hesitant to refer to himself as Messiah in Jewish contexts, but not here.

The turn of the conversation is naturally understood when Samaritan backgrounds surface. The woman does not sidetrack Jesus with her remarks. Rather, she begins to understand, from her past traditions, that someone expected in the future has indeed arrived—and that is a surprise. Samaritan traditions were expecting a Messiah-like figure. This prophet-like person, similar to Moses, could reveal secrets. When he appeared on the scene, he would restore true worship. This person was called a Taheb (similar to but not the same as the Jewish Messiah). Even so, Jesus fulfills Samaritan expectations too. The site of the destroyed Samaritan temple in the background on Mount Gerizim serves as an appropriate backdrop for the revelatory discussion of worship. On the brink of the turning of time, their worship is about to come to life, but in a new and unexpected way. Both the place and manner of worship are about to change.

The coming hour of Jesus in verse 21 is the point at which all worship—Samaritan and Jewish, even though Jewish is the appropriate one for now (cf. v. 22)—is transformed. Though it will be set in place at the cross and resurrection, in Jesus the end-time transformation is already present (v. 23: "Yet a time is coming and has now come"). This is one of many occasions when this Gospel emphasizes what is called realized eschatology. That is, along with the teaching on the life that comes with the future resurrection (called consistent eschatology), eternal life arrives now in this life in regeneration and the presence of the Spirit.

The author of this Gospel, more than any other New Testament writer, focuses on rebirth. It is this perspective that Jesus speaks about here. The presence of God will no longer be centered in a temple building. Rather, he will reside in believers, the new temple, who have the Spirit. This teaching is part of the significance of the first sign; these verses point back to 2:14–22 and are realized in 20:19–23, when Jesus breathes on the disciples and thus creates the church.

Various interpretations have been offered for verses 23–24. Some interpreters see in them a basis for a more spirited worship, different from a subdued, ritualistic type (i.e., formalistic worship). This view says that there is a certain way to worship, and when it is not done that way, it is not "true" worship. The small "s" in "spirit" of verse 23 (NIV) suggests this interpretation. Another interpretation refers to the Spirit who will make worship possible after the crucifixion and resurrection. (A similar difference of interpretation over the word "spirit" occurs in v. 24.)

I suggest that with "in spirit and truth" we have a figure of speech called a hendiadys (see comments on 3:3, 5). The two nouns should be taken together and form one concept. They act as an adverb modifying the verb "will worship." In other words, the translation should run, "will worship the Father in a truly spiritual manner." The meaning of "truly spiritual manner" pertains to the nature of the believer that Jesus through the Spirit has created. The reborn person takes on the spiritual nature of God and thus has the ability to communicate and fellowship with God. In an unregenerate state, no one understands the teaching of Jesus, who is from above. Further, "God is spirit" in verse 24 refers to the essence of God, but indicates that God is of a spiritual nature. In order for people to communicate with him, they must also have a similar nature. (I use the word "similar" here because John makes it clear that Christians are not the same nature as Jesus.)

The implications of this interpretation are great. John makes as the basis for Christian worship the new birth. This is a much needed balance in current worship theory, theology, and practice. Pentecostal and charismatic worship is dynamic, a valuable characteristic to be sure, but "dynamic" is not the basis of worship. Unless someone is regenerated, no matter what the form or style, worshiping God is impossible: "His worshipers *must* [emphasis mine] worship in spirit and in truth" (v. 24). Further, true worship is Christ-centered. Without Jesus and the new nature he gives, it is impossible to worship the Father, the object of fellowship. This kind of worship is a lifestyle of constant communication and fellowship (vv. 23–24).

When John uses the word "worship," he does so deliberately. He thus connects the material more tightly to chapter 2 and the idea of the new temple. This also helps explain why John has placed the cleansing of the temple at the beginning of his Gospel. He is saying that Jesus, through his own person and work, has brought an end to the earlier concept of temple. The new temple will not be impersonal, oriented toward any ethnic or religious preference or situated in a geographical site. Rather, his body of redeemed people will be the temple. Beyond the jarring thought (to a pious Jew) that Samaritans can be equal members in the temple, what about a Samaritan prostitute? Yet, this is exactly what John means: Such a one can partake of God's forgiveness and become a member of his body, the new temple.

"The Father seeks" (v. 23) carries with it a missionary thrust and an expanded meaning of worship. Through the work of Jesus, believers have the opportunity to be caught up in the whole fellowship that goes on among the members of the Trinity.

Earlier, Jesus went against custom by asking a Samaritan woman for water (v. 9). In verse 27, when his disciples return, they find Jesus talking with this woman. This catches them off guard. Here John does not mention that she is a Samaritan; rather, Jesus is talking with a woman (the readers already know that she is a Samaritan). This allows the author to bring out something about the disciples. In Jewish literature for a man to talk with a woman was a forbidden custom. The disciples are not necessarily against Samaritans (they have just gone into Samaria to buy food), just against women. This attitude adds to the tenure of the whole passage. Jesus sees their surprise and anticipates their concern, since they say nothing to him. They only urge him to eat what they have purchased. This is the setting for his strongly worded remarks to the disciples.

2.3.6. Jesus, His Disciples, and the Samaritan Woman (4:27–38). Before John records the disciples' encouraging Jesus to eat, he tells us about the woman's action of hastening to tell the townspeople that she has found the Messiah, though her faith appears to be less than complete (vv. 28–30). She leaves her jar by the well. This action allows the reader to anticipate her return and to connect with the jars in chapter 2. Her and the people's interest in Jesus contrasts sharply with the Jewish leadership and confirms the principle articulated in 3:19–21: Evil people do not come to the Light, for they do not want their evil deeds exposed; those who love the Light will come to the Light.

As the woman did not understand about living water earlier, so the disciples in the dialogue in verses 31–38 do not understand Jesus' statement about food. The use of "food" here resembles that in Jesus' citation of Deuteronomy 8:3 in Matthew 4:4. The nature of Jesus' response to his disciples here mixes both literal and figurative meanings. Verse 36, for example, states, "even now he [the reaper] harvests

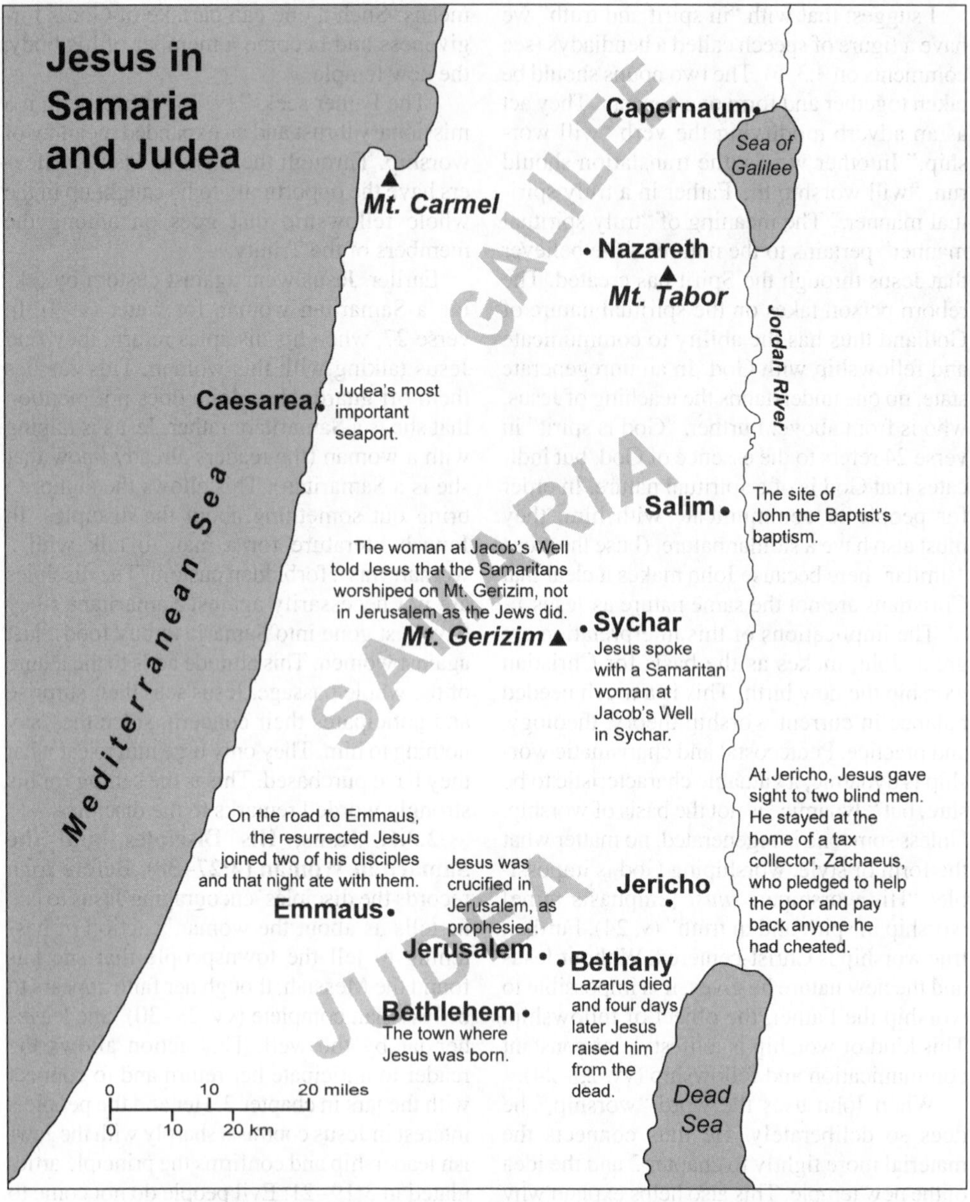
Jesus in Samaria and Judea
Capernaum
Sea of Galilee
Mt. Carmel
Nazareth
Mt. Tabor
GALILEE
Jordan River
Caesarea
Judea's most important seaport.
Mediterranean Sea
SAMARIA
Salim
The site of John the Baptist's baptism.
The woman at Jacob's Well told Jesus that the Samaritans worshiped on Mt. Gerizim, not in Jerusalem as the Jews did.
Mt. Gerizim
Sychar
Jesus spoke with a Samaritan woman at Jacob's Well in Sychar.
At Jericho, Jesus gave sight to two blind men. He stayed at the home of a tax collector, Zachaeus, who pledged to help the poor and pay back anyone he had cheated.
On the road to Emmaus, the resurrected Jesus joined two of his disciples and that night ate with them.
Jesus was crucified in Jerusalem, as prophesied.
Jericho
Emmaus
Jerusalem
Bethany
Lazarus died and four days later Jesus raised him from the dead.
JUDEA
Bethlehem
The town where Jesus was born.
0 10 20 miles
0 10 20 km
Dead Sea

The place of worship of the Samaritans was on Mt. Gerizim, just a short distance from Jacob's Well, where Jesus spoke to the Samaritan woman about the "living water."

the crop for eternal life." The "reaper," literal on one level of meaning, subtle on another, suggests Jesus. Thus, we have an allegory-like illustration coming from a farming situation. This illustration relates to what is happening here in Samaria. This dialogue revealed the shortsightedness of the disciples and, in contrast, God's love-driven and clear sight for the world.

In a real sense, this section contains a commission for world evangelism. At least two principles are clear here. (1) People are always ready for the gospel, but social custom and expectations may hinder the vision and task (the Samaritan harvest is some months away). The reference to the harvest can either be a proverb (four months was the accepted time between planting and harvesting) or it can be literal. Either way, it points out the lack of mission vision on the part of the disciples. Provocation of a vision may be necessary from time to time. (2) Evangelization occurs at different levels and requires different tasks, all involving teamwork over time. One plants, another harvests.

2.3.7. The Savior of the World (4:39–42). Verses 39–42 verify the results of Jesus' passing through Samaria and verifies the divine compulsion to stop there. With brief words the author paints a fitting conclusion to this episode. So much attention devoted to social outcasts such as Samaritans is significant in the New Testament. This chapter stands as a witness to the openness of John (the author) to everyone. The people of that village accept Jesus as Messiah and finally as "Savior of the world." This latter title is particularly significant according to Samaritan expectations. When they extend hospitality to him, he accepts. Their faith is placed on Jesus' word, not on the woman's witness.

We are not to see here a contrast between belief in signs as being negative (cf. 2:23–24) and belief in the words of Jesus (4:4–42) as being the proper way. Jesus' signs are divine acts of salvation, and they are not to be denigrated. People themselves make signs negative or positive. This Samaritan story clarifies and exemplifies the meaning of the first sign at Cana. That sign points to the work of Jesus on his cross and at his resurrection by which he creates a new temple, consisting of people who believe on him and who have received eternal life through the Spirit. What that sign points to is the true basis of faith. In a sense, his words are like the sign, too. They point to his work on the cross, the basis of God forgiving sinners. Through faith in Jesus, God forgives sins and creates a new people with new natures.

2.3.8. A Prophet's Own Country (4:43–45). Verses 43–45 are problematic. This small paragraph, containing a saying of Jesus about a prophet's lack of honor in his homeland (cf. Matt. 13:54–58; Mark 6:4–5; Luke 4:16–30), does not fit the chronology of Jesus' travels in John. He has gone from Samaria to Galilee in verse 43, but verse 44 seems to explain why he went there: He has no honor in his own country. In verse 45, the Galileans give him a warm reception when he arrives, having seen the signs he performed in Jerusalem "at the feast" (lit.).

In order to understand this section, we must note the additions John adds to what the other Gospels report. Note, for example, verse 45: "They had seen all that he had done in Jerusalem at the Passover [this word is not in the Greek, though perhaps implied] Feast, for they also had been there." This verse relates back to 2:23, where the people who saw Jesus' signs and believed in him are probably from Galilee. In 2:23, Jesus did not entrust himself to these people. If these are to be identified with the Galileans in 4:45, then John the author makes no further comment about their negative faith. John 4:43–45 recapitulates this teaching section on the first sign by referring to the same feast and to the people mentioned earlier.

In other words, Jesus goes from Samaria to Galilee, his home. But there he has a following of people who do not have the proper kind of faith. They receive him cordially but do not honor him or his mission. This explains verse 46: Jesus returns to the site of his first sign to get away from friendly people with the wrong kind of faith. We should note that verse 46 begins with the Greek word *oun*, which is usually rendered "therefore" (omitted in NIV).

2.3.9. The Second Sign (4:46–54). The NIV places verses 46–54 as the boundaries of the next paragraph. Interpreters are tempted to see here the beginning of a new section, attaching it to chapter 5. However, verse 54 appears more to bring closure to this section than do verses 43–45. Furthermore, verses 46–54 are connected with the first sign at Cana (note the expression "once more" at the beginning of verse 46, as well as the reference to Cana—a site that occurs only at 2:1, 11; 4:46; 21:2). John also mentions again the turning of water into wine. Note too that "some time later" in 5:1 indicates a sharp break in theme from chapter 4.

Verse 48 has the only use of the phrase "signs and wonders" in this Gospel. "Wonders" in the New Testament always occurs with "signs." Of the sixteen occurrences of the expression in the New Testament, only four are negative; this is one of them (the other three are linked with false prophets and with the signs and wonders they will perform in the end times). In John, "signs and wonders" are attached to false belief and discipleship and contrast with the "miraculous signs," which serve as powerful pointers to the death and resurrection of Jesus and which produce faith (cf. 20:30–31).

This section contains dialogue, which takes on a curious twist here. The "royal official" asks Jesus to heal his son, but Jesus responds curiously with a negative statement about signs and wonders. But the man seems to ignore Jesus' comment. This allows Jesus to further critique the false nature of the faith of those who are following him based on signs alone. This healing, then, becomes a commentary on the people from Galilee in 2:23–25 and 4:43–45, who do have not true faith.

Another indicator of the connection with the previous material is in the use of the ordinal "second" and word "sign" in verse 54 (cf. 2:11). The reference about "Judea to Galilee" in verse 54 connects with "in Galilee from Judea" in verse 47, which is Jesus' itinerary of chapters 2–4.

The royal official's son is about to die (vv. 46–47). His request pertains to healing but more precisely to restoring his child to life. Apparently, his faith is right and Jesus knows that, for verse 53 reads, "So he and all his household believed." This expression unites the official with the disciples in 2:11, who saw Jesus' glory (sign) and believed. This sign also attaches faith to life, and this life signifies eternal life, provided by Jesus' death and resurrection. This miracle also provides commentary on the first sign (see comments on John 2). True faith in Jesus brings eternal life. On the basis of this interpretation, one can note that signs in John contain a coherent significance—they point to the death and resurrection of Jesus.

But this man's faith differs in one way: He simply believes Jesus' word. He has not seen the miracle—he is some distance away from Capernaum when Jesus heals his son. In the words of verse 50b: "The man [obeyed and] took Jesus at his word and departed."

This is not to say that faith in a simple word of Jesus is superior to faith that is attached to miracles. The difference lies between what people think miracles are and how miracles function. For instance, it is one thing for a Christian to receive healing, quite another for a sinner, like this royal official, to experience it. It is also another matter to seek signs for personal aggrandizement or other gain. In the New Testament, signs and wonders are the gospel, along with proclamation of the kingdom. They are saving events in the same manner as "signs" in John are attached to the death and resurrection of Jesus. In John, life brings deliverance and salvation from sin, guilt, and death. In the Synoptics and Acts, as well as in Paul, signs and wonders bring deliverance from various kinds of oppression, sickness, demons, and other debilitating effects. This is part of what is implied above in the connection with these signs and the death and resurrection of Jesus.

John's commentary on the result of this miracle informs the reader about the social structure of this man's family as well as their Gentile background: "So he and all his household believed" (v. 53). Of all Mediterranean social structures, this description fits best the Roman family/household model. In Roman families, each person had special family relationships and roles and derived one's identity from the family. The father served as the head and carried power over every other member. Even household slaves and extended family members came under his authority. Decisions to believe in Jesus in the way this man and his household did are found throughout Acts (10:2; 11:14; 16:15, 31, 34; 18:8), indicating the conversion of similar households. If this father is a Gentile, he speaks here for all his household, who now believe in Jesus. The healing of this man's son, then, mirrors the inclusion of the Gentiles into the church.[2]

2.4. The Other Signs: Transformation of Holy Days (5:1–12:50)

We group this section together because of its focus and purpose. The content of this section, focusing on the holy days of Judaism, follows logically chapters 2–4. As the temple was a major contention between Christianity and Judaism, so were the holy days (the Sabbath and the Feasts of Passover, Tabernacles, and Dedication).[3] The important themes of these feasts centered around eternal life and light. These holy occasions brought time, space, and ritual together at the temple to restore order and harmony in the lives of adherents.

This section, then, sets forth Jesus' saving activity as other special signs signifying the transformation of these holy days. In Jesus, the Sabbath will become the first day of the week,

Passover will be replaced by the Lord's Supper (the Eucharist), and Tabernacles and Dedication (fall and winter festivals) will telescope into one celebration of the Feast of Tabernacles with Jesus as its fulfillment. These occasions were a major source of conflict for Jewish Christians in the latter part of the first century. In this Gospel, the conflict begins in chapter 5 and climaxes in 12.

2.4.1. The Healing at the Pool (5:1–47). The second sign at Cana has already introduced the third with "your son lives." By playing on the double-intentioned word "lives," which carries both the meaning of restoration to health and to life, John points toward the main point of eternal life in the next chapter. He thus conditions the reader's understanding of the next sign.

But with the third sign comes further tension and confrontation with the leaders in Jerusalem. The point of contention in this sign focuses on blasphemy and breaking the Sabbath, both of which are serious infractions of Jewish law. This healing of the paralytic provides the context for Jesus to address his right to transform the opposition's observance of the Sabbath.

Verses 1–5 introduce the setting of the sign, verses 6–9b note the sign, verses 9c–18 manifest the dialogue between the healed person, the Jewish leaders, and Jesus, verses 19–30 give the first interpretive discourse, and verses 31–47 the second.

2.4.1.1. The Lame Man at the Pool (5:1–5). We should note, first, that verses 1–5 contain some textual difficulties. (1) Regarding the name of the pool, several possibilities are given in the manuscripts: Bethesda, Bethsaida, and Bethzatha. Of these, Bethesda is preferred because it transliterates a Hebrew word meaning "house of flowing" (this name occurs in the Temple Scroll found at Qumran). (2) Verses 3b–4 are not found in many of the older, more trustworthy New Testament manuscripts (in the NIV, they have been placed in a text note).

Verse 1 provides the setting—there is "a feast of the Jews." Two observations are worth noting regarding this statement. (1) The word "feast" has no article; we therefore have no concrete clue as to which feast is intended. Presumably John wants to be vague so as to draw attention to the Sabbath, the point of the chapter.

(2) The only attachment is religious—it is a feast of Judaism ("Jews" here does not have an ethnic bias and should be translated Judaism). This identification of Judaism's holy days is typical in John's Gospel. But when Jesus performs his signs, they signify far more than their typical religious expectations of the holy days; they become something new. By placing this ambiguous feast as the backdrop of the Sabbath, John inaugurates this transforming activity of Jesus for all forthcoming holy days in this section.

The pool of Bethesda was near the northeast corner of the temple where the sheep were brought in for sacrifice ("the Sheep Gate"). This pool (now excavated) was surrounded by columns on four sides with a middle partition—thus five covered colonnades. Among these sit and lie the infirm, apparently waiting for the stirring of the water. The later addition (vv. 3b–4) attempts to explain the otherwise simple narrative: An angel comes down to trouble these waters, and the first one in is healed. One scientific explanation says that this was a wet-weather pool, which, when the ground water rose sufficiently, received water from an underground channel. In time people presumably attached healing properties to its seasonal water.

Jesus directs our attention to one particular man, "an invalid for thirty-eight years." He has divine knowledge of the man's condition, a theme found in other places in this Gospel.

2.4.1.2. Healing of the Lame Man (5:6–9b). This man is unable to walk, and Jesus asks if him wants to be whole (*hygies*). The paralyzed man does not provide a simple yes or no. Rather, he focuses on his plight and on the traditional healing process. Jesus seems to ignore his rather pessimistic reply—one can imagine how beaten down one would feel after thirty-eight years of lameness. He commands him to arise, take his pallet, and walk. "At once" the man becomes whole, takes up his pallet, and walks.

The word "whole" (*hygies*) occurs fourteen times in the New Testament, half of them in John's Gospel (six of them in 5:4–15). The standard New Testament lexicon says that this word in John (and elsewhere) refers to physical restoration and contrasts to sickness. However, on closer examination, the word takes on a more comprehensive meaning. "Wholeness"

The Pool of Bethesda was north of the temple. It was the site where Jesus healed the man who had been lame for thirty-eight years. Shown here (on the left) are ruins of the pool and, below, how the pool might have looked as depicted in the model of Jerusalem at the Holyland Hotel. John described the pool as being "surrounded by five covered colonnades."

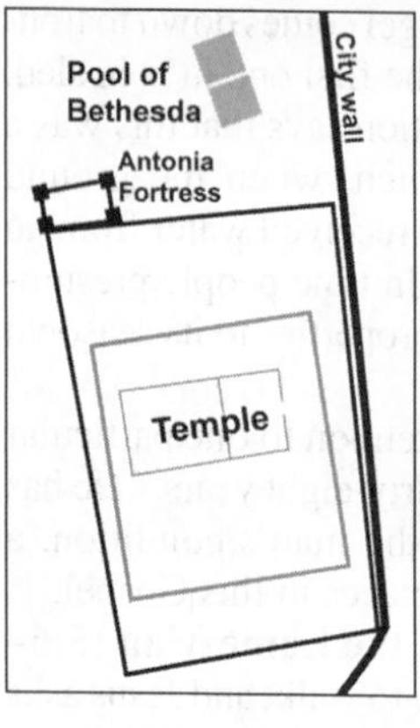

in the first century referred to the total welfare of the person, certainly to one's standing before God (cf. its use in Luke 5:31, a story unit that in Matt. 9:14–17 and Mark 2:18–22 bear out the connection between wholeness and righteousness). And the opposite was also true—to be sick was to be not whole, to be without God.

In John, therefore, this sign, with the rest of them, points to Jesus' death and resurrection, which provide for a person's wholeness. This is certainly brought out later in 5:14, where Jesus commands the man not to live a life of sin anymore ("Stop sinning or something worse may happen to you"). On the level of the healed man, however, the word probably means only health/healing (cf. v. 15). The wholeness that this man experiences manifests the true purpose of the Sabbath as it is fulfilled in Jesus—the rest of God. This miracle is indeed a true Sabbath work—bringing wholeness of life.

2.4.1.3. The Challenge to Jesus' Work (5:9c–18). The reader for the first time learns that this sign has occurred on the Sabbath. This prepares us for the forthcoming dialogue, in which the charges of Sabbath-breaking surface. Jesus apparently leaves quickly (v. 13), and the leaders of Judaism see this man carrying his pallet, an activity forbidden to do on the Sabbath. When questioned, the man passes on responsibility to the one who healed him. The ignorance of this man contrasts with the knowledge of Jesus in verse 6.

Jesus' contact with the man and his exhortation not to sin (v. 14) arms the healed man with the information the Jewish leaders seek (v. 14). This all the more incites them to persecute Jesus. Hence, we have the first major confrontation in the Gospel. Quickly, however, one charge of Sabbath-breaking becomes two, with the accusation of blasphemy from verse 18, where Jesus introduces the nature of the miracle he has worked on the Sabbath.

The Sabbath was one of the most identifying traits of the people of the Old Testament and Judaism. It ordered and structured the lives of a covenant people under God. Judaism added a number of regulations to the Old Testament guidelines. Carrying a pallet, as the healed man was doing here, was one of these, for in so doing, he was working on the Sabbath. Breaking the Sabbath in this manner was punishable by expulsion from the synagogue and even death. Such expulsion meant that the person had no life in the world to come (cf. *Keriothoth* 1).

In Jesus' time, Sabbath laws had become stringent, perhaps becoming less so when John wrote. Nonetheless, the Sabbath most identified Judaism; only circumcision seems to have been as important. Several requirements did override Sabbath observance, such as temple rituals, military action, saving a life, and circumcision (cf. *Mekilta* Shab. 1). Jesus appeals to this by using a rabbinic method of argumentation. If circumcision can be performed on the Sabbath, and this does great good, how much more then will the healing of a man do good (Jesus appeals to this in 7:23). Yet, the Jews lay claim to the work of carrying the pallet as breaking the Sabbath.

Judaism commonly believed that God continued working after he finished creating. After all, he continued as Lord over the world; else how would it keep on existing, even on the Sabbath? Moreover, people were born on the Sabbath, and only God gives life. These thoughts underlie verse 17—the Jews do not deny that God works on the Sabbath, but they do insist that Jesus has broken it and blasphemed. Clearly, Jesus claims to be divine as the Father is, which brings the charge: "[He] mak[es] himself equal with God" (v. 18).

2.4.1.4. The Gift of Life: Jesus' and the Father's Work (5:19–30). John has structured these verses in a tightly woven manner, elaborating on Jesus' statement in verse 17 about his doing the work of his Father and about the nature of that work. In making that man whole, Jesus is bringing eternal life, the Father's work. No longer is the Sabbath a special twenty-four-hour day; it is the time of God's salvation through Jesus. God calls us all to that rest through Jesus' work on the cross. This structure is in the form of repetitive statements—each building to a point and, then turning at the center point, working back in chiastic fashion to the starting point:

A vv. 19–20
  B vv. 21–23
    C v. 24
    C' v. 25
  B' vv. 26–29
A' v. 30

Some observations are in order. (1) Two comparative sentences ("as . . . so") in B (v. 21) and B' (v. 26) attribute divinity to Jesus in that he, like the Father, has unoriginated life in himself. (2) The center units (C and C') are each in the form of an "*amen amen*" saying (NIV, "I tell you the truth"), focusing on the ability of Jesus to give this life to those who believe in him. This new life is also resurrection life.

(3) The first half (vv. 19–24) contains verbs that are in the present tense, the second half (vv. 25–30), verbs in the future tense; this has led scholars to different conclusions about the nature of eschatology in this Gospel. (*Eschatology* means a study of or theory of the end times.) One scholar believes that John places all of his emphasis on the present time, as with the present tense in verses 19–24. According to him, the end fully arrives when people are born again. Furthermore, John does not say anything about the future end times. Verses 19–30, however, support the conclusion that John does teach both aspects of the end times. This information helps us to see that, in the reception of eternal life, the future has broken in and that the new birth is of the same nature as the resurrection ("he has crossed over from death to life," v. 24)—a fact that Paul also affirms. The content of chapter 5, especially this emphasis on life and resurrection, parallels the raising of Lazarus (ch. 11) and the themes of chapter 9.

New birth is a cause for celebration. It is a powerful experience, delivering believers from

sin and death, just like the lame man's condition—sin long held him in weary bondage. Eternal life, the new birth, needs emphasizing since it is the source of the Christian's power over sin and the way to take on a new nature and the character of God, the fruit of the Spirit; many of the gifts of the Spirit come by way of Spirit-baptism, especially power for witnessing. One flows out of the other in complementary fashion.

(4) Jesus' divine authority is not only indicated by his ability to give life but in his role as judge (vv. 26–30). Judgment dominates this part and other places in the Gospel. It is Jesus' divine prerogative. The title "Son of Man" is connected with this ability to judge.

2.4.1.5. Witnesses to Jesus (5:31–47). This section continues Jesus' monologue begun in verse 16 and returns to substantiate Jesus' claim to divinity and his right to show the true intention of the Sabbath. The key word here is "testify" (*martyreo*, 11 times in this section). "Testify" takes on legal connotations and is a theme found elsewhere in the Gospel (because of its purpose). John writes, in part, to demonstrate that Jesus is divine and that he has the right to transform holy days and institutions and to provide salvation to all who believe. Here, numerous witnesses come forth to affirm this right: John the Baptist (vv. 31–36), Scripture (v. 46), the works of the Father (v. 36), and the Father himself (v. 37). The works of the Father specifically connect the testimony theme to the healing of the lame man.

The chapter concludes by pointing out the unbelief of these leaders (v. 38). Again, they do not receive God because they do not receive Jesus, who has come in his Father's name. But it is the very Scriptures in which they claim to find life that accuse them (v. 39). If they were to believe them, they would believe Jesus, for they testify of him. Moses, the author of the Torah (the Pentateuch), stands as their accuser since he wrote of Jesus (vv. 45–47). Deuteronomy 31:26–27 may be in mind here: Moses is commanded to place the Book of the Law beside the ark as a witness against Israel's rebellion, implying that these leaders now participate in it (cf. John 7:19). If these leaders do not believe Moses' words, how can they believe Jesus' words? As in chapter 8:31ff., they do not have the Word (*logos*) abiding in them (5:38). Faith is only faith when its object is Jesus, and love for God through Jesus is faith at work (v. 42).

2.4.2. The Feeding of the Five Thousand and Consequences (6:1–71). Interpreters have noted that the geography does not flow smoothly from chapters 5 to 6, for the scene jumps from Jerusalem to the Sea of Galilee. Chapter 6 appears to flow more smoothly after chapter 4, where Jesus is already in Galilee. Displacement theories abound here. But once we consider that John does not so much write in chronological fashion as he does in sermonic order, the difficulty becomes less problematic.

John 6 may contain two signs, the feeding of the five thousand and Jesus' walking on water. Nonetheless, the theme of the chapter focuses on feeding the multitude and the eating of Jesus' body. This chapter has much in common with the other canonical Gospels (Matt. 14:13–21; Mark 6:32–44; Luke 9:10–17). The multiplication of loaves is the only public miracle recorded in all four Gospels.

Discussion arises here over whether John is sacramental. That is, does John suggest anywhere that he believes that the Lord's Supper/Eucharist or water baptism is the means of conveying in and of itself God's grace? Or does he emphasize faith and the Spirit apart from any such physical means?

It is also common to see behind this chapter the influence (content and form) of an extended midrash (i.e., Jewish method of interpreting Scripture) or a homily in narrative form (called Haggadah) on the concept of manna. Whatever the case, John does connect some elements of the Lord's Supper to the feeding of the multitude and to the Old Testament concept of manna.

2.4.2.1. Feeding of the Five Thousand (6:1–15). "Some time after this" (v. 1) moves the reader from the Sabbath theme to the Passover (v. 4) and to the next miracle; this phrase is common in John to indicate such shifts. This observation helps resolve the geographical difficulty of chapters 5 to 6.

The Passover, a feast of Judaism, has not arrived yet, though it is close. Since it is one of the three pilgrimage festivals, apparently the people are on their way to Jerusalem. Spring has arrived, and the grass is thick (v. 10) and green (cf. Mark 6:39) around the Sea of Galilee, probably on the east side near Beth-

saida (Mark 6:10?). The NIV renders this rather difficult geographical location as "the Sea of Galilee (that is, the Sea of Tiberias)" (v. 1). Tiberias (a Roman name) is the better known name for this lake in John's day.

Certain messianic expectations hang in the air (see v. 15). After performing the miracle of the multiplication of bread and fish (cf. 6:2), an expected sign of the Messiah (v. 14), the crowds wish to proclaim him king. But Jesus rejects their efforts because he is not the Messiah of their traditional expectations—he is radically different, and the kind of kingdom he brings requires a new way of salvation. What he does, therefore, transforms Passover because it is inadequate.

Some modern interpretations contend that the Jewish people reject Jesus and his kingdom and that he thus inaugurates the church age. However, this text tells us quite the opposite—Jesus rejects the Jews because their idea of kingdom is different (i.e., ethnic and political) from his (i.e., spiritual).

John, the author, connects this feeding miracle with the Passover, the walking on the water, and the manna story. The Old Testament figure of Moses and his activity occur in various ways in this chapter—such as Jesus' sitting on the mountain (v. 3), the people's following him (v. 2), and the expectation of the end-times Prophet (v. 14). At Passover services, Scriptures containing accounts of the manna were commonly used. Jesus' sitting on the mountain depicts a Moses-like situation of the great lawgiver teaching the people. The people follow Jesus as Israel followed Moses (v. 2). The mention of "the Prophet" (v. 14) echoes Deuteronomy 18:15, which calls for a prophet greater than Moses (a clearly messianic passage).

Also at Passover, 1 Kings 4:42–44 was read—that Elisha multiplied miraculously barley bread for one hundred men. All these Old Testament texts came together, as threads in cloth, throughout the Passover service and were understood with messianic overtones. John picks up on them and applies them to Jesus, who fulfills and transcends these expectations. In the multiplication of loaves and fish, then, Jesus is this greater than Moses, about whom the Scripture speaks. In fact, he is God, who supplies a greater food than Moses did—an abundant supply, enough to feed all the people and have twelve baskets left over! The manna he gives far exceeds the traditional Passover food. This is "the bread of life," which came down from above.

Furthermore, Jesus as the great divine Shepherd of Psalm 23 leads his new sheep in green pastures (cf. Mark 6:39), feeding and caring for them. The miracle happens when Jesus distributes the food to the people (note that the disciples do not touch the food in John's Gospel until they pick up the leftovers), whereas in the other three Gospels, Jesus hands the bread to his disciples. John records this account in this way to feature Jesus' divinity and authority in multiplying the food. The role the people serve here should be taken in a typological way because these people do not truly believe in Jesus. John intends to show that Jesus, the bread of heaven, has come to bring eternal life to all who receive him by faith. This is probably done for the sake of the disciples, who are on their way to receiving eternal life (see ch. 20). The feeding of the five thousand, then, focuses on this truth of Jesus.

John singles out two disciples by name here, Philip and Andrew. Verses 5–7 are devoted to the dialogue between Jesus and Philip. In his initial question, Jesus wants to test him by asking where they can get food for all these people. John adds a note about Jesus' previous determination to do what he is about to do, in order to help clarify why Jesus speaks to Philip. Philip's reply shows that he is looking to a natural and therefore impossible solution: "Eight months' wages would not buy enough bread for each one to have a bite" (v. 7). Philip may have had in mind the time in 4:7, when they went into a Samaritan town to buy food for Jesus and themselves; but this crowd is far too numerous to be cared for in a similar manner. In 1:43–45, Jesus called Philip to be a follower; Philip in turn told Nathanael that he had found the one about whom Moses wrote. Put this information together and we see that Philip had not yet realized the true nature of Jesus.

Without being addressed, Andrew, listening, manifests the same level of understanding as Philip. He differs in that he points out a boy with the five barley loaves and two small fish, allowing Jesus to use such a small thing, naturally speaking, to do his sign, and right in front of the disciples' own admission of an impossibility! Barley bread was less desirable than that made from wheat, and these were "small" fish. Such details heighten the miracle.

But what of the Lord's Supper in this? Can we find clues? Yes, and these conclusions are supported by the fact that in the normal place where the Supper occurs (the Upper Room scene, called by the Synoptics "the Passover"), John does not call that meal a Passover (cf. comments on ch. 13). John, in other words, attaches the Lord's Supper to a different situation in the life of Jesus—the miracle of feeding the five thousand (see also comments on ch. 20).

This paragraph concludes (v. 15) by noting that Jesus knows that the people are coming to make him their king by force. But he rejects their intentions and goes away to a mountain. They see his signs as portents of their Messiah, come to free them from foreign tyranny and to reestablish their kingdom on earth. His kingdom is not like that. They do not understand the nature of his signs. John 6:15 goes against the dispensational teaching that the Jewish people's rejection of Jesus causes God to establish a parenthetical and temporary era called the church age.

2.4.2.2. Jesus Walks on the Water (6:16–24). This next section details Jesus' walking on water. Should we consider it another sign? Surely, it is a miracle, but John does not call it a "sign" as he does the multiplication of food (v. 14). Rather, this walking on water further explains the previous miracle. "When evening came" (v. 16) intends us to understand this miracle in conjunction with the earlier one. Another element also connects them. In verses 22–24, the crowds seek Jesus the next day, returning to the place where he multiplied the food. What, then, is the relationship between these two miracles, the first of which is the leading one?

Jesus' walking on water substantiates further that he is indeed the divine Son of God, who has come from heaven with eternal life. Already in John, Jesus, like the Father, is said to have the ability to give life unoriginated, which only God can do (5:21). Chapter 1 has asked and answered who Jesus is. With each miracle and teaching block, John elaborates on Jesus' identity.

Two things in this section evidence Jesus' divinity. (1) The interpretation and recording of Jesus walking on the water (6:17–22) is done in a Jewish way, derived from one of Hillel's seven interpretative rules. Simply put, this principle says that whatever can be said of A can be equally said of B. In the Old Testament, Yahweh (NIV, "LORD") walked upon the water (see Job 9:8; Ps. 77:19). In *Exodus Rabbah*, a commentary on the book of Exodus, the same belief is extended. Thus, since Jesus walks on the sea, he is divine, too. In the environment of the Judaism of John's day, Jesus' walking on water would be connected immediately with Yahweh of their Scriptures. Further, this walking on water motif fits in with Passover times, since Judaism made such associations in their liturgy.

(2) In verses 19–20, when the fearing disciples cry out while Jesus is on the water, he replies, "It is I" (*ego eimi*; lit., "I am"; see comments on 4:26). On a surface level, *ego eimi* simply answers the disciples' unspoken inquiry of identification arising from their fear. On another level, however, it presents his divine name, reassuring them that he has control over the storm and sea. The most likely source of this understanding can be found in such places as Isaiah 43:10, 25. Though the "I am that I am" in Exodus 3:14 may play some part behind this name, it is the "I am" in Isaiah that precisely parallels the form of the name. This is one of God's names that brings assurance, promise, and revelation to his oppressed people (the background in Isaiah pertains to the scattered people of God needing salvation). The annunciation of this name in John 6:20 is the high point of this section.

The disciples leave the east shore at dark to cross over to the northwest side of Galilee (v. 17). As often happens, the wind whips up suddenly and turns the water into a dangerous situation. This sea's surface is about 686 feet below sea level. Winds can rush down the Arbel pass from the Mediterranean to churn its waters, almost like blowing vertically down onto the sea through a large pipe—causing calm to turn quickly into violent waters. The disciples find themselves on the sea when it becomes rough, suggesting that Jesus is further working on their faith, manifesting the same need displayed earlier by Philip and Andrew in the multiplying of food. Faith is often tested after God provides an outstanding miracle. Disciples of every era can be strengthened in the midst of a trial by reading this story and letting the Spirit speak through it.

Verses 22–24 reintroduce the eating of bread and transition to the next section, in which Jesus explains the multiplication of food.

2.4.2.3. Elaboration on Jesus the Bread of Life (6:25–59). The reader leaves familiar Synoptic-like material and steps back into John's uniqueness. This section explains the multiplication of food in verses 1–15. The people's question on how Jesus got there (v. 25) opens the way for his "*amen amen*" response in verse 26. John presents Jesus as the ultimate manna, the bread from heaven. But the manner of presentation leaves open the possibility of misunderstanding. Using both literal and figurative language, John explains what this new manna is, where it comes from, and how to apply it. Unless God gives revelation and the ability to understand, however, ignorance surfaces and the new manna becomes a stumbling block to faith.

In verse 26, Jesus pierces the people's true intention for following him: They seek him for reasons that perish instead of for reasons that last forever and that come from the Son of Man. These reasons are cast in the form of food. The food that lasts forever is Jesus, who brings eternal life. He is that superlative food, the manna of the end times. Work for this food, he says.

In response, the people ask, "What must we do to do the works God requires?" (v. 28). This question allows Jesus to define what "works" means. His response may address the concept of works in Judaism. There, faith is a virtue worthy of reward (this is not to say that Judaism is exclusively a religion of works—this is simply not the case). "Works" for Jesus refers to belief in Jesus, the One whom God has sent. But the people still do not understand the true nature of faith. They ask for a sign on which to base their faith. Jesus intends faith not to be placed on any signs, authenticating one's authority, but to be placed on a person, himself, God's Son. Their series of questions (v. 30) refers to Moses' giving of manna, which they call "bread from heaven" (v. 31).

Thereupon, Jesus plainly says that he is the true bread from heaven. Further, it was not Moses who gave them bread from heaven, but it was God. The true bread is Jesus, who has come down from heaven. It is he who gives eternal life.

Jesus now moves freely back and forth from one level of meaning to the other, mixing both without precise definition, letting spirituality (or its lack) do its work. Ultimately, bread refers to Jesus' work on the cross, and eating and drinking is believing, while the absence of hunger and thirst are the satisfaction that eternal life brings. This implies that God has created an innate desire in people for eternal life and that there exists in the unregenerate a lack of wholeness, a longing for completeness, a search to fill a void in the heart.

Originally, manna in Exodus was God's supernatural way of taking care of his people in the desert. In time, however, manna became spiritualized. For example, Psalm 78:24 reads that God gave his people "the grain of heaven"; 105:40 calls it "the bread of heaven." Later, Josephus noted that manna still came down in his day (*Ant.* 111.1.7). In a slightly different vein, Rabbi R. Eleazar said that the manna would come again in the age to come, and others taught that Elijah would bring manna. It was one of three things that the study of Torah would restore. The New Testament manifests similar understandings of the manna tradition. Paul in 1 Corinthians 10:3 writes that "they [our forefathers] all ate the same spiritual food." Revelation 2:17 likewise mentions that Jesus will give the hidden manna to the one who overcomes.

At verse 36, the mood shifts—Jesus announces their status: "You have seen me and still you do not believe." "Have seen" signifies a past event followed by its result; "do not believe" denotes an ongoing condition.

John then introduces the reader again to the sovereignty of God, a consistent theme in this Gospel—the work of God in drawing people to Jesus (v. 37). Jesus did the will and work of his Father by coming to earth. This work will bear the results of eternal life until the last day, the day of the resurrection. Until then, Jesus will keep all who believe him. The reference to the last day, the day of resurrection, repeats the theme in chapter 5 and manifests an element of future eschatology in the Gospel. Now, it is Jesus who resurrects the believer (vv. 39–40).

God's sovereignty continues into verse 40. The grumbling of the Jewish leaders in verses

41–43 mirrors the Israelites in the Exodus as they complained about the everyday and monotonous supply of quail and manna. This was a sign of unbelief, showing up now in Jesus' contemporaries. But Jesus explains that no one can come to him "unless the Father . . . draws him" (v. 44). It is not so much that God predestines apart from a conscious decision but that it is the new creation, which is a revelatory experience, that matters. To understand God's will requires this revelation from heaven, which comes from God by way of the new birth.

In verses 47–59, the language and the lack of spiritual discernment begin to distinguish among those present. Jesus speaks on two levels here. On one level, the lack of spiritual discernment shows itself in the people's taking the meanings of flesh, blood, and eating literally, and therefore harshly. On the other level, Jesus emphasizes the necessity and exclusivity of believing in him. Here, the literal meaning slips away into the mists of the mysterious heavenly language of faith, understood only by those who are born from above by faith in the Son of God.

2.4.2.4. Many Disciples Depart (6:60–71). Until now, the larger crowd of people have become disciples of one sort or another. They are still the same crowd, for they are murmuring about the harshness of Jesus' teaching. But many of them now stop following Jesus. Jesus then draws their attention to an even more difficult event—his ascension. This categorizes people into two states, flesh and spirit. "Flesh" refers to those who have not been born of the Spirit and are left in their earthbound condition, in their sin, not capable of knowing God; "spirit" consists of those who have eternal life, having been born of the Spirit from above. In the end, only the Twelve remain, for only they know that Jesus has the words of life, and they confess him to be the Holy One of God.

The sovereignty and foreknowledge of God come out again strongly (v. 64). From among the larger group, Jesus has chosen those who will follow him. But even among the Twelve, the chosen ones, there is one who has a devil (vv. 70–71). All this Jesus knows. He is in control, even over those, such as Judas, who choose not to follow the election of Jesus to eternal life. And the later events of Jesus' passion do not signify anything different. Jesus is in control; evil is on the run; he will rule triumphantly, even in death—for he has life.

What can we now say about the Lord's Supper? Is it here? Is it sacramental? To answer the last first, the way Jesus has moved to the upper level of meaning in the words "flesh," "blood," "body," etc., with his meaning of faith, suggests that he took a "spiritual" view, not a sacramental view, of the elements of the Lord's Supper. By looking at most of the words used in the Lord's Supper in the various places in Scripture, we can see how John relates to them. The chart at the bottom of the page shows a remarkable display of similarity.

The words of the blessing the bread in John in 6:11 and 23 are similar to the words of blessing in other places: "Jesus then took the loaves, gave thanks, and distributed to those who were seated as much as they wanted," and "where the people had eaten the bread after the Lord had given thanks."

	Matthew	Mark	Luke	1 Corinthians	John
took	26:26–27	14:22	22:17, 19	11:23, 25	6:11
bread	26:26	14:22	22:19	10:16–17; 11:23	6:51ff.
gave thanks	26:27	14:22–23	22:17	11:24	6:11
blessed	26:26	14:22		10:16	
eat	26:26	14:22	22:15	11:26	6:23, 51ff.
drink	26:27, 29	14:23, 25	22:18	11:25–26	6:53ff.
blood	26:28	14:24	22:20	11:25; 10:16	6:53ff.
body	26:26	14:22	22:19	11:24; 10:16–17	
flesh					6:53–56

Furthermore, in every case, words in a literal and figurative manner cluster around one concept. As we have seen, it is typical of John to work on two levels of meaning. For instance, "body ("flesh" in John)," "bread," and "eat" pertain to the same thing. It is Jesus' death, that is, his body, that is given. To eat his body means to believe in his substitutionary death/atonement. To eat the bread is the believer's celebration of receiving forgiveness of sins and of the presence of the Spirit. In the same way, the "drink," "blood," and "cup" are united. But with these words surrounding the blood, covenant language emerges, although "covenant" occurs only in Luke. The Lord's Supper, then, celebrates the new covenant, the one based on the bread of heaven, Jesus; the basis of the new covenant supersedes that of the old. In Jesus, the Passover has been transformed and nullified; whoever eats this new manna (bread) will never die!

At least one word differs in John from the other accounts. It is "flesh" (for "body"). This synonym, though, does not detract from identifying the Lord's Supper in John 6; it only shows some variety in the expressions.

In conclusion, the Lord's Supper supersedes the Passover and thus displays discontinuity, even though the latter has provided the ideas and language for the former. Christianity differs from Judaism. It is the heir of the old, as seen in its transformation of and continuity with the restoration of the true and better heavenly manna. But the Lord's Supper is not sacramental. It is not the means of grace that saves. The meal celebrates what does save—the atoning death of Jesus. Eternal life, flowing from the atoning work of Jesus, comes by the Spirit, the creative power of God. Further, Jesus works on two levels. On the one, he is the giver of the heavenly manna—he, as God, multiplies and gives the bread. On the other, he is the gift, the heavenly manna itself that brings life. As the book of Hebrews puts it, he is both priest and sacrifice.

2.4.3. Jesus and Tabernacles (7:1–12:50). We now come to one of the longest sections in this part of the Gospel, focusing on the Feast of Tabernacles. We will use this word because it has lodged itself in the sacred history of translations. However, this word can be misunderstood. "Tabernacle" may conjure up in our minds a picture of a large ornate church building. The Greek word for "tabernacles" occurs only in John 7:2. The corresponding Hebrew word means "booth" and refers to something like the old brush arbor of camp meeting days. On this feast, the Jews temporarily (seven days) built booths of branches and palm fronds and lived in them as they commemorated the time of their desert wandering after the Exodus (Lev. 23:42–43).

Sacrifices were offered each day of the Feast of Tabernacles (Num. 29:12–39; Ezek. 45:25 emphasizes a sin offering). It was a time of great celebration (Deut. 16:13–17). An eighth day was added, during which they held a special assembly (Num. 29:35). The contents and themes of Zechariah 14 arise from the Feast of Tabernacles. There, God will save his people from their enemies, after which the survivors of the nations will come to Jerusalem to worship the Lord and celebrate Tabernacles. Even in Zechariah, this is the most important end-times festival.

In Jesus' and John's day, the Feast of Tabernacles was one of several fall festivals (observed on the seventh month, September/October). By the first century, it was the most important festival—more important than Rosh Hashshanah (the new year), Yom Kippur (Day of Atonement), and even Passover. During this time, the people believed that Satan would accuse them of their sins, and they expected their enemies, such as the Romans in the first century, to assail them. But God would come to their defense. Abraham, their patriarch, who was considered full of good works, would also intercede mightily for his children and extend merits from his abundant supply of works to them on their behalf.

In the religious environment of God's covenant care and mercy, merits could be transferred from one person to another because of a certain social/cultural view. People within the covenant group could either benefit from or suffer from the actions of others. Benefits would move around—usually forward from Abraham to his descendants—through a religious system based on a bookkeeping process (cf. Rom. 4, where Paul uses the word "credited" to express the fact that Christ's death in our place allowed his benefits [i.e., righteousness] to be transferred to us). This principle of the transference of merits in Judaism was especially active during the Feast of

Tabernacles. This is precisely the function of Jesus' activity here during Tabernacles. He came to replace that aspect of Tabernacles in the religious system of Judaism, fulfilling all of its end-time expectations of deliverance and salvation.

Great messianic expectations and hopes arose from the liturgy, ritual, Scripture readings, and homilies of the celebrations of the Feast of Tabernacles. Especially important were the themes of light and water. The discarded underwear of priests was soaked in oil, wrapped around tall posts in the temple courtyard, and lit; they brightened up all Jerusalem. Daily, the priests led a procession from the pool of Siloam, carrying water to pour out on the altar, along with wine. The water rushed down funnels to the ground, eastward towards the Kidron Valley. This symbolized the coming of the Spirit and the arrival of the Messiah, when God would defeat his enemies and restore his fortune to Israel. Ezekiel 47:1–12 provided the scriptural background for this visual understanding. Rivers would flow down toward the Arabah (the desert) and on to the Dead Sea, bringing life in their wake. Trees would spring up and fish would thrive in abundant numbers.

For some time, the Feast of Tabernacles remained an important festival for Jewish followers of Jesus in the church. The book of Revelation, for example, bases much of its imagery and themes on this feast. Believers celebrated the victory over sin that Jesus brought and anticipated eternal Tabernacles. Christians celebrated the death and resurrection of Jesus through the Lord's Supper and the Feast of Tabernacles.

John 7:1–10:21 belongs together under Tabernacles, though only chapters 7–8 deal specifically with this feast. Yet no miraculous sign occurs in these two chapters; the sign for Tabernacles is the healing of the blind man in chapter 9—his restored sight is the arrival of light (a theme in Tabernacles). Also, the good shepherd allegory of 10:1–20 flows out of the discussion over the healing of the blind man of chapter 9. In other words, this section in John contains a sign within an extended narrative that explains the significance of Jesus and Tabernacles. Jesus fulfills and transforms the end-time expectations of this feast, bringing God's salvation to the world. He gives the water of life (i.e., the Spirit) and the revelation of God (light).

In spite of a seeming lack of unity of chapters 7–8, a close examination discovers various literary details holding them together demonstrating a carefully crafted unit. For example, the content focuses on Tabernacles; "hid" and "secret" (NIV) in 7:4, 10; and 8:59 (the same Greek word, *krupto*, occurs in all three verses) act as brackets to unify the section. Internal literary factors also connect as the narrative proceeds. This is the only place in this Gospel where the figure of Abraham shows up overtly, and he does so in harmony with its message and themes.

2.4.3.1. Jesus at Tabernacles (7:1–13). Verses 1–13 introduce this section, establishing the context with which to understand the relationship between Jesus' work and the Feast of Tabernacles. There is a minor break between verses 9 and 10. Verses 1–9 give the Galilean setting for the Tabernacles' narrative; verses 10–13 contain the Judean setting. Further, "hidden" in verses 4 and 10 and the Jewish leadership's desire to kill Jesus in verses 1 and 11 connect the two minor paragraphs.

"After this" in verse 1 is the typical way that John introduces new material—in this case the new feast and increased debate between Jesus and his opponents. Jesus purposely stays behind in Galilee (which had a friendlier climate for him than Judea) rather than going to the feast in Jerusalem (v. 1), for he knows that the Jewish leaders are seeking to kill him; on their part the Jewish opponents keep watching Jesus to see what he might be up to. They are still seeking him on the charge of blasphemy and Sabbath breaking.

Jesus is deliberate regarding the time when he will turn himself over to them, and this is not the right time (vv. 6–8). Moreover, his messiahship is quite unlike that which the Jews are expecting; this point is important for understanding this paragraph. The hint in this paragraph that these leaders are expecting him to show up suggests that more than the charges of blasphemy and Sabbath breaking are in mind—probably overtones of "Messiah" are intended here.

Verses 3–8 contain the dialogue between Jesus and his brothers. They speak first in verses 3–4, where they exhort Jesus to go to Jerusalem for this feast—the appropriate time for him to go public with his messianic claims, which, they think, should be made public in a bold manner: "Your disciples may see the miracles you do." Implied here is the notion that this is the way one collects followers—to perform signs. They conclude in verse 4 by exhorting him to manifest himself to the *world*.

The way Jesus' brothers speak clearly puts them into a category with unbelievers. Jesus further distinguishes between himself and his brothers. His brothers were last seen in 2:12. We now find out that in chapter 2 they are part of those who believed in Jesus because of the signs he had done in Jerusalem. Jesus did not commit himself to them then and he does not do so now. In these small paragraphs, these brothers play a major role and become Jesus' antagonists, showing up twice (vv. 3ff., 10). Though they relate closely with him biologically as his brothers, they stand with the world (which hates him) in their sin and inability to know spiritual things.

Later in 20:17, Jesus sends his brothers a message about going away to their Father, more than likely encouraging them to believe. They, as part of the "world" (7:4), cannot know him apart from what he will do for them at his hour and apart from faith in him as God's Son, who brings eternal life. This illustrates the fact that people without faith and the regenerative nature do not have spiritual understanding. Regeneration is a revelatory experience. Verse 5, somewhat parenthetical, makes plain that fact and serves as a transition to Jesus' reply in verses 6–8.

Jesus refers again to his "time" (v. 6) and distinguishes between his brothers and himself. They go on to join the world, but he is different and will not join them in this venture. This information about his hour, though, is important for understanding verse 10. Jesus' time (*kairos*) is not yet—*kairos* clearly refers to his death and resurrection, which are not to be connected with this feast. This word emphasizes the quality of the event towards which it points rather than the quantity aspect of time. Verse 6 implies that the time to inaugurate his messianic reign is not at Tabernacles but at Passover. This factor helps to resolve the issue in the next paragraph.

A problem emerges between verses 1–9, where Jesus says that he will not go to Jerusalem, and verses 10–13, where he goes anyway. The NIV resolves this problem by following a reading in some (less reliable) manuscripts and so translates verse 6: "The right time for me has not *yet* come." What Jesus is implying is that his hour of atonement for sins through his death and resurrection will come at Passover season. Clearly, his death is significant in light of Passover, because Jesus is the Lamb of God that takes away the sin of the world.

The verbs that John uses in this entire section add to the difference between Jesus and his brothers. In verse 3, his brothers say to him, "You ought to leave (*metabaino*) here and go to Judea." But Jesus refuses—he will not go up (*anabaino*, v. 8). In verse 10, the brothers go up (*anabaino*), then Jesus goes up (*anabaino*) "secretly," that is, by himself without anyone noticing. These verbs with the same root (*baino*) but different prefixes help to note the separate travel plans of Jesus.

The scene switches to Judea at verse 10. After John notes that Jesus and his brothers travel to Jerusalem separately, he immediately sets forth the different types of people and their responses to Jesus. The Jewish leaders are wondering where he is. On the other hand, various crowds have come to the feast and are disputing about Jesus. One group says that he is good (i.e., that he is the Messiah); the other, that he is leading the people astray. But none of them dare speak publicly for fear of the Jewish leaders. Thus, great conflict between these various groups, and between these groups and Jesus, arises.

2.4.3.2. Jesus' Teaching at the Feast (7:14–24). John places the teaching activity of Jesus in these verses in the temple courts during the middle of the feast, when Jesus finally came to Jerusalem. The section does not focus on the content of his teaching but on his right to teach (vv. 14–24) and on his origins (vv. 25–36). The themes parallel those of chapter 5 more closely than any other portion: healing on the Sabbath, his right to teach such things, and confrontation with the Jewish leaders. Various groups dialogue with Jesus throughout this section.

In the first paragraph (7:14–24) Jesus defends his right to teach. Beginning in verse 15, his teaching draws amazement from the leaders, and they ask, "How does this man get such learning without having studied?" This does not mean that Jesus was ignorant or did not know how to read. All Jewish boys learned to read by studying Scripture. Rather, Jesus had not come through any of the rabbinical schools, the means by which traditions were passed on and where learned teachers, who knew all the possible interpretations and positions of all the ancient rabbis, could give certain responses.

Jesus' response comes in verses 16–19 and focuses on the Jews' inability to comprehend. Certain principles emerge here. (1) Jesus does not speak/work for his own honor—he is a faithful envoy, who has come to honor God his Father, not himself. This person is truthful, then. This being established, the responsibility moves on to the One who sent him. They are accusing God of being deceitful. Therefore, if anyone wants to truly know, the next principle comes into play.

(2) The person who really chooses to do God's will, will truly know whether Jesus speaks on his own or not, since God has sent him.

(3) The Jewish leaders do not keep God's revelation that Moses has given them (i.e., the law). This fact condemns them and explains the source of their amazement (cf. v. 15): They lack the ability to know God. The word for "were amazed" (*thaumazo*) in John implies a lack of true faith. (The last time it occurred was in 5:20, 28, when this same group of leaders confronted Jesus.) Jesus then refers to their desire to kill him (7:19), picking up the same theme as 5:18.

Verse 20 carries their response, "You are demon-possessed." This is the same as crying, "You are crazy," for to be demented was to be demon-possessed in that culture. They deny that they seek to kill him. This charge will come up again and again in chapters 7–8.

Jesus' response in verses 21–24 avoids their denial in the form of a question. He returns to the sign he performed in chapter 5 and responds to it in a Jewish form of logic and interpretation that uses one of Hillel's rules of comparison (we have seen this before in John). The argument works like this: Circumcision took place eight days after birth. Sometimes a boy was born on the Sabbath, in which case he should be circumcised on the Sabbath. Circumcision took precedent over strict Sabbath keeping since it was important. Jesus points out that this ritualistic operation involved only part of the body. If the rabbis permitted that, how much more did he have the right to restore the whole body on the Sabbath?

The rabbis could have responded that they permitted treatment on the Sabbath only for emergencies. In contrast, the man healed in John 5 was no emergency; he had been lame for a long time. Yet it must be remembered that a greater person than Moses is here. Jesus reprimands them for evaluating things superficially, that is, "by mere appearances." In contrast, they should judge rightly. The implication of true discernment comes in John 3:17ff. in light of the meaning of "judge" there (*krino* in Greek). When they come to the light, they have passed out of judgment into life and are able to "see" clearly (i.e., "make a right judgment," 7:24).

2.4.3.3. Jesus as Messiah? (7:25–36). This paragraph contains dialogue between Jesus and a variety of people along with a variety of responses, focusing on the origin of Jesus and the question about his messiahship. Tabernacles was one of the annual pilgrimage festivals, and many visitors and guests have come to Jerusalem for its celebration.

First come some of the Jerusalemites. Their observation comes in the form of a question for John's readers. The Jerusalemites pick up on the identity of Jesus, his continued teaching, and the leaders' tacit approval of Jesus (i.e., their silence and lack of action stand as approval). After all, here is the one they seek to kill, and yet here he is teaching (vv. 25–26). They then must have concluded that he is the Messiah. This assumption, however, did not meet with their approval. These city people appeal to their tradition, a different one, that no one knows where the Messiah comes from. But they know where Jesus came from; how then can he be the Messiah?

We pause to note that chapter 1 contained two different groups seeking the identity of the Messiah. The Pharisees sent representatives to inquire of John (the Baptist) about his ministry, thinking he might be the Messiah. John answered them negatively and, in turn, pointed to Jesus; some of his disciples became followers of Jesus. The chapter concluded by answering who Jesus is. In each of his signs and subsequent discourses, Jesus, the Son of God, manifested himself. He is God's divine envoy, who came to lift judgment from the world and give it eternal life. As such he transforms traditional customs and expectations. Now, in chapter 7, we still have those who do not know who Jesus is. And they reject him here because they know his origins—they are quite earthly. They look for someone more "heavenly," a secret one more worthy to be their Messiah. Some Jewish traditions anticipated a secret Messiah, perhaps similar to the Son of Man thought reflected in the book of Enoch (the apocalyptic Messiah); that idea emerges here in 7:27.

Jesus responds with irony in verses 28–29—a literary device in which an opposite meaning appears alongside the literal, usually with a bit of sarcasm. The Jews' lack of understanding and spiritual condition is similar to that of Nicodemus in chapter 3. These people do know where he is from on one level; but on another, they do *not* know that he is from above. As is typical of unbelievers, they see Jesus as only a man; they cannot see that he is also divine. But this also brings to light their spiritual plight—they do not know the Father either. The only way to know the Father is by knowing who Jesus really is. John 1:18 is clearly in view: "No one has ever seen God, but God the One and Only, who is at the Father's side, has made him known." This role of Jesus and his opponents' ignorance is a significant motif in chapters 7–8.

In a terse way the author describes the futile response of the Jews and God's sovereign activity. "They [presumably the Jerusalemites] tried to seize him, but no one laid a hand on him." We are not told how, only that Jesus avoids their trap. Verse 30b contains a clause noting why they cannot catch him—it is not yet time for him to be arrested or killed. Though worldly circumstances seem powerful and determined, they will not prevail; God will have his way. What risk to put so much on the line in the midst of social and religious opposition, free will, and sinful nature! God's power and wisdom march on. His will is not thwarted. This also explains why in 7:1–13 Jesus said he was not going up to Tabernacles but went anyway. He was not going there to finish his work of salvation; his "time" is Passover, when he will die on the cross as God's Lamb.

Whereas the Jerusalemites do not believe on him because they know where he originated, the crowd in verse 31 do believe on him because of the signs he has performed. This "crowd" more than likely contains a number of different groups; "many" (though not all) of them believe. In contrast to the secret Messiah tradition of the Jerusalemites, the "signs" of the Messiah tradition were popular outside Jerusalem, showing up in the crowds who appear in the city for Tabernacles.

It might be useful to analyze the faith of these people at this point. We have seen earlier that some believed in his signs and that Jesus rejected their faith (2:23). This kind of "faith" will also be a factor later in 8:30–31. This type of faith is inadequate here as well. Note verse 31, where the people believe simply because of his ability to perform signs. This messianic expectation was rooted in the idea of a gifted human, perhaps even a holy man or a prophet. No one knew who might be the Messiah. During this period messianic expectation was extremely high, and many self-proclaimed saviors arose to claim followers for their cause. But Jesus hesitated to refer to himself as Messiah, for he knew he would be misunderstood as just another one of these. He came as a special Messiah—a fully divine and human Messiah, suffering and rising from the dead for the sins of the world. Of his kingdom there will be no end. And his kingdom is a spiritual one, not a political or worldly one. To enter it, human effort plays no part; the only way is for one to be born from above, by the Spirit.

"Believe" (*pisteuo*), an important word in John, bears some analysis. The noun "belief" does not occur in John at all, but the verb "believe" does occur nearly one hundred times. *Pisteuo* appears in a variety of ways with a variety of words to express its meaning. Sometimes it has no object with it (e.g., 6:36). In other instances, it takes the preposition "in" (*en*) (e.g., 3:15). A couple of times, it is followed by "through" (e.g., 1:7). More frequently, "believe" takes no preposition in Greek, but an object in the dative case (this was the typical construction in classical Greek); in English translation it is, "Then they believed the Scripture and the words that Jesus had spoken" (2:22). By far the most frequent accompanying word is the preposition *eis* ("into"; e.g., 2:11; 7:31).

An analysis does not show any significant difference in the meaning of these various uses. These constructions occur with believers, false believers, and unbelievers. For example, in 2:22, the disciples "believed" (no preposition), but in 2:23, people with the wrong kind of faith "believed *in* [*eis*] his name." What the evidence does suggest is that, with this preposition *eis*, a personal, knowing, and submitting relationship with potentiality, reality, and perseverance is present. It is potential because sincere people believed Jesus; but perseverance is also critical, since some did not persevere while others (like the disciples) did, even though they did not understand everything yet.

Furthermore, true faith makes believers one with God, as the Father and the Son are one. And one must believe the same way in the Son as in the Father (cf. 5:24, 53; 12:44; 14:1, 10–11; 16:27). Without believing in Jesus one cannot believe in the Father or even see him. Most often, faith comes later. The first sign preceded faith; also faith comes after the Scripture and Jesus' words (cf. 2:22). For the disciples, faith is based on the resurrection of Jesus and their having "seen" it (ch. 20). But for later generations and others who did not "see" such events, faith comes from their preaching of the gospel, from their testimony. Apostolic witness and word, therefore, become very important (e.g., see Thomas' account in 20:24–29).

But what else can we say about the crowd's faith in 7:31? It seems to be based genuinely but exclusively on miraculous signs. And their conclusion disturbs the Pharisees (v. 32), for the way the crowd's question is stated (v. 31c), they affirm Jesus as Messiah: "When the Christ comes, will he do more miraculous signs than this man?" This question anticipates a negative answer: "No, this man has done the most miraculous signs; he therefore must be the Messiah." It is the number of signs, then, that affects their decision to believe Jesus as the Messiah.

It was typical in the first century to accept a person as a King Messiah merely on the basis of what that person did. This helps explain how early Jewish converts, under differing circumstances, could later have doubts or confusion about such important doctrines as Jesus' divinity and the church. Initial faith is legitimate, but then as time and circumstances evolve, faith comes under pressure. As the church grew and had more and more confrontation with Judaism, such major issues as the divinity of Jesus, salvation, and the nature of the church became more acute.

It is one thing to accept and believe in a person and to accommodate that person into one's current worldview. It is quite another to believe and submit to that person to the extent that one radically alters one's worldview to become a servant and follower. The main issue is following Jesus unconditionally; he is the Lord who commands entire submission. Apparently, these crowds are not yet willing to commit publicly to him, for in verse 32, they are only "whispering" these things about him; that attitude says something about their faith.

Verses 25–36 help us understand a bit more about the situation of the various groups at the Feast of Tabernacles. Apparently the "crowd" includes most of the people mentioned here. Some among them believe; others (the Jerusalemites and the Pharisees), who hear the crowds murmuring, also form parts of the crowds. Either the chief priests or the Pharisees, who enter the narrative at verse 32, send word to the Jewish leaders about what the crowd is doing. Both of these groups, the power brokers of Jerusalem, feel threatened; they therefore send their officers to arrest Jesus before any further damage can be done.

The word "Jews" appears in verse 35. This word may have a different meaning here than earlier in the Gospel. It seems to be applied to the enemies of Jesus. It appears that the Pharisees of verse 32 are part of these Jews, together comprising the leaders who have opposed Jesus all along.

When the temple guards arrive, Jesus answers them, continuing the dialogue with the various parties during the Feast of Tabernacles. In his response, Jesus in a subtle manner (at least to the unbeliever), points toward his hour, although not mentioned in this specific context (vv. 33–34). What he means is that his remaining time on earth is short, his hour is inevitably coming, then he will ascend back to the Father from whom he came. These Jews are not able to go there.

What does "I go to the one who sent me" mean and why does Jesus phrase it this way? These questions can receive an answer at once. Clearly, this statement refers to his ascension, but it also includes more. Like a shorthand sentence, it refers to his whole passion week, suffering, death, resurrection, everything that leads up to and concludes in his return to heaven—this whole series of events that constitutes his end-times enthronement as messianic King, by which he sends the Spirit and creates and commissions the church to bring forgiveness of sins to the world.

Verses 35–36 close the first cycle at the Feast of Tabernacles, during which Jesus' authority and origins have undergone scrutiny and debate. "The Jews" pick up on what he has just said, and they ask among themselves where he will go that they cannot find him. Is he going to the Greeks in the Diaspora (NIV, "scattered among the Greeks"), a word that refers to the scattering of the Jewish people during the capture of northern Israel in 722/721 B.C. and Judah later in 587? Many Jewish people still lived outside the land of Israel, especially in Greek cities. "Greeks" may also refer to the common language spoken in the first century or to a way of life, characterized by the spread of Hellenism by Alexander the Great after 332 B.C.

2.4.3.4. The Gift of the Life-Giving Spirit (7:37–44). Verses 14–36 took place during the middle of the Feast of Tabernacles. When we come to verse 37, however, several days have passed. The scene opens on the last and greatest day of the feast (probably the seventh day). On this day the Torah reading cycle was finished and began again. The Feast of Tabernacles in part meant this: God put away the old and started over again with all things new—he had forgiven their sins. The water pouring looked forward to a bountiful year of harvest brought about through abundant rainfall induced by the water falling to the ground from the altar.

In this paragraph the reader is introduced to one of the great themes of Tabernacles, that of water. On this seventh day, the priests, leading a procession carrying water drawn from the pool of Siloam, circled the altar seven times before pouring it into the altar's funnels, where it flowed downward and eastward toward the valley running towards the Dead Sea. The image that this liturgical setting conjures up in the mind stands behind the description in Revelation 22:1–5, where water flows from the throne of the Lamb and God, bringing healing. Revelation 21–22 refer to the eschatological or eternal Feast of Tabernacles.

Theologically, this scene depicts what the actual rite meant. (For this particular context, I use "eschatological" instead of "end times." The latter puts stress on the last of a number of events in a sequence, such as viewing the number 10 as the last number in the list of 1 to 10, or 1900 introducing the last days of the second millennium after Christ. I intend "eschatological" to refer to a significant change in time and not to the numbering of events, the last of which is the "end times." In this case, the illustration would be: the 1900s introduced a significant change in the lifestyle of the people in America. In all other places, I use "end times" and "eschatological" as synonyms.)

At this time, "Jesus stood and said in a loud voice, 'If anyone is thirsty, let him come to me and drink'" (7:37). Jesus not only cries out loudly for everyone to hear but also intends to draw attention to the transformation of this feast. Jesus will transform Tabernacles expectation into an end-time realization, bringing about God's salvation and giving the Spirit, who in turn will give eternal life. The flow of water spoken about in Old Testament texts and in the liturgy of Judaism symbolized the coming of the Spirit in the day of God's salvation.

The coming of the Spirit here connects to Tabernacles and not to Pentecost (see Acts 2). As one notes the coming of the Spirit in John and in Acts, one can confuse or misunderstand the two events. In particular, Pentecostals and charismatics, believing in two works of the Spirit, have difficulty reconciling them. Pentecostals have played down the coming of the Spirit in regeneration (emphasized in John) while emphasizing (theologically) him in the Spirit-baptism experience (emphasized in Acts). For instance, some emphasize that holiness/sanctification and fruit of the Spirit come from Spirit-baptism. Rather, holiness and fruit are the result of the new nature while Spirit-baptism provides empowerment to witness about the exalted Jesus. Others tend to merge them into one experience. The experience about which John speaks refers to the comprehensive salvation event, which in God's economy includes the coming of the Spirit in Acts 2. The two are connected but distinguishable (see ch. 20 for further comments on this).

It appears as if John's community had a crisis over their identity and salvation, not a lack of empowerment as Luke, the writer of Acts, did in his community. When Jewish believers in Jesus celebrated this Feast of Tabernacles in the late first and early second centuries, they celebrated Jesus' victory over sin and the coming of the Spirit, and they looked forward to that eternal day when they would live with God and Jesus forever, celebrating the new and transformed Tabernacles.

Clearly, water symbolized the Spirit in Judaism and in this Gospel. For instance, in 3:5, both terms occur together, more than likely placing together and merging the meaning in the intended metaphor (water) and the literal referent (Spirit). Water is associated with the first sign, and it is explained further in 3:5 and in the temple references of chapter 4 (both elaborating the first sign). The healing of the lame man in chapter 5 also has water in its background. These usages suggest that John intends his reader to identify in some way water with the Spirit, either his person or work, whether or not he plainly says so. Note that the "Spirit" plays a major role in this Gospel, both in regards to the number of times the titles/names occur and to the significant role he plays in the Gospel's content.

Let us examine the logical flow of this brief paragraph. (1) Verse 37 contains the time setting—the last and great day of the feast and Jesus' statement. This is actually the interpretation of the water-pouring ceremony and its application. (2) Verse 38 connects the interpretation to Scripture and cites it. (3) Verse 39 is John's explanation of the whole event, referring to a later time when Jesus would give the Spirit—who had not been given yet—to those who would believe. This giving comes after Jesus' glorification, thus signifying the culmination of his work on the cross. (4) Verses 40–44 focus on the various reactions to Jesus' statement in verse 37.

These verses contain several major interpretive problems. The most crucial question is: Who is the person out of whom the water flows (v. 38)—the believer or Jesus? Contributing to the problem is the clause "whoever believes in me": Does it go with "if anyone is thirsty, let him come to me and drink"; or with the Scripture reference, as the NIV has it? Further, who is "him" in verse 39? And what does "as" refer to? It seems to leave something out; at least an incomplete thought persists if "whoever believes" does not go with verse 38. What does "drink" in verse 37 mean literally? And what is the meaning of "living water" in verse 38?

The original Greek manuscripts did not contain punctuation, so we cannot appeal to that. Does the order (i.e., syntax) of the elements of these verses contribute anything? "Whoever believes in me" occurs between the "drink" of verse 37 and "as the Scripture has said" of verse 38, coming in the middle of two logical concepts. In general in this Gospel, John uses the phrase "as it is written" *as a conclusion* to support an interpretation (see 6:30; 12:14). This is probably the style we are to see in 7:37–38.

Let us, then, analyze verses 37–39. Verse 37 begins with a conditional clause ("if anyone is thirsty"), which focuses on the need of the human heart. John uses the word "thirsty" in significant ways in his Gospel, usually in a figurative manner, referring to a person's perceived need of eternal life and forgiveness of sins (4:1–15; 6:35). The Samaritan woman and her people "thirsted" for the Messiah's salvation. Eternal life is the only thing that meets this thirst in the heart of every human. Some bury the thirst, like the Jewish leaders. Others ignore it in their quest for power and riches. But all thirst. Only Jesus can meet it through redemption and regeneration by the Spirit.

The "consequence" follows: "Let him come to me and let him drink." This clause contains parallel actions; whether or not they are synonymous remains to be seen. "Coming" and "drinking" are metaphors referring to the human response to the invitation and convey the action towards which "thirst" motivates. "Come" mirrors the action of John's disciples in chapter 1 when they pursued Jesus and went home with him. It is also used of the Samaritans, who trekked out to see the Savior of the world, and the royal official in 4:46–53, whose son lay at the point of death. "Coming" implies that faith is already at work, heading towards the only one who saves. It is not the act of "saving"; rather, it allows the Savior to do his work. "Drinking" completes the act of coming—both expressions are metaphors for "believe."

"Whoever believes" in verse 38 is a Greek participle. Without going into all the technical details, it seems best to see this phrase as summing up the previous metaphors. In essence, what Jesus is saying is this: "Let the thirsty one who believes in me come to me and drink." That is, "whoever believes in me" states literally what the three previous verbs ("is thirsty," "come," "drink") imply (see NIV note on this verse; also cf. above, where we pointed out how important belief in Jesus is in this Gospel). This process, then, is confirmed, in typical Johannine fashion, by the reference to Scripture that follows. The mental picture we have in verses 37–38a is this: Abundant waters flow out of Jesus. Anyone who thirsts may come to him and drink. Such a one simply has to believe; the waters flow out of Jesus.

This interpretation impacts how to take the next element in verse 38b: *Water is not flowing from the believer but from Jesus*. Our Lord is transforming the significance of the water-pouring ceremony at this Feast of Tabernacles, as he fulfills that feast. In verses 37–38a, Jesus refers to himself in the first person ("me," twice). When he gets to the scriptural basis (v. 38b), he refers to himself in the third person ("streams of living water will flow from within him," lit., "out of his stomach"). This quotation summarizes the theological significance implicit in a number of Scriptures.

Which ones? Where does the imagery of flowing streams of water originate? A number of Old Testament texts point in this direction, many of which were used as Scripture readings during Tabernacles. Here are some important ones. Isaiah 12:3: "With joy you will draw water from the wells of salvation." This verse figuratively expresses God's literal promise to restore and save his people. The rabbis identified this water with the Holy Spirit.

Again, in order to express God's deliverance of his people Isaiah writes in 43:19–20: "Now it springs up [as a gushing spring of water]; do you not perceive it? I am making a way in the desert and streams [*potamoi* in the Greek translation; cf. John 7:38] in the wasteland. The wild animals honor me, the jackals and the owls, because I provide water in the desert and streams [*potamoi*] in the wasteland, to give drink to my people, my chosen."

Note also Isaiah 44:3 here. Figurative elements stand side-by-side with the literal, connecting "water" with "Spirit." "For I will pour water on the thirsty land, and streams on the dry ground; I will pour out my Spirit on your offspring, and my blessing on your descendants." (See also 55:1a: "Come, all you who are thirsty, come to the waters"; cf. also 58:11.)

Ezekiel 47:1 is most significant for Tabernacles, "The man brought me back to the entrance of the temple, and I saw water coming out from under the threshold of the temple toward the east (for the temple faced east)." This text, along with the Zechariah references mentioned below, were part of the readings from the Prophets. In the conception of the new Jerusalem in rabbinic interpretations, there will be a spring in the temple from which water gushes (cf. *Meg*. 31a; Tosephta *Sukka* 3:3, 18). The stream of water flowing from the temple becomes larger, deeper, and wider, running towards the Arabah (desert in the south). The water, deep enough to swim in, brings life to the Dead Sea.

What is of further importance here is that this water comes out of the new temple, all of which is situated during the eschatological Feast of Tabernacles. In similar fashion, Joel 3:18b speaks of this salvation in figurative terms, "A fountain will flow out of the LORD's house and will water the valley of acacias" (note also 2:28, "I will pour out my Spirit on all people"). Likewise, the day of salvation (i.e., in terms of deliverance and judgment) in the context of Tabernacles is portrayed in Zechariah 13:1, "On that day a fountain will be opened to the house of David and the inhabitants of Jerusalem, to cleanse them from sin and impurity." And 14:8 reads, "On that day living water will flow out from Jerusalem, half to the eastern sea and half to the western sea, in summer and in winter."

We conclude, therefore, that the Old Testament portrays God as the source of water in these promissory salvation contexts, thus supporting the interpretation that John is focusing here on Jesus the source of eternal life. This interpretation then brings to light a common theme in this Gospel, that Jesus as deity performs the same function as Yahweh (God) in the Old Testament—he gives life.

These words and imagery are not only picked up in John's Gospel, they appear also in Revelation 21–22, the conclusion of all things in the context of the great Feast of Tabernacles. Note, for example, 21:6: "To him who is thirsty I will give to drink without cost [cf. Isa. 55:1] from the spring of the water of life"; Revelation 22:17: "Whoever is thirsty, let him come; and whoever wishes, let him take the free [Isa. 55] gift of the water of life." Further, the river flowing between the fruit trees (Rev. 22:1–3) figuratively is this river of living water about which John 7:37–39 speaks.

"*Living* water" in verse 38 bears some comment. "Water" here is clearly a metaphor for "Spirit"; "living/life" is what the Spirit brings to sinners who come to Jesus with faith. The word "rivers" refers to the abundant life that the Spirit brings. The Scriptures noted above speak of the work of the Spirit in salvation, often in terms of water. In dry climates (as in Palestine), the refreshing springs and periodic rainfalls are apt figures of speech for God's work in producing godly natures and actions in the spiritually barren lives of people.

Verse 39 explains Jesus' words in verses 37–38. The rivers of living water clearly refer to the Spirit, although he has not been given yet. His coming is connected to Jesus' glorification, to his hour that specifically arrives during his passion (see 17:1). This verse substantiates the interpretation given above, that "believers" receive—not give—the Spirit. It is the Father and Jesus who give the Spirit (cf. chs. 14–16). Note also John 3:34, which states that "God gives the Spirit without limit" (a comment parallel with "streams of living water").

We can note here also a comparison with Jacob's well in 4:6, 11. The water of that well is surpassed by the living water that Jesus gives, for that water satisfies believers eternally (4:13–14). To follow the analogy, believers become the "spring" into which Jesus puts water. Here in chapter 7, however, Jesus as the altar pours out water on the ground. The water gushes towards the Dead Sea, bringing life to everything in its wake. John 7:37 anticipates 19:34 both in the reference to the hour of his glory and in the pouring out of the blood *and water* from Jesus' side. Coming thus from the cross, Jesus' atoning death provides the basis for the giving of the Spirit in 20:22, where Jesus breathes on his disciples.

Finally, when John says that "the Spirit had not been given [lit., was not yet]," he means that Jesus has not yet experienced his atoning death and has not yet ascended, for it is he who gives the Spirit. John clearly tells us that Jesus must go to the Father before the Spirit will come (16:7). When he ascends, he will send the Spirit.

Pentecostals have had a tendency to misread John's emphasis here. His language here sounds similar to Lucan references to the baptism of the Spirit. Luke's expressions "full of the Spirit" and "baptism of the Spirit" have been interpreted as the additional gift of the Spirit that "finishes off" salvation, providing more of the Spirit in some way. The analogy used by Pentecostals has been that of a glass of water. At salvation, "some" of the Spirit is given (i.e., some water is in the drinking glass); but when the Spirit baptizes someone, water overflows the glass. At that time, the believer has the fullness of God.

However, this analogy does not hold up when all the biblical texts are appropriately and contextually considered. John has been read by Pentecostals through the eyes of Luke-Acts. Concepts such as "abundant life" and "streams of living water," significant for John, have been interpreted to mean the baptism of the Spirit. I would suggest that this analogy be modified. "Abundant life" and "streams of living water," expressions indicating "fullness," capture the coming of Jesus and his entire work of redemption/salvation, and they provide the framework for God's work in the world. Out of this (i.e., forgiveness and regeneration as a foundation) flows the baptism of the Spirit. Spirit-baptism is then essentially part of the plan of salvation. This makes Spirit-baptism an empowerment for evangelism in the world and min-

Water rushes to the Dead Sea, bringing a narrow green strip of life to an arid land.

.try in the church, both vitally part of God's 'ork of salvation as he moves his people ›wards their goal—heaven.

This suggestion unites the work of the pirit (regeneration, Spirit-baptism, and sanc- fication) in a way that the earlier model does ɔt. This suggestion allows for both unity in ıe work of the Spirit and yet biblical distinc- ons. Furthermore, it allows salvation, espe- ially Spirit theology, to be Christ-centered. ›hn, in concert with all other New Testament 'riters, is especially Christ-centered.

Jesus has cried in a loud voice (v. 37) so that number of people have heard him. Verses 0–44 contain various reactions to his words ertaining to the fulfillment of the Feast of abernacles. There are four general reactions › his words, which tell us about the end-time ope of the various groups of Jewish religious ·aching at this time. One group distinguishes etween *the* Prophet (cf. 1:21) and the Mes- ah; the "surely" of verse 40 informs us that ıey are convinced that Jesus is that Prophet. hey are not about to let him be harmed, pparently. A second group accepts him as *the* Iessiah (v. 41a)—although they do not accept im as the Messiah that he really is. The third roup wants to arrest ("seize") him (v. 44).

A final group holds firmly to the belief that ıe Messiah will come from David's territory, ethlehem, and from his family (vv. 41b–42). iblical traditions connect David and his final romised Son with southern Judea and Beth- ·hem (see 2 Sam. 7:12 and context; Ps. 89:3– ; Micah 5:2). Matthew 1–2 goes to great ·ngths to place Jesus in Bethlehem and sees im as a descendant of Abraham and David. 'his emphasis in Matthew played heavily in ıe missions enterprise to the Jewish people xpecting such a Messiah. Matthew serves ırgely as a missionary document with a Jew- h/Palestinian worldview. John's Gospel, by ɔntrast, was more of an apologetic, noting the arious reactions to Jesus.

The Davidic connection also plays largely ı Luke's Gospel, especially in the earlier hapters, although Luke differs from Matthew ı stressing that Jesus is from humble back- rounds (in Matthew he is a royal Messiah). :sus as Son of David also reached into Rome ia Paul in Romans 1:3, where the apostle uses ıis tradition to speak of Jesus' earthly and uman status. In the larger context of the Greco-Roman world, the Davidic connection became less important, except for those connected with Jewish religious backgrounds. For example, the environment of the book of Revelation plays out the conflict between Caesar and Jesus. Revelation points out that there is no contest—Jesus is Lord of all, including Caesar.

The mixed reaction in verses 40–44 and the same reaction in verse 25 bracket the sayings of Jesus regarding his origin and his fulfillment of Tabernacles and characterize Jewish responses to Jesus as Messiah, spreading from Sabbath observation to Tabernacles and beyond.

2.4.3.5. Unbelieving Jewish Leaders (7:45–52). The scene now turns to the response of the religious leaders, where several topics show up. The first of these pertains to an ethnic issue. We have seen that John uses the word "Jew(s)" (*Ioudaioi*) frequently in his Gospel. In this paragraph, we can see clearly what he intends with this word. The Pharisees are Jews, but they take an extremely prejudiced and hostile attitude against various other Jews, including Jesus. In other words, John's reference to *Ioudaioi* as enemies is limited to the Pharisees and other leaders who oppose Jesus *and other Jews*. Note that the Pharisees were the only group of Jewish leaders to survive the destruction of the temple (when this Gospel was written).[4]

The Pharisees play a major role in the rejection of Jesus in John. They set themselves apart from the common Jewish people, calling them a "mob," saying that they have a curse on them, and retorting that they are ignorant of the law (v. 49). These three characteristics belong together. The word "curse" (*eparatos*) in the New Testament occurs only here. The concept originates in the time of Ezra and Nehemiah, when the people became a mixture of pagan and Jews. Just before the time of Jesus, about 20 B.C., evidence exists of this hostility between a group of people called "the people of the land" (*'am ha-aretz*), who did not observe the strict customs of the law, and the Pharisees. In this time Rabbi Hillel noted that an uneducated man was quick to sin and that these common people were not pious (*Mishnah Aboth* 2:5). In the time of Jesus, this division was even sharper. The Pharisees even said that the reason why God would judge the world was because of the curse on these people (see Deut. 27:14–26; note also John 9:28).

The Pharisees belonged to the group that denied the Galilean origination of the Messiah, demonstrating a hostile posture against Galileans. Recent scholarship notes that possible revolutionary factors were more apt to be in Judea, especially in Jerusalem, than in Galilee. One reason for this is that this city controlled the power base for Judaism.

Nicodemus shows up here again (cf. ch. 3). We now learn that he is a Pharisee, though one with a different spirit. John implies here that when he came to Jesus, he did so as an earnest inquirer. The Pharisees have just slammed their own guards for not bringing back Jesus and accuse them of being cursed and ignorant, as were the crowds. They point to their own ranks, "Has any of the rulers or of the Pharisees believed in him?" (v. 48). The implied answer is "No!" But Nicodemus with irony shows them to be wrong. He speaks up for Jesus and draws a retort.

Finally, a comment on the topic of Jesus' speech is forthcoming. The Pharisees accuse the guards of being deceived (cf. 7:12). When asked why they do not have Jesus with them, they respond by saying that Jesus spoke in an unusual way. In Matthew 7:28, the crowds marvel over Jesus' teaching, noting that he had a certain authority and was therefore different from their scribes. In John 18:6, his authority emerges again, when, upon being asked his identity by those seeking his arrest, he answers, "I am." Thereupon, they fall to the ground, recognizing him to be divine. In other words, to those with the slightest quest for truth, Jesus has a certain presence that no one else has. Perhaps even for his opposition, they perceive something, too. Is that perhaps why they oppose him so violently?

This paragraph about the unbelieving Jewish leaders closes the second cycle at the Feast of Tabernacles, a cycle containing the proclamation that Jesus is the Giver of living water, the Spirit. The Son of God thus has fulfilled expectations of Tabernacles—the day of salvation has arrived, the end has come.

2.4.3.6. The Woman Taken in Adultery (7:53–8:11). Whether or not this section belongs in the Gospel of John is a matter of scholarly debate (see NIV note after 7:52).[5] Verse 53 appropriately provides a transition to that of the narrative of the woman caught i adultery. By saying that "each went to his ow home," followed by "but Jesus went to th Mount of Olives," (8:1), the text implies th Jesus has no home or place to go to. These su cinct sentences fit this section, leaving o details and moving right to the heart of th matter, the mercy of Jesus.

At dawn, Jesus appears in the temp courts, teaching the people. "At daw (*orthrou*) occurs only here in John's Gosp and this is the only place where "Mount Olives" occurs. John does refer to the ear hours of the morning elsewhere but in a di ferent way (see 20:1). Both of these expre sions sound more like Luke's Gospel, whic has them in the Passion narrative. Perhaps i reality this story happened during this week

Jesus is in "the temple courts" (8:2), vague place somewhere in the large temp precinct but outside the Holy Place. The sam expression provided the setting for Jesus' fi Tabernacles instruction in 7:14. In 8:20, h debate over his "light of the world" discour happens "in the temple area near the pla where the offerings were put."

The matter put before Jesus in 8:1–11 pe tains to adultery, a legal matter found in O Testament teaching and Jewish law. Th people gather around Jesus as he teaches, b soon the Pharisees and the teachers of the la appear with an adulterous woman. As fund mentalist adherents of the law and its inte pretation, application, and preservation, the are threatened by a new school of though Thus, they try to do away with Jesus with th situation.

Several observations will help us to unde stand this matter. It is not clear whether th Jewish authorities could decide capital cases this time. Scholars are not sure, either, wheth this woman has already been judged by the authorities; the context suggests that she h not. It appears that these teachers of the la and Pharisees have somehow entrapped th woman as a test case for Jesus. They hav caught her in the very act of illicit sexual inte course. Nothing is said about her husba ("adultery" refers to married people).

The Old Testament teaching on adulte occurs in several places in the Pentateuc Numbers 5:11–31 deals with cases having do with jealousy and a charge of adultery wit out witnesses on the part of either of the couple. In this case, where suspicion exists, care is taken to preserve the innocent. The wife is taken to the priest, who concocts a liquid to give to her to drink to discern whether she is guilty. If she survives, she is innocent; if not, she is worthy of her death. This is the only instance in the Pentateuch where both parties are not put to death. In this case, there is no way to determine the guilt or innocence of the man.

Leviticus 20:10 contains a one-sentence statement about adultery. This verse directs the sentence towards the sinning husband. If he should commit adultery with another man's wife, both are put to death.

Deuteronomy 17:1–7 provides controls for capital punishment, especially with respect to idolatry. At least two persons must have witnessed the act. The witnesses are to bring the charged person to the gate of the city (where legal events took place in the Oriental city) and cast the first stones (see Acts 7:57–58). Deuteronomy 22:13–26 refers to how to handle a variety of marriage situations surrounding adultery. The important thing here is that, in the face of overwhelming testimony, both partners are brought to the gate and stoned (cf. Ezek. 16:38–40). It is obvious that this commandment is not being followed in John 8:1–11. By the time of the first century, Jewish law came to favor the man; the woman bore the brunt of the affair.

We should also speak briefly about the type of legal system the Old Testament and Judaism embraced. In one sense it is similar to the type embraced in the Western world—that of following legal precedent. In other words, if a particular legal decision follows a course of action other than what has previously been written, that decision establishes a precedent for future cases. The law therefore can be both a deterrent and show mercy.

In John 8:1–11, then, we have a test case in which Jesus' enemies are trying to entrap him (cf. esp. v. 6). Logically, they are attempting to place Jesus on the horns of a dilemma. Only the Sanhedrin had the right to try capital offenses. Its members were counted in odd numbers so as to avoid a split jury. If the Romans did permit the Jewish court this type of authority at this time, then Jesus would be violating that pattern. If the court did not have this jurisdiction, then Jesus would be violating Mosaic law by releasing her, and he would be in trouble with the Romans if he voted to execute her. Jesus avoids this dilemma by turning his enemies' accusations against them. They have been the witnesses to her act and would have to throw the first stones. But they are likewise guilty of sin themselves and in no wise fit to judge. That all people are guilty of sin and under the sentence of death (condemnation) is assumed by John here (cf. 8:31ff.).

Jesus does not directly answer the question of verse 5. Rather, he bends over to write on the ground, but his enemies intently pursue him. He finally straightens up and answers in a rhetorical way. Jesus' comment in verse 7, when it comes to matters of guilt before God, is the question every person must face, and it brings everyone to the same level. All are sinners and ultimately unworthy to judge others. Only God can judge, except he does not—he forgives and removes condemnation through his Son. This is exactly what Jesus does to the woman when her accusers leave: "Neither do I condemn you." For any who do not believe, they remain under judgment. Though the Jewish leaders have come in force and together, they leave weakly and individually, each one personally receiving in his heart an arrow of conviction. Beginning with the oldest, they depart one at a time.

Jesus' final words to the woman are striking: "Go now and leave your life of sin." By setting her free from her guilt and shame, he releases her to a new life. Forgiveness brings what nothing else can—a new status to the sinner, regardless of its gravity. Her past adultery will no longer shame her. Its guilt is gone. The NIV appropriately brings out the significance of the present tense of the verb "sin" in this clause. This tense denotes a habitual action, to which one never again returns. In this case, it suggests one of two possibilities: Either the woman has been a prostitute (a lifestyle she will now leave), or John is referring to a lifestyle that a regenerate person has compared to that of an unbeliever. This is John's mandate of discipleship (see ch. 15).

2.4.3.7. The Light of the World (8:12–30). The third cycle at the Feast of Tabernacles focuses on Jesus as the light of the world, the second of two major themes in chapters 7–10 (the first one is water). Debate over Jesus' origin surfaces again.

"When Jesus spoke again to the people" (8:12) introduces a new section (and theme) and picks up on an earlier conversation (7:16) and theme (1:5, 9). "Light" in this section anticipates chapter 9, where the sign for this section occurs. Jesus is standing near the offering receptacles when he announces this topic: "I am the light of the world." Jesus, as God, in the manner he prescribes exists and acts in the manner he intends with the word "light."

This announcement is so appropriate for the Feast of Tabernacles. At the feast, wicks on tall poles in the courtyard shone brightly to all Jerusalem. "Light" had long been an important theme of Tabernacles (cf. Zech. 14:6). In Isaiah 9:2, darkness refers to oppression and death, salvation to light. In Isaiah 49:6, light is associated with the servant of Yahweh, who brings salvation to the Gentiles. Similarly in 60:1, 3, "light" and "glory" are synonymous, referring to the coming of God to Zion, which stands in the midst of the darkness of all peoples.

The theme of light is connected to God's day of salvation. Particularly in John, it is attached to wisdom and revelation. Both in turn flow out of and are part of what happens when the Spirit, who is from above, gives birth to blind sinners who now believe in Jesus. One can thus understand the relationship between the water-pouring ceremony and the lighted candelabras in these Tabernacles sections. Light is also related to truth, as in "the true light that gives light to every man was coming into the world" (1:9). "True" means the right and only One from God, who provides a unique salvation as opposed to others that many traditions expected. "Light" is also related to the bread of life (6:48), another "I am" saying. "Bread" emphasizes the means and source of life, whereas light emphasizes the result (the ability to know God and relate to him, what Jesus and the Spirit accomplish in salvation).

"Of the world" (v. 12) also helps the reader to understand light: It has come for the world. John is particularly fond of the word "world" (*kosmos*), which usually refers to the world of sinful people. Only when he mentions that the Word created the world does he imply that *kosmos* is something other than the order of fallen humans. But though God created the world through him, it has rejected his Son, because all people (Jew and Gentile alike) now are in sin. The world has a leader called the "prince" (12:31; 16:11). Its members, who are from the earth, kill, lie, and hate Jesus and his followers, who are from above, heaven. The world lies under condemnation as a result of its sin. But because he loved the world, God sent his Son into it to redeem it. It needs revelation about its status, so Jesus is its Light (i.e., revealer and standard). But the world rejects the Light, even though the Spirit has come to convict it of sin, righteousness, and judgment.

In the second half of verse 12, Jesus issues a call to discipleship, flowing out of his statement about the light. "Follow me" is a firm discipleship word, noting that Jesus is Lord and that the believer must submit and obey Jesus in all matters, especially righteousness. The one who follows Jesus, then, "will never walk in darkness" (i.e., will never live in sin). The consistent walk in faith affirms the identity and security of the believer.

A brief challenge from the Pharisees surfaces in verse 13, now in the recurring theme of seeking the validity of witnesses. The explanation of this comment lies at the end of verse 12. The Pharisees understand Jesus' statement in verse 12b as soliciting disciples. They fear his threat to their power and control. Verse 13 then implies something like this: "On whose authority can you ask anyone to follow you? You cannot do this on your own." Rabbis had their own pattern of discipleship, in which new rabbis passed on what they had been taught by prominent rabbis under whom they had learned. It was a great privilege to learn under a famous rabbi. Here the Pharisees attempt to discredit Jesus because of a technicality of the law regarding accreditation of a "witness." The law said that a witness was not valid if given by the person himself.

This testimony theme has occurred in 5:31–47, where Jesus said that he had numerous ones to testify of him: for example, John, the Father, and the Scriptures. He also admitted there that testimony from the person himself was not valid. Now, however, 8:14 seems to contradict that. We may respond in this fashion. (1) In chapter 5, Jesus was focusing attention on the other witnesses, appropriate for the argument there. In 8:14–18, he moves closer to the "bottom line" (vv. 23–24): He as the divine Son needs no other testimony. The " am" in verse 18, similar to the one in verse 12, subtly suggests his divinity, so that no higher court exists. (2) The Pharisees judge according to human standards because, in fact, they are human. (3) Without the aid of Jesus and the Spirit, no human can know spiritual things. But he is divine, and thus Jesus judges as God. Yet he does bring in the witness of the Father. (4) He and the Father, according to their law, supply a valid testimony. Jesus says in verse 17 that they refer to *their own* law. He knows of and appeals to a different law, one that does not violate Scripture.

When Jesus tells the Pharisees that his Father has sent him (v. 18), they immediately want to know where his father is (v. 19). This shows their spiritual state—they want to check out his father (asking such an earthly question), thus indicating that indeed they are in sin. The gap between them shows up sharply at verse 21, where Jesus once again mentions his passion and ascension with "I am going away," and their condition, "You cannot come." The word "Jews," which appears in verse 22, includes the "Pharisees" of verse 13. They pick up on Jesus' last statement and again show their spiritual condition by reaching the wrong conclusion through two strange rhetorical questions.

John, the writer, provides in verse 20 two editorial comments. (1) It may be significant that John notes where Jesus is teaching—near the offering receptacle. During Tabernacles, temple wardens collected and dispersed offerings to assist the people. Here Jesus can reach a variety of people to signify subtly that he is the One ultimately to meet their needs. (2) Jesus is in control—no one arrests him at this time, for the Father has reserved it for the later Passover.

Verses 23–24 state three things. (1) "Below" equals "this world," and "above," "not of this world." (2) Related to this is the essential nature of persons. The "below" category consists of unbelievers, who are sinful and blind and lie under condemnation. "Above," referring to Jesus, means divine, righteous nature. The phrases "from below" and "from above" indicate these essential natures. These are mutually exclusive, which explains why there is no communication between them. (3) The absolute use of "I am" occurs (i.e., there is no predicate; the NIV has in corner brackets, "I am ⌞the one I claim to be⌟"). This expression suggests the divine name.

Jesus' assertion remains consistent: What he has heard from his Father, he tells the world (vv. 25–26). Again, the Jews in their ignorance do not understand.

Verses 28–29 bring this section to a conclusion. In somewhat obscure language, Jesus points to his forthcoming passion and ascension and to their participation in his death. "When you have lifted up the Son of Man, then you will know that I am ⌞the one I claim to be⌟." "Lifted up" in John emotes positive feelings, for with it he conveys the most blessed benefit for the world: All can receive eternal life through this glorious event. Once again, the divine name "I am" occurs (cf. v. 24). On that occasion Jesus' enemies will know that he is divine and that he speaks for the Father, who sent him. That is, when he dies and ascends, he will judge them for their unbelief. This connects with verse 26 and the theme of judgment (cf. also chs. 14–16, on the coming of the Spirit and his judging function). The lifting up of Jesus (the cross through the ascension) directly relates to the coming of the Spirit and the continuation of Jesus' ministry.

The humble submissive attitude of Jesus comes through clearly in the final words of this section. He only speaks and does what the Father has taught him. In that, Jesus always pleases his Father. For this reason, the Father does not abandon Jesus.

Let us review the groups of people who have participated in this debate over the authority of Jesus and his statement regarding the light of the world. At first, "the people" are present for Jesus' statement in verse 12. "The Pharisees" jump in at verse 13, and at verse 22, "the Jews" show up. Finally at verse 30, "many [unnamed] put their faith in him." This may be the same group as those who believed in him in 7:31. In any case, this group becomes the focus of the final cycle at the Feast of Tabernacles (8:31–59), and there they change radically.

2.4.3.8. Jesus and Abraham (8:31–59). Translators and other scholars divide this section differently. One place is as the NIV has it, between verses 30 and 31; the other option is between verses 29 and 30, thus keeping verses 30–31 as a unit. The fact that two instances of the verb "believe" occur back-to-back in verses 30 and 31 generates a problem. This is one of those places where the literary seams in this Gospel appear to be a bit rough.

The construction of verses 30 and 31, however, suggests that they should be kept together. Verse 30 brings back into view a specific group that has sporadically appeared on the scene, both before this time and after (not the disciples). Let us now trace this group through the Gospel to determine if we can learn anything about them. The first time some believed in Jesus in this way was in 2:23. The reference to this group is as ambiguous there as in 8:30 ("many"). It is apparent, though, that they are Jews in Jerusalem and that they are at a Jewish feast. They believe Jesus because of his signs, but Jesus does not commit himself to them. Something has been fundamentally wrong with their faith from the start.

The next time this group appears is in 7:31, where the same kind of elements show up again. They are referred to as "many [from the crowd]," they are in Jerusalem at a Jewish feast, and they believe because of signs. In 8:30, "many" believe because of Jesus' words. What we have thus far is a growing group of Jewish believers who commit themselves to Jesus because of traditional reasons. Jesus performs miracles, which provoke their faith. But miracles are not of the same character as "the signs" in John. They have caught their attention to the extent that they are now listening to Jesus, but without the level of understanding that a true believer has. Their commitment has an inadequate basis for their call to discipleship.

This group appears two more times after chapter 8. In 10:42, a similar scenario exists: They are called "many," and by implication, miraculous signs also affect their belief in Jesus. But what is new here is the inclusion of John the Baptist's name. This group grows to include those who have been influenced by the Baptist. The last occasion is in 11:45. Here John notes that the "many" are part of the Jews. The reason for their belief is the raising of Lazarus from the dead. But they return to tell the Pharisees and chief priests what is going on. To this report the leaders exclaim, "Here is this man performing many miraculous signs. If we let him go on like this, everyone will believe in him, and then the Romans will come and take away both our place and our nation" (11:47–48). In other words, "Jesus is threatening our power—we have to stop him!"

Let us summarize. (1) The "many" who believe are Jewish and place their faith in Jesus' miracles, some of which are John's special signs. They are Jerusalemites and have some loyalties to the city power structures. (2) Their faith is not based as it should be; therefore, it is fundamentally wrong. (3) Like the Pharisees, they believe that Jesus is only a man. Note what the Pharisees say about Jesus in 11:47, "Here is this man." (4) The exact Greek construction for "believed in him" is the same in all four places. John wants his readers to understand that the faith that this group holds in common is totally inadequate. This conclusion is important for understanding 8:31–59.

The theological implications for the entire book of John, then, are great. This information suggests that many of the Jewish believers in John's church, who were wavering, have come to faith in Jesus like these "many" did. Unless they change the basis of their belief, they will be found wanting before God, just like these earlier ones, and they will break from the church, the true people of God. To be at one with God and his people, all must hold a common faith, rooted in Jesus the Son of God, the Savior of the world. Also noteworthy is that among those wavering in John's congregation are those influenced by the Baptist.

The real ardent enemies of Jesus (and John's congregation[s]), as is evident here, are the Pharisees and chief priests. This information suggests that the leaders of Judaism in John's day have been causing the trouble. In addition, a major issue focused on the person of Jesus. These leaders and these superficial believers look on Jesus merely as a man when, in fact, he was (is) fully God. John's emphasis on the divinity of Jesus, then, stems from the negative influence of Judaism, not Gnosticism. Let us return to 8:31 now.

The purpose of 8:31–59 is to distinguish these superficial believers and focus on why their faith is deficient. Jesus, here more than anywhere else in John, speaks most clearly about the essence and basis of faith. Interestingly, out of all the various groups that appear in this Tabernacles section, including those who seek to arrest and kill him, he finally turns and addresses those who have put their faith in him. And, we should hasten to add, in this sec-

JOHN'S TESTIMONY TO JESUS

A. The Seven Miracles of Jesus

"Jesus did many other miraculous signs in the presence of his disciples which are not recorded in this book. But these are written that you may believe that Jesus is the Christ, the Son God, and that by believing you may have life in his name."	John 30:20–31
Turning water into wine at Capernaum	John 2:1–11
Healing the official's son at Capernaum	John 4:46–51
Healing the sick man at the pool of Bethesda	John 5:1–9
Feeding the five thousand in Galilee	John 6:5–13
Walking on the stormy Sea of Galilee	John 6:19–21
Healing the man born blind in Jerusalem	John 9:1–7
Raising Lazarus from the dead in Bethany	John 11:1–44

B. The Seven Great "I Am's" of Jesus

"'You are not yet fifty years old,' the Jews said to him, 'and you have seen Abraham!' 'I tell you the truth,' Jesus answered, 'before Abraham was, I am!'"	John 6:57–58
"I am the bread of life."	John 6:35, 48; cf. v.51
"I am the light of the world."	John 8:12; 9:5
"I am the gate for the sheep."	John 10:7, 9
"I am the good shepherd."	John 10:11, 14
"I am the resurrection and the life."	John 11:25
"I am the way and the truth and the life."	John 14:6
"I am the true vine."	John 15:1, 5

C. The Seven "Greater Than's" of Jesus

"To this John [the Baptist] replied, 'A man can receive only what is given him from heaven. . . . He [Jesus] must become greater; I must become less.'"	John 3:27, 30
Jesus is greater than the angels.	John 1:51
Jesus is greater than Abraham.	John 8:56–58
Jesus is greater than Jacob.	John 4:11–14
Jesus is greater than Moses.	John 6:49–51
Jesus is greater than the law.	John 1:17; cf. 8:1–11
Jesus is greater than the Sabbath.	John 7:21–23; cf. 5:8–15; 9:14–33
Jesus is greater than the temple.	John 2:18–21

tion they turn vehemently against Jesus, seeking to kill him. Since this group had reached a significant size, it is time to speak to them about their faith; this certainly relates to John's congregations, and to ours today.

Jesus' words appear in the form of a conditional sentence, opening the dialogue. The conditional part reads, "If you hold to my teaching" (lit., "if you abide in my word"). "Abide" (*meno*) is a word that shows up frequently in this Gospel, emphasizing "holding to" or "living in." "My" emphasizes sharply whose word it is—the teaching of Jesus, which carries a stamp of approval from the Father, the

Spirit, his signs, and others. It sets him forth as the only One through whom God speaks in this manner. "Hold to" means to embrace wholly who he is and what he will do to save the world, to submit totally to him as his disciples. A believer in Jesus, then, should have a lifestyle that shows his Lordship in every way. This is what the consequence part of that sentence signifies, "You are really my disciples."

Verse 32 introduces further consequences and connects their present condition with the future. "You will know the truth" points to the moment at which the Spirit regenerates these disciples, bringing revelation and the capacity for it. The new birth is a revelatory experience. "Know" here is a spiritual experience, impacting the way one understands all reality. Through regeneration, the person becomes new and has a new worldview. The personal experience of "knowing" (not cognitive or intellectual), produced by the Spirit, results in freedom. But freedom from what? From the sinning nature, which no longer lords over the enslaved sinner. The theological stance of the two-natures theory, where the believer struggles as both a sinner and a saint, finds no place in John (cf. esp. 1 John 2:27–3:10, where the believer may sin, but sin does not dominate his or her life).

The truth has set the believer free. In John, freedom from sin, its power, and its influence is the consequence of the new birth. Freedom also means that the believer has passed from condemnation to life. Jesus has atoned for the world's sin, bringing a special, blood-bought victory. Death no longer has its power—eternal life now rules. To receive this consequence, one must continually "hold to [his] teaching [lit., word]." It is not a one-time experience.

Note one further thing: Those who believe are for the first time called "Jews" (*Ioudaioi*) (v. 31). John aims these words of Jesus towards the Jews, whoever they may be. We are not told of their status; we will find out from what follows that these people are steeped in the traditions of Judaism and have no intention of discarding them. This information may help the reader, in John's day and in these modern times, to know something about how Jewish people can initially believe in Jesus, even attend "Jesus" synagogues, but never be true followers of Jesus. Their expectations remain basically Jewish.

The response of these believers (v. 33) at first seems curious—they appeal to their cultural and religious heritage: "We are Abraham's descendants." Only in this section in all of John does Abraham appear overtly. (1) This adds to the significance of the section, adding to the importance of Jesus' address concerning the nature of faith.

(2) Abraham was the most significant figure in the history of Judaism, even more so than Moses. He was the beginning of Judaism, *the* patriarch (cf. Isa. 51:1–2, which calls him "the rock from which you were cut . . . your father"). In Jewish literature, all of his descendants, because of God's promises to him and his physical descendants, were virtually guaranteed a place in Paradise. This factor emerged in the Feast of Tabernacles; for during the feast, people prayed to the patriarch in much the same way as Christians do to Jesus, and expected to benefit from him. His merits could be transferred to all his children. He was literally Judaism's mediator.

(3) The idea of covenant lurks in the background with the mention of the patriarch. With Jesus replacing Abraham, we have the introduction of the new covenant. The attitude towards Abraham in John differs when compared with Matthew's Gospel and Paul in Romans. In both instances, Abraham is connected with the church in a positive way. Both Matthew and Paul appeal to current and potential Jewish adherents. In short, they are missionary documents. John's Gospel, however, is polemical and corrective in nature, shifting the theological status of Abraham below that of Jesus.

Furthermore, Judaism did not have a doctrine of salvation like Christianity. This comes out in verse 33, where this group cries out, "[We] have never been slaves of anyone." In a political sense, this statement is not true, for the Israelites had been slaves at various times throughout Old Testament history. Some, like the Zealots, even considered themselves slaves of Rome. But no doubt what is meant here is religious slavery. In their particular doctrine of salvation, they did not need to convert to some other system. In Abraham they had never been without salvation. God's promise to them had not been recalled. They were always under his covenant. Sacrifice, repentance, and all other such activity maintained their relationship with him. For them to have a need for conversion was unheard of, John the Baptist's ministry notwithstanding.

Those Jews who repented were preparing for the coming of their promised king. Their Messiah would come as a political and religious deliverer, quite unlike what Jesus' messiahship was. The real difference now emerges. These people begin to see that Jesus is no ordinary Messiah and that he teaches no ordinary view of salvation. He calls for something radically new, yet something connected with the past. The new transforms the old, rendering it obsolete. Their tenacity to the conflicting heir of the old, Judaism, emerges with, "How can you say that we shall be set free?" (v. 33).

Jesus now replies with the first of three "*amen, amen*" sayings in this section. It focuses on something else over which he and Judaism disagree—the doctrine of sin. The literature of Judaism displays, for the most part, a different view of sin from what Jesus espouses. Except for a few sectarian Jewish writings and the community of Qumran, sin was taken somewhat lightly. That is, sin was not inherent in a child of Abraham (see comments on John 1:29). If it did exist, it could be taken care of by human effort at obedience to the law, by repentance, or by some other work that balances the scales; and it could be atoned for by animal sacrifice (where, of course, God's mercy played a part).

In the Jewish way of thinking, one of the ways sin is present in human nature is in the doctrine of the two desires or impulses—the evil *yetzer* and the good *yetzer*. These two impulses fight against each other. In simplified form, the way to conquer the evil impulse is to train the good by doing good habits, following the Torah (law), whereby one can overcome the bad impulse. In spite of this, however, no Jewish person is without salvation. More than likely, this forms the background for the dialogue in John 8:31ff. Paul likely faced this same Jewish issue in Romans (esp. chs. 6–8), where the straw person he addresses (ch. 7) tries to deal with his evil nature by keeping the law. Paul says that sin has so much of a foothold in human nature that it cannot be broken with human effort. It takes the new birth and the power of Jesus' atonement. The Jewish people in John 8:31 are beginning to reject this new way outlined by Jesus.

The "*amen, amen*" saying in verse 34 proclaims the doctrine of sin in a new way: "Everyone who sins is a slave to sin." A better way to translate the Greek of the first part is as follows: "Everyone who practices the sin." This construction denotes the essence of sinful human nature: It is inclusive ("everyone"), and it is part of human nature. The word "sin" in Greek is a noun accompanied by a definite article "the," which functions as the object of "practices." This singular noun with the article specifies a certain sin (see also 1:29)—the sin that the first man and woman did, which separated all of their descendants from God. Their sinful nature passes on to all people. Jesus came to remove this chasm, to bridge it with his gracious work. This is why his atonement is so distinct, even from Old Testament systems. He came to do away with the sin that fractured the relationship between God and humans. All earlier approaches (i.e., in the Old Testament) only pointed to Jesus. He fulfilled them and thus transformed them, rendering them obsolete (cf. the book of Hebrews).

Verses 34–35 carry forward the concept of "slave." We possibly have a brief parable in this analogy of a slave and a son (cf. Heb. 3:2–6; see also the parable in Mark 12:1–10, which distinguishes between slave and heir/son). The Greek words for the NIV's "family" (*oikia*) in John and "house" (*oikos*) in Hebrews 3 literally mean "house." These words are virtually synonyms and have a variety of meanings in different contexts. In John, it has kingdom of God implications; in other words, this verse also touches on the doctrine of the church.

Verses 35–36 distinguish the length of participation in the household. The slave does not have the same status as a son. He may be part of the household for a while, but at some point a separation occurs. The point is, these "believing" Jews will be cast out unless they abide in Jesus' word (cf. v. 31). Furthermore, "if the Son sets you free, you will be free indeed" (v. 36). This is what it takes to be a member of the kingdom. Ethnic and religious backgrounds cut no deal with Jesus to enter the kingdom. The opposite of slavery is "freedom/free," and it occurs in John four times (all of them here). "Son" refers to Jesus; he is the one who frees all from sin.

In verse 37 Jesus acknowledges the ethnic background of these "believing" Jews, but he also points out their spiritual condition. The phrase "Abraham's descendants" needs some comment. John uses two words for the idea of "descendants" in verses 31–38, and they mean opposite things in John's worldview. Verses 33 and 37 use the word *sperma*, which refers to the patriarch's physical offspring (they are called "Jews" four times in vv. 31–59). The other word is *tekna*, which shows up only in verse 39. There Jesus gives this word a special meaning, referring to the spiritual offspring of Abraham; his descendants are those who act like him, regardless of their physical, genetic connection to the patriarch.

Teknon ("child") is conversion language in the New Testament and is used only for those who have a new Christ-like nature. In John, this word applies to Christians. The Greek word *huios* ("son") is never used of Christians in John (this word is reserved for Jesus, the "Son" of God). Thus, a believer is a *teknon* of God, not a *huios* of God. John in this way distinguishes between Jesus and believers. Only Jesus is divine. John makes this distinction because of the debate context of Christians and Jews during his time of writing.[6]

The idea of paternity, woven throughout verses 31–59, is a major motif in this section. When these "believing Jews" appeal to Abraham as their father, they inform the reader about their religious background. They are strict and conservative members of Judaism, appealing to their status as sons of Israel, even being a cut above other people. By their reactions, they distinguish sharply between Jewish boundaries and others, being intolerant of them. They look down on Samaritans, using that term to denote dementia and demon-possession (see v. 48).

But Jesus judges differently (see 8:15). He determines not on the basis of physical descent, but on the basis of what people do. He brings up their intent again in verse 37, in a seemingly surprising way, to kill him. They "have no room for my word" (see v. 31). Jesus' word will change their lives and remove hatred and murder from them. What Jesus says, then, is, "I know you are Jews, but you seek to kill me. Therefore, my word is not in you."

This thought continues in verse 38. Paternity is determined by what descendants do. And "doing" in that culture is connected with transmitting values. Transmission comes through modeling of parents, through teaching, and through vital relationships with family members. Consequently, Jesus acts in the manner he has "seen in [his] Father's presence"; the Jews act according to what they "have heard from [their] father." *Seeing* and *hearing* are significant comparisons. *Seeing* implies that Jesus and his Father are alive and currently in fellowship. It also suggests a dynamic, living relationship. In contrast, *hearing* intimates that the Jews only know about Abraham through word of mouth, that is, oral tradition passed on through centuries. They have no real paternity from him, even though they bear his ethnic likeness. He has been dead for a long time.

This implication becomes overt and gets reversed later in verses 52–54, where the Jews admit that Abraham has been dead for some time. And Jesus claims that the patriarch has seen Jesus? They are not even aware of what has transpired. Such irony! Further, what Jesus *has* "seen" (the perfect tense in v. 38) suggests his preexistence, his divinity, and the unchangeable character of God in contrast to the changeableness of humans. Jesus habitually "speaks" according to this divine nature—the verb suggests this with the present tense, indicating this customary practice. The Jews, on the other hand, merely "heard" (a simple past tense). But they habitually "do" it, referring to the life that flows from their nature.

The Jews come right back in verse 39, insisting that Abraham is their father. The phrasing of the answer suggests that they are referring to all the benefits and promises that belong to Abraham's offspring, especially available during Tabernacles. But Jesus quickly points to a person's actions/deeds and character in the form of another conditional sentence—this time, a contrary-to-fact condition. As far as he is concerned, the present condition of these Jews shows that they are not true children of Abraham. God has commanded the patriarchs' descendants to carry on faithful deeds; he threatens these children if they become unfaithful.

In verse 40 Jesus points out the difference between these "believing Jews" and Abraham. The "works" that Abraham performed and that his descendants are to do are love works. The heme of "love" (prominent in Deuteronomy) shows up in verse 42. It is God's nature to love, and apparently the patriarch's as well, for he oved God and others. Therefore, paternity proclaims that these people are not true children of Abraham. They follow their father (v. 41), whom Jesus will identify momentarily. In verse 40, Jesus also says that he heard things from God his Father, an activity for which they are determined to kill him.

Against Jesus' charge (v. 41b), these Jews continue to defend themselves, saying, "We are not illegitimate children" (lit., "we have not been born of adultery"). There may be here a subtle echo of a Jewish claim against Jesus' virgin birth. Or they may see in Jesus' charge a reference to idolatry. Their appeal to a monotheistic belief suggests that: "The only Father we have is God himself."

Verses 42–47 contain the lengthy response of Jesus, in which he shows that their actions reflect who their father is and, therefore, what their nature is. This, in turn, explains why they do not understand Jesus. He begins with another contrary-to-fact condition (v. 42). This sentence places together one's being (nature) and love (i.e., being and ethics): "If God were your Father [but he is not], you would love me [but you do not]." The rest of the verse shows the connection between paternity, origin, and ethics, returning to the theme of verse 38. Jesus has come from God and stands before them in that sense, not as one who has come on his own but as one who has been sent by God.

In verse 43, Jesus continues the theme of these people's sinful nature and spiritual ignorance. It contains a question and an answer. The NIV's "Why is my language not clear to you?" reflects the implication of the Greek. "Language" (*lalia*) suggests the heavenly origin of Jesus' speech. Now is a good time to elaborate upon "knowing" and "understanding" a bit.

At the heart of the matter in this Gospel is this issue: How does one know truth? The technical name for this issue is "epistemology." The answer to this question depends, to a great extent, on such things as one's previous experience, perspective, worldview, and philosophy. One's nature also impacts how one knows or understands. Nothing is objective in the strict sense of the word. For example, a cat "sees" things differently from a dog. Even dogs "see" things differently, though they still "see" as dogs. Whether or not one is regenerated has a great deal to do with how one knows and understands. Thus, verse 43b expresses the cause of these Jews' inability to "hear" Jesus' language ("hear" implies both understanding and putting into action). One cannot truly hear if one's ears are dull.

Verse 44a contains the conclusion of Jesus' argument up to this point: "You belong to your father, the devil, and you want to carry out your father's desire." Verse 44b elaborates on the ethical expression of his (and their) nature, connecting it with murder and lying. Jesus here alludes to the serpent's lie to Eve in Genesis 3:4 and to Abel's murder by Cain in 4:8 (cf. also Wisdom 2:4; 1 John 3:8, 11–15; Rev. 12). John, in both his Gospel and 1 John 3:15, equates hatred, an ethical attitude, with the ethical deed of murder. Hatred motivates one to murder. John also draws a connection between lying and murdering. If it is native for one to lie, then one cannot know the ultimate truth (see v. 45). Such a sinner is ready to defend oneself through lies and deception, and if necessary, through eradicating the opposition (i.e., murder).

Verse 46 contains a statement (actually a rhetorical question iterating the fact) about the sinlessness of Jesus. Certainly, according to the "Jews," beginning in chapter 5, Jesus broke the Sabbath and blasphemed. But in Jesus' own eyes, he committed no sin, and who were they to say they were sinless? "Sin" has no definite article and is singular, emphasizing the quality of Jesus' sinless nature. The word "prove" speaks of an arena into which these Jewish leaders hesitate to enter because they fear to have their own sin revealed (cf. 3:20). The accusers in 8:9 left because their sin was revealed. In 16:8, this revelation is the work of the Spirit.

Since this is the case and "if I am telling the truth" (v. 46b), "why don't you believe me?" asks Jesus. The type of condition Jesus uses here is one that affirms a truth; it can be translated, "since I am telling the truth." "Believe" surfaces here for the first time since verse 31 and points to the truth of the matter there and of the necessity of this focused debate in these verses. Therefore, "belief," related here to truth, is to be taken in the profound sense of being freed from sin, not in the sense of merely believing a spoken matter. Verse 47 summarizes Jesus' argument: The one whose origin is from God knows and understands his words, and because these Jews do not, it is evident that they are not from God.

At verse 48, we have a shift in the debate. The "Jews" respond by accusing Jesus of being a Samaritan (i.e., demented). This indicates the degree of ethnic prejudice and religious bigotry of these Jews towards Samaritans, for being a Samaritan was synonymous with being crazy and demon-possessed. This charge provides Jesus an opening to deny their charge (v. 49a) and to move the argument forward (v. 49b). He reintroduces the theme of "judgment" with honor and with dishonor.

Embedded in Jesus' response is the second of three "*amen, amen*" sayings in verses 31–59, focusing on what people must do to experience freedom from death (v. 51). This saying, another conditional sentence, resumes the opening theme of verses 31ff. about keeping Jesus' word. Two observations add to the significance of this saying: (1) "My" is in the emphatic form in Greek, signifying the uniqueness, authority, and power of Jesus' teaching, derived from the Father. (2) "Will never see" is an emphatic negation: "never ever." "Word" stands for the results of the person and work of Jesus, enlivened by the work of the Spirit, who is sent by the Father and the Son, and applied through true faith in him. "See" here reminds the reader of 3:3, where birth by the Spirit empowers the believer to "see" the kingdom. Eternal life asserts its full authority in this present age and causes physical death to lose its power and fear (cf. 1 Cor. 15).

But these Jews show their sinful condition and the accompanying ignorance of what Jesus means. In verse 52, they appeal to their earlier charge (v. 48)—"Now we know that you are demon-possessed"—and to the deaths of Abraham their biological father and the prophets. They think that Jesus is claiming something far greater than he is capable of with their reference to Abraham and the prophets. They repeat Jesus' conditional statement from above, but this time they change a few words. "My" is no longer emphatic, meaning that they have missed the point of Jesus' power and authority. Further, they substitute the word "taste" for "see" and thus show their spiritual condition and lack of faith. This is corroborated by further comments in verse 53: "Are you greater than our father Abraham? He died, and so did the prophets. Who do you think you are?" They think that Jesus is a charlatan, claiming authority as a false messiah.

Jesus replies in verse 54, returning to an earlier "Jewish" claim that God was their Father (v. 41). Here in another conditional sentence, he emphasizes that he does not glorify himself. In the spirit of a true apostle ("sent one"), which Jesus was, he represents perfectly the Father. It is God the Father who then glorifies Jesus. They lay claim to this same Father.

Verse 55 contrasts Jesus' and their positions; he strongly denies their claim in varying repetitive sentences. They do not know God—Jesus does. The first "I" in this verse is in the emphatic form and position, noting the important place of Jesus in God's strategy in this Gospel as Mediator and Revealer. In another contrary-to-fact condition, Jesus advances his argument to reiterate an earlier statement that they are liars, while he is not. Jesus emphasizes again that he knows the Father. This "knowing" also eventuates in the action of "keeping" his word. The reader's attention thus is brought back to verse 31, where the one who truly believes will "hold to my word" ("teaching," NIV). If one truly knows as Jesus knows the Father, then one's lifestyle will consistently show it in love and faithful works, just as Jesus' lifestyle did. Discipleship ultimately and simultaneously results in following Jesus and the Father.

In an abrupt manner, Jesus returns to Abraham, whose name binds this section together (v. 56). Jesus reaches a high point as he repositions, actually corrects, Abraham in this Jewish belief system. In contrast to being a guarantor of salvation and mediator between Israel and God, the patriarch functions merely as witness of Jesus' person and messianic mission in God's time ("day") of salvation. (Note the emphasis that Abraham is "your father"; he is not the father of Christians in John as he is for Paul [cf. Rom. 4:11].) In verse 39, Jesus appealed to Abraham as one who possesses the character of God, something the sinful Jews do not have. In John 1:18, Jesus has clearly replaced the role of Abraham for the Christian. That is, Abraham is no longer the one in the bosom of the Father as intercessor; Jesus is.

For John's audience and their conflict with Judaism, an intercessory role for Abraham is entirely inappropriate.

Just what is meant by "your father Abraham rejoiced at the thought of seeing my day; he saw it and was glad" (v. 56)? (The NIV adds to the Greek the phrase "at the thought of.") In Jewish literary traditions, Abraham was shown a number of visions about the future. In some stories he takes an active part on behalf of his children in the afterlife (cf. Luke 16:19–31, where the patriarch receives prayer from people in Hades and on earth and is a mediator between people and God). Jesus is more than likely referring to one of these traditions here, noting that the patriarch saw the day of the Messiah. It is not clear whether Abraham "saw" Jesus' day in his lifetime or later in Paradise. The Bible also indicates that Abraham was a prophet to whom God spoke and gave revelations (cf. Gen. 15).

The words "rejoiced" and "was glad" signify that Abraham had in mind the messianic era. This era will actualize the eschatological time of salvation, the time known as *shalom*, a time when divine joy will characterize all recipients of God's salvation. Abraham received an advance taste of the future.

Verses 57–59 contain a final interchange between Jesus and his opponents at the Feast of Tabernacles. The retort of the "Jews" shows their continuing depraved state, their ignorance of all things spiritual. Their absurd comment in verse 57 is a rhetorical question and turns around Jesus' statement of verse 56. Instead of "Abraham has seen my day," they say, "You have seen Abraham?" The number "fifty" in this verse more than likely heightens the absurd conclusion these people have reached in their sinful condition.

Jesus gives his final answer in a third "*amen, amen*" saying (v. 58). This time it focuses on Christology, affirming his preexistence: "Before Abraham was born, I am!" The Greek words here emphasize that Abraham was a created being, harking back to 1:3 by using the same verb (translated "made" there). In contrast, Jesus refers to himself as "I am," the absolute occurrence of this title, denoting his deity. This expression binds together 8:12–59, since "I am" occurs at both places (although in v. 12, "I am" does not occur in the absolute sense).

John completes this section (v. 59) by adding the note that these "Jews" take up stones to throw at him. They intend to stone him for blasphemy, for they take "I am" to refer to deity. People accused of this capital crime received stoning as punishment. Since they feel free to stone Jesus without any legal action, they have great power, implying that they are leaders of a kind.

But Jesus escapes their intention. John simply states that he avoids them, providing no details and thus emphasizing Jesus' sovereignty over them. This also provides information to clear up the somewhat ambiguous, if not seemingly contradictory, statements in 7:4, 10, in which Jesus said that he would not go up to the feast but then does. The Greek word translated "in secret" or "hid" occurs in both those verses and in 8:59. Jesus' "time" is not yet—it will come at Passover, when lambs are slaughtered to atone for the sins of the people, not at the Feast of Tabernacles.

There may be a subtle implication in verse 59 that he (and perhaps God) is abandoning the temple (cf. 2:13–21). In any case, Jesus will soon transform the whole temple enterprise, creating a new dwelling place for God.

2.4.3.9. Healing of the Man Born Blind and Consequences (9:1–41). This chapter contains themes running from chapters 5 through 10, with a particular number of connections with chapter 8. John 9:1 begins with *kai* ("and," omitted in NIV), which links it to 8:59. The "as he went along" of 9:1 also promotes smoothly the idea of connection and transition. In chapters 7–8, a rather lengthy series of debates occurred during the Feast of Tabernacles. In those debates Jesus presented transforming ideas, particularly concerning the Messiah and the water and light ceremonies of the feast.

But chapters 7–8 did not contain a sign. The healing of the blind man in chapter 9, then, presents the sign illustrating the significance of Jesus' transformation of Tabernacles and, at the same time, introduces new material. Jesus heals the blind man. He is the light of the world. The blind man has lived in darkness, representing the sinful person's condition of estrangement from God. The sinner is unable to know God. Jesus is the One who overcomes this darkness by bringing eternal life. This experience is then a revelatory one and expresses the salvation event.

Although this healing happens on the Sabbath (v. 16), it is still to be connected with the Feast of Tabernacles through the theme of light. Another feature connecting it with this feast is the pool of Siloam, where Jesus sends this blind man to wash. A daily procession carried water from there to the altar during Tabernacles. Thus the reader is to understand Tabernacles as the background.

2.4.3.9.1. The Healing of the Man Born Blind (9:1–7). These verses introduce the initial contact and healing of the blind man. He is congenitally blind—probably a defective gene, as we would scientifically describe it today. This is a tough issue for anyone to resolve—all of us struggle with it. Why do certain things far beyond our control happen? A popular way to handle this topic is with the simple answer, "It must be sin." His disciples give that answer (v. 2). Note that the disciples appeared in the Tabernacles section only in 7:3.

Many Jews associated suffering with sin and believed that these effects could be passed on from generation to generation. Even the fetus in a pregnant woman who worshiped in a pagan temple was guilty. Since the days of early Israel (Ex. 20:5), sin and its guilt were passed down through the generations. God spoke through the prophet Ezekiel's preaching against the abuse of this teaching, saying that the individual is guilty only for his or her own sin and its punishment.

At any rate, Jesus gives a different answer. Though the condition's origin and cause may be hidden to humankind, it is not to God, who offers another answer—this is an opportunity for him to reveal his grace and glory. Such complicated situations must be left in the hands of a loving and holy God, who does all things well, though not necessarily without pain. The benefit of sight and wholeness, though free, is not without great cost for the Son of God. In John, his suffering was glory.

Humans can identify with the blind man. We come with sin, Jesus comes with light and righteousness. The disciples focus on the cause (or beginning) of such a condition; Jesus focuses on the purpose and God's sovereignty (as he does elsewhere in this Gospel). Jesus' answer contrasts sharply with some modern theological systems. Much discussion arises over the origin and cause of sin. In this discussion, God's decrees usually begin with the Fall, redemption coming later in the plan. However, in God's plan in the Bible, redemption has always been the starting point, and the starting point is, at the same time, God's purpose.

Jesus' statement in 9:3 approximates Paul's comment on suffering in Romans 8:20–22:

> For the creation was subjected to frustration, not by its own choice, but by the will of the one who subjected it, in hope that the creation itself will be liberated from its bondage to decay and brought into the glorious freedom of the children of God.
>
> We know that the whole creation has been groaning as in the pains of childbirth right up to the present time. Not only so, but we ourselves, who have the firstfruits of the Spirit, groan inwardly as we await eagerly . . . the redemption of our bodies.

Thus we are encouraged—it is not just that people have been born in sin (see John 5:14), nor is it that humans are caught up in some mysterious and challenging process. No, God is at work, has been at work forever. Jesus as God's Son has always existed and has always been marked off as the Redeemer of fallen humanity. God longs to take us into his bosom as his children, and the only way to accomplish that is through the suffering of his Son, grace divine offered up through his unconditional love for a fallen race. This is the answer to life's biggest questions—"For God has bound all men over to disobedience so that he may have mercy on them all" (Rom. 11:32; see also Eph. 3:8–10).

Without interruption, Jesus continues in a way that is difficult to understand, probably urging his disciples to join him in this great salvation plan (v. 4). The use of two different pronouns in this verse points the reader in this direction: "*We* must do the work of him who sent *me*." "We" brings Jesus and his followers together in the world mission, while "me" points to the foundational provision of Jesus' unique work of salvation commissioned by the Father, which includes his death and resurrection. In verses 4–5, a time limit is prescribed. While the immediate context suggests that Jesus' earthly sojourn marks off this work, it probably takes on a larger meaning like that of a saying: Every person has a particular time in which to work; take advantage of this time, then (see Eph. 5:16).

In verse 5, Jesus again affirms himself to be "the light of the world." This theme connects chapter 9 with the Feast of Tabernacles in 8:12 and now bears additional comment. Light is one of the most fundamental metaphors in Scripture. Since 1:4, this image played largely in the significance of Jesus' person and work. In the frequent dualism of this Gospel, light and darkness illustrate contrasting forces. The blind man is in "darkness," the literal associating with the symbolical through its connection with sin. The disciples certainly make this association, and Jesus does not deny sin's presence. Instead, he talks about God's purpose in dealing with it. Later, in verses 40–41, "blindness" does refer to "sin" with its lack of spiritual sight/discernment. Thus the darkness of the world is invaded by the light of heaven.

In Psalm 44:3, light is associated with love and God's salvation (cf. also 43:3, where light is equated with truth and guidance). "Light" in rabbinic literature also takes on a figurative meaning, referring to Torah (law), temple, the souls of humans, and righteousness. This literature also connects the Messiah with light and his time of salvation. Likewise, "darkness" is connected with the darkness of the nations of the earth. It is King Messiah who provides light for them. Furthermore, the "light of the world" is an expression used of God (see *Numbers Rabbah* 15:5 on Ex. 8:2). "Light" in John also includes revelation and judgment. Jesus, then, at Tabernacles transforms, fulfills, and replaces all of these expectations and meanings of light.

"Works" (v. 4 NRSV) parallel in some cases the "signs" of this Gospel. They refer to the saving activity of God in Jesus and are miraculous in nature. In this instance, they are similar to some miracles in the other Gospels, which are also saving events.

The last part of verse 4 ("Night is coming, when no one can work") also challenges the interpreter (cf. also 5:17, 20; 11:9). But this statement continues the flow of thought of the previous sentence, particularly the note about the time of working: "as long as it is day." The time of Jesus' mission has its limits; a day will come when opportunity will no longer exist. The larger context suggests that the judgment is in view. Jesus' day of salvation, the work of the Father, will be over. It will then be judgment for all those who live in darkness. This interpretation is born out in verse 5, "While I am in the world, I am the light of the world."

These five verses, therefore, provide a basis for the healing that will now be described. Jesus mixes spittle and clay as a salve-like substance to place on the blind man's eyes. To mix these elements and put the mud on the blind man's eyes might appear to be magic. But Jesus is not performing magic here. Magic involves controlling unseen forces, and there is inevitably deception. With Jesus, the mixing of spittle and clay may subtly mirror the creation in Genesis 1:1–3, in that on the first day he made the heavens and the earth, i.e., earth and water, and light. Jesus is the One who brings new life and sight, themes of this Gospel.

Furthermore, Jesus tells the man to wash in the pool of Siloam. This pool connects this healing story with the Tabernacles celebration, important in chapters 7–8. Its name also connects with Jesus. Siloam is the Greek translation of the Hebrew *Shiloach*, which means "the sent one." The Hebrew word may be connected to "Shiloah" (cf. Isa. 8:6), which may in turn be *Shiloh* of Genesis 49:10 (cf. NIV note there). Both Jewish and Christian interpretations connected Shiloh with the Messiah. In John, Jesus is the "Sent One" (cf. 5:36–38; 8:16). He is the rock out of which comes the water (i.e., Spirit), who in turn brings life, spiritual sight, and physical healing.

2.4.3.9.2. Initial Reaction (9:8–12). These verses describe the first and least important reaction to the healing, but reinforce its point. The blind man's neighbors and others cannot agree over his identity. The various responses here are similar to earlier reactions to Jesus, reflecting a fundamental ignorance concerning him. The paragraph concludes with a testimony and a statement about the healed man's own ignorance regarding the whereabouts of Jesus.

2.4.3.9.3. Investigation of the Healing (9:13–34). The people bring this man to the Pharisees for interrogation. We learn now that the healing occurred on the Sabbath (v. 14), which has pricked the interest of this group because they are concerned whether or not Jesus has broken the Sabbath (v. 15). Two groups see the event from different perspectives. The Pharisees conclude that Jesus is not from God since he has broken the Sabbath.

Others look at the miracle itself and conclude that no sinner can perform such works. The people then appeal to the healed man, who gives a different answer—Jesus is a prophet. It is clear that this man does not yet know fully who Jesus is.

Another group called "the Jews," apparently part of the earliest group, is still not convinced that he is the same man who was blind, so they call on his parents. But the parents fear the Jews and put the responsibility back on their son (v. 22). In this verse many interpreters find evidence for the context of John's writing, both regarding the date and circumstances. To be put out of the synagogue, they claim, reflects the time when the twelfth prayer in the Eighteen Benedictions was lengthened to include a curse on the heretics, including believers in Jesus. At any rate, the "Jews" are trying to squash Jesus' influence before it gathers any more followers.

Verses 24–34 turn again to the healed man. This group intensifies its interrogation, attempting to force the man to recant any leanings he may have toward Jesus. But that does not work. On the contrary, their heated statements push him further toward Jesus. He concludes that Jesus has come from God since he performed such a miracle on him and since God does not listen to sinners: "Nobody has ever heard of opening the eyes of a man born blind" (v. 32). Neither the Old Testament nor intertestamental literature mentions a person born blind being healed. Indeed, this outstanding miracle appropriately demonstrates the saving work of Jesus.

But these Jewish leaders retort, "You were steeped in sin at birth; how dare you lecture us!" (v. 34). Their conclusion agrees with the question of 9:1. For them, the man's former blindness confirmed his sin, also evident in his budding affirmation of Jesus. "And they threw him out" suggests that these "Jews" were the religious leaders and that they have excommunicated him from the synagogue (cf. v. 22).

2.4.3.9.4. Confirmation of the Blind Pharisees (9:35–41). The next scene draws this healing to a conclusion by focusing on Jesus and the healed man and another confrontation between Jesus and the Pharisees. Jesus brings the faith of the healed man to fruition by having him precisely identify who it was that healed him and makes the point that he came to judge. That judgment will slice like a two-edged sword. On the one hand, those who are sinners (i.e., blind but responding in faith) will be saved (i.e., see), while those who can see (i.e., the religious unbelieving people) will become blind (i.e., be judged).

On the surface, this latter activity seems to contradict 3:17. But it does not. The coming of Jesus brings people to a crisis point, beyond which their decision makes clear where they stand. If they steadfastly refuse Jesus, they continue to stand under judgment. Jesus' answer to the Pharisees in 9:41 makes this clear, "If you were blind, you would not be guilty of sin; but now that you claim you can see, your guilt remains." They claim "to see" when they reject Jesus, manifesting blindness on another level. If anyone turns in faith as the blind man did, he or she will be saved from the path of judgment. John's Gospel assumes that all stand under judgment as a result of original sin.

This sign, therefore, works on two levels (as do the other signs in John). On the one level, there is the actual physical defect of blindness and its cure. On the other—and the one towards which it points—is the spiritual reality of revelation that faith and regeneration by the Spirit accomplishes. The difference between judgment/blindness and salvation/sight is faith.

Jesus used the title of "the Son of Man" here (v. 35), a somewhat rare occurrence in John (11 times) when compared to the other Gospels. Nonetheless, it is significant. (1) It depicts that Jesus is the worthy object of the man's faith. (2) As a result of coming to faith in the Son of Man, the healed person worships Jesus. In this Gospel the word "worship" (*proskuneo*) always refers to the worship of a deity (cf. 4:20, 21, 22, 23, 24; 12:20). Clearly, Jesus as God accepts worship. (3) It is the title by which Jesus reveals his judging and saving authority.

2.4.3.10. The Good Shepherd (10:1–42). This next section contains two parts: verses 1–21 and verses 22–42. While differing opinions exist about to which sections of the Gospel these parts should be attached, it is justifiable to connect them with the material in the Feast of Tabernacles. For example, verse 21 mentions the opening of blind eyes, the sign in chapter 9. The reference to the Feast of Dedication at verse 22 at first suggests new material, but this feast was considered a part of

Tabernacles, although it occurred later (in the month of December). At the same time, this material carries onward in a unified way the argument of the writer.

Some years ago, it was popular to distance John from the other canonical Gospels partly over the occurrence of parables. Indeed, John does not have any Synoptic-like parables. However, interpreters now talk about the form of parables differently. They recognize that people, including Jesus, used figurative language in a less precise way than modern technical specialists do. It is not fair to think that others, especially in antiquity and in a culture different from modern Western ones, should use them the same way. True, the Greek word *parabole* ("parable") does not occur in this Gospel. However, the Hebrew word in the Old Testament is *mashal*, and the Greek translation of the Old Testament used *paroimia* for this word. *Paroimia* is used in John's Gospel.

In chapter 10, then, we come across the first parable-like material in this Gospel. It does not matter whether or not these figures of speech are allegory or parable. They convey truths in a figurative manner. Still debated is the number of parables in these first verses.

2.4.3.10.1. The Good Shepherd and His Flock (10:1–21). The theme of this part is the good shepherd who rounds up the straying sheep of God. Pastoral imagery had long been used for spiritual messages, even though crop farming had also become an important way of life. Farming and herding are closely intertwined. In the Old Testament, God was the good shepherd (see Ps. 23). God's sheep were astray because of the failure of the leaders of Israel, who were portrayed as robbers, thieves, and strangers (e.g., Ezek. 34).

Thus, this section begins to culminate the confrontation between Jesus and Jewish leaders. Note how chapter 10 follows closely Jesus' response to the Pharisees in 9:40–41. Note too that nothing distinguishes sharply between these two chapters. These Jewish leaders are the false leaders of God's people. Jesus is the true shepherd, God's Messiah, who delivers and restores his people scattered across the landscape of sin.

Ezekiel 34 provides Scripture background for these parables. Half of this chapter was read during Tabernacles on the last and great day of the feast (7:36–37; another clue that we are to take this material together); the other half was read during the Feast of Dedication. In Ezekiel, God asked the prophet to speak against the shepherds of Israel (i.e., the leaders). They had mistreated the people, taken advantage of them, and scattered them abroad without a shepherd. God says that he himself will search out his sheep, restore, and care for them by binding up their wounds and leading them into abundant pastures and places of water.

Jesus in John 10 applies this situation to the current Jewish leaders and to himself. He uses Hillel's Rule 6: As God in the Old Testament was Israel's shepherd, in an equal way, Jesus as God's divine shepherd will seek out the lost sheep and will lay down his life for them—the sign of a true shepherd. Ezekiel 34 was understood as a messianic passage; such expectations ran high during Tabernacles.

Shepherding in the Near East even today is more similar to what took place in ancient times than it is to modern Western cultures. Thus, the Western reader may have to separate current ideas from those in the narrative of

The Good Shepherd tending his flock was an important theme in Jesus' teaching. Even today, sheep are tended in much the same way as in the time of Jesus.

John's Gospel. For example, in the Near East, shepherds walk before their sheep; in the West, they drive them. Leading (being an example) is a better discipleship model than driving (authoritarian model). Sheep in that culture are more like family, even being stalled near or in the home. The sheep also know the shepherd's voice and will not follow someone else. (Note that the healed blind man in ch. 9 knew only his shepherd's voice, the true one, and not that of the Pharisees.) Sheep are stabled during the night for protection and led out early the next morning by the shepherd for the day's care. It is common for flocks from different families to join for the day's forage, but then to be separated again at night.

A true story illustrates this activity. On the Mount of Olives just east of Jerusalem, a recent visitor to Israel enjoyed the early morning sitting on the veranda of a hotel. He was amazed as he watched shepherd boys with their flocks coming from various parts of the city to meet in an open field just below the hotel. Together they started out over the hills to the east, searching for pasture for the day. In the evening, this same group of sheep returned to the same field. As he watched, the shepherds left their bunched flocks and took up positions around but away from the flocks. Suddenly, one by one the shepherds started calling their flocks. The sheep responded by running to their shepherds. Each then went home for the night.

This may help to explain a difficulty in this section. Jesus is called both the door and the shepherd. In verse 1, he is distinguished from the door and its keeper (v. 3). But in verse 9 he is the door. "Door" here probably refers to the shepherd, who is the access of the sheep to the green pastures. In much the same manner as in this experience above, Jesus as the good shepherd leads the sheep out to abundant pasture and water. This is clearly brought out in verse 9, "He will come in and go out, and find pasture." But he is not the door of the fold (vv. 1–3).

Verses 1–18 can be divided into two parts: verses 1–6 and verses 7–18. Verses 1–5 contain the first parable, while verse 6 provides a comment about the listeners' response; verses 7–18 contain a mixture of literal and figurative elements. The latter section occurs in the first person, the former in the third person.

When Jesus finishes the first parable (vv. 1–5), John comments (v. 6) that his listeners do not understand him. Several observations are in order. (1) Though the word *paroimia* (v. 6), used to describe parabolic language, differs from that of the other canonical Gospels (*parabole*), in essence it refers to the same thing. It is a parable. (2) The hearers' response is also the same as that in the other Gospels; unbelievers simply do not understand this manner of speaking by Jesus. (3) Part of what contributes to their lack of understanding may have been that Jesus is speaking more in a subtle manner and uses the third person. He tells a simple story that anyone in the countryside knows. Without faith, a typical unbeliever's response will be: "So what?" They will miss the point that on another level Jesus is really judging and condemning them deeply. In this spiritual condition they are like thieves and robbers. They are the false shepherds. On the other hand, Jesus is the true shepherd because he does things the way God wants them done. He cares for his sheep. They know him and he knows them, and they will not follow a stranger's voice.

It is less than fruitful to try to discover the background of the words for "thief" and "robber." Evidence could be garnered from Palestine in the first century and earlier. Bandits and revolutionaries roamed everywhere, preying on people. The point is, these leaders who have dogged Jesus' trail all along the way are false and do nothing but lead the people astray. Speaking in figurative language, Jesus has come from the Father as his good shepherd to bring his people into green and abundant pastures and water.

Verses 7–18 contain an elaboration and clarification of the earlier parable. Here Jesus speaks in the first person and identifies himself in plain language. He elaborates on several areas. (1) He extends his identity. He is the gate. This figure emphasizes the uniqueness of Jesus as the Savior and our access to God. All religions fall short at this point. Only Jesus can bring people to God. Jesus also calls himself "the good shepherd" (three times). "Good" in this context refers to Jesus as the provider of salvation and care. It contains a deep relational significance, for he and his sheep are intimate, and they possess the same character and concern. They communicate only with one another.

His followers will not listen to the voice of others. This is the true meaning of discipleship, heavily stressed here.

(2) Jesus brings abundant life, as opposed to the marginalized "life" that the false shepherds bring.

(3) Jesus will lay down his life for his sheep. In this point we have at least two significant and new theological statements. (a) Jesus on his own is giving up his life. No one will take it from him. God is fully in control of these affairs through which he atones for the world's sin. The devil has no part. God's provision of salvation has always been a foregone conclusion in his mind. (b) Regarding the resurrection, the New Testament usually says that God the Father or the Spirit raised Jesus from the dead. But here Jesus says that he will raise himself, for he has the authority both to give his life and to take it up again.

(4) Jesus notes that there are "other sheep that are not of this sheep pen. I must bring them also. They too will listen to my voice, and there shall be one flock" (v. 16; cf. Eph. 2:11–22). A probable interpretation of this is that Jesus is transcending ethnic boundaries and including Gentiles among his people. This Gospel supports this in other places (e.g., John 11:52; 12:20–32). Jesus' atoning death and resurrection have destroyed all barriers between Jews and Gentiles. Sin has leveled the playing field for every human being, regardless of ethnic background. On the other hand, faith in Jesus, through which we receive God's mercy, lifts all to the same level.

At the end of Jesus' explanation of the parable (vv. 19–21), familiar responses surface. The "Jews" are split over what he has just said. These responses manifest the unbelieving attitude toward Jesus from among the various crowds at the Feast of Tabernacles. Some once again accuse Jesus of being demon-possessed (cf. 8:48). Others refer to the healing of chapter 9, thus connecting 10:1–21 with chapters 7–9.

2.4.3.10.2. The Feast of Dedication (10:22–42). The second part of chapter 10 focuses on what transpires during another feast of Judaism, the Feast of Dedication (now called Hannukah). This section of the Gospel is both new and connected to what went before, preparing for the climactic sign of the raising of Lazarus (ch. 11). This feast in some ways was linked with the earlier Feast of Tabernacles (cf. 2 Macc. 1:9). The Jews observed some of the same rituals, and light was important to both. The festival signified renewal or restoration. King Antiochus IV of Syria had desecrated Jewish practice and worship in 168/167 B.C. This brought about the Maccabean revolt. The Maccabees recaptured the temple in Jerusalem, and they cleansed it and rededicated it. The event is what was celebrated in the Feast of Dedication.

Jesus continues talking about his sheep in verses 25–30, thus linking this section with the preceding one. We have noted elsewhere that similar themes appear in chapters 5 onward, thus connecting all of them in some way. In 10:31–33 we see once again an attempt to stone Jesus for blasphemy (cf. 5:16–18; 7:44; 8:59).

Dedication occurred during "winter" (v. 22). Though several months have passed, John places the activities and dialogues of Tabernacles and Dedication closely together to get across his point about Jesus transcending the festivals of Judaism. The reader therefore knows that what happens in chapters 7–10 has a common significance. "Then" (v. 22) also connects these verses with 10:1–21. However, not since 8:59 has the temple shown up, where Jesus slipped out of it to escape his enemies. Now he walks in Solomon's Colonnade on the temple's east side (10:23).

The "Jews" surround him to press their claims (v. 24). Their question mirrors a much earlier quest (1:19–24). There, the "Jews" were identified as the religious leaders in Jerusalem; included among them were Levites, priests, and Pharisees. We should thus understand the "Jews" throughout the Gospel as referring to Jewish leaders made up of these several groups. In 10:24, these people are still in suspense about Jesus' identity. They ask him to tell them plainly, and Jesus clearly tells them that they are not among his sheep (cf. vv. 1–18). These leaders are the faithless, false shepherds.

Jesus' answer (vv. 25–30) greatly angers them, moving things to a head. But Jesus also provides consolation for his followers (vv. 27–29). He speaks of the security of the believer. This security is based on the personhood of the Father and Son and on their unity. Jesus gives them eternal life, an attribute of deity. The opposite of eternal life is to "perish." Life is that manner of existence that takes on the character of the one who gave it. In it there exists a wonderful dynamic relationship that is characterized as joy and peace.

It may be helpful to explore the relationship between human faith and divine act. John emphasizes that salvation is an act of God through Jesus. Salvation is strictly of God, resulting from Jesus' death and resurrection; people play no part in this provision. God offers this salvation to everyone. On the other hand, to receive it one must believe in Jesus, be born again by the Spirit, and follow Jesus. "Born again" is an event that results in a process, called in Semitic idiom, "walking in newness of life." When one believes in Jesus, therefore, while his or her faith does not participate in God's saving act (i.e., Jesus' death and resurrection), faith allows God to do his work.

As already mentioned, John emphasizes the divine act here. God is more than adequate to save and to keep those he saves. When people "lose" their salvation, they lose it because of their faith, not because of God's act. "Belief," while started and cultivated by the Spirit, still belongs to the believer. It is not God's faith. Note Romans 3:21–31 (esp. v. 22, "faith in Jesus Christ," and v. 25, "faith in his blood"); the NIV appropriately translates these verses to show that the object of faith is Jesus, not that this faith belongs to Jesus (i.e., "faith of Jesus"). The same holds for Galatians 2:20. Romans 12:3 is often quoted to support the coworking view, "in accordance with the measure of faith God has given you." But this context is not talking about saving faith; rather, Paul is discussing "charismatic" faith there.

Consequently, Jesus holds believers in his hand (v. 28), a metaphor for divine security. The believer need never doubt his or her salvation—it is secured by God alone. Is anyone greater (v. 29)? And Jesus and the Father are one (v. 30)! "One" in verse 30 is significant. Greek uses three genders for its nouns and adjectives: masculine, feminine, and neuter. The adjective must agree with the noun it modifies. Nothing but masculine nouns occur in this verse, but the numeral "one" here is neuter, emphasizing the "oneness" or "singleness" of purpose, power, and authority of Jesus and the Father. "One" does not blur the persons of the Father and Jesus into "one," but it does attribute "oneness" to their relationship and roles as articulated above.

Angered by these comments, the Jews take up stones to kill Jesus (v. 31), a theme occurring earlier (cf. 5:16–18). Jesus appeals to his miraculous signs as a witness to his authority, but they turn to the charge of blasphemy. Jesus answers them in rabbinic fashion, using one of Hillel's rules (vv. 34–36) and referring to Psalm 82:6 (he calls it "their law"). They and Jesus accept the infallibility of Scripture. The key word in Psalm 82 (John 10:34) is "gods." The Hebrew word *elohim* (Greek *theoi*) is plural in form, but when used of the one true God of Israel in the Old Testament, it is the plural of majesty and translated in the singular, "God."

However, this word can have several other meanings as well, as it does in this psalm. The word "gods" in Psalm 82:6 contains a double reference. The word specifically refers to kings or rulers; note verse 7, "you will fall like every other *ruler*." This may be the meaning of the word in verse 1, where God presides and gives judgment among the "gods." (An alternate meaning may be "angels.") But the other side of the meaning in verse 6 may contain what these rulers think of themselves; they may actually consider themselves to be divine. God, on the one hand, affirms that they are indeed rulers (i.e., "gods," v. 6). But the correction comes in what the psalmist notes of them. As "gods" they are "sons of the Most High." And the next verse proclaims, "you will die . . . you will fall." If this inspired writer can call people "gods," why cannot Jesus use the word to refer to himself, the one whom God has "set apart" for his saving mission and "sent into the world"?

Jesus continues to appeal to his right to be called God by referring to his miraculous works again (v. 38), as in chapter 5. His performance of his Father's works—they are, therefore, "one"—serves as the basis of his appeal and argument. In verse 39 the Jews repeat human futile efforts—they try to seize him "but he escaped their grasp." The astute reader remembers that God is still in control and that Jesus' hour has not yet arrived.

The chapter and section (and Gospel) reach a climax at 10:40–42. After Jesus eludes his enemies, he returns to more friendly climes—Jerusalem is still too unfriendly for him. He has avoided it before, now he does so again. This theme frames the large narrative section focusing on Jesus at Tabernacles (cf. 7:1 and 10:40–42). The reference to the friendly place where John baptized also recalls 1:28–29. There, Jesus finds a more receptive crowd among John's followers. They recognize that John had performed no signs but that he spoke the truth about Jesus. They therefore believe in Jesus. These three verses also inform the readers about John's function and status and encourage us likewise to follow Jesus. John simply pointed to Jesus; everyone must now follow him as the true Messiah.

2.4.3.11. Jesus Raises Lazarus (11:1–57). With the death and raising of Lazarus the reader comes to the pivotal sign that prepares for the climax of the Gospel, the passion and resurrection of Jesus. In this sign, the distance between the sign and its referent decreases. Death and life, eternal death and eternal life rub together.

This account is unique to John's Gospel and has distinct features. For example, the names of Mary, Martha, and Lazarus, all siblings, appear together only here. Lazarus as the brother of these sisters is found only in chapters 11–12. (In Luke 16:19–31 this name belongs to a certain beggar.) In Luke 10:38–42, a different story of the two sisters occurs.

Apparently, these three live in a common household without parents in Bethany, a small village several miles east of Jerusalem on the east slope of Olivet. This Bethany is to be distinguished from the one in John 1:28. John differentiates between them by adding after them either a geographical note (1:28: "on the other side of the Jordan") or attaching personal names (11:1: "the village of Mary and her sister Martha"). The order of the names of the sisters differs between Luke and John. "Mary," first in John, takes the initiative on several occasions, perhaps the most important one, seeing that she anoints the feet of Jesus (it is mentioned in 11:2, right after the names are given and a chapter before it is done).

2.4.3.11.1. The Death of Lazarus (11:1–16). In these verses, the death of Lazarus confronts the reader. Verses 1–3 set the stage, providing the characters, setting, and the opening situation—Lazarus is sick. His sickness is serious enough to cause his sisters to send a messenger to Jesus for aid, reminding him of his special love for their brother. They apparently can tell that if he does not receive help soon, he will die. This realization more than likely appears in their message to Jesus (cf. v. 4).

Verse 4 sums up Jesus' assessment of the situation and moves forward to the significance of his work, soon to be consummated in his passion and resurrection. This illness is for God's glory through the Son of God and "will not end in death." "Death" carries with it another meaning besides the normal one of physical death. To the astute and informed true believer, "death" refers to the judgment, eternal separation of sinners from God, a condition they already suffer. In fact, this account closely approximates the conditions of sinners: They are "sick," and their "sickness" will eventuate in this death. On the other hand, all who believe will have their sickness healed (i.e., sin removed), and it "will not end in death." Jesus' response is the same as in 9:3 and thus connects this sign with the healing of the man born blind.

The author adds verse 5 in anticipation of the harshness to come in verse 6, thus softening it for the reader with a tender but passionate note of Jesus' love for this little family on the brink of a personal tragedy, and in light of Jesus' forthcoming and seemingly careless action—he "stayed where he was two more days." No information is supplied about what Jesus does during those days, but the fact that he stays is important for the situation.

From verses 7–16, Jesus focuses on his disciples. After the two days, he tells them that they are headed back to Judea. They protest, citing negative feelings awaiting them there. Jesus, however, emphasizes a "golden window" of opportunity. More than likely this is what his difficult saying in verses 9–10 mean: "Are there not twelve hours of daylight? A man who walks by day will not stumble, for he sees by this world's light. It is when he walks by night that he stumbles, for he has no light." The reader last encountered a saying like this in 9:4 (another link with that sign). A person should take advantage of the daytime for a trip, for night will cause stumbling along the way.

This window of opportunity opens in the direction of the raising of Lazarus. Jesus' comment that their friend has "fallen asleep" and that he is going there to awaken him tells us about this window. For God to be glorified through the work of the Son of God, Lazarus must die (physically)—thus the two-day wait.

And the length of time between death and healing is significant. Jesus knows what he is doing—this does not upset the plan of God; rather, it is the plan. He is in control.

In reference to death, Jesus uses a figure of speech to soften this harsh reality. "Our friend Lazarus has fallen asleep" here means "he has died"; "to wake him up" refers to his healing. Scripture often speaks of death in this way. But the disciples miss the point. They take Jesus to mean literally that Lazarus is sleeping (v. 13). Their ignorance testifies about their spiritual condition, but it also speaks about the nature of faith. Though they follow Jesus and have a measure of faith, full faith will not come until its object is finished—the death and resurrection of Jesus the Son of God. This sign points in that direction.

Jesus then tells them plainly that Lazarus had died (vv. 14–15). But he also tells them why they must go there—so that they "may believe." Alas, one disciple does not get it (v. 16). Thomas's problem will show up again later (see 20:24). Apparently, he has great difficulty with faith, which impacts his spiritual insight (or his lack). This is a lesson for all to learn.

2.4.3.11.2. Jesus and Lazarus's Sisters (11:17–37). At this point, the narrative focuses on the sisters of Lazarus and the Jewish mourners and opens on a temporal note: When Jesus arrives, Lazarus has been entombed already four days (vv. 17–18). In typical Jewish fashion, the community has gathered to support the family and help them mourn. Four days leave no doubt about Lazarus's condition. Rabbis believed that the soul hovered near the body for three days. After that, no hope for coming back to life existed. Lazarus is beyond help, and the body has already started to decompose. In Jewish burial, no embalming was done. Burial happened quickly, and spices were used to cover for the odors of a decaying body.

When Mary and Martha hear that Jesus is approaching, Martha meets him on the way to talk with him. This appears similar to what she did in Luke 10:38–42; in both places she is quick to speak to Jesus, whereas Mary is more reserved. Martha's remark affirms that if Jesus had been there, her brother would not have died (v. 21). It also contains some ambiguity, for she is seemingly willing to submit to whatever he will do. This permits Jesus to respond with the appropriate word for the glory of God.

Jesus' answer (vv. 23, 25) contains two aspects of eschatology, current (or realized) and future. The future aspect points to the last day, the day when resurrection will occur (cf. v. 24). But Jesus also points towards a "realized" eschatology—to himself as the source of eternal life. The meaning of "life" in verse 25 transcends the human perception of resurrection and distinguishes between "natural" and "eternal" life. When Jesus says, "even though he dies . . . whoever lives and believes in me will never die," he is referring to a different kind of life, a qualitative life that characterizes the life that God has in himself. This life transcends both natural life and death; neither of these destroys eternal life.

Jesus' personal statement about himself in verse 25, "I am the resurrection and the life," is another one of his "I am" sayings. Here it signifies that Jesus in himself has the power and authority to resurrect and as such he is the source of this life. We have seen this teaching periodically in this Gospel. This attribute belongs exclusively to God.

Jesus also mentions the word "believe," which qualifies the reception of eternal life (see comment on 7:31). This word occurs three times in verses 25–26, signifying its importance. In all three instances, the verb is in the present tense, noting that faith is a lifestyle that goes beyond physical death. Note too that in verse 26 (which summarizes v. 25), the verb "lives" is also present tense. By constantly believing, one has eternal life; by having eternal life, one constantly believes. In verse 25, "live" is future, pointing toward (eternal) life after death.

This is the point Jesus wants to make about Lazarus's death and his delay in coming to raise him: Physical death does not matter if one has eternal life. Jesus will raise such a person from the dead, that is, will give eternal life.

Martha's confession in verse 27 identifies Jesus in the manner similar to what Nathanael did (1:49), with one addition of a final clause (which comes from 1:9; cf. NIV note there). She now confesses (using the perfect tense with "I believe"), "You are the Christ [i.e., the Messiah], the Son of God, who was to come into the world." If we take "who comes into the world" as a Jewish idiom for "humankind," n this clause connects Jesus with humanity 1 points towards him as the unique deemer and Revealer of God to humankind. tting together 1:9 and 11:27, we can pararase the matter in this way: "For all humanin the world, there is the true light, Jesus the essiah, God's Son, who also is in the world." artha's confession identifies Jesus for all aders who wish to follow in her steps.

The next paragraph focuses on Mary's ief, but at the same place where Martha countered Jesus. When Mary reaches Jesus, ong with other mourners who are following r, she falls at Jesus' feet and weeps. They, course, are also weeping. This sight deeply oubles Jesus (vv. 33, 38). The word (*embriaomai*) occurs only five times in the New estament, two of them in this Lazarus ccount. It expresses a deep feeling that arises ith several emotions and actions, such as urmuring (Mark 14:5), sternness (Matt. 30), or mourning (for a special person, John :33, 38). John employs another verb in verse 3 to convey this deep emotion, "troubled" *arasso*). His troubled spirit immediately oves Jesus to ask where they have buried azarus. He will no longer delay his activity. hey answer, "Come and see, Lord" (v. 34).

Several comments are in order here. Jesus sks "them" where "they" have buried Lazarus; they" answer. This impacts the meaning of Lord" in verse 34, which probably means omething like our English "sir," because of the nourners who have accompanied her. They do ot have the same faith or commitment as Aary. Furthermore, these are a mixed group, as een in their responses to Jesus' weeping in erses 36–37.

"Come and see" (v. 34b) points to a positive, empathetic invitation. Jesus gave a similar invitation to John the Baptist's disciples in :39. Jesus now weeps. Occasionally we find Jesus' emotion reported as we have it here e.g., Luke 19:41, where he weeps over Jerusalem's condition). In this emotion we have the coming together in Jesus of both a human and divine emotion. God is moved over the plight of lost humanity and desires to save it from death. Jesus weeps here in anticipation of confronting the scene before him and for what he is about to do.

2.4.3.11.3. The Raising of Lazarus (11:38–44). The next paragraph focuses on the raising of Lazarus. In verse 38 Jesus weeps again as he comes to the tomb, a cave with a stone in front of its entrance to seal it from animals. Martha is now present with them at the tomb and protests when Jesus commands to have the stone removed from the entrance, emphasizing the fact that her brother is surely dead. Now the condition of her faith (vv. 17–27) comes through, and Jesus reminds her of what he has said earlier (v. 40). The conditional sentence of verse 40 suggests that Lazarus's raising depends on her faith. But that is not the case. Jesus will do it to show the glory of God, not to predicate it upon her faith. Her faith will not cause his healing, it will simply allow her to see the glory of God. That glory refers to his resurrection power unleashed against humankind's enemy—death, the last enemy to be destroyed.

After they take away the stone, Jesus looks up and prays (apparently his eyes are open and his head lifted while praying), for the benefit of the people's faith who stand nearby (vv. 41–42). Their faith will be assisted by knowing that Jesus has a dynamic relationship with God, his Father. This miracle will substantiate his teaching that he comes from the Father. Furthermore, Jesus' prayer suggests that he always obeys his Father and does his will. Consequently, Jesus knows that God will answer his prayer. It is also significant that Jesus begins his prayer with a thanksgiving to his Father, in advance of the answer.

The tomb of Lazarus, in Bethany, is described by John as "a cave with a stone laid across the entrance." The story of Jesus raising Lazarus from the dead appears only in the Gospel of John.

Jesus then cries in a loud voice for Lazarus to come out. The loud voice is the authoritative command of God to the dead to arise (cf. 1 Thess. 4:16, regarding the great day of resurrection). In John 11 we should note that we do not have a resurrection as such but rather a resuscitation (even though the same Greek word is used for both concepts). A resurrected believer takes on a new body, never to die again. Jesus is the first one to have been resurrected—he is the firstfruits (1 Cor. 15:20). But Lazarus is simply brought back to life—truly a great miracle, but not a resurrection, for he will die again. Note that Lazarus still has on all the grave clothes, including the head wrapping, when he comes out of the cave. When Jesus came out of the grave, his burial clothes were undisturbed (20:5–7).

Note too that Lazarus comes out because he has life, not to receive life. Lazarus was dead—he could not do anything. This sequence is important for understanding in salvation the relationship between faith and God's activity. We obey God, not in order to get life, but because we have life. Obedience flows from the life that Jesus brings. Others have to take off Lazarus's grave clothes to release him (v. 44b).

2.4.3.11.4. A Plot to Kill Jesus (11:45–54). The Jewish leaders focus on a plot to take Jesus. In typical fashion, the crowd splits: One group believes in Jesus, the other carries news back to the leaders, his opponents. When they hear of this latest incident, they call a meeting of the Sanhedrin—the large council in Jerusalem that determined matters pertaining to capital punishment.

Among the Sanhedrin leaders are the Pharisees. Jesus was like the Pharisees in some respects. He not only believed but practiced what they believed—the resurrection. He upheld the Scripture and teachings arising from it. Both he and they were leaders of renewal efforts, though the methods of renewal were different. Jesus came to save sinners, that is, everyone, through being born again spiritually. The Pharisees sought a renewal of the Jews through Torah, including prayer, fasting, mercy, and faithfulness to God.

In this Sanhedrin meeting, the authorities note how Jesus is threatening their traditions and authority. They say among themselves that "if we let him go on like this, everyone will believe in him, and then the Romans will co and take away both our place and our natic (vv. 47b–48). Caiaphas, the high priest, th prophesies that Jesus will have to die for nation. John notes that his death will inde restore the nation and the scattered peo among the nations—Jesus will fulfill Old Te tament prophecies that God would bring ba the scattered of Israel, his method of salvati (cf. Ezek. 34; see comments on ch. 10).

Caiaphas's prophecy is not the norm prophetic mode. Rather, John sees in it a bit irony, that God will indeed take what peop intend for harm and make it turn out for h glory, an emphasis on his sovereignty a providence (vv. 51–52). It will be God's doin

Now since the Sanhedrin is plotting to k Jesus, Jesus no longer moves about public among these "Jews." He stays with his disc ples in the village of Ephraim in the dese Scholars are not sure where this Ephraim located. No doubt, it is somewhere north an perhaps east of Jerusalem, but not too far awa Soon Jesus will return to the city for his hou

2.4.3.11.5. Orders to Arrest Jesus (11:55 57). This brief paragraph moves the reader fo ward to the climactic moment when Jesu turns away from the world to concentrate o his disciples and to consummate his work. Fc a final time, he approaches the Jewish feast c Passover, for it is near. During this time, man pilgrims (v. 55) from the surrounding area travel to Jerusalem to observe it. This para graph focuses on the expectation of thes people and the leaders' increasing desire an plan to arrest Jesus. The verb tenses in verse 5 emphasize the fact that the people keep seek ing Jesus and discussing among themselves a they stand around the temple area whether o not he will appear. On the other hand (v. 57) the Jewish leaders have broadcast widely urgent "orders" to report his whereabouts sc that they may arrest him.

2.4.3.12. Appearance of the King (12:1–50). This is the last chapter of the manifestation of the light. The Passover is near, and Jesus remains close to Jerusalem, for his time is about to arrive. Chapter 12 focuses on Jesus' preparation for his forthcoming death, which in John is an anointing for his enthronement. This chapter also adds climactic information about his identity, a quest from the beginning of the Gospel.

To demonstrate that he is the King Messiah, anticipated from of old but different, Jesus follows the path of an enthronement ceremony as he enters Jerusalem. The enthronement ceremony celebrated a king's inaugural assumption of his right and power to rule. Two elements stood out: anointing and sitting down on the throne. This enthronement has roots in the Old Testament (see, e.g., 1 Kings 1:33–49; 2 Kings 11:1–20). Jesus will soon reign from his throne of power—the cross. He will soon become the divine King Messiah. The reader also understands in this section why some in Judaism, especially the Jewish leaders, reject God's Son.

2.4.3.12.1. Jesus' Anointing (12:1–8). Verses 1–8 provide some of the implicit details of Jesus' anointing for his kingship. The setting is Lazarus's house in Bethany. As in 1:28 and 11:1, John adds information to specify which Bethany. Martha, Mary, and Lazarus throw a dinner, probably in honor of what Jesus has just done for them. Lazarus serves as host, that is, he eats with others (v. 2b), while his sisters take the role of women (who normally did not eat with men). Martha serves (v. 2a) and Mary anoints Jesus (v. 3).

That Jesus is anointed is significant. Old Testament texts refer to the anointing of kings as well as the anointing of the Messiah. (In later Jewish traditions, however, probably in response to Christianity, rabbis left out any discussion about anointing when talking about the Messiah.) Oil was used for anointing in certain cases, usually when the identity of the king was in doubt and his right to the throne needed affirmation. Also in the Old Testament, oil was used when the kingship changed in some fashion.

This anointing in John 12 is not just for Jesus' death, though death is the heart of his work. In John, Jesus' feet are anointed instead of the head. It was unusual to anoint the feet, especially during a meal, and it was certainly improper for a woman to anoint feet. In Old Testament times, the head was anointed for an office, be it a king or a priest. The feet were anointed at death. But herein lies Jesus' unique kingship. He will conquer sin and death and will rule over his people through his resurrection. His cross will be his throne.

John emphasizes this by noting that Jesus will reveal his glory (see 11:40; cf. 12:27–36, 41). "Glory" (*doxa*) describes the aura surrounding a king's throne, indicating his worth, power, authority, and honor. His throne is more than a seat on which he rests. It involves his court, the furniture, attendants, and all the symbols in and around it that denote his glory. In the Old Testament, glory is associated with the presence of God. Jesus' glory and rule contrast sharply with that of the world. Through his death and resurrection he conquers the power of sin and death. This is the whole import of 12:27–36. He will judge the world and especially its ruler (12:31). That is, he will throw Satan out of heaven. He will rule over all as King Messiah. Note 12:13, where John cites Jesus as "the King of Israel" (cf. 1:49).

Many scholars believe that chapter 12 indicates the inauguration of Jesus' enthronement. According to the pattern for an enthronement ceremony, a dinner had to be given a certain distance from Jerusalem. Bethany's location suited this well. The king was anointed, as is Jesus here. The king then entered Jerusalem as a king (cf. Jesus in vv. 12–19, esp. 13–15). Finally, the day of the anointing had to be an ordinary day. John notes that this day is "six days before the Passover" (12:1)—that is, no special day.

The anointing substance used here is certainly for a king's anointing—it is "pure nard" (v. 3), very expensive and extraordinary, and its aroma fills the whole house. This scene shows great respect for Jesus. Mary anoints Jesus' feet, preparing for the burial of a corpse-to-be. This act signifies what Jesus' enthronement is to be: He will be lifted up on the cross. The fact that Mary pours oil on Jesus' feet, takes down her hair, and then wipes his feet with it is also unusual. This feature seems to be a part of the Gospel tradition, mirroring the extreme gratitude of a forgiven prostitute who came uninvited to a dinner where Jesus ate as a guest of a certain Pharisee (Luke 7:36–38). It is also unusual that a woman does the anointing of Jesus as king. This has parallels with the Samaritan woman in John 4. Because of Jesus, she, both a Samaritan woman and a prostitute (see comments on ch. 4), could be a part of the new temple.

The elements of the story roughly parallel those in Matthew 26:6–13 and Mark 14:3–9 (though there are major differences). Apparently, Jesus has begun to divulge information about his forthcoming death, which generates a flurry of anointing activity related to his crucifixion. Matthew and Mark do record that

Jesus has taught about his death. But John uniquely points to Jesus as the special eschatological King whose cross becomes his throne. His anointing for king comes before his entry into the city and his lifting up on his cross. Already in his anointing, his death is established.

Judas plays a major role in John's account. We are told only here that he is the treasurer (v. 6) and that he takes money from the treasury. The most trusted people of a group are often committed to caring for its money. Thus Judas acts in a particularly scandalous way. John explains that this is why he reacts negatively to Jesus' anointing. By not selling this expensive nard and "lifting" part of it, his "wages" are greatly diminished. Jesus, on the other hand, clearly says that Mary did this for his burial (v. 7).

Jesus continues, "You will always have the poor among you, but you will not always have me" (v. 8). Jesus does not deprecate the poor here. Following his culture, he notes that caring for the dead takes precedence over certain other social responsibilities. At the same time, he may have had Deuteronomy 15:11 in mind: "There will always be poor people in the land." He also calls attention to the importance of following and honoring him, quite befitting their King Messiah, something that Judas is not willing to do.

2.4.3.12.2. A Plot to Kill Lazarus (12:9–11). Jewish leaders who are planning to execute Jesus now also seek Lazarus's death. The reason for this is that many Jews are following Jesus because of Lazarus's revivification. Indeed, it looks as if Israel has a new leader. These Jewish leaders had better destroy all their opposition before they take over.

2.4.3.12.3. The Triumphal Entry (12:12–19). Jesus has become a popular messianic-like figure. Soon, however, the people will know that he does not fit the traditional and popular expectations of Messiah. In verses 23–26 he will announce the arrival of his hour—*the* Messiah will have to die for the sins of Israel.

It is a "great crowd" (v. 12) who, on the next day, hear that Jesus is coming, so they go out to meet him as he enters Jerusalem. It is not clear if they meet him before or after he has secured a young donkey. The narrative (esp. at v. 14) suggests that Jesus arranges for the donkey after seeing the people. At any rate, they respond to him by carrying palm branches and shouting parts of Psalm 118:25–26: "Hosanna [meaning lit., save us; cf. NIV note]! Blessed is he who comes in the name of the Lord."

The following clause is not found in the Old Testament: "Blessed is the King of Israel." While Jesus was on the cross (Matt. 27:42; Mark 15:32) his enemies taunt him as "the King of Israel." In John 1:49, Nathanael confesses that he is "the Son of God . . . the King of Israel." This clause is important, for it provides a clear interpretation and application of Psalm 118, both in terms of what the people think about Jesus and indeed what is affirmed in John 12:15, "See, your king is coming." This statement is a condensed recitation of Zechariah 9:9, which focuses on the arrival of the king, his assurance, and his nature. Instead of riding in as a conqueror on a horse of war, Jesus enters on a donkey, a beast signifying peace. King Jesus brings Israel's peace (*shalom*). There is no need, then, to fear, "O Daughter of Zion" (John 12:15). This parade certainly follows and thus supports the interpretation of his anointing in verses 1–8.

Both the Feasts of Tabernacles and Passover contained in their liturgy features about the Messiah. For example, palm branches were used (they were connected with the shout of "Hosanna"), and during Passover the temple choir sang Psalms 113–118. The New Testament never quotes Psalm 118:25–26 during Passover or immediately afterwards. It is always in a context of his Jerusalem entry, referring to his intended kingship (e.g., Matt. 21:9; 23:39; Mark 11:9–10; Luke 13:35;

For his triumphal entry into Jerusalem, Jesus rode a young donkey, fulfilling the prophecy in Zechariah 9:9, "See, your king comes to you . . . riding on . . . the foal of a donkey."

19:38; John 12:13). When Psalm 118:25 was reached, every person shook a palm branch and shouted "Hosanna" three times. A midrash on Psalm 118 applied "Blessed be he . . ." to the Messiah. Here these branches are appropriately strewn before Jesus to announce his arrival as they sing his greeting.

In verses 16–19, John adds personal insight as well as summarizes the content of verses 12–15. He notes (v. 16) that Jesus' disciples do not understand at the time the significance of what is being done, but later, after Jesus' resurrection and ascension, they do (see also 2:22). Their understanding of Scripture comes after Jesus' resurrection; that is, revelation comes only after one is born again. It is better, then, to think of this understanding as an act of revelation rather than as one of illumination. In the new birth, God provides a spirit that can communicate with him, which includes understanding the Scriptures.

In verses 17–18, John explains the people's action. Those who have been with Jesus when he raised Lazarus spread news about this event to others. As a result, many go out to see Jesus. This agitates the Pharisees all the more (v. 19).

2.4.3.12.4. The Arrival of Jesus' Hour (12:20–26). The theme of verses 20–26 is Jesus' recognition that his hour has come (v. 23). That arrival connects with the coming of "some Greeks" (v. 20), that is, Gentiles. A reference to the "Greeks" occurs earlier on the lips of the Jewish leaders, where they wonder if Jesus is about to go among the Greeks in the dispersion (7:35). The Greeks mentioned here have some attachment to Judaism, either as proselytes or simply God-fearers (people sympathetic to Jewish teachings but unwilling to commit themselves to circumcision). They have come to Jerusalem as pilgrims for this Passover Feast. These Gentiles may have come from Bethsaida in Galilee, the same city as Philip, Peter, and Andrew were from (see 1:43–46), for they seem to know Philip and seek him out in Jerusalem (12:21). Perhaps Philip and Andrew had been busy in Bethsaida in testifying to Jesus as the Messiah.

Chapter 2 links to this paragraph through the themes of the new temple (also known as Zion and Jerusalem), the climax of the old age, and the gathering of the people of God, especially the coming of the Gentiles to Jerusalem. Various Scripture texts initiate these ideas. Let us sample a few of the Old Testament texts. Isaiah 45:20, 22 and 55:5 tell of God's call to the nations. The nations await his offer of salvation in hope (55:5). Zechariah 2:10–13 reads:

> "Shout and be glad, O Daughter of Zion. For I am coming, and I will live among you," declares the LORD. "Many nations will be joined with the LORD in that day and will become my people. I will live among you and you will know that the LORD Almighty has sent me to you. The LORD will inherit Judah as his portion in the holy land and will again choose Jerusalem. Be still before the LORD, all mankind, because he has roused himself from his holy dwelling."

Isaiah 2:2 notes that the mountain of the Lord's temple will be raised above all other mountains and that all nations will stream to it. Isaiah 40:5, speaking of similar themes, adds, "And the glory of the LORD will be revealed, and all mankind together will see it." This last Scripture is important, for it connects the next paragraph in its reference to the glory of the Lord (John 12:28).

It is no coincidence that we find a connection here to chapter 2. Chapter 12 concludes the first major part of the Gospel. So this climactic chapter reaches backwards to the theme of temple replacement, framing the issue sharply as an important theme in John.

This information helps us to understand Jesus' seemingly abrupt reply in verse 23. As in 1:43–46, Philip finds someone else to inquire of Jesus (here it is Andrew); both go to Jesus and tell him about the Greeks. In his answer to his disciples, Jesus informs them that the time of salvation for all has come (cf. v. 32). Echoing the meaning of 2:16–22, zeal for his Father's house has consumed him—he is now making it a house for all nations. Using an "*amen, amen*" saying, this time in the form of a parable, Jesus illustrates his life's work with that of the single seed being planted and dying in the ground. From that single death comes new life and many more grains. So it is with Jesus' death.

Verses 25–26 bring out the ultimate significance of all of this—discipleship. Discipleship words abound here: "serve," "follow," "servant." All who would follow Jesus must believe in him, his atoning death and resurrection, and emulate him in order to receive eternal life. The Greeks come, wanting to *see* Jesus. But they must believe and follow him to be part of the new temple. When they say they want to "see" Jesus, there is a hint of "*see* the kingdom" in 3:3. It is, therefore, not just the taking on of a lifestyle and following someone around. Rather, being born again is suggested from 3:3–5 and carried forward to 12:25.

Present and future elements speak of a life of faithfulness in this world and its rewards in the next. For example, the present tense of "loves," "hates," "serves" (two times in vv. 25 and 26), and "must follow," coupled with "this world" in verse 25, establishes the necessity of discipleship and its relationship with the constancy of faith. The future tense of "will be" and "will honor" in verse 26 points toward the resurrection and the further work of the Father, the reward of honor for having given up one's life and having served Jesus.

2.4.3.12.5. The Heavenly Voice (12:27–36). The narrative moves on to focus on the "glorification" of the Son of Man, the theme of this paragraph. Serving as a bridge to verses 37–43, it brings to the surface both unbelief in the hearts of some and potential of belief for all.

Verse 27 expresses Jesus' state of being. Here his humanity surfaces—his soul (*psyche*) "is troubled" (NIV has "heart" here). This is an extremely troublesome and frightening time, and he reacts with deep emotion. His struggle, though framed with a rhetorical question whose answer he cannot avoid, affirms his mission. He has come for this very moment—so much hangs in the balance now—to save the world, and even more importantly, to glorify the Father's name (v. 28a). With that, the Father speaks from heaven: "I have glorified it, and will glorify it again."

Verse 29 provides several of the people's reactions to this voice. Some say that it thundered; others, that an angel spoke. We soon learn, however, that the voice was not for Jesus' sake; rather, it was for these people (v. 30; he addresses them there as "you" plural). The implication of this will become apparent later. Their different and indistinct hearing identifies them as unbelievers. Their inability to know the Father's voice manifests their hardhearted and unrepentant condition. The Father has just affirmed the arrival of his Son's hour, and they do not recognize his voice; they have not been born again and are unable to understand his revelation.

Verses 31–32 complete Jesus' response to the unbelievers' inability to understand. Verse 31 notes their status: Their response affirms that they rest in the state of judgment as members of this world. At the same time, its ruler, the devil (i.e., "the prince of this world"), has also been judged and cast out of heaven (see Rev. 12:9). "Now" refers to the hour of the lifting up of Jesus on the cross. It indicates that the time has come. Verse 32 speaks about the glorification of verse 28 and its results: Jesus will be lifted up and, as a result, will draw all to himself.

The expression "lifted up" suggests several things. It implies that this will be the moment when Jesus assumes his rule, that is, when he is enthroned (the theme of ch. 12). The expression also in a subtle manner refers to the entire process from his suffering, his death on the cross, his resurrection, to his ascension. "From the earth" particularly suggests this theme. "Will draw all men to myself" refers to his saving work applied to all peoples of the world. This clause particularly relates to the implication of the Greeks' seeking Jesus in verses 20–26.

Verse 32 contains language that is abstract in nature, suggesting several meanings. It can be misunderstood without explanation, so the author adds verse 33. This explanation focuses on the means of death, not its actuality or reality: He will be crucified on a cross. This verse also serves another purpose—it prepares for the crowd's response in the next verse. They will take Jesus' reference to being "lifted up" to mean "to be put to death."

The crowd responds to Jesus' comments in verse 34 and again manifests their status of unbelief. They say, "We have heard from the Law that the Christ will remain forever." "We have heard" implies that their knowledge of the Law came through the oral reading of Scripture. Usually, "Law" refers to the first five books of the Bible, called the Pentateuch. But here it refers to the entire Scriptures, for overt messianic references occur in the Psalms and the Prophets as well as the Pentateuch (cf. Luke 24:44). The idea that the Messiah will remain forever occurs in such texts as Psalms 89:4, 36; 110:4; Isaiah 9:7; Daniel 7:14. It is not clear whether this Jewish crowd believes in the eternal Messiah in this way or whether they have earlier heard Jesus.

Psalm 110 was particularly understood messianically by Christians. For example, the writer of the book of Hebrews used it as a major text for his teaching that Jesus is eternal. Other texts refer to the messianic line, the lineage of David rather than one person. The New Testament takes it both ways, that Jesus is in the lineage of David and that the promise of a king ends in Jesus. There will be no need for a successor to Jesus. This crowd understands that this "lifting up" will end his "career." They thus see a contradiction between the everlasting Messiah and the death of Jesus. This certainly was a major stumbling block to the Christian message among the Jews.

The crowd, however, fails to see two things: the fact that the atonement is needed and that God will resurrect Jesus. Their response (v. 34b) ends in a question focusing on the identity of Jesus: "Who is this 'Son of Man'?" This question serves as a bracket with 1:19–28, where the leaders from Jerusalem seek the identity of the Messiah. John and the first disciples there identify Jesus as the Messiah. Jesus specifically identifies himself at the end of chapter 1 in response to Nathanael as "the Son of Man" (1:51).

This question (v. 34) sets up Jesus' response in verses 35–36, where he encourages the people to believe in him as the light since he will still be with them for a little while. Verse 35 echoes 1:5 and 8:12. "Light" is identified with "life," "darkness" with "death." The word "walk" is Semitic for "live" and bristles with the discipleship significance of "follow." Another Semitic expression occurs in verse 36a: "sons of light." In its context it takes on the varied meaning of "to become children of God [i.e., to be like God]," "to have life," or "to be holy or righteous."

Verse 36b brings this part of the discussion to a close and marks a transition to the next paragraph. "When he had finished speaking, Jesus left and hid himself from them." This is similar to the "hidden" motif of 7:4, 10 and 8:59, where he hides himself from certain people.

2.4.3.12.6. Isaiah's Explanation of Their Blindness (12:37–43). These verses form a pause, where John comments on the place where these people and Jesus have now arrived. Despite the fact that Jesus has been with them for some time and has given them opportunity to believe in him, they have consistently refused. Verse 37 concludes, "Even after Jesus had done all these miraculous signs in their presence, they still would not believe in him." "Signs in their presence" refers to his entire ministry up to this point, including his miracles and his teaching. The Gospel is organized around the signs and Jesus' explanation of them. These two cannot be separated. That "they still would not believe in him" indicates the hardness of their hearts.

John then elucidates and underscores this hardening of the heart theme by citing an Old Testament text. The condition of these people fulfills the prophecy of Isaiah 53:1 (v. 38). Verse 39 and the subsequent reference in verses 40–41 to Isaiah 6:10 make it sound as if God has caused them to be blind so as not to heal them. This is not the case, however. Consider the context of this theme. John has made consistent reference to unbelief in the hearts of these people (e.g., vv. 27–36). Their condition is mirrored in the fact that they cannot understand God's revelation when it comes, even though it was for them (v. 30). Also, verses 35–36 show that they have had and still have opportunity to believe. These verses particularly impact the readers as they move on to the hardening of the heart theme. Isaiah's prophecies provide direction for the reader's understanding of these people's rejection of Jesus: They have blind eyes and hard hearts, and they are sick.

In contrast to their refusal to see the revelation of God (called his "glory" in v. 41), Isaiah did not see it, and yet he spoke of it. Note verse 42, however, which states that many of the rulers do believe in Jesus but publicly do not confess this belief because they do not want the Pharisees to excommunicate them from the synagogue. This verse may clarify who the secret believers are in John's Gospel. This may also reflect the time of writing, when leaders excommunicated from the synagogue worshipers who believed in Jesus. This verse would speak especially to them and encourage them in such difficult times.

The reason the Pharisees reject Jesus and excommunicate his Jewish followers is expressed in the last verse of this paragraph (v. 43): "They loved praise from men more than praise from God." The word "praise" is the Greek word *doxa*, usually translated "glory." The author plays on this word here in verse 43. The first *doxa* refers to the pride of self-centered sin, exalting oneself above God. The second *doxa* reflects the meaning in verse 41, where it alludes to the revelation of God in Jesus. What a tragic preference!

2.4.3.12.7. The Cry of Jesus (12:44–50). This paragraph ends this division of John's Gospel. Themes that appeared earlier do so again to summarize the narrative. The solemnity of this occasion is signified by the fact in verse 44 that "Jesus cried out." In 7:28 and 38 during the Feast of Tabernacles, he "cried out" in similar fashion, expressing similar themes. In 7:28, he identified himself with the Father and his teaching with that of his Father. In 7:38, Jesus cried out about the coming of the Spirit and the gift of eternal life, a theme also in this present paragraph, now connected with "command." "Belief" also occurs in the context of 7:38 and 12:44. But these themes were also part of the earliest verses of the Gospel.

Other significant themes appear here as well. Let us now list them.

(1) To believe in Jesus is also to believe in the Father.
(2) To see Jesus is to see the Father.
(3) Jesus as the light of the world came to remove the condemned from darkness.
(4) If people do not believe in Jesus, they remain under condemnation.
(5) Jesus came to save the world, not to condemn it.
(6) Jesus' word will judge the unbeliever on the last day.
(7) Jesus speaks the words of the Father.
(8) The Father's commandment is eternal life.

3. The Manifestation of the Light Among His Own (13:1–20:31)

This section contains the account of the Last Supper and large teaching blocks around it (chs. 13–16), Jesus' high priestly prayer (ch. 17), his betrayal and arrest (18:1–11), trial (18:12–19:16), crucifixion (19:17–37), burial (19:38–42), and resurrection (ch. 20). With chapter 13, Jesus turns from manifesting himself to the world to devoting attention to his disciples.

3.1. Dinner With His Disciples and Footwashing (13:1–38)

Chapter 13 contains the setting for dealing with two specific disciples and for the lengthy discourses that follow (chs. 14–17). This part of the narrative focuses on the last day of Jesus' life on earth. He will die during the time of the offering of the Passover lambs in the temple, the afternoon before the evening meal that is the Passover. He will therefore be the Passover Lamb that John announced in chapter 1.

3.1.1. A Pattern to Follow (13:1–17). The section begins with an emphatic expression about the time setting: "It was just before the Passover Feast" (cf. 12:1). The Greek expression used here distances this feast from the time during which Jesus and his disciples eat together and have fellowship. Jesus knows that his time has come "to leave this world and go to the Father." As mentioned before, this expression includes his death, resurrection, and ascension. Before he leaves, he wants to express to his disciples "the full extent of his love." In this footwashing scene we see the act of love in anticipation of his suffering on the cross for them. It is an extremely humbling act of self-giving love. The expression of this love also calls for affirming humility through modeling and handling betrayal.

Handling betrayal arises early in the text. In Greek verses 2–4 form one sentence. The main idea, that Jesus arises from dinner to wash the disciples' feet, is set in the context of betrayal. To eat with someone was a significant thing in that culture; being a host meant protecting all who came, and guests would respond accordingly. It was extremely shameful to treat a host in the manner that Judas will. Yet Jesus manifests his great love to all of them, even though he knows what will transpire.

Earlier in 6:70, Jesus knew that one of his disciples had a devil (lit., "one of you *is* a devil"). But he is in control here, for the Father has given him authority over all, even over his coming into the world and his going and what happens in between. This whole chapter should be read in light of this great love of Jesus for his own and of the fact that several of his close associates are to betray him.

Such a horrible deed as betrayal is not done by a human being alone. It is the devil who has placed the idea in Judas's heart, and the devil joined Judas with the religious leaders (8:44), who were murderers from the beginning. Now, in chapter 13, the devil has brought them together to accomplish this horrible deed. Sin is not just individual and personal; it can be religious and, certainly, is societal. But bringing these people together to kill Jesus is the devil's own undoing. Even he works out the plan of God. How wise God is to take what is meant for evil and turn it into great good! In this way the principle in the account of Joseph in Egypt surfaces again, to demonstrate God's glory and control of redemptive history. Note that in 1 John 3:8, John writes that Jesus came to destroy the works of the devil.

Verses 2 and 4 contain a somewhat general reference to the meal. The NIV has the "evening meal" (Gk. *deipnon*). This reference causes some problems among interpreters. A *deipnon* refers to a banquet or a regular meal, especially the evening one. John thus avoids the word for the Passover meal, which the Synoptics have (cf. Matt. 26:2, 14–29; Mark 14:1, 12–25; Luke 22:1–15). Scholars have given several explanations. John used a different calendar, such as the one the Qumran community used. Or perhaps a system was devised to extend the day of preparation for the Passover one day and make it two instead of one; this would allow those living away from the land of Israel some room to still observe the Passover properly, since communications were not as precise as they are today.

Whatever the explanation, one thing should be observed: Jesus is the Passover Lamb of God, and he was slain on the cross when the lambs were. Since the lambs were eaten later on in the evening, Jesus could not have eaten the Passover with his disciples—he was already in the tomb. He fulfilled what John the Baptist had said earlier in 1:29, "Look, the Lamb of God, who takes away the sin of the world!" John, then, substitutes "evening meal" for "Passover meal."

It is the emphasis on footwashing in the otherwise Passover setting that causes some to suggest that footwashing takes on the same character as that of the Lord's Supper. Footwashing, in this case, is more than a demonstration of humility in service—it is more sacramental. Jesus provides directions for it in verses 12–20.

Verses 1–3 have set the scene for the rest of the dramatic action. In verse 4, Jesus arises from the meal. He would have been reclining at the head of the table, since that is the way people positioned themselves to eat. Each person reclined on an elbow and extended the feet away from the table while eating with the other hand.

It is not clear about the order of events during this meal. Usually washing occurred well before a meal. A disciple rather than a slave should normally have done the job, since Jesus is alone with his followers. But they appear to have sat down already for the meal. At any rate, we must take the footwashing as an important part of the whole meal. Jesus takes the initiative. He stands up, takes off his outer clothing, and wraps a linen towel around his waist. The word "took off" is the same word as in 10:11, where Jesus "lays down" his life for his sheep. The reader should not miss the significance of the connection between these acts. In verse 5, Jesus pours water into a basin and begins to wash the disciples' feet. This act shows the servant-like attitude of Jesus and anticipates the laying down of his life.

Verses 6–17 focus on the washing of the disciples' feet and on its purpose. John does not report the order of seating or the order in which each pair of feet is washed, except later in verse 22. There, Peter is not close enough to hear what Jesus said. At any rate, we are to understand that John intended to set forth this as a lesson, focusing on Peter.

Verses 6–10 cover the dialogue between Jesus and Peter. Peter is the one who depicted ignorance and misunderstanding of Jesus' activity. With his supposed humility, he refuses to let Jesus wash his feet. Jesus' answer acknowledges his present ignorance and shifts attention to the instruction he will give when he finishes washing their feet (vv. 12–17). Peter's insistent refusal (v. 8) draws attention to the condition and seriousness of the act. Jesus' statement in verse 10, that most of the disciples have bathed bodies but need their feet washed, more than likely refers to their commitment to be his disciples and to the additional need of this lesson in servitude. The significance points towards the union of attitude between Jesus and those who want to follow him in service, as it is based on the impending and submissive death of Jesus on the cross. Thus Jesus replies in verse 8b, "Unless I wash you, you have no part with me."

We should mention that the water used in cleansing here subtly suggests the work of the Spirit in sanctification. In the interconnection of texts and ideas in this world, this association would be made. It is thus done in the Old Testament and in the literature of Judaism (see Craig S. Keener, *The Spirit in the Gospels and Acts: Divine Purity and Power*, 1997). In verse 11 John adds his own comment, clarifying the scene.

Verses 12–17 provide the reason for the footwashing. Having washed the disciples' feet, put on his clothing, and resumed his place at the meal, Jesus then can speak with new authority. This is brought out especially through the way he refers to himself. He is rightly their "Teacher," "Lord," and "master" (vv. 13–14, 16). He thus begins by asking a question, "Do you understand what I have done for you?" On their part, the anticipated answer is, "No, we do not." This is evident from Jesus' answer.

Verse 14 explains Jesus' motivation for the footwashing: "Now that I . . . have washed your feet, you also should wash one another's feet." Verse 15 plainly emphasizes the "example" factor involved—the servant attitude of discipleship modeled after Jesus' attitude and behavior. The word for "example" is *hypodeigma*; it refers to more than a mere "example," for it has an ethical and compulsory aspect. Yet one is not a servant of Jesus merely out of duty or compulsion; rather, servitude springs from love. Love motivated Jesus to give his life for the world and to wash the feet of his disciples. All service should be humble, regardless of status.

In this regard, both servant and master are on the same level (v. 16). Jesus sets in motion a pattern for true service for all time for all of his disciples. Footwashing in this context thus approaches the importance of other ordinances of the church. But its specific expression arises out of a cultural context in a different way from the ordinances. In our modern society, in other words, footwashing may need recontextualizing. That is, some other service may need to be done in the same attitude. To wash one another's feet, or to give one's life, can take many forms.

The significance of this instruction surfaces in verses 16–17 in two ways. (1) The importance appears in an "*amen, amen*" introduction to the saying in verse 16 (NIV, "I tell you the truth"). This introductory phrase elsewhere brings special attention and emphasis to a saying. (2) One of Jesus' beatitudes occurs at the end of this section. This brings humble and loving service under the canopy of Jesus' instructions in the Sermon on the Mount (cf. Matt. 7:24–27 with this concluding beatitude in John 13:17). The wise person is the one who obeys Jesus' instructions. The person who "washes the feet of others" will participate in the blessings and privileges of the kingdom.

3.1.2. The Betrayer (13:18–30). Jesus now focuses on Judas, who will complete the betrayal act. This horrible deed contrasts sharply with what has just happened. The Lord of all had demonstrated what true character is by washing his disciples' feet. Soon Judas, a recipient of Jesus' gracious action, will betray his Lord.

Jesus continues his instruction in verse 18. When he says that he is not referring to all of them, he either resumes what he said in verse 10 or else he wants to specify those who will be blessed by following his exhortations in verse 17. At any rate, this provides a transition to the topic of Judas's betrayal. Jesus uses no connectors in these first two sentences of verse 18, more than likely to emphasize what he says about Judas's betrayal in this paragraph.

These two sentences do go together, however. They stress the fact that Jesus knows in advance exactly who will betray him—the "I" in "I know" is emphatic in Greek. "Foreknowledge" connects to Jesus' divinity (v. 19) and not to his being merely a prophet. The same cluster of ideas occurred earlier in 6:70–71: foreknowledge, election, and choosing. Some see "choosing" and "election" as synonymous. Upon closer examination, however, they are distinct. "Choosing" here does not refer to salvation or to judgment; rather, it pertains to Jesus' selecting the Twelve as apostles. Among the Twelve, Jesus always knew that Judas would betray him and that he had a devil. This is the irony of chapter 13, that Jesus would select such a one as a close associate, even wash his feet, and then experience betrayal while eating this special meal together. Jesus has foreknowledge and is thus in control of his destiny and of salvation history.

Jesus shares this information with all of his disciples (esp. v. 19) so they may continue to believe in him when the moment of betrayal mes. That time will be most vexing (see ch. 8). This, then, is meant to unify him and his and of disciples rather than separate them and us cause God's plan to be thwarted. Further-ore, this verse relates to later persecutions of elievers, when they will be called upon to ve their lives.

Verse 20 is difficult to understand since it eems so vaguely connected to the surround-g verses. "I tell you the truth [*amen, amen*], hoever accepts anyone I send accepts me; d whoever accepts me accepts the one who nt me." This saying may be affirming in a sitive way the fact that in betraying Jesus, das is also rejecting God. There is no hope r this man.

In verse 18, Jesus uses Psalm 41:9 to direct e meaning of his remarks. This quote shifts tention away from the cluster of ideas to the cus of the fulfillment of Scripture. God is en both as the Lord of history and as the evealer of his plans to people through Scrip-re. Jesus' reference to this psalm is not in the rm of an exact quote. The psalmist, David, rites there of personal betrayal; this psalm ceives a Christological explanation here. sus draws attention to the betrayal of the ivine Son of God by a close associate. It is od himself who is being betrayed. This is ade clear by the title Jesus uses of himself at e end of verse 19. The NIV has "that I am le"; the Greek has only "that I Am." This is ne of the several occurrences of this title in hn's Gospel and is a title for God, based on aiah 40 and elsewhere, as we have noted ear-er (see comments on 4:26; 6:19–20).

A new scene moves into view with verse 1. Jesus is troubled in spirit as he affirms by stifying that one of his associates will betray im. Once again, this affirmation occurs in the rm of an "*amen, amen*" saying (NIV, "I tell ou the truth"). The troubled spirit of Jesus ontrasts with that of verses 18–19. We learn at Jesus is indeed deeply touched in his umanity over such adverse human situations f. also 11:33–35, where the same word *rasso* occurs).

Jesus' announcement in such a straightfor-ard manner causes a stir among the disciples. hey keep looking at one another in disbelief at one of them would do this. This scene, ough, is not to disclose in front of all who the ulprit is, for that is not shared (see v. 28). It was for the sake of those who would need to know at a later time, at the scene in the garden (see ch. 18). This information comes from the beloved disciple, more than likely John. Peter sits on the other side of John, away from Jesus, for Peter asks him to inquire of Jesus. But Jesus gives no names; he only refers John to the act of dipping the bread in the dish and handing it to someone. But the end of verse 26 provides full identity, apparently then unknown or at least unshared by John.

This context of the betrayal—the eating together of such close associates—drives home the awfulness and audacity of the betrayal. Judas would have been seated in a place of honor, next to Jesus. Furthermore, to dip bread and hand it to someone was an honorable act. How gracious and ironical! Jesus knows Judas will betray him but treats him with great respect. Perhaps all this is emphasized by the fact that, at the moment Jesus hands Judas the bread, Satan enters him (v. 27). This shows progression from 13:2, where Satan has placed it in the heart of Judas to betray Jesus. Now Satan enters Judas.

What should be noticed about this entire episode is that Satan has access to Judas's heart, probably to tempt him. But this is undoubtedly a special kind of temptation—one that sits on the edge between sinful human decision-making and the divine will (to die for people). Why is this meal the point at which Satan enters his heart? Jesus knows that Judas, with a weakness in his lust for money, is seriously considering this deed. He also knows that if this sin is not dealt with, it will eventuate in the act. He has recourse to observe that Judas is not handling it properly. We can now see why Jesus deals with it in this setting. His words themselves, as it were, "push" Judas at last to go forward with the act. Judas probably thinks, "Since he knows, I may as well get on with it now."

With the entering of Satan, Jesus instructs him to do his deed quickly. Jesus' hour has come—the cross awaits him (see vv. 31–38). However, no one understands; they simply think that Judas as the treasurer is going to buy something for the Feast or to give something to the poor. Verse 30 ends with Judas going out into the night. "It was night" suggests the mood of the hour, especially of the betrayal and of the sinfulness of humankind.

3.1.3. Intimate Self-Disclosure of His Glory (13:31–38). Verse 31 moves the narrative ahead from the dark hour of Judas's betrayal to that of the glory of the Son and the Father, and beyond that to the discourses in chapters 14–17. Verse 32, which goes along with verse 31, pulls together a number of statements about glorification that are difficult to interpret. Contributing to this difficulty is the fact that the first clause in verse 32 is missing in some manuscripts (see NIV note). Let us make a number of observations.

The title "Son of Man" in verse 31 occurs only here in chapters 13–21. In two ways its use is similar to the other Gospels. (1) The context denotes a time of suffering. This meal is placed within Jesus' hour of passion and suffering; he was heading toward his death. (2) Jesus uses it when referring to his glorification. This hour, too, includes glorification (this is the theme of vv. 31–32). Note also that the title "Son of Man" is found at 12:23 (see its similar context). Moreover, in John 13:31, "Son of Man" probably is equivalent to "Son of God."

"Now" begins Jesus' discourse as he turns to his own disciples in personal instruction, who are now without the traitor. This adverb is emphatic, drawing attention to another step in the progress of Jesus' time (lit., "hour"; see 13:1). "Now" and "hour" connect with 12:27 (see also 12:23 and context), the first time we see these terms. There, the Greeks sought Jesus, causing him to exclaim that his hour had finally arrived.

Glorification, the topic of verses 31–32, needs further discussion. The contexts where this expression occurs (cf. also 7:39; 14:13; 17:1, 4) suggest that it includes a number of events surrounding Jesus' last days before his crucifixion (i.e., his entry into Jerusalem before the Feast, cf. 12:23–33) until his ascension. All these events point toward the atoning work of Jesus, resulting in the believer's possession of eternal life and of a new relationship with the Father. This especially includes Judas's betrayal of Jesus. It is ironic that upon entering Judas to betray and thus kill Jesus, Satan seals his own doom. Satan will fall with Judas. For with this horrible plan (in the natural), Jesus will glorify the Father, who in turn will glorify Jesus.

This is a likely meaning of these five statements in verses 31–32, all containing the reciprocal glorification of the Father and the So The Father has sent the Son to reveal himse and to atone for the sins of the world; the Sc came to reveal the Father and to be the Father gift of salvation to the world. In the Son's con plete obedience, the Father is glorified; tl Father glorifies the Son in his complete obed ence.[7] The last sentence, "and will glorify him once," likely points to Jesus' impending cruc fixion, the next step in the hour of glorificatio

Verse 33 continues Jesus' instruction abo his impending death. (This verse supports tl interpretation of the last clause of v. 32.) Jes again talks about his going away, this tin directed exclusively to his disciples. Th going away refers to all he must experienc between now and his resurrection. There also a subtle reference to his ascension her though there is no overt part of the narrati in John discussing it. Jesus calls his discipl "children" (*teknia*)—the only time in th Gospel that this word is used (cf. the relate word *teknon*; see comments on 8:32–59). Th metaphor for disciples of Jesus expresses tl conversion experience.

Verse 33 anticipates verse 34, where Jes gives his disciples a new command directir their lives after he goes away and until the later follow him (see v. 36). Love is to be tl main ingredient binding them together. Jes refers to their mission in the world in verse 3: "By this [i.e., love] all men will know that yc are my disciples." This is the theme of tl beloved disciple—in this Gospel and in 1, : and 3 John. Love flows out of the new birth, tl creation of life that is like God's and that take on his character—God is love. Furthermor love is the principle that guides all Christia ethical behavior. It is the fabric of the kingdo of God. It is what fulfills all the commands (God (cf. Matt. 22:37–40). Jesus brings this in being with his coming. He has loved his disc ples fully (see 13:1). Love was the lesson of tl meal they have just concluded.

Verses 36–38 focus on Peter again, brin ing out Jesus' love for a trusted disciple wh will later deny him. Peter is closer to Jud than he realizes. Jesus' love is indeed fa reaching—for one who will betray him and fc one who will deny him.

In conclusion, verses 31–38 connect th "hour" of Jesus, running from chapter 12 to tl end of the Gospel. They also anticipate cha ers 14–17 in their use of certain terms. Finally, hey aid the transition from chapter 13 into the liscourse of chapter 14.

3.2. *Jesus' Impending Departure (14:1–31)*

Chapters 13–17 contain lengthy discourses by Jesus that the other Gospels do not have. Chapter 13, as we have noted, deals with Judas's betrayal and Peter's eventual denial of Jesus. The end of this chapter introduced again the hour of Jesus' glorification. Chapters 14–17 build on the implications of this glorification.

In summary form, here is the scene presented in these chapters. Jesus has come to do he work of the Father—to accomplish edemption for a lost world. To carry out that nessage to all peoples, he has selected a group of followers. At the completion of his work on earth, Jesus must return to the Father. The events of this work—especially the cross—will be difficult for the disciples. But Jesus must die on it, be raised, and ascend; and he wants his disciples to know that this is necessary. After Jesus ascends to the Father, he will not leave them alone. In fact, were he not to eturn to the Father and send the Spirit, the Father's work would not be finished. But Jesus and the Father will send them the Spirit. In him, Jesus will return. This will make the Father, Jesus, and believers one, though he and the Father will be in heaven and they on earth.

The disciples should pray to the Father, and he will send the Spirit, who will speak to them his will. Jesus is going away to build them a place where, after he returns to earth to get them, they can be together forever. Access to heaven is exclusively through Jesus, the Way. Meanwhile, believers will be left on earth to carry out the work of Jesus and the Father. This work exists in two related dimensions. 1) Believers will extend the work of redemption, that is, the work of the cross through proclamation and signs. (2) They will manifest a certain ethical lifestyle on the earth, especially characterized by love—the same kind of love that exists between the Father and Son. With these comments in mind, we now can work our way through the text.

3.2.1. The Promise of Comfort (14:1–14). These verses contain Jesus' encouragement of he disciples and his response to two of their questions. In verses 1–4 Jesus for the first time speaks to his disciples about what their future in heaven will be like. John has thus far focused more on the present life, on being born again. Now, however, as the time approaches for his departure, Jesus shares with them what he will do for them when he returns to heaven.

The paragraph begins with an exhortation by Jesus about the consternation they will soon experience. The exhortation (v. 1), "Do not let your hearts be troubled," comes from the lips of the Counselor (also known as the first Paraclete, the Comforter [cf. comments on 14:16]). As Jesus was troubled in 13:21, so his disciples will be; the Greek verb (*tarasso*) is the same in both places. Jesus encourages them in his great hour of glory and trial with the words of his exhortation in verse 1: "Trust in God; trust also in me." Here Jesus underscores the unity of the Father and himself. He is now enlarging the new thinking that will result from his coming. They will be introduced to a new facet of the Trinity, which is subordinate yet equal. These next chapters will spend some effort to emphasize the unity of the Father, Son, and believers.

In verses 2–4, Jesus speaks about the place where he is going. "In his Father's house are many rooms" has several implications. "Father's house" could refer to the kingdom of God or to the temple. "Kingdom" does occur in 3:3 and 5, but its reference there is to the present state of being born again. Here "Father's house" (*oikia*) seems to refer more centrally to the heavenly dwelling place of God. (Note that in 8:35, *oikia* refers to the people of God in their present and eternal state.)

"Rooms" translates the word *monai*. This word is related to the word John uses with some frequency, both in verb and noun forms, to speak of "remaining," "dwelling," and "living." It means literally "living rooms" or "dwelling places." In 1 Enoch 41:1, "kingdom" equals "dwelling places." In the Testament of Abraham 20, the patriarchs dwell in *monai* (cf. John 1:18 and the bosom of Abraham). In John, these "rooms" are in the Father's "house," and Jesus is going away to build these. What does this mean? Here is a suggestion. Scholars have long noted that chapters 14–16 pick up themes from the Feast of Tabernacles. "Rooms" here probably refers to eternal booths (booths means "tabernacles"). Attached to the celebration of Tabernacles was the expectation that in the future time (i.e., in the new age), the Messiah would come and build booths for an eternal celebration. Jesus, then, will go away to build these eternal booths, thus celebrating God's triumph over evil; he thus will dwell eternally with his people.

Verses 2–3 contain the word "place" (*topos*; "place" in NIV in v. 4 is not in the Greek text). *Topos* refers to the idea of "temple." Note that several of John's references to *topos* bear that significance (e.g., 4:20; 11:48; cf. also Matt. 24:15; Acts 6:13–14; 7:7; 21:28). All of this is important in John's themes. Through his saving work, Jesus will transform the temple and its feasts and move them into the spiritual realm. John 2, with the first sign and the cleansing of the temple, pointed toward this reality. Jesus will build these dwelling places by sending his Spirit to convict sinners of their sins and to regenerate them. These people, born from above, make up the new temple, God's dwelling place. This fact explains how unity between the Father, Son, and his people is achieved. Verse 4 concludes this presentation with Jesus saying, "You know the way to the place where I am going." Implicitly, Jesus refers to himself.

This statement causes questions to arise from two disciples, Thomas and Philip. Jesus answers them, providing more emphasis to his words (vv. 5–11). We have now heard from four disciples since 13:1: Judas, Peter, Thomas, and Philip. They have not come off very well. What comes through is that Jesus' disciples do not yet know much about spiritual or heavenly things. The reason for this John supplies for us—they have not yet been born of the Spirit.

Verse 7 contains a contrary-to-fact conditional sentence stating this very fact. The NIV has captured it well (I add my elements to the NIV). "If you really knew me [but you do not], you would know my Father as well [but you do not]." "Knowing" in John is connected with the ability to understand God's revelation, which only comes through the work of the Spirit in rebirth. In this Gospel, rebirth is a revelatory experience. "Knowing" fits among John's vocabulary of rebirth with such words as "entering" and "seeing" in 3:3, 5 ("seeing" occurs in parallel form with "knowing" at 14:7).

In chapter 3, John, using irony, shows Nicodemus to be blind because he has not been born again. There, John already pointed to the resurrection of Jesus for this experience. That section (2:1–4:54) focused on the first sign at the wedding, with its attendant implication of the cleansing of the temple. Jesus' discussion with Nicodemus is part of the sign narrative explaining the new temple. The new temple is connected with rebirth, which can only come after the resurrection of Jesus and after the Spirit has been given. In 7:39 John clearly says that the Spirit had not yet been given. Furthermore, as we have seen in the commentary on chapter 7, Jesus' atonement must be connected with Passover, not Tabernacles. Jesus' person and work climax with his resurrection and form the basis for the new temple. He is its foundation. The life and work of Jesus prior to his passion time is closely connected with his work on the cross but anticipates its consummation at the cross and resurrection. In other words, the Twelve were his disciples in some sort of way prior to his resurrection, but they were not born again until after he arose and breathed on them. This is what distinguishes Christianity from all other religions.

Furthermore, Gospel narrative works simultaneously on (at least) two levels. For example, when reading/hearing chapter 3 readers/listeners have in mind both crucifixion and post-resurrection times. Furthermore, by the time we arrive at chapter 14, we bring with us all we have read/heard earlier. So, the time for "knowing" has arrived. Thus verse 7 concludes with, "From now on, you do know him and have seen him."

The first question in verse 5 (in the form of a declaration) deals with the "way" (see v. 6). Jesus uses this to emphasize the uniqueness of his redeeming work. Only through him can one get to God. The "way and the truth and the life" of verse 6a flow together in one meaning.

The second question (v. 8) focuses on knowing the Father, the end of the way. This provides Jesus an opportunity to enlarge on the unity of himself and the Father. Whereas the first question used the word "know" and "see" (once, v. 7), Jesus' response turns to "believe" ("know" and "see" once each in v. 9). Both knowing and seeing probably denote the same activity. It is customary for John to use words like these interchangeably. But the unity of the Father, the Son, and believers from the human perspective depends on faith. Philip does not have that faith so he cannot see that Jesus has been revealing the Father all along. Jesus mplores Philip to believe the signs, even if he loes not believe his words.

After the resurrection, when that faith is resent, even the believer can do Jesus' and the ather's works—in fact, greater ones. Verses 1–12 focus on "works." Faith depends on elieving the "signs" Jesus has been doing. What are these "works"? The NIV uses several English words to translate *ergon/erga* (singuar/plural). The NIV has "work" (v. 10), "evilence of the miracles themselves" (v. 11), what I have been doing" (v. 12), and "things" v. 12). But we must see that there is one funlamental word behind these translations: the oun and verb form of *ergon*. The particular lause in verse 12 that is difficult to understand ut which heads toward the meaning of works" is: "He will do even greater things han these because I am going to the Father."

In several places in this Gospel, the singular oun *ergon* refers to the entire work of Jesus as e obeys the Father. In 4:34: "'My food,' said esus, 'is to do the will of him who sent me and o finish his work.'" The work in this context rises from the first sign and receives explicit xplanation in bringing salvation to the Samaritans. New temple and rebirth language bounds here. "Work" embraces the whole plan f redemption in John. Another one is in 17:4: I have brought you glory on earth by comleting the work you gave me to do."

John 6:26–29 presents another place where works" is the key word. Jesus tells his discisles to work for food "that endures to eternal ife," food that "the Son of Man will give you" v. 27). The Jewish leaders ask, "What must we o to do the works God requires?" (v. 28). esus explains what he means with "work": The work of God is this: to believe in the one e has sent" (v. 29). "Work," then, is connected o eternal life and true belief.

A cluster of texts helps us further undertand this concept. In 7:21, "Jesus said to them i.e., Jewish leaders], 'I did one miracle [i.e., vork, Gk. *ergon*], and you are all astonished.'" esus' "work" here refers to the healing of the rippled man in 5:1–28. The Jews accused esus of breaking the Sabbath and of blashemy. The context of this healing helps our nderstanding: "Works" refer to wholeness, ternal life, and resurrection. It is helpful to ote that "greater" occurs with "works" in 5:20 NRSV). The explicit reference is to the resurrection, not only of Jesus but of all who believe in him; these will receive life. John 9:4 and context bring out the same thing.

We can now summarize our analysis. "Works" and "signs" are interchangeable. They refer to the miracles Jesus performed in John. They are real but convey something beyond themselves. They point to the regenerating work of Jesus resulting from his work the last week of his life through his resurrection. The signs are chosen to appropriately convey what Jesus' saving activity does both physically and spiritually. For instance, the blind (e.g., sinners who cannot know spiritual things) are given sight. Lazarus is raised from the dead (i.e., sinners receive eternal life). These two signs come just before the death and resurrection of Jesus and speak clearly of his work. The "works" that believers will do, then, concern the proclamation of the gospel, in which all who believe will receive eternal life.

What then of miracles? They are part of the gospel as it does its work in overthrowing evil. But an ethical side exists as well. Since works flow from the unity of the Father, Son, and believers and since believers have eternal life from God, they also act like God. Especially is love emphasized—it is the motivating principle for spreading the gospel through word and miracle and through love for one another. What then of the "greater things" in 14:12? It refers to quantity rather than to quality. Jesus performed these "works," but his followers down through the centuries will bring millions more to the Father. This is what they do as they wait for the return of Jesus (cf. above).

Verses 13–14 contain the clearest place in the New Testament for praying in Jesus' name. To pray in his name is to ask for the Father's and Son's sake and glory. We are explicitly encouraged to pray to Jesus. He says he will give "whatever" and "anything" we ask for. But these words are not a blank check, for our requests must be qualified with reference to God's "glory." This kind of prayer is always answered.

3.2.2. The Spirit and the World (14:15–31). This section has three parts, all focusing on the distinction between the world and the believer: verses 15–21, 22–24, and 25–31. The believer will feel estranged because he or she, like Jesus, has nothing to do with the world. Each has a different life or existence.

The first part of this section is balanced by the second, and the final one summarizes and extends the thought of the first two.

The theme of verses 15–20 focuses on the coming of the Spirit to the side of the believer, who remains in a hostile world. Verses 15–16 present how the believer is to receive the Counselor, the Spirit. The Spirit will replace Jesus as the other Jesus-like Counselor. He will be with the believer forever. How does the believer receive the Spirit? He or she must keep the commandments. When one does, Jesus will pray to the Father, and he will answer that prayer and send the Spirit. This may seem strange for several reasons. (1) If th believer has the Spirit at regeneration, does i make sense in these verses to ask for more o the Spirit? (2) Is the coming of the Spirit con ditional on keeping commandments rathe than faith? (3) To what does this paragrap have reference—an unspecified future or Joh 20 (the post-resurrection appearances)?

Regarding the last question, one possible res olution is that this section pertains to the post resurrection appearances but with reference t time beyond that. As is typical with this Gospel Jesus is John's text to bring help and solution to his own audience.

THE WORK OF THE HOLY SPIRIT

Task	References
A. The Holy Spirit in Relation to Creation and Revelation	
1. Active in creation	Ge 1:2; Job 33:4
2. Imparts life to God's creatures	Ge 2:7; Job 33:4; Ps 104:30
3. Inspired the prophets and apostles	Nu 11:29; Isa 59:21; Mic 3:8; Zec 7:12; 2Ti 3:16; 2Pe 1:21
4. Speaks through the Word	2Sa 23:1–2; Ac 1:16–20; Eph 6:17; Heb 3:7–11; 9:8; 10:15
B. The Holy Spirit in Relation to Jesus Christ	
1. Jesus was conceived in Mary by the Spirit	Mt 1:18, 20–23; Lk 1:34–35
2. Was filled with the Spirit	Mt 3:16–17; Mk 1:12–13; Lk 3:21–22; Lk 4:1
3. Preached in the Spirit	Isa 11:2–4; 61:1–2; Lk 4:16–27
4. Performed miracles by the power of the Spirit	Isa 61:1; Mt 12:28; Lk 11:20; Ac 10:38
5. Will baptize believers in the Holy Spirit	Mt 3:11; Mk 1:8; Lk 3:16; Jn 1:33; Ac 1:4–5; 11:16
6. Promises the Holy Spirit	Jn 7:37–39; 14:16–18, 25–26; 15:26–27; 16:7–15
7. Is revealed to believers by the Spirit	Jn 16:13–15
8. Offered himself on the cross through the Spirit	Heb 9:14
9. Was raised from the dead by the Spirit	Ro 1:3–4; 8:11
10. Received the Spirit from the Father	Jn 16:5–14; Ac 2:33
11. Poured out the Spirit upon believers	Ac 2:33, 38–39
12. Is glorified by the Spirit	Jn 16:13–14
13. Spirit prays for his return	Rev 22:17
C. The Holy Spirit in Relation to the Church	
1. Dwells in the church as his temple	1Co 3:16; Eph 2:22; cf. Hag 2:5
2. Is poured out upon the church	Ac 1:5; 2:1–4, 16–21; cf. Isa 32:15; 44:3; Hos 6:3; Joel 2:23–32
3. Speaks to the church	Rev 2:7, 11, 17, 27; 3:6, 13, 22
4. Creates fellowship in the church	2Co 13:14; Php 2:1
5. Unites the church	1Co 12:13; Eph 4:4
6. Gives gifts to the church	Ro 12:6–8; Eph 4:11
7. Strengthens the church	Ac 4:30–33; 1Co 12:7–13; 14:1–33

Task	References
8. Appoints leaders for the church	Ac 20:28; Eph 4:11
9. Works through Spirit-filled people	Ac 6:3, 5, 8; 8:6–12; 15:28, 32; cf. Nu 27:18; Jdg 6:34; 1Sa 16:13; Zec 4:6
10. Empowers preachers	1Co 2:4
11. Directs the missionary enterprise	Ac 8:29, 39; 13:2–4; 16:6–7; 20:23
12. Guards the church against error	2Ti 1:14
13. Warns the church of apostasy	1Ti 4:1; cf. Ne 9:30
14. Equips the church for spiritual warfare	Eph 6:10–18
15. Glorifies Christ	Jn 16:13–15
16. Promotes righteousness	Ro 14:17; Eph 2:21–22; 3:16–21; 1Th 4:7–8

D. The Holy Spirit in Relation to Individual Believers

Task	References
1. Lives in every believer	Ro 8:11; 1Co 6:15–20; 2Co 3:3; Eph 1:13; Heb 6:4; 1Jn 3:24; 4:13
2. Convicts us of sin	Jn 16:7–11; Ac 2:37
3. Regenerates us	Jn 3:5–6; 14:17; 20:22; Ro 8:9; 2Co 3:6; Tit 3:5
4. Imparts God's love to us	Ro 5:5
5. Makes us realize God is our Father	Ro 8:14–16; Gal 4:6
6. Enables us to say "Jesus is Lord"	1Co 12:3
7. Reveals Christ to us	Jn 15:26; 16:14–15; 1Co 2:10–11
8. Reveals God's truth to us	Ne 9:20; Jn 14:16–17, 26; 16:13–14; 1Co 2:9–16
9. Enables us to distinguish truth from error	1Jn 4:1–3
10. Incorporates us into the church	1Co 12:13
11. Is given to all who ask	Lk 11:13
12. Baptizes us into Christ	Mt 3:11; Mk 1:8; Lk 3:16; Jn 1:33; Ac 1:4–5; 11:16; 1Co 12:13
13. Fills us	Lk 1:15, 41, 67; Ac 2:4; 4:8, 31; 6:3–5; 7:55; 11:24; 13:9, 52; Eph 5:18
14. Gives us power and boldness to witness	Lk 1:15–17; 24:47–49; Ac 1:8; 4:31; 6:9–10; 19:6; Ro 9:1–3
15. Gives us special gifts	Mk 16:17–18; 1Co 1:7; 12:7–11; 1Pe 4:10–11
16. Gives visions and prophecy	Joel 2:28–29; Ac 2:17–18; 10:9–22; 1Co 14:1–5, 21–25
17. Develops his fruit in us	Ro 14:17; 1Co 13; Gal 5:22–23; 1Th 1:6
18. Enables us to live a holy life	Ps 51:10–12; 143:10; Eze 11:19–20; 37:26; Ro 8:4–10; 15:16; Gal 5:16–18, 25; Php 2:12–13; 2Th 2:13; 1Pe 1:2
19. Frees us from the power of sin	Ro 8:2; Eph 3:16
20. Enables us to fight Satan with the Word	Eph 6:17
21. Enables us to speak in difficult moments	Mt 10:17–20; Mk 13:11; Lk 12:11–12
22. Gives us comfort and encouragement	Jn 14:17–18, 26–27; Ac 9:31
23. Helps us to pray	Ac 4:23–24; Ro 8:26; Eph 6:18; Jude 20
24. Enables us to worship	Jn 4:23–24; Ac 10:46; Eph 5:18–19; Php 3:3
25. Is our pledge of final redemption	2Co 1:22; 5:5; Eph 1:13–14
26. Makes us yearn for Christ's return	Ro 8:23; Rev 22:20
27. Gives life to our mortal bodies	Ro 8:11

The connection between obedience to Jesus' commands and the reception of the Spirit (vv. 15–16) can be explained in this way. Judaism taught this—God gives his Spirit to those who keep his commandments (cf. Acts 5:32). These verses, though, may be connected closely to verses 13–14 and may specify the rather ambiguous "whatever" and "anything." The prayer there may be for the coming of the Spirit. The condition of keeping the commandments may simply manifest whether or not one is a follower of Jesus. The "what I command" at verse 15 in the NIV in Greek is "keep my commandments" (note the plural). "Commandments" refers to the principle that governs them—love. Love serves a prominent role in these chapters. One other element to be mentioned is the matter about "you will obey." This verb is a statement (indicative mood), not a command (i.e., though, admittedly, sometimes the future functions as a command). The significance of this, then, is that once love for Jesus is present, commandments flow naturally. This naturally pleases God and makes an acceptable dwelling for him.

The role of the Counselor receives some attention. He is the one who will speak truthfully of Jesus (v. 16). He will not be recognized by the world, for it is an unacceptable habitation for him. One who has not been born again cannot understand the Spirit. Conversion and regeneration, as John teaches, are at the same time revelational and transformational. In contrast, the Counselor will live in the believer (v. 17). He, as the Spirit, will bring life, similar to what Jesus does (v. 19). The Spirit will also unify the Father, Jesus, and believers (v. 20). The Counselor will serve as a Father too, since his coming will not allow believers to be orphans (v. 18), although not in the same sense as Jesus is. It may be as well that "orphan" brings out the need for a teacher and guide, the work of the Spirit.

The word "another" in verse 16 means that the Spirit will carry on the work of Jesus in the same way as he did; that is, he will be as Jesus was in and among the believers. "On that day" (v. 20) probably refers to the post-resurrection appearance to the disciples (20:19–23).

Two observations should be made about "Counselor" here. (1) I use the masculine pronoun ("he," "him," etc.) for the Spirit, as does the NIV. The Greek has, for the most part, the neuter pronoun, simply because the noun i replaces ("Spirit") is neuter. Exceptions d exist (e.g., 14:26). Some of these may be du to the fact that "Spirit" is a neuter noun i Greek while "Counselor" is masculine.

(2) Different opinions occur among stu dents of Scripture over the meaning and origi of "Counselor" (Gk. *parakletos*). It can mea "comforter," "counselor," and "advocate. Strains of each of these occur throughout chap ters 14–16, where *parakletos* is used. It shoul also be noted that through the Counselor's rol of bringing Jesus to believers and comfortin them, this person functions messianically; tha is, he will work as the Messiah works when h appears and will bring peace and consolatio to God's people after all the centuries of bein estranged from land and temple.[8] *Parakleto* appears suddenly and without explanation fo the first time at 14:16, which suggests that thi term had significance among the original readers of this Gospel.

Verse 19 contrasts the world with th believer. "Before long" points towards Jesus death and the event beyond which the worl will not "see" Jesus. However, believers wil "see" him. "See," in the case of the latter expresses the ability to communicate with Go by means of the new birth and the presence o the Spirit. The basis of this ability is in the resurrection life of Jesus, which is now also th believer's.

Verse 21 recaps verse 15 and extends th conversation, thereby introducing the next paragraph. That new extension is in the wor "show." "Show" signifies a personal encounte between Jesus and the person who loves Go and lets obedience flow out of that love. Jesu responds and manifests himself in that situation.

In verse 22, another disciple named Judas (not the one who betrayed Jesus, John makes clear) shows his misunderstanding. He does not know why Jesus will show himself to them but not to the world. This manifests a misconception of God's kingdom, a view held by Jesus' brothers in 7:4 (see also Acts 1:1–7).

In verse 23 Jesus responds to the first part of the question and answers this in ways about which he has already spoken. Those who love him and keep his commandments (i.e., believers), he and the Father will love; they will come to them and "make [their] home with [them]." "Home" is the same Greek word as "rooms" in verse 2 (*mone*) and has a meaningful connection. As we have suggested, "rooms" refers to evangelization of the world. When someone believes, God comes to make his "home" in him or her. Thus, many "rooms" will exist. God's "house" is always under construction, with new "rooms" being added every day. Jesus answers the last part of the question in verse 24. The world does not love him or keep his commandments. It will not listen to his word, which is also the Father's word.

Verse 25 acts as a summary of the preceding verses: "All this I have spoken while still with you." He then speaks about the Counselor again (v. 26), who is now called the Holy Spirit. The Father will send him in Jesus' name. It is because of his redemptive work that the Spirit can now come and work in the world. This underscores the fact that Jesus and his work of salvation form the heart of all doctrine about the Spirit.

The Spirit's work is outlined in verse 26 as well. He will teach believers all things (i.e., about Jesus' words and deeds) and will empower the memory in regards to Jesus' teachings. No one can really know Jesus without the Spirit. Thus, it is not just cognitive but experiential, personal, and affective knowledge (i.e., knowledge that comes through personal acquaintance and fellowship). Jesus' words will bring assurance to the disciples that they are indeed his. Today, some speak of this experience as illumination, circumventing the direct and supernatural manifestation of God. Rather, it is best to call this acquisition of knowledge, revelation. The Spirit brings the Bible (i.e., the words of Jesus) alive in a powerful way.

In verse 27 Jesus leaves the disciples his peace. How does this fit with the preceding, and what is the meaning of "peace"? The Spirit comes through Jesus' name (v. 26), that is, through the redemptive work of Jesus. "Peace" in this context refers to what Paul calls "justification" and "reconciliation." That is, because of Jesus' work, people stand in a new relationship with God. Such a relationship is made actual when someone believes in Jesus.

This new relationship is expressed in two ways simultaneously. On the one hand, the person has a new standing before God because of Jesus' work. Jesus is in heaven with the Father, declaring that he has made peace with God for sinful people. (Note: This is the advocacy part of the Counselor, but in heaven.) On the other hand, the Spirit brings this peace to the believer. This is where reconciliation and justification become personal. (Note: This is the other part of the Counselor's advocacy, declaring and assuring the believer that he or she has a good standing with the Father in heaven. This also relates to the unity theme.) The new temple, a related theme, once again emerges in this context. Believers have heaven's presence in and with them. God no longer is separated from humankind because of unatoned-for sin, relegated to manifest himself behind closed curtains in a place called the Most Holy Place. Believers have the presence of God with and in them.

This idea of peace is embedded in the idea of *shalom* (the Hebrew word for "peace"), which has a lengthy history and is loaded with rich significance. This idea had gathered end-time meaning associated with the Messiah. *Shalom* meant the presence of God's salvation, of wholeness of mind, body, and soul, with persons being in right relationships with others. In the resurrection appearance in 20:19–23, Jesus speaks peace to the cowering disciples. There, as here, he comforts them in the midst of a most harrowing time. Thus, the second time (cf. 14:1) he says, "Do not let your hearts be troubled and do not be afraid" (v. 27b).

In the remaining verses (vv. 28–31), Jesus tells his disciples again of his going and its implications. He must go to the Father in heaven, for he is subject to him. There he must finish his work. This work will go on until he returns to earth. What Jesus implies here is that he must ascend to heaven to present his finished work to the Father. The same theme is taught in the book of Hebrews, whose ideas may well derive from Jesus' teaching here. There Jesus as the high priest returns to the heavenly temple to cleanse it and to offer himself there as a sacrifice—that is, to offer his work to God. This also suggests the mediatorship and intercession of Jesus, which is constant. Jesus works in the world and in the church from heaven through the Spirit (see his standing position in Acts 7:55).

Finally, Jesus divulges something about the devil: "The prince of this world is coming" (v. 30), but "he has no hold on me." His coming refers to the resurrection of Jesus coupled with his ascension, when, by his returning to the Father with his atoning power, Satan (the prince of this world) will be cast out of heaven and come to earth (see 12:31; cf. Rev. 12). "He has no hold on me" means that Jesus has him under control. The power that Satan has over people comes through sin and disobedience to God. God has taken care of that through the atonement of Jesus and the gift of the Spirit. People now must believe Jesus.

Chapter 14 and this discourse close with Jesus' request to change locations, "Come now; let us leave."

3.3. The True Vine (15:1–27)

John's style moves in a circular manner, repeating but moving forward. It is especially the case in chapters 13–16, making them difficult to outline. When we arrive at chapter 15, an extended allegory breaks into the narrative. But this allegory continues to feature themes of these chapters. It particularly focuses on the doctrine of the church, including ethics and discipleship.

We should examine John's presentation of the church. In this allegory of the grapevine lies some rather startling information, true to the teaching of this Gospel and its context. The Old Testament uses vineyard imagery as a symbol for Israel. In other words, this metaphor in many contexts stands for the people of God. Usually, however, this imagery is in judgment contexts. It is surprising to see what happens in this imagery in the New Testament. Paul in Romans 9–11 uses a fig tree as a symbol for the people of God. But he has the patriarchs as the root, and Israel extends upward until the unbelieving branches are cut off and the Gentiles are grafted in. The genealogies in Matthew and Luke show a similar interest in Israel.

In John, however, nothing is said about anyone earlier than Jesus. Jesus is the trunk, the Father is the gardener, believers in Jesus are the branches. John obviously wishes to show the unique position of Jesus in the plan of salvation. The patriarchs (see 1:18; 8:31–59 regarding Abraham; ch. 4 regarding Jacob and his well) and later Israelites have been removed. John will thus argue that Judaism does not make up the people of God, rather, only those who follow Jesus and are of the new creation of God. John clearly has this in mind, for in 15:25, Jesus speaks about those who hate and reject him and refers to these religious leaders in the following way: "But this is to fulfill what is written in their [Judaism's] law."

3.3.1. Pruning the Branches (15:1–10). Conflict surfaces in 15:1 with, "I am the true vine, and my Father is the gardener." In this verse, "I" and "true" in Greek are emphatic. Thus, in contrast to others (i.e., religious leaders) who claim to be part of God's true people, Jesus and his followers emerge as the true ones. This emphasizes the uniqueness of him as the way to God.

In verse 2, the point of this section emerges: sanctification. The word expressing this in the NIV is "prune," though the Greek word is usually translated "cleanse." This word belongs to the religious aspect of "making holy" or "sanctifying." What is assumed, then, is a view of the church discussed above, but what becomes obvious is that God cleanses the believer; and this allegory of the vine appropriately expresses that. It should be noted too that sanctification is a normal process of discipleship. The purpose of pruning is to increase fruitfulness.

Verses 3–5 speak of the union of Jesus and believers in figurative terms of the branch and the trunk. Jesus expresses the fact of this union with the words, "You are already clean because of the word I have spoken to you" (v. 3). But the result of that union is the growth process—in figurative terms, bearing fruit. Since a branch cannot bear fruit unless it is connected to the trunk (i.e., the person has to be [abide] in Christ), fruit has a certain meaning. In the context of chapters 13–17, fruit is love, a fundamental characteristic of God. To be able to love as God, then, one has to be born again (i.e., have eternal life) and to follow him. This love must be developed through the "pruning process."

This whole process is said to "remain" in him. "Remain" speaks of a life lived out in Jesus, something that is constant and habitual. One can readily see that this narrative pertains first to the disciples that manifest ignorance, and then to any disciple. As long as people love Jesus, he will be tender to help them grow and not cut them off. However, Judas is also alluded to in the verses coming up.

In verses 5b–6, Judas's type is implicitly addressed. If one separates from Jesus (the runk), one is cut off from the source of life and becomes like a branch cut off, good only for burning. This is the fate of all who follow in the betrayer's steps. Verse 6 teaches that believers can fall away. Chapter 15 thus becomes important for those in John's day who were considering leaving the church to return to the synagogue. The same danger appears in Hebrews.

This section concludes by noting that the abiding and pruning process results in answered prayer (v. 7). The ambiguous request in verse 7 is specified in verse 8. "Whatever you wish" is directed to asking God to help one love as he does, so that as a result, God may receive glory. To be a disciple is to love as God loves. Verses 9–10 recap what Jesus has said up to this point.

3.3.2. Love and Joy—Life in the Vine (15:11–17). This next paragraph repeats the theme of loving and keeping the commandment but adds another dimension. The NIV's "I have told you this" at verse 11 relates back to 14:25, where the same words occur in the Greek. In 15:11, joy is introduced. Joy goes along with "peace" mentioned in 14:27. "Joy" is what the Messiah will bring with him into his era. Peace and joy are kingdom realities that Jesus brings (cf. Rom. 14:17). But joy takes on a different characteristic, as did peace: Joy only comes from abiding in Jesus. In its context, joy comes from expressing the love that comes from God. We might add that this joy does not depend on circumstances. Rather, it comes when love is shown, even in spite of the most difficult circumstances as believers follow Jesus' pattern (v. 13). As he laid down his life for his friends, so believers lay down theirs.

In verses 13–17, Jesus introduces the word "friends" and its implications, contrasting it with "servant [slave]." It is true that slave is an important idea in the New Testament, especially in Pauline contexts. It expresses the believer's submission to the Lord, his rule over his disciples. Here, however, Jesus adds another important dimension to his relationship with his followers. This new term is a social one and is connected with John's major theme of the born again experience as a revelational one. Jesus hides nothing from the requirements of being a follower of his—his Father hid nothing from him (v. 15).

This straightforward manner of giving this kind of information makes a decision to follow Christ difficult because it offers and requires a self-sacrificing rather than a self-serving way. This is why Jesus said, "You did not choose me, but I chose you and appointed you to go and bear fruit—fruit that will last" (v. 16). Here "appointed" is added to "choose" to describe the eleven disciples who remain and who will carry on his work in the world. God's work and church do not rest on any human will or effort. What it took to rescue the human race from their dilemma was far beyond their ability. But Jesus' choosing and appointing provide the basis of joy and assurance for the troubled spirit.

A comment about "friendship" is helpful here. Friendship in the Old Testament, certain sects of Judaism in Jesus' day, and in the Greco-Roman world was significant. To be a friend meant to be loyal and trustworthy, even to death, and to share unreservedly in matters.

3.3.3. The Hatred of the World (15:18–25). This paragraph returns to elaborate on the disciples' relationship with the world and explains why they and the world are estranged. Here the religious leaders are identified as the "world" (see v. 25 and the statement containing "their Law").

The world (i.e., sinners) hates Jesus because he has come to speak to them about their sin (v. 22) and to show them miracles (i.e., the way of escape from their sins, v. 24; see also 3:17ff.). His disciples do not belong to the world because Jesus has chosen them out of the world (v. 19). "Chosen [them]" means "saved them." Since they have in this process identified with Jesus, the world hates them too (vv. 18, 21, 25). Jesus has said this before (v. 20) in the analogy of master and slave. The world will persecute Jesus' followers. This also is the context for the encouragement Jesus gives in chapters 13–16.

3.3.4. The Spirit's Testimony (15:26–27). Encouragement again surfaces in these final verses when Jesus returns to the Counselor theme. This time Jesus says that *he* will send the Spirit, who goes out from the Father. The Spirit, in turn, will testify about Jesus. The disciples will also testify of Jesus, "for you have been with me from the beginning." In verse 27, apostolic verification combines with the Spirit's witness concerning the life and teaching of Jesus.

It may also imply that they must testify about Jesus to the world that persecutes them. This element hints at the mission of the church with the presence of the Spirit. It also suggests that the Spirit will particularly be with them in times of persecution. This refers to the Spirit of prophecy that will come on them, fortify them, and inspire them to testify of Jesus.

We can now make a final observation on chapter 15. This chapter revolves around the allegory of the vine, speaking about the union of the Son and believers and the sanctifying process of the Father. The "pruning" process makes sense in the light of what Judas Iscariot, Peter, Thomas, Philip, and the other Judas did in the preceding chapters. The dinner at which Jesus showed them his love fully, connected with his dying, has given them an example they must follow. Judas Iscariot is the branch that has separated from the trunk. He cannot bear fruit (i.e., love). The others remain attached but need considerable pruning. But by remaining in him, they can do it.

3.4. The Work of the Spirit (16:1–33)

3.4.1. The Spirit's Work and Nature (16:1–16). Verses 1–4 are a small paragraph that begins with the same Greek word as 14:25 and 15:11: "All this I have *told* you." The paragraph also ends with the same phrase. This in effect brackets the unit. The topic of the paragraph contains a momentous admonition concerning persecution, which will come from the synagogue. Until the Passion week, it was not necessary for Jesus to warn his disciples of this; but now that his death is approaching, the time to do that has come. As his followers, they too will experience the same danger (v. 4—this element is an addition to the last bracket).

The word used only in John (three times) for this threat (*aposynagogos*) occurs for the last time (see comments on 9:22; 12:42). It literally means "put out of the synagogue." This reference reflects not only Jesus' day but also the heightened tensions coming at the official split of the church and synagogue somewhere around A.D. 85. It is this ingredient that gives this Gospel the appearance of being sectarian. That is, a small group believes that it bears the true religious nature that the larger body has abandoned, developing its own identity and exemplifying this true nature. Consequently, it draws the ire of this body. But the larger body believes it is protecting the truth by removing the threat. Jesus appropriately speaks to such situations: "A time is coming when anyone who kills you will think he is offering a service to God" (16:2). The reason for this is that they have not known the Father or the Son.

The last sentence in verse 4 serves as a transition to the next paragraph (vv. 5–16). Verse 5 in Greek begins with a contrasting connector. The statement about Jesus' return to heaven provides the reason for his informing them about persecution. "I am going" is in the present tense and suggests that in the events of his hour Jesus is already in the process of returning to heaven. This subtle fact pervades the Passion account and hints at his omnipresence.

Apparently, this news grieves the disciples greatly (v. 6). This further explains why several times Jesus has encouraged them. At 14:1, then, when he says, "Do not let your hearts be troubled," he is anticipating the impact of this news. But he has great news, too. In verse 7, he notes that he must return to heaven, or else the Counselor will not come. This supports what we noted earlier, that Jesus had to return to the Father to complete his redemptive work. The Spirit's (i.e., Counselor's) coming is based on Jesus' atoning work. All of the Spirit's work is thus connected with Jesus. Furthermore, the disciples cannot receive comfort without the Spirit, who will do his job on the inside and among them. This fact suggests that the word *parakletos* should in this context be translated "Comforter."

A noun from the same stem as "Counselor" appears in Luke 2:25. There, Simeon awaits the "consolation" of Israel. That is, Israel awaits the deliverance that the Messiah will bring from the painful condition. Israel will be consoled. However, there the Holy Spirit is already on Simeon, who yet awaits the consolation of the Messiah. However, it fits with John, for this consolation comes only through the redemption that Jesus the Messiah supplies. Note: Jesus himself sends the Spirit (v. 7).

Verses 8–11 describe the function of the Counselor. Written from the perspective of the earth, when he arrives he will convict the world of three things: sin, righteousness, and judgment. Up to now, the coming of the Counselor has been for the sake of believers. For example, he will be with them, will be as a father (i.e., not leave them as orphans), will testify to them, will instruct them, and will cause them to remember the things about Jesus. "Counselor" is an appropriate translation for *parakletos* heretofore. Now, however, the *parakletos* takes on a role similar to that of a modern prosecuting attorney. Perhaps no one name is adequate for the Spirit in John 14–16.

The reader is not left alone, wondering what these three things are that the Spirit will do as prosecuting attorney. (1) He will convict the world of sin. Though John assumes all are guilty of "original sin," this is not his emphasis. Recall John 3:16–21 (and other places), where Jesus says he has come not to judge sinners but save them. Yet unbelievers have already been judged because they have not believed (3:18). Jesus' coming confirms sinners in their state. In 3:20, the one who habitually practices evil refuses to come to the light lest he be convicted (note the same word as in 16:8–9; see esp. 15:22). But with the coming of the Counselor, he will convict them.

Jesus' function was to handle sin in a judiciary way. The Spirit's function will be to come to each sinner personally to speak to his or her heart and will. Now that the judiciary aspect has been taken care of, the Spirit can at last do his work. He will come and convict the world of sin, both in terms of original sin and separation from God (i.e., the singular form of "sin," in 16:8; cf. 1:29; 8:21; etc.), and of one's personal acts of sin (i.e., the plural form in 8:24; etc.). The occurrence of similar words and even clauses in chapters 3 and 16 tells the reader that both contexts speak about similar topics (e.g., cf. 16:8 with 3:18).

(2) The Spirit will convict the world of righteousness. The Counselor will convict of righteousness because Jesus has returned to the Father and they no longer see him. This, too, is a recurring refrain in this Gospel. Now that the world will be convinced of their sin, they will be drawn to its solution. Jesus will have done his work, beginning with the coming of the Greeks (cf. discussion on "hour" in ch. 12) until he returns to the Father and presents his finished work of atonement there. This is the only way of being made right with God—to accept Jesus as God's righteousness.

(3) The Spirit will convict the world of judgment because the prince of the world has been condemned. "The prince of this world" occurs in John 12:31; 14:30; 16:11. This prince rules over the world, which in John consists of all sinners. The place where this prince has been operating has been heaven. But in these three references, we find that with the inauguration of the *hora* ("hour") of Jesus, this prince has been judged and cast out of heaven to earth (cf. Rev. 12:13–17). This means that this prince no longer has access to God to accuse people before him.

Another name for this prince, "Satan," occurs only once in John (13:27). If Satan is the same as this prince, he also tempts people in the world so he can accuse them in the limited sphere he now inhabits. Because he is limited in a number of ways, he uses demons or spirits to help him; but he wants to take care of this situation personally (although in John's Gospel neither demons nor evil spirits appear). This is special warfare, then (cf. Rev. 12). Satan wants to destroy Jesus and thinks that his death will do it. This information makes us aware that Satan is not all-knowing and that he does not know or understand the resurrection. After all, no one has ever been resurrected before. This probably means that Satan did not understand creation either. Did not God create everything out of nothing? The only way Satan could know it was if it had happened so he could have experienced and "studied" it.

This kind of accusatory and tempting activity of Satan is noted in the Feast of Tabernacles (this is a theme that appears in its liturgy and the people's reflection). Why then did John use "Satan" in 13:27 instead of prince? Perhaps this is the answer. "Satan" means adversary and accuser (cf. Rev. 12:10). It is ironical, then, that Judas's adversary gets the best of him through temptation and deceit. But Satan gets more than he bargained for—both he and Judas meet their doom and are forever together.

These three objects of conviction are placed in a certain sequence: the human problem, sin; its solution, righteousness; and the source of sin's entry into the world and continuing provocation in his accusing people before God, judgment of the prince. God has now spoken in Jesus, providing at last the answer to the question of why there is evil. Several more observations are necessary. What does "convict" mean? Since Jesus did not come to condemn the world (3:16–17) but to save it, conviction must then involve the act of informing the sinner of the fact, nature, and consequence of sin (i.e., the cognitive aspect). It also involves drawing or wooing the sinner to the light (i.e., the emotional aspect). Finally, it includes convincing the sinner to move toward God (i.e., the volitional aspect). In these three objects of conviction lies a theology of world missions as well as an explanation of the presence of moral evil.

At verse 12, Jesus turns back to the disciples to indicate that they need the Spirit for further instruction—they can bear no more now. In this paragraph (vv. 12–16), "Spirit" replaces the name "Counselor," probably because Jesus wants to emphasize the truth aspect of the Spirit's instruction—that is the full name for him in verse 13. The Spirit's work is once again to guide into all truth. In the context (vv. 13–15), "all truth" is the communication about and from Jesus. The Spirit is the agent between the Son (and Father) in heaven and believers on earth. When Jesus says that "the Spirit will . . . make it known to you" (v. 15), he is not speaking about illumination but revelation. "He will tell you what is yet to come" (v. 13).

The Spirit's role, function, and nature are further elaborated upon here. The Spirit will not speak of himself but will glorify Jesus by making known what is his. The self-effacing nature and humility of the Spirit thus surface, even his submissive and servant-like attitude, just as Jesus demonstrated in the footwashing at the dinner.

Verse 16 caps this paragraph by returning to a recurring theme. As we have observed, the ascension is not plainly mentioned, but it is alluded to in the statement: "In a little while you will see me no more." Jesus' return through the Spirit comes from the phrase, "and then after a little while you will see me."

3.4.2. Exhortation to Ask for Joy/the Spirit (16:17–24). Since 14:22, Jesus has done all the talking. Now the disciples enter the dialogue by asking among themselves the meaning of verse 16. Verses 17–18 indicate that what Jesus said puzzles them. They "kept asking" themselves what this statement and parts of it mean. The particular point that makes them question is "a little while" (v. 18). It is this, then, that Jesus picks up on in the rest of this paragraph. And this point connects with chapters 14–17 and one of the meanings of "Counselor."

"A little while" means that the disciples will weep and mourn while the world rejoices. The "world" refers to sinners (all ethnic and people groups, including the Jews). This time of sorrowing covers the Passion week through the resurrection of Jesus. His disciples will sorrow during this time, whereas the people (the world) who kill Jesus will think they have done away with him and will therefore rejoice. They are under the influence and deception of, and have joined forces with, Satan. Like Satan and Judas, and even like the disciples, they have no perception of the resurrection. Jesus is warning and comforting them in advance.

But the disciples' sorrow will turn into joy. Verse 21 contains an illustration of pain turning to joy. It will be with them (vv. 20b, 22) as it is with a woman who gives birth to a child. After the baby is born, the anguish of birth is forgotten.

In verses 23–24, Jesus exhorts his disciples to pray to the Father in his name. They have not yet done this. Whatever they ask in his name, the Father will give. However, the context is clear. "Whatever" is not a blank check. Rather, Jesus is exhorting them to ask for the Spirit; he is the one who will bring joy. Jesus will give the Spirit, and they will receive him. He will bring the assurance that Jesus is alive, plus other revelation, and their joy will be full. The Spirit will bring the presence of the Father and Jesus to them. This points towards 20:19–23, when Jesus appears to the disciples behind closed doors. He breathes on them (i.e., gives them the Spirit), they are reborn, and joy floods their hearts.

Verse 22 alludes to this clearly in an interesting way. The Greek reads that Jesus said that he "will see" them and their hearts "will rejoice." The implications are these. (1) This presence of Jesus extends beyond his post-resurrection appearances. (2) Jesus "sees" them since he is divine but more so through the Spirit. They will experience him through the Spirit in the heart, the place where God is and rules.

3.4.3. At Last—The Disciples Understand (16:25–33). From verses 25–28, Jesus tells his disciples that he is no longer speaking to them in figurative speech. The time has come when they can understand what he has been saying all along—that they can relate directly to the Father as well as to him. It is important to note that Jesus' hour has come when his work is finished. This work includes the Spirit's work in the heart of the believer, resulting in understanding. Now his disciples understand that Jesus has come from the Father. The Father loves Jesus' followers because they love and believe Jesus. Jesus will return to the Father.

At this, his disciples declare that Jesus is speaking clearly without figures of speech and that they understand him (vv. 29–30). They need ask him no more questions (see vv. 17–18). The reference to "figures of speech" in verses 25 and 29 is the Greek word *paroimia* (see comments on 10:6). In John this word refers to parable-like language that is difficult to understand. In this sense, it is similar to the use of parables in the other Gospels. There too, hearers, including Jesus' disciples, often did not understand. *Paroimia* in John refers to the content and language that come from Jesus' lips and that people are unprepared spiritually to receive. In this case, the disciples receive insight that comes from the work of Jesus during the Passion week. Their ability will allow them to understand fully when the Spirit is given in 20:19–23. Their difficulty to understand, then, arises not from the type of language or from its content; rather, it points to their lack of spiritual capability.

Jesus' response in verses 31–33 concludes the dialogue. "You believe at last!" Some translators place a question mark here; others, a period. The NIV's exclamation mark fits the context best. But Jesus moves on to press the point about a matter, one that has been present throughout chapter 14 until now. Judas will not be the last to abandon Jesus; the other disciples too will scatter like sheep when the time comes. But the Father will not abandon them. The reader can draw great assurance from God's character. All may abandon, but God will never leave his children alone—"I will not leave you as orphans" (14:18).

Verse 33 concludes these three chapters of prolonged instruction from Jesus and dialogue between him and his disciples. This verse also provides another meaning of the title "Counselor": "Advocate." Jesus is telling his disciples in advance so they will have assurance of their standing with God—they will have peace. What is this peace? We have noted its presence and meaning earlier (see comment on 14:27). Fundamentally, it refers to a new and deep relationship between a believer and God. This relationship has come about through the work of Jesus in atoning for the sins of the world and providing righteousness and reconciliation to a world that has turned its back on its Creator.

Heretofore, the world lay under judgment. But now peace is possible to all who believe. Where it is found is also pointed out here: It is "in me" (v. 33). "Peace" and "in me" show up in the Pauline letters, expressing these powerful truths (see especially Rom. 5). "Take heart" also strengthens this meaning of "Counselor." In the midst of failure and sin, the believer can take heart in knowing that he or she has an advocate with the Father, even Jesus the Righteous and Faithful One (cf. 1 John 2:1–2). With this admonition and encouragement, Jesus turns now to his high priestly prayer (ch. 17).

We can now summarize the meaning and function of the word *parakletos*. In John 14–16, the *parakletos*, also called the Spirit, comes from the Father and the Son but through the Son. He represents both the Father and the Son to the world, especially to the believer. The world cannot and will not know him, and consequently, neither will it know the Father and the Son. Believers know him because they have accepted by faith the atoning work of Jesus. The Spirit then has taken up residence in them, who are now called his temple.

The Spirit not only lives in believers, but consoles, teaches, informs, assures, and directs them. On the other hand, the Spirit works through believers in the world to bring it to Jesus. There are thus two major functions of the *parakletos* in John 14–16: *in* believers to regenerate and build them up, and *through* believers to testify to the world that God has provided a solution to its sin through his Son. Though not in an explicit manner, these two broad functions parallel the work of the Spirit in Paul and Luke. Luke-Acts more explicitly emphasizes the second function—the empowerment for proclamation of the gospel to the world.

3.5. Jesus' Prayer for Believers (17:1–26)

Chapter 17 contains Jesus' prayer for himself and his followers. This prayer concludes the lengthy blocks of teaching and dialogue arising from the dinner in 13:1 and prepares for his betrayal in the next chapter. References to that betrayal (13:1ff. and 18:2ff.) bracket these blocks. Some interpreters of this Gospel have noted that this prayer has many parallels to the Lord's Prayer in Matthew and Luke, both in grandeur and content.

3.5.1. Jesus Prays for Mutual Glorification (17:1–5). "After Jesus said this" (v. 1) shifts the attention to his forthcoming prayer. The last such break came at 14:31, where Jesus said, "Come now; let us leave." Apparently still at the same spot where he just finished speaking, Jesus now looks "toward heaven and pray[s]." This gives Jesus' stance for this prayer—he is standing and looking upward as he prays (cf. Acts 7:55–56).

Verses 1b–5 contain the first part of the prayer, in which Jesus prays that both he and the Father may be glorified. The parallel structure of this paragraph may be seen as follows.

A Mutual glorification (v. 1b)
    B The granting of eternal life (vv. 2–3)
A' Mutual glorification (vv. 4–5)

Point A' elaborates on Jesus' request for glorification in Point A. He states in A' that he has come to earth and completed the work of the Father. Point B gives what Jesus' work has been. The Father has granted him authority over all people so he can give eternal life especially to those the Father has given him. This eternal life allows believers to know the Father and Jesus Christ (v. 3).

The paragraph concludes with Jesus' request to have the glory he had before the world began. This request alludes to Jesus' preexistence, a theme John introduced in 1:1ff. This is a common theme in John. In 17:5, however, it is put in a rather interesting way. This phrasing suggests that a change in Jesus' status came before his birth and that it started with creation. On closer examination, however, 1:1ff. does connect creation with the "Logos." This means, then, that with Jesus' work at creation, his glory had already been laid aside; his mediatorship had already started. Furthermore, this also implies that Jesus' person (divine and human natures) and atoning work were a foregone conclusion in God's mind before creation. Now Jesus is preparing to return home. This section speaks of his enthronement and the glory he is to receive, now already in progress in that his hour has come (v. 1).

Verses 1–5 parallel the first section of the Lord's Prayer (Matt. 6:9–10). These lines in Matthew pray for the coming of the rule of God (v. 10a) (equals the will of God in v. 10b) to earth so that the Father may be hallowed. This is what Jesus has done in his work; he has glorified the Father ("glorified" in John 17 equals "hallowed" in Matt. 6:9). To glorify the Father means that one has obeyed him fully in one's life. To "hallow" or "sanctify" means that one has devoted one's life fully to God. Such activity brings great glory to God.

3.5.2. Prayer for His Disciples (17:6–19). Jesus continues in these verses by praying for his disciples. As he did in verses 1–5, he prays in the first and second persons, denoting prayer between him and the Father. But the disciples are the reason for this part of his prayer. Consequently, Jesus refers to them in the third person. We have here a privilege to look into the private prayer life of Jesus as he communes with the Father about his disciples.

Key words in this paragraph are "keep" (i.e., preserve) and "give." These words signify the theme of the paragraph and the purpose of the prayer. Jesus asks the Father to preserve the disciples in the world as they live as God's people and as they witness of God and his work.

Perseverance is a concern of Jesus. The fact that he prays for perseverance suggests that it is not automatic for the believer; it depends on their continuing to believe in Jesus and to keep his word, and, especially and ultimately, on the power of God (see v. 11). The frequent use of reciprocal language throughout—that is, the theme of unity of Jesus and the Father (the Father sent Jesus, Jesus revealed the Father, etc.)—signifies how important the unity of God is. The Old Testament grounded Judaism and Christianity in this belief. For John's audience, this was important since it would have held off the charge of blasphemy—that of having two gods in Jesus and the Father. This unity is extended to believers in this prayer—that the Father, Jesus, and "they may be one" (v. 11). In verse 11, the word for "one" is neuter in gender, thus depicting in Greek what may be termed a dynamic unity.

This section can be divided into two parts, though just where it divides is debatable. One can break it at the end of verse 8 or after verse 11b. The reason one may want to divide at verse 11b is because Jesus says "Holy Father," as if he is beginning a special part of the prayer. In verse 9, however, Jesus does say, "I pray [to you, the Father] for them."

Verses 6–8 act as an introduction to the specific prayer beginning at verse 9 and acknowledge that the disciples have come to know and believe that Jesus and the Father are one. "Have obeyed" (Gk. *tereo*, "keep") in verse 6 connects with "they know" of verse 7. "Know" means more than "have knowledge." It refers to "believe" (see v. 8, where "believed" occurs).

Verse 6 begins with, "I have revealed you." The word "revealed" also occurs in John 2:11 and 9:3. In the first occurrence, Jesus has just performed the first sign. There, he made known the heart of the Father as outlined in his plan to transform the place of his dwelling from a physical place into a group of people who have believed in his Son's work on the cross. In the latter text, Jesus has just healed the blind man, performing another sign. This time he depicted what happens when one is born from above—from the darkness of sin to the revelational light from above. Thus from first to last, Jesus has made known to them that he has been doing the work of the Father in providing salvation for them and the world. The "you" in the NIV as the object of this revelation is literally "your name." "Your name" stands for the Father's character, plan, and work of revelation. It also means that the Father has become personal in his Son, Jesus.

"Sent" occurs at the end of verse 8. The disciples' awareness that the Father sent the Son serves as the basis for the assertion at verse 18 that Jesus will send them: As the Father sent Jesus, Jesus now sends his disciples. This commissioning, that is, for their invasion of the world, then connects with the theme of perseverance. As the disciples go out to evangelize, they must avoid becoming like the world again. They must persevere.

Jesus' specific petition begins at verse 9, praying for the disciples but not for the world. "World" in John refers to all people who are in sin and separated from God. When Jesus says that he does not pray for the world, he does not mean that he does not care for it. John 3:16–21 has already given God's attitude toward the world. What he means here is that he is particularly concerned for his followers. They are the ones through whom he will reach the world. In fact, he does not pray for their removal from the world (v. 15).

The success of the disciples depends on how much they are sanctified in the word of God (vv. 17–19). This sanctification implies alienation between the disciples and the world and informs of and directs his followers to the world's plight. The closer his followers are to the world, the less they will see and the more blind they will be to the world's situation. Thus, Jesus prays earnestly for his followers to remain sanctified, distanced from the world as he sends them. Jesus speaks of this alienation from the world in verse 14 (see also v. 16): "The world has hated them, for they are not of the world." "Of the world" denotes a similar nature, a common identity, and a common worldview that oppose Jesus. At verse 13 Jesus gives us the reason for his speaking these words: "so that they may have the full measure of my joy within them." This information draws the reader's attention to the theme of chapters 13–16.

In several places in this paragraph Jesus implies that he has already left this world (this is clearer in the Greek than in the NIV). (1) At verse 11 the NIV has, "I will remain in the world no longer"; the Greek literally translates, "I am no longer in the world." (2) At verse 12 the NIV reads, "While I was with them"; the Greek has, "When I was with them." (3) At verse 13, the NIV has, "I am coming to you"; the Greek has, "Now I come to you." The NIV translation for this last one is accurate, for the next clause aids in understanding what Jesus is saying. These sayings here and in the Passion narrative suggest that with the arrival of Jesus' hour, he had already begun his ascension.

Verses 17–19 recapitulate verses 6–16. All of the themes are found there (e.g., the word "sanctify" occurs three times). This word summarizes what he meant in the key word "keep."

Another parallel with the Lord's Prayer (Matt. 6:13) in this paragraph is John 17:15: "Protect them from the evil one." In John's economy, the evil one will be particularly active in the world since Jesus is casting him out of heaven. This action concerns Jesus about his followers—but his Father is able to keep them.

3.5.3. Jesus Prays for All Who Later Believe (17:20–26). Jesus now focuses his prayer on those who will believe the message of his disciples. This particularly refers back to the commission Jesus gave to his disciples in verse 18: "I have sent them into the world." The themes of the last part of this prayer are now repeated, but Jesus gives special attention to the preservation of his church throughout time until he returns. He prays that these new believers who come out of the world may be unified with those who have followed Jesus before (vv. 21–23). Furthermore, he prays that all believers may be unified with him and the Father, in the same way that he and the Father are unified (vv. 21–23, 25–26).

Jesus prays for this to happen, for he wants his followers to be with him and experience the glory he had before the creation of the world (v. 24). Though "glory" may contain other implications, it focuses its meaning in this paragraph on "love." This "love" theme shows up prominently here and in the context of unity and fellowship with one another and with the Father and Jesus. Indeed, the expression of this love among the people of God is "glorious."

We summarize it in this way. Jesus prays for the entire church age until he returns. He longs for the end to arrive, for he wants to have his followers with him in heaven to experience the glorious, full love that the Father shares with him. Jesus has come to share this message and demonstrate this love to a sinful world through his people—if only they will believe and follow him. He has come to bring back to heaven those for whom the Father has sent. Jesus' followers in turn carry on the mission of Jesus and the Father.

3.6. The Betrayal, Arrest, Crucifixion, Death, and Burial of Jesus (18:1–19:42)

Chapters 13–17 contain a large block of teaching. Not much time has elapsed, proportionately, given the lengthy discourses Jesus has just finished. John has slowed down time so as to put before his readers what he considers to be important information. With the conclusion of his prayer in chapter 17, Jesus moves toward the culmination of his hour. Here in chapters 18–19 also, time slows and events loom large in the stream of redemptive history.

3.6.1. The Arrest of Jesus (18:1–11). The setting of Jesus' arrest is given in verses 1–3. After Jesus finishes his lengthy discourses in chapters 13–17, he and his disciples cross, eastwardly, the Kidron Valley and travel a short distance to an "olive grove." It is still night; but they know their way in the dark, for it has been Jesus' custom to go there frequently (v. 2). Judas also knows the place well, and he leads "a detachment of soldiers and some officials from the chief priests and Pharisees." They carry torches, lanterns, and weapons—everything necessary to capture and retrieve a wanted person.

The narrative then springs to life with the dialogue between Jesus and those who have come searching for him. At this time when things seem to be out of control, John sets the stage by noting that Jesus knows everything that is going to happen (v. 4). In this confrontation, Jesus is firmly in charge. He does not wait for them to advance but goes out to them and asks (v. 4): "Who is it you want?" They respond, "Jesus of Nazareth." John adds a bit of information, connecting Judas the traitor with this activity (v. 5b). In this way the narrative moves forward the conflict in chapter 13 involving Judas. Jesus then says, "I am he."

"When Jesus said 'I am he,' they drew back and fell to the ground" (v. 6). Various opinions exist regarding what is going on here and why. Whether they are surprised or whether this is perceived as a response to an encounter with deity is not clear. "I am he" in Greek is *ego eimi* ("I am") and may be a name expressing divinity. This expression does fit the absolute form of the name occurring at other places in Greek in this Gospel (cf. 6:20; 8:24). Earlier these same guards had gone after Jesus but did not arrest him because "no one ever spoke the way this man does" (7:46). There they call Jesus a "man." What may have surprised them is that Jesus meets them as one whose time has arrived—and who is thus in control. He does not flee from his divine appointment.

Those planning to arrest Jesus have not recovered when he asks again whom they are seeking. Again, they repeat his name (v. 7). Jesus, following through on his mission, is nonetheless concerned for his followers and requests permission for them to go. Verse 9 is the author's commentary on Jesus' answer. He sees this request and its subsequent permission as a prophetic fulfillment of Jesus' earlier words in 6:39 and 17:12.

The statement about Jesus' keeping all whom God has given him (except Judas, who also was established beforehand), sets a frame for understanding what happens next. Verses 10–11 focus on blundering Peter. This connects with the matter of problematic disciples in chapters 13ff., especially Judas and Peter. It reveals God's keeping the power of those who really want to serve him but have great faults. Peter, in thinking he can fight off all these soldiers and thus help God out, finds himself going against his will (cf. also Matt. 16:21–28, where Peter wanted to keep Jesus from the cross; however, he received a stinging rebuke from Jesus—one has to be willing to give up one's life to serve God). Jesus therefore responds to Peter who has drawn his sword and cut off the servant's ear: "Shall I not drink the cup the Father has given me?"

3.6.2. Jesus Before the Religious Leaders (18:12–27). Verses 12–14 give the account of Jesus' arrest and appearance before Annas. Caiaphas, not Annas, is the high priest. The high priest is the one with the authority. So why do they bring him to Annas first? Here is a plausible answer. Annas became high priest around 6 B.C. and served as such until A.D. 15. After he was deposed, five of his sons, a grandson, plus a son-in-law (Caiaphas) became high priests. Until A.D. 41 this family of Annas exercised significant influence over all Sanhedrin cases. Thus it was typical for them to take Jesus first to Annas, the father-in-law of Caiaphas (see *DJG*, 845–46).

Verse 14 appears to be parenthetical. Yet Caiaphas, its subject, does not receive attention in John's Passion account. He appears in a minor way in verses 24 and 28, but he makes no overt determination about Jesus. However, verse 14 connects Caiaphas with a plot that has long been in process. In 11:49–53 Caiaphas advised that the arrest plan should include having Jesus killed for the people. John already saw there that this high priest prophesied about Jesus' substitutionary death for the whole Jewish nation. Such a death fits Old Testament prophecies about salvation, being described as the gathering of the people from the dispersion (cf. Ezek. 34).

Peter once again attracts attention (vv. 15–18). In these verses we learn that two of Jesus' disciples followed Jesus to Annas's house: Simon Peter and "another disciple." This nameless disciple is probably the author of the Fourth Gospel, the beloved disciple. Twice it is said that he "was known" by Annas (called here "high priest," vv. 15–16). The apostle, then a fisherman and a businessman, would have had contacts with people like Annas. Because of this he is allowed to go all the way "into the . . . courtyard" with Jesus while Peter stays outside. It seems as if Jesus is taken into a room while Peter remains outside the courtyard.

The other disciple comes out to let Peter in (i.e., into the courtyard), where a fire warms the servants and guards in the cold morning air (v. 18). They appear to be in a place different from the room where Jesus is being questioned. In this process of getting Peter inside, a servant girl, the gatekeeper, thinks she recognizes Peter and asks him if he is one of Jesus' disciples. She phrases the question in a way that expects a negative response. Peter answers appropriately.

The scene now shifts to Jesus' interrogation (vv. 19–24). The high priest asks him two questions: (1) What about his disciples, and (2) what does he teach? Jesus does not respond to the first question but goes right to the second one. He responds appropriately according to court procedure, saying in effect, "If you have to ask me what I am teaching, then you have no charges and you would be seeking testimony from witnesses." The way Jesus answers Annas highlights the trumped-up nature of the charges and the improper procedure—justice cannot prevail. Jesus protests the improper procedure of asking the accused of the charges against him rather than asking witnesses. One of the officials strikes Jesus when he finishes speaking. This blow does not hurt as much as it dishonors him. Jesus' second reply further shows up the injustice of the affair. Thereupon, Annas sends him on, still bound, to Caiaphas (v. 24).

Now the scene returns to Peter (vv. 25–27) for his second and third denials. For a second time the people there ask him a question, which again anticipates a negative response. The author of the Gospel, noting Peter's increasing anxiety, adds this time, "He denied it saying, 'I am not.'" The third time a relative of Malchus, whose ear Peter chopped off, challenges him with a question that anticipates a positive answer: "Didn't I see you with him in the olive grove?" John the writer avoids quoting Peter this time and simply writes that Peter denies it, providing the same response as before. "At that moment a rooster began to crow," signaling the end of Jesus' interrogation before the Jewish authorities. John does not mention that Jesus was brought before the Sanhedrin. They take him on to Pilate and the Romans.

3.6.3. Jesus Before Pilate and the Jewish Leaders (18:28–19:16a). This section contains seven scenes, alternating between inside and outside "the palace" (Gk. *praitorion*). After Pilate leads Jesus inside (v. 28), the inside/outside words interchange. Pilate:

(1) 18:29: "came out";
(2) 18:33: "went back inside";
(3) 18:38: "went out";
(4) 19:1: (inside implied) "had [Jesus] flogged";
(5) 19:4: "came out";
(6) 19:9: "went back inside";
(7) 19:13: "brought Jesus out."

The center and turning point of the seven scenes is the beating of Jesus (scene 4), thus emphasizing his mistreatment at the hands of Pilate at the instigation of the Jewish leaders. Furthermore, the other scenes show thematic parallels: scene 1 with scene 7 (the request for Jesus' death and granting his death); scene 2 with scene 6 (kingship and authority); and scene 3 with scene 5 (Jesus' innocence). Pilate, too, manifests persistent attitudes and actions—fear and Jesus' innocence. He gives in to pressure from these Jewish leaders.

3.6.3.1. The First Scene: Outside (18:28–32). In this first scene, the innocence of Jesus emerges. The Jewish leaders bring Jesus to Pilate, stopping outside the palace because they do not want to defile themselves before the Passover by entering a Gentile building. Pilate goes out to them and asks about charges. The dialogue between him and the Jewish leaders demonstrates only ambiguity regarding the charges. Pilate tells them to try him according to their own law. They do have certain authorities under Roman law, and rabbinic law did regulate capital punishment.

A short time later, however, this same Jewish group stones Stephen (Acts 7). We can make several comments about this. John suggests that Jesus' trial is an illegal one. Capital cases have to come before the Sanhedrin in Jerusalem. In John they have not met. In Acts 7, the Sanhedrin did meet and disposed of Stephen. What seems to be the case, then, is that the Jewish leaders desire Jesus crucified and want the Romans to do it, thus passing responsibility, knowing that the Romans exercised capital punishment in this manner. However, both they and Pilate pass Jesus back and forth, neither assuming the responsibility for his death.

Pilate cannot stand any more trouble from the Jews. These leaders have put him in a difficult place. However, John offers "the real" explanation in verse 32. This is happening according to God's plan; this kind of death fulfills Jesus' own words. Notice the several places where Jesus has spoken about this: (1) 3:14: "so the Son of Man must be lifted up"; (2) 8:28: "When you have lifted up the Son of Man"; (3) 12:32–33: "'But I, when I am lifted up from the earth, will draw all men to myself.' He said this to show the kind of death he was going to die."

3.6.3.2. The Second Scene: Inside (18:33–38a). Pilate, back inside, summons Jesus to inquire of him. But Jesus does not surrender his authority to Pilate in this time of inquiry. Instead of answering Pilate's question, Jesus simultaneously lets him know that he has nothing to fear from him since his kingdom is not of this world, and that he is a king. Pilate picks up on "king," however. Jesus responds to indicate the nature of his coming and of his kingdom.

In verse 37, Jesus speaks about his humanity: "For this reason I was born, and for this I came into the world." His kingship evidences God's holy nature, the sin of the world, and the need for atonement—all connecting to his sacrificial death on the cross. In order to die, he has to be human. Thus, he has been born to die. Pilate responds with the rhetorical question, "What is truth?" in verse 38a. This needs no response—it haunts sinful humanity throughout human history and leaves ringing in the ears the lingering assumption that, without God in Christ, no one knows the right answer.

3.6.3.3. The Third Scene: Outside (18:38b–40). Pilate returns to the waiting Jewish leaders with the words, "I find no basis for a charge against him," indicating his conclusion after talking with Jesus. Thinking that he may have a way to release this innocent man, he appeals to Caiaphas's earlier suggestion (i.e., "custom") that they release one prisoner at the time of Passover. But Pilate is still guilty of duplicity. Regardless of which one he suggests, these leaders will insist on the release of someone other than Jesus. Irony fills verse 40. Barabbas means literally in Aramaic, "son of the father." Furthermore, as a revolutionary he is guilty of a serious crime against Rome. If not for this irony, it would seem incredible for Pilate to release a proven threat to Rome, an insurrectionist.

3.6.3.4. The Fourth Scene: Inside (19:1–3). The description of this scene contains no mention of "outside" or "inside." Yet Jesus is the subject here, indicating that Pilate is "inside." As indicated above, this scene becomes the focal point of the trial. This means that what appears here is significant. Perhaps to flaunt the crowd outside, Pilate in mockery has Jesus appear as the Jewish king. This in realty is the truth—Jesus is king. Pilate has his soldiers flog Jesus (cf. Isa. 50:6). Of the three beatings that the Romans could administer, this was the second of three. John may have written it in this manner to suggest that this is an act of punishment in itself, rather than merely being part of capital punishment. Since Pilate before and after this episode believes Jesus to be innocent, he may have been working up to the point where he will try to release Jesus by means of applying this beating as punishment and to play on the sympathies of these people.

After administering this beating, the soldiers weave a crown out of thorns (John does not say from what plant or tree) and place it on Jesus' head. The soldiers put a royal (purple) robe on Jesus. Purple was the color of royalty. This highlights the kingly aspect of Jesus. When this is done, they go "up to him again and again, saying, 'Hail, king of the Jews'" (v. 3). When they are finished, they strike him in the face. Similar mockings were played out in various places throughout the Greco-Roman world on stages and in circuses.

3.6.3.5. The Fifth Scene: Outside (19:4–7). This scene parallels the third. Pilate comes out and brings Jesus with him, mockingly dressed as a king with a crown of thorns and a purple robe. He announces with that action that he has found no guilt in Jesus. With this ploy, Pilate more than likely tries to free Jesus. Yet the priests and officials refuse to accept it, calling for the death sentence: "Crucify! Crucify!" (v. 6). They appeal for this sentence from their law—he has blasphemed ("he claimed to be the Son of God," v. 7; cf. 5:18; 10:33).

Pilate is all the more afraid now. His fear shows implicitly the dilemma he is in—wedged between a certain type of Roman rule over the Jewish nation and his own failure and demise as governor. Underneath this in ironic manner, Jesus, who is really in control, thwarts Pilate's plan to release him. He has to die for the sins of the world. Ironically, Jesus is indeed king.

3.6.3.6. The Sixth Scene: Inside (19:8–11). This scene parallels the second and focuses on power and authority. Rebuffed, Pilate fearfully retreats into the palace and presses Jesus over his origins. But Jesus remained silent. Likely Pilate, licking his wounds, retorts concerning his authority, attempting to make Jesus see that he has control over him after all. Jesus now answers (v. 11), setting things into proper perspective for Pilate. Pilate's power comes from above, speaking of his Father; and these leaders are guilty of a greater sin than Pilate.

3.6.3.7. The Seventh Scene: Outside (19:12–16a). This final scene parallels the first. John summarizes what Pilate does as he goes out to these leaders. He is convinced that Jesus is innocent, but these leaders keep shouting and pressing their strategy. They want Jesus dead. To persuade Pilate to make the decision, they appeal to the historical and political situation Pilate finds himself in at this time. If he refuses to handle a situation in which one claims to be a king, he is no friend of the emperor of Rome. Pilate cannot withstand such a threat and gives in. To lose the status of friendship of Caesar was to court death. Further, if the Jews press this matter to Rome, Pilate's shortcomings are sure to surface.

Pilate then goes to the place where judgments are handed down (called *bema* in Greek) and has Jesus brought to him. This place in Aramaic was called Gabbatha ("the Stone Pavement," v. 13). Pilate still seeks to free Jesus, but these leaders press on relentlessly. This scene climaxes this trial in a dramatic fashion. The Jewish leaders give up their Davidic king by accepting Caesar (v. 15: "'We have no king but Caesar,' the chief priests answered"). Pilate does not have the power to release Jesus after all! He hands Jesus over for crucifixion.

John notes in verse 14 that this happened about the sixth hour on Preparation Day of Passover week. When he includes information like this, he intends something significant with it. This is the time when Passover lambs are slain and prepared for sacrifice and eating in an appropriate manner. At the time when Jesus is hanging on the cross, these lambs are hanging inside the temple mount. Jesus here culminates and fulfills what was claimed earlier in this Gospel: "Look, the Lamb of God, who takes away the sin of the world!" (1:29).

3.6.4. The Crucifixion, Death, and Burial of Jesus (19:16b–42). Some scholars see in these verses a similar arrangement as in the previous trial section, with seven scenes or acts. However, the evidence is not as clear-cut as in the trial scenes. Rather, these verses contain four sections, focusing on the decision made about Jesus by the Jewish leaders and Pilate in the preceding verses. The author provides the divine interpretation for his audience. In three of these sections, the author notes that Scripture has spoken of these events long ago.

3.6.4.1. Crucifixion (19:16b–27). Verses 16b–17 inform us what is done to Jesus after Pilate hands him over to the chief priests: The soldiers (not the Jewish leaders—this is Pilate's show now) take charge. They lead him outside the city to the place of crucifixion. Capital punishment by the Jews occurred outside the city (cf. Acts 7:58); so also here for the Romans. In Greek this place is called (literally) "the Skull Place" (NIV, "the place of the Skull"); in Aramaic, "Golgotha." Some say that this was a hill shaped like a skull. The place may well have been a typical place of crucifixion by the Romans—that is, a place where death hung heavy in the atmosphere. Verse 20 adds that this place is near the entrance to the city, where all who come and go can see.

Jesus carries his own cross (v. 17). John does not mention that anyone helps Jesus carry it (cf., e.g., Mark 15:21). John thus allows attention to fall on Jesus. "Cross" refers to the crosspiece that is to be fixed to the upper part of the upright beam upon arrival at the place of execution. This upright beam normally stood permanently at the place of execution. The soldiers would nail or tie the hands of the man to be executed to the crossbeam with outstretched arms, lift the beam with the attached victim up to the upright beam, fixing it in place. The feet would be nailed or tied with rope to the upright beam. His body would rest on a piece of wood protruding out of this beam. But John (and the other Gospel writers) simply say, "They crucified him" (v. 18). John notes that Jesus hangs between two others, though he avoids saying anything further about them, either about their crime or their mockery of Jesus. In so doing, he keeps the attention on Jesus.

For several verses, then, the kingship of Jesus is emphasized. Only in John do we read that the title over Jesus is in three languages, Aramaic, Latin, and Greek. Only in John do we read about the Jewish leaders' protest over this sign and Pilate's subsequent response (vv. 19–23). Only John refers to "Jesus of Nazareth," perhaps noting the mockery intended by Pilate and the importance for John's emphasis. "King of the Jews" alludes to the charge against Jesus.

This whole situation, however, drips with irony. In mockery, Jesus is their king. In fact, he is their messianic king, who in this event brings salvation to all who will receive him. In truth, they reject him (cf. 1:11–12). This scene completes what was started earlier, where Nathanael said, "You are the King of Israel" (1:49) and where he was anointed as king by Mary (see comments on 12:1–8). The cross becomes Jesus' throne—the place from which he unleashes his power as king to deliver from sin's clutch on human nature and from sin's condemnation before God. The title over the cross points to this as his throne in an obvious way. And the title in three languages suggests that Jesus is king of the world (cf. 3:16, "For God so loved the world").

Furthermore, none of the other Gospel writers mentions the seamless undergarment (vv. 23–24). The group of four soldiers (this is why there were four lots) decides not to divide this garment among themselves as they did his other clothing. While this garment, worn next to the skin, is not expensive, it may contribute to the overall impression of the narrative (perhaps that it is a priestly garment). In any case, here occurs the first reference to the fulfillment of Scripture, which evidences God's control of history, divulged to his people through his prophets. The life and death, and ministry of Jesus, then, is not to be perceived as accidental or fateful. It is the divine act of salvation history now coming to fruition.

This dividing of the clothes and casting of lots for the undergarment happens so that Scripture (Ps. 22:18) can be fulfilled. John has the plural for "clothes" in verse 23 (*himatia*), which matches the first line in Psalm 22:18. For "undergarment" in verse 23 he has *chiton*, matching what Psalm 22:18 has in the second line (though the word is different there, *himatismos*). John differs from the wording of Psalm 22:18 when reporting, "Let's decide by lot who will get it" (v. 24). The meaning is the same, nonetheless.

Here in the passion of Jesus, governors, rebellious crowds, and religious leaders do God's bidding. Not even death can stop the triumphant march of God in his gracious plans for a condemned and rebellious world.

This paragraph concludes with a personal reference (vv. 25–27). All the Gospels mention women and name at least some of them. It is difficult to identify some of these women and their relationships with any certainty. John helps us to understand a bit more about some of these relationships, especially when we compare information in all the Gospels. John mentions that Jesus' mother and her sister are present, along with the beloved disciple. Why are there no other men? Apparently, they have fled. John, the beloved disciple, did not have to run—the high priest knew him (cf. 18:15–18). The women and this disciple follow Jesus.

Jesus' mother's sister is likely the mother of John, the beloved disciple. In other words, this disciple and Jesus are cousins. Jesus' brothers are not there either, which explains why he commits his mother into the hands of the beloved disciple. Here, then, we can assume that Joseph is dead and that Jesus has until this time been responsible for Mary, his mother. Now Jesus places her in the care of her nephew. Since John is reticent to use his own name in this Gospel and that of his own mother, evidence mounts for Johannine authorship.

3.6.4.2. "It Is Finished" (19:28–30). It is useful to distinguish these two verses from the others because of their content. They focus on the completion of Jesus' work. The NIV's "later" (v. 28) may be a bit vague. The Greek suggests a more specific moment after the scene when he passes the care of his mother to the beloved disciple. It is at this moment that he knows that *all* has now been completed.

"Completed" refers to the finished work of Jesus, to his hour that started in 12:23. It is the full giving of love for his own mentioned in 13:1. In reality, it points to all that Jesus came to do. "Completed" means more than just "finished"; it signifies that his work is consummated. The death of Jesus is not the end of a long list of things. Rather, it is the goal and capstone of all that God has planned. The words in the NIV for this idea is "was ... completed" (v. 28) and "it is finished" (v. 30). However, in the Greek the same verb form is used: *tetelestai*. Thus, this word brackets and directs the significance of the entire paragraph. This verb denotes that the work of Jesus is finished but that the results are ongoing. Nothing more needs to be done regarding the plan of salvation. "It is finished" are the last words spoken by Jesus in John prior to his death.

Jesus becomes thirsty when he knows that his work is finished. He also knows that the completion of his work is the fulfillment of Scripture. What is the relationship between his thirst and his work? Certainly, what he has been through has been extremely demanding; thus, it is natural for him in his humanity to thirst. His work, that is, suffering atonement, has brought him to a moment of extreme pain. Only in his humanity can he experience that. This saying may parallel his cry of separation in the other Gospels, "My God, my God, why have you forsaken me?" (cf. Matt. 27:46).

Later, in John 19:34, blood and water pour out of Jesus' side. In this sacrificial moment, the paradox is outstanding—he thirsts greatly but furnishes life-giving water. He who is the source of the water of life now needs it. On the other hand, he is thirsty because of his own will—he knows that this is for the sake of fulfilling Scripture. This is what verse 28 means. Jesus' knowledge of his finished work comes from and fulfills Scripture.

Which Scripture does John have in mind when he comments on "I am thirsty" (v. 28)? Probably he has a number of passages together, the sum total of their teaching, such as we find in Psalms 22:15; 69:19–21. Psalm 22:15 is specific enough to underlie this statement. This is the second reference to the fulfillment of Scripture in John's record of the crucifixion. In verse 24, however, the word "fulfill" was *plerothe*, whereas here it is *tetelestai*. This may be a matter of John's using words synonymously, or it may be because the idea of "fulfillment" in Jesus' work is connected with his knowledge of Scripture. In a most suggestive way, then, *this* Scripture connects to this event.

Actually, Jesus' work is not finished until he drinks of the bitter drink they give him. This drink may suggest the awful cup of sin that he ingests for the sins of the whole world. This is hinted at already in 18:11: "Shall I not drink the cup the Father has given me?"

Jesus then bows his head and gives up his spirit (v. 30). Some see in this not only a reference to Jesus' death, but also a symbolic statement. Jesus with his death releases the Spirit to bring life to others. While this may be the case in other Gospels, it is probably not suggested in John, especially in light of his breathing life into his disciples in 20:22. Another interpretation may be possible in which these two events may be seen to connect his death and resurrection.

One other thing should be mentioned. The fact that Jesus dies a rather quick death is significant. The reason for this lies in the statement of his death. Jesus himself gives up his life; it is not taken from him (cf. 10:17–18). He thus offers his life up as a sacrifice.

3.6.4.3. Jesus' Death (19:31–37). Three elements stand out in this paragraph: the piercing of Jesus' side, the fact that the soldiers do not break Jesus' legs, and the testimony of the writer of this Gospel. The Jewish leaders—probably the same as those in verse 21—ask Pilate to take down from the crosses the bodies of those executed. It was Roman custom to leave people up for several days, even after death, mainly to act as a deterrent. Death by crucifixion was usually slow and extremely painful. But these Jewish leaders do not want these corpses to corrupt their holy days. Verse 31 notes that this day is "the day of Preparation" (i.e., Thursday evening to Friday evening). The next day, Passover, will run from Friday evening to Saturday evening. When the Passover fell on the Sabbath, it was a special Sabbath. Their request is rooted in this fact (v. 31), although it probably goes back to Deuteronomy 21:22. There, the body is to be impaled only for one day; it is not to hang out overnight, lest it desecrate the land.

To grant this request means that the soldiers have to break the legs (very painful but in a way, merciful) of the victims to hasten death. They do break the legs of the men on either side of Jesus. But when they come to Jesus, they find him already dead (vv. 32–33). Thus, they do not break his legs, but one of the soldiers does thrust a spear into the side of Jesus, probably toward the left side near his heart (v. 34a). Immediately, blood and water come out.

Only John provides this information, but for him it is important. While literal fact exists here, another level of meaning arises from the Gospel itself. Blood refers to the giving of a life for sacrifice. Water refers to the Spirit, which comes after blood (atonement) and brings life. In this Gospel, Jesus gives his life and then releases the Spirit. A number of themes cluster together to make this statement, such as the relationship between the Feast of Tabernacles and Passover. Jesus' death, as we saw in 7:1–9, was not to be associated with Tabernacles but with Passover. Tabernacles was associated with the giving of the Spirit. The Spirit, symbolized by water, flows out of the altar. The altar is Jesus' side—Jesus is the new temple. In other words, the flow of water from Jesus' side fulfills 7:38–39.

Verse 35 contains the written witness of the author, providing authentication for the death of Jesus and the fact that his legs were not broken. Though this particular verse does not say it, the context strongly suggests that this witness is from the beloved disciple, the author of this Gospel (cf. 19:25–27). This authentic witness gives the foundation for the belief of all Christians. This is the same kind of testimony that Paul supplies in 1 Corinthians 15:1–15. This verse of testimony introduces John 20, where faith surfaces as a major theme.

The final verses of this paragraph (vv. 36–37) use the third scriptural reference to speak of the unbroken leg bones and the pierced side of the Messiah. In typical rabbinic fashion John connects two different groups of texts. The first (Ex. 12:46 and Num. 9:12) gives guidance to not break the Passover lamb's legs. Psalm 34:20 speaks of God's protecting the righteous man in his troubles by not allowing any of his bones to be broken. The second (Zech. 12:10) stands behind the piercing. John's quoting, while it does not follow exactly either the Greek or Hebrew Scriptures,

Gordon's Calvary is a site some believe is the true Golgotha, where Jesus was crucified, because of two caves in the rocky face that look like the eye sockets of a skull. "Golgotha," in Hebrew, means "skull." The site was identified in 1883 by British General Charles Gordon.

Nearby is the Garden Tomb where some believe Jesus was buried. The traditional sites of the tomb and Golgotha are under the Church of the Holy Sepulchre.

does provide the sense. Zechariah 12 suggests a time when God will deliver the inhabitants of Jerusalem from their enemies by being pierced. Every clan of Israel will mourn at this piercing. Chapter 13 begins by saying that God will cleanse the inhabitants from sin (cf. Rev. 1:7 for similar wording).

3.6.4.4. Jesus' Burial (19:38–42). Later (v. 38), a certain Joseph asks Pilate for the body of Jesus, and Pilate grants his request. John tells two things about this man: He is from Arimathea and is a secret believer in Jesus. This Joseph only appears in the account of Jesus' burial in the Gospels. Luke 23:50–51 says that Arimathea was a city of the Jews. Joseph was also involved in the Sanhedrin and had a tomb near Jerusalem, meaning that he probably lived in Jerusalem at that time. Luke also tells us that he was a pious man. John emphasizes that he was a secret believer in Jesus out of fear of the Jewish leaders. These kinds of believers, who attended the synagogue, were numerous later, when leaders from Judaism persecuted them.

Nicodemus (v. 39; cf. ch. 3) accompanied Joseph, bringing a large supply of burial spices (about seventy-five pounds). Spices such as these were placed in the tomb to offset the odor from a decaying body. The sizable number suggests an extraordinary amount, that which is fit for a king. Nicodemus appears infrequently in this Gospel, indicating that he too was a secret believer in Jesus. He is also a leader among Jewish leaders (cf. 7:45–52).

The two men take Jesus' body and prepare it for burial according to Jewish custom. Preparation involved taking cloth and wrapping the body and then the head. With that finished, they place the body in a new tomb—again, one fit for a king. Since Passover is near (v. 42), they lay Jesus in this tomb in a garden, near the place of crucifixion.

3.7. Jesus' Resurrection (20:1–31)

Chapter 20 is the climax of this Gospel. Four of the five sections in this chapter contain similar states of being for the disciples. Each one begins with a state of fear and/or doubt (i.e., weak faith) and concludes with strengthened faith and joy. The resurrection appearances cause faith to come alive. In chapter 20, all of these appearances happen in Jerusalem.

3.7.1. Peter and the Beloved Disciple (20:1–10). This section begins with a note about the day of the week and the time of day: "early on the first day of the week," that is, early Sunday. Throughout his narrative John has noted that the religious feasts and the place where they occur (i.e., the temple) have been transformed. They belong to Judaism; Jesus' death and resurrection have transformed them, the One through whom all things were created (1:1–4).

This reference to time sets the tone for all that will now be considered. Sunday is the day of the new creation, serving to establish a reason for a new worship order and calendar system. For instance, Passover is no longer appropriate. John has handled references to it in his narrative so as to note that it belongs to the old order and not to the new. A new service, the Lord's Supper, now emerges from the resurrection and not from this outdated Jewish feast. This designation of time fits well with the purpose and tone of the book. The posture of John's Gospel is defensive, not evangelistic, though it concludes with a charge to pastor the church as God's flock and to evangelize outsiders.

In the heated debate with the synagogue over who the true people of God are, the proper response focuses on Jesus' person and work. It is the birth of the church by means of a suffering but triumphant Messiah, who sends the Spirit to cleanse and create. This Messiah King is thus the agent of the new creation in the same way that he was in Genesis 1 (cf. John 1:1–5). In this new creation, he has been more consciously involved. Just as God created originally (Gen. 1), so Jesus creates the church.

On this day, Mary Magdalene comes while it is still dark, that is, very "early." In that culture this day would be the equivalent of the Western world's Monday. It is not a holy day; it is a work day. The Sabbath has passed. So Mary comes out, apparently to pay homage. In all of the resurrection narratives, women play a vital role. Mary visits the tomb and finds the stone removed from the entrance. Upon her discovery, she returns to Peter and the beloved disciple with alarming news, showing that she has no idea about the possibility of the resurrection. She thinks that some unknown person or persons have carried Jesus' body away.

Let us reconstruct the scene. The movement from verses 3–9 is significant. At her news, two disciples (Peter and the beloved disciple) run to the tomb; the latter disciple outruns Peter and arrives first. He stands outside the tomb, bends over, and looks in. He sees the "strips of linen lying there but [does] not go in." Peter then arrives and goes into the tomb and sees "the strips of linen lying there, as well as the burial cloth that had been around Jesus' head. The cloth was folded up by itself, separate from the linen" (vv. 6–7). It is after Peter has gone in that the head cloth is seen. This detailed description of the inside of the tomb bears elaboration. John, the beloved disciple, is not only the one to witness Jesus' death on the cross, he is the first to see the empty tomb. But the significance of the scene before him does not dawn on him (or Peter).

A description of the tomb and burial clothing may help. Usually tombs were hewn out of a rock hill. The first act would be to cut a chamber. Tombs, or places to lay bodies, were carved out of the sides of these chamber rooms. Other chambers off of this original one could be cut out to expand burial sites as family members died and needed them. Since this tomb was a new one, it would have been a simple one, with likely only one tomb cut into the side of this chamber, visible from the opening. Access to tombs was controlled by cutting a large slot in the stone in front of the door to the chamber. In this slot was placed a large stone disc that would roll back and forth as needed. This trench or slot could be sloped to make it more difficult for persons, such as grave robbers, to enter.

Two common types of tombs were used: *arcosolium* and *kokim*. The first was cut at right angles into the rock of the chamber. It would be a ledge, wide enough to lay a body. Over the ledge, extending from the head and feet, the cut would arch and meet at the top, several feet above the ledge—thus the name *arcosolium*. The other kind of tomb was cut lengthwise into the rock. The height would not be as great since the cut would extend far back into the rock. The body would lie lengthwise, extending away from the viewer. What John describes is a simple *arcosolium*, cut into the side of a simple chamber, viewed from the outside, simply because in the darkness of the tomb, all the grave clothes could be seen.

The description of the linen body cloth and the head cloth is important. Both are lying in place, without disturbance, as if the body has suddenly disappeared from within them. Indeed, it has. This is the significance of the resurrection. The resurrected body slipped through this physical material without disturbing it. With nothing inside to hold the cloth up, it has collapsed upon itself. This is the nature of the resurrection body. Furthermore, the stone has not been rolled away so Jesus could get out; it has been rolled away so the disciples can get in. Note 20:19, which demonstrates that the resurrected Jesus has no need of doorways. But this is not the appearance of a phantom or spirit. John has already borne witness to the real death in chapter 19. Rather, the body has been changed; the grave clothes testify to that fact.

Note the movement from fear to faith. Some scholars rightly note the progression of Greek verbs to describe this change. The first verb occurs at verse 5 and describes the beloved disciple's status. The Greek verb is *blepo*—"looked in." He saw but understood nothing particularly significant at this point. The next verb (v. 6) is *theoreo* and describes Peter's point of reference as he comes into the tomb. This verb marks some movement in the process of spiritual understanding. But then the beloved disciple came in, "saw [*eidon*] and believed." This verb of "sight" denotes greater spiritual insight.

Belief comes, then, with this understanding of the resurrection. The resurrection is the basis of the Christian's faith. Paul in 1 Corinthians 15 also confirms this fact regarding the foundation of Christianity. Now faith can come into being. Its goal is in place. This is the reason people cannot be saved apart from Jesus and his resurrection.

It is important that these two most important apostles see the empty tomb and that their faith can come to completion, having begun in 2:11. This is apostolic witness. Yet John notes parenthetically (in the NIV) that they still do not understand the Scripture; in other words, something is still lacking, even though they have moved from fear to faith. In the New Testament, what becomes more important than the empty tomb are the resurrection appearances. It is not cold, apologetic, rational arguments that convince people of the resurrection. Rather, the post-resurrection appearances of Jesus solidify faith. It is the personal Jesus (i.e., his presence) that convinces people that he is alive. Peter and John then return to their homes (v. 10).

3.7.2. Mary Magdalene and Jesus (20:11–18). Apparently Peter and John are stunned as they leave. They do not say anything to Mary. But Mary Magdalene remains outside the tomb, weeping, showing her emotions of fear. Mary bends over, looks into the grave, and sees two angels—one sitting at the head of where Jesus had been, the other at the foot. They ask her, "Why are you crying?" But she does not recognize them as she answers.

Mary then turns and sees Jesus standing there but does not recognize him, thinking him to be the gardener. (Note: Jesus was buried in a garden tomb.) Jesus asks her the same question as the angels. But it is not until Jesus calls her by name that she recognizes him. This calls to mind 10:3–4: "He calls his own sheep by name and leads them out . . . and his sheep follow him because they know his voice." She responds in Aramaic "Rabboni," translated for Greek readers as "Teacher." Now her fear turns to faith at the presence of the resurrected Lord.

Then comes an interesting situation. Mary has apparently grabbed hold of Jesus, although John does not give us this information. Jesus, in a startling way, says, "Do not hold on to me, for I have not yet returned to the Father. Go instead to my brothers and tell them, 'I am returning to my Father and your Father, to my God and your God.'" Mary's personality shows up here. She is so grateful for what Jesus has done for her and is deeply moved and impacted by his imminent departure. The NIV's "Do not hold on to me" can be translated, "Stop clinging to me." The stress falls on the interruption of a constant and persistent action.

The next clause explains it further: "For I have not yet returned. . . . Go instead to my brothers and tell them." Her wanting to hold on to Jesus is preventing Jesus from finishing his task. Throughout chapters 14–16 he said that

RESURRECTION APPEARANCES

Event	Date	Matt.	Mark	Luke	John	Acts	1 Cor.
At the empty tomb outside Jerusalem	Early Sunday morning	28:1–10	16:1–8	24:1–12	20:1–9		
To Mary Magdalene at the tomb	Early Sunday morning		16:9–11		20:11–18		
To two travelers on the road to Emmaus	Sunday at midday			24:13–32			
To Peter in Jerusalem	During the day on Sunday			24:34			15:5
To the ten disciples in the upper room	Sunday evening		16:14	24:36–43	20:19–25		
To the eleven disciples in the upper room	One week later				20:26–31		15:5
To seven disciples fishing on the Sea of Galilee	One day at daybreak				21:1–3		
To the eleven disciples on the mountain in Galilee	Some time later	28:16–20	16:15–18				
To more than 500	Some time later						15:6
To James	Some time later						15:7
At the Ascension on the Mount of Olives	Forty days after the resurrection			24:44–49		1:3–8	

he had to return to the Father so that the Spirit could come. Jesus thus redirects her to a task, and so she, a woman, becomes the first evangelist (and to the disciples at that, including Peter and John).

The nature of Jesus' resurrected state is also given here: Mary can hold on to it. The verb "I am returning" in verse 17 is in the present (in process at that time) tense. (Jesus is already "quasi" ascended.) Mary has changed from a fearing, hopeless disciple to a faithful, testifying one. The difference is the presence of Jesus. This is what distinguishes between the earlier paragraph in which Peter and John play a role and the present paragraph. She has seen the Lord, whereas they did not. The intimacy between Jesus and his disciples comes through—Jesus calls them "my brothers" (v. 17). He thus continues to identity with them, something that began in chapter 13 when he washed their feet and in 15:14–15 when he called them "friends."

3.7.3. All the Disciples: The Creation of the Church (20:19–23). If chapter 20 is the climax of this Gospel, then this section is the epitome of this climax. Again, it shows movement from unbelief or faulty faith to that of new or strengthened faith. The foremost thing in this brief paragraph centers on the arrival of the era of *shalom* (peace) and the creation of the church.

The section begins by referring back to the first day of the week mentioned in verse 1, only evening this time. This note helps to establish the time setting for the paragraph. This connection with Sunday is thus important to what occurs here—it brings special emphasis to this day, making it the key to the chapter.

The disciples' mood also provides the setting for Jesus' appearance. They cower behind tightly closed doors in fear of the Jewish leaders. The simple reference of the plural "doors" tells us little about the type of building. The word "locked" is a perfect participle, used as an emphatic adjective. This situation addresses one that John's church has been experiencing. Pressed by Pharisaic leaders, their faith is threatened by these leaders' teachings, causing doubt to arise.

The time and mood establish a frame of reference in which to understand the main clause, which comes last in verse 19. "Jesus came and stood among them and said, 'Peace be with you!'" This verse focuses on the appearance of Jesus and on what he says. In other words, Jesus brings peace to his disciples on Sunday as they are cowering in fear.

What is the nature of this peace that he announces and brings? "Peace" occurs five times in this Gospel—three of them in this chapter (vv. 19, 21, 26) and all in the same clause: "Peace be with you!" The other two times are in 14:27 and 16:33. These five are closely related. In 14:27 the context is similar: Jesus promised the gift of his peace in the midst of a troubled and fearful situation; in 20:19, 21 he fulfills this promise. This peace differs from that of the world. Later, in 16:33, he assured his disciples that in him they would have this peace. They would not have it in the world, for the world only gives trouble.

It is important that this giving of peace coincides with the death and resurrection of Jesus and with his appearance to them. Peace is thus connected to the atoning work of Jesus. Paul likewise interprets "peace" in this way (Rom. 5:1, 11; in fact, peace serves as a bracket around verses 1–11 as a synonym of reconciliation). In Old Testament expectation and later Jewish background, this word group contained significant overtones concerning the doctrine of salvation. In fact, it can be understood synonymously with the term *salvation*. As recipients of this peace, disciples are unified with one another and with the Son and the Father. As such, they stand united against the opposition of the world (see esp. *EDNT*, 4:395–96).

Jesus' words are rooted deeply in the messianic hope of the people of Israel. When the Messiah came, he would bring peace with him—that is, he would bring salvation and healing, resulting in joy. Acts 2:46, a probable Eucharistic context, places joy, fellowship, and other messianic activity together. These people witness to the presence of the risen Christ. John 14:27–28 puts joy together with peace as gifts of Jesus. Also, 16:16–24 and the statement at its end, "and your joy will be complete," suggest the celebration of peace in the future age. In fact, in some places in Jewish literature, it is only God who brings peace. God's name is Peace.

John with this language uses one of Hillel's rules in order to equate the activity of God in the Old Testament with that of Jesus in the New Testament. As God has given peace, so

Jesus (as deity) gives peace. In the midst of persecution from their enemies, Jesus as God gives peace and joy to his people.

Verse 20 begins with, "After he said this," connecting the giving of peace with what follows. Jesus then shows his disciples his hands and side. In so doing, he shows that peace comes as a result of what has happened to him as reflected in his hands and side. In order to understand this action, we must discuss in greater length the words that describe it. This is the only place in the New Testament where this action occurs in this exact way. A similar description occurs in Luke 24:36–43, one of the few places where John parallels the other Gospels. (Scholars have also noted that both accounts have parts that resemble the Lord's Supper.) But Luke differs from John in one significant way: He has "hands and feet" in contrast to John's "hands and side."[9]

"Hands" and "side" together occur in the New Testament only here in John 20:20, 25, 27. "Hands" are found in all the Gospel accounts in the resurrection appearances. But why does John differ from Luke's "feet" and add, in contrast to all others, "side"? Several reasons can be given. "Side" (*pleura*) occurs five times in the New Testament, four of them in this Gospel (three times here and in 19:34). In John these occurrences are all connected, referring to the same body place and having the same theological significance. In 19:34 the soldier thrust his sword into the side of Jesus and water and blood gushed forth. "Side" thus ties together Jesus' death and resurrection appearances. It intertwines his death and his broken body with the blood and water.

"Side" with "hands" demonstrates the fact of atonement and its connection with the body of Jesus. "Side" also associates his body and blood with his life in this atonement. "Side" and "hands" become the identifying traits of his broken body in the Lord's Supper. Thus in 20:27, "he showed them his hands and side" (see also vv. 20, 25). The symbolic bread of communion not only point to his real bodily death (i.e., hands and side) and the instruments (cross and nails) used to bring it about; it also points to the bodily resurrected Christ with all its scars, preserved to show redemption's fact. The drink of communion represents Jesus' blood, here united with the broken body in atonement.

We have already noted that 19:34 fulfills 7:39 (see comment on 19:34). The water flowing from Jesus' side represents the Spirit that Jesus now gives to those who believe in him. Jesus' breathing out the Spirit on the disciples is the inaugural event of the age of salvation. The giving of the Spirit comes only as a result of Jesus' atoning work on the cross. This is the biblical order of the events of salvation: Jesus' death, his resurrection, and the giving of the Spirit. By John's taking notice of this breathing here, he shows that the giving of the Spirit comes as a result of Jesus and his work. This is significant. This ensures the reader that Jesus is the unique giver (divine as the Father is, the divine originator of life) and means (as the Father's submissive agent, the One who died) of salvation. This attachment makes Christianity an exclusive religion.

Verse 20 concludes with the impact that this revelation of Jesus' hands and side makes on his disciples: "The disciples were overjoyed when they saw the Lord." The NIV does not translate the Greek connector *oun*, which is inferential ("therefore"). This connector shows a cause-and-effect relationship between seeing the hands and side of Jesus and being "overjoyed." His work, as demonstrated by his hands and side, produces the effect of joy. John notes also that the disciples see the Lord, not that they see his hands and side. He has abbreviated this event, emphasizing how the presence of Jesus manifests his atoning work and produces the joy that only God brings.

Verse 21 marks another step in what Jesus is doing here in this appearance. Once again, the Greek text has the connector *oun* ("therefore"), untranslated in the NIV. As a result of their recognizing the Lord and receiving atonement, Jesus again announces to his disciples, "Peace be with you!" Then Jesus goes on to make a different connection from verse 19: He commissions them with the words, "As the Father has sent me, I am sending you." This is Jesus' commission as found in John's Gospel to evangelize the world (cf. Matt. 28:18–20; Mark 16:15–18; Luke 24:46–49; Acts 1:8). It is important to note that this commissioning comes after the disciples have received atonement, a new relationship stemming from the death and resurrection of Jesus.

This commission is characterized by a "sending" aspect. John uses another of Hillel's rules here, a similarity principle: As the Father has sent me, in a similar way I send you. "Sending," a word frequently used in John (he actually uses two Greek words, *apostello* and *pempo*), takes on special character in this Gospel. The authority and responsibility of mission that the Father gave the Son moves to believers. The Father and Son send the Spirit, who works in the world by giving life and sanctification to believers, thus empowering them; the Spirit in turn convicts sinners to whom they will preach (cf. 16:8–9).

When believers at conversion are brought into union with the Father and Son, they possess the same authority as the Father and the Son. Believers submit to the Father and Son in the same way as Jesus submitted to his Father, and they have the same Spirit who witnesses and effects in a dynamic way this authority. That this commissioning is the same as Jesus' is noted by the way he gives it: "As the Father has sent me, I am sending you" (v. 21). The "has sent me" signifies that Jesus is still under his commission, which includes the work and authority to send believers.

The work and responsibility of evangelization flows out of the work and person of Jesus, not out of the work and person of the Spirit. We will soon see that the Spirit is concerned with the work of evangelization in a profound and powerful way (v. 22), to be sure, but he is not its foundation. As taught in all the New Testament, especially as we have noted in John, Jesus is the center of all divine (i.e., Spirit) activity in the world. For example, he brings salvation and sends the Spirit. Jesus in John has already declared that he must go away so he can send the Spirit.

Verse 22 connects with what has preceded in a different manner. *Oun* does not occur in the narrative here (cf. comments above). Rather, John states that "when he said that" (NIV: "And with that"), Jesus breathes on them and says, "Receive the Holy Spirit." Let us attempt to explain what this meant to John's readers/hearers as he wrote this.

The verb "receive" is in the aorist tense and is an imperative. In ancient Greek liturgies, including New Testament prayers (e.g., the Lord's Prayer), this form of a verb occurs frequently. "Receive" occurs in the Synoptic Gospels (e.g., Luke 23:17) in the Eucharist, although not in Paul (cf. 1 Cor. 11:23–26). This imperative is not a regular command. When Jesus speaks these words, he is giving, not demanding a response.

Breathing on the disciples, however, precedes Jesus' statement regarding the gift of the Spirit. Yet, it should be noted that this act is connected with receiving the Spirit. Scholars debate over what this breathing means theologically. One interpretation says that this is merely symbolic. Another believes that John is recording the Acts 2 Pentecost event, making it the Johannine Pentecost. Others think that the writer of this Gospel places here both events (Jesus' breathing and the giving of the Spirit in Acts 2) together, molding them into one account.

Let us work our way through the evidence for a more probable interpretation. The themes of breath/breathing, the giving of life, creation, and the Spirit are associated in a number of texts, both biblical and extrabiblical. Note, for example the clustering of these themes in the following Old Testament texts: Genesis 2:7; 1 Kings 17:21 (in the Greek translation only); Psalm 104:29–30; and Ezekiel 37:4–10 (cf. 36:24–27). Outside the Old Testament canon, this biblical belief became an important theological concept: Wisdom 15:11; 2 Baruch 23:5. In Genesis Midrash Rabbah 14:8 two of these texts are commented on: Genesis 2:7 and Ezekiel 37:14. Breathing as a symbolic ritual, the accompanying giving of the Spirit, and the resultant life and/or creation were deeply rooted in biblical traditions. Jesus' words and actions would have been well understood. Moreover, with this one of Hillel's techniques appears again: What is true of God in the Old Testament is also true of Jesus. As God created Adam and, later, Israel, by giving the Spirit, so Jesus as God created the church here by giving the Spirit.

All the texts referred to above demonstrate the same thing: that God sends the Spirit, who creates and brings life. These texts are never merely symbolic. John (and Jesus) lived in this scriptural tradition. Beyond doubt the Jewish environment was also aware of these texts and their intention to refer to this divine activity. It is most natural, then, to take John 20:22 to refer to the creation of the church, that is, the impartation of eternal life.

John 20:22 contains these words: "He [Jesus] breathed on them." The Greek of John has the verb *enephysesen*. The Greek translation of Genesis 2:7 contains the same word, where God breathed into the first human being the breath of life. There it is not just a symbolic use but a real event. We have already noted that John appeals to Genesis, especially to the divine activity of creating (e.g., John 1:1ff.). That is the case here too. John wants us to believe this to be a real event. The reader/hearer with chapters 14–16 still in mind knows that Jesus' promise in those chapters to give the Spirit is coming to pass here. Furthermore, Jewish readers with this method of attributing divine activity and attributes to Jesus would clearly understand this.

Ezekiel 37:4–10 contains the same concepts as John 20:19–23. The train of thought begins in Ezekiel 36 (esp. beginning with v. 24). God has judged Israel for her sins. The nation has been scattered throughout foreign countries. But God will gather them (i.e., save them) and purify them by sprinkling clean water on them. He will give them a new heart and a new spirit. He will put his Spirit in them, and they will follow his commands (vv. 26–27). In 37:4–10, God addresses the prophet about dead Israel (i.e., dead bones), telling him to speak to the dead bones and "to the breath." Clearly "breath" here refers both to this new life and to the Spirit, who is the Breath of life. It refers to the promise of salvation of God's people in the future, which is being realized in John. This too is a real event that is both promised and realized.

In the Hebrew of Ezekiel several words convey this idea of the Spirit's bringing life. Notice the way the Hebrew slips back and forth between the words "Spirit" and "life," conveying a close connection. Ezekiel 37:5b reads, "I [i.e., God] will make breath [*ruach*, Heb. for breath, wind, spirit, Spirit] enter you, and you will come to life." The Hebrew is subtle. *Ruach* means both God's Spirit and the breath that denotes life (see *NIDOTTE*, 3:1073–77). We have here something typical in Semitic languages and culture—the same word used with several intentions. The Greek translation reads, "I [God] will bring on you the life-giving Spirit" (my trans.). In verse 6 the Greek also removes this Hebrew subtlety by translating "I [i.e., God] will put breath [*ruach*] in you" as "I will put my Spirit in you" (my trans.). At verse 8 the NIV has, "but there was no breath [*ruach*] in them." The Greek has for this word *pneuma*, the same as in the other references we have just examined. In both instances, the word clearly means "life."

The description of this future salvation event in Ezekiel is similar to the first creation account in Genesis. There are tendons, then flesh, then skin, but no life yet. Life only comes when God breathes it into them.

In Ezekiel 37:9, the NIV reads, "Prophesy to the breath [*ruach*]; prophesy, son of man, and say to it, 'This is what the Sovereign LORD says: Come from the four winds [Heb. pl., *ruchoth*], O breath [*ruach*], and breathe [*napach*] into these slain, that they may live.'" The Greek has, "Prophesy, son of man, prophesy to the Spirit [Gk., *pneuma*] and say to the Spirit, 'Thus says the Lord, from the four winds [Gk. pl., *pneumata*] come and breathe [*emphuseson*] into these dead and they shall live'" (my trans.). The NIV translates verse 10, "So I prophesied as he commanded me, and breath [Heb., *ruach*] entered them; they came to life." The Greek has, "And I prophesied as he commanded; and the Spirit [*pneuma*] came into them, and they came to life" (my trans.).

The verb used in John 20:22 (*enephysesen*) occurs in the Greek translation of Ezekiel 37:8–9. It also is in Genesis 2:7, as already noted. To connect these texts together, we make these further observations about this word. The Hebrew has two words for "breathe": *napach* and *nasham*. Genesis 2:7 has both of them together in parallel position; Ezekiel 37:4–10 has only *napach*. Nonetheless, they are connected in a significant way.

Some concluding and summary comments are in order. Ezekiel and Genesis are linked conceptually through using the same ideas and words. God gives life by his Spirit, and this life-giving event is described in terms of "breathing." "Life," breathe," and "Spirit" are inseparably connected, largely because life comes only from God; it is his Spirit that brings it; and the act of its impartation is in "breathing." One thing distinguishes Genesis from Ezekiel: Genesis refers to the creation of and impartation of "natural" life, while Ezekiel with the same language refers to the creation of the new order, the day of salvation, the impartation of spiritual life.

We should mention one other that corroborates our observations. Psalm 104:29–30 specifically speaks about God's Spirit sustaining and giving life. It also uses the Hebrew word *bara'* for creation, the same word used in Genesis for God's unique creating activity. We should also call attention to Ezekiel 36, the greater context of chapter 37. There, water for cleansing Israel's sins is used in the promise of this future salvation. Water and Spirit thus appear together as sanctifying and creating agents. This is important for the Gospel of John. When the Spirit in John causes one to be born again, one's sins are forgiven, that is, the Spirit cleanses them. The work of the Spirit and that of Jesus flow hand in hand. It is Jesus who atones for sin, the Spirit who in regeneration cleanses in a dynamic way (see Keener, *The Spirit in the Gospels and Acts*).

This breathing out the Spirit by Jesus is the ultimate and concluding sign, toward which all earlier ones point. This sign culminates all the events of Passion week, especially Jesus' death and resurrection. For example, the raising of Lazarus, the last of the signs, finds its meaning here. In this final sign, the use of one of Hillel's rules clearly specifies that Jesus is God, for he imparts the Spirit and gives life, a constant theme of this Gospel; he also gives *shalom*.

Verse 23 contains a rather difficult charge concerning the work of the new believers. This is the charge Jesus gives to the church: to forgive or not to forgive sins. This is the only time this command occurs in John, suggesting that only after Jesus' resurrection can the disciples do this. In contrast to the singular "sin" in some places (e.g., 1:29), this word here is plural. What is the difference? The singular "sin" refers to original sin; only Jesus can take care of that. The Spirit gives a new nature, which provides the power to walk in newness of life. "Sins" can refer to the sinful deeds that arise from the old nature. At any rate, the plural must be understood in this light. Forgiveness of "sins" is only possible because of the work of Jesus.

On the surface, forgiving and not forgiving in John 20:23 appears to be similar to binding and loosing in Matthew 16:19; 18:18. Upon closer analysis, they are not the same. Binding and loosing refers to the authority of the church to execute its affairs in differing situations. This procedure has its parallel in rabbinic circles. In Matthew, it occurs in a disciplining context. In contrast, John includes his comment in the commission for world evangelization. Here, the believer has this authority by virtue of having been sent. "Sending" in scriptural and in noncanonical contexts carries with it this meaning. Through Jesus' commissioning and authority, disciples can forgive sins because of the message they preach. If people do not receive the message, they remain in their sins. For example, in 6:28, the Jewish leaders asked Jesus what they must do to do the works of God. "Jesus answered, 'The work of God is this: to believe in the one he has sent'" (6:29). But they refuse. Therefore, "[their] guilt [Gk. sin] remains" (9:41b).

This third section has moved ahead the whole experience of faith that all the previous paragraphs have dealt with. Instead of individual faith, it has now broadened to corporate expression. Furthermore, the gift of the Spirit has made real this saving faith.

Arising from our analysis of this rich paragraph we can make some comments about the origins of some Christian practices. (1) It is now appropriate, for example, to explain how the church changed the worship day. This act of Jesus was the new creation spoken of in the Old Testament. Note, for example, Isaiah 42:5: "This is what God the LORD says—he who created the heavens and stretched them out, who spread out the earth and all that comes out of it, who gives breath to its people, and life to those who walk on it." Redemption/salvation is talked about in language of the first creation; it becomes the "second" creation.

Regarding the first creation, the Sabbath came afterwards, celebrating the completion of God's creative work. But the Sabbath has been changed in the second creation, though it is still connected with creation. It becomes the first day; as Hebrews puts it, it is the work of liberation, the entering in of the real rest, the day of salvation. Thus, it is the first day of the week, the day of the resurrection of Jesus, the foundation of the new creation that establishes a new worship order. This new creation also transforms the place of worship (cf. ch. 4). Real worship then goes on only in this new created order.

(2) Another comment pertains to the significance of the Lord's Supper. A similar scene to this appearance in John 20 is displayed in Revelation 4–6. Chapter 4 especially connects

creation with the Eucharist. These chapters are full of hymns to God, glorifying him for his wonderful acts of creation and redemption. In his Gospel, John, because of the conflict he finds himself in, serves as the apostle to distinguish theologically and experientially from a "sister religion"—Judaism—for the sake of his adherents. He is the spokesperson, the leader to prevent his congregation from aborting Jesus.

The church and the synagogue have been associated with each other in varying degrees, depending on geography and time. Now, the tension has progressed so as to threaten Jewish believers in Jesus. Christian observances are not those of Judaism. Thus John needs to show that and Jesus' transformation of them. Passover is not the basis for salvation. Rather, Jesus' death and resurrection are. The Lord's Supper, then, is not to be connected to the Passover. John makes a subtle suggestion about where it should be connected. By using the historical event of the exalted Jesus' appearance, he attaches the Supper to this event. Revelation 4–5 suggest that this association and observance has already happened.

(3) Furthermore, John 20:19–23 speaks about the founding of the church and the origin of its *authority* in evangelization; Acts 2 speaks about its *empowering* for evangelization. In John's Gospel, the church starts with Jesus in 20:19–23, allowing Jesus to be its foundation. John connects Jesus strongly with the church and thus subordinates the Spirit clearly to Jesus (and the Father). Upon closer examination, Luke-Acts does the same thing, especially when Acts 2 is seen as empowerment. The church starts with Jesus, not the Spirit.

Acts and John show different aspects of Jesus' activity, that is, empowering and creating. In Acts 2, Jesus is at the right hand of the Father, having received from him authority to send the Spirit to empower apostles for witness to him. In John 20, Jesus is on earth, though quasi-ascended already, creating the church. This is not to say that, in a more specific way, John does not include empowerment in his background. As a participant in Pentecost, he is well aware of it. But his purpose is not to highlight it. Moreover, in Old Testament texts such "blurring" of the lines between empowerment and the giving of life does occur. Most of the time, it is the latter that receives exclusive attention.

In both John and Luke, however, world missions flow from and focus on Jesus. In John continuity with Old Testament elements, such as the people of God and the temple, is not strong. Thus to have a *new* people is not so strange. This fits John's context. In this debate over who are the true people of God, John (over against Judaism) says that the church is the true people of God—because of Jesus. This setting strongly suggests a sectarian environment in which Christians (Jewish and Gentile) typify what the larger group (Judaism and its leaders) should be and do but fail. Both groups argue over who embraces the real. Judaism rejects Jesus. For this reason Judaism is not part of the real, in spite of its adherence to scriptural expectations and beliefs. "Jews" in John are like everyone else. They are part of the world and are thus in sin. Adhering to past traditions does not count since all are in sin. In this new order in Jesus, all have an opportunity to participate through faith in him and reception of the Spirit. Through the new creation and the new birth, people enter into this new order and become God's children.

3.7.4. Thomas and Jesus (20:24–29). The next paragraph contains the same movement as the earlier ones but with new dimensions. The previous paragraph involved faith and eyewitness. Now when we come to Thomas, we are informed that he was not present the week before (vv. 24, 28). The others have told him, "We have seen the Lord!" (v. 25). However, Thomas is the doubting one. The basis of his doubt lies in the fact that he has not seen the risen Lord. In other words, his faith rests on his immediate perception. Again, all the disciples are behind closed doors when Jesus appears (v. 26). Jesus says the same words to all as he did in verses 19 and 21: "Peace be with you" (v. 26). Then he turns and appeals to Thomas, showing his hands and side and bidding him to touch (cf. 1 John 1:1–3).

With the same words regarding peace, the hands and side, plus the fact that the disciples are all gathered in the same room a week later, we should take this to mean that this is another point at which John subtly reattaches the Lord's Supper.

Thomas moved from doubt to faith when he exclaimed (v. 28), "My Lord and my God!" In verse 29 we have the purpose for this paragraph. For successive generations who do not see and have not seen, they can still enter into the same relationship and demonstrate and experience the same faith. Thomas then represents all of these post-resurrection followers of Jesus. This sets up the final two verses of this chapter.

3.7.5. The Purpose of This Gospel (20:30–31). These two verses emphasize the death and resurrection of Jesus, moving towards the appearances of Jesus and the resultant rise of faith in disciples. The death and resurrection are the sign. Moreover, all earlier signs in the Gospel point to these events, connecting them in a profound manner. These also tell us, therefore, that John's selection of signs depended on their ability to convey the content and intent of the sign.

The purpose of all these signs is to produce faith, the consequence of which is life. But life only comes in Jesus' name. "Name" in verse 31 stands for all that "Jesus-is-the-Christ-the-Son-of-God" (v. 30) means. This name (representing its various titles) and what it has come to mean in this Gospel now answers the question of chapter 1, asked by Jesus' enemies and his first followers, and fleshes out what Nathanael declared in 1:49, "Rabbi, you are the Son of God; you are the King of Israel." This Gospel was written to believers to remain faithful in spite of various kinds of threats from Judaism.

4. The Epilogue (21:1–25)

Chapter 21 presents a problem for some scholars. For example, 20:30–31 look like a typical ending of a book. Also, the disciples, such as Peter, appear somewhat skeptical or at least uncommitted in chapter 21 in spite of the powerful appearances of Jesus in chapter 20. Nonetheless, chapter 21 contains a number of common threads with the Gospel as well as provides continuity of thought. The function of this chapter is to provide a more developed commission for evangelization, the role of Peter in the extension of the church, and the authentication of the witness of the author. With this chapter, John provides information about the location of Jesus' appearances. He appears in the south (Jerusalem) and in the north (the Sea of Tiberias). This chapter can be divided into four sections.

4.1. The Third Appearance: By the Sea (21:1–14)

Verse 1 summarizes chapter 21. "Afterward" typifies John's style, connecting this chapter with the previous one. Jesus will manifest himself to his disciples by the Sea of Tiberias. The name "Tiberias" came into popular use in the latter part of the first century A.D.

Verses 2–14 describe Jesus' appearance in the north. Verse 2 supplies the names of five disciples and mentions two others with reference to their father. Most of these disciples appear in the first chapter of John. By returning to them again in the final chapter, the author brackets his Gospel with them, thereby emphasizing discipleship. Nathanael's appearance is rather surprising—he is not a fisherman like Peter; it is added here that he comes from Cana. He shows up in John only in the first chapter, and though he makes a proper confession there, nothing is said about his becoming a follower of Jesus. This element thus furnishes evidence in a specific way about disciples other than the Eleven who see the Lord.

Dialogue fills this chapter as it has other chapters in John's narrative. After the first exchange in verse 3 between Peter and the other disciples, only Jesus and Peter talk (except for the beloved disciple, who calls once to Peter, v. 7).

In verse 3, Peter suddenly announces that he is returning to fishing and asks the others if they want to go. The brief statement that follows provides the setting for the dialogue and appearance. They are in the boat all night and have caught nothing. This information is puzzling for at least two reasons. (1) Peter has just had some dramatic encounters with Jesus. Why does he return to fishing unless he does not understand the reason for the appearances and commissioning? The tense of the verbs "I'm going" and "to fish" suggest that they are returning to a former occupation.

(2) In Luke 5:1–11, Peter had a significant meeting with Jesus, similar to this one; it pertained to the call to evangelize. More than likely, the futile fishing effort contrasts with the fruitfulness of their new vocation. It was common to fish at night, and the morning brought opportunity to sell freshly caught fish. But this time, the disciples fish in vain. They

need time for Jesus to teach them about what has happened. For instance, Acts 1 tells us that Jesus spends even more time with them before he ascended.

The scene focuses on the early morning after they have reached futility in their old way of life. Jesus appears to them from the shore, but they do not recognize him. Jesus calls and addresses them as "friends" (Gk. *paidia*; lit., "little children"; this is the only time this word is used for the disciples in John). The way Jesus phrases the question, he knows that they have caught nothing. When they respond with "No," Jesus directs them to let down their net on the other (right) side of the boat. They catch so many that they are unable to haul in their net.

At this point the beloved disciple recognizes Jesus (v. 7). Peter, as usual, acts. He is stripped down, working in his loin cloth, and he puts on what is probably his fishing jacket (a garment that went over the underwear), tucks it and ties it for action, jumps into the water, and swims to the shore. The other disciples come to shore in the boat, pulling the net of fish behind them. They do not have far to go, since they are about one hundred yards from shore. Jesus has a fire prepared for food when they arrive. We are not told where Jesus got the materials for the fire or the fish and bread that he prepared.

What happens next stirs debate. Jesus asks them to bring some of the fish they have just caught. Peter goes aboard and drags the net ashore without breaking the net. The net, we are told, had 153 large fish in it. A specific number is given. Why 153? Possible answers to this question vary from believing that John employs allegory, symbolism of numbers, gematria, geometry, or some combination. Gematria was Jewish in background. It attributed numerical value to each letter used in a word. In cases where one begins with the number, one has a difficult time to find the word that the writer had in mind with the number. Scholars have suggested several possibilities: (1) "the church of love" (*qhl h'hbh*); (2) Simon (76) plus *ichthys* ("fish") (77); (3) Engedi plus Eneglaim (names mentioned in Ezek. 47:10, the background for Tabernacles in John and Revelation).

The more probable meaning for this literal number of 153 fish is that they suggest the Jewish symbolism of the notion of universalism. This tradition believed that 153 species of fish existed in the world. This number, then, would represent the church's world mission. If this is correct, then we have in John a commission similar to the one given in Matthew 28. The context does emphasize the call to Peter to oversee God's entire flock. It certainly suggests a careful eyewitness observation.

Jesus then invites the disciples to breakfast. Yet none of the disciples dare to ask Jesus who he is—they know (v. 12). Jesus' actions and words in verse 13 mirror the Lord's Supper: "[He] took the bread and gave it to them, and did the same with the fish." Verse 14 supports this by saying this is now the third time Jesus has appeared, which also connects this chapter to chapter 20.

4.2. Jesus and Peter: The Call to Radical Commitment (21:15–19)

Jesus now focuses on Peter, pushing him for complete and final commitment. When they finish breakfast, Jesus dialogues with Peter on the theme of love and commitment. Peter's ego (and mood) is offended in this interchange as Jesus bears in and presses for a commitment that will drive out his indecisiveness to follow Jesus. Three times he asks Peter if he loves him. Three times Jesus calls Peter "Simon son of John." (This is the only place where we are given this name for Peter and the only chance to know his father's name.) Three times Jesus answers Peter's statement with "Feed my lambs" (v. 15); "Take care of my sheep" (v. 16); and "Feed my sheep" (v. 17). "Feed" occurs twice, the first and last; "take care" is in the middle. The word for "sheep" also changes: "lambs" (v. 15) and "sheep" (vv. 16–17).

The word for "love" also differs. The NIV has the following in the dialogue here:

(1) Jesus: "Do you truly love" (*agapao*); Peter: "I love" (*phileo*) v. 15;
(2) Jesus: "Do you truly love" (*agapao*); Peter: "I love" (*phileo*) (v. 16);
(3) Jesus: "Do you love me" (*phileo*); Peter: "I love you" (*phileo*) (v. 17).

Some interpretations (and translations) of "love" violate an interpretive principle and fall into the root fallacy. That is, they see different meanings of these two words based on their roots. However, meaning is never determined n this manner; context always contributes to a word's meaning. It is doubtful whether Jesus ntends something different in his last statement in pushing Peter to a full commitment, even though he uses *phileo*. By examining the way these two words are used in John and elsewhere (cf. Matt. 5:43–48; Luke 6:27–36), one can determine that John uses these words interchangeably, just as any good writer chooses synonyms rather than using the same word all he time. A good example of such variation occurs in this very paragraph with "sheep" and "feed."

The point of this dialogue between Jesus and Peter is that he presses Peter for a full commitment. Given Peter's history from chapters 13–19, this meeting has to occur. In these chapters, this disciple appears to vacillate and s weak in faith. Jesus presses him into his vocation. "Feed" and "take care of" pertain to eadership and nurture of the church. This dialogue also, along with other texts, places Peter nto a prominent role in the primitive church.

Verse 18, introduced by the typical affirming statement of Jesus in John ("*amen, amen*"; NIV, "I tell you the truth"), marks off a prophecy about the eventual death of Peter, suggesting that a time will come when he will no longer have his freedom but will be imprisoned and led away to his death.

The author provides an interpretation of this prophecy in verse 19. He also connects discipleship ("Follow me") with commitment that eads to death. This kind of martyrdom glorifies God. The use of shepherd language in this dialogue brings to memory chapter 10 and the material on the good shepherd. It is the good shepherd who lays down his life for the sheep. Peter will follow in the steps of his Lord.

4.3. Peter and the Beloved Disciple (21:20–23)

In these four verses, Peter and the beloved disciple are connected. Peter turns to inquire about his companion. (Compare ch. 13 for a similar position of John and Peter when Peter asks a question.) Jesus informs Peter that he should pay attention to his own call (v. 22). Discipleship language also shows up here: "You must follow me." Apparently, Jesus' statement to Peter has caused confusion among some in the early church. John thus takes the time in verse 23 to explain the rumor that has started. Jesus did not say that the beloved disciple will not die, but emphasized that Peter must do God's will for himself. Each one has a different calling. Jesus is Lord of all and of each.

4.4. The Author's Authentication (21:24–25)

These two verses close the Gospel. Verse 24 verifies the author's authenticity: He has been with Jesus from the start. He had a privileged place at the dinner, was present during the crucifixion, was the first to see the empty tomb, and was the first to recognize Jesus at the Sea of Tiberias. He also writes that he has information about Jesus that could fill many books (v. 25).

John (the apostle) never provides his name in this Gospel. He always refers to himself in other ways, mostly by "the disciple whom Jesus loved." This privilege belongs to all of us.

THE OLD TESTAMENT IN THE NEW

NT Text	OT Text	Subject
Jn 1:23	Isa 40:3	Voice in the wilderness
Jn 2:17	Ps 69:9	Zeal for God's house
Jn 6:31	Ex 16:4; Ne 9:15; Ps 78:24–25	Bread from heaven
Jn 6:45	Isa 54:13	All are taught by God
Jn 10:34	Ps 82:6	You are gods
Jn 12:13	Ps 118:26	Blessed is he who comes
Jn 12:15	Zec 9:9	Palm Sunday
Jn 12:38	Isa 53:1	Unbelief of Israel
Jn 12:40	Isa 6:10	God blinds the eyes
Jn 13:18	Ps 41:9	A double-crossing friend
Jn 15:25	Ps 35:19; 69:4	Hated without a cause
Jn 19:24	Ps 22:18	Dividing garmets by lot
Jn 19:36	Ex 12:46; Ps 34:20	No broken bones
Jn 19:37	Zec 12:10	Looking on one pierced

NOTES

[1]John uses "spring" (i.e., Jacob's well) here and "rivers" (the water-pouring ceremony of Tabernacles) in 7:37–39; this difference is significant. "Spring" refers to the work of the Spirit and his result in the believer, while "rivers" points to Jesus the source of the Spirit.

[2]It is possible, however, that this man belongs in the administration of Herod. If so, he may have been a Roman or a Jew. If the latter, he is then more open to Jesus and less attached to Jewish culture and its religious expression as indicated by the temple and synagogue.

[3]Notice the occurrence of these various holy days: 5:1 ("a feast"); 5:9ff. ("Sabbath"); 6:4 ("Passover Feast"); 7:1–10:21 ("Feast of Tabernacles"); 10:22 ("Feast of Dedication"); 11:55; 12:1ff. ("Passover").

[4]Note that the Sadducees are not mentioned in this Gospel. They had been connected with the temple and passed out of existence with its destruction in A.D. 70. Since they were not a part of the Jewish scene threatening John's community, he had no need of mentioning them in his Gospel.

[5]This section is one of the largest omissions in the New Testament. All scholarship recognizes that it is probably not part of the original text of John. But it has been part of the Bible long enough and used as Scripture in liturgical settings so that laypeople are used to having it before them. The NIV thus does a service for Christians to include it, but it is also true to the evidence to indicate that the earliest and most reliable manuscripts do not include it.

In university libraries and museums around the world, the New Testament is preserved in more than five thousand fragments or mostly whole manuscripts—all of which show minor variation among them. Through a scientific process known as textual criticism, a New Testament text of probable readings is assembled. John 7:53–8:12 is completely omitted in some of these manuscripts; in others it occurs after 7:36, after 21:24, or even after Luke 21:38. Many scholars do recognize that it is an authentic story that was written in the first century, but there is little consensus as to why it was eventually inserted here. Note how the text can flow directly from 7:52 to 8:12 without losing the train of thought.

[6]In a new context (1 John 3:9), *sperma* conveys an essential similarity between the believer and Jesus: "No one who is born of God will continue to sin, because God's *seed* [*sperma*] remains in him."

[7]In verses 31–32, of the five times the verb "glorify" is used, the first three (present tense) are probably not to be distinguished from the next two expressing the future ("will glorify").

[8]*Parakletos* also occurs in 1 John 2:1. There it differs considerably in meaning from its use in the Gospel—it is connected explicitly with a person who pleads a sinner's cause.

[9]Luke differs in other ways too. The disciples have a hard time believing, though they have joy (they also have "amazement," Luke 24:41). Luke also uses the same word for "show" as John does (*deiknymi* in Luke 24:40; cf. John 20:20). But this word does not contain the same significance in Luke as it does in John. Schneider rightly notes its special meaning in John: "In the Fourth Gospel and Revelation *deiknumi* has the meaning *reveal*, *unveil*" (*EDNT*, 1:281). Jesus thus reveals to the disciples the connection between atonement (i.e., peace) and his work on the cross (i.e., his hands and side).

MATTHEW

James B. Shelton

INTRODUCTION

The early church linked the writing of the Gospel of Matthew with one of Jesus' original apostles named Matthew, also known as Levi, who was a former tax collector in the employ of the Romans or the local puppet government. The Roman empire had taken power in the Holy Land by force of arms in 63 B.C., and since then it had imposed oppressive tax burdens on the people. Many of the populace considered the tax gatherers to be collaborators and traitors. Some, especially among the religious establishment, were scandalized that Jesus associated with and ministered to "tax collectors and 'sinners'" and that he had called Matthew to be his disciple. To this objection Jesus replied, "It is not the healthy who need a doctor, but the sick" (9:9–13). In response to Christ's call, Matthew eventually became a major teacher and preserver of the teachings of Jesus. For this reason the church honored the Gospel that bears Matthew's name with the first position in the canonical order of the New Testament.

When Matthew began writing his Gospel, several documents concerning Jesus had already been composed. Among them were letters from the apostles, a collection of the sayings of Jesus, early versions of the accounts of his life, and the Gospel of Mark. Why were they not enough? Why did Matthew feel compelled to write another version? In an era when a single piece of papyrus paper would cost several dollars by modern standards and the services of a scribe were costly, why did Matthew go to such expense? Furthermore, few churches could afford luxuries such as an extensive collection of hand-copied scrolls. Why, then, were the early Christians so willing to bear the expense when oral accounts, Mark, and other accounts of Jesus were already available? The answer lies in the nature of Christian revelation.

1. The Medium Is the Message

In other religions, accounts of revelations often involved the recipient being in an altered state in which the will was abrogated and the body became merely the mouthpiece of the god or spirit, with the recipient not even aware of what was being said or what it meant. This was not normative for Hebrew and Christian revelatory experience. Usually the prophet or inspired writer used all his physical, mental, and spiritual faculties to communicate what had been revealed to him. Often his own unique vocabulary was used as were expressions common to his community. Sometimes even bad grammar and awkward syntax were used; yet God in his sovereignty and choice of the recipient guaranteed that what he wanted expressed would be communicated fully and unhindered.

Christian revelation was based on an inspiration model, not a possession model. In fact, the Christians understood possession (i.e., complete control and violation of one's will and person) as evil—hence the idea of demonic possession. Even the apostle John, when he experienced the apocalyptic revelation of the heavenlies with all its otherworldliness, was not deprived of his will; on the contrary, in the midst of the experience he was expected to use it (Rev. 10:3–4). This divine-human reciprocity in revelation is exactly what one would expect in light of the Christian understanding of truth, for Jesus Christ is the Truth (John 14:6). He just did not speak truth; he was in his divine-human state Truth itself.

Thus, it is not surprising that Christian revelation should resemble the Incarnation of God with both human and divine components, which are neither to be confused nor separated. The words of God become the words of human beings. God is so comfortable with his sovereignty that he allows the will of humans to cooperate in his enterprise of communication, not unlike the description of the gift of prophecy as described by Paul, "the spirits of prophets are subject to the control of prophets" (1 Cor. 14:32). Not only is *what* God's Word says important but also *how* he communicates it; the medium also is a message. God wants human beings to cooperate with his plans of their own will. Possession and violation of his rational creatures are neither his method nor his message.

2. Faithful Witnesses

The writer of Matthew understood that God's revelation was not intended to be a monolithic monologue; the nature of the outpouring of God's Holy Spirit "on all people" precluded that (Acts 2:17). Jesus had promised the Holy Spirit so that the disciples would be witnesses (1:8), not just a single witness. They were not to be mere musical instruments upon which God played; they were not to be automatons, mindless robots. The prophetically endowed early church expected to hear more than one inspired witness; hence they would have been inclined to listen to Matthew's Gospel as well. In the preface to the Gospel of Luke, the closest thing in the Gospels to a bibliography, the evangelist lists the different kinds of sources he used: eyewitnesses and oral and written sources. Multiplicity in the witness was expected.

Since the ultimate Revelation of God, Jesus Christ, happened in time and in space (i.e., in history), he was seen by people with their eyes, heard with their ears, and touched with their hands (1 John 1:1–4). This revelation event was relatable through eyewitnesses, personal testimony, and written records. As a bearer of this historical record Matthew deserved an audience among his contemporaries. Yet the witness contained in his Gospel was not that of just anyone who happened to see the historical Jesus, but rather the witness of a believer, a disciple, one who bore an *apostolic* witness to Jesus.

The church accepted the testimony of Matthew's Gospel because it contained material that was recognized as the authentic teaching of those who had followed Jesus in his earthly ministry and who had been commissioned by him as the leaders of the church and trustees and interpreters of his message and ministry (Luke 24:44–49). The church included in the New Testament canon only those books that were written by a first-century apostle of Jesus or one closely associated with an apostle. The account not only had to be based on early sources but also had to be authoritative, that is, apostolic. The early church "devoted themselves to the apostles' teaching" (Acts 2:42). These essential teachings were in both oral and written form (Luke 1:1–4; 2 Thess. 2:15).

Furthermore, the church was considered the arbiter of these things as "the pillar and foundation of the truth" (1 Tim. 3:15). Although the Christian communities that had grown up around the apostles had a role in compiling and preserving their teachings, the apostles themselves were responsible for the teachings they had received from Jesus, which they explained, applied, and passed on to faithful successors. The origins of the basics of the Christian faith were "usually associated, not with anonymous communities but with well-known individual authoritative bearers of tradition" (Hengel, 1980, 26).

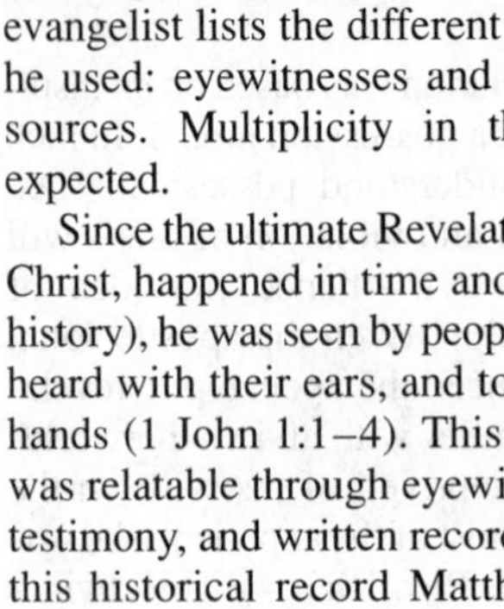

The Holy Land was only a small part of the Roman Empire at the time of the New Testament.

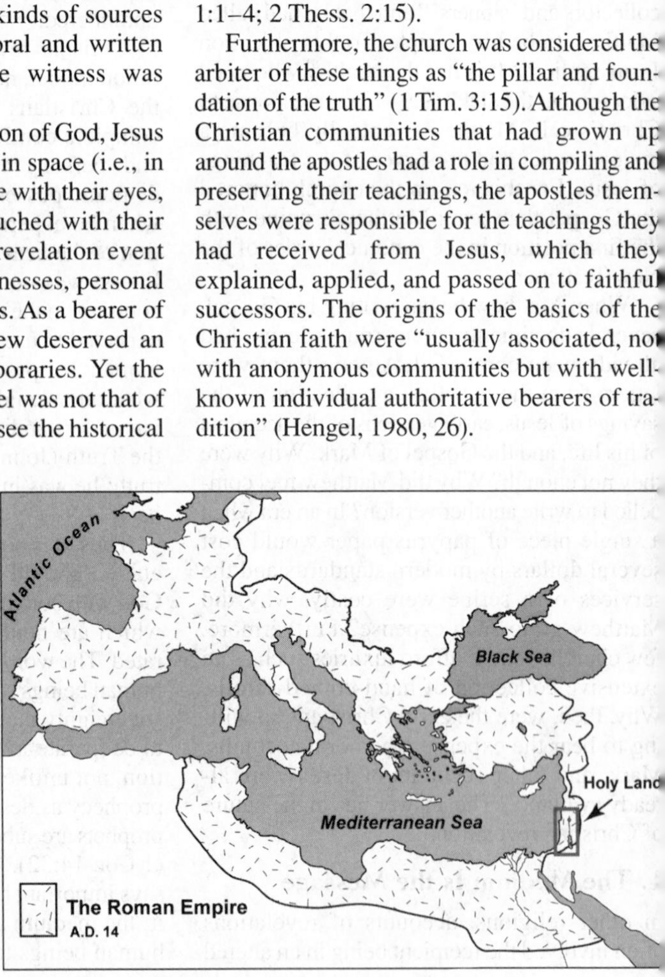

3. How and When Matthew Wrote

Matthew was written in Koine Greek. Its style is not polished Greek, in contrast to the classical style found in Luke and the letter to the Hebrews. Matthew's Greek evokes a Semitic flavor, which is probably due to his colloquial Greek, Hebraic/Aramaic sources, and his background. Matthew used oral and written sources. The author was trying to be accurate and use all resources available for the story of Jesus. One should not be put off with the idea of sources behind our Gospels. Jesus came to a literate world, and God used oral and written sources to proclaim and record his message (cf. Luke 1:1–4).

Most scholars believe that Matthew and Luke used the Gospel of Mark, the earliest extant Gospel, as a major source. According to Papias, writing at the turn of the century, Mark's Gospel records the teachings of Peter, which Mark wrote down after the apostle's martyrdom in the emperor Nero's persecution of the church in A.D. 64. If Matthew used Mark, then a date for his Gospel would be between A.D. 70–90. Cases have been made for a previous version of Mark that would have been available much earlier. Furthermore, Matthew presents Jesus' instructions regarding Jewish worship at the temple, perhaps indicating that the temple was still standing at the time of its writing, before its destruction in A.D. 70 (Matt. 5:23–24). The dating could be as early as the fifties. This commentator will not attempt to resolve the issue but will point out evidence for both early and late possibilities as they arise in the text.

Over 90 percent of Mark is reflected in Matthew and Luke. Hence the first three Gospels are called "synoptic," which means "to see together." Matthew and Luke also have another written source in common called "Q," coming from the German word *Quelle*, meaning source. Q consists of the material that both Matthew and Luke have in common but that Mark does not have. Matthew and Luke faithfully follow the Q material—often word for word, even to the point of awkward Greek word order. This unusual Greek syntax, probably the result of a Hebraic or Aramaic original being woodenly translated into Greek, reflects good Semitic usage.

Q consists primarily of the teachings of Jesus. Again, Papias's testimony is helpful. He records that Matthew wrote "the sayings [*logia*] of the Lord" in the "Hebrew dialect" (i.e., Aramaic), and others translated them as they were able. Note that Papias did *not* say Matthew wrote the gospel (*euangelion*) of Jesus but the sayings or teachings (*logia*) of the Lord. This may well be a reference to Q, a document no longer extant. The extant Gospel that bears his name may have been written by the apostle or his followers several years after the completion of Q. The Semitic flavor of Q may well speak of its antiquity and proximity to Aramaic, a cousin language of Hebrew and the language used in everyday life in the Holy Land in the first century.

Some scholars think that the passages Matthew and Luke have in common are a result of Mark and Luke using Matthew, though this is a minority opinion. An even smaller minority asserts the priority of Luke. Most scholars hold to "the four-source hypothesis" proposed by B. H. Streeter or some variation of it. It maintains that Matthew and Luke used Mark and Q and that Matthew and Luke had additional exclusive sources labeled "M" and "L" respectively. M and L may represent both oral and written sources. The following commentary assumes this scenario.

One might ask, why bother identifying sources since it does not affect the message. Three reasons arise. (1) It demonstrates the care the Gospel writers took in being faithful to the message. They did not blatantly invent stories about Jesus with no regard for the testimony of the early witnesses. (2) By knowing what sources Matthew used we can more readily identify his distinct, Spirit-led insights on the significance of the Jesus events that the Gospel writers have in common but of which they have unique understandings. (For example, all four Gospels mention the descent of the Spirit on Jesus, but each one posits a unique spiritual truth of its significance.) (3) By identifying the unique passages of Matthew we see the special concerns that motivated him to write yet another Gospel.

4. Why Was Matthew Written?

Each Gospel was written to a specific audience in order to accomplish specific goals.

They were not mere biographies or mere compilations of the teachings of Jesus; rather, they were written to express unique theological points as well as to present the basic message of Jesus. Matthew probably wrote to meet the specific needs of his readers. For example, he presupposes that his readers are familiar with Jewish customs while Mark, when relating the same events, explains the cultural practices to his Gentile audience (e.g., Matt. 15:1–9; Mark 7:1–13). Matthew's readers were probably Greek-speaking Jews who lived outside the Holy Land.

Matthew also emphasized persecution and church order in the passages unique to his Gospel (M material). This has led some scholars to suggest that Matthew's community (or that of his readers) was enduring persecution. Presumably Matthew selected those sayings of Jesus that were particularly attuned to this subject.

No doubt Matthew had help in compiling and writing even as Paul did in his letters (e.g., Rom. 16:22; Gal. 6:11). Mark served as Peter's scribe. The assistance of an amanuensis was not uncommon. Also, bear in mind that none of the Gospel texts bear the name of the author. In later copies the church identified the author in a title or sometimes with a preface giving biographical details. The church understood this Gospel to reflect the teachings that were associated with Matthew, the apostle of Jesus.

5. Matthew's Distinctive Issues

Matthew, like the other Gospel writers, has a specific agenda. There is commonality in the Gospels, but also diversity. Matthew, for example, emphasizes the teaching of Jesus while Mark emphasizes his actions, recording more miracles than the other Gospel writers. Matthew may raise a distinctive theological issue that he sees in an event in the life of Jesus, while the other Evangelists, commenting on the same event, emphasize a different ramification. In other words, Jesus' actions can have more than one significance. It is as though the four Gospel writers paint the same picture but use different colors. We often see color by contrast; thus, in the commentary we will often contrast the different issues of the Evangelists in common passages.

a. Jesus as King

Matthew's Gospel has been called the "Royal Gospel" and for good reason: The writer presents Jesus as the true King of Israel. This is why Matthew takes great care to present the genealogy of Jesus following the Davidic dynastic succession and emphasizes David the king as a major dividing point in his presentation. (Contrast this with Luke, who links Jesus in his genealogy with David through another progression of ancestors who did not sit on the throne at Jerusalem.) Often Matthew is preoccupied with Jesus as king when the other Evangelists at the same point do not mention it. For example, in his account of the birth of Jesus Matthew tells his readers about the Magi, who ask the question, "Where is the one who has been born king of the Jews?" (Matt. 2:2). Luke does not tell us about the Magi but about angels from heaven, who announce to the marginalized shepherds, not the birth of a king, but a Savior for all people, a theme that Luke frequently emphasizes (Luke 2:10–11). Throughout his Gospel Matthew underscores the royalty of Jesus.

Matthew also relates the Old Testament prophecies concerning the Messiah to Jesus. Messiah comes from the Hebrew word meaning "to anoint"; in the New Testament it is translated as "the Christ." In Old Testament times priests and kings were anointed with oil when they began their terms of service. This was to indicate that they were set aside for a holy purpose. The Messiah was the One whom God would raise up to bring Israel back to God, to lead them in true worship of God, and to rule not only Israel but the whole world. Since Jesus was the new King, Matthew also emphasized the nature of the kingdom of heaven as God's reigning over the hearts and minds of humankind.

b. Jesus as Teacher

Matthew presents more of Jesus' teaching than any of the other Gospel writers. He augments Mark's account with more of Jesus' teaching, thus making a crucial and necessary addition to the written record of the church.

Matthew not only presents Jesus as a king but also as a teacher (rabbi), hence a Teacher King. Jesus fulfills simultaneously the roles of Moses the lawgiver and David the king. It is no surprising, then, that he presents Jesus' teaching as the teaching of the kingdom or rule of God. He refers to the "kingdom of heaven" over thirty times, preferring this expression over "the kingdom," "the kingdom of God," or "the Father's kingdom" (all of which he does use on occasion). None of the other Evangelists use "kingdom of heaven"; they prefer "kingdom of God." The rule of God is the major characteristic of the teaching of Jesus. Matthew uses "kingdom of heaven" as a respectful way of referring to the kingdom of God in order to accommodate his Jewish audience, who out of reverence for God avoided speaking his name directly but instead referred to him indirectly by saying "Lord" or making some allusion to heaven (e.g., Dan. 4:26).

Some students of the Bible have tried to make a distinction between the "kingdom of heaven" as a solely future event and the "kingdom of God" as now present, creating two distinct epochs or dispensations in their view of salvation history. This is not the intent of the Evangelists. The parallels in Mark, Luke, and John clearly equate "kingdom of heaven" with the "kingdom of God"; furthermore, Matthew uses the terms interchangeably in 19:23–24. Jesus intends his ethical teachings to be lived out in the present and not in some distant era.

Matthew arranges his book differently from the other Gospel writers. He tends to group Jesus' teachings together according to their topics. He sets these blocks or sections of sayings between other blocks of narrative material that describe the works of Jesus and the advance of his mission. It is important to remember that the Gospels are not mere chronological biographies of Jesus; they are witnesses to who Jesus is. The Holy Spirit impressed each writer to present the same message in different ways so that different aspects of Jesus' ministry could be highlighted.

In portraying Jesus as teacher, Matthew presents five major groups of teachings, with Jesus as the new Moses. Some have suggested that Matthew's intent is to draw a parallel between Jesus' teachings and the first five books in the Old Testament, known as the Pentateuch. For this reason the teachings of Jesus have been termed "the new Torah" (i.e., new law). These teaching sections are framed with the beginning of the Gospel (chs. 1–4, including Jesus' genealogy and birth, the ministry of John the Baptist, and the commencement of Jesus' ministry) and the conclusion (chs. 26–28, including the plot against Jesus, the Last Supper, and Jesus' passion, death, and resurrection). The five teaching discourses are:

1. The Sermon on the Mount (5:1–7:29)
2. Call to Mission (9:35–10:42)
3. Parables of the Kingdom (13:1–52)
4. Jesus' Instructions to the Church (18:1–35)
5. The Olivet Discourse (24:1–25:46)

Each section concludes with words such as, "and when Jesus had finished these sayings . . ." (7:28; 11:1; 13:53; 19:1; 26:1). This scheme contains most of Matthew's teachings (see Bruce, 1972, 66–67).

c. Other Distinctive Interests

Jewish orientation. Matthew addresses his Gospel to the Jews. This orientation is reflected in his respect for the Jewish law and his frequent references to the Pharisees. Matthew acknowledges their wisdom and advocates that their instructions be kept (19:17–18; 23:2–3); yet he condemns them for adding to the commandments of God "teachings . . . taught by men" (15:9) and for preaching but not practicing the stipulations of God's law (23:1–3).

Emphasis on Gentiles. Matthew emphasizes the place of Gentiles. Ironically the Gospel that has the most Jewish flavor as well as a Jewish audience in mind is the one that also presents the message as a gospel for all nations and peoples. Initially the good news is reserved for the lost sheep of the house of Israel (10:6), but Matthew ends his work with a commission: "make disciples of all nations" (28:19). At times he is critical of the Jewish nation (e.g., 8:10–12; 21:43; 23:29–39; 27:24–25). Matthew struggles with the tension between the good of the old order and the greater program of the ever-expanding kingdom of heaven. It seems significant that only Matthew records the saying of Jesus, "Therefore every scribe who has been trained for the kingdom of heaven is like a householder who brings out of his treasure what is new and what is old" (13:52, RSV).

Scriptural proofs. Matthew constantly employs scriptural proofs. The phrase, "that it might be fulfilled which was spoken through the prophets," is one of his stock expressions. When the Evangelists mention the same event in Jesus' life, often only Matthew notes that it fulfills Old Testament prophecy. Frequently, it is the reference to geography, the place where the event occurs, that triggers Matthew's recognition that the event in Jesus' life fulfills an Old Testament event that occurred in the same location.

Ecclesiastical interests. Matthew is preoccupied with things ecclesiastical (i.e., relating to the church). Some examples are the Sermon on the Mount, the ethics of the kingdom (13:1–33), Peter's authority in the church (16:17–19), and the directions for discipline in the church (18:15–20).

Predictions of persecution. Matthew has several sections of warnings and instructions concerning persecution (5:1–12; 10:16–23; 19:30; 20:16; 24:9–13), probably because the people to whom he was writing were being persecuted (cf. above).

Infancy narrative. Of the four Evangelists, only Luke and Matthew give details of Jesus' birth. Only Matthew tells us about the angelic visitations to Joseph, the murder of innocent boys by Herod, the visit of the wise men, the Christmas star, and the flight to and from Egypt. In all of these events he presents Jesus either as king or as the fulfillment of Old Testament prophecy. Matthew concentrates on Joseph in the birth of Jesus while Luke emphasizes the role of Mary.

6. Matthew and the Holy Spirit

Matthew's presentation of the Holy Spirit is more extensive than that of Mark's, but it is not as developed as either Luke's or John's. The salient features of his pneumatology include the following:

(1) The Holy Spirit was the agent of Jesus' conception (1:18).

(2) The baptism in the Holy Spirit and fire distinguishes the ministry of Jesus from that of John the Baptist (ch. 3). Fire appears to be primarily a baptism of judgment. John refers to Jesus as a baptizer primarily to warn the Pharisees and Sadducees that Jesus will execute justice (3:11–12); Matthew, however, indicates here and elsewhere (28:19) that the baptism in the Holy Spirit and the baptism of fire are two different baptisms. The tw groups addressed in the preaching o John the Baptist in Matthew are (a) th truly repentant and (b) the Pharisees an Sadducees. As implied in the baptisma formula in 28:19, the baptism with th Holy Spirit is for repentant believers. Th fire is for the trees that do not bear fru (3:8–10).

(3) As in Mark, the baptism scene i Matthew identifies Jesus as the one asso ciated with the Holy Spirit and therefor as the great Baptizer. On this same occa sion the voice from heaven identifie Jesus as Messiah, the Anointed On (3:16–17).

(4) The Holy Spirit leads Jesus (4:1).

(5) The Spirit of God enables Jesus to pro claim judgment and lead justice to vic tory. Matthew considers this a fulfillment of prophecy concernin Jesus' ability to heal and/or his over avoidance of conflict with the Pharisee Matthew sees the Spirit as the source c Jesus' authority (12:15–21).

(6) The Spirit, the Holy Spirit, and the Spir of God are synonymous (ch. 12).

(7) The Spirit of the Father will spea through believers when they are co fronted by the authorities (10:19–20).

(8) To speak against the works of Jesus is t speak against the Holy Spirit, which i the capital sin (12:22–32).

(9) Like Mark, Matthew attributes Jesus power to perform exorcisms and to co front the devil to his empowerment b the Holy Spirit (12:28).

(10) The prophets spoke by the Holy Spir (22:43).

(11) Jesus' disciples are to perform baptism in the name of the Father, the Son, an the Holy Spirit. All authority is given t Jesus. Apparently, prior to the resurrec tion, Jesus operates by the authority c the Holy Spirit. Jesus dispenses power t the disciples in the Great Commissio (28:18–20).

Matthew's material on the Holy Spir serves two of his distinct interests well: the ro of the church (ecclesiology) and the identifi cation of Jesus (Christology). Matthew ofte speaks of the affairs of the church when oth

Gospel writers do not (e.g., 16:17–19; 18:15–20; 20:1–16; 28:18–20). Matthew views the Holy Spirit as the source of inspiration and authority for the church (10:19–20; 28:18–20). Following Mark's lead, Matthew emphasizes Jesus' link with the Holy Spirit to demonstrate his sonship. Matthew shows that although Jesus humbled himself by accepting baptism at the hands of John, Jesus is greater than the Baptist. The descent of the Holy Spirit as a result of Jesus' baptism proves John's prophecy: The one who would come after him would be his superior in the Holy Spirit (3:11–17).

The understanding of the work of the Holy Spirit common to Pauline and Johannine material and to Luke and Matthew indicates a widespread and basic pneumatology that exceeds the content presented in Mark (Shelton, 1991, –9).

OUTLINE

. **The Infancy Narratives** (1:1–2:23)
- **1.1.** The Genealogy of Jesus Christ (1:1–17)
- **1.2.** The Conception and Birth of Jesus (1:18–25)
  - **1.2.1.** Marriage and Betrothal in the First-Century Jewish Community (1:18a)
  - **1.2.2.** The Virgin Conceives (1:18b)
  - **1.2.3.** Joseph's Dilemma (1:19)
  - **1.2.4.** Joseph's Dream (1:20–21)
  - **1.2.5.** The Prophecy Fulfilled (1:22–23)
  - **1.2.6.** Joseph's Obedience (1:24)
  - **1.2.7.** Mary's Virginity Restated (1:25)
- **1.3.** The Wise Men, Herod, and the New King (2:1–23)
  - **1.3.1.** The Wise Men Come to Jerusalem (2:1–2)
  - **1.3.2.** Herod and Jerusalem React to the News (2:3–8)
  - **1.3.3.** The Wise Men Follow the Star to the New King (2:9–12)
  - **1.3.4.** The Flight to Egypt (2:13–15)
  - **1.3.5.** The Slaughter of the Innocents (2:16–18)
  - **1.3.6.** The Return From Egypt to Nazareth (2:19–23)

. **The Preparation for the Ministry** (3:1–4:25)
- **2.1.** John the Baptist Prepares the Way (3:1–12)
  - **2.1.1.** John as Baptizer (3:1–2)
  - **2.1.2.** John as Fulfiller of Prophecy (3:3–4)
  - **2.1.3.** The Fruitful and the Unfruitful (3:5–10)
  - **2.1.4.** John's Prophecy of a Spirit-Baptism (3:11–12)
- **2.2.** The Baptism of Jesus (3:13–17)
  - **2.2.1.** Jesus as Greater Than John (3:13–14)
  - **2.2.2.** Why Did Jesus Submit to Baptism? (3:15)
  - **2.2.3.** The Divine Witness at the Jordan (3:16–17)
- **2.3.** The Temptation of Jesus (4:1–11)
  - **2.3.1.** The Desert Wanderings (4:1)
  - **2.3.2.** The First Temptation (4:2–4)
  - **2.3.3.** The Second Temptation (4:5–7)
  - **2.3.4.** The Third Temptation (4:8–11)
- **2.4.** The Beginning of the Public Ministry of Jesus (4:12–25)
  - **2.4.1.** Jesus Leaves for Galilee (4:12–17)
  - **2.4.2.** Jesus Calls the First Disciples (4:18–22)
  - **2.4.3.** Jesus' Threefold Ministry (4:23–25)

3. **The Sermon on the Mount: Law of Kingdom** (The First Discourse: 5:1–7:29)
- **3.1.** The Beatitudes (5:1–12)
  - **3.1.1.** The Sermon Prologue (5:1–2)
  - **3.1.2.** The Poor in Spirit (5:3)
  - **3.1.3.** The Mourners (5:4)
  - **3.1.4.** The Meek (5:5)
  - **3.1.5.** The Hungry and Thirsty for Righteousness (5:6)
  - **3.1.6.** The Merciful (5:7)
  - **3.1.7.** The Pure in Heart (5:8)
  - **3.1.8.** The Peacemakers (5:9)
  - **3.1.9.** The Persecuted Because of Righteousness (5:10–12)
- **3.2.** Salt and Light (5:13–16)
- **3.3.** Jesus as Fulfillment of the Law (5:17–48)
  - **3.3.1.** Basic Principle (5:17–20)
  - **3.3.2.** Anger and Murder (5:21–26)
  - **3.3.3.** Adultery and Divorce (5:27–32)

6.1.2. Jesus Explains John the Baptist's Ministry (11:7–15)
6.1.3. Children in the Marketplaces (11:16–19)

6.2. Woes on the Galilean Cities (11:20–24)

6.3. Jesus Thanks the Father (11:25–27)

6.4. His Yoke Is Easy (11:28–30)

6.5. Jesus Confronts the Pharisees (12:1–50)
6.5.1. Jesus' Disciples Violate the Sabbath (12:1–8)
6.5.2. A Healing on the Sabbath (12:9–14)
6.5.3. The Gentle Healer (12:15–21)
6.5.4. Beelzebub and Blasphemy (12:22–37)
6.5.4.1. The Pharisees Attribute Jesus' Power to Beelzebub (12:22–24)
6.5.4.2. A Kingdom Divided Cannot Stand (12:25–30)
6.5.4.3. Blasphemy Against the Holy Spirit (12:31–37)
6.5.5. The Sign of Jonah (12:38–42)
6.5.6. The Return of the Unclean Spirit (12:43–45)
6.5.7. True Mothers, Brothers, and Sisters (12:46–50)

7. Parables of the Kingdom (The Third Discourse: 13:1–53)

7.1. The Parable of the Soils and Its Interpretation (13:1–9, 18–23)

7.2. Jesus' Reasons for Using Parables (13:10–17)

7.3. The Parable of the Weeds and Its Interpretation (13:24–30, 36–43)

7.4. Two Parables of Growth: The Mustard Seed and Leaven (13:31–33)

7.5. Jesus and the Use of Parables (13:34–35)

7.6. The Value of the Kingdom: Hidden Treasure and the Pearl (13:44–46)

7.7. The Fishnet (13:47–50)

7.8. The Parable of the Old and New (13:51–53)

8. Ministry and Opposition: Narrative (13:54–17:27)

8.1. Rejection at Nazareth (13:54–58)

8.2. Herod's Opinion of Jesus and the Death of John (14:1–12)

8.3. The Feeding of the Five Thousand (14:13–21)

8.4. Jesus Walks on the Water (14:22–33)

8.5. Jesus the Healer (14:34–36)

8.6. Tradition and Commandment (15:1–20)
8.6.1. The Pharisees' Accusation Against Jesus' Disciples: "Why do your disciples break the tradition of the elders?" (15:1–2)
8.6.2. Jesus' Counterattack: "Why do you break the command of God for the sake of your tradition?" (15:3–11)
8.6.3. Jesus' Private Explanation to the Disciples (15:12–20)

8.7. Jesus and the Canaanite Woman (15:21–28)

8.8. More Healings (15:29–31)

8.9. The Feeding of the Four Thousand (15:32–39)

8.10. The Opposition of the Enemies (16:1–12)
8.10.1. Pharisees and Sadducees Seek a Sign (16:1–4)
8.10.2. The Leaven of the Pharisees (16:5–12)

8.11. Jesus Is the Messiah (16:13–17:27)
8.11.1. Peter's Confession (16:13–16)
8.11.2. Jesus Blesses Peter (16:17–20)
8.11.2.1. Simon Becomes Peter (16:17–18a)
8.11.2.2. The Church (16:18b)
8.11.2.3. The Keys of the Kingdom (16:19–20)
8.11.3. Jesus Predicts His Death (16:21–23)
8.11.4. The Disciple Will Follow the Master (16:24–28)
8.11.5. The Transfiguration of Jesus (17:1–13)
8.11.5.1. Jesus Is Transfigured (17:1–2)
8.11.5.2. The Appearance of Moses and Elijah (17:3–4)
8.11.5.3. The Voice From the Cloud (17:5–9)
8.11.5.4. Elijah Comes First (17:10–13)

8.11.6. Jesus Heals a Boy Possessed by a Spirit (17:14–21)
8.11.7. Jesus Again Predicts His Passion (17:22–23)
8.11.8. The Messiah Submits to the Temple Tax (17:24–27)

9. Jesus' Instructions to the Church (The Fourth Discourse: 18:1–35)

9.1. The Greatest Is a Child (18:1–4)

9.2. Stumbling Blocks for the Little Ones (18:5–9)

9.3. Little Ones and the Lost Sheep (18:10–14)

9.4. Discipline in the Community (18:15–20)

9.5. Forgiveness Seventy Times Seven (18:21–22)

9.6. The Unforgiving Servant (18:23–35)

10. The Trip to Jerusalem: Narrative (19:1–20:34)

10.1. Jesus Begins the Journey to Jerusalem (19:1–2)

10.2. On Divorce (19:3–9)

10.3. On Celibacy (19:10–12)

10.4. Jesus Blesses the Little Children (19:13–15)

10.5. The Rich Young Man (19:16–22)

10.6. The Cost and Reward of Discipleship (19:23–30)

10.7. The Parable of the Merciful Employer (20:1–16)

10.8. Jesus Predicts His Passion for a Third Time (20:17–19)

10.9. Ambition and True Greatness (20:20–28)

10.10. Jesus Heals Two Blind Men (20:29–34)

11. Ministry in Jerusalem (21:1–23:39)

11.1. The Triumphal Entry (21:1–11)

11.2. Cleansing of the Temple (21:12–17)

11.3. The Cursing of the Fig Tree (21:18–22)

11.4. "By What Authority?" (21:23–27)

11.5. The Parable of the Two Sons (21:28–32)

11.6. The Parable of the Wicked Tenant Farmers (21:33–46)

11.7. The Parable of the Marriage Banquet (22:1–14)

11.8. Tribute to Caesar (22:15–22)

11.9. Jesus on the Resurrection (22:23–33)

11.10. The Great Commandment (22:34–40)

11.11. Son of David (22:41–46)

11.12. Woe to the Scribes and Pharisees (23:1–36)
11.12.1. General Indictment (23:1–4)
11.12.2. Phylacteries and Tassels (23:5)
11.12.3. Rabbi, Father, Teacher (23:6–12)
11.12.4. The Woes (23:13–36)
11.12.4.1. The First Woe: On Neither Entering Nor Allowing Others to Enter the Kingdom (23:13)
11.12.4.2. Interpolated Woe: On Stealing From Widows Under the Guise of Prayer (23:14)
11.12.4.3. The Second Woe: On Turning Proselytes Into Children of Hell (23:15)
11.12.4.4. The Third Woe: On Taking Oaths (23:16–22)
11.12.4.5. The Fourth Woe: On Tithing (23:23–24)
11.12.4.6. The Fifth and Sixth Woes: On Internal Impurity (23:25–28)
11.12.4.7. The Seventh Woe: On Building Tombs for the Prophets (23:29–36)

11.13. Jesus' Lament Over Jerusalem (23:37–39)

12. The Olivet Discourse (The Fifth Discourse: 24:1–25:46)

12.1. Prediction of the Destruction of the Temple (24:1–2)

12.2. Events Before the End (24:3–8)

12.3. Persecution Predicted (24:9–14)

12.4. The Abomination That Causes Desolation (24:15–22)

12.5. False Christs and False Prophets (24:23–28)
12.6. The Coming of the Son of Man (24:29–31)
12.7. The Parable of the Fig Tree (24:32–35)
12.8. The Sign of the Flood (24:36–42)
12.9. The Alert Householder (24:43–44)
12.10. The Parable of the Good and Wicked Servants (24:45–51)
12.11. The Parable of the Ten Virgins (25:1–13)
12.12. The Parable of the Talents (25:14–30)
12.13. The Last Judgment (25:31–46)

13. The Passion and Resurrection Narratives (26:1–28:20)
13.1. Events Leading to Gethsemane (26:1–35)
13.1.1. Jesus Again Predicts His Death (26:1–5)
13.1.2. The Anointing at Bethany (26:6–13)
13.1.3. Judas Sells Jesus Out (26:14–16)
13.1.4. Preparation for the Passover (26:17–19)
13.1.5. Jesus Predicts His Betrayal (26:20–25)
13.1.6. The Lord's Supper (26:26–29)
13.1.7. Peter's Denial Foretold (26:30–35)
13.2. Gethsemane, Arrest, Jewish Trial, and Peter's Denial (26:36–75)
13.2.1. Jesus in Gethsemane (26:36–46)
13.2.2. The Arrest of Jesus (26:47–56)
13.2.2.1. The Betrayal by Judas (26:47–50)
13.2.2.2. The Sword (26:51–54)
13.2.2.3. Jesus Forsaken (26:55–56)
13.2.3. Jesus Before the Sanhedrin (26:57–68)
13.2.4. Peter Denies the Lord (26:69–75)
13.3. Jesus Delivered to Pilate and the Death of Judas (27:1–10)
13.4. Jesus Stands Before Pilate (27:11–31a)
13.4.1. The Accusation (27:11–14)
13.4.2. Jesus or Barabbas? (27:15–18, 20–23)
13.4.3. Pilate's Wife (27:19)
13.4.4. Pilate Washes His Hands (27:24–25)
13.4.5. Jesus Is Scourged (27:26)
13.4.6. Soldiers Mock Jesus (27:27–31a)
13.5. The Crucifixion (27:31b–56)
13.5.1. Simon Carries the Cross of Jesus (27:31b–32)
13.5.2. Jesus Is Nailed to the Cross (27:33–44)
13.5.3. The Death of Jesus (27:45–50)
13.5.4. The Apocalyptic Witnesses to Jesus' Death (27:51–54)
13.5.5. Women Witness the Crucifixion (27:55–56)
13.6. The Burial of Jesus (27:57–61)
13.7. The Posting of the Guard at the Tomb (27:62–66)
13.8. The Resurrection of Jesus (28:1–20)
13.8.1. Women Witness the Empty Tomb and the Risen Jesus (28:1–10)
13.8.2. The Collusion of the Chief Priests and Guards (28:11–15)
13.8.3. Jesus Appears to the Disciples and Commissions Them (28:16–20)

COMMENTARY

1. The Infancy Narratives (1:1–2:23)

1.1. The Genealogy of Jesus Christ (1:1–17)

Matthew begins his presentation of Jesus in conformity with the Old Testament practice of linking significant personalities with their forebears, providing an uninterrupted flow of the saving acts of God in history. He does this not merely to conform to literary convention but to link Jesus with Abraham (the father of the nation of Israel), with David (the king of messianic promise), and with all of salvation history that preceded, in order to demonstrate that Jesus fulfilled them all.

Matthew's structure for the genealogical list is apparent: "Thus there were fourteen generations in all from Abraham to David, fourteen from David to the exile to Babylon, and fourteen from the exile to the Christ" (1:17). This arrangement of three groups of fourteen raises the question whether Matthew constructed it himself or whether he received it that way. Matthew could have used an existing genealogy, to which he added the names of Joseph and Jesus, and then was struck by the symmetrical character of the revised list (Brown, 1977, 70). It would appear that the list is a selection of some of Jesus' ancestors, for the three groups consist of 750, 400, and 600 years respectively.

When Matthew's list is compared to the succession of the kings in the Old Testament, we see that he has omitted Ahaziah, Joash, and Amaziah (cf. 1 Chron. 3:10–14). Some have suggested that these were left out because of their wickedness, but this is improbable since he retains the most nefarious king of all the kings of Judah, Manasseh, who even resorted to human sacrifice. The impression that Matthew was using an abridged list is also apparent when corresponding parts of Luke's genealogy have more generations listed (Luke 3:24–38). The mystery of the significance of the fourteens is further compounded when one realizes that Matthew's last grouping only has *thirteen* generations. This could be as a result of Matthew realizing that the fourteen of the last group is implied since the second group does not record Jehoiakim as the father of Jeconiah (Jehoiachin) and that Josiah was actually Jeconiah's grandfather (see 2 Kings 23:31–24:17).

In light of these anomalies one has to ask what Matthew was signifying in three groups of fourteen. It has been suggested that fourteen is a multiple of seven, which is considered the complete number. Both 3 times 14 and 6 times 7 equal 42; thus, Jesus commences the last epoch or the completion of the salvation history, which parallels a division of the ages found in the pseudepigraphal book of Enoch, but this is conjecture at best (Brown, 1977, 75). We cannot speak with certainty concerning the numerological significance of Matthew's presentation. Genealogies were important for the Jewish nation especially after the Exile, when racial identity and religious orthodoxy were major concerns.

Comparison of Genealogies in Matthew and Luke. Inevitably one notices the profound differences between Jesus as presented in Matthew 1:1–16 and Luke 3:23–38. The major differences are: (1) Matthew works forward in time while Luke works backward. (2) The number of names differs, Luke's list being longer: Matthew starts with Abraham while Luke goes back to Adam (and God); Matthew has forty-one names from Jesus to Abraham while Luke has fifty-seven. (3) Many of the names in the lists are not identical. For example, in Matthew the Davidic lineage emerges from Solomon and Rehoboam while in Luke the grandson of David is given as Matthat, the son of Nathan. This may be the result of Matthew's following the dynastic descent while Luke traces a more genetic descent. Either concept of "sonship" was acceptable to the ancient Near-Eastern mind.

Various explanations for the differences in the genealogies have been offered:

(1) Matthew lists the genealogy of Joseph while Luke follows Mary's family with Joseph's sonship being fulfilled by the fact that he is Eli's son-in-law. This idea has been popular for centuries, yet elsewhere Luke refers to the Davidic lineage of Joseph's family (1:27).

(2) The lists are incomplete. This is often the case in ancient Near-Eastern king lists in the centuries preceding the time of Jesus. Sometimes only significant ancestors are listed.

(3) Matthew's genealogy is a dynastic list, and Luke's is an actual descendant list (as mentioned above). Jewish genealogies were constructed primarily to demonstrate the family's Jewish origins and not necessarily to give an exhaustive accounting of every ancient relative.

(4) Some of the differences could be explained by levirate marriage. Under the Hebrew law, if a man died leaving no male heir to perpetuate his name among the Israelites, his surviving brother or other male relative was obligated to marry the deceased's wife and provide an heir to his brother's name (Deut. 25:5–10). This could explain some of the divergences, but generally it is not considered a solution for all of the differences. The prob-

lem is further complicated by the possibility of other types of adoption.

(5) The lists are fabrications with perhaps symbolic or numerological significance. Outright fabrication with no concern for historicity is unlikely in light of Jewish use of genealogies to establish bona fide pedigrees; however, the significance of various ancestors that may have been apparent to the early church may be elusive to the modern reader.

(6) The list is basically historical, but some points have been confused through transmission. This theory, while generally affirming the historical character of the genealogy, cannot incontrovertibly demonstrate that anomalies did indeed exist in Luke's and Matthew's source. Attempts to explain the nature and function of the genealogies to a modern audience are beset with difficulties. No solution is completely satisfactory.[1]

Significant Personalities and the Major Reasons for the Genealogy in Matthew. The people in Matthew's list make a strong theological statement about the mission of Jesus. (1) Abraham associates Jesus with the father of the nation of Israel, with whom the Jews identified (cf. 3:9). Jesus will bring forth a new people of faith. (2) Jesus is identified as a descendant of King David and the successor to his throne. Through David's family the messianic promises of restoration, prosperity, and fidelity to God were to be fulfilled. Israel lost her king in the Babylonian captivity because of her unfaithfulness, and apart from a brief historical moment of glory under the levitical, non-Davidic, Hasmonean dynasty (167–163 B.C.), the Jews remained largely subject to the will of foreign and pagan nations. Through Jesus the throne of David and the kingdom of God would be fulfilled on a scale beyond the comprehension of those expecting the restoration of Israel.

In the list of Jesus' ancestors, Matthew includes four women: Tamar, the daughter-in-law of Judah, who tricked him into making her pregnant to fulfill the levirate obligation to raise up sons to carry the name of her deceased husband; Rahab, the prostitute of Jericho, who hid the Israelite spies before the fall of that city to the Israelites as they took possession of the Holy Land; Ruth, the Moabite polytheist, who joined the community of Israel and became the great-grandmother of David; and Bathsheba, the wife of Uriah, with whom David committed adultery, and he later engineered her husband's death to cover his sin. Although women were occasionally mentioned in Hebrew genealogies, usually the male succession was emphasized.

One must wonder why Matthew presents these particular women, some of whom had less than sterling credentials. Some were identified as sinners; all were foreigners (or married to foreigners, i.e., Bathsheba, the wife of Uriah the Hittite). Possibly this reflects the goal of Jesus to save sinners, and this may also explain why such royal rascals as Solomon, Rehoboam, Ahaz, Manasseh, Jehoiakim, and other unfaithful kings of Judah are included. The presence of foreign women in the genealogy presages the extension of God's kingdom to Gentiles in the ministry of Jesus and his followers. What these women have in common is that all were involved in an out-of-the-ordinary union that contributed to the ancestry of the Messiah. In that regard the virgin birth of Jesus to Mary fits the pattern Matthew has recognized in Jesus' ancestors.

Modern readers should not expect this ancient document to conform to the modern concept of family trees, serve the same purposes, or have the precision that modern records provide. The major point Matthew stresses is that Jesus was in a Jewish family and had solid ties to the royal succession of David and ultimately to the original ancestor Abraham.

1.2. The Conception and Birth of Jesus (1:18–25)

1.2.1. Marriage and Betrothal in the First-Century Jewish Community (1:18a). The culture of the first-century Jewish community sheds much light on the relationship between Joseph and Mary. Women were usually married in their teenage years, often at an age that modern Western society would categorize as that of a girl. This would assure that women would be married at the beginning of their prime years for bearing children. They were married to older men, who were usually established in their trades and were able to care for the basic needs of the wife. We should keep in mind that lifespans were shorter, that romance was a peripheral issue, and that the survival and welfare of the family were primary concerns. Women were seldom seen in public and then only with veils, which made recognition of their facial features impossible. Only in her wedding procession was it considered proper that a woman appear in public without her veil. Jewish men seldom, if ever, spoke to a woman in public.

Proposals of marriage were made between the suitor and the father of the prospective bride. Girls younger than twelve-and-a-half years could be betrothed to any man without their consent. After that time the girls could have some degree of input on the proposed union. The betrothal usually occurred a year before the finalization of the marriage and was the process whereby the bride-to-be was transferred from the authority of the father to that of her husband. Often a bride-price was exchanged, with the father receiving payment and sometimes vice versa. At the time of the betrothal the woman was considered the legal wife of the husband even though the union had yet to be consummated; she could be divorced for unseemly behavior, such as appearing in public without a veil, excessive conversation with men, or infidelity (Jeremias, 1975, 359–76).

Mary, then, was probably in her teens when betrothed to Joseph, who was perhaps in his thirties or older and an established carpenter (see 12:46; 13:55, where Joseph is absent and presumably dead; also Mark 3:31; 6:3; John 2:1–12; 19:25–27; Acts 1:14, though John 6:42 may suggest that Joseph did survive to see the public ministry of Jesus). Joseph's trade probably involved more skills than the current meaning of carpenter or contractor implies. He may have been a widower when marriage to Mary was proposed since church tradition did not identify the "brothers" and "sisters" of Jesus as Mary's children; therefore they could have been Jesus' half brothers and sisters (Joseph's children from an earlier union). Furthermore, the words "brother" and "sister" can also refer to cousins and other relatives. An absence of any full brothers would explain why Jesus on the cross entrusted his mother to the Beloved Disciple and not to any of his kinsmen (John 19:26–27). Matthew's Gospel concentrates on Joseph's perspective in relating the accounts concerning Jesus' infancy while Luke emphasizes the role of Mary (Luke 2:51).

1.2.2. The Virgin Conceives (1:18b). "But before they came together, she was found to be with child through the Holy Spirit" (v. 18b). This amazing account cannot be properly appreciated by any worldview that precludes the possibility of the miraculous. Some have assumed that the doctrine of the virgin birth of Jesus was an awkward attempt by the early church to cover up his illegitimate birth. Others have suggested that the teaching is on a par with mythic accounts of sexual unions of deities with human beings, which resulted in offspring of phenomenal abilities (such accounts were current in the first century). Neither motive would get Matthew far with his Jewish-oriented readers. Matthew included this astounding account because he believed it true and essential to his message; otherwise, he would have started his work with the adult ministries of John the Baptist and Jesus, as Mark (his source) did.

1.2.3. Joseph's Dilemma (1:19). The news that Mary was with child left Joseph with several options. Under the old law he could have had her executed (Deut. 22:20–21). Or he could have instigated a publicized divorce, resulting in the humiliation of Mary. But Matthew describes Joseph as "a righteous [*dikaios*] man," a word that can also carry the meaning of just. Notice that righteousness does not demand the remorseless execution of the law; rather, it presupposes mercy as well. God never intended his law to be merely vindictive; his justice, even in its severe expressions, is designed to bring his people to salvation. In Joseph, justice and mercy meet.

1.2.4. Joseph's Dream (1:20–21). Dreams play a major role in communicating the divine will, and in Joseph's case it involves the appearance of an angel of the Lord, who explained that the child had been conceived by the Holy Spirit and instructed him to take Mary as his wife. The expression "angel of the Lord" may refer to a theophany. The angel addressed Joseph as "son of David," which reveals one of Matthew's major interests, the kingly ancestry of Jesus. It was crucial for Joseph to accept the child as his son in order to link Jesus with the royal line of David.

The angel also gave instructions to call the child Jesus. Jesus is a derivative of the name Jeshua, which means "God will save," and the angel followed with the reason, "because he will save his people from their sins" (v. 21). This would undoubtedly have been a surprise to Joseph and all of the Jews of his day. A Davidic Messiah delivering them from Roman oppression as a king they could understand, but a Davidic Messiah with some sort of priestly role, let alone a sacrificial function in the scheme of things, would have been a new insight on the role of Messiah that the people at large had not anticipated.

1.2.5. The Prophecy Fulfilled (1:22–23). These two verses contain the first occurrence of Matthew's oft-cited formula indicating fulfillment of prophecy in the life and ministry of Jesus. While all of the Gospel writers note prophetic fulfillment, this is one of Matthew's major emphases (see Introduction). The prophecy of the virgin with child in Isaiah 7:14 occurred at a time when the kings of Israel and Syria had united in an attempt to conquer the kingdom of Judah. In one of the bleakest moments in Judah's history, the prophet Isaiah brought good news to King Ahaz, predicting that the kingdoms of Israel and Syria would be devastated. The Lord invited Ahaz to ask for a sign that this would come to pass, but Ahaz refused to ask. Isaiah then responded that the Lord would give a sign:

> The virgin will be with child and will give birth to a son, and will call him Immanuel. He will eat curds and honey when he knows enough to reject the wrong and choose the right. But before the boy knows enough to reject the wrong and choose the right, the land of the two kings you dread will be laid waste.

In other words, by the time the promised boy was weaned and knew the difference between right and wrong, the threat to Judah would lie in ruins.

The Hebrew text reads *'almah* ("young girl"), while the Greek version (LXX) reads *parthenos* ("virgin"). The scribes that translated the Hebrew Old Testament into Greek understood that the woman was not yet pregnant—hence a virgin. Neither the Hebrew text nor the LXX were understood to mean that Isaiah was referring to a miraculous, virginal conception that would happen in the days of King Ahaz, nor did Isaiah in all probability have in mind a future conception without the aid of a human male. Both the Hebrew and Greek texts make it clear that a particular woman is intended. Perhaps Isaiah was predicting that the king's new wife would become pregnant and thereby provide the child of the promise. The fact that the sign meant one thing in the eighth century B.C. and another in the first century A.D. does not mean that Matthew has mishandled the Old Testament prophecy; God had much more in mind than either Isaiah or Ahaz could ever think or imagine.

Much misinterpretation and subsequent demeaning of prophecy have arisen because modern interpreters have not understood the nature of Jewish prophecy as interpreted by the rabbis, Jesus, and Matthew. It is crucial that we explore this issue to appreciate this passage and the rest of Matthew's announcements of Old Testament prophecy fulfillment. The Jewish community had a concept of the corporate man; that is to say, they believed that the experiences of the early patriarchs of Israel, such as the Passover and the Exodus, were actually experienced by the first-century Jews in the "loins of their fathers," and since God continues to work in similar ways with his people, these events of God's correction and salvation were reexperienced or repeated in history.

For example, God delivered the Israelites from captivity in Egypt when they miraculously crossed the Red Sea. Centuries later he allowed the Assyrians to take them into captivity to punish them for their infidelity. Predicting their return the prophet Hosea expressed the liberation in terms of the previous deliverance, the Exodus, "Out of Egypt I have called my son" (Hos. 11:1). Later Matthew sees the return of Joseph, Mary, and the baby Jesus from Egypt to the Holy Land as another fulfillment of the Exodus (Matt. 2:15).

The Jewish understanding of typology also depends on the idea of refulfillment of previous saving events. A *type* is a person, image, or event in the Old Testament whose role and significance is repeated and fulfilled in another person, image, or event later in the salvation history. For example, Matthew presents Jesus as the new Moses since he, like Moses, presents the code of ethics for the people of God. In this case Jesus fulfills and transcends the role of Moses. The Hebrews offered a lamb as sacrifice for their sins; Jesus as the Lamb of God fulfills the role as lamb and is much

CHRONOLOGY OF THE NEW TESTAMENT

		Birth of Jesus
Death of Herod; Archelaus successor	4 B.C.	
Tiberius Caesar (authority in provinces)	A.D. 11	
15th year of Tiberius	26	Beginning of Jesus' ministry
	30	Crucifixion of Jesus Friday, Nisan 15
	34	Conversion of Saul
Aretas in Damascus	37	Paul's first visit to Jerusalem
Death of Agrippa I	44	
Famine	46	Paul's second visit to Jerusalem
	47–49	First missionary journey
	51	Apostolic conference
Gallio, proconsul of Achaia (Corinth)	52	Second missionary journey
	54–57	Third missionary journey (Ephesus)
	58	Paul's arrest in Jerusalem
Festus succeeds Felix in Judea	60	
	61	Paul, prisoner in Rome
	62	Death of James, brother of the Lord
	63	Paul's release
Burning of Rome	64	
	67	Death of Peter and Paul
Fall of Jerusalem	70	
		John on Patmos
Death of Domitian	96	
	c. 98	Death of John

greater in the efficacy of his sacrifice. Therefore, Old Testament prophecy has the potential of multiple fulfillments—a *sensus plenior*, that is, a fuller sense that only God can reveal as he continues to act in time and space and in history to expand, complete, and bring to fullness the plan of the world's salvation.

Matthew's logic in declaring the birth of Jesus as fulfillment of the prophecy of Isaiah to Ahaz is this: If the birth of a baby who came into the world by ordinary means was a sign of God's promise of salvation, how much more is the supernatural conception and birth of Jesus a sign? If the son of Ahaz was called Immanuel, God with us, then how much more is God's Son, born of a woman, Immanuel? Given God's repetitive patterns acted out in salvation history, Matthew's observation that Isaiah 7:14 is fulfilled in the birth of Jesus is not a clever contrivance but nothing less than an apprehension of the mind and plan of God, which views Mary's supernatural child as the reason for being, the goal and consummation of all of God's previous prophetic words and saving acts.

It has been suggested that the doctrine of Jesus' virgin birth arose out of an imaginative use of this Isaiah passage through the creativity of the early church; that is, the church fabricated the account to explain away the alleged illegitimacy of Jesus' conception. Many have assumed that such a miracle is impossible, in keeping with a widely held modern worldview that confuses scientism with science. This view also suffers from a lack of reasonable rationale for such activity in the early church: Why would the early church invent such a phenomenal fabrication, which would draw more attention to the "awkward" details surrounding the conception of Jesus? Would it not have been better to have ignored the alleged illegitimacy and not mention the issue at all rather than to construct an explanation that would have offended the Jews and raised the eyebrows of the worldly-wise? All things considered, it seems more feasible that the virgin birth did in fact happen, and that then and only then did the early church see the prophetic parallel in the book of Isaiah.

1.2.6. Joseph's Obedience (1:24). Joseph's act of obedience was crucial for the fulfillment of the Messiah's coming. He accepted this woman and the onus of the community, who would assume the worst; in this way, Jesus could be called the Son of David and take up his rightful ministry as the Messiah-King. Scripture does not record a single word that Joseph uttered, only his mercifully righteous acts and his obedience. Followers of Jesus should follow the quiet example of the man who was for the human Jesus his first image of his heavenly Father.

1.2.7. Mary's Virginity Restated (1:25). This verse gives rise to the issue of the perpetual virginity of Mary, which maintains that Joseph and Mary never had sexual relations even after Jesus was born. Some object because there are scriptural references to the "brothers" and "sisters" of Jesus (e.g., Matt. 13:55–56; Mark 6:3) and because there is no explicit assertion of the idea in Scripture. Furthermore, our passage says that "*before* [*prin*] they came together, she was found to be with child . . ." (v. 18) and "he had no union with her *until* [*heos*] she gave birth to a son" (v. 25). It is assumed that the couple commenced conjugal relations after the birth of Jesus.

Others point out, however, that the pairing of *prin* and *heos* does not necessarily indicate the resumption of an activity following the before/after clause. Elsewhere in the New Testament in passages where *heos* is used, the state is assumed to have continued after the word *heos* with no change or suspension of that state (e.g., Matt. 5:18; 12:20; 13:33; 16:28; 18:22; 22:44); this is also true in the Septuagint (e.g., Josh. 4:9). *Heos* can also mean the state is never to cease (e.g., 1 Tim. 4:13). After a negative, it can mean either until or before (BAGD, 335). With the latter meaning the passage might read, "and knew her not *before* she gave birth to a son," which would put emphasis on the period of gestation during which there was sexual abstinence. K. Beyer notes that in Greek and Semitic languages such negations frequently imply nothing concerning what occurred after the time of the word "until" (Brown, 1977, 132).

As mentioned above, the "brothers" and "sisters" of Jesus may refer to cousins or other distant relatives (see comments on 1:18a). For example, John states that Mary, the mother of Jesus, and Mary her sister (*adelphe*), the wife of Clopas, were near the cross (John 19:25). It would be most peculiar if Mary's family had two daughters with the same name. Clearly "cousin" would be the better translation of *adelphe*. If Mary, the wife of Clopas, is the "other Mary" that Matthew and Mark note was at the crucifixion, then she would be the mother of James and Joses or Joseph (Matt. 27:56, 61; Mark 15:40). These men, along with Simon and Judas, are identified as the "brothers" (*adelphoi*) of Jesus (Matt. 13:55). If Mary, the wife of Clopas, was their mother, she would be Jesus' aunt or distant cousin, and her sons would be his cousins.

Matthew is not recording this information to deny or support the possibility of the perpetual virginity of Mary; that is not his reason for writing. Rather, he is emphatically asserting that in no way could Mary's baby be Joseph's, for he had no relations with her before or after his conception, even up to the time of his birth. Matthew's sole motive is to defend the doctrine of the Virgin Birth. Assuming that not all early teachings were inscripturated (as is intimated in 2 Thess. 2:15), then apostolic origin of the perpetual virginity is a possibility. It should not be a dividing issue among Christians; even Martin Luther and John Calvin subscribed to the doctrine. The more crucial issue that Matthew addresses is *the divine origin of Jesus*.

1.3. The Wise Men, Herod, and the New King (2:1–23)

1.3.1. The Wise Men Come to Jerusalem (2:1–2). The first event that Matthew recounts after the birth of Jesus is that of the wise men arriving in Jerusalem, asking the whereabouts of the newborn king and telling of the star that had alerted them to his birth. Stung with jealousy at the suggestion of another "king of the Jews," King Herod asks the chief priests and teachers of the law where the Christ, the Messiah, would be born. Ironically, these religious leaders, who later became Jesus' deadly enemies, were the ones who verified for Herod that Bethlehem was indeed the site where the Messiah was to be born. The establishment of Bethlehem as the location of Jesus' birth is crucial to Matthew not only because of its prophetic significance (vv. 5–6) but also because it serves his frequent theme of Jesus' kingship (Bethlehem is the city of David the king).

In the prophecy that named the Messiah's birthplace, Micah was predicting that once again God would use insignificant Bethlehem to lead Israel after she was delivered from the ensuing judgment from the malicious Assyrians and the later exile in Babylon (Mic. 5:2–4). To this Matthew includes the reference to "a ruler who will be the shepherd of my people Israel." Micah 5:4 records that the coming ruler "will stand and shepherd his flock in the strength of the LORD," but the actual words Matthew inserts at the end of the Micah prophecy are from the earlier Davidic prophecy, "You will shepherd my people Israel and you will become their ruler" (2 Sam. 5:2); typically Matthew makes the link with King David emphatic. It is significant that of the Gospel writers only Matthew records the account of the wise men and its fulfillment of prophecy. The themes of king and fulfillment, which dominate his theological agenda, motivate him to include this account in his Gospel.

Matthew helps provide a date for the birth of Jesus in the ominous phrase, "during the time of King Herod" (v. 1), whose reign as king of Judea and surrounding areas lasted from 37–4 B.C. Presumably Jesus was born near the end of Herod's reign since Matthew notes that the evil king's death took place before the holy family's return from Egypt (v. 19). This means that Jesus was actually born four to six years before Christ according to the calendar currently in use![2]

Herod the Great was an amazing politician; in the tumultuous first century he, like a cat, always seemed to land on his feet in spite of the fact that he was caught up in intrigues with such influential and dangerous people as Caesar Augustus, Cassius, Mark Antony, and Cleopatra. His father, Antipater II, an Idumean and convert to Judaism, supported the Hasmonean ruler Hyrcanus II and eventually became the real power behind the throne in Jerusalem. As a result Herod attained high positions in Jewish as well as in Roman government.

Herod had made a name for himself by constructing great buildings and cities, including Caesarea, which he named in honor of the emperor. He also built fortresses and pagan temples, amphitheaters, hippodromes, and other places in which Hellenistic activities were encouraged. His accommodation of pagan activities did not endear him to the conservative Jews, who saw them as abominations and a violation of God's law. When he rebuilt,

Caesarea, on the Mediterranean coast, was built by Herod the Great and named in honor of the Roman emperor.

enlarged, and beautified the Jewish temple in Jerusalem, however, he did garner some favor with his Jewish subjects. His reign brought much prosperity to the land, along with a sizeable tax burden and strife.

Herod proved to be a crafty and bloodthirsty despot whom even his relatives came to fear. He eventually killed his wife, sons, and relatives who he assumed were plotting against him. His subjects also had reason to fear him. Herod executed forty-five of the wealthiest aristocrats who had supported his Hasmonean predecessor and seized their property to fill his depleted coffers. Executions were common. This description, given by the Jewish historian Josephus, fits well with Matthew's account of Herod's duplicity with the wise men, his rage at being tricked, his attempt to kill the baby Jesus, and his heartless order to execute all the male infants in the vicinity of Bethlehem.

1.3.2. Herod and Jerusalem React to the News (2:3–8). Matthew tells us that when the Magi came inquiring about the new king, Herod was not the only one disturbed; so was "all Jerusalem with him." The people of Jerusalem had good reason to be concerned; not only was change of government often bloody, but they knew Herod would sacrifice many to hold onto power. Although the religious elite easily answered Herod's question on the place of the Messiah's birth, we have no record that they traveled the few miles to search for the Messiah—perhaps because they were too preoccupied with the complex and detailed ministry at the temple (Hannom, *The Peril of the Preoccupied and Other Sermons* [1942]). Although this indictment cannot be proved, the account of Jesus' birth seems to indicate that apart from a few poor folk, not many came to see the new king. The lesson has a sobering application to ministry in the church today: Do we minister to worship, or do we worship the ministry?

Herod might be mad and paranoid, but he was not stupid. He was wily and sly, with a deadly cunning and a disarming charm. His suggestion that the Magi report back to him that he might do homage to the baby was a smoke screen to cloak his murderous intentions toward the new baby. The reference to worship (*proskyneo* in vv. 2, 8, 11) can apply to a deity or a human being of high rank. We cannot say for certain what the wise men intended, though it was probably the latter. Herod, of course, intended neither. But given Matthew's advantage of hindsight and his Christology, he probably considered that worship of the divine is most appropriate here, for Jesus is to be adored by Jew and Gentile alike.

1.3.3. The Wise Men Follow the Star to the New King (2:9–12). The identity of the wise men (Magi) has been a mystery that has vexed exegetes and enchanted churchmen for ages. Herodotus (fifth century B.C.) wrote of priestly magi among the Medes, who were adept at interpreting dreams. The book of Daniel mentions Magi in conjunction with magicians, enchanters, diviners, sorcerers, and astrologers/astronomers. In that day the line between magic and divination on the one hand, and nascent science on the other was not clearly maintained. One cannot say for certain how much scientist and how much magician the wise men were. Suffice it to say that God could use even ancient pagan traditions and wisdom to provide a cosmopolitan witness to the birth of the Messiah.

In the transition of power from the Medes to the Persian empire, the Magi continued their activities, and reports of their practices continued during the Roman era. The reference to the "east" has led many to consider Persia/Parthia as the country of origin of the foreign visitors of Jesus. By the time of Jesus they may have been Zoroastrian priests. The gifts of the Magi—gold, frankincense, and myrrh—were products usually associated with Arabia. It is possible that they were Jews from the dispersion, who were scattered throughout the Roman and Parthian empires. There is ample archaeological evidence among the ruins of the synagogues of the era and in the rabbinical writings that the Jewish community was interested in astrology.

The Magi's identity and origin are further obscured when one notes that the phrase "in the east [*anatole*, lit., rising]" can refer to the rising of the star, which always occurs in the east because of the rotation of the earth and is the pattern of planetary advancement in the sky. Given the emphasis on the star in the account, the forte of these Magi appears to be the primordial astronomy of the day.

Like the identity of the wise men, the exact nature of the phenomenon that has come to be known as "the star of Bethlehem" remains a mystery. Matthew is attracted to the story of the star and the wise men who followed it not only because it confirms Jesus' royalty but also because it contrasts so vividly the devotion of the elusive foreigners with the unrighteousness of Israel's elite. Throughout the years commentators have tried to explain the star as a natural part of the universe. This is an appropriate and laudable effort, for God often uses ordinary means to express his supernatural message. Yet no common astronomical explanation (such as a comet, a supernova, the alignment of planets to appear as one heavenly body [a conjunction of Jupiter and Saturn occurred in 7 B.C.], a rogue asteroid) completely speaks to all of the evidence. Nor does the cynicism of a so-called "enlightenment" worldview, which assumes that the account is the fabrication of the Evangelist, explain for the phenomenon or apprehend the full significance of Matthew's message.

If the reference to "the east" (*anatole*) is figurative for "rising," then the text may not be saying that the wise men followed the star to Jerusalem. "Rather, having seen the rise of the star which they associate with the King of the Jews, they have come to the capital city of the Jews, for more information. Only in verse 9 is it clear that the star served as a guide—from Jerusalem to Bethlehem" (Brown, 1977, 174). It is precisely here that the suggestions cited above are deficient since these astronomical phenomena cannot explain how the wise men were led five miles south of Jerusalem to Bethlehem. Perhaps Matthew's understanding of the star's nature and movement is more dependent on the supernatural than the natural.

The more important and answerable question is: What is the significance of the star's appearance in Matthew's Gospel and in the overarching plan of God in salvation history? Most important, it attests to Jesus' role as king. Like the earthly genealogy in the previous context of chapter 1, the star provides a celestial witness to his royalty. The witness of the Magi leaves no room for speculation for its meaning: "Where is he who has been born king of the Jews? For we have seen his star in the East" (v. 2a, RSV).

A star was already associated with the advent of the Messiah. Numbers 24:17, part of the prophecy of Balaam delivered as the Israelites were about to begin their conquest of the Promised Land, reads: "A star will come out of Jacob; a scepter will arise out of Israel." Most scholars identify this stellar prophecy with King David, for the following verses, with their reference to the conquest of surrounding nations, were preeminently fulfilled in his military campaigns. That the passage was understood as messianic by Matthew's contemporaries is evident in the pseudepigraphal work The Testament of the Twelve Patriarchs, which associates a levitical, priestly messiah figure "with his star . . . [which] shall rise in heaven like a king" (T. Levi 18:3). Interestingly both Balaam and the Magi were foreigners, yet they both prophesied concerning the Hebrew Messiah (see Brown, 1977, 193–96 for more parallels). This also serves Matthew's greater program of presenting Jesus as King not only of the Jews but of all people.

The three treasures of the wise men—gold, frankincense, and myrrh—were all gifts associated with royalty, and this was probably Matthew's understanding and intent (v. 11). The later church, however, associated the gold with Jesus as king, the frankincense with Jesus as priest, and the myrrh as a spice to be used for embalming, thus related to his death and burial. Before the Magi leave, they are instructed in a dream not to return to Herod but to return home by a different route from which they came (v. 12).

1.3.4. The Flight to Egypt (2:13–15). After the departure of the Magi, Joseph has a dream, delivered by "an angel of the Lord" (v. 13), warning him to flee to Egypt. In the Bible angels sometimes appear as humans (e.g., Judg. 13:16); other times they appear as brilliant and fear-inspiring creatures, whose appearance and words humans can hardly bear (e.g., Ex. 3:2; Judg. 13:6, 19–21; 1 Chron. 21:12; Dan. 8:17). We are not told which form the angel took in Joseph's dream. Hebrew and Greek grammar suggests that the phrase "an angel of the Lord" can also legitimately be translated "*the* angel of the Lord." At times in the Old Testament, the angel of the Lord cannot be distinguished from God himself and should be considered as the Lord himself appearing and speaking (e.g., Gen. 16:11–13; Judg. 6:12–14). If this interpretation is Matthew's intent, then Joseph has a special revelation directly from God, a frightfully and powerfully overwhelming experience, a special revelation to a special man to accomplish the special and most urgent task of saving baby Jesus.

The force of the aorist participle (*egertheis*, "get up") together with the aorist tense of the imperative main verb (*paralabe*, "take") connotes great urgency and haste. In other words, "Get up out of your bed, get out of here now, and start your escape to Egypt . . . for Herod is about to start searching for the child Jesus." Notice that Joseph takes Mary and Jesus away by night to avoid detection by the agents of the king or by other witnesses.

There was a large Jewish community in Egypt, especially in the city of Alexandria, but where the holy family stayed and whether or not Joseph found work we are not told. It has been suggested that the precious gifts that the Magi gave them sustained them in exile. There they stayed until King Herod died. The fact that Jesus and his parents endured exile in a foreign land should promote Christian compassion to refugees near and far.

Matthew sees the return of Joseph, Mary, and Jesus from Egypt as a geographical fulfillment of prophecy and reenactment of historical events and theological types that have previously occurred in God's dealings with the Hebrews (see comments on 1:22–23). "Out of Egypt I called my son" is from Hosea 11:1, where the prophet describes the promised return from exile in Mesopotamia in

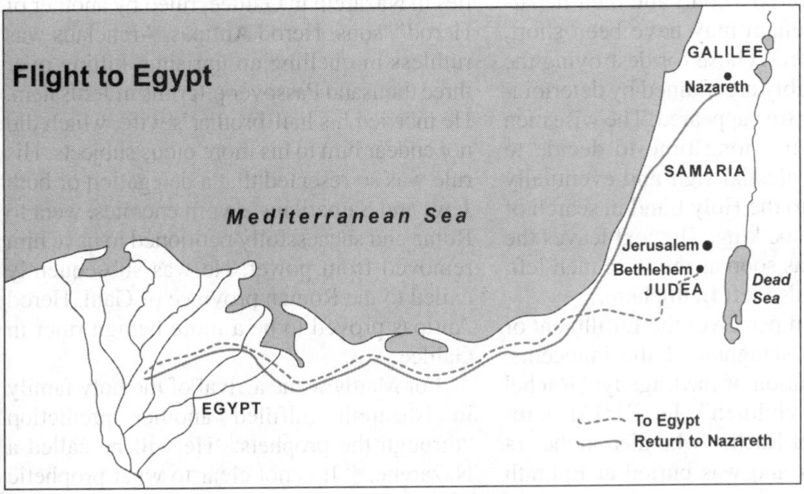

Joseph and Mary fled to Egypt with their son Jesus after being warned by an angel. They didn't return until after Herod the Great had died.

terms of the earlier deliverance from slavery in Egypt. Both of these events are seen as God's saving acts. Matthew sees the trip of the holy family from Egypt to the Holy Land as an even greater fulfillment of the first Exodus since the Savior himself is returning to the land of his birth. This reference to the Exodus presages Matthew's emphasis of Jesus as the new Moses, which he will further develop when he presents the teaching of Jesus.

1.3.5. The Slaughter of the Innocents (2:16–18). When the Magi did not return to reveal the location of his rival to the throne, Herod flew into a rage. He saw their disobedience as mockery; the word that the NIV translates as "outwitted" is later used in Matthew to describe the mockery endured by Jesus in the Passion Narrative (27:29, 31, 41). Given his reign of terror (see comments on 2:1–2), Herod's murder of all boys two years old and younger is not out of character. The estimates of the casualties, based on the probable population, are twenty to thirty infants.

Some have questioned the historicity of the event since it seems odd that the scheming and plotting Herod would allow the wise men and Jesus to escape his spy network. Further, the delay of his reaction, sometimes assumed to be a year or longer, seems equally improbable. But we cannot assume that Herod had the Magi followed; even if he did, we cannot assume that his intelligence organization was foolproof. Also, Matthew believes that divine providence had a hand in the escape of the wise men and Jesus. Moreover, the period of time between the arrival of the Magi at Jerusalem and Herod's court and their departure from Bethlehem may have been short. The age span Herod chose for destroying the babies was probably ascertained by determining when the star first appeared. The wise men could have taken a long time to decide to respond to the celestial sign and eventually make their way to the Holy Land in search of the child born to be king. The text leaves the impression that as soon as the wise men left, the holy family also left Bethlehem.

Matthew again perceives the fulfillment of prophecy in the slaughter of the innocents, based on the location of the tragedy: "Rachel weeping for her children" (Jer. 31:15). Jeremiah claimed that Rachel, who died in the era of the patriarchs and was buried at Ephrath (also called Bethlehem, cf. Gen. 35:19), would weep centuries later when her descendants would be force-marched into Babylonian captivity from the staging point at Ramah nearby. Ephrath is about eleven miles north of Jerusalem and south of Bethel, in the area of Benjamin and near Ramah. This is not to be confused geographically with Bethlehem of Judah, which is five miles south of Jerusalem. Later some Benjaminites of the Ephrath clan migrated to the area of the Bethlehem of Judah; hence the two towns were closely associated.

Matthew's understanding of the Jeremiah prophecy is that if Rachel wept after her death on the occasion of Judah's Exile, which destroyed so many of her descendants in the sixth century B.C., then she wept again when the infant victims of Herod were sacrificed in the first century A.D. Matthew once again demonstrates that the greater fulfillment of prophecy occurs in events associated with the life of Jesus. He also refers to the murdered boys in order to link the life of Jesus with that of Moses, whose role Jesus will complete as the new Lawgiver, for Moses too was saved from a despot's war on Hebrew children in ancient Egypt (Ex. 2:1–10).

1.3.6. The Return From Egypt to Nazareth (2:19–23). For a third time Joseph receives instruction from the angel of the Lord in a dream. The holy family returns to their homeland since Herod the Great is dead and no longer seeks the child's life. Then warned in yet another dream, Joseph prudently avoids settling in the Judean territory ruled by Herod's son and successor, Archelaus, and instead settles in Nazareth in Galilee, ruled by another of Herod's sons, Herod Antipas. Archelaus was ruthless in quelling an uprising, killing over three thousand Passover pilgrims in Jerusalem. He married his half-brother's wife, which did not endear him to his more pious subjects. His rule was so resented that a delegation of both Jews and Samaritans, sworn enemies, went to Rome and successfully petitioned to have him removed from power. He was subsequently exiled to the Roman province of Gaul. Herod Antipas proved to be a more benign ruler in Galilee.

For Matthew the arrival of the holy family in Nazareth fulfilled another prediction "through the prophets: 'He will be called a Nazarene.'" It is not clear to what prophetic work Matthew refers. He may be quoting from a work no longer extant and not included in either the Jewish or Christian canon. Not all references in the New Testament are from canonical books; Jude 9, for example, cites the Assumption of Moses. It also has been suggested that Matthew is making a play on words, linking "Nazarene" (*Nazoraios*) to Isaiah 11:1, where the prophet says that the Messiah will come from a "Branch" (*netser*) that "will come up from the stump of Jesse." *Nazoraios* and *netser* sound alike, though they are not from the same Semitic root word.

Another suggestion is that Matthew is linking the hometown of Jesus with the word "Nazirite." Although Nazareth and Nazirite (*nazir*) do not have the same etymological origin, it is argued that Matthew does not think it coincidental that the two words sound alike; it is providential and part of the divine plan to fulfill Scripture in a greater sense in the life of Jesus. The angelic announcement of the birth of Samson, the Nazirite judge, contains wording similar to the angel's announcement of the birth of Jesus (cf. Matt. 1:20–21 with Judg. 13:2–7). Although Jesus did function as a charismatic leader, endowed with the Holy Spirit, he did not fulfill all the dietary and ceremonial requirements in the Nazirite vow (Num. 6:1–21).

Since Matthew says the prophecy was spoken "through the *prophets*," he may have several meanings in mind for the significance of the term *Nazarene*. The Evangelist saw it as no accident that Jesus would grow up there and that the name of the hometown of the Messiah would be pregnant with allusions to earlier salvation history.

2. The Preparation for the Ministry (3:1–4:25)

2.1. John the Baptist Prepares the Way (3:1–12)

2.1.1. John as Baptizer (3:1–2). By the time Matthew wrote his Gospel John had received the title "the Baptist" and had a distinct following alongside the followers of Jesus (cf. Acts 19:1–4). Mark ascribes the participle *baptizon* to John, so that the text reads, "John came, baptizing in the desert region and preaching a baptism of repentance for the forgiveness of sins" (Mark 1:4). From these two activities the title "Baptist" gets its meaning. It is not just a reference to the ceremonial washing but a sign of repentance and reception of God's forgiveness and a cleansing and preserving grace. Hence baptism becomes a metonymy for the repentance message that was preached. Although *baptizo* can mean immerse or submerge, it can also refer to washing that does not necessarily imply total immersion (e.g., Mark 7:4). Furthermore, in regard to being baptized by the Holy Spirit, the verb "to pour out" is used in Acts (cf. 1:5 with 2:18, 33). The mode of baptism is not as crucial as a repentant heart and the gracious act of God.

2.1.2. John as Fulfiller of Prophecy (3:3–4). All four Evangelists record some version of the Isaiah 40:3–5 prophecy, which John fulfills. Repentance is paramount on Matthew's mind when presenting John's ministry as a necessary prerequisite for the impending kingdom of heaven, which Jesus is about to inaugurate (v. 2, note Matthew's preferred "kingdom of heaven" instead of "kingdom of God"; see Introduction).

Matthew considers John the Baptist to be the prophet who was to precede the coming of the Messiah and the messianic kingdom. He presents John's ministry in terms of the ministry of Elijah, the Old Testament prophet who uncompromisingly called for wayward Israel to repent and wholeheartedly follow the one true God. John's ascetic apparel and appearance are reminiscent of Elijah and other Old Testament prophets (Zech. 13:4; esp. 2 Kings 1:8). Like Mark, Matthew also follows the tradition that an Elijah-like figure would precede the advent of Messiah's kingdom (see Matt. 17:10–13; Mark 9:11–13; cf. Mal. 3:1; 4:5–6). Matthew explicitly identifies John as Elijah in Matthew 3:3; 11:14.[3]

Matthew delimits John and his ministry as the great culmination of the old prophetic age. Luke, by contrast, sees John operating in both the old and the new: the old in that John is the herald who prepares the way by repentance, the new in that John's witness to Jesus is described as "filled with the Holy Spirit," which is identical to the witness of the disciples after Pentecost.

2.1.3. The Fruitful and the Unfruitful (3:5–10). Like the Old Testament prophets, John the Baptist presents his message in poetic parallelism—saying one thing and then repeating the idea or its antithesis in the next line. This is characteristic of Hebrew poetry and reflects a Semitic origin of the Gospels. John presents two distinct and antithetical groups of people: the repentant and unrepentant, the fruitful and unfruitful trees, the wheat and the chaff (v. 12). The unrepentant group, condemned by John, are the Pharisees and Sadducees (v. 7; Luke identifies the truly repentant as the multitudes, tax collectors, and soldiers, Luke 3:10–14). The Pharisees and Sadducees are often paired together in Matthew's Gospel as clearly defined enemies of Jesus. Although these two groups disagreed sharply in politics and theology, they were for the most part united in their opposition to Jesus.

Repentance (*metanoia*) is often misunderstood as mere confession of sin; more accurately, it refers to the act of "thinking again" (*meta* plus *noia*), that is, reconsidering and changing one's lifestyle, often in sociologically observable ways: "Produce fruit in keeping with repentance" (v. 8). This is why John addresses his scathing rebuke, "brood of vipers," to the Pharisees and Sadducees. The Jews often observed ceremonial cleansing, from simple washing of hands to bathing the whole body in cisterns (as found in the archaeological sites in Jerusalem and at Qumran, the Dead Sea community). The Pharisees and Sadducees apparently assumed that since they were children of Abraham, they had a right to receive John's rite, but he was calling for them to repent as though they were Gentiles! The model of his baptism was proselyte baptism, which was required of all Gentile converts to Judaism. Such a demand would be considered crass presumption and an affront to those who thought that their pedigree and affiliation assured their access to the means of grace.

The force of John's language gives the impression that judgment is hovering and about to descend on the unrepentant. "The ax is already at the root of the trees," and the next stroke will rise, fall, and cut. Unfruitfulness will result in the fires of judgment.

2.1.4. John's Prophecy of a Spirit-Baptism (3:11–12). In verse 11 John contrasts his baptism with that of the coming Messiah. John's prophecy concerning the coming Messiah and his superior baptism also contains antithetical parallelism: John baptized in water; his superior will baptize in the Holy Spirit (*pneuma hagion*, which can also be trans. "holy wind") and in fire. Matthew probably intends a double entendre for the Greek *pneuma*, which can mean either spirit or wind (the same holds true for the Hebrew word *ruach*). With a winnowing fork the farmer throws the wheat and chaff into the wind to separate them, then uses fire to destroy the chaff (v. 12).

The focus of John's message to the unrepentant is the baptism of judgment, and to the repentant the baptism of repentance. Only Jesus will be able to give the Spirit (wind) and fire baptism—a fuller prophetic fulfillment of empowerment for mission and witness in the early church: "For John baptized with water, but in a few days you will be baptized with the Holy Spirit.... But you will receive power when the Holy Spirit comes on you; and you will be my witnesses ..." (Acts 1:5, 8). Luke presents the empowering aspect of Spirit-baptism when he presents Jesus' own baptism and empowering by the Holy Spirit (Luke 3).

John considers his role as one of a lowly and unworthy slave in contrast to that of the Messiah. The lowliest slave put the sandals on and took them off the feet of the master, and John claims he is not even worthy to do that! He makes it clear that he is not a candidate for messiahship. Luke and John further emphasize John's denial (Luke 3:15–17; John 1:20; 3:28).

2.2. The Baptism of Jesus (3:13–17)

When Jesus was baptized in the Jordan River, the heavens opened, the Holy Spirit as a dove descended on him, and a voice from heaven affirmed him as God's Son. The Synoptic Gospels each record this information; John mentions only the descent of the Spirit, not Jesus' actual baptism. Each Gospel writer presents this signal event to make particular theological statements about Jesus. Mark, for example, includes it because it provides an opportunity to affirm his reason for writing: to present the "gospel about Jesus Christ, the Son of God" (Mark 1:1). Luke emphasizes the empowerment that Jesus experienced as a result of the descent of the Holy Spirit (cf. Luke 4:1, 14, 18).

2.2.1. Jesus as Greater Than John (3:13–14). Unlike Luke, Matthew emphasizes the event of Jesus' baptism and draws particular

The Jordan River, where Jesus was baptized by John the Baptist, has become a popular choice for modern baptisms. This baptism took place at Yardenit.

attention to the fact that when Jesus asked for baptism at the hands of the Baptist, John was reluctant to do so (vv. 13–14). Matthew's interest includes Christology, but he also wishes to affirm who Jesus is in relation to John the Baptist. Remember that Matthew's audience was Jewish oriented, and perhaps they were asking: "How can Jesus be greater than John if John baptized him?" (Note that the Baptist sect continued to exist long after the time of John and Jesus; see Acts 19:1–4.) According to Matthew, Jesus is greater than John; even John himself acknowledged Jesus' superiority and was therefore reluctant to accede to the Messiah's request.

2.2.2. Why Did Jesus Submit to Baptism? (3:15). There are several ways to answer this question. According to Luke, it was necessary for Jesus to receive the Holy Spirit's power to fulfill his calling as Messiah. In Matthew, however, Jesus said, "It is proper for us to do this to fulfill all righteousness" (3:15). Was he in need of cleansing from sin? No, for the New Testament emphasizes that the early Christian understanding of the sacrifice required a spotless and sinless sacrifice, as in Jewish sacrifices. Jesus is presented as the spotless Lamb of God and the paschal sacrifice (e.g., Matt. 26:17–29; John 1:29; Rev. 5:6–8). Paul also understood Jesus to be sinless (2 Cor. 5:21); thus washing from sin is not the issue for Jesus.

Matthew's frequent theme of fulfillment holds the answer: "to fulfill all righteousness." Righteousness for Matthew is not merely keeping rules and regulations. True, Jesus does not set aside God's ethics, but rather intensifies them (e.g., 5:21–48). Yet true righteousness is based on a relationship with God that is predicated on his merciful forgiveness and a repentant recipient who wishes to fulfill God's righteousness and not one's own understanding of it (5:20; 6:33). A key to fulfilling God's righteousness is to extend mercy where mercy is not deserved (5:38–42; 18:21–35). Note that Jesus' earthly father, being a "righteous" man, did not wish to expose Mary to open shame when she was found with child (1:19). This merciful identification with those in need of mercy, tempered with an active respect for God's will, is characteristic of Jesus' righteousness as presented in Matthew (cf. 18:35).

In his baptism Jesus identified with those in need of forgiveness who, by the mere letter of the law, deserved stringent judgment. He identified with them so much that he entered their dirty bath water and stood with them even though he personally remained clean. Jesus fulfilled this surprising righteousness through obedience to his Father. Baptism is the catalyst that applies to us God's merciful righteousness, even the effects of the cross of Jesus and his life-giving resurrection (Rom. 6:3–7; 1 Peter 3:21). Christians join Jesus in baptism; he meets them there in the water.

2.2.3. The Divine Witness at the Jordan (3:16–17). Three major things occurred in this event: the heavens opened, the Holy Spirit descended, and a voice from heaven proclaimed Jesus as the Son of God. Each of these revelatory events merits attention.

The heavens were torn open (cf. Mark 1:10). The word "open" expresses the idea of revelation. Jesus' experience is reminiscent of the calling of the prophet Ezekiel, who was standing by the River Kebar when he saw the heavens opened and saw visions of God and God's Spirit entered him (Ezek. 1:1; 2:2).

The dove descended. The association of the Holy Spirit with a dove was infrequent in Hebrew and Jewish writing until after the time of Jesus. The dove symbol became a frequent image in Christianity. In Genesis 1:2 the Spirit hovered over the waters, which may be an allusion to a dove, as John Milton assumes so eloquently in *Paradise Lost*:

> Thou from the first
> Wast present, and with mighty
> wings outspread
> Dove-like satest brooding on the
> vast abyss
> And madest it pregnant.

The Holy Spirit often empowered the Old Testament prophets (e.g., Ezek. 2:2; Mic. 3:8; Zech. 7:12), and the prophecies regarding the Messiah often predicted an accompanying endowment of the Spirit (e.g., Isa. 42:1, 5; 61:1–3). Thus Jesus receives a special anointing and empowering by the Holy Spirit to proclaim God's message and to perform wonders. The coming of the Spirit on him is a sign that he is the Messiah, the Christ (lit., "the Anointed One"). This does not mean that this is the first time Jesus was involved with the power of the Spirit; he was conceived of the Holy Spirit (Matt. 1:20; Luke 1:35) and was obviously guided by the Spirit when he ministered in the temple as a youth (Luke 2:46–52). Nor does this mean that Jesus was "adopted" by the Spirit at the baptism and became the Messiah at that moment, for he was the Son of God before his baptism (Matt. 1:20; 2:15; Luke 1:35; 2:49; John 1:1, 14, 18; 3:16).

The voice spoke from heaven: "*This* is my Son, the Beloved, in whom I am well pleased" (Mark and Luke read, "*You* are my Son, the Beloved, in whom I am well pleased" [italics and trans. mine: Matt. 3:17; Mark 1:11; Luke 3:22]). This message reflects two Old Testament passages: "You are my son; today I have begotten you" (Ps. 2:7, NRSV), and, "Here is my servant, whom I uphold, my chosen, in whom my soul delights; I have put my spirit upon him" (Isa. 42:1, NRSV). Psalm 2 describes the enthronement of the Davidic king. In the ancient Near East the king was considered the son of the national god when he took the throne, and thus the power of the deity was invested in the king. At his coronation he was considered "begotten" of the god. Israel too considered their king to be invested with the power of Yahweh their God.

The second part of the voice from heaven alludes to Isaiah 42:1: "my Servant/Son, my Chosen One/Beloved, in whom my soul delights" (pers. trans.; see also Gen. 22:2). The word "servant, child, son" (Gk. *pais*) takes on a messianic sense in Isaiah. "Beloved" was used as a messianic title in Christian circles (cf. Matt. 17:5; Mark 1:11; 9:7; Luke 3:22; 2 Peter 1:17). The NIV translation of "whom I love" for *ho agapetos* (lit., "the Beloved"), though readable, does not treat the phrase as a messianic title. *Agapetos* could sometimes refer to an only son or daughter (e.g., Gen. 22:2, 12, 16; Judg. 11:34; Mark 12:6; Luke 20:13).

The combination of a Davidic enthronement psalm identifying the king as God's son and the use of the title "Beloved, with whom God is pleased," accompanied by the descent of the Holy Spirit, identifies Jesus for Matthew's readers as the messianic Son of David, the Son of God empowered by the Holy Spirit to inaugurate the reign of God and to speak his words.

Matthew's use of "*This* is my Son" instead of "*You* are my Son" raises a question: Was Jesus the only one who heard the voice, or did John and/or the people hear it too? We cannot know for sure. If the "this" reading is original, then many people would have heard it, and the idea that Jesus was Messiah would have become widespread; however, this apparently was not the case in the early part of his ministry. In fact, Jesus seems to have considered it classified information for a while. Inevitably the miracle ministry of Jesus led some to consider the possibility of his messiahship. It may be that the voice said "this," and the onlookers heard it; for Jesus, however, it would have had the meaning "you" since it involved him directly. If the voice addressed Jesus as "you" and there were onlookers who heard it, then to them it would have had the force of a witness referring to Jesus.

2.3. The Temptation of Jesus (4:1–11)

In Mark's account of Jesus' temptation, he writes that the Spirit "thrust" (*ekballo*) Jesus into the desert to be tempted, since Mark dwells on action in his Gospel account. Matthew and Luke, however, state that the Spirit "led" Jesus. These two Gospels also record the dialogue Jesus had with the devil, though the order of the temptations is different. Perhaps Matthew's order reflects a chronological order while Luke's version reflects a geographical procession from one traditional site of a temptation to another. Matthew and Mark both note that "angels came and attended him" (Matt. 4:11; cf. Mark 1:13) after his bout with Satan was over. The reference to "wild animals" (Mark 1:13) may allude to the Messiah's restoration of fallen nature (cf. Isa. 11:6–9; Ps. 91:11–13; T. Naph. 8:4).

2.3.1. The Desert Wanderings (4:1). Previous salvation history provides a context for Jesus' testing in the desert. The parallels between Jesus' temptation and the children of Israel's desert wandering after the Exodus are striking and provide a key to the reason Jesus was exposed to this testing. He was in the desert for forty days before he entered into his ministry, while the Israelites were in the desert for forty years before they entered the Promised Land:

> Remember how the LORD your God led you all the way in the desert these forty years, to humble you and to test you in order to know what was in your heart, whether or not you would keep his commands. He humbled you, causing you to hunger and then feeding you with manna, which neither you nor your fathers had known, to teach you that man does not live on bread alone but on every word that comes from the mouth of the LORD. (Deut. 8:2–3)

Jesus passed the test better than Israel. Here he fulfills the typology of Israel in the desert, which Matthew has already linked with Jesus: "Out of Egypt I called my Son" (2:15). Although Satan is the agent of temptations, God used them to test his people and later Jesus. The word *peirazo* can mean not only "to tempt" but also in the positive sense of "to try, test one's character" (e.g., Ps. 26:2; John 6:6; 2 Cor. 13:5; Heb. 11:17; Rev. 2:2). Note also the parallel of the manna and the stones into bread.

Traditionally commentators have emphasized the differences among the temptations. The temptation to turn the stones to bread tested him physically, the temptation to plunge from the temple heights tested his concept of the nature of his messianic ministry, and the temptation to worship the devil tested his spiritual allegiance to God. While no doubt each of these temptations did affect Jesus differently, together they had one crucial goal: to distract Jesus from or to break his relationship with God. The devil's suggestions unwittingly did a service for the cause of the kingdom: The steel of Jesus' resolve to follow God was tempered in the heat of temptation, the true nature of his messianic ministry was clarified, and the primacy of his relationship with his Father was maintained and given undivided attention.

2.3.2. The First Temptation (4:2–4). After forty days and forty nights of fasting Jesus was desperately hungry, his body craving food for its very survival. "The tempter" then suggested, "If you are the Son of God, tell these stones to become bread" (v. 2). This sentence in Greek is a first-class conditional clause, which indicates that the content of the "if" clause is assumed by the speaker to be true; thus the words of the tempter have the import of "*since* you are the Son of God." The devil was saying that since Jesus was Messiah, he should have no problem performing the miracle in order to eat.

The object of this first temptation was not so much to make Jesus doubt his relationship with the Father as it was to distract him from it. It is sometimes mistakenly assumed that for Jesus to have provided *miraculously* for his own needs would have been sinful. This is not the case since later Jesus miraculously multiplied the loaves and fish. God made food, and it is good. God made stomachs and the instinct to fill them. The Christian worldview does not deny the goodness of material things. But neither does the Christian just live for this life alone. C. S. Lewis, arguably the greatest Christian writer of the twentieth century, may shed some light on the issue in his *Screwtape Letters*. In it Screwtape, a veteran tempter, instructs a novice tempter in the dubious "art" of temptation:

> Never forget that when we are dealing with any pleasure in its healthy and normal and satisfying form, we are, in a sense, on the Enemy's [God's] ground. I know we have won many a soul through pleasure. All the same, it is his invention, not ours. He made pleasures: all our research so far has not enabled us to produce one. All we can do is to encourage the humans to take the same pleasures which our Enemy has produced, at times, or in ways, or in degrees which he has forbidden. (*Screwtape Letters* [1971], 41–42)

The question then is, "How was the suggestion to change stones into bread a temptation if it is not inherently evil?" Jesus' answer reveals the answer, "It is written: 'Man does not live on bread alone, but on every word that comes from the mouth of God,'" (v. 4). Jesus was not out in the desert for a picnic, but to listen to God. The Holy Spirit had sent him there to clarify the true nature of his messiahship and to prepare for his future ministry. To break his fast would have distracted him from the task to which the Holy Spirit had led him. It is important to note that Jesus overcame this temptation by differentiating between eating, which is generally considered a good thing, and fasting, which was God's best for that occasion.

The choice that confronted Jesus is similar to that of soldiers or athletes. In order to prepare for action athletes deprive themselves of good things, like rich foods or leisure, in order to attain their goal. They are often confronted with good possibilities, but they do not take all good options to be their calling. How did Jesus know what to do? His quotation of Deuteronomy 8:3 gives the answer: He was in a listening attitude in his relationship with his Father. An important lesson to apply is that it is not enough to choose a good thing but the best, God's best. Jesus hung on to the words of God already spoken to him. The context in Deuteronomy consisted of proving and testing the Israelites and teaching them to rely not on their own power to provide for needs but to trust and obey God. Obedience implies relationship, which is a key to understanding the rest of the temptations.

Three times Jesus responds to the temptations with the words, "It is written," using a perfect tense, which denotes, "It is written and still stands."

2.3.3. The Second Temptation (4:5–7). We are not certain if Jesus was taken physically to the high point of the temple in Jerusalem or if he experienced this event in a vision. The main point is that for him this was a real temptation. Again Matthew records the words of the devil, "If you are the Son of God," as something he does not doubt (a first-class condition). Thus the tempter is *not* saying, "Jump off and survive.... I bet you can't do it." Rather, he assumes Jesus could do it quite easily.

For Jesus to exercise such power in the temple precinct would have identified him as the supernaturally anointed leader whom the insurgents or extremists expected would lead them in religious reform and in rebellion against the Roman oppressors. This temptation haunted Jesus later (e.g., John 6:15). At his triumphal entry and in the cleansing of the temple, all Jesus had to say was, "To arms!" and his mission as Messiah would have been reduced to a military operation; as a result, the plan of spiritual salvation would have been lost. This temptation was always only a breath away. In Jesus' Gethsemane prayer, he expressed to his Father a hesitancy to fulfill his messiahship through self-sacrifice. Note Luke 4:13, that Jesus' temptations were not over in the desert but only that the devil "left him until an opportune time."

The secret of Jesus' victory was not in his rote memory of Scripture. Immersing oneself in the Word of God is good, but even Satan can "spout" Scripture. It was not just Jesus' head knowledge of Scripture that revealed God's plan but especially his relationship with his heavenly Father. The only proper center for rightly interpreting the Scriptures is a living relationship with God! What Jesus quoted merely revealed that preexistent relationship.

Some people today use the Scriptures as some sort of "wrestling hold" on God, that is, they quote a Scripture, God has to fulfill it. Mere "confession of the Word," like some magical spell, was not the secret of Jesus' success. The devil's citation of Scripture was to no avail. One must not presume to speak and apply the Word of God apart from God's will. This is what it means to speak in the name of God. How, for example, does one know the will of one's spouse? By frequent association. Only through relationship with God can we know his will.

2.3.4. The Third Temptation (4:8–11). The devil then took Jesus to a high mountain, showed him all the kingdoms of the world and their glory, and said to him, "All this I will give you ... if you will bow down and worship me." Jesus replied, "Begone, Satan! for it is written: 'You shall worship the Lord your God and him only shall you serve'" (RSV).

At first sight this hardly seems like a temptation. Certainly, it is bare of any frills, and the hook is quite exposed. Yet there is an attraction here. Frequently Old Testament prophets predicted that the descendants of David would rule over the entire world and that people would worship the one true God in Jerusalem. This prospect would be most attractive in order to spread the ethics of Judaism over the entire world. Yet to do so as a result of evil worship would ultimately spell doom for God's people. There is nothing as evil as good turned bad. Again, it was his relationship with the Father, not his mere proficiency in "confessing the Word," that pulled Jesus through. He conquered this temptation by avoiding any action that would diminish his relationship with God. Jesus was concerned with lifestyle as well as ends or goals. In many respects, his lifestyle—eternal communion with the Father—was his goal, for only in this relationship was he able to sacrifice himself for the likes of us!

Jesus, in addition to quoting Scripture, directly addressed the devil. Usually he avoided dialogue with demonic powers and forbade them to speak, but here he told the devil to leave. Jesus' practice stands in stark contrast to the popular practice of lengthy harangues of the devil even in the context of prayer.

The fact that Jesus underwent these temptations is part of his ultimate identification with humanity. He became a human being. He grew up and entered the cleansing waters of our baptism, even though he was without sin. He even endured temptation in his identification with us. He did not endure temptation merely as God, for that would be a sham. Jesus was completely God *and* completely human; therefore, his temptation was real, even though he was sinless. He *suffered* temptation; enduring and not giving in cause distress and pain. He did *not* have to have a "sin nature" to be tempted and to endure the pain of saying, "No." His temptation was similar to that of Adam and Eve who, though they had not sinned before, endured a genuine temptation.[4]

2.4. The Beginning of the Public Ministry of Jesus (4:12–25)

2.4.1. Jesus Leaves for Galilee (4:12–17). How each Gospel writer presents the beginning of Jesus' public ministry reveals a lot about the concerns and agendas of each Evangelist. Mark, for example, concentrates on Jesus' announcement of the nearness of the "kingdom of God" and his continuation of the message that John the Baptist had already proclaimed: "Repent and believe the good news" (Mark 1:15). Matthew follows Mark and presents these two messages of Jesus. In fact, he emphasizes the call to repentance all the more by moving it to the front of the quotation, "From that time on Jesus began to preach, 'Repent, for the kingdom of heaven is near'" (Matt. 4:17; on his use of "kingdom of heaven," see the Introduction). He also prefaces Jesus' announcement with the observation, "from that time on" (cf. 16:21), which indicates another major phase of Jesus' ministry is about to take place (Kingsbury, 1975, 7–25).

Matthew observes that the location for the beginning of this ministry fulfills prophecy, which is in keeping with his frequent and often exclusive geographically fulfilled prophecies (4:12–13; cf. 2:6, 15, 18, 23). The fact that Jesus withdrew to Galilee after the arrest of John to begin his public work is no coincidence for Matthew; he sees it as a fulfillment of Isaiah 9:1–2:

> Nevertheless, there will be no more gloom for those who were in distress. In the past he had humbled the land of Zebulun and the land of Naphtali, but in the future he will honor Galilee of the Gentiles, by the way of the sea, along the Jordan—
>
> The people walking in darkness
> have seen a great light;
> on those living in the land of the shadow of death
> a light has dawned.

Matthew sees Jesus as the obvious fulfillment of this prophecy of the Gentile enlightenment that occurred in Galilee and around Capernaum.

Jesus "withdrew" ("returned," NIV) when he heard of John the Baptist's arrest (4:12). The word *anachoreo* occurs fourteen times in the New Testament, with ten of these in Matthew. It can mean "return," but also "withdraw, retire, take refuge" (BAGD, 63). Matthew often uses it in this latter sense, especially after contexts where Jesus had come into conflict with his opponents or was in danger (2:12, 14, 22; 12:15; 14:13; 15:21). It is as if Jesus followed the advice that he later gave to his disciples: "If anyone will not welcome you or listen to your words, shake the dust off your feet when you leave that home or town" (10:14). Although Jesus could and did openly confront, he often avoided conflict, preferring to work among those open to the reign of God. Hence it is appropriate that when Herod Antipas, the mutual enemy of John and Jesus, arrested John, Jesus moved north to begin his ministry among the Jews in a Gentile-dominated region. Matthew anticipates the ministry of Jesus expanding to all nations (28:19).

2.4.2. Jesus Calls the First Disciples (4:18–22). Matthew places the calling of the disciples at this point because it follows the order set before him in Mark and because it identifies the primary audience for the Sermon on the Mount. It is also seen as a crucial part of the next phase of Jesus' work delineated in 4:17. He records the calling of only four disciples, three of whom will form his inner circle. Later he records the calling of Matthew, the disciple and former tax collector (9:9); he gives a complete listing of the twelve apostles in 10:2–4.

After Jesus left Nazareth, he settled in Capernaum, which is on the Sea of Galilee (4:13). While there he met several fishermen, whom he called to follow him. These men were probably not poor since they had a business and servants (Mark 1:20). The names of the disciples reflect the multicultural character of Galilee: Simon, John, and James are Jewish names while Andrew's name is Greek. Matthew also gives Simon's nickname, Peter (the Rock), given to him by Jesus in Matthew 16:17–19 (see comments). Matthew is anticipating that future event here.

It is striking that after these fishermen were called, they "immediately" (or "at once," vv. 20, 22) left both the work in which they were engaged and their families in order to follow Jesus. Given that Matthew often omits Mark's ubiquitous use of "immediately," it is all the more significant that he allows it to stand here. Later this complete renunciation of the respectable yet old ties figures prominently in the disciples' questions and in Jesus' teachings (8:21; 19:27–30). Note that these four men may have known about Jesus and had previous contact with him (cf. John 1:35–51).

Equally surprising are the words with which Jesus calls them: "Come, follow me . . . and I will make you fishers of men" (4:19). The inspiration of this metaphor probably comes out of the activity immediately before him. Jeremiah 16:16 refers to fishermen and hunters who track down sinners and exact double punishment for their sins. In contrast, Jesus calls his newly chosen disciples to fish for the salvation of souls, not for their destruction.

2.4.3. Jesus' Threefold Ministry (4:23–25). This summary of Jesus' ministry is one of many that Matthew gives his readers (e.g. 8:16; 9:35; 12:15; 14:35–36; 15:30–31; 19:1–2). This general description is programmatic for Jesus' ministry. For the most part, Matthew concentrates on Jesus' work in Galilee. He also concentrates on the Jewish population since Jesus' activity often was in synagogues (4:23). Jesus manifested a general reluctance to proclaim the good news to Gentiles and Samaritans at this time (cf. 10:5–6). Note also that Matthew is writing at a time when the schism between Jews and Christians is complete: "teaching in *their* synagogues" (4:23; see also Mark 1:39; Luke 4:15).

Teaching, proclaiming the good news of the kingdom, and healing every disease are the three major activities of Jesus and become a sign of his messiahship and of the eschatological in-breaking of God's new age, which will shake, destroy, or transform the institutions of the old age. These are the hallmarks of his work which will be capped by his ultimate work on the cross and in the resurrection and will be perpetuated in the community that he commissions to succeed him (10:1–40; 28:16–20).

Jesus' fame spreads throughout the surrounding territory, and many bring their sick to experience his compassionate power and to hear his preaching and teaching. This ministry serves to explain how in a few short years Jesus gathered the attention of the pagan, the Jew, the rich, the poor, and the temporal powers with which he collided. It also explains the origin of "the crowds" (5:1), who are present for the Sermon on the Mount that follows.

The illnesses that Jesus cured are listed in detail and merit discussion. Jesus healed people with diseases, with weaknesses or ailments, in severe pain or torment, and under attack or distress; he ministered to the demon possessed and those with seizures, as well as to those with paralysis or lameness. The "seizures" (4:24) may refer to the neurological malfunction of epilepsy, but in the New Testament this is sometimes associated with lemon possession. In 17:14–21, for example, vhat has the classic symptoms of an epileptic eizure is attributed to a spirit or demonic ictivity (cf. Mark 9:14–29; Luke 9:37–43). In he medical writings of the day many illnesses vere associated with a spirit (*pneuma*), and his may be a protoscientific description of the llness. It is probably inaccurate to describe nost epileptic-like symptoms in demonic erms, but some cases of thrashing or catatonic tates may have been understood by Jesus and iis contemporaries to be a result of evil spiriual influence. In such cases today medical olutions should be sought out as well as rayer for healing, and perhaps, in some cases, he classical first-century explanation should iot be ruled out. Elsewhere in Matthew lemonic exorcisms and healing are considered wo separate activities (e.g., Matt. 8:14–17).

. The Sermon on the Mount: Law of Kingdom (The First Discourse: 5:1–7:29)

3.1. The Beatitudes (5:1–12)

3.1.1. The Sermon Prologue (5:1–2). The ermon on the Mount is one of the most amous of Jesus' teachings. In spite of this, it is ot always easy to interpret and is frequently nisunderstood. It is radical, revolutionary, rovocative, simple yet profound. Previously Aatthew paralleled Jesus with Moses and the xodus (ch. 2). Here he makes further allusions o the penultimate prophet and teacher of the)ld Testament and shows that Jesus is greater nan Moses. It is perhaps no accident that Jesus egins his teaching on the ethics of the new ingdom on a mountain, just as Moses gave the aw from Mount Sinai. Furthermore, Jesus ites the old law in this sermon, proceeds to peak authoritatively on it, and expands it as iough he has greater authority than Moses e.g., 5:17–48). As Jesus teaches, he sits, and is disciples and the crowd sit around him—ie usual teaching posture for rabbis of the day.

Some (mostly dispensationalists) assume iat the requirements of Jesus' kingdom as xpounded in the Sermon on the Mount are npossible to keep and thus describe how iod's kingdom will be in its end-time fulfillient. They adopt this position by distinguishig between the kingdom of God, which exists ow, and the kingdom of heaven, which will be established in the future. This difference is alien to the mind of Matthew and the other Gospel writers (see Introduction). The consensus of the church, both ancient and modern, is that Jesus considered the ethic in this sermon possible to observe by the power of God's grace.

Much of the material in this sermon Luke presents in his Sermon on the Plain (Luke 6:17–49). Although Matthew and Luke presumably have a common source for these teachings, Jesus could have said them differently on more than one occasion. Matthew has collected the teachings of Jesus topically here as he did in the other teaching sections of his Gospel.

These pronouncements of Jesus get their formal name from the Latin *beatitudo*, a noun related to *beatus*, which is how the Vulgate translates the Greek *makarios* (vv. 3–11). This form of saying did not originate with Jesus; it frequently occurs in the Psalms and Wisdom Literature in the Old Testament, and even the Greeks had such sayings. The form seems to have originated in the Hebraic and Jewish literature with which Jesus was familiar (on this background, see Guelich, 1982; Young, 1989). While the form and spirit of the beatitudes come from the Jews, the uniqueness of Jesus' teachings shows that he brought their form and spirit to fulfillment. Each beatitude includes three sections: the state (i.e., "blessed"), the condition, and the reward.

What does *makarios* mean? It is difficult to express in English the force of this Greek word and its underlying Hebrew concept. Translations vary from "blessed" to "fortunate," "happy," "well off," and even "congratulations." It is not just a benediction or pronouncement of blessing that the speaker extends to the hearers who qualify, but a statement of reality or essence of those who exhibit the virtue mentioned in the pronouncement. "The beatitudes thus outline the attitudes of the true disciple, the one who has accepted the demands of God's kingdom in contrast with the attitudes of the 'man of the world,' and they present this as the best way of life not only in its intrinsic goodness but in its results" (France, 1985, 108). No single English word successfully expresses the nuances of either the Greek or Hebrew.

These beatitudes establish the tenor and substance of the rest of the sermon. The issues of poverty of spirit, mourning, meekness, righteousness, mercy, purity of heart, peace, and persecution are developed in the rest of the teaching. Therefore, we must carefully explore the meaning of each beatitude for Jesus, the Hebrew worldview, and the church. Care must be taken to distinguish these concepts from modern notions bearing the same name.

3.1.2. The Poor in Spirit (5:3). The phrase "poor in spirit" has many meanings. Suggestions are being humble, unassuming, or wretched, lacking in material things since the individual described is voluntarily poor for the sake of God's kingdom, or being devoid of materialism and covetousness. Interpretation is further complicated by the fact that Luke's version of the saying is, "Blessed are you who are poor, for yours is the kingdom of God" (Luke 6:20), which he contrasts with "But woe to you who are rich, for you have already received your comfort" (6:24).

The solution lies in the Hebrew understanding of the word "poor" (*ptochos*). The words in the Hebrew Old Testament translated "poor" shed light on the phrase. They can refer to a socioeconomic standing, but they also connote a dependency on another person, who can call one to account for his or her actions. The psalmists often express their dependency on God in terms of poverty. Even a king should see himself as poor when he stands before God.

Luke's use of "poor" appears at first sight to be saying that poverty itself (i.e., dire want) is a blessing. This is further heightened by his frequent contrast between the poor and the rich (e.g., Luke 1:53; 6:20–24; 12:13–21; 16:19–31). But one has to ask *why* Luke contrasts the rich and the poor. The rich are not rejected for having wealth per se but for reveling in self-sufficiency and celebrating the poverty of materialism (see 12:21). The rich man is condemned for his callous indifference to the plight of Lazarus (16:19–31). In Acts, also written by Luke, the Jerusalem church disposed of possessions to meet needs and held wealth in common (Acts 2:44–46), apparently on a voluntary basis (though private property was not completely liquidated in the church at large, for Paul was able to take up a collection among the Gentile churches in the dispersion for the poor Jerusalem church).

The "poor in spirit" are those who realize that they are morally, spiritually, and even physically bankrupt without the grace of God. They realize their ever-present need of God. How then are they blessed? They are blessed because they realize God is their source and that all other sources not sanctioned by God are empty idols. "My people have committed two sins: They have forsaken me, the spring of living water, and have dug their own cisterns, broken cisterns that cannot hold water" (Jer 2:13). Those who are desperate, who are not deluded by their self-sufficiency, and who throw themselves on God's mercy will find the resources of the kingdom of heaven in the hands of God.

"The kingdom of heaven" belongs to the poor in spirit. What is the kingdom of heaven (a term synonymous with "kingdom of God"; see Introduction)? When one is part of a kingdom, one has a king. The kingdom of heaven requires complete obedience to the king—physically, mentally, and spiritually. To pray "your kingdom come" implies, "May my kingdom go." The King of the kingdom of heaven requires us to acknowledge his complete sovereignty. It is hard for God to give us anything if our hands are full. The most precious thing this world can put in our hands is but rubbish compared to what God offers us.

Note that Jesus said the kingdom *is* theirs, not just will be theirs (France, 1985, 109):

> The tenses are future (for the beatitudes), except in the first and last, indicating that the best is yet to come, when God's kingdom is finally established and its subjects enter into their inheritance. But the present tense of vv. 3 and 10 warns us against an exclusively future interpretation, for God rewards these attitudes with their respective results progressively in the disciple's experience. The emphasis is not so much on time present or future, as on the *certainty* that discipleship will not be in vain.

Through Jesus the kingdom has already come in many respects, though the best is yet to be. The wedding has begun; the honeymoon awaits.

The symptom of a lack of poverty of spirit is a callous self-sufficiency and disregard for God's provision and the unconditional demands of his reign. This beatitude is not calling for a self-effacing false humility, as Bon hoeffer (1963, 118), the modern martyr, observed:

> He calls them blessed, not because of their privations, or the renunciation they have made, for these are not blessed in themselves. Only the call and the promise, for the sake of which they are ready to suffer poverty and renunciation, can justify the beatitudes.... The error lies in looking for some kind of human behavior as the ground for the beatitude instead of the call and promise of Jesus alone.

3.1.3. The Mourners (5:4). Each beatitude builds on the previous one, which is characteristic of Hebrew poetry. Instead of relying on meter or rhyme for structure, Hebrew poetry relies on parallelism. The second line repeats the idea of the previous line but gives added meaning. Those who thus realize that without God they are spiritually and morally bankrupt (5:3) have a natural response: mourning, that is, an expression of regret. This mourning refers to a religious response and not just regret of physical loss.

Much of the wording and concepts for Matthew's beatitudes comes from Isaiah 61. The historical context for this chapter is the exile of the Israelites in Babylon as a result of their disobedience and sin. The remnant who survived the destruction of Samaria (721 B.C.) and Jerusalem (587 B.C.) grieved over the loss of their land and nation. The persons and things precious to them, such as old friends, family, the city, and the temple, were destroyed. Although some Jews prospered in exile, many were in peril and destitute. The few Jews who remained in the Promised Land were equally devastated. While Luke emphasized the anointing of the Holy Spirit and the poor in his use of Isaiah 61 (Luke 4:18), Matthew concentrates on the themes of comfort for the grieving, restoration of prosperity, and the repossession of the land.

Many Old Testament psalms also express mourning and distress, and they call to God for deliverance, forgiveness, and restoration of right relationship with him (e.g. Ps. 22; 51). Like the exiles, the poor in spirit stand in grief, totally dependent on God's intervention. Jesus himself experienced mourning. He mourned over Jerusalem and her rejection of him and her subsequent destruction (Matt. 23:37–39). Jesus mourned over his dead friend Lazarus even though he was about to raise him from the dead (John 11:35). In Gethsemane he endured great agony over his impending sacrifice on the cross (Matt. 26:39). Jesus fulfilled Isaiah's description of the "Suffering Servant" as "a man of sorrows, and familiar with suffering" (Isa. 53:3). Someday he will wipe all tears from their eyes (Rev. 21:4).

To mourn is to have remorse over our sins and to repent of them, that is, to renounce and forsake them. It requires our complete reliance on God's mercy and complete impoverishment to all other resources. A symptom of the lack of this beatitude is a flippancy toward sin, a lack of seriousness about its consequences, and a presumption of God's forgiveness—"cheap grace," as Bonhoeffer puts it.

The mourners "will be comforted." Comfort is a major role of the Messiah in the restoration of the people, their land, and the establishment of his kingdom, as we saw in Isaiah 61. Also note Isaiah 40:1–2: "Comfort ye, comfort ye my people, saith your God. Speak ye comfortably to Jerusalem, and cry unto her, that her warfare is accomplished, that her iniquity is pardoned: for she hath received of the LORD's hand double for all her sins" (KJV; see also 49:13; 51:12; 66:13; Jer. 31:13). By the time of the rabbinic writing the Messiah was called *Menachem*, meaning "the Comforter."

3.1.4. The Meek (5:5). This third beatitude completes the first two and reveals the secret of living out the ethics of the new kingdom. E. Stanley Jones (1931, 51, 57) explains it well:

> The first Beatitude without the second ends in barren aloofness, but with it it ends in fruitful attachment. This verse cuts across those who would say that religion is an "escape mentality," a means of escaping from pain and sorrow. Here is religion now deliberately choosing sorrow for itself in order to cure it in others....
>
> The first two beatitudes corrected and supplemented by each other result in a synthesis of the two and become a third, namely, the meek who inherit the earth.

What is meekness? Meekness is one of the most misunderstood words in the English language. Its meaning in the text is further complicated by the nuances of the Greek and Hebrew words it attempts to translate. The Greek word is *praus*, a word the Septuagint uses to translate Hebrew words meaning "poor" or "humble." In other words, meekness had a wide connotation in Hebrew. Given the tendency to repeat ideas in synonymous parallelism, the primary meaning of *praus* is roughly equivalent to the meaning of "poor in spirit" in the first beatitude.

Many scholars believe that Jesus is alluding to Psalm 37:11, where the LXX translates the Hebrew word for poor as *praus*: "But the meek will inherit the land and enjoy great peace." In its Hebrew milieu "poor" did not just denote a person with no money. It was a religious term as well, meaning that the truly righteous acknowledge their moral and spiritual bankruptcy before a holy God and that any lasting merit is based on God's resources and graciousness. Thus it is a self-description of anyone in desperate straits, who knows that God alone can help (Ps. 40:17; 102:1; Isa. 41:17; 49:13; 66:2; Zeph. 2:3; 3:12).

Given the above definition, even a rich king who was righteous would consider himself poor and meek before God if he ruled kindly and justly. In Greek usage, Xenophon makes it clear that "meek" is not synonymous with "weak," for he describes a wild stallion that has been tamed as "meek." Aristotle defines it as the mean between excessive, explosive anger and no anger at all. In this application of humility the lack of power is not the only issue. In the triumphal entry of Jesus into Jerusalem, Matthew notes that Jesus fulfilled the prophecy of Zechariah 9:9 by being meek (*praus*, Matt. 21:5). Apparently by New Testament times "meek" had become a title honoring the Messiah, perhaps based on the description of Moses in Numbers 12:3, "Now the man Moses was very meek, above all the men which were upon the face of the earth" (KJV). In Sirach 45:4 we read concerning Moses: "For his faithfulness and meekness [*praus*] he consecrated him" (NRSV). Matthew presents Moses as the major prototype for the Messiah, who would be the new and better Lawgiver (cf., e.g., Matt. 5:43–44).

Clearly Jesus models meekness—not as weakness but, like Moses before him, as power under control (Phil. 2:3–11). Jesus was a person of power. He healed people, cast out demons, walked on water, and performed amazing miracles. He harassed his political enemies at will, and they often left him, routed in full intellectual retreat. He in his meekness demonstrated that righteous indignation naturally arises out of a humble concern for God and others. Yet he was the meekest person who ever lived! E. Stanley Jones (1931, 57–58) describes this aspect of Jesus' ministry as "the terrible meek," who has both great power and decisiveness and compassionate service. The meek are terrible because they cannot be bought or sold; their service to others outlives the bullying tyrant.

Paul provides valuable commentary on this beatitude when he includes meekness in his list of the fruit of the Spirit in contrast to the works of the sinful human nature (Gal. 5:22–23, KJV). He often associates meekness and gentleness together (2 Cor. 10:1; Eph. 4:2; Col. 3:11–12). Believers are to be gentle and to show perfect courtesy (*praus*; NIV, "humility") toward everyone (Titus 3:2); thus, gentleness is an integral part of meekness.

The promise to the meek is that "they will inherit the earth." To understand this part of the beatitude, one has to look at Israel's history, God's saving acts in that history, and the concept of Holy Land. Land has been an issue in salvation history since the Garden of Eden, when Adam and Eve were expelled from it and God promised an eventual return to Edenic paradise in the land of Israel (Gen. 49:8–12). When God redeemed Israel from Egyptian slavery, salvation came as a trip to the Promised Land. The same is true of the end of the exile from Assyrian and Babylonian captivity, which resulted in the return of the people and the restoration of the temple in Jerusalem (see Nehemiah). But real estate is not the only thing intended. The land was a promise given to those who trusted in God (Deut. 4:1; 16:20). The Promised Land and possession of it became a symbol of God's future action to save his people (Isa. 61:7).

The land takes on a greater significance since it is promised to the righteous meek, who humbly serve God. Only the righteous will eventually receive God's blessing while the prosperity of the wicked is short-lived (Ps. 37). The prosperity of the righteous is contingent on their love for God and their maintenance of the covenant out of love and loyalty. Although material prosperity often results for the meek follower of God, the inheritance of the earth ultimately represents God's final vindication of the meek. Those who exalt themselves will be abased, and those who humble themselves will be exalted (Matt. 23:12). Those who would seize the earth will lose it; it can only be received as a gift.

3.1.5. The Hungry and Thirsty for Righteousness (5:6). This beatitude reveals much about the nature of the kingdom of God. As we saw in the "poor in spirit" beatitude, this beatitude can also have a double meaning in both Matthew and Luke. Luke concentrates on the socioeconomic state of the church in his version of the poverty beatitude, and he follows the same pattern in his version of this beatitude (Luke 6:21):

> Blessed are you who hunger now,
> for you will be satisfied.
> Blessed are you who weep now,
> for you will laugh.

Luke often condemns the uncaring proponents of crass materialism. He does not condemn wealth but the abuse of it and its encumbrances in relation to spirituality.

Matthew, by contrast, emphasizes the spiritual aspect in his account by his reference to hungering and thirsting *for righteousness*. This is in keeping with the spiritual use of the word "poor" to describe one's need for God. God's righteousness, however, is not devoid of social ramifications; the righteous will alleviate suffering because righteousness is merciful (25:36). Many monastic orders have combined both meanings in vows of poverty in which they identify with the poor and are totally dependent on God's physical and spiritual provision.

The words "hunger and thirst" reveal much about Jesus' message. In the Greek text, both are present participles, denoting continual action, that is, a lifestyle of continually hungering and thirsting for righteousness. This kind of person seeks righteousness as a starving person seeks food or a lost desert wanderer craves water. The hunger and thirst are incessant; righteousness is the highest priority, the foremost need, the only thing that will satisfy.

This parallels the Old Testament Exodus account (Ex. 17:11–32; Deut. 8:15) in which both the physical and spiritual hungering and thirsting were present. When the Israelites sought God's will in obedience, bountiful provision followed, but the basic issue was spiritual. God said to Israel that he led them in the desert "to test you in order to know what was in your heart.... He humbled you, causing you to hunger and then feeding you with manna ... to teach you that man does not live on bread alone but on every word that comes from the mouth of the LORD" (Deut. 8:2–3). The Exodus became a repeated type or theme for divine provision in the future (e.g., Isa. 25:6; 41:17–18; 55:1–3). Thirst as a spiritual metaphor is used also in Psalm 42:1–4.

What does Matthew mean by the word "righteousness"? Apart from Luke 1:75, Matthew is the only Synoptic Evangelist who uses the word. He does not use it as mere legal justification; rather, he views righteousness both as an ethical requirement and as a gracious endowment to be lived out. The Hebrew understanding of righteousness involved behavior, life, and conduct—the understanding that Matthew faithfully preserves. Yet in this beatitude righteousness also includes the idea of grace and "the exercise of divine justice that finally results in the vindication longed for by the persecuted" (Gundry, 1994, 70).

Matthew does not intend for righteousness to refer merely to conduct, for in 5:20 he records Jesus' explanation that true righteousness must exceed that of the scribes and Pharisees. This is not a mere entrance requirement for the kingdom of heaven. Matthew's parable of the servant forgiven of an outrageous debt who refuses to forgive his fellow servant for a relatively insignificant debt sheds light on the meaning of righteousness (18:23–35). Unrighteousness is devoid of love and forgiveness, which are the medium of exchange in the new kingdom. All transactions are rendered void if any currency other than the righteousness of God is proffered.

The gracious act of God brings the recipient into a new relationship with God in which gratitude demands a similar response in keeping with the nature and will of the benefactor (5:6; 6:33). Like should beget like. Thus the kingdom brings a new relationship now between God and his creation, a relationship that issues in corresponding conduct in keeping with God's will. Guelich (1982, 86) notes that the context of Matthew reveals the "'gift'-character of righteousness." Righteousness is not so much an asset one has but an awareness of its lack and a driving desire for it. Thus the beatitude on mourning parallels and explains this one. Blessed are those who are aware of their wretched meanness and desperately seek God's resources of right.

Those who hunger for righteousness "will be filled." The verb for "filled" means "to eat until one has been filled." In secular literature it was used to describe cattle that had been fattened. Those whose lifestyle is righteousness-seeking will be fattened on it. God is not stingy to those craving the right things. Since the tense is future, it focuses attention on the coming messianic banquet; not all rewards of righteousness are immediate. At the same time, not all of the benefits of righteousness are in the remote future; some effects, such as God's provision, are in the here and now (6:33).

To receive God's gracious forgiveness and join the kingdom require renouncing the old, that is, repenting. True righteousness does not mean, nor was it ever in the old era, a mere eye-for-an-eye righteousness (5:38–42). God wants to write forgiving righteousness in people's hearts so that it becomes a part of their nature, thereby assuring that the ethical standards will be maintained (Jer. 31:33). This is not by merely keeping the Master's rules but by having the Master's heart and nature. God's righteousness is not merely forensic; it must be metamorphic. Forgiveness has not achieved its end if it does not create a thankful heart.

3.1.6. The Merciful (5:7). This beatitude approaches something of a law of reciprocity. Paul wrote, "A man reaps what he sows" (Gal. 6:7). Jesus himself testified: "Give, and it will be given to you.... For with the measure you use, it will be measured to you" (Luke 6:38).

Yet care must be taken not to reduce this beatitude to a mere law of the cosmos, some rarified natural law to be exploited by anyone. The law of reciprocity works only within a relationship with God and a submission to his Lordship. Everyone knows of instances where good has not been reciprocated with good in human experience, an exaggerated corollary to Murphy's law: "No good deed will go unpunished." Only in an obedient relationship with God in which he and his will are loved above all can this "law" be ultimately fulfilled in spite of wickedness in this world. The delayed harvest will only be a greater one.

To treat this truth as a formula to be manipulated is *not* Christianity, nor is it the spirit of the Hebrew religion; it is, instead, magic, the manipulation of a spirit or deity to get one's own way, paganism (Acts 19:15–16). Systems that emphasize these truths as laws to manipulate either leave God on the periphery of the equation or consider him their captive, who *must* do their bidding. They seem to think of Jesus the Lord as a cat who must do their will if they twist his tail. They have the Lion of Judah by the tail; they should put it down *carefully*.

To receive mercy, one must submit to and be in relationship with Mercy himself. We have received God's merciful invitation to salvation and union with his reign. Mercy is part of his agenda. As his agents and friends, we promote the program of mercy—even at our expense. To receive mercy is to become merciful. Like righteousness, mercy is metamorphic, character changing. If we have truly received God's mercy, we will be changed and show mercy; otherwise, we have not accepted God's merciful act in our lives.

What is mercy? In the Bible mercy has two major meanings. (1) It indicates that one has been pardoned for a wrong committed (Isa. 55:7). (2) It is the word used for kindnesses that help the needy (Luke 18:39). The giving of alms is called an act of mercy; in Greek "almsgiving" is in the same word group as "mercy." Both major meanings are used in Matthew, but mercy in the context of judging is the dominant intent in the Sermon on the Mount.

Often it is assumed that mercy and righteousness are opposites, that mercy is grace and righteousness is unbending law and justice. This was neither the Hebrew concept of mercy nor that of righteousness. The two are closely related: "Love and faithfulness meet together; righteousness and peace kiss each other" (Ps. 85:10). God's concept of righteousness is not hasty retribution, but one slow to anger and merciful (86:15). Even God's punishment of Israel for crass disobedience was not merely punitive; rather, it was designed to be corrective and therefore salvific. The goal of God's justice is a life-transforming and healing mercy. His concept of righteousness is merciful, not just remorseless laws (see Hos. 6:6). Modern definitions of mercy and righteousness need the mutual softening and tempering of each other. One must be "righteously merciful and mercifully righteous" (Guelich, 1982, 63).

The merciful "will be shown mercy." Apparently Jesus has in mind here the day of final judgment, yet in a sense the merciful also receive mercy now and are therefore able to give what they have received. This beatitude describes those who have received forgiveness from God for their failures and who in turn treat those offending them as God did when they were offensive to him. Mercy in the kingdom is like money in the economy: Only when it is in circulation does it do the most good. Often the fruits of mercy are visited upon the merciful in the present as an initial down payment of the end-time reward. Bonhoeffer (1963, 125) renders this beatitude as: "Blessed are the merciful, for they have the Merciful for their Lord."

3.1.7. The Pure in Heart (5:8). Purity of heart is often misunderstood in the contemporary church. Modern usage of the expression "pure in heart" often assumes that it means moral purity, clean motives, or even sexual purity. While this meaning is not alien to the biblical usage, the Hebraic use of the phrase expresses something more essential. The word "pure" (*katharos*) means clean, ceremonially pure, or morally pure (BAGD, 388). Hebrew usage gives the phrase its distinctive meaning in the Bible. Part of our misunderstanding stems from the fact that the Hebrews understood the "heart" as more than the seat of emotions; it was also the seat of one's spiritual and intellectual activities, the inner person, if you will. Hence in the Old Testament "heart" and "soul" are often used interchangeably.

In addition, the heart in Old Testament usage is the place where fantasies and visions occur (Jer. 14:14). Folly (Prov. 10:20–21) and evil thoughts also originate and develop in the heart, as do the will and intention (1 Kings 8:17) and the resolve to carry them out (Ex. 36:2). This Hebrew concept of heart is a comprehensive term for the human personality as a whole. It is the gyroscopic center of a person, where all thoughts, feelings, and intentions are either balanced or unbalanced.

The promise that the pure in heart "will see God" alludes to Psalm 24, in which "he who has clean hands and a pure heart" will "ascend the hill of the LORD" and "stand in his holy place" (vv. 3–4). "Clean hands and a pure heart" indicates outward and inward purity of the whole person before an all-seeing God. It is a single-minded orientation of one's whole person, like an internal compass or homing device that directs one constantly to God (v. 6; cf. Matt. 12:35).

But how can God be seen? The promise of seeing God here stands in stark contrast to the warning found in the book of Exodus that no one "may see [God] and live" (Ex. 33:20; cf. 3:6; 19:21). Yet God did appear to Abraham, Moses, and Isaiah (Gen. 17:1; Ex. 24:10–11; Deut. 34:10; Isa. 6:1, 5). Believers too have the hope of seeing God—on the last day (Heb. 12:14; 1 John 3:2; Rev. 22:4), when they will stand before God and are approved on the Day of Judgment (cf. Matt. 6:24, 33; 22:37).

3.1.8. The Peacemakers (5:9). Like some of the other beatitudes, English and Western concepts do not fit the words Jesus uses. Our word "peace" is a pitiful parallel for what Jesus meant. We often define peace as a state opposite of war and peacemaking as putting aside a conflict for a truce—a concept that also fits the classical Greek usage of the word. The Hebrew word *shalom* better reflects Jesus' intent. *Shalom* is a state of wholeness in individuals or nations, including safety, health, and wealth in the context of God's covenant with his people.

True peace is based on God's "covenant of peace" with his people (Ezek. 37:26). It is the nature of God's blessing for his faithful people, who are in right relationship with him. Mere absence of military strife and material wealth are not God's peace. For example, in the reign of Jeroboam II, Israel extended her frontiers, creating much material prosperity; yet the prophet Amos condemned the nation. Their wealth was ill-gotten gain at the expense of the poor, the product of greed, injustice, and lawlessness. The political good times turned out to be the calm before the storm, for they were about to succumb to the power that had made their neighbors weak, the ruthless and dreaded Assyrian empire, which destroyed Israel in 721 B.C.

God's peace is much deeper, more thorough, and more meaningful. Numbers 6:24–26 expresses it well: "The LORD bless you and keep you; the LORD make his face shine upon you and be gracious to you; the LORD turn his face toward you and give you peace." The reference to God's face speaks of his presence, which is the ultimate source of his peace.

God's peace comes from righteousness: "The fruit of righteousness will be peace; the effect of righteousness will be quietness and confidence forever" (Isa. 32:17). Peace and righteousness are often paired together (e.g., Ps. 72:7; 85:10; Isa. 48:18; 57:2; 60:17). Thus the one who is a peacemaker (more lit., a peace-doer) is upright (Mal. 2:6) and faithful (2 Sam. 20:19) and upholds the truth (Est. 9:30; Zech. 8:16). *Shalom* comes from obedience to God. It can never be achieved apart from relationship with him. The source of all peace is God's presence. *Shalom* has a perfective sense, as in the sense of being completely equipped, lacking nothing. Yet it is not mere material prosperity, for even righteous Josiah, who was killed in battle, is said to have died in peace because of his obedience (2 Kings 22:20).

This broad, all-inclusive meaning of peace continues in the New Testament (see its use in Rom. 8:6; 14:17; 15:13; Gal. 5:22; Phil. 4:7; Col. 3:15). The peace of Jesus is qualitatively superior to anything of this world: "Peace I leave with you; my peace I give you. I do not give to you as the world gives. Do not let your hearts be troubled and do not be afraid" (John 14:27). The dominant use of peace in the New Testament reflects its Hebrew heritage of wholeness, righteousness, and subsequent blessing for the individual and community who live humbly and obediently in the presence of God.

The role of Jesus as peace-doer was part of the Jewish expectation that the Messiah would establish universal peace, justice, and an Edenic paradise in the last days (Isa. 9:6–7; 54:10; Ezek. 34:25–31; 37:26; Mic. 5:4; Hag. 2:9; Zech. 8:12). Thus the coming Prince of Peace had an eschatological mission on a cosmic scale. Jesus began the establishment of the end-time peace. By his death and resurrection he became the peace between God and us (Rom. 5:1; Eph. 2:14–18; Col. 1:20). We receive this peace, though undeserved, as a gift from God, even while we are his enemies (Rom. 5:10; 2 Cor. 5:19; Col. 1:20–22). The peace Jesus gives to us is based on a relationship with him. Peace is found by being close to Jesus and by Jesus' closeness to us.

Peacemakers "will be called children of God" (NRSV). This blessing is in the future tense since it has in mind the final judgment. The verb is also passive because God is the One who makes us his children in nature, not just in name (5:45; Luke 6:35). Like God our Father, we will be makers of peace. This nomenclature "children of God" is Hebraic: Israel was God's child since they had been chosen by him, been given his covenant, and had a special relationship with him (Ex. 4:22; Deut. 14:1; Jer. 31:9; Hos. 1:10). The Messiah was, in a special sense, the Son of God (cf. Ps 2:7). The relationship between God and his children in this beatitude is not completely futuristic, for even now Christians are children of God (1 John 3:1–2).

Given the wide-ranging, all-inclusive nature of *shalom*, peacemakers are "wholemakers," whose work affects the entire community. They are more than reconcilers in that they work for healing and wholeness of society. This broader definition is supported in Jesus' call to "love your enemies" (5:44; cf Luke 6:27). The ultimate commentary on this aspect of peacemaking is Jesus himself, who died to reconcile God's enemies with him (Rom. 5:8). Thus we too, as children of God are called to love the unlovable and undeserving, and to reestablish wholeness in a fragmented, fallen world without which no lasting peace can exist. We have a part to play in the establishment of the kingdom.

3.1.9. The Persecuted Because of Righteousness (5:10–12). This beatitude links with the previous ones, especially the one on peacemaking. Peacekeeping is hazardous, but peacemaking, peace-doing, and justice-establishing call for even more sacrifice. Jesus' sacrifice on the cross is the ultimate example of the price of the Peace-doer. For real peace and wholeness, established conventions of society designed just to "keep the peace" or perpetuate injustice must go. As a child of the southern United States growing up in the 1950s and 1960s I have witnessed such changes. I often heard comments such as, "Why, we have always had two water fountains, one for blacks and one for whites," or "It's for their own good." To establish true peace, things had to change, and sometimes there was a price.

This beatitude parallels the status of the poor in spirit" in verse 3, who also receive the ingdom. Like the poor, the persecuted realize nat without God the cause is lost, but that with iod the cause will triumph regardless of hardhips. The beatitude about hungering and nirsting for righteousness also parallels this ne. One must seek wholeness as though life self depends on it, for it does—for both the ndividual and the community. To be a friend f God is to be an enemy of the world. Note nat the persecution is to be "because of righeousness," not for stupidity's sake or for egoaniacal stubbornness. As noted above, ighteousness is both a gift and a requireent—a gift that changes us and empowers us or change, but also an ethical code and festyle.

The persecuted—those who suffer at the ands and mouths of others for Jesus' sake—re like the bold prophets of old. The ultimate lessing is to be numbered with the faithful who will stand in God's judgment, feast ogether at the messianic banquet, and join in nceasing praise of God. Everything else is of econdary importance (6:33; Mark 8:36).

3.2. Salt and Light (5:13–16)

"Salt" is prized for two major attributes: aste and preserving. It cannot lose its saltiness f it is pure sodium chloride. This leads to the uggestion that Jesus meant that his disciples would cease being disciples if they lost their salty character. The unrefined salt mined at the Dead Sea was mixed with other minerals. From this crude salt the sodium chloride could leach out as a result of moisture, rendering it worthless (Jeremias, 1972, 169). Rabbinic teaching associated the metaphor of salt with wisdom. This was probably Jesus' intent since the word "worthless" has "foolish" as its root meaning. It is moronic for disciples to lose their character since then they are worthless to both the kingdom and the church and reap the contempt of both.

In the Old Testament "light" is associated with God (Ps. 18:28; 27:1), and the Servant of the Lord and Jerusalem are also clothed with God's light. The Servant will be a light to the Gentiles, and all nations will come to Jerusalem's light (Isa. 42:6; 49:6; 60:1–3). It is in this sense of being a light to the nations that Jesus identifies the disciples as light. It anticipates the conclusion of Matthew's Gospel: "Go and make disciples of all nations" (28:19). In the previous chapter Matthew identified Jesus as Isaiah's "great light" in Gentile Galilee (4:15–16). Now his disciples are called to be bearers of the light.

The "world" (*kosmos*) stands in contrast to the kingdom of heaven and is parallel to the word "earth" (*ge*) in verse 13. It refers to the habitation place of human beings. It can have a negative sense (18:7) and can refer to the present age in relation to the coming age.

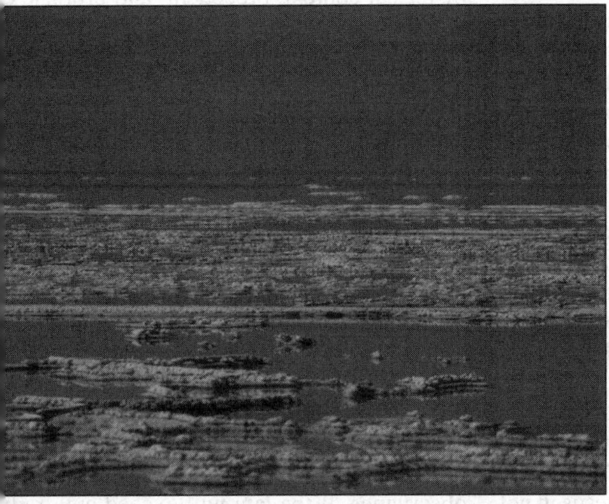

alt pans in the Dead Sea provide the salt needed for preserving ood. Jesus called his disciples "the salt of the earth." He also varned them that when salt loses its saltiness it is no longer good or anything.

"A city on a hill" may be inspired by Isaiah's description of Jerusalem clothed in God's light as a beacon to the nations (Isa. 60). Mount Zion also parallels the reference to the hill or mountain. The disciples are to carry out the commission of Jerusalem in the greater scheme of salvation history.

The "bowl" was about one peck in size. The issue is whether or not lights should be put in places of maximum visibility, such as on a lampstand. Christians are to be visible. Matthew makes this clear with his favored expression, "in the same way." The light of the disciples is the good works that they do. Not only are the disciples the light but they do the light.

It was not unusual for Jews to consider God as the Father of the nation of Israel, but for him to be the Father of individuals is a characteristic of Jesus' teaching and is well developed in the church's literature. "Your Father in heaven" often occurs in the Sermon on the Mount (5:45; 6:1, 9; 7:11). Our motive for good works is that people may glorify the heavenly Father, not us. Those who perform good for selfish motives receive the odious title "hypocrite" (6:1–4).

3.3. Jesus as Fulfillment of the Law (5:17–48)

3.3.1. Basic Principle (5:17–20). Often the opponents of Jesus criticized him for not keeping the minutiae of the traditional observances of the Jewish law. Here Jesus makes it clear that he is not out to destroy the law but to fulfill it and even intensify it. He sets higher standards. His major concern is why a law exists; he insists that keeping of law begins with the attitude of the heart. By this principle Jesus simultaneously affirms the value of the people and the law. In this respect he fulfills the law as anticipated by Jeremiah: "I will put my law in their minds and write it on their hearts. I will be their God, and they will be my people" (Jer. 31:33b).

As the successor to Moses, Jesus gives the final word on the law. But what does Jesus mean when he says he *fulfills* the law? It does not mean that he merely observed it. Nor does it mean that he annulled the Old Testament and its laws (as suggested by Marcion and the Gnostic heretics). The work of Jesus and his church are firmly rooted in previous salvation history. In one sense Jesus gave the law a fuller expression, and in another he transcended the law since he became the embodiment of its fulfillment. Matthew views fulfillment of the law in Jesus similar to the fulfillment of Old Testament prophecy: The new is like the old, but the new is greater than the old. Not only does the new fulfill the old but it transcends it. Jesus and his law of the new kingdom are the final intent, destination, and goal of the law.

Notice the emphatic wording of Jesus in not abolishing the law (v. 18). "I tell you the truth," "truly," or (as the KJV puts it) "verily" appears at the beginning of Jesus' most emphatic statements. This Greek word (*amen*) is simply transliteration from the Hebrew word Jesu spoke into Greek, and it has become special ized Christian language, denoting sacred affir mation. Jesus then asserts that not an iota, th smallest letter, nor a serif or a flourish on a let ter, will by any means pass away until all i accomplished.

It appears as if the manner in which Jesu fulfills the law varies according to the type c law. Many ritual laws are complete in Jesus sacrifice (cf. the letter to the Hebrews) an therefore no longer need to be observed. Jesu himself saw dietary laws as fulfilled sinc defilement comes from the heart (Mark 7:18 19; Acts 10:10–16; Gal. 2:11–14). Other law are fulfilled in Jesus' reinterpretation and reap plication in the spirit of an internalized heart felt law, as happens in his revolutionar interpretations of the old law set forth in th following sections of Matthew 5.

Those who minimize the significance of th old apart from Jesus' reinterpretation of the lav will be called least in the kingdom (5:19). Th word *lyo* (v. 19) can mean relax (RSV), brea (NIV), or annul (NASB). Later when Gnosticisr despised the material world and segregate salvation to a spiritual, mythical, or nonhistor ical venue, the early church fathers quickl insisted on the validity of God's working sal vation in time, space, and history as demon strated in the Old Testament. Without th historical context, precedent, and promise c the old, the declaration of the new can mea anything that any self-appointed prophet want it to mean.

Any presupposition that Jesus was perpet uating mere legalism and raising the legalisti ante evaporates in the heat of Jesus' warnin in verse 20: "For I tell you that unless your righ teousness surpasses that of the Pharisees an teachers of the law, you will certainly not ente the kingdom of heaven." The issue was th quality and end of the law, not its quantity.

3.3.2. Anger and Murder (5:21–26). Jesu also buries any assumption of antinomianisr on his part. He shows that fulfillment mus exceed the mere letter of the law and that thi fulfillment must come from the heart. Heartfel observance of the law will exceed any tradi tional formula for a punctilious observance.

The true battle for the law of the kingdor is not in mere outward actions or goin through the motions, no matter how detailed they are; rather, the battle is won or lost in the heart, the seat of the will. "The first step in becoming a saint is to will it" (Francis de Sales). Most sin is premeditated; early and sometimes drastic action is required to prevent the seed from taking root and giving a bitter harvest. Thus Jesus' remedies will seem to some extreme, but malignancy must be isolated and removed early for the best chance of recovery. Prevention is paramount.

The passive "it was said" (vv. 21, 28, 31, 33, 38, 43) is a deferential way of saying, "God said" (a Jewish way of respecting the name of God, an important issue for the Jewish community to which Matthew wrote). Jesus follows this phrase up with a portion of the Old Testament law. Then comes his startling statement: "But I [*ego* emphatic] say unto you . . . " (KJV), in which he intensifies the law. This is the structure for the next six sections. Jesus is functioning as the good teacher he describes later who brings out of his storeroom treasures old and new (Matt. 13:52).

The prohibition in verse 21 is not killing in general but murder, killing that is contrary to the law. Jesus intensifies the law by coming to the heart of the matter: the human will. Murder starts with anger; one must deal with the anger to avoid murder. One aspect of anger can be expressed through words. *Raca* is an Aramaic word that literally means "empty one" and was applied in uncomplimentary ways. Jesus forbids its use and says that this infraction makes one "answerable to the Sanhedrin" (i.e., to judgment). To use the word "fool" (*moros*) is to risk the "fire of hell [*geenna*]." Since *raca* and *moros* are presented in parallel structure and since elsewhere the Greek *moros* was used to translate the Aramaic *raqá*, it is not clear if one is more offensive than the other. To ruminate over the difference in intensity of the two words is to miss the point: Jesus forbids either.

Jesus takes this rule beyond the boundaries of his contemporaries. At the Qumran community, impudent or blasphemous speech could result in having a reduction of one's food ration for up to a year, being shunned, and in some cases being expelled from the community (1QS 6:23–7:5, 15–18). Jesus takes the offense to the precipice of hell. Matthew's use of *geenna* for hell is typically Jewish. In the Valley of Hinnom (from which *ge-henna* is derived) where human sacrifice to foreign gods once occurred, the Jews of Jerusalem burned their garbage; hence it became a symbol for a fiery, irrevocable curse.

Jesus expects his followers to deal quickly with strife. Before sacrificing at the altar in the temple, one is to leave an offering and go to those whom one has offended, settle things, and then return to sacrifice (vv. 23–24). Jesus then advises settling with one's legal adversary before a judge acts on the case. At first sight it appears that Jesus is merely offering good legal advice; but given the previous context, he is probably using an example of conventional legal wisdom to encourage his disciples to settle things before God's final judgment!

3.3.3. Adultery and Divorce (5:27–32). Jesus again addresses one of the Ten Commandments and asserts his greater authority to interpret it. Like some of his contemporaries he goes to great lengths to curb this vice. Some Pharisees would shut their eyes or walk with their heads bent down lest they look at a woman. But Jesus identifies the heart as the chief offending part of a human being, for the heart is the seat of the will, the imagination, and the intent of a person, although the eye does play a part. Jesus is not condemning natural sexual attraction but lust or lurid desire (v. 28). Jesus' message is clear: If one deals with the intent of the heart, then the eye will take care of itself.

To make his point, Jesus resorts to overstatement: "Gouge . . . out [the eye]," and, "Cut . . . off [the right hand]" (vv. 29–30). Jesus is not calling for dismemberment, for the battle is in the heart. Temptation is to be avoided because nothing less than the sacrifice of the whole person in hell is at stake.

Matthew presents the pronouncement of Jesus on divorce with the same formula he used earlier: "It was said . . . but I say to you. . . ." In Jesus' reassessment of the divorce laws of the day he shows his high view of marriage, its sanctity, and its indissolubility. He refers to the certificate of divorce from the Old Testament law (Deut. 24:1–4). Classically, the rabbinic schools of Hillel and Shammai demonstrate the antithetical positions that existed in Judaism. Rabbi Hillel said that a woman could be divorced by her husband for anything that displeased him, even burning his dinner! Rabbi Shammai said only sexual offenses attested by a witness could warrant a wife being sent away. Jesus identifies with Shammai, stating that any divorce on grounds other than unchastity (*porneia*) would be tantamount to being a party to adultery. *Porneia* can mean adultery, sex before marriage, incest, or the like; hence the NIV translates the exception clause of Jesus as "marital unfaithfulness." This exception clause is not a new proviso but expresses that discovered infidelity creates a de facto state of divorce (France, 1985, 124).

In the subsequent adulterous state of the woman who is remarried to a new mate, the fault is placed at the feet of the first man who, according to Jesus, gets a frivolous divorce. He precipitates an adulterous state of the remarried woman (who then may have had no say in the second marriage, given her social status). Later when Jesus pressed this stringent view of divorce, the Pharisees asked, "Why then . . . did Moses command that a man give his wife a certificate of divorce and send her away?" He responded that Moses tolerated this practice because "your hearts were hard." Jesus held to the precedent of natural law when he instructed the people that the Creator intended husband and wife to be one flesh and never to be separated (Matt. 19:4–11). In the present passage, Jesus says that any man divorcing his wife for any reason except marital unfaithfulness and then marrying another commits adultery. God's will is the permanence of marriage on this earth. Thus Malachi writes that God says that couples are one flesh and that he "hate[s] divorce," especially because of its effect on children (Mal. 2:14–16).

3.3.4. Oaths (5:33–37). Matthew presents the "it was said . . . but I say . . ." formula for a fourth time. In his comment on the old law Jesus makes a major adjustment. Oaths were allowed and in some instances demanded (e.g., Num. 5:19), but Jesus forbade the use of oaths. His use of the adverb *holos* ("at all," Matt. 5:34) indicates that he expected this activity to cease completely. Oaths alluding to God indirectly by referring to heaven, earth, and even one's self were forbidden, a stance that respects God's transcendence and immanence all the more. Jesus' moratorium on oaths and vows also eliminates the fulfillment of rashly taken and foolish vows. He strikes out at the heart of the issue: An honest person has no need to take an oath; a yes or no should be sufficient (see also James 5:12).

3.3.5. Retaliation and Rights (5:38–42). Jesus again intensifies the force of the old law, transcends it, and therefore fulfills the heart of it. The principle of an eye for an eye and a tooth for a tooth was common in the ancient Near East and was designed to keep blood feuds in check (Ex. 21:24–25; Lev. 24:20; Deut. 19:21). Jesus, however, calls for his followers not to assert their rights, to "resist not evil" (KJV). He is not instructing us to passively sit by while evil triumphs or to be an implicit accomplice in physical violence when one can keep it in check. The sense of Jesus' stand for good and attack on evil precludes such an idea. Given the context that follows, it appears that he is calling his disciples to reject their legitimate rights to property and redress of grievances. "Evil" in this context is not so much the devil or the opposite of the ideal good, but the one who wants to deprive the disciple of dignity or property unjustly.

The examples that follow are just that, examples of how to live out the principle. But what is that principle? It is not that disciples of Jesus are to be pushed around at will or that they are not as important. The answer lies in those crucial beatitudes, the keys to unlocking the meaning of the rest of the Sermon on the Mount. "Blessed are the meek, for they will inherit the earth." The meek, the poor in spirit, understand that they are totally reliant on God for sustenance and not on the ephemeral and illusory resources of this world's institutions. St. Basil, when threatened by Modestus, the emperor's henchman, with confiscation of his property, retorted, "How can you threaten a man who is dead to this world? Apart from my clothes and few books I have nothing. As to death it hastens me to where I desire to be" (Gregory's *Panegeric of Basil*).

The greater issue is not "my rights" but the affairs of God's kingdom. One can be legally correct in a lawsuit, yet end up totally enmeshed in materialism. "Something so good has happened to us that nothing by comparison can be as bad again" (Rev. Robert J. Stamps). The disciples can hold lightly to this world's goods because they know that God will provide for them. God is their source, their foundation; all else is shifting sand.

"Do not resist" can mean "do not take legal action against" and is probably the intent of the text. To strike on the right cheek refers to a backhand, which in the ancient Near East was most insulting, not to mention painful. To offer the other cheek would have been a most surprising response. Jesus suffered the same abuse in his trial (26:67) and fulfilled the abuse of the Suffering Servant of Isaiah (Isa. 50:6). Moreover, if a litigant wants to take your tunic (the inner garment), give him your outer garment as well (Matt. 5:40). This was specifically forbidden in the law so that no one would have to suffer from the cold (Ex. 22:25–27). Amos condemned the wicked rich in Israel for retaining the cloaks of the poor at night as surety on a debt (Amos 2:8). Yet Jesus in effect says, "Do not even avail yourself of your basic rights."

"To go one mile" refers to the much resented practice of the Roman occupying forces in the Holy Land who could require citizens to carry their pack 1,000 paces. Under this rule of forced labor Simon of Cyrene was compelled to carry the cross of Jesus (Matt. 27:32). When Jesus suggested that they willingly go two miles, he did not endear himself or his disciples to the Zealot revolutionaries, who practiced violent resistance to the Roman occupation. It was tantamount to collaboration with the enemy! On the heels of these unjust appropriations of property comes Jesus' command to give to the one begging from you. Christians are to be known for their generosity. God can be trusted to meet his children's needs; that is why acting like the merciful God who has forgiven them and provided for them is possible.

3.3.6. Love for One's Enemies (5:43–48). The Old Testament specifically calls for love of one's neighbor; Leviticus 19:18 makes it clear that the neighbor is a fellow Israelite. Luke 10:29–37 expands the definition of a "neighbor" to include anyone in need, even a despised foreigner. There is no explicit command to hate one's enemies, but the attitude is commended in Psalm 139:21: "Do I not hate those who hate you, O LORD?" (see also Deut. 30:7; Ps. 26:5; 137:7–9). The Qumran Manual of Discipline required all in the Dead Sea community "to love all the children of light . . . and hate all the children of darkness" (1QS 1:9–10; see also 1:4). The LXX version of Psalm 139:22 says, "I hate them with a perfect [*teleion*] hate." Contrast this with Matthew's conclusion of this passage, "Be perfect [*teleioi*], therefore, as your heavenly Father is perfect" (5:48). For Jesus perfection or completion included love of enemies.

Jesus includes traditional enemies as objects of love. These enemies are identified as persecutors in the parallel structure of verse 44. Matthew often raises the topic of persecution. More than avoidance of conflict Jesus calls his disciples to love those who want to destroy them, just as he did in forgiving his enemies from the cross (Luke 23:34), and just as Stephen did at his execution (Acts 7:60). Note the profound effect of both on Saul of Tarsus.

The mark of a true child "of your Father in heaven" (v. 45) is to have the heart of the Father. Note the indictment of the older brother in Luke's parable of the prodigal son because he refused to love his errant brother (Luke 15:25–31). So too Jesus calls for unconditional love. Loving forgiveness received from God requires that loving forgiveness be given to others (Matt. 6:12; 18:21–35). As proof that this is God's intent, Jesus relates that the Father sends needed sun and rain to both the righteous and unrighteous (v. 45). Liking one's own kind is not extraordinary, for even the nefarious "tax collectors" and "pagans" do the same (vv. 46–47).

"Be perfect" (v. 48) parallels Deuteronomy 18:13, that one should "be perfect [*teleios*, LXX] with the LORD" (KJV). The English word "perfect," defined as "faultless, incapable of error," has caused some Christians to despair over the teachings of Jesus, assuming that the standard is impossibly high for mere humans. Yet the problem is in the English, not in the Greek. *Teleios* means "completeness" or "wholeness," becoming what one was designed for. Jesus intends this as a summary or the goal of the previous passages. As children resemble their fathers so disciples are to resemble in miniature their loving heavenly Father. The issue is not infallible perfection but obeying and imitating the Father and thus fulfilling their reason for being.

This completion or goal of the old law is fulfilled in the disciples, who live out Jesus' completion of the old. We are called to be different in regard to anger, murder, lust, adultery, divorce, oaths, truthfulness, revenge, personal rights, and property in regard to both neighbors and those who hate us. We are called to be different not just in what we do but in our motives. The disciple of Jesus becomes complete as he or she exhibits the beatitude, "pure in heart."

3.4. Acts of Righteousness (6:1–18)

Only Matthew of the Gospel writers presents these sayings of Jesus concerning giving, praying, and fasting, all of which were basic requirements of Judaism: "Prayer with fasting is good, but better than both is almsgiving with righteousness" (Tob. 12:8, NRSV). These basic acts of righteousness were perpetuated in Christianity and assimilated in Islam. Jesus continues the theme he had in chapter 5, namely, righteousness (one of Matthew's major concerns). What he highlights on this issue hails back to the beatitudes, the DNA code for building the kingdom: purity of motive and integrity. The true subjects of God's kingdom are the poor in spirit, the pure in heart, the meek who solely serve righteousness. Jesus contrasts his understanding of righteousness with the popular notions of his day.

Jesus begins this part of the Sermon on the Mount with a solemn warning: "Be careful not to do your 'acts of righteousness' before men, to be seen by them" (6:1). In the Greek text the word "righteousness" (*dikaiosyne*) is moved forward for emphasis and the phrase is translated literally, "the righteousness of you not to do before men." Righteousness is not just a state of being, but also an action, something that one *does*. Given the negative context that follows, the NIV appropriately translates the reference to righteousness using quote marks in order to call its validity into question: Are good deeds done for self-aggrandizement true "acts of righteousness"?

3.4.1. Alms (6:1–4). Here Jesus is assuming that giving to the poor is the norm. He does not say, "*if* you give," but "*when* you give." His caution here is against giving to the poor with the wrong motives. The reason Jesus gives for low-visibility charity is that ostentatious largess does not result in a reward "from your Father in heaven." Matthew frequently raises the issue of payment and reward. The noun "reward" (*misthos*, sometimes trans. "wages"), occurring twenty-nine times in the New Testament, is found ten times in Matthew; the verb "to reward" (*apodidomi*, v. 4), occurring forty-eight times in the New Testament, is found eighteen times in Matthew. Usually these teachings on payment and reward for both good deeds and bad are set in the context of end-time judgment.

Jesus calls those who give for the wrong reasons "hypocrites" (*hypocrites*). This is strong language to describe the activities of his enemies even though earlier he warned against indiscriminate epithets (5:22). Self-deluding activities draw sharp criticism from Jesus, and he finds it necessary to awaken people to their peril. *Hypocrites* was originally used to describe actors—appropriate here since the ostentatious donor is playing to an audience. Pointing out such hypocrisy occupies much of Matthew's attention. Of the eighteen times *hypokrites* appears in the New Testament, fourteen are in his Gospel. It almost becomes a synonym for Jesus' enemies: "teachers of the law and Pharisees, you hypocrites" (e.g. 23:13, 15, 23, 25, 27, 29).

The verb "to be seen" (*theaomai*, v. 1) implies a "show"; it originates from the same word family from which comes the word "theater." This "theatrical righteousness" might deceive human beings, but the act is devoid of the pure motive of honoring God through right living (Bruner, 1998a, 229). To "announce it with trumpets" (v. 2) is a figurative expression meaning "to draw attention to someone," for there is no evidence that Pharisees ever came onto the public "stage" with literal trumpets blaring. In their almsgiving they sought their own glorification from other people rather than giving to the poor as an act of thankfulness made to the glory of God.

What follows in Matthew is quintessentially Jesus: "I tell you the truth [*amen*], they have received their reward in full" (v. 2). "They have received" has an accounting sense, indicating that full payment has been made and a receipt has been given. Their contract has been fulfilled; they have gotten what they bargained for—a deceived audience. But God is not deceived (Gal. 6:3, 7). The object of affection for the pure almsgiver is primarily God. The righteousness exceeding that of the Pharisees (cf. Matt. 5:20) preeminently seeks to please God.

Another subject that often appears in Matthew's presentation of Jesus' teachings and is repeated in our text is the word "hidden" or

JEWISH SECTS

Pharisees

Their roots can be traced to the second century B.C.—to the Hasidim.

1. Along with the Torah, they accepted as equally inspired and authoritative, all material contained with the oral tradition.
2. On free will and determination, they held to a mediating view that made it impossible for either free will or the sovereignty of God to cancel out the other.
3. They accepted a rather developed hierarchy of angels and demons.
4. They taught that there was a future for the dead.
5. They believed in the immortality of the soul and in reward and retribution after death.
6. They were champions of human equality.
7. The emphasis of their teaching was ethical rather than theological.

Sadducees

They probably had their beginning during the Hasmonean period (166–63 B.C.). Their demise occurred c. A.D. 70 with the fall of Jerusalem.

1. They denied that the oral law was authoritative and binding.
2. They interpreted Mosaic law more literally than did the Pharisees.
3. They were very exacting in Levitical purity.
4. They attributed all to free will.
5. They argued there is neither resurrection of the dead nor a future life.
6. They rejected a belief in angels and demons.
7. They rejected the idea of a spiritual world.
8. Only the books of Moses were canonical Scripture.

Essenes

They probably originated among the Hasidim, along with the Pharisees, from whom they later separated (1 Maccabees 2:42; 7:13). They were a group of very strict and zealous Jews who took part with the Maccabeans in a revolt against the Syrians, c. 165–155 B.C.

1. They followed a strict observance of the purity laws of the Torah.
2. They were notable for their communal ownership of property.
3. They had a strong sense of mutual responsibility.
4. Daily worship was an important feature along with a daily study of their sacred scriptures.
5. Solemn oaths of piety and obedience had to be taken.
6. Sacrifices were offered on holy days and during sacred seasons.
7. Marriage was not condemned in principle but was avoided.
8. They attributed all that happened to fate.

Zealots

They originated during the reign of Herod the Great c. 6 B.C. and ceased to exist in A.D. 73 at Masada.

1. They opposed payment of tribute for taxes to a pagan emperor, saying that allegiance was due only to God.
2. They held fierce loyalty to the Jewish traditions.
3. They were opposed to the use of the Greek language in Palestine.
4. They prophesied the coming of the time of salvation.

"secret" (*kryptos*) and the corresponding verb "to hide" (*krypto*). Eventually all things will be revealed, and the secrets will be known in God's final accounting (e.g., 10:26). Both hypocrisy and hidden righteousness will be revealed. "Do not let your left hand know what your right hand is doing" (6:3) is an obvious hyperbole. Its message is clear: Do not flaunt good deeds.

3.4.2. Prayer and the Lord's Prayer (6:5–15).

3.4.2.1. Secret Prayer (6:5–6). Again, Jesus uses the strong word "hypocrite" to show his disciples the antithesis of proper righteousness. Standing was an accepted posture for prayer among the Jews—that is not being condemned. Nor is public prayer the sticking point; Jesus prayed in the presence of other people (e.g., 11:25–26) as did the early church (e.g., Acts 4:24, 31). Jesus is more concerned about the contrived orchestration of religiosity. Apparently the ostentatious members of the Pharisees would engineer their appearances in crowded places to "show off" their piety at the appointed time of prayer. Jesus repeats word for word his solemn warning: "I tell you the truth [*amen*], they have received their reward in full" (v. 5).

Jesus calls his disciples to avoid the temptation of spiritual exhibitionism by retiring to their homes into the inner room (*tamieion*, usually the most central, secure, secluded room in a Jewish home), shutting or locking the door. There they are to begin to pray to their Father in secret, and the Father who continually sees will reward them (6:6).

3.4.2.2. Vain Prayer (6:7–8). Not only does Jesus warn his disciples against praying like the Pharisees, he also advises them against praying as the Gentiles do, "who keep on babbling," assuming that they will be heard "because of their many words" (6:7). Babbling (*battalogeo*) occurs only here in the New Testament. The NIV translators assume it means continual babbling because of the context that follows. Yet in the rare instances of it in other contemporary literature, it can mean foolish talk (BAGD, 137).

Jesus is not uttering a prohibition against all repetition in prayer; otherwise the Psalms would have to be discarded, and Jesus' prayer in Gethsemane would violate his own principle. Elsewhere Jesus taught that people "should always pray and not give up," in the context of repetitive prayer (Luke 18:1–8). He also said, "Keep on asking, and it will be given you," again in the context of prayer (Matt. 7:7 pers. trans.). The KJV does well when it translates Matthew 6:7, "Use not vain repetitions." The reference to Gentiles here (*ethnikos*, NIV "pagans") is often used in Matthew in a negative sense (see also 5:47; 18:17).

What great comfort it is to know that God knows our needs before we ask. The issue at stake here is not repetition but relationship. The prophets of Baal called and called on their god thinking their loudly repeated cries and self-mutilation would win his attention and favor. Elijah, who knew the true God, prayed simply and briefly, and fire came down from heaven (1 Kings 18:25–29). The pagans in Jesus' world often recited many divine names in their prayers in hope of contacting one sympathetic entity in an attempt to gain power over the deity. This practice of magic or manipulation is specifically forbidden in Judaism and Christianity. Current attempts to "use" the name of Jesus merely to get whatever one wants smacks more of this pagan practice than genuine attempts to pray (cf. Acts 19:13–17). Repetition and decibels do not make God better able to hear us. A god with an attention deficit and a hearing impairment is a pagan concept. A good father attentively stands ready to listen for the cry of his own children.

3.4.2.3. The Lord's Prayer (6:9–15). Jesus does not leave his disciples with just a list of prohibitions, nor does he leave them to their own devices in prayer. Rather, he gives a specific pattern for prayer. Some consider the Lord's Prayer a mere outline and therefore refuse to pray it as a rote prayer. Surely Jesus intended extempore prayers to grow out of his example, but there is nothing in this passage or the Lukan parallel (Luke 11:1–4) to prohibit using these words of Jesus in corporate and private prayer. The church that succeeded the apostolic era understood that this prayer was to be recited together in worship services and believed that they were preserving the pattern of worship established by the apostles.

The Lord's Prayer was an integral part of the communion service in the early church, as is attested by Jerome, Ambrose, Augustine, and Cyril. The Didache quotes the Lord's Prayer and instructs the faithful to pray in this manner three times a day (Didache 8:2–3). This document is usually dated at the end of the first century and the beginning of the second century.

Both Matthew and Luke include versions of the Lord's Prayer. Matthew's context is in the Sermon on the Mount, with the disciples and the crowds listening. Luke's version happens at an undisclosed place and apparently in a more intimate private time when the disciples, seeing Jesus at prayer, said, "Lord, teach us to pray, just as John taught his disciples" (Luke 11:1). Apparently Jesus' disciples were asking him to teach them a prayer that, like the Baptist movement's prayer, would identify them distinctively as followers of Jesus. In other words, what is the agenda for his kingdom in prayer? Luke's version is shorter than the one in Matthew, but both versions may have come directly from Jesus himself since he went from village to village teaching, undoubtedly with variations and inspired adjustments occurring as he spoke.

Some of what Jesus taught in this prayer was original while other parts were firmly grounded in the inspired practice of Judaism. The prayer's basic structure parallels the Aramaic Kaddish, which was used in the synagogue (see Jeremias, 1967, 98):

> Exalted and hallowed be his great name
> in the world which he created according
> to his will.
> May he let his kingdom rule
> in your lifetime and in your days and
> in the lifetime
> of the whole house of Israel speedily
> and soon.
> And to this say: Amen.

The first half of the Lord's Prayer (vv. 9–10) is concerned with honoring God and his kingdom. The second half (vv. 11–13) consists of requests for the personal needs of the disciples. This second part resembles the Jewish prayer of the Eighteen Benedictions in content and structure, yet Jesus' prayers are more concise and brief. We will note some of Jesus' unique contributions as each part of the prayer is analyzed.

3.4.2.3.1. "Our Father in heaven" (6:9a). It was not unusual for Jews to consider God as the Father of Israel, but as the Father of individuals in a special relationship was rather novel. This father/son experience was characteristic of Jesus' relationship with God. Jesus calls God "my Father" thirteen times in Matthew. Earlier in the Sermon on the Mount Jesus tells his followers that they share in a family experience with God as their heavenly Father and others as their brothers (5:9, 16, 22–23, 45, 47–48; 6:1, 3, 6, 8). Although it is a family word, Matthew's "our Father in heaven" is more august than Luke's simple "Father."

In reconstructing the prayer in the original language of Aramaic, Jeremias suggests that Luke's abrupt "Father" may have been "*Abba*" (a familiar term such as the English "papa" or "daddy"; cf. the use of *Abba* in Mark 14:36; Rom. 8:15; Gal. 4:6). This shows Jesus' unique intimacy with the Father. If *Abba* was the original word used by Jesus, then the context in Luke takes on greater meaning: Insofar as the disciples were asking for a special prayer that would identify them as kingdom followers of Jesus distinct from other groups, Jesus is saying that the unique way his followers address God is as their *Abba*. If *Abba* was also intended in Matthew's version, then God is simultaneously intimate and kind, yet powerful and transcendent. Christians at prayer are then climbing into the lap of the Builder of galaxies, stroking his cheek, and making their requests. The key to the relationship between Christians and their God is their approach to him as a loving Father.

3.4.2.3.2. "Hallowed be your name" (6:9b). The force of the word "hallowed" in Hebrew, Aramaic, and Greek is "to be holy" or "to be sanctified." Holiness primarily means to be set aside for a special purpose. In the case of God he is "wholly other." This reflects the Hebrew respect for God's name that is evident at the burning bush, when Moses inquired God's name and received as answer: "I AM WHO I AM" (Ex. 3:14). Moses was not given a name that he could use magically to manipulate God into acceding to his requests. Rather, God responded by affirming his existence. The Jews of Jesus' day trembled at the name of Yahweh and deferentially used *Adonai* (Lord) instead. The name of God and God's person are inseparable in Hebrew thought (e.g., Ex. 3:13–14; Isa. 52:6). Thus to profane God's name was to profane his person. Such pagan-like temerity was expressly forbidden in the Decalogue (Ex. 20:7).

Although Christians have been given the intimate and familiar right to address God as *Abba*, they do not do so presumptuously, for even that familiar name is sacred. He is not an overindulgent parent; as it has been said, "God is your Father, not your grandfather!" In the early church only after a person submitted to an extended period of instruction, prayer, fasting, and baptism were they allowed to pray the sacred prayer at their first communion and say, "Father!"

3.4.2.3.3. "Your kingdom come, your will be done . . ." (6:10). This parallel structure is what one would expect from a first-century Jewish teacher familiar with Hebrew poetry. In synonymous parallelism, the first line is repeated in the second, but the second line often adds reflection and insight on the original thought. So too in this verse. This petition also has a parallel in the Kaddish prayer quoted above. As seen in the parallel structure of the beatitudes, this verse arises out of the earlier parallel petition. God hallows his name by working out his kingdom in saving acts in history so that the inhabitants of earth say, "He is the living God and he endures forever; his kingdom will not be destroyed, his dominion will never end" (Dan. 6:26).

The phrase "your kingdom come" sets a clearly eschatological tone, orienting the hearers to the fulfillment of the end times in the final establishment of God's reign in the world. It calls for an end of any human institution not in conformity to God's will. This was a most revolutionary tenet uttered in the first-century Roman empire. Eventually its followers would defy the great Roman caesars. So too today if this prayer is spoken out and lived out earnestly, it pits the Christian against many accepted institutions and lifestyles.

It is incorrect to assume this call for the advent of God's kingdom to be a mere abdication to the present-day world order until, in the "sweet bye-and-bye," God will eventually get around to correcting the world system. (1) The force of the imperative mood and the aorist tense drives home the immediacy and irrevocability of the demands of God's rule: "*Let* your kingdom come, be it so now and forever." (2) The added phrase "on earth as it is in heaven" balances out the couplet structurally and thematically. The message of Jesus here is not that the kingdom is "somewhere, out there" in a spiritual dimension that does not affect the material, historical world in which we live. The kingdom conceived in the mind of the timeless Maker of time can, must, and will take form in this world even as the reader draws breath over this page. In each moment, in each borrowed breath we take from God, our Lord asks, "Will you let my kingdom come?" To pray sincerely "*Your* kingdom come," the disciple must say, "*My* kingdom go."

This radical kingdom revolution is not only to be visited out on the actions of world governments but also in the present life of each disciple, who is called to live out the life-transforming kingdom by doing the next right thing. The force of the grammar again is: "Let your will be done in my life *now*." This is characteristic of the dual nature of the kingdom of heaven as taught by Jesus and his successors: in one sense it is already, in another yet to come.

3.4.2.3.4. "Give us today our daily bread" (6:11). The first half of the prayer addresses the glory and will of God while the remaining petitions concern the physical needs and spiritual welfare of the disciples. Certainly Jesus intended this prayer to be a model of all Christian prayer not only in content but also in form and in order. It is appropriate that praising God and acknowledging his sovereignty in the world come first in the prayer. Without the first half it resembles a mere shopping list, and God is reduced in some minds to a mere bellhop, who is obligated to cater to every human whim. With all the familial familiarity of the Lord's Prayer, it does not compromise the all-encompassing rule of God. Requests, personal petitions, and intercession should be accompanied by the spirit of thanksgiving (1 Tim. 2:1).

The second half recognizes that the disciples are a needy people, totally dependent on God's gracious provision. Again, this part of the Sermon on the Mount hails back to the initial beatitude, "Blessed are the poor in spirit, for theirs is the kingdom of heaven" (5:3). The truly humble disciple recognizes that he or she is morally and spiritually bankrupt apart from God's example and resources of holy living.

Luke records the word "give" in the present imperative (*didou*) while Matthew records the aorist imperative tense (*dos*). Thus Luke's version means "continually give each day," while Matthew's version appears more urgent: "Give ow our daily bread *today*." The disciple then seen as totally at God's mercy for the next neal.

The word "daily" (*epiousios*) is a rare word oth in the New Testament and in secular writng of the day; it can also mean "tomorrow." The great Latin translator Jerome, writing in he fourth century, notes that the noncanonial Gospel to the Hebrews used the Aramaic vord for tomorrow at this point in the Lord's Prayer. If this is the correct rendering of *epiousios*, then several factors are at work. (1) It nay be an allusion to the end-time banquet of he Messiah. The petitioner is asking for the ulfillment of the kingdom now. The consummation of his kingdom results in food in abundance (e.g., Isa. 55:1–2; 61:1–6).

(2) The request for tomorrow's bread does not necessarily take the edge off the impression that the disciple is totally dependent on God. He has provided for today, may he also provide for tomorrow. A parallel to God's daily provision of manna in the desert is probably intended. In the practical aspect of a Palestinian household in that day, the provision of food the day before would be necessary in the preparation of the food for the coming day.

(3) Bread symbolizes all material need. Jesus explains the necessity of depending on God for basic needs in 6:24–34. Regardless of the original intent of *epiousios* (daily/ tomorrow), both the eschatological and the present application are apparent in Matthew's context.

3.4.2.3.5. "Forgive us our debts . . ." (6:12, 14–15). This part of the prayer expounds on several of the beatitudes. It reflects the initial message of John the Baptist and Jesus in the earlier section of the Gospel (3:8; 4:17). Confession and repentance from sin are marks of the true disciple; self-righteousness and spiritual smugness are severely criticized. The pervasiveness of sin as exposed by Jesus reminds the reader of the "poor in spirit" beatitude because they have committed sin and stand in need of daily forgiveness. This penitential prayer also assumes a sorrow for sins as well as an admission of guilt; thus the second characteristic of discipleship presented in the beatitudes, "Blessed are those who mourn" (5:4), is also evident.

The NIV translation of *opheilema* as "debts" is a literal translation of a word usually referring to financial obligations, but the Semitic original behind it used the word "debt" as an expression for sin. "Trespasses" is probably a better translation. Luke's account of the prayer says, "Forgive us our *sins*" (Luke 11:4), reflecting the original intent. Matthew 6:14–15 indicates that Jesus had in mind sins (*paraptoma*) and not mere financial debts. The Eighteen Benedictions of Judaism also asks for forgiveness from God, but it does not mention the forgiveness of others.

The teaching of Jesus is heavy not only with the good news of God's forgiveness but also with the call to his disciples to emulate the Father and forgive those who have offended them. If the program of the kingdom is forgiveness and restoration, then as ambassadors of the kingdom we are called to participate in the amnesty program even at our own expense (2 Cor. 5:18–20). The disciples' acts of forgiveness are those of the Father through the power of the Holy Spirit: "Receive the Holy Spirit. If you forgive anyone his sins, they are forgiven; if you do not forgive them, they are not forgiven" (John 20:22–23; see also Acts 7:60).

"As we also have forgiven our debtors" also builds on the beatitudes. The forgiving disciples hunger for God's concept of righteousness, which includes mercy and not hot-headed human retribution (5:6). Only the merciful ones will receive mercy (5:7). The ones with pure motives (5:8), the peacemakers (5:9) who may suffer persecution (5:10), will be called "children of the Father," for like him they forgive.

Some Christians have been uncomfortable with the import of this verse since our own forgiveness is apparently contingent on our forgiving others, but this is the significance of the comparative "as" (*hōs*). Furthermore, verses 14–15 make emphatic the cause and effect of forgiving and being forgiven: "Forgive . . . [and] your heavenly Father will also forgive you. . . . Do not forgive . . . [and] your Father will not forgive your sins." Jesus' sobering parable of the forgiven servant who was unforgiving makes the conclusion unavoidable (18:21–35). The forgiveness of the merciless servant is revoked: "This is how my heavenly Father will treat each of you unless you forgive your brother from your heart" (18:35; cf. also Mark 11:25–26; Luke 11:4; James 2:14–26). This is not, however, legalism or salvation by works, for such forgiveness requires a miraculous endowment of God's grace and an enabling that comes from a transformed heart (Rom. 12:1–2; 2 Cor. 5:17).

3.4.2.3.6. "And lead us not into temptation . . ." (6:13a). This request has a parallel in a Talmudic evening prayer, but whether it existed and was used by Jesus in his time we cannot be certain. As in the temptation account (4:1–11), the verb "tempt" (*peirazo*) can mean "test" in a neutral sense as well as "induce to do evil." The former seems more appropriate here. In the sense of proving one's faith, testing is initiated by God (e.g., Gen. 22:1–19; Ex. 15:25; 16:4; Deut. 8:2–6; Ps. 26:2). Testing also results in instruction, in edification, and in a tempering that produces character and results in reward (Sir. 2:1–6; Wis. 3:5; James 1:2, 12; 1 Peter 1:6; Rev. 2:10). Nevertheless, the origin of the testing is not always from God but from evil desires (James 1:14), enemies of the faith, and the devil (Matt. 4:1–11; Luke 4:1–13; 1 Cor. 7:5; 10:6–13); yet God can use it for good (Rom. 8:28).

Testing also has an eschatological dimension that logically follows the request, "Your kingdom come." The Day of the Lord results in a great and terrible judgment as well as great joy and reward. This theme of judgment, separation of the good and bad, frequently appears in Matthew; it is one of his major concerns and reasons for writing his Gospel (3:7–12; 13:24–30, 36–43, 47–50; 25:14–46).

The request to be spared the test is strong with the negated aorist subjunctive, which means, "Do not begin to put us to the test." The disciples wish to avoid temptation not because they do not trust God but because they realize that apart from God they have pitiful resources to resist evil. Hence they also pray for a timely deliverance or rescue from the possibility of temptation by "the evil" or "the evil one." This humble attitude was presented earlier in two of the beatitudes: "Blessed are the poor in spirit" (5:3), which acknowledges total dependency on God in the realm of righteousness, and "blessed are the merciful" (5:7), since the disciples realize that their will and perseverance are small and desperately in need of God's fortification.

3.4.2.3.7. "For yours is the kingdom . . ." (6:13b). The concluding doxology is not found in the earlier and better copies of Matthew, nor is it found in most manuscripts of Luke's parallel. It does appear after the Lord's Prayer in the Didache 8:2 (written c. A.D. 100). The doxology was probably a Christian response of praise and affirmation that followed the Lord's Prayer in worship. Its liturgical form appeared in later Greek copies of Matthew, which the translators of the KJV used.

3.4.3. Fasting (6:16–18). After this instruction on prayer, Matthew returns to the earlier subject of "acts of righteousness" (6:1). The introductory phrase and the structure of the present section resemble the preceding ones: "when you fast," "hypocrites," "I tell you the truth, they have received their reward in full," "obvious to [seen by] men," "your Father . . . will reward you." These are all key words previously occurring in his sections on alms and prayer. Thus Jesus links fasting with almsgiving and prayer. The Jews fasted on the Day of Atonement, New Year's, and a day for observing past national calamities. They also observed individual fasts. The Pharisees fasted twice a week, on Mondays and Thursdays (Luke 18:12; cf. Didache 8:1, which directs Christians to fast on Wednesdays and Fridays, in order not to be associated with "hypocrites").

Fasting was traditionally accompanied by dressing in sackcloth, not bathing, and not anointing the body or head with oil. Apparently some Pharisees were making a show of their fasts by covering the head or applying ample coats of ash and dirt to the face, making them barely recognizable. Jesus identified their motives as seeking human admiration of their extreme abstinence. (Jesus approved of sackcloth and ashes when it marked true repentance, cf. 11:21; Luke 10:13.) God rewards instead a fast that is observed to honor him (such as perhaps receiving ashes on Ash Wednesday as a mark of being a sinner in need of God's mercy).

Fasting is designed to improve one's relationship with God as a time of purging and refining motives. Jesus' experience of fasting in the desert proved to be a time of turbulence and testing. Saints have experienced this too, but they have also reported fasting as a time of purification, cleansing, great spiritual edification, and closeness to God. The crucial question is: "Whose attention am I trying to get in this fast?" Fasting should be more than a mere "crash diet." Those with serious medical conditions should fast only under medical supervision as should those who fast over an extensive period of time.

3.5. Wisdom Sayings (6:19–7:27)

3.5.1. Earthly and Heavenly Treasures (6:19–21). The teaching on doing righteousness has ended, and Jesus now begins a section of wisdom sayings. His first one relates to a favorite topic raised by Matthew. The word "treasure" (*thesauros*) occurs in this Gospel nine out of the seventeen times that it appears in the New Testament. It can refer to material wealth (e.g., 2:11; 13:44), but in most cases indicates a spiritual or heavenly wealth (e.g., 12:35; 13:52; 19:21). The parallelism in the passage bespeaks a Semitic background and may well reflect the antiquity of the saying. Jesus contrasts earthly treasures, which inevitably decompose, with the incorruptibility of heavenly riches. The expression in verse 19 literally translates, "treasure up treasures," intensifying the value of treasure. The thieves "dig through" (lit. trans. of *diorysso*) the earthen houses of the day to find the coins that were often in walls or under floors.

The things we treasure show what things we truly value. The "heart" refers to emotions, will, and intellect (see comments on 5:8).

3.5.2. The Good and Bad Eye (6:22–23). This is one of the more enigmatic sayings of Jesus, for how can darkness be light? The word "single" (*haplous*; NIV, "good") can refer to clear eyesight, the opposite of seeing double. Yet it is also used to connote generosity (e.g., Rom. 12:8; 2 Cor. 8:2; 9:11, 13; James 1:5). The "evil eye" indicates greediness, covetousness, or stinginess (the expression is trans. "envious" in 20:15). Coming on the heels of the treasure saying, Jesus appears to be explaining that one can lay up treasures in heaven by being generous (see on 6:1–4). Darkness being misunderstood as light denotes mistaken presuppositions and value judgments. "How great is that darkness" shows how dangerous this situation is. The chilling words of Milton's Satan come to mind: "Evil be thou my good!" If one persists in calling good evil or evil good, there is no hope for recovery.

3.5.3. Two Masters: God and Money (6:24). No one can be a slave (*douleuo*) to two masters. Only one will be loved, and to only one will the servant be inclined to give attention, especially when the two are God and Money. *Mamonas* ("Money") often bore a negative sense, though it also could refer to material things in a neutral sense. Certainly the love of money and its all-consuming lure are what Matthew has in mind. Again, the words of Milton from *Paradise Lost* (Book 1) enlighten us. When describing the fallen angels in hell building their capital, he personifies the vice:

> Mammon led them on,
> Mammon, the least erected spirit that fell
> From heaven, for even in heaven his
> looks and thoughts
> Were always downward bent,
> admiring more
> The riches of heaven's pavement,
> trodden gold,
> Than aught divine or holy else enjoyed
> In vision beatific. . . .

The reference to "love" and "hate" may be hyperbolic in that God is to be loved more (e.g., Gen. 29:30, 33). This appears to be the case since the money issues that follow are not inherently evil (Matt. 6:25–34). The disciple is not to hate the material world but to avoid materialism and love God above all things.

3.5.4. Care and Worry (6:25–34). "Therefore" (v. 25) identifies the preceding passage as the reason for this one. Since we have a good and caring Master in heaven, the disciples can be generous to others, knowing that he will take care of those who serve him. The word for "worry" (*merimnao*) occurs seven times in this Gospel. "Do not worry" is a message of great comfort from Jesus to the true believer. The present imperative negated here indicates that we should not continue worrying. The word also has the connotation of actively striving; Luke uses it in his account of busy Martha, who was concerned about many things but missed the most important thing (Luke 10:41). Note the use of the verb "run after" to describe this action in verse 32.

Jesus turns the attention of his audience to common and relatively insignificant birds (v. 26), who do not concern themselves with provisions as people do, yet for whom God provides. Since God values human beings more than birds, surely he will provide for the disciples. The description of God as "your heavenly Father" makes the assurance more intensive: Those in relationship with God as his children have his paternal concern and attention. Jesus is not providing rationalization for laziness or irresponsibility (see 25:14–30); rather, he is attacking a type of worry that arises from a lack of faith exhibited in a lifestyle obsessed with provisions.

This symptom of "little faith" (v. 30) betrays a spiritual malady that assumes and acts as though God does not care or is unable to provide. It reflects, in effect, an atheistic presumption, for one acts as though God is not there and aware. The Greek word *psyche* (v. 25; NIV, "life") can refer to soul, but it also refers to life in general, even though it is put in parallel with "the body."

The KJV translates *helikia* (v. 27; NIV, "life") as "stature," but it probably refers to age or life span since a cubit of height (eighteen inches) would be significant, but an hour added to a life span would not, and Jesus is showing here that excessive worry does not produce significant benefits. As medical science has since revealed, undue worry and stress actually reduce life span.

In verses 28–31, Jesus presents another reason for not worrying. Lilies do not work, yet God clothes them resplendently. "Solomon in all his splendor" was also mentioned in rabbinic writings. The marvels of Solomon's wealth amazed both Israelites and pagans (1 Kings 9:26–10:29), yet his robes were "shabby" in comparison to one lily clothed by God.

Jesus contrasts the short-lived yet well-clothed flowers and grasses used as fuel with the more valued disciples. The Old Testament expressed the temporary character of these plants in relation to the brevity of life (e.g. Ps. 37:2; 90:5–6; 102:11; 103:15; Isa. 40:6–8). Jesus promises that the Father will do "much more" for his children. He describes the worrying disciples as "you of little faith" (*oligopistoi*, lit., "little-faithed ones"). This word occurs five times in Matthew (six times in the entire New Testament); Jesus uses it to chide and correct his disciples. Little faith betrays ignorance, is ineffective, and creates great peril (see 8:26; 14:31; 16:8; 17:20). Faith essentially is trust here. St. Francis of Assisi trusted in God's provision so much that when he met a beggar with a cloak in worse shape than his own, he traded with him.

In verses 31–32, Jesus forbids the wringing of hands in worry, wondering how we will survive. With his assessment of such worry he chides his Jewish audience, "for the pagans [*ethne*, Gentiles] run after all these things" (v. 32). The implication is to quit acting like pagans. The present tense for "run after" or "seek" describes a lifestyle. "Your heavenly Father knows that you need them" identifies the pagan action as faithless with God. The intimate relationship with the good heavenly Father assures his children that he knows their every need and is quite willing to act out his love in providing for them.

In verses 33–34, the word "first," moved forward in the Greek to provide emphasis, shows that the issue is not whether one should work but rather what one's priority should be. The concerns of the kingdom must be foremost in the disciples' minds. The force of the present imperative "seek" shows it is a constant concern and activity of the disciple. Just as the pagan consumes all of his time pursuing financial security, the disciple constantly advances the kingdom above all else; the kingdom's cause becomes our passion. When this priority is established, the provision of the kingdom follows.

The goal of the kingdom is "righteousness" (see comments on 5:6). Jesus radically redefines this as more than legalistic justice. The righteousness of God allows for forgiveness and pardon. It offers mercy where it is undeserved, even to the greatest offenders. The world finds such a brand of justice scandalous. This lifestyle of seeking kingdom righteousness builds on the beatitude Jesus presented at the beginning of his sermon: "Blessed are the ones continually hungering and thirsting after righteousness" (5:6, pers. trans.); he promised that they would be "filled." We see that this fullness includes physical provision as well.

The disciple is commanded not to worry about tomorrow. Establishing the kingdom can be performed only today; tomorrow is not promised. The present, not the past or future, is where we come into contact with eternity. Each day has enough trouble or bad things (*kakia*, v. 34) to keep one busy. This does not mean the disciple is not to plan; even Jesus planned and moved toward a goal and destiny in Jerusalem.

3.5.5. Do Not Judge or Be Judged (7:1–5). This passage is one of the most misunderstood and misquoted sayings of Jesus. Often when one wants to preclude any criticism of one's attitudes, actions, or lifestyle, objections are met with "judge not." This clearly is *not* what Jesus intended. He expects value judgments to be made, right and wrong to be identified, and worthy and unworthy to be discerned, as can be seen in the verses that follow (esp. v. 6). The disciple must be able to see fault in a brother or sister so that such a person can be brought to kind yet uncompromising correction (cf. 18:15–17). Jesus never called for good and bad to be relative ideas determined by each person. The whole prophetic tradition calls for discernment and correction. God's offer of forgiveness does not involve unrepentant libertinism.

What Jesus does forbid in this passage is faultfinding, condemnation, and the spirit of hypocrisy. The present imperative here for "do not judge" (or "stop judging") indicates a lifestyle and a habitual attitude of condemnation. Such an attitude precludes mercy and subjects the participant to the same exacting, remorseless justice. The phrase "with the measure you use, it will be measured to you" (v. 2) connotes divine retribution and was used as such in Jewish rabbinic works (e.g., M. *Sotah* 1:7). This saying of Jesus hails back to the Lord's Prayer in the previous chapter, in which he made it clear that an unforgiving or condemning spirit revokes the forgiveness already received (6:14–15; cf. 18:23–35).

To expand his teaching against judging, Jesus uses the image of the speck and the plank (vv. 3–5). The plank, or wooden board, is a hyperbole Jesus uses to condemn a person with a plank in his or her eye (i.e., a major fault) trying to extract a bit of sawdust (a minor defect) from someone else's eye. This ridiculous image intensifies the faultiness and self-deception of hypocrisy. Usually Jesus reserves the title "hypocrite" for his enemies, but here he applies it to his disciples. No one is immune to this ethical myopia; thus one must frequently test one's spiritual depth perception.

3.5.6. Dogs and Pigs (7:6). "What is sacred" probably refers to the meat of a holy sacrifice of the temple, which was reserved for the priests and their families (Ex. 29:33; Lev. 2:3; 22:10–16; Num. 18:8–19). Dogs and swine were both unclean animals and were worthy only of unclean food. The early church applied this prohibition to the Eucharist and thus forbade non-Christians to partake. Matthew used the verb "trample" in 5:13 for the trampling of worthless salt. This saying probably has apostasy in view—that is, tainting the treasures of the kingdom with the mire of the world.[5] But with no context for the saying we must consider it one of Jesus' enigmatic sayings. What our context does reveal is that the previous prohibition against judging demonstrates that discernment between holy and profane, good and bad, is *not* to be prohibited.

3.5.7. A Good Father Gives Good Gifts (7:7–11). This passage bears two major messages: persistent prayer and a heavenly Father who wishes to give good gifts to his children. The force of the three present imperative verbs ("ask," "seek," and "knock"), along with the three corresponding present participles in verse 8, indicates that prayer is to be a continuing lifestyle for Christians. The early church imitating Jesus and his Jewish heritage prayed at least three times a day (Did. 8:3). Prayer should be a disciple's very breath. Persistent prayer will be answered (cf. also Luke 11:5–13; 18:1–8). This echoes the message of the persistence of the beatitude, "Blessed are those who hunger and thirst for righteousness" (Matt. 5:6).

Jesus argues from his audience's experience as parents and children to show the goodness of the heavenly Father and his generous attentiveness to the disciples. What parent on earth would meet a child's request for bread with a stone, or for a fish with a dangerous snake? Jesus' question, "Which of you, if his son asks for bread, will give him a stone?" is rhetorical. Sadly, in modern society, this cannot always be taken for granted.

The "evil" in verse 11 may be referring to the depravity of humanity, or it may simply stand to contrast hyperbolically the activities of humans with the ultimate goodness of God. Matthew's version says that the Father gives "good gifts" while Luke says he gives "the Holy Spirit," who is the power and source of all God's blessings (Luke 11:13; on this see Shelton, 1991, 96). The key to understanding this saying lies in experiencing the loving relationship expressed in the phrase "your Father in heaven." The heavenly Father's generosity to his children far exceeds that of the most loving human parent. This teaching reinforces the earlier promises of God's willing provision for the faithful disciple (6:11, 33).

3.5.8. The Golden Rule: The Summary of the Law (7:12). The Golden Rule is one of the best known of Jesus' teachings; many are not aware that it occurs in parallel forms in Greek, Roman, Oriental, and Jewish literature. Loving one's neighbor as oneself is part of the Old Testament law (Lev. 19:18; Matt. 22:39), and similar admonitions appear in the Jewish literature roughly contemporary with Jesus (e.g., Sir. 31:15; Tobit 4:15; 2 Enoch 61:1; Letter of Aristeas 20). Though Matthew and Luke both have versions of the saying, only Matthew includes "for this sums up the Law and the Prophets." Matthew's version closely resembles Rabbi Hillel's dictum spoken just before the time of Jesus: "What is hateful to you do not do to your fellow creature. That is the whole law; all else is commentary" (b. *Sabbath* 31a).

It has been suggested that Jesus was the first to put the saying in its positive form, but it also occurs in Jewish literature as both a positive and a negative commandment. The Christian Didache (c. A.D. 100) cites this saying of Jesus, calls it "the way of life," and links it with the summary of the law in Matthew 22:38–39 (Did. 1:2; see comments on Matt. 22:34–40). The reference to "the Law and the Prophets" stands for the entire Scripture. Jesus places the Golden Rule as the capstone on his description of doing "righteousness," which began with 5:17–20.

3.5.9. Two Ways: The Broad and the Narrow (7:13–14). The two ways of death and life appear in the Old Testament, intertestamental literature, the Qumran writings, and in early Christian literature (Deut. 11:26–28; 30:15–20; Ps. 1:6; 119:29–30; Jer. 21:8; 2 Enoch 30:15; T. Asher 1:3, 5; 4 Ezra 7:1–9; Did. 1:1; 5:1; 1QS 3:20–21). In the Qumran literature the two ways are described as the "way of light" and the "way of darkness." Jesus typically put the options before his audience in antithetical parallelism: a gate to life or a gate to death. The majority of people take the easy way out, which proves disastrous. The gate to life is difficult and restricting; the true disciples are a minority. Given the Matthean context, the difficulty of the narrow gate is the way of righteousness in which Jesus has just instructed the people.

3.5.10. True and False Prophets (7:15–23). Jesus' warning about false prophets has a timely lesson for the modern church. Only Matthew records the warning about false prophets, who are wolves in the clothing (*endyma*) of sheep (*probaton*). These two words are part of Matthew's preferred vocabulary: He uses *endyma* to describe clothing as a basic need (6:25, 28) and specifically to identify people wearing unique garments as part of the kingdom of God (3:4; 22:11–12; see also 28:2–3); he uses *probaton* to describe the elect or the people of Israel (e.g., 10:6; 15:24; 25:32–33). Jesus emphasizes here that sometimes false prophets cannot be discerned by words or actions alone. Even though they perform great miracles (7:22), they can be counterfeits.

Matthew's Gospel makes the fruit of the prophets the true test of their ministries. Character is essential. The Evangelist often discusses good and bad trees and their fruit; his interest in producing righteousness compels him to repeat these themes. John the Baptist describes the unrepentance of the Pharisees and Sadducees as a bad tree (cf. 3:8–12). In 12:33–35 Jesus links the Pharisees' accusation that he does good by the power of evil to bad fruit and calls it the blasphemy against the Holy Spirit.

First-century Christian communities frequently had to regulate prophecy (e.g., 1 Cor. 12–14; 2 Peter 2:1; 1 John 4:1–3). It was a part of the common life and worship of the early church and extended into subsequent centuries (see the Didache, Shepherd of Hermas, Ignatius, Ireneaus, Tertullian, Montanism, and Cyprian). In some communities the test for prophecy dealt with the proto-Gnostic denial of the flesh of Jesus Christ (1 John 4:1–3) or the spirit of legalism (Gal. 1:8–9). Here Matthew identifies the fruit of the error as antinomianism, calling these people "evildoers" (Matt. 7:23). Presumably false prophecy unaccompanied by the fruit of doing righteousness was a problem in Matthew's Christian community. The Didache also judges prophets as to whether they have or do not have "the behavior of the Lord." Even if they perform miracles, doctrine and lifestyle are the criteria for discernment (Did. 11:7–12).

The disciples will not be judged by what they say (e.g., "Lord, Lord") or by wonders they perform but by their character lived out in this world (see also the parable of the sheep and goats in 25:31–46). Jesus maintains that mercy given will be met with mercy (5:7; 6:14). This can never be mere works of righteousness since true believers know how desperately they too are in need of mercy, God's mercy (5:7; 6:12). Matthew probably intends the title of "Lord" (*kyrios*) to be more than a title of mere respect (i.e., "Sir"), since he is writing after Jesus' resurrection and since Jesus presumes the divine prerogative of the end-time judge (7:23).

The phrase "on that day" (v. 22) refers to the judgment day (cf. 24:36; Luke 10:12). Note also Matthew's characteristic "kingdom of heaven" (Matt. 7:21; see the Introduction and comments on 5:3). This "rule of God" requires acts of mercy as a sign that God's mercy has been received in the heart, for his kingdom of mercy is not only designed to extend juridical forgiveness but also to transform the nature, disposition, and character of the recipient.

3.5.11. The Wise and Foolish Builders (7:24–27). This parable is presented in classic parallelism: The wise man builds on rock; the foolish man builds on sand. The flood and storm probably represent both hard times and the end-time judgment (note that God's judgment is described as a flood in Isa. 28:17; Ezek. 13:10–16). Here again Jesus emphasizes behavior: "Everyone who hears these words of mine and puts them into practice is like a wise man" (v. 24). Doing righteousness is an indispensable part of preparing for life's difficult times and for the final judgment. Because we know we have a concerned and forgiving heavenly Father, we can forgive others and be concerned with the affairs of the kingdom of heaven. We know that the Father has our best interests in mind.

3.6. Sermon Epilogue (7:28–29)

That Matthew intends this to be the end of the first major section of Jesus' teaching is clear, for he concludes with the words, "When Jesus had finished saying these things . . ." (v. 28). Each of the five major teaching units that Matthew presents has such a narrative denouement (7:28; 11:1; 13:53; 19:1; 26:1). Jesus is the new Moses, who has five major presentations of the new law or Torah, just as Moses had five books of law in the Pentateuch (see Introduction).

What follows is an observation of the crowds' response to Jesus' teaching, which they recognize as being authoritative, unlike that of their teachers of the law (see also Mark 1:21–27; Luke 4:31–37). Matthew is directing the amazement of the people to Jesus' claims to be the definitive interpreter of the old law and the giver of the new law, whose words will be the basis of judgment in the end-time reckoning.

4. Jesus and Miracles: Narrative (8:1–9:34)

After the extensive section of teaching called the Sermon on the Mount (chs. 5–7), Matthew presents a series of miracles performed by Jesus. These dominate the narrative of chapters 8–9 and are punctuated with intermittent teaching. This is his attempt to flesh out the outline of Jesus' ministry provided earlier, "teaching . . . preaching . . . healing" (4:23). Matthew's attention is fixed more on Jesus' teachings than on his actions, augmenting the material he uses from Mark's Gospel (which is action-oriented). Frequently when more than one Evangelist includes a teaching section, Matthew's version is fuller and more detailed. By stark contrast he abbreviates the miracles from Mark's Gospel in chapters 8–9, providing the barest of details.

4.1. A Leper Cleansed (8:1–4)

Leprosy in the Bible was not just one illness; it included a variety of skin diseases. Jewish law required lepers to be quarantined until they recovered; only after being examined by a priest and making appropriate sacrifices could they be reassimilated into the community (Lev. 13–14). The leper "knelt" (or "worshiped," *proskyneo*) and addressed Jesus as Lord (*kyrios*). Both of these acts probably indicate respect or deference, as a subject bows before a ruler. The vocative *kyrie* can also mean "sir." The leper probably was not privy to the divine nature of Jesus, but for Matthew's readers the words would have greater meaning since they knew of Jesus' resurrection and had heard the apostles' witness to his Lordship.

MIRACLES OF JESUS

	Matthew	Mark	Luke	John
Healing				
Man with leprosy	Mt 8:2–4	Mk 1:40–42	Lk 5:12–13	
Roman centurion's servant	Mt 8:5–13	Lk 7:1–10		
Peter's mother-in-law	Mt 8:14–15	Mk 1:30–31	Lk 4:38–39	
Two men from Gadara	Mt 8:28–34	Mk 5:1–15	Lk 8:27–35	
Paralyzed man	Mt 9:2–7	Mk 2:3–12	Lk 5:18–25	
Woman with bleeding	Mt 9:20–22	Mk 5:25–29	Lk 8:43–48	
Two blind men	Mt 9:27–31			
Man mute and possessed	Mt 9:32–33			
Man with a shriveled hand	Mt 12:10ff	Mk 3:1–5	Lk 6:6–10	
Man blind, mute, and possessed	Mt 12:22		Lk 11:14	
Canaanite woman's daughter	Mt 15:21ff	Mk 7:24–30		
Boy with a demon	Mt 17:14ff	Mk 9:17–29	Lk 9:38–43	
Two blind men (one named)	Mt 20:29ff	Mk 10:46ff	Lk 18:35ff	
Deaf mute		Mk 7:31–37		
Man possessed, synagogue		Mk 1:23–26	Lk 4:33–35	
Blind man at Bethsaida		Mk 8:22–26		
Crippled woman			Lk 13:11ff	
Man with dropsy			Lk 14:1–4	
Ten men with leprosy			Lk 17:11ff	
The high priest's servant			Lk 22:50ff	

MIRACLES OF JESUS (cont.)

	Matthew	Mark	Luke	John
Healing (cont.)				
Official's son at Capernaum				Jn 4:46–54
Sick man, pool of Bethesda				Jn 5:1–9
Man born blind				Jn 9:1–7
Command Over the Forces of Nature				
Calming the storm	Mt 8:23–27	Mk 4:37–41	Lk 8:22–25	
Walking on water	Mt 14:25	Mk 6:48–51		Jn 6:19–21
5,000 people fed	Mt 14:15ff	Mk 6:35–44	Lk 9:12–17	Jn 6:5–13
4,000 people fed	Mt 15:32ff	Mk 8:1–9		
Coin in the fish's mouth	Mt 17:24ff			
Fig tree withered	Mt 21:18ff	Mk 11:12ff, 20–25		
Catch of fish			Lk 5:4–11	
Water turned into wine				Jn 2:1–11
Another catch of fish				Jn 21:1–11
Bringing the Dead Back to Life				
Jairus's daughter	Mt 9:18–19, 23–25	Mk 5:22–24, 38–42	Lk 8:41–42, 49–56	
Widow's son at Nain			Lk 7:11–15	
Lazarus				Jn 11:1–44

Jesus both sets aside and upholds the old law. (1) He touches the leper, which, for the good of the health of the community, was forbidden by Jewish law. Not only does he feel deeply for lepers (cf. Mark 1:41), but he also dares to touch them to show his compassion and to demonstrate his authority over the dreaded illness. Technically this act would have made Jesus ceremonially unclean. When he does so, the leprosy leaves the man immediately. (2) He orders the cleansed leper to show himself to the priest in conformity to the Mosaic law and to make the appropriate sacrifice (Lev. 14:1–32). Jesus fulfills the law by healing the leper, yet he submits to its conventions where appropriate (see comment on 5:17).

Curiously Jesus commands the man to silence (v. 4). Some have assumed that Jesus healed him privately, but the reference to the accompanying crowds render such an idea unlikely (8:1). Jesus frequently forbids recipients of healing to say how they were healed or who healed them. In nineteenth-century liberal scholarship some suggested that this was Mark's (and Matthew's) attempt to explain why Jesus did not claim publicly to be the Messiah in his ministry prior to his crucifixion. They referred to this as "the messianic secret." It seems more probable, however, that Jesus did not want to reveal his identity prematurely since it would—and eventually did—result in his expulsion from the synagogue, forcing his preaching into the open. In the triumphal entry into Jerusalem, Jesus deliberately and publicly did identify himself as the messianic successor to David's throne, and the word of his supernatural power did get out.

The phrase "as a testimony to them" (v. 4; lit., "unto a witness") can indicate: (1) mere compliance with the requirement of the law of Moses that cleansed lepers be examined by priests, (2) Jesus' respect for the Old Testament law, or (3) a witness (*martyrion*) to the ministry of Jesus. It is in this third meaning that Matthew uses the phrase in 10:18 and 24:14.

4.2. Healing of a Centurion's Servant (8:5–13)

Like the leper, the centurion would also have been viewed with disdain since he was a Gentile and part of the powerful military occupation forces of the Jews' hated overlords. Matthew, then, presents the centurion as yet another outcast in the ever-expanding plan of salvation. In Luke 7:4–5 the elders of the Jews intercede with Jesus on behalf of the centurion because of his sympathetic and supportive attitude toward Judaism.

It is unclear in Matthew's Gospel if Jesus responds to the centurion with a statement or a question; it can be read either way. If the former, the presence of the emphatic "I" (*ego*) would show that Jesus is eager to help: "even I will come to heal him." If the latter, the emphatic "I" would mean: "*I* will come to heal him?" expressing a strong reservation. Entering an unclean Gentile home was considered improper. Note that Jesus on several occasions was reticent to begin a ministry among the Gentiles since he was to go to the lost sheep of Israel first; the Gentile mission was to come later (10:5–6; 15:24; 24:14; 28:19–20). Most translations, however, assume that it is a simple statement giving Jesus' assent to accompany the centurion to his house.

The centurion perceives the nature of Jesus' spiritual authority; he sees that it transcends space and commands the obedience of lesser spiritual powers. He asserts that, like a military officer, Jesus only has to give the order and it will be carried out with or without his physical presence. Often the Gospels record that people marvel at Jesus, but here Jesus marvels at the faith of the centurion (8:10)—he has not found such faith in Israel. Jesus then anticipates the future ministry with the Gentiles in noting that many will come "from the east and the west," a phrase used to describe the dispersion of Israel being gathered back to the Holy Land (Ps. 107:3; Isa. 43:5–6; 49:12). These newcomers will sit and eat "with Abraham, Isaac and Jacob in the kingdom of heaven" while the "subjects of the kingdom" are cast out (Matt. 8:12).

Here the racially mixed character of the kingdom is revealed. For the patriarchs to eat with Gentiles would be odious to many Jews since they would be ceremonially unclean. The "feast" here refers to the messianic end-time banquet. The "weeping and gnashing of teeth" expresses ultimate judgment on the unrighteous. The lesson is clear: Faith (i.e., a complete trust and active reliance on Jesus) is the cardinal requirement for entrance into the kingdom. Tradition, racial pedigree, and social standing all give way to trust in the power and goodness of Jesus.

4.3. Peter's Mother-in-Law Healed (8:14–15)

After the healing of the centurion's servant, Jesus enters Peter's house in Capernaum (cf. Mark 1:29–31). This house was probably Jesus' headquarters for his Galilean ministry. Beneath an early Byzantine church in Capernaum, the ruined walls of a first-century Palestinian house have been found, which may well be Peter's house. Later Jesus singles out Peter as the leader of the disciples with singular authority. The point of this healing is that all humanity—Gentiles, Jews, men, women, young, and old—are objects of Jesus' love and merciful power.

4.4. The Sick Healed at Evening (8:16–17)

Matthew presents yet another summary of the character of Jesus' ministry (cf. 4:23–25). He observes that Jesus drove out evil spirits "with a word." Contrast this with the touching related to the earlier healing. Apparently Jesus' preferred method for exorcism was verbal with no physical contact. This is probably not coincidental and should be observed by the church when dealing with such situations. Jesus' worldview includes the possibility of demonic infestation and harassment, a view that today is often summarily dismissed as the product of prescientific superstition, overactive imagination, or mental instability. While some maladies that today are recognized as due to chemical or neurological imbalances were considered in Bible times the result of demon-possession (e.g., epilepsy), the modern world should reconsider the first-century cosmography in regard to the reality and pervasiveness of the supernatural, both good and evil. Reality cannot be limited to mere empiricism.

As Matthew adapts Mark's version of this summary (Mark 1:32–34), he adds a significant section that this event fulfills Old Testament prophecy (Matt. 8:17). Using his characteristic introduction, "this was to fulfill what was spoken through the prophet," he quotes one of Isaiah's Suffering Servant songs, "He took up our infirmities and carried our diseases" (Isa. 53:4; see Introduction: Matthew's Distinctive Issues; also comment on Matt. 1:22–23). Matthew's brevity in describing these miracles demonstrates that he wishes to affirm that Jesus is the teacher with divine authority and that his actions as well as his teaching fulfill prophecy.

4.5. On Following Jesus (8:18–22)

At the height of his popularity Jesus leaves the crowds and crosses the Sea of Galilee. As he prepares to leave, two would-be disciples approach him and declare their intent to follow him. Many scholars believe that for Matthew the trip across the lake is a symbol of true discipleship as distinguished from a fair-weather type, since this crossing the lake story is preceded by a teaching that concentrates on the radical demands of following Jesus.

The first would-be disciple is a teacher of the Mosaic law. As a general rule Matthew presents these teachers as enemies of Jesus. Some commentators see presumption and an overinflated self-assurance in this man's assertion to follow Jesus "wherever you go" (v. 19). On the face of it Jesus' response seems curt. Perhaps he wants to rebuff him to see if he is really sincere or to make it clear that, though God provides for the disciple (6:25–34), following Jesus is not easy.

The teacher of the law addresses Jesus as "teacher." This is in keeping with the use of the title "rabbi" in Jewish circles and with Matthew's emphasis on Jesus as a teacher. Moreover, in Matthew nondisciples usually address Jesus as "teacher" (see also 12:38; 22:16, 24, 36) while disciples call him "Lord." The teacher of the law was probably a prospective disciple, asserting his resolve to follow Jesus to the uttermost, although the possibility remains that he was already a disciple (cf. "another disciple," v. 21).

Jesus' response, "The Son of Man has no place to lay his head," has been interpreted in different ways (v. 20). Perhaps Jesus is completely destitute—that having left Capernaum he is now homeless; or Jesus may be alluding to the fact that he has been rejected by the people. The title "Son of Man" was sometimes used to denote humanity (see Ezek. 2:3; 3:1, 4). But by the time of the writing of Daniel, the expression took on a specialized use as a title for the Messiah, a heavenly Man, who would usher in God's apocalyptic, end-time kingdom.

(2) The other would-be follower is specifically described as a "disciple." He too wishes to accompany Jesus across the lake, but first he

says he must bury his father. Burial was a most important task that befell a son and had to be done within a day (Gen. 50:5; Lev. 21:2; Tobit 4:3; 6:14). Perhaps the father had not yet died, and the disciple was saying that as soon as he settled the estate, a duty incumbent on him by law, he would join Jesus. Again, Jesus' response is shocking: "Follow me, and let the dead bury their own dead." Following Jesus is more important than religious obligations and family loyalties.

Jesus' teaching is not without precedent, for during a Nazirite's time of dedication he could not be near a dead body, not even that of a relative (Num. 6:6–7). Similar restrictions applied to the high priest (Lev. 21:10–11). Dedication to Jesus was just as serious. "The dead" may have a double intent: the literal dead and spiritual dead (i.e., those who do not follow Jesus).

4.6. Even the Winds Obey Him (8:23–27)

After a brief teaching interlude (8:18–22), Matthew continues relating Jesus' miracles. His telling about the stilling of the storm seems to have two levels of meaning. Teaching is never far from his mind. We have already seen in the previous section that the trip across the lake served as an occasion for Jesus to provide a challenge to discipleship. This voyage into discipleship is a lesson in life, not just words; it demonstrates what it means to follow Jesus. The vocabulary that Matthew uses here also serves to make the storm say something about discipleship and to present Jesus as the Lord not only over the storm on the sea but also over the eschatological fury that will engulf the world at his death and in the last days.

Matthew's expression for "a furious storm" is literally "a great shaking [*seismos*]." Elsewhere he uses this word, from which is derived the English *seismic*, for an earthquake (24:7; 27:54; 28:2). This word often has an eschatological nuance, as is common in apocalyptic literature (such as the book of Revelation). Although storms frequently arose on the Sea of Galilee with little warning, this storm is not an ordinary one: The waves are so high that the boat is hidden from view.

The distraught disciples awaken Jesus with the address "Lord" (*kyrie*). Matthew's readers, reading the Gospel after the resurrection of Jesus, knew that this title certainly meant mo than "Sir," and it quickly becomes somethir more for the disciples who witness the stillir of this killer storm. The Old Testament asser that the sea obeys the Lord God (Job 38:8–1 Ps. 65:5–8; 89:8–9) and that he is the Lord the storm (Ps. 29). The Jews who accompan Jesus are aware of these Scriptures. It is n wonder that they express their amazement his power over nature and their salvation wi the words, "What kind of man is this? Even th winds and the waves obey him!" (v. 27). The are in the company of more than a mere huma being!

Matthew summarizes Mark's two questio of Jesus to the disciples regarding fear and lac of faith (Mark 4:40) with his favored expre sion, "you of little faith" (*oligopistoi*; see com ment on Matt. 6:30). The application t discipleship learned by the sailor-disciples an Matthew's readers is clear. Discipleshi involves danger, and one is totally depende on the Lord for salvation. Yet it is better to b with the Master in difficulty than to be els where in ease. As Corrie ten Boom has sai "To follow Jesus amidst the storm is safer tha a known way."

4.7. The Gadarene Demoniacs (8:28–34)

Matthew records only the bare essentials this exorcism, leaving out details from Ma 5:1–20 that show the severity of this posse sion, the terror to the whole community, and th instruction to the exorcised to witness to th people of Decapolis. But Matthew does add th there were *two* demoniacs (cf. also 9:27; 20:30 Perhaps the other Gospel writers center on ju one of them, or Matthew may be referring t two demoniacs in order to fulfill the Jewis requirement that legal testimony requires least two witnesses (Deut. 17:6; 19:15).

The phrase "before the appointed time (v. 29) refers to the commonly held idea i Judaism and Christianity that torment of th evil spirits will occur after the end-time judg ment (e.g., Rev. 14:10; 20:10; 1 Enoch 12:1 6; Jubilees 5:5–10; 10:1–13). The word fo "appointed time" here (*kairos*) indicates a cru cial moment, a momentous occasion, a tim ripe for fulfillment (see also the use of *kairo* in regard to the cross in 26:18 and judgment i 13:30).

The Gadarene country was on the southeastern shore of the Sea of Galilee. The city, part of the Decapolis (Ten Cities) confederation, was a few miles further to the southeast in the hills. The area was dominated by a Gentile population, hence the presence of pigs (unclean animals). Jesus usually did not tolerate communication with evil spirits. Rather, he silenced them and told them to depart. This instance was, therefore, an exception. Jesus asked their/his name, presumably to know with what and with how many he was dealing. When he received the answer "Legion" (cf. Mark 5:9), Jesus further tolerated the infestations' request to be thrown to the pigs. He allowed it because it was appropriate: unclean spirits for unclean animals. Jesus showed his authority over evil spirits here. In instances of demon-possession, ministers are well advised to follow the pattern of Jesus, keeping communication with evil spirits to a minimum. Arrogant railing at such spirits was not Jesus' practice, and the apostles forbade it (2 Peter 2:10–11; Jude 8–9).

The fate of the demons after the pigs drowned is not stated. Ironically, even though Jesus has presumably made the community a safer place, the population fears his goodness more than they had feared the evil in the demoniacs (see Luke 8:37). So great, so bright, so powerful is the salvation of God that many prefer to live with a less powerful and even malignant darkness. Some would rather hear the rattle of demonic chains in the night than to hear the liberating words of the Master in the light of the day.

4.8. The Healing of a Paralytic (9:1–8)

Jesus returns across the Sea of Galilee to Capernaum ("his own town"). In these verses he demonstrates his authority over another realm—human paralysis. Each of the miracles Matthew recounts says something about the nature and ministry of Jesus. Earlier the Evangelist has presented Jesus as the one who has control over sickness, demons, and nature, close up and from a distance, at home and abroad. Even asleep he is still the Master. When he stills the storm, the disciples ask the question, "What kind of man is this? Even the winds and the waves obey him!" (8:27). The Christological ramifications of that miracle are surprising, even shocking; and it shows the gravity of following Jesus.

On the occasion of the healing of the paralytic, in Matthew's haste to present who Jesus is, he declines to tell his readers that Jesus is preaching in a house crowded with people and that the friends of the paralytic tear the roof off the house and lower him into Jesus' presence (Mark 2:1–4; Luke 5:17–19). Matthew does, however, preserve the words of Jesus to the paralytic, "Take heart, son; your sins are forgiven" (v. 2). The man and his friends have come

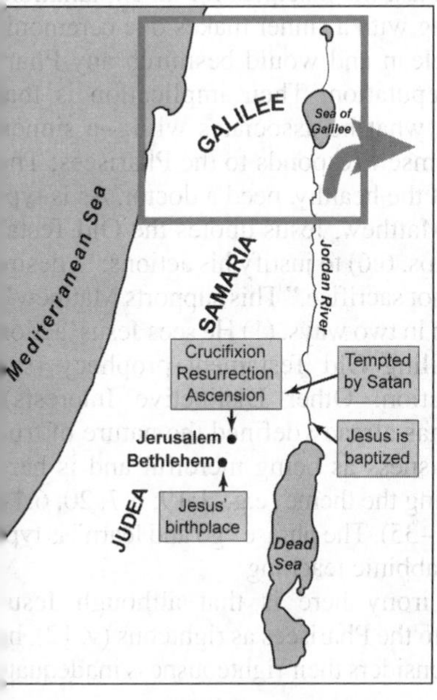

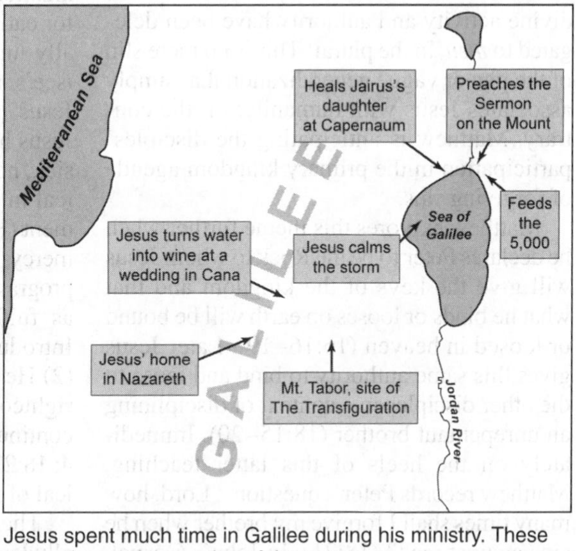

Jesus spent much time in Galilee during his ministry. These maps show only a portion of the events.

expecting a physical healing; they do not ask for or anticipate forgiveness.

The teachers of the law are scandalized, assuming that Jesus has blasphemed God. As Mark and Luke explain, they feel that only God has the authority to forgive sin and that Jesus has thus presumed to act as God. Jesus, "knowing their thoughts," counters their objection by intensifying the theological dilemma. Affirming that he knows that God alone forgives sin, he stands by his original statement, as if to say, "Go ahead, make the logical deduction that you find so offensive. I am about to prove it is a proper one!" His rhetorical question, "Which is easier: to forgive sin or to restore health?" needs no answer and forces the issue. To prove that "the Son of Man has authority on earth to forgive sins," he then heals the man. As in the calming of the storm, Jesus operates with the prerogatives of God; though human, he is more than a mere human being and greater than popular ideas of the nature and role of the Messiah.

The crowds "were filled with awe" (*phobeo*, lit., "afraid") and "praised God, who had given such authority to men." It would not be surprising for Matthew to point out how God has given authority to forgive to a *man*; this is in keeping with Matthew's theme that Jesus is the Messiah, God's Son, the successor to David the king (Ps. 2:7), with a divine mandate to save people from sin (Matt. 1:20–21). But note that Matthew says here that this divine activity and authority have been delegated to *men*, in the plural! This is no mere slip of the pen or vague generalization that simply associates Jesus with humanity; on the contrary, Matthew is anticipating the disciples' participation in the primary kingdom agenda of forgiving sins.

Matthew explores this theme further when he declares Peter to be the Rock to whom Jesus will give the keys of the kingdom and that what he binds or looses on earth will be bound or loosed in heaven (16:16–19). Later Jesus gives this same authority to bind and loose to the other disciples in a context of disciplining an unrepentant brother (18:15–20). Immediately on the heels of this latter teaching, Matthew records Peter's question, "Lord, how many times shall I forgive my brother when he sins against me?" (18:21). In John's Gospel, this theme is more emphatic: "If you forgive anyone his sins, they are forgiven; if you d not forgive them, they are not forgiven" (Joh 20:23). This ministry of forgiveness and rec onciliation is part of the disciples' job descrip tion, not because they are divine but becaus they have been divinely forgiven (Mat 18:23–35; 2 Cor. 5:18–20; 1 John 5:16; se also comments on Matt. 16:18; 18:18).

Jesus honors the faith of the paralytic' friends and forgives the man as well as heal his legs. The church has not always appreci ated the power and role of her faith. Our Go "is able to do immeasurably more than all w ask or imagine, according to his power that i at work *within us*" (Eph. 3:20). "This is the vic tory that has overcome the world, even ou faith" (1 John 5:4).

4.9. The Call of Matthew the Tax Collector (9:9–13)

Matthew now provides another interlude i his presentation of Jesus' miracles: the call o Matthew the tax collector (see also Mar 2:13–17; Luke 5:27–32). As a tax collecto and associate of sinners, Matthew stands i stark contrast to the two volunteer disciples i chapter 8, who receive a stern response fro Jesus; note that according to Mark, Matthe *immediately* leaves his post and follows Jesus

A short time later Matthew entertains Jesu in his house, along with some of his "sinner friends. The Pharisees witnessing this frater nization ask the disciples for an explanatio for eating with a sinner makes one ceremoni ally unclean and would besmirch any Phar isee's reputation. Their implication is tha Jesus is what he associates with—a sinne Jesus himself responds to the Pharisees: Th sick, not the healthy, need a doctor. As is typ ical in Matthew, Jesus quotes the Old Testa ment (Hos. 6:6) to justify his actions: "I desir mercy, not sacrifice." This supports Matthew' program in two ways. (1) He sees Jesus' actio as fulfilling Old Testament prophecy (se Introduction: Other Distinctive Interests) (2) He has already defined the nature of tru righteousness as being merciful and is her continuing the theme (e.g., 1:19; 5:7, 20; 6:1- 4; 18:23–35). The phrase "go and learn" is typ ical of rabbinic teaching.

The irony here is that although Jesu alludes to the Pharisees as righteous (v. 12), h really considers their righteousness inadequat since their very question betrays a deficiency of mercy. Earlier Jesus warned his followers that their righteousness must exceed that of the Pharisees (5:20). His brand of righteousness exceeds theirs in that he loves sinners and extends mercy to them, and he expects his followers to do the same. The image of the Messiah eating at table presages the eschatological banquet, which Jesus has already said will have some surprising guests and some surprising no-shows (8:11–12). Ironically, a tax collector like Matthew desiring to eat with Jesus is in better shape than the self-sufficient Pharisee. "Sinners who 'hunger and thirst for righteousness' are closer to true righteousness than the self-satisfied" (France, 1985, 168).

4.10. Fasting, Old and New (9:14–17)

Apparently the followers of John the Baptist fasted regularly. According to Mark 2:18, both the followers of John and the Pharisees were fasting at this time, but the followers of Jesus were not observing this fast. The New Testament says little about fasting, though the successors to Jesus practiced it, as did Jesus himself (4:1–2; Acts 13:2–3; 14:23; Did. 8:1b; see comments on 6:16–18). It is not clear whether the objections cited here refer to Matthew's dinner.

The "bridegroom" refers both to Jesus and to John. The absence of John, who had been imprisoned (4:12), was an occasion for sorrow and fasting for his followers. But Jesus is still with his own followers and expresses his joy by feasting. Jesus' allusion to the bridegroom's being taken away and the subsequent fasting of his followers anticipates his death.

The old and new cloth/wineskins parables are rather puzzling although their general meaning is clear. The new kingdom of Jesus is too "new" and too big for the old structure; only a new vessel can contain it. The images of a wedding, new garments, and wine are symbols of the eschatological celebration of God's salvation (cf. 22:11; John 2:11; Rev. 19:7–8; 21:2, 9; 22:17). Jesus as the bearer of the new era, the bridegroom who has come for his bride, calls for rejoicing. In one sense Jesus fulfills the eschaton, the end times, with his presence among his disciples before the resurrection and ascension. This realized eschatology, however, will have its greater completion in the cosmic culmination of the kingdom that is yet to come.

What is perplexing in this saying is that although Jesus perpetuates much of the old system, he calls simultaneously for a mixture of the old and new (13:52); furthermore, when he leaves, his disciples will practice the "old" fasting. This confusion arises, however, only if one considers this saying a description of Jesus' entire ministry rather than a direct answer to a question on a specific occasion: Jesus' eating and celebrating while the old order fasted.

4.11. Jairus's Daughter and the Woman With a Hemorrhage (9:18–26)

Matthew continues his account of Jesus' miracles. A comparison of his version of these two miracles with Mark 5:21–43 and Luke 8:40–56 shows that Matthew's is significantly shorter. He does not include Jairus's name or mention that his daughter died during the delay caused by the healing of the woman with the hemorrhage. Matthew simply presents the girl as dead.

As Jesus is heading for Jairus's house, a woman comes up behind him and touches "the edge of his cloak" (presumably a tassel on Jesus' garment). Jews often sewed tassels on their clothes to remind them to keep the law of Moses (see Num. 15:38–39; Deut. 22:12). The woman's bold action disregards the law because, according to it, her condition was unclean, and anyone she touched would become ceremonially unclean. This may be why, according to Mark and Luke, the woman was reluctant to admit touching Jesus. But Jesus told the woman to "take heart," for "your faith has healed [*sozo*, which in other passages means save] you."

When Jesus arrives at the deceased girl's house, the flute players and professional mourners—a required part of the Jewish funeral—are already there. When Jesus tells them to leave and insists that the girl is "asleep" and not dead, they ridicule him. Since sleep is a euphemism for death in Scripture, Jesus is probably saying that even though the girl is dead, the situation is only temporary. Again, Jesus disregards ceremonial taboos and touches the dead body, rendering himself ceremonially unclean in the eyes of many but making the girl alive before the eyes of her parents and Peter, James, and John (see Mark 5:37, 40–43).

4.12. Two Blind Men (9:27–31)

The presence of two similar accounts of Jesus' healing blind men in Matthew (here and in 20:29–34) seems puzzling since Mark and Luke mention only one version of this healing. Furthermore, Mark 10:46–52 and Luke 18:35–43 mention only one blind man whereas Matthew mentions two (see comment on Matt. 8:28–34).

As in 20:29–34, the blind men address Jesus as "Son of David" and beg him to "have mercy" on them. Unlike the Matthew 20 account, however, this miracle takes place in a house, where Jesus asks the blind men if they believe that he is able to restore their sight. When they respond affirmatively, Jesus restores their sight. As in earlier healing stories, this account supports the claim that Jesus speaks and teaches with authority.

4.13. The Mute Demoniac (9:32–34)

The exorcism of the mute demoniac has a parallel in 12:22–24, a healing of a demoniac who is both blind and mute. The structure and vocabulary of these two accounts are similar. Both note the amazement of the people and records a cynical assessment from the Pharisees (cf. also Mark 3:22; Luke 11:14–15). In the present account the Pharisees attribute Jesus' power to "the prince of demons" while Matthew's second account reads, "Beelzebub, the prince of demons." With this repetition of the accusation that Jesus is in league with the "prince of demons," one gets the impression that the conflict with his enemies is building and is about to come to a head. In the second account Jesus warns that the Pharisees are in danger of committing unpardonable blasphemy against the Holy Spirit (see comments on 12:31–37).

5. Call to Mission (The Second Discourse: 9:35–10:42)

This discourse is the second of five major units of Jesus' teaching, which Matthew has deliberately constructed to present Jesus as the new Moses (see comments on 5:21–22; see also Introduction: Jesus as Teacher). In this section Jesus presents instructions to his followers, who extend his work in a mission of their own.

5.1. Workers for the Harvest (9:35–38)

Matthew prefaces the saying about the plentiful harvest with a summary of Jesus' ministry, as he often does (see comments on 4:23–25). The threefold work of teaching, preaching, and healing is repeated here. This summary brings closure to the previous section on miracles (8:1–9:34) and provides transition to the ministry of the twelve apostles. It sets the stage for a major section of the teaching of Jesus (10:5–42).

Matthew describes Jesus' compassion for the shepherdless sheep to explain his ministry to the people as well as to define the harvest to which he is about to send the apostles (ch 10). The shepherdless sheep allude to Ezekiel 34, where the shepherds of Israel oppress the flock and leave them as prey to the wild beasts (see also 1 Kings 22:17; 2 Chron. 18:16). God himself promises to be their shepherd instead (cf. Num. 27:17; 1 Kings 22:17; Zech. 10:2–3). The people of Israel are described as lost sheep (e.g., Isa. 53:6), and the Messiah is described as a shepherd (Ezek. 34:23; Mic 5:4–5; Zech. 11:16). Matthew is fond of this motif and uses it frequently in his Gospel (2:6; 10:6, 16; 15:24; 25:31–46; 26:31).

The harvest metaphor carries the idea of judgment (Isa. 17:11; Hos. 6:11; Joel 3:13). Matthew previously referred to a harvest theme in John the Baptist's stark prophecy of judgment in the parables of the bad and good trees and the chaff and the wheat, where the ax, the winnowing fork, and fire are the tools of judgment (3:10–12). Here (vv. 37–38) the urgency of the situation compels Jesus to exhort his disciples to pray for laborers in the harvest. "The Lord of the harvest" is, of course, God.

5.2. The Commissioning of the Twelve (10:1–4)

Matthew lists the names of the twelve apostles when Jesus sends them on their first mission (v. 1). This gives his readers the impression that the selection of the twelve had occurred earlier. By choosing twelve apostles Jesus is making a deliberate statement. Just as Israel had twelve patriarchs in the sons of Jacob, who had jurisdiction over their corresponding tribes, so too the new kingdom ha twelve overseers to whom is entrusted the rule of the new Israel, the church. Note that the Qumran community, which believed they were the nucleus of the eschatological Israel, also had a council of twelve (1QS 8:1ff.). The selection of the twelve is not just for the mission at hand, but it also establishes them in ongoing positions of authority (see 16:18–19; 18:18–20; 19:27–28; 28:16, 18–20). Jesus defines the nature of the mission by the authority he gives to the apostles "to drive out evil spirits and to heal every disease."

This passage is the only time Matthew uses the word "apostle" (*apostolos*). Elsewhere he presents these men as the "twelve disciples," "the twelve," or "the disciples." *Apostolos* has a more general use elsewhere in the New Testament to indicate someone on a mission or a representative distinct from the twelve apostles (Rom. 16:7; 2 Cor. 8:23). The Didache (c. A.D. 100) calls itinerant preacher-prophets apostles (Did. 11:4, 6). Etymologically, the word means "sent one," but it is different than the simple action of sending someone on an errand. It connotes commissioning with authority. In secular literature *apostolos* described one commissioned as a captain of a ship. Note the reference to authority given to the apostles in Matthew.

The term *apostle* became a specialized term with a specialized function in the church. The early church recognized the unique role of the twelve apostles; in Acts 1, even before Pentecost, the church moved quickly to replace the office vacated by Judas Iscariot (Acts 1:15–26). Apparently Paul felt that he too had authority approaching that of the Twelve through a supernatural, yet belated call (1 Cor. 15:5–10). The "apostles' teaching" was the crucial link between the church and the teaching of Jesus (Acts 2:42). The apostolic church measured truth and falsity by the teaching, experience, and authority of the Twelve and those closely associated with them. The church of the late first and early second centuries understood that bishops were the successors of the twelve apostles, guardians of the faith, and shepherds of the faithful, although others had apostolic ministries analogous to the original apostles in that they were preachers, missionaries, and itinerant prophets.

The order of the apostles' names as listed in Matthew 10:2–4; Mark 3:16–19; Luke 6:12–16; and Acts 1:13b is much the same with a few variations. Matthew links Andrew with his brother Simon Peter, thus moving Andrew further up the list. In Acts John is in the second position while he is third in Matthew, Mark, and Luke. Luke lists Peter and John first in Acts, apparently to coincide with the prominent role they play in the first part of Acts. All the lists present the inner core of the apostles—Peter, James, and John—in the first three or four positions since Jesus selected them for a special role.

Matthew and Mark place Thaddeus in the tenth position while Luke and Acts name "Simon the Zealot" as number ten. It is sometimes assumed that Thaddeus is another name for Judas, the brother of James. It would also appear that Simon the Cananaean (which is the name given in the Greek text in Matthew and Mark) is the same man in the lists in Luke and Acts. The word "Cananaean" probably comes from the Aramaic word for Zealot.[6] The Zealots were Jews who advocated the violent overthrow of the Roman occupation and the establishment of a free and independent Jewish kingdom. Sadly appropriate, Judas Iscariot, the betrayer, is listed last.

Peter is always in the preeminent position. Matthew prefaces "Simon (who is called Peter)" with the word "first" (*protos*). This is more than a mere indication of the beginning of the list; rather, it serves to emphasize Peter's salient role in leadership and authority among the apostles, which is a major concern for Matthew. The nickname "Peter" ("Rock") anticipates Jesus' establishing him as a unique foundation for the building of the church. The evidence of his dominant role as first among equals is frequently seen in both the Gospels and Acts (see comments on 16:16–19). A reliable tradition notes that Peter died in the Neronian persecution in Rome, in which the emperor blamed the fire of Rome (A.D. 64) on Christians. Peter was crucified upside down at his own request since he deemed himself unworthy to die as Jesus did.

Several items are worth noting concerning the rest of the apostles in Matthew's list. Andrew, originally a follower of John the Baptist, is juxtaposed with Peter's name since they are related. He was the one who introduced Peter to Jesus (John 1:35–40). In John's Gospel Andrew brings several prospective disciples to Jesus (1:35–44; 6:8; 12:22). The brothers James and John, both sons of Zebedee, were known as the "Sons of Thunder" (Mark 3:17; see also 9:38–41; Luke 9:54–56). The latter is probably the beloved disciple of the Fourth Gospel. Tradition relates that after the fall of Jerusalem John went to Ephesus, where he had an influence on such future leaders in the church as Polycarp, Papias, and Ignatius.

Philip of Bethsaida should not be confused with the deacon in Acts. He had a minor role in the Fourth Gospel (John 1:44; 6:5–7; 12:21–22; 14:8–14). Polycrates, the second-century bishop of Ephesus, records that Philip ministered in the Roman province of Asia and was buried in the city of Hierapolis. Bartholomew is often identified with Nathaniel of Cana of Galilee, listed as a disciple in John's Gospel (1:45–49; 21:2).

Thomas was known for his doubt (John 20:24–27), but he courageously determined to go to Jerusalem to die with his beloved Master. After he was convinced of the Lord's physical resurrection, he declared Jesus to be "my Lord and my God" (20:28). He was also called "Didymus," which means "Twin." Tradition says that he was martyred in India, where he founded a church. After the Portuguese circumnavigated Africa in 1498 and arrived in India, they found a native church that claimed to have been started by St. Thomas.

Only Matthew's Gospel presents the apostle of the same name with the title "the tax collector," which may be a confession on the part of the writer (Matt. 9:9–11; 10:3). Judas Iscariot betrayed Jesus to the authorities. Iscariot could mean that he was from Kerioth, though some take it to be derived from the Latin *sicarius*, a term for a Zealot-like group of assassins. Others suggest it was from the Aramaic word for "falsehood" or meant "redhead." Judas serves as a constant reminder that the followers of Jesus should be on their guard that their words and actions never betray their Master. The rest of the Twelve serve to encourage the modern believer to imitate their devotion to the kingdom.

5.3. The Instructions to the Twelve (10:5–42)

Jesus' instructions to the apostles prior to their mission serve as an occasion for Matthew to present the second major section of the teachings of Jesus, the Giver of the new Torah for the new kingdom. That Matthew sees this passage as a separate section of Jesus' teaching is clear from his closing phrase found in 11:1a, "after Jesus had finished instructing his twelve disciples."

5.3.1. Directions for the Mission (10:5–8). Matthew alone records that this particular mission was limited to the "lost sheep of Israel"; Gentiles and Samaritans are, at this point, avoided (vv. 5–6). Having mentioned a few brief contacts with Gentiles earlier (8:5–13, 28–34; cf. 15:21–28), Matthew anticipates that the major outreach to the nations will occur after Jesus' resurrection (28:19–20). This exclusive Jewish interest is typical of Matthew's theological program. Also, only Matthew speaks in this context of proclaiming that "the kingdom of heaven is near [at hand, RSV]" (v. 7), the same message Jesus preached when he began his public ministry (4:17). His disciples are thus to continue that ministry. Jesus also commands the apostles to heal the sick, raise the dead, cleanse lepers, and perform exorcisms as the Master did (10:8). Jesus earlier gave them the authority to do so (v. 1).

5.3.2. Provisions for the Mission (10:9–16). Both Mark and Luke have essentially the same instructions for the apostles as here (Mark 6:8–11; Luke 9:3–5). The apostles are to take virtually nothing but their clothes with them on the mission. Jesus says, "Freely you have received; freely give" (Matt. 10:8). That is, since the apostles have received the benefits of the kingdom, they are to offer the gospel in its power without charge. Contrast this with the attitude of Simon, who thought the power of God could be bought and sold (Acts 8:19).

Does this mean that Jesus intends for missionaries not to provide for their needs? Apparently Paul and company on occasion did just that (1 Cor. 4:12; 2 Cor. 12:13–18). But Jesus is not forbidding all provisioning of missionary enterprises. If he were, then the Philippian church erred when they supported Paul in his endeavors outside his Philippian sojourn (Phil. 4:10, 14–16). The clue lies in Matthew 9:37–38, where Jesus noted that the "harvest is plentiful," and therefore workers are urgently needed to garner it. It seems that the urgency of the harvest compels Jesus to send out the apostles hastily without previous preparation and provisioning. Note how Jesus himself once sent his disciples to buy food and did not rely on local charity for sustenance (John 4:8). The Christian community represented in the Didache, however, did take these commands of Jesus to be normative for providing for itinerant apostles/prophets (Did. 11:3–6). In any event God provides for the needs of those truly commissioned and sent by him.

Matthew includes the blessing of peace on the homes of those who provide hospitality to the apostles (v. 13). To offer peace is to offer wholeness, health, and justice (see comment on 5:9). Receiving free room, board, and protection was a common aspect of ancient Near-Eastern hospitality (see Gen. 18:1–8; 19:1–8; Judg. 19:15–24).

The reference to shaking the dust off your feet (v. 14) alludes to a Jewish tradition. A Jew would dust off his clothes and feet when he departed from a pagan area so that he would not be tainted by the unclean land of the Gentiles. To suggest that such a symbolic action be directed toward a Jewish home would have been an outrageous affront, for it would be equating them with Gentiles. Matthew takes the issue further by comparing those who reject the message of the apostles with the people of Sodom and Gomorrah, cities symbolic of heinous sin and infamy. They will be worse off in the judgment than these two wicked cities, for they have received the gospel and rejected it!

Both Matthew and Luke mention the "sheep among wolves." Note the irony here: The Shepherd himself (Jesus) sends his flock into a pack of wolves (Carson, 1984, 246)! Matthew's version includes the warning, "Be as shrewd as snakes and as innocent as doves" (v. 16). In both the ancient world and modern Western culture the snake is often a symbol of evil, though the ancient world also considered it sly and intelligent (e.g., Gen. 3:1). Jesus' reference to doves prevents anyone from understanding this passage to be a justification of amoral slyness. The word "innocent" literally means "unmixed"; in figurative uses it means pure in relation to morality and motive. Richard France puts the meaning well: "Christians are not to be gullible simpletons. But neither are they to be rogues" (France, 1985, 182). Naiveté is neither a Christian attribute nor an asset.

5.3.3. Directions for Persecutions (10:17–42).

5.3.3.1. Be on Your Guard (10:17–18). Jesus warns his disciples not to go blithely into dangerous situations. Shrewdness avoids certain conflicts. Even Jesus avoided unnecessary conflict with his enemies and usually picked when and where he would confront them (e.g., 12:14–21; 21:12–17). He taught, "Blessed are those who are persecuted for righteousness' sake," not for stupidity's sake (5:10, RSV).

Inevitably, however, persecution comes for disciples as it did for the Master, such as floggings in the synagogues and among Gentiles (vv. 17–18). In mentioning both synagogues and Gentiles, Matthew is returning to one of his frequent themes, the Jewish-Gentile issue. The phrase "*their* synagogues" suggests that the division between the Jews and the new Christian sect is deep at the time of his writing. That this teaching of Jesus anticipates the later ministry of the church in evangelizing all nations (28:19–20) is reinforced by the fact that a few verses earlier Jesus had told the apostles to avoid Gentile contact during this campaign (10:5). Eventually the disciples, like Jesus, will endure the negative judgment of both Jews and Gentiles.

5.3.3.2. Words of Witness Supplied by the Spirit (10:19–20). In these trials before religious and civil rulers Jesus exhorts believers not to worry how to give answers, for the "Spirit of your Father" will speak through them (cf. also Mark 13:11; Luke 12:11–12; 21:15). These trials are not merely occasions to defend oneself but to provide witness (*martyrion*) to the faith.

5.3.3.3. Inevitability of Rejection (10:21–25). The material in verses 21–25 is, for the most part, found only in Matthew. The idea of division of the truly righteous from those who refuse to listen or live out the gospel interests Matthew greatly (e.g., 7:21–23; 13:24–30; 21:28–32; 22:1–14; 25:1–30). Jesus uses language from Micah 7:5–6, which describes the dissolution of Israelite society. The enemies of the faithful can be found in one's own house. The persecution is due to the offense that the name of Jesus brings (Matt. 10:22). This brings to mind the words of the apostles in a later persecution when they were flogged by the Sanhedrin and forbidden to speak in the name of Jesus; they rejoiced "because they had been counted worthy of suffering disgrace for the Name" (Acts 5:40–41). Salvation involves the disciples' steadfast endurance of rejection that comes even from one's family. Jesus warns later that salvation comes only to the disciple who patiently endures (Matt. 24:10–14).

The appropriate response to persecution is to move to another city (v. 23). Undue heroism was frowned upon in the early church; volunteer martyrs were often considered prideful. There would be opportunity enough to witness in times of danger. "Death does not make a martyr; it reveals a martyr" (Dan Beller). Martyrdom (from *martyrion*, "witness") means witness. To witness with one's blood is a gift, a crown given only by God. It is the ultimate witness.

The reference to "the cities of Israel" (v. 23) has perplexed some readers. Some have argued that the final consummation of the end times, the Second Coming, will occur before all the cities in Israel hear his message. Certainly the phrase about the coming of "the Son of Man" makes this interpretation possible. This would mean, as Albert Schweitzer in his famous *Quest for the Historical Jesus* maintained, that Jesus anticipated the final culmination of the kingdom within a short time, then realized he was mistaken when God did not deliver him from the cross. This, however, was not Jesus' intent in verse 23. When Matthew was writing, he in fact knew this was not the case. If it were, one must wonder why he did not omit rather than expand this alleged *faux pas* of Jesus. Moreover, the phrase "he who stands firm to the end" seems out of place if the eschaton was just days away in Jesus' mind.

It has also been suggested that the coming of Jesus in verse 23 has nothing to do with the remote end times; rather, Jesus is simply saying that the apostles are to get on with their mission at once since he will follow them and overtake them in their impending mission. This would fit in well with the context of the mission of the seventy-two disciples, whom Jesus sent "two by two ahead of him to every town and place where he was about to go" (Luke 10:1). In this case Jesus was using the title "Son of Man" simply as a Christological self-identification and not as a reference to an imminent consummation of the new kingdom along the lines of Daniel 7:13–14.

Other interpreters have suggested that the fulfillment of the end times will come in installments. For example, the "coming of the Son of Man" may be a synonym for the "coming of the kingdom," alluding to the destruction of Jerusalem in A.D. 70—an event that would fulfill the judgment Jesus promised as early as verse 17. In this interpretation the church replaces old Israel. With the destruction of Jerusalem "the temple cultus disappears, and the new wine necessarily takes to new wineskins" (Carson, 1984, 252). That the early church understood eschatological fulfillment as being realized in stages is clear in Acts 2:17–21, when Peter identified the phenomena at Pentecost as a fulfillment of the last days prophesied by Joel. Moreover, Jesus himself apparently recognized that some points of eschatology would be partially realized before the culmination of the ages (e.g., 4:17; 12:28).

Another crucial issue involves the identification of "the cities of Israel" (v. 23). Does this refer to the towns on the original mission's itinerary, all of the Jewish towns in the Holy Land, or all of the cities in Palestine *and* the Diaspora that have Jewish populations; or does Israel refer to the church both Jewish and Christian? This last suggestion fits in well with Jesus' comment in Mark's Gospel, "The gospel must first be preached to all nations" (Mark 13:10; cf. Matt. 24:14). If Jesus had in mind a larger group of cities than those on the itinerary of the first apostolic mission, then clearly he did not see the fulfillment of the end times as just days away from the first mission. All the above options are at best tentative attempts to interpret this saying of Jesus. Some of his teachings are never meant to be stripped of their mystery. Divination of the end times is dicey at best.

Suffice it to say, Jesus told his disciples to proceed expeditiously with the mission at hand, trusting God for provision, being wary yet bold concerning danger, and knowing that the student is not above his teacher. Having heeded Jesus' warnings, the humble and obedient disciple will not be taken by surprise when confronted with rejection, hatred, and persecution but will face it with courage and perseverance, based on the promise that God will bring about the fulfillment of the kingdom through Jesus.

5.3.3.4. Bold Witness (10:26–33). "Do not be afraid" is characteristic of Jesus' message, for God's provision and direction supports the true disciple. Jesus calls for the disciples to wit-

ess boldly. The kingdom message, which up
o this time Jesus has kept under wraps (note
sp. his instructions to healed people to keep
ilent, e.g., 9:30) is now to be proclaimed boldly
efore all (10:26–28). Nevertheless, Jesus does
anction fear in one case (v. 28). Its focus is to
e not on those who can execute the disciple but
ather on God himself and on his judgment. The
isciples' words should please God and not
nerely avoid the wrath of human authority.

This choice of ultimate allegiance to God ets the Christian against the might of the Roman empire and ultimately means that very Christian in some way must speak contrary to the *vox populi*, even under the most enign government. Peter and the other aposles lived this out, for when threatened by the erusalem authorities they declared, "We must bey God rather than men" (Acts 5:29). In the nidst of this sobering warning Jesus provides ssurance and comfort in terms reminiscent of he Sermon on the Mount (6:26–27). Sparrows re small birds and were used as food by the oor. Yet God is aware of each of them, and ince disciples are much more valuable to God e will take care of them. Not so much as a hair alls from the head of a disciple without the 'ather's notice (vv. 29–31).

On the basis of both great fear and great omfort, the disciple is to acknowledge Jesus efore other people. What the disciple says bout Jesus has an ultimate effect, for Jesus vill acknowledge that person before "my 'ather in heaven." The opposite is also true: Denying Jesus will result in a greater repudiation of the disciple in heaven (see also Luke 12:2–9). Luke equates failure to give witness or Jesus before the authorities as being tantamount to committing blasphemy against the Holy Spirit (Luke 12:8–12; see comments on Matt. 12:31–32).

5.3.3.5. The Sword and the Cross (10:34–39). Jesus does not leave the disciple any illuions about the price of following him. Allegiance to him and his Father is viewed by the lisciple's family as treason against them. Diviion and strife occur in families over the radial call to discipleship. Love of God must be preeminent.

Jesus describes discipleship in terms of leath. Some scholars insist that Jesus could not have known in advance that he would be cruified and that, therefore, the reference to the "cross" here has to be an early Christian phrase imposed upon his lips. But this is not a necessary deduction. (1) It assumes that genuine prophecy is, at best, unlikely. (2) Jesus no doubt saw or knew of crucifixions in Roman-occupied Palestine. He knew that if he did not lead the people in a military revolt, which was popularly expected, he would inevitably fall victim to the power brokers of the time, who saw him as a threat. In the Holy Land the Romans reserved the option of capital punishment to be carried out by themselves; hence a cross would not be far from his mind. Prediction of his death on the cross was not one of his more astounding predictions. What is more relevant here is the call for his disciples to follow him in sacrificial living.

The reason for such a radical demand of discipleship comes next (v. 39). Ironically the one who seeks to preserve life will ultimately lose it, while life lost for the kingdom will result in its ultimate preservation. As Jim Elliot, a missionary martyr in South America, put it, "Blessed is the man who gives what he cannot keep to gain what he cannot lose."

5.3.3.6. Reward (10:40–42). Jesus returns to the earlier subject of being rejected or accepted by people encountered in the mission. His saying provides a parallel couplet that assures that those who receive a "prophet" or "righteous man" will have the reward of the same. Matthew includes these instructions here not just because the apostles heard them from Jesus but because the later church needed encouragement to be generous with itinerant ministers (e.g., Phil. 4:15–17; Did. 11:1–4).

Giving "a cup of cold water" was considered a basic part of Near-Eastern hospitality, an act for which no recompense was expected; yet Jesus assures his disciples that even the most minuscule effort to assure the spread of the good news will in *no way* (the Greek in v. 42 contains an emphatic negative) go unrewarded. Thus, neither the apostle nor those who support him need fear for their lives or welfare while boldly witnessing for Jesus in this world.

6. Ministry and Confrontation: Narrative (11:1–12:50)

6.1. John the Baptist (11:1–19)

6.1.1. John the Baptist's Question (11:1–6). Verse 1 functions as a transition from the teaching section in chapter 10 to another part of Jesus' ministry (see comment on 7:28–29). Both Matthew and Luke record the event of the imprisoned John the Baptist's sending his disciples to inquire of Jesus concerning his identity as the Messiah (see also Luke 7:18–23). His question is indeed curious since he had witnessed the events at Jesus' baptism, and, according to the Fourth Gospel, had himself identified Jesus as the Messiah (John 1:24–34; 3:25–36).

At best we are left here with speculation. Perhaps John misunderstood the nature of the Messiah's ministry. The idea that the Messiah would be a military deliverer was popular, and John may have thought his cousin would soon raise an army, stage a *coup d'état*, and procure his release from prison. Perhaps the conditions of his imprisonment led to his doubts. Possibly John, like the Qumran community, anticipated more than one messiah. At Qumran they believed that there would be three messiahs: one of Aaron, one of Israel, and a third called the Prophet. John obviously saw Jesus as the end-time prophet but did not know if he would fulfill the other two roles. Earlier Jesus' followers, who did not fast, were contrasted with John's disciples, who did (9:14). Along with Jesus' association with disreputable folk this may have given him pause.

Both Matthew and Luke record Jesus' reply: "Go back and report to John what you hear and see: The blind receive sight, the lame walk, those who have leprosy are cured, the deaf hear, and the good news is preached to th poor. Blessed is the man who does not fal away on account of me" (vv. 4–6). Jesus response may well reveal the nature of John' question. Jesus' messianic program obviousl did not fit the generic populist expectations Yet Jesus considered these salvific and com passionate miracles as signs of his messi ahship. John earlier had presented Jesus ministry as an imminent, apocalyptic, escha tological consummation of the ages (3:7–12) Jesus' reference to offense in reference to Joh may well serve to indicate that John's concep of messiahship needed adjustment.

Questions concerning the Baptist's under standing of Jesus' ministry remain especiall in light of the Fourth Gospel, in which Joh describes Jesus as the Lamb of God (1:29), a unconventional concept of Messiah. W should note that Matthew does not share ou modern interest in the motives of John' inquiry; the Evangelist sees it as an opportu nity to show the compassionate yet powerfu nature of Jesus' messianic program.

6.1.2. Jesus Explains John the Baptist' Ministry (11:7–15). Jesus uses the occasio of John's questions to explain his ministry. H begins by noting the irony of the existing his torical situation: The crowds had not gone ou into the desert to see someone resplendentl clothed like Herod the king; on the contrary they had gone to see the roughly clad John The "reed swayed by the wind" may be trans

Ruins at the site of the Qumran community, on the shore of the Dead Sea. Ancient scrolls, now called the Dead Sea Scrolls, were found in 1947 in a cave in the hills behind these ruins.

lated as a rhetorical question that expects a negative response. John, though humbly dressed, was nothing like a reed that sways in the slightest breeze; rather, he was a strong, rugged figure, boldly proclaiming the truth in the face of those who had the ability to retaliate if they so chose, as one eventually did. In the midst of John's misgivings, Jesus is apparently defending him as he clarifies John's role in relation to his own.

Matthew identifies John as the messenger who prepares the way of the Messiah (the fulfillment of Mal. 3:1) as well as the precursor who comes before the great day of the Lord. If Jesus considers John the messenger who comes before the presence of God, the "Elijah" who appears before "that great and dreadful day of the LORD" (Mal. 4:5), then he considers himself "the manifestation of Yahweh [who is to bring] in the eschatological Day of Yahweh" (Carson, 1984, 264).

Of "those born of women," none is "greater than John the Baptist; yet he who is least in the kingdom of heaven is greater than he" (v. 11). This saying can be understood in two ways since "least" (*mikroteros*) can also mean "younger." It may mean that the lowest Christian in the new era is greater than John, or Jesus might intend the *mikroteros* to be a reference to himself as the one younger than John who is greater than John. The latter interpretation is least problematic.

The reference to violence and the kingdom in verse 12 is one of the most puzzling in the Gospels. Luke writes that since John, "the good news of the kingdom of God is being preached and everyone is forcing (*biazetai*) his way into it" (Luke 16:16). As a result of Jesus' preaching, people are "gate crashing" to get in. Yet the "everyone" appears hyperbolic since elsewhere Jesus says that few find the narrow gate and many reject him (Matt. 7:14; see Bruce, 1983, 116).

Matthew also uses *biazetai* in verse 12, which can be translated as middle ("forcefully advancing," NIV) or passive voice ("has suffered violence," RSV). The former option suggests that the kingdom is on the offensive, and "forceful [violent] men" counterattack. Brad Young argues for the middle voice translation by linking the saying with Micah 2:13, where the one who opens the breach delivers captive Israel. He assumes that, rather than breaching a city wall, a sheepfold is being opened. Shepherds controlled movement of the sheep to and from the rock-enclosed fold by filling or removing stones from the entrance. John is part of this outbreaking of the kingdom (Young, 1995, 51–53). If the passive reading is maintained, then the kingdom is being attacked, and violent men are seizing it. This latter meaning fits well with the imprisonment and subsequent execution of John the Baptist, the death of Jesus, and the persecution of his followers (even up to the point of time when Matthew writes his Gospel).

"All the Prophets and the Law prophesied until John" (v. 13). Matthew saw the division between the old era and the new as occurring at the end of John's ministry and the beginning of Jesus' ministry.[7] Of the four Gospel writers, only Matthew explicitly notes that Jesus himself identifies John the Baptist as Elijah. Luke does record that the angel Gabriel described John as preceding the Messiah "in the spirit and power of Elijah" (Luke 1:17). In John's Gospel the Baptist declined suggestions that he was Elijah (John 1:21), but Jesus saw the Baptist as fulfilling the role of the eschatological Elijah. At the same time, Jesus himself as the miracle-working Messiah resembles the ancient prophet.

6.1.3. Children in the Marketplaces (11:16–19). Jesus muses on the no-win situation in which both John and he found themselves. John, living the life of an ascetic, and Jesus, associating with sinners, stand condemned by the public, whom Jesus describes as unpleasable sulking children. Clearly the demands of the new kingdom and the universal amnesty it offers would be and still are offensive to the status quo of the old order.

The title "Son of Man" has a specific Christological import since Jesus associates his ministry with Lady Wisdom (e.g., Prov. 1:20–33; 7:4; 8:1–9:12; Sir. 24); Jesus identifies himself as Wisdom Incarnate. Apparently the Messiah as sage was less popular than the Messiah as military deliverer. Matthew concludes that wisdom is justified by "her actions"; that is, the miracles Jesus performs confirm his teaching.

6.2. Woes on the Galilean Cities (11:20–24)

The diatribe against the Galilean cities of Korazin, Bethsaida, and Capernaum is also found in Luke's Gospel (Luke 10:12–15), although Matthew relates the unrepentant cities not only to Tyre and Sidon but also to Sodom, the odious city whose name is the etymological root for sexual baseness in the English language to this day. The Old Testament prophets condemned Tyre and Sidon for their arrogant self-sufficiency and worship of Baal. Their commercialism was equated with harlotry (Isa. 23; Ezek. 26–28; Joel 3:4; Amos 1:9–10; Zech. 9:2–4). Jesus declares the Galilean cities more culpable than the Phoenician cities, for Tyre and Sidon would have repented had they seen the signs and wonders wrought by Jesus. The Galilean cities remain indifferent in the midst of their material prosperity.

Sackcloth and ashes are signs of mourning, great distress, or repentance (e.g., 1 Kings 21:27; Job 42:6; Dan. 9:3; Joel 1:8; Jonah 3:5–8). Jesus seems to believe here that there will be degrees of punishment in the afterlife (see also Luke 12:47–48). The applicability of this rebuke to modern Western Christendom is most chilling.

6.3. Jesus Thanks the Father (11:25–27)

The phrase "at that time" links these words of Jesus with the previous section (see also comments on 12:1; 14:1). Thus, in spite of Jesus' disappointment at the rejection in Galilee he rejoices that to his followers, the "little children," the Father has revealed "these things" while they are hidden from "the wise and learned." This revelation is based on the Father's "good pleasure." Jesus' unique relationship with the Father expressed here is similar to the relationship of the two expressed in John's Gospel (e.g., John 14–17). In Matthew the relationship of Jesus with his Father in heaven has already been mentioned (Matt. 2:15; 3:17; 4:3; 8:29) and will be noted again (14:33; 16:16–17; 17:5; 21:37).

The Father has committed all things into the hands of his Son (v. 27). Matthew uses similar language to explain how the authority given to the resurrected Jesus underwrites the witness of the post-resurrection disciples (28:18). The use of the word "know" (11:27b) implies more than mere knowledge; it indicates a close relationship. Only to those who do not reject Jesus does the Father and Son reveal this relationship (France, 1985, 200).

6.4. His Yoke Is Easy (11:28–30)

The yoke was a rabbinic symbol for the law of Moses. Jesus ben Sirach spoke of accepting the yoke of Lady Wisdom and advised his readers to do the same: "Put your neck under her yoke, and let your soul receive instruction.... See with your own eyes that I have labored but little and found for myself much serenity" (Sir. 51:26–27, NRSV). Jesus the Messiah is not requiring an oppressive observance of law, which he confronts in the next chapter (12:1–14) and elsewhere (23:4); for, like the personified Wisdom of Proverbs and Sirach, it is the person of Jesus that contains and is the true Wisdom. To take his yoke means that a relationship is established in which the disciple learns wisdom from the meek and lowly Master. This labor gives rest.

6.5. Jesus Confronts the Pharisees (12:1–50)

6.5.1. Jesus' Disciples Violate the Sabbath (12:1–8). This section is a commentary on 11:28–30, showing that the yoke of Jesus is easy and light compared to the oppressive legalism of the Pharisees in their attempt to obey God's law. The phrase "at that time" (v. 1) makes the connection clear. According to Jewish law, it was permissible for anyone to enter someone's field and take food as long as that person did not cut it with a sickle or carry it out in a container (Deut. 23:25). Thus travelers and the destitute did not need to go hungry. The Pharisees, however, objected to Jesus' disciples plucking grain *on the Sabbath*. Some rabbis took the prohibition of working on the Sabbath so seriously that they forbade spitting on that day lest it disturb the soil and thus be construed as plowing on the Sabbath. They limited Sabbath travel to three-fifths of a mile. Carrying belongings out of a burning house was forbidden on the Sabbath. Women were not allowed to look into a mirror on the Sabbath lest they be tempted to pull out a gray hair.

In contrast to the Pharisees, Jesus has a commonsensical approach to the law, embracing its inherent mercy rather than conforming mindlessly to every jot and tittle of its legalistic interpretation. Jesus defends the actions of his disciples by giving examples from the Scriptures in which religious conventions were set aside. Jesus' first example is the time when David and his men ate the bread of the Presence that sat on the table in the Holy Place. God's law allowed only the priests to consume this bread (Ex. 25:30; Lev. 24:5–9), yet David and his followers ate it when they were hungry (1 Sam. 21:1–6). Richard France suggests that Jesus cites this example not merely to justify his and his disciples' actions but also to show that his authority to interpret the law is greater than David's (France, 1985, 202–3). Three times in this chapter Jesus says that "one greater. . . is here": greater than the temple, greater than Jonah, and greater than Solomon (12:6, 41, 42).

Only Matthew records the second example of authority over the Sabbath: his allusion to the Old Testament priests who "desecrate" the Sabbath "and yet are innocent" (v. 5). Matthew includes this since his audience is more familiar with Jewish practices than the audiences of the other Evangelists (see Introduction). Jesus is referring to the sacrifices that priests were required to make on the Sabbath in addition to the usual offerings (Num. 28:9–10). He has a greater authority than that of the temple, in whose service the priests were required to work on the Sabbath in seeming violation of the law.

Jesus cites Hosea 6:6 to justify his actions, "I desire mercy, not sacrifice." Matthew earlier recorded Jesus' use of this verse to justify his association with the tax collectors and sinners, who needed his ministry (Matt. 9:13). Jesus makes it clear that the ancient law was designed to be beneficial and not odious to the people. The Mishnah allowed harvesting on the Sabbath only if death by starvation were imminent. In the present case the disciples were only hungry. But Jesus' main justification for the harvesting on the Sabbath is not his disciples' hunger but his own authority. Note what Mark records Jesus saying here: "The Sabbath was made for man, not man for the Sabbath. So the Son of Man is Lord even of the Sabbath" (Mark 2:27b–28; abbreviated in Matt. 12:8). Using the word "for" (*gar*), Matthew gives this as the reason for Jesus' actions and those of his disciples on the Sabbath: He is its Lord. Surely this statement would have been highly disturbing to Jesus' enemies since in the Jewish mind there can be only one Lord of the holy day, God! It is as though Jesus is implying, "If you knew to whom you were talking, you would not be asking that question!"

6.5.2. A Healing on the Sabbath (12:9–14). Matthew clearly connects this healing and the previous confrontation: "Going on from that place, he went into their synagogue" (12:9). This passage further proves that Jesus is "Lord of the Sabbath." Matthew, as we have noted, often arranges his material topically. Notice too the phrase "*their* synagogue," which denotes the Jewish house of prayer and worship. Apparently the rift between the Jewish and Christian communities was quite pronounced when Matthew took up his pen.

Matthew alerts his readers that a major event is about to take place, introducing it with his characteristic interjection, "Behold!" (*idou*; see 12:10). (Lamentably, this word is left untranslated in the NIV; *idou*, which occurs two hundred times in the New Testament, appears sixty times in Matthew.) The word "shriveled," describing the hand, literally means "dried," but it is used to describe paralysis.

Matthew emphatically brings the issue into the open when he notes that Jesus' enemies ask him if it is "lawful to heal on the Sabbath." Jesus shows the inconsistency of pharisaic Sabbath traditions, citing the rabbinic exception that allowed owners of animals in pain or peril on the Sabbath to rescue them (vv. 11–12). The Mishnah allowed for medical treatment in a life-threatening situation (*Yoma* 8:6). In another situation Jewish law allowed a person to be extricated from a collapsed building if he or she was still alive. But if the person was dead, no further work was to be done until the next day. Some even considered pouring cool water on a swollen sprained leg or arm as work and therefore forbidden on the Sabbath.

Jesus shows the inconsistency of a system of laws that offered aid to suffering animals on the Sabbath but refused it to humans. He moves to the heart of the issue—not the rule itself, but the reason for the existence of Sabbath. Is it designed to perpetuate misery, or is it a foretaste of the eschatological rest of the kingdom of heaven on earth? Jesus concludes that "it is lawful to do good on the Sabbath," echoing again Hosea 6:6, "I desire mercy, not sacrifice" (see comment on Matt. 12:7).

By healing the man Jesus proves that he is "Lord of the Sabbath" and that the Sabbath exists for the blessing of God and humankind.

Again, Jesus shows that his kingdom is different from what people usually expect. The Mishnah stipulated that two warnings for Sabbath violations were given before action was taken against the violator. Matthew has given two violations, which thereupon result in action against Jesus. The Pharisees take counsel against him, causing him to withdraw.

6.5.3. The Gentle Healer (12:15–21). Matthew gives another summary of Jesus' healing ministry (cf. 4:23–25) and adds insights into the significance of that ministry, especially in regard to fulfillment of prophecy. Why did Jesus avoid the plotting Pharisees, whom he has provoked? (1) Although Jesus can be confrontational, his ministry is not to "quarrel or cry out; no one will hear his voice in the streets" (v. 19). (2) The hostile reception in the synagogue gives occasion for Matthew to allude to Jesus' ministry among the Gentiles, which is one of his frequent interests (vv. 18, 21). Matthew cites Isaiah at this point, introduced with his often-used phrase, "This was to fulfill what was spoken through the prophet." Jesus' fulfillment of prophecy is ever on the mind and heart of Matthew. The "bruised reed" and "smoldering wick" correspond to Jesus' compassion on those who were healed and who followed him.

6.5.4. Beelzebub and Blasphemy (12:22–37).

6.5.4.1. The Pharisees Attribute Jesus' Power to Beelzebub (12:22–24). By the use of the word "then" (v. 22), Matthew links the healing of the blind and mute demon-possessed man with Jesus' earlier confrontation with the Pharisees; here he is about to clash with them again. The people who witnessed the exorcism suggested that it testified to Jesus' messianic royalty as "Son of David." It is not surprising that Matthew stresses this royal title since he often declares Jesus to be King.

The Pharisees, however, counter that Jesus does good by the evil power of Beelzebub (the prince of demons; some manuscripts read Beelzebul). Their accusation that Jesus derives his power from this demonic prince has already been raised (9:32–34; cf. also 10:25). Traditionally this title has been associated with Baal-Zebub, the Philistine god who is contrasted with the true God in 2 Kings 1:2–3. "Beelzebub" means "lord of the flies." Although its original meaning is uncertain, the latter is often assumed to be an insulting play on words, showing Israelite contempt for the evil gods of their neighbors. By the time of Jesus it was considered a synonym for the chief of demons, Satan.

6.5.4.2. A Kingdom Divided Cannot Stand (12:25–30). Jesus exposes the accusation of the Pharisees as both stupid and damnable. He attacks the logic of the Beelzebub accusation, pointing out that he is devastating the kingdom of Satan, not building it (vv. 25–26). He then demands that his enemies be consistent and apply the Beelzebub theory to their own exorcists. Finally, he asserts that it is by the "Spirit of God" that he performs exorcisms.

In attacking Jesus, the Pharisees are attacking the work of God because the source of his miraculous power is the Holy Spirit himself. Jesus has power over the associates of Satan not through collusion but by his having bound Satan and plundered his house (v. 29). Jesus asserts that those who raise these criticisms are not "with [him]" (v. 30). There is no neutral territory: If one is not with him, then one is against him. The implication is that his detractors are the ones who are guilty of what they have accused him; they are the ones in collusion with Satan.

6.5.4.3. Blasphemy Against the Holy Spirit (12:31–37). Jesus explains the potential seriousness of his enemies' accusations with a dire warning. Blasphemy or slanderous accusations against the Son of Man are forgivable, but speaking against the work of the Holy Spirit is particularly perilous. Over the years serious readers of this passage have been concerned over the possibility of their committing an unpardonable offense, and well they should; however, the offense of careless words is not necessarily hopeless. In Matthew and Mark the blasphemy against the Holy Spirit is calling Jesus' good works evil. Luke, preserving another tradition, identifies the blasphemy against the Holy Spirit as failing to give inspired witness before authorities and rulers and instead denouncing Jesus (Luke 12:8–12). Perhaps Jesus applied this sobering warning to different situations on separate occasions. Note that in Matthew and Mark the warning is directed to Jesus' enemies; in Luke it is directed to his disciples!

In the case of Matthew and Mark, if one persists in calling evil good and good evil, there is no hope for that person, any more than someone can survive who calls poison good and food bad. To persist in rejecting Jesus is ultimately to cut oneself off from the Holy Spirit, not unlike Milton's Satan who says, "Evil, be thou my good." If saying something against the works of God were irrevocably damning, then Paul would have been lost (Acts 7:57–8:3). Yet to speak against the work of the Holy Spirit, then and now, can be fatal (Acts 5:1–10).

In Luke's version, if failure to give witness before the rulers and authorities were a stringent law of retribution, then Peter, who denied the Lord three times, could never have been restored; yet he was (Matt. 26:33–34, 69–75; Luke 22:31; John 21:15–19). Early church history relates accounts of those who denied the Lord in the face of persecution and immediately died. The possibility of unpardonable offenses are real (Heb. 6:4); yet the power to avoid them is great (Luke 12:11–12). It is better to fear God than to fear human beings (Matt. 10:26–29; see Shelton, 1991, 102–9).

Matthew makes it clear that consistency of lifestyle and witness are the issues at stake when he next mentions the fruit of the tree (v. 33; see also 7:16–20). Jesus warns that the words of the mouth reveal the content and intent of the treasures of the heart (12:34–35). Yet every careless word makes one subject to judgment (vv. 36–37).

6.5.5. The Sign of Jonah (12:38–42). This section is one of Matthew's "doubles" (repeated in 16:1–4). Here the teachers of the law and the Pharisees address Jesus with the respectful title "teacher," yet their request draws a strong response from him. In asking for a sign, they are not just requesting a miracle, for Jesus has already performed miracles (as they concede, even though they question the source of his power; cf. 12:24). They are probably asking that Jesus prove the godly origin of his ministry by predicting some great event not unlike what the Old Testament prophets sometimes did (e.g., 1 Sam. 2:27–33; 1 Kings 20:1–43; Isa. 7:10–25).

Jesus rebukes the teachers of the law and the Pharisees for asking for specific miracles to prove his authenticity. He calls their generation "wicked and adulterous." In the Old Testament, adultery is used figuratively to describe the unfaithfulness of Israel to the love of her husband, God (Isa. 50:1; 57:3; Jer. 2:1–5; Ezek. 16:15; Hos. 2:16–23). The true follower of God is disposed to the unfolding ministry of Jesus. Says Suzanne de Dietrich (1961, 78), "Those who reject this love will not know how to recognize God when he comes to them."

Although it is only apparent later (16:4), Jesus cryptically gives his enemies a divine sign of his messiahship by comparing his forthcoming death and resurrection to Jonah's being in the belly of the great fish three days and three nights. By comparing the Pharisees to the citizens of the wicked city of Nineveh, Jesus shows his contempt for their opposition and arrogance. Nineveh was a capital city of Assyria, one of the most brutal, vicious rogue states of the ancient Near East. Under Assyria the Israelites suffered greatly. In fact, Jonah hated them so much that he did not wish to preach to them lest they repent and be spared judgment. Here Jesus is saying that his enemies will be worse off than the Assyrians when the day of reckoning comes.

Similarly Jesus mentions the "Queen of the South," or the Queen of Sheba, who visited Solomon. She too will condemn "this generation," for Jesus is greater than either Jonah or Solomon. Earlier Jesus asserted his power over the Sabbath because he is greater than King David or the temple (12:1–8).

By Jewish reckoning, even a partial day can be counted as a whole day; thus Matthew sees Jesus' time in the grave as three days even though it was not literally seventy-two hours. In the case of Jonah, his "resurrection" from the great fish preceded his message of repentance to the Ninevites while for Jesus the preaching preceded the resurrection; in both cases, however, the resurrection attested to the ministry. But Jesus' audience will be held more accountable since they are being visited by a greater prophet than Jonah and a greater king and sage than Solomon.

6.5.6. The Return of the Unclean Spirit (12:43–45). The presence of this teaching of Jesus here seems somewhat abrupt and disjointed. But remember that Matthew's approach in writing the Gospel is more topical than chronological. He understands this parable to be applicable to the previous audience, for he implies a comparison between "this wicked generation" (v. 45) and the plight of the foolish, repossessed man. It provides the logical denouement of Jesus' previous indictments against his sign-demanding detractors: "You are in worse shape than the Ninevites who believed Jonah. Your rejection of my present offer of deliverance will result in a greater ruin. Neutrality is not a possibility." Matthew intensifies this all-demanding allegiance in the following context when he records Jesus' teaching that even one's family is not an exception to the total allegiance demanded by the kingdom.

Traditionally demons were associated with the desert, hence the reference to "arid places." The reference to the additional seven demons probably means that it is a complete possession since seven is considered the number of completion. Matthew continues this theme of separation from God in the parables concerning end times and judgment (ch. 25).

6.5.7. True Mothers, Brothers, and Sisters (12:46–50). Matthew has several unique aspects in his presentation of this story, which shed light on family relations in the kingdom of heaven. (1) The context is unique; only in Matthew does this incident follow the warning of the return of the evil spirit. (2) Matthew binds this passage about his true relatives to the preceding one with the phrase, "while Jesus was still talking" (v. 46), and with his frequently used "behold" *(idou),* an attention-getter used to punctuate important events (see comments on 12:9–12). (3) Matthew alone notes that Jesus points to "his disciples" (12:49) as his mother and brothers.

Characteristically, Matthew follows the Jewish practice of avoiding the name of God out of holy reverence. Thus he says, "Whoever does the will of my Father in heaven" (v. 50). Matthew's reference to the Father completes the reference to the family as mother, sister, and brother. The only solution to being repossessed by the enemy (vv. 43–45) is discipleship—constantly following, listening to, and obeying Jesus. Matthew links these two events together, giving his audience the choice of either joining the family of discipleship or being ravaged by a sevenfold demonic possession. Those who call God "Father" are disciples only if they do the will of the Father. (For a discussion on the brothers of Jesus, see comments on 1:25.)

7. Parables of the Kingdom (The Third Discourse: 13:1–53)

In this third major teaching section in his Gospel (see Introduction and comments on ch. 5), Matthew continues to contrast the enemies of the kingdom and the true disciples, whom he has presented in chapter 12. Matthew connects this section with the preceding chapter by stating: "That same day Jesus went out of the house and sat by the lake. . . . Then he told them many things in parables" (vv. 1–3a). As mentioned earlier, Matthew typically presents Jesus as a teacher, and much of his Gospel consists of Jesus' teaching. This particular collection of teachings consists of eight parables and three explanations of parables.

The parable is the mode of instruction for which Jesus is best known. Often, the nature and the meaning of parables have been misunderstood. The word "parable" comes from the Greek verb *paraballo*, which means "to set beside" or "parallel with," and is used to compare one thing with another. But in the Septuagint, the Greek translation of the Old Testament, the Greek word *parabole* frequently translates the Hebrew word *mashal*. It is this Hebrew genre that we must grasp in order to understand what Jesus meant by "parable." The *mashal* can, it is true, denote a comparison but it also refers to an extended similitude or even a short wise saying or riddle. It was not a fixed form of literature and included various subgenres; yet it has its roots in the prophetic and rabbinic practice of teaching by telling a story (see Young, 1989).

Earlier interpreters often assumed parables were complex allegories, with most elements in the parables containing symbolic, often hidden meaning. Granted, parables can contain multiple symbols (e.g., the parable of the soils in our passage; cf. also Luke 19:11–18), but it is a mistake to assume that all parables have as many symbols as the rocks, birds, and thorns here. Multiple symbols in a parable are the exception, not the rule. To treat each element as symbolic, say in the parable of the good Samaritan or the prodigal son in Luke, will result in missing Jesus' point and reading into the story meanings never intended or, at best, remotely intended by Jesus. For example, to identify the innkeeper in the former parable as the church, the two silver coins as the law and the gospel, or the robbers as specific "bad guys" is going too far.

Adolf Jülicher and C. H. Dodd have demonstrated that Jesus told the parables *usually* to make one main point. For example, Jesus told the parable of the good Samaritan to answer the question, "Who is my neighbor?" (Luke 10:29). So too in Matthew, Jesus uses the parables of the householder, the faithful servant, the ten virgins, and the talents to call for constant vigilance and faithful service (Matt. 24:42–25:30). To demand a symbolic meaning for the oil, lamps, or the number of talents is in Jesus' purview. Even if the parables have multiple symbols, they still usually make one main point. This is not to say that parables were never intended to elicit new applications as people meditate on them, internalize them, and live them out.

One vital question to be asked of parables is, "Why did Jesus tell this story on this occasion?" The parables of Matthew 13 address the issue of the world order versus the disciples and the resulting nature of the kingdom of heaven.

7.1. The Parable of the Soils and Its Interpretation (13:1–9,18–23)

Ironically, when Jesus told this well-known parable about farming, he was in a boat in the lake since large crowds were pressing around him on the shore. It is one of the few parables for which Jesus explicitly provides an interpretation. Both the parable and the interpretation are found in each of the Synoptic Gospels (cf. Mark 4:1–9, 13–20; Luke 8:4–8, 11–15). The method for sowing may seem bizarre to modern readers, but ancient Near-Eastern farmers sowed first and then plowed (Jeremias, 1972, 11–12). The parable has been traditionally called "the parable of the sower," but the attention is focused on the soils.

In his interpretation of this parable Jesus explains how the four soils represent the various ways people receive the Word of God; the first three do not produce fruit while the fourth does. (1) The path on which some of the seed is sown represents those who hear but do not understand. Mere hearing is not enough; in this set of parables as in the previous context, understanding is to be demonstrated by action and its resulting fruit (e.g., 11:20; 12:12, 33, 41, 50; 13:8, 44–46).

(2) The soil with the substratum of rock represents those who initially accept the good news with joy, then shrink from producing fruit in the face of tribulation and persecution, seemingly normal events for followers of Jesus. (In certain plants, adversity often produces more and better fruit.) The desertion occurs at the first sign of trouble; it is immediate (v. 21).

(3) The ground with thorns represents the worries or cares of the age, the world, and the lure of wealth. Thus, the seed is unfruitful, or as Luke 8:14 puts it, "they do not mature." The story of the rich young ruler provides a chilling commentary on this type of soil: He declined to follow Jesus and "went away sad, because he had great wealth" (Matt. 19:22).

(4) The one receiving the Word as good soil "understands it," that is, produces fruit. Some assume that the hundredfold harvest is exaggeration for effect, but in some agricultural situations it is feasible. The important point is not whether this is hyperbole but that the obedient disciple brings forth much fruit while those who do not follow Jesus produce none. Luke defines the good soil as those who "hold [the word] fast in an honest and good heart, and bear fruit with patient endurance" (Luke 8:15, NRSV).

7.2. Jesus' Reasons for Using Parables (13:10–17)

Jesus' response concerning his use of parables underscores the continuing Matthean emphasis of the contrast between the disciples and the crowds. Apparently Jesus is no longer addressing the many but is speaking to his disciples alone. Only they are allowed to know the "secrets [*mysteria*] of the kingdom of heaven." In the Gospels *mysterion* occurs only here and in the parallel passages in Mark 4:11; Luke 8:10. Paul uses *mysterion* to indicate that the truth of the gospel comes only by revelation (France, 1985, 221). Without using this word, Matthew speaks of Jesus' revealing things to the babes that are hidden from the wise (Matt. 11:25–27).

Verse 12 describes the paradoxical nature of the kingdom of heaven: Those who are inclined to follow and obey Jesus receive more and more understanding, while those outside of the kingdom, for all their resourcefulness, will receive less and less. Obedience, to some extent, precedes understanding.

The issue of free will and predestination arises in verses 11–12. In verse 11 God has chosen to give the secrets of the kingdom to the disciples and not to unbelievers. Mark quotes Isaiah 6:9–10 to show that Jesus spoke in parables "so that" (*hina*) some could not understand (Mark 4:12). Matthew 13:13 appears to soften Mark's "so that" to "because" (*hoti*; cf. KJV). He does this perhaps to make room for the free rejection of Jesus on the part of the crowds and his enemies. Modern readers will have to accept that in the biblical literature the issue of free will and determinism is not resolved, and both philosophical models are used and held in dynamic tension—often by the same author (notably Paul).

In 11:20–24 (the passage on the rejection of Jesus by the cities of Korazin and Bethsaida), Matthew clearly endorses the concept of free will. He too maintains the tension between God's sovereign choice and human free will without resolving them. He presents both the "big picture" of God's grand design, which will be executed in spite of human rejection, and the individual responsibility of those who persist in "chronic unbelief" (for more on this, see Carson, 1984, 308–10). As we will soon see, Jesus had several reasons for constructing such ambiguities in his public addresses.

Although all the Synoptic writers allude to the Isaiah passage about seeing and not seeing, hearing and not hearing (Isa. 6:9–10), Matthew characteristically adds his favorite formula on prophetic fulfillment (Matt. 13:14) and quotes more extensively from this prophet than do Mark or Luke. God called Isaiah to prophesy to the inhabitants of Judah even though he knew that because of the callousness of their hearts they would not repent. To the disciples Jesus gives words of comfort by telling them that what prophets and righteous men longed to see and hear but did not, their eyes and ears have seen and heard. The words of Simeon, who blessed the baby Jesus in the temple, echo the sentiment: "Sovereign Lord, as you have promised, you now dismiss your servant in peace. For my eyes have seen your salvation" (Luke 2:29–30).

Another reason Jesus has for teaching in parables is that it keeps his accusers off guard as they listen for something with which to condemn him. It appears, however, that on other occasions he used parables to communicate clearly with his enemies, such as in the parable of the good Samaritan, which answered the lawyer's question, "Who is my neighbor?" Even later Jesus' enemies understood his parables enough to know that he was speaking against them (Mark 12:12). He also used parables to get his listeners to "drop their guard" and rethink their position, reassess their priorities, and examine their hearts (Stein, 1981, 35). (On 13:18–23, see comments on the parable of the soils, above.)

7.3. The Parable of the Weeds and Its Interpretation (13:24–30, 36–43)

Only Matthew presents the parable of the weeds. This is not surprising since the issues of end times and judgment occupy his attention more than the other Evangelists, and they often appear in the exclusively Matthean parables. The parable of the weeds also conforms to the overarching theme of Jesus' teaching in chapters 11–13: the contrast between the enemies, the would-be followers, and the true disciples of Jesus.

The weeds probably refer to the darnel plant, which in its early stages of growth is virtually identical with the young wheat. By the time the wheat and darnel can be identified, both species are well established, and extraction of the weeds will harm the crop. The themes of gathering grain and burning the chaff are reminiscent of the wheat/chaff imagery of end-time judgment that Matthew has presented in the sermon of John the Baptist (3:12).

As in the parable of the soils, Jesus provides an interpretation of the story of the weeds to his disciples privately (v. 36). The Messiah (the "Son of Man") is the sower of the good seed while the devil sows the bad seed. Jesus also identifies the Son of Man as the Lord of the harvest, the owner of the kingdom of heaven, and the end-time judge. The good seed are the "sons of the kingdom" while the bad seed are "the sons of the evil one." By identifying the wheat with the righteous and the similar-looking weeds with the wicked, Jesus makes the sobering point that it takes a long time to know which is which. This should cause his hearers to seriously scrutinize the character of their own lives.

The portrayal of the harvest as the end-time judgment complete with angels motivates Matthew, alone of the Gospel writers, to include this parable since he often presents Jesus' teachings concerning the end times. (For more on the end-time duties of angels see 16:27; 24:31; 25:31.) As in chapters 11–12 Matthew provides a stark contrast: Evildoers will suffer fiery torment (weeping and gnashing of teeth; see also 8:12) as a result of the judgment while the righteous will shine as brilliantly as the sun. Then the true nature and value of both species of plants will be clearly manifested.

The kingdom here is ascribed to both the Son of Man and the Father (vv. 41, 43). These are not two separated kingdoms, one on earth and one in heaven; rather, they are one and the same. The probable reason why the Son of Man and the Father are mentioned in tandem with the kingdom here is that both Jesus and the heavenly Father are prominent in the end-time judgment (see also 16:27–28; 25:31–46; see Kingsbury, 1969, 98). Jesus' conclusion of the interpretation of the parable calls for serious assessment and action: "He who has ears, let him hear" (13:43; cf. 11:15).

7.4. Two Parables of Growth: The Mustard Seed and Leaven (13:31–33)

Jesus calls the mustard seed "the smallest of all your seeds." This is hyperbole, intended to emphasize the minuscule nature of the seed. Among the rabbis this seed was used proverbially for smallness (M. *Niddah* 5:2). Jesus' point is that it becomes a shrub of significant size, even affording birds shelter. So too the kingdom of heaven has modest beginnings unnoticed by many but eventually has great effect. The advancement of the early church from its bleak beginnings to the transformation of the Roman empire provides appropriate commentary on the significance of the passage. The reference to a tree may indicate an expanding empire (e.g., Ezek. 17:23; 31:3–9; Dan. 4:10–12); the birds represent nations in the empire (Dan. 4:20–22) (France, 1985, 227).

The parable of the yeast reinforces the meaning of the mustard seed. Yeast often has a negative or evil image in the Bible, as in 16:6, 11: "Be on your guard against the yeast of the Pharisees and Sadducees." It is also used negatively in the Old Testament (e.g., Ex. 12:15; Lev. 2:11), though it also has a positive image (e.g., Lev. 7:13; 23:15–18). Here Jesus uses yeast to show how a small, unnoticed item can pervade the whole. Many do not see the kingdom at work because it is hidden and considered by many to be insignificant. But we should not despise the day of small things. Fruit follows faithfulness (Gal. 6:9). The work of the humblest disciple can have far-reaching effects.

7.5. Jesus and the Use of Parables (13:34–35)

Building on Mark 4:33–34, Matthew reiterates the reason for Jesus' use of parables. It deals with making hidden things clear, which, earlier in this chapter, Jesus reserves for his disciples. To the crowds he speaks in parables, which can only be understood by true believers.

As is typical for him, Matthew sees this reason for parables as fulfilling Old Testament prophecy; here he quotes Psalm 78:2, a psalm of Asaph. Asaph is regarded as a prophet because he is identified as a seer in 1 Chronicles 25:2 and 2 Chronicles 29:30. In Psalm 78 Asaph recounts the salvation history of the Israelites. The historical accounts are presumably common knowledge, yet Asaph says that he is revealing things hidden. In like manner Matthew sees Jesus' use of parables as both visible and cryptic. He is attracted to this psalm because of the use of the Hebrew word translated by *parabole* (i.e., *mashal*; see introductory comment to Matt. 13) and the reference to revelation of hidden things.

Matthew has a broad sense of the Old Testament's being fulfilled typologically in Jesus. As usual, the Evangelist prefaces the fulfilled Scripture with his favorite phrase, "So was fulfilled what was spoken through the prophet. . . ." Asaph's psalm comes to a fuller sense in Jesus. (On 13:36–43, see comments on the parable of the weeds, above.)

7.6. The Value of the Kingdom: Hidden Treasure and the Pearl (13:44–46)

Burying treasure was a common practice in the ancient Near East, where calamity, invasion, and looting happened often, and it became a popular theme in storytelling. Jesus uses one such story to emphasize the supreme value of the kingdom of heaven. Some people have questioned the ethics of the man who bought the land without informing the owner of the value. J. D. M. Derrett notes that in rabbinic law a day laborer who found a treasure on his employer's property could not extract it without giving it to the property owner. The discoverer circumvents this problem by buying the land (Derrett, 1970, 1–16). The ethics of the situation is a moot point, for Jesus is not addressing its legality but rather the value of the kingdom, which is so precious that the man joyfully sells everything he has in order to obtain it.

The message is effectively repeated in the next parable about the pearl of great price. Pearls were highly prized in the ancient world. Pliny the Elder writes that Cleopatra had a pearl worth five million dollars in modern currency (100 million sesterces—*Hist. Nat*. 9). What jeweler today would not liquidate all his assets to acquire the great Hope Diamond? The kingdom is worth much more than any sacrifice, so much so that the value of the pearl pales in comparison (see also Phil. 3:8–11). The kingdom of heaven is a "can't lose" proposition.

7.7. The Fishnet (13:47–50)

In the next parable Matthew returns to the theme of judgment and the division of the good and the bad. Jesus' explanation of the meaning of the parable is virtually identical to his interpretation of the parable of the weeds and wheat, with bad fish instead of chaff being thrown into a fiery furnace. This parallel structure reminds the reader of the warning in the previous parable (13:24–30, 36–43). The net here is a large one, probably handled by several men.

7.8. The Parable of the Old and New (13:51–53)

In this last parable Jesus not only instructs his disciples but also explains his intent in using parables. Jesus first asks if the disciples have understood his parables and their meaning. He describes his work—and subsequently their work—as that of a teacher of the law, who interprets and employs both the old and the new. A key to understanding this saying is found in verses 34–35. Like the psalmist, Jesus recounts salvation history and discovers its significance (Ps. 78). As a house owner Jesus brings out treasures that are both old and new. He assumes the message of his parables has authority, not unlike the earlier revelation of the Old Testament. Note that his teachings are not mere novelty but go back to "the creation of the world" (v. 35).

By way of application, Christians today should not just be enamored with the new but retrieve the precious things of previous generations of believers. The watchword for the teachers of the kingdom should be "ever old and ever new."

Matthew consciously concludes this major section of Jesus' teachings with a phrase similar to ones he used previously: "when Jesus had finished these parables" (13:53; see comment on 7:28–29). He deliberately presents these parables as a specific unit of Jesus' teachings in keeping with his overarching interest in Jesus as the new teacher of the law.

8. Ministry and Opposition: Narrative (13:54–17:27)

8.1. Rejection at Nazareth (13:54–58)

The Synoptic Gospels offer different emphases in their presentation of Jesus' rejection by his hometown (Matt. 13:54–58; Mark 6:1–6; Luke 4:16–30). Luke emphasizes Jesus' empowerment by the Holy Spirit and his ministry to the poor and to Gentiles (see Shelton, 1991, 63–70). Matthew continues the theme of the division between believers and unbelievers, which dominates chapter 13. The people at Nazareth have all the evidence they need to believe in Jesus, but because of his humble beginnings they refuse (cf. Mark 6:6).

Matthew identifies Jesus as "the carpenter's son" while Mark specifically calls him a "carpenter" (Mark 6:3). Jesus apparently followed Joseph in his profession. It may be better to translate *tekton* as a building contractor who works with more than wood. Justin Martyr (second century A.D.) relates that Jesus made plows and yokes in the home workshop in Nazareth (*Dialogue With Trypho* 88.8).

Jesus was rejected by the townsfolk of Nazareth and could do few miracles there (v. 58). Matthew explains their rejection in strong terms (*skandalizo*; v. 57, "took offense," a word that in 5:29 and 11:6 expresses rejection of Jesus and describes obstacles to true faith); that is, the Nazareth folk were "scandalized" by Jesus and his claims. They were not prepared to attribute his teachings and miracles to God. Their question, "Where did this man get this wisdom and these miraculous powers?" (v. 54), was answered by their lack of faith (v. 58). (Regarding issues raised by the reference to Jesus' brothers and sisters, see comments on 1:25.)

In spite of the fact that Jesus is the Messiah and that he performs miracles as a sign of his office, healing and miracles are often contingent on the faith of the beneficiary and/or the community of faith—as is the case in the healing of the centurion's servant, the paralytic lowered through the roof, the woman with the issue of blood, and the two blind men (8:10, 13; 9:2, 22, 28–29). Yet Jesus sometimes performed miracles apparently in the absence of faith in those around him—as in the stilling of the storm, the exorcism of the Gadarene demoniac, and the feeding of the thousands (8:23–27, 28–34; 14:15–21).

Jesus' power does not work automatically or magically. As part of God's mysterious plan he does not always execute his will on earth apart from humans and their faith. He allows and expects humans to participate in the working out of salvation history. He gives his disciples the dignity of causality in the kingdom and yet in doing so retains his sovereignty.

8.2. Herod's Opinion of Jesus and the Death of John (14:1–12)

Matthew continues the theme of acceptance or rejection of Jesus. He links the Herod material with the previous context by the phrase "at that time." Upon hearing about Jesus' ministry within his jurisdiction, Herod Antipas, tetrarch over Galilee, assumes that Jesus is John the Baptist come back to life, the man whom he had condemned to death after John had reproved him for marrying Herodias, his brother's wife. Herod attributes Jesus' miraculous powers to a supposed resurrection. The Synoptic Evangelists include the people's speculations concerning the true identity of Jesus as Elijah or one of the prophets (cf. Mark 6:14–16; Luke 9:7–9).

In Matthew, Herod seems fearful of the possibility that John might be alive again. This is in contrast to Luke's account, where Herod seems more perplexed and discounts the possibility that Jesus is John (see Luke 9:9). Both reactions are credible. Though dubious at one point, Herod may have become more fearful upon entertaining the thought that Jesus was the revived John whom he had executed, an act that had given him much anxiety (Matt. 14:3–12).

Why did Herod assume Jesus was John? Was it because both of them had performed miracles? According to the biblical record, John the Baptist "never performed a miraculous sign" (John 10:41); no Scripture records any miracle at his hands. But John's ministry was comparable to Jesus' in another respect: His basic message, a call to baptism and repentance, was repeated in Jesus' ministry; for this reason alone it comes as no surprise that Herod associated Jesus with John. Jesus' presence was as unwelcome to the unrepentant Herod as John's had been.

Josephus sheds light on why John was arrested when he notes that the people followed John and that Herod was afraid he might tell the crowds to rebel (*Antiquities* 18.5.2). Yet John's condemnation of Herod for his affair with Herodias, recorded in all three Synoptic Gospels, appears to be Herod's main grievance. John's arrest was an obviously controversial move, considering his popularity.

Both Matthew and Mark give a detailed account of the court intrigue and sordid subterfuge that sealed John's fate. The dance of Salome before Herod and her request for the head of John the Baptist at her mother's prompting have captured the imagination of artists and musicians. It bespeaks of the depravity of Herod's court, revealing how shallow his commitment to Judaism was. This incident also shows how pervasive the influence of Hellenism was among the Jewish ruling elite, for in obvious disregard for Jewish law, Herod ordered John executed without trial, exposing himself as a Near-Eastern tyrant with the principles of a pagan.

8.3. The Feeding of the Five Thousand (14:13–21)

After the death of John the Baptist Jesus withdraws by boat to a private location, perhaps to elude the murderous Herod (see comment on 15:21). Luke records this place as Bethsaida (Luke 9:10). But the crowds follow on foot, thus cutting short his respite. Having compassion on the leaderless crowds (cf. Mark 6:34), Jesus heals their sick. At day's end when the disciples suggest that the crowds be dismissed to the villages to buy food, Jesus tells them to feed the people. They report to Jesus that they have only five loaves and two fish, probably the contents of a boy's lunch (John 6:9). Despite the apparent lack of provision, Jesus orders the crowds to be seated, then proceeds to perform a miracle.

The twelve baskets of food left over are probably not a symbolic use of the number twelve but an indication that everyone was satisfied. That the feeding of thousands is a supernatural event is obvious; it is *not*, as some who have problems with the miraculous suggest, a result of the people sharing their lunches with one another.

The language and images of the miraculous feeding are pregnant with meaning. (1) It recalls the miraculous provision of manna in the desert after the Exodus (Ex. 16; cf. John 6). (2) It parallels the action of Elisha, who miraculously fed one hundred men (2 Kings 4:42–44). (3) Manna is associated with the Messiah in both Jewish and Christian writings (2 Baruch 29:8; Rev. 2:17). Through this miracle, therefore, Jesus is deliberately making a messianic declaration. His hosting a meal also anticipates the messianic banquet of the end time, which he will host as head of the community (Rev. 19:7–9). For now the sheep have a shepherd (see Mark 6:34).

Jesus' actions in performing this miracle strikingly parallel his actions at the Last Supper: He "took bread, gave thanks and broke it, and gave it to his disciples" (26:26–29; cf. Mark 14:22–25; Luke 22:15–20; 1 Cor. 11:23–25). These parallels also appear in the meal at Emmaus when the risen Lord was "recognized ... when he broke the bread" (Luke 24:35; cf. vv. 30–35). In John Jesus deliberately links the feeding of the five thousand with manna and with his words regarding his flesh and his blood (John 6:26, 31–58). It is significant that the apostles present the accounts of the Last Supper or communion in the "miracle language" of this feeding miracle. Apparently they intend for the celebration of the Lord's Supper to be seen in terms of miracle.

8.4. Jesus Walks on the Water (14:22–33)

It is not clear what destination the disciples have in mind as they embark again on the sea. In Luke the feeding miracle occurs at Bethsaida while Matthew and Mark place it in a solitary place (Luke 9:10; cf. Matt. 14:13; Mark 6:32). Yet after the feeding Mark says that the disciples went on "before him to the other side, to Bethsaida" (6:45, RSV). Perhaps the desert place mentioned in Matthew and Mark was in the countryside adjacent to Bethsaida and the disciples were taking the boat to the port of that city. Or they may have been headed to Capernaum to the west (John 6:16–17), with Bethsaida as the first stop.

Why does Jesus send the disciples and the crowds away? According to Matthew, he wants to pray alone (14:23). John refers to the messianic frenzy that engulfed the witnesses to the miraculous feeding, resulting in their wish to make Jesus king by force (John 6:15). To avoid the premature and rash act of the crowds and possibly even that of his disciples, he sends them away and sequesters himself in the hills.

The disciples find themselves in a fierce storm in the fourth watch of the night (from 3:00 to 6:00 A.M.). When they see Jesus walking on the water, they take him for a ghost and are terrified. Jesus assures them with the emphatic "It is I" (*ego eimi*). Matthew's Christian readers may well have understood this "I am" statement as identical to God's self-identification (see Ex. 3:14; Isa. 43:10; 51:12). The Gospel writers repeatedly use the phrase *ego eimi* to refer to Jesus in the contexts of revela-

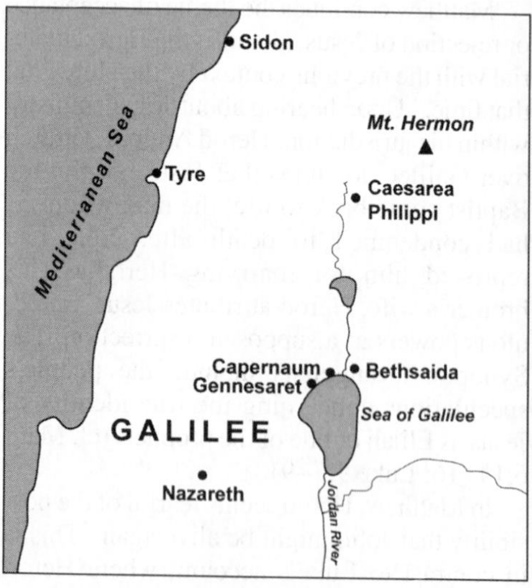

Jesus' actions in feeding the 5,000 at Bethsaida parallels his actions at the Last Supper.

.on and divine attestation (e.g., Mark 14:62; .uke 24:39; John 8:58; 18:5–6). After his resrrection and ascension Christians saw the tatements and actions of Jesus as having ,reater meaning when viewed in the "big pic-ıre" (cf. John 2:22).

Only Matthew records Peter's walking on he water (vv. 28–33). Either this is part of Aatthew's program of emphasizing Peter as he leader, albeit imperfect (cf. 16:17–19; 7:24–27), or he is presenting him as the typcal disciple. By the time Matthew's Gospel is eing written, the leadership of Peter (the Rock) has already been established (cf. also Acts and Paul's writings). The author of Aatthew, writing after Peter's death, is perhaps giving historical precedent for his preeminent ole and that of his successors.

Was Peter's request to walk on the water ıppropriate? Some say yes, since the disciples ıad been given power to perform miracles 10:1). Others, however, suggest that it was resumptuous for him to do so. Still others ıold that Peter was testing Jesus to see if the 'ghost" was indeed Jesus, saying in effect, "If you are really Jesus, then let me walk out to you." Thus Peter would be risking his life to est the hypothesis. This third interpretation loes not seem to be supported by the text. "If you are" is better translated "since you are," since the "if" clause is a first-class conditional clause, which assumes a fact (see also 4:3, 6). In other words, Peter appears to be saying, "You are truly the Lord, and I am coming out to you if you permit it."

Peter begins to sink because he doubts, putting more stock in the circumstances around him than in trusting the Lord who has said, "Come." After Jesus rescues him, he calls Peter "little-faithed one" (lit. trans. of *oligopistos*), a favorite phrase of Jesus in Matthew (6:30; 8:26; 14:31; 16:8; 17:20). Peter has faith enough to get out of the boat but not enough to walk through the storm to Jesus. Note the similar message in the stilling of the storm earlier in 8:23–27.

This miracle story not only establishes the fact that Jesus performed miracles but provides a spiritual lesson for believers. In the ancient Near East the sea was the domain of chaos and destructive forces. Already in the Old Testament the waters were viewed as dangerous and destructive, and God is the One who overcomes the waters and waves to preserve life (Job 9:8; 38:16; Ps. 77:19; Isa. 43:16). For Matthew's first readers the storm facing them may well have been persecution, a topic that frequently appears in his unique material. Christians are to step out and be bold, trusting Jesus in their vulnerability and knowing he is greater than any storm.

The endings provided by Matthew and Mark appear contradictory. Mark notes amazement (*existemi*), lack of understanding, and hardness of heart on the part of the disciples (Mark 6:51–52), while Matthew says that they "worshiped him saying 'Truly you are the Son of God'" (Matt. 14:33). In view of the miracle just witnessed, adoration and acknowledgment of the divine nature of Jesus would logically follow. D. A. Carson (1984, 345) notes that amazement can be used in contexts of "joyful worship (Lev. 9:24 [LXX] . . . Luke 5:26)"; in Mark *existemi* often "denotes amazement in response to some divine self-disclosure, but without fear."

As a harmonization of the two accounts, it appears that the disciples were in awe of Jesus; but given Peter's doubt about Jesus' saving power when he was in the middle of his walk on the water, "their hearts were hardened" (Mark 6:52). As Mark observes, they did not understand the significance of the feeding of the five thousand. The lesson of the loaves and fishes was more than mere social welfare; it was ultimately a revelation of the power behind all the forces of the cosmos. Jesus was not only their Source who could supply all their need but also Lord.

8.5. Jesus the Healer (14:34–36)

Jesus and the disciples landed at Gennesaret, which can either be the city or the fertile plain of that name, which lies on the northwest coast of the Sea of Galilee, consisting of a triangular-like shape about six miles long on the coast and extending two miles deep inland. This area is only about seven miles by water from the Bethsaida area. Apparently Jesus is well known at this time, for people recognize him and send for all the sick in the region to be brought to him.

The slightest contact with Jesus, such as touching a tassel on his prayer shawl, results in healing. Faith is not specifically mentioned as the agent of healing here, but presumably it has some effect since the lack of faith at Nazareth had greatly curtailed Jesus' ministry there (13:58). It appears as if Jesus' clothing was, to use Oral Roberts' phrase, a "point of contact for the releasing of faith" to effect healing. But the power resided in Jesus himself (Mark 5:30; Luke 8:46), and his will was involved (Matt. 8:2–3). The model for healing here is sacramental, for the power of God resides in the humanity of Jesus and everything he touches. Once an ordinary thing is touched by Jesus it is no longer ordinary! Special power is dispensed through apparently ordinary means.

Matthew elects to use a compound form of the word for healing/saving (*diasozo*; i.e., *dia* [through] plus *sozo* [save]). This makes the sense emphatic and complete, "to save through." Usually this word describes someone brought safely through as in a shipwreck, rescue, or protection from harm. In this context it emphasizes the completeness and thoroughness of Jesus' healing. The only other time this word is used in the Gospels it carries the same sense of healing (Luke 7:3).

Technically, whenever Jesus came into physical contact with an illness or with sinners, he was considered unclean by the Pharisees and other Jewish groups obsessed with keeping the ritual law. Perhaps that is why in the next story, the Pharisees and scribes complain that Jesus is too casual about ceremonial cleanness (15:1–2). The main issue, though, is not that what Jesus touches makes him unclean but rather that what *he* touches is made clean and whole (see also Acts 10:15). Getting in touch with Jesus through repentance, his Word, and the physical means of grace such as points of contact or sacraments is the key to healing and transformation. In one sense Jesus is the only healer in town, for all such grace ultimately comes from him.

8.6. Tradition and Commandment (15:1–20)

8.6.1. The Pharisees' Accusation Against Jesus' Disciples: "Why do your disciples break the tradition of the elders?" (15:1–2). Matthew uses the word "then" (*tote*) to link the demand of the Pharisees and teachers of the law for ceremonial washing (v. 2) with the healing account at the end of chapter 14, in which ceremonially unclean people were touching Jesus in order to be healed. *Tote* is one of Matthew's favorite transition words. Of the 160 times it appears in the New Testament, over 50 percent occur in Matthew's Gospel.

The "tradition of the elders" was composed of regulations designed to amplify the Mosaic law and facilitate keeping it. In accordance with tradition, Pharisees normally washed after being in a crowd, just in case they had touched a ceremonially unclean person; the issue for them was not health or hygiene. Caring more about ceremonial cleanness than the healing of the sick, they considered Jesus and his disciples unclean violators of the law (cf. Mark 7:3–4, which explains this tradition for a Gentile audience).

8.6.2. Jesus' Counterattack: "Why do you break the command of God for the sake of your tradition?" (15:3–11). Jesus does not answer the Pharisees' charge directly; rather he levels his own against them. He makes a clear distinction between God's commandments and his enemies' rather novel traditions, which did not observe the weightier matters of the law. He questions their standard operating procedures and presuppositions and shows how their traditions sabotaged the law of God for selfish ends. It is as if Jesus were saying, "Straighten out your own mess; then you can critique my practices." This is a bold counterattack since Jesus' opponents are from Jerusalem and probably represent the officials in their groups.

Jesus quotes the Mosaic law about honoring parents and speaking well of them, an infraction of which deserves death (see Ex. 20:12; 21:17; Deut. 5:16). He then cites the tradition of "Corban" (cf. Mark 7:11), in which things dedicated to God cannot be used for common things. Through legalistic subterfuge some Jews would shirk God's command to take care of their parents by saying the wealth they could have used to help them had been consecrated to God. One gets the impression that this money was to be given to the temple or synagogue. Thus, though the erring one did not actually curse his parents, refusal to meet their needs on a contrived religious technicality was tantamount to ill speaking and worse! "That this kind of shoddy transaction could be condoned by the same persons who professed shock at unwashed hands, this was the insufferable hypocrisy which revolted [Jesus]" (Vawter, 1967, 187–88). Matthew does not explain Corban, apparently assuming his readers have knowledge of Jewish customs.

At this point Jesus escalates his attack on his enemies, which increases in intensity until his arrest in Jerusalem. He seems to be provoking them and forcing their hand, a policy that contrasts sharply with his earlier habit of avoiding conflict. Jesus publicly labels the Pharisees and teachers of the law as "hypocrites," a favorite aspersion for Matthew.

Matthew's interest in fulfillment of prophecy motivates him to include Isaiah 29:13. In this citation he again makes it clear that obedience to God's law must be heartfelt and not merely verbal. Note that this is *not* a condemnation of all tradition but only that which does not keep the spirit of God's law of love.

Jesus concludes this confrontation by explaining to the people that what makes them unclean is not what goes into their mouths, but rather what comes out. Here he summarizes the nature of the law: The intent of the heart is the key to true spirituality. This is reminiscent of Jesus' exposition on the law in the Sermon on the Mount: Both righteousness and sin start in one's will and intent (5:17–48). Matthew will continue to drive home the point in later passages.

8.6.3. Jesus' Private Explanation to the Disciples (15:12–20). Jesus' disciples show concern over the fact that the Pharisees and teachers of the law are offended. This is understandable since these Jewish leaders are powerful and in times past Jesus tried to avoid confrontation with them. The reference to uprooting plants not planted by his heavenly Father calls to mind the parable of judgment concerning the wheat and the weeds (13:36–43). God calls Israel the plant he has planted. Those who practice superficial legalities that do not involve a pure intent are not the true Israel. Describing his enemies as the blind leading the blind, Jesus predicts the inevitable disaster that befalls those of impure intent. The command "Leave them" sounds like the order that the master of the field gave concerning the request to remove the weeds prematurely (13:28–30).

Peter as the spokesman for the disciples asks for an explanation of the parable (v. 15). Matthew already has and will continue to emphasize Peter's prominence among the disciples. Here he uses not the name Simon, Peter's given name, but rather the title "Peter" ("the Rock"), which Jesus has yet to give him in the narrative (16:18).

The private explanation of the parable to the disciples is characteristic of Jesus' practice of speaking obtusely in parables to the crowds and later providing a private interpretation for his disciples (13:1–52). However, on this occasion he is surprised that they require an explanation, which comes on the heels of his clash with the Pharisees. In the interpretation Jesus reiterates the essence of his teachings. Good and evil are not merely outward actions but come from the intent of the heart. The pure heart produces proper behavior.

Matthew concludes this passage by again citing Jesus' words on "unwashed hands," the issue that precipitated his teaching about true purity of heart in contrast to ceremonial cleanness (15:2). Mark, by contrast, sees Jesus' words as the rationale for the early church's laying aside of Jewish dietary restrictions: "In saying this, Jesus declared all foods 'clean'" (Mark 7:19). Matthew addresses the issues critical to his Jewish audience just as Mark addresses the issues critical to his Gentile audience.

8.7. Jesus and the Canaanite Woman (15:21–28)

Jesus withdraws into the area of Tyre and Sidon, two Phoenician cities that shared a religion and culture with the Canaanites, who controlled the Holy Land before the arrival of the Israelites. Hence he identifies the woman as "a Canaanite." Elsewhere when Matthew uses the word "withdraw" (*anachoreo*), it often indicates a tactical withdrawal in the face of hostility, which fits well with the previous context (e.g., 2:12–14; 4:12; 12:15; 14:13).

Matthew begins verse 22 with his characteristic attention-getting "behold" (*idou*), which he uses before momentous events (not translated in the NIV). In referring to the woman as a Canaanite, Matthew may be emphasizing that she is a Gentile from the land of Jezebel and Baal worship, a place traditionally hostile to exclusive devotion to Yahweh. She addresses Jesus as "Lord" (*kyrie*, from *kyrios*) three times (vv. 22, 25, 27), in contrast to Mark's one time. For Matthew Jesus' Lordship is a frequent theme. This word is a simple address of respect to superiors, but Matthew's readers, hearing it after the church has been established, would certainly understand it as having greater meaning, especially since Matthew describes the woman as falling at Jesus' feet in an act of homage or worship. Daniel J. Harrington (1991, 1:236–37) views this event as a paradigm for prayer and considers her great faith to be "praying faith."

The woman's use of the title "Son of David" not only serves Matthew's emphasis on Jesus as King but also acknowledges the Jewish nation as being the first agenda for salvation since salvation comes through a Jewish Messiah. Furthermore, it reminds Matthew's readers that the call to Israel to enlighten the nations still stands. The disciples' request that Jesus send the woman away can mean that they want him either to dismiss her immediately unsatisfied or to end her constant entreaty by healing her daughter.

The apparent brusqueness of Jesus' response seems uncharacteristic, but several factors are at work here. Apparently Jesus has entered the pagan country temporarily to avoid further conflict with his enemies. He does not intend this journey to be a mission to the Gentiles although such an option is mitigated by an earlier Gentile ministry (8:28–34). Jesus makes it clear that he is called to the "lost sheep of Israel" (15:24). Perhaps he is testing the woman, giving her an opportunity to prove her faith. Since Jesus has already healed at the Gentile centurion's request, it is clearly not a case of ethnic prejudice.

Whatever Jesus' motivation, the reader must recognize some tentativeness on his part. His indirect reference to the Gentile woman as a "dog" (the "dogs" in his statement being Gentiles and the "children" being Jews) may have the edge blunted when one notes that the word *kynarion* is a diminutive for a puppy or pet as opposed to a wild dog (v. 26). In any case, his statement remains stark. The woman is undaunted, however, and boldly answers that even household dogs are allowed to eat the crumbs that fall from their masters' tables. She is implying that for Jesus to heal her demonized daughter would take but a crumb of his power.

Jesus' amazed response that this pagan woman has great faith is reminiscent of his praise of the Roman centurion's great faith (8:5–13). This healing on behalf of a Gentile anticipates the universal ministry that the resurrected Jesus mandates at the end of Matthew (28:19–20).

8.8. More Healings (15:29–31)

Jesus leaves the area of Tyre and Sidon and goes to the region of the Sea of Galilee—probably to the eastern side of Galilee in the Decapolis (see Mark 7:31–37), which had a predominantly Gentile population. This puts him outside of Herod's jurisdiction, from whom Jesus has withdrawn since John the Baptist's execution (Matt. 14:1–13; see Carson, 1984, 356). Great crowds come to Jesus for healing, and he heals them. The listing of his miraculous healings (15:31) is similar to Isaiah's prophecies of healing: "Then will the eyes of the blind be opened and the ears of the deaf unstopped. Then will the lame leap like a deer, and the mute tongue shout for joy" (Isa. 35:5–6; see also 29:18–19).

Matthew's introductory phrase, "he went up on a mountainside and sat down" (v. 29), resembles his introduction for the Sermon on the Mount, where Jesus as a rabbi sat down to teach (5:1); here the teacher sits to heal. The compassionate miracles of Jesus are a part of his message. Here truly the medium *is* the message (see also Mark 1:27; Luke 4:36). The people's response of praising (*doxazo*, lit., "glorifying") the "God *of Israel*" supports the probability that Jesus is healing Gentiles, for why else would Matthew point out that Jews were praising the God of Israel (v. 31; cf. 9:8)? Ministry to the Gentiles helps to explain why another miraculous feast follows.

8.9. The Feeding of the Four Thousand (15:32–39)

This is the second miraculous feeding in this Gospel (see 14:13–21; cf. also Mark 6:32–44; 8:1–10). The guests for the second miraculous meal are Gentiles while the guests for the first meal were Jewish. Matthew and Mark are making the theological point that both groups are considered worthy of receiving the benefits of the kingdom of heaven. In the two meals we see the salvation of God offered both to all of Israel and to all the nations. In this miracle seven baskets are gathered up (attempts to see significance in the number "seven" here versus "twelve" in the earlier feeding have not been successful). The word for baskets here (*spyris*) is not the word used for Jewish food baskets, further heightening the Gentile overtones (BAGD, 447).

All four Gospels link the miraculous feedings to the manna that Israel received in the desert (Ex. 16:4–12) and to the eucharistic meal that Jesus instituted before his passion and death. The words Jesus spoke in performing these miracles are nearly identical to the words used to describe what he did at the Lord's Supper (see comments on 14:13–21; 26:26–29). Though fish are also part of the meal, they are not emphasized in either miracle feeding.

Matthew notes that the "four thousand" refers only to the men present (v. 38). With women and children, this could mean well over ten thousand people. The population of the country has been estimated to be a half million people. If so, the crowds fed in both miracles would have been a sizable portion of the population, and many more thousands would have heard about it.

It is not clear where Jesus goes next, for the exact location of Magadan (15:39) is unknown. Presumably it is on the western, Jewish side of the Sea of Galilee since in 16:1–12 he is confronted again by the Pharisees and Sadducees.

8.10. The Opposition of the Enemies (16:1–12)

8.10.1. Pharisees and Sadducees Seek a Sign (16:1–4). The controversy between Jesus and his enemies continues to escalate. This passage is similar to an earlier request by the Pharisees for a sign from Jesus (12:38–39). In both instances Jesus offers the "sign of Jonah," which refers to his death, burial, and resurrection. Here Matthew links the Pharisees and Sadducees in common cause against Jesus though they seldom agreed on theological or practical issues. Matthew is the only Gospel writer who links the two (3:7; 16:1, 6, 11–12; 22:34).[8] The later references to the Sanhedrin, controlled by both the Pharisees and Sadducees, undergird the fact that the two groups eventually presented a united attack against Jesus (e.g., 26:59). The word "tested" (*peirazo*) is the same word used for the temptation Satan engineered against Jesus in the desert (4:1–11), which thus links the enemies of Jesus with the evil one.

In verses 2–3 Jesus is criticizing the religious leaders of his day because they can predict the weather but cannot deduce from the signs and wonders that Jesus has already performed that he is the Messiah. It is improbable to assume that Jesus here intends the phrase "signs of the times" (v. 3) to refer to the end times; rather, it refers to the wondrous events unfolding in his critics' own day. In the Old Testament prophets adultery often represents unfaithfulness to God. (For more on this and on the sign of Jonah see comments on 12:38–39.)

8.10.2. The Leaven of the Pharisees (16:5–12). Yeast is used as both a positive and a negative sign (see comments on 13:33). Here it describes an influence that Jesus sees as negative, pervading his society. The disciples are at first confused since they tell him they have no bread to eat. Perhaps they misunderstand Jesus' warning to mean, "Do not buy any bread that contains yeast from the Pharisees and Sadducees," or perhaps their kosher laws are being scrutinized.

This is the fourth and last time the identification "little-faithed ones" (*oligopistos*) occurs in Matthew (6:30; 8:26; 14:31; 16:8). Faith here refers to a lack of understanding that can lead to a lack of trust. The lesson to be learned from Jesus' feeding miracles is that God will provide for his followers. Jesus makes it clear that his warnings have nothing to do with their immediate physical need; rather, it is the teaching of the Pharisees and Sadducees that concerns him.

8.11. Jesus Is the Messiah (16:13–17:27)

8.11.1. Peter's Confession (16:13–16). Few passages have elicited more controversy, and few bear such crucial importance regarding the nature of the church as Jesus envisioned it. The confession of Peter is found in each of the Synoptic Gospels; Matthew and Mark both note that it occurred in Caesarea Philippi, while Luke typically reports that Jesus asked the crucial question after a season of prayer (Mark 8:27–30; Luke 9:18–21). In light of the preceding context, Jesus rejects the authority of the Pharisees and Sadducees and confers a unique authority on Peter (Meier, 1990, 179).

Caesarea Philippi is at the southern edge of Mount Hermon at the source of the Jordan

River. It was a center of worship for the god Pan and was predominantly Hellenistic. Behind the city stood an enormous rock cliff, an appropriate locale for Jesus' "rock" saying.

Matthew's version of Jesus' question differs from either Mark's or Luke's. He refers to "the Son of Man" while the latter two ask who do people "say that *I* am." Is the expression "Son of Man" a way of referring to one's humanity, as used in Ezekiel (e.g., Ezek. 2:1, 3; 3:1; see also Ps. 8:4; 80:17), or does Jesus intend it to be a title for the Messiah, giving it a new meaning? The second option appears plausible since Jesus explained his mission in terms of the "one like a son of man" who appears in Daniel 7:13. It does not appear as a messianic title before the time of Jesus. Its titular use for the Messiah is used in all four Gospels, and given its Semitic character (*ben adam* and *bar nasha* in Hebrew and Aramaic respectively), it appears to have been an early title used for the Christ (Matt. 14:60; 26:63–64).

Matthew alone lists Jeremiah as one of the suggested identifications of Jesus in the minds of the people. Perhaps Matthew includes Jeremiah because he predicted God's judgment and suffered for it, grieving to tears over the plight of his people. He is an apt foreshadowing of Jesus' ministry.

Peter's response appears somewhat differently in each Gospel (see Mark 8:29 ["the Christ"]; Luke 9:20 ["the Christ of God"]; cf. John 6:69 ["the Holy One of God"]). Matthew's longer version ("the Christ, the Son of the living God") helps make it clear that Jesus' origin has nothing to do with the shrines of the pagan gods at Caesarea Philippi.

8.11.2. Jesus Blesses Peter (16:17–20). This blessing and commissioning of Peter appear only in Matthew. The passage has several characteristic aspects of Matthean style, but it also betrays several Aramaic and Semitic aspects that suggest its antiquity. Aramaic appears to be the language behind the Greek text as we have it today.

8.11.2.1. Simon Becomes Peter (16:17–18a). In giving the blessing, Jesus addresses Peter as "Simon son of Jonah" (*Simon Bariona*) and acknowledges that the only way he can know that Jesus is the Christ is through divine revelation and not by human speculation. *Bariona* ("*Bar Jona*") is Aramaic for "son of Jonah." Jesus then gives Simon the new name "Peter" (*Petros*), meaning "Rock," as they stand before the great rock behind the city with Mount Hermon in the visible distance. Upon this rock (Gk. *petra*) Jesus promises to build his church. Clearly Jesus intends the first rock, Peter, to be identified with the second rock.

Some scholars try to distance the two rocks by noting that Peter is *Petros* in Greek (a masculine noun), while the second rock is *petra* (a feminine noun). They maintain that the first denotes a little stone and the latter a sizable geologic formation. This interpretation asserts that the *petra* on which Jesus builds is the *confession* of Peter, not the man Peter.

It is reasonable, however, for *petra* to become *petros* when it refers to Simon because in Greek a man naturally bears the masculine form of a noun rather than the feminine. Otherwise it would be like calling Andrew, Andrea! Furthermore, the alleged difference between *petros* and *petra* evaporates when the original Aramaic is considered: "You are *Kepha*, and on this *kepha* I will build my church." (*Kepha* is the original of the name "Cephas," used for Peter.) The most obvious meaning of the text in Aramaic, Greek, or English is that Peter is the rock, and even most Protestant scholarship supports this. The use of *Petros/petra* in relationship with building in the context that follows reflects the teaching on the church where Jesus and the apostles are the foundation of the church (Acts 2:42; Eph. 2:20–21; Col. 1:18; 1 Tim. 3:15; 1 Peter 2:4–7).

8.11.2.2. The Church (16:18b). Matthew is the only Gospel to use the word "church" (Gk. *ekklesia*). The *idea* behind the concept "church" is in the Old Testament; *ekklesia* and other Greek words were used to translate the Hebrew word *qahal*, which distinguished God's righteous people from others. The Qumran community also held the idea of an elect community in the same era in which Jesus ministered. Therefore establishing a messianic community is not alien to Jesus the Jew.

It has been suggested that Jesus could never have envisioned establishing a church since he anticipated the imminent consummation of the end times. Several points mitigate against this suggestion. (1) It would seem remote that a Jewish Messiah would not establish an end-time community to partake of the messianic banquet. (2) Jesus was gathering disciples and ollowers in increasing numbers. Note here hat Jesus is establishing his church on the asis of apostolic authority. The eccentricity of ndividualism and the plurality of denominations that pervade Western culture would have een strange to Jesus and his followers. (For nore on Matthew's interest in Peter's role see omments on 10:2.)

8.11.2.3. The Keys of the Kingdom 16:19–20). Peter's receiving the keys appears o be a singular commission in light of the Old estament. In Isaiah the keys refer to the power f the majordomo, the prime minister of the ing. Eliakim received the key of David from ing Hezekiah, which he alone wore on his houlder. He was then the singular deputy of he king; to deal with him was to deal with the ower of the king. "What he opens no one can hut, and what he shuts no one can open" (Isa. 2:22). Although the other apostles receive a imilar commission later (18:18–19), they do ot receive the keys of the Messiah's right-and man. Also, rabbis were given a key as a ign that they were qualified to teach the law.

Binding and loosing can have a varied neaning in the experience of the church (e.g., xorcizing demons, extending God's forgiveess, pronouncing doctrines, and prescribing ertain practices). However, in the historical ontext of Jesus' day, binding and loosing eferred to the practice of rabbis requiring their ollowers to observe laws or to release them om obligations. Peter then becomes the chief eacher and executor of the teachings of Jesus. resumably Peter's office would not be exeuted apart from the direction of the Holy pirit (John 14:16–17, 26; Acts 4:8). His ntempered character exhibited in the next assage and at Jesus' arrest demonstrates that is fulfillment of his commission is only ccomplished through a special grace.

Here the office of Peter is a unique one. hroughout this passage Jesus is addressing eter personally (in the second person singur). He is not instructing the others yet (see 8:18). Jesus also gives him two other comissions later (Luke 22:31–32; John 21:15–7). Furthermore, in Acts Peter has a promient role as *primus inter pares* ("first among quals") among the apostles.

From this passage alone one cannot establsh that the successors to Peter were endowed ith his singular commission and primary authority in the church. Apparently Jesus intended some sense of hierarchy in his messianic community with the ascending order of disciples: the Seventy, the Twelve, the three (Peter, James, and John), and finally Peter (see also Acts 6:1–8; 8:4, 14; 15:4, 13–19; Titus 1:5). In light of the fact that most scholars think that Matthew's Gospel was written after Peter's death, Matthew may have had in mind Peter's successor. The church the first apostles left behind assumed that this singular power continued. Not everything the early church believed was written down (see 2 Thess. 2:15).

That Jesus commanded the disciples to secrecy concerning his messianic identity is not surprising. Earlier he had asked people he healed to remain silent lest word get out prematurely and his enemies arise. Here the command to be silent is best explained in the following passage.

8.11.3. Jesus Predicts His Death (16:21–23). Jesus reveals a new aspect of his ministry for which his disciples are not ready: his suffering, death, and resurrection. This was not the popular idea of the Messiah, who was to be a military leader freeing the Jews from Roman oppression and ushering in a new era of righteousness. Therefore, Peter begins to rebuke Jesus, for he does not wish nor can he imagine that his Master, the Messiah, will ever come to harm. The disciples cannot see the Messiah as Isaiah's Suffering Servant (Isa. 52:13–53:12).

Jesus' stinging counter-rebuke (v. 23) makes clear how crucial this role is. Identifying Peter with Satan reminds us of the temptations Jesus endured in the desert, where the role of the Messiah was one of the points of contention (4:1–11). Jesus calls Peter a "stumbling block," which contrasts him to the building block of the previous passage. If the disciples are unable to handle the death of the Messiah, then it is certainly wise to command them to silence (16:20).

8.11.4. The Disciple Will Follow the Master (16:24–28). In revealing the nature of the Messiah-King Jesus reveals the nature of the kingdom and the true disciple. If suffering and death await the Master, they surely await the disciple as well. The nature of discipleship involves a continual dying to things contrary to the kingdom. But this is not an exercise in masochism, for, paradoxically, the law of the kingdom is that only what is given up can be gained. To do otherwise would be to practice some form of idolatry. The disciple must be willing to die (Luke 9:23 adds "daily"). Some disciples will even be required to die physically for the kingdom.

The disciple is willing to die because the stakes are high: One's own soul is to be won or lost. The disciple sacrifices, knowing full well that the Son of Man will judge his or her actions at his coming (vv. 26–27, citing Ps. 62:12; Prov. 24:12; for the use of the expression *cross*, see comments on Matt. 10:38).

Verse 28 suggests that some of the disciples will not die before they see this fulfillment of end-time judgment. It is not clear what Jesus knew concerning the timetable for the end times (24:36). It appears, however, that Matthew, who records this saying of Jesus, has no problem also noting that the mission is to continue to all nations (28:19–20). In other words, the end times begin with Jesus' ministry, yet their complete consummation is yet to come.

It may be significant that this prediction of Jesus regarding his coming in glory occurs immediately before his transfiguration in 17:1–9. In one sense those "standing here" did not see death until they saw proleptically the coming glory of Jesus in that event. The nature of the end times is "already, but not yet," like a marriage before the consummation.

8.11.5. The Transfiguration of Jesus (17:1–13). The transfiguration of Jesus provides divine confirmation of Peter's confession that Jesus is the Messiah (16:16). It also confirms Jesus' understanding of messiahship as having a component not only of suffering and death (the cross) but also of glory. It is a proleptic fulfillment of Jesus' prediction in 16:28, a foretaste of the final establishment of the kingdom.

8.11.5.1. Jesus Is Transfigured (17:1–2). The reference to "six days" (v. 1) is reminiscent of the time between the appearance of the cloud of glory and the beginning of the revelation of the law to Moses on Mount Sinai (Ex. 24:16). Note that precise times between events are rare in the Synoptics. Luke says "eight days," which is a Greek expression of a week. The inner three disciples—Peter, James, and John—are the ones Jesus allows to see his private moments of communion with his Father as well as to participate in special revelatory events (see also 26:36; cf. Mark 5:37). This speaks of a nascent hierarchy in the early church (16:18–19; 17:24–27; 18:18; 20:20–23). Moses too had an entourage of three—Aaron, Nadab, and Abihu—at his experience on Mount Sinai (Ex. 24:1, 9).

The "high mountain" (v. 1) is also reminiscent of Moses' reception of the law, and in the Gospels revelations and theophanies occur on mountains (e.g., 5:1; 15:29; 28:16). Traditionally Mount Tabor has been identified as the location of Jesus' transfiguration, a place that is considerably south of Caesarea Philippi. Perhaps this event occurred among the heights of the area of Mount Hermon.

The word "transfigured" (*metamorphoo*, v. 2) is the origin of the English word "metamorphosis," indicating a profound change. The word is used in regard to believers in Romans 12:2 and 2 Corinthians 3:18, but here it refers to an external as well as an internal change

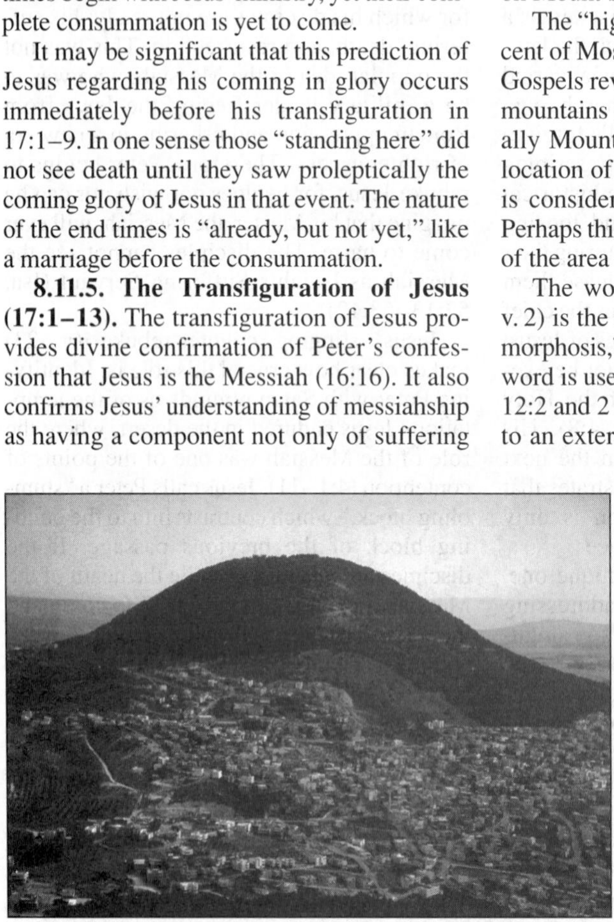

Mt. Tabor, the traditional site of Jesus' transfiguration, has two monasteries located on the mountaintop.

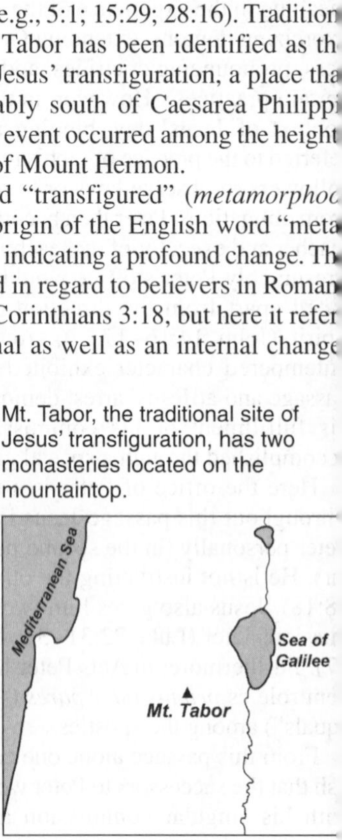

Even Jesus' clothes change in appearance. The shining of his face parallels the appearance of Moses after he was in the presence of God on Mount Sinai (Ex. 34:29).

8.11.5.2. The Appearance of Moses and Elijah (17:3–4). Moses and Elijah are the major figures of the Law and the Prophets (see also 5:17; 7:12; 11:13; 22:40). Thus these two Old Testament figures provide a heavenly witness to the revelation of Jesus. Elijah had ascended into heaven while Moses died; however, in later Jewish teaching his body was assumed into heaven. Luke says they also know about Jesus' impending "exodus." The saints in heaven, then, do not cease to exist, nor are they in a comatose state. They are alive and able to communicate with those on earth—in this instance with Jesus, Peter, James, and John. Although Jesus' transfiguration primarily reveals his nature as the heavenly Messiah, it also shows that departed saints are active participants in and witnesses to the ongoing work of God (Heb. 12:1). Death is not nonexistence for God's faithful.

In Matthew's version Peter calls Jesus "Lord" (*kyrios*), while in Mark he addresses him as "Rabbi" (v. 4; Mark 9:5). In Matthew Jesus' enemies address him as "Rabbi." Peter's suggestion that they build "three shelters" (*skene*, "tabernacle, tent") may suggest the Feast of Tabernacles, though it was probably not the time for it (Lev. 23:39–43). The Tent of Meeting in the desert indicated God's presence (Ex. 33:7–11). In Matthew it is unclear what Peter intended. Mark sheds light on Peter's remark with his statement: "He did not know what to say, they were so frightened" (Mark 9:6). What is manifestly clear in what follows is that three shelters for three prophets is not the issue here but *one* heavenly Son.

8.11.5.3. The Voice From the Cloud (17:5–9). These verses provide divine clarification. Even as Peter is speaking, a bright cloud overshadows them. Matthew uses his attention-getting "behold" (*idou*) twice in verse 5 (absent in the NIV), indicating a profound turn of events is about to occur. The bright cloud is reminiscent of the presence of God and his glory in the desert after the Exodus, in the giving of the law, and in the tabernacle and temple (Ex. 16:10; 19:9; 24:15–16; 33:9; 2 Macc. 2:8). This is the Shekinah, the glory of God visible. The disciples (Matt. 17:6) cannot stand in the presence of the glory-cloud, as was the case also with the priests when the Shekinah filled the temple of Solomon after the ark had been placed inside (1 Kings 8:10–11).

The voice from heaven is different in each Synoptic Gospel. Matthew records here the same heavenly words as were spoken at Jesus' baptism (for more on the title "Beloved" [NIV, "whom I love"], see comment on 3:17). The final answer to Peter's suggestion for three shelters is the singular sight of Jesus at the end of his transfiguration (v. 8). In verse 9 the disciples are again commanded to silence until the resurrection of Jesus.

8.11.5.4. Elijah Comes First (17:10–13). The appearance of Elijah with Jesus causes the disciples to ask how the roles of these two interact. The belief of "the teachers of the law" (v. 10) refers to Malachi 4:6 (see also Sir. 48:1–12). There is no explicit evidence that before Jesus the eschatological role of Elijah was seen as fulfilled by *both* a precursor to the Messiah *and* an Elijah-Messiah figure. The disciples probably understood that the Messiah would be the end-time Elijah. Since they had just seen Elijah in the transfiguration event as separate and distinct from Jesus, they naturally had some questions.

Jesus therefore reinterprets the eschatological Elijah role in terms of a precursor, whom he explicitly identifies as John the Baptist (compare 17:7–13 and 11:12–14 with Mark 1:2; 9:13; Luke 7:24–35; see comments on Matt. 3:3–4; 11:7–15). It could be that having seen the old Elijah the disciples expect the immediate advent of the Day of the Lord. Jesus' response is that they had seen Elijah even earlier and that their timetable for the end times needs correction; there is more to come before the end. Thus Jesus reiterates the announcement of his approaching death and resurrection (17:22–23).

8.11.6. Jesus Heals a Boy Possessed by a Spirit (17:14–21). After the mountaintop experience of the transfiguration Jesus and the three disciples are confronted with an evil spirit, who has thwarted the other disciples' attempts to dislodge it. Matthew's main concern here is to expose the unbelief of the disciples and to present Jesus' teaching on the power of faith. The son is literally called "moonstruck" (*seleniazomai*) or a lunatic (most modern translations see the situation here as a form of epilepsy). Matthew notes that the malady is demonic in origin, requiring an exorcism. The issue is further complicated in that Matthew refers to a healing (v. 16). (For more on the relation between spirits and illness in the first century, see comments on 4:23–25.)

Jesus rebukes the disciples, calling them an "unbelieving and perverse generation" (v. 17). Like Moses he too descends the mountain of revelation only to find faithlessness at the bottom (cf. Ex. 32). Jesus identifies the disciples with the spirit of the age, which he has already condemned as a "wicked and adulterous generation" (Matt. 12:38–45). He notes that the reason they failed in the attempted exorcism was their little or inadequate faith (*oligopistia*; see comments on the related adjective in 6:30; 8:26; 14:31; 16:8). Jesus states that a small amount of faith removes all impossibility (see also 13:31–32). Among the rabbis, moving a mountain was a figurative expression for a remote possibility (cf. Isa. 54:10; 1 Cor. 13:2).

8.11.7. Jesus Again Predicts His Passion (17:22–23). For the second time Jesus predicts his suffering and death, much to the heaviness of his followers. Here he adds that he will be delivered or handed over (*paradidomi*, i.e., betrayed) to his enemies (see also 26:15–21).

8.11.8. The Messiah Submits to the Temple Tax (17:24–27). Every male Jew was required to pay annually a tax for the maintenance of the temple (Ex. 30:11–16). As the King, Jesus is not obliged to pay it, but to avoid offense he does. His followers too should avoid unnecessary offense and fulfill the Lord's call to humility (Matt. 5:5). This account of paying taxes occurs only in Matthew, which is in keeping with the Gospel that bears the name of the former tax-collector-turned-disciple. Peter's acting in proxy for Jesus and paying the tax for both of them is in keeping with his newly acquired authority as Jesus' prime minister (16:18–19) and is yet another example of Peter's acting as spokesman for the disciples (e.g., 14:28–33; 16:16–17; 18:21–22).

9. Jesus' Instructions to the Church (The Fourth Discourse: 18:1–35)

This is the fourth major block of Jesus' teachings that Matthew presents in his program of presenting Jesus as the new Moses. As a parallel to the five books in the Old Testament ascribed to Moses, Matthew presents five major groupings of the teachings of Jesus (see Introduction and comments on 5:1–12). Here Matthew clearly identifies the beginning and end of the section: "at that time" (18:1) and "when Jesus had finished these sayings" (19:1). In this section he gives instructions to his disciples regarding the nature of greatness in the kingdom of heaven and further instructions on church discipline and authority. Though verses 15–17 have a certain legal tone to them, most of Matthew's narrative is more pastoral.

9.1. The Greatest Is a Child (18:1–4)

The question concerning who is the greatest in the kingdom arises from Jesus' acknowledgment that, though he is a king, he condescends to pay taxes to avoid risking offense. This troubles the disciples' more conventional understanding of greatness. In the midst of the great power and authority Jesus had given the disciples (see comments on 16:14–19), Jesus reveals that the nature of his kingdom is based on childlike humility. The word "child" (*paidion*) refers to a child twelve years old or younger, who in Jewish culture had no significant social status.

This is the paradoxical nature of the kingdom of heaven: The childlike and willing slave nature is the true essence of Jesus' reign. All true church government must serve and reflect these values (see also 20:25–28). Jesus has turned the values of the world upside down. Acceptance of Jesus is measured by acceptance of the truly humble members of the church (18:5–6; see also 5:3, 5; 10:40; 23:12; 25:31–46). The verb "change" (18:3) is literally "turn" (*strepho*), indicating a profound change of behavior on the part of the disciples.

9.2. Stumbling Blocks for the Little Ones (18:5–9)

The noun *skandalon* and the verb *skandalizo* are translated as "cause . . . to sin" in the NIV. Other translators use "offense" or "stumbling block" (cf. "offend" in 17:27). Of the forty-four uses of this word group in the New Testament, Matthew uses it nineteen times, often in contexts of accepting or rejecting Jesus or in contexts about judgment. It is to narrow to interpret it as "cause . . . to sin" when other offenses might be intended.

The context here is clearly judgment and potential damnation—a frequent theme for Matthew. Of the twelve New Testament uses of the Hebrew-based word for "hell" (*geenna*), Matthew uses it seven times (5:22, 29, 30; 10:28; 18:9; 23:15, 33). For the plucking out of an eye or amputation of a hand or foot and the fire of hell, see comments on 5:29–30. In this context these expressions may refer to excommunication of an offending member. "Woe" (18:7) is indicative of judgment as well.

9.3. Little Ones and the Lost Sheep (18:10–14)

The "little ones," the humble followers of Jesus, have what is commonly called guardian angels, who "always see the face of my Father in heaven" (v. 10). The reference to the "face" of God indicates his presence (see also Gen. 48:16; Dan. 2:28; 6:22; Heb. 1:4; Tob. 5:4). In other words, offenses to people of no status on earth are exposed before the very face of God.

Attempts to identify the angels of these little ones with their spirits that resemble their bodies (cf. also Acts 12:15) are not convincing and create other problems. Given that an angel frees Peter in Acts 12, "his angel" cannot be identified merely with his own spirit. Saints will be *like* angels, but they are not angels now nor will they ever be (Matt. 22:30; Luke 20:36; 2 Bar. 51:5).[9]

Matthew's version of the parable of the lost (or straying) sheep is found in a different context from Luke's Gospel (Luke 15:3–7). In Luke it is the first of three parables on lost things of value—the lost sheep, the lost coin, and the lost son (15:3–32)—and is addressed to Jesus' enemies, who fault him for associating with sinners (15:1–2). In Matthew it is addressed to his disciples and emphasizes the compassionate concern they should have for any erring person.

Apparently the shepherd here is God the Father (vv. 10, 14). Jesus' disciples, especially the Twelve, are to emulate the shepherd in caring for the little ones. This parable would have had significant meaning to the pastors in Matthew's audience. In Ezekiel 34 the shepherds of Israel were rebuked because they did not look for the sheep that had wandered away. God, instead, would shepherd the people. Here in Matthew the caution not to give cause or occasion for sin or offense among the little ones is directed to the pastors.

The word for "wanders away" (vv. 12–13) is *planao* rather than "lost" (*apollymi*), as in Luke 15. Of the fifteen times *planao* is used in the Gospels, Matthew uses it eight times. It often refers to deception practiced by false prophets and false christs (see also the use of related words *plane* and *planos* in 27:63–64). Matthew is deeply concerned about false leadership and deceit. His version of this parable is more ominous than Luke's because Matthew hints that the finding of the sheep is uncertain: "*if* he finds it" (18:13). The lost have God's special attention, and he wills that none be "lost" or "destroyed" (*apollymi*, v. 14).

9.4. Discipline in the Community (18:15–20)

Many of the important manuscripts omit the phrase "against you" in verse 15, which probably did not stand in the original text. Jesus is instructing the disciples how to handle not personal affronts so much as sins in general. This broader understanding regarding sins fits the theme Matthew presents at the beginning of the chapter.

Jesus follows the teaching of the Jewish law—the Torah—in instructing his followers how to confront sin. (1) The Torah taught that a neighbor be corrected when found in sin; to ignore sin was to "share in [the] guilt" (Lev. 19:17). Correction was made privately to save the dignity of both parties—the accused brother if guilty and the accuser if mistaken. (2) The Torah required two or three witnesses to sustain a charge if the offender refused to heed the initial confrontation (Deut. 19:15; cf. Matt. 18:16).

If the person in sin refuses to listen after the meeting with witnesses, Jesus instructs that the matter be brought before "the church" (v. 17). This demonstrates the juridical nature of his instructions; he is concerned with more than irksome personal affronts, namely, grave matters that can result in expulsion from the community. (For the use of the word "church" to describe the messianic community, see comments on 16:18.) To call an unrepentant fellow believer a "pagan or a tax collector" reflects the Jewish character of Matthew and his audience. (For the Christian practice of shunning the recalcitrant, see 1 Cor. 5:1–5; 2 Thess. 3:6–15; 2 John 10.)

This three-step procedure for dealing with sin is similar to that of the Qumran community (1QS 5:24–6:2). It is impossible to say whether Jesus assimilated this practice from the first-century sect who penned the Dead Sea Scrolls. His instructions concerning repentance and restoration are rather generous in contrast to the Qumran community's harsh punishments for infractions, including irrevocable excommunication.

In this context, "bind" and "loose" (v. 18) refer to the disciples' power to extend forgiveness or impose excommunication. Jesus had already given this authority to Peter (see comments on 16:17–19). Although the rest of the disciples now receive similar power, Jesus does not give them the keys to the kingdom, indicating that Jesus intended a special role for Peter.

The reference to "two or three com[ing] together" (v. 20) has a legal overtone since Jewish literature refers to this pattern for the study of the Torah: "If two sit together and words of the Law are between them, the Shekinah [the glorious presence of God] abides between them" (M. *Aboth* 3:2). Thus, the decisions of the community have the weight of God's authority behind them.

Regarding asking for "anything" in agreement with one other person (v. 19), the context of church discipline should be noted. This is not a *carte blanche* for fulfilling any whim we may have; one must speak in the will of and to the glory of God (John 14:13; 15:5, 16).

9.5. Forgiveness Seventy Times Seven (18:21–22)

The previous instruction concerning forgiveness (v. 18) raises a question in Peter's mind (note the connecting word "then" in v. 21). In light of the commission he has previously received regarding binding and loosing (16:17–19), Peter asks for clarification on how he should exercise his responsibility to pronounce forgiveness for a "brother . . . [who] sins against me." One cannot assume that sins against Peter or any other disciple are just personal affronts. Sins against people are sins against God, as the Ten Commandments suggest (Ex. 20:1–17; Deut. 5:6–21; cf. 1 John 4:20). Sin has both a horizontal and vertical effect, a slap in the face of both God and humankind.

Peter no doubt thought himself generous in offering forgiveness as much as seven times; traditionally the rabbis suggested three times. Jesus' response can be translated two ways: either as seventy-seven times or as seven times seventy (i.e., 490). If this is an antithetical reference to the vengeance of Lamech (Gen. 4:24), then seventy-seven is more likely. The more crucial issue is not the correct number but the correct attitude—being ever ready to forgive.

9.6. The Unforgiving Servant (18:23–35)

Jesus' call for willing forgiveness is the occasion for this parable. Matthew strongly links the two passages with his "therefore" (*dia touto*, lit., "for this reason"). Jesus begins by giving an example of extravagant forgiveness. That a servant (probably a court minister) owed ten thousand talents is incredible; Jesus probably exaggerates the astronomical sum for effect. A talent was a high denomination of money, equaling six to ten thousand denarii (one denarius was a laborer's average wage for a day's work). In terms of today's money, it would have been a debt in the billions of dollars. The servant could never hope to live long enough to accrue or swindle such an amount. So desperate is his plight that he and his family are to be sold into slavery (v. 25), but even that will hardly make a dent in the sum owed. Answering how the man can expect to repay it is beyond the function of the parable.

In pity the king writes off the outlandish amount (v. 26), which now is graciously referred to as a loan (*daneion*; NIV, "debt"). But after the servant leaves the king, he finds a fellow servant who owes him one hundred denarii (about three-months' minimum wage). His seizing the man by the throat stands in stark contrast to the king's compassion (v. 28). The forgiven servant rejects the very same plea he has just made to the king and throws his fellow servant into prison.

The other servants tell the king about the rascal's actions. The king calls the unmerciful servant "wicked," rescinds the forgiveness he has previously given him, and delivers him to the torturers in prison until he pays the impossible debt. Clearly this refers to eternal punish-nent—an item high on Matthew's agenda. Note also that the words "debt" (*opheiletes*) and "owed" (*opheilomenon*, vv. 32–34) are from the same word group as the word for sins used in the Lord's Prayer (*opheilema*; 6:12–15). This is a sobering commentary on the Lord's Prayer and the Sermon on the Mount, which say that forgiveness will not be given to an unforgiving person (see comments on 6:14–15; see also Luke 6:36). Clearly from the state of the first servant, forgiveness cannot be earned, "but we can lose it" (Meier, 1990, 209).

God's forgiveness is free and is, therefore, an act of undeserved grace; what one does in response to grace, however, determines where one will spend eternity. Forgiveness accepted changes the heart of the recipient if it is truly effective. The phrase "forgive your brother from your heart" (v. 35) precludes any pretext of legalism and self-salvation; nevertheless, God's requirement for obtaining a lasting forgiveness precludes any program of cheap grace that does not transform the recipient.

10. The Trip to Jerusalem: Narrative (19:1–20:34)

10.1. Jesus Begins the Journey to Jerusalem (19:1–2)

Matthew concludes Jesus' previous discourse (v. 1a; see comments on 7:28–29) and turns to his final trip from Galilee to Jerusalem. Like Mark, he records an itinerary that avoids Samaria by passing through the region beyond Jordan, a route most Jews took between Galilee and the Jewish capital (Mark 10:1). This differs from Luke's account, which speaks of Jesus going through a Samaritan village apparently on this same trip. Neither account, apparently, is a complete itinerary.

Matthew mentions healing at the beginning of the trip (19:2), but what predominate throughout the narrative are his teachings. Since this section does not end in 22:46 with the identifying phrase "when Jesus had finished sayings these things" (cf. 19:1 and comment on 7:28–29), it is not considered one of Matthew's five major teaching sections. The narrative heightens Jesus' conflict with his enemies, which intensifies the closer he gets to Jerusalem. There Jesus will deliver his fifth and final major block of teaching, known as the Olivet Discourse (24:1–25:46).

10.2. On Divorce (19:3–9)

The Pharisees test Jesus with a question on divorce. The word "test" (*peirazo*) is the same word used for the devil's temptation of Jesus (4:1). Mark's version records the Pharisees asking a simple question concerning the legality of divorce (Mark 10:2), while Matthew adds the phrase "for any and every reason" (Matt. 19:3). Their question appears irrelevant and inconsequential in the face of the pressing healing needs. Presumably the Pharisees have heard about Jesus' teaching on marriage and the stringent standard he set for his followers, which requires more than the Mosaic law (5:27–32).

The Pharisees are trying to draw Jesus into an ongoing controversy between two rabbinic schools of thought (Rabbis Hillel and Shammai) regarding divorce. Hillel allowed a man to divorce his wife for any shortcoming while Shammai allowed divorce only in the case of sexual immorality (see also comments on 5:31–32). Jesus' answer cuts through the controversy by examining what God intended for marriage (19:4–6). A man and a woman are to be united as one flesh (Gen. 1:27; 2:24; 1 Cor. 6:16; Eph. 5:31). Jesus concludes that God intends the union to be indissoluble, and it is not his will that humans try to undo the union of husband and wife.

The Pharisees next ask about Moses' permission to divorce, a question that plays into the logical ramification of Jesus' first answer: If God created the institution of marriage with a view to an irrevocable fusion of two into one, then any action that frustrates or ignores that divine intent is less than compliance with God's will. Jesus asks the better question: It is not, "What does the law allow?" but "What does God intend?"

Jesus assumes the existence of natural law. His rebuke for the people's hardness of heart is particularly strong. Hardness of heart indicates coldness, rebelliousness, and obstinacy, sometimes in the context of unbelief and mistrust of God (Prov. 17:20; Jer. 4:4; Ezek. 3:7; Sir. 16:9; Mark 10:5; 16:14). Jesus' reference to "your wives" drags the issue of impure motive and legal loopholing to his enemies' door! Such indictments infuriate them to the point that they will eventually kill him.

Jesus does not see the divorce exception as a *command* but as an *allowance* (contrast v. 7

with v. 8). In the case of adultery the forgiveness of the prophet Hosea for his wife, Gomer, demonstrates that even this impediment is not an impossible one. The effect of divorce on children is egregious and hardhearted. The indiscriminate use of divorce in recent Western civilization has become an epidemic of rebellion and self-will. "Has not the LORD made them one? In flesh and spirit they are his. And why one? Because he was seeking godly offspring. So guard yourself in your spirit, and do not break faith with the wife of your youth. 'I hate divorce,' says the LORD God of Israel" (Mal. 2:15–16).

It has been debated whether adultery is grounds both for divorce *and* remarriage. Note that only Matthew includes the words "except for marital unfaithfulness" (v. 9; contrast with Mark 10:11). It is not clear whether Jesus is condoning remarriage in the case of adultery. Matthew's exception juxtaposed with Mark's citation of Deuteronomy 24:1–4 makes it clear at least that remarriage on any other grounds is wrong. Given Jesus' remarks here and in the Sermon on the Mount (5:31–32) as well as Paul's teaching (1 Cor. 6:16; Eph. 5:31), the church has held her members to a higher view of marriage and has been loathe to countenance divorce and remarriage. The issue is not "What is permissible?" but "What is God's intent?"

10.3. On Celibacy (19:10–12)

The disciples express reserve about marriage in regard to its indissolubility. In verse 11 it is not clear whether the "word" that not all can accept refers to the teaching on marriage, the disciples' comments, or the celibacy saying here. The word "for" (*gar*) in verse 12 seems to link it with the last option. Jesus apparently uses the word "eunuch" both literally and figuratively here. The text more literally reads, "For there are eunuchs who have been so from birth, and there are eunuchs who have been made eunuchs by men, and there are eunuchs who have made themselves eunuchs for the sake of the kingdom of heaven" (RSV). Birth defects and human cruelty are literal, but "made themselves eunuchs" is probably figurative.

The law of Moses had a negative view of castration as ceremonially unacceptable to God (Lev. 22:24; Deut. 23:1). In Jewish society unmarried men were disparagingly called eunuchs, so that this saying may serve as defense of Jesus' unmarried state. Note th probable celibacy of John the Baptist an Paul. Also, the Essenes were known to remai unmarried, and perhaps some of the Qumra community were unmarried as well. The NIV therefore, translates "made themselve eunuchs for the sake of the kingdom o heaven" as "renounced marriage because o the kingdom of heaven." The optional natur of "the one who can accept this should accep it" is unusual in Jesus' teaching. Clearly Jesu approves both of celibacy and marriag (vv. 4–5). There are different callings and dif ferent gifts for the disciples.

10.4. Jesus Blesses the Little Childre (19:13–15)

Like the patriarchs of old, the rabbis blesse children (Mishnah, *Sopherim* 18:5). The dis ciples here rebuke those who are bringing the children to Jesus, though we are not told wh Children did not significantly figure in majo affairs. Jesus is not saying that children ow the kingdom of heaven, but those who are lik children compose the kingdom (see commen on 18:2–6). The laying on of Jesus' hands i associated with blessing (Gen. 48:8–20).

10.5. The Rich Young Man (19:16–22)

This incident occurs in all three Synopti Gospels, and each account provides addition information (Mark 10:17–22; Luke 18:18 23). Matthew describes the man wh approaches Jesus as young and wealthy (Ma 19:20, 22) while Luke calls him a ruler (Luk 18:18). Mark and Luke record that the ma addresses Jesus as "good teacher," whi Matthew makes the adjective "good" a sub stantive ("good thing" or "good deed," vv. 16 17). In Mark and Luke Jesus disavows himse of the title "good," reserving it to God alon by contrast, Matthew persists in speaking "the good" in general (v. 17).

Why does Matthew deviate from the oth Synoptics? While a firm answer to this que tion cannot be made, we should note that wo "good" here does not have an ethical impo but an ontological one. A good carpenter ca make a good house, and the goodness of th house derives from the good maker. The ult mate expression of good can only be God, an he is the measure of all good. Comparing the most godly saint to God is like comparing a candle to the sun. Seeing no diminution of the nature of Jesus, Matthew allows the final equation: "There is only One who is good" (v. 17). This statement is reminiscent of the Shema: "Hear, O Israel: The LORD our God, the LORD is one" (Deut. 6:4). Jesus' reference to a good God who controls all is meant as a corrective to any attempt at self-salvation.

The reason why Matthew concentrates on the good act rather than the good teacher is clear in Jesus' response: "If you want to enter life, obey the commandments" (v. 17b). Righteousness as something one must live out as well as receive is a major part of Matthew's message (e.g., 5:17–20, 43–48; 18:21–35). The young man is fixated on a penultimate good act that will cinch eternal life. He responds to Jesus' word about obeying God's commands with, "Which ones?" Jesus cites several commands, concluding with the general statement, "and love your neighbor as yourself." This final command is the justification for Jesus' requirement that the young man provide for the poor by giving his wealth away. The ruler's query, "What do I still lack?" (v. 20) indicates that he knows that the conventional concept of righteousness needs completion; he is seeking to do something beyond what is required.

What Jesus requires of the young man indeed is phenomenal—giving away his great wealth to aid the poor. However, the radical absolute goodness he seeks is God, and God will brook no rival for the young man's attention; his wealth impedes him. The ultimate good act of any human is to be wholly devoted to God. The word "perfect" in verse 21 is *teleios*, which indicates completion, not absolute perfection (see comment on 5:48).

Is this call to sell all required of all Christians? We have numerous examples of people, such as St. Anthony, St. Benedict, St. Francis, and St. Clare, who literally lived this out (cf. also Acts 2:45), but apparently not all are required to forego personal wealth (cf. Acts 5:4). Matthew 19:26 indicates that it is possible for the rich to be saved. The demands of discipleship vary, as the parable of the merciful employer in 20:1–16 demonstrates. One thing is clear: Every disciple must be willing to dispense with anything the Master thinks will impede his or her walk with God. The act of giving away all one's goods is not in itself complete, for Jesus adds, "Come, follow me" (v. 21; see also 1 Cor. 13:3).

The young man's response is sobering and chillingly paradigmatic for many today. He leaves grieving, wanting to follow Jesus but clinging to his addiction to materialism. Treasure in heaven lasts. The one thing that we preserve above all costs reveals our true affections and values (see comments on 6:19–21; 13:45–46).

10.6. The Cost and Reward of Discipleship (19:23–30)

The Jewish-oriented Matthew includes the Semitic word *amen* ("I tell you the truth") transliteration into Greek and uses "kingdom of heaven" in verse 23 rather than "kingdom of God." Note, however, that "kingdom of God" appears in verse 24 (see Introduction; see also Matt. 6:33; 12:25–28; 19:24; 21:31, 43). The two phrases are synonymous, not two separate eras or entities.

In verse 24 Jesus uses hyperbole to emphasize the difficulty wealth brings to discipleship (see also 13:22). Verse 26 makes it clear that Jesus is expressing what seems to be physically impossible. The disciples may have been surprised at Jesus' statement since traditionally wealth was seen as a result of God's blessing (Deut. 28:1–14), though the dangers of wealth are also noted in Judaism (Prov. 15:16; 30:8–9; Ezek. 7:19; Sir. 31:5–7). Here again Jesus has reversed the values of the world (see Matt. 20:24–28).

The disciples' question in verse 25, "Who then can be saved?" may carry that popular assumption that riches serve as an indication of God's blessing. If the rich are not going to make it, then how can any of the rest be saved? Here Jesus reveals that the true source of salvation is God, who can do all things (v. 26). "Eternal life" (v. 29) is linked with the verb "to save" (*sozo*) (v. 25), the verb often used in the Gospels to describe rescue from danger or healing. This shows the broader idea of salvation in relation to the fulfillment of the end times.

Peter's response seems almost self-seeking when he asks what the disciples will get for forsaking all to follow Jesus (v. 27). But Jesus' response is not rebuke; apparently he accepts it as a valid question. He promises eschatological reward in that the apostles will sit on twelve thrones and judge the twelve tribes. It is not necessary to identify these tribes either as Israel or as the church, the new Israel. Jesus goes on to promise that the cost of following him will bring great reward in terms of family, land, and houses. The expression "a hundred times as much" should not be reduced to a mere spiritual racing form with a hundred-to-one payoff. Formulas smack of magic or manipulation. Jesus simply means they will be greatly blessed (see comments on 13:8, 23). The rewards will be both earthly and eternal.

The saying regarding the first being last and vice versa (v. 30) can, in the context, mean that the final reckoning will surprise many. But it primarily serves as a lead-in to the parable of the merciful employer (20:1–16).

10.7. The Parable of the Merciful Employer (20:1–16)

Only Matthew records this parable (see comments on ch. 13 concerning Jesus' use of parables). He frames it by beginning and ending it with saying that the first will be last, and the last first (19:30; reversed in 20:16). In this way he leaves no doubt what the major point of the parable is. Coming on the heels of the story of the rich young man, "the first" clearly are those Jews who keep the law and are relatively wealthy; "the last" are the poor laborers who work for a denarius, the basic wage for a day's work.

The poor in Jesus' day often lived from day to day; a day without work meant a day without food. It is no surprise, then, that they tended to work even on holy days, which was an affront to devout observers of the law. The vineyard is probably an allusion to Israel, who was so described by the prophets (see Isa. 5:1–7; Jer. 12:10; Matt. 21:33–46). The harvest is often an image of judgment and end times, especially for Matthew (Matt. 3:12; 13:39, 47–50; 21:34).

The third, sixth, ninth, and eleventh hours are 9 A.M., noon, 3 P.M., and 5 P.M. respectively. The men are not idle because they are lazy but because they have not yet been offered work (v. 7). The reverse order of payment, in which the most recent workers are paid first, not only emphasizes the last-first point but also exposes the greed of the earlier workers. When those who have worked throughout the heat of the day see the master giving the workers who have worked only an hour a whole day's wage, they expect him to give them much greater reward, perhaps as much as twelve denarii! Their grumbling on receiving a just wage reveals their greed. The NIV renders verse 15 as "envious," but the literal translation is, "your eye is evil." The evil eye is an apt figure for greed and jealousy (see 6:23).

The master is being generous to the later workers, who, along with their families, would suffer without the basics for survival. These are the outcasts, those on the periphery of respectability, the "tax collectors and 'sinners'" befriended by Jesus (11:19). This also reminds Matthew's readers that Jesus came "not . . . to call the righteous, but sinners" (9:13). Mercy, not sacrifice, for those in need is Jesus' policy (12:1–7; 9:13, quoting Hosea 6:6). The rich young man does not get more but is rather required to give more in order to follow Jesus and attain eternal life. Thus Jesus is both just and merciful. Matthew's readers may have found it necessary to defend the practice of extending the kingdom to the marginalized (Harrington, 1991, 285).

10.8. Jesus Predicts His Passion for a Third Time (20:17–19)

For the third time Jesus predicts his suffering and death (see 16:21; 17:22–23); this time, however, there is a sense of urgency since he and his disciples are about to enter Jerusalem, where his death will occur. "Going up to Jerusalem" is mentioned twice here, apparently for emphasis (vv. 17–18). Jesus draws attention to the gravity of the impending event with his characteristic "behold" (*idou*, untranslated in the NIV in v. 18).

Jesus specifically identifies his death as a crucifixion, which is a Roman, not a Jewish, method of execution. Earlier Jesus has given hints of his foreknowledge of the cross (10:38; 16:24). He also elaborates on the nature of his martyrdom, which will not be glorious, neat, and tidy, but one of mockery and scourging. This third prediction provides the occasion for the cup of suffering passage that follows, in which Jesus' death is described as a "ransom for many" (v. 28). For more on the predictive nature of this saying, see comments on 10:38; 16:21–23.

10.9. Ambition and True Greatness (20:20–28)

This incident provides further explanation of Jesus' "first/last and last/first" saying (19:30; 20:16). The ambition of the Zebedee family provides a jolting contrast to Jesus' prediction of his death (vv. 17–19). Matthew links the two with his frequently used word "then." The incident provides an opportunity to explain further the role of Jesus' death as well as to correct the disciples' worldly ambition.

It may be that James, John, and their mother, under the assumption that Peter's preeminent position is slipping, consider Jesus' earlier rebuke and correction of Peter an opportunity for political advancement in the kingdom (16:22–23; 19:27, 30; see France, 1985, 292). The mother of James and John, perhaps understandably, asks for preferred positions for her sons in Jesus' "regime"; Mark writes that the men themselves make the request (Mark 10:35). To get sidetracked on who actually did the asking ignores the fact that Matthew's main point is that all three are standing before Jesus when the favor is asked. Whether the mother, the sons, or all three make the request, Jesus' words of correction hit the mark. Ambition lies just below the surface in the rest of the disciples as well (v. 24).

The mother of James and John kneels before Jesus. This is not an act of divine worship but a show of respect (cf. 2:2; 8:2), though on some occasions such kneeling acknowledged that Jesus was more than a mere man (14:33; 28:9, 17). For Matthew's readers with the advantage of hindsight, the mother unwittingly was showing proper honor. Her two sons, who have been sworn to secrecy, know that Jesus is the heavenly being who was transfigured before their eyes (17:1–8). James and John may well be thinking of the final messianic victory banquet when Jesus goes on to talk about "the cup" (v. 22).

Jesus, however, does not have the cup of messianic rejoicing in mind in this passage; the cup here is one of suffering, an image repeatedly used in the Old Testament (Isa. 51:17; Jer. 25:15; 49:12; 51:7; Lam. 4:21–22; Ezek. 23:32–33). The cup of the Last Supper will also be put in the context of suffering (Matt. 26:27–28, 39, 42). In other words, Jesus is asking whether the two disciples are ready to drink from this bitter draught. They are indeed: James was eventually killed by Herod (Acts 12:2), and John was imprisoned on Patmos (Rev. 1:9). The disciple is not above the Master (Matt. 10:24).

The reference to sitting at Jesus' right and left hails back to his promise of the disciples' sitting on twelve thrones judging Israel (19:28). The right and left positions would be the second and third seats of authority after Jesus. This clearly is a challenge to the position Peter has already been given (16:17–19). By the time Matthew wrote, Peter was likely dead, and his primacy may have been an issue. Here Matthew appears to support the primacy of Peter's successors. Only Matthew records "my Father," one of his favorite references to God on the lips of Jesus (e.g., 7:21; 10:32–33). To God alone is the choice of the leaders.

When the others become angry with James and John, Jesus addresses the nature of greatness in the kingdom (vv. 24–28). Echoing the "first/last and last/first" theme, he again turns the values of this world upside down. The Gentiles "lord it over" others and "exercise authority." They dominate their subjects. Jesus describes greatness in terms of service and, yes, slavery; the contrast between the world's concept of greatness and Jesus' concept is absolute.

Jesus is about to become the ultimate example of service in his sacrificial death. The word "ransom" (*lytron*) was used to describe deliverance from captivity through a purchase. "For [*anti*] many" means "instead of many," which clarifies that Jesus will die in the stead of the "many" (possibly the elect or the community of the covenant; see Dan. 12:2–3; 1QS 6:11–13). This saying alludes to the Suffering Servant figure of Isaiah (Isa. 53:11–12). That Matthew understands Jesus' upcoming death as a forgiving sacrifice is anticipated as early as 1:21, where he records that Jesus' name, "the Lord saves," indicates that "he will save his people from their sins."

10.10. Jesus Heals Two Blind Men (20:29–34)

Jesus' healing of two blind men at Jericho concludes his ministry prior to his entry into Jerusalem. Jesus knows he is on his way to die, yet he characteristically stops to heal two blind men. In the midst of messianic fervor and nationalistic hopes he puts the many on hold to minister to two needy people. No doubt Matthew intends this to be programmatic for his readers.

Matthew uses his attention-getting "behold" (*idou*, untransanted in NIV) to introduce *two* blind men (Mark 10:46 and Luke 18:35 record only one; cf. a similar phenomenon in Matthew with two demoniacs [Matt. 8:28], two other blind men [9:27], and two donkeys at the triumphal entry [21:2, 7]). Several suggestions have been made to explain Matthew's "doubling" tendency, none of which is entirely satisfactory. (1) Some have suggested that Matthew may have wanted to provide two witnesses to the miracle by having two recipients since multiple witnesses were required by Jewish law; however, this is unnecessary since others witnessed the miracle. (2) Others simply note doubling as a stylistic feature of Matthew's whose purpose escapes modern readers. (3) It is possible that Matthew is not using Mark as a source here.

The blind men address Jesus as "Son of David" (v. 30; cf. 9:27–31). This anticipates the messianic confession of the crowds when Jesus enters Jerusalem, deliberately repeating the act of Solomon, son of David, who rode on a donkey in the same valley where he was proclaimed king (1 Kings 1:33–53). There too the crowds in Jerusalem greet Jesus as "Son of David" (Matt. 21:9). Only Matthew records the use of that title, in keeping with his characteristic presentation of Jesus as king. But here in Jericho the "Son of David" is portrayed as the healer of the destitute (see also 9:27–31; 12:22–24; 15:21–28), while the crowd sees the blind men's needs as a hindrance to their understanding of the Messiah's program. In Jewish tradition Solomon, the son of David and the wisest man alive (1 Kings 4:31), also knew how to exorcize demons and heal people (e.g., Josephus, *Antiquities* 8.45–49; Testament of Solomon). Jesus fulfills the role of Solomon as exorcist and healer as well as wise man and king.[10]

The blind men address Jesus not only as "Son of David" but also as "Lord" (*kyrie*) when they cry, "Have mercy on us." As noted elsewhere, this may simply be a mere respectful address, but the readers have the advantage of hindsight, and use of the title "Lord" takes on heightened significance, more and more resembling prayer. The expression "have mercy" with "Lord" may have been a phrase used in the liturgy of the Matthean community (Meier, 1990, 230).

When the blind men are brought to Jesus, they again use "Lord" as they request that their eyes be opened (v. 33). Jesus' healing of these two men highlights his "compassion" (v. 34; see also 18:27), perhaps surprising insofar as he is aware that he is heading toward his death. The opening of the eyes may have a double meaning. The blind men ask that Jesus heal their physical eyes (*ophthalmoi*), but Matthew says that Jesus touches their *ommata*, another word for eyes (which occurs elsewhere in the New Testament only in Mark 8:23). Plato uses this word poetically to describe the eyes of the soul (see also 1 Clement 19:3). Perhaps Matthew wants to show that more than physical eyes are healed, for as soon as the two blind men are healed they follow Jesus—not only accompanying him to Jerusalem, but following him in discipleship.

Matthew is contrasting the "blind," avaricious ambition of James and John (vv. 20–28) with the humility, persistent faith, and insight of these two blind beggars, who follow Jesus unconditionally. He may also be contrasting the restored sight of the men with the spiritual blindness of Jesus' enemies, whom he will soon encounter in Jerusalem. Unlike the earlier healing of two blind men (9:27–31), Jesus does not demand silence. The time for silence is past. He is about to act out his role as King and receive royal acclaim from the people in his triumphal entry into Jerusalem (21:1–9).

11. Ministry in Jerusalem (21:1–23:39)

11.1. The Triumphal Entry (21:1–11)

Jesus makes his approach to Bethphage (meaning "house of figs"), a suburb of Jerusalem on the Mount of Olives. He deliberately proclaims his messiahship when he rides the donkey into Jerusalem. It is not clear whether Jesus has made prior arrangements with the owners to borrow the animals or whether the disciples were simply to take the donkey and her colt in obedience to Jesus. The latter seems more likely since he anticipates possible objections (v. 3). What could be construed as theft is probably a requisitioning of the animals for official use, which was the prerogative of both kings and rabbis. The answer the disciples are to use is clear: "The Lord needs them." "Lord" (*kyrios*) can mean "master" or "owner," but for the Christian reader it has greater meaning as a divine title.

Mark, Luke, and John record that Jesus uses *one* donkey while Matthew says that Jesus has the disciples procure a young donkey with its mother (Matt. 21:2; Mark 11:2; Luke 19:30; John 12:14). We have already observed Matthew's tendency to mention two people when the other Gospels mention only one (e.g., 8:28; 9:27; 20:30). Possibly Matthew has historically accurate information that two animals are there. Perhaps the mother is brought to keep the young one calm. The parallel reference from Zechariah 9:9 to a donkey *and* the foal of a donkey, obviously the same animal, may have been the inspiration for the two. Any suggested solution for Matthew's "twos" is not completely satisfying.

The more important issue is that Jesus deliberately identifies himself as Messiah and thus fulfills prophecy. So far in the Gospels no mention has been made of Jesus' traveling on an animal; he certainly would not need to ride a donkey the walking distance from Bethphage to the city gates. Of the Synoptic writers only Matthew notes that Jesus' actions fulfill prophecy (vv. 4–5; cf. also John 12:14–15). This is characteristic of Matthew's frequent recording of fulfilled prophecy with his introductory phrase: "This took place to fulfill what was spoken through the prophet." The first part of his citation is from Isaiah 62:11, the second from Zechariah 9:9. The Mount of Olives is the location of the Messiah's return (see Zech. 14:4).

In Matthew's use of Zechariah 9:9 he omits "righteous and having salvation" and the subsequent description of a victorious Messiah, preferring to emphasize Jesus as meek (*praus*; see Matt. 5:5; 12:18–21). The donkey is a conveyance of peace, not of war; the conqueror comes as a humble peacemaker. The Zechariah prophecy may hail back to the return of David from the east after the Absalom insurrection had been put down. Also, the fact that another "Son of David," Solomon, rode the donkey of his father David to his own coronation at the spring of Gihon through the same valley as Jesus is now riding (1 Kings 1:38) would not have been missed by Matthew's Jewish audience.

The garments on the donkeys serve as a saddle and festive decoration. Jesus sits on the garments on the donkey. The act of the crowds spreading their garments on the road before Jesus resembles the actions of the people when Jehu was declared king. He stood on the coats of the people as a sign that he was lord of the owners of those clothes (2 Kings 9:13).

Although cutting and spreading branches and shouting "Hosanna" are more reminiscent of the Feasts of Tabernacles and Dedication, this event clearly occurred at the Passover season (see also John 12:1, 12). Presumably some of the same activities occurred in a number of Jewish celebrations. The Hallel Psalms (Ps. 113–118) were regularly used at the festivals. "Hosanna" is a transliterated Greek version of the Hebrew expression, "Save us" (118:25), which was used more as an exclamation of praise than a prayer for help. Note that in Psalm 118 these words follow, "Blessed is he who comes in the name of the LORD" (118:26).

Of the Gospel writers only Matthew specifically records that the crowds address Jesus as the "Son of David" (v. 9), though it is implicit in Mark 11:10; Luke 19:38; John 12:13. This is in keeping with Matthew's emphasis on Jesus as the Davidic king and echoes the address of Jesus by the blind men in the previous passage (Matt. 20:31) and the later cry of the children when Jesus heals in the temple (21:14–15). Also Matthew alone says that all Jerusalem was "stirred" or "shaken" (v. 10). Although he intends a figurative meaning here, he uses this verb (*seio*; related to the noun *seismos*, meaning "storms, earthquakes, civil disturbances"). The coming of Jesus into Jerusalem, along with his death and resurrection, is literally and figuratively an event that shakes the foundations of the earth and of society (see also 24:7; 27:51, 54; 28:2, 4; Hinnebusch, 1980). Jesus' entrance into Jerusalem is an apocalyptic event. Note the similarity of this turmoil to Jerusalem's being "disturbed" at the coming of the Magi with the news of Jesus' birth (2:3).

The crowd also refers to Jesus as "the prophet from Nazareth of Galilee" (v. 11). This nomenclature may indicate the public's fluid opinion of who Jesus is (see 16:14). Matthew is probably asserting here as well that Jesus is the Prophet whom many Jews anticipated as part of the fulfillment of Moses' promise in Deuteronomy 18:15–18.

11.2. Cleansing of the Temple (21:12–17)

Even though Matthew may be writing after the destruction of the temple in A.D. 70, the historical record demands the inclusion of this incident. Perhaps he is trying to demonstrate that the church is the true temple community (Meier, 1990, 235–36), an issue crucial to believers both before and after the temple's destruction. He may also be providing a Christian response to the destruction, that even forty years earlier Jesus knew something was askew in the system. Some believe that Matthew would have not bothered relating the cleansing of a temple in ruins at the time of his writing; hence, he wrote *before* its destruction (see Introduction: How and When Matthew Wrote).

Jesus' actions occur in the court of the Gentiles, the outermost part of the temple open to Jew and Gentile alike. Here the necessary sale of sacrificial animals to pilgrims occurred. These transactions could take place only in the accepted Tyrian coins; thus, there was a lively exchange of currency. There is no explicit condemnation of the practices unless the reference to "den of robbers" is a blanket denunciation of common fraud. Jeremiah used this phrase not to denounce practices in temple worship but rather to criticize the people's lifestyles that defiled the holy place (Jer. 7:1–15).

Acting in his role as the Son of David, for so he has been acclaimed in his triumphal entry, Jesus wishes to revolutionize the use of the temple, which has been diverted from prayer to lesser practices. This monopolistic business controlled by the priests and Levites garnered much wealth, making corruption an ever-present possibility. Jesus' actions are presaged by Zechariah, who predicted that on the Day of the Lord no Canaanite or merchant would be in the "house of the LORD Almighty" (Zech. 14:21; see also Mal. 3:1–5; Psalms of Solomon 17:30). The temple had been cleansed after the abomination of desolation introduced by the pagan Antiochus Epiphanes (c. 168 B.C.) and the Roman Pompey's conquest of Jerusalem in 63 B.C. Here Jesus' stark action states that once again the temple has been desecrated, this time by the Jews themselves.

Matthew notes the appropriate use of the temple by the presence of the blind and lame

Jesus drove the money changers out of the large Court of the Gentiles that surrounded the temple and its sacred walled courtyards, shown here in a model of Jerusalem. He admonished the people, saying the temple was to be used for prayer.

there and by Jesus' healing them. His ancestor King David prohibited the blind and lame from entering the temple, but Jesus as the Messiah and reforming King reverses this edict (2 Sam. 5:8). Matthew earlier saw Jesus as "one greater than the temple" and therefore capable of its revision (12:6). Isaiah predicted the rescinding of ceremonial exclusions for the righteous, who would experience the temple as a "house of prayer" (Isa. 56:1–7).

The children then acclaim Jesus as "Son of David," presented here as a healer (cf. 9:27–31; 12:22–24; 15:21–28; see comments on 20:29–34). These children stand in contrast with the religious elite, the chief priests and teachers of the law, who are furious with the children's insight (see comment on 11:25 for the link between children and believers). Only once before has Matthew grouped the chief priests and teachers of the law together, when they unwittingly aided Herod in his attempt to kill the infant Jesus (2:4). Soon they will join the secular power to put Jesus to death.

This conflict between Jesus and his ever-increasing enemies has been steadily accelerating since he abandoned his policy of avoiding confrontation (12:13–21) and began counter-attacking (16:1–12). He knows that conflict with the chief priests and teachers of the law is inevitable (16:21; 20:18), and as the right time approaches, he relentlessly brings the battle to their doorstep. These willfully blinded groups stand in contrast to the sighted blind men of Jericho, who now follow Jesus (20:34).

Jesus answers his opponents in typical rabbinical fashion: "Have you never read . . . ?" (v. 16). He quotes from Psalm 8:2, that out of the mouth of children God has ordained praise. Again Matthew emphasizes fulfillment of prophecy. Although Jesus does not quote the rest of the verse, his learned enemies know what follows: "because of your enemies, to silence the foe and the avenger." Clearly a line has been drawn in the sand; even in the presence of supernatural miracles in the temple and the return of the Glory himself to the temple, his enemies do not see.

11.3. The Cursing of the Fig Tree (21:18–22)

The cursing of the fig tree is one of Jesus' most enigmatic actions. The destructive nature of this miracle is shocking and initially seems uncharacteristic of Jesus. However, it fits the aggressive stance Jesus takes upon entering Jerusalem for the last time, as is seen in the cleansing of the temple (21:12–16) and the subsequent confrontations with the Jewish leaders (21:23–22:46), and it serves well the major theme of Jesus' final teachings before his crucifixion: judgment (chs. 23–25). The timing is somewhat different in Mark (before the cleansing), though its significance is essentially the same.

The cursing of the fig tree in Matthew has at least two meanings. (1) Given its proximity to the temple cleansing, it is probably an indictment of the chief priests and teachers of the law, who oppose Jesus' actions. In Jeremiah 8:4–13 the fruitlessness of the people is due to "the lying pen of the scribes," deceitful prophets, and priests. As a result, Jeremiah writes, "there will be no figs on the tree, and their leaves will wither" (Jer. 8:13; see also Hos. 9:10–16; Mic. 7:1). Jesus is not the only one of his day to see the defects in the temple leadership; it is for this very reason that the Qumran community isolated themselves by the Dead Sea.

(2) Jesus also uses the withering of the fig tree as a lesson for the disciples on the power of faith and the efficacy of prayer (vv. 21–22). On previous occasions Jesus scolded his disciples for the ineffectiveness of their faith (6:30; 8:26; 14:31; 16:8; 17:20). The mountain Jesus refers to is probably the Mount of Olives, which Zechariah said would be split in the last days (Zech. 14:4). Jesus is not saying here that faith is a key to acquiring any trifling fancy. Theologies are to be avoided that reduce prayer and faith to a formula merely to get whatever one wants rather than to advance the kingdom of God. James, John, and their mother no doubt believed that their request would be granted, but it was not (20:20–28). The effectiveness of faith presupposes a trusting relationship with God, not a manipulation of God's goodness (8:10; 9:2, 22; 15:28). The former is a true, active, and effective belief; the latter is magic bordering on witchcraft.

11.4. "By What Authority?" (21:23–27)

Jesus now openly confronts "the chief priests and the elders" (Mark and Luke add "the teachers of the law"; Mark 11:27–33;

Luke 20:1–8). These groups controlled the Sanhedrin, the major Jewish governing body in Jerusalem. The elders represent the influential families. Before this, most of Jesus' conflict was with the Pharisees, who controlled many of the synagogues outside of Jerusalem. But soon they too will unite against Jesus with these other groups, along with the Herodians and Sadducees with whom they often clashed (21:45; 22:15–16, 23, 34, 41). With his entry into Jerusalem Jesus has changed his usual tactic of evasion to direct provocation, having deliberately performed actions that affirmed his messiahship. When his enemies counterattack, he advances still again, abandoning all reserve.

In an earlier skirmish Jesus' disciples expressed concern about the consequence of offending the local powers (15:12). How much more must they be disturbed now by the gravity of deliberately antagonizing the highest powers in the land in the capital city! This is the first of five confrontations between Jesus and his opponents, concluding at 22:46.

Jesus is teaching when the chief priests and elders confront him with a question on the source of his authority (v. 23). Using a typical rabbinical method, Jesus asks a counterquestion. He does not acquiesce to their power but assumes that his is the greater power. Their question is designed to maneuver him into a position where he can be accused of blasphemy (Harrington, 1991, 299), a charge that later surfaces at his trial (26:63–65).

Jesus' question concerning the origin of John's baptism (i.e., his preaching, see Mark 1:4; Luke 7:29–30; cf. Matt. 21:31–32) is a brilliant counterattack, which puts his enemies on the brink of a major political disaster; the enemies' move, "check," is answered with an immediate "checkmate." They are fully aware of their dilemma. If they say John was from heaven, then their rejection of John's baptism condemns them (see Matt. 3:7; Luke 7:29–30). Yet they dare not say John's message was wrong, for it was acclaimed by the people (Luke 7:29; cf. Josephus, *Antiquities* 18.118).

The approval of John and Jesus by the masses is the reason that the leaders cannot move against Jesus even in their strongest sphere of influence, the temple and capital city. Jesus' strategy of moving his ministry to the densely populated city is brilliant. Note that they dare move against Jesus only after the traitor Judas divulges when and where his master will be detached from the adoring mob.

The response of the Jewish leaders to Jesus' counterquestion is more diplomatic than straightforward: "We don't know." The truth is, they are afraid to say what they really think. Jesus' response shows that he is in control: "Neither will I tell you by what authority I am doing these things." He is not compelled by their authority to answer. By his refusal he in effect is saying that the source of his power is as obvious as John the Baptist's.

11.5. The Parable of the Two Sons (21:28–32)

Jesus continues his counterattack against his enemies with three parables dealing with the rejection of the leaders of Israel. Matthew introduces these parables with the phrase, "What do you think?" (cf. 17:25; 18:12). In keeping with the prophets, the vineyard in the first two of these parables represents Israel (Ps. 80:8–19; Jer. 2:21; Ezek. 19:10). In the parable of the two sons, the first son represents repentant sinners, who now serve the Father, while the second son represents the leaders, who honor God with their lips but whose hearts are far from him (Isa. 29:13). Earlier Jesus had associated with the tax collectors and sinners, and his enemies threw it in his face (9:9–13). Now he mentions the sinners to rebuke the chief priests and elders. John's call for repentance had a profound impact on the repentant sinners on the periphery of respectability (see esp. Luke 3:10–14; 7:29–30).

The use of the respectful "sir" or "Lord" (*kyrie*, v. 30) is typical of Matthew and probably has double meaning for both him and his audience. On the lips of the hypocritical son, it reminds the reader of Jesus' earlier words, "Not everyone who says to me, 'Lord, Lord,' will enter the kingdom of heaven, but only he who does the will of my Father who is in heaven" (7:21).

Earlier in his ministry Jesus explained his parables to his disciples privately (13:13–16, 36), but now he boldly explains the parable directly to the Jewish leaders, probably in order to force all who hear to choose him or reject him: "I tell you the truth, the tax collectors and the prostitutes are entering the kingdom of God ahead of you" (v. 31). Jesus leaves open the possibility that the "respectable" elite will follow the tax collectors and sinners into the kingdom of God, but given the parable's apocalyptic character, it sounds chillingly like words of final judgment.

11.6. The Parable of the Wicked Tenant Farmers (21:33–46)

Matthew intends this parable to expand the message of the previous one; hence he says, "Listen to another parable" (v. 33). "Servants" (v. 34) emphasizes the multiple witnesses God sent to Israel through the prophets. In the Old Testament Israel is depicted as the vine of God (Ps. 80:8; Isa. 5:1–7; Jer. 2:21; Ezek. 19:10). Hence the owner is God and the tenants are the leaders of Israel, that is, the chief priests and elders (Matt. 21:23). The tenants not only beat the servants but also kill and stone some of them (v. 35). This makes the story conform to the experience of the prophets that Jesus is about to endure.

The sending of the master's son is a distinct era ("last of all," v. 37), which inextricably links the son with Jesus. Like Jesus in his coming passion, the son is thrown out of the vineyard and then killed (v. 39)—just as Jesus was led out of the city of Jerusalem and then crucified.

The actions of the tenants do not appear so outlandish when one notes customs of the first century. One tradition said the tenants had right to land if the owner had not collected his share of the crop in four years; another one said that the land of a proselyte who died with no heir would be granted to the tenants. All efforts to explain such behavior are superfluous, however; greed and jealousy are the operating motives. The chief priests and elders recognize the actions of the tenants as heinous and, in condemning them, condemn themselves: "He will bring those wretches to a wretched end" (v. 41). The wording of this phrase is emphatic in Greek and includes a play on words. Matthew is emphasizing the surety of judgment on Jesus' enemies: "The bad ones he will destroy badly."

Here Jesus publicly identifies himself as the Son of God; previously only the disciples were privy to this (16:16). Perhaps this is the incident that gives his enemies the charge they will use at his trial: "Tell us if you are the Christ, the Son of God" (26:63).

Matthew frequently records that Jesus used the phrase, "Have you never read in the Scriptures" (v. 42) when identifying himself in an Old Testament passage (12:3; 19:4; 21:16; see also Mark 12:10). The image of the stone for Jesus the Messiah evokes several Old Testament allusions in addition to Psalm 118:22–23 (Isa. 8:14–15; Dan. 2:34–35, 44–45). This image is an important messianic one (Rom. 9:32–33; 1 Peter 2:4–8). The kingdom given to another nation (vv. 43–44) refers to the transfer of the kingdom of God to a "nation" (*ethnos*, NIV, "people who will produce its fruit"). This does not refer to Gentiles per se, which would be the plural "nations" (*ethne*). Although the predominant rejection of the church by the Jews and the destruction of Jerusalem assure a predominantly Gentile constituency for the church, here Jesus is saying that new leadership will be installed for God's kingdom.

The crushing stone in verse 44 is not in many important early copies of Matthew. If it belongs in this Gospel (cf. Luke 20:18), Jesus is predicting that the leaders' rejection of Jesus will lead to their own destruction as well as have disastrous results for many people. When the chief priests realize that Jesus is indicting them, they want to arrest him but cannot for fear of the people, who consider him a prophet (Matt. 21:45–46; cf. v. 11).

11.7. The Parable of the Marriage Banquet (22:1–14)

Jesus continues his counterattack against the chief priests and elders with a third parable. Matthew links it with the two preceding ones by the phrase, "Jesus spoke to them again in parables." Luke has a parable closely aligned to this one (Luke 14:15–24), which deals with a banquet prepared by "a certain man." Matthew's version involves a royal wedding feast, in keeping with his emphasis on the royalty of Jesus. While Luke reports the invitees making detailed excuses, Matthew simply says that they would not come.

Matthew begins the parable using one of his favorite phrases, "The kingdom of heaven is like. . . ." In it the son of a king is being married, a scene that has eschatological and final judgment overtones (see also 25:1–13; Rev. 19:7–9). The gravity of the invitation is shrugged off in busyness with lesser affairs

(Matt. 22:3, 5; see also 13:22; 19:16–26). As he does in the parable of the wicked tenants (21:35), Matthew records the persecution and murder of the servants, making the story parallel to the martyrdom of the prophets.

The spurned king becomes angry, so that the invitation is extended to anyone who will come; he destroys the city of those who have rejected his call and murdered his emissaries. This may be a reference to the future destruction of Jerusalem (A.D. 70). Although the leaders of the Jews are the ones being condemned, the entire nation of Israel suffers as a result.

The theme of judgment, however, does not end with the destruction of those who rejected the invitation. Jesus notes that both "good and bad" attend the feast (v. 10). One of these new guests is improperly dressed. We are not told why the king objects to this man. Whether special garments were provided or whether the man did not have the time or means to procure one is not answered and is irrelevant to the main point of the parable. As in the old covenant, so too it will be in the community of the new kingdom: The bad will be weeded out from the good (see 13:1–50). The "darkness" and the "weeping and gnashing of teeth" (22:13) represent final, irrevocable judgment. Both Israel of old and the church community will experience judgment.

Here Jesus is providing a Christian interpretation of salvation history. The leadership of God's elect community devolves from the conventional Jewish centers of power to the emerging church (cf. 21:43–45). The word "chosen" (*eklektoi*, 22:14) may be a term for the "messianic community of salvation" and is not intended as a statement on predestination. This word is used this way in the New Testament, Qumran literature, and the pseudepigraphal Book of Enoch (see Jeremias, 1971, 131). Election throughout Matthew is predicated both on God's action and a response from people (5:17–20; 18:23–35). Verse 14 should serve as a jarring warning to "make your calling and election sure" (2 Peter 1:10; see also Rom. 8:28–33).

11.8. Tribute to Caesar (22:15–22)

The Pharisees and the Herodians now come together to entangle Jesus in a trick question, although the Pharisees appear to be the primary aggressors. The Herodians were political supporters of Herod Antipas, who, as ruler in Galilee, owed his power to the occupying Roman forces. Here are two unlikely allies. The Pharisees normally viewed the Herodians as agents of a hated foreign government sympathetic to Hellenism, the mindset with which Antiochus IV had earlier threatened the very existence of Judaism.

This is the beginning of a new offensive against Jesus after he verbally attacked his enemies in the temple (21:12–16). What follows is a series of attacks and counterattacks on political, social, and theological issues. Feigning approval of Jesus, the Pharisees voice the reality of Jesus' popularity with the masses as an impartial "teacher" (22:16; see comments on 8:18–22). They then present Jesus with a question, "Is it right to pay taxes to Caesar or not?" (v. 17).

On the face of it, this question seems innocent enough, but it is a two-way booby trap. If Jesus answers yes, he stands to lose favor with the people, who find the tribute to the Roman occupying forces an egregious burden and reminder of their subjugated status. Such a response may well put Jesus on a "hit-list" of Zealot assassins. By contrast, a negative reply will please the people but raise himself in direct opposition to the Romans and their Herodian cronies and risk the possibility of arrest.

Jesus sees into the "evil intent" of his interrogators and inflames them by addressing them as "hypocrites" (v. 18), an accusation he repeats frequently in chapter 23. He then calls for a Roman denarius (see comment on 20:1–7), the coin used to pay tax. This coin had Caesar's image, name, and title, "Son of the Divine Augustus," a most offensive and idolatrous object to the Jews. While Jesus' request sounds innocent, it is really a countertrap; for when his enemies produce a denarius from *their* own purses, they betray how *they* stand on the issue! Since by law people were required to pay the tax with Caesar's coin and only his, Jesus is saying to "give [back]" (*apodidomi*) to the emperor what clearly is his to begin with. In other words, one should pay this tax, but Jesus avoids falling into his enemies' trap by raising a much more important issue: What does one owe to God?

Those hating the Roman occupation would approve of Jesus' more pressing question, for he is not saying it is proper to obey a secular power blindly. In some issues one must resist, but the tax is not one of them. Jesus is a master of discerning the more important issues and asking the better question (cf. 9:4–6; 12:1–13; 16:13–16; 20:22). Jesus does not use this ploy just to slip out of the trap, but offers it as a guiding principle for Christians. The hearers "were amazed" (22:22), both at the brilliance of Jesus' maneuvering out of a trap into a position of strength, and at the wisdom of knowing the difference between lesser and indispensable obligations.

11.9. Jesus on the Resurrection (22:23–33)

As yet another big gun in the growing array of Jesus' opponents, the Sadducees pose a question in an effort to entrap Jesus. This question occurs on the "same day" as the confrontation with the Pharisees and Herodians. The Sadducees also address Jesus as "teacher" (see comments on 8:18–22). Their question on the resurrection reflects their own theological position, which denies life after death—a doctrine that both Jesus and the Pharisees affirm (Acts 23:8). The Sadducees recognized only the Pentateuch as authoritative, and since the more explicit passages on resurrection are elsewhere (e.g., Isa. 26:19; Dan. 12:2), they denied this teaching.

Their question about the seven-times-widowed woman and the resurrection refers to the practice of levirate marriage, in which a brother of a deceased man could be called upon to marry the widow. Thus he would raise up sons to perpetuate his brother's name (Deut. 25:5–6; cf. Gen. 38:8). The Sadducees pick a practice specifically from the Pentateuch in their attempt to show that the concept of the resurrection is incompatible with the Torah and is not intended in the writings of Moses. In their minds the idea of one woman having seven husbands in the afterlife is absurd, and therefore they conclude that the doctrine of resurrection is untenable.

Jesus counters that the Sadducees misunderstand the nature of life after death, which has a different character than earthly life. He does not say that believers will become angels but that they will be *like* angels, whose normal activities do not include marriage (see 1 Cor. 15:35–50; cf. comments on 18:6–11). Such earthly complexities are not a problem for God's promise of resurrection; we are not given much detail but a sound assurance (1 John 3:2).

Jesus then refers to Exodus 3:6, which shows that life after death is neither incompatible with nor completely absent from the five books of Moses. There God speaks to Moses from the burning bush, saying, "I *am* the God of Abraham, the God of Isaac and the God of Jacob." Jesus finds it significant that God did not say "was." Apparently the patriarchs are quite alive. God continues to have a relationship with his faithful ones as "the God . . . of the living." Here Jesus assumes the role of ultimate interpreter and arbiter of Scripture (see comment on 5:17–48). This passage also anticipates Jesus' own resurrection (28:1–10). As in the previous section Matthew records the people's astonishment at Jesus' teaching (22:33).

11.10. The Great Commandment (22:34–40)

The question of the greatest commandment was a common topic among rabbis, and Jesus probably addressed it on various occasions (Luke records Jesus' comments on the summary of the law earlier in his ministry; see Luke 10:25–28). The Pharisees confer together after hearing how Jesus has silenced the Sadducees (Matt. 22:34). One of their number, a lawyer (*nomikos*; Mark 12:28 calls him a *grammateus*, "teacher of the law"), poses the question to Jesus, once again in an attempt to test or tempt (*peirazo*) Jesus (Matt. 22:35).

On the face of it, the question concerning which is "the greatest commandment in the Law" appears innocent as it had been a long-debated point among the rabbis; but here the intent is to trap Jesus. By getting him to identify *one* law as greatest, he can conceivably be accused of minimizing other crucial issues. Jesus sidesteps the trap by actually giving *two* commands that govern the use of all the others. Among the many regulations of the Hebrew law, the rabbis often distinguished between heavier and lighter matters of God's law. For example, how one treated one's parents was more crucial than how to treat a bird's nest or what kinds of fabric could be used to make clothes (Deut. 5:16; 22:6–12). Jesus also spoke against being concerned about the lighter laws while neglecting the "weightier matters of the law, judgment, mercy, and faith" (Matt. 23:23, KJV). Jesus' response provides important instruction for believers.

Once again Jesus' enemies address him as "Teacher" while his followers usually call him "Lord" (see comments on 8:18–22). Jesus responds by linking Deuteronomy 6:5, part of the Shema (which Jews recited daily), with Leviticus 19:18 to connect love of God with love of humanity. Jesus is not replacing the law with two guidelines. On the contrary, as he testified in the Sermon on the Mount, he intensifies the law (Matt. 5:17–20). These two love commands are the "constitution" of the kingdom, from which all other laws will be judged and all applications of the law deemed proper or not. These two commands guarantee that the entire law will conform to the spirit of the kingdom. The "heart," "soul," and "mind" are not separate parts of a person, but participate in overlapping areas involving emotions, will, and intellect (e.g., Ps. 14:1; 139:13–24; 140:2).

Although the popular "Golden Rule" was espoused in Judaism before Jesus' day (see comments on 7:12), Jesus may be the first teacher to link Deuteronomy 6:5 and Leviticus 19:18 as the ultimate expression of God's law. Love for God is not an excuse to neglect the needs of others on the premise that such love is the first law and loving others is the second. Jesus' teachings make it clear that love for God is expressed by loving one's fellow human beings (6:14–15; 18:23–35; Luke 15:3–32; cf. James 1:27; 1 John 2:10–11; 3:17; 4:20–21).

Jesus understands these two as the key to all the other laws since the others "hang" (*kremannymi*) on these two. *Kremannymi* may be a Jewish legal term for a lesser statute's dependence on a greater one. One is reminded of how the Jews wrote in that day. Letters were hung from a scribed line on the page like clothes on a clothesline. But whether this is the image Jesus has in mind, one cannot say for sure.

The Jewish-oriented readers to whom Matthew addresses this Gospel may have been in conflict with Jews who questioned the church's broader interpretation of the law. To answer, Matthew emphasizes the Pharisees' role in this passage and provides instruction on how to respond. Gundry (1994, 28, 447) suggests the reference to "got together" (from *synago*, v. 34) is an indirect reference to the Jewish synagogue and alludes to Psalm 2:2, where the nations and kings plot and "gather together" (*synago* in LXX) against "the LORD and ... his Anointed One."

11.11. Son of David (22:41–46)

Once again the Pharisees are "gathered together," which may also be a veiled reference to the Jewish synagogues (see comments on 21:34–40). Jesus enters into conversation with them concerning the sonship of the Messiah. The Pharisees—and presumably also the teachers of the law among them (cf. Mark 12:35–37)—respond to Jesus' question about the Messiah by saying, "The son of David" (Matt. 22:42).

In pursuing his question, Jesus quotes David in Psalm 110:1: "The Lord [*Yahweh*] said to my [David's] Lord [*Adonai*, i.e., David's descendant Jesus]...." This passage is difficult to understand unless one realizes that the psalmist is speaking prophetically of Jesus as David's descendant. From Jesus' perspective, David is not speaking of himself on the throne but of Jesus. Otherwise, the psalm stands simply as a royal enthronement psalm, in which a subject of the new king is saying that God will fight his battles. The ultimate meaning of the psalm is that the son or successor of David is greater than David. Yahweh is telling Jesus as David's successor to sit at his right hand until he has defeated all his enemies. To sit at God's right hand or power is to have God's power invested in the occupant of the throne. (For God's right hand or power in relation to Jesus, see Mark 16:19; Acts 2:34–35; Heb. 1:3; 8:1; 10:12.)

Here, as elsewhere in the Gospels, Jesus is being addressed as "Lord [*kyrios*]," an expression that has greater import here than just "Sir." Matthew has already used the title "Lord" with greater meaning (e.g., 15:21–28; 16:16 with 22, and the disciples' use after the transfiguration). In this interpretation Jesus links the Old Testament concept of a Son of David Messiah with the heavenly witness who spoke at Jesus' baptism and transfiguration that he is the divine Son of God (3:17; 17:5). Jesus has already declared that he is greater than David, the temple, Jonah, and Solomon (see 12:3–4, 6, 41–42). He probably also has in mind the heavenly figure in Daniel 7:14, who receives the kingdom from the Ancient of Days.

Although the assumption that David is speaking of Jesus may seem strange to some modern minds, the exegesis here is plausible to ancient rabbinic circles. When Jesus quotes Psalm 110:1, "The Lord said to my Lord," he is presenting a rabbinic antinomy that puts side by side two things that are true but appear contradictory. Usually this method resolves the conflict by demonstrating that both can be true. But here Jesus only poses the question and does not resolve it. Vincent Taylor (1966, 493) writes: "The allusive character of the saying half conceals and half reveals the 'messianic secret.'" Jesus leaves his opponents to make the deduction: "You agree that the Messiah will be the Son of David, and if I am, as the crowds say, 'The Son of David' (21:9, 15), then what does that make me?"

Recall that in 21:33–46 Jesus identified himself as the son of the master of the vineyard (God). Jesus is greater than a mere son of David; he is the Son of God! He is both (see Rom. 1:3–4). His enemies are unable to answer not because they are confused or do not know, but because they are afraid to take Jesus' reasoning to the logical end he proposes. They are not able to answer him a word. In fact, from that time forward "no one dared to ask of him any more questions" (v. 46). Matthew portrays Jesus as the master interpreter of the Scriptures who so completely defeats his enemies in this series of confrontations that the only move they have left is to wait for an opportunity to arrest him when his adoring crowds are not there to interfere.

11.12. Woe to the Scribes and Pharisees (23:1–36)

11.12.1. General Indictment (23:1–4). Jesus continues his counterattack on the teachers of the law and the Pharisees, but now his audience is the crowds and his disciples, who have just witnessed him besting his enemies. Earlier Jesus had confrontations with the Pharisees, but usually he withdrew to prevent a crisis (e.g., 9:1–9; 12:1–21). Since having revealed that he must go to Jerusalem and die, however, he has become more direct in his assault (16:1–12). Now the gale of his fury is unleashed. Most of the material in this chapter is found only in Matthew.

The teachers of the law ("scribes," NRSV) copied manuscripts for the government, temple, and synagogue; therefore, they were familiar with the Scriptures and provided commentary on how to live out the law and the Jewish traditions. It was Ezra along with his fellow teachers who established Judaism in the Holy Land after the Exile (Ezra 7:6, 11–13; Neh. 8:1, 4, 9, 13; 13:1–3). By the time of Jesus they were part of the Sanhedrin, the ruling body of religious affairs in the land. Although not all teachers of the law were Pharisees, many were associated with them as they are frequently mentioned together and identified with them (see esp. Mark 2:16; Acts 23:9).

The Pharisees, ironically, were close to Jesus in many theological issues. They believed in the resurrection of the dead and in angels and demons, and they accepted as authority the Torah (the Law), the Prophets, and the Writings of the Old Testament. By contrast, the Sadducees denied these beliefs and recognized only the Torah as Scripture. Where Jesus and the Pharisees disagreed was in the interpretation and application of God's law.

Jesus acknowledges the Pharisees as the successors to Moses in that they occupy his "seat" and speak with authority concerning the practice of the law (v. 2). He instructs the people to do what the Pharisees say but not to follow their example (v. 3). This verse can be taken several ways. (1) It can mean keeping *all* their regulations in minutiae but avoiding their hypocrisy. This interpretation is unlikely since Jesus has already challenged and done acts contrary to their traditions (8:3, 21–22; 9:1–18; 12:1–13). (2) It is conceivable that Jesus' approval of the Pharisees' rules is sarcastic; "if you want to try to observe them all, go ahead." (3) The best possibility is that Jesus generally approves of the system of regulations that show how to keep God's law. Many of the rules of the rabbis were wise: doing justice to others, respecting property, showing compassion, and honoring God. Yet he found some of their rules oppressive and counterproductive—especially those that encouraged keeping the letter of the law while purity of heart was absent. In spite of this, Jesus was not a reactionary libertine. He radically increased the requirements of the law to ensure the good intent of the heart (5:17–48). In contrast to their heavy laws, Jesus' "yoke is easy and [his] burden is light" (11:29–30).

11.12.2. Phylacteries and Tassels (23:5). Jesus' major grievance was that the Pharisees performed works for appearance and the approval of people rather than for God (see 6:1–8, 16–18). "Phylacteries" were small boxes or pouches of leather containing passages of Scripture, which were strapped to the forehead or arm in literal fulfillment of the command to keep the Scriptures ever before one's eyes (Ex. 13:9; Deut. 6:4–9; 11:13–21). Jewish men bound these to themselves during times of prayer. Apparently some were wearing big, ostentatious phylacteries with wide bands to appear especially pious. The law specifically commanded men to have fringe or "tassels" sown to the hem of their outer garments to remind them of the law (Num. 15:37–41; Deut. 22:12). The proud wore such tassels for ostentation and spiritual show.

11.12.3. Rabbi, Father, Teacher (23:6–12). Jesus criticizes the Pharisees for aspiring to hold the first place of honor at public events and to be addressed as "Rabbi" ("teacher"; lit., "great one"). Jesus forbids using that title, for he is the great Teacher, and all are brothers before him. We are also to call no man father or master, for God in heaven is Father and Jesus is the Master.

Some have used this passage to denounce the ancient practice of calling Christian priests of various churches "father." Two things need to be considered here. (1) If one takes this teaching to a literal extreme, then a male parent could not be called father or expressions such as "founding fathers" or Father Abraham would be forbidden. Moreover, those who insist on prohibiting this expression for spiritual leaders should be consistent and never use the word "teacher" to describe people who instruct others, and all managerial titles should be suspect as well.

(2) Paul himself uses the title "father" in relation to his converts (1 Cor. 4:15; see also Phil. 2:22). John also uses it to describe himself (implicitly) and others (explicitly) in the church (1 John 2:1, 13–14). That is, the early church did not understand Jesus' instructions here as prohibiting addressing spiritual elders as "fathers" and establishing instead an egalitarian anarchy. In fact, a family environment fostered such terminology. The context clearly does not prohibit use of these words for people in different offices; rather, Jesus is saying not to treat the Pharisees, the teachers of the law, or any other person as the *Ultimate Teacher* on the law, to the point of giving them honor and allegiance that is due only to God. In this sense Jesus is not deconstructing the authority he has already delegated to his apostles (16:18–19; 18:18).

What is more crucial than use of the titles is the attitude of humility and servanthood, for even in groups that forbid such titles can lurk the vices of prideful arrogance and presumption on the power of God. Here Jesus promises that the haughty will be humbled and the humble elevated. This does not support the view that no honor be accorded in the church. Jesus reiterates here his world-shaking dictum that in his kingdom the servant is greatest (cf. 20:25–28). Gregory the Great, a pope in the sixth century, chose the title "Servant of the servants of God."

11.12.4. The Woes (23:13–36).

11.12.4.1. The First Woe: On Neither Entering Nor Allowing Others to Enter the Kingdom (23:13). Jesus ceases addressing the crowd in general and lambastes the Pharisees directly, identifying them as "hypocrites" (see comments on 6:1–4; 7:5; 15:7; 22:18 on the meaning of "hypocrite"). Its meaning as actor is particularly appropriate here. Matthew uses his favorite phrase "kingdom of heaven," which his enemies will neither enter nor allow others to enter.

11.12.4.2. Interpolated Woe: On Stealing From Widows Under the Guise of Prayer (23:14). This verse is not in the better and earlier manuscripts and is probably a scribal interpolation from Mark 12:40 or Luke 20:47. Those copies that do have it in Matthew place it here or before verse 13. It condemns the teachers of the law and the Pharisees for covering their financial greed and theft with a camouflage of prayer.

11.12.4.3. The Second Woe: On Turning Proselytes Into Children of Hell (23:15). Jesus is not condemning the teachers of the law and the Pharisees for making converts (*proselytos*), for Israel was expected to be a light to win converts (e.g., Isa. 42:6; 49:6). What he hates is that the "converts" turn out worse than their converters.

11.12.4.4. The Third Woe: On Taking Oaths (23:16–22). In 5:33–37 Jesus asserted that oaths are not necessary for his disciples; rather, their words should be believed on their own because of their consistent integrity. Jesus lambastes word games that create loopholes to avoid filling obligations. Swearing by the altar, the gift thereon, the temple or its gold, or (as in 5:33–37) by one's head, earth, or heaven ultimately impinges on God and is therefore to be avoided out of reverence for him. Such a practice is absurd; truth needs no oath.

11.12.4.5. The Fourth Woe: On Tithing (23:23–24). The law required giving one-tenth of various goods, such as grain, wine, and oil (Lev. 27:30; Deut. 14:22–29). Apparently how extensive the tithe should be practiced was debated within the first century. Some even counted herb leaves in their gardens. Jesus does not condemn meticulous accounting but rather bothering with such minutiae while neglecting the "more important matters of the law" (see comments on 22:34–40). In the midst of opulent offerings, important issues go wanting, such as failing to "act justly and to love mercy and to walk humbly with your God" (Mic. 6:8).

The expression "strain out a gnat but swallow a camel" must have evoked laughter among the crowds since in Aramaic Jesus created the pun, "You strain at a *qamla* and swallow a *gamla*" (Black, 1954, 175–76). Since both of these animals were considered unclean, Jesus is calling their activities unclean, not fittingly Jewish. This is the central issue for these denouncements.

11.12.4.6. The Fifth and Sixth Woes: On Internal Impurity (23:25–28). The Pharisees were meticulous about ceremonial washing of cups and plates. Yet the greed and self-indulgence inside polluted them. The tombs were whitewashed or plastered so that people would avoid touching them and becoming ceremonially unclean (as happened when a person came in contact with the dead). Both look clean on the outside but are unclean on the inside (see Tobit 2:3–9, where performing a burial results in being forbidden to reenter the house that night).

11.12.4.7. The Seventh Woe: On Building Tombs for the Prophets (23:29–36). Jesus continues the theme of death by describing the magnificent monuments the Jews raised over the prophets. For example, Herod built a large marble edifice over the tomb of David (Josephus, *Antiquities*, 16.71). Jesus scorns his enemies' boast that they would have never killed the prophets as their ancestors had done. The "[full] measure" means that as their forefathers were punished, so too will the teachers of the law and the Pharisees be punished for persecuting and killing Jesus and his followers.

Clearly this woe reminds Matthew's readers of Jesus' death and of the strife between Jewish Christians and Jews, who are seen here as a separate synagogue (cf. 10:17). Given that Jews did not execute by crucifixion, Matthew anticipates a wider persecution, including the pagan hostility against Christians (as occurred in the reigns of Nero in A.D. 64 and Domitian c. 90). This also anticipates Jesus' warning of persecution elsewhere in Matthew (10:23; 24:9).

Jesus then addresses his enemies as a "brood of vipers," just as John the Baptist had done (v. 33; cf. 3:7). He compares the spilling of his innocent blood and that of his followers to the deaths of Abel and Zechariah. The Hebrew Old Testament ends with 2 Chronicles, in which Zechariah son of Jehoiada is killed; both deaths called for vengeance (Gen. 4:10; 2 Chron. 24:22). "This generation" anticipates impending judgment, which will soon occur in the destruction of Jerusalem (see also "generation" in 11:16; 12:39, 41; 16:4; 17:17; 24:34).

11.13. Jesus' Lament Over Jerusalem (23:37–39)

This lament provides a transition from Jesus' diatribe against his enemies to his prediction of judgment and destruction of Jerusalem in chapter 24. In Matthew these verses are Jesus' last major address to the crowds. The hen or bird gathering her young is reminiscent of God's giving refuge in the shadow of his wings (Ps. 36:7; see also Deut. 32:11; Ruth 2:12; Ps. 17:8; 57:1; 61:4; 91:4; Isa. 31:5). The "house" (Matt. 23:38) refers to the temple and is a reminder of the destruction of the first temple; once again God leaves his house (cf. Ezek. 10:18–19; 11:22–25). "Jerusalem" probably represents the entire country.

Jesus' grief here explains his earlier wrath; the dalliance of Israel's leaders and their rejection of Jesus have set judgment in motion. The force of the word "again" (*ap' arti* in v. 39; lit., "from here on out") shows that the apocalyptic judgment of Israel is near. Jesus is emphatic in the closing of the divine visitation; the double negative (*ou me*) emphatically shuts the door: "no more me will you see" (lit. trans.; "me" has been moved forward for emphasis).

Jesus' entry into Jerusalem is greeted with the acclamation: "Blessed is he who comes in the name of the LORD" (Ps. 118:26). Now as he is about to leave through death, he longs to hear it one more time but from a people truly prepared to enter his kingdom. That he will hear it again is not certain (*eipēte*, "you say," is an aorist subjunctive, v. 39). Thus the relationship of Jesus with Israel is a mystery yet to be deciphered (Rom. 9–11).

12. The Olivet Discourse (The Fifth Discourse: 24:1–25:46)

At the end of each of Jesus' five teaching sections Matthew adds the editorial comment, "When Jesus had finished saying these things," or something similar (7:28; 11:1; 13:53; 19:1; 26:1; see comment on 7:28–29). Some have suggested that this teaching section begins earlier with Jesus' disputes with his enemies (21:28–23:39). Although chapters 21–23 clearly flow into chapters 24–25 since they share similar themes, there are several reasons why chapters 24–25 are probably the intended unit to which the conclusion in 26:1 refers. (1) The audience in the earlier section is primarily Jesus' enemies; in Matthew's other teaching sections the disciples are the audience, as is the case here (24:3). (2) It is apparent that Jesus' chilling prediction, "You will not see me again," is his conclusion to his address to the teachers of the law, the Pharisees, and the crowd (23:39). (3) Jesus deliberately removes himself from the temple area and retires to the Mount of Olives to teach his disciples. He again assumes the traditional teaching posture of sitting (24:3; see also 5:1; 13:2).

This section is one of the most complex of Jesus' teachings. Whole systems of eschatology have been devised to explain this passage, with many bewildering points and counterpoints and opinions among the competing theories. It is not in the purview of this work to unravel them all and exhaustively critique them; rather, we will look at how this passage fits into Matthew's and Jesus' scheme of things and not try to wrest from the text facts that even Jesus himself did not know (24:36).

Each type of literature used in the revelation of the New Testament must be respected

The Mount of Olives, east of the Old City of Jerusalem, with the Church of All Nations at the base, shown here in the lower left corner. The Garden of Gethsemane is next to the church.

for its own characteristics. Here the dominant genres are *prophecy* and *apocalyptic*. Characteristically *prophecy* warns the unrepentant of impending judgment and promises blessing to the faithful. It also predicts future events. Often prophecy deals with God's judgment or deliverance, both of which occur through existing earthly institutions or persons within history.

Although prophecy can have apocalyptic characteristics, by the time of Jesus *apocalyptic* (from the Gr. word *apocalypsis*, "revelation") had become a distinct type of literature. It saw the judgment and promises of God coming through an invasion from a heavenly cosmos to the earthly world, engulfing and transforming it. Symbolism and figurative expressions are used to express the new heavenly, otherworldly age in terms comprehensible to the present one. Animals and metals represent kingdoms, and heavenly bodies such as stars, moon, and sun are symbolic of cataclysmic change. To make matters more complicated, in the apocalyptic experience, one can never be completely sure when any item is to be understood literally or figuratively or both.

Particularly helpful for interpreting this passage is Matthew's understanding of prophecy and its repeated use in salvation history. God repeats certain actions of judgment or salvation in dealing with his people; his righteousness and mercy demand it. Therefore, repeated "types" occur, are fulfilled, and then refulfilled as God interacts with Israel. As noted earlier, Matthew identifies repeated fulfillments of an earlier prophecy. For example, he presented multiple fulfillments of the exodus from Egypt in the return from Assyrian captivity as predicted by Hosea 11:1 and in the trip that the Holy Family took from Egypt back to Palestine (Matt. 2:15). He records other repeated fulfillments of prophecy in 1:23; 2:6, 18, 23. In this sense Jesus is the "fuller sense" or *sensus plenior* of earlier prophecy.

Thus, one should not be surprised that even the prophecies of Jesus presented in apocalyptic garb may have both a more immediate fulfillment in history and later fulfillments in the end times, the final judgment, and the final establishment of God's reign. One should look twice at interpretations that reduce the mystery of the consummation of all things to linear charts and rigid, brittle formulas. Apocalyptic means a *mystery revealed*, not necessarily a *mystery explained*. It should lead the reader to repentance, worship, and wonder, *not* to the exclamation, "Oh, I get it!" The central theme of the present passage is judgment dealing with the destruction of Jerusalem and the coming of the Son of Man.

12.1. Prediction of the Destruction of the Temple (24:1–2)

In Mark 13:1–2 the disciples are admiring all the temple buildings that Herod the Great had constructed. Many of the stones were huge, and to this day their placement is considered an engineering wonder. Jesus predicts that the wonders of the temple will be destroyed. This confirms that Jesus was referring to the temple when he said at the end of the previous chapter, "Your house is left to you desolate" (Matt. 23:38).

12.2. Events Before the End (24:3–8)

Jesus intentionally removes himself from the temple and the city and begins teaching on the Mount of Olives to the east, in full view of the city whose destruction he is about to foretell. This mountain is a most appropriate locale for his teaching on end times in light of Zechariah's prophecy: "On that day his feet will stand on the Mount of Olives, east of Jerusalem, and the Mount of Olives will be split in two" (Zech. 14:4).

The disciples ask a question about the sign of Jesus' "coming and of the end of the age" (v. 3). The structure of the Greek (one article for the two nouns "coming" and "end") shows that the disciples saw the "coming" (*parousia*) and "end of the age" as the same event. Jesus' answer corrects this, noting that various birth pangs will precede the kingdom's culmination in his coming. *Parousia* literally means "presence" and was used to describe official state visits of dignitaries; hence it became a technical term for Jesus' second coming. Jesus does not see the destruction of the temple as the time of his *parousia*. Note that he uses the same phrase "end of the age" in his post-resurrection instructions to his disciples to evangelize all nations (28:19–20).

Jesus warns his disciples to beware of assuming a premature culmination of the kingdom when he predicts that false messiahs will purportedly "come in [his] name" (v. 5). Before the end wars, famines, and earthquakes will occur in various places. (For "earthquake" [*seismos/seio*] as a favorite Matthean theme both literal and figurative, see 8:24; 21:10; 24:7; 27:51, 54; 28:2, 4.)

12.3. Persecution Predicted (24:9–14)

Matthew adds further commentary on these dire times with his warning of tribulation and death at the hands of "all nations" (v. 9). He links this passage with the previous section by his often-used "then" (*tote*). This reference to the nations demonstrates that Matthew does not anticipate an immediate return of Jesus.

The Evangelist is intensely concerned with persecution (see 10:17–22, where persecution at the hands of the Jewish community is emphasized). His is the only Gospel that records in the Olivet Discourse that the persecution will come from within the church as well as from without (24:10–12). Like Jesus, his followers will be handed over or betrayed (*paradidomi*) by Jew, Gentile, and church members (cf. 17:22). Many "will turn away from the faith" (see comments on 5:29; 13:21). As a result of false prophets leading many astray, lawlessness (*anomia*) will abound and cause the love of many to cool or be extinguished, just as water cools a fire.

Each of the Synoptic Evangelists warns that only by patient, continual endurance can salvation be procured (v. 13). The nature of salvation has three aspects: (1) immediate, at one point, (2) preserving, and (3) continual. In the New Testament one was saved, has been saved, is continually being saved, and will be saved (aorist, perfect, present, future tenses: e.g., Rom. 8:14; Eph. 2:8; 1 Cor. 1:18; Matt. 10:22 and Rom. 5:10, respectively). Apparently some of Matthew's readers expected a quick-fix salvation by an early return of Jesus, and others were not prepared to endure, obediently avoiding lawlessness; these will suffer the extinguishing of love (Meier, 1990, 279, 281). The Great Commission must be fulfilled before the end (24:14; 28:19–20).

12.4. The Abomination That Causes Desolation (24:15–22)

This desecration of the temple is predicted in Daniel 9:27; 11:31; 12:11. This event has had repeated fulfillments; in 167 B.C., for example, Antiochus IV Epiphanes, the Hellenistic ruler of Syria, offered a pig as a sacrifice to Zeus in the temple of the one true God (see 1 Macc. 1:21–29; 4:36–51; 2 Macc. 5:15–17; 6:1–5). The phrase "standing in the holy place" calls to mind Emperor Caligula's edict that a large statue of himself be set up in the Jewish temple, though this was not carried out because of his death (A.D. 40–41). The Jewish Zealots desecrated the temple in their uprising in A.D. 67/68 (Josephus, *War*, 4.6). Finally, the Romans destroyed the temple when they quelled the Zealot rebellion (A.D. 70). This image became an apocalyptic symbol for Christians of the end times (e.g., 2 Thess. 2:3–4). The parenthetical "let the reader understand" (Matt. 24:15) refers to Daniel 12:10, where the prophet calls his readers to see the relevance of his prophecy to their situation.

The calamity will be so sudden and severe that people will not have time to return to their houses to get anything. Only the unencumbered and swift of foot will escape. In the winter the roads of Palestine can be muddy and impassable. Flight on the Sabbath brings to mind the dilemma of the Jews in the Maccabean era. They refused to travel or defend themselves on the Sabbath and were slaughtered by the Seleucids. The freedom fighters then reasoned it would be better to break one Sabbath in order to keep many others (1 Macc. 2:29–41; 2 Macc. 6:11). This may indicate that Matthew's community held a strict observance of Sabbath regulations, or that Christian flight on the Sabbath would meet with Jewish hostility.[11]

Given that the tribulation described here is the worst ever to be in the history of the world (v. 21), it seems that multiple fulfillments are intended. The Roman destruction of Jerusalem is a symbol of apocalyptic judgment and final cataclysm, just as the "new Jerusalem" becomes a heavenly symbol of the end-time fulfillment of God's promises (Rev. 3:12; 21:2, 10). This cannot refer to first-century Jerusalem alone, for if God does not intervene, all of humanity will be destroyed (Matt. 24:22).

12.5. False Christs and False Prophets (24:23–28)

Messianic pretenders and false prophets were common in the first century (Acts 5:36; 21:38). Furthermore, Jesus earlier warned that he working of miracles is no guarantee that he practitioner is a true follower of the "Lord" (Matt. 7:21–23). Apparently false prophets can be so convincing that, "if that were possible," even the elect of God could be duped (24:24). Note the secretive locales of the false messiahs: in the secluded desert or the inner rooms of secretive, elite spiritual societies, such as occurred later in the Gnostic cults.

It was popularly assumed that the Messiah would be hidden; hence he was allegedly in the inner room (cf. John 7:27). By contrast, Jesus uses two images to emphasize the unmistakable, universally obvious nature of his coming. (1) It is like a lightning bolt in the sky; anyone with eyes knows it has happened. Given the earlier description of the times before the end as an extensive period, the emphasis in the lightning image is not that the Second Coming comes instantly without warning but rather that it will be clearly seen. There will be no need for "spiritually enlightened" diviners to reveal it.

(2) The coming of Jesus is described in terms of vultures; where one sees the vultures circling, there a dead body certainly is. In the Old Testament vultures and eagles are not clearly delineated. Some translate *aetoi* here as eagles and see in it an allusion to the eagle standards carried by Roman legions, but clearly this *parousia* event transcends the Roman-Jewish war of the first century. The image of the vultures in light of the carnage of the Roman massacre of the Jerusalem inhabitants in A.D. 70 becomes a chilling apocalyptic image awaiting a more cataclysmic fulfillment.

12.6. The Coming of the Son of Man (24:29–31)

"Immediately after the distress of those days" even the heavens will be shaken. Such imagery is frequently seen in Jewish and Christian apocalyptic writings (e.g., Isa. 13:10; Ezek. 32:7; Joel 2:10, 31; 3:15; Amos 8:9; Hag. 2:6, 21; Rev. 6:12–13; 8:12; 12:4). It definitely has symbolic meaning, but one cannot assume it is merely symbolic. This answers the original inquiry of the disciples concerning the "sign of your coming" (Matt. 24:3). The *parousia* of Jesus will affect all of the cosmos. Often in apocalyptic literature these astronomical calamities represent judgment on the nations. If the earlier judgment of Babylon and Edom shattered the heavens, how much more will the final one! Hence "all the nations of the earth will mourn" (24:30) at his coming, but the elect will be gathered. Earlier Matthew had recorded words about the wheat being gathered into the barn and the chaff destroyed (3:11–12; 13:24–30).

The sign of the "Son of Man coming on the clouds of the sky" (v. 30) comes from Daniel 7:13–14, a passage that contrasts the beastly kingdoms of earth with the heavenly rule of the Ancient of Days, who gives rule to the heavenly man figure. Note the presence of "his angels" at the final judgment (Matt. 13:39, 41, 49; 25:31–40). For the "loud trumpet" in calling the Jews scattered in exile back home, see Isaiah 27:13 (see also Rev. 8:2–9:21; 10:7). The elect are gathered "from the four winds" (Matt. 24:31).

12.7. The Parable of the Fig Tree (24:32–35)

The fig tree, unlike many trees in Palestine, sheds its leaves. Before the heat of summer it begins to produce new ones. That this occurs before the harvest indicates judgment.

"This generation" (v. 34) has raised many questions. Does Jesus expect both the destruction of Jerusalem and his second coming to happen within the life span of his audience? Does the expression "all these things" refer only to the judgment on Jerusalem, or does it include all the apocalyptic events, tribulation, succession of wars, famines, and earthquakes as well? Was Jesus mistaken in assuming his return would closely follow the fall of Jerusalem since he himself says that only God the Father knows the day (v. 36)? Was this a disclaimer?

In answer to these questions, one must first ask what Jesus meant by "generation" (*genea*). This word can mean the life span of a generation that achieves old age, or it can mean race (BAGD, 154). Thus, it can mean here that Jews will still exist when he comes again. Furthermore, what does Jesus mean by his appearing? Is it his resurrection? Here Luke says the "kingdom" is near (Luke 21:31). In one sense the Jews had seen and were about to see the fruition of the kingdom in installments—in Jesus' miracles, transfiguration, resurrection, and ascension. This would be in keeping with the *sensus plenior*, the repeated fulfillments that will eventually culminate in one final fulfillment. Jesus probably has in mind the immediate events of judgment on the Jewish nation when he refers to "all these things."

Most think that Matthew was written in its final form after the fall of Jerusalem (A.D. 70), probably in the 80s. If so, one must ask why the author would record an alleged "mistake" of Jesus if "all" refers exclusively to his second coming and the complete fulfillment of the eschaton. Obviously Matthew did not see "all these things" in that light. He probably has in mind the fall of the city and its calamities as the harbinger of the end. In the prophetic and apocalyptic writings, extended eras and fulfillments delayed are commonplace. The perspective of Jesus may be like that of earlier prophets, who apparently saw several later events as on the same horizon—as if they were two distant mountains that appear side by side when in fact they are miles apart.

On an apocalyptic scale "near" (v. 33) may not be as soon as human experience understands it (2 Peter 3:3–10). The kingdom is both already here and yet to be consummated. If Daniel 7:13–14 is the model for Jesus' words, then he may be speaking "not of a 'coming to earth,' but of coming to God to receive vindication and authority" (France, 1985, 344). No completely satisfactory answer can be given to what Jesus had in mind when he told the parable of the fig tree. In light of verse 36 he did not intend to give a play-by-play, blow-by-blow account of end times. He never intended us to make detailed end-time charts!

Sun-dried mud bricks are still used for building.

12.8. The Sign of the Flood (24:36–42)

Here the coming of the Son of Man resembles the destruction of Jerusalem (24:16–20); it will be sudden and unexpected, under the guise of peace, the calm before the storm. But his followers know better, for they have been given the signs. The days before Noah's flood become a sign or type of the days before the *parousia*. Those "taken" (vv. 40–41) are the ones saved, not the ones lost, since they are taken with Jesus (*paralambano*; see 1:20; 18:16; 20:17 for this meaning). Jesus gives no details about where they are taken. He is not answering this question; rather, he is emphasizing the radical division of the final judgment that he has already presented and continues later in this teaching section (13:24–30, 36–43, 47–50; 24:45–25:46).

Attempts to make this passage conform to other apocalyptic passages in the New Testament or imaginative reconstructions of the end times are too speculative to be taken seriously. Jesus here refuses to conform to a timetable. As noted above, his teaching is a mystery revealed, *not* a mystery explained; hence, the uncertainty of the meaning of the "this generation" pronouncement. What is not clear is when; what is clear is to what extent the judgment will be.

12.9. The Alert Householder (24:43–44)

Jesus immediately reinforces the suddenness of his coming with another parable: "Be ready" (v. 44). The word for "broken into" is literally "to dig through," reflecting the fact that the houses were made of sun-dried mud (see comment on 6:19). Although there are tumultuous signs of the Second Coming, it will also be accompanied by a dulling sense of false security in the day-to-day business usually associated with peace and a stable society (cf. Luke 12:39–40).

12.10. The Parable of the Good and Wicked Servants (24:45–51)

Jesus provides another parable on the theme of readiness (cf.

Luke 12:41–46). In this description the master, returning in an unexpected visit, finds his managing servant meeting or refusing to meet the needs of his fellow servants. Given Jesus' earlier critique of the Jewish leaders for their disregard of the welfare of the people, the oppressive, wasteful servant here provides commentary on the rejected rulers' actions (Matt. 23:1–4, 23–24).

The punishment of the wicked servant is severe. It is like that of "the hypocrites" (v. 51; see comments on 6:2–5, 16; cf. also 15:7; 22:18; 23:13–15, 29). Moreover, Jesus makes it clear that this is no mere earthly punishment but one of eternal judgment (for weeping and gnashing of teeth, see also 8:12; 13:42, 50; 22:13; 25:30).

12.11. The Parable of the Ten Virgins (25:1–13)

Matthew continues Jesus' last teaching section begun in chapter 24 with another parable (found only in Matthew) on the topic of perseverance as a prerequisite for ultimate salvation. This parable is in keeping with the author's recurring theme of judgment and the end times. One of his favorite phrases, "kingdom of heaven," is used here too.

This parable of the ten virgins is an additional commentary on the parable of the good and wicked servants (24:45–51). Note how Matthew connects the two parables with his frequently used connective "then" (*tote*). In the previous parable the servants are rewarded or condemned according to their righteous or abusive behavior. In this parable the wise and foolish virgins are admonished to persevere while they wait for the bridegroom. Since Jesus has left off condemning the Jewish leaders (23:39), he must intend the foolish and wise virgins to be his followers. Therefore, when Matthew records this parable decades after Jesus taught it, the foolish virgins are Christians who think Jesus' coming is so imminent that they are not prepared for a wait.

We are not told exactly what the oil represents here. Is it the good works of the previous parable? Clearly Jesus has not created an extensive allegory with many hidden meanings; yet the context demands that Jesus is the bridegroom, a popular theme in the early church (e.g., Matt. 9:15; John 3:29; 2 Cor. 11:2; Eph. 5:21–33; Rev. 21:2, 9; 22:17). It is not insignificant that Jesus uses an image that the Old Testament prophets identify as God himself, with Israel as the bride (Isa. 54:5; Jer. 31:32; Hos. 2:16). Here the virgins in the wedding party are church members, while the wedding feast symbolizes the end times (see also Matt. 22:1–14). To try to see more symbolism here is probably reading too much into the text (see comments on parables in ch. 13).

Traditionally, the bridegroom first goes to the house of the bride's father to finalize the contract and to bring her back to his house for the marriage feast. "Bridesmaids" is probably an inaccurate description of the ten virgins since they are not in the bride's entourage but are awaiting the groom's return to his house. The "lamps" could be oil-soaked torches used for the marriage procession; hence, the wise women carry jugs of oil to replenish them as needed. If the wise virgins were to share their oil, none of them would have light with which to greet the Lord. The door is shut, and exclusion from the feast is final. Given the presence of the eternal damnation in the parallel parables both before and after this one, clearly no reprieve is intended. Note the parallel with the wedding feast parable in 22:1–14, where the one without the appropriate garment is expelled from the wedding party.

Typically Matthew records the five foolish women addressing the bridegroom as "Lord, Lord" (RSV), one of his favorite titles for Jesus (see comment on 15:21–28). The response, "I don't know you" (v. 12), is hyperbolic since they are most likely in the groom's party. The "I don't know you" and the address, "Lord, Lord," anticipate the last parable of this section, in which the "goats" address the judging King as "Lord" (25:44). It also reminds the reader of the chilling warning of Jesus' first teaching section, "Not everyone who says to me, 'Lord, Lord,' will enter the kingdom.... 'I never knew you. Away from me, you evildoers'" (7:21–23). Faithful obedience, not a mere fascination with signs and wonders, is what will be rewarded.

12.12. The Parable of the Talents (25:14–30)

Jesus continues speaking of the delay of his second coming and of the need for doing his will. The Lukan parallel specifically records why Jesus told the parable: "The people thought that the kingdom of God was going to appear at once" (Luke 19:11). In Luke's version it is a nobleman who leaves to claim a kingdom (19:11–27). The inspiration for this parable may have arisen when Archelaus the son of Herod the Great went to Rome to receive the kingdom of Judah. The Greek word *talanton,* used only by Matthew, is a highly valued coin, depending on the metal of which it is made (in contrast with the *mna* of Luke, which had considerably lesser value, Luke 19:13). At one point a talent equaled 6,000 dinar, with a denarius being worth a day's wage for laborers (see Matt. 18:23–28). (The English use of the word *talent* for an individual's ability gets its meaning from this parable.) Both lending money to gain interest and burying hoards of coins were common in this era.

When the nobleman returns, each servant addresses him as "Lord" (*kyrie*, "master" in NIV). While it means "master" in the parable, for Matthew's readers it connotes the divinity of Jesus. Though all call him Lord, not all are faithful servants. Those who faithfully work at the business of the kingdom are approved and are invited to "share your master's happiness" (vv. 21, 23). The unfaithful servant claims that his inaction is a result of fear of the master, who would be angry had the servant invested the money in an unproductive enterprise. Rather than risk loss, he buries the treasure for protection (cf. 13:44). But he condemns himself by his own words. The Lord calls him "wicked" and "lazy" (25:26). Doing the work of the kingdom procures abundance in the eschaton while laziness is rewarded with eternal damnation (see comments on 24:51). Jesus taught that both the *practice* of righteousness and God's gracious forgiveness were indispensable for ultimate salvation.

12.13. The Last Judgment (25:31–46)

Jesus is the "Son of Man" here. When Matthew uses this messianic title, he usually does so either to predict Jesus' suffering and death or to portray his second coming. Of the approximately thirty times it occurs in Matthew, it occurs seven times in chapters 24–25. In this section the Son of Man's Parousia (second coming) and judgment dominate. It resembles Daniel 7:13–14, when "one like a son of man" receives the kingdom from the Ancient of Days. The attendant glory and angelic retinue heighten the apocalyptic finality of his coming (Zech. 14:5; Matt. 13:41; 16:27; 18:10; 24:31; 25:31).

Identification of the "nations" (*ethne*) is crucial for any interpretation. If this refers to Gentiles (and *ethne* often means peoples other than the Jews), then this judgment is separate from the judgment of the Jews already predicted by Jesus (23:37–24:3). In this scenario the Gentiles will be judged for how they treat Christian missionaries or Christians in general (for "least of these brothers of mine," see 12:48–50; 18:2–14; 28:10; for missionaries/apostles, see 10:40–42). Most likely, however, this is not a separate judgment but rather one of all nations, including Israel (e.g., 24:9–14). The separation of the sheep and goats represents not a judgment of those nations who are sympathetic to Christians from those who are not, but a judgment of the church from all nations. Note that both groups call Jesus "Lord." This division is reminiscent of the parables of the wheat and tares and the net in chapter 13, the wheat and chaff of 3:11–12, and the true and false disciples of 7:21–27. These are judgments on the Christian community.

Clearly what one does for others will have an effect on one's standing in the last judgment, but 7:23 makes it clear that this final winnowing of the elect is contingent on knowing Jesus as well. To be separated from Jesus is the ultimate punishment, one brought upon oneself. For judgment presented in terms of sheep and goats, see Ezekiel 34:17.

As in the previous parable, Jesus calls for an eternal punishment and an eternal reward. The good works here explain how one develops the talents given by the Lord in 25:14–30. Those who argue that the punishment is not eternal (*aionion*) but for a limited age or era are compelled to consider that the reward of life is limited too. Clearly Matthew is presenting an unending punishment and an unending life for the damned and the elect respectively (v. 46). The judgment is hell since fire represents hell (5:22; 13:42, 50; 18:8–9).

Here the Son of Man is described as a king (v. 34; cf. 13:41; 16:28; 19:28). The kingdom that the faithful inherit was prepared for them before "the creation of the world" (25:34), while hell was "prepared for the devil and his angels" (v. 41). Note the contrast between them and the angels of the Son of Man (v. 31). With verse 46, Jesus has finished his final teaching section (see comments on 26:1).

13. The Passion and Resurrection Narratives (26:1–28:20)

13.1. Events Leading to Gethsemane (26:1–35)

Matthew ends the fifth and last teaching section (chs. 24–25) with his typical conclusion: "When Jesus had finished saying all these things" (26:1; see comments on 7:28–29). Note the word "all" (cf. 7:28; 11:1; 13:53; 19:1), which indicates that the teaching of Jesus, the new Moses, is now complete. The Passion is about to begin. This terminology is reminiscent of the denouement of Moses' teaching: "When Moses finished reciting all these words . . ." (Deut. 32:45). After this Jesus is, for the most part, silent.

For the events leading up to the death of Jesus, Matthew by and large follows Mark. All three Synoptists place the final conspiracy against Jesus two days before the Passover and the Feast of Unleavened Bread; see Mark 14:1; Luke 22:1). By this they probably mean not forty-eight hours but "the day after tomorrow." Passover commenced with the slaughter of the lambs on Thursday afternoon, the fourteenth day of the month of Nisan, and continued on Friday, the fifteenth, which started at sundown (the same day by modern reckoning; remember that the Jewish new day started at sundown).

13.1.1. Jesus Again Predicts His Death (26:1–5). For a fourth time Jesus predicts to his disciples his impending arrest and death (16:21; 17:22–23; 20:18–19). In each prediction he gives more specific information. Here he again identifies crucifixion as the mode of execution. Thus, Jesus' death is part of a divine plan in which his enemies unwittingly participate. Matthew links the "Son of Man" with the Passover. Clearly he sees the role of Son of Man in sacrificial terms. He identifies the plotters as "the chief priests and the elders of the people" (cf. "the chief priests and the teachers of the law" in Mark 14:1; Luke 22:2).

These Jewish leaders develop their conspiracy in the palace of Caiaphas the high priest, who served in A.D. 18–36 (see comment on 26:57). In Matthew, in other words, it is the ruling aristocracy who finally act against Jesus, not the usual Pharisees and teachers of the law (who join later in 26:57; 27:41). Although the Jewish leaders wish to kill Jesus by stealth, they are hesitant because they fear a messianic riot might break out among the throngs of people gathered for the feast (cf. also John 11:47–48). But they unwittingly alter their plans to conform to the chronology of Jesus' prophecy of verse 2, for they cannot resist the opportunity that Judas's defection affords them during the feast.

Their reticence can also be understood as a fear to arrest Jesus *publicly* in the midst of the masses sympathetic to him. Luke simply writes that the leaders wanted to put him to death but were hesitant, "for they were afraid of the people"; he also notes Judas looked for a chance to betray Jesus in the absence of the crowds (Luke 22:2, 6). If this is the reason for their reserve, then they were shrewd to arrest Jesus at night outside the city in Gethsemane, far from the crowds.

13.1.2. The Anointing at Bethany (26:6–13). All four Gospels record a woman anointing Jesus (Mark 14:3–9; Luke 7:36–50; John 12:1–8). In Matthew Jesus is in the house of Simon the Leper, and a woman (apparently not a sinner) anoints his head. The disciples (esp. Judas, according to John) object to the waste out of concern for the poor. Jesus considers this anointing an anticipation of his burial. Because of the differences in the anointing stories, the church father Origen suggested that there were actually three anointings. Many modern scholars assume that there was only one. It seems likely that Luke's is an earlier anointing and the other three Gospels record the same anointing just prior to Jesus' death with varying details.

Curiously the host is identified as "Simon the Leper." Since lepers were ceremonially unclean and under quarantine, presumably he was formerly a leper, perhaps healed by Jesus; because of the length of his illness, he had acquired "the Leper" as a nickname.

According to Mark, the value of the perfume was three hundred denarii (see Mark 14:5). Alabaster is a translucent form of gypsum used to carve flasks for perfume. The narrow neck sealed the container and insured no evaporation. To open it one had to break it. The

PASSION WEEK
Bethany, the Mount of Olives, and Jerusalem

1. ***Arrival in Bethany—FRIDAY***
   Jn 12:1 — Jesus arrived in Bethany six days before the Passover to spend some time with his friends, Mary, Martha, and Lazarus. While here, Mary anointed his feet with costly perfume as an act of humility. This tender expression indicated Mary's devotion to Jesus and her willingness to serve him.

2. ***Day of Rest—SATURDAY***
   (Not mentioned in the Gospels) — Since the next day was the Sabbath, the Lord spent the day in traditional fashion with his friends.

3. ***The Triumphal Entry—SUNDAY***
   Mt 21:1–11; Mk 11:1–11; Lk 19:28–44; Jn 12:12–19 — On the first day of the week Jesus rode into Jerusalem on a donkey, fulfilling an ancient prophecy (Zec 9:9). The crowd welcomed him with "Hosanna" and the words of Ps 118:25–26, thus ascribing to him a Messianic title as the agent of the Lord, the coming King of Israel.

4. ***Clearing of the Temple—MONDAY***
   Mt 21:10–17; Mk 11:15–18; Lk 19:45–48 — The next day he returned to the temple and found the court of the Gentiles full of traders and money changers making a large profit as they gave out Jewish coins in exchange for "pagan" money. Jesus drove them out and overturned their tables.

5. ***Day of Controversy and Parables—TUESDAY***
   Mt 21:23–24:51; Mk 11:27–13:37; Lk 20:1–21:36 — In Jerusalem: Jesus evaded the traps set by the priests. On the Mount of Olives overlooking Jerusalem: (Tuesday afternoon, exact location unknown) He taught in parables and warned the people against the Pharisees. He predicted the destruction of Herod's great temple and told his disciples about future events, including his own return.

6. ***Day of Rest—WEDNESDAY***
   (Not mentioned in the Gospels) — The Scriptures do not mention this day, but the counting of the days (Mk 14:1; Jn 12:1) seems to indicate that there was another day concerning which the Gospels record nothing.

7. ***Passover, Last Supper—THURSDAY***
   Mt 26:17–30; Mk 14:12–26; Lk 22:7–23; Jn 13:1–30 — In an upper room, Jesus prepared both himself and his disciples for his death. He gave the Passover meal a new meaning. The loaf of bread and cup of wine represented his body soon to be sacrificed and his blood soon to be shed. And so he instituted the "Lord's Supper." After singing a hymn they went to the Garden of Gethsemane, where Jesus prayed in agony, knowing what lay ahead of him.

8. ***Crucifixion—FRIDAY***
   Mt 27:1–66; Mk 15:1–47; Lk 22:66–23:56; Jn 18:28–19:37 — Following betrayal, arrest, desertion, false trials, denial, condemnation, beatings, and mockery, Jesus was required to carry his cross to "The Place of the Skull," where he was crucified with two other prisoners.

9. ***In the Tomb—FRIDAY***
   Jesus' body was placed in the tomb before 6:00 P.M. Friday night, when the Sabbath began and all work stopped, and it lay in the tomb throughout the Sabbath.

10. ***Resurrection—SUNDAY***
    Mt 28:1–13; Mk 16:1–20; Lk 24:1–49; Jn 20:1–31 — Early in the morning, women went to the tomb and found that the stone closing the tomb's entrance had been rolled back. An angel told them Jesus was alive and gave them a message. Jesus appeared to Mary Magdalene in the garden, to Peter, to two disciples on the road to Emmaus, and later that day to all the disciples but Thomas. His resurrection was established as a fact.

containers were small and provided just enough perfume for one application.

The Greek does not make it clear whether Jesus supernaturally knew that the disciples were put off by the extravagant honor conferred on him. Jesus, however, does not consider it garish or wasteful but "beautiful" (*kalon*, v. 10). Earlier Jesus anticipated that the gospel would be proclaimed to the world (24:14; see also 28:19–20). Jesus promises that this woman's generous act, linked to his burial, will be continually proclaimed. This loving act stands in stark contrast to the plotting of the authorities (26:3–5) and Judas's joining the plot (26:14–16).

13.1.3. Judas Sells Jesus Out (26:14–16). Judas, one of the Twelve, seeks to betray Jesus to the chief priests. What his motives are we can only guess. Judas specifically requests money for his betrayal (v. 15). Perhaps Jesus' approval of the woman's "waste" of the precious perfume in the previous incident was particularly irksome. Perhaps Jesus' resignation to his death (v. 12) was a view of messiahship that ran counter to his triumphalist convictions. Or perhaps he, as presumably Saul/Paul originally did, now thought Jesus a false prophet. Both Luke and John write that Satan entered into Judas. Though he acted of his own will, he unwittingly cooperated with the devil and the eternal purposes of God (John 17:12).

The price, thirty pieces of silver, is a significant sum (approximately 120 denarii, or about four months of a basic wage). The sum was also the replacement price for a slave who was killed (Ex. 21:32). It was also the insulting wage offered to the true shepherd of Zechariah 11:12–13, who cast the sum back into the treasury (this anticipates the remorse and suicide of Judas in Matt. 27:3–10). Matthew uses the phrase "from then on" to identify major transitions in his account (e.g., 4:17; 16:21). Judas has now set into motion the events leading to the arrest, death, and resurrection of Jesus. It is a point of no return for them all, with dire consequences for Judas.

13.1.4. Preparation for the Passover (26:17–19). The Feast of Unleavened Bread, which lasted from the fifteenth to the twenty-first day of the month Nisan, overlapped with Passover. Passover began with the killing of the lambs at twilight on the fourteenth day and the Passover meal at twilight on the fifteenth (Ex. 12:1–8). This evening corresponds to our modern Thursday night, since, according to Western reckoning, midnight marks the end of one day and the beginning of another. In contrast, the Jews began their days at sundown. Thus, Jesus celebrated the Passover meal on the evening that *began* the fifteenth day of Nisan and died on the same day a few hours before it ended.

The Gospel of John, however, appears to have a different chronology for the Last Supper and death of Jesus (John 13:1 with 18:28; 19:14). In John's account Jesus presides at the Lord's Supper on the fourteenth of Nisan, on the evening that commences that day by Jewish reckoning. This makes Jesus' death fall on the same day in the following afternoon. In this chronology Jesus would have died at the same time as the lambs were being slaughtered in preparation for the Passover meal (see Mark 14:12). What then, in Johannine chronology, was the meal Jesus and his disciples had twenty-four hours before the traditional time for the Passover meal? Was it a Kiddish or Habburah, general ceremonial meals, or did Jesus deliberately celebrate the Passover meal a day early, perhaps because his enemies were moving quickly against him and he knew his time was short (Luke 22:15–16)?

Attempts to harmonize the Gospel of John with the Synoptics are complex and not without problems.[12] Suffice it to say that whenever Jesus celebrated the first Lord's Supper and was subsequently crucified, he saw both events in the context of the Passover with himself as the sacrificial Lamb.

13.1.5. Jesus Predicts His Betrayal (26:20–25). Matthew correctly observes that Jesus reclined at the table for the meal since guests rested on couches as they ate. Jesus introduces the announcement of his betrayal with the typically Semitic "truly" (*amen*) (RSV). That these words burned into the psyche of the early church is clear in the reaction of the disciples—they were "very sad" (*lypeo sphodra*, v. 22). Earlier Matthew used these words to express the consternation the disciples felt when Jesus foretold his death (17:23; cf. 18:31). Here again they are overwhelmed with the incredibly upsetting news; not only will Jesus die but one of their number will have a hand in it.

Each of the disciples asks if he is the one, addressing Jesus with the title "Lord" (*kyrie*) (see on 15:21–27). Judas, however, asks, "Surely not I, Rabbi?" (26:25). In Matthew's Gospel the enemies of Jesus often address him as Rabbi or Teacher (e.g., 8:19; 9:11; 12:38; 22:16, 24, 36). Here, in the case of Judas, Matthew is chillingly consistent.

Jesus' answer that "the one who has dipped his hand into the bowl with me will betray me" (v. 23) probably is not a clear identification of Judas as the traitor but is deliberately vague (see also Ps. 41:9). If Jesus had clearly fingered Judas, it is doubtful the disciples would have sat idly by and allowed him to leave unaccosted. John's Gospel seems to make it obvious that Judas was the traitor when Jesus gave him the piece of bread (John 13:26); yet the disciples think Judas has been sent by Jesus on an errand when he leaves (13:27–30). Apparently the action of Jesus and his words were somewhat cryptic. Jesus notes that the betrayal of "the Son of Man" is in accord with Scripture, and it would have been better had the betrayer not been born.

Jesus' response to Judas, "You have said" (*sy eipas*; NIV, "Yes, it is you"), is an indirect affirmation, perhaps necessary to avoid the disciples restraining him. At his trial Jesus will again use this expression (26:64; 27:11). For Judas's motives see comments on 26:14–16.

13.1.6. The Lord's Supper (26:26–29). The Passover meal consists of specific food, the paschal lamb with bitter herbs and greens, to remind the Jews of deliverance from slavery in Egypt. The Hallel Psalms (Ps. 113–118) were chanted. Interspersed in the meal are four cups of wine. The first one came after the thanksgiving prayer, the second with the main course, the third with another thanksgiving prayer, and the fourth with the chanting of the remaining psalms.

Jesus' blessing or thanksgiving probably occurs at the third cup. This blessing does not refer to the bread but to a blessing of God that occurred in the Passover ceremony. The verbs used in verse 26, "took bread, gave thanks [*eucharisteo*] and broke it, and gave," are the same ones used to describe the miracles of the feeding of the thousands (see comments on 14:19; 15:36). It is not insignificant that the early church presented the Lord's Supper in miracle language. Eucharist, the name of the supper, comes from the Greek word for "giving thanks."

Matthew's version of the Lord's Suppe includes the words "for the forgiveness c sins" (v. 28). This recalls 1:21: "because h will save his people from their sins" (see als 20:28). The Lord's Supper, then, has more tha just Passover implications; it draws on sever Old Testament events. As the Passover lam Jesus vicariously saves from death and usher in an era of liberty (Ex. 12). The "blood of th covenant" (Matt. 26:28) hails back to th blood-covenant sacrifice of Exodus 24:8, i which Moses threw half of the blood of th sacrificial animals on the altar of God an sprinkled the other half on the people (see als Zech. 9:11; Heb. 8:1–13; 9:11–10:18, 29 13:20). This established a new relationshi between God and his people. This nev covenant, as Luke and Paul describe it (Luk 22:20; 1 Cor. 11:25), was anticipated in Jere miah 31:31–34 and is qualitatively superior t the old (cf. Heb. 8:7–13). The vicarious suf fering is also alluded to in the Suffering Ser vant song of Isaiah 52:13–53:12. The pourin out of blood has sacrificial implications (Lev 1–7; 16).

13.1.7. Peter's Denial Foretold (26:30–35). The "hymn" (v. 30) refers to one of th concluding hymns of Passover celebration This verse serves as a transition, concludin the Passover meal and changing the venue t the Mount of Olives. Jesus predicts th "fall[ing] away" (v. 31, *skandalizo*) of all of th disciples. Matthew frequently uses this wor (e.g., 11:6; 13:57; 15:12). This desertion wi occur "this very night," showing how fas events are about to unfold (vv. 31, 34). It wi also fulfill the prophecy of Zechariah 13:7 regarding the striking of the shepherd and th dispersal of the flock of Israel into exile Zechariah 9–14 presents the shepherd-king a a messianic figure. Here Jesus predicts his res urrection and anticipates their reunion i Galilee (Matt. 26:32; see ch. 28).

Peter emphatically contradicts Jesus agai (vv. 33, 35), just as he did in 16:21–23. Jesus however, predicts Peter's threefold denial tha he ever knew Jesus (26:34; see 26:69–75).

13.2. Gethsemane, Arrest, Jewish Trial, and Peter's Denial (26:36–75)

13.2.1. Jesus in Gethsemane (26:36–46) Jesus and the disciples leave the city and retir across the Kidron, east to the Mount of Olives, specifically to Gethsemane (which means "olive press"). It is identified as a garden in John's Gospel (John 18:1, RSV), and Luke notes that Jesus frequented it often (22:39). Jesus takes with him Peter and the sons of Zebedee. Perhaps this is because Peter had been appointed the head apostle (see comment on Matt. 16:16–19) and because James and John had unwittingly offered to drink from Jesus' cup (20:20–23). These three also witnessed Jesus' transfiguration (17:1–8).

Matthew records three sessions of anguished prayer; he was "overwhelmed with sorrow" (*perilypos*, v. 38; see also Ps. 42:6; 43:5). Jesus then prostrates himself face down, demonstrating not only his agony of soul but also his total submission to his Father (Matt. 26:39). Jesus addresses God here as "my Father" and asks, "if it is possible," to have the cup removed. Here the cup is impending suffering and death (see comment on 20:20–23).

Jesus returns to his three disciples to find them sleeping, presumably exhausted from the tension of the last few days. He rebukes them by addressing Peter as the leader among them (see comment on Matt. 16:16–19). Even in his time of greatest need and agony Jesus expresses concern for his disciples, for his command to watch is as much for their sake as for his own. They are to pray to avoid temptation, referring to the trial they are about to experience, in which they will as a group perform rather poorly. Note the parallels between this occasion of prayer with that of the Lord's Prayer: "Father," "your will be done," and "lead us not into temptation" (Matt. 6:9–13). Jesus practiced what he preached; he prayed. Perhaps Matthew sees Jesus' three distinct prayers in contrast with Peter's three denials (26:69–75).

The word "hour" indicates that a crucial event is impending (v. 45). Typically the title "Son of Man" is linked with Jesus' suffering and death. Since he knows that Judas is about to betray him, he orders the disciples to "rise, let us go!" Jesus is in control of his betrayal, for it is a necessary part of the plan of redemption and fulfillment of Scripture. He is therefore saying in effect, "Rise, let us go meet my betrayer." No one will take Jesus' life; he lays it down on his own accord (John 10:18).

13.2.2. The Arrest of Jesus (26:47–56).

13.2.2.1. The Betrayal by Judas (26:47–50). While Jesus is still speaking, the entourage of the chief priests as well as a well-armed "*large* crowd" arrive, along with Judas (vv. 47–48). Why the large crowd? His enemies cannot seize him in the city for fear of the people (21:46); so they move against Jesus outside of the city and at night when fewer people are around him. Yet Jesus and the disciples are probably not completely alone. Many Passover pilgrims camped out on the Mount of Olives; thus for fear of the mob, the Jewish leaders bring a mob to capture Jesus.

The presence of numerous pilgrims in the vicinity explains why Judas must give his employers a cue identifying Jesus as their quarry. The kiss, a sign of respect and fealty, becomes a sign of hypocrisy and betrayal. Among some rabbis the disciple may only kiss the feet or face at a rabbi's bidding; thus, Judas's action might have been executed with an air of presumption and effrontery. His words to Jesus sound hollow and hypocritical. Once again, Judas addresses Jesus as "Rabbi" (see comments on 26:25).

Jesus' greeting of Judas as "friend" (*hetairos*)—a sting of ironic rebuke—is not the usual word for friend (*philos*). Socrates used this word to refer to his students, and it can mean comrade, neighbor, comrade-in-arms, political partisan, or one in a particular fraternity or organization. It was used in Judaism for those who scrupulously kept the law. The word occurs three times in Matthew (here; 20:13; 22:12). In each instance it "denotes a mutually binding relation between the speaker and the hearer which the latter has disregarded or scorned" (*TDNT*, 2:701). It also carries the meaning "table companion" (France, 1985, 375), which heightens Judas's treachery, since he had participated in the Lord's Supper, which ratified the new covenant and his alleged allegiance to Jesus.

Jesus' next words (v. 50) can either be translated as a question, "Wherefore art thou come?" (KJV), or as a command, "Do what you came for" (NIV). The latter is to be preferred since Jesus knows why Judas has come and Judas knows that Jesus knows. This command reemphasizes that Jesus is in charge of what is happening (see comment on 26:45).

13.2.2.2. The Sword (26:51–54). All four Gospels record a botched attempt to free Jesus by force, which results in the high priest's slave losing an ear (Mark 14:47; Luke 22:49–51; John 18:10–11). John identifies the assailant as Simon Peter. Given that Matthew frequently includes references to Peter, Matthew is most likely unaware of the identity of the attacker. Luke records that Jesus heals the wounded slave (Luke 22:51). Jesus instructs Peter to resheath the sword and adds words prohibiting violence (Matt. 26:52; see also 5:38–42; Rev. 13:10). Curiously in Luke Jesus had told the disciples to buy swords (22:35–38)! These two commands must be balanced; perhaps self-defense is tolerated but unprovoked attack is not. The example of Jesus and the practice of Jesus are characteristically nonviolent.

Jesus then asserts that he can ask his Father for twelve legions of angels to free him if he so wants to, indicating that heaven itself would come to his aid. This statement reinforces that Jesus is in charge and deliberately fulfills the Scriptures concerning himself. The Qumran community believed that angels would fight alongside them in the final end-time battle against the heathen (1QM 7:6). But Jesus refuses a cosmic quick-fix, such as Satan had offered him earlier in the temptation (Matt. 4:6–7).

13.2.2.3. Jesus Forsaken (26:55–56). Matthew makes it clear that the desertion of the disciples is a pivotal event by using the words "in that same hour" (KJV; "at that time," NIV). Jesus then addresses the hostile crowd. His rebuke exposes the treachery of his enemies. For days he taught publicly in the temple, yet now they surreptitiously move against him. He implies through his question in verse 55 that he is *not* "leading a rebellion." After all, by forbidding his disciples to defend him or themselves, he proves to his enemies that he is not a revolutionary. Matthew may be raising this issue because his community, composed of Jewish Christians, needed to answer the Jews who vilified their Messiah as a rabble-rousing impostor.

The disciples no doubt are confused at Jesus' acquiescence to the authorities despite his predictions. They were ready to fight (26:35), and they undoubtedly viewed his surrender as putting them all in peril; therefore, they quit the field without their leader. This fulfills Zechariah 13:7, which notes that when the shepherd is smitten, the sheep are scattered (see Matt. 26:31).

13.2.3. Jesus Before the Sanhedrin (26:57–68). Jesus is then taken before Caiaphas the high priest. Annas, his father-in-law, had earlier been high priest, but had been deposed; yet he continued to be the real power behind the office, ostensibly held by a succession of his sons and his son-in-law, Caiaphas. "Peter followed [Jesus] at a distance" in order to see what the outcome of the trial might be (v. 58).

The council met at night. Later Jewish law forbade capital offenses to be tried at night. Was this an illegal trial, or was this meeting an informal one that culminated in a formal trial in the morning? Inasmuch as the Roman occupation government prohibited the Jews to adjudicate cases involving the death penalty, any decision the Sanhedrin might make was at best provisional. Since the council was in the process of procuring false witnesses while the trial was going on, the whole affair appears ad hoc and tainted (v. 59).

According to Mark, the stories of the false witnesses do not agree (Mark 14:56). Like Mark, Matthew records the accusation that Jesus said he was able to destroy the temple and raise it in three days (Matt. 26:61; cf. 27:40). To this Matthew adds that *two* false witnesses affirm this; in capital cases Mosaic law required a minimum of two witnesses for a conviction (Deut. 17:6). This charge may have seemed credible in light of Jesus' hostility acted out in the cleansing of the temple (Matt. 21:12–13) and in light of his prediction of its destruction (24:2). John explains that Jesus' saying about the destruction of the temple referred to his death and resurrection (John 2:19–21). This charge against Jesus resurfaced at the trial of Stephen (Acts 6:14). But the ultimate focus for the young church's worship was not the temple but something greater than the temple (see Matt. 12:6).

Jesus refuses to answer this charge even when the high priest demands it. His silence may well have been in conscious imitation of the Suffering Servant of Isaiah: "He was oppressed and afflicted, yet he did not open his mouth; he was led like a lamb to the slaughter, and as a sheep before her shearers is silent, so he did not open his mouth" (Isa. 53:7).

Only when the high priest adjures Jesus by the "living God" does he respond to another charge, that of falsely claiming to be the Messiah (v. 63). The combination of "Son of God" and "the living God" is reminiscent of Peter's Christological confession (16:16). The charge that is ultimately written above Jesus' cross is that he claimed to be the Davidic Messiah (27:37). The high priest's question may have been presented in sarcasm or incredulity since no one there could have considered the apparently helpless figure of Jesus as the invincible Messiah.

Matthew records Jesus' answer to the charge as indirect, identical to his earlier response to Judas (lit., "you have said"); it is equivalent to "as you say" (see comment on 26:25). The rest of Jesus' response is more straightforward. He describes himself as the Son of Man from Daniel 7:14, who receives the kingdom from the Ancient of Days. He says to his enemies that later they will not see him seemingly helpless and bound but coming in apocalyptic glory. The NIV's "at the right hand of the Mighty One" is literally "at the right hand of Power." The word for "Mighty One" or "Power" is a respectful reference to God without using the sacred Name.

The high priest tears his robes as a sign of the gravity of the crime and insists Jesus "has spoken blasphemy," a crime punishable by death. He might have considered Jesus' words as an encroachment on the power of God and hence tantamount to blasphemy (Catchpole, 1971, 126).

The members of the council spit in his face, strike him with their fists, and slap him. The high priest himself may not only have approved the abuse Jesus received but even assigned the task to those at whose hands Jesus suffered. Mark's and Luke's accounts help clarify what is happening. In an effort to prove that their apparently hapless captive is not the Messiah, they blindfold him and ask the alleged messianic prophet to tell who is hitting him. Such prophetic abilities were expected of the Messiah (see Psalms of Solomon 17:37; cf. also Isa. 11:2).

13.2.4. Peter Denies the Lord (26:69–75). Matthew now picks up the story of Peter begun in 26:58. While the Jewish authorities examine Jesus, Peter is sitting in the courtyard, probably assuming he is unrecognized. The girl who first questions him is a servant of the high priest (v. 69; Mark 14:66). The diminutive *paidiske* carries the meaning "little." In other words, the disciple who swore he would die fighting for the Master cowers before a little slave girl! In his account of Peter's first denial, Matthew stresses that Peter denies the Lord "before them all," making it a public denial (Matt. 26:70).

Mark reports that the same girl asks again while Matthew notes that another slave girl asks the second time. This is typical of Matthew's use of "two" (see 8:28; 9:27; 20:30), perhaps to affirm the Jewish insistence of multiple witnesses for conviction. Upon this second identification of Peter as one of Jesus' disciples, he uses "an oath" to disavow any relationship with the Lord, a practice Jesus earlier had prohibited (26:72; cf. 5:33–37). The crowd then makes the same accusation because of Peter's Galilean accent. At this point Peter curses. The Greek can be translated that Peter pronounced a curse on himself or that he cursed his Lord, which later the Roman government would demand of Christians in exchange for their lives (France, 1985, 383).

There is a fourth witness to Peter's denial—a rooster. After this third denial all four Gospels record a rooster crowing; even nature raises its voice in protest to this denial of Jesus (Matt. 26:74; Mark 14:72; Luke 22:60; John 18:27). This brings to Peter's mind Jesus' prediction of his triple denial (Matt. 26:34), and he goes out and weeps "bitterly."

Peter becomes an example of hope for the sinner. No matter how grave the sin, repentance and restoration are always possible. Matthew will soon provide the contrast to Judas, who, though remorseful, does not return to God (27:3–10). Matthew does not, however, record Peter's restoration (cf. John 21:15–19). He probably assumes his readers know of the great role that the "Rock" performed in establishing the church.

13.3. Jesus Delivered to Pilate and the Death of Judas (27:1–10)

In the morning, at daybreak, the chief priests and elders decide to have Jesus put to death. According to Jewish law, this decision should not have been made at night (see comment on 26:59–66). Since by Roman law the Jews were forbidden to perform executions, they had to deliver Jesus to Pontius Pilate, the Roman governor in charge of Judea from A.D. 26–36. It is probably not insignificant that the word used for "handing over" Jesus to Pilate (*paradidomi*) is the same one used for Judas's betraying Jesus. Josephus relates that Pilate was a sly ruler, who on more than one occasion massacred Jews and Samaritans to impose his will and maintain order. Complaints had been made to Pilate's superiors regarding his brutality (*Antiquities*, 2.9.4; 4.1–2; 18.32; *Wars*, 2.9.2–4). It appears that Pilate was in Jerusalem during Passover to prevent disorder by providing a large visible military presence.

In the account of Judas's remorse and suicide (27:3–10), he realizes his guilt and regrets it, but his regret does not lead to repentance (see 3:8; Luke 3:8–14). When he tries to get rid of the blood money by returning it to the priests, who had originally given it to him, they refuse to accept it back into the temple treasury since it is tainted. Instead, they use the thirty pieces to purchase a field in which to bury strangers.[13] The main point here is that in contrast to the penitent Peter and his later restoration, Judas despairs of God's ability to redeem.

Matthew ascribes to Jeremiah a prophecy that is primarily from Zechariah 11:12–13 (with allusions to Jer. 18:2–3; 19:1–13; 32:6–15). Combined quotations were typical of rabbinic exegesis. For comments on Judas's fulfilling prophecy and on predestination, see 26:14–16, 21–26, 31.

13.4. Jesus Stands Before Pilate (27:11–31a)

Matthew calls Pilate "the governor." Although writing primarily from a Jewish perspective, Matthew does on occasion mention the role of the Gentiles. Here he exposes the role of the Roman government, the ultimate earthly political force in the Holy Land, in the unjust execution of Jesus. Recently scholars have tried to minimize or deny the role of the Jews in the death of Jesus for fear of the violence that has accompanied the scourge of anti-Semitism. Matthew, however, makes it clear that the Jewish leaders, and to some extent the Jewish people, were responsible for the death of Jesus (vv. 22–23). Yet he also asserts that the Gentiles, in the persona of Pilate and his soldiers, were guilty too.

The solution to the charge of anti-Semitism is *not* to change the text of the New Testament or to question its reliability, but to point out the stark guilt of *all* humanity, for everyone who has sinned in effect has helped to drive a nail into our Lord's hands and feet and then has danced defiantly beneath the cross, his blood dripping on them (Rom. 3:23; Heb. 6:6). The Jews were guilty not because they were Jews but because they were fallen human beings, even as Pilate and his associates were.

Jesus' standing before Pilate fulfills his own prediction, "You will be dragged before governors and kings for my sake, to bear testimony before them and the Gentiles" (10:17–18, RSV). What is true of the disciple is true of the Master (10:24). Note that Matthew mentions governors *and Gentiles* (cf. Luke 12:11–12). This serves his reminder that, like Jesus, Christians will suffer (Brown, 1994, 735). If Matthew is writing in the reign of the Emperor Domitian, then the mention of Gentiles refers to the Roman persecution of both Christians and Jews, which by comparison makes the Jewish violence against the church recorded in Acts look like a mere bee sting. Matthew is warning the followers of Jesus to be ready to suffer as Jesus did.

13.4.1. The Accusation (27:11–14). Pilate's question, "Are you the king of the Jews?" may be laced with sarcasm and irony since Jesus stands bound before him. Jesus' response, "You say" (lit. trans. of *sy legeis*; see comment on a similar expression in 26:25, 64) is an indirect affirmation. Matthew explicitly declares that at the Roman trial Jesus remains silent before the accusing chief priests and elders, just as he did in his Jewish trial (27:12–14; cf. 26:62–63; contrast Mark 15:3). Matthew probably has in mind Isaiah 42:2; 53:7: "He will not shout or cry out, or raise his voice in the streets"; and, "He was led like a lamb to the slaughter . . . he did not open his mouth." Pilate was amazed at his silence (cf. Isa. 52:15).

13.4.2. Jesus or Barabbas? (27:15–18, 20–23). At this point Luke records Herod's examination of Jesus and Pilate's subsequent declaration of his innocence (Luke 23:6–13); Matthew, by contrast, immediately proceeds to Pilate's offer of amnesty. Only in the Gospels do we learn of the Passover custom of offering freedom to a prisoner. Some think the Mishnah may suggest, albeit vaguely, the custom of release to a prisoner (*Pesahim* 8:6). Pilate may have been making a local accommodation to

ie Jews in order to placate them in the mat-
r. Under Roman law Pilate could release only
prisoner not yet convicted; presumably the
erdict on Barabbas had not been reached.

Who was Barabbas? Matthew calls him a notorious prisoner" (v. 16). From Mark and uke we learn he was a rebel and murderer vho was involved in an uprising in the city Mark 15:7; Luke 23:19). His name means son of the father." Some manuscripts of Iatthew record his name as "Jesus Barabbas" Jesus was a common name among the Jews in iat day). If this variant is correct, then it is ianifestly ironic: The people call for the lease of the rebel called "Jesus, son of the ather," while calling for the death of Jesus, the on of the Father! (Note Matthew's frequent ferences to Jesus calling God "my Father" in :21; 11:27; 16:17; 18:10; 26:42.) Pilate offers) release Jesus because he knows Jesus is nnocent and the victim of envy (27:18).

13.4.3. Pilate's Wife (27:19). Matthew ow records the dream of Pilate's wife as nother reason to release Jesus. She declares esus "that innocent [*dikaios*, lit., "righteous"] ian." Given Matthew's frequent use of the ighteousness word group (see comments on :15; 5:6), he probably intends double meanig. Matthew "is continuing the haunting motif f innocent blood that runs from Judas (27:4) irough this verse (27:19) to Pilate's attempt) wash his hands of it (27:24)" (Brown, 1994, 06). In spite of Pilate's attempts to have him reed, the leaders persuade the people to call or Jesus' death.

13.4.4. Pilate Washes His Hands (27:24–5). Pilate's washing his hands to declare his nnocence appears more a Jewish custom than Roman one (see Deut. 21:6–9; Ps. 26:6–10; sa. 1:15–16). Pilate may have been accomiodating a Jewish practice. Only Matthew ecords this action and the response of all of ie people: "Let his blood be on us and on our hildren" (Matt. 27:25). The people accept 'ilate's assertion that they are responsible for ie death of Jesus. No doubt the late first-cenry readers of the Gospel saw the destruction f Jerusalem as the fulfillment of this oath. 'his response by the crowd by no means exonrates Pilate; he was the supreme ruler of the gion in control of the military. He could have aved an innocent man; the buck stopped with im.

The crowd's rejection of Jesus fulfills his earlier words: "that upon you may fall the guilt of all the righteous blood shed on earth . . . upon this generation" (23:35–36, NASB). Matthew also wants to show the culpability of the Jewish community in the conflict with the first-century church. He presents Christianity as the legitimate successor of Judaism (see also Acts 3:13–14).

13.4.5. Jesus Is Scourged (27:26). Scourging was often part of the crucifixion process. The Old Testament limited beatings to forty lashes (Deut. 25:3; see also 2 Cor. 11:24), but Roman soldiers were not under such constraints. The scourge that was used in capital crimes was the *flagellum*, which often consisted of leather straps weighted with pieces of bone or metal. It often flayed to the bone and sometimes brought about the death of the victim before the crucifixion could be carried out (Josephus, *Jewish War*, 6.304).

13.4.6. Soldiers Mock Jesus (27:27–31a). The "Praetorium," once thought to be the Antonia Fortress, was probably Herod's palace (the Fortress was a barracks for troops). Part of the mockery Jesus endured at Roman hands was being stripped and having a "scarlet robe" placed on him. Luke records that Herod and his soldiers mocked Jesus by dressing him in an "elegant robe" before returning him to Pilate (Luke 23:11). Perhaps, then, Jesus' robe came from Herod, though this requires two mockeries by the soldiers, with the Roman soldiers removing the robe and then putting it on him again. Mark and John identify the robe as "purple" (Mark 15:17; John 19:2). The ancient color of purple does not necessarily correspond to the modern color; thus both scarlet and purple may have been closer to red than the modern color. Both colors were associated with wealth and rank (Rev. 17:4). Perhaps the cloak put on Jesus was a Roman soldier's cloak, which was scarlet (purple was also used to describe these cloaks; see BAGD, 694). This would be more in keeping with the impromptu farce that the staff and thorns suggest.

The "staff" acts a mock scepter; the soldiers use it to strike Jesus repeatedly on the head. The "thorns" probably mimic a Hellenistic crown, which had golden rays radiating from the monarch's head (commonly seen on ancient coins). With anything at hand the soldiers conspire to make Jesus look like a scarecrow king.

They mock him by standing him before their company as a monarch reviewing his troops, bowing before him and hailing him as "the king of the Jews"—the description of his crime placed above him on the cross. How surprising will it be to those who bowed once that they will bow twice! Those who mocked him as king will one day acknowledge him as Lord (Phil. 2:10–11), and the one they struck with a staff will one day rule them with a rod of iron (Rev. 19:15). By mentioning the staff, the soldiers' kneeling, and twice using the word "mocked," Matthew intensifies the shameful treatment Jesus endured at the hands of the Gentiles. He had predicted both the scourging and mocking at Gentile hands (Matt. 20:19).

13.5. The Crucifixion (27:31b–56)

Crucifixion was a Roman form of execution, reserved for slaves and noncitizens who had committed severe crimes. The usual Jewish mode of execution was stoning, but the Roman overlords reserved capital punishment as an imperial prerogative. Crucifixion was a most horrific instrument of torture leading to death. The victim was tied or nailed to a post and remained there until death ensued by asphyxiation. Hanging constricted the diaphragm, and breathing was only possible when the victim raised himself on the cross. The type of crosses and positions in which criminals were affixed were as varied as imaginations can be cruel. Sometimes blocks of wood served as crude footrests and narrow seats, prolonging the agony. Given that Jesus died in a relatively short time (it often took days for victims to die), he probably did not have a cross fitted with these "amenities."

Usually a crucified victim was naked, and this is probably the case with Jesus since his captors divided his garments (v. 35). Presumably the Romans had reclothed Jesus to march him to the execution site to accommodate Jewish sensibilities since usually victims were paraded naked to their cross. Whether Jesus had a loincloth on the cross (as is often depicted in art) is speculative at best. Jesus probably carried the cross beam only and not the whole cross to the execution site. The hands were lapped over the beam as it was borne on the prisoner's neck.

13.5.1. Simon Carries the Cross of Jesus (27:31b–32). Apparently Jesus' ill-treatment took its toll, and Jesus was too weak to carry the cross the entire distance. Thus, the Roman soldiers forced Simon of Cyrene to carry the crossbeam (v. 32), a common military practice (cf. 5:41). Cyrene was a Greek city in North Africa; Mark identifies this Simon as the father of Alexander and Rufus, persons his readers probably knew. Most likely the family became Christian, perhaps as a result of their father's bearing the cross of the Messiah. Luke gives further details regarding events on the way to the cross (Luke 23:27–32).

13.5.2. Jesus Is Nailed to the Cross (27:33–44). Jesus is crucified outside the city, a location that corresponds to the Hebrew injunctions regarding executions (Lev. 24:14; Num. 15:35–36; Acts 7:58; Heb. 13:12–13). The place was called Golgotha, from the Aramaic for "skull" (the Latin word for skull is *calvaria*, from which we get Calvary). Its exact location is not certain, but the most likely spot is near the Church of the Holy Sepulchre, north of the city.

Before the soldiers affix Jesus to the cross, they offer him wine mixed with gall. After Jesus tastes the drink, he refuses it. The wine/gall mixture would have been unpalatable and therefore a mockery of Jesus' thirst. Recognizing it as a cruel trick at his first taste, he rejects the insult. Matthew probably has in mind Psalm 69:21: "They put gall in my food and gave me vinegar for my thirst."[14]

The clothes of the condemned normally became the booty of the executioners. According to John, they gambled over Jesus' clothes, thus fulfilling Psalm 22:18 (John 19:23–24). The soldiers keep watch over Jesus (Matt. 27:36). Jesus is under constant guard; in no way could his followers have removed him from the cross. This anticipates the stationing of a guard at Jesus' tomb to prevent the disciples from stealing his body (vv. 62–66). All four Gospels present basically the same inscription of the charge that was placed over his head, "THIS IS JESUS, THE KING OF THE JEWS." This fits well with Matthew's emphasis on Jesus as King. John notes the inscription was in Hebrew, Latin, and Greek. According to Mark, Jesus is crucified at the third hour (9:00 A.M.).

To add to his shame Jesus is crucified with two "robbers" or insurrectionists, perhaps comrades of Barabbas. (For shaking heads a an insult see Ps. 22:7–8; 109:25; Lam. 2:15.) The crowds throw into Jesus' teeth his own words regarding destroying and rebuilding the temple in three days (Matt. 26:61; John 2:19; Acts 6:14). Their challenge for him to come down from the cross "if you are the Son of God" is reminiscent of the earlier temptations in the desert, set before him by Satan, to escape the rigors of his fast (Matt. 4:1–11).

The chief priests and elders add their taunt, mocking Jesus as "the King of Israel," who should be able miraculously to come down from the cross. Matthew's theme of Jesus as King is carried in the added words, "He trusts in God. Let God rescue him now . . . for he said 'I am the Son of God'" (v. 43). These words and Jesus' plight are astoundingly similar to those in Wisdom of Solomon 2:16–20, where the righteous is God's Son and the unrighteous torture him. The robbers crucified with Jesus also revile him. Luke, however, notes that one of the two affirms Jesus' innocence and is received by Jesus into his kingdom (Luke 23:39–43).

13.5.3. The Death of Jesus (27:45–50). Around noon ("the sixth hour") the land is

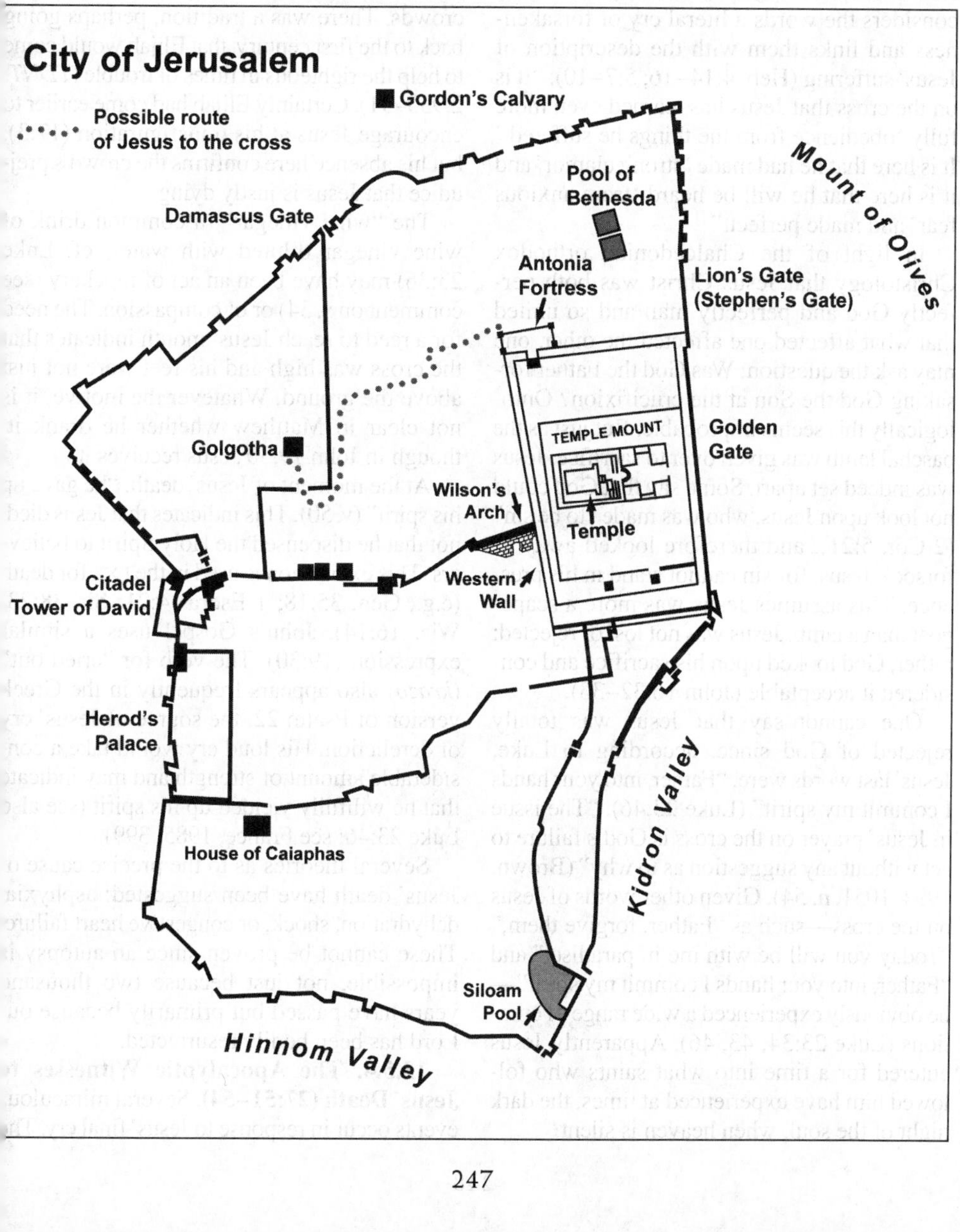

darkened until 3:00 P.M. ("the ninth hour"), when Jesus dies. This resembles the prophecy of Amos, "I will make the sun go down at noon and darken the earth in broad daylight" (Amos 8:9). The context in Matthew appears to be the same as that of Amos: judgment on the land.

Jesus cries out in the ninth hour, asking why God has forsaken him. He quotes Psalm 22:1, a psalm of dereliction. However, the psalm ends in hope, and this had led some to conclude that Jesus did not completely despair. Jesus' quote is a cry of desperation (e.g., "Sometimes I feel like a motherless child"; see also John 16:32–33). Brown (1994, 1047–51) considers the words a literal cry of forsakenness and links them with the description of Jesus' suffering (Heb. 4:14–16; 5:7–10): "It is on the cross that Jesus has learned even more fully 'obedience from the things he suffered.' It is here that he had made 'strong clamor' and it is here that he will be heard 'from anxious fear' and made perfect."

In light of the Chalcedonian orthodox Christology that Jesus Christ was both perfectly God and perfectly man and so united that what affected one affected the other, one may ask the question: Was God the Father forsaking God the Son at the crucifixion? Ontologically this seems improbable. But just as the paschal lamb was given over to sacrifice, Jesus was indeed set apart. Some say that God could not look upon Jesus, who was made "to be sin" (2 Cor. 5:21), and therefore looked away or forsook Jesus, for sin cannot stand in his presence. This assumes Jesus was more a scapegoat than a lamb. Jesus was not lost or rejected; rather, God looked upon his sacrifice and considered it acceptable (John 16:32–33).

One cannot say that Jesus was totally rejected of God since, according to Luke, Jesus' last words were, "Father, into your hands I commit my spirit" (Luke 23:46). "The issue in Jesus' prayer on the cross is God's failure to act without any suggestion as to why" (Brown, 1994, 1051, n. 54). Given other words of Jesus on the cross—such as "Father, forgive them," "Today you will be with me in paradise," and "Father, into your hands I commit my spirit"—he obviously experienced a wide range of emotions (Luke 23:34, 43, 46). Apparently Jesus entered for a time into what saints who followed him have experienced at times, the dark night of the soul, when heaven is silent.

Matthew's version of Jesus' God-forsaken cry is a combination of Hebrew and Aramaic words. This mixture can be accounted for in the Targums (Aramaic paraphrases of the Hebrew Scriptures), which did contain some blending of Aramaic and Hebrew. Or perhaps Jesus and his contemporaries spoke a mixture of the two languages (Gundry, 1967, 63–66). The crowd, however, misunderstands Jesus' cry of "*Eli, Eli*" (v. 46, cf. NIV note) as his calling to Elijah (v. 47). Such a misunderstanding is not unreasonable given that Jesus is no doubt dehydrated from the beating and mistreatment and given the circus-like din caused by the railings of the crowds. There was a tradition, perhaps going back to the first century, that Elijah would come to help the righteous in times of trouble (*TDNT*, 2:930–91). Certainly Elijah had come earlier to encourage Jesus at his transfiguration (17:3), but his absence here confirms the crowd's prejudice that Jesus is justly dying.

The "wine vinegar" (a common drink of wine vinegar diluted with water; cf. Luke 23:36) may have been an act of mockery (see comment on v. 34) or of compassion. The need for a reed to reach Jesus' mouth indicates that the cross was high and his feet were not just above the ground. Whatever the motive, it is not clear in Matthew whether he drank it though in John 19:30 Jesus receives it.

At the moment of Jesus' death, "he gave up his spirit" (v. 50). This indicates that Jesus died not that he dispensed the Holy Spirit to believers. This expression is used in the LXX for death (e.g., Gen. 35:18; 1 Esdras 4:21; Sir. 38:23 Wis. 16:14). John's Gospel uses a similar expression (19:30). The verb for "cried out" (*krazo*) also appears frequently in the Greek version of Psalm 22, the source of Jesus' cry of dereliction. His loud cry would take a considerable amount of strength and may indicate that he willfully yielded up his spirit (see also Luke 23:46; see France, 1985, 399).

Several theories as to the precise cause of Jesus' death have been suggested: asphyxia dehydration, shock, or congestive heart failure These cannot be proven since an autopsy is impossible, not just because two thousand years have passed but primarily because our Lord has been bodily resurrected.

13.5.4. The Apocalyptic Witnesses to Jesus' Death (27:51–54). Several miraculous events occur in response to Jesus' final cry. The curtain in the temple is torn from top to bottom (v. 51). There were two curtains in the temple: one separated the Holy Place from the court outside, and the other separated the Holy Place from the inner Most Holy Place, where the ark of the covenant stood. The inner one symbolized access to God for believers (in Hebrews the inner curtain is assumed: Heb. 4:16; 6:19–20; 9:11–28; 10:19–22).

The earthquake is a frequent element that Matthew uses both figuratively and literally (*seismos*/*seio*, see 8:24; 21:10; 24:7; 27:51, 54; 28:2, 4). It can be seen as a figurative apocalyptic symbol expressing the gravity of Jesus' death. Presumably there is an earthquake here, but it still has apocalyptic import. As a result of the opening of the earth, the saints of old rise from the dead (27:53). Apparently Matthew has lumped together several apocalyptic signs in this one passage, for he notes that they appear to people in Jerusalem *after* Jesus' resurrection.

Upon experiencing the earthquake the centurion and his men give witness that Jesus must have been the "Son of God." Some scholars have assumed that these men could not have uttered a statement with such theological import because they were pagan, not Jewish (see also Mark 15:39; Luke 23:47). Pagans, however, did have concepts of divine humans in their mythologies. Furthermore, it would be amazing if these Roman soldiers stationed in Judea were not aware of Jewish messianic expectations since their presence in Jerusalem was primarily to assure that rebellions arising from messianism would be short-lived. Of greater importance is the reason Matthew preserves the centurion's witness: It fulfills Jesus' predictions that Gentiles will replace the Jewish community as the followers of Jesus (e.g., Matt. 8:11–12; 21:43).

13.5.5. Women Witness the Crucifixion (27:55–56). Matthew makes a brief comment on the presence of women at the crucifixion and of their witness to the event from afar. All four Gospels record the faithfulness of the women disciples in contrast to the eleven remaining male disciples. John's Gospel includes an incident of the mother of Jesus and the beloved disciple at the foot of the cross (John 19:25–27).

13.6. The Burial of Jesus (27:57–61)

Knowing that his Jewish-oriented audience knows about the day of preparation before the Sabbath, Matthew does not explain this day as Mark does (Mark 15:42–47). He identifies Joseph of Arimathea as "a disciple," adding that he was "rich" (Matt. 27:57). Joseph hastily wraps Jesus' body in a shroud since the impending Sabbath prohibited any more activity. He places the body in his own tomb. Two Marys, identified by Mark as Mary Magdalene and Mary the mother of Joses (Mark 15:47), witness the burial. After the Sabbath the women plan to finish the preparation of the body (cf. Mark 16:1; Luke 23:56).

13.7. The Posting of the Guard at the Tomb (27:62–66)

Only Matthew records the posting of the guard and the controversy that led to it. Pilate allows the chief priests and Pharisees to post a guard to thwart any attempts to steal the body away in an alleged resurrection plot on the part of the disciples. Some think that the guards were the temple soldiers, who were Jews. Others suggest that they were Roman soldiers provided by Pilate. The latter is more probable since the Roman penalty for sleeping on watch was death, and the chief priests and elders promise to keep Pilate from acting on the soldiers' alleged dereliction of duty (28:11–15).

13.8. The Resurrection of Jesus (28:1–20)

13.8.1. Women Witness the Empty Tomb and the Risen Jesus (28:1–10). "Mary Magdalene and the other Mary" go to the tomb early on the day after the Sabbath. These two had witnessed Jesus' death (27:56) and burial (27:61); now they witness the empty tomb and the risen Jesus himself. Matthew uses their witness to corroborate that Jesus had indeed died and arose, thus refuting the anti-Christian rumor that his disciples stole his body (28:13–15). Mark records Salome as a third witness while Luke lists even more women (Mark 16:1; Luke 24:10).

Unlike Mark and Luke, Matthew does not say that the women were coming to anoint the body of Jesus (cf. Mark 16:1; Luke 24:1). Earlier Matthew recorded Jesus' anointing by an unidentified woman at the house of Simon the Leper, which Jesus said she did in anticipation of his burial (Matt. 26:6–13). It was the custom of the Jews to watch the tomb just in case the "deceased" revived, a victim of a premature burial (*Semahot* 8:1). Thus the women were coming to resume their watch over ("look at") the body after they had retired for the Sabbath.

On the way there is an earthquake (see comment on 27:51). The word for the guards being shaken (*seismos*) is from the earthquake/shaking word group; this is in keeping with Matthew's figurative and literal usage. He punctuates this extraordinary event with his attention-getting word "behold" (*idou*, absent in NIV).

An angel of the Lord, who is the cause of the earthquake, removes the stone. Matthew mentions an "angel of the Lord" only here and in 1:20; thus the beginning and the climax of his story of Jesus are explained by this special type of angel, whose appearance is sometimes equated with a manifestation of God himself (e.g., Ex. 14:19; Num. 22:22; Judg. 6:11–24; 2 Kings 1:3–4). The appearance of the angel is a brilliant white. After briefly noting that the guards are shaken and then paralyzed by fear, Matthew concentrates on the women's angelic encounter. Given his blinding brilliance, the angel's command, "Do not be afraid," is no surprise. He goes on to inform them that Jesus has indeed risen from the dead and invites them to "come and see the place where [Jesus] lay" (Matt. 28:6).

The angel then orders the women to return and inform the disciples to meet Jesus in Galilee—and to do so quickly (vv. 7–8). Filled both with fear and with great joy, the women obey the angel. Matthew emphasizes the Galilean appearances of Jesus in order to contrast his great rejection in Jerusalem and his subsequent condemnation of the city (23:38–39). Luke and John also record appearances of Jesus to the apostles in Jerusalem.

Along the way, the risen Jesus meets the women. Matthew again punctuates this encounter with his attention-getting "behold" (*idou*, "suddenly" in NIV). Notice that in his resurrected state he is corporeal; the women latch onto his feet (v. 9) The word for worship (*proskyneo*) can mean simply that they kneel before Jesus. It is used to express respect for both humans of high rank and for God. But their actions here seem to be more than merely expressing honor for an ordinary human ruler. Both here and in verse 17 *proskyneo* refers to expressing extraordinary honor to an extraordinary being.

Like the angel, Jesus calms their fears. Next he tells them to go tell his "brothers" to leave Jerusalem for Galilee in order to meet him there (v. 10). "Brothers" can refer either to the eleven remaining apostles or to his faithful followers in general. According to Paul, five hundred saw the risen Lord (1 Cor. 15:6). Earlier Matthew identified the followers of Jesus as his relatives (e.g., 5:22–23; 7:3, 5; 12:49–50; 18:15, 21, 35; 23:8).

13.8.2. The Collusion of the Chief Priests and Guards (28:11–15). Matthew recorded the posting of the guard at the tomb (27:62–66) and their incapacitating fear at the resurrection (28:4); now he records their false witness that the disciples stole Jesus' body. The chief priests were the ones who suggested the lie. If the guard detachment were Roman soldiers, their claim to have been asleep could have resulted in their execution; thus, it would have been necessary for the authorities to "keep [them] out of trouble" with Pilate, the Roman governor. Their claim of sleep was self-contradictory because their being asleep would have precluded their knowing that the body was removed and by whom! As in Judas's betrayal, money changed hands in order that Jesus and his kingdom might be defamed (26:15). This disparaging rumor was still circulating among the Jews at the time of his writing (28:15; late 80s in the first century?). According to Justin Martyr, it was still being told well into the second century.

13.8.3. Jesus Appears to the Disciples and Commissions Them (28:16–20). As promised, Jesus appears to the disciples in Galilee. Here the location for the appearance is a specific mountain—perhaps the mountain of transfiguration (17:1–8).

The disciples, like the women, worship or kneel (*proskyneo*) before Jesus. Some, however, doubt or are hesitant (the verb *distazo* can be translated either way). Although the Eleven are specifically identified as present, other "brothers" may also have been there (cf. 28:10). If the appearances to the Eleven in Jerusalem as recorded in Luke and John are taken into account, it seems unlikely that the Eleven would doubt Jesus' appearance since they have already seen him (Luke 24:36–53; John 20:19–29), nor would they be hesitant to bow and worship him. The doubters, in other words, are probably disciples other than the Eleven.

THE OLD TESTAMENT IN THE NEW

NT Text	OT Text	Subject
Mt 1:23	Isa 7:14	The virgin birth
Mt 2:6	Mic 5:2	Birth in Bethlehem
Mt 2:15	Hos 11:1	My son from Egypt
Mt 2:18	Jer 31:15	Crying in Ramah
Mt 3:3	Isa 40:3	Voice in the wilderness
Mt 4:4	Dt 8:3	Not by bread alone
Mt 4:6	Ps 91:11–12	Protecting angels
Mt 4:7	Dt 6:16	Do not test God
Mt 4:10	Dt 6:13	Serve God alone
Mt 4:15–16	Isa 9:1–2	Galilee of the Gentiles
Mt 5:21	Ex 20:13; Dt 5:17	Sixth commandment
Mt 5:27	Ex 20:14; Dt 5:18	Seventh commandment
Mt 5:31	Dt 24:1	Certificate of divorce
Mt 5:38	Ex 21:24; Lev 24:20	Eye for eye
Mt 5:43	Lev 19:18	Love your neighbor as yourself
Mt 8:17	Isa 53:4	Taking our infirmities
Mt 9:13	Hos 6:6	Mercy, not sacrifice
Mt 10:35	Mic 7:6	A divided household
Mt 11:10	Mal 3:1	Messenger sent ahead
Mt 12:7	Hos 6:6	Mercy, not sacrifice
Mt 12:18–21	Isa 42:1–4	The servant of the Lord
Mt 12:40	Jnh 1:17	Three days and nights
Mt 13:14–15	Isa 6:9–10	Seeing but not perceiving
Mt 13:35	Ps 78:2	Speaking in parables
Mt 15:4	Ex 20:12; Dt 5:16	Fifth commandment
Mt 15:4	Ex 21:17; Lev 20:9	Cursing parents
Mt 15:8–9	Isa 29:13	Hypocritical worship
Mt 16:27	Pr 24:12	God's fair judgment
Mt 17:10–11	Mal 4:5–6	Elijah comes
Mt 18:16	Dt 10:15	Two or three witnesses
Mt 19:4	Ge 1:27; 5:2	Creation of humans
Mt 19:5	Ge 2:24	Institution of marriage
Mt 19:19	Lev 19:18	Love your neighbor as yourself
Mt 21:5	Zec 9:9	Palm Sunday
Mt 21:19	Ps 118:26	Blessed is he who comes
Mt 21:13	Isa 56:7	God's house of prayer
Mt 21:13	Jer 7:11	A den of robbers
Mt 21:16	Ps 8:2	Children praising God
Mt 21:42	Ps 118:22–23	Rejected cornerstone
Mt 22:24	Dt 25:5	A brother's widow
Mt 22:32	Ex 3:6	The living God
Mt 22:37	Dt 6:5	Love God
Mt 22:39	Lev 19:18	Love your neighbor as yourself
Mt 22:44	Ps 110:1	At God's right hand
Mt 23:39	Ps 118:26	Blessed is he who comes
Mt 24:15	Dan 9:27; 11:31	Abomination of desolation
Mt 24:29	Isa 13:10; 34:4	The end times
Mt 24:30	Dan 7:13–14	Coming Son of Man
Mt 26:31	Zec 13:7	Striking the shepherd
Mt 26:64	Dan 7:13–14	Coming Son of Man
Mt 27:9–10	Zec 11:13	Thirty pieces of silver
Mt 27:35	Ps 22:18	Dividing garments by lot
Mt 27:46	Ps 22:1	God-forsaken cry

Jesus' commission to the disciples contains four uses of the word *pas* ("every, all"), which are not readily apparent in the NIV: *all* authority in heaven and earth has been given to Jesus (v. 18); the disciples are to go and make disciples of *all* nations (v. 19); the disciples are to teach *all* that Jesus had commanded them (v. 20); Jesus promises to be with them "*all* the days" (lit. trans.), even to the consummation of the age (v. 20). This all-inclusive commission provides an appropriate end for this Gospel, which emphasizes Jesus' teachings and authority. Jesus does not receive this authority because of his resurrection; he has been given this authority before. During the course of his ministry, he forgives sin (9:6), heals, has power over nature (14:22–34), and teaches with authority. "My words will never pass away" (24:35). After the resurrection, however, his authority has a wider application (Carson, 1984, 594–95).

On the basis of his authority Jesus commissions the Eleven to make disciples throughout the world. Discipleship is much more than merely having one's name on a membership list or espousing cultural trappings. It is doing the will of God as one's Father and submitting to a greater ethical accountability (e.g., 5:20–48; 12:48–50). "The nations" in Matthew refers to Gentiles (e.g., 4:15; 6:32; 12:18; 20:19, 25). "All nations" indicates that as a result of the rejection of Jesus by the Jewish authorities, the gospel is extended to the Gentiles (8:10–12; 12:21; 23:37–38). The time of the work limited to the Jews is over (10:6; 15:24).

It is reasonable to attribute the baptism formula, "in the name of the Father and of the Son and of the Holy Spirit," to Jesus himself as the touchstone of his teaching and not merely to a later church formula. Jesus often spoke of his relationship both with his Father and with the Holy Spirit (e.g., 10:32–33; 11:27; 26:39, 42, 53; cf. 1:18, 20; 3:11; 12:31–32). Such Trinitarian groupings occur in earlier New Testament works as well (e.g., 1 Cor. 12:4–6; 2 Cor. 13:14; 2 Thess. 2:13–14; see also Eph. 4:4–6; 1 Peter 1:2; Rev. 1:4–6). All three were present at Jesus' baptism; in the present passage, Matthew sees all three involved in Christian baptism (Matt. 3:16–17).

Teaching is as much a part of the discipleship process as is baptizing. The teaching of Jesus must be learned and observed as the Torah of the new kingdom (5:21–22, 27–28, 33–34). His words will outlast heaven and earth (24:35). Jesus asserts a demand for compliance to all his teaching not unlike God in the Old Testament (Ex. 29:35; Deut. 1:3; 7:11; 12:11–14).

Jesus' comforting promise of his presence with the disciples ("all the days"; NIV, "always") is emphatically expressed. This promise extends to the completion of this age, that is, to the return of the Lord (24:3). This stands as a greater fulfillment of the promise in the beginning of Matthew's Gospel that Jesus is "Immanuel . . . 'God with us'" (1:23).[15]

NOTES

[1]The above comparison of the genealogies of Matthew and Luke is taken from the author's work in *The Complete Biblical Library: The New Testament Study Bible, Luke*, ed. R. W. Harris, S. H. Horton, G. G. Seaver (1987), 105, 107.

[2]The reason for this anomaly is that after the fall of Rome, when the church began to convert its dating from Roman reckoning to B.C./A.D., its calculation was inaccurate by about four years.

[3]Luke includes Malachi 4:5–6 in the angel Gabriel's description of the role of John the Baptist (Luke 1:17). In general, however, he prefers to identify Jesus with Elijah since the old prophet, like Jesus, was well known for working miracles. Luke presents numerous parallels between Jesus' miracles and those of Elijah and his successor Elisha, of which Matthew and Mark say nothing (e.g., 4:25–27; 9:54; 12:54–56; 20:50–53; 24:49; Acts 1:9). John's Gospel notes that John the Baptist denied that he was the end-time Elijah (John 1:21).

[4]I would like to express my gratitude to the Oral Roberts University Center for Lifelong Education and the World Library Press for permission to use my previously published commentary *Study Guide for Luke-Acts*, 76–79; *The Complete Biblical Library: Luke*, 111–19.

[5]Elsewhere Matthew associates Gentiles with unclean dogs (15:26), but there the Canaanite woman is not condemned but approved for her faith.

[6]The meaning "Canaanite" is unlikely since this would make him a Gentile.

[7]In Luke's Gospel John's work is presented as, in some sense, a part of the new as well as the old since he links John with the Holy Spirit in post-Pentecost terms (see Shelton, 1991, 33–45, 165–77). Luke prefers to identify *Jesus* as the new Elijah with numerous allusions to the old prophet's work in his presentation of Jesus' ministry (cf. Luke 4:25–30 with 1 Kings 17 and 2 Kings 5; Luke 7:11–17 with 1 Kings 17:24 and 24:50–53; Acts 1:9, 11 with

2 Kings 2:11–12; 9:51 with 2 Kings 2:1; 24:49; Acts 1:4 with 2 Kings 2). The Elijah figure is a paradigm for describing Jesus as the messianic miracle worker.

[8]If a later date is accorded to Matthew's writing (c. A.D. 85), the presence of the Sadducees is somewhat perplexing since they ceased to be an influential power in Judaism when the temple (which they controlled) was destroyed by the Romans in A.D. 70. Why would Matthew reintroduce in the text a group no longer relevant to his readers? Some think this indicates an earlier date for the writing of the Gospel.

[9]Verse 11 does not appear in the earlier manuscripts of this Gospel. It may have originated from a scribal interpolation from Luke 19:10 or some other common source (see Metzger, 1971, 45).

[10]See D. C. Duling, "The Therapeutic Son of David: An Element in Matthew's Christological Apologetic," *NTS* 24 (1978): 392–410.

[11]Eusebius (*Ecclesiastical History* 3.5.3) relates that when the Zealots rebelled against Rome, the Christians in Jerusalem, warned by a prophecy, fled Jerusalem to the city of Pella in the Transjordan, thus escaping the carnage of the Roman siege of Jerusalem so graphically portrayed by Josephus (*War* 5–6).

[12]It has been suggested that one is following a solar calendar used by some Jewish sects while the other Gospel tradition is using a lunar calendar. This solution does not answer all the questions. Attempts to harmonize the two chronologies may be abetted when it appears that some Jewish groups reckoned the start of the day at *sunrise*, but simultaneously it further complicates any certainty in resolution. Further, the Sadducees and Pharisees may have had different dates for Passover. For a readable explanation of the various theories, see Marshall, 1980, esp. 62–75.

[13]According to Acts, Judas himself purchases a field into which he falls and is disemboweled (Acts 1:16–20). Here in Matthew he hangs himself. Efforts to harmonize the two accounts are problematic. Not surprisingly, on this confusing, traumatic, and horrific day, details may have been imprecise.

[14]Mark records that the drink was wine mixed with myrrh, which would have had a narcotic effect. Jesus refuses to drink the narcotic because he is willing to accept the cup of suffering put before him by God (Brown, 1994, 942).

[15]Appreciation is extended to the author's wife, Sally Moore Shelton, for typing, editing, and proofreading services so graciously given (Matt. 20:25–28). Thanks also to Mr. Trevor Bakhuis for his assistance.

BIBLIOGRAPHY

Matthew Black, *An Aramaic Approach to the Gospels and Acts* (1954); Dietrich Bonhoeffer, *The Cost of Discipleship* (1963); Raymond E. Brown, *The Birth of the Messiah: A Commentary on the Infancy Narratives in Matthew and Luke* (1977); idem, *The Death of the Messiah: A Commentary on the Passion Narratives in the Four Gospels* (1994); F. F. Bruce, *Message of the New Testament* (1972); idem, *The Hard Sayings of Jesus* (1983); Frederick Dale Bruner, *Matthew 1–12: The Christbook* (1998a); idem, *Matthew 13–28: The Churchbook* (1998b); D. A. Carson, "Matthew," *The Expositor's Bible Commentary* (1984), 8:3–599; D. R. Catchpole, *The Trial of Jesus* (1971); J. D. M. Derrett, *The Law in the New Testament* (1970); Suzanne de Dietrich, *The Gospel According to Matthew*, Layman's Bible Commentary (1961); Richard T. France, *The Gospel According to Matthew: An Introduction and Commentary*, TNTC (1985); R. Guelich, *The Sermon on the Mount: A Foundation for Understanding* (1982); Robert Gundry, *Matthew: A Commentary on His Handbook for a Mixed Church Under Persecution* (1994); idem, *The Use of the Old Testament in St. Matthew's Gospel* (1967); Daniel J. Harrington, *Sacra Pagina: The Gospel of Matthew* (1991); Martin Hengel, "The Sources of the History of Earliest Christianity," *Acts and the History of Earliest Christianity* (1980); Paul Hinnebusch, *St. Matthew's Earthquake: Judgment and Discipleship in the Gospel of Matthew* (1980); Joachim Jeremias, *The Prayers of Jesus* (1967); idem, *New Testament Theology: The Proclamation of Jesus* (1971); idem, *The Parables of Jesus* (1972); idem, *Jerusalem in the Time of Jesus: An Investigation Into Economic and Social Conditions During the New Testament Period* (1975); E. Stanley Jones, *The Christ of the Mount: A Working Philosophy of Life* (1931); Jack D. Kingsbury, *The Parables of Jesus in Matthew 13* (1969); idem, *Matthew: Structure, Christology, and Kingdom* (1975); I. Howard Marshall, *Last Supper and Lord's Supper* (1980); John P. Meier, *Matthew*, New Testament Message (1990); Bruce M. Metzger, *Textual Commentary on the Greek New Testament* (1971); James B. Shelton, *Mighty in Word and Deed: The Role of the Holy Spirit in Luke-Acts* (1991); Robert H. Stein, *An Introduction to the Parables of Jesus* (1981); Vincent Taylor, *The Gospel According to St. Mark* (1966); Bruce Vawter, *The Four Gospels: An Introduction* (1967); Brad H. Young, *Jesus and His Jewish Parables* (1989); idem, *Jesus the Jewish Theologian* (1995).

MARK

Jerry Camery-Hoggatt

INTRODUCTION

When I was asked to write this commentary on Mark "from a Pentecostal perspective," I was at first a little puzzled. What exactly is a "Pentecostal perspective"? How does it differ from other interpretations? Could the results of such a study be presented in a way that would be academically responsible, and yet ring true for pastors and laypeople whose experience of worship and church life is born and nurtured within the Pentecostal tradition, just as mine was?

1. Interpreting Mark

a. Approaches to Interpreting Mark

The issues raised by such questions will probably be clearer for the contributors to this commentary working with the Pauline literature and Acts, since that is where we find the texts that make sense of our own Pentecostal experience. But what of the narrative tradition in the Gospels? What of Mark, which has nothing direct to say about the operation of the charismatic gifts for believers (cf. here comments on 16:9–20)? This Evangelist does not mention tongues. The Holy Spirit itself is mentioned only five times (1:8, 12; 3:29; 12:36; 13:11), none of which are in the ways Pentecostals have tended to emphasize.

Mark has miracles to be sure, and these raise issues of interpretation to which Pentecostals will bring special sensitivities, but it is not adequate in a Pentecostal commentary simply to affirm what believing Pentecostals have always affirmed about miracles, namely, that they really happened. A close reading of Mark will indicate that his theology was not so much preoccupied with miracle as hesitant about it, or at least hesitant about the triumphalist notion that God will always in every way vindicate his people by miracle or move the gospel forward "by signs and wonders." The text itself says manifestly the opposite (8:11–13), and to the extent that we affirm miracle as God's primary and central means of showing "signs and wonders," we may find ourselves working with a worldview that is alien to one Mark himself took for granted.

Surely a Pentecostal interpretation of this Gospel is more than simply saying that because the Holy Spirit promises to guide us into all truth (John 16:13), whatever truth we discover in Mark is thereby uniquely spiritual (i.e., Pentecostal) truth. This verse in John does not mean that the Holy Spirit will intuitively lead us to a proper understanding of Scripture. It does not excuse us from the difficult task of studying in order to learn what God's Word means. Indeed, if we are to affirm the authority of Scripture, we must allow the Bible to control our understanding of the Spirit, rather than using our encounter with the Spirit to control our understanding of the Bible. Instead, the focus of John 16:13 is that the Spirit will lead us to a revelatory and life-changing encounter with Jesus, who is the Word of God.

Furthermore, we must recognize that different readers of Scripture may very well come to a text with good intentions and open hearts but reach incompatible understandings of what it means. While as Protestants we affirm that all believers have a right to determine the meaning of Scripture for themselves, that affirmation does not mean that all interpretations are equally valid. We may, in fact, draw wrong conclusions from our study of the Bible, and when we do so we contribute to our own destruction (cf. 2 Peter 3:16).

In other words, we must have some clear way of deciding which interpretations are valid and which are not. Otherwise, we will use Scripture to validate our own ideas, as though our ideas are inspired rather than need to be judged against the standard of God's Word itself. Our interpretations must work within boundaries; otherwise said, our interpretive frameworks (called "paradigms") have to be *critical*—not because they are hostile to the biblical text, but because they are careful ("critical") not to state claims that cannot be supported by the evidence of the biblical text itself. In order for a paradigm to be critical, its rules of evidence and its procedures of evaluation must be set out on the table so the reader who uses its results will know how those results were reached. There is an uncomfortable, but important benefit here: When we put our paradigms on the table, we also expose our secret biases and hidden agendas.[1]

Bible scholars use a number of critical paradigms to interpret Scripture, each designed to yield a different kind of information—e.g., source criticism, form criticism, redaction criticism, textual criticism, and social-science criticism. By and large, *evangelical* scholarship uses what is normally referred to as historical-grammatical exegesis—an interpretive method that attempts to discover what the author intended as he wrote the biblical text (see Fee and Stuart, 1982). The assumption here is that whatever the Bible means today must be consistent with the intention of the original author. And since authors intended their texts to be read and understood within specific historical, cultural, and linguistic contexts, exegesis concentrates on matters of history, culture, and language.

b. The Paradigm Used in This Commentary: Reader-Response Criticism

Recently, the method of interpretation that focuses on the author has been supplemented by a major shift of perspectives. Rather than asking directly what the author intended, we can ask the same question indirectly by focusing on the other end of the transmission process, the reader, and on the activities of reading by which readers uncover the meaning of texts. This paradigm is called *reader-response criticism* (see, e.g., McKnight, 1985; Camry-Hoggatt, 1995). In the following commentary I approach the Gospel of Mark from this perspective.

In order to eliminate misunderstanding, I must make it clear that there are patterns of reader-response criticism that allow the reader to see in a written text anything he or she wants to see. This is particularly prevalent in what is called postmodernism. For radical postmodernists, one's own historical and cultural context becomes the interpretive framework to discovering truth in a text, and they reject the idea that there is a single, right, normative reading of Scripture. Such an approach is incompatible with a clear commitment to the authority of the Bible.

Instead, the reader-response criticism I am proposing begins with the original readers of the biblical text (what I call "the authorial readers"). We need to, as it were, get inside the mind of these readers and seek to understand the text of the Scriptures in the same way as they would have first understood it. This approach to reading asks two main questions:

- What repertoire of information is the authorial reader of this text expected to know as a precondition of reading?
- How is the reader expected to use that information to inform and shape the reading process?

In principle, the procedure is quite simple: By answering these two questions the modern interpreter can clarify the sorts of strategies the author has used to engage his reader's attention and to manage his reader's responses to the text. But this is simple only in principle; in actual practice it can call for subtle interpretive work. Because we are distanced from the world of the first century by radical changes in culture, we must be careful how we go about answering the first question, and because the processes by which we manage language are complex we must be careful about how we answer the second.

For example, if Mark's authorial readers were part of a persecuted community, then he would have expected them to find in the words of the Olivet Discourse (Mark 13) a salve to their own wounds. If Mark wrote for Christians rather than non-Christians, that fact would have shaped and informed the way he worded his story. If the community for which Mark wrote was divided over questions of piety or theology, then the reader he had in view would come to the text with a position, with commitments and vested interests, perhaps even with family loyalties on the line. Indeed, the text may confirm or challenge the reader's existing commitments, but the reader is not neutral and detached. For some of Mark's readers, this Gospel must have been comforting and encouraging, while for others disturbing and perhaps even infuriating.

This method of interpretation also means deliberately bracketing information that Mark's authorial readers could *not* have known. For example, in 9:1 Jesus predicts that some of those standing there would "not taste death before they see the kingdom of God come with power." Those readers could not have known that two thousand years later we would be reading that prediction and that it would raise troubling questions. As legitimate as our questions may be—and such questions are certainly legitimate—this commentary will note when they would not have occurred to Mark's reader and will discount them as factors in the interpretive process.

Furthermore, we will be observing three interpretive constraints that are somewhat unusual for an evangelical interpretation of Mark. (1) We will bracket out of consideration the other Gospels and read Mark by itself. This is because Mark's reader could not have known the other Gospels and would not have used that information to understand what Mark wrote.

(2) We will respect the way Mark has sequenced his material. Earlier material may prepare the reader to read later material in a certain way, but we will assume that the reader does not know that he or she is being set up in this way. (The method of criticism that does this is rhetorical criticism, such as is used in this book in Aker's commentary on the Gospel of John.)

(3) We will respect the interplay of conventions and constraints as the text unfolds. Mark, for example, never expected his reader to dismantle the text into component parts or to evaluate the story for its historical accuracy—two typical modern-day questions asked of the Gospels. Where conventional scholarship tends to take the text apart, readers reading naturally try to understand the ways in which the parts work together. Where conventional scholarship tends to *analyze* the historical data about the characters, readers tend to *identify* with the characters.

The basic point here is that if we wish to understand the text the way Mark expected his authorial readers to understand it, we must, to the best of our ability, replicate what Mark expected his readers to do.

c. Reader-Response Criticism and Pentecostal Preaching

When we interpret this Gospel in this framework, we discover that Mark is more like a narrative sermon than a collection of historical details. It is a kind of preaching, and like all preaching it has a complex relationship to context: The preacher tries first to hear the text in its original context, but then to appropriate that same text for a new and different context, one in which the real issues of life may be profoundly different from those for which the text was prepared. What makes it legitimate that we do this for our congregations is that the Evangelists—Matthew, Mark, Luke, and John—and other early Christian preachers did it before us. From a reader-response perspective, what matters is not so much the details as the ways in which the details have been arranged to give the reader a fresh awareness of God at work in the world.

Note that this process is as much a matter of *proclaiming* as it is of *reporting*. The Evangelists do indeed report factual information about Jesus, but they use the facts in order to summon the listener to a fresh vision, a fresh encounter with Jesus, the Word of God. That fresh encounter is centrally the work of the Spirit! (With this we return to John 16:13!) The question is not only what the reader is expected to *know*, but also what the reader is expected to *do*.

Pentecostal preachers have always known this: Language is not only *in*formative, it is also *per*formative. That is, it does things. We judge a sermon not only by the accuracy of its exegesis, but also by the power of its delivery. No small part of the enormous impact of Pentecostal preaching lies in its respect for the power of the proclaimed Word. The language of the Bible is equally broad: Not only does the Bible tell us about God, it summons us into conversion.

Our approach to the Gospel of Mark has four advantages for Pentecostal preaching.

(1) Reader-response criticism may be understood as another way of discovering the author's intent. Authors do want their readers to respond to texts in certain ways. Our method of interpretation is also compatible with a richly developed doctrine of the inspiration and authority of Scripture.
(2) Reader-response criticism is compatible with a charismatic conviction that Scripture is life-changing. The text calls the reader to conversion, and those calls are central to the author's intent.

(3) Reader-response criticism approaches the text in ways that are close to the needs of the preacher, since the call to conversion within the text can become the trumpet-call of the sermon.
(4) Reader-response criticism of Mark affirms the supernatural and the miraculous as presented in the text. The author himself clearly expected his reader to believe in miracles, in demons, in voices from the sky, and in inspired prophetic words. Reader-response criticism insists that the modern interpreter must be willing to bracket any objection to miracle and read as though such things really did, and do, happen.

2. The Authorial Reader

From the foregoing, it is clear that the interpretive perspective taken in this commentary depends on a fairly specific definition of the term *authorial reader*. Who is Mark's "reader"? Surely not the modern reader, who brings to the text a completely foreign repertoire of ideas about the world. Nor is it the modern "charismatic" reader, who may rely on the Holy Spirit to fill in the gaps of the text and thus make critical exegesis irrelevant, but who has no criteria of validity by which to decide whether he or she has "understood" the Holy Spirit aright. The authorial reader Mark had in mind is also not to be confused with the characters of the story, who are "inside" the action and cannot hear the narrator's explanations of what is going on.

In this commentary we will envision as the authorial reader a real human being—or rather, a community of humans—to whom Mark addressed his narrative. This community brought to the reading a specific repertoire of skills and understandings, a certain knowledge of the world and how it worked. What then can we know of Mark's church? What did Mark expect his readers to know as a presupposition of the reading process?

a. General Cultural and Political Knowledge

We can know certain things about Mark's reader just from general knowledge of the ancient world. For example, he or she shared the cultural knowledge that was taken for granted throughout the ancient world—such as the fact that sowing preceded plowing (cf. 4:1–9), that for Jews work was prohibited on the Sabbath (3:1–6), and that edible precursors of figs (called *taqsh*) appear on fig trees long before the figs themselves (11:13). In Mark's taken-for-granted world, the dominant political power was Rome, a person's social status was fixed as a matter of morality, and the natural order was infested with demonic powers.

b. Jewish Knowledge

Mark also assumes that his reader possessed detailed knowledge of Judaism, both its literature and its daily practices. Thus, other significant elements of the ancient reader's repertoire of information can be gleaned from a study of contemporary Jewish literature. In recent years our understanding of first-century Judaism has been radically changed by new discoveries and by new ways of understanding old data.

In this area, three striking changes immediately jump out. (1) Because Jewish literature is primarily religious, and because our interests are motivated by a desire to understand Jewish theology as a background to the theological content of the New Testament, we have had a tendency to limit our observations to abstract questions of theology or to the day-to-day questions of religious practice. How far was a "Sabbath journey"? What did the rabbis believe about the coming Messiah? But this is distortive in that it highlights theological concerns at the expense of nonreligious ones. Jewish literature is theological, to be sure, but it expresses its theology in language, and language presupposes culture. We have seen an increase in interest in what might be called the "social" aspects of first-century Judaism. Like every other social group, the Jews observed certain kinship rules, rules of etiquette, assumptions about the relationship of parents to children, basic ideas about money and investments, and so forth.

Many of those practices and beliefs would seem strange to us, perhaps even objectionable, yet they are essential components of the interpretive task. The Jews' own reading of the theological content of their oral and written traditions sometimes depended on such ordinary knowledge as the proper way to construct a stone doorpost! Thus, the social dimensions of these texts are a matter of increasing interest among scholars.[2]

(2) Even within the religious sphere, the Judaism of the first century was much less unified than we had previously thought. Until recently it was common to assume that Jews were in agreement not only on fundamental questions, but also on the incidental details of daily piety. Thus, if an interpreter found a single quote from a single Jewish authority, that quote was taken as a representative picture of what all Jews believed. But this is profoundly wrong. In his recent book *Judaisms and Their Messiahs* (1988), Jacob Neusner has argued that first-century Judaism was more deeply divided, and its sects were more suspicious of one another, than previously thought. The plural in Neusner's title was chosen deliberately: There were Judaisms.

Indeed, it is no longer possible to say with certainty that "the Jews" completely agreed about any particular thing, except perhaps that there was one God and that God's people should be set apart by circumcision. If the biblical record is useful evidence, they were certainly divided in their decisions about what to make of Jesus!

(3) Older scholarship took for granted a deep division between Judaism and Hellenism, that is, between Hebrew and Greek modes of thought. This assumption too has crumbled under the weight of the historical evidence. In 1968 Martin Hengel demonstrated quite clearly that for ordinary Jews of the first century, daily life throughout the Mediterranean basin was more thoroughly Hellenized than anything we previously imagined.

c. Christian Knowledge

Mark's authorial readers were also Christians, who would have responded to his narrative from within a living experience of the church, with its real life concerns for working out the Christian faith in a hostile and pagan world. They did not know the future history of Christian faith, but they did know and understand Christian life and experience within a specific moment in time. Each of the three shifts in our understanding of first-century Judaism has been closely paralleled by shifts in our understanding of first-century Christianity.

(1) There is an increasing attention to the *social* dimensions of early Christian life. Like any social group, early Christian communities had to have effective ways of establishing borders between insiders and outsiders and of transitioning through these borders in either direction. They had to have ways of differentiating roles, of negotiating and enforcing lines of authority, of establishing norms of behavior, and of applying warrants and sanctions against group members who violated those norms. Increasingly scholars have been asking what those borders, norms, and warrants might have been, and the role the biblical writings played in defining and reinforcing them. This entails a fundamental change of paradigm: Instead of asking what the apostles said or thought, it is now becoming increasingly common to find scholars asking what ordinary Christians said and thought and what the experience of conversion to Christian faith might have been for someone who had been reared, say, in a pagan household, or whose decision to follow Jesus had meant expulsion from an orthodox Jewish home.

(2) First-century Christianity was considerably less unified than we have been accustomed to believe. There were arguments between Jewish and Gentile factions of the church (Acts 15; Gal. 2), arguments between Paul and other missionaries working in the same fields (Gal. 2:11–14; cf. 1 Cor. 1:10–4:21), arguments between Paul and his followers over to what extent he had the authority to make the extraordinary claims he made (2 Cor. 2:1–4), and even arguments over what criteria could be used to answer such questions. If Christians courageously faced martyrdom, sometimes it was because they had been betrayed by other Christians (e.g., Mark 13:12–13).

Indeed, if we were willing to read the Bible carefully, it would appear that the bulk of the New Testament literature is born out of tension. Clearly not all early Christians understood Jesus or the meaning of the Christ event in the same ways. They had conflicting approaches to circumcision, argued over tongues, and differed considerably on basic questions of right and wrong. In other words, early Christianity was more like the modern church than we would have guessed, as Pentecostal theologian Frank Macchia says, "God present in a confused situation."[3]

(3) Early Christianity was more profoundly affected by its exposure to Greek ideas than we

had previously thought. There is a simple reason why this was so. In the ancient world, the *paterfamilias*, the "head" of the extended family, usually decided the religion of his entire household. A good example from the New Testament is the story of the Philippian jailer in Acts 16:25–34. The jailer is converted and baptized, "he and his whole family" (v. 34). If, as seems likely, this conversion represents a standard pattern, then a significant number of new converts would have become Christians without a clear *personal* grasp of the issues of faith, such as what we have come to expect of converts in our own churches.

When family groups converted en masse, some of these people brought with them their pagan ideas, which would have posed significant challenges to the fledgling church. These raised important issues about purity of practice and even the nature of faith itself. An argument can be made that among the underlying reasons for the emergence of a specifically Christian body of literature was the need to make sense of the issues of faith for those converts whose fundamental ideas about life had been stamped out in a pagan press.

These three new understandings call both for a considerable rethinking of the issues to which the biblical writers addressed their attention and for a reexamination of the exegetical conclusions we have reached. As we will see in this commentary, Mark's authorial readers are not neutral, detached bystanders, but almost certainly come to the reading already committed to particular positions. Indeed, Mark's readers may well have been contenders in the fight.

d. Mark and His Church

What has been said thus far could be said of all early Christian literature. The most specific question is: Can we focus our attention more narrowly and develop a picture of the immediate situation to which Mark addressed his particular telling of the gospel? What specific events and experiences defined the issues of faith to which he directs his attention? In this section we will raise these questions, using two quite different interpretive paradigms. We will use a historian's paradigm to address the question of immediate historical background and a social-scientific paradigm to reconstruct the thought-world of Mark's community (both the things that were taken for granted and those that were under contention).

Authorship. The Gospel of Mark is technically anonymous, like the other Gospels. The usual title—"The Gospel According to Mark"—is the addition of an editor, not part of the inerrant Word of God. The questions of who wrote this Gospel, and why and when, are therefore subjects for historical inquiry. Our difficulty with Mark is that there are two very different early traditions, one claiming that Mark's Gospel was an abbreviation of Matthew's (championed especially by St. Augustine) and another, older theory claiming that it was dependent primarily on the preaching of Peter. The earliest reference to this second theory is a tradition cited by Eusebius, who refers to a volume (now lost) written by Papias, bishop of Hieropolis, around A.D. 140, that Mark was a translator and recorder of the preaching of Peter (see Eusebius, *Eccl. Hist.*, 3.39.15). Three other second-century witnesses establish the same connection: *The Anti-Marcionite Prologue* (c. 160–180), Irenaeus, *Against Heresies* 3.1.2 (c. 175), and *The Muratorian Canon* (c. 170–190).

It is also traditional, and to my mind highly probable, that the Mark in view here is the "John, also called Mark," of Acts 12:12—a sometime companion of Paul. His dual name (Heb. *Yohanan*; Latin *Marcus* [or Gk. *Markos*]) may indicate mixed parentage, though there is some indication that such names were common among Hellenistic Jews of the first century (e.g., Joseph Justus, 1:23). A resident of Jerusalem (12:12), Mark is identified as a cousin of Barnabas (Col. 4:10), a wealthy Cypriot landowner who figures prominently in the early chapters of Acts.

One tradition places the Lord's Supper in the Jerusalem home of Mark's mother, Mary, from which (it is suggested) he would have had occasion to follow Jesus' movements in Jerusalem rather closely. Note that the description of events in Acts permits the inference that this house was large and well appointed, since it had both a courtyard and space for "many" to gather for prayer (Acts 12:12–13a). The presence of a servant girl (v. 13b) and the connection with landowner Barnabas (4:36–37; Col. 4:10) combine to suggest that Mark's family was well-to-do, and the fact that Peter went there directly upon his release from prison

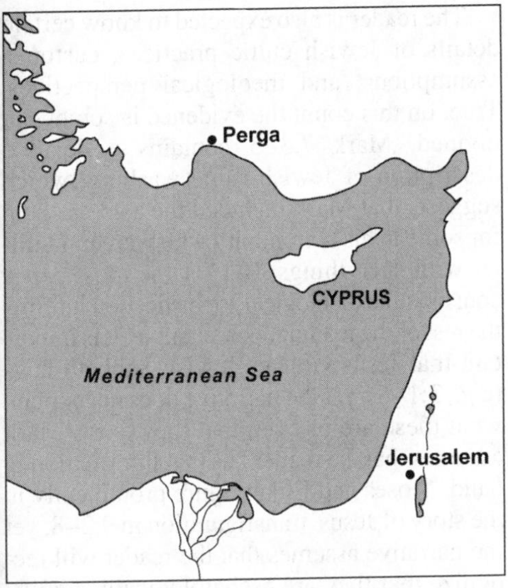

Mark traveled with Paul and Barnabas to Cyprus and to Perga on their first missionary trip. He then returned to Jerusalem. Tradition says Mark wrote the gospel of Mark after the fire in Rome in A.D. 64.

(Acts 12:12) suggests that this was a known meeting place for early Christian gatherings.

According to Acts 13:4–16, Paul and Barnabas took Mark with them on their first missionary journey to Cyprus (v. 13), then to Perga in Pamphylia (v. 13a), where Mark left them and returned to Jerusalem (v. 13b). The text does not give the reasons for his withdrawal, but it is clear from 15:39 that whatever they were, they were unacceptable to Paul. For several years Mark disappears from the historical record, only to reappear in Colossians 4:10 as a companion—and perhaps also attendant—of Paul (see also 2 Tim. 4:11; Philem. 24). Mark's connection with Peter and Rome is consistent with a reference in 1 Peter 5:13: "She who is in Babylon, chosen together with you, sends you her greetings, and so does my son Mark." The word "son" here cannot be intended literally and indicates instead a close personal relationship.

Both Irenaeus and the *Anti-Marcionite Prologue* report that Mark wrote following Peter's death. These citations permit the inference that Mark wrote following a fire that destroyed Rome in July of A.D. 64. That situation was clearly tragic for Christians. The Roman historian Suetonius charges that the fire was set by Nero, and though this is unproven, the historical record makes clear that the accusation found a ready hearing on the street. The rumor sparked the dry tinder of public resentment against Nero. To counteract it, Nero created a scapegoat by arresting and punishing Christians. A second series of traditions suggests that both Peter and Paul perished in this conflagration—Peter by crucifixion upside down, Paul by decapitation.

This, then, is the traditional reconstruction of the life situation that occasioned the writing of Mark: Mark, the Gospel to the Romans, was written in the years following the fire in Rome to a church under much duress, struggling with the problems of different theological and ethnic factions and grieving the loss of one of its pillars and perhaps many of its members.

Modern scholars have been cautious about taking this tradition at face value. Several elements within the Gospel do not seem to fit with the general conclusions reflected above. Perhaps foremost, Mark's Gospel characterizes Peter in the most uncomplimentary way, making him out to be little more than an oaf (9:6; cf. also 8:33; 14:66–72). Moreover, the traditional reconstruction understands the substance of the Gospel as coming primarily from Peter's preaching. But form-critical studies have shown that Mark, like the other Gospels, contains elements from a variety of sources—some oral, some collected already in smaller clusters, some associated by theme or "hookword." The Passion narrative is tied together by a series of tight chronological links, which suggests that it may have already been a connected sequence by the time Mark took it over. Thus, if Peter is a source for Mark, he may have played a somewhat narrower role than the tradition suggests.

This picture offers controls of its own that govern the reading process. For example, if Mark was written first, it does not do to supplement Mark's record with information from the other Gospels. It is highly unlikely, for example, that Mark's readers would have brought to their reading the high Christology of John 1:1–18, or the same formula for the Lord's Supper as the one we have grown accustomed from 1 Corinthians 11. In the commentary that follows, we will rigidly bracket such information unless it is suggested by the text itself.

As far as exegesis is concerned, this is the negative function of historical research: It can help us exclude from consideration theological or liturgical traditions that come from different sectors of church life. The positive function of historical research is that it can help us locate the text within specific historical contexts, and then bring in outside information from those contexts to clarify what the author was trying to say. Critical historical research is thus absolutely necessary if our reading of the text is to be informed by an appropriate literary repertoire.

Social-Science Perspectives. Until recently, historical research has only been able to provide us with bare-bones information. In recent years, however, scholars within the social sciences have asked if a careful reading of the biblical text itself could not put flesh on the bones and perhaps breathe a little of the spirit back into our grasp of early Christian life. Rather than being content with the witness of the church fathers and the direct statements that Scripture actually makes, we can also glean information from the kinds of arguments found within the Scripture itself. The narrative provides indirect clues about that taken-for-granted world; by looking carefully we can find these clues: what they explain, what they take for granted, what they assume the readers will already know.

(1) *A Believing Community.* Internal evidence makes it clear that Mark's reader is no stranger to the story of Jesus. The critical clue here is the way in which he relies on the reader's prior knowledge of Christian and Jewish traditions. Indeed, Mark often explains some element of the story by reminding the reader of some outside information, knowledge that the reader is expected to bring to the reading. This habit is illustrated by Mark's way of introducing characters. In 15:21, Simon the Cyrene is introduced as "the father of Alexander and Rufus," an introduction that reads awkwardly unless the reader somehow knew who Alexander and Rufus were. The introduction of Judas Iscariot is particularly telling: In 3:19 he is introduced as "Judas Iscariot, who betrayed him." The reader is clearly expected to know that there will be a betrayal, though this is the first mention of a betrayal in the narrative. The reader is also expected to know who Jesus' opponents are—Sadducees, Pharisees, and Herodians. These groups appear throughout the narrative without explanation, except for a note in 12:18 that the Sadducees do not believe in the resurrection.

The reader is also expected to know certain details of Jewish cultic practices, customs, assumptions, and theological perspectives. True, on this count the evidence is somewhat divided. Mark 7:3–5 contains a detailed description of Jewish ritual washing, which suggests that Mark included the aside as help for some in his community who were unfamiliar with such things. But for the most part a considerable theological sophistication informs the rest of the reading. For example, it is important that Jesus violates Jewish Sabbath laws (e.g., 3:1–6), yet the narrative does not explain what these are or even that they exist. Mark assumes that the reader has that information in hand. Moses and Elijah figure prominently in the story of Jesus' transfiguration in 9:2–8, yet the narrative assumes that the reader will recognize that they are eschatologically significant figures. Perhaps most telling, Mark expects his readers to recognize and understand massive and subtle allusions to the Old Testament and the intertestamental literature (see esp. 1:1–14; chs. 11–16). In the same vein, the tearing of the veil in the temple in 15:38 is a deeply theological moment in Mark's narrative, which would make no sense to someone unfamiliar with Jewish cultic practices.

(2) *A Eucharistic Community.* The central section of this Gospel yields another subtle theological nuance. In 1969, as the conclusion of a massive discussion of Mark 6:52, Quentin Quesnell argued that the primary issues in Mark have to do with the Lord's Supper, that is, the Eucharist. Mark 6:1–8:30 contains several subtle allusions to the Eucharist, but these would make no sense unless the reader brought into the reading a rich knowledge of Christian liturgical practices. This is especially so in 6:1–8:14, a section in which "bread" plays an important and symbolic role (see comments on this section). According to Quesnell, Mark implies what John later makes explicit: Jesus is the bread of life (see John 6:22–59). Though Quesnell perhaps overstates his case, this section of Mark does seem to stress the Eucharist as the eschatological meal that unites into one Body those two warring factors in Christendom, Jew and Gentile.

(3) *A Charismatic Community.* There are also traces in the narrative that at least suggest that Mark's church was a charismatic community. Here we must be especially cautious

because the historical evidence, which is quite slim, has been interpreted in a variety of ways, and Pentecostal interpreters must be especially careful to avoid reading into a text what is not there. Dispensationalists and cessationalists notwithstanding, however, the argument that the charismatic gifts died out at the end of Acts cannot be sustained. Yet any evidence in Mark's church of the ongoing presence of the Spirit is implicit and indirect, embedded in the structure of the rhetoric Mark uses to drive home his theological points; it would go too far to suggest that the charismatic gifts operated there in the same way that they operate in our churches today.

Let us examine this in some detail, discussing first the rhetoric of Acts as an illustration. The historical factors are these: Acts was written down some time after the events it describes. When Luke wrote down the traditions of the early church—certainly later, perhaps as late as the 80s—he tailored the way he reported them in order to teach his readers specific things about the working of God in the world and the ways in which he continues to work. That is, for Luke the events surrounding the early life of the church were like the rest of salvation history in that they continued to be theologically significant. (Indeed, the reason we *preach* from Acts, rather than merely cull information from it, is that we share the same conviction.)

Luke designed his telling of the story in order to bring out that significance, and in that way to appropriate its meaning for his own audience. For our purposes here, the important point is that the core of Luke's argument is that the presence of the charismatic gifts among Gentile believers validates the legitimacy of the Gentile mission (Acts 10:44–48; 11:15–18). This is why he takes pains to point out that the charismatic gifts were widely distributed, not only in Jewish, but also in Gentile churches.

The subtlety lies in the nature of Luke's argument. Within his narrative, Luke depicts events that took place during the early years of the church, but he expects his readers to understand and respond appropriately to the narrative when he wrote at a much later date. If the charismatic gifts had ceased to function by the time he wrote Acts—that is, if the presence of the Spirit were no longer clearly connected with identifiable signs—then the rhetorical force of the narrative would not only have been lost, it would have been counterproductive. For example, in Acts 11:15, Peter argues in favor of the Gentile mission by showing that "the Holy Spirit came on them as he had come on us at the beginning." He carries the point forward in verse 17: "Who was I to think that I could oppose God?" The point of the narrative—and the point that Luke surely intends that his readers hear and appreciate—is that the mission to the Gentiles is the work of God because it has been validated by the presence of the Spirit.

If, however, the charismatic gifts had been lost in the normal life of the church by A.D. 60 (as cessationists argue), the counterargument could have been made with equal force, perhaps greater force: The Spirit has abandoned the Gentiles, and the Gentile mission is thus no longer valid! But Luke assumes that this is not so. Indeed, the very success of his argument depends on the ongoing presence of the Spirit in the life of the church. If the charismatic gifts had died out, Luke's entire argument would be no longer valid or compelling.

This is an argument made in Luke's narrative, and thus the Christian community he addresses; but would it not have been heard the same way in Mark's narrative? We cannot say for certain, but there is some indication that Mark's rhetoric presupposes the same thing. For example, in Mark 9:23, during the exorcism of a demoniac boy, Jesus promises that "everything is possible," and in 11:22–24, following the withering of the fig tree, he promises that "whatever you ask for in prayer, believe that you have received it, and it will be yours" (v. 24). The only requirement is that we believe (v. 23) and that we forgive (v. 25). This evidence is somewhat stronger if, as Kee suggests, the attacks against Jesus had secondary rhetorical significance for Mark and his church. Kee (1977, 139) develops that thesis with specific reference to the Beelzebub controversy in Mark 3:22–29:

> The community, which saw itself as the extension of the ministry of Jesus—specifically in performing exorcisms (6.7; 9.14–29, 38f.)—is here appealing to a word of Jesus as a guarantee that it is carrying out its ministry by the power which comes from God. To attribute to

its members satanic powers is, as it was in the case of Jesus, a slander against God's spirit.

Kee goes on to argue (1977, 139) that "it is the Spirit who will sustain the followers of Jesus when they are summoned for trial before the authorities (13:11), just as he was." Here Mark's rhetoric, like Luke's, depends on the sustaining presence of the Spirit as a real and vital element of church life. If the Spirit proved absent in the moment of crisis, the extraordinary promise of 13:11 would have been instead evidence that the church had been abandoned! Thus, several elements combine to suggest that it is at least historically credible that Mark's church knew and appreciated the presence of the Spirit as a present reality in its daily life. What that presence would have been like and how it would have manifested itself remain unclear.

(4) *A Persecuted Community.* Internal evidence is also compatible with the tradition that Mark was written for a community experiencing persecution. If we begin with the tradition that Mark was written following the fire in Rome in A.D. 64, we then may ask whether the character of the book is consistent with that tradition (see article at sec. 2.5.7).

At the very least, the trauma of betrayal to the authorities (cf. 13:9–13) would have been deeply felt, since at least some of the members of the community would have already suffered rejection from within their families because of their decision to follow Jesus. In the ancient world, family was everything. To leave one's family was to dishonor one's very self, and to be repudiated by one's family was to be publicly humiliated. No doubt some within Mark's community had come to faith at great personal cost.

This issue is raised in 10:28–31, in which Mark's reader heard a word from Jesus that addressed his or her own situation: One loses one's family, but one gains a church. The classical text for exploring this situation is 13:9–13, and if as van Iersel (1988) suggests, the betrayal in view in 13:12 refers to members of the house churches, then the sense of betrayal would have been especially distressing. Time and again we will find that concern echoed within the narrative, and it has bearing on a surprising number of Mark's stories.

(5) *A Splintering Community.* Two elements of the text suggest that the community of Mark's Gospel was beginning to splinter. (a) Mark seems preoccupied with the factors that have led some Christians to abandon the faith and return to the Judaism or paganism of their youth. The parable of the sower (4:1–9) manifests this concern directly; and less directly but more importantly, Mark's analysis of the significance of the parable (4:10–20) shows that in his own reading, these were the elements that stood out. The terrible prophecies of end-time persecutions in the Olivet Discourse (ch. 13) contain the striking observation that "brother will betray brother to death, and a father his child" (v. 12a). If Mark's community is undergoing the intense persecution described above, one would expect such things to be happening.

Like Mark's reader, Jesus himself is rejected by the religious authorities (3:6), his family (3:31–35), his hometown (6:1–6), and his closest friends (14:50). When Peter says to Jesus, "We have left everything to follow you" (10:28), Jesus' response (10:29–30) contains both a word of comfort ("No one who has left home or brothers or sisters or mother or father or children or fields for me and the gospel will fail to receive a hundred times as much in this present age") and a word of caution (that with such things will come "persecutions").

(b) There is also evidence of splintering within the body of Christ. Like other early Christian communities, there seems to have been an ongoing controversy over the legitimacy and meaning of the mission to the Gentiles. In the commentary I will argue that the feeding of the five thousand (6:30–44) and the feeding of the four thousand (8:1–10) are told with special attention to symbolic numbers, to geographical details, and to the technical vocabulary of ethnic distinction. When these are taken into account, it seems especially significant that the second feeding takes place in Gentile territory. If these feeding narratives also allude to the Eucharist, Mark hints that they are of more than historical interest: The blessings of salvation are for Gentiles too. Once this organizing theme is recognized, a great many otherwise puzzling details in the central section (6:1–8:30) become clear. Other passages in Mark address the basic question of just how much Gentile converts can be expected to conform to the norms of Jewish piety.

In other words, within Mark's church we see hints of stresses that are visible throughout the literature of early Christianity. We know of conflict between Jews and Gentiles in the middle of the first century (Acts 15; Gal. 2) and at the end of the century (cf. Gospel of John). The failure to resolve the conflict in ways that satisfied Jewish believers perhaps led some to abandon their Christian commitments and return to traditional Judaism; such a scenario would explain underlying themes of Matthew, writing from one side of the issue, and Luke, writing from the other. Mark represents an earlier point in this chronology, coming as it does after Galatians but before Matthew and Luke. It is reasonable to assume that his readers are experiencing this conflict from the inside. Thus, an essential element of Mark's theological agenda is to validate the Gentile mission and to resolve the issues involved. If the community is divided over these fundamental issues, then it is a sure bet that the reader is not neutral, but comes to the reading with commitments already made; such prior commitments would surely have influenced the reading process.

(6) *An Apocalyptic Community.* Each of the major aspects of this portrait of Mark's reader discussed thus far is connected in some way with a pervasive apocalypticism. Indeed, Kee (1977) identifies apocalypticism as the primary orientation of Mark's community as a whole. Such a feature explains the prominent role Mark gives to eschatological images (see esp. the Olivet Discourse in ch. 13, which is riddled with the apocalyptic imagery). This large block of material may well have stood on its own as an independent unit, but its presence is buttressed by a wide-ranging collection of eschatological figures and imagery throughout the Gospel:

- Elijah is mentioned eight times explicitly (6:15; 8:23; 9:4–5, 11–13; 15:35) and alluded to twice (1:2–3, 6).
- Moses appears in the Transfiguration story (9:4–5).
- At Jesus' baptism the heavens are torn (1:10).
- The binding of Satan (3:22–27) carries eschatological significance.
- Both feeding stories (6:30–44; 8:1–9) suggest the great eschatological meal.

What is important is not the frequency and prominence of these images, but the fact that Mark expects his reader to recognize them without explanation. If Kee is right, these images and figures had long since been part of the vocabulary of faith by which Mark's church understood its common life. Indeed, Mark's famous aside in 13:14 ("let the reader understand") signals the reader that "*this* is *that*," as though the "abomination that causes desolation" Jesus has just mentioned is somehow connected to the present crisis.

There is one further apocalyptic nuance. Throughout the book the reader is reminded of realities beyond visible realities, truths beyond visible truths. Membership in Mark's community is a membership of *insight*, or rather, *revelation*. Insight is not taken by human beings so much as granted by God. This view of truth has close affinities with other Jewish apocalyptic movements. Susan Garrett (1998, 63) sums up: "In the apocalyptic view, events transpiring on the earthly plane are merely the reflection or outworking of events happening on a higher, unseen plane."

Summary. We have surveyed a number of aspects of early Christian life. Mark's "authorial readers" would have brought with them to the reading everything that was taken for granted in the ancient world, including a certain rigidly structured sense of social status, belief in demons, and an assumption that nothing is more important than family.

Mark's Christians would also have brought to bear certain Christian commitments, beliefs, and customs—though these were still in the formative stages and thus matters of contention. That contention reflects an uncomfortable mix of Jews and converts from paganism. They would have known about the Eucharist, but not about the other three Gospels. At least some of their members were probably engaged in research into the Old Testament as they formalized the theological underpinnings of their faith. As we read, we will constantly be asking how it might have sounded in the ears of a congregation such as that.

Mark's community also shows the inevitable signs of splintering under pressure, and we will read the Gospel as if it was written to deal with the sources and implications of those splits. These were hurting people, believers rather than outsiders, whose experience of life included intense persecution and who had lost family and friends to the arena of Nero, or worse, to apostasy. They eagerly awaited the end of time, in which the Son of Man would come again to set things right once and for all.

Anyone familiar with the social history of the Pentecostal movement will agree that there are uncanny parallels here between this portrait and ours. Like Mark's reader, we too have sometimes been hard beset for our faith; we have sometimes been persecuted for our convictions, convictions that have seemed strange and frightening to our tormentors. We have had to rely on the Spirit for guidance and power in our great struggle against the forces of Satan—whom we now call "The Enemy," but whose name we still know. We too have found that the good news of the gospel drives ministry across social, ethnic, and political boundaries in ways that have sometimes caused tension and difficulty, but that the bond of fellowship we find in Christ is greater than any differences that divide us. Like first-century Christians, we have sometimes found this a hard lesson. Finally, like Mark's Christians, we have had our fascination with the end times, when God will draw history to a close. In other words, although Mark composed his Gospel for a real historical congregation, for the Pentecostal believer his words somehow still ring strangely true.

OUTLINE

From the beginning, scholars have had difficulty forcing Mark's narrative into outline form. For our purposes, it is important to note that while outlines are useful tools of research, Mark did not expect his reader to have an outline in hand. An outline is rather like a bird's-eye view of a highway: The bird can see the beginning and end at the same time. A reader experiences the narrative more like a traveler on the road, never knowing what might be beyond the next bend. Part of the pleasure of a journey through a text is found in the surprises along the way, the gradual or sudden shifts of perspective or the fresh explorations through the narrative terrain. Indeed, the interpreter who relies strictly on an outline can miss the elements of surprise that may be central to the author's intent.

Because the reader is journeying through the text in sequence, the narrator/author must provide guidance for the reader, signposts to signal that he is moving on to a new section. Mark uses many of the standard literary devices to guide the reading and give direction: changes of character or locale, chronological markers, changes of theme, transitional comments, and summaries. Sometimes shifts of plot are signaled by the internal coherence of the story itself, especially when the story conforms to the usual structures of a genre known to the reader.

Three of Mark's stylistic techniques call for special attention. (1) Mark sometimes signals the end of a major section with a stylistic device known as *inclusion*. An inclusion occurs when a section begins and ends with thematically and structurally parallel stories. For example, a major section in 8:22–10:52 deals in part with the blindness of the disciples. This major section begins and ends with "book-end" stories about Jesus healing blind men—the twice-touched blind man (8:22–25) and blind Bartimaeus (10:46–52).

(2) Mark often begins a new section before he ends the last, creating a chain-like linking between the sections. The story of the twice-touched blind man in 8:22–25 launches a new section, but the prior section is not finished until Peter's confession in 8:27–30.

(3) Mark sometimes strings sections together with stories that seem as closely related to what precedes as to what follows. For example, the stilling of the storm in 4:35–41 is thematically connected to the collection of parables that precedes (4:1–34), but is similar in form to the miracles that follow (5:1–43). As such, it functions as a kind of bridge holding the two sections together and transitioning between them.

These three devices create a sense of the unity and coherence in the whole, but it is a unity that does not yield easily to systematic outlining. Even given Mark's habit of overlapping major sections, a careful reading of his standard transitional signals and inclusions yields an outline of two major sections (1:2–8:30; 8:22–15:39). The first is divided into seven large subsections, the second into four. As a general rule, chapters 1–10 tend to be organized by theme, while chapters 11–16 are organized by chronology. The book begins with a superscription (1:1) and ends with a short epilogue (15:40–16:8).

The Superscription (1:1)

Jesus the Messiah (1:2–8:30)

- **2.1.** Prologue (1:2–13)
  - **2.1.1.** John the Baptist (1:2–6)
  - **2.1.2.** John's Messianic Preaching (1:7–8)
  - **2.1.3.** The Baptism of Jesus (1:9–11)
  - **2.1.4.** The Temptation in the Desert (1:12–13)
- **2.2.** Opening Events (1:14–45)
  - **2.2.1.** The Ministry in Galilee (1:14–15)
  - **2.2.2.** The Call of the First Disciples (1:16–20)
  - **2.2.3.** Teaching and an Exorcism in the Synagogue at Capernaum (1:21–28)
  - **2.2.4.** Peter's Mother-in-Law (1:29–31)
  - **2.2.5.** The Sick Healed at Evening (1:32–34)
  - **2.2.6.** Jesus Departs From Capernaum (1:35–38)
  - **2.2.7.** First Preaching Tour of Galilee (1:39)
  - **2.2.8.** The Cleansing of the Leper (1:40–45)
- **2.3.** A Series of Controversies (2:1–3:6)
  - **2.3.1.** The Healing of the Paralytic (2:1–12)
  - **2.3.2.** The Call of Levi/Tax Collectors and Sinners (2:13–17)
  - **2.3.3.** The Question About Fasting (2:18–22)
  - **2.3.4.** Plucking Grain on the Sabbath (2:23–28)
  - **2.3.5.** The Man With the Withered Hand (3:1–6)
- **2.4.** More Controversies (3:7–35)
  - **2.4.1.** The Multitudes by the Sea (3:7–12)
  - **2.4.2.** The Choosing of the Twelve (3:13–19a)
  - **2.4.3.** Jesus Is Thought to Be Beside Himself (3:19b–21)
  - **2.4.4.** On Collusion With Satan (3:22–30)
  - **2.4.5.** Jesus' True Kindred (3:31–35)
- **2.5.** Parables (and a Miracle) of Promise (4:1–34)
  - **2.5.1.** The Parable of the Sower (4:1–9)
  - **2.5.2.** The Reason for the Parables (4:10–12)
  - **2.5.3.** The Interpretation of the Sower (4:13–20)
  - **2.5.4.** "He Who Has Ears to Hear, Let Him Hear" (4:21–25)
  - **2.5.5.** The Parable of the Seed Growing Secretly (4:26–29)
  - **2.5.6.** The Parable of the Mustard Seed (4:30–32)
  - **2.5.7.** Jesus' Use of Parables (4:33–34)
- **2.6.** Miracles (4:35–5:43)
  - **2.6.1.** The Stilling of the Storm (4:35–41)
  - **2.6.2.** The Gerasene Demoniac (5:1–20)
  - **2.6.3.** Jairus's Daughter/The Woman With the Hemorrhage (5:21–43)
- **2.7.** Salvation to the Gentiles (Subtheme: A Prophet and More Than a Prophet) (6:1–8:30)
  - **2.7.1.** Jesus Is Rejected at Nazareth (6:1–6a)
  - **2.7.2.** The Commissioning of the Twelve (6:6b–13)
  - **2.7.3.** Opinions Regarding Jesus (6:14–16)
  - **2.7.4.** The Death of John the Baptist (6:17–29)
  - **2.7.5.** The Return of the Twelve (6:30–31)
  - **2.7.6.** The Feeding of the Five Thousand (6:32–44)
  - **2.7.7.** The Walking on the Water (6:45–52)
  - **2.7.8.** The Healings at Gennesaret (6:53–56)
  - **2.7.9.** Defilement—Traditional and Real (7:1–23)
  - **2.7.10.** The Syrophoenician Woman (7:24–30)
  - **2.7.11.** Jesus Heals a Deaf Mute and Many Others (7:31–37)
  - **2.7.12.** The Feeding of the Four Thousand (8:1–10)
  - **2.7.13.** The Pharisees Seek a Sign (8:11–13)
  - **2.7.14.** The Leaven of the Pharisees (8:14–21)
  - **2.7.15.** The Twice-Touched Blind Man (8:22–26)
  - **2.7.16.** Peter's Confession (8:27–30)

3. Jesus Is the Son of God (8:22–15:39)

- **3.1.** Who Is This Man? (Subtheme: Discipleship Training) (8:22–10:52)
  - **3.1.1.** The Twice-Touched Blind Man (8:22–26)
  - **3.1.2.** Peter's Confession (8:27–30)
  - **3.1.3.** The First Passion Prediction (8:31–33)
  - **3.1.4.** "If Any Man Would Come After Me . . ." (8:34–9:1)
  - **3.1.5.** The Transfiguration (9:2–8)
  - **3.1.6.** The Coming of Elijah (9:9–13)
  - **3.1.7.** Jesus Heals a Demoniac Boy (9:14–29)
  - **3.1.8.** The Second Passion Prediction (9:30–32)
  - **3.1.9.** A Series of Hookword Stories (9:33–50)
    - **3.1.9.1.** True Greatness (9:33–37)
    - **3.1.9.2.** The Strange Exorcist (9:38–41)
    - **3.1.9.3.** Warnings Against Temptations (9:42–50)
  - **3.1.10.** Departure to Judea (10:1)
  - **3.1.11.** On Divorce and Remarriage (10:2–12)
  - **3.1.12.** Jesus Blesses the Children (10:13–16)
  - **3.1.13.** On Riches and the Rewards of Discipleship (10:17–31)
  - **3.1.14.** The Third Passion Prediction (10:32–34)
  - **3.1.15.** Precedence Among the Disciples (10:35–45)
  - **3.1.16.** The Healing of Blind Bartimaeus (10:46–52)
- **3.2.** Judgment on Jerusalem (11:1–12:44)
  - **3.2.1.** The Triumphal Entry (11:1–10)
  - **3.2.2.** Jesus Enters Jerusalem (11:11)
  - **3.2.3.** Judgment Against the Fig Tree (11:12–14)
  - **3.2.4.** Judgment Against the Temple (11:15–17)
  - **3.2.5.** The Chief Priests Conspire Against Jesus (11:18–19)
  - **3.2.6.** The Fig Tree Is Withered (11:20–26)
  - **3.2.7.** The Question About Authority (11:27–33)
  - **3.2.8.** The Parable of the Wicked Tenants (12:1–12)
  - **3.2.9.** On Paying Taxes to Caesar (12:13–17)
  - **3.2.10.** The Question About the Resurrection (12:18–27)
  - **3.2.11.** The Great Commandment (12:28–34)
  - **3.2.12.** The Question About David's Son (12:35–37a)
  - **3.2.13.** Woe to the Teachers of the Law (12:37b–40)
  - **3.2.14.** The Widow's Offering (12:41–44)
- **3.3.** The Olivet Discourse (13:1–37)
  - **3.3.1.** Prediction of the Destruction of the Temple (13:1–2)
  - **3.3.2.** Signs Before the End (13:3–8)
  - **3.3.3.** Persecutions Foretold (13:9–13)
  - **3.3.4.** The Abomination That Causes Desolation (13:14–20)
  - **3.3.5.** False Christs and False Prophets (13:21–23)
  - **3.3.6.** The Coming of the Son of Man (13:24–27)
  - **3.3.7.** "Take Heed! Watch!" (13:28–37)
- **3.4.** The Passion Proper (14:1–15:39)
  - **3.4.1.** Jesus' Death Is Premeditated (14:1–2)
  - **3.4.2.** The Anointing at Bethany (14:3–9)
  - **3.4.3.** The Betrayal by Judas (14:10–11)
  - **3.4.4.** Preparation for the Passover (14:12–17)
  - **3.4.5.** Jesus Foretells His Betrayal (14:18–21)
  - **3.4.6.** The Last Supper (14:22–26)
  - **3.4.7.** Peter's Denial Predicted (14:27–31)
  - **3.4.8.** Gethsemane (14:32–42)
  - **3.4.9.** Jesus Is Arrested (14:43–52)
  - **3.4.10.** Jesus Before the Sanhedrin (14:53–65)
  - **3.4.11.** Peter's Denial (14:66–72)
  - **3.4.12.** The Trial Before Pilate (15:1–14)
  - **3.4.13.** "Hail! King of the Jews!" (15:15–21)
  - **3.4.14.** The Crucifixion (15:22–39)

4. The Epilogue (15:40–16:8)

- **4.1.** Witnesses of the Crucifixion (15:40–41)
- **4.2.** The Burial of Jesus (15:42–47)
- **4.3.** The Women at the Tomb (16:1–8)

[The "Longer Ending" (16:9–20)]

COMMENTARY

1. The Superscription (1:1)

It is perhaps appropriate that Mark's opening should be problematic, just as his ending is problematic. Three major questions have occupied the attention of scholars here. (1) As to the actual text of this verse, some manuscripts include the words "Son of God," while others omit them. The evidence is not unequivocal, and cogent arguments could be made for either reading. We will follow the NIV and include them.[4]

(2) The nuance of the word "beginning" (*arche*) is an important issue. There are four options. (a) Mark uses this word to mean the Old Testament (referenced in vv. 2–3), so that his story about Jesus begins there. (b) Mark means the appearance of John the Baptist in the desert (introduced in v. 4). (c) *Arche* refers to the whole complex of events described in the Prologue (1:2–15). (d) The "beginning of the gospel" designates the entire narrative of Mark's Gospel.

Arguments have been made for each of these positions, though they are not all equally compelling. Option (a) is unlikely because it requires that the reader supply a verb; option (b) is unlikely because it overlooks the Old Testament allusion in verses 2–3; option (c) is questionable since Mark's reader would not have known at verse 1 that there was a prologue of fourteen verses immediately following. This leaves option (d), which seems to me to be the clear choice.

What the first three options have in common is that they neglect the sequence of the material. The position of verse 1 in the book and its lack of a verb suggest to the reader that it serves as a superscription for the entire book. The "lector," who read the text aloud in church, would have been expected to pause at this point before launching into the remainder of the narrative.

(3) This observation supports related conclusions about the meaning of the word "gospel" (*euangelion*) here. Though some maintain that the word can designate any "*historical event which introduces a new situation for the world*" (Lane, 1974, 43, a conclusion based on uses of this word in classical Greek), this interpretation fails to recognize that the church had already evolved its own narrower use for *euangelion*. Within Mark's community, pagan meanings would surely be superseded by Christian ones. For them the "gospel" is rooted in the complex of events and characters that is traced out in the narrative that follows and that flowers in the mission of the church itself. When Mark's audience first hears "the beginning of the gospel about Jesus Christ," any pagan associations with the word "gospel" are remote.

It is important also to note that the structure of verse 1 parallels the structure of the book as a whole. In this commentary we will follow the customary division of Mark into two halves. The climax of the first half is found in Peter's confession in 8:29: "You are the *Christ*." The climax of the second is found in the confession of the centurion in 15:39: "Surely this man was the *Son of God*!" These facts taken together suggest that for Mark the "beginning of the gospel about Jesus Christ, the Son of God" is the entire story about Jesus. This story is the beginning of the gospel, *but it is only the beginning*. By inference, the mission of the church that follows must be the *continuation* of the gospel, the story of redemption writ large in the life of the church.

Article: Irony

Important questions surround the rhetorical functions of verse 1. We can bring these into focus by asking what difference it makes for the reading process that this verse is here rather than somewhere else or missing altogether. With this verse, Mark places his readers on a privileged footing and thus distances them in important ways from the points of view of the characters inside the story.

The ironies thus created constitute a widely distributed rhetorical strategy in Mark's Gospel (for more on this topic, see Camery-Hogatt, 1992). In order to understand how this strategy works, we must remember that the characters within the Gospel do not hear the narrator's voice. They know nothing of the transitions and summaries, the allusions to the Old Testament, or the narrator's explanatory asides to the reader. The characters do not know that there is a crucifixion coming or that a church will continue "the gospel about Jesus Christ, the Son of God," after the narrative closes. But Mark's readers do know these things, which means that they bring with them critical interpretive clues that are lost on the story's characters until nearly the end of the narrative. In literary terms, we can say that the characters have no "up-take" on these events (see below, sec. 2.2.1).

In other words, Mark's *readers* have in hand a broad repertoire of information from which to evaluate and respond to the developments of the plot, and the conclusions reached by the *characters* (who are, after all, inside the story) will often appear baldly inadequate when seen against that repertoire. From time to time the narrator will create specific frames of reference in which the text can be understood in two ways. Inside the story, the characters see one thing while outside the readers see another. The point is not simply that the readers choose an alternative reading of the facts, but rather that the readers see both options, and from their privileged vantage point they pass judgment on the inadequate ideas held by the story's characters.

The underlying workings of this strategy of rhetoric can be subtle: In order for readers to pass judgment on the ideas of the characters, they must first embrace the narrator's point of view. We will see this effect again and again as we work our way through Mark's story of Jesus. A classic example may be found in the story of Peter's denial (14:54, 66–72), coupled as it is with the trial of Jesus (14:55–65; see secs. 3.4.11–12). The set-up comes in 14:26–31: Jesus prophesies that Peter will deny him three times. As Mark's readers sweep through the narrative, they hear this prophecy only minutes before they hear the story of Jesus' trial. At the climactic moment of the trial, Jesus' enemies strike him and demand, "Prophesy!" (14:65), but Jesus remains silent. What the priests cannot see, but Mark's readers can see, is that outside in the courtyard, at that very moment, a prophecy of Jesus is coming to pass!

The demand by Jesus' enemies that he prophesy is therefore theologically blind, but because of the way Mark has sequenced the disclosure of information, the readers can see that. If they respond with a word of judgment—"How blind these people are!"—they can only do so by sharing the narrator's point of view; they have been brought to faith on his terms. All of the ironies in Mark's Gospel begin with the information provided by the superscription (1:1). It is important, therefore, that this verse appears here, as the reader's first exposure to the story of Jesus.

2. Jesus the Messiah (1:2–8:30)

Traditionally, interpreters have divided the book into two halves (see comments on 1:1). Both halves begin with passages that are heavily loaded with eschatological imagery. Elements of the baptism story in 1:9–11 will be repeated in the transfiguration story in 9:2–10: Elijah will reappear, and the voice from the cloud will be heard again. Yet as balanced as these two halves appear, there are also important differences. After 8:30 the narrative takes a decided turn. The narrator's preoccupation turns to the cost of discipleship and the enormous price Jesus must pay if he is to fulfill his mission. It is not insignificant that the confession of the centurion that Jesus is the "Son of God" (15:39) will come not because of Jesus' miracles, but because of the manner of his death. But the first half of the book has a different agenda: It establishes the validity of Peter's confession in 8:27–30. Ignominious death notwithstanding, Jesus is the Christ!

2.1. Prologue (1:2–13)

The material found in these verses is commonly referred to as the Prologue of Mark. Several elements link this section of the narrative together. It both begins and ends with signals that locate the action "in the desert" (vv. 3, 4, 12, 13), a fact that is theologically significant because of the combined quotation from Exodus 23:20; Malachi 3:1; and Isaiah 40:3 in Mark 1:2–3. Except for the brief report of the temptation in the desert, John the Baptist appears as a central figure throughout (vv. 4–6, 7–8, 9–11, 14), then disappears after verse 14. The fact that he appears "in the desert" (v. 4) validates the connection with the Old Testament prophecy (vv. 2–3) and indicates that he stands in a kind of middle ground between the hope of a Messiah and the realization of that hope in the appearance of Jesus. Verses 14–15 are transitional and launch the narrative in an entirely new direction.

Commentators have often remarked on the blunt way in which Mark opens his narrative. There is no hint of the preexistent Christ (cf. John 1:1–18), no genealogy to tie the narrative to the Old Testament or to certify Jesus'

)avidic lineage (cf. Matt. 1:1–18; Luke 3:23–8), no angelic herald to announce the arrival f the newborn King (Luke 2:8–20), and no int of disaster (e.g., the massacre of the baby oys at Bethlehem, Matt. 2:1–18). Mark's narative simply launches, abruptly, with the ppearance of John the Baptist in the desert.

Or does it? A case can be made that variaons of the above-mentioned elements are preent in Mark's opening, but they are present only or those readers who possess the necessary epertoire of background knowledge. Certain lements of the Prologue give the narrative a nildly eschatological flavor, signaling the eader that this story has cosmic implications.)n the surface, John the Baptist (vv. 2–6) ppears like any other prophet in the Judean esert, but a direct and clear allusion in verse 6 nakes him out to be a sort of Elijah, an escha-)logical herald of the messianic age. The rendg of the heavens, the voice from heaven, and n allusion to intertestamental literature in the aptism story (vv. 9–11) identify Jesus as "Son f God," just as clearly as Luke's angelic hosts o in his later account. Subtle underlying literry allusions in the temptation in the desert (vv. 2–13) signal the presence of the second dam—more subtly than John's Prologue, but o less powerfully. For the reader who possesses ne appropriate repertoire of Old Testament and ntertestamental quotes, Mark's Prologue is ensely packed, perhaps even dazzling.

Article: Allusions

It is clear that Mark's rhetorical strategy elies heavily on the use of literary allusion, ut because the workings of that strategy are ubtle, it is worthwhile to note briefly the ways which they influence the reading process or more on this, see Camery-Hoggatt, 1995, 14–33). Literary allusions tend to make the eading process more challenging because they all for more intricate and complex mental ctivities. Whenever allusions appear, the secndary text—i.e., the source of the allusion—ntrudes on the reader's interaction with the rimary text.

Note, for example, Mark's description of ohn the Baptist (1:6): "John wore clothing nade of camel's hair, with a leather belt around is waist, and he ate locusts and wild honey." his description appears near the opening of Iark's narrative. Even so, already a number of allusive elements have primed a complex of schemas having to do with the appearance of the Messiah. The reference to "Isaiah the prophet" in verse 2a combines with the conflated quote from Malachi 3:1 and Isaiah 40:3 in Mark 1:2b–3 to evoke a series of visual images, all of which suggest the eschatological prophet Elijah. Moreover, the reader is likely to access within his or her mind the more specific information of Malachi 4:5: "See, I will send you the prophet Elijah before that great and dreadful day of the LORD comes."

Even though this reference is only implicit, it serves as background to the material that follows. Verse 6 nails the connection down solidly by describing John in the exact same language as a description of Elijah found in 2 Kings 1:8.

2 Kings 1:8a	Mark 1:6
He [Elijah] was a man with a garment of hair and with a leather belt around his waist	John wore clothing made of camel's hair, with a leather belt around his waist

For Mark's reader the allusion is clear. The narrator has identified the figure in the desert as John the Baptist, but the reader knows from the description that it is also Elijah the Tishbite, herald of the coming Messiah.

The allusions may have additional literary effects, not least of which is that they validate the narrator's skill in storytelling. In an oral culture, the ability to quote or allude to other traditional stories indicates the mastery of one's material, and when that tradition takes its bearings from sacred literature, it also indicates a high level of piety and thus of reliability. Allusions that refer to sacred literature also

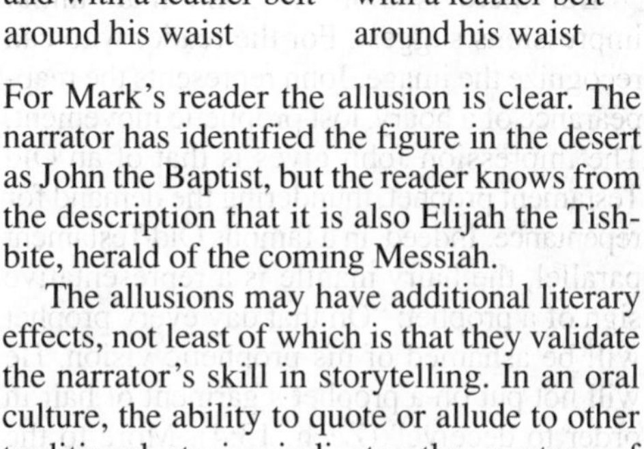

John the Baptist wore clothing of camel's hair with a belt around his waist and ate wild honey and locusts.

validate the theology of the narrative itself. Mark is telling his readers that the story he tells is somehow connected to the prophets of old.

2.1.1. John the Baptist (1:2–6). Mark begins his narrative proper with a combined quotation from Exodus 23:20; Malachi 3:1; and Isaiah 40:3. The sentence is incomplete, so that it looks for its verb in verse 4 (lit. trans.): "As it is written in Isaiah the prophet . . . John the Baptist appeared in the desert." This makes the quote in verses 2–3 into a functional parenthesis, a comment on the meaning of John's arrival on the scene. John is a man with a mission, a forerunner of the Christ—like Elijah, the expected harbinger of the Messiah.

Those images are deepened by Mark's depiction of John as a wild man in the Judean desert (vv. 4–6). Note the way in which he has taken pains to reinforce that imagery here. "Desert" is repeated four times in the Prologue (vv. 3, 4, 12, 13); John is roughly dressed, eating locusts and wild honey (v. 6).

But there is more to John than initial impressions suggest. For the reader who can recognize the image, John represents the reappearance of a hoary, lost prophetic movement. The impression John gives is that of an Old Testament prophet, thundering the demand for repentance. Indeed, in a famous Old Testament parallel, the hairy mantle is a representative sign of a prophet: "On that day every prophet will be ashamed of his prophetic vision. He will not put on a prophet's garment of hair in order to deceive" (Zech. 13:4). More to the point for our purposes, in 2 Kings 1:1–8 the prophet Elijah is specifically identified with a reference to his dress (see the article "Allusions" in sec. 2.1). When Mark's readers read the description of John the Baptist they cannot help but think: "It is Elijah the Tishbite!" Note that Mark will later validate that connection (9:11–13).

That allusion, coupled with the quotation from Malachi 3:1 in Mark 1:2, suggests a secondary reference to Malachi, this time from 4:5–6:

> See, I will send you the prophet Elijah before that great and dreadful day of the LORD comes. He will turn the hearts of the fathers to their children, and the hearts of the children to their fathers; or else I will come and strike the land with a curse.

Thus John's demand for repentance is fierce and the people stream into the Jordan to b baptized because they see in him the stirring o something deep within their collective dream Elijah has appeared! The Messiah will be next just wait.

It is important that John is fierce. Every thing in the narrative deepens that impression especially the reference to his dress and his die of locusts and wild honey. From time to tim interpreters have pointed to other traditions o desert dwellers eating locusts, but these leav us without an adequate explanation for wh Mark has included this note here. His point i different: John's odd diet is in keeping with th rest of the description given of the Baptist an thus deepens the impression of wildness.

The fierceness has its own kind of publi power because it reinforces the impression c an Old Testament prophet created by th description of John's dress and the allusions t the Elijah tradition. Verse 5 provides a vivi description of the public acclaim Joh receives. There will be a close verbal parall with verse 9, but Mark's reader does not kno that yet. Instead, the repetition of the Gree word *pas* in verse 5 ("whole," "all") places th emphasis on the great number of people wh responded. A similar enthusiasm will late build about Jesus (1:45; 2:1–2; 3:7–10), an the reference here may prepare the reader f the references there. The groundswell of sup port commanded by John will continue an deepen in Jesus' ministry. This may be part c a larger program of tying John's ministr closely to that of Jesus.

In 6:14, 16 and then again in 8:28 there wi be questions about John's identity, and popu lar sentiment will see Jesus as John revive from the dead. In 11:27–33, Jesus will defen his activities by raising the question of th legitimacy of John's baptism. Finally, in term of narrative technique, the fate of John antic pates and prepares for the fate of Jesus; th is, his arrest (1:14) and execution (6:17–2 foreshadow the arrest and execution of Jesu Indeed, death by martyrdom is another wa that John "prepares the way" for Jesus.

Thus, the image of John looms large in th background of Mark's narrative. It is reaso able to conjecture that Mark's community ha issues surrounding John: his identity, his co nection with Jesus, and his place in the eco omy of salvation. We will examine the historical background in our discussion of John's messianic preaching in verses 7–8. What emerges is a coarsely textured portrait that suggests—no, demands—that John the Baptist is a man to be reckoned with, someone who will brook no compromises. John is fierce for the kingdom.

2.1.2. John's Messianic Preaching (1:7–8). If verses 2–6 gave us John the Baptist as both the image of ferocity for the kingdom and as prophetic harbinger of the coming King, that portrait is now used as a contrasting image of the One who comes after John in verses 7–8. In his preaching John does not give us "gentle Jesus, meek and mild," but rather "the more powerful One." Thus the contrast is direct rather than inverse: If John is fierce in his proclamation, *how much more* fierce will be the One whom John proclaims!

In this summary of John's preaching, everything focuses on the contrast. The narrator presents us with two couplets. In the first (v. 7) John identifies the subject of his message as "one more powerful than I," and then he deepens that identification by indicating that he is not worthy to perform for that person the most menial of tasks—to loose the thong of his sandals (a task reserved for servants). Verse 8 carries the contrast one degree further, as the parallelism in the verse makes clear:

"I baptize you with water, but
he will baptize you with the Holy Spirit."

This is also something of a mixed image. John calls Jesus "one more powerful than I," but he also describes him as "he-who-comes-after-me." In Mark's vocabulary elsewhere, "to follow after [*opiso*]" is a technical designation for discipleship. Is Jesus presented as a disciple of John? This possibility is sometimes suggested, though the emphasis within the narrative directs the reader's attention in other ways.

It may well have been that Mark's community has encountered detractors, who could have argued with some measure of cogency that John, not Jesus, is the mouthpiece of God. Perhaps John is even the Messiah. After all, Jesus does come "after [John]," and he submitted to John's baptism. While we cannot know for certain, if Mark's church did face such challenges, the material in verses 7–8 would have formed a decisive response: The Baptist himself validates the claim of the church that Jesus is the greater of the two. If one is to be a true follower of John, one must follow him also in this. The logic of the comparison in verse 8 reinforces this dimension of the contrast: John only baptized in water, but Jesus is One who baptizes with the Holy Spirit. This is the significance of John's comment about the sandals in verse 7: John degrades himself to a point *below* that of a disciple of Jesus.

The Pentecostal reader is especially interested in John's reference to the Holy Spirit in verse 8. Clearly John did not have in mind the Christian experience of the infilling of the Spirit, typically characterized by tongues and by the charismatic gifts as we understand them from Acts. John did not live to see the events at Pentecost. Rather, everything in the context suggests that for John, the Spirit was the sign of the age of the end times, the very image of the coming judgment. It may be important that the Greek word here for "Spirit" (*pneuma*) means both "wind" and "spirit." For John the perfect image of the coming judgment is perhaps the desert sirocco wind, which whips up the sand and destroys everything in its path. Is this what a "holy *penuma*" does? If so, it would have been a disturbing image, but entirely in keeping with John's own ideas about "one more powerful" who will follow in the desert.

While this may be the image intended by John, an argument can also be made that Mark's reader heard nuances in John's language that the Baptist could not have intended. This would be especially true if, as I have argued earlier (see the Introduction), Mark's community experienced the Spirit as an integral part of its corporate life. Mark's reader would then have heard nuances of an especially potent kind: "I have baptized you with water, but he will equip you for a ministry of power." If so, John's threat to baptize a person with the Holy Spirit is also a promise, but a promise that is freighted with danger.

The two images are not easily resolved into one—the baptism of the Spirit as image of eschatological judgment, and the baptism of the Spirit as equipment for ministry. They function together only in the background. Yet as different as they are, they are probably more closely connected for Mark's readers than they are for us. The historical evidence tells us that

Mark's church found itself in conflicts of extraordinary, cosmic proportions. In Mark's context, ministry is a battle in which there are no minor skirmishes, and the rules of engagement are determined by the movements of supernatural powers (see sec. 2.1.4). For Mark, *everything* has eschatological significance.

2.1.3. The Baptism of Jesus (1:9–11). With the baptism of Jesus the cosmic dimensions of what has happened bursts on the reader full-blown. The NIV loses something of the force of Mark's Greek here: The heavens are "torn open" (*schizo*, lit., "torn apart"). This striking word reappears at the end of Mark's narrative with a comment that the curtain in the temple is "torn [apart]" at the moment of Jesus' death (15:38). This rending of the heavens has close literary parallels to a description of the expected Messiah found in the Testament of Levi 18:6 (an intertestamental Jewish work; see comments in Jeremias, 1971, 50–51):

> The heavens shall be opened, and from the temple of glory shall come upon him sanctification, with the Father's voice as from Abraham to Isaac. And the glory of the Most High shall be uttered over him, and the spirit of understanding and sanctification shall rest upon him.

The words from heaven in verse 11 carry weight for three reasons, which overlap and reinforce each other. (1) Their content represents a divine affirmation and call, and in that way validate any claims the narrator will later make on Jesus' behalf. This is the voice of God, after all. (2) Their form and structure evoke the whole complex of images connected with the Messiah, and in that way connect the narrative with older and hoarier traditions. (3) The words prepare the reader for the nearly identical affirmation that will come later at the moment of Transfiguration in 9:7 (though, of course, the reader does not yet know that).

All of this is lost on the story's characters, who are inside the story and—except for Jesus—cannot hear the voice of God or Mark's allusions in the story. God addresses Jesus directly, in the second person, and there is no indication that any other character in the narrative heard or understood him. The voice of God at the Transfiguration scene (9:7), however, will address the onlookers—Peter, James, and John–but here it addresses only Jesus.

Verse 9 closely parallels verse 5 in structure, a fact that is sometimes taken as an indication that Jesus identifies with fallen Israel even to the point of baptism (Lane, 1974, 55). But the verbal parallels are not apparent to the characters inside the story. Indeed, from their vantage point, Jesus appears no different from others who submit to John's baptism in the desert.

There is a practical application here that is sometimes overlooked by interpreters: The Messiah comes to Israel incognito; to the characters inside the story, his identity is hidden, something yet to be revealed. The hand of God may work like that; God is Master of the deft touch. He is at work, dramatically and vividly, but his work is visible only to those who have eyes to see and ears to hear. This theme reappears throughout Mark's story of Jesus.

2.1.4. The Temptation in the Desert (1:12–13). Careful readers have noted the relative brevity of Mark's temptation story in comparison with its parallels in Matthew 4:1–11 and Luke 4:1–13, both of which contain a long dialogue between Jesus and Satan that details out the temptation in terms of various dimensions of power. Jesus' responses to the devil have long served the church in its critical and devotional reflections on the meaning of temptation. Mark's temptation story, by contrast, appears truncated, with the result that his version has generally been overlooked. But this may be shortsighted. Throughout Mark, Jesus' assault on the demonic is a central and recurring theological theme. This means that the exorcisms are not incidental to his Gospel but are essential to its core.

Article: The Demonic in Mark

We could approach the evidence in several ways, and no matter how we begin or what leads we follow, we always arrive at the same conclusion: For Mark, exorcism is a major and central theological theme. Six elements support this conclusion. (1) Exorcisms are highlighted in Mark's summary statements. In four of the five times in which he summarizes Jesus' healing and missionary activity (1:34–39; 3:7–12; 6:53–56) or that of the disciples (3:14–15; 6:12–13), exorcism plays a critical and central role.

(2) Of nineteen specific miracles reported in Mark, four are clearly identified as exor

A monastery has been built in the cliffs on what is called Mt. Temptation. This rugged terrain is in the area believed to be the desert where Jesus was tempted by Satan.

cisms (1:21–28; 5:1–20; 7:24–30; 9:14–29), and several others include exorcism language (e.g., 1:40–45; 4:35–41).

(3) The call of the twelve disciples in 3:13–19 contains an explicit reference to their authority to cast out demons (v. 15).

(4) The brief dialogue about the strange exorcist in 9:38–41 suggests that wherever the work of exorcism goes forward in the world, there the work of Christ is also carried forward, even for those who are not part of the disciple band narrowly understood.

(5) Some of the references to demonic or satanic powers show curious relationships to their contexts. For example, Jesus' words to Peter in 8:33 ("Get behind me, Satan!") appears abrupt and out of keeping with Jesus' usual relationship with Peter.

(6) The entire Gospel is peppered with references to the "devil," "Satan," or "Beelzebub." Together this complex of words refers to the destructive power of the devil himself or to the work of his minions. By contrast, the work of redemption involves Jesus' own authority or the work of his representatives, the disciples.[5]

How, then, is this complex of references to be understood? While exorcism is clearly a dominating concern for Mark, some of the elements suggest that he envisions it differently from what we do. For us, the term *exorcism* is usually considered as a subcategory of *healing* or *miracle*. The evidence in Mark suggests that this schema should be reversed, so that the concepts of miracle and healing are subordinate to the larger category of exorcism (cf. Kee, 1986, 21–26). This explains the large quantity of material Mark has devoted to exorcism material (as mentioned above). For Mark, miracle is not a battle with natural forces but with unnatural ones. Even the healings are part of that battle, as is his teaching ministry.

Thus the temptation story in 1:12–13 holds significances that are larger and more programmatic than appear at first. Jesus' defeat of Satan here is a kind of thumbnail sketch of the Gospel as a whole. In its own way, this is as much a summary of the power of the gospel as verses 14–15 are a summary of its didactic thrust.

It is true that the modern reader may find this more pervasive image of the demonic disquieting (see also sec. 2.2.3). If so, it may be good to remind ourselves that for most of human history—indeed, even today for nearly all non-Western cultures—the reality and pervasiveness of demons is part of the taken-for-granted order of the universe. Mark's deep concern is to show not that demonic forces are everywhere, but that wherever they are found and however strong they may be, Jesus is stronger. It is an interesting and useful reflection on our culture that exactly those elements of the story that we find disquieting have provided our brothers and sisters from other cultures with comfort and reassurance. The devil will never win because his evil machinations have already been undone in the work of Jesus.

When this affirmation is linked to the opening thrust of the Prologue as a whole, it provides at least an echo of the apostle Paul (see 1 Cor. 15:22–23, 45–49): Here in the desert, Jesus plays out the role of the second Adam, reversing the catastrophe in which the first Adam fell victim of satanic powers.

2.2. Opening Events (1:14–45)

Although 1:14–15 is verbally tied to the Prologue (cf. sec. 2.2.1), Jesus' movement into Galilee (v. 14) drives the narrative into a whole new arena. The precise chronological links in verses 21, 29, 32, and 35 organize the stories in this section around a two-day period of ministry in Capernaum, from which Jesus' larger ministry will be launched (v. 39). The summary in verse 39 ("he traveled throughout Galilee") and the note in verse 45 that he "could no longer enter a town openly" together indicate the framework of extensive ministry that will form the context of the controversy stories that follow in chapters 2–3 (see secs. 2.3 and 2.4).

2.2.1. The Ministry in Galilee (1:14–15). These two verses are transitional. Several elements tie this section to what precedes. The word "gospel" (*euangelion*; NIV, "good news") is mentioned twice here, echoing the same word in verse 1. John the Baptist is still here. The phrasing and diction have the feel of a summary, which usually signals some sort of closure. That said, however, it is a closure that invites the reader to read on, to move forward into the next phase of the narrative. Clearly the intent of verse 14 is to remove John from the plot; indeed, from the clues provided in this Gospel, the reader will almost certainly conclude that the deliverance of John to prison is a reference to his death.

In the broader scope of Mark, verses 14–1 summarize and contextualize what follow more than what precedes. Perhaps most signif icant is the change of locale. Earlier Mark too pains to place the action in the desert (vv. 3 4, 12, 13); here the plot moves into Galile (v. 14). Thus, something new is afoot. What tha something new is, is summarized in verse 15 which is a thumbnail sketch of Jesus' whol program of preaching and teaching, not a ver batim quote of a single sermon or event: "'Th time has come,' he said. 'The kingdom of Go is near. Repent and believe the good news!'"

There are four parts to this verse, though th second ("the kingdom of God is near") is a elaboration of the first ("the time has come") Greek has two words for time: *chronos*, whic refers to time as an external reality, the sort o time that can be measured in fixed terms, an *kairos*, which refers to something more inte rior, something that can only be measured b a deep internal sense of urgency or sensitivit to appropriate *timing*. Here Mark chooses th latter word: It is the *kairos* that is fulfilled. Th kingdom is like a fruit on a vine, ripe for th plucking. There will be no second chances The time to act is now. To miss this time is t miss everything.

Yet this is not urgency for its own sake; it i urgency for "the kingdom [*basileia*] of God." One must act, but one must act *for the king dom*. This phrase conjures for the reader a raf of eschatological and messianic images (e.g. Ps. 103:19; 145:11–13; Mic. 4:7–8). While w normally think of the word "kingdom" as *place*, in Mark's vocabulary it implies th *authority* to rule in that place. The Scholar Version translates *basileia* as "imperial rule." Jesus' proclamation that the kingdom of Go is at hand is therefore a muscular word; i implies movement, a kind of stirring, a battl challenge to all who oppose God's authority.

By thus launching Jesus' ministry, Mar makes sure that the reader is on track for every thing that follows. The only adequate respons to the proclamation of the kingdom is repen tance and faith. These parallel notions denot not sorrow, but the wholesale turning of th self toward God. To accept the reign of God i to depose oneself from its centralized positio of authority and thus to move at last, not onl into right relationship with God, but into rela tionship with the self as well.

2.2.2. The Call of the First Disciples (1:16–20). This next section begins a cluster of four stories connected by chronological links (see 1:21, 29, 32, 35). There is a certain logic inherent in the connections between these stories; for example, the people bring their sick to Jesus after sunset (v. 32), presumably because they cannot do so earlier on the Sabbath.

Within this unit Mark gives us two call narratives. This is a form that will appear later in unlikely places (e.g., the healing of Bartimaeus in 10:46–52), and it is worth looking carefully at the way Mark has shaped these stories into that form. Verses 16–18 closely parallel verses 19–20. Both stories are sparse, bare-bone reports of Jesus' first encounters with his first disciples. The details that are included focus attention on the directness of the call and the immediacy of the response (indeed, in verses 20–21 the Greek word for "immediately" (*euthys*) occurs twice in successive sentences).

The fact that these call narratives are truncated is often noted. Mark does not tell his readers whether the four fishermen had any previous encounter with Jesus. What we *are* told is that they respond to the call "at once" (v. 18; cf. v. 20). Nothing yet narrated has prepared them for this moment. Thus, when they respond so readily, they do so on the force of the call alone. In this way, the focus shifts slightly from the fishermen's immediate and unquestioning response to the authoritative personality who can evoke such a response. While the disciples have much to learn about Jesus, Mark's readers already know enough to understand this enormous power over people.

Jesus' words are included as the single elaborated detail in the call of Simon and Andrew: "Come, follow me . . . and I will make you fishers of men" (v. 17). It is not clear what Simon and Andrew would have heard in such a statement. A clever wordplay on their vocation? A hint of missionary adventures? Perhaps something more weighty was in view: "Fishers of men" are also those who sort the catch, in the process deciding which fish to keep and which to discard (cf. Matt. 13:47–50). The expression may have intimations of power rather than evangelism: "Follow me, and I will give you authority over the fate of human beings." Perhaps that is what Simon and Andrew heard. In any case, Mark's reader would have heard more than they did, since at this point in the narrative Simon and Andrew know nothing of Jesus' messianic identity.

So this is a story about four fishermen, but it is also an example story, a call to the reader. If Mark's readers are to recognize the call as a general one and the response of the fishermen as an example, if they are to empathize with the story's characters and claim as their own the promise they have been given, then they too must drop everything and respond to a mysterious figure who simply appears and makes uncompromising and uncomfortable demands.

2.2.3. Teaching and an Exorcism in the Synagogue at Capernaum (1:21–28). It may not be insignificant that Mark opens his discussion of Jesus' mighty works with an exorcism. Clearly the demonic is a central Markan concern (see "The Demonic in Mark" in sec. 2.1.4). The modern pastor or scholar who works within the Pentecostal tradition will likely hear echoes of that concern in the questions posed by parishioners and students, though the passage of time and changes in science and culture have inevitably shifted the kinds of questions raised. For the modern interpreter, three questions seem to recur.

Jesus made Capernaum his base. He taught there and performed an exorcism. This synagogue, on the Sea of Galilee at Capernaum, was built in the third or fourth century.

(1) Do demons or demonic powers actually exist, and how is it that we do not experience them with the same frequency or visibility as what we see in the Bible? Has the devil changed strategies? (2) Is there a connection between demonic forces and what we have come to understand as physical or psychological illness?[6] (3) Can Christians become demon-possessed?

As important and as urgent as these issues are, they reflect a worldview and religious experience altogether different from those of Mark and his readers. The existence of demons was unquestioned in the ancient world, as was the connection between the demonic and disease (see Kee, 1986). The third question is simply not in view here or anywhere else in Mark. Instead, Mark's readers would have asked questions of their own: What is the relationship between the demonic and the various pagan deities and other supernatural powers? Is there an "evil eye," and how can it be warded off? Is there a connection between the demonic and the human urge toward evil, the so-called "evil *yetzer*" (see Garrett, 1998, 20)? And how are demonic forces to be brought under control? If Paul addresses the first of these questions in 1 Corinthians 8:4–8, Mark addresses this last indirectly in this first miracle, the exorcism in the synagogue.

Article: Miracle Form

While this is not the first indication of the supernatural in Mark, it is the first section that takes the form of a miracle story, and it is worth pausing momentarily to identify those elements that appear standard for this form in ancient literary convention. If we gather together the miracles of ancient literature—Jewish and Christian—they bear striking similarities in their format. The following general pattern, almost always occurring in the same sequence, is found throughout the traditions, over a long period of time, and in a variety of types of miracle stories: healings, raisings from the dead, exorcisms, and nature miracles.

1. *There is a description of the scene.* If there is a crowd, so much the better because the crowd can then serve as eyewitnesses to verify what the narrator describes.
2. *There is usually a description of the problem.* The more serious the problem, the more striking and impressive the miracle. An exception is often made in stories involving raisings from the dead, presumably because death is serious enough in its own right, though sometimes this too is heightened.
3. *There is the miracle itself.* Miracle stories in the Gospels often include the words that Jesus has spoken, which is unusual in ancient literature. I suspect this is because the focus of the miracle is not on the words themselves, but on the piety or authority of the miracle worker or on God, who ultimately performs the miracle. This distinction may be one of the ways in which we can distinguish miracle from magic.
4. *There is usually some "proof" that the miracle actually occurred*. The dead person talks (Luke 7:15) or eats (Mark 5:43). The man with the withered hand stretches it out and finds it restored (3:5). The wind ceases and there is a great calm (4:39).
5. *There is an acclamation from the onlookers,* declaring that this was indeed a great miracle. Acclamations may take several forms, but they usually affirm that the miracle has indeed taken place: "This [miracle] amazed everyone and they praised God, saying 'We have never seen anything like this!'" (2:12).

The common denominator here is the way in which these elements validate the miracle itself. Element 1 sets the scene. Element 2 shows the seriousness of the prior condition by including a detailed description. The more graphic the description, the more successful the miracle story. Element 4 describes a proof, and element 5 quotes eyewitnesses to verify the narrator's report. At the same time, data that would have drawn the reader's attention away from the effectiveness of the miracle are overlooked.

What is important here is that the form itself is widely attested in ancient literature and would have been widely recognized by any reader. It is not surprising that Mark would have taken over this form in the ways he tells the miracles of Jesus. What is surprising are the ways in which he modifies the form, or combines it with other forms, to shift the readers' perspectives or bring out special nuances in the story. A standard form shapes the read-ng process in two ways. (1) It helps the eader's imaginative latitude fill in the gaps of he text (see in the Introduction, "The Author-al Reader"). Different forms allow the reader ifferent degrees of freedom. A psalm or a oem gives the reader a different kind of lati-ude than, say, a letter or a recipe. (2) When a orm is widely recognized, it acts as a kind of emplate for the reading process. It tells the eader what to anticipate next.

These two functions of form are closely onnected to the sequence of the story because he reader has to discover what form is in view s the text unfolds, one word after another. The pening elements are most critical: Miracles end to begin in standardized ways. Those tandardized opening patterns I call *genre sig-als* (see Camery-Hoggatt, 1995, 106–9, 130–2). These are important in the reading of the Gospel literature because they tell the reader what interpretive strategies to use and set up series of expectations about what should hap-en next.

This is a critical aspect of reading, in part ecause it helps us understand what happens when the text deviates from standard form. The genre signals set up a series of expecta-ions in the reader, with appropriate interpre-ive strategies, and the reader is quickly moved n a certain direction. Deviations disrupt that novement and call for different strategies, ometimes creating areas of internal tension within the reading process. Disruptions lemand attention and thus may carry special weight. For this reason, a writer can create a ubtle form of emphasis by varying ways in which the elements of a story differ from or onform to the standard pattern. When these ariations reflect a consistent pattern or point f view, their combined weight may provide ritical clues about the Evangelist's primary nterests.

The exorcism in Capernaum deviates from he standard form for exorcisms in at least hree ways. (1) The words of the demon in erse 24 are unusual: "What do you want with s, Jesus of Nazareth? Have you come to lestroy us? I know who you are—the Holy One of God!" The words are unusual not only ecause such conversations are uncommon, ut because the demon appears to be attempt-ng to control Jesus. This impression is deep-ned because the demon addresses Jesus—the exorcist!—using exorcism language. It even attempts to assert control over Jesus by asserting that it "knows who Jesus is"! In most ancient exorcism stories, the exorcist controls the demon by identifying its secret names. These are words we would expect to come from the exorcist, not the demon.

Even though the demon here uses the language of exorcism, its words make clear who is the final authority and what his motives must be. The demon's opening question ("What do you want with us?") means, "We have nothing in common!" The second question ("Have you come to destroy us?") is clearer, but the Greek grammar permits one of two translations. (a) It can be read as a question, as most translations have it; (b) it can be read as an answer to the opening question: "What do you want with us? You have come to destroy us!" (note that the oldest Greek manuscripts have no punctuation marks). Read either way, the text makes clear that Jesus' appearance in the synagogue means the end of the rule of the demonic in human affairs.

(2) This general observation is deepened by the second way in which this story differs from standard miracle form. In the ancient world, exorcism stories almost always contain long and complex adjurations and incantation formulas. Pagan exorcism stories also often contain references to magical rings and amulets or potions made from the roots of certain plants. These are entirely lacking here. Jesus uses no special language beyond the command to silence. What is stunning is the directness and simplicity of his method: He simply commands, and the demon obeys. It shrieks (v. 26), to be sure, but the shrieking may serve as a secondary form of validation because it comes at the point in the miracle that the reader would expect some proof that the demon had in fact left.

(3) This story both opens and closes with expressions of astonishment at Jesus' *teaching*. The connection is clearest in verse 27, which can be punctuated to read as in the NIV: "What is this? A new teaching—and with authority! He even gives orders to evil spirits and they obey him." But it can also be punctuated to read this way: "What is this? A new teaching. With authority he even gives orders to evil spirits and they obey him!" Either way, the authority to perform the exorcism becomes a

dramatic validation of Jesus' authority to teach. By implication, the exorcism is itself a form of teaching. Mark will use this strategy of validation several times in the coming stories (e.g., 2:1–12; 3:1–6)—though to be sure, at this point the reader is unaware that those stories lie ahead in the narrative. Here the point is that although this story is bare of extraneous details, it stresses repeatedly the potency of Jesus' teaching ministry.

To sum up: The following four elements stand out because they deviate from standard exorcism form: (1) The demon dissociates itself from Jesus. (2) Its attempt to control Jesus ironically validates Jesus' identity as "the Holy One of God." (3) Jesus uses no incantations or devices, but simply commands the demon's obedience. (4) The entire miracle is housed within a discussion of Jesus' *teaching* ministry. When these four elements are taken together, they create a subtle but important highlight that Mark's reader would not have missed: Jesus' *teaching* is potent because it is supernatural, and his authority extends over the world of the demonic.

Mark drives home this highlight with a subtle barb in verse 22: Jesus teaches with authority, and not as their "scribes" (RSV; NIV, "teachers of the law"). In a single narrative sweep, Mark emphasizes the potency of Jesus' word and at the same moment makes the scribes out to be impotent in such matters. If he can exorcize demons and they cannot, perhaps they have no genuine authority to teach either.

This is Mark's first reference to teachers of the law, and they appear in the narrative without introduction. Indeed, in verse 22 they are mentioned offhandedly, as though the reader already knows who they are. These Jewish leaders appear in a number of Mark's stories, always in the role of opponents to Jesus. The offhanded note in verse 22, by which they are deftly shown to be without authority, will place all later references in a negative light. When these teachers later suggest that Jesus can only perform exorcisms because he is in league with Beelzebub (3:22–30), their suggestion will carry no weight and will appear to be a kind of sour grapes. When they wheedle him about his disciples' eating with unclean hands in 7:1–5, their objection will appear small-minded indeed.

2.2.4. Peter's Mother-in-Law (1:29–31). This is a simple miracle story, very close to standard form (see "Miracle Form" at sec. 2.2.3), sanded bare of extra details. It appears to have been included here as part of a series of stories connected by a chronological rubric (see vv. 21, 29, 32, 35). The story tells us several things indirectly: that Peter's home was near the synagogue in Capernaum, that he was married, and that his responsibilities extended to include care for his mother-in-law. These are small details, but they help the reader build a richer and more varied picture of the disciples, and they hint at what the decision to follow Jesus would have cost his new disciples. This, of course, remains only a minor concern at this point in the narrative, but it will surface later with greater clarity and force (see 10:28–31; 13:12–13).

At least three elements of this story stand out as unusual. (1) The transition from verse 28 seems strained because the summary of the previous paragraph has broadened out to include "the whole region of Galilee." (2) The mention of James and John (v. 29) seems unnecessary since they play no further role in the story. These two aspects reinforce the sense of simplicity and directness in the storytelling. The difficult transition from verse 28 appears to have been caused by the note that "news about him spread quickly over the whole region of Galilee." Mark may have included James and John because they can serve as eyewitnesses and thus as additional sources of validation for the miracle. Perhaps this also signals the reader that all four of the first disciples are aware that Jesus violated the Sabbath from early on in his ministry. (3) The fact that Peter's mother-in-law "began to wait on them"—i.e., she served them something to eat—is an unusual variation on the formal proof element of the miracle.

2.2.5. The Sick Healed at Evening (1:32–34). This is the third story in a series that depicts a day in the life of Jesus (see comment on 1:16–20). Verse 32 indicates that the townspeople brought the sick and the demon-possessed "after sunset," that is, after the Sabbath had passed. Because of Sabbath laws, they would not have transported the sick during the Sabbath. The impression Mark's reader gains is that this response to Jesus is further evidence of the report in verse 28 that "news about him spread quickly over the whole region of Galilee."

Verse 34 summarizes Jesus' response, but it adds a strange element: Jesus "would not let the demons speak because they knew who he was." Thus we are introduced to the problem of what scholars have called "the messianic secret."

Article: The Messianic Secret

The facts of the messianic secret are well known and need be rehearsed here only briefly. Jesus often commands silence from those he has healed (1:44; 7:36; 8:26) or who have witnessed a healing (5:43), from demons (1:34; 3:12), and from the disciples after they have seen some particularly significant clue to his identity (7:36; 8:30; 9:9). While he teaches the crowds general theological truths, he restricts his explanations to private discourses with his disciples (e.g., 4:10–12), often "in the house" and thus away from the crowds.

Scholars and pastors in various camps have offered a number of explanations for this secret. (1) One popular response is that Jesus was using "reverse psychology" as a way of actually spreading his message. There is, however, no other historical evidence to suggest this conclusion, and, perhaps more critically, it reflects a dangerous way of interpreting Scripture.

(2) An interpretation more commonly accepted among scholars is that Jesus himself never claimed messianic status; thus, his messiahship was never recognized during his ministry, even by his closest followers. According to this view, Jesus was a simple country preacher, and the idea that he was the Messiah was worked out in the church in the course of its mission. Mark is charged with the task of reconciling these historical realities—that Jesus made no messianic claims and that the church was making increasingly elevated claims on Jesus' behalf. The messianic secret is the result of that reconciliation. The primary difficulty here, however, is that the narrative constantly shows Jesus' followers disobeying the injunctions to silence. If Mark intended the messianic secret as a way of explaining the absence of rumors about Jesus' identity, then his narrative fails miserably in fulfilling that intention.

(3) Less common, but consistent with Mark's apocalyptic view of truth (see the Introduction), is the view that outsiders are simply incapable of grasping the meaning of these events. It is significant that the disciples are cautioned against saying anything about what they had seen *until the Son of Man had risen from the dead* (9:9; see sec. 3.1.6). This is subtle. The disciples may miss everything, but Mark clearly expects that his readers will not. This suggests that the messianic secret has close connections with both the apocalyptic ideas of a higher level of truth that must be *revealed* rather than *grasped*.

(4) An interpretation held more often by evangelicals is that Jesus was caught between competing misinterpretations of his mission. Clearly the crowds thought of Jesus only narrowly as a healer, teacher, prophet, or political messiah, while the authorities thought of him as a social renegade. The larger the crowds became, the more serious was the opposition from the religious authorities. The messianic secret was Jesus' way of slowing the growth of his movement until the disciples could be taught the way of the cross more adequately.

The payoff of this apocalyptic view of truth lies in the way Mark can turn the secret to good rhetorical effect. Until now, Mark's readers have not been made aware of the secret, but that does not mean they have not known the information the secret is designed to protect. Indeed, the Christian reader, who already knows the basic elements of the story line, has been in a privileged position since well before the narrative began; and even the reader who comes to the narrative as an outsider has been granted that special information in 1:1. That is, whatever the characters in the story know or do not know about the secret, the content of that secret—Jesus' messianic identity with all that that entails—is never a secret to the reader. As we saw in our discussion of verse 1, Mark will exploit this difference to bring his readers to a deeper and more appropriate level of faith.

2.2.6. Jesus Departs From Capernaum (1:35–38). Mark now presents us with a brief transitional scene that clarifies further the nature of Jesus' mission: "I came out" (RSV; NIV reads "have come") in order to preach (v. 38). The sentence is ambiguous, however: Is Jesus explaining to his followers his reasons for slipping out of Capernaum early that morning? Whatever his immediate intentions, the reader will be inclined to view this statement within the larger framework of the Gospel and will not miss its secondary nuances.

It is significant, therefore, that Mark connects Jesus' straightforward statement of mission with the first mention that he had slipped away for prayer. Mark will elsewhere find Jesus alone in prayer (e.g., 6:46; 14:32–40). This simple transitional story indicates in a plain way that Jesus' sense of mission is bathed in prayer, and it reminds the reader that even an enthusiastic public response to a remarkable day of healing can in its own way become a din that can drown out the voice of God.

2.2.7. First Preaching Tour of Galilee (1:39). Verse 39 is a short transition that follows naturally from verse 38. As a summary, it simply closes off the section with a light, generalized note about Jesus' activities. It is significant that Mark summarizes the miraculous element of those activities as "driving out demons," since this is the larger expression of which the nature miracles and healings are subordinate categories (see "The Demonic in Mark" at sec. 2.1.4).

2.2.8. The Cleansing of the Leper (1:40–45). Few stories in Mark have raised as many unresolved questions as this one. We will begin by tracing out the difficulties and then survey the options for resolving them. Each option leaves the plot complications unresolved in various ways, which explains why the history of interpretation has been long and frustrating.

An initial problem is found in the textual tradition of verse 41. The majority of the manuscripts read *splangchnistheis* ("filled with compassion"), while a small number read *orgistheis* ("in a passion of rage"). A fair case can be made both for and against either reading. The NIV, adopting the reading of the majority of witnesses, reflects the former option. If this is correct, it is clear who is performing the action: The leper prostrates himself, and Jesus responds with a compassionate touch. If, however, we take the second option, the pronouns are suddenly unclear. Who is touching whom, and who is enraged? The grammar of the Greek leaves that question open. It may well be that it is the leper who has touched Jesus in a rage. We will return to this problem.

There is no corresponding problem with the manuscripts in verse 43, where Jesus is clearly the subject of the sentence and where the anger is clearly evident in the terms Mark has chosen. The NIV translates this sentence in a way that disguises the force of the Greek words: "Jesus sent him away at once with a strong warning." The participle translated "with a strong warning" is unusually forceful. Herman Waetjen's translation (1989, 29, 85) expresses better the nuances here: "And being furious with him he immediately cast him out [the verb used here is the standard verb for exorcism], and says to him, 'Keep on seeing to it that you say nothing to no one.'"

Finally, the story fits its context only awkwardly. At this early point in the narrative why would Jesus caution the leper not to tell anyone what had happened (v. 44)? The only detail that prepares for this caution is found in verse 34, which at this point in the reading is cryptic in its own right. A conflict with the authorities has not yet been introduced.

We are therefore left with a number of puzzles: Did Jesus reach out and touch the man in a moment of compassion? Did the man touch Jesus in a fit of rage? Why was Jesus angry in verses 43–44? Was he angry at the man for touching him? Or perhaps for his (future) failure to obey the command not to say anything to anyone (vv. 44–45)? Was he angry at the ravages of the leprosy itself? Is this even to be understood as leprosy? Perhaps a demon has possessed the leper, so that verse 44 is addressed to it (see Kee, 1977, 35).

These are difficult questions, and no matter how one answers them, the answers raise questions of their own. Would Jesus upbraid the patient because he is angry at the illness? If he is angry because the man will disobey him, is he being prophetic? Is this preemptive anger? If a demon is involved here rather than an illness, why has Mark not said so more plainly? Clearly this story is not intended as a simple illustration of the healing activity that was summarized in verse 39, and one wonders why Mark has placed the story *here* rather than somewhere else.

One good suggestion is that this miracle story prepares for what follows in 2:1–12. It closes with the note in 1:45 that the man "went out and began to talk freely, spreading the news. As a result, Jesus could no longer enter a town openly but stayed outside in lonely places. Yet the people still came to him from everywhere." This explains the situation described in 2:2: "So many gathered that there was no room left, not even outside the door." In other words, the story of the leper looks forward rather than back; it is not an illustration of what precedes, but an anticipation of what follows. If the connection to what follows is what commended the story to Mark at this point, then for Mark at least, the central thrust of the story must have something to do with Jesus' growing fame and the problems that derived from it.

There is one other way in which this story prepares for what follows: The language is angry and raw, with unexplained rage. There are cautions against saying too much, especially to the wrong people. There are unresolved plot complications and unanswered questions. All of these, it seems to me, are a kind of narrative looking forward to the developing controversies that lurk just offstage in the wings, awaiting the narrator's cue. They set the reader's teeth on edge, and if—as I suspect—they speak to the urgencies of a church that must do its ministry in secret, they send a shudder down the reader's spine. What better way to prepare for the stories of anger and rage that follow in chapters 2–3?

2.3. A Series of Controversies (2:1–3:6)

Mark now includes a series of controversy stories. They share a common form and are connected by a developing theme rather than by clear chronological links. The attacks against Jesus increase in volume and in their proximity to him. In the first story (2:1–12), the authorities are enraged, but they say nothing (they are only "thinking to themselves" their objections, vv. 6–7). In the second (2:13–17), they raise objections but do not confront Jesus directly; instead, they question the disciples (v. 16). In the third (2:18–22) and fourth (2:23–28), they question Jesus, but only about the behavior of the disciples (vv. 18, 24). In the fifth and final story (3:1–6) we find them watching Jesus closely, looking for some way to accuse him directly (3:2). The series reaches a shuddering apex in 3:6, where Jesus' opponents reach a decision to destroy him.

The series has another kind of coherence. Note how both the opening story (2:1–12) and the closing one (3:1–6) use miracles to validate Jesus' position in the controversy. Thus, the entire unit forms an inclusion as these two parallel one another in rhetorical strategy and theme (on inclusions, see the Introduction). The closing comment in 3:6 forms a heavy ballast line, heavy enough to close the section, and the narrative immediately cuts to a summary section describing the now nearly fanatical public enthusiasm that accompanied Jesus' mission (3:7–12).

Article: The Form of Pronouncement Stories

Just as with miracle stories (see above at sec. 2.2.3), controversy stories tend to fall into a definite form, a subcategory of a larger group of stories that scholars call *pronouncement stories*. The general structure of pronouncement stories is simple: Everything in the story leads to a short, pithy saying (or *aphorism*) at the end, which "controls" the author's decisions about what to include and what to leave out—much the way a punch line controls a humorist's decisions about what to include and what to leave out of a joke. Once the story gets to the aphorism, it quits.

There are several types of pronouncement stories. *Biographical* pronouncement stories simply introduce the aphorism with some narrative context, and the aphorism is given in response to something in the context, rather than to some event (e.g., 10:17–31). Sometimes the aphorism comes in response to a question. If the question is placed by a disciple or follower of Jesus, the story is called a *scholastic dialogue*; if the question is hostile, it is a *controversy dialogue*.

In order to understand Mark's controversy dialogues correctly, we must bear in mind three further considerations. (1) Controversy stories were undoubtedly useful for the church as a way of answering challenges brought from outside. They are short, direct, and often clever; indeed, the aphorism is usually preserved because of its shrewdness or subtlety. As a result, careful attention to the finer details of their language may provide clues to the challenges that confronted the church.

(2) The biblical accounts leave out an important element of the stories—the effect of the dialogue on the audience. This sort of exchange is a kind of verbal duel (see Camery-Hoggatt, 1995, 140–42) fought before a gallery of onlookers. For a society in which one was publicly honored or shamed by one's performance in such a duel, the gallery is not only an audience of observers; by their very

presence they participate in the duel. If Jesus wins at thse duels, he humiliates his opponents in the all-important arena of public opinion.

(3) As with all literary forms, the author's intention can be signaled by the way in which a story deviates from the norm (cf. sec. 2.2.3). For example, the two stories that form the opening and closing of the series (2:1–12; 3:1–6) mix controversy and miracle forms; the resulting stories are especially powerful reminders that when Jesus acts, he does so with special authority.

2.3.1. The Healing of the Paralytic (2:1–12). Mark emphasizes the connection with what precedes by repeating several of the key words that drew the story of the leper to a close (1:40–45), though this is masked somewhat in translation. The opening of the scene in 2:1–2 echoes and develops the public enthusiasm of 1:45, clouded over by a lingering sense of danger.

Verse 3 signals that a miracle is coming. It is important to remember that Mark's reader is not consulting an outline or a commentary to tell him that this story opens a series of controversy stories. Chapter 1 has been packed with miracles, and this is what the reader expects here. Indeed, according to standard literary conventions, the story of the paralytic begins and ends with a perfectly formed miracle story. Nothing in the opening of the story itself even hints that there is trouble brewing. Mark takes pains to highlight the press of the crowds, a standard feature of miracle stories, presumably to provide eyewitnesses to the miracle itself. This fact provides occasion for the colorful detail that the paralytic was hauled to the roof by his friends (vv. 3–4)—an aspect that adds drama to the story. The miracle takes place, just as the reader expects, and the whole narrative closes on a note of acclamation in verse 12: "This [miracle] amazed everyone and they praised God, saying 'We have never seen anything like this!'"

Into the middle of the miracle, Mark has included a controversy with some teachers of the law. On the surface of it, the miracle and the controversy are joined together only awkwardly. Mark does not tell us where these scribes came from or what they are doing in the house. The rhetorical impact of the story lies, however, not in the controversy or in the miracle, but in the powerful shifts of imagery as the reader jostles the two images together.

The controversy aspect of this story, therefore, intrudes an alien element into the middle of the miracle story. Teachers of the law (appearing for the first time in v. 6) are set over against the unnamed friends who lower the paralytic through the roof (v. 4a). Their objections to Jesus' actions (vv. 8–9), unspoken though they are, stand in contrast with the actions of those friends, whose rash gesture of desperation is interpreted as an act of faith (v. 5). The religious scruples of these Jewish teachers look all the more paltry when compared to the faith of the paralytic's friends Why would anyone challenge someone who can perform miracles?

There are other significant interactions between the two parts of the story. Its impact turns on the relationship between the forgiveness of sins in verse 5 and the act of healing in verse 11. The point of connection makes Mark's general strategy clear: Jesus' ability to heal the man, which can be empirically demonstrated, confirms his right to forgive sins, which cannot. Thus the miracle validates Jesus' position in the controversy.

The question Jesus poses ("Which is easier ...") is a trick question, with a number of implications. He does not ask what is easier to *do*, but only what is easier to *say*. The teachers of the law have supposed that Jesus' act of pronouncing forgiveness is blasphemy since it usurps the authority of God (v. 7). From their perspective, Jesus is not only speaking empty words, easy to utter and impossible to perform but offensive words, words that should never be uttered. His words usurp the authority of God. But as the miracle shows, Jesus' word does have authority, which brings the matter back to verse 2: "He preached the word to them." The miracle, in other words, confirms the power and authenticity of Jesus' word.

The fact that through the miracle the teachers of the law are silenced is also significant. It establishes a sharp contrast between Jesus and his antagonists, a contrast that deepens as the controversy stories progress. But this silencing has ominous consequences. They are momentarily removed from the plot, but they will not be gone long; when they return, they will return with a vengeance.

2.3.2. The Call of Levi/Tax Collectors and Sinners (2:13–17). The short episode in verses 13–14 (on the surface, a simple "cal narrative" that parallels the call of the four fishermen in 1:16–20) occurs here primarily as a means of introducing Levi and moving the plot into his home. Even so, the call of Levi gives the reader momentary pause. This may be one of those moments where we must distinguish carefully between the several groups that make up Mark's larger community (on division in Mark's community, see the Introduction). For Jewish readers, it would be distressing to hear that Jesus calls a tax collector (who is, after all, a traitor) as one of his disciples. But for Gentile readers, the call of Levi would be a breath of fresh air, an open sign that Jesus ignores the old boundaries between acceptable and unacceptable people.

If a sound principle of interpretation implies that repeated elements signal the presence of significant themes, then surely the core of this story lies in its emphasis on Jesus' knowing association with disreputable people—sinners in general and tax collectors in particular. The repetition in verses 15–16 borders on tedium:

> . . . many *tax collectors and "sinners"* were eating with him and his disciples, for there were many who followed him. When the teachers of the law who were Pharisees saw him eating with the *"sinners" and tax collectors*, they asked his disciples: "Why does he eat with *tax collectors and 'sinners'*?" (italics added)

Mark has also taken pains to point out the large size of this contingent of Jesus' followers (note the repeated "many" in v. 15).

The translators of the NIV have placed the word "sinners" in quotation marks to indicate that the word has an unusual range of implications here. It designates a whole class of people, not just individuals who fail to keep the law in one point or another. The Semitic phrase is "*am ha-aretz*" (the "people of the land"), who are considered guilty because of their professions, their habits of dress, and their ignorance. Their very presence pollutes the land. According to the Pharisees (as reflected in rabbinic literature), it was a serious breach of scholarly decorum for Jesus to associate with such people. Everything in the story focuses the reader's attention on the two aphorisms on Jesus' lips recorded in verse 17, and they should be understood as the controlling elements of the story (see "The Form of Pronouncement Stories" in sec. 2.3).

These are issues that plagued the Gentile mission and presumably also Mark's conflicted community. If so, the objections voiced by the teachers of the law in verse 16 perhaps echoed a concern that troubled Mark's Jewish believers. That Jesus would even *be* in Levi's home is scandalous; that he would *eat* there is outrageous. It is not at all surprising that these teachers would raise questions. Even so, they remain circumspect: They direct their questions not to Jesus, but to his disciples. The two aphorisms in verse 17 are Jesus' reply to their question.

Unlike standard pronouncement stories elsewhere, the controversy stories in Mark often end with two aphorisms that reinforce one another, though they do not overlap completely. This is a prime example. The first aphorism ("It is not the healthy who need a doctor, but the sick") draws on a traditional folk saying. If it stood alone, it would indicate simply the legitimacy of Jesus' contact with "sinners." It is the second aphorism that drives the point to a different level. It contains a subtle ambiguity. Jesus could have meant that the zeal of the "righteous" stands them in good stead already, and that now the call of God is extended beyond them to include sinners. But the context of this aphorism militates against that view. The open hostility of the "righteous" sets them *over against* the sinners who are called, and thus over against the one who calls them (cf. Descamps, 1950, 98–110). Jesus' response is equally exclusionary. Put another way, he categorically accepts the outcast and the sinner and rejects those who think themselves righteous. If one is to respond appropriately to the call of Jesus, one can only do so as a sinner.

This story has wide implications for Mark. On a primary level, it raises and answers questions about Jesus' comportment. On a secondary level, it raises and addresses questions about the comportment of Gentile Christians, who like Jesus associate with the wrong kind of people, violate the Sabbath, and do not observe the calendar of feasts. No doubt some of Mark's Christians in Rome were themselves "the wrong kind of people." For those outcast Christians, this simple gesture of Jesus, this freedom to party with tax collectors and "sinners," obliterated the artificial boundaries of piety and defilement.

2.3.3. The Question About Fasting (2:18–22). The standard structure for pronouncement stories (see "The Form of Pronouncement Stories" at sec. 2.3) is that a brief narrative provides the context for a colorful aphorism. As noted in 2.3.2, Mark sometimes violates that form by giving two aphorisms; here he gives three. The last two are easily evaluated because they parallel one another in form and content.

The imagery in this section is straightforward. On its surface, the presenting problem in verse 18 has to do specifically with fasting, but the narrative hints at broader implications because the aphorisms in verses 21–22 have to do with the whole attitude of religious asceticism. Verse 18 does not tell who raised the question about fasting, and the question appears to be less hostile than the others in this section. Nevertheless, the question is a serious one. Is it that Jesus does not observe the fasts? Or is it something else?

The attitude of asceticism is clearly a religious issue. Fasts for religious purposes were common in the ancient world, though the observance of a liturgical calendar of fasts was a distinguishing feature of Judaism. Anyone familiar with that would know that feasting can equally be a religious act. What makes Jesus' behavior radical is that he ignores the disciplines of the liturgical calendar and feasts whenever and wherever the occasion permits, even if the calendar calls for fasting. This dimension of his religious life parallels his willingness to violate Sabbath laws.

The aphorisms in verses 21–22 provide one dimension of a response by drawing on common cultural knowledge. An old garment is presumably already shrunken from exposure to the elements, while a new patch is not. To repair the one with the other invites not only a later, larger tear, but shredding of the threads. A damaged older garment requires a repair with pre-shrunk cloth. The saying about the wine involves the same dynamic, though of course the image has to do with expansion of the wineskin from fermentation.

The two sayings are roughly parallel in meaning, though the first has a slightly larger dimension of judgment and the second more directly addresses the question. The old garment requires patching only when it has become damaged. This seems to be an implicit comment about Judaism, something that requires fixing. But what has that to do with the disciples' habit of ignoring the liturgical calendar? Jesus is suggesting that the festivities he and his disciples enjoy are not a repair of an old garment, but something altogether new.

The aphorism in verse 22 further addresses this old-versus-new question: The old wineskins clearly represent either Judaism or the formal disciplines of Jewish ascetic piety. Either way, they are no match for that new kingdom that Jesus and his disciples are celebrating. What Jesus is about is altogether new, and to measure it against the inflexible and uncompromising rules of Judaism is to get it all wrong. In fact, if the kingdom were to be poured into the old forms of piety, it would destroy them altogether.

So much for the two final aphorisms, but what of the first one in verses 19–20? Several elements are striking here: The context suggests that the word "bridegroom" identifies Jesus and that his disciples are the "wedding guests." A critical question to ask here is where the word "bridegroom" came from, and when and how it came to be applied to Jesus.

Wedding imagery is found distributed widely in the colloquial language of Palestine, and Jesus undoubtedly appropriated this saying from this repertoire of images. For wedding guests to fast while the bridegroom is with them would be an insult to the families of both bride and groom. This surely is the sense Mark's original readers would have made of the expression. It is helpful here to realize that the church used bridegroom language as it gradually came to terms with who Jesus was and what he expected (see John 3:29; 2 Cor. 11:2; Rev. 19:7; 21:2; cf. Eph. 5:23). The word "bridegroom" was elevated to a messianic title and describes the distinctive relationship between Christ and his church.

At the same time, the Christians in Mark's church—also disciples of Jesus—do fast. How are they to understand how verse 19 applies to them? Are they not like Jesus' opponents? Verse 20 answers that question neatly: The bridegroom has been taken away. Thus, although outwardly their behavior is the same as that of the Jews and the followers of John the Baptist, the inner reality of their motive is a different thing altogether. Even so, i remains a logical extension of the reason the original disciples *feasted* during Jesus' earthly ministry.

2.3.4. Plucking Grain on the Sabbath (2:23–28). A scholarly discussion concerning this passage has centered around the accuracy of verses 25–26. According to 1 Samuel 21:3–6, it was Ahimelech, rather than Abiathar, who gave the bread of the Presence to David for his men to eat. Two basic solutions to this dilemma have been proposed. (1) The apparent error is the result of a scribal gloss that crept into the manuscript tradition at an early date (there is no manuscript support for this theory). (2) Mark is intending only to indicate the general passage in which the appropriate Old Testament reference is to be found (see a similar use in 12:26; cf. Lane, 1974, 116). Presumably this problem would not have presented itself to Mark's authorial reader, especially if the text is quickly read aloud.

What is more to the point for our purposes is the rhetorical structure of the story and the way in which its various elements marshal the reader's understanding of Jesus' authority. Like the other stories in this section, this is a controversy dialogue (see "The Form of Pronouncement Stories" at sec. 2.3), this one concluding with three aphorisms. The first one (vv. 25–26) answers the question of verse 24 completely. The next two (vv. 27–28) appear as afterthoughts attached to the main body of the story to reiterate and round out its basic theme.

As is standard for such stories, we begin with a presenting problem: The disciples have offended the Pharisees by violating the Sabbath. It is difficult to identify the precise nature of the offense, but Mark clearly expected his readers to recognize some violation of Sabbath laws. What emerges later in the story is that the issue is not so much which Sabbath laws apply, but whether or not Jesus has the authority to overturn them.

By questioning the disciples' action (v. 24), the Pharisees implicitly challenge the orthodoxy of their teacher. The presence of witnesses—that is, the disciples—heightens the stakes involved in the game that the authorities have chosen to play with Jesus. He responds by calling attention to David's action of eating the bread of the Presence given him by Abiathar (or Ahimelech) in 1 Samuel 21:3–6. It is significant that the story in 1 Samuel does not mention Sabbath. If Jesus' strategy is to cite an Old Testament example of a Sabbath violation, then the strategy will fail. Rather, the point is that David exercised emergency authority over sacred things. Jesus is claiming to be David's equal.

Perhaps the story is making a claim on another level. The rabbinic logic used by Jesus here works like this: What applies in a lesser case surely applies in a greater case. Thus, if David could so arbitrarily appropriate sacred things, then surely Jesus—who is *greater* than David—can exercise similar authority. The assumption, which the reader is expected to share but the Pharisees would surely have questioned, is that Jesus is greater than David.

The narrative does not report the authorities' response to this argument; instead, it rushes forward into two buttressing aphorisms: "The Sabbath was made for man, not man for the Sabbath" (v. 27), and "the Son of Man is Lord even of the Sabbath" (v. 28). The first of these can stand in its own right as a response to the challenge brought by the Pharisees. But if Jesus were to leave the issue at this point, the saying would also generalize the authority to violate the Sabbath so that everyone had this authority. The presence of the final aphorism in verse 28, therefore, sharpens verse 27 into a transitional comment leading to Jesus' more specific and more significant claim that "the Son of Man is Lord even of the Sabbath."

Thus, Jesus declares for freedom from Sabbath rules. But that declaration does not relativize or minimize the importance of the Sabbath. Instead, it makes Jesus' special authority even clearer by showing that it transcends that of David, and that it extends even to that sacred Jewish observance of the day of rest.

2.3.5. The Man With the Withered Hand (3:1–6). The story of the man with the withered hand in 3:1–6 brings to a temporary end this section of controversies (controversy material resumes in 3:13). This story pulls the loose ends of the controversy series to closure with the announcement that the Pharisees had begun to plot with the Herodians to find a way to put Jesus to death (v. 6)—the first mention of a formal decision to take Jesus out. But it is not unexpected. We have seen the antagonisms of the authorities mount, at each step of the way becoming sharper and more directly pointed at Jesus. In this story, the authorities grow tired of the verbal sparring. They are silent, and in their antagonism instead execute a death thrust.

There is, however, a rhetorical counterdefense here that is so subtle it has escaped the notice of most of Mark's interpreters. We may bring it to the fore by focusing momentarily on the effect of the rhetorical question in verse 4: "Which is lawful on the Sabbath: to do good or to do evil, to save life or to kill?" Jesus' question is informed, of course, by the intention of his enemies to bring legal charges against him: "Some of them were looking for a reason to accuse Jesus, so they watched him closely to see if he would heal him on the Sabbath" (v. 2). They cannot answer his question in verse 4 because they have already colluded against him. Their silence is therefore ominous, an indication that they are unwilling or unable to answer positively, and that their intention—about which they have also been silent—cannot be reconciled with the principles of justice that the question implies.

We can state this matter differently. From the standpoint of the reader, the authorities have violated justice in their attempt to defend their Sabbath laws. There is a kind of subtle irony in this: They break the spirit of the law to prevent Jesus from breaking its letter. Their subsequent collusion with the Herodians makes that irony especially poignant: It is *on the Sabbath* that they hand down the decision that Jesus must be destroyed. Mark hardly needs to point out the irony of that decision. The second couplet of Jesus' unanswered question strains the irony almost to the breaking point. "[Is it] lawful on the Sabbath ... to kill?" In this way Jesus pronounces judgment on the authorities, or rather sets them up to pronounce implied judgment on themselves.

There are several other, perhaps less obvious, messages here. (1) The story mixes the miracle story form and the controversy story form in such a way that each deepens and enriches the other. Here the elements of controversy are clearly dominant, with the result that the story is a controversy in which the miracle plays the secondary but critical role of validating Jesus' right to make his audacious claims. In this the story forms an inclusion with the controversy about the rooftop paralytic, with which the controversy series formally began (2:1–12).

(2) The mixing of forms has one other significant effect: According to standard miracle form, the success of the cure is attested by the crowd of onlookers (see "Miracle Form" at 2.2.3). Here, however, where the reader expects an acclamation from the crowd, the story presents an abrupt reversal: The Pharisees and Herodians collude against Jesus, looking for some way to put him to death (v. 6). That decision is by no means unexpected. Everything has been leading up to it—the verbal sparring, the accusations becoming ever more open and ever more directly pointed at Jesus—and yet here even a miraculous cure fails to deflect the developing malice of Jesus' attackers! The decision to put Jesus to death forms an ironic acclamation in the sense that it would have been meaningless had the cure not actually taken place.

(3) Of course, there is a context in which this decision to kill Jesus makes perfect sense, and it may be useful to review these events *from the perspective of a righteous Jew*. Jesus is no innocent, facing charges trumped up out of thin air. He has behaved outrageously, but how should one understand that behavior? If he does not know what he is doing, he is a buffoon; if he does know, he is a social and religious renegade. A buffoon he is not. If he were, he would not have been able to silence his opponents so handily. The righteous Jew is left with only one alternative: Jesus is a renegade, who knows exactly what he is doing, and these are the acts of a dangerous man, staged affronts to the standing social and religious order.

He called Levi, not in *spite of* the fact that he was a tax collector but *because of* it. When his disciples, with Jesus' full knowledge, began working in the fields on the Sabbath (see 2:23–24), Jesus knew that there were Pharisees within sight, and he knew that they would take offense. With the story of the man with the withered hand everything is brought to a head. The authorities have watched for the chink in his armor, but Jesus is the one who chooses this place for the battle. Why would he choose this place and not somewhere less conspicuous? Why, if he were not grandstanding for the crowds? He has played the crowds as a magician does, using miracles as a kind of political sleight of hand to further his own dangerous ends. And he must be stopped.

(4) Mark, of course, has given us a different take on these scenes. From his point of

view, each of these stories raises questions of profound theological import. Jesus called Levi precisely to make a theological point. It is significant that he found Levi "sitting at the tax collector's booth" (2:14); if nothing else, this tells us that Levi was not one of the crowds who followed Jesus as he taught (v. 13). The call of Levi is instead an enacted parable, not a way of scoring a point with the crowd, but a way of illustrating one: The Kingdom of God that Jesus preaches does not recognize traditional boundaries of piety and defilement.

It is significant that the story of the man with the withered hand falls hard on the heels of the controversy about the Sabbath grain fields (2:23–28), in which the authorities have raised questions about the behavior of Jesus' disciples. The twin sayings that formed the conclusion of that story focus attention directly on the question of Jesus' authority; Mark's reader approaches the present story with this concern already brought into clear focus. Yet this story shifts the emphasis slightly. Rather than asserting his sovereign right as Lord of the Sabbath (as he could have done in 3:4), Jesus defends his actions with a more general ethical principle: It is right to do good on the Sabbath—right for anyone.

(5) The story of 3:1–6 is heavily embedded with the language of a law court. Thus, while the images evoked in the opening verse are all images of the synagogue at worship, the secondary images are those of a court of law. The mixing of images presents the reader with yet another subtle comment on the calumnies of a legal system Mark clearly took to be corrupt. By the judicious use of accusation and counterquestion, and by the inconsistency between Jesus' accusers' actions and the principles of justice implied in his question, Mark has indicted them. In the process he has summoned the reader—as jury—to hand down a verdict far different from the one for which Jesus' accusers watched.

2.4. More Controversies (3:7–35)

Unlike the controversies in 2:1–3:6, the series in 3:7–35 is loosely organized. In form, the report about the multitudes by the sea (vv. 7–12) is not a controversy at all, but rather a summary report of Jesus' growing fame. Verses 13–19 narrate the call of the twelve disciples. But these reports are punctuated by intimations of trouble: The crowds get out of hand (v. 10), there are demons (vv. 11–12, 15), and Jesus is accused of collusion with Beelzebub (vv. 20–30).

In the previous controversies we saw the Pharisees making incremental attacks against Jesus: saying nothing about their suspicions (2:6), asking Jesus' disciples about Jesus' behavior rather than addressing him directly (v. 16), and addressing Jesus, but only about the behavior of his disciples (vv. 18, 24). They approach Jesus himself at first with caution, then with increasing boldness. Finally, they reach the catastrophic decision to put Jesus to death (3:6), at which point the narrative shifts to an explosive description of Jesus' enormous popularity with the crowds. Clearly battle lines have been drawn. By narrating the call of the twelve in precisely this context (vv. 13–19), Mark makes it clear that the decision to follow Jesus is freighted with dangers. Indeed, one risks alienating not only religious authorities (vv. 22–30), but even one's family (vv. 21, 31–35).

2.4.1. The Multitudes by the Sea (3:7–12). This brief story tells the reader that much more happened that the narrator has not taken time to tell. Mark stresses here the "large crowd" (v. 7; cf. v. 8) that gathers around Jesus, giving a comprehensive list of places from which people have come. From among these multitudes, Jesus healed "many" (v. 10). A tumult of verbs describes the crowds and demoniacs. The diseased "were pushing forward" to touch him (v. 10); the evil spirits "fell down before him," crying out that Jesus was the Son of God (v. 11). In turn, Jesus cautioned them "much" (v. 12; NIV, "he gave them strict orders").

Mark uses quick, broad brush strokes to portray a situation of great energy and drama. In doing so, he splashes into his narrative a theme that has been slowly building since Jesus' appearance in the synagogue at Capernaum in chapter 1: His ministry was accompanied with wildly enthusiastic public acclaim (1:28, 32, 37, 39, 45; 2:1–2, 13). We will return to this theme again, but here for a moment it becomes the central focus of the narrator's attention.

Probably the most puzzling aspect of these verses is the presence of the boat in verse 9. Some commentators suppose that this is the same as the boat in 4:1, but Mark's reader would not yet be able even to ask that question because 4:1 lies ahead in the reading. At this point, the boat makes the scene more concrete and vivid, at the same time providing an occasion for the explanation in verses 9b–11: Everything, the boat included, heightens the sense of drama. The turmoil in the language reflects the turmoil in the plot.

Finally, a note about the significance of this story in Mark's overarching plot: This wild enthusiasm comes on the heels of the authorities' decision to put Jesus to death (3:6). The note that Jesus "withdrew" (v. 7) seems to imply that he slipped away to a place of safety. The line has been drawn in the sand, and if the enthusiasm of the crowds is contag*ious*, to the authorities it is also a contag*ion*—something to be contained. The light of the world casts a long shadow. Something of that shadow is hinted in Mark's language, for even though Jesus withdraws, he is unable to hide. The rumors fly, and he is found out, followed out into the desert. The crowds are so great he is in danger of being crushed (*thlibo*, v. 9), a word with ominous overtones. Jesus senses the danger and does not allow demons to tell who he is (v. 12; cf. 1:34, 40–45).

Yet the light of the world is still light, and verse 12 ends the story with a subtle twist. Despite the dangers that lurk in the wild enthusiasm, Jesus silences the demons, ordering them "not to tell who he was." The demons and the reader understand perfectly well that Jesus is not referring to public recognition but to his identity. Yet here, in the context of such commotion, the remark is almost humorous. The Greek in verse 12 permits a different rendering: "He silenced them much lest they should make him *famous*."

2.4.2. The Choosing of the Twelve (3:13–19a). The introduction of the list of disciples at this point has long interested the historian and excited the curiosity of the average reader. Who are these people? Why does Jesus choose them? Are they in any sense examples for others to follow? Mark does not try to answer such questions. Indeed, except for Judas Iscariot and the inner circle—Peter, James, John, and Andrew—the disciples are not even mentioned by name elsewhere in the narrative. Instead, Mark refers to them by the collective designation "the Twelve." They move through the narrative en masse, as though they were a single character.

The list of disciples itself poses several questions: Is James the son of Alphaeus (v. 18) the brother of Levi (2:14)? Is this another name for Levi himself? The modern reader is apt to add other questions, but these are unnatural for Mark's authorial reader, who did not have Matthew and Luke as points of comparison.

More to Mark's point is the opening in verses 14–15, which sets out clearly the nature of discipleship: "He appointed twelve ... that they might be with him and that he might send them out to preach and to have authority to drive out demons." Thus "appointed" for the task of preaching and exorcism, the twelve are termed *apostles* (v. 14). This sentence contains a subtle balance. Those appointed apostles were designated to two roles: to be with Jesus and to be sent out. The first is prerequisite to the second and reflects the profound importance of fellowship with Jesus as an aspect of the apostolic position. It is clear from the way Mark uses the phrase to "be with him" elsewhere that he understands discipleship in this way. One cannot hope to fulfill the commission of the Master without first having an intimate knowledge of the Master's strategies. Before one can be sent out, one first must draw close.

The grammar of the passage suggests that the single commission carries two balanced charges: to preach and to drive out demons. The fact that driving out demons is an integral part of the apostolic commission may give the modern reader pause, but we have already seen that Jesus' entire healing ministry should be understood as an act of vanquishing Satan. It would appear that for Mark's authorial reader, one could hardly hope to carry forward Jesus' program of the kingdom without in some way vanquishing Satan in Jesus' name.

This is an important theme in Mark, one that will reappear in his account of the Transfiguration in 9:2–10, where the disciples' inability to effect an exorcism places them in a precarious connection with the teachers of the law, and then in the story of the strange exorcist in 9:38–41, where it will have direct implications for Mark's own reader. This theme clearly catches Mark's own attention here, as an interpreter of the tradition he is passing along. He soon returns to this question with an account of a dispute with the teachers of the law over the nature of Jesus' activity of exorcism (3:22–30).

The Apostles	Who They Were	Other Names	What They Did	When They Died
PETER	A fisherman; brother of Andrew; born in Bethsaida; son of John; married, lived in Capernaum	Also known as Simon, Symeon, Cephas, and Simon Peter	Leader of the disciples; Peter and John became the leaders of the early church, especially in Jerusalem	Tradition says he died a martyr in Rome
ANDREW	A fisherman; brother of Peter; born in Bethsaida; lived with Peter in Capernaum; a disciple of John the Baptist		Preached in Schythia; tradition says he preached in what is now Russia	Crucified in Patras, Greece, on an X-shaped cross, now called a St. Andrew's cross
MATTHEW	Was a tax collector	Also known as Levi	Wrote the Gospel of Matthew c. A.D. 80 for Jewish Christians	
SIMON		Also known as the "Canaanite" and later as Simon the Zealot		
JOHN	A fisherman; a friend of Jesus; brother of James; son of Zebedee and Salome (sister of Mary, the mother of Jesus); from Galilee, probably Bethsaida; a disciple of John the Baptist		John and Peter became the leaders of the early church; John wrote five New Testament Books—the Gospel of John, the three letters of John, and Revelation	Tradition says he lived in Ephesus; died near the end of the first century
PHILIP	Born in Bethsaida		Among the disciples in the upper chamber before Pentecost	Tradition says he did missionary work in Asia Minor; tradition says he died a martyr at Hierapolis in Phrygia
THOMAS		Also known as Didymus, "the Twin," and "Doubting Thomas"		Tradition says he worked in India, Persia, and Parthia; died a martyr at Madras
JUDAS	Son of James	Also known as Judas of James and Jude	May have been the author of the epistle of Jude	
JAMES	A fisherman; brother of John; son of Zebedee			Executed by Herod Agrippa I c. A.D. 44
BARTHOLOMEW	Philip's friend	Also known as Nathanael		Tradition says he preached in Asia Minor and India; died a martyr when he was skinned alive in Armenia
JAMES	Son of Alphaeus			
JUDAS ISCARIOT	Son of Simon	Surname was Iscariot	Appointed treasurer for the disciples; betrayed Jesus	Killed himself, Matthew says he hanged himself, Acts says he "fell headlong, his body burst open"

2.4.3. Jesus Is Thought to Be Beside Himself (3:19b–21). This brief story is transitional in that it moves Jesus and the disciples off the mountain (v. 13). The "crowd" (v. 20) is the same word that had been repeated like a drumbeat in verses 7–12, so this story returns the plot to the tumult of activity surrounding Jesus.

In verse 21 the focus narrows to a specific group—Jesus' family. They set about to "take charge of him." But why? The subject of the next verb is unclear. Has Jesus' *family* said, "He is out of his mind"? Or has that accusation come from another quarter? The grammar seems to favor the former translation. Either way, Jesus' activity presents a public embarrassment for his family. Thus the scene is set. The curtain will remain up while Jesus engages a different challenge on the open stage: The teachers of the law from Jerusalem accuse him of collusion with Satan. Mark returns to the question of Jesus' family in verses 31–35.

2.4.4. On Collusion With Satan (3:22–30). This story uses the form of a controversy story that Mark momentarily abandoned after authorities had decided to put Jesus to death (3:6; see "The Form of Pronouncement Stories" at sec. 2.3). While the intervening material is not cast in the *form* of a controversy, it is still tension-ridden. By juxtaposing the enormous response of the crowds (vv. 7–10) with a generalized comment about demons (vv. 11–12), Mark cast the calling of the Twelve in a context of genuine and growing danger. The disciples stand to lose everything if they respond to this call.

Hard choices must be made. To reinforce the perils of discipleship Mark has sandwiched the controversy about collusion with Satan (vv. 22–30) into the middle of a confrontation between Jesus and his family (vv. 20b–21, 31–35). Verse 21 offers a natural human reaction from Jesus' family: "He is out of his mind." In verse 22 the teachers of the law carry the accusation to another level: "He is possessed by Beelzebub." The fact that these two passages are juxtaposed together prevents us from treating the questions as entirely separable, and the answer to one will reinforce the answer to the other. Thus, Mark points out that the issues of family relationships cannot be divorced from the question of one's spiritual commitments.

The accusation of the teachers of the law employs an archaic term, *Beelzebub* (NIV) or *Beelzebul* (NRSV). This compound term may derive from *baalzebul* ("lord of the flies") or "*baalzebub* ("lord of filth") and was the name of a Philistine deity (see 2 Kings 1:16). The parallels within this context make it clear that here the word refers to the lord (or *baal*) of the demons. Thus, the shift from Beelzebub to Satan in verse 23 represents only a minor shift of terminology, but it is one that sharpens the issues in the hearing of Mark's Gentile readers.

Jesus' response is clear. What is striking here is the repetition: The word "kingdom" (v. 24) is functionally parallel with the word "house" (v. 25), such that the latter must refer not to a physical house but to a ruling family.

What is less obvious is the logic of Jesus' response. This involves a rather audacious strategy of granting for the sake of argument the opponents' terms: "Suppose you are right that I am in collusion with Satan. The result of my ministry is that Satan's kingdom is now coming to an end. Does that not demonstrate that God's power is at work here?"

The reiterated elements of verses 24–26 specify the meaning of "strong man" in verse 27 as a reference to Satan. By implication, then, the binding of Satan refers to the exorcisms Jesus has been performing. (It is important to remember that for Mark, the entirety of Jesus' ministry is a battle with demonic forces; see 2.1.4.) But what is meant by the "possessions" of the strong man, which the exorcist "carries off"? In this context, what must be in view is the enormous toll demonic activity takes on human life, and thus the even greater triumph when Jesus (the plunderer) breaks the chains of the bondage and sets the prisoner free. Jesus binds the master to release the captive. The mission of the kingdom is more than espionage; it is rescue.

Jesus' language ties this claim to those that preceded in verses 24–26. There is a subtle shift between the first sentence and the second. In the first, Jesus uses a general word for "possessions"; in the second, he shifts to the specific word "house." Thus, verse 27 echoes the saying about the "house divided" in verse 25. In doing so, he reverses the argument in verse 26 and makes it clear that—rhetoric notwithstanding—Jesus is in no league with the devil.

At this point the defense ends, and Jesus takes up the cudgel: It is not enough to deny the charges brought against him. The very fact at one could bring such charges is itself a rious offense against the Holy Spirit. It is, verses 28–29 make clear, a form of blashemy (cf. v. 30), an "eternal sin."

Of all the passages dealing with spirituality, erhaps none has caused so much personal onsternation as Jesus' words about the unforivable sin in 3:28. Many a sincere Christian as wondered whether some personal flaw repesents that sin. But by placing this saying in is context, Mark has shown that the saying as both a narrow scope and a deep seriousess. T. W. Manson has described this passage terms that honor both of these constraints: He who blasphemes against the Holy Spirit as identified himself so completely with the ingdom of evil that for him evil is good, ugliess is beauty and falsehood truth; and so the vorkings of the Holy Spirit appear to him as nadness."[7]

How would this saying have been heard by Mark and his reader? This particular question as been explored as part of a wider inquiry bout the activities of early Christian prophets. Many scholars today hold that this saying was mportant in the early church as a warning gainst those who questioned the legitimacy of prophetic activity in the church. The early church, including the community Mark is addressing, was charismatic, and prophets were active in a variety of church contexts (see the Introduction). It is not difficult to envision a context in which the activities of early Christian prophets became points of contention. If so, this saying would have been heard with special urgency as a caution, not only against those who condemned the work of the Holy Spirit in the ministry of Jesus, but also against those who condemned the work of the Spirit in the life of the believer, particularly in its more visible prophetic and charismatic expressions.

When all is said and done, the saying about the unforgivable sin remains a disquieting reminder of the seriousness of the choices we make. Mark's Jesus is not averse to drawing hard lines, and he will later echo these sentiments by repeating Jesus' words to the apostles as he sends them out on a training mission: "And if any place will not welcome you or listen to you, shake the dust off your feet when you leave, as a testimony against them" (6:11).

But there is, oddly, a reverse side of this coin. In a context of great persecution and stress, where the confrontation is over eternal realities, sayings such as this one show clearly where the battle lines are drawn. At the moment that they identify who the outsiders are, they also identify and encourage those on the inside, those whose commitments have kept them on the right side of no man's land.

2.4.5. Jesus' True Kindred (3:31–35). Mark now returns to the tension between Jesus and his family (v. 21). Having just explored the seriousness of opposing the work of the Spirit, he now explores practical implications when one's commitment to the kingdom is opposed by one's immediate family. The earlier tensions with Jesus' own family erupt abruptly. Jesus effectively dismisses his nuclear family by redefining its import. Because this is a pronouncement story, everything focuses on the saying in verse 35: "Whoever does God's will is my brother and sister and mother."

It is important to recognize the critical role that family played in first-century sensibilities. The isolated individual, without family resources or family commitments, was unthinkable. One's personal identity was understood in terms of family connections. To reject one's family or to be rejected by one's family was social suicide because it alienated the very connections that made human experience possible. Thus, for Jesus to redefine the meaning of the family unit creates a shocking challenge against one of the taken-for-granted values of first-century society. The obvious first question is, "What would prompt this kind of shocking move?"

But perhaps this question is itself somewhat shortsighted. Rather, the commitments of Christian community in themselves redefined the nature of the family. In several places Mark describes tensions between Jesus and those closest to him (3:21, 31–35; 6:1–6). Related passages describe similar tensions between the disciples and their families (10:28–31). In the Olivet Discourse, a prophecy of Jesus will link this sort of tension to future persecution like that which we have supposed Mark's congregation had only recently experienced (13:12). The point here is that those tensions were already realities for Mark and his reader. In 10:29–31, Jesus will promise that those who have lost family will gain them again a hundredfold; here he promises that those who have lost family will gain it again in the person of

Jesus himself. With this great promise, Jesus tells those who have gathered around him, and implicitly the reader, that even though the cost of discipleship may be high, the compensations are higher still.

2.5. Parables (and a Miracle) of Promise (4:1–34)

This section of parables has been the subject of perhaps the most intensive efforts at interpretation of any other section of Mark except perhaps for the Passion Narrative. Clearly there are problems. The chronology is unclear, and there is intense debate about whether the allegory in verses 13–20 came from Jesus or was a Markan interpretation of Jesus' parable. The allegorical details of these verses appear to shift the emphasis from what is otherwise central in the parable itself. If these verses are removed, the remaining material illustrates a different point.

Furthermore, the parables of Jesus have received attention in their own right, an interest shared by all who want to understand his teaching, but which has led scholars to study them outside the literary context of the Gospels. This has often happened with the parables of Mark 4. The result is that the interpreters have imposed the conclusions of an abstract study of parables back onto the text of Mark.

A summary of that interpretive procedure goes like this: Remove verses 10–12 because they are depicted as taking place somewhere else (Jesus alone with his disciples). Remove also verses 13–20 because they are Mark's commentary on the tradition. What remains is a collection of parables that share a common theme: the overwhelming success of the gospel despite catastrophe—a theme found elsewhere in Jesus' teaching. The omitted sections are then treated as inconveniences to be resolved rather than as useful commentary by which Mark was prompting his reader to hear other nuances in Jesus' parable discourse.

The common theme of success in the teeth of tragedy is certainly to be found here. To that extent the procedure just mentioned has led to genuine clarity. But the standard procedure has also been distortive because it obscures another dimension of these stories, which to my mind is equally significant and probably closer to Mark's own understanding of his parables.

Let us approach this issue from a differe angle. Certainly Jesus told the parable of th sower. Mark passed along the parable basical as he received it. What elements in the para ble prompted the intrusion of verses 10–12 What caught Mark's attention was not the suc cess of the kingdom, but the many reasons wh people fall away. Indeed, this is a commo theme in Mark (e.g., 9:42–49; 10:29–3(13:12–13, 14–23; 14:27–31). Little wonde that this is what he heard here as he reflecte on the parable.

2.5.1. The Parable of the Sower (4:1–9 With the parable of the sower we are introduce to an entirely new section of the narrative. Sev eral elements call attention to the transitior most notably the heavy ballast line in 3:35 an mention of a fresh context and a new cast c characters in 4:1. Because of this marked tran sition and because the parable of the sower ha its own internally coherent rhetorical structure what follows has often been interpreted inde pendent of the narrative that precedes.

It is important to note that the parable i bracketed on either side by injunctions t attentive listening: "Listen!" (v. 3), and "h who has ears to hear, let him hear" (v. 9). Thi is a dominant concern for Mark. In the sectio immediately following, Mark includes a aside explaining why some people will fail t hear or grasp the "secret of the kingdom" (vv 11–12), and in verse 13, Jesus will move int an explanation of the sower with a rhetorica question: "Don't you *understand* this parable? How then will you *understand* any parable?" (emphasis added). That emphasis will be revisited in verses 23–24, 33. Clearly the intentior is that the entire discourse should be read with sensitivities attuned to deeper and less obvious nuances. But what?

One way to answer that question poses it within the context of Jesus' own ministry by identifying the elements of Jesus' opposition and assigning each a place within the unfolding parable. Terence Keegan (1994) provides a convenient summary:

> The Pharisees of Galilee are the seed that fell along the path; the disciples are the seed that fell on rocky ground; the crowds, prefigured by Herod, are the seed that fell among thorns; and the chief priests, scribes, and elders are the thorns responsible for choking the word.

Keegan's analysis is noteworthy for its attention to the place of the parable within the overall structure of the Gospel narrative, but it is limited in that it depends on the reader's rereading the story with elements in hand that only come later in the narrative.

John Paul Heil (1992) has defined the context of the parable somewhat more narrowly by asking only what has appeared *earlier* in the narrative to sharpen the readers' sensitivities. According to Heil, the farmer who "went out to sow his seed" (v. 3) recalls the many times the same verb (*exerchomai*) has been used already in Mark to describe Jesus' "going out" to conduct his ministry (see 1:35, 38; 2:13). That connection invites Mark's reader to understand that the farmer here metaphorically represents Jesus and his work, and that in turn gives a particular frame of reference for the meaning of the word "to sow seed," which has to do with God's work in the world. This impression is later confirmed in 4:14, where it is stated clearly: "The farmer sows *the word*"—Mark's standard word for Jesus' work of ministry (see 2:2). For now, however, it remains only an impression, but one so powerful that it provides the primary framework within which the parable should be understood.

If the reader has even subliminally understood that the farmer is Jesus, then the remainder of the parable will be connected to the rising and falling fortunes of Jesus' ministry. In this vein, Heil has correctly shown that the various ways in which the seed has failed will at the very least recall the hostility personified by the teachers of the law (2:6, 16; 3:22), the Pharisees (2:16, 24; 3:6), and Jesus' own family (3:21, 31–35). In the same way, the description of a bumper crop at the conclusion of the parable (v. 8) recalls the growing success of Jesus' ministry in the very teeth of opposition (cf. the *whole town* [1:33]; *many* were gathered [2:2]; a *large crowd* came to him [2:13; 3:7–8, 20; 4:1]). Thus, in its metaphorical movements the parable reflects the larger movements of Jesus' ministry, and the various soils represent the characters inside the story.

Whether we follow Keegan or Heil, the thrust of the story remains essentially the same: The parable encourages its audience—whether Jesus' listeners or Mark's readers—that even in the face of great trial and disappointment, the kingdom of God will succeed.

Whatever Mark and his reader might have thought of the characters within the story, no doubt they would also have brought to the reading their own memories of failed faith within the experience of their own church. If, as I argued in the Introduction, Mark's congregation is struggling with the aftermath of persecution, then the parable of the sower answers another, equally important question: Why do some people who have heard the word afterward fall away? The presence of the intrusion in verses 10–20 indicates that for Mark this question was the dominant one, a fact that gives us a clue to Mark's own reading of the parable. For this reading we should avoid making the categories too specific. The interpretation that follows in verses 13–20 will make it clear that for Mark at least, the various kinds of failure listed in the parable denote a variety of ways of losing faith, not various categories of specific people.

Thus, the parable offers not only comfort, but also caution. There may be one pathway to salvation, but there are many ways of getting lost. It is not insignificant, then, that the "the farmer sows the *word*" (v. 14), while the parable itself is bounded on every side by injunctions to "listen." In life, as in parables, more is going on than meets the eye.

2.5.2. The Reason for the Parables (4:10–12). Historians and theologians have long puzzled over this short passage. On the surface of it, the debated issue is clear: Did Jesus intend to say that he told parables in order to puzzle people, or did he use them to make his message clear? The fact that the discussion is so enduring and so passionate is evidence, I think, that there may be something awry in our method. Perhaps if we approach the question from a different angle we can reach clearer and more useful conclusions.

It is significant that the passage intrudes into the middle of the parable discourse. The chapter begins with a reference to Jesus in the boat in the sea (v. 1) and closes with a similar note (v. 36). Verse 10 locates Jesus and his entourage elsewhere, alone somewhere with his disciples. The chronological notes are unclear; Mark does not tell the reader when or how the story line reverts to the public scene on the beach. The presence of the disruption in verses 10–20 is therefore somewhat problematic: What prompted Mark to place it here rather than somewhere else? The obvious answer is that the substance of the parable of the sower has prompted him to recall another scene related by both theme and vocabulary, a practice common enough elsewhere in this Gospel (see sec. 3.1.9). The gist of this paragraph is connected in important ways with what Mark took to be the gist of the parable of the sower.

This observation allows us to place these two scenes in slightly different focus. Since in Mark's experience the two traditional stories shared a similar theme, then whatever the two have in common must be a clue to Mark's understanding of what that theme must have been. What the parable of the sower and the present passage have in common is that both provide an explanation of why some hearers have been scandalized by the word. Not all missionary activity reaps a positive harvest; indeed, some of those who have fallen away have already heard the word "and received it with joy" (v. 16), but the fact that they have fallen from faith shows that they "[had] no root" in themselves (v. 17) and were really among "those on the outside" (v. 11). People's hearts are blinded to the truth; everything is in riddles.

In other words, within this series is not only the commonly recognized theme of the success of the gospel in the teeth of disaster, but for Mark and his reader there is also the engagement with the disaster itself. The question is not only, "Will the work of God succeed in the world?" but also, "Why does it sometimes fail? Why have some who have heard the word and received it with joy abandoned it and fallen by the wayside?"

Though the state of the question does not support absolute certainty, I suspect that the allusion to Isaiah 6:9–10 in Mark 4:12 was known already in Mark's church, which would explain why he does not need to introduce the quote but can simply drop it in an offhanded way. Indeed, if the community was splintering under the pressures of persecution, the reference from Isaiah 6 would have provided an important way of making sense of apostasy. People in a social group often need some sort of explanation for those who have decided to leave. The words of Jesus in verses 10–12, packed so tightly with intimations of judgment, filled the bill perfectly: To those who are outside—to those who have been scandalized by the word—everything is in parables precisely in order that they see but not perceive and hear but not understand.

Whether or not Mark's readers would have noticed such subtleties, our conclusions about his redactional style help us come to better clarity about the concerns they brought to the reading process. They hear the parable of the sower and the saying about blindness, and they fill in the gaps with their experience: "Aha! This explains why some of our brothers and sisters in the faith have fallen by the wayside, or why the word, which is so compelling for us, seems to fall on deaf ears. They 'just don't get it'; the kingdom is a riddle they cannot penetrate."

Within the structures of the balanced phrasing, the term for parable (I translate it "riddle" here) is parallel to the term for "secret of the kingdom:"

To you has been given the secret of the kingdom	To those who are outside everything is in "riddles"

That is, the saying divides between insiders and outsiders, and the difference between them is one of clear perception. The secret (*mysterion*) of the kingdom is something *given*, not taken; *revealed*, not figured out. Try as they might, those outside experience everything as confusing, as a "riddle." The critical word here is *parabole*, which for Mark has a wide range of meanings. Originally the disciples have asked about "the parable," a reference that appears to be to the parable of the sower. Jesus' response is more expansive: Instead of explaining that particular parable, he explains that to outsiders *everything* is parabolic, *everything* is puzzling. One nuance of *parabole* is to see it as similar to the Hebrew word *mashal*, which may mean "dark saying, puzzle, riddle, or parabolic story."

We return now to the crux of the discussion. The word that has given most interpreters difficulty is *mepote*, which the NIV translates "otherwise":

> To those on the outside everything is
> said in parables so that
>
> "they may be ever seeing but never
> perceiving,
> and ever hearing but never
> understanding;
> otherwise [*mepote*] they might turn and
> be forgiven!"

On the surface of it, these verses explain the ;andal of the word by introducing a different ;andal. Interpreters have followed two basic rategies to remove the offense of the words ı verse 12. One is to reinterpret the verse as kind of ironic or sarcastic response, the oppo-te of Jesus' intention: "We wouldn't want ıem to be converted, now, would we?" A sec-nd way to remove the offense is to reinterpret *ıepote* as "unless," and in that way make the nderstanding conditional upon conversion:

That they may be ever seeing but
never perceiving,
And ever hearing but never
understanding,
Unless they turn again and are forgiven.

'his interpretation, however, is based on a sup-osed original Aramaic. It may correctly inter-ret Jesus, but his interpretation will not work ɔr Mark or his Greek-speaking reader, for ⁄Iark normally interprets Aramaisms for his ɜaders.

The critical question here is not what Mark ıtended by the term *mepote*, but what he vould have understood by "ever seeing but ıever perceiving" and "ever hearing but never ınderstanding." Our own tendency is to iden-ify these terms with cognitive understanding, vhile for Mark they must surely have identi-ied dispositions toward the gospel. We can ;ain a measure of clarity about this by look-ng at the parable of the wicked tenants in .2:1–12. Mark tells us that the listeners—pre-ıumably the chief priests, teachers of the law, ınd elders mentioned in 11:27—clearly under-.tood the meaning of the parable (v. 12), but ook offense at it "because they knew he had ıpoken the parable against them."

The point is that "grasping" a parable equires more than merely figuring out its ref-ɜrent or analogy. The parable lays claim on ɔne, demands a response, and sometimes does .o in quite startling ways. To "see" a parable ınd "perceive" its meaning is to respond ıppropriately to that claim. One may figure out vhat the parable is about and even understand ts metaphoric significance, but still be among he outsiders, who are "ever seeing but never ɔerceiving," and who are "ever hearing but ıever understanding." What is needed, Mark ıays, is transformation, not information; repen-ance, not mere assent.

This is not the last time Mark will deal out this kind of judgment. The language of seeing and not seeing will occur again in 8:14–19, in which the disciples are upbraided for their fail-ure to perceive or understand the significance of the loaves: "Why are you talking about hav-ing no bread? Do you still not see or under-stand? Are your hearts hardened? Do you have eyes but fail to see, and ears but fail to hear?" (vv. 17–18). The parallels between these two stories are hardly incidental, and the point of both passages is the same: To see and perceive is to penetrate beyond the obvious; to hear and understand is to listen with the ears of faith; and to have hearts that are not hardened is to be willing to respond with both a believing mind and a faithful heart.

Thus, the insistence on treating verses 10–12 as a matter of information is entirely mis-guided, as though the crucial issue was one of clarity of expression. For Isaiah, for Jesus, and for Mark—and for their listeners and readers too—the question was not a matter of *clarity*, but of *choice*: The parables force people to make their choices—just as life itself forces people to make their choices—and if they choose to oppose Jesus and his work in the world (or, in this context, they follow Jesus and then under the spell of some seduction or the pressure of some loss abandon him), they are ranked among those who "see but do not per-ceive, and hear but do not understand."

It is this which gives us a clue to the mean-ing of "everything" in 4:11. The question asked by Jesus' followers in verse 10 was about "the parables." Jesus' response is about "everything"; his answer covers more than the question. What Mark has in view is the role of the gospel itself in forcing people to their choice: Everything has parabolic significance. Mark's preoccupation with the factors in those choices prompts his own explanation of the parable of the sower, to which he will turn in the next section.

2.5.3. The Interpretation of the Sower (4:13–20). Scholars have debated whether these verses can be attributed to Jesus as authentic sayings. Some claim that Mark has falsely attributed this explanation to Jesus, but in fact it represents his own theological and pastoral agendas. The alternative view is that they are in fact authentic words of Jesus, but uttered at a later time. Either way, the standard method of interpretation removes these words from the immediate context and treats the parable of the sower without reference to them.

Neither of these approaches would have commended itself to Mark's authorial reader. Perhaps the best solution is a compromise of these two. The interpretation of the sower in verses 14–20 is not a word from Jesus. Greek has a clear way of indicating the beginning of a quotation, but no clear way to show where the quotation closes. So here. The quotation introduced in verse 11 continues, I argue, up to and including verse 13, but it closes before the interpretation of the parable in verse 14. The allegory reflects Mark's appropriation of the parable of the sower for the needs of his own community, and in that way implicitly displays the interpretive principles he used to appropriate the elements of the Jesus tradition.

We might approach this from a different angle: Mark himself is a "reader" of the parable of the sower. He did not create the parable, but himself "read" (or heard) it as it was handed down in the tradition. These verses tell us what elements stood out when he himself read the sower and thus offer clues to what he expected his own reader to make of it. Mark's reader would have taken these verses at face value, and thus would have heard here a particularly relevant way of understanding the meaning of the sower.

2.5.4. "He Who Has Ears to Hear, Let Him Hear" (4:21–25). The transitional phrase, "He said to them," is a frequent seam in Mark. At verses 21, 24, and 26 (the phrase in Greek is the same) it indicates that Mark has been assembling material into a collection. In the case of this small section, the exhortation to "consider carefully" in verse 24 ties the second set of aphorisms to the first. The mention of a "bushel basket" (NIV translates "bowl") in verse 21 probably prompted the inclusion of the saying about "measures" in verse 24, so that even though there are apparent shifts in sense, the whole collection is stamped with the sense of a theme.

In verses 21–23 the subject of that theme is the importance of attentive listening because there is more going on than meets the eye. Jesus uses the metaphor of a lamp to make this affirmation concrete. In this context, Mark's reader would no doubt have heard the word "lamp" as an extension of the metaphor of the "word," the subject of the parable of the sowe This is about the entire purpose of God. (I v. 26 Mark will supply the expression "king dom of God" for this same reality.) There i "something more" about God's purpose something that for now requires close atten tion. It is hidden inevitably from those wh have ears but who fail to listen.

Yet the parable also affirms the converse That "something more" is inevitably going t be revealed (v. 22), because that is the nature c things. It would make no more sense for Go to hide his purposes than for a homeowner t bring in a lamp and place it under a "bowl" (lit a "peck-measure," holding nearly nine liters) which would give no light, or under a "bed, which would run the risk of fire. There may b one further nuance here. According to Jose phus, one douses a lamp by smothering it unde a bowl to avoid filling the room with acri smoke (*Antiquities* 5.223). When Jesus asks th question, "Do you bring in a lamp to put i under a bowl?" the implication is that one doe not light a lamp merely to snuff it out.

Verses 24–25 press the metaphor in a dif ferent direction. If the thrust of verses 21–2 was that the purpose of God is now unclear bu will inevitably be revealed, the thrust of th present verses is that the amount of clarity on will have later depends in significant measur on what one grasps now. Indeed, the measur of one is the measure of the other. The sectio closes on a paradoxical note: How can one b stripped of anything if one has nothing at all The effect of the paradox is to render the state ment more radical, to turn logic on its head, t make the statement black and white. Jesus' lis teners, and Mark's readers, are confronted wit the reality that God's purposes cannot be cho sen in increments. This is all or nothing, nov or never, once for all.

2.5.5. The Parable of the Seed Growing Secretly (4:26–29). Mark now shifts to the phrase "kingdom of God" for the general real ity of the purposes of God (implied in "word" in v. 14 and "lamp" in v. 21). The parable of the seed growing secretly focuses attention on the fact that the sower, once he has done his work must wait for the seed to take root. The seed grows, "all by itself" (v. 28). The point is no that it grows without help—farmers still may tend their crops—but that its growth happens mysteriously even so. The farmer sows and the seed grows, "he does not know how." So it is with the kingdom.

Verse 29 closes the parable on an eschatological note that is comforting or ominous, depending on the hearer's disposition toward the kingdom: When the harvest has come, the farmer "puts the sickle to it." The growth of the seed—first the stalk, then the head, then the full kernel in the head (v. 28)—stresses what the attentive observer knows will follow as inevitably as harvest follows sowing. A time comes when the waiting is over. So it is with the kingdom.

2.5.6. The Parable of the Mustard Seed (4:30–32). The parable of the mustard seed merges two different images. (1) The first one revolves around a contrast between the smallness of the seed and the enormity of the shrub that grows from it. The seed itself is described as "the smallest seed you plant in the ground" (v. 31). This corresponds to other descriptions of the mustard seed, which is often used as a point of comparison to describe something minuscule (cf. Matt. 17:20; Luke 17:6). By contrast, when the seed takes root and grows, it becomes "the largest of all garden plants," with large branches, so that "the birds of the air can perch in its shade" (v. 32). This, of course, is a major theme of the parable discourse as a whole (see sec. 2.5). The kingdom begins inauspiciously, yet when it comes, it does so in full force.

(2) The parable also contains a vivid allusion to an Old Testament metaphor for a world-encompassing, redemptive move of God in Ezekiel 17:22–23:

> The is what the Sovereign LORD says: I myself will take a shoot from the very top of a cedar and plant it; I will break off a tender sprig from its topmost shoots and plant it on a high and lofty mountain. On the mountain heights of Israel I will plant it; it will produce branches and bear fruit and become a splendid cedar. *Birds of every kind will nest in it; they will find shelter in the shade of its branches.* (italics added)

The operative image here is of a large tree that shelters the whole earth. That image is not uncommon in the literature of apocalyptic Judaism (see also Ezek. 31:6; Dan. 4:10–12, 20–21).

Thus it is with the kingdom. Like the acorn that contains within it the promise of the oak—or, in Middle-Eastern terms, the tiny seed that contains the promise of the massive mustard shrub—the kingdom works its way unobtrusively. Grace and power come packaged in surprising, unexpected ways. Mark wants his readers to know that God will use even tiny and inauspicious beginnings, even when they are beginnings troubled by the tragedies and struggles of a church in crisis.

This is a timeless message. No doubt Jesus told this story to encourage his own followers in a time of trouble. Mark also repeated it afresh for his own congregation, facing troubles of their own. One cannot judge the power of the kingdom by the way things begin but by the way they come out. Often what looks like disaster will prove in the end to be the power of God at work in the world.

2.5.7. Jesus' Use of Parables (4:33–34). These two verses briefly summarize the parable section. Verse 34 appears to be an editorial reflection on the private teaching to "the Twelve and the others around him" in verses 10–20.

Before we leave the parables discourse, we should reflect on the common affirmations that tie them together. On the main, they contrast inauspicious and disastrous beginnings with sudden, staggering, overwhelming success (4:30–32). Despite the peril to the seed, the harvest comes as much as a hundredfold (4:3–20). What is hidden now will inevitably be revealed (4:21–23), with all its potential consequences for gain or loss (4:24–25). The kingdom will come mysteriously, but it will come as inevitably as harvest follows sowing (4:26–29).

The details of these parables are close to the Palestinian earth. No doubt they would have sounded a note of special encouragement to Jesus' disciples as they struggled to understand Jesus' failure to act, the subsequent delay of the kingdom, and the unexpected and sometimes harsh opposition they encountered from the religious authorities. Yet our focus has been on Mark's reader, struggling to come to terms with disasters that have become perhaps even more costly. Families have been destroyed; the church is divided; people have lost their lives for the faith. The opposition experienced by the disciples has erupted into open persecution for Mark's generation of Christians. When read against such a backdrop, the words of judgment expressed in Jesus' parables would have been sharper and more menacing, while the dimensions of comfort and encouragement would have been deeper still.

2.6. *Miracles (4:35–5:43)*

The limits of this section are difficult to establish. The section opens with the stilling of the storm (4:35–41), which is a miracle in form but much like a parable in content. Where does the section close? Commentators have almost universally closed it after the healing of Jairus's daughter (end of ch. 5). But if Mark's readers heard the text read aloud without consulting an outline, they would not have known that a new section had been introduced until 6:5, well into the story of the rejection of Jesus at Nazareth. When one reads the narrative naturally, the rejection at Nazareth appears at first to be one more miracle story. Part of its striking quality is the way it reverses the reader's expectations; the reader expects a miracle but gets the report that Jesus "could not do any miracles" in his hometown. That shock launches the next section. (Be sure to read sec. 2.7.1 in connection with the miracles in sec. 2.6.)

2.6.1. The Stilling of the Storm (4:35–41). This story bridges two major sections in Mark because it relates *thematically* to what precedes, but *formally* to what follows. Several times in Mark, Jesus' word or authority to teach is validated by miracles. The story of the exorcism in Capernaum (1:21–28) emphasizes that connection by identifying the exorcism itself as a kind of teaching—"with authority" (1:27). Even the controversy stories in 2:1–3:6 are bounded on either side by stories that intertwine miracle and authority (2:1–12; 3:1–6). Indeed, in the first story of the series (the healing of the paralytic), Jesus makes the audacious claim that the miracle demonstrates his authority to forgive sins (2:10).

This story of the stilling of the storm does precisely the same thing. The dominant theme of the parable discourse has been Jesus' assurance that the kingdom will indeed succeed; failure comes, but still there is a bumper crop (4:1–20). This may also be the underlying import of the parable of the candle (4:21–22): God does not light a candle merely to snuff it out or cover it up. The parable of the seed growing secretly (4:26–29) suggests something similar: The earth produces of itself automatically, without visible cause. Despite everything to the contrary, the kingdom is breaking in.

It is common to see this theme woven like a bright line throughout the parable discourse, but it is important also to see the darker underweave against which it makes such a bright contrast. As we have seen, Mark's readers brought with them sensitivities rent nearly to shreds by the pulling and pushing of faith against family, the politics of God against the politics of the nation. Persecution forces a church to consolidate its boundaries, and in doing so it sharply divides between insiders and outsiders. It is clear enough from the text itself that Mark's church was in crisis—father against son (13:12), Jew against Greek (6:1–8:30), perhaps even leader against laity. The parables have offered encouragement in this crisis. If this is the situation against which we should read the parables, it is also the situation against which we should read the stilling of the storm. Jesus' challenge to the disciples in verse 40 ("Why are you so afraid? Do you still have no faith?") challenges Mark's beleaguered Christians as well.

At the same time, however, this story deepens the thrust of the parable discourse by validating Jesus' words with a miracle. The storm becomes a metaphor for all those forces that oppose God's work in the world, and the stilling of the storm becomes an enacted parable in which Jesus accomplishes in deed what he had only moments before proclaimed in word.

In this way the stilling of the storm introduces the series of miracles that follows in chapter 5. It is clear from the circumstances that this is a historically credible account of a sudden squall on Galilee. Such storms often come up as late afternoon winds strafe the northern part of the lake. The boat (v. 36) would have been a long, shallow, relatively narrow affair, and thus particularly susceptible to swamping. The rowing of the disciples was presumably intended to keep the boat headed into the wind since a lengthwise turn would have capsized it almost instantly. Jesus is depicted as sleeping "on a cushion," a wooden affair usually kept under the coxswain's seat. If the disciples were rowing into the waves, then Jesus was sleeping in the part of the boat where the up and down movement was most violent. Almost certainly the disciples' cry of desperation in verse 38 was a call for help bailing water.

Of course, Mark has taken pains to structure the story according to the standard format for a miracle. Several elements of the story can be explained as variations on the miracle form, perhaps most notably the presence of "other boats" in verse 36. The other boats play no further role in the story, but miracle stories usually include additional eyewitnesses wherever that is possible. Perhaps these boats are included to serve that rhetorical purpose.

Nevertheless Mark abandons standard miracle form in three ways. (1) It is unusual that the miracle worker be sleeping. (2) A miracle worker does not usually upbraid the onlookers for their lack of faith. (3) Miracles usually end with a shout of acclamation from the crowd, while this story ends with an unanswered question, "Who is this? Even the wind and the waves obey him!"

When these three elements are taken together, they heighten the miraculous elements of the story, but they do so by transforming the meaning of Jesus' sleep in verse 38. At first glance, Jesus appears to be asleep because he is exhausted from the sheer physical work required to teach the multitudes by the lake. Verse 39 turns that impression on its head. Jesus sleeps the sleep of confidence that nothing can destroy God's work in the world. His question to the disciples—"Do you still have no faith?"—implies its converse: Those who do have faith have no reason to panic, even in a storm such as this one.

By its content, verse 39 hits the reader as a reversal. Mark first posits the understandable but natural perspective of the disciples and their fear (v. 38), then he subverts that perspective by showing that it is fundamentally flawed. Any reader who shares the disciples' perspective in the first instance will be trapped into Jesus' perspective by the second.

The miraculous elements of the story are heightened by three other considerations. (1) The story may contain a series of oblique references to Jonah 1:4–6, 11, 16. The language is inexact and the stories differ in their inner structures, but several parallels in concept suggest that an informed reader is expected to correlate these two stories. Both record a great storm at sea. In the Jonah story the sailors each repeatedly "cried out to his own god" (Jonah 1:5). Jonah, however, was below deck, asleep. The captain woke him up and challenged him: "How can you sleep? Get up and call on your god!" (1:6). In Mark's story Jesus is asleep, and the disciples cry out for his help, little knowing that they, too, are "crying out to their own God." It is possible, of course, that the average listener in Mark's audience may have missed these allusions.

(2) There may also be an allusion to Psalm 107:23–29, where merchants in a storm at sea "cried out to the LORD in their trouble, and he brought them out of their distress. He stilled the storm to a whisper; the waves of the sea were hushed" (vv. 28–29). The parallels in language are subtle here, but they may be enough to recall this dramatic passage. If so, there is a further subtlety. Just as Mark 1:3 transformed the quotation from Isaiah 40:3 by casting Jesus in the role of the "Lord," so the allusion to Psalm 107 casts Jesus in the role of "the LORD," whose redemptive acts are loudly and gloriously sung.

(3) The words of rebuke Jesus wields against the winds in verse 39 are imported from the technical vocabulary for exorcism. Do we have here mastery not only of nature, but of demonic forces as well? The winds that threaten the boat seem to howl with the fury of the demonic (note the exorcism of the Gerasene demoniac that follows in 5:1–20). Similarly, the stilling of the storm follows loosely but powerfully on the heels of Jesus' saying in 3:27 that "no one can enter a strong man's house and carry off his possessions unless he first ties up the strong man." Mark could hardly have made a more fitting transition to the story of the Gerasene demoniac.

Indeed, the connection between the two stories may be closer to the surface than even this thematic link. The stilling of the storm closes in 4:41 with an unanswered question: "Who is this? Even the wind and the waves obey him!" But by nature, readers are uncomfortable with questions left unanswered, so that the reader is prompted to provide the answer that has eluded the disciples' failing grasp: "This is Jesus, Son of God." That response—perhaps made subliminally—is echoed and validated by the words of Legion only seven verses later: "What do you want with me, Jesus, Son of the Most High God?" (5:7).

2.6.2. The Gerasene Demoniac (5:1–20). The story of the Gerasene demoniac is one of the longest and most frightening stories in the Gospel of Mark. All of the traditional elements of the miracle form are present here (see "Miracle Form" at sec. 2.2.3), though they are each distended beyond all norms. The story also contains unusual and striking elements. There is a strange exchange between Jesus and the demon(s), in which the demon uses the language of exorcism in an attempt to control Jesus: "Swear to God that you won't torture me!" (vv. 7–10). The townspeople are frightened at this miracle (vv. 14–17); certainly this twists the standard form of the "acclamation" into a strange new shape. Jesus seems to violate the messianic secret (see "The Messianic Secret" at sec. 2.2.5) as he sends the demoniac home to "tell them how much the Lord has done for you, and how he has had mercy on you" (vv. 19–20).

The result is a narrative that is both convoluted and spectral. It is as if Mark set about to sketch this exorcism in large strokes, and then went on to fill in the spaces with extra attention to detail. Not only does the wealth of detail slow the plot, it makes it more visual, so that the story that unfolds is striking for its descriptive imagery.

It is important that this story follows closely on the heels of the stilling of the storm. Because that miracle story contains echoes of exorcism language (see comments on 4:35–41), the reader is already attuned to the presence of the demonic. This is the setting in which the story commences in 5:1–5. As with most other miracle stories, this one begins with a description of the problem, a kind of "before" picture (vv. 3–5). This description is unusual for its vivid detail. That detail sets the stage for a contrast with verse 15, in which the demoniac is shown "sitting there, dressed and in his right mind." Thus Mark demonstrates the great power of Jesus' *word*, which is shown to be more powerful than the protective measures the townspeople had taken, all of which had failed to control the demon.

Between these two moments in the narrative stands the strange exchange between Jesus and the demoniac in verses 6–12. The fact that the demoniac "fell on his knees" before Jesus (v. 6, NIV) should not be taken as an expression of worship, but rather of obeisance or homage, an acknowledgment that one is in the presence of a greater power. The demon's language deepens the obeisance. It "begs" Jesus repeatedly, once in verse 7 ("Swear to God that you won't torture me"), again in verse 10 ("he begged Jesus again and again not to send them out of the area"), then again in verse 12 ("The demons begged Jesus, 'Send us among the pigs'"). The imagery is densely packed, with repeated references to submission and humiliation.

Mingled with the imagery of obeisance is the fact that the demon attempts to threaten and dominate Jesus by blurting out his name and title (v. 7) and by claiming to be named "Legion ... for we are many" (v. 9). Perhaps most conspicuous here is the demon's use of exorcism language in its address to Jesus: "I adjure you by God, do not torment me" (v. 7, RSV). This expression is a technical phrase usually used by exorcists in the performance of exorcism (e.g., Acts 19:13). How strange that such language should be used by a *demon*! And how strange that *Jesus* should grant the request of the demon in verse 13. These images are fused together in a kind of narrative puzzle: More is going on than meets the eye, but what?

That "something more" is the battle for a human soul. In the struggle between the townspeople, the man, and the demon, it is clear who has thus far been the victor. The savage power of the demonic is epitomized in the broken shackles and in this skulking human animal, who tears at his own flesh and howls out his agony in a graveyard at night.

The point is that Jesus does not see a human animal but a human being, who has been ravaged by this vicious and violent spirit. Mark allows that human voice to pierce the shrill exchange in verses 7–10. For example, the grammar leaves unclear who is speaking in verse 10: "And he begged Jesus again and again not to send them out of the area." Who is begging Jesus here—the demon or the man, or both? Perhaps behind the demon's voice Jesus hears the cry of the human being, a child of God who has been driven out of the city and left to rot in a cemetery.

Miracle stories usually end in some proof that a miracle actually happened and an acclamation of the crowd, both of which validate the storyteller's report by providing objective evidence and testimony. Here these two functions are served initially by the frenzied stam-

In this region east of the Sea of Galilee, Jesus healed a man possessed by demons by granting the demons' request to be sent "among the pigs." The pigs ran squealing down the hillside, into the lake, and drowned.

ede of the pigs (v. 13), the terror of the herds-en (v. 14) and townspeople (vv. 15, 17), and e dramatic change in the demoniac, who now ts quietly, "dressed and in his right mind" . 15). The reaction of the townspeople clearly iows a twist on the form of the acclamation: The people began to plead with Jesus to leave eir region."

Why are they afraid? On the surface of it, sus' presence here has exchanged one cata-rophe for another, and the loss of the pigs is equently cited as the reason for their desire to rid of him. But there is another reason, one oser to Mark's rhetorical strategy. Verse 17 arallels a pivotal verse in the stilling of the orm story: They wish to be rid of Jesus ecause they are terrified *of him* (cf. 4:40–41). oth the loss of the pigs and the shock of the emoniac, seated and in his right mind, are evi-ence that Jesus has superhuman power. Cer-inly his power exceeds theirs, but they do not now from whence it proceeds or what its dis-osition is toward them. The loss of the pigs is atastrophic from their point of view, and it sug-ests that the power is somehow malevolent. he fact that they are Gentiles who keep pigs, hile Jesus is a Jew, for whom pigs are offen-ve, only deepens their confusion and fear.

Thus, there are several lines of tension in this story—tension between Jesus and the legion of demons, tension between Jesus and the townspeople, tension between the demoniac and the townspeople. Each line strains against the others, so that from the moment Jesus appears on the scene the atmosphere is increasingly charged. Little wonder that the townspeople panic!

The complex of tensions is finally resolved when the former demoniac requests permission to "go with" Jesus (v. 18). The fact that this is the language of Christian discipleship (cf. 3:14) predisposes the reader to hear this request as an appropriate response to what has happened. But Jesus refuses and sends the man home. Why? Mark does not say. He leaves that matter to the reader's speculation. But he does offer guidelines in verses 19–20. In these verses, too, the language is clearly Christian. The message is to be proclaimed in the Decapolis, that is, among the Gentiles. Perhaps Mark wants to make clear that the message of the gospel—including liberation from the forces of demonic activity—is also for Gentiles. He wants to show his readers a Jesus who offers a living source of reassurance to the townspeople too, townspeople whose only encounter with Jesus had left them confused and terrified.

I have elsewhere argued that the mastery of the demonic is a controlling theme in Mark (see comments on 1:12–13; 3:22–30). This principle of the kingdom acted out in 5:1–20 in a moment of redemption is all the more compelling for its spectral and frightening overtones. God is not unaware of our fears. Jesus finds himself among the ravaged and the outcast, and even in his rage for order he takes care to reassure those whose experience of the kingdom leaves them frightened and confused.

2.6.3. Jairus's Daughter/The Woman With the Hemorrhage (5:21–43). This next section of Mark includes two miracles that are intertwined. This is the first instance of something Markan scholars identify as "intercalation," and more informally as "Markan sandwiches." Other instances are 6:6b–13 [14–29] 30–31; 11:12–14 [15–19] 20–26; 14:1–2 [3–9] 10–11; 14:53–54 [55–65] 66–72.

In each of these cases, one story is started (A^1), a second story is told in its entirety (B), then the first story is finished (A^2). The result is a complex narrative in which the two stories interact with one another in important ways. Sometimes the sandwiching technique allows one story to serve as a theological commentary on the other, such as in the story of the cleansing of the temple (11:15–17), which has been sandwiched into the middle of the cursing (vv. 12–14) and the withering of the fig tree (vv. 20–26).

Other times the interaction is rhetorical, as here. The Jairus story begins (5:21–24); the story of the hemorrhaging woman is told in its entirety (vv. 25–34); then the Jairus story is completed (vv. 35–43). There are incidental parallels between the two stories: Both involve females, both involve Jesus' coming into direct contact with someone or something that is ritually unclean, and both contain the number "twelve." These, however, are of secondary importance. More to the point is the effect of the encounter with the woman in verses 25–34, which stops the movement of the plot and in that way significantly heightens the tension of the Jairus story. The painfully slow march toward Jairus's house, the interruption, and the report of the servants that the girl has died all combine to make this a most suspenseful episode.

Several elements parallel details in the stor of the Gerasene demoniac (5:1–20). Jairus i "one of the synagogue rulers," but like th demoniac he prostrates himself before Jesu (v. 22; cf. v. 6; the woman with the hemorrhag also falls down before Jesus in v. 33). Like th demoniac Jairus is presented as pleadin "earnestly" (v. 23, written in the present tens and thus denoting continuous action). Thes lines of connection establish the demoniac an Jairus as literary foils, one from the lowe point on the social scale, the other from th highest, but both desperately in need of Jesu help. In his work with the demoniac, Jesu shows his compassion for the desolate, the rav aged, and the outcast; here he moves wit equal concern for the privileged and the elit

Verses 21–24 set the scene. Jairus's reque of Jesus is ironic in the sense that he asks f more than he knows: "My little daughter i dying. Please come and put your hands on h so that she will be healed and live." This is desperate request, and it is made in a conte of deep turmoil. The crowds press in. Jairus prostrate on the ground. Everything breath despair here, and the reader is invited to sha in the desperation Jairus must have felt. Th crowd begins a slow march to Jairus's hous

The arrival of the woman on the scene sto the progress of the march. In that way the su pense is considerably heightened. The disc ples feel it. The dialogue is terse, blunt, almo accusing: "You see the people crowdin against you . . . and yet you can ask, 'Wh touched me?'" (v. 31). When Jesus appears dawdle, the suspense thickens.

Of course, the story of the woman with th hemorrhage has its own internal movement Several of the standard elements for mirac stories have been modified, apparentl because of the indelicacy of her conditio There is no formal proof here, and we ca hardly expect eyewitness testimony to valida the narrator's claim. On the other hand, th assertion that a miracle has taken place is bu tressed in several ways. The woman "felt in h body" that she had been healed (v. 29). Sim larly, Jesus "realized that power had gone o from him" (v. 30a).

These are both "inside views," but they a strong enough to become externalized and th publicly visible. Jesus is willing to stop th movement of the crowd, even to delay his tr to an emergency, in order to find out what has happened (v. 30b); and the woman, despite her terror, comes forward to confess "the whole truth" (v. 33). Finally, the story ends with an authoritative pronouncement, validating both the woman's faith and the miracle (v. 34). The "proof" of the miracle is thus accomplished—first by repetition, then by agreement between the woman and Jesus, then by an authoritative pronouncement.

Jairus's servants now arrive. There is an urgent exchange. The story has by this time reached the level of frenzy. Jesus takes only the inner circle of disciples (v. 37) and makes his way to Jairus's house. The crowds have presumably been left behind (is such a thing possible?), and their place has been taken by mourners, already working the scene at Jairus's house (v. 38). Note the sudden reversal that takes place in verses 38–40. The mourners wail and lament; then, in response to the word that Jesus pronounces in verse 39 ("The child is not dead but asleep"), they instantly change to derision. Jesus' words may perhaps here be understood as subtle irony. True, the girl is literally dead; the whole movement of the plot depends on it. Jesus is not rejecting that notion, but is superimposing on it a secondary—or perhaps better, a new primary—frame of reference. Death is not final or ultimate. Tragedy may well be an occasion of mercy and grace, even when the situation is as hopeless as this is.

The fact that Jesus then expels the mourners may be symbolic, but in the narrative it also serves as a simple exclusionary tactic. Because of their disbelief they are prevented from viewing a miracle of immense significance. Here we may have a literal parallel to Jesus' explanation of the parables in 4:11–12: "To those on the outside everything is said in [riddles]" (see comments on those verses). Jesus' words are true not only figuratively, but also literally.

The intercalation of the two stories provides occasion for a different kind of literary foil. As the stories progress, the point of comparison for Jairus shifts from his differences from the demoniac to his differences from the woman. Both Jairus and the woman fall at Jesus' feet, although the effect of the gesture is somewhat different in each case. The woman falls at Jesus' feet out of fear of punishment for her unseemly act of having touched his clothes; Jairus falls as a way of expressing deference in a moment of extreme crisis. Yet the reader senses that Jairus, the ruler of the synagogue, must learn from the woman and must be prepared, by her healing, for the raising of his daughter.

2.7. Salvation to the Gentiles (Subtheme: A Prophet and More Than a Prophet) (6:1–8:30)

Two major themes are intertwined through the following narrative. (1) The first is the identification of Jesus as a prophet to the Gentiles. (a) Jesus identifies himself as a prophet (6:4). (b) The disciples go on a kind of "training mission" (6:6b–13), much like the schools of prophets in the Old Testament. (c) In the public's attempt to make sense of Jesus' identity (6:14–16), they see him as a new figure within the prophetic movement, similar to John (see secs. 2.1.1 and 2.1.2). (d) Like Elijah and Elisha, Jesus provides miraculous bread in the desert (6:30–44) and extends the blessings of salvation to Gentiles (7:24–37; 8:1–10). These affirmations come in response to the question raised in 6:3—"Isn't this the carpenter?"—and implicitly place Jesus within the framework of the restoration of the prophetic movement. As the reader already knows and as the disciples finally come to see in 8:27–30, the designation *prophet*, while true, is not the whole truth: Jesus is also the Messiah. He is a prophet, yet more than a prophet.

(2) Intertwined with this first theme is a set of allusions to the Lord's Supper. These references are clear when we consider the complex set of difficulties with which the section is riddled. (a) The first and most obvious is the apparent cipher in 6:52: The disciples were terrified when they saw Jesus walking on the sea because "they had not understood about the loaves." What is it about the loaves that, had the disciples understood it, they would not have been afraid to see Jesus walking on the water? Why does Mark ascribe their failure because "their hearts were hardened"? Mark does not tell his reader these things because he expects his reader to come to the story with that knowledge in hand.

(b) In 7:24–30 Mark tells us the story of a Syrophoenician woman who begged Jesus to exorcise a demon from her daughter. On the surface of it, Jesus' reply is offensive: "First let the children eat all they want . . . for it is not right to take the children's bread and toss it to their dogs." Is Jesus being racist here? And why does he say "bread" instead of "meat"? Dogs eat meat, not bread.

(c) In 8:4 the disciples ask Jesus "where in this remote place can anyone get enough bread to feed [the crowds]?" In this context their question makes little sense. Jesus had only moments before fed a larger crowd with fewer provisions (6:30–44).

(d) In 8:14 Mark tells us that the disciples had forgotten to bring bread, "except for one loaf they had with them in the boat." Yet in 8:16 they appear to have no bread at all. Which is it? One loaf or none?

(e) Finally, a series of rhetorical questions in 8:14–21 revisits the disciples' failure to understand something important about the bread in the two feeding miracles, and one has the distinct impression that the reader is expected to get what the disciples miss.

But what is that? Mark provides the reader with a series of clues. (a) Clearly the most visible clue is the preoccupation with "bread" (*artos*), a word that occurs seventeen times in this section and only three times elsewhere in Mark. Each of the problem passages listed above has something to do with bread. In the following discussion I will argue that for Mark and his reader, the *artos* of the two feeding miracles (6:30–44; 8:1–9) has become connected to the overarching theme of the communion table. *Artos* functions as a symbolic element in the narrative.

(b) Mark is preoccupied with elements that defile, which stands as the central movement of the plot in chapter 7 and thus forms a kind of turning point in the section as a whole. The narrative moves from defiled hands (7:1–8) to defiled hearts (7:14–23) to defiled people (7:24–30). An important expression of this concern is a subsidiary focus on Gentiles throughout this section of the Gospel.

(c) There is a heightened preoccupation with Jesus' identity in this section. Indeed, it opens and closes with this question, for the rejection at Nazareth in 6:1–6 forms an inclusion with the story of Peter's confession in 8:27–30. Although these two stories are quite different in their structure, they are parallel in their concern for Jesus' identity. In 6:2–3 the townspeople at Nazareth raise the question: "Where did this man get these things? . . . Isn't this the carpenter?" That question is raised again in 6:14–16 and is finally answered by Peter 8:27–30. "Who do you say I am?" Jesus asks; Peter replies, only half-insightfully, "You are the Christ" (v. 29).

These three clues to Mark's intent are closely intertwined. For example, there are subtle connections between the question of Jesus' identity and the theme of the Lord's Supper. For example, if the bread metaphorically represents the communion table and the informed reader knows that by breaking it Jesus "breaks his own body," then the preoccupation with the bread throughout the narrative is also connected in subtle but important ways to the question of his identity. Mark may be asking his reader to recognize by inference something that John tells his reader outright—that Jesus is "the bread of life" (John 6:35–40). Mark expects his readers to make that connection from these admittedly subtler clues. Jesus is himself the "one loaf" in the boat (cf. Mark 8:14 with John 6:25–59).

The question of the Lord's Supper is also connected in important ways to the question of defilement. It is important that the feeding of the five thousand takes place in Galilee, which is Jewish territory, while the feeding of the four thousand takes place in the Decapolis, which is Gentile territory. Indeed, Jesus has taken an awkward, contrived route, which appears deliberately to skirt the primarily Jewish territory of central Galilee (7:31). Mark seems to be signaling his reader that the blessings of salvation go also to the Gentiles, a critical narrative trap that validates the Gentile mission. Little wonder, then, that the opening of the section begins with the rejection of Jesus in his own hometown (6:1–6) and with Jesus' response: "Only in his hometown, among his relatives and in his own house is a prophet without honor" (v. 4).

To the modern evangelical reader all of this may appear unduly speculative. I suggest, however, that we come to the text with certain blind spots. (1) We bring our own repertoire of skills from our own church life, and these do not always overlap the skills Mark's reader would have brought to his stories. For example, almost all Protestant churches recite the elements of the Lord's Supper in the tradition

ınded down in 1 Corinthians 11:23–26, while
ſark's church appears to have observed a dif-
·rent tradition altogether (cf. Mark 14:22–
5). The language of the feeding stories closely
ırallels Mark's story of the Last Supper, but
ıis is harder for us to see because we are more
:customed to reading Paul's version.

(2) Our devotional and homiletical habits
ıve led us to read these stories in isolation
om one another and thus we miss the ways in
hich their messages share common themes
ıat resonate to bring out deeper theological
ıances. My argument here is that Mark
‹pected his reader to hear or read the narra-
ve as a connected, integrated whole, in which
ıe parts pile up on one another by the
ıevitable cadence of the lector's voice.

(3) Our preoccupation with the historicity
f the narrative makes us uncomfortable with
ıe idea that Mark himself may have been
ıore mystical. It is all right, we argue, to
elieve that the stories happened just as they
·e described, but it is more troubling to sup-
ɔse that Mark thought they might have been
ıeaningful on some other plane.

These are all difficulties to be overcome,
ıt when they are taken together, they give
ıape to and form the most basic issues of bib-
cal interpretation. They suggest that our stan-
ırd ways of reading the Bible may have
ıasked from us important and vibrant ele-
ıents of early Christian life. Those ele-
ıents—deep tension over Jesus' identity,
ıgorous discussion over the place of Gentiles in the economy of salvation, spirited wrestling over issues of taboo, law, right and wrong, uncleanness and defilement—all suggest a church in which such issues were taken with great seriousness. The sections that follow take their position on such questions; in doing so they address issues that may well have been close to the bone for Mark and his church.

2.7.1. Jesus Is Rejected at Nazareth (6:1–6a). The story of the rejection at Nazareth, by raising the question of Jesus' identity and by its heightened interest in his rejection, launches the next major section of Mark. But it is also intimately connected to the section that precedes. The context and the initial genre signals in verse 2 tell the reader to expect a miracle, but that expectation will be dramatically disrupted before the story reaches its climax in verse 6.

Everything depends on sequence here. The story will end with a stunning reversal of expectations, but the reader—taking in the story one element after another—does not know at first that this is coming. Instead, it begins on a positive note: Jesus has returned "to his own country" (RSV), accompanied by his disciples. We are accustomed to calling this story "the rejection at Nazareth," but Mark himself does not specify that this is where the visit took place. His reason for leaving the question open, I suspect, is that by using the word *patris* ("hometown") in verse 1, he can set the reader up to hear Jesus' aphorism about rejection in verse 4: "Only in his hometown [*patris*] . . . is a prophet without honor."

Though Nazareth was Jesus' home, the people of the city could not believe that "the carpenter" could teach at the synagogue and perform miracles. In fact, they were offended. Jesus said, "Only in his hometown . . . is a prophet without honor."

On the Sabbath Jesus "began to teach" in the synagogue (v. 2). Mark does not tell us the content of Jesus' teaching, but by this time the reader has come to understand that term in a broad sense as including everything about Jesus' ministry. In 1:22–28 teaching is specifically associated with an exorcism; in 2:13–15, with Jesus' embrace of religious and social outcasts. Perhaps the most vivid connections here are with the exorcism in the synagogue in 1:21–28. The two stories open with almost identical language:

Mark 1:21–22	Mark 6:1–2
They went	Jesus . . . went . . . accompanied by his disciples
to Capernaum	to his hometown
and when the Sabbath came	When the Sabbath came
Jesus went into the synagogue and began to teach	he began to teach in the synagogue
The people were amazed	and many who heard him were amazed

The point of the comparison here is that the parallels in wording show that the opening lines of the Nazareth story do not contain any intimations of the rejection that is coming, and they leave the narrative open to the broadest interpretation of Jesus' teaching. As chapter 6 opens, everything *appears* positive: When Jesus teaches, astonishing things happen. Drawing on these genre signals, the reader anticipates that a miracle will follow. Moreover, the present story comes after a series of miracle stories that have occupied the reader's attention since the stilling of the storm in 4:35–41. These stories set up a kind of rhythm in the narrative—the storm, the exorcism of the Gerasene demoniac (5:1–20), the raising of Jairus's daughter (5:21–24, 35–43), and the healing of a woman with a hemorrhage (5:25–34). Without any summary or ballast line to signal the reader that the miracle section has drawn to a close, the reader naturally anticipates another miracle here.

Thus, the astonishment of the townspeople appears at first to be simple wonderment. Note that they connect Jesus' *miracles* with his *wisdom* (v. 2b), both of which have thus far had positive associations in the narrative. The question about Jesus' family appears to be positive as well: This is the carpenter, one of o own, finally made good. All of that enc abruptly with a blunt Markan aside at the er of verse 3: "And they took offense at him The verb used here (*skandalizomai*) is a stror word in Mark (see 9:42–50).

The full force of the rejection now spring on the reader like a trap. The final line of ver 3 makes the reader scramble: The astonis ment is not admiration, but incredulity. Tl question about Jesus' family is an expressic of social outrage, outrage motivated perhap by social warrants against stepping beyor one's station. Jesus is a peasant after all, wh right has he to make such grandiose claims these? The remark about his parentage in ver 3 suddenly takes on a negative coloring: The call Jesus "Mary's son" rather than referring his father, as one would expect of a Semit patronymic. Are they intimating that there something suspicious about his parentage? H his father repudiated him, just as the oth members of his family appear to have repud ated him (see 3:21)? Is Jesus illegitimate? D we even *know* who his father is? These que tions are raised, but the narrative does answ them. The suspicions mount.

The reader's work now suddenly deepe in timbre and complexity, as noted by a shift genre signals. Instead of the expected miracl Mark writes a pronouncement story (see "Tl Form of Pronouncement Stories" at sec. 2.3 The shift does not drown out the intimations the miraculous, however. The pronounceme in verse 4 comes where the miracle should b but it comes as an explanation of Jesus' *failu* to do miracles! In this way, the story also pick up and deepens a dimension of the Jairus sto that it follows: There the people laughe (5:40), here they sneer (6:2–3). There, becau of their laughter, the onlookers were expelle from the house (5:40) and thus prevented fro seeing a miracle of truly astonishing propo tions; here, because of their disbelief, Jesu hands are tied almost completely: "He cou not do any miracles there" (6:5).

Mark drives the point home in verse 6 b evoking the standard form for miracle stori one last time, though here, too, with a dramat reversal. Miracles usually end with an expre sion of astonishment, which serves to valida the miracle by reporting the reactions of ey witnesses. Here, however, we have the absolu astonishment *of Jesus* at *their* failure to believe! Coming as it does immediately after the raising of Jairus's daughter, Mark's report that Jesus' hands are tied in Nazareth suggests to the reader that disbelief is more deadly than death itself.

The story of the rejection at Nazareth thus launches a new major section (see comments on sec. 2.6). Here we will discuss only those elements that connect with what follows as the narrative changes direction. There are two: (1) the question about Jesus' identity, raised here in dramatic terms (vv. 2–3); (2) the rejection itself, a clear preoccupation since most of the details about this story that have been preserved connect with it. Jesus' countrymen are amazed (v. 2a); they question his credentials (vv. 2b–3a); they take offense (v. 3b); Jesus interprets the rejection, using what is most likely a traditional folk saying (v. 4); his hands are tied (v. 5); and, in a dramatic reversal of miracle form, he himself is astonished by their unbelief (v. 6).

By interlacing the twin elements of the questioning after Jesus' identity and the theme of rejection, Mark nudges his reader in the direction of faith; there is, after all, a right way to ask the question of who Jesus is, and there is a wrong way. The reader who reads at cross-purposes may miss the point altogether and may find that, like the characters inside the story, he or she has tied God's hands. Both of these elements direct the reader's attention to questions that will become increasingly important as the narrative changes direction.

Before we leave this section, we should try to read it with sympathies attuned to the suffering of Mark's own church. When Jesus is rejected by his hometown, those readers who have experienced a loss of family or a disrupted friendship because of faith in Jesus bring special sensitivities to the reading; they understand what it means to be "without honor" in one's own house (v. 4). This is a theme to which Mark repeatedly turns. Modern readers may have difficulty understanding just how traumatic it would have been for an individual in the ancient world to have been cut off from family. To the ancients, one's very identity was embedded in the family unit, and to leave it voluntarily was not only dangerous; but disgraceful as well. One literally dishonored one's parents and one's self. In the same way, to be ostracized by one's family was to be publicly stigmatized (see comments on 3:31–35). Both internal and external evidence suggests that Mark's readers have experienced trauma of this sort. We can only guess at its magnitude.

This means, of course, that Mark's readers have been forced to declare loyalties and have had to make painful choices. In the face of this terrible shock, Mark offers an important word of comfort: What reader has lost everything, and Jesus has not also? What reader has been rejected by those who should know him best, and Jesus has not suffered the same? In the next major section (8:22–10:52), which focuses on the cost of discipleship, and in the Olivet Discourse (13:1–37), which places the sufferings of the Church in an eschatological context, Mark will raise again the question of lost family. The issue is never one of losing one's family for any frivolous reason, but always of responding to the higher claims of the gospel. Indeed, the point may be exactly that: If the most precious thing in the world, one's identity, is one's connection to one's family, how much must the gospel be worth if it is to be valued above even that!

In this context this section holds wider theological implications. Jesus has been rejected by Israel; as the Gospel of John would say, "He came to that which was his own, but his own did not receive him" (John 1:11). What better way to launch a section of the narrative that shows the legitimacy of Jesus' mission to the Gentiles?

2.7.2. The Commissioning of the Twelve (6:6b–13). The story of the commissioning of the Twelve was added here because of its importance to the general theme Mark is developing throughout this unit—the legitimacy of the mission to the Gentiles. The present section portrays the sharp edge that leads up to the point that one must have the freedom to cut one's losses, to walk away, to leave the unrepentant and unaccepting, and to let them live with the consequences of their decisions. In the rejection at Nazareth Mark dealt with what it is like to be rejected by one's family and friends. Here he turns the question of rejection on its head. In this respect, the thrust of verse 11 picks up the bitter tone of Jesus' proverb in verse 4.

For their part, the disciples must be without ulterior motives in the manner in which they conduct their mission. The refinement of motives is to be accomplished by a rather delicate balancing act: The instructions described in verses 8–9 are designed to make the disciples dependent on their hosts and thus without resources for manipulating social situations. At the same time, the prohibition against abandoning one's original host at each village is designed to make the disciples independent of pressure to move to more socially acceptable or influential housing should it be offered.

These two sets of prohibitions thus stand in a kind of dynamic tension. One prevents the disciple from manipulating the social situation, while the other prevents him from being manipulated. Taken together they enable the missionary to concentrate without distraction on the proclamation of the gospel, the care for the sick, and the casting out of unclean spirits (vv. 12–13).

This section has to do with more than social etiquette. Jesus' concern to transcend social pressures reflects an important dimension of the gospel. Two aspects of the cultural background combine to bring that dimension into clearer focus. (1) Throughout the ancient world hospitality for strangers was a universally binding social and moral obligation. (2) Also, the social order was taken with great seriousness because it was thought to mirror the natural order. One's social status was to be accepted, not only as the result of economic and political fortunes, but because it was somehow ordered into the structure of reality itself that there should be social classes. The moral thing was to remain where one was. Even today in the Middle East villages maintain social hierarchies going back generations. For a person to move up or down the social scale is shameful because it reflects an affront to the moral order.

These two social realities combine to provide the background of Jesus' concern that the disciples not abandon their original hosts. Indeed, in a world that took these obligations seriously, for a traveling evangelist to abandon an original host for a more influential house would impeach the adequacy of his hospitality and subject him and his house to public ridicule. This, of course, is contrary to the spirit of the gospel.

Verse 11 makes clear that Jesus' words are not without their sharper edge, and it is probably this sharper edge that accounts for the presence of the section at this point in the narrative: Where the host—or for that matter, anyone in a place—refuses to welcome the missionary, where they refuse to hear the gospel, they should indeed be brought into public condemnation. The symbolic act of shaking off the dust of one's feet represents the strongest possible form of public rebuke. The gospel is not only a word of grace, but in the movements of its emissaries it is also a parable of judgment.

2.7.3. Opinions Regarding Jesus (6:14–16). This brief section serves as a transition into the story of the beheading of John the Baptist. The basic elements will be repeated in 8:27–30. They permit the reader to sketch an impression of the rapidly growing public speculation about Jesus' identity and mission. Most interesting is Herod's speculation that Jesus was "John [the Baptist] ... raised from the dead" (v. 16).

It is well known that Herod was a superstitious man, and the comment recorded here may have been intended literally. It may well be, however, that the comment was a more generalized remark about how hard it is to rid the countryside of dangerous people like John. From Herod's perspective, the enormous popular support for Jesus is simply an extension of the support John had received. In any case, the remark offers a glimpse into the mind of an exasperated and apprehensive man. The death of John that follows (vv. 17–29) will demonstrate that Herod was the kind of man who barely maintained a kind of white-knuckled control over his own household, just as it shows all the more clearly the depths to which such a man could sink.

2.7.4. The Death of John the Baptist (6:17–29). This brief and horrifying story does not fit neatly into the section. Its inclusion here may have been prompted by the recounting of speculations about Jesus' identity in verses 14–16, especially the comment that some people thought Jesus was "John the Baptist ... raised from the dead." Mark nowhere else describes the events surrounding John's death. There is a hint of that in his comment in 1:14 that Jesus began his ministry "after John was put in prison," but this is only a hint (this verse can also be read that Jesus began his ministry "after John had been handed over *to the exe* *utioner*"). In any case, the death of John seems to have captured the imagination of the tradition.

This is a rambling and gruesome tale, but marvelously told. I have elsewhere described the rhetoric of this tale in terms of the development of its characterization of John and Herod (Camery-Hoggatt, 1995, 144–46). In this form of dramatic irony, the ironic hero is pitted against the pretender. The self-effacing character of the Baptist has been established already with respect to Jesus (1:7–8). He plays only a minor role in this story as well—his only spoken part is a remembered condemnation of Herod's adulterous relationship with his sister-in-law, Herodias. Yet the Baptist is a moral giant here; by contrast Herod is undone in the moral judgment of the reader. He is a moral idiot, stumbling headlong into his own undoing.

The story could also be analyzed in terms of its rhetorical style. Many scholars have suggested sensuality in the daughter's dance. If so, Mark has played that aspect down considerably. He reports only that "she *pleased* Herod and his dinner guests" (v. 22). One wonders why the sexual innuendo does not lie closer to the surface, but then the whole story is permeated with understatement: "Herodias nursed a grudge against John" (v. 19; she positively *hated* him); "it is not lawful for you to have your brother's wife" (v. 18; everybody knew that; surely John's language was stronger); "she *pleased* Herod and his dinner guests" (v. 22). Much has been left unsaid, but the attentive listener can hardly fail to hear behind the word "banquet" something crass enough for the tastes of military men (v. 21).

At the same time, there are touches of the preposterous here. Couched in the context of repeated understatement, Herod's offer to the girl becomes an unbelievable—and impossible—reward for a night's dance (v. 22). That is precisely the point. The "king" makes her an astonishing offer, unsolicited: "Ask me for anything you want, and I'll give it to you . . . up to half my kingdom." Or was it unsolicited? Was not the dance itself a solicitation? If that were the case, then the king's offer makes perfect sense. Mark would have us know that the old lecher is not rewarding her for a passing pleasure, he is asking her price for something more.

From her perspective and from that of her mother, a sword to the throat of the Baptist is a master stroke. John, it seems, is the one voice courageous enough to condemn Herod publicly for what he did. Herodias's daughter cannot with ease take Herod up on his offer; she cannot, that is, while John remains alive. With John dead, there may be other offers. With John dead, Herod's conscience dies, too. Herod equivocates, the tension mounts. The consequences are unbelievable. It seems equally unbelievable that Herodias would exploit a situation like that; this is her daughter, after all, and her husband. But that Herodias could promote such a liaison is no more incredible than her part in the dance. She appears not to have had any scruples at all.

There is another line of tension in this story that also requires comment before we leave: Herod and Herodias are set in contrast by the parallel between verses 19 and 20: "Herodias nursed a grudge against John and wanted to kill him," whereas "Herod feared John and protected him." These are both inside views. They inform the reader of critical tension in the story's underlying dynamic structures. It is this tension that establishes the backdrop of John's execution, in the process assassinating the character of Herod. The old king has been outfoxed, humiliated in a moment of passion and moral confusion; the fact that he went forward with the execution shows that he lacked both the moral clarity and the personal courage to extricate himself from his wife's trap.

Thus, the story stands on its own as a gruesome indictment of a political buffoon. Why has Mark invested this much space in such a horrifying tale? Why is this here? (1) Perhaps remotely, it may be the foreground for the controversy between Jesus and the Pharisees in 10:2–12. That controversy will focus on the same question—divorce—and it takes place in "Judea and across the Jordan," that is, in the territory of the same Herod Antipas. For the reader who knows that the traditional site of John's execution is the fortress of Machaerus, across the Jordan, the Pharisees' demand that Jesus take a public position on divorce *in that location* rings with greater danger because Mark has included *this* story *here*.

(2) More powerfully, as rambling and unedifying as it is, the death of John the Baptist somehow prepares for the death of Jesus. Jesus

and John are so intimately connected that the fate of the one foreshadows the fate of the other; John's plot is Jesus' plot in miniature. The death of John casts a deep and lasting shadow over the narrative, a shadow that only becomes deeper and more ominous as the opposition against Jesus mounts.

But the element of the ironic somehow also remains here. Like John, Jesus will assume the role of ironic hero, who will bring the opposition to its knees. Like John, he will be silent at his trial, but even his silence will speak volumes. More important, he will demonstrate by a supreme act of sacrifice the deeply ironic truth that in the power of God more is going on than meets the eye.

2.7.5. The Return of the Twelve (6:30–31). This brief transition returns the reader to the primary plot and prepares and sets the context for the feeding of the five thousand that follows. In only one other place are Jesus' disciples described as "apostles" (3:14). No doubt here the word is to distinguish Jesus' followers from the disciples of John the Baptist mentioned in the previous verse (6:29).

2.7.6. The Feeding of the Five Thousand (6:32–44). This miracle is closely connected with the feeding of the four thousand in 8:1–10 (see comments there). The present miracle is one of the most symbolically overloaded stories in the Gospel of Mark, though this is not immediately evident because the symbols grow on the reader gradually, accumulating a little at a time. The reading process is thus a process of discovery. Their cumulative weight will burst through as a fresh awareness that more is going on than meets the eye.

At the center of the symbols is the Greek word *artos*, which may be translated either "bread" or "loaf." As we saw in the opening discussion of the larger section (see above, sec. 2.7), this word eventually becomes a clear, though oblique, reference to Jesus, the Bread of Life, the One Loaf with the disciples in the boat (see 8:14–21). If we see Jesus as the "loaf," then the story takes on important nuances of the Last Supper. Those nuances are reinforced by nearly direct allusions to the language of the Supper—not in Paul's version, to which we are accustomed, but to the version found in 14:22–25, with which Mark and his reader would have been more familiar. It is worth noting that the set of parallels includes the language of Mark's other feeding story, the feeding of the four thousand, in 8:1–11. Indeed, the parallels are quite striking:

6:41	8:6	14:22
Taking the five loaves (*labon tous . . . artous*) and the two fish and looking up to heaven, he gave thanks (*eulogesen*) and broke the loaves (*kateklasen tous artous*). Then he gave them to his disciples (*kai edidou tois mathetais autou*). . . .	When he had taken the seven loaves (*labon tous . . . artous*) and given thanks (*eucharistesas*), he broke them (*eklasen*) and gave them to his disciples (*kai edidou tois mathetais autou*). . . .	While they were eating, Jesus took bread (*labon arton*), gave thanks (*eulogesas*) and broke it (*eklasen*), and gave it to his disciples (*kai edoken autois*). . . .

The reader of Mark is clearly expected to hear various allusions to the Lord's Supper in the stories of the two feedings. These elements will launch the reader into a reflection on the theological significance of the feedings, but it will do so by situating that reflection within the larger framework of a eucharistic Christology.

If this is so, then, Jesus' question to the disciples in verse 38 ("How many loaves do you have?") is a loaded question, just as the command in verse 37 that the disciples should "give them something to eat" is implicitly a command to mission. Though the disciples understandably miss the allusion, the reader is expected to catch it. Several details in the story combine to focus attention on the disciples' failure to recognize this aspect of their experience. In verses 35–36 the disciples themselves pose the question of how to feed the growing throngs, but what informs their question? Is it not that they failed to see Jesus himself in his identity as the Bread? His instruction in verse 37 prompts a similar uncomprehending response: "That would take eight months of a man's wages."

Mark later makes explicit commentary that indicates the manner in which he expected his reader to develop the hints. For example, in 8:4 Jesus is again confronted with a large crowd, and the disciples will ask another uncomprehending question: "Where in this remote place can anyone get enough bread to feed them?" Coming so soon after the miraculous feeding of more people with fewer provisions, the question is astonishing. Through such details

Mark tells how Jesus on two occasions miraculously fed thousands. He fed five thousand the first time with only five loaves of bread and two fish. The second feeding, Mark wrote, was for four thousand men. That time they started with seven loaves of bread and a few fish, yet had seven baskets full of food left over. This mosaic is at Tabgha, on the western shore of the Sea of Galilee.

Mark shows his reader something about Jesus' identity he fully expects the reader to understand. In 6:52, he says it directly: After the disciples are terrified when they see Jesus walking on the water, Mark explains their terror in terms of their failure to comprehend something about the *artous*: "They had not understood about the loaves."

There are two initial complications in this interpretation. (1) If Jesus is indeed the "one loaf . . . with them in the boat," why does the narrator go to such pains to note that there were *twelve* loaves left over after the first feeding and *seven* after the second? These numbers appear to be of major significance for Mark, because they stand at the center of the apparent riddle Jesus poses for the disciples in 8:14–21. (2) What are we to make of the fish, since so far as we know fish had no place in the early Christian Eucharist? Indeed, this is one of the ways in which the parallels between the feeding narratives and the Lord's Supper break down. But while the symbolic meaning of the fish remains an unresolved mystery, it is likely only a minor one.

The question of the multiplicity of leftover loaves of bread leads us to a different set of symbols. These have to do with ethnic differences between the two crowds, which Mark makes clear through a variety of details. The first feeding takes place in Galilee, Jewish territory; the second, in the Decapolis, Gentile territory (see 7:31). In the second feeding, Mark uses the word for general, all-purpose baskets (*spuridai*); in the first, the baskets are called *kophinoi*, typically identified as Jewish baskets. The *kophinos* was a kind of lunch basket, which orthodox Jews commonly carried to guarantee that their food was kosher. One could not, after all, trust what one might buy on the street. The Romans sometimes satirized the Jews for carrying their *kophinoi* everywhere (e.g., Juvenal, *Satires*, 3.14; 6.542). The word *kophinos* in Mark 6:43 is not to show the enormity of the miracle but to call attention to its Jewishness.

This is also a clue to the meaning of the numbers five and twelve (and, in the feeding of the four thousand, seven). Numerical metaphors are difficult for the modern mind to accept, perhaps because we use numbers as a tool of scientific precision. We ought to place ourselves in the position of Mark's authorial readers, who would have understood the numbers as metaphors. Elsewhere he has given clear indication that he expected this response (8:14–21). The number five is evocative of the five books of the Torah; the number twelve evokes the tribes of Israel; the number seven evokes the Jewish truism that seven is the number of completion, and (perhaps by extension) the belief that there are seventy nations on earth. Thus, Mark uses these numbers to reinforce this larger ethnic distinction between the two feeding narratives, in that the feeding of the five thousand was a Jewish feeding, while the feeding of the four thousand was Gentile.

Moreover, the imagery of Jesus miraculously feeding multitudes in the desert may evoke images of Elijah, who miraculously provided food for a widow and her son (1 Kings 17:8–16), and, more powerfully, of a famous miracle in which Elisha commanded his servant to give food to a hundred men (2 Kings 4:42–44). There are loose parallels between Jesus' command to the disciples in Mark 6:37 and Elisha's command to his servant to share with the people the twenty loaves of barley bread brought by a man from Baal Shalishah: "Give it to the people to eat" (2 Kings 4:42). In all three of these stories, the provisions were miraculously extended to the point of having food left over. In this way Mark places Jesus squarely within the prophetic tradition, a connection that prepares the reader for the question of Jesus' prophetic identity in the trial (14:53–65).

There are three additional nuances here. (1) The feeding of the five thousand broadens and deepens our understanding of what it means that Jesus "began teaching [the crowds]" (6:34). Indeed, the feeding is an enacted parable, with Jesus' identity as the Bread of Life serving as the parable's organizing core. (2) The fact that Jesus saw the Jewish crowds as "sheep without a shepherd" (v. 34) passes clear judgment on the Jewish authorities, who could not or would not care for the flock of God (cf. Ezek. 34). (3) The feeding of the five thousand prepares the reader to understand the feeding of the four thousand in an important way. One can say that, while the first feeding is not dependent on the second, surely the second does depend on the first.

Throughout this discussion we have moved back and forth through the narrative to sort out the repertoire of background nuances evoked by the secondary allusions to the Lord's Supper and to the literature of apocalypticism. For Mark's authorial reader, the nuances would have come down the linguistic pipeline unsorted, unfolding one element after another in a cumulative process of literary discovery. The feeding of the five thousand is an early movement in that process, and the discovery will continue to unfold as the narrative moves forward.

2.7.7. The Walking on the Water (6:45–52). This story is part of a larger complex of stories dealing with symbolic meanings in the feedings of the five thousand and the four thousand (be sure to read the comments on the entire section, beginning with 2.7).

In all four Gospels, the story of Jesus' walking on the water follows the feeding of the five thousand. The cryptic note in 6:51–52 that the disciples were "completely amazed, for they had not understood about the loaves" indicates that Mark sees a close theological connection as well. The note itself presupposes that the reader brings outside information to the reading, and I have elsewhere suggested that the outside information involves Jesus' identify as the Bread of Life. The nature and placement of 6:52 indicates Mark's expectation that by this point in the narrative the allusions to Jesus as the Bread of Life would have become conscious for the reader and could thus serve as keys to the riddle the disciples are unable to solve.

Everything in the narrative prepares for the riddle, but it does so by exploring a series of allusions and problematic questions. As the story unfolds, it begins to evoke memories of the stilling of the storm (4:35–41). It is the gist of that story, not the specific details, that come to the fore now. In the earlier story, Jesus had used exorcism language to still the storm. The fact that "the wind was against them" (6:48) reinforces the connection with the story of the stilling of the storm by recalling the exorcism language. In the earlier story, the wind is personified and hostile, perhaps even demonic.

This time, however, the disciples are alone when the wind kicks up. This may be the psychological background against which we should understand their fear at seeing a "ghost" (perhaps better, "apparition") on the water. Bear in mind that the disciples' were already disposed to interpret an apparition as an evil figure. In their mind, the demonic forces from the stilling of the storm have perhaps returned. What are they to do when Jesus is not with them? They have been given authority to cast out demons, but will it be enough?

Reference to the fourth watch of the night in verse 48 sets the time of the miracle about 3:00 A.M. More striking is the phrase "walking on the lake," which evokes a multitude of texts about the deity walking on water. When viewed against the background of these texts, the phrase connects with the reader's prior knowledge that Jesus is "Son of God," and in that way evokes the literary image of a theophany (divine appearance).

Several details of the story reinforce that image. The best known is Jesus' use of the divine name "It is I" in verse 50, to which we will turn shortly. The imagery of a theophany is the larger context in which we are to evaluate Mark's enigmatic saying that Jesus was "about to pass by them" (v. 48). This is especially odd since it appears to contradict the note in the prior sentence that Jesus "went out *to* them." What does "pass by" mean here? Several times in the Old Testament tradition, God is described as "passing by" in a show of divine majesty (e.g., Ex. 33:19, 22; 1 Kings 19:11). God "passes by" to permit a glancing view, or better, a glancing "awareness" because of the common belief that no one could look on the divine form without being destroyed. In the LXX of Amos 7:8 and 8:2, the same verb appears in a divine pronouncement that God will no more "pass by" the children of Israel, but will abandon them to their own devices.

Thus far what we have seen reinforces and deepens the impression of a theophany. What follows in verses 49–50 is therefore an implicit comment on the disciples' blindness to Jesus' true identity: They bring with them their memories of the exorcism language in chapter 4, and in their panic they conclude that what they are now seeing is an apparition of some sort. Ironically, they are seeing the opposite; although the disciples do not recognize Jesus, Mark's reader does.

Jesus calls out to the disciples, "Take courage! It is I. Don't be afraid" (v. 50). This functions on three levels. (1) At this point in the narrative it also recalls Jesus' words from 4:40: "Why are you so afraid? Do you still have no faith?" The recollection also reintroduces the disciples' unanswered question from 4:41: "Who is this? Even the wind and the waves obey him." (2) Within the narrative, verse 50 urges the disciples to recognize that their fears are unfounded. The structure of the narrative suggests that they can only do so by revising their understanding of who Jesus is. (3) The phrase Jesus speaks, "It is I," is probably an allusion to the divine name spoken by God to Moses in a theophany in Exodus 3:14, "I AM WHO I AM," which in the Greek of the LXX is spelled the same way.

When these three nuances are taken together, they suggest a subtle literary twist on an older literary form: The disciples are afraid, as people are generally afraid in theophanies, but they are afraid for the wrong reasons. Of course, the problem is not that one should be afraid for the right reasons, but rather that there is no reason for fear at all. Jesus' words to the disciples stress that fact both by repetition and by evoking a host of Old Testament texts that urge one to find faith and confidence in the victorious power of God.

Mark now supplies an explanation for what has prevented the disciples from seeing this great truth: "They had not understood about the loaves; their hearts were hardened" (v. 52). Of all the difficult passages in Mark, perhaps none is more enigmatic than this one. How do the *loaves* provide the key to the figure walking on the *water*? Roman Catholic interpreter Quentin Quesnell's conclusion (1969, 276) that the reference is a cipher pointing to the Eucharist (where life may be found) may strike Protestant sensibilities as overreaching. There is, however, much to commend it, not least of which is the series of allusions to the Last Supper embedded in the story of the feeding of the five thousand in the previous section (see comments on 6:32–44). Had the disciples seen the apparition through the eyes of faith, had they known that with God more is going on than meets the eye, had they grasped the ironic fact that even the threat of disaster does not separate one from the love of God—in Mark's terms had they "understood about the loaves"—they would have known that there was no reason for fear. Not here. Not ever.

2.7.8. The Healings at Gennesaret (6:53–56). Mark occasionally paints Jesus' movements with a broad brush and a few quick strokes (see also 1:32–34; 3:7–12; 4:33–34; 6:30–31; 7:31–37). Such summaries remind the reader that the story is representative rather than exhaustive, and they add a deep and rapid-fire quality to Jesus' movements.

2.7.9. Defilement—Traditional and Real (7:1–23). Before we launch an investigation of this long and complicated section, we should turn aside momentarily and examine one of Mark's compositional strategies: *organization by hookword*. Mark does not always follow a historical chronology in the arrangement of his material. While precise chronological notes tie the narrative together after the triumphal entry (11:1–16:8), such notes are rare in the first half of the gospel. The material appears more often organized by theme.

Sometimes in Mark, however, a thematically connected narrative is interrupted by an intrusion, prompted by some striking word or phrase in the story being told. As he wrote down a story, a certain word or phrase reminded him of another story with the same elements. Apparently he opted to include those elements right then, even though that meant disrupting an otherwise coherent theme. The phrase used for this process is *organization by hookword*. At some places it forms the major structural backbone of the narrative (see esp. sec. 3.1.9).

This organizational method tells us something of how Mark read the sources he had at his disposal. He was, after all, not only a teller of these stories but also a recipient, someone passing along a tradition that he had received, and he understood the tradition in particular ways. The long and complex section dealing with the question of defilement is bound together by the repeated hookword "tradition" (vv. 3, 5, 8, 9, 13). There is one larger, coherent narrative (in vv. 1–8 and 14–23), which is interrupted by a smaller aside (in vv. 9–13).

Let us begin with the larger story. What is at stake here is the true nature of defilement and, by implication, holiness. The explanation of Jewish customs in verses 3–4 has probably been included for the benefit of Gentile readers, some of whom would have needed an explanation. The chief actors in the story are certain Pharisees and teachers of the law "who had come from Jerusalem" (v. 1). The impression created is of a special "task force," come to investigate Jesus' practice in a somewhat formal way. The reader who knows that the end of the story is a crucifixion in Jerusalem may hear a hint of impending danger. Jesus has already done much to raise the suspicions of the authorities (see 2:1–3:6; 3:22–30). A formal inquiry will provide ammunition for later.

The present story is written as another controversy story, though Mark takes special pains to clarify the terms of the debate (see "The Form of Pronouncement Stories" at sec. 2.3). The question raised in verse 5 ("Why don't your disciples live according to the tradition of the elders?") sounds like a question that may have been raised against the members of Mark's own church. If so, Mark's readers would have a personal investment in Jesus' answer.

Jesus responds in verses 6–8 by quoting Isaiah 29:13. This language is unusually strong, even for Mark. By drawing this Old Testament text into the picture, Jesus indicates that the Pharisees and teachers of the law have abandoned a true perspective on the law and in its place have substituted a shallow, hypocritical posture. There may be a wordplay in the language here. Jesus calls the authorities "hypocrites" (from *hypocrites*, lit., "play actor"). This is a new term in Jewish religious vocabulary, perhaps derived from the introduction of theater into Jewish life. The religious leaders are "like actors [who] put on a performance for public adulation" (Batey, 1984, 564). This description is therefore consistent with what Isaiah says: "These people honor me with their lips, but their hearts are far from me." This is piety that dresses up and plays a part. It is script, but not Scripture, a masque of true piety.

As often happens in Mark, the saying is enigmatic, and the disciples receive a more concrete explanation in verses 14–23. Here Jesus declares the rules of kosher a violation of the law. In their place he substitutes an internalized ethic, rooted in the human heart rather than in external law. Jesus is convinced that the human heart or mind is the battleground of the spirits of truth and perversity (cf. also Rom. 1:29–31).

Thus the material in verses 1–8 and 14–23 stands together as an integrated and complex exploration of the nature of holiness and perversity. By opening with a challenge brought by Pharisees and teachers of the law, and by fingering these groups as the brunt of Jesus' sarcastic attack in verses 6–8, Mark makes crystal clear that he has in view a piety of a fundamentally different sort than that ratified by the Jewish authorities. The authorities have simply and profoundly asked the wrong questions; how can they hope to arrive at correct answers?

Between these two halves Mark has sandwiched a brief, almost vitriolic attack on the Pharisees for their tendency to use the letter of the law to manipulate their way around its spirit. Verse 9 opens with a wordplay: "You have a fine way of setting aside the commandments of God in order to observe your own traditions!" The irony here can be made more clear if we are permitted a few liberties in translation. The word "fine" may well ring in the readers' ears like this: "How beautifully you do an ugly thing!" or, perhaps, "You do illegality great justice."

The practice that Jesus is condemning here is documented from outside sources. The critical word is the Aramaic word *corban*, which Mark both transliterates and translates for his reader. This word may refer to a "curse," a "vow," or "something sacrificed [or given] to God." Thus, Mark translates *corban* into Greek as *doron*, which the NIV correctly renders as "a gift devoted to God." We do well to remember that these concepts are closely connected in Jewish thought. Something set aside for God is no longer to be used for any other purpose. It may even be destroyed to symbolize the totality of this principle. One can specify such a gift with a vow; just uttering the word *corban* constitutes a vow binding to God. On the basis of Numbers 30:2, such vows are binding, even if to keep them one must violate some other biblical statute.

In the case Jesus discusses here, there is a further consideration: The claims of God (i.e., those initiated by the vow) are higher than the claims of one's parents because, as is obvious, God is himself higher than one's parents. This attitude earns Jesus' excoriating remark in verse 13: "Thus you nullify the word of God by your tradition that you have handed down." The narrower point here is that the claims of God are better demonstrated in the whole of Scripture (which requires one to honor one's parents) than in the isolated instance of a personal vow.

But there is a larger point to be taken. While the discussion about *corban* is intrusive, its presence broadens out the question from a discussion of a particular instance of rabbinic food laws to include the question of law itself. Jesus' objection is not to one particular instance of rabbinic law, but to the entire interpretive framework by which that law is formulated, the tradition by which it is passed along, and the warrants by which it is enforced.

Four details of the passage reinforce this conclusion. (1) There is a generalizing comment in verses 3–4: "They observe many other traditions." (2) In verse 7 we read that Jesus is concerned about the "rules taught by men." (3) A similar theme appears in verse 13: "You do many things like that." (4) Finally, and perhaps most concretely, Jesus' own alternative ethic, his internalized ethic "of the heart," calls into question the ethic of rules that stood behind the objection of the teachers of the law and the Pharisees in the verses 2 and 5. While it does not do to read Mark in the light of Matthew, it may well be that here we have a rhetorical parallel to Matthew 5:20: "I tell you that unless your righteousness surpasses that of the Pharisees and the teachers of the law, you will certainly not enter the kingdom of heaven."

Let us pause here and consider the ways in which this story may have been heard by an ethnically mixed congregation. For Jewish members, the principles of piety Jesus sets forth would have sounded strangely familiar. Indeed, Jesus would have sounded much like a prophet, standing against the establishment but firmly within the tradition. For Gentile members, however, the thrust would have been the ways in which Jesus stands *over against* piety by legalism. The condemnation of the "teachers of the law who had come from Jerusalem" rings strangely like Luke's description of Christian Jews—Paul calls them "Judaizers"—who "came down from Judea to Antioch" to require Gentile converts to submit to circumcision (Acts 15:1–4) and adopt Jewish customs (Gal. 2:11–17).

While Luke's *account* of this conflict was written after Mark, the conflict itself came before, as the dating of Galatians demonstrates. Could it be that the contention continued and spread in the church? If so, Mark's Gentile reader would have heard Jesus' insistence on an internalized ethic with a kind of relief. Indeed, Mark himself interprets Jesus' language in the broadest possible way: "In saying this, Jesus declared all foods 'clean'" (7:19).

Overall, the thrust of this passage fits neatly into the wider theme of the progress of the gospel to include Gentiles. By definition they are considered defiled *people*. That progression will sharpen considerably in the following stories: Jesus will bring the blessings of salvation next to the family of a Greek woman, "born in Syrian Phoenicia" (7:26), and then, with a remarkable allusion to the Lord's Supper, to Gentile communities of the Decapolis (8:1–10).

2.7.10. The Syrophoenician Woman (7:24–30). This story merges two different forms by wrapping a miracle (vv. 24–26, 29–30) around a pronouncement story (vv. 27–28). The reader of this commentary is urged to review the discussions of those two forms (see "Miracle Form" and "The Form of Pronouncement Stories" at secs. 2.2.3 and 2.3, respectively). The story is also integrally connected to its literary context (review the general comments in sec. 2.7).

This unit in Mark has caused much confusion in the popular mind. The crucial words are in verse 27: "It is not right to take the children's bread and toss it to their dogs." Was Jesus being racist? Taking the details at face value, some early Christians may have interpreted it that way. Mark certainly emphasizes the fact that this woman was a Gentile. He situates the story in the Gentile region of Tyre and Sidon (v. 24) and identifies the woman as a "Greek, born in Syrian Phoenicia" (v. 26). Clearly this is a matter of some concern for Mark, and the forthright way in which he raises the question suggests that he does not want his reader to miss his point.

The point here is that verse 27 is ironic. To read only what lies on the surface of the narrative is to misread it. It is instead to be read as a bit of tongue-in-cheek. This is irony of a special kind, sometimes called "peirastic irony" (from the Greek term *peirazo*, "put to the test"). This type of irony is a verbal challenge intended to test the other person's response. It may in fact declare the opposite of the speaker's actual intention. An excellent example is found in Genesis 19:2, in which the angels of the Lord test the seriousness of Lot's offer of hospitality by declaring the opposite of their true intentions: "No . . . we will spend the night in the square."

There are clues that this is exactly how Mark understands this saying. (1) The first—and to my mind this is sufficient in itself—is the location of the story in this series of affirmations of the Gentile mission. If Mark thought the saying indicated Jesus' opposition to that mission, he could very well have left the whole episode out.

(2) Another evidence is the wit in the construction of the saying itself. It involves a set of metaphors and an allusion. The metaphors are "children" (surely denoting the Jews) and "dogs" (a common Jewish epithet for Gentiles). When Jesus poses his question, the reference to "bread" (*artos*) raises to consciousness the whole complex of meanings for that word that has been raised earlier in 6:1–8:30 (see comments on 2.7). It refers indirectly to the blessings of salvation, but in this context it also alludes to the Lord's Supper. The thrust of the peirastic irony is this: "The dogs—the Gentiles—will get theirs soon enough, but only afterward, when the scraps are thrown out as garbage. Jews first, Gentiles second. Right?" But Jesus' saying is cast as a challenge, a riddle to be solved, a witticism requiring a wittier response.

The woman's answer is brilliant. It extends the metaphor by adding the element of crumbs and by placing the dogs under the table. In the process it overturns the implication of the first part of verse 27. Crumbs fall to the dogs, and do so intentionally. Lane (1974, 263) is right: "If the dogs eat the crumbs under the table, they are fed at the same time as the children."

The combination of miracle form and pronouncement story form is not unusual in Mark (e.g., 2:1–12; 3:1–6). Elsewhere when this combination appears, the miracle serves the controversy; so it is here. The organizing principle of the passage is the exchange between Jesus and the woman (vv. 27–28). Indeed, while a number of elements are not necessary for a miracle, they serve as background for that exchange and thus deepen the significance of Jesus' question and the woman's response. The miracle itself serves that purpose. When Jesus heals her daughter, he demonstrates in no uncertain terms that all of the blessings of the kingdom are extended to believing Gentiles.

2.7.11. Jesus Heals a Deaf Mute and Many Others (7:31–37). In some sense this section serves a summarizing function (cf. also 1:39; 3:7–12; 6:53–56). The summary is made concrete and enlivened in two ways. (1) There is the problem of Jesus' circuitous route (v. 31): "Then Jesus left the vicinity of Tyre and went through Sidon, down to the Sea of Galilee and into the region of the Decapolis." This NIV translation disguises a serious problem. The Scholars Version retains something of the difficulty: "Then he left the regions of Tyre and traveled through Sidon to the Sea of Galilee, through the middle of the region known as the Decapolis." A quick glance at a map shows this to be awkward and even improbable, similar to this: "Then he left New York City and traveled through Boston to Washington DC, through the middle of the region known as the Deep South." What is more, the route does not correspond to the road system and leads across a mountain range, then a valley, then to the top of a high plateau.

Conservative scholars have held that the route is intentional, part of Jesus' larger efforts to keep his movements secret. What is more important, the language brings the plot directly into the region of the Decapolis (Gentile territory), which is the point of the larger section (see sec. 2.7). If Mark's original reader at all recognized the improbability of this route, that fact would simply reinforce the sense that Jesus' movements were deliberate. The healing of the deaf man, in other words, takes place in Gentile territory. Thus Jesus continues to act out the pattern of the prophets Elijah and Elisha in extending the benefits of salvation to outsiders. What better way would there be to prepare for the feeding of the four thousand that follows in 8:1–10?

(2) We should also note the manner in which Jesus heals the deaf man in verses 33–34. Sometimes Jesus heals by an authoritative word. Sometimes he heals at a distance. Sometimes, however, the healing includes a gesture or touch. Does this suggest that in those cases Jesus is using some "magical" technique? In my view it suggests instead a profound knowledge of human psychology and Jesus' ability to heal not only the body but also the mind and heart. There may be an important lesson here about the workings of grace. While the healing power of God does not require a touch to be effective, wounded people sometimes need a touch to recognize the presence of that power. A touch may aid belief.

Mark gives us Jesus' words, "*Ephphatha!*" together with a translation, "Be opened!" Here we have a violation of the norm for miracle stories, which tend not to record the words uttered by the miracle worker (see "Miracle Form" at sec. 2.2.3). Why does Mark include them here? Perhaps he wishes to provide a model for Christian healers. More likely, he wishes to show that the healing power does not reside in the words so much as in the healer. The reader is invited to try them, but will find that these words are not magic. This miracle is instead a representative healing, something that deepens the summary because it suggests that *all* of Jesus' miracles were as effective.

2.7.12. The Feeding of the Four Thousand (8:1–10). This miracle is closely connected with the feeding of the five thousand in 6:32–44 (see comments on that section; see also comments in sec. 2.7). The first feeding is for Jews in Galilee and the second for Gentiles in the Decapolis. Close verbal parallels with Mark's story of the Lord's Supper (see comments on 6:32–44; 14:22–25) suggest that both of these stories are to be understood in connection with the communion table; implicitly, the "loaf" (*artos*) that is broken for the multitudes is Jesus himself.

The most astonishing thing about this feeding is that neither the disciples nor the crowds here seem to be aware of the earlier feeding. Indeed, from a historian's point of view the disciples' question in 8:4 ("Where in this remote place can anyone get enough bread to feed them?") poses something of a puzzle. The disciples had witnessed the earlier breaking of the bread. And is it likely that none of these four thousand people were present on the earlier occasion? If we approach the two feedings from this point of view, the problems appear insuperable. Suggested solutions are that there was only one feeding whereas Mark mistakenly thought there were two. Or perhaps there was a natural explanation for the multiplication of the loaves and not a miracle at all. Note that neither miracle has any record of amazement at the multiplication of the food.

But perhaps the historical question is the wrong one to ask for this particular narrative. If we approach the narrative from a reader-oriented perspective, something altogether different occurs: The effect of 8:4 is to focus attention on the astonishing pigheadedness of the disciples. This is one of those important instances where Mark has sequenced the narrative to lead

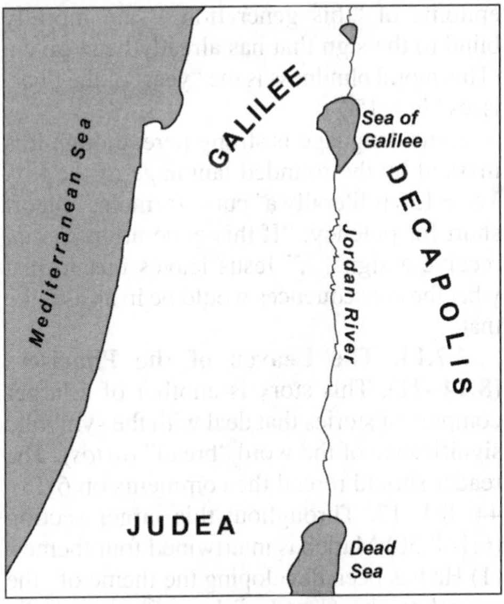

Jesus fed crowds of thousands twice, once in Galilee for Jews and a second time in the Decapolis for Gentiles.

the reader in a particular direction. By this time the reader is aware that Jesus is the *artos*, and the question implied in 8:2–3 is a theologically loaded one: "Is there enough of that *artos* to feed the Gentiles, too?" The correct response, of course, is that there is enough to feed the whole world, but the disciples have missed that implication altogether. The reader has not.

2.7.13. The Pharisees Seek a Sign (8:11–13). This section is closely tied to its context, both to what precedes and to what follows. Throughout 6:1–8:30 there have been repeated allusions and references to Jesus as the "bread" of life, the *artos* of the Lord's Supper (see initial comments on sec. 2.7). While each reference has been oblique, they have had a cumulative effect on one's reading, so that by the time the reader reaches this exchange with the Pharisees, he or she is fully aware that there is more to Jesus than meets the eye.

The crucial turn of phrase is in verse 12: "Why does this generation ask for a . . . sign? I tell you the truth, no sign will be given to it." Jesus could have meant this on several levels: "I will not perform miracles to prove my identity"; or, "There are plenty of miracles already"; or, "The 'sign from heaven' is standing here talking to you, and you are unwilling or unable to see it." No sign will be given this generation, not because there can be no such sign, but because the Pharisees—who are the epitome of "this generation"—are morally blind to the sign that has already been given. (This moral blindness is the "yeast of the Pharisees" in 8:15.)

Jesus' language is strong here, though it is masked by the rounded language of the NIV. Verse 12b is literally a "curse formula," cut off short for potency: "If this generation *should* receive a sign. . . ." Jesus leaves unsaid just what the consequences would be in a case like that.

2.7.14. The Leaven of the Pharisees (8:14–21). This story is another of a larger complex of stories that deal with the symbolic significance of the word "bread" (*artos*). The reader should reread the comments on 6:33–44; 8:1–13. Throughout this larger section (6:1–8:30) Mark has intertwined four themes. (1) He has been developing the theme of "the gospel to the Gentiles" by using symbolic numbers for Jews and Gentiles (see comments on 6:32–44), by carefully distinguishing the words for the baskets used in the two feeding stories (see comments on 6:32–44), and by tracing Jesus' deliberate movement out of Galilee and into Gentile territory, first to Tyre and Sidon (7:24–30), then by a roundabout route to the Decapolis (7:31). Indeed, if the point of this part of the narrative is that the gospel should go to Gentiles, then the explanation of 6:1–6 becomes an explanation for the section as a whole: "A prophet is not without honor, except in his own country, and among his own kin, and in his own house" (6:4, RSV).

(2) A second theme is intertwined with the first—the question of Jesus' identity. This question is first posed in the synagogue at Nazareth (6:2–3), but then posed again (6:14–16) by way of introducing the death of John the Baptist (6:17–29). The speculations of Herod and the crowds (Jesus is John the Baptist raised from the dead, Elijah, or another of the prophets) will all be repeated at the end of the section (8:27–30). In 6:49 the disciples wrongly think Jesus a ghost. In 8:11–13 the Pharisees will demand a "sign from heaven," not knowing that their demand is itself an ironical admission that they cannot recognize the "sign" who stands before them.

(3) We have had several occasions to demonstrate allusions to the Last Supper (see comments on 6:32–44). These have all had to do in one way or another with the symbolic meaning of the word *artos*, and Mark has included clues that the bread is Jesus himself.

(4) To all of this the disciples have been blind. When they saw Jesus walking on the water, they thought he was a ghost and cried out in terror (6:49). Mark has emphasized that the reason they thought Jesus was a ghost was that "they had not understood about the loaves; their hearts were hardened" (6:52). Indeed, like the Pharisees in 8:11–13, the disciples have been asking rather strange questions (e.g., those in 7:18–19; 8:4).

As important as these four themes are, for our purposes even more important are the responses they presumably evoked in Mark's original readers. Every important nuance missed by the disciples is noted and counted against them. When the townspeople asked, "Where did this man get these things?" (6:2), the reader answers, "From his Father." When they asked, "Isn't this the carpenter . . . Mary's son?" (6:3), the reader answers, "Yes, but he is also the Son of God." When the disciples suppose that Jesus is a "ghost" (6:49), the reader knows he is not. When Mark explains that the disciples "had not understood about the loaves; their hearts were hardened" (6:52), the reader is asked to share that judgment. When the disciples ask how they are to find enough bread to feed the multitudes in the desert (8:4), the reader knows there is enough "bread" there to feed the whole world. The disciples' questions and the readers' reactions stand in stark contrast. When Jesus therefore asks the disciples, "How many loaves do you have?" (8:5), the reader knows the correct answer: "One."

I have argued that the narrative invites this series of responses as a central part of its rhetorical strategy. These responses require a subtle shift of perspectives. In order for Mark's readers to accomplish this act of judgment, they must commit themselves to Mark's point of view. Indeed, from that point of view, clearly within the story of Jesus "everything" is in parables! Here I would argue that that shift of perspectives is as much a part of the background of this section as anything found within the narrative itself.

It is important that these reactions from Mark's readers come in series, that is, one after the other. The awareness of the four above-mentioned themes has been an accumulating awareness. In this story of the yeast of the Pharisees, everything is brought to a staggering climax. The last "gap" filled in by the reader immediately before this story is the reader's ironic reaction to the Pharisees' demand for a sign from heaven: "Jesus is himself the sign." The "yeast" of the Pharisees in verse 15 is habitual moral blindness, the sort of blindness that refuses to see the truth standing before it. As we noted regarding 8:12, Jesus' refusal to give a sign is an abbreviated curse formula. We will see that same stress burst forth on the disciples in verses 17–21, culminating in a sharply worded demand, "Do you still not understand?"

Mark will linger momentarily to prepare the reader for that final outburst by connecting the problem of the blindness to the symbolism of the bread. Note the odd comment about the bread in verses 14 and 16: "They had only one loaf with them in the boat" (v. 14, RSV). This "one loaf" does not play any role in the story itself. Why would Mark invest ink in preserving such an apparently insignificant detail? It does not move the story forward and seems to contradict the note that "the disciples had forgotten to bring bread" (v. 14), as well as the disciples' own comment that "we have no bread" (v. 16). Of course, that is precisely the point. They do have bread, just as the Pharisees had a "sign from heaven"; but they are unable to see it for what it is. The "one loaf . . . with them in the boat" is Jesus himself.

Thus the opening comment in verse 14a that "[they] had forgotten to bring bread" is a straightforward statement of fact; the narrator's aside in verse 14b that they had "one loaf . . . with them in the boat" is a theologically loaded comment on Jesus' identity; and the disciples' response in verse 16 that "we have no bread" is an ironic confession of blindness to that dimension of Jesus' identity. At this point the narrative becomes almost heavy-handed. Is not this blindness the very "yeast" Jesus is warning them against?

It is the disciples' ironic confession of blindness that prompts Jesus' response in verses 17–19: "Why are you talking about having no bread? Do you still not see or understand?" Understood in this way, this story is an extension of Jesus' refusal to provide a sign for the Pharisees and is thus a kind of ironic judgment on that demand for a sign, seeing that he is himself the sign from God. To miss it here, like there, is a form of "hardness of heart" (cf. v. 17).

2.7.15. The Twice-Touched Blind Man (8:22–26). With the story of the "twice-touched blind man" Mark introduces the largest transition in the book. Up until this point, Jesus has grown in public acclaim, and with it there has been a mounting opposition. Within the story itself no one knows who Jesus actually is except for the Father, John the Baptist, demons, and Jesus himself. For everyone else Jesus' identity and the nature of his mission have been mysterious and difficult, misunderstood by his opponents, the crowds, and even the disciples.

The fact that Jesus' opponents have misunderstood him is evident enough in their opposition to his work, but for Mark's readers their political machinations are evidence of their opposition to God as well. The crowds have understood Jesus in a variety of ways—a worker of miracles, a political contender, perhaps a revolutionary, a type of the old prophetic or wisdom tradition, a social demagogue. Whatever they think, Mark will make clear that any understanding of Jesus' identity and mission is incomplete and distorted until it takes into account the cross and the resurrection. The striking and ironic passage we have just left (8:14–21) makes clear that the disciples too have misunderstood Jesus' identity and the nature of his mission.

Throughout this litany of confused understandings, Mark has hinted that with Jesus more is going on than might seem apparent at first. There are important implications for understanding the true meaning of discipleship. It is not insignificant that this miracle of restored sight falls hard on the heels of Jesus' harsh words to the disciples: "Do you still not see or understand? . . . Do you have eyes but fail to see, and ears but fail to hear?" (vv. 17–18). As noted above, the failure to see and hear is evidence of a kind of moral blindness, an obtuseness of the spirit that prevents seeing and hearing. Jesus referred to that moral blindness as the "yeast of the Pharisees," and just at the moment that he cautioned the disciples against it, they ironically voice their failure to understand.

For Mark, the story of Jesus is an enacted parable that must be understood on two planes. By placing the story of the twice-touched blind man in exactly this context, he makes clear that the miracle of restored sight is also significant on two planes. Like other miracles in the book it is a kind of enacted parable. This literal blind man represents the blind disciples, who see but do not see, who hear but do not hear. This story is therefore also a literary subplot that mirrors the developments of the major plot: The story intimates that the disciples, too, will have a "second touch," but only after they have struggled with an incomplete and blurred vision of Jesus.

The next section (8:27–30) will introduce that blurred vision with striking clarity: In response to a direct question—"Who do you say I am?"—Peter will make a true but uncomprehending confession: "You are the Christ." Throughout the following section (8:22–15:39), the disciples' responses to Jesus will indicate that they simply do not understand the meaning of that confession. Mark's rhetorical strategies involve a subtle shift of identifications. He does not simply tell the reader about the disciples' failures; he passes judgment. In doing so, he wants the reader to take a position, to share the "enlightened" point of view from which the judgment proceeds. This is a subtle demand on the reader, but Mark offers no alternative; the reader who does not share the narrative's judgments falls under their condemnation.

Because this brief story of the twice-touched blind man functions as a narrative parable, it serves as the perfect transition into 8:27–30. It cautions the reader against making more of Peter's confession than is warranted; but at the same time it implicitly promises that the disciples, blinded perhaps by their unacknowledged aspirations to power, will someday have their own second touch of insight.

2.7.16. Peter's Confession (8:27–30). With this story we come to the apex of the first half of this Gospel (see comments on 1:1; 1:2–8:30). It is for this reason significant that at the precise moment of Peter's confession, the blindness of the disciples becomes explicit. They now know that Jesus is the Christ, but they do not know what that title will require of him or what it will require of them. If this is the pivotal transition in the narrative, it is also the narrative's supreme irony. Peter's confession is accurate only in its vocabulary. The political implications with which it is loaded run in entirely the wrong directions, and the reader is forced to a crisis of loyalties that mirrors that of the disciples.

Against the backdrop of the prediction of Jesus' passion in the next verses (8:31–32), Peter's confession is difficult. It signals to the reader the blind irony of his confession. As Peter intends it, the confession ("You are the Christ") is a shadow of the truth. He is dazzled by visions of splendor and blinded by a flash of false light. The realization that Jesus must suffer and die is true light, but it is searing, excruciating in its intensity.

So there is rhetorical tension here, deepened by a number of ironic movements. One would expect that the momentary identity of knowledge in 8:29 would lead to a common point of view, which would in turn eliminate further ironies. There are, in fact, fewer of them, but the ones that are there are more pointed. The disciples continue to blurt out double entendres, but now these entendres are ironies they should have known. Their continued blindness (a dominant motif of 8:31–10:52) has as its implied counterpoint the developing awareness on the part of the reader. At the point where the disciples appear muddled beyond redemption, the reader becomes crystal clear.

3. Jesus Is the Son of God (8:22–15:39)

With Peter's confession in 8:27–30 Mark's story takes a radical turn. Throughout the first half (esp. since 6:1), the focus of attention has been on the urgent question of Jesus' identity. That question has been asked repeatedly in the narrative (e.g., 1:22, 24; 2:7, 25; 4:41; 6:2–3, 14–15), and everything has been marshaled to confirm the first half of the author's opening salvo: "The beginning of the gospel about Jesus Christ . . ." (1:1). Not only has Mark shown the reader who Jesus is, he has also shown that Jesus' identity is lost on the other characters inside the story. This means in part that the other characters have possessed defective points of view from which to understand the meaning of the stories of which they are a part. Even the demons, who know that Jesus is "the Holy One of God" (1:24; cf. 5:7), appear to have no inkling of the great battle in which they are engaged.

But the clues that are missing for the characters are supplied for Mark's readers. The two groups cannot help but come at the story from different vantage points. The resulting dissonance in understanding between that held by the characters and that held by the readers represents a subtle but pervasive element of Mark's rhetorical strategy: As the characters stumble along through the plot, the reader cannot help but take a superior view, a view informed by dimensions of the narrative that the characters cannot hear. Indeed, it is the only point of view from which the inner workings of the narrative can function. But it is an emotionally and psychologically dissonant one, one that fairly cries out to the characters to pay better attention, to see what cannot be seen, finally to become *penetrating*—if that were in any way possible.

When Peter makes his confession in 8:27–30 the reader experiences a momentary relief: Peter has at last caught on. But has he? As the story continues to unfold, it becomes clear that his confession is a flash of insight but hardly sustained illumination. Jesus is indeed the Christ, but his ascent to power will come—to the characters inside the story it will come unexpectedly—by acclamation at the hands of a jeering and brutal gang of palace guards, and by a coronation that finds him impaled upon a cross. The fact that Jesus is the Christ is the shallower truth; the fact that it will cost him everything is the deeper one.

In the next section (8:31–15:39), Mark assists his reader in making the transition between these two apparently opposite affirmations. As he does this, he shifts the focus from Jesus' identity as "Christ" to his identity as "Son of God." Just as the first half culminates in Peter's confession that Jesus is the "Christ" (8:27–30), the second half culminates in the confession of the centurion that Jesus is the "Son of God" (15:39).

But something else is going on here. Throughout the book the critical point is not these two theologically loaded confessions. Mark has shown that it is entirely possible to get the facts right but misunderstand their meaning. That is the question to which he now turns, especially in the first unit of the second half (8:22–10:52), which explores the cost of discipleship. It is not insignificant that the centurion's confession that Jesus is the Son of God will come at the foot of the cross. Mark would very well have understood Dietrich Bonhoeffer's declaration, "When Jesus calls a man, he bids him come and die."

3.1. Who Is This Man? (Subtheme: Discipleship Training) (8:22–10:52)

As we saw in our discussion of the blind man at Bethsaida (8:22–26) and Peter's confession (8:27–30), it is not enough to know that Jesus is the Christ. One must also face the terrible consequences of that reality. There is more to Truth than truth; a *statement* of faith requires to be deepened into a *commitment* of faith, and a call to leadership must be transformed into a call to servanthood. Mark's narrative structure mirrors this double understanding, calling the reader first to share the statement of faith in Peter's confession, then to deepen and transform that statement with a theological reflection on the coming crucifixion. The subtheme of the previous section—"Who is this man?"—becomes the primary theme of the section that follows.

At 8:31 Mark introduces a new subtheme that carries with it a sobering implication: What happens to Jesus will happen to his followers too. The disciples must learn that for them, as for Jesus, leadership is service, defeat is victory, and death the pathway to life. Mark will accomplish this remarkable transformation by embedding the narrative with three specific predictions of the coming Passion (8:31–33; 9:30–32; 10:32–34). The predictions are explicit, but the narrative indicates with equal clarity that the disciples fail to understand their meaning. Following each prediction is a dialogue with the disciples that indicates they are blind to what he is saying. It is not insignificant, then, that this section is bounded by stories of blind men (at Bethsaida, 8:22–26; Bartimaeus, 10:46–52).

These exchanges are not merely reports of unsuccessful attempts at teaching. As the reader encounters the disciples' confusion, he or she must make some sort of judgment and come to a position, but the rhetorical structure of the narrative rigidly limits the kinds of positions the reader is free to take. Any reader who *agrees* with the disciples or shares their misunderstandings will come under the judgment of the story's implied point of view. Thus, Mark may be said to manage the reader's responses to the disciples here, and the methods by which that management takes place are clearly visible. While the narrative does not unfold in a coherent way (the parts would still make sense if they were arranged in a different sequence), it does seem to be bound together by an integrating thread. Mark accomplishes his ends by stating the point, then belaboring it and driving it home by repetition.

3.1.1. The Twice-Touched Blind Man (8:22–26). In the present commentary the story of this twice-touched blind man is discussed in two places. In some sense it reflects the theme of blindness that dominated the previous section (see sec. 2.7.15). Indeed, a major dimension of that entire section was a theological reflection on Jesus' identity, about which the disciples have been frustratingly undiscerning. A moment of relief comes when Peter makes his famous confession: Jesus is the Christ (8:29). Someone other than God and the devil knows who Jesus is. As it relates to what precedes, the story of the twice-touched blind man at Bethsaida suggests to the reader

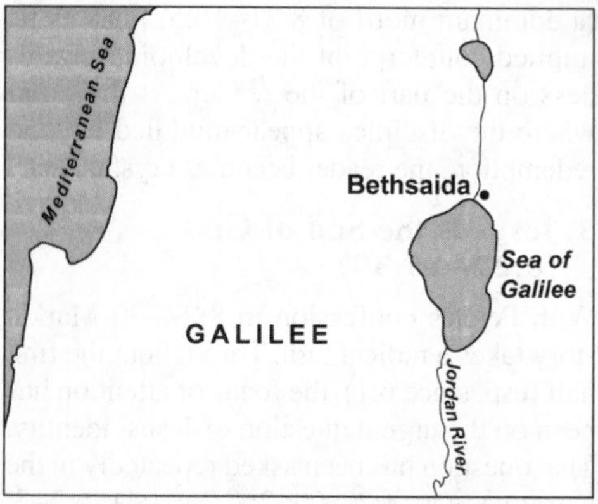

At Bethsaida, Jesus touched a blind man twice and the man then "saw everything clearly." What happened to that blind man will happen to the disciples. They will eventually see clearly that Jesus is the Christ.

that Peter, too, has finally come to *see* Jesus clearly at last.

But this will not prove to be so. This story is also oriented toward what follows. Together with the story of blind Bartimaeus in 10:46–52, it forms an inclusion that brackets a major section in which Jesus tries repeatedly but unsuccessfully to forewarn the disciples of the looming catastrophe that awaits them in Jerusalem. Despite everything—Peter's sudden recognition that Jesus is the Christ (8:27–30), the increasing machinations of the authorities, Jesus' intention to keep his movements secret, even the repeated predictions of the Passion (see sec. 3.1.3)—the disciples still fail to understand. Like the blind man at Bethsaida, they require a second touch.

Thus this puzzling little miracle story appears to be strategically placed. It mirrors what precedes in one way (see sec. 2.7.15) and what follows in another. Mark tells his reader that the man's "eyes were opened, his sight was restored, and he saw everything clearly" (8:25). What has happened to him will happen in its own good time to the disciples.

3.1.2. Peter's Confession (8:27–30). In the present commentary the story of Peter's confession is discussed in two places (see sec. 2.7.16). In one sense it culminates a long theological reflection on Jesus' true identity (6:1–8:30; see comments in sec. 2.7). Indeed, because of the structural balances in 1:1, Peter's confession that Jesus is the *Christ* draws to a close the entirety of the first half of the book, and is balanced by the confession of the centurion at the foot of the cross that Jesus is also the *Son of God* (15:39). These two themes are not discrete, but are mingled and contrasted throughout the book. What we have is a shift of emphasis. Thus, in a second sense Peter's confession launches the second half of the book (see also comments on 8:22–26 in sec. 2.7.15).

3.1.3. The First Passion Prediction (8:31–33). This is the first of three Passion predictions (see also 9:30–32; 10:32–34). The first and third are precise, the third more than the first. The phrase "he then *began* to teach them" (8:31) and the use of imperfect tenses for the verbs suggest that these moments in the narrative are three *representative* attempts at instruction. Apparently Jesus tried repeatedly to make this aspect of his mission clear to his disciples.

Why does Mark repeat this exchange three times? In order to answer that question we must explore the dynamics of reading aloud. By all accounts, ancient readers never read silently, even when alone. This means that some of the activities that are commonly part of silent reading would have been unknown, such as retrogressing or pausing to reflect on a striking phrase or an evocative image. It is these pauses that interest us here. Such lapses of sound and sense are fragile. A pause must not be drawn out too long. If it is, it can become intrusive and distracting. Indeed, even when one pauses to answer questions or offer explanations, the pauses can have a disruptive effect on the listening process. They must not be allowed to damage the listening experience. The reader must keep the narrative going.

Repetition is a way of overcoming this basic liability of reading aloud. Through repetition, the writer can create emphasis, drive home a point, or offer variety of explanations. So it is here. By repeating the Passion prediction three times, Mark is able to stress both the sheer deliberateness of Jesus' decision and the inability of the disciples to grasp what that decision will mean. The repetition also creates a kind of cadence in the narrative, so that Jesus' journey to Jerusalem becomes more than a journey—it is his death march.

Mark makes one thing clear: When Jesus began this march to Jerusalem, he knew exactly what would be the outcome. His crucifixion was no unexpected and tragic turn of events, but the result of a calculated and clear-headed choice. When Jesus calls his disciples—and indirectly the readers—to make the same choice (8:34–9:1), he asks them to follow only where he himself has had the courage to go before.

In 8:31–32, as with the other Passion predictions, the disciples do not understand. Here the objecting voice is Peter's "confession," which had been recorded only two verses earlier. The reversal is astonishing: Peter has at last grasped the basic fact that "Jesus is the Christ," but his response to this first prediction shows dramatically that he has no real grasp of what that means. Knowledge does not always translate into insight, even if accurate. Like the twice-touched blind man (see comments on 8:22–26), Peter requires a second touch. If one is to see beyond the truth to the Truth, one must learn to "have in mind the things of God," not "the things of men" (v. 33).

This is a serious challenge. Indeed, to the extent that Peter fails to have in mind the things of God, he may stand on the side of Satan himself. The fact that Jesus addresses Peter as "Satan" reminds the reader that the deeper concerns of the story have to do with matters of supernatural import, that the battle to be fought and won is a battle on the plane of the Spirit rather than the plane of politics, as Peter and the other disciples would no doubt have preferred.

3.1.4. "If Any Man Would Come After Me ..." (8:34–9:1). Throughout this commentary we have read the narrative against a backdrop of a church in crisis. No small part of that crisis has been driven forward by persecution. Several of Mark's stories about Jesus would have been heard with special urgency for various members of Mark's congregation: Families may have been set against families (3:31–35; 6:4; 10:28–31; 13:12–13), and Jews against Greeks (6:1–8:26). There may have been a great falling away (see comments on 4:1–20).

Indeed, throughout 8:31–10:52, Mark focuses attention on the cost of discipleship (see introductory comments on sec. 3). The present verses form part of a small complex of stories that sets the tone of the larger section. In 8:31–33 Jesus for the first time announces plainly to the disciples that he must go to Jerusalem and die, an announcement Peter clearly misunderstood (v. 32). Jesus' rebuke of

Peter in verse 33 is sharp. What now follows in 8:34–9:1 furthers Jesus' response to Peter's rebuke and carries the seriousness of the Passion prediction to a deeper level. The cost of messiahship will be death on a cross; the cost of discipleship may well be death in the arena. Jesus envisions a time in which his followers will have to make choices no less devastating, no less costly, than the choice he himself has had to make.

It is difficult to know what Jesus' listeners would have made of this soliloquy. What would Peter have heard? Perhaps the reference to the cross—mentioned here for the first time—specifies the manner of Jesus' death. Crucifixion was a Roman form of execution. Was Jesus sounding the battle cry of a political revolt by warning his followers that they may lose their lives in the fray? Is the question, "What good is it for a man to gain the whole world, yet forfeit his soul?" (v. 36), a cry for freedom, a kind of first-century version of the motto, "Live free or die"?

Mark's readers would have heard these words differently. For them, there are no intimations of danger here. Jesus' words do not tell them what to expect; rather, they interpret what has already happened. As the passage unfolds, all the horrors of this "prediction" are summoned to the reader's consciousness as memories—of family fortunes plundered, of friends lost to martyrdom, of other friends whose faith had failed them at the crucial moments of decision, of sons who have consigned fathers to the flames (see 13:12–13).

I suspect that for Mark's readers the recollections of personal loss would have made these verses the most emotionally wrenching of the entire book. Jesus has given a solemn pronouncement, the seriousness of which is deepened in two ways. (1) The basic themes are repeated. While the diction is not perfectly parallel, structural signals throughout the passage indicate partial stops and parallelisms:

Verse 34: If anyone would come after me …
Verse 35: Whoever wants to save his life …
Verse 35: Whoever loses his life …
Verse 38: Whoever is ashamed of me …
(lit. trans.)

(2) Verse 35 is structured in a chiastic manner, which deepens the sense of a solemn pronouncement:

A Whoever wants to save his life
B will lose it,
B' but whoever loses his life for me and for the gospel
A' will save it.

Perhaps most devastating of all is verse 38. For Mark's Roman reader, who heard these words in the aftermath of sacrifice and betrayal, this verse tells of a coming terrible judgment. Even in the heat of tribulation, Jesus brooks no compromises. For Christians who have failed the test of faith, these words of Jesus are pronouncements of damnation.

Thus far in our reading, this entire soliloquy has contained the most sobering words Jesus has spoken. But it is important to remember that the Gospel of Mark was not written to lapsed Christians but to those who had thus far survived the persecution. For them, Jesus' words redefine the meaning of their loss: One's friends and family who have been martyred in the arena have not died for naught. Death in the arena is a supreme form of discipleship, a way of following Christ. "Whoever loses his life for me and for the gospel will save it" (v. 35).

There is one other vantage point from which to read these terrible words of Jesus. The martyr who loses his life to the arena does not face the end alone, for Jesus has gone ahead. What sacrifice does Jesus require of his disciples that he himself has not already made? Yet that sacrifice is no less difficult for him than for his followers. Jesus is not glib about their loss. Because verses 34–37 clarify and interpret Jesus' prediction of his own death, they have a kind of self-reflective quality. What attentive listener can fail to hear the pathos in these words, coming so soon after Jesus has declared his intention to go to Jerusalem and die? Technically, the double significance of this declaration is ironic in that it means something for Jesus that is hidden from the listeners. The disciples should know, but do not.

Usually in Greek tragic literature, irony on the lips of the protagonist as he marches toward his doom evokes a deepening sense of horror in the audience. Here, however, the horror is mitigated by an almost tangible sense of the pathos of Jesus' words. In the prediction of his Passion he indicated that his approaching death is necessary (cf. "must," v. 31). Here he ponders death by martyrdom as a matter of active decision—a decision he himself has had make, a new "temptation" with which Mark ·gins the second half of the book. That pon- ·ring is masked by the direct address to the sciples and the crowds and by the general- ing "if anyone" in verse 34.

Regarding 9:1, from almost any vantage oint after the passing of the first generation of hristians, this saying has posed a major inter- retive problem. If the saying refers to the Sec- nd Coming, it would appear as if Jesus has ade a mistake. One typical way of resolving e difficulties thus created is the suggestion that y "the kingdom of God com[ing] with power" esus was referring either to his transfiguration):2–10) or to his crucifixion (ch. 15).

For Mark's reader the passage was read gainst the backdrop of their responses to the oliloquy in verses 34–38. They still had vivid emories of death by martyrdom in the arena. n psychological terms, the five verses have primed" the reader for 9:1. I suspect that vhen Mark wrote verses 34–38, the underly- ng theme of endurance under persecution eminded him of the saying about the kingdom f God coming with power. Indeed, we can be nore precise: The mention of "glory" and angels" in verse 38 has prompted Mark's rec- ollection. One of the traditions available to Mark associated these words with a third word, 'power" (see 13:26–27). There and here, the overwhelming image is power that comes after persecution. Indeed, the relevant parallel in the Olivet Discourse contains a similar promise see 13:30–31).

What, then, did Mark mean by this saying? The associations between power and suffering are clear, in that the sufferings associated with the end times will contain the promise of their opposite (13:3–37). But this is true of any suf- fering. If the reader reads about facing death and thinks of his or her own losses to the arena, the promise that the kingdom of God will come with power comes as great encourage- ment, as do Jesus' words in the Olivet Dis- course: "He who stands firm to the end will be saved" (13:13).

3.1.5. The Transfiguration (9:2–8). Let us begin with the broadest possible context: The reference to "six" days in 9:2 clearly ties the story of the Transfiguration to the narrative that precedes, but to what aspect of the narrative? A careful reading of the transitional signals in chapter 8 suggests that the three sections in 8:27–9:1 (the first Passion prediction [8:31–32a], Peter's rebuke [8:32b–33], and the exhortation to the multitudes [8:34–9:1]) are all extensions of Peter's confession and are construed as occurring on the same day. Thus, the reference "after six days" orients the reader back to the confession in 8:27–30, not to the enigmatic saying in 9:1.

Even in translation, the story of Jesus' transfiguration evokes a strong sense of the numinous. Mark has taken pains to reinforce that sense by placing this story directly between Jesus' soliloquy about taking up one's cross (8:34–9:1) and the disciples' inability to exorcise a demon (9:14–29). By sandwiching this story between these two painful reminders of the costs and the dangers of ministry, Mark heightens the impact of the scene on the mountain.

The mountain on which the Transfiguration occurs is not named. The focus of attention is on its *height*, not its *location*. Thus, the scene unfolding before the reader is elevated, literally and figuratively, to another plane. There Jesus is depicted as "transfigured" (v. 2b), and his garments are made "dazzling white" (v. 3). The extended comments about the whiteness demonstrate that the image the disciples now see is a supernatural one. The scene acquires a nearly visionary aspect—like something out of an Old Testament prophetic vision. The appearance of Moses and Elijah reinforces the image (v. 4) and gives an eschatological significance to the event, since both Moses and Elijah were expected to appear at the end of time. Both the cloud and the voice (v. 7) carry the image to a new depth, as does the sudden disappearance of everyone but Jesus (v. 8). When these elements are taken together, they create a powerful impression of a theophany, an appearance of a divine figure.

In its literary context, that image is reinforced and deepened by three other aspects of the text. (1) The reference to "six days" in 9:2 launches a series of oblique allusions to Exodus 24:16–18, which describes Moses' ascent of Mount Sinai, where he waited six days before receiving the tablets of stone containing the law and the commandments. The allusions are striking, but they do not appear connected in the narrative. Instead, they appear at first almost randomly, accumulating and gaining force as the narrative unfolds. The cloud, which forms the final and decisive connecting link with the Moses story, is withheld until verse 7.

(2) The allusions to the Sinai story are reinforced by other references to a wide range of Old Testament and intertestamental texts describing divine appearances. For example, the radiance itself vividly recalls the appearance of Moses' face in Exodus 34:29 (cf. also Dan. 12:3). Jesus' dazzling white garments (v. 3) recall the garments of the "Ancient of Days" in Daniel 7:9. The cloud (v. 7) recalls indirectly the many Old Testament references to God's manifesting his glory from a cloud (e.g., Ex. 16:10; 24:15–18; 34:5; 40:34–38). The author of 2 Maccabees 2:8 promises that the glory of the Lord will reappear, "and the cloud also, as it did in the days of Moses." In other words, the Transfiguration story is densely packed with supernatural imagery, like a series of fireworks going off in the reader's mind as the reading unfolds.

(3) This is the context in which we are to understand the appearance of Moses and Elijah. The reader will soon be reminded that in the end time Elijah will appear to "restore all things" (9:12–13), but the manner in which the reminder is introduced suggests that this is general knowledge, something even understood by the teachers of the law (v. 11). The probable context in which verses 11–13 is to be understood is the complex of images from Malachi (3:1; 4:5–6), in which Elijah appears in order to "prepare the way for the Lord" (Mark 1:3). What the disciples do not understand—and what is clearly understood by Jesus and Mark's readers—is that Elijah has already appeared in the person of John the Baptist. The reader already knows this because of the allusions in 1:4–8, and the reference in 9:12 will make this clear for the disciples as well.

Although Mark's audience may not have caught the complexity of these allusions as they *listened* to the reading of this Gospel for the first time, they would undoubtedly have perceived that on the mountaintop was a manifestation of God's glory. They would also have noted the mysterious voice from the clouds—a striking echo of the voice from heaven heard at Jesus' baptism (1:9–11). Note the sequence here: Mark has packed his narrative with an accumulating set of images, which finally reaches its critical mass in verse 7, in which everything comes together to focus on the voice from the cloud. This gives the voice the character of a thunderbolt; it occupies the central and controlling place in the story, much the way a punch line controls the structure of a joke.

With one exception: In the vortex of that swirling imagery, Mark pauses the scene at verses 5–6 to reinforce the disciples' failure to understand. These verses divert attention from the narrative's focus. From a compositional point of view, they pose a kind of narrative puzzle: Why would Mark interrupt the flow of movement of a majestic and numinous scene to intrude a picture of the disciples' stammering and failure to understand? If one reads this story without those two verses, it flows smoothly. Why this difficult and awkward intrusion?

One explanation is that the terror the disciples have experienced is a natural reaction to the numinous and therefore contributes to that dimension of the scene, rather than detracting from it. Clearly Matthew has portrayed the terror in that way (Matt. 17:6). For Mark's reader, however, the confusion and fear are more likely to be understood in the larger context of the disciples' failure to understand the nature of Jesus' ministry at all. Mark's Jesus has already indicted the disciples several times for this failure—most pointedly in 8:14–21 and most recently in Peter's rebuke of Jesus in 8:32. Thus, for Mark's reader, the failure to comprehend in 9:5–6 is part of that larger and more negative portrayal of the disciples.

The voice from the cloud in verse 7 returns the narrative to its primary focus. Its overall effect levels a stunning judgment on Peter for his failure to grasp the significance of what is taking place. The message spoken from heaven repeats almost verbatim the divine endorsement pronounced over Jesus in the scene at the Jordan, with two exceptions: (1) This time the verbs are placed in the second person, so that the disciples are addressed directly, and (2) the voice instructs the disciples to "listen to him." It may not be insignificant that the verb here is in the present tense and can be translated, "Keep listening to him." Does the voice from the cloud offer the solution to the disciples' ignorance? Is that solution offered also to the reader?

3.1.6. The Coming of Elijah (9:9–13). The gure of Elijah plays a significant role in the rama that is unfolding. Mark mentions him y name no less than nine times (6:15; 8:28; :4, 5, 11, 12, 13; 15:35, 36), and allusions to is activities have echoed through the feeding arratives (see comments on 6:1–8:30). Allu- ions to Elijah figured prominently in the pro- ogue (see comments on 1:2–15), in which oth the mission (1:2–3) and the clothing (1:6) f John the Baptist reminded readers of the ole of Elijah. Elijah will appear again at the rucifixion scene (15:34–36), in which the nlookers suppose that the words of derelic- on on the cross—*"Eloi, Eloi, lama abachthani?"*—address that Old Testament rophet.

Of the nine references to Elijah in Mark, ree appear in this section and two in the pre- eding story, the Transfiguration. Here the dis- ussion is prompted by Jesus' cautionary vords in verses 9–10: "Jesus gave them orders ot to tell anyone what they had seen until the on of Man had risen from the dead. They kept ne matter to themselves, discussing what 'ris- ng from the dead' meant."

For Mark's readers, this command to ilence contains an implicit injunction to its pposite, since they now possess a post-resur- ection perspective from which to grasp the neaning of all these things. The NIV translates erse 10, "they kept the matter [Gk. *logos*] to hemselves, discussing what 'rising from the ead' meant." The word *logos* here certainly oes not convey any reference to Jesus the ivine *Logos*, such as we find in John 1:1, 14. n this context the NIV has translated correctly. Yet the word *logos* is also Mark's shorthand vord for the gospel or for Jesus' ministry of reaching (see 2:2). Here, then, is the probable eason for Jesus' injunction to silence: They hould not talk about this matter until they ave a more adequate grasp of its meaning, vhich will only come after the Son of Man has isen from the dead, and the events of Jesus' ife—the Transfiguration included—are evealed in their true significance in the light of the cross.

The disciples seem to have difficulty plac- ng Jesus' words about his own death into their nore conventional ideas about the messianic kingdom (see sec. 3.1.3). Indeed, Elijah, who has appeared just moments before at the Transfiguration, entered into his heavenly glory without having suffered death (2 Kings 2:11). Thus, they find Jesus' words here puzzling (v. 10). Their question about Elijah (v. 11) attempts to connect his comments about the rising from the dead with the "great and dreadful day of the Lord" anticipated in Malachi 4:5–6 (see also 3:1–4). Based on this prophecy, the reappearance of Elijah as forerunner of either God or the Messiah was a common theme in popular eschatology, found widely distributed in Jewish (e.g., Sir. 48:10) and Christian literature (e.g., John 1:21, 25).

This widespread speculation is the context in which the disciples have understood both the appearance of Elijah at the Transfiguration (vv. 4–5) and Jesus' words about the resurrection from the dead (v. 9). All of this must anticipate the eschaton, and therefore be in the future. Any sense of that he is referring to his own death in the immediate future is lost on them, though not, of course, on Mark's reader.

Jesus responds in verses 12–13 that Elijah has *already* come, so the conditions required in the tradition have already been met. Indeed, the death of Elijah in the person of John the Baptist (6:17–29) not only serves as a precursor of Jesus' own death, but in a sad way it also fulfills Scripture (on which see, perhaps, 1 Kings 19:2, 10, 14). John, like Jesus, has met his death "just as it is written about him."

3.1.7. Jesus Heals a Demoniac Boy (9:14–29). Like several other of Mark's miracle stories, the story of the exorcism of the demoniac boy raises significant and unresolved questions. What is the controversy mentioned but not described in v. 14? Why does Mark mention the teachers of the law in verse 14b when they play no role in the remainder of the plot? Why are the crowds "overwhelmed with wonder" (v. 15)?

Moreover, why does Jesus appear exasperated in verse 19? Indeed, that apparent exasperation raises questions of its own: Jesus' questions in verse 19 remain unanswered. Why are they here? They do not move the story forward, and they give the reader serious pause. Whom is Jesus calling the "unbelieving generation"? The disciples? The father? The crowds? The teachers of the law? How are we to understand Jesus' response to the father—"if you can" (v. 23)? Is this a question, as the NIV translates? Or is the NRSV correct that it is an emphatic retort? If a question, is it rhetorical? If a retort, does it not belittle the father's cry for help? If verse 23 is structurally parallel to verse 19, the reader may suppose that Jesus is taunting the father; yet the response that the father makes in verse 24 ("I do believe; help me overcome my unbelief!") suggests that the father in his own desperate way takes the comment as encouragement to act on his own faith. (This element of the story may parallel Jesus' remark to the woman with the hemorrhage in 5:34 and to the Syrophoenician woman in 7:29.)

Why do the crowds come "running to the scene" in verse 25 when they appear to have been assembled already in verse 15? Why does the appearance of the crowds in verse 25 prompt Jesus to act? Perhaps Jesus wants to preempt the swelling of the crowds or to avoid arousing their hostility, as verse 25 implies; but the opening movements of the story in verses 14–24 seem to suggest that a large crowd was already present and that the preliminary crowd included a hostile contingent (v. 15).

These are difficulties in the *details* of the story, but there are also difficulties with the story's *structure*. Indeed, the story does not fall into the standard pattern for a miracle (see comments on "Miracle Form" at sec. 2.2.3), and the deviations seem to disrupt the normal flow of the plot. For example, the standard miracle form opens with a statement of the seriousness of the problem. Here, that function is served by Jesus' question in verse 21, but that comes in the middle of the story, while the boy is being convulsed. It seems unduly clinical, even unnatural or uncaring, for Jesus to ask such a question while the boy is suffering from an episode of demonic violence. Moreover, the length of time the boy has been tormented does not seem to have been a factor in Jesus' actual performance of the exorcism.

Thus, the story lurches along rather abruptly, raising questions that direct the reader's attention "off stage," as it were, to other issues not easily resolved. In answer to these questions, we will concern ourselves primarily with the rhetorical effect of the narrative on the original listeners to this Gospel. We begin by noting that although this story abandons the conventional structure for miracle stories, virtually every element of that structure is found here in heightened form. The nature of the problem is established in verses 17–1 then reinforced in verse 21. The convulsio itself (v. 20) has much the same effect. Star dard miracle form calls for the exorcist to utt appropriate adjurations, which Jesus does i verse 25. It may be important that Mark repor Jesus' actual words, which are not esoteri adjurations but simple direct commands. Th "proof" of the miracle in verse 26 contains th especially dramatic statement that the onlook ers thought the boy was dead.

Interwoven with these elements are thread of a different pattern—the inability of the di ciples to effect a cure on their own. Indeed, th story opens with the father's comment, " asked your disciples to drive out the spirit, bu they could not" (v. 18), and is brought to it close by the disciples' puzzled question, "Wh couldn't we drive it out?" (v. 28).

It appears as if the presence of the teacher of the law in verse 14 is in some way con nected to this theme. The teachers of the la and the disciples were "discussing somethin together" (a better translation than NIV's "argu ing"). Is the text aligning the disciples wit these scribes? If the disciples are at all in vie in Jesus' exasperated retort in verse 19, the the association may have more deeply negativ implications. The language of verse 19 is clos to Jesus' expression for the hostile Pharisee who sought a sign in 8:11–13, and to the "adul terous and sinful generation" in 8:38.

Furthermore, Mark had indicated earlie that the teachers of the law were impotent i matters having to do with the demonic (1:22 see also 3:22–30). Here, he extends that indict ment to include his own disciples, mentionin the indictment twice and reinforcing the indict ment by associating them with the teachers o the law. It is not clear why he does so, but th effect is striking: The whole weight of the pas sage turns on the impotence of the disciples t effect an exorcism. In Jesus' absence they hav reverted to old ways and have consulted wit scribes.

It is here that the point of the passage be comes evident. This story somehow forms powerful literary counterpoint to the story o the Transfiguration that preceded it (9:2–12). There the inner circle witnessed a theophan of Jesus—robed in stunning white, conversin with Moses and Elijah, attested by the voice o God. Here they are brought back to the reali ies of a world where unbelief and failure, argument, confusion, and even public disgrace remain ever-present dangers. The solutions offered by the teachers of the law are of no avail.

For many modern readers, the closing line in verse 29 ("This kind can come out only by prayer") is not weighty enough to answer the question the disciples have asked. But for readers with a high view of prayer, this response appears entirely adequate, not only for the disciples' question, but for the whole range of questions implied in this complex story. If we take Jesus' comment in verse 29 as a weighty ballast line, then the story fits its context nicely. In the shadow of the Mount of Transfiguration, in the daily grind of ministry pushed beyond human limits, for the disciples not privy to the theophany, for those whose knowledge of the story will forever rest on the testimony of witnesses, the answer to the issues of life is prayer. The solutions offered by the teachers of the law will prove worthless.

3.1.8. The Second Passion Prediction (9:30–32). This is the second of three Passion predictions (see also 8:31–33; 10:32–34; see comments on 8:31–33). The prediction forms the backdrop for the conversation in verses 33–50 about "true greatness" in the kingdom of God.

3.1.9. A Series of Hookword Stories (9:33–50). The following three stories are linked together as a single discourse between Jesus and the disciples, which took place in Capernaum. Jesus' question and the disciples' silence in verses 33–34 open the series by focusing the reader's attention on the subject of true greatness. One would expect that the subsequent verses would bring that attention to clearer focus. Yet it does not. Instead, the section ranges across a fairly wide terrain, raising and addressing questions unrelated to the presenting issue that opened it.

The passage contains a series of repeated phrases. The Greek word *skandalizo* ("to cause to sin") is repeated four times in verses 42–48, the word *pyr* ("fire") is repeated three times (vv. 43, 48–49), and the word *halas* and its derivatives ("salt") five times in (vv. 48–50). The final part of verse 50 ties the whole series back to the discourse on true greatness in verses 33–37 and reminds the reader that the initial problem was squabbling among the disciples.

Taken independently, the meaning of each of the sayings is clear; the difficulties of the passage have to do with the internal connections between the sayings. Verse 43 is only awkwardly connected to verse 42 because the opening lines of the paragraph have to do with one's offending against a child, while those that follow have to do with offending against one's own character. That is, verse 43 is connected to verse 42, not because they share a common theme, but because they share a certain striking vocabulary. A similar series of apparently awkward transitions connects the various elements of verses 47–50. Verse 50 ties the whole discourse back to the presenting problem in verses 33–37, but is not clearly connected to the saying about sin and scandal in verses 42–49. How are these to be explained?

It would appear that the entire assortment has been collected by *hookword* (see comments on 7:1–23). Mark decided to include the saying about Jesus' placing a child in the midst of the disciples in verses 36–37 because it illustrated in a practical and dramatic way Jesus' saying in verse 35: "If anyone wants to be first, he must be the very last, and the servant of all." The mention of welcoming a child in Jesus' name (v. 37) reminded the writer of two otherwise unconnected traditions. (1) The first is prompted by the reference to Jesus' name (vv. 38–41) in a dialogue between Jesus and John over people's casting out demons "in [Jesus'] name" (v. 38); this in turn prompts both Jesus' answer to the question (vv. 39–40) and another saying about Jesus' name (v. 41).

(2) The writer then returns to the original dialogue in verse 37 by picking up the saying about a child (v. 42). The structural parallel underscores a contrasting parallelism in content, where welcoming a child stands opposite to causing a child to sin. The striking element of verse 42 is the word *skandalidzo*, which serves as the mnemonic prompt for the series of sayings about the hand, foot, and eye causing someone to sin (vv. 43–48). That series ended with a reference to the unquenchable fire of Gehenna, where "their worm does not die and the fire is not quenched." Mention of "fire" (v. 48) then reminded the writer of another fire saying—"Everyone will be salted with fire" (attached in v. 49). Finally, mention of salt reminded him of a series of otherwise unconnected salt sayings (collected as v. 50).

3.1.9.1. True Greatness (9:33–37). This opening story sets the stage for the serious discussion that follows. Verse 33 identifies the scene in Capernaum, though the issue at hand is the discussion that had been going on beforehand, on the road. Here the important detail is the narrator's comment in verse 34 that after Jesus asked what they had been discussing, "they kept quiet" (lit., "they were silent"). This silence is critical to the potency of the story: Jesus "reads" their minds here, much the way he had read the minds of the teachers of the law in 2:1–12, and he responds to an error they have refused to state aloud. Their silence also suggests that they probably knew that their discussion about who was greatest was fundamentally out of keeping with Jesus' conception of his mission and their role within it.

In Mark's rhetorical strategy, both the question and the silence of the disciples pose the presenting issue of the passage: What does it mean to be "the greatest" in the kingdom of God? Indeed, as we have seen, this is the overall theme of 8:22–10:52. Mark revisits that theme with the brief illustration of the child, who serves as a sort of "embodied parable."

It is common to see this illustration as a kind of exhortation to childlike simplicity or trusting faith, but that is almost certainly not what is in view here. Instead, the example of the child is the direct, physical opposite of the presenting issue of the passage, the disturbing tendency of the disciples to jockey for position and status. Jesus is not enjoining them to be childlike in the sense of being simple; he is telling them to be childlike in the sense of being trivial, unimportant, and marginal. In the first century (and hence to the original readers of this Gospel), this is how children were viewed. In other words, the child symbolizes lowliness and lack of power.

The principle Jesus is illustrating is stated explicitly in verse 35: "If anyone wants to be first, he must be the very last, and the servant of all." Mark will return to this theme in 10:43–44, where he will remind his readers that "whoever wants to become great among you must be your servant, and whoever wants to be first must be slave of all." In that later passage, Mark offers a single further warrant for taking such a radical approach to greatness—Jesus' own example (10:45), embodied with distinctive power and clarity in his sacrifice. That warrant is implicit in the present context as well.

Throughout this section, the exhortations to servanthood have come point and counterpoint with Jesus' repeated attempts to tell the disciples that he is going to Jerusalem to die. This is a story told in the light of its ending. But the exhortations to servanthood have carried an implicit promise as well: "Whoever welcomes one of these little children in my name welcomes me; and whoever welcomes me does not welcome me but the one who sent me" (v. 37). Jesus builds a kind of stair-step accounting, ascending from the lowest order to the highest. Since the child is presented as an example, the disciples—and Mark's readers as well—are asked to believe that just as the catastrophe of the cross is not the final word, so also the demeaning positions of child and servant are the Christian's pathway to true greatness!

3.1.9.2. The Strange Exorcist (9:38–41). The phrase "in my name" (9:37) leads directly into this next section (see comments in 3.1.9). On the surface, the content of the sayings in 9:38–41 is split: The section opens with a question about exorcisms performed in Jesus' name by those who are not part of Jesus' band of disciples (vv. 38–40), while verse 41 leads in a different direction, about rewards for those who give a cup of water in Jesus' name.

What ties these two dissimilar subjects together is Jesus' openness to help from unexpected sources. True to form, the disciples have approached the matter from the standpoint of power: "Who controls the use of the name of Jesus?" Jesus approaches the question from the standpoint of the furthering of the kingdom: "To what uses has the name of Jesus been put?" (1) The very fact that someone can use Jesus' name in this way represents an implicit but important acknowledgment of his authority: "No one who does a miracle in my name can in the next moment say anything bad about me" (v. 39). (2) Perhaps more broadly, if the use of Jesus' name furthers the kingdom, then ultimately God's work moves forward in the world: "Whoever is not against us is for us" (v. 40). One is reminded of Paul's poignant comment from prison (Phil. 1:15–18a):

> It is true that some preach Christ out of envy and rivalry, but others out of good will.... But what does it matter? The

important thing is that in every way, whether from false motives or true, Christ is preached. And because of this I rejoice.

3.1.9.3. Warnings Against Temptations (9:42–50). This cluster of sayings is the conclusion of a series of sayings connected by hookword (see comments on 9:33–50). The parallels are inexact between the repeated elements, a fact that was cause for some consternation to the copyists, who apparently added the material in verses 44 and 46, but which has been removed from the NIV for lack of adequate manuscript support (see NIV footnotes).

The series of parallels actually begins with the promise in verse 37, which is balanced by the countervailing threats in verses 42–48. The thrust of the series is clear through verse 47, but a shift of images in verse 48 presents a problem: What is meant by the expressions "their worm does not die" and "salted with fire"? Are these unconnected sayings, attached here because of the hookword "fire" in verses 43, 48 and 49? Or are they integrally connected with the images presented in vv. 42–47? J. D. Derrett (1973) presents a compelling case for an intimate connection with what precedes. He argues that the entire section plays on the physical imagery of amputation carried out in ancient medicine. For obvious reasons, it would have been necessary to cauterize any wound from amputation; indeed, cauterization was a common, though desperate, treatment to stop the spread of infection. Where cauterization was ineffective, gangrene would set in, sometimes accompanied by maggots. The common treatment for gangrene and maggots was to rub salt into the festering wound.

It is important to grasp the cultural context in which such ghastly measures were considered necessary. Physical labor was often dangerous, and accidents happened. Medicine was primitive, and sanitation poor. Even a minor ailment could quickly become serious. Better amputation than death, even if amputation required such desperate measures as cauterization in an open flame. But this is precisely what the section is saying about sin: Better amputation than death. The language about worms, salt, and fire that permeates the passage is thus integrally connected with the imagery of amputation.

These elements, of course, create secondary frames of reference for these words, especially the word "fire" in verses 43 and 48b and "worm" in verse 48a. As terrible as such steps might be here, they prevent a more terrible consequence later on in hell (vv. 43, 46, 47). Here the worm is killed by the salt; there the worm "never dies" (v. 48a, NRSV). Here the fire is only temporary; there the fire "never goes out" (v. 43) and "is not quenched" (v. 48b). This last affirmation is drawn from Isaiah 66:24, which concludes the book of Isaiah with an especially vivid image of bodies decaying in the fires of hell.

This vivid imagery of amputation, freighted with its inherent dangers and inevitable deep suffering, serves as a ghastly reminder of the seriousness of the call to discipleship. What saves the day is the salt (v. 50), rubbed in an open wound as a last resort but serving as a curative. Christian discipleship is not always so simple or so joyful an affair as we would like. Sometimes the physician must amputate to heal, just as sometimes pain and trouble are the scalpels in the hands of that Great Physician who would ultimately see his people whole.

3.1.10. Departure to Judea (10:1). With Jesus' movement to Judea and the Transjordan, the plot moves within the sphere of Jerusalem and the dangers he has anticipated there. Those dangers become suddenly and strikingly evident in the ensuing controversy about divorce and remarriage (10:2–12). This short transition prepares for that controversy in two ways (for both of these, see comments in the next section). (1) It makes clear that the controversy about divorce takes place in the Transjordan. (2) It reintroduces the crowds and thus establishes a public forum for the verbal duel that follows.

3.1.11. On Divorce and Remarriage (10:2–12). The next three sections are tied to questions of family life: the question of husbands and wives (vv. 2–12), the treatment of children (vv. 13–16), and the issue of parents and siblings (vv. 17–22). A generalizing conversation between Jesus and Peter in verses 28–31 will tie the loss of family to the promise of the kingdom, bringing to its close the entire section of discipleship sayings. While the entire section presupposes important issues from Jewish law and culture, other details would have had special significance for the Roman situation to which Mark's Gospel is addressed.

There is no telling how Mark's Roman Christians would have heard this sharp exchange about divorce. Some see this section as stressing that women as well as men could initiate divorce. If so, Mark is not the first believer to have mentioned this in the Greek world, for Paul also balances instructions to men with instructions to women (1 Cor. 7:10–16). Paul's instructions on divorce inform us that at the very least some in Corinth struggled with this question. There is some evidence in classical writings that divorce was also a live issue in Rome. Divorce was common and easily obtainable throughout the ancient world. Taken at face value, Jesus' words restrict this common practice, and that in itself would require some explanation. Paul defends the restriction on the grounds that a believing spouse may somehow bring about the sanctification of an unbelieving one (1 Cor. 7:14–16). Here in Mark, Jesus defends the restriction with a reference to the creation mandate in Genesis 1:27 and 2:24.

However the passage may have been heard by the Gentiles in Mark's congregation, the basic lines of argument are Jewish and would have made their clearest sense to the Jews. But the narrative has prepared even the Gentiles to recognize a looming danger here. Twice Jesus has forewarned his disciples of impending judgment in Jerusalem (8:31–33; 9:30–32). The movement into Judea mentioned in 10:1 therefore brings that tragedy closer to its inevitable end.

Two aspects of the story deepen the sense of danger here. (1) The controversy takes place in the presence of a crowd (v. 1), a detail that heightens the stakes of the discussion. (2) The question about divorce is raised in the territory of Judea "and across the Jordan," that is, in the territory of that same Herod Antipas, who beheaded John the Baptist (see comments on 6:17–29). In a sense, that story has prepared for this one, so that when the Pharisees raise the question, "Is it lawful for a man to divorce his wife?" (10:2), the reader is prompted to recall both John's accusation against Herod (6:18) and Herod's superstition that Jesus was John himself, raised from the dead (6:16). According to tradition, John was beheaded at Herod's fortress in the Transjordan; one can hardly help but wonder whether the fortress of Machaerus was in view.

Jesus responds with a counterquestion i verse 3: "What did Moses command you?" N doubt this is good debater's strategy—to fin out the position of one's opponents. The posi tion that the Pharisees develop in verse 4 i based on an ambiguity particularly in the firs part of Deuteronomy 24:1–4:

> If a man marries a woman who becomes displeasing to him because he finds something indecent about her, and he writes her a certificate of divorce, gives it to her and sends her from his house. . . .

During Jesus' time a rabbinic debate ha crystallized around the interpretation of thes words. The more conservative school o Shammai focused on the phrase "he find something indecent about her," and argued tha the only legitimate grounds for divorce wa unchastity. The more liberal school of Hille focused on the phrase "who becomes dis pleasing to him," and argued that a man migh legitimately divorce his wife for virtually an cause. From Mark's comment that the Phar isees posed the question "to test him" (NRSV v. 2), and from their response to Jesus in vers 4, it appears that they are siding with Hillel. I is also clear that they expect Jesus will take th other view and condemn divorce. In th shadow of Herod's fortress at Machaerus, tha position is freighted with danger. Herod, afte

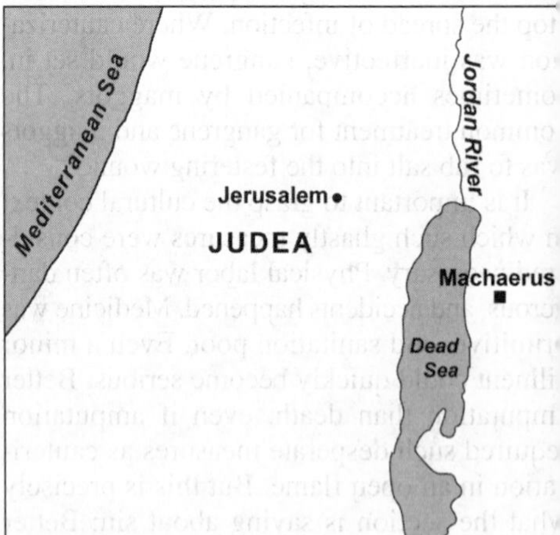

On his journey to Jerusalem, Jesus traveled in the region of the Transjordan, in the territory of Herod Antipas, who had had John the Baptist beheaded It is said that John was killed at Herod's fortress ir the Transjordan, which could have been Machaerus.

l, had arrested John for openly voicing oppo-tion to his marriage to his sister-in-law Hero-as (6:18), and he had later reacted to Jesus' owing popularity by recalling what he had one to John (v. 16). Thus the Pharisees' ques-on may have been intended to force Jesus into position of jeopardy.

This is the rhetorical function of Jesus' ques-on in verse 3. When he asks them for their ading of the law, he forces their position into blic view. Thus he exposes not only the dif-rences between them, but also their motives r raising precisely this question at precisely is place. At least figuratively, they have raised sword above him; the tension mounts.

Jesus does not sidestep the blow. Rather, he eets it head-on in verses 6–9. The Pharisees ve cited Scripture and argued from the tails of the law; Jesus cites earlier Scripture d argues from the creation order. They have terpreted Moses; Jesus interprets the intent God, arguing against divorce on the grounds at the one-flesh union at the heart of mar-ge is part of both the created order and the ill of God.

There is one other difference in their posi-ons. Although the Pharisees have asked about e right of the man to divorce his wife (v. 11), sus' response extends the prohibition to clude divorces initiated by the wives as well . 12). In extending his injunction to include omen, Jesus shows that women are also rectly responsible to God for their role in aintaining the health and viability of their arriages.

As different as Jesus' conclusions are from ose reached by his opponents, it is important note that he employs *their* principles of inter-etation. The interpretive strategy works like is: If two biblical texts share a common eme, they can be joined to make a new text at is larger and more encompassing than her. Jesus does this by joining together Gen-is 1:27 and 2:24 to create a new composite xt. In their new relationship, these two verses fine the source of the sanctity of marriage—e one-flesh union between a man and a oman is the will of God. Over against this, vorce—even divorce that is legally permitted Deuteronomy 24:1—represents a concession human sinfulness; it is a matter of failure.

This is a deadly serious game the Pharisees e playing, and it is their game, not his. They have made the rules. By employing rabbinic logic in the assembling of his responses, Jesus shows that he can beat them on their own territory. But the field of battle is also the territory of Herod Antipas and his sister-in-law, now wife Herodias, and the Pharisees' question is something of a strategically placed land mine. He strides across the trip wire, but the explosion does not come—not now, not here. Everything is moving much too quickly. Jesus' end will not come here, in the Transjordan, by a sword in the shadow of Machaerus. It will come later, in Jerusalem, on a cross in the shadow of the temple.

3.1.12. Jesus Blesses the Children (10:13–16). No clear narrative link ties this brief passage to the discussion of divorce that precedes it. Instead, it appears to have been included as part of a short collection of sayings that have to do with family life (see comments in the previous section). Yet the present section is not only about the treatment of children, as the surface of the story suggests. Like the famous passage in 9:33–37 (see comments), Jesus makes children an example to be emulated, not because they are innocent and trusting, but because they are vulnerable and powerless. "Anyone who will not receive the kingdom of God like a little child will never enter it" (v. 15).

3.1.13. On Riches and the Rewards of Discipleship (10:17–31). Verses 17–31 form a long, complex series of dialogues. Taken individually, each of these has the structure of a pronouncement story (see "The Form of Pronouncement Stories" at sec. 2.3), ending in an aphorism. This particular section could have closed at several places without loss of narrative sense. For example, verse 21 brings a satisfactory conclusion. So does verse 22. Verse 23 starts the series up again, and verse 25 brings a third closure. Verse 26 opens the series again, and verse 27 brings a fourth closure. Thus, the passage seems to conclude, then surge forward again.

What ties the entire section together are the extended sayings about leaving everything for the sake of the gospel (vv. 29–30) and the balanced aphorism of verse 31. The story about the rich man opens the series, and while it ends provisionally at verse 22, it will find its ultimate completion in the radical affirmations in verses 29–31.

Throughout this commentary we have read the text against a backdrop of crisis, in which Mark's Christians have lost everything for the sake of the gospel. Here a radical new element is introduced into the demands Mark places on his readers: *voluntary* poverty. Even in view of the extended comment about riches in verses 24–25, we should guard against viewing this as yet another commandment like those listed in verses 18–19, as though adding "sell everything you have and give to the poor" would complete the requirements that the rich man must meet if he is to "inherit eternal life" (v. 17). Instead, the conclusion of the series (vv. 28–30) generalizes the content to include leaving "everything" (v. 28) to follow Jesus. The focus of attention is placed on following Jesus and on leaving behind *anything* that prevents one from doing so.

Verse 31 carries the matter home with special clarity: "Many who are first will be last, and the last first." That is, one is asked to give up the sources of one's status and security, whenever that security is embedded in anything other than the will of God. Thus this story echoes the theme of the section as a whole, especially the series of sayings about true greatness (9:33–37). In the case of the rich man, the one obstacle between himself and his salvation was his dependence on his wealth.

But this message represents a fundamental disruption of values in ancient Judaism. The issue of wealth is closely connected to the question of Jewish piety introduced in verses 18–19. Indeed, without his wealth, the rich man would not have been able to make the claim he makes in verse 20: "All these [commandments] I have kept since I was a boy." In the mind of the righteous Jew, the sheer difficulty and expense of maintaining ritual purity positively excluded the poor from attaining the kingdom of God in this manner. Thus, Jesus has asked the rich man not only to abandon his wealth, but to embrace a radically different conception of what it means to be holy. How could a homeless disciple of an itinerant preacher hope to continue to meet the rigid demands imposed by Jewish legalism? Peter will later voice that same question in verse 26: "[If the rich cannot be saved], who then can be saved?"

Verse 22 brings the story to a provisional close. By continuing the scene into verses 23–31, Mark makes it clear that riches may pose a problem for faith in a way that poverty do not. Yet these verses also show that one's fai may be invested in many different thing Mark mentions family and property explicitl but it is clear that the list is representative, n exhaustive. The modern Christian may need be reminded that whatever claim to statu security, or power we might possess pales i the light of the gospel. To lose such things f the gospel is little loss at all; Jesus promises return of a hundredfold (v. 30a).

But with a catch: The hundredfold return tempered with a sobering comment. Suc things come "with . . . persecutions" (v. 30b Thus Mark's Jesus reminds the disciples—ar Mark's reader as well—that this is no mag cal formula that removes the reality of one loss; instead, it provides the larger context the kingdom of God as the defining frame reference in which one's loss can be unde stood. Mark's Roman Christian, reading t Gospel against the background of abando ment and betrayal, would have heard som thing strangely personal in Jesus' words abo leaving "home or brothers or sisters or moth or father or children or fields" for the sake Jesus and the gospel (v. 29).

Mark has already told his reader that to ga the whole world and forfeit one's soul is gain (8:34–9:1). Here he turns that formula its head: To lose everything and gain the kin dom, even "with . . . persecutions," is ul mately to gain everything that matters losing everything that does not.

It is difficult to see how stunning this fo mula actually is in its social and historical co text. We have already seen how central one family can be (see comments on 3:31–35). that earlier section Mark showed that whoev loses family for the sake of the kingdom regai the loss in the person of Jesus. Here he sho that whoever loses family for the kingdo regains the loss in the life of the church. T church is, after all, the family of God. In neith place does Jesus demean the family. Rather, uses what everyone understood as the high social good as a way of demonstrating the su passing worth of the kingdom of God.

3.1.14. The Third Passion Predicti (10:32–34). This is the last and most detail of three Passion predictions (see also 8:31–3 9:30–32; see comments on 8:31–33). Indeed, of the elements mentioned in verses 33–34 w

ater be precisely fulfilled within the narrative
self. Jesus and his disciples go up to Jerusalem
11:1), where he is delivered to the elders, chief
riests and teachers of the law (14:18–21, 43,
3–65), who condemn him to death (14:64) and
and him over to the Gentiles (15:1ff.), who in
ırn mock him (15:16–20), scourge him (15:15),
nd kill him (15:22–37). After three days he
ses again (16:1–8). For the most part the lan-
uage of the prediction is precisely repeated in
e moments of the fulfillment, so that when
lark's readers later come to the Passion proper
14:1–15:47), they remember that Jesus knew
eforehand that these events would take place.
'hat memory significantly affects the way they
espond to the actions of the characters inside the
ory (e.g., see comments on 14:66–72).

We might approach this question from a
ifferent perspective: How would the Passion
ead differently if these three predictions were
iissing? The most obvious answer is that
esus would appear as a victim, someone who
appened to be in the wrong place at the wrong
me. But that is precisely what does *not* hap-
en. Strangely—ironically—Jesus is in charge
f events, master of his own fate. It is the Pas-
ion predictions that make that irony clear.

The entirety of the Passion will later prove
be ironic because it holds dimensions for the
eader that are lost entirely on the characters
side the story. In some sense, those ironies
ad their beginning in 1:1 (see comments);
ere the third Passion prediction focuses those
onies, making sure that the reader under-
ands the deadly serious way in which Jesus
pproaches Jerusalem (v. 32).

**3.1.15. Precedence Among the Disciples
(10:35–45).** This extended dialogue says in
lear and precise terms what has been indirectly
inted after throughout this larger section
3:22–10:52): If Jesus himself must die for his
iission, so too must his disciples. Elsewhere,
e "death" is literal (e.g., 8:34–9:1), and the
isciples miss its meaning; here it becomes figrative, but crystal clear. There are many ways
"die" for the kingdom, and while taking
ne's place in the arena may well be one of
em, dying to one's self is another. In this way,
e injunction to "take up one's cross" is made
principle of Christian ethics, not a rule to be
llowed so much as a story to be acted out
gain and again in human relations. Little won-
er that Mark places this narrative at the apex of his section on discipleship training. Everything in this section comes to focus on the stunning words of Jesus in verses 42–44:

> You know that those who are regarded as rulers of the Gentiles lord it over them, and their high officials exercise authority over them. Not so with you. Instead, whoever wants to become great among you must be your servant, and whoever wants to be first must be slave of all.

Jesus made this same point earlier, using children as examples (9:33–37; 10:13–16). Here he makes the point by using his own sacrifice as an example. The reason his followers should do this is because "the Son of Man did not come to be served, but to serve, and to give his life as a ransom for many" (10:45).[8]

Mark accomplishes this goal *ironically*, that is, in the way he structures the presenting story. The ironies depend on the reader reading the story against a background of knowledge about the crucifixion, information that has not been introduced before in the narrative, but which must be brought in from outside. The outside details are specific: The reader is expected to know that the words "cup" (*poterion*) and "baptism" are oblique references to Jesus' death (see esp. *poterion* in 14:36). When these meanings are combined following the most explicit of the Passion predictions (10:32–34), they shape our understanding of the disciples' question in verse 37: "Let one of us sit at your right and the other at your left." The reader is expected to recognize this as another indirect reference to the two brigands who will be crucified with Jesus, "one on his right and one on his left" (15:27).

This is also the context in which we should understand the meaning of the word "glory" in 10:37: The "glory" of Jesus is the cross. When Jesus tells James and John that they will indeed "drink the cup" that he drinks, the reader may well know that James has already met a martyr's fate at the hands of Herod (cf. Acts 12:2)! The whole conversation totters on the edge of a precipice.

But the disciples in the story know none of this. Instead, they ask their question solely out of a personal drive for power, and they understand Jesus' responses solely within the context of the march to Jerusalem, which—quite naturally—they expect will end in an assault of some kind. What they intend and what they hear from Jesus have a more basic meaning. By "glory" they mean his coming position as head of state. "To sit at his right hand and at his left" is to take the positions of power when he holds court. When Jesus asks them, "Can you drink the cup [*poterion*] I drink?" they hear only, "Are you willing to serve as my wine tasters?" We cannot say for sure, but they would likely have heard the reference to baptism in a similar way, perhaps having something to do with the violence of the coming revolution.

The point of this discussion is that the conversation develops on two levels—one political, the other theological:

"Let one of us sit at your right and the other at your left in your glory" (v. 37).	*What the disciples intend:* "Let us have positions of honor at court."	*What Jesus hears:* "Let us be crucified with you."
"You don't know what you are asking. . . . Can you drink the cup I drink or be baptized with the baptism I am baptized with?"	*What Jesus intends:* "You are asking for a horrible death. Are you willing to be crucified with me?"	*What the disciples hear:* "Are you willing to serve as my special retainers, even my wine tasters?"

Mark's readers, on the other hand, are expected to hear both levels of meaning. The power of the story lies not in one level or the other, but in the nearly electric tension between them. The rhetoric of the narrative does not give the reader the option of taking the lower option here. The resulting ironic dialogue not only demands that the readers take the higher view; it forces them to recognize just how unlike Jesus the disciples have become, how unchristian is their grab for power. Any reader who began this narrative believing that Christian leaders should lead "the way the Gentiles do" will leave it knowing that among Christians "whoever wants to be first must be slave of all." Quite the remarkable thing is that Mark has used the rhetorical skills of the storyteller to teach his readers that truth long before verses 42–45 make it an explicit element of the text.

3.1.16. The Healing of Blind Bartimaeus (10:46–52). The story of the healing of blind Bartimaeus presents the reader with a subtle shift in emphasis. The reader's initial expectation—that this will be about a miracle—is not so much overturned as supplemented an in that way given a different meaning.

The narrative trick lies in the sequence o the story. The genre signals in the openin verses tell the reader to expect a miracle (se "Miracle Form" at sec. 2.2.3). Both the blin man and the crowd anticipate a healing mira cle. According to standard miracle form, wha *should* happen next is an encounter with th miracle worker in which the person is healed the "proof" demonstrated in some way, an then approved in the acclamation of th crowds. These things do happen, eventuall but for the moment they are suspended, and th reader is presented with elements of an entirel different form altogether.

What begins as a miracle develops into "call narrative" (see the double calling of th blind man in v. 49). The discarding of the cloa (v. 50) is a common element of a call narrativ Finally, this story ends with the note that whe Bartimaeus received his sight, he "followe Jesus along the road" (v. 52). This is subtl The fact that Bartimaeus followed Jesus serve indirectly in the place of the "proof" and pre sents a different emphasis. While the primar form and content signal the reader that this a healing, the secondary *form* indicates that is somehow also about discipleship, abo responding to the call of Jesus.

It is little wonder that Mark closes thi major section with a story such as this. Th section began with the healing of the twic touched blind man (see comments on 8:22 26), which foreshadowed the disciples' failu to understand Jesus' teaching that he must g to Jerusalem to die (see sec. 3.1). In the rheto ical structure of this story Bartimaeus, th blind man, saw clearly that Jesus was the "So of David" and "followed [him] along the road (vv. 47–52), which serves as another kind foil for the disciples, who should have see who Jesus was but did not.

3.2. Judgment on Jerusalem (11:1–12:44)

I have entitled this section "Judgment o Jerusalem," though in a sense that title appli to the book as a whole, and certainly to the enti Passion narrative. In a narrower sense, howeve this section brings the confrontation with th authorities into sharp focus and thus forms th backdrop for Jesus' trial and crucifixion.

The section is composed of two large ıovements. (1) Jesus stages what looks like an ıssault" on the city (11:1–10), laying claim ɔt only to its holy sites but also to its religious ıd political symbols. This Triumphal Entry is ɔllowed by an apparent inspection tour of the ity and temple (v. 11), and then by a fierce disɪay of prophetic passion in the temple (vv. 5–17). Mark sandwiches the cleansing of the ɛmple with the cursing (vv. 12–14) and withɛring of the fig tree (vv. 20–26), so that both ıe meaning and the power of Jesus' actions ecome clear. The authorities at last can stand no more. They recognize the threat against ıem and respond as they believe they must.

(2) The resulting series of confrontations in 1:27–12:44 sharpens the issues. Here Mark ɛintroduces the controversy form as a frameork on which to hang Jesus' authoritative ronouncements (see "The Form of Proɔuncement Stories" at sec. 2.3). We have seen ıis sort of encounter before, though now the ıthorities have Jesus on their own turf. As the arrative approaches its inevitable conclusion, ıe controversies heighten the stakes and refous attention on the seriousness of Jesus' ctions. There is one further sense in which ıese controversies move Mark's rhetorical rogram forward: Jesus presents another virıoso performance in the fine art of verbal ueling, so that later, when Jesus is silent at his ials (before the Sanhedrin [14:61]; before ilate [15:5]), the reader recognizes that his ılence is a deliberate choice.

3.2.1. The Triumphal Entry (11:1–10). Vhen Jesus and the disciples finally enter ɛrusalem, the narrative begins a new and more angerous phase. In a sense, everything ncountered thus far has prepared for this ıoment. The march to Jerusalem fills the ɛader with a sense of dread. This dread came s early as 1:14, when John the Baptist "was ut in prison" and perhaps handed over to the xecutioner. In 3:6 the Herodians and the Pharɛees held council against Jesus "how they ıight kill" him. In 6:1–6 Jesus was rejected in is hometown. The death of John the Baptist in :17–29 deepened the growing pall that now angs over the narrative like a menacing storm loud. After Peter made his famous confession 3:26–30), Jesus responded with the announceıent that he was going to Jerusalem to die 3:31–33), but Peter would have none of it (8:34–35). Jesus tried again to tell his disciples in 9:30–32, but again they failed to understand (9:33–50). He tried a third time in 10:32–34, this time unequivocally and precisely, but they refused to understand (10:35–45).

Mark has also stepped off the cadences of this great and somber march by intoning about Jesus' heading toward Jerusalem (8:27; 9:33; 10:32–33, 52). The counterbeats are the repeated calls to the disciples to "take up [their] cross" (8:34) and follow Jesus, to abandon all hope of political power (9:33–37), and to "drink the cup [he will] drink" (10:38). But of course, they have consistently failed to grasp what that meant.

When the Triumphal Entry is read against that great sense of dread, everything is suddenly reversed. Jesus' "victorious" entry into the city seated symbolically on a colt, the wild enthusiasm of the crowds, the waving palm branches, the loud hosannas, the victory song—all result in a grand shock of relief. There is no shadow here after all.

So much for its *effect*; what of its *content*? It is clear that the Triumphal Entry has been staged for its symbolic significance, perhaps even prearranged by Jesus himself. As such, it is a kind of enacted parable and thus an extension of Jesus' teaching ministry. Jesus—Son of David, conquering King—enters Jerusalem in fulfillment of Scripture (Zech. 9:9):

> Rejoice greatly, O Daughter of Zion!
> Shout, Daughter of Jerusalem!
> See, your king comes to you,
> righteous and having salvation,
> gentle and riding on a donkey,
> on a colt, the foal of a donkey.

The allusion to Zechariah 9:9 remains hidden within the narrative. Mark leaves the reader to discover that allusion from clues within the narrative itself. Other clues in the structure of the story suggest a secondary allusion to Genesis 49:10–11, itself a messianic text:

> The scepter will not depart from Judah,
> nor will the ruler's staff from between
> his feet,
> until he comes to whom it belongs
> and the obedience of nations is his.
> He will tether his donkey to a vine,
> his colt to the choicest branch. . . .

These, then, are the texts evoked by the story line. The crowds, who are inside the story itself and cannot hear the allusions, nevertheless pick up the significance of the donkey and stage a jubilant, if impromptu, demonstration. Here, too, everything has messianic significance. The spreading garments recall 2 Kings 9:12–13. The waving palm branches recall the triumphant arrival of Simon Maccabeus (1 Macc. 13:51), come to Jerusalem to assume the throne. The antiphonal singing in Mark 11:9–10 takes its cue from Psalm 118:25–26, one of the Hallel psalms, typically sung by pilgrims approaching Jerusalem. It is a moment of wild enthusiasm, in which Jesus takes the role of messianic king, come openly to recover what is rightfully God's.

3.2.2. Jesus Enters Jerusalem (11:11). This short transition ties off the story of the Triumphal Entry (11:1–10) and moves the plot to Bethany, a village on the far side of the Mount of Olives. The note that Jesus "looked around at everything" creates the impression of an inspection and thus completes the image of a conquering general or king, inspecting newly acquired territory.

Thus far in our reading of Mark, the material has been organized by *form* (e.g., miracle stories and pronouncement stories), by *theme* (e.g., the gospel to the Gentiles [6:1–8:30], or by *hookword* (see sec. 2.7.9). In 11:11 the chronological note "since it was already late" marks a shift to an organization loosely based on chronology. Hereafter, the chronological notes will become the predominant way of tying the parts of the narrative together and marking out its transitions. Because of this shift, the parts of the narrative are more closely bound up with one another, so that they ask to be read together as a single integrated account. This account, constituting nearly 40 percent of Mark, indicates that the events surrounding the crucifixion were of crucial significance in the Evangelist's theological program.

3.2.3. Judgment Against the Fig Tree (11:12–14). We must first examine this story as it would have been *heard* in an oral presentation of the Gospel. The entire episode is contained in only fifty-six Greek words and would have taken up little more than a minute or two. In that time, the listener is asked to hear and understand a story that has perplexed and troubled interpreters almost since the beginning of the church. It poses significant questions: If it was "not the season for figs" (v. 13), why did Jesus go seeking food in the first place? What is perhaps most troubling is the apparent arbitrariness—even violence—of Jesus' action against the tree.

The reader eventually learns (vv. 20–21) that the stories of the withered fig tree and the cleansing of the temple are "sandwiched" together, so that each story complements and deepens the rhetorical nuances of the other (see comments on 5:21–43). What is most striking is the abrupt way the fig tree story closes in verse 14. This raises terrible and violent images of Jesus, images that are not easy to reconcile with what else we know of Jesus' character. Then, without warning, the story quits, leaving the reader hanging. The failure of closure forces the reader to continue puzzling as the narrative moves forward to the cleansing of the temple (vv. 15–17). That is, the reader is asked to comprehend the temple story without having finalized an understanding of the fig tree story. These two activities of interpretation take place at the same time so that the one story becomes a comment on the other.

Mark has elsewhere treated the narratives of his Gospel as symbolic events, events that are embedded with theological significance (see comments on 4:10–12). The Triumphal Entry is a recent case in point: Jesus has seized on a grand occasion to *teach* by means of a symbolic gesture. In the present story the imagery draws on frequent Old Testament images of God as a landowner, who has returned to collect the yield from his crops. (This metaphor becomes explicit in the story of the parable of the wicked tenants in 12:1–12.)

One striking parallel here is Micah 7:1, in which the prophet laments the lack of righteousness in the land:

> What misery is mine!
>   I am like the one who gathers
>   summer fruit
>   at the gleaning of the vineyard;
> there is no cluster of grapes to eat,
>   none of the early figs that
>   I crave.

More in keeping with our own passage is Jeremiah 8:13, in which the Lord expresses anguish at the nation for its evil actions:

When I wanted to gather them, says the LORD,
  there are no grapes on the vine.
  nor figs on the fig tree;
even the leaves are withered,
  and what I gave them has passed away from them. (NRSV)

If the reader is able to hear such associations as these implied in the present story, the judgment against the fig tree is regnant with prophetic symbolism. It is a gesture of judgment that points beyond itself to a larger theological truth. The narrative now operates on two levels of reference—one literal, the other parabolic. At the end of verse 14 it is clear the literal brunt of Jesus' "curse" is directed at the fig tree: "May no one ever eat fruit from you again." What is the parabolic reference? Because of the Old Testament parallels, the reader sees this as a general reference to Israel and thus, in the experience of Mark's Christians, the Jews. When the narrative rushes forward to the cleansing of the temple (another prophetic act), the parabolic reference of this deeply symbolic act suddenly comes into focus: It is an explicit and damning judgment against the ministrations of the priests and the temple itself.

3.2.4. Judgment Against the Temple (11:15–17). The "sandwiching" of this story between the two halves of the story of the fig tree (vv. 12–14 and 20–26; see comments on 3:21–43) suggests that the two events be read together. As we saw in the previous section, the story of the fig tree leaves Mark's reader with a number of unresolved questions. More is going on here than an act of rage, but what? What does it mean that "it was not the season for figs" (v. 13)? If that is so, why did Jesus expect to find them? The story of the fig tree raises these questions, but stops cold without answering them; they linger in the reader's mind and bleed over into the reader's interpretation of the cleansing of the temple story.

Abrupt as it is, however, the judgment on the fig tree does not close without leaving these questions unaddressed. The context is filled with images of the Messiah—the wild enthusiasm of the crowd at the Triumphal Entry (vv. 1–10), the powerfully evoked language from the prophet Jeremiah and the cries of "Hosanna," the "inspection tour" of the city and temple (v. 11), and the suggestion of Israel in the image of the fig tree (vv. 12–14). The fact that the tree had no figs recalls imagery used by the prophet Jeremiah to describe Yahweh's lamenting the failure of faith in Israel (Jer. 8:13; see comments on 11:1–10). The point of this analysis is that the powerful layering of messianic images, coupled with the unresolved plot complications from the fig tree story, have primed the reader to expect an act of prophetic judgment against the temple, the seat of "official" Judaism.

No other story in Mark rivals the cleansing of the temple for its sheer furious drama. Jesus is a towering and turbulent figure here, overturning tables and chairs, arresting traffic, taking no prisoners. Notice the sequencing of the story. At first Jesus' outburst appears unprovoked. Reasons are given, but not until verse 17, after the tirade has exploded through the temple. What is happening here in the temple is an echo of what had happened to the fig tree outside on the highway. Why is Jesus doing this? The reader is prepared with an answer: For the same reason that he did what he did to the fig tree: He went looking for fruit, and found none.

By verse 16 the interplay of metaphors is clearly theological. In the person of Jesus, Yahweh, too, has come to his vineyard, looking for fruit, and has found none. Then, immediately following, verse 17 makes clear exactly what it means that Jesus "went to find out if it had any fruit . . . [but] found nothing but leaves" (see v. 13):

Is it not written:
  "'My house will be called
    a house of prayer for all nations'?
But you have made it a 'den of robbers.'"

There are several overlapping nuances here. The reference to a "house of prayer for all nations," taken from Isaiah 56:7, explains Jesus' reaction to the scene: The problem is not that buying and selling took place per se, but that it took place where it did, in the court of the Gentiles. By setting up shop within the temple compound, the merchants have commandeered the Gentiles' only legitimate place of worship. It may not be insignificant that Mark's church has been in contention over the place of Gentiles in the economy of salvation. At least *some* of Mark's readers would have heard these words with relief.

The second half of verse 17 contains an allusion to Jeremiah 7:11: "You have made it a 'den of robbers.'" The point of the allusion is not that the sellers and buyers in the temple have "robbed" people, perhaps by inflating their prices to take advantage of the crowded and stressful situation. Robbers do not rob people in a *den*. The robbers' den is the place of retreat and safety after robberies that have taken place somewhere else. The full text of Jeremiah 7:9–11 makes this point explicit:

> Will you steal and murder, commit adultery and perjury, burn incense to Baal and follow other gods you have not known, and then come and stand before me in this house, which bears my Name, and say, "We are safe"—safe to do all these detestable things? Has this house, which bears my Name, become a den of robbers to you?

The overlapping of the two stories has one other rhetorical effect: The overturning of the money-changers' tables and the scattering of their coins, the expulsion of the merchants, the prohibition against carrying "anything" through the temple precincts—all are made thematically parallel to the saying in verse 14: "May no one ever eat fruit from you again."

It is a shocking act, shocking in the same way that the withering of the fig tree was shocking, and for the same reasons: This prophetic act ends the ordinary business of the temple. That theme will echo again throughout the Passion narrative that follows. The reader will hear it perhaps most vividly in the opening of the Olivet Discourse: "Do you see all these great buildings? . . . Not one stone here will be left on another; every one will be thrown down" (13:2; see also vv. 14–23). It will sound again as one of the false accusations brought against Jesus at his "trial" before the Sanhedrin (14:58), and then again as a taunt, flung at him on the cross (15:29), and then finally—in a moment of supreme theological symbolism—in the rending of the temple curtain, from top to bottom, at the precise moment Jesus "breathed his last" (vv. 37–38).

Mark's reader does not need to wait for this pattern to feel the dread or the hope in Jesus' prophetic act against the temple. Everything is brought to an absolutely stunning conclusion in verse 20: "In the morning, as they went along, they saw the fig tree withere from the roots."

3.2.5. The Chief Priests Conspire Agains Jesus (11:18–19). Mark has sandwiche another story here—the brief episode about th authorities' conspiring against Jesus, place here to explore the effect of the cleansing o the temple story. Jesus' action against the tem ple has theological significance as a propheti act and as a step in the revisioning of redemp tion (see comments on 11:15–17), but the reli gious authorities cannot see that. Instead, the react to its social implications: What Jesus ha done wreaks havoc with the standing socia order. Turning over tables is the least of it. T the Jewish reader—for whom the temple wa the very center of the universe—he has turne the world upside down (see comments o 11:20–26).

Jesus has done this sort of thing befor (3:1–6), and the authorities' retrenchment ha begun to mount early on in the narrative (e.g 2:1–3:6, esp. 3:6). In the first half of th Gospel their movements were restricted t flanking actions. Since Peter's confession i 8:27–30, the authorities have largely disap peared from the narrative proper except withi Jesus' predictions that they will ultimately se him assassinated (8:31–33; 9:30–32; 10:32 34). They reappeared briefly in 10:2–12, i which they challenged Jesus on the question c divorce, but then disappeared again. In th story they reappear with a vengeance.

It is important to remember just ho socially disruptive Jesus' action in the templ really is. Throughout ancient society there wa a strong sense that people ought to keep in the *place*. One must never challenge one's better to do so could bring instant and seve reprisals. The technical expression for the issu here is the "honor-shame" social patter When one's honor is challenged, especially i public, one must *always* hit back. From th Jewish leaders' point of view, Jesus has cha lenged his betters in a display of incredib effrontery.

It is important that the effrontery also b public. The authorities must take action, whic must be decisive and absolute, though it mu be carried out cautiously for fear of the crow (11:18; see 14:1–2). The plot thickens. Th authorities begin to move their forces in position for a frontal assault.

3.2.6. The Fig Tree Is Withered (11:20–26). The withering of the fig tree is shocking ot only in its own right, but more importantly ecause it rounds out the symbolic cleansing f the temple (see comments on 11:12–17). Because of its connection with the fig tree, the emple cleansing is shown to be more than a imple corrective action; it is a symbolic closure of the temple. Jesus' words to the fig tree "May no one ever eat fruit from you again," . 13) are effectively addressed to the temple s well. By the same rhetorical strategy, Peter's vords to Jesus in verse 21 are also about the emple: "Rabbi, look! The fig tree you cursed as withered!"—withered "from the roots" v. 20), and thus beyond recovery.

It is difficult to describe just how chaotic—nd therefore terrifying—the world would ave seemed to a Jew without the temple. The normous size of its compound and the splendor of its ornamentation made the temple a ource of personal and national pride. More mportant, its religious functions made it the ornerstone of the world. The modern Christian mind conceives of God as everywhere present. The ancient Jew believed that too, but lso believed that there was a single *place* in ll the world where God was especially present—the Temple and its innermost sanctuary, the Most Holy Place. For this reason, the temple was the place where earth met heaven, the central point around which the rest of the created order turned. To remove the temple from one's map of the world was to shred the map itself. How could a person of faith live if there were no temple? Would God still hear one's prayers? How could forgiveness be found?

he story of the fig tree that bore no fruit and was ursed by Jesus is linked in Mark with the cleansng of the temple. In both cases, the "fruit" was nissing. On the tree, Jesus found "nothing but eaves." At the temple, he found "a den of robers." Jesus told his disciples, after they saw the vithered fig tree, that whatever they ask for in rayer "believe that you have received it, and it will e yours."

These are the questions Jesus addresses in verses 23–25. "Have faith in God," he tells his disciples in verse 23. The NIV misses an important grammatical detail here. The phrase "faith in God" is literally translated "faith [or faithfulness] of God." A paraphrase might get at this idea: "God himself is not dismayed by the destruction of the temple, so why should God's people be dismayed?" Moreover, the word translated as an imperative, "Have," can also be translated as an indicative, "You have." In other words, the sentence can read, "You have the faithfulness of God." Why, then, do you require a temple?

With the faithfulness of God in hand, the believer can then say to this mountain, "Go, throw yourself into the sea" (v. 23). Notice that Jesus is not referring here to just any mountain, but to "*this* mountain," that is, the temple mount, the Mount of Zion. In other words, Jesus is not speaking here about having faith to cast aside the great obstacles of life, but about having faith to live in direct dependence on God, without the temple or its cultic practices intervening. For the ancient Jewish mind, reared from childhood to revere the temple, this was a terrifying proposition.

Without a temple, will God hear our prayers? Jesus answers that question in verse 24. One may pray, Jesus suggests, even without the temple or its priests because one's prayers are based directly on the faithfulness of God.

Without a temple, how is forgiveness to be found? Jesus' response in verse 25 makes forgiveness with God dependent in important ways on believers' forgiveness of one another. On the surface, this is a "condition," added on top of faith in the grace of God. In its context, however, this "condition" carries reassurances. The temple may well be gone, just as the fig tree has withered away to its root, but one is not left in the world without God.

The cessation of temple worship is for us no longer even a memory, but for Jews and Christians in the first century it was a catastrophe of the first magnitude. Yet the question posed at that moment is not so far removed from the issues modern Christians and Jews must face. Jesus' reassurances are real reassurances still: God is still God and is still on the throne. God's faithfulness remains undiminished. God hears and answers prayer. God continues to forgive sins. Even in the face of catastrophe so large as the destruction of the temple, the world has not lost its center.

3.2.7. The Question About Authority (11:27–33). The presenting issue in this brief section is "authority" (*exousia*, vv. 28 [twice], 29, 33), though the levels of authority involved are not understood in the same ways by the readers and the characters.

What do the religious leaders mean by "these things" in verse 28? Clearly they intend the question on a political level, referring directly to the havoc Jesus has just wreaked in the temple, together with its social implications (see comments on 11:18–19). Mark's readers recognize a secondary level, however, and hear the question as a reference to the formal cessation of temple worship and the shift in the economy of salvation itself. The difference is rhetorically parallel to the Pharisees' demand for a "sign from heaven" in 8:11–13 (see comments), all the while blind to the fact that Jesus himself was the sign from heaven, standing before them in the flesh.

The Jewish leaders have challenged Jesus' right to take action in the temple. Since he is a peasant without formal theological training or recognized authority, his actions are shameful and disgraceful. The underlying logic is simple: In an honor-shame society, everyone is expected to keep within his or her social place. Their question is thus a serious thrust in a verbal duel, and the leaders cannot see how Jesus will be able to deflect the blow. Since he is a peasant who lacks both priestly credentials and formal theological training, he has no formal status to play any role in the temple but that of pilgrim and worshiper. There is no answer he can make to legitimate such outrageous behavior as what he has done.

To their surprise and dismay, Jesus is able to parry their thrust easily with a counterquestion. The logic of verses 30–33 is clear. In a single stroke he turns the thrust back upon itself, forcing them either to admit their blindness to the movement of God or to risk the condemnation of the gallery. Since the crowd connects Jesus with John (see 6:14–16; 8:27–28), any judgment the authorities make about John will apply automatically to Jesus. The leaders cannot condemn John without reaping the wrath of the crowd; but if they commend John, the people will wonder, "Why not also Jesus?"

For the reader, who watches the duel from a higher vantage point, the reply of the authorities in verse 33a carries a rich and ironic overlay of meaning: "We don't know." They do not know, indeed! Jesus' final response (v. 33b) is also ironic: "Neither will I tell you. . . ." It appears at first that this final thrust closes out the contest, but this turns out only to be a pause between rounds. In the parable of the wicked tenants that follows (12:1–12), Jesus opens the contest again, this time from a position of rhetorical advantage.

3.2.8. The Parable of the Wicked Tenants (12:1–12). How would this story have been heard in Mark's Roman church? Certain conditions are operative here. (1) The parable comes directly after Jesus' conflict with the authorities in 11:27–33, and the grammar of 12:1 makes it clear that it is directed to the "chief priests, the teachers of the law and the elders" in 11:27. In other words, the parable continues the verbal duel that began there. Like the controversy over authority, this section proceeds on two levels. The reader will no doubt understand this exchange within the context of the Triumphal Entry and the judgment against the fig tree and temple. That context includes not only the *text* of these great stories, but also its theological implications.

The "vineyard" is, of course, another metaphor for Israel, extending and deepening the imagery from Jeremiah that lay behind the fig tree story (see Jer. 8:13). Here that imagery is constructed onto the prophetic tradition of Isaiah 5:1–7. The parallels are striking, even in translation, and are reinforced by nearly verbatim language:

Isaiah 5:1–2	Mark 12:1b
My loved one had a vineyard on a fertile hillside.	A man planted a vineyard.
He dug it up and cleared it of stones	He put a wall around it
He built a watchtower in it	built a watchtower
and cut out a winepress as well	dug a pit for the winepress

The passage from Isaiah continues with a shift to a metaphor of disappointment and judgment: "Then he looked for a crop of good grapes, but it yielded only bad fruit" (Isa. 5:2b). This is not unlike the metaphor Mark's reader has already encountered in Mark 11. Both the literary context and the allusion to Isaiah suggest that the "man" in Mark 12:1 is God, who has come unsuccessfully looking for fruit (see 11:13 and comments on 11:20–26). The metaphor that unfolds is clear enough, even for the authorities inside the story; 12:12 makes it explicit.

The entrapment in this story is created by the *identifications* it evokes. Because of their political power, the chief priests, teachers of the law, and elders—who are *Jesus'* designated listeners—no doubt would have identified at first with the wealthy landowner whose property is at stake. But as the story unfolds, that identification becomes increasingly problematic. The allusion to Isaiah 5:1–7 in Mark 12:1 and the reference to the abuse of the first servant in verse 3 demand that they see themselves in the role of the wicked tenants. This shifts the claim of the story significantly, since it forces the recognition that the landowner here must be God. The story then develops the character portrait of the tenants, who abused the prophets.

At the same time, the authorities cannot entirely abandon their initial identification with the landowner—whose rights the rulers would very well have understood, and which they would have strenuously defended as a matter of law. The story thus leaves them with no option but self-condemnation. Furthermore, they cannot miss his implied claim to be the "beloved Son" (NASB) in verses 6–8, a son whom the tenants ruthlessly kill. Thus Jesus exposes their secret plot against him. How understandable but how ironic that they set about to arrest Jesus in verse 12. He accuses them of a miscarriage of justice, and they reply with a lynch mob!

Mark's reader observes this process of identification from the outside, hearing everything the authorities have heard, but more sharply. (1) When the story names the final emissary as a "son, whom [the landowner] loved" (v. 6), the language immediately evokes the voice of God from the cloud that identified Jesus with these same words at his baptism (1:11) and transfiguration (9:7). The authorities have not heard these two prior episodes, and they do not know that God has spoken from the clouds. But the reader *does* know these things; what is *implied* for the authorities is *explicit* for the reader. This subtle difference sharpens the reader's responses and in that way deepens the narrative's condemnation of the authorities in 12:12.

(2) The reader also has insight into the rhetorical question in verse 9: "What then will the owner of the vineyard do?" Indeed, what would the authorities themselves do in a similar situation? In a society without a functioning police force, the only legitimate response is to take personal action: "He will come and kill those tenants and give the vineyard to others."

From the reader's perspective this is no idle threat. If Mark's Gospel was composed after the fall of Jerusalem in A.D. 70, this has quite literally come true. Even if the book was written earlier, this is true prophetically. It is important that the threat in verse 9 comes *after* the complex of stories surrounding the "closure" of the temple in 11:12–26 (see comments on 11:15–17). Who are the "others" in view in 12:9? The text gives no clue. Perhaps they are the laypeople who will later assume leadership in the church. Perhaps they are the Gentiles, who are as far removed from Jewish religious authorities as one can get. Perhaps Mark's readers of all stripes will hear this as a reference to themselves.

(3) The saying about the rejected cornerstone in verses 10–11 comes as a final affront. On one level, this is clearly a quotation taken from Psalm 118:22. On another level, however, this Old Testament passage appears to have acquired the tenor of a folk saying, used to explain how a misfit person or thing in the end found its rightful place. The crucial stone is not the foundation stone, but the "capstone"—the one that forms the final piece in the construction of an arch, held in its place by its odd shape; it holds the rest of the construction in place. There is ample evidence that early Christians used this metaphor widely to explain how the work of Christ was the *finishing* work of faith (cf. Matt. 21:42; Luke 20:17; Acts 4:11; 1 Peter 2:7).

Lane (1974, 420) provides a summary of the meaning of this concept:

> The quotation of Ps. 118:22f agrees exactly with the LXX form of the text. The passage refers to one of the building blocks gathered at the site of Solomon's Temple which was rejected in the construction of the sanctuary but which proved to be the keystone of the porch.

Although there is no explicit biblical reference to an actual incident such as Lane describes in his commentary, there are noncanonical ones. For our purposes, perhaps the most useful reference is found in the Testament of Solomon 22:7:

> So Jerusalem was being built and the Temple was moving toward completion. Now there was a gigantic "cornerstone," which I wished to place at the head of the corner to complete the Temple of God.

The text goes on to describe the enormous difficulty the workers had in lifting the cornerstone into place. Finally, the stone is levitated into place by an angelic visitor (23:1–3), at which Solomon exclaims, "Truly the Scripture which says, '*It was the stone rejected by the builders that became the keystone*,' has now been fulfilled" (23:4). The Testament of Solomon is a late Jewish document (perhaps as late as the fourth century A.D.), but it demonstrates the use of the term *cornerstone* as the stone placed at the *peak* of the building. Later Jewish interpreters take great pains to point out that it was this stone that completed the building of the temple; perhaps in that way it acquired symbolic significance as the finishing work of faith.

But for the authorities, Jesus' use of this saying from the Psalms is clearly audacious, a word of rebuke leveled against them in public for actions they are trying to take in secret. They understand the accusation perfectly (v. 12), but they can take no action—at least, not yet. They first must find some way to undermine Jesus' popularity with the crowds. We are thus prepared for the controversy stories that fill the remainder of chapter 12.

3.2.9. On Paying Taxes to Caesar (12:13–17). This story once again uses the form of the controversy story (see "The Form of Pronouncement Stories" at sec. 2.3). It is important to remember that this is part of a series of such stories and that the tensions have been building for some time (see comment on 11:1–12:44). Mark's comment that the authorities were trying "to catch [Jesus] in his words" (v. 13) is unnecessary, but its presence here serves to sharpen the irony of verse 14. How ironic that Jesus' enemies should be duplicitous in their declaration that Jesus is "a man of integrity"! From the reader's point of view, such duplicity entraps *them* in *their* words.

These enemies pose their problem in verse 14b: "Is it right to pay taxes to Caesar or not?" The question is intended to impale Jesus on the horns of a dilemma. If he answers "yes," they can turn the crowds against him; if he answers "no," they have grounds to denounce him before a Roman court. Perhaps the presence of Herodians (v. 13a) facilitated just such a move (cf. 3:6).

The tension mounts, but Jesus' response threads this needle finely. By calling for a denarius and asking the rhetorical questions, "Whose portrait is this? And whose inscription?" (v. 16), he forces them into an acknowledgment that the coinage they themselves use is Roman. The very fact that one uses money of a certain origin is implicit affirmation of the authority that issued the money. Verse 17 then follows: Surely if one uses Roman coinage, one ought to "give to Caesar what is Caesar's." At the same time, one must not render to Caesar *more* than is his due; what is due to God must be denied Caesar. Indeed, with this deft turn of phrase, Jesus denies any imperial claim to deity and requires that there be no confusion about one's ultimate loyalties.

This reasoning may well have been too subtle for the crowds to grasp. It would be clear enough to them that Jesus had bested the authorities at their own game, but for the crowds Jesus' words may well have had a more sinister ring: "Caesar should get what he has coming to him!" As clear as its implications are, the saying is also a masterstroke of ambiguity. Any zealot *could* have greeted such a response with satisfied approval, and any Roman court *could* have heard the opposite. Thus Jesus impales the authorities on the horns of their own dilemma. Mark concludes by saying that his enemies were "amazed at him" (v. 17).

3.2.10. The Question About the Resurrection (12:18–27). This story continues to use the controversy form. Note once again that this is part of a series and that tensions have been building for some time (see comments on

11:1–12:44). Mark 12:18 indicates the position taken by the Sadducees and thus establishes the frame of reference both for their question (vv. 19–23) and for Jesus' response (vv. 24–27).

Despite addressing Jesus as "teacher" (v. 19), the question of the Sadducees is clearly hostile. They accepted as authoritative only the Pentateuch (the first five books of the Old Testament). Since explicit mention of the resurrection does not appear until Isaiah 26:19, they felt justified in questioning the legitimacy of this doctrine, even though belief in the general resurrection was the norm elsewhere in Judaism. Their question in Mark 12:19–23 is therefore posed as a riddle, for which they do not expect Jesus to have an adequate response.

The practice at issue is "levirate marriage," in which a surviving brother was expected to marry and father children with a deceased brother's widow (Deut. 25:5–10). The first son of such a union bore the name—and thus carried on the memory—of the deceased husband and in that way carried his name forward for posterity. The Sadducees use this practice of levirate marriage to frame their challenge to Jesus' view of the resurrection: If this problem repeats itself, then in the resurrection, whose wife will the woman be? The intention of the question is to demonstrate the absurdity of belief in the resurrection by connecting it to an absurd image of a woman in the afterlife, married to seven husbands.

Jesus' response moves forward in two parts. The first (vv. 24–25) describes conditions in heaven, setting aside their absurd image of a woman with seven husbands. The Sadducees' question does not represent an adequate picture of the afterlife, in which such concerns are transcended by the joy of communion with God. Those who rise from the dead are transformed in the resurrection; life in the afterlife is like that of the angels, and even so marvelous a state as marriage is made moot in the light of God's surpassing glory.

The second movement of Jesus' response involves an exposition of Exodus 3:6: "I am the God of . . . Abraham, the God of Isaac and the God of Jacob." The logic of this exposition is subtle and often overlooked in interpretation. On one level, Jesus' logic involves a claim about the implicit tense structures of the verse in question. God—who exists outside of time—is at one and the same time the God of these three men, each of whom lived at a moment in history. Furthermore, the sentence "*I am* that God" continues to be true even now. How can such a statement be true if Abraham, Isaac, and Jacob no longer exist?

On another level, the argument rests not on syntax but on "the power of God" (v. 24). Within first-century understanding, the phrase "the God of . . ." had come to mean, not "the God about whom one has beliefs," but "the God who offers help and protection." Thus, the claim "I am the God of Abraham, Isaac, and Jacob" can hardly be true if God had abandoned them at the time of that greatest of all afflictions, death. Belief in a God who does not raise the dead is, for Jesus, as self-contradictory and absurd as the hypothetical question the Sadducees posed.

For Mark's reader, of course, there is an additional ironic nuance here. The reader knows already that Jesus *himself* will be raised from the dead. This is knowledge brought in from outside, but it has been reinforced by Jesus' repeated predictions that he would be put to death in Jerusalem and afterward would rise again (8:31–33; 9:30–32; 10:32–34). Viewed from this vantage point, the Sadducees' question, though intended as a serious challenge, is ironically ludicrous. The fact that they can address such a question *to Jesus* makes them out to be buffoons.

3.2.11. The Great Commandment (12:28–34). This story, involving a reversal of expectations, concludes a series of controversy stories (see "The Form of Pronouncement Stories" at sec. 2.3), but it lacks the usual barbs and duplicity the reader has come to expect from such stories. The initial question posed in verse 28 appears not to have been motivated by the same duplicity as those raised in earlier stories in the section: "Of all the commandments, which is the most important?"

Jesus formulates his response by drawing first from the traditional Jewish confession of faith, the Shema (Deut. 6:4). In doing so he places the whole matter of law on a different footing. What matters is not one's exposition or performance of the law, but one's relationship to the living God. That is, what matters is not *obedience to Torah*, but *love of God*. So important is this love of God that its range is established through repetition: One should love God with one's *whole* heart, one's *whole* soul, one's *whole* mind, and one's *whole* strength (Mark 12:30). In making this affirmation, Jesus extends the Shema by adding "mind," an addition that deepens the rhetorical effect.

To this passage from Deuteronomy Jesus adds a similar comment from Leviticus 19:18: "Love your neighbor as yourself." Within Leviticus, this passage places the word "neighbor" in direct parallel with the phrase "one of your people," and this is how it was typically understood by first-century Jews, for whom "neighbor" excluded non-Jews. Jesus radically redefined this word in the parable of the good Samaritan (Luke 10:25–37). Paul also used a variation of this redefinition (Rom. 13:8–10), probably in anticipation of an argument for peace on the question of the "disputable matters" of the law (14:1–15:13). Indeed, the issue Paul addresses here has to do with the manner in which Gentiles are accepted into the family of faith. Mark's readers may have been hearing here, therefore, a reinterpretation of Leviticus 19:18.

The teacher of the law who poses the initial question in verse 28 hears Jesus' answer and repeats it at length, approvingly (vv. 32–33). In the reiteration, he makes a startling shift of content, interpreting Jesus' words in terms of concrete action within the sacrificial system. Where Jesus had said that "there is no commandment greater than" the twin duties of love of God and love of neighbor (v. 32), the teacher of the law says that these twin duties are "more important than all burnt offerings and sacrifices." With this shift, the teacher of the law takes a step in the direction of Jesus' more profound interpretation of the nature of law.

Mark has taken pains to cast this teacher of the law in a positive light. He was not part of the initial attempt to "catch him in his words" (v. 13), but came upon the scene unexpectedly (v. 28a); he approved of Jesus' answers to prior questions (v. 28b) and repeated his answer to this one with full approval (v. 32), extending its implications in concrete terms (v. 33b). For his part, Jesus describes the man's responses as "wise" (v. 34a) and pronounces a judgment of his own: "You are not far from the kingdom of God" (v. 34b). The response is ambiguous, for "not far" still implies "outside" and thus raises an unresolved question: What more must this man do to take that decisive step from "not far" to "inside"?

It is difficult to place verse 34c: "From then on no one dared ask him any more questions." Does this describe the responses of the authorities to Jesus' cordial but happenstance exchange with this teacher of the law in verses 28–34b? Or is it a ballast line that ties off all the controversy stories that began in 11:27? Or does it prepare for the exchange about David's Son that follows in 12:35? Hereafter Jesus teaches (vv. 35, 38), but not in response to direct challenges; indeed, it is Jesus who poses the difficult questions (vv. 35–37a) and makes the difficult accusations (vv. 38–40, 43–44), to the great delight of his listening public (v. 37b).

But verse 34c may also serve a different narrative function. Its language implies that Jesus has shown himself to be more than a match for his enemies in the public debates they themselves had initiated. Surely here (as in 2:1–3:35) the sword of Jesus' mouth is razor sharp. This portrayal of Jesus' dominating the debates in the temple will recur later in the narrative, especially in the Garden of Gethsemane, where he calls into question the action of the guards because they have arrested him in secret (14:49). The implication that Jesus enjoys tremendous popular support underlies the decision of the authorities to arrest Jesus by stealth and "not during the Feast . . . or the people may riot" (14:1–2). When in his trial Jesus remains silent (14:61), the reader knows that he very well *could* respond to the accusations they bring; his silence, then, stands in stunning contrast to his skill with words now. In other words, the controversy stories of chapter 12 prepare the reader for the Passion narrative that follows.

3.2.12. The Question About David's Son (12:35–37a). This story is preserved without context except for the note that Jesus said these things while teaching in the temple (v. 35). The implication is that the religious authorities who have been questioning him are somehow included in his audience. The question is posed as a riddle, which the authorities do not even attempt to answer. Perhaps their hesitation is connected in some way to the summary statement in verse 34: "From then on no one dared ask him any more questions."

The riddle juxtaposes two words in the context of Psalm 110:1: To be a "son" of some one is to come after, to be in some sense also subordinate; to be "Lord" of someone is to exercise greater status and power. So how can the Messiah ("the Christ") be both David's "son" and his "Lord?" Or, perhaps more correctly, *in what sense* is he both "son" and "Lord"? The reader, of course, knows the answer to this riddle. On the one hand, Jesus is "Son of David" (cf. the title as used in the story of blind Bartimaeus [10:47–48] and of the Triumphal Entry [11:10]). On the other hand, the reader knows that Jesus is "Lord" by virtue of his identity as Son of God, a frequent affirmation in Mark (see esp. 1:1).

There may be a further nuance here, in which Jesus' Lordship is connected not to his preexistent state or to the status reflected in the words spoken by God from the cloud (1:11; 9:7), but to the crucifixion and exaltation that still lie ahead in the narrative. The imagery of Psalm 110 is widely distributed in the New Testament (this Old Testament passage is frequently quoted in the New), which provides evidence that early Christians often referred to this psalm in their efforts to grasp the meaning of Jesus' life and work. In Acts 2:29–36, for example, Psalm 110 is interpreted Christologically in the light of Easter. The sense in which Jesus is Lord is the sense in which he passes through crucifixion to resurrection and to exaltation at the right hand of God.

The narrator also implies, however, that Jesus' question in verse 37 is left unanswered within the narrative because the authorities were unable to grasp these dimensions of Jesus' identity. Indeed, they do not even recognize that he is the "the Christ" about whom the riddle is posed in the first place. The reader is asked not only to respond to the riddle, but also to note the failure of the authorities to grasp what the riddle is ultimately about.

3.2.13. Woe to the Teachers of the Law (12:37b–40). Although this brief warning follows hard on the heels of a series of controversy stories (11:27–12:34), it is not cast in that form. It does, however, continue the condemnation of the religious authorities that has characterized nearly the entire section (except for 12:28–34). In doing so, it offers not only an explicit judgment against the piety of the teachers of the law, but also by implication an affirmation of those lay worshipers who have been displaced by the authorities. (That distinction is deepened by the note in v. 37b that "the large crowd listened to him with delight," which reiterates a similar comment in v. 18 and prepares for the subterfuge in 14:1–2.)

Over against the lay public Mark has placed "the chief priests," "the elders," and "the teachers of the law." The unusual phrase in 2:16 "scribes of the Pharisees" (lit.; NIV, "the teachers of the law who were Pharisees") and the frequent association of these teachers and the Pharisees elsewhere make it clear that in Mark's understanding, "teachers of the law" are associated with the movement of the Pharisees. In every instance but two (9:9–13; 12:28–34), Mark puts the teachers of the law in a negative light (e.g., 1:21–28; 2:1–12; 3:22–30; 7:1–23; 8:31–33; 9:14–29; 10:32–34). They are part of the Jewish conspiracy against Jesus, not recognizing who he is. All this prepares for the Passion, in which the teachers of the law continue to play a central role.

Here Jesus' condemnation of these teachers takes the form of a warning against their externalized piety, a warning that bears a remarkable similarity with an earlier word of judgment pronounced in Galilee (7:1–23). The customs referred to in verses 38–39 are well known. The teachers of the law enjoyed walking "around in flowing robes," a reference to the white linen robes that they wore as marks of distinction. They liked to "be greeted in the marketplaces," a reference to the honorific titles of "father," "rabbi," and "master" with which they preferred to be addressed. They also liked to "have the most important seats in the synagogues [i.e., facing the congregation and near the Torah] and the places of honor at banquets."

But their sheer "showiness" gives them away, as is especially evident in their treatment of widows. Traditionally in Judaism, widows and orphans were recipients of God's special care (Deut. 10:18; Ps. 68:5; Jer. 49:11), and the ways in which they were treated indicated the moral character of an entire people (Deut. 24:19–22; Job 22:9; 24:3; 31:16; Ps. 94:6; Isa. 1:23; 10:2; Mal. 3:5). The teachers of the law are guilty here not merely for confusing human recognition with divine approval, but for defrauding those who are socially vulnerable. Thus, Jesus' condemnation here reiterates the condemnation he made in 7:6–7, when he called them "hypocrites." The role they will soon play in the condemnation and execution of Jesus is also a scripted role, but one in which they act out what is really in their hearts.

3.2.14. The Widow's Offering (12:41–44). This brief story picks up and deepens the theme of the preceding paragraph, condemning the teachers of the law by comparing them with the inner piety and sacrificial love of God expressed by a simple Jewish woman: "She, out of her poverty, put in everything—all she had to live on" (v. 44).

Within the Jewish legal and social system, widows were not only without support, but also without a public voice. Women were not expected to speak on their own behalf, and a widow was left without an advocate. This situation was especially difficult if the widow had young children or was estranged from her husband's family. For this reason, care of widows and orphans was thought to be the special province of God, and abuse of widows was a particularly heinous but revealing indicator of a nation's lack of moral sensitivities (cf. 12:37b–40).

The woman's meager resources are represented by two *lepta*, the smallest copper coin in use in first-century Palestine. It is significant that the woman puts in *two* of such coins, for she could very well have divided them and kept one for herself. This fact increases the sense of the generosity in her gift and in that way sharpens the contrast with the teachers, whose self-serving and self-aggrandizing expressions of piety were called into question in the previous section.

3.3. The Olivet Discourse (13:1–37)

At first the Olivet Discourse appears to be an intrusion in the narrative. The movement of the plot stops completely. The discourse has its own internal structure, with a beginning, middle, and end, and the diction and vocabulary are unusual for Mark. For this reason, it is sometimes suggested that this long passage originally circulated independently of Mark. Even if this were so, the language of sacrifice and persecution is thoroughly Markan.

When we interpret the Gospel of Mark from the point of view of the *historian*, the meaning of these verses is clear. When we interpret it from the point of view of *Mark's reader*, the clarity is lost, and we are left with several options. Everything depends on the date of this Gospel. We know from Josephus that the temple compound was reduced to smoldering ruins in A.D. 70. In this commentary we have followed the traditional dating of the Gospel after the fire in Rome in A.D. 64, but we have no way of knowing exactly how long after the fire Mark wrote. If he wrote after the destruction of the temple, this dreadful prediction would have already been fulfilled. If not, the destruction of the temple was looming on the horizon.

In any case, the destruction of the temple is the central and dominating concern of this Olivet Discourse. It forms the presenting statement (vv. 1–2), which prompts the disciples' question (v. 4) and the exploration of implications (vv. 5–13). The desecration of the temple is alluded to in Jesus' comments about the "abomination that causes desolation" (v. 14), and this in turn leads to a recitation of the terrible apocalyptic signs that will accompany the end times and the appearance of the Son of Man (vv. 15–37; cf. vv. 7–8). The entire discourse closes with the repeated exhortations to "Watch!" (v. 37), for "no one knows about that day or hour" (v. 32), which return to the reader the initial questions the disciples asked in verse 4.

Other elements of the Olivet Discourse may have been more directly tied to the reader's own experience. For example, we have argued that Mark's congregation had suffered much persecution, with deep divisions in the church's corporate life (see comments in the Introduction). If so, the warnings in verses 9 and 12–13 would have been especially vivid.

But were these words heard as warnings or as memories? Did the Olivet Discourse steel its readers against the coming disaster? Did it offer specific—if coded—instructions: "Flee now to the mountains" (cf. vv. 14–19)? Or did it offer an accounting of the disaster that had already struck, and a promise that the next thing, the hopeful thing, would be the appearance of the Son of Man in the clouds (vv. 26, 32–37)? Perhaps Mark's readers are asked to see this long series of prophecies as *partially* fulfilled and thus find themselves on the fault line between this age and the age to come. If they are an *apocalyptic* community (see the Introduction), the fault line is already a chasm, open and moving, as the earth itself falls apart from its center.

Whatever connection the readers are expected to have made with their own experience, it is clear that the Olivet Discourse prepares in important ways for the Passion narrative that follows. In his trial, Jesus will be accused of having predicted that *he himself* would destroy the temple (14:58). The narrator will point out that this is false testimony, but leaves it to the readers to know why. The Olivet Discourse, terrible and vivid and sweeping in its language, is a powerful foreground for the false accusation at Jesus' trial (see also comments on 15:22–39).

3.3.1. Prediction of the Destruction of the Temple (13:1–2). In its immediate context, verse 1 functions as the presenting occasion of the Olivet Discourse. Note the way verses 2 and 4 transition into this discourse by raising the questions that Jesus will later address. The size and magnificence of Herod's temple were legendary, the compound itself covering more than 172,000 square yards, with walls extending eighty feet above the perimeter roads. While Herod made no modifications to the dimensions of the temple proper, he made massive and dazzling changes to the temple ornamentation. Josephus commented that onlookers were blinded by the reflection of the sunlight off the gold adornments.

If one may be permitted a bit of historical imagination, it is possible to reconstruct tentatively what this moment of 13:1–2 would have been like. The text of Mark does not indicate the time of day or the disciples' location when they made their famous comment in verse 1: "Look, Teacher! What massive stones! What magnificent buildings!" But one can easily imagine them looking back from a vantage point on the Mount of Olives (cf. v. 3) as they made their way to Bethany in the evening. If so, this moment may well have happened at sunset, and with the sunlight streaming through the temple complex, the image before them would have rivaled the splendor of any sight in the ancient world. This may also be the context of Jesus' damning words in verse 2: "Not one stone here will be left on another; every one will be thrown down." At such a moment, this comment is absolutely arresting.

The reader, of course, reads at a later time and encounters Jesus' comment within a different set of circumstances. Because we cannot be sure about the date of Mark's Gospel,

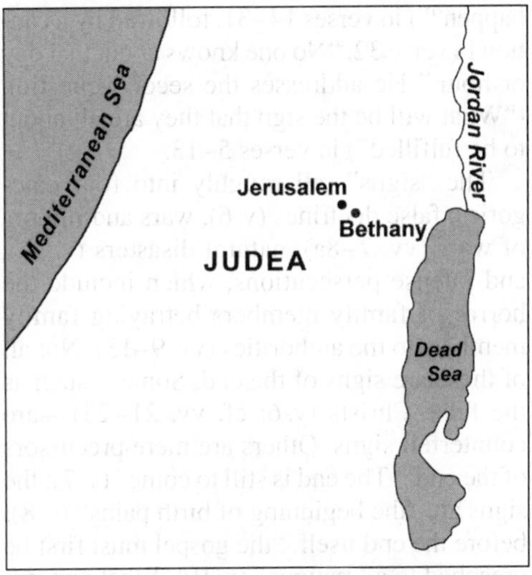

During his final visit to Jerusalem, Jesus and his disciples returned to Bethany at night. It was at Bethany that a woman anointed Jesus with an expensive perfume, pouring it on his head. When some rebuked the woman, saying money from the sale of the perfume could have helped the poor, Jesus defended her, saying that what she had done for him would be told wherever the gospel is preached in the world.

it is difficult to determine whether Mark's reader heard this statement as a prediction of impending disaster or as a prophecy of a *fait accompli*. Bas van Iersel (1988, 162) offers a moderating interpretation:

> The difference in time between the utterances of Jesus, the writing of the book, and the reading of it, on the one hand, and the interpolation addressed to the reader in 13:14, on the other, gives us every reason to presume that the narrator wishes to warn the readers through this section of a situation that already exists or may arise at any moment.

In terms of Mark's narrative itself, verse 2 may serve a secondary function of preparing for the accusations against Jesus at his trial (see comments in previous section).

3.3.2. Signs Before the End (13:3–8). In verse 4 the inner circle of disciples (Peter, James, John, and Andrew) pose two broad questions that form the framework within which the reader reads the Olivet Discourse. These two questions are answered in what is roughly reverse sequence. Jesus answers the opening question ("When will these things happen?") in verses 14–31, followed by a caution in verse 32: "No one knows about that day or hour." He addresses the second question ("What will be the sign that they are all about to be fulfilled") in verses 5–13.

The "signs" fall roughly into four categories: false doctrines (v. 6), wars and rumors of wars (vv. 7–8a), natural disasters (v. 8b), and intense persecutions, which include the horror of family members betraying family members to the authorities (vv. 9–13). Not all of these are signs of the end. Some—such as the false Christs (v. 6; cf. vv. 21–23)—are counterfeit signs. Others are mere precursors of the end: "The end is still to come" (v. 7); the signs are "the beginning of birth pains" (v. 8); before the end itself, "the gospel must first be preached to all nations" (v. 10). What appears as the genuine and definitive sign of the actual end is the desecration of the temple (v. 14), after which the disasters unleashed on human experience will make the former trials appear mild by comparison (vv. 19–20).

But at bottom, both the counterfeit signs and the repeated cautions serve as reminders that, as real and as horrible as the events before the end will be and as deeply connected with the end as they will be, they must not be taken as indicators by which to make predictions about what will happen next. Indeed, as the caution in verse 32 stresses, "no one knows about that day or hour." Instead, the reader, like the disciples, is urged to "watch" (vv. 33–37).

3.3.3. Persecutions Foretold (13:9–13). It is unclear how these verses fit into the general sequence. Are they part of the "counterfeit signs" described in verses 3–8? Or are they more directly connected with the apocalyptic events of the end described in verses 14–31? The fact that the text does not make that clear may be part of the wider program of caution that is laced throughout the Olivet Discourse. While the sufferings of Christians are in some way a precursor of the end, they are not a reliable basis for predicting what will come next.

It is widely recognized that verses 9–13 would have had special urgency for the members of Mark's persecuted church. But here again we must urge caution, for we cannot date this Gospel with precision. In this commentary, we understand its writing as following the great persecution of Christians in Rome in A.D. 64, and possibly as late as the destruction of the temple in A.D. 70. Mark's beleaguered Christians found themselves in stressful circumstances (see the Introduction; see also Heb. 10:32–34, which may have been written at about the same time and perhaps addressed to the same church). If these connections can be sustained, they provide insight into an extraordinarily painful time for Mark's readers. Could Christians in Rome have heard the terrible predictions of the Olivet Discourse and not have heard echoes of their own experience? If they did, Jesus' words offered comfort and encouragement in subtle and important ways (see comments on 13:28–37).

On first reading, the thrust of 13:9–13 is alarmist. Terrible things are in the air. Be forewarned. On closer reading, however, it is cautionary. It limits the tragedy, showing by a variety of devices that as terrible as these things are, they will ultimately be swallowed up in the redemptive activity of God. False Christs, wars, natural disasters, persecutions, and betrayals—all are real. Yet all are also limited, constrained and transformed by the encompassing power of God.

3.3.4. The Abomination That Causes Desolation (13:14–20). The prophecy of the "abomination that causes desolation" in verse 14 is one of those places in which Mark turns from his narrative and offers an explanatory aside to the reader: "Let the reader understand" (see also 7:3, 11, 19, 35; 15:34). But even the aside is cryptic, like the comment in 6:52: "They had not understood about the loaves." In both instances, the reader is expected to interpret the wording of the text in the light of information brought in from outside. But what is that here? What is the "abomination that causes desolation," and what is the reader expected to understand about the expression that the text itself does not say?

The expression itself has been taken over verbatim from Daniel 9:27, where the prophet predicts an event so terrible that it defiles the temple and makes it an unfit place for worship (see also Dan. 11:31; 12:11). But biblical prophecy can be repeatedly fulfilled. The writer of 1 Maccabees saw a literal fulfillment in 168 B.C., when Antiochus IV Epiphanes desecrated the temple, setting up an altar to Zeus and sacrificing a pig on the altar of burnt offerings (1 Macc. 1:54–59; cf. 6:7). The distribution of this phrase in intertestamental literature suggests that by the first century, it had become a technical reference to horrific events in the temple. Jesus' use of the phrase in Mark 13:14 indicates that in his view, Daniel's prophecy was not *ultimately* fulfilled in 168 B.C.; the trauma would happen yet again. Mark's aside to the reader in verse 14b prompts the readers to interpret the phrase "abomination that causes desolation" in the light of circumstances that were unfolding in their own context.

But what? If, as I have argued in the Introduction, Mark was written on the eve of, or perhaps immediately following, the destruction of Jerusalem in A.D. 70, the reader would likely have heard this prophecy in connection with that event. Technically, of course, the phrase "the abomination that causes desolation" does not refer to the destruction of the temple so much as to its desecration. True, there is no reference to the fire by which the temple walls were eventually razed. But the opening verses of the chapter provide clear evidence that this crisis was in some way placed within the context of the destruction of the temple precincts (esp. v. 2), and this larger context surely would have informed the reader's attempts to "understand" what the language of the prophecy in verse 14 meant.

Everything in the rhetorical structure of the passage focuses on the need to flee; indeed, the sacrilege in the temple is noted not primarily for its own sake, but as the decisive signal to "flee to the mountains." The repeated injunctions to flee (vv. 15–16), the concern about those most vulnerable at such a moment (v. 17), the increased dangers during winter (v. 18), the prophecy about the severity of the crisis (v. 19), and the prayer that the days be shortened (v. 20) all deepen the sense of urgency.

The instruction to flee itself is striking; in times of ancient war the most likely places of refuge were cities, especially those with sufficient provisions to withstand a siege. Verse 15 instructs those caught on rooftops not even to "go down," an idiom that probably means not to descend by an inner stair or, having gone down some other way, to return to the house to take anything away. A parallel injunction in verse 16 offers a similar warning to those in the field.

What is striking here is the immediacy of the flight. The abomination that causes desolation, when it happens, will come so suddenly that it will call for *instant* flight. There will not be time for provisions, a condition that surely deepens the sense of the severity of the disaster. That sense of disaster is reinforced in verses 19–20, in which the cataclysm is interpreted in the apocalyptic language of the end time. The prayer that the catastrophe "not take place in winter" (v. 18) similarly refers not to the hazards of weather but to a shortage of provisions.

It is important that this language specifically directs those who are *in Judea* to flee (v. 14); indeed, this may well be exactly what has happened. The church historian Eusebius records a tradition in which members of the church in Jerusalem fled to Pella and the Transjordan in response to "an oracle given in revelation" (*Ecc. Hist.* 3.5.3) in about the year 66, shortly before the siege of the city. If the "oracle" in view here is Mark 13:14–20, we have at least implicit evidence that some first-century Christians thought it referred to the Jewish war of A.D. 66–70 and to the Roman crusade that brought that war to its terrible end.

Certain aspects of the passage suggest that this is a disaster of cosmic proportions. The entire Olivet Discourse breathes the unmistakable air of Jewish apocalyptic, with its heavy emphasis on the portents in the heavens (esp. vv. 24–27), its use of the title "Son of Man" (a common term in Mark but here imbued with apocalyptic significance by the description of his appearing in the clouds of heaven, v. 26), its references to the gathering of the elect (v. 27), and its predictions of terrible tribulation (vv. 19–20). When these factors appear together—as they do here—they suggest in no uncertain terms that the events being described are in some way connected with the eschaton.

Yet other aspects of the passage urge caution against interpreting the abomination that causes desolation as the ultimate and definitive sign of the arrival of the end time. (1) Note that only those who are in Judea are exhorted to flee (v. 14). This at least suggests that the catastrophe will be localized, perhaps around the cities, certainly around Jerusalem. (2) Indeed, the very injunction to "flee to the mountains" implies the possibility that the disaster can be escaped. (3) More important, the apocalyptic language and the predictions of cosmic portents come hand in glove with repeated cautions against extrapolating a time line from the imagery provided in this chapter. The entire discourse closes on this exact note: "No one knows about that day or hour . . . [*not even*] the Son" (v. 32); Christians are not called to calculate the hour, but to be vigilant (vv. 33–37).

3.3.5. False Christs and False Prophets (13:21–23). Times of distress often make people more vulnerable to demagoguery, especially if the distress seems to match the expected tribulations of the end time. If the Messiah is to appear at all, then he will surely appear when his people need him most, when his appearance will fulfill prophecy, when he can validate his claims with signs and wonders (v. 22)! Yet that gullibility is precisely the opposite of the clear-eyed vigilance enjoined in the Olivet Discourse as a whole (esp. vv. 32–37).

This brief passage cautions the church not to panic at such moments. It does this by recalling a thread from earlier in the passage that urges cautions against the "many" who will come, saying "I am he," and in so doing will lead many astray (v. 6). The basis for urging caution here is that miracles are not infallible proofs of God's activity (see Deut. 13:1–3), though in the larger scheme of Mark's own Christology, the expectation of signs and wonders is itself a symptom of the moral blindness that fails to see the "sign" God has already placed (see 8:11–13). According to Mark, the true "sign" from heaven is Jesus himself, and the true "wonder" is the power of God displayed in Jesus' suffering and death on the cross. Any claim to be the Christ divorced from that death is a false claim; any "prophet" who supports such a claim is a "false" prophet; any believer who follows such a claim is being led astray (v. 22)—and all of that at precisely the moment of judgment and decision.

3.3.6. The Coming of the Son of Man (13:24–27). The language now becomes more consciously apocalyptic. The signs that follow "that distress [tribulation]" (v. 24) are drawn from conventional apocalyptic literature, and the imagery is more supernatural and cosmic than what appeared in verses 3–13. The very "powers in the heavens" (v. 25; NIV, "heavenly bodies") will be shaken, and the Son of Man will finally appear "in clouds with great power and glory" (v. 26).

There is some question about how to understand the phrase "Son of Man" in this section. Is this a reference to Jesus himself or to some other apocalyptic figure whom Jesus expected would come after him? If we read the expression within Mark's narrative, its meaning is absolutely clear. "Son of Man" appears fourteen times in Mark, nine of these at earlier points in the narrative. Those references are so obviously self-references to Jesus that Mark's reader has been schooled by the narrative to understand it here in only that way.

The Son of Man will appear "following that distress," an apparent reference back to the entire complex of events described in verses 3–23. Yet the imagery now extends that description by building on the natural disasters described in verse 8, which were just "the beginning of birth pains." These "birth pains" extend to other expected portents in the sky (vv. 24–25), to the appearance of the Son of Man in glory (v. 26), and to the gathering of the elect from the ends of the earth (v. 27).

Two things are striking here. (1) The imagery is heavily filled with allusions to the literature of Jewish apocalyptic, especially the title "Son of Man," which Jesus has used as self-designation, but which in this context also recalls Daniel 7:13–14. The Son of Man will appear "in clouds with great . . . glory" (cf. Mark 9:1; 14:62). These three references together evoke a range of cosmic images drawn from the Old Testament (Ex. 16:10; 19:9; 34:5; Ps. 104:3; Isa. 19:1). In the same vein, the image of the angels of God gathering the elect from the four winds and the ends of the earth in verse 27 draws on a widely ranging concatenation of Old Testament texts (Deut. 30:3; Ps. 50:3–5; Isa. 66:18–21; Jer. 32:37; Ezek. 34:11–16; 36:24; Zech. 2:6). These allusions remind the reader that the entire course of events, as disastrous as they may appear, is nevertheless part and parcel of God's great plan of redemption.

(2) The tribulation (vv. 3–23) is followed by the appearance of the Son of Man (v. 26); the elect of God, scattered to the ends of the earth, will be brought back home by the angels (v. 27). Little wonder that the heavens themselves will tremble at such an event (vv. 24–25)!

3.3.7. "Take Heed! Watch!" (13:28–37). The Olivet Discourse opened with Jesus' prediction of the final destruction of the temple (v. 2) and the question placed by the inner circle of disciples, "Tell us, when will these things happen? And what will be the sign that they are all about to be fulfilled?" (v. 4). Jesus returns at last to the first question they posed, only to tell them that he himself does not know the day or the hour (v. 32). The admission that even the Son does not know this aspect of the plan made by the Father is itself perhaps the single most striking aspect of the Olivet Discourse. Taken at face value it appears to erode the framework of apocalyptic predictions Jesus has just made about the end time.

But that may be the wrong way to read this admission. Instead, it should be read as a reinforcement of the caution against trying to calculate the events of the end time based on the imagery of the discourse. This chapter is shot through with cautionary notes. Verses 5–13 describe the appearance of false Christs, political and geographical upheavals, and great persecution and turmoil, but these are not to be taken as definitive "signs" of the end (see comments on 13:3–8).

Against that background, the apocalyptic elements must be understood to emphasize not so much the *timing* of the events as their *certainty*—their connection with God's ultimate plan of redemption and their reflection of the conviction that in the end, whatever else happens, God triumphs over his enemies. When Jesus assures the disciples in verse 29 that "when you see these things happening, you know that it [the end] is near, right at the door," he cannot be instructing them to calculate the end, but is rather assuring them that the end is certain. The promise that these events will take place within the lifetime of "this generation" (v. 30) should also be read within this larger context of certainty about the Christian's hope, but caution about its timing.

Jesus introduces the promise in verse 30 with a solemn pronouncement ("I tell you the truth") and buttresses the point with the equally solemn declaration that even though heaven and earth should pass away, his words will surely endure. What about the promise itself? Does Jesus' phrase "*this* generation" refer to the generation of his followers, or to the generation that is alive when these events begin to unfold, whenever that might be? One is tempted to take the latter course, if only because it seems to accord better with our own experience of nearly two thousand intervening years. But Mark's readers knew nothing of those intervening years and would no doubt have heard this as a reference to the first generation of Jesus' followers (see also comments on 8:34–9:1). For those readers, the words of this discourse would surely have spoken volumes about the course of events unfolding before them. What would they have heard?

(1) They would have heard here the assurance that these great tragedies are part of God's overall plan of redemption. The redemptive presence of God thus provides a larger context in which the tragedies can become meaningful. Even suffering—which Mark's Gospel has already told them is part of discipleship (8:34–9:1)—connects Christians with their Lord. Such things will happen, Jesus says, "on account of me" (v. 9); when everyone hates Christians, it will be "because of me" (v. 13a). Indeed, such things are connected in some deep and mysterious way to the moment of eschatological judgment in which all things are made right.

(2) Mark's readers would have heard here a reminder that they are not alone in the struggle. The prophecy about losing one's family in verses 12–13 recalls the striking description of losing one's family in 10:29–31, but being repaid "a hundred times as much" (though *with persecutions*, v. 30; see comments). Mark 13:11 makes clear that the Holy Spirit will accompany Christians to trial (a literal indication of the role of the Spirit as *parakletos*, or "counselor," though that word is not used). In the largest sense, Jesus is there with them because what is happening to them happened already to him. Indeed, the description of the troubles in verses 9–11 may well serve as a description of Jesus' own trial and execution. But these events are inseparably linked with the final justice of God. In the same way, the persecutions and sufferings of Christians are not a sign that they have been abandoned by God, but rather that their discipleship has been brought to its final test.

(3) Mark's readers would have heard that the tragedy will come to an end; it has a limit. The Son of Man will indeed appear, and the final judgment will come. The days will actually be shortened (v. 20); the end will come within the lifetime of "this generation" (v. 30), a phrase Mark's readers would no doubt have taken as a reference to their own lifetime. Indeed, the text says, "He who stands firm to the end will be saved" (v. 13b).

Yet throughout the Olivet Discourse Mark's readers would also have heard cautions against calculating a time line. No one but the Father knows the day and the hour. *No one*—not the angels in heaven, not even the Son. If even the Son does not know, then certainly the disciples (vv. 33, 35)—and with them Mark's readers—do not know.

For those certain of a coming judgment but uncertain of its timing, there can be only one response: not apocalyptic speculation, but vigilant attention. The Olivet Discourse closes with this urgent caution (vv. 35–37). The exhortation to watch is driven home in three ways. (1) The disciples and (and the readers! v. 37) do not know when the event will occur (vv. 33, 35). (2) *Four times* Jesus says: "Be on guard" (v. 33a); "be alert" (v. 33b); "keep watch" (v. 35); "watch" (v. 37). (3) In the parable of verses 34–35, the servant is watching for his master but does not know when he will appear. The result is an injunction to vigilance that can hardly be more dramatic in its rhetorical power.

3.4. The Passion Proper (14:1–15:39)

With the transition into the story of Jesus' Passion in 14:1 the narrative enters its closing phase. In a sense, however, the Passion narratives have been an overriding concern throughout the Gospel, and the reader's activities brought into play here involve the consolidation and execution of many elements introduced earlier.

Mark expects his readers to bring a certain repertoire of background information to bear on the text and to unpack the text in the light of that information. (1) They are Christians, whose convictions have been shaped by the life of the church, its history, its stories, and its liturgy. Since the readers already know the basic structures of the story line, it will not depend on surprises and plot twists to establish and hold their interest. Instead, it will engage their attention with a richly textured set of Old Testament allusions, with backward references to other places in Mark that have prepared for this moment, and with the strategic use of literary foils to highlight and contrast the actions of the story's characters.

(2) Mark also expects his readers to have a knowledge of the Old Testament and intertestamental literary traditions. The number of allusions here is striking, especially in the Lord's Supper and the crucifixion. Those allusions establish that the events surrounding the Passion are part and parcel of God's redemptive plan.

(3) Another source of background information that informs the reader's responses is what has gone before in the Gospel itself. That is, Mark does not expect his readers to launch their reading at 14:1, but rather at 1:1. He has frequently alluded to the coming Passion, and he completes the plot here. Such allusions include the subtle grammar of the arrest of John the Baptist in 1:14, the blatant decision of the authorities to have Jesus killed in 3:6, the death of John in 6:17–29, and the three explicit Passion predictions in 8:31–33; 9:30–32; and 10:32–34. The Passion itself is not a reversal of Jesus' intentions, but the completion of them.

The Passion narrative also continues Mark's habit of placing parallel and contrasting stories alongside one another so that they deepen one another by contrast (see comments on Mark's sandwiching technique at 5:21–43). The story of the anointing at Bethany (14:3–9) is sandwiched within the events surrounding Jesus' betrayal by Judas (vv. 1–2, 10–11), and the story of Jesus' "trial" in the house of the high priest (vv. 53–65) reads differently because it is set within the story of Peter's denial (vv. 54, 66–72).

There is one further sense in which the Passion narrative engages the reader's attention. Throughout this section, not only is Jesus' identity as *Messiah* and *Son of God* a matter of issue; his identity as *prophet* is at issue as well. The many references to Jesus' prophetic abilities establish his clear-eyed anticipation of the events that eventually engulf him. Jesus has predicted these events already; within the Passion proper he specifically predicts that the anointing will "be told in memory" of the unnamed woman at Bethany (14:9), that Judas will betray him (vv. 18–21), that all of the disciples will "fall away" (vv. 26–28, 31), and that Peter will deny him (v. 30). His prophetic ability becomes a point of issue at the trial before the Sanhedrin (14:58, 65), where it is profoundly and ironically vindicated, not only by Peter's denial in the courtyard, but also by the fact that the trial itself is a fulfillment of a prophecy he had made three times before.

Thus, through Mark's narrative preparation, the meaning of the events on the surface becomes a kind of mask of their deeper theological significance. When, for example, the authorities demand that Jesus "Prophesy!" (14:65) at his trial, they unwittingly and ironically fulfill the prophecies he himself made on his journey to Jerusalem. When they falsely accuse him of prophesying the destruction of the temple (14:58), they have no way of knowing that they are themselves fulfilling prophecies he has made about them, that he has already ended the ministrations of the temple by a grand symbolic gesture (11:20–26), and that the "temple made without hands" will indeed appear in the life and liturgy of the church. At the trial and again at the crucifixion, they will taunt him with the accusation that he cannot build a temple in three days, yet the reader knows that that is exactly what will happen. The self-serving accusation they apparently bring against him before Pilate—that he claimed to be "the King of the Jews" (see 15:2)—will be false, and yet ironically true: Jesus is indeed the King of the Jews! The soldiers will dress him up as a king in an act of refined brutality, and yet in the very act of doing so they will unwittingly become their own ironic victims.

The result of this series of double meanings is that the reader learns not only that Jesus' death is the propitiatory event par excellence, but also that beyond the observable truth there is another Truth, hidden and different from what the characters inside the story can grasp (on Mark's use of irony, see "Irony" at sec. 1). That deeper meaning is betrayed not only by what the text says, but also by the reactions it evokes in the reader. With God, more is going on than meets the eye. Mark's Passion account is thus an emotionally and theologically charged interpretation of the events of Jesus' death and burial, one by which the meaning of these events is made clear.

3.4.1. Jesus' Death Is Premeditated (14:1–2). This brief paragraph returns the narrative to its primary plot by reintroducing Jesus' opponents, "the chief priests and the teachers of the law." The chronological marker (v. 1a) sets the scene, and the mingled statements of hostile intentions (v. 1b) and caution (v. 2) call to mind a whole complex of impressions, among them Jesus' predictions in 8:27–30 and 10:32–34 about his rejection and crucifixion by the Jewish leaders (cf. 11:18; 12:12; on the Passion predictions, see comments on 8:31–33).

The stresses in the passage focus the reader's attention on the fact that these actions take place by stealth (the Greek for "some sly way" emphasizes deceit and treachery), and thus indicate that the atmosphere is politically charged. Jesus' influence with the crowds is enormous, so the authorities must move with caution. The plot thickens in its sense of impending danger.

Of course, to carry forward their plan the authorities need assistance, an implicit indication that Jesus kept his whereabouts secret. That assistance is forthcoming in the person of Judas Iscariot, something the reader knows from outside information and from prior asides in the narrative (3:19). For now, Judas waits in the wings (see 14:10), but at this point the authorities continue to plot, again not realizing that they are playing in a larger plot, already scripted in advance. The Passion predictions have demonstrated that, try as they might, the authorities have no control over the scenes in which they are about to find themselves; that control comes from an invisible Director, whose stage direction is crystal clear to the reader.

The reasons the authorities have for plotting also betray a serious rift between "official" Judaism and the popular support Jesus has found among the crowds in Jerusalem (see also 12:37). Soon enough, the crowds will turn ugly (15:11–15), but at this point their loyalties shield Jesus from the ugly machinations of the priests. This can only happen because the crowds are enormous. The chronological note in verse 1 ("the Passover and the Feast of Unleavened Bread were only two days away") is presented as a kind of hendiadys, coupling these two feasts into a single occasion. Technically, they were two events: Passover occurred on the 14th day of Nisan, and the Feast of Unleavened Bread on the seven days immediately following (see Ex. 12:1–20; Deut. 16:1–8). In common practice, the two events were so closely linked that either name could be applied to the combined celebration.

What is more important is that the Passover was one of three annual feasts in which every adult Jewish male was expected to appear in Jerusalem. Because of the Diaspora this did not happen, but it nevertheless prompted such a large number of pilgrims that the city overflowed and its boundaries had to be artificially extended to include the Kidron Valley and the Mount of Olives in order to accommodate them. Naturally, on such an occasion messianic fervor was in the air, the crowds were excitable, and the dangers attached to overt political action were intensified. What the authorities intend to do must therefore be done by stealth. The aura of subterfuge and treachery also leads to the secret arrangements Jesus must make for his own celebration of the Passover with his disciples (vv. 12–17).

3.4.2. The Anointing at Bethany (14:3–9). Like the previous paragraph, this touching story locates the action behind the scenes. Note that this story is "sandwiched" between the report of the authorities' plot against Jesus (vv. 1–2) and Judas' treacherous betrayal of Jesus for money (vv. 10–11). The placement suggests that the two stories be read together, each one commenting implicitly on the other (on the Markan "sandwiching" technique, see comments on 5:21–43). Judas's willingness to sell Jesus' whereabouts for money will stand in stark and painful contrast to the extraordinary generosity of this nameless woman.

Everything in the opening verses is calculated to establish and reinforce the extravagance of this woman's gesture. The flask was made of alabaster (v. 3a), a costly material in its own right, and it is broken to release its contents (v. 3b). The nard inside is "pure" and "very expensive" (v. 3b), worth as much as three hundred denarii (v. 5), a year's wage for a common laborer. The woman lavishes the nard on Jesus, pouring it over his head (v. 3c).

The whole episode violates every reasonable expectation for such a dinner party. The appearance of the woman in the room is itself unusual, since women did not ordinarily intrude on such dinner parties. Her gesture strikes a discordant note with some of the men in the room (v. 4). The attention shifts to their objection, which they base not on the strangeness of the gesture, but on the way it appears to violate the biblical mandate of care for the poor, a mandate taken with special seriousness at Passover (see also John 13:27–29). That objection again calls attention to the extravagance of the gift. Judas will shortly betray Jesus to the authorities for an unspecified sum of money, an act that will appear motivated by his own greed. Retrospectively, the objection in verse 4 appears to have been motivated by greed as well. The reader knows that it also reflects the disciples' failure to understand what is about to happen. Their loyalties are not divided so much as misdirected. Does the woman herself knowingly anticipate the Passion? The text does not say. Why is she here? Why is she doing this? The text does not say.

What the text does say is that Jesus interprets the woman's gesture in the light of the Passion that is to follow (vv. 6–9). He stamps it with meaning that runs beyond what the others at the table are willing or able to grasp. Thus, he saves face for the woman and at the same time solves a narrative puzzle that will appear later: Was Jesus' body prepared properly for burial after the crucifixion? On one level, clearly not. If it had been, there would be no need for the women to take spices to the tomb in 16:1–8. Yet on another level, clearly so, for this extravagant gesture from an unnamed admirer fulfills that necessary task symbolically but completely.

No doubt this story circulated in the churches, as verse 9 suggests. It is likely not new to the reader of Mark's Gospel, but is part of the complex of events surrounding the Passion. From the beginning the reader knows how this story will turn out. Yet it has surprising and disturbing detail: "The poor," Jesus says, "will always [be] with you, and you can help them any time you want" (v. 7). It is sometimes wrongly asserted that this means that Christians need not take immediate action in response to the needs of the poor, that the overriding concerns of holiness make concern for the poor a secondary matter. Yet Jesus' words contain an allusion to Deuteronomy 15:7–11 (esp. v. 11), a passage that commands generosity in the care of the poor. What better example of such generosity than this nameless woman, who out of her family's treasure provided for the burial of Jesus?

3.4.3. The Betrayal by Judas (14:10–11). If we were to read verse 10 immediately after verse 2, the transition would be smooth; we would be unaware that the story of the anointing of Jesus (vv. 3–9) was missing. The authorities require assistance (vv. 1–2); Judas volunteers his services (vv. 10–11). But Mark intends that the proper *narrative* context for the betrayal plot is not the need of the high priest, but the extravagant gesture of the woman with the ointment. Thus, Judas's motives appear to be connected in some way with the response of "some of those present" (v. 4) to the apparent waste of resources in the previous scene; more important, the extravagance of the woman's gesture is established as an important foil for Judas's greed.

Like the story of the anointing at Bethany (14:3–9), the brief account of the betrayal agreement by Judas does not come as a surprise to the reader. When Judas Iscariot first appeared in the narrative, his name was accompanied by an epithet: "who betrayed him" (3:19). Many plot details have already focused on the fact that Jesus will be betrayed to the authorities (e.g., 9:31: "The Son of Man is going to be betrayed into the hands of men"; 10:33: "The Son of Man will be betrayed to the chief priests and teachers of the law"). Each of these verses use the Greek verb *paradidomi* (lit., "to hand over"). The same verb is used in 15:1, in which the authorities "handed [Jesus] over to Pilate." What makes this an act of betrayal is that it is carried out by an insider, one of the Twelve (vv. 10a, 18a, 20a); this fact is deepened in verses 18b and 20b with the comment that the traitor was at that very moment sharing table fellowship with the Lord.

Thus Mark takes pains to establish that Judas is "one of the Twelve" (v. 10). Why is this important? On one level, it contributes to a literary allusion to Psalm 41:9, which will appear later at the scene of the Last Supper (vv. 18, 20). On another level, however, it openly faces the truth that Jesus was betrayed by an insider, handed over for money, and betrayed by a kiss. In that way it establishes a deep sense of treachery. The aura of secrecy continues to deepen, but the willingness of an insider to sell Jesus for an undisclosed sum of money colors the emotional air of the scene with a nearly impenetrable sense of sadness.

On yet a third level, the effect of these repeated references is a reminder to the reader of Jesus' prediction in the Olivet Discourse that his followers, too, will be betrayed. That passage contains the same verb, repeated like a drumbeat. Christians will be "handed over to the local councils and flogged in the synagogues" (13:9); they will be "arrested and brought to trial [*paradidomi*]" (v. 11); they will even be "betrayed" by their own brothers and parents (v. 12). If Mark's readers connected these words with their own situation, they would be recalled here with deep anguish. Mark's story of the betrayal by Judas would have grated raw on an open wound.

In some ways Judas is no different from the other disciples. None of them fully grasps the urgency of the situation. All will "fall away" (14:26–28, 50); even Peter, Jesus' closest friend, will abandon him (vv. 31, 66–72). The reader knows this from outside information or suspects it from the relentless dullness of the disciple band as a whole. They, like Judas, have little grasp of the events in which they have been caught up.

3.4.4. Preparation for the Passover (14:12–17). The chronological note in verse 12 moves the plot forward to the night of Passover. Technically, the celebration of Passover is completed before the Feast of Unleavened Bread is begun, though in common usage the two occasions are treated as a single celebration (see comments on 14:1–2). Mark makes clear that the events about to take place are in specific celebration of the Passover, but is careful also to connect this event to the Feast of Unleavened Bread, perhaps because the reader knows that Jesus is himself the "bread" being eaten here (see comments on 8:14–21), just as in John he is the "Lamb" of God (John 1:36) and the "bread of life" (6:26–59).

The need for secrecy has been explained by the events described in the preceding episodes: The authorities are plotting something by stealth (vv. 1–2), and an insider has fallen in with their plot (vv. 10–11). Jewish law required that the Passover be eaten within the city confines, so a retreat to Bethany is out of the question. In a scene that bears remarkable similarities to the Triumphal Entry story (11:1–10), he sends two of his disciples into the city to finalize preparations. It may be significant that he sends *two* disciples, since he knows that there is a traitor in their midst (vv. 19–21); a lone disciple might slip away and betray his whereabouts to the authorities. By sending two disciples, he prevents that from happening.

All the evidence here suggests subterfuge. A man carrying a water jar would be a ready signal, not only because it was unusual for a man to do this, but also because the natural place to carry such a jar would be on one's head and thus easily visible above the heads of the crowds of pilgrims that filled the city. No doubt Jesus has made these arrangements secretly to prevent any interruption of this last symbolic gesture with his disciples. Even the instructions are coded: "*The teacher* asks ..." (emphasis added). This is the only place where Jesus is identified as *the* teacher, and on the surface it no doubt reflects a popular term for Jesus. Here, however, it calls attention to the enormous symbolism with which Jesus has invested his activities; everything he does is a form of teaching—as it will turn out, the Supper especially. The reference to "evening" in verse 17 both closes this plot sequence and transitions into the next one. Passover was traditionally eaten late at night, and Jesus waits until dark to enter the city.

3.4.5. Jesus Foretells His Betrayal (14:18–21). Everything in the rhetoric of this brief section focuses attention on Jesus' being betrayed by an insider. It is impossible to overstate the seriousness of this fact. Jesus begins with a solemn expression, "I tell you the truth" (v. 18a). The traitor is one of the disciple band—"one of *you*" (v. 18b, emphasis added), "one of the Twelve" (v. 20; see comments on 14:10–11). The fact that the traitor is an insider is buttressed by the comment that he is at that moment sharing table fellowship with Jesus: He "dips bread into the bowl with me" (v. 20; cf. v. 18). This striking image recalls a particularly poignant expression of betrayal from the Psalms: "Even my close friend, whom I trusted, he who shared my bread, has lifted up his heel against me" (Ps. 41:9).

How did the disciples hear these extraordinarily painful words? Their responses in verse 19 indicate their confusion and sense of impending disaster. Perhaps they are being called upon to perform some service? The expression they use implies a negative response: "It isn't I, is it?" The text leaves it to the reader's imagination to grasp what Judas would have heard here. But he is surely present, a partner in a silent dialogue. The reader knows that he has taken action already (vv. 10–11). What Jesus is saying signals that he knows too. Verse 21 makes clear that Judas must bear full responsibility for the diabolical step he is about to take.

3.4.6. The Last Supper (14:22–26). The institution of the Last Supper is one of the most important events in early Christianity. For Jesus, it symbolizes the immolation of his own flesh on the cross, represented by the breaking of "bread" (v. 22), and the pouring out of his blood, represented by the wine (v. 24). The phrase "poured out blood," while a reference to the pouring of the wine into the cup, is also a common Semitic idiom for violent death. When Jesus says his blood is to be "poured out for many," the idiom refers in an understated way to the whole people of God (see also 10:45).

The second-floor Cenacle, in the Christian Quarter of Jerusalem, is one of two sites said to be the site of the Last Supper. It is located in the complex that contains David's Tomb. The other site is St. Mark's House on Ararat Street in the Armenian Quarter of the city.

Though they do not fully realize it at this point, for the disciples this meal will come to symbolize the participation of the believer in the suffering and death of Jesus (vv. 22–23), the unity of the body of Christ ("they all drank from it," v. 23), and the anticipation of the coming eschatological hope (v. 24). In the sense that the Supper is celebrated as a sacrament, it not only represents those realities but in a deep and unfathomable way it brings them into effect.

It is clear that Mark expected such meanings to be instantly evident to his readers precisely because they come to the text as Christians, with outside knowledge of these events. This in itself may account for the fact that this passage is told in lean, spare prose. It is not at all unlikely that Mark expects his readers to interpret this story within the larger framework of the Lord's Supper as they celebrated it as part of the liturgical life of their church. If that framework included other elements of the Passover meal, then certain details of Jesus' words become clearer. Such an occasion would have been opened perhaps by the symbolic breaking of the bread (represented in v. 22) and closed by the communal drinking of the cup (v. 23).

On the whole, the details have been overlaid already with a rich theological significance, on which Mark's readers are expected to draw. The opening of the Passover traditionally included a theological reflection on the meaning of the meal about to be eaten, a function taken over by Jesus' words of explanation in verse 22. The cup envisioned in verse 23 would have been the third or the last of the four cups of wine traditionally drunk during a Passover celebration. The singing of a hymn (probably from the Hallel Psalms [Ps. 113–118]) following the drinking of the cup suggests that this is the third cup and that Jesus left the final cup untouched. Either way, the cup recalls the promise of release from bondage made as part of the original Passover event (Ex. 6:6–7).

Jesus' solemn declaration in verse 25 ("I will not drink again of the fruit of the vine until that day when I drink it anew in the kingdom of God") reminds the disciples (and the reader!) that the work of the kingdom is yet to be completed, and it anticipates the hope that that day will in time be fully consummated.

Heard in the larger context of the Gospel of Mark, there may be two fresh nuances here. (1) The language of the Supper has appeared twice before already, in the feeding of the five thousand (6:33–44) and in the feeding of the four thousand (8:1–10). There the secondary nuances in the story stressed the inclusion of Gentiles in the economy of salvation (see comments on those passages). To the extent that this story calls to mind those previous feedings it also recalls the extraordinarily complex portrayal of Jesus as the "bread" that Mark had worked out in that larger section (see comments on 6:1–8:30).

(2) The reference to the "cup" from which they "all drank" (v. 23) has been given a secondary meaning by Jesus' conversation with James and John in 10:35–45. "Can you drink the cup I drink or be baptized with the baptism I am baptized with" (10:38)? That whole passage anticipated the Passion, concluding a section on discipleship training by reflecting on the Passion as the single warrant for Christian leadership: "For even the Son of Man did not come to be served, but to serve, and to give his life as a ransom for many" (10:45).

Thus, the elements of this Last Supper remind the believer that participation in the life of the community is predicated on participation in the death of Jesus. For some, it will work its way in practical terms by the Christian's willingness to abandon all aspirations of power and give one's self away in service (see comments on 10:35–45); for others it will work its way in the arena, a possibility of which Mark's Roman Christians may have been already painfully aware (see comments on 13:9–13).

3.4.7. Peter's Denial Predicted (14:27–31). This brief episode on the road to Gethsemane epitomizes a theme developed throughout the Passion narrative: When Jesus finally meets his end on the cross, he does so virtually alone (see comments on 14:32–42). Even this is anticipated in Scripture (v. 27), for the disciples' fleeing fulfills Zechariah 13:7. For those among Mark's readers who can recall the entire passage (Zech. 13:1–9), the quote evokes a fitting commentary on the events unfolding in the Passion narrative as a whole. It describes a necessary but violent process whereby the people are purified of sin and brought back into right relationship with God.

A particularly apt moment in that imagery is found in verse 6, in which the prophet laments violent treatment delivered at the hands of friends.

While the most striking elements of this episode center around Jesus' prophecy that Peter will deny him three times (v. 30), it is important that even in this Peter represents the entire disciple band. The statement that the disciples will "*all* fall away" in verse 27 is repeated in verse 29, and Peter's vehement assertion in verse 31 ("Even if I have to die with you, I will never disown you") is repeated by the band as a whole: "All the others said the same." Thus, Peter's denial of Jesus (vv. 54, 66–72) is a representative denial. Mark is careful to point out in verse 50 that "everyone deserted him and fled." Thus, on one level the present story represents an indictment in advance for their failure to keep faith.

On another level, however, this passage softens the hard edge of that indictment, in two ways. (1) It reminds the reader that these things are accomplished in fulfillment of Scripture and are therefore integral parts of the divine plan of redemption. (2) It promises the disciples, including Peter—*especially* Peter (see 16:7)—that after all things are accomplished, there is to be a reconciliation in Galilee (14:28). This prophecy, too, was eventually fulfilled (see Matt. 28:16; John 21:1–23). While its fulfillment came *outside* Mark's narrative as we have it, it is likely that the original reader of Mark's Gospel knew as much from Christian tradition. Even as Jesus' isolation grows, he takes it on himself to offer words of solace and encouragement. Thus, even as he is himself stricken, the shepherd sustains his scattered flock through the trials he knows that they, too, are about to face.

3.4.8. Gethsemane (14:32–42). With the exception of the actual crucifixion, no single image has impressed itself on Christian art and devotional reflection as much as the scene of Jesus' agony in the Garden of Gethsemane. What commends this image and invites prayerful reflection is the sheer pathos of the scene, the way it depicts Jesus prostrate in prayer before the Father, increasingly aware he must face this trial alone. The disciples have not abandoned him, not yet, but neither are they with him at this most painful hour. His prophecies have made his crucifixion a foregone conclusion, and yet here he hesitates, nearly falters, is moved to shuddering horror, but ultimately places his future in the care of the Father.

Three basic themes emerge from a study of Mark's text. (1) Mark carefully distances the disciples even further from Jesus as his "hour" approaches. This is part of a wider program by which he will finally present Jesus utterly alone as he dangles on the machine of his death. The religious authorities have opposed his work from the beginning (e.g., 3:6). He has been dismissed by his family (3:21) and rejected in his hometown (6:1–6). The crowds have enthusiastically endorsed his work, but in the end they will turn against him (15:11–15). Even God himself will finally turn aside (15:34). The only possible exception to this pattern is the women, who watch Jesus' death (15:40), but only "from a distance." When Jesus dies, he dies alone.

The emphasis in this account is on the abandonment of the disciples. It is not insignificant that this story is sandwiched between Jesus' prediction that the disciples "will all fall away" (v. 27) and the fulfillment of that prophecy in verse 50. In a similar but more complex way, it also falls between the prophecy of Peter's denial in verses 27–31 and the fulfillment of that prophecy in verses 66–72. As in other cases, the placement of the story here in the narrative calls attention to the distance that has been developing between Jesus and his disciples.

That distance is heightened by the repeated references to the disciples' sleeping (vv. 37, 40–41). While this is no doubt literal sleep ("their eyes were heavy" [v. 40], perhaps as much from the Passover wine as from the lateness of the hour), it nevertheless also characterizes their failure to grasp what is happening. They have no sense of the danger here.

With this we have the answer to a question that has puzzled interpreters of the Gospel of Mark: What did Jesus expect from his disciples here? Did he turn to them for comfort in his moment of trial, only to discover that because their "eyes were heavy," they could not even "keep watch [with him] for one hour" (v. 37)? This does not appear to be Mark's understanding. Rather, Jesus turns to the Father for solace at this moment of crisis and decision. He calls on God, using the most intimate term, "*Abba*" (which Mark translates for his reader as “Father,” v. 36). In fact, Jesus offers solace and comfort to the disciples rather than the other way around. What he expects from them is alert attention (cf. v. 34: “Stay here and keep watch”). At this most crucial hour Jesus does not wish to be interrupted.

(2) Another theme that dominates this passage is the deep humanity of Jesus, who faces his death just as any other human being faces death. Out of that humanity comes a shuddering horror (v. 33) and a crying out of his depths (v. 34). The language of verses 33–34 connects this moment with the lamentation of the psalmist (Ps. 40:12–13; 42:5, 9–11; 43:5; 55:5–6; 115:2; 116:3–4), but the allusions do not in any way diminish the fact that this is indeed Jesus' own response to the grim reality he now faces. When he prays for this “hour” to pass from him (vv. 35–36) and again that the “cup” might be removed from him (v. 39), the reader knows that these are real prayers, not artifices acted out to complete a prophetic scheme. The words “hour” and “cup” are interchangeable, referring in the Gospel of Mark to the impending judgment to be meted out on the cross.

(3) Thus we are introduced to the final theme here: Knowing full well the horrors that lie ahead and experiencing those horrors out of his full humanity, Jesus nevertheless abandons his own will in favor of God's will (v. 36). Commentators on Mark have occasionally remarked that Jesus' behavior at his trial and execution serves as a model of courage for Christians who face similar horrors. That courage is fully evident here, in the silence of the Garden of Gethsemane. The appearance of the traitor in verses 42–43 will turn the tide of events beyond recovery. It is here more than anywhere else that Jesus makes his decisive choice.

Viewed in this light, it may be possible to read Jesus' language differently. While references elsewhere in Mark make it clear Jesus' word “cup” in verse 36 evokes images of the terrible death on the cross (9:32; 10:38; 14:23), the word “hour” in verse 35 may refer not to the cross, but to the temptation to flee. When Jesus prays that the hour might pass from him, he may well be praying for the strength to resist the impulse to run. If so, then Jesus' prayer is indeed answered, though the answer is a reminder that tragedy may well be compatible with the will of God. When Jesus tells the disciples to “watch and pray so that you will not fall into temptation” (v. 38), he is speaking from his own experience. In just a moment his options will close. His own choice to stand his ground is a painful but courageous example for Christians who face similar moments of crisis and decision.

Thus this passage and the terrible consequence of the choices Jesus has made remind us of the warning in the Olivet Discourse: “All men will hate you because of me, but he who stands firm to the end will be saved” (13:13). The Holy Spirit sustains one in the hour of crisis (13:11). It is possible, though not certain, that “the spirit” in view in 14:38 is also the Holy Spirit rather than some higher human impulse toward God. In this sad story the face of human weakness is everywhere to be found, but the disciples will learn soon enough that the Spirit is with them as well. Jesus, too, is sustained in his moment of crisis by the abiding presence of the Spirit.

3.4.9. Jesus Is Arrested (14:43–52). With the appearance of Judas and an armed contingent from the religious authorities, Jesus' moment of decision is reached. The “hour” does indeed come (v. 42; see comments in previous section). Mark emphasizes three elements. (1) The details call attention to the inappropriateness of the arrest. Verse 43 notes that the contingent came armed with swords and clubs, a point that prepares for Jesus' dry remark in verse 48: “Am I leading a rebellion . . . that you have come out with swords and clubs to capture me?” The word for “leading a rebellion” (*lestes*) is variously translated “robber” or “brigand,” but here it clearly means “revolutionary.” The same word appeared earlier in 11:15–17, where an especially powerful allusion to Jeremiah 7:9–11 brought precisely this accusation against the religious authorities in the temple (v. 17; see comments).

The structure of Jesus' question in verse 48 implies a negative answer: “Of course not.” The denial of any pretensions toward revolution imbeds itself in the reader's mind in preparation for the charges of sedition that will be raised against him at the trial before Pilate (15:1–14). Later Pilate's soldiers will see that Jesus is crucified between two *lestai*, two revolutionaries, in order to complete their ironic parody of a king and his court.

The inappropriateness of the arrest is also emphasized by the detail in verse 49 that Jesus was "every day . . . teaching in the temple courts," yet without incident. Thus he calls attention to the fact that this arrest has taken place at night, in secret. The reader knows the story fully; Jesus' comment here recalls 14:1, that the authorities were seeking "some sly way to arrest Jesus." This expression implies not so much secrecy as deceit, so that the recollection of that verse here creates an implied judgment on the action taking place.

(2) On the treachery of the betrayal itself, when Mark points out that Judas is "one of the Twelve" (v. 43), he is hammering home something his readers already know. Indeed, because they are Christians, the readers knew this before the reading began, and Mark has recently belabored this point in Jesus' prediction of his betrayal (see comments on 14:18–21). That prediction evoked an allusion to Psalm 41:9: "Even my close friend, whom I trusted, he who shared my bread, has lifted up his heel against me." The prediction that the disciples will all fall away (vv. 27–31), with its allusion to Zechariah 13:7, may well have evoked a similar reference: "If someone asks him, 'What are these wounds on your body?' he will answer, 'The wounds I was given at the house of my friends'" (Zech. 13:6).

Thus the reader approaches the story of Jesus' arrest with a large repertoire of outside knowledge and literary allusions in hand, which deepen the act of betrayal beyond the point of treachery. It is the kiss that makes the treachery excruciating. The fact that it is repeated in the story (vv. 44–45) indicates its importance for Mark. Along with Judas's ironic address to Jesus ("Master!" v. 45, RSV), it signals that his betrayal is more than a self-serving act played out for money. At such a moment as this, Judas's choice to betray Jesus is made at the cost of his own soul (see v. 21). It would have been better, indeed, had he never been born.

(3) Yet all of this happens within the plan and foreknowledge of God. Like the Passion as a whole, the betrayal occurs in fulfillment of prophecy (8:31–33; 9:30–32; 10:34; 14:18–21). Jesus has made his choice, epitomized by his remark to the arresting soldiers in verse 49b: "The Scriptures must be fulfilled."

The passage ends with a puzzling episode about an unnamed "young man" who has somehow followed Jesus into the garden and has presumably observed what has taken place (vv. 51–52). It is impossible to say who this young man is or what his role is in the overall scheme of the Gospel. Why is it here? Some interpreters suppose that this is Mark himself, including a personal detail—a Markan "thumbprint." Other interpreters connected this young man with the angelic figure at the empty tomb in 16:1–8, though that is speculative. Perhaps it is best to leave the question open, just as Mark has done, on the assumption that this, too, may be a cipher for his audience that has been lost through time.

3.4.10. Jesus Before the Sanhedrin (14:53–65). What we have here is not a trial in the formal sense but a "hearing," held at night in a private residence (v. 53) and not in public, as the law required. The repeated elements of the narrative marshal the reader's attention around the illegalities involved in the "trial" and the illegitimacy of the charges; indeed, these questions have been dominant in the scholarly discussion of this important passage. The focus of those investigations has been on the actual historical event, but here we will focus on the rhetoric of the story and the strands of the reader's responses that tie this story to the larger narrative.

We begin with a question of minutia: Why does Mark focus attention on a single accusation, that Jesus had said that he would destroy the temple and then build another in three days (v. 58)? After all, verse 56 indicates that "many testified falsely against him." And in 15:3–4, when the Jewish authorities delivered Jesus to Pilate for formal trial, they "accused him of many things." Yet here Mark highlights only one charge, which will occur again as an epithet on the lips of Jesus' tormentors at the cross (15:29). Indeed, the destruction of the temple has come up before and appears to be a major preoccupation of the Olivet Discourse (13:1–2, 14). What is it about the charge that captures Mark's attention here?

Apparently, that accusation opens Jesus to the charge that he is both a false prophet and an enemy of the temple. Mark uses this moment of the trial to put both of these options to rest. Twice he writes, using an imperfect tense: "They were *continuously* giving false testimony" (vv. 56–57, pers. trans.). The effect here is a direct and clear disclaimer: Jesus never said that.

The disclaimer is reinforced in three ways. (1) Mark points out that the chief priests and the whole Sanhedrin cannot find any evidence to put Jesus to death (v. 55); what evidence they do find is twice identified as "*false* testimony" (vv. 56–57) and is shown to be conflicted (v. 59). (2) Jesus' silence in verses 60–61 implies that there need be no answer because the facts will speak for themselves. We can restate this from the standpoint of the readers: They are expected to know better and will recall other elements of the narrative that Jesus could very well have said in response. (3) Mark notes that the high priest seeks other charges against Jesus (vv. 62–65). This evidence suggests that even in the high council the charges of plotting against the temple have proven ineffective and need to be dropped.

The authorities cannot press their claim because the witnesses do not agree (vv. 56, 59). Mark says patently that the accusation is false. But in exactly what sense is it false? This would be clear if the reader could make a careful comparison with John 2:19. Jesus never said that *he* would destroy the temple, only that it was bound for destruction. But Mark's readers do not have the luxury of a direct comparison with John's Gospel. Instead, they must rely on resources from within Mark's narrative—or those they can bring in from oral tradition—to know why the quote is a *mis*quote. These Mark has supplied already in the Olivet Discourse. In 13:1–2 (and perhaps by implication in 13:14) Jesus predicted the destruction of the temple in the most striking terms. What reader will have forgotten the vividness and clarity of Jesus' language there? When Jesus is silent in 14:61, these are the expressions that come most readily to mind.

The more visible rhetorical strategies of the passage also deal with this same issue. Those strategies turn around the demand that Jesus "Prophesy!" in verse 65, which brings the section to its closure. Here is an ironical twist, created by the combination of several elements of the narrative. (1) The trial of Jesus is sandwiched into the middle of the story of Peter's denial (vv. 54, then 66–72; on Mark's "sandwiching" technique, see comments on 5:21–43). Jesus had already prophesied the denial in explicit form (14:27–31; see comments). It is important that Mark's Gospel is intended to be read in a single sweep, so the reader comes to the story of Peter's denial fresh from a reading of that prophecy. When the guards strike Jesus and demand that he prophesy, they cannot see what the reader can see: Outside in the courtyard, at that very moment, a prophecy of Jesus is coming to pass. The guards are their own ironic victims.

(2) We should also trace the shift of perspective Mark's narrative asks the readers to make. When the false witnesses accuse Jesus in verses 55–59 and when the guards strike him in verse 65, the reader is expected to respond with something like, "How blind they are!" In order to respond in that way, the reader must come round and share the viewpoint from which the narrative proceeds (see comments on 1:1). Just at the moment that "the chief priests and the whole Sanhedrin" (14:55) agree in condemning Jesus to death, they themselves come under the implied judgment of the narrative. They become guilty of the very charge they level against Jesus: This is blasphemy, and an ironic parody of the truth. Just who is on trial here, anyway? And who is the judge after all?

(3) That irony is deepened to a new level if the reader also remembers that Jesus had predicted the trial itself, with all of its attendant brutalities. The irony is dramatic in the extreme. The guards strike Jesus and demand that he prophesy, and the very scene dramatically acts out a prophecy he had made three times before (8:31–33; 9:30–32; 10:32–34).

(4) There is one final way in which this story of the trial is connected to the larger framework of Mark's story: The characterization of Jesus—silent, ironically in charge after all—forms a striking foil to the characterization of Peter in the high priest's courtyard below. Granite Peter (3:16). Peter of the great confession (8:26–31). Peter, who only moments before had nailed his confession to a cross: "Even if I have to die with you, I will never disown you" (v. 31). As the reader watches horrified, Peter's confession crumbles to sand and falls between his fingers and onto the cold palace floor. That stammering portrayal of Peter is all the more horrifying when seen against the backdrop of Jesus' coolheaded silence in his own trial.

3.4.11. Peter's Denial (14:66–72). The account of Peter's denial is one of the most dramatic and moving of all of Mark's great personal narratives. He has taken great pains to prepare the reader for this scene, so that this story must be understood in connection with what has gone before. Perhaps most important is the conversation on the road to Gethsemane (14:27–31), where Peter adamantly insisted, "Even if I have to die with you, I will never disown you" (v. 31). When he now repeatedly stammers out his three denials of Jesus (vv. 68, 70–71), the reader hears those denials against the backdrop of the bravado he had displayed in that tragic conversation. That bravado makes his repeated denials into a tragic turn of events.

Two things save the day. (1) Even the denial itself is an unwitting validation of Jesus' prophetic abilities (see comments on 14:53–65). (2) From outside knowledge the reader knows that in time Peter's confusion here will right itself to a confession once again. At the time of the original prophecy (vv. 27–31) Jesus softened the harshness of his comments with the promise that after everything had been accomplished, he would go before them into Galilee (v. 28). Indeed, he repeats that promise in 16:7, singling out Peter for special attention.

Inside the house, Jesus is on trial for his life before the highest religious authorities in the land. Yet in those frightful circumstances he plays the part of the falsely accused, letting his silence voice his judgment about the illegitimacy of the proceedings in which he finds himself. Jesus never loses his head. The prophecies he has made now make clear that it is he, not the authorities, who controls the unfolding movement of the plot. Outside, in the courtyard, Peter is also "on trial," only his accuser is a harmless servant girl. He plays out the role of fool and liar, stammering out his famous, "[I swear] I don't know this man you're talking about."

On a deeper level, the two stories are also connected rhetorically. One of the major issues at the trial is Jesus' refusal to prophesy (v. 65), but the reader is able to see what the authorities inside the house cannot: Outside in the courtyard, at precisely that moment, a prophecy of Jesus is coming to pass. In a way that is both metaphorical and ironic, Peter's denial is the overlooked evidence at the trial. The reader reads from the jury box and reaches the opposite conclusion from the chief priests and Sanhedrin: He is the prophetic Son of God. The reader who reads the narrative in this wa can hardly avoid being "entrapped" into con version.

3.4.12. The Trial Before Pilate (15:1–14 Mark's account of the trial before Pilate con tains three primary points of stress. (1) It con tinues Mark's program of fulfilled prophec which had been set in motion with the thre Passion predictions (8:31–33, 9:30–3 10:32–34). The third prediction had stated th matter in careful detail: "We are going up t Jerusalem . . . and the Son of Man will b betrayed to the chief priests and teachers of th law. They will condemn him to death and wil hand him over to the Gentiles, who will moc him and spit on him, flog him and kill hin Three days later he will rise" (10:33–34). Thi prediction and its precise fulfillment her reminds the reader that the events unfolding i the Passion are anticipated events, and tha everything about this terrible tragedy finds it meaning in God's plan.

(2) The charge and the trial revolve aroun the reiterated title "King of the Jews" (vv. 2, 9 12; see also vv. 18, 26). Clearly this title i important for Mark. Its significance will late be suggested in the farce of a coronation put o by the soldiers (vv. 16–20), who will dres Jesus in royal robes before stringing him up t die. Little do they know that Jesus is in fact th "King of the Jews," or that in God's larger pla this is the way such a king should mount hi throne.

(3) Mark also stresses the release of Barab bas, a convicted insurrectionist. To recogniz its significance in Mark's rhetorical strategies we should note that the charge brought befor Pilate about Jesus as "King of the Jews" implies a claim to revolutionary aspirations. I a sense, this is the logical extension of Jesus words to the high priest during the hearin before the Sanhedrin the previous night. Whe the high priest asked, "Are you the Christ, th Son of the Blessed One?" (14:61), Jesus ha replied in the affirmative, stating his claim i striking messianic language: "I am . . . and yo will see the Son of Man sitting at the right han of the Mighty One and coming on the cloud of heaven" (v. 62). The title "Christ" and "So of the Blessed One" have messianic overtones Later on, when the high priest and his com pany taunt Jesus at the crucifixion, they plac the first of these titles in parallel with the titl

'King of Israel" (15:32), a clear indication that n their understanding the terms overlap.

When the authorities bring charges against esus before Pilate, they focus on the claim to e king. In doing so they manipulate the proeedings by shifting the emphasis of the harge. The "crime" for which he was conlemned in the Sanhedrin was blasphemy 14:64), while here it is political sedition 15:2). This transposition is clearly intended to ranslate Jesus' claim to be the Son of the Blessed One into terms Pilate could not ignore. Thus they force Pilate's hand.

This shift is enough to expose the accusaion as malicious, but Mark is not content to eave it at that. Enter Barabbas (vv. 6–15). Barabbas provides a test, not of the judicial ystem, but of the integrity of the charge. From 'ilate's point of view, the choice he offers etween Jesus and Barabbas is a master stroke hat will offset the political maneuverings of he high priest's delegation by setting the rowds over against their own authorities. This hoice will prevent him from being manipuated by underlings he despises. He is, after all, ully aware that the execution of Jesus is a misarriage of justice (v. 10), and he expects the opulace to have different vested interests rom the authorities.

In the end, however, his choice of Barabbas r Jesus proves to be a tactical blunder because he crowds—at the instigation of the chief riests, who throw in their lot with rebels v. 11; cf. the implied accusation in 11:17)—lemand the release of Barabbas instead. When resented with an acknowledged insurrectionst, the people choose his release. Pilate is rapped by this countermove, and his options lose. Having committed himself to this course f action, he now must follow through, and he as Jesus flogged and remanded to the execuioner (v. 15).

3.4.13. "Hail! King of the Jews!" (15:15–1). There are three different scenes in which esus is subjected to humiliation: In 14:65 he s mocked by the Jewish authorities; in 15:16–1 he is mocked by the Roman soldiers; and in 5:21–32 he is derided by the passersby at the cene of the crucifixion. Here we deal only vith the mockery by the soldiers. Robert Tanehill (1979, 79) has pointed out that all three cenes are ironic in their overarching strategies on Mark's use of irony, see "Irony" at sec. 1):

> The rejection and scorning of Jesus, prominent in the passion announcements in chapters 8–10, are dramatized in the passion story by scenes of mocking. These scenes are systematically placed, one following each of the main events after the arrest.... The last two of the scenes are vivid and emphatic. All three are ironic and suggest to the reader important affirmations about Jesus.

The irony is developed in an almost allegorical fashion in verses 16–21. The mockery Jesus suffers at the hands of the soldiers represents a complex interplay of surface and deep significances. Who can miss the sarcastic pathos of the cloak, the crown of thorns, or the spittle? On the surface, this is gallows humor, pure and simple, a farce played out in a kind of refined brutality. But like the trial, it represents a perfect masque of the truth it parodies.

3.4.14. The Crucifixion (15:22–39). No single episode in history has occasioned such extensive comment as the story of the Crucifixion. Mark tells this story in 233 Greek words, and yet whole libraries have been written in an effort to understand its meaning. The approaches have been almost as wide-ranging as the number of commentators. Some interpreters have focused attention on the historical reconstruction of what actually happened, evaluating the similarities and differences between the canonical and noncanonical accounts and then discussing the details in terms of historical probability.

Other interpreters have focused on the sheer physical brutality of death by crucifixion—the size and shape of the cross, the placement of the nails through the bones of the wrist, the manner in which the body shuts down, the agonizing gasping for breath, the terror and anguish of a death by asphyxiation that can linger for days.

Other interpreters have focused on the legal issues surrounding the story—the legalities of the trial, the rights of Roman prefects, the relationship of the story to Roman habits of jurisprudence, or the uses of crucifixion as an instrument of government.

Other interpreters have focused on the political issues here—the shifting of the charge, the hidden motives, the subterfuge, Pilate's refusal to be bullied, the horrible consequences of a political stratagem gone awry.

Still other interpreters have focused on the theological nuances of the story, including its connections with Old Testament prophecy or the sacrificial system, the significance other New Testament writers found here, or the meaning of the story in Mark's own theological frames of reference.

Clearly Mark's reader would not have been able to conduct such a wide-ranging or deeply penetrating analysis of this brief story. Two hundred and thirty-three words would take perhaps three minutes to read aloud, three minutes to *hear*. And yet into those three minutes Mark packs the epitome of everything that has gone before. Here all of Mark's loose threads are finally woven into the fabric of the plot. Put one way, the crucifixion of Jesus is the point at which the meanings and anticipations generated throughout the Gospel are finally realized within the plot itself, woven into three minutes of densely textured narrative tapestry. Put another way, all of the loose ends and anticipations, all of the foregrounded images and prophecies, have prepared the reader to read the Crucifixion in a particular way. In the light of that preparation six major emphases seem to stand out here.

(1) The most immediately evident emphasis is that when Jesus dies, he does so with the title "King of the Jews" placarded above him (15:26). This is the charge brought before Pilate (15:1–2) and repeated over and over in the immediately preceding verses (vv. 2, 9, 12). Indeed, this is the intent of the mockery of the soldiers in verses 15–21. The crown of thorns, the purple robe, the spittle, the "acclamation," the homage, all deepen the impression of a kind of parody, a comic farce played out by brutal men intent on a ruthless joke (see comments on 15:15–21). The details of the Crucifixion carry the farce forward to include the execution of two *lestai*, "robbers" (NIV), or—more correctly—"brigands, revolutionaries." Perhaps having been denied Barabbas, the Romans consigned two of his cohorts to the gallows for no reason other than to complete the image of a king and his court.

Anticipations generated earlier in Mark's Gospel make clear how important it is that this "King" should lead "the Jews" in just this way. Throughout the story Mark has prepared the reader to see the Crucifixion as the single warrant for leadership among Jesus' followers. Indeed, this theme was the major thrust of the central section (see comments on 8:22–10:45). Perhaps most striking is the closing injunction of that major section (10:42–45), which epitomizes Christian leadership in terms of servanthood, self-sacrifice, and powerlessness. Those verses are now called to mind as a commentary on the meaning of the cross:

> You know that those who are regarded as rulers of the Gentiles lord it over them, and their high officials exercise authority over them. Not so with you. Instead, whoever wants to become great among you must be your servant, and whoever wants to be first must be slave of all. *For even the Son of Man did not come to be served, but to serve and to give his life as a ransom for many*. (italics added)

(2) The second major emphasis in the story is picked up in verses 29–32. Like the mockery of the soldiers in the previous paragraph, the taunts here are ironic. The passersby deride Jesus in two forms. (a) The first—"You who are going to destroy the temple and build it in three days . . ." (v. 29)—appears to have been carried over from the Sanhedrin trial (see 14:58), a detail that at least suggests that "those who passed by" were aware of what had gone on in the chief priest's private residence the night before. What they cannot know, of course, is that Jesus will indeed build another temple, not made with human hands, or that there will be a reader—a member of that temple!—who will listen to their taunt and hear theological nuances that they cannot have intended, indeed, that they cannot even have fathomed! For the reader, the reference to the "three days" that ends the taunt recalls the three Passion predictions (8:31–33; 9:30–32; 10:32–34), and—more critically—the resurrection that lies still ahead in the narrative.

(b) The other taunt, "Come down from the cross and save yourself," is also ironic, but it is a theological dead-end. For Jesus to "save himself" by coming down from the cross is precisely the thing Jesus cannot or will not do. Their stipulation in verse 52—"that we may see and believe"—is as ironically outrageous as the Pharisees' demand for a sign in 8:11 (see comments). The very Truth that brings belief hangs there before them and they cannot see it.

(3) Mark has also prepared his reader to recognize a third emphasis of the Crucifixion scene: It occurs in fulfillment of prophecy. This point must be made with special care. It is not that the death of Jesus replicates in detail the prophecies, but that the prophecies anticipate in detail the death of Jesus. The reality lies *here*. The prophecies anticipate in language what Jesus' death accomplishes in fact. It is the brutal reality of the Crucifixion that establishes the meaning of the prophecies that had gone before.

(4) When Jesus dies, he dies alone. As we have seen in our discussion of the events in the Garden of Gethsemane, the narrative has systematically distanced Jesus from the other characters (see comments on 14:32–42). The cry of dereliction from the cross (15:34–35) makes that isolation complete. This is arguably the most strikingly candid detail of the entire early Christian tradition, and efforts are often made to ease its harsh reality. Jesus' words themselves are the opening words of Psalm 22. Perhaps he is directing the onlookers—and the readers—to that psalm as a fitting Old Testament commentary on the agonies he now faces. But this strains the evidence, and to the extent that it diminishes the reality of Jesus' agony on the cross it sounds like special pleading.

The reader hears Jesus' cry of dereliction as a real cry, just as the prayers in Gethsemane were real prayers. At the same time, the narrative has also prepared the reader to provide the answer to Jesus' agonizing question. God has forsaken him, not because of his sins, but because only in this way can he bear the sins of fallen humanity. As Jesus himself had said, "The Son of Man did not come to be served, but to serve, and to give his life as a ransom for many" (10:45). Jesus' cry of dereliction holds in synecdoche all the nuances of a sacrificial offering. With a final outburst Jesus spends the last of his strength. In verse 37, he "breathed his last."

Thus far we have reviewed four major themes woven through Mark's tapestry of the Crucifixion: (1) Jesus dies as "King of the Jews," and thus implicitly as Messiah; (2) the taunts of the onlookers are ironic comments on the meaning of the scene unfolding before them; (3) Jesus' death occurs in fulfillment of prophecy; and (4) when Jesus dies, he dies alone. It is important to remember not only that these themes overlap and deepen one another, but that they unfold for the reader in *sequence*, as the details of the plot unfold during the reading. That is, the overlapping nuances here are *cumulative*, so that the narrative reaches a kind of epitome with the rending of the temple curtain in verse 38—"top to bottom"—and the "confession" of the centurion in verse 39—"Surely this man was the Son of God!" As shocking as it is, even the moment at which Jesus "breathed his last" (v. 37) lends its weight to these two theologically loaded statements. Everything comes down to this.

(5) Thus we are brought to the rending of the temple curtain in verse 38. The fact that the curtain is torn in two "from top to bottom" indicates in the clearest terms that this is a supernatural portent, something effected by God in response to the sacrificial death of Jesus in verse 37. (Another supernatural portent was the ominous darkness *over the whole land* in v. 33.) Mark's language here is vivid enough to evoke a memory of the rending of the heavens at Jesus' baptism: "The curtain of the temple was torn [*eschisthe*] in two from top to bottom" (15:38), just as Jesus "saw heaven being torn open [*schizomenos*] and the Spirit descending on him like a dove" (1:10).

In this context, however, the emphasis is on the fact that the torn curtain is the curtain *of the temple*. Mark's reader has been prepared for this moment not only by Jesus' prophecy in 13:1–2 that the temple would be destroyed, but also by the powerful overlay of symbolism in the cursing of the fig tree and the cleansing of the temple (11:1–26; see comments). If, as I believe is possible, Mark's Gospel is told on the eve of the destruction of Jerusalem in A.D. 70, these sections would have held powerful emotional content for Mark's readers, emotional content that would have driven home the symbolism involved. When the narrative reaches its apex with the rending of the temple curtain in verse 38, it evokes all of that symbolism and the emotional content that goes with it.

(6) The confession that Jesus was the Son of God in verse 39 forms the final major emphasis in Mark's story of the Crucifixion. This confession has been heard before in Mark's narrative, but always on the lips of a supernatural being. In Jesus' baptism (1:11) and then again in his transfiguration (9:7), it came from God himself, speaking both times

from a cloud. Jesus has also been identified as "the Son of God" (3:11) and "Son of the Most High God" (5:7), but these "confessions" are found on the lips of demons. Here for the first time, the confession comes on the lips of a human being, not coincidentally a Gentile: "Surely this man was the Son of God!" Thus the centurion brings Mark's narrative to its highest point by returning the plot to the point at which it was launched in 1:1: "The beginning of the gospel about Jesus Christ, *the Son of God*" (italics added).

But the story is not closed entirely. Verse 40 will shift the reader's attention to a short epilogue, in which Mark explores in rapid sequence the details of the burial and the empty tomb.

4. The Epilogue (15:40–16:8)

Following the crucifixion scene in verses 22–39, the plot of Mark winds rapidly down. Two basic emphases stand out in the final verses. (1) Many details appear to have been included for apologetic purposes. (2) The narrative closes with the strongest possible suggestion of a resurrection. Indeed, it *presupposes* the resurrection, without which none of the details that are included makes sense. Mark's epilogue is terribly abbreviated (see sec. 4.3 for comment on his rhetorical strategy of leaving the reader with an "unfinished work").

4.1. Witnesses of the Crucifixion (15:40–41)

After the story of the crucifixion reaches its shuddering apex with the centurion's confession in 15:39, the brief report of the women witnesses (vv. 40–41) appears almost as an afterthought. No doubt an actual historical reminiscence, at this place in the narrative it clearly serves apologetic purposes, just as the presence of Mary Magdalene and Mary the mother of Joses at the burial scene (v. 47) guarantees against the notion that the women returned to the wrong tomb. In this regard we should remember that the testimony of women was not well regarded in the ancient world, so this detail has the earmarks of an authentic eyewitness account. It is difficult to say who "James the younger" and "Joses" were. Perhaps they are known to the readers in the same way that "Alexander and Rufus" appear to have been known (15:21).

4.2. The Burial of Jesus (15:42–47)

As with the witnesses of the crucifixion in verses 40–41, these details have probably been shaped with apologetic interests in mind. While Joseph of Arimathea appears to have viewed with some urgency the rapid approach of sundown—and thus the Sabbath—Pilate's concern is that Jesus should have died so soon. Indeed, the manner of Jesus' death raises questions for which any governing magistrate would require answers. Normally, victims of crucifixion die by asphyxiation, a torment that could last for days. Pilate seeks the reassurance of the centurion, who offers a formal confirmation that Jesus has indeed died (v. 44). So important is this detail that Mark repeats it, emphasizing the official character of the inquiry and the directness of the response. Mark's reader would have heard here a useful apology against any notion that Jesus had been removed from the cross prematurely. Both the presence of the women as witnesses and the burial proceedings by Joseph reinforce the validity of the account.

Joseph is cast in the best possible light. He is "a prominent [or respected, cf. NRSV] member of the Council" (v. 43a). He was himself "waiting for the kingdom of God" (v. 43b), an expression of the depth of his piety. Throughout the ancient world it was considered a grave sacrilege against the gods—or against God—to fail to give corpses a proper burial. For the Romans the right of burial was a legal and moral obligation, though it was suspended in the case of prisoners who had been executed. The right of burial was instead left in the hands of the governing magistrate, who might well choose to leave a corpse in place as a warning to others.

Among Jews, the right of burial was a universal and sacred obligation. Joseph's concern that Jesus be properly buried reflects this common Jewish understanding. The fact that sundown is rapidly approaching adds urgency to the moment. He makes the necessary purchases—linen cloth, but not spices—wraps Jesus' body, and lays him in a tomb (v. 46).

Mark's apologetic interests continue in verse 47. "Mary Magdalene and Mary the mother of Joses" observe the place of burial. This comment guarantees against the objection that when they return on Sunday morning, they return to the wrong tomb.

4.3. The Women at the Tomb (16:1–8)

The ending of the Gospel of Mark is a matter of some debate among scholars. For reasons that are set out below, this commentary concludes its discussion of Mark at 16:8 (see below, final section).

Discerning readers of Mark's chronology sometimes wonder how a series of events that began late on a Friday afternoon and concluded early on a Sunday could be referred to as "three days" (10:34). The problem, however, is a problem of translation. In Greek, the expression "three days" includes partial days as factors of computation. A more precise translation would be "after three days or parts thereof." The statement that the women came to the tomb "when the Sabbath was over" means soon after sunrise on Sunday morning. They have purchased spices, presumably to complete the burial arrangements made by Joseph of Arimathea (15:46), which they knew from direct observation included only a linen burial shroud (15:47).

Repeated details in the story line continue to reflect Mark's attention to apologetic concerns. The note that the women "saw where he was laid" (15:47) has guaranteed that they have come to the correct tomb, as does the detail that they come to the tomb "after sunrise" (16:2), when there is adequate light. In 16:3–4 the repeated concern is with the size of the stone in front of the door and the difficulty the women would have had in moving it. This detail suggests that Joseph of Arimathea has used a family sepulcher, since burial arrangements of this sort were rare in Palestine. More important, it answers in advance the objection that the women may have moved the stone and somehow stolen the body of Jesus (cf. Matt. 28:11–15).

Verse 5 indicates a moment of discovery. The tomb is not empty, but where they expect to find the corpse of Jesus they find an unnamed "young man," whose presence, dress, and speech suggest an angelic figure. Mark's Gospel does not give us an account of the resurrected Lord but leaves that detail to the eyes of faith. The young man reminds the women of the prophecy Jesus had given on the road to Gethsemane: "After I have risen, I will go ahead of you into Galilee" (14:28). Here that prophecy is repeated nearly verbatim by the mysterious messenger, who directs them to report the same to the disciples (16:7). It is important that he specifies that the message be delivered "to [the] disciples *and Peter*" (italics added). Of all the disciples, Peter's failure has been the most profound, and yet in his failure he represented them all.

The young man, his apparently extraordinary knowledge, his solemn pronouncement that Jesus is not there but has risen, and his prophecy that Jesus will go "ahead of [them] into Galilee" and "there [they] will see him" all focus attention on the reality of the resurrection. Only the details of the actual resurrection have been left out of the narrative, not because it did not happen but because, had it not happened, the narrative itself would have made no sense.

The women fail in their commission "because they [are] afraid" (v. 8)—in its cultural context another apologetic detail. (Let it never be said that the resurrection of Jesus is the fabrication of women!) Thus the story ends as abruptly as it has begun.

Against the excruciating symbolism of the crucifixion scene, Mark's ending leaves the reader grasping for more. How has he brought his reader to this moment? In the first place, the plot has moved at a sustained clip, at each stage reaffirming Jesus' mastery over the situations with which he is confronted. We have followed his movements back and forth across the Sea of Galilee, in and out of Galilee, and in and out of the confused loyalties of his disciples. We have followed his inexorable and somber march to his death in Jerusalem, a march that has led him—in its own way triumphantly—across the open nerve endings of official Judaism. In Mark, Jesus has been the very soul of power. We have felt that dynamism at every turn.

Mark has been careful, however, to curtail any notion that Jesus' power is the result of personal charisma or collusion with satanic forces. It is nothing other than the embodiment of the "kingdom of God" bursting into the world. Even for the reader who has been schooled by the narrative to expect that this would happen, the empty tomb, the mysterious young man, and frightened silence of the women hardly provide an adequate closure for the book.

And that is precisely the point. The double meanings in Mark have left the reader with a deep sense that more is going on than meets the eye, that this story—including the crucifixion—is meaningful in a dimension not readily available on the surface. The reader is forced back into the book again. In the end, the unfinished business of the story line haunts the reader long after the story has drawn to a close. Have we fully grasped the meaning of this crucified Messiah, this empty tomb? What can be meant by the prophecy of a meeting in Galilee, found on the lips of a mysterious young man? What does this risen Lord require of me? Of us? What is the appropriate response? But perhaps these are best understood, not as unresolved questions, but as challenges to the reader: What sort of good news closes with, "They said nothing to anyone, because they were afraid"?

The "Longer Ending" (16:9–20)

It is well known that the ending of Mark is a matter of dispute. In this commentary we follow the lead of the NIV and end the Gospel after verse 8, with the explanation that "the most reliable early manuscripts and other ancient witnesses do not have Mark 16:9–20." Readers who wish to review the issues in depth will find a helpful introduction in Lane (1974, 601–5).

The Problem of the Manuscripts. The longer ending, well known to readers of the King James Version as 16:9–20, is not the only manuscript variation that follows verse 8, but these other endings are even less evident in manuscripts. What the NIV says is true: The so-called longer ending is lacking in the manuscripts noted for the reliability of the text of Mark. Moreover, the longer ending is theologically inconsistent with the rest of the book, contains non-Markan vocabulary and style, is unsupported by either Matthew or Luke, and appears to have been motivated by a desire to close off Mark's otherwise abrupt ending.

One of the basic principles for resolving the variations among the five thousand extant New Testament manuscripts is that, where all else is equal, any reading that can explain the rise of the others has a stronger claim to being the original. Clearly this is the case here. Without the longer ending, Mark ends on a note of fear and has no actual resurrection appearance. Even the grammar is awkward (v. 8 ends with the Gk. word *gar*, "for"). It is easy to see what would have motivated the addition of a longer ending, but difficult to see why that ending would have dropped out.

This conclusion itself raises other questions: If "Mark as we have it" ended at verse 8, does this mean that Mark intended to end there? Perhaps there was another ending that is now lost. Where did the substance of vv. 9–20 come from, and what can they tell us of early Christian tradition? Should we, or can we, preach from these verses, even if they were not contained in the earliest manuscripts?

Did Mark Intend to End at Verse 8? This question is more difficult to answer because we have no concrete historical evidence either way. For many years interpreters tried to account for the abruptness here by positing a "lost ending" or an interruption in the work. Perhaps Mark wrote in a situation of extreme peril and was interrupted before he could complete his work. This idea seems strained and it raises questions of its own: If Mark was interrupted, why was the rest of the manuscript not lost? Perhaps there was a longer ending, but it was torn off and lost through neglect. This does not seem likely because the exposed portion of a scroll is the opening rather than the end.

Since the question cannot be resolved from historical evidence, interpreters have recently approached the question of Mark's ending from a literary perspective, that the abruptness makes its own kind of literary sense. Thomas Boomershine and Gilbert Bartholomew (1981) have argued that the shorter ending is consistent with Mark's rhetorical style. Mark sometimes ends stories with a clause introduced by *gar* as an explanation of the characters' fear (6:45–52) or duplicity (12:1–12). According to these authors, the ending at 16:8 combines these elements in a kind of literary *tour de force*, an abrupt ending to be sure, but not a non-Markan one. Thus, while we cannot know for certain whether Mark's original manuscript contained additional elements, the literary evidence is at least compatible with the conclusion that it ended with verse 8. We should bear in mind that any different ending, however satisfactory, gives us a fundamentally different book.

Where Did Verses 9–20 Come From? If we grant that the longer ending is a later attachment, that possibility raises the question of where it came from. Close parallels in language and content suggest that it has been abstracted from material in Luke-Acts and perhaps from Matthew.[9]

Can We Preach From the Longer Ending? The answer to this question will depend on the reader's understanding of what constitutes an authoritative canon of Scripture. If by *canon* one means "a list of authoritative books, in the wording of their autographs," the options are limited. It is possible to defend preaching from the longer ending in either of two ways. (1) One can redefine the meaning of the term *canon* to exclude the reference to autographs and emphasize the "received text" (*textus receptus*). Sometimes this is done de facto by those for whom the standard of reference is the King James Bible, which includes the verses in question. (2) Or one can argue that the longer ending was indeed part of the autographs and is therefore part of the canon of Scripture and an appropriate text for preaching. It is the position of this commentary that neither of those options is correct.

What, Then, Do These Verses Mean? It is not inappropriate to make some observations about the meaning of this short postscript to the Gospel of Mark. As we do, we should bear in mind that it does not carry the authority of Scripture, and we should take care not to include those observations as factors in the interpretation of Mark's Gospel itself.

Many Pentecostal and charismatic readers of Mark have given special attention to the prophecy about miraculous signs accompanying Christian mission in verses 17–18 (cf. also v. 20). For those readers, the "loss" of the longer ending appears to diminish the promise of Scripture that the life of the believer will be accompanied by miraculous, charismatic signs. But those signs are attested elsewhere in Scripture, and perhaps more concretely in the real life of the community of faith. God has not failed to move redemptively or miraculously.

Furthermore, the longer ending itself suggests that faith that requires more than the testimony of the eyewitnesses is somehow defective faith (v. 14). The greater reality here—the reality that both opens and closes the longer ending—is that Jesus has risen from the dead (vv. 9–14) and is now seated at the right hand of the Father (v. 19).

THE OLD TESTAMENT IN THE NEW

NT Text	OT Text	Subject
Mk 1:2	Mal 3:1	Messenger sent ahead
Mk 1:3	Isa 40:3	Voice in the wilderness
Mk 4:12	Isa 6:9–10	Seeing but not perceiving
Mk 7:6–7	Isa 29:13	Hypocritical worship
Mk 7:10	Ex 20:12; Dt 5:16	Fifth commandment
Mk 7:10	Ex 21:17; Lev 20:9	Cursing parents
Mk 9:48	Isa 66:24	Unquenchable fire of hell
Mk 10:6	Ge 1:27	Creation of humans
Mk 10:7	Ge 2:24	Institution of marriage
Mk 11:9	Ps 118:25–26	Blessed is he who comes
Mk 11:17	Isa 56:7	God's house of prayer
Mk 11:17	Jer 7:11	A den of robbers
Mk 12:10–11	Ps 118:22–23	Rejected cornerstone
Mk 12:19	Dt 25:5	A brother's widow
Mk 12:26	Ex 3:6	The living God
Mk 12:29	Dt 6:4	Only one God
Mk 12:30, 33	Dt 6:5	Love God
Mk 12:31	Lev 19:18	Love your neighbor as yourself
Mk 12:32	Dt 4:35	No other God
Mk 12:36	Ps 110:1	At God's right hand
Mk 13:14	Dan 9:27; 11:31	Abomination of desolation
Mk 12:24–25	Isa 13:10; 34:4	The end times
Mk 13:26	Dan 7:13–14	Coming Son of Man
Mk 14:27	Zec 13:7	Striking the shepherd
Mk 14:62	Da 7:13–14	Coming Son of Man
Mk 15:34	Ps 22:1	God-forsaken cry

NOTES

[1]For a summary discussion of paradigms, see Jerry Camery-Hoggatt, *Speaking of God: Reading and Preaching the Word of God* (1995), 32–46.

[2]The social-science literature on early Christianity is now enormous. For a few representative discussions, see John H. Elliott, *What Is Social-Scientific Criticism?* (1993); Bengt Holmberg, *Sociology and the New Testament: An Appraisal* (1990); Richard A. Horsley and John S. Hanson, *Bandits, Prophets, and Messiahs: Popular Movements at the Time of Jesus* (1985); Howard Clark Kee, *Christian Origins in Sociological Perspective* (1980); Abraham Malherbe, *Social Aspects of Early Christianity* (1983); Bruce Malina and Richard Rohrbaugh, *Social-Science Commentary on the Synoptic Gospels* (1992); Wayne Meeks, *The First Urban Christians: The Social World of the Apostle Paul* (1983); Gerd Theissen, *The Sociology of Early Palestinian Christianity* (1978); idem, *The Gospels in Context: Social and Political History in the Synoptic Tradition* (1991); Derek Tidball, *The Social Context of the New Testament* (1984).

[3]Frank Macchia, "God Present in a Confused Situation," *Pneuma: The Journal of the Society for Pentecostal Studies*, forthcoming.

[4]For a discussion of this issue, see Bruce Metzger, ed., *A Textual Commentary on the Greek New Testament* (1971), 73.

[5]In an extension of this same observation into another arena, James Robinson (1982, 94) has pointed out close parallels between the exorcisms and the controversy debates between Jesus and the religious authorities.

[6]On this see S. V. McCasland, *By the Finger of God: Demon Possession and Exorcism in Early Christianity in the Light of Modern Views of Mental Illness* (1951). More recently, Walter Wink has raised the question of whether there is a connection between the demonic and the processes of *social* marginalization (*Unmasking the Powers: The Invisible Forces That Determine Human Existence* [1986]).

[7]For this quote I am indebted to Gordon S. Wakefield, "The Unforgivable Sin," *Exp Tim* 104 (1993): 143.

[8]We find a striking parallel to this logic in Paul's famous *kenosis* passage in Philippians 2:6–11. Commentators have often overlooked Paul's use of a presumed hymn to drive home a point about Christian discipleship. If Jesus, who was God, could humble himself in service, *how much more* should Christians, who are redeemed only by the grace of God, follow his example and humble themselves in service to one another (note 2:3–5, 14–17). That is precisely what Mark has in view in 10:42–45.

[9]Mark 16:9 appears to be an abbreviated form of Luke 8:1–2; Mark 16:12 may be a loose reference to the Emmaus story in Luke 24:13–35; the story of an exchange over their lack of faith (Mark 16:14) may hold echoes of a resurrection appearance in Luke 24:36–49. For a parallel reference to tongues (Mark 16:17), see Acts 2:4; to picking up serpents without harm (Mark 16:18a), see Acts 28:1–6; to laying hands on the sick for healing (Mark 16:18b), see Acts 2:43; 4:30; 5:12. The report of Jesus' ascension in Mark 16:19 seems to parallel Luke 24:50–53 and Peter's preaching at Pentecost in Acts 2:33. The commission to "go into all the world and preach the good news to all creation" (Mark 16:15) parallels Matthew 28:19.

BIBLIOGRAPHY

Richard Batey, "Jesus and the Theater," *New Testament Studies* 30 (1984): 563–74; T. E. Boomershine and G. L. Bartholomew, "The Narrative Technique of Mark 16:8," *Journal of Biblical Literature* 100 (1981): 213–23; Jerry Camery-Hoggatt, *Irony in Mark's Gospel: Text and Subtext* (1992); idem, *Speaking of God: Reading and Preaching the Word of God* (1995); J. Duncan Derrett, "Salted With Fire: Studies in Texts: Mark 9:42–50," *Theology* 76 (1973): 364–68; Albert Descamps, *Les justes et la justice dans les évangelies et les christianisme primitif* (1950); Gordon Fee and Douglas Stuart, *How to Read the Bible for All Its Worth* (1982); Susan Garrett, *The Temptations of Jesus in the Gospel of Mark* (1998); John Paul Heil, "Reader-Response and the Narrative Context of the Parables About Growing Seed in Mark 4:1–34," *Catholic Biblical Quarterly* 54 (1992): 271–86; Joachim Jeremias, *New Testament Theology: The Proclamation of Jesus* (1971); Howard Clark Kee, *Community of the New Age: Studies in Mark's Gospel* (1977); idem, *Medicine, Miracle and Magic in New Testament Times* (1986); Terence Keegan, "The Parable of the Sower and Mark's Jewish Leaders," *Catholic Biblical Quarterly* 56 (1994): 501–8; William Lane, *The Gospel According to Mark*, NICNT (1974); George McKnight, *The Bible and the Reader* (1985); Jacob Neusner, ed., *Judaisms and Their Messiahs at the Turn of the Christian Era* (1988); Quentin Quesnell, *The Mind of Mark: Interpretation and Method Through the Exegesis of Mark 6,52*, Analecta biblica 38 (1969); James Robinson, *The Problem of History in Mark* (1982); Robert Tannehill, "The Gospel of Mark As Narrative Christology," *Semeia* 16 (1979); Bas van Iersel, *Reading Mark* (1988); Herman C. Waetjen, *A Reordering of Power: A Socio-Political Reading of Mark's Gospel* (1989).

LUKE

French L. Arrington

INTRODUCTION TO LUKE-ACTS

Luke's Gospel is the longest book in the New Testament. It belongs with the book that we know as the Acts of the Apostles. Together these two make up 27 percent or a little more than a quarter of the New Testament. To say nothing of their theological significance, the length of Luke-Acts alone gives them prominence in the New Testament as the longest contribution made by any single author—including Paul.

1. The Holy Spirit and Luke-Acts

Luke's Gospel presents the life and teaching of Jesus. It opens by noting that his birth is in the atmosphere of the charismatic[1] activity of the Holy Spirit. Prior to Jesus' birth, the angel announces that John "will be filled with the Holy Spirit even from birth" (Luke 1:15). Moreover, John's parents, Elizabeth and Zechariah, are also "filled with the Spirit" (1:41, 67). And when Gabriel tells Mary about the miraculous birth of her son, he says, "The Holy Spirit will come upon you, and the power of the Most High will overshadow you" (1:35). Soon after the birth of Jesus devout Simeon is empowered by the Holy Spirit to recognize the infant Jesus as the Messiah and to speak prophetically about him as Savior of humankind (2:25–32).

At the outset of Jesus' public ministry Luke portrays him as uniquely a man of the Spirit. John the Baptist prepares the way for Jesus, who, as the Baptist says, is more powerful and will baptize in the Holy Spirit and fire (3:16). The One who is to baptize in the Holy Spirit must first himself be anointed by the Spirit. Jesus becomes the Christ, the Anointed One. Not only does he possess the Spirit but he is also subject to the leading of the Spirit and relies on the empowering of the Spirit (4:1, 14). Luke's entire account of Christ's public ministry, beginning with baptism until the day of Pentecost, portrays him as the charismatic Christ—the unique bearer of the Spirit (Stronstad, 1984, 39).

The presence and power of the Holy Spirit figure prominently in the three episodes of Jesus Christ—his baptism (3:21–22), temptation (4:1–13), and sermon at Nazareth (4:14–30)—that launch his public ministry. At his baptism "the Holy Spirit descended on him in bodily form like a dove" (3:22). This objective, physical manifestation of the Spirit was followed by Jesus' being led by the Spirit into the desert. Matthew and Mark also connect the temptation in the desert with Jesus' reception of the Spirit (Matt. 4:1; Mark 1:12), but only Luke describes Jesus as "full of the Holy Spirit" (Luke 4:1) and indicates that he "returned to Galilee in the power of the Spirit" (4:14).

Although all four Evangelists record the descent of the Holy Spirit on Jesus at his baptism, only Luke explains Jesus' self-understanding of this experience at the Jordan. After his return to Galilee he reads Isaiah 61:1–2 as the text for his inaugural sermon at a synagogue service (4:18–19). Then he announces to the congregation that that prophecy is fulfilled in their hearing. In other words, Jesus understands that the descent of the Spirit anointed him as the Messiah for a charismatic, prophetic ministry on the order of the ministry of Old Testament prophets such as Elijah and Elisha.

Though the other Gospels associate the Holy Spirit with the life and ministry of Jesus, Luke's record of the activity of the Spirit is distinct. He intends for us to understand that the Spirit's anointing, leading, and empowering are the marks of Christ's entire ministry. This Spirit-anointed ministry from his baptism to his ascension must be imitated by the church if it is to be faithful to its mission.

Just as the third Gospel relates the life and ministry of Jesus, who executes his mission in the power of the Holy Spirit, the sequel to Luke's Gospel, the Acts of the Apostles, records the life and ministry of the early church as it is empowered by the Holy Spirit to bear witness to the saving works of Jesus from Jerusalem to Rome. That is, Jesus and his Spirit-filled ministry is the model for the church; the charismatic ministry of Christ foreshadows and prepares for the worldwide mission of the church (Davies, 1966, 244). The same anointing of the Spirit that rested on Jesus is poured out on the community of believers at Pentecost (Acts 2). The anointed Jesus becomes the giver of the Spirit (2:33). That outpouring of the Spirit is pivotal to the future mission of the disciples, for they become heirs and successors to the Spirit-filled ministry of Jesus, in that they become empowered to continue to do and teach what "Jesus began to do and to teach" (1:1).

The empowering experience of the disciples is described in various ways: a clothing (Luke 24:49), a baptizing (Acts 1:5), a coming upon (1:8), a filling (2:4), a pouring out (2:33), a receiving (2:38), and a falling (11:15). These terms indicate that empowerment by the Spirit is a dynamic, complex experience; no single term adequately explains its meaning. At the heart of the Pentecostal experience lie a momentous event and a dynamic reality of the presence and power of God. The disciples experienced an intensity of the Spirit far beyond what they had experienced during the earthly ministry of Jesus.

Through the empowerment of the Spirit at Pentecost, God's people are able to execute the mission of the church. Throughout Acts, the Spirit is the source of guidance and of power for believers to witness to the saving grace of Christ. Furthermore, the deeds, teachings, and experiences of Christ provide the pattern for the deeds, teachings, and experiences of the church. Just as through the anointing of the Spirit Jesus became the charismatic Christ, so also at Pentecost by Spirit baptism the disciples become a charismatic community. Herein lies the significance of the day of Pentecost.

This analysis is clearly contrary to the traditional interpretation that the gift of the Spirit on Pentecost gives birth to the church. In no way can this day be rightly understood as the birthday of the church or as part of the process of the conversion of the 120 disciples (Stronstad, 1984, 62; Arrington, 1988, 6–7). The baptism in the Spirit is promised to *obedient believers* (Acts 5:32). Luke presents, therefore, the Pentecostal narrative not as the gift of the Spirit for salvation but as a charismatic anointing for witness and service. The same Holy Spirit anointing that came from God upon Jesus now comes upon the disciples. They become a charismatic community—heirs of the charismatic anointing that Jesus received. In essence, the outpouring of the Spirit at Pentecost is the pivotal pattern for the continuing charismatic activity of the Spirit among God's people.

2. The Unity of Luke-Acts

Although the Gospel of Luke and Acts deal with different persons, geographies, stories, and histories, together these form two volumes of a single work, conceived and executed as a unified literary effort by the author. To think of the third Gospel and Acts of the Apostles as two separate literary works is a distortion; they must be read together. The order of the books in the New Testament has obscured this intent, insofar as the Gospel of John has been inserted between the two. Thus, many readers overlook the literary and theological unity of Luke-Acts. But with the recognition that Luke and Acts are two parts of one work, a more comprehensive understanding of Jesus becomes possible.

The introductions to Luke (1:1–4) and Acts (1:1–2) show that these two books are parts of one continuous work. The longer introduction to Luke's Gospel suggests that both the Gospel and Acts are in view. The preface to Acts is briefer and secondary in importance since Luke 1:1–4 introduces both volumes; Acts picks up where the Gospel leaves off. Luke summarizes his Gospel's content as the historical basis of early apostolic preaching: "In my former book, Theophilus, I wrote about all that Jesus began to do and to teach until the day he was taken up to heaven." Acts records the subsequent process of apostolic preaching—the spread of that message from its Jewish beginnings in Jerusalem to the Gentiles at "the ends of the earth" (1:8; cf. van Unnik, 1960, 26–59).

There are other evidences that Luke and Acts form one story. Both books are dedicated to someone known as Theophilus (in the Gospel he is addressed as "most excellent Theophilus," but in Acts simply as "Theophilus"). Luke also has a sense of Greek style; of the four Evangelists he is the most polished in his use of the Greek language.

Prominent Lukan theological themes, such as salvation, forgiveness, the Holy Spirit, witness, mission, stewardship, and prayer, bind Luke-Acts together as one and give them a common theological perspective. Luke's one continuous story emphasizes Jesus Christ as the Spirit-anointed Savior, the gospel as a message of repentance and forgiveness, and the Holy Spirit as the power by which the church continues to carry forward the miraculous deeds of Jesus and to execute its mission.

3. The Author of Luke-Acts

To this point we have assumed that Luke wrote the third Gospel and the Acts of the Apostles, but the author does not identify himself by name in either book. Both works are anonymous, though modern scholars are almost unanimous that Luke-Acts has a common author because of the similar prefaces and the similar literary style and theological perspective.

From the work we conclude that the author was well educated but not an eyewitness to the ministry of Jesus. He had received the gospel tradition from "those who ... were eyewitnesses and servants of the word" (Luke 1:2). Yet he must have participated in some of the events narrated in the book of Acts (cf. the "we" passages; see below). He knows the Old Testament in the Greek translation, has a good knowledge of the social and political world in the middle of the first century, and admires the apostle Paul. Like Paul, he emphasizes a gospel for all humankind.

There is a well-established tradition that these books were written by Luke the physician, a traveling companion of Paul. The earliest witness to Lukan authorship comes in the Muratorian Canon, a list of New Testament books written about A.D. 170. Likewise, the Anti-Marcionite Prologue (about A.D. 160–180), which was attached to the third Gospel in a number of Latin manuscripts, attests Lukan authorship of the two-volume work. This latter document also records that Luke was a native of Antioch, a physician by profession, a disciple of the apostles, and an associate of Paul until his death in Rome. Irenaeus of Lyons (about A.D. 180) also identifies Luke as Paul's companion, as a follower of the apostles, and as the author of the Gospel and Acts (*Against Heresies* 3.1; 23.1). Other church fathers (such as Clement of Alexandria, Tertullian, and Eusebius) all hold Luke to be the author.

There seems to be no good reason to deny this early tradition. Had it been otherwise, it seems unlikely that the name of Luke could have become associated with books that tradition has ascribed to him (Caird, 1963, 17), for this person can scarcely be described as a prominent figure in first-century Christianity.

True, the author's name appears in neither of the books; nevertheless, we can infer from the text of Acts the identity of the author. The famous "we-passages" (Acts 16:8–18; 20:5–21:18; 27:1–28:16)—passages where the author shifts from the usual third-person pronouns ("they" and "them") to first-person pronouns ("we" and "us")—point to Luke as the author. The first such passage begins with these words:

> So they [Paul, Silas, and Timothy] passed by Mysia and went down to Troas. During the night Paul had a vision of a man of Macedonia standing and begging him, "Come over to Macedonia and help us." After Paul had seen the vision, *we* got ready at once to leave for Macedonia, concluding that God had called *us* to preach the gospel to them. (Acts 16:8–10; italics added)

The most natural explanation for this style is that the author of Acts joined Paul at Troas and accompanied him to Philippi on his second missionary journey (16:8–18). Apparently he remained there. When Paul came through the city near the end of his third missionary journey, the author joined him again and accompanied him to Miletus and then to Jerusalem (20:5–21:18). Finally, he sailed with Paul to Rome (27:1–28:16).

The "we-passages" are closely related in style and vocabulary to the rest of Luke's writing. This person could not have been any of Paul's traveling companions mentioned by name in these passages. Since this person accompanied Paul to Rome, he was most likely a companion during his two-year house arrest, during which time Paul wrote Colossians, Ephesians, Philippians, and Philemon. Among those who are mentioned in these letters as his companions is Luke—affectionately referred to as "our dear friend Luke, the doctor" (Col. 4:14), one of his fellow workers (Philem. 24).

Paul was probably released from his house arrest but was later imprisoned again in Rome. During the second Roman confinement Luke was again among his companions. Having noted that Demas had deserted him, Paul added, "Crescens has gone to Galatia, and Titus to Dalmatia. Only Luke is with me" (2 Tim. 4:10–11). Luke was a faithful companion of Paul and a coworker in the gospel. There is no legitimate basis for rejecting him as the author of both the Gospel and Acts. The conclusion of Morton and Macgregor has expressed it well: "There seems no sufficient reason to doubt the unanimous ancient tradition that the author was Luke, the fellow traveler of Paul and that the 'we' sections are extracts from his personal diary" (1964, 52).

We know so little about Luke's background. The second-century Anti-Marcionite Prologue to Luke's Gospel records that he was a Greek from Antioch in Syria, who had been a companion of Paul, never married, and finally died in Bithynia at the age of eighty-four. A number of scholars are inclined to think this tradition is authentic, while others assume Luke was from Rome. It does seem clear from Colossians 4:10–14 that he was a Gentile. In verses 10 and 11 Paul sends the greeting of some of his associates, of whom he says, "These are the only Jews among my fellow workers"; this implies that the rest whose greetings are sent, including Luke, were Gentile believers. The evidence is convincing that a Gentile named Luke, a companion of Paul, wrote Luke-Acts.

4. Luke As a Historian and Theologian

Luke is no longer regarded as merely a historian but as both a historian and a theologian. He writes history from a specific theological point of view. W. C. van Unnik says, "This discovery of Luke the theologian seems . . . the great gain of the present phase of Luke-Acts study" (Keck and Martyn, 1966, 24). Luke's account of the story of Jesus and of the early church is more than history; it is a theological interpretation of the life and ministry of both Jesus and the early church. The author's intent is not only to present "an orderly account" of historical events but to share with his readers what he believes and to show that the Holy Spirit, manifested in the ministry of Jesus and in the ministry of the early Christians, is the power for the proclamation of good news and for teaching, healing, and acts of compassion. Luke is writing history through the eyes of faith.

Moreover, the narratives of the two books express a message that is relevant for all time. Most biblical scholars now agree that biblical narratives express the theological views and concerns of their authors. Classical Pentecostal scholars had already come to the conclusion that biblical narratives not only have historical value, but, along with the doctrinal sections, are also normative for faith and practice. Pentecostals have through the years appealed to Luke-Acts as the basis for not only understanding the life of Christ and the ministry of the early Christians but also as the basis for their distinctive view of the baptism of the Spirit as subsequent to the experience of salvation.

Biblical authors use narrative as a legitimate vehicle of theology (1 Cor. 10:1ff.; 2 Tim. 3:16). Luke wanted Theophilus to "know the certainty of the things" that had occurred, but also the significance of those events for understanding personal faith. But since we read nothing more about this man in either book, Luke certainly must have had a wider audience in mind than a single individual. In other words, the third Gospel still calls men and women to become disciples of Jesus. Receiving the baptism in the Spirit cannot be adequately interpreted without asking what empowerment by the Spirit means for Luke and his readers and for us today. Note too that Luke's dedication of his two-volume work to Theophilus was according to literary conventions of his day.

It is true that the literary form of Acts is different from the Gospel, but Luke's purpose and methods are reflected in both volumes. These two volumes were separated mainly because each would have occupied a full-sized papyrus roll. Consequently, the same principles of interpretation should be applied to Luke as to Acts.

5. The Time and Place of Luke-Acts

When was Luke-Acts written and from where? One thing we can be sure about is that the Gospel must have been composed before Acts, the second volume. In the introduction to the Gospel Luke writes that a number of accounts about Jesus had been previously written (cf. Luke 1:1–3). One of those earlier accounts most likely was the Gospel of Mark, which Luke presumably used as one of his sources.

Mark was therefore written earlier, perhaps in the late 50s. Throughout his two volumes Luke includes information received from "eyewitnesses and servants of the word" (Luke 1:2), likely consisting of both oral and written sources. This evidence makes the early 60s as a possible date for the composition of Luke-Acts.

Some biblical scholars date Luke-Acts between A.D. 80 and 90. They insist that Luke's outlook reflects the church situation in the 80s and 90s rather than the 60s. It has been often assumed that Luke 21:20ff., a prophecy of the fall of Jerusalem, is "a prophecy after the event" and that Luke must have written after the fall of Jerusalem in A.D. 70. This assumption need not be the case, however. Predictive prophecy is common to the biblical message. There is no convincing reason why Luke 21 should not be taken as a genuine prophecy that Jesus gave before Jerusalem was destroyed by the Romans.

Another more radical suggested date for Luke-Acts is the second century, which comes from biblical scholars at the famous German university in Tübingen. These proponents build their case on the author's attitude toward Jews and Jewish Christianity and theological content of the book. On such a basis J. C. O'Neill suggests a date between A.D. 115 and 130 (1961, 4ff.). But Luke's attitude toward Jewish Christianity and his theological perspective provide no substantial basis that he wrote later than the first century.

Determining the exact date of books in the New Testament is difficult, but the tone of the two books implies an environment previous to both the destruction of Jerusalem by the armies of Rome and the death of Paul. The following considerations favor the early date: (1) Acts records nothing about the result of Paul's trial in Rome; he remains in prison at the end of the book. If he had already been released from prison, Luke would surely have mentioned it. (2) In Acts, there is no trace of the rebellion of the Jews and the Jewish War (A.D. 66–70) that led to the destruction of the Holy City. (3) Luke does record the fulfillment of the prophecy of Agabus (Acts 11:28), but says nothing about the fulfillment of Jesus' prophecy of the fall of Jerusalem (Luke 21:20ff.). (4) The Acts account gives no hint of Nero's persecution of the Christians (A.D. 64–67) and of his burning of Rome (about A.D. 64). Luke portrays Rome as a friend of Christians; the picture would certainly have been different after the persecutions sponsored by Nero began.

The early 60s of the first century is therefore a reasonably satisfactory date for the writing of Acts. As noted, the book of Acts draws to a close with Paul's preaching the gospel in Rome (Acts 28:16, 30). Is this the place where Luke wrote his Gospel and the Acts of the Apostles? Quite possibly, though we have little, if any, hard evidence for identifying the place(s) of composition. According to the Anti-Marcionite Prologue Luke wrote the Gospel in Achaia (southern Greece). Other possibilities are Antioch and Caesarea. Because of insufficient information, this question must remain open.

Luke lays claim to careful historical research as the basis for writing his Gospel (Luke 1:1–4). The same must hold true for Acts. Many of the eyewitnesses to the ministry of Christ and to the fulfillment of God's promise of the Spirit baptism to the followers of Jesus were still alive. Caesarea, the city where Paul was held prisoner for two years under Felix and Festus (Acts 23:23–26:35), could have been an excellent place and occasion for such research and the writing of the third Gospel and the first part of Acts. The latter chapters of Acts, especially the we-passages with their vivid biographical details, were probably written during the two years Luke stayed with Paul in Rome (Col. 4:14). Therefore, it seems likely that Luke finished the composition of Acts in that city (Arrington, 1988, xxxiii). Though this reconstruction comes short of absolute proof, it is a reasonable possibility.

6. The Purpose of Luke-Acts

Scholars have proposed many explanations as to why Luke wrote. At the opening of the Gospel he does give us a statement of his intention, namely, to make known "the certainty of the things you [Theophilus] have been taught." Luke desires to write a book that presents the saving significance of Jesus' ministry. He does it as a two-volume work that includes the story of the early church empowered by the Spirit to carry the gospel to the ends of the earth. He writes to instruct people who are removed in geography and time from the ministry of Jesus, to provide them (1) with an account of the story of Jesus so that they may be edified and have a reliable basis for faith, and (2) with an account of how God's plan in Jesus continues to unfold in the history of the early church.

In addition to a pastoral purpose, Luke-Acts reflects also an evangelistic concern. The evangelistic speeches, along with the emphasis on miracles as confirmations of the preaching of the word, serve Luke's desire to awaken faith (cf. Marshall, 1978, 35). He writes for the purpose of convincing, converting, saving, and spiritually edifying his readers.

a. The Evangelistic Concern

Luke summarizes the content of his first volume in Acts 1:1: "In my former book, Theophilus, I wrote about all that Jesus began to do and to teach" (Acts 1:1). The phrase "began to do and teach" encompasses Jesus' entire ministry. At the same time, it is a reminder that his mighty works and teaching are more than the ministry of a mere man. His activity is saving; his teaching brings salvation to the world. At Jesus' birth the angel announces the message of salvation: "I bring you good news of great joy that will be for all people. Today in the town of David a Savior has been born to you; he is Christ the Lord" (Luke 2:10–11). Simeon has been assured by the Holy Spirit that he will live to see "the consolation of Israel." Moved by the Holy Spirit, he goes into the temple courts. Upon seeing the child Jesus he declares, "My eyes have seen your salvation . . . a light for revelation to the Gentiles and for glory to your people Israel" (Luke 2:30–32). The mission of Jesus—summed up in what he did and said—is the means of the salvation for all people, Jew and Gentile. As the Savior himself says, "For the Son of Man came to seek and to save what was lost" (Luke 19:10).

Acts, Luke's second volume, has the same evangelistic emphasis. Its main message is the good news of salvation for people throughout the world. The two volumes show various aspects of the one great fact: "God's plan of salvation" (van Unnik, 1960, 26–59), which reached its fulfillment in Christ and flowed out of him through the early Christians as they were empowered by the Spirit. Acts, in other words, is a confirmation and continuation through his Spirit-filled witnesses of what God did in Christ as reported in the third Gospel. Indeed, Luke wants the gospel to be proclaimed in all the world so that those outside of the church may come to know the saving message of Jesus.

The emphasis in Acts on Spirit-filled preaching reveals the evangelistic outreach to the unsaved. The disciples are promised the power of the Spirit so they can become witnesses "to the ends of the earth" (Acts 1:8). When the disciples experience the baptism in the Spirit, the direct result is power so that they become witnesses and fulfill the global mission of the church. Clothed with extraordinary power (*dynamis*) to work miracles (*dynameis*) and to preach the gospel, they are fully equipped not only to proclaim the saving works of Christ, but also to convince unbelievers of its truth. An inseparable link exists between the power of the Spirit and the equipping of believers to proclaim that Jesus came to save all, regardless of race, sex, or social standing.

At Pentecost Peter expresses the heart of the evangelistic concern of Luke-Acts in his speech, which begins with Joel's prophecy. The outpouring of the Spirit is the clear sign that "the last days"—a new era—has been ushered in. The age of the Messiah, predicted by the prophets, has dawned; the Holy Spirit, who anointed Jesus and baptized his disciples, is the divine agent of these last times. These are days of universal salvation, in which "everyone who calls on the name of the Lord will be saved" (Acts 2:21), and everyone can be clothed with the power of the Spirit to bear witness to Christ (1:8; 4:8, 31). Jesus of Nazareth, rejected and crucified by wicked men, has been raised from the dead by God as Lord (2:23–28). There is no automatic participation in salvation, but only those who repent can be saved from this corrupt generation (2:38, 40). The hope for the entire human race is the crucified and risen Savior, because "everyone who believes in him receives forgiveness of sins through his name" (10:43). No one but those who trust him as their Savior will receive this forgiveness and escape the judgment that unbelief incurs.

b. The Pastoral Concern

Luke's evangelistic motive fails to give weight to the full scope of Luke-Acts. He also has his eyes on the practical problems of the church in his day. In addition to being a historian and theologian he is a pastor, who takes a pastoral approach to problems within the church, seeking to strengthen Christians in their faith and encouraging them to confront individuals with the demands of the gospel so that the number of believers may abound. For R. P. Martin, Luke's primary purpose is

> to aid the church in his lifetime by proclaiming the kerygma and by offering pastoral counsel and encouragement to his fellow believers who, to be sure, may well have needed some corrective teaching and have required a fresh retelling of the earthly life of their Lord. (1975, 1:249)

A frequent expression of Luke has to do with "certainty," "safety," or "security" (*asphaleia*, *asphales*, *asphalos*, Luke 1:4; Acts 2:36; 5:23; 16:23, 24; 21:34; 22:30; 25:26). Though the noun has a variety of meanings, in Luke 1:4 it refers either to factual accuracy of the Christian message or to inner assurance in regard to personal faith. Apparently Luke wants to give Theophilus and the other believers who read his two volumes a better understanding of Christian teaching so that they may have confident conviction as followers of Christ.

Obviously the church had a wide range of needs in Luke's day, and individual believers were vulnerable to the stress of living in a hostile world. Daily adversities and persecutions made Theophilus and other believers wonder whether the Lord was present and raised doubts in their minds about the claims of the gospel. They were tempted to lose confidence in their faith and perhaps to doubt the future of the church. Pastorally motivated, Luke writes biblical history to assure them that their faith and hope are well placed in God's mighty acts in Christ and that the message they believe is indeed God's word. Many of the pastoral problems Luke faces are apparent both in the third Gospel and in Acts.

(1) The Empowering Ministry of the Holy Spirit. The Spirit occupies a central place in Luke's theology. In his Gospel he refers to the Spirit seventeen times, compared with twelve references in Matthew and six in Mark. At the conception of Jesus, Mary is overshadowed by the Spirit (Luke 1:35). By the Spirit John is prepared for his ministry as the forerunner of Christ (1:15), and he "grew and became strong in [the] Spirit" (1:80). As a result of being filled with the Spirit, Elizabeth (1:41), Zechariah (1:67), and Simeon (2:25–27) prophesy. The Spirit came upon Jesus at baptism (3:22), led him into the desert to be tempted by Satan (4:1), and empowered him for his preaching and healing ministries (4:18–19). After his resurrection he predicted that the church would carry out its mission by the charismatic power of the Spirit (24:49). Acts vividly records the execution of the church's mission.

Of all the books in the New Testament, Acts mentions the Holy Spirit the most—more than fifty times. The charismatic power and work of the Holy Spirit manifested throughout Jesus' ministry subsequently go to work in the church as it carries out its evangelistic mission. As the One anointed by the Spirit, Jesus endues the disciples with power from on high by pouring out his Spirit so that they can carry out the church's mission (Acts 2:33). The Spirit, therefore, links the ministry of Jesus to the ministry of the church. As a result, the early disciples, strong in Pentecostal might, go forth as witnesses "to the ends of the earth." As a pastor Luke reminds his readers of the extraordinary power of the Spirit experienced by Jesus and by the first believers. He encourages them to maintain their confidence in the power of God and to remain faithful to the gospel.

The first believers experience the effects of increasing opposition and hostility, but the outpouring of the Spirit at Pentecost shows not only God's gracious design toward them but also toward the church of Luke's day. Throughout Acts runs a daily consciousness of the dynamic presence of the Holy Spirit, which comes not only from their initial Pentecostal experience[2] and from the miraculous manifestation of his power, but also from the guidance and fellowship of the Spirit. The Spirit's many and varied works attest that God is personally involved in the lives of Christians and directs the program of the church. By him Christians are strengthened and encouraged (Acts 9:31), are set apart for service (13:2), are guided in their deliberations (15:28), and are appointed as pastors (20:28). Especially noteworthy is 16:6–10, where Paul and his companions are "kept by the Holy Spirit from preaching the word in the province of Asia," but in a vision they learn that God has called them to Macedonia. For the first believers their baptism in the Spirit does not become merely an experience of the past but a dynamic reality in their daily lives, enabling them to face external adversities and to deal with problems in the church. Thus recounting the experiences, Luke encourages his readers to have confidence in the Spirit's power and the guidance to enable them to maintain unity in the church and to live as Christians in a gainsaying and unfriendly world.

(2) A Pronounced Compassion for the Outcasts and Sinners. Luke emphasizes Jesus' compassion for the disadvantaged and the outcasts of society. He shows Jesus as a friend of tax collectors and sinners. Sinners includes all who were guilty of wrongdoing and of failing to observe Jewish ceremonial laws. Tax collectors were hated because they collected revenues for the Roman government and many times lined their own pockets with some of the taxes. Luke alone records the parable of the Pharisee and the tax collector (Luke 18:9–14) as well as the story about the conversion of Zacchaeus, a tax collector (19:1–10). No other Gospel tells about the sinful woman (7:36–50), the good Samaritan (10:25–37), the prodigal son (15:11–32), and Jesus' pardon of the thief crucified with him (23:39–43).

A similar interest in outcasts is found in Acts: the healing of the lame beggar at the gate called Beautiful (3:1–10) and the deliverance of paralytics and the lame at Samaria (8:7). To the Samaritans (half-breed Jews), Philip proclaims the gospel and works miracles. The Jews normally have no dealings with the Samaritans (cf. John 4:9). But Peter and John's visit to Samaria confirms that the conversion of the hated Samaritans is God's will (Acts 8:14–25). Another example is the Ethiopian eunuch (8:26–39). As an imperfect human being he cannot enter the assembly of the Lord (Deut. 23:1). He remains an outcast of Jewish society, but he does become a full-fledged Christian (O'Toole, 1984, 146–47). With a pastor's heart Luke shows God's great compassion toward the disadvantaged and sinners. The death, resurrection, and teaching of Jesus form a message of salvation addressed to all people. The disadvantaged among Luke's readers have reason to take courage because Jesus, in particular, brings them salvation.

(3) A Marked Concern for the Poor. Luke has an inexhaustible compassion for people with troubles. His concern goes out especially for the plight of the poor. At the outset we read Mary's song of praise, where the hungry are satisfied with God's blessings (Luke 1:53). At Jesus' birth Mary and Joseph's presentation of an offering prescribed for the poor (2:24; cf. Lev. 12:8) shows that they are among the poor; in his sermon at Nazareth Jesus cites the prophecy of Isaiah to indicate that he has been anointed by the Spirit to preach good news to the poor (Luke 4:18; Isa. 61:1). Announcing the good news of salvation, he later says, "Blessed are you who are poor" (Luke 6:20). When Jesus describes his ministry for John the Baptist, he includes the clause, "the good news is preached to the poor" (7:22). His own living conditions are worse than that of foxes and birds since he has no place to lay his head (9:58). Luke alone records the parable of the rich man and Lazarus (16:19–31), Jesus' counsel to "sell your possessions and give to the poor" (12:33), and his advice to "invite the poor, the crippled, the lame, the blind" for a meal (14:13). Finally, only Luke tells the story of the conversion of Zacchaeus, who promises to give half of his possessions to the poor (19:1–10).

A similar interest in the poor appears in Acts. Luke writes about the early Christians sharing all things in common, selling their possessions, and distributing the money to the needy (Acts 2:44–45; 4:32–35). In the same spirit Peter says to the crippled man at the gate called Beautiful, "Silver or gold I do not have, but what I have I give you" (3:6). Against the background of the generosity of the early believers, especially that of Barnabas, Luke relates the story of Ananias and Sapphira (5:1–11). They pretend to give the full value of a piece of property to the church, but they hold back part of it. They want to appear to share all their things and to look good in the eyes of the church, but they have no real concern for the needy. Their fatal mistake is a failure to recognize the church as a Spirit-filled community. Inspired by Satan, they try to deceive not only the church but the Spirit in the church.

In contrast to the greed of Ananias and Sapphira, Luke calls attention to the correct use of wealth. God-fearing Cornelius gives "generously to those in need" (Acts 10:2). When the prophet Agabus predicts a famine in the Roman world, the church at Antioch sends help to the Christians in Judea (11:28–30). In his defense before Felix, Paul speaks of the relief fund in the Gentile churches for the poor Christians in Jerusalem (24:17). Paul urges the Ephesian elders to "help the weak" and supports this advice with a saying of Jesus, "It is more blessed to give than to receive" (20:35).

Luke champions the cause of the poor and shows Jesus' deep concern for these people, but he never makes poverty itself a virtue. There is no categorical condemnation of wealth, though its temptations are recognized. Jesus' concern for the poor is as it should be because of their great needs and general helplessness, not because of any particular virtue in poverty. The compassion of Jesus for the poor and that of the early Christians should serve as models for ministering to the poor and needy.

(4) A Strong Emphasis on Prayer. Luke recognizes the special significance of prayer. Of the nine prayers that the Gospel ascribes to Jesus, seven of them are recorded only in this Gospel. At crucial times prayer marks the ministry of Jesus. The Spirit descends upon Jesus after his baptism as he is praying (Luke 3:21). The temptation in the desert is in the context of prayer, since the testing occurs immediately after his baptism (4:1–13). Prior to choosing the twelve apostles Jesus spends all night in prayer (6:12–13). He prays on the Mount of Transfiguration and is transfigured while doing so (9:29). His practice of prayer inspires his disciples to request a model prayer, and he gives the Lord's Prayer (11:1–4). He prays for Peter (22:32) and for those who crucified him (23:34). In anticipation of the cross he prays three times (22:39–46). Luke indicates the intensity of Jesus' prayer: "He prayed more earnestly, and his sweat was like drops of blood falling to the ground." His last words on the cross is a prayer: "Father, into your hands I commit my spirit" (23:46). Three of the parables found only in Luke deal with prayer: the friend at midnight (11:5–10), the unjust judge (18:1–8), and the Pharisee and the tax collector (18:9–14).

The third Gospel reaches its climax with Jesus' return to heaven and the prayer and praise of the disciples (24:52–53). Along with the power of the Spirit, prayer is also vital to the life and growth of the church in Acts. As their Lord has done, the early believers "always pray and [do] not give up" (cf. 18:1). In preparation for the outpouring of the Spirit they devote themselves constantly to prayer (Acts 1:14). Seeking a replacement for Judas, the disciples pray before lots are cast (1:24). As Stephen is being stoned, he prays (7:59–60). Peter is praying when he receives clear directions to go to the house of Cornelius in Caesarea (10:9–20). Cornelius is also praying when the angel appears to him (10:3, 30). At the beginning of Paul's missionary journeys the church prays and fasts, and then sends Paul and Barnabas off.

A close link exists between the anointing of the Spirit and prayer in Luke-Acts. Only Luke tells that Jesus is praying when the Holy Spirit descends upon him at baptism and he is empowered for ministry (Luke 3:21). Throughout that ministry prayer is the effective means by which he apprehends the dynamic power of the Spirit. We also see this close link between prayer and the Holy Spirit at Pentecost and subsequent outpourings of the Spirit on the early Christians (Acts 1:13–14; 2:1–2; 4:31; 8:15). Just like their Lord they are praying when the Spirit descends upon them.

Luke sees prayer as vital to the unfolding of the divine plan for salvation. Prayer is God-centered and reaches far beyond the devotional life. It is at the center of salvation history. At significant moments God guides the unfolding of redemptive history through prayer. When an angel appears to Zechariah to announce the birth of John the Baptist, "all the assembled worshipers were praying" (Luke 1:10). Before the birth of Jesus Mary prays and worships God (1:46–55). As already indicated, many important events in Jesus' ministry are closely connected to prayer.

Likewise, prayer is at the center of the progress of the church in Acts. After Pentecost God's people face one crisis after another with prayer. So whatever the occasion—violent hostility, riots, imprisonments, the deceit of Ananias and Sapphira, the greed of Simon, the mockers among the Athenians, or the perils of Paul—the church continues to advance (Arrington, 1988, xlii). With confidence in the power of God they pray as Jesus has instructed

(Luke 18:1) and endure great adversity as they proclaim the divine plan of salvation for the world. Indeed, for them prayer is the fundamental means by which to experience the blessings of the kingdom.

7. The Sources of Luke-Acts

Luke speaks about receiving information from "those who from the first were eyewitnesses and servants of the word," though he does not name these eyewitnesses and servants (Luke 1:1–4). In addition Luke indicates there were written records, presumably at least the Gospels of Matthew and Mark. Luke has "carefully investigated everything from the beginning" in order "to write an orderly account." This means that he has done careful research and employed authoritative sources in writing his Gospel. It seems reasonable to assume that in composing Acts he has used both oral and written sources similar to those he used in writing his Gospel.

As a historian Luke chooses the best sources. It is generally agreed that he is selective in his use of them so that Luke-Acts includes only information that will demonstrate the origin of the Christian movement, its progress, and its triumph through the preaching of the gospel and the power of the Spirit. What does not serve Luke's purpose is omitted from his narratives. In all of this what is primary is the guidance of the Holy Spirit.

No consensus has been reached as to whether Luke's sources are primarily written or oral. Many scholars are convinced that a major source is the Gospel of Mark, for over one-third of Luke bears close similarity to Mark. Luke may have used some information from Mark if the Gospel had been written before or during the early months of Paul's Roman imprisonment. Another written source for Luke is the Greek Old Testament (LXX). Many stories of his Gospel have the style and flavor of the LXX. For example, Mary's song (Luke 1:46–55) is similar to Hannah's song (1 Sam. 2:1–10); Jesus as a boy in the temple (Luke 2:41–46) to the story of the boy Samuel in the temple (1 Sam. 3); Jesus' raising the son of a widow at Nain (Luke 7:11–17) to Elijah's raising the widow's son (1 Kings 17:17–24). In like manner Luke's literary style in Acts (especially chs. 1–12) echoes the language of the LXX. The life of Jesus and the church is, in other words, a continuation of the Old Testament story; through Jesus Christ the divine promises to Israel are extended to the world.

Oral information for Luke may have come from a number of his associates, some of whom were "eyewitnesses and servants of the word." For example, we know that Mary Jesus' mother, was present at Pentecost; she may have provided valuable information about the life of Jesus and the early church. Luke may have interviewed prominent people such as Mark, James the brother of the Lord, and Peter. He may have talked personally with some of the seventy-two disciples (Luke 10:1). Paul undoubtedly told Luke about his conversion on the road to Damascus. Luke stayed at the home of Philip the evangelist (Acts 21:8), who likely shared the story about the conversion of the Ethiopian (8:26–40). In addition Luke may have collected information through interviews with such persons as Timothy, Silas, and Gaius.

Luke does not, of course, identify his sources for Acts. But most likely written records were preserved by various churches and communities, such as Jerusalem, Damascus, Antioch, Caesarea, Philippi, Ephesus, Thessalonica, and Corinth. Conditions were conducive to the formation of traditions about the apostolic period and had their place in the preaching of the early church. Among the Pauline churches were those who had materials about the organization and spiritual triumphs of the churches (Jervell, 1972, 19–36). The letter sent by the Jerusalem Council may have been preserved at Antioch (Acts 15:30; 21:25). Another letter recorded in Acts was that of Claudius Lysias, sent to Caesarea (23:23–26:32). Luke presumably gathered a great deal of information in his two-year stay in Palestine during Paul's Caesarean imprisonment. Behind the "we-passages" probably stands a diary composed by Luke while he was with Paul.

Doubtless the sermons in Acts should be not viewed as word-for-word accounts; they are too short to be full sermons. Yet they are certainly reliable summaries of what the early believers preached. With great care Luke has selected from his sources information relevant to his purposes and molds it into a powerful and accurate account of both the life and ministry of Jesus and of the advance of the early church from Jerusalem to Rome within about thirty years. Luke knows his sources and bases what he writes not on rumors but on the truth.

8. The Plan and Organization of Luke-Acts

What provides structure for Luke-Acts is the travel motif and the various discourses. Just as the discourses of Jesus occupy a significant place in Luke's Gospel, for example, so also the apostolic speeches are prominent in Acts. Regarding the travel motif, in his Gospel Luke describes the ministry of the charismatic Christ from rural Galilee to the Jewish capital of Jerusalem; in Acts he traces the progress of the church from the Holy City to the imperial capital of Rome. The geographical scope reminds us of the breadth of Luke's plans and interest. The prevailing mood of the two volumes is summed up in Acts 8:4, "Those who had been scattered preached the word wherever they went."

Luke arranges his material so that great emphasis is placed on travel narratives. Following the preface (Luke 1:1–4), we have the accounts of the birth of both John the Baptist and Jesus (1:5–2:52). At the time of Jesus' birth the Holy Family journeys to Bethlehem and Jerusalem (2:4, 22); they go to Jerusalem again when Jesus is twelve years old (2:42). Jesus begins his itinerant preaching travels in Galilee with a sermon at Nazareth (4:14–30). His travels continue there until his Galilean ministry reaches its climax in his last journey to Jerusalem (9:51–19:44), beginning with the words: "Jesus resolutely set out for Jerusalem." The account of this journey indicates that the Spirit-anointed Jesus moves consistently toward Jerusalem to fulfill his mission on the earth. Some of the most memorable events and teachings of Jesus appear in these chapters: lessons on discipleship and its cost (9:51–62; 14:25–35), the good Samaritan (10:25–37), the Lord's Prayer and teaching about prayer (11:1–13), a lament over Jerusalem (13:31–35), the prodigal son (15:11–32), the rich man and Lazarus (16:19–31), and Jesus' triumphal entry into Jerusalem (19:28–44).

It is at Jerusalem that the final decision concerning the ministry and teaching of Jesus has to be made. So the suspense in Luke's Gospel builds toward this final crisis. Jesus' presence in Jerusalem (19:45–21:38) brings him into confrontation with his enemies. The chief priests and teachers of the law plot his destruction (19:47). Trying to trap Jesus, they ask him the question of paying tribute to Caesar (20:20–26), but the Spirit-anointed teaching of Jesus has a way of silencing his enemies (13:17; 14:6; 20:26, 40). Jesus assures his faithful followers that in similar crises they will be given "words and wisdom that none of your adversaries will be able to resist or contradict" (21:15). Israel's leaders' rejection of Jesus as their prophet-king will lead to divine judgment upon Jerusalem.

The stage is now set for the climax of Luke's Gospel: the trial, death, and the resurrection of Jesus (22:1–24:53). Luke records in rapid succession the events that lead up to the crucifixion. Judas' betrayal of Jesus (22:1–6), the Last Supper (22:7–38), Jesus' agony in prayer (22:39–46), his arrest and trials before the Sanhedrin, Pilate, and Herod (22:66–23:12) all precede his sentencing and crucifixion. His death is a fulfillment of prophecy (24:7, 26, 46) and has been ordained as a prelude to his resurrection (24:25–26). Luke emphasizes the reality of Jesus' resurrection and the difference it makes in the lives of his followers (24:1–49). With Jesus' concluding command that they wait in Jerusalem "until you have been clothed with power from on high," Luke prepares to continue his account in Acts.

One of the significant features of Luke is the inclusion of two great travel sections, one in the middle of his Gospel (Luke 9:51–19:44) and the other in the last third of Acts (Acts19:21–28:21). These sections are parallel and show that the outreach of the gospel is grounded in the Spirit-anointed ministry of Jesus and that of the church. In fact, the parallels are a significant structural feature of Luke-Acts. The others are:

(1) Preface with the dedication to Theophilus (Luke 1:1–4; Acts 1:1–5).
(2) Filled with the Holy Spirit (Luke 3:21–22; Acts 2:1–4).
(3) Forty-day period of preparation for ministry (Luke 4:2; Acts 1:3).
(4) The Spirit-anointed ministry, beginning with a sermon (Luke 4:16–30; Acts 2:14–40).

(5) Authoritative teaching and extraordinary deeds provoking conflict, unbelief, and rejection (Luke 4:31–8:56; Acts 3:1–12:17).
(6) The evangelization of the Gentiles (Luke 10:1–12; Acts 13:1–19:20).
(7) Journey to Jerusalem and arrest (Luke 9:51–22:53; Acts 19:21–21:36) (cf. Nickle, 1980, 127–28).

Though this list is only partial, the parallels are striking. Some of the most remarkable correspondences, however, are between Jesus and Paul. For example, three times Jesus comes to Jerusalem: once as an infant for presentation to God in the Temple; again at the age of twelve as a "son of the law"; finally the great travel narrative that takes up nearly 40 percent of the Gospel. The book of Acts records the three corresponding journeys of Paul, the last of which brings him to Rome. Such parallels suggest that the charismatic Christ is the model for the church if it is to be faithful to its mission. His Spirit-anointed acts and words provide the pattern for the ministry of the church. As we can surmise, many of the events described in Acts are either anticipated or predicted in Luke's Gospel.

The structure of Acts is inherent in its subject—the story of the church. Though the account is essentially chronological, scholars have suggested a number of outlines for the book, some of which are helpful to the interpreter. One approach sees Acts as falling into two major divisions (chs. 1–12; chs. 13–28). The emphasis is on the work of the Spirit within and through the church, first describing how he works in the churches in Palestine and second describing how he works in the establishing of the first Gentile churches. The earlier section centers around Jerusalem with the outreach of the gospel message to Judea, Galilee, Samaria, and Caesarea (8:1; 9:31; 10:1–48). The latter section centers around Antioch as a base for the missionary effort, and the church reaches into the Gentile world with its message (13:1; 14:26–27; 15:30ff.; 18:22). Each section has its central figure: Peter in the first and Paul in the second. In light of Luke's stress on the universal love of God in Christ and the recurring theme that includes the Gentiles in the plan of salvation, Jesus is "a light . . . to the Gentiles" (Luke 2:32), and his followers are to preach "to all nations" (24:47).

Another attractive and useful proposal is the organization of Acts around what has been called "six panels of progress" (1:1–6:7; 6:8–9:31; 9:32–12:24; 12:25–16:5; 16:6–19:20; 19:21–28:31). At the end of each panel is a summary that indicates the progress of the church.

Whether Luke had a specific outline before him as he wrote Luke-Acts we do not know. This commentary follows an outline that seeks to be simple and natural and to capture in Luke's two volumes the chronological and geographical movement as Jesus and the early church are empowered by the presence of the Holy Spirit to proclaim the gospel to the world.

OUTLINE OF LUKE-ACTS*

The Acts of Jesus (Content) **The Narratives of Jesus (Genre)**	**The Acts of the Apostles (Content)** **The Narratives of the Apostles (Genre)**
1. Preface (1:1–4)	**1. Preface** (1:1–11)
	1.1. Recapitulation and Summary (1:1–3)
	1.2. The Promise of the Holy Spirit (1:4–5)
	1.3. Jesus Announces the Empowering by the Spirit (1:6–8)
	1.4. Jesus Ascends Into Heaven (1:9–11)
2. The Origin of the Spirit-Anointed Christ (1:5–3:38)	**2. The Origin of the Spirit-Baptized/Filled Community** (1:12–2:41)
2.1. Announcement of the Birth of John (1:5–25)	**2.1.** The Community Awaits the Promised Spirit (1:12–26)

*I am indebted to Roger Stronstad for his assistance in preparing this parallel outline.

2.2. Announcement of the Birth of Jesus (1:26–38)

2.3. Mary's Visit to Elizabeth and Her Song (1:39–56)

2.4. The Birth of John and Zechariah's Song (1:57–80)

2.5. The Birth of Jesus (2:1–20)

2.6. Jesus As an Infant in the Temple (2:21–40)

2.7. Jesus As a Boy in the Temple (2:41–52)

2.8. The Anointing of Jesus (3:1–38)
- **2.8.1.** The Preaching of John the Baptist (3:1–20)
- **2.8.2.** The Baptism of Jesus (3:21–22)
- **2.8.3.** The Genealogy of Jesus (3:23–38)

3. The Ministry of the Spirit-Anointed Prophet: Christ in Galilee (4:1–9:50)

3.1. The Testing of Jesus (4:1–13)

3.2. Jesus' Inaugural Sermon (4:14–30)

3.3. The Authoritative Word and Healings (4:31–41)

3.4. Popular Acclaim (4:42–5:16)
- **3.4.1.** Summary (4:42–44)
- **3.4.2.** Simon Peter (5:1–11)
- **3.4.3.** Healing of a Leper (5:12–16)

3.5. Opposition (5:17–6:11)
- **3.5.1.** Pharisees: He Blasphemes (5:17–26)
- **3.5.2.** Pharisees: He Associates With Sinners (5:27–32)
- **3.5.3.** Pharisees: His Disciples Do Not Fast (5:33–39)
- **3.5.4.** Pharisees: He Breaks the Sabbath (6:1–11)
  - **3.5.4.1.** Disciples Harvest Grain (6:1–5)
  - **3.5.4.2.** Jesus Heals a Crippled Hand (6:6–11)

3.6. Jesus Chooses Twelve Apostles (6:12–16)

3.7. The Great Sermon on the Plain (6:17–49)
- **3.7.1.** Introduction to the Sermon (6:17–19)
- **3.7.2.** Blessings and Woes (6:20–26)
- **3.7.3.** Love for Enemies (6:27–36)
- **3.7.4.** Judging Others (6:37–45)

- **2.1.1.** The Community Devotes Itself to Prayer (1:12–14)
- **2.1.2.** The Community Chooses Matthias (1:15–26)

2.2. The Day of Pentecost (2:1–41)
- **2.2.1.** Sign: The Disciples Are Filled With the Holy Spirit (2:1–4)
- **2.2.2.** Wonder: The Crowd Is Amazed (2:5–13)
- **2.2.3.** Pneuma Discourse (2:14–36)
  - **2.2.3.1.** Explanation: The Three Signs Fulfill Joel's Prophecy (2:14–21)
  - **2.2.3.2.** Witness: Peter Proclaims Jesus as Lord and Christ (2:22–36)
- **2.2.4.** Response: About Three Thousand Are Saved (2:37–41)

3. The Acts of the Spirit-Baptized/Filled Community (2:42–6:7)

3.1. Fellowship Inaugurated: The Inner/Outer Life of the Community (2:42–47)

3.2. Example: Confirmatory Healing (3:1–26)
- **3.2.1.** Sign: Peter Raises Up a Lame Man (3:1–8)
- **3.2.2.** Wonder: The Crowd Is Amazed (3:9–10)
- **3.2.3.** Witness: Peter Proclaims Jesus As Servant (3:11–26)

3.3. Opposition (4:1–5:42)
- **3.3.1.** Priests–Sadducees Arrest Peter and John (4:1–22)
  - **3.3.1.1.** Peter and John Are Arrested (4:1–4)
  - **3.3.1.2.** Pneuma Discourse: Peter Addresses the Sanhedrin (4:5–12)
  - **3.3.1.3.** Response: The Sanhedrin Forbids Peter and John to Preach (4:13–22)
- **3.3.2.** Theophany: The Community Is Filled With the Spirit (4:23–31)
- **3.3.3.** The Spirit-Baptized Community Practices Fellowship (4:32–5:16)
  - **3.3.3.1.** Property Is Sold and Distributed (4:32–35)
  - **3.3.3.2.** Positive Example: Barnabas (4:36–37)
  - **3.3.3.3.** Negative Example: Ananias and Sapphira (5:1–11)

- **3.7.5.** A Picture of Two Houses (6:46–49)
- **3.8.** Jesus' Power Over Sickness and Death (7:1–17)
  - **3.8.1.** Healing of a Roman Officer's Servant (7:1–10)
  - **3.8.2.** Raising a Widow's Son From the Dead (7:11–17)
- **3.9.** John the Baptist and Jesus (7:18–35)
  - **3.9.1.** Messengers From John the Baptist (7:18–23)
  - **3.9.2.** Jesus' Estimate of John (7:24–30)
  - **3.9.3.** A Parable of Spoiled Children (7:31–35)
- **3.10.** Jesus Anointed by a Sinful Woman (7:36–50)
- **3.11.** Wise Teachings and Marvelous Deeds (8:1–56)
  - **3.11.1.** Women Share in Jesus' Ministry (8:1–3)
  - **3.11.2.** The Parable of the Sower (8:4–15)
  - **3.11.3.** A Lamp Under a Bowl (8:16–18)
  - **3.11.4.** The Real Family of Jesus (8:19–21)
  - **3.11.5.** Jesus Calms the Storm (8:22–25)
  - **3.11.6.** Jesus Delivers a Man With Demons (8:26–39)
  - **3.11.7.** Raising of Jairus's Daughter; Healing of a Woman With a Hemorrhage (8:40–56)
- **3.12.** Jesus and His Disciples (9:1–50)
  - **3.12.1.** Jesus Sends Out the Twelve (9:1–6)
  - **3.12.2.** Herod Hears Rumors About Jesus (9:7–9)
  - **3.12.3.** Jesus Feeds the Five Thousand (9:10–17)
  - **3.12.4.** Peter's Declaration and Jesus' First Prediction of His Death (9:18–27)
  - **3.12.5.** The Transfiguration of Jesus (9:28–36)
  - **3.12.6.** Flaws of the Disciples (9:37–50)

- **3.3.3.4.** Summary: Apostles Perform Signs and Wonders (5:12–16)
- **3.3.4.** Priests–Sadducees Arrest All the Apostles (5:17–42)
  - **3.3.4.1.** The Apostles Are Arrested and Released by an Angel (5:17–25)
  - **3.3.4.2.** The Apostles Are Rearrested and Peter Addresses the Sanhedrin (5:26–32)
  - **3.3.4.3.** Gamaliel Warns the Sanhedrin Against Opposing the Apostles (5:33–42)
- **3.4.** Fellowship Broken: Community Chooses Seven Deacons (6:1–7)

4. The Acts of Six Spirit-Filled Leaders (6:8–12:24)

- **4.1.** The Acts of Stephen: A Spirit-Filled Deacon (6:8–7:60)
  - **4.1.1.** Stephen Performs Signs and Wonders (6:8–10)
  - **4.1.2.** Stephen Defends Himself Before the Sanhedrin (6:11–7:53)
  - **4.1.3.** Stephen's Martyrdom (7:54–60)
- **4.2.** The Acts of Philip: A Spirit-Filled Deacon (8:1–40)
  - **4.2.1.** Persecution of the Jerusalem Church (8:1–3)
  - **4.2.2.** Philip Preaches in Samaria (8:4–13)
  - **4.2.3.** Peter and John Visit Samaria (8:14–25)
  - **4.2.4.** Philip Witnesses to an Ethiopian (8:26–40)
- **4.3.** The Conversion of Saul (9:1–31)
  - **4.3.1.** Saul's Vision of Jesus (9:1–9)
  - **4.3.2.** Ananias Visits Saul (9:10–19a)
  - **4.3.3.** Saul Preaches That Jesus Is the Christ (9:19b–22)
  - **4.3.4.** Jews Plot to Kill Saul (9:23–25)
  - **4.3.5.** Barnabas Befriends Saul (9:26–30)
  - **4.3.6.** Summary (9:31)
- **4.4.** The Acts of Peter: A Spirit-Filled Apostle (9:32–11:18)
  - **4.4.1.** Peter Heals a Paralytic (9:32–35)
  - **4.4.2.** Peter Raises Tabitha From the Dead (9:36–43)
  - **4.4.3.** Peter Preaches to the Gentiles (10:1–48)

4. Travel Narrative: The Journey of Jesus to Jerusalem (9:51–19:44)
- **4.1.** Jesus Sets His Face Toward Jerusalem (9:51–56)
- **4.2.** The Cost of Following Jesus (9:57–62)
- **4.3.** Jesus Sends Out His Seventy-Two (10:1–24)
  - **4.3.1.** Instruction to the Seventy-Two (10:1–12)
  - **4.3.2.** Pronouncement of Woes on the Unbelieving (10:13–16)
  - **4.3.3.** Return of the Seventy-Two (10:17–20)
  - **4.3.4.** A Prayer of Thanks and Blessing (10:21–24)
- **4.4.** Danger of Distraction (10:25–42)
  - **4.4.1.** A Lawyer and Parable of the Good Samaritan (10:25–37)
  - **4.4.2.** Mary and Martha (10:38–42)
- **4.5.** Jesus' Teaching on Prayer (11:1–13)
  - **4.5.1.** The Lord's Prayer (11:1–4)
  - **4.5.2.** The Parable of a Friend at Midnight (11:5–8)
  - **4.5.3.** The Assurance That Prayer Will Be Answered (11:9–13)
- **4.6.** Jesus' Power to Cast Out Demons (11:14–28)
  - **4.6.1.** Beelzebub Controversy (11:14–23)
  - **4.6.2.** The Return of the Evil Spirit (11:24–26)
  - **4.6.3.** The Outburst of a Woman (11:27–28)
- **4.7.** The Demand for a Miraculous Sign (11:29–36)
- **4.8.** Jesus Pronounces Woes on the Pharisees and the Teachers of the Law (11:37–54)
- **4.9.** Responsibilities and Privileges of Discipleship (12:1–13:9)
  - **4.9.1.** A Warning Against Hypocrisy (12:1–12)

- **4.4.4.** Peter Defends His Ministry (11:1–18)
- **4.5.** The Acts of Barnabas: A Spirit-Filled Prophet (11:19–26)
- **4.6.** The Acts of Agabus: A Spirit-Filled Prophet (11:27–30)
- **4.7.** The Imprisonment of Peter (12:1–24)

5. Travel Narratives: The Acts of Paul: An Itinerant, Spirit-Filled Prophet (12:25–22:21)
- **5.1.** First Missionary Journey (12:25–15:35)
  - **5.1.1.** Antioch: Barnabas and Saul Set Apart (12:25–13:3)
  - **5.1.2.** Cyprus (13:4–12)
  - **5.1.3.** Antioch in Pisidia (13:13–52)
  - **5.1.4.** Iconium (14:1–7)
  - **5.1.5.** Lystra (14:8–18)
  - **5.1.6.** Derbe to Antioch (14:19–28)
  - **5.1.7.** Aftermath: The Jerusalem Council (15:1–35)
- **5.2.** Second Missionary Journey (15:36–18:23)
  - **5.2.1.** Sharp Disagreement Between Paul and Barnabas (15:36–41)
  - **5.2.2.** Lystra: Timothy Joins Paul (16:1–5)
  - **5.2.3.** Call to Macedonia (16:6–10)
  - **5.2.4.** Paul Visits Philippi (16:11–40)
    - **5.2.4.1.** The Lord Converts Lydia (16:11–15)
    - **5.2.4.2.** Paul Casts Out a Demon (16:16–18)
    - **5.2.4.3.** Paul and Silas Are Imprisoned and Released (16:19–40)
  - **5.2.5.** Paul Visits Thessalonica (17:1–9)
  - **5.2.6.** Paul Visits Berea (17:10–15)
  - **5.2.7.** Paul Visits Athens (17:16–34)
  - **5.2.8.** Paul Visits Corinth (18:1–17)
    - **5.2.8.1.** Paul Joins Aquila As Tentmaker (18:1–4)
    - **5.2.8.2.** Paul Teaches for a Year and a Half (18:5–11)
    - **5.2.8.3.** Paul Brought to Trial Before Gallio (18:12–17)
  - **5.2.9.** Paul Returns to Antioch (18:18–23)
- **5.3.** Apollos Teaches in Ephesus and Achaia (18:24–28)

4.9.2. A Warning Against Greed (12:13–34)
4.9.3. Watchful and Faithful (12:35–48)
4.9.4. Family Divisions Over Christ (12:49–53)
4.9.5. Interpreting the Present Times (12:54–59)
4.9.6. Call to Repentance (13:1–9)

4.10. Preparation of the Disciples for Jerusalem and Events Beyond (13:10–35)
4.10.1. Healing of a Crippled Woman on the Sabbath (13:10–17)
4.10.2. Parables of the Kingdom (13:18–21)
4.10.3. Requirements for the Kingdom (13:22–30)
4.10.4. A Warning About Herod and Sorrow Over Jerusalem (13:31–35)

4.11. Table Fellowship With a Pharisee (14:1–24)
4.11.1. Jesus Heals a Sick Man on the Sabbath (14:1–6)
4.11.2. A Lesson for Guests at a Feast (14:7–11)
4.11.3. A Lesson for Hosts (14:12–14)
4.11.4. The Parable of the Great Banquet (14:15–24)

4.12. The Cost of Being a Disciple (14:25–35)

4.13. God's Love for the Lost (15:1–32)
4.13.1. The Parable of the Lost Sheep (15:1–7)
4.13.2. The Parable of the Lost Coin (15:8–10)
4.13.3. The Parable of the Lost Son (15:11–32)

4.14. Teachings on Wealth (16:1–31)
4.14.1. The Shrewd Manager (16:1–13)
4.14.2. The Function of the Law (16:14–18)
4.14.3. The Rich Man and Lazarus (16:19–31)

4.15. On Faith and Duty (17:1–10)

4.16. Teachings Leading to the Final Prediction of His Death (17:11–18:30)
4.16.1. The Grateful Leper (17:11–19)
4.16.2. The Kingdom and the Coming of the Son of Man (17:20–37)

5.4. Third Missionary Journey (19:1–22:21)
5.4.1. Paul Visits Ephesus (19:1–41)
5.4.1.1. Paul Meets the Twelve Disciples (19:1–7)
5.4.1.2. Paul Preaches for Two Years (19:8–20)
5.4.1.3. Paul Purposes to Visit Jerusalem and Rome (19:21–22)
5.4.1.4. Demetrius Stirs Up Opposition (19:23–41)
5.4.2. Paul Visits Macedonia and Greece (20:1–6)
5.4.3. Paul Visits Troas (20:7–12)
5.4.4. Paul Sails From Assos to Miletus (20:13–16)
5.4.5. Paul Addresses the Elders of the Church at Ephesus (20:17–38)
5.4.6. Paul Sails From Miletus to Tyre (21:1–6)
5.4.7. Paul Journeys From Tyre to Caesarea (21:7–14)
5.4.7.1. Paul Visits Philip the Evangelist (21:7–9)
5.4.7.2. Agabus Prophesies Paul's Arrest (21:10–14)
5.4.8. Paul Visits Jerusalem (21:15–22:21)
5.4.8.1. Paul Travels From Caesarea to Jerusalem (21:15–16)
5.4.8.2. Paul's "Triumphal Entry" Into Jerusalem (21:17–26)
5.4.8.3. Paul Enters the Temple (21:27–36)
5.4.8.4. Paul Asks to Address the Angry Mob (21:37–40)
5.4.8.5. Paul Makes His Defense Before the Mob (22:1–21)

4.16.3. Two Parables on Prayer (18:1–14)
4.16.4. Conditions for Entrance Into the Kingdom (18:15–30)
4.17. From Prediction of Death Until Entry Into Jerusalem (18:31–19:44)
4.17.1. Prediction of Coming Death (18:31–34)
4.17.2. A Blind Beggar Receives Sight (18:35–43)
4.17.3. Salvation Comes to Zacchaeus (19:1–10)
4.17.4. The Parable of the Pounds (19:11–27)
4.17.5. Jesus' Triumphal Entry (19:28–44)

5. Jesus: Rejected Prophet–King (19:45–21:38)

5.1. Cleansing of the Temple (19:45–48)

5.2. The Question of Authority (20:1–8)

5.3. The Story of Wicked Tenants (20:9–19)

5.4. The Question of Paying Taxes to Caesar (20:20–26)

5.5. The Question Concerning the Resurrection and Marriage (20:27–40)

5.6. The Question Concerning the Son of David (20:41–47)

5.7. The Widow's Gift to the Temple Treasury (21:1–4)

5.8. Prophecy Concerning the End of the World (21:5–38)
5.8.1. Destruction of the Temple (21:5–6)
5.8.2. Signs of Christ's Coming (21:7–19)
5.8.3. Destruction of Jerusalem (21:20–24)
5.8.4. Christ's Second Coming (21:25–28)
5.8.5. The Parable of the Fig Tree (21:29–31)
5.8.6. Readiness for Christ's Coming (21:32–36)
5.8.7. Summary (21:37–38)

6. The Trial, Death, and Resurrection of Jesus (22:1–24:53)

6.1. The Passover (22:1–38)
6.1.1. Conspiracy Against Jesus (22:1–6)

6. Paul's Arrest and Trials (22:22–26:32)

6.1. Paul Is Arrested (22:22–29)

6.2. Paul Defends Himself Before the Sanhedrin (22:30–23:10)

6.1.2. Preparation for the Passover (22:7–13)
6.1.3. The Last Supper (22:14–20)
6.1.4. The Farewell Discourse (22:21–38)

6.2. The Arrest (22:39–65)
6.2.1. Jesus' Prayer on the Mount of Olives (22:39–46)
6.2.2. Jesus' Betrayal and Arrest (22:47–53)
6.2.3. Peter's Denial (22:54–62)
6.2.4. Mockery of Jesus (22:63–65)

6.3. The Trial of Jesus (22:66–23:25)
6.3.1. Trial Before the Sanhedrin (22:66–71)
6.3.2. Trial Before Pilate (23:1–7)
6.3.3. Trial Before Herod (23:8–12)
6.3.4. Second Trial Before Pilate (23:13–25)

6.4. Crucifixion of Jesus (23:26–49)

6.5. Burial of Jesus (23:50–56)

6.6. Resurrection of Jesus (24:1–43)
6.6.1. Discovery of the Empty Tomb (24:1–12)
6.6.2. Appearance on the Road to Emmaus (24:13–35)
6.6.3. Appearance to the Disciples (24:36–43)

6.7. Christ's Final Message to His Disciples (24:44–49)

6.8. Christ's Departure for Heaven (24:50–53)

6.3. The Lord Encourages Paul (23:11)

6.4. Conspiracy to Murder Paul (23:12–22)

6.5. Paul Is Transferred From Jerusalem to Caesarea (23:23–26:32)
6.5.1. Paul and Felix (23:23–24:27)
6.5.1.1. Accompanying Letter Addressed to Felix (23:23–30)
6.5.1.2. Paul Is Transferred to Felix's Custody (23:31–35)
6.5.1.3. Paul Is Accused Before Felix (24:1–9)
6.5.1.4. Paul Defends Himself Before Felix (24:10–22)
6.5.1.5. Paul Is Detained in Custody (24:23–27)
6.5.2. Paul and Festus (25:1–26:32)
6.5.2.1. Jews Renew Charges Against Paul (25:1–5)
6.5.2.2. Paul Defends Himself Before Festus (25:6–12)
6.5.2.3. Festus Reviews Paul's Case with Agrippa (25:13–22)
6.5.2.4. Paul Defends Himself Before Agrippa (25:23–26:32)

7. Paul Is Sent to Rome (27:1–28:31)

7.1. Paul's Voyage and Shipwreck (27:1–44)
7.1.1. Paul Sails From Caesarea to Fair Havens (27:1–8)
7.1.2. Paul's Warning and Storm (27:9–26)
7.1.3. Shipwreck (27:27–44)

7.2. Paul Winters in Malta (28:1–10)
7.2.1. Paul Survives Viper Bite (28:1–6)
7.2.2. Paul Heals Many Maltese (28:7–10)

7.3. Paul's Arrival at Rome (28:11–15)

7.4. Paul Under House Arrest (28:16–31)
7.4.1. Paul Placed in the Custody of a Soldier (28:16)
7.4.2. Paul's First Meeting With Leading Jews (28:17–22)
7.4.3. Paul's Second Meeting With Leading Jews (28:23–29)
7.4.4. Paul Preaches the Gospel for Two Years (28:30–31)

COMMENTARY

1. Preface (1:1–4)

The preface serves to introduce both the Gospel and Acts; Luke has divided his work into two volumes. The preface of Acts (1:1–5) summarizes briefly the contents of the preceding volume: the life and ministry of Jesus. This division agrees with a common practice in the ancient world of dividing a longer work into more than one volume, with the first volume containing a preface for the whole work and secondary prefaces introducing other volumes. Luke 1:1–4 consists of one sentence that is carefully constructed and reflects the style and balance of excellent Greek.

From the outset Luke reveals that he is not the first to write about what God has done in Christ. He does not identify his predecessors or offer any criticism of their writings. We have no way of knowing how many may have written before Luke, though Mark's Gospel is probably one of them. Luke's predecessors wrote about "things that have been fulfilled among us," that is, in the midst of believers. The thought has to do with the events bringing salvation and empowering the church for ministry: the birth, ministry, death, and resurrection of Jesus, and the pouring forth of the Holy Spirit. These events had been promised by God and are now fully brought to pass. Here is a reminder of the working out of God's purpose.

Luke identifies his sources as "those who from the first were eyewitnesses and servants of the word." He himself was not among those with the Spirit-anointed Jesus during his ministry of teaching, preaching, and healing. The eyewitnesses, however, told what they had seen Jesus do and heard him say. By so doing they became "servants of the word." They "handed down" (*paradidomi*) in both oral and written form information about the deeds and teachings of Jesus. As servants of the word they proclaimed the gospel message, a message rooted in historical reality.

No doubt among these primary eyewitnesses were the apostles. Though Luke is not one of them, he does mention his own qualification to write. He has become acquainted with events, carefully investigating them in detail. The words "everything from the beginning" means the whole account, beginning with the birth narratives of John the Baptist and Jesus, moving to the mighty deeds of the Spirit-empowered Jesus in Galilee, Samaria, and Jerusalem, and concluding with the spread of the gospel from Jerusalem to Rome. Luke is interested in all the facts that have to do with his subject.

The aim of such painstaking research is to write an "orderly account for you, most excellent Theophilus." The word "orderly" (*kathexes*) means "one after the other, successively." Luke wants to write a systematic account of the story of Jesus and the church. His readers are Theophilus and any others who may read this story of Jesus and the church. We have no information that enables us to identify Theophilus. His name means "one who loves God." The title "most excellent" implies that he is a man of rank. Felix, the governor of Judea (Acts 23:26; 24:3) and his successor, Festus (26:25), are addressed in the same way. But it may be only a title of courtesy.

Much debated is the question of whether Theophilus was a Christian at the time Luke wrote. Luke does not address him as a "brother." Is he perhaps an influential unbeliever from whom Luke thinks he can gain his sympathy and support? We must keep open the possibility that he is more than an outsider (Morris, 1974a, 67). No doubt Theophilus knew something about the Christian faith, and Luke wants him to have a full and reliable account of the matters about which he has been informed. As he writes, Luke has in his audience those who have an insufficient grasp of their faith. Thus his purpose is pastoral as well as evangelistic—to strengthen believers and encourage unbelievers to accept Jesus as their Savior and Lord.

Luke has done careful research as a historian, but he makes it clear that he writes from the perspective of faith. The history Luke wrote is also theology—history with the greatest meaning and significance. It is the history of the Spirit-anointed Jesus from Bethlehem to Jerusalem and a Spirit-baptized church from Jerusalem to Rome. We should never fear honest scholarship. True, scholars with opinions, speculations, and prejudices against the supernatural have departed from the truth. We must not forget, however, that Jesus promised his true disciples that the Holy Spirit will lead "them into all truth" (John 16:13). Luke, a careful historian, was inspired by the Holy Spirit to persuade others to have faith in the Savior.

2. The Origin of the Spirit-Anointed Christ (1:5–3:38)

Each Gospel writer has his own way of presenting the story of Jesus. Mark begins with the preaching ministry of John the Baptist and with Jesus' baptism, thus revealing Jesus' eternal sonship and the power of the Spirit resting on his life. Matthew opens with the genealogy of Jesus and an account of the Virgin Birth of the Savior. John begins with the preexistent Christ, who enjoyed fellowship with God and was God himself but who became incarnate. In Luke the story of Jesus begins in Jerusalem with Zechariah, a country priest, and his wife, Elizabeth.

Luke provides us with information about the origin of John the Baptist and with information about Jesus' birth not found in Matthew's account. He draws significant parallels between the birth of John and of Jesus. The angel Gabriel announces the birth of both of them. Each birth is followed by circumcision and by prophetic utterances. Luke brings out in his account of John and Jesus the relationship between the old and the new era. At the close of the Old Testament, prophecy ceased; but now God is fulfilling his promise to send the Spirit-anointed Savior. Moreover, the gift of prophecy is also being renewed. John has a significant role as the forerunner of Jesus both in the birth narratives and later in the Gospel (7:28; 16:16). His person and ministry sum up the expectations of the Old Testament, and he stands at the beginning of the new era—the messianic era. A major concern of early chapters is, therefore, the relation of the roles of John and Jesus. John is the last and the greatest of all the prophets, but Jesus is the promised Redeemer, the very Son of God.

2.1. Announcement of the Birth of John (1:5–25)

As a historian, Luke makes it a practice to establish the times in which great events transpire. The events of the early chapters of Luke occur in the reign of Herod the Great (37–4 B.C.). Herod ruled Judea, which Luke usually understands to represent all of Palestine (4:44; 6:17; 7:17; 23:5). The events described in 1:5–2:40 occur near the end of Herod's reign.

The people of Israel believed that God was always in their midst, yet they looked forward to the time when he would come and they would enjoy his fuller presence (Mal. 3:1; 4:5–6). For them the temple was a symbol of God's presence. Temple worship provides an appropriate setting for the opening of the Gospel story. Luke introduces John's parents. His father, Zechariah, is a country priest (1:5–10) who belongs to the division of Abijah. Priests were divided into twenty-four groups, each of which served for two weeks a year, a week at a time. The large number of priests in each group made it necessary for duties of the morning and evening sacrifices to be assigned by lot, a method of discerning God's will. The most coveted service (to burn incense before the Lord) is chosen in this manner. Many priests never received this opportunity. No doubt it is a special occasion for Zechariah to be chosen on this occasion to burn incense on the altar in the Holy Place. The assembled worshipers at the temple pray as he burns the incense; the rising smoke symbolizes the rising of their prayers to God.

Both Zechariah and Elizabeth are descendants of Aaron, a devout couple known and respected highly in the temple community for their godliness. They walk in all that God requires in the Old Testament, and before their fellows they are blameless. They believe in and practice prayer. They look for the coming of the Messiah. They are not rich or famous by worldly standards, but they are by God's standards.

Yet Zechariah and Elizabeth have no children, and Elizabeth is well beyond the normal period of childbearing. Among the Jews having no children is a disgrace, even considered the result of divine punishment (Lev. 20:20–21; Isa. 4:1). Their lack of a child is their reproach and sorrow, and possibly they have given up hope for a child. Since they are "upright in the sight of God" (v. 6), their prayers for children have been unanswered not because of sin but in order that God's mighty work may be manifested in them (John 9:3). Like Abraham and Sarah, old and without children, Zechariah and Elizabeth are about to experience a miracle. What is humanly impossible and hopeless is possible with God. In extraordinary ways God answers the prayers of his people.

Daily at the temple priests offered sacrifices in the morning and evening. Luke does not tell

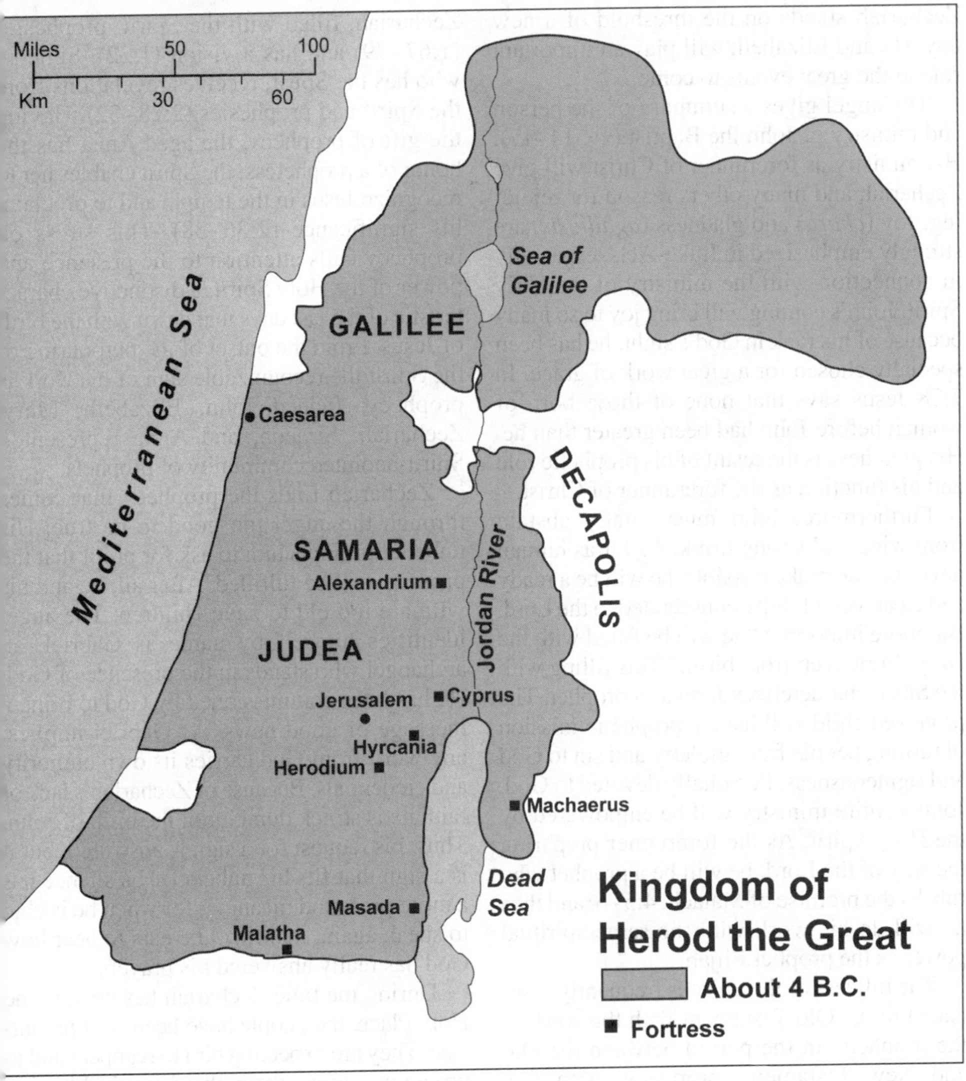

us which of these two Zechariah is officiating at. To perform his priestly duty he enters the Holy Place, where only priests could enter. It, along with the Holy of Holies, makes up the sanctuary. As he stands near the heated altar of incense, suddenly an angel appears to him. Not prepared for a visit from an angel, he is overwhelmed with fear. The heavenly messenger tells the terrified priest, "Do not be afraid, Zechariah; your prayer has been heard. Your wife Elizabeth will bear you a son, and you are to give him the name John" (v. 13).

What is Zechariah's prayer? The answer does not suggest that he has been using the opportunity at the altar to pray for a child. On many occasions, of course, he and Elizabeth prayed such a prayer. In addition, as he is now carrying out his priestly duties, most likely he prays for the coming of the Messiah—praying for the fulfillment of Israel's hope. Now his countless prayers have been heard; God is going to send the Messiah, the Anointed One, to redeem humankind. But also Zechariah and Elizabeth's personal prayer for a child is answered—he is to be the father of a son, who will be a prophet to bring back many people to the Lord by calling them to repentance. The child, therefore, will have a decisive role to play in God's plan of salvation: making "ready a people prepared for the Lord" (v. 17).

Zechariah stands on the threshold of a new day. He and Elizabeth will play an important role in the great events to come.

The angel gives a summary of the person and ministry of John the Baptist (vv. 14–17). His ministry as forerunner of Christ will give Zechariah and many others reason for rejoicing. Joy (*chara*) and gladness (*agalliasis*) are strongly emphasized in Luke-Acts, especially in connection with the ministry of the Holy Spirit. John's coming will bring joy to so many because of his rank in God's sight; he has been specially chosen for a great work of grace. In 7:28 Jesus says that none of those born of woman before John had been greater than he. His greatness is the result of his prophetic role and his function as the forerunner of Christ.

Furthermore, John must totally abstain from wine and strong drink. As far as human devotion can make possible, he will be a ready and clean vessel, fully consecrated to the Lord. But more important "he will be filled with the Holy Spirit even from birth." This filling with the Spirit characterizes John as a prophet. The promised child will have a prophetic mission of turning people from idolatry and sin to God and righteousness. Personally devoted to God, John's entire ministry will be empowered by the Holy Spirit. As the forerunner preparing the way of the Lord, he will be a prophet who fulfills the promise of Malachi 4:5–6, and thus he will do his work with the same spiritual power as the prophet Elijah.

The fullness of the Spirit is frequently associated in the Old Testament with the work of the prophets. In the period between the Old and New Testament, prophecy, with few exceptions, had ceased in Israel, though Joel had promised the outpouring of the Spirit and a rebirth of prophecy at the coming of Christ. In the Old Testament only a few people received the fullness of the Spirit—mainly prophets and other spiritual leaders—but Joel had announced the pouring forth of the Spirit on all people: "Your sons and daughters will prophesy, your old men will dream dreams, your young men will see visions. Even on my servants, both men and women, I will pour out my Spirit in those days" (Joel 2:28–29).

Luke records the beginning of the fulfillment of Joel's prophecy. John the Baptist will be filled with the Spirit (Luke 1:15). Elizabeth is filled with the Spirit and prophesies (1:41). Zechariah, filled with the Spirit, prophesies (1:67–79) and has a vision (1:22). Simeon, who has the Spirit, receives revelations from the Spirit and prophesies (2:28–32). Having the gift of prophecy, the aged Anna has the honor of a prophetess; the Spirit enables her to recognize Jesus in the temple and to proclaim his significance (2:36–38). This stress on prophecy calls attention to the presence and power of the Holy Spirit, a distinctive characteristic of the last days that dawn with the birth of Jesus. From the outset of the outpouring of the Spirit the recognizable sign of his work is prophecy. Indeed John, Elizabeth, Mary, Zechariah, Simeon, and Anna represent a Spirit-anointed community of prophets.

Zechariah finds the prophecy that comes through the angel too good to be true. His unbelief prompts him to ask for proof that the promise will be fulfilled. After all, he and his wife are too old to have children. The angel identifies himself by name as Gabriel, an archangel who stands in the presence of God. He has been commissioned by God to bring a message of good news. As Gabriel implies, any word from God carries its own authority and credentials. Because of Zechariah's lack of faith he is struck dumb until the birth of John. Thus, his request for a sign is answered, but it is a sign that fits his unbelief. His silence has a more profound meaning, for when he is able to speak again, there will be ears to hear how God has really answered his prayers.

During the time Zechariah has been in the Holy Place, the people have been waiting outside. They are expecting him to reappear and to pronounce upon them the Aaronic blessing (Num. 6:24–26). Because he delays so long, their patience is growing thin. But when he does return, they discern that he has had a supernatural experience, receiving a revelation from God. He tries to speak to them but cannot.

When the old priest has finished his priestly duties, he goes to his home. Soon after, Zechariah's wife conceives, fulfilling the divine promise. She has viewed her childlessness as a reproach, but now she begins to experience the joy and gladness that God has promised (1:14). Her reproach has been taken away and she has a child as a sign of God's blessings. God is working for the salvation of his people and blesses this righteous couple. God's word never fails; it will come to pass.

2.2. Announcement of the Birth of Jesus (1:26–38)

The similarities between the announcement of John's birth and that of Jesus are striking. The characters are not famous or wealthy. The angel Gabriel appears, provokes fear, promises the birth of a son who will play a crucial role in God's plan, and then names the son. But there are also differences between the accounts of the birth of John and Jesus. John is a prophet; Jesus is more than a prophet—he is the Messiah and Son of God. John is born to an aged couple; Jesus is born to a virgin. The announcement of John's birth comes to Zechariah while he serves as a priest at the religious center of Israel; the announcement that Mary, an average young woman, is to be the mother of the Messiah comes privately in the country. Mary's son will be far greater than John.

God takes the initiative when he sends Gabriel to an insignificant town in Galilee (a large province in northern Palestine). When he announces to Mary that she will give birth to the Savior of the world, she is a betrothed virgin. In verse 27 "virgin" (*parthenos*) is rendered "maiden" by Moffatt and by Goodspeed in their translations and by "girl" in the NEB. Yet this Greek noun regularly means "virgin," and this meaning is required by the context of Luke's Gospel. Mary is not yet married (1:34), but in the ancient world a betrothal, the first step to marriage, could be made when women were quite young. The period between betrothal and marriage was about a year. According to Jewish law betrothal established a relationship that was as binding as marriage itself; only divorce could dissolve the relationship. Joseph, the man Mary has been pledged to, is a descendant of David, providing Jesus with a legal connection to the house of David (1:32; 2:4). Long ago God promised David an heir whose rule would be remarkable (2 Sam. 7:13).

During the betrothal period the angel comes and greets Mary as the "highly favored." Then he adds, "The Lord is with you" (v. 28). She is a person of great integrity—obedient (v. 38), believing (v. 45), and dedicated to following God's law (2:22–51). It is not, however, because of her noble virtues that she has been chosen to be the mother of the Savior but because of the unmerited favor of God. God has greatly blessed (*kecharitomene*, 1:28) Mary not because she is particularly worthy but because she is an object of God's goodness. God has stepped into her life and chosen to use her in his service. Luke wishes to note her openness to God, but not unduly exalt her person. In fact, she is totally perplexed about the meaning of the heavenly visitor's message.

Mary's response prompts Gabriel to urge her to stop being afraid. He then goes on to give her a fourfold message (vv. 31–33): (1) She will give birth to a son named Jesus. (2) Her son's greatness will be without qualification; he will be the Son of God (cf. Ps. 2:7). (3) He will rule from the throne of David as the king of Israel (cf. 2 Sam. 7:12ff.; Ps. 89:29). (4) He will rule forever. This kingdom is not to be understood as an earthly realm; it is God's kingly rule, the promised messianic kingdom that Jesus clarifies in his teachings and through his miracles.

Mary has difficulty understanding what the angel has told her. As a virgin she has no idea how she can have a son. Her marriage has not been physically consummated. Gabriel says that the birth of Jesus will be brought about by the Holy Spirit's coming upon her and by the overshadowing of God's power. Luke typically links the Holy Spirit with the power of God (see esp. Acts 1:8). The verb "come upon" (*eperchomai* in Luke 1:35) is also used to refer to the promise of the Spirit's coming upon the disciples on the day of Pentecost (Acts 1:8). The overshadowing (*episkiazo*) refers to the presence of God (cf. Ex. 40:35) and reminds us of the overshadowing cloud as a sign of divine presence at the Transfiguration (Luke 9:34). God's powerful presence will rest on Mary so that the child she bears will be the Son of God. Conceived by the Holy Spirit, he will be holy as one specially anointed by the Spirit (4:1ff.). The language of Luke is clearly Trinitarian: the Most High, the Son of God, and the Holy Spirit.

Luke gives no indication exactly when Mary conceived Jesus; that miraculous birth has no parallel. Persons like Abraham and Sarah (Gen. 18:10–19) and Zechariah and Elizabeth (Luke 1:7–25), beyond the age of childbearing, were given children by God. The extraordinary power of God overcame the barrenness and age of those couples. But Jesus' birth does not fit that pattern. In his case God did not simply overcome inability of parents to have children but impregnated her in the complete absence of a human father (Brown, 1974, 360–62). The birth of Christ is an event of the last days, ushering in a new era that will culminate in the final judgment and the salvation of the redeemed. The glory of God's coming in flesh called for such a miracle as the Virgin Birth to indicate the mighty thing God was doing for our salvation. The Son stoops to our weakness, coming as a babe into our world. Though fully human, he has only one human parent; but we believe the One born of the virgin is God and Mary's Lord—absolutely unique; he is truly God and truly man.

When God calls Mary to be the mother of his Son, he puts her faith to an unusual test: Will she have the faith to believe that God is able to create life in her? Zechariah has not believed the lesser miracle of God in overcoming barrenness and age. Now God calls Mary to believe that she will give birth to the Savior and that he will enter the stream of our life by virginal conception. The angel gives her encouragement, however, pointing out that Elizabeth, who was thought to be barren, is going to have a child in her old age (v. 36). For six months new life has been stirring in the womb of this elderly woman. How is it possible for the aged Elizabeth to have a son? How is it possible for Mary, a virgin, to conceive? Gabriel assures Mary that "nothing is impossible with God" (v. 37; cf. Gen. 18:14). God can work miracles!

As "the Lord's servant" Mary humbly yields herself to God's word and says to the angel, "May it be to me as you have said" (v. 38). She is willing and ready to serve God and to be used of the Holy Spirit to give birth to the Savior.

The message Mary receives from the angel about the wondrous conception of a Son raises the question whether God can create life. The birth of Jesus through the miraculous work of the Holy Spirit answers with a resounding "Yes!" God, who creates life, recreates the life of those who come to faith in this virgin-born Son. The encounter with the angel leads Mary to the obedience of faith. It comes as no surprise, therefore, that she is among the believers when the Holy Spirit comes upon the entire community at Pentecost (Acts 1:12–14). She made the proper response to God's word and his grace—in humility, faith, and obedience.

2.3. Mary's Visit to Elizabeth and Her Song (1:39–56)

The stage has been set for the extraordina birth of Jesus. Mary hastens to an unnamed vi lage in the hills of Judea to visit Elizabeth. Th two women are related, but they also share common experience. Both are to have child—a most profound experience for them knowing that God is creatively at work. One old, and her son will bring an era to an end; th other is young and still a virgin, and her so will usher in a new era.

The two mothers meet, but also their tw unborn sons meet. When Mary greets Eliza beth, the child John leaps in his mother womb for joy (v. 41). John's reaction to th presence of Jesus begins his ministry as th forerunner to the Savior. His jumping is n ordinary stirring of an unborn child in th womb, for verse 44 states that the cause is jo The significance of the unborn child's jo becomes clear in light of his being filled wit the Spirit from birth (1:15). Luke records als that Jesus is "full of joy through the Hol Spirit" when he sees how God has revealed th truth to his disciples (10:21).

When John feels the presence of the Spiri the Spirit then also fills his mother, Elizabetl Under his inspiration, she speaks as a prophe ess, referring to Mary as "the mother of m Lord" (v. 43) and as blessed for believing wh God has said (v. 45). The gospel events begi in the midst of a revival of prophetic activity As a Spirit-anointed prophetess, Elizabet shows her excitement, crying out with a lou voice. What she utters goes far beyond anythin that Zechariah knew and could have told he By the charismatic enlightenment of the Spir she recognizes the unique blessedness of Mar and of her son (v. 42). Mary is blessed becaus God has chosen her to be the mother of his Sor her Son's blessedness consists of God's gra cious power and the favor that will rest on hin Elizabeth also expresses her unworthiness tha the mother of the Savior should visit her. He attitude provides an example that God desire all believers to follow. What a joy there is i sharing in the events of Jesus. Who can deserv such honor and blessings?

The joy of Elizabeth is shared by Mary who in a hymn of praise (vv. 46–55) speak about God's gracious work in her behal (vv. 48–49). She goes on to praise Go because he has acted in justice and mercy and will continue to do so, remembering the promise made to Abraham and his descendants forever (vv. 50–55).[3] This song of praise begins with Mary's celebrating what God has done for her and extends to how God has treated the righteous throughout the ages and how he will fully vindicate his own in the future. The language of the song resembles that of Hannah's song (1 Sam. 2:1–10) and gives a broad view of God's saving grace.

Mary begins on a note of joy—a joy that is brought forth by the Holy Spirit and by what God is doing. Elizabeth's prophecy was directed to Mary, but Mary's praise is to God and rightly so. God is always worthy of praise, and the Holy Spirit prompts the praise of God. Inspired by the Spirit, Mary magnifies God. We should not make a sharp distinction between soul (*psyche*) and spirit (*pneuma*); these words are poetic parallels, indicating that her praise is personal.

Mary knows her position before God and recognizes her humble state as his servant (v. 48). She is being exalted from her lowly state in the eyes of the world to greatness in God's sight. God reverses the positions of the proud and the humble in the new order introduced by the coming of Christ. He gives the proud no help. Also unless they become humble servants, the rich and mighty of the world receive no help from him; such people often feel they need nothing from God. But people like Mary, who are humble and open to his grace, God exalts from their low estate and puts a song in their hearts. His unmerited favor becomes the basis on which all future generations will honor her. It is also the reason for her praise. People from one generation to another will see her as a human touched by divine grace and used by God. Mary's humble spirit confirms her words to Gabriel, "I am the Lord's servant . . . may it be to me as you have said" (v. 38).

Contemplation of God's grace moves Mary to turn to God himself. She speaks about his power, his holiness, and his mercy. Though she feels insignificant, he possesses great power and has done and is still able to do great things. His name is holy. In the ancient world a name represented a person's whole character. God must be revered for, as Mary declares, his name is a holy name. God is a holy God. Furthermore, he is merciful. God's grace shows his love toward those who do not deserve it. But his mercy (*eleos*) shows his faithful love toward the unfortunate and the miserable. Mary is but one example. In every generation the blessings of God's mercy abound to those who show childlike reverence for him. Those who oppose him will face God's power and holiness as a warning against taking his commandments and mercy lightly.

Inspired by the Spirit, Mary continues to speak about God's mighty works. She uses six past tenses to speak of God's deeds (vv. 51–55). She looks prophetically forward to what God will do. As the Old Testament prophets frequently did, Mary is so certain of the things God will do that she speaks of them as though they have already been accomplished. The kind of power manifested by the strength of his arm at the Exodus, he will now show through the birth of Christ (Ex. 6:1; Ps. 89:13). No strength can match his strength.

By the wonderful display of his power he brings about astonishing reversals. The arrogant and the puffed up God scatters. He overthrows rulers who do not obey his will, but he exalts the humble. To those not rich in him God gives nothing, but the hungry are satisfied with the blessings he provides. God works in behalf of the poor, the hungry, and the humble—whatever station in life they have—if they look to God for care. Regardless of their plight, God promises his children that they will receive a great reward in the future. Those spiritually sensitive to God can count on that.

God keeps his word. He helped Israel, his servant, by "remembering to be merciful" (v. 54). It could have appeared to some that he had forgotten the promise made to Abraham (Gen. 12:1–3). But what God is doing now makes it clear that he remembers to be merciful and to care for Israel according to his covenant with Abraham and the fathers. Mary has full assurance that God will care for those open to his grace in Israel. She belongs to the holy remnant in the nation (Rom. 9:6). Because of God's act of remembering, she will give birth to the Savior not only of Jews but also of Gentiles. As Luke's story progresses, it becomes clear that God includes the Gentiles in his plan of salvation. A person like Theophilus can have the assurance that God remembers his promises to Gentiles as much as to Jews.

2.4. The Birth of John and Zechariah's Song (1:57–80)

With the birth of John God begins to fulfill what the angel has predicted in 1:13–17. God is never slack in fulfilling his promises, and thus he gives a son to Zechariah and Elizabeth. Verses 57–58 record the excitement and interest that center around John's birth. Elizabeth's friends and family have heard that God has shown her mercy and has removed her barrenness. Many of them share with her in the joy of the event and offer her congratulations. The way God deals with Elizabeth magnifies his mercy, a theme that runs through the opening chapters of Luke's Gospel.

According to Genesis 17:9–14 the custom of circumcision occurs on the eighth day after birth. Though children are frequently named at birth (25:25–26; 29:32–35), the official naming often takes place at the time of circumcision. The naming of John reveals two surprising things. (1) The crowd assumes that custom will be followed and John will be named after his father; they are attempting to call him Zechariah.[4] But Elizabeth will not hear of it. The name she has chosen is John, the one the angel had given in verse 13. Luke gives us no hint how she knows the name, but she probably has learned it from Zechariah. (2) This incident reveals the possibility of a clash between the divine plan and human desire (Weisiger, 1966, 23). The crowd is unaware of God's plan for this child. When God names a person, that gives special direction to one's life (Gen. 17:3–5; 32:28).

The crowd does not listen to Elizabeth, but Zechariah confirms his wife's decision. For nine months he has been silent, but when to everyone's amazement he writes, "His name is John," his tongue is loosed immediately and he begins to praise God. Just as the angel predicted in 1:20, Zechariah's handicap is removed with the fulfillment of God's promise. God never fails to fulfill his promises.

The neighbors experience deep awe, a profound sense of reverence from knowing that God is working here. The unusual events become known and are a topic of conversation "throughout the hill country of Judea" (v. 65). The people deeply affected ask a question—"What then is this child going to be?" Luke concludes with a comment: "The Lord's hand was with him"—the hand that directs and sus tains his chosen servants.

Zechariah's song (vv. 68–79) is yet anothe witness to the restoration of prophecy, and i provides a prophetic answer to the questio about John's destiny. When Mary visited Eliz abeth, a song of praise followed their meetin (vv. 46–55). Likewise, the birth of John is no followed by a song of praise. Both are th result of prophetic inspiration. Mary's Spirit inspired song took a broad view of God' mercy in dealing with his people, bu Zechariah focuses on the Messiah (vv. 68- 70),[5] his mission (vv. 78–79), and the role o John (vv. 76–77). Some have seen Zechariah' song as primarily political, with an emphasi on deliverance of Israel from its political ene mies, especially Rome (vv. 71–75). Bu Zechariah speaks prophetically, and the con tent of his prophecy is highly spiritual and reli gious. It is true that a close link can exis between the political and spiritual needs. I should be observed, however, that deliveranc from "the hand of our enemies" is in order tha we can "serve [God] without fear" (v. 74). Th song, in other words, speaks of spiritual rathe than political deliverance. We are able, as result of deliverance from our spiritual foes, t serve God "in holiness and righteousness (v. 75).

Zechariah's song/prophecy comes as result of his being filled with the Spirit (v. 67 The theme of his Spirit-inspired song is God' great plan of salvation and the events that hav already taken place. In his prophetic declara tion Zechariah praises God. The Lord has vis ited his people and has done so in the comin of the Messiah (2:26–32), but he comes t redeem *(lytrosin)* to rescue at a high cost. Th horn of an animal is a symbol of might an power; thus, God raises up a mighty Savio Jesus, a descendant of David (1:69). God' plan is being worked out because long ag through the prophets he had promised the Sav ior (v. 70). The promises include deliveranc of the people from their enemies and a remem bering of the covenant made with Abrahar (vv. 71–73). God had made promises both t David and to Abraham about the Messiah; bot sets of promises find their fulfillment in Jesu God does nothing for his people excep through Jesus Christ. Through him he deliv ers them from their enemies, such as Satan an he powers of darkness. This deliverance nakes it possible for them to serve the Lord n a holy and righteous manner (vv. 74–75).

The song began with the Messiah, but now Zechariah prophesies about the future ministry of his own son (vv. 76–77). He addresses him lirectly and says he "will be called a prophet of the Most High." There had been little or no prophecy for centuries, but now that is changing. As the forerunner to the Savior, the prophet John will tell people about salvation, which calls for repentance and offers the forgiveness of sins. Words about salvation seen as leliverance from enemies now give way to words about salvation that results in the sending away of our sins—as far as the east is from he west (Ps. 103:12). Forgiveness flows from he great fountain of God's "tender mercy." The "rising sun" (*anatole*) is a picture of the Messiah, who will visit us from heaven (v. 78). The result of that visit will be spiritual illumination, as a sunrise dispels darkness when the lay dawns. The coming of Christ will provide ight for those living in the darkness of sin and will drive away the hopeless shadow of death. That light will shine forever and "guide our eet into the path of peace"—a peace that alms our souls and strengthens our walk with God in a troubled world.

Luke closes this unit by summing up the hildhood of John the Baptist (v. 80). John xperiences normal growth to maturity, but he pends his youth in the desert. He remains here until the word of the Lord comes to him 3:2), and he is manifested as a prophet of God.

2.5. The Birth of Jesus (2:1–20)

Like the birth of John the Baptist, Jesus' irth fulfills prophecy. Gabriel predicted that Mary was to bear a son, but also the prophecies of Isaiah 7:14 and Micah 5:2–5 are fulilled in Jesus' birth. According to these rophecies (1) a virgin would have a son, and 2) the town of Bethlehem would host the birth f a child who would shepherd the flock of srael and whose authority would reach to the nds of the earth.[6] God does work in mysterious ways.

The time of the Savior's birth shows that God uses the affairs of nations, such as the issung of an imperial decree, to fulfill his prophetic romises. Luke connects sacred history with a lecree of Caesar Augustus (who ruled as sole emperor from 27 B.C. to A.D. 14) and sets the birth of Jesus on the world stage. The decree required all citizens of the Roman empire to register at their ancestral homes. This census took place during the administration of Quirinius, a governor of Syria (Luke provides the only record we have of this census, which probably sought to produce a registration list for taxes). Matthew 2:1 and Luke 1:5 indicate that Herod the Great is living at this time. Hence, Jesus' birth is before the death of Herod (spring of 4 B.C.) and after the census of Quirinius. Though difficult to pinpoint, the census probably is between 6 and 4 B.C.

As a result of the tax decree Mary and Joseph travel to Bethlehem, where the prophecy of Micah 5:2 said the Savior was to be born. God has been working out his purpose through Zechariah, Elizabeth, Mary, and now through the Roman government and Caesar Augustus. As a law-abiding citizen Joseph goes with Mary to Bethlehem, the town of David. Little is known about the regulations of taxation; but since his presence would suffice, Mary is probably not required to go to Bethlehem. She is now living with Joseph as his wife, though the marriage has not been physically consummated. This explains why Luke still speaks of her as "pledged to be married to him" (v. 5). By taking Mary with him Joseph protects her from slanderous tongues in Nazareth. As the couple arrives in Bethlehem, the time comes for Mary to give birth to her firstborn.

Christ's birth is described in the simplest of terms: "She gave birth to her firstborn, a son. She wrapped him in cloths and placed him in a manger, because there was no room for them in the inn" (v. 7). Most likely the manger was a feeding trough for animals, which now serves as a crib for the newborn child. The birth must have taken place in a stable or cave where animals were kept. Mary wraps her son in long strips of cloth (KJV "swaddling clothes") in order to protect him. God is working out his eternal purpose and doing it in such humble circumstances.

Shepherds in the nearby fields are the first to be informed about Christ's birth and to see him. An angel suddenly appears to them, and the glory of heaven shines around in beaming radiance. He proclaims to them "good news (*euangelizomai*) of great joy that will be for all

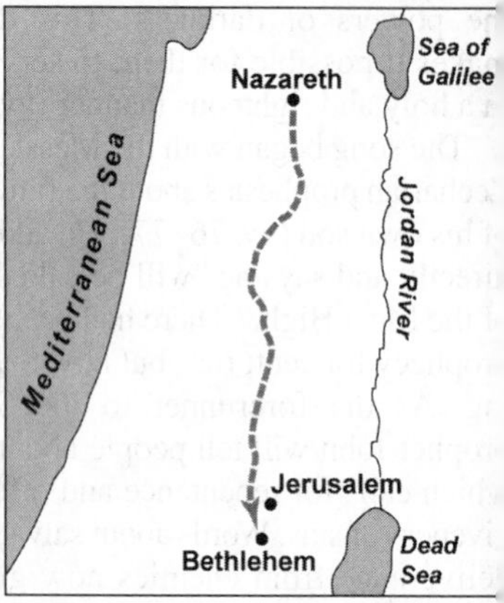

Joseph and Mary traveled from Nazareth to Bethlehem, Joseph's fam ily home, to be registered in a census of the Roman Empire. The cross-shaped church, at left, in Bethlehem's Manger Square, is on the site where Jesus was born.

the people" (v. 10). The gospel is "good news" and, therefore, brings joy, a theme that Luke keeps constantly before us. Since the gospel is for "all the people," God includes shepherds, who are on the lowest end of the social scale. The first people to hear the gospel, in other words, are ordinary, humble, and needy people. The prophecy of Isaiah 61:1 is already being fulfilled: The poor have the good news preached to them.

The salvation God provides is for all people; there are no racial, ethnic, social, or national boundaries. The message of the angel is for all humankind: "A Savior has been born to you: he is Christ the Lord" (v. 11).[7] With these three great titles—Savior, Christ, and Lord—the heavenly messenger identifies the child born under such lowly conditions and among such simple people. As *Savior* he acts as a special deliverer from sin and death for all who trust in him. As *Christ* he is the "Anointed One," the Messiah. The child is specially anointed to rule as King and to bring to fulfillment the hope of Israel. *Lord* is the word used for Israel's God (Yahweh) in the Greek translation of the Old Testament; it speaks of the divine nature of the one born of a virgin. Luke-Acts tells the story of Jesus as Savior, Christ, and Lord—how he saves all who believe in him from their sins.

Before the angel departs, he gives the shepherds a sign that will enable them to identify the child: "a baby wrapped in cloths and lyin in a manger" (v. 12). Perhaps other childre were born on that night in Bethlehem, but onl one will be lying in a manger. When the shep herds see it, they will know that the announce ment of the angel is true. The tiny babe has th poorest accommodations, a feeding trough, ye he is so great. Paul expresses it graphically i 2 Corinthians 8:9, "Though he was rich, yet fo our sakes he became poor, so that you throug his poverty might become rich."

Suddenly a host of angels join the ange who made the announcement. The praise o this angelic chorus leaves no doubt about th greatness of the child who has come to d God's work. Their song—"Glory to God in th highest, and on earth peace to men on whor his favor rests" (v. 14)—expresses what th birth of the Savior means in heaven and o earth. (1) The angels declare the glory of Go as shining forth in the coming of his Son in th flesh. The baby lying in a manger makes visi ble the majesty and grace of God. In this chil God has become incarnate. (2) On earth th meaning of the Christ-child is summed up i the word "peace" (*eirene*). This word encom passes more than the absence of strife and con flict, for it denotes all God's blessings th come through Christ. As the fruit of Christ' coming, peace brings about a situation char acterized by a new relationship between Go and those who trust in him. Christ has wo eace for all humankind (v. 10), but it is expeienced only by "men on whom his [God's] avor rests." That is, God's saving favor *eudokia*) rests only on those who personally ccept the Christ-child as the world's Savior.

After hearing the song of the heavenly host, he shepherds hasten to the city of David and ee for themselves the baby lying in a manger. 'hey are not only the first to hear the proclanation of the good news, but they also become he first humans to tell others about it (v. 17). 'hose who hear from the shepherds about what as happened are filled with amazement. By ontrast, Mary ponders the meaning of all these vents. They have been so miraculous that she ries to understand their significance. No doubt uke desires his readers to do likewise.

In the meantime the shepherds depart. The ngel's announcement to them of "good news f great joy" is no ordinary message. The sign f a baby lying in a manger is no ordinary sign. 'he birth of a Savior who is Christ and Lord s no ordinary birth. The shepherds go away glorifying and praising God for all the things hey had heard and seen" (v. 20). The presence f God permeates the story of Jesus' concepion and birth.

2.6. Jesus As an Infant in the Temple (2:21–40)

Mary and Joseph rear Jesus according to the aw of Moses. Five times in this passage Luke nentions that Jesus' parents act according to he law (vv. 22, 23, 24, 27, 39). These actions how their devotion and faith. As required by he law Jesus is circumcised on the eighth day. 3ut the emphasis is on the naming of the child ather than on circumcision. He is named 'Jesus," as the angel has instructed.

As devout Jews Mary and Joseph go to the emple again to offer sacrifices for Mary's urification after giving birth. According to eviticus 12 a woman who has given birth to son is unclean for seven days. After forty lays she has to come to the temple for purifiation. The ritual of cleansing includes offerng certain sacrifices. It is unclear what we hould make of the pronoun "their" in "their urification," but it may be that Joseph too is eremonially unclean. While at the temple, the arents of Jesus follow the instructions of Exolus 13:2, 12–15, to redeem every firstborn nale. This child belongs to God and can be redeemed by the offering of a sacrifice. The price paid by Mary and Joseph consists of "a pair of doves or two young pigeons" (Luke 2:24), the offering prescribed for a poor person (Lev. 12:8).

Mary and Joseph take Jesus with them to the temple to present him to the Lord for service. There is no requirement that the dedication take place in the temple, but the parents feel that it is appropriate. This presentation recalls the dedication of Samuel. At the temple a significant event occurs. Simeon, an old man known for his personal devotion, conducts himself properly in all matters. He has a vibrant walk with God, "waiting for the consolation of Israel" (a name for the Messiah). His eyes are set on a spiritual deliverance of God's people. Simeon is more than a devout man; he is a prophet. Resting on him is the Holy Spirit, who has assured him that before his death he will see the Lord's Anointed One. The text mentions the influence of the Spirit on Simeon three times (vv. 25, 26, 27).

The Spirit directs Simeon to the temple at the very time Mary and Joseph appear there to dedicate their infant son to the Lord. When Simeon sees Jesus, he knows at once that this child is the Messiah and takes him into his arms. Just as Elizabeth (1:41) and Zechariah (1:67) spoke Spirit-inspired prophecies before the birth of Jesus, so Simeon and Anna (vv. 36–38) speak prophetically when the child is brought into the temple.

With the Messiah in Simeon's arms the Spirit inspires the aged man to speak a prophetic prayer of praise (vv. 29–32). His prophecy is a mature expression of faith, similar to Mary's song of praise (1:46–55) and that of Zechariah (1:67–79). God has kept his promise to Simeon that he will see the Messiah before death. Now a new era of salvation has dawned, and he has actually seen the Christ-child, the source of life, through whom salvation will be offered to the world. The expectation to which he has devoted his life has been fulfilled. Now he can die "in peace" (*en eirene*)—with a deep sense of tranquillity and in harmony with God and his fellow human beings.

Simeon has personally seen salvation, which is none other than the baby boy he is holding in his arms. This salvation God has "prepared in the sight of all people" (v. 31), meaning that both Gentiles and the people of Israel will experience deliverance from sin. Simeon goes on to explain the nature of the salvation God has prepared—it is "a light for revelation to the Gentiles." Jesus is light and will bring light, which will serve as revelation that opens up the way of salvation to the Gentiles, which was unknown before his coming. But the coming of Jesus also spells glory for Israel (Isa. 40:5). The Old Testament speaks often about God's glory as his manifestations of himself to them, but the sending of his Son into the world is a unique manifestation of his visible presence for Israel. The Israelites are the people whom God has honored to give birth to the Messiah; no other people on the earth have such glory. The light given to the Gentiles in no way diminishes Israel's glory. The Messiah comes to lead both Jew and Gentile to glory.

Joseph and Mary are astonished at what Simeon is saying about Jesus. For the first time the parents hear about the significance of their child not only for Israel but also for the Gentiles—salvation for all humankind. But Simeon has not finished. With a prophetic anointing he predicts to Mary that the mission of Jesus will involve judgment on Israel. He "is destined to cause the falling and rising of many in Israel" (v. 34). Here we should not think of one group who will fall and then rise. Rather, those who reject Jesus will fall and be in danger of eternal judgment; others who accept him will rise and enter into salvation. Jesus will divide the nation of Israel—some for him and some against him. His extraordinary ministry is appointed by God as a sign of salvation, but it is "a sign that will be spoken against." Opposition to him culminates in his death on the cross, but it continues toward those who preach repentance and forgiveness of sin in his name.

In Acts we see Simeon's prophecy fulfilled. By preaching the crucified Jesus at Pentecost, Peter achieves extraordinary success. Yet because of the preaching of the gospel the church faces opposition. The authorities try to silence the missionaries (Acts 4:1–5:42), Stephen is executed (7:54–60), and Paul is arrested, almost losing his life at the hands of Jews who have sworn to destroy him (23:12–22). Jesus' teaching and life attract many to him, but they also provoke the ugliness of opposition and blasphemy. The thoughts of many hearts are revealed by his coming (v. 35a), either those of unbelief when he ha been rejected or those of faith when he i accepted as Savior and Lord.

Simeon also predicts that her Son's rejection will bring Mary grief and pain—"a swor will pierce your own soul too" (2:35b). Th "sword" is a symbol of suffering. At the rejection of her Son, which will culminate in hi death on the cross, she will experience grea sorrow. In Luke's Gospel this is the first hin that connects Jesus' mission with suffering The response to his suffering reveals wher each person is before God.

Present at the dedication of Jesus in th temple is another devout person—the age prophetess Anna, who had been married fo only seven years when she became a widow She keeps coming to worship at the templ probably never missing a service. Much of he time is spent there in fasting and praye Doubtless she has looked forward to the coming of the Messiah and has prayed many time that she will see him. She now offers heartfel thanks to God for the child's arrival. We are no told what Anna said in her Spirit-inspire prophecy, but she must have reinforce Simeon's message. Long after Joseph, Mary and Jesus leave, Anna continues to speak abou the newborn Savior to all who are expectin the redemption (*lytrosis*) of Jerusalem. Here Jerusalem is not political but spiritual, representing the whole nation of Israel. The Savic will at Calvary pay the price for their releas from spiritual bondage.

Having done all that the Mosaic la requires, the family returns to Nazareth. In tha obscure town God's incarnate Son, the Savio of the world, grows up. We can never penetrat the mystery of the development of Jesus, bu as he grows, he increases in strength and i filled with wisdom (*sophia*), gaining insigh into God's will and rule. God gives him grea favor (*charis*) and keeps on blessing him.

2.7. Jesus As a Boy in the Temple (2:41–52)

Angels have proclaimed the birth of th Savior (2:8–14). Prophetic voices have spoke messages of great hope over the infant Jesu and warned of suffering and judgment (2:28–38). The summary statement of 2:40 tells u about Jesus' growth, but we know very littl about his childhood. Luke stresses the myster f the divine and human in Jesus Christ. He loes record, however, one incident from his hildhood that indicates Jesus' awareness of is unique relationship with his heavenly ather and a clear sense of his calling.

At the age of twelve a Jewish boy becomes a son of the law" (*bar mitzvah*). At this time e accepts for himself the religious duties and bligations to which his parents committed im by the rite of circumcision (Caird, 1963, 6). For Jesus, this takes place when his parnts go up to Jerusalem to celebrate the assover. The Old Testament commanded that very male appear in Jerusalem for three fesivals: Passover, Pentecost, and Tabernacles Ex. 23:14–17; 34:23; Deut. 16:16). The disersion of the Jews throughout the world made t impossible for everyone to do this in the days f Mary and Joseph. Despite the distance, owever, devout Jews made the journey to erusalem once a year to attend at least the assover. Women were not required to be present, yet many did attend.

The Passover is held on the fourteenth day f the month of Nisan (about April 1) to celerate Israel's deliverance from slavery in gypt (Ex. 12:24–27). When Jesus is twelve ears old, his family makes the journey from Nazareth to Jerusalem (about eighty miles) to ttend the seven-day festival (Ex. 12:15; ev. 23:8). After it is over, Mary and Joseph lepart for home, assuming that Jesus is with riends or relatives in the caravan of pilgrims rom Galilee. Upon discovering that he has emained behind, they return to Jerusalem and earch for him. On the third day they finally ind him in the temple, listening to and asking uestions of the teachers. This twelve-year-old oy astonishes them (*existanto*, imperfect; lit., were standing out of themselves") with his nsight and answers. These teachers have never net a boy who has the grasp of the truth as he loes. His understanding involves more than imply being a bright student, for his mind and eart have been filled with divine wisdom v. 40). What an amazing and blessed child!

When Joseph and Mary find him, what they ee totally surprises them. Mary's question is atural, expressing a mother's concern about he pain that Jesus has caused them by remainng in Jerusalem. Here is the first fulfillment of imeon's prophecy to Mary: "A sword will ierce your own soul" (v. 35). The mild complaint of Mary leads Jesus to speak for the first time in Luke's Gospel for himself and to declare that the natural place for him is "in my Father's house" (v. 49), the temple (cf. John 2:16). Mary and Joseph need to understand his mission. He is absent from his earthly home because he has a strong sense of duty (*dei*, "it is necessary") to be in the house of his heavenly Father.

A key word here is "Father," which calls attention to a family characterized by an intimate, personal relationship. Jesus has a most profound relationship with his heavenly Father. At age twelve he asserts his unique sonship. God is his Father; he is God's Son. Jesus is not as other men; in a unique sense he is the Son of God. He is identified as such by the voice from heaven at his baptism and subsequently at his transfiguration: "You are my Son, whom I love" (3:22; 9:35). Jesus is the Son of God through the miracle and mystery of the Incarnation. The manifestation of God's Son in the flesh is a profound paradox. Jesus is fully God, yet he is fully human, who was born to a virgin and who experienced the normal processes of human growth. When his parents find him in the temple Jesus expresses a knowledge of who he really is. From this time on he has what scholars have called "a messianic consciousness"—an awareness of his person and mission.

Jesus does not become proud or rebellious because he has learned about his unique relationship with the heavenly Father. As an obedient son to his parents, he returns to Nazareth. But Joseph and Mary do not understand Jesus' remarks. They have marveled at the prophecy of Simeon (2:33) and are astonished by their son's words in the temple. Mary "treasured all these things in her heart," but apparently she has no clear understanding of how his mission will unfold. She has more questions than answers. In the meantime Jesus waits for God's time to begin his ministry. As he grows older, his development is perfect, growing "in wisdom and stature, and in favor with God and men" (v. 52). Luke wants his readers to do as Mary has done. It is good for us to ponder who Jesus is and what mission he will accomplish.

2.8. The Anointing of Jesus (3:1–38)

The main body of Luke's Gospel begins at Luke 4:14, with the ministry of Jesus. Luke

1:5–2:52 and 3:1–4:13 are two introductory sections, both of which record events before that ministry begins. The first section begins with the announcement of John's birth (1:5–25) and the second (3:1–4:13) with the ministry of John the Baptist (3:1–20), which prepares for the ministry of Jesus. In both introductory sections events in the lives of John and Jesus are closely connected.

2.8.1. The Preaching of John the Baptist (3:1–20). Luke's Gospel focuses on God's mighty saving work through Jesus Christ. John the Baptist has his role to play as the forerunner to Jesus. Luke places his prophetic ministry in the context of world history. It begins in the fifteenth year of the reign of the Roman emperor Tiberius (A.D. 14–37), that is, A.D. 28–29. Although not mentioned by name elsewhere in the New Testament, the emperor the Jews declare to be their king is this same Tiberius (John 19:15). Luke goes on to survey the political and religious leaders of the areas where Jesus will minister. The details here recall Luke's intent to investigate everything from the beginning and to write an orderly account (1:1–4). The list he provides here gives the religious and political setting for the beginning of John's ministry and helps the reader to date the events.

John initiates the beginning of the age of fulfillment, the age of the gospel. He stands between the old and new era, forming a bridge between them and thus belonging to both (Marshall, 1978, 132). John will be called "a prophet of the Most High" (1:76), but Jesus will be called "the Son of the Most High" (1:32, 35). John is filled with the Spirit while in the womb (1:15), but Jesus is conceived by the Holy Spirit (1:35). John's birth is proclaimed by neighbors and relatives (1:58), but Jesus' birth is proclaimed by angels (2:9–14). Jesus is heir to the throne of David and his rule will never end (1:32–33), and from his birth he is proclaimed as Savior, Messiah, and Lord (2:11). John himself cannot fulfill the hopes for the long-awaited Messiah, but he is anointed by the Spirit to prepare the way for the ministry of Christ.

While John is in the desert (the desolate region on the west side of the Jordan River), the word (*rhema*) of God comes to him as it had to other prophets (Isa. 38:4; Jer. 1:2). This word is more than a mere message from heaven. It has power to accomplish the purpose of God in the world and will not return void. God keeps his word. Luke employs two Greek terms for "word" (*logos*, *rhema*), but no rigid distinction should be made between them. They both have to do with salvation or the message of salvation (*rhema*: Luke 1:37–38; 2:11, 15, 17, 29–30, 48–50; 9:44–45; 18:34; 24:8; Acts 2:14; 5:20; 10:37; 11:14; 26:25; *logos*: Luke 4:22; 5:1; 9:26; 10:39; 11:28; Acts 13:26, 48; 14:3; 16:30–32; 18:5–11). God's message of salvation itself has power and is effective in bringing great blessings to those who receive the message and judgment to any who reject it.

John's ministry begins when he receives the powerful word of God. Like Old Testament prophets he is inspired by the Holy Spirit and proceeds under God's direction to proclaim "a baptism of repentance for the forgiveness of sins" (v. 3). Baptism in water is an outward rite that signifies the washing away of sins. Here it is described as "a baptism of repentance" (*metanoias*, a descriptive genitive), which literally means "a repentant baptism"—a baptism that is shot through and through with repentance. Only repentance prepares a person for baptism. In the phrase "for the forgiveness of sins" (*eis aphesin hamartion*), "for" (*eis*) indicates result, not cause (Dana and Mantey 1955, 105–6). That is, repentance results in the forgiveness of sins. Clearly John does not think baptism itself achieves forgiveness. Rather, it is a sign of forgiveness that results from genuine repentance and turning away from sin.

By his messianic preaching John fulfills the prophecy of Isaiah 40:3–5 (cf. Matt. 3:3; Mark 1:2–3; John 1:23). Isaiah's message has great spiritual and moral significance (vv. 4–6). All four Evangelists identify John with the voice crying in the desert, but only Luke includes the words "all mankind will see God's salvation" (v. 6)—words consistent with Luke's emphasis on salvation for all people and his forecast of the world mission of the church. As the Lord's coming approaches, the way must be prepared so that he can enter. Every valley must be filled and every mountain and hill must be leveled so that he may enter on a straight and true highway. That is, every moral hindrance and obstacle must be removed for the Lord's arrival. By the people turning from their sins the way will be prepared for the Lord's coming.

So God is about to establish his kingdom, and he has sent John to prepare the way. Matthew and Mark make it clear that John announces the nearness of God's kingdom (Matt. 3:2; Mark 1:14–15). The kingdom about which he speaks is not in the broadest sense God's rule from the beginning of creation. His announcement has to do with an aspect of God's rule that is now approaching, but has not yet become a reality. The kingdom that John proclaims is God's rule realized through the promised Messiah and through the extraordinary presence and power of the Holy Spirit.

As John preaches, he declares God's standard of righteousness to prepare the people for Messiah's coming. Crowds come out to be baptized by him, but they show no contrition for their sins. John's message is repentance, and baptism is only meaningful when it is a sign of sincere repentance. Repentance—never baptism—is what brings forgiveness. Apart from it all people stand under God's wrath as unbelievers. John knows that the people need repentance and forgiveness and thus calls them a "brood of vipers," exposing them as cunning hypocrites. They are as wicked as snakes and need to be transformed, since the fire of God's wrath draws near.

John demands the people to produce fruit—good works "in keeping with repentance" (v. 8). It is not enough for them to claim to have repented; they must prove their claims by conduct consistent with repentance. Genuine repentance (*metanoia*) involves more than regretting what we have done or wishing to do better in the future but with no real desire to stop sinning. In biblical terms, to repent is "to change our mind." This change produces a change of attitude toward God and sin, which leads to salvation and results in a new direction for our lives. "Godly sorrow brings repentance that leads to salvation" (2 Cor. 7:10; cf. also Acts 3:19; 26:20). The believers at Thessalonica manifested biblical repentance by their turning from idols, their primary sin being idolatry, to serve the living God (1 Thess. 1:9–10). God calls us to repentance so that he may transform our hearts and change the direction of our lives.

As the forerunner of Jesus, John warns his audience that their religious heritage will not save them from God's punishment of sinners (v. 8). They are Jews, descendants of Abraham, but that in itself does not make them God's children. A good heritage can be an advantage, but it cannot guarantee anyone a right relationship with God. No one is born a Christian; no one can inherit salvation. The only way to God is by repentance and faith in Jesus. A good home and roots may be a benefit, but they cannot yield salvation.

The experience of salvation is a matter of the creative power of God. From lifeless stones "God can raise up children for Abraham" (v. 8). This truth points to the creative power of God's grace, which drastically transforms the life of all who come to him in repentance. If God can produce new life out of lifeless stones, surely he can do it out of people.

Judgment is fast approaching. As the Baptist declares, "The ax is already at the root of the trees" (v. 9). Like an ax that has been raised, divine judgment is about to fall. Every unfruitful tree will be cut down and burned by God, while the trees producing good fruit, showing evidence of sincere repentance, will remain. Scripture frequently speaks of fire in reference to God's judgment of the wicked. The flames of divine judgment will consume those who do not heed the call of repentance. It is better to escape the coming wrath and not get burned.

John's urgent message has an impact on his audience. Three groups ask, "What should we do then" to escape the wrath of God? John's reply is simple. The first group, which consists of those who have two tunics (*chiton*, "undergarment"), are to share with him who has none. The same applies to food. Their duty is to share extra clothing in their wardrobe and food with the poor. They are to be generous and not be blind to the needs of others. The second group are the tax collectors; they are to be honest and just, collecting only the amount of taxes appropriate. The third group, soldiers, are to avoid such sins as robbing by the use of violence and accusing people falsely. Both these sins have to do with obtaining money by unlawful means. Thus John urges them to be satisfied with their wages. John has now explained "fruit in keeping with repentance" (v. 8) in practical terms. Unfortunately, there is the temptation for sinful human beings to be blind to the needs of the poor, to extort funds from others, and to take advantage of the powerless.

As great a prophet as John is, he knows his own limitations. He himself cannot fulfill the people's hopes for the Messiah. Their question concerning his identity (v. 15) allows John to distinguish between himself and the Coming One. In verses 16–17 he indicates three ways in which he differs from the One yet to come. (1) The Coming One is more powerful than John. In that day a slave was expected to remove his master's shoes. John indicates he is unworthy to be the servant of one mightier than he.

(2) John baptizes in water, but the more powerful One will baptize with (or "in") the Holy Spirit and fire. In the performance of any baptism there must be an agent who does the baptizing, the element in which baptism occurs, and the candidate who is baptized. When John baptizes, he is the agent, the water of the Jordan River is the element, and the candidates are those who repent and ask to be baptized. In the baptism of the Spirit, Jesus Christ is the agent, the Holy Spirit is the element, and the candidate is the believer. Acts 2:33 clearly teaches that Jesus is the agent in Spirit-baptism. Thus, the Holy Spirit is the element and the believer the candidate. At *conversion* the believer is spiritually baptized into the body of Christ (the church) by the Holy Spirit (1 Cor. 12:13). Then, *subsequently*, the believer in Christ can be baptized in the Holy Spirit by Christ. At one's conversion, the first baptism, the Holy Spirit is the agent; in the reception of the fullness of the Spirit, the second baptism, Christ is the agent.

(3) John does not just preach a baptism "with the Holy Spirit," but a baptism "with the Holy Spirit *and with fire*." Baptism with fire can refer to a second aspect of Jesus' ministry: purging and judgment. However, "fire" in verse 16 does not refer, at least primarily, to the final judgment and the fiery destruction of the godless, but to momentous events in the book of Acts. The anointing with the Spirit is not explicitly identified as baptism in the Spirit and fire. But Jesus does affirm John's promise of the baptism in the Spirit in Acts 1:5, and it is fulfilled as "tongues of fire" rested on each of the disciples at Pentecost: "All of them were filled with the Holy Spirit and began to speak in other tongues as the Spirit enabled them" (2:1–4). Thus "fire" is part of the Pentecostal experience as described in Acts 2. Tongues and prophecy are the recurring signs of the Spirit-baptism in Acts.

John the Baptist points to Jesus as one to whom we are all accountable. He is described as the ultimate judge in the preaching of Acts (4:10–12; 10:42; 17:31). Though John preaches many things, including judgment, his message is called "the good news" (v. 18). We may not think of judgment as a vital part of good news, especially in view of John's harsh warnings. But the good news of salvation demands that sinners repent and change their ways. Like a pill the message may be bitter to swallow, but preaching that exposes the moral and spiritual demands of the good news can bring healing to the soul. The gospel is a matter of life or death.

John continues to preach fearlessly righteousness and judgment. He rebukes Herod Antipas, the governor of Galilee, for marrying Herodias, his brother Philip's wife. Herod had persuaded her to leave her first husband to marry him, dismissing his own wife in the meantime. Aware of these evil deeds, John puts into words what many people felt about the royal couple. Herod strikes back by having the prophet thrown into prison and thus adds to his own sins. Sins that are unchecked often multiply and become magnified.

John's ministry overlaps with the early ministry of Jesus, but here Luke concludes it so that he can now focus on Jesus' ministry.

2.8.2. The Baptism of Jesus (3:21–22). John has pointed to Jesus, the Coming One, but now that Jesus has arrived, Luke turns to his empowerment for ministry by the Holy Spirit. Jesus' experience of the Spirit began with the angel Gabriel's announcement of the miraculous birth to Mary (1:26–34). But about thirty years later he begins a new relationship with the Holy Spirit in that he is anointed by the Spirit for ministry (cf. 4:18; Acts 10:38). The Spirit's descent on Jesus marks the beginning of his Spirit-filled public ministry (4:1, 14, 18–19). His Jordan River experience means that he is Pentecostal, charismatic—a man of the Spirit par excellence.

The Spirit descends on Jesus as John includes Jesus among those whom he is baptizing. By receiving John's baptism, Jesus identifies with the people. John's baptism is a sinner's baptism, to signify repentance, and Jesus has no sins from which to turn. But as the

Suffering Servant of Isaiah 53, he takes his stand with sinners, whom he has come to save. The anointing of Jesus by the Spirit is distinct from John's baptism so as to make it a prophetic empowerment for ministry. While Jesus is praying, he is filled with the Spirit. Throughout Luke's Gospel the critical events in the earthly life of Jesus unfold in the context of prayer (6:12; 9:18, 28; 10:21; 11:1; 22:32; 23:34, 46). He looks to the heavenly Father during every step of his mission (Bock, 1994, 78). Prayer is likewise the context in which the Holy Spirit is given (11:13; Acts 1:14, 24; 4:24–31; 8:14–17). The prayer life of Jesus and the early believers provides Christians an example to follow.

The anointing of Jesus is marked by the descent of the Spirit "in bodily form like a dove," and God's voice calls out of heaven: "You are my Son, whom I love; with you I am well pleased" (v. 22). This experience is both a visual and vocal fulfillment of God's promise to his servant in Isaiah 42:1. The coming down of the Spirit as a dove affirms by a visual sign the promise: "I will put my Spirit on him"; the voice out of heaven affirms the words: "my chosen one in whom I delight." The opening of the heavens recalls Isaiah's cry for God to rend the heavens and to come down in power (64:1). God intervenes in power at Jesus' baptism, and the Spirit equips him for his ministry of preaching, teaching, and healing. The heavenly voice proclaims Jesus, the Anointed One, as the Son of God, the true king of Israel (cf. Ps. 2:7). But he is not a son of God as the kings of old were, but is the beloved, unique, "only" Son of God (cf. Luke 10:21–22).

The events and words following Jesus' baptism reiterate that he is the Son of God: the genealogy (3:38), the temptations (4:3, 9), and the healing ministry (4:41). In only one other place in Luke's Gospel does God's voice break through and affirm Jesus as his Son (9:35), just after his first prediction that "the Son of Man must suffer many things" (9:22). Luke sees Jesus not only as a charismatic, but also as a person of the triune God.

The anointing of the Spirit extends throughout Jesus' entire ministry. From his baptism on he is full of the Spirit (4:1a), led by the Spirit (4:1b), and empowered by the Spirit (4:14). His experience at the Jordan River is programmatic for his ministry from its beginning to its conclusion. At the beginning of Jesus' ministry all the people try to touch him "because power was coming from him and healing them all" (6:19). As his ministry is drawing to a close, some of his disciples declare, "He was a prophet, powerful in word and deed before God" (24:19). Years later Peter speaks about "how God anointed Jesus of Nazareth with the Holy Spirit and power, and how he went around doing good and healing all who were under the power of the devil" (Acts 10:38). The future ministry of Jesus—all that he does and says—is directed, inspired, and empowered by the Spirit.

John has promised that Jesus will baptize in the Holy Spirit (v. 16). This promise, along with Jesus' experience at the Jordan River, emphasizes the importance of Jesus' first being anointed by the Spirit. Before he can bestow the Spirit on believers for anointing and service, he needs to be empowered by the Spirit himself. The fulfillment of John's promise that Jesus will baptize with the Holy Spirit and fire begins at Pentecost (Acts 2). Having received the Spirit at the beginning of his ministry, he becomes the giver of the Spirit (2:33). Both the descent of the Spirit on Jesus and the outpouring of the Spirit at Pentecost are anointings for ministry. The One anointed by the Spirit at the outset of his ministry subsequently equips and empowers his disciples for their ministry of teaching, preaching, and healing. They become the heirs and successors to his Spirit-anointed ministry after he ascends into heaven (1:9ff.).

2.8.3. The Genealogy of Jesus (3:23–38). Luke has stated that John the Baptist began to minister in the fifteenth year of Tiberius (3:1–3), which is A.D. 29. If John's ministry began early that year, Jesus' ministry gets underway soon after that, probably sometime between the summer of 29 and the Passover of 30. By then Jesus is around thirty-two years old. This fits well with Luke's observation: "Now Jesus himself was about thirty years old when he began his ministry" (v. 23). The length of Jesus' ministry is based primarily on evidence in John's Gospel, for John reports three Passovers Jesus attended (2:13; 6:4; 11:55). Because the Synoptic Gospels mention the disciples' plucking of ripe grain in Galilee (Matt. 12:1; Mark 2:23; Luke 6:1), a Passover likely occurs also between John 2:13 and 6:4. If so, that means a total of four Passovers during the ministry of Jesus. Hence, his ministry must have been about three and a half years in length.

Before describing the family line of Jesus Luke makes it clear that Joseph is not Jesus' father. Luke believes in the Virgin Birth and knows that normally a family line is traced through the father. Thus, to avoid any misunderstanding, Luke reminds his readers that Jesus is the son of Mary, not of Joseph as was supposed.

Matthew includes a genealogy of Jesus at the beginning of his Gospel (Matt. 1:1–17). A comparison of it with Luke's genealogy reveals several differences. Matthew's genealogy has forty-one names and Luke's seventy-seven; Matthew begins with Abraham, emphasizing that Jesus fulfilled God's promise to Abraham; Luke traces Jesus' family line all the way back to Adam, linking Jesus' Spirit-anointed mission not only to Israel but to all humankind. Not all the names correspond with each other. The discussion on this has been endless; several solutions have been proposed. A plausible explanation has been that Matthew traces Jesus' lineage through Joseph, who is the legal, though not the biological, father, and Luke through Mary, the actual mother.

Luke's genealogy makes a number of important statements: (1) It shows that Jesus is a real man with a family tree. A glance at his ancestry proves that he is not a demi-god of pagan mythology; he has his place as a member of the human race. (2) It affirms that Jesus is a son of David. According to Scripture the Messiah was to be an heir to David's throne (Ps. 110; Zech. 12:1–14; Mark 10:48; Luke 1:69; Acts 2:30; Rom. 1:3). As an essential messianic qualification Jesus has a claim to the throne of David. (3) It points to Jesus' relation to the entire human race by tracing his lineage back to Adam. He is a son of Adam as well as a son of David, stressing that his mission is ultimately to all humankind.

3. The Ministry of the Spirit-Anointed Prophet: Christ in Galilee (4:1–9:50)

Jesus' temptations in a desert place introduce the third major section of Luke's Gospel (4:1–9:50), which deal with a wide variety of subjects. The main theme of this section is the public, Spirit-anointed ministry of Jesus before he "resolutely set out for Jerusalem" (9:51). During this time Jesus remains in Galilee. His Galilean ministry is a traveling ministry, in which he preaches, performs miracles, awakens faith in the disciples, and arouses a growing opposition (Marshall, 1978, 175). Jesus devotes himself to walking with God wherever he leads, and to serving the people. This Galilean ministry provides a model for the life and ministry of the church.

3.1. The Testing of Jesus (4:1–13)

Soon after Jesus' anointing by the Spirit (3:21–22), Luke records that he is filled with the Spirit (4:1). Thereupon he commits himself to walking the path that will take him to Calvary. The empowering Spirit leads him into the desert, where for forty days he undergoes temptations by the devil. During this time Jesus communes with God through prayer and fasting. When the pangs of hunger reach great intensity, the devil begins an intense assault on the Son of God.

Jesus experiences three specific temptations. The first one involves his physical needs (vv. 3–4). The devil assumes Jesus is the Son of God—"If you are the Son of God" means "Since you are God's Son." Surely, then, Jesus can exercise God's power and turn a stone under his foot into a loaf of bread. The devil suggests that the use of this power to relieve his hunger will really prove him to be the Son of God. But should Jesus have turned a stone into bread, such a miracle would reveal his lack of faith in God's goodness. He would have obeyed the devil rather than God. He would have used his power to satisfy his own personal needs instead of using it for God's glory.

Jesus resists the devil's temptation by quoting Deuteronomy 8:3. The point of his reply is that human well-being is more than a matter of having enough food. More important is obeying the Word of God and trusting in the Lord to care for us. Jesus obeys God's Word even though it involves physical hunger.

The second temptation is the devil's offer to Jesus of authority over the kingdoms of the earth (vv. 5–8). In a moment of time the devil brings before him all the kingdoms of the world. He claims that they have been given to him and that he has the right to dispose of them as he wants. The devil's claim is a half-truth. Though he has great power (John 12:31; 14:30; 2 Cor. 4:4; Eph. 2:2), he does not have authority to give the kingdoms of the world and their glory to Jesus. The devil, however, promises Jesus that he can become the ruler of the earth only if he will worship him. Satan tries to lure Jesus to reach for political power and to set up a worldly kingdom greater than that of the Romans.

The kingdom Jesus has come to establish is very different, however. It is a kingdom in which God rules, and it is made up of men and women set free from the bondage of sin and Satan. To establish that kind of kingdom means a cross rather than a crown. Jesus again resists the devil by quoting the Bible (Deut. 6:13). Satan is not worthy of worship; only God deserves to be worshiped and served. Jesus puts worship and service together (v. 8); both are vital to the honoring of God. Just as worshiping the devil means selfishly grasping for power and glory, so worship of God means committing oneself to God's will in sacrificial service for others.

The third temptation has to do with proving the truth of God's promise (vv. 9–12). Jesus goes willingly with the evil one to the highest place on the temple. The precise location on the temple is uncertain, but from the temple's highest point Satan urges Jesus to jump: "If you are the Son of God . . . throw yourself down from here" (v. 9). The devil's suggestion is this: "Before you set out on your mission, you had better be certain of God's protection. So why not jump and assure yourself that God will care for you?" The evil one has been refuted twice with the Scriptures, so he quotes Psalm 91:11–12 to assure Jesus that God will protect him from any injury. This is an example of twisting the Scriptures to serve a purpose, for Psalm 91 does not guarantee that God will perform miracles on our own terms.

Once again Jesus resists the devil by citing the Bible: "Do not put the Lord your God to the test" (cf. Deut. 6:16). The verb "test" (*ekpeirazo*) is a stronger form than the word used in 4:2. It means "to put to test" and, therefore, to challenge God to prove that he really does care. Jesus refuses to test God's goodness by insisting on a miracle. In the desert the Israelites sinned by testing God (Ex. 17:1–7). It is as though they said to God, "If you do not give us water right now, this proves that you do not love us." Should Jesus have jumped off the pinnacle of the temple, that would have been the same as saying, "God, if you do not send your angels to keep me safe, this proves that you do not love me" (Bratcher, 1982, 61).

Jesus' quotation from Deuteronomy reminds us of Israel's sojourn in the desert. Israel failed the test there; but where Israel failed, Christ succeeds. He meets temptation with the Word of God and wins a decisive victory over the devil. He has tempted Jesus in every way, trying to make him sin; but Jesus, full of the Spirit and led by the Spirit, does not yield.

Having finished tempting Jesus, the devil leaves him for a while. In no way does this mean that Jesus will not be subject to further temptation (cf. 8:12; 11:18; 13:16; 22:3, 31). Each attack of Satan has failed, but this is only the first round of many victorious rounds Jesus will have with the devil. His success reveals that the Spirit-anointed Jesus is qualified for his mission. The desert experience establishes not only a pattern for his ministry, but also a pattern by which Christians should meet temptation. By the power of the Spirit and by using Scripture, we must face Satan in the same way as he did. Walking with God does not always take us along the easiest road. But God remains faithful, even during times when our spirituality and faith are sorely tested by Satan.

3.2. Jesus' Inaugural Sermon (4:14–30)

In verses 14–15 Luke summarizes the earliest days of Jesus' ministry. Filled with the Spirit Jesus comes into Galilee. For his ministry there he makes Capernaum his headquarters (4:31). News spreads throughout Galilee and surrounding regions about his teaching, arousing curiosity and excitement. As a result of his teaching in the synagogues, all the people have many good things to say about him (v. 15).

Jesus then returns to Nazareth, where he grew up. As was his custom during his boyhood, he goes to the synagogue on the Sabbath to worship. Not only does he attend the service, but he also participates. Synagogue services were rather informal, consisting of prayers, reading of Scripture, comments, and giving of gifts for the poor.[8] At his own request

Jesus is given the book of the prophet Isaiah. Having been filled with the Spirit at his baptism (3:22), he reads Isaiah 61:1–2[9] and identifies himself as an anointed prophet. He is the prophetic Messiah, anointed by the Spirit to proclaim good news.

The text from Isaiah announces the pattern of Jesus' total ministry of preaching and teaching, healing and deliverance. The promises of prophets like Isaiah are being realized, and the last days have begun. The era of salvation has arrived, bringing God's year of Jubilee—"the year of the Lord's favor." It is an evangel—the proclamation of the good news by mighty works and words. This good news offers God's favor to the poor and will set free prisoners in bonds, such as the demoniac in the region of the Gerasenes (Luke 8:26–39). The blind, such as the blind beggar at Jericho, will receive sight (18:35–43). As an anointed prophet Jesus will not only minister to the poor, the prisoners, and the blind but to all who are pulled down and oppressed, such as Lazarus or Zacchaeus, by sin, sickness, and poverty (5:31–32; 16:19–31; 19:1–10). Jesus is more than a prophet of the last days; he is the Messiah, who brings salvation.

As Jesus completes the reading of Isaiah, he sits down, taking the normal posture for preaching. The eyes of the congregation are fixed on him, expecting that he will begin his sermon. No one but Jesus can begin a sermon the way he does: "Today this scripture is fulfilled in your hearing" (v. 21). He claims himself to be the fulfillment of Isaiah's prophecy. As the congregation listens, the fulfillment of Scripture takes place in their hearing. The Anointed One about whom the prophet spoke is now present to carry out his mission. In Jesus' day many Jews did not doubt that the messianic reign would come in the future, but Jesus affirms that what they expected in a future age has just become a present reality. The time of salvation is "today." This is a "today" that continues; never does it become yesterday nor does it slip into a vague tomorrow.

At first the worshipers express approval, being impressed with the persuasive words (lit., "words of grace") coming from his mouth. But their admiration soon gives way to resentment. They become indignant at him for presuming to speak as a prophet. Their question, "Isn't this Joseph's son?" does not ask for information. It reflects the belief that he is no one but Joseph's son—certainly not an anointed prophet or the Messiah. He has grown up among them; in no way can he be the servant promised by Isaiah. Their earthbound eyes see him only as the carpenter's son.

Knowing their skepticism about his high claims, Jesus replies in three ways. (1) He cites the proverb: "Physician, heal yourself." This proverb anticipates that the people will insist that he should perform miracles in his home town to prove his claims. Jesus speaks about what has happened in Capernaum; yet according to Luke's Gospel mighty deeds are not done in that town until later. Therefore, Jesus is prophesying what the people of Nazareth will say in the future (Marshall, 1978, 187). The problem of these people is one of unbelief. Their response to Jesus' claims is "Show us." As powerful a witness as miracles are to Jesus, those who do not want to come to God remain unconvinced (16:31). People must be willing to believe the Word of God before they can see anything as God's work.

(2) Jesus observes that no prophet is welcomed in his own hometown. The nearer a prophet is to his home, the less acceptable and the less honored he is. The history of Israel's rejection of their own prophets leaves no doubt about this truth. Jesus knows that God's people in the Old Testament repeatedly rejected God's messengers (11:49–52; 13:32–35; 20:10–12; Acts 7:51–53). His observation serves as a prediction that he and his message will be rejected.

(3) Jesus refers to two notable Spirit-anointed prophets, Elijah and Elisha, from the Old Testament times (vv. 25–27), to whom he compares his ministry. He has just challenged his townspeople to honor him as an anointed prophet (v. 22), and he now uses these prophets to warn against rejecting God. Both Elijah and Elisha ministered to non-Jews (1 Kings 17–18; 2 Kings 5:1–4). In their day when idolatry and unfaithfulness abounded on every hand and rejection of God had become rampant, God's blessings went outside the nation of Israel to Gentile areas. Many widows lived in Israel, for example, but during a severe famine God sent Elijah only to a widow in the region of Sidon. Many in Israel had leprosy, but during the time of Elisha only Naaman the Syrian experienced deliverance. Jesus thereby warns his townsfolk

that if they reject him, he, like his prophetic predecessors, will turn to the Gentiles. The rejection of God's favor can be risky. God may withdraw it and offer his grace to others.

The worshipers at the synagogue have an opportunity to receive God's rich blessings, but Jesus' warning fills them with rage during the worship service. They do not appreciate his words and greet them instead with rejection, making a serious attempt to kill him. They refuse the gospel and suffer the tragic consequences.

3.3. The Authoritative Word and Healings (4:31–41)

Jesus embarks on a ministry like that described in Luke 4:18–19. After his rejection in the synagogue at Nazareth, he goes down to Capernaum, about twenty miles away. This town is on the shore of the Sea of Galilee and provides a base for Jesus' ministry in Galilee. "He went down" expresses appropriately the descent from Nazareth to Capernaum, located below sea level.

Luke's account of Jesus' ministry in Capernaum focuses on his mighty acts of deliverance accomplished by the power and authority of the Savior. The expulsion of a demon from a man (vv. 33–37), the healing of Peter's mother-in-law (vv. 38–39), and various other healings in the evening (vv. 40–41) are all deeds of compassion toward people in desperate need. The first two miracles involve power in the word of Jesus, and the others his healing touch. His teaching and miracles reflect his prophetic, charismatic authority.

Soon after arriving in Capernaum Jesus goes to a synagogue service and teaches with authority the word of God (vv. 31–32). The people are astonished by the way he teaches and by the content of his message. Jesus teaches as one who has authority himself. The rabbis often cited their famous predecessors to support their teaching. Jesus' authority depends on no external authority or position of power, but springs totally from himself, the truth he teaches, and his empowerment by the Holy Spirit (v. 14). His authority is absolute, and what he says is completely true. The people's amazement indicates the undiminished force of the word of God on them, but apparently its effect is only external and does not result in repentance and a change of heart. Their response to his teachings is the same as that to his miracles (cf. 9:43).

As Jesus delivers his authoritative message, there is present in the synagogue a man possessed by an evil spirit (lit., "a spirit of an unclean demon"). The demon stands in contrast to Jesus, "the Holy One of God" (v. 34). As is characteristic of demon possession, the evil spirit is in control of the man's personality. It is deeply disturbed by the presence of Jesus and his authoritative teaching. Speaking through the man, it interrupts Jesus by crying out wildly, "What do you want with us, Jesus of Nazareth?"

These words are more of a rebuke than a question and mean: "Do not meddle with us and involve yourself in our affairs. We have nothing in common with you." The man is indwelt by a single demon, but the pronoun "us" refers to all evil spirits as a group. From the outset of Jesus' ministry he finds himself in conflict with the spirit world. In fact, his mission is to destroy the works of the devil (1 John 3:8) and to set people free from the whole realm of demons. Thus the demon has grounds for being afraid. Jesus is "the Holy One of God"; conceived and anointed by the Holy Spirit for his holy work, he possesses power to destroy evil spirits.

Capernaum on the shore of the Sea of Galilee became Jesus' base for his ministry in the region. These ruins are all that remain of a synagogue that dates back to the third and fourth centuries.

Jesus speaks directly to the demon in the man and commands it to stop crying out (v. 33) and instead come out of the man (v. 35). The Greek says that he "rebuked" (*epetimesen*) the evil spirit. His rebuke indicates not only disapproval but also a subduing of that spirit. Jesus' powerful word prevails in silencing the demon and casting it out. As it leaves the man, it throws him in the midst of the people. Despite the violent departure, the demon does no permanent damage to him.

Jesus' power over unclean spirits amazes the people. Having seen Jesus set the man free, they discuss and deliberate with one another, "What is this teaching (*logos*)?" Here *logos* ("word") refers to his command, "Be silent.... Come out of him!" (v. 35). This command, as well as the people's statement about his power (*dynamis*) and authority (*exousia*), focuses on the power of Jesus' word. The terms *authority* and *power* have about the same meaning, though "authority" refers to Jesus' divine right to exercise his "power." Through his word he exercises his authority and power over evil spirits, and they have no choice but to obey him.

The deliverance of the man possessed by the evil spirit clearly demonstrates what Luke has in mind when he says that Jesus returns to Galilee "in the power of the Spirit" (v. 14). In addition, it implements for the first time his sermon at Nazareth (vv. 16–30). As a result of this miracle a report spreads throughout the region surrounding Capernaum. The people in the neighboring towns and villages talk about what Jesus is doing.

On the same Sabbath Jesus performs another miracle. Soon after leaving the synagogue, he goes to Peter's house, where his mother-in-law is suffering from a severe fever (vv. 38–39). Evidently the family of the woman requests that Jesus heal her. Since he has set the man in the synagogue free from an evil spirit, they have faith that he can deliver this woman from her hot fever. Standing over her, Jesus rebukes the fever in the same way as he did the demon. Luke does not connect her illness with demon possession, but just as the demoniac was set free from the evil spirit, Peter's mother-in-law is healed. Immediately she rises up and begins to go about her domestic duties, offering her guests food and drink.

By now the sun is almost set, marking the beginning of the first day of the week. Without violating the Sabbath, the people in Capernaum can now bring their sick to Jesus. They have heard of his spectacular ministry, and they bring numerous people with different diseases. On this occasion Jesus lays his hands on the sick and heals each one of them (v. 40). From the personal touch of the Spirit-anointed Jesus flows divine power. Many of those healed also have demons expelled from them, driven out by the healing hands of Jesus. As they leave their victims, they identify Jesus as "the Son of God." By his authoritative word he rebukes them and does not "allow them to speak, because they knew he was the Christ." The people in Capernaum may think that Jesus is merely a man, but the demons know better.

Jesus does not want the demons to reveal that he is the Messiah. After all, darkness cannot reveal light, but light reveals darkness. As God's unique Son, he does not want to be thought of merely as a miracle-worker or as a political Messiah. His miracles are acts of compassion and signs of the presence of the kingdom. The Spirit-anointed Jesus has the right to be publicly proclaimed as the Messiah, but never can he rightly be known apart from the Cross (9:20–23; 24:25–27).

3.4. Popular Acclaim (4:42–5:16)

Jesus has had a good day of ministry. He has healed Peter's mother-in-law and has delivered many others from various diseases and from demons (4:38–41). Word begins to spread about Jesus' power over sickness and evil spirits.

3.4.1. Summary (4:42–44). Early the next morning Jesus leaves Capernaum and goes to a place where there are no people so that he can pray (Mark 1:35). Because the people have been impressed by his deeds of power, they go in search of him. When they find him, they try to keep him from leaving the area. Their desire stands as a marked contrast to the people of Nazareth, who tried to kill him. But Jesus never allows others to dictate his ministry. So he explains the nature of his mission: "I must preach the good news of the kingdom of God to other towns also, because that is why I was sent."

For the first time in Luke we have mention of "the kingdom of God." This is the rule of God, which works through the ministry of Jesus in bringing salvation to the world. It is a present reality, but God will consummate his rule at the second coming of Christ. Jesus' offer of salvation and his power over sickness and demons demonstrate the presence of God's rule. He is under a divine imperative (*dei*, "it is necessary") to preach the rule of God and to call people to surrender to it. The good news of God's rule must be preached far and wide—not only in the cities of Nazareth and Capernaum—but throughout the country and ultimately "to the ends of the earth" (Acts 1:8). In Luke 4:44, "Judea" refers to the whole country of the Jews, including Galilee. So Jesus takes his message of God's rule to many other Jewish synagogues. Those who accept the gospel in repentance and faith become partakers of the rich blessings as God's rule fills their hearts.

3.4.2. Simon Peter (5:1–11). So far Luke has given a general account of Jesus' ministry, but now he singles out an event that calls attention to Jesus' gathering of disciples. He describes the call of several fishermen to discipleship, with the spotlight on Simon Peter. Peter has already had contact with Jesus (cf. 4:38–39), but until this incident he has devoted himself to his fishing business. He and his partners, James and John, probably own and operate a couple of boats. Jesus gathers his disciples from all walks of life: fishermen, tax collectors, zealots, and other common people.

Jesus has become a popular preacher. He is near the Lake of Gennesaret, better known as the Sea of Galilee. A crowd eager to hear the word of God presses around him as he speaks. Nearby are two boats, and fishermen are washing their nets. Among them is Peter, whose boat Jesus steps into. When he finishes teaching, he commands Peter to push the boat out from the shore and let his nets down for a catch of fish. This command takes Peter by surprise; a carpenter's son is telling a fisherman how to fish, especially after a night of fishing has proved fruitless. Nevertheless, Peter heeds the command of Jesus, and obedience brings great results. So many fish are caught that the nets are about to burst and the boats are in danger of sinking.

Peter and his partners have seen a manifestation of heavenly power. Reacting to the miraculous catch of fish, Peter falls on his knees before Jesus. The experience gives him extraordinary insight into Jesus' supernatural power. He calls him "Lord" (*kyrie*, v. 8), which can simply express respect in the meaning "Sir," but in the Greek Old Testament it often refers to God. Here "Lord" definitely has a deeper meaning than the respectful "master" in verse 5. In other words, Jesus is addressed as "Lord" in the full Christian sense. Before the Lord Jesus, Peter becomes aware that he is a sinful man. His confession reminds us of the words of Isaiah (Isa. 6:5). Like the prophet in God's presence, Peter is deeply aware of the difference between Jesus and himself. The power of God can produce a profound sense of our sinfulness and unworthiness.

When Peter has more success than ever in fishing, he has to stop and consider what God is doing. He and his companions recognize the extraordinary significance of the enormous catch of fish (v. 9). As a result Peter is deeply agitated and troubled in spirit. Jesus speaks reassuring words, "Don't be afraid," though a better translation is, "Stop being fearful" (v. 10). At this moment Peter receives the Lord's forgiveness and begins a new life. Jesus does not depart from this sinner (v. 8); rather, he accepts him and calls him to be a disciple. No longer will he catch fish, but "from now on you will catch men" (v. 10). Jesus prophesies that Peter will cast his net into a different sea, the sea of lost humanity, and that the catching of human beings will become his business.

The response of Peter and his partners is decisive. When the boats come to shore, they leave everything behind and set out on their

Fishermen still go out with their nets in small boats to catch fish, just as they did in the time of Jesus. It was on the Sea of Galilee where Jesus told Peter to go out to deep water and let down his nets. Peter and his partners caught more fish than they thought possible. When they returned, Jesus said, "Don't be afraid; from now on you will catch men."

new fishing expedition (v. 11) . Their experience with Jesus has brought them to total commitment. They cut their ties with the past and become disciples and followers of Jesus. By God's grace sinners are transformed into servants.

3.4.3. Healing of a Leper (5:12–16). Jesus now ministers a wonderful act of healing to a leper. In the ancient world a variety of skin diseases are called leprosy. Many of them were regarded as highly contagious and incurable. As the result of having such a disease, lepers were cut off from society, including their own families. At the approach of a person a leper was required to cry, "Unclean" (Lev. 13:45–46). The man Jesus meets is "covered with leprosy" (v. 12); he has the advanced stage of the disease and apparently is dying slowly.

Jesus has come to minister to the needy and is willing to show his mercy to a person on the lowest rung of society. Falling on his face, the leper declares that he fully believes that Jesus has the power to heal him: "Lord, if you are willing, you can make me clean" (v. 12). He is not certain about Jesus' compassion, but he does know Jesus has the ability to heal him. Touching the leper, Jesus speaks an authoritative word that has power to cause the leprosy to leave him. Jesus enters into this man's world of isolation and shame and gives himself to him. Among the signs that the age of fulfillment has dawned is that "those who have leprosy are cured" (7:22).

The man is ordered to tell nobody except the priest that he has been healed and then to offer a thanksgiving offering to God (Lev. 14:1–32). Beyond that, the man is to keep silence about his deliverance. Earlier Jesus forbade demons from saying anything (4:35, 41); now he also commands a healed leper to be silent. Why? (1) Jesus may want to avoid the crowds coming to him merely to seek healing. He does not want the people simply to define his ministry as a one-dimensional healing ministry. To be misunderstood has the potential of diminishing the effectiveness of his total work as outlined in 4:18–19. (2) Moreover, Jesus wants the man to avoid broadcasting his healing until he is formally pronounced clean by the priest, certifying the genuineness of the cure.

The healing of the leper bears witness to the people that the power of God is working through the Spirit-anointed Jesus. Word does get out, and news about the cleansing keeps spreading. As an inevitable result, crowds of people flock to hear Jesus as well as to receive healing for the sick. But they do not find him; he has already slipped away into lonely places for prayer (v. 16). The verbs "withdrew" and "prayed" both are present participles linked with an imperfect tense of the verb "to be"; they refer not to a single incident but to a pattern of customary behavior. Jesus often withdraws so that he can commune with God. He refuses to be carried away with the popular favor and demand. Prayer is the key to an effective, powerful ministry.

3.5. Opposition (5:17–6:11)

The wonderful ministry of Jesus and his rising popularity lead to opposition. When his parents presented Jesus in the temple, Simeon prophesied that the child would be "a sign that will be spoken against" (2:34). Although during his earthly ministry Jesus is without sin, his opponents charge him with a variety of sins. Luke 5:17–6:11 records confrontation that involves four issues: blasphemy, association with sinners, fasting, and the Sabbath.

3.5.1. Pharisees: He Blasphemes (5:17–26). The first sign of opposition comes from the religious leaders. Pharisees and teachers of the law come from Galilee and Judea, including Jerusalem, to hear and observe Jesus. The Pharisees were a leading Jewish party, known for their strict observance of the law of Moses. They sought to apply the regulations of Moses to all aspects of life. They defined each commandment as to how it applied in every possible situation. They sought to build a hedge about the law, but their rules had the effect of externalizing religion. They endeavored to separate themselves from any kind of defilement; their goal was to keep Israel faithful to God. Most of the teachers of the law, also called scribes, were Pharisees and had made their profession the study of the law. The Pharisees became the severest of Jesus' critics.

God's power rests on Jesus so that he can heal the sick. "The power of the Lord" (v. 17) is another way Luke has of speaking about his anointing of the Spirit. Jesus does not need any endorsement from religious leaders for his ministry; the Spirit grants him authority to heal the sick. We see this authority when four men bring a paralytic to him. Jesus is in a house, and the large crowd prevents access. But through the persistence of the paralytic's companions, he is let down through the roof of the house into Jesus' presence. No doubt the crowd is expecting a miracle; his reputation as a healer has already spread (4:40–44).

Instead of healing the paralytic, however, Jesus pronounces his sins as forgiven. Jesus recognizes the faith of the four companions, singling out for the first time the importance of faith to his miracles (7:9; 8:25, 48, 50; 17:19; 18:42). The focus is on the faith of these friends, but the paralytic's faith has a deeper lesson. He needs physical and spiritual help from Jesus. He does not receive merely healing for his body but also forgiveness of his sins. Full and complete salvation that encompasses both spiritual and physical blessings depends on faith.

Thus Jesus says, "Friend, your sins are forgiven" (v. 20). The Pharisees with their critical hearts hear these words and think in themselves that only God can set us free from sin. They must be given high marks for their theology. They rightly understand that Jesus claims to do something that only God can do. But in their hearts they are accusing him of blasphemy—violating the majesty of God. For a human being to claim to perform an act that only God can do is dishonoring to God. The issue raised, therefore, is this: Does Jesus have the authority to speak this way?

Jesus realizes what the Pharisees are thinking. It is not so much that he reads their faces, but he knows by the supernatural insight of the Spirit what is in their hearts (cf. John 2:24–25). So he confronts these religious leaders with their own thoughts. "Which is easier: to say, 'Your sins are forgiven,' or to say, 'Get up and walk'?" Neither is possible for a human being. But the Pharisees do not stop and inquire whether Jesus' relationship with God is such that he can forgive sins.

Since no one can see sins vanish, it would seem easier to say sins are forgiven. At the moment of Jesus' healing, however, all can see that the paralytic has been made whole. So Jesus links together the two acts. "But that you may know that the Son of Man has authority on earth to forgive sins . . . I tell you, get up, take your mat and go home" (v. 24). Immediately, the man walks away, demonstrating that Jesus does have authority to forgive sin. Both physical and spiritual healing have their source in God. Christ deals with the man's sins first because that is his basic need. He, however, is concerned about the total person.

We meet for the first time the title "Son of Man" in Luke's Gospel—a title Jesus applies to himself in all four Gospels. This title has an Old Testament background. In the prophecies of Ezekiel "son of man" means "person" or "human being," emphasizing that a human being is weak and mortal. Ezekiel stands in contrast to the power and the majesty of God. In Daniel 7:13–14, however, "son of man" is more than an ordinary human being. In the prophet's visions the Ancient of Days entrusts the Son of Man with "authority, glory and sovereign power; all peoples, nations and men of every language worshiped him. . . . His kingdom is one that will never be destroyed." Jesus uses the title "Son of Man" to deny that he is usurping divine authority, as the religious leaders accuse him. God has sent him on the great mission as the Son of Man to forgive sins and to heal the sick. At the moment he does this to the paralyzed man, he declares his divine authority for his ministry. His authority is unique—authority that only God has. As Son of Man he suffers and seems weak and powerless; on the other hand, he is vindicated and glorified by the power of God (Mark 13:26; Luke 9:26).

The forgiveness and healing of the paralytic have a profound effect on this man. He goes away praising God (v. 25), recognizing that God has worked mightily through Jesus Christ. His response to the authoritative work of Jesus is that of saying, "I thank you, God." The onlookers, too, see God's hand, for they praise God and are "filled with awe," saying, "We have seen remarkable things today" (v. 26). The miracle of healing, which confirms the man's forgiveness, moves them to praise God and to recognize God in Jesus. God has vindicated the claims and ministry of his Son.

3.5.2. Pharisees: He Associates With Sinners (5:27–32). After healing the paralytic, Jesus goes out—either out of the house or out of Capernaum. His attention now turns to a social outcast, Levi, a tax collector (called Matthew in the first Gospel; Matt. 9:9). Not all tax collectors were employed directly by Rome. Levi and his tax collector friends probably worked for Herod Antipas, who had been granted powers of taxation. But tax collectors became notorious for extortion, lining their own pockets and becoming wealthy. They were banned from the synagogue and treated as the scum of the earth. No respectable Jew would become a tax collector (Caird, 1963, 95). At the other end of the social scale stood the Pharisees, who regarded as sinners all who did not rigidly observe the ritual laws of cleanness.

The story of Levi shows the kind of people whom Jesus calls. He ministers to the needy, whether rich or poor. He associates freely with all kinds of people, but that puts him on a collision course with the Pharisees.

Jesus initiates contact with Levi, saying to him no more than, "Follow me." The power and authority of Jesus' word, previously noted in his teaching and casting out of demons (4:31–36), are demonstrated again. Levi's response is total, instantaneous. He makes a decisive break with his old life (aorist participle) and follows Jesus from that time on (imperfect tense), just as Peter and his fishing partners did (5:11). He walks away from his tax office, which involves no small financial sacrifice. But Levi becomes known the world over, and the Gospel of which he is the author continues to make many rich. For him Jesus must be given priority.

Rather than trying to make much out of his leaving his business and sacrificing for Jesus, Levi chooses to celebrate his call to Christian discipleship (v. 29) by hosting a great banquet for Jesus at his home and inviting many tax collectors and others to attend. No doubt he wants them to join him in the new life he has found in Jesus. Since the banquet takes place at his house, it shows that he still owns the house after leaving everything (v. 28). What Levi leaves behind is his way of life, not every one of his possessions. The rich and the famous need to hear the powerful word of Jesus. It, too, can change their lives.

At the splendid banquet are Levi's old associates—"tax collectors and others" (v. 29). These "others" are identified by the Pharisees as "sinners" (v. 30), which refers to common people who give little heed to the Pharisees' strict rules of purity. Levi does not invite the Pharisees and their experts in law, but they hear what is going on and complain to Jesus' followers about their eating and drinking with tax collectors and sinners. Neither of these groups can measure up to their standards. How can Jesus and his disciples claim to be religious when they have table fellowship with such people? But Jesus refuses to run and hide from the world and its needs. His friendship with people of low social standing and societal outcasts earns him the criticism of being "a friend of tax collectors and sinners" (7:34).

Jesus replies to the concern of the Pharisees by picturing himself as a physician who treats the sick, not the healthy. A physician cannot care for the sick if he stays away from them. His duty is to deal personally with his patients in order to cure them. At the same time he takes precautions to protect himself from their infections. That is, Jesus does not become a sinner, but he closely associates himself with such people in order that he may lead them to God and to a new life. His mission is not "to call the righteous, but sinners to repentance" (v. 32).

The "righteous" here are the Pharisees, who have a high estimate of themselves. In other words, Jesus has not come to call those who claim righteousness for themselves (though, to be sure, Jesus does not endorse their self-righteousness). Rather, he has come for those who know they are sick, for they will respond to a physician. Often the unrighteous are aware of their need, but the unrighteous "righteous" are not (Bock, 1994, 108). The Pharisees should examine their sickness and see that they too need to repent. Sinners do not need to be placed under a spiritual quarantine, as the Pharisees suggest, but under the medicine of God's forgiving grace. Such medicine is administered to all who have repentant hearts.

Jesus' compassionate concern for the outcasts of society offended the religious leaders of his day. Some today are still uncomfortable with an open and inclusive ministry, but it is true to the New Testament form of evangelism. It is true also to the kind of ministry that Jesus embodies and preaches. Can his followers do otherwise?

3.5.3. Pharisees: His Disciples Do Not Fast (5:33–39). On this same occasion, the Pharisees and teachers of the law question why Jesus' disciples do not conform to the widespread practice of fasting. This is another reminder that Jesus' disciples march to a different drummer. The Holy Spirit opens up new and fresh ways.

After Jesus and his disciples have left the house of Levi, his disciples appear too cheerful to the Jewish religious leaders. They do not practice fasting as do the disciples of John the Baptist and the Pharisees themselves (who go without food twice a week, 18:12). They therefore ask Jesus why. Nothing is said about Jesus directly, though their primary concern is with him. They know that he does things differently when it comes to practices like fasting and prayers at fixed hours.

Fasting had a significant place in ancient Judaism. It was regarded as an important act of worship. The Old Testament requires fasting only on the Day of Atonement (Lev. 16:29). Fasts could also be signs of remorse (1 Kings 21:27) or be associated with a solemn assembly (Joel 1:14) and with mourning (Est. 4:3). By the time of Jesus fasting had become a devotional exercise valued for its own merit. In no way did Jesus oppose fasting as long as its true meaning was observed (Matt. 6:17). Jesus himself fasted (Luke 4:2), as did the early church (Acts 13:2–3; 14:23).

Jesus answers the Pharisees, not only explaining why his disciples do not fast, but also explaining the significance of his presence. He compares himself to a bridegroom. No one expects a wedding party to fast as long as the bridegroom is still present. Thus, as long as Christ remains with his disciples, the time is not for fasting but for celebration. His presence marks the beginning of a new era. Jesus does, however, foresee the day when he "will be taken from them" (v. 35). This must refer to the cross; "will be taken" (*aparthe*) suggests violent removal by force and is another way of saying "will be killed." When that day comes, fasting will be appropriate. But even then fasting remains a voluntary spiritual discipline. Jesus never makes it a requirement, though it can be a beneficial discipline in the Christian life.

The question of fasting is part of a larger concern; the gospel expresses faith in Jesus in a new way of life. The good news calls for a life that is radically new. To make this point Jesus uses two illustrations, which he calls "parables." The first comes from the practice of patching clothes. No one takes a piece of new cloth and sews it on an old garment. Should someone do that, it creates two problems: The new patch with greater strength will make a tear in the old garment, and the new one will not match the old. Jesus introduces a new era of grace and faith. It demands new ways, different from the old ways of the Pharisees.

The second illustration involves wine and wineskins. Combining the old and new can be disastrous. New wineskins are elastic; but as they age, they become brittle and lose their quality. As new wine ferments in old wineskins, it bursts the skins and the wine is lost. New wine must be put into fresh wineskins (v. 38). The gospel brings a radically new approach to God. The teachings of Jesus and the new vision of God cannot be contained in the old practices of Judaism. Jesus knows that some, such as the Pharisees, will prefer the old (v. 39) and will refuse to taste the new wine of the gospel. In fact, they will reject the new teaching and the new ways of righteousness and purity.

One of the main issues the church in Acts struggled with was the new ways of the gospel versus the old practices of Judaism. What is required for salvation—circumcision and other Jewish rites, or faith alone? Under the direction of the Spirit the church concluded that faith is sufficient (Acts 15:22–29). Jesus has brought a new spiritual order that calls for a new life. It is not motivated by law and rigid traditions, but by the power and the guidance of the Holy Spirit. Relying on the Spirit brings a new dynamic and freshness to our walk with Christ.

3.5.4. Pharisees: He Breaks the Sabbath (6:1–11). Luke's account moves to another conflict between Jesus and the Pharisees, one that centers around what can be done on the Sabbath, the holy day of rest and worship. In all four of the controversies in 5:17–6:11 the Pharisees see Jesus as a threat, and on each occasion they question his authority. They fail to recognize that in him the promised kingdom of God has arrived and that he possesses a unique authority to forgive sins and to bring joy in the place of mourning and a deeper rest than the rest on the Sabbath.

3.5.4.1. Disciples Harvest Grain (6:1–5). Jesus' opponents ("some of the Pharisees," v. 2) accuse his disciples of breaking the Sabbath by picking and eating grain. On the other six days of the week, it would have been all right for them to do this as they walked through a wheat field, but not on the Sabbath. The issue here is not theft but work: The Pharisees insist that such activity is not permitted on the Sabbath.

Jesus replies that his disciples are fully consistent with what the Old Testament allows. According to 1 Samuel 21:1–9, when David was fleeing from Saul, he and his men became hungry. They entered the house of God at Nob and ate the consecrated bread that only priests were permitted to eat (cf. Lev. 24:9). Similar to David, Jesus has a responsibility for seeing to it that his disciples have enough to eat, and what the disciples are doing has been authorized by Jesus. David's authority equals that of the priest. Similarly, Jesus interprets the law of the Sabbath with equal authority to that of the teachers of the law and the Pharisees.

His authority, however, goes far beyond theirs: "The Son of Man is Lord of the Sabbath" (6:5). As "Lord" Jesus possesses authority over laws and religious institutions. If David can override the law of the consecrated bread without blame, how much more can the Lord of the Sabbath do the same! Superior to the Sabbath, Jesus can do what he wishes with the Sabbath. He can determine how, when, and where the Sabbath law applies. He interprets the law here to show that God is more concerned with the needs of his people than with rigid rules for holy days. Human needs override the outward form of religion.

3.5.4.2. Jesus Heals a Crippled Hand (6:6–11). The Pharisees' opposition to Jesus continues to build. These leaders have been observing him, but now their hostility reaches a greater intensity. They begin to "watch him closely" (*pareterounto*), which means that they are spying on him (v. 7). The occasion is another Sabbath (v. 6), and the Pharisees are waiting to see if he will heal a man with a crippled hand on that day. If he does, they will have grounds on which to bring charges against him.

Again, the Spirit-anointed Jesus discerns the evil thoughts of his opponents. He does not wait for them to launch their attack against him, but he takes the offensive by bringing it out into the open. Like spies they want to conceal their evil intent against him, but Jesus counters with a command that the man with the deformed hand step forward and stand with him. Then he poses a question: "Which is lawful on the Sabbath: to do good or to do evil, to save life or to destroy it?" These questions refute the Pharisees' assumption that to heal on the Sabbath violates the law. Love, which is the spirit of the law, calls for us to do good to one another at all times.

To defend their view of the Sabbath, the Pharisees are plotting to do harm to Jesus. Who, then, is transgressing the Sabbath? Who is sinning in the name of righteousness? The man before him has a handicap, and Jesus has an opportunity to minister to a need on the Sabbath and to enable the man to live free of his disability. Looking around to see if any of his opponents will reply, he commands the man to stretch out his hand. At once it becomes strong and healthy.

That is faith. That is manifestation of the healing power of God. But the Pharisees are more determined now to stop Jesus. They are filled with violent anger and do not know what they can do to stop his blasphemous actions. Though Jesus has done nothing but good to others, his ministry has attracted opposition. The opposition's resolve is building and becoming deadly serious. Often unrepented sin leads to more sin and blindly places blame on others.

3.6. Jesus Chooses Twelve Apostles (6:12–16)

The preceding events have demonstrated conflicts with the Pharisees and the increasing opposition to Jesus. As the hostility of the religious leaders mounts, Jesus withdraws to the hills and spends a whole night in prayer. Again we see how important prayer is to Jesus. He prayed as the Holy Spirit descended on him and filled him (3:21). When the crowds began to flock to him, he found it necessary to withdraw and have communion with his Father (5:16). Now he faces a momentous decision, the choosing of twelve men who will carry on the work after him.

As of yet, of course, there has been no clear-cut conspiracy to take his life. But he knows that when he is taken out of the picture, leaders must be in place to continue his ministry. In preparing to make the choice, Jesus spends an entire night in prayer, which stresses the importance of God's guidance in the selection of the Twelve. Later Luke tells about the commissioning of Barnabas and Paul, who were set apart for ministry in the context of fasting, prayer, and worship (Acts 13:1–3). In fact, the Holy Spirit specifically directed the church to consecrate them to the ministry for which God had called them. Without doubt the Holy Spirit has a role here in Jesus' choice of the Twelve.

The present passage reveals a number of significant facts. (1) Jesus chooses the Twelve from a larger group of disciples (v. 13). The number is significant; it recalls the twelve patriarchs of Israel and the twelve tribes. The Twelve represent the new Israel, the new people of God, whom Jesus is establishing. These people are new and distinct from the nation of Israel, but at the same time they experience the fulfillment of the promises made to the nation.

(2) The Twelve Jesus designates as "apostles." The term *apostle* (*apostolos*) refers to a person who is commissioned for a specific task and who exercises the authority of the one who sent him. It is the task of the Twelve to preach the kingdom of God, to cast out demons, and to heal the sick (9:1–2). Under the guidance of Jesus these twelve men will receive special training for leading the church. They will form a special core of eyewitnesses to the ministry of Jesus and his resurrection (Acts 1:21–22).

(3) Jesus chooses to work through ordinary people. Little or nothing is known about a number of the apostles as individuals. Among them are fishermen like Peter, Andrew, James, and John, and a despised tax collector, Matthew. Simon the Zealot has belonged to a radical revolutionary group dedicated to the violent resistance of Rome. Aware that Judas will betray Christ, Luke keeps before us the shadow that the cross casts upon the entire ministry of Christ (Marshall, 1978, 241). The fall of Judas reminds us that a person with great spiritual blessings can forfeit them by sin.

3.7. The Great Sermon on the Plain (6:17–49)

In this section Jesus' teaching provides a model for discipleship in the church. He teaches here "on a level place." This fact has influenced students of Scripture to call this unit the Sermon on the Plain. There are many similarities between this message and the Sermon on the Mount in Matthew 5–7. Each sermon includes some of Jesus' most important teachings on how disciples are to live and relate to others. So that the Twelve and others may build their lives around his teaching, Jesus wants them to understand the implications of discipleship.

3.7.1. Introduction to the Sermon (6:17–19). After a night of prayer in the hills Jesus ministers on a plain. He and the Twelve are joined by "a large crowd of his disciples" and "a great number of people" (v. 17). Many of these people have not yet become his disciples. Some have heard about his teaching and want to hear more; others want to be healed of their diseases and to be set free from evil spirits. Jesus carries on his preaching and healing ministry together. Indeed, the two are twin aspects of his ministry of compassion and love. His ministry of preaching is no less a sign of compassion than are his healing miracles (Matt. 9:36–38).

The people troubled by evil spirits are delivered and the sick try to touch him "because power was coming from him and healing them all" (v. 19). God accepts their faith, and out of the Spirit-anointed Jesus comes spiritual power for healing. Jesus' power, however, extends beyond the authority to heal, for he also teaches with great authority. Here the healings set the stage for the great sermon that follows.

3.7.2. Blessings and Woes (6:20–26). In general this sermon describes the life of the new people of God. This life is lived out in the kingdom of God, which is already breaking into the present through Jesus. In contrast to the Pharisees, his teaching emphasizes attitudes, motives, and purity of heart rather than religious ceremony and externals. Such spiritual health grows out of the experience of the kingdom, which transforms our lives by true repentance and faith.

Jesus begins by announcing four blessings and four woes. "Blessed" (*makarios*) means joyful, happy, or fortunate. Jesus pronounces as blessed the poor, the hungry, those who weep, and those who are persecuted for the sake of the Son of Man (vv. 20–22). Such people are fortunate because they receive the kingdom now and are promised blessings later, including satisfaction, laughter, and eternal bliss. Instead of grieving over the painful experiences of life, they will rejoice and leap for gladness (v. 23). They stand in the godly order of the prophets, who suffered greatly for righteousness. In God's bank in heaven is a great reward for all who suffer for Christ's sake. Commitment to Jesus can lead to rejection and persecution; the beatitudes serve to comfort all who belong to Christ and who live under the rule of God.

The four woes are the opposite of the beatitudes. "Woe" (*ouai*) expresses a combination of condemnation and regret. Jesus turns the world's values up side down and pronounces woes on those who are without the rule of God in their lives—the rich, the well-fed, the superficially happy, and the popular (vv. 24–26).

When Jesus says, "Blessed are you who are poor" but "woe to you who are rich," he is not making poverty a virtue and the possession of wealth a sin. But he knows the spiritual perils that wealth often brings to the souls of people. Many who are the rich in this world's goods think that they have no need of God and can do without pardon of their sins and the promise of heaven. They are satisfied with themselves and have no time for repentance and no desire to trust in Christ and his grace for salvation. Assuming that they have all that is worth having, they have no hunger for the things of God. They take life lightly and laugh at the blessings of the kingdom and the life to come. They are satisfied with their achievements and the applause of those who want their favor. But only false prophets enjoy the acclaim of the world. Thus Jesus warns those who are tempted to please the world and to win its applause: You are in the position of false prophets.

The values by which the world lives are not God's values. New life in Christ reverses the world's values. Blessed are those whose poverty, hunger, and sorrow make them open to the good news of the kingdom. God will reign in their lives. Their hunger for spiritual things will be satisfied. Their cause for sorrow will be removed, and they can laugh with joy again.

On the other hand, woe to those whose wealth, abundance of food, and trouble-free life blind them to their need of the peace and salvation of God. Their earthly possessions will be their only comfort. Though they are now well fed, they will remain spiritually poor and lost. Though they have a pleasant life now, the tables will be turned, and in the future they will mourn and weep. They may enjoy great popularity in the eyes of the masses, but woe to those who, like the false prophets, refuse to make a genuine commitment to God and serve him as true disciples. Ahead lies the terrible day of judgment—but also the day of reward for those who find God as their reward.

3.7.3. Love for Enemies (6:27–36). Jesus now addresses his disciples in particular, as distinct from the people alluded to in verses 24–26 and those whom he calls "sinners" (vv. 32–34). The Holy Spirit dwells in each of the disciples. As a result they have experienced a new life in the Spirit, and the Spirit has given them a new heart so that they can love even their enemies.

Love can easily be misunderstood and reduced to warm sentiment or affection. The Greek language has several words for love. *Eros* refers to sexual or romantic love, *storge* to family affection, and *philia* to affection of friends. But Jesus calls for none of these here. His call is for Christian love (*agape*), which is the way God loves us and desires us to love others. *Agape* is an active, gracious, persistent interest in the welfare of others. This dimension of love results from the Spirit's opening our eyes so that we no longer view people from a worldly standpoint, that is, whether they serve our interests or not (2 Cor. 5:16). We see them through the light that the Spirit provides to us and as people for whom Christ died. Such love remains viable, even in the face of hatred, cursing, and abuse.

Our supreme example for love is God himself: "God so loved the world that he gave . . ." (John 3:16). The followers of Christ can show God's love no better than by doing good to their personal enemies (v. 27). The fundamental requirement of love unfolds in the three commands: "Do good to those who hate you, bless those who curse you, pray for those who mistreat you" (vv. 27–28). Love does not call for emotion or feelings but for actions that give back good for evil. Normally enemies hurt us, but love absorbs the hurt. It involves more than not trying to get even; it responds to hate, cursing, and abuse with good, blessing, and prayer. Love demands that we deny ourselves and serve others. We are not to let personal enemies determine our lifestyle.

Jesus gives three concrete examples of genuine love. (1) "If someone strikes you on one cheek, turn to him the other also." The natural reaction is to strike back, but the followers of Christ must not seek revenge. They must minister to others and be willing to expose themselves to further injury. (2) "If someone takes your [outer garment], do not stop him from taking [your inner one]." The point is that the followers of Jesus must resist angry passion against the robber. They have the responsibility of manifesting generosity in all situations. Love must be ready to make great sacrifice and suffer loss if necessary. (3) Love expects nothing in return (v. 30). Jesus wants his followers to avoid ungodly passions and desires. They may suffer the loss of their things at the hands of evil persons, but they must bear no malice toward those who have wrongfully taken their resources. The highest example is the cross, where Jesus gave to those who had taken from him.

These three concrete illustrations must be taken seriously, but they are to be applied with wisdom. Love never fosters irresponsibility, abuse, dishonesty, or greed. For example, acting for the good of others at times may not call for turning the other cheek or giving them everything they demand (Dean, 1983, 51). Christian love, however, does require sacrificial action and far surpasses the world's standard of love. It is a giving to others with no demands or expectation they will return the favor. Jesus sums up his main point in the so-called Golden Rule: "Do to others as you would have them to do to you" (v. 31; cf. Lev. 19:18). How do we want others to treat us? Then treat them the same way, regardless of how they may respond.

Most sinners have an ethic of love! They "love those who love [them]" (v. 32). They will return good for good and evil for evil. But Jesus teaches us to return good for both evil and good. After all, what is so honorable about loving those who love us? Even sinners go that far. The children of God must go further. They have been transformed by the Holy Spirit to live in contrast to the way sinners live. Loving only those who love us is selfishness; there is nothing particularly praiseworthy in that. Jesus calls his followers to love enemies and the unlovable as well as lovable, and to expect nothing in return (vv. 34–35). To love like that is totally unlike the love of sinners.

We who reflect the love of God to the world are promised: "Your reward will be great, and you will be sons of the Most High." God will reward our love, and we will show ourselves to be his children. The Most High delights to reward those who yield to the Holy Spirit and have generous hearts like their heavenly Father. Our likeness to him will reveal that we are his children.

This call to radical love includes especially mercy (v. 36). God shows kindness to the unthankful and the evil. His very character is mercy, for he shows compassion toward all. Jesus urges his followers to be the same—merciful to everyone. As members of the heavenly family we must strive to pass on God's blessings, including mercy, to others.

3.7.4. Judging Others (6:37–45). Jesus' warning against being overly critical of others follows his call to be merciful as God is. We should not conclude that he wants us to close our eyes to sin. Being merciful makes no demand that we suspend moral judgment of wrongdoing. Jesus himself rebuked the Pharisees for their hypocrisy and sins (11:37–54). We must distinguish between good and evil. Resisting evil in ourselves and in others requires us to exercise judgment and discernment.

But Jesus does condemn hasty and harsh judgment of others. His followers must guard against a readiness to judge and condemn—literally, "Stop habitually judging" and "Stop habitually condemning" (v. 37). A critical faultfinding attitude makes ministry and reconciliation impossible. If we are gracious and forgiving of others, they will treat us likewise; but if we are constant critics of others, they will return the same. The words "you will not be judged" and "you will not be condemned" may refer to God, meaning that we will not be condemned in the final judgment. That is, those who refrain from becoming harshly judgmental will be treated mercifully on the Day of Judgment.

Jesus does not teach a salvation by works. He does, however, indicate that his true followers must be fair, not cruel, and must forgive, not hold grudges. The divine pattern is "Give, and it shall be given to you" (v. 38). If we forgive freely those who have inflicted personal insults and injuries on us, we are promised a divine reward. Forgiving such offenses against us is in accordance with God's grace and love. God approves of this kind of action and rewards generosity.

To the liberal giver God will give "a [full] measure, pressed down, shaken together and running over." This kind of language has in view the measuring of grain that graphically pictures a superabundance of blessings. The word "lap" (*kolpos*) refers to the fold in an outer garment, used as a large pocket. The practice of love and mercy will ensure us of a great reward in heaven: God will be as generous to us as we have been to others.

Jesus uses a number of illustrations. (1) He raises two questions (v. 39). Can a blind person show the way to another blind person? The particle (*meti*) expects the answer "No, the blind leaders will mislead their followers." The second question (introduced by *ouchi*) expects the answer "Yes, both will fall into a pit." Should the disciples place their trust in religious leaders like the Pharisees, the results will be spiritual disaster. Such leaders can see the sins of others, but they are blind to their own.

(2) Students depend on the guidance given by a teacher (v. 40). Thus, they must see to it that they choose the right teacher. Their progress is limited by the influence of the teacher's character as well as by the information they receive. A disciple never rises above his or her teacher. This reflects the days of Jesus, when a student had only his rabbi as a source of information. That has changed now, with libraries and other learning resources. Even so, disciples remain disciples, and a teacher still has great influence on them. For this reason they must choose the right leader and teacher.

Above all others Jesus' disciples must follow him and his message. Those who follow blind and hypocritical leaders, such as the Pharisees, can expect to be no different. The way to build a firm foundation for our lives is to follow the teachings and example of Jesus as set forth in God's Word. Those who do likewise are also worth listening to. We must be slow to judge but careful whom we follow.

(3) Jesus uses the humorous illustration of the speck of sawdust and the plank of wood (vv. 41–42). Here again he is warning against a judgmental attitude. It borders on the ridiculous for a person with a plank in his eye to try to remove a speck of sawdust from his brother's eye. Before trying to improve the spiritual condition of others by correcting their minor faults, we should consider our own faults and sin. Jesus is not warning here against examining the lives of others, but we are to do so with a careful eye on ourselves and our own failures. Nothing will make us more aware of our constant need of God's grace and of the help of the Spirit. Genuine humility cleanses the heart of false pride and a judgmental spirit.

Those who pretend not to see their own failures and mistakes—i.e., have a plank in their eye—but spend their time finding faults in others are "hypocrites." They are play-acting, pretending to be righteous and good when in reality their lives contradict their claims. They need to judge themselves and deal with their serious faults before trying to correct minor faults in others.

(4) Jesus continues with another illustration: the good tree and the bad tree (vv. 43–45). Trees are known for the kind of fruit they bear. Bad trees produce bad fruit and good trees good fruit. Thornbushes and briars cannot make figs or grapes. The fruit produced by a tree reveals its true nature. In like manner a good person will produce good fruit. The fruit one bears comes out of "the good stored up in his heart." His heart has been changed by God's grace, and he obeys God's Word. As a result he brings forth good in thought, word, and deed.

Those products reflect our inner character, which Jesus calls the heart, where good or bad things accumulate. Our words and deeds reveal what we have stored up in our hearts. If good, we bring forth good things; if bad, we bring forth bad things. What we say reveals our character. "For out of the overflow of his heart his mouth speaks."

3.7.5. A Picture of Two Houses (6:46–49). The Sermon on the Plain ends with a strong challenge to put into practice the teachings of Jesus. Matthew gives more details of this part of the sermon, but Luke makes clear that the major issue for the disciples is a firm commitment to obeying Jesus. Basic to obedience is walking with him. So discipleship does not rest on keeping rules but on a viable relationship with Jesus, from which should emerge a life of faithfulness.

If we claim to be faithful followers, our actions should not fail to match what we profess. Aware that actions may contradict words, Jesus issues a rebuke in verse 46: "Why do you call me, 'Lord, Lord,' and do not do what I say?" This rhetorical question warns against fake disciples, who by their deeds deny Jesus' prophetic authority over them. His authority goes far beyond that of a teacher; he is their *Lord*. "Lord" here has a deeper significance than merely an address of respect. As the divine, Spirit-anointed Lord, he has authority to command obedience. But Jesus knows that some who confess him as Lord fail to be faithful to him. The confession of Jesus as Lord is appropriate (Rom. 10:9; Phil. 2:9–11), but regardless of how fervent our confession is, there can be no substitute for doing his words. To live under his Lordship spells obedience.

Jesus concludes the great sermon with a parable about two houses, which reinforces the importance of putting his words into practice. One man builds his house on a solid rock. He knows what must go into a sound building. So he digs deep into the ground until he finds a solid rock on which to build. It takes time and is hard work, but the work is not in vain. The rock gives the house a secure foundation. In the winter when harsh weather comes and storms rage, this house stands. Nothing can move it. This house represents a life built on the solid rock of Jesus' words. In this life storms and trials will occur, but faithful followers of Jesus have divine strength to withstand its difficulties. By obeying Jesus they have built their lives on the most secure foundation.

In contrast, those who hear the words of Jesus but fail to accept him are like the man who builds his house on top of the ground without a firm foundation. Though the house may be attractive and appear strong, it cannot withstand bad weather. As soon as the river floods and torrents begin to beat against the house, it collapses, for there is no underlying rock to sustain it. The warning is clear: If we hear and do not obey Jesus' words, we are inviting disaster.

3.8. Jesus' Power over Sickness and Death (7:1–17)

Jesus' miracles reveal his compassion toward people. He acts out of compassion when he heals the centurion's servant (vv. 1–10) and raises a widow's son from the dead (vv. 11–17). These two miracles also demonstrate his authority over sickness and death and show that Jesus is a prophet like Elijah and Elisha, both of whom raised the dead.

3.8.1. Healing of a Roman Officer's Servant (7:1–10). After the Sermon on the Plain (6:17–49), Jesus goes back to Capernaum, his home base in Galilee. A Roman centurion stationed there has a servant who has become deathly ill, and he wants him healed. A centurion was in charge of about a hundred soldiers and was equivalent to an army captain in modern times.

This Roman officer, highly respected by local Jews, has heard about Jesus' miracle-working power. He sends some Jewish elders of the local synagogue to ask Jesus for this healing. In doing so, he is reflecting cultural sensitivity, for he is aware of some Jews' reluctance to associate with Gentiles. Knowing that Jesus is of Jewish heritage, he asks representatives of that same background to plead for his help. The Jewish elders make that request as a personal favor for the centurion. They present his case so as not to offend Jesus and to make the prospect of his help more likely. The cultural sensitivity of the centurion emphasizes the importance of respect for ethnic diversity and shows that people from different backgrounds can live and work together.

The Roman centurion is no ordinary soldier. While making their request, the Jewish elders refer to his worthiness rather than appeal to Jesus' compassion and character. As they present this case to Jesus, they do more than make him aware of the specific need. They insist earnestly that he should grant the request. They specify two reasons: (1) The centurion has a loving attitude toward the Jewish people and thus a deep appreciation for the nation of Israel; (2) he has expressed his love by building their synagogue in Capernaum. He must have been a man of considerable means; his love and generosity have prompted him to go far beyond the call of duty.

Jesus makes no comment about the merits of the Jews' appeal. Rather, he simply leaves with them immediately. This response demonstrates his positive attitude toward Gentiles. Although initially Jesus ministers to the lost sheep of the house of Israel, he makes no ethnic distinctions in his ministry. After his resurrection he empowers the disciples with the Holy Spirit and through them extends his ministry to the world (24:48–49; Acts 1:8; cf. Eph. 2:14–17).

As Jesus makes his way to the centurion's house, the Roman officer sends a group of his friends to Jesus to inform him that he does not want Jesus to bother to come all the way to his house; he feels unworthy to have this great teacher from God under his roof. He also may have thought that as a religious Jew, Jesus might have reservations about entering the home of a Gentile. The centurion also manifests a remarkable confidence in Jesus' power to heal his servant, for as far as he is concerned, the only thing necessary for Jesus is to say the word and his servant will be well.

This soldier knows something about authority. He is a man under his superiors and has authority over soldiers of lower rank. He knows firsthand what it is to give an order and have it obeyed. He needs only to speak to have his commands carried out; he does not even need to be present. Similarly, the centurion recognizes that Jesus receives his authority from a higher source, namely, God himself. He is convinced that Jesus needs only to speak a word and his servant will be healed.

Jesus is amazed at the faith of this Gentile. Only one other place in the New Testament are we told that Jesus' reaction is amazement. In Nazareth he performs only a few miracles and is amazed at their unbelief (Mark 6:6; cf. Matt. 8:10). The evidence of faith manifested by the centurion gives Jesus unexpected joy and moves him to issue this commendation: "I tell you, I have not found such great faith even in Israel." Jesus realizes that this Gentile recognizes the extraordinary power of Jesus, something that the Jews by and large have failed to acknowledge.

Luke does not indicate whether Jesus says anything regarding the healing of the centurion's servant. But when the messengers return to the house, they find the servant well. This miracle affirms the faith of a Gentile.

3.8.2. Raising a Widow's Son From the Dead (7:11–17). Soon after healing the centurion's servant, Jesus leaves Capernaum and travels about a day's journey to the town of Nain. Earlier in Israel's history, Elisha had raised a mother's son from the dead (2 Kings 4:18–37). No doubt the people remember that miracle performed by the prophet of God.

Jesus is enjoying popularity among the people, and a large crowd accompanies him and his disciples to Nain. As they approach the town gate, they meet a funeral procession. The procession is leaving through the gate to mourn and bury a widow's only son, who has probably died earlier that day. Jewish tradition encouraged a quick burial to avoid ceremonial uncleanness. The body has already been anointed and prepared for burial to prevent deterioration. As Jesus suggests in verse 14, the deceased is a "young man," probably in his late teens or early twenties. Thus he has suffered an untimely death.

The mother's grief is compounded by the fact that he is her only son. Being a widow, she now most likely has no means of support and no one to protect her. As we have observed Jesus shows deep concern for the poor and the outcasts of society. When he sees the grieving widow, he recognizes her intense pain. Moved with great compassion (*splanchnizomai*), he takes the initiative. First, he tells her, "Don't cry." These words come from his heart; they are not commanding words but words of comfort. God is the Father of the fatherless and a defender of widows (Ps. 68:5). As Lord, Jesus shows here his heavenly Father's compassion toward this woman now alone.

After speaking to the weeping widow, Jesus walks over and touches the wooden stretcher on which the body of the young man is lying. Immediately those who are carrying it stop. No doubt they expect something extraordinary to happen. Without hesitation Jesus speaks to the corpse with these words: "Young man, I say to you, get up!" Without divine authority Jesus' command would be the height of absurdity. But he speaks the word, and a miracle takes place. Because Jesus has authority over death, the young man responds by sitting up and talking. Death had taken the son away from his mother, but Jesus restores him to her. Jesus does not take the opportunity to instruct the crowd. He allows the miracle to speak for itself.

The people recognize that they have seen a miracle of God. Sensing God's presence, they are filled with fear and praise him. They also recognize that God has worked through Jesus and declare, "God has come to help his people." Possibly the crowd remembers Elisha when they call Jesus "a great prophet." This is a title of honor, and such a recognition is indeed important. But their estimate of Jesus is inadequate. He is more than a prophet; he is Lord and Savior. Because of his marvelous works his fame spreads throughout Judea and surrounding regions.

3.9. John the Baptist and Jesus (7:18–35)

Earlier Luke told about Herod Antipas locking up John the Baptist in prison (3:19–20).

This section speaks of John for the first time since the beginning of Jesus' Spirit-anointed ministry. John is still in prison and apparently unable to have any direct contact with Jesus, but John's disciples inform him about everything that Jesus has been doing in his Spirit-filled ministry (v. 18). Thus, in prison John the Baptist hears about Jesus' extraordinary ministry, such as the healing of the Roman officer's servant (7:1–10), the raising of the widow's son from the dead (7:11–17), and Jesus' Spirit-inspired teachings (6:17–49).

3.9.1. Messengers From John the Baptist (7:18–23). Hearing about Jesus' ministry, John sends two of his disciples with a question: "Are you the one who was to come, or should we expect someone else?" (v. 19). This question echoes John the Baptist's own preaching of Jesus as the "more powerful" Coming One (3:16). The title "Coming One" was not widely used for the Messiah; nevertheless, for John it refers to the Messiah. Like Jesus he probably avoids the term "Messiah" to guard against the people taking it in a political sense and trying to make Jesus a deliverer from Roman oppression.

What prompts the forerunner to ask whether Jesus is the one to come? He used to preach Jesus as the Messiah endowed with the Spirit, as one who would baptize God's people with the Spirit, and as one who would bring judgment, swinging a winnowing fork and burning up "the chaff with unquenchable fire" (3:17). Yet John has heard nothing about striking works of judgment. Though Jesus has performed miracles, his ministry has failed to measure up to John's expectation. Doubt begins to creep into his heart. Expecting Christ to destroy the power of darkness and to judge the wicked, the Baptist is disappointed and has doubts about the coming reign of God. As great a prophet as John is, Scripture pictures him as a fallible man. Prisons, disappointments, unfulfilled hopes, and shattered dreams can cast doubts in the minds of the great spiritual leaders like John. When God acts in surprising ways, we, too, can become perplexed.

When John's two disciples come to Jesus, he continues his preaching and healing ministry in their presence (v. 21). After a considerable time, he answers their question. He tells them to report to John what they have seen him doing and have heard: "The blind receive sight, the lame walk, those who have leprosy are cured, the deaf hear, the dead are raised, and the good news is preached to the poor" (v. 22). In the Greek all the verbs are present tenses, referring to what is happening regularly. As the Old Testament parallels reflect, Jesus' miraculous works and his preaching have messianic significance (Isa. 35:5–6; 61:1–2) and point to his Spirit-anointed authority. His ministry continues to follow the program that he announced in Luke 4:18–19.

True, John the Baptist has prophesied about the coming of divine judgment. But Jesus reminds him that the Old Testament speaks about the Messiah as one who ministers to the blind, the lame, lepers, the deaf, the dead, and the poor. Jesus is devoted to deeds of mercy. His ministry is filled with the power of God and is evidence of the fulfillment of messianic prophecies.

John the Baptist wants more proof. Jesus adds a warning: "Blessed is the man who does not fall away on account of me" (v. 23). The term "fall away" (*skandalizo*) means "to cause to stumble" or "to be offended." Here it refers to someone falling away as a result of being offended by what Jesus does or does not do. Jesus wants John and others to know that blessings come to those who are not offended by his ministry. We are to avoid taking offense at his extraordinary ministry. As Luke indicates, everyone who is not fully satisfied with what Jesus does finds himself or herself on the brink of unbelief (11:14–54). To be offended by Jesus shows nothing less than rejection of him (11:38, 52). Partial belief is never enough; doubts about the claims of Jesus as the divine Messiah can have disastrous results of forfeiting the blessedness of God's kingdom.

3.9.2. Jesus' Estimate of John (7:24–30). Because Jesus' ministry has failed to fulfill all John's expectations, the Baptist has doubts about Jesus as the Messiah. Jesus has given him a strong warning, but he does not say that John is out of the kingdom. In fact, after John's messengers have gone, Jesus delivers a powerful tribute to him as a courageous prophet.

The Savior raises a number of rhetorical questions to the crowd who have heard his warning to John. He does not want them to draw the wrong conclusions, so he takes the opportunity to tell them the kind of prophet John is and what God has done through him. When John was preaching in the desert, what did crowds go out to observe (v. 24)? They did not see a man like a reed that was swayed by the wind. Rather, they saw a man with strong convictions, not influenced by public opinion. John took a firm stand, the opposite of a reed that shakes at every puff of wind.

On the other hand, they did not look for a man wearing fancy clothes and living in luxury (v. 25). That kind of man might have been found in a king's palace but never in the desert. "But what did you go out to see?" (v. 26). Jesus answers his own question. "A prophet? Yes, I tell you, and more than a prophet." Should he have been ranked with the prophets of the Old Testament, John would be at the top. He is, however, more than a prophet; he fulfills the promise of Malachi 3:1 as the messenger who prepared the way of the Lord. His being the forerunner of the Messiah accounts for his greatness. He called the people to a change of heart and life so that they would be prepared for salvation. He pointed to Jesus as the Savior. John had an important role in announcing the presence of the Savior and his work of salvation.

Jesus praises a great man—greater than all the prophets. In fact, "among those born of women there is no one greater than John" (v. 28). Yet although he is the greatest of all the messengers sent by God, "the one who is least in the kingdom of God is greater than he." The most insignificant believer in Jesus towers above John. Not that John is excluded from the kingdom, but he is the forerunner only and stands between the old and new eras.

There is a great difference between the old era of the prophets and the new era tied to the redeeming work of Jesus. John belongs to the day of promise and does not have the privilege of the full light of the gospel. Being in prison, he has not witnessed the extraordinary ministry of Jesus, and he will die before the death and resurrection of the Savior. Those who share in the blessings of the kingdom enjoy absolute greatness. The age of fulfillment has begun, and to trust in Jesus—to have a place in God's kingdom—is more important than being a great prophet. In no way does Jesus deny John's importance, but he does show the supreme importance of membership in the kingdom.

Many take verses 29–30 as a comment by Luke. But the phrase "Jesus' words" (NIV) does not appear in the Greek text. These verses, therefore, can equally be taken as part of what Jesus says to the crowd about the various reactions to John's preaching.[10] When the common people and tax collectors heard John the Baptist, they acknowledged that God is right. That is, they "justified" (*edikaiosan*, "acknowledged as righteous") God—declaring God just and his ways right by accepting John's message of repentance and baptism. But the Pharisees and the experts in Jewish law rejected John's preaching. They refused God's plan and closed their hearts to his call for baptism. Often self-satisfied and smug people do not sense a need to repent. They reject God's way. But many common people respond to the call of the gospel to repent and be saved.

3.9.3. A Parable of Spoiled Children (7:31–35). The religious leaders and others among the people have refused to listen to John the Baptist and Jesus. Those who listen to neither are referred to here as "the people of this generation" (v. 31). There is no way of pleasing these people with their fickle notions and moods.

This generation's scornful rejection provides the springboard for Jesus' questions: "To what, then, can I compare the people of this generation? What are they like?" Answering again his own questions (cf. vv. 24–28), he observes that these people are like children who can never be pleased. Their playmates can never get these children to play with them when they make music in the marketplace. If they hear music suitable for a wedding, they refuse to dance; if they hear a funeral dirge, they do not mourn. No matter how hard their companions try to persuade them, they refuse to dance or weep.

Jesus applies this stinging illustration to this unbelieving generation (vv. 33–34). They complain about both John the Baptist and Jesus. John comes abstaining from bread and wine, eating only locusts and wild honey (Mark 1:6). Though he takes a disciplined approach to living, he does not have the favor of his fellows. They are uncomfortable with his preaching of repentance and coming judgment. They consider there must be something wrong with a man who lives as he does. So they link him with evil and write him off as demon-possessed.

At the same time, these same people are displeased with Jesus' association with all

PARABLES OF JESUS

Name of Parable	Matthew	Mark	Luke
Lamp under bowl	Mt 5:14–15	Mk 4:21–22	Lk 8:16; 11:33
Wise and foolish builders	Mt 7:24–27		Lk 6:47–49
New cloth on an old coat	Mt 9:16	Mk 2:21	Lk 5:36
New wine in old wineskins	Mt 9:17	Mk 2:22	Lk 5:37–38
Sower and the soils	Mt 13:3–8, 18ff	Mk 4:3–8,14f	Lk 8:5–8, 11ff
Weeds	Mt 13:24–30, 36f		
Mustard seed	Mt 13:31–32	Mk 4:30–32	Lk 13:18–19
Yeast	Mt 13:33		Lk 13:20–21
Hidden treasure	Mt 13:44		
Valuable pearl	Mt 13:45–46		
Net	Mt 13:47–50		
Owner of a house	Mt 13:52		
Lost sheep	Mt 18:12–14		Lk 15:4–7
Unmerciful servant	Mt 18:23–34		
Workers in the vineyard	Mt 20:1–16		
Two sons	Mt 21:28–32		
Tenants	Mt 21:33–44	Mk 12:1–11	Lk 20:9–18
Wedding banquet	Mt 22:2–14		
Fig tree	Mt 24:32–35	Mk 13:28–29	Lk 21:29–31
Faithful and wise servant	Mt 24:45–51		Lk 12:42–48
Ten virgins	Mt 25:1–13		
Talents (minas)	Mt 25:14–30		Lk 19:12–27
Sheep and goats	Mt 25:31–46		
Growing seed		Mk 4:26–29	
Watchful servants		Mk 13:35–37	Lk 12:35–40
Moneylender			Lk 7:41–43
Good Samaritan			Lk 10:30–37
Friend in need			Lk 11:5–8
Rich fool			Lk 12:16–21
Unfruitful fig tree			Lk 13:6–9
Lowest seat at the feast			Lk 14:7–14
Great banquet			Lk 14:16–24
Cost of discipleship			Lk 14:28–33
Lost coin			Lk 15:8–10
Lost (prodigal) son			Lk 15:11–32
Shrewd manager			Lk 16:1–8
Rich man and Lazarus			Lk 16:19–31
Master and his servant			Lk 17:7–10
Persistent widow			Lk 18:2–8
Pharisee and tax collector			Lk 18:10–14

kinds of people and will have nothing to do with the music he plays. Jesus comes "eating and drinking," and his critics call him "a glutton and a drunkard, a friend of tax collectors and 'sinners'" (v. 34). For them Jesus belongs to the swindlers and scum of society. They accuse him of the sins of those with whom he associates and rank him as no better than the undesirables. In other words, no matter what lifestyle God's messengers assume, this generation will complain. Should Jesus minister today as he did in the first century, some would say he gets too close to sinners and risks defiling himself.

Many of Jesus' generation have refused to dance to the music of either John or Jesus. But at the same time, some children are dancing to the tune of Jesus, the Son of Man. These children are the offspring of divine wisdom, and they prove by their lives that the wisdom of God is right (v. 35). They see what God is doing through Jesus and trust in the Savior as the path of wisdom. Among the children of wisdom are Peter, James, and John (5:9–11); Levi, the tax collector (5:27–28); the paralytic (5:17ff.); and the sinful woman (7:36ff.). They are the children of "wisdom." God's wisdom has been revealed to them through their faith in Jesus as the way, the truth, and the life. He is God's wisdom, the true guide for their life and ours.

3.10. Jesus Anointed by a Sinful Woman (7:36–50)

Luke gives us a glimpse of a Pharisee, Simon by name, and a sinful woman.[11] As is already apparent, the Pharisees oppose Jesus and scheme among themselves to put an end to his blasphemous claim to forgive sin (5:21–22). But not all Pharisees reject him. Among those who are portrayed as friends or at least sympathetic with his prophetic ministry is Simon. Jesus accepts the invitation to his home for a meal. Although Jesus is a friend to the outcast and sinners, his ministry to despised people does not exclude interest in the respectable members of society (Marshall, 1978, 308). They also need the gospel. Jesus wants to share it with people of all persuasions.

The account of Jesus' dining at the home of Simon the Pharisee illustrates his teaching about sin and salvation. A woman enters Simon's home as an uninvited guest. Luke calls her a *hamartolos*, best understood here as "a prostitute." She knows that Jesus is there; the meal he is attending is not private. As was common in those days, others had access to a meal in honor of a distinguished teacher, though this woman would never have been welcome in the house of a Pharisee.

No one seems to be shocked by her presence. She brings "an alabaster jar of perfume" (v. 37) and may have planned to anoint the head of Jesus. According to custom he is reclining on a low couch, with his feet behind him. As the woman stands behind him, she becomes overwhelmed with her deep emotions of gratitude and weeps profusely, wetting his feet with tears. Then she wipes his feet dry with her hair and kisses them, expressing her gratitude and respect to the Son of God. Finally, she pours the expensive perfume on them.

Obviously this woman has little or no concern about public opinion. She has forgotten that a decent woman does not let down her hair in public. It seems fair to say that she already knows Jesus as her Savior. She may have been among the people who listened to his teachings and was convicted of her evil ways. She repented, and he changed her life and put her on the road to self-respect. As a forgiven sinner, she knows the real meaning of sorrow for sin (Marshall, 1978, 309).

Simon the Pharisee has seen all that the woman has done and concludes that Jesus cannot be a prophet. A true prophet would have special insight as to exactly who this woman was and know that she was a sinner (v. 39). Moreover, a true prophet would never have allowed himself to be touched by this unclean woman. The Pharisee assumes that if Jesus had the gift of discernment, as true prophets have, he would see in the woman exactly what he sees. But as far as Jesus is concerned, the Pharisee does not have eyes to see the woman as she really is. Jesus sees her as a child of God forgiven of her sins and restored to fellowship with the Lord. Not only does he accept the touch of the woman, but he welcomes what she has done.

The Spirit-anointed Jesus has true prophetic insight. Perceiving the thoughts of Simon's heart, he proceeds to correct his false reasoning. He gives his evaluation of the woman through a parable about two debtors (vv. 41–42). The illustration is simple. There is a moneylender who has two debtors. One owes ten times more than the other (five hundred denarii versus fifty; a denarius is a day's wage of a rural worker). The lender forgives the debt of both. Each should be grateful, but one debtor has been forgiven much more than the other. So Jesus asks Simon which of these men would love his benefactor more. The Pharisee is intelligent and replies, "I suppose the one who had the bigger debt canceled" (v. 43). His answer is cautious but correct. When God forgives a notorious sinner like the woman, it provides opportunity for love. Awareness that God has blotted all the debts against us and grants us bountiful forgiveness should prompt us to great love and gratitude.

Jesus commends Simon for his judgment. Then he applies the parable by contrasting what he has not done with what the woman has done (vv. 44–47). Simon has provided no water for the washing of his feet (Gen. 18:4; Judg. 19:21), but she has washed his feet with her own tears and dried them with her hair. Simon has not given him a kiss as a sign of welcome (Gen. 29:13; 45:15), but in great humility she has showered his feet with kisses. Simon has not even anointed his head with cheap olive oil (Ps. 23:5; 141:5), but the woman has used expensive perfume to anoint his feet. In contrast to the Pharisee her gratitude and humility produce a tremendous response of love and devotion. The magnitude of her sins is beyond question, but "her many sins have been forgiven—for she loved much." She and others have felt their need for forgiveness, but Simon and others do not feel a need for forgiveness of sins like pride, self-righteousness, hypocrisy, and unbelief.

The woman's great love is evidence that she has been forgiven. The RSV and NIV translate verse 47 so that it implies that the woman's many sins have been forgiven because of her great love. The interpretation that love merited forgiveness, however, is contrary not only to the New Testament as a whole but also to verse 50: "Your faith has saved you." The woman's great love is a *result* of Jesus' forgiveness of her sins (cf. NRSV). The parable (vv. 41–42) itself indicates that the debtors are forgiven not because they love, but because of the goodness of the moneylender. Forgiveness produces their love. The woman's display of affection and gratitude leaves no doubt about the magnitude of her pardon. Her response is to divine grace, as the NEB brings out: "Her great love proves that her many sins have been forgiven."

The woman has been forgiven much and as a result loves much. By contrast, "he who has been forgiven little loves little" (v. 47). This seems to point to Simon, though it should not be taken to mean that he has already been forgiven by Jesus. Simon sees himself among the righteous and lacks an understanding of his own sins. Whether a person has sinned much or little, the better one understands sin and one's sinfulness, the more that person will love God and his forgiveness. Paul himself is an example. As he approached the end of his life, he marveled at God's forgiveness: "Christ Jesus came into the world to save sinners—of whom I am the worst" (1 Tim. 1:15).

In verse 48 Jesus addresses the woman directly. Consistent with the whole passage, he assures her of forgiveness. She may feel the scorn of Simon, but Jesus knows that she has moved from sin to repentance, and thence to gratitude and love. No matter what people like Simon think, her sins have been forgiven.

What Jesus says to the woman provokes comments by fellow guests at the meal. They understand the significance of the statement, "Your sins are forgiven." So they begin to ask among themselves, "Who is this who even forgives sins?" (v. 49). Simon has denied Jesus' prophetic authority, but any person who can forgive sins has to be more than a prophet. Jesus' pronouncement of forgiveness implies he has divine authority, for only God can forgive sin (5:21).

Jesus does not reply to what the guests say. But he does speak again to the woman, assuring her that she has been saved from the power of sin through faith (v. 50). She can now go in peace because of her personal trust in Jesus and her peace with God. God is always ready to blot out the guilt and sin of anyone who humbly turns to Jesus.

3.11. Wise Teachings and Marvelous Deeds (8:1–56)

Up to this point Luke has centered Jesus' Galilean ministry around the issue of his authority. Now he focuses also on response to that authority. After a brief reference to the women involved in Jesus' ministry (8:1–3), he turns to the preached word of Jesus: the parable of the sower (vv. 4–15), a lamp under a bowl

(vv. 16–18), and the real family of Jesus (vv. 19–21). Through his Spirit-anointed preaching, Jesus' authority becomes apparent. A series of miracles reveals that it extends into all realms. He controls nature by calming the storm (vv. 22–25), casts out demons (vv. 26–39), heals the sick, and even raises the dead (8:40–56). Jesus has unlimited authority.

3.11.1. Women Share in Jesus' Ministry (8:1–3). Jesus' ministry now becomes mobile. Growing opposition from the leaders of the synagogue may have made it necessary for him to abandon a settled ministry and go on a mission tour. He does not confine himself to a few cities in Galilee, but he makes his way from city to city and from town to town, announcing with authority the gracious rule of God that brings salvation to men and women. His itinerant ministry provides a model for missionary outreach. On the tour he is accompanied by the Twelve and some women.

The participation of the women in the mission tour reveals how revolutionary Jesus' ministry was. In his day rabbis declined to teach women and assigned them an inferior place (Morris, 1974, 149). For example, only males were allowed full participation in synagogue services. But Jesus treats women as persons and welcomes them into fellowship. They have equal access to grace and salvation, and many women become his followers. Among them are women of financial means, who minister to Jesus by giving their possessions to support him and his disciples.

Luke mentions three such women by name. First is "Mary (called Magdalene)," which means "from Magdala," a town on the west bank of the Sea of Galilee. Seven evil spirits had been driven out of her by Jesus. When she was set free from her wretched existence, she became a disciple of Jesus. Next is Joanna, described as "the wife of Cuza," who served as some kind of an administrator in the court of Herod Antipas. Joanna's dedication indicates the wide influence Jesus had because his ministry has already reached to some in the royal court. Both Joanna and Mary Magdalene are witnesses to the resurrection on Easter morning (24:10). Third is Susanna; nothing more is known about her.

These women give their earthly means to support the ministry of Jesus. Their generous help explains, at least in part, how Jesus and his disciples provide for themselves. Jesus had ministered to these women and set them free from the bondage of sin; out of deep affection and devotion they continue to "help" (*diekonoun*, imperfect tense signifying repetition) Jesus and his disciples "out of their own means" (v. 3). Money and possessions can seduce people and make them slaves to the things of the world. The generosity of these well-to-do women is commendable, but they show more than generosity here; they are sensitive to God's grace and to the guidance of the Holy Spirit. Blessed themselves, they in turn bless others by placing their money in submission to the gospel.

3.11.2. The Parable of the Sower (8:4–15). As Jesus travels, a large crowd gathers from different cities and villages, and he tells them the parable of the sower, also called the parable of soils (cf. Matt. 13; Mark 4). The emphasis is on the difference in the soils, not in the sower and his seed. Jesus has taught in parables before (Luke 5:36–39; 6:39–42; 7:41–42). Many of Jesus' prophetic predecessors, such as Ezekiel and Isaiah, also taught in parables. As Jesus uses this method of teaching, he knows that it fulfills what Isaiah is told to do: "Go and tell this people: 'Be ever hearing, but never understanding; be ever seeing, but never perceiving'" (Isa. 6:9).

Since Jesus places the parable of the sower at center stage, we must briefly review the nature and function of parables. The Greek word *parabole* ("parable") means "a placing of things side by side," usually for the sake of comparison. A parable is thus a short, simple story that expresses some teaching point. A. M. Hunter offers this definition: "A comparison drawn from nature or daily life and designed to illuminate some spiritual truth, on the assumption that what is valid in one sphere is valid also in the other" (1960, 8). As in his miracles, Jesus uses parables to confront his audience with the realities of God's kingdom—the miracles are for the eyes and the parables are for the ears (Dean, 1983, 59). The parable of the sower has a twofold purpose: (1) to assure the disciples that in spite of the disappointment and lack of success at times in preaching the gospel, they can have confidence that the good news will produce a rich harvest; and (2) to warn others against careless or casual response to God's preached word.

The parable of the sower records four reactions/ responses to Jesus' preaching—each described in terms of a different kind of soil. His hearers can relate to this story from their experience or observation. Farmers in Palestine sowed seed between October and December and harvested in June. The key to a successful harvest was the soil in which the seed was planted. There are four places where seed might fall: (1) on a narrow footpath through a field, where the seed could be stepped on by travelers and eaten by wild birds; (2) on the part of the field where only a thin layer of soil lay over a bed of rock—such soil had little moisture, and when the sun shone, the moisture evaporated and the plants withered; (3) among weeds with thorns—as the seeds tried to grow, the thistles took nutrients from the soil and made growth impossible; and (4) on good, fertile soil, in which the seed germinated and brought forth an abundant harvest—up to "a hundred times more than was sown" (v. 8).

To conclude the parable Jesus issues a call: "He who has ears to hear, let him hear" (cf. 14:35). This call does not put doubt on whether the listeners have ears, but it urges them to use their ears to hear the deep truths of the parable, which requires more than an outward hearing of words. It is an inward hearing that brings an understanding that God's message applies to the hearers, saves them from their sins, and produces much fruit in their lives. Nothing can be more important than hearing God's Word ourselves.

The disciples ask what the parable means (v. 9). In his answer, Jesus takes the opportunity to explain to them why he teaches in parables. He is not giving a lesson in farming; rather, the parable's meaning should be open to his disciples. God has made them able to know "the secrets of the kingdom" (v. 10), which refers to the plan of salvation and all the blessings that accompany his rule. The passive "has been given" speaks of divine giving. The grasp of the secret truths about the kingdom is not due to the disciples' discovery of them but to God's grace. By his Spirit, God has enabled them to grasp the profound truths revealed in Jesus Christ.

But parables have a double purpose: Not only do they reveal deep truths about the kingdom to the disciples, but they also conceal the deep meaning of their message from "others," that is, from unbelievers, whose minds remain closed to deeper truths. At this point Jesus refers to Isaiah 6:9, which teaches that people see with their eyes and hear with their ears, but they do not truly see or hear. They remain blind and deaf to the deep truths concerning the kingdom. There is real danger in exposure to the Word of God if we do not respond in faith. If a person willfully chooses to be blind and deaf to the gospel, God begins to withdraw it and hardness sets in; such people bring judgment on themselves. On the other hand, earnest seekers find great spiritual truths and significance in parables, for they go below the surface and discover their inner meaning. These words warn of the great danger of rejecting the good news of the kingdom. Nothing is more important than hearing and responding properly to the message of Jesus.

Now Jesus explains the parable to his disciples (vv. 11–15). The seed stands for the word of God, the preaching of God's kingdom and how to enter it. Obviously Jesus is the preacher. Luke does not identify him as such, so as to leave it open to include preaching by Jesus' followers. Jesus' interpretation of the parable draws attention to the different kinds of soil and what happens to the word of God when it falls on different types of ground. (1) Some seed falls on the hard footpath through the field (v. 12). Just as birds eat up the seed before they can germinate, so the devil snatches the word away and makes "those along the path" as though they never heard it. These people may hear the word, but before it can penetrate their hearts and change their lives, Satan persuades them to continue in unbelief.

(2) Some of the seed falls on rocks, where the soil is shallow (v. 13). As a result the plants cannot put down deep roots. This refers to the message that falls on hearers' hearts, but it does not penetrate deeply into their lives. At first they show promise—they "receive the word with joy when they hear it" and are excited about it. But that initial response does not last. "They have not root"—no depth of understanding or commitment. They are only temporary believers. Testing and temptations come to every believer in the form of troubles, difficulties, and persecutions. When that happens, "they fall away"; that is, they abandon their faith (cf. 1 Tim. 4:1; Heb. 3:12).

(3) Still other seed falls on soil with thorn bushes (v. 14). These people really do hear the word of God and understand its significance. It takes root in their hearts, and they experience salvation. Yet before long the thorns begin to do their work. Thorns represent such things as worries, riches, and pleasure. As time goes on, these gradually choke out any spiritual fruit in the lives of believers. These elements can distract us from spiritual matters, choke out our walk with God, and smother God's word in our lives. As a result we fail to reach maturity in Christ.

(4) The seed that fell on good soil is a picture of those who hear the word and bear abundant fruit in godly living. They have a "noble and good heart," which prepares them to accept the preaching of the word. It penetrates deep into their lives, where it flourishes. They retain the gospel message and hold on to it. But even more, "by persevering" they "produce a crop," an abundant spiritual harvest. The mention of "persevering" (*hypomone*, "patience") indicates that believers live under stress and face adversity. Holding on to the word, however, ensures that they bring forth fruit.

3.11.3. A Lamp Under a Bowl (8:16–18). Jesus' next parable is closely linked to the parable of the sower. The parable of the lamp fits the emphasis on bearing fruit in verse 15 and reinforces the message of the earlier parable. The main emphasis, however, is on the disciples' spreading the gospel message and becoming lights in the world.

This type of oil lamp was in use during the first century. In his teaching, Jesus told the disciples that they were to spread the gospel, make it known, just as a person lights a lamp and places it on a lampstand so that its light can be seen.

In the ancient world a lamp consisted of a wick in a small clay bowl filled with olive oil. A lamp provided light in a room or house. No one covered the lamp up or put it under a bed. Instead, it was put on a lampstand so that those who entered might see the light (v. 16). The lamp represents the light that Jesus has brought into the world. His followers should never hide the light of the gospel. He has enlightened their hearts with the word and has given them spiritual insight. They are to place their lights on lampstands and proclaim the word to others.

The light of the gospel will guide us through the darkness of this world. Light does more than illuminate the way; it also reveals what is hidden and makes things known as they really are (v. 17). That is the way the gospel works. As it is proclaimed, it exposes the secrets in human hearts. Its light should shine far and wide, for it not only illuminates believers, but it also shows others what they are like. The preaching of the gospel begins what God will complete in the final judgment (Lenski, 1946, 455). On that day everything will be "brought out into the open."

Everyone, therefore, should be careful to hear the word in the right way (v. 18). Those who respond in faith will receive more from God. Jesus is not encouraging those who have money to expect an increase in wealth but an increase in faith (v. 12), fruit-bearing (v. 15), joy, and knowledge of the gospel. If we use God's gifts, he will increase them. But those who do not receive the word will have taken away from them what they think they have. To reject the word of God means that we are left in a state of spiritual poverty (cf. also 19:26, which warns about the importance of the correct use of God's gifts).

3.11.4. The Real Family of Jesus (8:19–21). In this section Jesus emphasizes again the importance of hearing God's word properly. Mark tells us that Jesus' mother and brothers come to take charge of him because they think he has overextended himself in ministry and they want him to rest (Mark 3:21). Luke does not cite a motive, but he does show that their coming is an occasion for Jesus to teach that all who hear and obey God's word belong to his family.

Jesus' mother and brothers are unable to approach him because of the crowd (v. 19). He s devoting himself to the work that the Spirit as anointed him to do. When he learns of their resence, he shows no impatience or disrespect, but he does remark, "My mother and rothers are those who hear God's word and ut it into practice" (v. 21). Real kinship with esus is a matter of believing his word and beying all it tells us. Jesus does not disown is biological family or ignore them. On the ross, for example, he makes provision for his nother (John 19:26–27). But believers have closer relationship with him than do his nother and brothers. His family must enter the piritual family in the same way as any of his ollowers do. Through the indwelling presence f the Holy Spirit we are united with him and nade members of God's household.

3.11.5. Jesus Calms the Storm (8:22–25). esus now shows his power over the forces of ature. He has commanded evil spirits to leave eople (4:35, 41); he has ordered a fever to eave Peter's mother-in-law (4:39); he has leansed a man of leprosy (5:12–15); he has ealed a paralytic and forgiven him of his sins 5:17–26); he has raised the widow's dead son 7:11–17). In this section he orders a violent torm to stop. Jesus' control of the wind and vaves not only reveals his divine power, but lso his compassion toward those with all inds of needs. The calming of the storm is the irst of a series of four miracles in chapter 8.

Jesus and his disciples get into a boat to ross to the other side of the Sea of Galilee. As hey are sailing, Jesus drops off to sleep. Without any warning a violent windstorm blows lown on the lake. High waves begin to fill the oat with water. Some of the disciples are xperienced fishermen, but they are unable to revent the boat from filling with water. When hey see that the boat is in danger of sinking, hey become alarmed.

Undisturbed by the storm, Jesus continues o sleep until the disciples wake him with the vords, "Master, Master, we're going to lrown!" (v. 24). Having power over the elenents, Jesus rebukes the winds and raging vaves, and there is calm. The verb "rebuke" *epitimao*) is used also with evil spirits (4:35, 41) and with fever (4:39). This verb may thus mply that the evil one had a hand in the storm. But Jesus demonstrates his authority over ature. Furthermore, his followers can rely on is power to help them; he responds to their needs faithfully. This miracle teaches great spiritual realities about Jesus' power and compassion to minister to our needs.

The disciples have shown little faith during the storm, so Jesus rebukes them by asking, "Where is your faith?" (v. 25). They should not have been terrified, but trusted him. Their training under Jesus has not brought them to a strong, courageous faith, a faith that would have assured them of Jesus' care for them through the storm. Calming the winds and waves gives him an opportunity to remind the disciples of his care for them. Like all believers they need the kind of faith that will see them through perils and adversities. That kind of faith calls for holding on to the word of God (v. 15).

Filled with awe and astonishment, the disciples try to understand what they have seen. So they ask a question concerning Jesus' identity, "Who is this? He commands even the winds and the water, and they obey him." What kind of person is someone whom the wind and waves obey? No answer is given, but a student of the Old Testament knows that no one but God controls the wind and the seas (Ps. 18:15; 135:6–7; Nah. 1:4).

3.11.6. Jesus Delivers a Man With Demons (8:26–39). This next incident occurs on the east side of the Sea of Galilee in Gentile territory.[12] Jesus has revealed his power over the forces of nature by calming the storm, but he also has authority over the powers of the devil. He encounters a more severe case of demon possession than the incident recorded in 4:31–36. As Jesus steps on the shore, a demon-possessed man comes toward him. This man has been reduced to a sub-human level. He goes around naked and lives in burial caves. The demons have so infiltrated his personality that he finds himself powerless. They have stripped him of his sanity. Often when seized by the evil spirit, the man became violent. To restrain him people put chains on his hands and feet, but he would break them. All human means have failed to help him.

Something attracts the man to Jesus. As he approaches, he falls on his knees in front of Jesus. Then the demon speaks through his victim: "What do you want with me, Jesus, Son of the Most High God? I beg you, don't torture me!" (v. 28). The unclean spirit recognizes Jesus' authority to exercise judgment (4:34,

41) and addresses him as "Son of the Most High God." In a unique sense, Jesus is the Son of God, who has absolute authority over evil spirits. The demon knows Jesus' divine character and his purpose for coming (1 John 3:8).

Jesus inquires what the demon's name is, which brings the response "Legion" (v. 30). As a unit in the Roman army, a legion consisted of from four thousand to six thousand men. The man is thus possessed by a multitude of evil spirits. The victim cannot break their hold, but in the presence of Jesus the demons know they must leave the man. They dread the thought of being cast into "the Abyss," the place of the dead (Ps. 107:26; Rom. 10:7)—that is, the underworld, where evil spirits are kept until the final judgment. They prefer to enter humans or animals so that they can exercise their ungodly control. A herd of hogs is grazing nearby, and the demons request permission to enter them. Jesus allows them to do so. Once again, we see the power of the Spirit-anointed Jesus. He utters an authoritative word, and the demons can do nothing except what he allows.

The hogs react to the demons by rushing down a steep bank into the Sea of Galilee, where they drown. Thus, the deliverance of the man results in the death of swine. The owners suffer loss of the pigs, but an individual is worth far more than a whole herd of swine. Moreover, the community where the man has lived is now delivered from the dangers of this demoniac. But those caring for the hogs report to the townspeople what has happened (v. 34).

When the people come to see for themselves, they find the man completely free of demons, "sitting at Jesus' feet, dressed and in his right mind." The man has been transformed by the saving grace and power of Jesus and has become a disciple of the Savior. But rather than rejoice over his deliverance, the people are gripped with fear of Jesus' transforming power and request him to leave. Apparently the possibility of encountering the power of Jesus is seen as a threat. Jesus complies with their request. The healed man begs to go with him. But Jesus sends him home so that he can testify to what God has done for him. The man becomes an evangelist and goes all over the town, preaching what Jesus has done for him.

The deliverance of the man reminds us of some striking truths. (1) His deliverance brings out Jesus' absolute power and authority. The multitude of demons must obey his word. He overcomes the strongest demonic resistance and restores the man to full life.

(2) The man's response shows that Jesus should be first in our lives. He longs to go with Jesus and join the band of disciples. His devotion is praiseworthy, but Jesus directs him to go home and become a witness to his experience of God's saving power. That is what he does, and his preaching focuses on what Jesus has done for him.

(3) The deliverance of the man should reassure all believers that they share in Jesus' victory over principalities and powers (cf. 9:1; 10:17). Believers may be attacked by evil spirits and are expected to wage spiritual warfare against such spirits (Eph. 6:12). But while demons may influence, oppress, or vex believers, they cannot demonize or possess them. Each believer is indwelt by the Holy Spirit (Rom. 8:9; 1 Thess. 4:8); Satan and the Holy Spirit can never indwell or possess the same temple. And when Jesus returns in power and glory, he will put an end to the activities of the devil.

3.11.7. Raising of Jairus's Daughter; Healing of a Woman With a Hemorrhage (8:40–56). These two miracles are the last in the sequence of four. They occur on the same day and are interwoven. Luke does not identify the place, except that it is in Galilee, perhaps near Capernaum. The two miracles reveal Jesus' authority over a humanly incurable disease and even over death. It is significant that the raising of Jairus's daughter is the last of the four miracles. Even death, the most persistent and dreaded opponent, has to submit to the Lord of life. Ultimately Christ will overcome all disease and death. These miracles also teach us about the importance of faith (vv. 48, 50).

Jesus has delivered the man from a legion of demons (8:26–39). When he returns to Galilee, he finds a crowd eager to see him. Throughout his ministry in Galilee Jesus remains popular with the common people, though most religious leaders disapprove of him and his ministry. But on this occasion Jairus, a ruler in the local synagogue, expresses publicly his faith in the healing power of Jesus. Though he is a man of position in the community, he kneels at Jesus' feet, begging him to go home with him (v. 41). His only daughter, a twelve-year-old, is about to die. Convinced of esus' authority to heal the sick, the ruler leads with him for his daughter's life.

At once Jesus begins his journey to the ome of Jairus. Meanwhile, the crowd is so ıde that they press in upon him. This rudeness elays Jesus' journey, but it also gives a voman the opportunity to approach Jesus for ealing. She has been suffering from bleeding or twelve years, and physicians have been nable to help her. This woman's condition ıade her religiously unclean (cf. Lev. 15:19–1). As a result she has been treated as a social utcast, not allowed to attend temple worship r to have contact with other people. The social onsequences have added to her suffering and ıade her life even more difficult. Her only ope of touching Jesus is to do so secretly by oming up behind him. Should she try to pproach Jesus in any other way, the people vould not have allowed her to get near him. So he comes up from behind Jesus and touches ıe hem of his garment—that is, the tassels on ıe edge of the outer garment, which devout ews wore as a sign of their devotion to God. 'he moment she touches the hem, her bleeding stops (v. 44).

Aware that someone has deliberately ouched him, he asks, "Who touched me?" Jnder the circumstance that is a curious question. The people are all around him and pressng against him. They all deny any special ouching of Jesus. Astonished at the question, 'eter wonders how he can even ask that. Moreover, the question seems so insignificant since etting to the home of Jairus is a matter of leath or life.

But the Spirit-anointed Jesus insists that omeone has intentionally touched him. He nows he has ministered to a person and realzes that person has been healed, because he elt divine power go out of him (v. 46). There s a mystery here. Others in the crowd have ouched Jesus as they pressed against him, but o power went out from him. When the voman touched his hem, however, power lowed from him to her. This healing was not nvoluntary on Jesus' part. He willed her healng, and she was made whole. At the same time er deliverance was the Savior's response to er faith. Her faith has distinguished her from he crowd, but she now realizes that she canot keep herself concealed and slip away withut notice. Trembling with fear she comes forward and falls down at Jesus' feet. She testifies before all the people of what she did and of what Jesus did for her.

Jesus has no words of blame or rebuke. He addresses her affectionately as "daughter" and says to her the same thing as to the sinful woman of 7:50: "Your faith has healed [from *sozo*, "save"] you. Go in peace." The miracles of Jesus are accomplished by divine power that works through him. But another important element in miracles is faith. Her faith in Jesus prompts her to look to him for deliverance and draws from him healing power. Jesus' commendation, "Your faith has saved you," however, suggests something deeper than physical healing. Her contact with Jesus has been personal, and her healing must include both body and soul. She owes her new health and new life to the saving power of God. The woman has given her testimony, and she becomes an effective witness. So Jesus assures her that she has been cured by her faith and bids her to go in the peace of God. Both her illness and her sins are gone; salvation is hers, and she has peace with God.

This woman has caused a delay in reaching the house of Jairus. While Jesus is still speaking to her, a messenger arrives with news that Jairus's daughter has died. The one who brings the news has no hope that Jesus can do anything now for the child. His advice to Jairus is, "Don't bother the teacher any more" (v. 49). The messenger does not understand that Jesus' power extends beyond death. Likely Jairus, too, agrees with the messenger.

When Jesus hears the message, he promptly reassures the father with these words: "Don't be afraid; just believe, and she will be healed" (v. 50). Jairus must not draw any hasty conclusions. He has witnessed what Jesus did for the woman who trusted in his power. Knowing that she had been restored to health makes it easier to believe that Jesus can heal his daughter. Since she has died, Jesus urges him to have greater faith. The emphasis falls on the importance of faith. Without believing the ruler of the synagogue can have no real hope of seeing his daughter alive again. Only faith in the power of Christ can deliver her from the grip of death.

Jesus goes on to Jairus's house. He allows no one to enter except the child's parents and his three closest disciples. He wants to avoid a lot of publicity. Earlier he insisted that the woman healed of an issue of blood give public witness to what happened. No longer being viewed as unclean by the people will enable her to return to a normal religious and social life. Similarly here, Jesus does not want the young girl to become the center of an inquisitive crowd. Out of consideration for her he permits only a few people to enter her room.

By the time Jesus reaches the house mourners are weeping for the child. Among them must have been family and neighbors. Luke does not mention professional mourners, but likely they are there as well. Jesus interrupts the heart-rending mourning with a command: "Stop wailing." Then he explains, "She is not dead but asleep" (v. 52). To refer to death as sleep is a more pleasant way to speak of it. Jesus' intent, however, is not to contrast sleep and death, but to look at death from God's point of view. For us death is final, but for God a person can be awakened from it (Marshall, 1978, 347).

The mourners know that the young girl is not in a coma but has actually died. They think that Jesus is disputing her death and is speaking of ordinary sleep, so they laugh at his claim. By now Jesus is known as an anointed prophet and as one who has the gift of healing. But the mourners are so gripped by unbelief that they refuse to consider that he may be right. As Morris says, "what is death to men is no more than sleep for Jesus" (1974, 162).

The mourners feel that death always has the last word. They are wrong. Jesus has the last word when he takes the child by the hand and says, "Get up." The spirit returns to her lifeless body, and she immediately rises from the sleep of death. As the dead son of the widow of Nain, she experiences a stupendous miracle. From this time on she is to live a normal life. Out of tender concern Jesus commands them to give her some food (v. 55). Death has been robbed of its victim by the power of Jesus. The child's parents are amazed. Jesus charges them to tell no one about the miracle. What he has done is obvious to many, but he wants to avoid becoming known merely as a worker of miracles.

3.12. Jesus and His Disciples (9:1–50)

Luke 9:1–50 records the climax of Jesus' Galilean ministry, with an emphasis on his ministry among the people. He has shown his divine power through mighty works and his great compassion by ministering to people's needs. He has chosen the Twelve (6:12–16), who have traveled with him and observed what he did and said. Now Luke moves on to show that Jesus gives them power and authority to preach the kingdom of God and to perform miracles, just as he has done (vv. 1–6).

Meanwhile reports come to Herod about the activities of Jesus and his disciples (vv. 7–9). Herod's concern about who Jesus is, is followed by the feeding of the five thousand (vv. 10–17). Peter's confession identifies Jesus as Christ, God's Anointed One; this confession represents a significant turning point in the Gospel. Furthermore, Jesus declares for the first time the path of suffering that he and his disciples must walk (vv. 18–27). He is then transfigured while preparing the way for his final journey to Jerusalem (vv. 28–36). The section concludes with the disciples' lack of faith and emphasizes their preparation for Jesus' death (vv. 37–50).

3.12.1. Jesus Sends Out the Twelve (9:1–6). The Twelve have been with Jesus for most of his Galilean ministry. After the great miracle of raising Jairus's daughter, Jesus sends them out to do what he has done. Their commission seems to be the same as his (4:18–19). He gives them "power and authority to drive out all demons and to cure diseases." Furthermore, they are to proclaim the arrival of the kingdom. The redemptive rule of God has become a present reality, demonstrated by the preaching of the gospel and victory over evil through miracles and the casting out of demons. Like all ministers of the gospel, these disciples derive their power and authority from Jesus. They minister as his servants and stewards and thus are accountable to him. Prior to Pentecost their ministry serves as preparation for the work that they will be called to do in the power of the Spirit (24:49; Acts 1:8; 2:1ff.).

As the disciples travel, Jesus wants them to depend on God. He instructs them to take no provisions with them (v. 3). They are to focus on their ministry and not spend their time on elaborate preparations. Traveling as lightly as possible, they are to trust God and not take such things as a staff used on long journeys, a bag in which supplies are carried, money, or extra clothing. Jesus does not desire to afflict hardships on his disciples, but to teach them to devote their time to serving him and to warn them against worrying about their needs. The task that they have been assigned is urgent. They must simply go and trust God to provide for their needs as they proclaim the kingdom of God.

When the disciples enter a town, they must stay with the first family who welcomes them (v. 4) and avoid moving from house to house. They are to be satisfied with their food and lodging. If they look around for better accommodations, they would insult their host. Should they, however, enter a town where no one welcomes them, they must move on quickly to another town (v. 5). They need to take precautions against forcing themselves on a town that does not want them and their message. Upon leaving such towns, they are to do nothing more than "shake the dust off" from their feet. Jews observed this practice when leaving Gentile soil in order to rid themselves of Gentile pollution before they returned to their own land. The disciples are to adopt this as a symbolic act "as a testimony against them." It signifies that since a town as a whole has rejected the message of salvation, they do not belong to God's people. In other words, the disciples are not cleansing themselves, but warning the people of God's disapproval and condemnation for rejecting his messengers.

The disciples do as Jesus tells them (v. 6). Luke does not give the details of their journey, but they travel through all the villages, preaching the good news of the message of the kingdom and healing the sick. Ministry is their focus, not their own personal needs for the journey. Later Jesus does instruct his followers to take purse, bag, and sword (22:36). Even so, those who carry the gospel are to depend on God and be careful not to damage the credibility of the gospel. Yet God's people should provide for those who minister to them (10:7; 1 Cor. 9:3–14).

3.12.2. Herod Hears Rumors About Jesus (9:7–9). Luke places this brief passage between the disciples' departure (v. 6) and their return (v. 10). It helps provide background information to Peter's confession of Jesus as the Messiah (vv. 18–20). Luke records the reports and rumors that circulate as Jesus' popularity continues to increase in Galilee. Reports come to Herod Antipas, the ruler of Galilee (3:1, 19), about the cures and miracles performed by Jesus and his disciples. Along with Jesus' attracting the crowds, curiosity increases as to who he is. Rumors and conjectures become common. Many are puzzled by the gossip.

What Herod hears confuses him, especially the significance of Jesus' mighty works. He is most perplexed by the three different views of Jesus discussed at his court. Some believe that the miracles are being performed by John the Baptist, who has come to life again. Luke does not relate the story of John's death, but by now Herod has had him beheaded. Some of John's disciples may have difficulty accepting his death and could be responsible for the report of his resurrection. Others think that Jesus is the prophet Elijah. According to Malachi 4:5–6 Elijah (who had been taken up into heaven alive; see 2 Kings 2:11–12) was to return and prepare the way for the Messiah. The third view identifies Jesus as another prophet of long ago. Though this prophet is not named, some think that God has raised to life one of the ancient prophets.

Herod rejects the opinion that the one working miracles is John. He assumes that John and the others mentioned could not have risen from the dead, despite what popular opinion says. Still troubled, he wonders who the miracle-worker is. So he wants to see Jesus for himself and get to know him. His desire to meet him is prompted by curiosity, not faith (cf. 23:6–12). Faith, however, is vital for coming to grips with who Jesus really is. His identity can never be discovered from a distance or through secondhand information.

3.12.3. Jesus Feeds the Five Thousand (9:10–17). The feeding of the five thousand appears in all four Gospels (cf. Matt. 14:13–21; Mark 6:32–44; John 6:1–15). This miracle represents a turning point in Jesus' ministry. It recalls the feeding of the children of Israel in the desert at the time of Moses. In Luke's Gospel this event serves a fourfold purpose: (1) to reveal more about Jesus; (2) to provide a basis for Peter's confession of Jesus as the Messiah (vv. 19–20); (3) to prepare the disciples for teaching about his death and resurrection (v. 22); and (4) to teach his disciples to rely on him and his mighty power. Jesus intends the miraculous feeding as a lesson to his disciples. Luke tells us nothing about the response of the people to this miracle.

The disciples have been away preaching the kingdom of God. Upon their return they tell Jesus all that they have done. For a time of rest and refreshment Jesus withdraws in the direction of Bethsaida, a town located near the northeast shore of the Sea of Galilee. They do not enter that town but stay "in a remote place" (v. 12). The crowds go in pursuit of Jesus there, however. He and his disciples have only a little time of privacy before the crowds arrive. Yet he shows no irritation at the interruption; on the contrary, he extends to them a welcome. He cuts short the time of retreat with his disciples and devotes himself to giving a long message on the kingdom of God. At the same time he heals those who need it (v. 11). As Jesus proclaimed in the synagogue at Nazareth, preaching the gospel and healing the sick lie at the heart of his ministry (4:18–19).

When most of the day has passed, the disciples express a genuine concern about the people's welfare. So they remind Jesus that the crowd should be sent away into the nearby villages and towns so they can find something to eat and a place to spend the night. Jesus' answer is astonishing: "You give them something to eat" (v. 13). From their perspective it is impossible for them to feed such a large multitude. The only available food is five loaves of bread and a couple of cooked fish—insufficient to feed five thousand men (*andres*, as distinct from *anthropoi*, indicates women and children are not included in the number). Furthermore, even if food were available for purchase, the disciples do not have the financial resources to buy enough food. Under those conditions the feeding of the multitude is humanly impossible.

The disciples know that their resources are inadequate. They do not think about the power of Jesus to supply, nor do they consider his great compassion. He instructs the disciples to have the people to sit down in groups, with about fifty in each group. The disciples raise no objection and obey even though they have no idea where the food will come from to feed the multitude. Their sitting in groups makes it convenient to serve them.

Jesus then proceeds to work a miracle. Beginning as he would at a normal meal, he takes the five loaves and two fish and offers a blessing, thanking God for the loaves and fish and for what he is able to do to them. After the prayer the bread and fish are broken into pieces and given to the disciples for distribution to the people. The food miraculously increases, and there is plenty to satisfy the hunger of everyone. More is left over than a few crumbs and bits on the ground, for the disciples take up twelve baskets of leftover bread and fish—more than enough for all Israel. The people have enjoyed a full meal. What Jesus has done shows his ability to provide for human needs. Little is much in his hands.

Some see a link between the Lord's Supper and the feeding of the five thousand. The emphasis of the Supper is on spiritual food and the Lord's ability to minister to spiritual needs. The increase of the loaves and fishes teaches that Jesus is able to satisfy physical needs. This miracle may, however, be viewed as prefiguring the Lord's Supper (cf. John 6). Indeed Scripture makes clear that Jesus has the authority to minister to a full range of human needs, spiritual and physical.

3.12.4. Peter's Declaration and Jesus' First Prediction of His Death (9:18–27) Once again Jesus retires from the crowd for prayer. Prayer has a central role in his ministry. Though the disciples are close to Jesus, apparently they do not take part in the praying. Prayer signals that his ministry has reached a significant turning point. Of great importance is Peter's confession, which answers Herod's question, "Who, then, is this?" As well as identifying Jesus as the Messiah, the confession brings about a change in Jesus' teaching. He speaks for the first time about his coming suffering and begins to prepare the disciples for his death on the cross and for them to bear their cross daily.

After his time of prayer, Jesus begins a conversation with his disciples by asking: "Who do the crowds say I am?" (v. 18). The people in general do not think of him as the Messiah. Their answers are about the same as the rumors that came to Herod (vv. 7–8). They recognize the prophetic nature of his ministry and think that he may be John the Baptist, or Elijah, or some other ancient prophet raised from the dead.

Then Jesus asks his disciples the same question: "Who do you say I am?" The word "you" is emphatic in the Greek and stands in contrast to the crowds (v. 18). A genuine knowledge of Jesus comes through the work ng of God's Spirit (Matt. 16:17) and faith in him. Jesus has fulfilled the role of a Spirit-inspired prophet, but the raising of Jairus's daughter and the feeding of the five thousand revealed to the disciples that he is more than a prophet. Aware of Jesus' uniqueness, Peter speaks in behalf of the rest of the disciples when he answers, "The Christ of God." Peter confesses Jesus as the Anointed One, the Savior, whom God has promised to send; he is the One Israel has been looking for so long.

Hearing the words of Peter, Jesus immediately gives his disciples a strong command to tell nobody that he is the Messiah. Among scholars this is known as "the messianic secret." Jesus knows that for the Jews the term "Messiah" is associated with a political and military leader, who is expected to deliver Israel from Roman domination. He therefore forbids the disciples from saying anything in order to avoid a misunderstanding of his mission. Before his identity becomes public information, he wants his disciples to understand what kind of Messiah he is. Otherwise they too will fail to understand his kingdom and his purpose for coming.

So, using his title "Son of Man" (cf. 5:24), Jesus proceeds to explain the kind of Messiah he is and tells the disciples that he will not be the kind of Messiah the people expect. He "must suffer . . . be rejected . . . be killed . . . be raised to life" (v. 22). The verb "must" (*dei*) expresses that his suffering is a result of God's plan. No one enters life with the purpose of dying, but that is the purpose for Jesus' coming. In accordance with that divine purpose, the Son of Man will suffer by being rejected by the elders, chief priests, and teachers of the law. These groups form what is known as the Sanhedrin, the supreme council of the Jews. Within their own minds, the disciples have not yet associated the word "Messiah" with a violent death. It will take them a long time to understand this aspect of his mission. In fact, only the harsh reality of his death brings them to the point where they can no longer deny that he had to suffer many things (cf. 24:13–36).

Death, however, does not have the final word. On the third day the Son of Man must be raised to life (v. 22). His resurrection is as much a part of God's plan as his crucifixion. Jesus sees himself as the fulfillment of two great Old Testament prophecies. On the one hand, he is the Suffering Servant of Isaiah 53; on the other hand, he is the triumphant Son of Man of Daniel 7. The disciples and the people in general do not understand that Jesus is *both* the Suffering Servant *and* the victorious Son of Man. Had they done so, it would have been easier for them to accept him as the promised Redeemer. Many expected the Messiah to be only the second of these two—to have great power and glory. Thus when the lowly Jesus suffered and died, they were not prepared to receive him as Messiah.

Following Jesus calls for walking the path he walks and taking up a cross of self-denial. After Jesus' announcement to the disciples that he will die on the cross, he speaks of another cross—a cross that must be carried by all his followers (v. 23). His cross and his followers' crosses are different. The cross they bear is not literal and their suffering does not atone for sin. Yet the cross of the disciples is real. Like Jesus' cross, it is voluntary and calls for self-denial.

In verse 23 Jesus speaks to everyone, not just to his twelve disciples, reminding them of what is demanded of those who become his followers. First, they must deny self. All followers of Jesus need to understand that he offers them no easy trip to heaven. They must embrace the new life that pleases the Savior and brings glory to him. This requires that they renounce the old self and the old life with all the plans and wishes that go along with it.

Second, they must "take up [their] cross daily." When a person took up a cross in the first century, he was on his way to execution. Of course, Jesus wants his followers to be prepared to be persecuted and die as he must. But the addition "daily" shows that the call is not for physical death on a cross but for an attitude of continual self-denial. Taking up the cross means a daily resolution to deny oneself for the sake of the gospel. The followers of Christ must see themselves as having died to the old way of life, but they must renew every day their surrender of themselves to discipleship. As Paul teaches, cross-bearing is a matter of dying to self and sin (Rom. 8:36; 1 Cor. 15:31). It is not a momentary matter but a way of life. Christians can never be finished with bearing a cross.

Third, we must "follow [Christ]." The verbs "deny" and "take up" are aorist tense, calling for decisive action of denying oneself and taking up a cross day by day. But the verb "follow" is present tense, signifying a long and continuous course of action. Christians are on a journey. As we travel, we are constantly to follow Jesus and the path he has blazed.

Jesus goes on to explain more about cross-bearing discipleship (vv. 24–26). He contrasts two kinds of people. Those who try to preserve their life will lose it, but those who lose it for Christ's sake will preserve it. Here "life" (*psyche*) refers to the real person. Those who try to save themselves by refusing to deny the self and to take up their cross will lose their lives. By avoiding self-denial they may feel that they are getting the most out of life and that they are safe. But they lose what they try so hard to preserve, for they cut themselves off from the real Source of Life.

On the other hand, those who deny themselves for the benefit of Christ will have true life. Suffering loss of position, material things, and even physical life itself for following Christ may appear tragic, but at its worse such loss is minor. True life can never be measured by the things of this world. For the sake of Christ a person may find it necessary to forfeit the wealth, power, and glory that the world offers. But those losses are small in comparison to the great gain—eternal salvation. In contrast, people can gain the whole world and greedily have everything they want, but end up losing everything that really matters, including their very selves (v. 25). Great is the folly of losing our souls over a piece of this world. That is too high a price for anyone to pay (cf. 4:5–8). It is much better to make out with little of the world's goods than to lose our souls eternally.

The choice that we make now has eternal significance (v. 26), for the final judgment is coming. In light of that event Jesus warns his followers against being ashamed of the Son of Man and his Spirit-inspired message of salvation. To be ashamed of Jesus means to deny or reject him and his message. Through his powerful words he speaks to the hearts of people, but his message changes hearts only when it is received by faith. The ones who persist in unbelief and deny him, Jesus will deny "when he comes in his glory and in the glory of the Father and of the holy angels."

"Comes in his glory" refers to the Second Coming, when the Son of Man will come to judge all people (cf. 21:27). When he returns to judge, he will come with heavenly glory. The Father and angels live in heavenly glory. At his ascension Jesus will enter into that glory, and he will come again with the same glory. If we are ashamed of the Son of Man now, he will be ashamed of us on that glorious day. Rejecting Jesus Christ has serious consequences.

Jesus closes this section with a promise: "Some who are standing here will not taste death before they see the kingdom of God" (v. 27). He is speaking to the twelve disciples and others (v. 23). His words assure some of them that they will see the kingly rule of God come during their lifetime. The kingdom of God is already made present and visible in the powerful ministry of Jesus (11:20; 17:20–21). Apparently Jesus has in view the coming of the kingdom of God as a future event. It is, however, unclear what event he is thinking about. We can rule out the Second Coming, since then Jesus would be prophesying falsely here. Presumably he is referring to one or more events in the near future, such as the Transfiguration, the Resurrection, the Ascension, Pentecost, or the destruction of Jerusalem.

The kingdom of God comes in many ways; it is already present in Jesus' ministry if only the disciples have eyes to see. But we must emphasize "some" in "some . . . are standing" who will have the privilege before they die of seeing the kingdom of God. In context this must refer to the Transfiguration. On that occasion three disciples do in fact see the glory of God's rule as Jesus is gloriously transformed before their eyes (vv. 28–36). The disciples present at the Transfiguration, as well as those at Pentecost, receive a preview of the final arrival of the kingdom in its full glory.

3.12.5. The Transfiguration of Jesus (9:28–36). Luke dates this event about eight days after Peter's confession and Jesus' first prediction of his suffering. God's voice broke into the human realm when the Spirit anointed Jesus for his public ministry at his baptism (3:21–22). God now acknowledges him again as his Son (9:35). The occasion is the eve of his turning toward Jerusalem.

The Transfiguration comes at a time of a crisis in our Lord's life. Peter's confession that Jesus is the Messiah has signaled the end of his ministry to the multitudes. He has been widely

. Druze village in the foreground is dwarfed by the size of Mount
lermon, which remains snowcapped most of the year. Mount
lermon is considered a possible site where Jesus went with his
isciples to pray and where his Transfiguration took place. The
·aditional site is Mount Tabor.

eceived as a miracle-worker, but not as the ;avior. Soon he will begin his journey to erusalem to die for humankind. Thus, Jesus akes his closest disciples—Peter, James, and ohn—to a mountain. Likely it is Mount Hernon, located about fourteen miles north of Caesarea Philippi.

Seeking a place of solitude, Jesus and his lisciples go up the mountain to pray. It is not ard to imagine the content of the prayer. No loubt it has to do with his commitment to the vay of the cross (cf. v. 22). The Father does inswer the prayer, but the answer is not the emoval of the cross. Rather, God reveals the glory of his kingdom in its consummation. The livine glory on the mountain teaches the disiples that true glory and the cross go together. The Transfiguration is also designed to encourage Jesus as he makes his way to Jerusalem and to the cross.

The Transfiguration takes place while Jesus s praying. His whole appearance is changed. His face shines like the sun and his clothes glisen in a white glow (Matt. 17:2; Mark 9:3); the livine glory blazes through his clothing "as oright as a flash of lightning" (Luke 9:29). God's majesty shines through Jesus' whole oody (cf. Ex. 34:29–35; 2 Cor. 3:13). Later Peter writes: "We were eyewitnesses of his majesty. For he received honor and glory from God the Father when the voice came to him from the Majestic Glory, saying, 'This is my Son, whom I love; with him I am well pleased'" (2 Peter 1:16–17). John adds: "We have seen his glory, the glory of the One and Only, who came from the Father" (John 1:14; cf. Rev. 1:13–15). The Transfiguration provides a preview of Jesus' majesty when he returns to the earth "with power and great glory" (Luke 21:27).

On the mountain Moses and Elijah suddenly appear (vv. 30–31). These two men shine with the brightness of heavenly glory and speak about "his departure" that is about to be fulfilled at Jerusalem. The noun "departure" (*exodos*) alludes to Moses and Israel's going forth out of Egypt; here it clearly refers to Jesus' sacrificial death. It likely also refers to his resurrection, since both are the means by which Jesus departed from the earth. The verb "bring to fulfillment" (*pleroo*) speaks about the fulfillment of God's plan of salvation. Jesus will reenact the Exodus, this time leading the people out of *spiritual* bondage.

The presence of Moses and Elijah is significant. Moses is the great lawgiver; Elijah is the great representative of prophecy. Jesus has come to fulfill the Law and the Prophets, both of which testify of him. That is, Moses and Elijah point to the fulfillment of all the Old Testament shadows and prophecies about the Messiah. Their appearance is intended to assure the disciples what will happen in Jerusalem agrees with Old Testament prophecy. The disciples, however, fail to grasp the significance of the presence of these two men. Later as they approach Jerusalem, they still struggle with Jesus' prediction of his own death (18:31–34).

The three disciples are "very sleepy." It may have been night. But either the brilliant light or the conversation of the two heavenly visitors with Jesus awakens them. Only when they are fully awake do they see Jesus' glory and the two heavenly visitors in glorious splendor (v. 32). At this point Peter senses the greatness of the moment and wishes to prolong the event. When he observes that Moses and Elijah are leaving, he proposes to build three shelters (*skenas*, "booths, tents") for Jesus and his two heavenly visitors. In his appeal to Jesus he says, "It is good for us to be here." That is, "This experience is wonderful. So let us continue it so we can enjoy it as long as possible."

But, as Luke reminds us, Peter does not know what he is saying (v. 33). His proposal is out of place, reflecting his lack of understanding of the situation. This glorious experience is to last only for a little while. Jesus still has his mission to perform in Jerusalem. He can never atone for sin by staying on the mountaintop and celebrating that glorious experience. He must come down and set his face toward Jerusalem.

Before Jesus can respond to Peter, a cloud appears, and the heavenly Father interrupts Peter's senseless talk. The cloud, a sign of the presence of God, covers the disciples. As Jesus and the two heavenly visitors enter the cloud, the three disciples are terrified. The voice of God speaks from the cloud with words that are similar to those that came from heaven at the time of Jesus' baptism and anointing with the Spirit (3:21–22). On that occasion, the voice was directed primarily to Jesus, confirming him as the Messiah. This time the heavenly voice is directed primarily to the three disciples since they are commanded to obey Jesus (v. 35): "This is my Son whom I have chosen; listen to him." This authoritative testimony confirms Peter's confession of Jesus as "the Christ of God" (v. 20). He is the anointed King (Ps. 2:7), who will do the works of the Suffering Servant of the Lord (Isa. 42:1–53:12). The disciples must listen to him because he is a prophet who is much greater than Moses (Deut. 18:15–18). The disciples think that they know who he is, but he is greater than the most illustrious witness in the Old Testament. They need to sit at his feet and pay attention to what he says.

When the voice from the cloud stops, the two heavenly visitors are gone, and there remains only Jesus with the disciples. The experience has been so overwhelming that Peter, James, and John remain silent for months, telling no one what they have seen. Only after Jesus' resurrection do they come to understand his majesty and glory. He will be "declared with power to be the Son of God by his resurrection from the dead" (Rom. 1:4). His triumph over death makes the mysterious significance of the Transfiguration more apparent.

The Transfiguration has deep practical relevance to Christians. (1) As Jesus prays, he is transfigured. Worship and communion with God produce transformation of life, which touches the whole life of the believer—the inner and outer person, all one's habits and activities.

(2) The subject of Jesus' conversation with Moses and Elijah is his "departure." His own coming exodus has far greater spiritual consequences than the deliverance of Israel from Egypt. Moses led his people out of physical bondage to Pharaoh, but through Jesus' exodus (his death and resurrection), the prophet, like Moses, leads his people out of their spiritual bondage. He thereby makes them truly free (cf. John 8:34–36).

(3) The Transfiguration provides an example of the kinds of people who will inhabit the kingdom to come. Moses, a saint who died, and Elijah, a saint who was raptured without dying, appear with Jesus. These two heavenly visitors represent two types of believers, the ones who are resurrected from the dead and the ones who are raptured without experiencing death (cf. 1 Thess. 4:13–18).

(4) The Transfiguration points to the nature of the resurrected body. Jesus underwent a marvelous change; his people can expect to undergo a similar change. As Paul expressed it, when Christ returns he "will transform our lowly bodies so that they will be like his glorious body" (Phil. 3:21).

(5) Finally, the Transfiguration reminds us of "a mountaintop experience." Peter wants to stay on the mountaintop as long as possible. Great inspiration comes in the presence of God and meets deep spiritual needs. Worshipers are spiritually lifted up and edified when God moves in worship services and manifests his extraordinary presence through the power of the Holy Spirit and the operation of spiritual gifts. These kinds of experiences offer great encouragement and spiritual strength, but they are followed by routine and by commonplace work and service. Though the inspiration, the wonder, and the worship are tremendous, no one can live forever on the mountain of glory. There are peaks and valleys for all of us.

3.12.6. Flaws of the Disciples (9:37–50). Immediately after the Transfiguration Jesus and the three disciples descend from the mount of glory to the valley of human need. The four incidents that follow reveal the disciples' frailties: their lack of faith, ignorance, pride, and ıtolerance. This section concludes Jesus' ȷalilean ministry, but the flaws of the disciples o not make for a happy ending. They have ailed to listen to Jesus, so they have much to ·arn.

The first incident tells about the disciples' ıck of power to cast out a demon (vv. 37–43). esus and the three disciples are met by a huge rowd that has apparently been waiting for ıem. From the crowd shouts a man, crying out ɔ Jesus for help. In great distress he begs Jesus ɔ look on his son with compassion, explainıg that he is "my only child" (words that add ɔ the deep emotions of the situation). At times n evil spirit attacks his son and makes him cry ·ut with sudden screams. Pulled to and fro and hrown into convulsions, he foams at the nouth and is bruised from these attacks. The lemon will hardly leave him. The father's lescription emphasizes his great fear that this pirit will destroy his son.

The father had already appealed for help: "I ·egged your disciples to drive it out, but they ould not" (v. 40). The nine disciples left ·ehind during the Transfiguration were unable o drive the demon out. Jesus, however, had ;iven the twelve disciples power over devils ınd diseases (9:1–6). His response expresses ıis deep disappointment: "O unbelieving and ·erverse generation . . . how long shall I stay vith you and put up with you?" The word 'generation" (*genea*) is broad and may include ıll the people being addressed, but his rebuke ndicts particularly the nine disciples as mem·ers of an unbelieving and sinful generation cf. Deut. 32:5). Their unbelief has made them ɔowerless, and Jesus is frustrated.

Against the backdrop of the disciples' unbeief, Jesus acts with authority and out of comɔassion. He commands the boy to be brought o him. As the boy is coming, the demon nakes a last-minute attempt to afflict him and ɛnocks him to the ground. But Jesus is not noved by the power of the evil spirit. Where he disciples have failed, Jesus will succeed. The demon will no longer be permitted to conrol the boy. Spirit-empowered Jesus rebukes he demon and returns the boy to his father, ıealed. Everyone is amazed at this manifestaion of God's great power. There is a striking contrast here—the disciples are powerless in he face of demonic powers, but Jesus triımphs over all kinds of evil. They have become arrogant with success and have failed to sustain through prayer the faith and ministry of deliverance Christ gave them (9:1–6).

The second incident reveals the disciples' lack of understanding (vv. 44–45). Jesus has already told them clearly what lies in store for him (v. 22), but their traditional thinking has kept them from understanding and believing the truth. As people are still marveling at the deliverance of the boy from the demon, Jesus again discusses his forthcoming suffering with his disciples. To underscore the importance of what he is about to say, he asks for their complete attention and then informs them that the Son of Man will be handed over to others, betrayed, and put to death.

Jesus intends for the disciples to understand his coming passion, but they fail in this. Their thinking is still traditional. For them the Messiah will be a popular hero, a strong militaristic deliverer of his people. He will be a glorious, victorious person but never rejected and crucified. Unable in their minds to connect the Messiah with suffering, they fail to grasp the significance of Jesus' words. As a result, the importance of Jesus' passion remains hidden to them. And out of fear they ask Jesus no questions of clarification. Apparently they do not want to hear more about something that they do not want to hear at all (Marshall, 1978, 394). Yet their fear is a statement of mistrust and unbelief. Rather than understand the true plan of salvation, they cling to their traditional, idealistic views. We can only imagine the hurt of Jesus' heart that day.

The third incident exposes the pride of the disciples (vv. 46–48). An argument breaks out among them as to which one is the most important. Jesus has just predicted his own sacrificial suffering and death. The worldly aspirations of his disciples for position and prestige reflect that they have not comprehended his teaching on self-sacrifice and humility. Aspiring for great positions, they have fallen into the trap of pride and jealousy.

As the disciples argue, they are probably not within hearing distance of Jesus. But again Jesus shows prophetic, Spirit-anointed insight. Discerning what is going on in their hearts, he moves into action. He takes a small child and has him or her stand beside him—an act that places this child in a position of honor. But the child represents unimportant, weak members of society, those who have no status. It is not that Jesus sees children as insignificant. For him every person is important. A person with the attitude of a child can best accept Jesus and trust in him.

Jesus wants his disciples to adopt the attitude of a small child. Rather than contending for positions, they are to remember the poor, the weak, and the downtrodden. Whoever accepts and cares for these children, insignificant as they are in the eyes of society, welcomes Jesus himself and welcomes the One who sent him. As a climax, Jesus sets forth a principle that one who wants to be the greatest must consider himself or herself the least important. Greatness has nothing to do with rank, talent, or importance, but it has everything to do with humbling oneself in order to serve others. The person most willing to serve others regardless of origin, social standing, or color is the greatest; such people have abandoned all desire for greatness (Marshall, 1978, 397). An air of superiority in the church frequently hinders winning to Christ those who need him the most.

The final incident exposes the disciples' intolerance (vv. 49–50). This subject is closely tied to the preceding emphasis on humility and servanthood. The disciples have shown themselves to be competitive and arrogant, but they also show their desire to be a elite group. The case in point deals with a person who has driven out demons in the name of Jesus but is not a member of the Twelve. John, son of Zebedee, and the other disciples have tried to stop him because he does not belong to their group. They assume that they are the only ones approved to do wonders in Jesus' name.

John calls Jesus "Master" (*epistata*), showing respect for him, but he fails to realize whom he is addressing even after witnessing the Transfiguration. Obviously the disciples still see things as human beings see them and not as God sees them. They are cliquish, intolerant, and filled with ministerial jealousy, and they condemn the man driving out demons.

Jesus takes a different attitude. The disciples have no right to try to limit another person's ministry. So Jesus tells them, "Do not stop him." Then, with prophetic insight he adds, "For whoever is not against you is for you." This statement does not encourage a person to be neutral toward Jesus. The exorcist did not take a neutral position. In fact, he performed his ministry in Jesus' name—not by his own power but by Jesus' power. Jesus therefore endorses and empowers this man's ministry as he had done the Twelve. The man who opposes demons in Jesus' name is to be welcomed, not criticized.

Jesus' teaching here has implications for today. No group or denomination, no matter how holy or closely identified with the Savior, has an exclusive claim to divine power and ministry. Elitism has a way of showing its ugly head in our relationships with other believers. Many times brothers and sisters have pushed someone away because that person did not belong to a specific fellowship or denomination. We must realize that all who truly and faithfully use the name of Jesus are accepted as children of God. Furthermore, there is no middle ground. The disciples think of themselves as followers of Christ, yet they manifest worldly ways and attitudes. No one can be gripped by pride and jealousy and at the same time serve God. Adherence to Jesus' teaching by the help of the Holy Spirit purges us of such attitudes.

4. Travel Narrative: The Journey of Jesus to Jerusalem (9:51–19:44)

Jesus' ministry in Galilee is over. His rejection and death in Jerusalem lie before him. Luke 9:51–19:44, the longest section in this Gospel, records Jesus' journey to Jerusalem. During his journey he teaches and instructs the disciples and defends the gospel from his opponents.

Luke refers to Jesus as traveling to Jerusalem a number of times (9:51, 53; 13:22, 33; 17:11; 18:31; 19:11, 28), but he does not make a straight path to the city. At first he and his disciples seem to travel the shorter route through Samaria (9:51ff.). Later, however, we find him passing through Jericho, which lay on a longer route through Perea (19:1). In 10:38–42 he is at the home of Mary and Martha in Bethany, a village located about two miles from Jerusalem (cf. John 12:1–2). But Luke 17:11 has Jesus traveling in the north "along the border between Samaria and Galilee." Jesus is committed to go to Jerusalem but not by the shortest route.

Jesus knows what awaits him in the city. Near the end of his Galilean ministry he spoke plainly to the Twelve about his approaching death (9:22). On the mountain of glory Moses and Elijah talked with him about his "departure" that must be fulfilled in Jerusalem (9:31). He has descended from the mountain of glory to ascend a different one in Jerusalem, Mount Calvary. As he now makes his way toward that city, he has prepared his disciples to preach the gospel after his exaltation. If they are to share in his victorious resurrection and ascension, they must be willing to deny themselves and take up their cross daily. But they have been trying to promote themselves. So Jesus teaches them about discipleship and calls on them to be faithful whatever the cost.

4.1. Jesus Sets His Face Toward Jerusalem (9:51–56)

As Jesus begins the journey to Jerusalem, he knows he will face betrayal and death there in fulfillment of the divine plan. From there he is "to be taken up [*analempsis*] to heaven." This word refers to his ascension. His days on earth do not merely end with death and resurrection but culminate with his glorious ascension into heaven. The journey begins with Jesus' determination to do God's will regardless of the personal cost.

The most direct route to Jerusalem goes through Samaria. Jesus sends some of his disciples ahead to arrange a place for them to spend the night. The people in a Samaritan village know that Jesus is heading for Jerusalem. As a result, they refuse to welcome him. The Samaritans (regarded as half-breed Jews) did not get along with Jews and were usually unfriendly to pilgrims traveling to celebrate a festival at the temple in Jerusalem, a place they rejected as a true place of worship. For them, the holy site for worship was Mount Gerizim. Normally Jews traveling to Jerusalem avoided Samaria, but Jesus deliberately chooses this route. The Samaritans' rejection of him reflects the rejection he will experience in the Holy City, except that what he encounters there will be much worse.

When James and John learn about the Samaritans' refusal to welcome Jesus, these "Sons of Thunder" (Mark 3:17) are ready to take things into their own hands. They ask Jesus whether he wants them "to call fire down from heaven to destroy them." Their question assumes that they have the power to call down God's judgment on the Samaritans, and their desire to do this reminds us of the ministry of Elijah (2 Kings 1:9–10). Perhaps they are trying to copy Elijah, since Jesus himself has modeled his ministry after Elijah. The power they have received, however, is not for the purpose of destroying people, but for delivering them from sin and Satan.

James and John must be given higher marks for their zeal and devotion to Christ than for their understanding of his ministry and theirs. Earlier Jesus told them: "Love your enemies, do good to those who hate you, bless those who curse you, pray for those who mistreat you" (6:27–28). These disciples are unfit for ministry because of their vindictive and violent spirit (cf. also John 18:10–11). Jesus rebukes the two brothers for their overreaction to the Samaritans' refusal of hospitality (Luke 9:55). Their call for revenge shows that they have yielded to carnal desires. Elijah did call down fire out of heaven, but not because of revenge. It is easy to forget that human wrath does not work God's righteousness.

4.2. The Cost of Following Jesus (9:57–62)

Jesus has been rejected by a Samaritan village. So in the midst of rejection it becomes important to know what discipleship involves. As he goes on his way, Jesus meets three would-be followers. These men want to follow Jesus, but they fail to act on their desire. Meeting them gives Jesus an opportunity to show what is required for wholehearted discipleship. He spells out in specific circumstances what it means to pick up one's cross daily.

The first man offers to follow Jesus anywhere he goes, but he has not thought through what his offer means. He learns that Jesus is unwilling to negotiate terms of discipleship, but Jesus does want him to know the specific demands of following him. To go wherever Jesus goes means to be prepared to make the same sacrifices as he did. During his ministry the Savior was totally dependent on the hospitality of others. Both wild animals and birds have a place to call their own, but the Son of Man had no home. His true followers must count the cost of discipleship and be prepared to walk the path of self-denial and self-giving.

Jesus calls the second prospective disciple to follow him. But this man has something else to do before becoming a follower. He wants to return to his home so that he can bury his father. His request seems to be reasonable enough, but it has two possible meanings: (1) His father may have died already, and he wishes to take care of his father's funeral; or (2) his father may be very old and the man wishes to take care of him until he dies. He will then be free to go with Jesus.

If the father has already died, the call to follow Jesus is of greater urgency. Among the Jews the burying of family members had the greatest priority, taking precedence over such important matters as the study of the law, temple worship, preparing the Passover sacrifice, and the observance of circumcision (Morris, 1974, 180). For the pious Jew one of the most important duties was to provide a proper funeral and to show respect to one's parents.

To Jesus, taking care of the burial of a family member has its place, but it must not take precedence over the call to discipleship. Burial of the dead can be left to others. So Jesus says, "Let the dead bury their own dead." The man whom Jesus has called should not put discipleship off. As a disciple he has an urgent task: proclaiming the kingdom of God. The spiritually dead can handle the task of burying the physically dead; those made spiritually alive have a mission—to share the good news of God's rule so that others may be blessed and enjoy eternal life. Following Jesus deserves absolute priority.

The third man whom Jesus calls wants to go home and say good-bye to his family. This request also sounds reasonable, but apparently his request conceals some hesitation to cut his ties and become a follower of Jesus. He wants to avoid immediate and decisive action. Discipleship calls for wholehearted commitment and its demands are stringent. Jesus emphatically rejects the man's request and warns him that by looking back, he fails to measure up to the requirement for being used in the service of God's kingdom.

Jesus appeals here to the practice of plowing to make his point. A man held the handles of a plow as animals pulled it. He had to guide it with care in order to make a straight furrow. Should he keep looking back, he would not be able to do a good job of plowing. The same holds true for following Jesus. It calls for devotion and for concentration. Looking back distracts from wholehearted service. Jesus expects of us our best. Rendering to him our complete devotion makes us fit to be used in the service of God's kingdom.

4.3. Jesus Sends Out His Seventy-Two (10:1–24)

The account of Jesus' appointing seventy-two missionaries is similar to the mission charge to the Twelve (9:1–6). Luke treats this event rather extensively and shows that the task of ministry is not confined to the Twelve. All believers are called to represent Christ. Various New Testament letters teach that each believer has received a spiritual gift(s) for the work of the ministry (Rom. 12:3–8; 1 Cor. 12; Eph. 4:7–13; 1 Peter 4:10–11).

A sense of urgency characterizes this account. Jesus has set out for Jerusalem and does not have much time remaining for ministry, so the seventy-two must do their work quickly without distractions. Jesus equips with

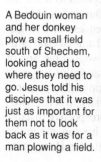

A Bedouin woman and her donkey plow a small field south of Shechem, looking ahead to where they need to go. Jesus told his disciples that it was just as important for them not to look back as it was for a man plowing a field.

power and sends out thirty-six pairs of disciples to places where he plans to go. They are to go ahead of him, preparing cities and villages for his ministry yet to come.

4.3.1. Instruction to the Seventy-Two (10:1–12). The urgency of the disciples' mission is seen as Jesus begins his instructions (v. 2). That "the harvest is plentiful" means that much work must be done to gather souls into the kingdom of God. People are ready to accept Jesus' message, but there are only a few workers. Many more must go out and win people to Jesus. Moreover, the seventy-two are to pray to God, the Lord of the harvest, that he will send more of his servants to share the good news and gather souls into his kingdom.

The harvest field, as Jesus understands it, includes the whole world. Thus his command to pray for more workers does not expire with the mission of the seventy-two. It applies as long as the harvest remains, that is, until all people in the world have heard the gospel. At the outpouring of the Holy Spirit at Pentecost Christ equipped the church to carry the gospel "to the ends of the earth" (Acts 1:8). The command to the disciples to pray for more workers implies that God may have to overcome the reluctance and apathy of those he wishes to send. Prayer for more laborers is the duty resting on those who work in the harvest. God does use our prayers to accomplish his purpose of evangelizing the world.

The ministry is no easy task (v. 3). As the seventy-two go out, they should see themselves as "lambs among wolves." This graphic phrase has a twofold meaning. (1) The word "wolves" refers to danger. As these people preach the gospel, they will face real danger. Jesus knows how violently people can respond when their religious pride and hypocrisy are exposed. These disciples need to count the cost involved in following Jesus (cf. 9:57–62). The world can be hostile to those who carry the gospel, but danger gives the disciple no excuse for withdrawing from it.

(2) The term "lambs" suggests the disciples will be defenseless before their enemies—like lambs before ravaging wolves. Like Jesus himself they are not to prepare to defend themselves or to minister in their own strength. They are to depend solely on God, taking with them no provision—no moneybag, knapsack, or extra pair of sandals. God will provide for their needs. Ministry must be their priority. They are to allow nothing to slow them down, especially greetings on the road. In Jewish culture greetings were long and elaborate. Jesus' desire is not for them to be impolite, but he does not want them to take too much time away from this urgent ministry. If the disciples are singular in purpose, they will be worthy of the support of those who receive their ministry.

The disciples are to use a simple strategy (vv. 5–7). When they reach a town or village, they must choose a house. The first house that extends hospitality is where they should stay during their ministry in that area. They should not think about their own comfort, moving from house to house and seeking better lodging. As they enter the house, they are to offer a blessing: "Peace to this house." This blessing involves much more than a custom or politeness. It is so real that God's presence can enter or depart from a house. Should the host be unworthy, the blessing will retreat from his house. If the host, however, is "a man of peace" open to the gospel, then the blessing of God's presence will rest on him. The position of that house is in one accord with God's kingdom.

The disciples' mission calls for single-mindedness and dedication to Jesus and his cause. The instruction to eat and drink what they are given means they are not to see themselves as a burden to their host. They earn their keep by preaching the gospel and healing the sick in that place. The workers deserve to be paid for their ministry (1 Cor. 9:7–14); the hospitality they receive is their payment. By staying in one house and being content with the hospitality they receive, the disciples are able to dedicate themselves to their primary mission.

Jesus then gives the seventy-two the procedure to be followed: First they are to receive hospitality, eating what is put before them, then heal the sick and preach the message of the kingdom. The food may not meet the requirements of the Old Testament food laws, but they are to be thankful for what is put before them. Like Jesus' own ministry, their healing of the sick is a sign that they have divine authority to carry God's message. Their preaching, as well as the healings, will serve to declare the presence of the kingdom.

The content of their preaching is specific: "The kingdom of God is near you." The verb "is near" (*engiken*, a perfect tense) indicates that

God's rule is present. The kingdom has become a reality through the ministry of Jesus and his disciples. Those who hear God's message can take part in the kingdom if they choose. True, the kingdom is a future reality, but it has broken into this world. The saving power of the gospel and the healing of the sick bear witness to its arrival. To say that the kingdom has arrived does not mean, however, that the kingdom has come in its fullness, for it will not fully come until Christ returns (Acts 1:6–8; 3:18–22).

Jesus continues his instructions. If the disciples enter a town or village where they are not welcome, they are to waste no time there. They must go into the streets where the townspeople are and publicly do two things. The first is to wipe the dust from their feet against them. This act shows the people that the disciples want nothing to do with that town. They have rejected the message of the kingdom and have missed their opportunity. Judgment will come upon such people. It is a fearful thing to fall into the hands of the living God. At the same time, they must warn them that the kingdom of God has come near and that their rejection of the message of salvation does not alter the reality of the presence of the kingdom. In rejecting these traveling preachers, they are rejecting more than just some humble men; they are rejecting the very kingdom of God.

There is an ominous note to the departing statement of the seventy-two: "Yet be sure of this: The kingdom of God is near." The townspeople have heard the message of the kingdom and have had the opportunity to embrace it. When that message of mercy and grace is rejected, it becomes a message of judgment. With the preaching of the kingdom comes accountability. The invitation is so generous and compelling that any town rejecting the witness of the disciples will fare worse in the coming judgment than the wicked city of Sodom did in Lot's time (v. 12). Jesus' charge must have impressed the seventy-two with the seriousness of their mission.

4.3.2. Pronouncement of Woes on the Unbelieving (10:13–16). The mission charge to the seventy-two disciples has been completed. But Jesus continues with the idea of accountability and judgment. He utters a Spirit-inspired, prophetic denouncement of cities where he has ministered and the gospel has been rejected. The statement, "Woe to you," expresses his deep regret over the fate of the cities of Chorazin, Bethsaida, and Capernaum—cities located near the Sea of Galilee, where Jesus performed many miracles.

Little is known about Jesus' ministry in Chorazin and Bethsaida, but he must have had an extensive ministry there. The mighty works he did in those two cities should have produced repentance. If Christ's ministry had reached to Tyre and Sidon, cities to the north of Galilee, the people there would have publicly turned from their sins by a deep, mournful repentance as indicated by "sackcloth and ashes" (v. 13).

Chorazin and Bethsaida come under the displeasure of Jesus, but not as much as Capernaum for its pride and wickedness. Jesus had made this city his base for ministry for a while, and he had performed many miracles there (4:23, 31–44; 7:1–10). The people of Capernaum thought highly of themselves, expecting to reach great heights of glory, but Jesus declares that they will be cast down into the depths of shame (v. 15).

The language used here is taken from Isaiah 14:13–15, where the prophet condemns the king of Babylon for his attempt to make himself God. "I will make myself like the Most High" means "I will become most powerful," and "You are brought down to the grave" means "You will be destroyed." In Luke "the skies" and "the depths" (*hades*) represent the contrast between heights of glory and the great depths of humiliation and shame. Hades is the place of the dead, but it is also a place of condemnation for the ungodly. God will throw down Capernaum into Hades because of their failure to respond properly to his message and miracles. Tyre and Sidon will be judged; but Chorazin, Bethsaida, and Capernaum, because of the greater opportunity they received, will be judged more severely.

Final judgment, in other words, will be based on degree of opportunity. It will be harder to bear for those who have rejected Jesus Christ. Verse 16 stresses the seriousness of accepting or rejecting the witness of the disciples. In his parting words to the seventy-two, Jesus tells them that they bear his authority and fully represent him: "He who listens to you listens to me; he who rejects you rejects me; but he who rejects me rejects him who sent me." Jesus draws a parallel between their authority from him and his authority from the Father.

These disciples speak with the authority of the One who sends them. Their mission is serious, and they can proceed with confidence to preach the gospel and do mighty works.

4.3.3. Return of the Seventy-Two (10:17–20). Luke gives us no hint how long the seventy-two are away. But when they return, they rejoice specifically because they have been successful in driving out demons (v. 17). They seem surprised that they were able to do this. In his charge Jesus did not tell them explicitly that they would have authority over demons, as he had earlier assured the Twelve (9:1). But to their amazement the seventy-two exercised great authority against the demonic powers in the name of Jesus. The Savior then explains why they have been able to exercise that authority: The chief of demons, Satan, has fallen and suffered defeat. Jesus has personally witnessed this defeat, though he gives no indication when he saw Satan fall.

There are three views of when Satan's overthrow took place: (1) The preexistent Christ witnessed Satan's fall based on Isaiah 14:12. (2) Jesus witnessed his fall in the desert temptation (4:1–12), when Jesus established his authority over all the forces of darkness. (3) Jesus had a vision while the seventy-two were ministering under his authority. This third option is most likely the correct explanation. As they were out on their mission, Jesus beheld Satan fall from heaven like the suddenness of lightning that comes down from the sky. This vision relates to the victories of his disciples over the powers of evil.

Similar to the Old Testament prophets, Jesus sees a spiritual reality: Satan, though still active on the earth, is powerless when confronted with the name and authority of the Son of God. The devil still directs his attacks, especially against Jesus' disciples (22:31ff.). They have been sent as lambs among wolves, but any concern that Jesus had about his lambs has now been diminished by this vision.

Jesus wants the disciples to have no question about their authority over all the power of the enemy, the devil. He gave them that authority when they were sent out, but he wants them to know that they continue to possess it. They have authority "to trample on snakes and scorpions." Jesus does not approve of handling snakes, but his words do give assurance of protection against poisonous snakes and the like (cf. Acts 28:3–5). The powers of evil cannot harm the disciples, though Jesus does not deny they will have to endure persecution for the sake of the gospel.

The seventy-two have, however, a greater cause for rejoicing than their victory over demonic spirits. First and foremost, they should rejoice because their names have been written in the books of heaven (v. 20; cf. Ex. 32:32; Dan. 7:10; Phil. 4:3; Rev. 3:5; 20:12). This must not be taken to mean that their status is incapable of being reversed, but they are secure in light of all the spiritual provisions to which they have access. Personal salvation is much more important than victory over demons. Access to God's power and gifts is exciting, but lasting joy comes in having our names recorded in the book of life. We must keep our priorities straight and guard ourselves against pride in spiritual gifts and victories. Spiritual successes are to be seen in light of God's reign and, since Pentecost, in light of the Holy Spirit empowering the church (Acts 5:3; 8:7, 18–24; 12:20–24; 13:4–12; 28:3–6).

4.3.4. A Prayer of Thanks and Blessing (10:21–24). As Jesus thinks about the glorious plan of his Father, he bursts forth into rejoicing. Nowhere else in the Gospels do we find such strong language used for the rejoicing of Jesus. Through the power and influence of the Holy Spirit he gives an inspired thanksgiving to God and turns to his disciples with blessings that remind them of the grace God has toward them. Thanksgiving and blessings go together in worship (Craddock, 1990, 147). Worship, as on this occasion, involves the triune God. Thanksgiving is offered to the Father by the Son through the power of the Holy Spirit.

At his baptism Jesus was filled with the Spirit (4:18). Inspired with joy by the Spirit, he now praises God that simple, humble men like the seventy-two are taking part in the wonderful work of the kingdom. He praises the Lord of heaven and earth for revealing "these things . . . to little children," that is, to childlike people (v. 21). "These things" refers to the gospel of the kingdom. The "wise" (people with great experience and practical knowledge) and the "learned" (those with great education and intellect) are for the most part unwilling to come to Jesus with childlike faith. They, therefore, fail to grasp the significance of the truth God has revealed in the gospel.

True discernment of redeeming truth, in other words, comes not through reasoning and well-informed intellect, but through the insight granted by the Holy Spirit (1 Cor. 2:14–16). The "wise and learned" probably refer to Jewish leaders, most of whom were rejecting the gospel. It may, however, include anyone with a proud spirit. The contrast is not between the educated and uneducated, but between those with an arrogant, self-sufficient attitude and those with a childlike attitude of trust.

After praising God the Father, Jesus directs words to his disciples, emphasizing the close relationship between the Father and himself (v. 22): "All things have been committed to me by my Father." The heavenly Father has given the Son the supreme place, withholding nothing from him, including the work of salvation and power over all evil spirits. The Son has absolute power and authority to reveal the Father on the earth. In his statement, "No one knows who the Son is except the Father," Jesus indicates that no human can fully understand his person. The character of the invisible God is revealed in him. The relationship between the Father and Son is unique and something of a mystery. They only have full and complete knowledge of each other.

By the same token, "no one knows who the Father is except the Son." But Jesus here makes a significant addition: "and those to whom the Son chooses to reveal him." By reason of his relationship with God, the Son can reveal the Father to whomever he wishes. People can come to know God the Father, but only through Jesus. The Son has no reluctance to reveal him and is never arbitrary in making him known. But it is to the "little children" spoken of in verse 21 that he wishes to reveal the heavenly Father. Truly knowing him is completely a matter of grace and faith.

The disciples are among those to whom Jesus is delighted to reveal the Father. So he turns to them and reminds them of their privileged position (vv. 23–24). They have received truths from Jesus about the Father and his kingdom that many of "the wise and learned" have rejected. They are blessed not only because they are coming to know the Father, but also because he has included them in saving the world. The kingdom has become real to them, and they have a part in it, though there is still a future aspect of that kingdom, which will begin with Christ's death and resurrection.

The disciples will actually witness these events as they come to pass. They are blessed because of the privilege of seeing what prophets and kings longed to see (1 Peter 1:10–12). The greatest of spiritual men desired to see the dawning of the new era but did not have the privilege. Because of their childlike humility and their role with Christ at this time in history, the disciples have the opportunity to take part in the dawning of the kingdom and to be servants of the gospel.

Jesus can still be a stone of stumbling today. It is easy to know much about Christianity and not see its Lord. According to the gospel human wisdom and divine wisdom clash. We will have to choose either to stumble with "the wise and learned" or humble ourselves as children and become servants of the Lord.

4.4. Danger of Distraction (10:25–42)

Jesus has emphasized that God bestows the blessings of his kingdom on those who have a childlike attitude rather than on "the wise and learned." The incidents of the lawyer (the expert in the Mosaic law) and of Martha and Mary warns against the danger of distraction. The lawyer has head knowledge of the law of Moses but lacks commitment to put it into practice. Martha receives Jesus into her home, but she too is distracted. Mary, her sister, chooses to hear Jesus' life-giving words.

4.4.1. A Lawyer and Parable of the Good Samaritan (10:25–37). Jesus tells the parable of the good Samaritan as a response to a question posed by a lawyer. This man, an expert in the first five books of the Old Testament, wishes to test Jesus' wisdom. His question is so important: "What must I do to inherit eternal life?" He is not seeking for information, however, but probably wants to gain an advantage over Jesus or is hoping Jesus will embarrass himself. His question assumes that he must do something to receive life after death. The thinking of the lawyer reflects a salvation by works rather than by divine grace.

Jesus could have emphasized to the lawyer that eternal life is a gift of God, but he does not try to correct the lawyer's thinking. He does probe, however, his understanding of the law by asking, "What is written in the Law? . . .

How do your read it?" Knowing that the man is an expert in the law of Moses, Jesus asks him how he understands the Scriptures. The lawyer answers by joining the commandments to love God with our whole being (Deut. 6:5) and to love our neighbor as ourselves (Lev. 19:18). Jesus agrees with his analysis, but he goes on to focus on the question of the "neighbor" (*plesion*). Jews limited the meaning of the term *neighbor* to members of their own nation, excluding Samaritans and foreigners (Marshall, 1978, 444). Jesus redefines the word, broadening its meaning. The love of one's neighbor grows out of love for God and must be equal to our love of ourselves.

Jesus then tells the lawyer, "Do this and you will live" (v. 28). To love God and neighbor is the proper response to the grace of God. But God never offers the law as a means of securing eternal life. The commandments of love are not a matter of earning salvation by works but of trust and devotion. If we really love God as Jesus teaches, we will rely on him, not on ourselves for salvation. But God's saving grace calls for a response from us. Our love—never the cause of forgiveness of sin—grows out of God's love and acceptance of us (cf. 7:40–47). So when Jesus tells the lawyer, "Do this and you will live," he does not endorse works as a way to obtain eternal life. Rather, God's love in our hearts prompts us to love him and neighbor. We live in the Spirit, which bears fruit in loving others and in living righteously (Rom. 8:1–11).

Jesus' response shows that the lawyer knows the answer to his own question. The Savior says to him in effect, "You do not need to ask about eternal life. You know what Moses teaches and you know the answer. Just practice what you know." But the expert in the law is not willing to let it rest there. So to justify his first question, he asks another one: "And who is my neighbor?" He wishes to show that his earlier question is not pointless and that the meaning of "neighbor" is unclear. To answer the lawyer's question about whom he should show love to, Jesus relates the story of a Samaritan who has compassion on a stranger.

A man is traveling on the rugged road between Jerusalem and Jericho. Robbers attack him, taking all that he has, beating him with clubs or sticks, and leaving him nearly dead. It just so happens that a priest comes along and sees the man lying there. Uncertain as to whether the man is dead, he fears defilement. Should he have touched him and the man was dead, the priest would have defiled himself (Lev. 21:1ff.). Exactly why he passes by "on the other side" of the road, Luke does not tell us. The point is that the priest has no heart; he does not bother to see if the sufferer is alive and needs help. A member of the priestly tribe of Levi does the same thing (v. 32). Normally, one would expect the priest and Levite, guardians of the religion of Israel, to render aid, but both have failed to be neighbors to the man.

A Samaritan (see comments on 9:51–56) also comes along. When he sees the wounded man by the side of the road, his heart is filled with compassion. He does not hesitate to help the man. On the spot he applies oil and wine to cleanse his wounds and to ease the pain. Since the injured man is unable to walk, he places him on his own donkey and brings him to an inn, where he can receive adequate care. His concern for the man does not stop even there. He gives the innkeeper money sufficient to cover several days of the man's board and instructs him to care for him as long as is necessary. Should the innkeeper have more expense, he will repay him on his way back.

Travel between Jericho and Jerusalem was through the rugged country of Wadi Kelt shown here. This donkey is on the old Roman road that connected the two cities.

A despised Samaritan proves to be a real neighbor to a wounded man.

This story of the good Samaritan teaches the lawyer that his neighbor is anyone he encounters who has a need. Thus Jesus closes the story with the question: "Which of these three do you think was a neighbor to the man who fell into the hands of the robbers?" The lawyer knows the answer, but he cannot bring himself to speak the despised word "Samaritan" and still wants to choose his neighbor. Thus he refers to him only as "the one who had mercy on him" (v. 37).

The lawyer's answer is correct, for the Samaritan is the one who acted as a neighbor. By showing compassion, he aligned himself with love for God and neighbor. Unlike the priest or Levite, he has submitted to the commandment of love that summarizes the entire law. Similarly, Jesus wants the lawyer to respond in a childlike manner to God and neighbor. So he tells him, "Go and do likewise." The lawyer too can fulfill the commandment to love God and neighbor by meeting the needs of others regardless of race, color, or gender.

4.4.2. Mary and Martha (10:38–42). The story of the Good Samaritan stresses the importance of caring for others in need. The incident of Mary and Martha shows that we need to listen to Jesus' word and not let other matters distract us. Although the focus of the story is on two women, the principles apply just as much to men as to women.

Martha and Mary, sisters of Lazarus, live at Bethany, a village a couple of miles from Jerusalem (John 11:1; 12:1–3). When Jesus and his disciples enter the village, Martha welcomes him into her home as a guest. Her sister, Mary, is described as sitting as a student at the feet of Jesus and listening to his words. In first-century culture Jewish teachers did not allow women to sit at their feet. What Jesus does on this occasion is highly unusual; he is the guest of a woman in her home and he teaches a woman. Without doubt he has an interest in all people.

While Mary listens to Jesus, Martha is hard at work preparing the best possible meal for him and his disciples. She is, however, displeased with Mary, who could help her in the kitchen. Martha, after all, would like to hear Jesus too. Becoming increasingly frustrated, she accuses Jesus of being insensitive to her situation. So she asks, "Lord, don't you care that my sister has left me to do the work by myself?" In Greek this question is asked in a way so that she expects a positive reply. Though she feels that he could have been more sensitive, Martha is convinced that Jesus does care and understands that she needs Mary's help. She expects Jesus to intervene.

But Jesus does not tell Mary to help Martha with the meal, though he does respond tenderly to Martha (v. 41). The double address, "Martha, Martha," expresses intense concern (cf. 2 Sam. 19:4; Luke 22:31). Jesus knows her anxiety, and he is concerned about her attitude: "You are worried and upset about many things." Jesus gently rebukes her for being distracted and troubled about the domestic responsibilities. Martha needs to establish some priorities. So he adds that "only one thing is needed." In light of the context this must refer to what Mary is doing—listening to Jesus' Spirit-anointed, life-giving teaching. Because Mary chooses to sit at the feet of Jesus, she "has chosen what is better." Not that Martha has done bad and deserves condemnation, but Mary has chosen what "will not be taken away from her."

In other words, the "meal" that Mary receives while at the feet of Jesus will last. No meal is as important and as satisfying as that meal. It is the anointed, saving, soul-satisfying word of Jesus Christ. No one can take that away from the children of God. Through the Holy Spirit his word saves and deepens our personal relationship with him. We must follow Mary's example and sit at the feet of Jesus, avoiding those distractions that leave no time for the study of the Scriptures, for prayer, and for praise and worship.

4.5. Jesus' Teaching on Prayer (11:1–13)

Luke brings to our attention the importance of prayer in two ways: by the example of Christ (see comments on 3:20–21; 5:12–16; 6:12–16) and by his teaching. On one occasion after praying, he receives from one of his disciples the request, "Lord, teach us to pray." In response Jesus gives the disciples a pattern for prayer (vv. 1–4), tells a story to illustrate the need for persistence in prayer (vv. 5–8), and assures them of God's answering prayer (vv. 9–13). He reminds them that God bestows the gift of the Spirit in response to prayer, linking, therefore, prayer to the Spirit, who empowers both Jesus (3:21) and the church (24:49; Acts 1:4–5, 8; 2:38).

4.5.1. The Lord's Prayer (11:1–4). Matthew's account of this prayer is longer and is part of the Sermon on the Mount (6:9–13). It is likely that Jesus taught the prayer more than once. As we consider Luke's account of the Lord's Prayer, two important points emerge. (1) Jesus gives it to his followers, making it "The Disciples' Prayer." (2) All the pronouns in the prayer are plural. Thus, it really is a community or corporate prayer. Jesus is forming a new community, and the prayer he gives will be one of its distinctives (Morris, 1974, 193).

The corporate emphasis is seen at the beginning of the prayer in the simple address, "Father" (*pater*). Jesus addressed God as Father in his prayer in 10:21–22 and did likewise in his later prayer from the cross: "Father, into your hands I commit my spirit" (23:46). For him and his disciples God is Father, with all that the term means. As the disciples address God as Father, they affirm their unity and their sense of belonging to his family. When they pray, the disciples are to be aware that they form a community before God. They share the same goals and love one another.

Beginning the prayer with "Father" also emphasizes an intimate, God-centered attitude. Jewish prayers tended to put a distance between human beings and the great God. Unlike them Jesus teaches his disciples to approach God as a small child would his earthly father. The word he uses for Father corresponds to the Aramaic *abba*—a word used by a child for his father. Generally, the Jews used another form in prayer, such as *abinu* ("Our Father"). They thought it too daring to speak with the King of the Universe as a child speaks with his father. But Jesus instructs his disciples to address God by his close family name. They have that right and privilege because they are sons and daughters in his great family (cf. Rom. 8:15; Gal. 4:6).

After the address, the prayer consists of five petitions. The first two focus on God and his great plan for the world; the last three requests deal with personal needs of the disciples. The content of the prayer reflects the basics of discipleship.

The first petition requests that God's name be hallowed. God's name stands for God himself and all that he has revealed about himself. His name sums up his whole character and purpose. The verb "hallowed" (*hagiazo*, "sanctify") emphasizes that God is holy and set apart. The petition is not for God to sanctify himself, but for people to acknowledge and treat God as holy, as One set apart and unique. God cannot become more holy, but worshipers can become more aware that there is none like unto him. When people respond to him as such, they acknowledge and worship him as the true God, above all creatures and things. Though his people have a close fellowship with God as Father, he is still to be revered as the High and Holy One. Their intimacy with him should never hinder their reverence for him.

The second petition is for God's kingdom to come. God's rule is a prominent theme in the teaching of Jesus; this petition expresses the desire for the future coming of God's reign. That kingdom has already arrived in the Spirit-empowered life and ministry of Jesus and in the lives of those who subject themselves to God and walk in his ways. On the other hand, it is yet to come in the fullness of its power and glory. When Christ returns, the kingdom will reach its fulfillment. All creation will be renewed and set free from the curse of sin (Rom. 8:18–21). Satan's rule will be brought to an end (Rev. 20:1–3, 7–10). Justice will prevail, and God's children will enjoy eternal salvation. It is for the final coming of the kingdom that we are to pray.

God can be trusted to provide for the needs of his people. So the second part of the prayer has to do with personal requests. Jesus begins with the most basic need, food. The Greek word translated "bread" (*artos*) includes all kinds of food, not just bread as such. The present tense of "give" (*didou*) means "keep on giving." Since it is linked with "each day" (*kath' hemeran*, "day by day"), we should look to God daily for provisions. Should God provide us with rations sufficient for a lengthy period, we may be tempted to forget him. Our heavenly Father desires that we live in a state of continued dependence on him as he cares for our physical needs.

The second request is for forgiveness of sins. By praying for forgiveness we confess that we are sinful and guilty of doing wrong. The

New Testament teaches that forgiveness comes by God's grace and that it is received through faith (Eph. 2:8); human merit has nothing to do with it. Jesus does, however, attach a condition to our asking God to forgive us of sin: We should be ready to "forgive everyone who sins against us" (cf. Eph. 4:32; Col. 3:13). The present tense expresses a constant readiness to forgive. Forgiving others fails to merit God's forgiveness for one's self, but we should never ask God to do something for us that we will not do for one another. Refusal to forgive closes our hearts to God's mercy.

The last petition is that God will not lead us into temptation. At first this petition may strike us as strange. Why should God tempt anyone to sin? After all, he does not tempt anyone (James 1:13–17). Nevertheless, he does allow Satan to bring us into trials and temptations in order to test and strengthen our characters (cf. Job). God's intent is never that we yield to temptation and fall into sin. But we as believers know that we are weak and can succumb to the flesh, sin, and Satan. We also know that God is able to protect us and keep us from falling into sin. So we pray to be delivered from circumstances where temptation assails us. Needless to say, God does not spare us of all temptations, but he does give victory to those who rely on him.

4.5.2. The Parable of a Friend at Midnight (11:5–8). Jesus continues to stress the importance of prayer with this parable of a friend at midnight. Here he emphasizes that prayer must be persistent and that God is always ready to answer. God's gracious response to prayer encourages us to go on praying.

The story reflects the culture of that day. There were two friends. One of them came to spend the night with the other, but did not arrive until midnight. Most food was prepared daily. Because the man's household had eaten their supply, he had nothing to offer his unexpected guest. But the man had to feed his guest since hospitality was a sacred duty. Therefore, he went to a neighbor who might be able to lend him three loaves of bread. But the neighbor and his family were asleep. Typically a humble Palestinian home had only one large room. At night mats were spread on the floor for the family to sleep. If the man were to get up for the bread, he would risk waking his family. Thus he refused the request, saying, "The door is already locked, and my children are with me in bed" (v. 7). Note that the basis of his refusal was not a refusal to give his neighbor bread during this time of need.

Jesus then brings it to a surprising conclusion. "I tell you, though he will not get up and give him the bread because he is his friend, yet because of the man's boldness [or persistence] he will get up and give him as much as he needs" (v. 8). The man will not go away, nor will he let his neighbor go back to sleep. Their mutual friendship does not prevail, but his refusal to give up does. The key word here is *anaideia* (shamelessness, boldness). The man's persistence and boldness bring results. The attitude reflected here is like that of Hebrews 10:19–22, where we are encouraged to draw near to God in prayer and worship.

This parable strongly encourages us to be persistent in prayer. We need not be ashamed to keep on asking. God will eventually respond to our persistence and answer our prayer because he truly loves us and cares about our needs. What better motivation can we have for being persistent in prayer? Our aim should not be to cajole God to change his mind when he has said "No." God withholds from us nothing that we need. He reserves his choicest blessings for those who value them and who keep on praying until they receive (Caird, 1963, 152).

4.5.3. The Assurance That Prayer Will Be Answered (11:9–13). Jesus concludes his teaching on prayer by stressing the way God answers our requests. He responds in a generous way and does not give grudgingly. He knows what we need ahead of time. But as we teach our children to do, he wants us to ask.

Jesus urges his followers to "ask ... seek ... [and] knock." The three verbs are present imperatives, emphasizing the need of continuous prayer. Prayer must be more than a single activity; we must keep on asking, keep on seeking, and keep on knocking. God will respond to deep, earnest, and persistent prayer (vv. 9–10). The three verbs—ask, seek, and knock—mean about the same thing, but there is progression from the general to the particular. To ask is general, but to seek is to search for a particular thing, and to knock is to go where the particular thing will be found. God will not let our needs go unattended, but this does not mean he will supply anything we equest. Jesus says nothing here about prayer prompted by wrong motives (see James 4:2–3). God can say "No" as well as "Yes." He answers according to what is best for us.

Because God wants what is best for us, we can rest assured that he is always ready to give good gifts to his children (vv. 11–13). Jesus underscores this truth with a couple of illustrations. A hungry son may ask his father for something to eat, such as a fish. What father would give him a poisonous snake instead? Or if the son should ask for an egg, would his father hand him a poisonous scorpion? No caring father puts his son in danger or gives his child harmful gifts. On the contrary, earthly fathers, even though they are evil, give good gifts to their children. Jesus assumes the sinfulness of humankind here. But with all their faults and imperfections, parents provide for the needs of their families. In contrast, our heavenly Father is perfect. How much greater, therefore, is his generosity, who gives the greatest gift, the Holy Spirit, to his children!

No gift can meet his children's spiritual needs better than the Holy Spirit. From conversion on, the Holy Spirit lives in believers (Rom. 8:9–11; 1 Cor. 6:19). After conversion God's children have a right to ask the Father to guide their lives by the Spirit and to empower them for the task of witnessing. At Pentecost the disciples waited in prayer to be filled with the Spirit and to be empowered for witness (Acts 1:8ff.; 2:1ff.). When they were persecuted and needed strength for witness, they prayed to be strengthened by the Spirit to preach the word (4:23–31). When Peter and John prayed, the Samaritan believers received the Holy Spirit (8:15–17).

The Spirit guided and empowered Jesus; when the Spirit comes upon his followers, they will be empowered to continue what Jesus began (Acts 1:1, 8). Believers are responsible to ask their heavenly Father for the Spirit's guidance and for his anointing power for service. Because of the kind of God he is, we can have absolute assurance that he "is able to do immeasurably more than all we ask or imagine" (Eph. 3:20).

4.6. Jesus' Power to Cast Out Demons (11:14–28)

The believer receives the Holy Spirit from the Father (v. 13); Luke now turns to a discussion of evil spirits under the authority of Satan. Jesus continues on his mission of casting out demons, demonstrating his power over the spirit world. Normally the time and place of Jesus' extraordinary works are indicated, but Luke tells us nothing here except that Jesus expels a demon that has caused dumbness. The rest of the account gives the controversial reaction to the miracle. From this point on opposition to Jesus from the religious leaders builds until it reaches its climax in Jerusalem, where he will suffer and die.

4.6.1. Beelzebub Controversy (11:14–23). Because of a demon a certain man is unable to speak. When Jesus drives the demon out, the man has no trouble talking. The miracle gives rise to three reactions. (1) Some are filled with amazement and deeply impressed. (2) Others seek to discredit Jesus, accusing him of driving demons out by the power of Beelzebub, a name given the devil as the ruler of demons. These people see Jesus as empowered by the devil rather than by the Holy Spirit. (3) Still others ask Jesus to show them "a sign from heaven," a miracle to prove he really has the power of God. These last two reactions show the danger of a made-up mind. Because their minds are closed, these people refuse to consider that Jesus drives out evil spirits by the power with which God has anointed him.

The Spirit-anointed Jesus understands the secret thoughts of his opponents (v. 17). They cannot deny his power. Thus, the issue is its source. Is it from Beelzebub or from God? Jesus answers the charge that it comes from the prince of devils in three ways. (1) Jesus makes a comparison by noting what happens when civil war occurs in a kingdom or when controversy exists in a household. A divided kingdom destroys itself and a divided household collapses. So how can Satan's kingdom stand if it is divided? No divided kingdom survives; it will come to a disastrous end. To charge Jesus with driving out demons by the power of the devil is ridiculous. It would point to civil war in Satan's kingdom, and it would fall apart.

(2) Jesus points out his opponents' inconsistency (v. 19) by raising the question of whose power their followers use to drive out demons. They are ascribing Jesus' power to Satan. If they are consistent, they must see their followers as doing likewise. Jesus recognizes that there are other Jewish exorcists, but

no one has accused them of driving out demons by Satan's hand. (We know nothing about the success of these Jewish exorcists and whether Jesus endorses their activity.) So if his critics are questioning his work, they must question the work of their own followers. Otherwise, they ascribe the same type of ministry to opposite causes: Satan and God.

(3) Jesus offers an alternative to his critics' charge. If Satan does not empower him, who does? It is by "the finger of God" (Ex. 8:19) that he drives out demons. Only God's power can break the grip of Satan. Jesus' power over demons therefore comes from God. His critics should thus consider the result: "The kingdom of God has come to you." Expulsion of demons is evidence of the presence of God's kingdom. Through the ministry of Jesus, God has already begun to rule and Satan's kingdom has been invaded.

Scholars debate the meaning of "has come" (*ephthasen*, from *phthano*) here, whether it signifies "has come near" or "has arrived." But along with the phrase "to you" (*eph' hymas*), it indicates that the kingdom has already arrived. God's kingly rule and saving power are evident in Jesus' power over demons. His mighty works announce the presence of God's power. As a result Satan's power on the earth is in the process of being overcome. But we must also remember that the consummation of the kingdom still lies in the future. It will take the return of Christ to bring the kingdom in its final form. Only then will the promise of the kingdom be brought to completion.

In the meantime, believers must continue to fight against Satan and the powers of darkness (Eph. 6:10–18). During his ministry on earth, the Spirit-empowered Jesus overcame sin, the flesh, and the devil. Jesus uses the illustration of the strong man to show his authority over Satan (vv. 21–23). The "strong man" refers to Satan and the "stronger" one to Jesus. Satan's having a well-fortified house represents the world under his control. He thinks his power is sufficient to repel God. But he is in control only until the stronger one overcomes him, taking his weapons and dividing his ill-gotten possessions. That stronger one has now come and is overcoming Satan by casting out demons. Satan still can do great damage, but his doom is sealed (cf. Eph. 6:10–18; Col. 2:14–15).

The kingdom of God and the kingdom of Satan, however, still confront one another in all-out war. Everyone who does not side with Jesus sides with the devil (v. 23). There is no place for neutrality. Those who do not help Jesus gather his flock together are scattering the sheep. The work of Jesus is to gather lost sheep; Satan seeks to scatter them.

4.6.2. The Return of the Evil Spirit (11:24–26). A person reading this short passage might conclude that the most important aspect of ministry is driving out demons. Although this theme is present, deliverance from the power of Satan is not enough. Our lives also must be filled with the power and presence of the Spirit, who indwells us.

Life must not be left empty. To drive this truth home, Jesus tells about a man out of whom an evil spirit has been driven. The spirit roams around in desert places, where demons like to live, but it finds no place to rest. So it decides to return to its house—that is, to the person out of whom it was driven. Upon arrival, the demon finds the house as it had been left—clean and everything in order. But the house is still empty. Therefore, the evil spirit brings in "seven other spirits more wicked than itself." As a result the man is in a worse condition than he was before.

The lesson is simple. After the man's deliverance from the evil spirit, he continues to live apart from God. The Holy Spirit does not occupy his heart. In other words, deliverance from the power of evil is not enough. The heart must be filled with the power and presence of the Holy Spirit. Getting rid of an evil spirit never means that we are immune to Satan's assaults. Satan is persistent, and unless our hearts are filled with God, the outcome can be tragic.

4.6.3. The Outburst of a Woman (11:27–28). A woman has been listening to Jesus speak about Satan and demons. She has been impressed by the power and the earnestness of his words. Because of her great admiration for him, she shouts out from the crowd a blessing on the mother who gave birth to Jesus and who nurtured him. She recognizes that every mother would like to have such a wonderful son. Her words of blessing are the beginning of the fulfillment of the prophecy of 1:48. She also affirms Jesus' messiahship and expresses goodwill toward him.

Jesus does not question the truth of her tribute, but he knows that praise does not ensure obedience to God's word. He proceeds to the real issue—obeying what God says. In verse 28 the term "rather" (*menoun*) stresses the greater significance of what follows (Reiling and Swellengrebel, 1971, 444). No doubt Jesus is aware that his mother is especially blessed of God. But considerably more significant is obedience to God's word as preached by the Savior. Obeying his message brings people to faith in Jesus and gives them a true spiritual relationship with him. Jesus always blesses those who accept his offer of the kingdom and believe the gospel. Heeding God's word results in being truly blessed.

4.7. The Demand for a Miraculous Sign (11:29–36)

Some of Jesus' critics have charged him with exercising power over demons by the help of Beelzebub. Others test him by insisting that he perform a miracle (v. 16). Jesus responds here to those "others," who want more signs that he is the Messiah.

People making such demands are described as "a wicked generation." They are wicked because they are demanding a sign rather than trusting God. The word "sign" (*semeion*) refers to the miraculous work of God. The people insist that unless God shows them special signs, they will not believe. Jesus promises them no sign "except the sign of Jonah" (v. 29)—a reference to the prophet Jonah's miraculous deliverance from death.

Some scholars insist that "the sign of Jonah" refers to his prophetic preaching of repentance rather than to resurrection. But Jonah spent three days in the belly of the fish before, so to speak, being restored to life (Jonah 1:17), and Matthew 12:40 clearly states that the sign of Jonah means resurrection. The difficulty with the view that this sign means Jonah's preaching is threefold. (1) The Scriptures never present the preaching of any prophet as a sign. (2) Jesus does not speak of Jonah's preaching but of Jonah himself as the sign. His presence in Nineveh was the sign that he had been miraculously saved from the huge fish. (3) Jesus uses the future (v. 30): As Jonah was a sign to the people in Nineveh, so the Son of Man *will be* a sign to this generation. The future points ahead to his resurrection. What happened to Jonah serves as a sign of Jesus' triumph over death. Thus, Jesus leaves no doubt that any signs he performs will be a matter of his own choosing. He will never give signs to satisfy the demands of an unbelieving generation.

The hearts of the faithless generation, the ones seeking for miraculous signs, are closed to the gospel message. Jesus emphasizes their guilt by referring to the Queen of Sheba (1 Kings 10:1–10). Though she was a Gentile woman, she traveled a great distance (from modern Yemen) to hear the wisdom of Solomon, the wisest man of that day. In the final judgment, this unbelieving generation will be condemned by her example of traveling so far to listen to Solomon's wisdom. For, as Jesus reminds them, one greater than Solomon has come to them, so that they do not even have to make a journey to hear him preaching the good news of salvation. Yet they are rejecting him and his message. On the Day of Judgment the Queen of Sheba will stand and condemn them for failure to believe in Christ for deliverance from sin.

The queen will not be the only witness against them in the final judgment. The men (*andres*) of Nineveh who repented at the preaching of Jonah will also condemn this generation for its unbelief. They believed his message and turned to God in sackcloth and ashes. On the other hand, the Jews of Jesus' day have the Messiah himself among them, yet most of them refuse to accept him as their Savior. Indeed, in their midst is one greater than Jonah. The very men who were saved in Nineveh will seal the fate of the people of Jesus' generation for refusing to hear the greatest of God's messengers, the Spirit-anointed Christ (v. 32).

Finally Jesus picks up on the theme of light (vv. 33–36). Some of those who do not believe demand a sign, but God gives Jesus and his message as a light. This light is sufficient to give light to all. As a result, no sign is needed to confirm his message. Jesus compares his preaching of the kingdom to a lamp. When it is lit, the lamp is put where the light cannot be hidden away—that is, on a stand, so that those entering a room can see where they are going. Jesus wants the gospel to spread in all its glory through his mighty works and words.

A lamp provides light in a dark room, but the human eye gives light to the body (that is, the entire person). Jesus says, "Your eye is the lamp of your body." The human eye can be either a source of light or darkness, depending on whether it is healthy or impaired. When the eye is "good," it lights up the whole body, and the person—body, soul, mind, and spirit—is "full of light," because the light dispels all darkness. On the other hand, when the eye is "bad," the person is "full of darkness," because that unsound eye hinders one from the full use of the light. Such a person cannot see where he is and where he is going.

Jesus has in mind two spiritual conditions. People can be either full of light or full of darkness. Their spiritual health rests on what they take into their souls. If their eyes are impaired and evil, they fail to receive the light of the gospel. But if their eyes are sound and pure, they take in all that God makes available in the gospel. As a result, their whole being is "full of light, and no part of it dark." When the wonderful light of the gospel enters our lives, it is like a lamp that shines on us in its full brightness. It dispels all darkness.

Some critics of Jesus have asked for a sign so that they might have more light. But the light that he has already provided is more than sufficient. Extra light never corrects poor eyesight. Since they have closed their eyes to the light of his mighty works and words, adding more light will not help their spiritual blindness.

4.8. Jesus Pronounces Woes on the Pharisees and the Teachers of the Law (11:37–54)

When Jesus finishes speaking about the importance of the body being full of light, a Pharisee invites him into his home for a meal. Like other Pharisees, this man has a keen interest in ritual purity. He notices that Jesus does not wash his hands before sitting down to eat. His concern has nothing to do with hygiene but with ceremonial purity. Washing hands was to get rid of ritual defilement caused by contact with Gentiles or ritually unclean objects. The Pharisee is offended by Jesus' crude manner.

This reaction exemplifies the growing hostility of the religious leaders toward Jesus. In his response Jesus goes on the offensive against religion that focuses on externals, such as washing hands before meals, but fails to deal with moral and spiritual needs of the heart. His attack reveals the dynamics of Jesus as a prophet and includes not only a general condemnation (vv. 39–41), but also six woes—three against the Pharisees (vv. 42–44) and three against the teachers of the law (vv. 46–52).

Luke gives no indication that the Pharisee says anything to Jesus, but the Spirit-anointed Savior discerns the thinking of his host. For the Pharisees, religion meant obedience to the law. They emphasized superficial matters like ritual washings rather than the cleansing of the heart from sin. Jesus declares that living such a life is like cleaning the outside of a cup or dish but leaving the inside dirty. The Pharisees may be ritually clean, but, as Jesus charges, inwardly they are "full of greed and wickedness" (v. 39). They harbor all kinds of sin in their hearts. They act as though the washing of their hands will cleanse their hearts and ensure a right relationship with God.

Wise people would not be so blind to think that God cares only for the outside. Therefore Jesus calls these religious leaders "foolish people." Fools think themselves to be wise, but in reality they are devoid of wisdom. If the Pharisees were wise, they would know that God made the inside as well as the outside. In fact, God has more interest in purity of heart than he does in washing hands and in other external matters of religion. The life that glorifies God springs from inner purity.

Next, Jesus adds a word about giving to the poor (v. 41). The Pharisees give more importance to keeping rules and regulations than they do to caring for the needy. The precise meaning of "give what is inside . . . to the poor" has been debated by scholars. Jesus seems to be emphasizing that giving to the needy is a matter of love and mercy, requiring action that issues from a clean heart. Acts of love stand in contrast to "greed and wickedness" (v. 39). Jesus calls for a new heart, filled with compassion for others. When we give out of hearts renewed by the Holy Spirit, the clean heart makes everything else clean (Lenski, 1946, 660). Cleansing must be internal.

Now Jesus begins the woes. Woes are not outbursts of anger; they are expressions of deep regret. Jesus is grieved by the practices of the Pharisees and teachers of the law. He has liberty in the Spirit, and with the directness of an Old Testament prophet he cries out against their hypocrisy and their neglect of things that really count.

Jesus directs the first three woes against the Pharisees. One of their practices was tithing (v. 42). This practice had its roots in the Old Testament (see Lev. 27:30–32; Deut. 14:22–23, which specify that a tenth of produce and of flocks and herds must be given to God). But Pharisees went beyond what the law required. They were so strict in obeying these commands that they paid tithes on the herbs produced by their gardens. They wanted to eliminate the possibility of transgressing any commandment and to provide themselves with a margin of safety. But in their efforts to give tithes on everything, they lost their sense of balance. They concentrated on the trivial, overlooking more important issues—doing right to others and obeying the commandment to love God (cf. 10:25–28).

Jesus does not want the Pharisees to neglect tithing. As far as he is concerned, they should give tithes, but without neglecting the other great commandments of God—notably, justice toward people and love for God. Zeal for the trivial can make us blind to what is most important.

The second woe addresses pride (v. 43). As well as failing to do the really important things, the Pharisees "love the most important seats in the synagogues and greetings in the marketplaces." Preoccupation with the outward and desire to be in the public eye go together. In synagogues the most prominent seats were those containing the sacred Scriptures. They were reserved for important people, and the Pharisees loved sitting in them. They knew that such seats drew attention to their importance and gave the impression that they were people of distinction. "Greetings in the marketplaces," such as bowing before the Pharisees and addressing them with titles of honor, also fed their pride. Showing respect has its place; but when carried to the extreme, it feeds vanity. Among religious leaders personal honor may be sought more than the honor of God.

The third woe accuses the Pharisees of corrupting others (v. 44). According to Jewish law, anyone who had contact with a dead body or touched a grave was considered ritually unclean for seven days (Num. 19:16). The Jews whitewashed tombs so that people could avoid touching them. Old, forgotten graves would be unmarked, so someone could easily step on one and become ritually unclean without realizing it. Though Pharisees thought of themselves as examples of purity, Jesus says that they "are like unmarked graves, which men walk over without knowing it." Indeed, the hearts of these religious leaders are "full of greed and wickedness" (v. 39).

In this wicked condition the leaders are sources of spiritual and moral defilement. Outwardly they appear to be righteous, but the external reveals nothing about the filthy condition of their hearts. Unfortunately few Jews realized just how deadly such leaders' influence could be. Having no idea of the danger, people became spiritually defiled by contact with them. As the proverb says, "Bad company corrupts good character" (1 Cor. 15:33). What Jesus describes here can be as true today as it was then.

At this point an expert in the law (*nomikos*, "lawyer") raises an objection. Many of these experts belonged to the party of the Pharisees. Jesus' condemnation of the Pharisees was, therefore, a condemnation of them as well. This man understands that Jesus' words apply to him and his fellow teachers, and he accuses him of insulting all of them. Luke does not indicate why the Pharisees have allowed Jesus to speak uninterrupted until now. Presumably 4:32 gives the answer: "because his message had authority." Anointed by the Holy Spirit, Jesus had a powerful presence and pronounced the woes with authority so that the character of these religious leaders was exposed.

It is unclear exactly what makes the expert in the law think Jesus' words apply to him and to his fellows. His objection moves Jesus to continue the woes and to draw attention specifically to the sins of this group. The first woe concerns their laying of burdens on others (v. 46). By their interpretations, these experts caused people to carry heavy burdens. They imposed duties that were difficult, if not impossible, to perform. Religion should make the burdens of life lighter, but the many rules and regulations of these law experts were making life a wearisome burden.

The second part of verse 46 says literally, "you yourselves do not touch the burdens with one of your fingers." This statement can be read in one of two ways. (1) The law experts were hypocrites, interpreting the religious traditions so that they could do whatever they wished. Knowing all the loopholes, they were able to evade the obligations of the law. They only pretended to observe its standards of spirituality. (2) These experts had no compassion, doing nothing to make it easier for the people to obey the law. Religion had become a burden because of legalistic demands. At the same time they refused to interpret and apply the law as it related to helping and showing mercy to the weak. The NIV translation makes the point well: "You yourselves will not lift one finger to help them." Cold and detached, they placed burden upon burden on other people and watched as the load crushed them.

Jesus' second woe for the experts in the law concerns rejecting God's Word (vv. 47–51). Jesus points out that these people have built monuments to the Old Testament prophets whom their fathers had murdered. The monuments, so they argued, were built to honor the prophets. Jesus takes exception with this argument. The only way the experts can truly honor the dead prophets is to do what they said. However, they disobey the message of the prophets and are, therefore, no better than those who put them to death. Their actions show that they give unconscious approval to the murders. The corrupt lives of the monument builders reveal that they are one with their ancestors.

Jesus goes on to speak about what God foresaw. In the past God's prophets were persecuted and murdered. At the present time experts in the law are erecting beautiful monuments where they assume the prophets have been buried, in order to honor them. "God in his wisdom" knows that in the future the prophets and apostles whom he sends will share the same fate as the Old Testament prophets. The leaders of Israel will persecute and kill them. The Pharisees and experts in the law are a true offspring of the enemies of God's messengers in the Old Testament.

Jesus, therefore, calls to their attention divine judgment. God will hold "this generation ... responsible for the blood of all the prophets that has been shed since the beginning of the world" (v. 50). They will have to account for all who have died for righteousness' sake, from Abel to Zechariah. Abel and Zechariah represent the first and the last martyrs in the Old Testament (Gen. 4:8; 2 Chron. 24:20–22). The people of Jesus' time will bear the guilt for the murder of all the prophets, since like their fathers they have disobeyed the prophets' message and show no signs of repentance. Only by repenting will they be spared the penalty for the guilt of past generations.

The last woe against the experts in the law deals with preventing others from knowing the Scriptures. These men professed to unlock Scripture. Instead, their interpretations distorted and misapplied them. God has provided the key to unlocking the Old Testament and to bringing people to a true knowledge of his plan of salvation. But these teachers of Israel have taken away "the key to knowledge." In essence, they have thrown the key away so that people cannot enter the kingdom of God. Their methods of interpretation add rigid requirements that go far beyond the Bible and make the teaching of Scripture so obscure that only the experts can understand them. They turn religion into mysteries and riddles and into impossible rules and regulations. They make no attempt to use the key for themselves. They choose to keep their hearts and minds shut to the gospel.

These woes of Jesus are strong, exposing the pride, the hypocrisy, and the lack of compassion on the part of the Pharisees and experts in the law. Their reaction to Jesus also is strong. After he leaves the home of the Pharisee who has invited him, his enemies begin "to oppose him fiercely and to besiege him with questions, waiting to catch him in something he might say" (vv. 53–54). That fierce hostility shows how accurately Jesus has spoken. They press in around him, asking him all kinds of difficult questions and hoping he will say something that they can use against him.

But Jesus, the Spirit-anointed prophet, continues on in spite of such attacks. Though under the careful eyes of his enemies, he will not allow them to distract him from fulfilling his mission. He sets his eyes constantly on doing the will that his heavenly Father has outlined for him.

4.9. Responsibilities and Privileges of Discipleship (12:1–13:9)

Luke now devotes a lengthy section to the nature of discipleship, consisting of teachings that Jesus directs primarily to his followers. He covers a wide range of subjects, concentrating on six main themes: (1) the coming judgment on those who live as hypocrites (12:1–12), (2) attachment and dependence on material hings (12:13–34), (3) being watchful and faithful servants (12:35–48), (4) Christ's being the cause of family divisions (12:49–53), 5) interpreting the signs of the time (12:54–59), and (6) the need for repentance (13:1–9).

Jesus presents these teachings as he is heading toward Jerusalem. On this journey a vast multitude of people is following him. As he speaks to his disciples, he wants these others to hear too. His teachings are not secret, and he desires that all learn what it means to be a disciple.

4.9.1. A Warning Against Hypocrisy 12:1–12). Among the common people Jesus' popularity is mounting, and the crowd has become so large that the people are stepping on one another. Jesus does not speak, as we might expect, to the thousands of people first, but to his disciples. They should not be misled by his present popularity; they need to remember the strong opposition that Jesus has already faced. So he first warns the disciples to keep their guard up against "the yeast of the Pharisees, which is hypocrisy."

Like yeast that causes a whole lump of dough to rise, the hypocrisy of the Pharisees can pervade all things. Hypocrisy involves acting a part that conceals the true person. Jesus charges the Pharisees with this sin because they are trying to hide behind masks of outward religious practices (11:39–44). They are insincere. It is better to be an honest sinner before God than a person who acts like a saint but is really corrupt.

The truth may be covered up for a while, but eventually everything will be known (vv. 2–3). In the final judgment every secret will be brought to the light and hypocrites will be exposed. The success of hypocrites depends on their ability to keep things hidden. But the things that they have concealed will inevitably be made known. Verse 3 explains it: "What you have said in the dark will be heard in the daylight, and what you have whispered in the ear in the inner rooms will be proclaimed from the roofs." All things are known by God. On the day of judgment every secret action, everything uttered in private, and even hidden motives and desires will be revealed (Rom. 2:15–16; 1 Cor. 5:6–8). Nothing will remain hidden.

As Jesus gives this prophetic warning, the Pharisees have things covered up. For example, some of them have given the impression that they are friends of Jesus. They have listened to his teaching and invited him into their homes (11:37). But they have refused to accept his Spirit-inspired teachings and to receive him as God's Son, and they are now trying to catch him in something he says (11:54). On the final day their hypocritical behavior will be exposed. We can never conceal our thoughts and actions from the eyes of God.

Hypocrisy can take a reverse form from that of the Pharisees. In times of persecution the disciples might be tempted to pretend that they are not followers of Jesus. Under pressure or threat, they may fear for their lives and try to conceal that they are believers. At the trial of Jesus, Peter pretended that he was not a disciple and denied Jesus three times (22:54–62). Aware that his disciples will come under persecution, he calls them "friends" and tells them not to fear men but to fear God (vv. 4–7). There are limits to the harm people can do to us. We are naturally inclined to fear those who may take our lives, but they cannot destroy anything more than the body. Once they have done that, their power has been exhausted. There is only one person to fear—God, who "has power to throw you into hell" (*geenna*, which denotes the place of eternal punishment).

Standing for God does not protect believers from persecution and rejection. Believers need to be prepared for the worst from evil people, but their destiny is in God's hands. Only the fear of God removes all fear of people. God has the right and power to judge everyone, but those who fear him can have assurance that he takes care of them, regardless of how bad the situation may be. A little sparrow, which is of no great value, does not escape God's attention. Five sparrows were sold for just a few pennies in an ancient market, yet God cares for these little birds—"not one of them is forgotten by God." In God's sight his people are much more precious than sparrows. He knows the smallest details about them, even the number of hairs on their heads. So we can be assured of his fatherly care and do not need to fear persecution.

Nothing is more important for believers than their loyalty to Jesus Christ (vv. 8–10). In adverse situations we must be on guard against failing to acknowledge him publicly as Savior and Lord. As he does frequently, Jesus calls himself the Son of Man. Those who acknowledge their loyalty to the Son of Man on earth will be acknowledged by Jesus in heaven. But those who deny him here he will deny in heaven. There are a number of ways to deny Jesus. We may deny his unique authority as the Son of God or explain his teachings so that they have little authority or relevance. We may reject his miracles and deity, insisting that he is only a great teacher or prophet.

How we relate to Jesus in the present determines our fate before God. As is clear in this passage, public confession of Jesus is important in our relationship with him. Jesus links such confession to discipleship. Believers who live as silent witnesses fail to be the best examples. They lead few people to the Lord. The book of Acts provides many examples of the power of the spoken word to the saving grace of Christ. Believers must bear witness to Christ by word and deed. To deny him here means that we will face rejection in the final judgment.

Acknowledging Jesus before men leads to the issue of blasphemy against the Holy Spirit, a sin that cannot be forgiven (vv. 10–11). Jesus has warned against the sin of rejecting him, but "everyone who speaks a word against the Son of Man will be forgiven." We should not assume that forgiveness for speaking against Jesus is automatic; it is granted only on the basis of repentance. People like Peter and Paul denied Jesus or refused to accept his claim to be the Redeemer of this world, but God forgave them when they repented of their sins (22:54–62; Acts 9:1ff.; 1 Tim. 1:12–14). Sin against Jesus is not to be taken lightly, but God does forgive that sin.

But anyone who insults the Holy Spirit will not be forgiven. Such a person is in a much worse condition. Jesus' statement has given rise to considerable debate. Does blasphemy of the Spirit refer to apostasy (Heb. 6:4–6)? Is it persistent rejection of the teaching of the apostles, since the Holy Spirit empowered their preaching of the word? Is it ascribing the works of the Spirit to Satan (cf. Matt. 12:24–32)?

Luke places Jesus' statement about blaspheming the Spirit in the context of times of hardship and persecution for believers. He warns them against denying him before other people (v. 9) and then adds, "When you are brought before synagogues, rulers and authorities . . . the Holy Spirit will teach you at that time what you should say" (vv. 11–12). Jesus encourages his disciples to be faithful witnesses under persecution as he warns against blaspheming the Spirit. He promises them power (*dynamis*) to bear witness and to endure hardship for the sake of the gospel (24:48–49; Acts 1:8; cf. 4:8). Should they yield to persecution and reject the help of the Spirit, they have committed the unpardonable sin. Injury and insult to the life-giving, empowering Spirit have dire consequences. Blasphemy against the Holy Spirit is a condition of the heart that prompts people to reject the Spirit's help at critical times in their lives. It is a rejection of God.

These words of Jesus have some clear implications. (1) God's grace in Jesus can be rejected. To deny Jesus is to reject the witness of the Spirit. The Spirit brings the truth of the gospel to the hearts of people. If they persist in unbelief, they run the risk of placing themselves beyond the reach of the Holy Spirit. Saving grace must be received, but persistent rejection of the Spirit's testimony has eternal consequences.

(2) The Spirit empowers believers for mission. Though he guides and directs lives (Acts 15:28), he is primarily for mission. Believers may plan missionary strategies and think they know where they are going and what they might say. But the Spirit may have other plans, as illustrated in the Spirit-directed mission of Peter to the house of Cornelius (Acts 10:1ff.). Note also how the Holy Spirit inspired the brilliant apologies that Paul delivered before rulers and authorities (Acts 21–26). As Jesus promises, "the Holy Spirit will teach you at that time what you should say."

Believers should be fortified against hypocrisy and fear of people, knowing that the Holy Spirit will come to their aid. They may face a hostile world, but his power is promised to obedient believers (Acts 5:32).

4.9.2. A Warning Against Greed (12:13–34). Greed shows itself in a strong desire to possess things. Jesus knows that attachment to possessions can hinder our walk with him. This section, therefore, deals with discipleship from the viewpoint of loving things (vv. 13–21) and worrying about having enough (vv. 22–34). These two subjects are closely connected. Wealth can pose a danger to those who do not have it as well as to those who do.

Jesus' warning against greed is prompted by two brothers' quarrel over their inheritance

One of the brothers asks Jesus to intervene and settle the dispute. He does not ask Jesus to serve as arbitrator and to consider the merits of the two claims. Rather, he wants Jesus to support his claim and persuade his brother to divide the inheritance (it was common for rabbis to be called upon to decide such matters). Discerning that greed was behind the family dispute, Jesus will have nothing to do with it; but he takes the opportunity to deal with the basic issue.

In his address to the crowd, Jesus warns against the danger of wanting more and more and stresses the importance of trust in God. He emphasizes that a person's true life and happiness cannot be measured by the amount of one's possessions. This truth points out the futility of all greed. Because greed makes material things a god, greed is idolatry (Eph. 5:3; Col. 3:5). Idolatry is bowing before something that is unworthy of honor and is unable to give life true meaning.

To drive this truth home Jesus tells a parable. It involves a wealthy farmer and how he uses wealth. This farmer has a bumper crop—so great that he has no place to store it. He therefore decides to dismantle his barns and use the materials to build larger ones. He feels that he is a very lucky man to have this kind of problem, but he does not thank God for his abundant harvest, nor does he think about needy neighbors. Once bigger barns have been built, he has confidence that his wealth will last for many years and plans for a secure retirement—to "take life easy; eat, drink and be merry." He assumes that he is the master of his life and he has many more years on the earth.

But God has a different point of view. "You fool!" he says. "This very night your life will be demanded from you" (v. 20). This man has lived as though he had no need of the true and living God. He disregarded the possibility of his being suddenly cut off, but on that very night God takes his life. In God's eyes anyone who trusts in material possessions rather than in him is a fool.

The rich man of this parable shows the wrong attitude toward wealth. Three of his blunders stand out: (1) He never saw beyond himself. Notice his frequent use of "I" and "my"—"This is what I'll do. I will tear down my barns . . . I will store all my grain and my goods. And I'll say to myself. . . ." Deeply ingrained in him is self-interest. He has made his money and intends to spend it on himself. He shows no interest in others and has no sense of stewardship.

(2) He believed that the future was in his control. As it turned out, however, he had no control at all. What he stored up for himself did not benefit him. He was unable to take any of his wealth with him. So God asked this man, "Then who will get what you have prepared for yourself?" His attitude toward his possessions gave him a false sense of security. Until it was too late, he never realized the uncertainty of the future. "Do not boast about tomorrow, for you do not know what a day may bring forth" (Prov. 27:1; cf. James 4:13–16).

(3) He had no hope in God. His life was filled with earthly things and gave no place to God. Anyone who is like this man, holding on to his possessions for personal use only, is not open to trusting in God. Possessions are not evil in themselves, but we can turn them into our gods. We determine the place and value they have in our lives.

Jesus continues the theme of material possessions in verses 22–34. He knows that greed is never satisfied. It leads individuals, whether rich or poor, to become preoccupied with material things. To help his followers avoid this trap, Jesus urges them not to worry about their physical needs. But how are they to deal with their needs of food and clothing? After all, everyone needs something to eat and to wear. Jesus' answer is simple: Trust God, who knows your needs and will provide for them. Real life consists of more than what we eat and put on (cf. 4:4). True, food and clothing are important, and believers may give reasonable forethought to such needs. But since God provides, we should refrain from worrying about them. Life involves so much more than the material aspects that sustain it. Our concern must be about life as a whole.

In a convincing way Jesus then gives three reasons why it is futile to be preoccupied with material things. (1) The heavenly Father cares for the ravens. These birds were unclean (Lev. 11:15) and were viewed as some of the lowest of God's creatures. They did not plant seed or harvest grain. They had no place to store anything for later use. Yet God cares for them by providing them food day by day. Will this God forget his people? Of course not!

They are of greater value than birds of the air. God certainly does provide for us (though Jesus' reference to birds that do not work should not be taken to mean that we can avoid work; he does not encourage us to be lazy).

(2) Anxious grasping for things is unproductive. No one by worrying can add a single hour to the span of his or her life. In fact, worrying can be counterproductive; anxiety can affect our health and shorten life. The rich fool was unable to add a moment to the length of his life when God called him. Jesus speaks about adding to the span of our lives as a "very little thing." Living a little longer may be important to us, but from God's point of view it is a small matter. If we are unable to do anything about a small matter, why bother worrying about bigger matters?

(3) God adorns the lilies and the grass of the field, which can teach us to depend on God for our clothing. The beauty of the lilies is not the result of their making garments, as people do. Without any effort on their part, they just grow and come to bloom. God clothes them with a beauty that exceeds the splendor of Solomon arrayed in his finest robes. Similarly, the flowers (*chorton*, "grass") of the field blossom only for a short time and then are used for heating clay ovens. Yet these flowers are gloriously clothed by God. Certainly he will take greater care of his children. People of little faith show anxiety, but that is unnecessary.

Worry is pointless. Jesus therefore commands his disciples not to invest their energy in something that yields nothing: "Do not set your heart on what you will eat or drink; do not worry about it" (v. 29). This instruction may seem to be hard in our culture, where unemployment can be high and many do not have job security. It is not that these concerns have no place in our lives. Believers need to work and make plans for the future, but they should not become anxious and fretful about tomorrow. By worrying about food and clothing we become like those who do not trust in the true God.

Unbelievers are worried about these things. Believers, on the other hand, have a heavenly Father and can be assured that he knows they need food, drink, and clothing. They are not to run after such things. Instead, they are to seek God's kingdom. This godly pursuit puts all things in their proper perspective. Our priority becomes living in fellowship with God and under his rule, serving him, and preparing ourselves for the coming of his kingdom in its full glory. In addition to the blessings of the kingdom, God will provide these other things as well. We can count on him.

Jesus closes this discourse with a comment on material possessions and faith in God's goodness (vv. 32–34). He is still talking to his disciples and compares them to a small flock of sheep. In doing so, he reminds them that he is their Shepherd and that they can expect such care from him. Sheep are weak and can be easily frightened in the face of danger, but Jesus commands his little flock not to be afraid. They may be scattered by persecution, but they can rest assured that God cares for them and is pleased to give to them his kingdom.

Here Jesus' emphasis is probably on the kingdom as it is seen at the end of the world. When that kingdom finally comes in its fullness, God's people will rule with him. But even now believers can be confident that God cares and will provide kingdom blessings. These blessings are best understood by what God does now and will do to enhance his rule among them. He offers no promise of abundant, material blessings, but he does desire sufficient provisions for his people.

Jesus' words forbid us to understand kingdom blessings as stockpiling material things, for his very next statement is this: "Sell your possessions and give to the poor." The stress here is not on giving up possessions, but on how we use them. Jesus does not command us to literally sell all our earthly possessions. That would reduce us to poverty and make us dependent on others. But his concern is that we not become slaves to our possessions and that we use them to help others. Confident of God's care, we can be generous with what he provides. If we are not attached to the world, it is easy to become servants of the kingdom and to consider the needs of others.

The rich fool in the parable (vv. 16–21) stands in sharp contrast to the generous person. That man preoccupied himself with accumulating wealth and security and had no intention of using his possessions for anybody but for himself. To guard against such greed, followers of Jesus are to make an investment that neither time nor circumstances can destroy. In so doing they will have "purses . . . that will not wear out, a treasure in heaven that will not be exhausted." These kinds of purses will not cause their owners anxiety. They will never perish and their contents will be the inexhaustible treasures in heaven.

Such treasures are real riches and are absolutely secure. No thief can break in and steal them. They are also secure from damage by moths, which can ruin earthly riches. Those who seek to store up treasures in heaven by sharing some of their resources show that their hearts are heavenbound. On the other hand, those who pile up earthly riches and refuse to share them reveal that their hearts are earthbound. What we do with our treasures tells us where our hearts are.

4.9.3. Watchful and Faithful (12:35–48). Continuing his discussion on discipleship, Jesus now turns to being prepared for the return of the Son of Man. Freedom from the cares of the world and assurance that the heavenly Father cares for his own can tempt his followers to become lazy and have a carefree attitude. But as Jesus makes clear, true discipleship includes being faithful in service and ready for his return. Life on the earth is uncertain, but the coming of the Son of Man is sure. Jesus gives three parables here to stress the importance of spiritual preparation: the parable of being prepared for the coming of the Son of Man (vv. 35–38), the parable of expecting the Son of Man (vv. 39–40), and the parable of the faithful manager during the master's absence (vv. 41–48).

The first parable opens with an emphasis on being ready for service (vv. 35–38). Jesus uses two pictures. The NIV renders the first as "Be dressed ready for service," but the Greek literally says, "Girding up your loins stand." In the East men wore long flowing robes, but to do work it was necessary to tuck the robe into a belt around the waist so that it did not get in the way. Jesus calls on his disciples to keep themselves ready for service.

The second picture, lamps burning, adds the emphasis of watching for the Second Coming. The disciples are to be like servants whose master has gone to a wedding feast. They do not know at what moment he will return. But if they remain ready, they will open the door as he knocks and provide whatever service he desires. Jesus' disciples should live so that they are ready for his appearing at the door at any moment. The time of his return is unpredictable.

Jesus then pronounces a blessing on those servants who are watching and ready when the master returns (vv. 37–38). The master will be so pleased that he will reverse the normal roles. Rather than having the servants wait on him, the master will serve them. He will put on his apron, place them at the table, and serve them a meal.

In verse 38 Jesus repeats the blessing, but he adds, "even if he comes in the second or third watch of the night." The Jews divided the night into three periods and the Romans into four. It is unclear which of the schedules Jesus has in mind, but either way the second watch is midnight or even later. The point is clear: The disciples need to be ready always because they do not know at what moment their master (the Lord) will return. He may come at a late hour of the night when he is not expected. They must stay awake and be prepared. Those who are watchful and ready will receive an extraordinary blessing: The master will make a great feast for them.

Normally a master never served his slaves, but the grace of God does the unexpected. This is not the first time in Scripture that the concept of a master serving his servants is introduced. At his first coming Jesus, "who, being in very nature God," took on "the very nature of a servant" (Phil. 2:6–7). Jesus served his people, and he will do no different when he comes again. At that time he will serve his faithful people and bless them far beyond what they can imagine.

The second parable teaches the need to expect the coming of the Son of Man (vv. 39–40). This parable offers a strong warning to people not ready for the return of Christ. If the owner of a house knew when a thief was planning to come and rob his house, he could protect his home. He would not leave it exposed and would be prepared for the thief. Of course, he could not constantly be on guard, staying awake twenty-four hours a day to watch for thieves. So as he slept, the thief broke in and stole all he wanted.

The coming of Christ will be similar to the sudden and unexpected arrival of a thief. But unlike the man whose house was robbed, Jesus' followers can be constantly ready for their Lord's coming. They cannot always be awake, of course, but they can be prepared for the sudden return of Christ. We do not know when that will occur, but we cannot afford to be unprepared.

The third parable stresses faithfulness during the master's absence (vv. 41–48). As Peter often does, he takes the lead among the disciples. He has heard Jesus' teaching and wants to know if what the Savior has been saying applies only to the disciples (the ones with leadership responsibilities) or to all the listeners. Jesus does not answer the question directly. He asks another question to encourage Peter to think: "Who then is the faithful and wise manager?" (*oikonomos*, "steward"). In verse 43 the manager is also called a "servant" (*doulos*, "slave"). The parable is an indirect reply to Peter's question and provides insight into what a good manager or steward is like.

A manager in the ancient world was given responsibility to watch over the whole estate while the master was away. One of his major tasks was to see that the members of the household received their allotment of food. He might hand it out daily, weekly, or monthly. The point is that his job called for him to serve, not to exercise power. His master might return at any time. When the master does come, a "faithful and wise manager" should be found discharging his duties.

Jesus praises the servant who serves faithfully in his master's absence. For his efficiency his master will reward him (v. 44) with a promotion, giving him responsibility not only over the house and its servants but also over his entire estate. Jesus leaves unexplained how this promotion theme applies to his disciples. Certain biblical texts indicate that Christ will reign for a period of time on earth after he returns (19:17; 1 Cor. 6:1–3; Rev. 20:1–6). During that time he will need assistants, who will serve with him as he reigns. The reward probably involves this future reign of Christ, at which time faithfulness will be rewarded with larger opportunities for service.

God promises to reward the faithful, but the outcome can be different. The same manager may think that it will be a long time before his master returns. He thus becomes careless and develops a false sense of independence. Instead of caring for the servants under him, he abuses them and indulges himself by eating, drinking, and getting drunk. His master's return then comes as a complete surprise to him. The master will catch him in his folly and see his wickedness, and the arrogant and unfaithful servant will be held accountable for his sins.

The NIV expresses the severity of his punishment: "He will cut him to pieces and assign him a place with the unbelievers" (v. 46). The picture is that of dismemberment, indicating the punishment is more than a mere beating. It involves execution, death. He will share the same fate as unbelievers. According to Matthew 24:51, this servant will be assigned "a place with the hypocrites, where there will be weeping and gnashing of teeth."

This outcome should serve as a warning especially to those who have authority and leadership positions. Even in the church, a leader may be tempted to abuse others and to pursue personal interests. Jesus has emphasized faithfulness, but now he emphasizes the responsibility that rests on those who know God's will. The servant who knows what his master wants but fails to do it will be assigned a place with unbelievers. This servant cannot plead ignorance; he has a clear understanding of his master's will. Because he had failed, he "will be beaten with many blows."

But there is another servant. Unlike the first one he does not know what his master wants. In ignorance he disobeys his master's will. His punishment is less severe than the previous two, in that he receives a "few blows." The point is that it is worse to disobey God's will when we know it than to be ignorant and disobey. No one can plead absolute moral ignorance (Rom. 1:20; 2:14–15). But privilege and blessings do bring greater responsibility. God expects much from those to whom he has given much. The person blessed with opportunity and privilege should act accordingly. It is certain that judgment will be according to blessings.

4.9.4. Family Divisions Over Christ (12:49–53). In these verses Jesus speaks of his mission, how it will be accomplished and what its outcome will be. His mission is designed to bring salvation and peace; but in another sense, it also brings judgment and division. He will throw fire on the earth. The term "fire" can stand for: (1) divine judgment (3:9, 17; 9:54; 17:29; Acts 2:19), (2) purification (Mal. 3:2–3; 2 Peter 3:10–13), or (3) the power of the Holy Spirit (Acts 2:1–4). In this context "fire" must refer to judgment. Yet judgment is connected to the Holy Spirit. The salvation experience involves judgment with the Holy Spirit communicating the convicting, judging message of the gospel to the human heart.

The Holy Spirit condemns sin and unbelief. Jesus, however, looks ahead to the fire of God's judgment being kindled. From the outset of his ministry, the fire began to burn as families became divided because their members responded differently to the gospel. But it will not be fully kindled until his death, resurrection, and exaltation, and the outpouring of the Holy Spirit. As Jesus makes his way to Jerusalem, he longs for his saving work and its outcome to be accomplished. The Cross is not an attractive prospect. He knows that through it he will bear judgment on behalf of others and that his suffering is necessary to fulfill his mission.

Aware of what is awaiting him, Jesus speaks of the Cross as "a baptism" (v. 50). This baptism will plunge him into the waters of suffering and death as when a person is baptized in water. Knowing that he will come under judgment for the sins of humankind, Jesus becomes filled with distress. He longs to see the fire of judgment fully burning, but knowing the severity of his coming "baptism" makes him wish that he has already accomplished his mission.

Because Jesus is referred to as the Prince of Peace (Isa. 9:6), one might assume that his sole mission is to bring unqualified peace. He does bring real peace to the hearts of those who trust him, but his mission also includes the throwing of fire on the earth (v. 49). He makes that clear here. His coming will create dissension and split families. Jesus calls to faith members of the same family, but they respond differently. Some embrace him as their Savior, while others choose to persist in their unbelief. Some are for him; others against him. Some love him; others hate him. Jesus predicts that divided families will exist "from now on"—from his first coming to the end of time (v. 52). Opposition should come as no surprise to us. The gospel is a challenge to take up our cross and follow Jesus. To accept this challenge may result in rejection by members of our own family.

4.9.5. Interpreting the Present Times (12:54–59). At this point "the crowds" get Jesus' attention. He has urged his disciples to be ready for the coming judgment of the Son of Man (vv. 35–48). Now in harsh words Jesus castigates the crowd for blindness to the signs of God. They can interpret signs of the weather as clouds form or as a heat wave is on its way. From a few observations they can accurately forecast the weather, but their spiritual dullness prevents them from discerning "this present time" (v. 56)—the ministry of Jesus in their midst. They are completely oblivious to the signs.

They fail, in other words, to see that God is at work in his Spirit-anointed Son. They interpret the weather signs, but they do not bother to try to understand the signs of the times. Since the signs were prominent in their lifetime, they could have easily interpreted them. The works of God in Jesus are as plain as "a cloud rising in the west" or the wind blowing from the south. Signs included the preaching of John the Baptist, who declared that Jesus would baptize with the Holy Spirit and fire (3:16), and the anointed preaching of Jesus and his extraordinary works.

The crowds ignore what is truly important. Because they devote themselves to the superficial and pretend to know how to interpret the present time, they are, in fact, "hypocrites" (v. 56). Their failure to discern God's mighty signs of salvation in Jesus has nothing to do with their ability but with their will. They deliberately refuse to recognize the meaning of his saving mission and his Spirit-anointed message (cf. 11:30). Their rejection prevents them from understanding the clouds and winds of God. They do not see that in the days of Isaiah God used the Assyrians to bring judgment on his people, and now he is about to use Rome as an agent of his judgment (A.D. 66–70). They fail to see the significance of Jesus and to understand that he is their only hope.

Jesus' presence and teaching require the crowds to make a decision: "Why don't you judge for yourselves what is right?" (v. 57). They are on their way to judgment, but it is not too late to turn back. God has given them the gospel, and under its influence and that of the Holy Spirit they can believe in Jesus and flee from the wrath to come. The time for them to give attention to their relation to God is now. To illustrate the urgency of this need Jesus refers to a legal dispute. A debtor is being dragged into court. His only hope of avoiding time in prison is to settle his case out of court before a judge. Otherwise he will face utter ruin. Once in prison, he will have no opportunity of earning money to repay his creditor and thus will have no prospect of being released.

Through this story Jesus warns sinners not to allow themselves to be lulled into a sense of false security. By their disobedience they have withheld from God what he rightfully expects—obedience. As a result they are debtors and should spare no effort to settle their accounts with God by repenting of their sins and casting themselves on his mercy. Should the accounts not be cleared, the consequences will be tragic and eternal: They will lose everything when they stand before God in the final judgment. Only Jesus can settle our accounts with God and pay our debts. To avoid eternal disaster, we must repent and trust him. Wise people will do that before it is too late.

4.9.6. Call to Repentance (13:1–9). The gospel offers repentance and forgiveness of sins (24:47). After his warning about the danger of divine judgment (12:54–59), Jesus issues a call to repentance in order to avoid God's wrath. This message is a message of grace. God graciously offers everyone the opportunity for repentance.

Jesus emphasizes the urgency for repenting and turning to God by focusing on two tragedies. In his first he discusses Pilate's slaughter of some Galileans, about which he has just been informed. A group of Galileans had gone up to Jerusalem to worship. While they were in the temple offering animal sacrifices, Pilate's soldiers rushed in, cut them down, and mixed their own blood with the sacrifices at the temple. We know nothing about this incident except what Luke tells us. The violent death of these Galileans may have been the result of a plot to set Palestine free from Roman domination or of Pilate's abuse of his power. The horrible way they were executed points to Pilate's own personal rage against them.

But why was this terrible piece of news brought to Jesus? Those who reported it assumed that the Galileans received what they deserved. Many at that time believed that tragedies reflected God's judgment on people for their sins. In response Jesus emphatically denies (*ouchi*) this popular notion (v. 3). This tragic incident does not prove that these Galileans were greater sinners in God's eyes than others. The self-righteousness of the reporters caused them to draw wrong conclusions.

In this life sin sometimes results in conspicuous punishment, making us aware of the connection between sin and its consequences. But God's rule and providence are deeply mysterious. There are no simple explanations for the stoning of Stephen or the death of James by the sword. Our financial and physical conditions do not always reflect our spiritual condition. Jesus makes no attempt to explain the tragic death of the Galileans, but he does use their deaths to remind each person of his or her own sin and of the need to repent: "But unless you repent, you too will all perish" (v. 3). A more fundamental issue than the connection of the Galileans' deaths to their sin is that all people are sinners and must repent. Otherwise one's end will be more tragic than the violent death of the Galileans. Those who remain unresponsive to the call of Jesus risk spiritual disaster.

Jesus goes on to speak of another tragedy (vv. 4–5). The first one involved death as an act of human evil, but this second tragedy was a natural disaster—eighteen people "died when the tower of Siloam fell on them." Siloam was a suburb of Jerusalem; we know nothing about the fall of the tower apart from this reference. Probably the tower was connected to the wall that surrounded Jerusalem. For some unforeseen reason the tower collapsed.

Many devout Jews must have regarded the accident as evidence of God's judgment, because popular theology of the day ascribed tragic events to divine wrath against the victims. Jesus emphatically denies this conclusion. The death of these eighteen does not prove they were the worst sinners living in Jerusalem. As with the Galileans, Jesus refuses to speculate about what caused the tower to fall. Nevertheless, the important thing is repentance. The tower tragedy warns everyone of the urgency of repentance. After all, life can come to an end at any moment, but Jesus Christ has made repentance a way for us to escape the eternal consequence of death.

Up to now Jesus has stressed the importance of repenting in order to avoid divine judgment. His next parable, of the unfruitful fig tree, also teaches the need of repentance and God's patience in dealing with sinners (vv. 6–9). Although the opportunity for people to repent has not yet passed, it will not be present forever. Thus Jesus illustrates the result of failing to repent.

The scene involves a fig tree in a vineyard. The owner from time to time goes looking for fruit on the tree, but he finds none. He has every right to expect it to bear fruit, for it has grown to full maturity. The owner has been patient for three years, but patience is wearing thin. Therefore he tells the man who has cared for his vineyard to cut down the tree. The ground it occupies can be put to more fruitful use. But the vineyard keeper asks the owner to let it stand for one more year, during which time he will loosen the soil around it and add fertilizer. Perhaps the extra care will make it productive. If it fails to become fruitful after another year, however, drastic measures can be taken to remove it.

The parable of the barren fig tree reminds us that God is watching over his vineyard. He gives us opportunity to turn to him and to bear fruit worthy of repentance. God's willingness to give us time to turn to him shows his patience and mercy. According to 2 Peter 3:9, "He is patient . . . not wanting anyone to perish, but everyone to come to repentance." If we do not repent, we will remain unfruitful and in the end suffer great loss. There are limits to divine patience.

4.10. Preparation of the Disciples for Jerusalem and Events Beyond (13:10–35)

After focusing on the urgency of repentance, Jesus again enters a dispute about the proper use of the Sabbath (vv. 10–17). Luke then records two short parables Jesus told—about the nature of the kingdom (vv. 18–21) and about how to enter it (vv. 22–30). He ends this section with a warning about the murderous intent of Herod Antipas (cf. 9:7–9) and with Jesus' weeping over Jerusalem (vv. 31–35). In the middle of this section Luke mentions that Jesus continues to set his face toward Jerusalem, the city where he must die (v. 22; cf. 9:51). As the journey progresses, he prepares the disciples for what will happen there.

4.10.1. Healing of a Crippled Woman on the Sabbath (13:10–17). This miracle brings Jesus into conflict once again with the religious leaders. It occurs while he is teaching in a synagogue on the Sabbath (this is the last occasion in Luke where Jesus appears in a synagogue). As he is teaching, "a woman [is] there who had been crippled by a spirit for eighteen years. She was bent over and could not straighten up at all" (v. 11). The mention of the spirit is significant because the woman's deformity is not due to the process of aging or a disease, but to an evil spirit. The demon's control has had a crippling effect, making it impossible for her to stand up straight. The length of time she has lived with this condition shows its severity.

Likely this woman has come to the synagogue to worship. She does not approach Jesus nor petition him to heal her. Nothing is said about her believing in him. When his eyes fall on her, the Spirit-anointed Jesus has compassion on her. Immediately he takes the initiative by calling out to her, laying his hands on her, and pronouncing her cured. The perfect tense (*apolelysai*) stresses that her healing is permanent. She now stands erect in front of everyone, freed from the power of Satan, who caused her infirmity. Her heart is filled with gratitude, and she begins to praise God for his mighty works. She connects God's power with what Jesus has done for her.

The healing of this woman shows that God delivers his people from the power of Satan by his grace. It demonstrates the presence of his kingdom. But the miracle also reveals the hypocrisy of the Jewish leaders and their growing opposition to Jesus. The ruler of the synagogue becomes angry because Jesus healed the woman on the Sabbath. In his eyes Jesus has violated the fourth commandment. In Jewish tradition, such deeds of mercy were permitted on the Sabbath only if the person's life was in grave danger. Since this woman has needed help for eighteen years, obviously her sickness was not an emergency.

But the synagogue ruler avoids attacking Jesus to his face. Instead he speaks to the people and complains to them, "There are six days for work. So come and be healed on those days, not on the Sabbath." He has no appreciation for what he has just seen. All that he can think about is the desecration of the Sabbath, ignoring the woman who has been set free from her pain. He disregards the healing power of God manifested through Jesus and shows no compassion or joy about the miracle. But not daring to attack Jesus directly, he reprimands the people for coming on the Sabbath for healing. They can receive healing on the other six days of the week.

The synagogue ruler has really aimed his rebuke at Jesus. The Spirit-anointed Savior meets this indirect attack with a direct response, calling him and all his colleagues "hypocrites." As a stinging rebuke, Jesus asks two questions. He asks if a man is allowed to care for his animals on the Sabbath. In their teachings the rabbis express great concern for the care of animals. Even on the Sabbath they could be looked after. Water could be drawn for cattle and poured in a trough without transgressing the Sabbath. Jesus' second question makes the point: If animals can be cared for on the Sabbath, why should a crippled woman have to wait another day for healing? She is "a daughter of Abraham," a member of God's people. Surely she is more important in God's sight than animals and ought to be set free from Satan.

The phrase "should . . . be set free" literally means "it was necessary (*edei*) to be loosed." This clause expresses a necessity far more important than watering an ox or donkey. Jesus insists that there is a moral obligation to do good on the Sabbath. In effect, this woman must be liberated; what day could be more appropriate than the Sabbath? Satan does not stop his work on the Sabbath, and by healing her on the Sabbath Jesus has revealed Satan's impotence. God had given Israel the Sabbath for release from the bondage of work and as a sign of liberation (cf. Deut. 5:15; Mark 2:27). No day could be more fitting for men and women to be released from the rule of Satan and to come under the gracious rule of God. By his works of mercy Jesus is consecrating the day.

The synagogue ruler has tried to hinder the people's response to Jesus' mighty deed. Jesus' response puts his opponents to shame. He has exposed their hypocrisy, and they have lost face in the eyes of the people in the synagogue. By contrast, the people are thrilled with his mighty works. They rejoice because of all the glorious deeds done by Jesus.

4.10.2. Parables of the Kingdom (13:18–21). Jesus follows this miracle up with two short parables to illustrate what the kingdom of God is like. Presumably he is still in the synagogue. The healed crippled woman has been a sign of the powerful presence of God's kingdom, his rule of grace. In both these parables Jesus explains the kingdom as a present reality. He wants his hearers to think about God's rule and to understand its nature and characteristics.

In general the Jews expected the messianic kingdom to come suddenly and decisively. But Jesus insists here that the kingdom in its initial form may seem to be very small and can hardly be recognized. It is like a tiny mustard seed or yeast in dough, but it spreads and produces something much larger. Though the kingdom is almost invisible at first, the mighty works of Jesus show its powerful presence and that eventually it will become dominant.

According to the parable of the mustard seed, the kingdom is making a decisive impact. It is like a mustard seed planted in a field, from which grows a tree. Normally a mustard seed grew into a bush about four feet high, but under favorable conditions some have been known to grow as much as nine feet tall (Marshall, 1978, 561). In other words, Jesus has supernatural growth in mind here. In this tree birds build their nests and roost in its branches, a fact that likely represents the nations of the world (Ps. 104:13; Ezek. 17:23; 31:6). A small beginning produces a great result, depicting the worldwide growth of God's kingdom. That kingdom will become universal and will provide a peaceful resting place for people from all nations.

The parable of yeast has a similar emphasis on the tremendous growth of the kingdom and on the transforming power of God's grace. A woman wants to make a lot of bread. So she takes "a large amount of flour" (Greek: "three measures," probably about fifty pounds) and adds a tiny amount of yeast to it. The yeast slowly permeates the large mass of dough and causes it to rise. In the Scriptures yeast often represents evil influences, but here it refers to the all-pervading and powerful influence of God's kingdom. It begins with Jesus' preaching and healings as a small movement and often works in an invisible way, as yeast does. As it begins to permeate and influence lives and society, the future results far exceed its present size. We see this kind of powerful influence in the book of Acts as the gospel permeated the Roman world.

God's people can take courage when there seems to be a lack of success. Opposition whether satanic or human, cannot stop the kingdom's impact on the world. God is at work advancing his plan and purpose. Do no become depressed by the opposition or by the greatness of the task. As yeast works mysteriously, invisibly, and secretly, so does God's kingdom. The immense power of God guarantees that his kingdom will reach to the ends of the earth.

4.10.3. Requirements for the Kingdom (13:22–30). The preceding two parables affirm the power and influence of the kingdom. Luke reminds us again that Jesus is on his way to Jerusalem (v. 22). As he travels, he evangelizes "towns and villages." Someone in the crowd suddenly asks, "Lord, are only a few people going to be saved?"

This question gives Jesus an opportunity to summarize the demands for entrance into the kingdom of God. His teaching has probably left the impression that only a few will be saved. As he often does, he gives no direct answer to speculative questions. He points out to those present that they should not spend their time discussing how many will be saved. Far more important is the consideration of questions such as these: Are you among the saved? Have you been delivered from sin and divine judgment and been received into God's kingdom? Using a parable Jesus deals with the man's question in a practical, personal way, warning the people not to speculate about the fate of others but to make sure that they themselves have received eternal life.

The door to the kingdom, to salvation, stands open, but it is narrow. Though people do not need to open the door, they must "make every effort to enter through the narrow door." The verb "make every effort" (*agonizomai*) means "to agonize," suggesting that everyone must strive diligently to enter the narrow door to the kingdom. God offers only one door into heaven, and it is narrow. It can never be a matter of choosing from a variety of doors, nor is the door wide like an interstate highway. The only way to pass through that door is by personal repentance.

Many obstacles can stand in the way of our repenting and turning from sin. Among them are our own pride, self-righteousness, indifference to God's grace, and the works of the flesh. But to enter the narrow door into the kingdom demands agonizing before God and turning away from careless living. It demands self-denial and commitment to the way of the cross (9:57–62).

The door will not remain open forever. Many who fail to enter the narrow door will try one day, but they will not succeed because the door will have been shut (v. 25). They have turned a deaf ear to the gospel and have allowed the day of salvation to pass them by. A day is coming when there will no longer be a door of opportunity for personal repentance and faith in Jesus Christ. People may knock and seek to enter, but the owner of the house (the Lord) will shut it and never reopen it. His patience and mercy will come to an end, and the unrepentant will stand in the final judgment condemned for their unbelief and sins.

On that final day the Lord will tell them, "I don't know you or where you come from." The issue here is a matter of relationship with the Lord. Such people are strangers to him, and he does not even know from where they have come. They will claim to have enjoyed table fellowship with him and heard him preaching in streets, but their claims will be empty. They may have eaten meals in Jesus' presence, but they had no real fellowship with him. They may have listened to his teachings, but they failed to accept them. Outward exposure to and contact with the Savior mean little; inward acceptance of him means everything. Faith in him brings us into personal fellowship with him and brings us a real knowledge of him. Otherwise we remain strangers.

The pleading of these people will be futile. They have let the time of grace pass them by. Jesus' verdict is, "Away from me, all you evildoers." Their sinful works provide the basis for their rejection. They have persisted in unbelief, and it leads to "weeping . . . and gnashing of teeth." Having to endure the torment of outer darkness, they will experience overwhelming pain and despair. Jesus reminds his audience that everyone will see the kingdom of God at the end of time. Those who persist in unbelief will behold the Hebrew patriarchs and prophets enjoying the joys and glories of that heavenly kingdom, but they themselves will be on the outside.

The words "thrown out" may suggest a previous entrance, but the context indicates these people have never actually entered the kingdom. Since the word used here (*ekballomenous*) is a present participle, it emphasizes that their rejection continues. Thus the translation "barred" is better than "thrown out." When they try to enter, they will fail to succeed. They must remain outside and be numbered with the evildoers. For now, of course, the door remains open, and there is still time for those headed for judgment to alter their course. The only thing God seeks is for them to accept the invitation of the gospel to trust Jesus as their Savior.

When the kingdom comes in its fullness, the Jews will be in for a surprise. They rightly assume that the patriarchs and prophets will be in heaven, but they also believe that Gentiles will be shut out. To counter this popular belief the anointed Jesus predicts: "People will come from east and west and north and south, and will take their places at the feast in the kingdom of God." In other words, people from all nations, races, and languages will take their places at the heavenly banquet at the end of time (cf. Isa. 25:6–7; Matt. 22:2–10; Mark 14:25; Luke 14:15; Rev. 19:7–9). Those who stand at the closed door will experience deep regret as they see large numbers admitted. The saints from all the ages, having believed in Christ, will be united completely with him in this great feast. "Blessed are those who are invited to the wedding supper of the Lamb!" (Rev. 19:9).

Everyone now has equal access to God's blessings through Christ (Eph. 2:11–22), but this access will not last forever. God is presently adding to his kingdom those who repent and believe the gospel. No doubt, there will be surprises in the heavenly kingdom, for there will be some among the redeemed whom we did not expect. Thus, as Jesus closed his parable, he calls attention to the reversal that will occur in the last day: "There are those who are last [Gentiles] who will be first, and first [Jews] who will be last."

Some scholars have erroneously taken "first" and "last" to refer to time, making the latecomers first in the kingdom of God. But Jesus' emphasis here is not time, but rank or position. The Jews supposed themselves to rank first and to be more favored, while they ranked Gentiles last. So Jesus warns his audience that the first will be last, meaning that they may not enter the kingdom at all. Yet people coming from all over the world will be inside. Some have great opportunity for salvation, but they fail to take advantage of it. Others have no opportunity for salvation at the beginning; but as soon as they get it, they take full advantage of it. At church, people may have much exposure to Christ, but they may turn out to be barred from the kingdom because they have not accepted Jesus' offer of eternal life. There is no substitute for knowing Jesus personally.

4.10.4. A Warning About Herod and Sorrow Over Jerusalem (13:31–35). Soon after Jesus has urged the people to make sure they are among those who are saved, he receives a warning from some Pharisees that he should leave Galilee, the territory governed by Herod Antipas. Herod had beheaded John the Baptist and had been perplexed about Jesus to the point of wanting to see him (9:7–9). Now, apparently, Herod wishes to have Jesus put to death. This warning prompts Jesus to express his love for Jerusalem. He is on his way there and knows that it has a history of killing prophets like himself. As he thinks about his death there, he is deeply saddened by the hardness of the people's hearts and the final fate of the city.

Why do the Pharisees warn Jesus about Herod's threat? They have had strong differences with him regarding the interpretation of the law (11:37–53), but a few of them have appeared to be friendly toward him (7:36; 14:1). But overall Luke describes them as hostile to Jesus. Are these Pharisees sincere, or are they trying to trap Jesus by getting him to go into Judea, where they have more authority and influence?

We have no way of knowing exactly what their motives are. But Jesus takes their report as accurate and gives them a message for Herod. Without fear of the governor he calls him "that fox." At times the fox was portrayed as being an insignificant animal in comparison to the lion. But the fox was also considered to be a crafty and destructive creature (Marshall, 1978, 571). Likely both ideas apply to Herod, showing that he is neither a man of true greatness nor one of genuine honesty. By calling him a fox Jesus shows contempt for him.

Later Jesus and Herod do meet in Jerusalem, but Jesus has no respect for him and refuses to answer his questions (23:8–9). He will not run from Herod, but he will go on with his ministry and not be prevented from fulfilling his mission at Jerusalem. Jesus therefore reminds Herod that he continues his ministry of driving out demons and healing the sick. His mighty works reveal his divine power and majesty. He remains undisturbed by the threats from "that fox."

Jesus also recognizes that his ministry will go on yet for only a limited period of time. The phrase "today and tomorrow, and on the third day" should not be taken literally, but refer to a short period of time. His death does not occur three days after he spoke these words. Rather, Jesus is stressing that he does not have much time left. Soon a decisive point will be reached and he will complete his ministry in death. Until then, his ministry will continue, and Herod can do nothing to interfere with Jesus' reaching his goal.

As Jesus suggested in 4:40–44, he "must keep going today and tomorrow" through the towns and villages, preaching, driving out demons, and healing the sick. It is a divine "must" (*dei*, "it is necessary") that he go to Jerusalem, "for surely no prophet can die outside Jerusalem!" (v. 33). God established that city as Jesus' goal from the start, and in a short time he will fulfill his mission in death. Jerusalem was famous for its murder of prophets (though Jesus' words should not be pressed to mean that no prophet ever perished outside Jerusalem; cf. 9:9; Mark 6:14ff.). Since it was the capital of the nation and many prophets had been killed there, it was fitting for the greatest of all divine messengers to die there (Deut. 18:15, 18). Empowered by the Holy Spirit and deeply committed to the saving purpose of his heavenly Father, Jesus pursues his mission with no fear of Herod.

Jesus' prophecy of his destiny in Jerusalem leads him to be deeply saddened. The people there are rejecting God's love and are refusing to repent and turn to him (v. 34). That is the true tragedy, not his death. In a prophetic lament Jesus cries out to all the house of Israel and its capital city: "O Jerusalem, Jerusalem." That city's history of rejecting God's messengers will lead to judgment. Jesus wanted to protect the people there from the coming judgment not just once but many times. The words "how often" refer to the several visits he made to the holy city (cf. John's Gospel). He desired to gather the people as a mother hen shelters her little chickens under her wings, but they were not willing." Entrance into God's kingdom is always on the condition of a personal response. Saving grace can be accepted or rejected; God forces no one to be saved.

Rejection of God's love inevitably results in judgment (v. 35). So Jesus predicts that their house will be left desolate. Many take "house" to be the temple, but here it refers to the entire city. What he says does not describe Jerusalem at that time, but it is a prophecy of what will happen. Contrary to the NIV, the verb (*aphietai*) should be translated "will be left desolate" instead of "is left desolate." God will abandon the city to its enemies. No longer will he protect the people there. As we know, Jerusalem came under judgment at the hands of Romans in A.D. 70 (cf. 19:41–44). Sin and rejection of God's grace will bring disaster.

Jerusalem will be ruined, but its desolation will not last forever. Jesus goes on to say that these people will not see him again until they greet him in the words of Psalm 118:26: "Blessed is he who comes in the name of the Lord." His visit to the Holy City will be the last time they will see him until he returns with great power and glory. As a whole, Jerusalem and the nation will reject Jesus as the Messiah, but the Jews who in Christ's day and throughout the ages have repented and believed will welcome him as the true Messiah at his second coming. There is hope for the Jewish people. Now is the "time of the Gentiles," but in Romans 11 Paul says that the original branches (the Jews) broken off from the olive tree can be grafted back in. The door to the kingdom has not been permanently shut to them. When Jesus returns to this earth, many will turn to him and greet him as their Savior.

4.11. Table Fellowship With a Pharisee (14:1–24)

For the early Christians eating together had profound religious, social, and economic significance (24:28–32; Acts 1:4–8; 10:9–16; 11:1–18; 1 Cor. 11:17–34; Gal. 2:11–16). Jesus uses a meal at a Pharisee's home as an opportunity to perform a miracle and to do some teaching. The opening incident deals with the healing of a man on the Sabbath (vv. 1–6). Included also are a lesson for guests at a meal (vv. 7–11) and for a host on his choice of guests (vv. 12–14). The section concludes with a parable about a great banquet (vv. 15–24).

4.11.1. Jesus Heals a Sick Man on the Sabbath (14:1–6). Luke records another healing on the Sabbath (cf. 4:31–44; 6:6–11;

13:10–17). As a result of the miracle, Jesus again finds himself in conflict with the religious leaders. This healing occurs during a meal at the home of a prominent Pharisee—probably soon after a service in the synagogue of which he was the leader. Luke tells us nothing about the man's motives for inviting Jesus. As in 7:36ff., it is evident that Jesus includes everyone in his circle of concern; he has come to save Pharisees also.

The account gives us no details about the place or time of the meal except that it is on the Sabbath. Presumably many other Pharisees are also present. Everyone keeps watching Jesus closely to see what he may do. They are deeply suspicious of him and hope that he will say or do something that they can use against him. The conversation at the meal is not the normal table talk.

Present is a man suffering from dropsy, a condition in which the body accumulates fluids and arms and legs swell. Luke does not indicate whether the man has come wanting to be healed, but Jesus cannot help noticing him since he is right in front of him. The Spirit-anointed Jesus is aware that all eyes are fixed on him, so he asks the Pharisees and experts of the law a theological question: "Is it lawful to heal on the Sabbath or not?" This question calls for reflection: Is it in harmony with God's law to heal on the day of rest? According to rabbinic teaching it was not lawful. Healing could only take place on the Sabbath when life was in danger. This man would probably be no worse off to wait another day.

Not one of the religious leaders speaks up and answers the question. Confronted by silence Jesus gives a decisive answer. He heals the man, thereby declaring that indeed it is lawful to help people on the Sabbath. After the man has gone, Jesus points out (cf. also 13:10–16) to the religious leaders that they would offer aid to a son or an ox that fell into a well on the Sabbath. By opposing healing on the Sabbath, they reveal how inconsistent they are. Healing on the Sabbath ceases to be an academic question for them when it involves their own family or possessions. God has much more compassion than human beings do.

Jesus' critics also know that the law allows deeds of mercy on any day of the week. Loving our neighbor demands that we help people when they are in need. The miraculous work Jesus does on the Sabbath is a work of love but also a work of God. In the face of the evidence, the critics can say nothing. They have seen the miracle with their own eyes, but deliberately refuse to see it as the power of God. Sin blinds their eyes and makes their hearts stubborn and resistant to God's grace.

Jesus exposes the hypocrisy of the Pharisees. Their opposition to healing on the Sabbath warns us against rigid views of the day of rest. Sunday should not be reserved for our own personal interests. It is a day in which we place ourselves at God's disposal so that we may help to relieve spiritual and physical suffering. Human needs demand the ministry of God's people without delay.

4.11.2. A Lesson for Guests at a Feast (14:7–11). As the meal at the Pharisee's house continues, Jesus observes the social behavior of the guests. In particular he notices "how the guests picked the places of honor at the table." Thus, he uses a parable to teach humility. His advice to the Pharisees scrambling for chief seats consists of more than etiquette rules, for he uses the occasion to teach a lesson on the coming of God's kingdom. Life in the kingdom will not be marked by self-assertion and pride but by humility and unselfishness. The position of a person in the kingdom of heaven depends on God rather than on the exaltation of self and personal honor.

The parable is really a rebuke of many at the dinner table. In most cultures there are honorable and less honorable places at a meal (Bratcher, 1982, 244). People of higher social standing usually have places closer to the host. To teach them the order of God's things, Jesus begins by urging them, if they are guests at a wedding feast, to take the lowest places. A person more distinguished than they may be invited. Should a guest arrive before this person and grab the seat nearest the host, he runs the risk of being humiliated. The host will ask the one holding the seat of honor to move. The presumptuous guest may find that if most of the seats are occupied, he will have to take the least desirable seat. His self-promotion leads to shame and humiliation.

Jesus does not recommend the practice of false humility, but the guest who takes the lowest seat at first does not risk embarrassment. In fact, when the host sees him sitting in a lower seat, he will invite him to move up. This brings honor to him in the eyes of all the wedding guests.

Right before his eyes Jesus sees the Pharisees seeking positions of prestige and honor. What he has said can be taken to mean that they should be subtle in trying to get what they want. That is, in order to get the seat of honor first take lower seats. Such an understanding makes Jesus endorse selfish motives, which, of course, he never did. He is simply telling the Pharisees that their whole approach is wrong and can only result in their humiliation. The great principle is: "For everyone who exalts himself will be humbled, and he who humbles himself will be exalted" (v. 11). They need to realize that honor cannot be seized; it can only be given. The Pharisees expect to receive the best places in the kingdom of God, but they have no claim to them. Those places are not reserved by God for proud, aggressive people, but for those who humbly trust in Jesus. True disciples of Jesus are marked by humility. Church leaders will do well to heed Jesus' message about humility and his warning against the sin of self-worship.

4.11.3. A Lesson for Hosts (14:12–14). Jesus has addressed the guests. Now he turns to the host. What he says to him applies also to religious leaders. The Pharisees excluded the poor, the crippled, the lame, and the blind from full participation in religious life. To counter this practice, Jesus indicates that hospitality should be extended to all and cautions against including only friends, relatives, the rich, and the famous.

The temptation is to entertain only our own kind. When a host invites others to his house for a meal, he should include those who cannot repay the favor. If he feels that his guests will invite him later to a meal, what has he given? Nothing! There is only a trade, but no generosity is involved. His hospitality is motivated by his desire for reward. But true hospitality and kindness occur when there is no possibility of a "payback." Those who want to please God must reach out to the poor and the handicapped. Jesus does not forbid our hosting those who are able in turn to host us. But he does forbid forgetting those who are not in the position to repay. Generosity and kindness should not be used to gain power over others and to put them in debt to us. True hospitality, prompted by genuine love, will have no strings attached.

Breaking bread with the needy and disabled will never go unnoticed by the heavenly Father. Though they can offer us no recompense, God can and does. What the poor and the handicapped cannot do for us, he will do "at the resurrection of the righteous." That is, on the day the righteous rise from the dead, God will give a splendid reward to those who have been generous to the needy and weak. Such people have shown by their loving service that they have learned to live the kingdom life on the earth, and they will be rightly rewarded in the end time.

4.11.4. The Parable of the Great Banquet (14:15–24). The table talk at the house of a prominent Pharisee (v. 1) ends with the parable of the great banquet, which Jesus tells as a response to the remark made by one of the guests: "Blessed is the man who will eat at the feast in the kingdom of God." Apparently this comment is prompted by Jesus' assurance that unselfish hospitality will be rewarded "at the resurrection of the righteous" (v. 14). No doubt this man understands that Jesus has been talking about the feast in the kingdom of God (vv. 7–14). His remark about future blessedness shows that he is fully confident of being there.

Jesus therefore takes the opportunity to issue yet another warning. He challenges the complacency and pride that lead people to presume that they will break bread at the feast in heaven. No one can be at that feast by his or her own efforts but only by responding to the invitation. All who accept God's gracious invitation will indeed be blessed; those not present at the great heavenly feast will be lost, but it will be their own fault.

The parable begins with a certain man inviting a large number of guests to a great feast. As was the custom, he sends the invitation out in advance. Apparently all of them accept and are planning to attend. When the hour for the feast approaches, the host has his servant go to the invited guests and announce, "Come, for everything is now ready" (v. 17). The host here represents God, and the servant is Jesus. Through the promises of the Old Testament he has sent out an invitation in advance. The feast represents the kingdom of God, and Jesus is the one extending the final invitation. The gospel banquet has been made ready by his perfect saving work. Now is the time for the guests to take their places and to receive salvation with all of its present and future blessings.

When the invited guests hear that it is time for the banquet to begin, a surprising thing happens. They all beg to be excused, sending their regrets to the host. Of their excuses Jesus mentions three, which reinforce his warnings about allowing earthly interests to interfere with the call to discipleship.

The first excuse involves the inspection of a field recently purchased. Who would buy some land without first carefully inspecting it? Assuming that he has done this, nothing compels him to see what it looks like at this particular time. But the new owner pleads that it is a necessity (*ananke*), but the excuse is false. The fact is, he does not want to come to the banquet.

The second excuse involves the purchase of five pairs of oxen. The man claims that he is on his "way to try them out." But it is a little late to hitch each yoke to a plow to see if the two oxen work well together. No sensible person buys oxen and then tries to satisfy himself that they can do the job. Even if he did, there is no rush to find out this particular day if they work well. He simply does not wish to join the celebration.

The third excuse involves a man who has recently married. It is unclear why it is impossible for him to be present at the banquet. Marriage carries with it obligations, but it does not cancel out other obligations (Morris, 1974, 234). His excuse makes sense only if he cannot take his new bride along. But if so, he can go without her. Like the other two men his excuse is weak. These excuses represent excuses for not becoming members of the kingdom.

When the servant reports the refusals, the master becomes rightfully angry at the invited guests—a picture of God's wrath against all who reject his offer of salvation. The responses to his invitation have come as a surprise to him. But the feast has already been prepared, so he decides that the party must go on. He directs his servant to go into the streets and alleys of the city, bringing in the poor, the crippled, the blind, and the lame (cf. v. 13). The servant follows his master's instructions and reports back that many have come, but there is still room for more.

As a result, another invitation is sent—this time to people outside the city. The servant is to find the guests in rural areas, on country roads and lanes where tramps and beggars come and go, and must "make [*anankason*, compel] them come in." The master wants his banquet hall full. This command refers to the drawing power of saving grace. The invitation is urgent, though these people outside the city, too, may reject the invitation. The emphasis here provides no basis for the teaching that God has determined who will and will not enter the kingdom. God invites everyone. People may condemn themselves by their own choice to remain outside the kingdom. On the other hand, people do not save themselves; a person is saved only by God's grace.

The first invitation went out to the people through the promises and prophets of the Old Testament. Now Jesus himself offers the second invitation. Many of the religious people of his day are refusing it, but there is room at the banquet for people outside the city. The Spirit-anointed Savior predicts that his invitation will be carried to the Gentiles—to people, so to speak, who live on the country roads and lanes. What Jesus foretells here begins to be fulfilled in Acts as the Holy Spirit empowers believers to preach the gospel to the ends of the earth.

Jesus concludes the parable by rebuking those who were first invited but made excuses (v. 24). For them the day of opportunity had passed; they will not have a second chance to attend the banquet. To experience the saving power of God's kingdom depends on our responding to his invitation to the gospel banquet and relying on Jesus as Savior. The party goes on and remains open to all who will come. "Come, for everything is now ready" (v. 17).

4.12. The Cost of Being a Disciple (14:25–35)

Jesus returns to the road again, making his way toward Jerusalem (cf. 9:51; 10:38; 13:22). He has become amazingly popular among the people and is followed by large crowds. Many of them do not understand the demands of being a disciple. In light of what he will face in Jerusalem, he tells them what it means to follow him and urges them to consider carefully the cost of sharing in his suffering. No one can remain a true disciple without coming to grips with the price that must be paid to bear the cross (cf. 9:57–62).

Becoming his disciple involves great sacrifice (vv. 26–27). A disciple must be prepared to put devotion to Jesus before any earthly ties. In a Semitic way of speaking, he says that his disciples are to hate their families and life itself. On the lips of Jesus "hate" (*miseo*) does not refer to feelings of aversion and malice. After all, his disciples are to love even their enemies. Rather, "hate" here expresses preference (cf. Gen. 29:30–31; Deut. 21:15–17; Rom. 9:13). That is, should there be conflict between family loyalty and one's desire to follow Jesus, one must choose Jesus; family and life itself (i.e., personal desires, designs, and expectations) may only have second place in our affections. Nothing may interfere with absolute commitment to Jesus Christ.

The heart of discipleship is carrying one's cross and following Jesus in self-denial. Verse 27 refers to Jesus' own experience. The disciples must be prepared to share in the ordeal of the cross that awaits him in Jerusalem. To achieve moral excellence and discipline requires denying ourselves of certain things, but cross-bearing demands more than self-denial. It involves surrender—surrender of self to Jesus. To become a disciple means that we say no to the self-life and yes to a new life with Christ.

From the beginning of fellowship with Jesus we meet the cross and the demands of discipleship. It is possible to have been a disciple for some time, yet still not discover the deepest dimensions of discipleship (cf. 9:18–27; Matt. 10:38). Peter himself demonstrates that it is possible to be a disciple and to fail to grasp that cross-bearing is the essence of discipleship (Luke 22:54–62). Each disciple must bear his or her own cross: "Anyone who does not carry his cross and follow me cannot be my disciple."

Salvation comes as a free gift, but discipleship is costly. Those who follow Jesus must be willing to pay a high price. He wants people to realize that counting the cost before making a decision is a serious matter. It calls for repentance and total commitment to Jesus. To drive this point home he uses two parables.

The first parable tells about a man who wants to build a tower. Before he begins, he sits down and calculates the cost. To ensure success he does careful planning by estimating "the cost to see if he has enough money to complete it." Otherwise, he may lay the foundation but be unable to bear the total cost and never finish the job. His failure would make him a joke in front of others.

The second parable tells about a king who finds that the forces of an enemy outnumber his army by two to one. He debates whether or not he should engage in war. It is unlikely that an army of ten thousand soldiers can defeat one with twenty thousand. Therefore, before going to battle, he sits down to consider his options. In light of the prospect of defeat, he sends messengers to the king with the larger army and inquires as to what they must do to make peace.

The two parables make similar points; they look at discipleship in different ways, though in both cases it is serious business. The first one teaches that no one should blindly become a disciple of Jesus. Any sensible person should consider carefully if he or she can afford to follow Jesus. We ought to reflect on the demands of cross-bearing. This emphasis does not deny that there is risk in faith; total commitment includes confidence that Jesus is sufficient for whatever the future brings.

In the second parable the sensible person needs to consider whether one can afford not to follow Jesus. We must come to terms with the stronger enemy before war breaks out. Facing overwhelming forces, a wise king will make peace and avoid plunging his army into destruction. The stronger foe we must deal with in life is Satan. It is wise to count the cost of fighting him alone, for he is much stronger than we are. The only way to be successful against him is by allying ourselves with God through faith in Jesus (Eph. 6:10–17).

Jesus closes his discourse by once again warning against underestimating the cost of discipleship and embarking halfheartedly on following him. Those who fail to manifest the character of a true disciple are like salt that loses its saltiness (v. 34). No one can make it salty again. Having lost its taste, it is worthless and has to be thrown away. Just like salt that becomes tasteless, one's initial commitment to Jesus can fade in due time. Failure to manifest the life of a true disciple renders one useless in God's kingdom.

There is no place in the ranks of Jesus' disciples for anyone lacking the qualities of discipleship. Even when nurtured by prayer, worship, fellowship, and study of God's Word, commitment to Jesus will be severely tested. As devotion to following him to the cross wanes, position, family, and job try to become first once again. The salt gradually loses its taste. Many followers do not notice what is happening until it is too late. Jesus' warning against underestimating the cost should be heeded. For as Jesus concludes, "He who has ears to hear, let him hear."

4.13. God's Love for the Lost (15:1–32)

Chapter 15 consists of three parables with a common theme: God's love for the lost. Jesus speaks them in response to criticism made by the Pharisees and teachers of the law regarding his welcoming tax collectors and sinners and having table fellowship with them. In the opinion of these religious leaders, such people are "undesirables" and have little value in God's sight (cf. 5:29–32; 7:34; 19:1–10). They believe that separation of good and bad people must be preserved to have a proper sense of righteousness. In the parables Jesus shows the Father's attitude toward those accepting the invitation of the kingdom: He rejoices at the repentance of one sinner. They also show Jesus' mission as shepherd, woman, and father to seek and to save the lost.

4.13.1. The Parable of the Lost Sheep (15:1–7). Jesus has announced judgment on the Pharisees and teachers of the law (14:15–24). They return the compliment by complaining that Jesus "welcomes sinners and eats with them." The religious leaders normally rejected sinners as immoral and treated them as "unclean." Now the tables are turned. Jesus is the host and at his table he decides who are fit and "clean." He receives as his guests tax collectors and other "sinners" (see comments on 5:27–32). Such are the people Jesus invites to his table and into his kingdom. The Pharisees, however, do not understand Jesus' mission—to save those kinds of people.

Jesus begins with a picture depicting a common experience for a Palestinian shepherd. The shepherd has a hundred sheep, and one of them strays away from the flock and gets lost. When he counts his sheep at the end of the day, he discovers that one is missing. The shepherd loves the sheep so much that he leaves the ninety-nine and goes in search of the lost sheep. If not found, the sheep could starve to death or be killed by predators, and the shepherd will not allow that to happen. Sparing no effort, he searches until he finds his lost sheep. When he does, he joyfully puts it on his shoulders and carries it home. Wanting others to share in his joy, he invites his friends and neighbors to celebrate with him.

Jesus concludes the parable with an explanation. The shepherd's joy at his recovery of the lost sheep and the celebration that follows at his home give us a picture of the great joy "in heaven over one sinner who repents." This heavenly joy stands in contrast to his critics, who are complaining about Jesus' eating with sinners. They are blinded by their pride and fail to realize what causes celebration in heaven. One repentant sinner causes more joy than do "ninety-nine righteous persons" who think they do not need to repent. "Righteous persons" refer to the Pharisees and teachers of the law. As much as anyone, such people do need to repent. Nor should it be forgotten that Jesus

In the parable of the lost sheep, Jesus describes the shepherd who leaves the ninety-nine sheep to search for the one that is missing at the end of the day. Jesus compares the shepherd's joy at finding that one lost sheep with the joy "in heaven over one sinner who repents."

is the good shepherd, who lays his life down for the sheep (John 10:11). God provides salvation through the death of his Son and draws sinners to himself through the Spirit.

4.13.2. The Parable of the Lost Coin (15:8–10). This second parable parallels the preceding one. Here a silver coin (*drachme*, about a day's wage for an average worker) has been lost rather than a sheep. This parable focuses on a woman who lives in a peasant's house. Normally such homes have no windows, so as soon as she loses her coin, she begins to search for it. She lights a lamp and sweeps the house, looking carefully until she finds it. She is greatly relieved, and like the shepherd (v. 6) she invites friends and neighbors over for a celebration meal. Jesus' application of this parable is similar to the previous one, though this time "there is rejoicing in the presence of the angels of God over one sinner who repents" rather than "rejoicing in heaven" (v. 7). Both parables refer to God's joy when a sinner returns to him.

Jesus does not want his critics to miss the point. Like the shepherd and the woman he seeks out the lost and receives sinners who repent. His mission is to bring such people into fellowship with God. Dining with Jesus is never enough. True repentance is necessary for salvation.

4.13.3. The Parable of the Lost Son (15:11–32). The third story tells about a son who is lost and later found. Of all parables, this story is the favorite of many people.

The parable portrays repentance, love, forgiveness, and joy. It gives more attention to the father's forgiving love than to the return of the son. We see the lost son's sin, his need, his repentance, his return, and his older brother's response. The purpose of the parable is to show God's attitude of pardoning love toward sinners, stressing divine mercy that exceeds all expectations. While there is no direct reference to the saving power of the Cross, the parable shows the great love that moved God to give his Son for sinners. God's saving purpose depends on the Cross, and this parable powerfully sets forth his love for the lost.

The parable opens with a man who has two sons. From the outset the story points to the father's relation with his sons. The father represents God; the prodigal son represents the lost, particularly tax collectors and sinners; and the older son represents the self-righteous, such as the Pharisees, the teachers of the law, and people in the church without faith.

At the beginning of the story the younger son wants to leave home. He may have been in his late teens or a little older. Instead of waiting until his father dies, he requests his share of the inheritance (which would be half as much as the older son would receive; see Deut. 21:17). Normally the estate would not be divided until the father's death (Marshall, 1978, 607), but the younger son wants it now. The father does what his son asks and divides his property (*bios*, "living, subsistence") between his two sons. At this point the younger son decides he does not want to live in his father's house any longer, and the father allows him to leave with his inheritance. God allows sinners to go out on their own, though his goodness tries to lead them to repentance (Rom. 2:4).

The younger son gives no reason for his request, but his desire for the pleasures of the world becomes clear soon after he has control of his inheritance. He gathers together everything he has, probably by turning it into cash, and then departs for a distant country. He makes a clean break, apparently leaving nothing behind that would cause him to want to return. Out on his own he begins to waste his money in wild, extravagant living. Jesus gives none of the details, but the Greek says that he scatters (*diaskorpizo*) his funds in many directions.

After he has thrown his inheritance away by wasteful extravagance, however, he has to face a natural catastrophe. A severe famine falls on the whole country and increases his difficulties. Food becomes scarce and as a result is costly. He is about to starve. When he set out from his father's house, it never entered his mind that he would find himself in such desperate need. Having nothing to eat, he gets a job on a farm feeding pigs, which Jews considered to be unclean (Deut. 14:8). No job was more degrading to a Jew (Lev. 11:7; 14:8; Isa. 65:4; 66:17), but he had to make this choice in order to avoid starvation.

Though employed, his misery remains about the same. He gets to the point where he wants to eat the pods that the pigs eat. These pods are the fruit of the carob tree, used for fodder and eaten by only extremely poor people (Marshall, 1978, 609). He is willing to eat hog feed (though it is unclear from the passage whether he really does or not). No one, however, gives him anything to eat (v. 16). Whoever his so-called friends were when he had wealth, they offer him no help. His condition is worse than death. He is a lost soul, experiencing hell on earth.

The young man reflects on his condition and comes to his senses (v. 17), recognizing that he has done wrong. Hardship makes him face the facts. He realizes that at his father's house the hired servants have more food than they can eat, but here he is dying of hunger. The prodigal realizes that his desperate condition is the result of his sin. He does not want to be lost anymore and live in such a forlorn place. He decides to act decisively and go back home.

The young man rehearses what he will confess to his father: "Father, I have sinned against heaven and against you. I am no longer worthy to be called your son; make me like one of your hired men." The Greek "against heaven" is a way of speaking about God. He has sinned against God and his father by disobeying the fifth commandment (Ex. 20:12). He recognizes that no longer does he deserve to be treated like a son, but he hopes his father will take him back as one of his hired servants. His plea expresses deep humility. Sinners have nothing to rely on but the Father's mercy and pardoning grace.

The prodigal sets out for home, not as a demanding son but as a humble servant. From afar off his father sees him coming, but will have nothing to do with treating his rebellious son as a hired servant. Instead, his heart goes out to him. It is obvious that the old man has been looking and hoping for his son's return. He is so pleased to see him that he runs out to meet the young man. With warm affection he puts his arms around him and kisses him (*kataphileo*, which means "to kiss fervently," a sign that the prodigal is already forgiven). What an unexpected welcome! Nevertheless the son begins his confession, declaring his sin and unworthiness to be considered his father's son.

But before the son can ask to be treated as a hired servant, the father interrupts. Rather than treat him as a hired servant, he wants to restore him to full sonship and treat him as a guest of honor. The father gives him a most beautiful robe appropriate for his position as a son, a ring symbolizing his authority, and sandals for his feet as a sign of a free man (it was fitting only for slaves to go barefoot). He even orders that the fattened calf, which has been carefully fed and saved for a special occasion, be killed. What occasion could be more special than this one? It calls for a full celebration, not just an ordinary party. "For this son of mine was dead and is alive again; he was lost and is found" (v. 24; cf. Eph. 2:1). It is indeed amazing how the heavenly Father welcomes repentant sinners. He takes them back with no questions asked.

This is not the end of the story, however. The father's older son has stayed home and remained faithful. But like his younger brother, he too is lost, even though he lives in his father's house. He has been out in the field working; and when he returns, he hears music and dancing. A celebration is in full swing, but he has no idea what it is about until a servant explains to him: "Your brother has come . . . and your father has killed the fattened calf because he has him back safe and sound" (v. 27). Needless to say, the older brother is less than pleased with his father. He becomes angry and refuses to go in. This reaction represents that of the Pharisees and the teachers of the law in verse 2. Like the older brother, in their pride and self-righteousness they refuse to enter the feast of God's kingdom.

The father also loves his older son and has no false pride. He has already gone out to one son; now he goes out and begs repeatedly (*parekalei*, imperfect tense) to the other one to come in and join the celebration. The older son vents feelings that have been building up for years and shows the old man little respect. We can almost hear him shouting that his father has never appreciated what a wonderful son he has been. He has been a model son, slaving for his father many years and never disobeying him. Yet what has his father given him? Nothing—not even a young goat (cheap by comparison to a fattened calf) so that he could have a feast with his friends.

Showing obvious contempt, the older son refers to the prodigal not as his brother but as "this son of yours." So proud and self-righteous, he speaks about the younger man as spending his father's money on prostitutes. Then he accuses his father of being unfair: "You kill the fattened calf for him," the good-for-nothing brother. In no way does the prodigal, the elder brother thinks, deserve this kind of treatment. He is right, but he fails to understand a father's love. Moreover, he has no understanding of forgiveness and compassion.

Again the father takes the initiative, and his reply shows great compassion. He could have been angry and denounced his older son for his harsh words and attitude. Just the opposite, he remains patient, as he was with his younger son. He offers to his older son, who is also lost, necessary grace: "My son . . . you are always with me, and everything I have is yours." The younger son has received his share of the estate; the rest will go to the older son. But like the Pharisees, who have criticized Jesus for receiving unclean people (prodigals) and have forced him to defend his practice of eating with them, the older son fails to realize his privileges and forces his father to give account for the feast that is celebrating the return of his brother.

But feasting is the right thing to do, explains the father; "we had to [*edei*] celebrate and be glad." How could they not celebrate this happy occasion? "This brother of yours was dead and is alive again; he was lost and is found." A great transformation has occurred in the life of not "my son" but "this brother of yours." The father does not want the older brother to overlook his relationship to the prodigal. A wonderful thing has happened, and he ought to join in the rejoicing.

The father loves both of his sons. Embracing the younger son does not mean that he rejects the older one. God's love of tax collectors and sinners by no means negates his love for Pharisees and self-righteous sinners. Such love of the heavenly Father reminds us of the radical nature of divine grace. Being lost is dangerous, but being found is a matter of grace. Like the prodigal some people get lost by running away, but no place is too far to keep God's grace from finding them. Others, like the older son, get lost when they stay at home and fail to see grace all around them.

We may see in ourselves the prodigal and the elder brother. Like the prodigal we rejoice in the welcoming grace of God. On the other hand, when individuals fail to live up to our standards, we may become critical through self-righteousness, similar to the self-righteous pride of the older brother and the Pharisees. Let us remember that we are all in desperate need of grace; we ought not have trouble giving grace to those who are undeserving. The fact is that none of us deserves the honor of living in God's home, so God must give grace to us if we are to make our way to his kingdom.

4.14. Teachings on Wealth (16:1–31)

This section in many respects serves as a contrasting study to the previous chapter regarding the lost and dispossessed. Jesus now addresses his message to those with abundant, or at least sufficient, possessions. Such people have the responsibility to meet the material needs of others. The broader reference is to those who possess God's Word (both the disciples of our Lord and the Pharisees) and who, because of this more valuable commodity, have the means and responsibility to meet the spiritual needs of others.

The issue Jesus addresses is not simply wealth, but the attitude of spiritual condescension that prevails when the personal accumulation of wealth is seen as a sanction by God. Jesus challenges his hearers not only to be generous, but to rethink the meaning of their wealth in a needy world. In this sense, the section does not so much contrast the preceding section on the lost as build upon it and address the responsibility that we as believers have toward the lost.

4.14.1. The Shrewd Manager (16:1–13). Few passages in the New Testament, and arguably no parable of Jesus, engender so many varying interpretations as the parable of the shrewd manager. The crux of the problem is that Jesus appears to uphold a criminal act as an example for his followers to emulate (vv. 8–9). As a result, interpreters have disagreed both on what the steward is doing and on what primary point Jesus intends to convey in this story.

Among the many interpretations of this parable, two bear mention. (1) The shrewd manager behaves as a scoundrel throughout the story. By this reckoning, the manager misappropriates his master's possessions; when confronted with his deceit, he proceeds to falsify the accounts of his master's debtors by lowering their balances in order to obtain their favor. The dilemma for the Christian reader is that by this interpretation the parable lifts up an unscrupulous character as an example to follow. Though this interpretation is problematic, it is not insurmountable. Jesus elsewhere uses sinful people as examples (11:31; 18:2–7). In addition, the manager is not praised by his master (or Jesus) for his thievery, but for his forethought in making provision for the future.

(2) Other scholars suggest that interest is being charged the debtors, and the original amount includes the interest due. Though the Old Testament law expressly forbade charging interest (Lev. 25:36), research into the legal and financial practices of the first century suggests that Jewish law had worked loopholes around this biblical admonition. Thus the manager, when confronted with the loss of his livelihood, acts within the law and reduces the balances on the debtors' accounts by forgiving the interest due, winning the favor of the debtors. At the same time, his master is cast in a generous light and so can enjoy an undeserved reputation for benevolence.

Note that Jesus addresses this story to his disciples (v. 1). This intended audience is of paramount importance for determining which interpretation of the parable makes the most sense. In the first option the theme of the parable can only be the wise use of money. But from the second perspective, the parable has two equally important themes: the wise use of money and repentance. It is only when the shrewd manager shows his repentance through his acts of charity that he is able to use money wisely. And it is only in the context of this theme of repentance that the absolute contrast of serving God and serving money in verse 13 makes sense. Thus, the second interpretation is to be preferred. The broader message for the disciples is, therefore, one that challenges them to rethink their worldview, using the realm of finance as an illustrative tool.

It is clear from the outset that the charge levied against the manager is not false, for he offers no defense of himself. The master takes the charge so seriously that he has already decided to dismiss the manager (v. 2). The question that the master poses in verse 2, "What is this I hear about you?" is not a true query about the manager's actions. He knows already the answer. This is essentially a rhetorical question, which reveals the master's sense of disappointment and betrayal that he must have been experiencing: "How could you have done this to me?"

In addition, the master instructs the manager to prepare a final accounting, giving him time to devise a course of action. The shrewd manager takes action at once. Like the lost son of Luke 15:11–31, he is faced with a choice of begging or harsh physical labor. Being too ashamed to beg and believing himself too weak to dig (v. 3), he dismisses those options. Unlike the lost son, he never considers the option of pleading for mercy. Instead, he chooses a course that will endear him to his master's debtors (v. 4) and that he can quickly implement.

In verses 5–7, we see this plan in action. The two encounters depicted here are to be taken as representative of his dealings with all of his master's debtors. Three points deserve mention. (1) The transactions occur "quickly" (v. 6). (2) The transactions occur one by one in secrecy. For the manager, time is of the essence. The stealth and haste with which he carries out his plan is essential. He wants to avoid having the master intervene before his plan can be brought to a successful conclusion. (3) The amounts discussed by the shrewd manager and the debtors are vast. The goodwill engendered by forgiving such debts will be great indeed.

The parable concludes with the surprising and attention-getting response of the master (v. 8). Upon learning of the manager's shrewd dealings, the master commends his resourcefulness. Just as we find the master's response surprising, so must the audience of Jesus' day. It is at this point, having corralled the attention of his hearers with this surprising conclusion, that Jesus begins to make application.

His initial point is made in the conclusion of verse 8. Yet another surprise is in store as the sinful "people of this world" are favorably compared with the "people of the light." It is their resourcefulness and their dedication to the achievement of their intended goals that are held up as examples for emulation. The implication is that the "people of the light," whose goal is infinitely more valuable, should be all the more resourceful and dedicated as they work toward their goal of a "treasure in heaven that will not be exhausted" (12:33).

Next, a more direct application is offered, which speaks directly to the use of money (v. 9). Money is referred to as "worldly wealth" (RSV, "unrighteous mammon"). But being an inanimate and morally neutral tool, which Jesus is here instructing his disciples to use, why does the Lord call money "worldly" r "unrighteous?" There are perhaps three enses in which money can be thought of as vorldly or unrighteous: because it tempts us to cquire it by unrighteous means, because it empts us to use it for unrighteous ends, and ecause it will fail us when we come before God for judgment. We must be reminded, owever, that it is not money per se but "the ove of money," which Paul warns Timothy is "a root of all kinds of evil" (1 Tim. 6:10).

But if money is to be understood as a vehicle for temptation and a false sense of security, hen how is it that money can be used to secure welcome "into eternal dwellings"? The answer to this question is found in the opportunities for almsgiving afforded the rich man of 16:19–31. In this story we are introduced to a person with great "worldly wealth" who uses that wealth to secure for himself a sumptuous lifestyle. But he ignores the plight of Lazarus, a wretched beggar who lies at his gate. Later, after death, the rich man finds himself in Hades and learns that he could have secured an entry into the "eternal dwellings" had he used his wealth to provide for and befriend Lazarus.

In verses 10–12, Jesus offers a third and much broader application of this parable. Money, indeed all possessions, are pictured as resources with which we are entrusted by God. It is not our money, our home, our property; but it is God's money, God's home, God's property, which he has entrusted into our care. The shrewd manager commended earlier is here chastised for his unfaithfulness to his master. This application is then extended to Jesus' hearers, who are further told that more important than money is their handling of "true riches" (v. 11).

The application of this parable concludes with a verse striking for the way money is set up as an adversary to God. Already Jesus has called money "worldly," but now he depicts money with human attributes, calling it a master set up in opposition to God (v. 13). This application is surprising, given the foregoing comments that money can be used to secure a heavenly dwelling. The Lord's point here, however, is that money can be a god. The one who serves money is no less than an idol worshiper (cf. Eph. 5:5), and the Lord leaves no middle ground on this issue.

Each person must choose to be a manager in service to money or a manager in service to God. Just as the shrewd manager's love for money made service to his master impossible, the rich man's love for money makes service to the poor and to Jesus impossible (16:19–31). The Pharisees' love for money (v. 14) makes service to God impossible, and our love for money makes service to the Lord impossible too.

4.14.2. The Function of the Law (16:14–18). Although the intended audience for the preceding parable is the disciples (v. 1), we now learn that some of the Pharisees have been listening and have taken offense to the implications of Jesus' message (v. 14). The Pharisees, whom Luke tells us "loved money," viewed wealth as a reward from God for faithful observance of the law. Knowing this, Jesus pauses in his teaching on wealth to address the topic of the law with those who reputedly held it in the highest regard.

From the Pharisaic perspective, the poverty of Jesus testified to his rejection by God; thus, his teaching engenders their derision and sneers. In their view, it is all too easy for someone like Jesus, who has nothing, to ridicule the wealthy. But the Spirit-anointed Jesus strikes at the fundamental sin of the Pharisees—that their self-exaltation as law observers is a hypocrisy covering their sinful greed (v. 15). People they can fool, Jesus tells the Pharisees, but God, who looks on their heart, is not fooled by their pretense of holiness.

But just what is it that Jesus says is "highly valued among men" and also "detestable in God's sight"? In this context Jesus must be referring either to the Pharisees' love for and relentless pursuit of wealth or to their hypocritical self-justification before others. In fact, both may be in mind. But what is doubly important is that the Pharisees should know better. Solomon addressed the vanity of the love of money (Eccl. 5:10–12). Knowing the law as they claim, the Pharisees should recognize the self-deception and hypocrisy in promoting material riches as evidence of God's approval. Jesus' remark should not be taken as an isolated saying. Elsewhere, Paul insists that the love of money is a deterrence to faith and a gateway to sin (1 Tim. 6:9–10; 2 Tim. 3:2), as does the writer of Hebrews (Heb. 13:5).

Recognizing the challenge to his authority, Jesus now proceeds to trace the origin of his authority and to delineate his superior devotion to the law. He presents the "Law and the Prophets" (i.e., the Old Testament) and the preaching of John the Baptist as a unit (v. 16). John heralded the coming of the new age and participated in it. It is "since that time" (v. 16), that is to say, beginning with John, that the kingdom of God is preached. Jesus' point is that neither John nor the Old Testament prophets are needed to confirm the other but that both serve as forerunners, leading to Jesus' preaching of the good news of the kingdom of God.

At this point is an interesting but difficult saying: "Everyone is forcing his way into [the kingdom of God]" (v. 16). What does this mean? (1) For Jesus' hearers the kingdom of God is no longer a future hope but a present reality available to them. Although sometimes the kingdom is portrayed as future, the emphasis here is clearly placed on its presence. (2) One must strive to enter God's kingdom. To enter this kingdom calls for courage and resolution, and obstacles to entry are many. Indeed, Luke has already alluded to the religious authorities, including the Pharisees, as obstacles to entry into God's kingdom (13:10–17, 24–30; 15:11–32).

If the challenge from the Pharisees is that Jesus is an object of derision and a renegade from God's law, then verse 17 serves as the summary of our Lord's response. Surely the kingdom of God is now manifest on earth, but this reality in no way sets aside the law. For Jesus' hearers, who are pondering whether to accept his challenge to force their way into the kingdom of God, this is no way abrogates their devotion and responsibility to God's law. They are not required to abandon their religious heritage as sons of Abraham in order to become disciples of Christ.

The teaching on divorce that follows (v. 18) is therefore offered not as an out-of-context all-inclusive statement of Jesus' position on the matter (cf. Matt. 19:9), but as an allegation against the Pharisees. They accuse Jesus of defying God's law. He now shows that while he adheres to "the least stroke of a pen" of the law (v. 17), the Pharisees manipulate God's Word in order to lead lives of open and unrepentant sin. Surely Jesus has in mind the prevailing Jewish idea of the day, which as a liberalization of Deuteronomy 24:1 held that a man could put away his wife with little provocation. Examples are Hillel's teaching that a spoiled dinner is adequate justification for divorce, or Abihu's notion that finding someone prettier is suitable grounds. Having been rebuked by the Pharisees for keeping the company of sinners (15:2), Jesus replies that the sinners are those who disregard God's law by so readily entering into and dissolving marriage.

At first glance, it would seem that 16:14–18, sandwiched between two parables on the use of material possessions, is awkward and out of place. There is a tendency to interpret this passage in isolation from the two adjoining parables. But then we miss something of the message that Luke may be trying to communicate. If it is presupposed that Luke 16 forms a unity, then how are verses 14–18 related to the parables of the shrewd manager and of the rich man and Lazarus (vv. 19–31)?

Perhaps we learn something of the church community to which Luke addresses his Gospel, and by extension something about our own church communities. Just as the Pharisees, "who loved money" (v. 14), resented the implications of Jesus' parable, it may be reasonable to assume that Luke knows there are rich members within his own Christian fellowship who do not believe that almsgiving is important (cf. Acts 5:1–11). In fact, perhaps they believe, like the Pharisees, that riches are an indication of favor from God (Luke 16:15). If so, the greater and indeed more dangerous problem may be that these members are attempting to justify their avarice on theological grounds. Such people destroy the fellowship of love and compassion that God wants in the church community (cf. Acts 2:42–47; 4:31–35).

As a result, in the midst of Luke's presentation of Jesus' teachings on wealth, he must address the function and authority of the law. The placement of this brief passage thus serves to underscore the admonition to the Pharisees, to the rich members of Luke's community, and to the members of our own day who insist that material things are sure signs of God's blessings. God's Word cannot be used to justify sinful greed. In this regard, verses 14–18 are directly linked to 16:29–31, which reemphasizes that "the law and the prophets" are sufficient to lead us to the conclusion that God requires repentance from a self-centered lifestyle.

4.14.3. The Rich Man and Lazarus (16:19–31). Jesus' teachings on the dangers of ealth conclude with a parable unique to uke's Gospel. The consequences of a life ved in dedication to material pursuits are xpressed here with a stark sense of finality not een before in Luke's Gospel. The rich man oved money, not God, and was thus found detestable in God's sight" (16:15).

The broader implication of this parable is est understood by recognizing that it climaxes ot only the wealth teachings but also the preious section on God's love for the lost (ch. 15). he rich man is condemned not because of his ealth but because he ignores the opportunity rovided him in the beggar Lazarus. Abraham, whom the rich man turns when he finds himelf in torment, was also rich, but he is not conemned for this. Instead, it is the rich man's ailure to notice Lazarus that is the issue at take—he loves money instead of God (16:13), nd he does not share in God's love for the lost.

The parable opens with an introduction to he rich man (v. 19). From the outset, the xcesses of this man's life are made clear: He s luxuriously dressed in purple (the color of oyalty and the gods) and in fine linen (expenive, imported garments). He indulges himself daily in this luxuriant lifestyle. But equally mportant is what is not said about the rich man. He is not pictured as a cruel, vindictive character; he is simply wealthy and self-indulgent.

In the first of a series of contrasts between he two main characters, Luke describes the miserable state of the beggar at the rich man's gate (vv. 20–21). He is lame, penniless, and ill. Even his meager desire to eat the crumbs from he rich man's table is unfulfilled. The only attention he receives is from dogs, who lick his sores. There is some dispute as to whether this licking is a painful aggravation to the poor man, which he is too weak to fend off, or whether the sores are cleansed and soothed by the dogs' soft tongues. In either case, the poor man's only companions are dogs, ritually unclean animals, which places him outside the realm of God's mercy.

Jesus tells of the reversal of fortunes at the deaths of these two men. Lazarus, without help in this life, is lavished with divine care as he is transported by angels to Abraham's side (v. 22). Never offered a place even to eat remnants from the rich man's table, he now sits in the seat of honor at Abraham's side at the heavenly banquet table. The rich man receives a proper burial; thus, all earthly preparation is made for this affluent man. But just as there is no mention of care taken to bury the body of Lazarus, there is no mention of care taken for the soul of the rich man.

The contrast between the two men continues as Jesus tells of the rich man's fate. He now finds himself in "hell" ("Hades"). Though "Hades" has more than one meaning in the Bible, it here refers to a place of torment. The fortunes of the two men are now reversed. Everything the rich man once enjoyed he now lacks; everything Lazarus once lacked he now enjoys.

In his torment, the rich man looks up to see Abraham with Lazarus (cf. 6:23). Not recognizing that earthly values have been overturned, the rich man calls upon his lineage as a child of Abraham to have his torment relieved. He wants "Father Abraham" to have mercy on him and relieve his thirst by sending Lazarus to his aid. The rich man, who never had to beg and never heeded the begging voice of Lazarus, now finds himself begging. Just as Lazarus had not asked to eat from the rich man's table but only to eat the crumbs that fell from it, the rich man does not ask to be taken to Abraham's side to enjoy the fountain he must see there but simply to have Lazarus bring a few drops of water to ease his thirst.

Abraham responds to the rich man's request (vv. 25–26). His address, "Son," is tender and confirms his claim to be a physical descendant of the patriarch. But the careful use of the pronoun "your" (v. 25) shows the rich man that by the choices he made in his life, he forsook the blessings that he could have enjoyed as a child of Abraham. The rich man chose material blessings; thus, Abraham calls his riches "your good things." He had not consciously rejected God, but in his lovelessness he ignored Lazarus; and because he ignored Lazarus, he also ignored God.

Lazarus, on the other hand, chose God. The evil things he received in his life were not the result of his own choices. Now, the inequities of life are addressed. In the life to come, there is no need for a psalmist to bemoan the fact that evildoers flourish while the righteous are left to suffer. The imbalances of life are rectified on the basis of choices made.

But there is another factor, the great chasm, that lends a sense of finality to the fate of the two men. No one may cross the gulf that separates them. In his insensitivity to the fate of the poor man at his gate, the rich man is the one who created this great chasm. He had an opportunity and had the capability of spanning the abyss between the two. But in his death, this great chasm has now been made permanent. As hopeless as the fate of Lazarus was on earth, the fate of the rich man in hell is even more hopeless. As a result, far from easing his anguish, the "far away" sighting of the poor man with Abraham multiplies his agony.

The rich man's pain is now not only from the torments of hell, but also from knowing that he deprived himself of the abundance of heaven. The contentment that he always sought and that his earthly riches could never fulfill, he now sees Lazarus enjoying, and he is faced with the stark reality that he never will. Heaven is that moment when the one thing that you have been searching for all your life becomes manifest, and hell, in its sense of deprivation, is knowing that you will never experience it. The rich man now knows that eternal life is beyond his reach.

This parable reminds us of some noteworthy truths about the hereafter that should not be dismissed. (1) The dead are neither annihilated nor unconscious but are fully cognizant of their surroundings and their fate. (2) The plight of the dead is fixed by the choices made in this life. There is no second chance afforded beyond the grave. Thus, opportunities we receive to minister to the lost and needy bear eternal implications and must not be squandered.

At this point, the subject abruptly changes as the rich man asks that Lazarus be sent to warn his five brothers (vv. 27–28). It is interesting to note that even now, having learned of his eternal fate, the rich man still thinks of Lazarus as the poor man at his disposal. It may seem surprising that the rich man in his anguish is thinking of others, but this should not be taken to mean that he now has a repentant heart, full of compassion and grace. Rather, he is thinking not of the poor but of his own, his family. Moreover, in his request he apparently feels he is being unjustly tormented. If a sufficient warning had been given him (as he now requests for his brothers), the rich man is sure that he would not be in this predicament.

In the concluding exchange (vv. 29–31), Abraham spurns the rich man's request by saying that his brothers have the Law and th Prophets, that is, the Scriptures (v. 29). Whe the rich man says that surely a miracle wi convince his brothers (v. 30), Abraham als rejects this assertion (v. 31). Faith arises n from an encounter with the dramatic but fro an encounter with the word of God. A miracl may lead someone to marvel at the power o God, but it will not lead to faith and repentanc apart from God's Word.

This parable emphasizes the far-reachin consequences of this present life and the cen tral role that faith plays in directing the out come of that life. Possessions will neither sav nor condemn the soul. Likewise, poverty i neither a sin nor a virtue. It is the repentant o unrepentant nature of the heart in the contex of both riches and poverty that determines person's fate. The rich man, by his disdain an neglect for the poor, reveals the sinfulness o his heart. But whether rich or poor, those wh surrender all they have and all they are to th Lord and whose lives bear the mark of a repen tant heart will find themselves in the compan of Lazarus at the side of Abraham. The mes sage is not that the material inequities of thi life will be balanced in the afterlife but that life of faith with love and charity is the key b which eternal destination is determined.

Two points must be made that are pertinen to the Pentecostal and charismatic communit of believers. First, the error of a "health an wealth," "positive confession," or "name-it claim-it" gospel is exposed here. Jesus doe not preach that wealth is a sign of God' approval. While the Lord teaches that possessions can be used for noble purposes (10:29–37), he repeatedly warns that possessions are also a danger, which can serve as a serious distraction to discipleship (12:15–21; 18:18–23). In the worst case, possessions can be an irresistible and life-destroying temptation, as Ananias and Sapphira learned (Acts 5:1–11).

Second, it is important for Pentecostals and charismatics, who enjoy firsthand the working of signs and wonders, to recognize that Jesus refuses to fulfill the onlookers' demand for a miraculous sign (cf. Matt. 16:1–4; Mark 8:11; Luke 11:29–32). Likewise, it is impertinent for believers today to "put a fleece before the Lord" and request a sign regarding a matter to which the Scriptures have already spoken. When the Lord brings a person with need into r lives and has blessed us so that we are able meet that need, we are not justified in ask-g the Lord for a sign to show us whether we ould help. Just as the rich man and his broth-s should have already known, we should ready know that it is God's will to minister henever the opportunity arises.

4.15. On Faith and Duty (17:1–10)

Jesus' attention shifts now to his closest fol-wers. He offers advice to them on four aspects f discipleship: (1) the danger of causing others sin (vv. 1–3a); (2) the need to forgive (vv. 3b–); (3) the power of faith (vv. 5–6); and (4) the uty of a servant (vv. 7–10). As disciples of hrist, believers are free, but they must be sponsible to their Lord and the community of ith. Christian freedom needs to be curbed by ve for the members of the community. Faith cludes forgiveness of those who sin against us nd leads to performance of duty, expecting no pecial treatment.

(1) Jesus warns against leading others stray into sin and apostasy. Satan has a strong nfluence in the world. Enticements to embrace alse teachings and temptations to sin are cer-ain to occur. Those who yield to these temp-ations experience spiritual disaster. The word *kandalon*, translated in the NIV as "cause . . . o sin," means "stumbling block," "cause of ffense," or "pitfall." Jesus pronounces a woe n anyone responsible for leading others to sin r to renounce the faith (v. 1). A person doing hat would be better off to have suffered a vio-ent death, such as drowning with a heavy mill-tone around the neck.

The prospect for judgment is fearful and the onsequences severe for someone causing piritual harm to "one of these little ones." esus characterizes his disciples as "little nes," meaning all who believe in him (cf. Matt. 18:6). This warning equals the fire of esus' rebuke of the Pharisees in 16:15. The eading astray of God's children is not merely omething to worry about in the future. On the ontrary, the danger is real now among the dis-iples themselves. Jesus reinforces his warn-ng: "So watch yourselves."

(2) The next aspect of discipleship involves orgiveness (vv. 3b–4). Rather than leading thers into sin, believers must guard them-elves against sin. Sin always threatens the fel-owship of believers. When one believer sins against another, the wronged believer should rebuke the offender. This does not mean one should adopt a critical, self-righteous attitude, for the context emphasizes forgiveness. It means, however, that such a person must be strong, reprimanding the fellow believer for wrongdoing and urging him or her to repent. Responsible love is always compassionate, but such love rebukes in order to correct (Craddock, 1990, 199).

If the offending person repents, he or she must be forgiven so that good relationships can be restored promptly. Should that person sin again and again, forgiveness should be repeated. "Seven times in a day" refers to a countless number of times; Jesus sets no limits on forgiveness. True forgiveness prevents an insulted believer from holding grudges and resenting the offender. No matter how many offenses, forgiveness must be the practice.

(3) Jesus then focuses on an increase of faith (vv. 5–6). The apostles are conscious of their role as leaders among the disciples. Apparently they feel they need more faith to be able to forgive the repentant and to combat strife and jealousy among them. So they say, "Increase our faith." It has been debated as to what is meant by "faith," whether it is the spiritual gift of miracle-working faith (1 Cor. 12:9; 13:2) or simply stronger faith. Since the request assumes that the apostles have faith, it seems to refer to the charismatic gift of faith to perform miracles.

Jesus' answer turns his disciples' attention away from greater faith to its true nature. What is crucial is not the amount of faith, but its reality. If the disciples have faith as a mustard seed, the smallest of all seeds in Palestine, they could pull out of the ground a huge mulberry tree standing nearby and stand it in the sea. A small faith can do impossible things, for with it they can tap into the miraculous power of God. After the outpouring of the Spirit at Pentecost the disciples did humanly impossible things. Trusting in God's power and enabled by the Spirit, they performed many mighty deeds. So whether great or small, faith can accomplish great things for God.

(4) Finally, Jesus addresses the standard of servanthood (vv. 7–10). Out of faith may flow mighty works. Believers who are blessed with an extraordinary ministry may feel that they deserve special treatment and can fall into

spiritual pride. Jesus appeals to the slave-master relationship as the pattern God's servants should follow. In Jesus' day a servant had duties in both the field and the home. After he had a long day plowing or caring for the flock, his master did not invite him to sit down and have dinner. On the contrary, he expected the slave to prepare the meal and serve him while he ate. The slave received no gratitude or praise from the master for the faithful performance of his duty (v. 9).

The same principle applies to the servants of the Lord. We should not expect to receive thanks or special favors for doing our duty before God. When we have done what we ought to do, we remain "unworthy servants." The word "unworthy" (*achreioi*) expresses the servant's humility, indicating that we do not deserve praise, thanks, or reward. This attitude stands in sharp contrast to that of the Pharisee in 18:11–12. Jesus warns his followers against an attitude that expects special recognition. God has called and equipped us for service, and we are obligated to him. Our best service fails to make God our debtor; we are always undeserving servants. Even after obeying all his commands, we must say, "We have only done our duty."

4.16. Teachings Leading to the Final Prediction of His Death (17:11–18:30)

Jesus continues his charismatic ministry of healing and teaching. As he goes "on his way to Jerusalem," he heals ten lepers (vv. 11–19) and gives a long discourse in which he predicts the future coming of the Son of Man and the decisive manifestation of the kingdom (vv. 20–37). Following the discourse Jesus gives two parables dealing with prayer (18:1–14). This section closes with qualifications for entering God's kingdom (vv. 15–30). All that Jesus teaches here serves to encourage believers like Theophilus (cf. 1:1–4).

4.16.1. The Grateful Leper (17:11–19). Jesus is on the border between Samaria and Galilee. As he heads toward his destiny in Jerusalem, a group of ten lepers meet him. Treated as outcasts, lepers could not live in a village (see comments on 5:12–16). They address him as "Master," which shows that they understand that he has authority to perform mighty deeds of mercy; it does not mean they consider themselves his disciples, thoug later one of them does become a followe They want to be healed, so they appeal t Jesus' compassion.

Jesus does not lay his hands on them n does he declare them healed. Instead, he tes their faith and obedience by telling them to g and show themselves to the priests. The pries served as health examiners and could certif that they had been healed of their diseas (Lev. 14:2ff.). The obedience of these ten lep ers before they are healed shows their faith i the miracle-working power of Jesus. As the go, they are made whole (v. 14). So Jesus hea them from a distance (cf. 7:1–10). No longe will they be outcasts; they can resume the place in society.

What Luke emphasizes is the reactions of th lepers to their healing. One of the lepers stand out from the others because he returns to Jesu to offer him thanks, praising God for the mirac ulous cure; this man is an outsider, a Samarita Apparently the other nine are Jews, who do n bother to show their gratitude for their healing When the Samaritan reaches Jesus, he throw himself at Jesus' feet and submits himself to th Master's authority (vv. 15–16).

The Samaritan appreciates God's blessings Of the ten healed he would certainly be the las one whom a person might expect to return an express thanks to a Jewish healer. The "n show" of the other nine disappoints Jesus, a indicated by his question: "Were not all te cleansed? Where are the other nine?" In th Greek the first question (introduced by *ouchi* expects the answer: "Yes, all ten were healed!" None have returned, however, to express thanks except the foreigner, seen in Jewish society as a social outcast and a religious heretic. A man who does not belong to God's chosen people is the only one who returns to give thanks to God (v. 18).

Jesus appreciates the Samaritan's sensitivity and praises him for his response to God's blessings. So often God's grace is taken for granted and ignored. Some people may be thankful, but they fail to take time to praise God for his blessings. Like the Samaritan, however, a surprising number of people praise and worship God in appreciation for his wonderful grace.

The nine lepers have faith, but it is incomplete. The Samaritan's gratitude reveals that his faith is complete. It is not only an instrument of miraculous healing but also personal salvation, and Jesus sends him off with the assurance that it is as well with his soul as it is with his body (Morris, 1974, 259). Only the Samaritan hears these reassuring words: "Your faith has made you well" (v. 19)—literally, "Your faith has saved [*sesoken*, from *sozo*] you." The man's trust in Jesus brings him more than cleansing; it also brings him into a right relationship with God. Only those who accept what God has done in Christ receive the full blessing of salvation. The other nine have been healed, but their lack of gratitude demonstrates, by contrast, how God wants his chosen people to respond to his mighty saving work in Christ.

4.16.2. The Kingdom and the Coming of the Son of Man (17:20–37). The Spirit-inspired Jesus speaks prophetically about the coming of God's kingdom, including his own second coming and the final judgment. Luke records two of Jesus' major discourses on end-time events (17:20–37; 21:5–36). The kingdom, the reign of God, is a present reality (see 10:9, 11; 11:20). Jesus' life and ministry declare in a powerful and new way the presence of God's kingly reign. But the coming of that kingdom is also a future event. Jesus refers to both prongs of God's sovereign reign here. In verses 20–21, in response to a question posed by the Pharisees, he explains the present nature of the kingdom. Then in verses 22–37, he explains to his disciples the future coming of the kingdom.

Some Pharisees ask Jesus when God will establish his kingdom on the earth. No doubt they have been impressed with Jesus' prophetic gifts, so now they wish to know the moment when God will begin to exercise his royal rule over humankind. They want a timetable, and they assume that visible signs will precede the coming of the kingdom. Jesus explains that God's kingdom is unlike the kingdoms with which the Pharisees are familiar. Its coming will not correspond with visible signs, so that no one can predict the exact time of its arrival. People misunderstand the character of God's kingdom when they say, "'There it is,' or 'Here it is.'" Such predictions are arrogant and prove false and disappointing to people persuaded by them (cf. Acts 1:6–7).

Jesus affirms that the initial phase of the kingdom does not come that way; in fact, it has already come (v. 21). Jesus uses the word *entos* to describe its presence—a word that means either "within" you or "among, in the midst of" you. Jesus is speaking to Pharisees, who no doubt have rejected him. He would not say that God's rule is within their hearts. Yet the kingdom is a fact of history. Thus, Jesus means that the kingdom is "among you"—present in what he does and says—even though the Pharisees remain blind to it (cf. 11:20). They expect to see signs of its coming sometime in the future. But there is no need to look for future signs of the coming of God's rule. Now it can be entered into, though its final consummation will come later.

In the New Testament God's kingdom has an "already" and "not yet" dimension. Already it is present, but it has not yet come in the fullness of its power and glory. The disciples are concerned about the future manifestation of God's reign. So turning to them, Jesus begins to speak about the kingdom in its final glory with the words, "The time is coming." He predicts that his disciples will yearn for "one of the days of the Son of Man," which refers to the period in which God's kingdom is established on the earth (on "Son of Man," see comments on 5:17–26). The disciples will long for the day when God will vindicate his people and put down his enemies.

That day, however, will not come immediately (v. 22), so the disciples must not be misled by false prophets who insist that the Messiah has already returned. They will say, "'There he is!' or 'Here he is!'" pointing to some man as the Messiah. Jesus' followers are not to allow themselves to be deceived by these claims. In theological terms the view that Christ has already returned is called "over-realized eschatology." This error teaches that the kingdom of God has already fully come and now believers enjoy all the benefits of heaven, including the life of resurrection (cf. 1 Cor. 4:8; 2 Tim. 2:17–18).

Individuals will falsely conclude that the Son of Man has returned and will claim that no one has knowledge of the event except them. But the return of the Son of Man will be as visible as a flash of lightning that lights up the entire sky (v. 24). His second appearance will be sudden and visible to all. The glory of his presence will be manifested everywhere on that wonderful day. Before he comes with glory, other things must happen first. Just ahead lies the Cross. Jesus must (*dei*, "it is necessary") endure suffering and even be rejected "by this generation," the chosen people who should have accepted him (v. 25).

According to the divine plan his rejection must precede glory (24:26). The Son of Man is walking a path to glory and honor through suffering and rejection. There can be no resurrection without the Cross. There can be no Second Coming without the first coming. His final coming will establish God's kingdom, and his glorious presence will be witnessed throughout the world. But for now he must go on his way to Jerusalem, the place of suffering and rejection.

Jesus compares the day of his return to the times of Noah and Lot. Before the Flood people lived normal lives. They kept on eating, drinking, and marrying. They failed to take seriously Noah's preaching of judgment. When the Flood did come, they were unprepared, and everyone perished (Gen. 7:11–23).

Something similar happened in the days of Lot. People were devoted to earthly pursuits. They ate, drank, bought, sold, planted, and built. These people were preoccupied with their own pursuits, unaware that they were on their way to judgment. They too were unprepared when God rained fire and sulfur from heaven (Gen. 19:23–25). Opportunity for salvation passed them by and divine judgment overtook them. When Christ returns, that same indifference and complacency will prevail (Luke 17:30). People will not discern the times in which they live because of being weighted down with the cares of life.

When judgment does come, it will be swift and decisive. On the day of the glorious appearing of Christ, human beings must guard against devotion to their own concerns. A man on a housetop where he is resting or out in the field working may think that he has time to go into his home and gather up his possessions. That will be impossible.

Everyone must be free from attachment to earthly things and committed in heart to the kingdom of God. The coming of the Son of Man calls for wholehearted devotion to him. Worldly concerns and love for material possessions have fatal consequences. Lot's wife serves as a warning against becoming attached to worldly pursuits and possessions. She came close to escaping from the doomed city of Sodom; but she looked back, longing for the delights that she was leaving behind. As a result, she got caught up in the judgment upon Sodom and perished (Gen. 19:26).

Now is the time to set our hearts on Christ and on eternal treasures. We run a high risk if we wait until the last hour (cf. 12:35–40). To try to preserve our life (*psyche*) is to lose it, but to lose our life is to gain it (v. 33). In other words, to seek the fullness of life in earthly things has fatal consequences. Devotion to Christ and self-sacrifice, however, bring true happiness and life. To follow Christ now and to persevere in the faith ensure us of life in the most glorious sense of the word. The world may see us as throwing our lives away, but God will vindicate his people.

At his final coming, Jesus says, there will be a division between the saved and unsaved. On that day two people, husband and wife, will be in the same bed. One will be taken away; the other will be left behind. Again, two women will be grinding grain together; they also will be separated. Jesus does not explain what he means by "taken," but Noah was saved by being taken away in the ark (v. 27). Evidently the people left behind are unbelievers, who will face judgment. Christ will take away the believers from the earth, the scene of judgment, to be with him in heaven.

The apostle Paul speaks about this event as "the day of the Lord," which will come suddenly and unannounced. First will be the resurrection of "the dead in Christ," and then the believers "who are still alive and are left will be caught up together with them in the clouds to meet the Lord in the air." This transformation of believers, whether dead or living, is usually called the "rapture" of the church (1 Thess. 4:16–17). When Christ returns, judgment will come suddenly upon the unsaved, "as labor pains on a pregnant woman, and they will not escape." Yet his coming again will hold no terror for believers, for Christ will remove us from the scene of judgment and "we will be with the Lord forever" (1 Thess. 4:17–5:3). We must be watchful and ready for the return of Christ.

In response to Jesus the disciples want to know where the events of verses 31–35 will take place (v. 37). Rather than telling them directly where this separation will occur, he cites a proverb: "Where there is a dead body, there the vultures will gather." When vultures fly around in the sky, a dead body is somewhere nearby. So when the moral and spiritual conditions of the world get ripe, Christ will come and judgment will follow. There will be no sign by which we can know exactly the time of the Second Coming. On that day, however, everlasting judgment will come on those who are spiritually dead as swiftly as vultures swoop down upon a dead prey. The situation will be grim for them, but for those entering into eternal life it will be glorious.

4.16.3. Two Parables on Prayer (18:1–14). Following his teaching about the final coming of the kingdom, Jesus returns to the subject of prayer by telling two parables. As we have noted, Jesus himself provides us with a model for the practice of prayer (3:21–22; 6:12; 11:5–13). He is aware of the disciples' temptation to sin and to "give up" (18:1) before the kingdom comes with triumphant power. In light of their weakness, he encourages them to pray and to maintain their faith even as he will soon face rejection in Jerusalem.

A careful reading of the two parables reveals that both are about God's vindicating, justifying, upholding, and saving his people. The first parable shows God's attitude toward his people; he will hear their cries, vindicate them, and save them (vv. 1–8). The second parable emphasizes that the one who humbles himself and confesses his sin is justified and accepted by God. God does not vindicate those who claim that they are holy, but those who confess that they are sinners. Discipleship demands a humble, childlike faith.

Jesus has already taught his disciples to pray and emphasized the importance of persistence in prayer (11:1–13). Aware that they will face persecution and hardship, he urges them to "always pray and not give up" (v. 1). Luke probably includes these parables in his Gospel because he wants the Christians of his day to persist in prayer and not lose heart in the face of suffering and abuse. The parable of the corrupt judge and the widow focuses on persistent prayer. Jesus, of course, is not teaching that God is like an unjust judge. The parable is cast in a "how much more" style. If a wicked man finally responds to the cries of a widow, how much more will a righteous God hear the prayers of his children.

The parable talks about a real-life situation. The judge has no reverence for God or respect for people's rights. A poor widow involved in a lawsuit in the same town pleads with the callous judge to rule in her favor against an adversary (v. 3). For a long time he does nothing, ignoring her cries for justice. Like other widows in that society, she is powerless and among the most vulnerable of people. She is dependent on others for her care.

Because she goes again and again to the judge, he becomes willing to grant her justice. Her persistence tests his patience. He fears that her continued pleas will "wear me out" (*hypopiazo*)—a verb that comes from prize fighting and literally means "to strike under the eye." To prevent her from continuing to bother him, he decides to vindicate this woman against her adversary. Constant intercession brings her success.

The Lord Jesus then applies the parable. We must not think that we have to wear God down with persistent prayer before he will pay attention to us. God is the *righteous* Judge, a champion of the needy and the weak. He hears the cries of his chosen people and brings about justice for them. These people are precious in his sight, and God has called them for service. When they seek his face in prayer night and day and depend entirely on him, he will vindicate them. Because of persecution and affliction they recognize their great need and know God is their only hope. They cry out to him in prayer. He has compassion on them and immediately answers their prayers (v. 7).

God does vindicate his people and does it "quickly" (v. 8). In contrast to the unjust judge, the righteous God does not delay in responding to his people and lightening their suffering. Many believers have experienced a delayed response from God to their prayers. God's ways are mysterious, and with him "a day is like a thousand years, and a thousand years are like a day" (2 Peter 3:8). It is a certainty that God will act quickly to vindicate his people when the time arrives for Jesus to return. Jesus is not promising that he will return soon according to our timetable; but it will be soon in God's time, because the Second Coming is the next major event on God's calendar.

Believers may be tempted to give up their faith because their prayers have not been answered. But God has not forgotten them, and they must not become discouraged. Jesus then asks, "When the Son of Man comes, will he find faith on the earth?" That is, will God's people be praying and looking for his return? Like the poor widow we must persevere and keep asking. Unlike the unjust judge God does not grudgingly answer our prayers. He delights in granting our desires and in vindicating us.

The second parable tells about the attitudes of two men as they pray (vv. 9–14). It emphasizes that God accepts only those who have a childlike faith and trust. The Pharisee's pride stands in contrast to the tax collector's humility. The sin denounced is characteristic of the Pharisees, but is by no means restricted to them.

Jesus does not address the parable specifically to his disciples, but to the self-righteous people who have contempt for everybody else (v. 9). He intends the parable for those who perform their religious duties out of a sense of pride. Pride is dangerous, for it leads us to trust in ourselves and our abilities, and it influences us to be insensitive to the needs of others.

Two men enter the temple to pray. One is a very religious Pharisee, a member of the party of the religious elite, which was known for its careful observance of the Jewish law; the other is a sinful tax collector (v. 10), someone on the outer bounds of Jewish society and one who did not follow the law. Religious people tended to avoid any association with such an outcast.

The prayers of these two men stand in contrast. The Pharisee has an aura of arrogant self-confidence. As the normal position for prayer, he stands and announces to God the kind of person he is: "I am not like other men—robbers, evildoers, adulterers—or even like this tax collector. I fast twice a week and give a tenth of all I get." He fails to offer thanks to God for his blessings. His prayer simply records his activities in a self-glorifying manner; he reminds God of the vices from which he abstains and the pious practices in which he engages.

God's law called for one annual day of fasting, on the Day of Atonement (Lev. 16:29; 23:27), and for a tithe to be paid on certain crops (Lev. 27:30–32; Deut. 14:22–27). But the Pharisee has gone beyond those requirements, fasting *twice a week* and giving tithes *on everything*. But his statements reflect that he does not rely on the grace and love of God. Rather, he is proud and insensitive. He does not ask God for anything nor does he express gratitude to him. He wants God to appreciate what a marvelous man he is.

The tax collector, whom the Pharisee despises, stands in the temple too. But in contrast to the Pharisee, he is under conviction for the wrongs he has done. Though normal in prayer, the tax collector does not so much as "look up to heaven." As a sign of sorrow and repentance, he throws himself on God's grace and prays, "God, have mercy on me, a sinner" (v. 13). The verb "have mercy" (*hilaskomai*) means "be propitiated." He asks God to remove his anger against him for sinning. He knows that he has sinned and in pleading for forgiveness he knows what he deserves.

Jesus concludes the parable by declaring that the tax collector goes home justified before God. In humility he has cried out for mercy and receives God's approval by being forgiven of his sin. On the other hand, the self-righteous Pharisee is not justified. Thus, Jesus concludes, "everyone who exalts himself will be humbled, and he who humbles himself will be exalted."

We should come to God like the tax collector, recognizing our sinfulness and repenting of sin. After repentance, however, we should not go through life continually looking at the ground, beating our breast, and crying out, "God, have mercy on me, a sinner." We are sinners saved by grace, but dwelling on that can easily become a way to avoid responsibility for our actions. Celebration of grace has its place, but grace calls for responsible living.

4.16.4. Conditions for Entrance Into the Kingdom (18:15–30). Jesus continues giving the requirements for entering the kingdom of God (cf. 13:22–30; 18:9–14); it rests solely on divine grace and faith in Jesus. Childlike faith and trust are demanded of everyone (18:15–17). The rich ruler refuses to show such attitudes (vv. 18–23); he represents any who have confidence in their own goodness, as the Pharisee had (vv. 11–12). The ruler's attachment to his wealth identifies him with the Pharisees (cf. 16:13–15). The disciples have fulfilled the condition that the rich ruler fails to fulfill. Thus Jesus assures them that since they have made sacrifices for the kingdom, they will be repaid (18:26–30).

The account of Jesus' blessing the children warns against adult indifferences. Little chilren, even infants (*brephe*, "babies," NIV), are ;ood examples of discipleship and of how the :ingdom is to be received. Parents are bring- ng their babies to Jesus so that he will lay his ıands on their heads. Apparently they believe esus has the power to bless. The disciples, ıowever, like most people in their culture, do ıot see the importance of children. They think little ones" are not old enough to be useful nd that Jesus does not have time for them. 'herefore, they rebuke the parents.

It is not clear why the disciples see this ttempt as inappropriate. Perhaps they think esus is too busy to be bothered with children.)r children are not important and Jesus needs ɔ use his time for more important matters. In ny case, the disciples are dangerously close to ɔllowing the Pharisee in verses 10–12 and thers who looked down on everyone else v. 9). By turning away the parents and chil- ren, the disciples are showing a false notion f adult importance. Their action also reveals ıat they do not understand the nature of the ingdom. Little children possess the qualities ecessary to enter the kingdom: openness, ust, humility, and dependence.

Jesus rebukes the disciples with a double ommand: "Let the little children come to me, nd do not hinder them." Calling the children ɔ himself, he says, "The kingdom of God elongs to such as these" (v. 16). People who, ke children, show trust and dependence are ccepted into the kingdom of God. Children re models for the way adults are to enter iod's kingdom. No one enters it by his or her wn works and merit. Rather, we enter the omain of God's rule by his work and grace. mall children bring nothing; neither can we ı receiving God's kingdom. We must receive with the same attitude as a child when a pre- ent is offered, that is, with delight and trust.

Without childlike trust, entry into the king- om of God is blocked. An example is the rich ıler (vv. 18–25), who is unwilling to respond ı Jesus in humility and faith. Matthew escribes him as young (Matt. 19:20), and uke identifies him as a ruler, perhaps of a syn- gogue (cf. Luke 8:41). Like the Pharisees, he as confidence in his good deeds. He also has 'ealth, to which he is attached.

This ruler assumes that some work he is not oing at the present is required for eternal life. Ie recognizes Jesus as an authority figure and asks him, "Good teacher, what must I do to inherit eternal life?" The young man presents his question to the greatest authority on the subject, but he greets Jesus as simply a "good teacher." His understanding of Jesus is shallow. He regards him merely as a man and has no idea that Jesus is the Messiah, the Son of God. His esteem for the Savior is no higher than what he would have for any distinguished teacher. The way he addresses Jesus seems to be nothing more than flattery.

The Savior rebukes this rich young ruler, asking, "Why do you call me good?" Knowing that the ruler sees him as no more than a man, Jesus reminds him that only God can be called good in the absolute sense. He wants the young man to reflect on his use of the word "good" and to avoid using it lightly. By raising the question Jesus is not denying his own sinlessness or deity. Should the ruler have recognized him as the Son of God, the Savior would have accepted the designation "good." The young man has cheapened the idea of goodness, since he sees Jesus as no more than a man. Moreover, he already shows he will not take the teacher's advice seriously.

In response to the ruler's specific question, Jesus calls his attention to that portion of the Ten Commandments that deals with our duty toward others: avoiding adultery, murder, stealing, and false testimony, and one's honoring parents. These commandments had been summed up in the words, "Love your neighbor as yourself" (10:27; cf. Matt. 19:19). Jesus' appeal to the commandments that express how we are to relate to others is significant in this context. The issue is clearly the ruler's love of his money and possessions. Attachment to things tends to make us treat others as means to an end rather than as persons. Jesus is concerned about the young man's love (or lack thereof) for others. His mention of honoring parents may imply that one should take financial responsibility for them in their old age (Bock, 1994, 300).

The rich ruler's problem then begins to surface. He is confident that he has kept all five commandments dealing with his duty to others. Ever since his boyhood (probably referring to the age of twelve, cf. 2:42), he claims that he has kept these commandments and can stand before God on his own merit. Such a claim is outlandish and reveals that he has not given much thought to what keeping the commandments really means. He has no sense of the broadness and inner spirituality of the commandments.

According to Paul, the law convicts people of sin, with the result "that every mouth [is] silenced" (Rom. 3:19). A right understanding of the law makes us see our sin. The law prepares us to come to Christ (Gal. 3:24). That is, those who take seriously its demands will realize their true spiritual condition and come to trust Jesus for salvation. But this young man, by focusing on what he considers are his good works, sees no need for repentance. Instead of seeking a reward, however, he should cry out for mercy, for "all have sinned and fall short of the glory of God" (Rom. 3:23).

The Spirit-anointed Jesus does not condemn or praise the man for claiming to have kept the commandments. As the perfect discerner of the human heart, he perceives the ruler worships his earthly possessions and reminds him that he has to do one more thing: "Sell everything you have and give to the poor, and you will have treasure in heaven. Then come, follow me." Jesus has put his finger on the sin in this man's heart—his love of his material possessions. His earthly wealth stands between him and God. Since he has not put God first in his heart, Jesus demands that the man part with his money.

This requirement is the negative aspect of Jesus' response; the positive side is that he "will have treasure in heaven." His heart will no longer be attached to earthly things but to God and to heavenly things. So the way to salvation for this man—as well as for everyone—is through repentance. Jesus does not always ask us to give all our possessions to needy people. He does not oppose personal ownership of wealth, but he warns against our trusting in riches instead of in God. The special case of the rich young ruler is an example of the spiritual peril of the love of material possessions. Because of his priorities, he is challenged to sell his possessions. Such an act would be the first evidence of true repentance and of his becoming a faithful follower of Jesus.

The challenge is too much for the young man. He goes away deeply grieved when he hears Jesus' words, for he loves his great wealth (v. 23). That wealth is the obstacle separating him from God. That attachment t riches reveals how superficial his claim to hav kept the commandments is. He chooses mammon over God and violates the first commandment: "You shall have no other god before me" (Ex. 20:3). In short, the young ma is an idolater, his great wealth being his go He has enjoyed the earthly pleasures, ease, an security that wealth offers.

Unwilling to obey Jesus, the rich youn ruler departs without eternal life. As he doe so, Jesus observes how hard it is for the ric to enter into the kingdom of God (v. 24). Thei temptation is to rely on earthly things. The find it difficult to cast themselves on the merc of God and to choose the kingdom. To illustrate how hard it is, Jesus insists that it is n easier for the rich to enter the kingdom of Go than for a camel to get through the eye of needle. This vivid illustration teaches ho impossible it is for the rich on their own merits to enter the kingdom of God. Humanl speaking, it is impossible. Any attempt to se oneself free from a demonic love for earthl things will fail.

Both the disciples and the crowds who hea the conversation are shocked. If a rich perso cannot enter into the kingdom of God, "Wh then can be saved?" If what Jesus has said i true, their conclusion is that no one can b saved. If those with wealth—thought to be sign of God's blessing—cannot enter the kingdom, who can? Since those at the top of th economic ladder cannot get in, is there an hope for anyone?

Jesus reminds his audience that although is impossible for a person to save oneself, Go can. He can do what is impossible for huma beings. He can redirect the heart from a lov for earthly things to a love for the eternal, an he can work the miracle of conversion in th hearts of both rich and poor. People cann change their own hearts; but when we respon to God by faith, the Holy Spirit transforms ou hearts and provides us with salvation. We cannot be righteous enough, religious enough, o rich enough to save ourselves (Dean, 198 115). Only the gospel, the power of God unt salvation, can save us (Rom. 1:16–17).

The conversation now takes another direction. Peter reacts to Jesus' command to the ric ruler to sell his possessions and follow him. H and the other disciples want assurance the will be rewarded for the sacrifices they have made in following him. They have done what Jesus asked the ruler to do; they have invested a lot in the kingdom of God and have made personal sacrifices. Will they "have treasure in heaven"?

Jesus reassures Peter and the disciples of the treasures of eternal life, "the age to come," as well as assures them of blessings "in this age." Those who make sacrifices "for the sake of the kingdom of God" will inherit everlasting life, but in addition will receive rich blessings in this life. In fact, they will "receive many times as much." Heavenly riches are a matter of pure grace, and people should not follow Jesus with gain in mind. Their blessings will far exceed their sacrifices.

The fulfillment of Jesus' promise of blessing provides no real support for "the gospel of prosperity." God often blesses his people spiritually rather than materially. On the other hand, poverty by itself is not a virtue, and every believer is not called to leave family and possessions.

4.17. From Prediction of Death Until Entry Into Jerusalem (18:31–19:44)

Jesus has been preparing the disciples for Jerusalem. Luke relates four final events in his ministry that take place before he enters the city: the last prediction of his death (18:31–34), the healing of a blind beggar near Jericho (18:35–43), the conversion of Zacchaeus in Jericho (19:1–10), and the parable of pounds (19:11–27). After these events Jesus journeys the seventeen miles from Jericho up to Jerusalem. As he approaches Jerusalem on a colt, he prophesies the destruction of the city and laments his coming rejection there (19:28–44).

4.17.1. Prediction of Coming Death (18:31–34). The journey of Jesus to Jerusalem is near completion. He now gives a final prophecy about his death—an event he has already referred to six times in this Gospel (see 5:35; 9:22, 44; 12:50; 13:32–33; 17:25). This emphasis indicates that Jesus has been in the process of preparing his disciples to continue his ministry after his physical departure from the earth. The prediction of his coming rejection is yet another example of discipleship. Following Jesus must be motivated by self-giving. He himself is the supreme example of one who forsook all to do God's will and to serve the good of others.

Jesus takes the disciples aside and tells them privately that he must suffer and die, giving them more details than he did in his earlier predictions (9:22, 44; 13:33). He also assures them that all that has been foretold by the prophets concerning him will be fulfilled (18:31). God has a plan, which will be worked out regardless of what people may do. At the heart of that plan is the suffering of the Son of Man, the Anointed One, for the salvation of the world. All that the prophets have said about the Savior's suffering (e.g., Ps. 2; Isa. 50:6; 52:13–53:12) will be accomplished at Jerusalem.

Jesus be will handed over to the Gentiles, the Roman authorities in Jerusalem. The verb "will be handed over" (*paradothesetai*, a theological passive) suggests divine permission; God allows the Jewish nation to hand over the Savior to the Romans. Jesus does not speak of the cross directly, but he does describe his treatment at the hands of the authorities. They will ridicule him (22:63; 23:11), insult him (22:65), and even spit on him. They will flog him, punishment reserved for those condemned to die (Bratcher, 1982, 224). Then they will put him to death. But the life of Jesus will not end at the cross. Three days later he will rise again and triumph over death.

The disciples do not understand what Jesus is trying to communicate (v. 34). The meaning of his prophecy is hidden from them (cf. 9:45). One wonders why, since his words are so clear that he is going to die and rise again. What they mainly fail to grasp is how Scripture will be fulfilled and why the Messiah must suffer. Human logic breaks down when it comes to God's purpose and work.

The meaning of Jesus' death and resurrection cannot be grasped fully by the human intellect. Understanding these events is a matter of revelation and only comes as the Holy Spirit makes known to us the deep things of God (cf. 1 Cor. 2:10–15). After the resurrection of Christ the Holy Spirit will open the disciples' eyes and minds. At that time they will grasp that the death and resurrection of Jesus fulfill Scripture (24:13–49).

4.17.2. A Blind Beggar Receives Sight (18:35–43). Earlier Jesus asked the question: "When the Son of Man comes, will he find faith on the earth?" (18:8). The blind beggar demonstrates that there is faith on the earth. Continuing his way to Jerusalem and now approaching Jericho, a town in the Jordan Valley (about 700 feet below sea level), Jesus meets a blind man. Mark tells us that his name is Bartimaeus (Mark 10:46), and Matthew reports that he has a blind companion (20:29–34). The healing of Bartimaeus is the final miracle of Jesus on the journey to Jerusalem.

Though he is physically blind, Bartimaeus has excellent spiritual vision. He calls Jesus "Son of David," affirming him as the Messiah. He has the same kind of spiritual vision as the tax collector in Jesus' parable (18:9–14). Bartimaeus stands in sharp contrast to the rich ruler, who had everything but was spiritually blind (18:18–25). The beggar has nothing, not even eyesight, but he sees spiritual things well.

At the beginning of his ministry Jesus announced that he was anointed by the Spirit to give sight to the blind (4:18). Bartimaeus has heard about Jesus' ministry of healing the sick and casting out demons and believes Jesus does have power to heal. By calling him "Son of David," the blind man indicates he has already begun to believe in him as the Savior. He wants Jesus to heal him so that he can see the flowers and trees. People ahead of Jesus try to quiet down the man, but he persists in call ing out to Jesus.

We should not be surprised at this effort t hinder the man. A little earlier the disciple attempted to prevent little children from com ing to Jesus (18:15–17). For Jesus, howeve the beggar's persistence is evidence of hi faith. He stops and commands "the man to b brought to him" (v. 40). When Jesus inquire what he wants, the beggar does not ask fo money but expresses his faith: "Lord, I want t see." The Spirit-empowered Savior gives hir what he asks for: "Receive your sight; you faith has healed you." As the man hears th authoritative words of Jesus, he receives hi sight. Faith always gets the attention of the So of David. Faith is the hand by which a perso lays hold of divine power for healing.

This miracle illustrates divine power i response to faith. Jesus has power to open th eyes of those suffering from physical as wel as spiritual blindness. From the moment o his healing the man becomes a disciple o Jesus, and he honors and praises God. Whe those present see what has happened, they to praise God. That response is proper, for all th deeds of Jesus are to glorify the heavenl Father. This healing of the blind beggar is bu

At Jericho, on his way to Jerusalem for the final time, Jesus healed a blind beggar, Bartimaeus. It was the last miracle Jesus performed on that trip. Shown in the foreground is the area of the Old Testament city.

›ne example of the Lord's willingness to hear ›ur cries.

4.17.3. Salvation Comes to Zacchaeus 19:1–10). Jesus continues to minister by the ›ower of the Spirit to the needs of people. He ıas been making his way from Galilee toward 'erusalem. As he traveled, he has been a friend o tax collectors and sinners. Jesus now passes hrough Jericho. Along the way he meets a tax :ollector named Zacchaeus. The account of his man's conversion reflects many of the hemes prominent in Luke's Gospel.

Zacchaeus is employed by the Romans to :ollect taxes in the territory (see comments on ;:27–32). Overall Luke portrays tax collectors n a positive light (3:12–14; 5:27–30; 18:9–14). Jnlike the other tax collectors that we have met hus far in Luke's Gospel, Zacchaeus is not sim›ly a tax collector; he is "a chief tax collector." \pparently a tax office is located in Jericho, and 'acchaeus employs others to do the actual col›ecting of the taxes. This man is at the zenith of ıis despised profession, overseeing the work of number of tax collectors. Furthermore, he is vealthy, for whom it is humanly impossible to nter the kingdom of God (18:18–27). He thus tands in marked contrast to the blind beggar 18:35–43). Yet this rich tax collector is also aved by God's grace (cf. 18:27).

Zacchaeus is "a short man." His smallness s significant because he is unable to see Jesus n the crowd of people. Earlier Jesus has varned against causing "little ones" to sin 17:2), and we have seen the disciples hinder the little children" from coming to Jesus 18:15–17). Though Zacchaeus is too short to ee Jesus, a powerful urge moves him to step utside of the crowd and climb up in a ycamore tree to see the event.

When Jesus passes under the tree, he stops. ,ikely by supernatural knowledge he knows ıat Zacchaeus is there. He takes the initiative nd calls him to come down. "I must," he says, stay at your house today." Jesus' stay with ;acchaeus is a divine "must" (*dei*, "it is nec›ssary"). He has been sent by his heavenly 'ather and sees his lodging with Zacchaeus as art of his divine mission. Zacchaeus responds y coming down out of the tree with haste and velcoming Jesus into his home. Similar to the ervants who wait for their master's return 12:36–38), Zacchaeus is ready to open the oor to Jesus, the Lord, and does so with great joy. This response is always appropriate to God's initiative.

All Zacchaeus, the chief tax collector in Jericho, wanted when he climbed into a sycamore tree was a better view of Jesus. But it changed his life. Jesus became his guest for the night and Zacchaeus decided to give half of all he owned to the poor and would pay back anyone he had cheated with an amount four times what he had taken.

All who watch Jesus enter the house of Zacchaeus begin to grumble (v. 7). They brand the tax collector as a "sinner" and criticize Jesus for being the guest of a man who, though Jewish, does not keep the law of Moses. Like the Pharisees (15:1–2) these people are repelled by Jesus' eating and drinking with a sinful man. Zacchaeus, however, standing before Jesus, declares his intention of living a new life, a clear sign of repentance. His action also expresses gratitude to Jesus for his kindness.

As evidence of his changed life, Zacchaeus announces the gift of half of his assets to the needy. Furthermore, he promises to pay money back fourfold to whomever he has cheated (Ex. 22:1; 2 Sam. 12:6). As a tax collector Zacchaeus has probably charged more duty on goods than was required. He now humbles himself

(Luke 14:11; 18:14), and by his repentance shows that he will serve only one master (16:13)—note the contrast to the rich ruler (18:18–30). His generosity demonstrates his love for God and his neighbor (10:27). Jesus did not call on Zacchaeus to sell everything. Yet he has his heart in the right place when it comes to earthly possessions and is a marvelous example of a disciple who retains wealth. Zacchaeus produces "fruit in keeping with repentance" (3:8).

Jesus then says to Zacchaeus, "Today salvation has come to this house" (v. 9). Zacchaeus's actions reveal that he has become a man of faith and is therefore saved. Now as a believer he is a *true* "son of Abraham." Sharing in the faith and works of Abraham, he has become a child of God (Rom. 4:12; Gal. 3:9, 29). Here we see the miracle of saving grace. Zacchaeus has received God's blessing simply by faith. He is the kind of person for whom the heavenly Father has sent Jesus, the good shepherd.

Jesus has come to seek and to save people like Zacchaeus (v. 10). Before Jesus found him, he was "lost" and in need of rescue. With joy he welcomed Jesus into his home and into his heart. The whole life of this man has been changed by Jesus, and no longer is he among the lost. The precise purpose for Jesus' coming is so that lives may be changed: "The Son of Man came to seek and to save what was lost."

4.17.4. The Parable of the Pounds (19:11–27). The journey to Jerusalem will soon reach its climax. Many of the people with Jesus still do not recognize the kingdom in their midst. Thus, in verse 11 he tells them a parable. His purpose in telling this final parable before they reach Jerusalem is twofold. (1) He wants to correct the misunderstanding that when they arrive in Jerusalem, the kingdom of God will appear in its fullness immediately. In the crowd are those who believe that the sovereign reign of God will take place immediately and that they are about to receive the joy, peace, and freedom associated with the kingdom of God (cf. Acts 1:6). They must recognize that the consummation of the kingdom is still in the future.

(2) Jesus also wants to emphasize the disciples' stewardship between his death and return to this earth. After his departure they must be accountable servants until the final coming of the kingdom. What is about to happen in Jerusalem will not be the end of th story. They are to stay in the city until the "have been clothed with power from on high (24:49) and then preach repentance and for giveness of sins "to all nations, beginning a Jerusalem" (24:47).

The parable of the pounds is simple enoug and may reflect the circumstances of Arche laus's claim to kingship soon after the death o his father, Herod the Great (Josephus, *Jewis War* 2.6; *Antiquities* 17.8.11). A man of hig rank goes into a distant land to be appointe king, but he already has subjects who hate hin (v. 14). Before he departs he calls ten of his ser vants and entrusts to each a gold coin (a *mna* valued at about three months' wages), so tha they can engage in trade on his behalf. His ser vants hate him. So while the man is away, the send a delegation to prevent him from gainin more authority over them, with this message "We don't want this man to be our king (v. 14).

Upon returning the master calls each servan to give an account of his stewardship. Two c them have made a handsome profit and receiv a reward for their faithfulness. They are prc moted and placed in charge of cities in propor tion to their profits. The third servant has bee slothful. Having hidden his share, he has gaine nothing. He sees his master as a ruthless busi nessman, taking what is not rightfully his an reaping what he does not sow. According t him, his master runs over people to get what h wants. This servant is condemned.

The lessons in the parable are clear. (1) Th Jewish leaders reject Jesus as their Kin (vv. 14, 27). They reject all that he stands fc and do not want him to rule over them. Whil on his way to Jerusalem, they have sought t hinder his authority.

(2) The Jews' rejection of the Savior wi not prevent him from being installed as Kin with great power and glory. When he reache Jerusalem, this rejected prophet will be cruc fied. But after the resurrection he will be take up to heaven to the right hand of God (9:5 Acts 2:33). Later, he will return in judgmen like lightning flashing across the sky (Luk 17:24–35; 21:27). The reminder of his retur is a warning to those who reject his lordshi He has gone away, but he will return wit kingly authority to judge all who have rejecte God's rule in their hearts.

(3) Each of Jesus' servants will be judged as to how well he or she has served him and his cause. The first and second servants in the parable have been faithful while their master was away and have made good use of their opportunities to serve him. They are richly rewarded upon his return by receiving greater opportunities for service—one is placed over ten cities, the other over five cities. Those who acknowledge Jesus as their King and faithfully serve him will be richly rewarded when he returns. They will find themselves with more opportunities to serve him and to share in the authority of their eternal King.

On the other hand, those who reject Jesus as their King will be treated like the third servant in the parable. In light of his attitude, his failure to be a good steward comes as no surprise. He has been afraid of his master as a hard taskmaster. Such words are sufficient grounds for his condemnation. At least he could have put the master's money on deposit so that it would earn a little interest. This servant ends up with nothing. His gold coin is taken from him and given to the servant with ten gold coins.

At the Second Coming those who are spiritually rich will be made even richer, but those who have neglected their opportunities to serve Christ will become spiritually impoverished (Geldenhuys, 1951, 475). The unfaithful will give an account for their poor stewardship and will suffer loss. What determines the well-being of Jesus' servants is the manner in which they have managed his wealth prior to his return. Thus, Jesus teaches that a day is coming when we must give an account of our stewardship. Our Master will ask us what we have done with the gospel and with our lives and spiritual gifts. All Christians ought to strive to be useful to their Lord.

Jesus concludes on a grim note (v. 27). What about those enemies of the master who sent a delegation with the words, "We don't want this man to be our king" (v. 14)? Their rejection of the Savior was total. Since they have refused to repent and accept his rule, the master says, "Bring them here and kill them in front of me." This reminds us of the reality of God's judgment. Those who persist in unbelief will have no choice but to take the consequences. It is a dangerous thing to reject the living God.

4.17.5. Jesus' Triumphal Entry (19:28–44). Jesus is approaching Bethphage and Bethany, both located about two miles from Jerusalem. Yet the people in the city are blind to the real meaning of his royal visit. When he then enters Jerusalem, his followers, not the crowds or the residents of that city, hail him as King. The people in general do not want him as their King (cf. v. 14). They remain blind to his unique authority and lordship. They reject, therefore, his attempts to gather together the children of Jerusalem (13:33–34).

The Spirit-anointed Jesus has almost reached the place where he will be rejected and crowned with thorns. The crowning of him as our Lord requires more than merely riding in triumph into Jerusalem. He must bear the full burden of our sins, climbing up a hill to the cross and giving himself to death. The account of Jesus' entrance into Jerusalem has two parts: the entry itself (vv. 29–40) and the lament over Jerusalem (vv. 41–44).

A few miles east of the city, Jesus makes preparations to enter it as the Messiah, though not as the Messiah his countrymen expect—they want a military man, one who will free them from the oppression of the Romans. Jesus instructs two disciples to go to a nearby village and get a young colt for him (cf. Zech. 9:9). They will find the animal, which has never been ridden, tied. If someone inquires why they are taking the colt, they are to reply, "The Lord needs it." The title "Lord" applies to Jesus in this Gospel (Luke 5:8).

The owner of the colt must already know Jesus as "Lord." When he allows the disciples to take his colt, he honors him as such. This incident reminds us that Jesus is the divine Lord. Some have suggested that Jesus has made prior arrangements to get the animal. But the Spirit-anointed Jesus uses his divine knowledge in instructing the disciples how to find the colt. The disciples obey their Lord, and their experience matches what he has predicted (vv. 33–34).

Jesus is placed on the colt, and the procession into Jerusalem begins (v. 35). His royal ride on a lowly colt is similar to the animal on which Solomon rode at his coronation a thousand years earlier (1 Kings 1:32–40). Jesus' followers spread their garments on the road, making a carpet for his triumphal ride (cf. 2 Kings 9:13). As the procession nears the Mount of Olives, a multitude of disciples erupt in praise. They praise God for all the mighty deeds performed by Jesus. Many of the people from Galilee have seen his miracles. He arrives in Jerusalem at the Passover season, and they hail him as the promised King in the words of the Passover Psalm 118:26: "Blessed is the king who comes in the name of the Lord!" (cf. 9:18–20).

It is a happy occasion, and the enthusiasm runs high. The crowds are seeing what many of the prophets have longed to see but did not (1 Peter 1:10–12). Yet on this day they rejoice only about the miracles that they have seen Jesus perform. There is a hollow ring to their praise. Earlier the seventy-two disciples also rejoiced over the miracles they had seen. But Jesus reminded them that they should be rejoicing over their salvation (10:19–20). Furthermore, Zacchaeus (19:8) and the father of the lost son (15:15–24) rejoiced over demonstrations of power. They stand in contrast to these followers because they also rejoiced in the saving power of God. Their enthusiasm was over acts of confession and repentance, not just miraculous healings.

Miracles have had a significant place in Jesus' ministry. He frequently reminded his followers, however, that their celebration should first be over their salvation (10:20; 11:28; 13:28–29; 15:3–32; 16:22; 18:9–14). Luke goes on to indicate that Jesus' followers include in their praise thanks for "Peace in heaven." These words remind us that God is at peace with humankind and now offers people peace, that is, salvation. God saves through Christ, and to him redounds glory in the highest places as the author of salvation.

The Pharisees do not want Jesus proclaimed as the Messiah (v. 39). They have heard the acclaims and ovations of the crowds, and they do not go along with this estimate of Jesus. "Some of the Pharisees," therefore, try to silence the people. They know that the crowd has spontaneously expressed their hope that Jesus is the Messiah according to Zechariah 9:9. They recognize that he has been hailed as the one who comes with the authority of the Lord (13:35). But the Pharisees are still attempting to stop the growing enthusiasm for Jesus as the Messiah. They see him as only a "teacher," and they urge him not to tolerate such misguided zeal. Using the aorist imperative (*epitimeson*), they call for decisive action, that Jesus stop the outbursts of praise.

Jesus' response is that the shouts and praise are inevitable. If his disciples become silent, he replies, "the stones will cry out." The stones on the road there understand God's ways better than the blind religious leaders. God will always have witnesses, even if he has to provide them through inanimate creation. Should Jesus' followers stop their praise, lifeless stones will acclaim him as the Savior (cf. Gen 4:10; Hab. 2:11).

After the attempt by the Pharisees to dampen Jesus' acclaim, the royal procession draws within sight of Jerusalem. The praise of the disciples does not divert Jesus' eyes from the spiritual condition of the city. He prophesies (vv. 42–44) and laments his coming rejection by the disobedient nation, who had come to Jerusalem for the Passover. The irony of his visit to the city is clear: Jesus weeps over his rejection even as he is hailed by his followers as King.

Jesus was anointed by the Holy Spirit after his baptism and was sent forth to proclaim salvation and to perform mighty works in the power of the Spirit. But as he now nears Jerusalem, the persistent opposition to his authoritative ministry becomes overbearing. His deep frustration and compassion for the people leads him to weep over a city that has no real understanding of his royal visit, that it is for their salvation. He knows they are recklessly headed for judgment.

The fact remains that God visits his people either for salvation or for judgment. Those who do not acknowledge Jesus as Lord and Savior will face God's judgment. Jesus prophesies the irrevocable consequences of their rejection of him. Recognizing the people's ignorance, he expresses his sorrow that they do not know what will bring them "peace" (*eirene*, v. 42). Here peace is more than the absence of conflict. It is God's gift of salvation, which puts an end to strife between God and his people. But peace is hidden from the eyes of the people of Jerusalem. Their rejection of Jesus has blinded their eyes to peace.

Jesus proceeds to predict the siege and destruction of Jerusalem by the Romans (vv. 43–44). He foresees in grim detail its coming devastation. According to historical accounts, in A.D. 70 the Roman armies of Titus and Vespasian surrounded the city for over a year. The people were shut up in it, and star ation and thirst killed thousands. The armies then moved in and destroyed the city. As Jesus predicted, not one stone was left on another. The city and temple were destroyed (cf. 3:34–35). Josephus's description of the war shows the truth of Jesus' prophecy (*Jewish War* 5.11.4; 5.12.2; 7.1.1).

The reason for the destruction is simple: "You did not recognize the time of God's coming to you." God visits his people for salvation in the person of his Son. Because they are blind to his visit, disaster will befall them. Although they will soon cry out for Jesus' crucifixion (23:13–25), Jesus now draws near to Jerusalem with grace and pardon. But the people there do not want him and what he offers them. By rejecting him, they choose judgment rather than salvation.

5. Jesus: Rejected Prophet-King (19:45–21:38)

Jesus has no illusions about the outcome of his final visit to Jerusalem. On a number of occasions he has specifically predicted his rejection and death (9:22, 44; 13:33–34; 18:31–34). Once in Jerusalem Jesus continues his teaching ministry. He warns the people against their leaders, comparing them to wicked tenant farmers (20:9–19). In reaction to Jesus' cleansing the temple, the religious leaders try to trap him with questions about his authority (20:1–8), about paying taxes to Caesar (20:20–26), about the resurrection and marriage (20:27–40), and about the Son of David (20:41–47). Jesus also contrasts the devotion of a poor widow with the false piety of teachers of the law (21:1–4) and prophesies concerning the end of the world (21:5–38).

These events occur in the temple. Luke's Gospel opened with Zechariah going into the temple to burn incense before the Lord (1:5–23); now Jesus is teaching in the temple, and Luke's Gospel concludes with the disciples in the temple continually praising God for the gift of his Son (24:50–53; cf. also Acts 2:46).

5.1. Cleansing of the Temple (19:45–48)

All four Gospels record Jesus' cleansing of the temple, the center of Jewish religious life and worship and the place where God's presence was manifested among his people. John presents the cleansing at the beginning of his Gospel. Likely Jesus cleansed the temple a couple of times. This event demonstrates the relationship between Jesus and the Jewish leaders.

The first thing Jesus does when he arrives in Jerusalem is to go to the temple. There he finds merchants carrying on their business in the court of the Gentiles, the section where non-Jews could pray. The merchants make it convenient for worshipers who come from distant places to buy sacrificial animals and salt, wine, and oil used in the sacrifices (Bratcher, 1982, 314). Jesus takes exception to what is going on. He exercises his prophetic authority and drives out the merchants. Luke says nothing about moneychangers, though Matthew and Mark refer to them as well.

Jesus condemns these traders, using Jeremiah 7:11 and Isaiah 56:7. He points out the difference between the merchants' dishonesty and the temple as a place dedicated to prayer. They have been making the temple a place where thieves hide out rather than a place of worship. Using the house of God to carry on their dishonest business, they are desecrating it. Jesus rids the temple of these scoundrels and reclaims it for God; he then continues to teach there (v. 47).

By cleansing the temple Jesus has raised the issue of his authority in the minds of the leadership. The chief priests, teachers of the law, and leaders among the people plot against him. They know that the followers of Jesus have hailed him as King—a confession he has accepted (vv. 38, 40). His cleansing of the temple was prophetic in character. Jesus has, in effect, indicted the Jewish authorities for allowing the purpose of the temple and its worship to be obscured. He has also warned against the danger of combining religion and making money at the expense of bringing people near to God. The authorities cannot tolerate such a challenge to their authority, and they decide Jesus must be stopped.

But despite their constant effort to find an opportunity to kill Jesus, the Jewish leaders are unsuccessful. The people are fond of him, and he is constantly surrounded by a large number of those listening to his teaching.

5.2. The Question of Authority (20:1–8)

Representatives from the Sanhedrin—the chief priests, teachers of the law, and elders—arrive to interrogate Jesus. They find Jesus teaching and preaching the gospel to the people in the temple. Although his death is approaching, he continues to declare the good news of the kingdom.

These Jewish leaders interrupt Jesus with a question about his authority. The temple is, after all, the place where they exercise their authority. This place of worship is totally in their hands. Jesus is in their territory, attracting large audiences with his teaching. His popularity is such that they do not dare to take action directly against him. Their plan is to trap him into a statement that will get him in trouble with the Roman authorities or discredit him in the eyes of the people.

Jesus' opponents therefore ask, "Tell us by what authority you are doing these things." They are referring to his cleansing the temple and his teaching and preaching. What religious authority does he have? How can he justify what he has been doing? Jesus has had no official training since he never studied under a rabbi. Does he claim prophetic authority?

Often prophets and preachers claim authority that comes directly from God. This kind of authority is not as easily certifiable as authority that results from position in a church or a corporation. Not everyone who has claimed to have been sent by God has been empowered by the Holy Spirit. So where did Jesus get the right to do these things? Anyone who has read Luke's Gospel knows the answer. After his baptism he was filled with the Holy Spirit, anointed not only for a prophetic ministry but also as the Messiah (3:21–4:1). Later he "returned to Galilee in the power of the Spirit" (4:14). In his inaugural sermon he declared that his ministry was empowered and directed by the Holy Spirit (4:18–19). Throughout his ministry he acted with divine authority. He is the charismatic Christ—the unique bearer of the Spirit.

Jesus responds to the question of his opponents with a question—not in an attempt to be evasive but to give the religious leaders an opportunity to answer their own question. His question is simple: "John's baptism—was it from heaven, or from men?" Like Jesus, John came in the name of God. Did his authority to preach the kingdom of God and to baptize come from God? Was there evidence that God stood behind his prophetic ministry?

The Jewish religious leaders have only two options: either God gave John his authority or he did not. If they reply that John's ministry was from heaven, then they must explain their failure to accept his message, for John testified that Jesus is the Messiah. On the other hand, if the religious leaders deny that John was sent by God, then they run the risk of being stoned (Deut. 13:1–11). The people know that John came from God and that he was a true prophet of God.

The religious leadership recognize their dilemma. They are in a no-win situation. Thus, they refuse to take a position and resort to a plea of ignorance, claiming that they have no idea where John received his authority from. The private dialogue among these leaders reveals their hypocrisy. They are fully persuaded that John had nothing but purely human authority. Lacking the integrity to speak the truth, they refuse to give an honest answer to Jesus.

Because of their refusal, Jesus will not respond to their question. His own actions reveal the source of his authority, but their rejection of him affirms their blindness. Their attempt to trap him has failed, and their hypocrisy has been exposed. But nothing has been resolved.

5.3. The Story of Wicked Tenants (20:9–19)

The religious leaders have rejected John the Baptist and Jesus as messengers of God. Jesus responds by telling a parable. This parable has features more like an allegory since the parable refers to the history of Israel and the rejection of God's messengers by its leaders (Marshall, 1978, 726). In it Jesus rebukes the current religious leaders for their rejection. He addresses the parable to the people in the presence of those leaders, so that they are able to overhear what he says. Two themes are prominent here: (1) a warning to the religious leaders for their refusal to recognize the messengers of God, and (2) Jesus' claim of unique authority as the Son of God.

Jesus begins the parable by referring to a vineyard, which represents the nation of Israel (cf. Isa. 5:1–7; Jer. 2:21). The owner (God) rents the vineyard to some tenant farmers. These farmers represent the Jewish leaders to whom God has entrusted the care of his people. The rent that they are to pay is to be part of the harvest. The owner sends servants to collect what is due him. Each time one of them goes to collect the rent, the wicked farmers behave outrageously. Instead of paying what they owe, they beat up the representative and send him away, bleeding, with nothing. This part of the parable represents the persecution of the prophets whom God sent throughout Israel's history (Jer. 7:25; 25:4; Zech. 1:6). But the owner is patient, sending someone three times in hopes that the farmers will mend their ways—all to no avail.

The owner of the vineyard still remains compassionate toward the wicked tenants. He decides to send his son, whom he loves, hoping that they will respect him (v. 13)—"whom I love" (*agapetos*) is the same word used of Jesus when the Spirit descends on him and anoints him for ministry (3:22). The tenants reason that killing the son will be to their advantage, for with the heir gone, they can take possession of the vineyard. This is precisely what they do, throwing him out of the vineyard and killing him (v. 15).

Jesus is here predicting how the religious authorities will treat God's own Son, whom he has sent into the world. He knows that these leaders have rejected him and are determined to put him to death (cf. 19:47). When the Jewish leaders see the heir, God's unique Son, they reason that killing him will be to their advantage. His death outside the vineyard points to Jesus' death outside of Jerusalem (John 19:17; Heb. 13:12–13).

The owner cannot overlook what has been done to his son. The evildoers must face the consequences of their deeds. So Jesus asks, "What then will the owner of the vineyard do to them?" The wicked tenants have failed to consider the determination of the owner. Judgment will come on them, they will be destroyed for their deeds, and the vineyard they have coveted will be given to others.

In other words, killing Jesus, the beloved Son of the Father, will make the Jewish leaders liable to divine judgment. The vineyard will not stay in their hands, not even in the hands of the nation of Israel. God remains the owner, and he will place the vineyard under the supervision of "others"—Gentile believers. The book of Acts tells us how rejection of the gospel by God's chosen people led to powerful preaching of the good news to the Gentiles. Many accepted it and became the new tenants of the vineyard.

When the people hear Jesus' words, they are shocked. To them it is unthinkable that God will give the privileges of his chosen people to the Gentiles. Alarmed at what Jesus has said about their leaders and about the owner's reaction, they respond, "May this never be!" These words express their outrage and horror that their leaders will act this way toward God. Yet in a few days the murder of God's Son will take place.

The destruction predicted by Jesus must occur because it accords with Scripture. He cites Psalm 118:22: "The stone the builders rejected has become the capstone." Jesus' followers had just taken words from this messianic psalm as he made his triumphal entry into Jerusalem (19:38; cf. 13:35). Eventually the stone that the builders (religious leaders) were rejecting as worthless did become the most important stone in the building. "Capstone" (*kephalen gonias*) literally means "head of the corner." This stone was placed at the corner of the foundation where two rows of stones came together. It was absolutely indispensable to a building. Jesus is the rejected stone, but he is crucial to the new spiritual structure God is raising up. He is destined to be made the cornerstone of God's plan. He can even be called the foundation (1 Cor. 3:11). No one can ever replace this precious and chosen stone.

The picture changes in verse 18. The emphasis is no longer on the great importance of the stone, but on its destructive power against those who reject it. Jesus speaks of two possibilities. When someone falls on the stone, that person is dashed to pieces. On the other hand, when the stone falls on someone, that person will be crushed by it. In either case, the result is fatal. Rejecting God's Son and persisting in unbelief have grave consequences. Jesus is the cornerstone of God's plan of salvation, but he is also a stone of judgment for those who reject his authority.

The leaders know that Jesus has aimed the parable at them. His words provoke them to want to take action against him immediately. They see him as a real threat to their authority and would like to arrest him, but they lack the courage. He remains too popular with the people. His arrest could lead to a riot, and where that would lead no one knows.

5.4. The Question of Paying Taxes to Caesar (20:20–26)

The way Jesus deals with the religious leaders provides valuable lessons in handling conflict. The next controversy centers around the matter of paying taxes to Caesar. His opponents have been defeated in the two previous encounters (vv. 1–19). Now they attempt to trap Jesus into saying something that can be interpreted as political treason. Should they succeed, they would have grounds for bringing him before the Roman governor, Pilate.

This time Jesus' opponents send "spies," who pretend to be "honest" (*dikaios*, "righteous") but are full of malice and hypocrisy. They look for an opportunity to get information they can use against him so that they can hand him over to Pilate for trial. Hoping that Jesus will let his guard down, they attempt to flatter him and try to convince him that they are sincere in their questions. These men address Jesus as "Teacher," as one who speaks the truth and shows no partiality to anyone, regardless of rank or social standing. They ascribe to him unique authority, noting that he truly teaches God's way. The spies speak the truth, but with the wrong motives.

The spies go on to insist they are struggling with a question and want an authoritative answer: Should taxes be paid by Jews to the Roman government (v. 22)? In truth, however, they are setting a trap for him. If he says that they should not pay taxes to Caesar, then he will be in trouble with the Roman authorities. If he says Jews should pay Roman taxes, he will be in trouble with the people, especially those who are convinced that paying taxes to a pagan power goes against God's will. Jesus sees "through their duplicity" (*panourgia*, "craftiness, trickery," v. 23). Guided by the Spirit, he knows that the question is not an honest one.

Jesus thus asks them to show him a silver coin (*denarion*, the average pay for a day's work). When he inquires as to whose inscription is on the coin, they reply, "Caesar's," implying that the Jews accept the emperor's rule as a practical reality. It was generally understood at that time a ruler's power extended as far as his coins (Geldenhuys, 1951, 504). Without pausing Jesus answers their question—not with a "Yes" or "No" as they hoped, but in these words: "Then give to Caesar what is Caesar's, and to God what is God's." This answer goes beyond the payment of taxes (cf. Rom. 13:1–7; 1 Peter 2:13–17). What things belong to Caesar should be paid to him; what things belong to God should be paid to God. Obviously the coin belongs to Caesar; therefore, taxes should be paid to the emperor.

Issues centered around duties to God and duties to Caesar can become complex. When the affairs of the state conflict with God's will, God's people must obey God (cf. Acts 5:29). As Jesus teaches, there are two kingdoms: an earthly and a heavenly kingdom. God's people owe loyalty to both—loyalty to the kingdom of Caesar is conditional, but loyalty to the kingdom of God is absolute. Jesus' enemies have directed a tough theological question to him. His response means that God's people must remain faithful to God and obedient to civil authority as long as their actions do not conflict with the law of the Lord.

Again, the attempt to trap Jesus has failed. Having great spiritual insight, he handles their question with ease. He is much wiser than those who try to trap him. His opponents are silenced.

5.5. The Question Concerning the Resurrection and Marriage (20:27–40)

Jesus now confronts a different group of people, the Sadducees (the name appears to be derived from Zadok; cf. 1 Kings 1:8; 2:35); this section records the only appearance of this group in Luke's Gospel. The Sadducees were priestly and lay aristocrats, who controlled much of the religious life of Israel in the first century. At that time most Jews believed in the resurrection, but the Sadducees rejected any hope of resurrection. They held in high veneration the first five books of the Old Testament (the Pentateuch), but not the rest of the books (in this they differed from the Pharisees).

The Sadducees bring to Jesus a question about the resurrection, a significant question for all people who reflect on life after death. Their aim is to make belief in the resurrection look ridiculous, and they want to make Jesus look ridiculous in the eyes of the people because he believes and teaches the resurrection (cf. 14:14). In their question, the Sadducees appeal to the practice of levirate marriage, a legal provision that prevented a man's name and family from dying out. According to this practice, when a man died and left no children, his brother was to take the widow as his wife and raise up children to the deceased brother (cf. Deut. 25:5–10). We have no record of this being practiced in New Testament times.

The Sadducees tell Jesus a story about seven brothers. The first one marries and dies but leaves behind no children. Each remaining brother in turn marries the same woman and dies, but she bears no children. Since the woman has married the seven brothers, the Sadducees pose the question of whose wife she will be when the dead are raised to life.

A usual answer to this question would have been the first husband. Should Jesus have given this answer, however, he would have failed to deal with the Sadducees' disbelief in the resurrection. They think that they have made their theological point. They assume that Jesus' view of resurrection is the same as that of the Pharisees, who believed in normal human functions and relationships in heaven. They hope that it will become clear how foolish Jesus is for believing in the resurrection of the dead.

Jesus' reply has two parts. The first one deals with the kind of life God's people will have after the resurrection (vv. 34–36). The Savior contrasts this present age with the age to come. In the latter, human relationships will not continue as they are now. In heaven all will have put on immortality (1 Cor. 15:50–54) and will have no need to get married and have children to continue human life and the family line. The Sadducees, therefore, completely misrepresent life after resurrection. The question they pose is irrelevant: People do not get married in heaven.

Jesus is speaking here only about the redeemed children of God, referred to as "considered worthy of taking part in that age and in the resurrection from the dead," which reminds us that our own merit or position in life has nothing to do with our place in the age to come. Not all people will share in the life of the new age. God is the one who accounts people worthy. The phrase "resurrection from the dead" (v. 35) explains "that age." These two phrases do not refer to different events. When the redeemed are raised from the dead, they will take part in "that age."

Jesus goes on to describe two further elements about the resurrected righteous in addition to their not getting married. (1) "They can no longer die." The redeemed will be free from death. Life in the age to come will be of such quality that death cannot touch it. Not only will people not die, but "they can no longer die." The redeemed will live forever and will have no need to procreate to preserve the human race. (2) "They are like the angels" and "are God's children." The Greek (*isangeloi*) means "equal to the angels." The Sadducees denied the existence of the spirit world. Jesus not only believes that angels exist, but also that in the age to come God's children will be like the angels, especially since dying will become impossible for them.

Being immortal like the angels, believers will be recognized as God's children. In this age believers are already children of God. We have been born again. God has adopted us into his family. But in the age to come we will receive our full inheritance as God's children. At our resurrection our intimate relationship with God will be revealed, and we will be recognized as "children of the resurrection" (v. 36). At the resurrection we will also be transformed.

The second part of Jesus' reply shows that the resurrection is consistent with the writings of Moses (vv. 37–38) and that the Sadducees have it wrong. He appeals to the account of the burning bush in Exodus 3:1–6, a passage that formed the foundation of the miracle of Israel's deliverance from Egypt. In this passage, Moses alludes to the doctrine of the resurrection of the dead. Years after the death of the patriarchs "he calls the Lord 'the God of Abraham, and the God of Isaac, and the God of Jacob.'" God remains the God of the patriarchs, even though they have died. Fellowship with the living God is eternal. "Death may put an end to physical existence, but not to a relationship that is by nature eternal. Men may lose their friends by death, but not God" (Caird, 1963, 224). After death the patriarchs and all believers remain alive and will one day share in the resurrection.

Jesus' conclusion is clear: The Lord "is not the God of the dead, but of the living." Like the patriarchs, believers do not die to God because "to him all are alive." That is, in the eyes of other human beings, people die, but in relation to God they remain alive by virtue of their relationship with the living God and the author of the resurrection. To deny the resurrection is to deny the teaching of God's Word.

After Jesus refutes the Sadducees, some of the teachers of the law (Pharisees) tell Jesus he has answered their question "Well." It is not that they are favorably disposed to him, but they are gloating over the embarrassment of their rivals, the Sadducees. On this occasion the Sadducees back off from challenging Jesus with more questions. They realize that he could reveal their faults and do not want to appear foolish again or to be put in a humiliating situation.

5.6. The Question Concerning the Son of David (20:41–47)

Jesus has silenced his opponents. They have decided it is useless to try to trap him with hard questions. Such attempts only give him more opportunities to win victories. Jesus now takes the initiative and poses his own theological question. His purpose is to challenge a popular view of the Messiah, especially that of the teachers of the law. Many of Jesus' contemporaries believed that the Messiah would be merely a son of David and similar to David in outlook and accomplishments. Jesus does not deny the Messiah is a descendant of David, but insists that he is much more. He speaks here to a general audience (v. 45), though likely teachers of the law are part of it (v. 39).

To emphasize that the Messiah is superior to David, Jesus cites Psalm 110:1. In this verse "The Lord" (*Yahweh*) is the God of Israel and "my Lord" (*Adonai*) is the Messiah. A possible translation is: "The Lord God said to the Messiah." God invites the Messiah to sit at his right hand—the place of honor and authority. The Messiah is to exercise divine power until he puts his enemies as a footstool under his feet.

Although he is a son of David (1:27, 32, 69; 2:4), the Messiah is more than a descendant of Israel's greatest king because "David calls him Lord" (v. 44). In other words, David recognized the Messiah as the divine Lord. The nature of Jesus' birth and the events around it, as recorded in Luke, have shown him to be greater than David. The teachers of the law and others need to change their expectations of the Messiah. They think that he will triumph over all of Israel's enemies and enjoy military successes, similar to what David did. But the Spirit-anointed King of David's line will establish an eternal kingdom that will far exceed the glories of ancient Israel. The Messiah is far more than an earthly successor to David. He is the divine Lord.

After challenging the theology of the teachers of the law, Jesus goes on to warn his followers against them (vv. 45–47). He criticizes their way of life and repeats the charges he has made against the Pharisees and teachers of the law in 11:37–54 and 14:1–24. He again exposes their pride, greed, and hypocrisy.

The teachers of the law wear long robes in public as a sign of their distinction and love to have people bow and greet them with titles of respect. They want to look good in the eyes of the people. At any public gathering, these Jewish leaders take the most important seats and places of honor. Their hypocrisy becomes evident in their treatment of others. They take advantage of helpless widows, evidently robbing them of their possessions. They make long prayers to create the impression that they love God and others. To cover up what they do and who they really are, they try to appear to be very religious. So Jesus again warns his followers against such attitudes. True devotion flows from a heart marked by humility and love of others. People who persist in pride and greed will come to no good in the end.

5.7. The Widow's Gift to the Temple Treasury (21:1–4)

This next incident stands in contrast to the pride and hypocrisy of the religious leaders. While still in the temple, Jesus moves to the Court of the Women, where he points out the difference between a poor widow and the rich contributors to the temple. The woman in this story manifests a greater devotion to God than do the wealthy.

In this court are thirteen trumpet-shaped boxes for the people to put in their various gifts (Marshall, 1978, 751). As Jesus sits there, he observes the rich putting large gifts in the treasury. But his attention is drawn to a poor widow, who puts in "two very small copper coins." At that time such a coin was the smallest piece of money; its value was only a fraction of that of a denarius, the average wage for a day's work. To say the least, her gift is very small. Nevertheless, Jesus calls this woman's gift the greatest of them all and says that her generosity exceeds that of the rich. She "has put in more than all the others. All these people gave their gifts out of their wealth; but she out of her poverty put in all she had to live on" (vv. 3–4). Jesus literally says that the widow's gift is more than all of the others put together.

How can this be? Jesus' words provide the answer. (1) The rich gave out of their abundance. Jesus does not condemn them for their gifts, but they were not sacrificing in their giving. Their large gifts represented only a small portion of their great wealth. But the widow has given everything she had. In other words, after the rich have given, they have much left. But the widow has nothing left after depositing her two coins. Real giving involves giving until it hurts. (2) The amount of a gift is not everything; what matters most is the spirit in which it is given. The widow gives money that she needs, which demonstrates that her gift is the inevitable outflow of a loving heart. Generosity does not depend on the amount, but on the spirit of sacrifice and wholehearted devotion to God.

This poor widow serves as an example of true greatness in the kingdom of God. The disciples are to beware of the hypocrisy and greed of the religious leaders. They are to follow the widow, who has given sacrificially to honor God.

5.8. Prophecy Concerning the End of the World (21:5–38)

Jesus' public ministry reaches its climax as he gives a discourse about future events. He is still in the temple, and his disciples and the people are present. According to verse 5 his disciples observe the beauty of the temple. In response to their observation, Jesus implies a link between the destruction of the temple and the end of the world. In Jesus' day both events are in the future. From our perspective, of course, the temple is a matter of past history, for it was destroyed when the Romans conquered Jerusalem in A.D. 70. What connection does the fall of Jerusalem have to the return of Christ? Both events are the fulfillment of prophecy and are events of the last days.

But because these events are separated by thousands of years, this explanation fails to explain adequately their relation. The answer lies in the way the prophets grasp patterns in divine history. For the prophets the events of salvation and judgment follow certain patterns. One event mirrors another. For example, the Old Testament prophets compared the deliverance of God's people from Babylon or Assyria to the going forth of Israel out of Egypt. Also, in the New Testament the Exodus provides the basic pattern for God's mighty saving work in Christ. As a prophet like Moses, Jesus reproduced many of the characteristics of the great patriarch. Stephen also brought out the parallels between Moses and Jesus (Acts 7:20ff.; cf. Deut. 18:15).

The history of salvation reveals that many events are linked together and that they mirror one another. Following this practice Jesus links the destruction of Jerusalem and his return to the earth. The divine judgment of the city of Jerusalem mirrors God's judgment when Christ returns. Both events are part of God's plan; Jerusalem's fall becomes a picture of the end.

As a Spirit-anointed prophet, Jesus unfolds future events in God's plan. His prophetic discourse deals with a number of events. He foretells the destruction of the temple (vv. 5–6) and goes on to speak of worldwide troubles and the persecution of his followers as signs of his return to the earth (vv. 7–19). He predicts the destruction of Jerusalem (vv. 20–24) and tells again about his second coming (vv. 25–28). He then uses the parable of the fig tree to announce the certainty of the visible and full manifestation of God's plan (vv. 29–31) and concludes with a warning to be ready for his return (vv. 32–36). A short summary follows (vv. 37–38).

5.8.1. Destruction of the Temple (21:5–6). Some of the disciples call Jesus' attention to the grandeur of the temple; in his response, the Lord addresses all of the disciples (cf. vv. 10–19). Like all who visited the temple, they are impressed with its grand structures, "adorned with beautiful stones and with gifts dedicated to God" (v. 5). Many of these gifts came from other countries, and its doors and gates were of the finest materials and craftsmanship.[13] Throughout Israel's history, the temple stood as a symbol of God's presence.

Since the temple was so beautiful and was the place where people worshiped God, surely it would never be destroyed, the disciples think. Jesus responds by repeating the prophecy of

19:41–44, where he predicted the total destruction of Herod's temple and judgment on the nation for its unbelief, rejection of the gospel and the Messiah, and slaying of God's Son (cf. 9:22; 13:33–34; 18:31–33; Acts 13:46–48; 18:5–6). Jesus' prophecy was fulfilled in A.D. 70, when the Roman armies overthrew Jerusalem. Some of the defenders took refuge in the temple, expecting God to come to their rescue; but they perished, and the temple and the city were devastated.

5.8.2. Signs of Christ's Coming (21:7–19). The disciples accept Jesus' prophecy of the destruction of the temple as the truth and inquire as to when "these things" will happen, apparently understanding that Jesus has spoken about end-time events. They also want to know what "sign" or great event will warn them of the coming events. Jesus never gives dates, nor does he give anyone a sign of the temple's destruction along with the fall of Jerusalem (except for Jerusalem's being surrounded by armies, 21:20). Any judgment of Jerusalem that leaves the temple in ruins would be a great catastrophe and a disaster for God's chosen people.

The signs of verses 8–19 have recurred through the ages, but they especially take us forward in time and mirror conditions that will exist before Christ returns to the earth. In verses 20–24 Jesus comes back to a description of Jerusalem's fall and the period of the Gentiles. This discourse is typical of biblical prophecy, in which one event foreshadows another. When Jerusalem falls, it is part of the outworking of God's plan toward the fulfillment of his promises and points to the time just before the return of the Son of Man.

The way Jesus begins his response to the disciples shows his deep concern for them. He warns them against allowing themselves to be led astray by false messiahs, claiming that the end is at hand. Such people will come, professing to be the Christ and predicting that God's appointed time for the end has arrived. The disciples are to keep their eyes open so as not to be led to believe such claims. The sad thing is that many people are deceived by false prophets.

Furthermore, Jesus predicts political upheavals (vv. 9–11). The disciples will hear of wars and revolutions among nations, but they must not be terrified and think that the end of the world has come. These events "must happen" (*dei*, a divine necessity), for they are part of God's plan. When such events do happen, "the end will not come right away." Obviously Jesus does not expect the end of the world during the lifetime of his disciples.

In addition to political troubles, there will be mighty earthquakes, famines, and pestilences that bring death. Strange and fearful events will occur as "signs from heaven." In short, worldwide signs and chaos will precede the end.

These days will also be troubled times for believers. Prior to all these things happening, the disciples will experience cruel persecution. The church will go through great troubles, and the enemies of the gospel will offer strong opposition. Jesus' followers can expect that people in authority will imprison them and force them to appear before synagogues, kings, and governors.

The reference to synagogues reminds us that Jesus has the period of the early church in view here. The first followers of Jesus can expect to stand trial in synagogues, places where the law is administered (cf. 12:11) and local trials are held. Opposition and persecution will come from the Sanhedrin (Acts 4), governors (Acts 23:24ff.), and kings (Acts 12:1–2). They will suffer for the sake of Christ, but persecution will give them the opportunity to testify to their enemies about the gospel. Suffering for Jesus' sake is a testimony, but to testify in the face of persecution to what God has done makes our witness most effective. Stephen is a marvelous example (Acts 7).

When they are tried in the synagogue, Jesus does not want his followers to worry about how to defend themselves (v. 14). They are to devote no time to preparing a defense before Jewish and pagan authorities, for Jesus himself promises to empower their testimony. Through the Spirit (Mark 13:11) he will give them "words and wisdom" (Luke 21:15) that none of their opponents can withstand or contradict (cf. Acts 4:1ff.; 6:10; 13:8–12). Jesus' words have nothing to do with sermons and lectures that faithful preachers and teachers must prepare. His followers, however, can have the assurance that when they face persecution, the Holy Spirit will give them the power and the wherewithal to bear witness to God.

In addition to persecution by the authorities, the disciples will suffer at the hands of their nearest relatives and friends who reject Christ (v. 16). Blood relationships are strong and so is friendship, but hatred of Christ can destroy the closest of relationships. At times the gospel divides families and alienates friends. Thus Jesus predicts that family members and former friends will betray believers to the hostile authorities, and some of them will be killed by their adversaries. But believers can rest assured that God is in control and will work out his plan for their good (Rom. 8:28–39). Though some may die for the gospel, they will triumph through the final victory of God.

Persecution will also come from the world at large: "All men will hate you because of me" (v. 17). The true disciples will receive the same kind of treatment as their Savior did (John 15:18–21). The world rejected the Savior and hates those who love him. Once again, however, Jesus offers his followers comfort with a solemn promise: "But not a hair of your head will perish" (v. 18). The double negative in this sentence (*ou me*) emphasizes God's care to the last hair on their heads.

This promise does not mean that believers will never suffer and even die for Christ (cf. vv. 12–16). Rather, it points to God's providence and to his being with them even in death. No real spiritual harm can come to them. In the book of Acts God did sometimes miraculously deliver his believers. But whether he does or not, he is always with them. They are spiritually safe, and no physical harm can come to them unless God permits it.

In no way does God's sovereign rule deny the importance of believers remaining faithful. Thus, Jesus exhorts his followers to stand firm in faith and in God's Word (v. 19; cf. 8:15; 14:25–33). By enduring to the end they acquire eternal life for themselves.

5.8.3. Destruction of Jerusalem (21:20–24). These verses refer to the coming judgment of Jerusalem, not to the second coming of Christ (cf. 19:43–44). Here Jesus emphasizes the danger that believers will experience in the disaster. Luke's account does not include all the details provided in Matthew and Mark. Nothing is said, for example, about "the abomination that causes desolation" (Matt. 24:15; Mark 13:14) and about these days of judgment being cut short for the sake of God's people (Matt. 24:22; Mark 13:20). In verse 6 Jesus has predicted the destruction of the temple; this section focuses on the violent end of the city.

How will the faithful know that Jerusalem's destruction is at hand? When they see the city being surrounded by hostile armies, they will realize the time of devastation is near. The invading armies will be the sign for the faithful in and around the city to flee to the mountains. Its walls and towers will provide no protection from the enemy forces. That coming judgment will be "punishment" (v. 22) for the city's unbelief and sins against the gospel, fulfilling also the warnings of Jeremiah and Micah against the nation's unfaithfulness (Jer. 7:14–26; 16:1–9; Mic. 3:12).

The capture of Jerusalem will bring suffering to all, especially to pregnant women and new mothers. The destruction will be dreadful, and God's wrath (*orge*, "anger, punishment") will come upon "this people," the Jews. When Jerusalem falls into the hands of the Gentiles, some of the defenders of the city will die in battle, while others will be taken as prisoners to foreign countries. It will remain under their control "until the times of the Gentiles are fulfilled." God has ordained how long the Gentiles will rule Jerusalem. When that time ends, the city will be returned to the custody of the Jews. This prophecy of Jesus has already been partially fulfilled in our time, for the Jews have repossessed the city. But only God knows when "the times of the Gentiles" will run out. Whenever it happens, Christ will come and establish his kingdom on the earth.

The "times of the Gentiles" is the present time, as the gospel is being carried to all parts of the earth. Empowered by the Spirit, the church moves out into the world to make disciples of all nations (cf. the book of Acts). God, however, will not forget Israel. Those people have a particular future in his plan. Paul explains the fulfillment of the divine plan in the end time: "Israel has experienced a hardening in part until the full number of the Gentiles has come in. And so all Israel will be saved" (Rom. 11:25–26). The hope of Israel is Jesus Christ. The day is coming when they will accept him as their Savior. So "what will their acceptance be but life from the dead?" (11:15).

Jesus' prophecy of the overthrow of Jerusalem has been fulfilled. The Roman army completely destroyed the city in A.D. 70. The historian Josephus wrote that more than a million Jews perished in the assault of the Roman General Titus and his army. Almost a hundred thousand were deported to other countries (*Jewish War* 6.9.3). God's judgment of the Jews warns all nations and individuals of the danger of rebelling against him and of refusing to believe his Son.

The terrifying destruction of Jerusalem and the temple foreshadow the last days and the final judgment. The fulfillment of Jesus' prophecy is prophetic of worse things to come upon an unbelieving world. God judged the nation of Israel, but the destruction of the city and the temple is not the final stage of his plan. There remains one more decisive stage.

5.8.4. Christ's Second Coming (21:25–28). After the times of the Gentiles are fulfilled, the final stage of God's plan begins with the return of Christ. Both dead and living saints will be caught up in heaven to be with the Lord (1 Thess. 4:16–17), and those who do not believe the gospel will be judged (2 Thess. 1:6–8; 2:8; Rev. 19:11–16). Jesus never gives a calendar for these end-time events, but he does speak of "signs" that will occur as his return draws near. Many servants of God have felt that they were living at the end of the age and that Christ would return in their lifetime. Their mistaken conclusions should not prevent us from taking seriously the signs that will set the stage for the Second Coming.

Jesus describes end-time conditions that will affect the whole world (vv. 25–26) just prior to the new order of his eternal kingdom. The heavenly bodies will shake and be darkened (cf. Mark 13:24–25). The extinguishing of the sun, moon, and stars will indicate that the present natural order of things is breaking up and that the end is near. Violent storms at sea will result in destruction on land. These alarming signs will create panic on the earth. People of many countries will be anxious and will become desperate because of what they expect is coming on the earth. What happens will terrify and overwhelm people unprepared for the coming of Christ.

On the contrary, the signs of Christ's return are reasons for God's people to rejoice. When they see the signs of judgment, believers are to lift up their heads because their full redemption is drawing near (v. 28). Christ is hidden from the human eye now, but there will someday be a visible and full revelation of him. At his second advent people "will see the Son of Man coming in a cloud with power and great glory" (v. 27; on the "Son of Man" title, see comments on 5:17–26). Jesus will come in judgment and salvation at the end of time and will unveil his power and glory. He will usher in the fullness of the kingdom. He will rule on the earth and will exercise judgment in behalf of God's people (Rev. 19:8–20:15).

In the beginning God created the world, and he will eventually bring it to its end. His kingdom began to break into this world in the person of his Son (11:20), and God will bring about its fullness when his Son returns to the earth. Thus, the present sinful condition of the world is not going to continue forever. Wars and violence, prejudices and hatreds, suffering and heartbreaks, and fears and death—all will be abolished when Jesus ushers in the final rule of God. Our "redemption" from all darkness, sin, evil, and death will finally come. That is why the signs of Christ's return are cause for rejoicing.

5.8.5. The Parable of the Fig Tree (21:29–31). Jesus now draws a comparison between a fig tree beginning to bud and the signs of his return to the earth. No special meaning should be attached to the fig tree, especially since Luke adds "all the trees." Through this parable Jesus indicates the events of verses 25–26 are sure signs of his second coming. In the springtime a fig tree begins to put on leaves; that new growth is a sign that the winter has passed and summer is near.

Likewise, the signs of the times will proclaim that the end is near. When believers see these signs, they can be filled with joy. True, Jesus' return will be like a thief in the night (12:40). No one will be able to establish the precise time of his arrival. Nevertheless, the predicted events (21:25–26) will be signs to believers that his coming is at hand (cf. 1 Thess. 5:4). They may not know the day and hour, but by the things that happen they can "know that the kingdom of God is near." In its initial phase the kingdom is already present, but Jesus has in view here its future, yet-to-come phase.

Many have become sign-watchers. They have tried to fit together prophecies and biblical chronology to find the key to end-time events. The New Testament warns against getting too specific with our predictions, for no ne knows precisely when he will return—not ven the angels of heaven or the Son himself Mark 13:32). Needless to say, we should be xtremely suspicious of anyone who makes xact predictions about Christ's return.

5.8.6. Readiness for Christ's Coming 21:32–36). The kingdom will someday arrive n its fullness. God will complete what he has egun in Christ. There are signs that announce ts arrival, just as tender leaves on a tree signal the approach of summer. Knowing that the ingdom is coming, most Christians have a egitimate concern concerning timing.

All three Synoptic Gospels record Jesus' nswer to this concern: "I tell you the truth, this eneration will certainly not pass away until all hese things have happened" (v. 32; cf. Matt. 24:34; Mark 13:30). This prediction is made mphatic with the strong negation in the Greek *ou me*). The phrase "all these things" refers to he signs of the end (vv. 25–26).

It might appear that Jesus predicts his generation will live to see all these things happen. The interpretation rests on how the word "generation" (*genea*) is to be understood. Does it efer to a specific length of time, such as thirty or forty years (cf. Deut. 2:14; Ps. 95:10)? Should we define generation in that way, then Jesus is wrong in his prediction. Such an understanding of Jesus' prophecy is unacceptable. But since Jesus gives the prediction in the 30s and Luke probably writes in the 60s (thirty years later), it is unlikely that Jesus (or Luke) has in mind his own generation.

In the Old Testament "generation" often refers not to a number of years but to a kind of people, either evil (Ps. 12:7) or good (14:5). In light of this meaning, "this generation" can include several lifetimes and refer to people who form part of every generation. Using the term with this ethical significance, Jesus predicts that throughout the ages evil and unbelieving people will remain. In no way will such people pass away. Their kind will be present when Christ returns, and they will not escape the judgment. His arrival will mean redemption for the faithful and judgment for the unbelieving.

The followers of Jesus can rest assured that everything Jesus has said will come true. His prophecies—all his teachings—will be fulfilled. His word is more permanent than creation itself, for "heaven and earth will pass away" at the end of the world (cf. Rom. 8:19–23; 1 Cor. 7:31; Rev. 21:1–5), but "[Jesus'] words will never pass away" (Luke 21:33). His words are identical to the Word of God, which does not return to God void. God's Word accomplishes the purposes and mission of the Lord of heaven and earth (Isa. 55:11; cf. 40:8). Believers, therefore, know that every word of Jesus will be fulfilled completely. He has promised the fullness of the kingdom, and someday it will arrive. At present we live between his birth at Bethlehem and his return in glory. Our security rests on the absolute truth of Jesus' words.

Convinced that the kingdom is coming, what kind of people should we try to be (cf. 2 Peter 3:11–13)? Jesus' followers must live holy lives in light of these exciting events to come and not yield to the temptations of the world. No people have as much to look forward to as we do. We know what the outcome of history will be—the establishment of God's eternal kingdom. We know who will greet and bless us when Christ returns with great power and glory. We even know what he will be like because we read about his character throughout the Gospels. We know, therefore, that his ways must shape our behavior and relationships and influence our lives.

The Lord's return makes it urgent that we guard ourselves against earthly cares and worldly interests. Jesus calls for faithful living until we see him face to face. "Be careful, or your hearts will be weighed down with dissipation, drunkenness and the anxieties of life." This warning is against the sins of carousing, heavy drinking, and worrying constantly about the affairs of life. Such a lifestyle destroys our faithfulness and causes the heart to be "weighed down" by worldly concerns.

Many people are tempted to resort to orgies and to strong drink to deal with their troubles. Coupled with the anxious cares of life, the emotional load can become too much for them. Such people cannot be looking for the return of the Lord and are unprepared for his coming. The day of his return will come upon them when they least expect it, as a trap catches a bird. One thing is certain: The return of Christ will impact all who dwell on the earth (v. 35). No one can escape God's judgment.

The final word of Jesus here admonishes believers to expect him at any time. "Be always on the watch, and pray that you may be able to escape all that is about to happen, and that you may be able to stand before the Son of Man" (v. 36). "Watching" and "praying" stress the responsibility of his followers. We must constantly be on the alert against sin and pray that God will give us strength to withstand the temptations and distress that will precede the Second Coming. Each person who endures to the end will "be able to stand before the Son of Man" as one of the redeemed.

We may stand before the Lord Jesus at any time—perhaps tomorrow morning. When we do, let us remember that in no way will our righteousness enable us to inherit the kingdom. Our only hope is that of the tax collector who prayed, "God, have mercy on me, a sinner" (18:13). Just as God forgave the tax collector of his sins, he accepts every sinner who repents and relies on his mercy revealed in his Son, Jesus Christ. Though fearful things will precede the end of history, for faithful Christians the coming of Christ will be a time of great gladness and celebration.

5.8.7. Summary (21:37–38). Luke closes his account of Jesus' public ministry in Jerusalem. During the day the Savior teaches the people in the temple, but at night he withdraws for lodging to a hill called the Mount of Olives. He is still popular with the people, many of whom come early in the morning to hear him. The Jewish authorities continue their opposition to him, but do not have the courage to forbid his appearance in the temple or to arrest him. But even his popularity with the people will not last long. His rejection and death are drawing near.

6. The Trial, Death, and Resurrection of Jesus (22:1–24:53)

The last major section of Luke's Gospel deals with the Last Supper, the arrest, the trial, and the crucifixion of Jesus (chaps. 22–23); in the closing chapter (chap. 24), the focus is on Jesus' resurrection, his empty tomb, his appearance to his disciples, and his ascension. The section opens with Judas's agreement to betray Jesus and Jesus' observance of the Passover with his disciples. Throughout the account Luke emphasizes the Savior's innocence and his fulfillment of Old Testament prophecies. As the righteous sufferer, Jesus follows the path marked out for him by God, a path that leads him through suffering to glory.

Luke continues the story in his second volume, the Acts of the Apostles, with the disci-

The Mount of Olives may have been where Jesus stayed at night during his last week in Jerusalem. The Church of All Nations, at the base of the hill, is next to the Garden of Gethsemane, where Jesus went to pray after the Last Supper and where he was arrested when betrayed by Judas.

ples' endument with power by the Holy Spirit to take the gospel to the ends of the earth (Acts 2:1ff.).

6.1. The Passover (22:1–38)

The scene now changes from Jesus' teaching in the temple to the events before his arrest and trial. Many Jews have come to Jerusalem for the Passover. All four Gospels indicate that Jesus died during this season. As the festival of the Passover approaches, the religious leaders are determined to find a way to kill the Lord (cf. 19:47).

6.1.1. Conspiracy Against Jesus (22:1–6). Jesus was arrested and crucified during "the Feast of Unleavened Bread, called the Passover." The Passover was a one-day festival, observed on Nisan 14. "The Feast of Unleavened Bread" lasted seven days (from Nisan 15 to 22); its name derived from the practice of making bread without yeast (leaven) during that week. Together the two festivals celebrated the deliverance of the Hebrews from their slavery in Egypt. Since they were observed at the same time, they could be regarded as one festival.

The ultimate significance of the Passover lies in the death of Christ. The link between the Passover and Jesus' death is not chance, for it happens according to the divine plan. The lamb slain the night that Israel departed from Egypt prefigured the redemptive work of the Lamb of God and the power of his Cross to deliver people from the bondage of sin. Jesus fulfills all that the exodus from Egypt represented. Reflecting on the crucifixion, Paul writes, "For Christ, our Passover lamb, has been sacrificed" (1 Cor. 5:7).

The religious leaders plot against Jesus, the pioneer of a new exodus. They enlist Judas, one of the Twelve, in their scheme. By now he has given his heart and mind over to Satan (v. 3). This mention makes it clear that more than wicked men are involved in Jesus' betrayal and death. Satan is interested in the outcome and inspires Judas to sell his Lord for a few pieces of silver (Matt. 26:14ff.). Under Satan's control he confers with the Jewish religious leadership ("the chief priests and the officers of the temple guard"). They are pleased to learn that someone among Jesus' trusted friends is willing to hand him over to them. Judas has joined the camp of the enemy.

The Jewish leadership and Judas strike a bargain immediately. A sum of money is exchanged, though Luke says nothing about the amount. The chief priests are glad to pay him for his assistance, for this transaction greatly simplifies the execution of their plot to kill Jesus.

The religious leaders are concerned that they arrest Jesus in private. If they are able to take him without the people knowing about it, they will not risk an uprising. These leaders reveal that sin is a powerful reality in the human heart. They plan murder under the guise of righteousness. Indeed, sin distorts our perception of reality.

6.1.2. Preparation for the Passover (22:7–13). The Passover meal was an important part of the festival. It required the sacrifice and roasting of a lamb, unleavened bread, bitter herbs, and wine. The Passover meal was to be eaten reclining and after sundown (at the beginning of the fifteenth of Nisan). So, before the Passover meal could be celebrated, careful preparations had to be made.

Luke recounts how Jesus prepares to eat the last Passover meal with his disciples before his death. The expression "the day of Unleavened Bread" probably refers to the day before the meal, the fourteenth of Nisan, when the Jews removed all leaven from their homes in preparation for the festival. Jesus instructs Peter and John to make the necessary arrangements, but they have no idea where he wants to have the celebration. Because Jesus knows that Judas has agreed to turn him over to the religious leaders (vv. 21–22), he has kept the place of the meal a secret. During the Passover meal all Jewish people would be indoors, and such an occasion would offer a convenient time for Judas to turn Jesus over to the authorities. But Jesus will be arrested at the time of his own choosing, not when his enemies choose (Morris, 1974, 304).

Apparently Jesus and the Twelve are outside of Jerusalem, perhaps on the Mount of Olives or in Bethany. Jesus tells Peter and John to look for "a man carrying a jar of water" as they enter the city. This sign is unusual because the carrying of water jars was normally the work of women. The man will make his way to a house, and the two disciples are to follow him. The owner of the house will show them the guest room where their celebration will be held. This room will be furnished and filled with the necessary tables and cushions on which the disciples can recline.

Peter and John obey Jesus and find everything as he has said. From the account we may get the impression that Jesus made arrangements earlier for the room, but Luke never says that the room has been reserved by Jesus. This incident seems to demonstrate again Jesus' divine authority and Spirit-directed knowledge (cf. 19:29). His ministry has been charismatic from its beginning (3:21–22; 4:13–19). He has manifested repeatedly prophetic authority and supernatural knowledge.

6.1.3. The Last Supper (22:14–20). Everything has been prepared for the celebration. Jesus and the Twelve assemble in the room and sit down for the Passover meal. Taking his place at the table, Jesus expresses how intensely he has longed to eat this meal with the disciples before he suffers. He knows that the Passover mirrors the greater redemption that his own death will secure. Having now only a short time left, he will not be able to celebrate another Passover with the disciples—not until the consummation of God's kingdom. At that time the full significance of the Passover will be fully realized, and God's people will have complete freedom and blessedness.

Passover celebrations foreshadow the messianic banquet, the wedding supper of the Lamb (Rev. 19:9), when Christ will celebrate with all the redeemed final victory over all sin and evil. As believers we live between Christ's first and second coming. The celebration of this supper between Jesus and his disciples mirrors the inexpressible joy we will experience at the heavenly wedding feast and intensifies our expectation of the glorious return of Christ.

The Last Supper begins. Jesus takes the bread and offers a prayer of thanksgiving to God. As a regular feature of the Passover, he breaks the bread into pieces, but he distributes them with these words: "This is my body given for you; do this in remembrance of me." The point is not that the bread actually becomes his body (transubstantiation) or that he enters the bread and is present in it (consubstantiation). Jesus does not hold his own body in his hands. Rather, the broken bread is a symbol for the death of Christ. On the cross his body will be broken by death for the sins of the world (cf. Isa. 53:12; 1 John 2:2). At the celebration of the Supper, Christ is present as the host. The elements proclaim his atoning death, but they remain unchanged (1 Cor. 10:15–18; 11:17ff.).

The disciples must not forget the sacrificial death of their Savior. Clearly indicating the symbolic character of the meal, Jesus calls for future celebrations of the Supper so that he will be remembered. The Supper thus serves as a reminder of our deliverance from the bondage of sin by his death. The word "remembrance" (*anamnesis*) refers to a past event. When the church celebrates the Supper, it looks back to the death of Christ; but more is involved than merely recalling the Cross. "Remember" also signifies that Christ's death brings spiritual renewal and blessings into the present. The Supper is a profound act of worship.

A short time after the Passover meal Jesus takes the cup and passes it to his disciples, saying, "This cup is the new covenant in my blood, which is poured out for you." By giving the bread and the cup, Jesus indicates that his followers share in the blessings of the new covenant. This covenant stands in contrast to the old covenant made at Mount Sinai (Ex. 24:7–8).

The new covenant is a prominent theme in the New Testament (Matt. 26:28; Mark 14:24; 2 Cor. 3–4; Heb. 8–10). The old covenant was ratified by sprinkling the blood of sacrificed animals on the people (Ex. 24:7–8). The new covenant will be ratified by the blood that the Savior pours out at his death. By his death he will bring about a superior covenant, which establishes a new way to approach God and introduces a new era of fulfillment. His sacrifice provides forgiveness of sin for all who trust him and opens the way for the outpouring of the Spirit (Luke 24:44–49; Acts 2:1ff.).

Paul speaks of the Lord's Supper in terms of fellowship (*koinonia*, "partaking, sharing"). One dimension of this fellowship is "a participation in the blood of Christ" (that is, his saving benefits) in a spiritual way (1 Cor. 10:16). Only by faith in Christ and through the Holy Spirit do we have fellowship with him and share in the saving benefits of his death. Another dimension of fellowship in the Supper is that of believers with one another. To use the words of Paul, "And is not the bread that we break a participation in the body of Christ?" (1 Cor. 10:16). The "body of Christ" refers to the church, the fellowship of believers. Sharing in the saving benefits of Christ's death is expressed in our fellowship with each other. The Supper is thus a visible sign that we are spiritually nourished by Christ and that we have fellowship with other believers.

6.1.4. The Farewell Discourse (22:21–38). Before Jesus leaves the table where the Last Supper has been celebrated, he mentions the presence of the traitor (Judas). He emphatically states that the betrayer has received the bread and cup from him. Judas's participation in the Last Supper makes his betrayal even more horrible. Jesus' coming death and Judas's role in it come as no surprise to him.

The path to the cross has been determined by God, but that does not mean those responsible for his death will be guiltless. God does overrule the evil of human beings and at times brings good out of their evil deeds, but it does not make them less evil nor less accountable. Through Satan's influence Judas has plotted with the religious authorities to betray the Lord. One of Jesus' own disciples has willingly chosen to let Satan rule his heart and to hand the Savior over to his enemies. He is responsible, and woe will befall the traitor. The disciples are startled by what their ears have just heard. Evidently Judas has been able to conceal his terrible deed from the other disciples.

Before the disciples leave the upper room (v. 12), a dispute breaks out among them as to who will have the highest position in the kingdom of God. Evidently they expect the kingdom to come soon in its fullness, and they quarrel about who among them will have the most important positions in it. Their argument shows how out of touch they are with the Savior. In a few hours he will die on the cross, but they are far from the spirit of the Cross, the spirit of self-giving and love for God and others. They are still full of personal ambition (cf. John 13).

In response Jesus contrasts leadership in the world with leadership in God's kingdom. It was normal for pagan kings to be authoritarian, exercising lordship over their subjects. They found their greatness in acting as supreme lords with all their people under them. As proof of their greatness, a number of kings in the ancient world assumed a title such as "Benefactor." They had everyone call them by that title because they wanted to be regarded as great and generous.

Christian greatness stands in sharp contrast. The greatest among Christ's followers are the humblest. Disciple-leaders must be different from leaders who exploit others. Though they may be older, they must regard themselves as younger in regard to position and honor. With that attitude they must always take the lowest place. Also, though they are leaders, they must regard themselves as servants, always carrying out their tasks as people who serve.

A person who sits down to a meal would be considered greater than the one who waits on him. That is, a superior person is the one who enjoys privileges. Jesus, however, is a contrast. The disciples recognize him as their leader, but among them he does the work of a servant (v. 27). Jesus uses the verb "serves" (*diakoneo*) three times in verses 26–27. This verb can refer to the serving of tables (12:37), but Jesus has in mind here the general meaning of lowly service. He is a humble servant, providing a model for all church leaders. Anointed by the Spirit, he is a person of authority and power, but he exercises his authoritative ministry by humbly serving God and others.

Jesus has rebuked the disciples for their argument about the best place in the kingdom and urges them to be content as humble servants. But unlike Judas, they have been faithful to him in the hard and trying times of his ministry. Jesus expresses appreciation for their standing by him and promises them they will share in the authority and joys of the coming kingdom. The Father has given Jesus authority to rule over his people. The Savior shares his authority with these disciples. When the kingdom finally arrives, they will sit on twelve thrones and judge the tribes of Israel in the sense of ruling over them. They will also celebrate the great messianic banquet with Jesus (Rev. 19:6–9) and have the most intimate fellowship with him, eating and drinking at his table.

The disciples, in other words, are not to expect worldly pleasure and power as their reward, but heavenly authority and the joy of dining with the King in the eternal kingdom. They will be greatly rewarded, but Jesus does not promise to place one over the other nor to give more honor to any one of them. The authority given to them will be unique, but all his followers are promised a reward and a place at the messianic feast.

Jesus goes on to mention that Satan is continuing his sinister work against him. But he is a powerful opponent not only of Jesus but also of his followers; he is trying to defeat both him and his disciples. To impress Peter with the seriousness of the matter, Jesus addresses him as "Simon, Simon" and warns him that Satan wants to sift all the disciples like wheat (cf. the use of the plural "you" [*hymas*] in v. 31, cf. NIV note). As he did in regard to Job, Satan has requested God to let him test all of Jesus' followers by tribulations and adversities. They will all be in the coming conflict, and Satan will spare no effort in trying to break up their circle. The Savior is especially aware that Peter's faithfulness will soon be severely tested and that Peter will deny Jesus. Thus, in verse 32, Jesus focuses his concern on Peter.

Satan does not have unlimited authority to do what he desires to God's people. Satan is permitted to test Peter, but Jesus has prayed that Peter's "faith may not fail." Peter, in other words, has an advocate who, by prayer, comes to his defense. But notice that Jesus has not prayed for Peter's freedom from trouble. Bearing the cross is the Christian way. Soon Peter may lose his courage, but he will not make a total renunciation of the Savior. Satan will be unable to destroy Peter's faith. The testing will not achieve the end he desires. Peter will turn from his denial and will be restored by his Lord.

The Father, in other words, will answer Jesus' prayer for Peter. Not only will his failure be temporary, but when Peter returns to Jesus, he will be able to strengthen his fellow disciples. Peter's ministry to others is the ultimate focus of Jesus' prayer: Having learned through his own experience that the flesh is weak, Peter will be able to help other believers. Filled with the Spirit at Pentecost, he will become an especially encouraging voice (Acts 2).

Peter realizes neither the seriousness of what he has just heard nor his own weakness. Without hesitation he claims to be ready to go to prison with his Lord or even to die with him. Peter's self-confidence may seem commendable, but human strength alone is never sufficient to withstand severe temptation (1 Cor. 10:12–13). No doubt he intends to be faithful to Jesus. In fact, when the soldiers come to arrest him, Peter draws his sword to defend Jesus (v. 50; cf. John 18:10). But what does Peter do when those who are hostile to Jesus ask if he is a disciple of the Galilean (Luke 22:56–62)? The Spirit-anointed Savior knows much about human weakness and knows Peter better than Peter knows himself. Thus, he prophesies about Peter's threefold denial of him.

We should remember that it is nighttime, after the Last Supper. Jesus says, "I tell you, Peter, before the rooster crows today, you will deny three times that you know me." He has predicted the number of times that Peter will deny him and that each time will be marked by the crowing of the rooster. This prophecy, with its supernatural knowledge, is in keeping with that of Isaiah: "The Spirit of the LORD will rest on him—the Spirit of wisdom and of understanding" (Isa. 11:2).

The final words of Jesus to his disciples in the upper room remind them of trouble ahead (vv. 35–38). Earlier he had sent them empty-handed to preach the gospel (9:1–6; 10:3–4). They had traveled lightly and had taken with them limited provisions, but their needs had been supplied. In the peaceful days of the Galilean mission they had relied on the hospitality of the people. Now times have changed, and they will face troubles as they have never known before. Soon Jesus will be executed as a criminal, and his disciples will be seen as his associates in crime. God will still be with the disciples, but from here on they must take provisions and protection for travel. They will have to defend themselves against enemies of the gospel, against Satan, and against the forces of darkness. They are to procure a sword.

Some take the word "sword" literally, meaning that the disciples are to buy swords to use in physical conflict. Later some are prepared to defend Jesus with swords, but he stops that attempt in its tracks (vv. 49–51). What Jesus really intends here is that his disciples are to provide for themselves and to protect themselves without shedding blood. They will find themselves thrown more and more into a spiritual and cosmic struggle. The purchase of swords thus is to remind them of that coming battle. To wage that kind of warfare requires special weapons, including "the sword of the Spirit, which is the word of God" (Eph. 6:11–18).

The disciples do not seem to understand (v. 38). They report that they have two swords. Jesus says, "that is enough," probably intending it as an ironic rebuke for thinking that way.

They will engage in a cosmic warfare; human resources are never sufficient for that kind of struggle.

6.2. The Arrest (22:39–65)

The Last Supper was celebrated on Thursday night. Having concluded the farewell discourse, Jesus departs from the upper room with his disciples. The following morning he is formally tried by the Sanhedrin (vv. 66–71). Before that trial Jesus prepares himself in prayer for what lies ahead (vv. 39–46); he is then arrested (vv. 47–53), denied by Peter (vv. 54–62), and mocked (vv. 63–65).

6.2.1. Jesus' Prayer on the Mount of Olives (22:39–46). It is still night. Jesus knows that his enemies will soon come to arrest him. He leaves the city of Jerusalem with the eleven faithful disciples and makes his way to the Mount of Olives.

They go to a place where he and his disciples regularly gather for prayer. There he urges them to pray that God will keep them from falling into hard trials and temptations that are now at hand. Then he withdraws a short distance ("a stone's throw"—about 100 feet). Kneeling in prayer he lays his heart open to God: "Father, if you are willing, take this cup from me." He knows that ahead of him lies great suffering, the cup of wrath (cf. Ps. 11:6; 75:7–8; Isa. 51:17) for the salvation of others. He recoils at the thought of drinking that cup and prays that if possible the Father remove it. Utterly distressed, he fills the night with crying and prayer, and his sweat falls on the ground like great drops of blood (v. 44). It is as though he is already beginning to shed his blood.

Christ in Gethsemane confronts us with a profound mystery. Why does he have such great anguish? Some have suggested that he is experiencing more than an ordinary attack by Satan, but the biblical accounts (Matt. 26:36–46; Mark 14:32–42) give no hint of this. Nor can it be because he anticipates the great physical pain and suffering of the crucifixion. Scripture provides no basis for the view that Jesus is afraid of physical pain and death. Throughout his ministry his courage has been undiminished, even when in great physical danger. Furthermore, the death of many Christian martyrs often involved more intense physical pain than Christ's crucifixion, yet they appeared calmer than Christ in Gethsemane. Surely the martyrs were not greater than their Lord.

No doubt the deep agony of Jesus in Gethsemane lies in bearing the divine penalty for the sins of the world (cf. Isa. 53:10). In Gethsemane he begins to taste spiritual death for every person. His agony comes from his paying the debt for our sins, and even now in the garden he feels the excruciating pain of being made sin for us (2 Cor. 5:21).

But Jesus never wavers in his obedience to the Father. He submits himself to God's will: "Yet not my will, but yours be done." His commitment is to carry the divine plan for the salvation of the world. If it means death, so be it. And Jesus does not have to face this dark hour by himself. An angel comes from heaven, strengthening him and enabling him to pray "more earnestly." The distress in his heart is overcome by help from heaven and by his persevering in prayer. He has affirmed his desire that the Father's will should prevail and accepts what now faces him.

In the meantime the disciples have fallen asleep. They are presumably worn out from sorrow. Nor should we forget that it is midnight or even later. They have no understanding of the struggle that Jesus has just gone through. Instead of praying with him and for him, they have slept. But knowing the circumstances that they will soon have to face, Jesus wakes them. He expresses his astonishment by asking, "Why are you sleeping?" and then urges them to get up and to pray for God to keep them from falling into temptation (cf. v. 40). Only by continuing in communion with the living God will they be able to withstand the distress and persecution of the coming days.

6.2.2. Jesus' Betrayal and Arrest (22:47–53). The arrest takes place on the Mount of Olives, the same night as the celebration of the Last Supper. Jesus is speaking to his disciples when Judas and others arrive. Luke does not provide as many details as do Matthew and Mark, but focuses on the essentials of the Savior's betrayal. Judas takes the leading role and kisses Jesus on the cheek, a sign of friendship. The betrayer knows the lodging place of Jesus and the eleven disciples and has led representatives of the Sanhedrin to the place. The customary greeting with a kiss makes Jesus aware of the enormity of Judas's hypocrisy. He perceives that the kiss is a signal to his enemies that he is the one they are to arrest, and he rebukes Judas: "Judas, are you betraying the Son of Man with a kiss?"

The disciples are ready to defend their Lord by the power of the sword. Earlier he had spoken to them about swords (v. 36); now they inquire whether they should use them to prevent his arrest. Before Jesus can forbid the use of violence, Peter takes matters in his own hands and cuts off the right ear of "the servant of the high priest." The servant must have seen the blow coming and ducked his head to avoid being killed. Jesus urges his disciples to permit events to take their course, including his arrest. He does not want any more violence (cf. John 18:36). So he touches the ear of this avowed enemy and heals him. Jesus will not live by the sword. This remarkable miracle is a reminder that the Spirit-anointed Savior takes advantage of all opportunities to minister. Jesus is a man of peace.

Until this point Jesus has not spoken to those who have come to arrest him. Now he rebukes the Jewish leaders for coming so heavily armed—with swords and clubs, weapons suitable to seize an outlaw. They are treating him, a man of grace and gentleness, as though he were a dangerous criminal. Thus, Jesus raises a question: "Am I leading a rebellion?" He sees through what they are doing and confronts them with the truth.

Some of the temple authorities had most likely been present in the background as Jesus taught in the temple. These officials did not lay so much as a hand on him at that time. "The forces of law and order do their work publicly and in the light of day" (Caird, 1963, 243). But something sinister and demonic is now afoot. The Jewish leaders have come under the cover of night to arrest him and are determined to treat him as a criminal, regardless of how unjust it is.

Jesus knows, however, that more than human players are in this drama. He knows why Judas and the religious authorities are acting in this manner: "This is your hour—when darkness reigns." It is the designated hour for the enemies of Christ to act. In the Fourth Gospel "hour" is a time ordained by God (cf. 17:1) and has a similar meaning here. The time chosen by God for Jesus to be arrested has arrived. The forces of darkness are behind this human activity and are attacking God. Satan is the ruler of the kingdom of darkness. The religious leaders belong to his kingdom and are doing his work. The forces of evil have their way or "reign" for a while.

6.2.3. Peter's Denial (22:54–62). It is now late at night. The officers of the temple guard take Jesus captive and lead him to the house of the high priest, where they keep him in custody until daybreak (v. 66). The high priest is not named here, but Luke refers to Annas and Caiaphas as high priests at the beginning of the ministry of John the Baptist (3:2; cf. Matt. 26:57). Jesus is kept under guard at the house of the high priest until his trial before the Sanhedrin. During this time Peter denies his Lord, and the guards entertain themselves by mocking their prisoner.

After the arrest evidently none of the disciples follow Jesus except Peter. This disciple, who has been overly confident, follows "at a distance," staying far enough away so that he is not in danger of being arrested too, but close enough that he can see where they take Jesus. Peter makes his way to the courtyard of the high priest's house and joins those sitting around a fire there.

By the firelight a woman identifies Peter as one of Jesus' disciples (v. 56). At her first glimpse of him she is not certain, but upon taking a harder look she has no doubt that he is one of the disciples. She announces, "This man was with him." Peter sees himself at risk, and his reaction is one of denial—not only that he is a follower of Christ but also that he has any acquaintance with him.

A while later another person also identifies Peter as a follower of Jesus (v. 58). He is emphatic: "You also are one of them." Peter flatly denies it: "Man, I am not!"

Then a third person identifies Peter. His charge is more serious, for he supports it with evidence: "He is a Galilean." By his distinctive accent the man probably knows that Peter is from Galilee (cf. Matt. 26:73). John identifies this man as a relative of the slave whose ear was severed in the Garden of Gethsemane. Having seen Peter in the garden, the man's testimony has weight. But Peter denies that he understands what the man says. "I don't know what you're talking about!" Matthew and Mark tell us that this denial reaches its climax in Peter's cursing and swearing.

As Peter is denying his Lord, the rooster crows. He remembers what Jesus had pre-cted (v. 34). Luke does not indicate where sus is at this time, but he can see Peter. ophetically aware of what is taking place, sus turns his head and looks straight at Peter. hose eyes and the crowing of the rooster mind Peter of what the Savior said. He is erwhelmed with sorrow and goes outside in tter tears; the over-confident Peter has failed s Lord. He has learned the lesson that faith-lness depends on our reliance on the power the Holy Spirit. Later Peter is restored, and ter the outpouring of the Spirit at Pentecost becomes a courageous witness for his Lord Acts 2). From his experience he knows how asy it is to fall. Having learned that the flesh weak, he becomes able to strengthen fellow elievers.

6.2.4. Mockery of Jesus (22:63–65). It is ill night, and Jesus is kept under guard by a roup of soldiers. These guards take advantage f their prisoner by taunting, insulting, and eating him. After being forsaken by his dis-iples, he is now abused by his enemies. These rutal men know that many think of him as a rophet, so they play a little game to get him o show his prophetic gifts. Having blindfolded im, one of them strikes him, and they call on im to prophesy and tell them who struck him. As far as they are concerned, Jesus does not now what is going on around him. But Jesus as a knowledge that none of them have—that e is walking the path of God's will. Without single word he endures their outrageous nsults and violence.

The headquarters of the Sanhedrin is shown in this model of Jerusalem on display at a hotel in the city. The morning after the Last Supper, Jesus was brought before the members of the Sanhedrin to be formally tried.

6.3. The Trial of Jesus (22:66–23:25)

The Jewish leadership spares no effort to have Jesus executed. Because of his obedience to God's will, they put him on trial. He is tried before religious leaders who claim to be righ-teous, but in reality are examples of injustice and evil. The true character of these people has been shown throughout Luke's Gospel. They stand condemned by Jesus' righteousness, a righteousness that involves fellowship with sinners and outcasts. His innocence has been reflected in his entire public ministry. His pre-sent suffering from the leaders' abuse without just cause reminds us that he is the righteous servant of Isaiah 53. Note how both Pilate and Herod Antipas, secular rulers, pronounce him innocent, in spite of the religious leaders' con-demning him to death.

Luke gives a longer account of Jesus' trial than he does of his crucifixion. The trial sheds light on the meaning of Jesus' death. This Gospel focuses on the examinations before the Sanhedrin (22:66–71), Pilate (23:1–7, 13–25), and Herod (23:8–12). Despite his accusers' lack of evidence, the trial proceeds relentlessly toward his condemnation.

6.3.1. Trial Before the Sanhedrin (22:66–71). Jesus' mockery took place in the courtyard of the house of the high priest, Caiaphas. Shortly after sunrise he is brought before the elders, chief priests, and teachers of the law. Together they form the Sanhedrin, the supreme council of the Jews, who exercise authority over all aspects of daily living, including legal matters. According to rabbinic law the Sanhedrin could not try a capital case at night. Thus, they hold an early morning meeting to make legal what they have already decided to do (Matt. 26:57–68; Mark 14:53–65).

After the Sanhedrin has as-sembled, the trial begins. They demand that Jesus tell them if he is the Christ. They focus on one of the primary themes of Luke's Gospel: the identity of Jesus (see 1:32, 35; 3:22; 4:3, 9, 41; 8:28; 9:35). This Gospel depicts Jesus as the Messiah-King. When he approached the Mount of Olives, he refused to silence his disciples when they acclaimed him as the

Messiah (19:37–40). As Messiah he then entered the temple to teach and to cleanse it (19:45–48). So the question the religious leaders raise is significant. But they have already made up their minds that he is not the Christ. So they want Jesus to incriminate himself by telling them he is the Messiah. Nothing would please them more than for him to say, "Yes, I am."

Jesus does not play into their hands so they can exploit the implications of his being a political messiah. His response is twofold. (1) If he tells them that he is the Messiah, they will not believe him. Although they should be impartial judges, they have already determined not to believe him. Then he adds: "If I asked you, you would not answer." That is, if he asked them penetrating questions concerning himself, they would decline to answer (20:1–8, 41–44). (2) He claims, "From now on, the Son of Man will be seated at the right hand of the mighty God." What he says here is the key to his claims. They are unwilling to believe his claim to be the Messiah, but he assures them that as the divine Son of Man (Dan. 7:13) he will reign with God in power and glory.

As Messiah Jesus is not the political liberator that Israel is expecting, but he points to the time when he will take his seat at the right hand of God and rule from heaven. The phrase "from now on" means "in the near future," indicating that a change is at hand. Indeed it is, for the death, resurrection, and ascension of Jesus will change everything (Morris, 1974, 318). Thus, what will happen soon will make the Sanhedrin's trial of Jesus irrelevant. They see his fate as being in their hands, but the resurrected Son of Man will rule from God's side, and his judgment is what counts.

The religious leaders have enough theological discernment to know that Jesus claims to share God's rule and power. A position at "the right hand of the mighty God" is much higher than what they expect the Messiah to occupy. They conclude that he claims to be the divine Son of God. If he will say so, they will then be able to charge him with blasphemy. So they ask him, "Are you then the Son of God?" (v. 70). At the time, men were called "sons of God," but the "the" (*ho*) means the religious leaders are asking him if he claims a unique relationship with God.

Avoiding the direct answer "Yes," Jesus gives an indirect reply: "You are right in saying I am." As far as the Sanhedrin is con cerned, this statement is blasphemy and ha come "from his own lips." His admission t being God's Son makes him guilty of blas phemy. These men only want his death and ar willing to use the most feeble evidence to jus tify their condemnation of him.

6.3.2. Trial Before Pilate (23:1–7). Th Sanhedrin takes Jesus to Pilate, the Roma governor. According to Roman law a subjec people cannot pass the death sentence, exe cuting persons who may be Rome's loyal sup porters. Only the governor has the power t institute the death penalty. So the religiou leaders need the support of Pilate. But the also know that the charges must be formulate so that Pilate sees Jesus as a threat to Rome an to his own future as governor. Jesus' claim t be the Son of God would not be grounds fo execution.

Luke records three of their charges in vers 2. (1) Jesus is "subverting our nation." Bu Jesus has not tried to stir up armed revolution The issues here are Jewish traditions and laws Jesus has been calling for radical social chang and has criticized traditional practice observed by the religious leadership. Fron their perspective, in gaining the support of th people he has been stirring up unrest. Publi affirmation of Jesus might possibly lead t rebellion. So they find some justification fo this accusation.

(2) Jesus has been opposing "payment o taxes to Caesar." The Romans placed poll an other taxes on their provinces. This charge i clever since it was a major responsibility o Pilate to collect the taxes. The religious lead ers have already tried to trap Jesus on the issu but without success (20:20–26). This secon charge is entirely false.

(3) Jesus claims "to be Christ, a king." Thi charge could be understood as Jesus attempt ing to rise to a position of political authorit and would be, therefore, a concern to Rome On the grounds of his claim to be a king, Jesu could be accused of treason or rebellion. The issue is sensitive, for Pilate's administratio would be placed in jeopardy if he did not dea with a man depicted as a dangerous revolu tionary. He has an obligation to the empero to stop Jesus.

Both the second and third charges are seri ous. Pilate picks up on the accusation that has the greatest significance to Rome and asks Jesus if he is "the king of the Jews." Again, Jesus refuses to give the unqualified answer "Yes" (cf. 22:70). He is a king, but not in the sense that Pilate understands the title (cf. John 18:33–38). There is truth in the charge, but Jesus' kingship is not the kind that his accusers want Pilate to believe that it is.

Jesus' response satisfies Pilate. The governor makes a public statement that he finds no reason for condemning this man. Likely he has some knowledge of the malice of the chief priests toward Jesus and their motives for desiring his death. For the first time in this trial the "crowds" are said to be present. Though they may not agree with the charges, they will not be free from a share of the responsibility for his death, though the large share belongs to the Jewish leadership.

Unhappy with Pilate's judgment, the chief priests insist that Jesus has been stirring up riots that started in Galilee and have now spread to Jerusalem itself. When Pilate hears mention of "Galilee," he realizes that Jesus is under the jurisdiction of Herod Antipas and tries to shift the responsibility to this tetrarch of Galilee. Because he is present in Jerusalem to observe the Passover, it is convenient for Pilate to refer the case to him. But sending Jesus to Herod is a mistake, for from this point on Pilate loses control of the case.

6.3.3. Trial Before Herod (23:8–12). Pilate hopes to achieve two things by having Jesus go to Herod. He will rid himself of a difficult case and will make a step toward reconciliation with the tetrarch. Although born in Bethlehem, Jesus is considered a Galilean because of his parents. Also, Galilee is the region where Jesus has spent most of his life.

Herod has heard about Jesus' charismatic ministry of miracles and of teaching (cf. 9:7; 13:31). He is delighted to see Jesus since he has been longing for this opportunity. He is also hoping to see him perform a miracle. Now Jesus is actually standing before him, but he has consistently refused to do miracles to be spectacular (4:9–12; 11:16, 29). Not only will he not provide entertainment now, but he also chooses to remain silent. The many questions that Herod directs to Jesus go unanswered. His response recalls Isaiah 53:7, which Luke quotes in Acts 8:32. The chief priests and teachers of the law do not want to take any chances of Herod's releasing him. They make many strong charges against him, but they are unsuccessful in getting Herod to condemn him.

Irritated by Jesus' silence, Herod takes the opportunity to show his contempt for Jesus. Along with his soldiers he resorts to making fun of the prisoner. They array him in a bright royal robe, which likely serves to mock Jesus' claim to kingship. Herod's behavior shows that he does not take seriously the Jews' charge that Jesus claims to be a king. Herod then returns Jesus to Pilate, but without any substantiated charges. Because Pilate has shown respect for Herod's position, these two enemies are reconciled. Jesus has been used as a political pawn.

6.3.4. Second Trial Before Pilate (23:13–25). This incident is the real turning point in the Passion account. Pilate summons together not only the chief priests and the rulers but also the people, who with one voice cry out for Jesus' death (v. 18). Until now the people have stood in sharp contrast to their leaders in support of Jesus. No longer do they offer resistance to the religious leaders' attempts to entrap the Savior. The dynamics have changed, and the people join their leaders to stop Pilate from releasing him.

Pilate has found nothing in Jesus worthy of death, and he announces Jesus' innocence in the presence of the people. This verdict is not only his own decision, but Herod's as well. Pilate expects Herod to know more about Jewish matters than a Roman governor and sees Herod's dismissal of him as equivalent to acquittal.

Yet Pilate still does not set Jesus free. He offers instead to have his soldiers whip Jesus and then release him (he always released a prisoner at the Passover to win favor with the people). This offer is probably Pilate's attempt to appease the Jews. Pilate has committed a grave injustice by sending him to Herod for trial when he has already declared Jesus to be innocent. But the compromise he now proposes brutalizes an innocent man and makes him suffer greater injustice.

No compromise can be reached, however. In one voice the people and their leaders cry out instead for the release of Barabbas. They prefer an insurrectionist and a murderer over Jesus. But Pilate does not give up easily, and he appeals to them again to allow him to flog

Jesus and then set him free. In desperation he declares Jesus' innocence for the third time (vv. 4, 14, 22). By now mob psychology has taken over. The shouts of the crowd drown out all reason. Rather than listening to Pilate, they keep shouting back at the governor, "Crucify him! Crucify him!" The verb "kept shouting" (*epephonoun*) is imperfect, stressing that they are repeatedly crying out for his death.

The situation has grown increasingly ugly. Pilate decides to offer no more resistance to the mob and to allow them to do with Jesus what they want to. He sets free the man they ask for (Barabbas) and hands over "Jesus to their will" (v. 25), emphasizing the perverted choice of these people. They demand the freedom of a rebel and murderer so that they can crucify their Messiah. The release of a guilty man from prison and the dying of an innocent man in his place strongly points to the substitutionary atonement (cf. Morris, 1974, 324).

Throughout the Gospel of Luke the leading opponents of Jesus have been the Pharisees and the teachers of the law. As a Roman governor, religious leaders, the people, and even a disciple now have a hand in condemning Jesus to death, it becomes clear that the leaven of the Pharisees has carried the day (Moessner, 1989, 196–97). The people who have hung to every word of Jesus have become a ruthless mob, determined to nail their Messiah to a Roman cross.

6.4. Crucifixion of Jesus (23:26–49)

For about three years Jesus has ministered to many people, healing their infirmities and offering true life to all who believe in him. Now his public ministry has reached its end, and he is led away to be crucified. His crucifixion stands at the heart of the gospel as an act of divine love on behalf of sinners. Luke's account of Jesus' death focuses on the journey to the place called "the Skull" (vv. 26–32), the crucifixion (vv. 33–38), the conversation with the two thieves (vv. 39–43), and extraordinary signs in creation along with people's reactions to Jesus' death (vv. 44–49).

The Roman soldiers lead Jesus from Pilate's hall. As was customary for a condemned man, he is forced to carry the cross on his back to the place of execution. Jesus starts the journey, but he has been weakened by his flogging, and the cross becomes too heavy. Someone is seized from the crowd—Simon from Cyrene in North Africa—to carry the cross for him to Golgotha.

A large crowd of people follow Jesus. Included in their number must have been the curious and those who have called for Jesus' death. But there are still those who admire

The Arch, right, is on the Via Dolorosa, the route Jesus took on his way to Golgotha. At bottom is a game scratched into stone that was played by Roman soldiers. The lines have been painted red to make them more visible.

Jesus. Among them are women who weep profusely over him (they are not the women who have followed him out of Galilee; cf. v. 49). In prophetic-sounding words, Jesus calls them "Daughters of Jerusalem," meaning women who live in that city (cf. Isa. 37:22; Zech. 9:9). The text implies that their weeping is sincere and admirable. These local women are behaving this way over the torture and the approaching death of one who has done so many good deeds.

As Jesus makes his way to Golgotha, he is not thinking of himself but of them. He insists that they should be weeping for themselves and for their children, not for him. Jesus knows that bitter days of judgment are coming (vv. 29–30)—the fate of Jerusalem has already been predicted (13:34; 19:41–44; 21:20–21). The Jews saw children as blessings of God, but during the awful days of judgment it will be better not to have children than to see them suffer. To escape this dreadful time women will cry to the mountains and hills to fall on them and kill them.

To support what he has said Jesus appeals to a proverb: "For if men do these things when the tree is green, what will happen when it is dry?" Jesus is the green wood; the dry wood is Jerusalem in judgment. If God does not spare the innocent Jesus, what will be the fate of those who reject the Son of God? Jesus bears God's judgment of sin so that forgiveness may be offered, but the fire of divine judgment will be worse for such people. Green wood is never consumed by fire as easily as dry wood. The tragedy is not Jesus' death, but refusal by the people to accept forgiveness.

The soldiers also lead two others out to be crucified with Jesus. Luke describes them as "criminals," but Matthew and Mark call them "robbers" (Matt. 27:38; Mark 15:27). They crucify the three men at "the place called the Skull." We are uncertain as to why it has this name; it may have been a hill shaped like a human skull. Here Jesus is nailed to a beam that is placed across another piece of wood. The cross is then lifted up and dropped into the ground. Crucifixion was the most cruel kind of punishment known to the Romans. It was also a public event.

Jesus has come "to seek and to save what was lost" (19:10). Thus, in spite of his desperate situation, he continues his mission of offering forgiveness of sin. He prays for those who have executed him and pleads for God to forgive them because they have acted out of ignorance in crucifying the Son of God; but ignorance never removes guilt. Following his Lord's example Stephen later also prays for those who do him wrong (Acts 7:60). The soldiers cast lots for Jesus' clothes, leaving him to die with nothing on his back.

The crowd offers various reactions to Jesus as he suffers on the cross. Many watch out of curiosity; others weep. The first reproach comes from the religious leaders. They speak to one another as they challenge Jesus to come down from the cross: "He saved others; let him save himself." They are mocking his miracles, assuming that his healings and raising of the dead must not have been real. Otherwise, Jesus would use his power to help himself. The religious leaders are persistent to the end and address him with contempt as "the Christ of God, the Chosen One." They are convinced that the Anointed One, chosen by God, would never suffer and die on a cross (but cf. Isa. 52:13–53:12). Suffering has no place in their theology of the Messiah. Instead, these leaders see the Messiah as one who would act with power to destroy his enemies.

The second reproach comes from the soldiers: "If you are the king of the Jews, save yourself." Before his death they offer him "wine vinegar" (*oxos*), a cheap wine drunk by Roman soldiers. They are not showing compassion by offering Jesus something to drink. To offer a king that kind of wine is to insult him. Picking up on Pilate's idea, they ridicule him as the king of the Jews and shout at him to save himself. On the vertical beam above Jesus' head they have put these words: "THIS IS THE KING OF THE JEWS." By having the inscription placed on the cross (John 19:20) Pilate may have sought revenge against the Jewish leaders for pressuring him to condemn an innocent man. Nevertheless, the inscription is a testimony to the royalty of Jesus. He is the one and only King of the Jews—the King of an eternal kingdom.

The final reproach comes from one of the criminals: "Aren't you the Christ? Save yourself and us!" This man expects that the reply to his question will be "Yes," but he raises it as a way of mocking and insulting this innocent man. The other lawbreaker, however, rebukes him for railing against Jesus. He accuses him of not honoring God and reminds him that all three of them are under the same sentence. The two criminals deserve their punishment and are paying for their sins against society, but he has seen and heard enough about Jesus to know that the Savior "has done nothing wrong." Many must have recognized the innocence of Jesus.

Then this thief turns to Jesus and says, "Jesus, remember me when you come into your kingdom." Here "remember" means more than thinking about him. He wants Jesus to be gracious toward him when he begins his reign. This man has confessed his faith and casts himself on Jesus' mercy and saving power. He comes empty-handed to the Savior and has nothing to offer him—no moral life, not even service after conversion. But as death approaches, he finds that the free grace of Christ is sufficient for salvation. This thief hopes to share one day in Jesus' kingdom when it finally comes in its fullness. The Savior will begin to reign as King when he ascends into heaven, but the penitent thief looks beyond that time to the Second Coming and the resurrection of the dead. He knows that his death will not be the end and expresses his desire to have a place in that kingdom.

Jesus promises the repentant thief more than what he asks for: "I tell you the truth, today you will be with me in paradise." He assures him that even "today" he will find himself in paradise, the place of the redeemed in heaven. The suffering of this crucified thief will soon be over. Immediately after death he will enjoy fellowship with his Savior. At death believers depart to be with Christ (Phil. 1:23; 2 Cor. 5:6–8) and enjoy intimate fellowship with him. Between death and resurrection their souls remain in a state of heavenly bliss. As the Messiah Jesus opens the doors of paradise to all who trust in him and wraps his arms of mercy around them. Like the penitent thief all true believers will share in the glory and power of the kingdom at Christ's second coming.

As Jesus hangs on the cross, signs in creation and reactions from onlookers mark the significance of his death (vv. 44–49). (1) The first sign is that the sun stops shining and darkness comes over the whole country—beginning at noon, when the sun normally shines the brightest, and continuing for three hours. The failure of the sun to shine shows God's displeasure at the Jews' rejection of Jesus. Likely more is involved because darkness and judgment go together (Joel 2:31; 3:14–15; Amos 8:9). Jesus comes under God's judgment for the sins of the world.

(2) The second sign is the tearing of the temple veil in two. This veil is the heavy curtain that separates the Holy Place from the Most Holy Place. This miracle may be a forewarning of the destruction of the temple about which Jesus has prophesied (21:5–6). It points to Jesus' atoning death as opening a new way into the presence of God (cf. Heb. 9:3, 8; 10:19–25). For the penitent thief Jesus has opened the way to paradise and gives all believers equal access to God.

Just before he dies, Jesus expresses his trust in God, his Father. In the words of Psalm 31:5 he cries out, "Father, into your hands I commit my spirit." He had begun his ministry with trust in the Father. His trust had remained constant, and in death he now hands himself over to the Father. Both in life and death Jesus shows that he is at one with the will of a trustworthy Father. He has spent his entire ministry doing good, trusting God every step of the way. Finally, with serenity and trust he gives himself to death.

His death has an effect on those who are watching—especially on the Roman centurion who had the responsibility for executing Jesus. After observing what has happened, he is moved to glorify God. Pilate and the penitent thief have declared the innocence of Jesus. This soldier adds his testimony: "Surely this was a righteous man." He has seen the brutality Jesus has suffered and the extraordinary events of the day. As a result he confesses that Jesus is a righteous man, not guilty of any crime worthy of death.

Many people from Jerusalem have come to witness the execution. They have no special interest in or attachment to Jesus. Leaving that place to return to their homes, "they beat their breasts." They came to see a show and to be entertained, but they go away saddened and grieved. They must have realized that wicked men have crucified an innocent person (cf. Acts 2:22–24).

Present also are Jesus' friends. Among them are not only the disciples but also women who have come from Galilee (8:2–3). Unlike the eople from Jerusalem, they know Jesus well. 'hey have seen the mocking and the soldiers asting lots for his clothes. They have seen him anging between the two criminals and the arkness that covered the country. They have eard his loud cry from the cross and have seen im die. These people remain after Jesus' eath, but they stand "at a distance" (cf. Ps. 7:12, LXX). Luke gives no indication whether eir distance from Jesus is due to the soldiers' reventing them from coming closer, but their anding there highlights the loneliness of the avior. In the hour of his greatest suffering, ven his friends stand aloof, frightened and ven embarrassed by what is happening (cf. a. 53:2–4). Jesus therefore has only God to all upon.

6.5. Burial of Jesus (23:50–56)

Jesus had been rejected and crucified, but e is given an honorable burial. Among the ystanders is a member of the Sanhedrin, oseph of Arimathea (a town in Judea). He was disciple of Jesus (Matt. 27:57; John 19:38) nd did not agree with the leaders' conviction f the Savior. Since the vote of this group to xecute Jesus was unanimous, he must have een absent at that time. Known as a devout erson, he was looking forward to God's establishment of the kingdom on earth. His interest Jesus' burial reveals the presence of a few elievers among the Jewish leaders.

Joseph goes to Pilate and gets permission to ive Jesus a decent burial. He takes the body own from the cross, wraps it in a linen cloth, nd places it in a tomb cut out of solid rock ithout any delay, because the Sabbath is pproaching. At that time tombs had space for everal bodies (Marshall, 1978, 880), but no ne had been buried in this tomb (Deut. 21:22–3). The burial takes place between 3:00 P.M. nd sundown.

Luke explains that it is "Preparation Day," riday, on which Jews prepared things for the abbath. Women from Galilee who had given nancial support to Jesus (8:2–3) observed is burial of their Savior. As the Sabbath raws near, they decide to return to their omes in Jerusalem and to prepare spices to noint his body. Corpses were not embalmed y Jews, but aromatic spices were applied to revent stench. Since these women are devout ew, the spices have to be prepared before sunset, when Sabbath begins. The women rest on the Sabbath and plan to return to the tomb.

6.6. Resurrection of Jesus (24:1–43)

The death and burial of Jesus are not the end of his story. Jesus has trusted in God, his Father. In his darkest hour God does not abandon him. As an answer to Jesus' complete trust in him, the Father raises him from the dead and pours out the Spirit on the church at Pentecost. The depth of Jesus' humiliation is matched by the height of his exaltation.

Luke's account of the resurrection draws attention to the empty tomb (vv. 1–12), Jesus' conversation with two disciples on the road to Emmaus (vv. 13–35), and his appearance to the disciples (vv. 36–43). In this Gospel the appearances take place around Jerusalem, but we read nothing about appearances of the risen Lord in Galilee. Jesus died in Jerusalem, and Luke shows that this city is the place of the Lord's victory and where the church receives the power of the Spirit to evangelize the world. Jesus' disciples are surprised at his triumph over death. Even they have to be convinced that he has risen.

6.6.1. Discovery of the Empty Tomb (24:1–12). At dawn of the first day of the week (our Sunday), the women make their way to Jesus' tomb. They expect to find his remains and to anoint them with spices. The first hint they have that something unusual has happened is that the stone at the entrance of the tomb has been rolled away. They enter the open tomb, and to their surprise they do not "find the body of the Lord Jesus."

The women are perplexed, wondering what has happened. While they are in the tomb, two men in bright shining clothes stand beside them. Their description makes it clear that these visitors are angels (cf. v. 23; Acts 1:10). Their presence startles the women. Out of respect for them, the women bow their faces to the ground. Rebuking them mildly, the angels ask why they are looking for the Living One in a tomb, among the dead. They should know better. Jesus has risen and is no longer there. He himself had told them in Galilee what was going to happen: "The Son of Man must be delivered into the hands of sinful men, be crucified and on the third day be raised again" (cf. 9:22; 18:32–33). This empty tomb is empty according to Jesus' prophecy. The key word is "must"

Herod's family tomb in Jerusalem, near the King David Hotel, clearly shows how tombs were sealed with a stone rolled across the entrance. The slot was usually slanted toward the entrance to make it easier to close, harder to open.

(*dei*), which indicates the divine will at work in Jesus' life and experiences. There is no need for the women to anoint his body with spices. God has taken care of it once and for all.

The women then remember Jesus' words spoken in Galilee. They had seen him die on the cross, and now they are seeing the literal fulfillment of his prophecy that on the third day he would rise from the dead. These women leave to share with the disciples what they have seen and heard.

A large group of women apparently saw the empty tomb, but Luke identifies only three by name: Mary Magdalene (8:2), Joanna (8:3), and Mary the mother of James (Mark 16:1). Trying to convince the eleven apostles of their story, they relate (*elegon*, imperfect tense) their experience repeatedly. But in accord with Jewish prejudice against women acting as witnesses, their message is dismissed as "nonsense" (*leros*, "idle tale"). Like the women, the apostles had heard the prophecies from the lips of Jesus, but they are utterly skeptical. They refuse to believe. Nothing but undeniable evidence will convince them of the reality of the resurrection.

Among the skeptics is Peter. Upon hearing the report he immediately runs to the tomb and bends down to look where the body had bee placed. He sees only the grave clothes "lying b themselves," which confirms the fact of th empty tomb. But the absence of the Lord's bod fails to convince him of the resurrection. H departs, "wondering to himself what had hap pened." He knows something marvelous ma have taken place, but he cannot understand it.

6.6.2. Appearance on the Road to Emmau (24:13–35). This incident on the road to Emmau gives further evidence of the disciples' difficul in believing the resurrection. On Sunday, the da that the tomb was discovered to be empty, tw disciples are journeying from Jerusalem Emmaus. As they walk, the recent events giv them plenty to talk about. Not only do they di cuss, but they also debate the meaning of th events connected with Jesus' trial and crucifixio and the women's report of the empty tomb. The question one another intensely (as the verb *syz teo* suggests, v. 15). Their debate reveals what going on in the hearts of all the disciples. The are bewildered by what has happened and a feeling great despair over Christ's death.

As the two disciples are speaking with or another, Jesus walks up. Their intense conve sation has slowed their pace and allows the re urrected Jesus to overtake them. As he joir them, they are unaware of who he is. God in control and keeps their eyes from recogni ing him (vv.16, 31). Jesus asks the two me about their animated discussion. He wan them to share with him their thoughts and fee ings. This question brings them to a halt, an they stand with "their faces downcast." Lik the other disciples, these two do not expect resurrection. They were discouraged and fe hopeless after the crucifixion. One of the tra elers (identified as Cleopas) expresses surpri that anyone in Jerusalem needs to be told abo what has happened. Jesus of Nazareth is on th lips of everyone in the Holy City.

To get them to talk, Jesus asks, "Wh things?" This question leads them to open the hearts and to summarize the story of Jesus four points (vv. 19–24). (1) They refer to hi as a prophet, a popular understanding of Jes (4:16–30; 7:16; 13:31–35). Indeed, in regar to his ministry Jesus can be compared to prophet like Moses (Acts 3:14–26; 10:38–39 Anointed by the Spirit, throughout his minist Jesus was "powerful in word and deed" ar approved both by God and the people. The recognition of him as a prophet is correct, but their understanding of his person is limited (Morris, 1974, 337). He is much more than a prophet.

(2) The religious leaders, the chief priests, and the rulers handed Jesus over to death. This good man suffered a most shameful and cruel form of execution. These disciples place a large part of the blame for Jesus' death on the Jewish leadership.

(3) They express disappointment. Before Jesus died, they had hoped that he would redeem Israel. But his death has put an end to their hopes. They point out that it is the third day since the trial and crucifixion of Jesus. Their understanding of redemption, however, is political—deliverance from their enemies, the Romans. Jesus did in fact provide redemption for Israel through his death.

(4) They confirm that that very morning the tomb was found empty and that angels said he was alive. Reporting what the angels said shows that they want to believe the heavenly messengers. But they have reservations about believing because him no one actually saw (v. 24). The pronoun "him" is emphatic. If the disciples had actually seen him, things would be different.

The two disciples still do not recognize Jesus. That lack of recognition allows this stranger to teach them the necessity of his death and resurrection and to show that these events fulfill Scripture (vv. 25–28). He has listened to them and now speaks. He first rebukes them for lacking spiritual perception and for being slow to be convinced of the truth. They have failed to believe "all that the prophets have spoken!" The root of their problem is failure to believe the teaching of Scripture—passages like Deuteronomy 18:15; Psalms 2:7; 110:1; Isaiah 52–53; Daniel 7:13–14. Otherwise, they would know that Jesus' suffering and his entrance into glory are according to the plan and promise of God. The disciples have embraced the idea of Jesus' establishing an earthly kingdom, but they have forgotten all the prophecies concerning his suffering.

Jesus, therefore, starts with Moses and goes through all the prophets, explaining what the Scriptures say about him. The approach that he takes to interpreting Scripture is important. Without reservation Jesus accepts the authority of Scripture. Failure to believe its teachings is "foolish." Moreover, Jesus' interpretation is based on the entirety of Scripture. In verse 27 the repetition of "all" is not accidental. Last, Jesus understands Scripture to be primarily Christ-centered. From beginning to end, the Old Testament is a prophetic witness to the life of the Messiah (Soderlund, 1987, 2–3).

As the two disciples approach their village, the stranger appears to be going on. But they urge him to stay with them. It is near sundown, so they give him a compelling invitation to spend the night. As he sits down at their table for the evening meal, this guest behaves in an unusual manner. He takes over as the host. Taking the bread, he thanks God for it and gives a piece to each of them. At once they recognize the risen Christ, and the condition of verse 16 is reversed. After their eyes are opened, he vanishes from their sight. They may have observed the manner in which he broke the bread or saw the nail scars in his hands, but the opening of their eyes is a divine act. Only the risen Christ makes himself known to us.

Suddenly, the discussion that Jesus had with them on the road about the Scriptures makes sense. They ask themselves, "Were not our hearts burning within us?" The expression indicates the powerful effect of the dawning of new truth on the hearts of these two people. When the Savior first appears to them, they do not understand or believe in his saving death and resurrection. As he explains to them the Scriptures, the Holy One kindles a flame in their hearts and opens their eyes so that they understand everything that happened to Jesus is in agreement with the prophetic word and that Jesus is the promised Redeemer (Arrington, 1994, 76).

With a flame lit in their hearts by the Holy Spirit, they want to share with others the good news that Jesus is alive. Without any delay they return in the dark to Jerusalem to tell the Eleven and others about their experience. The lateness of the hour does not discourage them (Morris, 1974, 371). The news they have is too good to keep to themselves. But when they arrive, they find that the truth is already known: "The Lord has risen and has appeared to Simon." The report that these two disciples from Emmaus then give falls in two parts: (1) events on the road to Emmaus, and (2) recognition of the risen Savior at the breaking of bread.

This Emmaus road experience affirms for us that Jesus is alive and assures us that he draws near to those who have lost their hope. People become discouraged when they fail to place their trust in his Word. Jesus invites people to tell him their troubles. He listens carefully and ministers to their needs through the Scriptures. The Holy Spirit causes our hearts to recognize and embrace truth and opens our eyes so that we can see the risen Christ. When we see him, our first reaction should be to tell others about him.

6.6.3. Appearance to the Disciples (24:36–43). The two disciples had reached Emmaus before sundown. After the evening meal, they returned to Jerusalem, about seven miles away, and joined the disciples there. As they are telling about their encounter with the living Christ, Jesus himself appears and pronounces "peace" upon them. But the disciples have not yet come to grips with the physical reality of the resurrection of Jesus. Thus, his greeting fails to bring peace to their hearts. They are terrified, thinking that they are seeing a "spirit" (*pneuma*, "a ghost," NIV). The empty tomb and the numerous reports of his appearance have failed to convince them.

Jesus recognizes that they are deeply troubled and still have grave doubts about the resurrection of his body, which had been placed in the tomb. So he shows them his hands and feet and invites them to touch him. No one can handle an apparition or a ghost. The One who stands in their midst has "flesh and bones." Bearing the marks of nail prints in his hands and feet, the crucified Jesus is really alive. He stands in their presence in his body, having overcome sin and death.

All that the disciples have seen and heard is too much for them. After Jesus shows them his hands and feet, they still do not believe. Their reaction seems to be a mixture of unbelief, joy, and amazement, though their joy and amazement at what they see before them hints that they are slowly coming to faith in the risen Savior. Knowing that they still have some doubt, Jesus offers them a final proof. He asks for food, and they give him a piece of broiled fish. As they watch him, he eats it. His eating destroys the disciples' view that what they are seeing is a ghost or spirit.

The risen Jesus, therefore, has a real visible body that can be touched. Yet his resurrected body is marvelous and extraordinary, for he i able to appear and disappear at will (v. 31). Th body placed in the tomb was miraculousl raised, changed, and endowed with supernat ural qualities. Though it is substantial and ca be touched, it is doubtless "a spiritual body (1 Cor. 15:44).

6.7. Christ's Final Message to His Disciples (24:44–49)

Luke now records Jesus' final instruction to his disciples. The risen Savior summarize what he has taught during his time with then on earth. He must have emphasized thes truths throughout the period of his resurrectio appearances, since he will soon depart fron the earth.

One of Jesus' main messages is that every thing in Scripture relating to him must be ful filled according to the divine plan. The Ol Testament has a threefold division: "the law o Moses, the Prophets and the Psalms [the Writ ings]." All parts of Scripture bear witness t Jesus. The fulfillment of what God ha promised completely centers in him. As he di on the road to Emmaus (v. 32), he again open the minds of the disciples to a genuine under standing of the prophetic Scriptures. He give them spiritual insight so they understand hov prophecy is fulfilled in him.

What God promises, he brings to pass. Th risen Lord calls the disciples' attention to wha Scripture predicted. (1) The Christ (Messiah must suffer. His death had been anticipated i Scripture (Ps. 22; 31:5; 69; 118; Isa. 53).

(2) The Christ must be raised on the thir day (Ps. 16:10; 110:1; 118:22–26). The Ol Testament predicts both his death and resur rection—events that have already taken place As Jesus speaks to the disciples, they are expe riencing the reality of the resurrection.

(3) The mission to the Gentiles must b undertaken (Isa. 42:6; 49:6). Like Christ' death and resurrection, ministry to the Gentile will fulfill Scripture. The disciples must tak their message to all nations, starting fron Jerusalem. They are to go "in [Jesus'] name, that is, with his authority and with this mes sage: "Repent of your sins, and God will for give you." They must proclaim it first i Jerusalem and then to people everywhere Jesus is the Savior of all, so the message mus go to all.

But before the mission of preaching repentance and forgiveness of sins begins, the believers are to be empowered by the Spirit. Jesus assures them that he will send to them the power that his Father has promised. As a result, they will be "clothed with power from on high." They are not to begin the task of evangelism in their own strength, but only after they have received the promise of the Father, the fullness of the Spirit.

Many promises are given in the Bible, but "the promise of my Father" (v. 49, RSV) deals directly with the outpouring of the Holy Spirit. The prophet Ezekiel spoke of God's pouring out the Spirit in the house of Israel (Ezek. 39:29). Joel promised that the outpouring will be on all flesh (Joel 2:28). The charismatic outpouring of the Spirit, in other words, is as much a part of the divine plan as Calvary and the empty tomb. God had promised through the prophets to fill all believers with his Spirit so that they would be empowered for divine service. God fulfills this promise first at Pentecost (Acts 2:1ff.), but the outpouring of the Spirit there is only the beginning of its fulfillment (2:39). The Pentecostal gift of the Spirit reaches beyond the first Pentecost. It is "on all people" (2:17), meaning that the outpouring of the Spirit is universal.

It is a promise of "power [*dynamis*] from on high." The power is a heavenly power—power that comes only from God. It is a power for service—a power granted by the Holy Spirit for believers to give testimony to Jesus Christ and to influence others to accept Christ. The experience is described by Jesus as being "clothed [*enduo*] with power." As people are clothed with garments, so believers will be clothed with supernatural power. This experience is not a general increase of supernatural power, but charismatic power that equips believers for divine service and enables them to be more effective in their ongoing service to the risen Christ.

This promise of power from on high has a direct link to the story of Pentecost (Acts 2:1ff.). As the unique bearer of the Spirit, Christ assures his disciples that he will send "what my Father has promised." Believers need the special power of the Holy Spirit to accomplish their difficult mission. It is the exalted Christ who sends this blessing (Acts 2:33) so that we may preach the kingdom of God, exercise power over demons, and heal the sick (cf. Luke 9:1–6).

6.8. Christ's Departure for Heaven (24:50–53)

As the climax to his Gospel, Luke describes briefly Jesus' ascension into heaven (cf. also Acts 1:1–11). Luke has recorded in this Gospel only half of his story, beginning with Jesus' birth and concluding with his resurrection-ascension; the sequel comes in Acts. The link between the two volumes is Jesus' resurrection-ascension and the outpouring of the Holy Spirit. Before he departs for heaven he confirms the promise of verse 49: "In a few days you will be baptized with the Holy Spirit" (Acts 1:5). And after his exaltation at the right hand of God, the Savior pours out the promised Holy Spirit, which those present at Pentecost see and hear (Acts 2:33). Thus, the way is paved for the ministry of the church.

Before Jesus departs from the earth, he leads his disciples out to Bethany. Lifting up his hands, he prays for God to bless them. As he is praying, he departs from them and is taken into heaven by his heavenly Father. His ascension means that he has entered into his glory (24:26), exalted and enthroned at the right hand of the Father.

Christ's departure completes his work on earth. His followers will not see him on earth as they have in the past. He has taken the humanity that he assumed when he came to the earth into heaven. Despite his departure, the disciples are filled "with great joy" and worship him. They have come to understand much more than before. Rather than this final parting being a time of grief, it is an occasion for joy, gratitude, and praise. Now they recognize that he is the Messiah, the divine Son of God, and they worship him as Lord and King.

The disciples expect to be filled with the Spirit. So they obey the Lord's command and return to Jerusalem to wait until they are "clothed with power from on high" (v. 49). While there they spend much of their time in the temple, worshiping and praising God. Luke begins his Gospel in an atmosphere of worship: People are at the temple in Jerusalem at the hour of prayer. So he fittingly concludes with the disciples in the temple, worshiping God with great joy and fervor. What can be a more appropriate response to God's grace?

THE OLD TESTAMENT IN THE NEW

NT Text	OT Text	Subject
Lk 2:23	Ex 13:2, 12	Dedication of the firstborn
Lk 2:24	Lev 5:11; 12:8	Offering of the poor
Lk 3:4–6	Isa 40:3–5	Voice in the wilderness
Lk 4:4	Dt 8:3	Not by bread alone
Lk 4:8	Dt 6:13	Serve God alone
Lk 4:10–11	Ps 91:11–12	Protecting angels
Lk 4:12	Dt 6:16	Do not test God
Lk 1:18–19	Isa 61:1–2	God's Spirit on me
Lk 7:27	Mal 3:1	Messenger sent ahead
Lk 8:10	Isa 6:9–10	Seeing but not perceiving
Lk 10:27	Dt 6:5	Love God
Lk 10:27	Lev 19:18	Love your neighbor as yourself
Lk 12:53	Mic 7:6	A divided household
Lk 13:35	Ps 118:26	Blessed is he who comes
Lk 19:38	Ps 118:26	Blessed is he who comes
Lk 19:46	Isa 56:7	God's house of prayer
Lk 19:46	Jer 7:11	A den of robbers
Lk 20:17	Ps 118:22–23	Rejected cornerstone
Lk 20:28	Dt 25:5	A brother's widow
Lk 20:37	Ex 3:6	The living God
Lk 20:42–43	Ps 110:1	At God's right hand
Lk 21:27	Dan 7:13–14	Coming Son of Man
Lk 22:37	Isa 53:12	Numbered with transgressors
Lk 23:30	Hos 10:8	Hills falling on us
Lk 23:46	Ps 31:5	I commit my spirit

NOTES

[1]The term *charismatic* has been used in a broad sense to refer to a transdenominational movement that spans the entire spectrum of Christianity and that emphasizes spiritual gifts in the life of the church, but I use the term to mean that a person is empowered by the Holy Spirit for ministry. In this sense Luke's theology is charismatic with an emphasis on the Holy Spirit's empowerment of the church for the fulfillment of its mission.

[2]Pentecostals do not distinguish themselves from evangelical Christians in regard to the fundamentals of the Christian faith except in one aspect of the doctrine of the Holy Spirit. They emphasize the "Pentecostal experience," which they understand to be an experience in the Spirit subsequent to conversion and to be an enduement with power for service. The evidence of this experience is speaking in tongues as the Spirit gives the utterance. To be Pentecostal is to identify oneself with the experience that came to Christ's followers on the day of Pentecost.

[3]The aorists of 1:51–55 are best understood as prophetic aorists, stating what is yet to happen as though it has already happened, or as gnomic (timeless) aorists, stating what God does at all times. It is also possible that Mary is looking back to specific occasions when God did things, so that the verbs can be taken as ordinary historical aorists; but likely Mary is prophesying of help that will come through the Messiah. Understanding the verbs as prophetic aorists reminds us that what God has done in the past will be essentially no different from his action through Jesus Christ in the future.

[4]The verb used in verse 59 (*ekaloun*) is best understood as a conative imperfect, emphasizing a lack of attainment.

[5]The verbs of Luke 1:68–69 should be understood to be prophetic aorists.

[6]Matthew also records the Virgin Birth (1:18–2:23). Matthew and Luke exclude any possibility of misunderstanding the nature of our Lord's birth by recording it at the outset of their Gospels. Their birth narratives were not written in collaboration, but the fact that they agree points to the accuracy of the records. They agree that Christ was born in Bethlehem, that he was the son of Mary who was betrothed to Joseph, and that he was a descendant of David. More important is the fact that the two narratives affirm that Mary conceived him by the Holy Spirit while she was still a virgin. Luke speaks of the manner of conception by simply saying that the Holy Spirit overshadowed Mary (Luke 1:34–38). It is true that he later refers to Jesus' father and mother as "his parents" (2:33, 41), and he reports what Mary said to Jesus, "Your father and I have been

anxiously searching for you" (2:48). But Luke's record of Christ's birth indicates how these statements are to be understood. Matthew also attests to the Virgin Birth by saying that Mary, who was pledged to be married to Joseph, was found with a child *through the Holy Spirit* before they came together (Matt. 1:18). The Greek preposition translated "through" (*ek*) indicates source. The Holy Spirit was the originating source, attesting to the fact that Mary was the only human parent.

[7]The Greek literally reads, "Christ Lord," but the phrase is probably best understood to mean "Christ the Lord."

[8]This account is the oldest record of a synagogue service. At later times lessons were read from the Law and the Prophets, but it is debatable whether this practice existed in the first century (Morris, 1974, 11–37).

[9]Apparently one line of the quotation comes from Isaiah 58:6, "to release the oppressed."

[10]The participle (*akousas*) has no object in the Greek. The NIV adds "Jesus' words" as the object, but it is just as plausible to understand the object of the participle as John the Baptist.

[11]Luke's account of the anointing by a sinful woman does not parallel the anointing stories in the other Gospels. This nameless woman should not be identified as Mary Magdalene or Mary of Bethany (Matt. 26:6–13; Mark 14:3–9; John 12:1–8). These three accounts indicate events that occur late in the ministry of Jesus, and a comparison of them with Luke's account reveals other differences.

[12]The Greek manuscripts differ as to the name of the place. Some have the region of the Gadarenes or of the Gergesenes. A number of the modern translations follow the manuscripts that read Gerasenes (cf. NIV, NEB, RSV, Phillips).

[13]In Jewish history there were three temples. The first was Solomon's, of which Jeremiah predicted the destruction (Jer. 7:1ff.). The Babylonians destroyed it in 587 B.C. A second temple, known as the Temple of the Return, was built by Zerubbabel about 515 B.C. Herod the Great began to build his temple in 20 B.C. Therefore, it is Herod's temple that Jesus' disciples admired. Josephus gives descriptions of its beauty (*Antiquities* 15.11.1–7; *Jewish War* 5.5.1–5).

BIBLIOGRAPHY

F. L. Arrington, "The Indwelling, Baptism, and Infilling With the Holy Spirit: A Differentiation of Terms," *Pneuma* 3/2 (1981): 1–10; idem, *Christian Doctrine*, vol. 3 (1994); idem, *The Acts of the Apostles* (1988); D. E. Aune, *The New Testament in Its Literary Environment* (1987); C. K. Barrett, *Luke the Historian in Recent Study* (1961); E. M. Blaiklock, *The Acts of the Apostles* (1959); D. L. Bock, *Luke* (2 vols.: 1994 and 1996); R. G. Bratcher, *A Translation Guide to the Gospel of Luke* (1982); R. E. Brown, "Luke's Description of the Virginal Conception," (1974): 360–62; F. F. Bruce, *The Acts of the Apostles: The Greek Text With Introduction and Commentary* (1952); idem, *Commentary on the Book of Acts* (1956); G. B. Caird, *The Gospel of St. Luke* (1963); F. B. Craddock, *Luke* (1990); H. E. Dana and J. R. Mantey, *A Manual Grammar of the Greek New Testament* (1955); W. D. Davies, *Invitation to the New Testament* (1966); R. J. Dean, *Layman's Bible Book Commentary* (1983); D. S. Dockery, K. A. Matthews, and R.B. Sloan, eds., *Foundations for Biblical Interpretation* (1994); H. M. Ervin, *Spirit Baptism* (1987); J. A. Fitzmyer, *The Gospel According to Luke I-IX* (1981); H. Flender, *St. Luke: Theologian of Redemptive History* (1967); E. Franklin, *Christ the Lord: A Study of the Purpose and Theology of Luke-Acts* (1975); W. W. Gasque and R. P. Martin, eds., *Apostolic History and the Gospel* (1970); W. W. Gasque, *A History of the Criticism of the Acts of the Apostles* (1975); N. Geldenhuys, *Commentary on the Gospel of Luke* (1951); T. George, *Galatians* (1994); E. Haenchen, *The Acts of the Apostles* (1971); C. J. Hemer, *The Book of Acts in the Setting of Hellenistic History* (1990); M. Hengel, *Acts and the History of Earliest Christianity* (1979); idem, *The Acts of the Apostles* (1951); idem, *Between Jesus and Paul* (1983); S. Horton, *What the Bible Says About the Holy Spirit* (1976); A. M. Hunter, *Interpreting the Parables* (1960); J. Jervell, *Luke and the People of God* (1972); D. Juel, *Luke-Acts* (1983); R. J. Karris, *What Are They Saying About Luke and Acts?* (1979); L. E. Keck and J. L. Martyn, eds., *Studies in Luke-Acts* (1966); G. M. Lee, "Walk to Emmaus," *ExpTim* 77 (September, 1966): 380–81; R. C. H. Lenski, *The Interpretation of St. Luke's Gospel* (1946); I. H. Marshall, *The Acts of the Apostles* (1980); idem, *Commentary on Luke* (1978); R. P. Martin, *New Testament Foundations*, vol. 1 (1975) and vol. 2 (1978); G. B. McGee, ed., *Initial Evidence* (1991); D. P. Moessner, *Lord of the Banquet* (1989); D. Moody, *Spirit of the Living God* (1968); L. Morris, *Luke* (1974); idem, "Luke and Early Catholicism," in *Studying the New Testament Today*, ed. J. H. Skilton (1974); A.Q. Morton and G. G. H. Macgregor, *The Structure of Luke-Acts* (1964); W. Neil, *The Acts of the Apostles* (1973); B. M. Newman and E. A. Nida, *A Translator's Handbook on the Acts of the Apostles* (1972); K. F. Nickle, *The Synoptic Gospels* (1980); J. C. O'Neill, *Theology of Acts in Its Historical Setting* (1961); R. F. O'Toole, *The Unity of Luke's Theology: An Analysis of Luke-Acts* (1984); A. Plummer, *A Critical and Exegetical Commentary on the Gospel According to St. Luke* (1896); R. B. Rackham, *The Acts of the Apostles* (1953); J. Reiling and J. L. Swellengrebel, *A Translator's*

Handbook on the Gospel of Luke (1971); A. T. Robertson, *A Grammar of the Greek New Testament in the Light of Historical Research* (1934); E. Schweizer, *The Good News According to Luke* (1984); W. G. Scroggie, *The Acts of the Apostles* (1976); W. H. Shepherd, *The Narrative Function of the Holy Spirit As a Character in Luke-Acts* (1994); A. N. Sherwin-White, *Roman Society and Roman Law in the New Testament* (1963); S. Soderlund, "Burning Hearts and Open Minds: Exposition on the Emmaus Road," *Crux* 2 (March, 1987): 2–4; R. Stronstad, *The Charismatic Theology of St. Luke* (1984); idem, "The Influence of the Old Testament on the Charismatic Theology of Luke," *Pneuma* 2 (1980): 32–50; C. H. Talbert, *Literary Patterns, Theological Themes and the Genre of Luke-Acts* (1974); W. C. van Unnik, "The 'Book of Acts': The Confirmation of the Gospel," *NovT* 4 (1960): 26–59; C. N. Weisiger III, *The Gospel of Luke* (1966).

ACTS OF THE APOSTLES

French L. Arrington

INTRODUCTION AND OUTLINE

See the introduction and outline to the Gospel of Luke.

COMMENTARY

In the book of Acts, Luke continues the history that he began in his Gospel. The Gospel concluded with Jesus' telling his disciples to wait in Jerusalem for the promise of power so that they might preach the gospel to all nations. Then Jesus led his disciples to a place near Bethany, a town on the Mount of Olives (cf. Luke 24:50; Acts 1:12) overlooking Jerusalem from the east. As he lifted up his hands and blessed them, he ascended into heaven. The disciples responded by worshiping their exalted Lord and returning to Jerusalem filled with joy (Luke 24:50–52). Jesus had brought the disciples to a point of expectation, confidence, and sustained worship. Luke's final words indicated that the disciples were staying in Jerusalem, praising God in the temple and awaiting God's promised power to come on them.

The promise of power and the commission to a vast evangelistic enterprise have set the stage for the book of Acts, Luke's second volume, which tells about the marvelous spread of the gospel from Jerusalem to what the prophets call "the ends of the earth" (i.e., the entire Gentile world). In this book Luke also interprets the theological significance of the powerful spread of the gospel message.

1. Preface (1:1–11)

1.1. Recapitulation and Summary (1:1–3)

Luke writes Acts as a continuation of his former book, the Gospel of Luke. The Third Gospel records what God accomplished through the deeds and teachings of the Spirit-anointed Jesus, whereas Acts emphasizes the continuing work of Jesus through his Spirit-empowered witnesses. The preface of Acts links this book to the Gospel of Luke and provides a short summary of it.

In Acts 1:1 Luke refers to his Gospel as a record of "all that Jesus began to do and to teach"; he then looks back at the main events of Luke 24: (1) the appearances of the risen Christ to the disciples, (2) the promise of the baptism in the Holy Spirit, and (3) the ascension of the risen Christ into heaven (Acts 1:2–11). It is significant that the Holy Spirit is spoken of twice in the preface—in terms of "instructions" given to the apostles and of the Spirit-baptism they will receive (vv. 2, 5). Christ's exaltation into heaven does not mean that he is absent; the risen Lord continues to be present in the church and in his word (2:38–39; 3:22–23; 4:29–30; 10:43; 16:6–7, 18; 22:17–21), and he carries on his work in many ways. One of the most prominent ways in which he does so is through Spirit-empowered believers.

Acts, then, records the continuation of the ministry of Jesus. From the outset to the conclusion of his earthly ministry, all that Jesus did and said was directed and empowered by the Spirit. Luke's second volume narrates a similar story, which focuses on a Spirit-anointed community of disciples continuing to do and teach the things Jesus had begun to do and teach during his time on earth (Stronstad, 1984, 9).

Luke begins by reminding Theophilus of Jesus' ministry up to his ascension (vv. 1–2). Theophilus (meaning "Lover of God") must have been a distinguished Gentile, either a high-ranking government official or a respected middle-class Roman citizen (see comments on Luke 1:1–4). By the word "began" Luke reminds Theophilus and others of Jesus' continuing ministry through the church. That ongoing ministry is accomplished through the Holy Spirit by his disciples as the gospel spreads from Jerusalem to Rome, and Luke specifically points out how the Lord is actively present in such events as Paul's conversion and captivity (9:3–6; 23:11).

Before Jesus' departure for heaven, we are told that "through the Holy Spirit" he gave instruction to the apostles. These men had been chosen by him, and he instructed them to continue his work through the power of the Spirit. His instruction must have included what we call the Great Commission (Matt. 28:16–20; Mark 16:15–18; John 20:21–23). As part of his instructions, he spoke about the kingdom of God, the sovereign rule of God, and told them to remain in Jerusalem until they received "the gift my Father promised" (Acts 1:4), which is the same as being "baptized with the Holy Spirit" (v. 5) or being "clothed with power from on high" (Luke 24:49). After his exaltation to the right hand of God, the apostles, empowered by the Spirit, are to preach forgiveness of sins to all nations.

During the interval of forty days between Christ's resurrection and ascension, he frequently appeared to the apostles (Acts 1:3). After experiencing tremendous public suffering, including hostility from the Jews, an unjust trial, and crucifixion, Jesus was able to demonstrate the reality of his resurrection by "many convincing proofs." The risen Savior made a number of personal appearances to the apostles, which became an essential credential for their ministry (Luke 1:2). He appeared not only to individuals but to groups, not only to men but also to women. As his disciples now fulfill their commission to go into all the world, a vital part of their message is Jesus' triumph over death (Acts 2:22–36; 4:8–11, 33; 10:37–43). They have physically touched the resurrected Christ and have listened to him teach about the kingdom of God.

Unlike earthly kingdoms, God's kingdom does not refer to the control of a territory and the people in it, but to God's gracious rule over his people that began in the historical life and ministry of Jesus (cf. Mark 1:15; 3:20–30; Luke 10:23–24; 11:17–23). Christ gave his people new insight into God's rule, demonstrated in the saving events of his own life, death, and resurrection. He illuminated the Scriptures about his suffering, death, and resurrection for his disciples and charged them to preach repentance and forgiveness of sins to all nations (Luke 24:45–47).

Through Christ a new era has dawned, and God's reign has become a powerful, saving reality among men. What will come in its fullness at the Second Coming began in his mighty deeds. The church, following the preaching of Jesus, emphasizes God's rule with "a new emphasis as Jesus himself becomes part of the message" (Marshall, 1980, 57; cf. Acts 28:31). To proclaim the facts of Christ's ministry, death, and resurrection is to proclaim the message of the kingdom.

1.2. The Promise of the Holy Spirit (1:4–5)

One of the "convincing proofs" of Jesus' being alive after his crucifixion was his presence at a meal with his disciples (v. 4). The word translated as "was eating with" (*synalizomenos*) literally means "to eat salt with," probably referring to Christ's eating with the disciples in Luke 24:42. On that occasion he urged them to remain in Jerusalem, the city where he died, until they received the promised Holy Spirit (24:47).

The fullness of the Spirit is called "the gift my Father promised" (lit., "the promise of the Father"). Many promises are given in the Bible, but this specific promise has to do directly with the outpouring of the Spirit. Prophets like Ezekiel and Joel had pointed to a future outpouring of the Spirit on the house of Israel (Ezek. 39:29) and even on all flesh (Joel 2:28; cf. Isa. 32:15; 44:3). So God, through the prophets (including John the Baptist), had promised the outpouring of the Spirit.

John the Baptist had administered baptism in the waters of the Jordan as an outward sign of God's cleansing power from sin to those who repented. During his ministry, John spoke of a Spirit-baptism that would be administered by Christ and through which believers would be empowered (Matt. 3:11; Mark 1:8; Luke 3:16; John 1:33). Later Jesus promised the disciples that they would be baptized with the Spirit in just a short time (Acts 1: 5).

In the performance of any baptism there must be an agent who does the baptizing, an element into which baptism occurs, and a candidate who is baptized. When John the Baptist baptized, he was the agent, the waters of the Jordan the element, and the candidates those who repented and desired baptism. In baptism with the Spirit, Christ is the agent, the Spirit is the element, and the candidate is the Christian. Like the NIV, most modern translations use the phrase "with the Holy Spirit," but the preposition "with" (*en*) may be rendered "in." "Baptized in the Spirit" identifies clearly the Holy Spirit as the element of this baptism, whereas the phrase "baptism with the Spirit" may suggest being in the company of the Holy Spirit.

What is baptism with or in the Spirit? The verb "baptize" (*baptizo*) literally means "to dip" or "to immerse." It is an intense spiritual experience through which the lives of believers are immersed into the Spirit of God. They are surrounded, covered, and filled with the power and presence of God. Like a garment that has been dipped in water, they find themselves surrounded, covered, and filled with the power and presence of the Spirit.

The experience of baptism in the Spirit is distinct from the experience of regeneration, which believers have at the time of conversion. Note that the disciples to whom Jesus is speaking here have already experienced the renewal of their hearts by the regenerating work of the Spirit (cf. Titus 3:5). Spirit-baptism is not the same as the new life that accompanies repentance and faith. We are born again by the Spirit and indwelt by the Spirit from the time of conversion (Rom. 8:9; 1 Cor. 6:19). Spirit-baptism, on the other hand, is a supernatural, charismatic empowerment that equips the church to fulfill its mission in the world (Acts 2:4, 17; 8:17–19; 9:31; 10:38, 44–45; 11:15–16; 13:2, 4).

In his sermon on Pentecost Peter does not allude to Old Testament prophets such as Isaiah (Isa. 61:7–9) and Ezekiel (Ezek. 37:1–14), who announce inward renewal of the heart. Rather, he quotes Joel, who promises charismatic and prophetic manifestations of the Spirit for the last days. So Luke sees the outpouring of the Spirit as ushering in the last days and as the supernatural anointing of believers for service. This empowering experience is similar to, but more intensive than, the anointing that the disciples enjoyed during Christ's earthly ministry. The Holy Spirit came to dwell in the disciples at the time of their conversion, but not until Pentecost are they fully empowered to proclaim the gospel and to do the works of God.

1.3. Jesus Announces the Empowering by the Spirit (1:6–8)

During the forty days between his resurrection and ascension, Jesus has spoken to the disciples concerning the kingdom (v. 3). The disciples mistakenly think that in the kingdom Israel is destined for world dominion. They anticipate the fulfillment of Jesus' promise that they themselves will exercise authority over the tribes of Israel (Luke 22:30). At a fellowship meal, therefore, they ask Jesus if he is going to restore the kingdom to Israel at this time. They hope for an earthly order in which Israel rules over other nations, as in the period of David and Solomon. They also, according to apocalyptic expectation, see the outpouring of the Spirit as a sign of the new world order.

Obviously the kingdom of God cannot be defined in terms of merely an earthly order in which Israel has political supremacy. The disciples fail to understand its nature, for God's rule has already been initiated through the ministry, death, and resurrection of Jesus. But they are right about one thing: A strong link exists between the Holy Spirit and the kingdom of God. The rule of God was initiated and exercised by the Holy Spirit in the last days through the ministry of Christ. Jesus does not deny the restoration of the kingdom to Israel, but he rejects his disciples' efforts to determine when that will occur.

The disciples' question about how soon the end will come is inappropriate. The time in which Israel is restored to statehood and the kingdom comes in its fullness has to be left to God. No one needs to know the times or dates the Father has set by his own authority (v. 7). Note Jesus' words: "No one knows about that day or hour, not even the angels in heaven, nor the Son, but only the Father" (Matt. 24:36). That is, it is not important to be able to mark on the calendar the date when the kingdom will be finally established, nor should God's people speculate about the nearness of the end of the world. What they must do is wait and receive the power of the Holy Spirit so that they may bear witness to Christ's death and resurrection until he does return.

Once again the Spirit-anointed Jesus promises the disciples that they will be empowered by the Holy Spirit (v. 8). Rather than changing the subject when the disciples ask about the kingdom, he does give them an answer. His answer does not indicate the time of the consummation of the kingdom, but rather that the gospel must be preached to all nations before the true blessedness for Israel and the whole world will come (cf. Matt. 24:14).

The disciples are promised "power"—not political power but power for service. The word for "power" (*dynamis*) comes from a verb that means "to be able" or "to have strength." In Acts power refers to the working of miracles (3:12; 4:7; 6:8), power for bearing witness to Christ (1:8; 4:33), and power over the devil (10:38). Jesus, then, promises to equip the disciples to be his "witnesses." The basic meaning of the word "witness" (*martys*) is "one who testifies"; the power for such comes from God, a "power from on high" (Luke 24:49), a power granted by the Holy Spirit to give testimony to Jesus Christ, a power to influence others to accept Christ.

Jesus' words "you will be my witnesses" has often been taken as a command, but it is not so much a command as a promise. This promise is linked to their receiving the baptism in the Spirit. When they receive the fullness of the Spirit, the power they receive will inevitably transform them into witnesses. And bearing witness to Jesus will identify them as the people of God. The empowerment for witnessing is described as the Holy Spirit's coming on them (v. 8; cf. 19:6)—an expression closely tied to the idea of "clothed with power" (Luke 24:49). The Holy Spirit will enter them in a fresh way, suggesting the continuing powerful presence of the Holy Spirit.

The witness of the apostles is to begin in the same city in which Jesus was condemned and will not conclude until they have reached "to the ends of the earth." Their mission can be summed up in three stages, which form the geographical framework of the book of Acts: first, Jerusalem, where Jesus was crucified (chaps. 1–7); next, Judea and Samaria, where people had heard Jesus' preaching and seen his miracles (chaps. 8–12); and finally, to the ends of the earth (chaps. 13–28). The book tells of the journeys of God's people as they fulfill their mission (1:15–5:42; 6:1–9:31; 9:32–12:25; 13:1–15:35; 15:36–19:20; 19:21–28:31). Each of these sections indicates the movement of the church along the path announced in verse 8.

As they make their journeys, the people of God are Spirit-empowered and follow the example of their Spirit-anointed Savior (Luke 4:18–19) by proclaiming the kingdom of God (1:3; 8:12; 14:21-22; 19:8; 20:25; 28:23, 31). The rule is to preach the gospel "first [to] the Jew, then [to] the Gentile" (Rom. 1:16). The church makes a significant advancement in its mission when the Samaritans hear the gospel. Its model for mission is the Servant of the Lord, who brings light to the nations and salvation "to the ends of the earth" (Isa. 49:6)—a phrase meaning distant lands in Acts 13:47. Though this phrase may mean "Rome" to Jesus' disciples, it is prophetic of church growth and focuses on the spread of the gospel in the last days, until Jesus returns.

1.4. Jesus Ascends Into Heaven (1:9–11)

The third Gospel closes with the ascension of Jesus, and the book of Acts opens with the ascension. Everything in the Gospel of Luke moves toward the ascension, and everything in Acts moves out from the ascension.

After Jesus has promised the disciples the power of the Spirit to fulfill their mission, God the Father takes him up into heaven before their eyes (vv. 9–11). At Luke 9:51 Jesus began his great journey to Jerusalem, where he was to make his departure from the earth. His journey was not complete until he reached heaven. We can define this journey as the way to the ascension. On the Mount of Transfiguration Moses and Elijah spoke about Jesus' departure (*exodos*, "exodus," Luke 9:31). His "exodus" encompasses his transit from earth to heaven, including his death, resurrection, and ascension (cf. chap. 24). His departure for heaven marks the end of an era and the beginning of another, in which believers are empowered by the same Spirit who anointed Jesus' life and mission.

As Jesus makes his entrance into glory, a cloud hides him from the sight of the disciples. They can no longer see him, but the real significance of the cloud is to signify that Jesus has been received now into God's glory. The Shekinah, God's presence, had rested on the Tent of Meeting in the days of Moses (Ex. 40:34). When Moses and Elijah departed from the Mount of Transfiguration, they were enveloped with the cloud of God's presence (Luke 9:34). The cloud on that occasion and the cloud at Christ's ascension indicate that the last days have dawned in the life and ministry of Jesus. Jesus now departs from the earth into God's glorifying presence.

The cloud also foreshadows the manner in which Jesus will return—on a cloud of glory. In fact, the two angels who appear at the ascension declare that Jesus will return as the disciples have seen him go into heaven—visibly, bodily, and personally (Acts 1:11). Their focus is on the manner of his return, not on its time.

Christ is now enthroned in heaven as king, sitting at God's right hand. Elevated into God's presence, he has completed his journey and taken the final step to his exaltation in glory. The Christ, born of a woman, who lived a human life and died on the cross, now sits at God's right hand. At the Jordan the Holy Spirit had descended on Christ and made him the anointed Prophet, Priest, and King (Luke 3:21–22). Jesus fulfills his royal office in his ascension. As King he will pour out the promised Holy Spirit and will finally come again.

2. The Origin of the Spirit-Baptized/Filled Community (1:12–2:41)

At Pentecost the community of believers experience a totally new dimension of the Holy Spirit. The disciples already enjoy spiritual renewal through the indwelling of the Holy Spirit in their hearts. The "little flock" formed by Christ during his earthly ministry stands between the Old Testament economy and Pentecost.

According to the Gospels, the process of forming the community of believers involved two stages. The first stage consists of the disciples of John the Baptist becoming followers of Christ (John 1:35–37; cf. 3:30); the second stage incorporates an additional group of devoted disciples that gathered around Jesus (see comments on Acts 1:15). Among these disciples were most of the twelve apostles, the seventy, and about five hundred Jews (1 Cor. 15:6). In other words, the Christian church already existed before Pentecost. The outpouring of the Spirit at Pentecost does not mean a new church but an empowered church, an anointed community of believers, who are closely linked to the people of God in the Old Testament (Acts 7:38). As previously promised, soon they will be baptized in the Spirit and become an anointed community of believers.

This section records the disciples in the upper room (1:12–14), the replacing of Judas (1:15–26), the outpouring of the Holy Spirit (2:1–13), and Peter's discourse to the crowd (2:14–41).

2.1. The Community Awaits the Promised Spirit (1:12–26)

2.1.1. The Community Devotes Itself to Prayer (1:12–14). The ascension occurs in the vicinity of the Mount of Olives, east of Jerusalem across the Kidron valley. From that place to Jerusalem is about three-fourths of a mile, the distance a pious Jew was permitted to walk on the Sabbath (Ex. 16:29; Num. 35:5). The disciples now return to Jerusalem "with great joy" (Luke 24:52). Any sorrow that they have at the parting of Jesus is turned into joy at the thought of seeing Jesus again. They go to the upper room. The location of the particular room is uncertain. It must be either the place of the Last Supper (Mark 14:15; Luke 22:8, 12) or the house of Mary, John Mark's mother (Acts 12:12). There they wait for the promise of power from on high.

Among the believers are four groups: (1) the eleven apostles, who are confirming the exclusion of Judas from their number and preparing for his replacement; (2) certain devout women, including Mary the mother of Jesus and probably those from Galilee who had been healed by Jesus—women who supported his ministry out of their means (Luke 8:2–3) and beheld his crucifixion (23:49); (3) the brothers of Jesus, who earlier were skeptical (Mark 3:21; John 7:5) but now are convinced that Jesus is the Messiah; and (4) other followers of Jesus. Judas is conspicuously absent from any of the groups.

As we should expect, the ten days that the disciples spend waiting for God's power are marked by steadfast prayer. The place of prayer is probably not only the upper room, where they are staying, but also the temple (cf. Luke 24:53: "They stayed continually at the temple, praising God"). All present are "joined together," a word meaning they are of one mind and purpose (cf. Rom. 15:6). The early Christians do experience tensions in their fellowship, but they overcome them by their response to the crucified, risen Lord.

The disciples join in prayer with great frequency and singleness of purpose. They pray, expecting Spirit-baptism. Jesus had earlier assured them that the Spirit's empowerment would be an answer to prayer: "How much more will your Father in heaven give the Holy Spirit to those who ask him!" (Luke 11:13). Their constancy in prayer and praise prepares them for receiving the baptism in the Holy Spirit (cf. Acts 4:29–31; 8:14–17). Believing and expectant prayer provides the spiritual environment for receiving the fullness of the Spirit.

2.1.2. The Community Chooses Matthias (1:15–26). As their leader, Peter assumes the role of spokesman for the apostles. He speaks to about 120 believers and relates the facts of Judas's betrayal and terrible end. This number does not mean that these are the only disciples Jesus has at this time. Paul says that more than five hundred brothers at one time saw the risen Jesus (1 Cor. 15:6). These 120 are likely all who are present in Jerusalem on this occasion.

Judas had been one of the twelve apostles and shared in their ministry, but he had forfeited his ministry and suffered a tragic death. The prophetic Scripture makes it necessary that the disciples choose a successor to him.

Peter's description of Judas's death differs in two ways from the account of Matthew 27:3–10. (1) Matthew records that remorseful Judas hung himself, but Peter says that Judas fell head first and burst open. It is possible for both accounts to be true, for when Judas hung himself, the rope presumably broke and he hit the ground with such an impact that his abdomen burst open. (2) Peter says that Judas purchased a field, whereas Matthew records that the chief priests bought a piece of land with the thirty pieces of silver that Judas returned to them. It is likely that the priests bought the potter's field with the money. But the land really belonged to Judas since it was purchased with his money, and his heirs would have legal claim to it (Bruce, 1956, 49). The field apparently derives its name, Akeldama (Aramaic for "Field of Blood"), from the thirty pieces of silver given to Judas for betraying the Savior. This field, purchased with blood money and located somewhere near Jerusalem, is where Judas is buried.

Judas's tragic end is predicted in Psalms 69:25 and 109:8 (LXX). Both passages deal with the enemies of Israel in the time of David, but Peter applies them to Judas. Through the mouth of David the Holy Spirit predicted the fate of wicked people who persecute the servants of God. This prophecy applies in the case of Judas in two particular ways. (1) His dwelling place, that is, either his home or the field he purchased, will be deserted; it will be under a curse and nobody will live in it (Ps 69:25). (2) His place of leadership will be taken by another (Ps. 109:8). The place he has had as an apostle is now vacant. The administrative role the apostles will have in the coming kingdom (Luke 22:28–30) makes it imperative to appoint a replacement.

A man needs to be chosen to succeed Judas as an apostle (cf. 1:26). The word "apostle" has a rich and varied significance. The verb from which it is derived (*apostello*) means "to send" or "to dispatch"; thus, literally, an apostle is an envoy or ambassador. The Christian office of apostle is possibly derived from the Jewish concept of the *shaliach*. This term occurs in rabbinic sources and refers to a person who acts in behalf of another. A *shaliach* has delegated authority, similar to what we call the power of attorney.

In the New Testament the term *apostle* is used in both a general and restrictive sense. Examples of the general meaning are Hebrews 3:1, where Jesus is referred to as "the apostle and high priest whom we confess," and Acts 14:14, where Paul and Barnabas, missionaries sent out by the congregation at Antioch, are called "apostles" (cf. Rom. 16:7; Phil. 2:25). Luke here, however, uses it in its restrictive sense to designate the twelve individuals Christ chose from the larger band of disciples (Luke 6:12–16) as his special representatives. By the end of his earthly ministry, the Twelve form that special group, even though Judas is no longer one of them (cf. 1 Cor. 15:5).

The apostles must be witnesses to the life and ministry of Jesus, especially his resurrection. As Acts makes clear, the replacement for Judas has to meet two qualifications. (1) He must have been associated with Jesus throughout his ministry. The baptism of Jesus by John the Baptist and his anointing with the Spirit mark the beginning of Jesus' ministry; the ascension is the conclusion of his earthly ministry. Having been with the Lord from the outset of his ministry to his exaltation, Judas's successor can testify with great authority to Christ's mighty works and words. As an eyewitness he can speak about Jesus' healing the sick, setting free the demon-possessed, and delivering sinners from the bondage of sin (Luke 1:2).

(2) The essential qualification is to have seen Jesus after his resurrection (cf. 1 Cor.

9:1). The apostles testify only to what they have seen and heard (Acts 4:20). Between Jesus' resurrection and ascension he gave many convincing proofs that he was alive (1:3). Having seen the Lord in this period, Judas's replacement can declare that Jesus has risen from the dead and lives forever. The gospel events must be central to the witness of the church.

After Peter's speech the believers choose two men, Joseph, called Barsabbas, and Matthias. Both have been among Jesus' earliest disciples and are well-qualified to succeed Judas. The Bible tells us nothing else about these two. After putting their names forward, the disciples pray for the Lord's guidance to show them which of the two he has chosen: "Lord, you know everyone's heart. Show us which of these two you have chosen to take over this apostolic ministry, which Judas left to go where he belongs" (vv. 24–25). They address the "Lord" as one who knows all things, including the innermost desires of the human heart.

After prayer the disciples cast lots, understanding that the one on whom the lot falls is the Lord's choice. In the ancient world the casting of lots was widely used for determining God's will (Lev. 16:8–10; Josh. 18:6, 8). We have no way of knowing the precise method used. Probably rocks with names inscribed on them were put in a vessel and shaken until one fell out. By casting of lots the disciples show their strong belief in divine providence. God was the one who guided the outcome of something that seemed as accidental as the casting of lots. When the lots are cast, it falls on Matthias. God has already chosen this man as Judas's successor; the lot simply confirms that decision. The human factor is thus excluded in filling the empty place among the twelve apostles (Haenchen, 1971, 162).

The exaltation of Jesus and the filling of the vacant place of the traitor have now set the stage for the outpouring of the Spirit.

2.2. The Day of Pentecost (2:1–41)

Acts 2 gives an account of the first Pentecost after the resurrection of Christ. The day of Pentecost (*he pentecoste*, "the fiftieth [day]") occurred fifty days from Nisan 16, the day after the Passover. It was also called "the Feast of Weeks," because it occurred seven weeks after the Passover. On account of the wheat harvest occurring in that period, it was a celebration of the grain harvest (Ex. 23:16; 34:22; Lev. 23:15–21). By the time of Luke, it may also have become an occasion for the Jews to

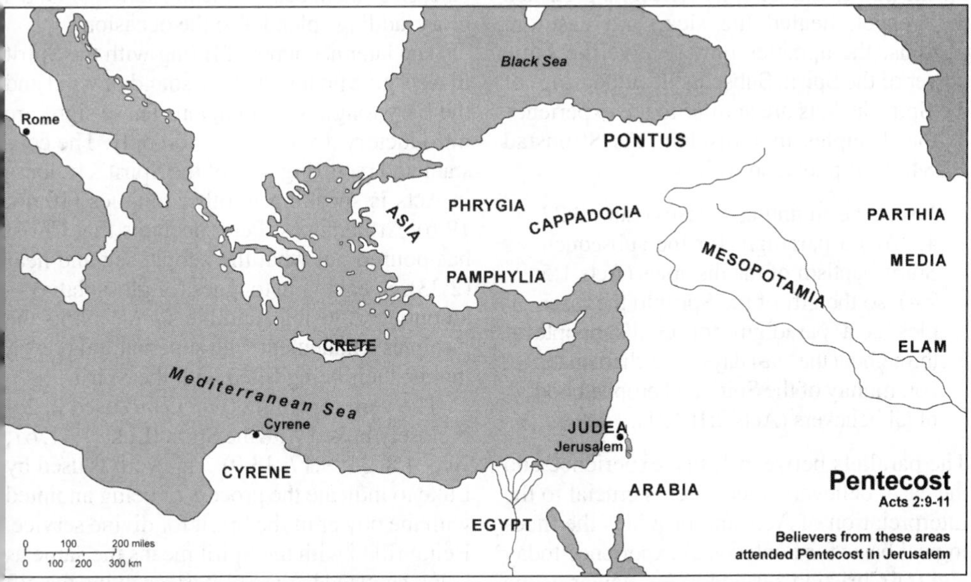

At the Feast of Pentecost in Jerusalem, the Holy Spirit descended on the disciples as a violent wind and what appeared to be tongues of fire that touched each one. The disciples then began speaking to the people who had come from the different foreign countries using the different languages—languages the disciples had never spoken before.

celebrate the giving of the law on Mount Sinai. There is, however, no authority for this tradition in the Old Testament, nor is there any known Jewish tradition as early as the first century that connects the giving of the law with the feast of Pentecost. Many devout Jews from a number of countries came to Jerusalem to observe the Feast of the Passover and stayed until the Feast of Pentecost.

The Jewish festival of Pentecost takes on a new significance in Acts 2, for it is the day on which the promised Spirit descends in power and makes possible the advance of the gospel to the ends of the earth. The apostles' baptism with the Spirit at Pentecost serves as the foundation of the church's mission to the Gentiles. That experience corresponds to Jesus' anointing with the Spirit at the Jordan (Luke 3:21–22).

Similarities exist between these two events. The Spirit descended on Jesus after he prayed (Luke 3:22); on the day of Pentecost the disciples are also filled with the Spirit after praying (Acts 1:14). Physical manifestations accompany both events. At the Jordan the Holy Spirit descended in the bodily form of a dove, and at Pentecost the Spirit's presence is evident in the parting of the tongues of fire and in the disciples' speaking in other tongues. Jesus' experience emphasized a messianic anointing for his public ministry, by which he preached the gospel, healed the sick, and cast out demons; the apostles now receive the same power of the Spirit. Subsequent outpourings of the Spirit in Acts are similar to the experience of the disciples in Jerusalem. As Stronstad (1984, 8–9) puts it so well:

> Just as the anointing of Jesus (Luke 3:22; 4:18) is a paradigm for the subsequent Spirit-baptism of the disciples (Acts 1:5; 2:4), so the gift of the Spirit to the disciples is a paradigm for God's people throughout the "last days" as a charismatic community of the Spirit and prophethood of all believers (Acts 2:16–21).

The parallels between Jesus' experience and the early believers, therefore, is crucial to the interpretation of Acts and provides the theological basis for Pentecostal experience today and for Christian service in the power of the Spirit until Jesus returns.

2.2.1. Sign: The Disciples Are Filled With the Holy Spirit (2:1–4). On the day of Pentecost the disciples are praying and waiting, ready to be baptized in the Spirit. A striking characteristic of them is their unity. Luke has already described them as being united in prayer, suggesting they have one mind and purpose (1:14). The day of Pentecost begins with them "all together in one place" (2:1)—mostly likely in the temple, where they gathered daily (Luke 24:53; Acts 2:46; 5:42; cf. 6:13–14). In view of the context, they are not merely in the same place, but they are in fellowship with one another. Their real sense of community centers in their personal knowledge of the risen Christ and their devotion to him.

When the day of Pentecost dawns, the time of praying and waiting is over for these 120 disciples. At first there is a supernatural sound out of heaven, as of a violent wind. As the sound fills the house (temple) where they are sitting, tongues like fire rest on those present. Miraculous signs introduce Pentecost as at Sinai (Ex. 19:18–19), Bethlehem (Matt. 1:18–2:12; Luke 2:8–20), and Calvary (Matt. 27:51–53; Luke 23:44). The wind and fire emphasize the greatness of the occasion and are audible, visible evidence of the presence of the Spirit—the sound of the mighty wind signifying that the Holy Spirit is with the disciples, and the tongue-like flames of fire that rest on each of them being a manifestation of God's glory, adding splendor to the occasion.

The later accounts of filling with the Spirit in Acts give no hint that the sound of wind and the fiery tongues occur again. These signs are introductory, for that occasion only. The constant and recurring sign of the Spirit's fullness in Acts is speaking in other tongues (10:46; 19:6). At Pentecost Peter declares that Christ has poured out what the people see and hear (2:33). Speaking in tongues (or glossolalia)—an outward, visible, audible sign—marks the disciples' enduement with supernatural power, that is, their being filled with the Spirit.

The verb for filling (*pimplemi*) used in 2:4 is closely linked with the Spirit (Luke 1:41, 67; Acts 4:8, 31; 9:17; 13:9). This verb is used by Luke to indicate the process of being anointed with the power of the Spirit for divine service. Being filled with the Spirit means the same as being baptized in the Spirit or receiving the gift of the Spirit (cf. 1:5; 2:4, 38).

The Holy Spirit enables the disciples to "speak in other tongues." Speaking in tongues is not merely a matter of human will, for the Holy Spirit initiates this manifestation. In full submission to the Spirit ("as the Spirit enabled them"), they speak and act as the Spirit leads them. Such utterances are not ecstatic speech or mere gibberish; but, as the term "to speak" (*apophthengomai*) suggests, they are mighty and authoritative (cf. 2:14; 26:25). This verb refers in the Greek Old Testament to the activity of soothsayers and prophets who claim divine inspiration (Ezek. 13:9, 19; Mic. 5:11; Zech. 10:2) and points to a divinely inspired proclamation.

Tongues at Pentecost can properly be described as prophetic and confirm the pattern of Acts 2:17–18: "Your sons and daughters will prophesy." In Spirit-baptism, inspired utterances originate with the Holy Spirit. Believers are the mouthpieces of the Spirit, though they remain in full control of their faculties. The Spirit respects their freedom and seeks their cooperation. He speaks through them, but they are actively speaking in tongues and are able to stop at will. Peter, for example, speaks in tongues, but stops when he addresses the multitude. So the manifestation of tongues can be understood as an active response and obedience to the Holy Spirit.

The experience of the disciples at Pentecost has a fourfold significance. (1) The main feature of baptism in the Spirit is primarily vocational in purpose and result. As in Old Testament times, the anointing with the Spirit is primarily vocational rather than salvific (i.e., leading to eternal life). Spirit-baptism does not save and render a person a member of God's family; rather, it is a subsequent anointing, an infilling that equips with power for service. At Pentecost the disciples become members of a charismatic community, heirs to the earlier charismatic ministry of Jesus. They are initiated into a Spirit-empowered and Spirit-directed service for the Lord.

(2) Speaking in tongues is the initial sign of baptism in the Spirit. It serves as an outward manifestation of the Spirit and accompanies the baptism or immersion in the Spirit. For Peter this miraculous sign demonstrates the fullness of the Spirit. He accepts tongues as the evidence that the 120 have been filled with the Spirit. As the initial sign, tongues transform a profound spiritual experience into a knowable, audible, visible event. Believers receive assurance that they have been baptized in the Spirit. Jesus himself did not speak in tongues, not even at the Jordan. His special anointing there was normative for his ministry, but the Acts 2 outpouring of the Spirit is normative for believers. The distinction between Jesus and believers is that he initiates the new era as its Lord.

(3) Tongues provide the disciples with the means by which they praise and worship God. These disciples speak in languages that they have never learned, but their celebrating the mighty works of God is fully intelligible to the onlookers (v. 11). All those witnessing what is happening recognize that the disciples are praising God. In the various languages they magnify and thank God for the great things he has done.

(4) Speaking in tongues is a sign to the unbelieving hearers (cf. 1 Cor. 14:22). The words of praise on the lips of the disciples serve as a sign of judgment to unbelievers. On the basis of the miraculous manifestation Peter declares, "Let all Israel be assured of this: God has made this Jesus, whom you crucified, both Lord and Christ" (Acts 2:36). Speaking in tongues is a means by which the Holy Spirit condemns the Jews for their act of crucifying Jesus and for their unbelief. As well as the initial evidence of Spirit-baptism, tongues may be a sign of God's displeasure.

2.2.2. Wonder: The Crowd Is Amazed (2:5–13). At Pentecost the disciples have an international audience, for devout Jews from Jerusalem and outside of Palestine have gathered for this Jewish festival. Many hear the disciples speaking about the wonderful works of God in a variety of languages. By this time the disciples must have left the temple and have gone into the streets. The God-fearing Jews behold the work of the Spirit and hear the Galilean disciples speaking in languages of the national groups present—a great miracle indeed! Knowing that the disciples do not know these languages, they have no reasonable explanation for this phenomenon. Luke describes the response of these groups to this miracle as bewilderment, amazement, and perplexity (vv. 6, 12).

In no other place does the New Testament (e.g., Acts 10:46; 19:6; 1 Cor. 12; 14) describe glossolalia as speaking in foreign languages. The genuineness of the manifestation does not depend on the presence or the absence of speaking in foreign languages. Paul emphasizes that the gift of interpretation must accompany tongues for the local church to be edified (1 Cor. 12:7–10; 14:1–5). According to Paul, tongues is a language, but without the companion gift of interpretation a message in tongues remains unintelligible to both the speaker and the hearer. Therefore, the gift of tongues must be interpreted in the local church.

On this day a miracle occurs that has never before been witnessed. The following question has been asked: Are these inspired utterances a miracle of speaking or a miracle of hearing? The miracle is in speaking, since it is more logical to think of a miracle in believers rather than in unbelievers. A defense of the miracle only as a matter of the ear of the multitude is difficult to make, especially since Acts 2 emphasizes Spirit-inspired utterances ("they . . . began to speak," v. 4). Moreover, the account of tongues in 10:45–46 does not emphasize hearing but speaking in tongues (see also 19:6).

The people recognize the miraculous nature of what is happening. Some are amazed and are troubled by what the Spirit's manifestation means. They have no idea of what purpose the miracle serves. Others make fun of the event by accusing the disciples of being drunk. Not recognizing some of the particular languages in which the disciples are speaking, they mistake them for nonsense.

But what some claim is the result of drunkenness is actually a manifestation of the outpouring of the Holy Spirit. The disciples have had a profound spiritual experience, and with joy and vigor they express their thanksgiving and praise to God for his mighty saving work in Christ and for their Spirit-baptism. The same Spirit who guided the patriarchs and empowered the prophets has come to guide and empower the church to carry the gospel to all nations.

The presence of "Jews from every nation under heaven" at Pentecost, beginning with Parthia in the east and reaching as far as Rome in the west (vv. 9–11), indicates that the gospel is universal in scope. The Christian mission has begun already to reach out "to the ends of the earth" (Haenchen, 1971, 170). The gospel must be preached in many languages and dialects. The universal audience anticipates Peter's promise that God will pour out his Spirit on "all people" (v. 17).

2.2.3. Pneuma Discourse (2:14–36)

2.2.3.1. Explanation: The Three Signs Fulfill Joel's Prophecy (2:14–21). The apostle Peter is now filled with the Spirit and "addresses" the crowd in a Spirit-inspired utterance. Having heard what those mocking the disciples have said, he responds to the question "What does this mean?" (v. 12) with great prophetic authority. He first denies that the disciples are drunk: "It's only nine in the morning!" Men may be intoxicated at any hour, but the early hour makes it highly improbable. Nine o'clock was the hour of prayer, and Jews normally did not have breakfast until ten o'clock. Instead, these disciples have been filled with the Spirit.

To show the falseness of the charge of drunkenness and to explain the meaning of the Spirit's manifestation, Peter links the events of Pentecost with Joel 2:28–32. The multitude is seeing the prophecy of Joel fulfilled before their eyes. What was expected "in the last days" has come to pass: the outpouring of God's Spirit. Speaking in tongues is an eschatological sign that the last days have dawned.

In the Old Testament the expression "last days" refers to the coming of the Messiah (Isa. 2:2; Mic. 4:1). In the New Testament these "last days" are initiated by the coming of Christ, and the mighty outpouring of the Spirit signals that the messianic era is here. The last days encompass the period between the first and second comings of Christ. The age of fulfillment has begun, though the final consummation still lies in the future. The hearers at Pentecost are now living in these last days. The use of the plural in "last days" indicates that the outpouring of the Spirit encompasses more than just one day.

The age of the Spirit was long ago predicted by the prophets: "This is what was spoken by the prophet Joel" (v. 16). In the Old Testament only a few people experienced the Spirit. From Pentecost on, God makes available to *all* his children the fullness of the Spirit. The charismatic power of the Spirit is no longer limited to the leaders of God's people. Basing his message on Joel's prophecy, Peter promises that the outpouring of the Spirit is for "all people." It is universal in scope—on young men as well as old, on daughters as well as sons, even on those of low estate, both men and women. Instead of just on kings, priests, and prophets, the Spirit is to be poured out on believers of every race, nationality, and gender.

Upon receiving the baptism of the Spirit people are to prophesy. Tongues that accompany the experience of immersion in the Spirit have the character of prophetic speech, and Peter links the power of the Spirit with the universal outburst of prophecy. The same connection is made between the charismatic power of the Spirit and prophecy in Numbers 11:24–29, where the elders prophesy after the Spirit has been transferred from Moses to them. Moses then expresses the desire that all God's people might prophesy. Joel 2 promises the fulfillment of Moses' desire, and the events at Pentecost potentially fulfill that desire. The age of the prophethood of all believers dawns with the outpouring of the Spirit in prophetic power, thus creating a community of prophets in the last days.

The initial fulfillment of Joel's promise at Pentecost baptizes the disciples for a prophetic ministry of bearing witness to the saving work of Christ. But this baptism of the Spirit for prophecy is not confined to the believers at Pentecost. The words of Peter, "your sons and daughters will prophesy," point to the continuing prophetic activity of the church. Further evidence of the works of the Spirit will be seen in "dreams" and "visions." These kinds of experiences were ways of receiving prophetic revelation (Num. 12:6). Through dreams and visions the Holy Spirit revealed divine truth to God's people (Luke 1:22; 9:28–36; Acts 7:55–56; 8:29; 9:10; 10:10; 11:5, 28; 16:9; 22:17–21; 27:23).

The purpose of this outpouring of the Spirit is to prepare God's people for "the coming of the great and glorious day of the Lord" (v. 20). As a prelude to the day of the Lord, "wonders in the heaven above" and "signs on the earth below" will occur. Cosmic signs, such as war, fire, hail, and the coloring of the sun will precede the Day of the Lord, that day when history as we know it will end. First comes "the last days," introduced by the first advent of Christ and the outpouring of the Spirit. Then comes the great apocalyptic terrors in heaven and on earth (Rev. 8:5, 7; 20:9). Finally comes the "glorious day of the Lord," the second coming of Christ.

The church exists in "the last days," between two events: the outpouring of the Spirit and the return of Christ. The coming age has become a reality in the lives of God's people. The new era has dawned with the death and resurrection of Christ and the events of Pentecost, but the old age of sin and death will remain until Christ comes the second time. As a result of the baptism of the Spirit, God's people have received power to accomplish their prophetic mission of bearing witness to the gospel. Our message should be, "Everyone who calls on the name of the Lord will be saved" (v. 21). Only those who call out to the Lord in prayer for salvation will escape the terrors of the final judgment. Until the Day of the Lord, people can look to the Lord Jesus for salvation (Rom. 10:13–15).

2.2.3.2. Witness: Peter Proclaims Jesus as Lord and Christ (2:22–36). Inspired by the Spirit, Peter's sermon and character now stand in contrast to his previous denials of his Lord (Luke 22:54–62). After the outpouring of the Spirit, he becomes courageous and bold. His first sermon reflects his clear-cut convictions. He no longer has any doubt about his Savior and his Savior's mission and interprets the significance of Jesus' life and ministry.

(1) Peter calls their attention to Jesus, a man "of Nazareth" (v. 22). His ministry was clearly empowered and approved by God, and his miracles were evidence that the Spirit had anointed him (cf. 10:38). Through him God performed mighty miracles (*dynameis*), wonders (*terata*), and signs (*semeia*). These terms do not mean three different kinds of action, but they describe the same divine work. The miracles of Jesus are mighty works because they were performed by the power of God. As wonders, they excited amazement in those who witnessed them. As signs they signified God's approval of what Jesus had taught in connection with them.

Jesus' ministry was public. Many of the hearers of Peter's sermon had been eyewitnesses to what God accomplished through Jesus: "as you yourselves know" (v. 22). The miracles had occurred among them, and they are well aware that they singled Jesus out as an unusual person. During his earthly ministry Jesus' opponents ascribed his power to cast out demons to Beelzebub (Luke 11:15). They remained unconvinced that his ministry was the work of God, but his disciples know differently (note, for example, Luke 24:19).

(2) Jesus' death on the cross occurred according to God's plan. Rather than recognize him as a man of God, the Jewish leaders crucified him. Yet what happened was no accident; it was according to the purpose of God that Jesus had been delivered to them. Included in his plan to save the world was Judas's betrayal, the Jews' plot, and Pilate's decision.

The Jewish leaders instigated the death of Jesus, but by "the help of wicked [*anomoi*, lawless] men" they had him crucified. The "lawless" men were the Romans, who had not received the law given at Sinai; they were the ones who nailed Jesus to the cross. Without knowing it they were doing God's will (Acts 13:27). Here in a profound way the eternal purpose of God and human will are joined together. Having Jesus crucified, the Jews fulfilled the will of the sovereign God. Even so, that does not lessen the crime and the guilt of those responsible.

(3) God raised Jesus from the dead. Wicked men killed Jesus; in contrast, God took decisive action and caused him to live again. The divine plan took Jesus through death to exaltation as Lord and Savior. Raising him from the dead, God set him free from "the agony of death"—*tas odinas tou thanatou*, which literally means "birth pangs of death." The purpose is not to show that Jesus suffered any pangs after death, but to indicate in a descriptive way how he was released from the bonds of death. The words "it was impossible" (v. 24) mean that death could no longer hold him in bonds as a prisoner.

As proof of Jesus' resurrection, Peter cites the prophecy of David in Psalm 16:8–11, a passage that predicted the resurrection of a person. David spoke in the first person, as if he meant himself. Rather than referring to himself, however, he was referring to God's Holy One, the Messiah. David did in fact die and was buried; his grave remained in Jerusalem (v. 29). No one assumed that God had delivered him from the world of the dead and that his body was no longer in the grave. Psalm 16 did not, therefore, apply to David but to the Messiah.

Psalm 16 is the prayer of a godly man who has confidence that the Lord is at his right hand and will not abandon him in the world of the dead or permit his body to decay, but that he will rejoice in the presence of God one day. As Peter explains, its ultimate meaning lies in Jesus Christ, whom God did not abandon in the grave or allow his body to decay (Acts 2:31). Before his crucifixion Jesus had great confidence in the Father (v. 26), and after his resurrection he was filled with gladness in God's presence (v. 28). Appealing to these words of David, Peter gives a Spirit-inspired interpretation of Scripture and proves that both the resurrection and the death of Christ occurred according to God's plan.

As a gifted prophet of God, David not only foresaw Christ's resurrection but also the Savior as "one of his descendants," who would sit on his throne (v. 30; cf. Luke 1:69). By a divine oath the patriarch received assurance that his family line would continue to occupy the throne. The promised Messiah would be a descendant of David and would rule from his throne. God's promise referred to a particular type of descendant: a true son of David, whose resurrection demonstrates that he is the Spirit-anointed Messiah.

Throughout his earthly ministry Jesus was the Messiah. Thus, Peter's argument does not mean that Christ's resurrection made him the Messiah. Peter does disclose, however, that God raised Jesus from the dead as the Messiah to sit on his throne. Filled with the Spirit, Peter can declare: "God has raised this Jesus to life, and we are all witnesses of the fact" (v. 32).

(4) God has poured out the Spirit. After establishing Jesus as the Messiah who must be raised from the dead, Peter shows that the Savior has actually been exalted to the throne of God (v. 33). Although Peter and his companions have seen Jesus ascend into heaven, for him to allude to their having seen Jesus disappear into the cloud (1:9) would be unconvincing. Therefore, his appeal is to what his audience has seen and heard—Peter and his colleagues speaking in tongues, tongues of fire sitting on their heads, and a sound like a great wind from heaven. For Peter this outpouring of the Spirit is proof that Jesus has been "exalted to the right hand of God," meaning that he is at a place of honor at God's side. Another possible translation is "exalted by the right hand of God," emphasizing the power of God in the exaltation of Jesus.

Having ascended into heaven, "Jesus ... received from the Father the promised Holy

Spirit." Immediately after his baptism in water Jesus was filled with the Spirit (Luke 3:21–22), and during his entire public ministry he was the bearer of the Spirit par excellence (Acts 10:38). He did not need the Spirit as an endowment for himself; but when he ascended into heaven, the Father gave him the Holy Spirit for distribution to the church (Haenchen, 1971, 183). As a result, Jesus, the Lord of the church, pours out the Holy Spirit. All that is seen and heard at Pentecost flows from the ascended Christ. He is absent in body from the earth but present with the Father in heaven. As the exalted Christ, he continues to distribute to believers the power of the Holy Spirit and the gifts he has received from the Father.

In Ephesians 4:8–11 Paul connects the ministries of the church with the ascension of Christ: "When he [Christ] ascended on high, he . . . gave gifts to men." Apparently Paul has the day of Pentecost in mind, when the exalted Christ poured out the Spirit on the church for witness and gave spiritual gifts to persons, such as apostles, prophets, evangelists, and pastor-teachers. From Pentecost on, the ministries of the church have been charismatic in character. There is no hint in Scripture that the Spirit-led character of ministry should change. Through the power of the Holy Spirit, Christ continues to equip the church with a variety of ministries and offices (cf. Acts 13:1–2; 14:14; 21:8).

(5) Jesus is the Messiah, but he is also Lord. He has ascended into heaven and is sitting on the heavenly throne. Since David himself had not gone up into heaven, he could not be speaking of himself when he wrote in Psalm 110:1: "The LORD says to my Lord: 'Sit at my right hand until I make your enemies a footstool for your feet.'" The Pharisees themselves admitted that this passage refers to the Messiah (Luke 20:41–44). In the present context, "the LORD" refers to God the Father and "my Lord" to the exalted Jesus. David's calling the Messiah his Lord, therefore, indicates that Jesus is much more than a son of his.

Taking nothing for granted, Peter declares that God has exalted Jesus as Lord and Christ (v. 36). From the time of his birth Jesus was both Lord and Messiah (Luke 2:11). During his public ministry he exercised functions as Lord (cf. 1 Cor. 7:10, 12, 25; 9:5, 14; Heb. 2:3) and died as the Messiah (Acts 3:18; 10:38). He "was declared with power to be the Son of God by his resurrection from the dead" (Rom. 1:4). The outpouring of the Spirit at Pentecost confirms to Jesus' disciples his power and authority. The one whom the people nailed to the cross God has exalted. Jesus' present reign in heaven proves who he really is.

The people have committed a terrible crime and should tremble at the thought that they are numbered among the enemies of the Lord Jesus. He has taken possession of his throne at God's right hand and will continue to reign until he overcomes and defeats all his enemies. The mighty campaign to subdue them has already begun (Col. 2:15).

2.2.4. Response: About Three Thousand Are Saved (2:37–41). Peter's inspired message reaches the hearts of the people. They understand that his words apply to them personally, for many of them had agreed with the actions of their leaders against Jesus. As they listen to Peter, they are "cut to the heart." Being deeply troubled and convicted of their sins, namely, that they have killed their Messiah, they inquire, "Brothers, what shall we do?" A change has taken place in their convictions, and they feel a keen sense of remorse. They believe that Jesus is the Christ, and their hearts are broken at the thought that they have murdered him. Convicted by the Holy Spirit of their sins, they are ready to receive salvation.

Peter tells them to do two things: repent and be baptized in the name of Jesus Christ. The basic meaning of "to repent" here involves both a change of mind and remorse for errors and sins (BAGD, 512). Repentance demands the forsaking of the old life of sin and living a life of obedience to God.

Persons who repent should also "be baptized" in water. Faith is the means by which God grants forgiveness. The ordinance of baptism itself is ineffective in washing away sin. The phrase following Peter's double command to repent and be baptized can be literally translated, "unto [*eis*] the forgiveness of sins." The Greek may express either result or cause. Here "unto" indicates result, not cause (Dana and Mantey, 1955, 103–5). Repentance results in the forgiveness of sins; baptism takes place because sins have been forgiven.

The New Testament does not teach that a physical act such as baptism produces a spiritual change. John the Baptist refused to baptize people until they showed that they were repentant (Matt. 3:8; Luke 3:8). Jesus taught that repentance precedes forgiveness of sins (Luke 24:47). In the Great Commission the disciples were told to make disciples of people before baptizing them (Matt. 28:18–19). And now in his sermon Peter puts repentance before baptism (Acts 2:38). Water baptism must be preceded by repentance and faith.

Sacramental theology insists upon the ordinance of baptism as the instrumental cause of salvation. An external rite such as baptism is not the objective basis for blotting out sin; only Christ's atoning death on the cross can do that. Neither can baptism mediate salvation, for the Holy Spirit is the only carrier and agent of salvation. Water can never wash away our sin; on the other hand, people who have sincerely repented of their sins must not regard water baptism as an unnecessary and valueless rite. Peter calls not only for repentance but also for baptism. From the beginning of the church's mission in Acts, baptism has its place in the preaching of the gospel and fulfills the Great Commission.

The ordinance of baptism is to be performed "in the name of Jesus Christ." This phrase may be used as a baptismal formula, but it has greater significance than that. Baptism administered in Jesus' name recognizes his authority and Lordship. By the act of water baptism believers express their faith and devotion to Jesus Christ. It serves as a sign that sins have been forgiven and as a sign of commitment to Jesus Christ as Lord. As a result of faith in Christ, the Holy Spirit renews and indwells every believer (cf. Rom. 8:9; 1 Cor. 6:19).

Peter goes on to promise those who repent and are baptized "the gift of the Holy Spirit." This promise must be understood in the context of the outpouring of the Spirit at Pentecost, which Peter and his colleagues have just experienced. The initial work of the Spirit follows repentance and issues in a new life in Christ. Peter's promise here refers to a subsequent free gift of the Spirit, fulfilling Joel's promise of charismatic, Pentecostal power. Such power equips believers to be witnesses for Christ and empowers them to do miracles (cf. 2:43). This baptism is a clothing with power; it is a gift that Jesus encourages his disciples to pray for (Luke 11:13).

Pentecostal power is promised to all believers: "for you and your children and for all who are far off" (i.e., Gentiles). Baptism in the Spirit is a potentially universal experience, as Cornelius and his household (Acts 10) and the disciples at Ephesus (19:1–7) demonstrate. The promise of a special endowment of the Spirit is not only to Peter's immediate audience, but to all who come to faith in Jesus Christ and follow him in obedience (cf. 5:32). There is no restriction of time—from generation to generation (v. 39); no social restriction—from young to old, from female to male, and from slaves to free people (vv. 17–18); no restriction of geography—from Jerusalem to the ends of the earth (1:8).

God desires that all his people have the same momentous experience that the disciples received at Pentecost. The fulfillment of his promise of the Spirit, given in the Old Testament, is not exhausted in the book of Acts as the church reaches out to the Gentiles. It remains a present, universal blessing, "for all whom the Lord our God will call," including "all who are far off."

In his sermon Peter has answered the question, "What shall we do?" The phrase "with many other words" (v. 40) indicates that Luke has only provided a summary of the sermon. Peter continues to warn, exhort, and plead with his audience to save themselves from the wicked generation to which they belong (cf. Luke 9:41). The literal meaning is "be saved" (*sothete*, a passive voice). There is a way to be delivered from the judgment that unbelievers will inevitably face, but people can do nothing to merit their own salvation. Faith and repentance is the only prescribed way to receive forgiveness of sin.

The response to Peter's message is overwhelming. About three thousand people receive his preaching as the truth. Adopting it as their rule for action, they submit to baptism and thereby give a public expression to their faith in Jesus as the anointed Savior. Now they are joined to the other believers and recognized as members of the church. The outpouring of the Spirit at Pentecost has established the disciples as a Pentecostal, charismatic community. The church enjoys impressive growth after Jesus transferred his Spirit to the disciples and Peter preached an inspired message. Through anointed preaching the Holy Spirit increases the number of believers.

3. The Acts of the Spirit-Baptized/Filled Community (2:42–6:7)

3.1. Fellowship Inaugurated: The Inner/Outer Life of the Community (2:42–47)

In addition to growth in numbers, the outpouring of the Spirit brings about other changes. There begins to emerge among the believers what may be described as a "Pentecostal lifestyle." Luke pictures the life of this community in four ways.

(1) The new converts are committed believers who devote themselves steadfastly to everything taught by the apostles. The apostles were eyewitnesses to the ministry of Jesus, and their teachings provide the foundation for the church. Jesus had commanded the apostles to teach those who became disciples (Matt. 28:19–20; cf. Luke 24:45–48). So they execute their commission to teach, and these new believers give themselves to the essential truths vital to a strong faith and abide by their teaching. Solid doctrine provides a sound basis for Christian living. "If you hold to my teaching," Christ said, "you are really my disciples" (John 8:31). This is precisely what these believers do. Knowing and trusting Jesus does not become abstract for them. They continue daily in the apostles' teaching.

(2) The believers devote themselves to "the fellowship." The word "fellowship" (*koinonia*) expresses the unity of the early church. No single English word fully translates its meaning. Fellowship involves more than a communal spirit that believers share with one another. It is a joint participation at the deepest level in the spiritual fellowship that is "in Christ." On the human side believers share with one another, but the quality of their fellowship is determined by their union with Christ. They have been called into fellowship with him and jointly participate in his saving work. Their mutual participation in him is effected by the Holy Spirit (2 Cor. 13:14), and "so it becomes a fellowship of the Holy Ghost. And where the Son and Spirit are, there is the Father, so it is a fellowship with the Father" (Rackham, 1953, 35). These first disciples are one by faith in Jesus Christ and by their fellowship with one another. They express their love and harmony. They are united in mind and heart.

(3) The new believers continue "the breaking of bread"—a phrase used only by Luke. Does it refer to ordinary fellowship meals or to the Lord's Supper? An ancient Jewish custom involved breaking a loaf of bread with the hands rather than cutting it with a knife, but the breaking of bread was also an essential feature of the celebration of the Lord's Supper. Obviously more is involved here than simply having meals together. Such a meaning would be out of place with weighty matters such as "teaching," "fellowship," and "prayer" (cf. 20:11). Luke is relating here only significant actions of the three thousand believers, so most likely the breaking of bread refers to the observance of the Lord's Supper.

Christ himself broke bread in the upper room and commanded his disciples to do likewise. After giving thanks, he broke the bread and said, "This is my body, which is for you" (1 Cor. 11:24). These words provide the basis for calling the Lord's Supper "the breaking of bread." The breaking of the loaf represents Christ's giving himself to suffering and death. As the bread and fruit of the vine are received, believers see them as signs that the spotless Lamb of God has been slain. The observance of this Supper points to Christ's death, but it also reminds us that Christ's blessings are constantly appropriated, that his strength is the source of our strength. The Holy Supper also calls us to look forward to Christ's return to the earth. It anticipates the blessings and joy of all who will participate in the marriage supper of the Lamb (Rev. 19:9).

(4) The daily devotions of these new believers include prayer. In addition to special times of prayer and praise together, they also pray in the temple (3:1). After Jesus ascended into heaven, the disciples returned to Jerusalem and made the temple a place of worship (Luke 24:51–53). They observed the Jewish hours of prayer, and before Pentecost they were united together in prayer for baptism in the Spirit (Acts 1:14). After the outpouring of the Spirit, they continue steadfastly in prayer. Thus, prayer and praise mark the life of the church in addition to the other three elements. All four elements confirm the power and the presence of the Spirit in the church.

The single-hearted devotion of the disciples does not go without notice. The miracles performed by God through the apostles and the dedication of the disciples to holy living inspire a profound reverence among the Jewish people for them (v. 43). These believers manifest a remarkable fellowship, and out of spontaneous love for God and their fellows they share their possessions in common. Rather than neglecting the poor, they voluntarily sell their "possessions and goods" to relieve the distress of those in need. There is no suggestion that they give up everything they own to a common community fund, but they do give goods to a common storehouse in order to meet specific needs in the Christian community.

The fact that Barnabas is later singled out for selling some property indicates that this practice is not something that all the believers are doing (4:36–37). The new believers are willing to share their possessions when needs arise (v. 45). The term communism does not describe this practice. Rather, they are expressing spontaneous love, and it is completely voluntary.

These humble believers meet daily in the temple. Their single-hearted devotion brings them to the house of God, a sacred place. Likely the temple is more than a meeting place for them. Their presence there implies that they participate in daily worship there (Marshall, 1980, 85). Their fellowship with one another is strong because they meet in different homes for meals. These meals are joyful occasions. The admirable lives that they are leading and the miracles that are done are visible tokens of the Spirit's power in their midst.

The Greek verbs in vv. 43–47 have the force of repeated or continuous action. That is, all the people keep on being filled with awe, the disciples keep on selling their goods as individual needs arise and keep on sharing all things in common, and God keeps on adding to their fellowship those who are being saved. Completely dedicated to Christ, they continue to praise God and worship him in the temple. They have experienced the blessings of the last days: the joy, liberty, and power of the Holy Spirit, and a profound sense of being the people of God.

The influence and respect in which the disciples are held give them an opportunity for witness. Their evangelistic efforts continue, and there are daily additions to the church. As people are forgiven of their sins, they are joined to the church. Only the forgiveness of their sins entitles them to church membership. Their fellowship continues to grow too. Day after day God continues to add to the Christian fellowship those who become believers.

3.2. Example: Confirmatory Healing (3:1–26)

This miracle of physical healing illustrates the supernatural power that the disciples received at Pentecost. It is one of the many signs and wonders mentioned in 2:43 and results in a serious conflict with the Jewish authorities.

3.2.1. Sign: Peter Raises Up a Lame Man (3:1–8). Because of the circumstances in which the miracle occurs, it attracts extraordinary attention. At three o'clock one afternoon, Peter and John son of Zebedee go to the temple. This is one of the regular times for prayer in the temple—the time for the daily evening sacrifice (Ex. 29:38–41; Num. 28:2–8). The temple has a number of gates; the gate called Beautiful must have been either the Nicanor Gate (named in honor of its donor, Nicanor of Alexandria) or the Corinthian Gate (because of its Corinthian bronze doors; see Hengel, 1983, 102–4; *TDNT*, 3:236). Apparently the gate was a favorite passageway into the temple court.

Many of the Jewish Christians continue the religious practices they observed before their conversion (vv. 1–3). Though the temple is no longer for them a place of sacrifice, since Jesus made atonement for sin "once and for all," it does remain a place of prayer. The recipient of this miraculous cure has been a cripple all his life. Cripples were not allowed to enter the temple precincts beyond the court of the Gentiles. So the crippled man is placed daily at the Beautiful Gate, where he begs from people on their way to worship. As Peter and John are about to enter the sanctuary, they come upon him, and he makes strong appeals to them for money.

Both Peter and John fix their eyes on the crippled man. Looking intensely at the beggar, Peter says, "Look at us!" The words of Peter give the crippled man encouragement, and he feels confident that these two men will give him a monetary gift. The words, "Silver or gold I do not have" are emphatic and must have been disappointing to the beggar.

But immediately this disappointment is dispelled because Peter offers the man something nly God can give—something much better, amely, healing for his body. Peter commands im "in the name of Jesus Christ" to walk. As in :38, "name" signifies the authority and power f Jesus exercised by his followers to heal the ick and lame (3:16; 4:10). As Peter speaks his vords, he takes the beggar's right hand and aises him to his feet. Immediately the miracle akes place, and his legs are made whole.

The miraculous power of healing enables ie cripple not only to stand up but also to valk. He leaps in joy, praising God (that is, eclaring how great and wonderful God is). 'his miracle is a manifestation of the power of ie Holy Spirit bestowed on the disciples by esus at Pentecost (2:33). Though Peter has no silver or gold" to give the beggar, he is able o get at the root of this man's physical need. 'he healing is done in the name of "Jesus Christ of Nazareth," which identifies the ource of Peter's power and authority.

3.2.2. Wonder: The Crowd Is Amazed 3:9–10). The healed man accompanies Peter nd John into the temple. As the people see im leaping and shouting, no one needs to ask he meaning of his conduct (vv. 9–10). They ave often seen him sitting at the temple gate nd begging, but now they all see the man eaping with childlike joy, using his whole ody to express his happiness. Twice it is noted hat he is "praising God" as he goes into the ourts of the temple.

The reaction of the people to this miracle s that of "wonder and amazement" (cf. Luke 1:36; 5:9; 7:16). The man has been lame from he time he was born, but now he has encoun-ered the power of God. The people are over-whelmed at what God has done for this unnamed beggar. This great sign confirms the ruth of Jesus' message and God's power to heal. Spiritual triumphs depend on the mani-festation of God's presence and power. They are designed to meet human needs. Luke, how-ever, gives no hint here that the people's reac-tion prompts them to have faith in Jesus' grace and power.

3.2.3. Witness: Peter Proclaims Jesus As Servant (3:11–26). Great attention generated by the miracle gives Peter the opportunity to explain that the power of Jesus has healed the man. What follows is a summary of his expla-nation of the wonderful event and his procla-mation of the gospel, which focuses on the centrality of the Cross. Like the sermon at Pen-tecost, this second sermon (vv. 12–26) has its basis in the Christian kerygma. In this sermon Peter also speaks about the second coming of Christ and the blessings associated with that event.

The healing has been done simply "in the name of Jesus Christ" (v. 6). The infirm man immediately became strong in his feet and ankles, and his every step is now a leap of childlike joy. The man clings to Peter and John. His behavior attracts a crowd of people, and he tells them that Peter and John are responsible for his healing. The people gather at Solomon's Colonnade, probably a porch that ran along the east side of the temple (cf. 5:42; John 10:23).

The admiration of the people is directed toward two apostles as though their own power has healed the man. Peter thus turns the people's thoughts in the right direction. He denies that his and John's godliness and power have made the crippled man strong. Rather, Peter is only a channel for the remarkable power of the Holy Spirit. Peter points the people to the true source of the extraordinary healing—the God of their ancestors, the God of the great patriarchs (Abraham, Isaac, and Jacob); Peter has performed the miracle through "his servant Jesus."

The word "servant" (*pais*) brings to mind Isaiah's prophecies about the Servant of the Lord, who was to redeem Israel through his suffering (Isa. 52:13–53:12). Jesus is that Suf-fering Servant. He obeyed God, and God has shown the greatness and glory of Jesus by healing the lame man. By "faith" in the name of the crucified and risen Savior the man has been made whole (Acts 3:16). Without the human response of faith in Jesus' power and authority, the man would have remained a crip-ple. Whether it is the faith of Peter and John or of the healed man is difficult to say with cer-tainty. At any rate the man is strong because of the name of Jesus Christ.

Peter then goes on to describe the enormity of the crime committed against Jesus in three ways (vv. 13b–18). (1) The people handed him over to Pilate to be killed. The governor desired to let him go, but the people and their leaders refused to release him.

(2) The people demanded that Barabbas, a murderer, be released rather than "the Holy

and Righteous One" (v. 14; cf. Luke 23:18–25). Here Peter continues the theme of the innocent Suffering Servant. Isaiah had described the Suffering Servant as the "Righteous One": "By his knowledge my righteous servant will justify many, and he will bear their iniquities" (Isa. 53:11). Like Isaiah, Peter combines the themes of suffering and innocence and identifies Jesus as that righteous one, who in no way deserved to be treated as a criminal (cf. Luke 23:47). Before Pilate the people had denied Jesus' moral uprightness.

(3) Their demands caused the Romans to crucify "the author of life" (v. 15). The word "author" (*archegos*) can have the meaning of "leader," as in a later sermon of Peter's (Acts 5:31). Here, however, "author" in the sense of "originator" or "source" fits the context (cf. Heb. 2:10; 5:9; 12:2). They put to death the very author of life itself.

The climax of their evil, however, is not what they expected—"God raised him from the dead." The triumph of Jesus over death was an action of God, and Peter declares himself and John to be witnesses to this undeniable reality. To avoid any misunderstanding, Peter emphasizes that by the power of the risen Jesus the miracle was wrought. That is, by faith in the Savior's name the lame man at the gate of the temple "was made strong." With their own eyes the crowd can see that he has been healed. This proclamation of Jesus' power should make it desirous for people to believe.

At this point Peter addresses the people as "brothers," not in the Christian sense but as a fellow countryman and as a change of tone. He has already spoken about the people's guilt in betraying and rejecting Jesus. Now Peter places the sovereignty of God and the free agency of humans side by side (cf. 2:23). He recognizes that the people and their leaders have acted out of ignorance (v. 17) and that they have failed to understand the significance of what they have done. Sin has had a blinding effect and has robbed them of the power to correctly discern their condition and acts. He points out, however, that their failure to perceive the significance of their crime does not make them innocent, for they acted willfully. Their mistreatment of Jesus did fulfill what God had foretold through his prophets about the suffering and death of Christ. The crucifixion was no accident. But neither their ignorance nor God's eternal will frees them of gui for crucifying Jesus.

Yet it is not too late for them to repent an make things right with God. Peter therefo exhorts them to turn to God (v. 19). Repe tance involves a turning away from the old li of sin and rebellion against God to the new li of faith and obedience to God. The immedia result of repentance is that their sins will b blotted out or erased. The apostle makes n mention of faith, but his command carries th assumption that they believe if they repent.

To urge them to turn from sin to faith i Christ, Peter mentions two additional benefit (1) "Times of refreshing [will] come from th Lord." For years the Jews have been expectin the messianic age, the golden age of blessing The prophets themselves spoke about the com ing of spiritual strength and blessings. Thi new age has dawned with the coming c Christ. Peter's "times of refreshing" is one wa of speaking about the baptism in the Spirit. Th people can now experience the renewal o "refreshing" of their souls through the joys an the power of the Holy Spirit. As a result of thei repentance, not only will their sin be forgive and they will receive relief from their guilt, bu they will also experience spiritual renewa through the Holy Spirit.

(2) The second benefit of turning from si to Christ is the return of Jesus from heave (vv. 20–21). God appointed Jesus beforehan to be the Messiah of the Jews. Peter remind his hearers that as Jesus taught, his secon coming will not take place immediately. A period of time must lapse before his return t this earth. Until that day Jesus makes his hom in heaven. But when he comes again, God wil "restore everything, as he promised long ag through his holy prophets." Then will tak place the fullness of renewal—the restoratio of all things.

Through his prophets God announced his promise to restore the original order of creation (Isa. 11:6–8; 35:1–10; 65:17–25). As a result of Adam's sin in Eden, creation was subjected to disorder, decay, and death. But at the return of Christ all things will be brought under his lordship, and the physical world will be brought back to its original and perfect order. Christ will redeem the world order and set it free from the curse of Adam. Creation will be restored to the beauty, fruitfulness, order, and unity that existed before the Fall (Matt. 19:28; Rom. 8:19–23; 2 Peter 3:13; Rev. 21:5).

Peter has warned the people against rejecting the matters of which he is speaking (vv. 13–18) and has urged them to repent and believe on Jesus. Now he cites the well-known prophecy of Moses, in which the Lord promised that the coming Messiah would be a prophet like Moses (Deut. 18:15–19; cf. Num. 11:29). Moses is distinguished from all the other prophets in that he was a deliverer and ruler over God's people. Like him Jesus is both a deliverer and ruler, but his deliverance is far more glorious, and his lordship will be absolute at his return: "Anyone who does not listen to him will be completely cut off from among his people" (v. 23). He is more than a Spirit-anointed prophet; he is the promised Messiah, the risen, glorified Savior.

Other prophets of the Old Testament also spoke about the Savior (v. 24). Several of them had predicted "these days" discussed in Acts and the important events in the ministry of Jesus. Beginning with Samuel, many of the prophets included in their message an element of future hope. Peter has already cited a number of their predictions, all of which find their ultimate and final fulfillment in Jesus Christ.

Peter makes a final appeal to the hearers as "heirs of the prophets." They should expect the prophetic promises to be fulfilled and that they will be personally blessed by their fulfillment. They are also heirs "of the covenant God made with your fathers." God made this covenant first with Abraham, and through the covenant he promised blessings not only to Abraham's descendants but also to "all peoples on earth" (v. 25; cf. Gen. 12:3; 22:18). In reminding the people of the blessings promised to Abraham, Peter suggests that these blessings are offered in Christ, the true offspring of Abraham. The blessings are so great that they embrace all nations and peoples. God sent the risen Savior first to bless Israel because of their relationship to the prophets and to Abraham. For this reason the gospel was first preached to the Jews. As God's people they have the opportunity of being blessed before the rest of humanity.

Those listening to Peter have seen the promises of the prophets fulfilled in the life and ministry of Jesus. The very blessings promised to Abraham can now be received by any who turn from their wicked ways (v. 26). The sole purpose of the first coming of Jesus is that people may repent of their sins and receive the promised blessing of salvation. Such a blessing enables them to depart from the ways of sin and to be renewed by the Holy Spirit and empowered for service.

3.3. Opposition (4:1–5:42)

Chapter 4 tells about the first persecution of the church. The healing of the lame man and Peter's second sermon make a favorable impression upon the people. News of the healing spreads throughout the entire city of Jerusalem. The miracle along with Peter's appeal (3:12–16) arouse the opposition of the Jewish leaders, especially the Sadducees. They arrest Peter and John and bring them before the Sanhedrin.

Immediately following the discussion of this external problem, chapter 5 records an internal problem within the Christian community, the selfishness of Ananias and Sapphira (vv. 1–11). After the exposure and punishment of this couple, the apostles perform a great number of miracles. Those miracles and the increase in the number of believers prompt the Sadducees to have all the apostles arrested and put on trial before the Sanhedrin (vv. 12–42). Yet despite opposition, the church continues to preach the gospel and keeps on growing.

3.3.1. Priests–Sadducees Arrest Peter and John (4:1–22). Earlier the Sadducees had opposed Jesus (Luke 20:27–40). Taking the lead against the apostles, these Jewish leaders are now responsible for the arrest of Peter and John (see also 5:17; 23:6–10).

The theological and political differences between the Sadducees and the Pharisees are well known. Contrary to the Pharisees, the Sadducees did not believe in the resurrection, angels, and spirits (Luke 20:27; Acts 23:8). They were not an official body as were the priests, but they were a priestly, aristocratic party, to which the high priestly families belonged. As representatives of the official theology of the temple, they rejected oral tradition and adhered only to the written law. Politically, they sympathized with Rome, supporting the status quo since it ensured them of remaining in power. Their hostility toward the Christians shows that they are bitter opponents of the church (cf. *TDNT*, 7:35–54).

3.3.1.1. Peter and John Are Arrested (4:1–4). The first outbreak of persecution against the church comes from the temple authorities in charge of the area of the temple where the lame man was healed and the people had gathered. As Peter and John are speaking, the "captain of the temple guard," accompanied by temple priests and Sadducees, approach them. Being next in authority to the high priest, the captain of the temple guard was responsible for good order in the temple (5:24, 26).

The healing miracle has attracted a lot of attention. The authorities are particularly opposed to the apostles' "proclaiming in Jesus the resurrection of the dead" (i.e., Jesus' triumph over death). The issue at hand here is the resurrection of Jesus, not the general resurrection. His victory over death is, however, the basis of the resurrection of all believers. The apostles' preaching of Jesus' resurrection strongly implies that people in general will rise from the dead. Since the resurrection is directly contrary to the doctrine of the Sadducees, they will not tolerate the claims of Peter and John. Their response here implies that at this time all temple politics and theology were controlled by them.

Until this incident the ministry of these apostles has been without interruption, but now they are abruptly seized by the temple authorities. Because it is already evening, the authorities put them in prison until the next day (v. 3). The arrest of the disciples must have created great excitement among many of the believers, who are possibly reminded of similar scenes that led to the death of Jesus.

Nevertheless, empowered by the Spirit, Peter and John's preaching of the good news of salvation has had a decided effect. Because of the healing of the lame man and Peter's Spirit-baptized preaching, many believe the message of salvation. Thus, in spite of opposition, the church continues to grow. On the day of Pentecost three thousand accepted the gospel, but now the church has increased to about five thousand men. This present attack on the apostles does not keep the church from growing. The increase of believers since the outpouring of the Spirit shows that the church has been growing daily (2:47) and that opposition does not hinder evangelism.

3.3.1.2. Pneuma Discourse: Peter Addresses the Sanhedrin (4:5–12). The Sanhedrin meets the next morning in order to decide what should be done with Peter and John. This body of seventy-one men was the highest political and religious court of the Jews. It was composed of "rulers" (sometimes called chief priests), "elders" (laymen who represented experience and who were the heads of aristocratic families), and "teachers of the law" (the official interpreters of the law, many of whom belonged to the party of the Pharisees).

Among those in the Sanhedrin is Annas, who served as high priest from A.D. 6 to 15. Once a man had been the high priest he retained that title for the rest of his life. Despite the fact that Annas was deposed by the Romans, he was still recognized as a high priest (Luke 3:2) and had great influence. The official high priest is Caiaphas (A.D. 18–36), the son-in-law of Annas. Nothing is known of John and Alexander, also members of the Sanhedrin, except that they are men of great authority. Others present at the meeting are "men of the high priest's family," who hold various positions in temple administration.

The official high priest, Caiaphas, presides at the meeting. When the Sanhedrin assembles, Peter and John are brought in. The healed man is also present. The Sanhedrin asks the two disciples by what authority or in whose name they have healed the cripple.

The question provides Peter an opportunity to present the gospel. The apostles had witnessed about the gospel before Pentecost when Jesus sent them on a preaching tour (Luke 9:1–9), but after Pentecost there is a new power and quality in their preaching. What Jesus had promised them is now fulfilled in the Pentecostal experience (12:11–12; 21:12–19; 24:49). Having been filled with the Spirit, Peter, who earlier denied his Lord three times (22:54–62), stands before the authorities with boldness. His powerful message reflects his strong convictions and parallels the sermon at Pentecost.

Peter declares that the man has been healed by power in the name of the crucified, risen Jesus Christ of Nazareth. Realizing that the Jewish leaders cannot deny the miracle with the man standing before them, Peter goes on to speak about Jesus' death and resurrection, pointing to Psalm 118:22 for evidence. The Crucified One is the One the builders (i.e., the leaders of the Jews) rejected, but in raising him from the dead, God made him the capstone. The stone that the builders thought was no good has become the most important stone. Exalted into heaven, Jesus is now indispensable to the foundation of God's building. "Salvation is found in no one else, for there is no other name under heaven given to men by which we must be saved" (v. 12).

Both the noun "salvation" and the verb "saved" (cf. v. 9) can have a double meaning. They can refer to physical healing, but also to deliverance from sin and the final judgment. In his declaration Peter claims that no one but Jesus can offer people salvation in the fullest sense. Only in the rejected but now exalted Jesus can salvation be found—not merely deliverance from physical affliction, as the man at the Beautiful Gate experienced, but also deliverance from bondage to sin and from condemnation. There is no salvation for anyone except in the name of Jesus, whom they crucified. The gospel demands faith in Jesus and obedience to him.

3.3.1.3. Response: The Sanhedrin Forbids Peter and John to Preach (4:13–22). Empowered by the Holy Spirit, Peter has preached Jesus. The members of the Sanhedrin are amazed at these two simple Galilean fishermen (vv. 13–14). They recognize that Peter and John have not had any special education in theology and rhetoric, nor have they had formal training in the Jewish law. Yet these two men, inspired by the Holy Spirit, have boldness and courage before their judges. The Holy Spirit has enabled them to speak freely and with confidence. The Council rightly recalls "that these men had been with Jesus." They were followers of Jesus, and his character has left its marks on them. The renewing grace of God and anointing of the Spirit have made Jesus visible in their lives.

When Peter and John were asked by the Sanhedrin what power they had used to heal a crippled beggar, Peter said it was by the name of Jesus, "the stone you builders rejected, which has become the capstone." This huge lintel stone supports a wall of Nimrod, a thirteenth-century Syrian fortress in the Golan, built in the time of the Crusades.

At the close of Peter's sermon there is total silence—"There was nothing they could say" (v. 14). None of them can contradict anything that has been said. So what can they do? The man who has been healed stands there with Peter and John. The Council is in a quandary.

The silence is broken by the proposal that the prisoners be removed from the chamber of the Council. The extraordinary miracle is known throughout Jerusalem (v. 16). In their deliberations the Sanhedrin decides to place a ban on any preaching about Jesus. How Luke learns about the particulars of the Council's discussion we are not told, but later "a large number of priests became obedient to the faith" (6:7). It is possible that some in this group shared the details of the proceedings.

As soon as this solution is adopted, the Sanhedrin summons the apostles back and issues a stern warning against their speaking about Jesus in any circumstances, whether public or private. This is the best the Jewish court can do, for they have not broken any law.

As servants of the gospel Peter and John know that they will not obey this command for silence, and they tell the court that they cannot do so. The important issue is to whom they owe their obedience. Should they obey God or the command of a human institution? For the apostles, where there is conflict between these two, God must always be obeyed rather than human beings. They have been called by God and empowered by the Holy Spirit to preach the gospel. Not for a moment will they stop talking about what they "have seen and heard" (v. 20). They have been eyewitnesses to the ministry of Jesus and are duty bound to continue to bear witness to his deeds and teaching, especially to his resurrection. The deliverance of the lame man testifies that Jesus is still alive and healing people. No one can prevent the apostles from preaching what they know to be true. They are willing to die for the gospel.

The Sanhedrin can do little about such defiance. The people enthusiastically have accepted the miraculous cure of a man who had been lame for over forty years, and they praise God for this great sign. With the desire to conciliate the people and perhaps afraid of these apostles through whom God has worked the miracle, the Jewish court restrains its anger. Because the authorities have no legal grounds to arrest Peter and John, their only recourse is to let them go. Before doing so, however, they repeat their threats of what will happen if they appear before the court again.

3.3.2. Theophany: The Community Is Filled With the Spirit (4:23–31). After the release of the apostles, the focus falls on prayer by the believers and on the answer to that prayer, that they be refilled with the Spirit. Peter and John go to a large group of fellow Christians, probably at the temple, and inform them about the threats of the Jewish authorities. The immediate reaction is to join "together" (v. 24) in prayer. These Christians are united in the Spirit as they worship God (cf. 1:14; 2:44). Their minds and hearts are one as they pray to the Creator. They move as one body, in unity in Christ.

Of all the prayers recorded in Luke-Acts, this one is the longest. It reminds us of Old Testament prayers such as 2 Kings 19:15–19 and Isaiah 37:15–20. The prayer is worthy of study and imitation. (1) These believers begin by recognizing God as "Sovereign Lord." They recall his mighty power in creation and are confident that he controls everything in earth and heaven.

(2) They refer to a prophecy that the sovereign Lord gave through David under the inspiration of the Holy Spirit (Ps. 2:1–2), and they apply it to the suffering of Jesus (cf. also 13:33; Heb. 1:5; 5:5). Long ago David had predicted the persecution of Christ by his enemies. Jesus did suffer at the hands of "the nations" (Romans), the people of Israel, and the rulers (who included Herod and Pilate). The Jews plotted against God's Anointed One. Even though Pilate found him innocent three times (Luke 23:4, 14, 22), he still turned him over to be crucified. Like David Jesus is described as God's "servant" (Acts 4:27), but the description of him as "holy servant" emphasizes his innocent suffering as the Suffering Servant of Isaiah 53 (cf. Acts 3:14).

At his baptism Jesus was anointed by the Spirit as the Messiah (Luke 3:22; cf. 4:1). The plotting of his adversaries against the Spirit-anointed Savior was under God's sovereignty (Acts 4:28). What the authorities did to him in condemning him was in full accordance with God's purpose. The sovereign Lord remained in control and used the free but evil deeds of human beings to accomplish salvation. His ruling hand should reassure his people in the face of persecution; like Jesus they can expect to be vindicated by their Lord.

(3) The believers call attention to their present circumstances (vv. 29–30), with the threats made against them (*TDNT*, 4:1122). The church finds itself in a difficult situation. The believers are not in danger of losing political power or privileges but something far more precious—their freedom, even their lives. But rather than pray for deliverance from danger, they ask for boldness to preach the "word." God's word is the message of Jesus Christ and God's saving work in him. The word "boldness" (*parresia*) refers to courage and freedom of speech that results from being empowered by the Spirit (cf. Luke 21:15). The believers want to be inspired by the Holy Spirit so that they will have the courage to boldly present the message of salvation without any regard for the threats of their enemies.

At the same time these believers are aware that signs and wonders aid the preached word. So they also ask that God act directly and by his own hand heal the sick and perform miracles by the power of Jesus. It becomes clear why the Sanhedrin's orders against mighty deeds are ineffective: They are trying to stop God's own work. The disciples' witness to the gospel cannot be suppressed, nor can the signs and wonders that attest divine approval of their ministry.

(4) God answers their prayer (v. 31). He gives them a visible sign of his presence: the place (*topos*) where they are meeting is shaken. Luke does not identify the place where they have gathered, but the evidence points to the temple mount, which would have accommodated a gathering of thousands. There are other examples in Scripture of pivotal events that probably occurred on the temple mount. After Christ's ascension into heaven, the disciples "stayed continually at the temple, praising God" (Luke 24:53). After the day of Pentecost Peter and John went into the temple to pray (Acts 3:1). A little later the disciples "meet

together in Solomon's Colonnade" (5:12), and they continue to meet daily in the temple courts (5:42). Both in Acts 4:31 and 6:13–14 "place" (*topos*) refers to the temple mount.

In other words, the way Luke uses the term "place" confirms that the large group of disciples are gathered at the temple when they experience a great theophany—the shaking of the temple mount (cf. Ex. 19:18; 1 Kings 19:11). This external manifestation of God's power reassures the believers that the sovereign Lord is still with them. God has heard them pray for the boldness needed to bear witness to the gospel as well as for signs and wonders.

The believers also experience an internal filling with the Spirit. These believers, including Peter and John, already received their initial filling with the Spirit at Pentecost (2:4). But Scripture teaches that to be filled with the Spirit is not a once-for-all experience. A person already filled with the Spirit may receive a fresh filling, especially when particular needs and challenges arise. The repetitive character of this experience is demonstrated by the fresh filling of Peter, John, and other Christians as they pray.

According to our Western understanding something full cannot be filled more, but from the standpoint of the Bible a Spirit-filled believer can receive additional fillings with the Spirit. These new fillings give the disciples extraordinary spiritual power needed to face the threats of the authorities. With boldness and great power, they continue to speak the word of God and to bear witness about the resurrection of Jesus (Acts 4:33).

Jesus promised that the heavenly Father would fill his children who ask him for the Spirit (Luke 11:13). Therefore, God does not fail to answer the prayer of the believers in Acts 4. This prayer is a model for Luke's readers and for us. The church must faithfully proclaim the message of salvation; through prayer God guides the course of events in history.

3.3.3. The Spirit-Baptized Community Practices Fellowship (4:32–5:16). After the account of the first arrest of the apostles, Luke turns attention once again to the internal condition of the church (cf. 2:42–47). The unity of the believers and their sharing of possessions with the needy show the continuing presence of the Holy Spirit. This passage also introduces Barnabas. This man's spirit of generosity places him in contrast to the conduct of Ananias and Sapphira. The exposure of the deception of this couple, the fellowship the disciples have, and the powerful proclamation of Christ's resurrection are the results of the Spirit's presence. The generosity of Barnabas and the incident of Ananias and Sapphira also show the proper and the improper use of possessions.

3.3.3.1. Property Is Sold and Distributed (4:32–35). Unity and generosity prevail among the believers (cf. the expression "one heart and mind"). In Jewish thought "heart" (*kardia*) is not only the center of affections but also of intellectual thought, and "mind" (*psyche*; lit., "soul") is the seat of life and will. A hard and fast distinction between the two words is impossible. So "heart and mind" refers to the center of personality that determines a person's conduct. Despite their large numbers, therefore, the believers remain united in purpose and in devotion to their Lord. No divisions, no schisms, and no dissensions exist among them. These believers are also willing to use some of their possessions to relieve the needs of others. Brotherly love created by the Holy Spirit prompts them to consider the welfare of the needy among them.

It is significant that the word "power" is described as "great" (v. 33), indicating the manifestation of God's power in signs and wonders. Miracles accompany and confirm the apostles' preaching of the resurrection of Christ, just as miracles accompanied the ministry of Jesus. At the same time God pours out "much grace" on the community of believers (v. 33), meaning that they are showered with rich blessings. The evidence of divine grace is seen both in the preaching and the relief of material needs of the poor.

The Old Testament ideal that there should be no poor among the Israelites (Deut. 15:4) is realized in the church through the members' generosity with their wealth. As needs arise from time to time, those who are better off sell some property and bring the proceeds to the apostles. The phrase "at the apostles' feet" (v. 35; 5:2) indicates that the apostles are sitting and perhaps teaching. The phrase also points to their authority, for as the money is turned over to them, they serve as the administrative authorities for its distribution to each person according to need.

3.3.3.2. Positive Example: Barnabas (4:36–37). Luke introduces Joseph, who is called Barnabas by the apostles, and singles him out as a prime example of the fellowship that exists through the generous sharing of property and possessions. "Barnabas" conceivably means "son of a prophet" or "son of Nebo" (a god). Why Luke interprets "Barnabas" to mean "Son of Encouragement" is not clear. It may be a second name and reflects the notion that he has the spiritual gift of encouraging his fellow Christians. This man certainly gives encouragement (9:27; 11:23; 15:37).

A native of Cyprus, Barnabas may have moved to Jerusalem when he was a young man. He belonged to the tribe of Levi. In New Testament times the Levites were an order of temple officials, but Luke gives no indication whether Barnabas had any function in the Jerusalem temple (cf. *TDNT*, 4:239–41). The law of Moses did not make provision for Levites to be landowners (Num. 18:20; Deut. 10:9), but no particular law prevented them from acquiring land. Whether the tract of land owned by Barnabas was in Palestine or Cyprus is unknown, but this excellent man voluntarily gives the proceeds from his land to the Christian community. From this fund the apostles distribute assistance to the needy. As far as we know, such distribution remained in the first century a practice of the local church in Jerusalem.

The "community of goods fund" does not provide support for an argument against private ownership. No such practice became universal or compulsory in the first-century church. What prompted the generosity of the early believers is hard to say. It may have been a new worldview, in which they had a deep sense of accountability to God for the way they used their possessions.

3.3.3.3. Negative Example: Ananias and Sapphira (5:1–11). Every noble virtue in the human character has its counterfeits. Ananias and Sapphira are negative examples of fellowship and stand in bold contrast to the generosity of Barnabas. They too sell a piece of land, but unlike Barnabas this married couple keeps some of the proceeds for themselves while pretending to give all the money to the church. This account of their greed and hypocrisy is similar to the Old Testament story of Achan (Josh. 7:16–26).

Ananias and his wife feel confident that they can deceive the apostles and the whole church. They have the freedom to do whatever they want with the money from the sale. They claim to give all the proceeds and lay it at the apostles' feet, but Ananias keeps "back part of the money for himself" (v. 2). His deception is detected at once. Under the prophetic inspiration of the Spirit, Peter exposes his falsehood. Ananias is not only lying to the church and its leaders, but also to the Holy Spirit present in the community of believers.

In contrast to Jesus and his disciples, who are full of the Spirit (Luke 4:1; Acts 2:4), Ananias is filled with Satan. Yielding to Satan, he lies to the Holy Spirit, which is identical with lying to God (vv. 3–4). This story points to the relationship of the triune God to the church. This couple has lied to the Holy Spirit and God and put to test the Spirit of the Lord Jesus. The holy Trinity—Father, Son, and Holy Spirit—are active in the life of the Christian community.

The presence of the Holy Spirit in the church is not a temporary thing. He has brought the church into existence by his life-giving power, and he exercises constant oversight over the community of believers. By the authority of the Spirit, Peter thus rebukes Ananias: "What made you think of doing such a thing?" (v. 4). The entire passage portrays Peter as someone who knows. His knowledge of Ananias's attempt at deception is not the result of human insight but insight imparted by the Holy Spirit.

Peter's recognition of the hypocrisy of Ananias and Sapphira is an example of "the message [*logos*, word] of knowledge" (1 Cor. 12:8). The Spirit-anointed Jesus exercised this spiritual gift while on earth. Without being told by anyone, he knew the name, character, and the prior location of Nathanael (John 1:44–49; cf. 4:39). Similarly, Peter is thus able to unmask Ananias as a liar. In questioning him, Peter does not expect answers, for his questions are really declarative statements. As soon as he stops speaking, the heinousness of Ananias's sin becomes apparent. By divine power he is smitten with instant death. The sins of dishonesty and hypocrisy are always serious. It is no small matter to sin against the Holy Spirit.

Three hours after the sudden death of her husband and his burial, Sapphira arrives. No word about the fate of her husband has reached her ears. She has collaborated fully with Anaias and is prepared to act out the part agreed n between them (v. 2). Peter begins with an mperative and a question: "Tell me, is this the rice you and Ananias got for the land?" (v. 8). Ier answer reflects her total agreement with Ananias. Her reply only condemns herself.

In his second question Peter asks Sapphira, How could you agree to test the Spirit of the ord?" (v. 9). By their mutual agreement Anaias and Sapphira have shared totally not only 1 the decision but also in the guilt of their sin. 'hey are guilty of testing "the Spirit of the ord," thinking that they could get away with ieir deception. In verse 4 Ananias has lied to iod, but here Peter charges the couple with utting the Spirit of the Lord to the test.

The phrase "Spirit of the Lord" does not ccur frequently in Luke-Acts. Jesus speaks of ie Spirit of the Lord as being upon him (Luke :18). In this passage "Lord" refers to God ince Jesus is the recipient of the Spirit's nointing (cf. Acts 8:39). There are good reaons, however, for understanding "Lord" in cts 5:9 as referring to Jesus. (1) Verses 1–11 how the triune God at work in the church. 2) At Pentecost Peter declares that God has iade the crucified Jesus "both Lord and 'hrist" (2:36). (3) The apostles "testify to the esurrection of the Lord Jesus" (4:33). (4) The Ioly Spirit is later referred to as "the Spirit of esus" (16:6–7). The Holy Spirit was proment in Jesus' earthly ministry, and through the xalted Lord the Holy Spirit is poured out to quip the church for ministry (2:33).

The same verb (*peirazo*) that expressed the mptation of Jesus in the desert is used by 'eter for Ananias and Sapphira's testing of the pirit of the Lord. Both accounts deal with aving integrity before God and involve an ncounter with Satan.

Upon Sapphira's affirming her husband's e, Peter knows what is about to take place. nmediately he issues a solemn prophetic roclamation: "Look! The feet of the men who uried your husband are at the door, and they 'ill carry you out also" (v. 9). This prophecy s spoken directly to her and has her death writn all over it. At once she collapses at the feet f Peter. The same young men who had buried er husband find her dead, and they bury her eside Ananias.

Peter carries no fault for the deaths of either nanias or Sapphira. Those deaths are the result of God's direct intervention. Neither an apostle nor the whole Christian community has received power to kill someone. The end of Ananias and Sapphira is tragic. As they were united together in deception, so now they are together in death and the graveyard.

What prompted Ananias and Sapphira to allow Satan to enter their hearts and fall into the deceitful use of possessions? At least two unholy desires seem to have motivated their hypocrisy. (1) The first is love of money. They were governed by a passion for money. Like Achan, Ananias kept "back part of the money for himself," and his wife had full knowledge of this. At the same time, they pretended to give it all to God. Their conduct reminds us of those who hear the word of God, "but as they go on their way they are choked by life's worries, riches and pleasures" (Luke 8:14). A number of sins and failures recorded in Acts illustrate the love of money or the trust in its power (Acts 1:18; 8:18; 16:16–19; 19:23–41).

(2) The second unholy desire motivating Ananias and Sapphira's deception is the love of praise. They desired to have praise, such as was bestowed on Barnabas. The Greek verb translated "got" (*apedosthe*, v. 8) means "you sold for your own interest" (Robertson, 1934, 810). The action of Barnabas was based on sincerity, but theirs on hypocrisy, because they acted out of self-interest. They wanted to be admired and to hear words of praise and commendation from the followers of Christ. Selling their land was motivated by the desire to gain a reputation for generosity rather than by a genuine concern for the needy among them.

In verse 11 the term "church" (*ekklesia*) appears for the first time in Luke-Acts. Here this word is a technical term used to describe the Christian community in Jerusalem—the community of the redeemed. Throughout history the church can be identified as the people of God (Ex. 19:5–6; Ps. 22:22). The disciples who gathered around Jesus during his earthly ministry were the church, so that one should not assume that the church has just come into existence in Acts 5:11. Those who heard Jesus during his public ministry and responded were the "little flock" to whom the Father was pleased to give the kingdom (Luke 12:32). This flock was his church and was to be the kingdom's heralds (9:60; 10:9). Even before Pentecost Jesus sent the disciples to undertake missionary work (9:1–6; 10:1–16), affirming that they were in fact the church. As redeemed people, they took up the church's mission to the world prior to Jesus' death and resurrection.

On the day of Pentecost the 120 believers became a Spirit-anointed community of prophets. Before that day ended the number grew to about three thousand (Acts 2:41). As the apostles continued their witness in Jerusalem the number of believers swelled to about five thousand (4:4). After such growth Luke ceases to count and speaks of the believers simply as "the multitude" (*to plethos*). Finally, he identifies them as "the church" (5:11).

The word *ekklesia* first appears in the Bible in reference to the nation of Israel (Deut. 4:10; 9:10; 18:16 LXX). At this point the growing number of Spirit-filled prophets had achieved the theological status of a nation, even though they had not achieved such a status geographically or through their numbers. The prophet Joel had promised a general outpouring of the prophetic Spirit on the nation of Israel (Stronstad, unpublished material). Now in Acts this outpouring of the Spirit on "all flesh" is being worked out in the experience of the Spirit-anointed community of believers. The fatal mistake of Ananias and Sapphira is that they failed to recognize that the church is a Spirit-filled community and that deceiving the church is, therefore, tantamount to deceiving the Holy Spirit.

As a result of God's punishment on the couple, "great fear" comes on the whole church and everyone who hears about the event (vv. 5, 11). These two deaths warn against the love of money and unholy desires for recognition. Even unbelievers who hear about the incident tremble at the thought of the removal of the two impostors from the church.

But the primary interest for Luke in recounting this story is not to strike fear in the human heart, but to teach that the Holy Spirit is active in the church. Victory over these two individuals is more a victory over Satan than over a couple of impostors. God assures the church that they will enjoy and benefit from the presence and power of the Spirit. The Holy Spirit protects the church's integrity and guards it against such divisive sin as that of Ananias and Sapphira. This account, therefore, offers encouragement to Luke's readers and to Christians today.

3.3.3.4. Summary: Apostles Perform Signs and Wonders (5:12–16). This summary of the church's situation is similar to 2:43–47 where Luke emphasizes the apostles' magnificent ministry of signs and wonders, the awesome respect of the people for God's presence and the harmony and unity of the Christians. Here in chapter 5 he covers more fully the effects of the exposure and punishment of Ananias and Sapphira: a great number of signs and wonders, a greater reverence felt by the people and conversion of more people.

God continues to answer the prayer of 4:29–30 for power to preach the gospel with boldness and for the preached word to be accompanied by signs and wonders. The apostles continue their powerful ministry in Solomon's Colonnade, a large portico of the temple (cf. 3:11), and make a deep impression on the people.

Nevertheless, a paradoxical situation develops: "No one else dared join them, even though they were highly regarded by the people" (v. 13). Apparently unbelievers keep themselves at a distance from the Christians because of fear resulting from the deaths of Ananias and Sapphira. They may have been frightened by the possibility that half-hearted commitment could also lead to their judgment. At the same time, these people have high respect for this new community, knowing that the conduct of Ananias and Sapphira has not been tolerated by the church. They can only praise them for their commitment to holy living.

In spite of this hesitancy, those men and women who earnestly desire salvation are saved and become members of the church (v. 14). Here the Greek may mean either that the new converts believe in the Lord (cf. NIV) or that they are added to the Lord. In any case an increasing number of converts make the church their spiritual home. News of what is happening spreads throughout Jerusalem and even to "towns around Jerusalem" (v. 16). As a result, the reputation of the Christians grows and more people bring the sick and those troubled by demons for deliverance. They place the sick in the streets, believing that healing power works through the apostles.

Again the focus of attention is on the apostles' leader, Peter, whose shadow serves as the medium of healing power. The placing of the sick so that the shadow of Peter can fall on

em must not be passed off as popular super-
ition, especially in light of the fact that "all
' them were healed" (v. 16). In Luke 1:35 and
34 "overshadow" refers to God's presence
d power. The healings through Peter's
adow are similar to the healing power of
sus' clothing (Mark 6:56) and cloths touched
Paul (Acts 19:12). Again, God's power
ves those who believe the gospel, heals the
ck, and sets free those with demons.

3.3.4. Priests–Sadducees Arrest All the postles (5:17–42). Earlier the religious thorities commanded Peter and John to stop oclaiming the good news about Jesus (4:18). ut Peter and John and the other apostles never op preaching and healing the sick in the name ' the Savior. Once again their many successes ouse the hostility of the religious leaders.

3.3.4.1. The Apostles Are Arrested and eleased by an Angel (5:17–25). Most of the position comes from "the party of the Sad- icees" and is driven by the jealousy of the iief priests, of whom Caiaphas is leader (4:6). he disciples are filled with the Spirit, but the dducees are "filled with jealousy" and have ecome the real foes of the church. They are ow more determined than ever to stop the read of this new movement in Jerusalem. As result, they arrest all the leaders of the church d put them in jail overnight. Caiaphas plans have them brought before the Sanhedrin the ext day.

Their arrest and imprisonment do not come a surprise to the apostles. They know that e Sanhedrin is controlled by men who are kely to carry out their threats. What happens uring the night, however, must come as a reat surprise to the apostles and to all rusalem. Before daybreak the angel of the ord delivers them from prison. In the Old estament this angel acted as an agent for God :30, 38). In the New Testament he brings nportant messages (Luke 1:11; 2:9; Acts :26) and performs miracles (Acts 12:8–11, 3). On this occasion the angel miraculously ts the apostles free from prison so that they n continue their Spirit-inspired ministry.

Contrary to the command of the Sanhedrin :18), the angel instructs the apostles to return the temple and to teach "the full message of is new life" (v. 20). The phrase "this new life" fers to the life initiated by the death and res- rrection of Jesus. The apostles obey the angel's command and once again preach the message of salvation that leads to the Christian life. Ironically, the apostles are miraculously set free by an angel, whose existence is denied by these adversaries (see comments on 4:1).

Early the next morning Caiaphas and his associates call a full meeting of the Sanhedrin. The temple guards are then sent to get the prisoners, but they find the prison empty (v. 22); all twelve have vanished. When the authorities hear of the disappearance of the apostles, they are distressed and feel helpless, not knowing what will "come of this" (v. 24); they do not know what to do or say. Some of them, such as Gamaliel (cf. 5:34–40), may have considered that the supernatural was at work, especially since miracles had been performed through the hands of the apostles. Later a messenger informs them that the apostles are in the temple. As the angel had instructed, they are telling the people about "this new life" of salvation provided in Jesus Christ. This miracle of deliverance demonstrates that the gospel cannot be stopped by bonds or prisons (cf. 12:6–11; 16:26–27). God is able to open prison doors and set his people free.

3.3.4.2. The Apostles Are Rearrested and Peter Addresses the Sanhedrin (5:26–32). When news comes that the apostles are in the temple, the temple guards go at once to the escaped prisoners and arrest them. Their rearrest is peaceable, indicating that the authorities recognize that the apostles are popular and that the use of force may result in a violent reaction from the people. The apostles are brought before the Sanhedrin. Caiaphas repeats the earlier injunction "not to teach in this name" (4:18), but he also introduces a new theme: the apostles' attempt to make the Jewish council "guilty of this man's blood" (v. 28).

The high priest avoids mentioning the name of Jesus. The Jewish leaders are aware that they are accused directly of murdering the Messiah (2:23; 3:14–15). This charge is a sensitive point. God has vindicated the claims of Jesus by raising him from the dead and has implicated the Jewish authorities in the crime of shedding innocent blood. Now the Jewish leaders find themselves branded as murderers, and the Christians are in effect publicly calling for God to judge them for their crime. Caiaphas fears that the Christians may seek to avenge Jesus' death.

The disciples have prayed for Spirit-inspired boldness to speak the word (4:29); God continues to answer their prayer. As the spokesman for the apostles, Peter speaks boldly to the Sanhedrin's charge of disobedience: "We must obey God rather than men!" (5:29). This moral obligation assumes the divine command of the angel that set them free, as well as the commission of Christ to preach the gospel to the ends of the earth (Luke 24:45–49; Acts 1:8). Peter concedes that the apostles are guilty of disobeying the Sanhedrin. But God's authority is above that of human beings. With great candor Peter goes on to stress that the Jewish leaders are personally responsible for the death of Jesus—they have shed innocent blood.

In his speech, Peter uses three of the major elements normally emphasized in early Christian preaching (i.e., the kerygma). (1) Christ's death—"whom you had killed by hanging him on a tree." Peter again reminds the religious leaders that they are responsible for killing Jesus by crucifixion. They could offer Jesus no greater insult than to crucify him. Here the death of Christ is described in terms of Deuteronomy 21:23 (cf. Acts 10:39; 13:27, 29; Gal. 3:13), which refers to the Jewish practice of hanging the corpse of a criminal after execution on a beam and thereby declaring it to be cursed. The expression "hanging him on a tree" applies to the crucifixion of Christ and emphasizes the shame of his death. Any person impaled on a cross was deemed cursed by God. Thus, the religious authorities inflicted on Jesus the death of a criminal. But he did not die under the curse of God, as some no doubt thought. His death was a vicarious atonement for sin. Christ has purchased the church with his own blood (see 20:28; cf. 1 Peter 1:18–19).

(2) Christ's resurrection—"The God of our fathers raised Jesus from the dead." The person whom the authorities crucified is the one whom the God of their ancestors restored to life. What the Jewish leaders did to Jesus was an act against God; but despite their violent rejection of Jesus, God by his mighty hand raised him from the dead. No wedge is driven between the death and resurrection of Christ in early Christian preaching. Biblical writers regard his cross and triumph over death as vital components of redemption (cf. Rom. 4:24; 1 Cor. 15:3–5). Eternal life is rooted and grounded in his humiliation and exaltatio Earlier in Acts, Jesus was identified as "th author of life," whom God raised from th dead (3:15). He has been divinely appointe and empowered by the Spirit to be the Savio of the world. Since Jesus is the author of life his resurrection is a pledge to all believers tha they will share in his triumph over death.

(3) Christ's ascension—"God exalted him t his own right hand as Prince and Savior." Go exalted the crucified Jesus not only by raisin him from the dead but also by enthroning hi in heaven. Being exalted to sit at God's righ hand signifies a place of honor (Acts 2:34; c Ps. 110:1). Through Jesus, the Prince (*archego* "leader") and Savior, God offers Israel th opportunity to repent and to receive forgiveness God has prepared the way for the salvation o humankind. As the crucified and risen Lord Jesus Christ is the Author of salvation, offerin eternal life to all who repent of their sins.

Peter and his fellow apostles are eyewitnesses to the death, resurrection, and ascensio of Jesus, but the Holy Spirit is also a witnes to these gospel events. The outpouring of th Spirit at Pentecost attests the reality of th exaltation of Jesus (2:33), and, according t Peter, God gives the Holy Spirit to those wh obey him (5:32). Walking in the obedience o faith prepares believers to be baptized o immersed in the Spirit. God bestows th charismatic gift of the Spirit on those who ar people of faith, people who give themselves i obedience to Christ.

3.3.4.3. Gamaliel Warns the Sanhedri Against Opposing the Apostles (5:33–42 As the spokesman for the apostles, Peter provokes the anger of the Sanhedrin. "They wer furious" translates a Greek word that literall means "sawn asunder" or "cut to the quick The NEB renders it, "This touched them on th raw." Luke later uses the same word t describe their reaction to Stephen (7:54 These men, who have crucified Jesus, a ready to commit murder again. Their violen rage to kill the apostles foreshadows what the will do to Stephen.

At least Gamaliel, a member of the Sanhedrin, dares to offer wise counsel to this eli group to which he belongs. Gamaliel was th grandson of the famous Rabbi Hillel and wa himself a distinguished Pharisaic rabbi (v. 34 at whose feet Paul studied (22:3). Though th

Pharisees were a larger party and had stronger support among the people, the Sadducees were the majority in the Sanhedrin. Luke's presentation of Gamaliel reflects the more positive attitude of the Pharisees toward the Christian movement in contrast to the hostility of the Sadducees (Luke 7:36; 11:37; 14:1; Acts 15:5; 23:6). Thus, it is not strange for Gamaliel to caution the Sanhedrin against taking hasty action in dealing with the Christians.

Gamaliel's motives for speaking before the Sanhedrin are unclear. His interest may have been more in scoring points against his opponents, the Sadducees, than in defending the apostles. This highly respected Pharisee does, however, express a favorable attitude toward the believers. Before he speaks, he orders the guard to remove the prisoners. He advises his colleagues to restrain their rage and to consider the possibility that the movement is "from God" (v. 39). He suggests that no direct action be taken against the leaders of this movement. Should they do so, they run the risk of "fighting against God" (v. 39).

Gamaliel's argument runs like this: If this movement, as it is thought by the Sanhedrin, is not blessed of God, it will come to nothing. On the other hand, should it prove, as the Christians believe, to be the work of God, nothing would succeed in stopping it. Any such efforts to end it would be futile. Still worse, the Sanhedrin would not only be opposing human beings but also God and would be standing under his judgment. By taking no action against the Christians, the Sanhedrin would avoid the risk of becoming "God-fighters."

Gamaliel cites two examples of messianic movements without the blessing of God, which therefore proved unsuccessful. The first is the false messianic movement led by Theudas. The mention of this man has raised a question about the accuracy of Scripture. Josephus does speak about a rebel by the name of Theudas (*Ant.* 20.55.1), but according to him this Theudas led his rebellion well after the time that Gamaliel gave his speech to the Sanhedrin (ca. A.D. 45 or 46). One explanation is that Theudas was a common name and that there may have been another religious leader named Theudas. The details are insufficient to support the identity of the Theudas of Luke and the Theudas of Josephus. On the other hand, perhaps Josephus's dating of the revolution of Theudas is wrong. When Herod the Great died in 4 B.C., a number of insurgent leaders arose in Palestine. Some scholars have concluded that the Theudas of Acts 5:36 was among them (Bruce, 1952, 125).

The second unsuccessful movement cited by Gamaliel is the one led by Judas the Galilean. This movement was also unfruitful because of its strictly human origin. This Judas led a revolt against the Romans in A.D. 6. At this time Rome took a census to assess the amount of taxes to be paid by the province of Judea. Convinced that God was the true king of Israel, Judas insisted that there was no reason for his people to pay taxes to the heathen Romans (*Ant.* 18.1–2;.; 20.5.2; *Jewish War* 2.8.1). This movement was crushed by the Romans and Judas perished. Though his movement died out, his cause may have lived on after his death in the party of the Zealots (Bruce, 1952, 43).

The fate of Theudas and Judas provides the basis for Gamaliel's proposal of a hands-off policy. He insists that the Christian movement will come to the same end, as did these men's movements, if it is not inspired by God. Without God's blessings a messianic movement lacks enduring stability.

We err today if we take Gamaliel's advice as a general rule to allow everything to go its way unopposed. To wait to see if a religious movement proves successful can have devastating consequences. Every lover of truth should investigate a movement's claims without any regard for its probable success. Note especially that Gamaliel's main concern is whether the Christian movement should be suppressed *by violence*. Gamaliel was not a prophet or an apostle, but his viewpoint (although it serves a purpose in God's plan) is really a statement of truth. Evil movements can prosper a long time on earth but not forever.

The advice of Gamaliel does restrain the Sanhedrin from taking the lives of the apostles (vv. 40–42). But before they are released, the authorities have them beaten, each receiving forty stripes less one (Deut. 25:1–3; 2 Cor. 11:24). This punishment is more severe than the earlier imprisonment and threats (4:21). Again, the Council forbids them from preaching about Jesus.

The flogging conforms to what Jesus had told his disciples to expect (Luke 21:12), but the Sanhedrin does not succeed in discouraging them. The apostles go away, "rejoicing because they had been counted worthy of suffering disgrace for the Name." In the midst of persecution the apostles are full of joy because they consider it a great honor to suffer for the sake of Jesus Christ. They are glad for the opportunity to show that Christ's confidence in them is not misplaced. Refusing to heed the threat of the Sanhedrin, the apostles continue to teach and preach daily that Jesus is the true Messiah. As before they preach publicly in the temple, but now they also teach in private homes. Persecution does not diminish their Spirit-anointed witness. Their devotion and methods provide a marvelous example for evangelizing a community.

3.4. Fellowship Broken: Community Chooses Seven Deacons (6:1–7)

The believers have devoted themselves to forming a community of fellowship (2:42), which finds expression in sharing their possessions with the needy. As a positive example of fellowship Luke has called attention to Barnabas (4:36–37); in contrast, Ananias and his wife are negative examples (5:1–11). In chapter 6 Luke reports a breakdown in fellowship because of the community's neglect of its Grecian widows. In the midst of tremendous progress of the church this problem places the unity of the church in serious jeopardy.

At this time the Christian community consists of two groups: the Grecian Jews (*Hellenistai*, "Greek-speaking believers") and the Hebraic Jews (*Hebraioi*, "Aramaic-speaking believers"). The Grecian Jews of Acts 6 are believers who have been strongly influenced by Greek culture, probably while living outside of Palestine, while the Hebraic Jews are Christians who have lived in their native land of Palestine.

Many devout Jews who lived outside of Palestine most of their lives moved to Jerusalem in their old age so that they could be buried near this city. When the men died, few of the widows were capable of supporting themselves. They depended on the benevolence of religious groups for survival. Because these widows were not well known, it was easy for the leaders of the community to overlook them (v. 1; *TDNT*, 3:389–90). The widows of the Aramaic-speaking Christians were more likely to have been better known and thus less likely to be overlooked in daily distribution of assistance.

More seems to be involved than language difference between the two groups, however. Social circumstances and theological differences may also have played a part in the friction between the two groups. The Aramaic-speaking Christians seem to have been more entrenched in their Palestinian religious traditions and showed more restraint in their attitude toward the Jewish law and the temple. Being more aggressive in their approach, the Hellenistic Jews incited anger. On at least one occasion the aggressive preaching of a Greek-speaking believer in the Hellenists' synagogue in Jerusalem leads to his stoning. The Hellenistic Jews present the gospel with such zeal that their opponents eventually compel them to flee Jerusalem for their lives (8:1–3).

The Christians have set aside funds for the needy (2:45; 4:34–35, 37), but they have not adequately administered it to take care of the widows of the Greek-speaking believers. The apostles' immediate response indicates that this neglect is an oversight, not intentional discrimination. Their responsibility to preach the gospel, to devote themselves to prayer, and to govern the church make it impracticable for them to administer relief to the poor. It is not that caring for widows is "beneath" them, nor do they consider it to be a lower level of ministry. Rather, their primary burden is to offer the bread of life that brings salvation and to administer the affairs of the church.

As Spirit-led leaders, the apostles call a general meeting of "all the disciples" and propose a solution to the problem—that the church select seven men to whom is given the responsibility to care for the widows (vv. 2–3). Their function will be "to wait on tables" (*diakonein trapezais*; lit., "to serve tables"). Luke does not use the word "deacon" (*diakonos*) to describe the seven men, but the words for "serve" and "deacon" come from the same Greek root. "Deacons" are mentioned in Philippians 1:1 and 1 Timothy 3:8–13. Thus it seems appropriate to use this title for the Seven, especially in light of the work performed by deacons in later times (which included the handling of finances, caring for the needy, and other practical matters of ministry).

If this plan is followed, the apostles will then be able to devote themselves "to prayer and the ministry of the word" (v. 4). Luke does not state how the choice of the Seven is made, but the congregation as a whole sees the wisdom of the apostles' proposal (v. 5) and participates in the selection of these deacons. The basic qualification is spirituality, but they are to be distinguished in two ways. (1) They are to be "full of the Spirit." Rather than being merely good administrators or managers of funds, this qualification requires them to be empowered by the Spirit on the order of the disciples at Pentecost. That is, they should have the power of a miracle-working faith.

(2) They are also to be "full of . . . wisdom." Complementary to acts of power is Spirit-inspired speech. The deacons are, therefore, to be powerful in works and word. As competent and mature people who are inspired by the Spirit, they must have good practical sense and be able to properly handle delicate problems. Their ministry includes business affairs and the distribution of assistance to the needy, but it is also to be spiritual and charismatic. They are to exercise whatever spiritual gifts God has bestowed on them.

Among the seven men chosen to serve as deacons are Stephen and Philip (the only two whom Luke describes in any detail). Philip emerges as a charismatic preacher (8:4–8, 26–40; 21:8); he is the first to plant a church among the Samaritans. Stephen is described as "a man full of faith" (v. 5), no doubt meaning miracle-working faith. He does "great wonders and miraculous signs" (v. 8), and his opponents are unable to cope with his preaching (v. 10). The ministry of these two men illustrates the ministries of the charismatic deacons, which extend far beyond the practical day-to-day concerns of the church.

The seven men that are chosen all have Greek names, but this does not prove they are native Greeks. At this time many Jews had Greek names. Undoubtedly these men speak Greek and are equipped spiritually and also linguistically to deal with the problem to which they have been assigned. Stephen's name appears first in the list and is followed by the words, "a man full of faith and of the Holy Spirit." These words are not repeated after the other names, but we should understand them to describe all seven deacons.

The appointment of the Seven as deacons leaves the apostles free to preach, teach, and pray. At their installation, the new deacons are presented by the entire congregation to the apostles. The NIV indicates that only the apostles pray and lay hands on them, but the Greek text fails to make that explicit. Apparently the entire community participates. The laying on of hands ratifies the community's choice and signifies the giving of responsibility and the imparting of strength and blessings for the task.

The appointment of the seven deacons provides a good model for ministering to minorities in the church. As in the early church, we should be concerned about how minorities—the poor, widows, orphans, and people of different racial origins—are treated. Similar to the widows of the Greek-speaking believers, such people are often powerless, and their needs can be overlooked. Each congregation should have a proper plan to minister to the disadvantaged and minorities and commit this ministry to those who are spiritually gifted and committed to caring for them.

Upon the resolution of a potentially dangerous rift, the church again enjoys a spirit of unity and rapid growth (v. 7). An impressive number of new converts join the group, including especially for the first time "a large number of priests." Through the power of the Spirit the word of God spreads and increases in its effects so that even the priesthood is being transformed by the gospel. Luke underscores the striking effect of the gospel on these priests. They become "obedient to the faith," indicating that faith in Jesus Christ demands a course of life in accordance with what one believes. To follow this course is to obey the faith (cf. Rom. 1:5).

4. The Acts of Six Spirit-Filled Leaders (6:8–12:24)

Luke has emphasized the disciples as a community of Spirit-baptized prophets and has reported the acts of this Spirit-filled community. Once the neglect of the widows of the Greek-speaking believers has been addressed, the attention shifts to six charismatic leaders, beginning with Stephen and ending with Paul (6:8–28:31). From this point on Luke devotes his narrative to these six leaders: Stephen, Philip, Barnabas, Agabus, Peter, and Paul. These men are Spirit-anointed prophets. Their deeds and words are inspired by the Holy Spirit, and their ministry typifies the ministry of the prophethood of all believers.

4.1. The Acts of Stephen: A Spirit-Filled Deacon (6:8–7:60)

All seven deacons are full of the Spirit and wisdom (6:3). The word "full" (*pleres*) implies duration and refers to a quality of spiritual fullness that enables them to speak under great inspiration and to perform signs and wonders (vv. 5, 8). The success of these Christian witnesses in Jerusalem arouses opposition, as it had on two previous occasions (4:1–22; 5:17–41.). But on this particular occasion, the opposition extends beyond the Sanhedrin and temple authorities to include members from a Greek-speaking synagogue (v. 9; cf. 24:12) and the people in general (v. 12). Stephen becomes the victim of their resistance to the gospel.

4.1.1. Stephen Performs Signs and Wonders (6:8–10). Luke has described Stephen's charismatic life and ministry as one "full of the Spirit and wisdom" (v. 3) and him as "a man full of faith and of the Holy Spirit" (v. 5). Now he further describes Stephen's charismatic gifts in terms of his being "full of God's grace and power," enabling him to do "great wonders and miraculous signs among the people." The coupling of grace (*charis*) and power (*dynamis*) indicates that divine grace confers on him spiritual gifts to perform miracles.

Miraculous works empowered by the Spirit are typical of Stephen's ministry. These marvelous manifestations along with his preaching stir up opposition. The Greek-speaking Jews of the Synagogue of Freemen (probably prisoners of war set free by the Romans) argue with Stephen. Some of these Jews came from Cyrene and Alexandria, others from the provinces of Cilicia and Asia. There must have been an inclination for Greek-speaking Jews to gather together in particular synagogues in Jerusalem. But none of Stephen's adversaries can "stand up against his wisdom or the Spirit by whom he spoke" (v. 10). As he speaks, Stephen is empowered by the Holy Spirit, and his message manifests the spiritual gift of wisdom. It is theologically informed, and his opponents cannot answer his arguments or repudiate his logic (cf. Ex. 4:14; Luke 21:15).

This occasion is the first time that believers confront their opponents in open discussion. The conflict has become an intellectual struggle—arguments that center around the question of the validity of the law and temple. Stephen measures arms with his foes in open debate, and they are unable to cope with the prophetic deeds and words of this Spirit-filled deacon.

4.1.2. Stephen Defends Himself Before the Sanhedrin (6:11–7:53). Stephen's adversaries charge him with blasphemy. Being more interested in vindicating themselves than in the truth, they resort to obtaining false testimony from witnesses, who accuse him of blasphemous attacks "against Moses and against God" (v. 11). For the first time the people are stirred up against the Christians. The authorities have so far been restrained in their actions against the disciples because of their fear of the people (cf. 2:47). But the false witnesses poison the minds of the people against the disciples, distorting certain utterances of Stephen.

The dispute between Stephen and the Greek-speaking Jews focuses on his interpretation of the law of Moses and of God's purpose for temple worship. (1) As the bearer of the law, Moses represented God's revelation given to the Jews at Mount Sinai. He symbolized all that was holy and valued in rabbinic religion; to deny Moses was to assault the divine authority and validity of the worship and practices of the Jews. Stephen is thus accused of changing the customs handed down by Moses (v. 14), which probably not only includes the written law but also the oral tradition that gives the scribal interpretation of the law (Marshall, 1980, 130). (2) Temple worship prescribed the divine order of worship for the people of Israel. To question temple order was seen as a violation of God's power and majesty.

A similar charge had been made against Jesus. He had predicted the destruction of the temple. The Fourth Gospel records the prophecy and its significance: "Destroy this temple, and I will raise it again in three days." But, as John explained, "the temple he had spoken of was his body" (John 2:19, 21; cf. Matt. 26:61; Mark 14:58). It is possible that Stephen during his debate in the synagogue cited this prophecy. Twisting Stephen's words as blasphemous, his enemies charge him with teaching that Jesus would destroy the temple and abolish its services (v. 14).

What Stephen actually taught did accord with Old Testament prophecy that God does no dwell in temples made by hands (7:48–49). The eternal and spiritual substance of the Old Testament is preserved in the gospel, but Stephen sees the saving work of Christ as bringing to an end the temple order with its ceremonial and sacrificial worship. A new dimension of fellowship with God has been introduced through Jesus. Such fellowship with God far exceeds the temple and its worship.

In other words, the old temple is being replaced by a new temple, the Christian church (cf. 15:16–18). The exclusivism of Judaism is passing away, and God is replacing it with the universalism of the Christian movement. The One greater than the temple has come (Matt. 12:6), and the whole world is to be drawn into the higher life of the Spirit. The replacement of the temple "made with hands" means that God's people can have a dynamic, creative fellowship with God. This transition makes clear that the last days have dawned. Through the power of the Spirit, Stephen proclaims salvation universal in scope. But the Greek-speaking Jews, zealous defenders of tradition, see his prophetic preaching as a threat to sacrificial worship and the ceremonial law.

By misrepresenting what he has said as blasphemy (6:12, 14), his enemies stir up the people, the elders, and the teachers of the law against him. They arrest him and bring him before the Sanhedrin for trial. As charges are made against him, his face appears to the court "like the face of an angel" (v. 15). That is, his countenance is aglow with God's glory like that of Moses (Ex. 34:29–30) and of Jesus (Luke 9:29). The glorious radiance of Stephen's face indicates that just as Jesus had promised to his disciples, the Holy Spirit continues to inspire him to proclaim the gospel (Luke 12:11–12; 21:14–15). After the high priest's question, "Are these charges true?" a silence falls on the Sanhedrin until Stephen completes his defense (Acts 7:2–53).

Stephen stands where his Master stood when he was condemned to die. The Sanhedrin has come together to condemn him on a similar charge of blasphemy. Spirit-filled Stephen must know that he will suffer the same fate as did his Savior. In his speech before the Council he gives a remarkable discourse. He recites Israel's history from Abraham to Solomon, rehearsing God's dealings with his people. He selects from the Old Testament events that confront his hearers with two themes. (1) God has repeatedly sent persons to serve as deliverers of his people, but God's messengers have been rejected (vv. 2–43). (2) The Jews mistakenly believe that God actually dwells in the temple (vv. 44–50).

The old temple in Jerusalem was replaced by a new temple, the Christian church—the believers. This early Christian church in the Golan was destroyed by an earthquake about A.D. 747. Note the single direction of the broken pillars.

Both of these themes reoccur throughout the speech. Although Stephen is responding to charges made against him, his speech can be more accurately described as a frontal attack on his audience for rejecting, as their fathers had, the messengers sent to them by God (vv. 51–53). The speech has six major divisions, concentrating mainly on the history of God's people as found in the Pentateuch (the only part of the Scriptures the Sadducees accepted as authoritative).

(1) After a courteous salutation to those present as "brothers and fathers" (cf. 22:1), Stephen proceeds to this first topic, God's creation of a nation through the call of Abraham (vv. 2–8). He begins by describing God as "the God of glory" (Ps. 29:3). This description

emphasizes the majesty of the God who cannot be confined to a temple made with human hands. As Spirit-filled Stephen speaks, his own face radiates with divine glory.

God appeared to "our father Abraham" while he was living in Mesopotamia. In other words, when God called Abraham, the father of their nation, the patriarch was living outside of the Holy Land in Mesopotamia. His call started him in the direction of Canaan, the land that God would show him. Note that Abraham received divine revelation in a pagan country, demonstrating that God is not limited to the land of Palestine.

Obeying God, Abraham, with his father, Terah, left the land of the Chaldeans (that is, Mesopotamia) and made his home in Haran. Apparently Stephen understands that the patriarch remained there until Terah's death (cf. Gen. 11:27–12:4). Abraham then migrated to Canaan, the land God promised to him and the very land in which Stephen's audience now lives. But the complete fulfillment of God's promise did not come quickly with Abraham's settlement in Canaan because he owned none of the land, "not even a foot of ground" (v. 5). God's promise must have appeared to him to be impossible, especially since God had assured him that he and his descendants would possess the land, but at this point he had no heir. Abraham did have a son before Isaac, but he was not the promised heir.

The land remained only a promise for Abraham, but it becomes "a possession" for his descendants after they spend four hundred years in Egyptian bondage. God delivered those descendants from their oppression. Only then did they journey to Canaan and become heirs of the Promised Land. As in verse 7, the land was more than a mere place to live; it was "in this place" (Palestine) that they were to pray and worship God.

God's promise set in motion Abraham's faith. Abraham believed that his descendants would inherit the Promised Land, but God told him that only after a period of bondage would his posterity be blessed. A further indication of Abraham's faith was his acceptance of the covenant, by which God's promises made Abraham and his descendants special objects of his love and care. God gave circumcision as the external sign of this covenant, which was to show their commitment to God. Being strong in faith, Abraham transmitted the covenant to the next generation by circumcising Isaac (Gen. 21:4). The covenant line continued through Jacob and through his twelve sons. In contrast to Stephen's audience, Abraham, the founder of the Jewish nation, is an example of faith and obedience.

(2) After his discussion of Abraham, Stephen summarizes the story of Joseph, telling about Jacob's journey into Egypt with his sons and their deaths in that foreign land (vv. 9–16). Throughout Stephen's speech runs the theme of conflict in the family (vv. 23–29, 35, 39, 51–53). He introduces this theme by referring to the patriarchs' jealousy of Joseph, which prompted them to reject him and sell him as a slave to the Gentiles. Through what happened to Joseph, God fulfilled his promises of enslavement and mistreatment (v. 6). Stephen's implication is that just as the high priest and his associates were jealous of the disciples (5:17), so were Joseph's brothers jealous of him. But God was with Joseph in his bondage in Egypt and delivered him from his afflictions by giving him wisdom (cf. 6:3). This spiritual gift enabled him to interpret dreams, led to his elevation as governor of Egypt, and enabled him to prepare for a famine.

When the famine came upon Egypt, it had a devastating effect on the world (Gen. 41:57), particularly on Canaan (42:1–5). Therefore, Jacob sent his remaining sons to Egypt in search of food. On the first visit they did not recognize Joseph. When they came the next time, he revealed himself to them and became their deliverer. When Pharaoh learned about Joseph's family, he invited them to settle in Egypt. Jacob's family of seventy-five persons traveled to Egypt and were strangers in a Gentile country (cf. Gen. 46:27, LXX). Although Jacob and the patriarchs later died in Egypt, they were not buried there, but in the land that God had promised as an inheritance to their descendants, the land of Canaan. They themselves had no inheritance in Canaan except for a burial plot purchased by Abraham at Shechem, so their bodies were brought and buried in that place. Their tombs at Shechem bear witness that these men died with faith in the promise.

Because God was with Joseph in Egypt, the evil efforts of his brothers served to further

God's plans. Once again Stephen insists that God cannot be limited to the temple. Down in Egypt he used Joseph to save his people from starvation. In spite of their ill-treatment of him, his brothers recognized him as the divinely anointed deliverer of their family and people.

(3) Stephen then turns to the history of Moses, the man whom God raised up to deliver the children of Abraham out of Egyptian bondage (vv. 17–38). After the death of Jacob and his sons, the Israelites remained in Egypt and continued to multiply until the time for the fulfillment of the promise to Abraham was near. At this time a new king who did not know Joseph came to the throne of Egypt. Until now the memory of Joseph and of what he had done brought favor to the people of God. Under the administration of the new king that favor changed, and they were oppressed by his cruel policies.

Stephen mentions only the worse part about the cruel treatment of the Hebrews, the destruction of their male children. To prevent the Israelites from growing in number and being a threat to his rule, Pharaoh ordered that all male babies be put outside their homes so that they would be exposed and die (Ex. 1:15–22). At this time Moses came on the scene. Moses was "no ordinary child." Contrary to the king's edict, his parents kept him at home for three months. Finally, they did expose him to death, but in a marvelous way he was saved and was adopted by Pharaoh's daughter as her own child. As a member of the king's own family, Moses was brought up in a Gentile palace and received the best of an Egyptian education. Such magnificent training did not go to waste; it produced a man who was "powerful in speech and action" (Acts 7:22).

God had appointed Moses as leader and deliverer. Stephen tells about the people's first rejection of him (vv. 23–29). At age forty Moses visited his fellow Israelites. Although he had grown up in a Gentile court, he had not become an Egyptian in heart. On his visit he saw the oppression of his people and witnessed an Israelite being mistreated by an Egyptian. Not only did Moses come to the defense of the slave, but he also exacted vengeance by killing the Egyptian. According to Exodus 2:12 he hid the body in the sand so that nobody would know what he had done. Apparently he did not want the Egyptians to learn about the incident; but, as Stephen indicates, Moses also hoped the Israelites would recognize him as their friend and the one who was divinely appointed to bring them deliverance (*soteria*, "salvation") from slavery.

The day after his killing of the Egyptian, Moses saw two Hebrews fighting. Moses tried to settle the feud but was unsuccessful. He was "pushed . . . aside" and vehemently rebuked by the wrongdoer: "Who made you ruler and judge over us? Do you want to kill me as you killed the Egyptian yesterday?" The answer to the first question is provided: "He was sent to be their ruler and deliverer by God himself" (v. 35). Moses already felt that he was an instrument of God to deliver the Israelites from the brutal oppression of the Egyptians, but he was rejected by his own people, as Joseph before and Jesus afterwards.

Moses therefore had to flee to the land of Midian, located in northwestern Arabia. He was not only an outcast from his people, but also an exile in the foreign land, where he settled down and raised a family. After forty years in Midian, he had a decisive experience in the uninhabited area of Mount Sinai. There he was confronted by an angel "in the flames of a burning bush" (v. 30). The burning bush served as a symbol of God's presence, through which God got Moses' attention. As Moses looked closely at the burning bush, he heard the voice of the Lord coming from it, calling him to deliver his people from Egypt. The voice corresponded to the heavenly voice that Jesus later heard at his baptism (Luke 3:22).

From the bush the Lord identified himself as the God of Moses' ancestors, who had made a covenant with Abraham, Isaac, and Jacob. This astounding encounter caused Moses to tremble with fear, and he did not dare raise his eyes to look at the bush unconsumed by the flames. God assured him that he was standing on "holy ground." God's presence made that place sacred; once again, Stephen is reminding his audience that God's revelation of himself is not confined to Jewish soil. In fact, in the Old Testament the most important place of revelation is not in the Promised Land but at Mount Sinai.

God had seen the cruel suffering of his people in Egypt and had sent Moses to be their ruler and deliverer, but they had already rejected him (v. 35). Moses' task began in earnest when he returned to Egypt. Not only do we see a parallel between Moses' and Jesus' rejection, but also like Jesus, Moses performed mighty works as Israel's God-appointed redeemer, which prefigured God's mighty saving act from our bondage of sin through Christ. Israel's journey to the Promised Land was accompanied by miraculous signs from God. Furthermore, Moses also spoke mighty words, which predicted the coming of the Messiah—a prophet and deliverer like himself but one who would be much greater than himself (v. 37; cf. Deut. 18:15). His prophecy was fulfilled in the coming of Jesus Christ.

A final feature of Moses' ministry that Stephen stresses is his work as mediator (v. 38). Moses mediated the old covenant just as Jesus served as mediator of the new covenant. Stephen singles out Moses' role in the giving of the law. At Sinai Moses was with "the assembly in the desert" (v. 38). The word translated "assembly" is *ekklesia* ("congregation, church"). On the mountain Moses received the "living words," a phrase that refers to the divine revelation of the law. It is "living" because the divine message given at Sinai has power to consummate life (cf. Heb. 4:12) and is an enduring message that encompasses God's grace and his promise of salvation. Exodus 19:19–25 indicates that God spoke directly to Moses, but Stephen understands that God revealed his message through an angel (cf. Gal. 3:19; Heb. 2:2).

(4) At this point Stephen becomes more specific in his description of Israel's rebellion (vv. 39–43). The Israelites' first rejection of Moses (cf. vv. 27–28) foreshadowed what later happened in the desert. The people had witnessed the miraculous manifestations of God's presence in Egypt, at the Red Sea, and in their journey to Mount Sinai. Yet in spite of everything that they had seen God do for them under Moses' leadership, the people refused "to obey him." While he was on Sinai receiving the law, "they . . . in their hearts turned back to Egypt," and they demanded that Aaron make idols for them to worship.

Their rebellion is well summarized in the account of the making of the golden calf (v. 41; cf. Ex. 32), to whom they offered sacrifices, and they rejoiced in the work of their hands. It was bad enough for them to reject Moses—the man anointed by God as their leader and deliverer—but to make things far worse, these people fell into pagan idolatry. They did not want to walk by faith. Dissatisfied with the invisible presence of God, they built themselves a golden calf so they could have a god to go before them.

Stephen then cites Amos 5:25–27 (LXX), which begins with the question, "Did you bring me sacrifices and offerings forty years in the desert?" The fact is the people had not offered sacrifices to God during the desert wanderings. That generation abandoned the worship of God. As a consequence God gave them over to the worship of heavenly bodies (Acts 7:42; Rom. 1:24–28). During the desert journey they offered sacrifices not to God but to various idols. Their idol worship began at the foot of Mount Sinai and continued for the next forty years. They offered sacrifices to Molech, the Canaanite deity of sun and sky, and to Rephan, an Egyptian god associated with the planet Saturn. Furthermore, the Israelites also made images of these gods and worshiped them.

In the days of Amos (the eighth century B.C.), the people's hearts worshiped Molech and Rephan, members of the host of heaven. Because of the Israelites' history, dealing with the problem of idolatry is not a new problem. Stephen discerns that the bad religion Amos condemned reached back to the desert. So just as it was written in the book of the prophets, God gave a rebellious people over not only to idolatrous worship but also to Babylonian captivity (v. 43). In other words, divine judgment had been a fact of Israel's past, even as far back as the Exodus journey to the Promised Land.

(5) Stephen's next point ends his historical survey and introduces a new topic: the tabernacle and its successor, the temple (vv. 44–50). The Greek-speaking Jews have charged him with blasphemy against the temple. Instead of denying that charge directly, Spirit-filled Stephen proceeds to explain the true value of the temple. He begins by discussing the tabernacle, which eventually was replaced by the temple. He refers to the tabernacle as "the tabernacle of the Testimony" because the law was kept in the sacred ark (Num. 17:7). It was also the place where God often revealed himself to his people. God gave Moses the blueprints for its construction (Ex. 25:9), and it became part of Israel's life.

Under the leadership of Joshua the tabernacle entered into the Promised Land. There it remained the focal point of Israel's worship until the time of David. Since it was only a movable tent, David desired to establish a more permanent dwelling place for the God of Jacob (v. 46). But it was Solomon who replaced the tent with the temple as God's house.

The people mistakenly think that God's presence can be contained in a man-made building. As grand a structure as was Solomon's temple, it was too small to hold the living God. Stephen shows from Isaiah 66:1–2 the error of Israelite thinking: No building can contain the Ruler of earth and heaven. It is therefore not blasphemy to say that the temple is to be set aside and destroyed. Stephen's attack is not against the grand temple itself but against the theology that limits God's presence to the temple. Like Solomon (1 Kings 8:27), Stephen knows that since the highest heaven cannot contain God, nothing made with hands can.

The divine name "the Most High" (v. 48) emphasizes the transcendence of God. Israel should have known that such a God cannot be confined to a temple. Isaiah clearly prophesied that the Creator does not dwell in handmade structures: "Heaven is my throne. . . . Where will my resting place be? Has not my hand made all these things?" (Isa. 66:1–2). Consequently, God must not be treated as an idol and be seen as housed in a temple. Never can he be limited to any temple, whether in Jerusalem or Palestine. Such limits are false, for God can be worshiped anywhere people turn to him with faith in Jesus Christ. God does now have a dwelling place; it is the community of believers, the church, where his Spirit resides and his presence is at work.

(6) Stephen concludes his speech with scorching words directed at his accusers and the members of the Sanhedrin (vv. 51–53). Deeply stirred by his convictions and inspired by the Holy Spirit, Stephen uses vivid language to denounce them for their hardness of heart. They are "stiff-necked" (Ex. 33:35) and have "uncircumcised hearts and ears" (Lev. 26:41; Deut. 10:16). Among Jews "uncircumcised" was a term of reproach and contempt. David denounced Goliath as "this uncircumcised Philistine" (1 Sam. 17:26), and Ezekiel called foreigners "uncircumcised in heart" (Ezek 44:7, 9). Moses and the prophets had hurled these same two expressions at pagan nations and apostate Israel. No words could be more accurate for Stephen's opponents, who are following in the steps of their fathers by closing their minds to the message of God and resisting the Holy Spirit (cf. Isa. 63:10), under whose inspiration Stephen is speaking.

There is nothing new about the Jewish leaders' rejection of Spirit-inspired leaders. Their predecessors had persecuted the prophets and killed those who prophesied of Christ's first coming (v. 52). But now the leaders of Israel are guilty of having betrayed and murdered "the Righteous One," the Messiah himself. A definite pattern of disobedience runs throughout Israel's history. Israel has been blessed, receiving the law through the hands of angels, but they have transgressed the law. Thus, Stephen is justified in applying Moses' words to the people before him. Because the leaders oppose the Holy Spirit, they show themselves not to be the true people of God. They, not Stephen, are denying their spiritual heritage.

Many in the Christian church have fallen into the same error of rejecting the Holy Spirit through their own actions. As the Pharisees rejected the Spirit-anointed ministry of Jesus, so church leaders in the name of sound doctrine are tempted to reject the demonstration of the Spirit's power and the manifestations of his gifts.

4.1.3. Stephen's Martyrdom (7:54–60). Stephen has presented ample evidence to stress his prophetic denunciation of the nation's leaders. In the climax of his speech he has touched the hearers on a tender spot. As a result, his prophetic words provoke the Sanhedrin to great anger. They have been portrayed as belonging to a nation of idolaters and are charged with being guilty of crucifying the Messiah. The charges against them have been sustained by a number of Scriptures. An outburst of rage arises against Stephen, and they gnash their teeth at him. He has presented a great defense; but even though the Sanhedrin convicts him, they are unable to withstand the wisdom and the Spirit in which Stephen speaks.

Spirit-filled Stephen behaves as a prophet. Through the Holy Spirit, he sees God's blazing glory and Jesus exalted at the right hand of God (vv. 55–56; cf. Luke 22:69). During his vision the Trinitarian pattern appears. Stephen, full of the *Holy Spirit*, looks up into heaven and sees the *Lord Jesus* standing at the right hand of *God the Father*. That vision leaves no doubt about Jesus' place in the Godhead.

Only here in the New Testament is Jesus portrayed as standing rather than sitting at God's right hand. The most satisfying explanation of this stance is that he is acting in the role of intercessor, advocate, and witness. His position suggests that he is confessing Stephen before the heavenly Father, even as he had promised, "Whoever acknowledges me before men, I will also acknowledge him before my Father in heaven" (Matt. 10:32). Jesus is the exalted Lord, and his people have access to God through him (cf. Rom. 8:34). As the Righteous One (v. 52), the Son of Man is qualified to represent God's people and to bear witness on their behalf.

Stephen now for the first time confesses the risen Lord before the Sanhedrin, declaring that he sees Jesus Christ sharing in God's glory as the exalted Son of Man. These words are blasphemous to the religious leaders. They cover their ears, indicating that they will no longer listen to the blasphemer. Their refusal to hear reflects a much deeper problem: fighting against their ears being opened by the Holy Spirit (v. 52; *TDNT*, 5:556). They drown out Stephen's voice by "yelling at the top of their voices" (v. 57) and rushing to grab him.

These violent reactions suggest a lynching rather than an official act. The Sanhedrin had no right to impose the death penalty without the consent of the Roman governor. The reference to witnesses (v. 58), who were expected to cast the first stones at a condemned person (Deut. 17:7), may suggest a trial procedure; but the outburst of rage in verse 57 indicates that Stephen has fallen victim to fanatical mob action. They rush him outside of the city and proceed to stone him, the punishment prescribed for a blasphemer (Lev. 24:14–16; Num. 15:32–36). His death is brought about by injustice and the mob violence.

Among the witnesses to Stephen's death is "a young man named Saul" (v. 58). When those who hurl the stones remove their outer garments to give themselves more freedom to throw the stones, they place their garments at Saul's feet. Here in Acts Saul is identified by name for the first time, though he may have been among the Jews at Jerusalem referred to as being from the province of Cilicia (6:9). Saul is among Stephen's opponents, and Stephen's address may have prompted him to take part in his murder. The death of Stephen made a deep and lasting impression on the young man Saul. Years later he recalled it with sadness (22:20). Still later, however, Saul becomes a friend of Christians when he is miraculously transformed by God's grace. He eventually becomes the main character in the expanding mission of the church.

The account of Stephen's death reminds us of the passion of his Lord. Like Jesus he is rejected by his own people. Stephen's prayer as he dies bears a striking resemblance to Jesus' prayer as he faced his own death: "Lord Jesus, receive my spirit" (v. 59). There is a difference, however. Jesus committed his spirit into the hands of the Father (Luke 23:46), but Stephen looks to the Lord Jesus and commits his spirit to the greatest vindicator of God's people.

Next Stephen kneels in prayer and echoes still another utterance of Jesus on the cross:

Inside the Lion's Gate in Jerusalem, also called St. Stephen's Gate. When brought before the Sanhedrin, Stephen recounted the history of Israel, saying the people had persecuted and killed their prophets and disobeyed God. When he accused the crowd of killing Christ and disobeying God, he was dragged outside the city and stoned, the beginning of the persecution of Christians.

Lord, do not hold this sin against them" (v. 60). With the calm confidence of a prophet he follows the example of Jesus and remains faithful to his teaching: "Pray for those who mistreat you" (Luke 6:28). Before Stephen dies, all hear this inspired witness offer a prayer of forgiveness for his executioners. Only the power of the Holy Spirit can enable Stephen to pray as he does. Like Jesus he is rejected by his own people—a rejected prophet.

Describing what is characteristic of a believer's death, Luke simply says, "he fell asleep." The death of this charismatic deacon stands in contrast to the fanatical frenzy of the mob. His death becomes a major transition. Now the persecution of the church widens, and it is scattered throughout Judea and Samaria (cf. 1:8).

4.2. The Acts of Philip: A Spirit-Filled Deacon (8:1–40)

The death of Stephen raises theological questions about the continuing authority of the law and temple worship among God's people (6:10–14; 7:46–50). Stephen and other Christians have tied their challenge to the betrayal and death of Jesus at the hands of the religious leaders (cf. 2:23–24; 7:51–53). Now many in Jerusalem are enraged against the Christians and violently reject the gospel.

4.2.1. Persecution of the Jerusalem Church (8:1–3). The execution of Stephen signals a new wave of persecution. Mob violence against believers forces the church to become a missionary church. The great community of believers scatters "throughout Judea and Samaria," though the apostles remain behind in Jerusalem. They are not forced to flee, probably because the intense persecution is directed against Greek-speaking (Hellenistic) Christians rather than Aramaic-speaking believers (cf. 6:1–4). The suffering of these Christians, however, leads to the growth of the church. Many of Luke's readers were probably also suffering. The suffering of these first Christians makes them aware that suffering for the sake of the gospel does have a purpose, which gives them encouragement and hope.

The death of Stephen was a great loss for the community of believers, and they mourned greatly for him. "Godly men" bury Stephen. In this case, these "godly men" may have been Christians, though the word "godly" (*eulabes*) elsewhere in the New Testament refers to devout Jews (2:5; cf. Luke 2:25). It is used later to describe Ananias as "a devout observer of the law." Like many early Jewish Christians, because Ananias continues to obey the law (Acts 22:12), he is referred to as *eulabes*. Though the hearts of Christians are grief-stricken, Stephen's execution provides an example for them of how faith in Christ can sustain them in the face of death.

After Stephen's burial, Saul takes a leading part in persecuting Greek-speaking believers. Luke does not tell us whether he acts as an agent of the Sanhedrin or as a representative of one or more of the synagogues. He does indicate, however, that before Saul departs for Damascus, he secures letters of authority from the high priest (9:2). His persecution of Christians in Jerusalem is fierce and violent. He goes to their homes and drags them away to prison. He does not even spare the women. Later, after Saul became a Christian, the memory of what he did lingered with him. He recalled how extremely zealous he had been for his ancestral traditions, how violently he persecuted Christians, and how he had relentlessly sought to destroy the Christian movement (Gal. 1:13–14; cf. 1 Cor. 15:9; Phil. 3:6; 1 Tim. 1:13).

As the Christians flee from Jerusalem, the church begins to fulfill Jesus' mandate to be witnesses to the ends of the earth (1:8). The enemies of Christ have sought to destroy the church; but as Christians scatter, they go everywhere preaching the gospel (8:4). The first believers may have been prone to settle down in Jerusalem, but rejection of the gospel in that city forces a wider proclamation of Jesus Christ. The Christians now catch the worldwide vision of the gospel and begin the work of evangelism.

4.2.2. Philip Preaches in Samaria (8:4–13). The real significance of the preaching of the gospel in Samaria cannot be explained in terms of numerical success, but in the fact that the work there is a step in the church's commitment to evangelize the Gentiles. The Samaritans were a racially mixed people and were viewed as semi-pagans (see comments on Luke 9:51–56). The missionary mandate of Acts 1:8 included Samaria as a place where the good news was to be preached. Preaching the gospel there begins the Christian mission to non-Jewish communities.

Among the Christians who flee Jerusalem is Philip, one of the seven charismatic deacons (6:5) and a spiritually gifted evangelist (21:8). He goes to the capital city of Samaria, also called Samaria. As a Greek-speaking Christian, he is probably more open to the Samaritans than a person with a strict Jewish background. When he enters the city, he finds that these people are ready for the gospel. The crowds there show a real interest in Philip's preaching about the Messiah. The coming of the Messiah was apparently a vital part of their hope (see John 4:25). Their expectation was based on Deuteronomy 18:15–18, and they looked for the Messiah to be more like a teacher rather than a ruler.

The Samaritans listen intently to Philip's preaching, but their interest is especially aroused by what they see. Like Jesus, the apostles, and Stephen, Philip is mighty in work as well as word. His Spirit-anointed preaching is accompanied by powerful miracles, which confirm his prophetic word. The Holy Spirit working through Philip makes evil spirits powerless, forcing them to come out of their victims. Many who are lame and paralyzed receive healing for their bodies. As a result, the Samaritans believe Philip's message and are saved (v. 12), and they experience "great joy." This joy is the direct consequence of the power of the Holy Spirit and their experience of salvation.

Luke then draws attention to something that happened in Samaria before the arrival of Philip and the conversion of the Samaritans. For some time they had been under the influence of a magician by the name of Simon (vv. 9–11). Simon probably combined astrology with magic to promote himself as a person with great authority and power. Many had been deceived by his tricks and were thus convinced he had supernatural power. His followers acclaimed him as "the divine power known as the Great Power." Apparently among them he had immense prestige, for they saw him as a deity on earth or the incarnation of great godly power.

But Simon's tricks and claims of supernatural power are now surpassed by Philip's Spirit-filled ministry of preaching and healing the sick. Philip announces the good news about Jesus and tells the people that the kingdom of God has dawned through Christ. His acts of healing confirm his message and the presence of God's rule. Philip explains that the age of fulfillment has arrived. The miracles the people are witnessing are the signs foretold by Isaiah (Isa. 35:5–6), and they attest to the powerful presence of the Holy Spirit.

The prophetic words and deeds of Philip triumph over magic and the tricks of sorcery. Even Simon is amazed by Philip's mighty works, and along with others, he believes Philip's message and is baptized. The verb "believe" (*pisteuo*) is used for the faith of both Simon and the Samaritans. But Simon's subsequent behavior reveals that he remains in bondage to his sins, unregenerated. He is still "full of bitterness and captive to sin" (v. 23) and tries to purchase the power of the Holy Spirit (v. 18). His faith is superficial, resting apparently on miracles alone (Bruce, 1952, 179). He has failed to experience genuine repentance and lacks a real spiritual understanding of the gospel. He has not become a true child of God; his faith is centered in human beings, not in Jesus Christ.

At first Simon attaches himself closely with Philip, being captivated by the great wonders and miracles. Though he does not repent, he wants to escape the threats of judgment pronounced by Peter and requests that the apostle pray for him (v. 24). In other words, even after hearing the gospel he has no understanding of repentance before God and of faith in Jesus Christ.

In contrast to the half-hearted faith of Simon, the inspired biblical text makes clear the sincerity of the Samaritans' faith in Jesus Christ. (1) Since they receive Christian baptism, their faith is acknowledged as valid by Philip (v. 12) and later by the Jerusalem church (v. 14). (2) Although Simon was baptized, unlike the Samaritans he fails to bear fruit of genuine repentance and faith. (3) They experience the joy (*chara*) of salvation (v. 8; cf. 8:39; 13:52; Rom. 14:17; 15:13). (4) They receive the charismatic fullness of the Spirit when Peter and John lay their hands on them (Acts 8:15–17). The Spirit-baptism is for those who are already "in Jesus Christ" and is a distinct work of the Holy Spirit.

4.2.3. Peter and John Visit Samaria (8:14–25). The people of Samaria receive salvation through the ministry of Philip. News reaches Jerusalem that the Samaritans have received "the word of God." The spread of the gospel into a new area is a remarkable event, and the apostles send two of their number, Peter the spokesperson and John his associate, to see what is happening. Through Peter and John's ministry the Samaritan believers receive a full immersion in the power of the Holy Spirit. The Spirit-baptism of these believers begins the fulfillment of Peter's prophetic words: "The promise is . . . for all who are far off" (2:39).

When Peter and John arrive in Samaria, they affirm their approval of Philip's ministry by praying for the Samaritan believers to be baptized in the Spirit (cf. Luke 11:13). These people have been saved and baptized in water in the name of the Lord Jesus, but they do not receive the Pentecostal fullness of the Spirit until Peter and John lay hands on them and pray. Note that the two apostles do not pray for them to be saved, but only to be filled with the Spirit. As believers they already have faith in Christ and are indwelt by the Holy Spirit as the source of salvation, love, and joy. Peter and John do not question the quality of their faith but their reception of the fullness of the Spirit as a separate experience, subsequent to their receiving salvation.

This experience of the Samaritans shows that people can come to faith in Christ and be baptized in water without being endued with the power of the Spirit. The Samaritan narrative confronts us with a clear chronological separation between the belief of the Samaritans and their being immersed in the Spirit. Not only does their initial faith fail to effect the reception of the Spirit's fullness, but their baptism in water likewise fails to be the means of receiving it (Stronstad, 1984, 64).

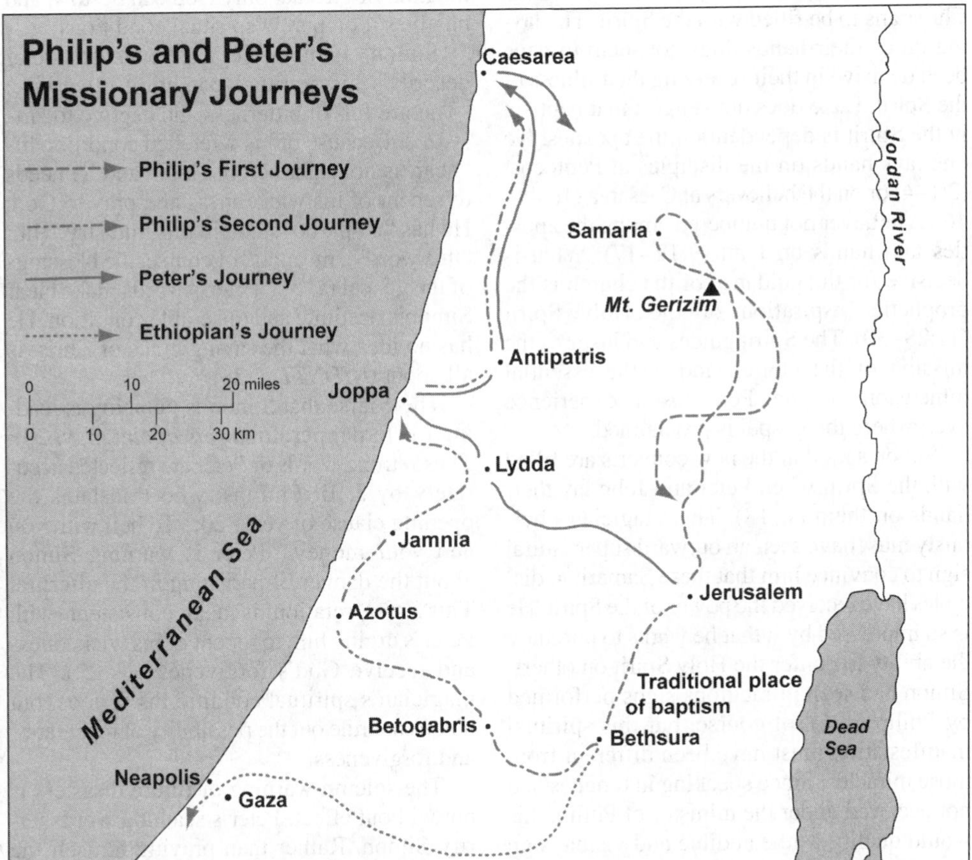

After hearing that the Samaritans had received "the word of God" through Philip's ministry, the apostles sent Peter and John to Samaria. Through their ministry, the people received the Holy Spirit, beginning the fulfillment of the prophecy: "The promise is . . . for all who are far off."

A Roman theater at Samaria. The city was rebuilt by Herod the Great. Its name was changed to Sebaste.

tongues as the Spirit gives the utterance fits the details of the stories of Spirit-baptism recorded elsewhere in Acts (cf. 2:1–4; 10:44–45; 19:1–7).

Simon's response to seeing the Samaritan believers receive the Spirit of prophecy and tongues reveals that he is not a true believer. When he offers money for the power to confer the Spirit, Peter rebukes him for thinking he can buy "the gift of God" (v. 20). Like Ananias and Sapphira (5:1–11), Simon fails to understand the true nature of the Spirit. He mistakenly thinks that the Spirit and his fullness are transmitted by an individual and that the power to do it can be bought and sold. Spirit-baptism is the kind of gift that only God can bestow, and he gives it on purely spiritual conditions.

The primary purpose of Peter and John's visit, therefore, is to pray for the Samaritan Christians to be filled with the Spirit. The laying on of their hands does not seem to have been decisive in their receiving the fullness of the Spirit. Luke does not suggest that baptism in the Spirit is dependent on the apostles. No one lays hands on the disciples at Pentecost (2:1–4) or on the believers at Caesarea (10:44–46). A believer not numbered among the apostles laid hands on Paul (9:12–17). What is decisive for the guidance of the church is the prophetic inspiration of the Holy Spirit (11:28–30). The Spirit guides and inspires the mission of the church and is the essential dimension of the Pentecostal experience everywhere the gospel is proclaimed.

Simon sees that the new converts are filled with the Spirit when Peter and John lay their hands on them (v. 18). This magician obviously must have seen an outward supernatural sign to convince him that these Samaritan disciples have received the power of the Spirit. He is so impressed by it that he wants to purchase the ability to confer the Holy Spirit on others. Simon had seen miraculous signs performed by Philip (v. 6), of course, but this spiritual manifestation must have been different from those miracles. Since speaking in tongues had not occurred under the ministry of Philip, this would qualify as the audible and visible sign the magician sees, though Luke does not specifically affirm or deny this. However, accepting that the Samaritan believers speak in

Simon claims to be a believer, but Peter describes his spiritual condition otherwise: "You are full of bitterness and captive to sin" (v. 23). Because of his wretched condition his "heart is not right before God," and he needs to repent of his wickedness and pray to God. He has "no part or share in this ministry" (lit., "this word"), meaning, of course, the blessings of the gospel (v. 21). Peter's words make clear Simon's destitute and miserable condition. He has no idea what the saving grace of Christ is all about (*NIDNTT*, 2:28).

The course that Simon is pursuing is leading to eternal perdition (*eis apoleian*, v. 20). These strong words of Peter are reflected accurately by J. B. Phillips, who translates the opening clause of verse 20: "To hell with you and your money." Peter is warning Simon about the danger of perishing in the afterlife. This interpretation is also consistent with Peter's urging him to repent of his wickedness and receive God's forgiveness (v. 22). The magician's spiritual condition is serious, but it does not rule out the possibility of repentance and forgiveness.

The solemn warning of future disasters is not without effect. Peter's scathing words terrify Simon. Rather than praying himself, he calls on the two apostles to pray for him. But he limits his request to escaping the consequences of his evil ways. True repentance does not seem to have prompted his plea. Although Peter's words do influence him, we have no assurance of Simon's repentance and salvation.

After Peter and John's successful ministry in Samaria, they return to Jerusalem. As they go, they evangelize many Samaritan villages, and the gospel continues to make progress.

4.2.4. Philip Witnesses to an Ethiopian (8:26–40). Philip probably returns with Peter and John to Jerusalem as they preach the gospel in a number of Samaritan towns. From there he is called to another field of labor. A heavenly messenger directs him southward on the road from Jerusalem to Gaza, which leads through an uninhabited area of the country. He has been a Spirit-inspired witness in the city of Samaria, performing prophetic signs of power; now the Lord directs him to bear witness to a single individual. Immediately this evangelist obeys and sets out on this lonely route.

Along the desert road leading to Gaza, Philip sees a chariot, a two-wheeled vehicle drawn by horses, on its way southward. Riding in it is a man from Ethiopia, probably a God-fearing Gentile. Philip knows nothing about this man, but apparently he is a distinguished court official since he serves as treasurer to Candace, a dynasty of queens of Ethiopia and North Sudan. Being a eunuch he is seen as an imperfect human and is not allowed to enter the congregation of Israel (Deut. 23:1) or the Jewish court in the temple. His condition does not bar him from the court of Gentiles, however, where all people, clean or unclean, have liberty to worship. This Ethiopian must have been on his way home, and he is occupying himself by reading aloud, apparently a common practice in ancient times (Acts 8:30).

The man has been to Jerusalem to worship and is now studying the book of Isaiah. When Philip sees him, the Holy Spirit directs him to go and stay close to the chariot. Now he understands why the angel instructed him to go toward Gaza. Again Philip promptly obeys and discovers that the Ethiopian is reading Isaiah 53. He asks, "Do you understand what you are reading?" (Acts 8:30). The man confesses that he needs help. Like the risen Lord (Luke 24:25–27), Peter (Acts 2:14–36), and Stephen (7:2–53), Philip's task is to interpret properly the Scripture as it relates to Christ. The Spirit has brought the two men together, preparing the eunuch's heart to receive the gospel and empowering Philip to "do the work of an evangelist."

The Ethiopian is puzzled whether Isaiah is speaking about himself as the Suffering Servant of the Lord or about someone else (v. 34). At that time Isaiah 53 was a much-disputed text in Jerusalem. The eunuch had been to the city where, no doubt, debate was raging between Christians and Jews regarding the identity of the Servant. Many of the Jews argued that the prophet was describing his own experience, but the Christians insisted that the reference was to someone else, namely, Christ.

The Ethiopian's lack of understanding gives Philip an opening. He begins at Isaiah 53:7–8, where the eunuch is reading, and gives him a Christ-centered interpretation (Acts 8:35). The first thing Philip does is to show that Jesus in his life and death fulfilled the prophecy of Isaiah.

This word of Isaiah provides Philip with a scriptural basis to explain the betrayal, trial, death, and resurrection of Jesus. As a sheep remains silent when about to be slaughtered or sheared, Jesus expressed no protest in his humiliation and death (v. 32). His life was taken from him by violence. He received an unfair trial and was condemned. Moreover, no one can speak about his descendants, for he had no physical offspring when his life was cut off (v. 33). God, however, vindicated him by raising him from the dead.

The heart of Philip's message is that the death of Jesus as the Suffering Servant takes away the sin of the world and brings redemption to humanity. The specific words cited from Isaiah 53 do not mention that Jesus bears the sins of others, but this truth is expressed elsewhere in both Luke's Gospel (22:19–20) and Acts (20:28). Moreover, it is implied in the verses of Isaiah just prior to the ones quoted in the text (Isa. 53:4–6). And Jesus, the Suffering Servant, had himself spoken of his ministry in terms of the prophecy of Isaiah 53, when he said that the Son of Man came "to give his life a ransom for many" (Mark 10:45; cf. Isa. 53:12).

Philip's instruction to the eunuch most likely includes some teaching regarding baptism. He probably speaks about the ordinance along the lines that Peter did in his Pentecostal sermon—that is, that baptism is the proper response to the gospel (Acts 2:38). The

Ethiopian believes the gospel; and when they come to a stream of water, he expresses his desire to be baptized. Stopping the chariot, they go down into the stream, where Philip baptizes him. As a result of this experience the eunuch is full of joy. He has received the correct understanding of Scripture and has accepted Christ as his Savior. Though he is viewed by the Jews as an imperfect human being and as an outsider, he has become a Christian. With Jesus as his newly found Savior, he returns to his native land, rejoicing in the forgiveness of his sins and the hope of eternal life. His joy may imply that he goes away baptized in the Spirit (cf. 13:52; 16:34).

Having fulfilled his mission, Philip, like his prophetic predecessors Elijah and Ezekiel, is suddenly and miraculously carried away by the Holy Spirit (vv. 39–40). The Spirit has empowered Philip's ministry from its beginning (6:3). The Spirit of the Lord had presumably directed Philip to Samaria, where he was powerful through the Spirit in word and deed (8:6–7, 13). Later the Spirit directed Philip to go near the chariot on which the Ethiopian eunuch was riding (v. 29). After Philip baptized the man, the Spirit of the Lord transported him physically for further evangelistic work. He put Philip down in Azotus, about twenty miles north of Gaza.

These types of miraculous experiences indicate that Philip is more than a charismatic deacon. His experiences of the Spirit demonstrate that he is a prophet as well. This prophet of God continues his ministry, evangelizing the cities on the coast from Azotus to Caesarea, where he makes his home (21:8).

The gospel has thus spread beyond Judea and Samaria to the coastland, including Gaza, Azotus, Caesarea, and even to more distant Ethiopia. The enemies of Christ are trying to destroy the church, but their persecution of the believers leads to a wider proclamation of the gospel, and the ministry of the church is broadened. Thus, progress is being made so that outsiders are included in the church. The gospel crosses racial, geographical, and religious boundaries as the church continues to grow.

4.3. The Conversion of Saul (9:1–31)

Earlier Luke introduced Saul as a young man who received the outer garments of those who stoned Stephen (7:58). Their clothing lay at his feet as Stephen died. Soon after that martyrdom, Saul attempted vehemently to destroy the church. He threw both men and women in jail (8:3) and went from synagogue to synagogue in Jerusalem, trying to make the Christians blaspheme the name of Jesus (26:11). As Peter did earlier, however, Saul becomes the Spirit-filled, charismatic apostle Paul. Whereas Peter is the central figure in the first twelve chapters of Acts, Paul dominates chapters 13–28. His conversion marks a major turning point in the narrative of Acts and is one of the most remarkable events in the history of the church.

4.3.1. Saul's Vision of Jesus (9:1–9). This passage is the first of three accounts of Paul's conversion in Acts (cf. 22:3–16; 26:9–18). More verses in Acts are devoted to this event than to any other subject, leaving no doubt about its importance. The appearance of Christ to Saul on the Damascus road involves both his conversion to Christianity and his commission to be the apostle to the Gentiles. Though these are interlocking realities, the emphasis in Acts falls more on his calling than on his conversion (9:6; 22:10; 26:16–18).

By this time Saul's anger at the Christians knows no bounds. Like a raging bull he breathes out violent threats of murder against them, but he is not satisfied to limit his persecution to Jerusalem. Because many Christians have fled the city, he is determined to pursue them and bring them back to Jerusalem as prisoners. Saul goes to the high priest (Caiaphas) and secures letters authorizing him to arrest and extradite the followers of "the Way" who have fled Jerusalem after the death of Stephen (v. 2; 26:11).

Only in Acts is the term "the Way" used as a designation for Christians (19:9, 23; 24:14). We do not know what prompted the followers of Christ to be referred to as "the Way." Perhaps it stemmed from such Old Testament expressions as "the way of God" or "the way of righteousness," or it may have come from Jesus' calling himself "the way" (John 14:6). When Paul later confesses that he persecuted "the Way" (Acts 22:4), he means the Christian community and its message of the death and resurrection of Jesus. In Acts, therefore, "the Way" refers to the Christian community and its proclamation of Jesus, and to a particular way of life summed up as Christian discipleship (cf. *NIDNTT*, 3:941–42).

Having obtained letters apparently from the Sanhedrin, Saul heads for Damascus, a city about 140 miles north of Jerusalem and the home of a large Jewish community. He knows that many Christians will be found worshiping in Jewish synagogues. The implication here is that the Sanhedrin had power over the members of synagogues outside of Palestine, but scholars have disputed whether the high priest had authority to intervene in the affairs of those synagogues. Luke does not tell us, but perhaps Saul's traveling companions are officers of the Sanhedrin.

As Saul and his companions draw near to Damascus, he is dramatically stopped in his tracks. Without any warning he has an encounter with the risen Lord. He is suddenly surrounded by a blinding light out of heaven and hears a voice speaking to him in Aramaic (26:14). These two manifestations are characteristics of divine revelation. The light shows forth the glory of the exalted Lord. It is not surprising that it blinds Saul since no one is able to physically look at God. The voice out of heaven is also characteristic of revelation (Luke 3:22; 9:35).

The risen Jesus is the one who appears to Saul (cf. 1 Cor. 9:1; 15:8) and speaks to him: "Saul, Saul, why do you persecute me?" (Acts 9:4). That question is directed at Saul's immediate purpose to destroy the church. Attacking Jesus' disciples is not, as Saul thinks, mere persecution of people worshiping in a heretical manner. It is an attack upon their heavenly representative himself, in the person of his people. To persecute Christians is to persecute Christ (Luke 10:16), who himself was rejected but now is risen and continues to be active in history.

At first Jesus does not identify himself. Thus the persecutor asks, "Who are you, Lord" (v. 5). The address "Lord" used here may be simply a title of respect meaning "Sir." But there is strong support for understanding it in the Christian sense as "Lord" (cf. 1:6, 24; 4:29; 7:59–60; 9:10, 13; 10:14; 11:8; 22:19). Saul acknowledges the one who is speaking as Lord, recognizing that he is speaking to a heavenly person.

The exalted Lord then identifies himself as Jesus, the one whom Saul is persecuting. There on the road to Damascus the Crucified One, revealed to Saul in his divine glory, transforms him. The archenemy of the church dies spiritually to his former life and is made a new man (cf. Gal. 2:20). At the time of his miraculous change he receives a prophetic call, with a task to perform: He must get up and go into Damascus, where he will be given instructions about his future ministry. Saul offers no resistance, though just a short time ago he was "breathing out murderous threats against the Lord's disciples" (Acts 9:1).

Saul's companions stand speechless; they hear the sound of the Lord's voice, evidently not understanding what he is saying (cf. Arrington, 1988, 95–96), but they do not see him. They are puzzled. The risen Lord has appeared only to Saul and given him a command. Obeying it, he arises to go into Damascus and discovers that he is unable to see. As a result, he has to be led into the city by his companions. There he fasts for three days. Luke does not tell us why, but his abstinence from food and drink may have been due to his state of shock or his waiting to be told what to do. This zealous opponent of the church has been rendered helpless by the Lord.

4.3.2. Ananias Visits Saul (9:10–19a). While Saul is fasting and praying, the risen Lord prepares to let him know that his calling is to preach the gospel. The Lord speaks to a Jewish Christian in Damascus named Ananias, who is "a devout observer of the law and highly respected by all the Jews living there" (22:12). Nothing more is known about him, but he may have been among those who fled Jerusalem after the death of Stephen. In a vision the Lord directs Ananias to a house on Straight Street, a street that runs east to west in Damascus. In that house he will find Saul of Tarsus, engaged in earnest prayer. Saul is expecting the visit because he has been granted a vision of a man called Ananias laying "his hands on him to restore his sight" (9:12). The Lord is working on both ends by speaking to Saul and to Ananias (cf. 10:1–23).

God has prepared Ananias to minister to Saul, but at first he is reluctant because he has heard about Saul's persecution of God's people. According to reports, Saul was throwing believers into jail in Jerusalem (8:2–3), and he now had letters authorizing him to arrest Christians in Damascus and to extradite them to Jerusalem. Ananias speaks of the believers in two significant expressions: as "saints" and as "all who call on your name." (1) "Saints"

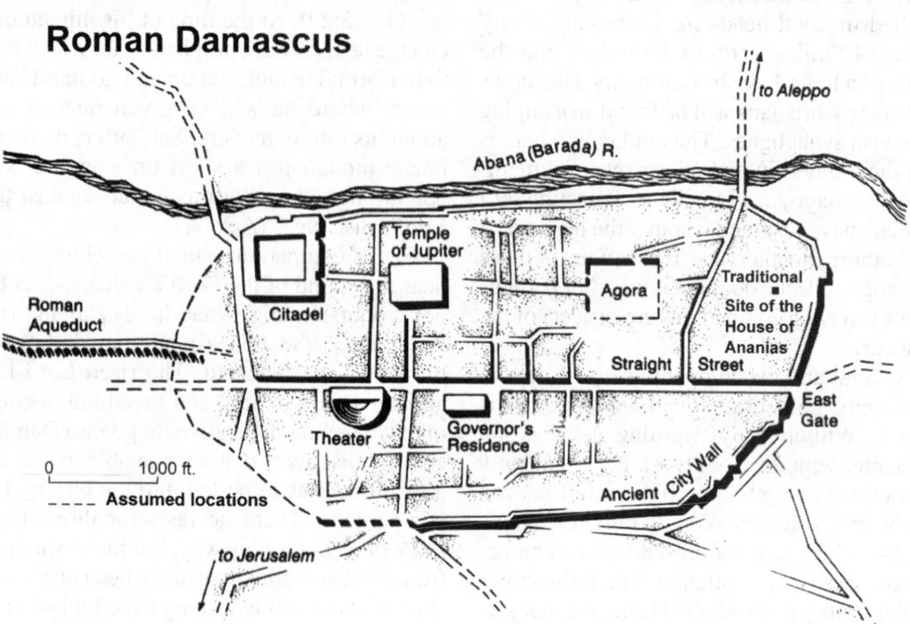

Damascus represented much more to Saul, the strict Pharisee, than another stop on his campaign of repression. It was the hub of a vast commercial network with far-flung lines of caravan trade reaching into north Syria, Mesopotamia, Anatolia, Persia, and Arabia. If the new "Way" of Christianity flourished in Damascus, it would quickly reach all these places. From the viewpoint of the Sanhedrin and of Saul, the arch-persecutor, it had to be stopped in Damascus.

The city was a veritable oasis, situated in a plain watered by the biblical rivers Abana and Pharpar. Roman architecture overlaid the Hellenistic town plan with a great temple to Jupiter and a mile-long colonnaded street, the "Straight Street" of Acts 9:11. The city gates and a section of the town wall, as well as the lengthy bazaar that runs along the line of the ancient street, may still be seen today.

The dominant political figure at the time of Paul's escape from Damascus (2 Cor 11:32-33) was Aretas IV, king of the Nabateans (9 B.C.-A.D. 40), though normally cities of the Decapolis were attached to the province of Syria and under the influence of Rome.

is a term used frequently in the New Testament for Christians; it describes them as being consecrated to live holy lives in the service of the Lord. (2) "All who call on your name" means they are people who pray and worship in the name of Jesus Christ (cf. 2:21; 22:16).

In light of the terrible suffering Saul has been causing the Christians, Ananias's initial response is entirely natural. But that response introduces a further statement from the Lord about his calling of Saul. "This man is my chosen instrument" (v. 15; cf. Gal. 1:15–16), a statement that emphasizes the divine initiative in calling him. Despite what Saul has done in the past, God has future plans for him. His task is to proclaim the name of Jesus to Gentiles, to their kings, and to the people of Israel. Like the other disciples, he is to bear witness to the ends of the earth (Acts 1:8).

The fulfillment of Saul's mission will involve suffering for the sake of Jesus (v. 16). The list of his sufferings in 2 Corinthians 11:23–29 gives us a good commentary on this facet of Jesus' message. Saul's conversion and call bring about a radical change in his life—the persecutor becomes the persecuted. Here we see in sharp contrast what Saul intended to be and what he becomes as a chosen servant of the Lord. It is no easy matter to bear witness to the Savior. To say the least, it is costly.

The East Gate of Damascus still opens onto Straight Street. It was in Damascus, in the house of Ananias, that Saul fasted for three days after he was blinded by his meeting with Jesus on the road into the city. Saul, who became Paul, had been on his way to Damascus to arrest any Christians he found there, but became a Christian instead.

The word Ananias receives from the Lord removes his fear of the former persecutor. He therefore goes to where Saul is staying. When he comes into his presence, he addresses Saul as "Brother"—not meaning fellow Israelite but fellow believer. As a Christian Saul has accepted Jesus as his Savior and Lord and has been renewed and indwelt by the Holy Spirit. He is now a brother in Christ. The Lord has sent Ananias so that Saul's sight may be restored and that he may "be filled with the Holy Spirit" (v. 17). As Ananias prays for him, a flaky substance falls from Saul's eyes, and he recovers his sight.

Saul had been motivated by zeal to persecute believers, but now he needs more than zeal to fulfill his prophetic task of preaching the gospel to the Gentiles. He must be "filled with the Holy Spirit," just as the disciples were on the day of Pentecost. The Acts account does not state precisely when he receives the fullness of the Spirit. Most likely he receives the Pentecostal experience as Ananias lays his hands on him.

Saul's subsequent ministry in Damascus clearly indicates that he is full of the Spirit. After his healing he is baptized by Ananias, which may imply that he has already been filled with the Spirit. He then ends his fast. But he does not leave Damascus. "At once" Saul begins to proclaim the gospel in the synagogues of that city that Jesus is the Son of God (v. 20). His inspired preaching is a clear sign that he is full of the Spirit. He grows "more and more powerful," baffling "the Jews living in Damascus by proving that Jesus is the Christ" (v. 22).

By healing Saul of his blindness the Lord gives him a powerful sign of his calling, and through baptism in the Spirit he empowers him to proclaim the gospel to everyone (v. 15). This experience demonstrates that God gives the fullness of his Spirit to those who obey him (5:32) and to those who earnestly pray for it (Luke 11:13). Note how after his encounter with the Lord on the road, Saul obeyed the heavenly voice by going into Damascus, where he spent three days in intense prayer and fasting.

Luke is silent not only about the time when Saul is filled with the Spirit but also about any manifestations that may have accompanied the experience. He makes no mention, for example, of his speaking in tongues. But in his first letter to the Corinthians Paul affirms that he does speak in tongues, an experience he ascribes to the Spirit (1 Cor. 12:10–11; 14:18). His charismatic experience in Damascus most certainly included speaking in tongues. Luke's primary concern is to describe Saul's call and the empowering he received for preaching the good news. His experience, therefore, is consistent with the outpouring of the Spirit on the believers at Jerusalem and Samaria.

Paul's charismatic experience, according to Acts, parallels that of Peter. Both Paul and Peter are empowered by the Spirit to carry the name of Jesus (2:4; 4:8, 31; 9:17; 13:9, 52). The most important factor in their success is that they are guided and enabled by the Holy Spirit. As Luke has noted, the Spirit has already worked through Peter in powerful ways (2:14–41; 3:11–26; 4:8–12; 5:1–11), and those ways are the same as the pattern for later events in Peter's ministry (10:1–11:18; 12:1–17). Consistent with Paul's charismatic anointing, the Holy Spirit is present in a powerful manner to make him succeed as an apostolic missionary. Because he is filled with the Spirit, he bears witness to Jesus by works of power such as healing the sick (14:8–20), casting out demons (16:16–18), and raising the dead (20:7–12). He also bears witness by words of power, such as his pronouncement of a curse on Elymas the magician (13:6–12) and his powerful testimony before the Sanhedrin (23:1–11). Like Peter, Paul's special anointing has great significance for his ministry that lies ahead.

4.3.3. Saul Preaches That Jesus Is the Christ (9:19b–22). Saul stays several days with the Damascus Christians, who apparently receive him at once into their fellowship. Soon after his baptism in water and in the Spirit, he begins to fulfill the mission God has given him by preaching that Jesus is the Son of God. The title "Son of God" refers to Jesus' messianic sonship in accordance to Psalm 2:7 and is a key in Paul's theology (cf. Rom. 1:4). Like Peter at Pentecost, he is empowered by the Spirit to proclaim to unbelieving Jews that Jesus is the initiator of salvation and that his death is the only means of reconciling people to God (cf. Rom. 5:10; Gal. 2:20; Col. 1:13–14). Evidently on this occasion Saul has only a short ministry in the city.

Saul's preaching has a strong effect upon his hearers. All who hear him are amazed at this man who had sought to destroy the church in Jerusalem and had come to Damascus with a similar purpose. The word translated here "raised havoc" (*portheo*) means to sack or ravage a city (cf. Gal. 1:13, 23, where Paul uses this word to describe his efforts to destroy the church). Now in the synagogues in Damascus he bears witness to the same faith he had tried to destroy. Saul had seen the risen Christ in his glory and thus preaches as an eyewitness (cf. 1 Cor. 9:1).

The Jews in Damascus find themselves baffled by Saul's arguments that the crucified Jesus is the Messiah promised by the Old Testament prophets. Inspired by the Holy Spirit, he becomes more and more powerful in his preaching, and his opponents are thrown into confusion and are unable to refute him. This increase in power speaks of the dynamic work of the Spirit. Such spiritual power is basic to the Pentecostal experience and is basic to Paul's entire ministry, which begins here in Damascus and continues for the next twenty-five years or more.

4.3.4. Jews Plot to Kill Saul (9:23–25). Luke makes no mention of Saul's visit to Arabia soon after his conversion and his subsequent return to Damascus (see Gal. 1:17). Where he went in Arabia and how long he stayed, we are not told. At that time the area designated as "Arabia" applied to the whole territory of modern Arabia, Sinai, and inland up to Damascus. Saul probably spent most of the three years in and around Damascus, preaching in various cities and villages.

"After many days had gone by," the Jews plot to assassinate Saul (Acts 9:23). These "many days" likely make up the three years mentioned in Galatians 1:18 as lapsing before Saul goes up to Jerusalem. That plot may have been the result of his powerful missionary activity in Arabia. Luke does not tell us how Saul learns about the plot against his life. According to 2 Corinthians 11:32 the governor of Damascus under Aretas, the king of Arabia, cooperates with an attempt to arrest the apostle. His would-be assassins keep constant watch of the city gates, waiting for him to try to leave the city. This activity becomes known to Saul's Christian friends, and they enable him to escape the clutches of his enemies by letting him down in a basket outside the city wall.

Already Saul has begun to suffer for the name of his Savior (cf. v. 16). His prophetic proclamation of Jesus as the Son of God has met strong resistance, but God's deliverance of him from Damascus suggests that this Spirit-filled apostle is destined to preach the gospel to the ends of the earth. None of the efforts to obstruct his path will succeed, and finally because of God's grace and power this "chosen instrument" (v. 15) will emerge as one through whom God's purpose is fulfilled (28:31).

4.3.5. Barnabas Befriends Saul (9:26–30). Compelled to flee from the scene of his first labors in the gospel, Saul returns to Jerusalem. The twelve apostles had remained in the Holy City when Saul set out on his murderous mission. They and other disciples had not forgotten his persecution. When he arrives, he encounters doubt and suspicion. The believers have heard about his conversion (Gal. 1:23); but knowing his history, they are fearful of him and doubt that he is a genuine disciple. They do not rule out the possibility of a grand plot to take advantage of them. It seems incredible to them that such a violent persecutor has become a Christian. Thus, the Christians reject Saul when he attempts to join them.

Barnabas seems to be the first to have been convinced of Saul's sincerity. He introduces him to two of the apostles, Peter and James (Gal. 1:18–24). This "Son of Encouragement" (Acts 4:36) is familiar with the details of Saul's conversion and his evangelistic work in Damascus. He apparently convinces the Christian community not only of the genuineness of this Pharisee's conversion but also of the Lord's calling and equipping him for ministry. Because of Barnabas's commendation Saul is accepted as a genuine disciple and a preacher of the gospel.

Now having a close association with the apostles and the power of his ministry recognized by them, Saul preaches with the same boldness as he had in Damascus (v. 28). Following in the footsteps of Stephen, he preaches to the Greek-speaking Jews (*Hellenistai*) and debates with them. They find their new opponent just as invincible as Stephen had been. Since they cannot repudiate Saul's reasoning from the Scriptures, they resolve that his fate will be the same as Stephen's. When the Christians learn that Saul's life is in peril, they send him to Caesarea. He makes a short voyage north on the Mediterranean into the region of Tarsus, the place of his birth (21:39; 22:3).

Saul disappears at this point from Luke's account and reappears about ten years later (11:25–30). This is known as a "silent period," but obviously it is silent only to us. During this period, according to his own account, he went into the regions of Syria and Cilicia, preaching to people there the faith he had once tried to destroy (Gal. 1:21–24).

4.3.6. Summary (9:31). Luke moves from the labors of Saul to Peter's mission to the Gentiles by summing up the state of the expanding church. The "church" (a singular word) refers to the churches in Judea, Samaria, and Galilee as one spiritual body. All the believers belong to one brotherhood. The church has advanced in the land of the Jews, and Luke will soon focus on a new stage in the church's mission under the constant guidance of the Holy Spirit—the coastal regions of Lydda and Joppa (9:32–43) and then Caesarea (10:1–11:18).

The church enjoys peace since persecution has ceased. Freedom from sufferings allows believers through the help of the Spirit to build up the church spiritually and numerically. Their faith is strengthened and their way of life is determined by their reverential fear of the Lord. They are aided by the encouragement (*paraklesis*) of the Holy Spirit. That is, the Spirit inspires anointed preaching and teaching so that the church is enriched and its number grows.

4.4. The Acts of Peter: A Spirit-Filled Apostle (9:32–11:18)

In this section the focus shifts back to the charismatic apostle Peter. The conspicuous weaknesses he manifested in the Gospel period are no longer evident. His baptism in the Spirit accounts for the change between the Peter of the Gospels and the Peter of Acts. The outpouring of the Spirit of prophecy (2:14–17) has empowered him and the other disciples to bear witness to Jesus Christ by works and words.

After Pentecost everything that Luke tells us about Peter identifies him as a prophet powerful in words (2:14–39; 4:8–12; 5:29–32) and works (2:43; 3:1–10; 4:29–33; 5:12–16). Like his Lord, Peter has an itinerant ministry and heals people who are crippled and raises the dead. As he had done earlier in Jerusalem, Peter now performs miracles in Lydda (9:32–35) and Joppa (9:40). He reaches out to people of various races—Jews, Samaritans, and eventually Gentiles.

Although the Ethiopian eunuch, a Gentile, had been converted prior to Peter's travels, his conversion had not permanently affected the policy of the church in regard to the admission of Gentiles. During the Palestinian portion of Peter's tour, by the leading and inspiration of the Holy Spirit, the apostle witnesses for Christ to the Gentile Cornelius and his household (10:9–11:18), thus continuing the spread of the gospel to the "ends of the earth" (1:8). The outpouring of the Spirit on this family raises the difficult issue of evangelizing the Gentiles.

4.4.1. Peter Heals a Paralytic (9:32–35). Luke describes Peter's travels throughout Judea, to places outside Jerusalem where there are Christian communities. He arrives in Lydda, located west of Jerusalem on the road leading to the coastal town of Joppa. There he visits the Christians who either fled from Jerusalem when Saul was persecuting the church or who were converted by Philip when he was evangelizing from Azotus to Caesarea (8:40).

At Lydda, Peter finds a man by the name of Aeneas, who has been bedridden for eight years with paralysis. Peter's words to the man make it clear that Jesus works miracles through him: "Jesus Christ heals you" (v. 34). This healing reminds us of the miracle performed by Jesus on a paralytic man, brought to him by four friends (Luke 5:17–26), and of the healing of the lame man at the Beautiful Gate in Jerusalem (Acts 3:1–10; 4:22). The healing of Aeneas shows that Jesus' healing ministry did not cease with his death on the cross.

The effects of Jesus' power are visible. At Peter's command Aeneas gets up, leaving no doubt about the reality of his healing. The Jews in Lydda and in the surrounding plain of Sharon see that the man has been made whole. The man is widely known, and this prophetic deed causes many of them to become believers in the Lord Jesus.

4.4.2. Peter Raises Tabitha From the Dead (9:36–43). From Lydda, where the gospel has triumphed, Peter goes to Joppa, a seaport serving Jerusalem located only about thirty-five miles from the Holy City. There two men approach Peter regarding Tabitha, a Christian woman, who has been ill and recently died. Tabitha is known in Joppa for her ministry to the poor and to widows. During her life, she clothed widows with garments made with her own hands. The phrase "all the widows" in verse 39 may suggest that although widows were not officially recognized as an order in the church, they may have been treated so by those ministering to them. Regardless, Tabitha's ministry to the widows is seen as a vital part of the ministry of the church.

At the time of Tabitha's death, according to Jewish custom of the purification of the dead, her body is washed (m. *Shabbath*, 23:50) and laid in an upper chamber (cf. 2 Kings 4:32–37). The normal practice was a speedy burial so that the corpse would not lie overnight. Her friends, however, delay her burial in hopes that Tabitha may be raised from the dead. They send two men to Peter in Lydda with the urgent request: "Please come at once!" Tabitha's friends have sufficient faith to believe that Peter might possibly raise this saint from the dead.

When Peter arrives in Joppa, he encounters a touching situation. People are mourning in the house where the body of Tabitha lies in the upstairs room. A group of poor widows shows Peter the clothing that Tabitha had made for them and their children. Peter sends all the people out of the room (cf. Mark 5:40). He kneels and prays the prayer of faith for a miracle. Then, with a voice of authority, the apostle commands the dead woman to stand up. She responds to Peter's call by opening her eyes and sitting up. He then reaches out his hand and helps her to her feet.

Once again the effects of the power of Jesus become visible and demonstrate charismatic power working through Peter. This mighty act of healing is closely associated with Spirit-empowered prophets such as Elijah, who raised the widow's son from the dead (1 Kings 17:17–24), and Elisha, who raised the Shunammite woman's son from the dead (2 Kings 4:8–37), as well as with Jesus, who raised several people from the dead. This miracle strongly confirms that Peter's ministry is both prophetic and charismatic.

Like many events in Luke-Acts the miracle of raising Tabitha from the dead is an answer to prayer. Her resurrection shows that Jesus is the Lord of life and that he is able to overcome the power of death. This event must have brought great joy to the Christians in Joppa. It gives us also a foretaste of the joy we will experience when the dead in Christ will rise. No wonder this great miracle of resurrection and healing becomes known throughout all Joppa and leads many Jews to believe in the Lord as their Savior.

4.4.3. Peter Preaches to the Gentiles (10:1–48). The scene shifts from Joppa to Caesarea, an important seaport on the coast of Palestine. At that time Caesarea, primarily a Gentile city, was the Roman capital for Judea and Syria. Luke focuses attention on Cornelius, undeniably a Gentile and a rough Roman soldier, but at the same time a godly man, who devoted himself to constant prayer and to generosity with his neighbors. He is a "God-fearer"—someone who is devoted to Judaism, but in the eyes of the Jews is still a pagan and unclean because he has not accepted baptism and circumcision.

The importance of this story is evident by e space that Luke gives it (10:1–11:18). The count of the outpouring of the Spirit on Cor-·lius falls in line with the plan and purpose of ıke-Acts. Luke emphasizes three main truths this particular episode. (1) God approves of e ever-widening evangelistic outreach, cluding now outreach to the Gentiles (cf. 8). This outreach ministry embraces prayers, sions, angels, conversions, and ministry of e Spirit, all of which are the direct result of vine guidance and empowerment.

(2) Emphasis on God's initiative in ministry ›es not deny personal decisions or make Peter ıd Cornelius robots. As occurs throughout cts, the divine initiative calls for human sponse. It is a matter of divine direction and ıman obedience, as Peter's response to the ords of the Holy Spirit in 10:19–20 illustrates.

(3) When Peter reports what happened while : was praying in Joppa and later at the home Cornelius, Luke writes that the believers at rusalem approve of receiving Gentiles in the ıurch (11:17). This approval is significant for ‹tending the mission to the Gentiles, but it fails settle the issue of receiving uncircumcised entiles into the church (cf. 15:1–29).

As a Roman centurion Cornelius is in ıarge of a hundred soldiers, about one-sixth f a regiment. His regiment is :signated "the Italian Regi-ıent," which was probably a spe-al body of Roman troops. He is prayerful man, and, though a entile, he observes the tradi-onal Jewish hour of prayer . 3). His prayers do not fall on eaf ears, for one afternoon while : is praying, an angel of God ppears to him in a vision.

The presence of the angel ·ightens Cornelius, a natural reac-on to being confronted by the ıpernatural. He addresses the eavenly visitor as "Lord" and ıquires what he wants. There is no :al reason for this devout man to : alarmed. The angel calls Cor-elius by name and assures him ıat his prayers have been heard nd that God has taken note of his eeds of kindness to the poor. The hrase "come up as a memorial offering" (v. 4) is the language of sacrifice (cf. Lev. 2:2, 9, 16). God has accepted Cornelius's prayers and gifts to the poor as fitting sacrifices. They are like burnt offerings and ascend like incense. God is now about to answer his prayers.

The angel calls upon Cornelius to act out his faith through obedience. He must send for a man in Joppa "named Simon who is called Peter." At this time Simon Peter is staying at the home of a tanner, also named Simon. Promptly Cornelius obeys the word of the angel and sends two household servants and a devout soldier to Joppa. The Jews regarded the job of a tanner, which involved preserving pigs' hides, as a despised and unclean occupation (Num. 19:11–13).

The scene shifts from Caesarea to Joppa, to the home where Peter is staying and where the Lord will now prepare him to preach the gospel to Gentiles. Peter has an indispensable work to do so that Cornelius may be brought into deeper fellowship with God and be baptized with the Spirit. As the messengers from Cornelius approach Joppa, Peter goes up on the roof of the house to pray. The flat roofs of Palestinian houses are favorite places for solitude and prayer. Like so many events in Luke-Acts, prayer provides the setting for a special revelation from the Lord (Luke 1:13; Acts 9:4).

Flat-roofed housing, seen here in a model of Jerusalem, was typical in the Holy Land. It was on the roof of a house in Joppa that Peter, who had always carefully obeyed Old Testament food laws and would not eat any meat considered unclean, falls into a trance in which God tells him, "Do not call anything impure that God has made clean." Peter soon understands God's message to mean the acceptance of Gentiles into the church.

It is noon and Peter is hungry, which, in fact, prepares him for the vision. While the meal is being prepared, he prays, falls into a trance, and has a vision. Peter's praying indicates that he is in the condition to receive a message from God. In his vision heaven opens, and Peter sees a great sheet being gradually lowered from the sky by four ropes. The sheet contains all kinds of unclean animals, reptiles, and birds (v. 12; 11:6), and he hears a heavenly voice urging him to kill the unclean animals and prepare a meal (10:13, 15). Consistent with the importance of this event, the sheet appears to Peter three times.

Though Peter is in a trance, he is completely in touch with his thoughts and feelings. Eating meat considered unclean is strongly objectionable to him. He recoils at the thought of violating the Old Testament food laws (Lev. 11; Deut. 14:1–21) and protests the command from heaven. Never in his life has he eaten anything unclean, and by abstaining he is obeying the laws given to his ancestors. Peter fails to consider that God is now abolishing such laws.

Three times Peter is rebuked by the words: "Do not call anything impure that God has made clean." This divine corrective emphasizes the cleansing power of God's saving grace. The vision, therefore, involves more than setting aside food laws and attitudes toward ritual purity. It shows especially that the Jewish distinction between the clean and unclean has no place in the church. Gentiles, cleansed by the renewing grace of God, are to be included in the fellowship of God's people. The church has no right to declare certain animals or people as defiled and to avoid them as unclean (*TDNT*, 9:298). Abolishing the food laws is God's token of the removal of a major barrier that kept Jews and Gentiles apart and indicates that God has introduced a new order in the church (cf. Eph. 2:11–18).

Peter understands that the vision challenges his traditional beliefs about the distinction between clean and unclean animals. But he is perplexed and ponders the possibility of a secondary meaning of the vision (vv. 17, 19). His mind is going this way and that (lit. meaning of *dienthymeomai*, "thinking about," in v. 19), but he is unable to come to any understanding or conclusion. But he does not remain in doubt for long, for the delegation from Cornelius arrives. The Holy Spirit reveals to Peter that has three visitors and bids him to go with ther

In other words, this entire episode has bee directed by God, and now the Holy Spi shows Peter the significance of the vision. T coming of the three men is no accident. Co vinced, the apostle goes downstairs to meet t guests. The messengers make themselv known and tell Peter of their mission. To mal a favorable impression on the apostle, the describe their master as "a righteous and Go fearing man, who is respected by all the Jev ish people." They have come because a ho angel instructed Cornelius to invite Peter preach in Caesarea. Their mentioning of Co nelius's desire to listen to what Peter has to sa introduces for the first time the idea that Pet will preach to the centurion (see vv. 34–43)

Since it is too late that day to return to Ca sarea, Peter treats the visitors as his guests. B inviting them to spend the night, it becom clear that he recognizes the truth of the visio No longer does he recoil from fellowship wi Gentiles. He sees now that he has bee divinely called to go into the home of a Ge tile and to preach the word of the Lord ther Nothing but an undeniable divine call cou have induced Peter to do this. By the Ho Spirit working through obedient servants, th way is being opened to receive Gentiles in the fellowship of the church.

Convinced that he is being led by the Ho Spirit, the next day Peter and the delegatio begin their journey to Caesarea. Six Jewis Christians from Joppa accompany them. Thes Christians probably go along because of inte est in what is happening. Later they becom crucial witnesses to God's acceptance of Ge tiles into the church and to the outpouring o the Holy Spirit on the Gentiles (11:12). Sinc they go to Caesarea with Peter, they are lat able to confirm Peter's account in Jerusalem o what happened at the home of Cornelius.

It takes Peter and the others a full day an part of the next one to reach Caesarea. Co nelius is expecting them; he has already gath ered an audience made up of his relatives an close friends (vv. 24, 27). These people hav been informed of what the centurion has don and are eager to hear Peter's message. The must have known how long the journey woul take and thus are ready and waiting for th arrival of the visitors.

As Peter enters the house of Cornelius, the enturion meets him and kneels at his feet as if) worship him. This act shows his personal umility and his great respect for the apostle as iod's messenger. Peter refuses to accept Cor-elius's respect, however, which demonstrates is own noble character. Throughout the New 'estament no one but God should receive such onor (14:14–18; Rev. 19:10; 22:9). Peter eels that the centurion's homage is excessive, nd he promptly helps him up, saying, "I am nly a man myself," making it clear that he is ot an angel. Thus the two men enter the house nd converse together as equals.

Once inside, Peter finds a group of Gentiles ssembled together to hear him. The vision hat he received dealt with certain foods as mpure or unclean, but from it Peter has dis-erned the deeper meaning that he is not to egard any person as impure or unclean. His ewish religion had taught him that Jews were ot to visit Gentiles or take meals with them, ut this is no longer valid. The presence of 'eter in the home of the Gentile Cornelius eflects a radical departure in his attitude oward the Gentiles. The Holy Spirit has pre-ared Peter to preach the gospel and Cornelius o receive it. Both men have responded to ivine direction in their own respective ways. s a result, the old barriers between Jews and Gentiles are collapsing.

The messengers have told Peter the purpose or which Cornelius invites him (v. 22), but the postle determines it appropriate to ask for a tatement as to why he has been summoned. Cornelius answers Peter's question in a direct nanner by summarizing and emphasizing ome of the facts of the vision. He was pray-ng when suddenly a man stood before him "in hining clothes"—a common way of describ-ng heavenly messengers (Matt. 28:3; Luke 4:4; Rev. 15:6). He retells what the angel said bout his prayer and gifts and that the angel nstructed him to send for Peter in Joppa. Hav-ng promptly complied with the angel's orders, e thanks the apostle for coming so quickly.

All those gathered in Cornelius's house ave gathered "in the presence of God," imply-ng that when people come together to hear the gospel, they do so in God's own presence. This gathering is not merely a meeting; it is for the urpose of hearing everything the Lord wants 'eter to tell them. The apostle has an ideal congregation, which has a marvelous attitude toward God, his word, and his messenger. They do not know what Peter will tell them, but they are willing to receive God's word from him and obey it.

Peter immediately begins his sermon. As we have noted several times, he has been empowered by the Spirit to give witness to Jesus by words (2:14–39; 4:8–12) and works (4:29–33; 5:12–16). Although Luke does not remind us again here that Peter witnesses to Cornelius and his household as a Spirit-filled apostle, obviously what he says to that Gentile household is a Spirit-inspired, prophetic message (vv. 19–20; 11:15–17). This message has three major parts.

(1) Peter begins by addressing the specific situation (vv. 34–35). He declares that God treats all people on the same basis. God does not judge a person on such factors as nationality or race but on character—he "accepts men from every nation who fear [God] and do what is right." Peter goes on to teach that salvation is only possible through faith in the gospel of the death and resurrection of Jesus Christ. Following moral rules fails to make a person acceptable to God. This gospel is offered to all without restriction, provided they are willing to repent of their sins and trust in Jesus for forgiveness. In God's sight those who fear him and do what is right are those who are marked by faith in the Savior.

(2) Peter describes the personal career of Jesus, providing a commendable summary of the Gospel of Luke (vv. 36–41). God does not discriminate, for he sent the message through Jesus Christ, who is the Lord of all people, not just Israel (v. 36). The content of God's message is the "good news of peace," which Jesus preached to the people of Israel. "Peace" refers to peace with God or reconciliation offered to all people and made possible through the atoning death of Jesus Christ. Peace is more than the absence of strife and enmity with God; it includes experiencing the positive blessings of salvation. Although Jesus first preached the good news to the Jews, the message was not intended for Israel alone.

Devout people like Cornelius and his friends know about the ministry of Jesus that began in Galilee after John the Baptist preached his baptism, and the good news of peace filled the land of Judea (v. 37). Peter's use of the words "you know" seems to indicate the people present have already heard the gospel before Peter preaches to them. In light of the narrative of Acts we could assume that these people are hearing their first Christian sermon from Peter, but Philip, an evangelist living in Caesarea (8:40; 21:8), or some other believer may have actually introduced them to the gospel on an earlier occasion. At the conclusion of Peter's sermon he simply declares that everyone who believes in Christ receives forgiveness of sins (v. 43).

The reference in 11:18 that "God has granted even the Gentiles repentance unto life" fails to indicate whether this repentance happened before or after Peter arrived. Cornelius is reported in 11:14 to have been told to send for Peter in order that he and his people may be "saved." Yet nothing is mentioned here explicitly concerning the repentance and conversion of Cornelius and his friends. Peter's preaching may have only confirmed their prior faith in Jesus. But Luke does not state explicitly anything to this effect. Rather, he simply describes Cornelius in Jewish terms as "God-fearing" and as a follower of the Jewish practice of almsgiving and prayer (10:2).

Another possible interpretation is that as Peter preaches to the people of Cornelius, they believe the gospel and are subsequently baptized in the Spirit. This interpretation, like the previous one, maintains a distinction between the indwelling of the Holy Spirit and the baptism of the Spirit. According to this view, their immersion in the Spirit comes immediately after their conversion. Their double experience occurs concomitantly. One matter is clear: As Peter preaches the gospel, the Holy Spirit comes upon the God-fearing Gentiles (v. 44; 11:15).

Continuing the second part of his sermon, Peter gives a brief outline of what happened to Jesus. (a) "God anointed Jesus of Nazareth with the Holy Spirit and power." After Jesus' baptism in the Jordan, the Holy Spirit anointed Jesus for his ministry (Luke 3:21–22; 4:1, 14–21). The power of the Spirit enabled him to do truly good deeds for the people. By his miracles he demonstrated God's rule over the devil and the forces of evil. His mighty deeds show that God was with him and was working through him (Acts 10:38). The apostles had been with Jesus from the very beginning of his ministry (1:21–22), so they were eyewitnesses of what he did in the city of Jerusalem and the rest of the country of the Jews (Luke 4:31–44). As witnesses of Jesus' whole ministry, Peter and his companions affirm the full truth of the gospel.

(b) Jesus was put to death by the Jews, who hung "him on a tree" (see comments on 5:17–32). But God brought him back to life on the third day and allowed a select group of witnesses to see him alive on earth for a period of forty days (Luke 24:13–53; Acts 1:3–11). These witnesses were "chosen" by God beforehand. Jesus, therefore, did not appear to all the Jewish people, but only to those who had been prepared to be witnesses through their long and intimate association with the Savior. Their testimony rested especially on the fact they had meals with Christ after his resurrection (Acts 10:41; cf. Luke 24:13–43). Now Peter bears witness to these Gentiles about this central truth of the gospel—the resurrection of Christ.

(3) Peter speaks about Christ's mandate to the apostles to preach to the people. As part of their message they are to declare that God has appointed Jesus "as judge of the living and the dead" (v. 42; 2 Tim. 4:1; 1 Peter 4:5). He is destined to judge all persons of both the past and present. At the end of the world some will still be alive on the earth; they as well as the dead will face the Spirit-anointed Christ as their ultimate judge (cf. John 5:21–22). To this One the Old Testament prophets testify, and their witness agrees with the apostolic preaching "that everyone who believes in him receives forgiveness of sins through his name" (Acts 10:43; cf. Isa. 33:24; 53:4–6; Jer. 31:34). All who believe in Jesus, both Jew and Gentile, will have their sins forgiven.

Peter's sermon is suddenly interrupted by the Gentile believers' receiving the charismatic gift of the Holy Spirit (vv. 44–48). A favorable response of Cornelius and his friends to the sermon is indicated: "all who heard the message" (v. 44) and "praising God" (v. 46). God takes the initiative by letting the Holy Spirit fall upon (cf. *epepesen* in v. 44) these uncircumcised believers as Peter preaches to them. They receive the same Spirit-baptism as did the believers at Pentecost. As the audible, visible, initial evidence of being filled with the Spirit, Cornelius and his friends speak in tongues—a manifestation that later causes the hurch leaders to glorify God and to acknowl-dge that "God has granted even the Gentiles epentance unto life" (11:18).

The six Jewish Christians accompanying 'eter to Caesarea are surprised by the falling f the charismatic gift of the Spirit on these ientiles. Clearly God here pours out his Spirit n the household of Cornelius in the Pente-ostal fashion. The similarities between the utpouring of the Spirit at this occasion in Cae-area and on the Day of Pentecost in Jerusalem re striking.

- On both occasions the Spirit fills people who are already saved. Before they receive the fullness of the Spirit, they are already children of God and are indwelt by the Spirit. The reception of the Spirit's power for ministry and service is therefore distinct from the Spirit's reception by faith for salvation.
- The disciples at Pentecost and the believ-ers at Caesarea respond in similar ways: speaking in tongues (2:4; 10:46) and praising God (2:11; 10:46).
- When the church at Jerusalem questions Peter about visiting Cornelius, he declares that "the Holy Spirit came on them as he had come on us at the beginning" (11:15). Later he tells the Jerusalem Council that God gave the Holy Spirit to the household of Cornelius "just as he did to us" (15:8). Without the evidence of speaking in tongues, Peter, the six Jewish Christians, and the leaders of the Jerusalem church would never have acknowledged that the uncircumcised Gentiles were baptized in the Spirit and accepted into God's family.

After the interruption Peter continues the iscourse. The baptism in the Spirit indicates aat these Gentiles are as acceptable to God as re Jewish believers. Cornelius and his house-old "have received the Holy Spirit" as did the elievers at Pentecost (v. 47). God, of course, ook the initiative in bestowing the Pentecostal ift of the Spirit, but the verb "received" active voice) indicates the necessity of a uman response to this divine initiative. efore his ascension into heaven Jesus romised the disciples that they would receive ower after the Holy Spirit had come upon em (1:8; cf. 2:38; 8:15; 19:2). The household f Cornelius has received the power of the Spirit, clearly indicating concomitant human response to God's initiative.

On the basis of their Spirit-baptism the apostle challenges anyone to deny the Gentile believers water baptism, the ordinance that serves as an outward sign of conversion and thus of cleansing from sin. Since no one raises an objection, Peter commands the Gentiles to be "baptized in the name of Jesus Christ" (v. 48). They belong to Jesus and can rightly be baptized in his name, for they owe allegiance to him as their Lord.

Baptism in the Spirit normally follows water baptism (see Acts 2:38; 8:14–17), but here empowerment by the Spirit precedes it. The work of the Spirit is not tied to water bap-tism. Only after the household of Cornelius has been saved and empowered by the Spirit to be prophetic witnesses does Peter administer to them the rite of water baptism. The vision at Joppa convinced Peter that "God does not show favoritism" (v. 34)—that even people like Cornelius are accepted by God. But the Gentiles' receiving Spirit-baptism teaches Peter a second lesson: God's impartiality applies not only to salvation; it applies to all his gifts (Stronstad, 1984, 67).

God makes no difference between Gentile and Jewish believers. Without becoming con-verts to Judaism, Cornelius and his family enter the church on equal standing with the Jewish Christians, and they receive the same prophetic gift of the Spirit bestowed on the believers at Pentecost, on the Samaritans (8:14–17), and on the apostle Paul (9:17). The outpouring of the Spirit on the Gentile house-hold of Cornelius becomes a decisive turning point in the mission of the church. The Chris-tian church now begins to reach out to Gentiles as well as Jews.

At the end of Peter's meeting with Cor-nelius, rather than leaving immediately, Peter stays with the Gentile believers "for a few days." His brief stay shows the full member-ship of Gentiles in the Christian community. The gospel makes it possible for people of dif-ferent backgrounds and racial origins to have fellowship with one another.

4.4.4. Peter Defends His Ministry (11:1–18). The gospel has broken through to the Gen-tiles, and the household of Cornelius has been filled with the Spirit. Peter has had a signifi-cant role in this development (Acts 10). The news travels, so that Jewish believers and the apostles in Jerusalem hear that the Gentiles in Caesarea have received the gospel.

When Peter arrives in Jerusalem, he faces criticism from "the circumcised believers" (v. 2). Among the Jewish Christians these critics apparently constitute a sub-group who favor the circumcision of Gentiles, requiring them to become Jews before they can become Christians. Though they probably have reservations about Peter's launching a mission to the Gentiles, they do not attack him directly for preaching to them but rather for engaging in table fellowship with them—that is, for entering the home of uncircumcised Gentiles and eating with them. He has disregarded both the law of circumcision and the Jewish food laws.

In his defense, Peter describes the events that took place in Caesarea (vv. 4–15; cf. 10:24–48). Likely those Jewish Christians had received an inaccurate report, but by relating the events as they actually happened, Peter points out that God had led him to do what he did. He therefore tells them about the vision, the hearing of the voice, and the command of the Holy Spirit to go with the men to Caesarea. The message that accompanied that vision was that no one may regard as unclean what God has made clean. In other words, not only did God approve but he actually initiated Peter's preaching to the Gentiles and associating with them. The vision nullified the old laws of separation and justified Peter's willingness to have social contact with Gentiles.

The relating of this story underscores the great importance of the outpouring of the Holy Spirit on Cornelius and his household. In retelling it Peter mentions the "six brothers" for the first time (v. 12)—earlier referred to as "some of the brothers from Joppa" (10:23). They had accompanied Peter to Caesarea, were eyewitnesses to the outpouring of the Holy Spirit on the Gentiles, and can presumably verify everything. Peter does not mention his baptizing the Gentiles in water, but he does point out that the angel's message to Cornelius included the assurance of salvation for his household (11:14). In other words, Peter's actions have served God's great saving purpose. Whether Cornelius found salvation before or as Peter preached is not addressed.

Peter then tells the Christian Jews that before he could finish his sermon to the Gentiles, they experienced precisely what Jesus' followe experienced "at the beginning," that is in th upper room, on the day of Pentecost (vv. 1 17). Cornelius and his household received th baptism in the Spirit, and they were thu empowered for ministry subsequent to salva tion. Having experienced the transformin grace of the Spirit, they were empowered a prophetic witnesses to the gospel. The outwar sign of tongues confirmed that God ha accepted and anointed them to be his servants

According to chapter 11, Peter does nc explicitly mention tongues as part of what hap pened at Caesarea, but this sign of the Spir is strongly suggested to the Jerusalem believ ers by his allusion to the events of Pentecos "The Holy Spirit came upon them as he ha come on us at the beginning" (v. 15); God gav to the Gentiles "the same gift as he gave us (v. 17). The mention of tongues in 10:46 make any reference to them unnecessary in chapte 11. The Jewish Christians would have recog nized such inspired speaking as the inevitabl sign of the Spirit-baptism. The Gentiles at th house of Cornelius, therefore, have entered th church on a par with the Jewish believers an were anointed with power for ministry.

The outpouring of the Spirit at Caesare reminds Peter of the words of Jesus in 1: "John baptized with water, but you will be bap tized with the Holy Spirit" (v. 16). This promis had been fulfilled at Pentecost and now also a Caesarea to Gentiles. The gospel had broke through to the Gentiles, and Peter saw that Go had given them "the same gift" with the sign c tongues as on the day of Pentecost.

For Peter the manifestation of glossolali has important apologetic value. Because th Spirit had manifested himself in this manne on Pentecost, tongues provided significan proof that Cornelius and his friends had bee immersed in the Spirit. The outpouring of th Spirit at Caesarea was just as decisive as a Pentecost. No one could deny that these Ger tiles had been filled with the Spirit and tha God had opened the doors of the church t them. Failure to recognize that God had fille them with the Spirit—but even more th refusal to act accordingly—would have bee tantamount to opposing God.

Thus, Peter asks his critics if they think tha he should have prevented God from doin what he wanted to do (v. 17). The obviou swer is no. Peter was, therefore, certainly stified in going into the house of the Gen-es, eating with them, and baptizing them; for od intended there to be no distinction tween these Gentile believers and the Jew-n believers.

Upon hearing these facts from Peter, his ponents, the Jewish Christians in Judea, stop eir criticism (v. 18). The Pentecostal mani-station of tongues was undeniable proof of e Gentiles' immersion in the Spirit. They cept the truth and, without complaining, mediately praise God, acknowledging that od has granted even the Gentiles repentance to life." The door of the church had been ened to the Gentiles by God's giving them e opportunity to repent and receive eternal e. Accordingly, Gentile Christians must be elcomed, and believers must praise God for ving them and giving them the fullness of the irit.

This account provides a striking example of sus' promise that the Holy Spirit will lead lievers into all truth (John 16:13). Peter did t know that God had planned that uncir-mcised persons could enter the church. But obeying the command of the Holy Spirit cts 11:12), he was guided into this new truth. s subsequent recounting of these events also ought his critics in Jerusalem the same light. e Spirit illuminated their hearts and minds; ey could clearly see the evidence that had nvinced Peter. The Spirit still works in this anner; he reaches the hearts and minds of ople through the Scriptures and spiritual fts (cf. 1 Cor. 12:8–11).

We are not told how far the implications of ter's actions reach in Jerusalem. His expla-tion silences his critics, but it is unclear ether Jerusalem is willing to follow Peter's d. The question of whether Gentiles can come Christians without first becoming ws seems to have been fully settled here, but e same question becomes an issue once again Acts 15.

4.5. The Acts of Barnabas: A Spirit-Filled Prophet (11:19–26)

The Gentile mission now shifts to Antioch Syria. Earlier Luke had mentioned how the es of persecution ignited against the first lievers in Jerusalem after the stoning of ephen. That persecution had the effect of multiplying rather than silencing their witness: "Those who had been scattered preached the word wherever they went" (8:4).

Some of these first Christian missionaries came to Antioch, a city about three hundred miles north of Jerusalem. Its political importance was due to the fact it served as the capital of the Roman province of Syria. Syrian Antioch, the third largest city of the Roman empire (after Rome and Alexandria), became the home base for the expansion of Christianity outside of Palestine and figured significantly in Christian missions to the Gentiles (13:1–3; 14:26–28; 15:22–35; 18:22).

The march of the gospel does not stop in Samaria and Caesarea. Some of the missionaries evangelize as far north as Phoenicia (modern Lebanon); others to the island of Cyprus, the home of Barnabas (11:19–20; cf. 4:36). This means that there were Christians on the island before Paul and Barnabas preached the gospel there (13:4–12). Still other missionaries venture even further to the north, to the famous city of Antioch, with a population that has been estimated to be about 500,000 (Marshall, 1980, 201) and the Jewish community of some 65,000 during the New Testament era (George, 1994, 170).

Apparently most of these scattered believers preached "only to Jews" (v. 19), but a few believers from Cyprus and Cyrene take a bold step and preach the good news of Jesus "to Greeks also," that is, to pagan Gentiles in Antioch (v. 20). It appears that they reached Antioch at a later time than those who preached only to Jews. Something may have taken place during the interval to cause them to be so courageous and revolutionary, such as the outpouring of the Holy Spirit at Caesarea. They put into practice what the Spirit led Peter to do with Cornelius and his friends.

The preaching of the gospel in Antioch has numerical success, which is ascribed to "the Lord's hand" (v. 21). That is, God blesses their ministry, and his power enables the disciples to bring many Jews and Gentiles of that city to faith in Jesus Christ. Peter's ministry had opened the doors of the church to the Gentiles in Caesarea, but the preaching of the gospel in Antioch is the beginning of a vigorous effort to evangelize the Gentile world.

When the church in Jerusalem learns of the spiritual awakening in Antioch, they send

This first-century cave church, right, at Antioch was the first Christian church outside of Jerusalem. It was started by Paul, Peter, and Barnabas. Followers of Jesus became known as Christians. The Roman period stela, below, still stands to the left of the entrance.

Barnabas as their representative to assist the new believers there. Evidently he is chosen because of his qualifications: "a good man, full of the Holy Spirit and faith" (v. 24). Earlier Luke introduced him as a Levite from Cyprus and explained the meaning of his name as "Son of Encouragement" (4:36). Moved by generous impulses Barnabas acted as a supporter of the former persecutor and the newly converted Saul (9:26–30). Barnabas is also identified as one of the charismatic prophets at Antioch (13:1). Along with some other disciples he is "continually filled with joy and with the Holy Spirit" (13:52; author's trans.).

When this Spirit-anointed leader arrives in Antioch, he sees already manifested in the church "the grace of God" (v. 23). He cannot help seeing the effects of divine grace apparent both in the growth of the church and in the manifestations of the Spirit (cf. 10:45). The evidence of grace at Antioch makes him gl
and true to his name he encourages the n
believers to purpose with all their heart
remain faithful to the Lord. In this context
fullness of the Spirit's anointing is the catal
behind Barnabas's inspired exhortation. T
quality of his character and the Spirit's anoi
ing of his ministry equip him well to tak
leading role in the Jewish-Gentile church
Antioch.

Barnabas is the only person in Acts wh
Luke describes as "good" (Marshall, 19
202). As a Spirit-filled man he strengthens
new converts, recognizing that God's plan
the church is being fulfilled at Antioch. A
result of his ministry and presence there, a s
ond wave of conversions occurs. "A gr
number of people" come to faith in Je
Christ without any legalistic demands be
placed upon them. God's servants who

rong in faith and full of the Spirit are well-juipped for mission.

Soon after his arrival in Antioch, Barnabas cognizes the great potential of the situation or church growth and feels the need of more elp in evangelism and teaching. His thoughts rn to Saul, the man whom he had befriended Jerusalem and who had been filled with the pirit to bear witness about Jesus to the Genles (9:15–17). Because of persecution, Saul ad fled Jerusalem and returned to his home-own, Tarsus (9:28–30), where he had mained for about ten years (cf. Gal. 1:21–24; :1). Perhaps Barnabas heard more about him nce coming to Antioch.

Barnabas is convinced this Spirit-filled postle is a suitable person to serve as a leader the mixed congregation at Antioch. Saul ould be able to meet Jews and Gentiles on qual terms. He had been reared in the Jewish aditions (Gal. 1:14; Phil. 3:4–6), and his irthplace was Tarsus, a university town influ-nced by Greek thought. When Barnabas trav-ls to Tarsus to recruit him, Saul is already an xperienced missionary. For a whole year ese two men work together at Antioch.

It seems apparent that Antioch required a ifferent contextual response to Christianity an Judea did. Christianity in the Judean envi-onment was influenced by the presence of the mple in Jerusalem, by the Pharisees and ealots, and by a law-oriented interpretation of e Christian faith. On the other hand, Antioch ood at a geographical, political, and cultural rossroads of the East and the West. In this city f great cultural diversity, Barnabas and Saul erve as pastors for a year. Their work includes oth evangelism and building up existing con-erts. They meet with the church (probably for orship) and teach large numbers of people v. 26). Many people receive Christ, and Barn-bas and Saul teach the gospel to them.

Another significant result of this year-long ninistry at Antioch is that Jesus' followers ecome known by the new name "Christians" v. 26; 26:28; 1 Peter 4:16). The word "Chris-an" refers to a follower of Christ. Outsiders dentify the believers as such because they onfess Christ as their Lord. They are the eople of the Messiah. By referring to them as Christians, unbelievers can thereby distinguish ne church from the Jewish community. It is atural and proper to call the believers Christians, but coming from unbelievers the term may have contained an element of ridicule and contempt.

4.6. The Acts of Agabus: A Spirit-Filled Prophet (11:27–30)

In his report about the ministry of Barnabas in Antioch, Luke introduces Agabus. He relates that after Saul arrives in the city, "some prophets [come] down from Jerusalem" (v. 27), among whom is Agabus. In the early church prophets were individuals with the charismatic gift of revealing God's will. They did so in the interest of the well-being of the Christian community. They were inspired as mouthpieces of the Spirit to promote and guide the church in its mission of spreading the gospel.

In Acts, Luke describes prophecy as the power of the Holy Spirit in the last days (1:8; 2:17, 33). At Pentecost the manifestation of tongues was identified as prophecy (2:4, 11, 17). In the early church any member of the Christian community could prophesy, but prophecy was mainly associated with those who had a prophetic ministry that included prediction of future events (11:28; 20:23–31), pronouncement of divine judgment (13:11; 28:25–28), the use of symbolic actions (21:11), the proclamation of God's word (13:1–5; 15:12–18), and strengthening of believers (15:32).

The first mention in Acts of the prophetic ministry of Agabus (cf. also 21:10–11) has to do with his inspired prediction of a famine to extend over the Roman empire (11:28). Luke's reference to Claudius, emperor of Rome from A.D. 41–54, provides a point in history for dating events in Acts. We have from other sources information that during the reign of Claudius famines occurred in various parts of the Roman world (cf. Suetonius, *Life of Claudius* 18.2; Tacitus, *Annals* 12.43). There was a severe famine in Judea about A.D. 46, the year Josephus reports that a famine reached its climax. That could be the year in which Paul and Barnabas take relief funds to Jerusalem.

The prophetic words of Agabus inspire the Christians at Antioch to send an offering (collection of money) to the mother church in Jerusalem to aid in the coming crisis. The Antiochian Christians believe implicitly his prophecy and make immediate provision to gather funds for the Jerusalem church. This famine likely proved to be more distressing there because of the crowded region of Judea and the prevalence of poverty. Sending a gift also served to deepen the fellowship of believers with those in Jerusalem.

The members of the congregation at Antioch voluntarily take part in this joint undertaking to avert the harm threatening the Christians in Judea. There must have been at least three reasons for their action: (1) to express their gratitude to the Jerusalem church from which the message of the gospel had come, (2) to show unity with the mother community, and (3) to demonstrate Christian love. Because God has blessed the Antiochian church numerically and materially, they are able to send a substantial love gift to the Judean Christians. All the members of the young congregation contribute whatever they can (v. 29).

Paul has been at Antioch for only about a year when the church sends him and Barnabas to Jerusalem with the love gift. Paul's first visit to Jerusalem occurred three years after his conversion (Gal. 1:18). The next visit recorded in his letters (2:1–10) has been identified with the visit either of Acts 11 or of Acts 15. The events of the famine visit of Acts 11:27–30 parallel better the Galatians 2 visit. Luke focuses his account on the love gift from Antioch without any hint of the issue of admitting Gentiles into the church (cf. Paul's comments in Gal. 2:1–10).

Barnabas and Paul deliver the gift in person to "the elders" of the church in Jerusalem. This is the first mention of Christian elders in Acts. They probably functioned similarly to the elders of a Jewish synagogue in that they presided over the Jerusalem church (cf. 15:13). The word "elders" does not necessarily mean that they were "old men," though it seems likely that the leadership of a congregation was in the hands of older people. No doubt the organization of the church was still developing, but with elders to manage the local affairs of the church the apostles were free to devote themselves to the preaching of the gospel. When the elders of the church in Jerusalem receive the love gift, they see to its proper distribution to the needy.

The church at Antioch manifests real Christian generosity. Their love gift shows to the Christians in Jerusalem that God's grace is at work at that city. Their gift not only relieves the distress of famine victims, but it also serve to strengthen the fellowship of Jewish an Gentile believers in Christ. Moreover, the disposition of this new congregation toward possessions reflects the genuineness of their faith

4.7. The Imprisonment of Peter (12:1–24)

Luke introduces a new story. He does nc indicate its precise time, but suggests it "wa about [the] time" of Barnabas and Saul's visi to Jerusalem (v. 1). The events recorded her transpire in Jerusalem. Prior persecution an opposition to the gospel came from the Jewis religious authorities (4:1–6; 5:17–18, 21–2 6:12–15; 7:54–8:3; 9:1). Until now the religious leaders, especially the Sadducees, hav persecuted the believers without the assistanc of the civil authorities. But now persecutio intensifies, and the ruler of Palestine, Hero Agrippa I, takes the lead.

Herod Agrippa was the son of Aristobulu and the grandson of Herod the Great, wh ruled Galilee at the time of Jesus' birth (Mat 2:1). Like a number of the members of Herod' family, Agrippa served as a puppet ruler ove the Jews under the Roman occupation c Palestine. He grew up in Rome, where he live in extravagance and wasted what he had inherited. In A.D. 41 Emperor Claudius made hir king of all the territory ruled by Herod th Great, though his reign lasted only three year When he returned to Palestine, he became popular and lived in luxury. He constantly sougl the favor of the Jews and presented himself a a devotee of their religion, though the Hero family were non-Jews from Idumea. Awar that Jewish opinion was against the churcl Agrippa took steps to persecute the believer to enhance his popularity.

Agrippa begins to persecute (*kakoo*, "t hurt, mistreat") "some who belonged to th church" (v. 1). Those who carry out his orde persecute the believers so intensely that the suffer more than they did earlier at the hands c the Sanhedrin. Agrippa's main target seems t have been the leaders of the church. He strike at Jesus' inner circle of disciples by having th apostle James son of Zebedee executed. N reason is given for selecting James. He is th first apostle to suffer martyrdom. He dies by th sword, apparently his head being placed on block and cut off by an executioner.

The Jews as a whole take pleasure in Agrippa's persecution of the apostles. The situation in Judea has certainly changed from the earlier days, when persecution involved only the Jewish leaders. Hostility toward the gospel has spread. The support that Agrippa receives from the populace encourages him to press forward in his actions against the other apostles. So he has Peter arrested, clearly intending to do to him what he had done to James. Evidently Agrippa is seeking to destroy the Jerusalem church by beheading its leaders.

Peter is seized during the Festival of Unleavened Bread, a seven-day feast after Passover (Ex. 12:14ff.). By the New Testament times these festivals had become one celebration, so that the two terms were synonyms (cf. Luke 22:1). During this time Jerusalem was full of Jews who were enthusiastic for the law. To avoid creating a disturbance or alienating the Jews, Agrippa has Peter placed in prison until after the Passover week. Should he have held a public trial or an execution during the festive week, the Jews would have felt that the feast was desecrated.

Determined to make sure that Peter will not escape, Agrippa places a guard of sixteen soldiers (v. 4). He must have heard about the previous imprisonment of the apostles and their escape from prison in the night without the knowledge of the guards (5:17–23). Divided into four squads, each squad of four guards is on duty for three hours for around-the-clock watching. Two of these guards are chained to Peter while the other two stand duty at the entrance (v. 6).

While Peter is in prison, the church prays on his behalf. The intensity of their prayers is indicated in two ways in verse 5. (1) The verb "was . . . praying" (imperfect tense) reflects their persistence in prayer; they keep on praying, knowing that human impossibilities are possible with God. (2) The adverb "earnestly" (*ektenos*, "intently") signifies they recognize the urgency of the situation; they pray with words that they feel intently in their hearts. We do not know whether this prayer of the church is for Peter's deliverance or for his faith not to fail. They may have remembered that earlier Peter had faltered in the face of danger (Luke 22:54–62). Furthermore, they probably did not expect Peter to be delivered since both Stephen and James had become martyrs. In any case, God's mighty act of delivering Peter takes place in the context of prayer.

The detailed description of deliverance emphasizes that it is wholly a miracle (vv. 6–11). On the last night of Passover week, Peter must have been expecting to die the next morning. He lies sleeping between two guards, chained to both of them. God suddenly intervenes in the situation by sending an angel, who fills the prison cell with the light of divine glory. The very thing that Herod wants to prevent is about to occur. The angel wakes Peter up by slapping him on the side, and the chains fall off. Peter obeys the angel by fastening his belt and slipping on his sandals, and then he follows the heavenly visitor.

While he is being delivered, Peter has the impression that he is dreaming and does not realize that he is actually leaving the prison. He thinks that what is happening is only a vision, and he fails to comprehend the reality of it. Peter and the angel pass the two guards stationed at the cell door, evidently without these men recognizing Peter (v. 18). As they come to the heavy iron gate of the prison, it miraculously opens without any visible cause. The angel accompanies Peter down a street until he is beyond the pursuit of the guards. The angel then disappears.

King Agrippa has taken great precautions to prevent Peter's escape. Those efforts to restrain God's Spirit-filled messenger only make the miracle more dramatic. When Peter realizes what has happened, his own words interpret the significance of his deliverance (v. 11). What he has seen was no vision. God has sent an angel and miraculously rescued him from the hand of Agrippa (cf. Dan. 3:19–27). Divine intervention has frustrated opponents of the church. It is true that no angel delivered James from the executioner's sword. His death must be placed in the larger perspective of God's inscrutable will and seen as the cross's casting its shadow in the cruel cutting off of the apostle's life. Luke offers no theological explanation for it, but the great miracle of Peter's deliverance demonstrates God's saving power and help.

The Christians have been praying for Peter, but his miraculous deliverance astonishes them (vv. 12–17). After his release Peter immediately decides to inform his Christian friends about what has happened. Thus, he goes to the house of Mary, the mother of John Mark (mentioned for the first time here; cf. also 12:25; 13:5, 13; 15:37–39). Many believers have gathered at Mary's house to pray on what appears to be the last night of Peter's life. Peter enters the gateway that leads from the street to the courtyard and begins to knock on the outside door, interrupting the prayer of those on the inside.

A servant girl named Rhoda answers the door and is excited when she recognizes Peter's voice. Forgetting to unlock the door, she rushes inside in amazement to tell the others. The Christians in Mary's house do not believe Rhoda's report that Peter is at the door. They insist that Rhoda is crazy, but she confidently maintains that Peter is there. The Christians then suggest that she has seen an appearance of Peter's angel, who has assumed his voice and appearance. A common belief among the Jews was that each person had a guardian angel (see Strack and Billerbeck, 1:781f.; cf. Matt. 18:10; Heb. 1:14). But they are wrong; Peter is really standing at the door, continuing to knock. When the Christians open the door, they are shocked.

After Peter finally gains entrance, with a motion of his hand the people become quiet. He satisfies their curiosity by explaining that God has set him free. Since the other leaders of the church are not present, Peter requests that "James and the brothers" be told about the miracle. James here is the brother of Jesus (Mark 6:3). The manner in which he is mentioned indicates his prominence in the church. Both Luke and Paul indicate that James served as the head of the Jerusalem church (Acts 15:13; 21:18; Gal. 1:19; 2:9, 12).

After Peter has asked the believers to pass on the news to other church leaders, he leaves in the night for "another place," which may have been another house in Jerusalem or, most likely, another town outside the city for safety reasons. He must have expected a vigorous effort to rearrest him, making it difficult for him to hide himself safely in Jerusalem. After a few years Peter does appear again in Jerusalem (15:4, 7), though he may have returned sooner than that since Agrippa lived only a short time after Peter's departure (12:20–23).

The next morning Peter's escape becomes known publicly (vv. 18–19). By then he is safe in a secret hiding place. When the guards to whom he was chained are awakened by daylight, they see that their prisoner has escaped. There is great confusion among the guards, not knowing what happened to Peter. They have no idea of how he got loose from his chains and how the guards standing watch did not see anyone pass them. All that they know is that Peter is gone.

When Agrippa hears the news, he has his officers make a thorough search, but they fail to find any trace of the prisoner. Although their inability to find Peter confirms that a stupendous miracle has occurred, Agrippa refuses to acknowledge the miracle. He interrogates the four guards on duty at the time of Peter's escape. After questioning them, the king charges them with negligence and has them, as the text literally reads, "led off" (*apachthenai*), probably not to prison but to execution (v. 19; cf. NIV). When Roman soldiers allowed a prisoner to escape, customarily they received the same punishment due the prisoner. Accordingly, the innocent guards become victims of Agrippa's violence.

God has vindicated Peter. Luke continues the story with further proof of divine vindication in the death of Agrippa (vv. 20–23). The king goes to Caesarea to meet with a delegation from Tyre and Sidon. At that time antagonism developed between Agrippa and the people of those two cities. Luke gives no explanation for the dispute, but it seems to have been an economic dispute. The cities of Tyre and Sidon depended on the grain fields of Judea for much of their food. Apparently Agrippa diverted grain exports destined for Tyre and Sidon to Caesarea, thereby diminishing their food supply.

As a matter of public policy good relations with the king are desirable. Thus the people of these two large cities think it best to conciliate the king, so they send a delegation to Caesarea to make peace. They secure the favor of Blastus, a servant in charge of the king's private quarters. Through this trusted servant they obtain a public audience with Agrippa. Josephus gives a more detailed account of what follows. At the time of the meeting Agrippa is at a festival celebrated to honor the Roman emperor Claudius. He is arrayed in his royal apparel; his splendid robe glistens in the morning sun. On the second day of the festival the eople present are happy because the grievances of those from Tyre and Sidon have been esolved. They flatter the king and address him s a god. According to Josephus, because King Agrippa accepts the acclamation as a god, he s overcome with violent pain and dies in gony a few days later (*Ant.* 19.8.2).

Luke explicitly states that "an angel of the ord struck him down," and bluntly explains, he was eaten by worms and died" (v. 23). To e eaten by worms is a characteristic way of ncient writers to describe a painful death esulting from divine judgment (cf. 2 Macc. :5–9; Josephus, *Ant.* 17.6.5). The death of Agrippa I reminds us of the deaths of Ananias nd Sapphira. Like that couple, Agrippa shows isrespect for God and is struck dead. He is not atisfied to oppose God, but he competes with im by claiming divine honors. The fatal misake of this arrogant tyrant is that he "did not ive praise to God" (v. 23). As a ruler he is subect to the Supreme Ruler of the universe. His buse of power and arrogance bring divine vrath on him. Consistent with what had been redicted (Luke 1:52), God's swift judgment rings him low.

Agrippa I boldly executed the persecution f the church, but it did not stop the advance of he gospel. This defiant opponent of God's eople died, "but the word of God continued o increase and spread" (v. 24). Another great eversal has occurred. The gospel thrives under ersecution because more and more people ear the truth and believe.

5. Travel Narratives: The Acts of Paul, an Itinerant, Spirit-Filled Prophet (12:25–22:21)

The stage is now set for the preaching of the ospel throughout the Gentile world. From this oint on Luke confines his narrative to the rominent events in the life of Paul. Peter has een the dominant spokesman in Acts 1–12, ut from here on the focus centers on Paul's ninistry. Through him and his coworkers, who re empowered by the Holy Spirit, the gospel s preached and the boundaries of the church ontinue to extend far beyond Palestine. As we ave observed, the Holy Spirit has directed the ffairs of the church up to now, and Luke's ccount of Paul's travels makes it clear that the pirit continues to direct and empower God's eople.

5.1. First Missionary Journey (12:25–15:35)

Having fulfilled their mission to Jerusalem (cf. 11:27–30), Barnabas and Saul, taking with them John Mark, return to Antioch. Here Luke introduces Mark (12:25). It was to the house of his mother, Mary, that Peter went when released from prison. Soon after their arrival in Antioch, the church in that city begins a new phase of missionary activity. Through its efforts, Antioch becomes a vital center for Christian missions. Luke's account of what has been called Paul's first missionary journey begins with the Holy Spirit's selection of Barnabas and Saul for a special work.

5.1.1. Antioch: Barnabas and Saul Set Apart (12:25–13:3). The church at Antioch is being served by prophets and teachers. In the early church both prophets and teachers were Spirit-filled people, often mentioned as prominent preachers of the word (Rom. 12:6–8; 1 Cor. 12:28–29; Eph. 4:11). The New Testament does not draw a clear distinction between these two, and the same person could be both. In general, however, a prophet was more spontaneous in his or her utterance, speaking by inspiration to people on the basis of revelation with attention directed toward the purposes of God for the future; an inspired teacher was more didactic and expounded the Scriptures and fundamentals of the faith. He sought to give guidance to the church on the basis of what had happened in the past (*TDNT*, 6:854).

Luke lists five men as prophets and teachers. He gives no indication which were which; likely no clear dividing line could be drawn between the ministry of any of them. All five were probably involved in the exposition of Scripture and had charismatic gifts for inspired utterances. Numbered among these spiritual leaders are Barnabas and Paul (Saul). Barnabas stands first in the list, suggesting that he was considered the most prominent.

Luke makes an important reference to worship in verse 2. He does not indicate that the congregation is present, but that may be assumed. The new initiative for outreach with the gospel, in other words, occurs in the setting of worship of the Lord Jesus, fasting, and prayer. The prophets and teachers were sensitive to spiritual needs and spent time together in worship and fasting. The word for worship (*leitourgeo*) has to do with a religious service, such as occurred in the temple. The idea communicated by this word is that of rendering service and worship to the Lord, but in the Septuagint the word is used for doing service, especially by praying (*BAGD*, 470–71). A major element of their worship must have been prayer.

The prophets and teachers demonstrate the earnestness of their prayers by fasting (cf. 14:23). During one of these periods the Holy Spirit reaffirms the truth revealed to Peter (10:9–20) and directs the church to enlarge its witness. He commands that Barnabas and Saul be "set apart" (*aphorizo*, "consecrate"). This word was used in the sense of the consecration of the Levites to the work to which God had already called them (Num. 16:9). It also refers to Paul's separation to become an apostle (Rom. 1:1; Gal. 1:15). Presumably this message from the Holy Spirit is communicated through one or more of the prophets.

The clause "for the work to which I have called them" (v. 2) indicates that both men had been called before this time. That is, God had already made a decision about the work of Barnabas and Saul. Saul, we know, had been commissioned by the Lord at the time of his conversion to evangelize the Gentiles (26:16–18). His experience on the road to Damascus included both a profound transformation of his life in coming to know Jesus Christ as Savior and a profound revelation that he was called to be an apostle to the Gentiles. Exactly when Barnabas received his call, we have no way of knowing.

The work of Barnabas and Saul originates with God—not with plans devised by humans—and is undertaken in obedience to the voice of the Spirit. Consequently, the church at Antioch formally commissions Barnabas and Saul as missionaries. Before they do so, the church fasts and prays, and then lays hands on the two men. The laying on of hands here is not their ordination to ministry but their consecration to a special work. It gives them a solemn responsibility, imparting to them strength and commending them to the grace of God. Barnabas and Saul are then sent off as representatives of the church at Antioch.

5.1.2. Cyprus (13:4–12). The first missionary journey begins at Antioch with the Holy Spirit speaking through the prophets. Luke emphasizes again that the Holy Spirit is directing this mission and is sending out the missionaries (v. 4), a procedure that proves t be programmatic for Paul's three journeys. A the beginning of each one Luke observes th work of the Spirit and shows how Paul doe the work of a Spirit-filled apostle and prophe (cf. 13:4; 16:6–8; 19:1–7).

As they set out on their journey, Barnaba and Saul go to Seleucia, the seaport of Antioch From there they sail to the port of Salami located at the eastern end of the island c Cyprus. This island was the birthplace of Barn abas and a suitable field for missionary work since it had a large Jewish population. Evi dently the gospel has already been preached i Cyprus with some success (11:19–20). Th missionaries' strategy is to begin preaching th gospel in the Jewish synagogues.

Preaching in the synagogues becomes char acteristic of Paul's mission work (13:14, 4(14:1; 17:1, 10; 18:4, 19; 19:8). By startin there, Barnabas and Saul follow the principl of offering the gospel "first for the Jew, the for the Gentile" (Rom. 1:16; cf. Jesus' com ments in John 4:22). Practically speaking, th synagogue also provided an opportunity fo establishing a point of contact for the gospe Ordinarily Jews, proselytes, and God-fearin Gentiles could be reached there. John Mar accompanies the two missionaries as "helper" (*hyperetes*, "attendant"), probabl assisting them in every way, including teach ing converts the elements of the faith. Little i known about the success of the missionaries preaching in Salamis.

After a short stay at Salamis, the mission aries travel to Paphos, the capital city c Cyprus, about ninety miles from Salamis on th western end of the island. Luke pauses his nar rative to relate the missionaries' encounter wit two particular men: Sergius Paulus, the Roma governor (NIV "proconsul," *anthypatos*, head c a senatorial province) of Cyprus; and Elyma a magician, known also by the Jewish nam Bar-Jesus. Luke characterizes Sergius Paulu as an "intelligent man," meaning that he ha mental capacities and is not taken in by th magician (v. 7). As was common in the ancie world, the governor was attracted to magic an had consulted sorcery and fortune-telling abou important matters.

Among the attendants of Sergius Paulus i the Jewish magician, Bar-Jesus. Bar-Jesus dab bles in magic and apparently thinks of himse

'his fourth-century
:hurch in Paphos,
elow, the oldest
:hurch on the island
f Cyprus, is associ-
ted with Paul's first
nissionary trip.
.ocal legend states
'aul was tied to this
olumn, above, and
vhipped.

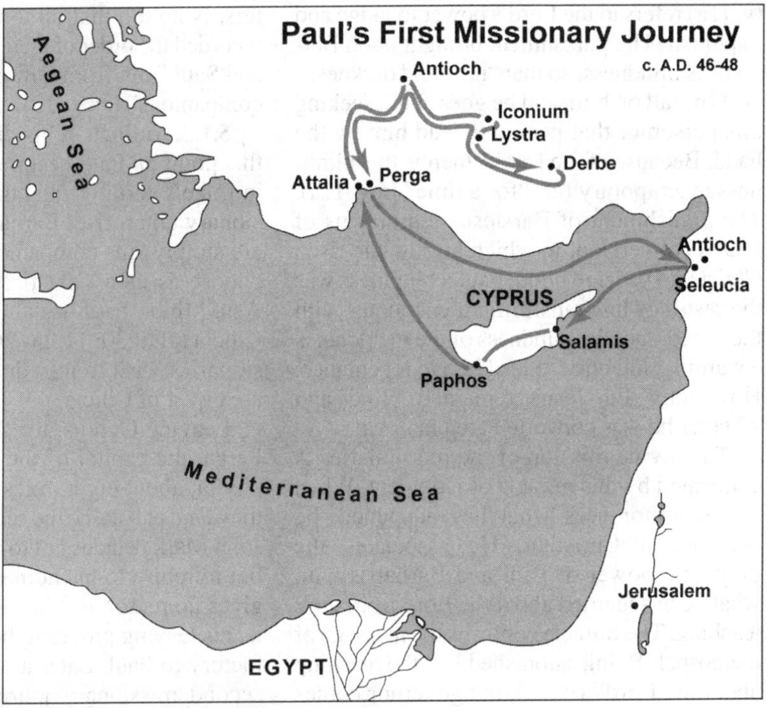

s a prophet, claiming to be inspired. Even hough Sergius Paulus is attracted to magic, he hows a remarkable openness to the gospel by sking to speak with Paul and Barnabas. When e learns that these two men bring good news bout Christ, the governor sends for them so hat he can hear what they have to say. We can ssume that Sergius Paulus is impressed with heir message.

The success of Paul and Barnabas con- inces Bar-Jesus that his influence on the gov- rnor may come to an end; thus, he becomes earful that he will lose his position. So Bar-Jesus tries with his greatest efforts to turn the governor aside from the Christian gospel. The magician's open opposition results in a confrontation between Paul, the true prophet (13:1), and the false prophet. This exchange is the second confrontation of Christianity with magic (cf. 8:9–24).

Knowing that Bar-Jesus is trying to obstruct the true word of God, Paul takes strong, prophetic action against him (vv. 9–11). He is "filled with the Holy Spirit" (v. 9; cf. v. 4) and through the Spirit's power pronounces judgment on this enemy of the gospel. He describes the character of Bar-Jesus as "a child of the devil." That is, the magician is filled with satanic power and deceit, and his magic is inspired by demons rather than by the Spirit of God. He is "an enemy of everything that is right" and is "perverting the right ways of the Lord" (v. 10). "Right ways" refer to God's plans and his teachings that lead to faith, especially to the advancement of the mission of the church (cf. Prov. 10:9; Hos. 14:9). The false prophet is attempting to twist and pervert the truths of God into lies.

As a prophet of God and filled with the Spirit, Paul pronounces a curse upon this agent of the devil. The expression "hand of the Lord"

(v. 11a) refers to the Lord's power to judge and to punish. The punishment brought upon Bar-Jesus is blindness, so that "mist and darkness" (v. 11b) fall on him, and he goes about seeking this person or that person to lead him by the hand. Because of the Lord's mercy, this blindness is temporary (cf. "for a time" in v. 11a). The punishment of Bar-Jesus reminds us of Paul's conversion, in which he saw the risen Christ and became blind. Paul's blindness was the result of his transforming encounter with the Savior, but the blindness of the magician is a warning, intended to lead him to repentance. How long Bar-Jesus remained blind and whether he was converted are unknown.

The divine mission of the missionaries is confirmed by this miracle of judgment. When the governor sees what has happened, he becomes a Christian. He associates the prophetic power of Paul and Barnabas with what he has learned about the Lord from their teaching. The miracle confirms the message of the gospel. Being astonished by "the teaching about the Lord" (v. 12), the governor comes to faith. Most likely "Lord" refers to Jesus (cf. vv. 10–11). In Acts Luke never speaks of the teachings of the Father, but only of the teachings of the Son, Jesus Christ.

From this account two particular facts are evident. (1) The missionary journey begins with the confrontation of a practitioner of magic, a false prophet. Victory over the magician parallels Peter's encounter with Simon the sorcerer (8:9–25). Bar-Jesus, an agent of the devil, cannot stop the march of the gospel. The first stage of Paul and Barnabas's journey is successful because they have been endowed with the fullness of the Holy Spirit and because the power of the gospel is superior to the demonic power of the world.

(2) The clause "Saul, who is also called Paul" (v. 9) reflects that Luke will now refer to Paul by his Roman name rather than by his Hebrew name, Saul. Many Jews who lived outside of Palestine had both a Hebrew and a Roman name. As a Roman citizen, he likely acquired his Roman name earlier. Luke mentions the other name here because from this time on, Paul becomes a more prominent leader in the church. Moreover, it is more fitting to identify Paul by his Roman name now since he has begun his ministry to the Gentile world, and it is the name Paul uses in his letters. Note too that up to this event Luke has recorded the order of their names as "Barnabas and Saul," but from now on it is "Paul and his companions" (cf. v. 13).

5.1.3. Antioch in Pisidia (13:13–52). From this point on Paul becomes the central figure in Luke's narrative and the leader of the missionary enterprise. Barnabas and John Mark are simply "his companions." The three men choose as their next field of labor southern Asia Minor. Paul has already evangelized in Cilicia (cf. 9:30; 11:25–26), but now the missionaries wish to introduce the gospel to the area west of Cilicia.

Leaving Cyprus, the three of them sail to Perga, the capital of the region called Pamphylia, about eight miles inland. Most likely they land at Attalia, the seaport of Perga. There John Mark decides not to continue the journey but to return to his home in Jerusalem. Luke gives no reason for this decision. Whatever it is, his leaving proves to be extremely unsatisfactory to Paul. Later at the beginning of the second missionary journey Paul refuses to allow Mark to join the missionary party, and Paul and Barnabas have a bitter split (15:37–39). Years later, however, Paul wrote to the believers at Colosse these words of approval "If he [John Mark] comes to you, welcome him" (Col. 4:10; cf. 2 Tim. 4:11).

After a short stay at Perga, Paul and Barnabas go to Pisidian Antioch, the capital and military center of southern Asia Minor. This city, about a hundred miles northeast of Perga was just outside the province of Pisidia. It had attracted a considerable number of Jewish people. In accord with the missionaries' normal practice, they begin their work in the city by preaching the gospel in the local Jewish synagogue. On the Sabbath Paul and Barnabas take modest seats in the congregation among the people.

Luke does not provide us with a full description of the synagogue service, but normally such meetings begin with readings from the Law of Moses and the Book of the Prophets and move on to prayer; then a sermon, usually hortatory in nature, is given by anyone present who is able to preach. It may have been known that Paul and Barnabas are visiting teachers. Perhaps the leaders of the synagogues have had some contact with them before the synagogue service begins. The invite these two missionaries to offer "a message of encouragement" (*paraklesis*, "exhortation"). They are addressed as "brothers," that is, as fellow Jews, not as fellow believers. Paul accepts the friendly invitation and arises to address the congregation.

Among the Gentiles it was customary to stand to address a group. Standing, Paul gestures with his hand to get the attention of the congregation. He acknowledges the presence of not only Jews but also Gentiles, God-fearers (cf. 10:2), who desire to worship the God of Israel.

Paul's message at Antioch is the first and longest example of Paul's missionary preaching. Luke's record of it should not be taken as a full transcript of Paul's sermon delivered that day. His Spirit-inspired message follows a similar pattern to both the preaching of Peter (2:14–36; 3:12–26; 10:34–43) and that of Stephen (7:2–53). Paul outlines the main features of salvation history, showing how God has worked out his plan for Israel. (1) He begins with a brief account of the history of God's goodness to Israel (vv. 16b–22); (2) he argues that according to Old Testament prophecies, Jesus proved to be the Savior by his death and resurrection (vv. 23–37); (3) he presents forgiveness of sin as being available only through Jesus Christ (vv. 38–41).

(1) After addressing the crowd as "men of Israel and you Gentiles who worship God" (v. 16b), Paul summarizes Israel's glorious history, speaking of God's goodness to Israel from the Exodus to the time of David (vv. 17–22). Going back to the patriarchs, the first of whom was Abraham, he says, "The God of the people of Israel chose our fathers." While the Israelites lived as foreigners and slaves in Egypt, God caused them to prosper, increasing their number and strength so that they became a mighty nation. Miraculously God stretched forth his mighty arm and set his people free from the bondage of Egypt. In spite of the Israelites' failings and the way they treated God during the forty-year journey to Canaan, God put up with his people (v. 18). He then defeated seven nations in Canaan and gave that land to his people.

God did all that is recited here in 450 years. This period is hard to calculate. Presumably this period covers 400 years spent in Egypt, 40 years of wandering in the desert, and another 10 years for the time of the entry into Canaan to the time the land was divided among the tribes.

Paul then continues his story, discussing the time from the entrance into Canaan through the era of the judges to the end of Saul's reign as king. The phrase "after this [time]" (lit., "after these things," v. 20) refers to the series of events that Paul talked about in verses 17–20, which concluded with the defeat of the seven nations by Joshua. Soon after Israel's entry into the Promised Land, God gave them judges, who were charismatic leaders—spiritually endowed individuals who enabled the Israelites to overcome their enemies.

Although the judges provided inspired leadership, the Israelites eventually asked for a king. In response to their request God gave them Saul as their king. According to historical records this man from the tribe of Benjamin ruled them for forty years, though the length of his reign is not given in the Old Testament (cf. Josephus, *Ant.* 6.14.9). God removed Saul because he was unfit for the task and anointed David as king in his place.

Paul cites the divine testimony regarding David: "I have found David son of Jesse a man after my own heart; he will do everything I want him to do" (v. 22; cf. 1 Sam. 13:14; Ps. 89:20). These words refer to the character of David as a whole. True, David committed some great sins, but his sins did not change God's estimate of him because David repented. Saul failed in obedience and worship of God, but by doing the divine will and repenting, David proved himself to be the kind of man that God wanted him to be. Paul concludes the first part of his sermon, therefore, by pointing out that David established himself as the ideal king of Israel.

(2) In the next section of his sermon, Paul immediately shifts to his major theme: Jesus, the promised Son of David. Jesus is much greater than David because he is the anointed Savior (vv. 23–37). Before Jesus' public ministry John the Baptist preached a baptism of repentance, calling on the people of Israel to repent and be baptized. His ministry was the beginning of a new era and introduced Jesus as the Messiah. As the forerunner of Jesus Christ, John was the crucial link between David and Christ. Before he completed his ministry, he denied that he was the promised Messiah.

Rather, someone coming after him would be greater than he was. Jesus was so great that John did not feel worthy to perform the slave's task of washing Jesus' feet.

After addressing his audience again (v. 26; cf. v. 16), Paul moves directly to Jesus' suffering and death on the cross (vv. 27–29). He explains that the Jews of Jerusalem and their leaders did not recognize Jesus as the Messiah, nor did they understand the prophetic witness in the Old Testament, which they heard read in their synagogues each Sabbath. The Jews unknowingly fulfilled God's plan that had been proclaimed by the prophets concerning the Messiah. Neither the Jews nor Pilate could find any legal grounds on which to condemn Jesus. Although the Sanhedrin charged him with blasphemy, they were unable to prove it. Even so, the Jewish people and their leaders condemned Jesus and put him to death on the cross.

Paul refers to the cross here as a "tree," just as Peter did (5:30; 10:39; 1 Peter 2:24). He makes no distinction between Christ's enemies who crucified him and his friends. The second "they" of verse 29 must include friends such as Joseph and Nicodemus, who took him down from the cross and buried him in a tomb. But Jesus did not remain in the grave, for God raised him from the dead. That is, God set his seal upon Jesus as the Savior by making him alive after his crucifixion. This resurrection vindicated his claim to be the Christ. The cross and the resurrection must not be separated; they belong together as God's mighty redemptive act.

The risen Savior then appeared to the disciples, who had been with Jesus throughout his public ministry, over a period of "many days" (v. 31; cf. Luke 24:13–53; Acts 1:3–9). They knew him well and could not have been deceived. Having seen the risen Jesus again and again, they were well qualified to bear witness to the reality of his triumph over death "to our people" (i.e., to the Jews). Paul has in mind primarily the apostles' preaching the gospel to the Jews in Palestine and perhaps also his own position as God's chosen witness to the Gentiles. His main point is that the proclamation of Jesus' resurrection did not rest on rumors or human traditions but on the testimony of men and women who had seen with their own eyes the risen Savior.

As Paul proclaims the good news, he wants to make his Jewish listeners willing to accept the promise given to their ancestors (v. 32). No longer is the good news just a matter of promise, but one of fulfillment, because God has fulfilled the promise given to the patriarchs. The pronoun "us" in the phrase "for us" (v. 33) includes the Jews who are present and Paul, but the presence of God-fearers in the audience (vv. 16, 26) may suggest that these people are seen as spiritual descendants of the Jewish ancestors (cf. Rom. 4:11–25). The ancient promise of the Messiah had been fulfilled in the life and ministry of Jesus, including his glorious resurrection.

The truth of God's raising Jesus from the dead is new for Paul's audience. Because of their lack of knowledge, he appeals not only to eyewitnesses but also to the testimony of Scripture as proof of Jesus' resurrection. First he cites Psalm 2:7—"You are my Son; today I have become your Father." When a man was anointed king in Israel, he was understood to be a representative of the nation and, as such, he was in a new relationship with Yahweh, the Lord. After Jesus' baptism in the Jordan, he was anointed by the Holy Spirit for his ministry, an experience similar to the anointing of a king, who is to represent his nation before God. When the Spirit empowered Jesus for his charismatic work, a voice spoke to him out of heaven in the words of Psalm 2:7, "You are my Son" (Luke 3:22). This Scripture affirmed the divine sonship of Christ.

Jesus' victory over death proved him to be the Son of God. Although Jesus' sonship was already a reality and did not begin at his resurrection, the first Easter affirmed him to be the divine Son of God (cf. Rom. 1:4; Heb. 1:5). Some have insisted that at Jesus' resurrection God adopted him as his Son, appealing to Psalm 2 as a basis for their interpretation. But during his earthly ministry Jesus was already the Son of God (Luke 3:22; 9:35; John 1:14). Jesus' followers declared him to be what he had always been—the Son of God. The reality of his resurrection simply gave final proof that he was Savior and King forever.

Paul cites two other closely linked passages as prophecies of Christ's resurrection, Isaiah 55:3 and Psalm 16:10. Isaiah suggests that at Jesus' resurrection he entered a new existence, in which he would "never . . . decay" or die again (Acts 13:34). His resurrection involved more than his being restored to life. Centuries before Christ died on the cross, God had promised David an offspring to rule upon his throne *forever* (2 Sam. 7:8–16). This promise was renewed in Isaiah 55:3; Paul points out that God has now fulfilled that promise by raising Jesus from the dead to sit on David's throne (cf. Luke 1:32). God has bestowed on Jesus "the holy and sure blessings promised to David"; the word "you" (plural, Acts 13:34) refers not only to Jesus but to all those who put their trust in him. Believers receive the sure manifestations of God's grace promised to David, such as the forgiveness of sins and eternal life through Christ.

The risen and exalted Christ will reign forever because God will not let his "Holy One see decay" (Ps. 16:10). The "Holy One" refers to Jesus, the Messiah, not David, who died and whose body saw decay by remaining in the grave (cf. Acts 2:25–32). In contrast to David, Jesus' body did not stay in the grave. The prophecy of Psalm 16:10, therefore, refers not to David but to Jesus, who triumphed over death and will never die again. Once again, more than Jesus' resurrection is involved here. The promised blessing of Psalm 16:10 applies to "you" (plural), the believers (Isa. 55:3). The fulfillment of God's blessings to David through Jesus Christ assures believers also of their resurrection. Jesus' resurrection makes possible and leads to ours.

(3) In the conclusion of Paul's sermon, he emphasizes that forgiveness of sin is made possible by faith in the risen Christ (vv. 38–41; cf. 2:38; 3:19; 5:31; Luke 24:47). He again addresses his audience as "my brothers," including both fellow Israelites and Gentile God-fearers. He then explains to them the significance that Jesus' resurrection has for those who put their trust in him. Salvation comes "through Jesus," meaning that only through Jesus' death and resurrection can the forgiveness of sin be proclaimed and offered to the people.

Paul's use of the word "justified" (*dikaioo*) here gives the sermon a distinctive Pauline emphasis and basically means "declared not guilty." The word is a legal term that was used in the courts to express a verdict of acquittal. Paul uses it here to describe the condition of those who believe in Christ. The divine verdict is guilty (Rom. 3:23), but believers are acquitted because the penalty for their sin has been paid by another, Christ. He remits their sins and treats them as though they have never sinned, putting them into a right relationship with himself.

Verse 39 summarizes this doctrine of justification. On the negative side, no one can secure forgiveness of sin or justification by observing the rules and regulations of the Mosaic law. The way this verse reads in the NIV can erroneously be taken to mean that the law of Moses can set us free from some sins though not from others. This verse must not be weakened to mean that Christ provides a remedy for those sins that the law does not. Paul's point is that the law offers no remedy. The law of Moses cannot justify us or set us free from sin at all.

On the positive side, verse 39 emphasizes that both justification and forgiveness of sin are offered through faith in Christ. Although the Mosaic law cannot justify us, faith in Christ sets us free from all sins. God has a universal way of salvation: "everyone who believes," Gentile as well as Jew, "is justified." God declares as righteous in his sight all who put their faith in Christ. Any human effort to secure forgiveness of sins through the works of the law is futile.

Paul concludes his sermon with a prophetic warning from Habakkuk 1:5. The content of the words he cites from the prophet shows that the prophet is referring to the impending invasion and destruction of Judah by the Babylonians (about 605 B.C.). He appeals to this prophecy as a warning against rejecting the gospel he is preaching. Doubtless Paul's remarks about the law of Moses must have aroused concern from some of his Jewish hearers. If they reject God's justifying grace offered in Christ, they identify themselves with those to whom Habakkuk spoke his fearful words, when God was doing mighty deeds that no one would believe. The unbelievers' rejection of the gospel in Paul's day is as inexcusable as the unbelief of those scoffers at the time of the Babylonian invasion in the days of the prophet (Hab. 1:5–11).

Luke's narrative of the synagogue experience continues with the people's response to the sermon (vv. 42–49) and the persecution and departure of the missionaries (vv. 50–52). Paul's Spirit-inspired sermon makes a profound impression on the majority of the audience. As Paul and Barnabas begin to leave the synagogue, many express interest in hearing them speak on the next Sabbath.

After the dismissal of the congregation, Luke records that "many of the Jews and devout converts to Judaism" follow the missionaries. As already indicated, some of those present in the synagogue service were "Gentiles who worship God" (vv. 16, 26). These God-fearers were Gentiles who worshiped the Lord but who had not become full converts to Judaism. The phrase "devout converts to Judaism" (lit., "worshiping proselytes") refers to the Gentiles who were full converts to Judaism; they had accepted circumcision and felt a strong attachment to the Jewish form of worship. As they leave, many of these devout Gentiles and Jews continue to talk with Paul and Barnabas and express deep interest in his message.

As they talk to the people, Paul and Barnabas encourage them to remain faithful to "the grace of God." Grace here must not be taken in the technical sense of receiving salvation offered through Jesus Christ. These people have not yet believed the gospel; therefore, they have not yet been saved. But Paul urges them to continue to rely on the goodness and favor of God and to remain earnest seekers after the truth by believing that Jesus is the fulfillment of God's promises in the Old Testament.

During the following week, word about the missionary sermon in the synagogue spreads throughout the city of Antioch. As a result, "almost the whole city" comes out to the synagogue the next Sabbath to hear the Christian message, "the word of the Lord," preached by Paul. The apostle then delivers a sermon, not recorded by Luke, in which he sets forth the truth proclaimed on the previous Sabbath in greater detail. Most certainly, then, he declares again the inadequacy of the law to justify anyone in God's sight and the sufficiency of Christ to set us free from sin and bring us into a right relationship with God (v. 39).

When the Jews (probably the leaders of the synagogue) see the large crowds eager to hear Paul, they are "filled [*pimplemi*] with jealousy [*zelos*, envy]" (v. 45). The same verb "filled" that appears here was used to speak of the disciples being filled with the Spirit at Pentecost (2:4) and the disciples at Antioch as being filled with joy and the Holy Spirit (13:52). But the Jewish authorities are not moved by the Holy Spirit but by an envious spirit. They desire to preserve the sanctity of the law and fear that the gospel will draw away the God-fearers from the synagogue. They have doubts about what Paul is preaching and are unable to see God at work in their midst, just as the prophecy of Habakkuk anticipated (v. 41). In order to halt the religious movement, they take issue with what Paul says and declare his teachings to be a lie.

At this point it appears useless to reason with these leaders. They are becoming abusive in contradicting the Christian message and give little thought to what they are saying. The missionaries have spoken out boldly and openly, no doubt inspired by the Holy Spirit. But their bold utterance has increased the opposition of the Jewish authorities. That rejection of the gospel gives Paul and Barnabas opportunity to state the principle of their mission: "We had to preach the word of God to you first" (v. 46). According to the divine plan the gospel must be presented to the Jews first and then to the Gentiles (Rom. 1:16; 2:10). From place to place even in Gentile lands, their practice was to go first to the Jews. Now that these Jews have rejected the gospel, the missionaries are free of their obligation to them and turn to the Gentiles.

Because the Jews refuse to believe the gospel, they have pronounced upon themselves the judgment that they are not "worthy of eternal life." The word "worthy" (*axios*) does not refer to their personal worthiness, but to their disqualifying themselves through unbelief from receiving eternal life. Such life is life in the age to come, offered only through Christ, and is solely a matter of God's grace. No one within oneself is worthy of it.

Since the Jews have rejected the gospel, Paul and Barnabas now openly announce the Gentile mission (vv. 46–47), and the Gentiles present are delighted to hear that the gospel is intended for them (v. 48). They respond by rejoicing and honoring (lit., "glorifying") "the word of the Lord." The Gentile mission is a direct fulfillment of the prophecy of Isaiah 49:6 (quoted in Acts 13:47). Empowered by the Spirit, Jesus, the Servant of the Lord, brings the light of salvation to the Gentiles (Luke 2:32). Likewise, the missionaries are empowered by the Spirit to take the light of the gospel to "the ends of the earth" (Acts 1:8).

Then Luke adds: "All who were appointed for eternal life believed" (v. 48). The verb "were appointed" has been understood to endorse predestination and to teach that personal salvation of individuals is the result of God's eternal decree. The context helps us in understanding Luke's meaning here. The Jews were indifferent to eternal life and refused to believe the gospel, whereas the Gentiles believed the good news and received the gift of eternal life. Clearly human choice does have a part in saving faith. The response of believing or refusing to believe is not determined by an eternal decree. The Scriptures place the responsibility for one's response to the gospel on that person and never on God. No one receives resurrection life apart from a conscious act of faith in Christ. What Luke is teaching here is that God's great plan of salvation includes Gentiles and that it is irrevocably unfolding in the preaching of the gospel to the Gentiles. By believing the gospel they were "appointed for eternal life"—that is, the life of the age to come, which has dawned in Christ. It is resurrection life that God has ordained that all who believe in Jesus Christ should receive (Arrington, 1988, 137).

The Jews at Antioch have rejected the gospel, but they cannot keep it from spreading throughout the region (vv. 49–52). More and more people in the surrounding territory hear about the word of the Lord. Because of the triumph of the gospel the Jews intensify their opposition to Paul and Barnabas (cf. v. 45). A number of the local Gentile women had become adherents to Judaism. Among these God-fearing women were those who were probably wives of prominent Gentile citizens. The Jews now turn these socially important women against the missionaries.

Women have always been among the most steadfast supporters of the gospel, but these women with their husbands are induced to take hostile action against the missionaries. Paul and his coworkers are therefore forced to leave the city. They are not without indignation and show that they know the Jews are responsible for their expulsion. Thus, before making their departure, they shake off the dust from their feet as a symbol that they are free of any responsibility for those who have rejected the gospel (cf. Mark 6:11; Luke 10:16).

Apparently after the missionaries leave Antioch, the new believers encounter persecution. Nevertheless, the hearts of these new converts are not filled with grief and fear. Rather, the Holy Spirit ministers to their spiritual needs. As a result they are filled with joy and the Holy Spirit. The verb "were filled" (*eplerounto*, an imperfect tense) refers to linear action in past time ("were being filled"), describing the charismatic empowerment and inspiration of the Holy Spirit that these disciples experienced daily. The Spirit continually fills and empowers the believers during this period of spiritual duress.

Earlier these new believers had most certainly received the initial Spirit-baptism, but like the disciples at Pentecost they are refilled with the Spirit (cf. 4:31). The initial experience may be described as baptism (immersion) in the Spirit or filling with the Spirit, but there are refillings for specific needs or tasks. The filling with the Spirit is, therefore, not only an initial experience; it should be an ongoing reality and the normal condition of Pentecostal believers.

5.1.4. Iconium (14:1–7). After leaving Antioch, Paul and Barnabas take a road leading southeast until they reach Iconium, about ninety miles. Luke gives only a brief summary of their ministry in that city (v. 3), but what they experience there becomes the typical response to the gospel in future missionary endeavors. When they arrive in Iconium, they go to the local synagogue, where, as was their custom, they begin their work. At the synagogue the missionaries find people prepared to hear the good news.

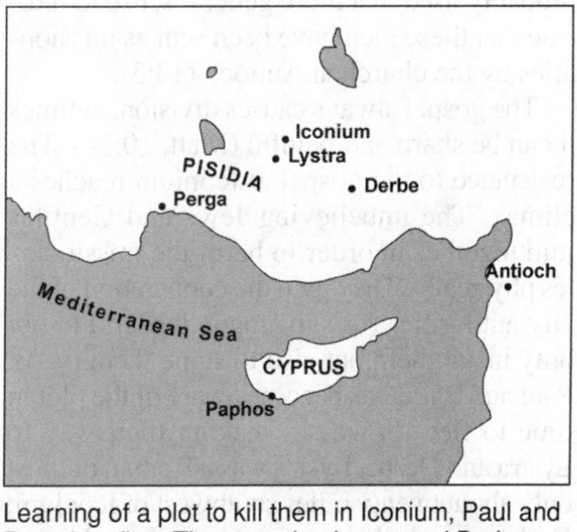

Learning of a plot to kill them in Iconium, Paul and Barnabas flee. They travel to Lystra and Derbe.

According to the pattern established on the first missionary journey (13:46; 14:1), the preaching is directed first to the Jews. Inspired by the Spirit, Paul and Barnabas speak with great persuasion. Their preaching carries conviction and leads to the conversion of a great number of Jews and God-fearing Gentiles (v. 1). Their missionary message does not fall on deaf ears as long as it is judged on its own merits and without interference. But trouble is not long in coming. Unbelieving Jews stir up the feelings of Gentiles (unattached to the synagogue) against "the brothers" (believers). They poison the minds of these Gentiles, most likely by using false and malicious slander. As a result, opposition to the gospel arises, from both Jews and Gentiles within the city.

Paul and Barnabas spend "considerable time" preaching in Iconium. In spite of the resistance they do it "boldly," a characteristic way of describing preachers as inspired by the Spirit (cf. 9:27; 18:26; 19:8; 26:26). Their Spirit-inspired, prophetic witness about the saving grace of God revealed in Christ has God's approval. God confirms their inspired message by "enabling them to do miraculous signs and wonders." God himself bears witness to his word in miracles, just as he had done at Jerusalem (5:12).

Luke does not give any details about these miracles, but both the preaching and the miracles have a decisive effect on people in the city. They are divided in their loyalties. Some are loyal to the Jews and others to Paul and Barnabas, who are identified as "apostles." For the first time in Acts, Luke speaks about both of them as apostles. This designation here is probably used in a more general sense to indicate that these men have been sent as missionaries by the church at Antioch (13:3).

The gospel always causes division; at times it can be sharp and painful (Matt. 10:34). The resistance to the gospel at Iconium reaches a climax. The unbelieving Jews and Gentiles join together in order to harm the missionaries physically. They gain the cooperation of the city authorities (or synagogue leaders) to not only insult them but also to stone them (v. 5). Paul and Barnabas become aware of the plot in time to flee for safety, making their way to Lystra and Derbe. Lystra was a Roman outpost only about twenty miles southwest of Iconium; Derbe was a little over fifty miles from Lystra. In these cities and "the surrounding country" the missionaries preach the good news about Christ. The opposition they have encountered has not diminished their commitment to declare the word that brings life and salvation.

5.1.5. Lystra (14:8–18). Lystra was a rather insignificant town. When Paul and Barnabas arrive there, they find no Jewish synagogue. It is possible that the population of Lystra consisted only of Gentiles. Here Paul preaches the gospel in the open, probably either in the streets or in a space near a city gate. Again we see a twofold witness of prophetic words (sermon) and deeds (signs and wonders).

Luke's account shows us the response of pagans to the gospel. Evidently Paul's preaching includes some reference to the healing ministry of Jesus and the power of the Holy Spirit, and the Spirit enables the apostle to perform similar healings as proof of his divine mission. He observes a man listening to him who has been lame from birth and has never walked (v. 8). By the Holy Spirit Paul discerns that this disabled man has faith to be healed. Empowered by the Spirit, Paul orders him to stand up. Instantly the man is healed, jumps up, and begins to walk. A similar healing of a cripple by Peter (cf. 3:1–10) aroused the hostility of the Jews, and the one in Lystra prompts a confrontation with pagan religion and superstition.

The people are amazed at what has happened before their eyes. Their excitement causes them to begin shouting in their local tongue, the language of Lycaonia (of which little is known). Neither Paul nor Barnabas can understand what they are saying, but the people jump to the conclusion that two gods in the likeness of men have come down from heaven to them. They arrive at this conclusion as a result of Greek legends about the gods coming to earth in the form of men.

In a local legend, Zeus and Hermes once visited the area of Lystra disguised as beggars. At first no one offered these deities hospitality but finally two old peasants, Philemon and his wife Baucis, were kind to them without knowing that they were gods. All the people were destroyed except for this elderly couple (Ovid *Metamorphoses*, 8.626–738). When the missionaries therefore heal the helpless man, these people conclude that they are gods. They see in Paul and Barnabas features that remind them of their supreme deities. Barnabas must have been noble in appearance and is taken to be Zeus, the chief god of the Greeks. Since Paul does the speaking, they identify him as Hermes, the god of eloquence and speech.

Consequently, the local people want to show proper honor to these two gods, whom they assume are disguised as men (vv. 13–14). Because of a language barrier, Paul and Barnabas are unaware of what is going on, but the local priest of Zeus makes arrangement to offer sacrifices to them as gods. Apparently the temple to Zeus was located just outside of the city near the city gates. In order that the people can show proper honor to their visitors, the priest brings oxen and wreaths of flowers near where Paul and Barnabas are standing.

As the priest moves toward the altar at the temple, the two missionaries realize that his intent is to bestow divine honors on them by offering them animal sacrifices. In other words, Paul and Barnabas find themselves as objects of idolatrous worship. They are shocked beyond measure. As a protest against what the people are about to do, they tear their clothes. The tearing of clothes in Jewish tradition is a proper reaction to blasphemy (Mark 14:63), but here it probably is a sign of distress and agitation. The two apostles then explain that they are mere men and not gods. Because it was the Lord God who wrought miracles through their hands, they emphatically deny any right to divine honor and insist that they have the same nature, limitations, and infirmities as any human being. Only the true and living God deserves to be worshiped.

Without hesitating Paul takes the opportunity to explain to the people the nature of the true God. On this occasion his sermon reflects features characteristic of early Christian preaching to Gentiles. The people in Lystra have no Jewish background to which Paul can appeal, so he makes no reference to the Old Testament. He begins by condemning idolatry, urging them to turn away from "worthless things" (v. 15), meaning the worship of idols. There is no longer an excuse for worshiping such objects because God has revealed himself in the gospel. The good news he proclaims instructs people to turn to the living God, who has revealed himself in creation.

The people of Lystra should do as Paul later exhorted the Thessalonians, who "turned to God from idols to serve the living and true God" (1 Thess. 1:9). Paul's main emphasis here is on God as Creator, noting the goodness and power of God revealed in his works of creation and providence. In creation the living God has revealed himself visibly to all people at all times and places (cf. Acts 17:24–31; Rom. 1:20). The Gentiles can see with their eyes evidence of God's existence. God has given proof of himself by doing good things and shows what kind of God he is by giving crops at the right time, by providing food, and by filling people's hearts with joy. This God is the true object of worship, but idolaters worship creation and blur the distinction between the Creator and the creature.

In the past generations the living God allowed the Gentile nations to "go their own way" (v. 16). Living as they pleased, they walked in the ways of idolatry, worshiping the creature rather than the Creator. At that time they had no specific revelation of his will in Jesus Christ. Because of their ignorance God overlooked their idolatry. He has now revealed himself in Christ, making their ignorance inexcusable and obligating them to turn from idols to the living God.

God has left a witness to himself in the created universe, though sin has marred creation (Gen. 3:17–19; Rom. 8:18–25), and as a result it now reflects imperfectly God's glory. General revelation offered through creation can never bring anyone into a saving relationship with God. Only through Jesus Christ, God's Son, is there revelation that saves. Although the death and resurrection of Jesus are what is required for personal salvation, these distinctive elements are missing from Paul's sermon as recorded here; Paul presumably explained the gospel to the people at Lystra before he concluded his sermon.

Luke's purpose here is to show that Paul's missionary preaching to pagan Gentiles included not only an emphasis on the saving work of Christ, but also on his revelation through the created universe. The emphasis on God as Creator and Sustainer serves to introduce the proclamation of the gospel. Paul mentions "good news" in verse 15. He does not develop it at the moment, but he does speak about what God had done "in the past" by permitting the Gentiles to live in their own ways (v. 16). This fact strongly implies that God has now done something in a new way to reveal himself. He did it through his Son, Jesus Christ.

Paul's words prevent the crowd from bestowing divine honors on him and Barnabas by offering them sacrifices (v. 18), but restraining them is not easy. They are deeply entrenched in pagan superstition, and the healing of the crippled man has made a strong impression on them. They are still uncertain as to who Paul and Barnabas might be.

5.1.6. Derbe to Antioch (14:19–28). While Paul and Barnabas are facing the situation in Lystra, word about their activities reaches the ears of their enemies, and soon the Jews who forced Paul and Barnabas to leave Iconium and Antioch arrive in Lystra. The distance from Antioch to Lystra was about 130 miles, and it was about forty miles from Iconium to Lystra. These Jews have come a great distance to cause the missionaries trouble.

Thus, the scene at Lystra changes abruptly. Paul and Barnabas now become objects of the hatred of Jews, who want to put them to death. At Iconium Jews and Gentiles were prepared to stone them (v. 5), but the missionaries fled. So persistent and intense is their hatred that the Jews from Antioch and Iconium are determined to carry out their earlier plans. Desiring to silence the gospel, these Jews, along with the cooperation of citizens of Lystra, stone Paul and drag his body outside of the city, where they leave him for dead. There is no data in the narrative to explain why only Paul becomes a victim of stoning, and not also Barnabas.

Paul's ministry in Lystra has been fruitful. The people who have become disciples gather around him after his attackers leave. Nothing is said about how long they have to wait before Paul shows signs of life. His recovery implies that Paul may have died and come back to life. Bruce says that his recovery "has the flavor of a miracle" (1952, 296). Later Paul writes that he bears in his body the marks of Jesus' passion and death (Gal. 6:17)—possibly a reference to the effects of the brutal stoning he received in Lystra. The believers there would have known firsthand about the "marks." As soon as he is able to walk, he gets up and returns to the city. Paul's recovery vindicates the gospel. Opposition and violence do not diminish the commitment of these Spirit-filled men to their God-assigned mission.

The next day Paul and Barnabas go on to Derbe. In contrast to Antioch, Iconium, and Lystra, the apostles seem to suffer no persecution here. They are successful in evangelizing the people, filling the city with the good news of Christ, and winning many new disciples. The first missionary journey reaches its climax with an abundant harvest of souls.

An important feature of the Pauline mission is the revisiting of newly established churches. Taking their lives in their hands, Paul and Barnabas return to Lystra, Iconium, and Antioch of Pisidia (v. 21). In these places they provide pastoral care by strengthening the souls of believers and encouraging them to remain faithful to what they believe. The believers must be prepared to face hostility and persecution. Only through many tribulations and hardships will they enter the kingdom of God. Here the kingdom of God is God's future rule in the age to come, at the second coming of Christ. The way to that kingdom is not easy. Those who set out on the path that leads to life in the age to come can expect to suffer (cf. Luke 21:12–19; 1 Thess. 3:2–4; 2 Thess. 1:5). Suffering is not only the lot of early Christians but of Christians in general. It is part of the journey into the kingdom. The prize at the end of the journey makes the endurance of hardships worthwhile.

The ministry of "strengthening" (v. 22) involves more than just pastoral care. It also includes some organizational structure, consisting of the appointment of elders "in each church" (v. 23). Paul and Barnabas's organization of church leaders is similar to the leadership of the Jewish synagogue. Elders served as local church leaders, like those who supervised the synagogue and its worship. The appointed elders in these new churches were responsible for worship, instruction, administration, and discipline of the congregation (cf. 1 Tim. 3:1–7; Titus 1:5–9).

For Paul and Barnabas the appointment of elders is of great importance, and so they do it "with prayer and fasting" (v. 23). As we have seen, the seven deacons of the church in Jerusalem were set aside for their ministry with prayer and the laying on of hands (6:6). When the Holy Spirit appointed Paul and Barnabas as missionaries, the church at Antioch prayed and fasted, then laid hands on them and sent them on their first missionary tour (13:2–3).

True appointment to ministry involves more than the approval of human beings. The Holy Spirit calls people to ministry and empowers them so that they can fulfill their call. After elders are appointed in the newly established churches, Paul and Barnabas commit the new converts to the care of "the Lord, in whom they had put their trust" when they became Christians (v. 23).

Having spiritually fortified the new churches and properly organized them, the missionaries descend from Antioch of Pisidia to Perga, which was the first place they visited on their voyage from Cyprus (13:14). On their prior visit to Perga they had passed through without preaching. Waiting for a vessel bound for Antioch of Syria, they evangelize the city for the first time. Nothing is said about the fruits of their labor there. Paul and Barnabas then set sail from the nearby seaport of Attalia to Antioch of Syria.

Upon returning to Antioch, the missionaries give a report to the entire congregation that had commissioned them. Likely no one had heard from Paul and Barnabas since the church had sent them forth by a special service of prayer and fasting. These apostles are eager to tell the church about the progress of the gospel among the Gentiles. They want the congregation to know what has been accomplished and how.

In their report, Paul and Barnabas do not dwell on the hardships and violence they have encountered, nor do they boast about their dedication and strength in the face of persecution. Their report emphasizes two things: (1) "All that God had done through them." It is significant that the emphasis falls on what God did. Their success was due to God because he worked through them. The Holy Spirit initiated, empowered, and sustained them on their mission. The apostles endured great adversity, but the Spirit's work through them explains their successes.

(2) God "had opened the door of faith to the Gentiles." An open door of faith means that the Gentiles have access to the blessings of the gospel (cf. 1 Cor. 16:9; 2 Cor. 2:12; Col. 4:3). When God opens a door, no one can shut it (cf. Rev. 3:7). Faith in Jesus Christ is the only door into the kingdom of God. His opening the door of faith always has far-reaching consequences. A considerable length of time, probably weeks rather than years, passes between the report of Paul and Barnabas and their journey to the council at Jerusalem (v. 28; cf. 15:2).

5.1.7. Aftermath: The Jerusalem Council (15:1–35). On the first missionary journey a large number of Gentiles had been brought into the church. The initial success of the Gentile mission was bound to raise concerns among conservative Jewish Christians, especially since Gentiles were received as having full Christian status without being required to observe any Jewish rites and rituals. Strict Jewish believers insisted that Gentile converts had to undergo circumcision, the chief badge of Judaism, for full admission to God's people. They began to teach: "Unless you are circumcised, according to the custom taught by Moses, you cannot be saved" (v. 1). Salvation by grace alone became a pastoral problem that centered around doctrine and cultural differences.

As a result, the acceptance of Gentiles without circumcision became a theological issue that the church found necessary to address at a later meeting in Jerusalem. Peter had successfully defended his acceptance of uncircumcised Gentiles of the house of Cornelius, but that discussion had not completely settled the matter (11:18). The problem became acute and made clarification of the missionary message necessary. A meeting is therefore called at Jerusalem to settle the theological question of the relationship of Gentile believers to the law of Moses. This meeting is known as the Jerusalem Council. Present at the meeting are representatives from the two local churches—Antioch and Jerusalem.

The meeting is recorded in Acts 15, which is a significant turning point in the book of Acts. In this chapter Peter is mentioned for the last time, and after this chapter Luke focuses exclusively on Paul and his ministry. But more important is the decision of the council that commits the church officially to preaching the gospel to Gentiles and admitting them into the Christian fellowship on the basis of faith alone.

The importance of this decision may be difficult for Christians today to grasp. In the light of the New Testament, the proponents of circumcision had a weak case. At the time of the Jerusalem Council, however, there was no New Testament canon to which they could refer. Furthermore, the leaders of God's people from Abraham to Paul's day had been circumcised, and the Old Testament teaches that circumcision was an everlasting requirement (Gen. 17:9–14). Jesus himself never explicitly taught that circumcision was no longer necessary. The weight of this evidence should not be denied.

Nevertheless, the church at the Jerusalem Council decides that circumcision—the work of the law—is no longer required. The Holy Spirit guides and directs the affairs of this important meeting. Luke's account of the Jerusalem Council has a number of features: (1) introduction of the circumcision issue in Antioch (vv. 1–2); (2) the scene of conflict at Jerusalem (vv. 3–5); (3) the speeches (vv. 6–21); (4) the council's letter to Gentile believers (vv. 22–29); and (5) the report to the church (vv. 30–35).

(1) Luke's account of the circumcision controversy begins at Antioch in Syria (vv. 1–2). The unity of the church there is threatened by the arrival of some Judean Christians who want all Christians to follow the Law of Moses. This incident may be the same as the one referred to in Galatians 2:12. These Judean Christians have been called "Judaizers," because they believe that anyone who receives the gospel should convert to Judaism and keep the Law of Moses, particularly circumcision.

The teaching of the Judaizers creates division in the church. They come in a spirit of Jewish exclusivism and pronounce that uncircumcised Gentile believers are not saved and that faith in Christ is not enough for salvation. These agitators dogmatically insist that circumcision must be added to faith in the Savior. Verse 24 indicates that they claim to be an official delegation from Jerusalem, acting in behalf of the apostles and elders; but Luke does not give the impression that they are official representatives, for he identifies Judea rather than Jerusalem as the place from which they came (v. 1).

These unauthorized teachers meet strong resistance in Antioch. Their effort to Judaize the church creates a heated debate and has the potential of dividing the church into two factions, one with headquarters at Jerusalem and the other at Antioch. The integrity of the gospel as well as the unity of the church is at stake. The word translated "sharp dispute" (*stasis*) in the NIV literally means "uprising, faction, discord," whereas the word translated "debate" (*zetesis*) means "quarrel, strife." These two words describe a conflict-ridden situation that is provoked by anger, disunity, and strife. Paul and Barnabas seem to be at the center of controversy. The issue cannot be resolved by letting it smolder or by sweeping it under the rug, hoping it will go away.

Because of the danger of schism and the importance of the missionary message, a delegation is sent to Jerusalem to resolve the matter. Among the delegates are Paul and Barnabas, whose missionary work could be especially affected by the Judaizers' attempt to impose the Jewish law on Gentile believers. They are to present this dispute to "the apostles and elders"—a group mentioned five times in the chapter (vv. 2, 4, 6, 22, 23). They serve as an established part of the organizational structure of the church.

In the Greek the phrase "apostles and elders" is modified by only one article "the," indicating that they should be regarded as one group rather than two, although their functions may overlap. This group is the highest body of leaders in the church. No doubt their ministry must have been a manifestation of their spiritual gifts. Being led by the Spirit, they and others will have the wisdom to resolve the matter so that the integrity of the gospel can be maintained.

(2) The delegates depart for Jerusalem (v. 2). As they travel, Paul and Barnabas take the opportunity to report the progress of the gospel among the Gentiles. Although Luke has told us nothing about the preaching of the gospel in Phoenicia, evidently there are Christian communities in both Phoenicia and Samaria. This omission is a reminder that Luke is selective in what he records. Rather than presenting an exhaustive account of the growth of the church in the first century, he shows the universal nature of the faith, emphasizing the spread of the gospel from Jerusalem to Rome.

As the delegates recount again and again the Gentiles' turning to God, the news brings great joy to the hearts of the believers. In contrast to the Judaizers, the congregations in Phoenicia and Samaria rejoice in the triumphs of the gospel in the Gentile world. The churches in Phoenicia (composed of Jewish believers) and the Samaritan Christians seem to share Paul's attitude toward circumcision. Support for the Gentile mission is widespread. Most certainly, the rejoicing of these churches gives Paul and Barnabas assurance of support for the gospel as they have preached it and for their missionary activities.

The delegation from Antioch receives a warm reception from the church and its leaders (v. 4). The word "welcome" (*paradechomai*) means "to receive as guests." Such an enthusiastic welcome would not be possible if the leaders at Jerusalem already agreed with the Judaizers. Paul and Barnabas give a report about their first missionary journey, which they undertook at the direction of the Holy Spirit (13:2). They emphasize "everything God had done through them." Divine approval of their ministry was attested by mighty miracles and the conversion of large numbers of Gentiles. Their report must have brought joy to the hearts of those sympathetic to the Gentile mission.

But in the audience are believers who belong to the party of the Pharisees (v. 5). Like the Judaizers who had come to Antioch, these converted Pharisees are convinced that Gentiles must undergo circumcision in order to be saved. In the Gospel of Luke the Pharisees, for the most part, are among the opponents of Jesus, and in the earlier chapters of Acts they also manifested hostility toward the church. But now some of them have become believers. There are enough of them to exert a strong influence. They have clung tenaciously to some of their earlier beliefs about the law, and it comes as no surprise that they are on the wrong side of the debate.

As they listen to Paul and Barnabas's report, the ex-Pharisees take the opportunity to point out what they regard as a serious defect in the missionaries' instruction. They insist that Gentile converts should be circumcised. After the ex-Pharisees have stated their position, the apostles and elders take charge of the situation. They adjourn the meeting without discussing the matter but imply that they intend to give the matter more formal consideration.

(3) The second meeting appears to be more formal. The apostles and elders gather to clarify the missionary message. This appears to be a general meeting, including not only the leaders but also the congregation (vv. 12, 22). At the heart of the controversy is the fundamental theological question: What is required of salvation—must Gentiles become Jews to be saved or is faith alone sufficient? As the meeting begins, things are tense; several speeches are given on each side of the issue. The speakers express strong and opposing convictions. "After much discussion" the debate reaches its peak. It is then that Peter stands and gives the first of three speeches crucial to the resolution of the issue.

(a) Peter's speech (15:5–11). Peter emphasizes that there is only one way of salvation—"through the grace of the Lord Jesus" (v. 11). He supports this truth by appealing to the experience of Cornelius (10:1–11:18). His argument contains three points. (i) God himself took the initiative in making known the gospel to the Gentiles. At the beginning of the mission to the Gentiles, about ten years earlier, God chose him to preach the gospel to Cornelius and his friends and to assure them of their acceptance into the church. On a very practical level, the conversion of Gentiles is due to this divine initiative.

(ii) Visible evidence of God's approval is that Cornelius's family received the baptism in the Spirit. Peter insists that God gave the household of Cornelius the Holy Spirit "just as he did to us" at Pentecost (v. 8). The Gentile believers at Caesarea spoke in tongues as the sign of being empowered by the Spirit (10:45–46). God knew their hearts as he does the hearts of all people; that is why he filled them with the Spirit. Their experience equipped them to be witnesses, just as the outpouring of the Spirit did on the disciples at Pentecost.

(iii) God made no distinction between "us" (Jews) and "them" (Gentiles) (v. 9). By faith the hearts of both Jewish and Gentile believers had been cleansed of sin. Cornelius and his friends had been purified from sin the same way Jewish Christians had. Neither Gentile nor Jewish believers had been saved by circumcision and obedience to the law (v. 11). God had granted them inward purity by their act of faith and also had filled them with the Spirit. All that mattered in God's sight was faith in Jesus Christ. Likewise, we should make no distinction between Jews and Gentiles.

Peter goes on to warn against testing God by trying to add requirements for salvation (v. 10). To test God is to go against his revealed will (cf. 5:9; Ex. 17:2; Deut. 6:16), and God has revealed that he accepts Gentiles by faith alone. Therefore, demanding observance of the law puts God to a test and challenges his acceptance of Gentiles by faith in Christ. Any attempt to modify the divine plan of salvation will provoke God's anger. How can the church put an unnecessary "yoke" on the necks of the Gentiles?

Peter knows that the keeping of the law for salvation is an intolerable burden. On this issue he makes two observations: (a) The Jews themselves have found the law too heavy to bear and have been unable to keep it. No one has ever been saved by obedience to the law, not even Jews who have devoted their lives to trying to keep it. (b) There is only one way of salvation—"through the grace of our Lord Jesus." God saves through grace and faith, not through the law.

(b) Paul's speech (15:12). The evidence presented by Peter carries weight, and the Pharisees begin to soften. Doubtless Luke has recorded only a summary of what has been said. Everyone has spoken freely. But as Peter speaks, the Holy Spirit quiets hearts, for the meeting, highly charged with dissension, settles down into silence (v. 12). With the Pharisees holding their peace, the Holy Spirit prompts Barnabas and Paul to stand to their feet and to speak to the issue. They tell again the story of how God blessed their ministry among the Gentiles and placed his approval on their labors by performing "miraculous signs and wonders" by their hands. They tell about God's striking a Cyprus magician blind (13:8–11), healing a crippled man at Lystra (14:8–10), and delivering Paul from a stoning (14:19–20). God has been guiding the Gentile mission.

The testimony of Barnabas and Paul must not have been limited to miracles, but also included how God's saving grace had visited the Gentiles. God had worked through Barnabas and Paul to bring the Gentiles to accept Christ as their Savior (13:12, 44, 48). As the missionaries preached to the Gentiles and organized them into congregations, they did so without circumcision and without requiring the converts to keep the law.

(c) James's speech (15:13–21). After Peter's speech calms the council and Barnabas and Paul have given a report of what "God had done among the Gentiles through them," James, directed by the Holy Spirit, proposes a decisive solution (vv. 13–21). James appears to have been the chief leader in the church (12:17; 21:18), though Luke does not identify him as such. He appears to be James, the brother of the Lord. James was a pillar of the church (Gal. 2:9) and presides at this meeting. Luke's silence regarding his credentials shows his undisputed authority.

Like Peter, James also calls attention to the divine initiative (cf. vv. 7, 14), expressing his approval of what Simon (Peter's Jewish name) said about God's visitation of the Gentiles. He states the theme of his discourse in verse 14: God's purpose is to take "from the Gentiles a people for himself." He goes on to insist that the idea of Gentiles being included among God's people is not a new truth. The prophets had predicted their conversion, and Gentile presence in the church is a fulfillment of Old Testament prophecy (cf. Isa. 56:3–8; Zech. 2:11). The task of James is twofold: (i) to show from Scripture that God always intended to save the Gentiles; and (ii) to propose a practical solution to the problem raised by the believing Pharisees.

(i) For scriptural proof James cites the Greek version (LXX) of Amos 9:11–12 (cf. also Jer. 12:15; Isa. 45:21), which shows that Old Testament prophecy agrees with the gospel message. In previous verses Amos predicted the destruction of Israel, which would be the overthrow of the tent or house of David. Through the prophet God promised to rebuild "David's fallen tent." David's descendants reigned as kings, and so the building of his house can be accomplished only by an offspring of David, who will once again ascend to the throne.

After the destruction of Jerusalem in 586 B.C., no one from David's family occupied the throne until Jesus was raised from the dead and enthroned in heaven. God fulfilled the promise through the resurrection of the crucified Son of David. Through his triumph over death, David's house (*skene*, "tent, tabernacle") is rebuilt from its ruins. This rebuilding has been followed by "the remnant of men" (Gentiles) seeking after the Lord, which has been going on ever since Peter visited the home of Cornelius. Through the Savior, God has created a new people, the Christian church, which includes Gentiles as well as Jews. A new era of salvation has dawned. "For ages" God had made known through sacred Scripture his purpose to call all people to salvation (v. 18). James believes Amos was confident that God would carry out what he had promised (v. 19).

(ii) On the basis of Amos 9:11–12 James submits two proposals as a solution to the controversy. The first is that no one interfere with God's plan of accepting the Gentiles. James emphasizes his authority with his opening remark: "It is my judgment" (v. 19). The basis for his authoritative judgment is Peter's testimony, Scripture, and the special guidance of the Holy Spirit (cf. v. 28). Determined not to compromise the gospel, he calls on the council not to heed the demands of the Pharisees. Troubling the Gentile disciples by requiring circumcision and the keeping of the law must stop. Through the preaching of the gospel, Gentiles have been saved and baptized in the Spirit without observing the law of Moses. As Peter has declared, imposing law on the Gentiles will prove to be an oppressive burden and make it difficult for them to turn to God. Thus James rejects the Judaizing demand that Gentile believers become Jews (proselytes) in order to be saved.

James's second proposal reveals a deeper understanding of the law than that of the believing Pharisees. The law itself provides a solution because it imposed certain regulations on Gentiles living among Jews (Lev. 17–18). James appeals to these prohibitions. He does not urge the Gentile believers to submit to circumcision or to keep the many legal prescriptions of the law, but on the basis of Leviticus 17–18 he recommends that they avoid certain pagan practices.

These practices include: [a] Abstinence from food used in the worship of idols. Many Gentiles ate meat that had been offered to heathen gods. As believers they are to avoid eating sacrificial meat (cf. 21:25), which was considered as defiled by its connection to idolatry. They must be sensitive to the convictions of the Jews.

[b] Abstinence from sexual immorality. This prohibition has strong moral implications, forbidding promiscuous relationships that were part of pagan worship and feasts. Including illicit sex as part of religion makes the sin more repulsive, though this prohibition probably refers more to the unlawful sexual relations of Leviticus 18:6–20. Many Gentiles did not view illicit sex as a sin, but only as a function of the body. It is, however, a moral transgression. Abstinence from such is required for purity of life.

[c] Abstinence from flesh of animals not properly slaughtered, and [d] abstinence from blood. These last two prohibitions can be treated together since they are closely related. In conformity to certain food laws (Lev. 17:10–15; cf. Deut. 12:16, 23), the Jews avoided eating any animal from which the blood had not been drained. Among Gentiles, animals used in sacrificial worship were strangled or choked to death (*NIDNTT*, 1:226). Animals killed in this manner retain their blood and were not to be eaten. Because of the feelings of many Jewish Christians, Gentiles are to abstain from meat of animals that have been strangled.

In addressing the requirements for Gentile Christians, note that James does not propose that they be required to be circumcised. He asks only that they avoid certain practices that offend Jews and states that certain requirements should be conditions of fellowship for Gentiles who associate with Jewish Christians. Recognizing that God has accepted both, James recommends the two groups make concessions to one another to preserve the unity of the church. His solution does not abolish the law, but by the aid of the Spirit he interprets more correctly the law.

Jesus had promised that "the Holy Spirit … will teach you all things and remind you of everything I have said to you" (John 14:26; cf. 16:13). The Spirit inspires insight into Scripture. His works and power are fundamental to the preaching of the gospel to the Gentiles (Acts 8:29, 39; 10:19–20, 44–46; 11:12; 13:2; 15:28). Because James's insights are Spirit-inspired, Gentile believers should not be offended by the regulations or see them as arbitrary and burdensome. To the Jews scattered among the Gentiles, the Mosaic Scriptures have been read and preached weekly in the synagogues. As a result, these regulations will be well known by the Gentiles, and they should be willing to observe them out of respect for the Jewish believers. In so doing, they avoid creating schism in the body of Christ.

In light of the rest of the New Testament, these regulations, with the exception of the regulation requiring abstinence from immorality, were never binding on Gentile Christians. Paul, for example, leaves the question of eating meat sacrificed to idols to the Christian conscience (1 Cor. 8). On the other hand, because no principle is at stake, he himself submitted to ritual purification to keep from offending Jewish Christians (Acts 21:17–36).

(4) The proposals of James have a firm basis in Scripture and are motivated by the Holy Spirit. They prevail. As James has recommended to the Council (v. 20), a letter to the Gentile churches is drafted, announcing the decision of the apostles and elders (v. 23). The community of believers choose two men highly respected among them, Judas and Silas, to accompany Paul and Barnabas back to Antioch. The letter is addressed to believers in Antioch, Syria, and Cilicia, showing the scope of Jerusalem's influence. It is primarily intended for Antioch, however, the city in which circumcision had become an issue. Antioch was also home of the church that was the stronghold for the Gentile mission (11:20–26). The letter contains three significant points.

(a) The Judaizers who went to Antioch had no authority to tell other churches what to do (v. 24). This repudiation of having any responsibility for the Judaizers' teaching suggests that the Judaizers are not to be linked with the believing Pharisees in Jerusalem. Apparently the believers among the Pharisees comply with the council's decision. But the Judaizers who left Jerusalem and caused trouble in other churches had acted on their own initiative; their demands were alien to the gospel. These self-appointed emissaries had done great damage. The word rendered "disturbed" (*anaskeuazo*) means "to destroy" or "to tear down what has been built." Their false teaching had misrepresented the Jerusalem church badly and caused believers to doubt that salvation is a matter of grace and faith alone.

(b) The community of believers is sending official representatives to explain the decisions reached in Jerusalem (vv. 25–27). Among those chosen to go with Paul and Barnabas are Judas and Silas. The church at Antioch had sent Paul and Barnabas to Jerusalem as their representatives; now the church at Jerusalem sends two men as their representatives. The Jerusalem Christians describe Paul and Barnabas as "dear friends" (*agapetos*, "beloved"), expressing their high regard for them. As these Christians also recognize, Paul and Barnabas had encountered great dangers on the first missionary journey (13:50; 14:2, 5, 19). The risking of their lives for the sake of Jesus Christ made them dearer to the mother church. No doubt the Judaizers held an altogether different opinion of the two missionaries, but nothing is said in the apostolic letter about that.

The church manifests great wisdom in sending highly respected men, Judas and Silas. Both of them are described as prophets (v. 32), which is no doubt the basis of their ministry. They must have had strong prophetic influence as leaders in the Jerusalem church (v. 22). In addition to carrying the letter, these prophets are given strict orders to explain by word of mouth its contents. The letter is brief and will need some explanation should anyone have questions. Judas and Silas will also be able to vouch for the agreement and affirm that the believers are united in the handling of the whole matter.

(c) The decision the Council of Jerusalem made is inspired by the Holy Spirit (v. 28). Since Pentecost the Holy Spirit had empowered and guided the actions and decisions of the early Christians. Here Luke provides another example—the Holy Spirit's directing of the church in regard to doctrine affecting the salvation of souls. The decision made at Jerusalem was approved by the Holy Spirit and the church. The Spirit's work here is described in terms of counsel. The words "seemed good to the Holy Spirit and to us" suggest that the Holy Spirit took those believers in counsel with himself.

Jesus had promised that the Spirit would lead the disciples in their decisions (John 16:13). James is certainly correct in calling attention to the Spirit's active role in the decision-making process of the church. The letter is a product of the combination of divine and human authority, though the emphasis falls on the guidance and authority of the Holy Spirit. The Spirit himself has brought the church to this decision (Shepherd, 1994, 218). The Spirit directed the community to reach out beyond Jerusalem and Judea through the ministry of Philip (8:29, 39). The Spirit directed Peter to Caesarea and baptized Cornelius with prophetic power for witnessing. The Spirit was directly responsible for the missionary tour of Paul and Barnabas (13:1–3). The Spirit opened the door of the church to the Gentiles without requiring them to become Jews.

The minimum requirements are repeated in the letter sent to Antioch (v. 29). The keeping of them is endorsed by the Spirit, though the

Spirit never approves of any compromise of basic and essential things. With the exception of the prohibition of sexual immorality the others are minor burdens necessary for fellowship in the church. The letter has a firm tone of authority. If observed, this policy will help maintain and enrich fellowship within the Christian community.

The message concludes with a courteous appeal to follow the advice of the council. The words "you will do well" can be taken to mean doing what is right and commendable. As a result, those believers who do what is right can expect to be blessed.

(5) After the authorized delegates have received instruction from the church, they depart for Antioch (v. 30). On arrival they gather together the local congregation and present the letter. As they read it to the church, the Gentile believers are "glad for its encouraging message" (v. 31) and burst forth in exultant joy. A joyful response is typically associated with the work of the Spirit (Luke 1:41–44; 10:21; Acts 8:8; 13:52); their great joy is a Spirit-inspired joy. Furthermore, the message encourages the believers. They recognize the letter as a *paraklesis*, an "exhortation." It gives them the assurance that they can remain uncircumcised and still be accepted as full Christians, maintaining their unity with Jewish believers (Haenchen, 1971, 454).

Likewise, Judas and Silas encourage (*parakaleo*, same root as *paraklesis*) the Christians (v. 32). These men are prophets, whose Spirit-inspired instructions and exhortations encourage and strengthen the church. By prophetic power they are able to give a detailed explanation of the letter and urge the believers to comply with it. No doubt they declare that circumcision is unnecessary and affirm the spiritual significance of the law of Moses. Their authoritative exhortations regarding this divisive issue serve to build up the Christians in their faith.

Judas and Silas stay in Antioch for "some time" and encourage the believers on numerous occasions. When they decide to return to Jerusalem, the church sends them "with the blessing of peace" (v. 33) and with its prayers. The controversy is behind them; the letter has brought peace and sealed harmonious relationships in the body of Christ. Paul and Barnabas stay in Antioch, and with many other Christians they continue to preach the word of the Lord. Because of a number of teachers and preachers in the congregation, Paul and Barnabas are free to resume their work elsewhere, but to the best of our knowledge, they never do so together again.

From this account of the ministry of the Jerusalem Council we learn that the Holy Spirit guides the church and enables Christians in each generation to deal with new problems and issues as they arise. As well as resting on the Spirit's guidance, the decision of the council rested on Scripture. All that the Old Testament prophets had said as summarized by Amos (Acts 15:16–18) agreed with the invitation to everyone for salvation. James was clearly led by the Spirit in applying that prophecy of the last days to the missionary message. His interpretation binds together Christian experience (15:7–11), Scripture (15:15–19), and the Spirit (15:28), showing that all are indispensable to the church in addressing fresh pastoral and doctrinal issues.

5.2. Second Missionary Journey (15:36–18:23)

The second missionary journey takes Paul to Europe. He travels westward to the area of the Aegean, first focusing on the two provinces of Greece, Macedonia and Achaia, and then moving briefly to Asia Minor, mainly Ephesus. The narrative of the European mission begins with an emphasis on the leading of the Holy Spirit (16:6–10). Asthe first journey, Paul, directed by the Holy Spirit, continues his work as a charismatic apostle and prophet.

5.2.1. Sharp Disagreement Between Paul and Barnabas (15:36–41). Paul's mission to Europe begins with a modest proposal to Barnabas "some time later" (v. 36) to revisit the churches established in Asia Minor on their first journey (13:13–14:20), in order to see how their converts are doing spiritually. Paul and Barnabas had remained in Antioch after returning from Jerusalem (v. 35). Nothing is said here about preaching the gospel in new areas.

This proposal sets off a bitter quarrel between Paul and Barnabas. The best of friends can differ concerning matters of personal preference, but now we observe that Spirit-filled persons may also have such differences. The two missionaries disagree regarding John Mark, a nephew of Barnabas,

On his second missionary trip, Paul extends his work to Europe, traveling as far west as Corinth in what is now Greece. In Philippi in Macedonia he and Silas are held in prison overnight.

who had deserted them on the first journey at Pamphylia (cf. 13:13). Because of Mark's withdrawal on that occasion (we do not know why he did so), Paul refuses to have him along as part of the new mission.

Barnabas, however, wants to give Mark a second chance. For his part, Paul is concerned about the effect Mark will have on their work. He apparently is unwilling to risk taking Mark along a second time, who may prove to lack the courage and self-sacrifice necessary for a missionary. As a result of this argument, the two missionaries part ways.

This conflict illustrates the problem of whether the interest of the individual or the work as a whole should be first. There is no simple way of dealing with such disagreements, and no easy answers are offered here. In spite of their strong disagreement and separation, Paul and Barnabas do not allow the cause of the gospel to suffer. Deciding to revisit the Christians on Cyprus, Barnabas sails with Mark to the island. Paul takes Silas along as his companion, one of those who had come from Jerusalem to Antioch bearing the apostolic letter (v. 32).

Some scholars think that the strong influence exerted by legalistic Judaizers on Barnabas at Antioch (Gal. 2:11–13) contributed to the sharp disagreement over the suitability of John Mark a missionary partner. But it is uncertain hether there was a lingering friction between e two men after the incident at Antioch in hich the church had been divided over issues garding the role of the law. Certainly no peranent rupture took place, though we have no cord that Paul and Barnabas met again in this fe. Later, Paul does associate himself with arnabas in a positive manner (1 Cor. 9:5–6). e also acknowledges the value of Mark and ees him as a colleague in the ministry (Col. :10; 2 Tim. 4:11). Barnabas acts wisely by takg Mark under his wing and giving him the pportunity to develop as a missionary.

Before Paul and Silas depart, the Christian ommunity by prayer and probably the laying n of hands commends them to the grace of od. They then go north and revisit the Genle churches in Syria and Cilicia. They carry ith them the letter from the Council at erusalem that had been specifically addressed the churches in the region (15:23). As Paul nd Silas travel, they strengthen the believers in heir faith by instruction and exhortation. This eriod of helping the people to be strong in their aith begins the most fruitful period in Paul's ninistry and is a decisive turning point in the istory of the church (Hengel, 1979, 123).

The revisiting of areas already evangelized eads to a full-scale missionary campaign nder the direction of the Holy Spirit. No menion is made about the guidance of the Spirit luring the first stage of this journey. It is nlikely that Luke wants to link the Spirit with he dispute over Mark. But Luke does undertand that the Spirit is at work even when he s not specifically mentioned.

5.2.2. Lystra: Timothy Joins Paul (16:1–5). Paul and Silas go westward over land, revisting Derbe and Lystra. Luke omits the details of their ministry in Syria and Cilicia and begins with their arrival in Derbe, the last city in the province of Galatia that Paul and Barnabas reached on the first missionary journey. The missionaries then go on to Lystra, where Paul had also preached and established a church.

At this point in the narrative Luke introduces a new person—Timothy, who already is a Christian. Paul calls him "my son whom I love, who is faithful in the Lord" (1 Cor. 4:17), which implies that he was one of Paul's converts. Apparently Timothy was converted during Paul's earlier visit to Lystra. He was a child of a mixed marriage. His mother was a Jewish Christian woman and his father a Gentile. From 2 Timothy we learn that his Christian mother's name was Eunice, and his grandmother, Lois, was also a Christian (2 Tim. 1:5).

During Timothy's childhood these two godly women had instructed him in the Scriptures (2 Tim. 3:14–15). Timothy, therefore, had been raised in his mother's religion, but his father remained a Gentile and had not converted to Judaism. Jews were not to marry Gentiles. When they did, the children were legally regarded as Jews and normally would be circumcised soon after birth. But Timothy had never been circumcised. Perhaps his father refused to approve it. Whatever the reason, not being circumcised gave Timothy an irregular status.

Despite his irregular upbringing, the young man Timothy had a good reputation among the Christians at Lystra and Iconium (v. 2). Being well spoken of is an indispensable qualification for Christian leadership (1:21; 6:3; 1 Tim. 3:7). Paul discerns that Timothy could prove to be a valuable companion and assistant, perhaps doing the work that was assigned to Mark on the first journey. But Paul knows that in their travels they are bound to come into contact with Jews and that the Jews will not look favorably on a man of Jewish blood who is uncircumcised. So to give Timothy and himself credibility among the Jews, Paul has the young man circumcised.

This act shows Paul's sensitivity to Jewish concerns and puts into practice the principle of 1 Corinthians 9:20: "To the Jews I became like a Jew, to win the Jews." Paul is not insisting that Timothy be circumcised in order for him to be saved. Its purpose is not to bring him under the law as a means of salvation. In the case of Titus, the Judaizers had insisted that circumcision was necessary to receive salvation (Gal. 2:3), and they promoted circumcision at the Jerusalem Council as a requirement for all Gentile believers. In both instances Paul categorically refused to tolerate the rite as grounds for a person's relation to Christ and for salvation.

But no such principle is at stake in the case of Timothy. What Paul does is in the interest of the greater influence of the gospel among unsaved Jews, hoping to avoid any unnecessary offense to them. Since Timothy is a half-Jew, he knows that Jews will look on the young man as they do Gentile believers, and he will most likely become a hindrance to the progress of the gospel. Paul, therefore, has Timothy circumcised so that he can be received by the Jews as an accredited missionary.

Continuing now his narrative, Luke tells us about other work done by the missionaries in towns they visit (vv. 4–5). The decisions that were reached by the apostles and elders in Jerusalem (15:22–29) are intended for all the Gentile churches, not just Syria and Cilicia—the two regions that made up the area to which the apostolic letter was initially addressed (15:23). As Paul and Silas travel from church to church, they explain to the believers what the council decided and urge them to obey these decisions. No doubt they tell them that circumcision is unnecessary for salvation and state the concessions demanded of the Gentile Christians.

The decisions of the Jerusalem Council are needed to unite in harmonious fellowship Jewish and Gentile believers. The missionaries' explanation of the decisions has a tremendous effect. The faith of the believers is strengthened, and daily the churches receive new members. The result is true success: Believers are made stronger in doctrine and practice, and the churches become more effective in evangelism.

5.2.3. Call to Macedonia (16:6–10). Luke gives few details of the Phrygia/Galatia part of the journey, though the journey through that area must have taken months. He does not indicate where Paul preaches or the precise route that he takes through "the region of Phrygia and Galatia." The Greek indicates that only one region is in view, for the words should be rendered "the Phrygian and Galatian region." Presumably, therefore, the missionaries travel through a border area shared by both Phrygia and Galatia (cf. 18:23).

Evidently Paul and his group intend to evangelize the large cities of Asia (the official name for the western part of Asia Minor). With Ephesus as its capital this province embraced the richest and most densely populated region in the eastern Roman empire. But human initiative and plans are not enough, for the Holy Spirit prevents them from preaching there. The verb "kept" (*koluo*, v. 6) means "to cut short, hinder, restrain." It signifies a forceful intervention, as though the Spirit flung a barrier across the road into Asia. The great cities of Ephesus and Laodicea would have been fruitful fields for evangelistic work, but the guidance of the Holy Spirit is more important than favorable conditions and human initiative. For the first time the missionaries are overruled by the Holy Spirit. The mission of the church must always be directed by the Spirit.

Paul therefore goes northward, intending to enter into Bithynia, a rich and important Roman province. Once again his plans are overruled by the Spirit. Here the Spirit is referred to as "the Spirit of Jesus." No other place in the entire New Testament uses this phrase. The Holy Spirit is the Spirit of Jesus (v. 6) most likely because the Spirit anointed Jesus at the Jordan (Luke 3:22) and was active in his earthly ministry (4:1, 18-19). Moreover, the exalted Jesus bestows the Spirit on believers to equip them for ministry (24:49; Acts 2:33). Throughout his earthly ministry the Spirit empowered Jesus himself; but ever since his ascension into heaven, Jesus has worked and will continue to do so through the power and presence of the Spirit.

The missionaries therefore turn in a northwestern direction and pass through the province of Mysia without stopping. They come down to Troas on the coast of the Aegean Sea, near the site of ancient Troy. They must have been puzzled why the Holy Spirit directed them away from these inviting fields, and they are uncertain where the Lord is leading them to. During their stay in Troas a third dramatic intervention occurs, this one in the form of a vision, through which they receive God's call to Macedonia. In the vision Paul sees a Macedonian man urging the missionaries to come to his country and help them. Paul and his traveling companions interpret the vision to mean God is calling them to take the gospel to Macedonia, thereby initiating a new area of work, the European mission.

The earlier messages of the Spirit may have come through the prophetic voice of Silas. Those messages had been negative and prepared them for God's gracious guidance through the vision of the Macedonian man. At times visions are granted in the daytime (10:11), but Paul had a number of visions while he slept (18:9; 23:11; 27:23). These are not mere dreams but supernatural means of divine communication. Paul and his companions promptly comply with the call to Macedonia. The vision does not render their decision superfluous, but it shows that their crossing to Macedonia is an act of obedience.

At this point Luke indicates his own presence by his shift from third person pronouns "he" and "they" to the first person pronoun "we" (v. 10). Evidently Luke joins the missionaries at Troas. Verse 10 begins the first of four we-passages in Acts (16:10–17; 20:5–15; 21:1–18; 27:1–28:16). The traveling companions are now Paul, Silas, Timothy, and Luke. As a member of the group, Luke writes from the perspective of an eyewitness.

5.2.4. Paul Visits Philippi (16:11–40). Determined to obey the heavenly vision, the missionaries do not waste time in departing from Troas.

5.2.4.1. The Lord Converts Lydia (16:11–15). Paul and his companions set sail directly to Samothrace, a mountainous island halfway between Troas and Neapolis. After spending the night there, they continue on to the seaport city of Neapolis. From there it was only about ten miles inland to Philippi, the main city of the district of Macedonia and "a Roman colony" where the emperor Augustus had settled a large number of veterans.

Normally upon entering a city, Paul started his mission in a Jewish synagogue, but in Philippi there is no synagogue where the missionaries may preach. Philippi is mostly populated by Gentiles and has only a small Jewish population (fewer than ten adult male Jews). Because there is no synagogue, the few Jews in the area meet for worship "outside of the city" (v. 13). Paul's strategy is to first plant a church in Philippi, and from it the gospel will spread into the surrounding area.

On the first Sabbath after their arrival in the city, they visit a place of prayer outside the city gate. They have probably heard that some women go to this place by the river for worship each seventh day. There Paul and his coworkers meet them. After they sit down, their conversation turns to the gospel.

Among those present is Lydia, a woman who dealt in purple cloth worn by the rich and who was from the city of Thyatira, the center of trade for this expensive purple cloth. Though she is a businesswoman and a Gentile, Lydia is a devout worshiper of the God of Israel. Since Philippi has no synagogue, she observes the Sabbath as a holy day in prayer on the river bank. Her fidelity to God has not been diminished by unfavorable circumstances. In a mysterious way the Holy Spirit has directed the missionaries' journey by land and sea to this dealer in purple.

When Lydia hears Paul's message, the Lord opens her heart, meaning that he removes any misconception that she has that may prevent her from receiving Christ. Consequently, she pays attention to what Paul says and is converted. Another way of putting it is that the gospel comes to her through the Holy Spirit, and in joy she responds to it (cf. 1 Thess. 1:6). Her conversion is due to God's action, but this emphasis in no way denies the responsibility of the hearer to repent and believe on Jesus Christ. Upon the profession of her faith, Lydia and the people who live with her are baptized (Acts 16:15).

Baptism is a visible expression of the salvation she has received; she has died with Christ and been raised to a new life. Those who advocate infant baptism appeal to verse 15 and other verses (11:14; 16:33; 18:8; 1 Cor. 1:16). In none of these passages, however, is there any indication that the households included small children. Since Lydia is a businesswoman, she may have been single or a widow. The members of her household might have been relatives or servants. But one thing is certain: Immediately after her conversion she offers Paul and his companions hospitality. She insists that they stay with her if they deem her to have genuine faith.

5.2.4.2. Paul Casts Out a Demon (16:16–18). At the place where the Jews regularly gather for prayer (cf. v. 13), Paul and his companions confront a slave girl. This girl had been sold into slavery and is described by Luke as having "a spirit by which she predicted the future." Literally the Greek indicates she has "a python spirit" (*pneuma pythona*). The word *python* was originally used in Greek mythology for the snake that guarded the sacred place at Delphi, where divine prophecies were given. The *python* had been slain by Apollo, the god of prophecy. Later the word was used to designate a person who had power to foretell the future and who was thought to be inspired by the serpent called Python (cf. 1 Sam. 28:7, LXX).

Luke recognizes that the slave girl has an evil spirit that enables her to tell fortunes and predict the future. No doubt this case is an example of demon possession. Because she is able to prophesy, she is in great demand and provides a lucrative income for her owners. The slave girl behaves as the demoniacs did in the presence of the Lord (Mark 1:24; Luke 4:41; 8:28). Inspired by the evil spirit, each day she follows Paul and the other missionaries as they minister. She recognizes who the missionaries are and repeatedly shouts out, "These men are servants of the Most High God, who are telling you the way to be saved" (v. 17).

The slave girl's prophetic power and insight actually come from the evil spirit, which inspires her to speak oracles. This evil spirit does announce the truth to the people, for the missionaries are obedient servants of God who proclaim the way of salvation (cf. v. 31). The title "Most High God" was also used by a Gentile (Luke 8:28) and the Gerasene demoniac (Mark 5:7). The phrase was often used by both Jews and Gentiles for the God of Israel. The Gentiles likely borrowed it from the Jews to speak of Israel's God, who is higher and more important than all other gods.

The proclamation of the slave girl goes on for several days. No explanation is given as to why Paul waits many days before dealing with her. At first he may have seen her as being harmless, or it is possible that the Holy Spirit did not direct him to cast out the evil spirit. When she persists in following the missionaries, Paul becomes deeply troubled. Full of the Spirit he casts out the *python* spirit "in the name of Jesus Christ" (v. 18). As in the case of other healings (3:6, 12, 16; 4:10), the slave girl is miraculously set free by the power of Jesus Christ. The risen Savior continues to work as he had during his earthly ministry (Luke 4:35, 41; 8:29), and he drives out the evil spirit.

Paul's exercise of the spiritual gift of discernment and the exorcism bring an end to the girl's exploitation for profit by her owners. What becomes of her, we are not informed; but out of gratitude for so great a deliverance she must have come under the influence of Paul and women such as Lydia (vv. 13–15). Luke's interest is to show that the Lord continues to work through Paul as he had through the other apostles in earlier years (cf. 3:6; 4:10). Luke also uses the account to call attention to the repercussions the miracle will have on Paul and his associates.

5.2.4.3. Paul and Silas Are Imprisoned and Released (16:19–40). The deliverance of the slave girl results in trouble for Paul and his missionary companions. We do not know whether her owners are present when she is set free from the evil spirit, but they soon discover that "their hope of making money was gone." Luke here makes a humorous play on words. The verb "left" (*exelthen*, "went out") that Luke uses when the spirit leaves the girl is the same one he uses to describe the masters' hope of monetary gain "being gone." That is, when the evil spirit "left," the masters saw their hope of gain "leaving." They realize that their business of exploiting the girl for profit is ruined, and they know who is responsible for their loss.

As in a later case in Ephesus (19:23–29), the unconverted are prone to react violently when the gospel threatens their income. So these owners are enraged at Paul and Silas. With the assistance of some bystanders (cf. v. 22), they seize the two men and drag them into the marketplace before the authorities. The marketplace was the city square where public court was conducted. City life centered around the marketplace, and it was used regularly for political meetings, judicial hearings, and business. The girl's owners present their case against Paul and Silas before the magistrates (*strategoi*), the chief Roman officials of Philippi.

The two missionaries are referred to by their accusers as Jews, not as Christians. They suppress the real cause of their complaint: the girl's deliverance from the demon, which had put an end to their profit-making enterprise. They make a false charge against Paul and Silas, which falls into two parts. (1) The missionaries have caused trouble in the city. To support this they identify Paul and Silas as Jews, thereby appealing to anti-Jewish sentiments. At that time it was easy in a predominantly Gentile city like Philippi to arouse strong feelings against the Jews. The accusers know that there is prejudice against this religious minority, so they charge them with creating public confusion. The disturbance of the peace is serious enough, but the implication that Jews have caused the disturbance makes the accusation even worse.

(2) The missionaries are also charged with introducing unlawful customs (*ethe*, v. 21). It is unclear what customs are involved, but most likely this accusation refers to the missionaries' proselytizing of Roman citizens. Though the Romans were tolerant of the Jews' practicing their religion, they did not permit them to evangelize Roman citizens. Romans were forbidden by law to become converts to Judaism. So any

In Philippi, Paul and Silas are arrested, beaten, and jailed after Paul orders a demon to come out of a slave girl. These ruins are said to be the inner jail cell where the two men were held, their feet fastened in stocks. An earthquake shook the prison, releasing door locks and chains, but they didn't leave and were released the next morning.

evangelistic preaching by the missionaries would be seen as going contrary to that law. Like the charges made against Jesus by the Sanhedrin, the charges against Paul and Silas are motivated by rage and revenge.

The outcry of the slave owners against Paul and Silas has an effect on the crowd that had gathered in the city square to hear the proceedings. Excited by these charges, the anti-Jewish crowd joins with the slave owners and cries out against Paul and Silas. No one gives the missionaries an opportunity to defend themselves.

After the girl's owners make this formal complaint, the Roman authorities have them arrested. The Greek may suggest here that the magistrates tore off with their own hands the clothes of the prisoners, but more likely they ordered soldiers standing nearby to strip them of their clothes. After the prisoners' garments were ripped off (according to the Roman practice), their naked bodies were beaten with rods by the lictors, who normally accompanied the magistrates. In his catalogue of apostolic hardships in 2 Corinthians 11:25 Paul says, "Three times I was beaten with rods." Doubtless this is one of the occasions.

A beating should not have been imposed on a Roman citizen, especially without a trial. Neither Paul nor Silas assert their rights here as Roman citizens. As 22:25 points out, the lictors would not have ignored claims to Roman citizenship. The magistrates are ignorant of the

status of the missionaries (cf. vv. 35–39). Jewish law restricted punishment to forty blows save one; no such limits were in Roman law, so that the severity of the punishment depended on the authorities. The Greek states simply that these men received "many blows" (v. 23). The severe beating followed by imprisonment shows that the magistrates assume the guilt of the innocent missionaries. Paul and Silas are suffering for doing good—for delivering a slave girl from being taken advantage of by her owners.

The jailer is not only told by the authorities to lock the prisoners up but also to guard them carefully so that it is impossible for them to escape (v. 23). He locks them up in "the inner cell," the best-guarded cell in the prison. In addition to that, he adds torture by fastening their legs in stocks. The Romans used stocks as an instrument of torture. They were made of wood with two holes for the prisoner's legs. The holes were placed so that the legs of a prisoner could be forced apart causing great pain. By placing Paul and Silas in such an instrument, the jailer makes it humanly impossible for Paul and Silas to escape.

Despite their imprisonment and pain Paul and Silas manifest a firm trust in God. Unable to sleep, they express their joy that God considers them worthy to suffer for the sake of the gospel. At midnight the other prisoners hear the missionaries offering prayers to God and singing hymns to him. Here we have a concrete example of the Christian practice of rejoicing in the midst of suffering (cf. Rom. 5:3; Col. 1:24; James 1:2; 1 Peter 1:6).

The prayers that Paul and Silas offer must have been simply praise to God; there is no hint that they are praying for release, though the other prisoners may regard the coming of the earthquake as an answer to the missionaries' prayers. This incident of suffering and prayer shows that Paul learned by experience what he later taught the believers in this same city: "Do not be anxious about anything, but in everything, by prayer and petition, with thanksgiving, present your requests to God. And the peace of God, which transcends all understanding, will guard your hearts and your minds in Christ Jesus" (Phil. 4:6–7).

While Paul and Silas pray and sing, the other prisoners listen attentively. In answer to their joyful prayer-hymns there comes an earthquake, which shakes the foundations of the prison and throws open the doors (vv. 25–26). Then another miracle occurs in which the chains on the prisoners are unfastened. This direct divine intervention has a paralyzing effect, for no prisoner tries to escape.

The jailer is awakened at midnight by the violent earthquake and by the slamming of the doors. Aroused from sleep he is confused by the miracle, and his heart is filled with fear. He knows that if the prisoners escape, he will be charged with neglect of duty and receive the same punishment due the prisoners (cf. 12:19; 27:42). Most likely some of the prisoners have been slated to be executed, and the jailer assumes that he will be killed if they escape. Greatly troubled, he is about to plunge his sword into himself and commit suicide, when Paul shouts, "Don't harm yourself! We are all here!" How does Paul know that none of the prisoners have escaped and that the jailer is about to kill himself? This may be another example of supernatural insight, or Luke may have felt it unnecessary to include all the details of the miracle.

As soon as the jailer can collect his senses, he remembers that Paul and Silas are preachers of the "Most High God" (v. 17). They have gained a reputation for preaching the way of salvation, and now he sees that their God has miraculously delivered his servants. The jailer has heard that supernatural power works through Paul and Silas and perceives that their God has caused the extraordinary event. Since it is midnight, the jailer calls his aids to bring torches.

Trembling with fear, the jailer falls at the feet of the missionaries and wants to know what he must do to be saved (v. 30). Exactly what he means by this question is uncertain, but Paul and Silas take the question in its full theological meaning. They give him a summary of the doctrine of salvation: "Believe in the Lord Jesus, and you will be saved—you and your household" (v. 31). If he had heard the missionaries before, he would know what to do for salvation. Some modern preachers may leave their congregations in doubt regarding this supreme question, but not the first preachers of the gospel. They inform the jailer that salvation occurs only through faith in Jesus as Lord.

At first the missionaries give the jailer the gospel in a nutshell: Salvation is only by faith in Jesus. Then they speak the word of the Lord to all the other members of the jailer's house. They explain who Jesus is and how one can be saved by believing in him as Lord. Just as the jailer has done, his family puts their trust and confidence in Jesus. The promise of salvation to his household does not mean that one person can believe for others. Rather, salvation is available to his family on the same terms as it is to the jailer. Kinship relationships do offer favorable circumstances for evangelism.

The jailer shows his change of heart and the genuineness of his discipleship by taking the missionaries to his home. He tends to their wounds, a result of the beating they had received the previous day. After the jailer and his household are baptized, the jailer feeds the missionaries as an expression of his hospital ty and appreciation for his and his family's alvation. They are filled with joy and cele-›rate their faith in God. Their joy is sure proof ›f the presence and the work of the Holy Spirit n their hearts.

Earlier God had intervened and delivered ›eter from prison by an angel (12:5–9); now ›aul and Silas have been delivered by a violent arthquake of the Lord. This miracle serves as he background to the conversion of the jailer nd his household and shows that God can frus-rate attempts to stop the gospel. Paul and Silas ave suffered for the sake of Christ, but their uffering is not in vain, for a jailer and his fam-ly have been converted. The Roman authori-ies who had Paul and Silas beaten and thrown n prison have no knowledge of what has taken lace during the night. The earthquake proba-ly did not extend beyond the prison.

After the miraculous deliverance of Paul nd Silas from prison, they are vindicated in ne Gentile city during the final scene of the ccount (vv. 35–40). Just the day before, they ad been flogged severely and locked up in jail v. 24). The next morning the Roman authori-es, convinced that the missionaries had been dequately punished, send the lictors to order ne jailer to release Paul and Silas from prison. 'he jailer is pleased to bid the missionaries, ›ho are now back in prison apparently at their wn insistence, to go in peace. By using the ›ord "peace," he takes up the Jewish form of reeting, pronouncing on Paul and Silas God's lessings as they continue their journey (cf. uke 8:48).

But both Paul and Silas are Roman citizens, nd the ruling authorities have violated their ghts under Roman law. No citizen was to be eaten and locked up without a trial. The mis-ionaries had not been found guilty of any rime. The authorities had exceeded their uthority by their arbitrary treatment of Roman itizens. On the previous day Paul and Silas id not protest their flogging and imprison-ent on the basis of Roman citizenship. Per-aps they did not want to leave the impression at they desired to avoid suffering for the sake f Christ. But now, knowledge of their Roman itizenship may ensure that the believers left ehind will receive better treatment.

Paul speaks directly to the officers and efuses to leave without a personal apology om the magistrates themselves. The apostle reminds the officers that the authorities' treatment violated his and Silas's personal rights as Roman citizens. They have suffered serious wrong by being beaten and imprisoned as though they were criminals. Paul refuses to be dismissed quietly without any public acknowledgment of the wrong the authorities have done. Therefore Paul demands that the magistrates come in person and admit the wrong they did to their prisoners.

When the authorities hear of Paul's demand and of the fact that the missionaries are Roman citizens, they are justifiably alarmed, knowing that persons violating the rights of Roman citizens often received severe punishment. To make the best of a bad situation, they come personally to the prison and humbly ask Paul and Silas to leave the city. The two men take their time in complying with the request. They make a final call on Lydia, whose house by now has become the headquarters for the Christians at Philippi. They encourage the members of the infant church. Their mission has been vindicated against the hostile actions of the Roman authorities, and they depart from Philippi in triumph. The pattern of triumph through suffering, which took place in the Lord Jesus, is reproduced in the experience of his servants.

5.2.5. Paul Visits Thessalonica (17:1–9). After departing from Philippi, the missionaries travel southwest along a well-established road (the Via Egnatia) to the capital city of Macedonia, Thessalonica (modern Salonika). The city was about a hundred miles from Philippi. Luke does not indicate whether the missionaries travel by animal or foot, but they pass through Amphipolis, about thirty miles southwest of Philippi, and Apollonia, about thirty miles southwest of Amphipolis. Luke apparently stays behind to continue the work in Philippi (see comments on 16:10). Since neither he nor Timothy were imprisoned in Philippi with Paul and Silas, both of them may have remained behind.

Paul's strategy of spreading the gospel becomes clear as the missionaries pass through two cities and settle in Thessalonica. This city was a center of trade, where people came and went. Therefore, it was a strategic place for establishing a church. Empowered by the Spirit, Paul preaches the gospel to Jews and Gentiles and plants churches in strategic metropolitan centers.

When the missionaries arrive in Thessalonica, in keeping with his normal practice Paul first goes to the Jewish synagogue. The synagogue there indicates the presence of a considerable Jewish population with a number of Gentile God-fearers and proselytes. It provides an open door for the introduction of the gospel in the city. For three Sabbaths in the synagogue Paul reasons with the Jews from the Scriptures, explaining how Christ has fulfilled the Old Testament (v. 2).

Paul's letters suggest he may have spent more than three weeks in the city. We know that he had to work there to provide for his livelihood (1 Thess. 2:9; 2 Thess. 3:7–9). We also know that the Christians at Philippi sent him money for his support a number of times, for they had sent aid "again and again" to him while he was in Thessalonica (Phil. 4:16).

In his preaching in the synagogue Paul focuses on three themes: the necessity of Christ's suffering, the necessity of his resurrection, and the Messiahship of Jesus. (1) The necessity of Christ's suffering. The suffering of Jesus included his death on the cross, according to God's plan. In his writings Luke has emphasized the necessity of Christ's death (Luke 9:22; 17:25; 24:7, 26, 46; Acts 2:23). The Jews expected the Messiah to be a conqueror. Paul's preaching that Christ had to suffer offended them because it appeared to be inconsistent with the glorious reign of the Messiah as they interpreted it in the prophets (cf. Dan. 7:13–14). But Paul opens the Scriptures, showing the Jews that the promised Messiah had to suffer (cf. Ps. 2:1–2; Isa. 53).

(2) The necessity of Christ's resurrection. The Messiah conquered death, but only after he had come under the power of death. Like other early apostolic preachers Paul emphasizes also the necessity of the resurrection of Christ, which lay in the will of God and his plan of redemption (cf. Ps. 16; 110). No doubt Paul also proclaims the evidence for Jesus' triumph over death, such as the testimonies of the original eyewitnesses, who saw him alive after his crucifixion. For Jesus to die and rise again fulfilled prophecy.

(3) Jesus is the Messiah. Since Jesus fulfilled the conditions of Scripture, Paul declares that Jesus is the Messiah. Paul undoubtedly also points out the extraordinary miracles and signs that have been performed in Jesus' name, demonstrating that he is the living, divine Lord; note 1 Thessalonians 1:5: "Our gospel came to you not simply with words, but also with power, with the Holy Spirit." That is, the Holy Spirit worked miracles before the Thessalonians and gave them the assurance of the resurrection and glorification of Jesus, in whose name the miracles were done. The life and ministry of Jesus produced a new understanding of the Messiah as the crucified and risen Lord.

Paul convinces only "some of the Jews" that Jesus is the Messiah. Their response stands in sharp contrast to the conversion of Gentiles, including a few important women in the city (v. 4). The great majority of the converts, therefore, are devout Gentiles, who had learned to worship the God of the Jews but were not fully converted to Judaism. These converts join Paul and Silas, forming a new group apart from the synagogue, evidently meeting at the house of Jason (v. 5).

Paul's success among the local Gentiles arouses the anger and jealousy of the unbelieving Jews. Apparently they took pride in the attachment of devout Gentiles to the synagogue and see Paul and Silas as stealing their sheep. The Jews therefore collect loafers and troublemakers, who hang around the marketplace, and incite them to give Paul and his friends trouble. These loafers, being extremely hostile toward the missionaries, form a mob and start a disturbance in the city. They gather outside of the home of a man named Jason, thinking that Paul and Silas are there. When the unruly mob fails to find the two missionaries there, in their frustration they drag Jason and some other Christians before the city magistrates.

The mob accuses Jason of sheltering these men who cause "trouble all over the world" and violate the decrees of Caesar. No doubt these two charges were previously leveled against the missionaries by the Jews and perhaps by the Gentiles. The first charge is true. The gospel was impacting individuals and society in a revolutionary way through its redemptive power. There was a consistent tendency for the gospel to disturb the peace everywhere it was preached (16:20; 24:5, 12). Apparently news came from Philippi (and perhaps elsewhere) about the hostile action taken against the missionaries (16:20–24).

The second charge is that the missionaries have preached sedition against Rome. The have declared that there is "another king" besides Caesar (Claudius), namely, Jesus. In proclaiming him as king, they do not intentionally act contrary to Caesar's decrees, which include Roman laws against rebellion and treason. The missionaries' claims of Jesus' kingship, however, did cause the Roman authorities to perceive Christianity as a political threat.

Note how a similar charge of sedition had maliciously been made by the Jews against Jesus before Pilate. They accused him of high treason—perverting the people from loyalty to Caesar and declaring himself to be "Christ, a king" (Luke 23:2). A common practice of the Roman emperors was to claim divine honors. Thus the proclamation of Jesus as king could easily be misinterpreted by Paul's enemies as an attack on the emperor and as incompatible with his claims. The missionaries have no intention, however, of inciting rebellion in response to the Jews' malicious charges. Paul's letters to the Thessalonians reveal that his preaching dealt with the kingdom of God (1 Thess. 2:12; 2 Thess. 1:5), not with matters of politics. Jesus' kingdom is not of this world. He is a spiritual king, not a political one; therefore, his rule is radically different from the rule of the Roman emperor.

Though false, the charge of treason against the emperor does have serious effects. A crowd gathers as a result of the violence done to Jason and other Christians by the previous mob. The city authorities and crowd recognize the serious political implications of the charge. Knowing what the consequences of plots against Caesar could be, the authorities are alarmed by the accusation made against Paul and Silas.

In this case the city leaders do not rush to judgment, assuming that the missionaries are political agitators. Instead, they conduct an investigation, upon which they determine that the charge put forward by the Jews against the Christian preachers lacks real substance. Because of the false charges and arrest, the authorities attempt to ensure that Jason and his Christian friends are not inclined toward political insurrection. The city leaders require them to post bond, presumably cash, and then they go free. This action vindicates the missionaries once again.

Paul and his friends have preached that Jesus is the Christ (v. 3), and their success among the Gentile God-fearers at the synagogue has led to their being falsely charged with preaching political revolution. In the midst of all this, Paul and his friends have preached the gospel in the power of the Spirit. Though the conversion of the Thessalonian Christians involved great suffering, these people received the gospel with joy inspired by the Holy Spirit (1 Thess. 1:5–6). Opposition to the gospel seems to have been an exercise in futility.

5.2.6. Paul Visits Berea (17:10–15). Apparently the Christians in Thessalonica realize that the continuance of Paul and Silas in the city could bring personal violence to themselves and possibly result also in the forfeiture of the bond posted by Jason and the others. Jason has given his word to the authorities that the missionaries will cease preaching in the city. Somewhere in Thessalonica the Christians meet secretly at night, suggesting that they are still in danger. Paul and Silas are sent on their way to Berea, a city fifty miles to the southwest (now called Véroia).

When Paul and the missionaries arrive in Berea, it becomes clear that their recent experiences in Philippi and Thessalonica have not discouraged them. Berea has a flourishing

On his trip to Macedonia, Paul would have passed by this fourth-century B.C. funerary sculpture, the Lion of Amfipolis, which guards a bridge over the Strimon River, east of Thessalonica.

Jewish community. In keeping with their previous pattern of ministry, they find a synagogue and make it the starting point for their preaching. Paul finds the Jews in Berea are "of more noble character," which indicates that they are more open-minded than the Jews at Thessalonica and are willing to listen to the gospel and to examine it as mature human beings. Proof of their open-mindedness is their strong desire to listen to Paul's message and their daily examination of the Old Testament in order to see if Paul is preaching the truth.

Paul's message, which must have included the cross of Christ, would have been disturbing to the Jews, for according to Jewish tradition anyone crucified is accursed of God (Deut. 21:23). But the apostle appeals to the Old Testament to prove that the crucifixion is scriptural (Isa. 53). Many Jews as well as a number of Greek men and women of high social standing accept Paul's message and believe in Christ. It is not surprising that "many of the Jews believed" in the Lord Jesus, since they have investigated thoughtfully and critically the Scriptures for themselves, keeping open minds while examining the claims of the gospel.

The response of these people to the gospel makes an important theological point: Faith comes by hearing the Word of God. The Jews' open-minded response to the missionary message corresponds to their willingness to give the Scriptures a fair hearing. A common error of unbelievers is to stop up their ears when God speaks and close their eyes to the truth of Scripture. The impressive response of the Berean Jews and Greeks is not only to be highly commended but also carefully imitated.

At Berea there seems to have been no serious obstacle to the gospel. The missionaries may have hoped to turn the whole city to Christ. But before long the enemies of the gospel attack them from the rear. The Jews in Thessalonica hear about Paul's success in Berea. Like the Jews of Antioch and Iconium who pursued Paul to Lystra (14:19), they come to that city and repeat their tactics by stirring the crowds up to mob action against the missionaries. As at Thessalonica they probably accuse them of preaching political insurrection and rebellion, hoping to stop Paul's work. The results are the same—a popular uproar in the city and the forming of mobs. Paul, who is obviously at the center of the attack, has to flee for his life again. The Jews seem to keep pursuing him as long as he stays in Macedonia.

Feeling that it is wise for Paul to leave the city, the Christians send him along with others to the coast to sail for Athens. Timothy and Silas, however, stay behind so that they may further instruct and encourage the Christians in Berea (v. 15). Timothy may have been left with Luke at Philippi earlier (16:40); but since he appears here in the narrative, he has caught up with the missionaries. He and Silas are instructed to follow Paul as soon as possible. Shortly after Paul leaves, Timothy and Silas do go to Athens; but upon arriving there, they are sent back to Macedonia to encourage the Thessalonian believers (1 Thess. 3:1–3). They rejoin Paul after he goes from Athens to Corinth (Acts 18:1, 5).

Paul has left behind three congregations: Philippi, Thessalonica, and Berea. If the Christians in these churches prove to be committed to evangelism, the gospel could successfully spread throughout the province. Later Paul writes the following about the Christian witness of the Thessalonians: "The Lord's message rang out from you not only in Macedonia and Achaia—your faith in God has become known everywhere" (1 Thess. 1:8). No doubt much of their zeal and faithfulness were due to Timothy and Silas's having been left behind for that purpose.

5.2.7. Paul Visits Athens (17:16–34) Luke does not tell us how long Paul remains in Athens, but he shows how the apostle engages popular pagan religion and preaches to educated pagans. At the time of Paul's arrival (about A.D. 50), Athens was still an important cultural and intellectual center. It was "a quiet little city of about 5,000 citizens" (Haenchen 1971, 517). Greece was no longer a military superpower, and Athens was politically insignificant. In spite of this, the city still served as a place of lively intellectual interest.

No doubt Paul knows the reputation of Athens. But we have no record of his saying anything about the city's cultural and intellectual achievements, most notably represented by such philosophers as Socrates, Plato, and Aristotle. Paul's interest is not in the past glories of Athens. What strikes him is the extent to which the people are devoted to idolatry. The Spirit-filled apostle preaches the gospel in that city in spite of his message being rejected by the wise. The experience of Paul in Athens focuses attention on two incidents: preaching in the marketplace (vv. 16–21) and a sermon before the council of the Areopagus (vv. 22–31).

(1) Paul expects Timothy and Silas to arrive soon. As he waits for them, he observes that the city is "full of idols" (*kateidolon*), which literally means "thick with images." Paul is greatly upset to see idols all over the city and to realize how thoroughly idolatrous the Athenians are. He recognizes their spiritual condition for what it is. At first he divides his ministry between the synagogue, where he reasons with Jews and Gentile God-fearers about Jesus, and the marketplace, where he preaches to those who happen to be present. Daily he speaks in the marketplace where philosophers, idlers, and people of leisure often gather for conversation and discussion. Because of Paul's persistent efforts he attracts the attention of the Epicureans and Stoics, representatives of two schools of philosophy.

The Epicureans taught that the highest good of human existence was pleasure, but for them pleasure could be best secured by avoiding excess. They interpreted pleasures not as the prudent gratification of every desire and inclination but as being free from disturbing passions and emotions. The ideal life was a life of tranquillity that caused no pain and was based on prudence, honor, and justice. They strongly attacked superstitious belief in gods but recognized the existence of certain gods. Even so, they were materialistic in outlook and atheistic in practice.

On the other hand, the Stoics believed that the good life was attained through a total indifference to both the sorrows and pleasures of the world. For them God was a living force embodied in nature rather than a person, and everything had been predetermined. God is in all things, and everything that happens has to be accepted as God's will. Human reason determines what is good and what is evil. Thus, the Stoics were rationalists and fatalists in their religious views, advocating the apathetic acceptance of the natural course of events.

Paul's persistence in preaching the gospel prompts the Epicureans and Stoics to engage him in argument (v. 18). Some of the philosophers mockingly characterize Paul as a "babbler" (*spermologos*, "a seed picker"). This word was first used of birds that pick up seed and then of people who collect bits of information and truth without really grasping their meaning. To them Paul is nothing more than an incompetent plagiarist, who teaches second-hand fragments of knowledge that cannot be fashioned into a philosophical system.

Other philosophers in Athens claim that Paul preaches "foreign gods," because he preaches Jesus and the resurrection (including not only Jesus' resurrection but probably also the hope of resurrection of the dead to everlasting life). This charge may indicate the philosophers think that he is speaking about two deities: Jesus and *Anastasis* (*anastasis* is the Greek word for "resurrection"). Though Paul may have been misunderstood, he does preach a wonderful new message concerning Jesus and the resurrection. He does not present foreign gods but the only true God, the One who has revealed himself in Jesus Christ.

(2) In spite of their contempt for Paul, some wish to learn more about his teaching and so satisfy their curiosity. They do not arrest him, but they do lead him from the noisy crowd of the marketplace to "a meeting of the Areopagus." "Areopagus" means "the hill of Ares," named for Ares, the god of war, whom the Romans called Mars. It is uncertain whether Luke has in mind the hill where the Athenian council met or the actual meeting of the council. The NIV supports the latter, suggesting that Paul expounds his teaching before that venerable council. This ancient council, which lost most of its power in the fifth century B.C. with the growth of Athenian democracy, had regained much of its authority under the Romans. In the first century, it apparently exercised control over public lecturers.

It could be expected, therefore, that Paul in Athens with a new message should be invited to explain it before the council (Bruce, 1943, 88). The mention of "Dionysius, a member of the Areopagus" (v. 34), suggests that Paul appears before the council in public session. Though the accusation that he advocates foreign gods may have seemed serious, Luke gives no hint that Paul's presence before the council involves a formal trial. This council is responsible to hear and evaluate public speakers in Athens and allows the Spirit-filled apostle to explain his message.

As indicated by his parenthetical statement in verse 21, Luke has a low opinion of the religious discussion and debate that normally went on at meetings of the Areopagus. The council sought merely to gratify their curiosity and take advantage of every opportunity to discuss any new idea on philosophy. But the informal character of the proceedings gives Paul the opportunity to preach a sermon, spelling out his views (vv. 22–31). In it he strongly attacks the Athenians and their religion. Paul's defense of the Christian faith contains a classic statement on what is described as "natural theology" (cf. 14:15–17), which emphasizes the distinction between revelation in creation and providence and special revelation in the Scriptures and Jesus Christ.

Paul begins by addressing his audience as "Men of Athens." He then admits that these people are "very religious," which he probably intends as a compliment for their piety. Their religious devotion cannot be denied, for any visitor to Athens could see the many idols and shrines, among which Paul has seen an altar erected in honor of an unknown god (v. 23). The Greeks commonly dedicated altars to unknown gods out of fear of overlooking a god that would otherwise be offended. The altar to an unknown god was probably a type of "insurance," to ward off judgment from a god demanding attention about whom they knew nothing. Inscriptions have been found "to unknown gods," but so far no altar has been discovered dedicated "to an unknown god." There is no doubt, however, that such an altar existed in Athens in Paul's day.

This inscription gives Paul an opportunity to introduce the true and living God, whom the Athenians do not know. They seek to worship him even though they are ignorant of who he is (v. 23). Obviously Paul is not trying to draw a direct connection between the unknown god and the true God, but he uses the inscription of the altar as a means to begin telling the Athenians about the living God, the Creator—an excellent strategy for not offending pagan sensibilities.

Since the Athenians do not accept the authority of the Scriptures, which speak about the long-expected Messiah, and do not know Jewish history, Paul has to adapt his message to his audience. Therefore, to acquaint the Athenians with the Lord God, he reasons from God's revelation of himself in creation. His sermon is firmly rooted in the Old Testament, especially its presentation of God as Creator and sovereign Lord of heaven and earth. Paul's goal is to introduce the Athenians to God's saving purposes and to bring them the joy of salvation. The sermon provides a pattern for presenting the gospel to those not anchored in the biblical tradition.

Paul makes a number of statements about God, each of which presents God as the true and living God in striking contrast to the gods of the Greeks. (1) God is both Creator and "Lord of heaven and earth" (v. 24). He brought the universe into existence and governs it. He, therefore, cannot live in sanctuaries made by human hands, such as the magnificent Parthenon, where the Greek gods of Athens dwelt. Regardless of how splendid temples might be, no building can contain the Lord of the universe (cf. 7:49–50). This thought lifts the Lord God above the deities of the Athenians.

(2) God is self-sufficient (v. 25; Isa. 42:5). Since God has created everything, he is not served by human beings as though they can supply him something he needs. Helpless man-made idols, unlike God, topple over unless secured, and the priests present to them sacrificial gifts, even offerings of food and drink. In contrast, God stands in need of none of these things. He is the absolute self-sufficient Creator and is completely independent. All people are dependent on him as the ultimate source of all life and breath. Our very existence is a gift that flows from the Creator and Preserver of all life.

(3) God has created humanity (v. 26). Paul's emphasis falls on the way he created humankind; he made all nations from a single person, Adam. All human beings share the same nature because they have one common ancestor (Gen. 1:26–28). The unity of the human family lies in that fact. The Creator of the human race also rules human history. His hand has been evident in the history of individual nations, making them settle all over the earth. He has given humankind the earth for a home and in his wise providence has "determined the times set for them"—probably meaning the seasons of the year, indicating the continuance of God's goodwill and favor. Furthermore, he has established the national boundaries, determining exactly where each nation should live on the earth. It is, therefore, wrong to identify God with a particular city or a single nation. He is only one infinite Creator and Ruler, and his hand and work have been revealed in history and still are.

At this point Paul explains the supreme purpose of God's revelation of himself in creation and his providential dealing with humankind: "God did this so that men would seek him and perhaps reach out for him and find him, though he is not far from each one of us" (v. 27). God has disclosed himself so that human beings will "seek him" and "find him," the very thing Paul wants the Athenians to do. The verb "reach out" (*pselaphao*) expresses the idea of feeling around for God in darkness as a blind person who feels around to identify an object or to determine where he is. A tone of uncertainty is introduced with the phrase *ei ara ge* ("perhaps," lit., "if perhaps"); but finding God is a real possibility, seeing that "he is not far from each one of us."

The Athenians are blindly reaching out for the living God, who stands so close to them and who desires to be found; but finding him is not inevitable, nor is it something that happens automatically. Though they seek God, so far they have failed to find him. But it is still possible for them to know him because, despite his greatness and transcendence, he is near every one of them. In creation the living God reveals his glory, power, wisdom, and goodness (cf. Rom. 1:19–22). Revelation in creation discloses God's existence, but it cannot save. Only God's revelation in Jesus Christ can deliver from sin.

From God's revelation in creation, people such as the Athenians can come to a knowledge of his unlimited power and beneficent rule. Paul appeals to Greek literature to illustrate the relationship of the living God to humankind. His first quotation is presumably from the philosopher-poet Epimenides of Crete (sixth century B.C.) and emphasizes the nearness of God: "For in him we live and move and have our being" (v. 28). In contrast to idols, which have no life and lack real existence, God is Creator and Sustainer of life. Without him we cannot live, move, and have existence. This truth reminds us of providence as well as of God's wonderful presence in all times and in all places. He is not withdrawn from the world, as the Epicureans believe, but is ever present in creation.

The second quotation, ascribed to the Cilician poet Aratus (third century B.C.), states that as God's creatures "we are his offspring." This poet acknowledges a resemblance between human beings and God. Thus, the relationship is not simply that of Creator and creature but that of Parent and child. Human beings are not divine, but as God's offspring, we are created in his image (Gen. 1:26). Since we are living creatures, God must be much greater than his creation and, therefore, unlike lifeless idols. He is the living God. All people are united by their kinship to him.

Since human beings are the offspring of God, Paul concludes that idols are unsuitable representations of God. We should not think of God as being like something made by human hands. Lifeless idols of gold, silver, and stone—no matter how skillfully and beautifully made—are mere human productions. They cannot truly represent God nor are they appropriate for the worship of the living Creator. Out of self-respect for ourselves we should not think of him from whom we derive life as being like the dead works that our hands produce. The One who made heaven and earth and is the source of all life cannot be worshiped by man-made images.

At this point Paul directs the attention of his audience away from revelation in creation to the plan of salvation revealed in Christ (v. 30). The coming of Jesus Christ into the world was a decisive event. Before that time God "overlooked" humanity's ignorance of him. In the former age of ignorance he had not punished them as they deserved. God made allowance for their misguided efforts to worship him, not because they were innocent but because he was merciful and patient.

But things have changed. Now the age of salvation for all humankind has dawned through Christ. By his coming God has "now" demanded a fundamental change, that "all people everywhere [should] repent." The mention of repentance implies the Christian idea of sin. People must repent of their idolatry and evil ways and turn to the true God. The gospel message is for all people everywhere (28:22).

Paul then presents the motivation for their repentance, the solemn fact of future judgment (v. 31). All human beings have a moral responsibility to God and stand under his judgment. So, as Paul reminds the Athenians, God "has set a day when he will judge the world with justice" (v. 31). All people can have the assurance that at God's designated time they will be judged "with justice" and fairness. He will make no mistake in judging the sins and idolatries of the unrepentant.

Their fate will be in the hands of Jesus Christ, a human being appointed by God to judge the world. He is the one through whom justice will be mediated to all people (John 5:22–29). The proof that Jesus will be the judge is that God has raised him from the dead. In contrast to lifeless idols, Jesus, like God the Father, is now alive. He died that all may repent and be saved, but his resurrection, a monument to his deity (Rom. 1:4), seals him as judge on the last day.

Paul's audience at the meeting of the Areopagus has been listening to the apostle's sermon until he mentions the resurrection. The Christian doctrine of the resurrection is a stumbling block for them (vv. 32–34). The Greeks believed in the immortality of the soul, but generally they refused to believe that someone could rise from the dead. They regarded the body as earthy and evil in contrast to the soul, which they saw as the seat of divine life in human beings. Those present at the meeting tolerate Paul's reference to the folly of their idolatrous worship, but they interrupt him as he speaks about the bodily resurrection of the dead. That idea is offensive to them.

Luke records three responses to Paul's sermon: (1) Some members of the audience are negative, sneering at the thought that dead people may be resurrected. They dismiss the resurrection as preposterous, convinced, no doubt, that the soul will live on but not the body. (2) Others are more positive, telling Paul they want to hear him speak more on the subject. It is not clear whether they are serious about wanting to hear more about this doctrine or whether, in a polite way, they dismiss the apostle. (3) Some believe and receive Christ as Savior. Luke in his account identifies two of these believers by name: Dionysius, a member of the Areopagus, and Damaris, a woman. Neither is mentioned elsewhere in the New Testament, but they have the honored status of being among the first converts of the province of Achaia (1 Cor. 15:16).

Paul abruptly concludes his sermon and departs from the Areopagus. His ministry has not been as successful in Athens as in other places, but it does bear some fruit in that citadel of Greek culture. As Paul departs, he leaves behind a few worshipers of the true and living God.

5.2.8. Paul Visits Corinth (18:1–17). When Paul leaves Athens, he travels southwest to Corinth. This city had a Roman as well as a Greek flavor. It was the capital of the southern province of Greece, known as Achaia. Corinth was located on the western coast of a narrow isthmus that connected northern and southern Greece. This neck of land was on the sea route between Asia Minor and Italy, and the distance across it was only nine miles. Corinth, therefore, offered many commercial advantages, being situated between the two ports of Cenchrea and Lechaeum.

Being an important trade center, Corinth also had a notorious reputation for loose morals. Many cults found a home in that city. In 146 B.C. the city had been burned down by the Roman general Lucius Mummius, but Julius Caesar, recognizing its strategic military value, had it rebuilt in 46–44 B.C. The new Corinth was about three and a half miles northeast of the old city.

More is known about the church that Paul established in this city than any of the other Pauline churches. He wrote four letters to the Corinthian congregation, only two of which, 1 and 2 Corinthians, have survived. Little is known about the other two letters (see 1 Cor. 5:9; 2 Cor. 2:4; 7:8). Acts 18:1–17 tells about the founding of the church and illustrates Paul's work in still another situation on the second missionary journey. Certain features of his ministry are familiar, such as his beginning his preaching in the synagogue to the Jews and then witnessing later to the Gentiles; but some aspects of his experience in the urban center of Corinth were distinctively different from those in other cities.

5.2.8.1. Paul Joins Aquila As Tentmaker (18:1–4). The apostle arrives in Corinth about A.D. 50. There he meets Aquila and Priscilla, a Jewish couple, who play a vital role as coworkers in the gospel (Rom. 16:3; 1 Cor. 16:19; 2 Tim. 4:19). In A.D. 49 the emperor Claudius had issued a decree expelling Jews from Rome because of riots in the city. The trouble was over the teaching of "Chrestus" (a latinized form of "Christ"). Among those expelled were Aquila and Priscilla, who probably were converted under the preaching of Roman Jews who had been present in Jerusalem at the outpouring of the Spirit on Pentecost (Acts 2:10).

Luke introduces Aquila as being from Pontus in Asia Minor, but evidently Aquila later became a resident of Rome. When Claudius made the decree that compelled Jews to leave Rome, Aquila and Priscilla settled in Corinth. Once the trouble subsided in Rome, many Jews returned to the city. After Aquila and Priscilla visit Corinth and Ephesus (18:18–28), they return to Rome and are living there when Paul writes Romans (Rom. 16:3).

Paul's ministry in Athens seems to have discouraged him, but it is certain that the immediate Christian fellowship of Aquila and Priscilla gives him tremendous encouragement. Not only do Paul and they share the same faith, but also the same trade—they are tentmakers. The word "tentmaker" (*skenopoios*) is probably more accurately rendered "leatherworker." Tents were made out of goat's hair or leather. Paul finds it necessary to earn his living, so he resides with Aquila and Priscilla, enjoying Christian fellowship with them and sharing in their work. At the same time he also begins to evangelize the wicked city.

As usual, Paul first preaches in the synagogue, but he seems to limit his ministry to "every Sabbath." Through the week he works at his trade, but each Sabbath he preaches to Jews and God-fearers at the synagogue. For several Sabbaths he reasons with the Jews, and from the outset, his ministry at Corinth proclaims the simple gospel in full reliance on the power of the Holy Spirit (cf. 1 Cor. 2:2–5). The verb "persuade" (*epeithen*) may be translated as a conative imperfect as in the NIV ("trying to persuade"), but it may be also rendered "was persuading"—that is, Paul convinces both Jews and Gentiles who attend the synagogue to believe the gospel.

5.2.8.2. Paul Teaches for a Year and a Half (18:5–11). As Paul continues his ministry, Silas and Timothy come from Macedonia to Corinth. They had remained behind in Berea until now (17:15). Seeing these friends again must have encouraged the apostle. As a result of their arrival, Paul begins to devote himself entirely to preaching the word (v. 5). Likely Silas and Timothy have brought a financial gift from the Philippian believers that enables Paul to give himself totally to the proclamation of the gospel. The substance of his message is "that Jesus was the Christ [Messiah]." The Jews know about the predictions of the Messiah from the Old Testament, but the new information for them is that "Jesus" is the Messiah. The issue is whether or not Jesus, who suffered and died on the cross and rose again, is the Messiah.

The increase in evangelism and Paul's claims about Christ prove to be fruitful and lead to intense opposition from the Jews (cf. 13:45; 17:5, 13). Once again they reject the gospel. As Paul departs from the synagogue, he shakes out his garments as a sign that he is breaking off fellowship with the callous Jews at Corinth and that the Jews in Corinth bear full responsibility for rejecting the gospel (cf. 13:46; 28:28). For Paul unbelieving Jews are no more part of the true people of God than are Gentiles who reject the gospel. He has discharged his responsibility in preaching the gospel to the Jews. Any blame for their condemnation and separation from God cannot be placed on the apostle. With a clear conscience he solemnly declares: "Your blood be on your own heads!" (v. 6).

Paul then devotes his energies to preaching to the Gentiles. Obviously, Paul can no longer minister in the synagogue. But next door to the synagogue lives Titius Justus, a God-fearing Gentile, who must have become a convert under Paul's ministry. Paul accepts this man's hospitality and begins to conduct his mission in his house. The rival meeting place right next to the synagogue can hardly have helped relations between Paul and the synagogue leaders, but no doubt it is a strategic location for influencing worshipers at the synagogue.

This bold venture proves to be highly successful. Many Corinthians believe and are baptized in water. Among them is Crispus, the synagogue ruler, with his entire household. Along with Gaius, Crispus is mentioned as being baptized by Paul in 1 Corinthians 1:14. For such a prominent synagogue official to become a Christian must have been galling for the unbelieving Jews. His conversion occurs at a time when the Jews are intensely opposed to and abusive toward Christians (v. 6); it must also have been influential on the God-fearers, for the number of Gentile converts to the gospel continues to increase (v. 8). In spite of strong opposition, many—both Jews and Gentiles—come to believe in Jesus as Savior.

By the power of the Holy Spirit, Paul has taken bold steps in establishing a mission next door to the synagogue. But although the success since leaving the synagogue has been a source of comfort for him, he knows that trouble is brewing and that he will likely face reprisals from the Jews for drawing away their leader and other adherents from the synagogue. Furthermore, when the apostle arrived at Corinth, it was "in weakness and fear, and with much trembling" (1 Cor. 2:3). He may still be feeling as he did then. If so, Paul now needs spiritual encouragement to continue his ministry in Corinth.

Christ therefore appears to Paul in a nighttime vision to strengthen him for his future work and any new circumstances he may face. In that vision the Lord urges him not to become silent but to continue proclaiming the gospel as he has been doing without fear of his Jewish opponents. Paul receives assurance of the Lord's presence and the promise that the protective hand of the Lord will allow no one to harm him. This kind of assurance of personal safety dispels Paul's fear.

The Lord also gives a second reason for Paul to be confident: "because I have many people in this city" (v. 10). The term "people" here does not refer to Jewish people as it so often does in the Old Testament but to people who will receive the gospel. Since these people are not yet converted, the Lord speaks on the basis of foreknowledge that many are ready to hear the gospel message of salvation. He foresees that under Paul's preaching many will believe. Now Paul has the assurance of being kept safe from persecution (cf. vv. 12–17) and that his work will not be in vain (v. 11).

This message from the Lord breathes courage into Paul's spirit, so that he continues his work in Corinth for eighteen months. This length of time may constitute the total time he spent in the city or be the length of time after he received the vision. Some feel that he stayed there for two years. In any case, it is clear that because of the vision Paul has an unusually long stay in this city. Many of the Corinthians did respond to the gospel. Perhaps the Corinthian congregation became Paul's largest church.

5.2.8.3. Paul Brought to Trial Before Gallio (18:12–17). As predicted in the vision, Paul has success in evangelism, but also the hand of the Lord protects him as the Jews try to suppress his preaching of the gospel (vv. 12–16). When Gallio becomes the proconsul of the Roman province of Achaia, Paul's Jewish opponents take advantage of the arrival of a new governor by attacking Paul. Gallio was brother of Seneca, the Stoic philosopher an tutor of Nero. According to an inscription dis covered at Delphi, another city in the provinc of Achaia, he served as governor between A.D 51 and 53. This inscription was recorded in th form of a letter from Emperor Claudius.

At the beginning of Gallio's governorshi (around July, A.D. 51), the Jews in Corinth tr to enlist the power of Rome on their sid against the Christian movement. Unite together, Paul's opponents haul him before th tribunal ("court") of Gallio. The tribuna (*bema*) was a raised platform in the marke place of the city, from which Gallio preside and rendered judgment (cf. vv. 16–17). Th Jews charge Paul with seducing people "t worship God in ways contrary to the law."

It is unclear in verse 13 whether Paul i being accused of breaking Roman law or Jew ish law, but likely their charges have to do wit the law of the Jews. If Roman laws had bee in question, Gallio could have been expecte to listen and to enforce them. The governo sees the charges against the apostle as squab bles about the Jewish religion (vv. 14–15) Paul's vindication is swift. Before he can eve speak in his own defense, Gallio shows hi impatience with the Jews, reminding them tha Paul has committed no crime against the la of the Romans. His alleged crimes involve n fraud or deception from the standpoint o Roman justice. Paul's opponents have no lega case against him. As far as the governor ca see, the dispute is religious and centers aroun theological words and claims such as "Jesus i the Messiah."

Gallio goes on to explain that if the Jews charge were to focus on crimes against th state, then he would deal with the case. As Roman official, it is not his duty to investigat matters concerning Jewish religion. He is no about to involve himself in issues for which h has no interest. So the governor promptl rejects the charge and tells the Jews he will no bother trying to settle this religious dispute Such matters must be resolved by the Jew themselves.

Apparently Gallio becomes impatient wit the Jews. His vigorous and prompt actio against them is indicated by the verb "ejected (*apelauno*), which is stronger than just "sen away." He has his soldiers force the Jews awa from the tribunal. The stage is set for what follows. Since the tribunal is in the open air, the hearing has excited public interest, and a crowd of spectators gathers. Until now there is no indication how the Gentiles in the city feel about Paul, but the crowd of Corinthians that witness the governor's decision realize that they can take advantage of his refusal to interfere in Jewish matters.

The crowd indulges its feelings against the Jews by beating up Sosthenes, the synagogue ruler and probably the successor of Crispus (v. 8). Apparently he had taken a leading role in bringing charges against Paul. Sosthenes is beaten before the tribunal of Gallio, an act that demonstrates the hatred of the Jews prevalent in the ancient world. This flagrant act happens before Gallio, but he shows "no concern whatever" (v. 17). He has had the Jews driven away from the tribunal and now allows the crushing humiliation of the leader of Paul's adversaries.

5.2.9. Paul Returns to Antioch (18:18–23). The apostle stays in the city "for some time" after his arraignment before Gallio (v. 18). Because the governor has refused to support the Jews against the gospel, Paul is encouraged to continue. When he feels his work is complete, he decides to return to Antioch in Syria. In verses 18–22 Luke compresses the journey of Paul from Corinth to Ephesus, then to Jerusalem, and finally to Antioch.

Accompanied by Priscilla and Aquila, Paul goes to Cenchrea, the eastern port near Corinth. In the narrative here, the order of the couple's names suggests that Priscilla had been more important to the work of the Corinthian church. Before joining Paul this couple's destination had been Ephesus, which seems to explain why Paul sails to Ephesus rather than directly to Caesarea. The apostle had let his hair grow for a period. It seems that he had taken a Nazirite vow, during which the hair was permitted to grow. When he arrives in Cenchrea, he has his hair cut, which, together with an offering, marks the conclusion of the vow. For a person taking a Nazirite vow, the cutting of hair was permissible anywhere (m. *Nazir* 3b; 5:4), but the sacrifice could only be offered in the temple at Jerusalem, where Paul is now headed.

This Nazirite vow shows that Paul does not hesitate to observe Jewish practices and to continue to be faithful to his Jewish heritage as long as such practices are not insisted on as grounds for salvation (cf. 21:23–26). Luke gives no direct hint as to why Paul had taken the vow, but likely God's goodness to him in Corinth prompts him to take the vow and express his gratitude for the success of the gospel among the Gentiles. Such action does not place Christians under obligation to take similar vows, but it demonstrates Paul's Jewish piety. His action also illustrates that he is prepared to become "like a Jew, to win the Jews" (1 Cor. 9:20).

Paul sails to Ephesus, the major city in the Roman province of Asia and a city that had a large Jewish population. When he and his companions arrive there, he makes his way to the synagogue. We do not know whether there were Christians in Ephesus before this time, but apparently there is no organized body of believers in the city. At the synagogue Paul speaks to the Jews and proclaims Jesus as the Messiah. Although he is free to preach in Ephesus, he does not take the opportunity to evangelize the great city.

Earlier the Holy Spirit had prevented Paul from preaching the gospel in Asia (where Ephesus was located; see 16:6). He now decides it is time for him to return to Antioch. When the people at the synagogue invite him to stay longer, he declines but promises that he will return, if it is God's will (18:20–21). Thus, his visit here is a brief one.

The apostle embarks on a ship in the harbor of Ephesus. Parting company with Priscilla and Aquila, he sails to Palestine. He disembarks at Caesarea and "goes up" to Jerusalem and greets the church. Jerusalem is not specifically mentioned here (v. 22), but the verbs "go up" and "go down" were regularly used for traveling to and from Jerusalem, seeing that the ancient city was built on a hill. This location also fits the suggestion that Paul could only end his vow by offering a sacrifice in Jerusalem. He probably arrives there near the celebration of the Passover in April of A.D. 52, and he evidently gives a report of his work to the church.

From Jerusalem Paul returns to Antioch, from where he had begun, thus completing the second missionary journey. There he gives a report of the progress of the gospel to the church that had commended him and Silas "to the grace of the Lord" (15:40). After a period of time in Antioch, this Spirit-filled apostle begins his next campaign—his third missionary journey. Earlier he had declined an invitation to stay in Ephesus (v. 21), but now that city is his goal. He takes the opportunity first to visit the region of Galatia and Phrygia for the third time. This region probably is the area in south Galatia he had evangelized on his first missionary campaign (Acts 13–14). The apostle finds the churches in good condition and has a short visit, consisting of giving spiritual encouragement to the believers. Luke picks up this third missionary journey in 19:1–22:21.

5.3. Apollos Teaches in Ephesus and Achaia (18:24–28)

Priscilla and Aquila remain in Ephesus after Paul leaves for Jerusalem and Antioch. Before he returns to Ephesus, Apollos arrives on the scene. Later Apollos becomes an important person in the church at Corinth (1 Cor. 3:1–9), but in the church at Ephesus some controversy centers around him. When Apollos arrives there, though he has "been instructed in the way of the Lord" (v. 25), his knowledge seems imperfect. Priscilla and Aquila explain "to him the way of God more adequately" (v. 26), and he comes to share Paul's theological outlook. Here we see how early Christians dealt with those in need of a fuller understanding of the faith.

Luke describes Apollos in positive terms. (1) He is an Alexandrian Jew. Born in Alexandria, Egypt, he comes from one of the leading cities in the ancient world and an important center of learning. Little is known about the beginning of Christianity in Alexandria, though presumably it began during the outpouring of the Spirit at Pentecost, at which time people from Egypt were present (2:10). The first recorded Christianity in Alexandria was characterized by Gnostic tendencies. The instruction received by Apollos may not have been in the mainstream of apostolic Christianity and, therefore, may account for his inadequate understanding.

(2) Apollos is a learned man, who knows the Old Testament Scriptures. It is difficult to decide with certainty the exact meaning of "learned" (*logios*). Some scholars take this word to mean "eloquent," emphasizing the great capacity of Apollos as a speaker; others understand it to mean "a man of learning," stressing the extent of his knowledge. It is possible to combine the two meanings and understand that Apollos is an eloquent and learned Alexandrian, especially in light of his knowledge of the Old Testament.

(3) Apollos speaks fervently in the Spirit. Some authorities take *pneuma* ("spirit," cf. NIV note) to refer to Apollos's own spirit and thus to mean that he speaks with great enthusiasm. This interpretation is reflected in the NIV's "with great fervor" and the RSV's "being fervent in spirit." Since Apollos's natural gifts are emphasized in verse 24, however, verse 25 seems to speak about his spiritual endowment. He is powerfully equipped by the Spirit for ministry. It is his practice to preach under the inspiration of the Holy Spirit and with the same prophetic authority associated with Peter's ministry at Pentecost.

(4) Apollos accurately teaches the facts about Jesus and is thus well informed about the life of Jesus and perhaps also his teaching, probably hearing it from those present during the outpouring of the Spirit at Pentecost (2:10). He is acquainted with the baptism of John and must have received that baptism, which John the Baptist administered from the perspective of the redeeming work of Christ (John 1:29ff.; cf. Matt. 3:1ff.; Mark 1:4ff.; Luke 3:1ff.). It is unlikely that Apollos was rebaptized since Luke says nothing about it. Luke knows that the experience of charismatic fullness of the Spirit does not depend on baptism in water (Acts 10:44–48).

Unlike the twelve disciples at Ephesus (19:1–7), Apollos has already been filled with the Spirit. Though he preaches accurately the story of Jesus with great charismatic inspiration, he comes short—"upon the further question of the bearing of the deeds and works of Jesus upon the present life, he is silent" (Rackham, 1953, 343). It is possible for a person who has received the baptism in the Spirit to be defective in some aspect of his faith. As 1 Corinthians illustrates throughout the letter, charismatic experience does not ensure adequate understanding of Christian doctrine and practice.

At first Apollos carries out the Christian mission in the synagogue. He preaches with great boldness, but he comes short in his understanding of the faith. Hearing him, Priscilla and Aquila soon realize that this powerful preacher needs more instruction in "the way of God" (v. 26). So they take him aside in the privacy of their home and explain to him a more accurate understanding of the faith. Evidently they give Apollos more instruction in the distinctive Pauline doctrines, with an emphasis on Jesus as the Messiah.

Apollos must have been an eager student and a man of deep spirituality. His advance in understanding becomes apparent. A little later he sounds a new note in his preaching—"for he vigorously refuted the Jews in public debate, proving from the Scriptures that Jesus was the Christ" (v. 28). Understanding the faith better, he now proclaims that messianic salvation is a present experience through faith in Jesus as well as a future hope. "His charismatic message becomes messianic" (Moody, 1968, 78).

For a reason not given, Apollos decides to visit the churches established by Paul in Achaia. The Christians, who have been converted under Paul's brief ministry in Ephesus and the ministry of Priscilla and Aquila, express full confidence in Apollos. As he departs for Achaia, they encourage him and are pleased to write a letter of introduction, urging the believers of Achaia to welcome this man.

In the apostolic age letters of recommendation were common (cf. Rom. 16:1; 2 Cor. 3:1). Apollos lives up to his recommendation. On his arrival in Corinth, he is a great blessing to the believers and is successful in building them up in their faith (see v. 28). Among the Christians at Corinth, Apollos becomes a prominent leader, his followers ranking him with Peter and Paul (1 Cor. 1:12). Paul speaks about Apollos as watering what he had planted (3:6). He does not regard Apollos as a rival, as some Corinthian believers assumed, but as a fellow worker (4:1–7). Apollos's success as a pastor and evangelist shows that he has a variety of spiritual gifts.

5.4. Third Missionary Journey (19:1–22:21)

Paul ended his second missionary journey in Antioch in Syria and began his third journey (see comments on 18:18–23). Luke begins his formal account of Paul's third missionary journey with the outpouring of the Holy Spirit as the apostle lays hands on some disciples at Ephesus. In Ephesus, he appeals to the Jews in the synagogue and argues "persuasively [i.e., through the power of the Spirit] about the kingdom of God" (vv. 8–10). His Spirit-anointed ministry is also marked by extraordinary miracles and exorcisms (vv. 11–20).

At the beginning of each journey, therefore, Luke emphasizes the fundamental importance of the Spirit's power and guidance to Paul's ministry and shows that it follows the programmatic pattern of Jesus' ministry (Luke 3:22; 4:1, 14, 18) and that of the disciples (Acts 1:8; 2:4, 14–41). The first missionary journey was initiated by the Holy Spirit's speaking through a prophet (13:1–3). The second journey began by the Spirit's leading the missionaries contrary to their own inclination (16:6–8). At the start of the third journey, Paul bestows the fullness of the Spirit on others, speaks as an inspired prophet to the Jews, and performs prophetic deeds. From the beginning to the end of his ministry, Paul is a charismatic apostle and prophet, made powerful in both word and deeds by the Holy Spirit.

5.4.1. Paul Visits Ephesus (19:1–41). After Apollos departs for Corinth, Paul comes to Ephesus from Antioch, having visited the churches in the region of Galatia and Phrygia (18:23). He remains in Ephesus for about three years. This city was one of the most important in the Roman empire. It was the capital of the Roman province of Asia and a major seaport and commercial center, located at the western end of the great highway that ran across Asia Minor. It was famous as a pagan religious center, being the site of the temple of the fertility goddess Artemis, that temple being one of the seven wonders of the ancient world. Her temple was the largest marble structure in the Hellenistic world. Magic played an important part in the religious life of the Ephesians as well as the cult of the goddess.

5.4.1.1. Paul Meets the Twelve Disciples (19:1–7). When Paul arrives in Ephesus, he meets twelve disciples. Like Apollos these disciples have received the baptism of John the Baptist, but there is a distinct difference between these disciples and Apollos's experience. According to the prophecy of Joel (2:28–32; cf. Acts 2:17–21), Apollos had received the Pentecostal baptism in the Spirit (18:25), but the twelve disciples at Ephesus have not been filled with the Spirit. Luke still refers to them as "disciples," however—that is, true Christian believers.

Some interpreters contend that the description of the twelve as "some disciples" (v. 1) indicates that they did not belong to the Christian

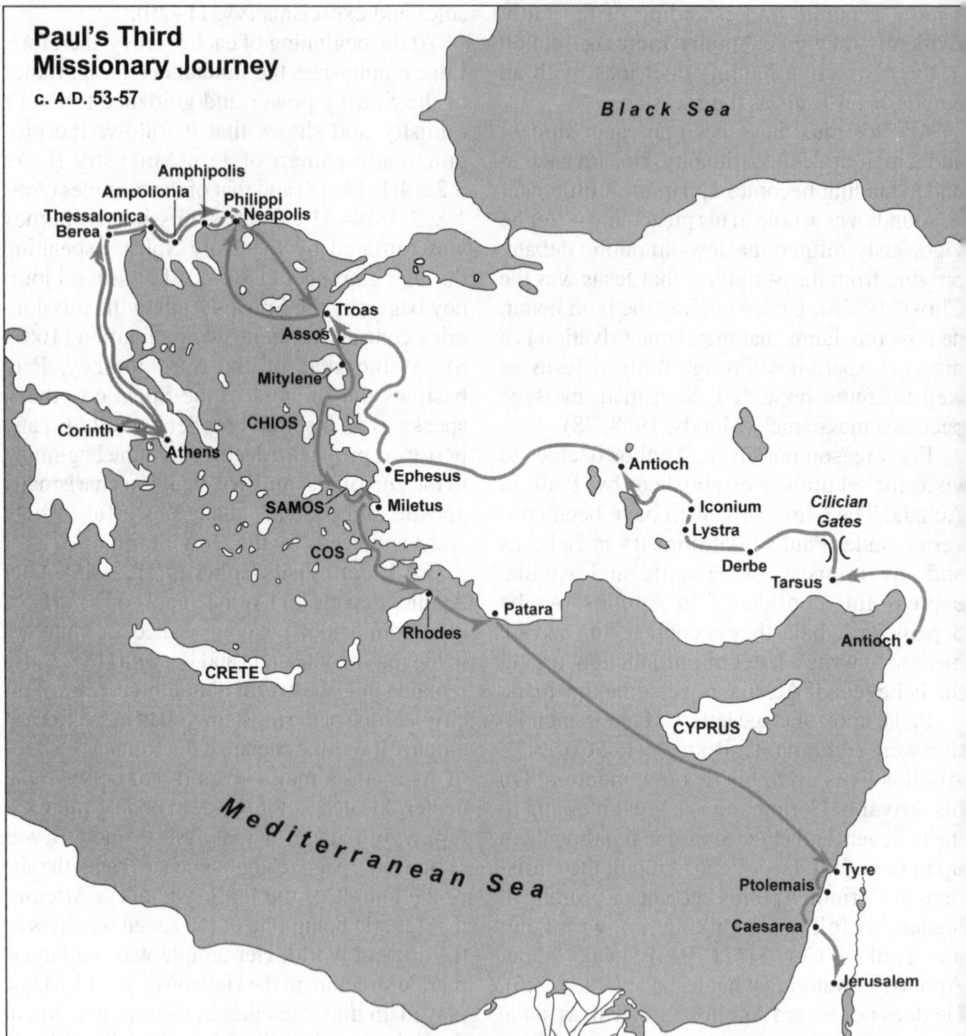

Paul stays in Ephesus for three years during his third missionary trip.

group at Ephesus but were rather a group of John the Baptist's disciples. This argument rests in large measure on the absence of the definite article ("the") before "disciples" and the assumption that the indefinite pronoun "some" (*tines*) implies they are disciples of John the Baptist. The book of Acts, however, fails to support the view that passes the twelve off as being completely distinct and separate from the Christian community. Whether with or without the article, Luke consistently uses "disciples" (*mathetai*) to refer to Christians (6:1, 7; 9:1, 19, 26; 11:26; 14:21–22). Moreover, the word *tine*, does not provide a commentary on the spiritua standing of these men. Luke uses the same pronoun in three passages to refer to known Christians: Ananias (9:10), Tabitha (9:36), and Timothy (16:1). Whether singular or plural, this indefinite pronoun describes the followers of Christ. These twelve men were pre-Pentecostal Christians. They were converted but not filled with the Spirit.

Apparently John's baptism was still prescribed and practiced in some places, but there was no uniformity of experience among those who had been influenced by this tradition. Because Paul addresses these Ephesian disciples as believers (*pisteusantes*, v. 2), we know that they, like Apollos, were already Christians before Paul's arrival. However, they had not received subsequent to salvation the anointing of the Spirit for ministry.

Paul perceives their need for the anointing and asks, "Did you receive the Holy Spirit when you believed?" (v. 2). This question deals with their experience of the Spirit. The aorist participle (*pisteusantes*), which the NIV renders "when you believed," can also be translated "after you believed." Paul's question does not deal with their receiving the Holy Spirit at the moment of conversion. From the time the Ephesian twelve were converted, they were indwelt by the Holy Spirit, as all Christians are (Rom. 8:9). Thus, the question is not about receiving the Spirit in salvation, but about what is basic to Luke-Acts and to the immediate context, namely, the Spirit's anointing with power subsequent to the experience of salvation.

We do not know exactly what prompts Paul to ask the question. The sermons and conversations in Acts are summaries, and Luke's purpose is to focus on the power of the Spirit rather than to present exhaustive accounts. Presumably Paul's questioning of these disciples was preceded by a longer conversation. In any case, their reply to Paul's question is negative. They had not so much as heard about the outpouring of the Spirit at Pentecost. The Ephesian disciples, no doubt, had heard about the Holy Spirit, since he is discussed prominently in the Old Testament and in John the Baptist's preaching. What they are ignorant of is the specific anointing of the Spirit for ministry subsequent to conversion. Influenced by John the Baptist's tradition, they had heard about Jesus and believed in him, but they had not been filled with the Spirit.

Paul recognizes, therefore, that the Ephesian twelve are lacking in regard to the charismatic gift of the Spirit. As Paul explains to them, John the Baptist's preaching was a saving ministry and was according to God's plan. He had called the people to repentance and to faith in Jesus, the Coming One. The purpose of his preaching was so that those who heard him might believe in Jesus, the same focus and goal of Paul's own preaching. John administered baptism as a symbol of the washing away of sins by the Holy Spirit.

Having heard Paul's explanation of baptism, the Ephesian disciples want to make sure their spiritual relationship with the Lord rests on a proper foundation. They therefore request baptism. Luke gives only a brief account of this event, but most likely Paul's message prompts the Ephesian disciples to make the request. Paul complies and baptizes them. This is the only place where rebaptism is mentioned in the New Testament.

Just as Ananias laid his hand on Paul and the apostle was filled with the Spirit (9:17), so Paul now lays his hands on the twelve men, and they also are filled with the Spirit: "The Holy Spirit came on them, and they spoke in tongues and prophesied" (19:6). It should be noted that the terms "came" (from *erchomai*) and "on" (*epi*) parallel the precise language of Acts 1:8. It firmly connects the experience of the Ephesian disciples with the promise of Jesus. This outpouring of the Spirit at Ephesus shows that Spirit-baptism is subsequent and distinct from conversion in the theology of both Luke and Paul.

The immediate consequences of this Spirit-baptism are charismatic manifestations of tongues and prophecy. The phrase "and prophesied" must not be assumed to indicate an additional sign. It stands parallel to the phrase "praising God" in Acts 10:46. Prophetic activity is realized in the last days (cf. the events of Pentecost, which shows a close relationship between speaking in tongues and prophesying via Joel 2). Similar to the disciples at Pentecost and Caesarea, these people at Ephesus speak in tongues and give inspired praise to God after receiving the Pentecostal power of the Spirit. Like earlier outpourings of the Spirit, the initial evidence of the charismatic experience of the Ephesian believers is speaking in tongues (cf. 2:4; 10:44–46). Paul instructs, baptizes, and lays hands on them, but through the sovereign action of the prophetic Spirit they are endowed with power for ministry.

The Ephesian Pentecost marks not a conversion experience but an enduement of the Spirit's power for the spreading of the gospel. The entire book of Acts emphasizes this charismatic experience of receiving power for evangelism. The Ephesian twelve receive the fresh vital power of the Spirit so that they, like the disciples at Pentecost, Samaria, and Caesarea, will be equipped to fulfill the commission of Acts 1:8.

Paul expects believers to be filled with the Spirit. The outpouring of the Spirit on the Ephesian twelve makes it clear that his teaching and practice are consistent with the charismatic theology of Luke. No doubt this incident is an example of how the apostles ministered to many who had become believers but had never heard about Pentecost.

5.4.1.2. Paul Preaches for Two Years (19:8–20). After the apostle ministers to the twelve disciples, he continues his work at the synagogue. If the twelve had not already been Christians, then Paul likely would have followed his usual practice and begun his ministry by first preaching at the synagogue rather than by talking with "some disciples."

Empowered by the Holy Spirit, Paul goes regularly to the synagogue to preach. Over a period of three months he speaks "boldly" to the people there. That boldness is a characteristic indication that he is inspired by the Spirit (9:27). Paul's approach is persuasive, the theme of his message being the kingdom of God that is fulfilled in the life and ministry of Jesus. His focus has not changed; it remains on the kingdom (14:22; 20:25; 28:23) and on Jesus as the Messiah.

Paul's ministry in the synagogue is brought to an end by the Jews who harden their hearts against the gospel and refuse to believe that the promises of the kingdom are fulfilled in Jesus. These unbelievers speak against "the Way," the Christian movement that centers in Christ and his teachings (cf. 9:2; 19:23; 22:4; 24:14, 22). The opposition makes it necessary for Paul and the other believers to withdraw from the synagogue as a base for evangelism.

At Corinth when Paul was persecuted, he moved from the synagogue to the private home of Titius Justus (18:7), but on this occasion he moves to "the lecture hall of Tyrannus," a room for lectures and other gatherings. Either Tyrannus owns this place or gives lectures there; Paul uses it daily during times that Tyrannus is not using it, to discuss with the people the Christian Way. For two years he conducts discussions in this new meeting place. Including the three earlier months at the synagogue (19:8), Paul stays in Ephesus for about three years (20:31).

During this time the ministry of Paul and his colleagues reaches beyond Ephesus. Though not always delivered directly by Paul, the gospel is preached at Colosse, Laodicea, and other places, "so that all the Jews and Greeks who lived in the province of Asia heard the word of the Lord" (v. 10). Equipped for ministry by the Spirit, the missionaries evangelize the entire region and are used in the ever-widening influence of the gospel.

In addition to his anointed preaching, Paul also performs miracles (vv. 11–12), described as "extraordinary" because they are special charismatic manifestations of the Spirit. Equipped with the power of the Spirit, he ministers to human needs by incredible miracles, healings, and exorcisms (cf. Rom. 15:18–19; 2 Cor. 12:12). God performs these unusual miracles directly through Paul's laying on hands on the sick, but also through handkerchiefs and aprons that have touched his body. People unable to come to the apostle are healed by indirect contact with him. Such healings clearly parallel the charismatic ministry of Jesus (Luke 8:43–45) and of Peter (Acts 5:12–16). Because Paul is a Spirit-anointed prophet and apostle, these mighty deeds glorify Jesus Christ, advertising and sealing the saving power of "the word of the Lord."

Paul gains fame for performing miracles and casting out evil spirits. At that time the practice of driving out demons was widespread in the ancient world and was practiced by people using various kinds of formulas, incantations, and clairvoyant powers. Paul's miracles are curious because he performs them in Jesus' name. Some Jewish magicians observe the miracles that Paul does in Christ's name (vv. 13–20), and they conclude that the powerful charm is in that name. Seeking to capitalize on Paul's success, they also try to cast out demons using that name. The formula they use is: "In the name of Jesus, whom Paul preaches" (v. 13).

Among those attempting to cast out demons in the name of Jesus are the seven sons of a Jewish high priest named Sceva. There is no record of a high priest in Jerusalem by that name. Sceva may have been a member of a high priestly family or he may have been a renegade Jew who had assumed the title to impress others and deceive the public. The exorcists themselves could have falsely claimed to be the sons of the high priest. Evidently, they do not know much about the life and the ministry of Jesus. These unbelieving brothers are simple magicians, and they fail to recognize that the name of Jesus is powerful only when it is pronounced by his authority and with faith in him as their Savior (*TDNT*, 5:463).

On one occasion these exorcists meet a demoniac in a house and attempt to cast the demon out of the man "in the name of Jesus, whom Paul preaches." The evil spirit in the man confesses to know Jesus and Paul, but he challenges their right to use the name. Why should he obey them? They are neither disciples of Jesus nor colleagues of Paul. He recognizes no power in the name of Jesus as pronounced by the sons of Sceva (v. 15). An alarming thing then happens. The demon becomes enraged at these false exorcists, and the demoniac leaps on them. They find themselves powerless against such demonic power, and the man with the spirit single-handedly whips them. Beaten, bleeding, and naked, the seven flee from the house into the street.

With the sons of Sceva wounded, clothes torn off, and running away from the house, the account may strike us as humorous, but it is no laughing matter for the people in Ephesus. As news spreads about what has happened, holy fear grips their hearts. They recognize that this defeat of the seven exorcists comes from misuse of the name of Jesus. Many Ephesians are devoted to the practice of magic and realize how dangerous a thing it is to use the name of Jesus lightly. Because of the dramatic failure of the sons of Sceva, the people honor and magnify the name of Jesus more highly.

The exposure of the sons of Sceva has striking results. Those who are already believers confess their evil deeds and abandon all pagan practices. Some believers had brought trappings from their pagan past into their Christian experience and continued to practice magic and pagan superstitions. They now realize the sinfulness of such practices and publicly confess their use of magic in casting spells on people and deceiving them. They bring their scrolls that tell them how to practice sorcery and magic and burn them as people watch. The word "sorcery" (*perierga*) is a technical term for magic arts. The root meaning involves interest in other people's business (it is translated as "busybodies" in 1 Tim. 5:13). Thus, this term in Acts 19:19 means interfering with other people through magic arts. Practitioners tried to control spirits to carry out their own wishes or to develop psychic powers so they could control a person or situation (*NIDNTT*, 2:556–61).

The scrolls of spells, invocations, and magic formulas have become charred rubbish; but if they had been sold, their value would have been approximately equal to the wages that 50,000 workmen received for a day's work (v. 19). These believers have made a decisive break with their pagan past. Their response shows the purifying power of the gospel to change pagan ways of thinking about God.

Both then and now, the tendency is to let bad religion and crippling superstitions influence our ideas of God. Many areas of modern life are gripped by magical practices and philosophical views of God that are clearly banned in Scripture (Deut. 18:10–14). The success of Paul's ministry in Ephesus shows the importance of purifying Christian thinking from paganism. Anointed by the Holy Spirit, the word of God transforms lives and the church experiences new growth and strength. According to this account Paul once again has a direct encounter with demonic power and magic (cf. Acts 13:6–12; 16:16–18). God gives him a tremendous victory, demonstrating that the power of Jesus is superior to that of demons and magic.

5.4.1.3. Paul Purposes to Visit Jerusalem and Rome (19:21–22). After the public burning of the scrolls, the triumph of the Lord's word makes Paul realize that the Ephesian church has gained strength. He can now think about leaving Ephesus and focus on his future travel plans. The clause "Paul decided to go" (NIV) may be translated, "Paul purposed by the Spirit to go" (*en to pneumati*) (cf. NRSV, "Paul resolved in the Spirit"). This latter translation is consistent with the entire narrative of Luke and sets the tone for Paul's travels from Ephesus until he arrives in Rome. His future travels are prompted by the same divine initiative as his first missionary journey from Antioch (13:2, 4). The readers can, therefore, have assurance that the Holy Spirit is at work in Paul's trials and tribulations as well as in Paul's victories.

In other words, when Paul forms his plans for future travels, he does so with the help and approval of the Holy Spirit. His decision to revisit Macedonia and Achaia, then go to Jerusalem, and then on to Rome is inspired by the Spirit. Verse 21 summarizes the remainder of Acts and states clearly that the objective of Acts is to describe Paul's journey to the imperial city of Rome. It serves as a prophetic announcement of what will follow (19:22–28:31).

No doubt Paul wants to accept the monetary offering that the Gentile churches have given as a gift for the poor Christians in Jerusalem (24:17). As Jesus did, Paul decides to go first to Jerusalem, a city known for killing prophets (Luke 9:51; 13:34). In spite of warnings he receives along the way that Jerusalem is a dangerous place for him, Paul continues on as the Holy Spirit directs him (Acts 20:22–23; 21:4, 11). This visit will be his fifth and final one to the Holy City.

Paul knows that it is the will of the exalted Lord for him to bear witness to the gospel in Rome. That is why he states that he must (*dei*, "it is necessary") take the gospel to Rome. Luke lets us see that God's purpose is to lead Paul to the capital of the Gentile world. His mission will culminate in Rome, the final stage of his missionary outreach "to the ends of the earth" (1:8). Luke devotes one-third of his account of the apostolic church in the book of Acts to that journey. (Note that Luke does not mention any plans for missionary work in Spain, Rom. 15:23–29.)

But before heading to Jerusalem, where as part of the divine plan he will be arrested, imprisoned, and make his appeal to Rome, Paul first plans to return to Greece. He does not want to forget the churches he has established in Macedonia and Achaia and feels that he must first revisit and strengthen them. Near the end of his stay at Ephesus, Paul sends two of his colleagues, Timothy and Erastus, on ahead to Macedonia to prepare for his visit.

5.4.1.4. Demetrius Stirs Up Opposition (19:23–41). Paul has already made preparations to leave Ephesus, but before he departs, an anti-Christian riot breaks out. The riot is led by Demetrius, a silversmith who makes silver models of the temple of the goddess Artemis, and it results in a direct encounter between the gospel and pagan religion. Although idolatry and superstition have been crippled by the power of the gospel in the region of Ephesus, the powers of darkness are still present. People involved in pagan religion and witchcraft are prepared to wage a desperate struggle to protect their own financial interests.

Luke does not give us all the details of Paul's experiences in Ephesus. But in 1 and 2 Corinthians, written from Ephesus, Paul helps us to understand better the persecution that occurred there. He writes about his life being in danger every hour and even says, "If I fought wild beasts in Ephesus" (1 Cor. 15:30–32)—the type of conditional clause used here suggests Paul is speaking of something that actually happened. Later in the same letter he writes: "I will stay on at Ephesus until Pentecost, because a great door for effective work has opened to me, and there are many who oppose me" (16:8–9). And in 2 Corinthians, Paul goes so far as to say about what happened in Asia: "We were under great pressure, far beyond our ability to endure, so that we despaired even of life. Indeed, in our hearts we felt the sentence of death" (2 Cor. 1:8–9).

Many of Paul's troubles came from Jewish opponents, but the riot at Ephesus comes from pagan religion and the vested interest of makers of miniature shrines. The growing influence of the gospel has caused their business to suffer. No doubt the burning of scrolls of spells and magical charms greatly have diminished the sale of idols and shrines (v. 19). The silversmiths, led by Demetrius, connect the loss of their trade to "the Way" (v. 23).

Ephesus was the center for the worship of the goddess of fertility, identified by the Greeks as Artemis and by the Romans as Diana. Her magnificent temple was one of the seven wonders of the ancient world and the glory of Ephesus. It had gold between its stones instead of mortar and housed some of the magnificent sculptures of antiquity. From all parts of Asia Minor pilgrims came to Ephesus to see the splendid building. The rendering "silver shrines of Artemis" is misleading, because it suggests that Demetrius makes silver figurines of the goddess herself. Rather, he makes small shrines representing the famous temple of Artemis. Countless numbers of these replicas were sold to the pilgrims and taken home as objects of worship.

Seeing his profits from the sale of miniature shrines diminish, Demetrius, ringleader of the opposition to Paul, organizes a protest demonstration. He calls together those who are in the

Ephesus, an important port and a center for a cult that worshiped the goddess of fertility, was in decline by the time of Paul's visits. The Temple of of Vespasian, below, dates back to the first century. The Mercantile Agora, left, was built in the third century B.C.

same trade as he is. He is shrewd enough to know how to stir up the silversmiths and others against Paul by appealing to economic self-interest and zeal for the magnificence and worship of Artemis. His appeal to the profit motive warns the silversmiths of the danger of suffering financial ruin. Most of the people would probably not have been concerned if Demetrius went out of business, but for the temple to cease to be a popular attraction and worshipers to lose faith in the goddess is an entirely different matter. So his outcry against the danger of the great goddess Artemis being discredited appeals to a wider audience.

Paul's ministry has had a widespread and penetrating effect. According to Demetrius, the apostle's preaching against idolatry, declaring "that man-made gods are no gods at all" (v. 26), has spread throughout the province of Asia. The conversion of many worshipers of Artemis to Christianity has reduced the sale of miniature shrines. More than profits are in danger (v. 27), however. Christ has been offered as a genuine alternative to Artemis, and a large number of people have been convinced to turn "from idols to serve the living and true God" (1 Thess. 1:9). The success of the gospel has endangered the cult of Artemis and "her divine majesty." In other words, Paul's ministry has affected not only economic concerns in Ephesus but also their religion. Artemis may lose her position of honor in the eyes of the people.

Demetrius proves to be an effective spokesman. The craftsmen become enraged at Paul. They begin to give vent to their excitement by acclaiming the deity of the goddess with the cult shout: "Great is Artemis of the Ephesians!" (v. 28). This outcry of the shrinemakers prompts a massive riot. The excitement spreads quickly and the city is filled with confusion. A huge crowd sympathetic with the silversmiths gathers. Acting as a mob, they grab two missionaries, Gaius and Aristarchus, "Paul's traveling companions from Macedonia" (v. 29), and drag them to the great amphitheater. This open-air theater with space for about 25,000 people was used as a place of entertainment as well as for city meetings. They gather there on this occasion for the purpose of persuading the city officials to take action against the missionaries.

Paul hears about the mob's dragging his two companions to the theater. He assumes that their lives are in grave danger and decides that he should go before the crowd. He probably hopes to reason with them. Evidently it is Paul that they want rather than his fellow missionaries. His Christian friends are convinced that if Paul goes into the theater, his life will be in danger.

Therefore, in fear of his safety, they refuse to allow him to do this (v. 30). Acting out of friendship toward Paul, even some of the "officials of the province" (Asiarchs) warn him against placing his life in danger. The Asiarchs were important officials in the cities of the province of Asia, appointed by Rome to oversee athletic games and to promote the worship of the Roman emperor as a god. They formed a provincial council with religious and political responsibilities and belonged to the most influential families. It is significant that Paul has friends among the Asiarchs and that they are concerned about his safety before the mob. His preaching and his personal influence have reached to the highest circles of pagan society.

Luke now turns to the actual meeting in the amphitheater. Many people in the mob have no idea why they are there (v. 32); this is typical of mobs. Some of the Jews present must have feared the wrath of the mob and want to prevent the confusion from turning into an anti-Jewish riot. It was generally known that Jews strongly opposed idolatry and that Paul himself was a Jew. So the Jews put forward as their spokesman Alexander, possibly a friend of Demetrius. His task is presumably to explain that Paul is an apostate from the Jewish faith, that Jews are not Christians, and that they should not be held responsible for what Christians say.

Alexander tries to get the mob to listen, but in their hysterical state of mind they are in no mood to listen to a Jew. They drown out his voice with their cultic shout: "Great is Artemis of the Ephesians!" Once it starts, the shouting continues with momentum for two hours. Typical of mob psychology, no one is ready to listen to reason.

At first the city authorities do not interfere. But after two hours of continued outcry, the authorities intervene. The city clerk is finally able to restore quiet. He was an important city official, responsible for issuing decrees prepared by public assembly. Once he takes control of the assembly and silences the crowd, he warns them against taking rash action against the missionaries (vv. 35–40). There is no need for the people to get excited about the decline of the reputation of their goddess. After all, everyone is aware of the devotion of Ephesus to the worship of Artemis, since the city is the guardian of her temple (the title "guardian of the temple" was originally applied to individuals but was later used to indicate cities).

Moreover, Ephesus can also claim divine accreditation for the cult of Artemis. A statue seems to have been carved from a stone that the people considered to be sacred, possibly the fragment of a meteorite that had fallen out of heaven on their area. The statue was a female figure with many breasts, representing the fertility of the goddess. The town clerk reassures the crowd of the certainty of Ephesian devotion to the goddess and the well-known origin of her image. He emphasizes that none of these facts can be denied, even though some may try to contradict them. Since nothing can damage the prestige and the worship of Artemis, the people should quiet down and do nothing reckless.

As a defender of law and order, the town clerk then addresses the cause for the uproar in the city. He asserts that the crowd has acted rashly by dragging "these men" (referring to Gaius and Aristarchus, v. 29) into the theater. He does not mention that the missionaries have denied that images made with hands are gods (cf. v. 26), but declares that Paul's coworkers are not temple robbers, nor have they spoken evil of the goddess (v. 37). Apparently it was common for Jews to be accused of stealing sacred items from pagan temples and of blaspheming other gods. Clearing them of these charges appears to those who "did not even know why they were there" (v. 32) to vindicate the two missionaries.

The city clerk goes on to remind Demetrius and his fellow silversmiths that if they have serious, legitimate charges against the Christians, they can settle these matters in the courts before the "proconsuls." Each Roman province had a proconsul (governor). The plural, "proconsuls," seems to be a general way of referring to court authorities. Normally in the Asian cities a representative of the governor held court and administered justice. If there were matters not covered by existing laws or charges not suitably dealt with in these courts, such concerns "must be settled in a legal assembly," that is, a lawfully called assembly presided over by the city clerk (in contrast to the riotous gathering described in vv. 32–34). The city clerk implies that the charges against the Christians are unfounded because Demetrius and the others who have grievances have failed to use the courts.

Finally, the city clerk expresses his fears that gatherings that almost become riots can have drastic consequences (v. 40). This gathering no doubt has been an ugly scene. Much more could have been lost than profits from the selling of shrines, for the people are risking losing their freedom. As the city clerk reminds them, the Roman authorities are sensitive to unruly gatherings. No reasonable excuse can be given to them for the commotion. As punishment, the Roman authorities might limit the city's freedom. Loss of freedom for the city of Ephesus would mean its losing any rights to self-government. The missionaries are not the real threat to peace and stability but the people themselves.

The crowd listens to the sound arguments of the city clerk, and reason prevails. His moderating voice has quieted the uproar. He then dismisses the crowd, and they go quietly to their homes. As far as we know, Demetrius takes no further action against Paul and his fellow missionaries. No doubt, Gaius and Aristarchus realize that their lives have been in grave danger, and God has spared them. Again Paul has been vindicated by the authorities.

5.4.2. Paul Visits Macedonia and Greece (20:1–6). Paul's long stay in Ephesus comes to an end. He has accomplished much in the city and in the province of Asia in spite of his many adversaries (cf. 1 Cor. 16:8–9). With the guidance of the Holy Spirit he has made his plans to return to Jerusalem (Acts 19:21). Luke gives only a brief summary of Paul's subsequent activities in Asia and Greece. Two of Paul's letters, 2 Corinthians and Romans, fill in some of the details not included in Acts.

The trouble started by Demetrius in Ephesus has died down; but before Paul leaves the city, he calls together the church and gives them a message of encouragement, the content of which was probably similar to the exhortation recorded in 20:18–35. Then, as planned, Paul departs for Macedonia (fall of A.D. 56 or 57, because he plans to reach Jerusalem by Pentecost, v. 16). First he goes north to Troas, where he hopes to meet Titus, who is to bring news from Corinth. The door is open for him to preach the gospel there, but he is so disappointed because Titus has not arrived that he foregoes the opportunity (2 Cor. 2:12–13). The apostle decides to take a ship for Macedonia, where according to his practice, he probably revisits the Christians in Philippi, Thessalonica, and Berea and strengthens them in their faith.

Somewhere in Macedonia Paul meets Titus, perhaps in Philippi. The good news from Corinth relieves his intense anxiety and worries. The majority of the believers at Corinth have repented of the injury done to the apostle, and now they are longing for him (2 Cor. 7:5–7). During his stay in Macedonia he writes 2 Corinthians, expressing his thankfulness for their "godly sorrow" to repentance (7:8–16) and his concern about a few personal enemies still trying to undermine his authority as an apostle (10; 11:13–15). Paul sends the letter by Titus and two others whose names are not given; they are to supervise the collection of money for the poor saints in Jerusalem (8:16–24).

Paul then moves on to Greece (v. 2). Here "Greece" refers to Corinth, the main city of the Roman province of Achaia. He stays there for three months, probably during the winter. During this time he must have written his letter to the Romans (cf. Rom. 15:22–33). Luke makes no mention here of the offering for "the saints in Jerusalem" (but cf. Acts 24:17). Likely Paul devotes much of his energy to this project during his time in Macedonia and Corinth. Before he departs to deliver the monetary gift, the apostle requests that the Roman Christians pray that this offering will be received by the saints in Jerusalem (Rom. 15:30–32).

Once again Paul becomes aware of a Jewish plot against him (v. 3). A number of Jews are heading for Jerusalem to attend Passover or the Feast of Pentecost. Since these enemies hear that Paul is about to embark on a ship headed for Syria, Paul knows it would be easy for them to attack him and rob him of the money he is carrying to Jerusalem. Therefore, he decides to change his plans and take a much longer route by going overland through Macedonia.

At this point Luke lists Paul's seven traveling companions (v. 4). These seven were from the various regions of Paul's Gentile mission and could bear witness to the success of Paul's preaching of the gospel. This group carries with them the offering (probably in gold) collected from the Gentile churches for the saints in Jerusalem. For reasons that Luke does not tell us, the seven men go ahead of Paul and cross over to Troas, where they wait for the apostle to join them.

We know that Luke, who was among Paul's traveling companions, must have rejoined Paul at Philippi, because a "we" passage begins at this point in the narrative (see comments on 16:10). It seems as if Luke had spent several years ministering in Philippi and had remained in that region ever since Paul and Silas's departure (16:40). Now Luke again becomes one of Paul's traveling companions and provides an eyewitness account of the events. After Passover (20:6), Paul, Luke, and perhaps others of his traveling party sail for Troas. The voyage takes five days, apparently because of adverse winds (on an earlier occasion a trip from Troas to Philippi took only two days, 16:11–12).

5.4.3. Paul Visits Troas (20:7–12). A seven-day stay in Troas ends "on the first day of the week," the Lord's day. According to Jewish reckoning, the first day of the week began Saturday at sundown and continued until sunset on Sunday. Luke does not mention how this congregation was founded, but the believers have gathered together "to break bread," that is, to celebrate the Lord's Supper (cf. 1 Cor. 10:16–17; 11:20–34).

This passage is significant regarding the early church's practice of worship. It shows that there were three central elements in the worship of the Pauline churches: preaching of the gospel (vv. 7, 11), healing (vv. 8–10), and the celebration of the Supper (vv. 7, 11). The first day of the week is already being observed as a day of worship (1 Cor. 16:2; Rev. 1:10). The breaking of bread conforms to earlier apostolic practice (Acts 2:42, 46). Significantly, the church at Troas breaks bread on the same day as Christ arose from the dead (cf. John 20:1, 19).

Just like the disciples at the Last Supper, the Christians at Troas celebrate the Lord's Supper in an upper room (v. 8). At this worship service Paul preaches until midnight. This is a long time by Western standards, but the length of his sermon is likely due to his plans to leave the next day. During the sermon "a young man named Eutychus" is seated in a window. The atmosphere in the room is probably hot and stuffy because of the "many lamps in the upstairs room" that are burning (v. 8). Finding it impossible to stay awake, Eutychus goes to sleep and falls out of a third-floor window to his death. Luke could easily have said that he appeared dead, but he says that the young man was "picked up dead" (v. 9).

Paul goes down to Eutychus and embraces his lifeless body. After the same fashion of Elijah and Elisha (1 Kings 17:21; 2 Kings 4:34–36), the apostle raises him from the dead. Urging the Christians to stop being alarmed, Paul says, "He's alive!" By this he does not mean that Eutychus had not died, but that his life returned when Paul embraced him. This astonishing miracle of Paul's raising the dead corresponds to Peter's raising of Dorcas (9:36–42). It also documents Paul's charismatic, prophetic powers.

After the miracle, Paul goes upstairs and breaks bread. Whether this phrase refers to a communion service or a common meal, presumably the entire congregation participates. The apostle may have eaten for the sake of nourishment before departing, but the way Luke uses the phrase "to break bread" makes it more likely that the reference is to the Lord's Supper or to a fellowship meal that often accompanied it. Paul then continues to preach until sunrise and departs. As the Christians leave, they had expected that Eutychus would be taken home dead. But now they are "greatly comforted" since he is still alive, and they can tell their friends and neighbors about the great miracle.

5.4.4. Paul Sails From Assos to Miletus (20:13–16). The apostle continues his travels. All of his companions (v. 4), including Luke, sail to Assos, about twenty miles by foot south of Troas but longer by boat. Paul chooses to travel directly by land to Assos. Luke gives no reason why the apostle wants to travel on foot. Perhaps he desires to be alone and think through the dangers of his journey to Jerusalem. In several of the cities he has already received prophetic warning of bonds and imprisonment awaiting him (vv. 22–23). Only in solitude can he find time for meditation and prayer.

At Assos Paul joins the others on board. Then they sail to Mitylene, the main town of the island of Lesbos. After spending the night there, they arrive off the coast of Kios but do not enter the harbor. The following day they ome to Samos, an island off the coast south of phesus. A short run on the fourth day brings nem to the important seaport of Miletus. They ave passed by Ephesus, where Paul had spent hree years but where he had also had encountered great opposition. Evidently he fears that f he stops in Ephesus, he will spend too much ime in Asia and fail to arrive in Jerusalem in ime for Pentecost. He is anxious to reach the Ioly City as quickly as possible to present the offering for the poor saints and also to observe Pentecost, demonstrating to Jewish Christians his faithfulness to his Jewish heritage.

5.4.5. Paul Addresses the Elders of the Church at Ephesus (20:17–38). The ship on which Paul is traveling anchors for a while in the harbor of Miletus. He takes advantage of the delay by sending for the elders of the church at Ephesus—a distance of about thirty miles. He could have gone to Ephesus, but there may have been some uncertainty about the ship's departure. How long before they arrive is unknown, but Paul may have had a considerable wait. His message to the elders emphasizes his own personal integrity as a preacher of the gospel, and it is also his farewell to them. This address is the only one in Acts in which Paul speaks to a Christian group. It has special relevance because he stresses here aspects of pastoral care and unfolds his theology of ministry.

This address serves as a challenge for the church and its leaders. Its great message can be divided into four parts: (1) Paul's discharge of his pastoral duties, (2) his present situation and impending future, (3) a pastoral exhortation, and (4) his commitment and example.

(1) A review of Paul's faithful discharge of his pastoral duties (vv. 18–21). The Christian elders from Ephesus are the leaders of the Ephesian congregation. These men know the manner in which Paul lived and worked from the day he set his foot in Asia until the day he left. He reminds them that he was a model minister. He "served the Lord with great humility and with tears," meaning that he was always a humble servant of the church but that he also suffered distress and grief out of concern for his converts.

Many trials had befallen him because of his countrymen, the Jews. Though he suffered greatly at their hands, he had declared the whole truth and did not keep back anything that was beneficial to his hearers. He preached and taught in public and in private homes. He declared what was necessary for salvation, faithfully warning both Jews and Gentiles that, to be saved, they had to turn from their sins to God in repentance and believe on Jesus as Lord and Messiah. The apostle had devoted himself to evangelism and to the edification of the church. His review of his ministry in Asia reflects the prophetic pattern of service and suffering.

(2) Paul's present situation and his impending future (vv. 22–27). The apostle's plans to go to Jerusalem have been made in the Spirit (cf. 19:21; 23:11). Paul graphically characterizes his journey to the city as "compelled by the Spirit" (lit., "having been bound in the Spirit"). In a sense, he is a prisoner of the Holy Spirit. Under the Spirit's constant constraint, he knows he is being guided by God and must obey. In spite of uncertainty as to what may await him, he is willing to go to Jerusalem. The Spirit has already revealed through prophets in several cities some of what will happen to him, such as imprisonment and hardships. He understands these solemn prophetic warnings as the Lord's definite guidance to go to Jerusalem. Thus, he is confident that the trials and tribulations that await him there are part of God's plan.

The unfolding of these adversities becomes the fulfillment of the Spirit's predictions. He is ready even to give his life for the gospel. His overpowering desire is to complete the mission and work that he has received from the Lord Jesus. He characterizes his ministry as bearing witness "to the gospel of God's grace," which means that salvation is God's free gift. At his conversion Christ had given him the task of declaring the grace of God (9:10–16). Now what matters is faithfully fulfilling his part of the mission to evangelize the world.

Paul does not expect that his present audience will see him again (v. 25). He feels that his work in this location is complete (Rom. 15:23). He has already preached the kingdom of God in Ephesus and the surrounding areas, and he is satisfied with what he has done. The kingdom has become present in Jesus Christ and through the outpouring of the Holy Spirit (cf. 1:6–8; 19:8; 28:23). Paul has also preached "the whole will of God" (20:27). That is, he has faithfully declared the full gospel, including divine judgment of sin and salvation through Christ.

Because Paul has discharged his duty to the utmost, he is "innocent of the blood of all men"

(v. 26). In other words, since he has been faithful in his presentation of the message that brings salvation, he should not be held responsible for the eternal death of anyone. The apostle never loses sight of his responsibility before God.

Acts concludes with Paul's preaching the gospel in Rome during his imprisonment there (28:17–31). Most likely Paul was released from this Roman imprisonment. After his release, he seems to have returned to Ephesus, as Paul's movements as recorded in the Pastoral Letters suggest. He apparently visited several cities: Ephesus (1 Tim. 1:3), Crete, Nicopolis (Titus 1:5; 3:12), Corinth, Miletus, Troas, and finally Rome (2 Tim. 1:17; 4:13, 20). On the present occasion in Miletus, however, Paul feels that it is unlikely that he will revisit Ephesus and see these people again. Evidently, those fears were not realized.

(3) Paul's pastoral exhortation to the Ephesian elders (vv. 28–31). Paul urges the elders to be concerned about their own spiritual welfare and to care for "the flock." Paul uses the familiar Old Testament term "flock" for God's people (cf. Ps. 100:3; Isa. 40:11; Ezek. 34:22, 31). Aware that he will no longer be able to care for that congregation, Paul urges these church leaders to give attention to their own personal godliness and to discharge faithfully their pastoral duties.

He reminds them too that the Holy Spirit is responsible for the leadership positions they hold (v. 28). He has appointed them as overseers and given them spiritual gifts, equipping them to serve as shepherds of the church of God. The same leaders whom Luke calls "elders" (*presbyteroi*) in verse 17 Paul calls "overseers" (*episkopoi*) in verse 28. The two terms are used interchangeably. *Elder* describes the person of the church leaders; normally, they were the older people in the congregation. *Overseer* indicates their function, which was to superintend the work of the local congregation and to exercise oversight over the spiritual life of God's people.

Earlier Paul and Barnabas's appointment of elders had been accomplished with prayer and fasting—that is, with dependence upon the Holy Spirit—in each church they established (cf. 14:23); but now Paul ascribes the appointment of the Ephesian elders directly to the Holy Spirit (cf. 13:1–4). As in Paul's own ministry, the Holy Spirit provides strong endorsement of the ministry of the Ephesian elders.

Having been made overseers by the Spirit, these elders are responsible to serve as the pastoral and prophetic leaders of the congregation. The phrase "keep watch over yourselves" does not imply that elders should look out for themselves, but that they should be concerned about their own spiritual welfare as well as those whom the Holy Spirit has entrusted to their care. The Spirit had equipped them to be "shepherds of the church of God" (v. 28). They were to care for the church in the same way as shepherds care for their flocks. The phrase "church of God" means that the church belongs to God. Through the blood of his own Son, shed on the cross to atone for sin, God purchased the church, the whole company of all the redeemed of all ages and places. "He . . . did not spare his own Son, but gave him up for us all" (Rom. 8:32). The great price God paid to acquire the church should motivate the elders to make the needed sacrifices for its welfare.

With prophetic insight Paul goes on to warn the Ephesian elders that heretical teachers will enter the congregation of believers. They are depicted as "wolves," a common term for heretics (Matt. 7:15; 10:16; John 10:12). As "savage" wolves, they will seek to destroy the flock. Not only will they come from the outside (v. 29), but heretical Christians will also rise up within the church itself (v. 30) and introduce dangerous doctrines into the church. Their purpose will be to pervert the truth and draw away believers from the flock to their camp. The activities of these people will be a mortal threat to the life of God's flock.

So the elders, like shepherds, are first to guard their flock from these fierce wolves. Staying on guard will enable them to discern the threat of trouble and to stop it before the flock is scattered. They are also told to remember Paul's own example (v. 31). The word "remember" (*mnemoneuo*) refers to more than the mental act of recalling; it means to give heed and so be encouraged. The Ephesian elders are to draw strength and courage from the example that Paul had set during his time with them and to imitate that example. During his three-year stay among them, Paul effectively led the believers by constantly warning and instructing them. That stay had not been without adversity and suffering.

(4) Paul's commitment of the elders to God and his example (vv. 32–38). Before he leaves

his friends, Paul points them to their only source of courage and strength by committing them to God and "to the word of his grace." He puts them in God's hands and submits them to the message of God's unmerited favor, which he had preached to them. God's grace will make them strong and mature spiritually and give them a great future inheritance, which belongs to all God's holy people. At the second coming of Christ all believers will enter the inheritance of God's people (Eph. 1:14; Col. 1:12; 3:24). At that time the elders and the people as a whole will share in the full benefits of God's kingly rule. Holiness is the condition for receiving the inheritance, and that condition is met by standing under the Word of God and being led by the Holy Spirit (Rom. 8:14; Heb. 12:14).

During his stay in Ephesus the apostle had set a good example for the Ephesian elders. He had not coveted anything that belonged to others (v. 33). On the contrary, while among them he worked with his own hands and earned enough to provide for the needs of himself and his companions. He had declined to exercise his right to receive financial reward for his ministry (cf. 18:3; 1 Cor. 9:3–18). His reason for supporting himself was not only to avoid being dependent on others, but also to show the elders by example that they must provide for themselves and others, especially the "weak," that is, the sick and needy.

Jesus himself had taught the responsible care of the needy who depend on help and gifts from others. If the elders follow Paul's own example, they will fulfill a saying of Jesus: "It is more blessed to give than to receive" (v. 35). This saying appears only here in the New Testament. It may be a summary of Jesus' teaching in Luke 6:38, or it may have been preserved in oral tradition. This treasured teaching of the Lord can be misunderstood. Its intent is not to teach that those who bestow gifts are more blessed than those who receive them; rather, this saying of Jesus shows that Paul is not only faithful to the mission to which Jesus has called him, but through his giving, he is also faithful to the teachings of the Savior. The elders are to keep in mind that those who give are happier than those who seek to amass wealth for themselves.

Paul ends his farewell address with this saying of Jesus. Appropriately, he follows the saying with a prayer, during which all of them kneel down and pray together. His departure from them is a sad occasion. The depth of their grief and their affections for Paul are evident. As an expression of their love, the elders hug and kiss him. Their hearts are filled with grief and their eyes with tears. This hour of parting is a touching scene, and they do not expect to see Paul again, thinking his journey to Jerusalem will result in certain death.

The elders then accompany Paul to the ship that is about to sail from Miletus; thereafter, they return to their homes. We can imagine their sorrowful conversation as they return to Ephesus while Paul sails for Jerusalem, where bonds and afflictions await him.

5.4.6. Paul Sails From Miletus to Tyre (21:1–6). After Paul and his traveling companions tear themselves away from their beloved friends from Ephesus, they leave Miletus by boat. According to Acts their departure marks the end of Paul's ministry in the Aegean area. Luke narrates the stages of the voyage from Miletus to Tyre, noting that the ship stops at various ports. He seems to outline the journey day by day.

The first day takes them to the small island of Cos, about forty miles from Miletus. Apparently the wind is favorable, and the ship sails due south to that island. On the second day they reach the large island of Rhodes, southwest of Asia Minor, and on the third day they sail east to the port city of Patara, on the southeast coast of Lycia. At Patara they transfer to a larger ship on its way to Phoenicia. They then sail directly across the open sea to the port of Tyre. Paul and his companions pass south of Cyprus, where Paul and Barnabas had preached on the first missionary journey (13:4–12). They dock at Tyre, where they stay for a few days. They may have stayed there because of delays caused by the unloading of the ship's cargo or because of the need to transfer to a ship headed for Caesarea.

The delay in Tyre gives Paul and his companions an opportunity to find the believers there. Likely the church in that city had been established as a result of the scattering of Christians by persecution (see 8:1–4; 11:19; cf. Luke 6:17; 10:13–14). The Christian community there must have been small since a few days later, when Paul and his friends prepare to leave, "all the disciples and their wives and children" accompany them to the beach to see them off (v. 5).

After finding the believers, Paul and his traveling companions stay with them for seven days. Some of them have the gift of prophecy, and they warn Paul about what he is to face in Jerusalem. "Through the Spirit" they urge him not to go there (v. 4). Their inspired warnings seem to be opposite of the earlier guidance of the Holy Spirit (20:22–23). The best way to interpret this is that the Spirit revealed to these prophets Paul's imminent suffering in Jerusalem, and they of their own accord urge him not to go. It is the prophets, not the Spirit, who tell the apostle not to press on to the city that kills prophets (Luke 13:34).

In spite of the warnings, Paul recognizes a higher constraint to proceed. His decision to go to Jerusalem was made under the Spirit's guidance, and now the Spirit continues to impel him forward toward that dangerous city. Paul knows that captivity awaits him there, and he has counted the cost. Though the dangers are great, he must follow the leading of the Spirit.

When the time comes for Paul and his companions to resume their journey, the scene of departure is filled with tenderness and emotion. The entire Christian community—men, women, and children—escort them to the ship. These believers kneel with Paul and his companions and pray fervently that Paul will be brought safely through the approaching dangers. After an affectionate farewell, the two Christian groups go their separate ways: "We went aboard the ship, and they returned home." The parting scene must have remained a cherished memory of the Christians at Tyre.

5.4.7. Paul Journeys From Tyre to Caesarea (21:7–14). From Tyre Paul sails south to the port of Ptolemais. Luke does not indicate why Paul chooses to wait seven days at Tyre for a ship, for he could have traveled the distance on land in much less time. Moreover, it is unclear whether Paul goes from Ptolemais to Caesarea by water or land; the verb (*dianyo*) in verse 7 may mean either "finish" or "continue" (contrast NIV with NRSV). Although it is possible they finish their boat journey at Ptolemais, most likely they reach Caesarea by sea.

5.4.7.1. Paul Visits Philip the Evangelist (21:7–9). The apostle and his companions arrive at the port of Ptolemais, about forty miles south of Tyre. This city was the ancient city of Acco (Judg. 1:31) and had been renamed in honor of the Egyptian ruler Ptolemy II. It was located directly across from Mount Carmel, a mountain connected with Elijah and Elisha, two great prophets of Israel. Ptolemais had probably been evangelized at the same time as Tyre (Acts 11:19, which indicates that the gospel had been preached throughout Phoenicia). Paul also finds a Christian community there and stays overnight, enjoying the fellowship of believers.

The next day Paul moves on to Caesarea, another forty miles directly south. Here the apostle and his fellow travelers become guests in the home of Philip the evangelist. Philip is "one of the Seven" charismatic deacons, who had been chosen in Jerusalem (6:1–6). He had become an effective evangelist, preaching the gospel in Samaria and in all the cities from Azotus to Caesarea (8:4–40). He probably established the church in Caesarea, where he now resides.

Earlier Luke showed that Philip was a Spirit-filled prophet (6:5); here he indicates that this prophet also has four unmarried daughters, all of whom have the gift of prophecy. Nothing is said about them prophesying on this occasion. The NIV rendering of the present participle (*propheteuousai*) as "prophesied" implies that they occasionally exercise their prophetic powers. But the present tense refers to an ongoing or repeated activity. Philip's daughters exercise the gift of prophecy regularly; their prophetic ministry is not an occasional manifestation. Under the inspiration of the Spirit they are devoted to preaching the gospel. The reference to Agabus in the immediate context (v. 10) may suggest that they are prophetesses on the order of Agabus and like him have prophesied about future events. The New Testament does not fail to note the ministry of women in the early church.

5.4.7.2. Agabus Prophesies Paul's Arrest (21:10–14). Paul and his fellow travelers spend several days at the home of Philip. They have plenty of time to get to Jerusalem for the celebration of Pentecost. During their stay Paul receives a final prophetic warning regarding the dangers awaiting him in Jerusalem—this one from Agabus.

Agabus has just come from his home in Judea. Luke introduces him as though he has not mentioned him before. But he is, no doubt, the same prophet who, as a mouthpiece of the pirit, had predicted the worldwide famine uring the reign of Claudius, which prompted ne Christians in Antioch to send relief to the Christians in Judea by the hands of Paul and arnabas (11:27–29). Nothing more is known bout Agabus than what we are told in Acts 11 nd here, but he does stand close to the rophetic tradition in ancient Israel. As a strik-ng parallel to some of the Old Testament rophets, he expresses the Spirit's message in vords (similar to "This is what the LORD ays") and symbolic actions (cf. Isa. 20:2–4; er. 27:1–11; Zech. 11:7–14).

When this spiritually gifted prophet arrives n Caesarea, he goes straight to Paul and, in a ramatic manner, grabs his belt and ties him-elf up with it. He speaks for the Spirit (v. 11) nd declares that binding himself with Paul's elt demonstrates the bondage that awaits the postle in Jerusalem (cf. 20:22–23). Agabus xplicitly announces that the Jews will hand 'aul over to the Gentiles (21:11). When Paul rrives in Jerusalem, the hatred of the Jews oes lead to Paul's arrest by the Roman author-ties and to the fulfillment of this prophecy. Though the Jews do not actually deliver him o the Romans, they are responsible for his mprisonment. The prophecy that Paul will be lelivered to the Gentiles echoes Jesus' predic-ion of his own fate (Luke 9:44; 18:32; cf. Mark 10:33). The way Agabus words his prophecy learly brings out the close parallel between the ates of Jesus and his servant, Paul.

Agabus's prophecy has a powerful, dra-natic effect (vv. 12–14). When Paul's com-anions and the local Christians hear it, their ourage fails. Presumably when the earlier rophecies had been given about Paul's fate, is traveling companions had remained silent. But on this occasion, they join in with local elievers in urging Paul to cancel his trip. Out of great love for the apostle everyone pleads with him not to go to Jerusalem.

The grief these people manifest makes it more difficult for Paul to do God's will. He knows that what he is about to do will hurt those whom he loves. He is already bearing a heavy burden, but the effect of their grief makes the burden even heavier and breaks his heart. Yet, in spite of his personal distress, Paul remains steadfast in his purpose. Not only is he prepared to be imprisoned (as has been prophesied), but he is also ready to face death in Jerusalem. It is not that he sees any virtue in suffering for its own sake, but whatever he suffers will be "for the name of the Lord Jesus" (v. 13)—that is, as part of his devotion to Jesus and of his Christ-ian service. The apostle feels compelled to fol-low the prophetic pattern (cf. Luke 9:51–53; 13:22, 33–34; 18:31–33; Acts 20:22–24) and die in Jerusalem if it is God's will.

Among these believers are undoubtedly Spirit-filled prophets. They and Paul disagree on whether he should go to Jerusalem. Both apparently claim the inspiration of the Holy Spirit. This incident clearly shows that Spirit-filled believers can disagree as to what is the will of the Lord. When there appears a contra-diction in divine guidance, it becomes imper-ative for the church to exercise spiritual discernment. It is seldom easy to distinguish divine revelation from human interpretation. An appeal to divine guidance fails to provide an easy escape from the uncertainties and ambiguities of human life.

What resolves the issue is Paul's appeal to the example of Jesus and the prophets who go to Jerusalem only to suffer and to die. That convinces the believers. This powerful exam-ple brings the two sides of this community together again. Paul's Christian friends then stop trying to persuade him not to go to Jerusalem. Convinced of the guiding hand of the Lord, they exclaim, "The Lord's will be done." The Spirit is still guiding Paul. It is God's will that he go to Jerusalem. What hap-pens there will be according to the divine plan.

5.4.8. Paul Visits Jerusalem (21:15–22:21). We come now to the final stage of Paul's journey to Jerusalem. In a sense this journey is a miniature of the much longer travel narrative in Luke of Jesus' journey from Galilee to Jerusalem (Luke 9:51–19:44). Some elements of the scene at Caesarea parallel inci-dents in the Lukan record: Paul's resolution to go to Jerusalem (21:13; cf. Luke 9:51) and Paul's being handed over by Jews to Gentiles (Acts 21:11; cf. Luke 18:32; 24:6–7).

Things turn out differently, however, for Paul than they did for Jesus. Paul does not die in Jerusalem. Luke's account does not include all the details of the arrival of Paul and his friends in the city. No mention is made of the apostles being there, the celebration of the Feast of Pentecost, and the offering for the poor Christians (though see 24:17). These omissions show that Luke's main goal is to record the events that move Paul toward Rome. His last visit to the Holy City is decisive in bringing him to the capital of the Roman empire.

5.4.8.1. Paul Travels From Caesarea to Jerusalem (21:15–16). After spending several days in Caesarea, Paul and his friends leave for Jerusalem, a trip of about sixty-five miles. It takes about two days for them to reach the Holy City. Some of the Christians at Caesarea accompany Paul and his companions so that they can introduce them to their host, Mnason.

Mnason appears nowhere else in the New Testament. He was apparently a member of the church in Jerusalem and either lived in the city or near it. Like Barnabas he was from the island of Cyprus and was "one of the early disciples" (v. 16). As a Christian of long standing, he may have become a believer after the resurrection of Jesus and been among the disciples when the Spirit was poured out at Pentecost. Mnason provides lodging for Paul's party during their stay in Jerusalem. The Christians who accompany them must know Mnason well and are aware that he is glad to accommodate these guests.

5.4.8.2. Paul's "Triumphal Entry" Into Jerusalem (21:17–26). The Christians in Jerusalem give Paul and his companions a warm reception. In verse 18 Luke refers to "James, and all the elders," who now have assumed the full leadership of the Jerusalem church. Most likely the elders are presided over by James, the brother of the Lord (12:17; 15:13–21; 1 Cor. 15:7; Gal. 1:19–20). At this time Peter and the other apostles are not in Jerusalem. Accompanied by his traveling companions, Paul meets with these leaders on the day following his arrival in the city. At the meeting the apostle must have presented the offering from the Gentile churches to the Jerusalem church, but Luke makes only a brief allusion about it later (24:17).

Reminiscent of his earlier reports to Antioch (14:24–28) and at the Jerusalem Council (15:4, 12), Paul gives an account of his missionary work to the Jerusalem church leaders. Undoubtedly he includes such details as the Gentiles' forsaking the worship of idols, the generous gift from the Gentile churches, and the outpouring of the Holy Spirit on the Gentiles. God has greatly blessed his work among the Gentiles. The church leaders receive Paul's report enthusiastically. They glorify and prais God for what he has done through Paul's min istry—a fact that shows these leaders are i full accord with Paul's teaching and practice The success of the mission is ascribed to Go

After James and the elders have thanke God for working through Paul, they urge hi to recognize a sensitive situation: Some Jewis Christians are still "zealous for the law" (v. 20 They report that "many thousands" of Jewis believers, probably in Judea and Jerusalem, ar devoted to the law of Moses. These believer are intensely suspicious of the apostle becaus they have heard that he teaches Jews living out side of Palestine not to circumcise their chil dren and to disregard such Jewish customs a the food laws and eating with Gentiles (v. 21 Moreover, rumors have circulated about Paul' preaching of a law-free gospel.

The apostle's opponents had twisted hi words, for Paul had not ceased to be a Je once he became a Christian. When the mis sionary situation called for it, he was willing t conform to certain Jewish practices for th sake of the gospel (cf. 21:26; 1 Cor. 9:19–23 He had never taught Jewish Christians not t circumcise their children. He himself had cir cumcised Timothy (Acts 16:3) and taken Nazirite vow while in Achaia (18:18). He i now in Jerusalem for the Feast of Pentecost, Jewish festival. In observing such rituals h never compromised the gospel or Christia freedom. James and the elders recognize th rumors and charges are false (v. 24).

Like the converted Pharisees in 15:5, thes Jewish Christians are zealots for the law Unlike them, however, they are not objectin to the policy of admitting Gentiles into th church or having fellowship with them. Thes issues have been settled (15:19–21, 23–29 and the provisions of the Jerusalem Counci are fully acceptable to them. Rather, thes zealots are worried about the implications o Paul's teaching for the believers who wish t remain faithful to their Jewish lifestyle. The are enthusiastic for the law as a gift of God t Israel and for the traditional Jewish way of life

Paul himself had once been "extremely zealous for the traditions of [his] fathers" (Gal 1:14), but after he met Jesus Christ he gave u the law as a means of obtaining salvation (Phil 3:8–9). Some Jewish believers, however, have not found it easy to abandon their previous wa of life. As upholders of God's law revealed in the Old Testament, they continue to practice circumcision and follow Jewish customs. They see Paul as a threat to the vitality of Jewish Christianity, especially among Jewish believers who live outside of Judea (v. 21).

We know from Acts and Paul's letters that the apostle did teach justification apart from the law (Rom. 3:21–22) and from circumcision (2:25–29). It is easy to see how his opponents could take some things he had said and use them to convince these disciples, "zealous for the law," that he was a threat to the cultural expressions of Judaism. These Jewish believers are not trying to make Gentile Christianity Jewish, but they want to prevent Jewish Christianity from becoming Gentile so that they can continue to practice the traditions of their fathers.

James and the elders inquire what should be done (v. 22). What they mean is, "Can anything be done to show the rumors are unfounded?" The problem cannot be solved by silence. The Jewish Christians who believe the false rumors will hear that Paul is in Jerusalem. Not wanting to risk any trouble with them, the church leaders propose something practical in order to prove the rumors are false. Paul should submit to the purification ritual of the temple and pay the expenses of four Jewish Christians who have taken a Nazirite vow.

According to Jewish custom, at the end of a Nazirite vow it was necessary for a Jew to go through a purification ritual, offering expensive sacrifices and shaving their heads (Num. 6:2–21). The request is not that Paul take the vow along with these men, but that he go through the rite of purification with them and underwrite their expenses. Luke does not say why Paul undertook the ritual of purification, but Diaspora Jews often underwent purification when they came to the temple to worship. Paying for sacrificial animals for the poor was considered a supreme act of religious devotion. These acts would prove to those "zealous for the law" (v. 20) that the rumors are untrue and that Paul is a law-abiding Jew.

However, James and the elders give Paul the assurance that his observance of Jewish customs on this occasion will not compromise the liberty of the Gentiles. The fundamental freedom of the Gentiles from the law had already been established in the provisions of the Jerusalem Council (15:20). In verse 25 James cites the terms of the council verbatim. Since Paul was a participant in the Jerusalem Council, he is well acquainted with that decree. This part of James's address must be for the benefit of Paul's companions and shifts attention from Jewish believers to Gentile believers and their freedom in Christ.

Paul complies with the request. On the next day, to show that he is ready to conform to the rituals of Jewish piety, he goes to the temple to begin a period of ceremonial cleansing and to give notice when he and four men will complete this period. He pays the stipulated fees so that each of the Nazirites may offer a sacrifice. In doing so, the apostle reassures believers in Jerusalem of his personal compatibility with Jewish traditions as long as they involve no compromise of the gospel.

Many of the Jewish believers observed their traditions as a duty; Paul does not share their convictions. The sacrificial death of Christ not only made temple sacrifices and purification rites unnecessary, but exposed their real meaning. But according to the principle of 1 Corinthians 9:20, Paul was prepared to live under the law in order to win unconverted Jews to the gospel. On this occasion he accommodates himself to an extreme right wing of Jewish Christianity in order to deal with negative press and the harsh feelings they have for him. While the apostle is free from the law, he does not allow his liberty in Christ to become a form of bondage. His exercise of his freedom serves the integrity of the gospel and the unity of the church.

5.4.8.3. Paul Enters the Temple (21:27–36). The troubles that develop for the apostle in Jerusalem are not from Jewish believers but from a second source of opposition—non-Christian Jews from Asia. Agabus had prophesied that "the Jews of Jerusalem will bind" Paul (v. 11). Like Stephen earlier, Paul is attacked by Jews visiting Jerusalem from the Diaspora (cf. 6:9–11; 9:29). Over the next five years he is put on trial before various judges and is carried to Rome in chains. The rest of Acts describes Paul's imprisonment and defense.

Apparently the four who had taken the Nazirite vow have contacted some ceremonial defilement and need to undergo the ritual purification. Before a person could be purified, seven days had to pass after the defilement. On the seventh day he was required to shave his head and on the eighth day offer a sacrifice

(Num. 6:9–12). When the seven days of purification are almost completed for the four Nazirites, "Jews from the province of Asia" see Paul in the temple. These Jews are probably from Ephesus because they recognize "Trophimus the Ephesian" (v. 29).

Likely these Jews are pilgrims who have traveled to Jerusalem to celebrate the Feast of Pentecost. It is also likely that Paul has already suffered from their plots during his three years of ministry in Ephesus (20:19). They turn out to be Paul's real opponents. When they see him in the temple, they stir up a crowd to mob action against him and level charges similar to those brought against Stephen (6:13). Urging the people to join them, they allege that Paul has attacked the covenant people of Israel, undermined the law of Moses, and defiled "this holy place," the temple (v. 28). These charges cause the people to become angry at him. He is charged with teaching "all men everywhere" against the three symbols of Jewish unity: the people, the law, and the temple.

The Asian Jews in particular insist that Paul has defiled the temple. Earlier they saw Trophimus, an uncircumcised Gentile from Ephesus, going around with Paul in Jerusalem. They draw the hasty conclusion that Paul has taken him into the temple (v. 29) and thus defiled it. The temple was divided into a number of courts. Gentiles were allowed into the outer "court of Gentiles," but were forbidden to proceed into the "court of women" and especially into the "court of Israel." There was an official barrier in the temple that warned Gentiles that it was a capital offense to go beyond the court of Gentiles. Their presence beyond the barrier would make the temple unclean, and the offense was punishable by death.

The Sanhedrin had no authority to invoke capital punishment, but the Roman authorities, to conciliate the Jews, usually ratified the death penalty for this offense (cf. Josephus, *Jewish War*, 6.2.4; Bruce, 1952, 433). On occasion the authorities may have looked the other way. But the apostle Paul would not have defiled the temple. He himself is undergoing purification and would not have provided Jews with grounds for charging him with disregard for the law.

The Asian Jews have no evidence to believe that Paul had actually brought an Ephesian Gentile into the Holy Place. These partisan Jews see this charge as the easiest way to incite the wrath of the people against him. News of their outcry against Paul travels fast, and they succeed in arousing the entire city. A lynch mob seizes Paul, but they do not kill him in the temple. Rather, they drag him outside (probably out into the court of the Gentiles), and the doors are shut by the temple authorities. These doors are probably the ones that separated the inner courts from the Gentile court rather than the outer doors to the entire temple complex.

Almost immediately, news about the violent disturbance reaches the Roman garrison in Jerusalem. This garrison was a cohort of a thousand men, commanded by an officer with the rank similar to our colonel. It was kept ready for emergencies during the feasts. These Roman troops were stationed in the tower of Antonia, which overlooked the entire temple area from the northwest corner. This tower had a flight of steps that led down into the court of the Gentiles.

Upon receiving news of the disturbance, the commander of the garrison quickly takes a strong force of soldiers down to the scene where the furious mob is trying to beat Paul to death. The term for "beating" (*typto*, v. 32) means the uncontrolled and unrestricted battering of someone with a view to killing him. When the mob sees the commander and his troops, they stop attacking the apostle. Again the Romans rescue him from the hands of his countrymen (cf. 18:12–16), only on this occasion he barely escapes with his life.

Even though the Roman officer rescues Paul, he assumes that Paul is the cause of the trouble and orders each of his hands to be chained to a soldier, fulfilling the prophecy of Agabus (v. 11). From this point to the end of Acts Paul remains a prisoner. The commander asks the crowd who the prisoner is and what he has done so that he may know how to deal with him. The result is nothing but confusion. "Some in the crowd shouted one thing and some another" (v. 34).

The confused answers from the angry mob make it clear to the commander that he must seek the truth some other way. He orders the soldiers to do the sensible thing and to take the prisoner to their barracks, where under more peaceful conditions the Roman authorities can examine him. The soldiers promptly obey the order of their commander. As they reach the steps that lead into the fortress of Antonia, the violence of the angry mob makes it impossible for Paul to walk up the stairs safely. Therefore, for his own safety the soldiers carry him up the stairway. The mob keeps shouting, "Away with him," just as the angry mob had done at the trial of Jesus (Luke 23:18). Their recurring shouts underscore their murderous intentions to kill him. Rather than urging the Romans to put him to death, they want to do it themselves.

5.4.8.4. Paul Asks to Address the Angry Mob (21:37–40). The soldiers are about to take Paul into the fort so that he can be interrogated, but the apostle wishes to speak to the mob. He turns to the commander and asks if he may say something to him. Paul surprises this Roman soldier by addressing him in Greek. In the ancient world Greek was a *lingua franca*, but the commander had misjudged Paul as a Jew and as a rough character without any education.

Hearing him speak fluent Greek, the officer changes his mind about his prisoner and concludes that he has on his hands a revolutionary Egyptian who recently had led a group of terrorists against Jerusalem and was defeated by the Romans. No doubt the man to whom the commander refers is the Egyptian false prophet mentioned by Josephus (*Jewish War* 2.13.5; *Ant.* 20.8.6). According to Josephus this Egyptian revolt took place at the time of the governorship of Felix (A.D. 52–59).

True to his well-known tendency to exaggerate, Josephus reports that the Egyptian had led 30,000 men to revolt against Rome. The terrorists were extreme Jewish nationalists, enemies of the Romans and all Jews sympathetic to Rome. Members of this fanatical group were known as "daggermen" (*Sicarii*); they got their name from the small dagger they carried with them to execute their enemies. They were "cutthroats," devoted political terrorists and murderers. This Egyptian rebel, posing as a prophet, had recently incited a group of terrorists to revolt against the Romans and had stirred up 4,000 of his followers in the desert to go to the Mount of Olives and attack Jerusalem (cf. v. 38), claiming they would see the walls of the city fall before their eyes. Felix, the Roman governor of Judea at that time, put down the rebellion. Most of the prophet's followers were killed or taken prisoner, but he himself escaped. Since the revolt took place recently, the Roman commander naturally assumes that Paul is that false prophet, who has returned to cause another revolt against his government.

Paul's response to the commander makes it clear that there is no connection between Christians and Jewish terrorists. He draws attention to two facts: He is a Jew by nationality, not an Egyptian; and he is a citizen of Tarsus. As a Jew Paul has every right to go into the inner court of the temple. Because of his Jewish heritage, he is certainly not the kind of person who would cause a riot in the temple. Therefore, he should not be identified as the Egyptian false prophet. And as a citizen of Tarsus, the apostle comes from an illustrious city located outside of Palestine. It was "no ordinary city" (v. 39), for Tarsus had a university

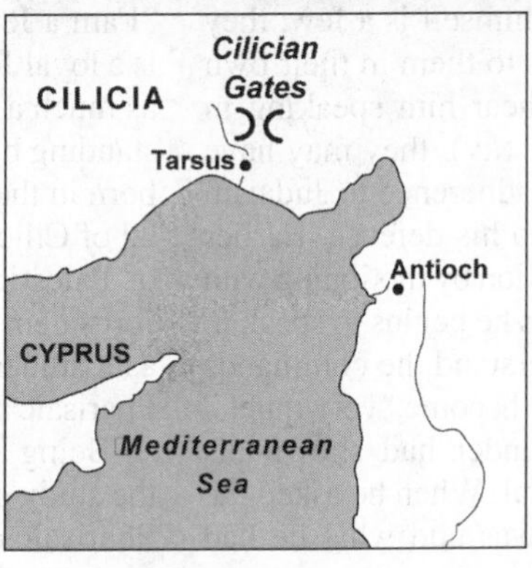

The mountains of Tarsus, Paul's homeland. This view is toward the mountain pass called Cilician Gates that Paul, on his second and third missionary trips, would have passed through. Armies moving north and west would also have used this pass.

and was a self-governing city. The city was noted for its cultural, intellectual, and political significance. Paul is proud to be a citizen of that well-known city.

Empowered by the Spirit, Paul desires to speak to those who have tried to kill him. The commander grants him his request. Standing at the top of the stairs and surrounded by Roman soldiers, he waves his hand to the mob to secure silence and then speaks to them "in Aramaic" (v. 40). The phrase Luke uses is *te Hebraïdi dialekto* (lit., "in the Hebrew dialect"), but a number of biblical scholars are convinced that it was the popular Semitic tongue known as Aramaic. The Dead Sea Scrolls, however, show Hebrew as a living language in the first century; thus, Paul may have given his address in Hebrew (cf. 22:2; 26:14).

5.4.8.5. Paul Makes His Defense Before the Mob (22:1–21). Luke records four speeches that Paul makes in defense of himself and his ministry. These speeches are biographical in character, but each is made to a different audience: (1) the Jewish mob (22:1–21); (2) the Sanhedrin (23:1–6); (3) the Roman governor Felix (24:2–23); and (4) King Agrippa (26:1–29). Prior to his first speech, he was accused of speaking against the Jewish people, the law, and the temple (21:28). As is customary for Paul, he answers the charges leveled against him but also takes the opportunity to bear witness to the transforming power of the gospel.

Paul begins by addressing his audience as "brothers and fathers," the same greeting Stephen used in his speech (7:2). "Fathers" would be appropriate for the priests and members of the Sanhedrin. Nothing is said about them, but some of them may be present on this occasion. By addressing them as "brothers," Paul reinforces that he himself is a Jew; they are brothers. He speaks to them in their own language. When they hear him speaking in Hebrew ("in Aramaic," NIV), they may have been impressed by his adherence to Judaism and listened carefully to his defense. Earlier Paul got the mob's attention by motioning with his hand (21:40); now as he begins to speak in the language they understand, he commands their attention, and they become "very quiet."

The Roman commander had shown his misunderstanding of Paul. When he asked the mob who the apostle was and what he had done, many of them were equally ignorant (21:33–38). Knowing that the people believe the charges, such as the claim that Paul opposed the law and had brought a Gentile into the forbidden courts of the temple, the apostle provides his Jewish audience with information they ought to know about him. The three expressions—"born in Tarsus," "brought up in this city," and "under Gamaliel ... thoroughly trained"—speak of Paul's background. In light of the setting of the speech, "this city" more likely refers to Jerusalem rather than to Tarsus. If Paul was referring to Tarsus, he would have used the expression "that city."

The punctuation of verse 3 is an issue here. The NIV puts a period after "city," thereby separating "brought up" from "under Gamaliel" and suggesting that Paul was raised in Tarsus. Although he was born in Tarsus, Paul most likely grew up in Jerusalem. The NRSV rendering links "brought up" with the training he received under Gamaliel: "brought up in this city at the feet of Gamaliel, educated strictly according to our ancestral law. . . ." His rabbinic education would have begun in his early teens.

In other words, Paul came to Jerusalem at an early age and did not, as some have assumed, spend his childhood in Tarsus. The word "brought up" (*anatrepho*) was used for nurture within a family. Leaving Tarsus at an early age, he came to Jerusalem, where he may have lived at his sister's home (23:16). Despite having spent his boyhood and adolescence in Jerusalem, through his family he maintained contact with Tarsus. After his conversion he concluded his first visit to Jerusalem by returning to the city of his birth (9:30; 11:25; Gal. 1:21).

Paul's brief biographical sketch of himself draws attention to his strong Jewish heritage. "I am a Jew" sets the tone of his defense. He is a loyal Jew, not an alien nor an apostate, but as much a Jew as anyone in the hostile crowd standing before him. He is proud to have been born in the illustrious city of Tarsus, the capital of Cilicia. Though his birthplace is outside of Palestine, he explains that he grew up in Jerusalem and spent much of his youth there as a student of Gamaliel (5:34), a renowned Pharisaic rabbi from the school of Hillel.

Being a Pharisee, Paul devoted himself to the study of the law according to rabbinic and Pharisaic exegesis (*TDNT*, 5:619). From his acher he had learned how to observe carelly "the law of our fathers," meaning not ıly the law of Moses but the traditions that ıd developed around it (cf. Gal. 1:13–14). ıul had been "just as zealous for God" as any his listeners. He acknowledges the sincerity their devotion to God. His religious zeal pressed itself in the meticulous observance the law and Jewish traditions. Paul's devoon to Judaism is also confirmed by his scription of his background in Philippians 5–6: "circumcised on the eighth day, of the ople of Israel, of the tribe of Benjamin, a ebrew of Hebrews; in regard to the law, a ıarisee; as for zeal, persecuting the church; for legalistic righteousness, faultless."

Paul then goes on to talk about his extreme al in persecuting the church, which shows at his religious zeal exceeded that of his audiıce (vv. 4–5). He wreaked havoc on the ıurch and unrelentlessly persecuted the hristians. The persistence and horror of his rsecution of the church is seen in such words : "I persecuted the followers of this Way to eir death" (v. 4); "Saul was still breathing out urderous threats against the Lord's disciples" :1); "When they were put to death, I cast my ote against them" (26:10). Because of Paul, ome Christians had been thrown into prison ıd evidently released, but others had been ecuted.

The high priest and the entire Sanhedrin can onfirm that Paul is telling the truth. His reliious zeal prompted him to ask the high priest r letters authorizing him to bring Christians om Damascus to Jerusalem so they could be unished. At the time Paul made his request, aiaphas was the high priest, though now the gh priest is Ananias (23:2; 24:1). Though he ad been deposed, Caiaphas may have still een alive. Perhaps Paul is appealing to the resent Sanhedrin's recollection of what their redecessors had done.

The apostle then describes his conversion ıd prophetic call so that the mob will know ow he became a follower of the Lord Jesus. s he went to Damascus with credentials to tradite Christians in that city, at "about oon" he experienced a heavenly light shining ound him. This light was no delusion; it was righter than the midday sun, implying that ıis was no ordinary night vision but the ppearance of the risen Lord. The miraculous light blinded him. He fell to the ground and heard a heavenly voice speaking to him.

The conversation that follows (vv. 7–10) is identical with 9:4–5, except that Jesus here describes himself as being from "Nazareth" (2:22; 3:6; 4:10; 6:14; 26:9). The common designation of the Savior as "Jesus of Nazareth" appears only in this account of Paul's experience on the way to Damascus (cf. 26:15). By referring to Jesus in this manner Paul makes clear to the Jewish mob the precise identity of the heavenly speaker (Luke 24:19). The despised and crucified Nazarene was now alive and was the real object of Paul's persecution of the church. Jesus had been raised from the dead and is the Lord of glory. Otherwise, he could not have spoken out of heaven. To put it simply, it was God himself whom Paul was attacking.

Paul interrupts the account of his conversation with the risen Lord to describe his companions (v. 9). They saw the light, but were unable to understand the heavenly voice. His companions recognized this as an extraordinary event, but only Paul received divine revelation. They saw the bright light and heard only the sound of a voice, but they did not hear the specific words spoken. A comparison of the three accounts in Acts of Paul's conversion and call to ministry reveals slight differences (9:3–19; 26:12–18). These variations have been ascribed to traditional sources available to Luke, but Luke may have varied the accounts to maintain the interest of his readers.

Paul's conversation with the Lord continues. Paul raised a second question, "What shall I do, Lord?" (v. 10). The question indicates that his overwhelming experience had made him realize the significance of what he had been doing; he knew he had to change his way of life. His calling Jesus "Lord" meant that he had a new estimate of Jesus. He had known Jesus as only a man, but from this time on, no longer did he see Jesus as a renegade Jew or revolutionary rabbi who was rightly crucified. This same man Jesus was now his Lord.

The Lord's reply is similar to 9:7. Paul was told to go to Damascus, where he would receive additional instructions. The brilliant light of divine glory had blinded him, so his companions had to lead him by the hand into Damascus (22:11). In that city lived Ananias, a devout and law-abiding Jew, who was respected by all the Jews in that city (v. 12). As Paul tells this story to the Jewish mob, he wants them to know about Ananias's piety and obedience to the law. It was this kind of man that the Lord sent to Paul (9:12–19) and used to effect instant recovery of his sight. It was this kind of man who told the apostle that "the God of our fathers" had commissioned him to be a prophetic witness to all men (22:14–15).

The miracle of Paul's recovered sight served as a divine confirmation that the message of Ananias was from the Lord. Paul's emphasis on "the God of our fathers" as being the one who had called him stresses to his Jewish audience that his revelation through Jesus Christ is compatible with God's revelation recorded in the Old Testament. The God of Paul and other Christians is the God of Israel.

On the Damascus road Paul not only heard the voice of the Lord (cf. 26:16), but he saw "the Righteous One," a direct reference to Jesus, emphasizing the Savior's innocence (cf. 3:14; 7:52). God revealed the risen Savior to Paul, and the purpose of the revelation was to commission him to be a witness. He was summoned to faith by the living Savior and to bear witness to "the Righteous One," who died and arose for the salvation of the Jews and Gentiles.

Paul's call reminds us of earlier calls to prophetic ministry (Jer. 1:4–5; cf. Gal. 1:15–16; also Acts 26:16). This ministry required him "to know" what God wanted him to do and "to see the Righteous One" (22:14). Like the first apostles Paul was a qualified "witness" to the risen Christ (v. 15), and he proclaimed what he had heard from the mouth of the Savior. Thus, Paul was commanded to tell all people what he had seen and heard, "with all that implied that Jesus of Nazareth, crucified by men, exalted by God, was Israel's Messiah, glorified Son of God, and the Savior of mankind" (Bruce, 1952, 443).

By a miracle Paul's sight was restored. God openly declared his conversion and his prophetic call to his ministry through Ananias. Paul was filled with the Spirit (9:17). Ananias went on to assure him it was proper for him to be baptized "and wash yours sins away" (22:16). A close connection exists between water baptism and the forgiveness of sins, but the New Testament does not teach that baptism is a means by which our sins are forgiven. Paul was to submit to baptism as an outward, visible sign of his repentance and the washin away of his sins by the grace of God (see comments on 2:38).

According to 2:38, his baptism was "in th name of Jesus Christ." Here it involved als "calling on his name" in prayer. The empha sis on the Lord's name not only distinguishe Christian baptism from other baptisms, but signifies commitment to the entire paradigm c Christian discipleship. By baptism Pa declared his faith in Jesus Christ, the Righteou One, as the Messiah, and he likely acknow edged his loyalty to the Lord through prayer

Now Paul relates the third part of his expe rience (vv. 17–21). He tells about his visio in the temple at Jerusalem, which is omitted i the previous narrative (9:26–31). Just ho soon he went up to Jerusalem after his Dam ascus experience is not indicated by Luk According to Galatians 1:18 three years ha passed. When he came to the Holy City, th call to spread the gospel among the Gentile was reaffirmed. He stayed in Jerusalem onl fifteen days, during which time his rigorou debate aroused the hostility of the Grecia Jews. When the disciples learned that the Jews were seeking an opportunity to kill hin they escorted him to Caesarea and put him c a ship bound for his hometown of Tarsu (9:28–30).

Paul tells the people that before he departe from Jerusalem, he entered the temple to wo ship, and there the risen Lord made his secor appearance to him. While praying he "fell in a trance," in which Jesus spoke to him (c 10:10; 11:5). This visionary experience has a the features of a prophetic call (cf. Isa. 6:1–13 Earlier "the God of our fathers" had mediate the call through Ananias, in which Paul wa appointed to testify "to all men" (Acts 22:14 15). Now in this temple vision it was Jesus wh directed him to leave Jerusalem (v. 18) and se him to witness to the Gentiles (v. 21).

The fact that he was told *in the temple* leave the city helps to refute the charge that t apostle had spoken against the temple (21:28 He departed from Jerusalem because the Jev would reject his message. Characteristicall the unbelief of the Jews led to Paul's preac ing of the gospel to the Gentiles. It is ironic th while in the temple, the very heart of Israel religion, Paul was specially instructed preach to the Gentiles, his prophetic ministr

Paul also informs the mob that he was actu-
lly inclined to minister to his own people
/v. 19–20). He was convinced that he was the
ıan that the Jews should hear. After all, they
new his record as a former persecutor of
'hristians and his terrorist acts against the
hurch (7:54–8:3). Surely they would listen to
ıe very man who had imprisoned and beat
'hristians in the synagogues. Furthermore,
ıany remembered the part he had in the ston-
ıg of Stephen. Here Stephen is described as
martyr" (*martys*, "witness"). This word was
lready acquiring the particular meaning of a
'itness unto death (Rev. 1:5; 2:13; 3:14).
tephen had told the people in Jerusalem about
esus and as a result was put to death. Paul's
ıvolvement in that murder and other atrocities
gainst the church were common knowledge.

As a converted blasphemer and persecutor 'aul assumed that his testimony to the gospel vould carry special weight in Jerusalem, vhere he had been known as the leading oppo-ıent of the church. "But as a matter of fact their nowledge of his former record made them the nore unwilling to hear him at all" (Bruce, 952, 443). His former Jewish colleagues had trongly respected him, but now they saw him s a deserter and as a traitor to their cause. His lea with the Lord to allow him to remain in erusalem to preach the gospel to the Jews did ıot avail. Paul was Jesus' chosen prophet "to ll men," specifically "to the Gentiles.")espite Paul's reluctance to leave Jerusalem, he Lord had work for him elsewhere, among he Gentiles. The events of 9:28–30 emphasize he human circumstances that prompted him to eave the city.

). Paul's Arrest and Trials (22:22–26:32)

n 22:22–26:32, Luke describes what happens o Paul after he addresses the angry mob. Ear-ier our Lord had set his face toward Jerusalem Luke 9:51–52), and likewise the apostle had esolved to go to the city (Acts 21:12–13). 'aul knew the fate expected of God's faithful rophets in Jerusalem (Luke 9:51–53; 18:31–33). As he made his way to the city, he was ıware of the imprisonment and troubles that ay before him. Along the way he was eminded of them by the Holy Spirit at each tep: Miletus (Acts 20:22–24), Tyre (21:4), ınd Caesarea (21:11). Finally, Paul's friends conceded that his going to Jerusalem was "the Lord's will" (21:14). In Jerusalem it becomes evident that their fears are well founded. Although Paul is arrested, Luke leaves no doubt that what occurs conforms to God's plan (9:15; 19:21; 23:11).

6.1. Paul Is Arrested (22:22–29)

The mob has listened to Paul's speech; but when he mentions the burning topic of his divine call to a Gentile mission, they interrupt him and break out in a rage. They have heard him describe his conversion and speak about the crucified and risen Jesus. But because of his claim that he has been commanded by God to preach to the Gentiles, they assume all the charges made against him are justified (21:28–29). The thought of religious equality between Jews and Gentiles triggers their hostility, and they will listen to Paul no longer. He is not worthy to live. Renewing their demands that he be put to death, the mob breaks their silence with shouts, "Rid the earth of him! He is not fit to live" (v. 22).

To give vent to their rage and to add force to their demands, these people throw off their outer robes and cast dust in the air. At Lystra, Paul and Barnabas tore off their clothes when they learned that the people wanted to offer sacrifices to them (14:14). Throwing off the garments and casting dust into the air here express the mob's horror at what they consider to be blasphemy—Paul's claim that he was called by God to preach to Gentiles. The whole scene bears a striking resemblance to the violent madness of the mob that stoned Stephen (7:54). They consider Paul a blasphemer and a renegade Jew and demand that he be removed from the earth. No blasphemer is "fit to live!" Fortunately for him, there are no loose stones in the outer court of the temple.

The Roman commander does not understand the situation. Since he probably speaks neither Hebrew nor Aramaic, he is confused more than ever by Paul's speech. Even if he had understood the gist of Paul's defense, it is unlikely that he would have comprehended the real issues of the case. The violent anger of the mob has probably frightened the commander. He decides to question his prisoner in the barracks and to extract the truth from him by torture. So he instructs his soldiers to lead Paul into the barracks and, as Pilate had beaten

Jesus, orders Paul to be flogged. The truth is to be whipped out of him by a scourge, consisting of leather straps with pieces of bone and metal attached. The typical form of Roman punishment had dreadful effects on the victim's back and was much more severe than undergoing a beating from the Jews (see comments on 16:22).

As soldiers are preparing Paul for a beating, he realizes what is about to happen. According to Roman law, it was illegal to submit a Roman citizen to this kind of torture, especially before a proper trial. Aware of that, Paul lays claim to his rights as a Roman citizen. He asks the centurion in charge of the scourging: "Is it legal for you to flog a Roman citizen who hasn't even been found guilty?" (v. 25).

Paul's claim of Roman citizenship prompts a delay in the procedure. Immediately the centurion goes to the Roman commander to report to him what Paul has said. The commander knows and respects Roman law. He immediately goes to Paul and inquires about his claim to be a Roman citizen. The officer does not doubt Paul, but he sarcastically remarks that he had to pay a high sum of money for his citizenship. The implication is that the privilege of citizenship is losing its value and anyone can afford to buy the right for himself. His point is that the apostle does not look like the kind of person who could pay much. Paul must have presented "a battered and undignified spectacle" at this time (Bruce, 1952, 446). He has been dragged into the outer court of the temple and is about to be tortured. He has suffered many of the indignities that had been inflicted on his Lord.

The cost mentioned by the commander probably does not refer to an amount paid to the Roman government but to the officials of the government as a bribe. But Paul had no need to purchase citizenship, for he had been a Roman citizen from birth (v. 28). The tables are turned on the commander. In respect to citizenship the prisoner stands superior to the officer who is about to have him flogged. Purchased citizenship bows before natural citizenship.

The disclosure of Paul's citizenship promptly halts the effort to question him by torture (v. 29), and the soldier assigned to do the scourging withdraws. The commander realizes that he has put a Roman citizen in chains and is about to commit a grave violation of Roman law, and he becomes fearful. He knows that what he has already done could cost him dearly, especially if the procurator hears about it. Once again the Romans tremble before this Roman citizen (16:38). No doubt Paul's experience encouraged Luke's Christian readers who were Roman citizens to claim their rights as such.

Paul's family had obtained the distinction of Roman citizenship lawfully in one of three ways: (1) The Roman senate conferred it for meritorious service; (2) a person could receive it as an inheritance from a father who was a citizen; and (3) a person could get it as a birthright of being born in a free city, that is, a city that had rendered some special service to the empire and was rewarded by granting citizenship to all born in it.

6.2. Paul Defends Himself Before the Sanhedrin (22:30–23:10)

The Roman commander is still puzzled as to the precise charges made against Paul. He has inquired of the mob (21:33–34) and has listened to Paul's speech (22:1–21). He does recognize that Paul is unpopular with the Jews and that the accusations involve matters of the Jewish law. The officer wants to "get at the truth" (21:34; cf. 25:26–27) and determines to make one more effort to discover the precise nature of the charges.

Though the commander has been informed of Paul's Roman citizenship, he keeps him in custody over night. The next day the officer releases him from prison and has Paul brought before the Sanhedrin. It is not clear that this Roman commander has the authority to call an official meeting of this Jewish council. He may have been authorized to call such a meeting in the absence of the procurator, or the meeting may not have been official. The commander's main goal is to send some kind of report to his superior officer. What Paul did to provoke the Jews to riot is not clear to him. But if the Jewish leaders decided there are no real grounds for charges against Paul, then the officer can set him free. So he consults with the Sanhedrin to find out why the Jews have reacted so violently.

As Paul stands before the Sanhedrin, we might expect his accusers to state their case and bring charges against Paul. But they do not. Perhaps Luke wants to focus on Paul and omits the charges since we already know wha they are (21:28). The apostle shows no anxiety before the Sanhedrin, but manifests a prophetic boldness. He looks straight at his judges and begins his defense by declaring he has discharged his duty to God with a good conscience to that very moment (23:1). Paul must not be thinking of incidents of long ago, such as the murder of Stephen and other Christians, but of events of the more recent past. He is rejecting the charges of speaking against the Jewish people, the law of Moses, and the temple (21:28). With God as his witness, Paul has remained faithful to the messianic and resurrection hope that he embraced as a Pharisee. The charges brought against him have no foundation; he is innocent.

At this time Ananias was the high priest. He was appointed in A.D. 47 and removed from office in A.D. 59. At the beginning of the Jewish war against the Romans (A.D. 66–70), he was assassinated (probably by zealots) as an unscrupulous politician and supporter of Roman politics. As Paul is speaking to the Sanhedrin (about A.D. 58), Ananias interrupts him and orders those nearby to strike him. By this action the high priest protests Paul's bold claim of innocence. For the prisoner to declare that he has lived with a good conscience before God appears to him to be a lie. No doubt it is easier to have Paul struck on the mouth than to disprove what he has said.

The rude interruption and the blow anger Paul. With prophetic boldness the apostle cries out, "God will strike you, you whitewashed wall" (v. 3). This pronouncement is a prophetic curse, indicating Paul's authority as a Spirit-anointed prophet of God. To describe Ananias as a "whitewashed wall" is simply to declare that he is a hypocrite (cf. Matt. 23:27–28). His real character is hidden by generous coats of whitewash. His actions disclose his hypocrisy and reveal that his loyalty to the law is only an outward show. As high priest Ananias should have dispensed justice according to the law, but he has violated biblical prescriptions for impartial judgment by his harsh treatment of Paul (Lev. 19:15; Deut. 1:16–17). The apostle denounces this man's superficial sanctity in the name of God (cf. Acts 13:10).

Members of the council are alarmed when they hear Paul pronounce a curse on the high priest. As they understand it, this man has been appointed by God to his office. They ask how Paul dares to insult this chosen servant of God (v. 4). He replies that he did not know that he was speaking to the high priest. His failure to recognize the high priest has been explained as the result of supposed bad eyesight, the high priest's not wearing his distinctive dress, or Paul's unawareness that Ananias was now the high priest.

Paul's reply is probably spoken with sarcasm (v. 5). He does not mean that he is ignorant of pronouncing judgment on the high priest, but sarcastically he reminds Ananias that his conduct is unworthy of his office. Never would the apostle insult him if Ananias behaved himself as a high priest. This man wants to appear as a devout observer of the law, but he breaks the law by having an uncondemned man hit in the face. The behavior of Ananias fails to reflect the true character of a high priest, and Paul refuses to show him the respect due to a true high priest.

Paul knows that the Scripture teaches the importance of respect for the leaders of Israel, for he quotes Exodus 22:28: "Do not speak evil about the ruler of your people." In contrast to Ananias's disobedience to the law, Paul expresses his willingness to live by it. The apostle would have shown respect for any high priest who executed his office properly. To have denounced a high priest who was upright would be tantamount to blasphemy (*NIDNTT*, 3:347). But giving the order to strike Paul was out of character for a high priest. It makes Ananias unrecognizable as the high priest and shows that Paul is not likely to receive justice.

The Sanhedrin is made up of both Sadducees and Pharisees (see comments on 4:1). The Sadducees were the priestly aristocracy and in theology were the more conservative, accepting only the Pentateuch. Politically they were aligned with Rome. On the other hand, the Pharisees were silent opponents of Rome and were the theological progressives. They accepted the scribal interpretation of the Law and saw the Prophets as authoritative as the Pentateuch. They believed in the resurrection of the dead, while the Sadducees did not.

Although Paul introduces the general concept of resurrection in this Sanhedrin meeting, the real issue is the resurrection of Jesus. In Acts 4:1–2 the Sadducees objected to the apostles' proclaiming that the resurrection had begun with Jesus' triumph over death. The fundamental beliefs of the Christians have a close link to the theology of the Pharisees. True, the Pharisees' legalistic understanding of the law was different from the Christian understanding of the law. Not denying these differences, there were similarities in Pharisaic belief in the resurrection and God's promises to Israel that find their fulfillment in the risen Messiah.

Paul perceives some of the Sanhedrin members are Sadducees and others are Pharisees. He knows about the ill-feeling that exists between the two parties and the party feuds that characterize the council's deliberations. Aware that he is not likely to get a fair trial before this body, Paul declares that he is a Pharisee and that he believes a central doctrine of Pharisaism—the doctrine of the resurrection of the dead (v. 6). It is for his confident and patient expectation that people will rise from the dead, Paul points out, that he is on trial.

Paul's hope of the resurrection was not the immediate cause of his arrest, of course (see 21:27–29), but this hope was the ultimate ground for the Sadducees' hatred of the apostle. His aim here is to enlist the sympathy of the Pharisees and to defend himself on the basis of his belief in the resurrection. The Pharisaic expectation of the resurrection had prepared him to believe in the risen Savior. Paul remains a Pharisee because he has found fulfillment of the messianic hope of resurrection in the resurrection of Jesus. The Savior's victory over death is the central doctrine of his apostolic gospel and has strong implications for the resurrection of humankind (13:30, 34; 1 Cor. 15; cf. Acts 2:32; 3:15; 4:10).

Paul testifies boldly that he is still a Pharisee with a Pharisaic heritage. He speaks of himself not as "a son of a Pharisee" (NIV) but "of Pharisees" (*Pharisaion*), meaning that both of his parents were pharisaically inclined. (Women, of course, were not allowed as members of the Pharisees.) The Sanhedrin knows that Paul is a Christian, but he still regards himself as both a Jew (22:3) and a Pharisee. As he admits elsewhere, however, his Pharisaic past no longer has real significance for him. He is prepared to count it as useless for Christ's sake (Phil. 3:7).

Paul's claim to be a Pharisee provokes controversy within the council (v. 7). He stands with the Pharisees in their points of antagonism with the Sadducees. As a result, the Pharisees in the meeting quickly turn in favor of th apostle. The dispute that breaks out betwee the two parties produces schism. The Roma commander has called together the council t learn why they have demanded Paul's death But now the council finds itself in an awkwar position, being divided and in an uproar.

For the benefit of his readers Luke describe the Sadducees as skeptics who are rationalisti and worldly in their outlook; they "say tha there is no resurrection, and that there are nei ther angels nor spirits, but the Pharisee acknowledge them all" (v. 8). It is uncertai what the reference to "angels" and "spirits" means. "Angels" appear in the Pentateuch which the Sadducees embrace as authoritativ Scripture; "spirits" cannot include the Spirit o God (also in the Pentateuch). The Pharisee may have argued that the resurrection occurs i a spiritual body similar to an angel or pur spirit, assuming, therefore, that "angels" an "spirits" are synonyms. Since the Sadducee reject the hope of the resurrection, they natu rally also deny the possibility of a post resurrection existence in either of these form (Marshall, 1980, 365). Though the Phariseee do not endorse Paul's understanding of Jesus resurrection, they are more tolerant of the Chris tians than are the Sadducees (cf. 5:34–40).

As the debate in the Sanhedrin unfolds, th lines are sharply drawn between the Pharisee and Sadducees. The Pharisees come short o recognizing Jesus as the risen Messiah, bu some of them vigorously support Paul. The insist that this man has done no wrong o which he can be condemned and defend hin on the basis that a spirit or an angel may hav spoken to him (v. 9; cf. 27:23; also 13:2; 16:6 21:11). Since the Sadducees believe in neithe this comment only adds to the commotion an clash of opinion. The meeting breaks up in violent dispute, and bedlam almost become a scene of lynching. The Roman commande realizes that Paul's life is in grave danger an that he is about to be torn apart limb by limb To rescue him from the fury of the Sanhedrin the officer orders his soldiers to take him b force back to the barracks.

Again the commander is disappointed. Hi efforts to learn the truth about Paul's case hav been unfruitful. Little progress has been mad toward helping the officer understand th charges against the apostle.

6.3. The Lord Encourages Paul (23:11)

At critical times in Paul's ministry he receives divine guidance through visions (9:5; 18:9; 22:17–18). Such an occasion occurs on the night following Paul's deliverance from the hands of the Sanhedrin by the Roman soldiers. After the stress and strain of the last two days, the risen Lord appears to him and reaffirms him as a witness. Earlier Paul had expressed his desire to preach the gospel in Rome (19:21; Rom. 1:11–13). Now the exalted Lord assures him that as he has testified of his Lord in Jerusalem, the center of Judaism, so will he preach in Rome.

This prophecy of the risen Lord serves as programmatic until Paul stands before Caesar in Rome. What happens in the next few years follows the divine plan. The words "take courage" look to the events to follow: Paul will encounter every kind of danger, opposition, oppression, and affliction on his journey to Rome and during his stay in the city. Because of what he has already suffered—arrest in Jerusalem, the threat of death and scourging, and rejection by the members of the Sanhedrin—he needs encouragement now. The vision must have given him new courage for the present and future. In the Lord's own way and time, he will escape this present danger and preach the gospel in the capital of the Roman empire.

6.4. Conspiracy to Murder Paul (23:12–22)

Though Paul's vision of the risen Lord encouraged him, the next morning it becomes clear that he should expect to receive no justice from the hands of the Jews. A group of Jewish fanatics plan to murder Paul. Luke does not identify them. They are not members of the priesthood or of the Sanhedrin, but they have the disposition of zealots who are inclined to resort to violence to achieve their ends. These conspirators may have belonged to the secret society of terrorists known as the Sicarii (cf. comments on 21:37–38).

The hatred of this group for Paul prompts them to take a common vow against his life. They pledge to abstain from food and drink until they have killed him. This group, including over forty conspirators, put themselves under a divine curse or voluntarily declare their lives forfeited if they fail to put forth every effort to fulfill their vow (*TDNT*, 1:355). Fortunately for these fanatics, the Mishnah made it possible to be released from such vows. Thus, it is not likely that these people died of starvation or thirst because of their failure to destroy Paul.

After taking the solemn vow, the conspirators appeal to the chief priests and elders to help them to carry out their plot. On the previous day the Sadducees in the council had been enraged at Paul (vv. 6–10). Therefore, unscrupulous members of the Sanhedrin are ready to join the religious fanatics in their effort to murder Paul. Their scheme is to request of the Roman commander that the council wishes to secure more information from Paul so that they may come to a more informed decision about his case. Under this pretext the plotters will get Paul out of the fortress of Antonia. As Paul is being led to the council by unsuspecting soldiers, the group of more than forty conspirators will ambush and murder the apostle.

This conspiracy is known by too many people. News about it leaks out, and it reaches the ears of Paul's nephew who, for some unknown reason, is in Jerusalem. This reference to Paul's family is the only one made by Luke. The presence of Paul's sister and her son may suggest that they lived in Jerusalem, but they may have been among those who had come there to celebrate the Feast of Pentecost. When the young man hears what the conspirators are planning, he goes directly to Paul and tells him the story (v. 16). Paul wants the commander to know about the plot and asks one of the centurions to take the boy to the commander so that he may know the urgency of the situation. Paul's abrupt instructions to the centurion may indicate that he has the favor of the commander.

Immediately the centurion takes the young man to his superior. Showing him kind consideration, the officer takes the lad's hand and leads him aside. In private the Roman inquires what Paul's nephew has to tell him. His message is essentially the same as is already known about the plot. He speaks of the conspirators as "the Jews," meaning a group of fanatics and the Sanhedrin. We also learn that they intend to execute their plan the following day (v. 20). The plotters have no intention of fasting for a long period. Before the boy is dismissed, he urges the commander to refuse the request to hand over Paul to the Jews, and he makes it clear that the officer should do whatever is necessary to ensure Paul's safety. His opponents are ready to kill him and are only waiting for the commander to grant their request (v. 21).

The plot is aborted through the efforts of the young informant and the commander (v. 22). The Roman commander believes what he has been told and decides that the proper course of action is to refer Paul's case to his superior officer. He lacks the judicial authority to handle it himself. But desiring that the conspirators not know what he is about to do, he sends the lad away with the charge: "Don't tell anyone that you have reported this to me." Furthermore, if the young man were to breathe a word about it, he could lose his own life.

6.5. Paul Is Transferred From Jerusalem to Caesarea (23:23–26:32)

Having received the information from Paul's nephew, the commander tries to protect Paul and avoid bloodshed. Promptly he prepares to send his prisoner to Caesarea, the headquarters of Roman authority in Palestine. As a Roman soldier he does not have authority to deal judicially with prisoners once he has restored order, but he chooses a course of action that is both just and prudent. To avoid risking the life of an uncondemned Roman citizen in his custody, the officer is willing to deploy half the city's garrison to protect Paul.

The commander's instructions to the two centurions reflect that he wants every precaution taken to foil the plot and to prevent Paul from falling into the hands of the Jewish fanatics. The centurions arrange for 470 soldiers on foot and on horses. The troops are to be ready to march by 9:00 P.M. so that their departure from Jerusalem will be under cover of darkness. Such a large bodyguard may be due to the riot that occurred in the temple (21:35) or the number of conspirators (23:13). Sending a formidable body of armed guards will ensure Paul's safety even if his departure is discovered by the Jews. No doubt the Roman commander is greatly relieved when Paul arrives safely in Caesarea.

6.5.1. Paul and Felix (23:23–24:27). The apostle is to be transferred to the custody of the governor of Judea (v. 24). At this time he is Antonius Felix (A.D. 52–59), who holds the same position that Pontius Pilate held in A.D. 26–36. He is portrayed by the Roman historian Tacitus as arrogant and corrupt (*Annals* 12.54 *Histories* 5.9). Emperor Nero relieved him of his duties in Judea because of well-founded complaints from the Jews about mismanagement and injustices. Because of Felix's cruelty corruption, and lust, Tacitus summed up his character in a single biting comment: He exercised the power of a king with the mind of a slave. Until Felix was set free, he had been a slave of Antonia, the mother of Emperor Claudius. Evidently he never rose above his lowly origins.

6.5.1.1. Accompanying Letter Addressed to Felix (23:23–30). A formal letter addressed to Felix accompanies Paul to Caesarea, written by the Roman commander Claudius Lysias. For the first time the officer is identified by name. The form of the letter reflects the characteristic letter form in the first century. In it Lysias explains to Felix why he has sent the prisoner to him. The officer wants the governor to understand what led to this action and includes the important elements of the story:

- He puts the blame squarely on the Jews for the hostile action against Paul.
- The officer rescued Paul because he was a Roman citizen. Here Lysias bends the truth slightly; strictly speaking, he did not recognize Paul to be a Roman citizen until he was about to have him scourged. No doubt this is an accurate report of what Lysias wrote, but this small embellishment makes Lysias look good and is typical of bureaucratic correspondence.
- Lysias followed proper procedure in trying to determine the nature of the charges against this Roman citizen. Thus, he brought the prisoner before the Sanhedrin so that his accusers could face him directly. The Jewish proceedings resulted in a violent uproar.
- Lysias discovered that the charges against Paul brought by the Jews were due to theological differences that centered around their law. (At first Paul was charged with bringing a Gentile into the temple [21:28] but the Asian Jews who made this charge have disappeared from the narrative [cf 24:18–21]. The actual charges before the

Sanhedrin had to do with Paul's teachings on the resurrection, angels, and spirits [23:6–9].)

- The commander categorically declares Paul's innocence in regard to any capital offense. He has done nothing that makes him deserve to be thrown into prison or be put to death. Convinced that Paul had committed no political crime, the Roman would have soon released him if it had not been for the plot of the Jews.
- News of that plot prompted him to send Paul to the governor so that the case can be settled properly. The accusers had been informed by Lysias that if the Jews wish to press charges against Paul, they can best present them to the governor (v. 30) and settle them once and for all in a court of law.

6.5.1.2. Paul Is Transferred to Felix's Custody (23:31–35). The commander's instructions are carried out as outlined in verses 23–24. The military escort with Paul departs from Jerusalem by night and arrives the following morning at Antipatris, a town about thirty-five miles northwest of Jerusalem. It was named after the father of Herod the Great, Antipater, and was more than halfway to Caesarea. Luke leaves the impression that the distance of thirty-five miles is covered overnight. This distance would be difficult for foot soldiers to

Paul was taken to Caesarea when a plot to kill him was discovered. Paul had been arrested on a claim that his teachings violated Jewish law. Built by Herod the Great, Caesarea was a major Mediterranean seaport. Part of the aqueduct is from Herod's time, as is the theater. The fortress on the harbor was built later.

accomplish in a night's march. The normal day's march for a group of soldiers was twenty-four miles. But in a rapid forced march and in the cool of the night the troops could possibly cover more distance.

Of course, we may not have all of the details of the journey. Possibly after the troops were beyond the danger of attack, the foot soldiers turned back, leaving the cavalry to complete the journey. The danger from the plotters was most acute in and near Jerusalem. Once they were beyond that threat, the full force would not have been needed. Seventy horsemen would be sufficient escort the rest of the way to Caesarea.

In any case, the infantry eventually does turn back and return to Jerusalem. From Antipatris the escort travels by the way of the coastal plain. This part of the journey is not as hazardous, and Paul is only lightly protected at this time. Paul arrives safely in Caesarea and is delivered into the hands of Felix by the cavalry (v. 33). After the governor reads the letter, he has the prisoner brought before him for preliminary questioning.

During the brief interrogation Felix asks Paul about his home province. This question may have been prompted by Felix's curiosity, but most likely he intends to send the prisoner to the governor of that province for trial. In that way he can rid himself of the responsibility of dealing with this difficult case. But Felix does not choose this course of action. When he learns that the apostle is from Cilicia, he decides to hear the case himself. If he decided otherwise, then "not only would it have caused bad relations with the Jews (who would have had to travel to Cilicia to make charges), but also Cilicia at this time was not a full province. It was part of Syria and came under the jurisdiction of the legate of Syria, who would not want to be bothered with minor offences" (Marshall, 1980, 373).

Felix has no way to avoid his duty without offending others. So he promises to hear Paul's case upon the arrival of his accusers. In the meantime he confines Paul to the palace built by Herod the Great, but now used for the governor's headquarters. Paul is kept in the palace with soldiers guarding him. Felix has carefully followed Roman protocol.

6.5.1.3. Paul Is Accused Before Felix (24:1–9). Though the Jews are unsuccessful in carrying out their plot, they still hope to secure Paul's death. Five days after Paul's arrival, a delegation of the Sanhedrin, led by the high priest Ananias, arrives in Caesarea to present their case against Paul. They are represented by a lawyer named Tertullus. This man is an attorney who knows both Roman and Jewish law. He may have been a Jew who had lived abroad and had taken a Roman name. Note how he identifies himself with his clients by using the pronouns "we" and "us" (vv. 2, 3, 4)—either because he is a Jew or simply because he is their attorney. The Jewish delegation needs the services of a man like Tertullus. They are now in a Roman court, and they must have someone familiar with the proceedings of such a court to represent them.

The proceedings against Paul remind us much of our modern courts. The apostle is brought into court. A formal statement of the charges is made by the prosecuting attorney, Tertullus (vv. 2–8). His statement is followed by an equally formal response from Paul (vv. 10–21). Luke's report of Tertullus's speech is brief. Like other speeches and sermons recorded in Acts, we have only a summary of what is said.

Acting in behalf of Paul's accusers, Tertullus begins his speech in the customary way of addressing government officials. His introductory remarks make up almost half of his speech and are nothing but pure flattery, designed to win the favor of Felix. By devoting a large part of his speech to flattery, the prosecutor hints that the Jews really have a weak case against Paul. Tertullus praises the governor for suppressing terrorism and establishing peace. Ironically, Felix's administration had been marked by unrest rather than peace and major reforms. Living conditions had not improved under his leadership, and the relationship between the Jews and Rome continued to deteriorate. No doubt Luke's readers, who know of Felix's incompetence and scandalous reputation, recognize Tertullus's opening words for what they are.

After the ingratiating introduction, Tertullus states the Jews' charges against Paul. He tries to denigrate the apostle on three counts. (1) Paul is "a troublemaker," that is, a messianic revolutionary, who excites the Jews in many places to insurrection. He is portrayed as the cause of unrest and riots not only in Palestine but beyond. This accusation makes Paul responsible for dissensions and uprisings throughout the Roman world among the Jews. Tertullus implies that Paul is like the Egyptian revolutionary who led four thousand terrorists (21:38)—note that it was Felix who had put this Egyptian down. Paul is, in other words, a threat to Roman stability and peace.

(2) Paul is the "ringleader of the Nazarene sect." This charge has broad religious implications. It depicts Paul as the leader of a new and, therefore, illegal religion. The apostle had been in the vanguard of the Christian movement, preaching the gospel everywhere he went. Even now he is in prison for spreading what Tertullus describes as "the Nazarene sect." In no other place in the New Testament are the followers of Jesus called Nazarenes. The Jews referred to Jesus as the "Nazarene," seeking to discredit his claim of being the Messiah. It was a widely held view that nothing good could come out of the lowly village of Nazareth (cf. John 1:46). So with similar contempt, Tertullus designates the Christian movement as "the Nazarene sect."

(3) The first two charges have been general, but now Tertullus makes a specific charge: Paul has attempted to desecrate the temple. The reference here is to the rumor that Paul had brought the Gentile Trophimus into the sacred court of the Israelites (21:28–29). That is, Paul had tried to make unholy the center of Jewish piety and the symbol of the nation. Tertullus here tries to provide a concrete example to show that Paul is a Jewish renegade who is insensitive to the customs and practices of a well-established religion. As the charge stands, the Jews "seized him" in order to prevent the profaning of the temple (v. 6). What Tertullus does not say is that the Jews were ready to lynch their enemy.

The NIV omits verse 7, but some editors and commentators think that it is part of the authentic text. This verse explains the situation in greater detail, indicating that Tertullus lays the blame for violence on the Roman commander, Lysias. The reader can infer this from the context, and the manuscript evidence is not strong for including verse 7. The inclusion of the verse, however, is in keeping with the Jews' desire to present themselves in a good light.

Tertullus closes his speech with an appeal to Felix to examine the evidence (v. 8). The governor is assured that an examination of the prisoner will prove the truth of the charges. The delegation of the Jews join in and support the charges against Paul by affirming that they are true (v. 9). The hearing of the case does not seem to involve the formal calling of witnesses for the plaintiff. The Jews have no solid evidence on which to base their case against Paul. The three charges have strong religious and theological overtones, but they are calculated to make Paul appear to the governor as a political agitator and a danger to civil order and peace.

6.5.1.4. Paul Defends Himself Before Felix (24:10–22). The apostle conducts his own defense. Point by point he intends to convince Felix that he himself is innocent of all political charges and that the real issue between him and the Jews is theological, centering around the doctrine of the resurrection (vv. 20–21). Paul limits his remarks to his conduct in Jerusalem, noting that he came to the city as a devout pilgrim to worship God. His defense is carefully crafted, but he has had no previous notification of the charges so that he may prepare a defense against the accusations. In this crisis and similar ones the Spirit-inspired apostle finds that Jesus' words are fulfilled in himself: "For I will give you words and wisdom that none of your adversaries will be able to resist or contradict" (Luke 21:15). On this promise he relies.

With the nod of his head Felix invites Paul to speak for himself (v. 10). In sharp contrast to the flattering introduction of Tertullus (vv. 2–4), Paul simply recognizes that Felix has had several years of experience in Jewish matters as governor of Judea. In Judea the governor has had to deal with seditions and insurrections. So the apostle is glad to appear before one who is well acquainted with Judea and its problems.

In his reply to the charges Paul observes that he had been in Jerusalem a total of twelve days, several of which have been spent in Roman custody. He had not had time to stir up sedition and insurrection, at least not in Jerusalem. He would not have had sufficient time to plot against the government, and therefore he denies any responsibility as a troublemaker. His purpose for going to Jerusalem was for lawful business: to worship God (v. 11) and to deliver the money collected from Gentile churches for needy believers in the city (v. 17). While he was in Jerusalem, he did not engage in arguments with anyone in the temple, in the synagogues, or in any place in the city (v. 12). None of his accusers can prove that he disrupted the peace. On this particular visit to Jerusalem he did not preach to or evangelize anyone.

Paul gladly identifies himself as a worshiper of the God of his fathers according to "the Way," which his enemies contemptuously call "a sect" (v. 14), but he does not identify himself as its ringleader (cf. v. 5). "The Way" is used in a technical sense to describe the Christian movement (cf. 9:2; 18:25–26; 19:9, 23; 22:4; 24:22), but it echoes the Old Testament expectation for the true people of God to walk in the way of obedience (cf. Ex. 32:8; Deut. 5:33; 9:12, 16). As a Christian he believes that he rightly worships the God of Israel. For him there is an essential unity between the Old Testament message and the Christian faith. The Law and the Prophets find their fulfillment in the message of the gospel (Luke 24:44). His loyalty to the entire Scripture remains firm, as is demonstrated in his exchange with Ananias (23:1–5).

Believing the Law and the Prophets, like the Pharisees, he has hope in the resurrection and the judgment of "both the righteous and wicked" (v. 15). By implication he aligns himself again with the Pharisees against the Sadducees (23:8; cf. Luke 20:27–40). Because of his hope for the resurrection, he strives to have a blameless conscience before God and humankind. The biblical doctrine of resurrection not only includes the hope of final transformation, renewal, and blessedness, but also the expectation of judgment. In Scripture judgment is bound up with resurrection (Matt. 25:31–46; John 5:28–39; Rev. 20:12), at which time the righteous will be rewarded and the wicked punished. Paul endeavors "to keep [his] conscience clear," that is, to have a conscience that does not condemn him. He lives a circumspect life in the presence of God. He therefore has a clear conscience regarding the charge of being a political troublemaker.

As Paul continues his defense, he mentions that a number of years have lapsed since he visited Jerusalem (cf. 15:1–29). At this point Paul speaks of "gifts for the poor" (v. 17). He brought a substantial sum of money to Jerusalem for the poor Christians, collected from the Gentile churches as a token of their love and as an expression of the church's unity (Rom. 15:25–26; 1 Cor. 16:1–4; 2 Cor. 8–9)—this is the only reference to the collection in Acts. This collection is a donation to "my people" (*to ethnos mou*, "my nation"), which can mean a gift to the Jews generally. The reference, however, must be not to funds for the nation generally but to the relief fund for the poor Christians in Jerusalem. In other words, Paul did not come to the city to cause riots; he was not a rabble-rouser and had no desire to act irresponsibly and overturn the beliefs of his ancestors.

While he was in Jerusalem, he also presented "offerings" (v. 17), referring to his payment of expenses for four men so that they could complete their Nazirite vow by offering appropriate sacrifices (21:23–26). On that occasion the Asian Jews found him in the temple after he had completed the ritual of purification to avoid defiling the Holy Place (vv. 18–19). Paul mentions this incident to refute the final charge of profaning the temple (v. 6; cf. 21:28). When the Jews from Asia came upon him, he was ceremonially pure (v. 18). Contrary to his opponents' allegation that he had defiled the temple, they found him in a holy state. He was quietly attending the ritual of purification and was not gathering people around him or causing a disturbance. The clear implication is that Jews from Asia were the real disturbers of the peace.

Certain Asian Jews had claimed to be eyewitnesses to Paul's supposed crime. They are the only ones who claim to be witnesses to his desecrating the temple. But these Asian Jews are not even in court today to testify to what they saw. Paul's conclusion, therefore, is that they have no case against him (v. 19). Otherwise, they would be present.

In fact, no one has any evidence that Paul has committed a crime. Even Ananias and his delegation did not find him guilty of any criminal charge. When he appeared before the high priest in the Sanhedrin, the only thing he was guilty of was shouting out, "It is concerning the resurrection of the dead that I am on trial before you today" (v. 21). That was no crime, though it did involve a point of doctrine and created confusion in the Sanhedrin. Ananias and his Sadducean friends resented the Pharisaic confession of belief in the resurrection. The result was a fierce quarrel between the Sadducees and Pharisees. Different Jewish groups had different convictions about the hope of the resurrection.

In other words, at the heart of the dispute between Paul and the Jews is the conflict over the interpretation of Scripture (vv. 14–15). It is a debate over theology, with the focus on the resurrection. Why, therefore, should Paul be judged on a doctrinal matter over which the Sanhedrin itself is divided? It is outside of Roman authority to deal with theological issues and to condemn a man for heresy. Paul's reference to the resurrection stresses a vital link between Judaism and Christianity. By believing that the dead will rise, the Pharisees are just a short step from the central Christian doctrine—the resurrection of Jesus. His triumph over death demonstrates that he is the Messiah and Savior of Israel and the fulfillment of the prophetic promises of the Old Testament (v. 14).

6.5.1.5. Paul Is Detained in Custody (24:23–27). Felix defers Paul's case and makes no formal decision. That decision is not uninformed; he is "well acquainted with the Way" and is not deceived by Ananias and his delegation. He has heard nothing that would indicate the apostle is a criminal. The charges against him could have been dismissed, but to avoid annoying the Jews (cf. v. 27) Felix postpones his judgment.

The motives ascribed to his adjourning the proceedings without a decision are twofold. (1) He has an accurate understanding of the Christian movement. How he acquired this information is uncertain. His wife Drusilla may have been his source, but the governor has been in Judea long enough to learn the religious parties into which his subjects are divided and to know what Christians believe. As Luke's account stands here, Felix's decision suggests that he is acting out of sympathy for the Christians and does not want the Jews to mistreat them. He seems to be sympathetic toward Christians, though his later behavior reveals that he is unwilling to treat them justly if there is the danger of repercussion from the Jewish authorities (v. 27).

(2) Felix wants to confer with Lysias, the commander who sent Paul to him, before he makes a decision. It may have been his genuine intent to get more details about the case, but we have no evidence that the governor sent for Lysias or sought his advice.

The decision to postpone the case implies that Felix is convinced of Paul's innocence. But he does not release him, as he should have. He does, however, treat him as a Roman citizen who has not yet been proved guilty of a crime. As a prisoner Paul enjoys a measure of freedom. He is allowed to receive visitors and medical attention. The Christians who live in Caesarea and elsewhere can visit him and bring him food, letters, and writing materials. This humane treatment reveals where Felix's sympathies are.

Apparently after the adjournment of Paul's trial, Felix leaves Caesarea. When he returns, he brings his Jewish wife Drusilla to the city. She was the youngest daughter of Herod Agrippa I (cf. 12:18–23), who at the age of fourteen had married Aziz, king of the small Syrian state of Emesa. Two years later she was induced by Felix to abandon her first husband.

The governor brings Paul from prison so that he and Drusilla can listen to this Christian missionary speak about what it means to believe in Christ (v. 24). Paul had been the defender, but now he becomes the preacher. At the invitation to speak "about faith in Jesus Christ," Paul chooses topics for his message that have direct reference to the spiritual condition of Felix and Drusilla. He never compromises the gospel before those who have power to set him free. His message is exactly what the couple need to hear—the moral demands of the gospel with the focus on "righteousness, self-control and the judgment to come" (v. 25).

"Righteousness" requires that everyone be treated justly, but Felix's administration had been marked by injustice. He had been a cruel, tyrannical, unjust ruler. He had not practiced "self-control," but had given himself to unbridled lust. He had become enamored with Drusilla's beauty, and their marriage was the result of his enticing her away from her first husband. Along with all who fail to repent, Felix will stand under condemnation in "the judgment to come" for his failure to administer justice, for his love of money, and for his uncontrolled passions.

The governor has enough conscience left that the moral demands of the gospel strike fear in his heart. The truth reveals his guilt, but even though he is deeply disturbed by Paul's message, he does not repent and turn from his evil ways of injustice, greed, treachery, ungodly passions, and bloodshed. Felix is terrified at the prospect of judgment, but he smothers his conscience and fails to believe the gospel that offers the forgiveness of sins.

How genuine is Felix's interest in the gospel? It is difficult to say, but he does not manifest a deeply spiritual interest, especially in light of his subsequent conduct of hoping to receive a bribe from Paul (v. 26) and of wanting to grant a favor to the Jews (v. 27). The governor probably had only a superficial interest in the "strange teachings" of the Christians (Marshall, 1980, 381). But the message he and Drusilla have heard is far from superficial. It has been a stirring message; he wants no more of it at the present time. So with haste, he sends Paul away, explaining that he will find time to send for him again.

Felix continues to have frequent interviews with Paul, but they are not due to a genuine interest in the Christian faith. Rather, he hopes that Paul will take the hint and offer him a bribe for his release (v. 26). At his trial Paul had reported that he had brought money from the Gentiles to the poor Christians in Jerusalem and paid purification expenses for four men. Felix hopes that the bold preacher will raise a large sum of money for his release from prison. He assumes that either Paul has funds or can get them from his friends or relatives. Roman law prohibited bribery, but it was not uncommon for officials of government to receive bribes anyway. Paul will take no part in such a crime.

Paul spends two years in prison at Caesarea (v. 27). Festus succeeds Felix as the new governor of Judea. During those two years, Paul remains a prisoner because Felix wants to win the favor of the Jews and so maintain his position as governor. To avoid antagonizing them further, he is willing to sacrifice an innocent man. But he does not succeed in his effort. When he eventually does return to Rome, Emperor Nero replaces him with Festus.

6.5.2. Paul and Festus (25:1–26:32). Luke has shown that Paul is innocent of any serious charges. The next phase of the proceeding takes place before Porcius Festus, the successor of Felix. This man was appointed by Nero, probably about A.D. 59. As a desirable contrast to his predecessor, Festus was a wise and just governor. He died in office in A.D. 62.

Paul's fortunes remain unchanged before Festus. There is, however, an interesting contrast in regard to the characters. Felix had had little to say, and Paul had spoken on his own behalf. But now in the proceedings before Festus, Paul is more in the background, and the Roman governor speaks and acts in his behalf.

We have noted many parallels between Jesus and Paul, but these parallels reach their high point in the proceedings recorded in Acts 25–26. The resemblances are striking between Jesus' appearance before Pilate and Herod Antipas (Luke 23:1–25) and Paul's appearance before Festus and Agrippa II. Like his Savior, the Spirit-filled apostle is declared by the Roman governor as having "done nothing deserving of death" (Acts 25:25; cf. Luke 23:13–15). Agrippa desires to hear Paul (Acts 25:22), just as Herod Antipas had wanted to see Jesus (Luke 23:8). So Paul comes before governors and kings, just as his Lord did.

6.5.2.1. Jews Renew Charges Against Paul (25:1–5). When Festus becomes governor of Judea, he immediately goes up to Jerusalem. On the third day after he takes up his duties, he decides to visit the city, coming from Caesarea, the seat of the civil government. This visit is a courtesy visit to the religious center of the Jews, though Festus must know that there had not been the best relations between Felix and the people in Jerusalem. No doubt the new governor wants to meet the Jewish leaders and learn from them matters that need his attention.

Members of the Sanhedrin take advantage of the occasion to inform Festus of their charges against Paul (v. 2). His long imprisonment has not moderated in the least their hatred of the apostle. Being as determined as ever to destroy him, they renew their charges to Festus. They appeal to him to press the case against the apostle. The Jewish leaders do not simply ask, but they "urgently request" Festus to bring Paul to Jerusalem for trial (v. 3).

As Paul's archenemies suggest, if their request is granted, it would be a special favor or kindness to them. But a trial in Jerusalem among Paul's enemies would not be in his favor. Either at Caesarea or at Jerusalem the apostle could have been tried in a Roman court, though perhaps the Jewish leaders entertain the possibility of the trial before the Sanhedrin without Festus having any role at all. The real intent of their request for the transfer of the prisoner, of course, is so that they will have an opportunity to kill him on the way to Jerusalem.

Earlier, more than forty men had plotted to take Paul's life (23:12–15), and now his enemies hope they will have another opportunity to carry out their plan. Of course, Festus knows nothing about the plan to ambush Paul, but the governor refuses to be taken in by the Jews. Paul remains a prisoner in Caesarea, and the governor insists that the trial must take place here. So in a polite way he refuses their request and tells them that they must fit their plans to his.

But since the chief priests and Jewish leaders have left the impression that they want to bring the trial to conclusion as quickly as possible, the governor invites the Jewish leaders to accompany him to Caesarea (v. 5). "Your leaders" (*hoi en hymin dunatoi*) literally means "men of power among you." It may suggest the ability for debate as well as the power to act as representatives of the Sanhedrin. Such a delegation can state their charges against the prisoner in a public and formal way.

6.5.2.2. Paul Defends Himself Before Festus (25:6–12). Festus remains in Jerusalem for only eight or ten days and then returns to Caesarea (v. 6). Without delay he makes arrangements for the trial. The following day Paul is brought before Festus. When he appears in the courtroom, his accusers lodge "many serious charges against him" (v. 7), but because the case is two years old, it is difficult, if not impossible, to secure eyewitnesses to support any specific accusations. Thus, the delegation from Jerusalem has to be satisfied with generalities.

On this occasion the accusers do not have a lawyer to speak in behalf of them as Tertullus had in Paul's trial before Felix (24:1–22). By his brief statement Tertullus had made the best of a bad case. Before Festus, Paul's enemies succeed in making the charges sound very serious, but they cannot support them with any real evidence (v. 7). This lack of evidence shows the folly of Paul's accusers and the extent to which they will go in trying to accomplish their ends. Luke does not state what the "serious charges" are, but in light of Paul's defense, they are similar to the old charges made by Tertullus before Felix, only stated more forcefully.

As the defendant Paul pleads "not guilty" to every one of the charges lodged against him (v. 8). (1) He has done nothing against the law of the Jews (24:14–16; cf. 21:21; 23:5). There is no ground on which to accuse him of heresy. He is a Pharisee, faithful to his Pharisaic heritage, especially his belief in the risen Messiah (23:6; 26:4–23). (2) He has not profaned the temple (21:28; 24:7, 18). He has done nothing to violate the sanctity of that place of worship. (3) He denies committing any offense "against Caesar" (cf. 16:21). Originally "Caesar" was a proper name, but later it was used as a title for the Roman emperor. As a theological concept in the New Testament, it refers to the legitimate power of political authority (*NIDNTT*, 1:269).

This last charge is a new formulation of 24:5, where Paul was accused of being a "troublemaker, stirring up riots among the Jews all over the world." Charges of sedition against the emperor and Rome have serious political implications. Paul has preached Jesus as the Messiah. This message could be understood by Festus as a threat to peace and to allegiance to Caesar. Even so, the apostle is so confident that he is not guilty of causing rebellion against Rome that he eventually appeals his case to Caesar (v. 11). The Jews make allegations, but they fail to show that what they say about Paul is true.

After Festus has heard both sides, he should have released his prisoner unconditionally. But like his predecessor (24:27), he sees Paul's case as an opportunity to gain the favor of the Jews. At this point, the case takes a new turn. Festus, as a newcomer to Judea, wants to ingratiate himself with the Jews, and he is perplexed as to how to deal with these charges, which are of a religious nature (cf. v. 20). Thus, he asks Paul whether he is willing to stand trial in Jerusalem (v. 9), since that was where Paul's accusers said he committed the crimes. It may have appeared to Festus that more facts about the case and its background could be gathered there.

Earlier Festus had refused to hold his court in Jerusalem (vv. 4–5); now he is willing to try the case in that city. Should the trial be transferred to Jerusalem, the governor assures Paul that his case will not be turned over to the Jewish authorities. As a Roman citizen Paul can only be tried by a Roman court ("before me," v. 9), not before the Sanhedrin. The governor probably does not know about the Jewish plot to kill Paul (v. 3), but we cannot clear him of blame even though he carefully follows the legal procedure of the Romans. He does yield to the pressure of the Jews and, therefore, bears the responsibility for continuing Paul's trial.

But Paul is unwilling to submit to a trial in Jerusalem even before Festus. If he agrees to go there, he will be playing into the hands of his bitter enemies, suggesting that they perhaps do have a case against him. Moreover, his life will be in grave danger, and he probably suspects that the Jews' insistence on a trial in Jerusalem is prompted by a sinister plot. As indicated in verses 18–19, Festus is convinced that the charges made against Paul are due entirely to his opponents' theological prejudice.

Paul then reminds the governor that he (Festus) knows that he is innocent, based on the trial in Caesarea. This reminder shows that Paul suspects Festus is trying to win the favor of the Jews. As the governor knows, his prisoner has done the Jews no wrong, nor has he committed any crime against Rome, for which the penalty is death. The Spirit-filled apostle shows himself resolute, convinced of his rights and refusing to be intimidated by government officials willing to yield to political pressure. Therefore, he insists, he should be tried before the present court, which is a Roman one.

Fearing that he will become just a political pawn in Festus's hands, Paul refuses any sort of trial before the governor in Jerusalem. So that justice may be served, he has only one option: to appeal his case as a Roman citizen to Caesar (v. 11). In conferring with his advisers (v. 12), Festus perceives that the appeal stops the local proceedings and transfers the case to the imperial court in Rome. The exact details of the appeals process are unknown (see Sherwin-White, 1963, 57–70). But because of the appeal Festus is required to send his prisoner to Rome for trial.

Through this legal procedure God's plan for Paul to bear witness in Rome is being carried forward. Because of God's will, Paul has felt that he must take the gospel to Rome (19:21). Already in a vision the Lord has confirmed Paul's mission to preach the gospel in Rome (23:11). By honoring Paul's appeal, Festus unknowingly makes it possible for the apostle to be a witness in that great city. God's hand is directing the course of events.

6.5.2.3. Festus Reviews Paul's Case With Agrippa (25:13–22). Before Paul is sent to Rome, Agrippa arrives in Caesarea to pay the newly appointed Festus a courtesy call. This was Herod Agrippa II, the only son of Herod Agrippa I, who had murdered the apostle James (12:1–2). He also was the great-grandson of Herod the Great and the brother of both Drusilla, the wife of Felix (24:24), and Bernice, who accompanies him to Caesarea. After the husband of Bernice, the king of Chalcis and her own uncle, died, she lived for a while in the home of her brother. Later she became the mistress of the Roman general Titus.

The Romans had given Agrippa II the right to appoint the high priest and to supervise the temple and its funds. He was also king of some districts in northern Palestine and was regarded as an expert in Jewish affairs. So as a somewhat important political figure, he goes to Caesarea to give Festus an official welcome. This visit gives Festus an opportunity to mention Paul's case and to appeal to the king's knowledge of Jewish religion and ways. The case is now beyond the governor's authority; he simply wants to get information that can be sent to the imperial court.

Festus has a private conversation with King Agrippa II, where he tells the king about an interesting man whom Felix had left behind as a prisoner. In explaining Paul's situation to the king, Festus recounts the events from the time he had gone up to Jerusalem, including Paul's trial he held in Caesarea. Festus first learned about the charges of the Jews against Paul on that visit to Jerusalem (v. 15). The Jews urged him to settle this long-standing case by condemning the apostle. From a Roman point of view Festus had emphasized to Paul's accusers the impartiality of Roman law in legal proceedings (v. 16). Roman law demanded a fair trial for the accused, in which both the defendant and the accusers could present their cases.

His predecessor, Felix, had been lax in handling the case; in contrast, Festus reminds Agrippa that he had not lost any time (v. 17). As soon as the Jewish authorities arrived in Caesarea, he acted as quickly as possible and brought the prisoner before his court. Festus had expected Paul's accusers to bring charges of serious crimes against him (v. 18), but the charges revealed only their ill-will toward the prisoner and a determination to treat him as a criminal.

Festus is convinced that Paul's accusers grossly overstated the seriousness of their charges. When examined by Roman law, he appeared innocent. He might have been thought to be mad, but not a criminal. The judgment of Festus is that Paul has committed no grave crimes and that the dispute is about trivial matters of their own religion. The governor, therefore, sees Paul and his opponents as belonging to the same camp and their dispute as being over matters within the Jewish faith. In other words, Paul is not an outsider trying to stir up trouble, but an insider who wants to be heard.

Festus also introduces a distinctive feature of Paul's position. He discerns that a specific issue of the dispute is not the general resurrection of the dead, which the Pharisees affirm and Sadducees deny. The real issue is the resurrection of a particular person—Jesus. The charge that Paul had defiled the temple (21:28–29) has disappeared from sight. Now the question is whether Jesus is alive or dead.

The cardinal Christian truth of Jesus' resurrection was a specific application of the Pharisees' doctrine of the general resurrection of the dead. Even so, this application demanded more than what the Pharisees could believe or allow. These staunch advocates of a general resurrection denied the Easter faith—that Jesus, who had died on the cross, is now alive (v. 19). Paul had described to a Jerusalem crowd his encounter with the risen Jesus on the road to Damascus (22:6–21).

When Paul stood before the Sanhedrin or before Felix, none of his opponents raised the point about Jesus' resurrection (23:1–10; 24:1–27). Yet Festus can see what the central issue is. This pagan has heard Paul talk about Jesus, a man who had died but is now claimed as alive. He knows that the apostle has tried to convince the Jewish people that the risen Lord is the fulfillment of the promised Redeemer in their own Scriptures. Here we have an example of an outsider having a better understanding of the truth than do Paul's enemies (cf. 5:38–39). The cardinal truth of Jesus' resurrection has penetrated his mind.

Like a man of the world, Festus admits to his confusion about this religious debate, claiming that he does not know how to go about investigating such matters (v. 20). He pleads ignorance of the religious ideas of the Jews and implies that the debate has provided more heat and fog than light. His confusion is not due to ignorance, but to his unwillingness to set an innocent man free. Enough light had been thrown on the case for Festus to declare Paul free of guilt, and he had sent his accusers back to Jerusalem. Of course, Festus wants to present himself in a good light to his royal guest. So he does not admit to Agrippa that he wanted to transfer the trial to Jerusalem to win the favor of Paul's accusers, but does tell his guest that he approached Paul about being tried in Jerusalem.

Festus then tells Agrippa that Paul refused the offer to move the trial to Jerusalem and exercised his right of appeal to the emperor (v. 21). When the apostle insisted that his case be heard in the highest court of the empire, Festus ordered his soldiers to keep him in custody until he could be sent to Rome.

Festus's description of Paul's case intrigues Agrippa. Most likely the king has heard before now about Paul and Jesus. His father, Herod Agrippa I, had tried to suppress the Christian faith by killing the apostle James and imprisoning Peter for the purpose of putting him to death (12:1–19). In 25:22 the verb "would like" literally means "I was desiring" (imperfect tense), suggesting that Agrippa had entertained the desire to hear Paul for some time (cf. Luke 23:8).

Festus will gladly gratify the curiosity of his royal guest by granting him an audience with the prisoner. Furthermore, such a meeting may give some assistance to Festus and provide information for his official report to the emperor (vv. 26–27). So like his Lord, Paul stands before a Roman governor and a Jewish king; unlike his Lord, of course, Paul has appealed to Caesar for protection against what amounts to religious persecution (*NIDNTT*, 1:269).

6.5.2.4. Paul Defends Himself Before Agrippa (25:23–26:32). The stage is set for the grandest defense speech given by Paul, in which the apostle gives another account of his conversion and call to ministry. He stresses again that his faith in Christ is in line with his Jewish beliefs as a Pharisee and that the risen Lord has commissioned him to offer salvation to both Jews and Gentiles. On this occasion

Paul appears before King Agrippa II, the most important dignitary before whom he formally speaks in Acts. As a prominent Jew, Agrippa, well-versed in the Jewish religion and ways, may be able to give advice on the case (Marshall, 1980, 387).

Paul's meeting with Agrippa takes place the next day, after Festus has spoken about him to the king. This occasion is one of pomp and ceremony, with a splendid audience and all the fanfare of oriental kings in public gatherings. The event is held in "the audience room" (v. 23), which apparently was located in the palace built by Herod the Great for magnificent gatherings. Agrippa and Bernice are there in their royal robes. Military officials and civil dignitaries are also present. The scene is set, whereupon Festus orders the soldiers to bring the prisoner into the hall.

The humble apostle is a glaring contrast to the pomp and pride of this dignified audience. Nevertheless, he stands center stage as the main actor on this auspicious occasion, and for the Christian readers he is the most important person present. Without intending to honor Paul, Festus provides him with an audience of dignitaries to whom he preaches the gospel.

The proceedings are conducted with formality and dignity. Festus opens the meeting with a brief statement. He recognizes the presence of his royal guest, King Agrippa, and then introduces the apostle's case to his august audience. This scene fulfills Jesus' prophecy of Luke 12:11–12. In the introduction Festus states that the "whole Jewish community," not merely the Jewish leaders, have brought charges against this man (v. 24). Jewish mobs have called for Paul's execution (21:36; 22:22). Apparently on this basis, Festus claims that the Sanhedrin had represented the sentiments of the Jewish people in their demand that Paul be put to death.

Festus then makes a response to this petition from the Jewish community that Paul should die. In his judgment Paul has done nothing to deserve death. This unqualified declaration of Paul's innocence confirms the earlier declarations made by Paul himself (22:25; 23:1; 24:12–13, 16, 19–20; 25:8, 10–11). Festus admits that the apostle should have been released when his accusers presented no evidence of his wrongdoing. He even hints that he was going to release him; but because of Paul's appeal to Caesar, Festus feels politically obligated to send him to Rome (Sherwin-White, 1963, 65).

Paul's appeal now presents a difficult problem for the governor. He has to submit to the emperor substantiated charges against the prisoner (v. 26), but the absence of evidence once again makes the point of Paul's innocence. Festus does not know what to write to "His Majesty" (*sebastos*—a designation for the Roman emperor with more of an official ring to it than "Caesar"). Any statement will have to state the charges against the prisoner; otherwise, Festus will get himself in trouble at Rome.

Festus could, of course, describe the earlier proceedings, which would include the Jews' charges against Paul. But if he asserts the prisoner's innocence to Caesar, then why did he not set him free? Festus will then expose himself to the charge of incompetence and will have to explain in the imperial court why he kept the prisoner in custody. The problem is real, and his audience can see that the governor is in a bad predicament. But it is a problem of his own making; he has held as a prisoner a man entitled to his freedom.

To get himself out of the dilemma, Festus hopes to receive advice from Agrippa about the case. As he explains, the prisoner has been brought before King Agrippa so that he can examine Paul with the intent of uncovering other facts about Paul's supposed crimes. Festus knows the prisoner has committed no crimes, but Agrippa will save him great personal embarrassment if the king can determine that Paul is guilty of a crime. Should that be the result of this proceeding, Festus can then write a sensible letter to the emperor, complete with charges (v. 27).

By the courtesy of Festus, King Agrippa takes control of the meeting. Acting more or less as the chairman of the proceedings, the king gives Paul permission to speak (26:1). The apostle stretches out his hand, perhaps as a gesture of respect for the distinguished audience, and then begins to speak. As was customary in such proceedings, he politely acknowledges King Agrippa and indicates that he considers himself fortunate to have the opportunity to be heard by such an expert in Jewish customs and questions (vv. 2–3). Unlike Lysias, Felix, and Festus, the king is acquainted with the faith of the Jews. In fact, the emperor entrusted him with oversight of the religious affairs in Jerusalem. Paul implies that Agrippa's knowledge of the Jewish religion will enable him to understand the case and see that he is innocent. The apostle does not want to be disturbed by angry outbursts and interruptions; so he asks Agrippa to listen to him with patience (v. 3), since he expects his defense will be some length.

After this brief introduction there follows Paul's defense, which is autobiographical in style and consists of three sections: Paul's past life (vv. 4–11), his conversion (vv. 12–15), and his commission and ministry (vv. 16–23). This is followed up by an interchange between Festus and Paul (vv. 24–25) and one between Paul and Agrippa (vv. 26–29). The meeting comes to a close with the judgment of the distinguished audience (vv. 30–32).

As Paul begins his defense, he is aware that his audience consists mostly of Gentiles. But he directs his speech to Agrippa and, therefore, primarily to the Jews. His intent is not to deal with the charges of the Jews. He has no need to deny their accusations on this occasion. Festus himself has declared that the apostle has not transgressed Roman law and has in essence found him innocent. The occasion gives Paul an opportunity to affirm his loyalty to what he considers to be true Judaism and to underscore his Pharisaic heritage.

With this purpose in mind Paul summarizes his life and work, emphasizing the victory of the risen Christ over death (v. 23). The story of his early life is generally known by his people (v. 4). Ever since he was a youth, they have known how he spent his life in his "own country, and also in Jerusalem." Here "country" can be taken to refer to Cilicia, covering his life in the community of Tarsus; but it more likely refers to the land of Judea, especially since Paul seems to have grown up in Jerusalem (see comments on 22:3). This whole verse, therefore, applies to Paul's residence at Jerusalem, and the Jewish nation living in Judea is more precisely defined by "in Jerusalem." It is difficult to understand how most Jews could have known about Paul's life if he were referring to the distant city of Tarsus.

Being known among his people as a man who was zealous for the ancestral traditions (cf. Gal. 1:14) gave Paul a prominence among the Jews. Many of his fellow countrymen have known him a long time and can testify that he has been a member of the Pharisees. The Pharisees were a group that pledged to live strictly according to the traditions, customs, and religious observances of the Jews (Acts 26:5; cf. 22:3; 23:6).

Now Paul is on trial, but he has committed no apostasy. As he had believed when he was a Pharisee, he still believes what God has promised to "our fathers" and "our twelve tribes." It is for his hope in the fulfillment of the divine promises given to the ancestors of the Jews that he now stands on trial (v. 6). Maintaining his faithfulness to his Pharisaic heritage as a Christian, he holds fast to the same messianic hope that God gave to Israel in the promises and prophecies of the Old Testament. He believes the promises to the fathers—Abraham, Isaac, and Jacob—and for him these promises have been and will be fulfilled in Jesus Christ.

When he lived as a zealous Pharisee, no one would have thought that later he would be on trial for his belief in the fulfillment of God's promises, but that has brought him into his present circumstances. So again Paul states that it is a travesty for him to be put on trial by the Jews for "this hope" (v. 7). The whole Jewish nation, which Paul refers to as "our twelve tribes," has ardently hoped to receive that which God has promised. Jewish devotion has been expressed as the people have habitually worshiped God day and night, especially in the temple.

Hope has inspired many devout people, who have faithfully observed the commandments and religious practices of Judaism (Luke 1:6; 2:25; 23:50–51; Acts 10:2). Anna, a superb example of such devotion, ardently looked for the Messiah and, without leaving the temple, worshiped God with fasting and prayer night and day (Luke 2:37). For the Jews to condemn one of their own for adhering to the great hope of their faith raises the question of whether they truly believe in the fulfillment of God's promises (Marshall, 1980, 392). The way Paul has been treated implies that they deny "this hope."

Paul is a defender of the resurrection hope and makes the victory of the risen Christ over death the basis of his message. So taking the offensive, he asks the question why it is thought incredible for God to raise the dead

(v. 8). To this point Paul has been addressing Agrippa, but now he speaks to the entire group of Jews present ("you" in v. 8 is plural). Many Jews, especially the Pharisees, have hoped in the resurrection of the dead. But the real issue is not the general resurrection of all people at the end of history, but the resurrection of Jesus. For Paul the denial that God raised Jesus from the dead is tantamount to denying belief in the general resurrection.

Paul's reference to the resurrection defines the content of his hope and indicates, too, that Israel's hope is in God's promises of resurrection. This hope was fulfilled by Jesus' resurrection, which proved him to be the Messiah. The Jews have no valid reason for denying the resurrection of Jesus. That God raised him from the dead might seem incredible to the Gentiles, but it should not be for the Jews. As a Christian, Paul's faith centers in the resurrection of Jesus. So why should he be branded by the Jews as a heretic?

Continuing to describe his past life, Paul gives a brief review of his career as a persecutor of the church (vv. 9–11). Before his conversion he had held the same viewpoint of Christ and Christians that his opponents now have. His statement about the persecution of those who confessed the risen Christ is described in more detail here than in previous accounts of it in Acts (cf. 9:1–2; 22:4–5). When he heard Christians preaching that Jesus had risen from the dead and is the Lord and Messiah, he wanted to do everything possible to oppose them. As he states it, his aim was "to oppose the name of Jesus of Nazareth." That is, he acted as his opponents are doing, who have tried to have him condemned as a criminal; and just as they, he rejected what the Christians said about Jesus.

At that time Paul shared their blindness of heart. In his zeal he sought to suppress the Christian movement in Jerusalem, and with the authority of the chief priests he put many of God's people in prison. As an aggressive opponent of Christianity, he was not simply a consenting bystander, as in Stephen's death (8:1; 22:20), but he also cast his vote in the death of many Jerusalem Christians. These words strongly suggest that not only did Paul cast his vote for the death of Christians but that he had also been a member of the Sanhedrin in Jerusalem.

This interpretation raises a problem. The Jews did not normally have the authority to put people to death (John 18:31). An isolated death, as in the case of Stephen, is conceivable; but we are not able to say how the Sanhedrin could execute many Christians without the intervention of the Roman authorities. Perhaps Paul is speaking figuratively and means only that he was favorable to their execution, as in the death of Stephen. Yet the statement, "I cast my vote against them," suggests that he did not just give his approval but voted for the death sentence.

In any case, it is clear that Paul was unrelenting in his persecution of the Christians in Jerusalem. Many times he went to all the synagogues throughout Jerusalem to have believers punished, and he tried to compel them "to blaspheme," that is, to deny their faith in Jesus Christ. Whether he was successful or not we are not told; the only thing Paul says is that he "tried to force" them to recant. No doubt those who stood firm were put to death (v. 10), but those who blasphemed had their lives spared. Paul did not confine his efforts to Jerusalem. Being obsessed with the desire to harm the followers of Christ, he took his campaign not only to Damascus but to "foreign cities." We know that he visited Damascus, but what other cities we are not able to say.

Like King Agrippa's father, Herod Agrippa I (12:1–19), and his great-grandfather, Herod the Great (Matt. 2:1–18), Paul had tried to suppress the cause of Jesus Christ. He is not giving this witness to brag about the evil deeds of his past life, as some converts do. His intent is rather to magnify the saving grace of Christ. This former fierce enemy of Christ and bloody persecutor of Christians now stands before Agrippa as a dedicated apostle of Jesus. Wishing to explain what brought about the radical reversal in his life, Paul gives a third account of his conversion (vv. 12–18; cf. 9:3–19; 22:6–16).

The details of this account vary slightly from the others. As the other accounts, this one begins with Paul's journey to Damascus. He had received his commission from the chief priests and was armed with authority to arrest the Christians (9:2 talks about official "letters"). As he made his way to Damascus, about midday when the sun is at its greatest intensity, he saw a light from heaven brighter than the sunlight shining around him and his traveling companions (26:13). The light was a revelation of the Lord (*TDNT*, 5:542–43). Not only Paul but also his companions were overwhelmed by the miraculous light and fell to the ground. Nothing is said about his companions falling to the ground in 9:4 and 22:7, nor does Paul say anything here about his being blinded.

Paul then draws attention to what the Lord said to him. A voice spoke to him in Aramaic, as in the other accounts, "Why do you persecute me?" Here there is added, "It is hard for you to kick against the goads" (v. 14). These words reflect a rather common proverb of a stubborn ox futilely kicking at a sharp pointed stick its owner uses to guide it. The point could be that Paul was struggling against the haunting doubts of conscience and the memory of Stephen, but the proverb in Greek and Latin often signified fighting against the will of the gods. Likely, therefore, the proverb refers to Paul's resistance of the divine will. The heavenly voice implied that the persecutor was not going to have his way. He had met his Master, and his obstinacy is challenged by the heavenly voice.

As in 9:5, Paul's response to the voice was, "Who are you, Lord?" The reply to him was also the same: "I am Jesus, whom you are persecuting" (26:15). Jesus revealed the real meaning of Paul's persecution of the Christians. In his attacks against them Paul was wounding Christ himself, a reality he never forgot (1 Cor. 8:11–13) and one that is probably the basis of his understanding the church as Christ's body (1 Cor. 12:12). Here the persecutor identified Jesus as "Lord." Since Jesus addressed Paul out of heaven, it was proof that he was the risen, glorified Lord, who now occupies a position of authority alongside of God. The apostle condenses the accounts of the events that follow. He omits the exalted Lord's instructions to go into the city of Damascus and what God said to him through Ananias (9:6–19).

Paul's dramatic encounter with the living Lord transformed his life. The experience was a judgment of his past life and a new beginning, which he elsewhere describes as "a new creation" (2 Cor. 5:17). In his darkness and misdirected zeal Paul and his companions were caused to fall to the earth by the risen Lord. The zealous persecutor's resistance was broken, but he was not to remain in the posture of humility. The risen Savior instructed him to stand on his feet and do the work of the Lord, just as the prostrate Ezekiel was told when God commissioned him to preach to Israel (Ezek. 2:1–3). Thus, as part of his Damascus road experience, Paul received a divine commission on the order of prophetic calls in the Old Testament (Jer. 1:6–10; Ezek. 2:1).

The Lord's purpose for appearing to Paul was to appoint the persecutor as "a servant and as a witness." The combination of "witness" (*martys*) with "servant" (*hyperetes*) is likely explanatory, so that "witness" defines more specifically Paul's role as a servant of Jesus Christ. The first "eyewitnesses and servants of the word" handed down the things about Christ (Luke 1:2). Among eyewitnesses the risen Lord includes Paul, who had not been numbered among the disciples during Jesus' earthly ministry. Paul's witness was to rest on whom he had seen—the glorified Christ—and on what he would see through visions in the future (18:9; 22:17–21; 23:11; 27:23; 2 Cor. 12:1–4, 7). Like the prophets of old, he was promised divine protection from Jews (26:17; cf. 9:23–25; 14:19–20; 17:10) and Gentiles (26:17; cf. 16:19–40; 19:23–41).

Paul's prophetic mission was to preach the gospel to both Jews and Gentiles, with special attention to the Gentiles. He was to open the eyes of people, turning them from the realm of darkness to light, and to cause them to leave the area of Satan's power and enter the realm where God reigns (v. 18). Christian conversion involves two aspects: (1) a turning away from darkness and from the power of Satan, and (2) a turning to light and to God. Conversion is a surrender of the whole life to God. The coming out of darkness into light requires a change of lords. At conversion a person under the lordship of Satan comes under the lordship of God.

God forgives the sins of those who are converted and gives them "a place among those who are sanctified by faith" in Jesus Christ (v. 18). Agrippa probably does not comprehend the full significance of the theological language, but it reflects the fundamental nature of conversion. Those who believe in Christ find their place among those who are sanctified. The emphasis on faith in Christ as the condition for forgiveness shows that sanctification (*hegiasmenois*, a perfect tense) must be viewed in a broad sense of separation to God. It denotes the state of holiness in which Christians are consecrated to God. It involves all that delivers us from darkness and from the power of Satan: repentance, justification, forgiveness of sin, holy living, and a place among God's chosen people.

Paul's thought is revolutionary in that now, through faith in Christ, Gentiles can have an equal place among God's chosen people. Conversion leads to the complete transformation of the entire life of the believer and to a place in the new society of Christ's people. From the experience of conversion issues a new outlook and power for living, but it is all the result of the work of the Holy Spirit (*NIDNTT*, 1:355).

Paul has described to Agrippa his vision of the risen Christ, in which he received a divine commission to preach the gospel. Next, he tells the king how he has executed the divine orders (vv. 19–23). In fact, obedience to his call has brought him before Agrippa. Paul did not disobey the call of God, which is an emphatic way of stating that he obeyed the revelation given to him on the road to Damascus. For him the vision was a compelling and decisive experience. As a result he became a faithful servant and began to fulfill the mission given to him.

His ministry began in Damascus, continued in Jerusalem (9:20–29) and the land of Judea, and reached into the Gentile lands, a special field of labor (22:19–21). Grammatically the phrase "in all Judea" does not seem to fit the sentence. This phrase is in the accusative case and does not, as is expected, stand parallel to Damascus and Jerusalem, both in the dative case. Perhaps "in all Judea" is the gloss of a scribe, but the account of Paul's ministry in Acts does not rule out his preaching in Judea. Acts 9:30 suggests that he was sent to Tarsus and passed through Judea on the way, though nothing is said about a mission in Judea. Galatians 1:22, where Paul states that he was personally unknown by the churches in Judea, seems to deny such a mission, though his evangelistic work there may have been done at a later time than the period covered in Galatians 1:18–24.

In any case, the apostle fulfilled his prophetic commission by preaching to both Jews and Gentiles that they should repent and turn to God. Salvation was offered to both groups on the same basis—repentance and turning to God by faith in Jesus. The thrust of Paul's message was conversion—a fundamental change of the whole life. Such a change required deeds that demonstrated genuine repentance (v. 20). This expectation is reminiscent of John the Baptist's preaching (Luke 3:7–9) and indicates that a life characterized by good works is the sign of a living faith.

The narrative of Acts has shown that the Jews resisted Paul's missionary efforts. As an example of such resistance, Paul refers to the incident in the temple (v. 21). Because of his dedication to his mission, the Jews seized him in the temple and actually tried to kill him (21:27–35). The ultimate reason for their attempt to destroy him was his preaching of the gospel. But the Jews failed in their efforts to take his life in the temple. He was rescued from their hands by the intervention of the Romans. But behind Paul's deliverance from the Jews' attack was the special help of God. Human beings could not do more harm to him than what God allowed. God's protection continues "to this very day," as Paul is now testifying before Agrippa.

Throughout his ministry, the apostle has been empowered by God to "testify to small and great alike." At the present moment he is carrying out his commission as a witness to people of every rank in society, and he preaches the same truth to the ones small in importance and the ones great in importance, even a governor and a king. What he preaches agrees with what Moses and the prophets predicted was going to happen: redemption, the outpouring of the Holy Spirit, the new covenant, and the final judgment.

Paul emphasizes two prominent themes in his preaching: (1) God ordained the death of the Messiah (cf. 2:23; Luke 24:25–26). The divine promise was fulfilled in the suffering and the death of Christ. Paul does not state here where this promise appears in Moses and the prophets, but likely he has in mind the Suffering Servant of Isaiah 53. Since the crucifixion of Christ was promised in Scripture, it was willed by God and was thus a divine necessity.

(2) As the first to rise from the dead, Christ proclaimed light to Jews and Gentiles. His resurrection is also a matter of inspired prophecy and reflects Paul's teaching that Christ is the firstfruits of the resurrection (1 Cor. 15:4, 20). Again Paul implies that Christ is identified with

ıe Suffering Servant, who, though "cut off om the land of the living" (Isa. 53:8), "will … rolong his days" (v. 10). As the risen Lord, he as now sent forth his witnesses to proclaim the ght of salvation to everyone (cf. Isa. 9:2).

Christ's triumph over death was itself the ıessage of liberty and is a pledge of believers' ictory over sin and death. So, as the first to xperience resurrection, he was proclaimed as the author of life" (Acts 3:15). In his death nd resurrection Jesus of Nazareth fulfilled the)ld Testament expectation of the Messiah. By nplication Paul identifies the Messiah and the uffering Servant with Jesus, who died, arose, nd enlightened Jews and Gentiles. The aposıe is therefore no apostate, but his Jewish pponents are. He has preached exactly what ıad been foretold in the Old Testament and has ccepted the prophecies as fulfilled in Jesus, vhereas his accusers have repudiated the witıess of Moses and the prophets and the hope of God's people.

The message of Paul arouses a strong outburst from Festus (v. 24). It may seem that Paul s suddenly interrupted as he is speaking. More ikely, however, the message has reached its :limax with the emphasis on the resurrection. As a pagan, Festus is still unable to understand Jewish theology with its reference to resurrec:ion (cf. 25:19–20). What Paul has said about :he crucified, risen Jesus and about his commission to preach the gospel is beyond him. Belief that a dead man arose from the dead is incredible to him. Thus, in a loud voice the governor declares that Paul is out of his mind, completely deranged and nothing more than a religious fanatic.

True, Paul is a wise and learned man, but Festus pronounces that "great learning" is a real danger to sanity. Could anyone who can think straight endorse a teaching such as the resurrection of the dead? Festus does not think so. It is unknown what precisely Festus means by suggesting that much learning can be bad for a person, but perhaps he thinks Paul is insane because of his learning in the Old Testament and his efforts to penetrate the ultimate mysteries of life. Festus shows that he is out of his depth by attributing Paul's supposed insanity to great learning. Clearly the governor is not open to the gospel and thus disqualifies himself from rendering proper judgment in this matter.

Paul denies the charge of insanity (v. 25). What he has said about Christian teachings and experience is "true and reasonable." That is, no one but a sane person can utter words that are marked by truth and can be confirmed by reason. The gospel makes no claims to be irrational in the sense of being contrary to reason. But there is much in the gospel that is above human reason and can only be known by faith.

Paul's message is an enigma to Festus, but Agrippa's knowledge of Jewish matters enables him to appreciate what the apostle has said. Therefore, Paul appeals to the king for confirmation (vv. 26–27). He is confident that Agrippa knows about "these things"—the death and resurrection of Jesus, and the ensuing mission of the church. Since the king knows about Jesus and his apostles, Paul can "speak freely to him," that is, he can speak with complete openness and confidence to Agrippa. None of the events has escaped Agrippa. These events are public knowledge, and the king is fully cognizant of them. In fact, using a well-known Greek expression, Paul insists to Agrippa that these events have not happened "in a corner."

Luke's account of the Christian movement shows that it occurred in the public domain. From its beginning Christianity did not take place in an unknown location. Rather, it occurred in world history and is open to examination; it is not wrapped up in vague myths and legends, nor is it the result of the speculations of a deranged mind. The Christian movement was no secret in Palestine, and many knew the believers' claim that the crucified Jesus had risen from the dead. At Pentecost thousands witnessed the outpouring of the Spirit and accepted the gospel (2:41).

Being himself a Jew, Agrippa had to have been well acquainted with the events that centered around Jesus. Paul therefore presses his appeal to the king by asking if he believes the prophets. Paul never describes Agrippa as Jewish, but his remarks imply that the king is a Jew. Thus, he surely believes the prophets and their oracles about the death and resurrection of the Messiah. Paul's question in verse 27 calls on Agrippa to bear witness to the truth of the prophetic oracles and to accept the Christian view that they have been fulfilled in Jesus. It is not, therefore, information that Paul seeks from Agrippa. He assumes that the king is a devout Jew and answers his own question with the words: "I know you do." These words cannot mean that Agrippa has accepted Jesus as the Messiah. Paul affirms only that the king believes what the prophets predicted about the coming of the Messiah.

The Christians understand these prophecies as fulfilled in Jesus of Nazareth, but Agrippa is unwilling to view them as the Christians do. To void the answer demanded by Paul's question, Agrippa pushes it aside with a lighthearted remark about the apostle's attempt to make him a Christian so quickly (v. 28). The KJV renders Agrippa's reply as, "Almost thou persuadest me to be a Christian." The exact translation is difficult, as is seen by consulting various translations. His words have been translated as a serious declaration, as a question, or as sarcasm, but Paul's phrase "short time or long" (v. 29), picking up on Agrippa's reply, seems to indicate that in a relatively short time of speaking the apostle is trying to make the king a Christian.

By using the word "Christian" Agrippa reveals that he does know something about the Way (9:2; 19:9, 23; 22:4; 24:14, 22), but he chooses to remain an unbeliever. The king knows that it is unthinkable for a loyal Jew to deny belief in the prophets. If he affirms his belief in what they say, then the obvious follow-up will be, "Surely you accept Jesus as the Messiah, then, right?" Agrippa sees clearly the aim of Paul and gets himself out of the dilemma with a jest about the attempt to convert him. The king's response is not an outright rejection of Paul's witness, but he does turn aside the gospel that can save him from the power of sin.

Paul does not deny the king's charge that he wants him to become a believer, but in his response he expresses the desire for all in his illustrious audience to become Christians like himself (v. 29). He prays that they will receive the blessings that he enjoys in Christ, but without having to wear chains as a result. Again the apostle leaves no doubt that it is senseless to treat people as criminals for being Christians. Even though he stands in chains before Agrippa and a distinguished audience, he is in fact better off than they are, for he has met the Lord, who forgave him of his sins, opened his eyes, and delivered him from the tyranny of Satan. Knowing the blessedness of being a Christian, Paul is ready to expend the energy to make his audience true believers in Jesus as Savior, whether it takes a "short time or long" to persuade them.

Agrippa concludes the interview. When the king and others on the platform stand, the meeting comes to a close (vv. 30–32). In it people of rank and power have heard the apostle. As these dignitaries leave, they engage in lively conversation based on what they have heard, especially the tone of sincerity and of honesty of Paul's speech. Agrippa and Bernice confirm what Festus had already declared (25:25), that they too are strongly convinced of the prisoner's innocence of anything deserving death or imprisonment.

Speaking from a Jewish point of view, Agrippa expresses his regret that Paul had not been released before he made his appeal to Caesar. This is a reminder that Festus had not acted wisely in proposing the continuation of the trial (25:9). The governor finds himself in the same predicament as when he stated the case to the illustrious audience (25:24–27). He is under obligation to send the prisoner to the emperor, but does not know how to state the charges against Paul.

No one knows what Festus eventually wrote to Caesar, but he must have been compelled to say that Paul was found to be innocent by him and others who heard the charges against him. The question still remains: Why then did Festus not set Paul free? He had not released him earlier because he desired to win the favor of the Jews, but why did he still keep him in prison? Only a technical obstacle stands in Paul's way to freedom. This technicality is political rather than legal: Festus had formally accepted Paul's appeal to the emperor (25:12).

If a prisoner had done nothing worthy of being sent to Rome, it seems as though the emperor would have preferred not to have the bother of a trial. Roman law did not prohibit acquittal after an appeal to Caesar, but to have acquitted Paul would have offended both the emperor and the province of Judea (Sherwin-White, 1963, 65). The apostle bears no blame for not being released, but his appeal to Caesar did remove the case from the hands of Festus. The governor is not about to offend the emperor and commit political suicide.

The apostle is God's appointed servant and witness (26:16). For some time he has wanted to go to Rome, the capital of the Gentile world, hough no doubt under different circumstances (Rom. 1:10–13; 15:25–28). He goes in chains as a prisoner of Rome. In a vision he had been promised that he would testify of Jesus in that city (Acts 23:11). Because of divine guidance of circumstances, Paul is now about to begin his journey to Rome. He will enter the city as a prisoner who has appealed his case to Caesar, not as a condemned criminal. The apostle has been pronounced entirely innocent by both Festus and Agrippa.

7. Paul Is Sent to Rome (27:1–28:31)

Soon after the speech before Agrippa, Paul begins his voyage to Rome. His journey from Palestine to Italy, including his shipwreck in Malta, is one of the most dramatic parts of Acts. A distinctive feature of the narrative is the geographical and nautical details, but the real significance of the account is the emphasis on God's guidance and protection of Paul. It is God's will that Paul stand trial in Rome and bear witness there to the gospel (23:11; 27:24). Interpreting history theologically, Luke discerns that the hand of God brings Paul to the capital of the Gentile world. The same Pentecostal might that anointed his ministry on the missionary journeys will enable him to be an effective witness in Rome.

7.1. Paul's Voyage and Shipwreck (27:1–44)

While on his way to Rome, Paul demonstrates great faith and courage. God had commissioned him to preach the gospel to the world, but he has learned through personal experiences that God allows his servants to undergo great adversity before delivering them (2 Cor. 1:8–11). Through the adversity of a storm at sea and a shipwreck, God brings Paul safely to Rome. He finds God as he has in the past, as one who keeps his promises and answers prayer (Rom. 15:30–32).

7.1.1. Paul Sails From Caesarea to Fair Havens (27:1–8). Festus has decided that Paul should be sent to Rome. His two friends, Luke and Aristarchus, undertake the journey on their own initiative. Luke is not identified by name, but the significant "we" (v. 1) shows that he is in Paul's company as they sail to Rome. The word "we" has not appeared since Paul's arrival in Jerusalem (21:19). The strong probability is that Luke was among Paul's companions in Jerusalem and had remained close to him during the two-year imprisonment at Caesarea. Luke may have written his Gospel during the first part of Paul's imprisonment there.

Aristarchus, from Thessalonica (cf. 19:29), had also been among those who accompanied Paul to Jerusalem (20:4). After the apostle arrives in Rome, he refers to Aristarchus as a fellow prisoner in his letter to the Colossians (Col. 4:10) and as a fellow worker in his letter to Philemon (Philem. 24). Both letters are thought to come from the period of Paul's Roman confinement.

The vivid account of the journey begins with Paul and a few other prisoners being put on a ship that had come from Adramyttium, a port not far from Troas. Festus has them "handed over to a centurion named Julius" (v. 1) and some of his soldiers (v. 42). Nothing more is known about this centurion except his identity as belonging to the Imperial Regiment. Probably this regiment consisted of auxiliary soldiers who had been stationed in Syria in the first century. Normally regular regiments were not given such an honorary title as "Imperial" (*sebastos*, "worthy of reverence"), but it was frequently given to auxiliary troops (BAGD, 745).

The Romans treat Paul kindly. As they sail, he makes a favorable impression on Julius. The day after setting sail they arrive at Sidon, on the coast of Syria, about sixty-nine nautical miles from Caesarea. Because of Julius's friendliness toward Paul, he is given permission to visit "his friends" (*tous philous*) in the city—likely a technical designation for Christians, as in 3 John 14: "The friends here send their greetings. Greet the friends there by name." Such a designation suggests the intimacy of fellowship among believers at Sidon.

Luke has recorded nothing about the establishment of a church in Sidon. While Paul spends a few hours on shore with believers there, the other prisoners are probably kept on the ship for security purposes; presumably Paul goes ashore under military guard. He is refreshed by the Christians' hospitality, and they give him perhaps a meal and whatever else he needs.

From Sidon the ship sails northwestward and avoids striking out into the open sea. The next place they land is at Myra, the chief city in the province of Lycia. A more direct route to that city across the Mediterranean would have been to the west of Cyprus; but because of winds from the west and north, the sailors choose the less dangerous route around the eastern side of the island. By keeping close to the coast of the Mediterranean Sea, they hope that the island will break the force of the winds from the west and therefore make it easier to sail eastward toward Cyprus on the lee side, that is, the sheltered side of the island. This late in the season, boats normally took this route and then headed westward along the southern coast of Asia Minor. Breezes from the mainland also helped offset any stormy turbulence.

Myra is likely the ship's home port, and the ship must have been a small vessel. Normally grain ships were put into this harbor to avoid a direct route across the Mediterranean in the stormy season. The centurion in charge of Paul and the other prisoners intends to catch such a ship for the remainder of the journey to Rome. When they arrive at Myra, a vessel from Alexandria is about to sail for Italy. This ship had sailed due north from Alexandria to Myra to take advantage of the coast of Asia Minor for the next stage of the journey. Julius transfers Paul and the other prisoners to this Egyptian grain ship bound for Italy (v. 6).

Julius and his prisoners sail toward Cnidus, a port on the southwest tip of Asia Minor about 130 miles from Myra. From the outset they encounter adverse weather conditions. Because of strong, prevailing northwesterly winds, the sailing is slow and turbulent. As a result, it takes them several days to arrive off Cnidus. From there the ship continues to have difficulty proceeding. The normal route from Cnidus would have taken them to the north of Crete, but the windy conditions prevent the ship from continuing westward. The sailors change their course and turn sharply to the south, sailing by the eastern end of Crete and along its southern shore.

After they go around the eastern tip of Crete, the wind constantly threatens to drive the vessel out into the open sea. But by hugging the shore, with difficulty they creep along. Using breezes from the land, they are able to sail into the small bay of Fair Havens, a few miles west of the town of Lasea (v. 8). Fair Havens was an open bay and served as a harbor for protecting ships, but in bad weather it offered little protection.

7.1.2. Paul's Warning and Storm (27:9–26). So far the voyage has been difficult and has consumed a great deal of time. Now winter is

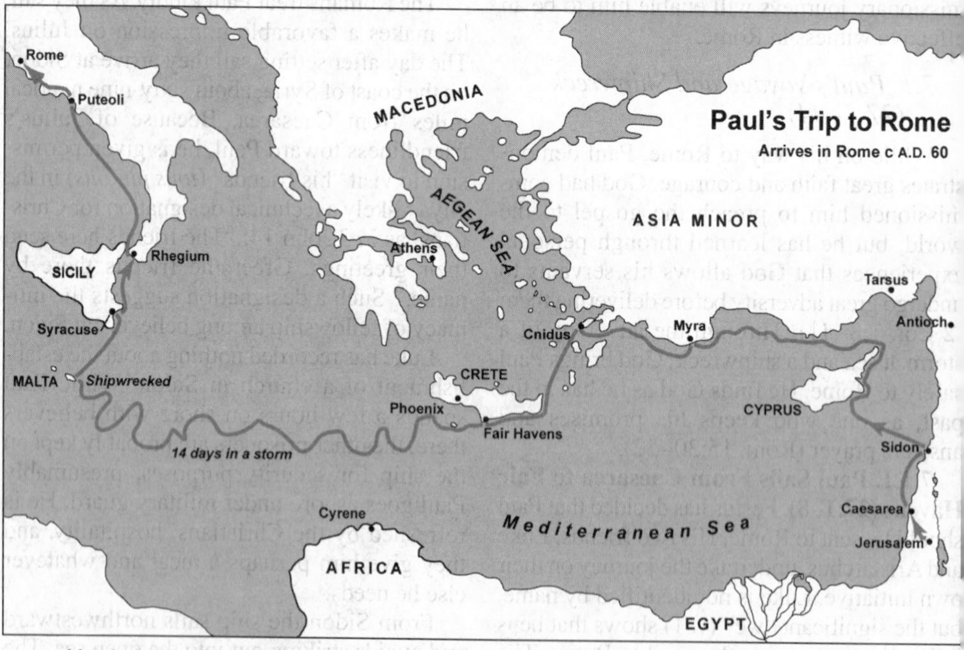

After being held at Caesarea for two years, Paul is sent to Rome, still a prisoner, though he has not been found guilty of anything. Blown off course by a storm, the ship is wrecked on a sandbar at Malta. Everyone makes it safely to shore.

proaching, and it was unsafe to try to complete journey before spring. The question is, therere, whether to spend the winter in Fair Havens to try to reach a more desirable winter port.

"The Fast" mentioned in verse 9 is the Jewh fast on the Day of Atonement (Lev. 16:29–; 23:27–32). The exact day on which the Day Atonement was celebrated differed from year year, but it would have been either in late Sepmber or early October—the beginning of the ormy season. Sailing in the Mediterranean as risky after mid-September and impossible ter mid-November (Haenchen, 1971, 699–00). Most likely the year was A.D. 59, and the ast came in this year on October 5.

Paul knows from personal experience the erils of a shipwreck (2 Cor. 11:25). Aware that continue could mean disaster, he gives a rophetic warning. No doubt Paul is inspired y the Spirit and predicts disastrous results if e voyage continues. His reference to the cerinty of disaster indicates that the warning is e result of divine revelation. He therefore rges the men in charge of the voyage to remain t Fair Havens for the winter, rather than risk e loss of both cargo and vessel, as well as peraps the lives of those on board (v. 10).

Apparently the crew and passengers discuss ogether what to do. The centurion has listened o Paul's advice, but he is in charge of only the risoners and has no decisive word in the mater. Not knowing how reliable Paul's advice is, he Roman officer agrees with the pilot, the fficer in charge of navigation, and with the hip's owner, a man evidently serving as capain of his own ship. These two men presumbly asked the centurion for his opinion. No oubt he recognizes that they have more expert nowledge about sailing conditions, so natually their words carry more weight with him han Paul's advice.

What weighs in the decision to sail on is hat Fair Havens is not a suitable port for proection from winter storms (v. 12). Evidently ome want to press on to Italy, but most of the hip's crew favor a more cautious plan of tryng to reach a decent port for spending the winer somewhere on the coast of Crete. They ave in mind Phoenix, located about forty niles to the west. Luke's description of this arbor as "facing both southwest and northvest" has created keen debate about its idenity. Some identify it as modern Lutro, but the Greek literally means "toward the southwest and toward the northwest." That is the way modern Phineka faces—a harbor to the west of Lutro just around a ridge jutting out into the sea. Though it is not far from Fair Havens, sailing to the harbor proves to be extremely risky.

After the majority has decided to spend the winter in the harbor at Phoenix rather than in Fair Havens, a gentle wind from the south begins to blow. With this change of the wind, they assume it is safe to sail to Phoenix, which can be reached easily in a day, and hope to make it there before nightfall. They weigh the anchor and sail as close as possible to the coast of Crete to prevent being blown out to the open sea (v. 14).

The ship sails smoothly for a while over the sea, but that is just a prelude to a fearful change. Just a few miles west of Fair Havens a mighty northeast gale sweeps down suddenly from the mountaintops of Crete. The name of this gale is "northeaster" (*eurakylon*), a sailor's term used to indicate the direction of the wind. The ship is struck by the gale and blown off course out to sea. The water is very rough, and the sailors try to head the vessel into the wind in the direction of Phoenix. Finding that impossible, they have to allow the wind to carry the ship away from the land.

Driven by the violent winds and waves, the ship passes the southern side of the small island of Cauda, off the southwest coast of Crete. On that side of the island the vessel is sheltered briefly from the wind. The sailors take the time there to make emergency measures. Apparently a lifeboat in tow has either become waterlogged or is in danger of being dashed to pieces against the ship. The sailors have difficulty pulling the lifeboat up on board. They also pass "ropes under the ship itself to hold it together" (v. 17).

The Greek word for "passed under" (*hypozonnymi*, "to be undergirded") is a technical nautical term for bracing or reinforcing a ship, but it is unclear exactly how the sailors strengthen the ship. The undergirding seems to have consisted of passing ropes around the hull of the ship and drawing them tight to prevent its timbers from parting. Two other explanations are: (1) stretching cables tightly from side to side below the deck, and (2) stretching cables from stem to stern and tightening them with posts secured on the deck. The experts disagree, but the Greek verb for undergirding favors the placing of ropes underneath the ship and pulling them tight to keep the hull from coming apart in the storm.

As the ship is driven by the gale across the Mediterranean, the sailors are afraid they might be blown southwest, to the northern coast of Africa into the Syrtis. This area just off of the coast of Libya had dreaded sandbars and quicksand and was notorious as a danger to shipping. The ship is still more than 380 miles from the area, but the sailors, aware of the great hazard, do not want to take any chances (Marshall, 1980, 409). They lower "the sea anchor," the meaning of which is uncertain. It may refer to lowering the mainsail or throwing spare gear overboard, but most likely the sailors try to reduce the speed of the ship toward the dangerous sandbars by dropping a board dragged at right angles to the direction the ship sails.

The ship continues to be carried by the violent winds, but it drifts more to the north than toward the area of danger. Getting no relief from the storm, the crew begins to lighten the ship by taking the cargo and throwing it into the water (v. 18). All the measures taken so far are inadequate, and the ship remains in peril. On the third day they throw off the ship's tackle, the ropes, pulleys, sails, poles, furniture, and material carried for the purpose of making repairs. The phrase "with their own hands" may appear strange since the sailors have no other means than their hands to lighten the ship. Likely it is an emphatic way of stating that they throw overboard everything on which they could lay their hands.

In spite of their efforts the situation continues to worsen. The sailors are dependent on the sun and stars to know the direction in which the ship is sailing. Because of the heavy cloud cover for several days, they have no navigation points to determine where they are, and as a result they lose their bearings. The storm continues to rage, and all on board finally give up hope of surviving. Their present plight confirms the accuracy of Paul's warnings (v. 10). They have already lost the cargo, and now the vessel and their lives are in grave danger.

Fear and despondency settle on the ship. They have food (cf. v. 36), but because of a deliberate fast or despair or preoccupation with trying to protect themselves, they go a long time without eating. The men on board are now more prepared to listen to Paul, since his earlier prediction has come so near to being fulfilled. A God's own direction Paul stands in the midst c the crew and passengers and gives them a divin word of comfort. Again he speaks as a prophe insisting that if his advice to spend the winte in Fair Havens had been heeded, they woul have been spared the risk and suffering (v. 21 As a result of their mistake they now find them selves in this desperate situation, but he urge them not to despair. He predicts that none of th persons on board will lose their lives, but onl the ship will be lost (cf. vv. 41–44).

This qualification of his former prophec about the possibility of the loss of lives enable him to encourage all on board the ship. In vision the previous night, an angel of Go appeared to Paul, urging him to stop fearin and confirming an earlier promise that h "must stand trial before Caesar" (v. 24; cf 28:14). "Must" (*dei*) once again emphasize God's plan for Paul to bear witness in the pres ence of the emperor (23:11). This occasion i at least the third time an angel has appeared t Paul during a crisis (18:9; 23:11). Paul and hi traveling companions' lives will be spared s that he can reach Rome to fulfill God's plan. I fact, the angel assures the apostle that God ha graciously granted him the lives of those sail ing with him (v. 24). The implication is tha God has answered Paul's prayers for them an their lives will be spared.

The apostle emphasizes to the despairin hearts of the sailors and passengers the impor tance of maintaining their courage. He is full confident that what God has promised wil come to pass, and he wants everyone on boar to share his conviction (v. 25). Paul not onl predicts that no life will be lost, but also tha they will strike an island and the ship will b destroyed (v. 26). Their running aground on a island is also according to God's plan (cf "must" [*dei*] again). Only by God's direc intervention will the lives of Paul and his fel low travelers be spared. When human hope i exhausted, there is only hope in the Almighty

7.1.3. Shipwreck (27:27–44). Paul's prophecy of safety does not result in immedi ate deliverance from peril, but the fulfillmen of what he has predicted begins to happen. Th fourteenth night, presumably after the shi sailed from Fair Havens, the wind continues t blow Paul and his fellow travelers across th Adriatic Sea. In ancient times the Adriatic Se was the sea between Sicily and Crete, the whole mid-Mediterranean area. It is not the same as the current Adriatic, which is applied to the waters between Italy and Yugoslavia (cf. NIV note on v. 27).

As the ship makes some headway in the strong northeast gale, about midnight the sailors become aware of drawing near to land. They probably hear the roar of the breakers on a rocky shore. At first the noise of the breakers is so faint that the sailors are uncertain what it is. They drop a rope with a weight tied to it to determine how deep the water is under the vessel. At their first sounding they find that the depth of the water is about a hundred and twenty feet; the second sounding is only ninety feet. The decreasing depth indicates that the ship is approaching land. Because of the shallower water the ship is in danger of running on to the rocks. In such a powerful storm, that would result in the destruction of the ship and the loss of all on board.

The shallowness of the water and the sound of the breakers demand that the sailors take safety precautions. So they put out four anchors from the stern (v. 29). By lowering these four heavy weights from the back of the ship, they hope to slow its speed and keep its bow headed toward land in the driving wind. If the storm swings the ship around and turns its broadside to the waves, the result will be fatal (Haenchen, 1971, 705). With these safety measures taken in the dark, the only thing they can do now is hope and pray for daylight to come soon. It is a time of great anxiety as they approach the island of Malta (28:1). This Mediterranean island lies directly south of Sicily, about a hundred and fifty miles from the "toe" of Italy.

Thinking only of their own safety, the sailors decide to lower a lifeboat to escape from the ship (v. 30). Their circumstances convince them that they will be safer on a small boat in a raging storm than staying on board the ship in the darkness. Feeling that the ship will most likely be destroyed before morning, the sailors resolve to risk their lives in an attempt to get ashore. Because of the stormy conditions and darkness, they must have lost their heads and are willing to do a foolish thing, which could have resulted in their deaths. The crew's attempt to reach the shore is done under the pretense of putting other anchors out from the bow. They want it to appear as if they are going to drop anchors from the lifeboat out in the front of the ship. Perhaps this was thought to be more effectual than dropping the anchors from the bow itself.

Paul, however, is not deceived. After the sailors lower the lifeboat, he becomes aware of their foolish intention of escaping in stormy, pitch-dark conditions to reach an unknown coast. The ship's passengers are now the apostle's responsibility. He warns the centurion that unless the crew remains on board, he and his soldiers will perish—thus appealing to their sense of self-preservation (v. 31; the word "saved" here means deliverance from physical danger). If the crew leaves the ship, there will be no one to bring it to shore. Disaster is sure to follow without skillful sailors to run the ship ashore in such a storm (cf. vv. 39–41).

By the time the centurion hears Paul's warning, the crew has already lowered the little boat and is about to enter it. The ropes that fasten the boat to the ship are cut by the soldiers so that the lifeboat is blown away by the storm. This prompt action prevents the sailors from deserting the ship.

As the day begins to dawn, the ship remains anchored; but the danger has not passed. Paul reminds everyone on board that they have not eaten for two weeks. For that period of time they have been preoccupied only with their own safety. It is difficult to determine exactly what is meant by the statement that they have not eaten for fourteen days. Out of fear and anxiety the people on the ship may have fasted to appease the anger of their pagan gods. The sea had been rough, and many on board may have become seasick and eaten little. Paul's observation may be a forceful way of stating that they had not eaten properly for several days. Also, despair had set in on the ship, and their failure to take proper meals may have been the result of their state of mind. In any case, aware that they need strength for the strenuous task of getting to shore, Paul urges the people to eat some food. They need it in order to survive; the Greek says, "This is necessary for your salvation" (*soteria*), meaning their physical safety or survival.

Again Paul assures all on board that no harm will come to them, recalling the prophetic promise that only the ship would be lost (v. 22). Using a biblical proverb, he says, "Not one of you will lose a single hair from his head" (v. 34;

cf. 1 Sam. 14:45; 2 Sam. 14:11; 1 Kings 1:52; Luke 21:18). God has graciously given to Paul all who are sailing with him (v. 24). But the apostle is just as careful to watch over those who are committed to his care as though the prophetic promise of their escape had not been given.

After assuring them of protection from harm, Paul takes bread as Jews and Christians normally do and offers thanks to God in the presence of the crew and passengers (v. 35). As a Jewish practice of devotion, he breaks off a piece of bread and begins to eat it. All are encouraged by Paul's words and actions, and they eat as well. In times of great danger even people with strong hearts can be overcome with fear, but the apostle manifests great courage in the presence of the whole ship's company. Strengthened by the Holy Spirit, he conducts himself as a man of God under the most difficult circumstances. He is a true witness to his God on the ship.

The language of giving thanks and breaking bread has led a number of commentators to think that Paul is dispensing the Lord's Supper. His actions do remind us of the Last Supper (Luke 22:19; cf. 1 Cor. 11:17–34), but this should be seen as an ordinary meal, since they all partake. Luke and other Christians are present, but Paul's action does not go beyond the normal Jewish practice at a meal. Most of the 276 aboard the ship are not believers. Since a mixed company of people are present and a large number of them have no understanding of the Lord's Supper, most likely Luke is describing a common meal.

Paul's offering of thanks is a fitting expression of gratitude to God for food and drink. When all have eaten a hearty meal, they prepare to beach the ship by making it as light as possible. They have already thrown much of the cargo overboard (v. 18), but they have kept the grain as long as they could. Now they need to take measures to make the vessel float as high as possible so that it will not run aground before reaching the beach. So they begin throwing the remainder of the cargo overboard. To make the ship lighter required the renewed strength imparted by the food they took.

As daylight comes Paul's prophetic predictions are more fully realized (v. 39). The crew and passengers are able to see land, but they do not recognize the coast. This is not surprising since the storm has carried them away from the usual route of sailing; ships normally did not go by the island of Malta. The light reveals a bay with a sandy beach. Today this inlet is called St. Paul's Bay, located on the northeast coast of the island. Seeing the bay and sandy beach, the sailors feel that under the circumstances it is the best place to land the vessel.

The task of steering the ship safely to shore demands navigational skills. The difficulty of steering the ship reveals the wisdom of Paul in keeping the sailors on board when they tried to desert the ship the night before. The sailors prepare to maneuver the ship toward the beach (v. 40). They cut the ropes that hold the anchors, leaving them in the sea and setting the ship adrift. At the same time they release the two large oar-like rudders. These steering paddles, one at each side toward the back of the ship, had earlier been lifted out of the water, and their handles had been pressed down on the deck and fastened there with ropes for safety during the storm. They are now slipped back into the water for steering. The sailors also hoist a sail on the forward mast, which gives the vessel forward movement through the water.

Having prepared to control the ship by the use of both the sail and rudders, the sailors head for the beach in the gale. In spite of their skill, things do not go as planned. As they guide the ship toward the shore, it strikes a sandbar at the entrance of the bay. The front of the ship plows deep into the sand so that no one can move it (v. 41). While the bow of the ship rests on the sandbar, the hind part is in deep water and exposed to the violent force of the waves. The ship is still a considerable distance from the beach, and the strong waves put strain on the timbers of the vessel, dashing against the stern and doing great damage to it (v. 41). The breaking of the stern into pieces confirms Paul's predictions that the ship would be destroyed (v. 22).

If the crew and passengers hope to escape, they cannot lose any time in leaving the ship. Before the soldiers try to swim to shore, they want to kill the prisoners (v. 42). Under the conditions of shipwreck the prisoners are probably not in chains. If they swim to shore, they might flee into the countryside, and it would be difficult for the soldiers to recapture them. Being responsible for their prisoners, the soldiers know that they could be charged with negligence.

But the centurion is kindly disposed toward Paul. Once again, therefore, Paul is the reason why the lives of his fellow passengers are spared. Wanting to prevent Paul from being killed, the Roman officer stops the soldiers from carrying out their plan to slaughter the prisoners (v. 43). Nothing is indicated about the centurion's attitude toward the other prisoners, but he refuses to put Paul's life in danger. Evidently the events of the voyage must have increased his admiration for the apostle. He has developed a genuine gratitude for Paul's conduct of himself on board under terrifying circumstances.

The ship is still in water too deep for wading. Because of the waves and the depth of the water, it is no easy task to reach the beach. But the centurion orders everyone to try to make it to shore, either by swimming or by floating on wreckage from the ship. The ship's crew and all the passengers reach the beach (v. 44). Their safety is truly remarkable, even more so in that it fulfills the prophecy of verse 24: "God has graciously given you the lives of all who sail with you."

The safe arrival of crew and passengers on the island is a tribute to the faithfulness of God, who has caused his servant Paul to triumph. God had declared that not a single person would be lost; but as he often does to accomplish his purpose, he used people such as Paul, the centurion, the soldiers, and the crew. It is not unusual for God to use individuals to fulfill his promises. We should diligently carry out God's will and mission as though we have no promise of his help. On the other hand, we should always be confident of his help as though all will be done by God.

7.2. Paul Winters in Malta (28:1–10)

As soon as daylight appears, likely a number of the local people on the island see the distressed ship and watch as the sailors try to guide it to the beach. The shipwrecked travelers learn from the inhabitants that the name of the island is Malta. It is about sixty miles south of Sicily; its length is seventeen miles, with a maximum width of nine miles. Their safe arrival fulfills Paul's prophecy that they would run aground on an island (27:26). Every prophetic word he spoke on the ship has proved to be true. While he is on Malta, we see two other aspects of Paul's portrait: God's protection of him, and a demonstration of his prophetic deeds.

7.2.1. Paul Survives Viper Bite (28:1–6). Luke calls the people on Malta *hoi barbaroi* (lit., "barbarians"; NIV, "the islanders"). This designation does not mean that they were uncivilized, but that they did not speak Greek. They were descendants of the ancient Phoenicians, a highly civilized people, and probably spoke a dialect of Punic or Phoenician. Except for themselves, the Greeks considered all people as barbarians; but these barbarians, probably rustic, simple people, are far from savages. Such people could be expected to be suspicious of strangers and even hostile toward them. Paul and his fellow travelers, however, are pleasantly surprised that the natives are hospitable and receive them in a friendly manner.

When Paul and his companions reach the beach, it is raining and cold. The natives show their kindness by building a fire and welcoming them to the island (v. 2). It is no small task to build a fire in the rain, and one large enough so that 276 people can get near it. The extraordinary kindness of the Maltese prompts them to build that fire and to care for the shipwrecked travelers for about three months (v. 11).

Among those who gather wood for the fire is Paul. Making himself useful, he picks up an armful of brushwood. As he is putting it on the fire, a poisonous snake darts out of the hot fire, bites his hand, and keeps hanging on. When the Maltese natives see what happens, they quickly conclude that Paul must be a murderer (v. 4). Though he has escaped from the ship, they are convinced that he is a marked man and now has been overtaken by a more terrible fate. The attack by the snake, so they think, is a visit from a god called Justice (*dike*).

Greek mythology has a goddess of Justice. The people of Malta probably have a similar deity. They are aware that good people may be bitten by a snake, but they also know that Paul has escaped from drowning at sea, and they have probably learned that he is a prisoner. What they know about him contributes to their conviction that this man is a murderer and that the snake bite is an act of divine judgment. Seemingly unperturbed, Paul shakes off his assailant and shows no side effects of the snake bite. Nevertheless, the natives think that the attack will prove fatal, so they expect him to swell up and fall dead suddenly (v. 6).

Realizing after a long time that Paul really has no ill effects from the snake, the Maltese change their minds and conclude that he is a god rather than a murderer. At Lystra Paul was first thought to be a god, and afterward was stoned (14:8–20). Here he is first taken as a murderer and then as a god. What they have seen is a marvel in their eyes.

Though there is no disclaimer here of Paul's being a "god," he obviously does not consider himself as divine (14:15). God's miraculous power works through him, and his survival of the snake bite clearly confirms that he is under divine protection. That protection is not from the gods of pagan religion but from the God who has revealed himself in Christ, to whom Paul belongs and whom he serves (cf. 27:23–24). By protecting Paul from the harm of a snake bite, the Lord directs attention to his servant and fulfills in him the promise of Luke 10:19.

7.2.2. Paul Heals Many Maltese (28:7–10). Paul and his fellow travelers are fortunate to have landed where they did, for they are treated kindly by the people on the island. Near where they went ashore is the estate of the chief official of the island. His name is Publius, and the title given to him in the Greek here suggests that he is the governor of Malta. He is either the leading Roman official on the island or a native official. Likely he is a Roman in charge of the island.

The governor manifests the same warmth toward Paul and the others as the Maltese have done. If "us" (v. 7) refers to the entire shipwrecked party, the governor entertains with food and lodging 276 men. That kind of hospitality is worthy of commendation. Whether the governor extends his invitation to all the men we cannot be certain, but it certainly includes Paul and Luke. It may be that Publius provides lodging and food for the entire shipwrecked party for three days.

While Paul is on Malta, many of the sick are miraculously healed. His prophetic power is first demonstrated in his healing the father of Publius. At this time the governor's father lies sick, suffering from attacks of fever and dysentery (v. 8). Paul goes to the room of the sick man. Through his prayer of faith and the laying on of hands, God heals him (cf. Paul's own healing in 9:17). This healing shows that the apostle is empowered by the Spirit and that the miraculous power of Jesus continues to manifest itself through this charismatic prophet (c Luke 4:40; 13:13; Acts 5:12; 14:3; 19:11).

Word about the miracle spreads througho the island. The sick of Malta come to Paul, ar as the Spirit-filled apostle prays and lays han on them, many are healed. The entire islar benefits from Paul's presence and ministr Those who are healed show their gratitude and respect for Paul and his companions by pr senting them with gifts. They also express the thanks by tending to the needs of the compar when it comes time for them to resume the journey to Rome. Expressions of their gratitud confirm the reality of Paul's prophetic deeds.

Luke reports nothing about Paul's preac ing of the gospel on Malta. But it is hard t imagine that he healed the people of their di eases without mentioning the name of Jesu During his three-month stay there, the nam and the power of Jesus must have becom known throughout the island. Often miracle are the seal of the gospel.

7.3. Paul's Arrival at Rome (28:11–15)

Paul and his shipwrecked companion spend three months on Malta, probably fror mid-November to mid-February. As soon a sailing is considered safe, they continue the voyage. In the early spring they embark on a Alexandrian ship, which may have docked a Malta during the severest part of the winte Like the one that was wrecked, it must hav been loaded with wheat for the Italian marke It is distinguished by the insignia of the twi brothers Castor and Pollux, sons of Zeus. I Greek mythology these twin gods were con

MIRACLES OF THE APOSTLES

Miracle	Acts
Lame man cured (by Peter)	3:6–9
Death of Ananias and Sapphira	5:1–10
Saul's sight restored	9:17–18
Healing of Aeneas	9:33–35
Raising of Dorcas	9:36–41
Elymas blinded	13:8–11
Lame man cured (by Paul)	14:8–10
Demon cast out of a girl	16:16–18
Raising of Eutychus	20:9–10
Unharmed by viper	28:3–5
Healing of Publius's father	28:7–9

lered special guardians of sailors and were ten worshiped by them. Egypt had a wide-read cult to them. Such an insignia must ve been regarded as a protective charm.

On the final stage of the journey the apos- proceeds with remarkable freedom. They op first at Syracuse, a flourishing city on the utheastern coast of Sicily, about a hundred iles from Malta (v. 12). The ship remains re for three days because of either adverse nds or the unloading of cargo. Then they sail to Rhegium, on the toe of Italy in the straits Messina (v. 13). From the southern extrem- of Italy they sail north with favorable winds the city of Puteoli, near modern Naples. This smopolitan city was the regular seaport for ips from the east and the place where grain ips from Alexandria usually unloaded.

A church had already been established in teoli, proof that the gospel had been preached Italy before Paul arrives in Rome. Such urches remind us that the gospel spread to rts of the Roman empire, including Rome, by named missionaries. Paul and his compan-ns stay for a week with the Christians at Pute-i (v. 14). No explanation is given why they op here for seven days, but Paul must have joyed a week of rest and fellowship with the ristians there, including a day of worship on e Lord's Day. In the meantime the Christians Rome hear of Paul's arrival at Puteoli.

It is puzzling to find Luke writing, "And so e came to Rome" before they actually do . 14). The effect is that he refers twice to their rival at Rome (v. 16). Likely "so" (*houtos*) in rse 14 should be translated "as follows," dicating that under the following circum-ances they make their way to Rome, the goal the entire journey.

The route that Paul takes from Puteoli to ome is about 150 miles. Christians from ome travel south on the famous Appian Way, ancient paved road from Puteoli to Rome. welcome the apostle some Roman Chris-ans walk to the Three Taverns, a frequent eeting place for travelers. Three Taverns was little more than thirty miles from Rome. Oth-s walk another ten miles to the Forum of ppius, a market town. Before Paul reaches ome, in other words, he has been welcomed penly by two groups of Christians from ome. When he sees them, he thanks God and encouraged to know that he has friends in the city of Rome. These Roman believers receive him as God's "servant and . . . witness" (26:16).

Paul has many reasons for being grateful to God. Among them is his safe arrival after a long, difficult journey. At sea he has experienced many dangers, and he must have had some anxiety about what he will encounter in Rome. He will enter the city as a prisoner in chains. Until the Roman Christians meet him on the final leg of his journey, he most likely has apprehension about their reception of him.

But the Roman believers show themselves to be people of true Christian compassion and become for Paul a source of comfort. Their mutual bond "in Christ" has brought them forth to meet the author of the letter written to them. He must have realized that his letter had been well received by the Roman church. He now has a thrilling story to tell these faithful Christians about what has finally brought him to Rome and how on the journey the sovereign God had protected him from a storm and the bite of a venomous snake.

7.4. Paul Under House Arrest (28:16–31)

The apostle has arrived at Rome for his trial. The travel narrative of Acts has come to its conclusion. Paul's arrival in Rome is according to the prophetic pattern established by Jesus and conforms to the programmatic outline of Acts 1:8: "to the ends of the earth." The scope of the task of the church is worldwide. For this task of evangelism the disciples, including Paul, had received the promised power of the Holy Spirit (Luke 24:49; Acts 1:4, 8; 9:17–19). The Holy Spirit has directed and empowered them for ministry from the center of Judaism to the imperial city of the Gentile world.

7.4.1. Paul Placed in the Custody of a Soldier (28:16). Paul is handed over to the Roman authorities. But instead of being placed in a common prison, the authorities extend him an unusual courtesy: They allow him to live by himself in a private house under the guard of a single soldier. He is also given considerable freedom, including permission to have visitors. The treatment he receives from the Roman government may be due to the report of the centurion Julius about Paul's conduct on the journey.

7.4.2. Paul's First Meeting With Leading Jews (28:17–22). Paul's entrance into Rome was different from what he had hoped (Rom.

15:24, 30–32). He had come to the city as a prisoner and remains a prisoner for two years. Though the Romans have placed him under house arrest and have given him a measure of freedom, he is not allowed to visit the synagogues or to participate in a public forum. He is kept under military guard day and night.

Nevertheless, Paul's missionary strategy does not change at Rome. His first focus is on unbelieving Jews. Throughout his missionary work he always made his first appeal to the Jews; when they rejected the gospel, he turned to the Gentiles. Thus, after Paul has been in Rome for three days, he invites non-Christian Jews to meet with him so that he can explain the nature of the gospel to them. The brief account of his activities in the city over the two years centers on his relationship with these Jewish leaders. He gives them an opportunity to respond to the gospel as he had preached it over the years. No doubt, they are already familiar with the message from those in Rome who were present in Jerusalem at the outpouring of the Holy Spirit (2:10).

Nobody really knows why Paul's trial is delayed. Perhaps Paul's Jewish accusers from Palestine delayed their coming, or there was difficulty in finding a slot on Caesar's calendar for the trial. The documents sent by Festus specifying the charges may have been lost in the shipwreck (27:27–41) Securing duplicates would have taken time and would have also caused a delay (Blaiklock, 1959, 194). For whatever reason, Luke gives no hint that Paul became discouraged during his two-year imprisonment. Rather, he took advantage of his stay in Rome to do the work of an evangelist among those who visited his dwelling place.

Those who respond to Paul's invitation to meet with him are apparently unfamiliar with his case, so he explains to them why he has been brought to Rome as a prisoner. He addresses these representatives of a large body of Jews in the city as "my brothers" (v. 17; cf. 22:1). What he says to them can be outlined in four points. (1) He has done nothing to harm the Jewish people or to violate the religious practices handed down by their ancestors. However, he had been "handed over to the Romans" by the leaders of Jerusalem. Some scholars think this statement contradicts the earlier account of the Romans' rescue of Paul from the Jews, who wanted to put him to death (21:30–36). But Paul's speech to the Jews i Rome is highly abbreviated. Luke is, therefor concerned with the essentials and does not tr to give all the details.

(2) After the Romans questioned him, Pa insists they wanted to release him (v. 18). The found that he had done nothing that made hi worthy of death. Paul here makes clearer th intentions of the Romans than has previousl been stated. King Agrippa was the one wh declared that Paul should be released, and Fe tus apparently agreed with him (26:32). Th Jews, however, insisted on pressing charge against him.

(3) Opposition from the Jews compelle Paul to appeal to Caesar (v. 19). Even thoug they had opposed his being released, Paul appeal was not due to any bitterness or charg against his people. He is in Rome to preach th gospel and to defend himself, not to mak accusations against the Jews. He tries to b conciliatory toward them and wants them know why he is a prisoner in Rome (v. 20 That is why he has called them together t meet with him.

(4) Concluding his remarks, he declares th it is "because of the hope of Israel" that he now in chains (cf. 23:6; 26:6–7). This is the re issue of his trial. He wants the Jewish leade to learn firsthand that he is a loyal Jew and th he is a prisoner. Like any devout Jew, h believes in the coming of the Messiah and th resurrection. Jesus' triumph over death is co vincing evidence of both his messiahship an the doctrine of the resurrection. He is in chai because he accepts the crucified and risen Jes as the fulfillment of his nation's greatest hop

The Jewish leaders know that it is n uncommon for their people to be persecute for their faith, even though Judaism w legally permitted by the Romans. When Pa completes his explanation, the Roman Jew candidly state that they know nothing abo Paul's case. They have not received any wri ten reports from Judea that could be used i court against Paul. Neither had any messeng come with an oral report, denouncing the apo tle. Evidently the authorities in Jerusalem ha not pursued the case. They must have realiz that they had little ground on which to build case against Paul in Rome.

Nevertheless, the Roman Jews do want hear what Paul has to say. They know som ing about "this sect" that he represents. oman Jews present at the outpouring of the oly Spirit in Jerusalem on the day of Pente- ost returned home with the gospel, and the urch in Rome has some Jewish Christians Rom. 2:17). But the information that these ncoverted Jews have is general. They also now that the church in Rome is often under tack and that the Christian movement is spo- en against everywhere (v. 22). Most of what ey have heard is negative and prejudicial. So ey want to learn more about why Christian- y is out of favor, especially with the authori- es in Jerusalem.

7.4.3. Paul's Second Meeting With Lead- g Jews (28:23–29). Paul has treated the oman Jews with courtesy. He has spoken to em in a conciliatory manner, and they seem illing to listen to new points of view. Before ey leave Paul, they make an appointment to ear him speak at length on the subject of the ospel of Jesus Christ. They come in "even rger numbers" (v. 23) on the appointed day the place where Paul is staying for a second eeting.

Luke gives us only a brief summary of aul's testimony to them. The discourse is a ng one, for Paul devotes the whole day to xplaining to them the kingdom of God. The hrase "the kingdom of God" means essen- ally the reign of God, though it can refer to e entire Christian message (cf. also 19:8;):25; 28:31), including the future reign of od, to be realized at Christ's second coming 4:22; cf. Luke 22:30; 23:42). To his Jewish sitors Paul emphasizes the breaking in of od's new reign in the person of Jesus Christ. od's rule has been established by his mighty ts in the death and resurrection of Jesus.

As always in his preaching to the Jews, he ppeals to the Old Testament. Paul represents esus as the fulfillment of God's promises in e Scripture (Luke 24:27; Acts 2:25–36; 3:18;):43). What the Law of Moses and the rophets had predicted about the Messiah is lfilled in Jesus' death and his resurrection. hese Scriptures provide the main evidence r his arguments, but some of the Jews are not nvinced that his interpretation is correct.

As Paul had frequently experienced on ear- er occasions, the response of the Jews to the ospel is mixed (vv. 24–25; 13:43; 14:4; 17:4, ; 18:4–8). Some are favorable to the gospel and believe what he has said is true. Others completely reject his message. Again, God's people are divided into two camps. The meet- ing breaks up with the Jews arguing among themselves. As they are about to depart, Paul applies the prophecy of Isaiah 6:9–10 to the unbelieving portion of his audience, a text that strongly indicates Jewish rejection of the gospel (Acts 28:25–28). The reference to "the Holy Spirit" (v. 25) summarizes the Spirit's prophetic function in inspiring the Scriptures. The direct action of the Spirit caused Isaiah to prophesy, and the Spirit is now speaking to the unbeliev- ing Jews through the words of the prophet.

Isaiah's prophecy explains why many Jews have not accepted the gospel. God has poured out his judgment on them because they refuse to hear the message and believe. The ones who reject the gospel do not comprehend the mes- sage; "they hardly hear with their ears, and they have closed their eyes." If they were truly open to the gospel, they would "see with their eyes, hear with their ears, understand with their hearts" (v. 27; cf. Matt. 13:13–15). On the other hand, their eyes and ears are not closed by some power above them. They themselves have chosen voluntarily not to understand and perceive what God is saying to them.

Spiritual insight is the work of the Holy Spirit, but the unbelieving Jews' lack of insight is due to their stubbornness. They have made their hearts callous to God's Word. If they open their eyes and ears to what Paul has presented, they will indeed turn to the Lord and be saved. The authoritative word is painful to perceive and hear, for it pronounces judgment on sin and unbelief. As the word condemns sin and wounds the conscience, it also intends to heal us—not only physical healing but also spiritual transformation. Receiving the gospel causes us to be well again, but the consequences of reject- ing the gospel can be disastrous. "Once a per- son deliberately refuses the word, there comes a point when he is deprived of the capacity to receive it. It is a stern warning to those who tri- fle with the gospel" (Marshall, 1980, 425).

God is no respecter of persons. To all who hear the gospel he extends through the Holy Spirit the gift of salvation. No one can ascribe his or her final ruin to God. The Jews' stubborn rejection of the gospel fulfills Isaiah's prophecy. They refuse to listen to the prophets, but God continues to speak to them through the prophetic Spirit, urging and calling them to repent and accept salvation. The Spirit does this not because they deserve it, but because God is faithful.

The unbelief of Paul's countrymen prompts him to make a solemn pronouncement, consistent with his pattern throughout Acts: "Therefore I want you to know that God's salvation has been sent to the Gentiles, and they will listen!" (v. 28). As a result of Jewish resistance to the gospel in 13:46–48 and 18:6, Paul turned from the Jews to the Gentiles. Here Paul's break with his fellow Jews seems sharper than his earlier turnings to the Gentiles. The message of salvation is now going to the Gentiles, and they will respond more favorably. No longer does he feel that God's message of salvation must first be preached to the Jews (cf. Rom. 11:11–24). Nothing, therefore, can stop the gospel in its forward march "to the ends of the earth"—not even the persistent unbelief of God's chosen people, the Jews. Paul does envision the conversion of Israel at a later time (Rom. 11:25–32), but for now the real hope lies with the mission to the Gentiles.

Verse 29 is omitted in modern translations, including the NIV. It appears in the Western text and is simply a repetition of verse 25.

7.4.4. Paul Preaches the Gospel for Two Years (28:30–31). The narrative of Acts ends abruptly with Paul still a prisoner. If Luke knows what happened after this period (including the outcome of his trial before Caesar), he does not tell his readers about it. That conclusion satisfies neither the curiosity of many modern readers nor their literary taste. References such as 20:25, 38; 21:13; and 25:11 may imply that Paul finally died as a martyr for the sake of the gospel. Some are convinced that after two years Paul was tried and executed, but it seems more likely that he was acquitted and released. Evidence in the Pastoral Letters suggests that he had a post-Acts ministry and was then rearrested (probably during the Neronic persecution).

Luke has shown how the gospel has spread from Jerusalem to Rome through the power of the Holy Spirit. Many Gentiles have accepted the message of salvation, but the Jewish people as a whole have grown increasingly hostile toward the gospel. Yet their opposition does not stop the gospel's advance. Acts has traced the power of the Holy Spirit working in the church until Paul comes to Rome. The Spir has empowered God's servants to preach th gospel and has sovereignly brought the "apos tle to the Gentiles" to that imperial city.

Luke gives few of the details of the tw years Paul spends in Rome. As the apostl lives in a house at his own expense, he is wai ing for trial in Caesar's court and "boldly an without hindrance" preaches the gospel to a who come to him. The last word of the Gree text of Acts is "without hindrance." This wor refers to both the theological freedom of th gospel from Jewish constrictions and th preaching of it "without hindrance" in the cit of Rome. The word of God freely enters th hearts of those who believe: "Everyone wh calls on the name of the Lord will be saved (2:21; cf. 13:39). All the obstacles and hir drances of salvation are removed in Christ.

As Luke has shown, the gospel is goo news for everyone, regardless of where a pe son comes from. The good news is not for onl one nation but for believers of all nations in th forgiving grace of Christ (Luke 24:47). In spi of obstacles and hindrances, the gosp remains unhindered for those who believe it. is an irrepressible message, and Paul has co fidence in it, preaching the good news "boldly to everyone who comes to see him.

The unhindered proclamation in the cent of the Gentile world strikes a powerful note o the triumph of the Christian mission. Notwit standing his chains, Paul is free to preach th gospel of salvation. At the beginning of h ministry Jesus declared, "The Spirit of th Lord is on me, because he has anointed me t preach good news to the poor" (Luke 4:18 The Spirit-empowered Savior devoted h entire ministry to proclaiming the gospel. Ju before he ascended to the Father, he instructe his disciples as a consequence of his death an resurrection to preach "repentance and fo giveness of sins . . . to all nations" (24:47). Th third Gospel closes with him speaking abo what his Father had promised and givin instruction to "stay . . . until you have bee clothed with power from on high" (24:49).

Acts continues the story of Luke's Gospe It opens with the promise of power for wi nessing and a program for extending th gospel to the ends of the earth (Acts 1:8). Th remainder of the book shows the continuou advance of the preaching of the gospel. Not g could hinder its progress and ultimate victory. Persecution and imprisonment could not inder the march of the gospel. Both Peter and aul were delivered from jail (5:19; 12:6–11; 6:26–40). Human barriers of racial prejudice d separation did not stop the gospel.

The Gentiles received the baptism in the pirit exactly as did the Jewish believers at entecost. Aware that God had bestowed on the entiles the Spirit's power, Peter challenged yone present to "keep these people from eing baptized with water" (10:47). The Greek ord "keep" (*kolysai*) derives from the same ot as the last word of Acts, "without hinrance" (*akolytos*). Not allowing the gospel to e hindered, the Spirit opened the doors of the urch to all, and regardless of sexual and age ifferences believers were baptized with his ower (2:17). The physically handicapped man ould not get beyond the temple door (3:2–11), d the Ethiopian eunuch because of his physal condition could not be accepted by the Jews as a full convert (8:26–39), but the saving power of God was available to both of them.

Without being limited by a narrow nationalistic outlook, the church, empowered by the Spirit, preached the gospel beyond the border of Palestine. The gospel continued to triumph over all barriers when Paul, a Spirit-inspired missionary and apostle, arrived as a prisoner in Rome. Near the end of his life he remained confident of the triumph of the gospel. Thus, he could write that he suffers "even to the point of being chained like a criminal. But God's word is not chained" (2 Tim. 2:9). During his imprisonment the gospel continued spreading and reached "those who belong to Caesar's household" (Phil. 4:22). The good news that began in the Jerusalem temple (Luke 1:5–20) has marched to the imperial city of Rome—"the ends of the earth." What could be a more appropriate conclusion to Luke-Acts than an affirmation of the power of the gospel to triumph over all opposition and barriers?

THE OLD TESTAMENT IN THE NEW

NT Text	OT Text	Subject
Ac 1:20	Ps 69:25	Judgment on Judas
Ac 1:20	Ps 109:8	Replacement for Judas
Ac 2:17–21	Joel 2:28–32	God's Spirit poured out
Ac 2:25–28, 31	Ps 16:8–11	Resurrection of Christ
Ac 2:34–35	Ps 110:1	At God's right hand
Ac 3:22–23	Dt 18:15, 18–19	The prophet
Ac 3:25	Ge 22:18; 26:4	Nations blessed in Abraham
Ac 4:11	Ps 118:22	Rejected cornerstone
Ac 4:24	Ex 20:11; Ps 146:6	God the Creator
Ac 4:25–26	Ps 2:1–2	Kings against the Lord
Ac 7:3	Ge 12:1	Call of Abraham
Ac 7:6–7	Ge 15:13–14	Prophecy to Abraham
Ac 7:18	Ex 1:8	King who did not know Joseph
Ac 7:27–28, 35	Ex 2:14	Moses in Egypt
Ac 7:32	Ex 3:6	The living God
Ac 7:33	Ex 3:5	Moses at the burning bush
Ac 7:34	Ex 3:7–8, 10	God promises to deliver Israel
Ac 7:37	Dt 18:15	The prophet
Ac 7:40	Ex 32:1, 23	Asking for idols
Ac 7:42–43	Am 5:25–27	Sin and judgment
Ac 7:49–50	Isa 66:1–2	No temple contains God
Ac 8:32–33	Isa 53:7–8	Jesus as the dying Lamb
Ac 13:33	Ps 2:7	You are my Son
Ac 13:34	Isa 55:3	Blessings of David
Ac 13:35	Ps 16:10	Resurrection of Christ
Ac 13:41	Hab 1:5	Judgment for sin
Ac 13:47	Isa 49:6	Salvation of the Gentiles
Ac 14:15	Ex 20:11; Ps 146:6	God the Creator
Ac 15:16–17	Am 9:11–12	Restoration for everyone
Ac 23:5	Ex 22:28	Cursing rulers
Ac 28:26–27	Isa 6:9–10	Seeing but not perceiving

BIBLIOGRAPHY

F. L. Arrington, "The Indwelling, Baptism, and Infilling With the Holy Spirit: A Differentiation of Terms," *Pneuma* 3/2 (1981): 1–10; idem, *Christian Doctrine*, vol. 3 (1994); idem, *The Acts of the Apostles* (1988); D. E. Aune, *The New Testament in Its Literary Environment* (1987); C. K. Barrett, *Luke the Historian in Recent Study* (1961); E. M. Blaiklock, *The Acts of the Apostles* (1959); D. L. Bock, *Luke* (1994); R. G. Bratcher, *A Translation Guide to the Gospel of Luke* (1982); R. E. Brown, "Luke's Description of the Virginal Conception," *T S* (1974): 360–62; F. F. Bruce, *Are the New Testament Documents Reliable?* (1943); idem, *The Acts of the Apostles: The Greek Text With Introduction and Commentary* (1952); idem, *Commentary on the Book of Acts* (1956); G. B. Caird, *The Gospel of St. Luke* (1963); F. B. Craddock, *Luke* (1990); H. E. Dana and J. R. Mantey, *A Manual Grammar of the Greek New Testament* (1955); W. D. Davies, *Invitation to the New Testament* (1966); R. J. Dean, *Layman's Bible Book Commentary* (1983); D. S. Dockery, K. A. Matthews, and R. B. Sloan, eds., *Foundations for Biblical Interpretation* (1994); H. M. Ervin, *Spirit Baptism* (1987); J. A. Fitzmyer, *The Gospel According to Luke I-IX* (1981); H. Flender, *St. Luke: Theologian of Redemptive History* (1967); E. Franklin, *Christ the Lord: A Study of the Purpose and Theology of Luke-Acts* (1975); W. W. Gasque and R. P. Martin, eds., *Apostolic History and the Gospel* (1970); W. W. Gasque, *A History of the Criticism of the Acts of the Apostles* (1975); N. Geldenhuys, *Commentary on the Gospel of Luke* (1951); T. George, *Galatians* (1994); E. Haenchen, *The Acts of the Apostles* (1971); C. J. Hemer, *The Book of Acts in the Setting of Hellenistic History* (1990); M. Hengel, *Acts and the History of Earliest Christianity* (1979); idem, *The Acts of the Apostles* (1951); idem, *Between Jesus and Paul* (1983); S. Horton, *What the Bible Says About the Holy Spirit* (1976); A. M. Hunter, *Interpreting the Parables* (1960); J. Jervell, *Luke and the People of God* (1972); D. Juel, *Luke-Acts* (1983); R. J. Karris, *What Are They Saying About Luke and Acts?* (1979); L. E. Keck a J. L. Martyn, eds., *Studies in Luke-Acts* (1966); M. Lee, "Walk to Emmaus," *ExpTim* 77 (Septer ber, 1966): 380–81; R. C. H. Lenski, *The Interpr tation of St. Luke's Gospel* (1946); I. H. Marsha *The Acts of the Apostles* (1980); idem, *Commenta on Luke* (1978); R. P. Martin, *New Testament Fou dations*, vol. 1 (1975) and vol. 2 (1978); G. McGee, ed., *Initial Evidence* (1991); D. P. Moes ner, *Lord of the Banquet* (1989); D. Moody, *Spi of the Living God* (1968); L. Morris, *Luke* (197 A. Q. Morton and G. H. C. Macgregor, *The Stru ture of Luke-Acts* (1964); L. Morris, "Luke a Early Catholicism," in *Studying the New Testame Today*, ed. J. H. Skilton, 1974; W. Neil, *The Acts the Apostles* (1973); B. M. Newman and E. A. Nid *A Translator's Handbook on the Acts of the Apo tles* (1972); K. F. Nickle, *The Synoptic Gospe* (1980); J. C. O'Neill, *Theology of Acts in Its Hi torical Setting* (1961); R. F. O'Toole, *The Unity Luke's Theology: An Analysis of Luke-Acts* (198 A. Plummer, *A Critical and Exegetical Commenta on the Gospel According to St. Luke* (1896); R. Rackham, *The Acts of the Apostles* (1953); J. Re ing and J. L. Swellengrebel, *A Translator's Han book on the Gospel of Luke* (1971); A. T. Roberts *A Grammar of the Greek New Testament in t Light of Historical Research* (1934); E. Schweiz *The Good News According to Luke* (1984); W. Scroggie, *The Acts of the Apostles* (1976); W. Shepherd, *The Narrative Function of the Holy Spi As a Character in Luke-Acts* (1994); A. N. Sherwi White, *Roman Society and Roman Law in the Ne Testament* (1963); S. Soderlund, "Burning Hear and Open Minds: Exposition on the Emma Road," *Crux* 23 (March, 1987): 2–4; R. Stronsta *The Charismatic Theology of St. Luke* (1984); ide "The Influence of the Old Testament on the Chari matic Theology of Luke," *Pneuma* 2 (1980): 32–5 C. H. Talbert, *Literary Patterns, Theologic Themes, and the Genre of Luke-Acts* (1974); W. van Unnik, "The 'Book of Acts': The Confirmati of the Gospel," *NovT* 4 (1960): 26–59; C. Weisiger III, *The Gospel of Luke* (1966).

ROMANS

Van Johnson

NTRODUCTION

. Author

n order to enhance our reading of Romans, a ew pertinent matters about the author—Paul, he Jewish apostle to the Gentiles—will be lealt with briefly:

a. Paul's Calling

"Christianity is not a religion; it is a relaionship" is a favorite saying of evangelicals. 'aul would have had no quarrel with this charcterization of the Christian life, since Chrisianity for him was intensely personal. What lse might we expect, considering the nature f his own "conversion"? He was not won ver in the midst of debate or through hearng the testimonies of believers. Even watchng Stephen being stoned for his faith did not hange Paul's belief about Christianity (Acts :54–8:1). He was seized by Jesus himself, vho confronted him on the road to Damascus nd called him (9:1–9). Consequently, he haracterizes himself as a "called . . . apostle" nd "a servant of Christ Jesus" (Rom. 1:1).

Paul's Jewish past had already predisposed im to view faith in relational terms. Nowhere s this more apparent than in the idea of the ovenant. God entered into a covenant with \braham; that is, he established a relationship vith Abraham in order to create a people for imself. The Old Testament concept of the ighteousness of God, which is the overarchng theme of Romans, concerns the manner in vhich God acts to fulfill the terms of this ovenant relationship. Israel was to respond in ove and obedience to the One who not only nitiated the relationship, but also maintained t by his righteousness.

This relational understanding of faith was ntensified for Paul when he met the living Christ. That the truth of the gospel came to 'aul through a personal encounter affected the nanner in which he later describes it. To cite xamples from every section of Romans:

- The aforementioned theme of the righteousness of God (e.g., 1:17) emphasizes God's saving acts to bring people into relationship with himself (e.g., 3:21–31).
- The wrath of God falls on those who have rejected the relationship he offers (1:18–23; 2:4–5).
- Peace with God (5:1), which results from justification by faith, refers to the restoration of relationship between humanity and God.
- Paul depicts life as either being related to Adam or related to Christ (5:12–21).
- Our relationship with Christ is such that we actually share in his life in a manner that goes beyond the nature of human relationships—we have died with Christ, and we will be raised with him (6:2–10).
- The indwelling Spirit causes the presence of Jesus to be made real to us (8:9–10). We have been adopted into the people of God, and that adoption is confirmed to us by the witness of the Spirit (8:14–17) and secured by the saving work of God and Christ (8:31–39).
- The paraenesis section of the letter begins with the premise that we live our lives in response to the mercy of God (12:1–2).
- The paraenesis section goes on to describe how our relationship with God and Christ is to be lived out in our relationships with others (12:3–15:13). In other words, we live in response to the relationship that he has graciously initiated.

Paul's calling was not only personal, it was specific: He was to be an apostle to the Gentiles (1:5; cf. Gal. 1:15–16). Although Peter, John, and James recognized that Paul had been called to this type of ministry (Gal. 2:9), his message to the Gentiles about freedom in Christ, without regard for Jewish observances, led to criticism from Jews both inside and outside of the church. As a result, in the course of dictating Romans Paul takes great pains to defend the nature of his apostleship (e.g., see Rom. 1:1–6). The apostle not only affirms his love for his own people (9:1–3; 10:1), but also discloses that he views his Gentile mission as a means of stirring the Jews to jealousy that they might come to Christ (11:13–15).

TIMELINE OF PAUL'S LIFE

5 A.D.	Birth of Saul between 6 B.C. and A.D. 10, but probably about A.D. 5 (based on the terms "young man," Ac 7:58, and "old man," Phm 9)
35	Martyrdom of Stephen (Ac 7:57–60)
	Conversion of Saul (Ac 9:1–19)
35–38	Arabian trip (Gal 1:17) fits in at Ac 9:23, during the "many days"
38	Two-week visit to Jerusalem (Ac 9:26–29; Gal 1:18–19)
38–43	Ministry in Syria and Cilicia (Ac 9:30; Gal 1:21)
43	Arrival in Syrian Antioch (Ac 11:25–26)
43/44	Famine visit (Ac 11:27–30; 12:25; Gal 2:1–10?); Herod's death, which occurred in A.D. 44, is sandwiched between the trips to and from Jerusalem (Ac 12:19–23)
46–48	First Missionary Journey (Ac 13:2–14:28)
48/49	Writing of Galatians (?) from Syrian Antioch
49/50	Jerusalem conference (Ac 15:1–29; Gal 2:1–10?)
50–52	Second Missionary Journey (Ac 15:40–18:23)
51	Writing of 1 Thessalonians from Corinth
51/52	Writing of 2 Thessalonians from Corinth
51/52	Appearance before Gallio (Ac 18:12–17)
51/52	Writing of Galatians? from Corinth
52	Return to Jerusalem and Syrian Antioch (Ac 18:22)
53	Writing of Galatians? from Syrian Antioch
53–57	Third Missionary Journey (Ac 18:23–21:17)
53–55	At Ephesus (Ac 19:1–20:1)
55	Writing of 1 Corinthians from Ephesus
55	Writing of 2 Corinthians from Macedonia
57	Writing of Romans from Cenchrea or Corinth
57	Arrest in Jerusalem (Ac 21:27–22:30)
57–59	Caesarean imprisonment (Ac 23:23–26:32)
59	Shipwreck voyage to Rome (Ac 27:1–28:16)
59–61/62	First Roman imprisonment (Ac 28:16–31)
60	Writing of Ephesians from Rome
60	Writing of Colossians from Rome
60	Writing of Philemon from Rome
61	Writing of Philippians from Rome
62	Release from Roman imprisonment
62–67	Fourth Missionary Journey including ministry on Crete (Tit 1:5)
63–66	Writing of 1 Timothy and Titus from Philippi
67/68	Second Roman imprisonment (2 Ti 4:6–8)
67/68	Writing of 2 Timothy from the Mamertime dungeon (2 Ti 4:6–8)
67/68	Trial and execution

b. Paul's Apocalyptic Eschatology

The eschatological viewpoint (the term *eschatological* has to do with the end times) of Paul was a decisive factor in the formation of his theology. There are points of similarity between his eschatology and apocalyptic eschatology, which came into its own within Jewish circles in the second century B.C. and remained influential until the beginning of the second century A.D. There is no room to give a full treatment to the topic of apocalyptic eschatology, but some of its aspects and their relationship to Pauline ideas will be briefly drawn out here.

Apocalyptic eschatology stressed that the end of time would bring the solution for Israel's woes. Unlike a prominent theological view in the Old Testament, which tended to see the outworking of God's rewards and punishments within the course of history, apocalyptic eschatology was more inclined to view the dispensing of divine justice in the age to come. Certainly this view of the afterlife had its roots in the Old Testament (e.g., Isa. 26:19; Dan. 12:1–2), but many of the ideas surrounding the nature of the afterlife were debated and developed by the apocalyptic writers. They wrote of future hope to give consolation to the oppressed and to exhort them to be faithful in the meantime (cf. Rom. 5:3–5; 8:18–25; 13:11–14). In particular, it was their emphasis on the imminent end of this age that gave their writings such power to console and encourage.

In almost all of the Jewish apocalyptic writings the final judgment figured prominently as the moment when God's justice would be meted out. At that time the righteous would be rewarded and sinners punished. The judgment would be the moment of vindication for those who were faithful to God, when the whole world would see who were and were not the truly righteous (cf. Rom. 8:19). Paul's emphasis on justification occurring at the judgment corresponds with this view (3:20; 5:9–10, 19; cf. also Isa. 45:25; 50:8–9). At that time the divine judge will give his ruling about who is acquitted and who is condemned. This means that while justification can be said to be something that has already occurred for the believer (Rom. 5:1), it is only a present benefit because it is guaranteed to be a future reality.

Dualism is another trait of the apocalyptic worldview. Reality is depicted in one of two modes: There is a present age and an age to come, and there are only two types of people—sinners and the righteous. Similar to this, Paul will argue that one is either in Adam or in Christ (5:12–21), one is either under the power of sin or alive in Christ (ch. 6), and one is either in the flesh or in the Spirit (ch. 8).

But it is in terms of temporal dualism, the division between this age and the next, that Paul's eschatology differs from that of the popular apocalyptic conception. For Paul the future age has already broken into the present age. Until the Lord returns, we live in the overlap of the ages. His understanding of the work of Christ causes him to move the beginning of the future age *into the present*. Although the completion of God's saving work will come at the end of this age, the death and resurrection of Christ provide benefits in the here and now. Because of his death, those who are in Christ are already saved: They have died to sin and been brought into a new relationship with God. Because of his resurrection, those in Christ already experience something of his resurrection power in the midst of a dying world (chs. 5–6). This view of the two ages is commonly referred to as "the already/not yet" structure of eschatology. In other words, God's end-time work has already begun, but it will not be complete until the new age arrives when the present one ends.

c. Paul's View of the Law

One of the primary revolutions in New Testament studies over the last few decades is a new view of Second Temple Judaism and the role that the law played within it. The former understanding of Judaism as a religion of works-righteousness has been largely abandoned. Although this reevaluation of Judaism began earlier in this century, it was E. P. Sanders's *Paul and Palestinian Judaism* (1977) that set New Testament scholarship on a new course. Sanders argued that one can analyze a religion by looking at how one gets into that religion and how one stays in. By examining early Palestinian writings, he concluded that the law functioned in Judaism not as a means of gaining entry into the covenant (salvation), but as a means of maintaining a place within the covenant people. The Jews, therefore, understood that they were in a covenant relationship with God because God had elected them. Accordingly, observance of the law was seen as a response to God's gracious initiative. Sanders typified this pattern of religion as "covenantal nomism." This was not, then, a legalistic religion, if we understand legalism to be a system in which God's favor is gained by works.

The problem for the interpreter of Paul—and particularly for the reader of Romans, where discussion of Judaism and the law is pivotal to the argument of the letter—is to evaluate what he wrote in light of this new perspective on Judaism. The viewpoint that has dominated Protestant exegesis in the post-Reformation era is that Paul was criticizing the belief that one could gain righteousness by observing the law. In other words, Paul was attacking the very type of Judaism that Sanders argued never existed.

A number of solutions have been proposed to the current debate about Paul and the law. (1) One suggestion is that Paul did not understand Judaism. The obvious difficulty with this idea is that it proposes that we in the twentieth century can now comprehend what Paul, a participant in it, did not.

(2) Paul intentionally distorted Judaism to differentiate Christianity from its Jewish roots. By representing Judaism as a religion of works-righteousness, he was able to show that Christianity's message of salvation by grace through faith is unique—and superior. How Paul thought this tactic of misrepresentation might succeed when writing to congregations where there were Jews present, however, is difficult to explain.

(3) The most popular approach in the last few decades has been to see the problem lying not in how Paul viewed Judaism, but in how we have viewed Paul. According to this line of thinking, the shadow of Reformation teaching looming in our theological past has caused us to carry on a misunderstanding of Paul's argument against the law. The Reformers interpreted Paul's critique of Judaism in light of their battle with the Roman Catholic Church. Thus, they interpreted Paul as if he were arguing against the same type of religious system that they were: a system in which works are tied to salvation. In short, Judaism did not teach obtaining righteousness through works; the Roman Catholic Church did.

Although there are a wide variety of interpretations that maintain that Paul's view of the law and Judaism has been misunderstood, many share the idea that Paul was attacking a Judaism characterized by "covenantal nomism." I will describe in brief the argument of one prominent New Testament scholar who advocates this. J. Dunn argues in his commentary on Romans (see esp. pp. lxiii–lxxii) that the issue in Romans is not about how one gets into the covenant people of God through keeping the law (which is a misunderstanding of Judaism and Paul's approach to it). Rather, the Jews held that certain works, or covenantal markers, were critical for them to *maintain* their place within the covenant. These identity markers served to separate the Jews from the rest of the world as God's chosen people. It was the observance of these works—circumcision, food laws, and the observance of the Sabbath and other Jewish holy days—that Paul was attacking. Paul's argument, then, is this: Now that Christ has come, the Jews can no longer assume that those who observe these works will be declared righteous. In other words, they cannot assume that membership in the people of God grants them an advantage at the judgment over all other nations.

(4) But there is another approach in the current debate about Paul and the law, and one that seems preferable: Judaism was more pluralistic in its understanding and practice of the law than what the concept of "covenantal nomism" conveys. This is not to dispute the existence of first- century covenantal nomists, who saw observing the law as a means of expressing love for the God who made them his people by his grace. But there is reason to question whether this view of the law was universally held and practiced. After all, almost all scholars agree today that there was not one single type of Judaism in the first century. Moreover, the argument of Paul in Romans does not easily lend itself to the interpretation of Dunn, who argues that Paul was attacking a system in which doing the works of the law was becoming increasingly associated with keeping certain practices. Of the practices that Dunn identifies as the main three—circumcision, food laws, and Sabbath—only the first comes up for discussion where he argues against law-keeping (ch. 2).

Before Sanders's landmark work was published in 1977, R. Longenecker's identified two approaches to the law in Second Temple Judaism, one of which was that of the "reacting nomist." Similar to the idea of "covenantal nomism" that Sanders would go on and make famous, Longenecker wrote that the reacting nomist was the Jew who kept the law in response to God's mercy. Many first-century expressions of Jewish piety show an understanding that grace precedes works, that is, that keeping the covenant is a loving response to God's mercy. There are other writings, however, which show another motivation for doing works of the law—to *gain* righteousness or the favor of God (66–70). This is the approach of the "acting legalist."

A law-based religion like Judaism would have been prone to such diverse responses, even with an impressive body of literature that proclaimed the law as a response to grace. Evangelicals should be able to understand this. Despite the fact that salvation by grace is proclaimed from their pulpits, there is a tendency for those who hear and accept the message to fall into legalism, as if what they do gains or preserves their place in the kingdom. Any faith can degenerate into legalism, particularly those in which law and holiness codes are central to the expressions of piety.

The common element for the "reacting nomist" and the "acting legalist" is the keeping of the law, from whatever motivation. For both, righteousness is associated with the law. Paul's argument in Romans addresses both groups in that it separates righteousness from works of the law altogether, whether these be understood as achieving righteousness or as the proper response to God's grace. That is, his argument is that with the coming of Christ, the role of the law in terms of righteousness has come to an end (10:4).

2. Recipients

Paul was only one traveler among many who made the resolution, "I must visit Rome also" (Acts 19:21). Rome, the center of the Roman empire, attracted visitors and settlers from all across the empire and beyond. The composition of the company of believers that met in that great city reflected its status as an imperial and cosmopolitan city. In fact, the various human distinctions that Paul declared to be invalid in Christ—"there is neither Jew nor Greek, slave nor free, male nor female" (Gal. 3:28)—aptly describe the audience Paul addressed. For instance, judging from the high percentage of those in Rome who had either been slaves, or were still slaves and from the number of slave names that appear in the list of Roman believers in chapter 16, the Christian contingent of those with a slave background was probably fairly large (see the comments on 6:15–23).

The first contingent of Roman believers was predominantly Jewish. As was the pattern elsewhere, the establishment of a Christian church there occurred within the Jewish community. We know from Acts that the Christian mission was initially centered around the synagogue whenever and wherever possible (e.g., Acts 11:19–21; 13:5, 14). Of the estimated one million people living in Rome in the first century A.D., somewhere between forty and fifty thousand were Jews. From the evidence of the Jewish catacombs in Rome, it appears that the Jewish population was segregated into a number of communities, each centralized around a local synagogue and with its own governing body (Schürer, 3:95–96).

This was the milieu in which Christianity grew in Rome. The early Christian Jews would have remained associated with their local synagogues, with the result that various house churches would have grown up around the Jewish quarter. This legacy is still evident when Paul writes Romans. In his greetings to the believers in Rome he identifies various groupings of people that presumably represent house churches (16:5, 10–11, 14–15). That there was not one body of believers in Rome may explain why Paul never refers to the Roman believers as a church.

Early church tradition notwithstanding, Peter did not establish the Roman church. There is no biblical evidence to support this theory. Instead, Acts leads us to believe that the ministry of Peter remained centered around Jerusalem during the time when Christianity began to penetrate the imperial city in the period after Pentecost. Furthermore, if Peter had founded the church, then one would expect some reference to this in Paul's introductory letter to them.

The appearance of Christianity in Rome was likely preceded by reports from Jews traveling from Judea to Rome of what was being said and done by Jesus of Nazareth. As well, there were Roman Jews in Jerusalem to celebrate Pentecost just after the crucifixion of Jesus.

Some of them witnessed the result of the Holy Spirit coming upon the one hundred and twenty believers (Acts 1:15; 2:1–4, 10–11), and they surely would have reported what they saw and heard back home. Indeed, there may have been some Roman Jews among the three thousand who were baptized in response to Peter's sermon that day (2:41). In any event, it would not be long after that other Jews who had come to believe in Christ would travel to Rome. This was almost certainly how a Christian community was established in the capital city.

That is not to say that the earliest phase of Christianity was entirely Jewish or that it remained primarily Jewish for long. Connected to the synagogues were Gentiles attracted to Judaism. These "God-fearers" would have been open to the gospel, because it was connected with the Jewish faith and proclaimed acceptance by God without all the requirements of the law.

By the time of Paul's writing of Romans the house churches were taking on an increasingly Gentile character. If we are correct in placing the time of the letter in the mid-50s, then this is the period in which many Jews, Christians included, were returning to Rome and attempting to reintegrate themselves into Roman society. In A.D. 49, Emperor Claudius had decreed that the Jews be expelled from Rome on account of some disturbance in the Jewish quarter. As the Roman historian Suetonius wrote some seventy years after the event, "because the Jews of Rome were indulging in constant riots at the instigation of Chrestus he expelled them from the city" (*Claudius*, 25.4). Since it is widely believed that "Chrestus" refers to "Christ," the disturbance probably had something to do with the opposition among certain Jews to the gospel message. Acts 18:2 records that two of the Jews expelled were Aquila and Priscilla. The decree would have lapsed with the death of Claudius in A.D. 54, if not sooner, and so those Jews predisposed to return would have begun to do so. One of the challenges Paul faced in this letter was to address the problem that these Christian Jews would have had in returning to churches that had become less Jewish in their absence.

3. Date and Place

It is far simpler to establish the place of Romans within Paul's life and work than to be specific about the time when the letter was written. There is, however, a general consensus that the writing of Romans occurred sometime in the middle to late 50s A.D.

There is widespread agreement that Paul was in Corinth when he dictated Romans to Tertius (16:22). Paul was likely in the region of Macedonia and Achaia at the time of writing since he had just completed his collection for the saints of Jerusalem from the churches in that region, but he had not yet begun his journey to Jerusalem (15:25–28). Moreover, some of the people he mentions in his list of greetings suggest that he was in Corinth when he wrote. (1) Phoebe, the messenger who brought Paul's letter to Rome, was a deaconess from Cenchrea—the eastern port of Corinth, some seven miles away (16:1–2). (2) Gaius, Paul's host at the time of writing (16:23), may be the same Gaius whom Paul baptized at Corinth (1 Cor. 1:14). (3) Erastus, who sent greetings along with Gaius to the Roman church (Rom. 16:23), may be the individual associated with Corinth in Acts 19:22 and 2 Timothy 4:20.

For the interpreter of Romans, an understanding of where this letter fits into the context of Paul's life and ministry is of much greater importance than a solution to the problem of where and when Romans was written. Before he wrote this letter, the apostle had already expressed to the Corinthians his desire to preach the gospel in the lands beyond them (2 Cor. 10:16)—presumably, Paul meant the regions further west of Achaia. One of the reasons why Paul writes to the Roman church is to inform them that this long-held desire is about to happen. In Romans 15:17–24 Paul explains that he would have traveled west to Rome sooner, but has been delayed because of his goal to complete his preaching to the east of them, that is, the region from Jerusalem to Illyricum (part of the area of the former Yugoslavia). As to whether Paul actually ministered in Illyricum (no mention in Acts), or only as far as its border, is a moot point.

But before the apostle goes to Rome, he must deliver to the saints in Jerusalem the collection that he has assembled from the predominantly Gentile churches in Macedonia and Achaia (15:25–26). We know from Paul's correspondence with the Corinthians that he attached great importance to this collection

(1 Cor. 16:1–4; 2 Cor. 8–9). It is not surprising, then, that he is somewhat anxious about the trip to Jerusalem now that it is immediately before him. He requests the prayers of the Roman believers for the trip because he has enemies in Judea and because he is apprehensive that the collection might not be considered acceptable by the saints there.

Behind his concern that the gift from the Gentile churches be deemed acceptable by its recipients is the lingering tension between Paul, the apostle to the Gentiles, and other Jewish believers who disagreed with Paul's missionary practices. Paul faced earlier opposition from Jewish Christians that was centered in Jerusalem (Acts 15; Gal. 2). Of significance here is the fact that one of the results of the Jerusalem Council—a meeting convened to discuss the whole matter of what Gentiles should be obligated to do after conversion—was that they be required to remember the poor (Gal. 2:10; i.e., the poor in Jerusalem). Before Paul embarks on a new phase of ministry, he is anxious to fulfill that requirement and bring to a fitting conclusion his ministry in the east by offering a generous expression of the Gentile churches' concern for their Jewish brethren. This, Paul hopes, will set relations between the Diaspora churches and the church in Jerusalem on a solid foundation before he leaves the region.

Paul does not envision when he writes Romans that he will someday arrive in Rome in chains. But his misgivings about his trip to Jerusalem are well-founded. Certain Jews from Asia stir up enough opposition to Paul within Jerusalem that Paul is arrested and eventually sent to Caesarea as a prisoner to be tried by Felix, the procurator of the Roman province of Judea. Paul remains in Caesarea as a prisoner for at least two years (Acts 24:27), at which time Felix is replaced by Festus. Paul appeals to Caesar in his appearance before Festus, and so Paul finally arrives in Rome as a prisoner awaiting trial (chs. 25–28).

4. Occasion and Purpose

Before we discuss why Paul wrote Romans, it should be emphasized that Romans is a letter. Since the work of A. Deissmann (1912), which compared the New Testament documents with the texts of the Greco-Roman world, it has been common to differentiate between an epistle and a letter. An epistle is an essay written in letter form, but unlike an actual letter, it does not address the specifics of a local situation. Even though Romans bears a closer resemblance to an epistle than any of Paul's other letters, it remains a letter. It was occasioned by the situations of both the apostle and the Christian community in Rome. In fact, as we will see, the reason why Romans so closely resembles an epistle relates directly to the circumstances of the writer and the recipients.

There is no consensus among scholars about the purpose for Romans. The confusion begins with Paul: He cites different reasons for writing at the beginning of the letter than he does at the end. Scholars often differ over which of these reasons is the real purpose for the letter. But if the presumption is removed that there must be one single purpose for Romans, then the task becomes simplified. Why should we presume that Paul has only one reason in mind for drafting this letter? After all, his purposes derive from both his situation and that of the Roman believers.

Paul is a missionary with aspirations of future evangelistic work in Spain. The Roman house congregations are important to Paul because he wants Rome to serve as a support base for this new project (15:23–29). But Paul does not have apostolic authority over the Roman community of believers since he has never ministered there. One of the purposes of this letter, then, is to introduce his ministry and message. This is why, as we noted earlier, much of Romans is so systematic. Paul is developing a lengthy and logical explanation of his message. Still, it is not a systematic treatise, for he never loses sight of his Roman audience. His awareness of them and his own particular concerns come out at various points even when he is in the midst of an extended argument.

Paul hopes that this letter will be well received and pave the way for his arrival. He has no guarantee of a positive reception, however, since criticism of his ministry and message has circulated widely as a result of opposition from fellow Jews. Thus, this letter is more than an explanation of his message; it is also a defense.

But Paul has something more in mind than just using the Roman church as a point of departure or as something of a home base for his evangelistic endeavors elsewhere. There is a pastoral purpose behind this correspondence. At the outset of the letter he informs them of his intention to impart to them a spiritual gift. As will be discussed in the commentary itself, Paul's letter represents the beginning of his apostolic ministry to them. Paul is aware of the tension between Jewish and Gentile Christians in Rome, and this is why he feels compelled to offer them the type of ministry for which he, a Jewish apostle to the Gentiles, has been called. Surely he has their situation in mind as he argues in chapters 1–11 about the equality of Jew and Gentile in terms of righteousness. And he makes his knowledge of the tension among them explicit when he applies the message of chapters 1–11 in chapters 12–15, where the relationship between Jew and Gentile is the focal point of these latter chapters.

5. Theme

Since the Reformation it has been common to identify justification by faith as the theme of Romans and the center of Pauline theology. This is, however, to overstate its role in Romans and its importance for Pauline thought. Justification by faith is central to Paul's argument in 1:18–5:21 that both Jew and Gentile stand equally guilty before God, with the result that both can only be saved by faith. It is on the basis of faith in Christ that the individual will be declared righteous, or will be justified, at the judgment.

Justification by faith is a dominant concept in only two Pauline letters: Romans and Galatians. There is a reason for this. Justification is an Old Testament concept, and it is applicable in these letters because both deal with issues of particular importance to the Jews. For the same reason, Paul makes extensive use of Old Testament quotations and allusions in both letters (see esp. Rom. 9–11, where the topic is God's righteousness toward Israel). When Paul addresses a Gentile congregation, or at least one in which Jewish issues are not significant, he prefers to speak of believers as those who are in Christ rather than those who have been justified by faith.

If we are looking for the one theme that overarches the entire letter, then it is the concept of God's righteousness. In fact, justification by faith is an aspect of this broader theme. In 1:16–17 Paul lays out the subject of the letter: "In the gospel a righteousness from God is revealed." What Paul does in Romans, then, is to describe the nature of God's righteousness or saving work (see comments on 1:16–17). We may summarize the content of the letter in this way:

- God's righteousness to cancel the penalty of sin (1:18–5:21)
- God's righteousness to break the power of sin through the death of Christ and the empowerment of the indwelling Spirit (6:1–8:39)
- God's righteousness now and in the future toward his chosen people (9:1–11:36)
- God's righteousness, his saving work, lived out by Jew and Gentile alike (12:1–15:13)

6. Original Form of Romans

There is a theory that chapter 16 was not originally part of the letter to the Romans. Among the various reasons given for this position are the presence of a benediction at the end of chapter 15 and the fact that chapter 16 contains a lengthy list of people greeted by Paul, which suggests that this chapter could not have been written to Rome, a place that he had never been. It has been argued that the extensive list of acquaintances points to a church where he had spent time in ministry, such as Ephesus. Thus, the Ephesian theory maintains that chapter 16 was a separate letter sent to the Ephesians, which at some early point became attached to the Roman letter.

Against this theory are a number of decisive factors. (1) The various elements contained in chapter 16—greetings, doxology, and final notes—are typical of the final section of a letter written by Paul, and it would be surprising if Romans did not contain them in its conclusion as well. (2) C. H. Dodd (14) has observed that when Paul writes a church he only greets individuals if he is writing to an assembly that he has not visited (e.g., Colossians). By greeting specific individuals Paul establishes points of contact with the church. In other words, these individuals are his personal references. That Paul knew so many people who had moved to Rome is a result of that city's status as a primary destination within the empire ("all roads lead to Rome"), with good roads and political peace facilitating frequent travel in and out of the capital.

Methodology

A few points should be made about the approach that is being taken in this section of the *Full Life Bible Commentary*:

(1) In a short commentary tough decisions must constantly be made in terms of what will and will not be covered. Romans is so rich in content that these decisions are particularly difficult, and, of course, all of Romans is God's Word. The reader should be aware that there are many good full-length commentaries that give greater detail and explanation of all the critical issues that surround certain texts (see Bibliography). My approach has been to give certain chapters more attention because of (a) their critical role within the argument of the letter as a whole, and/or (b) their relevance for Christians entering the third millennium. In particular, chapters 3, 6–8, 12, and 14 are dealt with more extensively than the others.

(2) The fact that Romans is a letter raises a few hermeneutical considerations. The primary resource for interpreting Romans is the letter itself. When Paul writes the congregations in Rome, he does not presume they have a collection of his letters at their disposal—indeed, this is his first direct contact with them. He presumes that what he writes will be understood from the context of the letter itself. Therefore, where I make reference to similar topics and phrases in Paul's other letters, it will be for the sake of comparison rather than interpretation. Although other letters aid us in our attempts to fill out the nature of Pauline thought, priority must always go to understanding an individual letter on its own terms. For instance, we should not assume that Paul argues the same way in all of his letters, or that he uses words and phrases in only one way from one letter to another. Letters are occasional documents in which the type of communication they contain is determined by the situations of the writer and recipient.

There is another hermeneutical consideration here. We will pay attention to the letter structure of Romans. There are clues here that help us determine Paul's emphases in the letter, as well as his purpose in writing to Rome (see opening comments on 1:1–17).

(3) This is not a critical commentary. It does not attempt to engage in extended argument or to interact with the world of scholarship to any great extent. It does attempt to give a clear and relevant commentary on Paul's letter to the Roman believers. But to give the reader some idea of the controversies and debates that are in circulation today, I will interact with a couple of modern and influential commentaries in particular throughout the exposition. This will provide the reader with some sense of the various positions that are presently being argued. Special attention will be given to the commentaries of D. Moo and J. D. G. Dunn, and to Fee's *God's Empowering Presence,* which is an exposition of every Pauline passage that deals with the Holy Spirit.

(4) Regarding the means of notation, page numbers will not be given for the commentaries if the content being referred to appears in those volumes under the verse that we are discussing. That is, if I am explaining Romans 8:28 and I cite Moo, the reader can find the reference in Moo's commentary under the same chapter and verse. Pages numbers will be used for books or for introductory material in the commentaries.

OUTLINE

1. Letter Opening (1:1–17)
- **1.1.** Salutation (1:1–7)
- **1.2.** Thanksgiving Prayer (1:8–10)
- **1.3.** Travelogue # 1 (1:11–15)
- **1.4.** Letter Theme (1:16–17)

2. Body of the Letter: God's Righteousness Revealed in the Gospel (1:18–15:13)
- **2.1.** God's Righteousness Cancels the Penalty of Sin (1:18–5:21)
  - **2.1.1.** The Plight of Humanity Under the Wrath of God (1:18–3:20)
    - **2.1.1.1.** The Wrath of God on Humanity (1:18–32)
    - **2.1.1.2.** The Wrath of God on the Jews (2:1–3:20)
      - **2.1.1.2.1.** God's Impartial Judgment (2:1–11)
      - **2.1.1.2.2.** Judgment and the Law (2:12–16)
      - **2.1.1.2.3.** Jewish Predicament (2:17–24)
      - **2.1.1.2.4.** Judgment and Circumcision (2:25–29)
      - **2.1.1.2.5.** Objections (3:1–8)
      - **2.1.1.2.6.** Sum: All People Are Subject to Wrath (3:9–20)

2.1.2. The Salvation of Humanity Through Faith in Jesus Christ (3:21–4:25)
- **2.1.2.1.** Salvation Through the Death of Christ (3:21–26)
- **2.1.2.2.** Salvation by Faith (3:27–4:25)
  - **2.1.2.2.1.** Basic Concept of Faith (3:27–31)
  - **2.1.2.2.2.** Illustration: The Faith of Abraham (4:1–25)

2.1.3. The Sphere of Grace (5:1–21)
- **2.1.3.1.** Life Within the Sphere of Grace (5:1–11)
  - **2.1.3.1.1.** Benefits of Grace (5:1–5)
  - **2.1.3.1.2.** Ultimate Expression of Grace (5:6–8)
  - **2.1.3.1.3.** Goal of Grace (5:9–11)
- **2.1.3.2.** Triumph of Grace Over Sin and Death (5:12–21)

2.2. God's Righteousness Breaks the Power of Sin (6:1–8:39)
- **2.2.1.** Power Over Sin (6:1–7:6)
  - **2.2.1.1.** Dying to Live (6:1–14)
  - **2.2.1.2.** Dying to Serve (6:15–23)
  - **2.2.1.3.** Dying to the Law (7:1–6)
- **2.2.2.** The Law and Sin: A Defense of the Law (7:7–25)
  - **2.2.2.1.** Death Through the Law (7:7–12)
  - **2.2.2.2.** Powerlessness of the Law and the Flesh (7:13–25)
- **2.2.3.** The Spirit of Life Gives Power Over Sin and Death (8:1–13)
- **2.2.4.** The Spirit of Adoption (8:14–17)
- **2.2.5.** The Hope of Glory (8:18–39)
  - **2.2.5.1.** The Hope of Glory: Present in Suffering (8:18–27)
  - **2.2.5.2.** The Hope of Glory: Guaranteed by God's Righteousness (8:28–39)

2.3. God's Righteousness Toward Israel (9:1–11:36)
- **2.3.1.** The Problem (9:1–5)
- **2.3.2.** God's Purpose (9:6–29)
- **2.3.3.** Israel's Failure (9:30–10:21)
- **2.3.4.** Saving the Remnant; Hardening the Others (11:1–10)
- **2.3.5.** God's Present and Future for Israel (11:11–32)
  - **2.3.5.1.** Purpose in Hardening (11:11–16)
  - **2.3.5.2.** How to View the Jews (11:17–24)
  - **2.3.5.3.** The Salvation of Israel (11:25–32)
- **2.3.6.** In Praise of God (11:33–36)

2.4. God's Righteousness Lived Out by and Between Jew and Gentile (12:1–15:13)
- **2.4.1.** Living in Response to God's Righteousness (12:1–2)
- **2.4.2.** Relationships in the Church (12:3–13a)
  - **2.4.2.1.** Right Thinking About Relationships (12:3–5)
  - **2.4.2.2.** Individual Gifts (12:6–8)
  - **2.4.2.3.** General Exhortations on Relating to Others in the Church (12:9–13a)
- **2.4.3.** Relationship With the World (12:13b–13:14)
  - **2.4.3.1.** Relationship With the World in General (12:13b–21)
  - **2.4.3.2.** Relationship With the Government (13:1–7)
  - **2.4.3.3.** Relationship With One's Neighbors (13:8–10)
  - **2.4.3.4.** Living Out One's Relationships With Eschatological Urgency (13:11–14)
- **2.4.4.** Relationships Between Jew and Gentile (14:1–15:13)
  - **2.4.4.1.** Accept One Another; Don't Judge (14:1–12)
  - **2.4.4.2.** Act With Love Toward One Another; Don't Scandalize (14:13–23)
  - **2.4.4.3.** Christ the Model for Weak and Strong (15:1–6)
  - **2.4.4.4.** Summary (15:7–13)

3. Letter Closing (15:14–16:27)

3.1. Travelogue #2 (15:14–33)
- **3.1.1.** Paul's Mission (15:14–22)
- **3.1.2.** Before Spain: The Collection for the Saints (15:23–33)

3.2. Commendation of Phoebe (16:1–2)

3.3. Greetings to Paul's Acquaintances (16:3–16)

3.4. Final Warning (16:17–20)

3.5. Greetings From Paul's Associates (16:21–23)

3.6. Closing Doxology (16:25–27)

COMMENTARY

1. Letter Opening (1:1–17)

As was customary in the first century, the letter opening of Romans begins with a salutation and a thanksgiving. Paul not only adopts these epistolary conventions but adapts them according to his apostolic purposes.

1.1. Salutation (1:1–7)

The elements and their order in the salutation of Romans conform to the common conventions of the Hellenistic letter—the identification of the sender, the naming of the recipients, and a greeting. Paul adapts these formal elements by packing in and around them theological themes and personal matters of concern, which serve to indicate what is to follow in the letter.

The salutation, which is not only much longer than the typical salutation of the day, is also the longest by Pauline standards. It is significant that the other two Pauline letters where the salutations are longer than the Pauline norm (1 Corinthians and Galatians) are letters in which Paul expresses acute concern about the congregations being addressed. Therefore, the long salutation in Romans warns against viewing this letter simply, as is sometimes done, as a systematic and dispassionate treatment of theological issues.

This letter opening betrays a pressing concern on the mind of the writer, not so much with the Roman situation itself, as with Paul's own standing vis-à-vis the Roman churches in light of his impending visit. The apostle had opponents, and the salutation reveals that he assumed that their criticism of him had spread to Rome. The opening section is so lengthy, then, because Paul immediately interjects into its structure a defense of his gospel and apostleship. His concern about the visit becomes explicit in the travelogues that bracket the body of the letter (1:11–15 and 15:14–33).

In a departure from his established epistolary form, Paul identifies himself in verse 1 in a twofold manner: "a servant of Christ Jesus" and a "called . . . apostle." More typical is his singular self-definition as "apostle" (see 1 Cor. 1:1; 2 Cor. 1:1; Eph. 1:1; Col. 1:1; 2 Tim. 1:1; in Phil. 1:1, however, he calls himself "servant," and in Philem. 1, "prisoner"). The only other place that the twofold designation of servant and apostle appears is in Titus 1:1, but there "apostle" stands without the word "called." (Paul will also address the Roman believers with a twofold definition in v. 7.)

The emphatic double reference to Paul's status as apostle and servant is appropriate for an introduction, or—in light of the criticism being leveled against Paul's gospel—an apologetic, to a church that he is about to visit for the first time. These terms merit brief comment, for they tell us the manner in which Paul wished to be understood. (1) Most important, Paul is a "servant," or "slave" (Gk. *doulos*), of Jesus. In using the "servant" terminology familiar to him from biblical references to Moses, David, and many of the prophets, Paul shows his identification with the work of God begun among the Jews. In his clarification that he is a servant of Christ Jesus, he shows his absolute devotion to the Messiah.

(2) He is "called to be an apostle." Behind this phrase lies the dramatic calling of Paul on the Damascus road (Acts 9), when the risen Lord appeared to him and commissioned him. This experience would permit Paul to include himself among the apostolic band, because being an eyewitness of Jesus was a prerequisite for membership (cf. 1 Cor. 9:1; 15:7–8).

After introducing himself in verse 1 and before naming the recipients—which typically followed immediately in the first-century letter—Paul proceeds to address any misconceptions that might be circulating in Rome about him and his preaching. According to many modern commentators, the short, balanced phrases in verses 3–4 are taken from an early Christian confession. Paul's inclusion of a confessional statement serves first notice to his audience that his gospel—despite what they might have heard—was in line with the gospel tradition handed down to him.

The gospel for which Paul was set apart (v. 1) declares the fulfillment of what was promised in the Old Testament through the prophets (v. 2) concerning Jesus the Messiah, who is described in two complementary clauses. "As to his human nature," he was of the line of David (v. 3; cf. Isa. 11:1). As to his spiritual existence in heaven, he lives "with power" (instead of the weakness associated with the human form; cf. 1 Cor. 15:35–55).

The NIV translation suggests that "the Spirit of holiness" (the Holy Spirit) played a role in the exaltation of Christ. Perhaps it is better to understand this phrase (lit., "according to the Spirit of holiness")—as we have done above—as functioning in parallel with the phrase in verse 3 (lit. "according to the flesh") to contrast two realms of existence. The earthly state is lived according to human limitations, whereas the post-resurrection state is a spiritual existence characterized by power. It is a "Spirit life par excellence" (Fee, 1994, 481). This latter theme will be explored later when Paul describes the present implications for those who live in the age of the Spirit (chs. 5; 8).

The resurrection effected Christ's passage from one state to the other. Not that this sequence of events brought about his Sonship, as the beginning of verse 3 makes clear, but that his full status as Son—or, as "our Lord"—is now inaugurated, for he rules from heaven alongside of the Father.

It is from this Lord that Paul received (the "we" is probably a stylistic reference to himself) "grace and apostleship" (v. 5). The two are closely related. "Grace," a predominant theme in Romans, denotes here the act of God whereby a persecutor of the church was commissioned by the risen Lord to be his apostle. Paul's particular apostolic mission was to call the Gentiles to the same submission to Christ that he himself first experienced in his encounter with Christ on the road to Damascus. So he addresses the Romans as those who have been called to faith in Jesus Christ from among the nations (v. 6).

When he comes to the second formal element in the salutation in verse 7, the naming of the addressees, he uses two descriptive phrases (which balance the two designators he used for himself): "loved by God" and "called to be saints." The second phrase parallels Paul's self-definition as "called to be an apostle." As he was a called apostle, so they have been called to be saints, that is, those who on account of God's summons have been set apart for his service.

"Grace [*charis*] and peace to you" is Paul's standard greeting, combining a variation on the Greek *chairein* ("greeting") with the Greek word for the typical Hebrew salutation, *shalom* ("peace").

1.2. Thanksgiving Prayer (1:8–10)

In the first-century letter the salutation was customarily followed by a thanksgiving and a prayer wish, typically for the health of the one addressed. It was also Paul's custom to include at this point an expression of thanks to God for the recipients of the letter (except in Galatians). This included not only matters that the apostle had been praying about for the congregation he is writing to, but also topics that he now wants to address. That is to say, the thanksgiving prayer served the reader with early notice about what was ahead. The fact that in Romans Paul moves quickly from his word of thanksgiving to his travel plans is not a break from form. Rather, it indicates the significance of Paul's travelogue for the purpose of the letter.

Paul's commendation of the Roman believers for their widespread reputation for faith is expressed as a thanksgiving to God through Jesus Christ. "As it is through Christ that God's grace is conveyed to men (verse 5), so it is through Christ that men's gratitude is conveyed to God" (Bruce, 1985[1]). That Paul would highlight the faith of the Roman Christians in verse 8 is not surprising because of his missionary preoccupation with bringing Gentiles to a point of faith (1:5). What is surprising is the abrupt change of tone that is introduced by the oath of verse 9: The apostle calls God as a witness for his assertion that he has prayed for them constantly. Behind such a solemn formula lies the apostle's apprehension that his declaration of concern for them might not be believed since he had never visited them.

Therefore, Paul immediately makes known his prayer request that "now at last by God's will the way may be opened for me to come to you" (v. 10). Paul was sensitive to the criticism, which had been leveled at him before (2 Cor. 1:17), that what he says he does not always do. The inference Paul wants drawn from his prayer request is that God himself was the one who had delayed his trip to the capital city of the Roman empire. His earnestness about the whole matter surfaces again in verse 13, where he uses a disclosure formula—"I do not want you to be unaware, brothers"—to stress that his repeated plans to come had been prevented.

Also of note here is Paul's qualification in verse 9 that he serves God "with my spirit" (NIV "with my whole heart"). What he means by this phrase is probably explained by the contrast he sets up in 12:1, where Paul uses imagery taken from the Old Testament sacrificial system to show the differences between the spiritual dynamics under the new covenant and those under the law. A similar contrast is in the background of verse 9, where "with my spirit" signifies that the requirements of God are now internalized to a much greater degree than was the case under the written requirements of the law.

1.3. Travelogue #1 (1:11–15)

The travelogue was a common feature in the Pauline letter. It served to inform his readers about his travel plans or that of his associates. It is particularly prominent in Romans, coming in both the letter opening and the letter closing (15:14–33), because his reason for writing the letter is closely tied to his impending visit.

Paul's expressed purpose for longing to see them is that he might impart to them "some spiritual gift" (*ti charisma pneumatikon*, v. 11). "Gift" (*charisma*), which is formed from *charis* ("grace"), is best defined as a concrete expression of God's grace. This grace may refer to something as broad as God's work in Christ (e.g., Eph. 2:8) or to the provision of eternal life (Rom. 6:23). It may also express, as it does here, a form of grace that is individualized for the one who receives it. We often call these spiritually enabled abilities "spiritual gifts" (they are listed in Rom. 12, 1 Cor. 12, and Eph. 4; cf. Fee, 1993, 339–47).

The indefinite pronoun "some" (*ti*) implies that Paul does not have a specific "spiritual gift" in mind. Nevertheless, the combination of grace and apostleship in verse 5—an association that would still be ringing in the ears of the listeners—would suggest to them that the spiritual gift he wants to impart relates to his apostleship. Presumably, he means the type of ministry that his calling and authority as the apostle to the Gentiles enables him to bring them. He is, therefore, already sharing his gift with them in this letter (cf. Fee, 1994, 486–89).

Paul anticipates that by sharing his spiritual gift with them a "harvest" (*karpos*, lit., "fruit") will be produced. In other words, he hopes that his work with the Romans will have the same positive results that it has had among other Gentiles. For as he makes clear, his mandate is to reach all Gentiles, whether "Greek" or "non-Greeks" (lit., "barbarians"), "wise" or "foolish." The apostle's contrast here is not just about race or geography, but also about class. The word "barbarian" had come to designate, in derogatory fashion, all peoples within the empire who were not "Greek" in training and culture. Paul is declaring, then, that the gospel is for everyone.

Lest it sound presumptuous that they alone needed his ministry, he immediately qualifies his stated intention to give them a gift with "that is, that you and I may be mutually encouraged by each other's faith" (v. 12). This is more than a polite way of speaking. As his teaching in 12:3–8 illustrates, Paul views each member of the body of Christ as functioning in a mutually interdependent relationship. To put it simply, Paul is putting into practice his conviction that believers need one another.

To summarize, this letter was more than a letter of introduction to gain the approval of a congregation whose aid he needed for his mission to Spain. It was also the beginning of the type of ministry emphasis, or spiritual gift, that he intended to bring to Rome—his message of the unity of Jew and Gentile in Christ.

1.4. Letter Theme (1:16–17)

Paul concludes this extended letter opening, in which he has taken pains to introduce himself and the gospel he preaches, with a thematic statement about the nature of his gospel. Because of the opposition his message has stirred, both within Christian circles (cf. 3:8) and without, he prefaces his statement with a strong affirmation: "I am not ashamed of the gospel." By using this phrase, Paul identifies his preaching with the same gospel that Jesus commanded his followers not to be ashamed of (Mark 8:38//Luke 9:26).

Paul is not ashamed of the gospel because it is nothing less than the vehicle of the "power [*dynamis*] of God," enabling all who believe to be saved from his wrath, both now (cf. v. 18) and at the end. The gospel, the proclamation of God's work in Christ, effects the salvation it describes. As Wright puts it: "The gospel . . . is not just about God's power saving people. It *is* God's power at work to save people" (1997, 61). When the gospel is preached, lives are touched and transformed by God's power.

The order of salvation given at the end of verse 16, "first for the Jew, then for the Gentile,"

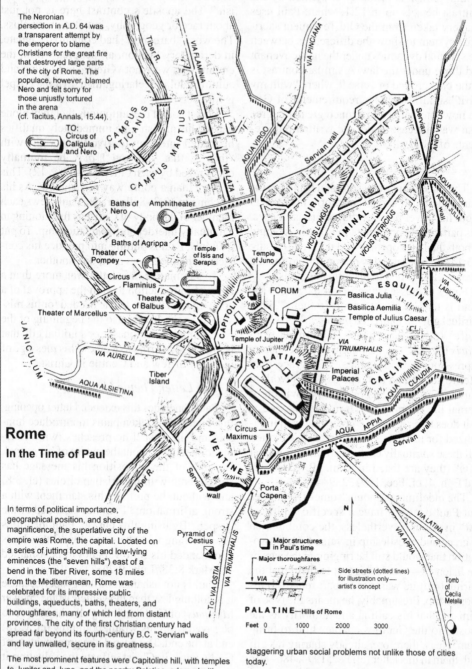

The Neronian persection in A.D. 64 was a transparent attempt by the emperor to blame Christians for the great fire that destroyed large parts of the city of Rome. The populace, however, blamed Nero and felt sorry for those unjustly tortured in the arena (cf. Tacitus, Annals, 15.44).

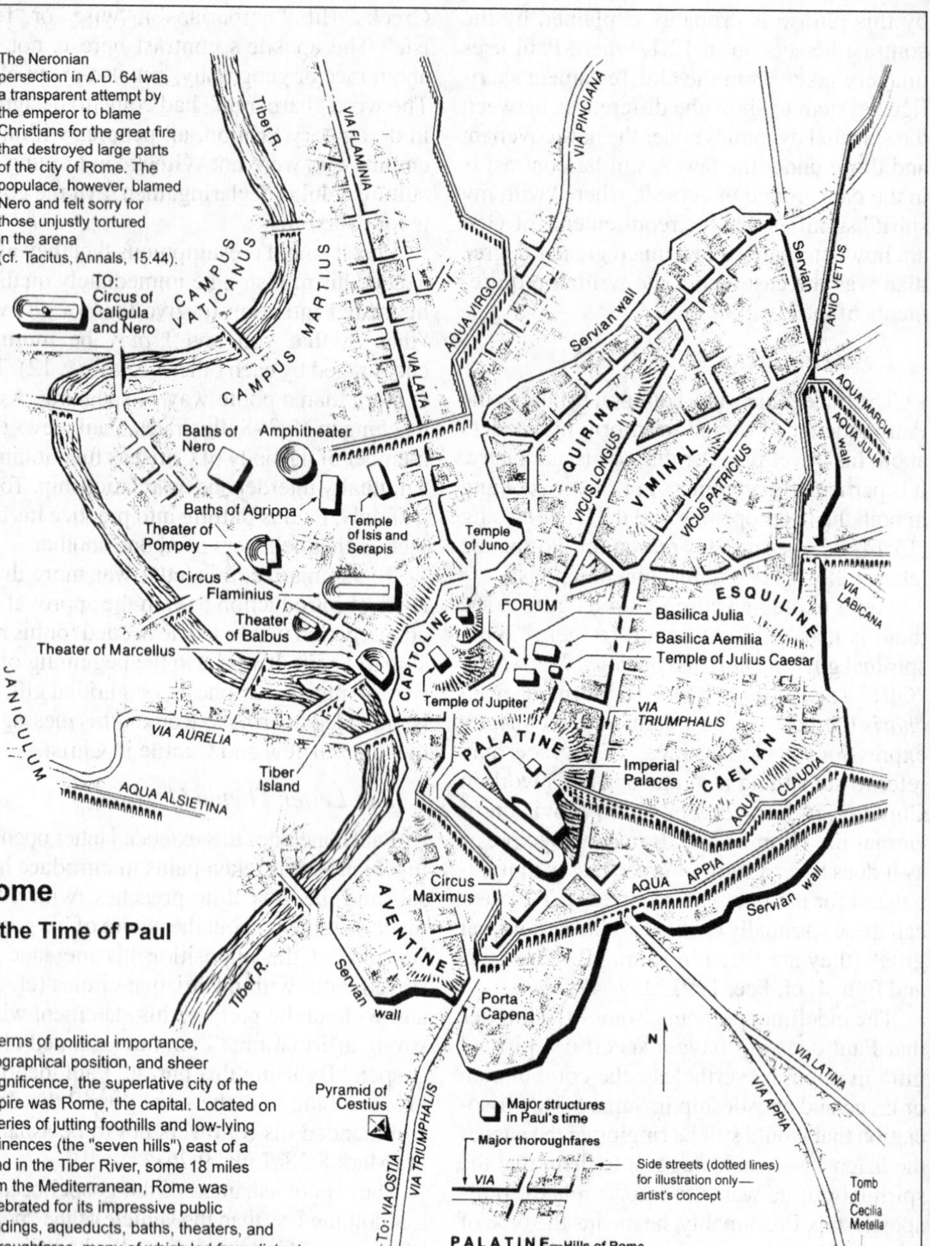

Rome

In the Time of Paul

In terms of political importance, geographical position, and sheer magnificence, the superlative city of the empire was Rome, the capital. Located on a series of jutting foothills and low-lying eminences (the "seven hills") east of a bend in the Tiber River, some 18 miles from the Mediterranean, Rome was celebrated for its impressive public buildings, aqueducts, baths, theaters, and thoroughfares, many of which led from distant provinces. The city of the first Christian century had spread far beyond its fourth-century B.C. "Servian" walls and lay unwalled, secure in its greatness.

The most prominent features were Capitoline hill, with temples to Jupiter and Juno, and the nearby Palatine, adorned with imperial palaces, including Nero's "Golden House." Both hills overlooked the Roman Forum, the hub of the entire empire.

Alternatively described as the glorious crowning achievement of mankind and as the sewer of the universe, where all the scum from every corner of the empire gathered, Rome had reasons for both civic pride in its architecture and shame for staggering urban social problems not unlike those of cities today.

The apostle Paul entered the city from the south on the Via Appia. He first lived under house arrest and then, after a period of freedom, as a condemned prisoner in the Mamertime dungeon near the Forum. Remarkably, Paul was able to proclaim the Gospel among all classes of people, from the palace to the prison. According to tradition, he was executed at a spot on the Ostian Way outside Rome in A.D. 68.

reflects the primacy of the Jews as God's chosen people. The order appears in this context not so much as a statement of priority, however, but as a proclamation of the inclusiveness of the gospel. To put it another way, Paul is saying that this is the sole means of salvation for the Jew as well as the Gentile. What he means by this will become evident in the letter: The law is no longer a factor in the equation of righteousness.

Verse 17 elaborates on what makes the gospel the power of God. It reveals a "righteousness from God," in other words, his saving activity. The concept of the righteousness of God in Paul's letters has been variously understood by New Testament commentators (see Wright, 1997, 100–110). The common view found in Reformation writings was that God's righteousness refers to a righteousness we receive from God. In other words, it is his righteousness imputed to us. By contrast, the view taken by many scholars today is that Paul's understanding reflects the Old Testament concept of God's righteousness, which puts the emphasis on God's acting in faithfulness to the covenant. In other words, the revelation of God's righteousness in verse 17 signifies the revealing of his saving activity.

There is another aspect to God's righteousness, however. Although the emphasis of the phrase is on God's saving activity, the Old Testament background warns us against making too hard a separation between what God does and the result of his action. In the Old Testament God's faithfulness to the covenant is expressed by his acting to maintain the relationship that he initiated with his people. God's righteousness results in relationship. The righteousness of God that is being revealed, then, is his activity to bring men and women into relationship with himself and to sustain that relationship by his grace (see Dunn; Moo).

How should we understand the revelation of the righteousness of God? What is being revealed? Is it content about God's saving plan in Jesus Christ? There is certainly background for this view in Jewish apocalyptic, where God is seen to disclose aspects of his plan for heaven and earth that were not known previously and could not be known otherwise. One could make a good argument that what is being unveiled is the mode of salvation in Christ that completely bypasses the law and is received by faith alone.

Or, in line with the concept of the revelation of God's wrath that appears in verse 18—which refers to the dispensing of wrath—is the revelation of his righteousness in verse 17 a manifestation of his saving work? In other words, is God in action being revealed? As we argued above when we looked at the gospel as the power of God, both senses are probably involved here. In the gospel the righteousness of God is being explained, that is, his saving ways are revealed. But what is being explained is what God is actually doing, and his righteousness may be experienced through faith.

The centrality of faith as the means by which one responds to God's saving work is emphasized in verses 16–17. Salvation is for "everyone who believes" (v. 16). Indeed, because it is actualized by faith rather than by any other criteria that might exclude some, such as law or race, God's righteousness is accessible to all. The importance of faith is summarized in the phrase "by faith from first to last" (v. 17). Habakkuk 2:4 (which also appears in Gal. 3:11 and Heb. 10:38) is brought forward to substantiate its critical role. It affirms that the righteous person is the one who lives within the context of faith. Habakkuk 2:4 is rendered differently in the Hebrew text than in the Septuagint (or LXX—the Greek translation of the Old Testament). In the former it is a human being's faithfulness that is in view, whereas in the latter it is God's faithfulness or righteousness. The reference in the preceding phrase to our response of faith suggests that the Hebrew text is in Paul's mind.

2. Body of the Letter: God's Righteousness Revealed in the Gospel (1:18–15:13)

The thematic statement in verses 16–17 about how the gospel reveals the righteousness of God is now fleshed out in detail in the body of the letter:

- God's righteousness, or his saving work, to cancel the penalty of sin (1:18–5:21)
- God's saving work to break the power of sin through Christ's death the empowerment of the indwelling Spirit (6:1–8:39)
- God's saving work now and in the future toward his chosen people (9:1–11:36)
- God's saving work, his righteousness, lived out by Jew and Gentile alike (12:1–15:13).

2.1. God's Righteousness Cancels the Penalty of Sin (1:18–5:21)

2.1.1. The Plight of Humanity Under the Wrath of God (1:18–3:20). As the main argument of the letter begins in verse 18, the reader is abruptly brought down to earth from the lofty heights of the declaration in 1:16–17 about the saving power of the gospel. For another process is working simultaneously with the revelation of the righteousness of God: the revelation of his wrath on those who suppress the truth in unrighteousness. Both processes are ongoing realities that anticipate the final judgment, when both will be brought to a point of completion—either in final salvation or final condemnation. It is informative that Paul exposes the divine indictment on sinful humanity (1:18–3:20) before he discusses the divine plan of salvation (3:21–5:21). One cannot comprehend salvation without first confronting judgment.

The theme of God's wrath is developed in the next few chapters, where the apostle turns his attention first to the Gentiles and then to the Jews. What occupies him as the argument progresses is a concern that the Jews might misinterpret their status as God's chosen people to mean that they have been given a special exemption from God's wrath that the Gentiles do not enjoy.

2.1.1.1. The Wrath of God on Humanity (1:18–32). Paul begins his argument by explaining that the divine indictment on the human race is a result of humanity's rejection of God's revelation to them. Indeed, the destiny of each individual pivots on the acceptance or rejection of divine revelation. The nature of God's revelation and the consequences of rejecting it are now described.

Because God has revealed himself (for he is otherwise unknowable) through his creation, men and women are morally responsible for what may be known about him (1:19–20). This is what theologians call "natural revelation," that is, the revelation of God through the physical world. What is revealed is the "eternal power" and "divine nature" of the Creator. This "truth," that is, the reality that there is a Creator to whom creation must respond, is suppressed by his creation as men and women live in ways that reject the supremacy of God.

In short, they are "without excuse" (v. 20) and deserve the wrath that is poured out on them. Humanity is not indicted because of a failure to find God, but because of a failure to respond to God's initiative. As Käsemann writes (42), "rebellion is seen as the signature of human reality before and apart from Christ."

What the modern reader would miss in 1:18–32 is the echo of arguments being used during Paul's time by Jewish apologists, who were attempting to convince the Gentiles of the truth of Judaism. In verses 18–20 Paul draws on this material as he interacts with a popular form of Greek philosophy—Stoicism. The expression "have been clearly seen, being understood" (v. 20) appears to be a direct reference to the Stoic belief that the existence of the invisible God could be understood through the rational mind (cf. Dunn). Paul adopts this idea in order to make his assertion that the Gentiles have failed to live up to what they know.

For many modern readers Darwinism casts a shadow of doubt on an apologetic such as this one. Notwithstanding, the signature of the Creator on the physical world has been a witness to his existence for centuries, and even in this age the testimony of what has been made still demands a response.

Humankind's rejection of the revelation of God and its disastrous consequences are now chronicled in some detail (vv. 21–32). The downward spiral of human sin begins with humanity's rejection of the knowledge of God in their possession. It continues as people act out their rejection by exchanging the divine for the profane. This pattern of willful rejection followed by rebellious action is repeated as men and women sink further into depravity.

What is particularly noticeable about this process is the degree to which God is active in it rather than passive. The thrice repeated "God gave them over" (vv. 24, 26, 28) reinforces the point made in verse 18 that God's wrath is being dispensed, and it also specifies how it is dispensed. That wrath is meted out as he releases humanity to the effects of sin.

In the background of verses 21–22 is the primal sin of Adam, who knew God but did not act accordingly. The result of his attempt to elevate himself to a new level of wisdom independently of God doomed him to a lesser state. So Paul summarizes the history of Adam's race in these verses as the commission of this primal sin over and over again. Each time the esult is the same—"although they claimed to be wise, they became fools" (v. 22).

The penalty for not responding with honor and praise to the revelation of God is to suffer a paralysis of one's God-given faculties. With a rejection of truth, thinking becomes futile; with a rejection of the light of revelation, the heart, or the essence of the human being, becomes darkened (v. 21). Without God, the human race is doomed to grope in the dark; without God, life is "meaningless, a chasing after the wind" (Eccl. 2:26).

The practice of idolatry (prohibited in the second commandment) figures prominently in this passage. There was an established polemic within Judaism (originating in the Old Testament and carried on throughout the Second Temple Period, e.g., Wisd. Sol. 11–14) against the pagan practice of idolatry. Paul draws on it here and in the remainder of the chapter, because idolatry serves to illustrate the depth to which men and women fall when they reject the revelation of the true God. They exchange "the glory of the immortal God" (v. 23), which is seen in creation (v. 20), for images (or likenesses) of created things, whether of a human being or a beast.

There is no better contemporary illustration of how the practice of idolatry continues today than that afforded us by the philosophy of the New Age movement. In total disregard for the true God, it champions a godlike potential in every human being, which is said to permit each person to become the creator of his or her own reality.

The combination of "glory" and "image" in verse 23 recalls 1 Corinthians 11:7, where man is depicted as "the image and glory of God." The original couple marred the image of God in which they were created (Gen. 1:27–28) by attempting to become gods through eating the forbidden fruit. Their rebellious response to the revelation of God caused that image to be tainted. If a person adopts a false image of God, then the falsification of God's image in that person inevitably results. The following verses illustrate this truth.

God's judgment on humanity's substitution of created images for the image of God is carried out as God releases them ("God gave them over") to the effects of their rejection—"the degrading of their bodies with one another," or "sexual impurity" (vv. 24–25). That "God gave them over in the sinful desires of their hearts" does not mean that he creates sinful desire. Rather, he responds to it. For example, Pharaoh hardened his heart repeatedly to God's command (Ex. 8:15, 19, 32) before God released him ("the LORD hardened Pharaoh's heart," Ex. 9:12; 10:20, 27; cf. 10:1) to the consequences of his sinful resolve.

Paul repeats the reason for the desperate plight of humanity. "The truth of God"—what God has made plain to them (cf. 1:20)—has been exchanged "for a lie." The consequence of accepting the lie that there is truth outside of the revelation of God (a repetition of the sin of Adam and Eve) is this: Creation is served rather than the Creator himself. Noteworthy is Dunn's observation that this verse reveals the human predisposition to serve something or someone.

The creation account teaches that men and women were created to live in relationship with their Creator and with one another. Humankind's rejection of a relationship with their Creator results in the perversion of all their other relationships. What God declared good, namely, that man and woman would live together in relationship as one flesh (Gen. 2:18–25), is exchanged for relationships in which men engage in sexual relations with other men, and women with other women (vv. 26–27). Therefore, these deeds are "unnatural," that is, they contravene the created order. The phrase in verse 27, "committed indecent acts," shows that what is condemned is the homosexual or lesbian act, not the temptation itself. The context also makes clear that the reason that homosexuality is raised here is not because it is more perverse than other types of sexual sin. Rather, Paul uses it to show how sin perverts the created order of male and female.

Verse 28 follows the same pattern we have seen above: Humankind's rejection of the knowledge of God available to them leads to divine retribution. There is a play on words in the Greek that reinforces Paul's argument that the punishment suits the sin. Because "they did not think it worthwhile" (*dokimazo*) to retain a true knowledge of God, "he gave them over to a depraved [*adokimos*] mind."

The list of vices that follows denotes the sorry effects of the loss of humanity's capacity to see the truth. The introductory line to the list of evil behaviors, "they have become filled with every kind of wickedness" (v. 29), indicates that the apostle wants the list to be heard as a whole. The point of verses 29–31, therefore, is not to be found by examining each deed that is mentioned. Instead, the emphasis is on how the whole range of human depravity can be traced back to the willful rejection of God. Vice lists such as this were common in writings of the period, both in Jewish and Hellenistic writings.

Three points will round off our discussion of chapter 1. (1) It strikes the modern reader that these vices are just as common today as they were in the apostle's day. (2) Paul has taken great pains to trace sin back to the decision made about God. What one thinks about God and how one then responds to this knowledge determine the cycle of behavior. This is just as true for us today as it was for the Romans and as it was for Adam and Eve. (3) The concluding verse aptly summarizes the downward cycle of sin described in verses 18–32: While men and women know God's indictment on their sin, they continue on in their sin nonetheless. But verse 32 also makes an additional point: The human condition has sunk to a new level when people not only do what is wrong, but even "approve" of it. Unfortunately, such a condition is a modern epidemic.

2.1.1.2. The Wrath of God on the Jews (2:1–3:20). Although Paul continues his discourse about the revelation of God's wrath in 2:1–3:20, the chapter division at 2:1 marks an abrupt change of style. He switches from the third person to the second as he addresses an imaginary dialogue partner, or interlocutor. The man with whom Paul directs his conversation is a Jew, whose identity is made explicit in verse 17. This dialogical form of argument, known as the diatribe, was practiced regularly in the philosophical schools. (The most definitive study to date of Paul's use of diatribe in this letter is that of S. K. Stowers [1981]).

The change of style in 2:1 marks a different stage in the argument. In chapter 1 Paul has described the deception prevalent among the Gentiles about the nature of God and the sinful behavior that resulted. In 2:1–3:20 he turns to address the deception prevalent among the Jews that their status as the elect of God granted them a more lenient standard of judgment. While knowing the righteous decrees of God and the grave consequences of disobedience, the Jews not only continued to disobey but actually excused themselves in the process (cf. 1:32). By the time the apostle concludes in 3:20, he will have argued repeatedly that Jews and Gentiles stand on an equal footing before the judgment seat.

2.1.1.2.1. God's Impartial Judgment (2:1–11). At the outset of chapter 2 Paul abruptly singles out a member of his audience—the Jew who was standing in total agreement with Paul's condemnation of Gentile practices in 1:18–32. The Jewish members of the audience would have recoiled in disgust at the mention of idolatry and homosexuality. They would have nodded their approval at Paul's argument that these Gentile behaviors show that God's wrath is already upon them. In fact, they would have recognized that Paul was making his case by drawing on traditional Jewish arguments against the beliefs and practices of the Gentiles. Thus, the Jewish contingent in Rome would have been startled by such a quick and unexpected reversal of the argument. Paul now turns to the Jew and accuses him of unjustly condemning others for what he himself practices.

While the "righteous" Jew could distance himself from such sins as homosexuality and idolatry, the deeds listed in 1:29–31 represent the broad array of human sin committed by Jew and Gentile alike. Consequently, when the Jew condemns the Gentile for sinful practices, he condemns himself in the process. Paul knows his audience must agree that the judgment of God rightly falls (NIV "based on truth") on evildoers (v. 2). As the prophet Malachi warned the Jews of his day: It is one thing to call for God's judgment on one's enemies; it is another matter to be ready to face it personally (Mal. 2:17–3:5).

That Paul is attacking Jewish presumption based on their covenant relationship with God is readily apparent from the rhetorical question in verse 4. The Jews were making the fatal error of misinterpreting the fact that they had been spared from the wrath of God as proof of their righteousness. Paul accuses them of showing contempt for God's mercy by taking advantage of it through sinful behavior. God's kindness is meant to give opportunity for repentance, not license for sin. A similar thought appears in Wisdom of Solomon 11:23—where God's grace is expressed as his willingness to "overlook people's sins, so that they may repent" (NRSV)—but there the writer meant the mercy of God toward the nations. Paul is directly challenging a Jewish presupposition that it was the Gentiles *alone* who needed such a gracious extension of divine mercy.

The temptation to condemn in others what one excuses in oneself is universal. One can always find a reason to justify oneself or one's group, but that action is never justified. For the Jew it had to do with being God's elect. For the Christian it may be that one's Christian heritage is misunderstood as a credit that allows one to engage in certain sins without having to pay the consequence. Or it may be an inappropriate understanding of grace, such that freedom in Christ is used as an excuse to engage in actions that are condemned in others (cf. Gal. 5:13).

Although judgment is temporarily postponed for God's chosen people, its eventual severity increases in the interim as Jews with unrepentant hearts store up wrath against themselves (v. 5). The Old Testament warned repeatedly that a hardened heart is a grave condition, which must be avoided through repentance (e.g., Deut. 10:16). "The day of God's wrath" (an Old Testament expression for judgment, e.g., Isa. 13:9; Zeph. 1:14–15) is the Day when God "will give to each person according to what he has done" (Rom. 2:6; cf. Ps. 62:12; Prov. 24:12).

Verses 7–10 are tightly constructed in a chiastic fashion. That is, verses 7 and 10 speak of reward, whereas verses 8 and 9 of condemnation. Two points in this section are reiterated from verses 1–6: (1) Both Jew and Gentile are on an equal footing at the judgment, and (2) the judgment is based on deeds. The order of salvation given in 1:16—the Jew first, then the Gentile—reappears here with a new twist. On the one hand, they are first in line for eternal life (v. 10); on the other hand, they are first in line for judgment (v. 9).

The contrast in verses 7–10 is between those Jews and Gentiles who, "by persistence in doing good," seek what God desires for humanity—"glory, honor and immortality" (cf. Ps. 8:5)—and those Jews and Gentiles who, through their selfish ambition, bring about what is evil. The text does not describe the postmortem conditions that face these two groups. This is noteworthy because speculation about the nature of the realm of the dead was widespread in some sectors of Second Temple Judaism. The Jewish apocalyptic writers of this period presented various and often detailed descriptions about the nature of the afterlife. Paul, however, is content to stop with the assertion that there is reward and punishment for all after death.

This passage raises the question as to how a judgment by works relates to a central theme in Romans—justification by faith. Before making comment on this, however, the central point here must not be missed. Both verses 6 and 11 state clearly that God is an impartial judge. Deeds are evaluated without regard to religious or ethnic status. The Jew, then, must not imagine that there is a separate standard in place for him or her.

The idea of a judgment according to works is a New Testament concept as well as an Old Testament one. It is found in the Gospels (Matt. 16:27), in the Petrine letters (1 Peter 1:17), in Revelation 2:23, and elsewhere in the Pauline correspondence (2 Cor. 5:10). This concept is not at odds with the doctrine of salvation by grace through faith. Instead, the prevalence in the New Testament of teaching about a judgment by works reflects the widespread understanding that deeds are an indispensable component of the Christian life. Works do not earn salvation (3:20), but they are the normative response by believers to the work of God's grace in their lives (ch. 6), and such righteous living is only possible by the Spirit (8:4, 10, 13).

2.1.1.2.2. Judgment and the Law (2:12–16). The first reference to the law (*nomos*) in Romans appears in this section, as Paul continues the discussion begun in 2:1–11 about the impartiality of God's judgment. He makes his main point in this section at the outset: Judgment falls on everyone who sins regardless of whether one possesses the Mosaic Law or not (v. 12). Those who live under the law are judged by it; those who live without the law are judged in accordance with their response to the demands of the law written on their hearts (vv. 14–15).

Paul's statement that the Gentiles "are a law for themselves" (v. 14) does not mean that the Gentiles become their own law. He is not arguing that there are two laws in operation—the

Mosaic Law for the Jew and a natural law for the Gentile. Rather, the requirements of God's one law are reflected in the moral conscience, which every man and woman has "by nature." Proof of the existence of the law written on the heart (cf. Jer. 31:33) is the manner in which the conscience condemns certain activities and even defends others (v. 15).

The discussion in 2:12–16 is not about natural law or the fate at the judgment of the Gentile who has been faithful to that law through the guidance of his or her conscience. Therefore, this text does not address the issue of the eternal destiny of the morally upright individual who has never heard the gospel message. Paul's concern here is to establish that *the Jew* cannot claim special standing on the day of wrath as a result of possessing the law.

This is the reason why Paul raises the situation of the Gentiles. They illustrate that there are those without the advantage of having the law who nevertheless show a moral sensitivity that reflects the requirements of the law. Possession in and of itself has no salvific value. Only those who do the law, rather than those who only hear it or possess it (cf. Gal. 3:12; James 1:22–23), will be "declared righteous," that is, will be acquitted on the Judgment Day (v. 13).

This future aspect to justification—that is, the acquittal that comes at the final judgment—does not nullify the present or realized aspect of it. The believer has been justified through faith (5:1). But there remains a future aspect, when at the judgment the final sentence of "not guilty" is read. Similarly, salvation is something we receive at the point of faith, but Paul often prefers to speak about salvation as a future event (cf. Rom. 5:9–10: salvation from final wrath). What this tells us is that the work of God with the believer is ongoing. Believers are not left to their own devices after the initial salvation event. God continues the work of salvation for those who trust him (see 5:1–11).

In a short commentary such as this, the reader must be alert to the fact that the simplicity of explanation I have given here of necessity disguises the complexity of some of the questions raised by the text. One such question, which continues to be hotly debated, is whether the idea discussed in 2:13—that there is a righteousness that may be obtained by doing the law—actually circulated in first-century Judaism. The Introduction should be consulted on this matter (see "Paul's View of the Law"), as well as the longer commentaries. Suffice it to say for our purposes, what Paul raises as a theoretical possibility in 2:13 is discounted as unattainable because of human weakness in chapter 3. The conclusion given there, which the reader does not yet see, is that *all* attempts at finding favor with God ultimately come up short without Jesus Christ.

2.1.1.2.3. Jewish Predicament (2:17–24). Whereas the previous section attacked the misconception that possession of the law granted some sort of immunity from God's wrath, this section takes issue with Jewish pride over being the people of the law. The diatribe style introduced in 2:1–4 reappears as Paul resumes his conversation with a representative Jew. Paul rehearses for his conversation partner various attitudes that the Jews held as people of the law (vv. 17–20), and then contrasts these attitudes with their actual performance (vv. 21–24).

Paul employs a rhetorical device to emphasize the disparity between their profession and their performance. Verses 17–20 form an anacoluthon, or an unfinished sentence—indicated in the NIV by the dash at the end of verse 20. This sharp grammatical break, coming directly after a listing of their attitudes, underlines the discontinuity between what the Jews thought of themselves and how they lived.

Paul identifies various aspects of Jewish pride: pride in knowing that having the law allows them, in distinction from all other nations, to know God and discern his will (vv. 17–18), and pride in their role as teachers to the nations (vv. 19–20). There is no doubt that these characterizations give an accurate portrayal of Jewish self-perception at the time of Paul. Philo's identification of Israel as both prophet and priest for all nations (*On Abraham* 98) is only one reference among many that can be cited in this regard. The phrases in verse 19, "a guide for the blind, a light for those who are in the dark," echo the role given the Servant of the Lord in Isaiah 42:6–7, a role that the Jews readily took as their own (cf. 1 Enoch 105:1; Wisd. Sol. 18:4). The statement made in verse 20 that knowledge and truth are embodied in the law reflected their belief that the wisdom sought by the nations had been graciously given to them by God (e.g., 1 Bar. 4:1–4).

While Paul does not dispute the unique role f Israel within the plan of salvation, he does ring the indictment, in a series of rhetorical uestions (vv. 21–23), that she has failed in her ssignment. For what the Jews condemn, they emselves practice. Paul now expands on the arlier charge made in 2:1 (they "who pass dgment . . . do the same things") by menoning some specific sins.

Of the ones mentioned (stealing, adultery, nd robbing temples), it is the last that is difcult to understand: "You who abhor idols, do ou rob temples?" The difficulty lies in deterining what the offense of robbing temples efers to, and what the relationship might be etween this offense and idolatry. "Robbing mples" may be taken literally as signifying e use of precious metals that came from ems pilfered from pagan temples (Moo). Or e charge may be understood metaphorically s some sort of sacrilege. For example, itzmyer interprets this sin as the elevation of e law to an improper level.

At any rate, the point is clear and ironic. aul's point concerns the disparity between the ational standard and the actions of individal Jews. The irony is that Judaism was known or its high moral standards, and it was this feaure that had attracted some Gentiles to the ynagogue. What others lauded and the Jews xulted in, Paul attacks.

The twentieth-century Christian can easily dentify with this predicament. On the one and, Christianity is known for its high moral tandards. Those standards, which are often irectly in opposition to societal norms, draw oth praise from some quarters of society and riticism from others. On the other hand, the ccusation that is often leveled against Chrisians is that they do not practice what they reach. Unfortunately, the oft-repeated barb hat "the church is full of hypocrites" has some asis in fact.

To seal his argument Paul quotes Isaiah 2:5 (cf. Ezek. 36:22), which testifies to the erision that was brought on the name of God s a result of his people's state of exile (Rom. :24). The quotation reinforces the declaration f v. 23 that God is being dishonored by his eople's disobedience. But this summary verse lso brings the reader back to the main point: What matters to God is doing the law rather han possessing it. The reference to the Exile in this Old Testament quotation has the particular effect of reminding the Jews that the Exile itself was due to Israel's sin (e.g., Ezek. 36:17–23). Being the people of the law did not prevent the Exile; it will not prevent the final judgment either.

2.1.1.2.4. Judgment and Circumcision (2:25–29). Having discussed the law, Paul raises the topic of circumcision—the other great symbol of the covenant that the Lord made with the Jews. Circumcision was instituted as a sign of the covenant in the time of Abraham (Gen. 17:10–11), and the importance of this rite for the Jews had only grown in importance in the period following the Maccabean War (early second century B.C.). It had become a symbol of national resistance against Hellenism. It had also become a safeguard against hell. The rabbinical writings contain numerous assurances that the circumcised individual would avoid Gehenna (e.g., *Gen. Rab.* 48 [30a]; *Exod. Rab.* 19 [81c]).

According to Paul, however, circumcision plays no direct role in determining one's fate on the Judgment Day. He develops his position in stages. (1) Circumcision in and of itself has no spiritual merit. Its value is tied to keeping the law (v. 25). In the same way that possessing the law is only of ultimate value if it is obeyed, so being circumcised is valueless unless it is accompanied by obedience. By separating the doing of the law from the rite of circumcision, the apostle is challenging any thought that one had kept the law by being circumcised. Paul would have made the same argument about other acts considered defining characteristics of the Jews, such as observing the food laws and keeping the feasts and holy days.

(2) Circumcision is no guarantee of a favorable ruling at the judgment. The one who keeps the law without being circumcised (cf. 2:14–15) is better off than the one who is circumcised but fails to keep it: "The one who is not circumcised physically and yet obeys the law will condemn you who . . . are a lawbreaker" (v. 27). The background to this statement needs to be appreciated before its force may be heard. It was a common belief in Jewish literature that the unrighteous would stand condemned and that the righteous Jew would be vindicated in the presence of his enemies (Dan. 12:2–3; 1 Enoch 62–63; 104; 108:11–15; 2 Bar. 49–51). And it was a common

assumption during Paul's day that "the righteous" were the observant Jews who resisted compromise with the Hellenistic world and that "the sinners" were the Gentiles and those Jews who had become like them. The apostle is challenging these categories.

(3) There is another type of circumcision that does mark the people of God (vv. 28–29). While it is certainly true that Paul was not the first Jew to call for a circumcision of the heart as a complement to the physical rite (Deut. 10:16; 30:6; Jer. 4:4; Jub. 1:23; 1QS 5:5–6), it is his insistence that circumcision in and of itself has no salvific value that sets his approach apart.

To this point in the chapter the focus has not been on the means of salvation, even though the possibility of salvation through works was raised more than once. Instead, the discussion has been about the equality of all individuals before the judgment; verses 25–27 reiterate this. In the final two verses of the chapter, however, Paul hints at what he will go on to develop later. There is a standard for being the people of God that is internal rather than external, which has to do with the circumcision of the heart—a circumcision performed by the Spirit rather than by the written law. Thus, the chapter ends with the idea that the one whom God accepts as one of his own, a true member of the chosen people, has undergone a spiritual work that supersedes all physical works.

2.1.1.2.5. Objections (3:1–8). The dialogue partner now responds to Paul's argument with questions of his own. In the rhetorical dialogue that follows in 3:1–8 we hear the echo of Paul's debates with the Jews, both those inside and outside of the Christian camp. Paul was criticized by Jewish opponents because of his "accommodation" to the Gentiles in matters that were deemed essential to the covenant relationship God had made with the Jews (cf. Gal. 1:10). His devaluation of law observance and, in particular, his refusal to command Gentile converts to be circumcised or to keep food laws meant that opposition hounded him wherever he went. Paul's response to Jewish objections about his gospel is found here and in chapter 6; his explanation why the Jews have rejected the gospel comes in chapters 9–11.

The first question responds to the case, made in chapter 2, against Jewish presumption (3:1). If there is no special standing for the circumcised Jew in relation to the judgment, the what advantage is there in being a Jew? I other words, does Paul's gospel do away wit the benefits of God's election entirely? In ligl of the preceding discussion, Paul's answer th the advantages of being a Jew are "much i every way" (v. 2) is somewhat surprising. B his response alerts us to the fact that the apos tle's polemic is not about the covenant as suc Rather, it is about the presumption that th covenant ensures some type of national immu nity from the wrath of God.

The first advantage (there is no second men tioned here—the list continues in 9:4–5) is th the Jews have been "entrusted with the ver words of God" (v. 2)—that is, the inspired utte ances of the Scriptures. Paul is affirming wh his fellow Jews held to be a special privileg (e.g., 1 Bar. 4:4 proclaims: "Happy are we, (Israel, for we know what is pleasing to God")

The second question from the Jewish objec tor is prompted by the previous answer. This i readily evident in the Greek text, where th second question (v. 3) plays on the wor "entrusted" (a form of *pisteuo*) in verse 2 b using other words that derive from this sam Greek root (*pist-*); they may be translated a either "faith" or "faithfulness" in verse 3a an as "lack of faith" or "unfaithfulness" in vers 3b. In light of the previous verse, which iden tified the Jews as those entrusted with God' words, the follow-up question probably con cerns their faithfulness in carrying out th responsibility attached to this privilege. Th point of the question is, then, what happens t the privilege of being entrusted with the word of God if "some Jews" (not all) have not prop erly handled what they were entrusted with.

With two Old Testament quotes (Ps. 116:1 and 51:4) Paul replies that the truth of God (c 1:18, 25; 2:8), or his faithfulness, stands regard less of the falsehood, or faithlessness, of hi chosen people (Rom. 3:4). That is to say, Go remains true to the Abrahamic covenant. Bu this does not mean, as the reference in Psaln 51:4 to God's judgment makes clear, tha because he is faithful he will not judge them.

The juxtaposition of God's faithfulnes with the unfaithfulness of the Jews raises a fur ther objection, which is repeated twice (vv. 5 7). If God's faithfulness is seen more clearl against the backdrop of the people's failure then why are they punished for something tha 'increases his glory"? Paul's curt response points to the character of God. God could not judge the world if that was an unjust act. Even mentioning the possibility that God is unjust causes Paul to add a disclaimer, "I am using a human argument."

That Paul introduces into his discussion about God's covenant faithfulness the fact that his preaching was being criticized for promoting an immoral lifestyle (v. 8) is informative. It shows us that this portion of the dialogue was more than a hypothetical construct. Jewish Christians had leveled the charge against the apostle that his preaching about salvation by faith, without works of the law, amounted to a license for sin (Gal. 1:10; 2:17). Their objection appears here: If God's grace covers it all, then why not do evil so that God's grace is seen even more clearly? (Does not the end justify the means?) Paul takes up this objection in earnest in 6:1—"Shall we go on sinning so that grace may increase?"

2.1.1.2.6. Sum: All People Are Subject to Wrath (3:9–20). Paul, having completed his digression on God's faithfulness (3:1–8), now sums up his lengthy discourse on God's wrath. His summation introduces concepts and expressions that he will take up later in the letter: "under sin" (3:9; cf. chs. 6–7), "by observing the law" (3:20; cf. chs. 3–4), and the role of the law in making one aware of sin (chs. 4–5; 7).

The question in 3:9 is difficult to translate, let alone interpret. Much of the difficulty surrounds the verb *proecho*, which appears only here in the New Testament. The translation "Are we any better?" is preferred by some commentators (e.g., Barrett; Cranfield; Käsemann) and found in many of the versions, including the NIV. The NIV puts an alternate translation in the footnote: "Are we any worse?"

There is another way to read this verb that gives the verse a different sense. Among others, Stuhlmacher and Dunn translate it in such a way that the question has to do with making excuses or constructing a defense. For instance, Stuhlmacher's translation reads: "Are we making excuses?" There are problems with all of these translations, and no attempt will be made here to weigh out the arguments for each reading (Cranfield has a detailed discussion).

If we follow the NIV, then the point of the question and answer in verse 9 appears to contradict what we read in verses 1–2: "What advantage, then, is there in being a Jew? ... Much in every way!" (3:1–2); "Are we any better? Not at all!" (3:9). The tension produced by this reading of verse 9 is one of the reasons why Dunn rejects this translation. The latter part of verse 9, however, clarifies what Paul means when he says that the Jews are not at an advantage: "We have already made the charge that Jews and Gentiles alike are all under sin." Although the Jew has certain advantages as God's elect, these advantages count for nothing before the judgment seat of God. As Barrett concludes, Paul is being paradoxical, not contradictory.

The expression "under sin"(v. 9), describing the common condition of Jew and Gentile, is noteworthy. It expresses a central aspect of Pauline theology. Men and women do not just sin; they are *under the power of* sin. They need more than forgiveness; they need deliverance. What liberates humanity from such domination is yet to be described.

In order to establish the universal indictment that all are "under sin," Paul recites in verses 10–18 a string of biblical quotations taken mainly from Psalms. Note the following points about this section. (1) Moo has noted that this is the longest string of Old Testament quotes in the Pauline letters. On so crucial a point, on which the rest of Paul's gospel message stands, Paul piles up biblical proof texts.

(2) The repeated occurrence of "no one" in these Old Testament texts reinforces the assertion of verse 9 that "all [are] under sin."

(3) These quotes cover a broad range of human sin.

(4) Some of these Old Testament references were taken from contexts in which their indictments of sin were directed against Gentiles, not righteous Jews. Paul's reuse of them to describe the condition of the Jew as well as the Gentile furthers his agenda of establishing that all fall under the same indictment.

(5) The last quotation sums up the cause of human sin: "There is no fear of God before their eyes" (Ps. 36:1). When God is not acknowledged as God, sinful behavior results. This reminds us of the earlier indictment of the Gentiles (Rom. 1:18–32), who "suppress the truth by their wickedness" (1:18).

In verses 19–20, by way of final summary before moving on to God's prescription for the human predicament, Paul depicts a courtroom in which first the Jews ("those who are under the law") and then the rest of humanity ("the whole world") are identified as the defendants. God is both the one offended and the Judge of the offense. Cranfield explains the apostle's reasoning here: "With the proof that the Jews (the people who might seem to have reason to regard themselves as an exception) are in fact no exception, the proof that the entire human race lies under God's judgment is finally completed." Their collective guilt is exposed when they are given opportunity to speak on their own behalf. But they are speechless before God, because the testimony of the law (given in vv. 10–18) leaves them without any defense.

What the law says about the sinfulness of all people (as the long series of Old Testament quotations has shown) must apply to those who are "within the law" (a preferable translation to the NIV's "under the law"; the preposition is *en*, not *hypo*). Paul is condemning any thought that those within the law—that is, those who live within its boundaries—are to be treated differently before the judgment of God. The same point is reiterated in verse 20: "No one will be declared righteous in his sight by observing the law" (cf. Ps. 143:2: "for no one living is righteous before you").

The phrase "by observing the law" (v. 20; *ex ergon nomou*) literally translates "by works of law," which denotes the service required by the law (cf. Gal. 2:16). What are these works? Dunn argues that the "works of law" refer to those particular works that were seen to distinguish the Jew over against the Gentile (e.g., circumcision, 2:25–29). It is the keeping of these sort of laws that Paul is attacking.

The previous references in this letter to observing the law, however, are not restricted to observing certain laws that were considered distinguishing traits of the Jewish people, such as circumcision and food regulations. For instance, the distinction in 2:25–26 between circumcision and practicing the law warns us against equating what Paul has in mind when he speaks about keeping the law with circumcision and some other distinctive practices. (For more on this, the section in the Introduction, "Paul's View of the Law," should be consulted.)

What strikes the reader is the contrast that this summary creates with the previous discussion about obtaining eternal life through doing what is right (2:7–10, 13–16). It now appears that gaining salvation through such means, while a hypothetical possibility, is a practical impossibility because of human fallibility.

The answer to the human predicament, then, is not in keeping the law. This does not undermine the value of the law, however. The law exposes the need for salvation that comes through another channel.

2.1.2. The Salvation of Humanity Through Faith in Jesus Christ (3:21–4:25)

2.1.2.1. Salvation Through the Death of Christ (3:21–26). Paul's preceding presentation of the desperate plight of sinful humanity before a just God creates a sense of despair. This is the intended effect. For the full glory of God's plan of salvation can only be appreciated fully from the point of despair. Paul now reveals, albeit in condensed form, a summary of the righteousness of God, that is, his saving activity on behalf of men and women.

The fact that the section about God's wrath on the human condition is much longer (1:18–3:20) than his presentation of the righteousness of God requires comment. It must be borne in mind that this is a letter, not a systematic treatise (see "Occasion and Purpose" in the Introduction). Although Paul is describing his gospel message in somewhat systematic fashion, he never forgets that among his audience are Jews who might object to his presentation. Paul's conviction that the Jew could claim no special advantage over the Gentile in terms of sin and judgment had drawn opposition before. Thus, he pursues this line of argument in extended fashion in 2:1–3:8.

But when he turns to describe how God's righteousness was expressed in Jesus Christ, he presents a theological understanding of the meaning of Jesus' death that was shared by Jewish and Gentile Christians alike. As a result, this topic commands less attention. Indeed, the curt manner with which he describes the means of salvation in 3:21–26 suggests that he is repeating material that was familiar to these believers. It is commonly supposed that Paul is drawing on creedal expressions of the early church in verses 25–26a, and perhaps also in verse 24 (one of the reasons for this view is the number of non-Pauline words in this section). The reader will note, however, that the one aspect of salvation that Paul will go on to emphasize is that it comes by faith alone (3:27–4:25), since this matter *was* controversial.

Paul's opening statement (v. 21) that God's node of salvation is both "apart from law" and lso in line with what "the Law and the 'rophets testify" indicates his concern that his osition on the law be properly understood. On he one hand, righteousness is not to be btained through the system defined by the aw or through being one of the people of the aw. On the other hand, the Old Testament criptures do testify about God's righteousness nd how it may be obtained. The present tense f "testify" denotes that the witness of the criptures continues to speak to the Jews and veryone else who will hear it (cf. 1:2; 3:2; :23–24), even in our own day.

In 1:17–18 God's righteousness and his vrath were introduced as two simultaneous nd ongoing divine activities being revealed to he world. Here, as Paul opens the topic of the ighteousness of God, he specifies that it "has een made known" (v. 21). He is referring now ot to the process, but to that pivotal event that naugurated it—the crucifixion of Christ, vhen "God presented him as a sacrifice of tonement" (v. 25).

The translation of *hilasterion* (NIV "sacriice of atonement") continues to be a matter of ebate. The NIV rendering of this word sugests that Christ is the means of atonement (see Dunn; Morris, 1955–56, 33–43), whereas nany commentators prefer "place of expiaion/propitiation" or "mercy seat" (e.g., 'itzmyer; Stuhlmacher; Gundry-Volf, 282–3)—which is what it means in its only other ppearance in the New Testament (Heb. 9:5). t is difficult to choose between these two ptions. In fact, Black and Dunn urge that hese two options should not be seen as mutully exclusive.

Fortunately for us, even though the actual eferent of *hilasterion* is difficult to determine, he theological truth being conveyed is not. Vhether *hilasterion* refers to the mercy seat the cover of the ark on which the blood of the in offering for the nation was sprinkled annully on the Day of Atonement—Lev. 16) or to he sacrifice offered to God for atonement, the ewish sacrificial system is being called to nind. It is clear, then, as the reference to "in is blood" confirms (v. 25b), that the sacrificial eath of Christ is being represented by this nagery. As that which was offered on the altar vas sacrificed to pay the punishment for the one who had sinned, so Christ was offered to bear the penalty for the sin of humanity.

We call this the doctrine of substitutionary atonement. Christ was put to death as the substitute for all men and women. Our sin is transferred to him; his life, or righteousness, is given to us (cf. Rom. 8:3; 2 Cor. 5:21; Gal. 3:13). This understanding of Christ's death was that of the early church. Paul told the Corinthians that the tradition he had received declared "that Christ died for our sins according to the Scriptures" (1 Cor. 15:3b).

The sacrifice of atonement is "through faith in his blood" (v. 25). Although the NIV does not use a comma to separate "through faith" and "in his blood," it is best to understand these phrases separately. As Käsemann argues, "through faith in his blood" is without parallel in the New Testament, and in Paul's letters *pistis* (faith) is not followed by *en* (in). What Paul is saying, then, is that the "sacrifice of atonement" is appropriated through faith, and it is achieved in his blood, that is, by Christ's sacrificial death.

Debate continues in theological circles about whether the sacrifice of atonement should be understood as "expiation" or "propitiation." Expiation refers to the removal of sin; propitiation to the appeasement of God or the satisfaction of his wrath. C. H. Dodd has argued that the concept of propitiation had all but been lost in the LXX usage of *hilasterion* and its cognates, and that the notion of propitiation was more a pagan concept than a biblical teaching. The sacrifice of Christ, according to Dodd, is to be understood as an expiatory sacrifice that dealt with human sin and guilt.

Dodd's argument has met with much opposition. One of his primary critics is L. Morris (1955, 167–94), who defends the more traditional view that *hilasterion* involves propitiation. Among the various arguments he makes is one taken from the preceding context. After three chapters about the wrath of God, *hilasterion* must give some indication about how that wrath is diverted away from the believer.

It seems inconceivable (in light of 1:18–3:20) that the solution to human sin Paul presents would not address this reality. And certainly we are to understand that the sacrifice of Christ is sufficient to turn away God's wrath from the believer. Yet, Gundry-Volf (281–82) argues that it does not necessarily follow that we should understand this process as achieving a change in the disposition of an angry God. This is because the repeated message in Romans 3 is that God in his mercy took the initiative to provide an effective solution: "*God presented him* as a sacrifice of atonement" (v. 25a, italics added).

The idea that his saving activity is presented, or put on public display, represents a significant transition in salvation history. The locus of God's work of salvation has moved beyond the old boundaries of the nation of Israel. No longer is his method of dealing with human sin confined within the Most Holy Place of the temple, where only one man could go once a year. His righteousness has been moved out into the open, where all have access to it; up on a hill, where everyone can see it; on a cross, where everyone can kneel at its foot.

Another distinction is made in this passage between the nature of the temple sacrifice and the sacrifice of Christ. Christ's death accomplished what all the repeated offerings of the past were unable to do: to deal with sin in a definitive and final manner. Paul says that God passed over the sins of the past (v. 25). In other words, God, "in his forbearance" (i.e., restraint), did not exact the penalty for sins committed. While the former *hilasterion* was sufficient for a time, the full payment for sin was made on the cross.

As Paul comes to the end of this condensed treatment of the meaning of Christ's death, he asserts twice that it was "to demonstrate his justice" (vv. 25b, 26a) that God presented Christ as a sacrifice of atonement. The Gk. word *dikaiosyne,* translated here as "justice," is also the word for "righteousness."

What did God demonstrate about his righteousness? It deals both with the past and with the present, and in such a way that it is seen to be "just" (v. 26b). (1) He is shown to be right in his actions toward the covenant people in the past because God "left the sins committed beforehand unpunished" (v. 25). That is, the offering of the perfect sacrifice, Jesus Christ, was the appropriate measure to deal definitively with those transgressions that had been handled through the sacrificial system, but that had in some sense remained unpunished (see Dunn). (2) But God is also shown to be right in his actions in the present. For the sacrifice of atonement is the full provision for the si of everyone, not just the Jew.

Our focus to this point has been on th motif of *hilasterion*, with its background in th temple sacrifice. There are two othe metaphors that Paul uses here to explain th meaning of Christ's death. (1) One, taken fron the law court, is the language of justificatio or acquittal (v. 24). Because of the cross, th believer is declared "not guilty."

(2) The other comes from the world of slav ery. The believer's release from sin's captiv ity is conveyed with the term *redemptio* (*apolytrosis*). Common to the first-centur concept of redemption was the idea of freein someone from bondage through the paymen of a price or ransom (L. Morris, 1993, 785) Within the Old Testament God is depicted a the Redeemer of his people from bondage whether from Egypt (e.g., Deut. 7:8) or Baby lon (e.g., Isa. 52:3). In such references th aspect of the metaphor that is conveyed is th idea of deliverance rather than that of a ranson payment. This is also the case in Paul's usag of the term. Morris makes a helpful distinctio here: There is nothing in Paul's thought abou the one to whom a payment might be made But that does not mean that there was n cost—the cost was the life of Christ.

Faith is the means whereby every individ ual without exception comes into the salvatio offered by God through Jesus Christ. This i because every individual has no other mean available. Human effort is insufficient, for "a have sinned and fall short of the glory of God (v. 23). The glory of God has figured promi nently in the letter so far, as that which ha been rejected by the many (1:21) and sough by the few (2:7, 10). Romans 3:23 reveals tha this search, stemming from human initiative is in vain.

What is this glory that humans seek but fal short of? Within Second Temple Judaism glory had come to be associated with the righ teousness that the original couple knew in th Garden before the Fall (e.g., in Apoc. Mos 21:6, Adam says to Eve, "You have estrange me from the glory of God"). Consequently, th apocalyptic writers depicted the hope of faith ful Jews in terms of the restoration of glor (1 Enoch 50:1; 4 Ezra 7:122–5; 2 Bar. 51:1 This is the background of "glory" in Roman 3:23. The glory that people fall short of is tha ate of right relationship with God that char- :terized the Garden of Eden experience of dam and Eve.

2.1.2.2. Salvation by Faith (3:27–4:25). It significant for us that Paul returns to the ›pic of faith in 3:27–31 and in chapter 4. It not the ransom theology of verse 24, or the crifice of atonement imagery in verse 25, or ıy of the other ideas in the preceding section at he revisits for the sake of additional expla- ation and validation. This is significant ecause it shows which aspect of his salvation essage the apostle considered contentious— at of faith.

It was not the message of faith or trust in od in and of itself that was controversial. ather, it was Paul's insistence that the mes- ge of faith meant that *the attainment or aintenance of righteousness was completely sassociated from the practice of the law*. This what had stirred the opposition of some Jews d the Gentiles whom they had influenced. nd it is with this audience in mind that Paul ghlights the centrality and biblical nature of ith.

2.1.2.2.1. Basic Concept of Faith (3:27–). In these verses, Paul returns to the dialogic yle. The listener therefore anticipates that the llowing "conversation" is once more tween Paul and a representative Jew. Unlike e preceding dialogues, however, distin- uishing between the two voices has become ore problematic. Nevertheless, this does not nder our understanding because the meaning nerges in the dialogue itself.

The opening question and answer about the gitimacy of boasting ("Where, then, is boast- g? It is excluded," v. 27a) brings the discus- on back around to the subject of Jewish pride being people of the law—an attitude that ul attacked as dangerous and misguided in 17–24. What is interesting here is the man- r in which the dialogue in verse 27b is rased: "Through what law?" (NIV: "On what inciple?"); "Of works?" (NIV: "On that of ›serving the law?"). Paul's typical use of aw" (*nomos*) to this point in the letter has en in reference to the Mosaic Law. It is ely the case here as well since there is no ›od reason to interpret it otherwise.

But it is in the response to this question— hich translates literally: "No, but through ıe] law of faith"—that Paul appears to be making a play on the word "law" to denote something different. What Paul seems to be saying is that boasting is not excluded through the law of works, that is, the Jewish law, but through the "law," or principle, of faith.

While many commentators take "law of faith" as a reference to the Old Testament law (e.g., Dunn—"the law understood in terms of faith"; Cranfield—"the law that summons people to faith"), this interpretation runs into difficulty when we get to the question in verse 31. If Paul is affirming the value of the Jewish law by defining it as the "law of faith" in verse 27 then why ask in verse 31 whether the law is nullified by faith?

Boasting is not permitted according to the principle of faith because it rules that a person is justified (made righteous) on the basis of faith without observing the law (v. 28). In other words, boasting only comes into play with human effort. In Barrett's words, "Boasting and faith are mutually exclusive."

Verse 28 has played a pivotal role in Protestant theology. It was to this verse that Luther added the word "alone" in his translation of the phrase "justified by faith." (He was not the first to add this term [see Fitzmyer for a list], but the addition has become attached to his name.) The teaching of this verse, which is summarized in the Reformation axiom *sola fide* ("through faith alone"), continues to define the Protestant understanding of salvation. Thus, evangelical preaching has made the case that if even the law that God gave to the Jews cannot save, certainly no other law or religious-based system has any salvific merit before a righteous God either.

Paul now presses the validity of justification by faith by arguing from the Jewish belief in monotheism (v. 29). Because there is only one God, the Jews would concede that God is the God of the Gentiles in that he is the Creator and Judge of all. Nevertheless, their covenantal relationship with God meant that the Jews viewed God as particularly *their* God. Paul is directly challenging the exclusivity of this view by arguing that God could not be the God of the Gentiles unless he provided for them the same means of justification as he provides for the Jews (vv. 29–30). It follows, then, that such a means of righteousness could not be law-based, for that would exclude the Gentile world.

The final question of this exchange comes to the heart of the matter for the Jew or the Jewish Christian. Does the gospel of faith nullify the law (cf. Matt. 5:17)? Paul responds to the question with his characteristic *me genoito*, a strong negation that translates literally as "may it not be" (cf. Rom. 3:4, 6; 6:2, 15; 7:7, 13; 9:14; 11:1, 11; 1 Cor. 6:15; Gal. 2:17; 3:21). His cryptic answer, "Rather, we uphold the law" (3:31), leaves us wondering exactly what Paul meant by this phrase. Nevertheless, by refuting the notion that his gospel nullifies the law, he affirms some continuing function for the law.

Moo categorizes three different ways that the ongoing role of the law may be understood. (1) It testifies to faith (Cranfield); (2) it convicts so that one sees the need for faith in Christ (cf. 3:19–20; Harrison); (3) it commands obedience—that is, faith fulfills the demands of the law (cf. 8:4; Moo). The second option has in its favor the preceding reference in verses 19–20 to the convicting work of the law. But the third option must also be considered. The idea that faith fulfills the demands of the law is made explicit later in 8:4: "that the righteous requirements of the law might be fully met in us." That 8:4 is so far removed from 3:31 should not immediately cancel out the applicability of this interpretation. As we have already seen, the author does not hesitate to introduce a subject in brief and then leave its development until later (e.g., the advantage of the Jew: 3:1–2; 9:4–5).

2.1.2.2.2. Illustration: The Faith of Abraham (4:1–25). The chapter division marks a transition rather than a change of subject. Paul's defense of justification by faith continues as he calls to the stand an impressive witness: Abraham, the father of the nation of Israel. If the examination of this great patriarch proves that his righteousness was accorded on the basis of his faith rather than his works, then Paul's case for the biblical nature of his gospel—that it is a gospel "to which the Law and the Prophets testify" (3:21)—becomes compelling.

But there is another reason why Abraham is singled out for such attention. He was important within Judaism because he was the one who first accepted the covenant and its conditions; he was the one who accepted circumcision as a sign of the covenant (Gen. 17). According to Jewish tradition, to him God granted righteousness because of his *faithfu*-*ness* (not his faith), a faithfulness he demo-strated by his willingness to offer Isaac as sacrifice (Sir. 44:20; 1 Macc. 2:52). Abraha was also the one, according to that same tr-dition, who kept the Mosaic Law even befo it was written down (e.g., Jub. 16:28; 2 Ba 57:1–2).[2]

To argue against this characterization of t patriarch and the nature of his righteousnes Paul adopts the type of methodology used b his opponents. The extended exposition o Genesis 15:6 given here conforms to the pri ciples and practices of biblical exegesis in t Second Temple Period. The exposition of Ge esis 15:6—"Abram believed the LORD, and l credited it to him as righteousness"—focus on two key words: "believed" and "credited

Since Paul is arguing against a Jewish inte pretation of Abraham, the dialogic style that l has been using to interact with a Jewish co versation partner continues in chapter 4. As the previous section (3:27–31), however, it becoming more difficult to identify whether is Paul or the Jewish interlocutor who is as ing the questions. It does seem that Paul is no not only answering the questions, but also po ing them.

The opening question asks what Abraha "discovered in this matter" (v. 1). That is, wh did Abraham discover about the means of rig teousness? Dunn notes that the verb Paul us for "discovered" (*heurisko*) appears frequent in the LXX in the phrase "to find favor [grace]" (esp. in Genesis, e.g., Gen. 18:3). Co sequently, Paul appears to be giving advan notice as to what he will argue was the natu of Abraham's discovery (see Rom. 4:4).

That Abraham did not discover rig teousness by works is substantiated with a cit tion from his principle text: Genesis 15: Contrary to the Jewish view that this text co cerned Abraham's faithfulness or obedienc Paul argues that the crediting of righteousne was in response to his faith. Genesis 15 defin Abraham's faith as a belief in the promise th God gave him that he, although still without heir, would be the father of a great nation. T point is, then, that if Abraham could not boa in his works (cf. Rom. 2:17, 23; 3:27)—t one who according to Jewish tradition kept t law before it was given to Moses—then w can (Calvert, 7)?

In verses 4–8 Paul commences his exposi-ion of Genesis 15:6 with an explanation of the mport of the word "credited" or "reckoned" *elogisthe*, a form of the verb *logizo*). To illus-rate its meaning in Genesis 15:6, Paul takes dvantage of the commercial sense of this vord current in the Greco-Roman world in rder to draw an analogy from the business ealm. The comparison he draws is not plainly vident, however, because he has not fully pelled out the corresponding components. 'he key to interpreting Romans 4:4–5 is in oting the antithesis at the end of verse 4 etween "gift" (*charis*; lit., grace) and "oblig-tion." A person who works earns a wage. In ther words, the employer is obliged to credit e worker with a wage. But righteousness is ot so earned. Rather, it is credited as a gift to e individual who believes. Paul has here pro-ided the answer to the question he raised in erse 1. What did Abraham discover? He ound that it is by grace that a person is ccepted by God.

The nature of faith is given some definition verse 5: It is believing in the "God who jus-fies the wicked." It is hard to imagine a more rring expression of grace. After all, Paul had eclared earlier that the wrath of God is poured ut on the wicked (1:18). Furthermore, those 'ho were familiar with the Old Testament and ubsequent Jewish literature were accustomed hearing about how God justifies the pious nd punishes the wicked (Ex. 23:7; Ps. 1; Prov. 7:15; Isa. 5:22–23; 1 Enoch 108). It is none ther than Abraham, the father of the Jews, 'ho is the justification for such an expression f grace. He was, according to Jewish tradi-on, the Gentile who turned from his idolatry follow the one God (Jub. 12:1–21; Apoc. br. 1–8).

The wondrous gospel proclamation that od justifies the wicked still jars the hearer. veryday life constantly reinforces the prin-iple that a person gets what is coming to him r her: "You get what you pay for"; "there is o free lunch." But the eyes of faith must see eyond the world of recompense to fix on the od who rewards with grace those who do not eserve it.

In order to expand further on the nature of race, Paul cites Psalm 32:1–2 in Romans :7–8, which is another text in which the reek verb *logizo* ("count," v. 8) appears: "Blessed is the man whose sin the Lord will never count against him." This methodology of interpreting one verse by another containing the same key word was common in Jewish exegesis. Paul's citation of a few lines from David's psalm of contrition, then, reinforces the point just made that "credited" in Genesis 15:6 has nothing to do with human merit or repayment of debt. The relationship between forgiveness of sins in Psalm 32 and crediting of righteousness in Genesis 15 is just this: Both come by grace. As forgiveness comes regardless of human action, so does righteousness.

In verses 9–12 Paul picks up on the word "blessed" in the quotation from Psalm 32 and asks who might know such blessedness? The remainder of the argument in this chapter seeks to establish that such blessedness is available to Jew and Gentile, to the circumcised and the uncircumcised. He proceeds to do this by focusing on the second of the two words from Genesis 15:6 that he has chosen to examine: "believed" (Gk. *pisteuo*). For it is by believing, or through faith, that all may be credited with the righteousness of God.

As the apostle continues his attack on the Jewish presumption that the righteousness of God was exclusively for those within the covenant, he returns to the subject of circumcision (see Rom. 2:25–29). This is no surprise in a discussion of Abraham. He was the one who accepted the sign of the covenant (circumcision) in response to the covenant God had made with him (Gen. 17). That observing circumcision was integral for obtaining righteousness was presumed among the Jews. The Pauline agenda here is to sever this connection.

The apostle does this with a chronological argument: Righteousness was credited to Abraham *before* he accepted the rite of circumcision. Circumcision, then, cannot be said to be grounds for his righteousness. Rather, circumcision was given as a sign, or distinguishing mark, of the fact that Abraham had already been made righteous. It was, to borrow Dunn's words, "a ratification that Abraham had been accepted by God."

Stuhlmacher observes that Paul's argument follows the principle of Jewish exegesis that priority in time indicates priority of importance. In the life of Abraham believing was the crucial event rather than circumcision. Consequently, Abraham should be considered "the father of all who believe" (v. 11), whether that be a believing Gentile or a believing Jew (v. 12). The inflammatory nature of such a remark is evident from W. D. Davies's comment (177) that "even proselytes were not allowed to call Abraham 'our father.'"

Paul goes on to argue that to justify Abraham in this manner was God's purpose all along ("in order that" in v. 11 indicates purpose), because this was also to be his means of justifying all others. The identifying mark of God's people is faith.

The broader context of Genesis 15:6, the promise God gave to Abraham that he would be the father of a great nation, is brought into view in Romans 4:13–17. The reference to Abraham as "heir of the world" in verse 13 reflects common Jewish belief (Sir. 44:21; Jub. 22:14; 32:19). Having argued in Romans 2–3 for the separation of law and righteousness, Paul now goes on to argue that the promise also functions independently of the law. On the basis of Genesis 15:6 Paul asserts that the promise came to Abraham through his faith, not through his obedience to the law (Rom. 4:13). For what Abraham believed when he was credited with righteousness was the promise.

This is still the manner in which the promise comes to his offspring—both Jew and Gentile (vv. 13, 16). Just as it came by faith according to divine design, so it continues to come by faith, in order that its terms may always be understood as stemming from God's grace rather than human achievement (v. 16). And because both Jew and Gentile are his seed, it may be said that the promise of Genesis 17:5 is fulfilled, which says "I have made you a father of many nations" (Rom. 4:17a).

For the Jew, the fulfillment of God's promise was tied to observance of the law, since the law provided the means whereby the Jew worked out the terms of the covenant and so became an heir of the promise. But Paul argues that "if those who live by law are heirs, faith has no value and the promise is worthless" (v. 14). God credited righteousness to the one who *believed* the promise. To remove faith and substitute works is to make faith irrelevant and to nullify the original promise.

In fact, the role of the law is not to convey the promise but to condemn. The subject of the function of the law, last referred to in 3:31, has reappeared. The statement that "where there is no law there is no transgression" (4:15b) hold significance for the discussion of the wrath o God in 1:18–3:20. It is the presence of God' law that explains his wrath.

The God in whom Abraham placed his fait was characterized in 4:5 as the "God who jus tifies the wicked." God is defined further i 4:17 as "the God who gives life to the dead and the one who "calls things that are not a though they were." Calvert (7) points out th both of these phrases in verse 17 were curren within Jewish literature. God was depicted a one who had "creative ability to call into bein that which existed from that which did no exist" (e.g., 2 Bar. 21:4; 48:8; 2 Macc. 7:28 The second phrase held particular relevanc for Paul's advocacy of the view that the Gen tiles were included among the righteou through the criterion of faith. The idea of giv ing life to the dead had already been used as metaphor for the conversion of Gentiles (Jo Asen. 27:10).

The two phrases used in verse 17b t describe God emphasize that his power func tions in the realm of human impossibility. Th fulfillment of the promise that God had mad to Abraham was humanly impossibl Advanced in age, the reproductive abilities o Abraham and Sarah were "as good as dead (see Gen. 18). But Abraham was "fully pe suaded that God had power to do what he ha promised" (Rom. 4:21), and "Abraham i hope believed" (v. 18), giving "glory to God (v. 20). Abraham was unlike the sinful on described in Romans 1:21, who refused t respond to God as God and give him glory.

It was precisely because of Abraham's tru at the point of human impossibility that Pa uses that situation to attack the understandin of righteousness current within Judaism. It wa not Abraham's faithfulness, or works, th gained him the credit of righteousness. Rathe it was his trust in God alone—his trust in God who would do what only he could do. was precisely because it was humanly impo sible for Abraham to have a son that his situa tion depicts the nature of faith. Biblical faith trust in the ability of God to do what we ca not do. In light of 3:21–4:25 it is our faith i his ability to do what only he can do—mak us righteous.

In verse 22 Paul quotes Genesis 15:6 agai by way of summary. Reciting the verse agai as the effect on the hearer of allowing him or er to hear it a final time with the significance at the previous argument has given it. What ould be heard is that the righteousness of God as credited to Abraham, not because of his orks, but because he trusted in the God who ad the power to do what he had promised. The gument of this chapter is summarized in one f Paul's later letters. "For it is by grace you ave been saved, through faith—and this not om yourselves, it is the gift of God—not by orks, so that no one can boast" (Eph. 2:8–9).

In the closing verses of Romans 4 (vv. 23–5) Paul applies the exposition of Genesis 15:6 his audience in the Roman house churches. s teaching is "also for us." Abraham's faith is e prototype for the faith of all believers in od. As Abraham believed in the God who ould bring life out of death (Rom. 4:17–1)—that is, give them a child when it was hysically impossible for pregnancy to ccur—so the Christian believes in the God ho brought Jesus to life from death (v. 24; cf. 0:9). What Paul has done is to draw out the arallel between two events that are "in salvaon-history terms ... literally epoch-creating vents" (Dunn). These two events celebrate od's life-giving power. In the case of Abraam the emphasis was on the fact that God graiously performed what no human could erform. Abraham could only believe. What braham discovered (v. 1) was grace; so must e. All we can do for salvation is believe that y God's grace he makes the unrighteous righous, giving life to the dead.

A final statement about Christ's work ounds out the discussion, bringing back into entral focus the subject with which Paul egan his discussion of God's righteousness in :21. The first phrase in 4:25 reflects the early hurch understanding about Christ's death. esus "was handed over" (NRSV). The use of e verb (*paradidomi*) in the passive voice here ay be taken two ways. (1) Most important, is to be understood as a divine passive: God as the one who handed Jesus over. The influnce of Isaiah 53:12 (in the LXX), "and was anded over because of their iniquities," is kely in the background. (2) The passive voice lso reflects the betrayal of Judas, who handed hrist over to the authorities.

The second phrase in verse 25 pairs justifiation and resurrection. Although the pairing is rather unusual—justification is typically spoken of in terms of the cross—it fits the context, in which the story of Abraham's justification is linked with his belief in God's ability to bring life out of death. This pairing also reminds us that the salvific work of Christ extended beyond the cross to the empty tomb. While it is true that this work is often explained from the perspective of the cross, the resurrection is always there in the background as the completion of that work.

2.1.3. The Sphere of Grace (5:1–21). Romans 5 marks a turning point in the letter. It functions as a summary of previous arguments about sin and God's wrath, and about faith and justification. It also serves to give advance notice that Paul is about to shift gears as he moves his attention to the life of the individual believer. Dunn has observed that the movement in the two sections of this chapter—from a focus on the individual believer (vv. 1–11) to the global perspective of salvation history (vv. 12–21)—sets the order for what follows in chapters 6–11: The individual believer is the subject of chapters 6–8; humanity, both Jew and Gentile, the focus of chapters 9–11.

There is a correspondence between the two sections in chapter 5. For instance, a similar phrase appears at the end of each section: "through our Lord Jesus Christ" (v. 11) and "through Jesus Christ our Lord" (v. 21). What is particularly striking is the repeated emphasis that Paul gives to the theme of grace throughout the chapter. Although grace has played an important role in the letter so far—especially in describing how God's righteousness comes to men and women (3:24; 4:1–4, 16)—the focus on it in this transitional chapter, designed to both summarize and preview, gives it particular prominence. Paul returns to the topic of grace at this strategic point in order to emphasize that it is nothing short of "amazing grace" that defines our existence as believers.

2.1.3.1. Life Within the Sphere of Grace (5:1–11). The benefits that belong to the one who has been justified, that is, to the one who has entered into the sphere of grace, are described in two parts (vv. 1–5 and 9–11), both of which open with "since we have been justified." Separating the two parts is an account of the objective ground on which these experiential benefits are based: the death of

Christ as the ultimate expression of God's grace (vv. 6–8).

2.1.3.1.1. Benefits of Grace (5:1–5). With the point made in chapter 4 that we are justified in the same manner as Abraham (4:23–25), Paul now draws out the benefits that all of us who have entered into a state of righteousness enjoy. The first is "peace with God" (cf. Isa. 32:17: "the fruit of righteousness will be peace"). Two points should be made here. (1) This peace is not an inner feeling of well-being, though that is certainly one of the by-products of peace with God. Peace with God refers to the restoration of relationship; we are no longer enemies of God, subject to his wrath (cf. Rom. 5:9–11). God took the initiative to deal with the division caused by human rebellion through the death of his Son (cf. Col. 1:21–22).

(2) In the Old Testament peace was often defined in national terms, that is, what God would bring about between Israel and her neighbors. Paul's teaching redirects the concept of peace vertically toward God. Nevertheless, the horizontal dimension of peace is not disregarded, on account of the fact that our peace with God establishes the basis for peace with others (Eph. 2:14).

The entry of the believer into a new state of existence, having been described with the concept of justification in verse 1, is reexpressed in verse 2 with the language of grace. This is because grace is the basis on which justification (3:24), as well as all other benefits, come to the believer. Through Christ, Paul declares, "we have gained access by faith into this grace in which we now stand." Unlike those without faith in Christ, we do not stand under wrath. We stand in the sphere of grace.

For the Jew the imagery of gaining access to God would suggest that the heavy curtain in the sanctuary, which concealed the presence of God, had been drawn back. For the Greek the imagery would have more readily suggested the royal court. One only gained access to the king through his favor or grace. The favored individual would be led into his presence with the aid of the royal chamberlain. Indeed, Christ was the one who led us into the presence of God, "introducing us as those who belong to him and so to the Father" (Harrison).

Standing within the sphere of grace means experiencing the continual activity of the power of God, and standing there gives us hope tha the future will be a completion of the work o God already in progress (v. 2). The hope of th Christian is this: that what humankind lost i the Garden of Eden—the glory of God—wil be restored in men and women as they ar brought back into conformity to the image o God, which was marred by sin (cf. 8:29).

The Greek verb "rejoice" (*kauchaomai* picks up on earlier appearances of variou forms of the same word, where it was trans lated as "brag" or "boasting" (2:17, 23; 3:27) Since boasting was discouraged earlier on, deliberate contrast is being made here betwee two types of boasting. On the one hand, it i illegitimate to boast in human achievement Thus, Paul criticized the Jewish boast in thei special standing before God. It is legitimate however, to boast in what God accomplishe for those who live within the sphere of grace

Life is transformed for the one standing i the sphere of grace. Even suffering is radicall affected. It is for this reason that Paul can mak suffering as well as hope a reason for rejoicin (vv. 2–3). Suffering, which is viewed in th New Testament as "the normal experience of Christian" (Bruce, 1985), is viewed positivel here because it produces results. Within th sphere of grace suffering is not meaningless because it initiates a process through whic character is formed. Suffering produces perse verance, and perseverance, character, and char acter, hope (vv. 3–4). The theological term fo this process in which the character of a perso is brought into conformity with the image o God is called *sanctification*, which Paul wi deal with extensively in the next chapter.

Paul knows from his own experience tha there is value in suffering. Through his thor in the flesh he experienced the grace of Go (2 Cor. 12:7–10). Grace is only fully experi enced when we come to a place of desperatio to a place where we find ourselves completel dependent on him. Pentecostal theology ha rightly stressed the power of God to delive from distress. What it has not always stresse however, is the power of God unleashed to bo ster a person's endurance. This continuou work of grace is just as miraculous, if not mo so, than the singular act of deliverance that lif a person out of difficulty. God always deli ers the believer, but sometimes he delivers u through the affliction rather than out of it.

Paul says "we know" (v. 3) from experience that enduring trials produces in us the quality of "perseverance"—a quality highly prized in Paul's day by Stoics and Jews alike. Perseverance is an active quality, not a passive resignation to fate. It involves standing one's ground during duress. It is apparent from Paul's many references to this quality that he saw it as indispensable for the Christian life (see 2:7; 5:3–4; 8:25; 15:4–5; also, e.g., 2 Cor. 6:4; Col. 1:11).

Perseverance produces "character" (*dokime*)—"the quality of being approved" (BAGD). The imagery evoked by the term is that of the testing of gold through fire. The idea here, then, is that the trials of life, if met with perseverance, purify one's character.

The end result of this process is the production of "hope" (v. 4). The reappearance of hope makes it apparent that the juxtaposition of hope and suffering in verses 2b–3a was suggestive of an integral relationship between them. Hope for the final restoration of the glory of God in our lives (v. 2) is fortified in the present because the believer sees what is hoped for already initiated in his or her life by the process that begins with suffering. As the Christian lives within the sphere of grace, suffering is transformed, character is built, and hope is increased that God will finish the work that he has started.

But there is something else in our experience that also builds our confidence that our future hope is sure: The love of God has been "poured out . . . into our hearts" (v. 5). The verb "to pour out" (*ekcheo*) portrays love descending on us like a downpour. The medium of such a deep experience of love is, as we might expect, the Holy Spirit, for the Spirit is the person within the Godhead who applies the work of the Father and Son to us.

Paul assumes that this downpour of love is a vivid enough experience for believers that it can serve as a source of assurance about the future work of God in their lives (cf. Gal. 3:2–5). What is this experience to which he refers? The background to the association of *ekcheo* with the Holy Spirit is found in Joel 2:28–30, where the promise is given concerning the Spirit's being poured out on all flesh (see Fee, 1994, 497, n.70; Dunn). Indeed, this Old Testament prophecy was quoted by Peter on the day of Pentecost as an interpretation of what had happened on that day (Acts 2). This same association appears in the description of the Spirit's coming on the house of Cornelius in Acts 10:45.

Consequently, it would appear to be the case that Paul is describing what Pentecostals call "Spirit baptism." The verb *ekcheo* appears in the perfect tense here. This Greek tense signifies a present state that has resulted from a past event. What Paul means, then, is that the impact of the initial outpouring of love continues to reverberate in the Christian's day-to-day life. Fee comments that the effect of Spirit baptism on the people he knew from his Pentecostal upbringing had the same effect that Paul writes about here in verses 2–5: It gave an assurance "of God's love and of their own future glory" [1994, 497, n.71).

2.1.3.1.2. Ultimate Expression of Grace (5:6–8). While verse 5 spoke of the love of God as a subjective experience, verses 6–8 make it clear that it is more than that. God demonstrated his love for us tangibly through the death of Christ (v. 8). Talk of death dominates this passage. While not apparent from the English text, each of the four phrases in this section ends with the word "die" (*apothnesko*). This is because the death of Christ represents the ultimate act of grace and the most compelling proof of God's love.

What Paul shows us here in a series of contrasts is the nature of "amazing grace." (1) There is a total contrast between what God gives and what is actually deserved. The cross represented the extension of his love to those who least deserved it. Christ's death occurred "at just the right time," that is, to borrow Bruce's words (1985), "at the time of greatest need"—when we were still weak and powerless because of our ungodliness (v. 6).

(2) There is a complete contrast between divine and human love. Human love tends to be conditional; divine love, unconditional. Although someone might die for another person who has some sort of merit (v. 7), Christ died for those with no spiritual merit—he died for sinners (v. 8; cf. 4:5). The phrase "Christ died for us" (5:8) expresses his sacrificial death on our behalf. This traditional understanding of Christ's death ("For what I received I passed on to you . . . that Christ died for our sins" [1 Cor. 15:3]) was expanded on in 3:21–26.

2.1.3.1.3. Goal of Grace (5:9–11). After establishing in verses 6–8 that our standing within the sphere of grace was made possible by Christ's death, Paul now resumes his discussion about the benefits that belong to those who live within that sphere. Verses 9–10 emphasize, through the use of a rabbinic form of argument known as *a minori ad maius* (from the lesser to the greater), that the believer's future salvation is assured. In other words, if God has already begun his work for believers in justification, then he certainly will complete that work with salvation in the future (v. 9). Paul makes a similar point in the next verse, but this time with more pointed language: If God reconciled his enemies—if he did that much—surely he will save those same ones in the future (v. 10).

While evangelicals tend to speak of their salvation as a turning point in their past, it is significant to note Paul's perspective. Typically in his writings, salvation is depicted as an ongoing work that comes to completion at the end of this age. It is certainly appropriate to speak of having been saved, but it is even more correct to say that we are being saved. Within the sphere of grace the power of God continues to act beyond the point of initial conversion.

Many North American Pentecostals hold to an Arminian understanding of salvation, which includes the conviction that a Christian can lose his or her faith, that is, can backslide. The point is raised not to dispute this doctrine, but to remind those of us within this theological camp that we must not underestimate the keeping power of grace. Those believers who presume that the onus is on them for maintaining their salvation once they are saved, or those believers who respond repeatedly to an invitation for salvation after a difficult week, have missed the point of grace. We are saved by grace and we are kept by grace.

Paul finishes this section in the same way he began—with the subject of reconciliation. As always in the New Testament, our reconciliation with God, or our peace with him, is depicted in verses 10–11 as a divine initiative. The work of reconciliation was done by God through Christ; our role is only to receive it. There is a theological term for this: grace. It is for this reason that our boast is not just in our future hope (v. 2), nor in our present sufferings (v. 3), but in God himself, who through Christ is solely responsible for the advantageous position of the one who stands in the sphere of grace.

2.1.3.2. Triumph of Grace Over Sin and Death (5:12–21). Paul shifts his focus away from the individual believer to humanity in general in this section in order to recount the history of sin and salvation. This history is divided into two eras: the era of Adam and the era of Christ. By comparing these two men and their effects on humankind, Paul sums up the content of the letter to this point concerning the desperate plight of all humanity and God's gracious provision of salvation. This section also works in continuity with 5:1–11 as it reviews, now on a cosmic scale, the truths of justification and grace. Indeed, the central idea of this portion of the letter is the triumph of grace over sin and death.

Paul begins a comparison between the work of Adam and that of Christ in verse 12 that remains uncompleted until verses 18–19. After laying out the first element, the sin of Adam, he immediately digresses to discuss the relationship of sin and death and its disastrous effect on the human race. Then, as he prepares to take up the comparison of Adam and Christ at the end of verse 14, he pauses to make the qualification in verses 15–17 that Christ's work supersedes that of Adam. After finally resuming the comparison begun in verse 12, he completes it with two parallel sentences (vv. 18–19), then summarizes the whole in verses 20–21.

The "just as" clause that begins verse 12 introduces Paul's overview of salvation history. He immediately becomes sidetracked, however, as he decides to expand on the content of the opening clause regarding the nature of sin and death.

The interrelationship between sin and death has a long history. The connection made in verse 12 between sin and death (cf. 1:32)—sin enters the world first, and then through sin death—recounts the Genesis story of the fall of humanity (Gen. 2–3). The story of human rebellion Paul chronicled in 1:18–32, which was characterized as the repetition of Adam's sin (see comments on 1:21–22), is being given its historical background in 5:12–19.

Sin in the Garden of Eden resulted in the breakdown of the intimate relationship that existed between God and the original human pair. Their expulsion from that garden, where they had walked with God, conveys a graphic illustration of the loss of intimacy. Having lost the perfect relationship they had known with God, the loss of their lives became their eventual fate. In other words, spiritual death resulted in physical death.

According to biblical thinking, life is more than the presence of vital signs, and death more than their absence. Life is living in relationship with God; death is the absence of that relationship. Death, then, may be experienced on this side of the grave (Ps. 6:5; 9:17; 30; 115:17). For example, in the Old Testament some people were described as being in the sphere of death while still alive because their relationship with God had broken down (Ps. 88; Isa. 38:10–19; Jonah 2:1–9; for more on the topic of the biblical view of life and death see Johnson, 25–34, 84–95). In line with biblical teaching, Paul is speaking of death in Romans 5 as a spiritual phenomenon with physical consequences.

Romans 5:12, along with verses 18–19, are the primary New Testament texts for the concept of "original sin," that is, that all people are born into sin because of the sin of Adam. Or, as it is often said, everyone inherits a depraved nature. This is not the place for an extended discussion on original sin or for a review of the debate that surrounds the topic. For this the longer commentaries and theological texts should be consulted.[3]

Without becoming bogged down in debate, there are some conclusions from this text that we may draw with confidence. (1) Paul establishes a connection between Adam's sin and ours (v. 19a: "through the disobedience of the one man the many were made sinners"). He does so, however, without specifying the nature of the connection. It is clear, at the very least, that he meant to teach that Adam's sin released the power of sin into the world. This power—however its transmission is understood—has proven impossible for anyone to resist.

(2) Paul also asserts that each of us is responsible for the state we find ourselves in—"death came to all men, because all sinned" (v. 12). None of us is released from personal responsibility because of Adam. None of us can say, "Adam made me do it." We are born into a world tainted by sin and death, yet we cannot say, "Society made us do it."

(3) This tension between the inherited effects of Adam's sin and individual responsibility reflects a similar tension within the Jewish writings of this same period. The idea of individual responsibility is found in Sirach 15:14–15; 2 Baruch 54:19; 1QS 4; that of inherited depravity in Sirach 25:24; 4 Ezra 7:116–126; 1QS 11. To cite one example, 2 Baruch 54:15, 19 (c. A.D. 100) reads: "For, although Adam sinned first and has brought death upon all who were not in his own time, yet each of them who has been born from him has prepared for himself the coming torment. . . . Adam is, therefore, not the cause, except only for himself, but each of us has become our own Adam."

(4) Paul is more concerned in 5:12–21 with what we might call original death than he is with original sin (see Dunn). Because of Adam all people are born into and imprisoned within the sphere of death. This passage shows that death was not the original plan for humankind. Adam and Eve were created to have a relationship with their Creator extending into eternity. But this fact of sinful life does not bring us to a point of despair. Rather, as this passage as a whole affirms, through Christ's death the sphere of grace has overcome the sphere of death.

In verses 13–14 Paul enters a clarification about the law's role in relation to sin (see 5:20). The advent of the Mosaic Law did not bring about the appearance of sin and guilt, for sin and guilt had been present since the time of Adam. Consequently, the phrase "sin is not taken into account when there is no law" (v. 13) does not mean that people living in the period before the law was given on Mount Sinai were not held responsible for their actions. Rather, the advent of the law meant that sin was now to be evaluated by a different scale. This interjection about the law shows that Paul never lost sight of the Jewish members of his audience in Rome and the dominant role that the law played in their understanding of sin and salvation.

The last phrase of verse 14 identifies Adam as "a pattern," or type (*typos*), of Christ. That is, there is a similarity between the two men. Both Adam and Christ inaugurated an era in salvation history, and their actions determined the nature of existence for those living in each era. This Paul will develop in a full comparison in verses 18–19, but before he explains the typological relationship he enters a qualification. He wants it understood that the deeds of the two are not to be seen on equal terms.

Therefore, two contrasts are given in verses 15–16. (1) "The gift [*charisma*] is not like the trespass" (v. 15a). The gift, which stands for the death of Christ (vv. 6–11), comes to men and women as a superabundance of grace. Note the piling up of "grace" words here in verse 15b: "grace" (*charis*—repeated twice) and "gift" (*dorea*). "Characteristic of his understanding of 'grace' is that it is abundant, more than enough" (Dunn). The action of Adam, by way of contrast, simply brought about what was deserved—death.

(2) The gift is not like the result of Adam's sin (v. 16a). This second contrast highlights the eternal consequences facing those who belong to Adam as opposed to those who belong to Christ (vv. 16b–17). Condemnation and judgment are set over against justification. The contrast of condemnation with justification in the context of the final judgment shows that justification is understood here as acquittal. As in verse 15b, the grace of God comes to the fore in this second contrast. While one sin received its just desserts, centuries of accumulated sin were graciously covered over by the act of Christ (v. 16b). One sin led to the reign of death; God's provision of grace permits those who receive it to reign in life—a reference to the age to come.

The reader will notice how Paul freely switches from "all" to "many" throughout this entire section. Paul was probably influenced in his use of the word "many" by Isaiah 53:11: "My righteous servant will justify many." The use of *many* as opposed to *all* is not significant, because Paul uses the terms interchangeably. The "many" who died by the trespass of one man (v. 15) is certainly a reference to all people. And the parallel nature of verses 18–19 suggests that the "all" of verse 18 is equivalent to the "many" of verse 19.

In verses 18–21 Paul finally completes the "just as ... so" comparison that he left unfinished in verse 12. In two largely parallel sentences Paul sets out the typological relationship of Adam and Christ—a relationship that he has been qualifying since verse 15. Paul here shows the manner in which Christ's act reversed the consequences of Adam's act.

In verse 18 the act that brought condemnation is countered by the righteous act that brought justification (see comments above on vv. 16–17). Justification brings life for all, which—in light of the preceding context (vv. 9–10, 17)—represents life in the new age. In verse 19 it is the act of disobedience (Adam's sin) that is countered with an act of obedience (Christ's death; see vv. 6–10; cf. Phil. 2:8—"and became obedient to death").

There are two spheres of existence—one associated with Adam and the other with Christ. Those who have not received God's grace exist solely within the sphere of sin and death. Although believers are still affected by the sphere of death that dominates this age, they are not dominated by sin and death. The primary influence on the Christian in the interim period before the Lord returns is the sphere of grace, in which the power of God is expressed in gracious acts.

The use of "all" and "many" to describe those who stand in solidarity with both Adam and Christ has led some to conclude that Paul is teaching universal salvation. For instance, verse 18 says that Adam's sin brought "condemnation for all men," but "justification ... brings life for all men" through Christ. Why should we not understand, so some argue, that salvation is just as universal as condemnation or death?

In answer to this, some scholars have argued that what is provided for all people is the *provision* for their justification, not justification itself (e.g., Lenski; Meyer). Moo makes a strong argument, however, that the language of justification in verse 18 suggests (as it usually does) not a potential state based on the work of the atonement, but a "status actually conferred on the individual." Moo argues that Paul's use of universal language indicates that he wanted to emphasize that the results of Christ's work extend just as surely to all his followers as does the work of Adam to those who follow him. Paul's point, to quote Moo, is "that Christ affects those who are his just as certainly as Adam does those who are his."

Two additional arguments may be made against interpreting these verses as teaching universal salvation. (1) Verse 17 stipulates that the condition for reigning in life comes only to those who receive the gift of righteousness. Whereas everyone finds himself or herself automatically under the reign of death as a matter of being born into the human race, the reception of God's act of grace does involve individual choice. (2) It is hard to make sense of the extended discussion about God's wrath on sinful humanity and about salvation from that wrath through an act of faith (1:18–4:25) if universal salvation is what Paul really had in mind all along.

In verse 20, for the second time in this chapter, the subject of the law is abruptly introduced (cf. v. 13). Here Paul anticipates further discussion in chapter 7 as he remarks that the law was given "so that the trespass might increase" (cf. Gal. 3:19). This would have been a shocking statement for the Jew, for whom God's law was understood as his gift to them so that they might know God's will and so avoid sin (2:17–24).

Instead of expanding on the role of the law at this point, however, Paul returns to the central theme of grace overcoming sin through Jesus Christ our Lord (v. 21). What Paul wants to affirm is that the law was not the antidote for sin. Rather, it was grace: As sin increased, so did grace. To borrow the words of Harrison: "The apostle waxes almost ecstatic as he revels in the superlative excellence of the divine overruling that makes sin serve a gracious purpose."

2.2. God's Righteousness Breaks the Power of Sin (6:1–8:39)

Paul's discussion now moves to the topic of how God's righteousness, his saving activity, effects a change in the believer's lifestyle. God acts not only to bring a person into right relationship with himself, but also to enable that person to act in accordance with that relationship. This means that God deals with the power of sin through Christ and the Holy Spirit.

We can readily appreciate that Paul's "law-free" gospel message could have been misunderstood by its hearers. For there is an inherent danger in the preaching of the gospel of grace—a danger that is as real for the twentieth-century Christian as it was for the first-century believer. It is that those who hear the gospel message with its emphasis on grace might interpret it as minimizing the gravity of sin and its consequences. If God freely forgives, if his grace meets us at the point of our failure, then why strive to avoid sin?

In chapters 6–8 we find Paul's refutation of such a misunderstanding about the relationship between sin and grace (cf. Gal. 5). Grace not only deals with the penalty of sin (ch. 5), but, as we will see in this section, with its power. It is by grace that the penalty of sin is canceled through justification by faith. And it is by that same grace that the power of sin is dealt with through what we call sanctification, the work of God in us to produce increasing conformity to the image of Christ (cf. 8:29).

Specifically, Paul will show in chapter 6 how the work of Christ made righteous living possible and in chapter 8 how the Holy Spirit makes it a reality in the experience of the believer. Through the work of the Holy Spirit the process of sanctification occurs. In chapter 7 he will explain the relationship of the law and sin—a topic raised earlier but not fully developed.

The processes of justification (right standing before God) and sanctification (right living before God), while conceptually distinct, must not be distinguished too sharply. The temptation to divide them temporally, as if justification is a completed work and sanctification a perpetual one, misses Paul's emphasis on salvation as a continuous act of God's grace. God's salvific work or righteousness encompasses both what we call justification and sanctification. That justification is more than a fait accompli is seen in 6:16, where justification, or the attainment of righteousness, is a future event for all believers. Final justification occurs when Christ returns.

There is also a temptation to see justification as a divine initiative and sanctification as a human endeavor. What Paul will make clear in chapter 6 is that we become like Christ only as we are joined to him, or as we are in Christ. In other words, the grace of God continues to be available through Christ, and that grace effects the change in us. In chapter 8 the apostle will specify that it is the Spirit who transmits this transforming grace. Having said all this, the imperatives in chapter 6 to right thinking and right acting stress our responsibility to respond to grace and cooperate with the work of the Holy Spirit.

2.2.1. Power Over Sin (6:1–7:6). Three similar questions about the nature of sin and grace structure this chapter. (1) Should we engage in sin so that the amount of glory God might receive will be increased as he responds

GREAT DOCTRINES IN PAUL

The apostle Paul has often been called the first great Christian theologian. His writings have shaped Christian doctrine from the time that he wrote his letters. The following chart lists many of the great doctrines of the church and the main passages in Paul that explore these doctrines. There are, of course, many other passages in Paul, not listed here, that touch on these doctrines, and there are many other passages of the Bible, not written by Paul, that also explore these teachings. The ones listed here are the main ones of Paul.

The Inspiration of Scripture	Gal 1:11–12; 2Ti 3:14–17
Divine Election	Ro 8:29–30; 9:6–33; Eph 1:3–14
God's Plan for Israel	Ro 11:1–32
The Universality of Human Sinfulness	Ro 1:18–3:20; 3:23; Tit 3:3
Victory Over Sin and Satan	Ro 6:11–7:6; 8:31–39; Eph 6:10–18
The Twofold Nature of Jesus Christ	Ro 1:3–4; Php 2:5–11
The Sacrificial Atonement of Christ	Ro 3:25–26; 5:6–10; Gal 3:10–14
Reconciliation Between Human Beings and God	Ro 5:10–11; 2Co 5:16–21; Col 1:19–23
Christ as the Second Adam	Ro 5:12–21; 1Co 15:20–22, 42–49
The Supreme Lordship of Jesus Christ	Ro 10:9–13; Eph 1:15–23; Php 2:9–11; Col 1:15–20; 2:6–15
The Old and New Covenant	2Co 3:1–18; Gal 3:15–4:7; 4:21–31
Justification by God's Grace through Faith	Ro 1:16–17; 3:21–4:25; Gal 2:16–3:14; Eph 2:1–10; Php 3:7–11; 1Ti 1:12–16; Tit 3:4–8
Life Through the Holy Spirit	Ro 8:1–17, 26–27; Gal 5:16–26
The Christian's Life of Love	Ro 12:9–21; 13:8–10; 1Co 13; Gal 5:13–15; Col 3:12–14
The Gifts of the Holy Spirit	Ro 12:3–8; 1Co 12:1–11, 27–31; 14:1–40; Eph 4:7–12
Marriage in Christ	1Co 7:1–40; Eph 5:22–33; Col 3:18–19
Christian Freedom	Ro 14:1–15:13; 1Co 8:1–13; 10:23–33; Gal 5:1–12; Col 3:16–23
Unity in the Church	1Co 1:10–17; Eph 2:11–21; 4:1–16
Baptism	Ro 6:1–10; 1Co 12:12–13; Col 2:11–12
Lord's Supper	1Co 10:14–22; 11:17–34
Death for Believers	2Co 5:1–8; Php 1:19–26
The Resurrection	1Co 15; Php 3:20–21
The End of History	1Co 15:23–29; 2Co 5:10; 1Th 5:1–11; 2Th 1:5–2:12; 2Ti 3:1–9
The Second Coming of Jesus Christ	1Co 15:51–57; Php 3:20–21; 1Th 4:13–18; Tit 2:11–14

to sin by dispensing more grace (v. 1)? In response, Paul insists that continuing in sin is impossible for Christians because we have died with Christ to sin. We are no longer under its power. In fact, we walk in newness of life because of the resurrection of Christ. Yet Paul will caution in verses 11–14 that what Christ's work achieved must be appropriated by each individual. (2) In the absence of the law, has sin become permissible (v. 15)? Should one sin because of grace? No, the apostle answers, for believers have moved from slavery to sin to slavery to righteousness. The lordship of Christ demands that we serve him rather than sin. (3) What is the role of the law in the believer's life (7:1–6)?

2.2.1.1. Dying to Live (6:1–14). The appearance of a question at the beginning of this section returns us to the dialogue format used earlier (3:1–9, 27–31; 4:1–12). And the subject matter of the question returns us to the objection raised by his dialogue partner in 3:7–8. Thus, Paul is once more addressing the charge made against him that his proclamation of the gospel of grace was promoting sin. This time, however, the matter is dealt with more definitively.

In response to the objection of verse 1 that sin may as well be encouraged if it brings about more grace—an objection arising out of the statement in 5:20 that as sin increased, grace increased all the more—Paul comes to the heart of the matter immediately: The believer cannot remain in sin because he or she has died to sin (v. 2).

"How can we live in it any longer?" (v. 2b) is not a moral plea but a statement of fact. Paul is not asking: "How can we?" Rather, his question implies, "We can't!" Yet Paul is not arguing that the Christian is incapable of committing sin (see vv. 11–14), because the "we can't" derives from his understanding of sin as a reigning power (5:21). As he will go on to explain, the death of the believer to sin means that the domination of sin has been broken. In short, Paul's initial response to the charge that his gospel promotes sin is that grace, instead of encouraging sin, actually provides the means to escape its fatal grip.

What follows (vv. 3–14) is commentary on the believer's death to sin. Paul uses water baptism, practiced by believers since the inception of the church (Matt. 28:19; Acts 2:37–41), to explain how the Christian has died to sin (vv. 3–4). Paul's line of argument proceeds from the presupposition that the rite of baptism is closely tied to the act of placing one's trust in Christ.

The reader will find in commentaries a broad array of interpretations concerning the function and significance of water baptism based on this passage. Indeed, it is an important text for formulating a theological understanding of the rite. Unfortunately for us, Paul does not engage in a full discussion of it because (1) he presumes that the Romans are already familiar with its significance, and (2) he is concerned to draw out only those aspects that support his argument that the believer has died to sin. Part of the reason for the diversity of interpretation of this text is the partial treatment of water baptism that Paul supplies here.

What can we glean here about the significance of water baptism? A common interpretation is that being lowered into and then raised out of the water symbolizes the participant's dying and rising with Christ. That is, it is a metaphor for conversion, which illustrates the end of the old life and the beginning of the new. This understanding goes back at least as far as Tertullian (see Moo), but it is not certain that this was the first-century conception. A careful reading of Romans 6 reveals that Paul links baptism with being buried with Christ, but he does not say that the convert has been raised with Christ in baptism—that remains a future event (see comments on vv. 5–10). Thus, at the very least, this passage teaches that baptism symbolizes the believer's participation in Christ's death. Still, the fuller symbolism of dying and rising with Christ may be in the background here, for Paul may have chosen only that part of the tradition that refers to Christ's death because his argument concerns death to sin.

The essence of Christian baptism is expressed in the phrase "baptized into Christ Jesus" (v. 3). To be baptized "into" (*eis*) Christ signifies union with him or the establishment of relationship. Beasley-Murray (61) argues that this is the meaning behind being baptized into the name of Jesus: "In baptism ... the Lord appropriates the baptized for his own and the baptized owns Jesus as Lord and submits to his lordship."

Our conception of how a believer participates in the life of Christ must be understood in relational terms. To quote Beasley-Murray again (62), "Because baptism signifies union with Christ, Paul saw it as extending to union with Christ in his redemptive actions." Since we have been brought into relationship with him, we share in the benefits of his life: We have been crucified with him (v. 6), we died and were buried with him (vv. 4, 5, 8), and we will be raised with him (vv. 5, 8). This is not to say that we have shared in his substitutionary work or that in some mystical sense we were actually there with Christ when he was crucified. Our Lord suffered and died alone. But it does have something to say about the way that Paul views the connection between the Lord and his followers.

An analogy may be drawn from human relationships. When a person enters into a relationship, he or she becomes involved in another's life. The more intimate the relationship, the greater the degree of involvement. Similarly, when one enters into a relationship with Christ, he or she begins to share his life—albeit in a different manner than is the case in even the most intimate human relationships. For as with any this-worldly analogy for spiritual realities, this one also falls short of the glory it intends to convey. (1) When the believer is joined to Christ, he or she is joined to the Lord himself. This requires complete submission, not mutual submission or friendship (and so the call for obedience starts in v. 11). (2) The one drawn into the world of his or her Lord shares fully in the consequences of the deeds of Christ to a degree unparalleled in human relationships. He is more than one we relate to; he is also our representative.

It is certainly appropriate to say, as many modern commentators do, that we participate in the benefits of Christ's life because he is our representative. As we were in Adam and thus shared the consequences of his sin, so by being in Christ we share the results of his work. Our solidarity with him as our representative transfers his acts to us. But we must not miss the more personal relational sense behind this idea. It is because we know him that we share his life.

To summarize, Paul begins chapter 6 by arguing that believers cannot remain under sin's power because they have died to sin. He refers to his readers' experience with water baptism to establish this point. As he did in 5:5 (in which he used their experience with Spirit baptism to assure them about their future hope), so here he has chosen a vivid experience to convince them of a spiritual reality. The water baptism of believers signifies that their union with Christ is also a union with him in his death.

When does death with Christ occur in the life of the convert? Since Paul uses baptism to convey this idea, and since baptism is associated with the beginning of a Christian's life, presumably this occurs at the moment of conversion. It is "through [*dia*] baptism" (v. 4) that one is buried. Paul says "through baptism" not because the rite itself effects death with Christ. Rather, the rite represents in public fashion one's decision to begin life with Christ.

Within those traditions that view baptism as a symbol of the salvation experience (e.g., Baptists, Pentecostals), rather than sacramentally as a means of saving grace (e.g., Roman Catholics, Lutherans), there is a danger that the importance and imperative of the rite will be downplayed. What is at stake is a loss of water baptism's connection with and significance for the beginning of the Christian life.

The reason we have been buried with Christ is given at the end of verse 4: so that "we too may live a new life" (lit., "walk in newness of life"). This is not the wording we might expect. To complement the statement that we have died with Christ, we expect Paul to say, after a reference to Christ's resurrection, that we have also been raised with him. But he says that because of Christ's resurrection we now walk in newness of life. Although we are yet to be resurrected with him, we presently share in resurrection life. We are living in the conditions of the age to come to the extent that they may be enjoyed while still existing within the constraints of the present age.

This is Paul's "already/not yet" way of understanding Christian existence in this transitional period between our past death with him and our future resurrection. (The role of the Holy Spirit in mediating the life of the risen Christ to believers will be explained in ch. 8 [see also 7:6].) The age of Christ has broken into the age of Adam, and the believer is transferred into this new age through the death of Christ. Our orientation is forever altered because grace has transformed our past, present, and future.

Nevertheless, the conditions of the new age will not be experienced fully until after the future resurrection of believers, when the old age will have completely passed away. In the meantime we are still influenced by the worldly conditions set in motion by what Adam did. We are still subject to physical death, and we are still tempted by sin. Paul's perspective on the overlapping of the two ages (5:12–21) reflects the worldview of apocalyptic eschatology (see "Paul's Apocalyptic Eschatology" in the Introduction).

In verse 5 the baptismal imagery is left behind, having served its purpose as an illustration of the believer's death to sin. To the fore comes the motif of dying and rising with Christ. Twice in verses 5–10 Paul states that just as surely as identification with Christ means dying with him, so it also means being raised with him (vv. 5, 8). His focus, however, remains with the former aspect, as he continues to discuss the nature of the Christian's death to sin.

Note how the apostle depicts the eschatological situation of the believer with the use of different tenses. The verb translated "have been" in verse 5a is in the perfect tense (*gegonamen*), signifying that our union with him in his death is a past event with continuing effect. That effect is our freedom from the power of sin. The union of the believer with Christ's resurrection, however, is in the future ("we will ... be"). Some have argued (eg., Fitzmyer) that this is a logical future (logical in the sense that it follows our dying with Christ and thus really denotes our present state). This is not the best interpretation, however. Nor is the future to be taken as a moral imperative (the type of future tense we see in most of the Ten Commandments)—that is, that we must be conformed to Christ's resurrection in our present behavior (Cranfield). Rather, this is a real future, expressing the truth of the final resurrection (Tannehill; Dunn; Käsemann). That is why Paul does not place our resurrection with Christ in the past (cf. Eph. 4:22–24 and Col. 3:9–11, where he does speak of a spiritual resurrection).

Tannehill (12) explains the present and future aspects of rising with Christ in this way:

> The believer participates in the new life in the present, but Paul is careful to make clear that it does not become the believer's possession. It is realized through a continual surrender of one's present activity to God, a walking in newness of life, and at the same time it remains God's gift for the future.

The imperatives of verses 11–14 show that the benefits of both Christ's death and resurrection must be appropriated in the present.

How the believer has died to sin is explained in verses 6–7. The death that the believer experiences in union with Christ means that the individual is transferred out of the age of Adam and into the age of Christ. Or, as Paul expresses it here, the "old self" (lit., "our old man") is crucified (cf. Gal. 2:20). The old self is what one was in Adam (Barrett; Moo), and that person has been put to death. Consequently, we should not understand, as some do, that a Christian has two natures that constantly wage an internal battle for supremacy. The language of crucifixion is intended to leave no doubt that what the person was in his or her association with Adam has ceased to be. Although not named here, the new self—what one is in Christ—has replaced the old one (see Col. 3:9–10). The believer lives, then, in the new realm associated with Christ.

The old self was crucified so that the "body of sin might be rendered powerless" (cf. NIV note on v. 6). The expression "body of sin" does not teach that the physical body itself is sinful. The interpretation of the Greek word *soma* ("body") has been the subject of some debate in this century. Since the time of R. Bultmann, it has been common to view this word as referring to the whole person. By contrast, a deemphasis on the physical body in the contemporary understanding of *soma* led Gundry to a monograph-long defense of this word as denoting only the human body.

The mediating position of Harris is helpful. While he recognizes the validity of Gundry's criticism of the equation of *soma* with the whole person, Harris (120) argues that the word may still serve to signify a person as a whole, but with the emphasis on the person's corporeal or outward aspects. In other words, *soma* denotes the person in interaction with this world. The "body of sin," then, is the person who stands in solidarity with Adam. But in Christ that person who was enslaved to sin is no more.

Verse 7 is commonly thought to be a general maxim, which may explain why a phrase that is unusual for Paul appears here: (lit.) "to be justified from sin." The NIV translation of this phrase, "has been freed from sin" (cf. also BAGD, Käsemann), fits the context well, because it reinforces the argument that sin's power has been broken. The justification terminology, however, may signify that Paul has in mind freedom from the penalty (the topic of ch. 5) rather than from the power of sin. Thus Dunn suggests "declared free from sin." That is, the Christian is no longer in bondage to a crushing debt from the past. The introduction of the notion of freedom from guilt into a discussion about the destruction of sin's power is not out of place. Both aspects of sin's domination of humankind have been dealt with in Christ.

The repetition of the same point in verse 8 that Paul made earlier in verse 5—the believer has died with Christ and will live with him–occurs for emphasis. Paul wants to leave no doubt that the gospel of grace provides the solution to the problem of sin—both its penalty and its power. The penalty and power of sin were dealt with historically in the death and resurrection of Christ. He has broken out of the realm of sin and death; sin has no hold on him, death no mastery over him (v. 9). He lives to God now; he cannot die again (v. 10). What the reader should hear, then, is that the same is true for him or her. The Christian has died to sin in being joined to Christ. And once you are dead, you are dead. The problem, of course, is living in accordance with this death. To this dilemma Paul now turns.

In verses 11–14 the discussion takes a different direction. It moves from a declaration of *what is true* about the believer who is in Christ (conveyed in vv. 2–10 by verbs in the indicative) to *what should be true* in terms of everyday living (the verbs are now in the imperative). Paul switches to the second person as he exhorts the Roman believers to act in accordance with who they are in Christ. In other words, to quote the widely repeated phrase, "Become what you are." Dunn suggests a modification, "Become what you are becoming," because this phraseology captures the sense that we cooperate with what the Holy Spirit is bringing about in us. Sanctification, then, is no more the result of human effort than is salvation. We are to respond in obedience to his grace, "which precedes and makes possible all moral effort" (Dunn).

That believers need to appropriate what is already the case is made necessary because of the time in which we live. We live in the overlap of the two ages of Adam and Christ, in that period between the death and resurrection of Christ and the resurrection of all humankind. Within this period our lives are shaped by new realities: We already share in Christ's death and in the newness of life based on his resurrection, but we continue to be affected by old realities as well: the presence of sin and the inevitability of death. This is why believers are responsible to appropriate the benefits of being in Christ. We must act in accordance with our death to sin. And we experience the benefits of his resurrection life in the present as we respond in obedience.

Romans 7 is a popular chapter since it seems to describe the common experience of believers with an ongoing struggle with sin. Paul's talk about the inevitability of performing those actions that are not desired rather than what is desired (7:14–25) certainly does reflect the experience of many Christians. But it is here in chapter 6 that the moral struggle that continues to be fought by those who have died to sin is explained. We are still in the world, and we are still tempted by the power that we previously served.

The first word in verse 11 (*houtos*, "so then"; NIV, "in the same way") identifies what follows as practical conclusions from what Paul has been declaring about the believer's relationship to Christ (Cranfield). Those who have died with Christ must count themselves dead to sin and alive to God. The word "count" (or "reckon") is a present imperative, which means that the apostle is calling for a continual decision to view oneself in this manner. Paul used the same word in his discussion of the righteousness of Abraham in chapter 4 (where it is translated "credited"). Barrett notes the similarity between the two texts: As Abraham was *credited* with righteousness when he was not so visibly, so believers should *reckon* that they are dead to sin even though their death with Christ did not occur in the visible realm.

Verse 11 conveys the absolute necessity that the believer's self-perception be based on spiritual realities. Right action flows from right thinking (Phil. 4:8–9). This is not mere mental gymnastics or an exercise in positive thinking or a determination to look on the bright side of things; no, this is thinking on the right side of truth. How we consider ourselves should be based on the fact of our participation in the historical deeds of Christ. It is for this reason that the end of verse 11 specifies that this type of reckoning is appropriate for those who are "in Christ." It is in Christ that power over sin becomes a true possibility rather than an impossible dream.

What it means to consider oneself dead to sin is explained in verses 12–13 with two prohibitions and two positive commands. The fact that the apostle commands certain behavior while warning against other courses of action reveals his presupposition that those who are in Christ have the choice to obey or disobey. The old person had no such freedom, being unable to break free from the dominance of sin. But to have died with Christ makes living in newness of life possible.

That it remains possible for a believer to allow sin to continue its dominance is readily apparent from the text, as it is from our own experience. To offer the parts or members of the body to sin is not about the submission of one's physical appendages, but the offering of one's natural capacities (Cranfield). Those who are in Christ are not to offer their capacities "as instruments [*hopla*, weapons] of wickedness," but "as instruments of righteousness." The military sense of *hopla* may be in view here. Not only is Paul prone to use this word to mean "weapons" (Rom. 13:12; 2 Cor. 6:7; 10:4), but the context, with its overriding theme of power and dominance, suggests that he has chosen the word for this purpose. The idea, then, is that we are no longer to offer our abilities to defend or advance the interests of the kingdom of wickedness, but to offer them in the service of God and his righteousness.

Indeed, Paul calls on individuals to present themselves to God "as if" (*hosei*; NIV, "as those who have been") they have been brought from death into life (v. 13). Again we see his hesitation to depict believers as fully sharing in the resurrection experience of Christ. We do walk in newness of life because of his resurrection (v. 4), but complete liberation from sin's temptation and death's claim on our mortal bodies will only be ours after the resurrection. In the interim period, however, we are to live in anticipation of our future resurrected state and act accordingly.

The reason we should do so is contained in verse 14: "For sin shall not be your master, because you are not under law, but under grace." Once more Paul refers back to the change of eras depicted in the latter half of chapter 5. The age of grace has replaced the age of the law (cf. John 1:17). Paul certainly does not mean to contrast grace and law in absolute terms, as if before Christ there was only law, and since then, only grace. After all, Paul has argued in chapter 4 that Abraham found grace. Rather, law is referred to because it functioned within the old era to increase sin (5:20).

To be in Christ means that we have crossed over into the age of grace, where grace reigns rather than sin. It is because we are in the age of grace that Paul can declare with such assurance that sin will no longer master us. This declaration provides the definitive answer for the question raised at the beginning of the chapter. It is unthinkable to argue that sin may as well continue if it promotes grace. After all, under the law sin is increased; under grace its power is annulled.

2.2.1.2. Dying to Serve (6:15–23). Similar to the opening question of chapter 6, the one asked in verse 15 also concerns the relationship between sin and grace. This time, however, the question makes specific reference to the law—a topic that was reintroduced into the discussion in the previous verse. If grace is now the standard rather than the law, then what prohibits sin? Such "law-lessness" would seem to invite sinful behavior.

The two dominant motifs of verses 15–23 are slavery and freedom. Paul will argue repeatedly that release from slavery to sin does not mean freedom to live as one might choose. Instead, freedom from sin entails slavery to God. Although "sin shall not be your master" (v. 14), *God will be*. Rather than encouraging sin, grace actually binds one in holy service to God.

The metaphor of slavery to represent Christian existence in the two ages would have been particularly poignant in the context of the Greco-Roman world. A. Rupprecht (881) estimates that in the first and second centuries A.D. as high as "85–90 percent of the inhabitants of Rome and peninsula Italy were slaves or of slave origin." It stands to reason, then, that the majority of Paul's audience in Rome had a similar background. In fact, some of the names that appear in the list of greetings in chapter 16 were typical slave names (e.g., Andronicus and Urbanus; see Ruprecht, 882). Even though the lot of many slaves within Rome would have been far better than the conditions we associate with slavery in the United States before the Civil War, Paul's contention that freedom means another type of slavery would have been jarring indeed.

Paul builds his case in verse 16 that the believer is either a slave to sin or to God by repeating a well-known fact. "Don't you know that" is a phrase Paul often uses to raise a point familiar to his audience. He seems to be referring to the practice whereby an individual under financial duress would offer himself as a slave to avoid ruin. As this individual became a slave to the one he gave himself to, so it is with those who offer themselves to either sin or obedience. To put it another way, what one does has consequences. To continue in sin is to return to bondage all over again.

The result of slavery to sin is death—both now and eternally; the result of slavery to obedience is righteousness. We expect that Paul would speak of slavery to God or Christ rather than to obedience, but as Barrett points out, the appearance of obedience here shows the stress that he wants to put on this aspect of the Christian life. Also curious is the fact that righteousness is named as the end product of obedience. After his forceful argument about salvation by faith in the preceding chapters, he obviously felt there was no danger of being misinterpreted as advocating some type of righteousness that is gained by works. His point is that within the sphere defined by grace and faith, there is also the critical element of human response to all that God has done and continues to do for us in Christ. That is why he proclaims that obedience leads to righteousness, that is, final justification (Cranfield; cf. 2:13; Gal. 5:5).

In verse 17, for the second time in this chapter, Paul refers to the conversion experience of the Romans in order to set up an exhortation (which comes in v. 19). This time, however, he does not use baptismal imagery as a symbol of their initiation into the Christian faith (vv. 3–4). The manner in which he proceeds here deserves particular attention.

(1) Paul returns in verse 17, as he will again in verse 18, to the central point of verses 1–14: the believer's death to sin. This constant repetition was meant to drive home to his hearers a point that he knew was pivotal to their self-understanding—as it is to ours. We are constantly bombarded by temptations—so much so that at times it seems overwhelming, and our resistance too often succumbs to sin's lure. But the fundamental temptation to be avoided is the one that encourages the Christian to regard the fight against sin as hopeless. Those who are in Christ must not give in to despair, since the rule of sin is history. In the words of the hymn "This Is My Father's World": "That though the wrong seems oft so strong, God is the Ruler yet." His rule is established in those who are in Christ, in those who have died to sin with him. We must constantly hear Paul's reminder: We are dead to sin.

(2) Note the prominence of the theme of obedience in the description of what transpired at the moment of conversion. Paul makes no distinction between accepting Christ in faith as Savior and submitting to him as Lord. To believe in Christ is to respond to who he is: the Lord himself. A relationship with Christ, then, demands obedience.

(3) Obedience is defined as obedience to "the form [or pattern, *typos*] of teaching to which you were entrusted" (v. 17b). If Paul is simply referring to Christian teaching, then what is the significance of the word *typos*? Many commentators understand "pattern of teaching" to refer to an early Christian body of truth to which converts committed themselves (e.g., Fitzmyer, a "succinct baptismal summary of faith"). Dunn wonders, however, whether there was an established pattern of teaching this early in the history of the church that would have been known to Paul and the Roman community of faith. The phrase may not be referring to a specific body of teaching as much as setting up a contrast with another pattern of teaching, that of Judaism. The point being made, then, is that the gospel message, despite what its Jewish critics are saying, is not without its own authoritative teaching.

(4) That the believer is said to be entrusted to this authoritative form of teaching is a turn of phrase that was meant to catch the reader's attention. Although the word *paradidomi* ("hand over, entrust") may be used in the sense of handing down tradition (e.g., 1 Cor. 11:2; 15:3), within Romans it has been conveying the idea of transfer from one authority to another (e.g., from God's protection over to sin's domain [1:24, 26, 28]; Christ was handed over to the authorities to be put to death [4:25]). Within this context where slavery is the central motif, this type of language is apropos. Whereas unbelievers are handed over to

the authority of sin, believers have been handed over to the authority of the teaching of the gospel.

Verse 18 clarifies what Paul has been driving at since the question in verse 15. Being set free from slavery to sin means going into slavery to righteousness. Replacing the old power is a new authoritative power—righteousness, which is God's power at work in the life of believers.

Paul was certainly aware of the impact that his juxtaposition of freedom and slavery would have had on his audience. This pairing is no less shocking for the modern reader. Freedom is prized as a supreme value in North American society. On a societal level it has become the rallying cry for countless causes. On a personal level it has become the goal of many individuals who find themselves in situations that they desire release from. Unfortunately, freedom is often valued above responsibility, with the result that people are quitting their jobs, fleeing their families, and even breaking their marriages in its pursuit.

According to this section of the letter, however, a life of freedom from all constraints is illusory. As Nygren wrote: "It is quite characteristic of bondage to sin, that he who lives in it thinks himself free and his own master." Or, to quote Bob Dylan's song, "It may be the devil, or it may be the Lord, but you gotta serve somebody." The privilege of the Christian, who has been set free from sin, is having the freedom to give service to the Lord.

The boldness of the statement in verse 18 concerning freedom from sin and slavery to righteousness elicits an immediate disclaimer in verse 19a. The apostle was obviously somewhat uncomfortable with characterizing the Christian life as slavery. Nevertheless, he carries the imagery on through to the end of the chapter. His rationale for doing so is somewhat cryptic: "because you are weak in your natural selves [lit., flesh, *sarx*]." Is this intellectual weakness—a problem with self-deception (Cranfield)? Or is this a problem of the will—the tendency of people to demand autonomy from such constraints (Käsemann)? Either way, Paul judges such imagery necessary to combat the human tendency to avoid submission.

The exhortation toward which the preceding verses have been building comes in verse 19b. On the basis of the believer's release from sin and relocation under the authority of righteousness (v. 18), Paul exhorts his hearers with a pointed comparison. As you once served impurity, now in the same way (or as Moo remarks, with the same zeal) serve righteousness. Life outside of Christ is characterized by a cycle of increasing wickedness. This is the tragic result of the rejection of God's revelation (1:18–32). But that cycle has been broken by grace. Within the sphere of grace, life consists of a progression into increasing holiness.

Verses 20–23 function to support the urgency and the eternal importance of this exhortation. Although the unbeliever does know a certain freedom, it is only a freedom from God's righteousness (v. 20), which allows a person to accrue a "benefit" (lit., "fruit") of shame. The believer, however, reaps the fruit that leads to holiness, and holiness leads to eternal life.

The final verse (v. 23) aptly summarizes the argument of the chapter, while picking up on the emphasis in chapter 5 on God's gracious gift. The eternal consequences of the two modes of living are again contrasted: life and death. Also contrasted are the ideas of merit and grace: "wages"—which had come to be used in Paul's day for any type of wage paid with money—is set opposite "the gift." In the realm of sin, we get what we have earned. But in the realm of grace, we receive what we have not earned—in fact, cannot earn. Any lingering thought the reader might have from verse 16 that obedience might lead to eternal life is here dispelled. The gift comes to us "in Christ Jesus our Lord"—a phrase similar to the one Paul used to frame his previous discussion about the gift of Jesus Christ (5:11, 21).

2.2.1.3. Dying to the Law (7:1–6). Chapter 7 continues the discussion begun in 6:1 about how sin is counteracted in the age of grace. The role of the law in this process is now clarified. Paul expands on earlier statements about the law (3:19–20, 27–28; 4:13–15; 5:13–14, 20) and, in particular, picks up on the unexplained phrase in 6:14 that the one under grace is not under the law. To depict the transition from being under the law to being under grace, Paul again uses the motif of dying and rising with Christ, which was prominent in ch. 6.

The first structural break in chapter 7 comes early. Paul has made his central point of the chapter by verse 6, namely, that death with

Christ means death to the law. The argument of verses 7–25 functions only to clarify what he has been saying about the law. It is, as Sanders argues, more than that the law "crops up . . . on the bad side of the dividing line between those under sin and those under Christ" (72). Rather, unlike Galatians 3–4, the role of the law in the old age is intensified in Romans 6–7, where Paul argues it serves as an agent of sin (ibid., 70–73). But this does not mean that Paul's intention is to demean the law. Instead, chapter 7 is a defense of the law.

From the outset of this discussion it seems clear that Paul is contending for his view of the law against the criticisms that had arisen against it in Jewish and Jewish-Christian circles. If Paul is going to find a base for his missionary operation to Spain in Rome, he knows he must bring the Roman believers to understand and accept his view on the law.

We see Paul's concern that his view of the law be accepted by (1) his use of "brothers" (vv. 1, 4), a term of endearment that last appeared in 1:13, and (2) his reference to them as those "who know the law" (v. 1). The latter reference does not imply that Paul's audience is primarily Jewish (Barrett; Cranfield). Many of the early Gentile converts to Christianity were familiar with the law because they had been "God-fearers" when they heard about Christ—that is, they had been regular worshipers in the synagogue. Paul appeals to his audience on the basis of their knowledge of the law. In other words, he suggests that their familiarity with it should lead them to agree with his presentation.

The phrase "do you not know" indicates that Paul takes for granted that these people are familiar with the point he is about to make. That the law has authority over a person only to the point of death is known from the Jewish writings (b. Shabbat 30a; Pesiqta Rabati 51b). "The law has authority" (lit., "the law rules") means that at least to some degree, the law is in the same league with the other ruling powers of the old age (death [6:9] and sin [6:14]). Such a perspective on the law must be borne in mind when we interpret what Paul means by saying that we have died to (v. 4), or been released from (v. 6), the law.

Death as a release from legal obligation is illustrated with the example of the marriage bond (vv. 2–3). According to Jewish law (not Roman law; see Dunn) a married woman remained under the authority of her husband for as long as he lived (cf. Deut. 24:1). She was free to remarry someone else without being condemned as an adulteress only after her former husband's death. The term used here for married woman, *hypandros,* means "under a husband" which continues the theme of ruling power from verse 1.

The point is straightforward: As death dissolves a marriage bond, so it also breaks one's bond to the law (v. 4). Interpretive problems only arise if one attempts to turn the illustration into an allegory, in which the husband represents Torah and the wife the believer. For in the application (v. 4) it is not Torah (husband) that dies, but the believer (wife). Nevertheless, Paul has chosen this particular illustration from marriage because he wants to affirm in verse 4 more than the mere termination of the law's authority at the point of death. As the end of verse 3 indicates, he also wants to say that the dissolution of a marriage bond permits remarriage.

In verse 4 Paul applies the logic of verses 1–3 to the situation of the believer vis-à-vis the law. Since the believer has died (i.e., through participation in Christ's death, cf. 6:3), then he or she has died as far as the law is concerned. The rule of the law is identified with the old age. Therefore, to be out from under the law means that one has been transferred through death out of the realm in which it held sway.

Freedom from the law means freedom to "belong to another," that is, to Christ. Here Paul picks up the idea of remarriage from verse 3. As a women is free to remarry only after the bond to her husband is completely broken by death, so it is only those whose bond to the law has been severed by death who may belong to Christ. The marriage metaphor as a description of relationship with Christ appears elsewhere in Paul (1 Cor. 6:17; 2 Cor. 11:2; Eph. 5:22–33).

Christ's death ("through the body of Christ") and resurrection ("raised from the dead") serve, as they did repeatedly in chapter 6, as defining events for the nature of Christian existence. Although we have died with Christ (6:2), once more Paul stops short of saying that we have been raised with him (see 6:1–14). At the resurrection the believer will enjoy fully the benefits of the new age, which may only be enjoyed partially in the here and now.

The purpose of transference out of the age of the law and into the age of Christ is "that we might bear fruit to God" (v. 4). The language of fruit-bearing recalls 6:21–22, in which two types of fruit ("benefit" in the NIV) were contrasted. In 6:22 the fruit of those who are slaves to God is said to lead to holiness. So also here fruit has to do with godly character (cf. Gal. 5:22–23) and the behavior that results.

Consistent with Paul's pattern of bringing one line of thought to a conclusion while simultaneously anticipating a future one, verses 5–6 expand on verse 4 while bringing together ideas and terms that will be discussed in the next chapter and a half. In particular, his introduction of the active role of the law in the old age as the agent of sin leads into verses 7–25, while the mention of the new way of the Spirit in contrast to the old way of the written code anticipates the argument beginning in 8:2.

Two modes of existence—one in Adam, one in Christ—are contrasted again, but this time with particular attention to the role that the law played in the former, which is what is meant by the phrase "when we were controlled by the sinful nature." The NIV translation "sinful nature" (lit.: "flesh," *sarx*) gives the impression that Paul is referring to a part of a person. Within Paul's extended discussion of the two realms that we find here, however, "the flesh" denotes life in the realm of Adam.

We should understand the contrast of Spirit with the old written code in the same fashion (v. 6; cf. 2:27–29). "In the new way of the Spirit" represents life in the new age; "in the old way of the written code" typifies life in the old age. The means of transfer (i.e., the release from the law) is once more said to be achieved through our dying with Christ (cf. 6:3–4). The idea that new life comes through the Holy Spirit is introduced here, though it is not described in its glorious detail until chapter 8. Before coming to this topic Paul wants to say more about the law.

Paul previously connected the law with an increase of sin and wrath (3:20; 4:15; 5:20). He now argues that the law actually works to the advantage of sin. Sinful passion is aroused by the law, an idea that will be explained further in verses 7–12.

2.2.2. The Law and Sin: A Defense of the Law (7:7–25). Paul has had much to say about the negative role that the law played in God's plan of salvation. This portion of the letter serves not only to expand on what he has been arguing about the law, but also to clarify that the law is holy and good despite its association with sin. His defense of the law consists of putting the blame for the connection between sin and the law squarely on the shoulders of sin—a power capable of manipulating the law for its own purposes—and on the "fleshliness" of humanity.

A couple of introductory comments need to be made about this section, with a more detailed discussion about its difficulties in the exposition below. (1) The immense popularity of this part of the letter derives from the fact that Christians can readily identify with its depiction of the struggle with sin. Interpreting this section as the dilemma of the Christian has had a long history within the church. The Reformers saw it this way; in particular, Luther used chapter 7 to argue that this passage reflects the situation of the one who has been justified by faith. Since justification changes one's standing before God but does not change one's character, the struggle with sin is to be expected (Luther, 327). Those in denominations with roots in the Holiness Movement of the nineteenth century have likewise identified with the struggle depicted here, for they see in it their own battle to adhere to whatever holiness code they live under.

(2) The central theme of verses 7–25 is not the human struggle with sin, but a defense of the law. In other words, the key to unlocking the teaching of chapter 7 does not lie in determining the identity of the "I"—the one who despairs of an inability to do what is desired. Regardless of the debate about the identity of that speaker, the message of this portion of the letter is plain since it has to do, as we have said, with the law. And what chapter 7 says about the law is clear.

(3) That being said, we are not content to leave unresolved the question of who is being depicted in 7:7–25. We all share a personal interest in knowing whether Paul is expressing the dilemma of an unregenerate or of a regenerate person. If Paul is speaking as a believer, then it assists us in coming to grips with our own inabilities and frustrations.

Moreover, for pastors and teachers, the manner in which this text is explained is of significant import. If we teach that a constant inability to do what God desires, accompanied by a sense of despair because sin is in control, is normative for believers, it will affect the determination and hope with which they pursue holiness. But if we teach that this is the dilemma of those outside of Christ, then what chapters 6 and 8 say about sin may be taken at full value: Sin no longer holds believers captive and there is freedom in Christ. In other words, those who picture the victorious Christian as normative rather than the defeated believer will tend to pursue holiness with greater faith and vigor. The truth, as Jesus said, will set you free (John 8:32). But which interpretation reflects the truth Paul was communicating?

(4) Although there are points to be made for both interpretations, the view that 7:7–25 is about the believer faces, to my way of thinking, a formidable obstacle. How the speaker in chapter 7 characterizes his situation stands diametrically opposed to the description of the Christian life given in chapters 5–6. The Christian is "[dead] to sin" (6:2); once a slave to sin (6:17), he or she is now "set free from sin" (6:18). Contrarily, the subject of the latter half of chapter 7 identifies himself as "sold as a slave to sin" (7:14).

Furthermore, while the believer is no longer under the authority of the law (6:14; 7:4–6), the struggle of the one in 7:13–25 has to do with an inability to keep the law. Why would Paul describe a Christian's attempt to satisfy the demands of the law? Therefore, I conclude that the subject of 7:7–25 is a non-Christian who struggles unsuccessfully to fulfill the law.

(5) The text divides into two sections: verses 7–12 and verses 14–25, with verse 13 functioning as a transitional verse between them. In verses 7–12 the Adam tradition is brought forward to explain how sin manipulated the law to bring sin and death into the human realm. Verses 14–25 show that the law's purpose was not only controverted by sin, but also by the weakness of human flesh. In both sections the inability of the law to bring life is vividly portrayed. By speaking in the first person Paul forcefully conveys the desperate condition faced by all those under the law.

2.2.2.1. Death Through the Law (7:7–12). Paul's repeated association of the law with sin evokes the question in verse 7: "Is the law sin?" That is, is the law evil? The answer comes in verse 12: No, the law is "holy, righteous and good." That is to say, the law reflects the one who gave it. In between the question and the answer is the explanation about how the holy law has remained untainted despite its association with sin and death. Sin manipulated the law, which resulted in the introduction of death into the world.

To make this argument Paul draws on the Genesis account of Adam's fall (Gen. 2–3). The Garden of Eden incident has had a determinative effect on the relationship of the law with sin and death within the human sphere. The discussion here is similar to 5:12–21, where Adam's act of disobedience was depicted as dooming all of his descendants to the sphere of sin and death. Unlike 5:12–21, however, Paul shows his identification with Adam through the use of "I." Although the name is not mentioned, it is apparent from the text that Paul is narrating Adam's story: for example, "Once I was alive apart from law" (v. 9a); "For sin . . . deceived me" (v. 11).

This is certainly not the only interpretation of "I" in Romans 7. Indeed, the most natural reading of "I" is that Paul is narrating his own story. But the autobiographical interpretation leaves open a number of questions. What experience in his past is he describing in verses 7–11? His *bar mitzvah*, when he became responsible for the law (e.g., Deissmann, 1927, 91)? His preconversion state as a Pharisee (e.g., Hodge, 224)? And what spiritual crisis is he recounting in verse 14–25? Is he describing his moral dilemma as a non-Christian (e.g., Wesley, 543–44), or his current struggle as a Christian with sin (e.g., Calvin, 264–75)?

Since a 1929 study by Kümmel it has become widely accepted that the use of "I" need not be autobiographical; that is, Paul need not be recounting his personal story. Kümmel (124, 132) argued that Paul had adopted a current practice of using "I" as a rhetorical device to describe a universal condition. There are examples of such a generic use of the first person in Paul (e.g., Rom. 3:7; 1 Cor. 13; Gal. 2:18–20) and elsewhere (e.g., Philo, *Somn.* 1.176–77; for more examples, see Dunn and Stuhlmacher). This does not mean, however, that Paul is describing an experience that is personally unrelated to him. His use of "I" is consonant with the Jewish idea of corporate identity, in which the action of one representative figure is considered to be definitive for those related to him (see 5:12–21). Paul speaks in identification with Adam, and in so doing, he speaks for all of us born into the realm of Adam. To summarize, Paul reintroduces the subject of the Fall (referred to implicitly in 1:21–23 and explicitly in 5:12–21) to describe the common condition of humanity under the law.

Verses 7–11 explain in detail the nature of the relationship between law and sin by recounting Adam's fall, noting how sin controverted the purpose of God's law. As argued above, Paul speaks in the first person to reflect his, and our, solidarity with Adam.

The law is not sin, as the question in verse 7a suggests, but it did bring an awareness of sin (v. 7b), because the law defines what constitutes right and wrong before God. Paul gives the example of the tenth commandment in verse 7c, but in abbreviated form. Unlike Exodus 20:17 and Deuteronomy 5:21, where various possessions of one's neighbor are specified as the objects of covetousness, there is no object given in verse 7. The consequence of this shortened form is to broaden the commandment to include any type of illicit desire.

The relevance of this commandment for the purpose at hand is twofold. (1) It suits the temptation of Adam and Eve. They were being tempted with desire for what was forbidden: the knowledge of good and evil. By the time of Paul, the breaking of the tenth commandment was commonly seen as the root of all sin (Apoc. Mos. 19:3: "Covetousness is the origin of every sin"; Apoc. Abr. 24:9; cf. James 1:15). (2) A complementary notion was also in circulation about this time, namely, that this commandment was a summation of the Mosaic Law (e.g., Philo, *De decalogo* 142–43, 173; Josephus *Ant.* 1.41–47; 4 Ezra 7:11).

In light of this evidence, it seems that Paul views the command given to Adam and Eve as representative of the law that would one day be given to Israel. In fact, earlier in 5:14 Paul drew a comparison between Adam's transgression and the breaking of the law (see Dunn). As Adam represents us, so the tenth commandment represents the law. In short, Adam's act of disobedience defined the relationship of sin with the law and set in motion the conditions that would pertain for all of his descendants under the law.

In verse 8 Paul becomes more specific about how sin manipulated the law. The command given to Adam provided the "opportunity" (*aphorme*) that sin needed to gain entrance into the human sphere. The word *aphorme* was often used for a military base of operations or a bridgehead. Considering the personification of sin in these chapters as a power, this nuance of the word is probably present here as well. It should be noted that whatever power sin has over men and women, it is derivative. Unlike the power of God, which functions independently of all circumstances, sin needs an opportunity to launch its attack. It is dead without the law; that is, "sin had no vital energy of its own" (Stuhlmacher).

It was the serpent in the Garden of Eden who seized the opportunity afforded it by the prohibition about not eating from the tree of the knowledge of good and evil (Gen. 2:17). The command that was intended to keep the original pair from doing what was sinful was used by sin to produce the desire for disobedience. As Paul found this to be true in his own experience, so we know it as well. It is indicative of the human condition as defined by Adam that desire for something or some activity increases at the moment that it is prohibited. Kids illustrate this well. Say no, and a child wants what is prohibited all the more. For that matter, big kids illustrate this too. We, like Adam and Eve, resist limitations; we, like Adam and Eve, seek independence from the One who made us. Tragically, what we covet is fatal.

The force of this argument against a Jewish understanding of the law as the solution for sin should not be missed. Paul declares in verse 10 that "the very commandment that was intended to bring life actually brought death." If Adam and Eve had kept God's command, then, presumably, they would have been able to eat of the tree of life (Gen. 3:22–24). With the coming of sin, however, what was intended to promote life was now the means by which death exercised its power over human existence. The same point is made in verse 11. Repeating the phrase from verse 8a, Paul states that sin seized "the opportunity afforded by the commandment" given to Adam. The result was that sin, which is represented by the serpent, "deceived me, and through the commandment put me to death."

Two eras are thus contrasted in verses 8c–10a. Before the law, sin was dead and "I" was alive; after the law, sin sprang to life, and "I" died. That is, before God gave the command to

Adam, he was fully alive, that is, he experienced unbroken relationship with God. After God gave the command, with the requisite condition for temptation in place, sin sprang to life. With his act of disobedience, Adam experienced death (see 5:12–21), that is, spiritual death—broken relationship with his Creator. Consequently, physical death became his destiny and ours, for Adam had been warned that "when you eat of it you will surely die" (Gen. 2:17).

We should note again that through Christ the conditions that existed prior to the breaking of God's command will be restored. The age is coming when sin and death will be no more. In the meantime, the believer is alive to God, and although sin still exists, he or she is dead to sin (6:2).

2.2.2.2. Powerlessness of the Law and the Flesh (7:13–25). Although the topic remains the same in verses 13–25 as it was in verses 7–12 (the relationship of law and sin) and the narrator is still the "I," the perspective changes. More emphasis is put on the role that "flesh" (*sarx*) has played in the history of the relationship of law and sin. While sin took advantage of the law, it was able to do so only because of the complicity of the flesh. What we have here, then, is a continuation of Paul's defense of the innocence of the law.

But that is not all. As the argument progresses it becomes increasingly apparent that Paul's concern at this stage of the letter extends beyond just defending the law. He is also furthering the discussion of chapters 6–8 concerning the manner in which sin is dealt with in the age of grace. Paul declares that only grace, not the law, could deal with the power of sin.

We now encounter verbs in the present. Whereas verses 7–11 described the initial impact of Adam's sin on our relationship to God's law and how his sin has defined the interrelationship of law and sin in the Adamic era, verses 13–25 lay out the conditions that now face his descendants. The human predicament is told from the perspective of the "I." That is, Paul assumes the voice of all those who are in Adam (those who are under the law *and without Christ*). Although there are times when what he narrates is particularly true of the Jew (e.g., v. 22), this is the universal dilemma of all who face God's command.

This section (vv. 13–25) begins, as the one before it (vv. 7–12), with a curt question: "Did that which is good, then, become death to me?" The "good" is the law (cf. v. 12). To paraphrase the question: Should it not be said, on the basis of what has been argued, that the law is to blame for the condition of humankind? Didn't it produce death?

While the answer reiterates from verses 7–11 the goodness of the law and the culpability of sin, the sovereignty of God is now brought into the discussion. One of the questions not yet addressed in this discussion about sin's use of the law is: Where is God in all of this? Two clauses in verse 13 (both beginning with *hina*: "in order that" and "so that") show how the divine purpose supersedes sin's intent. By allowing sin to use the law, God lays bare the true nature of sin. This "is part of God's fuller and deeper strategy to bring out the character of sin and of its end product and payment—only death" (Dunn).

Verse 14 is a summary statement about how sin was able to produce death through the law. The weakness that sin exploited was not in the law, but in the "fleshiness" of humanity. Paul's characterization of the law as spiritual (*pneumatikos*) is unprecedented in the Old Testament and somewhat unexpected, considering its affiliation with sin in this discussion. By using "spiritual" he affirms the divine nature of the law and sets up a strong contrast with the "I" as "fleshly" (*sarkinos*; NIV, "unspiritual"). The latter expression, the equivalent of being "in the flesh" (v. 5), characterizes the non-Christian. That the unbeliever is in view here rather than the Christian (contra Cranfield; Murray) is apparent from the final phrase of the verse: "sold as a slave to sin." To be under the dominion of sin is the condition of those outside of Christ (see 3:9; 7:6; see also the imagery of slavery to sin in ch. 6). In other words, to be fleshly is to be in Adam.

Verses 15–20 expand on verse 14 by focusing on the inner conflict that plagues the person in Adam: the conflict between willing and doing. Because the non-Christian is "fleshly," it is impossible for him or her to do what the spiritual law commands.

The dilemma is portrayed with emphatic language. (1) Instead of doing what is desired, the person in Adam does not just commit what is undesirable. He does what he hates; she does what she detests (v. 15). Such is the awful power of sin. (2) The inability to perform what the law calls for leads to a dogmatic conclusion: "I know that nothing good lives in me" (v. 18). Such is the awful realization that one controlled by sin is brought to at a moment of God-given insight.

Undoubtedly most Christians have expressed similar sentiments about an inability to follow through on the intention of the will. But this passage is not about the struggle of a believer. The "I" depicted here expresses such absolute desperation, stemming from an imprisonment to sin, that it is inconceivable that this is the testimony of a Christian. Although all Christians struggle with carrying out the intent of their will, this text describes the situation of one who sees no hope of deliverance from the power of sin.

Paul's qualification in verse 18 that he means that there is nothing good "in my flesh" requires comment. As I did above in verse 5, I take issue with the NIV translation here of "in my sinful nature" (lit., "in my flesh"). This NIV translation suggests that "in my flesh" denotes a part of a person's constitution. Instead, "in my flesh" designates something external—a realm. Being in the flesh (= being fleshly [v. 14]) is to be in Adam. It is to be controlled by the realm of sin and death—and in this realm there is nothing good.

Paul draws a number of conclusions from the mental conflict he describes. (1) In an interesting twist, he argues that his inability to do what he wants is not proof that he rejects the law, but that he accepts its validity. That he does what he does not want to do attests to the fact that he acknowledges the law as good and desires to obey it. The problem for Paul, then, is not about the will. This leads to the next conclusion.

(2) His inability (as a man in Adam) to do what is desired is proof that there is another power at work. The disparity between thought and action is the product of indwelling sin (vv. 17, 20). How else can Paul explain why the will is consistently thwarted? To blame the problem on indwelling sin is not to shift the blame away from the sinner. The argument of the letter about sin and salvation presupposes that all people are individually responsible before God. But it does serve to explain the utter failure that attends the attempt to be consistent.[4]

The vivid depiction that we find here of the divided self who cannot do what the law demands is Paul's reflection on his Pharisaic past from his Christian present. In other words, this is probably not the way he would have described his life when he was still a Pharisee. More representative of that former period would have been the self-assessment he offered in Philippians 3:6: "as for legalistic righteousness, faultless." After being blinded by Christ on the Damascus road, however, he saw his previous experience with the law in a new light.

In verse 21 Paul concludes the discussion about the battle that rages in the non-Christian who is "confronted with the Law, but ruled by sin" (Stuhlmacher). Paul reports that he has discovered a "law" (*nomos*). Although Paul has been consistent in the letter in using *nomos* for the Mosaic Law, in this verse and the next few he varies the definition of that Greek word for effect. The most natural reading of verse 21 is to understand "law" as a "principle" or "rule," with the definition of that rule being given in the remainder of the verse. What Paul discovered, then, is this: The inevitability that evil is present when he wants to do good.

As the argument moves toward its climax, the depiction of the conflict between willing and doing becomes even more dramatic. For one thing, the "I" delights in the law of God in the inner being (v. 22). Two comments are pertinent here. (1) One of the arguments raised against the view that the non-Christian is the subject of verses 13–25 is that only a believer can say that he or she delights in God's law. This argument misunderstands the nature of Jewish piety. Rather than viewing the law as a burden—which is how we might see it—the law was revered among the Jews because it was seen as God's gift to the nation of Israel.

Psalms 19:7–11 and 119, for example, convey this delight, and Paul mentions the giving of the law to Israel as one of the nation's advantages (Rom. 3:2; 9:4). Now, this is not to say that every Jew evidenced such delight in the law, but Paul is representing his people at their best. He is representing them as the type of Jew Paul himself was before he met Christ. And such a representation sets up a strong contrast. It is precisely the one who delights in the law, even that one, who suffers from an inability to express that love with concrete action.

(2) The "inner being" (v. 22) and the "mind" (v. 23) are synonymous expressions for the source of the desire for good that Paul has been

describing since verse 15. Jeremias has shown that the expression was used in the Greek world for a person in his or her "Godward, immortal side" (*TDNT*, 1.365). It is this sense of a person's "spiritual" inclination that we find here. If Paul was depicting the dilemma of a Christian in verses 13–25, then "in my spirit" (rather than "in my inner being") would have been the natural phrase to describe the source of a Christian's longing for God. But Paul avoids "S/spirit" language throughout this whole passage since it does not apply to the one who does not belong to Christ (cf. 8:9).

Since Paul began to refer to different types of laws in verse 21, the expression "God's law" in verse 22 (= "the law of my mind," v. 23) is necessary to clarify that Torah is once more in view. This is the law in which the inner man delights. But there is "another law" mentioned in verse 23, which is defined later in the verse as the "law of sin." Dunn has argued that all of the references to *nomos* in Romans 7 are to the Mosaic Law. The contrasting views of *nomos* reflect, not different types of laws, but the same law seen from different angles. Thus, for Dunn, the "law of sin" is the Mosaic Law seen from the perspective of its manipulation by sin.

Yet this is unlikely, considering (1) Paul's belabored attempt throughout this chapter to preserve the innocence of the law over against sin, and (2) the fact that the more natural reading suggests Paul has two laws in mind. Would Paul have expected the Romans to interpret these contrasting descriptions of the law as two sides of the same law? Paul is distinguishing God's law, which is holy and good (v. 12), from the "law" (or the authority or principle) of sin.

Military imagery—"waging war" and "making me a prisoner"—functions in verse 23 to bring to a climax Paul's diagnosis of the human condition under the law of sin. Human optimism might view the battle with sin as ongoing. It might proclaim that it is within the grasp of every individual to rise and conquer the power of sin. But the war is over. Sin won its battle with Adam, taking all of his descendants into captivity. The desperate cry in the next verse is the cry of the captive. In other words, both the law and the person in Adam are powerless against sin. The solution to sin's power must come from somewhere outside of the realm of human striving and the realm of the law.

In verse 24, the meaning of the term "wretched" ranges from "an expression of despair or condemnation" to "the state of a man pulled in two directions" (Dunn). Either nuance fits the context well. This is the cry of one who is imprisoned and feels no way out. The question, "Who will rescue me from this body of death?" is, as Moo points out, unusual if this is a Christian expressing despair over the struggle with sin. What is unusual is the fact that chapter 7 finishes on a solemn note, with a reiteration of the human dilemma without Christ. Such an ending resets the problem before the solution is given in the next chapter.

The rescuer is "God—through Jesus Christ our Lord" (v. 25), which brings us back to the previous discussion about the deliverance effected for believers through the cross (3:21–26). It is interesting that Paul mentions the other two members of the Trinity just before the focus shifts in chapter 8 to the Spirit. The work of the entire Godhead is involved in bringing salvation to humanity.

2.2.3. The Spirit of Life Gives Power Over Sin and Death (8:1–13). The cloud of despair that hung over much of chapter 7 suddenly vanishes with the opening declaration of chapter 8 that there is no condemnation for those who are in Christ. The cry of desperation in 7:24—the cry of one who is outside of Christ and under the law, the cry of one who is subject to "the law of sin and death" (8:2)—is met with a response. The cry of desperation fades into the background as Paul declares that there is freedom for those who are in Christ. There is life in the Holy Spirit—both now and forever. And there is no threat of separation from God and his love.

Chapter 8 works at a number of different levels to draw together various theological threads from earlier parts of the letter. It picks up where 7:6 left off, which contrasted the old way under the law with the new way of the Spirit. Paul will now describe in glorious detail what life in the Spirit is about. As he describes the role of the Holy Spirit in actualizing the work of Christ for the individual believer, he revisits concepts found in chapters 5–7. Romans 8:1–17 continues the argument begun in chapter 6 that the age of grace does not spell the demise of righteousness, for the Holy Spirit makes possible the life of righteousness. The twin themes of hope and suffering, which were xtaposed in 5:3–4, become the dominant otifs of 8:18–39. Life is so transformed in e age of grace that even suffering is set ithin the realm of hope.

The first thirteen verses follow a pattern miliar to us from chapter 6. A discussion out what is true of believers—the new stas given to those who have been transferred it of the age of Adam and into the age of hrist—is followed by a declaration of what ould be true of them in practice. Unlike apter 6, however, the Holy Spirit's role in inging about the benefits of the death and surrection of Christ to believers is now ought to the fore.

"Therefore, there is now no condemnation r those who are in Christ Jesus" (v. 1). Therefore" is stating a conclusion, but to hat? It is hard to pin down which part of the eceding argument Paul has in mind. Is he inking back to 7:7–25, to 7:6 (Barrett), or to e argument of chapters 5–7 (Moo)? Or is this summation of the overarching theme of the tter (i.e., the righteousness of God) that xtends back to 1:17? The role that chapter 8 lays as a summary and climax of the explaation about God's righteousness to Jew and entile, before Paul's focus narrows to God's ghteousness toward Israel, suggests that this ection summarizes the letter's dominant eme.

"Condemnation" (cf. also 5:16, 18) is a idicial term, which in this context denotes the esult of God's judgment. Like death, with hich it is linked in 5:12–21, it refers to eteral separation from God. Those who are "in Christ Jesus" may rejoice that no such horror waits them at the judgment. Indeed, chapter 8 inishes with a powerful declaration that nothg can separate us from God and Christ—othing in the present and nothing in the uture.[5]

The basis of the declaration that there is no ondemnation is given in verse 2. Believers do ot face the consequence that awaits those nder the power of sin (i.e., death or condemation) because they have been "set . . . free rom the law of sin and death." As in 7:21–25, where Paul used "law" to denote something ther than the Mosaic Law, he varies the meanng of this word to drive his point home. The aw of sin and death is not the Jewish law, seen rom the negative side (so Dunn), but a "power" or "authority" that brings men and women into slavery. Similarly, "the law of the Spirit of life" represents the power of the Holy Spirit, who frees humanity from the tyranny of sin and death. The phrase "the law of the Spirit of life" appears nowhere else in Paul's letters. It must be the case, then, that Paul coins this phrase here because he is continuing the wordplay on "law" that he began in the previous chapter.

The ideas of slavery and freedom, and of sin and death as ruling powers, are familiar to Paul's listeners from chapters 5–6 (and to a lesser extent, from ch. 7). In chapters 5–6 the emphasis was on the death of Christ as the event that enables one to be transferred out of the realm of sin and death. Here Paul relates the role of the Holy Spirit to the saving work of Christ. In fact, the phrase "through Christ Jesus" is likely included with "the law of the Spirit of life" to clarify that it is not the Spirit who effects this transfer independently. What the Spirit does is predicated on the death and resurrection of Christ.

The law of Moses comes into view again in verse 3. We can be sure that it is the Jewish law that Paul has in mind in this verse because, unlike verse 2, there is no modifying phrase attached to the word "law" (*nomos*) to suggest otherwise. Also, the content of the verse recaps what Paul said about the law in chapter 7. What the Mosaic Law could not do was deal with the sin problem; this is what God did through the sending of his Son—that is, his sending of Christ to die for our sins. Through the cross God "condemned sin in sinful man" (lit., "in the flesh").

It is difficult to decide which "flesh" Paul has in mind here: Is it Christ's flesh (Cranfield) or, as the NIV suggests, our own sinful flesh? Perhaps this question attempts to divide what Paul viewed as two parts of a whole. Christ, as our substitute, bears the condemnation in his flesh due us. As a result, the condemnation that faces all people in the flesh is removed.

The sacrificial death of Christ is also referred to by the phrase that the NIV has translated as "to be a sin offering" (lit., "concerning sin"). The NIV translators concluded, as we do here, that "concerning sin" denotes a sin offering, since this expression was often used in the LXX in this way (see Moo, Fee). In short, condemnation will not fall on those who are in

Christ because God's wrath has already fallen somewhere else—on Christ.

This theologically dense verse needs two more comments. (1) Significant is Paul's qualification that Christ came "in the likeness of sinful man [lit., flesh]" rather than, as he might have said, "in sinful flesh." The Greek word *homoioma* ("likeness") is being used to preserve a distinction. Paul wants to affirm that Christ was an appropriate substitute for humanity because he came in human flesh, but he also wants to avoid any thought that Christ became sinful in his incarnation. Consequently, he says that Christ came in the *likeness* of sinful flesh.

(2) The idea that the law "was weakened by the sinful nature [lit., flesh]" picks up the discussion in chapter 7, where Paul argued that the law was unable to deliver us from sin. In fact, the appearance of the law gave sin the opportunity to become entrenched in the human sphere (7:7–11). Similarly here, although the law is holy and good (7:12), humanity is not. Human "flesh" is in bondage to sin and death, and such a bondage the law is powerless to break.

The purpose for condemning sin in the flesh is that the "righteous requirements of the law might be fully met in us" (v. 4). Any impression that Paul may have given that God's purpose in giving the law had been completely circumvented by human sinfulness is now dispelled. As Dunn argues, "Paul here deliberately and provocatively insists on the continuity of God's purpose in the law and through the Spirit."

There are two primary lines of thought about how this fulfillment ("fully met") occurred or occurs. They divide over whether it is Christ or the believer who is active in fulfilling this requirement. (1) In one view, Christ fulfilled the requirements of the law by his perfect obedience. By his death he took our condemnation. This allows an "interchange": "Christ becomes what we are so that we might become what Christ is" (Moo).

(2) Christians fulfill the law as they live "according to the Spirit" (v. 4b). According to this view, the second part of the verse explains how the fulfillment is accomplished. It is not that we now obey the law, but we fulfill its purpose, which was to bring about righteousness (Fee, 1994, 534–58). While there is much to be said for the first view, it does seem that the most natural reading of the verse is to take t subordinate clause beginning with "who do n live . . ." as an explanation of the type of fu fillment he means. This position does n move the emphasis away from what God do to what men and women do. As Fee argues, t emphasis is still on what the Holy Spirit do to enable or empower us to live in rig teousness (1994, 535).

In the next nine verses (vv. 5–13), the co trast between "flesh" (*sarx*) and "spiri (*pneuma*) dominates the discussion, as the di ference between walking according to the fle as opposed to according to the Spirit (v. 4b) explained. The focus in verses 5–8 is on tho who live in the flesh; the emphasis shifts to t believer in verses 9–11. The flesh/spirit dua ism is eschatological, not anthropological. Th is a contrast between states of existence in tw eras—the era of Adam and that of Christ (se 5:12–21). This is not about two conflictir natures within the individual, but a compar son of those who live in Christ with those wh do not.

The before and after pictures displaye here—of life before and outside of Christ an then of life in Christ—are depicted as extrem opposites. Such a stark contrast fixes vivi images onto the mind of the reader. Paul wan the Roman Christians to have a clear picture o what they were as opposed to what they hav become. The purpose of the contrasting image in verses 5–11 is to compel them to adopt lifestyle commensurate with their new statu (vv. 12–13).

Paul begins by comparing the differing or entations of the mind or will (vv. 5–6). Wha is being discussed is what the mind is "se on"—not so much what a person thinks abou but rather what his or her orientation is. The ori entation of someone in the flesh is this-worldly the mind is set on the values of a world that ha rejected God. The non-Christian, in othe words, may be defined as one who is "hostil to God" (v. 7). This does not mean, obviously that all unbelievers act consciously out of hos tility toward God. But in the stark contrast o the two modes of existence presented here, on is either directed toward the world of the flesh or the world of the Spirit (cf. Matt. 12:30, "H who is not with me is against me"). Pau depicted a similar, worldly orientation in 1:18– 32: Humanity has rejected the knowledge o

God available to them, resulting in a cycle of thought and action that is a perversion of all that he intended for humanity. In sum, the person with such an orientation "cannot please God" (v. 8).

It should be noted that pleasing God has nothing to do with being a "good" or "bad" person per se. There are unbelievers of good character and integrity, and there are those who are evil. The point here, as it has been since 1:18, is that pleasing God is ultimately related not to what we do, but to what he has done for us in Christ. Or, to put it differently, it is his righteousness, or saving activity, that is the basis for the relationship that we have with God.

The fate of those who are hostile to God is "death" (v. 6), which is a spiritual death with physical consequences (see 5:12–21). Spiritual death (or separation from God) may be experienced on both sides of the grave. Estrangement from God in the present becomes an eternally fixed state for those who remain outside of Christ. The word of Christ from the cross, "My God, my God, why have you forsaken me?" (Matt. 27:46), suggests that Christ knew not only physical death, but also spiritual death, that is, separation from God's presence. He experienced death fully so that we do not need to.

The mode of existence of those who are in Christ is opposite that of those who are in Adam. Those whose orientation is toward God, or "what the Spirit desires" (v. 5), know life and peace (cf. 5:1, 12–21). Having been set free from the law of sin and death, they live in relationship with God through "the Spirit of life" (v. 2). There is peace rather than hostility between them and God (cf. 5:1). Peace and life characterize what we may enjoy now and what we will know forever, for not even death can separate us from our relationship with God (cf. 8:35–39).

In verses 9–11 the emphasis shifts to those who walk according to the Spirit. Whereas unbelievers are characterized as being in the flesh, believers are "in the Spirit" (which the NIV translates as "controlled . . . by the Spirit"). This is a new type of existence where the power of the Spirit, rather than the power of sin and death, is at work. And, as the middle of verse 9 states, believers are those in whom the Spirit, rather than sin (cf. 7:20), dwells. We conclude, then, that the Spirit takes the place of sin, both as the sphere in which we live (i.e., the power that controls us) and as the presence that indwells us.

The shift from "the Spirit of God" (v. 9a; cf. v. 11) to "the Spirit of Christ" (v. 9b) reflects the emphasis in verses 9b–10 on the work of Christ. The phrase "if Christ is in you" (v. 10a) does not mean that both Christ and the Spirit indwell the believer, nor that the two are indistinguishable. Rather, with Cranfield we understand that "through the indwelling of the Spirit Christ himself is present to us." To say that Christ is present to us through the Spirit is not to deemphasize the personal nature of our relationship with Christ. The Spirit is able to represent Christ so completely because the Spirit is a person as well. We are not indwelt by a force but by a personal being.

The central point of verses 9–11 is to elaborate further on "the law of the Spirit of life" (v. 2a), which is the power of the Holy Spirit at work, giving life now and forever to those who are in Christ. Verse 10 speaks of life in the present, whereas verse 11 deals with life in the future. Even though the "body is dead because of sin," the Spirit is life because of righteousness. The body is subject to death because of sin; death came to all people through the sin of Adam (5:12). Yet the Spirit is life because of righteousness; life comes to all people through the righteousness of Christ (5:18).

The interpretation of *pneuma* ("spirit") in verse 10 as the Holy Spirit (see Dunn; Moo) rather than the human spirit (NIV) is preferable. Barrett argues that we would expect Paul to say that "the spirit is alive" if he meant the human spirit. What we read instead is "the spirit is life," which immediately reminds us of "the Spirit of life" (v. 2). As well, verse 11 explains the meaning of the phrase we are examining, and there it is the Spirit that is being discussed (Moo).

Regarding life in the future (v. 11), we know from 6:5 that because we have died with Christ, we will also be raised with him. Here the role of the Spirit of life in making this future certain for the believer is identified. God effects the resurrection of believers through the agency of the Holy Spirit. Paul specifies that the resurrection involves even our "mortal bodies"—those same bodies that were said to be destined for death in verse 10. Resurrection involves the whole person, not just the spirit.

A "spiritual" resurrection is what the Corinthians imagined, probably a result of the influence of the Greek idea of immortality of the soul. It was believed that at death the soul/spirit was freed from the body, which was then discarded (1 Cor. 15). Writing from Corinth, with that location serving as a reminder of a previous controversy, Paul affirms that even the body is raised. (The transformation of other aspects of the physical world are described in vv. 19–21.)

That an imperative (vv. 12–13)[6] serves as a summation to an extended discourse about what is now true of believers (vv. 1–11) is a familiar pattern in Paul. As in 6:1–14, the apostle begins by describing what God/Christ has done for us (8:1–11) and ends with discussing what we must do in response to his gracious acts (8:12–13).

The imperatival idea, in line with what has preceded, is framed by contrasting Spirit and flesh (NIV, "sinful nature") as well as life and death. And, in line with the preceding argument, Spirit and flesh refer to two contrary modes of existence. That is to say, this section of the letter does not concern the internal struggle within a believer between the God-ward side and the sin-ward side. To be in the Spirit as opposed to being in the flesh is to be a Christian as opposed to being a non-Christian.

The importance of what Paul is about to say is conveyed by the reappearance of the word "brothers" (see 7:1, 4). He is writing about an obligation incumbent on believers, which is not the same obligation that once pressed on them under the rule of sin and death. To return to the former life—that is, to live according to the flesh again—means death, now and forever (v. 13a). This is not to say that death awaits the Christian who commits a single sin. The present tense of "live" in the phrase "if you live according to the sinful nature [flesh]" applies the warning to the one who *continues in sin*, who constantly behaves as if he or she were still in the flesh.

The obligation of the believer is to live like one who is in the Spirit. Therefore it is imperative that "the misdeeds of the body" be "put to death." We expect to read "the misdeeds of the flesh," since Paul has been using flesh in connection with sin and death. Fee comments that "body" is appropriate here because Christians are no longer in the flesh (1994, 558).

If we are to avoid despair because of ou continuing temptation to sin and our all-toc frequent practice of giving in to temptation, w must pay particular attention to the phrase "b the Spirit." The notion that one is saved b grace, but kept by one's own effort, is foreig to this text. If it were so, then we would be liv ing precariously, not joyfully, as we constantl teeter on the brink of the abyss. But just as w have not earned our salvation, so we do nc keep it through our own initiative either. O our own we are powerless to do what Go requires, but the Spirit enables us to put t death evil deeds. The answer to the problem c the power of sin, which was raised in 6:1 an has been at the forefront of the discussio since, is now given: It is the Spirit.

2.2.4. The Spirit of Adoption (8:14–17) Although the topic suddenly shifts to adoptio or "sonship" in verse 14, the connection witl verse 13 should not be missed. What verse 1. stated in the negative, verse 14a states in th positive: To put to death the deeds of the bod is to be "led by the Spirit." To be led of th Spirit is a popular concept in Pentecostal charismatic circles. What this text tells us i that the Spirit's leading has to do, first an foremost, with the manner in which he guide us into righteous living. Like the phrase "b the Spirit" (v. 13), the concept of being led b the Spirit reminds us again that in terms of ou sanctification—that is, our walking appropri ately in the relationship God has establishe for us by his righteousness—the Holy Spirit i fundamental. We work only as he works; w follow as he leads. "The daily, hourly puttin to death of the schemings and enterprises o the sinful flesh by means of the Spirit is a mat ter of being led, directed, impelled, controlle by the Spirit" (Cranfield).

In 6:16–23 Paul spoke of Christians as thos who have been transferred from slavery to si to slavery to God. The harshness of the slaver imagery was used there to press the point tha being under grace instead of the law does no entail freedom to sin. In 8:15 slavery is pre sented as the antithesis of life in the Spirit because Paul wants to contrast life outside o Christ with life in Christ. To receive the Spiri is not to receive a "spirit that makes you slave" (this is not an actual spirit, but a phras coined to make a point), which results in a fea of condemnation. Instead, the Spirit comes tc s as the "Spirit of sonship [or adoption]." To ceive the Spirit is to be adopted as a child of od (cf. Gal. 4:4–6). We are led by the Spirit to the type of behavior that is appropriate for ose who are part of God's family (Rom. 8:14).

The apostle is describing the believer with rminology that was understood by the Jew to fer to his exclusive status before God. Israel as God's son, and God his Father (e.g., Ex. :22–23; Deut. 32:6; Isa. 63:16). It was Israel at was adopted: "Theirs is the adoption as ons" (Rom. 9:4). The gospel reveals that rough Christ membership in the people of God as been opened to all, both Jew and Gentile.

The warmth of familial imagery impresses e reader with the truth that the Spirit gives us omplete assurance about our present and ture standing with God. We are sons and aughters now; we are heirs of future glory as ell. The cry of "*Abba*" comes from the lips of elievers as they are prompted by the Holy pirit (v. 15; cf. Gal. 4:6). In other words, the dwelling Spirit confirms to us the reality of ur relationship to God, and we proclaim it oud. According to the law (Deut. 19:15), two itnesses were required to settle a matter. here are two witnesses that establish the truth f your relationship with God—the Holy pirit and your spirit.

Paul's choice of "*Abba*, Father" (v. 15) was eant to echo the form of address used by od's only begotten Son when he prayed Mark 14:36). Although it is true that Jesus was ot the only one of his day to pray this way see Fitzmyer), Jesus' use of it is significant. reveals to us the level of intimacy that the on had with the Father, and its reappearance ere conveys that those who are adopted into e family of God are now invited to share a imilar relationship.

The present nature of our adopted state falls hort of the full realization of "sonship" that ill be ours someday. True, "we are children" lready, but we have not yet received the future heritance (v. 17). As 8:10–11 affirmed that e presence of the Spirit of life in us now is a uarantee of fullness of life at the resurrection, o the present "sonship" of believers, effected y the Spirit, is our assurance that the full benfits of inheritance will accrue to us.

This talk of family and its privileges folows hard on the heels of his warning about the eath penalty for those who resume the practices of their old life (vv. 12–13). How do we integrate the harshness of the one with the sense of security evoked by the other? What kind of "family" is this, where the children face a constant threat of expulsion into the realm of death? To understand how we should view the interplay of these two, an analogy may be drawn from a typical family relationship. An act of disobedience on the part of a son or daughter, or even a series of them, does not normally result in expulsion from a family. But a family member may choose to rebel, rejecting the responsibilities of family life altogether. In such a case the individual must face the consequences.

Verse 17 recalls several earlier themes. (1) We are identified with the Son, an identification implicit in verse 15 with its reference to our privilege of crying out to God as Jesus did ("*Abba*"). We, the adopted ones, are placed alongside Christ as coheirs of the promises of God. (2) The inheritance is now available beyond the borders of Israel (4:13–17; Gal. 3:16–18); all who have the Spirit are heirs. (3) Eschatological hope is juxtaposed with present suffering (see Rom. 5:3–4). To be glorified with Christ in the future entails suffering with him in the present. To be in relationship with Christ means to share in his life. We have died with him in the past and will be raised with him in the future (6:3–5); in the meantime we share the same hope he had while we endure suffering as he did (cf. Heb. 12:2). Suffering in the midst of hope is the focus of the next section of the letter.

2.2.5. The Hope of Glory (8:18–39). The pairing of suffering and glory dominates the following discussion, along with the theme of hope. Hope depicts our posture as we endure present suffering while awaiting future glory.

2.2.5.1. The Hope of Glory: Present in Suffering (8:18–27). The stipulation given in verse 17 that sharing in his glory requires sharing in his suffering elicits an immediate qualification in verse 18. Although the two are both part of the Christian life, they are not comparable. In fact, Paul says, they "are not [even] worth comparing." The magnificence of future glory renders present suffering insignificant (cf. 2 Cor. 4:17). The glorification of believers will restore them to the perfected state that Adam and Eve knew in the Garden before the Fall. Or, to put it in the terms of Romans 8:29, glory is to be "conformed to the likeness of his Son." Sin and death will be history; unbroken relationship with God the Father and Christ the Son will be the eternal reality.

The phrase "our present sufferings" (lit., "the sufferings of the present time," v. 18) are those difficulties we endure in this transitional era, when the new age of Christ is overlapping with the old age of Adam (Michaelis, 934). We belong to the era of Christ, yet we still live in a world whose conditions have been defined by the sin of Adam. What Paul means by suffering extends beyond the idea of persecution for the sake of Christ, though it certainly includes that idea. Suffering is the result of the pressure placed on us by the continuing effects of sin and death in this world. In a sense, then, we experience some of the same types of suffering as non-Christians. But in another sense, our experience of them is different, for our sufferings are transformed by the sphere of grace (5:1–5) and work for the good of God's calling (8:28–29).

It is not just believers who experience the tension between the "already" and the "not yet," between what God has done and what he will do. Creation itself, the nonhuman world, awaits with eager anticipation "for the sons of God to be revealed" (v. 19). Revelation concerns the making known of some aspect of God's plan that was previously hidden. The revelation of the sons of God refers to the time at the return of Christ when the whole world will see who really are God's children.

The belief that the end of time will reveal to the world the true identity of those who were faithful to God and those who were not was a common conviction in Jewish apocalyptic writings. Indeed, for at least one writer this public revelation involved a transformation of all people to expose their true identities. The writer of 2 Baruch envisioned that at the end the wicked would be made to look even more evil, while the righteous would be glorified in resplendent beauty (2 Bar. 51:1–6; cf. Dan. 12:3). Similarly, the redemption of our bodies (Rom. 8:23) is also about eschatological transformation from earthly bodies into heavenly ones (cf. 1 Cor. 15:51–52).

The reason why creation is said to anticipate the revelation of the sons of God is explained in verse 20: "Creation was subjected to frustration." The word "frustration" (*mataiotes*, "emptiness, purposelessness") indicates that creation was unable to fulfill i original purpose (see Cranfield). Once mor as in 1:21–22; 5:12–21; 7:8–11, the traditic of Adam comes into play in Paul's argumen Creation's original purpose was thwarted b the sin of Adam and Eve (Gen. 3:17–18). Th consequence of the introduction into creatic of the foreign element of sin was that the wor fell into "bondage to decay" (Rom. 8:21). "Th one who subjected" creation to this state (frustration, while also giving it a reason f hope, was God. That is, with the curse– "cursed is the ground because of you" (Ge 3:17)—came a promise about the defeat (Satan—"he will crush your head" (3:15). (Th theme of hope surfaces again in Rom. 16:20

In the meantime, the earth groans "as in th pains of childbirth" (v. 22). The birth pang imagery, used elsewhere to describe conditio in the last days (Matt. 24:8; John 16:21), is a apt metaphor because it conveys both the sens of present difficulty and the hope that there a definite end in view. Groaning is also used t describe the expectation of believers (Ron 8:23), as well as the manner in which the Spir intercedes on behalf of expectant saints (v 26–27).

Verse 23 marks the return, after the descrip tion of the cosmic dimensions of eschatolog cal anticipation in verses 19–22, to the subje of verses 17b–18: the believers' anticipation (future glory in the midst of present sufferin Like the inanimate world, they also groa while awaiting the final end of this age and th full consummation of the next one. Groanin expresses a deep longing for the fulfillment (God's promises.

The "adoption"/sonship described in vers 23 is a future hope instead of, as in verse 1 a present reality. This is not contradictory: W are sons and daughters now, but a day is com ing when we will enjoy that status fully. Th tension we experience in the interim is wh we should expect, Paul says. For "in this hop we were saved" (v. 24). In other words, hop for what is not seen (which is the only true de inition of hope) defines Christian existenc from the moment one comes to know Christ

Living in hope means exercising enduranc in the interim (v. 25). This is more than wai ing "patiently," if we understand patience to b a passive resignation to wait it out. It is bette to translate the word *hypomone* as "endurance.

/e wait by continuing steadfastly in the work which God has called us. Indeed, we can ıdure because a glorious end is in sight.

The role of the Holy Spirit, so prominent verses 1–17, now comes into view again at vo points related to the "groaning" motif. The esence of the Spirit in our lives causes our oaning, and the presence of weakness in our ves causes the Spirit's groaning. Let us take ese in turn. (1) Although we might underand the clause "we … who have the firstfruits the Spirit" (v. 23) as concessive, that is, ven though we have the firstfruits" (Godet), is preferable to understand this clause in a usal sense (Dunn). That is, we groan *ecause* we have the firstfruits." In this conxt firstfruits (*aparche*) designate the beginng of the eschatological harvest. When used a harvest, *aparche* refers to the first part of crop that is brought in—the first sheaves. ne firstfruits in verse 23 represent the Holy pirit. The idea, then, is this: Because we have e firstfruits, because we already have the pirit's presence with us, we long for the cometion of his work in us. An initial taste makes long to enjoy it all.

There is another aspect to this metaphor as ell. The firstfruits signal that the harvest has gun and that the rest of the crop is going to me. The presence of the Holy Spirit is the arantee that what God has begun in us will completed. Dunn observes that the early urch made a connection between the firstuits and the Spirit. The feast of Pentecost was celebration of the firstfruits of the harvest, d this was when the Spirit was poured out on e one hundred and twenty gathered in the pper room (Acts 2).

(2) The weakness we experience as those ho belong to this age causes the Spirit to oan in intercession (vv. 26–27). The dwelling Spirit is not only a guarantee for us future life; he is also a participant in our prent life. The unusual description of prayer as oaning is suited to a context where the groangs of believers and of creation have been the pic of discussion. The Spirit assists us by terceding on our behalf because of our weakss. The context, with its emphasis on sufferg and on the groaning that arises in our spirits anticipation of what is yet to come, leads us think that this weakness describes our curnt condition in this period of anticipation.

So the problem is not that we do not know *how* to pray, but our circumstances are such that we often do not know *what* to pray. There is a certain confusion that accompanies living in two realms simultaneously. What do we pray when the conditions of the present age, to which we no longer belong, seem so much more real and pressing than those of the world we can only experience partially in the here and now? Although we are assured of deliverance from death and release from temptation at the resurrection, how do we pray in the meantime when sin and death still confront us? We have this assurance, however, that the Spirit is praying for us "in accordance with God's will." Furthermore, though we do not comprehend what the Spirit is praying, God certainly does because he "knows the mind of the Spirit" (v. 27).

We now turn to the question about how the Spirit aids us in prayer. Is Paul saying that we pray with the help of the Spirit, or that the Holy Spirit prays for us? Or does Paul perhaps have in mind a combination of these two? That is, is the phenomenon described here what we know as praying in tongues (which Paul calls praying in the Spirit in 1 Cor. 14:14–15), in which the Holy Spirit prays through the individual? If it is the latter, then this is of particular interest to those readers for whom this experience is real, especially since the biblical texts about it are few in number.

An initial objection to this approach is that Paul uses the terminology of groaning rather than of praying in tongues or in the Spirit. Yet, as noted above, Paul's terminology throughout this section is influenced by the groaning motif that he introduced in verse 22. Consequently, we might expect him to express himself here in a way that he does not elsewhere. There are other objections to this interpretation. Moo argues against seeing tongues in verse 26 because (1) in his view, 1 Corinthians 12:30 limits speaking in tongues to certain individuals, while this text presupposes that all believers have the experience being described. (2) Moreover, he interprets the Greek word *alaletois* (NIV "that words cannot express") as meaning "unspoken," which would rule out speaking in tongues. What Paul is describing, according to Moo, is the Spirit's "language of prayer," which "takes place in our hearts (cf. v. 27) in a manner imperceptible to us."

There is no room to discuss this issue to any great extent. Nevertheless, there are some points that should be raised. (1) To begin with, there is no standard Pentecostal/charismatic interpretation of this text. Some Pentecostal writers (e.g., Lim, 140, n.3) agree with the majority of New Testament scholars that something other than glossolalia is being discussed here. Fee, on the other hand, has made a strong case for seeing the activity described here as praying in the Spirit or speaking in tongues (the interested reader should read his detailed argument: 1994, 575–86). This line of interpretation is not new or Pentecostal in origin—Origen taught it (*De oratione* 2) and others have since then, most notably E. Käsemann (although the nature of his argument has not won many converts).

(2) The word *alaletois* ("that words cannot express"), which Moo translates as "unspoken" and others understand as "inexpressible" (e.g., Fitzmyer), Fee interprets as "without words" (1994, 583). The groanings are not understandable to the human mind, according to Fee, because they are not expressed in intelligible words. This interpretation suggests that what Paul is describing here is the same phenomenon as praying in the Spirit or praying in tongues. There are two similarities between what we know of the Spirit's groaning and praying in the Spirit: They are expressions in prayer that the mind cannot comprehend (1 Cor. 14:2, 6–11, 13–19), and it is the Spirit who prays. In 1 Corinthians 14:2 Paul speaks of mysteries uttered "by the Spirit" (the NIV reads "with his spirit," but this is not the best translation—see Fee, 1994, 218, n.525). Both texts, then, depict the Spirit praying through the believer as he or she prays in tongues.

(3) Finally, Romans 8:26–27 is a commentary on the statement in 1 Corinthians 14:4 that "he who speaks in a tongue edifies himself." We are aided in our weakness, that is, we are edified, as the Spirit intercedes through us in accordance with the will of God. The nature of his will for us is the subject to which he now turns in verses 28–29.

2.2.5.2. The Hope of Glory: Guaranteed by God's Righteousness (8:28–39). The grammatical subject of verse 28 is unclear in the Greek text. The KJV makes "all things" the subject: "And we know that all things work together" (so also Barrett; Käsemann). The majority of scholars, however, supply "God as the subject, despite the fact that his nam does not appear in the first part of the vers (e.g., NIV; Bruce, 1985). Thus, God works i all things for the good of the believer. Fe argues that "the Spirit" is the subject, eve though, as with taking God as the subject, on has to read the Spirit into the verse. He make the point that because the Spirit has been th subject in the preceding verses, the most na ural reading sees him as the subject of th verse as well (1994, 589–90). As Dunn note Paul may not have been concerned to remov the ambiguity since the meaning is the sam regardless of the subject of the verse.

We must not miss the connection of verse 28–29 with the preceding discussion about th Spirit's intercession for the will of God to b effected in our lives. These verses not onl state what the will of God is, they also assu us that what the Spirit prays for on our beha is working out in our daily lives. The good which all things work is related to the purpos to which we have been called: conformity the likeness (image) of Christ. His will is th we be conformed to Christ.

It is Christ's righteousness that guarantee this glorious result. His continual saving acti ity in us is his active intervention to make a aspects of our lives work toward this goal. T put it differently, in the sphere of grace life transposed to a higher key (see comments c 5:2–5). Life is no longer a series of meanin less events, a series of trivial pursuits, or a su cession of acts determined by fate. Althoug not everything that we experience is good— for example, our sin and its results—all life's events are made to contribute toward th good, which is the formation of Christ's imag in us. We will be completely conformed Christ at the resurrection. Yet, by divine gra and through the events of our lives, the qua ity of Christ is already being formed in us (c 2 Cor. 3:18).

The particular words Paul uses in ver 29—"foreknew" and "predestined"—hav engendered debate about whether this descri tion of salvation leaves any room for the fre will response of people to God's salvific wor This is not the place to attempt to solve th debate between Calvinists and Arminian What should be noted, however, are a fe basic points.

(1) The main point of these verses is to proide certainty about the believer's eternal
uture based on God's sovereignty. What he
as purposed will come about. To that end,
aul brings in the idea that it was God's plan
rom the very beginning to save men and
vomen. Lest there be any thought that cir-
umstances on earth might circumvent God's
lan, the apostle shows that God determined
is course of action before we had any oppor-
nity to respond.

(2) The necessity of human response is
iven in verse 28—things work "for the good
f those who love him."

(3) Similar to Galatians 4:9, where the
tatement that we know God is immediately
ollowed with the clarification that we are
nown by him, and in line with the emphasis
n Romans on God's initiative in salvation,
aul qualifies "of those who love him." In the
ext phrase he specifies that those who love
im are the ones whom he has already called.
His calling in love (cf. 1:5–7) precedes our
oving response.

(4) Finally, Paul does not explain what he
neans when he writes that God "foreknew"
nd "predestined" us. I agree with Dunn that
hese two words are hard to distinguish. Per-
aps the second is meant to clarify the first
Bultmann, *TDNT*, 1.715). What is certain, as
nentioned above, is that these words show
od's predetermination to save humankind
nd that such predetermination guarantees its
ccurrence. Perhaps it is best to say that free
ill and God's foreknowledge are both com-
atible. That is, we may affirm both ideas withut compromising the validity of either one.
The topic of predestination returns in ch. 9.)

Verse 30, beginning with the second verb in
erse 29, resumes Paul's description about the
rder in which God's righteousness is carried
ut. The call is the call to salvation (1:5–7), to
hich people must respond. Justification, the
redominant theme of 3:21–5:21, describes
hat God does as he declares us to be righous in his sight. Glorification is the culmi-
ation of the process of salvation, in which we
gain the glory lost in the Garden by the first
dam by becoming like Christ—the second
dam (1 Cor. 15:45).

The last section of chapter 8 (vv. 31–39) is
triumphant summary of Paul's description of
od's righteousness or saving activity. These verses evoke a mood of celebration as they pile up resounding exclamations about the security of the believer within the sphere of grace. They offer a final answer to the sense of despair with which the first major section of the letter ended (3:9–20). They also provide the reader with a brief oasis before the detailed argument of chapters 9–11.

This section will be dealt with rather succinctly because the themes are by now familiar to us. Like a work of art or a piece of music, this section is best appreciated by taking it all in as a whole and experiencing its emotional impact. My temptation—which I resisted—was simply to repeat verses 31–39 here without comment. But there are certain elements of this text that we will appreciate more with some explanation.

In this section Paul begins with a quick succession of brief responses to rhetorical questions about the believer's assurance of future glory (vv. 31–34), after which he offers his final extended proclamation about the power of the love of God and of Christ (vv. 35–39). Having made the transition already in verses 28–29 away from a particular focus on the work of the Holy Spirit, the remaining part of chapter 8 celebrates the work of God and Christ.

The answer given in verse 31 is not only the first but also the most definitive response to these questions about the believer's assurance in Christ. There is no need to say more than: "If God is for us, who can be against us?" But this is the time to celebrate, and Paul is just getting warmed up.

The cross is the most convincing demonstration of the conviction that God is for us (v. 32). Is there any possible room for doubt when the cross is the starting point? The only deduction to be made is that his grace will continue toward us (cf. 5:8–9). Indeed, his grace is what gives us confidence that we will receive a favorable ruling before the divine court. There will be no successful charge raised against any believer because God is the judge and the ones being charged are his chosen (cf. Col. 3:12)—those whom he will justify (see Rom. 8:30).

In verse 34 the theme of condemnation reappears from verse 1, but this time with further elaboration. Behind the confidence that we will not receive what our sins deserve when we stand before God—that is, that we will be justified (v. 33)—is not only the death of Christ. There is also his intercession on our behalf (the Holy Spirit also intercedes for us, vv. 26–27). It is not that the work of the cross was incomplete. Jesus' death was sufficient. What is being addressed here is the question of whether we may be confident that his salvific work will apply to each of us on the day of judgment. We may have complete confidence because Christ has an exalted position in heaven alongside of God (being at the right hand signifies authority; cf. Ps. 110:1), and he uses his position to be our advocate. The verb "intercedes" in the Greek is in the present tense, indicating that this is a continuing work.

In 5:2 Christ was pictured as the one who leads us into the presence of God at the time of our salvation (through Christ we "gained access" into the sphere of grace). In 8:34 he stands before God so that we may be able to stay in the presence of God for all of eternity. There will be no condemnation or separation from God at the final judgment. Christ as our great High Priest (Heb. 7:25; 1 John 2:1) is effective in his intercession because he is the one who died and rose on our behalf. As Pelagius commented, the type of intercession that Christ offers is a presentation of himself (113).

Verses 35–39, which contain two lists, are bracketed by the thought that nothing will separate us from divine love, whether that be the love of Christ (v. 35) or of God (v. 39). The first list of things that cannot separate us from Christ's love (v. 35) are all, save the last ("sword"), conditions that Paul had endured (2 Cor. 11:26–27; 12:10). With the confidence that comes from personal experience Paul declares that "in all these things we are more than conquerors" (Rom. 8:37). Paul would discover later that even death by the sword could not separate him from Christ (cf. Phil. 1:20–23). The quotation in verse 36 from Psalm 44:22 is intended to remind the hearer that this great confidence is the hope of the one who suffers (Rom. 8:17–18).

This great confidence is now reexpressed in verses 38–39, as Paul enumerates every possible element that might threaten the believer's security in Christ. The second list begins the way that the first one ended: with death. That death is featured prominently at the climax of one list and the starting point of the other is significant. For the one in Adam, death mea separation from God; death is the final salvo sin. But for the one in Christ, death is powe less to destroy one's relationship with God.

The final element in the second sequenc "nor anything else in all creation," is a catch phrase. Paul is saying in essence here: If I ha left anything out, include it here as anoth thing that cannot separate us from God's lov When you read this verse, then, put in he whatever aspect of life gives you the greate cause for concern regarding your relationsh with Christ.

How do we summarize such a wonderf chapter? By answering the question given verse 31—"What, then, shall we say in respon to this?"—with one word: "Hallelujah!"

2.3. God's Righteousness Toward Israel (9:1–11:36)

It is somewhat jarring to be moved so su denly from celebration to lamentation. T abrupt change in mood from the conclusion chapter 8 to the beginning of chapter 9 signa a change of topic. Having discussed in the fir eight chapters the righteousness of God towa Jew and Gentile alike, Paul now focuses God's righteousness, or his saving activit toward the nation of Israel. Why does he di cuss Israel when what he has already argu applies to the Jew? The response of the Jev to the gospel—the very ones to whom t gospel was "promised beforehand through h prophets" (1:2)—was lagging far behind th of the Gentiles. This situation raised question If these are God's chosen people, then wl have they not responded to God's chosen Me siah? Why are Gentiles coming into the kin dom in increasing numbers, while t proportion of Jews within the church conti ues to decline?

In 9:6 Paul draws out a possible implicati of this state of affairs in order to refute Although it might seem as if God's word (h covenantal promises to the Jews) has come naught, Paul will contend in chapters 9–11 th the reverse is true. It is of the utmost impo tance for the apostle to demonstrate th Israel's rejection of the gospel does not ca doubt on the legitimacy of what God promis this nation. Such a conclusion would be challenge the very nature of God and to sa that his righteousness toward Israel had faile

And it would be to misunderstand the gospel message itself, which is rooted in the purposes of God first proclaimed to the prophets. Paul's exegesis of the Old Testament is critical to his argument, then, because he wants to show that this current state of affairs is actually in line with God's promises.

This discussion would have had relevance for both the Gentiles and the Jews in the house churches in Rome. In the Introduction ("Occasion and Purpose") we explained that Paul wrote this letter in order to familiarize the Christians in Rome with his ministry and message in preparation for his first visit there. His intention was to gain their support for his missionary trip to Spain. He was clearly aware that distortions and criticisms of his message had already reached the capital city. And, of course, he could not know exactly what they had heard or how much of it they had believed. So this letter is an attempt to set the record straight.

The type of attack Paul faced had moved beyond a criticism of his message. It had become more personal. The heartfelt and earnest manner in which he declares his love for his own people in 9:1–3 and 10:1 implies that the apostle to the Gentiles was accused of having forsaken those of his own race. Because Paul was one of the key players in the rapid entry of the Gentiles into the church, he had become a prime target for the resentment among Jewish believers that the church was losing its Jewish roots.

It wasn't just the shift in numbers, however, that had created the animosity. It was also the manner in which Paul had "accommodated" the Gentiles by removing covenantal markers such as circumcision and food laws from his gospel message. It is no wonder, his Jewish detractors would have concluded, that so many Gentiles are being attracted to Paul's gospel. To them, Paul was a threat and a traitor. We see, then, the significance of Paul's counterclaim that he actually envisions the success of his mission to the Gentiles resulting in the salvation of the Jews (10:19; 11:13–14).

What Paul is doing in chapters 9–11, then, is providing both Jew and Gentile with the information they need to judge him fairly and, as Paul hopes, favorably. The apostle has other concerns as well. He knows about the precarious position of the Jews in Rome. He is aware of the difficulty that the reentry of Christian Jews back into their house churches in Rome, after Claudius's expulsion of the Jews from that city lapsed, created for them. He also intends that this section will help the Jews come to grips with the theological reasons for the rejection of a vast majority of their own and give them hope that a brighter future for the nation is in view—"all Israel will be saved" (11:26).

But, no doubt, he wants the Gentiles to hear this discussion too. This is most apparent in the last section of chapter 11, where Paul deals with an inappropriate attitude that has arisen among the Gentiles because of their ascendancy within the expanding church. Their situation predisposed them to look down on the Jews within their midst. Thus, Paul warns them about taking their adoption as God's children for granted. This concern carries over into 14:1–15:13, where he comes at the problem of attitude again as he discusses the sensitivity that Jew and Gentile should have toward one another in terms of the observance of food laws and the like. There, however, he is especially concerned with the unchristian attitude of the Gentiles (note esp. 15:1–9).

In terms of structure, 9:1–5 forms an introduction to the whole section, as it lays out the dilemma of the Jews' rejection of the gospel. In 9:6 Paul enters a thesis statement that much of the remainder of these three chapters sets out to defend: "It is not as though God's word had failed." He then shows the plan of God in salvation history (9:6b–29) and argues that the greater part of Israel has not accepted the gospel, whereas the Gentiles have done so (9:30–10:21). Nevertheless, the election of Israel means the eventual salvation of Israel, despite the temporary hardening that has occurred (11:1–32). The sovereignty of God in all of this leads to the climactic doxology of 11:33–36. In short, God's righteousness toward Israel has not ceased, but will result by his grace in a glorious day of salvation, which will include all Israel, both the remnant and those now hardened.

2.3.1. The Problem (9:1–5). The problem Paul raises, as we have noted above, is how to explain the rejection of Christ by the very ones to whom God gave the promises of a Messiah in the first place (1:2). He takes up the subject on a personal note by entering a passionate lament for Israel. Reminiscent of the plea that

Moses made to God that he might spare his people (Ex. 32:30–32), Paul offers himself as a substitute for the sake of the Jews. That is, he expresses the desire to be accursed (*anathema*) and cut off from the "Christ" (i.e., the Messiah) in order that his fellow Jews might be saved (9:3). How exactly Paul thought that this might happen, or if he actually conceived of it as a possibility, is beyond our knowing. Nevertheless, he communicates clearly his anguish for the state of his own race (see also 10:1).

Another aspect of Paul's frame of mind comes through in verse 1: his determination that his expression of intense concern be believed. Thus he states it in the form of an oath (cf. 2 Cor. 11:31; Gal. 1:20; 1 Tim. 2:7). Note that the role of the Holy Spirit as a witness to the truth of Paul's attestation is similar to what we saw in Romans 8:16 (the Spirit bears witness with our spirit that we are children of God).

By recounting in 9:4–5 the many covenantal privileges given to Israel, Paul lays bare the heart of the problem that he is grappling with here. Despite the fact that Israel has been given all of these prerogatives, she still remains opposed to the plan of God in Jesus Christ. This list of benefits continues what Paul began to enumerate in 3:1–2, where, after asserting that the privileges of election are many, he mentioned only the giving of the law.

Without examining each of these covenantal privileges individually (and certainly Paul meant them to be heard as a whole to impress on the hearer all that the Jews had been given), a few of them jump out at us because of their significance in the letter. (1) The mention of the law reminds the reader once again that for Paul the law was intended by God as a blessing to Israel (cf. 7:12). (2) The inclusion of adoption as a privilege of the Jews, despite his argument that adoption is for all those in Christ (8:13–17, 23), serves notice that the adoption of Israel continues to have significance. There is no thought here, in other words, that the church has supplanted Israel, the one whom God chose as his son (e.g., Ex. 4:22–23; Deut. 14:1–2). In reality, God's plan for his chosen son is not yet fulfilled (Rom. 11). (3) By concluding his list with the fact that Christ's human ancestry was through the Jews, he highlights the paradox that they are rejecting the very one given to them.

2.3.2. God's Purpose (9:6–29). Some see in this section a strong argument for Calvinism, in which God's sovereignty in election is seen to predetermine the eternal destiny of all individuals, either for salvation or damnation. Unlike 8:29–30, however, the election of individuals is not the topic here.[7] Rather, the election of God in chapter 9 concerns the election of nations and of peoples (Klein, 197–98; Ellison, 43).

The individuals named in verses 7–13 are those whom God elected to fulfill roles necessary for the advancement of his work with the nations. The emphasis, therefore, is not on the individual destinies of the ones named, but on the historical roles they played for the nations they represent. We may add, then, that God's election of nations is not determinative for the people within those nations. For example, whereas the election of Israel was God's decision, the participation of a particular Israelite in the covenantal blessings depended on his or her individual response to God. In short, God will achieve his purposes for the nations. The inclusion of a particular individual within his saving grace hinges on one's personal response to God's mercy.

The central theological statement of chapters 9–11 is made in 9:6; what follows is a defense and elaboration of this proposition. To claim that God's word has not failed is the primary issue for Paul. As Stuhlmacher comments, only after showing that the gospel is effective for Israel "does his message really deserve to be called the power of salvation for *all* who believe, for the Jews first, but also for the Gentiles, as he designated it in 1:16f."

The first stage of Paul's defense that God's word or promise to Israel has not been proven false by her rejection of Christ comes in verse 6b. With the phrase "for not all who are descended from Israel are Israel" the apostle makes a distinction between national Israel and true Israel. This is a crucial point for his argument. If this distinction is recognized, then it allows Paul to contend that even though national Israel has rejected the promised gospel, the true Israel is presently the recipient and beneficiary of the promises of God.

To defend this distinction from Scripture, Paul recalls two similar moments in salvation history, from two successive generations (vv. 7–9, 10–13), when God chose between two brothers to advance his salvific plan. As was ne case when Paul discussed Adam and Christ and their roles in salvation history, these two ets of brothers serve as representatives. Jnlike 5:12–21, however, where the emphasis was on what Adam and Christ did and how heir actions defined the old and new ages, the mphasis here is solely on the sovereign election of God. When God selected one brother nd rejected the other, it was not on the basis f what either had done, nor did it have to do vith their personal salvation or damnation. His lection of these individuals was based on his wn purpose, and it concerned the destinies of ational entities.

One cannot, Paul contends, define Israel on ne basis of ancestry from Abraham alone. Such n assertion, of course, was a direct challenge to he Jews' belief that the members of the ovenant people were so defined. (1) His first iblical proof of this proposition is this: Abraham had two descendants, Isaac and Ishmael, ut only Isaac was selected to represent the chilren of God, the children of promise. As Gensis 21:12 declared: "It is through Isaac that our offspring will be reckoned" (Rom. 9:7).

God's promise to Abraham of a son, which vas a focal point in Romans 4, figures promiently in 9:8–9. We recall the discussion of hapter 4 concerning the justification of Abraam through grace rather than by works. God rought about the promise through his initiaive, since Abraham and Sarah were past childearing years. The only stipulation pressed on Abraham was that he accept the promise in aith. By now reintroducing the promise made o Abraham, Paul recalls the discussion of it in hapter 4 and the overriding theme of grace ound there—a theme that will become increasngly explicit as the argument progresses.

(2) Paul's second proof that ancestry alone s insufficient to define the people of God conerns God's election of Jacob over Esau (vv. 0–13). Lest anyone think that there were rounds for a distinction between Ishmael and saac because they were half brothers, Paul ives the example of two individuals who not nly had the same mother and father, but who vere also "twins." God chose one brother to ontinue the line of promise solely on the basis f his will. In fact, his selection of Jacob over Esau reversed the standard pecking order, in vhich the younger would be expected to serve he older (cf. v. 12, which cites Gen. 25:23).

The rather startling statement in verse 13, "Jacob I loved, but Esau I hated" (a quote from Mal. 1:2–3), deserves some comment. (1) Let us remember the context here: to show that Israel cannot presume that being the elect of God has anything to do with ancestry or any other type of merit. (2) The love and hatred of God depicted here are not expressions of emotion. They have to do with the actions of God in choosing one over the other (cf. Matt. 6:24). (3) Jacob and Esau represent Israel and the Edomites. The phrase "the older will serve the younger" is taken from Genesis 25:23, which begins by identifying Jacob and Esau as two nations. Furthermore, the context of Malachi 1:2–3 is also about the Edomites and Israel. (4) The selection of Jacob did not mean that God refused to act graciously toward the descendants of Esau. For example, the Lord prohibited the Israelites from making war or taking advantage of the Edomites when they passed through their region during their exodus pilgrimage (Deut. 2:4–6).

The double emphasis in verses 11–12 that God's election was uninfluenced by human deeds ("before the twins ... had done anything good or bad"; "not by works") underscores the sovereignty of God. I agree with Dunn that by mentioning "works" Paul is bringing the idea of the law back into view. Paul has just recalled the content of chapter 4 (in 9:7–9), where law and works were contrasted with grace and faith. It is this association of ideas from earlier on that explains the question in verse 14.

"What then shall we say?" (v. 14) appears once again in a context in which Paul's Jewish dialogue partner raises an objection (cf. 3:5; 6:1; 7:7). The question that follows is not about the ethics of election. The language of righteousness here indicates that the objector is asking about God's faithfulness to the covenant (Wright, 1980, 211). This is an objection to Paul's argument as a whole (9:6–13). That is, if God is making a distinction about the identity of true Israel that is not based on being a descendant of Abraham, and if this distinction has nothing to do with works (i.e., keeping the covenantal law), then is God being faithful to the covenant?

The answer is framed by "God's mercy" (vv. 15–16). Verse 15 quotes what God said to Moses after the golden calf incident. In response to Moses' request that God reveal himself, God complied by speaking of his compassion and mercy. Paul cites Exodus 33:19 here to make the point that God's mercy, rather than human considerations, explains his election. God is acting rightly toward his covenant people because he is acting in accordance with his mercy, which is how they were formed in the first place (Rom. 9:7–13). And, as he will argue below, it continues to explain how God has expanded the people of God to include Gentiles with Jews (vv. 24ff.).

The purpose of God in salvation history is also illustrated by the way God used Pharaoh (v. 17). Pharaoh was raised up by God so that his divine power might be displayed and his name proclaimed in all of the earth. God's name was revealed to the nations through his dealings with Pharaoh. Pharaoh's magicians recognized the finger of God (Ex. 8:19); some Egyptians left with the Israelites when they were set free (Ex. 12:38); and the Philistines heard about the power of God because of the plagues (1 Sam. 4:8). In short, even God's hardening is informed by his mercy. Later Paul will argue that Israel has suffered a similar hardening, but her hardening is temporary because of God's mercy (Rom. 11).

As mentioned earlier, Romans 9 is often used to defend the doctrine of predestination. Pharaoh's hardening is often taken as evidence that God has mercy on some to save them and hardens others to damn them. It should be borne in mind, however, that in the Exodus account it was Pharaoh who hardened his own heart repeatedly (Ex. 7:13, 22; 8:19; 9:7) before God finally seconded the motion (Ex. 9:12). Moreover, what God did with Pharaoh was not about determining his final destiny, but about bringing glory to his name and setting his people free.

Verse 19 enters another objection to Paul's argument. If God elects, if he determines his purpose for the nations, then why should the peoples be blamed? After all, no one can resist what God has determined to accomplish. Paul's response (vv. 20–21) begins with a series of rhetorical questions, which derive mainly from the Old Testament metaphor of the potter and the clay (Isa. 29:16; 45:9; Jer. 18:1–6). Questioning the Creator about his designs for the different parts of his creation is as inane as the pot demanding an explanation from the potter.

Verse 22 begins the application of the potte illustration, but the presence of *de* ("but"; nc in NIV) at the beginning of this verse inform the hearer that the ways of God wit humankind are somewhat different than th ways of a potter with a lump of clay. Wherea the potter forms the clay for purposes that rang from the noble to the common (v. 21), God doe not create some vessels for destruction.

However, as the phrase "prepared in advanc for glory" denotes his election to salvation, th phrase "prepared for destruction" has bee taken to mean that God does elect some t damnation (Moo). But there is a significant dif ference in the way Paul describes God's deal ings with the vessels of wrath (v. 22) and th vessels of mercy (v. 23). It is only the vessel of mercy that are "prepared in advance [*proe toimazo*] for glory" (cf. 8:17, 30). The verb th Paul uses in verse 22, which is also translated a "prepared" in the NIV, is *katartizo*. As Dun points out, Paul's usual use of this verb, whic means "fit together" or "restore" (e.g., 1 Co 1:10; 2 Cor. 13:11; Gal. 6:1; 1 Thess. 3:10), doe not lend itself to the idea that these vessels hav actually been created for destruction. Rathe they are being fitted for destruction. In othe words, the emphasis is not on what made thes people unrighteous, but on how God is respond ing to their unrighteousness.

Romans 1:18–28 helps explain what Pau means here. The wrath of God is currently bein poured out on sinners as he releases them to th results of their evil desires. They are being fit ted for destruction as they continue in the down ward spiral of sin. There is still a final wrath t come (which is what "destruction" [*apoleia* denotes), and there is still time to avoid it.

Indeed, it appears as if Paul has his intro ductory statements from 1:16–18 in view as h dictates these verses. The dual aspect of th purpose of God given in 9:22—"to show hi wrath and make his power known"—mirro this earlier text. The gospel is the power o God for salvation (1:16), and this is what Go is revealing to the world; but he also manifest his wrath on unrepentant sinners. In order tha the world might know his saving power, Go bears with "great patience the objects [lit., ves sels] of his wrath" (9:22). That is, his patienc allows opportunity for repentance (see 2:4). I is this opportunity for repentance, it is thi expression of mercy, that God is holding ou not just to the Gentiles, but to the Jews as well (11:23–24).

The answer to the objection in verse 19 is similar to the one given to the objection of verse 14. Both focus on the mercy of God, which is the context in which God's elective plans are conceived and carried out. To the critic of God's dealings with humankind comes the response that he deals with men and women not as they deserve, but with mercy. We deserve our just punishment; there is no necessity that demands God's patience with us.

The ones who have been "prepared in advance for glory" (v. 23) are those whom God has called, both Jew and Gentile (v. 24). The argument in 9:6b–24 has established that God's calling is not bound by race or works, but flows out of his mercy. He is free, therefore, to call Gentiles as well as Jews, as the following Old Testament texts demonstrate.

The Old Testament texts prove what Paul asserted in 9:6a—the word of God has not failed. Although the majority of the Jews have rejected the gospel message and the Gentiles are the ones who are receiving it with joy, this situation is not an indication that God's promises have been broken. His word has not failed because the prophets spoke of (1) only a remnant of Israel being saved (vv. 27–29), and (2) the salvation of the Gentiles (vv. 25–26).

The two references that Paul selects to show the calling of the Gentiles are both from Hosea (Hos. 2:23 and 1:10). What makes them remarkable is that Hosea was writing about the redemption of the northern tribes of Israel, not the Gentiles. But Paul sees in Hosea the principle that God gathers people who were not his people, that is, those who were estranged from him, into relationship with him through his gracious calling.

2.3.3. Israel's Failure (9:30–10:21). Paul's first line of defense for the thesis statement in 9:6a that God's word has not failed was to focus on God's purpose (9:6b–29). The objection that God's word has failed, Paul argued, fails to understand what that purpose actually is. Yet, that argument does not tell the whole story. Now Paul examines the other side of the equation. The reason that the Gentiles rather than the Jews are flooding into the kingdom of God also has to do with Jewish failure.

Although the chapter division suggests that 10:1 is the point where the argument takes on a new direction, 9:30–10:21 forms a cohesive unit of thought. The new line of argument is initiated with the by-now-familiar phrase, "What then shall we say?" which has been used to signal that another objection to Paul's teaching is about to be dealt with. Verses 30–31 state the great paradox that Paul is attempting to explain. The Gentiles, who were not seeking righteousness, have obtained it; the Jews, who were pursuing "a law of righteousness," have not attained their goal.

This is not to contradict what Paul said earlier in 2:14–15 that there are some Gentiles who engage in commendable behavior. Righteousness for Paul is not simply a matter of ethics. It pertains less to right living than it does to right relationship, because righteousness is only obtained in relationship to God—a relationship that he makes possible by what he does, that is, by his righteousness. What Paul means here, then, is that the Gentiles were not seeking righteousness because they were outside of the covenant relationship. It was only within the covenant that relationship with God was possible. But they have now obtained it because the gospel proclaims that God's righteousness is bringing people into relationship with himself outside of the old covenantal boundaries. To put it another way, the people of God are no longer defined by race, but by faith in Jesus.

The Jews, on the other hand, have been pursuing a law that promised righteousness and doing so with zeal (10:2), but have been unsuccessful in their pursuit because they do not know ("their zeal is not based on knowledge") that righteousness from God comes through his Son (10:2–3). They have been pursuing it by works rather than by faith in Jesus Christ (cf. 3:20). It is one's reaction to Christ—the stone in 9:33—that is crucial. Paul conflates two passages from Isaiah (28:16 and 8:14) to establish this. In Isaiah 8:14 it is the Lord God who is the stone, and stumbling over him is a sign of judgment. For Paul, to stumble over Christ is to fall off the path that leads to righteousness.

That the Jews do not know God's righteousness (10:3) seems a strange statement to make about the people to whom God has given his law. But the reference to God's righteousness here is not a reference to an ethical standard. God's righteousness, as we have

PASSAGES INDICATING THE DEITY OF CHRIST

Many passages in both the OT and NT help to demonstrate that Jesus Christ is fully God, a teaching often denied by sectarian groups and cults. This chart compiles the major passages that support this important Christian doctrine.

In the Old Testament

God's Son is to rule on the throne at God's right hand, equal in power with the Father	Pss. 2:7–12; 110:1–2
The promised Messiah will be "Immanuel" (i.e., "God with us")	Isa 7:4 (cf. Mt 1:23)
The promised Messiah will be "Mighty God," ruling eternally	Isa 9:6–7
The ruler born in Bethlehem has origin from all eternity	Mic 5:2
The righteous Branch of David is called "The LORD Our Righteousness"	Jer 23:5–6; 33:15–16
The one who will appear in the temple is "the Lord"	Mal 3:1

Self-Affirmations of Jesus

His is "Lord" of the Sabbath, having created it	Mt 12:8; Mk 2:28; Lk 6:5
He is the "I am" of Ex 3:14	Jn 8:57–58
He is one with the Father	Jn 10:30
He is the judge of the living and the dead	Mt 25:31–32; Jn 5:22, 27 (cf. Ps 98:9)
He deserves the same honor as the Father	Jn 5:23
He made himself equal with God	Jn 5:16–18; 10:33
He, like God, is everywhere present	Mt 28:20
He, like God, is all-powerful	Mt 28:18
He, like God, is all-knowing	Jn 1:47–50 (cf. 2:22–23)
He has the authority, which belongs only to God, to forgive sins	Mt 9:2–7; Mk 2:5–12; Lk 5:20–25
Believing in him and believing in God are the same	Jn 14:1
To know him is to know the Father, and vice versa	Mt 11:27; Lk 10:22
He is the only way to the Father, and to see him is to see the Father	Jn 14:6–10

Other Testimonies in the Gospels and in Acts

Jesus is the eternal Word of God	Jn 1:1
Jesus was present at the time of creation	Jn 1:2–3
Jesus is the One and Only God	Jn 1:18
Thomas confessed Jesus as "My Lord and my God"	Jn 20:28
Evil spirits recognized Jesus as "the Holy One of God" (an OT term used for God)	Mk 1:24 (cf. Isa 6:3; 30:15)
Jesus is "Lord" (the same Greek word as translates "Yahweh" ("LORD") in the LXX	Ac 2:36; 10:36

Jesus is "the Holy and Righteous One"	Ac 3:14 (cf. Isa 6:3; 30:15; Jer 23:6)
Jesus is the coming Judge	Ac 10:42; 17:31 (cf. Ps 98:9)
The Testimony of Paul	
Jesus is "God over all"	Ro 9:5
Jesus is in very nature God and equal with God	Php 2:6
Jesus is "Lord" (the same Greek word as translates "Yahweh" ["LORD"] in the LXX)	Ro 10:9; 1Co 2:8; Php 2:11; Col 2:6
Jesus is the fullness of the Deity	Col 1:19; 2:9
Jesus was present at the time of creation	Col 1:16
There is only one God and Lord	1Co 8:5–6; Eph 4:5–6
Jesus is "our great God and Savior"	Tit 2:13 (cf. 1Ti 4:10; 2Ti 1:10)
The Testimony of the Other New Testament Letters	
The Son is "the exact representation of God"	Heb 1:3
The Son is God	Heb 1:8
God commands the angels to worship the Son, an act that belongs only to God	Heb 1:6 (cf. Mt 4:10; Rev 19:10; 22:8–9)
Jesus, like God, is unchanging	Heb 13:8 (cf. Mal 3:6)
Jesus is "our God and Savior"	2Pe 1:1
Jesus is "our Lord and Savior"	2Pe 1:11; 2:20; 3:18
Jesus Christ is "the Righteous One"	1Jn 2:1 (cf. Jer 23:5)
To acknowledge the Son is to acknowledge the Father	1Jn 2:23
The Son Jesus Christ is "the true God"	1Jn 5:20
The Testimony in Revelation	
Jesus is "the Alpha and Omega," "the First and the Last" (a term ascribed to God in the OT)	Rev 1:8; 2:8; 21:6; 22:13 (cf. Isa 44:6; 48:12)
Jesus is "the Almighty"	Rev 1:8
Jesus is "the Living One"	Rev 1:18 (cf. Jos 3:10; Pss 42:2; 84:2)
Jesus holds the key of David (ascribed in the OT to God)	Rev 3:7 (cf. Isa 22:22)
Jesus is "Lord of Lords"	Rev 17:14; 19:16
Jesus received worship from people, an act that belongs only to God	Rev 5:11–14 (cf. 19:10; 22:8–9)

interpreted it throughout the letter, is his saving activity that brings people into relationship with him. What Israel does not understand is that God's saving activity is now in Christ. They do not realize that "Christ is the end of the law" (10:4). Not that he brings the value of the law to an end. All Scripture, certainly including the Old Testament, is intended to teach us (1 Cor. 10:6, 11; 2 Tim. 3:16). Moreover, there are aspects of the law that Christ affirms in his ministry, giving them continuing relevance in the New Testament age (see, e.g., Matt. 5:17–48, where Jesus strengthened individual laws by broadening and deepening them).

Rather, Christ is the end of the law *in terms of righteousness*. That is, the law no longer has a role to play in either obtaining or maintaining righteousness. This is what verse 4 teaches. Christ is the end (*telos*) of the law so that, or with the result that, righteousness may come to everyone through faith. The law is no longer a barrier that separates those who have access to righteousness and those who do not.

"The righteousness that is by the law" is mentioned in verse 5, where Paul cites Leviticus 18:5 in order to set up a contrast with "the righteousness that is by faith" (Rom. 10:6). It is with the latter that his interest lies in the next few verses. "Do not say in your heart" is taken from Deuteronomy 9:4, a passage in which the Israelites were being cautioned about their reaction when they took possession of the Promised Land. They were not to assume that their success had anything to do with their own righteousness.

What follows in 10:6b–8a is adapted from Deuteronomy 30:12–14, where the Israelites were told that the law was not too difficult for them to obey because it was present with them. The law was not beyond their reach; it was not in heaven or on the other side of the sea. Paul substitutes the Greek word *abyssos* ("abyss, the deep") in Romans 10:7 for the Old Testament reference to "the sea." Paul is following the popular conception that *sheol* (the word for the realm of the dead in Hebrew) was associated with the deep.

Paul cites Deuteronomy 30:12–14 because of its applicability for describing the gospel of the One who brought the law to an end (cf. Rom. 10:4). It is now the revelation of Christ that is immediately accessible to them. There is neither a need of ascending to heaven to find the Messiah (he came in the Incarnation), nor of descending to the realm of the dead (he rose from there). As the word of the law was said to be in the mouths of the Israelites and in their hearts, even more so is this true of "the word of faith" (10:8), that is, the gospel proclamation that calls for faith (Cranfield).

Jeremiah had predicted that in the new covenant the law would be written on the human heart (Jer. 31:31–34). What this prophet foresaw about the day when God's will would be more immediate to his people is now made possible in the age of Christ. He who fulfilled the law becomes present for us as the Holy Spirit reveals him. Indeed, Christ actually indwells us through the presence of the Holy Spirit (see Rom. 8:9–11).

Paul carries forward two expressions from Deuteronomy 30:14, "in your mouth" and "in your heart," into Romans 10:9–10 and maintains the same order in which these expressions appear in Deuteronomy. He wants to clarify the two things that "the word of faith" proclaims. (1) Salvation comes to those who "confess with [their] mouth, 'Jesus is Lord.'" This has been the confession of the church from the very beginning (Acts 2:36; 1 Cor. 12:3; 16:22; Phil. 2:11). It is likewise the confession of those about to begin life with Christ, who acknowledge that Jesus alone is to be worshiped and served.

(2) In addition, salvation comes to those who "believe in [their] heart that God raised him from the dead." To believe from the heart is to believe from the depths of one's being. To believe that God raised Christ from the dead is to believe that he has conquered death and hell and to believe as well that those who have faith in him will also conquer death and hell, for they are joined to him (6:2–10). The focus on the resurrection of Christ is not to ignore the cross, but to place the emphasis on the event that culminated the salvific work of Christ.

Here we need to remember that Paul is fashioning these verses on the model of Deuteronomy 30:14. Therefore, while confession and belief are both necessary responses to the gospel, we should not understand that they are the two steps to salvation or that confession somehow precedes belief. Paul always emphasizes faith or belief as the criterion of receiving salvation. Nevertheless, public confession is the necessary response to an inner commitment, and there is a sense in which a believer's decision to trust Christ is solidified in his or her mind at the point of confessing to another.

In verses 11–13 Paul revisits a central theme of Romans: the equality of Jew and Gentile in regards to salvation. As they are on an equal footing before God in terms of his wrath (1:18–3:20), so they are in terms of salvation (3:21–4:25). Christ is the Lord of Jew and Gentile (cf. 3:29–30); salvation comes to both by calling on him. By grace our call is returned with his spiritual blessings. He placed the first call (8:28–29; 9:24–26), and we respond by calling back.

In 10:14–21 Paul returns us to the discussion begun in 9:30 about the failure of the Jews to respond to the gospel. If everyone who calls on Jesus is saved (10:1–13), then why are the Jews not calling? Paul traces back the steps that precede calling on the Lord in verses 14–15. Before calling, one must believe; before believing, one must hear; before hearing, someone must preach; before preaching, someone must be sent to preach.

This is how Paul the apostle understands his ministry. He has been called, or sent out by Christ—an "apostle" is one who has been sent—to preach the gospel (1:1, 5; 1 Cor. 15:8–11). But despite the fact that he and others have been preaching the good news, "not all the Israelites" have accepted it. "How beautiful are the feet of those who bring good news" was written by Isaiah (Isa. 52:7) as a proclamation of deliverance from exile. Paul sees in the gospel a proclamation of salvation for the Jews through Messiah, but it is this message that they are not receiving. Thus, Paul recites Isaiah 53:1: "Lord, who has believed our message?" (a verse that was also used in John 12:38 to describe the Jews' unbelief).

Paul returns to the matter of hearing in 10:17–18 to establish that the refusal of the Jews to accept Christ cannot be explained as a result of ignorance. The gospel has gone out "to the ends of the world" (Ps. 19:4). Paul knows there are peoples yet to hear—for example, he wants to bring the gospel to Spain—but his point is that the message of the gospel is being proclaimed far and wide. Therefore no one can say they are ignorant for lack of hearing.

Nor can the failure of the Jews to accept Christ be attributed to a lack of understanding. What Paul says they know is detailed in the Old Testament quotations in verses 19–21. They should understand several things from Scripture. (1) God will use another people, a "no nation" with no understanding, to make them envious (v. 19; cf. Deut. 32:21)—Paul raises this idea again in Romans 11:11. (2) God will reveal himself to those who are not seeking him (Rom. 10:20; cf. Isa. 65:1). (3) Finally, what is keeping the Jews from receiving the salvation being offered them is their own obstinacy (Rom. 10:21; cf. Isa. 65:2).

The chapter concludes with a strong note of grace: "All day long I have held out my hands" (v. 21). As the next chapter shows, those hands will be outstretched to the Jews again.

2.3.4. Saving the Remnant; Hardening the Others (11:1–10). The opening question of chapter 11 informs us that Paul is still concerned with defending the statement he made in 9:6—God's word has not failed. To paraphrase the question: If God has revealed himself to the Gentiles and they are responding, but the Jews—to whom God has stretched out his hands—are not (10:19–21), then is God done with the Jews? Paul is not the first Jew to ask, during a dark hour in Israel's history, whether God has rejected her—nor would he be the last (cf. 2 Kings 21:14; Jer. 7:29). The response of Paul the Jew is emphatic, since he is living proof that the contrary is true: *God has not rejected him.* He is part of the remnant of Israel (see Rom. 9:27–29), and there are others as well, as the story of Elijah illustrates (11:3–5).

The Israelites are still God's people, Paul argues, because God foreknew them (v. 2; cf. 8:29). That is, their status rests on his election rather than their performance (see 9:10–16). The conclusion we are to draw, then, is this: If God chose them without regard for their deeds, then he will not reject them on that basis either. There is a theological term for this action on God's part, and Paul uses it four times in 11:5–6: *grace*. By his grace alone a remnant is being preserved.

The figure of Elijah is one whom Paul can readily identify with (see Dunn). For as Elijah was opposed by most of his fellow Jews ("I am the only one left, and they are trying to kill me," 11:3), Paul also is being opposed by his nation. Moreover, both of their lives were threatened. And finally, like Elijah, Paul has been called by God at a critical moment in the nation's history.

What was hinted at in chapter 9, that Paul was raising the idea of Pharaoh's hardening to explain what occurred to national Israel, is now made explicit. As God hardened Pharaoh's heart to advance his sovereign purpose (9:17–18), so now he is causing the nation to suffer a loss of spiritual sensitivity (11:7–10), which Paul explains here.

In accordance with rabbinic argument, Paul justifies his position by citing texts from what were considered the three parts of the Old Testament: the Torah (Deut 29:4 is quoted in Rom. 11:8b, beginning with "eyes so that . . ."); the Prophets (Isa. 29:10 supplies the phrase "God gave them a spirit of stupor" in Rom. 11:8a); and the Writings (Ps. 69:22–23 is quoted in Rom. 11:9–10). These Old Testament texts serve as proof that God's word has not failed (9:6); the rejection of the gospel by Israel is in line with the revelation of Scripture.

2.3.5. God's Present and Future for Israel (11:11–32). This last major section brings a number of surprising turns to the argument begun in 9:1. (1) Most important, Paul begins a new line of argument in defense of the thesis of 9:6 that God's Word to the Jews has not failed. The apostle has already argued that God shows himself faithful to his Word by preserving a remnant of Israel. Now he advances the claim that God's future plan for the restoration of the rest of Israel also establishes the truth of God's covenant word (see Donaldson, 177).

(2) It becomes obvious that the author's target audience in this extended exposition about Israel is not only the Jews. In verse 13 he notifies his readers that it is the Gentile contingent in Rome whom he is now addressing. Paul shows a deep concern about the Gentiles' attitude toward the Jews. The nature of his argument suggests that he is aware that the increasingly dominant role that the Gentiles are assuming in the growing church has negatively affected their response to Jewish Christians and non-Christians. This is one of the reasons why Paul declares repeatedly throughout these chapters that he has a personal passion for the state of his fellow Jews (9:1–3; 10:1). And it is for this reason that he tells the Gentiles that he diligently pursues his work as an evangelist to the Gentiles because he believes that his success there will lead some Jews to become jealous (11:14). What Paul wants to correct is any misconception that the apostle to the Gentiles has rejected his own people.

2.3.5.1. Purpose in Hardening (11:11–16). It is safe to assume that the Gentiles who heard this section of the letter being read presumed that this was primarily a discussion between Paul and fellow Jewish believers. Anticipating this, Paul dictates verse 13 to Tertius (cf. 16:22): "I am talking to you Gentiles. . . ." The apostle to the Gentiles wants them to take notice of and be affected by his approach to the Jewish people, and he keeps their attention by using "you" throughout the rest of this section. After arresting their attention, Paul declares his hope that the success of his ministry among the Gentiles will further the goal of Jewish acceptance of the gospel.

Paul then restates (vv. 14–15) what he declared in verses 11–12 in order that they will all hear it: Jewish rejection of the gospel has meant blessing for Gentiles (the gospel has been proclaimed to them), but God is not yet finished with the Jews. In fact, the future of Gentile believers, as well as creation itself, remains bound up with that of the Jewish nation. When the Jews come to accept Christ, it will result in an even greater blessing for all Christians—the resurrection.

Four points need be made about these significant verses. (1) The opening question (v. 11) allows Paul to declare that the hardening spoken of in verses 7–10 is not permanent. The salvation of the Gentiles is not the final result of (or God's only purpose for) Israel's hardening, because God will use the salvation of the Gentiles to restore Israel (v. 11). Paul draws the idea from Deuteronomy 32:21 (quoted in Rom. 10:19) that the extension of God's mercy to the Gentiles will provoke Israel to jealousy. To summarize, the hardening of the hearts of the Jews is a temporary phase in God's broader plan to bring Gentiles to salvation, which in turn will result in the eventual salvation of the Jews.

The two metaphors in verse 16 serve to reemphasize that what God has begun with the Jews he will carry on to completion. Commentators disagree over the referent for each metaphor (e.g., do the "firstfruits" refer to the patriarchs, as "the root" in the corresponding metaphor appears to do? [Moo]; or, do they represent the remnant of Christian Jews? [Cranfield]). Nevertheless, the overall point is clear. The surety of the future salvation of the Jews rests on what God has already initiated among his people.

(2) Paul does not elaborate how the hardening of the Jews leads to the salvation of the Gentiles (v. 15). One common theory understands that God removed the Jews so as to make room for the Gentiles to come in—"the spatial logic of displacement" (Donaldson, 223). But it is difficult to understand why there isn't enough room for both Jew and Gentile within God's kingdom. Preferable is Donaldson's own view that Israel's rejection made salvation available to the Gentiles because it gave them time to repent before the end of the age—"the temporal logic of delay." The Jews' acceptance of Christ is associated in verse 15 with the resurrection. Therefore, Donaldson argues, it is the delay in their acceptance of Christ—this period of hardening—that has given the

Gentiles a window of opportunity to come into the kingdom before the resurrection and the end of the age. If the Jews had accepted Christ immediately, the end of the age would have arrived and the Gentiles would have had no such opportunity.

(3) The relationship described here between the nation of Israel and the Gentiles in God's plan of salvation suggests that Paul thinks that the Jews will fulfill their divinely appointed role to bring blessing to the nations (Gen. 12:3b) in two different ways. (a) As was already occurring, their transgression will provide a time of salvation for the Gentiles. Certainly Israel envisioned that it would be their faithfulness to God, and his blessing of them in response, that would draw the nations to her Lord. But even in her transgression the centrality of Israel for God's salvation of the nations is preserved.

(b) Israel's acceptance of Christ will mean even greater riches for the nations (v. 12), that is, the resurrection (v. 15). The great and final blessing of Israel to the world will be to trigger the end of this age and the commencement of the world to come.

(4) The apocalyptic concept of "fullness" (*pleroma*) is applied to both the Jews (v. 12) and the Gentiles (v. 25). We can understand this word in either a qualitative sense, as fulfillment, or in a quantitative sense, as the full number. It is certainly the latter meaning that is appropriate regarding the Gentiles' fullness, since verse 25 refers to their fullness as coming in. This word suggests that there is a predetermined number of Gentiles who must come to salvation before the period of Jewish hardening closes. If Gentile fullness is related to a foreordained number, then we may presume that the same is the case with the fullness of the Jews in verse 12. Thus, a certain number of Jews must be saved before the world can be brought to a conclusion. It was a common conception among the apocalyptic writers that the inauguration of the world to come hinged on reaching the number of the elect whom God had predetermined would be saved (e.g., 4 Ezra 4:35–37; 1 Enoch 47:4).

2.3.5.2. How to View the Jews (11:17–24). Paul continues in this section to deal with the Gentiles' attitude toward the Jews—both those in and outside of the church. It seems as if the apostle is targeting a spiritual arrogance, born of the fact that the Gentile presence in the church is growing while that of the Jews is declining. It may be tempting for the Gentiles to conclude by the present pattern of church growth that God himself has moved his salvific attention away from the Jews to the Gentiles. What disturbs Paul, then, is that the Gentiles might fall into the same sin of spiritual pride that plagued the Jews (see 2:17).

He challenges the Gentiles' attitude of superiority with three considerations. (1) They owe a debt of gratitude and respect to the Jews who came before them. They are the root; they are the ones God chose to be his people and with whom he established a covenantal relationship. It is through the Jews that God now extends privileges to the Gentiles once exclusive to the covenant people. Thus, Paul contends that the Jews are the ones who support the branches (the Gentiles) being grafted in (vv. 17–18).

(2) Since the Gentiles have become a part of God's people by faith, they can equally be removed by a lack of faith (vv. 19–22). Consequently, fear rather than arrogance is the posture the Gentiles should assume (v. 20). To fear God is not to live with a sense of terror (see ch. 8, with its assurances regarding our adoption into the family of God). But it does connote, along the lines of the Old Testament concept, the reverential stance of one who never forgets that the Lord is God and everyone else is not. Note also in this regard that faith expresses itself by responding to God's grace—"provided that you continue in his kindness" (v. 22). This was dealt with theologically in chapters 6–8 and will be dealt with in practical terms in chapters 12–15. Romans 12:1 declares that the mercy of God is the altar on which the sacrifice of our lives is to be offered.

(3) If God has performed the miracle of grafting Gentiles (wild olive branches) onto a Jewish base, then is there any reason why God cannot graft the Jews back onto their own tree (cultivated olive tree)?

The application of all this for us is obvious. Perhaps the temptation that those early Gentiles faced is even more acute for us. At least the believers in Rome could look around and see a healthy contingent of Jewish Christians, which would have been a continual reminder that the foundation of the church was laid on God's work with the Jews. How much more difficult it is for us to remember this when we live in a Christian world almost entirely Gentile! But remembrance is not enough. We need a passion similar to that of Paul. If God has not forgotten about the Jews, then neither may we.

2.3.5.3. The Salvation of Israel (11:25–32). As a conclusion to the discussion of chapters 9–11, Paul reveals what has been revealed to him—a "mystery" (*mysterion*). Paul frequently refers to the revelation of a mystery when he speaks about some aspect of God's plan of salvation (e.g., Rom. 16:25; Eph. 1:9–10; Col. 1:26–27; 2:2). The term *mystery* in Paul does not denote something mysterious, beyond human comprehension. Rather, it refers to something previously hidden from mortals in the counsel of God that now being revealed in the last days to his people.[8]

It is not obvious what Paul considers the content of this mystery to be. Is it the hardening of Israel, the full number of the Gentiles coming in, or the eventual salvation of "all Israel"? If we assume that the apostle is here revealing what he has not discussed previously in the letter, then we should probably think that the mystery involves the Gentile role in the end-time revival among the Jews. After all, the hardening of Israel and her eventual restoration was discussed earlier in this chapter. Paul is revealing, then, the concept that the full number of the Gentiles must be reached before the hardening of the Jews will cease.

As mentioned in the comments on 11:12, Jewish apocalyptic writers commonly noted that God had a number of the elect in mind who would be saved before the end came. But to them the elect were the Jews; it was their salvation that initiated the end. Paul, it is true, did speak about the fullness of the Jews preceding the moment of resurrection (11:12, 15), but here it is the pivotal role of the Gentiles in salvation history that is highlighted. The Jews will not come into salvation in large measure until the Gentiles have already done so.

Paul is pressing the point on his Gentile audience that his Gentile mission, which he hopes they will support as he moves on to Spain, furthers a larger facet of God's plan. Their salvation is not the climax of salvation history, but its penultimate event. Thus, the Gentiles are being given the opportunity to be a spiritual blessing to the Jews. As they further the gospel, the number of the Gentiles moves closer to the total needed for all Israel to be saved.

"All Israel" is Israel as a whole, that is, not just the remnant of Israel, but the rest as well—the branches that have been cut off (11:17). The quotation in verse 26 combines Isaiah 59:20–21a with a phrase from Isaiah 27:9 ("when I take away their sins"). The one modification to this quote, which is close to some manuscripts of the LXX, is that in Romans 11:26 the Redeemer comes *out of* Zion, whereas in the Hebrew text of Isaiah 59:20 he comes *to* Zion. This may be an attempt to reinforce the point made at the outset of this whole discussion in Romans 9:5, that the one whom the Jews were rejecting was one of their own. But Paul gives the assurance that the day will come when they will realize that Jesus is Messiah. At that time the Lord will complete his covenant relationship with the Jews, established with the patriarchs (11:28–29), by forgiving them of their sins (v. 27).

In verses 28–32 we find a succinct summary of chapters 9–11. Paul resets the paradox that launched the discussion. The ones to whom God made an irrevocable call to be his people, and to whom he gave gifts of covenant privilege (see 9:4–5), these are the ones who are set against or are enemies of the gospel (11:28–29). Paul restates how God is using the disobedience of the Jews to bring the Gentiles in, and how, in turn, he will use his mercy to the Gentiles to extend his mercy to the Jews. Note that in verses 30–31 the means by which God extends mercy is Jewish disobedience, but it is God's mercy rather than Gentile obedience that figures in on the other side of the equation. It is not the righteousness of the Gentiles that achieves God's purposes, but God's mercy alone.

Paul's expectation that the temporary period of Jewish hardening may end soon is indicated by the phrase "they too may now receive mercy" (v. 31). It is with this conviction in mind that Paul determines to "make much" of his ministry to the Gentiles "in the hope that I may somehow arouse my own people to envy and save some of them" (11:13–14). To that end, he is on to Jerusalem, then Rome, and then Spain.

In one final statement, which introduces a doxology, Paul declares the merciful plan of God: to bind "all men over to disobedience so that he may have mercy on them all" (v. 32). In one phrase he summarizes three chapters and reinforces a dominant theme of the letter: the equality of Jew and Gentile in terms of God's wrath and in terms of his grace. And mercy sounds the first note of the paraenesis section of the letter that begins in 12:1.

2.3.6. In Praise of God (11:33–36). Paul typically uses doxologies to punctuate parts of his letter rather than to conclude them (e.g., Gal. 1:5; Eph. 3:21; Phil. 4:20; 1 Tim. 1:17; 2 Tim. 4:18). In fact, the only letter where a doxology forms the conclusion is Romans (16:25–27), although there is some dispute as to whether this doxology actually concluded the original letter. Paul's letters were read publicly when the believers were gathered for worship; thus the doxologies, as well as his benedictions, would have functioned to enhance the worship service.

The doxology in Romans 11:33–36 expresses praise to God and wonder at the mystery and wisdom of his judgments. Even though Paul has received a revelation about the unfolding of God's salvific plan (11:25), it is but a partial glimpse into the great mystery of his will. Dunn observes that giving praise to God for receiving an insight into his ways was a typically Jewish response.

2.4. God's Righteousness Lived Out by and Between Jew and Gentile (12:1–15:13)

Paul now begins the section of the letter (12:1–15:13) where the preceding theological discussion receives practical application. The theme of Romans, the revelation of God's righteousness in the gospel (1:17), carries on into this last major section. God's righteousness is his power extended to save from the penalty of sin through Jesus Christ (1:18–5:21), as well as to transform the individual into the image of Christ through the indwelling Spirit (ch. 8). In other words, righteousness is not a static concept. It describes not only what God did through the death of Christ, but also what he continues to do for those he has brought into relationship with him. Thus, the righteousness of God affects the everyday life of the believer.

The term often used for the section in which Paul engages his readers with moral exhortation aimed at their everyday lives is *paraenesis* (from the Gk. word meaning "advice"). Sometimes paraenesis appears in a block toward the end of a Pauline letter (e.g., Gal. 4:12–6:10; Eph. 4:1–6:20; Col. 3:1–4:6). At other times, Paul's practical exhortations are scattered throughout the letter (e.g., 1 Cor.; Phil.). The paraenesis in Romans explains how the new relationship of Jew and Gentile before God—a relationship inaugurated by the work of Christ and lived out in the Spirit rather than under the conditions of the law—is to work out in their relationships with one another (12:3–13a; 14:1–15:13) and with the surrounding world (12:13b–13:14).

In order to reflect the emphases of this part of the letter, two sections will receive particular attention: 12:1–2, because it sets the theme for the entire paraenesis; and 14:1–15:13, because it is the climax of Paul's exhortation, where he addresses at length a problem between Jewish and Gentile Christians that was threatening the survival of the early church in Rome. Indeed, it is a problem that still threatens the life of the church.

2.4.1. Living in Response to God's Righteousness (12:1–2). In these two verses Paul sets out the theme for the entire paraenetical section: The mercy of God compels a continual response of personal sacrifice, that is, a life of worship. The conduct required by such a daily sacrifice is informed by the renewed mind.

The opening imperative derives its force from God's gracious acts: "Therefore, I urge you, brothers, in view of God's mercy, to offer your bodies as living sacrifices" (v. 1a). Paul sets his exhortation within the context of God's mercy, not as some polite form of address—i.e., the theological equivalent of saying "please"—but out of theological necessity. The whole story of God's interaction with the human race follows the same pattern: God acts; we react. God acts, not out of compulsion, but according to his gracious love; we react, compelled by the acts of God, either to reject or to accept his merciful advances.

Note similarly how when Paul summarized his brief discourse on the history of God's election of the Jews, he did so in this way: "It does not, therefore, depend on man's desire or effort, but on God's mercy" (9:16). When he depicted God's salvific plan for the whole world, he declared: "While we were still sinners, Christ died for us" (5:8b). Consequently, it is theologically correct for Paul to build his exhortation in 12:1–15:13 on the foundation of God's mercy—a recurring theme in the preceding sections of the letter (e.g., chs. 4–6), and one that dominates the last half of ch. 11 (11:25–32).

The appropriate response to God's mercy is to "offer your bodies as living sacrifices, holy and pleasing to God—this is your spiritual act of worship" (v. 1b). Although the sacrifice of animals and produce was common in the Greco-Roman world (e.g., the problem of meat-eating in Corinth was related to the presence of pagan sacrificial cults [1 Cor. 8; 10]), the background for this sacrificial language is in the Old Testament. By choosing this metaphor to express the nature of Christian service, Paul is able to contrast life under the law with life in the Spirit.

The "spiritual ... worship" called for here—or the worship appropriate for one who lives in the Spirit—transposes worship to a higher key. Whereas the Jewish sacrificial system required the worshiper to offer an animal or produce at the temple, life in the Spirit requires the worshiper to offer himself or herself. For those who bring something to an altar, the act of worship ends when the offering is consumed; for those who offer themselves, the sacrificial act is just the beginning. The Christian is a "living sacrifice," which means that worship is transferred out of the temple and into the streets. In short, the degree of personal responsibility is heightened for the one who walks in the Spirit instead of according to the law.

What Paul means by "spiritual [*logiken*]" worship is debated. The word *logikos* (the lexical form of *logiken*), which Paul uses nowhere else in his writings, was widely used by Greek philosophers. It often denoted "rationality," that is, the characteristic distinguishing human beings from animals. "Reasonable service" (KJV) preserves this sense. Other scholars (e.g., Bruce) prefer "spiritual," for they see in this use of *logiken* a contrast with the "externalities" of the sacrificial cult—that is, a contrast of spiritual worship and religious ritual. It would seem, however, that if this was Paul's point, he would used *pneumatikos*, the more unambiguous word for "spiritual" (cf. "spiritual sacrifices" in 1 Peter 2:5).

In other words, Paul appears to be arguing for a worship that is logical or appropriate for those living in the Spirit (cf. Fee, 1994, 601), who, as we will see in the following verse, are guided into appropriate behavior by the renewed mind. The contrast Paul is conveying is with those sinners described in 1:18–32 who, by ignoring the evidence of natural revelation, are futile in their thinking (see Thompson, 79–83). We may say that the body of the letter begins with a description of those who walk in futility; the paraenesis, with those who walk in the Spirit.

The sacrificial language of verse 1 also serves to reinforce an earlier contrast made between those who serve God and those who serve sin. The exhortation to "offer your bodies" reminds the reader of the earlier injunction in 6:13, where the same Greek word for "offer" appears twice: "Do not offer the parts of your body to sin ... but rather offer yourselves to God, as those who have been brought from death to life."

In verse 2 Paul states the means by which the imperative thrust of verse 1 is to be realized. It is the transformation effected by the renewed mind that enables the Christian to live sacrificially day in and day out. The renewed mind—which, although not stated here, results from the work of the Holy Spirit (cf. 2 Cor. 3:18; Titus 3:5; see Dunn; Bruce; Fee, 1994, 602)—is able to discern God's will as it applies to everyday life. Whereas God's judgments in his dealings with humankind are "unsearchable" (11:33–34), the mind that is "being renewed" (the use of the present tense suggests an ongoing process) is able to determine his "good, pleasing and perfect will" for daily living.

In short, the heightened responsibility of the Christian not only involves a life of worship that extends beyond particular times and places of sacrifice, but also entails a personal responsibility to determine how such a life is to be lived. In contrast to Judaism, in which the law prescribes righteous conduct, Christianity requires a greater degree of personal discernment.

Consequently, it is by means of an internal change rather than through adherence to an external code that the Christian is to avoid conformity to the pattern of this world. Christian transformation works from the inside out. In the next section Paul will begin to demonstrate how renewed thinking is to be applied to various areas of the Christian life.

2.4.2. Relationships in the Church (12:3–13a).

2.4.2.1. Right Thinking About Relationships (12:3–5). The first matter that concerns the renewed mind is right thinking about relationships within the Christian community (vv. 3–5). Conformity within the church to a worldly mindset about human relationships produces a distorted view of other members of the body of Christ. Worldly thinking in the Roman congregations involved both the Jews and the Gentiles overrating their status in comparison to the other (v. 3a)—one because they had the law, the other because they did not.

The issue does not appear to be the same one as in Corinth, where the problem stemmed from an illegitimate ranking of the value of various *charismata* (spiritual gifts). Those exercising the gift of tongues accorded themselves superior status over those exercising "lesser" gifts (1 Cor. 12–14). Paul's warnings in Romans to both Jew (Rom. 2–4) and Gentile (ch. 11; 14:1–15:13) about an attitude of superiority or arrogance toward the other suggests that the call for sober thinking in chapter 12 addresses ethnic/religious tension rather than charismatic enthusiasm.

The type of renewed thinking in view here is sober judgment that functions in accordance with "the measure of faith God has given" (v. 3b). The "measure of faith" recalls a recurring theme: God's grace preempts human boasting. The cross is the great equalizer: Everyone must kneel in the same dirt at the foot of the cross in order to receive forgiveness. Consequently, no one can claim any other standing in the body of Christ than the position of humility with which he or she entered the body of Christ in the first place. Each individual comes in by faith and stays in by faith rather than by personal merit.

To illustrate the point, Paul uses the metaphor of the human body to represent the church—a common image in his letters (1 Cor. 12:12–31; Eph. 1:22–23; Col. 1:18; 2:19). The closest parallel to what we find in Romans 12:3–8 is in 1 Corinthians 12:12–31, where Paul also employs an analogy from the human body as part of his discussion about spiritual gifts. There he emphasized that each member of the body of Christ, no matter what his or her spiritual gift, is equally vital to the life of the church, in the same way that each bodily part is necessary for the proper functioning of the entire physical body. Here Paul insists that one with a renewed mind should look at the diversity of Jew and Gentile in the body of Christ not as an opportunity for posturing oneself over against another, but as an opportunity to assume the posture of a servant. Membership in the body of Christ has its responsibilities, for "each member belongs to all the others" (Rom. 12:5).

What unites the body of Christ is its diversity. Each member is dependent on every other because the gifts are distributed throughout the body in such a way that no member is self-sufficient. Consequently, the body of Christ functions effectively only when all members utilize whatever gifts they have for the benefit of the rest.

2.4.2.2. Individual Gifts (12:6–8). Before examining the individual gifts, it should be emphasized that for each gift the point is the same: If you have this gift, use it. That is why the list of gifts is incomplete—in fact, none of Paul's gift lists is exhaustive (1 Cor. 12:8–10, 28; Eph. 4:11). Although the passage before us provides some phrase-length explanations about how some of these gifts are to be used, Paul's primary purpose here is motivation, not instruction.

This is not unusual. Paul does not define the various gifts in any of the passages where he lists them. Rather, he assumes a common understanding on the part of his audience about the nature of these gifts, which they would have gained from previous teaching and from observation of the gifts at work. The exception—that is, the extended discussion about the nature of prophecy and tongues in 1 Corinthians 14—is not an attempt to introduce and define these two gifts, but to correct the Corinthians' perception and usage of them.

The list of seven gifts is divided in two by the grammatical structure of the passage, which changes abruptly with the fifth gift. For each of the first four gifts, the phrase in which they appear begins with "if"; the last three begin with "the one who" (the NIV uses "if" for all seven). This structure will be of aid in our interpretation of the sixth gift.

What is noteworthy here is that "prophesying" tops the list—a position that accords with the emphasis Paul gives to this gift elsewhere (1 Cor. 14; 1 Thess. 5:19–20). In particular, in the lists in 1 Corinthians 12:28 and Ephesians

4:11 the ranking of the prophet is second only to that of the apostle. The gift of prophecy—the only gift to appear in every Pauline list of spiritual gifts—is the ability to give an immediate message or revelation from God to his people. As is the case with Old Testament prophecy, New Testament prophecy is chiefly concerned with addressing the situation of God's people in the present rather than predicting the future.

Prophecy is qualified with an unusual stipulation—that it be used "in proportion to his faith." This is not the same type of faith referred to in verse 3 (the "measure [*metron*] of faith"). Here it is the "proportion" (*analogia*) of "the faith" (not "his faith," as in the NIV). "The faith" seems to signify the gospel (cf. 14:1). This is an option that Käsemann accepts and Fee finds attractive but ultimately rejects, because he sees this as an unprecedented admonition for the prophet to test himself (1994, 608–9). Nothing here, however, requires such an interpretation. Paul here gives the criteria by which a prophecy is judged, not the one who does the judging (for that, see 1 Cor. 14:29). "In proportion to the faith" is the acid test of a prophecy: It must be *in line with the gospel tradition*. In sum, the importance of the gift is seen in its prominent place atop the list; the potential dangers of prophecy, in the test of authenticity that regulates it.

"Serving" (*diakonia*; lit., "service") may be defined as the supporting role of ministry. Our word "deacon" derives from this Greek word. The critical role of service in the church was recognized early on: In order to provide proper care for the widows in the Jerusalem church, while at the same time freeing the apostles to fulfill their calling of prayer and preaching, the apostles appointed seven Spirit-filled men to oversee this work (Acts 6:1–6).

Unlike prophecy, no evaluative criterion accompanies the gift of "teaching" (v. 7b). Käsemann's suggestion that it was understood that the teacher was bound to the received tradition of the early church may explain why this is the case. While the teacher is tied to the disciplines of study and systematic presentation of the truths handed down, the prophet speaks divinely inspired, impromptu messages. The freedom that the prophet enjoys to claim authority based on divine inspiration (and the possible abuses of such a claim) explains the reservation that teachers often have toward those who practice the prophetic gift.

The next word (*paraklesis*, "encouraging" in NIV; from the same word group as Paraclete, a title given to the Holy Spirit in John 16:7) has a range of meanings encompassing, based on the root verb *parakaleo*: (1) invite, summon; (2) exhort; and (3) comfort, encourage (G. Braumann, 1.570). The latter two meanings are common in Paul (*paraklesis* as comfort in Rom. 15:4; 2 Cor. 1:3–7; *parakaleo* as exhortation in Rom. 12:1; 15:30; 1 Cor. 4:16), and both should probably be seen as different modes of expressing this gift. This whole section of the letter (12:1–15:13) is Paul's exhortation to the Romans, which is apparent not only from the content (exhortations to Christian living in response to God's mercy), but also from his initial "I urge you, brothers" (12:1).

The last three gifts, each of which is given a one-phrase description about their use, involve acts of practical concern. Giving is the sharing of one's personal resources for the good of others, whether food, money, or possessions. It is probably not so much a giving of time, for that is presupposed in the use of every gift. The gift is to be given "generously" or, perhaps better, "with simplicity." That is, the one who gives must not do so from mixed motives; simplicity in giving means to do so without any motive for personal gain. Dunn writes: "The sense here may be extended to embrace the thought of 'generosity, liberality' ... though if so it should be remembered that it is a liberality which arises out of and expresses the simplicity and single-mindedness of the person of faith."

The second gift in this final grouping of three, *proïstemi*, is usually translated as "leadership." The word means "to set before, set over." It denotes leadership, but also the related function of guardianship or responsibility for those placed under one's jurisdiction. The latter sense of caring for or giving aid appears to be what Paul intended (see Dunn). Not only does the word come between two other gifts that express similar functions, but the structural device that Paul uses in grouping these three—each gift is introduced in Greek by "he who ..."—associates these three acts of caring even more closely. This gift is to be exercised "diligently" so that the various needs of a congregation may be met.

The last gift in the list, "showing mercy," is the ability to put empathy into concrete action. The one exercising this gift extends mercy to those in need. While this may refer to any general act of mercy (see Cranfield: "tend the sick, relieve the poor, or care for the aged and disabled"), Paul may have had a more limited activity in mind, considering that he has already mentioned "giving." The requirement that "showing mercy" be done "cheerfully" may indicate that giving alms to the poor is in view here. In Jewish tradition cheerfulness is regularly enjoined as the manner in which one should do this (cf. 2 Cor. 9:7).

2.4.2.3. General Exhortations on Relating to Others in the Church (12:9–13a). The structure of 12:9–21 is tightly organized. The entire section is subsumed under the initial exhortation to love without hypocrisy (v. 9). What follows are two sets of brief exhortations, bracketed by the theme of good and evil (vv. 9b, 21). The first set (12:9b–13a) continues the previous application of the concept of renewed thinking to life within the Christian community. The second (12:13b–21) directs Christian thinking toward the marketplace.

The call for sincere love in verse 9 stands over the remainder of the chapter. Each set of exhortations is introduced by a compound word(s) formed with the Greek word *philos*, "love": *philadelphia* (brotherly love) and *philostorgos* (devotion) in verse 10, and *philoxenia* (love of strangers) in verse 13. That Romans was written from Corinth is significant for our understanding of the prominence given to love. In his first extant letter to this congregation Paul addressed their abuse of the gifts of the Spirit, insisting that love must accompany the gifts to make them effective (1 Cor. 13). So it is not coincidental that love is the first topic following a discussion about gifts in Romans. As we will see in the following verses, love serves to shape the believer's relationships inside and outside the church.

The phrase in the latter part of verse 9, "hate what is evil; cling to what is good," complements what precedes and prefaces what follows. (A similar injunction comes after the mention of prophecy in 1 Thess. 5:20–22.) To cling to the good and detest what is evil challenges the charismatic community to work together without hypocrisy, without selfishness, without pride. In other words, the church should function with a renewed mind in every aspect of her life, whether that be in the use of the gifts mentioned above or in the actions named below. The strong terminology that Paul employs here for evil (*poneros* rather than the more typical and less severe *kakos* [used in v. 21]) may be another indication that the memories of his history at Corinth were still fresh in his mind as he wrote the Roman believers.

In verses 10–13 are nine consecutive phrases, most of them participial and all but the last beginning with a dative. The first four appear to be instrumental datives (vv. 10–11b), that is, "with brotherly love," "with honor . . ."; the last four seem to be locative datives (vv. 12–13a), that is, "in hope rejoicing," "in affliction steadfast," and so forth. The only puzzle concerns the fifth (v. 11c): Is it instrumental (like the previous phrases)—"serving by means of the Lord"—or locative (like the following datives)—"serving in the Lord"? Or should it be translated, as it usually is, "serving the Lord"? The structure of the passage makes one of the first two options more likely than the third.

The love called for in verse 10a is family love. With "brotherly love" (*philadelphia*) the Christian is to express the type of devotion that a parent has for a child (*philostorgos*). This involves preferring others by giving them honor (v. 10b), which reinforces the idea addressed earlier in the chapter concerning sober self-evaluation of one's standing in the body of Christ. The temptation to demean others who are different—whether, for example, by virtue of their gifts or their race—must be overcome by an aggressive approach that actually puts others ahead of oneself in terms of honor and respect (cf. 12:3, which calls for sober thinking on this matter).

Verse 11 specifies that loving acts within the community must be done with zeal, with the fire of the Holy Spirit, and with the graces and gifts of the Lord (i.e., serving by means of the Lord). As Fee notes (1994, 611, n.419), commentators tend to prefer a reference here to the Holy Spirit, whereas the translations favor the human spirit, as does the NIV—"keep your spiritual fervor." The fervency Paul has in mind is a combination of personal discipline (lit., "with zeal, not slothful") and the power of the Holy Spirit (cf. Acts 1:8; 1 Thess. 5:19).

The threefold responsibility of the Christian to maintain this zeal is given in verse 12: "Be joyful in hope, patient in affliction, faithful in prayer." These are not unrelated exhortations. The hope that gives joy is our future hope in Christ. This hope supplies the mental toughness to be able to endure earthly affliction. And persistent prayer relates to both: It focuses one's hope on the glorious future as opposed to the difficult present, and it opens one to the continual refreshment of the Lord's strength and wisdom in the interim.

Familial love is brought to the fore again in verse 13a, as it will be in the next chapter (13:8–14). Providing for the practical needs of members of the family of God is one of the ways that we assist them in being "patient in affliction" (v. 12). Moreover, it demonstrates once more that our reasonable service is expressed not just with hands raised, but with hands extended.

2.4.3. Relationships With the World (12:13b–13:14).

2.4.3.1. Relationship With the World in General (12:13b–21). The latter half of verse 13 marks the transition from Paul's exhortations about acts of loving service within the church to his counsel regarding interaction with those outside the family of God. The command "practice hospitality" connects the sections in that hospitality (*philoxenia*, lit., "love of strangers") calls for acts of love to be extended to those outside of the immediate family of believers. Because of the bad reputation of many inns, traveling Christians would count on the hospitality of believers. Indeed, the practice of hospitality was presupposed by Jesus when he sent out his disciples (Matt. 10:11).

But hospitality would also include demands that might be made on local believers from fellow countrymen, especially in such a frequent destination like Rome. Another indication that with "practice hospitality" Paul has begun to turn his attention to the believer's interaction with the unbeliever is his use of the word "practice" (lit., "pursue") in both this verse and the next. In verse 14 this same verb means pursue or persecute.

When Paul addresses the Roman believers' relationship with the world, he does so with sensitivity to the threat that the Roman house churches were facing in the capital city. The Romans had expelled the Jews in A.D. 49 during the time of Claudius. Paul knew that the early Christians, probably seen as a Jewish sect by the authorities, would have no assurance of better treatment if they were perceived as a threat to society. Paul was right to be concerned, because the great persecution under Nero would soon come. Consequently, his admonition in this section, as in the next chapter, is to avoid all possible provocation—"if it is possible, as far as it depends on you, live at peace with everyone" (v. 18).

But his counsel goes further and is in line with the teaching of Christ (Luke 6:27–28). He exhorts the Roman Christians to bless those who persecute them (v. 14). This is not passive resistance, but an active response to persecution that returns good for evil (vv. 17–21). Christians are called to bless those they interact with by identifying with them in their joy and sorrow, rather than rejoicing in their difficulty and resenting their successes (v. 15). The injunction in verse 16 to associate with people in all stations of life, even those perceived to be of lower status, is an application to the marketplace of the principle of preferring others above oneself (cf. vv. 3, 10).

In verses 17–21, the believer is to return good for evil rather than to respond in kind. God will avenge injustice (v. 19). Such action is intended to overcome evil (v. 21). The citation in verse 20 from Proverbs 25:21–22, which in Paul's letter ends with the statement that the extension of an act of kindness to a foe is equivalent to heaping coals of fire on his head, must be interpreted in line with this emphasis. That is, Paul is not suggesting that this is the Christian way to get some revenge while dressing it in the guise of kindness. The coals of fire are not meant to be punitive but redemptive. The shame that an enemy experiences in this scenario is intended to bring him or her to a point of repentance. It is significant that there was an Egyptian custom that one would carry burning coals in a dish on one's head as a public declaration of true repentance (cf. Käsemann; Dunn). In short, within the capital city of Rome, where the actions of a growing church would be watched suspiciously, Paul desired that the Christian community become known for its love.

2.4.3.2. Relationship With the Government (13:1–7). In these verses we have Paul's most extensive discussion of the relationship between the believer and earthly authority. Its insertion at this point of the letter places it at the heart of his discussion of how renewed thinking informs the believer's interaction with the world. The occasion for this treatment stems primarily from the sociopolitical environment of the Roman house churches. As we will note below, Paul formulates this section with an awareness of the social and political realities that faced the Christians in Rome, which necessitated a judicious response from believers to their environment in order to avoid unnecessary persecution.

Paul's view that government has been ordained by God has generated much debate over the applicability of this passage for believers suffering under repressive political regimes. For instance, there was a lively debate about Romans 13 in German-speaking areas in the aftermath of the atrocities of the Third Reich (Käsemann). A traditional interpretation of this text (e.g., Conybeare and Howson, 529, n.2; Reasoner, 722) insists that Paul's favorable stance toward the state reflects the period in which Romans was written, that is, the earlier period of Nero's reign—a time when the evil impulses that would later manifest themselves in the emperor were kept in check by his mother, Agrippina (whom he later killed), and by the influence of the great statesman and Stoic philosopher Seneca (who later retired). Käsemann, however, has argued that the particular character of Roman rule at the time Paul wrote is irrelevant for interpreting this passage. For Paul was not speaking about the Roman empire or even the state as such, but about the local authorities, that is, the police, tax collectors, and magistrates.

While space prevents a full discussion of this text and its ramifications for believers under various political regimes, a few matters must be addressed before we give a brief interpretation of the text itself. (1) The context for the topic of the believer's relationship to government is Paul's development of the idea that the righteousness of God transforms all earthly relationships. Therefore, renewed thinking must be applied to every facet of a Christian's life, whether it is life in the gathered assembly of believers or in the marketplace, for all of life is worship. As Paul described the nature of a worshipful response to other members of the church (12:3–13a) and to one's enemies (12:13b–21), he now prescribes the way in which a Christian may bring glory to God by his or her conduct toward the state.

(2) The question concerning the extent to which Christians should submit to a state that abuses its power is not addressed here. Paul certainly would have qualified his statement in verse 2 that "he who rebels against the authority is rebelling against what God has instituted" if he had been writing in A.D. 64, when the lights from burning Christian corpses, deployed by Nero as human torches, were flickering in the streets of Rome. Since 13:1–7 prescribes how a Christian can bring glory to God by the manner in which he or she responds to authority, it follows that any action on the part of the state that prohibits the Christian's expression of love for God should be resisted. Indeed, the disciples, when forbidden by the Sanhedrin from preaching the message of the resurrected Lord, responded: "We must obey God rather than men!" (Acts 5:29). The inherent tension of a Christian under secular authority finds some resolution in Bruce's comment that "Christians will voice their 'No' to Caesar's unauthorized demands the more effectively if they have shown themselves ready to say 'Yes' to all his authorized demands" (1985).

(3) Finally, Käsemann has warned us against interpreting Paul's positive attitude toward political authority solely on the basis of the favorable climate that existed in Rome when he wrote the letter. The import of Paul's counsel extends beyond the context of a benevolent political regime. To refer to Bruce again, although Paul's "happy experience of Roman justice is no doubt reflected" in 13:1–7, "the principles laid down here were valid even when the 'higher powers' were not so benevolent towards Christians as Gallio had been towards Paul."

Paul is drawing on an established tradition, developed in the Old Testament and circulated in the writings of Second Temple Judaism, that God's people should give due respect and obedience to earthly kings and rulers, whether those rulers were Jewish kings or foreign monarchs. This tradition had its genesis in the belief that God appoints human leadership. Daniel 2:21 declares that "he changes times and seasons; he sets up kings and deposes them." In the wisdom literature of the Second

Temple period are found restatements of the same tradition (e.g., Wisd. Sol. 6:3; Sir. 17:17: "He appointed a ruler for every nation").

Accompanying the idea that God appoints leadership is the tandem belief that he also holds them accountable for their stewardship of the authority given them. Daniel 4 affirms not only the divine authority granted to King Nebuchadnezzar to rule, but also the judgment that would fall on him because of his arrogance. The parables of Enoch (contained within the composite work 1 Enoch), probably written in the New Testament era, warn in 46:5 that God "shall depose the kings from their thrones and kingdoms. For they do not extol and glorify him, and neither do they obey him, the source of their kingship."

This posture toward the secular state was widely adopted by the early church. First Peter 2:13–17 exhorts believers to submit to king as well as to magistrates (cf. 1 Tim. 2:1–2). First Clement—a letter written to Corinth from the bishop of Rome around A.D. 100—contains a prayer that, even though written in the aftermath of the persecutions of both Nero and Domitian, repeats the twin themes of earthly authority as appointed by God and the necessity for Christians to obey them.

It is significant that Paul saw this tried and tested political stance as a necessity for the Roman believers, not because of the benevolence of the state, but on account of the constant threat that Rome posed for the Christian church. If Claudius expelled Jews from Rome in A.D. 49 for what appears to have been a conflict that arose within the Jewish quarter over the claims of Christ (see "Recipients" in the Introduction), then the Christian community could expect the same treatment if it was perceived to be a threat to society. After all, the relative peace that the Christian church had enjoyed in those early years was a result of the Roman authorities' perception that the Christians were a sect of Judaism, a religion recognized by Roman law (see Bruce, 1985).

Paul wrote elsewhere about God-ordained authority in the church (Eph. 4:11–12; 1 Tim. 3:1–7) and in the home (Eph. 5:22–6:3). Here in Romans 13:1–5 he teaches that God has also instituted authority within society as an act of grace to uphold the moral order. So for Paul "there is no authority except that which God has established" (v. 1b).

Paul portrays the role of government in verses 2–5 in largely negative terms as a restrainer of evil. Rulers have been handed the sword "to bring punishment on the wrongdoer" (v. 4). Although believers are not to seek vengeance (12:19), God has appointed civil authority to mete out his wrath on evildoers. There is, it is true, a more positive aspect to their God-ordained function: Rulers commend the one who does right (v. 3c). Nevertheless, the emphasis of the text on wrongdoing—particularly the sobering admonition that Christians will also face the state's wrath if they transgress (v. 4b)—betrays Paul's concern for the precarious position of the church within the capital of the Roman empire. Persecution for doing right must be faced, but persecution brought on by a flagrant disregard for the law of the land may be avoided.

Paul warns his readers against any thought that as subjects of the kingdom of God they are released from the political realities of being subjects of the kingdom of this world. The key word that describes the believer's response to God-ordained authority is "submit" (*hypotasso* in v. 1). Submission involves "putting one's own interest below what is required for relationships with the civil authorities" (Mott, 142). Since "there is no authority except that which God has established" (v. 1b), submission to governing authorities is the appropriate response of the believer. Paul therefore concludes that "it is necessary to submit to the authorities, not only because of possible punishment but also because of conscience" (v. 5).

Submission defines much of the Christian's life. Consequently, Paul's call for submission to earthly authorities brings us back to the worship context of Romans 12:1–2: All of life is to be lived in worship to God. As the earthly Jesus submitted to his heavenly Father (John 14:31), we are to submit to the lordship of Christ (John 15:10). This, in turn, entails service to others. Jesus defined himself as a servant and commanded the disciples to view themselves in the same manner (Mark 10:43–45). The believer's submission to all earthly authority, then, is an extension of his or her submission to Christ (see, e.g., Col. 3:23).

In verses 6–7 Paul continues his discussion of the believer's relationship to government by addressing the topic of taxation. Some commentators see this issue as the climax of 13:1–

(Dunn; Furnish, 131–35) rather than as an dditional consideration or a specific illustra- on of the preceding argument about submis- on to God-ordained authority. In other words, e pressing concern behind Paul's repeated dmonition against civil disobedience in erses 1–5 may have been about paying taxes.

Paul's interest in the subject of taxation— unusual topic for him—may have origi- ated from reports that he received about rowing unrest in Rome over high taxation vels. Based on a report from Tacitus in *nnals* 13.50–51 that there was a popular out- y against the taxation system in A.D. 58, unn argues that there was a growing dissat- faction among the populace in the years lead- g up to the protest, which was the period in hich Paul wrote the Roman church.

The statement "This is also why you pay xes" (v. 6a) makes the connection between erses 6–7 and the argument about God- rdained authority explicit. Paul spells it out: The authorities are God's servants, who give eir full time to governing" (v. 6b). The long- anding principle that God's servants are to be ompensated (applied in the Old Testament to e priest, and by Paul to the preacher of the ospel [1 Cor. 9:13–14]) is extended here to ivic authorities. Paul's governing point—that ll of life is to be lived in worship to God 12:1–2)—lies behind this text. "Subordina- ion to civil government, particularly in the ymbolic act of paying taxes, is an aspect of e call to spiritual worship in the everyday life f the world" (Mott, 142).

The echo of our Lord's teaching on taxation n Mark 12:13–17 is heard in the imperative f verse 7: Give to each person whatever you we, whether that be "taxes" (*phoros*), "rev- nue" (*telos*), "respect" (*phobos*), or "honor" *time*). Jesus' response to the thorny question of aying taxes to a foreign government was that ne should "give to Caesar what is Caesar's nd to God what is God's" (Mark 12:17a). As Bruce writes, "Paul sees in the rendering of Caesar's dues to Caesar one form of rendering o God what is due to God" (1977, 109).

There is a careful balance preserved in the ist of four obligations in verse 7 between mon- etary debt and the attitude of deference that is owed. The distinction between *phoros* and *elos* may differentiate *phoros* as tribute (cf. Luke 20:22)—that which subjected peoples within the empire were required to pay, but from which the populace in the capital was exempt—from *telos* as taxes, which included customs, duties, and tolls (Harrison; Dunn). Paul's point is not in the distinction, however, but in the manner in which the two terms work together to suggest all forms of taxation. Respect (*phobos*, lit., "fear"; cf. vv. 3–4) and honor (*time*), in light of the context, are owed to all to whom God has given authority (cf. Käsemann). By deferring to God's representa- tives, one worships God.

2.4.3.3. Relationship With One's Neigh- bors (13:8–10). Having dealt with how Chris- tians should be guided by renewed thinking in their interactions with those who persecute them and the governing authorities, Paul finishes his discussion about a Christian response to society by turning to the believer's relationship with neighbors (13:8–10). While the believer owes respect and tax dollars to the government, his or her "continuing debt" to a neighbor is love (v. 8). Paul reintroduces a theme he used to define the Christian response to persecution. Love defines a Christian's interaction with the world whether or not that love is reciprocated.

Paul intertwines the two themes of love and law—the former the dominant theme in the paraenetical section, the latter, a major theme in the earlier part of the letter. The idea that love is the fulfillment of the law brackets 13:8–10. It reflects the pronouncements of Jesus con- cerning, on the one hand, his own mission to fulfill rather than abolish the law (Matt. 5:17– 20), and, on the other, the essence of the Old Testament law as the love of God and neighbor (Mark 12:28–34). Jesus cited Leviticus 19:18b to make his point that love of one's neighbor is one of the two most important command- ments (Mark 12:31). Thus, in this section, where Paul is concluding his teaching on the believer's interaction with the world, he calls on this same verse to define the manner in which the believer might fulfill the law by act- ing with love in everyday life (cf. Rom. 8:4).

In order to defend his assertion that "he who loves his fellowman has fulfilled the law" (v. 8), Paul refers to four commandments (the prohibitions against adultery, murder, theft, and covetousness) that pertain to social rela- tions, and he argues that these four are sum- marized in the command to "love your neighbor as yourself" (vv. 9–10).

2.4.3.4. Living Out One's Relationships With Eschatological Urgency (13:11–14). "And do this, understanding the present time" (v. 11a). Before Paul turns his attention once more to relationships within the Christian community (14:1–15:13), he heightens the intensity of his preceding admonitions by alerting the Romans to the urgency of the time they are living in. Throughout his letters Paul reinforces ethical imperatives with eschatological urgency by highlighting various impending events on the end-times calendar: for example, the imminent return of Jesus (Phil. 3:17–4:1; Col. 3:4; 1 Thess. 5:1–11), the nearness of the resurrection (1 Cor. 15:51–58), and the coming judgment (Col. 3:6).

This same mode of exhortation appears frequently in the writings of the early church fathers—a corpus of some fifteen compositions penned between A.D. 90 and 140. These documents, which "may be considered a fairly immediate echo of the preaching of the Apostles" (Quasten, 40), are replete with ethical exhortations set within an eschatological context (e.g., 1 Clem. 21–23; Did. 16; Ign. Eph. 11; 2 Clem. 3:2–4).

The particular interest of this for Pentecostals lies in the fact that the modern Pentecostal movement began within an environment of heightened expectation of the nearness of Christ's return. The restoration of the gifts of the Spirit were seen by early Pentecostals as a sign that the last days had arrived; the prophecy of Joel, cited in Peter's Pentecost sermon, was being fulfilled in their lifetime—"In the last days, God says, I will pour out my Spirit on all people" (Acts 2:17). As a result, the emphasis on holy living, which was brought into early Pentecostalism through its roots in the nineteenth-century Holiness Movement, was sustained in Pentecostal circles through the constant theme that believers must purify themselves before the imminent return of Christ.

Paul calls on the Roman believers to offer the sacrifice of love in the marketplace because "our salvation is nearer now than when we first believed" (v. 11c), and "the night is nearly over; the day is almost here" (v. 12a). This double emphasis on the imminent return of Christ shows that Paul had retained in his later ministry a theme that marked the ministry of Jesus and that appeared in the apostle's earlier letters (e.g., 1 Cor. 7:29; 16:22; 1 Thess. 4:13–5:11). The night, which represents this evil age, is in its final stages; the day, which signifies the inauguration of the kingdom, is impending (cf. John 1:4–5).

The "salvation" that believers await is final salvation (see 8:18–25). There is a sense in which the believer has already been saved, which began at the point "when we first believed" (13:11c). Yet there is another sense in which the believer is being saved, as God's righteousness or saving activity continues to work on his or her behalf. This process of salvation will be completed when Christ returns (see 5:9–10).

Behind this "already/not yet" view of salvation lies Paul's eschatological understanding that we live in the period of human history in which two ages are overlapping: The age of Christ has broken into the age of Adam (5:12–21). As believers we experience some of the blessings of the age of Christ now, which is yet to come in its fullness, while we remain affected by the conditions of the age of Adam, which is passing away. Paul summons believers to live according to the reality of the age of Christ despite the continued presence of the age of Adam.

In this transitional period, the believer is to "wake up from . . . slumber" so as to live as if the day has already arrived. This means casting off "the deeds of darkness" and putting on "the armor of light" (v. 12b). These deeds are given in a vice list of three couplets (v. 13); these six sins represent the range of temptations that the Roman believers must resist. The provision given to believers while awaiting the consummation of their salvation is the armor of light (cf. Eph. 6:11; 1 Thess. 5:8). Although the decisive battle against sin was won on the cross (Rom. 3:21–26), and we have died to sin with Christ (6:2), we continue to be influenced by the sinful conditions of our age. In this interim period, we engage in repeated skirmishes with sin.

To complete his comments on what enables us to fight successfully, Paul returns in verse 14 to the concept of putting on clothes (cf. the earlier reference in v. 12). This time the apostle names the ultimate battle garb for the believer: the Lord Jesus Christ (Gal. 3:27; Eph. 4:24). Paul is using this imagery to convey the continual responsibility we have of living in ccordance with the image of Christ, to which we will be completely transformed some day (Rom. 8:29).

The phrase "sinful nature" (v. 14b) is the NIV rendering of "flesh" (*sarx*). As we have argued in previous instances where *sarx* has appeared (e.g., 7:5–6), it is preferable to understand flesh as denoting, not a part of us—as if there is still a sinful nature within us—but the power of the old age of Adam. This power continues to entice us to exist within its destructive realm. Once we lived in the flesh, but now we are in Christ. It is only by living out our association with Christ that it is possible to respond with sacrificial love, which is the antithesis of selfish gratification.

2.4.4. Relationships Between Jew and Gentile (14:1–15:13). The paraenetical portion of Romans began in 12:1–2 with a definition of Christian living, namely, that all of one's life is to be offered back to God in worshipful response to his mercies. This thematic statement is now brought to bear on the remainder of the paraenesis in 14:1–15:13, which returns us to the subject of 12:3–13: relationships within the community of faith.

What follows is an extended discussion about how liberty and love are to function together to maintain unity in a community made up of Jewish and Gentile believers. The amount of space given to this topic and its position at the end of the paraenetical section indicate the special concern it held for Paul. To say that the whole of Romans serves as a preface to the problem addressed in 14:1–15:13 (Watson, 97–98) overrates the importance of this section in relation to the rest of the letter. Still, it is certainly appropriate to say with Fee (1994, 616) that what is at stake in this text is "the glory of God." That is, "the gospel must work out in real life, at this intersection of real differences among them, if it is going to count for anything at all."

Paul had staked his ministry as an apostle to the Gentiles on the principle of the equality of Jew and Gentile in their standing before God. Indeed, this is a central theological assertion of Romans. But this principle must result in a church where Jew and Gentile actually stand together in unity before a world that is skeptical of the gospel. Unity expressed through love is a sign to the world that Jesus is still present in the church (cf. John 13:35).

This section is a pastoral response to a specific situation in Rome, not (as some have argued) a general discourse that grew out of the Corinthian conflict described in 1 Corinthians 8–10 (see Karris, 65–84). The length of the discussion in Romans and the differences between the arguments in 1 Corinthians 8–10 and Romans 14–15:13 imply that Paul is responding here to an actual problem rather than dealing in generalizations from a past conflict. For instance, there is no hint in Romans about the Corinthian concern with meat offered to idols.

Moreover, a historical situation provides the context for Romans 14:1–15:13. When the Jews returned to Rome in the mid-50s after the lapse of Claudius's edict, which had expelled them in A.D. 49, Jewish believers began to reintegrate into the various believing communities in Rome. Paul was certainly aware of this situation from his contact with Aquila and Priscilla, who had been part of the Jewish contingent expelled from Rome (Acts 18:2). The fact that Paul evidences greater concern for the Gentiles' reaction to Jewish believers than he does for the Jews' response to Gentile Christians is revealing. It shows that Paul is aware of the disadvantage the Jews faced in reentering a church that had taken on a more pronounced Gentile character during their absence. Here, then, is a practical application of the concern expressed in 11:17–21: The Gentile believers must not be arrogant in their position vis-à-vis the Jews.

That the problem confronted here stemmed from Jewish-Gentile differences in Rome is evident from the text (see Moo for a review of various other options). (1) Although neither Jew nor Gentile is addressed by name throughout 14:1–15:6, the concluding part of this section (15:7–13), with its explicit reference to these two groups, makes this assumption sure (Cranfield). (2) Much of the discussion in chapter 14 concerns whether certain types of food are unclean. The word *koinos* ("unclean") was used by the Jews to typify what was profane as opposed to sacred (see Mark's use of this word regarding clean and unclean foods in Mark 7:2, 5). The prominence of this concept in Romans 14 also suggests that the food dispute among Roman believers was being carried on between Jews who wished to observe food regulations and Gentiles who had no interest in such a restriction on their freedom (cf. Dunn).

The controversy in the Christian community in Rome revolved around the practices of eating meat, observing certain days as more holy than others, and drinking wine (the latter activity receives less emphasis in the text). Those who ate meat, drank wine, and disregarded the particular value attached to certain days are called the "strong" (15:1); those who did the opposite are the "weak" (15:1), or those whose "faith is weak" (14:1). The association of the weak with those who abstain from eating meat because of the categories of clean and unclean (14:2, 14) shows that the Jews were the ones Paul considered weak and the Gentiles, the strong.

This is, of course, a simplification of the matter. The divisions in the Roman house churches would not have been so neatly drawn on ethnic lines. There certainly were Jews like Paul who sided with "the strong." Conversely, there were likely some Gentile converts to Christianity, who, having come into the church through the synagogue as God-fearers or even as Jewish proselytes, favored the retention of Jewish practices they had already adopted. These people would naturally have expected other Christians to follow that same pattern of obedience to God's law. Nevertheless, the generalization used here that this dispute was between Jews and Gentiles remains helpful; it reflects the overall situation, and it is true to the distinction Paul makes between these two parties in 15:8.

The concern of the weak was with the preservation of certain practices that they held to be necessary expressions of Christian faith. The issue, as Paul sees it, is not about legalism—if that is understood as a system in which certain rituals are observed as a means of obtaining grace—because Paul approaches the weak as those who have already been accepted by God (14:3; 15:7). The only means to God's acceptance, as Paul argued repeatedly in 3:21–5:21, is through justification by faith, not through doing works of the law.

The issue, in other words, is not about how to become a believer, but how to act like one. In the words of Cranfield, these Jewish believers felt that "it was only along this particular path that they could obediently express their response of faith to God's grace in Christ." Dietary laws and the observance of sacred days, whether these be Sabbaths or feast days were identifying marks of the Jews in Palestine and the Diaspora. It was difficult for them to conceive that these identifiers, which had been so critical to their self-understanding as the covenant people of God, were now to be abandoned.

Indeed, although there were other Jewish practices that distinguished the Jews from other peoples in the Hellenistic world, the importance of dietary laws and the observance of certain days as holy had actually increased in importance in the Maccabean and post-Maccabean periods, that is, the periods immediately preceding the one in which Paul wrote (cf. Dunn). The concern about sacred days is seen in the calendrical disputes that were occurring over the proper dating of Jewish feasts (e.g., 1 Enoch 74:10–12; Jub. 6:32–35; 1QS 1:14–15). In fact Josephus tells us that even before the Maccabean era "eating unclean food and violating the sabbath" were considered the two primary acts of disobedience to the covenant (*Ant* 11.346).

The issues confronting Paul, therefore were not trivial matters. The Jewish believers still saw themselves as God's chosen people with their status as Christians in direct fulfillment of promises given by God to their ancestors. This self-understanding explains why issues surrounding Old Testament food laws kept resurfacing in the early church (Acts 10; 15; Gal. 2:11–14).

For most Gentiles, of course, these practices held neither cultural relevance nor theological weight. The refusal of Gentile Christians, who saw themselves as free in Christ, to observe Jewish practices had the backing of the apostle Paul. Yet Paul knew that something more than liberty was at stake.

Before proceeding to the interpretation of the text itself, a few comments should be made about the specific issues causing conflict among Roman believers, beginning with the controversy over eating meat. Vegetarianism was practiced by various groups in antiquity (see Dunn). It is interesting to note the fourth-century record of Eusebius that James, the brother of Jesus, was a vegetarian (*Eccl. Hist.* 2.23.5). Why it was adopted by some in Rome is difficult to determine.

If the background for the prohibition against eating meat was the same in Rome as t was in Corinth, then the problem was related o idol worship. The weak maintained that neat should not be eaten if it had been tainted y its presentation to an idol (1 Cor. 8:7). The roblem for the scrupulous Christian or Jew vho desired to avoid such meat was knowing vhether a certain piece of meat had been so ffered. Meat not burnt or eaten within the emple precincts might end up in the local maret. Since there was no tag identifying its preious whereabouts, the only way to be 100 ercent sure of not eating tainted meat was to bstain from it altogether.

If this sensitivity to meat lay behind the egetarian stance taken by a faction in Rome, hen the prohibition against drinking wine may e explained in similar fashion. For wine was lso offered in the pagan temples as a libation o the gods. Yet Paul never specifically speaks n Romans 14–15 about "meat sacrificed to an dol." It is hard to explain why it is never menioned if the situation in Rome was the same as n Corinth.

Perhaps the issue in Rome was about the roper preparation of meat. While there were ertain meats that the Jews were not to eat at ll, regulations governed the preparation of neats that were allowed. The problem with his interpretation is that Paul seems to be dealng with a group that refused meat of any kind. till, although the Old Testament law permited the eating of certain types of meat, a Jew ould not be sure if a particular piece of meat ad been prepared in a *kosher* manner by the ocal butcher. Was this, then, a conviction that ll meat should be avoided in light of the difiiculties with determining the status of a paricular piece of meat?

As with keeping food laws, observance of ertain holy days was widely practiced among ews—not only within Palestine, but also outide the region—as an expression of Jewish dentity. The dispute in the Christian community in Rome may have had to do with keeping ither the Sabbath or the feasts of the Jewish alendar, or both. Whatever the situation, the eeping of certain days above others did preent a barrier to fellowship with those Gentile elievers who had no inclination to celebrate ewish holy days.

In sum, the problem Paul attempts to esolve in 14:1–15:13 stemmed from the tenion between Gentile and Jewish Christians over the issue of the continuing relevance of certain Jewish practices that the Jews deemed critical for remaining within the people of God. Although his discussion deals with incorrect attitudes and actions on the part of both parties, the apostle's pastoral concern focuses on the inappropriate responses of the Gentiles. For it is with them that he sees the greater hope for a solution.

This pastoral response bears great relevance for the church today. Whenever there is a move away from a traditional form of Christian expression or a reevaluation of what constitutes proper behavior for a believer, there is likely to be tension within the body of Christ. On the one side will be those who insist on the old ways, and on the other, those who espouse the new.

Evangelical churches have long championed a Christianity that is marked by the dynamic of relationship rather than the ritual of religion. More specifically, Pentecostal/charismatic churches have been long-standing proponents of freedom in worship expression. It is ironic, then, how certain rituals or forms of piety have become so entrenched within both evangelical and Pentecostal/charismatic circles. The Holiness traditions of many Pentecostal groups make them prone to "canonize" certain Holiness practices as the only proper means of living out one's Christianity. The forms of worship so indicative of Pentecostal/charismatic worship—for example, raised hands, dancing feet, praying in the Spirit—may also come to be viewed as the only truly "spiritual" means of worshiping God. Where certain "religious" forms become normative, the church needs the renewing touch of the Spirit. Factions made up of "those who do" and "those who do not" still threaten the unity of the church.

Paul's argument can be summarized as follows: (1) Accept one another; don't judge (14:1–12); (2) act with love toward one another; don't scandalize (14:13–23); and (3) act like Christ; don't please yourself (15:1–13).

2.4.4.1. Accept One Another; Don't Judge (14:1–12). Paul's opening statement is an exhortation to the strong to accept the one "whose faith is weak," that is, the one whose conscience is not "strong" enough to allow a greater freedom of action (which in this first section means a lack of liberty to eat meat).

The reason for this appeal is given in verse 3c: "God has accepted" the weak. That the same Greek word for "accept" appears in both verses 1 and 3 underscores the reciprocity between our relationship with God and with each other. We are to accept one another because God has accepted each one of us. That this word appears two more times in a similar exhortation toward the end of the discussion (15:7)—Jew and Gentile are to accept one another as Christ has accepted both of them—indicates that mutual acceptance is an undergirding theme of the entire section.

Because of God's acceptance there is no place for condemnation in the community formed by grace. Christ, whose death on the cross effected the believer's acceptance before God (5:10), will make the weak to "stand" (v. 4)—that is, able to live without condemnation before the Lord, both now and at the end (8:1). Because we are servants of God, each of us "stands or falls" before him alone (v. 4). His judgment is ultimately all that matters. Therefore, the appropriate question for every member of the church is: "Who are you to judge someone else's servant?" (v. 4a).

Even though Paul's primary concern in 14:1–15:13 is with the Gentile reaction to Jewish believers, in verse 3 Paul shows his awareness that there were injurious attitudes in both camps. Both were passing judgment on the behavior of the other in different, but equally damaging ways. Thus, Paul calls for the strong not to "despise" (KJV) the abstainer, and for the weak not to "judge" the one who eats whatever he or she wants. The strong were looking down on those who did not take advantage of their liberty; the weak, who saw themselves as the only righteous ones because of their stricter code of behavior, condemned those who did not have the same scruples. Perhaps behind the weak believers' condemnation of the strong lay the presupposition that the strong were not Christians at all.

We find here an accurate depiction of the nature of factionalism in the modern church. Meat-eating is no longer a compelling issue for the contemporary church, but divergent attitudes toward other amoral areas of behavior continue to divide those who do and those who don't. You do not have unity when one faction considers itself superior to another, or when one faction questions the very Christianity of those who do not comply with certain codes of conduct.

In the second paragraph (vv. 5–8), Paul continues to build his case by introducing another source of friction—the issue of sacred days (v. 5). The practice in question here (as argued above) is likely a Jewish-Christian insistence on the continued observance of certain days deemed holy or sacred within Judaism, such as the Sabbath, or Jewish feast days, or both.

Paul then sets this dispute about special days, as well as the meat-eating controversy, within a worship context (vv. 6–8). Since all of life is to be offered in worship (12:1, the programmatic statement given at the outset of the paraenesis section of Romans), the conduct of each believer must be evaluated accordingly. "Each one should be fully convinced in his own mind" about the appropriateness of his or her actions (v. 5c), so that whatever one does or does not do might be done "to the Lord." That is why the one who eats and the one who abstains are both pictured in verse 6 as offering a blessing before their meal (cf. Acts 27:35; 1 Cor. 10:30). This vividly illustrates that the believer who condemns another for what he or she eats is in the dangerous position of condemning, not a sinful act, but rather someone else's act of worship.

Paul reiterates his concern for the type of renewed thinking that sees all of life as worship in verses 7–8, which is summarized by the phrase: "So, whether we live or die, we belong to the Lord" (v. 8c). Paul will later adapt this same principle to the situation of the Colossian believers: "Whatever you do, work at it with all your heart, as working for the Lord, not for men. . . . It is the Lord Christ you are serving" (Col. 3:23–24b; cf. 1 Cor. 10:31).

In short, the function of verses 5–8 is twofold. It reinforces the point made earlier—that the Christian should accept rather than judge someone who is a servant of God—by emphasizing the fact that to criticize another believer's action is to criticize that person's worship. As well, it implies what will become explicit later: Every servant of God is responsible to determine if his or her action may actually be offered to God as an act of worship.

The mention of Christ's death and resurrection in verse 9—those events that enabled Christ to become "the Lord of both the dead nd the living"—is prompted by the previous ssertion that we both live and die to the Lord. 'he reference to Christ's lordship raises the uestion first posed in verse 4: "You, then, why lo you judge your brother?" (v. 10). If Christ s Lord, then we have no right to judge the one vho is responsible to him. The judgment is oming soon enough, when each will receive is or her due. The believer has no right to surp the authority of God to judge or to ttempt to advance the day of judgment.

That is not to say that there is no judgment or the one who is in Christ, "for we will all tand before God's judgment seat" (v. 10c). 'he Old Testament quotation in verse 11, a ombination of Isaiah 49:18 and 45:23, reinorces the argument that each servant is esponsible and accountable to the Lord. God vill judge other believers, but he will also udge the individual who has appointed himelf or herself as a judge of others. It is one hing to hope for justice to be served on others; : is another to be prepared to face one's own udgment. The introduction of the theme of ersonal responsibility prepares the reader for e next stage of the discussion.

2.4.4.2. Act With Love Toward One nother; Don't Scandalize (14:13–23). Vhereas the first stage of Paul's argument ealt with judgmental attitudes, the second rods the hearer to consider what type of ctions are appropriate in a community formed y God's gracious acceptance of all believers. 'here appears to be a rough chiastic structure ere; that is, the points made in the first part f verses 13–23 are dealt with again in reverse rder in the latter part (see Thompson, 201–4). Vhat we observe, then, is a repetition of hemes from verses 13–15 in verses 20–23, nd the "center and therefore the point of mphasis" (Fee, 1994, 617) is in the middle of e passage (vv. 16–19). Different from verses –12, where the apostle's exhortation was irected to both weak and strong, is the maner in which Paul focuses his attention for the emainder of the chapter on the latter. What ollows is his directive to the Gentile members f the Roman church that one's liberty must be onstrained in the interests of love.

Verse 13 marks a transition in the discusion. It summarizes the preceding argument: Therefore [i.e., on the basis of each believer's esponsibility to Christ as Lord and to God as judge] let us stop passing judgment on one another" (v. 13a). And it calls for a new resolution: "Instead, make up your mind not to put any stumbling block or obstacle in your brother's way" (v. 13b). This call for a change of attitude is reinforced by a play on words: The apostle uses the same word *krino* ("to judge") in verse 13a and verse 13b. The literal translation of the Greek reads: "Therefore, let us no longer judge one another, but rather judge [i.e., decide or determine] this—not to put any stumbling block. . . ." Renewed thinking rejects judgmental attitudes and embraces those thoughts that promote the welfare of others in the body of Christ (cf. 12:3–9).

The terms *stumbling block* and *obstacle* are used synonymously as metaphors for something that causes someone to lose faith. The "stumbling block" is something that might cause someone to trip; an "obstacle," which referred originally to the piece of wood that held open an animal trap, is used frequently in both the Old and New Testaments as something that might entice one to sin. The imagery is clear: The open exercise of liberty by the strong presents a temptation to the weak that could result in a fall into sin.

To hear the force of this word combination, however, we must recall the use of these two concepts in 9:33, where they appeared in a quotation from Isaiah 8:14. There the stumbling block ("a stone that causes men to stumble") and obstacle ("a rock that makes them fall") referred to Christ. The Jews stumbled over Christ; that is, they were offended by him, and in their rejection of Jesus as Messiah they rejected God's saving initiative. Similarly, in Romans 14 Paul exhorts the Gentiles to avoid any action that might cause other Jews to lose their faith in Christ. This time the stumbling block is the eating of meat or the nonobservance of certain holy days.

Paul's pronouncement that "no food is unclean in itself" (v. 14) is prefaced with a justification: "As one who is in the Lord Jesus, I am fully convinced. . . ." The combination of these two phrases to introduce the apostle's conviction about this matter betrays his feeling that his thoughts here would elicit strong opposition from the weak, for whom food regulations held covenantal significance. Some understand the phrase "as one who is in the Lord Jesus" as equivalent to the Pauline expression "in Christ," which is Paul's "most characteristic way of defining his relation to the Saviour" (Murray). According to Dodd, Paul is affirming that his conviction "is inseparable from his Christian experience."

Nevertheless, the use of the word "Jesus" distinguishes this expression from the phrase "in Christ" or the variant expression "in the Lord." In other words, Paul cites the name "Jesus" because he is thinking about the earthly ministry of Jesus, not about his relationship with the risen Christ. The apostle is here staking his position on the teaching of Jesus, which is preserved for us in Mark 7:15–23 (cf. Harrison; Fee, 1994, 619). In Jesus' debate with the Pharisees over their tradition regarding clean and unclean, occasioned by their criticism of the disciples' failure to wash their hands before eating (7:1–5), Jesus made the pronouncement that nothing that goes into a man makes him unclean, but rather what comes out (7:15). What Paul is convinced about "in the Lord Jesus" (Rom. 14:14) is that the weak have no theological leg to stand on in their insistence that food laws be observed by the Christian community.

The apostle then immediately qualifies the applicability of his sweeping statement of Christian liberty that "no food is unclean" with the standard set by the individual conscience. While eating meat is neither right nor sinful in and of itself, it is morally wrong for the one who believes in abstaining on spiritual grounds. To put it another way, Christian morality has a subjective component. There is no thought here, of course, that all ethical conduct is subjectively determined. Romans 13:13, to take one example, contains a list of activities prohibited to anyone who claims to walk in the light of the day.

From the premise that the individual conscience plays a role in determining one's ethical conduct comes at least two implications for the strong. (1) The conscience of the weak must not be despised or disregarded, but rather taken into account because of the command to love. To eat in front of someone who considers the practice wrong is to make the mistake of placing the principle of liberty in front of the *agape* principle. "Love," as Paul wrote in 13:10, "does no harm to its neighbor."

(2) For the strong to disregard the feelings of the weak is not only offensive, but potentially destructive. Paul could not ha expressed his warning to the strong about su misguided behavior with greater force than does at the end of verse 15: "Do not by yo eating destroy your brother for whom Chri died." In one phrase Paul both confronts t strong with the supreme example of love, t sacrifice of Christ, which exposes the selfis ness behind their open display of liberty, ar reminds them of the inestimable value of tho for whom Christ paid with his life.

That a brother might be destroyed by a fl grant abuse of liberty reveals the critical ro that the conscience plays in the Christian lif When the conscience is undermined in one are it becomes vulnerable in other areas as we Other beliefs may become open to doubt; oth practices, previously taboo, may begin to l entertained and then enjoyed—even those pra tices that are intrinsically evil. The end of t process may mean the destruction of the soul

The paraenesis in Paul's letter to t Romans opened with a call to each member the body to assume responsibility for oth members by using his or her gifts for the be efit of the whole body (12:3–8). The call f sensitivity to the convictions of fellow belie ers in chapter 14 shows us another way of ta ing responsibility for the welfare of oth Christians.

In verses 16–19, the center of the argume of verses 13–23, come several statements th both summarize and ground what precedes an what follows. The vagueness of verse 16, "D not allow what you consider good to be sp ken of as evil," has resulted in various inte pretations. Dunn, for example, sees in th statement a warning that the non-Christian wi come to despise the gospel because of disha mony in the church. He understands "what yo consider good" to refer to the gospel and view the switch from the second person singular i verse 15 to the plural "you" in verse 15 as a indication that both weak and strong are bein admonished to live in such a way that th church will not be reviled by an onlookin world.

The switch from the singular to the plura however, is too subtle to serve as an indicatio that the intended audience is now the entir church instead of just the strong. It is prefe able to view the switch as a stylistic device t add emphasis (Cranfield). Moreover, th ireek phrase translated "your good" (NIV, 'what you consider good") is an awkward xpression for the gospel; it more naturally lescribes what the strong understood as their reedom within the will of God (cf. 12:2).

The strong are to avoid having their free-om—or what they know is good before God—"be spoken of as evil" (lit., "blas-hemed"). The thought of blasphemy relates ack to verse 6, where acts of eating and bstaining were set within a worship context. he problem Paul anticipates is that what the trong consider part of their spiritual worship 12:1) the Jew considers profane. This is sim-lar to Paul's discussion of eating meat in 1 Co-inthians 10:30: "If I take part in the meal with hankfulness, why am I denounced [lit., blas-hemed] because of something I thank God or?" Paul is not only concerned about how the trong view the weak, but also how the weak erceive the strong, and this concern extends nto Romans 14:17.

The theological basis for what Paul has een arguing is given in verse 17: "The king-om of God is not a matter of eating and drink-ıg, but of righteousness, peace and joy in the Ioly Spirit." The phrase "the kingdom of iod" appears infrequently in the Pauline let-ers, which is rather surprising considering its requent occurrence in the Gospels. Instead of sing kingdom terminology, Paul tends to efine the sphere of Christian existence with uch phrases as "in Christ" and "walking in the pirit." The significance of "the kingdom of iod" here, as Dunn rightly notes, is indicated y the reference to the Holy Spirit at the end of e verse. The connection of the Spirit with the ingdom of God is that "for both Jesus and aul the Spirit *is* the presence of the kingdom, till future in its complete fulfillment."

The phrase "the kingdom of God is not a iatter of eating and drinking" sends a message both Jew and Gentile. For the Gentile, this ieans that the essence of Christianity is some-ing other than insisting on one's liberty to eat nd drink. To put it in more modern terminol-gy, the kingdom is not about fighting for ne's individual rights. What Paul prescribes what he himself regularly practiced: Though I am free and belong to no man, I ake myself a slave to everyone, to win as any as possible" (1 Cor. 9:19). This stance eveals the true freedom that the apostle has discovered. As Bruce aptly summarized: "So completely emancipated was he from spiritual bondage that he was not even in bondage to his emancipation" (1985, 243).

Even though Paul's address in this section continues to be to the strong, verse 17 would have caught the attention of the weak as well. If Paul can say to the strong that the kingdom is not about eating and drinking, then the implication is that the kingdom is not about abstinence either, that is, not eating and not drinking. The law no longer has any role to play in prescribing the terms of righteousness because Christ is the end of the law (10:4). Righteousness is not gained or maintained through food regulations or any other practice of law-keeping. If the Jewish believers are continuing to be observant of certain laws, their only reason for doing so is cultural pref-erence rather than divine requirement. While insisting that the Gentiles graciously accept the practices of the Jews, Paul is simultaneously insisting that the Jews have no theological basis for an attempt to alter the eating habits of the Gentiles.

Having established what the kingdom of God is not, the apostle goes on to define it in terms of relationship: "righteousness, peace and joy in the Holy Spirit" (v. 17b). "In the Holy Spirit" modifies the three nouns that pre-cede it (cf. Käsemann) rather than just the last noun "joy." Consequently, these nouns describe various aspects of living in the Spirit. The prob-lem is determining whether these aspects of life in the Spirit are to be understood as expressions of our vertical relationship to God or of our hor-izontal relationship with others.

If we interpret righteousness, peace, and joy vertically, then this final occurrence in Romans of the word "righteousness" refers to forensic righteousness, that is, the result of God's jus-tification of the believer that places him or her in right standing before him (cf. Cranfield; Käsemann). "Peace" is then our peace with God (cf. 5:1), and "joy" our response to God's work on our behalf.

If, however, we understand these three aspects to be describing our interaction with others in the body of Christ, then righteousness in the Holy Spirit is "right action" (Sanday and Headlam; Barrett; Murray). Peace in the Holy Spirit is the peace that we are to have with one another, with joy being the result. As many commentators have noted, the parallel for this reference to peace and joy in the Spirit is the list of the fruit of the Spirit in Galatians 5:22–23.

The context suggests that these three aspects of life in the Spirit have to do with horizontal relationships. The whole of 12:1–15:13 is intended to explain how the theological arguments of chapters 1–11 are to work out in the life of the Christian community in Rome. Moreover, the verses that follow (vv. 18–19) stress serving and doing—that is, what Christians are supposed to do—which suggests that verse 17b is also about right living. Finally, the phrase that is in parallel with "righteousness, peace and joy in the Holy Spirit" is concerned with human behavior: eating and drinking (v. 17a). Fee even finds in Paul's use of the modifier "Holy" with "the Spirit," a rare combination for him, another indication "that righteousness essentially involves conduct" (1994, 621, n.450).

Thus, Paul is addressing the need for community action that is indicative of life in the Spirit, rather than the divisive type of action that places liberty ahead of love. Paul's definition of the kingdom of God in the here and now is acting rightly, pursuing peace with others, and living in the joy that arises when right action leads to peaceful coexistence with other members of the body of Christ. It should be noted, however, that although the focus in verse 17 is on ethical righteousness rather than forensic righteousness, we would be unwise to separate them completely. For it is God's work in Christ, which sets the individual in right relationship with God, that forms the basis for relationships within the body of Christ.

The idea that renewed thinking reveals God's "good, pleasing and perfect will" (12:2) is revisited in verse 18. To add force to his exhortation in verse 17, the apostle specifies that a community that lives rightly in the pursuit of peace is "pleasing to God." That Paul reintroduces such a statement at this point in the letter suggests that, to his mind, this area was in particular need of renewed thinking. That we live in a day when the themes of personal rights and freedom are often championed above the virtue of sacrificial love suggests that we need the same constant renewing of our minds.

Verse 19 calls believers to pursue actions that promote "peace" and "mutual edification." As this combination suggests, peac among believers is more than the absence o conflict; peace is actualized in the church a members live together in a unity that strength ens all believers. This recalls 12:3–8, wher Paul counseled against the divisive nature o pride, exhorting the believers in Rome to buil each other up through the use of the gifts of th Spirit.

In the remaining verses of chapter 1 (vv. 20–23), earlier points from verses 13–1 are repeated and expanded on. The repercus sions of offending another Christian are no described on a broader scale: Not only is th offended individual's soul at risk (v. 15), bu also "the work of God" (v. 20). In the body o Christ an effect produced in one membe affects the rest of the body.

The category of offensive acts is broadene beyond eating and observing special days wit the introduction of wine drinking (v. 21) as possible offense to the weak conscience. (Fo the background on this, see introductory com ments to ch. 14.) More significantly, Pau writes that "anything else" that might cause brother to fall must also be avoided. Thi important qualification will alert the Roma church to the dangers of future areas of con flict. It also serves to warn us against an thought that a passage dealing with the histo ical problems of a first-century church has n relevance to us. Our schisms may not b between meat-eaters and vegetarians, but th church has never lacked for new issues aroun which to argue and divide.

Verses 22–23 contain a brief summary c the argument to this point: The strong ar indeed in the right to enjoy the freedom the have—they are "blessed" to be able to act wit a clean conscience. Nevertheless, for the sak of the body this liberty should not be flaunte in front of the weak or lobbied for in order t change the habits of others. The strong are t keep their convictions between themselves an God (v. 22).

The weak, on the other hand, are con demned if they transgress their conviction and as the letter makes explicit in verse 23 such infractions are not just personal offense but actual sins against God. Whatever cann be offered to God in worship, whatever "doe not come from faith," is nothing less tha "sin." This drives us back to the decree c

2:1–2, that life for the Christian is not deter- ıined by law but by relationship—established y the work of God in Christ and lived in the pirit. It is for this reason that Paul can say that wo believers can engage in the same activity, hile for only one it is a sin. A law-bound reli- ion would allow no such deviance; a faith- onstituted relationship with God must allow or such.

2.4.4.3. Christ the Model for Weak and trong (15:1–6). The chapter division at 15:1 isguises the fact that the discussion begun in hapter 14 about the relationship between the eak and strong continues in this chapter. Paul ow summarizes and reinforces his earlier oints.

The function of 15:1–2, as Käsemann has oted, is the same as that of 14:13: It recaps the receding section of the argument while focus- ıg attention on the strong in the process. The pening phrase, "We who are strong," reveals 'aul's identification with the theological tance taken by the strong. He continues to ıake it perfectly clear, however, that he does ot side with the manner in which they were ıteracting with the weak. The strong are urged) "bear" the "failings" of the weak.

The word translated "failings" denotes 'eakness rather than moral failing. The weak re those whose faith is too weak or too lim- ed to allow themselves greater freedom of onduct. In line with Galatians 6:2, the strong re called upon to do more than "bear with" (or put up with") the scruples of the weak; the erb used here has a broader range of meaning ıat includes the idea of bearing or carrying.

The type of support that the strong are to rovide for the weak is expressed negatively, ıot to please ourselves" (v. 1), and then pos- ively, to "please his neighbor" (which recalls ıe injunction of Lev. 19:18, cited in Rom. 3:9) and "to build him up" (v. 2). Paul rein- ›rces this second call for love (cf. 14:15) and ıe strengthening of others (cf. 14:19) by plac- ıg the greatest model of selflessness before ıem, Christ: "For even Christ did not please imself" (15:3a). The motif of Jesus as the xample for Christian faith and practice recurs equently throughout the New Testament :.g., Mark 10:35–45; John 13:1–17; 1 Peter :21; 1 John 3:16). Like Philippians 2:1–8, here the humility of Christ that extended ven to death on a cross is set against the pride of the Philippians, Romans 15:3 makes its point by contrasting the ultimate sacrifice of Christ with the selfish attitude of the strong. Paul's choice of the messianic title "Christ" heightens the contrast even further. The point is, if the Christ did that much, how can you not do even this much? Every sacrifice of one's own rights pales in comparison when set against the cross.

Christ's sacrifice is conveyed with a quotation in verse 3 from Psalm 69:9, a psalm that was widely understood as messianic by the early church (Mark 15:23, 36; John 2:17; 15:25). This verse from the Psalms expresses the plight of the one who, because of his faithfulness to God, endures the insults intended for God; in Romans 15:3 the psalm conveys the passion of Christ, who, because of his faithfulness to God, endured the shame of the cross (cf. Phil. 2:8).

The rationale for using Psalm 69 is given in the next verse: The Old Testament "was written to teach us" (cf. 1 Cor. 10:6, 11; 2 Tim. 3:16). This statement (which also explains Paul's frequent use of the Old Testament throughout the letter) is just as pertinent for believers today as it was for the letter's original audience. Although the law is no longer in effect for those who are in Christ, the Old Testament continues to have direct relevance for us. The Scriptures provide encouragement for believers through the sure promises of God contained within them, and they inspire endurance through the examples recorded of those who persevered because of their faith in God.

Such endurance and encouragement produce "hope" within us (v. 4c). Christian hope is future-oriented; it is focused on the completion of God's plan at the end of the age (e.g., 8:18–25; Col. 1:5; 1 Thess. 1:3). Hope is often linked to endurance in the Pauline letters, particularly in Romans (2:7; 5:2–4; 8:24–25; 12:12; cf. also 1 Thess. 1:3), as that which bolsters courage to endure present hardship. The connection between hope and endurance here, however, is different. It is the believer's endurance that allows him or her to participate in that future hope, which is pictured in verses 5–6 as that eschatological moment when Jew and Gentile are united in worship "with one heart and mouth." The certainty of that great day is confirmed by the witness of the Old Testament references in verses 9–11. That Jew and Gentile will one day enjoy together the culmination of God's righteousness was the conclusion of his lengthy discussion in chapters 9–11 about God's faithfulness to Israel (11:25–32).

R. Jewett (18–34) has labeled verses 5–6 a "homiletic benediction"—a form of prayer request normally used at the end of a sermon, but which Paul uses here in Romans (also in 15:13) and in the Thessalonian correspondence (1 Thess. 3:11–13; 5:23; 2 Thess. 2:16–17; 3:5, 16) to summarize arguments in prayer form. He capsulizes his thoughts about the weak and strong, about the Jew and Gentile, by expressing a prayerful request: May the Roman Christians, despite their differences, participate in that glorious future when Jew and Gentile will be united in worship by living together now in "a spirit of unity." Living in love and in mutual dependence as an expression of ultimate unity is a necessary prelude to the grand finale, in which praise of "the God and Father of our Lord Jesus Christ" is the final chord.

2.4.4.4. Summary (15:7–13). It is not readily apparent whether we should understand these verses as the conclusion of the argument about Jew-Gentile relations in 14:1–15:6, of the entire paraenesis (12:1–15:6), or of the whole body of the letter that began in 1:16. The confusion results from the fact that 15:7–13 pick up themes from each of them. We would be wise, then, to see a conclusion that sums up the whole letter, but with particular reference to what has immediately preceded.

The ties between 15:7–13 and 14:1–15:6 are numerous. The subject of the relationship between strong and weak ends the way it began, with a charge that believers accept one another (14:1; 15:7). It is significant, however, that this final admonition—unlike 14:1, which was directed solely toward the strong—reminds *both* parties of their shared responsibility. The body of Christ can only function in unity if all sides graciously accept the other "just as Christ accepted you" (v. 7). This appeal to Christ's example is the second link with the preceding verses (cf. 15:3).

A third link is the appearance of Paul's call for unity within a worship context. That God be glorified is the theme that both concludes 14:1–15:6 and dominates 15:7–13. Jews and Gentiles are to be united in praise to God (vv. 5–6); their acceptance of one another ascribes honor to him (v. 7); Christ's work enables the Gentiles to glorify God for his mercy (vv. 8–9); and the collection of Old Testament references in vv. 9–12 reiterates the theme of praise to God. This theme also brings us back to the opening of the paraenesis in 12:1–2. The hope expressed in 12:2—that all Christians offer themselves in worshipful response to his mercy—is depicted in its eschatological fulfillment in 15:7–13.

Yet, there is a broader perspective in this section that revisits many of the recurring themes in the letter as a whole. The four Old Testament references in verses 9–12 all envisage a future in which Gentiles respond to the Lord God with faith and worship, that is, a future that reverses the past in which the Gentiles "neither glorified him as God nor gave thanks to him" (1:21). These Old Testament texts represent the Torah, the Writings, and the Prophets—Deuteronomy 32:43 (v. 10), Psalm 117:1 (v. 11), and 2 Samuel 22:50 (v. 9) and Isaiah 11:10 (v. 12), respectively.

In a rabbinic style of argumentation, an interpretation was often defended by selecting proof texts from each of these sections of the Hebrew Scriptures. This was surely not the first time that Paul drew on such verses in defense of his mission. The last Old Testament text (v. 12) prophesies the day when the Gentiles will place their hope in the Jewish Messiah, the root of Jesse. That this aspect of the eschaton is stressed reflects the calling of the apostle, for whom "the acceptance of the Gentiles is . . . the decisive eschatological event" (Käsemann).

By pointing to Christ as "a servant of the Jews [lit., of the circumcised] on behalf of God's truth" (i.e., God's faithfulness to the promises made to the patriarchs; cf. 11:28–29), Paul reminds the Roman believers of what he argued earlier: God is not finished with Israel (ch. 9–11). The order of salvation, "first for the Jew, then for the Gentile" (1:16), has not been forgotten. Christ was sent to the circumcised; and when he came, he came as a servant to fulfill the covenant promises. It is incumbent on the Gentiles, then, to serve these brothers and sisters as well, by foregoing aspects of Christian liberty for their sakes.

This section closes with another "homiletic benediction" (cf. 15:5–6), that the "God of ope" will fill these Christians with all joy and eace so that they might overflow with hope v. 13). The final clause "by the power of the Ioly Spirit" modifies the entire verse, indiating that the Spirit's operation is involved in ne production of both fruit and hope. The nention of "joy and peace" in the context of ne Spirit's work revisits the pivotal argument n 14:17. The peace envisioned here, in light of s usage in 14:17 and the surrounding verses, s peace between Jew and Gentile, and the joy eferred to is the result of this state of peace. 'he stipulation that these qualities develop as ne individual exercises his or her trust in God s not to deny their supernatural source, but to ighlight the manner in which the individual is alled on to respond to the Spirit's work by valking in faith.

The power of the Holy Spirit also produces n overflowing of hope in the life of the eliever. Fee (1994, 624) has noted the rather nusual combination of "power" and "Holy pirit": "For Paul and the early church the pirit and power belong together; one cannot nagine the one (Spirit) without the other. Hence it is so seldom put in those terms." For ne to abound in hope in a world largely evoid of it represents a miraculous work of ne Holy Spirit and a sign to the world of the ower of God.

3. Letter Closing (15:14–16:27)

3.1. Travelogue #2 (15:14–33)

3.1.1. Paul's Mission (15:14–22). As the etter opening ended with a travelogue (1:8–5), the final section of the letter opens with nother travelogue. Paul's travel plans figure o prominently in Romans because they have o do with his purposes for writing the letter. At the outset Paul declared that he was intending to visit Rome in order to preach to them 1:15) and so impart to them some spiritual gift 1:11), with the hope that he might reap a harvest among them as he had among other Gentiles (1:13).

Much more explicit, and at the same time pologetic, is the explanation of his future ravel plans in 15:14–33. Is it that after writing t such length he now feels compelled to justify, as Fee says, "that he should write such a ong letter to *them*, as though they needed his nstruction at all" (1994, 625)? This seems ikely because Paul begins by adding another tribute to the one he gave them earlier about their reputation for faith (1:8). He now credits them with being "complete in knowledge and competent to instruct one another" (15:14). This accolade necessarily elicits the clarification that his letter, although written "quite boldly on some points" (referring to 14:1–15:6?), serves "as if to remind" them (15:15). But then the apostle immediately justifies his interest in them on the basis of his unique, God-appointed role as the minister to the Gentiles. It is the grace of God, referred to earlier as the basis for his ministry (1:5; 12:3), that gives him his authority.

Here is an attempt, then, both to recognize the independence and maturity of the Roman congregations, which he lauds, and to assert their need of his ministry, which he introduces with the letter. Romans, however, represents more than an overview of his ministry. Paul's teaching and exhortation in this letter function as the beginning of his ministry to the Roman believers—what he would have said to them in person if he had not been delayed so long in coming.

What Paul describes in verses 15b–16 is his role in bringing about the vision presented in verses 9–12 of Jews and Gentiles worshiping together. He symbolizes his part in this grand scheme with imagery drawn from the Jewish sacrificial system. The apostle depicts himself in verse 16 as a *leitourgos* (NIV "minister"), which in the context of the passage denotes the priestly office. He depicts his ministry as being a priest of Christ Jesus for the nations, with a view to preparing the Gentiles to be a holy sacrifice to God, that is, an "offering . . . sanctified by the Holy Spirit" (note the involvement of the Trinity). The Holy Spirit's work in incorporating a convert into the body of Christ is depicted (cf. 1 Cor. 12:13), again with priestly imagery, as setting the Gentiles apart as a holy sacrifice. Implicit within this phrase is a rebuttal to any Jewish assertion of Gentile uncleanness or unworthiness. The sustained use of sacrificial imagery betrays Paul's understanding of his ministry to the Gentiles as "wholly in continuity and succession with the main line of salvation-revelation in the OT" (Dunn).

Having described his personal calling, he now writes of the nature of his ministry, that is, "what Christ has accomplished through me in leading the Gentiles to obey God" (v. 18; cf. 1:5).

PERSONAL GIFTS OF THE HOLY SPIRIT

Gift	Definition	General References	Specific Examples
Message of wisdom	An utterance from the Holy Spirit applying God's Word or wisdom to a specific situation	Ac 6:3; 1Co 12:8; 13:2, 9, 12	Stephen: Ac 6:10 James: Ac 15:13–21
Message of knowledge	An utterance from the Holy Spirit revealing knowledge about people, circumstances, or Biblical truth	Ac 10:47–48; 13:2; 15:7–11; 1Co 12:8; 13:2, 9, 12; 14:25	Peter: Ac 5:9–10
Faith	Supernatural faith imparted by the Holy Spirit, enabling a Christian to believe God for the miraculous	Mt 21:21–22; Mk 9:23–24; 11:22–24; Lk 17:6; Ac 3:1–8; Ac 6:5–8; 1Co 12:9; 13:2; Jas 5:14–15	A centurion: Mt 8:5–10 A sick woman: Mt 9:20–22 Two blind men: Mt 9:27–29 A Canaanite woman: Mt 15:22–28 A sinful woman: Lk 9:36–50 A leper: Lk 17:11–19
Healing and miraculous powers	Restoring someone to physical health or altering the course of nature by divinely supernatural means	Mt 4:23–24; 8:16; 9:35; 10:1, 8; Mk 1:32–34; 6:13; 16:18; Lk 4:40–41; 9:1–2; Jn 6:2; 14:12; Ac 4:30; 5:15–16; 19:11–12; Ro 15:19; 1Co 12:9, 28, 30; 2Co 12:12;Gal 3:5	Jesus: See chart on "The Miracles of Jesus" Apostles: See chart on "The Miracles of the Apostles"
Prophecy	A special temporary ability to bring a word, warning, exhortation, or revelation from God under the impulse of the Holy Spirit	Lk 12:12; Ac 2:17–18; 1Co 12:10; 13:9; 14:1–33; Eph 4:11; 1Th 5:20–21; 2Pe 1:20–21; 1Jn 4:1–3	Elizabeth: Lk 1:40–45 Mary: Lk 1:46–55 Zechariah: Lk 1:67–79 Peter: Ac 2:14–40; 4:8–12 Twelve men from Ephesus: Ac 19:6 Four daughters of Philip: Ac 21:9 Agabus: Ac 11:27–28; 21:10–11

PERSONAL GIFTS OF THE HOLY SPIRIT (cont.)

Gift	Definition	General References	Specific Examples
Distinguishing between spirits	Special ability to judge whether prophecies and utterances are from the Holy Spirit	1Co 12:10; 14:29	Peter: Ac 8:18–24 Paul: Ac 13:8–12; 16:16–18
Speaking in tongues	Expressing oneself at a level of one's spirit under the direct influence of the Holy Spirit in a language he or she has not learned and does not know	1Co 12:10, 28, 30; 13:1; 14:1–40	Disciples: Ac 2:4–11 Cornelius and his family: Ac 10:44–45; 11:17 Ephesian believers: Ac 19:2–7 Paul: 1Co 14:6, 15, 18
Interpretation of tongues	Special ability to interpret what is spoken in tongues	1Co 12:10, 30; 14:5, 13, 26–28	

The Christocentric character of Paul's work is apparent: Not only did Christ's faithfulness to his role as servant to the Jews prepare the way for the Gentile mission (see 15:8–9), but it now advances only as Christ does the work. Consequently, the Romans are to view his apostolic mission as that of the Lord himself, who works through him by the power of the Holy Spirit.

Paul categorizes his mode of ministry as twofold: in word and deed (v. 18; cf. 2 Thess. 2:17). Two modifying phrases in verse 19 explain the manner in which he has conducted this mode of ministry. They read, literally: "in the power of signs and wonders," and "in the power of the Spirit." The first clarifies what Paul means by deed—the miraculous occurrences that accompanied the preaching of the word. As Murray explains, "signs and wonders" designate not two types of phenomena, but the same acts seen from different points of view: "As a sign it points to the agency by which it occurs and has thus certificatory character; as a wonder the marvel of the event is emphasized" (see Dunn for the use of this phrase in Old Testament and Jewish writings of the Second Temple period).

We know from the New Testament that the miraculous regularly accompanied the preaching of the gospel. In order to provide his readers with evidence that Jesus was the Messiah, John reports in his Gospel some of the various signs (miracles) that Jesus performed (John 20:30–31). Luke records for us the manner in which the miracle served to bring attention to the message being preached, both among the apostles (Acts 2:5–41; 3:1–4:4; 4:29–30; 5:12–16; 8:13 [Philip]) and in the ministry of Paul (13:9–12; 14:3, 8–18; 15:12; 16:25–34; 19:11–20). It was the miraculous that seized the attention of people for whom there was no lack of religious and philosophical options.

The second modifier, "in the power of the Spirit," specifies how these deeds were performed. But there is no reason to limit the applicability of "the power of the Spirit" to the "signs and wonders" (see Dunn; Murray; Fee, 1994, 629). While "signs and wonders" clarify the deeds that Paul has in mind, "the power of the Spirit" explains the spiritual dynamic behind his entire ministry of word and deed.

Unfortunately, such a combined ministry emphasis is often lacking in North American evangelism. The New Testament mode of ministry is still applicable in our modern, pluralistic world. Will it not be a return to such dynamic ministry—in which the powerful proclamation of God's Word is accompanied by a demonstration of his power in the marketplace—that will bring the gospel onto the main stage of a world distracted by religious and pseudo-spiritual sideshows?

The details about Paul's missionary strategy in verses 19b–22 explain why, in light of his concern for the Romans conveyed in this letter, he is only now seeing his way clear to visit Rome. For one thing, he had been preoccupied with evangelizing the region "from Jerusalem all the way around to Illyricum." The latter was a region on the eastern shore of the Adriatic Sea, to the north of Macedonia. Although there is no biblical record of any Pauline ministry in this region, Paul may have gone there during his time in Corinth or during the missionary journey referred to in Acts 20:1. On the other hand, Paul may have used Illyricum to designate the border of his activities, since neighboring Macedonia had been an area of service for him.

Behind Paul's declaration that he had "fully proclaimed" the gospel in this area is not a claim that the whole area had been completely evangelized. Instead, the statement reflects his understanding that he had laid a foundation for the gospel in this region. His missionary strategy involved targeting urban centers in strategic locations, which would then serve as launching points for evangelism by others in the surrounding areas (cf. 1 Cor. 3:10; 1 Thess. 1:8–10).

The other detail given about his missionary strategy is his determination not to build "on someone else's foundation" (supported by a quotation from Isa. 52:15), which is significant for Paul's explanation of both his delay in coming to Rome—where there was an established church already—and his motivation for the impending visit. His visit is not to be perceived as an attempt to exert authority over them, which would contravene the just-stated principle. Rather, he comes to them on his way to an unevangelized field to the west of Italy.

3.1.2. Before Spain: The Collection for the Saints (15:23–33). With the completion of his work in the region from Jerusalem to Illyricum, Paul's long-range itinerary comes into view: a much-anticipated visit to Rome where he hopes to gain support from them for his final destination, Spain (vv. 23–24). The anticipated support may have entailed anything from money to the recruitment of believers willing to accompany him on his journey from Rome to a region with which he was totally unfamiliar. The reason why Paul had chosen Spain for his next missionary journey is not stated. Dunn suggests that Roman influence in Spain in the preceding centuries may have made that region more attractive to a Roman citizen like Paul than other areas, such as Gaul to the northeast. There is no firm evidence that Paul ever reached Spain, despite the report given in 1 Clement 5:7 that he preached to "the farthest limits of the West."

But Paul cannot commence his trip to Spain via Rome until he has delivered to the saints in Jerusalem a collection gathered among the churches he has founded and served. This trip to Jerusalem is the final stage in a lengthy project commonly referred to as "the collection for the saints" (vv. 25–28; see McKnight, 143–47).

Some background information is necessary in order to appreciate the pertinence of this trip for the apostle and for the church in Jerusalem. In Galatians 2:1–10 Paul describes a visit he made to Jerusalem fourteen years after his conversion (or perhaps, after his first visit to Jerusalem), where a significant agreement was reached between the apostles and Paul as to the legitimacy of his missionary endeavors among the Gentiles. The apostle reports that James, Peter, and John sent Barnabas and him on their way with "the right hand of fellowship," but with the stipulation that they would "continue to remember the poor," meaning the poor in Jerusalem (Gal. 2:9–10). Whether because of famine (Acts 11:27–30) or the burden that the Jerusalem assemblies may have faced in hosting visitors to the city, or perhaps as a result of the church's early attempt to share all things in common, the Jerusalem church was in need. Paul's long-standing concern with fulfilling this obligation is evident from his letters (1 Cor. 16:1–4; 2 Cor. 8–9), and its significance from the size of the delegation accompanying him (Acts 20:4–6).

This collection also held great theological import for the apostle. He viewed this offering gathered from predominantly Gentile churches as a means of giving recognition to the spiri tual debt they as Gentile believers owed the Jews (Rom. 15:27). Paul reminded the Gentiles in chapter 11 that they had not supplanted the Jews in the salvific plan of God: "You do not support the root, but the root supports you" (11:18). Moreover, Paul saw the delivery of these funds as an illustration of the mutual dependence between believers that Paul argued for in the paraenesis (12:5; 14:19; 15:2). In other words, it was a practical expression of unity in the body of Christ.

Undoubtedly, this collection had also consumed so much of his time and energy for more personal reasons. The delivery of funds to Jerusalem would have proven Paul's faithfulness to the agreement made between him and the apostles and would have served as a vindication of his work among the Gentiles. At least, Paul hopes that the collection will be perceived in such a positive manner.

But as his prayer request in verses 30–32 betrays, he has no such assurance. The forceful language used to express this request ("I urge you . . . to join me in my struggle") reveals his deep-seated misgivings about the reception that awaits him. He is not only concerned about his enemies there ("the unbelievers"), who attempted to kill him some years previous (Acts 9:29–30), but also about the Jewish believers and their reaction to the gift. Is this why he stresses not just the obligation of the Gentiles to support the Jewish saints, but also mentions twice that the northern Mediterranean Gentiles have contributed with gladness rather than from a sense of compulsion (vv. 26–27)? Is this his way of refuting any notion that the gift is simply an obligation that the Jerusalem church is owed, instead of, as Paul intends, the demonstration of the Spirit's love at work in the body?

The misgivings of the apostle to the Gentiles about his arrival in the center of the Jewish world are well-founded. The optimistic statements that lie alongside his expressions of concern—"I know that when I come to you, I will come in the full measure of the blessing of Christ" (v. 29)—and his prayerful wish that he might arrive "with joy" (v. 32) after his watershed experience in Jerusalem strike a note of sadness for the modern reader. For we know what the apostle only suspects. Paul will be imprisoned in Jerusalem and eventually arrive in Rome, not as an evangelist about to embark on the next phase of his missionary work, not "in the full measure of the blessing of Christ" (at least not in the manner he anticipates it), but in shackles.

Something of Paul's reaction to his arrival in the capital as a prisoner is seen in the letter he wrote the Philippians from his cell in Rome (Phil. 1:12–18). To his joy he discovered that his presence in Rome as a prisoner had inspired some to preach with new boldness because of their regard for him. To his dismay he also heard that Christ was being preached with new vigor by others because they viewed his confinement as an opportunity to gain converts at his expense. He came to a point of personal resolution to this situation by focusing on the resultant surge in evangelistic preaching, whether from motives of love or rivalry. Indeed, Paul declared that he would rejoice because of it (Phil. 1:18). Paul found himself in a position where he had to live out the principle of Romans 8:28—that in all things God works for good—in front of the very ones to whom he had originally penned it.

Romans 15 ends with a benediction (v. 33), but, like the homiletic benedictions given earlier (15:5–6, 13), it functions as a point of summary and transition rather than as a conclusion. When Paul uses a benediction to close out a letter, it is typically in the form "the grace of the Lord Jesus Christ be with you" (with minor variations; see 16:20b). What is noteworthy is Paul's selection of the expression "the God of peace" in 15:33 (cf. 2 Cor. 13:11; Phil. 4:9), for it reveals the outcome he desires from his trip to Jerusalem.

3.2. Commendation of Phoebe (16:1–2)

The first matter of final business for Paul is to commend Phoebe, the woman who is carrying this letter to Rome (there was no public mail system). Presumably, Phoebe will pick up the letter from Paul in transit through Corinth from her home in Cenchrea, the eastern port of Corinth. Paul's commendation is important because it opens doors of hospitality and Christian fellowship to her, which will also mitigate the dangers facing a woman traveling alone.

Some intriguing, but unfortunately cryptic, details are given about Phoebe. She is identified as a deaconess (*diakonos*) of the church in

Cenchrea. The NIV translates *diakonos* as "servant," which seems to miss the more official role suggested by the grammar (see Dunn; Käsemann). The time when offices were first recognized in the history of the early church is a moot point. We know that at least by the time of the writing of Philippians some years later the office of "deacon" had appeared (Phil. 1:1); 1 Timothy, written later still, lists requirements for deacons, although without specifying their role. Nevertheless, what seems clear in Romans 16:1 is the somewhat formal role that Phoebe held within her church. Käsemann argues, "Insofar as Phoebe has a permanent and recognized ministry, as is emphasized by the participle and the place name, one may at least see an early stage of what later became the ecclesiastical office."

Phoebe is also identified as a "patron" (NIV "a great help to"), that is, an individual of some means who offered her influence and financial resources to others. The NIV translation once more moves away from any type of recognized role here, but Dunn argues well that the term *prostatis* indicates a position in the Christian community. As a patron in Cenchrea, her work benefited both local believers and Christians who traveled through that Corinthian port, including the apostle himself (v. 2). Presumably the local body of believers met in her house. By stressing her value to the saints as deacon and patron (perhaps these were intertwined), Paul is commending her as a person worthy of respect.

3.3. Greetings to Paul's Acquaintances (16:3–16)

The greetings in this section are not just about keeping in touch. While the apostle certainly wants to be remembered to those he knows, some quite well, the list of people named serves to establish points of contact between himself and the Roman communities of faith. He uses what was by this time a standard form of greeting. Despite appearances in the English translation, the form was used to extend greetings directly to the one named; that is, Paul is saying "greetings to . . ." (Gamble, 93).

For the sake of space, we will not examine each of these greetings individually. Instead, a few particular points of interest will be raised. (1) At the head of the list we encounter a married couple, because they held a certain priority in Paul's missionary work. Priscilla (here Prisca, a diminutive form; see NIV note) and Aquila, as they did in Ephesus (1 Cor. 16:19), are again hosting a church in their home in Rome. They worked closely with the apostle in Corinth, where they first met him (Acts 18:2–3). They then accompanied him to Ephesus (18:18–19). Perhaps it was there, during the riot mentioned in Acts 19:23–41, that they risked their lives for him (Rom. 16:4). Paul was the sort of individual who could attract such fierce loyalty and, conversely, provoke fierce opposition (15:31).

(2) There are other local assemblies of believers identified in this list (v. 10—"the household of Aristobulus"; v. 11—"the household of Narcissus"; v. 14—"the brothers with them"; v. 15—"all the saints with them"), which shows that what we often refer to as the church in Rome was actually a number of house churches across the city (see "Recipients" in the Introduction).

(3) Also noteworthy is the prominence of women in this list, where Paul "lists about twice as many men as women, but commends more than twice as many women as men" (Keener, 589)—a testament to their vital importance in the early church. Of particular interest in this regard is the reference in verse 7 to Junias, who is called, along with Andronicus, "outstanding among the apostles." There is good reason to render this name as the female name Junia, even though many commentators translate it Junias, taking it as a contraction of the masculine name Junianus. Up until the modern period, however, it was presumed that this was a female name. Significant is the fact that "Junia" is well attested in inscriptions of the period, but there is no such evidence for the existence of the male form "Junias."

Beyond its common designation of the Twelve, the term *apostle* had a wider range of meaning that included those who had distinguished themselves in the early church (1 Cor. 15:5–7 differentiates between the two groups). What we have here, then, is evidence that a woman was numbered among the larger group of "apostles" (see Stuhlmacher).

(4) The types of names that appear in this list reveal something of the social composition of the Roman assemblies.[9] Many of these are

names one would find among the lower classes of Roman society, that is, slaves, freedmen, and freedwomen.

(5) Finally, it is touching to see the reference to the mother of Rufus, whom Paul also calls "a mother to me" (v. 13). Noteworthy for our understanding of the character of Paul is not only the fact that this woman, in some way, treated the apostle as her own son, but also that Paul recognizes it and proclaims it publicly.

3.4. Final Warning (16:17–20)

Paul uses the opportunity afforded in the closing section of the letter to sound a warning. The sudden shift in mood—from cordial greetings to earnest warning—is not unprecedented in his letters (Gal. 6:11–15; Phil. 3:2–21). The mention of the reputation of the believers in Rome for obedience (Rom. 16:19) indicates that this threat has not yet penetrated their churches. The brevity of Paul's treatment of the issue and its postscript location also give evidence that this warning is a preventative measure.

Although it is common for interpreters to identify a particular party or philosophy that occasions this warning, the various solutions remain speculative. Paul warns against false teachers without specifying whether he has in mind other "Christians" or unbelievers, and without explaining the content of their teaching. It has been suggested that the Judaizers are in the background—that is, those Jewish Christians who insisted on obedience to certain Jewish practices as a necessary part of the Christian life.

There is no clear indication in the text, however, that Paul is reacting to a Jewish-Christian agenda. In fact, Käsemann argues that the lack of any explicit reference in verses 17–20 to the overriding concern of Romans with Jew-Gentile relations is another reason to doubt that chapter 16 was part of the original copy of Romans (see the Introduction, "Original Form of Romans"). Others, however, have argued that the general nature of this warning is meant to compensate for Paul's preoccupation with Jew-Gentile relations in Romans. On coming to the end of the letter, he is now reminded of another threat facing them (Dunn, 901–2).

The phrase "such people are not serving our Lord Christ, but their own appetites [lit., belly]" (v. 18) offers a contrast between those who serve Christ and those who serve their own desires. This phrase may indicate that Paul is concerned about an antinomian philosophy that might lead believers into exercising a sinful liberty. Such a concern has appeared in chapters 6–8, where Paul takes pains to show that his message of freedom from the law is not an antinomian manifesto.

There are similarities between the warnings given here and in Philippians 3. But this fact alone does not allow us to settle the question about the nature of the threat to the Roman believers. For (1) it is difficult to determine who the opponents of the gospel were in Philippi, and (2) the presence of some similarities (cf. "their god is their stomach" [Phil. 3:19] with Rom. 16:18) is not sufficient to establish that the same type of opponent is in view in both situations.

All this being said, it is probably best to take this section as a general warning against any teaching "contrary to the teaching you have learned" (v. 17). The general nature of the warning, however, does not permit us to ignore its importance for the Romans and for us. The Christian faith is built on the revealed truths that have been handed down through the centuries. With each new generation there is the same danger that the message of the gospel will be abandoned in favor of some new approach that, while packaged in enticing phraseology and culturally relevant symbols, is simply self-serving and thus ultimately destructive. The test of each religious trend and "new revelation" is its consistency with the teaching of the gospel preserved for us in the Scriptures.

The final prayer wish in verse 20—that "the God of peace will soon crush Satan under your feet"—brings this brief warning into eschatological perspective. Although the believer must be on guard against evil now, the time is soon coming when Satan himself will be crushed by God and held underfoot (which is the symbolic stance of the conqueror over the vanquished). But note that it is under the feet of the Christian that Satan will be placed. By God's grace the church will share in the divine victory. An allusion to Genesis 3:15 lies behind this text: Not only does the idiom of crushing under one's foot recall the prophecy that the offspring of the woman will crush the serpent's head, but the warning against being deceived is reinforced by alluding to the serpent's deception of Eve.

When will this crushing of Satan occur? Commentators differ on the chronology of this event. Some view it as coming after the Parousia (Käsemann; Black), while others see it as a present event. That is, there is a speedy victory for the believer over Satan in the here and now (Harrison). An understanding of apocalyptic eschatology is helpful here. One of its primary functions was to encourage those in distress by means of a revelation of some imminent event. The stunning image of Satan, the great nemesis of the church, soon being held under the feet of believers when Christ returns strengthens one's resolve to continue to engage the enemy in the present. We are fighting a battle that we know we are going to win.

3.5. Greetings From Paul's Associates (16:21–23)

In a second set of greetings, various coworkers with Paul in Corinth are now remembered to the Roman community of believers. Paul regularly passed along greetings from others at the end of his letters. Sometimes he simply identified the parties in mind as a group: "the saints" (2 Cor. 13:13; Phil. 4:22), "the brothers" (1 Cor. 16:20; Phil. 4:21), or "everyone" (Titus 3:15). At other times, as here, individuals are mentioned (Col. 4:10–14; 2 Tim. 4:21; Philem. 23–24).

The greetings to particular individuals given in the letters to the Romans and to the Colossians share the common function of establishing contact with an assembly that Paul has not visited. Not only is this the case with the greetings that Paul sends (16:3–16), but also with the ones his associates pass along. These two letters are the only ones Paul wrote to churches in which specific individuals are mentioned who send greetings. In other words, the naming of people (probably some of them known among the assemblies addressed) furthers his aim of building a connection between himself and those assemblies.

At the head of the list is Timothy, who had been a great help to Paul in his ministry in Macedonia and Achaia (Acts 17–18). His role in dealing with the opposition Paul faced from the Corinthian congregation is known to us from 1 Corinthians 4:17; 16:10–11. He is appropriately given the noteworthy title of "my fellow worker." Three individuals, who are impossible to identify with certainty, are all called "relatives": Lucius, Jason, and Sosipater. As in verses 7 and 11, this word probably denotes fellow Jews, who, as Dunn suggests, may have been part of the entourage accompanying Paul on his mission to deliver the Jerusalem collection.

That the man who wrote down this letter, Tertius, puts in his own greeting is unusual (v. 22), but not the fact that Paul employed a secretary. This was common practice for the apostle. In several of his letters he picked up a pen at the end in order to put a more personal touch on the ending (1 Cor. 16:21; Gal. 6:11; Col. 4:18; 2 Thess. 3:17; Philem. 19).

Listed also among those who desire to be remembered to the saints in Rome are Gaius, Erastus, and Quartus. Even though connecting these names with individuals known elsewhere in the New Testament is speculative, we can be reasonably sure that the Gaius mentioned here, who is commended for his generosity in allowing his house to accommodate the believers in Corinth, is the same man Paul names as one of the few he baptized in water during his ministry in Corinth (1 Cor. 1:14). Erastus is identified as *oikonomos* (from which we derive "economist") of the city, which may be a lesser position than what the NIV credits him with—"the city's director of public works." What is certain is that he held some type of financial post in Corinth; perhaps he is included here because of his contacts in Rome.

3.6. Closing Doxology (16:25–27)

There is some dispute as to whether this closing doxology was original to the letter. Its varied positions in the manuscripts (consult the longer commentaries) and the non-Pauline nature of the idioms used have suggested to some interpreters that this doxology comes from a hand other than Paul's. Moreover, all of Paul's other New Testament letters end with a benediction. There is another textual problem here as well: the status of the benediction in verse 24. Because the manuscript evidence for its inclusion is rather weak, the NIV places it in a footnote.

These matters return us to the issue of the history of this letter. There is some evidence that this letter, because of its great value, may have circulated in a number of different forms

THE OLD TESTAMENT IN THE NEW

NT Text	OT Text	Subject
Ro 1:17	Hab 2:4	The righteous live by faith
Ro 2:6	Ps 62:12; Pr 24:12	God's fair judgment
Ro 2:24	Isa 52:5; Eze 36:22	God's name cursed among Gentiles
Ro 3:4	Ps 51:4	God's righteous judgment
Ro 3:10–18	Ps 5:9; 10:7; 14:1–3; 36:1; 53:1–3; 140:3; Ecc 7:20; Isa 59:7–8	Sin of humanity
Ro 4:3, 9	Ge 15:6	Faith of Abraham
Ro 4:7–8	Ps 32:1–2	Blessings of forgiveness
Ro 4:17	Ge 17:5	Abraham as a father of many
Ro 4:18	Ge 15:5	Offspring of Abraham
Ro 4:22	Ge 15:6	Faith of Abraham
Ro 7:7	Ex 20:17; Dt 5:21	Tenth commandment
Ro 8:36	Ps 44:22	Sheep for the slaughter
Ro 9:7	Ge 21:12	God's choice of Isaac
Ro 9:9	Ge 18:10, 14	Promise for Sarah
Ro 9:12	Ge 25:23	God's choice of Jacob
Ro 9:13	Mal 1:2–3	Love for Jacob, not Esau
Ro 9:15	Ex 33:19	Mercy of God
Ro 9:17	Ex 9:16	Purpose of Moses
Ro 9:20	Isa 29:16; 45:9	Potter and clay
Ro 9:25–26	Hos 1:10; 2:23	Now God's people
Ro 9:27–29	Isa 1:9; 10:22–23	The remnant
Ro 9:32–33	Isa 8:14	A stone on which people stumble
Ro 9:33	Isa 28:16	Trust in the cornerstone
Ro 10:5	Lev 18:5	Living by the law
Ro 10:6	Dt 30:12	The word not in heaven
Ro 10:7	Dt 30:13	The word not in the deep
Ro 10:8	Dt 30:14	The word near you
Ro 10:11	Isa 28:16	Trust in the cornerstone
Ro 10:13	Joel 2:32	Salvation in the Lord
Ro 10:15	Isa 52:7	Beautiful feet
Ro 10:16	Isa 53:1	Unbelief of Israel
Ro 10:18	Ps 19:4	General revelation
Ro 10:19	Dt 32:21	Making Israel envious
Ro 10:20	Isa 65:1	Salvation of the Gentiles
Ro 10:21	Isa 65:2	Obstinate Israel
Ro 11:3–4	1Ki 19:10, 14, 18	A saved remnant
Ro 11:8	Dt 29:4	A misunder-standing mind
Ro 11:8	Isa 29:10	God seals the eyes
Ro 11:9–10	Ps 69:22–23	Judgment on enemies
Ro 11:26–27	Isa 59:20–21	Deliverer from Zion
Ro 11:27	Isa 27:9	Full removal of sin
Ro 11:34	Isa 40:13	The mind of the Lord
Ro 11:35	Job 41:11	God owns all
Ro 12:19	Dt 32:35	God avenges sin
Ro 12:20–21	Pr 25:21–22	Treating one's enemies
Ro 13:9	Ex 20:13; Dt 5:17	Sixth commandment
Ro 13:9	Ex 20:14; Dt 5:18	Seventh commandment
Ro 13:9	Ex 20:15; Dt 5:19	Eighth commandment
Ro 13:9	Ex 20:17; Dt 5:21	Tenth commandment
Ro 13:9	Lev 19:18	Love your neighbor as yourself
Ro 14:11	Isa 45:23	Every knee shall bow
Ro 15:3	Ps 69:9	Insults on Christ
Ro 15:9	2Sa 22:50; Ps 18:49	Praise among the nations
Ro 15:10	Dt 32:43	Rejoice, O nations
Ro 15:11	Ps 117:1	Nations praising God
Ro 15:12	Isa 11:10	The root of Jesse
Ro 15:21	Isa 52:15	Gentiles hear the gospel

during the early church period. This would explain the differences in the endings contained in the manuscripts. It is certainly possible that the doxology we find here was appended at a later time.

Still, the argument frequently made that the language and idiom of the doxology are not Pauline is difficult to sustain for two reasons. (1) One should not expect Paul to use the same phraseology in composing a doxology, with its poetic structure, as he does when writing the rest of the letter. (2) The connections between the doxology and the letter are so close that it suggests that one author composed both.

Stuhlmacher makes a strong case that Paul wrote the doxology in order to recall the opening of the letter in 1:1–7. That is, this concluding praise to God reiterates the original intention of the introduction: an explanation of "the gospel of Christ which had been entrusted to Paul." The doxology (1) summarizes the nature of the gospel, here described as a "mystery"—the plan of God to bring salvation to all the nations, which was prophesied beforehand (cf. 1:2) and is now being made clear in the preaching of Jesus Christ (cf. 1:3–4); and (2) restates its goal: that everyone, Jew and Gentile alike, might come to a point of faith and obedience (cf. 1:5).

The tight structure of the doxology shows the careful manner in which it was crafted. The brief, balanced phrases suggest that this was designed to be used liturgically. In fact, the final line—"to the only wise God be glory forever through Jesus Christ! Amen"—may have been the response of the congregation (Cranfield; Käsemann; Stuhlmacher). Such a note of praise at the conclusion of this magnificent letter does deserve a response: Amen, so be it!

NOTES

[1]When references to other commentaries on Romans are made, page numbers will not be given if the quote in question can be found in the discussion of that same verse in that commentary.

[2]For more on the depiction of Abraham in both canonical and noncanonical writings, see N. L. Calvert, "Abraham," *DPL*, 1–9.

[3]One can find in the commentaries of Moo and Bruce, for example, a traditional defense of the doctrine of original sin. Moo does concede, however, that one must take Romans 5:12 together with 5:18–19 to defend the idea that when Adam sinned, all of humankind did so as well. Conversely, Stuhlmacher argues that no such doctrine can be found here or elsewhere in Paul.

[4]The idea that an evil desire was resident within an individual was found in the Judaism of Paul's day (see T. Jud. 20:1ff.; T. Ash. 1:3–4).

[5]For those familiar with 8:1 from the KJV, it is immediately apparent that the NIV translation is shorter. There is a good reason for this. Earlier manuscripts than the ones available to the translators of the KJV do not include the longer ending—"who walk not after the flesh, but after the Spirit." It seems as if the longer ending was added at one point in the history of the transmission of this letter, probably to bring this verse into line with the ending of verse 4.

[6]Strictly speaking, there is no imperative in the Greek in Romans 12:12–13, but there is an imperatival idea present.

[7]For a vigorous defense of the idea that chapter 9 does have applicability for the eternal destiny of individuals, see the commentary of Moo on this section.

[8]Similar was the understanding of the Jewish apocalyptic writers, who believed that God was revealing to his people in the last days information about the time of the end.

[9]See the analysis of the various names and their associations in the longer commentaries, such as those of Dunn, Harrison, and Käsemann.

BIBLIOGRAPHY

C. K. Barrett, *A Commentary on the Epistle to the Romans*, HNTC (1957); G. R. Beasley-Murray "Baptism," *DPL*, 60–66 (1993); M. Black, *Romans* NCB (1973); G. Braumann, "Exhort," *NIDNTT* 1.567–71 (1975); F. F. Bruce, *Paul: Apostle of the Heart Set Free* (1977); idem, *The Letter of Paul to the Romans*, TNTC (1985); R. Bultmann, *TDNT* 1.715–16 (1964); N. Calvert, "Abraham," *DPL*, 1–9 (1993); J. Calvin, *Commentaries on the Epistle of Paul the Apostle to the Romans* (1947); J Charlesworth, ed., *Old Testament Pseudepigrapha* 2 vols. (1983, 1985); W. Conybeare and J. Howson *The Life and Epistles of St. Paul* (1899); C. E. B Cranfield, *A Critical and Exegetical Commentary on the Epistle to the Romans*, ICC (1975, 1979); W D. Davies, *The Gospel and the Land* (1974); A Deissmann, *Paul: A Study in Social and Religious History* (1912; rev. ed. 1927); C. H. Dodd, *The Epistle of Paul to the Romans*, MNTC (1932); T. Donaldson, *Paul and the Gentiles: Remapping the Apostle's Convictional World* (1997); J. D. G. Dunn *Romans 1–8; Romans 9–16* (1988); H. L. Ellison *The Mystery of Israel: An Exposition of Romans 9–11* (1966); G. Fee, "Pauline Literature," *Dictionary of Pentecostal and Charismatic Movements*, 665–83 (1988); idem, "Gifts of the Spirit," *DPL*, 339–47 (1993); idem, *God's Empowering Presence* (1994)

. A. Fitzmyer, *Romans*, AB (1993); V. Furnish, *The Moral Teaching of Paul* (1979); H. Gamble, *The Textual History of the Letter to the Romans* (1977); . Godet, *Commentary on Romans* (1879; repr. 977); R. Gundry, Soma *in Biblical Theology With Emphasis on Pauline Anthropology* (1976); J. Gundry-Volf, "Expiation, Propitiation, Mercy Seat," *DPL*, 279–84 (1993); M. J. Harris, *Raised Immortal: Resurrection and Immortality in the New Testament* (1983); E. F. Harrison, "Romans," *EBC* 1976); C. Hodge, *Commentary on the Epistle to the Romans* (1886; repr. 1950); J. Jeremias, *TDNT*, .364–67; R. Jewett, "The Form and Function of the Homiletic Benediction," *Anglican Theological Review* 51 (1969): 18–34; V. Johnson, "The Development of Sheol in the Jewish Apocalyptic Writings" (Th.D. thesis, Wycliffe College, University of Toronto, 1996); R. Karris, "Romans 14:1–15:13 and the Occasion of Romans," *The Romans Debate*, 55–84 (rev. ed. 1991); E. Käsemann, *Commentary on Romans* (1980); C. S. Keener, "Man and Woman," *DPL*, 583–92 (1993); W. W. Klein, *The New Chosen People: A Corporate View of Election* 1990); W. G. Kümmel, *Römer 7 und die Bekehrung des Paulus* (1929); R. C. Lenski, Interpretation of St. Paul's Epistle to the Romans (1945); D. Lim, *Spiritual Gifts: A Fresh Approach* (1991); R. Longenecker, *Paul, Apostle of Liberty* (1976); M. Luther, *Lectures on Romans: Glosses and Scholia* 1972); S. McKnight, "Collection for the Saints," *DPL*, 143–47 (1993); H. A. W. Meyer, *Critical and Exegetical Handbook to the Epistle to the Romans* (1884); W. Michaelis, *TDNT*, 5.930–35; D. Moo, *The Epistle to the Romans*, NICNT (1996); L. Morris, "The Meaning of *hilasterion* in Romans 3:25," *NTS* 2 (1955–56): 33–43; idem, *The Apostolic Preaching of the Cross* (1965); idem, "Redemption," *DPL*, 784–819 (1993); S. Mott, "Civil Authority," *DPL*, 141–43 (1993); J. Murray, *The Epistle to the Romans*, NICNT, 2 vols. (1959, 1965); A. Nygren, *Commentary on Romans* (1944); Pelagius, *Pelagius's Commentary on Romans*, ed. by M. De Bruyn (1993); J. Quasten, *The Beginnings of Patristic Literature* (1950); M. Reasoner, "Political Systems," *DPL*, 718–23 (1993); A. Rupprecht, "Slave, Slavery," *DPL*, 881–83 (1993); W. Sanday and A. C. Headlam, *A Critical and Exegetical Commentary on the Epistle to the Romans*, ICC (1902); E. P. Sanders, *Paul and Palestinian Judaism* (1977); idem, *Paul, the Law, and the Jewish People* (1983); E. Schürer, *The History of the Jewish People in the Age of Jesus Christ* (1973–87); S. K. Stowers, *The Diatribe and Paul's Letter to the Romans* (1981); P. Stuhlmacher, *Paul's Letter to the Romans* (1994); R. C. Tannehill, *Dying and Rising With Christ. A Study in Pauline Theology* (1967); M. Thompson, *Clothed With Christ: The Example and Teaching of Jesus in Romans 12.1–15.13* (1991); F. Watson, *Paul, Judaism and the Gentiles: A Sociological Approach* (1986); J. Wesley, *Explanatory Notes Upon the New Testament* (1950); N. T. Wright, "The Messiah and the People of God" (Ph.D. diss., Oxford University, 1980); idem, *What Saint Paul Really Said* (1997).

1 CORINTHIANS

Anthony Palma

INTRODUCTION

1. Paul and the Corinthian Church

On his second missionary journey, Paul visited Corinth (Acts 18:1–18) after preaching in the chief cities of Macedonia and in Athens. He remained in the city for one and a half years (18:11). He may have reached Corinth in the spring of A.D. 50 and departed in the fall of A.D. 51.

Shortly after arriving in Corinth, Paul met Aquila and Priscilla, with whom he stayed. He bore witness to Christ each Sabbath in the synagogue until Jewish resistance forced him to withdraw, but not before Crispus, the ruler of the synagogue, was converted along with his household. Paul then turned to the Gentiles; among the converts would have been proselytes to Judaism and God-fearers, as well as pagan idolaters.

Jewish opposition culminated in the Jews bringing charges against Paul before Gallio, the proconsul of Achaia. Gallio had the Jews "ejected from the court" (Acts 18:16) because he judged it was a matter internal to Judaism, which they ought to settle among themselves. The mention of Gallio provides one of the few New Testament dates that can be ascertained with reasonable accuracy. Based on an inscription found at Delphi, his proconsulship probably began in July of A.D. 51. The Jews likely appealed to him shortly after he took office.

After leaving Corinth in the fall of 51, Paul made a brief stop at Ephesus before returning to Antioch in Syria. He revisited Ephesus in the summer of 52 and remained there about three years (Acts 20:31).

2. The Corinthian Correspondence

We know that Paul wrote at least four letters to the Corinthians. (1) During his lengthy stay in Ephesus, he wrote a letter prior to 1 Corinthians, to which he alludes in 5:9. This letter is lost unless, as some believe, part of it is found in 2 Corinthians 6:14–7:1. (2) He later wrote 1 Corinthians, possibly in the spring of A.D. 55, sometime prior to Pentecost (1 Cor. 16:8). (3) In 2 Corinthians he refers to a letter he had written "out of great distress and anguish of heart and with many tears" after he wrote 1 Corinthians (2 Cor. 2:3–9; 7:8). (4) His last letter was 2 Corinthians, written possibly in the fall of A.D. 56.

3. Occasion for Writing

First Corinthians is probably the most "occasional" of all Paul's letters, primarily because of the circumstances under which it was written. The apostle was motivated to write the letter after receiving reports about disturbing conditions in the Corinthian assembly. One source of information was members of Chloe's household (1:11); chapters 1–6 are a response to their reports. Another major source of information was Stephanas, Fortunatus, and Achaicus, members of the Corinthian church, who delivered a letter from the church to Paul in Ephesus (16:15–17). Most of chapters 7–16 responds to questions asked in that letter. The variety of problems Paul was compelled to address accounts for the sometimes abrupt changes from one topic to the next.

The numerous and serious problems in the Corinthian church were probably not typical of all the churches Paul founded. They serve, nevertheless, to disabuse the contemporary believer of any romanticized, idealized view of the early church. The *types* of problems, if not the specific problems themselves, have surfaced in the church throughout its history.

The various problems in the Corinthian assembly resulted in tremendous benefit to the church at large. Were it not for their problems, for example, we would be without a theological treatment of the Lord's Supper, the great love chapter, the extended treatment of spiritual gifts, the classical passage on bodily resurrection, and instructions related to church discipline, marriage, and Christian ethics.

4. The City of Corinth

In New Testament times, Corinth was probably the third largest city of the Roman Empire, next to Rome and Alexandria. Its population is variously estimated, but may have numbered

Corinth

In the time of Paul

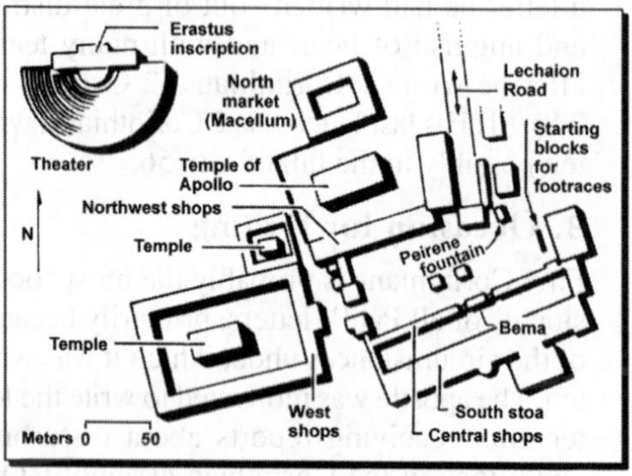

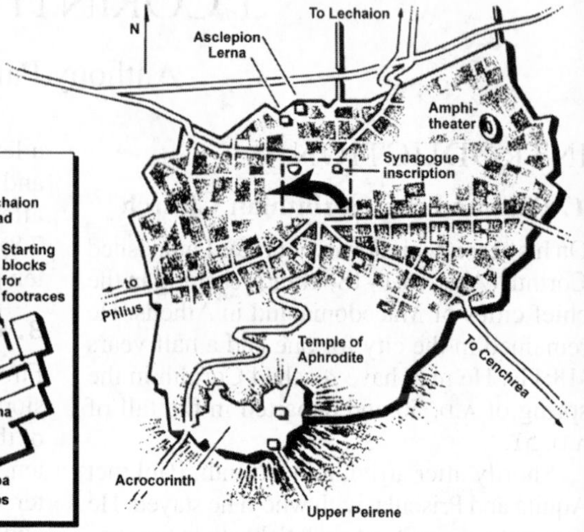

The city of Corinth, perched like a one-eyed Titan astride the narrow isthmus connecting the Greek mainland with the Peloponnese, was one of the dominant commercial centers of the Hellenic world as early as the eighth century B.C.

No city in Greece was more favorably situated for land and sea trade. With a high, strong citadel at its back, it lay between the Saronic Gulf and the Ionian Sea and ports at Lechaion and Cenchrea. A *diolkos*, or stone tramway for the overland transport of ships, linked the two seas. Crowning the Acrocorinth was the temple of Aphrodite which was served, according to Strabo, by more than 1,000 pagan priestess-prostitutes.

By the time the gospel reached Corinth in the spring of A.D. 52, the city had a proud history of leadership in the Achaian League and a spirit of revived hellenism under Roman domination following the destruction of the city by Mummius in 146 B.C.

Paul's lengthy stay in Corinth brought him directly in contact with the major monuments of the *agora*, many of which still survive. The fountain-house of the spring *Peirene*, the temple of Apollo, the *macellum*, or meat market (1Co 10:25), and the theater, the *bema* (Ac 18:12), and the unimpressive synagogue all played a part in the experience of the apostle. An inscription from the theater names the city official Erastus, probably the friend of Paul mentioned in Romans 16:23.

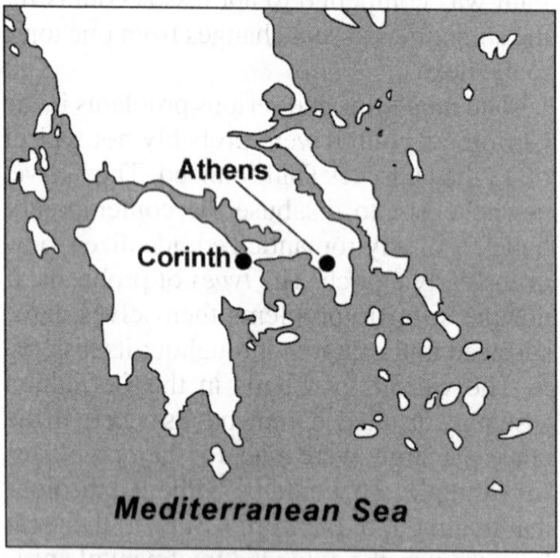

After preaching in Macedonia and Athens, Paul visited Corinth and stayed for a year and a half.

about half a million. It was located on the Peloponnesus, a small land area connected to the Greek mainland by a narrow isthmus. It lay about a mile and a half south of the isthmus.

Corinth reached the peak of its glory and prosperity around 600 B.C. It was destroyed by the Romans in 146 B.C. In 46 B.C. Julius Caesar rebuilt it, designated it a Roman colony, and settled it with many Roman freedmen. Augustus, the first Roman emperor (died A.D. 14), made Corinth the capital of the province of Achaia. When Paul first visited the city in A.D. 50, the population consisted of native Greeks, Romans, and Jews, as well as slaves.

Because of its ideal location, Corinth was a crossroads of much trade and travel between Rome and the East. It was inland but had two nearby seaports on the isthmus—Cenchrea leading to the Aegean Sea (Acts 18:18; Rom. 16:1) and Lechaeum to the Adriatic Sea. Sea captains chose to take their cargo across the isthmus rather than travel around the Peloponnesus. Smaller ships would be dragged by special devices across the narrow isthmus—about three and a half miles. The cargo of larger ships would be unloaded on one side and reloaded onto another ship on the other side. A canal, completed in 1893, now cuts across the isthmus.

The most prominent landmark of the city is the Acrocorinth, which rises to the south at a height of about 1900 feet. It served as an effec-

Paul visited the Roman city of Corinth on his second trip. Its most visible landmark, Acrocorinth, rose to a height of about 1,900 feet and had a temple to Aphrodite at the top. The columns in the foreground are from the fifth-century B.C. Temple of Apollo. Corinth had a reputation as an immoral city.

tive fortress by controlling the trade routes into and across the Peloponnesus. The temple of Aphrodite was situated on it. Other temples of note in the city were dedicated to the gods Apollo and Asclepius. Temple prostitutes were common and account in part for Corinth's reputation as an immoral city. A verb was coined, *korinthiazomai* (corinthianize), to describe a licentious lifestyle.

Archaeological items of interest include: (1) an inscription containing the Latin word *macellum* ("market," see 1 Cor. 10:25); (2) a shop in the marketplace with a doorstep bearing the inscription "Lucius the Butcher"; (3) an ornate structure where public officials addressed the people; (4) an inscription near that building with the Latin word *rostra*, the equivalent of the Greek *bema* ("judgment seat," Acts 18:12)—probably where Paul was brought before Gallio, the proconsul of Achaia.

The Isthmian Games, which honored Poseidon, the Greek god of the sea, were held every two years. They were second in importance only to the Olympic Games. Their proximity to Corinth accounts for Paul's references to athletics in the Corinthian letters.

OUTLINE

1. **Introduction** (1:1–9)
   - **1.1.** Salutation (1:1–3)
   - **1.2.** Thanksgiving (1:4–9)
2. **Response to News from Corinth** (1:10–6:20)
   - **2.1.** Wisdom and Division at Corinth (1:10–4:21)
     - **2.1.1.** Church Divisions (1:10–17)
     - **2.1.2.** The Wisdom and Power of God (1:18–31)
     - **2.1.3.** Paul's Testimony (2:1–5)
     - **2.1.4.** False and True Wisdom (2:6–16)
     - **2.1.5.** Spiritual Immaturity (3:1–4)
     - **2.1.6** Paul and Apollos: Fellow-Servants (3:5–15)
     - **2.1.7.** The Temple of God (3:16–17)
     - **2.1.8.** Foolish and Wise Thinking (3:18–23)
     - **2.1.9.** The Work of the Lord's Servants (4:1–5)
     - **2.1.10.** True Apostles (4:6–13)
     - **2.1.11.** Paul: Their Spiritual Father (4:14–21)
   - **2.2.** Sexual Immorality and the Church (5:1–13)
     - **2.2.1.** The Incestuous Brother (5:1–8)
     - **2.2.2.** Associating with Immoral Believers (5:9–13)
   - **2.3.** Lawsuits Between Believers (6:1–11)
     - **2.3.1.** Christians and the Civil Courts (6:1–6)
     - **2.3.2.** The Proper Attitude When Wronged (6:7–8)
     - **2.3.3.** Inheritors of the Kingdom (6:9–11)
   - **2.4.** Teaching on Sexual Immorality (6:12–20)
     - **2.4.1.** The Nature of Sexual Immorality (6:12–17)
     - **2.4.2.** The Temple of the Holy Spirit (6:18–20)
3. **Response to a Letter from Corinth** (7:1–16:4)
   - **3.1.** Marriage and Related Questions (7:1–40)

3.1.1. Proper Behavior Within Marriage (7:1–7)
3.1.2. The Unmarried and Widows (7:8–9)
3.1.3. The Christian Married Couple (7:10–11)
3.1.4. Mixed Marriages (7:12–16)
3.1.5. Remaining in One's Present State (7:17–28)
3.1.6. Reasons to Remain in One's State (7:29–35)
3.1.7. Virgins and Widows (7:36–40)

3.2. Food Sacrificed to Idols (8:1–11:1)
3.2.1. Superiority of Love Over "Knowledge" (8:1–8)
3.2.2. Sinning Against a Weak Brother (8:9–13)
3.2.3. The Rights of an Apostle (9:1–27)
3.2.4. Israel's History: A Warning (10:1–13)
3.2.5. The Lord's Supper and Idol Feasts (10:14–22)
3.2.6 Eating Meat Market Food (10:23–11:1)

3.3. Christian Worship (11:2–34)
3.3.1. The Veiling of Women (11:2–16)
3.3.2. The Lord's Supper (11:17–34)

3.4. Spiritual Gifts (12:1–14:40)
3.4.1. Basic Teaching Concerning Gifts (12:1–11)
3.4.1.1. General Criterion for Determining Gifts (12:1–3)
3.4.1.2. Variety and Basis of Gifts (12:4–6)
3.4.1.3. Sample Listing of Gifts (12:7–12)
3.4.2. One Body, Many Members (12:12–27)
3.4.3. Additional Gifts (12:28–31a)
3.4.4. Love and Its Relation to Gifts (12:31b–13:13)
3.4.4.1. Introductory Comments on Love (12:31b–13:3)
3.4.4.2. Characteristics of Love (13:4–7)
3.4.4.3. Love in an Eschatological Context (13:8–13)
3.4.5. Need for Intelligibility in Worship (14:1–25)
3.4.5.1. The Groundwork (14:1–5)
3.4.5.2. Strengthening the Argument (14:6–12)
3.4.5.3. Need for Interpretation of Tongues (14:13–19)
3.4.5.4. Appeal to the Corinthians (14:20–25)
3.4.6. Need for Orderliness in Worship (14:26–40)
3.4.6.1. Variety and Spontaneity in Worship (14:26–33a)
3.4.6.2. Women in Worship (14:33b–35)
3.4.6.3. Conclusion on Spiritual Gifts (14:36–40)
Article A: Was Jesus Accursed?
Article B: Spiritual Gifts
Article C: The Working of Miracles
Article D: The Gift of Prophecy As Revelation
Article E: Distinguishing of Spirits
Article F: Glossolalia—Do Luke and Paul Agree?
Article G: Baptized *by* and *in* the Holy Spirit
Article H: The Groanings of Romans 8:26

3.5. The Resurrection (15:1–58)
3.5.1. The Elements of the Gospel (15:1–11)
3.5.2. Denial of the Resurrection (15:12–19)
3.5.3. Christ, the Firstfruits (15:20–28)
3.5.4. Arguments from Experience (15:29–34)
3.5.5. The Nature of the Resurrection Body (15:35–49)
3.5.6. The Believers' Triumph Over Death (15:50–58)

3.6. The Collection (16:1–4)

4. Conclusion (16:5–24)
4.1. Paul's Personal Plans (16:5–9)
4.2. Requests Concerning Some Believers (16:10–18)
4.3. Final Greetings and Benediction (16:19–24)

COMMENTARY

1. Introduction (1:1–9)

1.1. Salutation (1:1–3)

The opening words of the letter have the essential elements of a salutation in first-century letters: identification of the writer, identification of the recipients, and well-wishing.

Paul reminds the Corinthian believers that e is "called to be an apostle" (*apostolos* neans "sent one"). He is not an apostle by his wn choosing, but rather "by the will of God." Ie must have recalled many times that prior to is conversion, he had been appointed by the ewish elders in Jerusalem to be their "sent ne" to Damascus to investigate and appre-end Christ's followers (Acts 9:1–3). Here vas a divine irony: The "sent one" of the Jew-sh high priests against Christians became the 'sent one" of Christ Jesus. As Christ's apos-le, he has the full backing, endorsement, and uthority of Christ. He will return to this theme of his apostleship at several critical points in he letter.

Paul is accompanied by "our brother Sos-henes" (lit., "Sosthenes, the brother"). "The rticle implies that he was well known to some Corinthians" (Robertson and Plummer, 2). He s possibly the Sosthenes who was the syna-gogue ruler in Corinth when Paul preached in hat city and who was beaten by the Jews who vere hostile to Paul (Acts 18:17). Early Chris-ians often identified themselves as brothers, which highlighted both their close association with one another and their being children of God (cf. Rom. 16:23; 1 Cor. 16:12; 2 Cor. 1:1; Col. 1:1; Philem. 1; Heb. 13:23). The term, however, was used in a religious sense also in Jewish and pagan circles.

The terms Paul uses to identify the recipi-ents of the letter are important: They are "the church of God," "sanctified in Christ Jesus," and "called to be holy." Later in the letter he deals at length with various aspects of the church. The Greek word translated "church" (*ekklesia*) was common in the Greek-speaking world. It had already been used in the Septu-agint as a designation for Israel (Deut. 4:10; see also Acts 7:38). It was used generally for an assembling of people or specifically for the gathering of community officials for the pur-pose of conducting civic business (Acts 19:32, 39, 41). Early believers adopted this word as a common designation for a local gathering of Christians (e.g., 1 Cor. 4:17; 7:17; 11:16; 14:33; Gal. 1:22) or for the universal body of believers (e.g., 1 Cor. 15:9; Eph. 5:25). It is the church "of God"; that is, it belongs to him. In view of the Corinthians' attachment to various leaders, Paul may be hinting that the church does not belong to any of them.

Believers are also "called to be holy." Just as Paul was specifically called by God to apos-tleship, so all believers are called to holiness. "Those who have been sanctified" (NASB) is in the Greek perfect tense, indicating both a past action and a continuing state. The designation of Christians as saints is often misunderstood. The word "saint" in Greek (*hagios*) is really an adjective and means "holy." When it describes a person and no noun is used, it means "holy one" or "saint." It derives from the verb *hagiazo*, whose basic meaning is "to separate." Consequently, Christians are ones who have been separated by God from their life of sin and rebellion to one of service and devotion to him. Paul later tells the Corinthians, "you were sanctified," along with the parallel expressions "you were washed" and "you were justified" (6:11). Ancient Israel was "a holy [separated] nation" (Ex. 19:5–6) in spite of its imperfections. Believers are also holy ones, in spite of their imperfections. In fact, Peter calls believers "a holy nation" (1 Peter 2:9).

Not only have the Corinthians believers been called by God; they, along with all believ-ers everywhere, have called "on the name of our Lord Jesus Christ" and have thus been saved (1:2; cf. Joel 2:32; Rom. 10:13). To call on the name of the Lord Jesus Christ means to confess faith in him and to appeal to all that he is, for in biblical usage one's name often designates that person's nature or character.

Paul wishes "grace and peace" for the church. A non-Christian Greek normally sent greetings (*chairein*) to a friend—a word found in the salutation of the letter the Jerusalem council sent to the Gentile churches (Acts 15:23; cf. also James 1:1). Paul's word "grace" (*charis*) is derived from it. The New Testament concept of grace can often be traced to the Old Testament idea of God's steadfast love (lov-ingkindness, KJV); its basic meaning is that of undeserved blessing bestowed by God. The wish for "peace" reflects the common Jewish greeting of *shalom*, which embodies the idea of wholeness and well-being. According to Barrett (35), when Christians wish grace and peace to another believer, they are praying "that he may apprehend more fully the grace of God in which he already stands, and the peace he already enjoys." Robertson and Plummer (4) suggest that grace is the source and peace is the consummation.

Grace and peace come from both "God our Father and the Lord Jesus Christ," his Son. The Father is the source and Christ is the mediator or agent by which they come to us.

1.2. Thanksgiving (1:4–9)

In this thanksgiving section, Paul anticipates matters about which he will soon write, such as speech, knowledge, spiritual gifts, the concept of the church, and the coming of the Lord. He compliments the Corinthian believers, even though much of the letter will be corrective in nature. He takes them back to their conversion experience, talks about their present endowment with spiritual gifts, and emphasizes God's enablement in keeping them steadfast until the coming of the Lord.

Paul thanks God for the Corinthians because of God's grace that they have experienced. Several points about divine grace are worth noting. (1) It is given by God, not earned (Rom. 12:3, 6; 15:15; 1 Cor. 3:10; Gal. 2:9; Eph. 2:8; 3:7). (2) It is "in Christ Jesus"—a reminder that all God's blessings are centered in his Son. In this connection, they "have been enriched in every way." On several other occasions Paul speaks about the spiritual wealth of the Christian life (2 Cor. 6:10; 8:2, 7, 9; 9:11). (3) They "do not lack any spiritual gift" (*charisma*). A *charisma* is a gift that is received as the result of God's grace (*charis*).

The Corinthian believers were placing considerable importance on matters related to "speaking" and "knowledge" (v. 5), especially as they related to spiritual gifts. They were captivated by the gift of tongues and apparently evaluated it above the other gifts. They also rated prophesying, another gift of utterance, highly. Moreover, they prided themselves in having knowledge (*gnosis*), a word that receives much attention in Paul's correspondence with them (8:1, 7, 10–11; 12:8; 13:2, 8; 14:6; 2 Cor. 2:14; 4:6; 6:6; 8:7; 10:5; 11:6). When he returns to these themes, he does not speak disparagingly of the gifts of speech and knowledge, but he does give corrective teaching because the Corinthians overemphasized and misunderstood them. It would be anachronistic to say that the Corinthians were influenced by the philosophical system that came to be known as Gnosticism, but one can certainly detect the influence of incipient gnostic thought, which "may be described as 'gnosticizing' rather than 'Gnostic'" (Bruce, 31).

The statement that the Corinthians "do not lack any spiritual gift" (v. 7) has been understood in several ways. (1) It may mean that they, as a congregation, possessed all the spiritual gifts. (2) Closely related is the idea that, potentially if not actually, all the gifts could be theirs (cf. Robertson and Plummer[6], who maintain the Greek construction "points to a *contemplated* result"). (3) Or it may mean that the Corinthians were boasting that they possessed all the gifts and that Paul is being sarcastic by repeating their claim. But it is unlikely that Paul rebukes them at this point. In view of what he writes in chapters 12–14, the second option is best.

"The day of our Lord Jesus Christ" (v. 8) refers to the return of Christ, which Paul calls "the revelation of our Lord Jesus Christ" (v. 7, NKJV) and which speaks of his coming in glory (4:5; 15:23). This may be intended as a corrective to the mistaken idea of some Corinthians that they had already experienced end-time fullness, a matter to which Paul will return several times. In the Old Testament it is sometimes called "the day of the LORD" (Joel 2:31; Amos 5:18). Rather than being terrorized by the idea of the coming judgment, Christians may be encouraged by the thought that the Lord "will keep you strong [firm] to the end" (v. 8). Paul's words to the Philippians parallel this: "being confident of this, that he who began a good work in you will carry it on to completion until the day of Christ Jesus" (Phil. 1:6).

Being blameless or irreproachable at the coming of the Lord (Col. 1:22) does not depend on the worthiness of Christians but on one's faith in Christ, who has become "our righteousness" (1 Cor. 1:30). This is grounded in the truth that "God is faithful"—a favorite expression of Paul (10:13; 1 Thess. 5:24; 2 Thess. 3:3; 2 Tim. 2:13; see also Heb. 10:23; 11:11). "If they fail, it will not be his fault" (Robertson and Plummer, 7). One final blessing a Christian enjoys is that of being called by God "into fellowship" (*koinonia*) with his Son; it means sharing in and with Christ.

2. Response to News from Corinth (1:10–6:20)

Throughout the letter, Paul deals with problems in the Corinthian congregation. One source of his knowledge of the problems was members of Chloe's household who had visited him in Ephesus. He had also been visited by several brothers from Corinth (16:15–18).

2.1. Wisdom and Division at Corinth (1:10–4:21)

2.1.1. Church Divisions (1:10–17). Paul deals first with the problem of divisions within the congregation, but Fee (47) rightly cautions that because divisions and quarrels are "the first item to which Paul speaks, most people tend to read the rest of the letter in light of chaps. 1–4." Paul addresses the Corinthian believers as "brothers" (*adelphoi*, a word he uses thirty-nine times in this letter). It indicates his own spiritual identification with them in their being children of the Father. But he uses it even more to imply that a brotherly spirit should prevail among the members, rather than the divisions that existed. This word is meant to be gender inclusive (see Fee, 53, fn.22).

In verses 10–12 Paul states the nature of the problem, which he identifies as "divisions" and "quarrels." Even though the Greek word for divisions (*schisma*) might suggest fragmentation, the idea is that of dissension. The problem might be expressed by the more contemporary idiom "cliques." The Greek word for quarrels (*eris*) means strife or discord. Paul lists it as one of the acts or works of the sinful nature (Gal. 5:19–21). He is the only New Testament writer to use this word.

In verse 10, Paul appeals to the Corinthians to "agree with one another" (lit., "to all speak the same thing"), because they had divided themselves into groups attached to different leaders. Speaking the same thing will have two results: It will eliminate the divisions that exist, and the believers will be "united in mind and thought." The word for united (*katartizo*) is appropriate. It is used for the mending or restoring of nets (Matt. 4:21; Mark 1:19), and for Paul's desire to supply or complete what is lacking in the faith of the Thessalonians (1 Thess. 3:10; see also 2 Cor. 13:11; Gal. 6:1; Heb. 13:21).

The unity for which Paul appeals is internal in nature. To speak the same thing means more than simply uttering the same words; it is to be "in the same mind and the same purpose" (1 Cor. 1:10, NRSV). This is possible only as believers relate themselves not only to one another but to the Lord Jesus Christ, into whose fellowship they have been called (v. 9) and in whose name Paul makes his appeal (v. 10).

The identity of Chloe (v. 11) is uncertain. She was apparently wealthy, since the persons from her household were probably slaves or employees. They may have been members of the Corinthian congregation or perhaps had visited it. It is not clear whether Chloe lived in Corinth or in Ephesus, or whether she herself was a Christian. But the report of the messengers was clear and disturbing. The specific nature of the problem evolved from a common tendency of Christians to identify themselves with a human leader. Literally, the statements of the groups read, "I am of Paul," "I of Apollos," etc. Some versions translate, "I follow Paul," etc. (NIV); others, "I belong to Paul," etc. (NRSV). The problem was not that some preferred one leader over the others; it was that their attitude was divisive.

Some identified with Paul, probably feeling a special attachment to him as the founder of the congregation. But such attachment implies that there were those in the church who opposed him. Opposition to Paul becomes evident later in the letter, insofar as some challenged his claim to apostleship (ch. 9). It is "altogether likely that the quarreling over their leaders is not just *for* Paul or Cephas, but is decidedly *over against* Paul at the same time" (Fee, 49). Paul flatly rejects the partisan spirit evident in a "Paul party" (see vv. 13–17).

Apollos first appears in Acts 18:24–28. He was a Jew from Alexandria, Egypt, who visited Ephesus and met Priscilla and Aquila there. "He was a learned [eloquent, NRSV] man, with a thorough knowledge of the Scriptures" (v. 24). He had previously become a Christian, but had an incomplete knowledge of the gospel. He had been instructed in the way of the Lord and taught accurately what he knew about Jesus (v. 25). Priscilla and Aquila, however, "explained to him the way of God more adequately" (v. 26). We should note that "the Way" was a special designation for the Christian movement in the book of Acts (9:2; 19:9, 23; 22:4; 24:14, 22).

From Ephesus, Apollos traveled to Corinth, where he greatly helped the Christians by powerfully refuting the church's Jewish opponents, proving from the Scriptures that Jesus was indeed the Messiah, the Christ. It is little wonder, then, that some in the congregation felt a special attraction to this eloquent defender of the faith. Yet Paul nowhere suggests that there were any theological or personal differences between himself and Apollos. He later makes a point of saying that he and Apollos are fellow workers and fellow servants of the Lord (3:5–9). But since Paul was not an eloquent speaker (2 Cor. 10:10; 11:6) and since some of the Corinthians were probably converted through Apollos's ministry, a group within the congregation attached themselves to Apollos.

Cephas is the Aramaic form of the Greek name Peter. When referring to him, Paul usually opts for his Aramaic name (e.g., 3:22; 9:5; 15:5; Gal. 1:18; 2:9, 11, 14). There is no clear indication that Peter ever went to Corinth. But the Cephas party may have preferred him over both Apollos and Paul because of his early association with Jesus and his acknowledged leadership among the original apostles and in the early church (Acts 1:15–17; 2:14, etc.). Peter was recognized as the apostle to the Jews, Paul as the apostle to the Gentiles (Gal. 2:7–8). In Galatians 2:11–21, Paul recounts how he confronted Peter in Antioch on the matter of Jewish Christians eating with Gentile Christians. But there were no significant theological differences between the two men. It may be that some in the Corinthian church preferred Peter over Paul because, in their judgment, Peter's claims to apostleship were indisputable. Perhaps this group represented a Judaizing tendency that insisted on the food restrictions mentioned in Acts 15:28–29 (cf. 1 Cor. 8; 10:25). Héring (5) says that "this party must have been made up of Jewish Christians from Palestine, who had perhaps been baptized by Peter."

What about the fourth group, which is characterized as saying, "I follow Christ"? Perhaps this group represents those who looked disdainfully on the other three and self-righteously proclaimed themselves as following Jesus (Fee, 59). But in so doing, they were themselves creating a fourth party and thus adding to the divisive spirit that had invaded the congregation. Furthermore, this group may have had some distinctive teachings about Christ that had been influenced by the Hellenistic culture in which they lived (Bruce, 33).

Leon Morris (41) capably summarizes these few verses by saying that Paul does not attack the teaching of any of these parties, but simply the fact that there were such parties. There is nothing inherently wrong with Christians identifying themselves with human leaders. The spiritual danger is in deeming one's choice to be superior to all others. One may feel a certain affinity for Martin Luther, or John Calvin, or John Wesley, or Menno Simons. That is understandable, but spiritual snobbery is not. We ought to regard Christians in traditions other than our own as fellow believers, even while recognizing points of difference. In the body of Christ, diversity is permissible; divisiveness is not (see also 1 Cor. 12 on this issue).

In verses 13–17 Paul reinforces what he said with the question: "Is Christ divided?" Some understand this to be a statement rather than a question: "Christ is divided!" This is possible, since the manuscripts did not have punctuation. If so, it would indicate Paul's exasperation with the situation by telling the Corinthians that they had, in effect, divided Christ. This interpretation, however, is unlikely. The verb *merizo* means "divide up" (cf. Rom. 12:3; 1 Cor. 7:17; 2 Cor. 10:13; Heb. 7:2). Paul is pointing to the absurdity of thinking that Christ is divisible; his answer to the question is a resounding no. He will later talk about the indivisibility of Christ and of the church (esp. 1 Cor. 12).

"Paul was not crucified for you, was he?" "You were not baptized into the name of Paul, were you?" These are more accurate translations of the next two questions, both of which imply a negative answer. He will speak a little later about "Christ crucified" (v. 23). In the New Testament, baptism was usually administered in the name of Jesus Christ (see Acts 2:38; 8:16). One was baptized in (*en*) or into (*eis*) his name; the prepositions suggest entering into fellowship with him. Baptism was on the authority of Jesus' name, for in biblical usage a person's name often stood for who or what the person was. Jesus himself commanded baptism to be in the name of the Father, the Son, and the Holy Spirit (Matt. 28:19). Baptism also portrays the believer's participation in the death and resurrection of Christ (Rom. 6:3–4). It is possible, based on Paul's discussion in 1 Corinthians 10:1–6, that the Corinthians held a highly mystical view of baptism (see Héring, 7).

In view of the partisan situation that had developed, Paul expresses gratitude that he had baptized few members of the Corinthian congregation. At best, only these few could misguidedly claim they had been baptized into Paul's name (v. 17), an idea abhorrent to Paul. Crispus is probably the synagogue ruler who became an early convert in Corinth (Acts 18:8). Several persons in the New Testament bear the name of Gaius (Acts 19:29; 20:4; Rom. 16:23; 3 John 1); the one mentioned here is probably the man who was hospitable to Paul and all the church (Rom. 16:23). Paul recalls that he also baptized the household of Stephanas (see 1 Cor. 16:15–18); he was possibly present at the writing of this letter.

Who were included in the "household" (*oikos*) of Stephanas? The Greek word is not precise; it could include all the members of a family plus servants or slaves. Does this imply that Paul baptized infants or young children? No details are given, but a later reference to the household concept is instructive: Paul says that Stephanas's household (*oikia*, a synonym) "have devoted themselves to the service of the saints" (16:15). This, of course, would exclude infants and young children from the meaning of household here.

Did Paul think baptism was relatively unimportant, since he baptized so few converts and also says, "Christ did not send (*apostello*, i.e., commission) me to baptize, but to preach the gospel" (v. 17)? The evidence indicates otherwise. Acts 19:1–6 records how Paul explained Christian baptism to certain men in Ephesus who had already participated in the baptism associated with John the Baptist. They agreed to be baptized in the name of Jesus, and Paul did the baptizing. In 1 Corinthians 1:13–16 he has already used the verb *baptizo* five times. In 10:1–2 he speaks of the Israelites being "baptized into Moses," the typological fulfillment of which is Christian baptism. Baptism was indeed central to his doctrine of salvation, for he says we were buried with Christ through baptism into his death (Rom. 6:3–4; Col. 2:12). Furthermore, in some passages it is difficult to separate the thought of being baptized into Christ, by which believers become members of his body, from what is sometimes called "water baptism" (Gal. 3:27; 1 Cor. 12:13; Eph. 4:5).

In other words, Paul, like Jesus, placed considerable importance on baptism. Yet Jesus himself did not baptize his followers; instead, he delegated the baptizing to his disciples (John 4:1–2). Likewise, Paul must have had considerable help (e.g., from Silas and Timothy) in ensuring that new converts were baptized. Baptizing did not require any special or personal gifts, but preaching did. The absence of this requirement does not belittle baptism, which must be preceded by the preaching of the gospel (Robertson and Plummer, 15).

Christ sent Paul "to preach the gospel" (*euangelizomai*). This word means "to bring good news." It was used in the angel's announcement to the shepherds: "I bring you good news of great joy" (Luke 2:10), and is found throughout the New Testament as the message of the gospel spread throughout the Mediterranean world. Paul emphasizes that his preaching was not "with words of human wisdom" ("in cleverness of speech" [NASB]; "with eloquent wisdom" [NRSV]; "with wisdom of words" [NKJV]). He does not claim to be an orator, nor does he aspire to be one. The apostle speaks this way because of the Greeks' high regard for wisdom, which, he will show shortly, is misplaced and is actually a hindrance to their receiving the gospel. His primary concern is communicating the *content* of the good news, not the manner in which it is done.

The good news is the message of "the cross of Christ." This expression does not refer to the wooden instrument of execution on which Jesus hung. It is a figure of speech—a metonymy—in which a word or term is used

The sign of the cross quickly became a "shorthand" for the message of Christ. This cross is on a column at a chapel at Kursi, the site of the story of "Legion," the demons that Jesus sent into a herd of pigs that ran into the Sea of Galilee and drowned.

for something readily associated with it. It is theological "shorthand" for the redemptive death of Jesus and occurs frequently in Paul's writings either as "the cross" or "the cross of Christ/our Lord Jesus Christ" (Gal. 5:11; 6:12, 14; Eph. 2:16; Phil. 2:8; 3:18; Col. 1:20; 2:14; also Heb. 12:2; cf. "tree" in Acts 5:30; 10:39; 13:29; Gal. 3:13; 1 Peter 2:24).

2.1.2. The Wisdom and Power of God (1:18–31). In verses 18–25, Paul divides unbelieving humanity into two groups: Jews and Greeks. Often in the New Testament the designation "Greeks" is a way of referring to all Gentiles (cf. v. 23), since the New Testament world was largely Greek-speaking (see Rom. 1:16; 10:12; Gal. 3:28; Col. 3:11). Throughout the paragraph Paul focuses on Jews and Gentiles. However, the designation "Greeks" has special significance since Corinth was the provincial capital of Achaia, a part of present-day Greece, and in all likelihood most of its citizens were ethnic Greeks.

The message of the cross has a twofold effect on the hearers. To those who accept it, it means salvation; to those who reject it, it means destruction. There is no middle ground; a person is either saved or not saved. More accurately, Paul speaks of "those who are perishing" and "[those] who are being saved." Salvation is not experienced in its completeness in this life, nor is spiritual destruction irreversible in this life. There is an eschatological aspect to each. Both salvation and judgment have present as well as future aspects.

To the Jews and Greeks, the message was "foolishness" (v. 18). It was foolishness to the unbelieving Greeks because it did not coincide with their notion of wisdom. It was weakness and a stumbling block to unbelieving Jews because it did not coincide with their notion of power. To a Jew, a crucified Messiah was a contradiction in terms, since hanging indicated God's curse on the crucified one (Gal. 3:13; cf. Deut. 21:23).

The Corinthians placed considerable importance on wisdom. Ancient Greece prided itself on its history of illustrious philosophers (a word that lit. means "lovers of wisdom"). Note Luke's comment on the Greeks' preoccupation with wisdom in Acts 17:21: "All the Athenians and the foreigners who lived there spent their time doing nothing but talking about and listening to the latest ideas." The idea of a crucified Savior did not make sense to them, since it did not square with their idea of a leader. "Where," asks Paul, "is the wise man? Where is the scribe? Where is the debater of this age?" (NASB). The wise man is the Greek philosopher; the scribe is the Jewish scholar of the law; the debater (disputer) is applicable to both Greek and Jew. "This age" [*aion*] was a Jewish designation for the time preceding "the age to come," that is, the messianic era (Luke 18:30; 20:35). Paul speaks of "this age" only in negative terms (1 Cor. 2:6; 2 Cor. 4:4; Eph. 2:2).

Human wisdom is the wisdom "of the world"—a phrase synonymous with "of this age." Such wisdom does not lead to God. The fundamental difference between religion and the Christian faith is that religion is humanity's attempt to reach up to and know God; but the world through its own wisdom cannot know God (v. 21; see Rom. 1:18–31). The Scriptures stress that God has taken the initiative by reaching down, through the cross, to bring us up to himself.

John's Gospel records an incident in which some Greeks requested an interview with Jesus (John 12:20–25). There is no indication that Jesus granted the interview. Instead, he spoke about his impending death. One may infer that Jesus responded as he did because these Greeks (presumably Hellenistic Jews) were attracted to him only as a philosopher and great teacher.

The unbelieving Jews demand miraculous signs as proof that Jesus was indeed the Messiah. Following Jesus' feeding of the four thousand, the Pharisees asked Jesus for a sign from heaven (Mark 8:11–12), but Jesus did not accommodate them. On another occasion some Pharisees and teachers of the law said to Jesus, "We want to see a miraculous sign from you" (Matt. 12:38; see also 16:4; John 4:48; 6:30). Again, Jesus did not comply with their wishes. Instead, he said that the only sign to be given to "a wicked and adulterous generation" was the sign of the prophet Jonah, which pointed to his death and burial (Matt. 12:39–41). The lesson is clear: No amount of miracles will convince a person who refuses to believe. The hard-hearted Jew found it impossible to believe in a crucified Messiah.

The means by which individuals are saved is "the foolishness of what was preached"

(1:21). Foolish, yes, from a human point of view. Paul is not here talking about the act of preaching, but the subject matter of the preaching—Christ crucified (v. 23; see 2:2; Gal. 3:1). "Christ was not preached as a conqueror to please one [Jew], nor as a philosopher to please the other [Greek]" (Robertson and Plummer, 22). God "was pleased" (*eudokeo*) to ordain the death of Christ as the means by which people can be saved (v. 21). The theme of God's good pleasure (verb, *eudokeo*; noun, *eudokia*) is found elsewhere in Paul's writings (Gal. 1:15; Eph. 1:5; Phil. 2:13; Col. 1:19); it stresses God's sovereignty as well as his good pleasure in ordaining certain things.

As a conclusion to verses 18–25, Paul says to the Greek, Christ is "the wisdom of God," and to the Jew, Christ is "the power of God." The cross is a demonstration of divine wisdom in that it brings together both God's justice and his love. By means of the cross, God is both "just and the one who justifies those who have faith in Jesus" (Rom. 3:26). The cross is also a demonstration of divine power in that it has triumphed over the forces of evil and provides redemption and deliverance for all who respond in faith.

In verses 26–31 Paul goes on to give an insight into the composition of the Corinthian congregation. To illustrate the truth of what he has just written, Paul asks them to consider the makeup of their church. At the time they were called, not many were "wise by human standards," or "influential" ([lit., powerful), or "of noble birth." The early church was not without these types of converts (see Acts 17:4, 12, 34; Rom. 16:23), but that was not the makeup of the church in Corinth (cf. also 1 Cor. 7:21). Even though people from all walks of life and all social and economic strata became believers, it is a matter of historical record that in New Testament times the gospel was most readily received by the lower classes of society.

God's sovereignty again appears in the occurrence three times of the word "chose" (vv. 27–28). God chose the foolish things of the world and the weak things of the world to shame the wise and the strong; he chose the lowly and despised things of the world and the things that are not to nullify the things that are. His purpose in all this is "that no one may boast before him." God has determined that he alone will receive the glory for humankind's salvation, for it is a demonstration of his grace and is not based on human efforts (Eph. 2:8–9).

Believers are both "of [God]" and "in Christ Jesus" (v. 30). God is the source of their spiritual life (John 1:12–13; 2 Cor. 5:17–18). In addition, they enjoy an intimate relationship with Christ. "In Christ" is a favorite expression in Paul's writings and is closely associated with the concept of being a part of the body of Christ.

The believers' close identification with Christ makes them recipients of wisdom, righteousness, holiness, and redemption. Christ is indeed the "wisdom of God" (v. 24), and in him "are hidden all the treasures of wisdom and knowledge" (Col. 2:3). We may go so far as to say that he is the personification of God's wisdom. In Proverbs, Wisdom is personified and is closely associated with creation (Prov. 8:22–31). This concept is remarkably parallel with what John says about the role of the Logos in creation (John 1:1, 3). Wisdom is no longer an abstraction or a human pursuit, about which Paul has already spoken a number of times (1 Cor. 1:17, 19, 21). It is a person, and Christ as the wisdom of God is now the possession of Christians.

The words wisdom (*sophia*), righteousness (*dikaiosyne*), holiness (*hagiasmos*), and redemption (*apolytrosis*) (v. 30) may coordinate with each other and represent various benefits that a believer receives. But it is also possible to accept the NIV translation, which takes the last three as an elaboration of Christ as the wisdom of God (Robertson and Plummer, 27).

Christ is indeed the "righteousness" of the Christian because "God made him who had no sin to be sin for us, so that in him we might become the righteousness of God" (2 Cor. 5:21). Christ is the Righteous One (Acts 3:14; 22:14; 2 Tim. 4:8; 1 Peter 3:18; 1 John 2:1, 29; 3:7). Because of our identification with him, we participate in his righteousness. Righteousness is a legal or forensic term, which calls to mind the imagery of the courtroom with a transgressor facing a judge. He is found guilty and must be punished, but a third party intervenes and pays the penalty. So it is with sinners before God. The righteousness of Christ is applied to them so that they have right standing before God. When they accept Christ's offer in faith, their faith is counted to them as righteousness (Rom. 1:17; 4:3; Gal. 3:6).

Christ has also become the believer's "holiness" or sanctification. Paul has already called believers "those sanctified in Christ Jesus and called to be holy" (1:2). He has much to say in this letter about God's requirement of holy conduct for Christians (see also 1 Thess. 4:3–7), but the word here refers to a believer's identification with Christ as the Holy One (Mark 1:24; Luke 1:35; 4:34; John 6:69; Acts 3:14; 4:27; Rev. 3:7). It speaks of our initial experience of holiness at the time of conversion, whereby we share in the holiness of Christ (1 Cor. 6:11). Holiness suggests the imagery of the temple as God's holy place.

Finally, Christ is also "redemption" for the believer. Redemption involves two ideas: being set free from something and the price paid for the freedom. Later in this letter Paul writes: "You were bought at a price" (6:20; 7:23). Elsewhere he says, "In [Christ] we have redemption through his blood" (Eph. 1:7). Peter also emphasizes the cost of redemption when he says we were not redeemed with perishable things like silver or gold, but with the precious blood of Christ (1 Peter 1:18–19). The aspect of release or freedom goes back to Israel's deliverance from Egyptian bondage; it also calls to mind the Old Testament provision for manumission of slaves. Paul alludes to this in Galatians 4:3–7, when he reminds believers that they were once in slavery but have now been redeemed, so that they are no longer slaves but children of God. The imagery is that of the marketplace in an ancient city, where slaves were often sold on the auction block.

In view of all that he has said, Paul appeals to believers to acknowledge their complete indebtedness to the Lord. Nothing that is theirs spiritually is cause for self-boasting (1:31). On the contrary, the only basis for boasting is "in the Lord" (see Jer. 9:23–24).

2.1.3. Paul's Testimony (2:1–5). Because of the Corinthians' preoccupation with human wisdom, Paul now makes it clear where he stands on the relation between human wisdom and the preaching of the gospel. He cites himself as an example of one who relied on the Holy Spirit for his message to be effective, not on human eloquence or wisdom. In line with what he has just said at the end of chapter 1, his boasting is in the Lord.

The first word in the Greek text is emphatic: *kago* (lit., "and I"). Paul did not come to the Corinthians originally with superior wisdom (the processes involved in thinking) or eloquence (the manner of expression). The nature of his message was a proclamation of "the testimony about God" (cf. "our testimony about Christ" in 1:6). God and Christ were at the center of his message, not human or philosophical speculation.

Paul had previously talked about preaching the gospel (*euangelizomai*, 1:17) and preaching (*kerysso*) Christ crucified (1:23). He now uses another synonym: "I proclaimed (*katangello*) to you the testimony about God." The first Greek word embodies the idea of the good news of salvation; the second, the activity of a herald in making an announcement; and the third, the idea that the communication is a message.

Paul emphasizes again that his central message is Jesus Christ, and especially his crucifixion (v. 2). "Crucified" is a perfect participle in Greek (cf. also 1:23). This form of the verb is significant because it portrays Christ as crucified in the past, with the benefits of his death continuing to the present. "The crucifixion is permanent in its efficacy" (Morris, 46).

Paul visited Corinth (Acts 18:1) immediately after he left Athens, where he had encountered opposition and ridicule. There the results were small compared to those in other cities he had visited. Because of this, some interpret his comments in 1 Corinthians 2:3–4 as defensive on Paul's part, implying that he arrived in Corinth depressed and defeated, having realized that his attempt in Athens to be wise and persuasive had failed and determined not to repeat those mistakes. This interpretation, however, is not necessary. Paul is contrasting his state of mind and manner of delivery not with his experience in Athens, but with the arrogance and assumed wisdom and eloquence that appealed to many of the Corinthians. For him, preaching the gospel was an awesome and daunting responsibility; it is small wonder that he did it with a feeling of "weakness and fear, and with much trembling." These words describe his usual frame of mind when he preached (cf. 1 Thess. 1:5). It was a feeling of complete inadequacy in the face of evangelizing cities such as Corinth. "This is the background of the encouragement given to him in Ac. 18.9f." (Bruce, 37).

Far from depending on his own resources or persuasive powers, Paul relied on the Holy

Spirit. His message was not conveyed in "wise and persuasive words." Rather, it was "with a demonstration [*apodeixis*] of the Spirit's power [lit., of Spirit and power]." *Apodeixis* may be translated "manifestation" (NASB); its meaning here is "proof of spirit and power, i.e. proof consisting in possession of the Spirit and power" (BAGD, 89; cf. Acts 2:22; 25:7, where the verb form of this word group appears, meaning "prove" or "attest").

A number of other New Testament passages link the Holy Spirit with power (e.g., Acts 1:8; 10:38; Rom. 15:13; 1 Thess. 1:5). The phrase "Spirit and power" (here and in Acts 10:38) may be understood in a number of ways: "Spirit's power," "Spirit, that is, power," or "powerful Spirit." The writers are not talking about two separate ideas, but rather are giving one thought in which two nouns are so closely related to each other as to form one idea (the technical term is hendiadys). Note that this identification of the Spirit with power is parallel to the phrase "God's power" (1 Cor. 2:5), which implies that the Holy Spirit is God. This identification of the Spirit with God recalls Peter's statements to Ananias in Acts 5:3–4: "You have lied to the Holy Spirit," and "You have . . . lied . . . to God."

Paul concludes the paragraph by saying that effective proclamation of the gospel in the power of the Holy Spirit will produce "faith" in the hearers. Such faith will rest not on human wisdom, which can and does change regularly, but on the power of God. These verses contain the first reference to the Holy Spirit in this letter. Paul will say much more about him in the rest of this chapter and at other key points in the letter.

2.1.4. False and True Wisdom (2:6–16). The word "wisdom" (*sophia*) occurs fifteen times in the first two chapters of the letter and only twice elsewhere (3:19; 12:8). In 3:19, the phrase "the wisdom of this world" is in line with Paul's comments here in contrasting it with the wisdom of God in the cross; in 12:8, it occurs as one of the spiritual gifts.

Verses 6–9 have several points worth noting. Paul and other true proclaimers of the gospel (note the "we" in v. 6) speak wisdom "among the mature [*teleioi*]." Who are "the mature"? One view is that this group is being distinguished from "infants in Christ" (3:1), and therefore refers to Christians who have attained a higher degree of spirituality (Héring, 15–16; Robertson and Plummer, 35). If this was Paul's meaning, then he is rebuking the Corinthians for their erroneous concept of spiritual maturity in which they placed themselves above other Christians. True maturity, he says, is acceptance not of human wisdom but of the wisdom of the cross. Alternatively, the phrase may refer to all who have accepted the cross as the wisdom of God. In this case, the contrast is not between spiritually superior and inferior Christians, but between those who accept and those who reject the message of the cross (Fee, 101–3). Of these two interpretations, the second one is preferable.

Humanly generated wisdom is characterized negatively in two ways: it is "of this age [*aion*]" and "of the rulers of this age." These phrases probably refer to the origin of this wisdom. Paul had already characterized human wisdom as belonging to this *aion* (1:20). He used a synonymous word (*kosmos*) in talking along the same lines (1:20–21, 27). Elsewhere he characterizes "this age" as evil (Gal. 1:4). As a Jew, he sometimes contrasted "this age" with "the age to come," which Judaism identified as the messianic era. But since for Paul the Messiah had already come, he can speak of Christians as those "on whom the fulfillment of the ages has come" (1 Cor. 10:11; see also Heb. 6:5).

Who are "the rulers [*archontes*] of this age"? Opinion is divided. Some identify them with demonic or spiritually negative forces. Jesus himself called Satan "the prince [*archon*] of this world [*kosmos*]" (John 12:31; 14:30; 16:11); Paul calls him "the god of this age [*aion*]" (2 Cor. 4:4) and "the ruler [*archon*] of the kingdom of the air" (Eph. 2:2; cf. the related word *arche* for demonic forces in Rom. 8:38; Eph. 1:21; Col. 2:15). Héring sees them as supernatural powers that are not evil by nature (16–17; cf. also Bruce, 38–39). On the other hand, the phrase is specifically used for earthly rulers in Acts 3:17; 4:5, 8, 26; 13:27; 14:5; and Romans 13:3. Furthermore, verse 8 of this chapter says that "the rulers of this age" did not understand the wisdom of God and consequently crucified Jesus (cf. Acts 3:17; 13:27). This cannot be said of demons, since they knew who Jesus was (Mark 1:24). It is possible, however, to see a connection between these two interpretations when we observe that Paul said,

"The god of this age has blinded the minds of unbelievers, so that they cannot see the light of the gospel of the glory of Christ" (2 Cor. 4:4).

The rulers of this age "are coming to nothing" (2:6). The word Paul uses here, *katargeo*, occurs nine times in this letter and sixteen times in his other writings. In this passage it means "bring to nothing, render ineffective, nullify" (as in 1:28). It is important to note that the rulers of this age are in the process of coming to nothing. Their end, along with the wisdom they represent, is certain. Paul is confident that the message of the cross will triumph ultimately over the wisdom and the rulers of this age.

"God's secret wisdom" (v. 7) is literally "God's wisdom in a mystery." We note several points with regard to this expression. (1) There is a secret quality about God's wisdom; it is something that is enigmatic, unable to be understood. It is hidden to those who reject the gospel (2 Cor. 3:14; 4:3). (2) This was all in God's plan. It was foreordained, or predestined, by him "before time began" (lit., "before the ages"). God's redemptive purpose in Christ was not an afterthought (Eph. 3:2–6). (3) General usage of the word "mystery" (*mysterion*) in Paul's writings is something that at one time had been hidden but has now been revealed by God (Rom. 16:25–26; Eph. 3:2–6; Col. 1:26–27). He attributes this revealing to the Holy Spirit (1 Cor. 2:10).

God's purpose in all this is "for our glory" (v. 7), an expression related to the end times. Ultimately we will conform to the image of God's Son (Rom. 8:29), who is the Lord of glory (1 Cor. 2:8; cf. James 2:1). "Lord of glory" occurs a number of times in the noncanonical book of 1 Enoch as an expression for God (22:14; 25:3, 7; 27:3, 4; 63:2; 75:3); Paul applies it to Christ. Complete conformity to the image of the glorious Son of God will take place at his return (1 John 3:2) and will include the transformation of the believer's body so that it will be like the glorious body of Jesus (Phil. 3:20–21; see also Rom. 8:18, 21; 2 Cor 4:17). Paul elaborates on this theme in 1 Corinthians 15; but even in the present, believers are in the process of being transformed into the likeness of Christ "with ever-increasing glory," reflecting "the Lord's glory" (2 Cor. 3:18).

Paul now appeals to the Scriptures for support (v. 9): "No eye has seen, no ear has heard, no mind has conceived what God has prepared for those who love him." The recurring formula "it is written" indicates how deeply rooted the New Testament is in the Old—though it is sometimes difficult for us today to see a connection between a quoted Old Testament text and the New Testament context in which it appears. To the question, "Where in the Old Testament is the passage quoted in verse 9?" the answer is uncertain. "Most likely the 'citation' is an amalgamation of OT texts that had already been joined and reflected on in apocalyptic Judaism" (Fee, 109; see Isa. 64:4; 65:17; also 52:15). First-century writers did not feel obligated to give a verbatim rendering of Scripture; what was important was to do no violence to the original text.

To the first-century reader, "no mind [lit., heart] has conceived" represented a number of internal processes, one of which was the human "mind." Paul's general thought here is clear: Humanity, apart from the Spirit's help, is unable to apprehend sensually or intellectually the glory that God has prepared for those who love him. A significant turn takes place in Paul's reasoning with the Corinthians. Their emphasis had been on knowledge, wisdom, and oratorical skill; his emphasis is on loving God. Love is all-important (8:1; 13:2). "Not *gnosis* [knowledge] but love is the touchstone of Christian maturity and spirituality" (Barrett, 73).

Verses 10–16 focus further on the role of the Holy Spirit in all that has preceded. He is mentioned six times in these verses. (1) The Spirit is the means by which God reveals himself and his purposes (v. 10). On our own, we as human beings are incapable of discovering God or his purposes. (2) The Spirit searches the deep things of God (v. 10); there is nothing beyond his knowledge. Since the Spirit alone knows the thoughts of God (v. 11), we see a hint again of his deity. The analogy of a human being and his thoughts is appropriate. No one external to a person can know what is within that individual; that can be done only by the person's own spirit. So it is with God and his Spirit. (3) Closely related is the ministry of the Spirit in enabling believers to understand what God has so freely given them. These things are already in existence; the Holy Spirit reveals them.

Much of what Paul says about the Holy Spirit reminds one of Jesus' thoughts about the activity of the Paraclete, the Spirit of truth. "[He] will teach you.... [He] will remind you" (John 14:26). "He will guide you into all truth" (16:12). "He will bring glory to me" (16:14). "The Spirit will take from what is mine and make it known to you" (16:15).

Christians have received "the Spirit who is from God" (Rom. 8:14–16; Gal. 3:2; 4:6), not "the spirit of the world" (cf. also Rom. 8:15; 2 Tim. 1:7). "The spirit of the world" is sometimes understood to be Satan, especially since the two spirits are here contrasted (see notes on 1 Cor. 2:6, above). Paul certainly believed in Satan and demons, but more likely the phrase refers to the attitude characteristic of those who rely on human resources and wisdom. The Greek word for *spirit* (*pneuma*) may mean, like the English word, either an entity in the nonphysical realm or an attitude or disposition. Christians are those, ideally, who have not allowed themselves to be influenced by the prevailing attitudes of an unbelieving world. Barrett (75) notes that "the spirit of the world" is almost indistinguishable from "the wisdom of this age" (1 Cor. 2:6). Both expressions "suggest a self-regarding wisdom" that is "man-centered," and is a condition that prevents one from understanding the divine truth manifested in Christ crucified.

The closing words of verse 13 have been translated in a number of ways. For example:

> expressing spiritual truths in spiritual words (NIV)
> comparing spiritual things with spiritual (NKJV)
> combining spiritual thoughts with spiritual words (NASB)
> interpreting spiritual things to those who are spiritual (NRSV)

Two Greek words are the points of discussion in this variation. The first is *synkrino*, which the NIV translates "expressing"; it may mean (1) bring together, combine; (2) compare; (3) explain, interpret (BAGD, 774). The second word is *pneumatikos*, which the NIV translates "spiritual words." Because the specific form of the word (dative plural) may be either masculine or neuter, it can be variously translated as "to/for spiritual things," "spiritual persons," or even "spiritual words" (since "word" [*logos*] is masculine). The main point is that these are truths attributable to the Holy Spirit, which are communicated either (1) by means of spiritual words or (2) to spiritual persons. If it is indeed "spiritual persons" who are the recipients of these spiritual truths, then this leads naturally to the verses that follow.

In verses 14–16, Paul contrasts "the spiritual man" (*pneumatikos*, a word based on *pneuma* [spirit]) with "the man without the Spirit." The phrase "without the Spirit," however, is an NIV interpretation rather than a translation of the Greek word *psychikos*, a word based on the word *psyche* (soul, life). Lexicons suggest the meaning "an unspiritual man, one who lives on the purely material plane without being touched by the Spirit of God" (BAGD, 894). "The *psychikos* is the 'unrenewed' man, the 'natural' man"; he is "distinct from the man who is actuated by the Spirit" (Robertson and Plummer, 49). In passages like this, *psyche* and *pneuma* are antithetical. The natural person lives apart from the Spirit of God and, consequently, is unable to welcome the things that come from the Spirit, regarding them as foolishness. Furthermore, he or she is unable to understand them because they are "spiritually discerned" (*anakrino*). This verb occurs ten times in 1 Corinthians, often with the meaning "assess, appraise, examine, scrutinize, judge" (as in 14:24).

The spiritual person, by contrast, has the capability of judging or appraising all things because of the indwelling Holy Spirit, who guides in decision-making. This does not imply infallibility in making judgments, but it does highlight that in spiritual matters such a person moves in a completely different sphere from that of the natural person. Yet, Paul says, the spiritual person "is not subject to any man's judgment." This does not, however, place the individual above criticism. Later, Paul will stress that presumably inspired utterances must be judged by other believers (14:29). Thus, in the present passage, "any man's judgment" must be understood as "any *natural* man's judgment"; that is, anyone who lives apart from the Spirit of God is unable to evaluate matters that are in the realm of the Spirit.

To buttress this point, Paul appeals to Isaiah 40:13, in which the Hebrew text speaks of "the Spirit of the LORD [Yahweh]." But the Greek text of 1 Corinthians 2:16 reads "mind of the Lord," following the Greek (Septuagint) rather than the Hebrew text. The transition from Spirit to mind is an easy one, since in 2:10 Paul already said, "The Spirit searches all things, even the deep things of God," which is another way of speaking about the mind of God (cf. Rom. 11:34).

The conclusion is that "we [emphasized in the Greek] have the mind of Christ." The Spirit/mind of Yahweh in the Isaiah passage now becomes the mind of Christ. Here is an implicit equation of Christ with the God/Lord of the Old Testament; if this is so, then it speaks of his deity. The Holy Spirit is the Spirit of God; he is also the Spirit of Christ (Rom. 8:9), who lives in believers (1 Cor. 3:16) and reveals Christ. Because believers are so indwelt, they do not have the mind or the spirit of the world. Ideally, they are controlled by the mind or Spirit of Christ.

The doctrine of the Trinity lies just beneath the surface in this chapter, with its mention of God, Christ, and the Holy Spirit. Often in the New Testament, and especially in Trinitarian passages, *God* refers to the Father and *Lord* refers to the Son (e.g., see 12:4–6; 2 Cor. 13:14; Eph. 4:4–6).

2.1.5. Spiritual Immaturity (3:1–4). Paul attributes the problems in the Corinthian church—specifically their fascination with worldly wisdom and their divisive spirit—to spiritual immaturity. In order not to encumber the following exposition, attention is first given to three important adjectives used to describe spiritually deficient persons: *psychikos*, *sarkinos*, and *sarkikos*.

Psychikos occurred in 2:14 to describe the person who is incapable of receiving or understanding the things that come from the Spirit of God (see discussion above). This word is contrasted with "spirit" in a number of passages. In the context of the resurrection of believers, the "natural [*psychikos*] body" is contrasted with the "spiritual [*pneumatikos*] body" (15:44, 46). James says that human wisdom "does not come down from heaven but is earthly, unspiritual [*psychikos*], of the devil" (James 3:15). Jude uses the word to describe persons who "do not have the Spirit" (Jude 19). This adjective, when applied to persons, designates those who have not experienced the regenerating, renewing work of the Holy Spirit—that is, unbelievers.

The adjectives *sarkinos* and *sarkikos* derive from the noun *sarx*, often translated "flesh." *Sarkinos* occurs four times in the New Testament (Rom. 7:14; 1 Cor. 3:1; 2 Cor. 3:3; Heb. 7:16); *sarkikos* is found in six passages (Rom. 15:27; 1 Cor. 3:3; 9:11; 2 Cor. 1:12; 10:4; 1 Pet. 2:11). Some see no distinction between them in 1 Corinthians 3:1, 3 (e.g., Barrett, 79, fn. 1; Héring, 22). Others maintain that a distinction should be observed (e.g., Morris, Fee, and Robertson and Plummer), such as that *sarkinos* is a neutral term, meaning "made of flesh, fleshly, belonging to the realm of the flesh" (cf. 2 Cor. 3:3, where it is translated "human"). *Sarkikos*, on the other hand, often has ethical implications and means that which is weak or sinful (cf. 1 Pet. 2:11, "abstain from sinful [*sarkikos*] desires"). This distinction will be observed here.

Pneumatikos (spiritual) is the adjective contrasted with all three of the above (1 Cor. 2:13–15; 3:1). The unbeliever is *psychikos*; believers may be either *sarkinos* or *sarkikos*, even though they may regard themselves as *pneumatikos*. *Pneumatikos* is applicable to all believers, even though in practice some may not demonstrate that they are completely controlled by the Spirit.

Paul again addresses his readers as "brothers" (cf. 1:10), which he does twenty times in this letter. In three instances it is "my brothers" (1:11; 11:33; 12:39) and in one instance "my dear [beloved] brothers" (15:58). This is especially significant in view of his corrective and sometimes harsh tone in the letter. Notwithstanding all the faults of the Corinthian believers, they are still his brothers.

Spiritual Christians are mature Christians; they are first distinguished from fleshly (*sarkinos*) Christians, who are infants in Christ (v. 1). Paul is here pointing to his original sharing of the gospel with them. The problem is not that spiritually immature believers are in the church, for all new converts begin as spiritual infants. As such they need milk and cannot be faulted for not yet being ready for solid food (cf. the similar metaphor of milk in Heb. 5:11–12; 1 Pet. 2:2). But the problem arises because certain Corinthians are guilty of arrested spiritual development: They are "still not ready" for solid food because they are "still worldly [*sarkikos*]" (1 Cor. 3:2–3).

Their spiritual immaturity is evidenced by "jealousy and quarreling" (v. 3). The Greek word *zelos* has both positive and negative meanings. Positively, it means zeal or ardor (Rom. 10:2; 2 Cor. 7:7, 11; 9:2; Phil. 3:6); negatively, it means jealousy or envy (Rom. 13:13; 2 Cor. 12:20). Jealousy is coupled with quarreling (*eris*, cf. 1 Cor. 1:11). "Both terms point to self-assertion and unhealthy rivalries" (Morris, 62). Paul includes both words in the acts of the sinful human nature ("discord, jealousy," Gal. 5:20; see also Rom. 13:13; 2 Cor. 12:20). Quarreling represents the result of an inner disposition (*zelos*).

The Greek wording of Paul's compound question in verse 3 requires a yes answer: "You are worldly [*sarkikos*], aren't you, and walking according to men, aren't you?" (pers. trans.). He is asking the same question in two different ways. Walking is a common metaphor for one's conduct (7:17; Gal. 5:16; Eph. 2:2; 4:1). Walking or acting "like mere men" (NIV, NASB) gives the sense of Paul's question. The conduct of these people is on an earthly or human plane, not on a spiritual plane.

"When" (*hotan* in v. 4) implies that the divisive expressions of "I follow . . ." is an ongoing problem. Paul does not mention Cephas here because (1) he is merely giving examples of the divisive spirit, and (2) he and Apollos were both involved in ministry in Corinth, a matter he will now discuss.

2.1.6. Paul and Apollos: Fellow-Servants (3:5–15). Paul now emphasizes that neither he nor Apollos (nor any other person apart from Christ) is worthy of a following, because no one can take credit for the birth and growth of the congregation in Corinth. This emphasis is followed by a strong reminder of the final day of reckoning when each person's works will be tested.

Verses 5–9 focus on the ministries of Paul and Apollos and serve as guidelines for anyone involved in ministry. "What . . . [not who are] Apollos . . . and . . . Paul?" They are "servants" (*diakonoi*), following in the footsteps of Jesus who came not to be served, but to serve (Mark 10:45; Luke 22:25–27). *Diakonos* originally meant someone who serves tables (e.g., a waiter) and implies a status lower than that of those being served. It is often used in Scripture for the service (*diakonia*) one must render to God. Paul and Apollos are, therefore, first and foremost servants of the Lord (1 Cor. 3:5), even though there is a sense in which they are also servants of the Lord's people (2 Cor. 4:5). It was by means of them that the Corinthians first believed.

We note the implication that Apollos, as well as Paul, was instrumental as an evangelist. Paul's initial visit to Corinth is recorded in Acts 18:1–18, that of Apollos in Acts 18:27–19:1. "The Lord has assigned to each [*hekastos*] his task" (NIV paraphrase of the literal "the Lord gave to each") is probably a correct understanding of Paul's intent and is in keeping with what follows. It recalls different ministries of the Word which Paul mentions elsewhere, wherein the Lord "gave some to be apostles . . . prophets . . . evangelists . . . pastors and teachers" (Eph. 4:11). Robertson and Plummer (57) observe that *hekastos* (each, every) occurs five times in verses 5–13, emphasizing that God deals separately with each individual.

Paul emphasizes that he and Apollos have had and continue to have complementing, not competing, ministries since they are "God's fellow workers" (v. 9), not in the sense of working together *with* God (though that certainly is true) but working with each other *for* the Lord in his service (Bruce, 43). He makes this point crystal clear by using two metaphors—"God's field" and "God's building." The metaphors of planting and building are combined in Jeremiah 18:9; 24:6; and Ezekiel 36:9. They also occur together in the Qumran literature: "The Community council shall be founded on truth, like an eternal plantation, a holy house for Israel" (1QS 8:5; cf. 8:7).

The answer to the questions "What . . . is Apollos?" and "What is Paul?" (v. 5) is nothing (v. 7). God alone receives credit for the existence of the congregation, for in the final analysis God's people are "a planting of the LORD" (Isa. 61:3). In pursuing the agrarian imagery of the church as God's field, Paul considers himself the sower and Apollos the waterer (v. 6). He is the evangelist planting the seed, while Apollos is the teacher tending the plants. But this application cannot be pressed too far, since Paul often functioned as a teacher as well and Apollos, by implication, served as an evangelist. The main point is that they have complementing ministries with respect to God's people, but the life in the seed comes from God, not from them. And God is the One who effects the germination and growth of the seed (vv. 6–7).

Paul emphasizes the unity and interdependence of one servant on the other. They have different ministries but "one purpose" (lit., "are one thing"). "One" is neuter in gender (*hen*) and may also mean that they are united in spirit. The same word occurs in Jesus' statement that he and the Father are one (John 10:30). Thus, Paul and Apollos are coworkers, fellow servants, colleagues, not rivals. These related themes of diversity and unity will be developed later in the extended treatment of the church as the body of Christ (1 Cor. 12:12–27).

Another important principle is that each will receive a reward (*misthos*) from God "according to his own labor" (v. 8). This reward is not based on any human concept of success. Its nature is not specified, but the basic meaning of the Greek word is pay or wages. The time when the reward or wages are awarded is not given, but it certainly includes the blessing awaiting those who are the Lord's faithful servants (cf. Matt. 25:19–23).

Verses 10–15 develop the metaphor of the church as "God's building" (v. 9). In some respects it is analogous to the metaphor of the field. Paul sowed the seed; he laid the foundation. Apollos watered the seed; he built upon the foundation.

Paul attributes to God's "grace" (*charis*) anything he has accomplished in his ministry (v. 10). In a general sense grace speaks of God's favor on those who do not deserve it. In a more restricted sense it is God's enablement under pressure ("My grace is sufficient for you" [2 Cor. 12:9]). God's enabling power is part of the meaning here. In addition, the word is sometimes linked with *charisma* (gift), whose root idea is something that has been received as the result of grace (see Rom. 12:6; also v. 3). Paul's gift, in our passage, is that of the evangelist, that is, laying the spiritual foundation on which a church will be built. (We note in passing that Paul's policy was not to build on another's foundation [Rom. 15:20].)

Paul describes himself as an expert or skilled (*sophos*) master builder (*architekton*—see Isa. 3:3, LXX). The basic meaning of *sophos* is "wise," though here the extended meaning of expert or skilled is more appropriate (cf. the LXX's use of this word to describe the men who worked on the tabernacle, Ex. 35:10, 25; 36:1, 4, 8); but Paul's use of this word may also be an indirect attack on the Corinthians for their own vaunted wisdom (cf. ch. 2). An *architek ton* is one who oversees the work of buildin and should be differentiated from the worker themselves. But in no sense should Paul' autobiographical statement be taken to mea that he himself was not fully engaged in th work of laying the foundation.

The church's one and only foundation i Jesus Christ (see Isa. 28:16; Rom. 9:33; 1 Pete 2:6). He himself is the rock on which he wi build his church (Matt. 16:18). Note that "o this rock" must go back to Peter's confession o Jesus as "the Christ, the Son of the living God (16:16; see comments on this verse). As som suggest, it is possible that a group of th Corinthians claimed allegiance to Peter becaus they regarded him, in some way, as the founde of the church in a general sense. Paul's empha sis that Christ is the only foundation unde scores the exclusive claims of Christianity th Jesus is the only Savior (John 14:6; Acts 4:12

The foundation is secure; how one build on it may or may not be. "Each one should b careful how he builds" (v. 10). The expressio "each one" also occurs twice in the Greek tex of verse 13; it underscores the awesome, indi vidual responsibility of believers for their ow actions. "Each of us will give an account o himself to God" (Rom. 14:12). "We must al appear before the judgment seat of Christ, tha each one may receive what is due him" (2 Co 5:10). The word of caution mentions *how* on builds, not *what* one builds, implying tha proper motivation is the basis on which one' deeds will ultimately be evaluated.

The imagery of the building continue Though the foundation has already been lai once for all, the superstructure is in process o being erected on a personal basis (v. 12). Th building materials a believer uses fall into on of two categories—one of which will with stand the heat of God's fiery judgment, whil the other will be consumed. Gold, silver, costl stones (decorative jewels [see Isa. 54:11–12 Rev. 21:18–21] or, perhaps, valuable buildin stones like marble) will endure on the day o judgment. Combustible materials like wood hay, and straw will be destroyed. To try t identify what each of the six materials repre sents goes well beyond Paul's purpose. Hi concern is simply to discuss two basic classe

The time of testing is called "the Day (v. 13), shorthand for the Old Testament co cept of the Day of the Lord (Isa. 2:12; Jer. 46:10; Ezek. 7:9–10; Amos 5:18). Comparable expressions occur frequently in Paul's writings, often as "the day of Jesus Christ" (e.g., see Rom. 2:16; 1 Cor. 1:8; 5:5; 2 Cor. 1:14; 1 Thess. 5:2, 4; 2 Thess. 2:2). That day will be revealed "with fire" (cf. Isa. 26:11; 31:9; Dan. 7:9–10; Mal. 4:1; 2 Thess. 1:7–8; 2:8), the purpose of which is twofold: to bring to light the valuable materials and to destroy the corrupt materials.

Paul once again mentions reward (see v. 8), this time for those whose building materials survive the fire. The nature of the reward is not given (see Matt. 25:21, 23 for a suggestion), though note that Paul is not referring here to one's entrance into heaven. Conversely, the persons whose works are burned up will "suffer loss." It is important to observe that the fire consumes the person's works, not the person. Such an individual will still be saved, "but only as one escaping through the flames" (v. 15). Paul may have borrowed the imagery from Old Testament passages that speak of being snatched from the fire (Amos 4:11; Zech. 3:2). These persons forfeit the reward that could have been theirs had they built with gold, silver, and costly stones.

The purpose of the fire is to test the works of believers, not to cleanse or purify them. Those who appeal to this passage for a doctrine of purgatory have seriously misinterpreted Paul. The judgment of fire is not purificatory, beginning with the moment one dies. Rather, it is the final one that takes place on the Day of the Lord, when Jesus returns. Nor is there any indication of a period of preparation before a believer is entitled to enter into the full bliss of God's presence. Jesus said to the repentant thief, "Today you will be with me in paradise" (Luke 23:43).

2.1.7. The Temple of God (3:16–17). The transition from the church as a building to the church as a specific building, "God's temple," is easy. Paul begins with a question that conveys the idea, "You know, don't you?" This translation conveys the Greek method of wording a question in such a way that the expected answer is yes. He uses this structure ten times in the letter, as a mild reprimand (3:16; 5:6; 6:2, 3, 9, 15, 16, 19; 9:13, 24).

The New Testament employs two Greek words for temple. *Hieron* is a broader term and includes all that is in the temple precincts. *Naos* (the word used here) is the sanctuary itself; its root is *naio* (to dwell). This word, by etymology as well as usage, means the dwelling place of a deity. In Scripture its roots are in the book of Exodus; the tent in the desert, the tabernacle, was the precursor to Solomon's temple. The presence of God lived in it in a special way, as it did in the temple. At the dedication of both buildings, the glory of God descended (Ex. 40:34–35; 1 Kings 8:10–11).

These Old Testament institutions, however, were fulfilled typologically and superseded in the New Testament. When the Logos became flesh, he lived (*skenoo*—lit., tented or tabernacled) among us (John 1:14). Jesus himself indicated he was the fulfillment of what the Jewish temple foreshadowed when, in the context of his cleansing of the temple (John 2:19–21), he referred to his body as a temple. In effect, God's special presence on earth was now centered in his Son, not in the temple building.

Paul now makes the bold statement, "You yourselves are God's temple and . . . God's Spirit lives in you" (v. 16). The two statements are complementary. The close identification of the Holy Spirit's indwelling with the spiritual temple cannot be overlooked, for the Spirit, in a real sense, *is* the presence of God (note the parallelism in Ps. 51:11; 139:7)—the means by which God indwells his people. Paul will have other occasions to use the temple metaphor (1 Cor. 6:19; 2 Cor. 6:16; Eph. 2:21–22; cf. also 1 Peter 2:5).

"You" is plural, "temple" is singular (v. 16; note also the end of v. 17, where "you" is also plural). Because "temple" does not appear with a definite article, two options are possible: The finer points of Greek grammar indicate that the noun may still be understood to mean "*the* temple" because of its position in the sentence; alternatively, the noun may be saying something about the character or nature of God's people—that of temple. Collectively, believers constitute the one temple of God. This is Paul's emphasis (cf. also 1 Peter 2:5); the only exception is Paul's reference to the individual believer's body as a temple of the Holy Spirit in 1 Cor. 6:19).

"If anyone destroys" seems at odds with Jesus' assertion that the gates of Hades will not overcome the church (Matt. 16:18). But in the present passage, in light of the context, God's temple is the Corinthian congregation, which is a local expression of the one universal temple. The "if" clause may be interpreted in two ways. It may mean that it is indeed possible for a local congregation to be destroyed. It may also mean, "If anyone sets out, or tries, to destroy the temple." In view of the situation in Corinth, Paul maintains that partisanship and preoccupation with worldly wisdom may well result in the ruination of a local assembly of believers.

The verb *phtheiro* (destroy) is repeated as the judgment that comes on one who destroys God's temple. This can certainly be understood as referring to God's final and sure judgment on such a person, even though the more common New Testament word for this is *apollymi* (as in 1:18; 8:11; 15:18). But the meaning of *phtheiro* is varied. Paul's basic idea is that fearsome consequences await those who destroy or try to destroy God's temple. The punishment, whatever its specific nature, will fit the crime. One should not dismiss the possibility of "terrible ruin and eternal loss of some kind" (Robertson and Plummer, 67). The reason is that God's temple is "sacred" (*hagios*), a word previously used to designate God's people (1:2).

2.1.8. Foolish and Wise Thinking (3:18–23). This paragraph summarizes, adds to, and concludes Paul's treatment of the Corinthians' twofold problem: their improper attachment to human leaders and their fascination with worldly wisdom.

The basic problem of the Corinthians is self-deception (v. 18). The verb Paul uses here has the additional meaning of "cheat" and, as Paul will indicate shortly, is a fitting way to speak of the Corinthians' folly: They are cheating themselves. His use of the present tense has the force of, "Stop deceiving yourselves." True wisdom is attained only when one becomes foolish in the eyes of the world—that is, accepts the message of the cross as God's wisdom (1:18).

Not only is the wisdom of God foolishness in the estimation of the world, but conversely, the presumed wisdom of the world (1:21; 2:6) is foolishness to God (3:19). Paul now appeals for support to two Old Testament passages, though the quotations are not verbatim. (1) "[God] catches the wise in their craftiness" (Job 5:13). "Craftiness" (*panourgia*) denotes cunning or trickery; Paul's use of this word suggests he may have suspected some underhanded activities directed against him (Barrett 94). It is clear later that some were contesting his apostolic calling and leadership. Even if their craftiness is viewed positively (the word may have that connotation), it is still a human attempt to apprehend spiritual reality. But human beings cannot reach up to God; the message of the cross is that God has reached down to us.

(2) "The Lord knows that the thoughts of the wise are futile" (v. 20, a quote from Ps 94:11, which reads "man" rather than "the wise"). "Futile" (*mataios*) means "idle, fruitless, useless, powerless" (BAGD, 495). Although the word for "thoughts" (*dialogismos*) is often used in a neutral sense, it may also have a negative connotation (Matt. 15:19; Luke 5:22; 6:8; James 2:4). This negative connotation suggests a tie-in with Paul's statement in Romans 1:21, using these same two words, that the Gentiles did not glorify God or give thanks to him and that "their thinking became futile and their foolish hearts were darkened."

In view of all this, there is no room for boasting about human beings—whether the wise of this world or leaders in the church (v. 21). The only basis for legitimate boasting is "in the Lord" (1:31) or "in the cross of our Lord Jesus Christ" (Gal. 6:14). In boasting about and attaching themselves to human beings, the Corinthians were actually shortchanging themselves. "All things are yours," says Paul, and he proceeds to elaborate on the all-inclusiveness of believers' possessions. The separate leaders to whom they had attached themselves belong to them, because these leaders are servants through whom the Corinthians had come to faith (1 Cor. 3:6)—servants of the Lord but also, in another sense, servants of the Lord's people (2 Cor. 4:5). This idea is a reversal of their partisan spirit ("I belong to Paul," etc., 1 Cor. 1:12, NRSV).

The world, life, death, present, and future things—these, too, are theirs because of their relationship with Christ, who is Lord over all (v. 22). A similar list in Romans 8:38–39 assures believers that no force—physical, spiritual, temporal, cosmic—can separate them from God's love in Christ. Consequently, they must respond as though they really belong to him and not to themselves or some human leader.

Believers can be "of Christ" only because Christ is "of God" (v. 23). The phrase does not indicate an inferior status for Christ, for Paul amply indicates in his writings that Christ is of the same essence or nature as the Father (e.g., Phil. 2:6; Col. 1:16–19) and on a par with him (2 Cor. 13:14). Nor can it apply only to his earthly state in which, as a human being, he was often dependent on and answerable to the Father, for Paul later says that at the consummation of the ages, "the Son himself will be made subject to him who put everything under him" (1 Cor. 15:28). The relationship of the Son to the Father must be viewed as one of subordination rather than inferiority of essence. This subordination is functional, focusing on his *role* in the divine plan; it in no way impinges on his deity and equality with the Father (see also 8:6; 11:3).

2.1.9. The Work of the Lord's Servants (4:1–5). Chapter 4 concludes Paul's extensive treatment of the two general and interrelated problems in the congregation: their mistaken view of wisdom and their divisive spirit in claiming allegiance to one leader in opposition to other leaders. Now he aims to show how their assessment of leaders is mistaken, because it is at odds with God's. It becomes increasingly clear that some in the church were rejecting his authority and thereby also his teaching.

Paul picks up the argument of chapter 3 by saying, "So then" (v. 1). He proceeds to tell them what their proper attitude ought to be toward spiritual leaders. His comments in this chapter give indispensable guidelines for evaluating one's ministry. At best, he says, he and the other leaders should be regarded as Christ's "servants" (*hyperetes*, not *diakonos* as in 3:5). In recounting his conversion experience, Paul quoted Jesus saying to him, "I have appeared to you to appoint you as a *hyperetes*" (Acts 26:16). These two Greek words are synonyms with different shades of meaning. In Paul's day, *hyperetes* meant "servant, helper, assistant" (BAGD, 842). John Mark, who was with Barnabas and Saul on their first missionary journey, is called their "helper" (Acts 13:5). Both Greek terms direct attention to the subordinate role of the servant. Paul and his fellow ministers are servants "of Christ."

In addition to being servants, they are also "stewards [*oikonomos*] of the mysteries of God" (v. 1, NASB). An *oikonomos* was one who managed or supervised a large estate (Luke 12:42; 16:1), but the administrative responsibilities of such a trusted person are not Paul's emphasis in this self-designation. It is rather on the accountability of the steward to his master; he must prove himself faithful or trustworthy (*pistos*). Jesus asked the question, "Who . . . is the faithful and wise manager [*oikonomos*]?" and then answered it (Luke 12:42–44). Faithfulness, in its broadest sense, is required of all God's people (Rev. 2:10) and is among the fruit of the Spirit listed by Paul (Gal. 5:22–23), where the word *pistis* (noun form of *pistos*) is best translated "faithfulness, reliability, trustworthiness." This is predicated on the truth that God himself is faithful, a recurrent statement in Scripture (cf. 1 Cor. 1:9; 2 Cor. 1:18; 1 Thess. 5:24; 2 Thess. 3:3; 2 Tim. 2:13). He who is always faithful will enable his people to be faithful.

Just as a household steward was entrusted with his master's resources, so, says Paul, are he and his ministerial colleagues entrusted with "the secret things [mysteries] of God." The word *mystery* occurs twenty times in his writings. He uses the plural only in this book (4:1; 13:2; 14:2), and it is not certain that the meaning in the last two occurences coincides with the meaning in 4:1. The plural form of the word here does not differ materially from the meaning of the singular (see on 2:7). Perhaps in Paul's mind the plural includes the various aspects of God's redemptive plan that have now been revealed.

Paul's expression "stewards of the mysteries of God" (NASB) is interpreted by some to mean the role of the minister in administering the sacraments, or ordinances, of the church. But this informs the term *mysteries* with a meaning alien to the New Testament and probably reflects a reading back into the New Testament of a later "mysterious," mystical interpretation of these observances. Certainly no such meaning is found in Paul's treatment of baptism and the Lord's Supper in this letter (e.g., 1:13–17; 10:1–4; 11:23–32), where the word *mystery* does not occur.

Paul goes on to deal with the question, "To whom is the servant-steward of God responsible?" The answer is obvious, but he feels compelled to elaborate in view of the prevailing problems in the congregation. Verse 3 begins with "to me"; its position at the beginning of the statement makes it emphatic. The Corinthians may have considered it a matter of considerable importance to examine (NIV, judge, *anakrino*) Paul's claim to apostolic authority. This verb was sometimes used in a law court for the process of examining and cross-examining a witness. This meaning is highlighted by his addition of "or by any human court" (lit., "human day"). The apostle will wait for the Lord to make the ultimate judgment on his ministry in the Day of the Lord (3:13). Note how he later wrote to the Romans, "Who are you to judge someone else's servant? To his own master he stands or falls" (Rom. 14:4; see also 2:1, 19–21).

The injunction not to "judge" anyone must be understood in context. Earlier Paul used this word for a legitimate act by a spiritual person (2:14–15), and later he uses the similar word *krino* (e.g., 5:3, 12–13). He also uses another cognate word (*diakrino*) when instructing believers to assess properly the Lord's body (11:19, 31) and prophetic utterances (14:29). In other words, believers are not required to suspend evaluation or judgment in all cases. The present context enjoins it because it was being motivated by pride and self-righteousness. This is behind Jesus' command, "Do not judge" (Matt. 7:1); one who has a plank in one eye must not fault a brother who has a speck of sawdust in his eye (vv. 5–6). Yet Jesus also said, "Make a righteous judgment [lit., judge righteous judgment]" (John 7:24).

Surprisingly, Paul goes on to say, "I do not even judge myself" (4:3). This seems to contradict his later statement, in connection with observing the Lord's Supper, that "a man ought to examine himself [*dokimazo*—a synonym for *anakrino*] before he eats of the bread and drinks of the cup" (11:28). He does not rule out self-examination or evaluating one's own spiritual walk, but the context of 4:4 speaks of the Lord as the ultimate Judge at his coming (2 Cor. 5:10). Paul says that his own self-assessment may be faulty, even though his "conscience is clear."

Contrary to popular opinion, a clear conscience does not necessarily mean that the person is blameless. There is always the possibility of unintentional self-deception or of one's "conscience" being an expression of the mores and morals of this world. So, says Paul, a clear conscience "does not make me innocent" (lit., "by this, I am not justified"). The verb used is *dikaioo*, "to declare not guilty, to acquit." This is a favorite word in Paul's writings, when he magnifies God's grace in justifying people, contrasting it with their own attempts to earn justification on the basis of their own good works. It is a forensic, legal term and is appropriate in a context that portrays Jesus as the ultimate Judge. It is wise, therefore, to leave judgment in the hands of the Judge par excellence. He is, after all, "the righteous Judge" who "on that day" will award the crown of righteousness "to all who have longed for his appearing" (2 Tim. 4:8).

The word *conscience* (*syneidesis*, a noun Paul uses eighteen times; e.g. Rom. 2:15; 9:1; 1 Cor. 8:7, 12; 10:25, 27–29) does not appear in this paragraph, but the translation is based on the verb from which it derives—*synoida*, which means "share knowledge with" (BAGD, 791). The NASB translates, "I am conscious of nothing against myself" (cf. also Job 27:6, LXX). The noun's basic meaning is that of consciousness or, by extension, moral consciousness. However one defines it, conscience ideally is the ability to discriminate between good and evil; in that regard it may be considered a function or aspect of the image of God in humankind. But because of the Fall that image has been marred (some say "effaced"). Consequently, it cannot be an infallible guide even for Christian believers, since they are not yet fully restored to the divine image (Rom. 8:29; 2 Cor. 3:18; 1 John 3:2).

The upshot is that the Corinthians must "stop judging" (the force of the Greek present tense), an indication that they were guilty of doing it. Believers are to judge nothing "before the appointed time" (v. 5), that is, the end of the age, when the saints will judge the world and angels (6:2–3). The "time," then, is identified with the Day of the Lord (1:8; 3:13), that is, when "the Lord comes."

The ultimate Judge "will bring to light what is hidden in darkness"; that is, he "will expose the motives of men's hearts" (see Ps. 139:11–12). Inner thoughts and motives, not just deeds, will be exposed and judged in that Day—another indication that human beings, with their limitations, are unable to read huma earts. At that time, "each will receive his raise from God," not from other people, for e Corinthians were guilty of bestowing praise n Cephas, Apollos, Paul, etc. All that matters, ltimately, is that one is praised by God.

2.1.10. True Apostles (4:6–13). Paul again ddresses the Corinthians as "brothers," even ough he must continue admonishing and ebuking them for their personal pride and ille-itimate pride in leaders. He must remind them at whatever a Christian has is by God's grace. le proceeds with biting irony to make his case y comparing their smug, self-satisfied attitude ith the hardships endured by him and other postles.

Verses 6–7 present a translation difficulty the opening clause because of the unusual erb Paul uses (*metaschematizo*). It occurs nly four other times in the New Testament. alse apostles, Satan, and Satan's servants all ansform ("masquerade," NIV) themselves Cor. 11:13–15); Christ will transform our wly bodies (Phil. 3:21). All have the idea of ansforming or changing the form of some-ing. Here are sample renderings of the clause verse 6:

I have applied these things to myself and Apollos (NIV)
I have applied all this to Apollos and myself (NRSV)
These things . . . I have figuratively applied to myself and Apollos (NASB)
These things . . . I have figuratively transferred to myself and Apollos (NKJV)

he translation given in BAGD (513), with its xplanatory note, will be sufficient here: "*I ave applied this to Apollos and myself* = I ave given this teaching of mine the form of n exposition concerning Apollos and myself." hat is, Paul has used Apollos and himself as lustrations of what he had previously indi-ated constitutes a true servant of the Lord. he purpose of this is "for your benefit, so that ou may learn from us"—certainly the prin-ple of "leadership by example."

Paul implies there was a saying, "Do not go eyond what is written," whose meaning the orinthians should learn (v. 6). "It is written" as a common expression introducing Old estament quotations (e.g., 1:19, 31; 2:9; 19). Thus, Paul is likely alluding to Old Tes-ment teaching on the subject, even though he does not quote a passage. Certainly much of what he has said is found in essence, if not in exact words, in the Old Testament. He is, then, exhorting them to live in accordance with the Scriptures. It is not necessary to interpret Paul's statement, as some do, as referring to some well-known secular saying known to him or to the Corinthians.

Having learned this basic lesson, the Corinthians will then "not take pride [*physioo*—become arrogant, NASB] in one man over against another." This verb basically means "to blow up, puff up, inflate." It occurs only seven times in the New Testament: six in this letter (4:6, 18, 19; 5:2; 8:1; 13:4) and once elsewhere (Col. 2:18). The sin of pride was a genuine problem among the Corinthian believers. Up to this point in the letter their pride was in their distorted view of wisdom and their attachment to selected leaders. Shortly Paul will charge them with pride in the area of moral and ethical indifference (1 Cor. 5:2), in their "knowledge" (8:1), and, implicitly, in their lack of love (13:4). In the present context, their pride is in "one man over against another"—that is, their inclination to pit one leader against another, though more generally it is a caution against a believer's feeling of spiritual superiority over other believers.

Differences do indeed exist among God's people, but they are God's doing. If one seems to be superior to another, it is not to that person's credit. "What do you [singular in v. 7] have that you did not receive?" asks Paul. He previously stated that as a congregation they do not lack, or need not lack, any spiritual gift (1:7); but as he explains in detail in chapter 12, gifts and functions of members of the body of Christ are by divine distribution. Consequently, no one ought to "boast" (*kauchaomai*—a frequent word in 1 and 2 Corinthians, along with the noun *kauchema*). "Who makes you different from anyone else?" The answer is God. "What do you have that you did not receive?" The answer is nothing. "Why [then] do you boast?" The question is rhetorical; the answer is obvious.

Verses 8–13 contain some of the most ironic, perhaps even sarcastic, comments in Scripture. Is this unworthy of Paul? If the design of such language is simply to hurt or give pain, then it is morally questionable. But since Paul is speaking to his spiritual children

(vv. 14–16), whom he also addresses as "brothers," he uses irony to jar them into right thinking. "I am not writing this to shame you, but to warn you" (v. 14).

The key to understanding this paragraph is the word "already" (*ede*), which occurs twice in verse 8, along with the tenses of the two verbs. "You have all you want" is in the Greek perfect tense, indicating a completed action whose results continue to the present. You were, and are now, satiated. "You have become rich" is in the Greek aorist tense (lit., "You became rich"). The Corinthians had, in their own thinking, "already" attained complete fulfillment; they needed nothing further. Their feeling of self-sufficiency was similar to the ideal of Stoicism, but it was completely contrary to the spirit of the New Testament. They could join the church at Laodicea in saying, "I am rich; I have acquired wealth and do not need a thing" (Rev. 3:17).

In other words, the Corinthians felt there was no future aspect to their salvation. They had reached the zenith of spirituality; there was nothing further for them to expect. This viewpoint of what can be termed *over-realized eschatology* is at variance with the correct concept of redemption, which is often expressed in terms of "already/not yet." Believers are indeed saved at the present time ("by grace you have been saved" [Eph. 2:8]), but there is also the future aspect (see 1 Cor. 15; cf. also Rom. 8:23; Phil. 3:20–21). Believers have already received the Holy Spirit, but that is only a "deposit" of their inheritance, "guaranteeing what is to come" (2 Cor. 1:22; cf. Eph. 1:13–14). The kingdom of God is a present reality (1 Cor. 4:20), but also future (6:9). The feeling of self-sufficiency on the part of the Corinthians was undoubtedly responsible for their stunted spiritual growth (3:1–4). How unlike Paul, who confessed he was still "straining toward what is ahead," pressing on toward the goal to win God's approval (Phil. 3:13–14).

The Corinthians felt they had already entered the age to come. They were already ruling with Christ. "You have become kings," says Paul, "and that without us." "Without us" may be mean without our help, or apart from us. Preference should be given to the latter in view of the statement that follows: "so that we might be kings with you!" It seems as if the Corinthians were laying claim to something neither Paul nor the other apostles had ye[t] achieved.

Verses 9–13 detail some of the hardship[s] Paul had endured and was presently experi[en]cing in Ephesus. How unlike the presume[d] reigning of the Corinthians! How he wishe[d] such reigning could be true of him (v. 8)! Bu[t] God, instead, has placed the apostles in th[e] arena, figuratively. They are like condemne[d] criminals destined to die, either at the hands o[f] other people or by wild beasts (see 15:32). I[n] Paul's day, condemned criminals often wer[e] paraded before a bloodthirsty crowd and wer[e] objects of derision. The apostles have becom[e] a spectacle "to the whole universe." The uni[]verse (*kosmos*) here includes all intelligen[t] personal beings—angelic as well as huma[n]. Angels are sometimes portrayed in Scriptur[e] as observing human events (e.g., 11:10; 1 Ti[m.] 3:16; 5:21; 1 Peter 1:12).

Paul continues his irony with three con[]trasting pairs of statements (v. 10). (1) Th[e] apostles are "fools" on account of (*dia*) Chris[t] (see comments on 1:18–25; 3:18; see als[o] 2 Cor. 4:11; Phil. 3:7); the Corinthians ar[e] "wise in Christ." In the latter statement Pau[l] is sarcastically repeating their claim. (2) Pa[ul] continues: The apostles "are weak"; th[e] Corinthians "are strong." A Christian's admis[]sion of weakness is a confession of need fo[r] divine assistance. It provides God with a[n] occasion to display his own strength (2 Co[r.] 12:9), and it enables believers to say they ca[n] do all things through Christ, who strengthen[s] them (Phil. 4:13). On the other hand, th[e] alleged strength of the Corinthians is reall[y] weakness, since it is independent of God an[d] is mere talk (1 Cor. 4:19–20). (3) They "ar[e] honored"; the apostles "are dishonored." The[y] are honored by their own standards, wherea[s] the apostles are despised.

One sees in this trilogy that the Corinthian[s], through their self-estimate, conferred on them[]selves wisdom, strength, and honor. Paul, o[n] the other hand, evaluates himself and his fellow apostles in terms that are distasteful to unspi[r]itual persons—foolishness, weakness, and dis[]honor. They may be characterized, perhap[s] caricatured, in this way by those who measu[re] by human standards, but in God's sight they ar[e] the truly wise, strong, and honored.

"To this very hour," says Paul, he and oth[]ers are "hungry and thirsty . . . [and] are i[n] rags" (v. 11). They are brutally beaten (*kolaphizo*), as was Jesus (Matt. 26:67); he uses the same verb when speaking of the messenger of Satan who tormented him (2 Cor. 12:7). They are also "homeless," reminiscent of Jesus' words that "the Son of Man has no place to lay his head" (Matt. 8:20; Luke 9:58). We may compare these statements with similar listings (for example, 2 Cor. 6:4–10). The apostles are in good company with their Lord!

As a further disgrace in the eyes of the Corinthians, Paul reminds them, "We toil [*kopiao*], working with our own hands" (v. 12, NASB). Manual work was despised by the Greeks, and it was especially reprehensible for a teacher to be so engaged. But Paul is not out to ingratiate himself with his readers. In his missionary journeys he plied his trade as necessary in order to support himself (Acts 18:3; 20:34; 1 Cor. 9:6,12,15–18; 2 Cor. 11:7–9; 12:13; 1 Thess. 2:9; 2 Thess. 3:8). In stark contrast to the Greek concept, manual labor was considered honorable in Judaism. *Kopiao* means to work hard, toil, struggle; Paul often uses this word when speaking of the work of ministry (e.g., 15:10; 16:16; Gal. 4:11; Phil. 2:16; Col. 1:29).

The ministry of the apostles has resulted in their being cursed, persecuted, and slandered (vv. 12–13; cf. Jesus' teaching and example in Matt. 5:11–12, 39–45; Luke 6:28; 23:34; cf. Rom. 12:14–21). They bless those who curse them, they endure persecution, and they speak kindly to their slanderers. They have become "the scum [*perikatharma*] of the earth, the refuse [*peripsema*] of the world." These two Greek words are similar in meaning. The first is based on the word for cleanse or purify, and by extension came to mean scapegoat. It was used in the pagan world "to denote the means by which a people or city might be morally or religiously cleansed," sometimes with a voluntary human sacrifice. The most worthless men came to be used as sacrifices (Barrett, 112; see also Héring, 31). Morris (79) writes: "It is the refuse after a thorough cleaning, the filth that is thrown out." The second word means dirt or offscouring. Paul is emphasizing the extremely low opinion the world holds of messengers of the gospel.

2.1.11. Paul: Their Spiritual Father (4:14–21). Paul reverses his severe tone. In this closing paragraph of the first segment of his letter, he addresses his readers as "my dear children" (v. 14). He has written, not to make them ashamed, but to warn, or better admonish (*noutheteo*), them (cf. Rom. 15:14; Col. 1:28; 3:16; 1 Thess. 5:12, 14; 2 Thess. 3:15). It is "criticism in love" (Morris, 80), of a father to his children (cf. Eph. 6:4); this is appropriate in this context because, as Paul says, "in Christ Jesus I became your father through the gospel" (v. 15). As their spiritual father he feels an obligation to correct them; in fact, as their only legitimate spiritual father, he alone has this responsibility. He would not discount the idea that others who came after him had been instrumental in the conversion of some of them. But his point is that a unique bond exists between him and the Corinthians.

The Corinthians may have "ten thousand guardians [*paidagogos*]"—an obvious exaggeration to make a point (v. 15). In those days a *paidagogos* (cf. also Gal. 3:24) was a trusted slave who was responsible to look after a boy or boys in the household. He was, literally, a "'boy-leader'... whose duty it was to conduct the boy or youth ... to and from school and to superintend his conduct generally" (BAGD, 603). The word must not be understood to mean teacher, even though it is the root of our English word *pedagogue* (teacher). Paul does not mean to belittle others who have nurtured the Corinthians; that would be contrary to his emphasis on complementing ministries (see comments on 3:6–9). But he does want to stress that as their spiritual father, he is uniquely entitled and qualified to correct them.

Paul is not at variance with Jesus' command, "Do not call anyone on earth 'father'" (Matt. 23:9). The word "call" in this verse (*kaleo*) has the meaning of address. No spiritual leader is to be addressed in this manner because "you have one Father, and he is in heaven." No one should arrogate to oneself a religious term of address that belongs to God alone. But 1 Corinthians 4:15 does not detract from a spiritual father-child relationship among believers.

In view of the special relationship between him and the Corinthians, Paul now urges them to imitate him—a common theme in his writings (11:1; Gal. 4:12; Phil. 3:17; 4:9; 1 Thess. 1:6; 2 Thess. 3:7, 9). He would not subscribe to the common dictum, "Do as I say, not as I do." His leadership was by example, though it is qualified by a later statement: "Follow my example, as I follow the example of Christ" (11:1). In another context, Paul says, "Be imitators of God" (Eph. 5:1). Why could not the Corinthians simply follow the example of Christ directly? One possibility is they did not know enough about his life, character, and teachings. But a more obvious reason is that the example set by Christ was concretized in Paul, and thus Paul's example, as it reflected Christ, was easier to follow.

Timothy has been dispatched by Paul "for this reason," that is, to "remind you of my way [lit., ways] of life in Christ Jesus" (v. 17). Timothy is Paul's spiritual child, whom Paul loves and who is faithful (*pistos*—see comments at 4:2) in the Lord. He was one of Paul's closest associates in the ministry (Acts 16:1–13; 1 Tim. 1:2; 2 Tim. 1:2–6) and is mentioned frequently in his writings, as well as in Acts and Hebrews. He may have assisted Paul in founding the church in Corinth (2 Cor. 1:19). "Way" (Hebrew, *halakah*) was a common Jewish metaphor for one's conduct, the moral path one followed. Timothy was already on his way to Corinth by way of Macedonia (NIV's "am sending" is a past tense). This route would take longer than the sea route from Ephesus to Corinth by which Paul would have sent the letter.

Even though Paul is here dealing with problems peculiar to the Corinthian congregation, he requires no more of them than he does of others. What he tells them is also "what I teach everywhere in every church" (v. 17; see also 7:17; 11:16; 14:33, 36).

It is important to note that "some" of the Corinthians had "become arrogant" (cf. v. 6), thinking that Paul would not return to them and therefore that they were free to conduct themselves as they pleased (v. 18). The apostle is quick to tell them he will come "very soon," with the proviso "if the Lord is willing" (cf. 16:7; also Acts 18:21; Heb. 6:3; James 4:13–16). "Only divine restraint . . . will stop him" (Morris, 81). The plans and movements of the child of God are always subject to revision, postponement, or cancellation by God.

Returning to the arrogant Corinthians' fascination with "talk," Paul now contrasts it with "power" (v. 20). Does their way of life demonstrate the power of the gospel in righteous living, or is it merely a matter of words? Words and deeds are contrasted elsewhere by Paul (2:4, 13; 1 Thess. 1:5). Note also Jesus' statement, "Not everyone who says to me, 'Lor Lord,' will enter the kingdom of heaven, bu only he who does the will of my Father wh is in heaven" (Matt. 7:21). John speaks simi larly when he says, "Let us not love with word or tongue but with actions and in truth" (1 Joh 3:18). Put simply, actions are more importar than words, and righteous conduct shoul measure up to any claims of spirituality. It i not difficult to contrast Paul's comments on th kingdom with the Corinthians' claim to thei own kingship (1 Cor. 4:8). For Paul, the king dom of God was both present (Rom. 14:17 and future (1 Cor. 15:28).

The essence of the kingdom of God i power, not talk. The kingdom of God is a fre quent topic of Jesus' teaching in the Synopti Gospels, in which it is often associated wit power (e.g., Luke 11:20). Divine power i linked with the Holy Spirit (see note on 2:4 who, according to Romans 8, is the means b which the child of God can live acceptably The kingdom of God is not a prominent con cept in Paul's writings (mentioned only eleve times, including here; 6:9–10; 15:24, 50), an the kingdom of Christ is mentioned only fou times (Eph. 5:5; Col. 1:13; 2 Tim. 4:1, 18 Even though he does not often use "kingdom terminology, what he does say accords with th teaching of Jesus. In all things, God (an Christ) must be supreme.

The Corinthians will decide the mood i which Paul will come to them (v. 21). Th alternatives are clear-cut: He can come "wit a whip," to rebuke them sternly, or "with gentle spirit" and "in love" (see Matt. 5:5 11:29; Gal. 6:1). The choice is theirs. Perhap the imagery of coming to them with a whip i to prepare the way for his stern tone in the nex chapter.

2.2. Sexual Immorality and the Church (5:1–13)

A distinction is sometimes made betwee sins of the spirit and sins of the flesh. Jesus di not make this distinction, however, as we se in his teaching about murder and adultery o the one hand, and anger and lust on the othe (Matt. 5:21–22, 27–28). Nevertheless, such distinction may be useful in differentiatin between sins of the disposition and overt sins But this should not suggest a hierarchy of sins in which some are "worse" than others.

Up to here Paul has dealt with "sins of the spirit"—a partisan spirit, arrogance, and fascination with worldly wisdom. He must now address a question of sexual immorality in the congregation. If it be asked how the Corinthian church could tolerate such conduct by one of its members, one does not need to look far to see that the contemporary church may be as guilty.

2.2.1. The Incestuous Brother (5:1–8). This passage deals with the disciplining of a sinning brother. A valid assumption is that the woman was not a believer and therefore need not be censured by the congregation. Strictly speaking, this sin cannot be called incest (Barrett, 121), since that sin implies a blood relationship between the sexual partners. The woman is the man's "father's wife"; she is not called his mother (i.e., she is his stepmother). Most likely the father had divorced her or he had died. Paul does not even call the sin adultery (*moicheia*), since adultery involves at least one married partner.

Verses 1–2a cover the problem as Paul sees it. The report he received was that there was "sexual immorality" (*porneia*) in the Corinthian assembly. In the New Testament *porneia* includes all kinds of illicit sexual activity. In this case, "a man has his father's wife" (v. 1)—a euphemism for sexual union (John 4:18; cf. also 1 Cor. 7:2–3). The present tense of the verb "has" indicates it was not a one-time sin. The partners were regularly engaging in sexual activity; marriage or concubinage were likely involved (Barrett, 122; Robertson and Plummer, 96).

The Old Testament clearly forbade sexual activity between a man and his father's wife (Lev. 18:8; 20:11; Deut. 22:30; 27:20), a sin punishable by death. Such conduct was so reprehensible that even pagan Gentiles, both Greek and Roman, were offended by it. Roman law forbade such activity even after the father's death (Héring, 34). This does not mean it did not occur among them, but it does say that they condemned it. Strange, indeed, that conduct condemned by the Gentiles was tolerated by the Corinthian church.

In this matter, says Paul, "You have become arrogant" (v. 2, NASB). He has already censured them for their arrogance (see comment on 4:6) in setting up "one man over against another." It now manifests itself in another way. To them, in their self-exalted spiritual state, "everything is permissible" (see comments on 6:12; 10:23). They had reached the pinnacle of spirituality; therefore, what they did with their bodies was inconsequential. They were guilty of what is called libertinism or antinomianism. They placed themselves above any law. There may be intimations here of an influence of early Gnosticism (see comments on 1:5). Since Gnostics taught that all matter is evil, some of its devotees believed that what they did with their bodies could not adversely affect their superior spiritual state.

Verses 2b–5 deal with Paul's resolution of the problem. Rather than priding themselves in their misguided freedom, the Corinthians should have taken two related actions in this deplorable situation. (1) They should have been filled with grief; this was an occasion for mourning, not boasting. (2) If they had truly been grief-stricken, they would have disfellowshiped the sinning member by handing him over to Satan (vv. 2b, 5).

Although the church has not taken action, Paul has. He is, of course, not physically present, but he is with them "in spirit." In Paul's writings it is sometimes difficult to know, when he uses the word "spirit," whether he means the human spirit or the Holy Spirit (e.g., 14:15); in some instances it may be a case of both-and. But in this passage it likely refers to his own spirit in contrast to his body. The idea seems to be that his thoughts are with them (see also v. 4; Col. 2:5). The concluding clause of verse 3 is better translated "being present" rather than the NIV's "just as if I were present." Paul is indeed present, in spirit (see Fee, 204–5, fnn. 39, 41).

Though the Corinthians have placed themselves above criticizing or judging the immoral man, Paul says he himself has already passed judgment (*krino*) on him (see comments on 4:5). He has evaluated the situation and has concluded that the man is guilty before God and must be disciplined. Leon Morris (84–85) lists seven possible ways of understanding this passage. It will serve our purpose to observe the following key elements:

1. Any action taken against the man must be by the entire congregation, not by Paul: "when you are assembled."
2. The Lord Jesus is prominent. Whatever takes place must be in his name (i.e., with his authority) and with his power or enabling.

3. Ideally, the authority the congregation exercises will be directed by Christ and so will be endorsed by him.
4. Paul will be with them "in spirit."

Paul's thoughts on disciplining a church member are consistent with Jesus' more extended teaching on the matter (Matt. 18:15–20). Both place the matter in the context of the assembling of believers, and both speak of a community action. Both deal with a believer who refuses to repent. Both call for the exclusion of the unrepentant sinner from the community of believers. And in both passages the Lord is present to honor the decision made by the congregation. In the background is the Jewish practice of expelling some followers of Jesus from the synagogue (John 9:22; 12:42; 16:2).

The expression "hand ... over to Satan" (v. 5) occurs also in 1 Timothy 1:19–20: "Some ... have shipwrecked their faith. Among them are Hymenaeus and Alexander, whom I have handed over to Satan to be taught not to blaspheme." It is the idea of excommunication, that is, expelling a person from the community of believers (cf. 1 Cor. 5:7, 13). Such an individual is returned to the dominion of Satan from which he or she had once been delivered (Col. 1:13), for there is no middle ground for a recalcitrant, unrepentant, sinning believer. Nothing could be more decisive than Paul's concluding words in this chapter, "Expel the wicked man from among you." He then becomes like the pagans, vulnerable to Satan (1 John 5:19), in a manner that Christians cannot be (Robertson and Plummer, 99).

Satan, for Paul, is a personal spiritual being unalterably opposed to God and his people. The word is Hebrew in origin and means "adversary." In addition to other designations for him, the name Satan appears ten times in Paul's letters (Rom. 16:20; 1 Cor. 5:5; 7:5; 2 Cor. 2:11; 11:14; 12:7; 1 Thess. 2:18; 2 Thess. 2:9; 1 Tim. 1:20; 5:15).

The sinning brother is to be handed over to him "for the destruction [*olethros*] of the flesh [*sarx*]" (NRSV, NKJV). The word *sarx* has been interpreted to mean either (1) sinful nature, or (2) the physical body. The NIV opts for the first: "so that the sinful nature may be destroyed," and Fee concurs (210–12). The word often does convey that meaning, especially in Paul's writings. It is difficult, however, to see how Satan, the attempted destroyer (Apollyon) of God's people and purposes (Rev. 9:11), would be used by God to destroy a person's sinful nature. It is easier to understand the word as a synonym for body (15:39). With this interpretation, Satan would be God's instrument in the physical chastisement of the disfellowshiped person.

"Destruction" (*olethros*) has a note of finality about it. It probably refers to death (Bruce, 55); at best it means grave physical sickness. Paul will speak later about Christians who are sick or who have died because of unconfessed sin (11:30). The death of Ananias and Sapphira is often cited as an example of such "destruction of the flesh" (Acts 5:1–10). One may also think of Job's experience, in which God allowed Satan to attack him physically (Job 1:9–12; 2:1–7), even though it was not punishment for sin. Or consider Paul's thorn in the flesh, which he describes as "a messenger of Satan, to torment me" (2 Cor. 12:7). For the sinning Corinthian, if death is not in the mind of Paul, then surely suffering at the hand of Satan is.

This "destruction of the flesh" is the immediate consequence of expulsion from the community. Although it is punitive in nature, it is also designed to bring the man to his spiritual senses; unfortunately, Paul does not explain how this might happen. But the goal is that the man's spirit will be "saved on the day of the Lord" (cf. 1:8; 3:13). Some see a sequel to this incident in 2 Corinthians 2:5–9, that the sinning brother did in fact repent and was seeking restoration to the fellowship. Others, like Bruce (55), think this is doubtful. In any case, the purpose of Paul's recommended drastic action is the ultimate salvation of the unrepentant brother, not his eternal destruction at the time of the final judgment.

Verses 6–8 emphasize the permeating effect of serious sin in a member's life on the entire congregation if it is not dealt with. Once again, Paul reprimands the Corinthians for their pride in not dealing with the problem (v. 6; see comment on v. 2). The immoral man must be expelled for his own good, but there is an additional reason for doing so: They should have known (lit., "You know, don't you?") that, like yeast in dough, sin will spread throughout the congregation. Like the proverbial rotten apple in a barrel, eventually the whole batch will be contaminated if the one apple is not removed. Some suggest that the leaven is the Corinthians' boasting (v. 6); as long as they continue to boast about their tolerance of sinful situations, that pride will eat through their hearts like a cancer and destroy them from the inside.

"A little yeast works through the whole batch of dough" seems to have been a well-known proverb (Gal. 5:9). With some exceptions (e.g., Matt. 13:33; Luke 13:20–21), yeast (leaven) in Scripture signifies evil (e.g., Matt. 16:6, 11–12; Mark 8:15; Luke 12:1). The metaphor recalls the time of the Exodus and the first Passover, when the Hebrews were told to make unleavened bread (Ex. 12:15–16, 34–39; 13:3; 23:15). Later Jewish custom dictated that at the Passover season a household was to dispose of all traces of yeast, so that the Feast of Unleavened Bread could be observed. After the feast, the household could once again bake and eat leavened bread. Now the Corinthians are commanded to "get rid of" the old yeast, in order that they might be "a new batch without yeast" (1 Cor. 5:7). This seems simple enough to understand, except that the last statement is followed by the seemingly contradictory statement, "just as you are in fact unleavened" (NASB).

In its present situation, how could Paul characterize the Corinthian congregation as both leavened and unleavened? There is a motif, especially in Paul's writing, that can be captured in the common, paradoxical saying, "Become what you are." It is often expressed in terms of the indicative and imperative moods (see Barrett, 128; Fee, 217). In general, it says that since one is a child of God, that person ought to behave like one. To illustrate, Paul says that Christians have died with Christ (Rom. 6:8), but he then goes on to say, "Count yourselves dead to sin" (v. 11). The Corinthian Christians are indeed unleavened—cleansed from their sins (6:11)—for whom "the old has gone, the new has come" (2 Cor. 5:17). Now they must act like it, by purifying their community of the leaven that found its way into it.

Following through on the Old Testament analogy, Paul says that "Christ our Passover lamb [*pascha*], has been sacrificed" (v. 7). *Pascha* can mean both the Passover Feast and the Pascal lamb (BAGD, 633). Certainly Christ is the fulfillment of the Passover sacrificial animal (1 Peter 1:19); his death coincided with the death of the Passover lambs (John 19:14, 31; cf. Ex. 12:16; Deut. 16:6). Moreover, Christ fulfilled all that the original Passover foreshadowed, including cleansing from sin and deliverance from death and bondage. In view of this, the church is exhorted (Paul includes himself—"let us") to keep on celebrating (the significance of the present tense here) the Feast. It is to be celebrated not with old yeast, which signifies malice and wickedness (two closely related synonyms), but with unleavened bread, which signifies sincerity and truth (synonyms involving the idea of purity, v. 8).

Though not necessarily related to Paul's theological comments on the Feast of Unleavened Bread and Passover, it is interesting to conjecture that Paul wrote this at the Passover season. Since he was writing from Ephesus and said he would remain there until the Feast of Pentecost (16:8), it is possible that this letter was written some fifty days prior to that feast.

2.2.2. Associating with Immoral Believers (5:9–13). It seems as if the Corinthians misunderstood something Paul had written in a previous letter on the matter of not associating with sexually immoral people (v. 9), a letter that is now lost (though some think that 2 Cor. 6:14–7:1 may be part of it). He clearly meant immoral members of the Christian community, not immoral people of "this world" (v. 10). The unusual Greek verb for "associate" occurs only here (vv. 9, 11) and in 2 Thessalonians 3:14 in the New Testament. Its literal meaning is "mix up together."

The people of this world are described as sexually immoral persons, greedy people, swindlers, and idolaters (v. 10; cf. 6:9–10 for a more complete list). For Christians to separate themselves completely from such people is neither possible ("you would have to leave this world") nor desirable, since they must associate themselves with them in order to proclaim to them the gospel. Like Jesus, they must be "a friend of tax collectors and 'sinners'" (Matt. 11:19).

Religious communities throughout history have often felt the need to withdraw from society. Some do it in protest to the evil of the world; others, to protect themselves from that evil and thereby achieve piety; still others, to pursue a contemplative lifestyle, whether individually or communally. The Judaism of Paul's day had the Essene communities, known to us primarily from the Dead Sea Scrolls as the Qumran community, which withdrew to the

Judean desert to escape the corruption of the world around them and to protest their perceived corruption of mainstream Judaism. The Christian church has also had its share of separatists. However, as is evident from the Gospels, withdrawal for a limited period from the world and even from fellow believers is sometimes appropriate in order for one to be refurbished physically and spiritually.

To further clarify his previous letter, and in unmistakable language, Paul goes on to say: "But now I am writing you that you must not associate with anyone who calls himself a brother but . . ." (v. 11). The inescapable conclusion is that a person in the Christian community whose lifestyle is one of sexual immorality, greediness, idolatry, slandering, drunkenness, or swindling has forfeited the right to be called a brother; his conduct betrays his profession of faith. The word "slanderer" (NIV) is found elsewhere in the New Testament only in 6:10. The related Greek noun for the act of reviling occurs in 1 Timothy 5:14 and 1 Peter 3:9 (cf. the verb at John 9:28; Acts 23:4; 1 Cor. 4:13; 1 Peter 2:23); the basic idea is that of verbal abuse. "Slanderer" more properly is associated with the word *diabolos*, used in the New Testament to describe either humans (e.g., 1 Tim. 3:11; Titus 2:3) or the devil (e.g., Matt. 4:1).

The "greedy and swindlers" (v. 10) are one class; they not only covet but sometimes seize what they covet. Paul will deal with actual idolatry later (chaps. 8; 10), but he also considers covetousness figuratively to be idolatry (Eph. 5:5; Col. 3:5). A drunkard is one who imbibes to excess; drunkenness was not frowned upon in the Mediterranean world among the pagans, except in the case of women or if it was responsible for vices detrimental to society.

Christians are to withdraw, not from the world, but from unrepentant Christians guilty of such overt sins. To be sure, all attempts must be made to restore a fellow believer who "is caught in a sin" (Gal. 6:1); but when such attempts are resisted, exclusion from the community is the proper course of action. But by all means, the sinning, unrepentant brother or sister must be distinguished from one who sincerely struggles to overcome sin and experiences periodic setbacks, but is genuinely repentant. Such an individual needs the encouragement and support of fellow believers.

To "not even eat" with the unrepentant person seems unrelated to casting that person out of the congregation. But so serious is this matter that the Corinthian believers should have no social intercourse with such an individual. Note that in the biblical world, gathering around a table involved more than simply partaking of food and drink. Eating together was virtually synonymous with enjoying fellowship. This concept applied not only to private meals, but also to meals shared by believers in conjunction with the Lord's Supper. In chapters 10–11 Paul will elaborate on the connection between the church's communal meals, including the Lord's Supper, and the concept of fellowship. The disciplined person is thus deprived of a meaningful way in which believers share fellowship with each other. It is therefore not necessary to think of the expulsion action as physical, though that may be. It is rather a barring of the person from all contact with the community of believers.

It is implied, however, and will be stated more clearly later, that the Corinthian believers are free to eat with their pagan neighbors (10:27).

In concluding this matter, Paul speaks of two groups—"those outside" and "those inside" (vv. 12–13). After "those outside," the NIV has added "the church," which is not in the Greek text. The thought is correct, however, since the phrase is used elsewhere of pagans (Col. 4:5; 1 Thess. 4:12). God will judge such people, for he is "the Judge of all the earth" (Gen. 18:25). The Greek for "will judge" may also be rendered in the present tense—"judges" (NASB, NKJV). The spelling for both tenses is the same; the difference is in the type of accent used. But since the early manuscripts did not have accent marks, translators are free to make their own decision. In effect, both meanings apply. God certainly does judge in the present, and his final judgment will be in the Day of the Lord.

Paul goes on to ask, "You are to judge those inside, are you not?" (pers. trans.). The Greek wording requires an affirmative answer. Since this is true, "expel the wicked man from among you" (v. 13). Paul quotes here from Deuteronomy 13:5 and 17:7: "You must purge the evil from among you." Being barred from the Christian community, the immoral person will then be numbered with those "outside the church" and consequently be subject to God's judgment.

The instructions to the Corinthian church are relevant for the church of God at all times and in all places. Sin must be identified for what it is—rebellion against God. Professing but unrepentant Christians who persist in sinning must be excluded from fellowship in the community of believers.

2.3. Lawsuits Between Believers (6:1–11)

Paul has just dealt with the problem of a sexually immoral member, concluding it with the verb "judge" (*krino*) three times in 5:12–13. The word is a link with the next problem he addresses—Christians taking Christians to court, allowing themselves to be judged by pagans. The apostle presumably received this information from members of Chloe's household (1:11) or from the three Corinthian brothers who visited him (16:17). He concludes his treatment of the problem by saying the Corinthians cheat and wrong one another (6:8). This leads to statements about who will inherit the kingdom of God (vv. 9–11).

2.3.1. Christians and the Civil Courts (6:1–6). The opening word of the Greek text (*tolmao*) is a strong one, meaning to dare, to presume: "How dare anyone of you, having a case against another, allow it to be judged before the unrighteous and not before the saints?" (v. 1, pers. trans.). At the outset, Paul strongly implies that it is inappropriate, indeed wrong, for one believer to litigate against another in the civil courts. Those courts, after all, are staffed by the unrighteous (*adikos*)—those who have not experienced the justification that comes from God. Paul is not using *adikos* in a pejorative sense, but rather to distinguish them from believers. It is a scandal for those who have been declared righteous by God ("justified," v. 11) to "air their dirty linen" before the world.

It is wrong to infer that Paul held the Romans in contempt. Quite the contrary is true. This system was one of the areas in which the Romans distinguished themselves. Paul himself appealed to it when appropriate (Acts 16:37–39; 25:10–12). His views on the role of civil authorities in maintaining law and order are clear (Rom. 13:1–5): They "hold no terror for those who do right, but for those who do wrong" (v. 3), and they are "God's servant[s]" (v. 4).

Notwithstanding, legal disputes between members of the Christian community ought to be taken for judgment before their own people, "the saints" (*hagios*—see comment on 1:2). Believers are indwelt by the Holy Spirit (6:19); they have "the mind of Christ" (2:16). Thus, they are in a superior position to judge such disputes. The practice of members of a religious community settling their own internal disputes is found in the Judaism of New Testament times. The Gospels and Acts show various times when the Romans allowed Jews to adjudicate their internal disputes, and throughout the Roman Empire every Jewish community had its own court for dispensing civil justice. The Qumran community also had its own procedures for settling internal problems.

Paul again asks, "You know, don't you . . . ?" (v. 2), a question repeated five more times in the chapter (vv. 3, 9, 15, 16, 19). It implies that the Corinthians are acquainted with the matter that follows. To further strengthen his case, Paul uses argumentation that proceeds from a major premise to a minor premise. The major premise is that the saints will judge the world. This does not contradict his previous statement that neither he nor they should judge those outside the church (5:12); there he was talking about the present. The saints' participation in the judgment of the world is a future event (see Dan. 7:18, 22; Wisd. Sol. 3:7–8; 1 Enoch 1:9, 38; Jub. 24:29; cf. also the Qumran community, 1QpHab 5:4). Jesus also taught something similar; there, however, the judgment is of the twelve tribes of Israel (Matt. 19:28; Luke 22:29–30; see also Rev. 20:4). Paul is more inclusive when he says that the saints will judge the entire world (*kosmos*).

Since believers will participate in a judgment of such magnitude, Paul then asks, "Are you not competent to judge trivial cases?" (NIV). Translations differ at this point, and valid arguments may be made in favor of this or other options, such as:

> Are you not competent to constitute the smallest law courts? (NASB)
> Are you incompetent to try trivial cases? (NRSV)
> Are you unworthy to judge the smallest matters? (NKJV)

Reasons for the different translations revolve around two words. *Anaxios* may mean either incompetent, unfit, or unworthy; *kriterion* may mean law court or tribunal, or lawsuit or legal action (BAGD, 58, 453). The main point is clear, however. If believers will participate on such a grand scale in the judgment of the world; surely they ought to be able to settle disputes among themselves that are relatively trivial.

Paul uses the same basic reasoning when he says, "You know, don't you, that we will judge angels?" (v. 3, pers. trans.). By including angels, he is saying that believers will ultimately judge all intelligent beings, human and angelic. Angels in Scripture are either bad or good; presumably, Paul is talking here about the former. The New Testament speaks elsewhere of the judgment of evil angels at the consummation of the age (Matt. 25:41; 2 Peter 2:4; Jude 6). Once again arguing from the greater to the lesser, Paul says, "How much more [should you judge] the things of this life?"—that is, ordinary, everyday affairs.

The emphasis now is on the Corinthians' failure to settle disputes internally (v. 4). "If you have disputes [*kriterion*] about such matters" appears in some translations as "If you have law courts . . ." (cf. comments above on *kriterion*). The difference is not critical; Paul's main point is clear. When there are these types of problems, believers must "appoint as judges even men of little account [*exoutheneo*] in the church." If this NIV translation is accepted, Paul is calling some Christians "men of little account." The verb *exoutheneo* means to despise or disdain. It is improbable that Paul would refer to believers in this way. A better translation would be: "Do you appoint as judges those who have no standing in the church?" (NRSV; note that "appoint" may be translated as either a command, a statement, or a question).

It is to the shame of the Corinthian Christians that they have resorted to the civil courts to settle their disputes. Are they so completely lacking in wisdom that "there is not among you one wise man who will be able to decide between his brothers" (v. 5, NASB)? These people were immensely proud of their wisdom, yet they seemed unable to produce one member who could arbitrate between disputing believers! The shame, the disgrace, is that they as believers make public to unbelievers the problems they have in getting along with one another.

2.3.2. The Proper Attitude When Wronged (6:7–8). Underlying all that Paul has said on this subject is a fundamental element of New Testament ethics: Christians should not seek reparations or retaliation against someone who has wronged them (Rom. 12:17; 1 Thess 5:15). By instituting lawsuits and obtaining judgments against fellow believers, the Corinthians "have been completely defeated already." They may win a legal case, but they are morally defeated by doing so because they have not lived up to God's ideal. The high road Paul prescribes is the one Jesus commanded: not an eye for an eye, but turning the other cheek; not surrendering only your tunic when someone sues for it, but giving your cloak as well (Matt. 5:38–40). "Why not rather be wronged? Why not rather be cheated?" The questions answer themselves.

It seems as if the Corinthians were more concerned about their own "rights" than the rights of others. Although they were accusing fellow Christians of wronging and cheating them, some were themselves wronging and cheating others (v. 8).

Paul here makes no exceptions in dealing with the problem of lawsuits instituted by Christians. Is it because there are none? Or is it because the situation among the Corinthians had deteriorated so badly that he felt compelled to speak in absolute terms? These and other questions will continue to be asked, but it is important to remember his dominant emphases: (1) It is a shameful, disgraceful testimony to the world when Christians institute legal action against other Christians. (2) The church is responsible for setting up its own system of adjudicating differences among believers. (3) It is better to suffer wrongdoing than to appeal even to a church court.

2.3.3. Inheritors of the Kingdom (6:9–11). "You know, don't you, that the unrighteous [*adikos*, see comment on 6:1–6] will not inherit the kingdom of God [see comment on 4:20]?" (pers. trans.). The unrighteous do not participate in the present aspects of the kingdom, and those who die in a state of wickedness will never inherit it. Paul calls on the Corinthians not to be deceived in this matter, for it is all too easy to rationalize that God cannot be so demanding.

The apostle then proceeds to give a sample list of unrighteous people (see also Gal. 5:16–

21). His thought is that of lifestyle, not an occasional lapse into sin (cf. 1 Cor. 5:2). He is certainly implying that if members of the Christian community practice such lifestyles, they will forfeit their eternal inheritance. All Christians are heirs, but heirs may be disinherited (Robertson and Plummer, 118; Fee, 229,242). Paul does not seem to be concerned about the questions later theologians have raised, namely, whether such people were saved in the first place, or whether such Christians lose a reward but not their salvation. We note again that, contrary to the mistaken view of some of the Corinthians that they were in full possession of the kingdom (cf. 4:8), Paul here is speaking of the kingdom in its future aspect.

Each of the ten types of lifestyles mentioned merits a study of its own. This commentary will, however, make some basic and general comments. Idolatry is linked with sexual sins. This is not unusual. Though idolatry is a sin in its own right, idolatrous worship was often associated with sexual immorality (cf. Rom. 1:21–28). Pagan religions in biblical times often combined sexual acts with worship. Temple prostitutes were dedicated to pagan gods. Historically, heathen religion in Corinth was notorious in this regard. It was previously noted that *porneia* was a catch-all word for almost any kind of sexual irregularity and could, by extension and application, include sins like rape and pedophilia (see comments on 5:1). The list also includes adulterers, that is, married persons guilty of sexual relations with someone other than their spouse. "Male prostitutes" and "homosexual offenders" are, respectively, the passive and active partners in homosexual activity.

Thieves, greedy persons, and swindlers are all persons who covet or take what is not rightfully theirs, whether by theft, by thought, or by deceit and force, respectively. Drunkenness existed even in the Corinthian congregation (11:21), and Paul was compelled to tell the Ephesian Christians, "Do not get drunk on wine" (Eph. 5:18). Slanderers (see comment on 5:11) are verbally abusive people.

The contemporary Christian ought not look with disdain on the Corinthian congregation for some of its low ethical standards and its tolerance and commission of sins. Note that they were largely from raw pagan backgrounds, and that moral snobbery on the part of current Christians may be just as objectionable, perhaps worse, in the sight of God. Nor are the sins in this listing peculiar to the Corinthian context. They are prevalent today, and some of them, sadly, are being condoned in some quarters of the church. The sexual revolution of the 1960s has taken its toll not only on society in general, but also within the walls of the church. How else can one account for the ordaining, as yet infrequent, of practicing homosexuals by some denominations? And the emergence of congregations led by a homosexual pastor whose membership is largely and overtly homosexual?

Paul, however, will not conclude the discussion on this negative note, even though some of these sins existed within the Corinthian community of believers. He reminds them of their preconversion days: "And that is what some of you were" (v. 11). With all its imperfections, the Corinthian church still stood as a testimony to the power of the gospel in effecting a radical change in the lives of converts. The strong Greek conjunction *alla* introduces each of the next three statements and contrasts their present state, however deficient, with their former state: "But you were washed, but you were sanctified, but you were justified . . ." (NASB). This trio presents, in three different ways, the work that took place in their lives at the time of faith in Christ (see comments on 1:30 for a similar treatment).

They "were washed" (*apolouo*) of their sins. The imagery calls to mind the Corinthians' baptism at the time of conversion (1:13–16). Paul knew, from his own experience, that baptism symbolized the removal of sin. He could easily recall the words of Ananias to him, "Get up, be baptized and wash your sins away, calling on his [Christ's] name" (Acts 22:16). These words of Ananias contain the only other New Testament occurrence of *apolouo*. Its noun form (*loutron*), used symbolically, occurs in Ephesians 5:26, which speaks of Christ's having cleansed the church "by the washing with water through the word," and Titus 3:5, which says that God "saved us through the washing of rebirth." The basic verb form (*louo*) occurs in a number of passages that speak of a literal washing in water (e.g., John 13:10; Acts 9:37; 16:33; 2 Peter

2:22). In the words "you were washed," there is certainly an allusion to baptism, but it is noteworthy that Paul did not here say, "You were baptized." Perhaps he wanted to avoid the misunderstanding that baptism actually removed sin, rather than its being a symbol of that removal.

John teaches that the blood of Christ is the agent that cleanses (*katharizo*) from sin (1 John 1:7, 9; cf. also Heb. 9:14), meaning that his death is the means for removing sin. This verb is a synonym for *louo* (wash); Paul uses both when he says that Christ cleansed the church by the washing with water (Eph. 5:26). But he does not make a direct connection between the blood of Christ and cleansing from sin. For him, the blood of Christ is the means by which the wrath of God is averted (Rom. 3:25), the believer is justified (Rom. 5:9), the price of redemption is paid (Eph. 1:7), the basis for drawing near to God is provided (2:13), and peace is established between God and sinners (Col. 1:20). John and Paul have complementing thoughts on this subject: The *means* is the blood of Christ; baptism symbolizes that cleansing.

"You were sanctified." This statement is also in a Greek past tense. In this context, sanctification is not an ongoing process but an accomplished fact (see comments on 1:2). The position of this statement between "washed" and "justified" dictates that it be understood as the specific act of God in separating to himself those who have come to faith. In spite of their shortcomings, the Corinthian Christians are still saints—holy ones, sanctified.

"You were justified" (cf. comments on 1:30) harks back to the time of the Corinthians' conversion, when God acquitted them of their past sins and placed to their credit the righteousness of Christ.

This threefold action of God on their behalf is "in the name of the Lord Jesus Christ" (see 1:10; 5:4). It is on the basis of all that his name signifies—his character, his authority, his Saviorhood (Matt. 1:21).

This divine action is also "by [means of] the Spirit of our God." An alternate translation would be "in the Spirit of our God," indicating that God's work in the believing sinner takes place in the realm of the Spirit. Although that is indeed true, the first translation is preferable since it calls attention to the ministry of the Spirit in conversion. Note how in Titus 3:5, "the washing of rebirth" is parallel to "renewal by the Holy Spirit." Jesus spoke of being born of the Spirit (John 3:5–8). Likewise, sanctification is a work of the Holy Spirit (Rom. 15:16; 2 Thess. 2:13). The same can be said for justification, for Paul says, "the law of the Spirit of life [i.e., the Holy Spirit] set me free from the law of sin and death" (Rom. 8:2).

Once again, we notice Paul's "quite unconscious Trinitarianism" (Barrett, 143), his "unobtrusive Trinitarianism" (Morris, 95), his "latent Trinitarianism" (Fee, 246). In the closing words of the paragraph, he mentions "the Lord Jesus Christ," "the Spirit," and "our God."

2.4. Teaching on Sexual Immorality (6:12–20)

Paul has already dealt with the matter of sexual immorality with respect to the incestuous brother; he has also given instruction concerning believers associating with the sexually immoral (ch. 5). In 6:9–10 he has mentioned several types of sexually immoral people. He must now deal with the problem of sexual immorality in more detail.

2.4.1. The Nature of Sexual Immorality (6:12–17). "Everything is permissible for me" is probably a saying of the Corinthian Christians, which Paul quotes twice here and twice in 10:23. Since first-century Greek did not have the concept of quotation marks, they are supplied by many commentators who interpret the statement in this way. The same is true of the "food . . . stomach" statement in verse 13.

Some of the believers in Corinth had placed themselves above moral restraints. They had "arrived" spiritually; they were arrogant; they felt free to do with their bodies whatever they pleased because, they rationalized, they were living in the realm of the Spirit. If there was an early Gnostic influence behind this saying, it was based on the idea that truly spiritual persons may, with impunity, do whatever they wish with their bodies since the body, being material, is inherently evil anyway. But while Paul does indeed teach that the Christian is free, he also says, "Do not use your freedom to indulge the sinful nature" (Gal. 5:13).

In principle, Paul agrees with the Corinthians' saying. But "all things" (NASB) must be understood in the context of love—love for God and love for one's neighbor. For example, ove for God means abstention from matters he as clearly forbidden, such as sexual immorality. So Paul qualifies his tentative agreement with them in two ways. "Not everything is beneficial" implies that some things, like immorality, are spiritually harmful. What is beneficial is love (cf. 8:1). The believer's conduct must be guided by what is spiritually beneficial, not by what is "permissible." In a matter that God has not specifically proscribed and that may not in itself be sinful, the question believers must ask themselves is not, "Is it permissible?" or "Is it all right?" but "Is it beneficial?"

Paul's second qualification is: "I will not be mastered [*exousiazo*] by anything." This verb occurs also in 7:4 and Luke 22:25. The apostle will not allow bodily appetites to dictate his conduct. His only master is Christ, to whom he has enslaved himself (Rom. 1:1; see also 1 Cor. 7:22). The irony, according to Paul, is that the person who exercises unbridled freedom actually becomes a slave to that freedom.

Another apparent watchword of the Corinthians was, "Food for the stomach and the stomach for food" (v. 13). Paul does not qualify this statement, though later he will argue for abstention from certain foods in a given situation on the basis of love for one's fellow believers. Morris suggests that in their thinking "one bodily function is much like another. Fornication is as natural as eating" (96). This interpretation is probably so, since the saying is in the middle of a section on sexual immorality. But their reasoning is faulty. Both stomach and food are perishable, destined to be destroyed by God. The human body, on the other hand, is "for the Lord, and the Lord for the body." God intended the human body to be devoted to him, not used for sexual immorality. A strict translation reads, "The body is not for sexual immorality, but for the Lord." But the Lord is also "for the body." The stomach will be destroyed; the body will not. In fact, God is so much "for the body" that he will transform it at the coming of the Lord.

"By his power" God raised the Lord Jesus from the dead (v. 14), and he will do the same for believers (15:44, 51; cf. Rom. 1:4; 8:11; Phil. 3:20–21). So important is this concept that Paul discusses it at length in chapter 15, where he argues that the resurrection of Jesus is foundational for the believers' hope of their own resurrection from the dead. Jesus' resurrection was of paramount importance in the preaching of the early church; Acts demonstrates that it was an indispensable element in the proclamation of the gospel.

Pursuing a further line of reasoning, Paul asks, "You know, don't you, that your bodies are members [*melos*] of Christ?" (v. 15, pers. trans.). *Melos* is a word used for parts of the human body (Rom. 6:13, 19) and metaphorically for parts of the body of Christ. Paul uses this metaphor of the body and its members in a number of different ways when speaking about the relation of believers to Christ. In 12:12–27, each person is a member of the body (see also Rom. 12:5). There is only one body, the body of Christ (Eph. 4:4), of which Christ is the head (Col. 1:18, 24).

The Corinthians must understand that their bodies do not belong to them; they belong to the Lord because he purchased them (v. 20). Their bodies, as Christ's members, are an integral part of him. It is unthinkable to "take the members of Christ and unite them with a prostitute" (lit., "make them members of a prostitute"). The mere thought causes Paul to react by saying, "Never!" ("God forbid," KJV). The Greek expression used here, *me genoito*, literally means, "May it not be." It can be paraphrased by "Perish the thought" or "On no account whatever." The idea would be especially abhorrent if the prostitute were attached to a pagan temple.

In verse 16, Paul appeals to Scripture for support, which says that "the two [the man and his wife] will become one flesh" (Gen. 2:24, LXX). He again asks, "You know this, don't you?" God's will is that sexual union will take place only within marriage. When it occurs with a prostitute, the man becomes "one body" with her. In some New Testament passages there is an important theological difference between "flesh" (*sarx*) and "body" (*soma*), but in this passage they are used interchangeably. The immoral man thus "unites himself with a prostitute." Conversely, "he who unites himself with the Lord is one with him in spirit." The believer enjoys a spiritual union with Christ because he has received the Spirit of Christ (Rom. 8:9). Paul's point is that it is impossible to belong to two bodies at the same time. This impossibility is not just numerical; it is moral (Héring, 46).

2.4.2. The Temple of the Holy Spirit (6:18–20). Paul's command, in view of all the preceding, is "Flee from sexual immorality" (cf. his later command, "flee from idolatry," 10:14). In both instances the form of the verb means either "keep on fleeing" or, as Morris suggests (98), "make it your habit to flee." Sexual temptations were so common in Corinth that this was the only course Christians should take. They must put as much distance as possible between themselves and the occasion to sin, whether it be a house of prostitution, a temple of prostitution, or a soliciting prostitute. The story of Joseph fleeing from Potiphar's wife readily comes to mind (Gen. 39:7–12).

Paul's admonition to flee must be distinguished from his previous admonition that believers not disassociate themselves from "sexually immoral people" (5:9–10). In the present instance, they are told to flee from sexual immorality, not from unbelievers who may be sexually immoral. They must abstain from sexually irregular conduct, but they must not avoid normal social intercourse with all people, including the sexually immoral.

Scholars agree that Paul's next statement is one of the most difficult to interpret: "All other

From the height of the Acrocorinth, at right, you can look down on the old city of Corinth. The ruins of the fortress are a mix of different eras, including the Roman. The Romans destroyed the city in 148 B.C., then rebuilt it as a colony. Below are the remains of the Temple to Aphrodite, the Greek goddess of love and beauty. Paul warned the Corinthians not to associate with sexually immoral people.

ns a man commits are outside his body, but e who sins sexually sins against his own ody" (v. 18). Is this really a valid distinction? re not many other sins also against one's ody—drunkenness, drug addiction, gluttony, c.? (Note that the word "other" is not in the reek text and does not appear in the NKJV and RSV; it is added in the NIV and, in italics, in the ASB.) The following are sample explanations:

1. Comparatively, sexual sins are more sinful than other sins.
2. Other sins against the body often involve something that comes from outside the body, whereas sexual sin comes from within.
3. The first part of the sentence is a slogan of some Corinthian Christians who, in their spiritual arrogance, felt that the category of sin did not apply to them: "All sins a man commits are outside his body." It is based on the idea that the word "body" means one's entire being, one's "personality," one's innermost self; therefore, anything that is classified as sin does not apply to them.
4. Paul is writing in a general way, "rather loosely," and not as a moral philosopher (Barrett, 150). Barrett quotes John Calvin, "These other sins do not leave anything like the same filthy stain on our bodies as fornication does."
5. The "special character" of sexual immorality is that a man removes his body, the temple of the Holy Spirit which is "for the Lord," from union with Christ, making it a member of the woman's body (Fee, 262).

The last two options seem to present the ewest problems. But however one undertands Paul on this matter, the main point is bvious: the body is sacred and is valued by God, so much so that he will resurrect it.

Paul's last question of "You know, don't you?" concerns the relationship of the believer o the Holy Spirit. The believer's body is destined for resurrection, but in the here and now t is a temple of the Holy Spirit (v. 19). This act provides another reason for maintaining sexual purity: One must not defile that which s God's sanctuary. In this context, the individual believer is a temple (*naos*) of the Spirit, whom believers received at the time of faith in Christ (Rom. 8:15–16; Gal. 4:6). Previously, Paul had stated that Christians collectively are God's temple, indwelt by him (see comments on 3:16–17). The two ideas are complementary; both the individual believer and the corporate church (local or universal) are God's special dwelling place on earth.

There is an interrelationship in this context between the bodily resurrection of believers and their being indwelt by the Holy Spirit. The Spirit is the earnest, the down payment, on our eternal inheritance (Rom. 8:23; 2 Cor. 1:21–22; Eph. 1:13–14; 4:30), and it is by the power of the Spirit that we will be raised from the dead (Rom. 8:11). Some of the Corinthians believed that because they had received the Spirit, the body was inconsequential. Paul's argument is just the opposite.

"And you are not your own" (pers. trans.) may be an additional statement (NIV), or it may be a continuation of the "Or do you not know?" question (NRSV). In either case, the point is that believers now belong to the Lord, who "bought [them] at a price." They are his slaves, not their own masters. The imagery of a ransom price is one important way in which the New Testament portrays God's saving work (see comments on 1:30), for Jesus himself said he would give his life as a ransom [*lytron*] for many (Matt. 20:28; Mark 10:45). Another form of the noun (*apolytrosis*) is found in passages that say the purchase price of redemption was the blood of Christ (Rom. 3:24–25; Eph. 1:7; see also *lytroo* in 1 Peter 1:18–19). The verb for "bought" in 1 Corinthians 6:20 is *agorazo* (also used in 7:23; 2 Peter 2:1; Rev. 5:9; 14:3–4; cf. also Gal. 3:13; 4:5, which uses an intensified form, *exagorazo*).

The line of reasoning that Paul follows here was revolutionary. According to Jean Héring (47), "we are probably witnessing here the first attempt in the history of moral thought to refute libertinism in some other way than by the arguments of an ascetic, legalistic or utilitarian type which are so common in Greek philosophy."

"Therefore," Paul concludes, "honor [glorify] God with your body" (cf. Rom. 12:1, "offer your bodies as living sacrifices"). "Therefore" translates the little word *dē*, which gives "greater urgency" to exhortations or commands (BAGD, 178). There should be no delay in the matter. The negative command to flee from sexual immorality (v. 18) is now balanced by this urgent, positive command. Paul broadens this final exhortation later when he says, "Whether you eat or drink or whatever you do, do it all for the glory of God" (10:31).

3. Response to a Letter from Corinth (7:1–16:4)

Paul has addressed problems brought to his attention by members of Chloe's household and others. He now focuses on questions contained in a letter he received from the church in Corinth. The phrase "now for" (*peri de*), which occurs six times in chapters 7–16, introduces each separate topic (7:1, 25; 8:1; 12:1; 16:1, 12). The issues include matters related to marriage, virgins, food sacrificed to idols, spiritual gifts, the collection, and Apollos.

3.1. Marriage and Related Questions (7:1–40)

Paul's extended treatment of sexual immorality in chapters 5–6 leads easily into a discussion of marriage. Chapter 7 is the most comprehensive passage in Scripture on the subject of marriage and related matters. In the following notes, the term *celibacy* means abstention from sexual relations, whether within marriage or outside of marriage. This clarification is necessary because one meaning of celibacy is simply abstention from marriage, with no necessary implication of sexual purity. The term *continence* might better serve our purpose, but it is not widely used today. *Chastity* might be a good alternative, especially as it applies to the unmarried.

3.1.1. Proper Behavior Within Marriage (7:1–7). In matters related to sexual behavior, Paul was fighting on two fronts. One element among the Corinthians—the libertines or antinomians—claimed it was morally indifferent what a person did with his or her body. But another element went in the opposite direction—that of asceticism. This may have been due to a pre-Gnostic influence that maintained that because our bodies, being physical, are inherently evil, one must deny oneself physical pleasure. Others seem to have thought that since they had reached the pinnacle of spirituality, they had fully entered into the "age to come" (see comments on 4:8). Thus they had no need for sexual satisfaction; they were "above" such things.

Part of the problem was the "eschatological women" who, according to Gordon Fee, were denying conjugal rights to their husbands. They thought of themselves as having alread realized resurrection from the dead "by bein in spirit" and consequently were already as th angels (11:2–16; 13:1), neither marrying no giving in marriage (Fee, 269). This passag immediately following Paul's condemnatio of those who visited prostitutes, lends suppo to the idea that some husbands felt compelle to seek sexual satisfaction outside the home.

"It is good for a man not to marry" (v. 1, NIV is not a translation but an interpretation (proba bly correct) of the Greek text, which reads li erally, "It is good [well, NRSV] for a man not t touch a woman" (NASB, NKJV). "Touching woman" is an Old Testament euphemism fo sexual relations (see Gen. 20:6; Prov. 6:29 Verses 2–7 justify the interpretation that mar riage is in view, although the statemen expresses a generally ascetic mentality. The sen tence containing "not to touch a woman" wa probably a quotation from the letter fron Corinth addressed to Paul. It is also possible however, to translate verse 1 as a question: "I it good for a man not to touch a woman?" In tha case the Corinthians were asking for an opinion

Several points may be made by way of pre viewing the chapter. (1) Paul does not disagree entirely with the statement about not touching a woman. Several times in this chapter he wil indicate why he thinks the unmarried, celibate state is preferable to the married state. It is so on pragmatic grounds but is not morally supe rior, as though the married state is evil Celibacy is a gift from God, but so is marriage (v. 7). Paul knew well that "it is not good for the man to be alone" (Gen. 2:18) and that mar riage was divinely instituted.

(2) In giving seeming preference to the celi bate, unmarried state, Paul diverges from con ventional Jewish thinking. In Judaism marriage for men was not an option but a vir tual obligation; it was expected that a young man would be married.

(3) Paul's attitude toward sex is realistic Celibacy, as opposed to marriage, should be more the exception than the rule. Marriage is the divinely appointed means for giving expression to the sex impulse. "The man who wrote Eph. 5:22, 23, 32, 33 had no low view of marriage" (Robertson and Plummer, 133).

(4) A marriage without sex is a contradiction in terms. There can be no such thing as a purely "spiritual" marriage.

(5) Marriage involves rights and obligations for both husband and wife.

Sexual immorality was not uncommon among the Corinthian believers. "Since there is so much immorality" (lit., "on account of the acts of immorality"), men and women ought to be married since sexual intercourse is permissible only within marriage. Marriage, therefore, should be a deterrent to sexual misbehavior. There are, to be sure, other reasons for getting married, but this is the one Paul must mention here. Marriage is the norm; more than that, it is a command, even though there can be exceptions (v. 7). Furthermore, monogamy is implied since "each man should have his own wife, and each woman her own husband." The verb "have" is also a euphemism for sexual relations (see comments on 5:1).

Verses 3 and 4 present a remarkable advance over prevailing social ideas in both Gentile and Jewish circles. Husband and wife are addressed in parallel fashion; what applies to one applies equally to the other. Through marriage husband and wife become "one flesh" (6:16; Gen. 2:24). Therefore, they must fulfill their sexual obligation to each other. The verb tenses used here suggest that this should be a continuing pattern of behavior. The emphasis is on giving oneself to the other, not on receiving something or demanding one's "rights" from the other.

Consequently, the general rule is that marriage partners must not "deprive [*apostereo*] each other" of sexual expression. The verb also means "defraud" ("cheat" in 6:7–8). "Stop depriving one another" (NASB) more accurately translates the Greek tense; that is, some were already guilty of withholding sex from their partners. There is one allowable exception, but the guidelines are clear: Abstinence from sex must be (1) by mutual consent, (2) temporary ("for a set time," NRSV), (3) for the purpose of husband and wife devoting themselves to prayer, and (4) on condition that they "come together again." There is Old Testament precedent for this temporary abstaining for spiritual purposes (Joel 2:16; Zech. 12:12–14). To conclude this matter with a suggestive comment: It seems plausible, in view of the abstinence, the time limitation, and the connection with prayer, to construe this as a form of fasting.

The resumption of normal sexual activity is "so that Satan will not tempt you because of your lack of self-control." Lack of self-control in sexual matters is mentioned in verse 9 as legitimate grounds for marriage. Here the married couple must not allow the Adversary, Satan, to tempt them into expressing that drive in sinful behavior by having intimate relations with someone other than their marriage partner.

"I say this as a concession, not as a command" (v. 6) is variously interpreted, depending on what Paul means by "this." Several options are possible: (1) It applies to what follows in verse 7, that all men might be as he is. (2) It applies to the temporary suspension of sexual relations by the married couple, which would be a partial concession to those who advocated no sex in marriage at all (Héring, 50). (3) It applies only to the statement at the end of verse 5, that the couple are to come back together. (4) It applies to verses 2–5, so that Paul is saying that he does not command everyone to be married but allows it as a concession to those who cannot remain celibate (Robertson and Plummer, 135). The last option presents the fewest difficulties.

Paul now expresses his preference by wishing "that all men were as I am" (v. 7). The likelihood is that Paul, as a pious Jew, had at one time been married. This would be especially true if he had at one time been a member of the Sanhedrin (as some understand Acts 26:10), since it is generally understood that members of that body were required to be married. But it is not known for certain whether at this time he was a widower, whether his wife had left him, or whether had ever been married. Since Paul was a rabbi, however, the last possibility is ruled out. He recognizes, however, that not all are able to live a celibate life, for celibacy is a "gift [*charisma*—see comments on 1:7] from God" (cf. Matt. 19:11–12). But Paul implies that marriage is also a gift from God when he says, "the one in one way, the other in another" (BAGD, 597–98). (The concept of *charisma* will receive detailed attention in chs. 12–14.)

3.1.2. The Unmarried and Widows (7:8–9). Paul has dealt with marriage in general; now he gives attention to specific categories of people. "The unmarried" are, in contemporary terminology, the "singles" (cf. also vv. 11, 32, 34). The word has a broad meaning: (1) Even though it is masculine, it is gender-inclusive in accordance with Greek usage; (2) it includes all who are not presently married—

the never-married, the divorced, and the widowed. But why would Paul then add "and the widows"? One possibility is that they are mentioned specifically "because of their particular vulnerability and the consequent temptation to remarry" (Morris, 105). A parallel grammatical construction occurs in 9:5, where Paul speaks of "the other apostles . . . and Cephas"; Cephas, an apostle, receives special mention (see also Mark 16:7). A second possibility is that widows at this time already formed a distinct group in a congregation, and their status had given rise to discussion (see 1 Tim. 5:3–16; cf. Héring, 51).

Paul's recommendation is that "it is good for them to stay unmarried, as I am" (v. 8). Once again, this does not imply that it is sinful to marry (see comments on v. 1), but only that the recommended course of action is to remain single—depending, of course, on whether they have the gift of celibacy (v. 7). "But if they do not have self-control" (NASB), or, "But if they are not practicing self-control" (NRSV) are more accurate translations than "if they cannot control themselves" (NIV), since "cannot" is not in the Greek text (v. 9). It seems that some of the unmarried and widows were indulging their sexual passions. Such persons should marry (v. 2), "for it is better to marry than to burn" (v. 9, NASB).

The NIV reads here "than to burn with passion." This interpretation may be correct, since Paul uses the same word (*pyroo*) figuratively on another occasion when speaking of his own intense feelings (2 Cor. 11:29), though not in the context of the sex drive. Paul later gives similar advice to younger widows (1 Tim. 5:11–15). An alternative is to understand the burning as the eternal punishment of hell (Gehenna) that awaits immoral people, since they will not inherit the kingdom of God (1 Cor. 6:9–10). Bruce quotes two relevant rabbinic passages: "Whoever multiplies conversation with a woman . . . will in the end inherit Gehenna"; and, one rabbi comments to another as they see a woman walking ahead of them, "Hurry up and get in front of Gehenna" (Bruce, 68). There is truth in both interpretations; it may be wise not to accept one to the exclusion of the other.

3.1.3. The Christian Married Couple (7:10–11). Paul issued no command to the previous group; he does, however, to this one. Indeed, it is not he but the Lord who speaks (v. 10), for what he says echoes Jesus' basic teaching on the subject of divorce and remarriage (Mark 10:2–12). Paul is speaking here to a married couple who are both Christians.

His instruction is clear: The wife must not be separated (*chorizo* in the passive voice) from her husband; the husband must not divorce (*aphiemi*) his wife. The two verbs are used interchangeably, as we see later when *aphiemi* is a wife's action and *chorizo* a husband's. The modern distinction between divorce and separation does not apply here, since the context says that the woman who separates will be unmarried (v. 11). Paul makes no exceptions, as Jesus does in permitting divorce on the grounds of sexual immorality (Matt. 5:32; 19:9). One explanation is that Paul is addressing a unique situation in which a Christian wife feels she has risen above the sexual obligations of marriage (vv. 3–5). Another is that Paul is giving general teaching and does not deal with specific problems. In any event, if the woman does separate from her husband, she must either remain unmarried or be reconciled to him.

Paul does not amplify his comments about the Christian husband who divorces a Christian wife; but in view of everything else in the chapter that stresses the equality of marriage partners, what applies to the wife's action applies equally to the husband's. He, too, must either remain unmarried or else be reconciled to his wife.

We note in passing that Paul does not comment on whether or not the partner who did not initiate the divorce is free to marry.

3.1.4. Mixed Marriages (7:12–16). The "rules" are different when only one marriage partner is a Christian. "To the rest" means the others in the congregation (v. 12). An application of the principle to "not be yoked together with unbelievers" (2 Cor. 6:14) is that a believer must not marry an unbeliever. It is not known whether the "mixed" marriages referred to here were the result of a believer marrying an unbeliever, or whether they were "mixed" because one partner of a pagan marriage subsequently became a believer.

Paul's statement, "I say this (I, not the Lord)" is open to three interpretations: (1) He is expressing his own opinion, not the Lord's, and therefore what he says is by way of suggestion rather than command; (2) he is giving his own opinion, not the Lord's, but his teaching is nevertheless authoritative; or (3) Jesus did not say anything on the subject of mixed marriages since his ministry was almost entirely within Judaism, and therefore Paul cannot appeal for support to anything Jesus said (Bruce, 69). The last option is certainly true and ought to be combined with the second, since Paul later bases his "judgment" (*gnome*) on his trustworthiness (v. 25) and also appeals to the Spirit of God in support of his "judgment" (*gnome* again) (v. 40).

The counsel to believing partners is that they must not initiate a divorce if their unbelieving partner is willing to live with them. Greek and Roman law permitted a wife to divorce her husband; Jewish law did not. The immediate reason Paul gives is that the unbeliever "has been sanctified through" (i.e., by means of) the believing partner (v. 14). Contrary to the thinking of some, a pagan spouse does not contaminate the marriage. The believer is not defiled; rather, the unbeliever is sanctified. The believer is already sanctified, a saint, separated by God and for God (see comments on 1:2, 30; 6:11), and the unbeliever participates in that sanctification, though not in a saving sense. According to Morris (107), it is a principle of Scripture that "the blessings that flow from fellowship with God are not confined to the immediate recipients, but extend to others (e.g. Gn. 15:18; 17:7; 18:26ff.; 1 Ki. 15:4; Is. 37:4)." Bruce (69) calls it "holiness by association."

The mixed-marriage unbeliever is in a category distinct from and superior to that of an unbeliever in an entirely pagan marriage. Paul may be suggesting the mixed-marriage unbeliever is more likely to be converted (v. 16). The perfect tense of the Greek verb indicates that the mixed-marriage unbeliever was sanctified at the time of the partner's conversion and continues to be separated. The believer's sanctification likewise extends to the children of the marriage; they are "holy," not "unclean." Paul does not say whether they may be regarded as saved, at least until they are old enough to make a responsible decision, but in some way they are part of the community of faith.

The initiative to sever the marriage bond must come from the unbeliever who is unwilling to live in such a situation (v. 15). The Greek text is expressive: "If the unbeliever separates himself [*chorizo*, as in v. 10], let him separate himself" (pers. trans.). The masculine gender of "unbeliever" is used inclusively, as the rest of the verse indicates. In such circumstances, the believer is "not bound." Not bound in what sense? The answers vary: (1) not bound to "a mechanical retention" of a relationship the other partner wishes to forsake (Barrett, 166; Fee, 302); (2) not bound to try to preserve the marriage at the cost of domestic harmony, for "God has called us to live in peace"; or (3) not bound to remain unmarried but free to remarry (Héring, 53; Bruce, 70). While there is truth in the first two, the last interpretation may be the best since Paul does not explicitly forbid remarriage here as he does in the case of a Christian who divorces a Christian marriage partner.

The ideal solution to the problem of a mixed marriage is that the unbeliever become a Christian (v. 16). The expression "how do you know . . . whether" has a virtual counterpart in the Septuagint and is the equivalent of "perhaps" (see 2 Sam. 12:22; Est. 4:14; Joel 2:14; Jonah 3:9) (Bruce, 70). The Christian partner's godly example and lifestyle, it is hoped, will result in the salvation of the unbeliever (see 1 Peter 3:1). "Whether you will save your husband . . . wife" must be understood to mean, "whether you will be the means of saving" (see 9:22 for similar language). There is no guarantee, however, that the unbelieving spouse will be saved.

What Paul says cannot be used as a rationalization for a believer to marry an unbeliever; but if such a union does take place, the believer must live in accordance with his teaching.

3.1.5. Remaining in One's Present State (7:17–28). Paul now shifts from teaching related specifically to marriage to a discussion of remaining content in the state in which the Lord has placed one. His broad advice is, "Stay where you are. You should not feel compelled to change your occupation or station in life simply because you have become a Christian" (cf. v. 17) Apart from a situation that is incompatible with Christianity, a believer need not feel obligated to seek change. Paul's personal statement is appropriate here: "I have learned to be content whatever the circumstances" (Phil. 4:11).

What the apostle prescribes for the Corinthians he prescribes for "all the churches" (see also 11:16; 14:33). It is based on the fact that "the Lord [has] assigned" to each one a specific place in life. "As God has called each" (NASB) supplements the previous statement. The divine call here is the call to salvation, but it seems to include the vocation or place in life in which people were at the time of their conversion (vv. 20, 24). "In this manner let him walk" (NASB) is a better rendering than "each one should retain the place in life" (NIV), since "walk" (*peripateo*) is figurative language for one's manner of conduct (see comments on 3:3).

Paul goes on to illustrate his point by relating the Christian walk to circumcision and slavery, "the great religious and social distinctions which divided the world of his day" (Morris, 108), as well as to virgins.

(1) The circumcised should remain circumcised, and the uncircumcised, uncircumcised. Circumcision was the distinguishing mark of male Jews, dating back to God's command to Abraham (Gen. 17:10–14); for most Jews, it symbolized obedience to the entire Law. A circumcised man "should not become uncircumcised." Jewish history records incidents of some Jewish youths undergoing a surgical procedure that would "uncircumcise" them (1 Macc. 1:14–15; Josephus, *Ant.* 12:241).

Conversely, uncircumcised males should not seek to be circumcised. Paul is not dealing here, as he does especially in Romans and Galatians, with the theological and soteriological implications of circumcision raised by the Judaizers in early Christianity. What he is saying is that Jewish male converts to Christianity should not deny their Jewishness, and Gentile male converts should remain Gentiles and not desire to tie into Judaism, possibly on the grounds of Christianity's Jewish roots. Note that the circumcision of Timothy was a special case because his mother was Jewish, and his uncircumcised state was an unnecessary obstacle in reaching Jews (Acts 16:1–3).

Neither circumcision nor uncircumcision is of ultimate significance in the sight of God. What really counts is (a) "keeping God's commands" (7:19); (b) "faith expressing itself through love" (Gal. 5:6); and (c) "a new creation" (6:15). Jewish opponents might demur and insist that circumcision is one of God's commands that must be kept. Paul would respond that the "law of Christ" supersedes other laws (1 Cor. 9:21; Gal. 6:2), and that Jews, whether Christian or not, could submit to circumcision with impunity as long as it was not regarded as essential for salvation for themselves or Gentile believers. The concluding note is that these two groups of people should continue (lit., "let them remain") in their present state.

(2) Paul now turns to slaves and free people (vv. 20–21). Slaves should not be troubled by the fact that they were slaves at the time of their calling. "Calling" here has shifted in meaning from one's station in life or vocation (v. 17) to a term related to conversion. Slaves ought to remain where they are since God, who called them to himself, can give them the grace needed to be good slaves. Differences in understanding Paul's next statement are reflected in the following:

> Although if you can gain your freedom, do so. (NIV)
> If you are able also to become free, rather do that. (NASB; cf. Bruce, 71–72)
> But if you can be made free, rather use it. (NKJV; cf. Robertson and Plummer, 147; Fee, 317))
> Even if you can gain your freedom, make use of your present condition now more than ever. (NRSV; cf. Héring, 55)
> Even though you should be able to become free, put up rather with your present status. (Barrett, 170)

The most reasonable interpretation is that Paul is saying, "If you can obtain your freedom in a legitimate way, take advantage of it. You are already the Lord's freedman, though a slave, and if you can also become a societal freedman, well and good." Throughout this chapter Paul generally allows for exceptions to the rules he lays down. Why would he object to a Christian slave becoming free? Why would he object to Christians bettering themselves? What is of ultimate importance is one's relationship with the Lord (v. 22), not one's station in life. Yet Paul is clear that the Christian, while a slave, must render due service to one's master (Eph. 6:5–8; Col. 3:22–24; cf. 1 Peter 2:18–20).

Paul distinguishes between a freedman (an ex-slave) and a free man (one who has never been a slave). To make a point, he states that a slave is Christ's freedman, whereas a free man is Christ's slave. But the paradox is really that all Christians are freed by Christ and also enslaved to him. This is how Paul regarded himself (Rom. 1:1; Phil. 1:1; Titus 1:1). Our freedom has been obtained at a price, the blood of Christ (see comments on 1 Cor. 6:20). Because of this, we should not become "slaves of men" (7:23). This phrase should be taken in a religious sense, as being free from spiritual bondage (2 Cor. 11:20; Gal. 5:1; Col. 2:20–22). People cannot be the spiritual slaves of both Christ and human beings, thereby having two masters (see Matt. 6:24).

Apart from the allowed exception, this paragraph concludes with: "Brethren, let each man remain with God in that condition in which he was called" (1 Cor. 7:24, NASB).

(3) Virgins form the third category of those who ought to remain in their present state (vv. 25–28). The Greek noun *parthenos* can be either masculine (Rev. 14:4) or feminine (all its other occurrences in 1 Cor. 7 have the feminine article—vv. 28, 34, 36, 37, 38). In verse 25 Paul is likely referring to young women, even though the noun and its accompanying article (genitive plural) are ambiguous (either masculine or feminine; it could include both). "Now about" occurs for the second time (cf. 7:1), an indication that the Corinthians had written to Paul about the status of virgins. Virgins here are probably young women who have been betrothed but are not yet married. The apostle does not give a command but a "judgment" ("opinion"—NASB) based on his trustworthiness (*pistos*, "trustworthy"—see comments on 4:2, 17), which he attributes to "the Lord's mercy."

The NIV has not translated verse 26b well: "It is good for you to remain as you are." The Greek text more properly reads, "It is good for a man [*anthropos*] so to remain" (pers. trans.). Paul again enunciates a general principle and, in accordance with Greek usage, uses the masculine in a gender-inclusive way. *Anthropos*, while it can mean "man," is also a generic term for a human being and sometimes simply means "one" or "a person" (e.g., see 11:28, where Paul does not mean to exempt women from examining themselves at the Lord's Supper). The statement might legitimately be rendered, "it is good for one to so remain." "Good" must not be understood in a moral sense, as though getting married were sinful. Paul says plainly that if a virgin marries, she has not sinned (v. 28). "It is advisable" would be a valid paraphrase.

As far as Paul is concerned, both men and women ought to remain unmarried "because of the present crisis [*ananke*]." Opinion is divided on the nature of the crisis. A common viewpoint is that it refers to troubles that will precede the return of Christ (cf. the use of this word in Luke 21:23). Paul is implying they are already at that point, since "present" may mean imminent or impending (2 Tim. 3:1). Furthermore, he does say further on that "the time is short [lit., has been shortened]" (1 Cor. 7:29; see Mark 13:20). But Morris observes that Paul speaks often about the coming of the Lord but never uses *ananke* in connection with that event. An alternative viewpoint is that the crisis consists of some type of unexplained hardship, compulsion, or distress that the church was experiencing (for this noneschatological use of *ananke*, see v. 37; 9:16; also 2 Cor. 6:4; 9:7; 12:10; 1 Thess. 3:7). It is not necessary, however, to choose one interpretation to the exclusion of the other, though the first seems preferable.

In this context of "the present crisis," Paul repeats his earlier instructions on remaining in one's present state. A married person should not seek a divorce; an unmarried man should not look for a wife. But even if one does marry, he or she has not sinned. The apostle's concern is pastoral: He is trying to spare the unmarried Corinthians "many troubles in this life [lit., flesh—*sarx*]" that will come if they marry. Whatever the nature of "the present crisis," it will compound problems for one who has marital and family responsibilities.

3.1.6. Reasons to Remain in One's State (7:29–35). Two interrelated themes dominate verses 29–31: (1) the transitory nature of this world, and, in view of it, (2) the believer's nonattachment to the world. The paragraph begins with "the time is short"; that is, time is running out, for the Second Advent is near (Rom. 13:11). Paul concludes this section with a related statement (v. 31), that "this world in its present form is passing away" (see 1 John 2:15–17). In view of this, the apostle makes specific recommendations.

A believer must not be preoccupied with the things of this life. An expression this writer heard in his younger days is especially apt: "Live your life in the light of eternity." Paul does not mean that Christians ought to abandon or deny the marital relationship and responsibilities. But marriage is a temporary, earthly arrangement; it will not exist in heaven (Mark 12:25). The same principle applies to the transitoriness of earthly mourning and joy or to the acquisition of earthly possessions. Although Christians must live in the world, they ought not to be "engrossed" (NIV) in the things of the world. To use the words of the NASB, it is legitimate for Christians to "use [*chraomai*] the world," but they must "not make full use [*katachraomai*] of it."

Paul elaborates on this theme in verses 32–35, centering on the thought of anxiety. The verb *merimnao* (used four times in these verses) basically means "care for, be concerned about"; but it can also mean "have anxiety, be anxious, be (unduly) concerned" (BAGD, 505). In light of the context that Christians must not be preoccupied with the things of this world, the latter meaning applies here. Paul echoes Jesus' teaching in the Sermon on the Mount, that his disciples ought not to be anxious about earthly things (Matt. 6:25–34; cf. also 1 Peter 5:7: "Cast all your anxiety on him [God] because he cares for you"). Paul wants the Corinthians to be "free from concern" (*amerimnos*—the negative adjective equivalent of the verb *merimnao*).

This commentary takes the viewpoint that Paul desires all four classes to be worry-free: the unmarried man, the married man, the unmarried woman or virgin, and the married woman. Otherwise the verb *merimnao*, which he applies to all four, would vary in meaning from one occurrence to another—at one point being used in a positive sense, at another in a negative sense. The controlling thought is his opening statement that all the Corinthians be free of anxiety.

The unmarried man must be free of his anxiety about the Lord's affairs. Anxiety, however, must not be confused with eagerness. It is possible for an unmarried man to be so desirous of pleasing the Lord, certainly a laudable objective, that he loses all perspective and, unlike the married man, is undivided in that pursuit. Barrett (179) suggests that such a person is anxious "to win God's favour by pleasing him through the performance of meritorious religious works." In that case his motives must be redirected.

The married man, by contrast, is "concerned about the affairs of this world—how he can please his wife." But he is a Christian and also wants to please the Lord. Thus, "his interests are divided" (lit., "he has divided himself," or "he has been divided"). Paul advocates neither detachment from the world nor neglect of one's wife, but he does imply that the married man is forced to divide his time and energy between his wife and the Lord. In doing so, he will exhibit some anxiety. What he says about the married man applies equally to the married woman (v. 34b), except that in her case he does not say that she is divided. That undoubtedly will be true, but the inference may be that the man, as the head of the household, bears a heavier responsibility in regard to "the affairs of this world."

An unmarried woman or virgin is also concerned about the Lord's affairs. The distinction Paul intended between these two persons is not clear. "Unmarried woman" probably means any single woman who is not a virgin—one who never married, a widow, or a divorcee; "virgin" may mean a betrothed young woman (Bruce, 76). An alternative possibility is that the words "the unmarried woman and the virgin" (not "unmarried woman *or* virgin" as in NIV) could validly be translated as "the unmarried woman, that is, the virgin." The first suggestion, however, is better.

The aim of these women is to "be holy both in body and spirit" (NASB). Their goal is commendable, but they may be overly concerned about it and, like the unmarried man (v. 32), may be in danger of trying to establish their relationship to the Lord on the basis of their own efforts. Some interpret the reference to body to indicate abstinence from sexual relations as an indication of one's holiness, that is, separation to God. But Paul had previously called on all Christians to glorify God in their bodies by abstaining from illicit sexual relations (6:20). A married woman who was sexually faithful to her husband would also be holy in body.

Paul's concluding comment in verse 35 is to all he has addressed in verses 32–34.The pronoun "you" throughout the verse is plural. He again expresses his pastoral concern for the Corinthians' welfare. This strengthens the iewpoint that all four groups could in some 'ay be deficient. He has said these things for ieir own "good" ("benefit," NASB). He does ot mean to "restrict" them—the Greek expres-on used here (*epiballo brochon*) means "to irow a noose over"; in nonbiblical literature is found in contexts of war and hunting 3AGD, 289). Rather, his motivation is posi-ve: He wants believers to "live in a right way i undivided [undistracted, NASB; unhindered, RSV] devotion to the Lord." In one way or nother, each of the four groups was in danger f insufficient devotion to the Lord.

3.1.7. Virgins and Widows (7:36–40). aul has twice given general counsel concern-ıg virgins (vv. 25–26, 34). He now addresses specific problem that was probably raised by ıe Corinthians (vv. 36–38). It involves a vir-in, but the comments are directed to a man 'ith whom she has some kind of special rela-onship. These verses are the subject of con-iderable discussion and difference of opinion. ven some translations have resorted to inter-retation; uninformed readers may thereby be ıisled into thinking they have before them 'hat Paul actually said. For example, the ireek text in verse 36 says simply "his virgin" :f. NKJV) but sample versions read:

the virgin he is engaged to (NIV)
his fiancée (NRSV)
his virgin *daughter* (NASB, italics indicate an added word)

There are three main interpretations of erses 36–38. (1) The man and the virgin are artners in a "spiritual marriage" (Héring, 63). 'hey are living together but are united only in pirit since both of them have taken a vow of bstinence from all sexual relations. But sex-al abstinence is becoming difficult, especially or the man. If he can no longer restrain him-elf, Paul's advice is that he should marry the irgin—that it should be a genuine marriage ıat will include sexual relations. This situa-on may reflect the thinking of some Corinthi-ns who felt either that all sexual relations, ven within marriage, were wrong (cf. 7:1) or ıat it was a mark of genuine spirituality to ave risen above the need for sex. Against this ıterpretation of a "spiritual marriage" is the act that there is no evidence that this was prac-ced in the first-century church. Furthermore, : runs counter to everything Paul has already said about the nature of marriage, and it would be uncharacteristic of him not to condemn such an arrangement.

(2) "His virgin" is speaking about the relationship between a virgin and her father or guardian (NASB, Robertson and Plummer, Morris). Customs of the day, both Jewish and pagan, dictated that the father or guardian would decide if and to whom a young woman would be married. The following points are in favor of this position: (a) "Acting improperly" toward her means that he has not made a marriage arrangement and now has misgivings about it. (b) The reason is that "she is getting along in years" (NIV). The NASB reads, "If she should be of full age." One exegetical problem is that this clause does not have an expressed subject, which could be either male or female. If it is female, the meaning of the adjective is "past one's prime ... past the bloom of youth" (BAGD, 839; Bruce, 76). If, however, the subject is male, the adjective means "with strong passions" (BAGD); Barrett suggests the not-so-elegant "over-sexed" (182)—if this is Paul's intent, then it is a point in favor of the next position. (c) Verse 38 uses *gamizo* twice—a verb that means "give in marriage" (e.g., Matt. 22:30; 24:38; Mark 12:25; Luke 17:27; 20:35). It differs from *gameo*, which means "marry" (used in verse 36; see also vv. 9, 28, 33, 34). The NRSV reads here, "Let them marry." The NASB, reflecting the difficulty of its "virgin daughter" rendering, reads, "Let her marry," with a marginal note that "her" is literally "them."

This last observation leads to at least two objections to this position: (a) "They" ("Let them") in verse 36 cannot mean the virgin and her father or guardian. Attempts to make this apply to the virgin and a possible husband are strained since, according to this view, the man had not even been mentioned previously. (b) "His virgin" is an unusual way (though not impossible) to refer to a father and his daughter.

(3) "His virgin" refers to a man and his fiancée (the position of NIV and NRSV). In favor of this position: (a) The counsel "Let them marry" is most easily understood as referring to these two persons in the phrase "his virgin" (v. 36, NKJV). (b) The strict meaning of the verb *gamizo*, which is not found outside the New Testament, is "give ... in marriage," but it may also mean "marry" (BAGD, 151), and is so understood by some reliable commentators

(e.g., Barrett, Fee). The reason for the change from *gameo* to *gamizo* may simply be stylistic (Fee). (c) "Acting improperly toward [her]" may mean that the man has been depriving her of sexual fulfillment until now; she is "past her prime, past the bloom of youth," and he has misgivings about it. (d) If the adjective *hyperakmos* applies to the man's own strong sexual drive, then he ought to marry rather than burn (v. 9).

Against this view: (a) "His virgin" is an awkward way of saying "his fiancée." Barrett, however, suggests it might be the equivalent of "his girl." (b) Engagement, as often practiced in Western culture, was not a custom in that culture, even though a betrothal was usually arranged by a young woman's father or guardian. It may well be, however, that a young man and young woman would be attracted to each other and, without necessarily entering into a "spiritual marriage," would have a mutual understanding of sexual abstinence.

The various interpretations to verses 36–38 by equally competent scholars should deter one from taking an inflexible position. In the judgment of this commentator, however, the last option presents the fewest difficulties.

Consonant with what Paul has said previously in the chapter, he enjoins neither marriage nor remaining single. With his realistic approach, he counsels marriage for those who have difficulty maintaining sexual purity in the single state. For those who can, he recommends remaining unmarried.

While there is some uncertainty about Paul's instructions concerning virgins, there is none in what he says regarding Christian widows (vv. 39–40). But he must first reiterate, in different language, the thought that a Christian wife must not seek a divorce (vv. 11, 27). She is bound to her husband as long as he lives, but is free to marry if he dies (see also Rom. 7:1–3). "If her husband dies" reads, in the Greek text, "If her husband falls asleep [*koimao*]." This was a common euphemism for death, especially a believer's death (e.g., Matt. 27:52; John 11:11; 1 Cor. 11:30; 15:6, 18, 20, 51; 1 Thess. 4:13–15). Death cancels the marriage bond; the widow is therefore "free to marry anyone she wishes."

This is an incidental, though not necessarily unimportant, indication that the Old Testament law of levirate marriage (Deut. 25:5–10) does not apply to Christians. The widow is not obligated to marry a brother of her husband. But if she does remarry, it must be "only in the Lord" (NASB, a lit. trans.). The NIV takes liberty in rendering the phrase, "but he must belong to the Lord." Although Paul would agree that a widow's remarriage should be to a Christian, "only in the Lord" applies to the woman and is better interpreted to mean that all her motivation and decisions pertaining to remarriage must be controlled by her relationship to the Lord.

Paul again expresses an opinion ("in my judgment"; see comment on v. 25). As he did earlier in the chapter (v. 8), he advises the widow to remain unmarried, to stay "as she is." In light of everything he said previously in comparing and contrasting the unmarried state with the married, she will be happier in that state. Though he does not command in this matter, he does appeal to the backing of the Holy Spirit: "I think that I too have the Spirit of God" (see v. 25). "I too" may be an indirect response to the claim of some Corinthians that what they believed and practiced came from the Holy Spirit.

Paul does not speak to widowers, perhaps because the letter from Corinth asked specifically about widows. But in view of the thrust of the entire chapter, what he says to widows ought to apply equally to widowers.

3.2. Food Sacrificed to Idols (8:1–11:1)

For the third time Paul says, "Now about." The question raised here by the Corinthians deals with the proper Christian attitude toward "food sacrificed to idols [*eidolothutos*]." This is the word Jews and Christians would normally use for pagan temple sacrifices. A related but neutral term, *hierothutos* (food sacrificed in a temple, or temple food), occurs in 10:28 and is the pagan counterpart. This matter is so important that 8:1–13 and 10:14–11:1 are devoted to it.

Priests received a share of any sacrificed animal. The meat that was left over was taken home for private meals, was sold in the markets, or was eaten at temple banquets—social occasions to which Christians were sometimes invited and which some attended. This topic has special relevance today for Christians living in cultures where non-Christian and sub-Christian religion permeates everyday life and holiday observances.

The question goes deeper than whether a Christian ought to associate with non-Christians in the ordinary course of things. Paul has already expressed himself on this issue (see on 5:9–10). The problem was twofold: (1) Chapter 8 deals primarily with a Christian's participation in a social event that was clearly identified with pagan idolatry since it was a community dinner held in the temple complex. Should a Christian attend these dinners and eat meat that had been sacrificed to idols? A Jew, and some Jewish Christians, would not hesitate to answer "No." But the Corinthian congregation was divided on the matter; the "strong" believer said "Yes," while the "weak" believer said "No."

(2) A related problem dealt with the eating of meat sold at the market (10:14–11:1). Most such meat would originally have been part of a pagan sacrifice in a temple or elsewhere. Were Christians at liberty to each such meat, whether in their own home or at an unbeliever's home? And how could one know whether a particular item of such meat was part of a pagan sacrifice?

3.2.1. Superiority of Love Over "Knowledge" (8:1–8). "We know that we all possess knowledge" is probably a quotation from the Corinthians' letter. They had previously prided themselves on speech or rhetoric (*logos*) and wisdom (*sophia*); knowledge (*gnosis*) is now a third source of their pride. It had become an "in" word in Corinth (Fee, 366).

Paul does not disagree with the idea that we all possess knowledge, since all rational beings have some knowledge. But he will disagree with them on two related counts: (1) Their attitude regarding knowledge is wrong because "we all" refers only to themselves, and (2) the content and extent of their "knowledge" are wrong. Their brand of knowledge results in their being arrogant, puffed up (*physioo*; see 4:6, 18–19; 5:2). Love, on the other hand, does not make one puffed up (13:4) but rather builds up (*oikodomeo*) (v. 1). In light of what Paul says later, this building up relates to the community of believers (14:3–5, 12, 17, 26), in contrast to knowledge, which inflates the individual claimant. Certainly Paul is not saying that love and genuine knowledge are incompatible. He himself is a prime example that the two may indeed be, and ought to be, typical of a Christian.

It is not far afield to say that those who claimed "We all possess knowledge" also implied "We possess all knowledge." This attitude may be behind Paul's next statement, "If any one supposes that he knows [*egnokenai*] anything" (v. 2, NSAB). This form of the Greek word *ginosko* is in the perfect tense, suggesting that the person supposes he has known and continues to know something. But incomplete and imperfect knowledge are characteristic of this life (13:9), even though a misguided "spiritual" person may claim otherwise; such a person does not really know the extent of his or her ignorance. Furthermore, it is noteworthy that this person claims to know "something," whereas true knowledge consists in knowing God, which, in its biblical sense, means enjoying a relationship with him (John 17:3).

The person who claims to know something is contrasted with the one who loves God and "is known by God" (v. 3). Paul does not say that loving God results *in* God's knowing us, but rather that our loving God results *from* God's knowing us. The Greek for "is known" (*egnostai*) is more properly translated "has been known"—an action prior to one's loving God. Paul repeats this theme elsewhere in slightly different language: "Now that you know God—or rather are known by God" (Gal. 4:9; see also 2 Tim. 2:19; cf. Ps. 1:6; Isa. 49:1; Jer. 1:5; Nah. 1:7). He is fond of reminding readers that it is God who took the initiative in establishing the relationship between himself and humankind (Rom. 5:8). The implication of Paul's statement is that only the person who loves God, and consequently loves fellow believers, is the one who can settle the question about food offered to idols.

The opening words of verse 4 show that the problem was not in the food itself but in the *eating* (*brosis*) of the food at temple meals. "We know that an idol is nothing at all in the world" may be another quotation from the letter, and perhaps included the following statement, "and that there is no God but one." Because of the parallel grammatical construction of these two statements, a preferred translation would be, "that there is no idol in the world, and that there is no God but one" (Robertson and Plummer, 166).

This was the rationale adopted by the Corinthians, who saw no harm in eating food sacrificed to idols because idols were representations of nonexistent gods. Even if they ate, they still believed in the one true God. They readily agreed that there is no god alongside the God of Israel and had no difficulty reciting, with pious Jews, the Shema found in Deuteronomy 6:4, "Hear, O Israel: The LORD our God, the LORD is one" (in Paul, the terminology "one God" is found also in Gal. 3:20 and 1 Tim. 2:5). Some of the more sophisticated Greeks also believed in only one supreme deity. Thus, the Corinthian Christians could appeal both to the Old Testament and to contemporary philosophical thought as the basis for their belief in one God.

Paul cannot agree that an idol "is nothing at all," for he says later that behind the idols are demons (10:20). But for the moment, for the sake of argument, he concedes that there are "so-called gods, whether in heaven or on earth." "So-called," however, indicates he does not accept the existence of these gods, even though they were a subjective reality to the worshipers. It is well known that most deities of the Greco-Roman world had their abode in the heavens and that at times they visited humans. Note the account of Paul and Barnabas at Lystra (Acts 14:8–18), where the natives cried out, "The gods have come down to us in human form!" They identified Barnabas with Zeus and Paul with Hermes.

Everett Ferguson makes several enlightening comments on Paul's statement about "so-called gods ... on earth" (v. 5). He suggests a possible reference to deities whose abode was not Mount Olympus but the earth or the underworld, citing Hades (the Roman Pluto) as an example (142). The expression may also refer to the worship of "someone who was supposed to have existed but after death remained powerful enough to protect those on earth and thus was someone worthy of homage.... Their power was associated with their remains and the place of their burial" (148–49). In addition, not far from Paul's mind would have been the practice in Hellenistic-Roman religion of offering divine honors to kings (185).

Paul will concede that in the minds of the pagans there were "many 'gods' and many 'lords,'" but he is quick to point out that for Christians "there is but one God, the Father," and only "one Lord, Jesus Christ" (v. 6). Paul may have had in mind Old Testament passages that speak of Yahweh as the God of gods ar Lord of lords (Deut. 10:17; Ps. 136:2–3 According to Fee, the terms "gods" ar "lords" reflect two basic forms of Greco Roman religion: "Gods" refers to the trad tional deities and "lords" to mystery-cu deities.

God is the Father certainly in his relation the Son, but he is also Father in the sense being the Source and Creator of all thin ("from whom all things came"), as well as t Father of those who serve him ("for whom w live"). The Lord Jesus Christ is the agent of cr ation, "through whom all things came" (Joh 1:3; Col. 1:16; Heb. 1:2); he is also the agent the new creation (2 Cor. 5:17–18) "throug whom we live" spiritually. Paul is not co cerned here with reconciling the idea of on God with the mention of two whom he regar as God; that was for later theologians to wre tle with. His main point is that, contrary to th many gods of the pagans, there is only on God; and contrary to their many lords, there only one Lord. The title *Lord* as applied Jesus points both to the word's common usag Old Testament and otherwise, in reference God, as well as its connotation in the Greco Roman world of divinity or superiority.

The problem of the Corinthian Christia was both theological and practical. Some we theologically correct in these matters, but the were lacking in love and consideration fo other believers who did not possess this know edge (v. 7). Not everyone acknowledged wh Paul had just said about the nonreality of paga gods. Some had been so steeped in idolat (12:2) that they could not shake it off com pletely. Consequently, when they ate food th had been sacrificed to an idol, they could n escape its idolatrous implications. Therefo their conscience, which was weak, becan defiled—not because of the food they ha eaten, since food itself cannot defile (Ma 7:18–19), but because they had done som thing their conscience did not allow.

In light of this, Paul must now give son clear guidelines. (1) "Food will not commen us to God" (v. 8, NASB). This is preferable to th NIV's "food does not bring us near to God Manuscript evidence favors the future tens which could be an allusion to the final jud ment, as seen in a parallel passage (Ro 14:10–12), which contains the same ve *paristemi*; cf. also Rom. 6:13; 2 Cor. 4:14). "Present" is a better translation of the verb, since it implies either approval or condemnation. In principle, neither what we eat nor what we refrain from eating, in and of itself, affects our relationship with God. In the matter under discussion, the "weak" person is no worse for not eating, and the "strong" person is no better for eating. Christians are not saved because they are "advanced" with liberal views, nor are they damned because they obey their overscrupulous conscience (Barrett, 195). Elsewhere Paul says, "I am fully convinced that no food is unclean in itself" (Rom. 14:14). And Jesus said, in another context, "What goes into a man's mouth does not make him 'unclean'" (Matt.15:11; cf. 15:17–20; Mark 7:15).

3.2.2. Sinning Against a Weak Brother (8:9–13). (2) "Strong" believers must not exercise their "freedom" (*exousia*, "right") to eat at the expense of "weak" believers' spirituality (v. 9). Their freedom in eating may not harm *themselves*, but it may harm *others*. The strong must not become a stumbling block to the weak—a means for the downfall of fellow Christians (cf. also Rom. 14:13). If weak believers see a strong fellow Christian eating at a meal in a pagan temple, they might be "emboldened [*oikodomeo*] to eat what has been sacrificed to idols" (v. 10). This Greek verb normally is used in a positive sense, "to build up" (see on v. 1), but the irony is that the strong Christian's "knowledge" strengthens (builds up) weak believers to sin. Paul makes his point once again: "Knowledge puffs up, but love builds up" (v. 1). Rather than contributing to the genuine building up of the weak, the strong believer contributes to their ruin.

If the weak believers eat, they will violate their conscience and consequently be "destroyed" (*apollymi*) by the other's loveless conduct (v. 11; cf. also Rom. 14:15). "Ruined," rather than "destroyed," may be a preferable translation in these verses. Paul does not necessarily have in mind eternal destruction; the word is in the Greek present tense, conveying the idea that the weak believers are in process of being ruined. They will sin by acting contrary to their conscience, for Paul says in a similar context that "the man who has doubts is condemned if he eats, because his eating is not from faith; and everything that does not come from faith is sin" (Rom. 14:23). Yet the idea of eternal ruin or destruction cannot be ruled out, since *apollymi* is often used in this sense. Occurrences of the word speak of spiritual and even eternal destruction (see Rom. 2:12; 1 Cor. 10:9–10; 15:18; 2 Cor. 2:15; 4:3; 2 Thess. 2:10).

The strong Christians have also sinned in that their conduct was influenced by a faulty view of freedom rather than by love for their weaker fellow believers (v. 12). "If your brother is distressed because of what you eat, you are no longer acting in love" (Rom. 14:15). Barrett (96) cites, with approval, an observation by Adolph Schlatter that many Greeks of that day had abandoned belief in the gods and the efficacy of sacrifices, but nevertheless continued to take part, for social reasons, in rites associated with pagan religion. Some of the "enlightened" believers might have reasoned similarly—that their participation was purely social since they denied the existence of the gods. But this exercise of their liberty resulted in a number of adverse effects on weak Christians, whose consciences became defiled (1 Cor. 8:7) and wounded (v. 12). They had been influenced to sin by violating their conscience (v. 13). The so-called strong Christians should be willing to forgo something that in itself may not be sin and which their conscience permitted them to do, if such action would be damaging to a fellow believer.

The action of the Jerusalem council is instructive. Gentile Christians were requested "to abstain from food polluted by idols" and from the meat of animals that had not been killed in compliance with Jewish custom (Acts 15:20, 29). They were asked to do this out of consideration for some Jewish Christians who, as a matter of conscience, adhered to those restrictions.

(3) "When you sin against your brothers ... you sin against Christ" (v. 12). There is a hint here of what is found elsewhere in Paul's writings on the church as the body of Christ. Since it is his body, whatever harm or good is done to one member is done to him. We see this concept in Jesus himself, for on the last day he will say to those who appear before him: "Whatever you did for one of the least of these brothers of mine, you did for me" (Matt. 25:40; see also Mark 9:37; Luke 10:16; John 13:20). And his words to Saul, the persecutor of Christians, are especially instructive: "Saul, Saul, why do you

persecute me?" (Acts 9:4). The application of this concept to the church at large should be so obvious as to require no further comment.

Paul's concluding remarks are personal rather than directive: If eating meat will cause his fellow Christian to "stumble [*skandalizo*]" (NASB; note Jesus' use of this word in Mark 9:42), he will deny himself that freedom and never again eat meat. The expression "never again" is one of the strongest possible ways to express a negative idea, essentially meaning "never forever." For Paul's extended treatment of principles pertaining to these and similar matters, the reader is directed to Romans 14. His basic stance on these matters is reflected in what he says regarding winning the lost to Christ: "To the weak I became weak, to win the weak" (1 Cor. 9:22).

3.2.3. The Rights of an Apostle (9:1–27). Chapter 9 is a defense (*apologia*, v. 3) by Paul of his apostleship, with the emphasis on his voluntary surrender of certain rights or privileges to which an apostle was entitled. Some in Corinth were questioning his apostolic call and authority. Much of their argument, curiously, was that since Paul did not avail himself of apostolic privileges, that negated his claim to an apostle. He began the letter by stating he was "called to be an apostle of Christ Jesus by the will of God" (1:1). In chapter 4, he wrote much about how he and other apostles had been mistreated for the sake of Christ. He now devotes more time to the matter of his apostleship.

This chapter seems to be an intrusion into the subject of food offered to idols, which receives attention in chapters 8 and 10. But he uses this occasion to give a lengthy defense of his apostleship. One emphasis in chapter 8 is the theoretical right (freedom) of a Christian to participate in pagan temple feasts. His last thought in the chapter is his personal approach to the problem, which is a self-denial of his freedom in the interests of a weak Christian's welfare. He picks up this theme of freedom at the beginning of chapter 9 and pursues it throughout much of the chapter. He concludes this chapter with a warning of the fearful consequence of not practicing self-denial or self-restraint with regard to one's liberty. He then begins chapter 10 by illustrating this consequence from Israel's history, which included a lapse into idolatry (10:1–13). This leads him to return to the subject of food offered to idols (10:14–33).

Verses 1–12a are Paul's clear statement
that he is entitled to the same privileges tha
other apostles enjoy. Verse 1 contains a serie
of questions. Paul seems to be following th
procedure of Greek philosophers, who ofte
used argumentation by means of questions. I
their Greek form, all the questions expect th
answer "yes": "I am free, am I not?" etc. H
is free in the sense that all Christians are free
but in the wider context he says that as an apos
tle he has not always availed himself of apos
tolic privileges.

The last three questions are interrelated: "
am an apostle, am I not? I have seen Jesus ou
Lord, have I not? You are the result of my wor
in the Lord, are you not?" (pers. trans.). Hi
claim to apostleship is based on his havin
seen Jesus, and the very existence of th
Corinthian congregation is a testimony to hi
apostolic ministry. It was actually Jesus wh
appeared to him on the Damascus road (Act
9:3–6, 17, 27; 22:8, 14; 26:15–18), and late
in the letter he includes himself among al
those to whom the risen Lord had appeare
(1 Cor. 15:3–8). He may be referring also t
other appearances of Jesus to him (Acts 18:9
22:17). He is therefore a witness to the resur
rection of Jesus, which was a qualification fo
apostleship (Acts 1:22; 2:32). But it was no
the only qualification, since many others ha
also seen the risen Jesus. As the word *aposto*
los ("sent one") indicates, a divine commissio
was an integral part of an apostolic call.

Any attempt to define the word *apostle* wit
absolute precision is doomed to failure, for
number of reasons. (1) The Greek word *apos*
tolos is used in both a restricted sense ("th
Twelve") and in a broader sense. For exampl
Paul unquestionably placed himself on th
same level as those who were indisputabl
regarded as apostles. Moreover, James, th
Lord's brother, seems to be classified as a
apostle (Gal. 1:19), and Andronicus and Junia
"are outstanding among the apostles" (Ro
16:7). Also, Barnabas, along with Paul, i
called an apostle in Acts 14:4, 14.

(2) A common idea is that an apostle is on
whose ministry is to preach Christ to th
unevangelized and whose ministry wa
accompanied by signs and wonders (2 Co
12:12). But Philip, the evangelist to Samari
through whom miracles occurred, is neve
called an apostle (Acts 8:5–24). Furthermor

here is no clear record in Scripture that all the postles were evangelists in virgin territory.

(3) Peter's qualifications for the person to eplace Judas in the apostolic circle pose some roblems. This person was to be one who had een with the original Twelve throughout the arthly ministry of Jesus, beginning with ohn's baptism and ending with Jesus' ascenion (Acts 1:21–22). These qualifications canot apply in all cases, since they clearly xclude Paul and all others who at a later time re called apostles. It may be that these qualiications were Peter's idea alone, his thoughts eing accurately recorded but not necessarily xpressing God's will. If it was indeed a equirement, then Jesus waived it in the case f Paul and others.

(4) In some passages the word *apostolos* nay simply mean messenger, as in the case of paphroditus (Phil. 2:25).

The foregoing is not meant to strip the word *postolos* of any special meaning it had for aul in the Corinthian letters, where he is esponding to a challenge that he is not on a par vith "original" apostles like Peter. Among the ifts he lists in 12:28, for example, he does ssign priority to apostles (see also Eph. 4:11). nd in the letter to the Ephesians, there is no uestion that the apostles had a unique role in ne first-century church (2:20; 3:4–5; 4:11). Whatever else may be said about apostles—nd much remains to be said—Paul will not etreat from his claim to be every bit as much n apostle as Peter and others.

Practical proof of Paul's apostleship is the xistence of the Corinthian church (v. 2; see lso Rom. 15:15–21). They are the result of his ninistry. He planted the church, that is, he ounded it (1 Cor. 3:6, 10). Others may queson the validity of his claim, but how could the Corinthians? They were "the seal of [his] aposeship"—a seal being a sign of both ownerhip and authentication (2 Cor. 1:22; Eph. :13; 4:30; 2 Tim. 2:19). In this passage the mphasis is on authentication. And who are the others" to whom Paul "may not be an apose"? They might be other churches that he imself did not establish, or they might be outiders who had come to Corinth to undermine im (1 Cor. 4:15; 9:12).

"This is my defense" (v. 3) may apply to vhat precedes (Bruce, 83; Robertson and lummer, 179) or to what follows (Héring, 76; Fee, 401). Opinion is divided, but it seems better to apply it to Paul's previous comments. The reason why Paul speaks so strongly is that there are those who "sit in judgment [*anakrino*]" against him. The word was used of judicial hearings, and several translations render it "examine" (NASB, NRSV, NKJV). "Defense" (*apologia*) also suggests the context of a court of law (Acts 22:1; 25:16; Phil. 1:7, 16; 2 Tim. 4:16).

The next three questions speak of privileges that were commonly accorded apostles: food and drink, accompaniment by one's wife, and freedom from "secular" work (vv. 4–6). The key word is "right" (*exousia*). Paul willingly waived those privileges, and for that his claim to apostleship was being challenged. We note in passing the shift from "I" to "we," since Paul includes Barnabas (v. 6). Barnabas was Paul's friend and colleague in the ministry (Acts 9:27; 11:25–15:39; Gal. 2:1). He was an early member of the Jerusalem church (Acts 4:36–37), and Luke specifically calls him an apostle (Acts 14:4, 14).

The first matter, dealing with food and drink, is a bridge to the preceding chapter, implying that apostles are as free as other Christians to make decisions about what it is proper to eat and drink. But it goes beyond that. It implies that visiting apostles usually received sustenance at the church's expense or from local believers.

The second matter deals with taking along "a believing wife" (lit., "a wife [who is] a sister"). The implication is that the wife would be included in the church's provision for an apostle's needs. "The other apostles" suggests that most, if not all, of them were married. We know this for certain about Peter (i.e., Cephas) (Mark 1:30). He receives special mention here because of his leadership role in the early church and also because some of the Corinthians had set him in opposition to Paul.

The words "the Lord's brothers" should be interpreted at face value (Mark 3:31; 6:3; John 7:5; Acts 1:14), especially because they are often mentioned in conjunction with Mary. Except for those whose exegesis is dictated by dogma, there is no reason to believe that Mary would not have had children after Jesus. Luke calls Jesus "her firstborn" (Luke 2:7), implying others. Furthermore, Matthew says that Joseph "had no union with [Mary] until she gave birth to a son [Jesus]" (Matt. 1:25). It is speculative to say that these brothers had to be either Jesus' stepbrothers (Joseph's by a previous marriage) or his cousins. The only New Testament occurrence of the word "cousin" (*anepsios*) relates Mark to Barnabas (Col. 4:10). One can only wonder whether those who deny that Mary had other children are unwittingly saying that she, like some of the misguided Corinthian women, was too spiritual to have had sexual relations with her husband.

By including Barnabas in the third item, that of working for a living, Paul implies that Barnabas, too, is an apostle (see Acts 14:4, 14). It is well established that Paul often worked at his trade during his travels so as not to be a burden to the church (1 Cor. 4:12; cf. Acts 20:33–34; 1 Thess. 2:9; 2 Thess. 3:8). By contrast, Greeks thought it was inappropriate for a teacher to work manually.

To further strengthen his case, Paul illustrates from everyday life that compensation is to be expected for one's work, citing the soldier, the farmer, and the shepherd (v. 7). The needs of a soldier are met by those who engaged him. The planter of a vineyard eats its grapes (Deut. 20:6; Prov. 27:18). The shepherd drinks (lit., "eats") the milk of the sheep; apparently, milk was considered a food, not a beverage.

On these three matters, Paul was speaking "from a human point of view" (*kata anthropon* in v. 8—also in 3:3; 15:32). But there is a higher authority, the Scriptures, for God's law says the same thing. The term *law* is sometimes used in the New Testament in an inclusive sense for all the Hebrew Scriptures, but often it refers to the Torah, the first five books. Paul quotes Deuteronomy 25:4 here: "Do not muzzle an ox while it is treading out the grain." The procedure was for an ox to trample the grain in order to separate the grain from the husks. The ox was unmuzzled in order to allow it to eat some of the grain for sustenance while it worked. The application is again obvious.

But Paul's next question, which expects a negative answer, raises an interpretive problem: "God is not concerned about the oxen, is he?" (pers. trans.). Some say the Deuteronomy passage may be figurative and therefore deals with people rather than animals. Even if this is so, it would be incorrect to infer from this that God is not concerned about animals (see Matt. 6:26; 10:29; Luke 12:6–7). If the quoted passage is taken literally, then Paul is arguin from the minor to the major: God made pro vision for an animal to be fed for its work; hov much more an apostle for his work? Elsewher Paul can take an Old Testament passage liter ally and at the same time make a spiritua application (e.g., Hagar and Sarah in Gal. 4:24 Moses' shining face in 2 Cor. 3:13; Israel' desert experiences in 1 Cor. 10:1–11).

Paul follows with another question: "Or i he speaking altogether for our sake?" (v. 10 NASB). The wording of the question in Gree leaves the answer open. "Altogether" (*pantos* has a range of meanings: "by all means, cer tainly, probably, doubtless" (BAGD, 609) When Paul responds with "Yes, for our sake (NASB), he does not repeat "altogether." Thi leaves the door open to include the literal inter pretation and its specific application to th apostle's ministry. Paul has given a mor extended meaning to the Old Testament pas sage. He follows his application by giving th reason why God commanded that the ox not b muzzled—so that the plowman and th thresher will share in the harvest. The thought of plowing and threshing may be metaphor for different stages of missionary wor (Robertson and Plummer, 185).

Continuing further with agrarian imagery Paul talks in terms of sowing and reaping. "I we have sown spiritual seed among you, is i too much if we reap a material harvest fron you" (v. 11). "We" in both clauses is in th emphatic position in the Greek text. "If other share the right [of support] from you, we shoul all the more, shouldn't we?" (v. 12a—per trans.). Paul had this same idea in mind whe he told the Galatians, "Anyone who receive instruction in the word must share all goo things with his instructor" (Gal. 6:6). The infer ence in the present passage is that the Corinthi ans had indeed supported other apostles.

Verses 12b–18 are a further step in Paul' defense of his apostleship. He has argued tha he has the right to be supported by th Corinthians. Now he emphasizes his voluntar waiving of that right (vv. 12b, 15a) and hi main reason for doing so: "We endure a things, that we may cause no hindrance to th gospel of Christ" (v. 12b, NASB). He had pre viously mentioned some of the things he ha endured: hunger, thirst, lack of proper cloth ing, beatings, homelessness (4:11; cf. 2 Co

1:23–29). He will not bring discredit on the ;ospel by insisting on his right to be supported, or will he risk being accused of profiteering rom his ministry. Insisting on rights only erves to turn people away from the gospel, vhereas Paul's paramount concern is the furherance of the gospel of Christ by winning as nany people as possible (vv. 19–23). The xpression "the gospel of Christ" suggests that 'aul wishes his whole life to be conformed to Christ, who himself endured similar hardships nd did not insist on rights (Rom. 15:3).

Verse 13 introduces another illustration, this ime appropriately from religious practices, vhich expects a positive answer: "Those who vork in the temple get their food from the temle, and those who serve at the altar share in vhat is offered on the altar." It is not necessary o limit what Paul says about those who serve t a temple and its altar to a Jewish context Levites and priests, respectively), though it ertainly does apply to them (e.g., Lev. 7:6, 8–0, 28–36; Num. 18:8–32; Deut. 18:1–8). It vas and is common practice in most religions hat those who perform ritual duties get their ivelihood from doing so.

But as he did in verse 8, Paul appeals to a igher authority; this time, however, it is not he Hebrew Scriptures but the Lord Jesus himelf, who commanded that "those who preach he gospel should receive their living from the ;ospel" (v. 14; see Matt. 10:10; Luke 10:7). 'hat is, those who receive the gospel ought to ake care of the one who brought it to them. Although Paul's immediate concern is to stablish the principle as it relates to apostles, esus' words have a wider application since in Matthew they are addressed to the twelve postles and in Luke to seventy disciples. It is vorth noting also that in 1 Timothy 5:18 Paul ombines the Old Testament quotation about ot muzzling the ox (cf. 1 Cor. 9:9) with this aying of Jesus.

So far Paul has appealed to everyday expeiences in the secular realm (vv. 7, 10), the Hebrew Scriptures (vv. 8–9), common reliious practice (v. 13), and Jesus himself (v. 14) o support the idea that those who minister the ;ospel ought to be provided for by those who eceive it. The irony is that some Corinthians vere insisting that a legitimate apostle is *equired* to accept their assistance, not merely hat he is *entitled* to it. Therefore, they maintained, one who declined their support could not be a genuine apostle.

Thus, Paul must again remind the Corinthians: "I have not used any of these rights" (v. 15). "I" is in the emphatic position in the Greek text; Paul contrasts himself with others. But it is important to note that Paul nowhere faults those who are fed by the community, take along their wives, and choose not to work in a secular occupation. Furthermore, the Corinthians must not understand him as hoping that he wishes now to be supported by them. He then starts to give another reason for his decision to maintain his present status, but seems to be so overcome with emotion that he does not complete the sentence. This is reflected in the NRSV: "Indeed, I would rather die than that—no one will deprive me of my ground for boasting!" (v. 15b). In Paul's writings, boasting may be either negative or positive. He uses it in a positive sense when he relates it to Christ crucified (1:30–31), his own weakness in light of the Lord's strength (2 Cor. 12:3–5), and his sufferings (Gal. 6:14).

The precise nature of Paul's reason is unclear, but it is related to his preaching of the gospel. Preaching is not a cause for boasting because for him it was not a matter of choice. He is "compelled" (v. 16—lit., "compulsion lies upon me"). He did not *choose* to preach the Gospel, but he *must* in view of the divine call. His words are reminiscent of Jeremiah's: "If I say, 'I will not mention him [the LORD] or speak any more in his name,' his word is in my heart like a fire, a fire shut up in my bones. I am weary of holding it in; indeed, I cannot" (Jer. 20:9). Paul was commissioned in this manner at the time of his conversion (Acts 9:6, 15; 22:21). If he does not preach, it will result in "woe" for him. He does not explain the nature of the woe; it is enough to realize that failure to preach the gospel will be calamitous for him.

Verses 17–18 are difficult to interpret with absolute precision, but the general tenor is clear. It is the relationship between preaching the gospel and rewards for doing so. If Paul's preaching were voluntary—he has just said that it is not—then it merits a reward, presumably from God. But since it is done involuntarily, he has "a stewardship [*oikonomia*] entrusted to" him (NASB). He had spoken previously of the obligations of "stewards [*oikonomos*] of the mysteries of God" (4:1,

NASB). This is slave language, a steward being a trusted slave who managed a household. Such a person is simply discharging his responsibilities and is not *entitled* to reward or wages. "What then is my reward?" (v. 18a) may be taken as a completion of the last part of verse 17: "if . . . I am simply discharging the trust . . . what then is my reward?" Or it may be independent of verse 17 and ask a question that Paul will proceed to answer. This latter alternative seems preferable: Paul's reward is to preach the gospel "free of charge." "His pay is to serve without pay!" (Morris, 135). It is his privilege not to invoke his right to receive compensation for his ministry, "not to make full use of my right in the gospel" (v. 18, NASB).

Verses 19–23 are a classic in missiological studies. The main thought is that of adapting, perhaps accommodating, oneself to the context in which one ministers. To do so is to join Paul in the free man/slave paradox (v. 19). He is free (cf. v. 1) and "belong[s] to no man." The meaning is twofold. (1) As a Roman citizen and a free man, Paul is no one's slave. (2) In the situation at hand, he is free to eat or not eat, to receive support or not receive support. Yet, as it relates to the focus of his ministry, he voluntarily enslaved himself to everyone, even the Corinthians (2 Cor. 4:5). His focus was to win (*kerdaino*) as many as possible (*hoi pleiones*).

The verb *kerdaino* occurs four times in this paragraph, an indication of its importance. *Hoi pleiones* means "the larger part" or "the largest possible number" (Héring, 82; the same phrase occurs in 10:5). Paul did not expect to win everyone. His posture of adaptation or accommodation, however, must not be construed as compromising the purity of the gospel. When necessary, he attacked both Jews and Gentiles on matters like righteousness by works or idolatry. Yet, "he could find in all men something with which he could sympathize, and he used this to win them" (Robertson and Plummer, 191).

Why did Paul, a Jew, say he "became like a Jew" (v. 20), since he never denied his Jewish ethnicity and heritage (2 Cor. 11:22; Phil. 3:5)? The key is in the threefold repetition of both "Jew" and "under the law," and the identification of one with the other (v. 20). The apostle was not under the law of Moses but under the law of Christ, who is "the end of the law" (Rom. 10:4). Note his careful wording: He became "*like* a Jew"; he did not "become a Jew," which in this context would have meant a denial of Christ. The same is true of his comments on the Gentiles: He became "*like* one not having the law" (v. 21). There may be implicit in these statements the idea that humankind is divisible into three groups: Jews, Gentiles, and Christians.

To return to Paul's thought on winning Jews: At least two incidents in his ministry illustrate his point. He himself circumcised Timothy (considered to be a Jew because his mother was Jewish) "because of the Jews who lived in that area." In an attempt to "win Jews," Paul removed an unnecessary barrier to their receptivity to the gospel (Acts 16:1–3). But in Paul's mind, becoming circumcised is unrelated to one's salvation. By contrast, he refused to have Titus circumcised, because Titus was Greek. By doing so he would have capitulated to the Judaizers, who taught that circumcision was necessary for salvation (Gal. 2:3–4). With Timothy, it was accommodation; with Titus, it was refusal to compromise the truth of the gospel of grace.

The second incident relates to Paul's participation in, and sponsorship of, a vow undertaken by four Jewish men (Acts 21:19–24). He did it for the sake of recent Jewish converts who perceived him as being against the Law of Moses. They did not understand that in Paul's thinking the Law was holy, righteous good, and spiritual (Rom. 7:12, 14), but that it was not meant by God to be the means of salvation. These people could be compared to the "weak" in this discussion of 1 Corinthians 8–10. Paul was willing to accommodate them in order to win them over. But again, we must note that his involvement in the Jewish vow had nothing to do with his salvation or that of the four men. In technical terminology, the vow was an *adiaphoron* (lit., a matter of indifference), as was circumcision, with respect to personal salvation.

With regard to Gentiles, "those not having the law," Paul became like one of them (v. 21). His preaching to Gentile audiences demonstrates his adaptable style (Acts 14:15–17; 17:22–31). Since they did not have the law of Moses, Paul quotes only once from the Hebrew Scriptures (14:15), though he does not hesitate to quote Greek writers in his address to the Athenians.

Paul characterizes Gentiles as *anomos*. The ord often means "lawless," but in contexts :e this it has the meaning "outside of law" "not having the Mosaic law" (cf. Acts 2:23; om. 2:14). When the apostle goes on to state at he became *anomos* in order to win Gen-es, he is quick to explain what this means. does not make him lawless, free from God's w. Rather, he is subject to the law of Christ. e is *ennomos Christou*—under the law of nrist. For the law of Christ, we may turn to veral passages for suggestions (Mark 12:28– ; Luke 10:25–28; Gal. 6:2). Jesus' summa-on of God's law—loving God and loving e's neighbor—can justifiably be called his w. It dovetails with Paul's emphasis in this tter (e.g., 8:1; ch. 13).

Paul then says he became weak in order to in the weak. "The weak" are probably Chris-ns, such as those in chapter 8, who are overly rupulous to the point that they are bound by galism. They may be like those new converts, entioned above, for whose benefit Paul par-:ipated in the vow of the four men (Acts :19–24). His aim in doing so is to "win" em. While this may refer to conversion for me, in a more general sense Paul means that wants to "win them over" to a fuller under-anding of Christianity or, even better, that he ants to "*keep* them for the church," instead driving them away by violating their con-ience (Barrett, 215). By saying he became eak for their sake, he considers himself nong the strong (Rom. 15:1).

In all these matters, Paul is not like the overbial chameleon, which changes its color conform to its environment in an attempt to eserve itself. The apostle adapts himself to ese varying situations "so that by all possi-e means I might save some" (v. 22; "save" d "win" are interchangeable in this para-aph). His driving motivation is the salvation his hearers. For some it means the initial ep of saving faith (Eph. 2:8), for others con-uance and perseverance in their faith. He es all this "for the sake of the gospel" (1 Cor. 23), not for self-aggrandizement or self-eservation.

Yet Paul does express the desire that by inistering in this manner he "may become a llow-partaker of it" (NASB). Some transla-ns speak of participating in the "blessings" the gospel (e.g., NIV, NRSV), which, though not a strict translation, is probably Paul's meaning. By calling himself a "fellow-partaker," Paul identifies himself with all those he has won. Not far from his mind is the idea of the blessing that awaits believers at the con-summation of their faith.

Verses 24–27 focus on the necessity of self-discipline in the life of a believer. Once again Paul introduces this discussion with a question that expects a positive answer: "You know, don't you?" (pers. trans.). The Corinthians were familiar with the Isthmian Games, the biennial athletic contests that were held in their vicinity, second in importance only to the Olympic Games. Imagery of athletic games to illustrate the Christian life is common in Paul's writings (e.g., Phil. 3:12–14; 2 Tim. 2:5; 4:7–8) and elsewhere (e.g., Heb. 12:1–2). His main point here is that the Christian life requires self-control (*enkrateia*) if the spiritual athlete is to persevere to the end. This word denotes a virtue that ought to be characteristic of all Christians (Gal. 5:23; 2 Pet. 1:6) and, in its adjective form, is listed among the qualifica-tions for an elder (Titus 1:8). Its verb form occurs in this passage (v. 25—"goes into strict training" [NIV]; "exercises self-control" [NASB]) and in 7:9, which mentions the inabil-ity of some unmarried women to control their sexual impulses.

Most figures of speech do not correspond at every point with what they symbolize. This is true of the race metaphor. Its main point is that the runner, to be successful, must have con-siderable self-discipline. The fact that only one runner can win and receive the crown is irrel-evant to Paul's purpose, for theoretically every Christian can receive the crown. Yet Paul also has in mind that entrance into the race is no guarantee that one will complete it.

Self-discipline was mandatory prior to the race; athletes were expected to train vigorously for the preceding ten months, but it was also imperative during the race (Acts 20:24; Phil. 3:14; 2 Tim. 2:5; 4:7–8). The crown was a wreath made from pine branches and, some-times, from celery. By its nature, it "will not last." By contrast, the crown awaiting the believer "will last forever." It is a symbol of victory—variously called "the crown of righ-teousness" (2 Tim. 4:8), "the crown of life" (James 1:12; Rev. 2:10), and "the crown of glory" (1 Peter 5:4).

The self-discipline Paul enjoins includes concentrating on the goal. "I do not run like a man running aimlessly; I do not fight [lit., box] like a man beating [*dero*] the air" (v. 26). BAGD (175) suggests that *dero* is used of unskillful boxers, who miss their mark. The thought is that of unfocused, wasted energy. Continuing the boxing metaphor, Paul says that he beats (*hypopiazo*) his body and makes it his slave (v. 27). This Greek word basically means "strike under the eye, give a black eye to" and, symbolically, "treat roughly, torment, maltreat" (BAGD, 848).

We must not interpret Paul to mean that the body is inherently evil, even though he knows it may be put to sinful use. That is why he calls on believers not to let sin reign in their mortal body and not to present the members of their body to sin as instruments of wickedness (Rom. 6:12–13; Col. 3:5). Nor is he talking about the practice, common in some non-Christian religions and some segments of Christianity, of abusing one's body as an indication of remorse in an attempt to atone for one's sins. Paul says he subjugates his body because he does not want to be "disqualified for the prize." In preaching to others, he does not want to overlook the responsibility for his own spiritual welfare. He allows for the possibility that if he is neglectful or undisciplined, he might not receive the imperishable crown of life.

3.2.4. Israel's History: A Warning (10:1–13). A major theme of chapter 9 was the Christian's need to exercise self-discipline in order to avoid the risk of being disqualified for the eternal prize (9:27). Paul now illustrates this amply by citing ancient Israel's failures. Much of chapter 10 dovetails with Paul's statements in chapter 8 regarding the eating of meat at temple feasts. But he now introduces a new element: Israel's Exodus experiences as types of the Christian observances of baptism and the Lord's Supper. (Because of his theological commitment, this commentator will not use the term *sacrament*; his preferences are *ordinance*, *rite*, *observance*.)

Apparently some Corinthians had a magical view of the ordinances, feeling they were secure in their salvation as long as they observed them. For them, proper or improper Christian conduct had no bearing on their eternal salvation. Paul must disabuse them of this ruinous misconception. He does so, not so much by intricate theological argumentation, but by using Old Testa-ment Israel as a prime example of those wh[o] failed to gain the "prize" (9:24, 27).

Verses 1–5 focus on Israel's participation [in] events that have clear associations with th[e] church's ordinances. "I do not want you to b[e] ignorant" (v. 1) is used numbers of times b[y] Paul to call attention to something that [is] important and perhaps new (Rom. 1:13; 11:25; 1 Cor. 12:1; 2 Cor. 1:8; 1 Thess. 4:13). Th[e] Corinthians probably knew the stories abo[ut] Israel, but Paul does not want them "to b[e] ignorant" of the application of those narrativ[es] to their own lives.

The apostle begins, significantly, by callin[g] the Israelites "our forefathers." The Corinthia[n] Christians, even though most were Gentile[s,] are nevertheless identified with Israel. Th[e] church, in Paul's view, is the true Israel (Ga[l.] 6:16); all believers are Abraham's spiritu[al] descendants (Rom. 4:16–17; Gal. 3:6–9, 29[).] True Jews are those, including Gentiles, wh[o] have undergone spiritual circumcision (Ro[m.] 2:28–29). The church is now defined in term[s] that once applied to ancient Israel (1 Peter 2:[9;] see Ex. 19:5–6). A full treatment of this them[e] is beyond the scope of this commentary; it w[ill] suffice to say that these observations do n[ot] necessarily exclude national or ethnic Isra[el] from any involvement in God's plans for th[e] future.

The ancient Israelites experienced th[e] equivalents of baptism and the Lord's Supp[er.] The Greek word *pantes* ("all"), significantl[y,] occurs five times in verses 1–4. No one w[as] excluded; all participated. This is contraste[d] with God's not being pleased with "most [of] them" (v. 5). All participated; most incurre[d] divine displeasure. They "were all under th[e] cloud" (v. 1; cf. Ex. 13:21–22), which sign[i]fied God's guiding presence. Note Psal[m] 105:39, which says that the Lord "spread ou[t a] cloud as a covering." The same idea is foun[d] in the noncanonical Wisdom of Solomo[n,] where there is the idea of enveloping the[m] (Wisd. Sol. 10:17; 19:7).

They also "all passed through the sea" (v. [1;] cf. Ex. 14:21–22), certainly a type of baptis[m] (1 Cor. 10:2). Paul's analogy, however, do[es] not emphasize the correspondence between t[he] sea water and the waters of Christian baptis[m.] We should recall that the Israelites walked [on] dry land when they crossed the sea. The po[int] f contact with Christian baptism is that they ›ere all "baptized into Moses." Minimally, the hrase serves to identify the people closely ›ith their leader. Its New Testament counter-art is that believers are baptized "into Christ" Rom. 6:3; Gal. 3:27) or "into one body Christ's]" (1 Cor. 12:13). It seems that Paul, ›orking backwards in time, adapted the "into Christ" phrase to Moses.

While one's approach to typology must be uarded and conservative, it is easy to see Ioses here as a type of Christ, who leads his eople out of bondage, for it is a New Testament ommonplace that Jesus is the antitype of Ioses as well as his superior (e.g., Heb. 3:1–6). his typology is implied in the only New Tes-ment occurrence of the Greek word *lytrotes* edeemer, deliverer), which Stephen applies to Ioses (Acts 7:35), even though the concept of demption through Christ occurs throughout e New Testament. Stephen does make clear nmediately afterward that Jesus is the Moses-ke prophet whose coming was foretold by Ioses (Acts 7:37; cf. Deut. 18:15, 18–19).

In addition to their baptism, the Israelites ll ate the same spiritual food and [all] drank e same spiritual drink" (vv. 3–4). The adjec-ve "spiritual" (*pneumatikos*) is variously terpreted, but it cannot mean that Paul garded the food and drink as nonmaterial. ome take the word to mean "typological" or symbolic," foreshadowing the elements of the ord's Supper. Others take it to mean "super-atural"—that the bread and water were mirac-ously provided. Elsewhere it is called "the ain of heaven" and "the bread of angels" (Ps. 3:24–25). Similar expressions are found in the Visdom of Solomon 16:20. Neither interpreta-on excludes the other. The food is the manna Ex. 16:4, 14–18); the drink is the water from e rock (Ex. 17:6; Num. 20:7–13). The food is piritual/miraculous because it came from eaven; the water is spiritual/miraculous ecause it came from a spiritual/miraculous ck (1 Cor. 10:4).

A rock supplied water at the beginning and ward the end of the desert experience (Ex. 7:1–7; Num. 20:2–13). Jewish legend, not e Old Testament, said that the rock accom-nied the people throughout the journey. Paul ay be alluding to the legend, without neces-rily subscribing to it, to make a point. It ould not surprise us if he had said that the rock "typified" Christ, but his statement that the rock "was" Christ is startling.

Several points may be made in this regard. (1) The statement implies that Christ accompanied the Israelites throughout their journey. (2) This being so, it speaks of his preexistence (in Paul's writings, also in Rom. 8:3; 2 Cor. 8:9; Gal. 4:4; Phil. 2:5–7). (3) Yahweh in the Old Testament is "the Rock" (Deut. 32:4, 15, 18, 30–31; Ps. 18:2), and Christ is here identified with him. There are obvious implications for later developments in Christology. (4) Many theologians have identified the angel of Yahweh, who accompanied Israel in the desert (Ex. 14:19; 23:20–23; 32:34; 33:2), with the preincarnate Christ. (5) In an interpretation of John 7:38–39 to which this commentator subscribes, Jesus' statement about "streams of living water" flowing from within someone refers not to a believer but to himself as the antitypical rock in the desert. This viewpoint is strengthened by his immediately preceding statement that the one who is thirsty should "come to me and drink" (v. 37), since he is the source of the living water (John 4:10, 13–14).

"Nevertheless" (*alla*) is a strong conjunction that introduces a radical shift in direction. All the Israelites were blessed and sustained by the miraculously supplied bread and water, but this did not guarantee their survival in the desert and eventual entrance into the Promised Land. "God was not pleased with most of them," with the result that "their bodies were scattered over the desert" (v. 5). The Lord "slaughtered them in the desert" (Num. 14:16; cf. Heb. 3:17). Paul will shortly give reasons for God's displeasure. The word "most" is an understatement; only two Israelites of that generation, Caleb and Joshua, survived (Num. 14:30–32)!

Verses 6–13 return specifically to the theme of idolatry and idol feasts. Israel's desert experiences "occurred as examples [*typos*] to keep us from setting our hearts on [craving, NASB] evil things as they did" (v. 6). "Evil things" refers primarily to idolatry and whatever is associated with it. The Israelites' craving might refer to the fleshpots of Egypt (Num. 11:4–34), which were associated with idolatry. It might also include sexual immorality, often associated with idolatry. The analogy with the current situation in Corinth is all too clear. Some of the believers were flirting with idolatry by participating in the temple feasts. God did not

Paul warned the Corinthians to not make the same mistakes as the ancient Israelites who wandered in the desert for forty years. "We should not test the Lord, as some of them did," he said. This area is at the foot of Mount Sinai. A camel is in the foreground. Grain is drying in squares on the ground.

spare the Israelites, and he will not spare idolatry-inclined Christians, notwithstanding their participation in the ordinances of the church. For the Israelites, participation in these "rites" was no substitute for obedience motivated by faith in the Lord; so also with the Corinthians.

Paul now selects four sins of Israel that reflect the shortcomings of the Corinthians: idolatry, sexual immorality, testing the Lord, and grumbling (vv. 7–10). (1) "Do not be idolaters" more properly means, because of the Greek tense, "Stop being idolaters" (v. 7). A later command says, "Flee from idolatry" (v. 14). The negative example of the Israelites follows. In the presence of the golden calf, they "sat down to eat and drink and got up to indulge in pagan revelry [*paizo*—play, amuse oneself, dance]" (quoted from Ex. 32:6, 19, which in the LXX speaks of dances [*choroi*]). The last item may be a euphemism for sexual immorality (mentioned by Paul in the next verse). Such immorality was often associated with the eating of food offered to idols (Acts 15:29). In Corinth, as in other cities, prostitute were often found at the temples. While Pau does not mention it, three thousand Israelite were killed on that occasion.

(2) The next Old Testament incident t which Paul refers is recorded in Number 25:1–9. Because of Israel's involvement i idol worship and attendant sexual immoralit with Moabite women, twenty-four thousan Israelites perished. Paul says the number wa twenty-three thousand. Several explanation for the apparent discrepancy have been pro posed: (a) There is a copyist's error in the LX which took the abbreviation for four (*trs*) t mean three (*treis*). (b) Numbers 25:5 seems t record a selective slaying of one thousand b the judges; this may account for the differenc in figures. (c) Twenty-three thousand wer slain in one day. (d) The two numbers hav been rounded off for a figure that was som where between the two.

(3) Paul goes on to admonish, "We shoul not test the Lord" (v. 9), and cites another Ol Testament example: the fiery serpents sent t chastise the people for "testing" the Lord (Nun 21:4–7; Ps. 78:18; also 95:8–9). Such testin took the form of complaining about the foo God had been supplying miraculously; the complaints resulted in some being destroyed b the serpents. "To test the Lord" is to see how fa one can go in stretching God's patience befor experiencing his judgment (Deut. 6:16). Ana nias and Sapphira are prime examples of peopl who agreed "to test the Spirit of the Lord" (Ac 5:9). Some Corinthians, it is clear, were testin God by compromising with idolatry.

(4) The final incident is cited in gener terms. "Do not grumble [lit., stop grumbling] says Paul, "as some of them did" (v. 10). Isra had a history of grumbling. Is Paul referring a specific incident? Two possibilities exis (a) This may refer to Korah's rebellion in cha lenging Moses' leadership (Num. 16:1–35 God's judgment came in the form of a chas opening up and swallowing Korah and tho associated with him. Subsequent murmuring b the people over the incident resulted in 14,70 additional persons dying by a plague sent b the Lord (vv. 41–50). (b) Numbers 14 recor grumbling in general, which resulted in th Lord's pronouncement that only Joshua ar Caleb of that generation would enter Canaa while the rest would perish in the desert.

The agent of judgment is here called "the estroyer" (*ho olothreutes*). This Greek xpression occurs in the LXX in reference to the ngel who destroyed the firstborn of Egypt Ex. 12:23; see Heb. 11:28). This may be the asis for the NIV's rendering, "the destroying ngel." Other Old Testament passages speak bout angels who destroyed the Lord's eneies (2 Sam. 24:16; 1 Chron. 21:12, 15; Chron. 32:21; Isa. 37:36; see also Acts 12:23; leb. 11:28).

Paul repeats that Israel's experiences serve s examples to believers and indeed "were writn down as warnings for us." He indicates that ey are not merely stories about Israel that ave no relevance for New Testament believrs. Christians are those "on whom the fulfillent [lit., the ends] of the ages has come" . 11; see also Heb. 9:26; 1 Pet. 1:20). All preious periods of history culminated in the comg of Christ to earth. They "are the ages past their totality" (Bruce, 93; see also Robertson nd Plummer, 207). They have reached their oal (Fee, 459). Paul speaks of it elsewhere as e time that had fully come (Gal. 4:4).

Those who are in Christ have already enred the messianic age, known to Jews as "the ge to come." Believers are those who have tasted ... the powers of the coming age" Heb. 6:5). Peter, on the Day of Pentecost, lentified the coming of the Spirit with the last days" (Acts 2:17), which in Jewish thinkg was contrasted with "this age," that is, the ge preceding the coming of the Messiah.

Even though believers have entered into the ew age of the Messiah, they must not be spirually overconfident. "If you think you are anding firm, be careful that you don't fall" . 12). They have begun the race but, like aul, must not risk being disqualified (9:27). ıst as Israel fell in the desert, they too may fall piritually.

If some feel insecure because of these arnings, Paul assures them that the temptaons and trials they experience are those that e common to all (v. 13; the word *peirasmos* eans either trial or temptation). But "God is ithful" in not allowing them to be tempted eyond their ability to resist. Believers may epend on him, for he is reliable and trustorthy. But this security is contingent on their wn faith in, and faithfulness to, God. They ust not put God to the test (v. 9) by edging as closely as possible to idolatry and its accompanying sins. But they can withstand temptations they are exposed to that are not of their own choosing. For each trial or temptation, the Lord provides *the* way of escape (the definite article is in the Greek text).

3.2.5. The Lord's Supper and Idol Feasts (10:14–22). In these verses Paul is less tolerant of Christians who eat meat sacrificed to idols than he appeared to be in chapter 8. Here, for reasons he will give, such eating is forbidden.

Verses 14–17 relate verses 1–13 to the Lord's Supper, with which Paul will deal at length in chapter 11. "Therefore" translates a strong adverbial conjunction that shows the logical connection between what precedes and what follows. Paul addresses these comments to "my dear friends" (*agapetos*—lit., "beloved"). The designation occurs elsewhere in this letter (4:14, 17; 15:58). He uses it also in 2 Corinthians 7:1, which follows a passage that deals with two closely related topics—the incompatibility between idols and those who are the temple of God, and the appeal to the beloved to separate and purify themselves (6:14–18).

The Corinthians had previously been urged to "flee from sexual immorality" (6:18; see also 2 Tim. 2:22). They are now told to "flee from idolatry" (1 Cor. 10:14). As with the previous admonition, the Greek present tense means "keep on fleeing" or "make it a practice to flee." Believers ought not to go knowingly into temptation and then expect to be delivered. "They must not try how near they can go, but how far they can fly" (Robertson and Plummer, 211). It has been pointed out several times that idolatry and sexual immorality were closely associated in the Corinthians' pagan world; it is not accidental that Paul's only uses of "flee" in this letter have these two sins as its object. Rather than rationalize why it was all right for them to participate in pagan temple feasts, the Corinthians ought to distance themselves as far as possible from them.

Paul appeals to them as sensible people (v. 15). Earlier, he noted that they prided themselves in their wisdom (1:18–2:16); now he says that if they are truly wise they will be able to judge for themselves the correctness of what he will say.

The two questions of verse 16, which deal with the Lord's Supper, must be answered in the affirmative. Yes, "the cup of thanksgiving for which we give thanks [is] a participation in the blood of Christ." Yes, "the bread that we break [is] a participation in the body of Christ." The expression "the cup of thanksgiving [*eulogia*, lit., blessing]" was the term Jews gave to the cup of wine that was drunk at the end of a meal and also to the third cup of the Passover meal, at which time a prayer of thanksgiving (or blessing) was offered. Paul uses this expression probably because it refers to the blessing, or thanksgiving, that Jesus pronounced at the Last Supper (11:24). It is the cup "blessed by the Lord, which we bless in our turn" (Héring, 93–94). The Communion cup is a "participation" (*koinonia*) in the blood of Christ, the Passover lamb (5:7). Some prefer the translation "fellowship" rather than "participation."

Paul does not say that Christians, at the Lord's Supper, in some way drink the blood of Christ. The phrase "the blood of Christ" is another way of speaking about his death, the pouring out of his life blood. Drinking the cup, therefore, means identification with Christ in his death and reception of its benefits.

The same general ideas apply to the bread. Bread was a necessary part of the Passover meal. In the Lord's Supper, it stands for the body of Christ, which was "broken" (or abused) just prior to, and also at, his crucifixion. Eating the bread therefore symbolizes participation in the benefits of Christ's death. Some do not interpret the bread in this way. In light of the following verse (v. 17), the bread and "the body of Christ" are both taken to mean the church (cf. 12:17; Rom. 12:5), which means that verse 16 is speaking about the common bond that Christians share among themselves.

While this may be true, the following should be noted: (1) Drinking the cup and eating the bread are parallel to each other (v. 16); each ought to be interpreted consistently with the other. (2) Paul later uses the term *body* to mean Christ's physical body, in the more extended passage on the Lord's Supper (11:24, 27). (3) The word for bread/loaf (*artos*) is not used anywhere else as a metaphor for the church, even though "body" (*soma*) is so used (12:12–27). The paradox in verse 17 is that believers constitute one body (the body of Christ) because they all "partake of the one loaf," which is his crucified body. Therefore the rendering of NIV (cf. also NASB, NRSV) is to be preferred: "Because there is one loaf, we, who are many, are one body, for we all partal of the one loaf." The loaf represents the cr cified body of Christ.

In verses 18–22, Paul notes that particip tion in the Lord's table and in pagan table feas are mutually exclusive (v. 21). He appeals aga to historic Israel for an example. "Do not tho who eat the sacrifices participate in the altar (v. 18). The Greek wording requires the answ "Yes." It is an accepted fact from Israel's hi tory that those who ate sacrificial food we related in a special way to all that the altar re resented. Both priests (Lev. 10:12–15) a those not priests (see 1 Sam. 9:10–24) ate suc food. It was an identification with the Lor who was present at the sacrifice. Paul th applies this to the present situation. Is meat sa rificed to an idol anything? The answer is n "Is an idol anything?"(v. 19). The answer aga is no (see 8:4). No change takes place in t meat itself; that is why, under certain cond tions, it is all right to eat it (v. 27). Likewise, t wood or stone material of an idol does not hav any reality in itself.

At best, pagans think they are sacrificing their gods. Paul now corrects this misconce tion. Their sacrifices "are offered to demon not to God" (v. 20; cf. Deut. 32:16–17; P 96:5; 106:36–37). Therefore those who e meat at the pagan altar or temple where it w sacrificed are identifying themselves—ente ing into fellowship with—the evil spirits which the meat was offered. Paul does not co tradict himself here. The material out of whic an idol is made is nothing, but the object wo shiped through an idol is a demon. Just Israel's authorized sacrifices united them wi God, so pagan sacrifices unite the worshipe with demons. Just as ancient Israel had choose between worshiping God and wo shiping pagan deities (demons), so th Corinthians must choose between "the Lord table and the table of demons" (v. 21).

"You cannot" occurs twice in verse 2 Worshiping at the Lord's table and at the tab of demons are mutually exclusive; there is n middle ground. In biblical usage, "table" an "food" are synonymous with fellowshi Christians must decide whether their fellov ship will be with the Lord or with demons. Th expression "the Lord's table" (see Luke 22:3 goes back to Malachi 1:7, 12, where it mea "altar" (cf. Ezek. 41:22; 44:16).

"Are we trying to arouse the Lord's jeal-
usy?" (v. 22) recalls the admonition not to test
e Lord (see comments on v. 9). God will not
are his glory with anyone or anything else.
e alone must be the object of worship. When
trong" Christians (8:9) participate in pagan
asts, they imply they are stronger than God,
ho forbids it.

3.2.6. Eating Meat Market Food (10:23–:1). Verses 10:23–24 give general guidelines
the entire subject of meat offered to idols, hich, by extension, apply to all matters of hristian conduct. "Everything is permissible" . 23) again repeats a saying of the Corinthi-s (see comment on 6:12). Paul may agree ith this in principle, but he also qualifies it. 'hatever a Christian does must be "benefi-al" and "constructive" (see comment on 8:1). must not be in the person's own interests, at is, insisting on one's freedom to do some-ing. Literally, Paul says, "Let no one seek his vn thing" (v. 24; Phil. 2:4). Rather, Christians ust seek the good of others. And ultimately, 'erything must be done "for the glory of od" (v. 31).

Verses 10:25–30 deal specifically with the estion of eating food *away* from temple asts that *may* have been offered to idols. bout this Paul says, "Eat anything sold in the eat market without raising questions of con-ience" (v. 25). All food originates with God, nce "the earth is the Lord's, and everything it" (v. 26, quoting Ps. 24:1). "Everything od created is good, and nothing is to be jected if it is received with thanksgiving" Tim. 4:4). Consequently, the Christian is etter off not trying to determine whether a articular item was part of a pagan sacrifice. he reason is that there is nothing inherently vil even in meat offered in pagan sacrifices, nce the meat does not undergo any change. he Christian is free to purchase and eat what-'er is sold in the marketplace without raising e question "of conscience." In other words, hristians ought not to be overly scrupulous in is matter.

But once again, the believer is not always ee to eat such meat (vv. 27–30). A believer ight be invited to an unbeliever's home for meal. (While not relevant to the main point, e see here that Christians could and did have ocial intercourse with pagan neighbors and iends; cf. 5:9–10.) The Christian was free to eat whatever was served (see Luke 10:7–8) and should not ask whether the food had been offered to idols. The situation was altered, however, if someone at table should say, "This has been offered in sacrifice [*hierothuton*]" (10:28). This Greek word differs from *eidolothuton*, the word previously used in 8:1, 4, 7, 10; 10:19 (which means something offered to an idol). This second term would have been used by Christians. The first term is neutral and would have been used by pagans or by diplomatic Christians not wishing to offend pagans. In this event, the instructions are clear: "Then do not eat it."

Who would have made the statement about the meat having been offered to idols? Possibly a considerate host who might not know the scruples of his Christian guest, possibly a pagan guest, or possibly a "weak" Christian. Of these three options, most likely it was the weak Christian, who, being overly scrupulous, might have inquired about the origin of the meat; after all, the word "conscience" would hardly apply to a pagan host or pagan guest. Thus Paul again appeals to "strong" Christians to defer to the weak Christian by not eating that food (see Rom. 14:13–16, 20–23; 15:1). Otherwise, if they eat, their freedom will be condemned ("judged," NIV) by the conscience of the weak Christian (1 Cor. 10:29b).

The thought continues in verse 30. Theoretically, Paul "may take part in the meal with thankfulness [*chariti*, from *charis*]," but he will be "denounced because of [it]." *Chariti* may also be translated "by grace," meaning that he may eat such meat because God's grace allows him to do so with thanksgiving. But he will not risk being "denounced" (*blasphemeo*) by exercising his liberty. This Greek verb may mean "slandered" (NASB), being "evil spoken of" (NKJV), or blasphemed, reviled (BAGD, 142).

Verses 10:31–11:1 conclude Paul's lengthy treatment of food offered to idols. He broadens the principles he has outlined to apply to "whatever you do." Whatever the Christian does, whatever decisions are made—all must be "for the glory of God" (v. 31; cf. 6:20; Col. 3:17), not for one's self-satisfaction in having asserted one's "rights."

Paul then broadens his comments by saying, "Give no offense" (v. 32, NASB, NRSV, NKJV; for a similar idea, see 8:13). Of special interest are the three groups a Christian must not offend—"Jews, Greeks or the church of God." A review of chapters 8–10 shows how Paul himself deferred to all three groups with a view to winning them (e.g., 9:19–22). His comment that "I try to please everybody in every way" must be understood in its context (see Rom. 15:1–3). When the truth of the gospel was the issue, Paul decisively did not try to please human beings (Gal. 1:10). In the present context, however, he seeks "the good of many, so that they may be saved" (1 Cor. 10:33; cf. 9:22), not his own good (10:24). Pleasing others is evil when the motivation is to curry their favor; it is good if its object is to lead them to the truth (Barrett, 245).

Paul had previously called on the Corinthians to imitate him (4:16; see also Phil. 3:17; 2 Thess. 3:7, 9). He now says, "Be imitators of me, just as I also am of Christ" (1 Cor. 11:1, NASB; see Eph. 5:1; 1 Thess. 1:6). A specific aspect of Christ's example they ought to follow relates to not pleasing oneself in matters of another's conscience (see Rom. 15:1–2 in light of ch. 14).

3.3. Christian Worship (11:2–34)

Most of the material in chapters 10–14 relates, in some way, to the subject of Christian worship. But chapter 11 focuses on two specific problems in the Corinthian church: (1) the veiling of women in public worship (vv. 2–16), and (2) the Lord's Supper (vv. 17–34
Before correcting the church on these two ma
ters, however, Paul begins by praising them

3.3.1. The Veiling of Women (11:2–16
Verse 2 may reflect the Corinthians' ow
claims to remembering Paul *in everything* an
holding to the traditions he passed on to ther
If so, it may be a mark of graciousness by hi
to accept their comments at face value, eve
though he has had to correct them all along an
will continue to do so (note v. 17). "Tradition
is a better translation of *paradoseis* tha
"teachings." It was a term used in Judaism fo
the oral transmission of religious teaching th
was sometimes (often?) contrary to the lett
and spirit of the written Word. Jesus called
"the traditions of men" (Mark 7:8; also c
Matt. 15:6). In the present context, the wo
refers to the essentials of the Christian fai
that were handed down orally (2 Thess. 2:1
3:6; 2 Tim. 1:5) and which eventually becan
part of Holy Scripture. The related verb *para*
didomi occurs here and in 1 Corinthians 11:2
"what I also passed on to you." Paul emplo
this verb when he talks about the Lord's Su
per (v. 23) and the resurrection (15:3).

Verses 3–6 introduce the problem of "li
erated" Christian women who felt no need
wear the conventional head covering in wo
ship. Paul does not begin his discussion of th
subject with the usual "now about" phra
(which indicates a matter abo
which the Corinthians had wri
ten him—cf. 7:1, 25; 8:1; 12:1
he may have learned of th
problem from a member
Chloe's household (1:11)
from the Corinthian men wh
had visited him (16:17).

Two explanatory notes mu
be made at this prelimina
stage. (1) The noun *veil/coverin*
(*kalymma*) does not occur in th
chapter, but related forms d
(*katakalypto*—cover [vv. 6–7
akatalyptos—uncovered [vv.
13]). (2) Even though the idea
a head covering is present,
need not be interpreted to mea
a covering of the face. "Shaw
might better convey the ide
Among both Jews and Greek
this customary covering for

Bedouin women still wear the shawl type of head covering that was traditional in the time of the New Testament. Describing propriety in worship, Paul writes to the Corinthians that "every woman who prays or prophesies with her head uncovered dishonors her head." He calls a head covering "a sign of authority on her head."

oman was regarded as modest and was espe-
ally appropriate in worship.

Paul begins with theological and biblical
ıalogies, focusing on the word "head"
ephale). The word has several meanings:
) literally, the uppermost part of the human
ody; (2) figuratively, someone in authority,
.ch as "the head of a government"
supremacy"; cf. Robertson and Plummer,
27); (3) figuratively, source or origin, such as
ıeadwaters," which means the source of a
ver (Fee, 503). The concept of a man having
ıperiority over a woman does not appear in
is chapter (though Héring sees it here [102]),
ıt woman owing her origin to man does (vv.
12). Thus, the third meaning applies in verse
"the head of the woman is man."

Even though *aner* may mean either man or
ısband and *gyne* either woman or wife, the
ontext clearly does not exclude unmarried
en and unmarried women. The passage
erefore deals with the man-woman, not the
ısband-wife, relationship. The threefold anal-
gy may be rearranged in descending order:
od is the source of Christ; Christ is the source
every man; man is the source of woman.

In an analogy, one must not look for logical
orrespondence at every point. Paul does not
tend to say that the Son has a historical ori-
n in the Father. Nor is he concerned here with
e fine points of later Trinitarian theology (see
omments on 3:23 and 8:6). If "God" in verse
is taken in the general sense of Deity and is
ot restricted to the Father, there will be less
fficulty in saying that the source or origin of
hrist is God. Nor can "Christ" mean the Son
nly in his earthly state, since "the head of
very man is Christ." This must refer to the
gency of the eternal Son in the creation of all
ings (8:6; Col. 1:16). Alternatively, it may
ıean that God is the head of Christ in refer-
ıce to Christ's incarnational work (Fee, 505).
inally, woman owes her origin to man (see
en. 2:18–23, which states that the woman's
rigin was Adam's rib). Paul says twice in this
ection, "Woman [came] from man" (1 Cor.
1:8, 12).

Even though the "liberated" women are the
roblem, Paul's discussion involves men as
ell—more by contrast, it seems, than as
eing part of the problem. "Every man who
rays or prophesies with his head covered [lit.,
aving down from the head] dishonors his
head" (v. 4). Some interpret the Greek clause to mean having long hair, like a woman's, arguing that Greek men had short hair. Others deduce that Paul is contending against a "unisex" hairdo, with possible undertones of homosexuality. Against this is the general context that speaks in terms of a man's cover or lack of cover (e.g., v. 7) for his head. Fee (506) cites Esther 6:12 (LXX), which says that Haman rushed home "with his head covered" (the same Greek phrase used here by Paul). Man "is the image and glory of God" (1 Cor. 11:7; cf. Gen. 1:26–27; Ps. 8:5) and therefore ought not to cover that image and glory when he prays or prophesies publicly. At this time it may not have been customary even for Jewish men to wear a cap or shawl when they prayed.

What is the "head" that man disgraces when he covers it? The answer may be twofold. He disgraces his own actual head, just as the woman who prays or prophesies with uncovered head disgraces her head (v. 7). But he also disgraces his metaphorical head—Christ (v. 3); some see a connection with 2 Corinthians 3:13–18, which speaks of the veil over Moses' face and of the unveiled face of the Christian, who is being transformed into the image of Christ.

Paul does not disapprove of Christian women praying or prophesying in public worship. He would not have hesitated to correct this practice if he felt it was irregular. But as he does later on the general subject of spiritual gifts in public worship (ch. 14), he must set down guidelines. Although Paul is chief among New Testament writers in contending that in Christ there is neither male nor female (Gal. 3:28), this "does not obliterate the distinction given in creation" (Barrett, 251). Therefore, the uncovered/unveiled (*akatakalyptos*) woman who prays or prophesies is like a woman whose head has been shaved (v. 5). Such a woman in those times was an object of disgrace; she disgraced her head, her husband, by wanting to be like him (Héring, 105). The Greek adjective could have the thought of loosed hair coming down over the shoulders and back; there is evidence that some pagan religions had frenzied women with "dishevelled hair and head thrown back" (cited by Fee, 509, fn.75). Paul is even stronger in the following statement. A woman who does not cover her head "should have her hair cut off"

(v. 6). Since a shaven head or short hair were both disgraceful, a Christian woman ought to cover her head.

Verses 7–16 compare and contrast men and women on the basis of creation. Paul's appeal has been that Christian women must not defy prevailing custom in the matter of a head cover, but his argument goes beyond the conventions of the time. Man is the glory of *God*, woman is the glory of *man* (v. 7). The thought seems to be that God will not share his glory with someone else; thus, the glory of man (the woman's head) must be covered in worship.

Pursuing the biblical basis for his restrictions, Paul says that man did not come from woman; he was a direct creation of God (v. 8). Nor was he created for (*dia*, "for the sake of") the woman, but the woman came from man and was created for his sake (v. 9). She was taken from his side (Gen. 2:21) for the purpose of being "a helper suitable for him" (v. 18). While Paul may be understood here as assigning a subordinate and perhaps inferior role to woman, his *main points* are that distinctions between the sexes must be maintained and that man is the origin of woman. Oneness in Christ does not override the reality of the created order.

"For this reason [the one just given]," says Paul, "and because of the angels [an additional reason], the woman ought to have a sign of authority on her head" (1 Cor. 11:10). The reference to angels has been variously interpreted. (1) Some say they are the clergy, a viewpoint difficult to hold, though some interpret the angels of the seven churches of Revelation 2–3 as the pastors.

(2) Some identify the angels as fallen angels or evil spirits, who will lust after women if they do not wear coverings. These scholars appeal to Genesis 6:1–2, which says that the "sons of God" married the daughters of men—sons of God being understood as fallen angels. This interpretation is inadequate, however. Not all interpreters agree that these sons of God are fallen angels; some identify them as godly descendants of Seth. Furthermore, why would uncovered women *in church*, and not everywhere, be a temptation to them? And would the mere wearing of a veil be a deterrent to such spirits?

(3) The viewpoint that they are "guardian angels" (i.e., that an angel protector is assigned to each believer) may also be discarded sin this interpretation has no scriptural basis.

(4) Others suggest that the phrase "becau of the angels" means "because the angels so" in the presence of God, their superior, covering their faces (Isa. 6:2), and that wom should therefore cover themselves in the pre ence of their superior, man (Robertson a Plummer, 235).

(5) Perhaps the best explanation is to s these beings as good angels who are prese at worship. Angels are indeed presented Scripture as "ministering spirits" to Christia (Heb. 1:14) and are themselves often assoc ated with worship. They may function observers, if not participants, when Christia gather for worship. An unveiled woman worship would offend them since she has vi lated the divine order of things (Robertson a Plummer, 233). Though not determinative f this interpretation, it is nevertheless interesti that the Dead Sea community of Qumr believed that certain imperfect individua such as the diseased and crippled, were to excluded from the assembly because "t angels of holiness [holy angels] are among t congregation" (1QSa 2:5–9).

Paul repeats the requirement that a woman head be covered, but he speaks of it as her ha ing "a sign of authority on her head" (v. 10 Some versions read "a symbol of authority her head" (NASB, NRSV, NKJV). A common expl nation, which may be correct, is that the Chri tian woman's veil, in contrast to that of a Jewe or pagan woman, was not a sign of subjectio but rather an indication of the authority she ha to pray and prophesy publicly. This is a attempt to explain the Greek text, which, how ever, does not contain the words "a sign/symb of." It reads simply, "the woman ought to hav authority. . . ." The preposition following th word "authority" (*exousia*) is *epi*, which may b translated "over." This commentator prefers simple explanation of that last clause of vers 10: The woman ought to have "authority (co trol)" over her head in the sense that *she* mu decide that it will be covered. This combinatio of the same two Greek words (*exousia epi*) found in a number of passages (e.g., Luke 9: Rev. 2:26; 6:8; 11:6; 14:18; 16:9; 22:14), ofte with the meaning of "control over."

Paul moves on to balance his previous com ments, which seem to have assigned a subo inate or inferior status to women. "In the Lord" (v. 11) there is basic equality and interdependence between men and women. Neither can exist or function apart from the other because, even though woman came from man originally (v. 8), every man comes into the world by means of a woman. But even though the sexes owe their existence to each other, ultimately "everything comes from God," to whom they are both accountable.

Paul had previously called on the believers to judge wisely on the matter of idolatry (10:15). He now says in regard to the matter at hand, "Judge for yourselves" (11:13), placing responsibility on their shoulders. A literal and stilted rendering, translating both pronouns in the Greek text, might be, "Judge among you yourselves." The matter to be judged is whether it is proper for a woman to pray with her head uncovered. It should be noted that the matter is one of propriety, not sin. Throughout this lengthy discussion, Paul never says that the woman who prays or prophesies with head uncovered is sinning. He has argued the matter on theological grounds; he now speaks on the basis of what is culturally acceptable.

Verse 14–15 begin with a question: "Nature [*physis*] itself teaches, doesn't it, that if a man has long hair, it is a disgrace to him?" (pers. trans.). *Physis* occurs a number of times in Paul's writings (Rom. 1:26; 2:14, 27; 11:21, 24; Gal. 2:15; 4:8; Eph. 2:3), but it is difficult to assign a uniform meaning to all the occurrences. Even though a strict translation reads "nature itself," the NIV rendering may well capture Paul's thought: "the very nature of things." Paul is appealing to the common, everyday customs of the times; it was considered culturally "natural" that a woman's hair would be long, a man's short ("nature," of course, has not endowed only women with the possibility of long hair). Furthermore, Paul well knew that in the animal kingdom, such as with lions, "nature" has endowed the male with longer and more abundant hair. The entire discussion ends with the idea that a woman's long hair is her glory, because it is given to her as a covering (*peribolaion*—a different word from that previously used, but having the same basic meaning).

Paul assumes that not everyone will be convinced by his reasoning; someone may want to be "contentious" about this matter (v. 16). Thus, his concluding remark is that "we have no other practice." It is not clear who is meant by "we"—whether Paul means himself (using the "editorial we"), or those with him at the time of writing, or all the apostles. But he is inclusive when he adds, "nor do the churches of God" (see on 1:2 for comments on "church"). The norm in all the churches was that women who prayed or prophesied had to be covered. Throughout his letters, Paul often uses the plural of the word "church." He probably has in mind the churches he himself founded, but the general thought is that all churches constitute the one universal church. He is careful to say that they are God's churches, not his. They are God's because the Lord purchased them "with his own blood" (Acts 20:28).

Based largely on this passage, some present-day Christians teach that it is wrong for a woman to cut her hair or for a man to have long hair. Others insist that a woman must have her head covered during times of worship. This commentary has mentioned several times that we must interpret this passage in light of current cultural expectations. One emphasis is that a Christian ought to conform to prevailing customs of his or her culture if such customs are not incompatible with Christianity. Another is that distinctions between the sexes ought to be maintained. These general principles should be observed regardless of the specific context in which Christians find themselves. On the other hand, Christians should be respected if they believe that for them it is wrong for a woman to cut her hair, for a man to have long hair, or for a woman to worship with head uncovered.

3.3.2. The Lord's Supper (11:17–34). This passage continues the theme of proper worship, with focus on the Lord's Supper—the only New Testament passage of any length on this observance. It is the earliest record of a Communion Service Liturgy as well as an important source for the theology of the observance. The Corinthians' abuses of the Lord's Supper gave rise to this treatment.

Verses 17–22 introduce the problem. The opening words are a bridge between the two sections of the chapter: "But in giving this instruction [about the veiling of women], I do not praise you" (v. 17, NASB). The NIV rendering ("In the following directives I have no

This mosaic of the Last Supper is in Jerusalem, at St. Peter in Gallicantu Church. Paul writes to the Corinthians about the proper observance of the Lord's Supper. He chastises them for eating regular suppers at the church, rather than in their homes, while ignoring the needs of the poor among them.

praise for you") fails to translate the connective "but" (*de*) and adds "following." Two observations are important: (1) Paul really says, "In commanding [*parangello*] this"—a verb used previously in 7:10. It has a note of authority. (2) Paul began the chapter by praising the Corinthians generally, but now he says he does not praise them in the matter just discussed. And after stating the current problems related to Communion, he says, "Shall I praise you for this? Certainly not!" (v. 22).

Paul's condemnation of their services is unqualified: "You come together not for the better but for the worse" (v. 17, NASB). What ought to be an occasion for mutual edification has instead become destructive to the unity of the church. Word has reached Paul about divisions (*schisma*) among the people when they come together as a church (v. 18). Again, we do not know the source of his information, but it distressed him even though he believed the report only "to some extent."

These divisions are different from those mentioned earlier, which were personality centered (1:10–12). Prior indications are that the congregation included the rich and influential as well as the poor and slaves (1:26–29). The differences in socioeconomic status were trag ically evident in their "coming together" fo worship (see also James 2:1–4). The divisions however, served one useful purpose: The showed which believers had God's approva by their not contributing to the scandal (v. 19 cf. also 2 Thess. 2:11–12). Paul had previousl said that he himself did not want to incur God' disapproval in the Christian race (1 Cor. 9:27) But the factionalism displayed by some coul only be ranked with "acts of the sinful nature listed in Galatians 5:19–21, the practice o which could disqualify someone from th kingdom of God.

The basic problem grew out of the custom of celebrating the Lord's Supper in conjunc tion with a "church supper" (vv. 20–21). In al likelihood the Communion observance wa informal, though details are lacking. Since th Christians did not have church buildings, thei meetings were often held in the larger home of the wealthy. They would come together "i one place [*epi to auto*]" (NKJV—a phras unfortunately not translated in some versions see also Acts 1:15; 2:1, 44). They cam together physically, but were divided spiritu ally. Meals for large groups were eaten in th ning room and the atrium, and the wealthy embers provided most of the food. The problem was that each of the wealthy "takes his own supper first" (1 Cor. 11:21, NASB), leaving little or nothing for the poor, who constituted most of the congregation. The rich could arrive early; the poor and the slaves could come only after completing their day's work. Thus the rich were filled and some were even drunk, while the poor remained hungry (v. 21).

The rich failed to understand that the meal was intended to be "the Lord's Supper," not their own. In the New Testament, the adjective *kyriakos* ("Lord's") occurs only here and in the phrase "the Lord's day" (Rev. 1:10). It entails the basic idea of possession; Paul goes on to explain in more detail why the Supper is indeed the Lord's. Paul remonstrates with the rich in several ways. He instructs them to eat and drink in their own homes prior to the scheduled time of the church dinner and observance of the Lord's Supper if they are so hungry, rather than eating their own dinner at the gathering and leaving little or none for the others (v. 21). By their misconduct they "despise the church of God and humiliate those who have nothing" (v. 22). Paul is saying the same thing in two different ways: (1) They are showing scorn for the church by the way they humiliate other believers, their conduct being motivated not by love but by self-interest; the suppers were anything but "love feasts" (Jude 12). (2) They fail to grasp the communion (fellowship, sharing) aspect of the Lord's Supper.

Verses 23–26 deal with the institution of the Lord's Supper. What Paul says on the matter is what he "received [*paralambano*] from the Lord" and also "passed on [*paradidomi*]" to the Corinthians. The two verbs used here are the language of tradition (see comment on v. 2). The subject "I" is emphatic—"I myself." Paul may have learned some *facts* of the Last Supper from others, but his *interpretation* of it probably came directly from the Lord. Such direct, unmediated communication from the Lord was not unknown to him (Acts 18:9–10; 22:18; 23:11; 27:23–25; 2 Cor. 12:7–9; Gal. 1:12; 2:2). He speaks of the night on which Jesus was betrayed (*paradidomi*); this verb seems to refer primarily to Judas's betrayal. But Paul also uses the verb when he says that Jesus was "delivered up because of our transgressions" (Rom. 4:25, NASB) and that God gave Jesus up for us all (8:32; cf. also Gal. 2:20).

Jesus "took bread, and when he had given thanks [*eucharisteo*], he broke it" (vv. 23–24). In the Synoptic accounts, Luke uses this same word for giving thanks; Matthew and Mark use *eulogeo* ("bless"). The difference in verbs is not significant, since the Jewish blessing over the Passover bread and wine was an expression of thanksgiving to God. The mention of thanksgiving is the reason why some Christians prefer to call the observance the Eucharist.

"This is my body" (as well as "This is my blood") qualifies as one of the most vigorously debated passages in all of Scripture, with interpretations ranging from the Roman Catholic view of transubstantiation to the Zwinglian view that the Supper is simply a remembrance of Jesus' death. These statements must be understood metaphorically: The bread signifies the body of Jesus, the cup his blood. Morris rightly observes that the gender of the demonstrative pronoun "this" in verse 24 is neuter, whereas the word "bread" is masculine. Jesus therefore could not mean that "this bread is literally my body." "It may refer to the whole action, as the second *this* does" in this verse (158).

Paul then adds two important statements about Jesus. Jesus' body, represented by the bread, is "for [*hyper*] you." The preposition *hyper* is used frequently in connection with the sacrificial death of Jesus; its basic meaning is "on behalf of, for the sake of"; Jesus died on our behalf. In addition, Jesus said, "Do [keep on doing] this in remembrance of me" (see also v. 26). As believers participate in the Lord's Supper, they are to recall the meaning of his death and be edified by doing so. But note that Jesus said "in remembrance of *me*," not "in remembrance of my death." Robertson and Plummer (246) suggest that this includes remembering his resurrection as well, implied in that the memorial was to be observed on the first day of the week. This remembrance is more than an intellectual exercise; it involves "a realization [experiencing] of what is remembered" (Bruce, 111). The Jewish Passover was a time for remembering God's deliverance of his people (Ex. 12:12; 13:9; Deut. 16:3); we note again that Christ, in his death, is our Passover (1 Cor. 5:7).

Much that has been said about the bread applies equally to the cup. But it is significant that Jesus did not say, "This cup is my blood," but rather, "This cup is the new covenant in my blood" (v. 25). The doctrine of transubstantiation is hard put to explain how "this cup" (itself a metonymy meaning "the contents of this cup") can literally be transformed into a covenant—the new covenant. The Old Testament predicted a new covenant that would supersede the old (Jer. 31:31–34; Ezek. 36:25–27; cf. Heb. 8:7–13; 9:18–20). The old covenant was instituted by means of a sacrifice, "the blood of the covenant" (Exod. 24:5–8). So the new covenant was inaugurated by means of the blood of Christ.

"As often as" (vv. 25–26, NASB) suggests that the observance is an important part of a congregation's life. Apart from the personal benefit believers receive, they also "proclaim the Lord's death" when they observe the Lord's Supper. The verb used here is often used for the proclamation of the gospel (e.g., 2:1; 9:14; cf. Acts 13:38; Col. 1:28). Robertson and Plummer comment: "The Eucharist is an *acted* sermon, an *acted* proclamation of the death which it commemorates" (249). It is to be a continual proclaiming of that death (the verb is in the present tense) until the Lord comes. This eschatological aspect of the Lord's Supper is not original with Paul, since Jesus himself at the Last Supper told the disciples that he would not again drink of the fruit of the vine "until that day when I drink it anew with you in my Father's kingdom" (Matt. 26:29; cf. also Mark 14:25; Luke 22:18).

Verses 27–34 begin with "therefore." Paul now makes clear what is required of those who sit at the Lord's table: They must not partake "in an unworthy manner," for in doing so they are "guilty of sinning against the body and blood of the Lord." The preceding context (esp. vv. 18–22) describes the *type* of person who partakes unworthily, though Paul will presently be more general in his application. The emphasis, however, is not so much on the spiritual state of the individual as it is on the *manner* in which one partakes. In one sense, no one is truly worthy of eating and drinking at the Lord's table, apart from appropriating God's grace and forgiveness by faith, whereby a person's heart becomes right with God. A person is unworthy only as long as he or she persists in sin. And sinning, specifically in this context, is against fellow believers, and consequently against Christ himself (see 8:12). Therefore, such a person shares in the guilt of those who crucified the Lord (see Heb. 6:6).

In view of this, believers ought to examine or prove themselves before partaking, lest they partake in an unworthy manner. "It is important to conduct a rigorous self-examination" (Morris, 161), as Paul admonishes in 2 Corinthians 13:5–6 and Galatians 6:4. This does not imply that Christians must be morally perfect or continually in a state of contrition and admission of unworthiness; it does mean that those who are unwilling to evaluate themselves spiritually should not participate. Otherwise they will participate "without discerning [*diakrino*] the body" (1 Cor. 11:29 NRSV)—presumably, the body "of the Lord" (words added in NIV; cf. v. 27).

Because the verb *diakrino* may also mean "distinguish," there is some merit in the view that some Corinthians failed to see a difference between this sacred meal and an ordinary meal. Another viewpoint is that by "body" Paul means the church as the body of Christ. While Paul does deal with this concept of the church elsewhere in the letter (10:17; 12:12–27), throughout this chapter the word "body" refers consistently to the crucified body of Christ.

By not properly discerning the body, such persons are not only guilty of the body and blood of the Lord; they also eat and drink judgment on themselves (v. 29). The judgment may take the form of weakness, sickness, or death (sleep). Such consequences are indications of the Lord's disciplining of his children (Heb. 12:5–11). The message is clear: Spiritual sickness may result in physical sickness and even death, though the manner in which this takes place is not given (cf. comments about the incestuous man at 5:5). Barrett (275) suggests (based on 10:20–21) that Christians who abuse the Lord's table expose themselves to the power of demons and that the demons are the cause of physical disease.

Regardless of the means by which the Lord's discipline takes place, it is wrong to generalize by saying that unrepented sin is the cause of all weakness, sickness, and death among Christians. Note again that the death of Christians—even chastened Christians—is called sleep (see comment on 7:39; see also

5:6, 18, 20, 51). As with the incestuous man, ›od's judgment is meant to be redemptive ıther than punitive. We are judged and disci-'lined by the Lord "so that we will not be con-emned with the world" (v. 32). On the other and, if we keep judging ourselves (*diakrino* ı the imperfect tense) rightly, "we [will] not ome under [God's] judgment" (i.e., his con-emnation, v. 31).

The severity of Paul's remarks is tempered s he once again addresses the Corinthians as my brothers," which is followed by some ımmarizing admonitions (vv. 33–34). They re simple and practical: When you come ›gether for the love feast, wait for one another. f you are so hungry that you cannot wait, then at at home prior to coming to the gathering.)bserving these basic guidelines will prevent ıeir coming under God's judgment. Paul has ıore to say about the Lord's Supper, proba-ly on matters of a less serious nature, which an wait until he comes to them in person (4:9; 6:5–9).

3.4. Spiritual Gifts (12:1–14:40)

This commentary gives a disproportionate mount of space to the subject of spiritual gifts. 'he reason is twofold: (1) Paul himself com-ıented more extensively on this topic than on ny other in the letter. (2) The nature of *The 'ull Life Bible Commentary* lends itself to an xtensive and intensive treatment of the sub-ect. The burgeoning Pentecostal and charis-ıatic movements of our day make a lengthy tudy both desirable and necessary.

Paul's reason for addressing this topic is wofold: (1) the Corinthians' misplaced mphasis on spiritual gifts rather than spiritual irtues, and (2) their overvaluation of certain ifts and virtual neglect or ignorance of others. 'hapter 12 is a general treatment of the subject f spiritual gifts; it includes the classical treat-ıent of the church as a body. The commentary vill indicate how these two topics interrelate. 'hapter 13, the classic love chapter, is egarded by some as an interruption in the flow f Paul's thought. The commentary will show hat the chapter is strategically placed to under-core the role of the primary virtue of love in elation to the gifts. Chapter 14 is essentially comparison and contrast of the gifts of ›ngues and prophecy, especially in the con-ext of corporate worship.

Rather than interrupt the flow of the exposition, this writer has chosen to append a number of articles at the end of chapter 14. Indication of an applicable article will be given at the appropriate juncture in the commentary.

3.4.1. Basic Teaching concerning Gifts (12:1–11). Paul gives a general criterion for determining the validity of inspired utterances (vv. 1–3). He then emphasizes the idea of the variety of gifts and their Trinitarian basis (vv. 4–6). He follows by giving a sample list of spiritual gifts, emphasizing that each believer receives something, as determined by the Holy Spirit (vv. 7–11).

3.4.1.1. General Criterion for Determining Gifts (12:1–3). The first three verses introduce the subject of spiritual gifts in an unusual way. "Now about" (see comment on 7:1) suggests that Paul is addressing a topic about which the Corinthians had inquired and about which he wants them to be fully informed (v. 1). He again addresses them as "brothers," even though the discussion of chapters 12–14 is largely corrective in nature.

Paul does not want the Corinthians to be ignorant about "spiritual gifts" (*pneumatikon*), a plural adjective meaning "spiritual" and used here absolutely. Because of its case ending, the Greek word may mean either "spiritual matters" (neuter) or "spiritual persons" (masculine). Most exegetes prefer the former. Even though the concept of "gifts" is not inherent in the word itself, the usage and context of the word in chapters 12–14 justify that interpretation for this word. (See Article B for a study of New Testament terms used for spiritual gifts.)

Paul calls attention first to the preconversion spiritual experiences of some of the believers in Corinth (v. 2; Eph. 2:1–3). The best exegetes differ on the precise translation of the original text, but the meaning is clear. The following translations are from sample versions:

> You know that when you were pagans,
> somehow or other you were influenced
> and led astray to mute idols. (NIV)
> You know that when you were pagans,
> you were led astray to the dumb idols,
> however you were led. (NASB)
> You know that when you were pagans,
> you were enticed and led astray to
> idols that could not speak. (NRSV)

> You know that you were Gentiles, carried away to these dumb idols, however you were led. (NKJV)

It is well known that in pagan religions the devotees were sometimes swept away in ecstasy. This is the meaning of "carried away" (*apago*), a word used elsewhere in the New Testament for leading someone away to trial, prison, or execution (Mark 14:44; Luke 23:26; Acts 12:19). At times such worshipers would also utter some kind of inspired speech, prompted by the spirit (demon) behind the mute idol (e.g., see Acts 16:16, the slave girl who followed Paul in Philippi; see also comments on 1 Cor. 10:20–21 for equating mute idols with demons). The Greek god Apollo was especially identified as a source of ecstatic, sometimes frenzied, utterances. In their pre-conversion days some believers were led by evil spirits; Paul teaches that, by contrast, believers are led by the Holy Spirit (Rom. 8:14; Gal. 4:8–9).

The apostle's comments at this point are an indirect rebuke to those Corinthians who placed inordinate value on utterance gifts like glossolalia and prophecy. He indicates that seemingly inspired utterances, in and of themselves, are not a mark of genuine spirituality since even pagans sometimes have such experiences. As he will show, the source and content of an utterance determine its genuineness, not the manner in which it is given.

The relation of the Holy Spirit to inspired utterances now receives attention (v. 3). Two examples are given. The first is that "no one who is speaking by the Spirit of God says, 'Jesus be cursed [*anathema*].'" To the contemporary believer, Paul's statement is a truism; the Spirit exalts, never maligns, Jesus (John 16:14).

Some say that Paul is speaking hypothetically here in order to balance his next statement ("Jesus is Lord"), and that in reality no Christian would conceivably make such an utterance. For those who see the statement as actually having been made, explanations are not lacking. "Jesus be cursed" may have been uttered by:

- an unbelieving Jew
- a Christian Gnostic, who rejected the man Jesus because of a philosophical belief that all matter, including the human body, is evil (such a person would curse the hi torical, human Jesus while blessing th spiritual, pneumatic "Christ")
- a recanting Christian brought before civ or religious (Jewish) courts
- a non-Christian speaking out in a Chri tian worship service
- a Christian inspired by a demonic spirit
- a Christian who resisted the Holy Spir coming on him or her, thinking it woul lead to a state of ecstasy or a trance c which the person was fearful (Barrett, 28(
- a Christian who misunderstood Paul' teaching that Christ became a curse for u (Gal. 3:13) (Morris, 165).

This last explanation may be the most reasor able. (See Article A for a study of "curse" a it relates to Christ.)

The second example, by contrast, is th "no one can say, 'Jesus is Lord,' except by th Holy Spirit." The confession that Jesus is Lor (Acts 2:36; Rom. 10:9; Phil. 2:11) may be th earliest creedal expression of the church. Pau is not saying that a simple, mechanical utter ance of those words is tantamount to divin inspiration (a parrot might be taught to spea the words!), but that whatever purports to b said by divine inspiration will exalt the Lor Jesus. We have here a suggestion that inspire utterances must be evaluated; Paul will sa more on this in chapter 14.

3.4.1.2. Variety and Basis of Gifts (12:4 6). Verses 4–11 present some basic aspects c spiritual gifts. In verses 4–6, one notice immediately the threefold recurrence of *diaire sis*, whose basic meaning is apportionmen variety, difference—hence "varieties" (NASB or "different kinds" (NIV). In the New Testa ment the word occurs only here. Its verb cog nate (*diaireo*) speaks of the Spirit "distributin to each one individually just as He wills (v. 11, NASB). This distribution of gifts by th Spirit to each member was designed to pro duce unity and harmony, in contrast to the divi sions that existed at Corinth (1:10; 11:18–19 12:25). By highlighting the thought of variety Paul implies that the Corinthians needed t expand their understanding of the nature, iden tity, and number of spiritual gifts.

Paul employs three terms for thes bestowals of the Spirit: gifts (*charisma*—v. 4) services (*diakonia*—v. 5), and working (*energema*—v. 6). Some see here a threefold categorization of spiritual gifts. It is generally acknowledged, however, that Paul is not suggesting such a division (see Carson, 34; Martin, 11; Bruce, 118). He is instead presenting three aspects of spiritual gifts (Fee, 586–87; Bittlinger, 20).

Charisma is used specifically for one gift of the Spirit, the gifts of healings (vv. 9, 28, 30), but it is also an inclusive designation for all the gifts (v. 31). It emphasizes that the gifts are the result of divine grace (*charis*), and consequently are not based on the recipient's worthiness. (See further in Article B.)

Diakonia stresses the purpose of spiritual gifts—service to the community of God's people. They are for "the common good" (v. 7), not for the recipient's personal benefit. This aspect is emphasized in chapter 14 in the recurring theme of edification of others as the divine purpose in bestowing gifts.

Energema is found in connection with only one gift—"effecting of miracles" (v. 10, NASB). The word directs attention to the source of gifts, God's "energy."

Each of the three terms is associated with a member of the Trinity—one of several Trinitarian passages in Paul's writings (e.g., 2 Cor. 13:14; Eph. 4:4–6; see also notes on 1 Cor. 2:7–16; 6:11). Even though these gifts are distributed by the Holy Spirit (vv. 7, 11), Paul places them in a Trinitarian context—"the . . . Spirit" (v. 4), "the . . . Lord [Jesus]" (v. 5), "God [the Father]" (v. 6). It is "the Spirit who gives, the Lord who is served, the God who is at work" (Barrett, 284). The caution is implied that one must not be preoccupied with the Spirit's role to the neglect of the other members of the Godhead.

3.4.1.3. Sample Listing of Gifts (12:7–11). Verses 7–11 contain a list of nine spiritual gifts, bracketed by significant statements about the role of the Holy Spirit in this matter. We note, first of all, the phrase "the manifestation of the Spirit" (v. 7). "Of the Spirit" could mean either that the Spirit is the source of the manifestation (subjective genitive) or that the gifts manifest the Spirit (objective genitive). Though both aspects are true, the general context favors the Spirit as the source. Paul does not speak of "manifestations"; rather, he speaks of "nine forms of spiritual 'manifestation'" (Bruce, 119). The singular form of the noun, plus the definite article, suggests that this is a comprehensive term for the gifts, analogous to the singular "fruit of the Spirit," which includes the nine virtues enumerated by Paul (Gal. 5:22–23).

The manifestation of the Spirit is given "to each one." The consensus of New Testament writers is that every believer receives at least one gift (Rom. 12:3; 1 Cor. 1:7; 3:5; 12:7, 11; 14:1, 26; Eph. 4:7, 11; 1 Peter 4:10; cf. Matt. 25:15). But the gifts are given to individuals not for their personal benefit, but for the benefit of others ("for the common good"). One exception would be the self-edificatory function of uninterpreted tongues (1 Cor. 14:4).

Before the gifts listed in verses 8–10 are discussed individually, some general comments are in order. (1) Gifts are given *to* individuals *for* the church. This comment would be unnecessary if it were not that some maintain the gifts are given to the church, not to individuals.

(2) The list is by no means exhaustive. A comparative study with other lists of gifts makes this obvious (vv. 28–30; also Rom. 12:6–8; Eph. 4:11). Perhaps Paul selected these nine gifts because they had a bearing on the situation in Corinth (Martin, 13).

(3) There is no special significance to variations in the phrases that mention the Spirit—"through [*dia*] the Spirit" (v. 8a), "by means of [*kata*] the same Spirit" (v. 8b), "by [*en*] the same Spirit" (v. 9a), and "by [*en*] that one Spirit" (v. 9b) (cf. Carson, 37). The reason for the changes is stylistic, for literary variety, rather than to point out distinctions in meaning.

(4) The individual gifts are not in airtight compartments. Sometimes they overlap, as with gifts of healings and workings of miracles. In other instances it is not easy to distinguish sharply one gift from another, as between a word of wisdom and a word of knowledge.

(5) Paul's use of the two related adjectives for "another" (*allos* and *heteros*) is, in my judgment, for stylistic reasons (Barrett, 285) and not to suggest a threefold classification that uses *heteros* to introduce the second and third groups that begin with faith and tongues, respectively. It is more natural to group prophecy and distinguishing between spirits with tongues and interpretation than with faith, healings, and miracles. Paul's list of nine gifts

divides more easily into the following three groups: (a) a word of wisdom, a word of knowledge; (b) faith, healings, miracles; (c) prophecy, distinguishing between spirits, tongues, interpretation of tongues. Martin concurs in this threefold division (12–14).

The first group (v. 8) consists of two closely related gifts. The Greek text does not have the definite article *ho* ("the") before *logos* (word) in either instance. Unfortunately, most English versions have inserted it. The NIV, for example, reads "the message of wisdom" and "the message of knowledge." Moreover, the NIV rendering of *logos* by "message" is also unfortunate; even though this is a valid meaning for *logos*, here it may convey something not intended by Paul. It is more advisable to translate *logos* with the basic meaning of "word" or "saying."

It is virtually impossible to establish a rigid distinction between these two gifts, even though the difference might have been clear to the Corinthians. It seems best to follow the advice of Rudolf Bultmann that "as a rule the distinction between related gifts must not be too precisely made" (*Theology of the New Testament*, 1951, 1:154). Nevertheless, one must still seek to understand what Paul is saying.

Attempts are often made to relate these gifts to the proclamation of the gospel or to insight into the plan of salvation, and to set them in contrast to the Corinthians' vaunted claim of having wisdom and knowledge. The early chapters of the letter, as well as chapter 8, address that issue. More specifically, some associate one or both of these "word" gifts with the gift of teaching (Lim, 65). It may not be necessary, however, to relate them to Paul's previous discussions of wisdom and knowledge but to look elsewhere for their meaning.

It is important to observe that the gifts are not wisdom and knowledge, but a "word of wisdom" and a "word of knowledge" (NASB). The first gift could validly be understood as "a wise saying" or "speaking wisely" (BAGD, 477). "In a difficult or dangerous situation a word of wisdom may be given which resolves the difficulty or silences the opponent" (Bittlinger, 28). The decision of the Jerusalem Council is a case in point: "It seemed good to the Holy Spirit and to us" (Acts 15:28). And Jesus promised that the Holy Spirit would speak through his disciples at times of persecution, to give them the right thing to say (Matt. 10:17–20; Luke 21:14–15). See, for example, Peter's response to his persecutors after being filled with the Spirit (Acts 4:8) and their astonishment at his defense (v. 13). Stephen provides another example. His persecutors "could not stand up against his wisdom or the Spirit by whom he spoke" (6:10).

The gift of a "word of knowledge" (NASB) may be understood as a knowledgeable saying. In one view, it is not knowledge that results from instruction guided by reason and that requires no illumination, but rather "the use of this knowledge, in accordance with the Spirit, for the edification of others" that constitutes the gift (Robertson and Plummer, 265). It is thus closely related to the ministry of teachers (Lim, 73).

According to Fee (59), this gift is most likely "'a special utterance' of some revelatory kind," suggested in part by its place between "revelation" and "prophecy" in 14:6. Still another view maintains that it is a "higher knowledge" that can be obtained only through revelation, a concept closely related to that of the Gnostics. The argument is based partly on the position of *gnosis* ("knowledge") between "revelation" and "prophecy" in 14:6 as well as its mention beside mysteries in 13:2, thus giving the term the significance of "supernatural mystical knowledge—a meaning which the word has in Hellenistic Greek, especially in the mystery cults" (BAGD, 163–64). Those who receive this higher knowledge would constitute an elitist group in the church—a concept rejected by Paul in his discussion of the gifts.

It is not necessary, however, to construe this gift in the above-mentioned ways. Instead, it seems more appropriate to understand "word of knowledge" as a receiving of knowledge of facts or events unobtainable or unknowable except by a revelatory act of the Spirit, which will in some way serve the community of believers. How, for instance, did Peter know that Ananias had withheld part of the money (Acts 5:1–4)? In any event, the revelatory aspect of this gift tends to associate it with the gift of prophecy (1 Cor. 14:24–25).

The second group comprises three interrelated gifts, sometimes called power gifts. "Faith" (*pistis*) as a spiritual gift must be distinguished from faith as trust and commitment, which includes saving faith as well as faith in the ordinary course of every believer's life. The one who receives the gift of faith has a divinely given conviction that God will reveal his power in a specific instance; it is an assurance that draws the supernatural into the natural world. As such it manifests itself in deeds; it is the type of faith that can move mountains (13:2; cf. Matt. 17:20; 21:21; Mark 11:22–24). This gift may be regarded as the antithesis of the "little faith" of which Jesus speaks.

The gift of faith does not function in isolation. It is a means to an end—usually miraculous healings and other displays of divine power (Gal. 3:5; see Matt. 15:28). Paul expresses the former of these gifts by using plural forms for both nouns—lit., "gifts of healings." "Gifts" could indicate that every healing is a special gift (Bittlinger, 37; Fee, 594); "healings" possibly calls attention to different types or categories of healings that involve "restoration of health to the whole man, body, soul and spirit" (Bittlinger, 34). The Gospels and Acts bear ample testimony to the wide diversity of healings effected by Jesus and his followers (see Mark 1:32–34). It is not necessary, however, to conclude that the plural implies that a specific gifted individual has a disease or group of diseases that he or she could cure (Robertson and Plummer, 266), or that it means different gifts for different kinds of sickness (Morris, 168).

The gift of "miraculous powers" (lit., "workings of miracles"; note again the plural in both nouns) is another way in which the gift of faith is manifested. The concepts of power and Spirit are closely associated in the writings of Paul and Luke (Luke 1:35; 24:49; Acts 1:8; 10:38; Rom. 15:19; 1 Cor. 2:4; Gal. 3:5; 1 Thess. 1:5; see also 2 Tim. 1:7). This gift appears to have been one of the marks of an apostle (Rom. 15:19; 2 Cor. 12:12; see Heb. 2:4), but was not restricted to them.

Healings are indeed miracles, but Paul has in mind divine interventions apart from healings since "miracle" (*dynamis*) is a general, comprehensive word for wonder-inspiring works of all kinds. Exorcism in particular could be one function of this gift (see Acts 16:18; 19:12) and was among the "extraordinary miracles" that God performed through Paul (19:11). Bittlinger (41) suggests it could include raising the dead (9:36–42; 20:7–12) and nature miracles (28:3–4). It would also include events such as the judgment of blindness on Elymas the magician (a reverse healing!) (13:9–11). The early disciples prayed for the Lord to perform healings as well as "signs and wonders" (4:29–30). The book of Acts is ample testimony that their prayer was answered.

Georg Bertram observes that the noun *energeia* ("working") is used in the LXX and the New Testament, along with the cognate verb *energeo*, almost exclusively for the work of divine or demonic powers (*TDNT*, 2.652–53). It may well be that this gift, perhaps more than any other, is bestowed for a "power encounter" with the forces of Satan. (See Article C for an additional treatment of this gift.)

The third group consists of four gifts that receive lengthy attention in chapter 14. "Prophecy" and "distinguishing between spirits" constitute one related pair, "speaking in . . . tongues" and "the interpretation of tongues" another related pair. Both prophecy and speaking in tongues are gifts of inspired utterance, the former in a language at the command of the speaker, the latter in a language unknown to the speaker.

The gift of "prophecy" (or the word "prophet") is the only gift that occurs in all of Paul's listings of gifts, an indication of its importance and priority in relation to other gifts (Rom. 12:6–8; 1 Cor. 12:8–10, 28–30; Eph. 4:11). It is both continuous and discontinuous with the Old Testament phenomenon of prophetic utterances. Its primary function is not foretelling the future but rather a telling forth of God's message. It is a spontaneous, intelligible utterance, usually delivered in the assembly of believers. Héring, mistakenly, says that because prophecy is to edify, exhort, and encourage (1 Cor. 14:13), "it coincides therefore to a large extent with what we call a sermon today" (127). (See Article D, plus the commentary on 1 Corinthians 14.)

The gift of "distinguishing between spirits" is a corollary of the gift of prophecy. Its primary function is the assessment of prophetic utterances, though it may be applicable in other situations as well. It is the ability to discern between human, divine, and demonic influences in a purported prophecy. Allusions to it are in other key passages: "Do not treat prophecies with contempt. Test everything. Hold on to the good" (1 Thess. 5:20–21). "Do not believe every spirit, but test the spirits to see whether they are from God" (1 John 4:1). The Didache, a late first-century writing on church life, says that "not every one that speaks in the Spirit is a prophet, but only if he has the ways of the Lord" (*Did.* 11:8). (See Article E and the commentary on 14:29 for a further treatment of this gift.)

"Kinds of tongues" (*gene glosson*) refers to the gift of speaking in languages unknown and unlearned by the speakers, often called glossolalia (a combination of two Greek words: *glossa*, "tongue/language," and *lalia*, "speech"). "Kinds" (*genos*) may mean two basic types of languages—human, identifiable languages and spiritual, heavenly, or angelic languages. Paul expresses this phenomenon in a number of ways: to "speak in tongues"/*lalein glossais* (12:30; cf. 13:1; 14:5, 6, 18, 23, 39); to "speak in a tongue"/*lalein glosse* (cf. 14:2, 4, 5, 13, 27); "kinds of tongues"/*gene glosson* (12:10, 28); "tongues"/*glossai* (13:8; 14:22); "tongue"/*glossa* (14:9, 14, 19, 26). The expression *lalein glossais* occurs elsewhere (Mark 16:17; Acts 2:4; 10:46; 19:6).

The gift of "interpretation of tongues" interprets or translates a glossolalic utterance for the edification of the congregation. It may be given either to the person who has spoken in tongues (1 Cor. 14:5, 13) or to someone else (12:10; 14:26–27). (See Article F and the commentary on chapters 13 and 14 for a discussion of tongues and interpretation of tongues.)

According to some commentators, Paul considers tongues to be the least of the gifts because, together with interpretation of tongues, it is listed last. If this were the case, then the first gift—a word of wisdom—would be the most important gift, the second gift would be next in importance, etc. Prophecy, about which Paul speaks highly, would be rated only sixth in importance. This rationale of assigning relative importance to gifts goes contrary to the general thrust of Paul's argumentation when he talks about the members of the body (vv. 12–17). A simpler and more natural explanation accounts for the position of the last four gifts in the list: They are the ones with which Paul will deal in detail in chapter 14 and so are placed in a literary position closer to that discussion.

Paul concludes his foundational remarks on spiritual gifts with the statement, "But one and the same Spirit works [*energeo*—see v. 6 for the noun form] all these things, distributing to each one individually just as He wills" (v. 11, NASB). The apostle highlights several aspects of the Spirit and his ministry: (1) He is the "one and the same Spirit," suggesting that it is the one Holy Spirit who energizes all the gifts. The implicit appeal to the Corinthians is for unity in this matter, rather than the divisions to which they were prone. (2) The Spirit distributes "to each one individually." There is a suggestion that the gift is suited to the person to whom it is given; in a sense, each gift is "personalized." The gifts are not distributed indiscriminately. In addition, each believer is the recipient of a gift (see also v. 7). (3) The distribution of the gifts is according to the sovereign will of the Spirit.

3.4.2. One Body, Many Members (12:12–27). This extended section, bracketed by two passages that focus on spiritual gifts (vv. 1–11 and 28–31), seems to be an intrusion. But, as Martin (15) notes, the gifts "act as a bridge between 'one Spirit' [v. 11] and 'one body' [v. 12]." Previously in the letter, Paul presented the church under the imagery of a field and a temple (3:9–17). He now devotes considerable space to the metaphor of the human body (see also Rom. 12:4–8; Eph. 1:22; 4:4, 15; 5:23; Col. 1:18; 2:19).

In the ancient world, the human body was used by the Stoics as an analogy for the world or the state, composed of individual citizens. For Paul, the church is Christ's body (1 Cor. 12:27), which speaks of an indissoluble and inseparable link between him and his people. This is akin to the Hebrew concept of corporate personality, in which one individual represents and is considered to be the embodiment of a group. There is a hint of this in Jesus' words to Paul on the Damascus road, "Why do you persecute me?" (Acts 9:4; also 22:7; 26:14), as well as Paul's statement that "when you sin against your brothers . . . you sin against Christ" (1 Cor. 8:12).

Verses 12–13 introduce the metaphor and lay the groundwork for what follows. How does this metaphor relate to the preceding and following contexts that deal with spiritual gifts? Lim asks, "Is not Paul talking about the different functions of the gifts in his analogy between believers and the human body?" (66). In Paul's treatment of gifts, the emphasis is on the complementing themes of unity and diversity; the various gifts are "for the common good." They originate with "one and the same Spirit," who distributes them to each believer. The same ideas carry over in his discussion of the human body, which is composed of many different members, each of which is necessary for the well-being of the body (v. 12). The concepts of the body of Christ and of spiritual gifts in the church must be placed side by side. In a meaningful sense, individual members of the body represent individual gifts or functions in the church. When Paul says, "so it is with Christ," Fee (603) may be correct in saying that "Christ" is a shorthand form for the "body of Christ," the church, and he finds "clear evidence" for this in verses 27–28.

Verse 13 is the most disputed passage in this section. The discussion revolves around the meaning of the two clauses and how they are related to each other: "We were all baptized by one Spirit into one body" (clause 1), and "we were all given the one Spirit to drink" (clause 2). In a nutshell, what is the connection, if any, of this verse with John the Baptist's prediction that Jesus would baptize in the Holy Spirit? The main interpretations follow.

(1) Both clauses refer to the Spirit's work in conversion and are an example of Hebrew synonymous parallelism. The baptism is the same as that predicted by John the Baptist. It is the view of most scholars (among others, Bruce, 121; Carson, 42–49; Martin, 24; Robertson and Plummer, 272). This interpretation is rejected by most Pentecostals.

(2) Both clauses refer to the Spirit's work in conversion and are an example of Hebrew synonymous parallelism—but this baptism is different from the one predicted by John. This is the position of the writer of this commentary and some other Pentecostals. (See Article G, which opts for "by one Spirit" rather than "in one Spirit.")

(3) Clause l refers to conversion and clause 2 to a subsequent work of the Holy Spirit. This would be a case of Hebrew synthetic parallelism. It is the position held by some Pentecostals, including Howard Ervin in *Conversion-Initiation and the Baptism of the Holy Spirit* (98–102).

(4) Both clauses refer to a work of the Spirit subsequent to conversion—also, therefore, an example of Hebrew synonymous parallelism. It is the position of some Pentecostals.

(5) Clause 1 refers to baptism in water, and clause 2 to the Lord's Supper. But the aorist (simple past) tense of "drink" as a completed action eliminates an allusion to the Lord's Supper.

Those who have been baptized into the one body include Jews or Greeks as well as slave or free (Gal. 3:27; Col. 3:11). Social and ethnic/religious distinctions within the church disappear when believers become members of the body of Christ. But at what point does the incorporation take place? Does baptism into Christ occur at the time of "water" baptism? The New Testament church would not have asked these questions, since new converts were baptized immediately after placing faith in Christ, or as soon thereafter as possible. The two events took place in such close proximity that for all practical purposes they were regarded as one and the same. Many today, whether sacramentalists or not, take the position that "water" baptism is necessary for salvation and indeed is the means by which one becomes a member of Christ's body. This, they maintain, accords with Paul's statement that there is "one baptism" (Eph. 4:6).

Others maintain a distinction between the two baptisms, saying that one becomes a member at the time of faith in Christ and that baptism in water, though commanded by Jesus, does not effect membership in the body of Christ but rather depicts it. In other words, one is already a member at the time of submitting to water baptism. Their response to the question about "one baptism" is that Paul in Ephesians is speaking about the one indispensable baptism for becoming part of the "one body," which is the work of the Spirit at the time of initial faith. The same line of reasoning is followed by virtually all Pentecostals, who also teach a baptism in the Spirit distinct from both baptism into the body of Christ and water baptism.

The language of "we were ... given ... to drink" recalls Jesus' invitation to the thirsty to come to him and drink, and John's identification of water with the Holy Spirit (John 7:37–39).

Verses 14–20 stress the importance of all members of the body as well as the necessary diversity that exists within the body. Even though the body is a unity, it is made up of many parts (vv. 14, 20), and no one part ought to feel inferior to the others. Apparently the dissensions within the congregation had a depressing effect on some members, who thought they were not as gifted as others. Paul's remarks are designed to encourage such members. The foot, hand, ear, eye—each is essential to the well-being of the whole (vv. 15–17). No member should be discontent with his or her function and feel unworthy to be in the body, nor should such a member covet someone else's function in the body.

God has appointed ("arranged," NIV) the members of the body "just as he wanted them to be" (v. 18). This links with what Paul said previously, that the Spirit gives gifts to each one "just as he determines" (v. 11), as well as with what he says in the next section, that God "has appointed" (same verb) the various leaders and other gifts in the church (v. 28).

The body would be unable to function properly without one of its members (v. 17). Furthermore, it would not be a body, but a monstrosity, if it consisted of only one member (v. 19). So even the member that seems to be lowly contributes to the whole. The repetition of the idea of unity in diversity concludes this part of the discussion (v. 20). Since the body is an organism, the key thought is that of unity, not uniformity.

Verses 21–27 are addressed to those members who feel superior to other members. The previous paragraph emphasized that every member is important; this paragraph cautions against an arrogance that wishes to dismiss others as unimportant or unnecessary. No one member can say to another, "I don't need you!" (v. 21). The various members are dependent on one another.

Paul proceeds to speak of parts of the body that "seem to be weaker" but are nevertheless "indispensable" (v. 22). The reference most likely is to the internal organs. In an ancient fable, certain members of the body discovered this truth when they tried to starve the stomach because, they thought, it did not work as they were required to do. They learned, to their distress, that the stomach was indeed dependent on them, but that they in turn were dependent on the stomach. Sometimes in society, the humbler workers are as necessary and even more necessary than those in higher positions (Robertson and Plummer, 275).

The parts that we think are "less honorable" we treat "with special honor" (v. 23a), and the parts that are "unpresentable" are treated "with special modesty, while our presentable parts need no special treatment" (vv. 23b–24). Morris (173) suggests that the "special honor" we give to the less honorable members is to clothe them in seemly fashion, and that our treament of the unpresentable organs probably refers to the reproductive and excretory organs. This variety is by God's design; he has "combined [blended, mixed] the members of the body" (v. 24).

What Paul has said applies, to be sure, to the church on a universal level, but his primary concern is with the local Corinthian church. The purpose of the body-members discussion is twofold: (1) "that there should be no division [*schisma*—see 1:10] in the body," and (2) "that its parts should have equal concern for each other" (v. 25). The two clauses are joined by the strong adversative conjunction *alla* ("but"): no division (the negative), but equal concern for one another (the positive). These concerns have a specific application to what Paul said previously about the problems connected with the Lord's Supper (11:17–34) and are reflected in members' sharing both the sufferings and the joys of another member (12:26). Members of the body cannot distance themselves from other members. Whether they realize it or not, they, as fellow members of the body, share in the suffering of others. Likewise, when one member is honored, the entire body benefits.

Verse 27 is transitional, encapsulating verses 12–26 and leading into verses 28–31. The Greek text begins emphatically with the plural pronoun *hymeis* ("you"); the first clause may be paraphrased: "And you all constitute Christ's body." Then, says Paul, you are "individually members of it" (NASB). His use of the pronoun in the second person plural, rather than the first person plural ("we"), indicates that the primary application of what he has said is to the Corinthian congregation—and any other local congregation.

3.4.3. Additional Gifts (12:28–31a). Paul introduces the nine gifts in this list with the words, "in the church God has appointed . . ." (v. 28; see v. 18). "In the church" may be understood either universally or locally. The universal meaning applies at least in the case of apostles, who were itinerant (Barrett, 295). The other gifts would function primarily, if not entirely, on the local level. Some, however, contend that the primary meaning is the universal church, of which a local congregation is an "outgrowth" (Martin, 31).

The list includes some gifts—apostles, prophets, teachers, helps, administration—that are not in the previous list (vv. 6–8). The first three ("apostles . . . prophets . . . teachers") are clearly distinguished from the others on three points. (1) By their identification as "first," "second," and "third," they hold chronological and functional priority over all other gifts, for by them the church is founded and built up (Barrett, 295). (2) They are separated from the rest of the gifts by the Greek particle *men* ("on the one hand"), while the adverb *epeita* ("then") introduces the others. The numerical sequence is dropped after the first three. (3) The triad is presented in terms of persons; the rest of the gifts in verse 28, contrary to some translations, are activities. Bruce says that the first three exercise the three most important ministries (122), and Barrett calls them "the threefold ministry of the word" (295).

Paul occasionally uses the word *apostolos* ("apostle") in a wide sense to denote the function of having been sent (Rom. 16:7; 2 Cor. 8:23; Phil. 2:25), but generally he uses it in the more restricted sense of Christ's witnesses who have seen the risen Lord and have been definitely commissioned by him to preach the gospel (see comments on 1:1 and 9:1). The term *apostle*, in its more restricted sense, implies a nonrepeatable, once-for-all ministry of certain individuals (usually understood to be "the Twelve" and Paul). This restricted meaning is clearly seen in Ephesians 2:20, where "apostles and prophets" jointly have a unique ministry. They are the foundation of the church (cf. also Rev. 21:14), the ones to whom and through whom the mystery of the gospel was revealed (Eph. 3:4–6), and the ones who, like the current list, head up the list of leadership gifts (4:11).

The word *prophetes* ("prophet") does not have a uniform meaning in the New Testament. It may represent a distinct group in a congregation (Acts 13:1), or it may be used broadly for anyone on whom the prophetic impulse comes. Even though in practice the gift of prophecy is limited to a relatively small circle, Paul indicates that, at least theoretically, it is available to all (1 Cor. 14:5, 24, 31) (Fee, 621). Some passages indicate that prophets moved about (e.g., Matt. 10:41; Acts 11:27–28 with 21:10; 15:22, 32). The *Didache* also talks about peripatetic prophets, though this should not be generalized to mean that all prophets did so (Morris, 175; Barrett, 295).

The gift of prophecy is not restricted to men. Joel's prophecy, quoted by Peter on the day of Pentecost, said, "Your sons and daughters will prophesy" (Acts 2:17). Philip had four unmarried daughters who prophesied (21:9), and Paul spoke previously in this letter about women in the church who prophesy (1 Cor. 11:5). (Additional comments on the gift of prophecy will be found in the notes at 12:10 and throughout chapter 14, as well as in Article D.)

"Teachers" (*didaskalos*) constitute another important group of leaders in the church. They are referred to both in personal terms as "teachers" (1 Cor. 12:28–29; Eph. 4:11; cf. also Acts 13:1; 1 Tim. 2:7; 2 Tim. 1:11; James 3:1) and in impersonal, more general terms as "if [a man's gift] is teaching" (Rom. 12:7; cf. Gal. 6:6). Teachers presumably were mature Christians who instructed others in the meaning of the Christian faith. Included in this might be an exposition of the Old Testament Scriptures (Barrett, 295; Héring, 133).

In Ephesians 4:11, does Paul combine the gifts of pastors and teachers into one leadership role? Does he mean "pastor-teachers" or perhaps "teaching pastors," or is he speaking about two distinct ministries? Equally competent scholars disagree on the interpretation of this verse. This may be another example of the imprecision with which some charismatic terminology is used. But there is sufficient indication elsewhere, as noted above, that teaching constitutes a distinct ministry. Nevertheless, the pastor also has a teaching role. Note how one qualification for an elder/pastor is that he be "able to teach" (1 Tim. 3:2). This, then, is another example of overlapping in spiritual gifts. Similarly, it is possible that the "prophets and teachers" of Acts 13:1 are not two distinct groups but one group exercising both ministries.

Two previously unmentioned gifts are included in the remainder of the list—helps (*antilempsis*) and administrations (*kybernesis*). *Antilempsis* conveys the basic idea of help or support (Gerhard Delling, *TDNT*, 1.375–76; Barrett, 295). Héring speaks of "works of charity" (133). In its verb form the New Testament uses the word for the serious concern of a right relationship with a fellow believer (1 Tim. 6:2) or for regard for the weak (Acts 20:35) (Delling,

1.375). The gift of *kybernesis* enables one to serve as a helmsman (the basic meaning of the word is steering or piloting) to the congregation (the related noun *kybernetes* denotes the pilot or captain of a ship; see Acts 27:11; Rev. 18:17). But the precise scope of this activity is undefined. The gift likely is the same as the gift of leadership (see Rom. 12:8; 1 Thess. 5:12; Heb. 13:7, where, however, different words are used).

Likely, these last two gifts foreshadow the work of bishops/overseers and deacons, whom Paul does not mention in his earliest letters (Barrett, 296; Héring, 133; Robertson and Plummer, 281; Martin, 33; Fee disagrees strongly, 622, fn. 22). They are mentioned for the first time in Philippians 1:1.

Verses 29–30 are a series of questions, each of which requires a negative answer. The clearest way to translate the questions is: "Not all are apostles, are they? Not all are prophets, are they?" etc. No one gift is given to everyone, nor can one person lay claim to all the gifts.

This series of questions contains one that is more controversial than the others: "Not all speak in tongues, do they?" This seems to contradict the classical Pentecostal teaching that all will speak in tongues at the time they are baptized in the Spirit. The Pentecostal response is that Paul's questions here deal with ministries and gifts as they relate to fellow believers and perhaps to outsiders. His question about the following gift, the interpretation of tongues, relates both it and glossolalia to a worship context. Speaking in tongues, in the sense of an audible expression in a congregational setting that must be interpreted, is indeed not given to all. But this does not rule out speaking in tongues on a personal, noncongregational level. Paul does speak later of the self-edificatory function of tongues. Would God deny to any Christian any means of spiritual edification? It is at least suggestive, if not programmatic, that Luke reports in Acts 2:4 that on the day of Pentecost, all who were filled with the Spirit spoke in tongues, since the Greek adjective *pantes* ("all") is the subject of both clauses.

Verse 31a ("Eagerly desire [*zeloo*] the greater [*meizona*] gifts [*charisma*]") is the subject of considerable discussion, occasioned largely by the verb form *zeloute* (which may be a command, a statement, or a question) and the adjective *meizona*.

A basic question is: Are there indeed "greater" gifts? The concept seems to militate against much of what Paul said previously, especially in his analogy of the body. But on the other hand, he does assign priority to some gifts. In a parallel passage, for instance, his command is to earnestly desire especially the gift of prophecy (14:1). If some gifts are indeed greater than others, it would be on the basis of their ability to build up the church. One emphasis in chapter 14 is that, in the church, gifts that are intelligible are superior to those that are not (such as tongues unaccompanied by an interpretation).

Perhaps the simplest as well as the most common interpretation of verse 31a takes the words at face value: Paul is urging the Corinthians to eagerly desire the gifts that are truly greater, that is, those that will edify the body. In favor of this understanding is Paul's parallel statement, "Eagerly desire spiritual gifts, especially the gift of prophecy" (14:1).

Another interpretation, which translates the clause as a statement rather than a command, is that it is a rebuke: "You are eagerly desiring the greater gifts." In other words, the Corinthians are earnestly seeking what *they* consider to be the greater gifts (cf. 14:12). The last three words could be enclosed in quotation marks to indicate *their* terminology. Even if some gifts are indeed greater than others, the Corinthians are mistaken as to the identification of those gifts and their striving after them (Bittlinger, 73). Martin endorses the essence of "this eminently reasonable suggestion" (34–35).

A related interpretation is that Paul is quoting from the Corinthians' letter in which *they* say, perhaps reflecting an exhortation of the "spiritual" persons to those less "spiritual": "Eagerly desire the greater gifts." In their judgment the greater gifts would include glossolalia.

A final suggestion is to translate the sentence as a question: "Are you earnestly desiring the [truly] greater gifts?" In this interpretation, Paul is indirectly rebuking them that the gifts they desire are not the greater ones.

While all of the above interpretations are possible, the first is the best. Paul is appealing to the Corinthians to eagerly desire the gifts that will most edify others.

Verse 31a requires two other comments. (1) The verb *zeloo*, while it may denote envy, is properly understood here in its other basic meaning—"be zealous for, earnestly desire." But Paul's appeal seems to contradict earlier statements that the Spirit/God decides on the distribution of gifts (vv. 11, 18, 28). A resolution is not difficult: Believers may express their desire in this matter, trusting that God will honor them while at the same time being receptive to whatever gift(s) he chooses to bestow. (2) The occurrence of *charisma* (see v. 4) indicates that it and *pneumatikon* (v. 1; 14:1) are interchangeable words for spiritual gifts (see Article B).

3.4.4. Love and Its Relation to Gifts (12:31b–13:13). The great Love Chapter of the Bible is not a digression. Neither is it the interpolation of an already existing composition, whether written by Paul or someone else, into the discussion of spiritual gifts. Its references to a number of spiritual gifts would have made little sense if it had already existed in isolation. That is, its mention of tongues, prophecy, mysteries, knowledge, and faith indicates it was written for this specific occasion and that it formed a necessary bridge between the existence of the gifts (ch. 12) and their operation (ch. 14).

Several preliminary notes are in order: (1) The word for love, *agape*, was not in common use prior to the first century. The New Testament writers, however, present it as the cardinal Christian virtue. It occurs about 115 times in the New Testament.

(2) Love is not a spiritual gift, given alongside those Paul discusses in this context and elsewhere. It is, instead, a virtue, an aspect of the fruit of the Spirit (Gal. 5:22–23). "Love is not a *charisma* [gift] but an entire way of life" (Carson, 57).

(3) The essence of love is sacrificial giving of oneself, sometimes on behalf of an unworthy object. The supreme examples are God himself (John 3:16) and Jesus (Eph. 5:25).

(4) Paul does not place love in opposition to the gifts, implying that one must choose between the two. Properly understood, he teaches both-and. In 14:1, the Corinthians are urged to pursue both love and the spiritual gifts.

(5) Paul does not question the validity of the gifts but the loveless manner in which they may be manifested.

(6) The chapter division between verses 31a and 31b is unfortunate. Chapter 12 is better terminated with verse 31a.

3.4.4.1. Introductory Comments on Love (12:31b–13:3). These verses are introduced by, "And I show you a still more excellent [*kath' hyperbolen*] way" (v. 31b, NASB). The comparative "more" better suits the context than the superlative "most." "The most excellent way" (NIV) is a questionable rendering, for at least two reasons: (1) The article "the" is not in the Greek text; (2) Jesus is *the* way (John 14:6), not love. The phrase *kath' hyperbolen* may be translated "a far better way" (BAGD, 840).

Verses 1–3 stress the indispensability of love, saying that possession of gifts as well as self-sacrificing acts do not benefit a Christian who does not have love. The gifts and other acts, however, are not nullified by its absence. Paul speaks in the first person to make his point more effective: "I am only a resounding gong or a clanging cymbal" (v. 1), "I am nothing" (v. 2), "I gain nothing" (v. 3)—these are the results of the manifestation of gifts and the performance of sacrificial acts by a person without love. The individual will not benefit from them, even though others may.

Tongues, prophecy, knowledge (shorthand for "word of knowledge"?), mysteries (which are understood perhaps by "word of wisdom and/or knowledge"), faith—these are mentioned in the preceding chapter. In the present passage, tongues is mentioned first and receives the lengthiest treatment, probably because its abuse was a serious problem in the Corinthian church.

"Tongues [languages] of men and of angels" has been variously interpreted. (1) It is poetic language for all consummate verbal communication. The Jerusalem Bible translates it, "All the eloquence of men or of angels." (2) "Tongues of men" means eloquent communication not inspired by the Spirit in understood languages; "tongues of . . . angels" means glossolalia (Barrett, 300; Martin, 43). (3) The entire expression refers to speaking in tongues (Morris, 177; Bruce, 125; Héring, 135), either in human languages ("tongues of men") or in spiritual/heavenly languages ("tongues . . . of angels") (Fee, 630). This third option is the position adopted by this commentator (see further in Article F).

"Tongues . . . of angels" may refer to the belief, found in some extrabiblical literature, that angels have their own languages. In the Pseudepigrapha, Job's daughters are said to have spoken in the various languages of angels (*T. Job* 48–50). The rabbinic tradition refers to Johanan ben Zakkai, a pious man who was able to understand the speech of angels. In addition, some see angelic or heavenly languages in a few New Testament passages (e.g., 1 Cor. 14:2; Rev. 14:2–3).

"Gong" was a musical instrument, but it is not certain that gongs were used at this time in pagan worship. Cymbals, however, were so used, some think to gain the god's attention or to drive away demons (Barrett, 300). Their sounds would have been familiar in Corinth from their use by worshipers of Dionysius and Cybele (Morris, 178). Cymbals were also used in Old Testament worship (2 Sam. 6:5; Neh. 12:27; Ps. 150:5). The two instruments make noise, but produce no melody; so also does the glossolalist lacking in love.

Possession and exercise of spiritual gifts, even the most dramatic, do not in themselves constitute an endorsement of the person. Prophetic utterance, comprehension of "all mysteries and all knowledge," and all "faith that can move mountains"—these are genuine works of the Spirit, but they can be manifested without love. If so, the individual is nothing (v. 2). ("All" occurs in the Greek text before mysteries, knowledge, and faith; the NIV omits it before the last.)

Although sacrificial giving is the essence of love, it is nevertheless true that self-sacrificing may be improperly motivated. Giving all that one possesses and surrendering one's body to fire are not necessarily acts of love (v. 3). If the person doing these things does not have love, "I gain nothing." Such a person may give all, but will receive no spiritual compensation.

Two additional notes on verse 3: (1) The words "to the poor" do not occur in the Greek, though that may well be implied. (2) Manuscripts differ between giving the body "to be burned [*kauthesomai*] (NASB)" and giving it "so that I may boast [*kauchesomai*] (NRSV)." Assuming that Paul meant the former, scholars have suggested three interpretations: (a) He may have had in mind the three Hebrew young men who "yielded up their bodies" (Dan. 3:28, NASB) or those martyred under Antiochus Epiphanes, who gave up "body and life" (2 Macc. 7:37, NRSV). In the mid-first century, Christians were not yet martyred by burning, though Paul may be speaking in extreme terms to make a point. (b) Paul may be speaking of self-immolation (Barrett, 301). (c) Paul may be speaking about being branded as a slave, that is, selling oneself into slavery, in order to help the poor with the money received (though this is unlikely).

The manuscript evidence for "boast" is stronger and so is preferred by some scholars (Morris, 179; Fee, 624). Bruce (126), however, recommends *burn* "on grounds of intrinsic probability: it is certainly by far the more forceful of the two meanings." In either case, loveless motivation behind the act results in no benefit to the individual.

3.4.4.2. Characteristics of Love (13:4–7). These verses give characteristics of love in fifteen brief statements. It is not difficult to see them as a characterization of both Jesus and the Father. Love:

(1) "is patient," especially with regard to people. "Long-suffering" is an older translation that is close to the etymology of the Greek word; it bears the idea of "far from wrath" (Martin, 47) or "long-tempered" (Lim, 118). This virtue is the enduring of personal injury without the thought of retaliation (see Rom. 2:4; 1 Peter 3:20; 2 Peter 3:9, 15). It is an aspect of the fruit of the Spirit (Gal. 5:22–23).

(2) "is kind"—another aspect of the fruit of the Spirit. Patience is inward; kindness is outward (see Rom. 2:4; 11:22; 2 Cor. 6:6; Col. 3:12).

(3) "does not envy." The negative meaning of the verb is intended here, involving the thought of jealousy.

(4) "does not boast." BAGD suggests the meaning "behave as a... braggart, windbag" (653).

(5) "is not proud." The idea is that of arrogance, of becoming puffed up or conceited (see 4:6, 18–19; 5:2; 8:1).

(6) "is not rude." It does not "behave disgracefully, dishonorably, indecently" (BAGD, 119); the only other New Testament occurrence of the Greek word used here is in 1 Cor. 7:36 ("acting improperly"). The opposite meaning, using the same verb stem, occurs in adverbial form in 14:40, "Everything should be done in a fitting . . . way."

(7) "is not self-seeking" (lit., "does not seek its own things"). It may be understood as insisting on one's own way or being selfish (Morris, 180).

(8) "is not easily angered." "Easily" (NIV) is not in the Greek text. Properly understood, anger per se is not wrong (Eph. 4:26). The thought here is that of hypersensitivity or irritability (see Acts 15:39).

(9) "keeps no record of wrongs." Love does not maintain a list of personal injuries inflicted by another person, with a view to repaying in kind. The Greek phrase used here is found in Zechariah 8:17 (LXX), where there is the added idea of plotting evil.

(10) "does not delight [rejoice] in evil." Love is not judgmental with respect to the wrongdoing of others, nor will it self-righteously place one above the wicked.

(11) "rejoices with the truth" (the positive side of the preceding statement). One suggested translation is, "Love joins [with others] in rejoicing at the truth" (Barrett, 298; Martin, 63). Truth and unrighteousness are set against each other elsewhere (2 Thess. 2:10, 12). Truth is more than propositional statements about the Christian faith. In the present context, in contrast to unrighteousness it speaks of righteous conduct, which is doing "the truth" (John 3:21). In the final analysis, truth is Jesus himself (John 14:6).

(12) "always protects." The Greek verb *stego*, used here, can mean cover, pass over in silence, keep confidential (BAGD, 765–66). BAGD suggests that this statement speaks of "love that throws a cloak of silence over what is displeasing in another person" (766). A second meaning of the verb is to endure, bear, put up with, and is preferred by some.

(13) "always trusts." Love believes the best, not the worst, about people and their actions. This does not suggest selective blindness to the sins and faults of others, but it does caution against an attitude of censuring others.

(14) "always hopes." In relation to others' failings, love is optimistic that such persons will ultimately overcome their deficiencies. In the New Testament, the term *hope* does not, as in contemporary English, contain an element of uncertainty. Faith/trust and hope are closely related. Hope may be thought of as faith in the future.

(15) "always perseveres." This is related to the first in the series, that "love is patient." One distinction of the word used here is that it implies actively enduring circumstances rather than resigned long-suffering with regard to people.

3.4.4.3. Love in an Eschatological Context (13:8–13). The opening and closing statements of this section underscore the eschatological context: "Love never fails"; faith, hope, and love "remain . . . but the greatest of these is love."

Verses 8–10 highlight the permanence of love and the impermanence of spiritual gifts. "Love never fails [*pipto*]" (v. 8). *Pipto* means to fall, collapse; in context, it here means that love will never cease to exist. On the other hand, prophecies, tongues, and knowledge (word of knowledge?) will cease "when perfection comes" (v. 10). They function, nevertheless, in the here and now to contribute to the upbuilding of God's people. "Knowledge and prophecy are useful as lamps in the darkness, but they will be useless when the eternal Day has dawned" (Robertson and Plummer, 297). The termination of these gifts is expressed by two different verbs: *katargeo*, used with "prophecies" and "knowledge," means to render ineffective or inoperative, to cease or pass away; *pauo*, used with "tongues," means to stop or cease. Paul is not suggesting a subtle difference between the two words; the variation is for rhetorical reasons (see Carson, 66–67).

The reason for the cessation of gifts is that knowledge and prophesying (also tongues?) are only "in part" and are consequently imperfect (vv. 9–10); they will no longer be needed when "the perfect" (NASB) comes. Knowledge in this present life, whether acquired by human effort or by revelation, will never be complete. The statement about the coming of the perfect must be understood here in an eschatological sense, as the consummation of all things (Héring, 141–42). At the coming of the Lord, we will be like him (1 John 3:2) and will transcend the need for partial, imperfect, and temporary insights and revelations.

Verses 11–12 illustrate the imperfect-perfect contrast in two ways. (1) Speaking in the first person, Paul says that childhood speech, thinking, and reasoning are appropriate for a child, but the child must not remain a child. There is a twofold purpose in what Paul says: (a) The Corinthians are in a state of arrested spiritual development (3:1–3), particularly in the present context in their understanding of spiritual gifts. (b) In this present life all Christians are immature to some degree. Complete maturity will take place at the Parousia.

(2) Paul draws on the analogy of a mirror. "Now we see in a mirror dimly [*en ainigmati*]" (NASB). The English word "enigma" (riddle) transliterates the Greek noun *ainigma*; in using it Paul probably had in mind Numbers 12:6–8. First-century mirrors were polished metal; some of the finest were made in Corinth. Only the more wealthy could afford a mirror of good quality, and even those were not always free of imperfections. Furthermore, a mirror by its nature distorts because its reflection is the reverse of the person or object before it. But someday we will see "face to face," which is "almost a formula in the Septuagint for a theophany" (Carson, 71, who cites Gen. 32:30; Deut. 5:4; 34:10; Judg. 6:22; Ezek. 20:35).

The now-then motif continues: "Now I know [*ginosko*] in part; then I shall know fully [*epiginosko*], even as I am fully known [*epiginosko*]." *Epiginosko* is a compound form of *ginosko* and here denotes knowledge that is full and complete. For the believer such knowledge will take place at the coming of the Lord. The last clause is best understood to mean, "as I was fully known [by God]" (see comment on 8:3). God's full knowledge of Paul is already complete; Paul's full knowledge of God is yet future.

Throughout this chapter Paul corrects the mistaken notion of some Corinthians that they had already entered the age to come. Applications of his teaching on love to that situation are obvious, though chapter 14 will make some of them specific.

Verse 13 is a fitting climax to the chapter. "And now" can be taken temporally, "at the present time," or logically, "in conclusion." The three things that remain are "faith, hope and love"; the verb "remain" is in the singular, suggesting that the three are a unity. The triad is found frequently in the New Testament (Rom. 5:2–5; Gal. 5:5–6; Eph. 1:15–18; 4:2–5; Col. 1:4–5; 1 Thess. 1:3; 5:8; Heb. 6:10–12; 10:22–24; 1 Peter 1:3–8, 21–22).

"Faith" is not the gift of faith but basic trust in the Lord and commitment to him. "Hope" is confidence in the future. It is sometimes a synonym for the return of the Lord (1 John 3:3), which the Christian regards as a certainty. It is worth observing that in this chapter faith and hope in respect to others are expressions of love (v. 7). "Love" is the supreme virtue, "the greatest of these" three. But Paul does not say that love alone will endure forever, even though faith will one day turn to sight and the coming of the Lord will fulfill all hope. The verb "remain" is spelled the same for both the present tense and the future tense; the only difference is in the placement of an accent mark over the word. But since the New Testament manuscripts do not contain accents, the thought behind the verb may be future rather than present. Even though faith, hope, and love remain and will remain, love, the essence of God (1 John 4:8, 16), forever has pride of place.

3.4.5. Need for Intelligibility in Worship (14:1–25). The two gifts most closely associated with worship, tongues and prophecy, now receive special attention. Paul's overarching concern is that of intelligibility in the public exercise of these gifts, which will in turn contribute to the upbuilding of God's people. For this reason he must compare and contrast the two gifts.

3.4.5.1. The Groundwork (14:1–5). The first five verses lay the groundwork for Paul's discussion. The opening statement establishes a link with both preceding chapters: "Pursue love, yet desire earnestly spiritual gifts [*pneumatikon*]" (NASB). The two verbs used here are synonymous. Chapter 13 is basically descriptive in its treatment of love; now comes the imperative that love must be actively pursued, since the qualities of love detailed in that chapter do not come to Christians automatically. But they must also earnestly "desire spiritual gifts"; the similarity of this imperative with that of 12:31 is obvious, with two differences. (1) "Eagerly desire the greater gifts" (12:31) now becomes eagerly desire "especially that you may prophesy" (NASB). The verb in both statements is the same. (2) "Gifts" in 12:31 is *charisma*; in 14:1 it is *pneumatikon*. But the terms are interchangeable.

Paul here disabuses his readers of two misunderstandings, namely (1) that love and the gifts are antithetical, and so one ought to pursue only love, and (2) that glossolalia is the gift par excellence. He proceeds to show why, in corporate worship, prophecy is superior to glossolalia.

Although tongues and prophecy are both Spirit-inspired speech, the glossolalist "does not speak to men but to God" (v. 2; also vv. 14–16). On the other hand, "everyone who prophesies speaks to men" (v. 3). This basic distinction is essential for understanding much of what Paul proceeds to say. "No one understands" the glossolalist; "he utters mysteries with his spirit [*pneumati*]" explains why. "With his spirit" is an interpretation, not a translation, since "his" is not in the Greek text. A preferred rendering of the word *pneumati* would be "in the Spirit" or "by the Spirit" (Barrett, 315; cf. NIV note); some take it to mean "in spirit," that is, the speaker's own spirit as distinct from his understanding (Morris, 187).

If "no one understands" is interpreted strictly, it implies that tongues are heavenly, not human, languages. But this may be a general statement and, given the multiplicity of human languages, the odds are that no one present will understand the glossolalic language. Since no one understands, the content of tongues is "mysteries." Here the word does not have the theological import it carries elsewhere, but rather the basic meaning of secret, that is, something that is not understood. The two statements in verses 2–3a are then parallel: The glossolalist speaks *to* God, the prophet speaks *from* God (Martin, 66).

Prophecy is directed to men "for their strengthening [*oikodome*], encouragement [*paraklesis*] and comfort [*paramythia*]" (v. 3b). Paul may have intended the last two to be the means by which the first is accomplished. Because *paraklesis* may also mean comfort, it is difficult to find a sure criterion by which it differs from *paramythia*, since both involve admonition and comfort. In the New Testament, admonition becomes genuine comfort and comfort becomes admonition (see Phil. 2:1; Col. 2:2; 4:8; 1 Thess. 5:11; cf. Stählin, *TDNT*, 5.820–21). Stählin notes that one distinction between the two, in accordance with Old Testament and rabbinic usage, is that *paraklesis* is used for eschatological comfort and consolation, whereas *paramythia* is often in a contemporary context (related forms occur in Phil. 2:1; 1 Thess. 2:12).

Paraklesis is here treated as a function of the gift of prophecy, but in the gifts listed in Romans 12:6–8, it is separate from prophesying. Apparently Paul thought it was important enough to be listed as a gift in its own right. Nevertheless, it functions as well within the gift of prophecy (see also 1 Cor. 14:31). This is an instance of the overlapping of some spiritual gifts.

Strengthening/upbuilding (*oikodome*), together with the related verb *oikodomeo*, is a dominant theme of the chapter (vv. 3, 4, 5, 12, 17, 26). It is the equivalent of "for the common good" (12:7). Intelligible utterances contribute to the upbuilding; unintelligible utterances do not.

Uninterpreted tongues do not edify the church, but they do edify the speaker. Therefore tongues without an accompanying interpretation should not be manifested in corporate worship. Yet Paul does not downplay the self-edificatory function of tongues. "Contrary to the opinion of many, spiritual edification can take place in ways other than through the cortex of the brain" (Fee, 657). There is no sarcasm in the statement that the one who speaks in tongues edifies himself (Robertson and Plummer, 307). This is evident from Paul's next statement, "I would like every one of you to speak in tongues" (v. 5). Together with verse 18 ("I thank God that I speak in tongues more than all of you"), this statement seems to contradict the required response of "No" to the question of whether all speak in tongues (see comment on 12:30 for a possible resolution). "But," Paul adds, "I would rather have you prophesy." The contrast is not between tongues and prophecy per se, but between uninterpreted tongues and prophecy in a worship setting, in which case only prophecy is permissible.

Interpreted glossolalia and prophecy are equally valid for edifying the congregation. "He who prophesies is greater than one who speaks in tongues, unless he interprets." Paul does not say here that tongues plus interpretation is the equivalent of prophecy or, to phrase it differently, that the interpretation is a prophecy (as Barrett holds, 316). That view, in effect, obliterates any substantive difference between these gifts (Lim, 144). According to

Carson, "it appears as if tongues can have the same *functional* significance as prophecy if there is an interpreter present.... This does not mean that there is no difference between tongues-plus-interpretation and prophecy. Verses 18–25 are still to come" (102–3). Bittlinger adds, "The gift of tongues when interpreted is *equal in value* to prophecy in the building up of the church" (101, italics added).

The words "unless he interprets" indicate that the glossolalist may be his or her own interpreter (see v. 13). But the normal pattern is that someone else will be given the gift of interpretation (12:10). Because of this, some choose to translate the Greek phrase, "unless someone interprets," which is a possible rendering (Héring, 146–47).

3.4.5.2. Strengthening the Argument (14:6–12). These verses strengthen and illustrate the argument. Paul shifts to the first person singular to lend added force to what he says. "If I come to you speaking [only] in tongues, what shall I profit [cf. 13:3] you?" (v. 6, NASB). ("Only" is required by the context.) The answer is obvious. But how do the four elements mentioned here—revelation, knowledge, prophecy, instruction—relate to this question? There are two main suggestions: (1) They represent different forms an interpretation may take (cf. Barrett, 317). But since prophecy is one of the four, this view would erase the difference between tongues and prophecy—the difference being the very thrust of the chapter. (2) Morris's suggestion (188), that there is an ellipsis in the Greek text, is more acceptable. After the first complete question, there is another question: "[What shall I profit you], except I speak . . . ?" The appeal again is for intelligible communication by one of four means.

Attempts to make absolute distinctions among the four expressions of spiritual gifts are doomed to failure. Some suggest a pattern of a-b-a-b: Revelation and prophecy form a pair (see Article D); knowledge and instruction/teaching are another pair. Carson suggests that the first two probably refer to content and the latter two to the form of the content (103). Worded somewhat differently, the first two are "internal gifts" of which the latter two are the "external manifestation" (Robertson and Plummer, 308). Paul is not here concerned with fine distinctions, but rather the idea that these four means of expression are given in intelligible language and consequently are superior to uninterpreted tongues in corporate worship. Fee regards these four items as another list of gifts (662).

Verses 7–11 illustrate the need for intelligibility by two examples: musical instruments and foreign languages. Even "lifeless things that make sounds, such as the flute or harp," convey a message only when "there is a distinction in the notes" (v. 7). The flute may represent wind instruments generally, the harp stringed instruments. And in a military context, the trumpet must "sound a clear call" in order for the soldiers to prepare for battle (v. 8).

The answer to the questions of verses 7–8 is obvious. Paul then makes the application: "So it is with you. Unless you [in the emphatic position] speak intelligible [*eusemos*] words with your tongue . . . you will just be speaking into the air" (v. 9). This clause is more accurately translated, "Unless you give an intelligible saying/message with the tongue." *Eusemos* occurs only here in the New Testament and means "easily recognizable, clear, distinct" (BAGD, 326), hence "intelligible." "Into the air" recalls Paul's imagery of a boxer "beating the air" (see 9:26).

Paul's next illustration involves human languages. "Undoubtedly there are all sorts of languages [*phone*] in the world, yet none of them is without meaning" (v. 10). Paul probably chose *phone* rather than *glossa* "because the latter is used throughout this passage to refer to 'speaking in tongues,' that special 'utterance' inspired by the Spirit" (Fee, 665). The implication is that glossolalia also has meaning; but as with any language, the meaning is lost if the hearer does not understand it or it is not interpreted, for "speech without meaning is a contradiction in terms" (Robertson and Plummer, 310). The speaker is a foreigner (*barbaros*) to the hearer, and the hearer a foreigner to the speaker (v. 11), if the hearer does not "grasp the meaning" of what is said. *Barbaros* (barbarian) is an onomatopoeia used by Greeks for someone "whose language sounds like 'bar bar,' i.e., whose language makes no sense" (Morris, 189). It was used most often in a derogatory sense. This thought is a veiled rebuke to those Corinthians who prized glossolalia so much that they were concerned only with displaying it publicly, with no regard for its meaning being understood by the hearers. This is confirmed by Paul's next statement, "So it is with you" (v. 12a).

"Since you are zealots [*zelotes*] for spirits" is a literal translation of verse 12b (*zelotes* is the noun form of *zeloo*, "eagerly desire" [12:31; 14:1]). "Spirits" is generally understood to be shorthand for spiritual gifts or "manifestations of the Spirit" (Bruce, 131). "The building up of the community is the basic reason for corporate settings of worship; they should probably not be turned into a corporate gathering for a thousand individual experiences of worship" (Fee, 667). The Corinthians' zeal is commendable, but it must be channeled properly; they must "seek to abound for the edification of the church" (NASB), not for their own gratification.

3.4.5.3. Need for Interpretation of Tongues (14:13–19). This next section focuses on the need in corporate worship for speaking in tongues to be interpreted (see 12:10). It also highlights the essentially vertical aspect of tongues: Their content consists of prayer or praise to God (see further in Article F). "Anyone who speaks in a tongue should pray that he may interpret" (v. 13) places responsibility on the glossolalist to interpret what he has audibly spoken (v. 5). It may be inferred that since the interpretation is normally given to another person, the glossolalist is obligated to interpret the utterance if no one else does so.

The person who prays in a tongue prays with one's spirit, but the "mind is unfruitful [*akarpos*]" (v.14). One suggested understanding of *akarpos* is that praying in tongues does not benefit the mind (Fee, 669). But BAGD suggests that the mind is "unproductive, because it is not active" (29). The person's intellect does not contribute to the glossolalic utterance, which is the product of the Holy Spirit's working with and through the human spirit. Paul here gives the modus operandi of tongues; he is not speaking slightingly about the role of the mind in worship, nor is he concerned with a fine anthropological distinction between spirit and mind. Neither is he suggesting that the glossolalist is in a trancelike state. "The mind is not blanked out and put into neutral, as may be the case in some Eastern religions" (Lim, 149). If the individual were truly beside himself ("ecstatic"), the later restrictions on tongues would be meaningless (vv. 27–28).

In prayer and praise, the spirit and the mind are not antithetical but rather complementary (vv. 15–17). "The spirit" implies glossolalia; "the mind" implies either the interpretation of glossolalia or prayer and praise in one's language in the course of corporate worship. Praying "with my spirit" may be compared with Paul's statement about "groans that words cannot express" (Rom. 8:26; see Article H).

Singing with the spirit (v. 15) suggests the possibility of spontaneous, improvised singing by a worshiper. This activity may not be specifically glossolalic in nature, but the entire discussion in this context strongly suggests this possibility; that would distinguish it from singing "with my mind." There are parallels between singing with the spirit and the "spiritual songs" of Ephesians 5:19 and Colossians 3:16 (Martin, 70–71). The contrast between being drunk with wine and being filled with the Spirit appears not only in Ephesians 5:18 but also in another "charismatic," glossolalic context (Acts 2:4, 15). The more unusual verb *laleo* rather than *lego*, both of which mean "speak," is always the verb used with glossolalia, and it occurs in Ephesians 5:19: "Speak to one another with psalms, hymns and spiritual songs." The verb "sing" is another point of contact (1 Cor. 14:15; Eph. 5:19).

Praying and praising God in uninterpreted tongues precludes "the one who fills the place of the ungifted [*idiotes*]" from saying a concurring "Amen," "since he does not know what you are saying" (v. 16, NASB). Two notes are in order: (1) "Amen," derived from the Hebrew word for confirm, was the vocalized concurrence to a prayer in both Jewish and early Christian circles (Deut. 27:14–26; 1 Chron. 16:36; Neh. 5:13; 8:6; Ps. 106:48; Rev. 5:14; 7:12; 19:4).

(2) Identification of the *idiotes* defies unanimity among New Testament scholars. Bruce suggests he is an outsider, an "uninitiated person" (131–32). BAGD (370) says the word is used of proselytes and catechumens and may mean "inquirer." A related view is that the *idiotes* is a member of the congregation who is not endowed with the gift of tongues or interpretation of tongues (Schlier, *TDNT*, 3.217; Héring, 151; Carson, 105).

In the judgment of this commentator, these views are unsatisfactory. An outsider would not be expected to say "Amen," since this was the response of believers to a prayer. The other interpretations are too restrictive, since Paul said earlier that "no one" understands uninterpreted tongues. The simplest and most adequate interpretation is that, under the circumstances, *anyone* present is an *idiotes*, and therefore an "outsider." This may be the meaning of Bittlinger (103) when he says, "Neither the Christian nor the unbeliever is edified through speaking in tongues in church without interpretation." The meaning of the word shifts in verses 23–24, where Paul speaks of "*idiotai* or unbelievers" and "an unbeliever or an *idiotes*" entering a worship service. In those instances *idiotes* may mean "outsider" with respect to the Christian faith, and two translation options are open: "an unbeliever, that is, an outsider" or "an unbelieving outsider."

Paul does not question the *authenticity* of uninterpreted glossolalia, for he says, "You may be giving thanks well enough" (v. 17). What he does question is its *propriety* in corporate worship.

Paul then becomes personal about his own practice of tongues. Lest the Corinthians think he belittles the gift, he tells them, "I thank God that I speak in tongues more than all of you" (v. 18). He exaggerates, for how could he know how much or how often they spoke in tongues? Nevertheless, he assures them that they may consider him to be the arch-glossolalist. But he must balance this comment with another exaggeration to emphasize again the necessity of intelligibility in congregational worship: "In the church I would rather speak five intelligible words to instruct others than ten thousand words in a tongue" (v. 19).

3.4.5.4. Appeal to the Corinthians (14:20–25). In this section Paul appeals to the Corinthians to think maturely about the gifts. Up to this point, his primary focus has been on the function of gifts for the edification of the congregation. He now relates the gifts specifically to their effect on unbelievers. "Do not be children in your thinking; yet in evil be babes, but in your thinking be mature" (v. 20, NASB). Preoccupation with tongues is a mark of immaturity or childishness. Yet childlikeness, innocence, is required with regard to evil. Paul calls on his "brothers" to advance from immature thinking to mature (adult) thinking.

Verses 20–25 teach, in part, that tongues are *not* a sign for or to believers, contrary to the thinking of some Corinthians. For confirmation, Paul appeals to "the Law" (here an inclusive term for the entire Hebrew Scriptures). Paul quotes from Isaiah 28:11, and his applied instruction must be understood from the historical background of that passage. It is a message of coming judgment on the northern kingdom of Israel for its continual disobedience to the Lord. The judgment would be in the form of the Assyrian invasion of the land (which took place in 721 B.C.). The foreign languages that the Israelites heard would be the sign of God's displeasure and judgment on them. Isaiah's own words might have sounded like babbling to them, since the Hebrew text reads, "*ṣaw laṣaw ṣaw laṣaw, qaw laqaw qaw laqaw, zᵉʿêr šam zᵉʿêr šam*" (Isa. 28:10, 13). They refused to heed the Lord's warning when it was given to them by Isaiah in elementary Hebrew; now they would hear it by means of the foreign speech of the Assyrian invaders, which they would not understand (Bruce, 132).

Although a totally clear exegesis of 1 Cor. 14:21 may be elusive, the main point "is that a divine communication in strange tongues addressed to the deliberately disobedient will but confirm them in their disobedience: they will remain all the more unbelievers" (Bruce, 133). (See Article F for a further discussion of the Isaiah passage.) In light of this, tongues are "for a sign . . . to unbelievers," not to believers (v. 22, NASB). Most commentators make a one-on-one application of the Isaiah passage and consider tongues to be a sign of divine judgment on unreceptive unbelievers. The tongues they hear confirm them in their unbelief, because tongues are a sign of the presence and activity of God, which they continue to reject. Prophecy, on the other hand, is "for believers"; perhaps by ellipsis Paul meant, "a sign for believers."

If everyone in the congregation speaks in tongues, unbelievers who are present will say, "You are out of your mind [*mainomai*]" (v. 23). Paul is not necessarily referring to everyone speaking in tongues *at the same time*, though that is a possible interpretation. The idea may be more that of a rapid succession of utterances in tongues, with no attendant interpretations (Robertson and Plummer, 317). Concerning the charge that the glossolalists are out of their mind, the New Testament writers refrain from ısing *mainomai* and related words when peaking either of a prophet or a glossolalist. 'hose words were applied in classical Greek ɔ persons in a frenzied or "possessed" state, uch as the slave girl in Philippi (Acts 16:16).

The statement that "prophecy is for believ-rs" may be understood in two, not necessar-ly contradictory, ways: (1) It is "for the benefit f believers," for their edification, encourage-nent, and comfort (cf. 14:3). (2) It is "for elievers" in the sense that it produces believ-rs (Bruce, 133). The expression Paul uses for believers" denotes "those coming to faith" Martin, 73) or "those in the process of becom-ng Christians" (Héring, 153). Justification for he latter interpretation is found in verses 24–5. If everyone prophesies (not necessarily all n one service and certainly not simultane-usly), the effect on an unbeliever may be pos-tive in that such a person will worship, xclaiming, "God is really among you!" "He vill fall on his face" (NASB), an attitude of wor-hip that "bears witness to a profound sense of nworthiness, as well as of the immediate resence of God" (Barrett, 326–27; Gen. 17:3; uke 5:12; Rev. 7:11; 11:16).

Prophetic utterance, therefore, may be the ıeans by which an outsider is "convinced *elencho*] by all that he is a sinner and will be ıdged [*anakrino*, cf. 2:15] by all" because the secrets of his heart will be laid bare." *'lencho* is the work of the Holy Spirit in con-icting or convincing of sin (John 16:8). The evelatory role of prophecy is especially ointed here (see Article D), and is a departure rom the usual functions of prophecy in a wor-hip context. However, "the aim of prophets is *ot primarily* evangelism: they speak to nstruct,' and their hearers are in their pres-nce to 'learn' (v. 31; cf. v. 35)" (Martin, 80). See notes on 14:16 for comments on *idiotes*.)

3.4.6. Need for Orderliness in Worship 14:26–40). Paul now embarks on another ıajor theme. Not only must the exercise of tterance gifts be intelligible; the worship ser-ices themselves must be orderly within the ee working of the Spirit implicit in the gifts. he gifts must be regulated (vv. 26–33a); omen worshipers must not be disorderly 33b–35); Paul's apostolic authority in all the receding instruction on gifts must be recog-ized, in order for corporate worship to be fit-ng and orderly (vv. 36–40).

3.4.6.1. Variety and Spontaneity in Worship (14:26–33a). In these verses Paul gives an insight into worship in the Corinthian church. Even though what he says is corrective and restrictive, he wishes to emphasize the general ideas of variety and spontaneity. No one gift should predominate (Lim, 164). When the church gathers for worship, it is proper, and expected, that each member will manifest a gift *if prompted by the Spirit to do so* (v. 26). "Everyone has" does not mean that everyone *must* or *will* manifest a gift, but it does underscore that each member, potentially, *may*.

Some regard the five elements ("a hymn [*psalmos*], or a word of instruction, a revelation, a tongue or an interpretation") as another list of gifts. Like the others, it is ad hoc; "most likely, they [the five items] represent various *types* of verbal manifestations of the Spirit that should occur in their assembly" (Fee, 690). It is strange that "a prophecy" is not included, but "a revelation" is tantamount to the same (again, see Article D). *Psalmos* occurs in other worship passages (Eph. 5:19; Col. 3:16). It may refer to one of the Old Testament psalms, but it is a general word for "song" and could be related to "sing [*psallo*] with my spirit" (see 1 Cor. 14:15). "Church meetings in Corinth can scarcely have suffered from dullness" (Barrett, 327).

The Corinthians must again be reminded that "all of these must be done for the strengthening [*oikodome*; see comment on 14:3] of the church." This will be accomplished, in large measure, by observing the guidelines that follow. But they are "more than corrective. They are positive principles to encourage the exercise of gifts" (Lim, 163). Paul places considerable emphasis on the controllability of utterance gifts; this aspect separates them effectively from any activities in the pagan religious world that were phenomenologically similar.

Glossolalic utterances must observe three guidelines (v. 27): (1) There can be no more than three in any one worship service. No one gift may overshadow or preempt the others. The Corinthians must be open to the reception and manifestation of other gifts in worship. (2) The utterances must be "one at a time." Otherwise, confusion will result. (3) An interpretation must follow each utterance. "Let one [*heis*—the numeral one] interpret" (NASB) literally translates the Greek text. Two explanations are offered: (a) "One" means only one person does all the interpreting (Martin, 78). (b) "One" means no more than one person must attempt to interpret an individual utterance; otherwise the result will be confusion (Robertson and Plummer, 321). In this view, three different persons might interpret three utterances. It is the more congenial view and accords well with the general emphasis on the wide distribution of gifts.

"If there is no interpreter" (v. 28) implies that interpreters were regularly used in the worship setting. In the absence of such a person, the glossolalist should keep quiet in church, restraining the impulse to speak audibly, and should speak "to himself and God." He should perhaps do so in a subdued voice that will not disturb others. Some suggest that "to himself" means he must do it privately, that is, when he is alone (Robertson and Plummer, 321).

What ought to happen if one speaks in tongues audibly and no interpreter is present? The glossolalist should pray to receive the interpretation (vv. 5, 13).

Restrictions apply as well to prophetic utterances (v. 29). "Prophets" is used in a broad sense for anyone who gives a prophetic utterance and does not mean persons who had the title or office of prophet. Naturally, such utterances should not be given simultaneously. (1) That "two or three prophets should speak" places the same numerical limitation that applied to tongues utterances: "three at a meeting" (Robertson and Plummer, 321). Fee, differing from most commentators, interprets the expression to mean "no more than three at a time before 'the others weigh carefully what is said'" (693); he allows for an unlimited number of prophetic utterances.

(2) "The others should weigh carefully what is said." Prophecies must be evaluated; the means is the gift of distinguishing between spirits. (See details in Article E.) Some understand "the others" to mean the other prophets (Robertson and Plummer, 322), and verse 32 is used to justify this position: "Spirits of prophets [those giving utterances] are subject to . . . prophets [those evaluating them]." But it is more natural to take the expression to mean any worshipers to whom the distinguishing gift is given (Morris, 195; Barrett, 328; Büchsel, *TDNT*, 2.947). This may be the same as Martin's comment that "the others" means "the church as a whole" (120).

(3) "If a revelation comes to someone who is sitting down, the first speaker should stop [lit. be silent]" (v. 30). Apparently, prophets stood when giving utterances. Someone in the process of giving a prophecy should defer to another who is also moved upon. How this comes about is not clear, but the implication is that no one should monopolize worship or think he or she alone can give prophetic utterances. The theme of variety is again emphasized.

"You can all prophesy in turn" (v. 31) is open to several interpretations: (1) "All" means all the prophets (Morris, 195–96). (2) "All" does not mean every person in the church without exception, "but every person in the church without distinction—men, women, slaves, noble, and so forth, provided he or she has the gift" (cf. Martin, 117). (3) Every believer has the capacity and potential for prophesying (Fee, 695). Prophesying by all participants in the new covenant is predicted by Joel (2:28–29; see Acts 2:17–21, esp. Peter's addition of "and they will prophesy" in v. 18; see also Num. 11:29). This third view is the most tenable, since it is unlikely that an unlimited number of prophetic utterances would be permitted.

A strict translation of verse 32 reads, "And spirits of prophets are subject to prophets." All three nouns are without the definite article, which makes the sentence read like a proverb (Morris, 196). Interpretations vary: (1) As noted above, it means that prophets are subject to other prophets. (2) The "spirits" of prophets are "their 'spiritual gifts' or 'manifestations of the Spirit,' as in verse 12" (Bruce, 134–35; Barrett, 329). (3) Prophets are able to discipline their own spirits and to keep silent under certain conditions. This view underscores the controllability of the prophetic impulse; it is the simplest interpretation and is most in accord with the general tenor of the chapter.

The reason prophets ought to control themselves is that "God is not a God of disorder but of peace" (v. 33a). Undisciplined believers, not God or the gifts per se, are the cause of disorder and confusion in worship. The gifts, properly exercised, will result in harmony among believers, because they come from the God of peace. Fee says aptly, "The character of one deity is reflected in the character of one's worship" (697).

3.4.6.2. Women in Worship (14:33b–35). These verses are among the most disputed in the entire letter, for two reasons: (1) What Paul says here seems to conflict with what he said earlier (ch. 11) about the role of women in worship. (2) Some question the genuineness and authenticity of the passage, on the grounds that it interrupts the flow of the discussion. A related argument is that in some manuscripts the verses appear at the end of the chapter. Nonetheless, most authorities consider them to be genuinely Pauline.

Verse 33b begins the discussion, though some authorities would append it to the preceding verse. Paul is appealing to a practice common in all the churches, which ought to be true of the Corinthian church as well. If the discussion said only, "Women should remain silent [*sigao*] in the churches" (v. 34), that, along with the following statement, "They are not allowed to speak," would clearly conflict with a previous statement about women who pray and prophesy in church (11:5). In light of the context, Morris is surely right when he says, "Paul is not discussing whether and how qualified women may minister, *but how women should learn* (v. 35)" (197, italics added). Paul's use of *sigao* provides a helpful clue. In two previous occurrences of the word, absolute silence is not enjoined, only silence under certain conditions. The glossolalist should keep silent *only* if an interpreter is not present (v. 28); a prophet should keep silent *only* when another must be given the opportunity to speak (v. 30).

Under what circumstances, then, must women be silent in church? The answer is clear: "If they desire to learn anything" (v. 35, NASB). Any interpretation that misses or ignores this important clue about learning cannot be taken seriously, as, for example, the position that "their primal error is . . . a wrongful aspiration to be charismatic teachers" (Martin, 87). This view is exactly the opposite of what Paul says. The women want to learn; there is no indication they want to be teachers. Those who say the women want to be teachers, whether "charismatic" or otherwise, appear to import into the Corinthian text what Paul says in 1 Timothy 2:12–14—a passage that certainly must be interpreted in its own right and in its own context, but which must not be superimposed on the passage at hand.

Some commentators relate Paul's injunction to silence to the preceding verses, maintaining that women are not allowed to participate in evaluating prophetic utterances. But there is nothing in the context to suggest that this is the problem. The problem, once again, is that the women "want to learn," not that they want to evaluate prophecies. Furthermore, since the gift of distinguishing between spirits functions primarily in connection with prophecies (see comment on v. 29), there is no indication it is for men only. If this were indeed the case, Paul could easily have said, "The men should weigh carefully what is said" (v. 29). This conclusion, however, does not rule out two possibilities: (1) Some women might indeed be inquiring audibly about something in charismatic utterances, but this is not the same as wanting to evaluate them formally. (2) Women, more than men, might be more inclined to ask for information.

Most women of that day were uneducated, but the assembly of believers was not the place for them to express questions vocally, even questions about spiritual matters. Instead, they should ask their husbands at home. We must understand Paul's instructions in the larger context of wanting order and harmony in a church meeting. Talking women would be a distraction. A contemporary application ought to be obvious: Unnecessary talking should not take place in a meeting where God's people are gathered for worship.

The disgrace accompanying the talking in church would be that of both the woman and her husband. It should be understood in terms of violating the conventions of society, which frowned on woman creating a disturbance in a public place.

Paul appeals to "the Law" for his statement that the women must be in submission. He has in mind passages that talk specifically about the relation of the woman to the man (Gen. 1:26–28; 2:21–23; 3:16, especially the first two), but the general thought is that of submission, especially submission to the practice common in all the churches (v. 33b). That submission would express itself in the woman asking a question of her husband in their home.

3.4.6.3. Conclusion on Spiritual Gifts (14:36–40). Paul is ready to conclude his lengthy discussion of spiritual gifts. But he feels constrained, even in his closing comments, to chide the Corinthians for their arrogant spirit. The word of God did not originate with them, nor are they the only people to whom it came (v. 36). Therefore, they need to acknowledge his apostolic authority and the practices of other congregations (11:16; 14:33b). They cannot be a law to themselves, but must recognize that what he has written is the Lord's command (14:37).

Paul assumes that anyone who is truly "a prophet or spiritually gifted [*pneumatikos*]" will acknowledge the superiority of what he has said over any of their utterances or claims. *Pneumatikos* is taken by many to be a glossolalist, Paul using the word tongue-in-cheek for one who regards speaking in tongues as the apex of spirituality. But the term may be understood generally of anyone who considered himself or herself to be spiritual. But if such a person ignores what Paul has taught, that person will be ignored (v. 38).

The Greek text of verse 38 is not clear, however, and can have other meanings. The NASB, for example, reads, "If anyone does not recognize this, he is not recognized" (cf. also NRSV). Paul may mean he does not recognize such a person as inspired (Barrett, 334). Fee interprets the passage to mean, "Failure to recognize the Spirit in Paul's letter will lead to the person's failure to be 'recognized' by God.... It is a prophetic sentence of judgment on those who fail to heed this letter" (712). The NKJV reads: "But if anyone is ignorant, let him be ignorant." For this reading, Bruce comments, "Let him remain in his ignorance" (137).

A summation of all Paul has said is expressed in three commands: (1) "Be eager [*zeloo*] to prophesy" (see v. 1). He has discussed at length the superiority of prophesy in corporate worship. (2) "Do not forbid speaking in tongues." He wants to avoid an overreaction or misunderstanding by some who misinterpret him as proscribing tongues altogether in the assembly. His purpose is to regulate, not to suppress (Bittlinger, 117). (3) "Let all things be done properly and in an orderly manner" (NASB). The first two commands are especially applicable to the Corinthian congregation and summarize verses 1–25. This last command summarizes verses 26–35 and applies to churches everywhere.

Articles

In the following articles, note that all Scripture quotations are from the NASB, unless otherwise noted.

Article A: Was Jesus Accursed?

Paul seems to make contradictory statements about the concept of curse as it relates

Lecheon Road in Corinth, which dates back to the time of Paul. Among Paul's instructions to the Corinthians were to be eager to prophesy, to not forbid speaking in tongues, and to do things properly and in an orderly manner.

to Jesus. On the one hand, he says that "no one speaking by the Spirit of God says, 'Jesus is accursed [*anathema*]'" (1 Cor. 12:3). On the other hand he speaks of Christ's "having become a curse [*katara*] for us" (Gal. 3:13). These two Greek words are synonyms, so that one cannot resolve the apparent contradiction by appealing to the fact that different words are used. The simplest resolution is to see that Christ's becoming a curse is expressed as an event in the past, whereas the disapproved statement in 1 Corinthians 12:3 is expressed in the present. Historically, Christ *became* a curse for us on the cross; he is *not now* accursed in any sense of the word.

A look at the two Greek words will be instructive. *Anathema* is a word whose original meaning underwent a change in the course of time. Its root meaning suggests something which is "set up" or dedicated, and in the LXX it is often used in relation to God. In its original form, it meant "votive offering" and this form of the word is so translated in Luke 21:5. But in time it took on the meaning of that which is dedicated or handed over to God for destruction.

The Hebrew translated by *anathema* is *ḥerem*. Often this word carried the meaning not only of the banning but also the destruction or extermination of a nation, person, or thing (Lev. 27:29; Deut. 13:16–17). Simply stated, that which is *anathema*/*ḥerem* is the object of divine wrath. We see this nuance especially in several New Testament passages in which *anathema* occurs. (1) Paul states, "For I could wish that I myself were accursed, separated from Christ for the sake of my brethren, my kinsmen according to the flesh" (Rom. 9:3). The apostle is saying he would actually be willing to sacrifice his own salvation and become an object of God's wrath, if by doing so it would mean the salvation of his fellow-Jews.

(2) In another significant passage Paul writes, "Even though we, or an angel from heaven, should preach to you a gospel contrary to that which we have preached to you, let him be accursed" (Gal. 1:8, also v. 9). Anyone who distorts the gospel by teaching that salvation is not by faith alone but by a combination of faith and works comes under the wrath of God. Paul is clearly talking about Judaizers as the purveyors of false doctrine, but what does he mean by "an angel from heaven"? Perhaps he is referring to a spirit being who purportedly is a divine messenger but in reality is not. One thinks of Mohammed's claim that he was visited by the angel Gabriel, or Joseph Smith's story of being visited by the angel Moroni. Echoing a similar thought, Peter says that false prophets are "accursed children [*kataras tekna*]" (2 Peter 2:14).

(3) In a third passage Paul simply states, "If anyone does not love the Lord, let him be accursed" (1 Cor. 16:22). It is not clear why this statement is in the concluding remarks of the letter, but the thought it expresses is nevertheless clear: A person who has not committed himself or herself to the Lord is placed under the wrath of God.

The most significant passage in which *katara* occurs is Galatians 3:13: "Christ redeemed us from the curse (*katara*) of the Law, having become a curse (*katara*) for us—for it is written, 'Cursed [*epikataratos*] is everyone who hangs on a tree.'" The quotation is from Deuteronomy 21:23, where the word for curse is *qelalah*. This Hebrew word is used a number of times along with its antonym, bless (*barak* and cognates like *berakah*). The antithetical pair occurs in Jacob's fear expressed to Rebekah that if the dying Isaac discovers his deception, "I shall bring upon myself a curse and not a blessing" (Gen. 27:12; see also Deut. 30:19, "life and death, the blessing and the curse").

The contrast between the two words is highlighted in Deuteronomy 11:26–29, which speaks of blessing associated with Mount Gerizim and curse with Mount Ebal. In chapters 27 and 28 of that book, where the ideas of blessing and curse are amplified, the word for curse is *'arur*, a synonym of *qelalah*.

What is the meaning of Christ's having become a curse "for us [*hyper hemon*]" (Gal. 3:13)? The preposition *hyper* means "for our benefit/on our behalf." But it also incorporates the idea of substitution, as the context indicates. Verse 10, referring to Deuteronomy 27:26, says, "Cursed [*epikataratos*] is everyone who does not abide by all things written in the book of the Law, to perform them." Christ took on himself the curse, the condemnation, the judgment that we deserved. This thought is paralleled in 2 Corinthians 5:21, which states that God "made Him [Christ] who knew no sin to be sin on our behalf [*hyper hemon*]."

In the context of Galatians 3:10–14, we see once again the meaningful contrast between curse and blessing, for Paul states that Christ became a curse for us "in order that in Christ Jesus the blessing of Abraham might come to the Gentiles" (v. 14).

Is Jesus accursed (1 Cor. 12:3)? The answer is an emphatic "No!" *Was* Jesus accursed (Gal. 3:13)? The answer is an emphatic "Yes!" New Testament authorities differ as to the precise meaning of the first passage, but under no circumstances can it mean that Jesus is in disfavor with God. But with respect to the second passage, we know that on the cross Jesus cried out, "My God, My God, why hast Thou forsaken Me?" (Matt. 27:46). He died (and rose again!) in order to reverse the curse that had befallen the human race because of the sin of our first parents. Because Jesus became a curse for us, in the New Jerusalem "there shall no longer be any curse [*katathema*, a synonym for *anathema*]" (Rev. 22:3).

Article B: Spiritual Gifts

This article focuses on the terms the New Testament uses for what are commonly called "spiritual gifts" or "gifts of the Spirit." Surprisingly, the former term is found only once in the New Testament (Rom. 1:11) and the latter not at all (see the comments on Heb. 2:4).

***Charisma*—An Emphasis on Grace.** The Greek word *charisma* (plural *charismata*) occurs seventeen times in the New Testament; except for 1 Peter 4:10, all occurrences are in Paul's writings (Rom. 1:11; 5:15,16; 6:23; 11:29; 12:6; 1 Cor. 1:7; 7:7; 12:4, 9, 28, 30, 31; 2 Cor. 1:11; 1 Tim. 4:14; 2 Tim. 1:6). It is not found in the LXX and occurs rarely in nonbiblical literature.

The linguistic basis for the word is the common noun *charis* ("grace"), to which was added the suffix *ma*, which conveys the idea "result of." Consequently, although the general meaning of the word is gift, specifically it is something that has been received as a result of God's grace. *Charismata* are not received on the basis of merit; though perhaps redundant, the phrase "free gift" properly conveys the nature of this divine bestowal.

Charisma in and of itself does not mean "spiritual gift." It is used of salvation: "the free gift [*charisma*] of God is eternal life in Christ Jesus our Lord" (Rom. 6:23). Paul uses it when referring to the gifts God bestowed on Israel (Rom. 11:29) and when speaking of being rescued from mortal danger ("the favor bestowed [*charisma*] upon us through the prayers of many," 2 Cor. 1:11). He also refers to the unmarried, celibate life and the married life as *charismata*: "Each man has his own gift from God, one in this manner, and another in that" (1 Cor. 7:7).

Yet by common usage today, the word *charisma* has come to mean "spiritual gift." Paul's statement to the Corinthians that "you are not lacking in any gift" (1 Cor. 1:7), in the overall context of the letter, refers to spiritual gifts. In writing to the Romans he says, "For I long to see you in order that I may impart some spiritual gift [*charisma pneumatikon*] to you" (Rom. 1:11). The precise nature of this gift is not mentioned, but Paul undoubtedly has in mind the kinds of gifts he describes in Romans 12:6–8; 1 Corinthians 12:8–10, 28–30; and Ephesians 4:11.

Paul uses *charisma* five times in 1 Corinthians 12, where he speaks of "varieties of gifts" (v. 4), "gifts of healing [lit., healings]" (vv. 9, 28, 30), and earnestly desiring "the greater gifts" (v. 31). In a similar listing of spiritual gifts he says, "We have gifts that differ according to the grace given to us" (Rom. 12:6). Peter's solitary use of the word parallels Paul's teaching: "As each one has received a special gift, employ it in serving one another, as good stewards of the manifold grace of God" (1 Peter 4:10).

Two passages in the Pastoral Letters are related to the preceding statements. Timothy is admonished, "Do not neglect the spiritual gift [*charisma*, 'spiritual' is not in the Greek text] within you, which was bestowed upon you through prophetic utterance with the laying on of hands by the presbytery" (1 Tim. 4:14). Later Paul again admonishes him "to kindle afresh the gift of God which is in you through the laying on of my hands" (2 Tim. 1:6).

***Pneumatikon*—Emphasis on the Spirit.** *Pneumatikon* is an adjective whose basic meaning is "spiritual." It is used often in the New Testament with that general meaning (e.g., 1 Cor. 2:13, 14; 3:1; Eph. 1:3). But it is also used as a designation for the *charismata*. Since in 1 Corinthians 12–14 it is used absolutely (the noun it modifies is not expressed), a noun must be supplied. The most logical choice is "gifts." A comparison of two statements clearly shows the equivalence of the two words. "Earnestly desire the greater gifts [*charismata*]" (1 Cor. 12:31) is parallel to "desire earnestly spiritual gifts [*pneumatika*]" (14:1). In the introduction to his lengthy treatment of the subject, Paul says: "Now concerning spiritual gifts [*pneumatikon*—genitive plural], brethren, I do not want you to be unaware" (12:1, see comments on that verse).

Although *charismata* and *pneumatika* are used synonymously in 1 Corinthians 12–14, the emphasis is different. The former term calls attention to the aspect of grace in the bestowal of gifts; the latter directs attention to the Holy Spirit as the source of the gifts, highlighted by Paul's statement: "But one and the same Spirit works all these things, distributing to each one individually just as He wills" (12:11). Related to this is verse 7, "But to each one is given the manifestation [*phanerosis*] of the Spirit for the common good." The phrase "of the Spirit" likely denotes source—that is, "from the Spirit." *Phanerosis* is a collective term for the gifts.

***Dorea/Doma*—The General Idea.** The basic, most common Greek verb for "give" is *didomi*. Cognate nouns as well as the verb are found in Ephesians 4:7–11, another important passage dealing with spiritual gifts. Excerpts follow: "But to each one of us grace [*charis*] was given [*didomi*] according to the measure of Christ's gift [*dorea*]" (v. 7); "He gave [*didomi*] gifts [*domata*, plural of *doma*] to men" (v. 8); "And He gave [*didomi*] some as apostles . . ." (v. 11). No special meaning attaches to this family of Greek words other than the broad idea of "give/gift," but a comparison of this passage with those previously cited shows the interchangeability of all three terms.

***Merismoi*—Distributions.** Hebrews 2:4 reads, "God also bearing witness with them, both by signs and wonders and by various miracles and by gifts [*merismois*] of the Holy Spirit according to His own will." Many translations render the Greek word similarly. But the noun properly means "distribution, apportionment" and parallels the verb in 1 Corinthians 12:11, which says that the Spirit distributes (*diaireo*, distribute, divide) the gifts. While the idea of spiritual gifts is certainly present in Hebrews 2:4, the translation "gifts" for *merismois* is not accurate. The only other New Testament occurrence of this word is in 4:12, which speaks of the "division" of soul and spirit.

Summary. The New Testament uses a variety of terms when it speaks of spiritual gifts. *Charisma* emphasizes the grace, free-gift aspect. *Pneumatikon* directs attention to the Holy Spirit as the source, and *merismos* to him as the distributor, of the gifts. *Dorea/doma* broadly emphasize the "gift" aspect. Each term makes its own contribution to a fuller understanding of the concept of spiritual gifts.

Article C: The Working of Miracles

The word translated miracles is *dynamis*, whose basic meaning is power and which is so rendered in passages like Acts 1:8, "You shall receive power when the Holy Spirit has come upon you." This close connection between *dynamis* and the Holy Spirit is made in a number of ways. There are passages where the two seem to be used coordinately—"Holy Spirit and . . . power" (Acts 10:38; cf. 1 Cor. 2:4). But in these passages we do not have two separate entities. Instead, this is a grammatical construction called *hendiadys*, in which the second noun modifies the first noun so that the phrase means "powerful Holy Spirit." The New Testament makes two other connections between these nouns. Paul speaks of the "[S]pirit . . . of power" (2 Tim. 1:7) and the "power of the Spirit" (Rom. 15:19). There emerges the idea of an indissoluble link between the Holy Spirit and the manifestation of God's power.

Because *dynamis* is a demonstration of the power of God, the word in Scripture often connotes a miracle. An extraordinary manifestation of God's power apart from a healing (which, of course, is a miracle) is an example of the gift of workings of miracles. The plural *workings* suggests that this is a multifaceted gift, which manifests itself in many ways.

An important clue emerges when we investigate the New Testament usage of *energema* ("working") and its cognates. This word group is used, almost without exception, of the activity of God or of Satanic forces.* This suggests the possibility of conflict between these two forces. It is especially in this context that we can look for one important manifestation of the gift. As one writer has put it, these are "acts of power invading the kingdom of demons" and vanquishing them. In light of this, it is appropriate to include the casting out of demons with the "working of miracles" because of the encounter between the power of God and the power of Satan. In our day, with the power and presence of Satan so evident through Satanism and occultism, it is heartening to know that God has provided the means to counteract and overcome these forces.

One should not be unnecessarily restrictive by limiting the scope of this gift to the above considerations. Any extraordinary manifestation of the power of God, apart from miracles or a "power encounter" with Satan, could be included in this gift.

Atricle D: The Gift of Prophecy As Revelation

A prophet is one who communicates a divine revelation to others. In the Old Testament the common word for "prophet" (*nab'*) has the basic meaning of spokesman or speaker. In classical Greek writings a *prophetes* was one who spoke for a god and interpreted his will to others. In the LXX and the New Testament, the basic meaning is a proclaimer and interpreter of a divine revelation.

First Corinthians 14 demonstrates how the words "prophecy" (*propheteia*) and "revelation" (*apokalypsis*) may be used interchangeably. Paul, enumerating specific contributions to a service by worshipers, speaks of a psalm, a teaching, a revelation, a tongue, and an interpretation (v. 26). It is strange that prophecy is not mentioned in this verse, especially since the chapter is a lengthy treatment of the gifts of tongues and prophecy. But this difficulty is resolved when one looks at verses 29–30: "Let two or three prophets speak, and let the others pass judgment. But if a revelation is made to another who is seated, let the first keep silent." No one person has a monopoly on the gift of prophecy; another prophet may also receive a "revelation."

In 14:24–25 Paul refers to an unbeliever or unlearned person who is present in a service and says that through prophecy "the secrets of his heart are disclosed" (*phanera*, the synonym for *apocalypsis*). Even in verse 6, where Paul lists revelation, knowledge, prophecy, and teaching, he is probably relating these to one another on the pattern a-b-a-b—a common literary device (see comments on this verse). In other words, revelation is imparted by means of prophecy, and knowledge by means of teaching.

Although *apocalypsis* is a virtual synonym for *propheteia*, the gift is not intended to be a means of providing new truth in the sense of adding to the Scriptures. This is a continuing danger among people who experience the charismatic, spontaneous working of the Holy Spirit. "Revelation" must be understood as a disclosure by God of his will for his people at a particular point in time. It is to meet a special need among believers, the specific nature of which may not and need not be known to the prophet. But it will result in "edification and exhortation [encouragement] and consolation" (14:3).

Article E: Distinguishing of Spirits

"Distinguishing of spirits [*diakriseis pneumaton*]" is one of nine *charismata* listed in 1 Corinthians 12:8–10. Two preliminary observations are important: (1) The gift is listed immediately after the gift of prophecy, suggesting a connection between the two. (2) In the Greek text, the first noun is plural; it should be translated "distinguishings." In addition, attention needs to be given to the identity of the "spirits" who are the object of this evaluation process.

Relationship to the Gift of Prophecy. Significantly, while this gift is revelatory in nature, it is not listed with a "word of wisdom" and a "word of knowledge," but rather after the gift of prophecy. The connection between these two gifts is clear in 1 Corinthians 14:29, which reads: "And let two or three prophets speak, and let the others pass judgment [*diakrino*]." This verb *diakrino* and the noun *diakriseis* used in 12:10 are cognates. In effect, 14:29 is a commentary on those two gifts listed in 12:10. Therefore the primary function of the gift of distinguishings of spirits is related to the gift of prophecy. Just as the last two gifts in Paul's list—tongues and interpretation of tongues—are corollaries, so are the two gifts under consideration. The second gift in each pair is a follow-up of the preceding gift.

Parallel Passages. Injunctions to evaluate/appraise/ assess prophetic utterances are found in other New Testament passages. For example, "Do not quench the Spirit; do not despise prophetic utterances. But examine [*dokimazo*] everything carefully; hold fast to that which is good" (1 Thess. 5:19–21). John echoes the same thought when he says, "Beloved, do not believe every spirit, but test [*dokimazo*] the spirits to see whether they are from God; because many false prophets have gone out into the world" (1 John 4:1). *Dokimazo* is therefore synonymous with *diakrino* in passages that deal with the evaluation of prophetic utterances.

Who Evaluates? Who are the "others" in the statement, "let the others [*alloi*] pass judgment" (1 Cor. 14:29)? Some say it refers to other prophets who are present—that prophetic utterances should be evaluated by fellow prophets. A strict meaning of the adjective *allos* is pressed to mean "another of the same kind." But such a distinction between this adjective and its synonym *heteros* (another of a different kind) does not always occur in New Testament usage. In my judgment it is impossible to press this distinction in the very passage that enumerates spiritual gifts (12:8–10), where *allos* occurs six times and *heteros* twice.

It is better to understand *alloi* to mean the other persons present. This view is in keeping with the biblical principle that God wishes to use all believers in the exercise of spiritual gifts. Furthermore, in the 1 Thessalonians and 1 John passages quoted above, there is no indication that the evaluating or testing is to be done by persons who are themselves prophets.

Who/What Are the "Spirits" to Be Judged? The New Testament uses the Greek word "spirit" (*pneuma*) in a variety of ways. It may refer to the Holy Spirit (Rom. 8:32), to an evil or angelic spirit (Mark 5:2; Heb. 1:14), to the aspect of a human being other than his soul and body (1 Thess. 5:23), or to a person's disposition (2 Tim. 1:7). The purpose of the gift of evaluation is to enable one to perceive the source or impetus of a prophetic utterance.

From a practical standpoint, one must be cautious about labeling an utterance as demon-inspired. On the other hand, there is the possibility of the speaker's own spirit injecting itself to a degree—albeit innocently—because the ministry of the Spirit is mediated through a human channel. In transmitting a genuine message from the Lord, the speaker may unconsciously include one's own feelings or interpretation of the message. This, in my judgment, is the only satisfactory way to understand the statement that the disciples in Tyre "kept telling Paul through the Spirit not to set foot in Jerusalem" (Acts 21:4). Apparently their personal feelings for him were included as part of the prophecy. A collation of related passages shows that the Spirit did indeed forewarn Paul of trouble in Jerusalem (20:23; 21:10–14); yet the believers in Caesarea, after begging him not to go to Jerusalem following the prophecy of Agabus, finally acquiesced to his determination to do so and said, "The will of the Lord be done!"

In addition, allowance must be made for the possibility that an entire "prophecy" may be neither directly from the Lord nor from Satan, but that it is an expression coming from the spirit of a well-intentioned speaker who honestly feels he or she has a message from the Lord.

The Means of Evaluation. This gift of distinguishing between spirits may be considered a subjective criterion by which members of the congregation know intuitively whether a prophetic utterance is genuine. Externally, there may be no discernible difference between a divinely inspired person and one who is demonically or "self-" inspired. But in a manner not clearly explained in Scripture, the gift operates in such a way that "the others" somehow know in their own spirits whether the Holy Spirit is the source.

In addition, and following the lead of the Old Testament (Deut. 13:2–6; 18:21–22), Paul claims that content is the objective criterion by which prophecies are to be assessed. He says no one speaking "by the Spirit of God" will say "Jesus is accursed" (1 Cor. 12:3). In a parallel passage the test is also doctrinal: "By this you know the Spirit of God: every spirit that confesses that Jesus Christ has come in the flesh is from God" (1 John 4:2). These passages must be understood in the light of the specific theological problems the authors were addressing, but we may extrapolate and say that doctrinal tests should always be applied to prophetic utterances.

Other Relevant Matters. The focus of this article has been the connection between the gift of distinguishing and prophetic utterances, but this gift has other functions, which may be why its designation is in the plural. It can be linked with the gift of a word of knowledge, by which something otherwise unknowable is made known to a person by the Spirit of God.

And it has a clear application in the area of demon possession. As is well known, similar physical symptoms may be present both in cases of physical, organic sickness and in cases of demon possession. Spiritually sensitive persons can be assured that the gift will enable them to discern whether to pray for the person's healing or to engage in a power encounter with Satan.

Article F: Glossolalia—Do Luke and Paul Agree?

The word glossolalia is a coinage based on two Greek words: *glossa* ("tongue") and *lalia* ("speech") and literally means "tongue-speech." It is the one, unique phenomenon associated with the outpouring of the Holy Spirit on the Day of Pentecost. In the Old Testament, wind and fire were common manifestations of God's presence. But speaking in tongues does not occur there, even though some try to identify it with some prophets' utterances.

The purpose of this article is to see how the expression "speaking in tongues" (*laleo glossais*) is used in Acts and in 1 Corinthians. The study is prompted primarily because some maintain that the phenomenon in Acts (especially ch. 2) differs from the one mentioned by Paul. In the former, it is held, the languages are human, foreign, and identifiable; in the latter, they are ecstatic vocal expressions that cannot really be called languages. Consequently, the glossolalia of Acts 2 is superior to the glossolalia of 1 Corinthians.

The Expression *Laleo Glossais*. This expression is found only in the New Testament, in both Acts (2:4; 10:46; 19:6) and 1 Corinthians (12:30; 13:1; 14:5, 6, 18, 23, 39). It seems to occur nowhere else in Greek literature. It is a technical term in Scripture for Spirit-inspired utterance in a language not at the speaker's command.

The verb *laleo* ("speak") occurs throughout Scripture and is a synonym for *lego*. Yet only *laleo* is used when the writers speak of this phenomenon—an indication that we are dealing here with a technical term. The word *glossais* is the dative plural of *glossa*; the dative case shows the means by which the speaking takes place—languages. The basic meaning of the word *glossa* is that of the organ of speech, the tongue. An extended meaning is that of language—that which the tongue produces. Just as in English and in a number of other languages the term *tongue* has both these meanings, so also in Greek. The meaning "languages" is obvious from the contents of Acts 2, where the synonym *dialektoi* also occurs (vv. 6, 8, 21).

Both Paul and Luke use the identical technical term *laleo glossais*. Since they were close associates who undoubtedly discussed "theology," it is improbable that they would use the same unusual expression with disparate meanings.

"Other" Tongues. Acts 2:4 states that the disciples "began to speak with other [*heteros*] tongues." Luke's choice of *heteros* rather than its synonym *allos*, both of which mean "other," may have been influenced by Isaiah 28:11 (see below). In any event, the context unmistakably identifies the *glossais* as languages unknown to the speakers. Since this is the first occurrence of glossolalia in biblical history, it is significant that Luke gives this detail about its nature.

Is Paul in agreement? Does he view glossolalia as a speaking in languages? Or is he to be understood as saying that vocal expressions may take place without their being languages? In his discussion of the gift of tongues, he quotes Isaiah 28:11, "'By men of strange tongues [*en heteroglossois*] and by the lips of strangers [*en cheilesin heteron*] I will speak [*laleo*] to this people'" (1 Cor. 14:21). *Heteroglossois* is simply a combination of *heteros* and *glossa*. It is not accidental that forms of the Acts 2:4 adjective *heteros* occur twice here, as does the verb *laleo*, which is used consistently in the expression *laleo glossais*.

The Isaiah quote by Paul is not from the LXX, which reads "through stammering lips and a foreign tongue [*glosses heteras*]," but the similarities between his quote, the LXX, and Acts 2:4 are striking. The context of the Isaiah passage deals with the coming of the Assyrian invaders, whose language would not be understood by the Israelites. The point is that Luke and Paul both think of glossolalia as a speaking in languages.

A simple yet adequate definition of language is that it consists of words, their pronunciation, and the methods of combining them used in communicating to someone. Should we press the meaning of glossolalia to include only human, identifiable languages?

Or is it possible that *laleo glossais* can be extended to mean some type of "spiritual" language? The general tenor of 1 Corinthians 14 suggests the possibility of a spiritual, or heavenly, language. This speaking is directed to God, since no one "understands" (14:2). Allusion to this idea is also found in the phrase "tongues . . . of angels" (13:1). One must allow for the possibility of glossolalia including a nonhuman but nevertheless spiritual, heavenly, or angelic language. Could this be part of the meaning of "kinds of tongues [*gene glosson*]" (12:10, 28)?

The Interpretation of Tongues. The corollary gift of the interpretation of tongues (*hermeneia glosson*) strongly implies that glossolalia is indeed a speaking in languages (1 Cor. 12:10). Throughout the New Testament, *hermeneia* and its cognates apply to the interpretation or translation of an unintelligible language (e.g., Matt. 1:23; John 1:38–39, 42–43; Acts 4:36; the only exception is Luke 24:27, which speaks of explaining the Scriptures). Again, Paul regards glossolalia as languages needing interpretation or translation.

Glossolalia as Praise/Prayer. Another similarity between Luke and Paul is related to the content of glossolalic utterances. In Acts 2:11, the disciples were heard "speaking of the mighty deeds of God." In 10:46 Cornelius and his household were "speaking with tongues and exalting God." The second verb here is a commentary on the first; the word "and" (*kai*) can be translated "that is." In 1 Corinthians 14, Paul speaks of praying in a tongue (v. 14), blessing in the Spirit (v. 16), and giving thanks (vv. 16–17)—all related to the content of speaking in tongues. Thus both writers point to the Godward direction of glossolalia.

Luke and Paul indeed agree on important matters related to *the nature of glossolalia*. Other aspects of the phenomenon are beyond the scope of the article.

Article G: Baptized by and in the Holy Spirit

Does the New Testament distinguish between being baptized *by* the Holy Spirit and being baptized *in* the Holy Spirit? Seven passages contain the verb "baptize" and the noun "Holy Spirit" or "Spirit." Do all these verses teach the same thing about the relationship between the baptism and the Holy Spirit?

No "Baptism *of* the Spirit." The New Testament writers never speak about a "baptism *of* the Holy Spirit." The term is ambivalent and could be used for either of two experiences of the Spirit. One is a baptism *by* the Spirit, which makes one a member of the body of Christ (1 Cor. 12:13). The other is a baptism *in* the Spirit, which empowers a believer for service (Matt. 3:11; Mark 1:8; Luke 3:16; John 1:33; Acts 1:5; 11;16; see also Luke 24:49; Acts 1:8). Is this distinction valid?

Baptized *in* the Spirit. The experience of the Spirit mentioned in the Gospels and Acts passages is one of baptism "*in* [*en*] the Holy Spirit." This rendering most clearly translates the Greek and adequately conveys the meaning of the experience. It is preferred for two reasons.

(1) The preposition *en* is the most common preposition in the New Testament and may be variously translated (*in*, *with*, *by*, *among*, *within*), depending on the context. We may eliminate the last two as not suitable in any of the passages we are discussing. We may also eliminate *by* since Jesus, not the Holy Spirit, is the One who does the baptizing. It is a baptism *by* Jesus *in* the Holy Spirit.

(2) *In* is preferable to *with* because it is associated with the imagery of baptism. The verb *baptizo* means to immerse or dip. If we substitute *immerse* for *baptize* in the Gospels and Acts passages, it would be awkward to say, "He shall immerse you *with* the Holy Spirit." The more natural rendering is "*in* the Holy Spirit." Versions that read "baptize *with* water" and "baptize *with* the Holy Spirit" may reflect the unconscious bias of nonimmersionist translators. Note too that John baptized people at the Jordan River; why, if the baptisms were not to be *in* water? Thus, just as John immersed *in* water, Jesus immerses believers *in* the Holy Spirit.

A preference for *in* as the correct translation of the Gospels and Acts passages involves more than semantic hairsplitting. It reflects a correct understanding of the nature of the baptism in the Holy Spirit foretold by John the Baptist. It emphasizes that this is an experience in which a believer is totally immersed in the Spirit.

Baptized *by* the Spirit. Being baptized *in* the Holy Spirit should be distinguished from being baptized *by* the Spirit *into* the body of

Christ (1 Cor. 12:13). The same preposition *en* occurs in this verse, the first part of which reads, "For by [*en*] one Spirit we were all baptized into one body." "By" indicates that the Holy Spirit is the means or the instrument by which this baptism takes place. The experience Paul speaks of is different from the experience mentioned by John the Baptist, Jesus, and Peter in the other six passages. Some, however, argue that Paul would have used the preposition *hypo* or *dia* instead of *en* if he meant the Holy Spirit is the agent in that baptism rather than its element.

The two groups of passages do indeed have some common terms. But it is questionable to insist that because certain combinations of words occur in different passages, their translation and meaning must be the same. Apart from the few similarities, the two groups of passages have little in common. For instance, Paul mentions the *one* Spirit; he does not use the full two-word designation "Holy Spirit"; he talks about being baptized "into one body." Furthermore, the prepositional phrase "*en* the one Spirit" precedes the verb *baptize*; in all the other passages it follows the verb (except for Acts 1:5, where, curious to some, it comes between *Spirit* and *Holy*).

Since *en* is the most versatile of the Greek prepositions, context must determine how to translate it. Therefore one needs to see how Paul himself uses expressions similar or identical to "*en* the one Spirit." The immediate context, 1 Corinthians 12, contains four such phrases.

Verse 3 reads, "Therefore I make known to you, that no one speaking by [*en*] the Spirit of God says, 'Jesus is accursed'; and no one can say, 'Jesus is Lord,' except by [*en*] the Holy Spirit." Verse 9, which continues Paul's list of spiritual gifts, reads, "to another faith by [*en*] the same Spirit, and to another gifts of healing by [*en*] the one Spirit." This last phrase is identical to the one in verse 13, the only exception being that the Greek contains the article *the*. One may also look at 6:11—"justified .... by [*en*] the Spirit of our God" (NIV). In this connection, Schweizer writes, "It is probable that *en pneumati* of v. 13a is to be taken instrumentally [= "by"] as in 1 Cor. 6:11" (*TDNT*, 6.418).

In all the occurrences in 1 Corinthians where *en* is linked with the Holy Spirit, the translation "by" comes much more easily and is more readily understood than any other translation. Furthermore, in chapter 12 Paul emphasizes the activity of the Holy Spirit; it is axiomatic that this activity will be in the sphere or realm of the Spirit. Therefore the reading "by one Spirit" is preferable.

This concept of being baptized into the body is mentioned in a slightly different way in Romans 6:3 and Galatians 3:27, which speak about being "baptized into Christ [Jesus]." This baptism differs from the baptism mentioned by John the Baptist, Jesus, and Peter. According to John the Baptist, it is Jesus who baptizes in the Holy Spirit. According to Paul, it is the Holy Spirit who baptizes into the body of Christ, or into Christ. If this distinction is not maintained, we have the strange idea that Christ baptizes into Christ!

Summary. The distinction between being baptized *by* the Spirit and being baptized *in* the Spirit is not due to a Pentecostal hermeneutical bias. A comparison of the translation of *en* in 1 Corinthians 12:13 in major versions shows a decided preference even by non-Pentecostal scholars for the rendering *by*. The following have the word *by*: KJV, NKJV, NASB, NIV, RSV, Living Bible, TE, The New Testament in Modern English. The translation *in* appears in the following: ASV, NRSV, NEB, NAB.

There is a clear distinction in the purpose of each of the baptisms. Incorporation, or baptism, into Christ or his body is found in 1 Corinthians 12:13. This differs from the baptism in the Holy Spirit, the primary purpose of which is the receiving of power (Luke 24:49; Acts 1:8).

Article H: The Groanings of Romans 8:26

The two-word phrase *stenagmois alaletois* in Romans 8:26 is the subject of much discussion and difference among scholars. Here are sample translations:

> groanings which cannot be uttered (NKJV)
> sighs too deep for words (NRSV)
> groans that words cannot express (NIV)
> groanings too deep for words (NASB)

This article focuses on the noun *stenagmos* and its modifier *alaletos*. For ease of discussion, the singular, nominative forms will be used.

The Noun *Stenagmos*. The meaning of *stenagmos* is simple: sigh, groan or groaning. It occurs only twice in the New Testament and about twenty times in the LXX, where it translates six different Hebrew words. Related verb forms occur eight times in the New Testament and about twenty times in the LXX, where it translates nine different Hebrew words. The verb, like the noun, generally means to sigh or groan.

The noun occurs in Acts 7:34, where Stephen quotes Exodus 3:7: "I have certainly seen the oppression of My people in Egypt, and have heard their groans." Examples of usage in the LXX include the intense pain felt by a woman in labor (Jer. 4:31) and the groaning that takes place when one is in distress (Ps. 38:8). The verb in the LXX expresses a number of different but related ideas: crying out for help (Job 30:25), sighing as an expression of grief (Ezek. 9:4), mourning (Isa. 19:8), groaning of the wounded (Ezek. 26:15), sighing or groaning (Isa. 24:7; Lam. 1:8, 21). New Testament examples include grumbling, complaining, or groaning against someone (James 5:9), and grief in contrast to joy (Heb. 13:17).

Jesus, in his humanness, is twice the subject of this verb. When a deaf man was brought to him, Mark says that "looking up to heaven, he sighed [*stenazo*] and said to him, 'Ephphatha,' that is, 'Be opened'" (7:34, NRSV). In the next chapter Mark records Jesus' reaction to the sign-seeking Pharisees: "And sighing deeply [*anastenazo*] in His spirit, He said, 'Why does this generation seek for a sign?'" (8:12).

The verb occurs twice in the immediate context of Romans 8:26. Verse 22 states, "The whole creation groans [*sustenazo*] and suffers the pains of childbirth together until now." The next verse says, "even we ourselves groan [*stenazo*] within ourselves." These three occurrences of the *stenagmos/stenazo* words are in an eschatological context that must be understood in the light of the original creation and the fall of humanity. In their present, not fully redeemed state, Christians, along with the rest of creation, groan for the ultimate reversal of the curse.

A close parallel is 2 Corinthians 5:2, 4. In talking about the redemption of the body, Paul says that "in this house, we groan [*stenazo*], longing to be clothed with our dwelling from heaven," and further, "while we are in this tent, we groan [*stenazo*], being burdened, because we . . . want . . . to be clothed, in order that what is mortal may be swallowed up by life." This is reminiscent of the eschatological note struck by Isaiah, which, while applying strictly to Israel's return from captivity, foreshadows the ultimate redemption of God's people: "They will find gladness and joy, and sorrow and sighing [*stenazo*] will flee away" (Isa. 35:10; also 51:11).

The Modifier *Alaletos*. *Alaletos* generally means "unexpressed, wordless" (BAGD, 34). It, along with its cognates, is a negative of the verb *laleo*, to speak. This modifier occurs only once in all of Scripture. Since it is virtually impossible to think of groans/sighs being inaudible or silent, it is important to investigate the connection between *alaletos* and *stenagmos*.

A related adjective (*alalos*) describes persons who are mute or dumb (Mark 7:37; 9:17, 25); the idea is that of speechlessness. But it is the verb form (*alalazo*) that occurs most frequently in Scripture, with meanings such as wail or lament (Jer. 4:8; 25:34; Mark 5:38), ring loudly or clang (Ps. 150:5; 1 Cor. 13:1 ["clanging cymbal"]), utter a joyful shout (Ps. 47:1; 66:1), repeat frequently the cry *alala* (a battle cry) (Josh. 6:20). The last passage says that "the people shouted [*alalazo*] with a great shout [*alalagmos*]" just prior to the walls of Jericho falling down.

All the foregoing militates against the idea that Paul is speaking about silent groaning—an obvious oxymoron. *Alaletos* and its cognates involve some kind of vocalization, though it may be in sounds and not words—or at least words not understood by the speaker or the hearers. At this point the activity of the Holy Spirit comes into play.

Speaking in Tongues? Equally competent scholars are divided as to whether the expression *stenagmois alaletois* refers to speaking in tongues, exclusively or partly, or to some unrelated phenomenon. The phrase is unique in Scripture; therefore it will be helpful to look at a passage that is conceptually parallel. Since Romans 8:26 is related to the ministry of the Holy Spirit in prayer on behalf of believers, it can be associated with Paul's statements in 1 Corinthians 14:14–15, where he says, "If I pray in a tongue, my spirit prays, but my mind is unfruitful. . . . I shall pray with the spirit." Romans 8:26 says that the Holy Spirit "helps our weakness . . . the Spirit Himself intercedes for us with groanings too deep for words."

Eminent scholars like E. Käsemann identify these groanings as "glossolalic utterances." F. Godet, well-known Swiss exegete of the late nineteenth century, makes the same identification: "We here find ourselves in a domain analogous to that of the *glossais lalein, speaking in tongues*, to which 1 Cor. xiv. refers; comp. vv. 14 and 15." Others, like F. F. Bruce and C. K. Barrett in their commentaries on the book of Romans, allow for the possibility that the expression includes speaking in tongues. Of special interest is that these scholars were not identified with the Pentecostal/charismatic movement.

Responsible exegesis requires restraint in making an absolute and exclusive identification of the groanings in Romans 8:26 with glossolalia, but the evidence points in that direction. *Alaletos* may indeed mean that the groaning is wordless to the speaker, since he does not understand what the Spirit is praying for and through him. This interpretation would be parallel to Paul's statement that when he prays in tongues, "my mind is unfruitful" (1 Cor. 14:14).

3.5. The Resurrection (15:1–58)

Chapter 15 is the most extensive biblical passage on the doctrine of the resurrection of the dead. Why did Paul, certainly under the inspiration of the Holy Spirit, devote so much space to this teaching?

As with so much in this letter, what Paul writes is either a response to questions raised by the Corinthians themselves or a reaction to reports he had received. At least two situations among the believers motivated him to write at length. One is that some saw no need for a resurrection of their bodies; they had restricted the concept of their own resurrection to the new spiritual life they had in Christ. They felt they had already "arrived," that they had already entered fully into all the blessings of the new age (see comment on 4:8). They might not necessarily have denied the actual, bodily resurrection of Jesus. In fact, they might possibly have argued that his physical resurrection was the basis for their own spiritual resurrection.

Another situation Paul addresses relates to a common Greek idea that ridiculed the concept of bodily resurrection. The belief was that the body is the prison of the soul and that at death it is freed from that prison. Why would anyone want to be reimprisoned in a body? Undoubtedly some of the congregation held this belief even after their conversion. Paul's experience in Athens reflects this common Greek notion (Acts 17:16–34, see comments below).

The Greeks believed in immortality but not in resurrection. Immortality pertains to the soul and is the belief that the soul persists after death. In Greek thought, the dead had some kind of undefined, shadowy existence. The idea of the survival of the soul after death is an almost universal religious belief. But it must be distinguished from the biblical doctrine of the afterlife, which teaches not only that the soul/spirit continues to exist after death (immortality), but also that it will some day be reunited with the body (resurrection).

Nowhere in this chapter does Paul mention the resurrection of the unrighteous dead, but it is unwarranted to infer from this that he did not believe in it. The most simple, and probably most satisfying, explanation is that his concern is to correct the Corinthian believers' misconception or denial of a bodily resurrection for themselves. Nevertheless, there are hints in the letter that unbelievers will indeed be resurrected. The saints will judge the world (6:2), which Paul places in an eschatological context. It is unlikely that this judging will be only of souls and not of embodied spirits. In addition, he says to those who are unable to control themselves sexually that it is better to marry than to burn (see comment on 7:10). This may well include the idea of hell, which involves bodily torment of some kind. And there is at least one unambiguous statement by Paul recorded in Acts 24:15: "There will be a resurrection of both the righteous and the wicked."

Luke's account of Paul in Athens is instructive. "Paul was preaching the good news about Jesus and the resurrection" (Acts 17:18). Luke does not say "his resurrection," though this is a possible rendering. Some Athenians understood "the resurrection" to mean a god in addition to Jesus, which indicates they did not identify it as Jesus' own resurrection. Later, Paul spoke about the final judgment of the world, basing it on the resurrection of Jesus (v. 31). Some sneered "when they heard about the resurrection of the dead" (v. 32)—that is, not Jesus' resurrection specifically, but the eneral idea of resurrection. Since the peeches in Acts are only summaries of the ctual addresses, at some point Paul must have poken to his Athenian audiences specifically bout the resurrection of all, both the righteous nd the unrighteous.

3.5.1. The Elements of the Gospel (15:1–1). This opening section of Paul's lengthy discussion of the resurrection focuses on the ssential elements of the gospel (v. 1). The vord "gospel" (*euangelion*) literally means good news." The concept is so important that 'aul also uses the related verb *euangelizomai* 'preach the good news") twice in verses 1–. An indispensable element of the gospel mesage is the resurrection of Jesus, for it could not e good news if the message ended with only is death and burial.

Paul begins by addressing his readers as brothers." In spite of their many shortcomings vith which he has had to deal, he will not xclude them from the family of God, nor will e regard them as lesser children of God than imself. "I want to remind you" does not accuately translate the verb *gnorizo*, which means I make known." Yet the thought of reminding s there, since the present tense of the verb may uggest the meaning, "I continue to make nown." Morris (200) calls the word "a gentle rebuke," because some Corinthians evidently did not appreciate the meaning of the gospel (see Gal. 1:11 for a similar use of the vord). Paul had initially spent eighteen months n Corinth, "teaching them the word of God" Acts 18:11). He will now rehearse the basic elements of the gospel he preached and taught.

In verses 1–2 Paul makes several important tatements about the gospel: (1) He had preached it to the Corinthians; (2) they had eceived it; (3) they have taken their stand on t; (4) they are saved by means of it. This last verb is in the present tense, indicating an ongoing process. Their salvation began when they irst received the gospel; it will continue as hey "hold firmly to the word" Paul preached o them. This progressive aspect of personal alvation is found in 1:18 ("to us who are being aved") as well as in other passages (e.g., Acts 2:47; Rom. 5:9; 2 Cor. 2:15; 1 Thess. 5:9–10).

The remainder of verse 2 is grammatically difficult, because it is not clear to what element n the sentence the conditional clause "if you hold firmly" should be attached. The simplest solution is to connect it to the idea of "being saved"; that is, the Corinthians will continue being saved if they "hold firmly to the word I preached to you" (NIV; cf. also NASB, NRSV, NKJV). If they fail to do so, they "have believed in vain [*eikei*]." *Eikei* may mean either "to no purpose" or "without due consideration, in a haphazard manner" (BAGD, 222). As Paul will demonstrate shortly, this consequence is because they have rejected an indispensable element of the gospel by means of which they believed—the resurrection of Jesus.

In verses 3–8 Paul encapsulates the gospel in four events: the death of Jesus, his burial, his resurrection, and his post-resurrection appearances. We note at the outset that Paul twice uses the phrase "according to the Scriptures" (vv. 3–4). The heart of the New Testament proclamation of the Gospel is grounded firmly in the Old Testament, which foretold the key events of Christ's death and resurrection. Paul makes clear that he is not the originator of the gospel. He says, "What I received [*paralambano*] I passed on [*paradidomi*] to you." He used these same verbs to introduce his instruction on the Lord's Supper (see comment on 11:23). Therefore, what he shares with the Corinthians is the basic message proclaimed by the early church (cf. 1:21; 2:4). This matter is "of first importance." There may be additional elements, but the starting point and the focal point of the gospel are these four events.

Paul here seems to contradict what he says elsewhere, that he received (*paralambano*) the gospel "by revelation from Jesus Christ" (Gal. 1:11–12). The contradiction, however, is apparent, not real. Jesus revealed himself to Paul on the Damascus road, and on the basis of that experience Paul proceeded immediately to preach Christ (Gal. 1:15–17). But as with the Lord's Supper, there were many details about the death, burial, resurrection, and post-resurrection appearances of Jesus that Paul could not have known apart from consultation with men like Peter and James (Gal. 1:18–19). In that sense, he was the recipient of the traditions concerning Jesus. The main point is that Paul did not invent or originate what he passed on to them. Barrett comments: "Paul was a Christian rabbi, handing on a body of established truth within the circle of his pupils" (337). Most scholars regard verses 3b–5 as an early Christian creed that Paul quotes.

(1) "Christ died for [*hyper*] our sins according to the Scriptures" (v. 3). Paul had previously written about the death of Jesus (1:18–25; 2:2; 7:20; 8:11; 11:23–26). He now says that it was "for our sins"—a common theme in his writings (see Rom. 3:24–26; 4:25; 8:3; 2 Cor. 5:21; Gal. 1:4). His death was an atoning death, and it was in accordance with the Scriptures. It was not an afterthought in the mind of God, nor was it accidental or unanticipated.

Paul does not quote from the Old Testament, but he must have had in mind Isaiah's statement, "He bore the sin of many," which concludes the passage on the Suffering Servant (Isa. 52:13–53:12). The identification of Jesus with Isaiah's Servant of the Lord (Isa. 42:1; 52:13; 53:11) is made a number of times in the early speeches of Acts (Acts 3:13, 26; 4:27, 30; see also Matt. 12:18). Moreover, Paul must surely have related the atoning death of Jesus to the Old Testament sacrifices offered as atonement for sin, in anticipation of the one eternal sacrifice to be made by "the Lamb of God, who takes away the sin of the world" (John 1:29). Then, too, our attention goes back to Paul's statement that "Christ, our Passover lamb, has been sacrificed" (see comment on 1 Cor. 5:7). Even though this verse does not mention Christ's dying for sin, the concept of his death is nevertheless a fulfillment of the Old Testament type.

(2) "He was buried" (v. 4a). Possibly the Old Testament background for this is Isaiah 53:9, "He was assigned a grave with the wicked, and with the rich in his death." Why even mention the burial of Jesus? It was, of course, the intermediate step between his death and his resurrection; and it underscores both the certainty of his death and the reality of his resurrection. It is recorded in all four Gospels. Peter, on the day of Pentecost, preached that "the patriarch David died and was buried, and his tomb is here to this day" (Acts 2:29). By contrast, Peter then speaks of the resurrection of Christ, the Son of David, who "was not abandoned to the grave, nor did his body see decay" (2:31). Since he was buried, his resurrection had to be the reanimation of a corpse.

(3) "He was raised [*egegertai*] on the third day according to the Scriptures" (1 Cor. 15:4b). A shift in tenses takes place. Paul used the simple past (Greek aorist) tense in speaking of Christ's death and burial; he follows with the Greek perfect tense in speaking of his resurrection. This tense suggests that the event took place in the past and is still in effect. A valid paraphrase would be, "He was raised and continues in that state." So important is this concept that Paul uses the word *egegertai* six more times in this chapter (vv. 12, 13, 14, 16, 17, 20). Christ was and is the risen Lord. "He always lives" (Heb. 7:25). "I am the Living One; I was dead, and behold I am alive for ever and ever!" (Rev. 1:18). Note also that this key verb is in the passive voice. It stresses the activity of the Father in raising the Son (v. 15; cf. Rom. 8:11), even though it may also be said that Jesus raised himself (John 2:19–22) or that he was raised by the power of the Holy Spirit (Rom. 1:4).

The phrase "according to the Scriptures" probably modifies "was raised" rather than "on the third day." The Old Testament contains no clear reference to a resurrection on the third day, though some cite Hosea 6:2 (doubtful) and Jonah 1:17 (possible). Jesus, in predicting his resurrection, did indeed liken himself to Jonah and his three days in the fish (Matt. 12:40). Some find a prophecy of his resurrection in Isaiah 53:10, which reads: "Though the LORD makes his life a guilt offering, he will see his offspring and prolong his days." Others see it in Psalm 16:10, quoted in Acts by both Peter and Paul: "You will not abandon me to the grave, nor will you let your Holy One see decay" (Acts 2:27–31; 13:35–37). Bruce (140) suggests that Paul, in light of 1 Corinthians 15:20, 23, was more likely thinking of the presentation of the firstfruits of the spring harvest (Lev. 23), prescribed for the Sunday following Passover.

(4) "He appeared" to three individuals and three groups (vv. 5–8). This list of post-resurrection appearances is not exhaustive. No appearances to women are mentioned, perhaps because their testimony, in the eyes of the culture, would not be considered reliable. Jesus' appearance to Cephas (Peter) is recorded in Luke 24:34 (see also Mark 16:7). It was appropriate that the leader of the early church should receive a personal visitation from the risen Lord. Moreover, Jesus probably wanted to assure Peter of his mercy after the latter's threefold denial.

Jesus then appeared to "the Twelve." The phrase is not to be taken literally to mean twelve persons. It was rather a general designation for the group of men who had been closest to Jesus (Mark 3:14). His appearances to them included one occasion when only ten were present (John 20:19–20) and another when eleven were present (Matt. 28:16–17; John 20:26).

Jesus also appeared "to more than five hundred of the brothers at the same time" (v. 6). The Gospels, however, contain no record of such an event. How and when did Paul learn of this and other appearances he mentions? Probably when he visited Peter and James three years after his conversion (Gal. 1:18–19). Paul adds that most of the five hundred men were still alive, more than twenty years afterward, "though some have fallen asleep." He again applies the euphemism of sleeping to believers who have died (1 Cor. 7:39 [lit.]; 11:30; 15:18, 20, 51; 1 Thess. 4:13–15).

James was also privileged to see the risen Jesus (v. 7). He is mentioned together with Peter as those whom Paul had visited in Jerusalem (Gal. 1:18–19). Most scholars agree that he is a brother of Jesus. Along with his other brothers, he was not a follower of Jesus prior to the crucifixion (John 7:5). More than likely, his conversion was the result of this resurrection appearance to him. Within forty days of the resurrection of Jesus, James and his brothers were among the company of believers (Acts 1:14). He later became the leader of the Jerusalem church (ch. 15) and was recognized as an apostle (Gal. 1:19). He is the author of the letter of James.

Jesus then appeared "to all the apostles" (v. 7). Does Paul here mean only "the Twelve" plus James? That is possible, but he may have a larger group in mind (Héring, 162). The extended meaning of the term *apostle* (see on 4:9; 9:1) may here include a group of missionaries, larger than the Twelve but smaller than the group of five hundred mentioned previously (Barrett, 343). If this is true, there is no sure record of this appearance in the Gospels or in Acts.

"Last of all," says Paul, Jesus appeared also to him, "as to one abnormally born" (v. 8). "Last of all" may mean that, to Paul's knowledge, there were no appearances of the resurrected Jesus after his own experience. His encounter with Jesus on the Damascus road was not a vision; it was Jesus himself who appeared to him. He had stated earlier, "Have I not seen Jesus our Lord?" (9:1). This encounter clearly placed his experience on the same level with that of Peter, the Twelve, and James, and consequently qualified him to be an apostle.

In what sense was Paul "one abnormally born"? Other translations read "one born out of due time" (NKJV) and "one untimely born" (NASB, NRSV). Barrett suggests, "one hurried into the world before his time" (344). BAGD says the word used here, *ektroma*, means "untimely birth, miscarriage" and suggests, "So Paul calls himself, perhaps taking up an insult . . . hurled at him by his opponents" (246). They called him an "abortion" of an apostle, implying he was "an ugly parody of a true apostle," just as an aborted fetus is of a healthy infant born at the full term of gestation (Bruce, 142). Indications are that Paul was not a handsome man (2 Cor. 10:10). His opponents may have combined an insult to his personal appearance with a criticism of his claim to apostleship (Morris, 204; for Paul's lengthy defense of his apostleship, see 2 Cor. 10–13).

In verses 9–11 Paul continues to defend his calling as an apostle. The paragraph begins with the emphatic pronoun "I." He calls himself "the least of the apostles" and says he does not even deserve to be called an apostle (cf. Eph. 3:8; 1 Tim. 1:15). He seems to make a concession to his critics, but that is not the reason for his self-deprecating remarks. In fact, he says later, "I do not think that I am in the least inferior to those 'super-apostles'" (2 Cor. 11:5). His purpose is really to magnify the grace of God bestowed on him. This depreciating of himself is because of his preconversion persecution of "the church of God" (1 Cor. 15:9; cf. Acts 8:1–3; 9:1–5; 22:4–5; 26:9–11; Gal. 1:13, 22–23; Phil. 3:6; 1 Tim. 1:12–14). His expression of unworthiness is therefore in relation to the Lord, not to his critics.

Paul is what he is "by the grace of God" (v. 10). Grace (*charis*), the bestowal of divine favor, is especially manifested in Paul. First and foremost, it was the means of his personal salvation (Eph. 2:8). But secondarily, and especially in this context, it is the basis for his divine call to apostleship. *Charis* is the root of *charisma*, a gift that is a concrete manifestation of grace (cf. Article B, above). The two words are used almost interchangeably in

Romans 12:3 (*charis*) and 12:6 (*charisma*). Paul includes apostles among the gifts (*charismata*) (1 Cor. 12:28).

He assures his readers that his call to be an apostle "was not without effect." Indeed, he "worked harder than all of them." The record of Acts 13–28 is indisputable proof of Paul's tireless labors on behalf of the gospel. Yet his missionary successes are attributable not to himself but to "the grace of God that was with me." God's grace was *with* him, the preposition suggesting that grace is "a fellow-laborer, working alongside him," thus emphasizing that Paul cannot receive credit (Morris, 205). Fee (736) comments that even though Paul's labor is in response to grace, it is more properly the effect of grace; "all is of grace; nothing is deserved."

In verse 11, Paul returns to the thought with which he began the chapter—the preaching of the gospel, which the Corinthians had originally believed. The message he preached and continues to preach is the same as that proclaimed by the other apostles. They, as well as he, preached not only the death and burial of Jesus, but also his resurrection, which was attested by his appearances to them. Therefore the Corinthian Christians must accept the doctrine of the resurrection because it is a teaching held by all the apostles.

3.5.2. Denial of the Resurrection (15:12–19). For the Corinthians' general attitude toward the idea of resurrection, see the comments that introduce this chapter. It is important to note that Paul says *some*, not *all*, of the Corinthian believers denied the concept (v. 12). His argument in this paragraph may be summarized as follows: If the dead don't rise, then Christ could not have risen. If Christ did not indeed rise, then (1) the apostles' preaching is useless and they are false witnesses; (2) the faith of the Corinthians is futile and they are still in their sins; (3) Christians who have died are lost eternally; (4) Christians are the most pitiable of all people.

A more accurate translation of verse 12 would begin, "But if Christ is preached that he has risen from the dead." Paul contrasts the apostolic word with the faulty thinking of some of the believers when he completes the sentence by asking, "How can some of you say that there is no resurrection of the dead?" The answer is that they had allowed current pagan thought or the idea of their own super-spirituality to contradict the apostles' message of the resurrection.

We should note that Paul says Christ has risen "from the dead" (*ek nekron*). A more accurate rendering of these two Greek words is "from among dead persons" (also v. 20). This phrase must be distinguished from "resurrection of the dead" (*anastasis nekron*), more accurately translated as "resurrection of dead persons" (vv. 12, 13, 21, 42). This distinction is not accidental. Jesus died and for three days was one of the dead; then he was resurrected *from among* them as "the firstfruits of those who have fallen asleep" (v. 20). The New Testament expresses this concept in another way when it designates Christ as the firstborn from the dead (Col. 1:18; Rev. 1:5). On the other hand, "resurrection of dead persons" refers to the raising of all and does not mean the raising of some and the nonraising of others.

Paul's argumentation in verses 13–19 is somewhat repetitious, but it is his way of hammering away at the truth with a succession of "if" clauses. He proceeds to detail the drastic consequences of not believing in a resurrection of the dead. (1) Such disbelief is a denial of the resurrection of Christ (v. 13). Paul argues from the general to the specific: If there is no such thing as resurrection from the dead, "then not even Christ has been raised." Verse 16 repeats this idea. Furthermore, the resurrection of Christ is "the source of Divine Power which *effects* the Resurrection in store for His members" (Robertson and Plummer, 348).

(2) Both Paul's preaching (*kerygma*) and their faith are "useless" (v. 14). In verse 17 he says that their faith would be "futile." In the Greek text, both adjectives are in the emphatic position at the beginning of their respective clauses. Their faith (*pistis*) refers to their trust in and commitment to Christ, not to the body of truth sometimes called "the faith." The reason is that Christ's resurrection demonstrates God's approval and validation of his atoning death, for without his resurrection there can be no justification from sins (Rom. 4:25).

(3) Paul and his fellow preachers "are then found to be false witnesses about God, for we have testified about God that he raised Christ from the dead" (v. 15). The second "about God" is better translated "against God" (Morris, 207), conveying the idea that they were

aying God did something which in fact he did ot do. In simple words, they would be liars.

(4) The Corinthians "are still in [their] sins" v. 17). "Christ died for our sins" (v. 3) has no alidity if his death was not followed by his esurrection, which, once again, was the ather's seal of approval on his atoning death. The Corinthians would still be dead in their respasses and sins (cf. Eph. 2:1, 5), since a lead Christ would be unable to save them from leath, which is the penalty for sin (Robertson nd Plummer, 349).

(5) "Those also who have fallen asleep in Christ are lost [*apollymi*]" (v. 18). "They had erished irretrievably, being eternally cut off rom God" (Bruce, 145). Paul used *apollymi* vhen he contrasted those who are perishing vith those who are being saved (1:18; cf. also Cor. 2:15). This strong word occurs four ther times in the letter (1:19; 8:11; 10:9–10). f there is no resurrection, then "those who ave fallen asleep in Christ" is a contradiction n terms. They could not be "in Christ," since hat phrase means participation in the life of Christ. Nor can it be said that they have "fallen sleep," since the expression presupposes a ime of awakening.

(6) Christians "are to be pitied more than all nen" if "only for this life we have hope in Christ" (v. 19). The Greek words mean, more iterally, "we are ones who have set our hope nd continue to hope." Paul does not deny that n this present life there are compensations for elievers (1 Tim. 4:8), but his point is that if his world is all that exists for us, then we are leluded. We would be "martyrs to an illusion" Héring, 163). What then would be the point of uffering the loss of all things for the sake of Christ (Phil. 3:8) or of struggling to win the mperishable crown (1 Cor. 9:25)?

3.5.3. Christ, the Firstfruits (15:20–28). Paul now changes course from the "if" statenents of verses 12–19 to a series of certainties bout the resurrection of Christ and its implications for believers. Much of what he now ays is grounded in the Old Testament. He egins by affirming, "But Christ has indeed een raised from the dead" (v. 20). He likens he resurrection of Jesus to the offering of "the irstfruits" of the harvest (Lev. 23:10–11). In hat annual event, the sheaf was offered to the Lord as the first installment of the crop, and it vas a guarantee of the coming harvest. The crop, of which Jesus was the firstfruits, consists of "those who have fallen asleep." It may be significant that this particular offering was made on the day after the Sabbath and that Jesus was raised from the dead on the day after the Sabbath.

Paul goes on to give the basis for the hope of resurrection by placing Adam and Christ alongside each other (vv. 21–22; he returns to this Adam-Christ analogy in vv. 44b–49; cf. also Rom. 5:12–21). This is an important theme in Paul's writings, even though these are the only passages where Adam is mentioned by name. In the verses at hand, the points of comparison and contrast are as follows: (1) Death came through Adam; resurrection of the dead comes through Christ. (2) In Adam, all die; in Christ, all will be made alive.

Adam was the means by which death made its entrance into the world. It was the penalty for his sin (Gen. 2:17; 3:22–24; Rom. 5:12). The death was both physical and spiritual—physical in that his body would return to the earth, spiritual in that he was excluded from the presence of God in Eden. But Adam's sin adversely affected all his descendants in a manner not clearly delineated in Scripture. A clue, however, lies in the Hebrew word for Adam (*'adam*). Not only was it the name of the first man; it is also the Hebrew word for humankind. Genesis 5:2 says that when God created male and female, "he called them 'man' [*'adam*]." The historical figure Adam, then, is representative of all humanity. As the head of the human race, his sin affected all his descendants so that all die. The precise manner in which this happened, however, is not given in Scripture and is debated among theologians.

But Christ is the head of another humanity, by virtue of his incarnation. He was as fully human as Adam. As a human being, he died; but through his death he destroyed death by rising from the dead (Heb. 2:14–15). Christ, who is later called "the last Adam" (1 Cor. 15:45), reversed the effects of the first Adam's sin—death by Adam #1 and life by Adam #2. Just as Adam's sin had such far-reaching consequences, so Christ's sinless life and atoning death have far-reaching consequences.

All who are "in Adam" die (v. 22); their death is both spiritual and physical. All who are "in Christ" will be made alive; they will suffer physical death, but will overcome that death by participating in the benefits of the resurrection of the last Adam. A distinction, therefore, must be made between "all" as it relates to Adam and "all" as it relates to Christ. Paul does not imply that the entire human race will be saved on the basis of Christ's overcoming of death, for he has already spoken in this letter of those who will perish (1:18; 3:17; 5:13; 6:9–10; 9:27). His point is that only all those who have identified themselves with Christ will be raised. Paul's remarks are addressed to Christians, so that his concern is with the resurrection to life that the righteous may anticipate (Dan. 12:2; John 5:29; Acts 24:15). It is the "dead in Christ" who will be raised at his coming (1 Thess. 4:16), not all the dead.

Paul has based the resurrection of believers on the resurrection of Christ. Then he says, "But each in his own turn [*tagma*]" (v. 23). *Tagma* was a military term meaning rank. In the present context, Paul speaks of two ranks in chronological order. The first is Christ, the firstfruits (see comment on v. 20). After him will be the resurrection of those who belong to him, at the time of his coming (*parousia*). This Greek word was often used in the secular world for a royal visit. In the New Testament, it is used frequently for the return of the reigning Christ. Especially related to the present context are Paul's words in 1 Thessalonians 4:15–17, which speak of the resurrection of believers at the time of the Parousia.

"Then the end will come," says Paul (v. 24). The Greek text simply reads, "Then the end [*to telos*]." Some take *to telos* to mean "the rest" and see here a third group, unbelievers, to be resurrected at the very end. There is no basis, however, for translating the Greek noun this way. Its general meaning is that of aim or consummation, and it is comparable to the expression "the end of the age" (Matt. 13:40, 49; 24:3; 28:20). Just as there will have been a time lapse between the first and second stages, so there will be one between the second and the third.

Verses 24–27 speak of events that will take place between the Parousia and the Consummation. Christ will abolish "all dominion, authority and power." It is unnecessary to determine how these nouns differ from one another. They represent, collectively, all the hostile forces that oppose Christ and his people. He will render them ineffective and inoperative; they will be deprived of their power and influence. The same is said about death. Death is the last enemy to be abolished (Heb. 2:14–15; Rev. 20:14); it, together with Hades, will be cast into the lake of fire. Elsewhere these hostile forces, including death, are treated as though they have already been disarmed and abolished (Col. 2:15; 2 Tim. 1:10; 1 Peter 3:22). The reason is that "the death and resurrection of Christ constitute the decisive battle in the war that ends victoriously with the resurrection of his people" (Bruce, 147). This is another example of the already/not yet principle observed previously in this letter (see comment on 1:18; 4:8).

All the enemies of the Lord will be subdued; they will be "under his feet" (vv. 25, 27). Paul alludes to two messianic psalms. Psalm 110:1 reads, "The LORD [Yahweh] says to my Lord . . . 'I make your enemies a footstool for your feet.'" This verse is applied elsewhere to Jesus (Mark 12:35–37; Acts 2:34–35). The apostle then cites a related passage, Psalm 8:6, which reads, "You [Yahweh] put everything under his feet." This psalm refers to humankind in general and to Adam in particular, to whom God originally gave dominion over everything. Paul now applies it in a fuller sense to Christ, the last Adam.

Paul calls the period between the Parousia and the End "the kingdom" (v. 24) and says that Christ "must reign until [God] has put all his enemies under his feet" (v. 25; cf. v. 27). The words "must reign" point to the certainty of his rulership, which will be over everyone and everything, with the obvious exception of God himself. After Christ has so ruled, he then "hands over the kingdom to God the Father" (v. 24). Then he who subjected everyone and everything to himself "will be made subject to [the Father] who put everything under him" (v. 28). Disobedience to God characterized the first Adam; obedience to God the Father characterized and will eternally characterize the last Adam.

Inevitably, the question of subordinationism arises here. As noted previously (see comment on 3:29), the Son's subordination to the Father is functional and relates primarily to his role as Redeemer. This must be distinguished sharply from any notion of inferiority to the Father, since both he and the Father share the same essential nature.

The purpose to which all these events lead is "so that God may be all in all" (cf. also Rom. 11:36; 1 Cor. 15:54–57). "God will be supreme in every quarter and in every way" (Fee, 760). It is best to understand "God" comprehensively to mean the Godhead (Father, Son, and Holy Spirit), rather than simply the Father.

3.5.4. Arguments from Experience (15:29–34). Paul now directs attention to Christian practices and experiences that are meaningless if there is no resurrection of believers. (1) He begins with the question, "What will those do who are baptized for the dead?" (v. 29). The words "baptized for the dead" form one of the most puzzling clauses in all of Scripture. Attempted explanations are too numerous to list (there may be as many as forty!). Only two of the most viable interpretations will be given.

(a) At face value Paul is talking about proxy baptism or what some call vicarious baptism. Note that he says "those [not 'we'] do who are baptized for the dead." Apparently some believers engaged in this practice on behalf of unbaptized deceased believers. It is unlikely that deceased unbelievers were the intended beneficiaries. The practice would be based on a sacramental or mystical view of baptism that assured ultimate salvation for departed believers.

A major problem with this interpretation, apart from its theological unsoundness, is that church history does not record such a practice in the first century; at best, it was practiced in the second century only by some heretics. Moreover, it is unusual that Paul neither condemns nor condones the practice. He mentions it in passing "in an *ad hominem* argument with neither praise nor blame" (Bruce, 148). The probable reason is his concern to show how illogical and useless proxy baptism is if there is no resurrection of the dead anyway. Thus he asks, "If the dead are not raised at all, why are people baptized for them?" Since this is the only reference in Scripture to such a practice, it is improper to base on it a doctrine and practice of proxy baptism. Morris is surely right when he says, "The language points to vicarious baptism," adding that we are left to conjecture if we try to interpret otherwise (215). Héring agrees, adding that the preposition *hyper* has the sense of "on behalf of" or even "instead of" (170).

(b) As a point of interest, a different interpretation of "baptized for the dead" is that the dead are deceased, baptized believers and that the persons being baptized are loved ones or friends who submit to baptism to ensure being reunited with the departed. Robertson and Plummer call this "one of the best" interpretations (360–61).

(2) Paul refers to his own experience (vv. 30–32): "Why do we endanger ourselves every hour," he asks, if there is no hope of resurrection, if death ends everything? In 2 Corinthians 1:8–9; 11:23–28, he lists some of the hardships he endured for the sake of the gospel.

Verse 31 is an oath or a solemn statement. It contains the word *ne*, which is a "particle of strong affirmation" and is translated "by," followed by the "person or thing by which one swears or affirms" (BAGD, 537). Barrett's translation captures this idea: "By the boasting that I have of you in Christ Jesus our Lord, brothers" (365). The statement can mean either Paul's boasting regarding the Corinthians or their boasting regarding him. The former choice is better suited to the letter (see also Phil. 2:16; 1 Thess. 2:18), since many Corinthians were critical of him. Not surprisingly, Paul's boasting is grounded in the Lord, not in his own achievements.

The statement "I die every day" is based on Paul's solemn affirmation. The context dictates that he is speaking about the possibility of martyrdom, which threatened him constantly (see also Rom. 8:35–36; 1 Cor. 4:9; 2 Cor. 4:10–12). In other words, Paul is not referring to some daily self-mortification as a means to attaining complete sanctification. He then cites one example of the daily jeopardy in which he lived. "I fought wild beasts in Ephesus" (1 Cor. 15:32). "Wild beasts" must not be interpreted literally. (a) Paul makes no mention of fighting actual wild beasts in the list of trials he endured (2 Cor. 11:23–28). (b) Roman citizens were exempt from such punishment. In exceptional circumstances when they were so condemned, they lost their citizenship even if they survived. Paul was still a Roman citizen at the time he wrote this letter. (c) Had Paul actually fought wild beasts, he likely would not have survived to write about it.

"Wild beasts" is thus a metaphor for those who sought his life, possibly the rioters in Ephesus (Acts 19:23–29; cf. also 2 Cor. 1:8–10).

Or, since he was writing this letter from Ephesus (1 Cor. 16:8), he may be referring to the opposition he was encountering in that city. This metaphorical use of wild beasts is found in a number of biblical passages (e.g., Ps. 22:12–13; 2 Tim. 4:17; Titus 1:12).

Paul asks, "What have I gained?" if he fought "for merely human reasons [*kata anthropon*]" (NIV). This Greek phrase means "according to man" and has been translated in a number of ways: "from human motives" (NASB); "with merely human hopes" (NRSV); "in the manner of men" (NKJV); Barrett suggests "on purely human terms" (365). The thought is that there is neither earthly nor eternal gain if such suffering and impending death are the end of all. "If the dead are not raised, [then] 'Let us eat and drink, for tomorrow we die.'" Paul quotes Isaiah 22:13 and also perhaps has in mind Ecclesiastes 2:24; 9:7–10.

(3) If there is no resurrection of the dead, not only will there be little motivation to pursue the Christian life with all its perils, but also this absence of hope easily leads to relaxed moral standards and an attitude of gratifying oneself with the pleasures and pleasure-seekers of this world. So Paul admonishes, "Do not be misled" (v. 33). The command is better understood as, "Stop being misled." He then quotes a proverb going back to Menander, a Greek dramatist: "Bad company corrupts good character [*ethe*; better trans. 'habits']." (For other quotations of secular writers by Paul, see Acts 17:28; Titus 1:12.) But Paul does not advocate a Christian's complete disassociation from unbelievers (1 Cor. 5:9–13; 10:27). He may be implying that believers ought to separate themselves from other believers, not unbelievers, who live immoral lives (see comment on 5:1–8).

The admonition to stop being misled is followed by two interrelated ones (v. 34). (a) "Come back to your senses as you ought." In blunt language, Paul says, "Get sober," referring not to drunkenness but to wrong reasoning. (b) "Stop sinning." Morris (217) comments, "Doctrine leads to conduct, and unsound doctrine in the end must lead to sinful behaviour." Failure to live rightly connects with failure to think rightly. The reason Paul gives for these two commands is that "there are some who are ignorant of God." "Ignorance" is *agnosia*, a lack of spiritual discernment (BAGD, 12), and should be distinguished from *agnoia*, lack of knowledge. Earlier in the letter the apostle had criticized those who claimed to have special spiritual knowledge (2:5; 8:1; 13:2, 8). In reality, such persons are ignorant of God and need to come back to their senses. It is to their shame that they continue to be misled and to sin.

3.5.5. The Nature of the Resurrection Body (15:35–49). Paul has argued for the reality of the resurrection. He now turns to the nature of the resurrected body and the manner in which the resurrection will take place. He must do this partly to correct a Jewish belief that the resurrection body will be identical with the body that died. This passage may be summarized by the statement: "While there will be identity there will also be difference" (Morris, 218).

Verses 35–44a illustrate Paul's main point by the analogy of sowing and reaping and then the analogy of different kinds of bodies in the universe. The passage answers the questions "How are the dead raised? With what kind of body will they come?" (v. 35). We do not know whether these questions were asked by some in Corinth, or whether Paul is following the rhetorical style of a diatribe, in which the speaker poses an assumed objection and then answers it (e.g., see Rom. 9:19; 11:19). In either event, the questions are foolish ones (v. 36).

In verses 36–38 Paul begins his response by bluntly addressing as "You fool!" (NASB lit., "foolish one") the one who asks the questions. He then uses the illustration of a seed and a plant: "What *you* [emphatic position] sow does not come to life unless it dies." Death is the necessary antecedent to life; life emerges only when there is first a death. Paul's words are reminiscent of those of Jesus: "Unless a kernel of wheat falls to the ground and dies, it remains only a single seed. But if it dies, it produces many seeds" (John 12:24). The seed must die, that is, be buried, before it "is . . . made alive" (NKJV). This last verb is in the passive voice, pointing to an agent external to the seed, God, as the life-giver. This thought permeates the remaining discussion of the resurrection body. There is continuity between the seed and the plant ("body") that emerges, even though there is also considerable difference (vv. 37–38). God gives to the individual seed "a body as he has determined."

Paul now moves to his second point: There re different types of bodies (vv. 39–41). Bod-›s exist in many different forms, and each ›rm is appropriate for its particular type of xistence. Not all flesh is the same—the flesh f human beings, animals, birds, and fish all ifferering from each another (v. 39). It is not lear why Paul switched from "body" (*soma*) verse 38 to "flesh" (*sarx*) in verse 39. It may e simply for literary variety. Héring suggests iat *sarx* is "the sort of matter from which a ody is composed" (174).

There is also a difference between heavenly odies and earthly bodies, and the splendor *loxa*) of one differs from that of the other ⁄. 40). "Heavenly bodies" may mean the sun, ıoon, stars, etc., but Paul mentions these pecifically in the next verse. Likely he refers ere to celestial beings (angels, etc.), whose odies are of a different nature from those of uman beings. The point is that each group pos-ɛsses bodies proper to their sphere of exis-›nce. Paul then speaks of heavenly bodies as 'e commonly use that term, making the point ıat the sun, moon, and stars each have their wn unique splendor or brightness (*doxa* gain). In summary, Paul implies, since there re so many different kinds of bodies in the uni-erse, why should we suppose that there can be nly one kind of human body (Bruce, 151)?

In verses 42–44a Paul draws on the previ-us analogies (vv. 35–41) to summarize his rgument about the nature of the resurrection ody. In verses 42–43, "the body" is the sub-ɛct of all the clauses. The contrast between the arthly body and the resurrected body is raphic. The body is sown "in corruption" NKJV), in dishonor, and in weakness; it is aised "in incorruption" (NKJV), in glory, and ı power. The former is sown a natural body, ıe latter is raised a spiritual body. "Natural" escribes the body as animated by the soul; spiritual" describes the body as animated by ıe Holy Spirit and may also mean "supernat-ıral" (see 10:3–4).

Paul speaks elsewhere of this transforma-ion as "the redemption of our bodies" by the ctivity of the Holy Spirit (Rom. 8:23, cf. . 11), the result being a body like the "glori-›us body" of the Lord Jesus Christ (Phil. 3:20–1). The change that takes place is more than reanimation or resuscitation of a dead body. t is a transformation by which the body is raised "in incorruption"—that is, no longer subject to death and decay.

Verses 44b–49 elaborate on the Adam-Christ analogy of verses 21–22 and apply it to the concepts of the natural body and the spiritual body (v. 44a). It will help to place this material in parallel columns.

Adam	*Christ*
natural body came first	spiritual body follows
first man	last Adam
became a living soul	became a life-giving spirit
origin is the dust of the earth	origin is heaven, and he is heavenly
those of the dust are like him	heavenly ones are like him
we have borne the likeness of Adam	we will bear the likeness of Christ

The background for this comparison is Genesis 2:7, "The LORD God formed the man from the dust of the ground and breathed into his nostrils the breath of life, and the man became a living being [Heb. *nephesh*, 'soul']." From the beginning, all persons have been characterized by "soul" (*psyche*, Greek equivalent of *nephesh*). Christ, however, is the "last Adam." "There will be no other Head of the human race" (Robertson and Plummer, 373). All persons receive their "soulish" (*psychikos*) nature from Adam; they share his earthly origin—the dust of the earth. The righteous receive their "spiritual" (*pneumatikos*) nature from Christ; they share his heavenly origin, so that they are "those who are of heaven [*epouranios*]" (v. 48). It is possible that Paul here means that Jesus both had a heavenly origin and that he is now "heavenly," that is, in a glorified state. Paul says elsewhere that believers are "in the heavenly realms [*epouranios* again] . . . in Christ" (Eph. 1:3, 20; 2:6). Using somewhat different imagery, Jesus said, "Flesh gives birth to flesh, but the Spirit gives birth to spirit" (John 3:6).

"Just as we have borne the image of the man of dust, we will also bear the image of the man of heaven" (v. 49, NRSV). A variant and possibly original reading of the Greek text makes the main clause a type of command: "Let us also bear" (see NIV and NRSV notes). Paul would then be exhorting believers to be conformed to the image of Christ (cf. Rom. 8:29; 2 Cor. 3:18), appealing to them to prepare themselves for the future. Complete conformity to Christ's image, however, cannot be realized in this life. It will happen at the Parousia. The apostle John says that "when he appears, we shall be like him, for we shall see him as he is" (1 John 3:2).

3.5.6. The Believers' Triumph Over Death (15:50–58). Paul concludes his lengthy resurrection discourse with one of the most triumphant notes in all of Scripture. The word "victory" occurs three times in verses 54–57. He alludes to themes previously mentioned and introduces new elements.

Verses 50–57 relate the concepts of resurrection and transformation to the return of Christ. Paul declares that "flesh and blood cannot inherit the kingdom of God, nor does the perishable inherit the imperishable" (v. 50). The two statements suggest Hebrew synonymous parallelism: flesh and blood = the perishable; the kingdom of God = the imperishable. Barrett (379), however, following Jeremias, suggests that the first clause refers to the living at the time of the Parousia and the second to those who died before the Parousia.

In any case, "flesh and blood" refers to humankind in distinction from God and points to the limitations and frailty of earthly existence (Matt. 16:17; Gal. 1:16; Heb. 2:14). The two elements form a single entity, since "cannot" is singular in the Greek. Both are perishable, subject to decay (1 Cor. 15:42, 53–54). On the other hand, the kingdom of God is imperishable. Paul had previously said that the unrighteous will not inherit the kingdom of God (6:9–10). He now says that what is only physical (flesh and blood) cannot inherit the kingdom. His point in the present passage is that a radical change must take place in a believer's body prior to its entrance into the kingdom. It must be transformed from a "natural body" to a "spiritual body" (vv. 42–44).

The miracle of the resurrection of believers is a "mystery" (v. 51). The New Testament concept of a mystery is that something that at one time had not been fully revealed has now been made known to God's people (see 2:7; 4:1). "We will not all sleep" might better be understood as, "Not all of us will sleep," meaning that some will be alive at the time of the transformation. "We will all be changed" denotes a change for deceased as well as liv ing Christians.

The speed with which the transformatio will take place is captured in the expression "in a flash" and "in the twinkling of an eye" (v. 52). For the latter expression, Morris suggests, "the time it takes to cast a glance, or perhaps to flutter an eyelid" (228). The resurrection will occur "at the last trumpet" (see Matt. 24:31; 1 Thess. 4:16; Rev. 8:2). Trumpets are often used in Scripture to herald special events, to call to arms, or to signal victory over enemies. The adjective "last" is better understood as describing the time period when the trumpet will be sounded, that is, the End, rather than that it will be the last in a series of trumpet blasts.

In verses 53–54, Paul likens the resurrection event to being clothed with a spiritual body, which he says "must" happen. The metaphor suggests that the earthly body is the clothing of the soul and spirit; at the resurrection moment the believer will receive a different attire. Paul makes the same basic point under different imagery when he likens the earthly body to an earthly tent and the resurrected body to an eternal house (2 Cor. 5:1–4). Some see two groups in the word pairs "perishable-imperishable" and "mortal-immortality," the former being deceased believers and the latter living believers. If Paul did not intend this distinction here, he did allude to it earlier (see comment on 1 Cor. 15:51) and clearly mentions it in 1 Thessalonians 4:15–17.

In typical fashion, Paul sees his teaching as a fulfillment of Scripture: "Death has been swallowed up [*katapino*] in victory" (v. 54) is from Isaiah 25:8. In a parallel passage, he speaks of "what is mortal" being "swallowed up [*katapino*] by life" (2 Cor. 5:4). "Where, O death, is your victory? Where, O death, is your sting [*kentron*]?" (v. 55) is an adaptation of Hosea 13:14, in which Death and Sheol are personified. Paul is taunting death, implying that for the believer its sting and victory are only temporary. A *kentron* may be either a goad to drive oxen (Acts 26:14) or the sting of an animal, such as a scorpion (Rev. 9:10). Paul explains that the sting is not death itself, but sin (v. 56).

For the believer, therefore, whose sin has been forgiven, death has no sting. Death is gain, not loss (Phil. 1:21, 23). In addition, si ınd the law are closely associated, "[for] hrough the law we become conscious of sin" Rom. 3:20; cf. 7:7–11). But Christ redeemed ıs from the curse of the law (Gal. 3:13). Death, long with the enemies that brought death to ll (sin and the law), has been overcome by esurrection (Fee, 805).

In a paean of praise, Paul exclaims, "But hanks be to God! He gives us the victory [over leath] through our Lord Jesus Christ" (v. 57). 3od "gives," not "will give," the victory. 3elievers participate in Christ's victory even luring their earthly existence, since death has ost its terror. Death, though still an enemy, is "disabled one," because Christ overcame it Bruce, 156–57).

Not surprisingly, Paul concludes this argely theological treatise with an exhortation o his readers, who are still his "dear brothers" n spite of their many shortcomings (v. 58). He ncourages them to be "steadfast, immovable, lways abounding in the work of the Lord" NASB). He wants them to know that their work n the Lord is not in vain (see 9:26–27; 15:10; 3al. 2:2; Phil. 2:16), which it would be if there vere no resurrection (cf. 1 Cor. 15:14–19).

3.6. The Collection (16:1–4)

"Now concerning the collection for the aints" (NASB) introduces another item about vhich the Corinthians had inquired (v. 1; see omment on 7:1). The NIV incorrectly renders e last phrase "for God's people." Though the vord "saints" applies to all believers (see comıent on 1:2; also 16:15), the recipients of this ollection are the poor Jewish Christians in erusalem (Acts 24:17; Rom. 15:26; 2 Cor. :1–11; 9:1–2). The Corinthians had heard bout this special collection and apparently 'anted to contribute to it.

On a previous occasion Paul and Barnabas ad collected funds in Antioch of Syria that ey took to Jerusalem to assist the Christians uring a time of famine (Acts 11:30). They 'ere requested by the Jerusalem leadership to continue to remember the poor," which, says aul, was "the very thing I was eager to do" Gal. 2:10). He knew that fellow believers ıere could expect no help from Jews. He new also that there were religious communies among the Greeks that looked after their wn (Morris, 232). Surely, believers could and ould help other believers.

The contributions of the Gentile churches would be a means of showing their spiritual solidarity with the Jewish Christians. They would also be an expression of gratitude to them, to whom they owed so much spiritually. Consequently, Paul solicited funds from the churches he had established. Mentioned specifically are those in the provinces of Macedonia (2 Cor. 8:1–5) and Galatia (1 Cor. 16:1). The identity and specific locations of the "Galatian churches" are relatively unimportant for Paul's present purpose. His specific aim is to ask the Corinthians to do what he had requested other Gentile churches to do. The contributions Paul solicits are voluntary.

Evidently the Jerusalem church was poorer than the churches Paul had founded. It is not clear why this was the case. Perhaps there were periodic famines (Acts 11:28–30). Morris (232) suggests they may have suffered the aftereffects of pooling resources in the early days (4:34–35).

Paul's instructions are that "on the first day of every week let each one of you put aside and save, as he may prosper" (v. 2, NASB). It is not certain that "the first day" refers to the weekly worship of Christians on Sundays, though there is evidence that believers, at an early stage, did meet on that day for worship. This is undoubtedly what John means when he says, "On the Lord's Day I was in the Spirit" (Rev. 1:10; see also John 20:19, 26; Acts 20:7).

"Each one of you" emphasizes that all were expected to participate. They were to "put aside" the money, which means it was to be held in the home (Fee, 813). It is not known whether, in the first century, monetary offerings were received during a church service. The amount set aside should be in proportion to how much the individual "may prosper." Paul is careful to instruct his readers in this way "so that when I come no collections will have to be made." He wants to avoid "impulse giving" resulting from an emotional appeal.

Fee (812) observes that Paul speaks of this collection elsewhere in terms that are "full of theological content": fellowship (Rom. 15:26; 2 Cor. 8:4; 9:13), service (Rom. 15:31; 2 Cor. 8:4; 9:1, 12–13), grace (2 Cor. 8:4, 6–7, 19), blessing (9:5), divine service (9:12). The collection was more than a matter of money; it was a ministry both to God's people and to God himself.

Paul then details how the money will be handled (v. 3). When he arrives, he will give letters of introduction to men approved by the Corinthians to take the gift to Jerusalem. Some translations suggest that the Corinthians would write the letters of introduction, but it is more natural to regard Paul as the writer. We note that Paul will not participate in the choice of the men; he wishes to avoid any suggestion that he might tamper with the offering. It would be handled exclusively by the Corinthians.

Paul says that the men will accompany him, not that he will accompany them, "if it seems advisable" for him to go also (v. 4; NASB and NKJV read "if it is fitting"). The Greek word used here basically means "worthy" and is interpreted by some to mean that Paul will join the men if the collection comes to a sum worthy of an apostle to deliver (Morris, 234; Robertson and Plummer, 387). This, however, seems unlikely. He may mean simply that he will go if circumstances permit.

4. Conclusion (16:5–24)

4.1. Paul's Personal Plans (16:5–9)

Paul definitely planned to return to Corinth, but the timing was uncertain. Twice, in verses 2 and 3, he uses the indefinite conjunction *hotan* ("whenever") when speaking of his next visit. He will stay with them, perhaps for the winter, but he cannot leave Ephesus until he has completed his work there.

Paul had previously indicated his intention to revisit Corinth (4:19). He now says definitely, "I will come to you" (v. 5). But he will do so only after going through Macedonia, making brief visits to the churches he had established in that province (Acts 16:1–15). This would require a mostly overland, longer route from Ephesus, as opposed to a direct sea route across the Aegean from Ephesus to Cenchrea, Corinth's port city. He once again uses "whenever" (*hotan*; NIV "after"). But his plans are still uncertain and flexible: "Perhaps I will stay with you awhile, or even spend the winter." He would spend the winter with them, partly because navigation in the Mediterranean Sea was hazardous during the early fall and was suspended from late fall to early March. Therefore, it will not be "a passing visit."

Paul will stay with them for several months "so that you can help me on my journey, wherever I go" (v. 6b). To "help on one's journey" or "send on one's way" (*propempō*) is euphemism for helping someone meet th expenses of an upcoming trip (Acts 15:3 Rom. 15:24; 1 Cor. 16:11; 2 Cor. 1:16; Titu 3:13; 3 John 6). Paul asks the Corinthians t do the same for Timothy after he visits them (1 Cor. 16:11). Paul's intimation that they hel him seems to contradict his contention i chapter 9 that he has chosen not to receiv assistance from God's people, but Fee sug gests that "this has all the earmarks of bein a peace offering on this matter" (819). Even tually, Paul did go from Ephesus to Macedo nia, then on to Greece, where he stayed fo three months (Acts 20:1–3). "Wherever I go seems like indecisiveness, but it expresse Paul's commitment to "if the Lord permits (v. 7; cf. Acts 18:21; 1 Cor. 4:19; Heb. 6:3 James 4:13–15).

Paul plans to remain in Ephesus "until Pen tecost" (v. 8). Even though the Jewish Feast o Pentecost may not have been observed by th Corinthian Christians, it served as a chrono logical benchmark for both Paul and them i anticipation of his arrival. The reason he wi remain in Ephesus is that "a great door fo effective work has opened to me" (v. 9; "a wid door for effective service," NASB). "Door" is metaphor for "opportunity" (2 Cor. 2:12; Co 4:3). Perhaps at that time Paul was witnessin a spiritual breakthrough in Ephesus and felt hi presence was needed there a while longer.

One is not prepared for the anticlimacti ending of the sentence: "and there are man who oppose me." These opponents may be th "wild beasts" he had previously mentione (1 Cor. 15:32). It is a reminder that the work o the Lord does not often go unopposed, espe cially during times of unusual opportunity fo the gospel.

4.2. Requests Concerning Some Believers (16:10–18)

Paul had spoken earlier of sending Timoth (4:17), who had worked with him in the found ing of the Corinthian assembly (Acts 18:5). H now says, "If [*ean*] Timothy comes, see to that he has nothing to fear" (v. 10). Timothy visit is not in doubt, however (but see Rober son and Plummer, 390–91, who consider th *ean* to indicate uncertainty). The particle *ea* sometimes means "whenever" or "when," an that is the sense here.

Timothy, with Erastus, went first to Maceonia (Acts 19:22). Paul is apprehensive that ıe Corinthians will not treat Timothy well /hile he is with them, because of Timothy's outh and shy disposition (2 Tim. 1:7–8). Even ome years later, Paul admonishes him, "Don't t anyone look down on you because you are oung" (1 Tim. 4:12). If the Corinthians did ot hesitate to attack Paul, what might they do) his young associate? Paul tells them Timoıy is carrying on the work of the Lord, just as e is. Therefore no one should refuse to accept im. Rather, they should "send him on his way *ropempo*—see comment on v. 6) in peace."

Paul expects Timothy to return to him in phesus, but it is not clear what he means by, I am expecting him along with the brothers.")oes he mean, "I, along with the brothers [in phesus], am expecting him"? Possibly, but the osition in Greek of the phrase "along with the rothers" favors the NIV translation. The brothrs would include Erastus and others who might ave accompanied Timothy to Ephesus, as well s some brothers from the Corinthian church.

Verse 12 begins with the final occurrence of ıe familiar phrase "now about" (see comment n 7:1). It concerns another of Paul's assocites, Apollos (mentioned in 1:12; 3:4–6; 4:6). ll indications are that the two men were on the est of terms with each other. Perhaps the orinthians had asked Paul whether Apollos ould visit them again. Paul urged him to go long with Timothy and the brothers to Maceonia and then to Corinth, but he "was quite nwilling to go now." A literal translation of the reek reads, "And there was not at all a will ıat he should go now." Whose will? The Greek xt does not say. Perhaps Apollos was indeed luctant to make the trip (Robertson and Plumer, 392; Fee, 824). But "will" could refer to od's will, as it does in Romans 2:18 (Bruce, 50). This seems more in keeping with Paul's ommitment to divine direction for his own ovements. In either event, Apollos "will go hen he has the opportunity," though we do not now whether he ever again visited Corinth.

Verses 13–14 consist of five short exhortaons. They are all in the Greek present tense, ggesting that they are to be continuing, not ıe-time, actions. (1) "Be on your guard" is an hortation to remain alert. The verb Paul uses re often appears in connection with the secd coming of Christ (Matt. 24:42–43; 25:13; Mark 13:37; Rev. 3:3), though it is not restricted to that context (Acts 20:31; 1 Peter 5:8).

(2) "Stand firm in the faith" is capable of two interpretations. "The faith"—the article is in the Greek text—suggests the body of Christian truth (as in Acts 6:7; Jude 3). Some, however, take the expression to mean a Christian's personal trust in Christ.

(3) "Be men of courage" translates *andrizomai* ("conduct oneself in a manly or courageous way" [BAGD]). This verb and the following verb occur in Psalm 31:24.

(4) "Be strong" may also be translated "be made strong," which points to the Lord as the source of one's strength.

(5) "Let all that you do be done in love" (NASB) directs our attention back to 8:1–3 and chapter 13. Love is "the very atmosphere in which the Christian lives and moves and has his being" (Morris, 238).

Verses 15–18 focus on three members of the Corinthian congregation who had visited Paul in Ephesus—Stephanas, Fortunatus, and Achaicus—and who presumably delivered the Corinthians' letter to him. His comments about them are commendatory, much in contrast to what he has had to say about many of the Corinthians.

Paul had previously mentioned that he baptized the household of Stephanas (1:16). He now makes two important comments about these people: (1) "The household of Stephanas were the first converts in Achaia." A more accurate translation reads: "The household of Stephanas ... is the firstfruits [*aparche*] of Achaia" (NKJV). This statement is slightly problematic, since there had been converts in Achaia, in the city of Athens, prior to Paul's initial visit to Corinth (Acts 17:34). Perhaps the emphasis is on the conversion of a household rather than on individuals, as was the case in Athens. *Aparche* (see comment on 1 Cor. 15:20) suggests that the conversion of this household was a harbinger of a harvest to come in Achaia (Morris, 239). (For similar uses of "firstfruits," see Rom. 16:15; 2 Thess. 2:13.)

(2) "They have devoted [*tasso*] themselves to the service of the saints." *Tasso* also means "appoint." Stephanas and his household were not appointed by Paul or the church; they appointed themselves, that is, they voluntarily dedicated themselves to ministering to the saints (Barrett, 393–94). The "saints" are

God's people generally, not the Jerusalem Christians mentioned in verse 1. Paul thus calls on the Corinthian believers to submit to them and to others of like commitment, who not only work but "labor" on their behalf (v. 16; cf. 1 Thess. 5:12–13).

Fortunatus and Achaicus are not mentioned elsewhere in the New Testament. Their presence in Ephesus along with Stephanas made Paul rejoice, "because they have supplied what was lacking from you" (v. 17). Apparently Paul missed the Corinthian believers, and these three men "have filled the gap of your absence" (Héring, 185). By their visit they had "refreshed [his] spirit" as well as the spirit of the Corinthians, since they carried the church's letter to Paul, which contained the questions they had raised (v. 18; cf. 7:1). In view of this, these men "deserve recognition" by the congregation.

4.3. Final Greetings and Benediction (16:19–24)

Verses 19–20 convey greetings to the Corinthians from four sources. (1) The "churches . . . of Asia" send greetings. The Roman province of Asia was in the western part of Asia Minor, which is part of present-day Turkey. Ephesus was its main city, but Paul evangelized the entire province during his two-year stay in that area (Acts 19:10, 26).

(2) Aquila and Prisca ("Priscilla," NIV) send warm greetings "in the Lord." The wife's name appears in its diminutive form Priscilla in Acts (18:2, 18, 26), but Paul always calls her Prisca (Rom. 16:3; 2 Tim. 4:19). They were Jews who had at one time settled in Rome. When Emperor Claudius expelled all Jews from the city in A.D. 49, they went to Corinth, where Paul made their acquaintance and lived and worked with them (Acts 18:1–3). When Paul left Corinth, they accompanied him and settled in Ephesus (18:18–19). Paul says of them, "They risked their lives for me" (Rom. 16:4); this incident may well have occurred in Ephesus. They were evidently mature believers, for they were able to instruct Apollos in a fuller understanding of the Lord (Acts 18:26). The couple were probably people of means, for they traveled freely and also had a large enough house in Ephesus in which Christians met for worship.

(3) "The church that meets at their house" sends greetings as well (see also Rom. 16:3–5). House churches are mentioned elsewhere (Col. 4:15; Philem. 2). It is not likely that th entire company of Ephesian believers met fo worship in the home of Aquila and Prisca since the "living room" of a moderately well-to-do couple might accommodate only abou thirty persons (Morris, 241). Therefore, ther may have been a number of such hous churches in the city.

(4) "All the brothers here" may refer t Paul's fellow missionaries, to Christians othe than those who met in Aquila and Priscilla' home, or to the men from Corinth who visite Paul. Their identity is not of major importanc

Paul instructs the Corinthians to "greet on another with a holy kiss" (v. 20; see also Ron 16:16; 2 Cor. 13:12; 1 Thess. 5:26; 1 Pete 5:14). Kissing relatives and friends as a forn of greeting was common in the culture of th day. The kiss is not to be perfunctory, artificia or forced; it is to be "holy." The saints (lit "holy ones") should greet one another in a hol way. In view of the problems within th Corinthian congregation, this exhortation i especially relevant.

Verses 21–24 contain Paul's concludin remarks. He sends his personal greeting wri ten in his own hand (v. 21). The usual custo of the day was that an amanuensis (a scribe would write a letter dictated by the sende (Rom. 16:22) and that the sender woul include a personal note at the end in his ow handwriting (Gal. 6:11; Col. 4:18; 2 Thes 3:17; Philem. 19).

Paul includes a jarring note in his conclu ing remarks: "If anyone does not love [*phile* the Lord—a curse [*anathema*] be on him (v. 22). He uses *phileo* for "love" only or other time (Titus 3:15), but it is speculative seek here any subtle difference between it ar *agapao*, his usual word (cf. 1 Cor. 13). (F *anathema*, see comments on 12:3.) Some su gest that this statement is a Christian formu related to the liturgy of the early church (Ba rett, 396; Bruce, 162). In any event, Paul ma be implying that the many problems in th Corinthian assembly stem from the absence genuine love for the Lord.

"Come, O Lord" is a translation of an Ar maic expression *Maranatha*. This expressi goes back to the early days of the Jerusale church. It is one of a few transliterated ar untranslated words in use to this day (alo with Amen, Hallelujah, and Hosanna). Sin he earliest New Testament manuscripts did ıot separate the words, *Maranatha* lends itself o two possible translations, depending on how ne divides the letters. *Maran atha* means 'Our Lord has come" or "Our Lord comes"; *1arana tha* means "Our Lord, come." The later option is preferable, being a prayer similar o "Come, Lord Jesus" (Rev. 22:20). It xpresses a longing for the Lord to return.

Paul includes a benediction typical of his etters: "The grace [*charis*] of the Lord Jesus e with you" (v. 23; see comment on 1:3–4 for *haris*). The Corinthians have already experinced divine grace; now he prays for its conınuance in their lives. He then adds: "My love e with you all in Christ Jesus" (v. 24, NASB). n spite of the harsh tone of much of the leter, the apostle loves even those who have creted the greatest problems. The reason is that is love is "in Christ Jesus" (a better undertanding of the phrase than having it modify you all"). It is fitting that, according to some eliable manuscripts, the last word of the letter . "Amen"—"So be it!"

BIBLIOGRAPHY

Divine activity: Matt. 14:2; Mark 6:14; 1 Cor. 12:6, 11; Gal. 3:5; Eph. 1:9; 3:7; 4:16; Phil. 3:21; Col. 1:29; 2:12. Satanic activity: Eph. 2:2; 2 Thess. 2:7, 9.

C. K. Barrett, *A Commentary on the First Epistle to the Corinthians* (1968); Arnold Bittlinger, *Gifts and Graces: A Commentary on 1 Corinthians 12–14* (1968); F. F. Bruce, *1 and 2 Corinthians.* (NCC, 1971); D. A. Carson, *Showing the Spirit: A Theological Exposition of 1 Corinthians 12–14* (1987); Gordon Fee, *The First Epistle to the Corinthians* (NICNT, 1987); Everett Ferguson, *Backgrounds of Early Christianity* (1987); Jean Héring, *The First Epistle of Saint Paul to the Corinthians* (1962); David Lim, *Spritual Gifts: A Fresh Look* (1991); Ralph P. Martin, *The Spirit and the Congregation: Studies in 1 Corinthians 12–15* (1984); Florentino Garc'a Mart'nez, *The Dead Sea Scrolls Translated: The Qumran Texts in English* (1996); Leon Morris, *The First Epistle of Paul to the Corinthians* (TNTC, 1985); Archibald Robertson and Alfred Plummer, *A Critical and Exegetical Commentary on the First Epistle of St. Paul to the Corinthians* (ICC, 1914).

THE OLD TESTAMENT IN THE NEW

NT Text	OT Text	Subject
1Co 1:19	Isa 29:14	Worldly wisdom perishes
1Co 1:31	Jer 9:24	Boasting in the Lord
1Co 2:9	Isa 64:4	What no eye has seen
1Co 2:16	Isa 40:13	The mind of the Lord
1Co 3:19	Job 5:13	God and the crafty
1Co 3:20	Ps 94:11	God knows human thoughts
1Co 5:13	Dt 17:7	Purge evil
1Co 6:16	Ge 2:24	Institution of marriage
1Co 9:9	Dt 25:4	Not muzzling an ox
1Co 10:7	Ex 32:6	Sin of idolatry
1Co 10:26	Ps 24:1	The earth is the Lord's
1Co 14:21	Isa 28:11–12	Through strange tongues
1Co 15:27	Ps 8:6	Everything subject to Christ
1Co 15:32	Isa 22:13	Tomorrow we die
1Co 15:45	Ge 2:7	Creation of Adam
1Co 15:54	Isa 25:8	Death is swallowed up
1Co 15:55	Hos 13:14	Victory over death

2 CORINTHIANS

James Hernando

NTRODUCTION

1. Author

'ew scholars have challenged the Pauline uthorship of 2 Corinthians. Even critics who ontend that the letter contains fragments of ther letters (see "Literary Unity") usually redit Paul with writing those sections. Internal and external evidence both demonstrate he genuineness of the letter.

Twice within the letter Paul is identified as ts author (1:1; 10:1). Such self-disclosures ecome more credible when placed alongside he content of the letter. For example, it has een correctly pointed out that a "pious imitator" of Paul would hardly portray the apostle s "in danger of losing his apostolic authority nd struggling to preserve the Corinthians from postasy" (Harris, 306). Furthermore, the internal character of the letter points to its authenticity. It often reads like a one-sided telephone onversation. It is difficult to imagine a forger onstructing a letter so full of oblique and bscure references to situations and details bviously well known to the author and his udience. Even an inartful imposter would ave taken more care to make himself clear.

What appears most convincing of Paul's uthorship is that we encounter not only his haracteristic vocabulary and style, but quinessential Paul in his passionate pastoral "concern for all the churches" (11:28). Present is the ame humble gratitude (1:3–11; 2:14; 8:16), varm affection (2:1–4; 6:11–13; 7:2–4), passionate jealousy over Christ's church and his harges (11:1–4; 12:14–21), compassion oward a struggling sinner (2:5–11), and bold ndignation toward those who defy his apostolic authority (2:17; 4:2, 5; 10:1–18; 11:5–2:13) as are visible in Paul's other letters.

With regard to external evidence, the letter was known and used at the end of the first entury A.D. While unknown to Clement of Rome (ca. A.D. 95), verbal allusions to the letter appear in two documents of the Apostolic 'athers—the letters of Barnabus and Diognetus (both ca. 70–135). It is quoted by Polycarp ca. A.D. 105), Irenaeus (ca. 180), Clement of Alexandria (ca. 200–210), Tertullian (ca. 210), and Cyprian (ca. 230). In addition, Athenagorus (ca. 180) and Theophilus of Antioch (ca. 170–180) seem to have known the letter. It appears in Marcion's canon (ca. 140) and the Muratorian Canon (ca. 170).

2. Date and Place of Writing

Both the date and place of 2 Corinthians hinges on the date of 1 Corinthians and the historical reconstruction of events that transpired between these two letters (see "Occasion and Purpose"). The date of 1 Corinthians is tied historically to the proconsulship of Gallio in Corinth, which a famous inscription helps us date from July 1, A.D. 51, to July 1, A.D. 52 (see Carson, Moo, and Morris, 223–31). As Acts records, some time during that tenure the Jews "made a united attack on Paul" and dragged him before the Roman proconsul (Acts 18:12). If, as seems likely, the Jews took advantage of the changing administration, Paul's appearance before Gallio took place early in his proconsulship (i.e., in the fall of A.D. 51). Paul spent a short but indeterminate period in Corinth after this event, then sailed for Syria (18:18), probably in the spring of A.D. 52. He stopped briefly in Ephesus (18:19–20) before setting sail again and landing in Caesarea (18:22).

After "spending some time in Antioch" (Acts 18:23), Paul embarked on his third missionary journey, passing through the regions of Galatia and Phrygia and coming again to Ephesus (19:1), where he stayed at least two and a half years (cf. 19:8, 10; 20:31). Adding the numbers and allowing for travel time, his stay there ended late in A.D. 55. Paul wrote 1 Corinthians from Ephesus probably some time in the spring (before Pentecost, cf. 1 Cor. 16:8) of A.D. 55. Second Corinthians was probably written a year or so after that (mid to late 56); we must allow for an intervening visit and other correspondence (see "Occasion and Purpose") to occur and for Paul to travel to and minister in Macedonia (2 Cor. 2:12–13; 7:5; 8:1–5; 9:2). Possibly Paul wrote this letter from the Macedonian city of Philippi, since "Macedonia" in 11:9 appears to designate Philippi (see Phil. 4:15).

3. Occasion and Purpose

Determining the occasion of this letter requires careful sifting of 1 and 2 Corinthians and Acts for details that will enable us to reconstruct Paul's relationship to the church of Corinth. The difficulty with such a reconstruction is that we encounter numerous gaps. For example, Acts records no correspondence with Corinth, yet from the letters we learn there were several. Acts records two visits of Paul to Corinth (Acts 18:1; 20:2), while 2 Corinthians 13:1 suggests a third visit (about which Acts is silent). These gaps must be cautiously filled in because they allow for more than one configuration of the data we possess. Despite the difficulties, we must venture such a historical reconstruction in order to understand 2 Corinthians.

Paul first visited Corinth during his second missionary journey (Acts 18). He had come there following a string of trying circumstances in Macedonia and Achaia. At Philippi (Acts 16) he and Silas were miraculously delivered after being beaten and imprisoned. He narrowly escaped similar treatment in Thessalonica and Berea (17:1–15), being hounded and driven out by the Jews. At Athens (17:16–34), surrounded by a rampant idolatry that vexed his soul, his gospel was met with scorn, ridicule, and a meager response. It is little wonder that he approached Corinth shortly afterwards "in weakness and fear, and with much trembling" (1 Cor. 2:3).

Encouraged by Christ in a dream-vision (Acts 18:9), Paul labored in Corinth for eighteen months (18:11), along with Priscilla and Aquila, who had recently come to Corinth from Rome as a result of the persecution of Jews under Emperor Claudius (18:2). After seeing the church established, Paul set sail for Syria, via Ephesus, where he left Priscilla and Aquila (cf. 18:26). Landing at Caesarea he traveled to Jerusalem and greeted the church, then shortly went on to Antioch, from where he began his third missionary journey. After crossing Asia Minor and strengthening churches en route (18:23), he arrived again in Ephesus (19:1). There Paul stayed the better part of three years (19:8, 10; 20:31). Sometime during that stay he received disturbing news about affairs in Corinth. The following outline is offered as a historical reconstruction of his correspondence and contacts with the city:

(1) Paul writes a letter (referred to in 1 Co 5:9) in response to the troubling news The contents of this "previous letter" ar largely unknown, but include a warning t the Corinthians not to associate wit immoral people. His instructions probabl concerned church discipline and wer apparently misunderstood (5:10–13).

(2) Sometime later (or perhaps at the sam time) Paul hears reports from members o "Chloe's household" (1 Cor. 1:11) of othe disorders in the church. In addition Stephanus, Fortunatus, and Achaicus (per haps an official delegation from Corinth arrive (16:17), bearing a letter (7:1) con taining several questions the church want Paul to answer (cf. also "now about [o concerning]" in 7:25; 8:1; 12:1; 16:1 16:12). To these inquiries Paul write 1 Corinthians and sends the letter via Tim othy (4:17; 16:10–11; cf. Acts 19:22).

(3) Paul had intended to stay in Ephesus unt the Feast of Pentecost, then travel acros the Aegean Sea to Macedonia. There h would visit churches as he traveled sout to Corinth, where he hoped to spend th winter (1 Cor. 16:6–8). However, he appar ently changes his plans, intending to vis them twice, landing at Corinth on his wa to Macedonia and again on the way back sailing from Corinth to Judea (2 Cor. 1:16

(4) Paul's plans are disrupted by bad new from Corinth, whether by Timothy him self or some other messenger. Apparently the apostle's letter was not well received in fact, the situation is serious. Pau decides not to delay his visit and goe immediately to Corinth for what he cal a "painful visit" (2 Cor. 2:1). This visi results in an emotionally charged and dis tressing confrontation—the type that Pau earlier warned them not to provok (1 Cor. 4:21). What seems to have hap pened is that prior to this visit, Corinth ha welcomed into its midst certain teacher who mounted a formidable challenge t Paul's authority and undermine his teach ing. Paul is forced to withdraw in th midst of the turmoil.

(5) Upon his return to Ephesus Paul sends letter to the Corinthians "out of great dis tress and anguish of heart and with man tears" (2 Cor. 2:4) in an attempt to corre

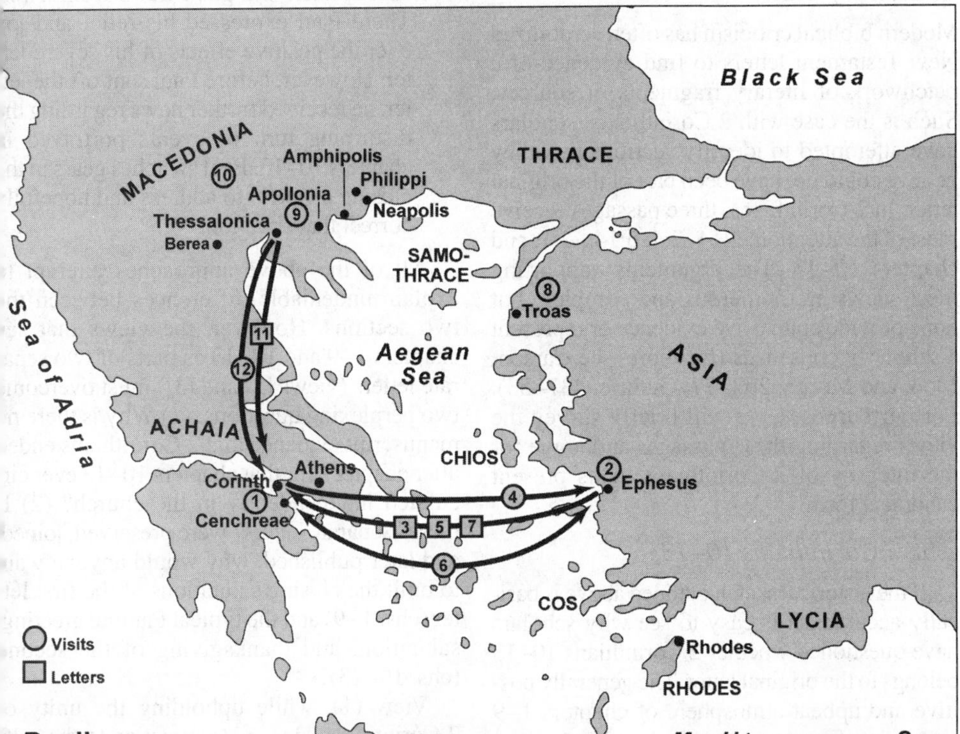

Paul's Interaction with Corinth

1. A.D. 50-51: Paul establishes the church at Corinth (Acts 18:1-18).
2. 53-56: Paul establishes the church at Ephesus (Acts 18:23; 19:1, 8-10).
3. 54: Paul hears about immorality at Corinth and writes a brief letter (see 1 Cor 5:9).
4. 54: People from Chloe's household (1 Cor 1:11) and later Stephanas, Fortunatus, and Achaicus (1 Cor 16:17) visit Paul in Ephesus; one of these groups brings a letter (1 Cor 7:1).
5. 54: Paul writes 1 Corinthians and sends it to Corinth—perhaps with Stephanas, Fortunatus, and Achaicus.
6. 55: Paul hears about further problems in Corinth and pays a brief, painful visit to the church (2 Cor 2:11; cf. 12:18; 13:2).
7. 55: Paul fires off a third letter to Corinth, called the "severe letter" (2 Cor 2:3-4, 6, 9; 7:8, 12). He sends it with Titus, who is also told to organize the collection in Corinth (2 Cor 8:6).
8. 56: Paul leaves Ephesus and has an opportunity to evangelize Troas, but he does not do so (2 Cor 2:12-13).
9. 56: Paul crosses over into Macedonia and begins evangelistic work there (Acts 20:1-2; 2 Cor 2:13; 7:5).
10. 56: Titus meets Paul in Macedonia (Thessalonica or Philippi?) and reports on his successful stay in Corinth (2 Cor 7:6-16).
11. 56: Paul writes 2 Corinthians 1-9 and, after hearing of further problems, writes chapters 10-13; he sends the whole letter to Corinth with Titus (2 Cor 8:16-24).
12. 56: After evangelizing more, going all the way to Illyricum (west of Macedonia, (see Rom 15:19-21), Paul visits Corinth and spends the winter there (Acts 20:2).

the situation. This so-called "sorrowful letter" is probably carried by Titus (2 Cor. 8:6), who is also given charge of completing the benevolence collection for the saints in Jerusalem.

(6) Sometime later Paul leaves Ephesus and goes to Troas, where he awaits news from Titus (2 Cor. 2:12). Disappointed when Titus does not arrive (2:13), Paul goes on to Macedonia, where he encourages the churches (Acts 20:1–2) and continues to conduct his benevolence offering for the Jerusalem church (2 Cor. 8:1–4; 9:2). While there Titus finally arrives with good news from Corinth. Paul's previous letter, although causing pain "for a little while" (7:8), has been well received. In fact, it has led the Corinthians to repent (7:9). Paul is greatly relieved and elated (7:6–7).

(7) Paul then writes the major portion of 2 Corinthians (chs. 1–9) to express his relief that the "sorrowful letter" and Titus's mission had been a success. Residual resistance causes him to write chapters 10–13.

4. Literary Unity

Modern biblical criticism has often scrutinized New Testament letters to find evidence of a patchwork of literary fragments or sources. Such is the case with 2 Corinthians; scholars have attempted to identify sections that they believe could not have been part of the original letter. In 2 Corinthians, three passages receive most of the attention: 2:14–7:4; 6:14:–7:1; and chapters 10–13. The arguments supporting these views are numerous and complex, but none provide conclusive evidence or represent a scholarly consensus (for more, see Carson, Moo, and Morris, 267–77; Guthrie, 437–53). For our purposes, we will briefly survey the views regarding these passages and argue for the integrity of 2 Corinthians in its present canonical form.

a. 2 Corinthians 10–13

If the historical sketch outlined above is basically accurate, it is easy to see why scholars have questioned whether 2 Corinthians 10–13 belongs to the original letter. The generally positive and upbeat atmosphere of chapters 1–9 seems out of sync with the harsh and censorious tone of chapters 10–13. Several approaches to explain these chapters have been offered.

(1) Second Corinthians was written by Paul in its present canonical form. The striking change in tone between these two sections is explained by an appeal to the humanness of Paul, being given to emotional mood changes and outbursts. Some have argued that too much is made of alleged differences between these sections and that there is no grounds to the charge of inconsistency (see Hughes, xxxi–xxxv).

(2) Given the allusion to an earlier "painful visit" to Corinth and the "tearful letter" that followed, the letter Paul penned after receiving Titus's good report was 2 Corinthians 1–9. Chapters 10–13 belong to the earlier letter mentioned in 2:4.

(3) After Titus's report Paul wrote chapters 1–9. Shortly thereafter he received discouraging news and responded with another, separate letter, which included chapters 10–13; it dealt with more recent challenges to and criticisms of his ministry.

(4) Paul wrote 2 Corinthians over an extended period of time. Chapters 1–9 were written shortly after the good news from Titus. There Paul expressed his relief and joy over the positive effects of his severe letter. However, before Paul sent off the letter, he received further news regarding the disturbing turn of events portrayed in chapters 10–13. Paul switches gears in the closing chapters to address and hopefully correct that situation.

All of the above approaches attempt to explain undeniable differences between the two sections. However, the views that see chapters 1–9 and 10–13 as parts of two separate letters (views [2] and [3]) must overcome two perplexing questions: (1) Why is there no manuscript evidence that 2 Corinthians ended after chapter 9, or that chapters 10–13 ever circulated independently in the church? (2) If these "separate letters" were preserved, joined, and later published, why would anyone want to omit the closing salutations of the first letter (chs. 1–9) and the typical Pauline greeting, salutation, and thanksgiving of the second (chs. 10–13)?

View (1), while upholding the unity of 2 Corinthians, does not do justice to the self-evident differences that exist between the two sections. For example, if both sections were composed at the same time, certainly the joy expressed over the news from Titus (7:6–16) would have been offset by the imminent threat and dire situation expressed in chapters 10–13. In this author's estimation, view (4) most reasonably explains how two such disparate sections could have been combined in a single letter.

b. 2 Corinthians 2:14–7:4

It is often noted that if you omit this section, 2 Corinthians 7:5 follows 2:13 quite naturally, since both deal with Paul's trip to Macedonia after being disappointed in not finding Titus (2:12). Consequently, some have supposed that 2:14–7:4 was originally part (or the whole) of a separate letter later inserted into the text by some editor of Paul's letters. The alleged insertion is seen as a major digression from Paul's travelogue to a description and discussion of his apostolic ministry.

This interpretation of the text we must reject for several reasons. (1) We should quickly point out that lengthy digressions in Paul's letters are not without precedent (see

Rom. 9–11; Phil. 3:2–21). In addition, Paul's words in 7:5, "For when we came into Macedonia," hardly seem to be what would have immediately followed those of 2:13, "So I said good-by to them and went on to Macedonia." The second mention of Macedonia in 7:5 looks more like Paul is returning to the travelogue after an intentional digression. (2) Others have pointed out that there are verbal and thematic features that tie the contents of the disputed passage to what follows. Such seems unlikely if this passage represents the insertion of foreign material from another letter.[1] (3) It must again be noted that no Greek manuscript supports the independent existence of 2:14–7:4, nor does any copy of 2 Corinthians leave this passage out.

c. 2 Corinthians 6:14–7:1

This passage is surely one of the most contested ones in 2 Corinthians. It is viewed not only as an insertion into the text, but some deny that Paul even wrote it. The reasons for the former charge we have met before. These six verses interrupt the personal exhortation formed by 6:13 and 7:2 with a unit of thought that does not fit the context. But we should again recognize that Paul's mind is capable of digressions, which, while on the surface appearing out of context, when given a closer look have profound relevance to Paul's larger purpose.

It is, therefore, possible to argue for the cogency of this passage. Paul has concluded a description of his apostleship in 6:3–10 as one filled with hardship and sacrifice. He has spoken openly to promote and encourage a mutual love and intimacy between himself and the Corinthians (6:11–13). But, as we are to learn in chapters 10–13, the authority and character of Paul's apostleship is being challenged by other self-claimed apostles. The Corinthians are here faced with an all-important choice as to whom to listen to. The digression, whether intended to define the moral and theological significance of that choice (Barrett, 192–203; Hughes, 244–60) or to return to an area of teaching that the Corinthians have failed to embrace (see Fee, 1977, 140–61), serves to underscore the gravity of what is at stake. To reject Paul and his apostleship is to reject the gospel of Christ itself as modeled in Paul's apostolic ministry.

Those who argue against Pauline authorship of these verses base their position on words and concepts that they allege Paul would not use or could not hold. Six words, for example, appear in this passage that are found nowhere else in the New Testament. But such words are characteristic of 2 Corinthians as a whole (see Hughes, 242, who counts fifty such words), and five of the six words find related terms elsewhere in Paul's writings (Fee, 1977, 144–45). In any event, arguments based on word usage are inconclusive, for they assume a static rather than a dynamic and flexible vocabulary on the part of the apostle.

Others point to fundamental theological concepts in this passage as uncharacteristic of Paul: for example, the dualism of light versus darkness, righteousness versus iniquity, and Christ versus Belial, considered to be more characteristic of the Qumran community than Paul (Fitzmyer, 271–80). Paul places "body" (*sarx*, lit., "flesh") alongside "spirit" (*pneuma*) in a complementary way here (7:1), whereas elsewhere he presents them in opposition to one another (Gal. 5:16–21). Betz (88–108) argues that the exclusivism of this passage (denial of fellowship) is said to be more characteristic of the Pharisees than Paul.

At first glance these arguments seem to have weight. However, the above observations are not entirely accurate. For example, while the precise form of dualistic terminology found in 6:14–15 may be absent in Paul, the concepts are not. Light and darkness do have moral and spiritual significance and are contrasted elsewhere in Paul's writings (Rom. 2:19; 13:12; 1 Cor. 4:5; 2 Cor. 4:6; Eph. 5:8). Similarly, while the Christ-Belial comparison is unique to this passage, Paul surely presents Satan in an adversarial relationship to the Lord Jesus on a number of occasions (Rom. 16:20; 1 Cor. 5:5; 2 Cor. 2:10–11; 11:13–14; 2 Thess. 2:8–9). Again, while the precise phrase "righteousness [*dikaiosyne*] and wickedness [*anomia*]" (6:14) appears nowhere else in Paul, both terms serve as moral opposites in two prominent Pauline passages (Rom. 4:1–13 [esp. vv. 6–8]; 6:15–23 [esp. vv. 18–19]).

The charge that the exclusivism of this passage could not have come from Paul's pen ignores such passages as Galatians 1:8–9; 1 Corinthians 6:9–10, 15–20; 10:14–21. When Paul was addressing a threat to the spiritual life and survival of the church, such exclusivism was not only possible but necessary.

Finally, the contention that the expression "body and spirit" (7:1) is non-Pauline suffers from the same lack of scrutiny. True, Paul usually contrasts these terms (see Gal. 5:16–25). But we must recognize that the Greek term *sarx* ("flesh") in the Galatians 5 passage is being used to represent the sinful human nature, whereas in 2 Corinthians 6:14 the word is morally neutral and represents the physical or bodily aspect of a person. Together "body and spirit" refer to the whole person (Carson, Moo, and Morris, 275).

In summary, the reasons for seeing this passage as non-Pauline are inconclusive at best and often weak and unconvincing.

5. The Opponents of Paul

Even a casual reading of Acts indicates that Paul's missionary career was marked with conflict. It is not surprising, then, to turn to his letters and find reflections of those conflicts. Paul's letters were written in response to specific life situations that had developed in his churches. Many of those problem situations came about as a result of individuals who undermined (or misrepresented) Paul's teaching or opposed his ministry in some fashion. Such was certainly the case at Corinth. Consequently, the identification and analysis of Paul's opponents at Corinth is essential to understanding so much of the content of the Corinthian correspondence (see Barnett, 644–53).

a. Identity of Paul's Opponents

Identifying Paul's opponents is a difficult task because, as with all his letters, we are privy to only one side of a dialog. However, the manner in which the apostle expresses himself often reveals he is addressing antagonists. Even so, precise identification is not always possible because what he says can plausibly be interpreted to represent different groups. Usually those groups fall under two broad categories: Jews or Hellenists (Greeks) (see Martin, 279–89). Before moving toward more specific identification we must heed a few cautions.

(1) We must not assume that we are dealing with the same opponents in 1 and 2 Corinthians or that the opponents represent a single group. We must allow for the possibility that opposition to Paul's ministry could have come from a variety of fronts or factions within the church. One major distinction between the two letters seems clear. Most of the problems addressed in 1 Corinthians seem to have been generated from *within* by their own members (e.g., the internal divisions alluded to in 1 Cor. 1:10–16; 3:21–22; see also comments on 1 Cor. 7:1). In 2 Corinthians, however, the opponents of Paul, arrived with letters of recommendation (2 Cor. 3:1) from *outside* Corinth (10:14–16; 11:4), and his comments are addressed to an identifiable group (2:17; 3:1; 10:2, 10–12; 11:4–5, 13–15, 18, 20). Clearly the opposition front has shifted between the writing of 1 and 2 Corinthians.

(2) We should avoid being forced into opting for an exclusively Jewish or Hellenistic identification of Paul's opponents. Proponents of the former make much of the emphasis Paul places on his Jewish credentials (11:16ff.) and tend to link the "super-apostles" (11:5; 12:11) with the pillars of the Jerusalem church (i.e., the apostles). Others, however, draw attention to the Greek literary character of chapters 10–13 and to the criteria by which these "super-apostles" criticize Paul's apostleship and exalt their own—criteria that reflect more the priorities of the Hellenistic world (Martin, 282–83). This polarity of choices may not be necessary for two reasons. (a) As will be more fully discussed in the commentary, the "super-apostles" may or may not refer to the same group as the "false apostles" (11:13). If they are not identical but represent another group of opposition, then both Jews and Greeks may be numbered among Paul's opponents. (b) Our present understanding of Judaism supports the probability that Jews in and outside Palestine held ideas closely associated with the Hellenistic world (see Brinsmead, 9–22).

(3) We must avoid too quickly using labels such as *Judaizers* or *Gnostics* to identify the opponents of Paul. The former term is often used to designate Jewish Christians who insisted on circumcision and the keeping of the Law of Moses as a prerequisite for salvation (e.g., see Acts 15:1, 5; Gal.

2:1–4). It is clear that at least one group of Paul's opponents ("the false apostles") were Jewish (11:22), but nowhere in 2 Corinthians do we find circumcision mentioned or implied. Nevertheless, a careful reading of the letter shows that one segment of Paul's opposition did measure righteousness by the law (see 11:13–15; cf. 3:6–18). In the fullest and technical sense, then, the opponents cannot be labeled Judaizers. However, the term would be appropriate if it were applied to Jewish Christians who tried to impose on Gentiles some measure of law-keeping as a necessary expression of their Christian faith.

As for the label *Gnostics*, we must recognize that Gnosticism was a second-century religion of the larger Greek world. It was highly syncretistic and borrowed its concepts from a variety of sources. Scholars now recognize that the religious ideas and terminology of *gnosis* long preceded the religion of Gnosticism (see Nash, 203–24). For example, Paul did not need to have Gnostics in mind simply because his writing contains what appears to be a dualism of body and spirit. Such a dichotomy was found in the Greek world from the time of Plato. In addition, a careful examination of 1 and 2 Corinthians uncovers none of the essential features of full-fledged Gnosticism. Thus, it is safe to conclude that among Paul's opponents were Gentiles who shared many of the religious and philosophical ideas of the Greek world.

b. Analysis of Paul's Opponents

Above we cautioned against assuming that the opponents of Paul were singular or that they were the same people in both 1 and 2 Corinthians. We also noted that the primary opponents of Paul in 2 Corinthians are singled out in chapters 10–13. It is our contention that the opponents addressed in these chapters are the same self-proclaimed Christian leaders who had earlier arrived in Corinth, causing Paul to make a hasty visit (2:1) and later to write the "sorrowful letter" (2:4). Apparently, the good news from Titus, which caused Paul to rejoice (7:7), was short-lived. Later news necessitated Paul to write chapters 10–13 in order to address a new challenge from his antagonists. What do we know about these opponents? A more detailed analysis will follow in the commentary, but for now the following outline will serve.

Who were they, and what were they doing at Corinth?

(1) While their connection with the Jerusalem church remains uncertain, it seems clear that Paul's opponents were Jewish and proud of their Hebrew culture and heritage (11:22), although not unfamiliar with Greek culture.

(2) As previously noted, they were "outsiders" who had come to Corinth and coopted the title "apostle" for themselves (11:13). To establish the credibility of their claim they flaunted letters (perhaps from the Jerusalem apostles; see 11:5; 12:11) of recommendation (3:1) as proof of their pedigree.

(3) They were proud and arrogant, whose importance was self-declared. They were fond of "commend[ing] themselves" (3:1; 10:12; cf. 12:11) and boasting about themselves (cf. Paul's sarcasm as he refers to the opponents prideful and misdirected boasts; 10:8, 15; 11:6, 10, 12, 16–18, 30; 12:1, 5–6, 9). They were also interlopers, who took credit for the labors of others (esp. Paul's; cf. 10:15–16).

(4) As teachers they were overbearing and authoritarian (11:21), who set themselves up as the standard to follow and measured everyone else by that standard (10:12).

(5) To undermine the influence and authority of the apostle Paul, these opponents embarked on a campaign of criticism aimed at calling his apostleship into question.

What were Paul's opponents contending about Paul?

(1) They claimed that Paul did not preach like an apostle; that is, he lacked the rhetorical eloquence and power of a true apostle. This explains Paul's frequent admission of this fact (10:10; 11:6; cf. 1 Cor. 1:17; 2:1, 4, 13) and his suggestion that personal integrity (10:11) and knowledge of the truth (11:6) are more important than the oratorical skill.

(2) They insisted that Paul did not carry himself like an apostle; he was weak, lacking boldness and the authoritative bearing of a

true apostle (10:1–2). Paul counters this charge by affirming that his demeanor among them was modeled after the meekness and gentleness of Christ. Rather than deny his weakness, Paul admits it and glories in it as the means of securing the power of God (11:30; 12:9–10; 13:3–4, 9).

(3) The opponents claimed that Paul did not act like an apostle. Apparently they objected to his practice of preaching the gospel without charge or of expecting to be supported by his converts (11:7–12). Paul boldly declares his freedom to do so and makes this practice the object of his own boast.

How does Paul regard the opponents and their ministry?

(1) Paul regards his opponents as "false apostles" (11:13). The grounds on which he makes this judgment is clear. There is only one, true apostolic gospel (cf. Gal. 1:6–8), and these men were not preaching it. In its place they taught a Jesus and gospel different from the one the Corinthians had first received from Paul (2 Cor. 11:4). Furthermore, the whole inner character of the opponents' ministry was foreign and at odds with Paul's. Paul saw in his opponents a denial of a conscious identification with the weakness and sufferings of Christ (11:23–33; 12:7–10), which Paul considered a failure to understand and fully embrace the cross of Christ (13:1–6).

(2) Paul sees his opponents as deceivers. This is evident by the terms he uses to describe them. They were "masquerading" as apostles of Christ (11:13). Their alien gospel and Jesus were aimed at deceiving the Corinthians and leading them away from a simple and pure faith in Christ (11:3). Twice Paul compares their preaching with the work of Satan, going so far as to suggest they are Satan's agents, doing his deceitful work (11:3, 14).

(3) Paul describes his opponents as "carnal" or "worldly," both in the way he distances himself from conduct done "in a worldly manner" (1:17; cf. 5:17; 10:2) and in the way he condemns the prideful boasts of his opponents as "the way the world" acts (11:18), even as he sarcastically illustrates this carnality with boasts of his own (11:18ff.).

OUTLINE

1. **Introduction** (1:1–11)
   - **1.1.** Salutation (1:1–2)
   - **1.2.** Praise for God's Comfort in Affliction (1:3–7)
   - **1.3.** Thanksgiving for God's Deliverance in Asia (1:8–11)
2. **Explanation of Paul's Recent Conduct** (1:12–2:13)
   - **2.1.** Paul's Only Boast—His Integrity Among Them (1:12–14)
   - **2.2.** Paul Defends His Change of Plans (1:15–2:4)
     - **2.2.1.** It Was Not the Result of Vacillating (1:15–17)
     - **2.2.2.** They Can Rely on the Sure Word of God (1:18–22)
     - **2.2.3.** It Was to Avoid a Painful Confrontation (1:23–2:4)
   - **2.3.** Paul Urges Forgiveness for an Offending Brother (2:5–11)
     - **2.3.1.** Paul's Gracious Attitude of Detachment (2:5)
     - **2.3.2.** Paul's Concern for Restoration (2:6–11)
   - **2.4.** Waiting for News From Titus (2:12–13)
3. **Digression from Travelogue: Description of Paul's Apostolic Ministry** (2:14–7:4)
   - **3.1.** Paul's Grateful Confidence (2:14–17)
     - **3.1.1.** In God to Lead in Triumph (2:14–16a)
     - **3.1.2.** In the Integrity of His Ministry (2:16b–17)
   - **3.2.** The Greatness and Glory of Paul's Ministry (3:1–4:6)
     - **3.2.1.** Every Believer's Becoming a Letter of Christ (3:1–3)
     - **3.2.2.** Paul's Confidence in and Enablement by God (3:4–6a)
     - **3.2.3.** The Greater Glory of the New Covenant (3:6b–11)
     - **3.2.4.** The Veil That Conceals (3:12–16)
     - **3.2.5.** The Life-Giving and Liberating Spirit (3:17–18)
     - **3.2.6.** The Gospel That Brings Light (4:1–6)

3.3. The Trials and Triumph of Apostolic Ministry (4:7–5:10)
- **3.3.1.** The Paradox of Paul's Sufferings (4:7–11)
- **3.3.2.** Paul's Confidence in Sufferings (4:12–15)
- **3.3.3.** Paul's Hope in Sufferings (4:16–18)
- **3.3.4.** Paul's Hope in the Face of Death (5:1–10)

3.4. The Nature and Function of Apostolic Ministry (5:11–7:4)
- **3.4.1.** The Motivation of Apostolic Ministry (5:11–16)
- **3.4.2.** The Message of Apostolic Ministry (5:17–6:2)
- **3.4.3.** The Sufferings of Apostolic Ministry (6:3–10)
- **3.4.4.** The Intimacy and Joy of Apostolic Ministry (6:11–7:4)

4. Return to Travelogue: Good News From Titus (7:5–16)

4.1. Paul Comforted in Macedonia (7:5–7)

4.2. The Harsh Letter and Its Effect—Reasons to Rejoice (7:8–16)

5. The Macedonian Collection for the Jerusalem Saints (8:1–9:15)

5.1. Paul Urges the Grace of Giving (8:1–15)
- **5.1.1.** The Macedonian Example (8:1–5)
- **5.1.2.** Paul's Appeal for Generous Giving (8:6–12)
- **5.1.3.** The Goal of the Appeal (8:13–15)

5.2. Paul Arranges for the Integrity and Success of the Offering (8:16–9:15)
- **5.2.1.** Paul Sends Praiseworthy Delegates (8:16–24)
- **5.2.2.** Paul Commends Their Willingness to Give (9:1–5)
- **5.2.3.** Paul Teaches Principles About Giving (9:6–15)

6. The Affirmation and Defense of Paul's Apostolic Ministry (10:1–13:14)

6.1. Paul Answers His Critics (10:1–18)
- **6.1.1.** Concerning Apostolic Authority and Presence (10:1–11)
- **6.1.2.** Concerning Legitimate Boasting (10:12–18)

6.2. Paul Exposes His Critics (11:1–15)
- **6.2.1.** By Revealing His Spiritual Passion for the Corinthians (11:1–6)
- **6.2.2.** By Contrasting Them with His Willingness to Preach the Gospel Without Charge (11:7–12)
- **6.2.3.** By Denouncing Them As Masquerading Impostors (11:13–15)

6.3. Paul Defends the Legitimacy of His Apostolic Ministry Through Foolish Boasting (11:16–12:13)
- **6.3.1.** Paul's Right to Engage in Such Boasting (11:16–21)
- **6.3.2.** Paul Boasts in Natural Qualifications (11:22)
- **6.3.3.** Paul Boasts of Trials and Sufferings (11:23–33)
- **6.3.4.** Paul Boasts of Weakness Due to Great Revelation (12:1–10)
- **6.3.5.** The Proof of Paul's Apostolic Ministry (12:11–13)

6.4. Paul Plans a Third Visit (12:14–13:14)
- **6.4.1.** Paul's Intention Not to Be a Burden (12:14–18)
- **6.4.2.** Paul's Fears and Misgivings Over the Coming Visit (12:19–21)
- **6.4.3.** Paul Warns of Possible Discipline (13:1–4)
- **6.4.4.** Paul's Plea for Self-Examination to Avoid Discipline (13:5–10)
- **6.4.5.** Paul's Closing Greeting (13:11–14)

COMMENTARY

1. Introduction (1:1–11)

1.1. Salutation (1:1–2)

As in most of his letters, Paul opens by identifying himself as an "apostle of Christ Jesus." Paul's apostleship designates him as an authoritative messenger or bearer of the gospel. As we know from Acts, he owed his status as an apostle to God's choice of him (Acts 9:15) and to God's intervention in his life. Consequently, Paul adds here "by the will of God."

Paul's mention of "Timothy our brother" may simply be his way of mentioning someone well known to his audience. However, we recall that Timothy was the bearer of 1 Corinthians

(1 Cor. 16:10) and that neither he nor the letter was well received (see "Occasion and Purpose" in the Introduction). Perhaps sending a rather young (1 Tim. 4:12) and timid (2 Tim. 1:7) person as Paul's representative had something to do with the failure of the mission. In any event, following his "painful visit" Paul chose Titus to carry the "tearful letter" to Corinth. Thus, Paul's endearing reference to Timothy may be his way of bolstering his damaged image among the Corinthians.

With Timothy Paul greets God's church "in Corinth" and "throughout Achaia." The Christians of Achaia would likely have opportunity to read the letter as it circulated in the province. Paul is fond of referring to believers as "saints" (he uses the word thirty-seven times in his letters). The Greek expression *hoi hagioi* (lit., "the holy ones") designates God's people as those set apart or consecrated as his very own. It is not hard to see behind this term Paul's Hebrew understanding of Israel as "consecrated/holy to the LORD" (Ezra 8:28; Jer. 2:3; cf. also Lev. 11:44–45; 19:2; 20:7, 26).

In characteristic fashion Paul greets the Corinthians with "grace and peace to you." Here he shows his ability to fuse elements of two cultures. Typically Greek letters began with the word *chairein* ("greetings"; see Acts 15:23; 23:26). But Paul does not simply wish to greet the saints, but to convey his desire that God's unmerited favor (*charis*, "grace") or blessings in Christ be their portion. Behind his use of "peace" (*eirene*) undoubtedly lies the Hebrew word for peace (*shalom*). It speaks of blessings and a state of well-being that come from God as a result of standing in covenant relationship with him. Thus, Paul can speak both of peace *from* God (Rom. 1:7; 1 Cor. 1:3) and peace *with* God (Rom. 5:1).

With respect to this greeting one important theological observation should be made. Paul is not expressing a casual wish, but invoking a blessing or benediction upon the church. Implicit in this greeting is an affirmation of the deity of Christ. Nowhere in his writings does Paul invoke a blessing and present "grace" as coming from anyone other than God and/or Jesus Christ. Furthermore, it would have been unthinkable for a devout Jew such as Paul to call upon anyone but God for the bestowal of *shalom*. In Paul's thinking God the Father and the Lord Jesus Christ were the divine source of grace and peace.

1.2. Praise for God's Comfort in Affliction (1:3–7)

Following his opening greeting, Paul usually commends the church to which he writes. He often accomplishes this by thanking God for some demonstration of their faith or new life in Christ (see, e.g., Rom. 1:8; 1 Cor. 1:4; Eph. 1:15–16; Phil. 1:3–7). But it seems that the memory of a recent deliverance (1:8–11) is so intense that Paul begins instead by praising God for his sustaining grace in the midst of trials.

Paul testifies from personal experience that God is a source of boundless mercy and comfort for Christians who are suffering. God's character of "compassion" (or "mercy," see Ex. 33:19; Ps. 111:4) and "comfort" (Isa. 40:1; 66:13) was well known to his people in the Old Testament. God's comfort (*paraklesis*, 2 Cor. 1:3) refers to his help and carries the idea of consolation or encouragement. Compassion (*oiktirmos*) is that quality of God that moves him to respond with kindness and mercy toward those who are suffering or in distress.

Paul's identification of God as the "Father of our Lord Jesus Christ" is also noteworthy (cf. Rom. 15:6; Eph. 1:3; Col. 1:3). God is the source of mercy and comfort, but his comfort overflows through Christ. Believers undergoing afflictions are said to be experiencing "the sufferings of Christ" (2 Cor. 1:5). In context it seems that Paul has in view a unity of divine action. Believers who endure affliction for the cause of Christ can be assured that God the Father *and* the Lord Jesus Christ stand ready to provide aid and comfort.

Paul goes on to offer a positive perspective concerning afflictions. In verse 4 his words reveal that enduring trials through divine comfort is part of God's plan for equipping us to be his comforting agents. Paul's own afflictions (v. 6) and the comfort he received from God were the means of preparing him to offer divine encouragement to the Corinthians when they encountered trials. Such encouragement ensured their deliverance (*soteria*, lit., "salvation"; this word can designate both eternal salvation and physical rescue from danger) by enabling them to persevere in faith through the very "same sufferings" endured by Paul. Certainly Paul understood that the bond between sufferer and comforter is never stronger than when forged by a common experience of pain

Paul offers two words of hope here. (1) Verse 5 suggests that God administers his comforting grace in proportion to the sufferings we are called to endure for the sake of Christ. If we are called to suffer greatly for Christ, we can be assured of God's abundant comfort. (2) Paul's own experience has given him a confident hope (v. 7) that the Corinthians will emerge victorious from their trials. Since they are called upon to endure the same sufferings as Paul, they will certainly partake of the same comfort from God. Paul's confidence rests securely in the consistent and proven character of God to visit his suffering saints with his comforting grace.

1.3. Thanksgiving for God's Deliverance in Asia (1:8–11)

Paul now tells of his own recent deliverance from a near-death trial while in Asia. We know virtually nothing of the "deadly peril" (v. 10) about which Paul speaks. It must have taken place during one of his two stays in Ephesus in Asia (Acts 18:19–21; 19:1–20:1), but beyond this we are uninformed. He recalls the experience partly to encourage the Corinthians to trust God and embrace hope when they undergo trials. His main motive, however, is to silence the accusation of his opponents who, because of his delay in coming and a recent change of plans (1:15–2:4), have accused him of vacillating and not keeping his promise. Paul wants the Corinthians to know that nothing less than the severest of trials could have prevented him from coming as planned. The burden of the trial was so far beyond his ability to cope that he "despaired even of life" (v. 8). Indeed, he felt as if a "sentence of death" had already been passed on him, and he truly expected to die (v. 9).

But Paul's account serves to illustrate another positive purpose of trials for the Christian (cf. vv. 4, 6). Paul saw a divine purpose behind his near-death trial. Through it he and

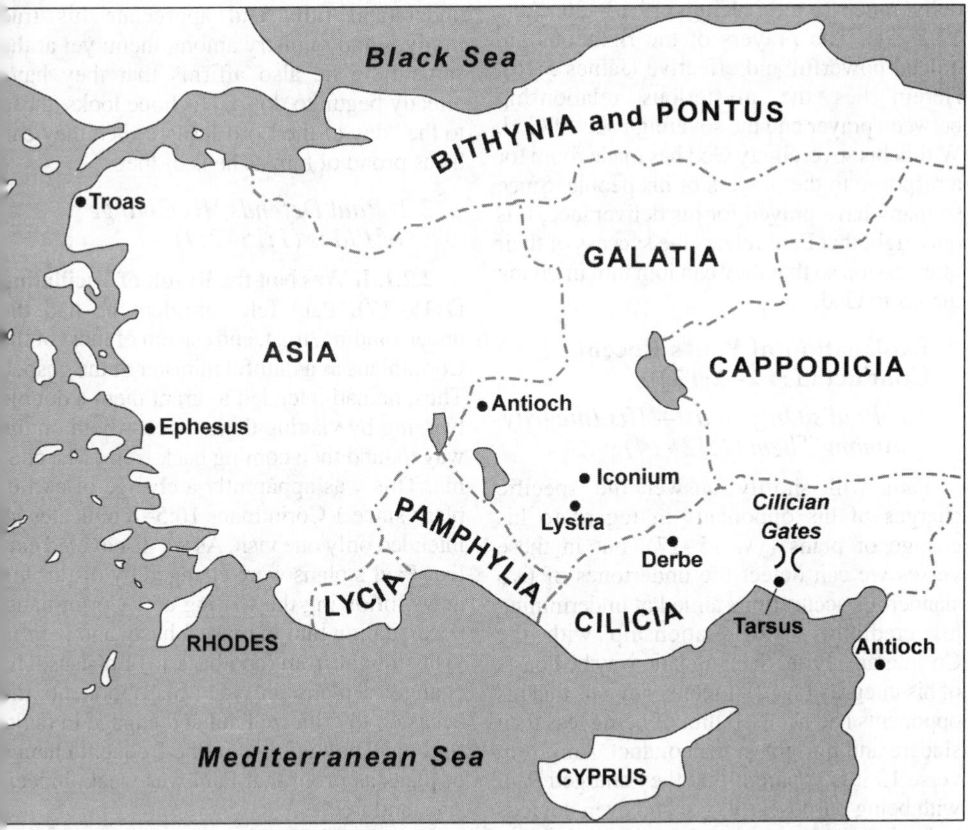

Paul wrote to the Corinthians of the hardships he had suffered in Asia. Asia was a Roman province in the western part of Asia Minor.

his companions had learned to trust God more fully. It had stripped them of their independence and self-reliance, and they were forced to look beyond themselves to the "Father of compassion" and the "God of all comfort" (v. 3). In his mercy God rescued them from that "deadly peril" (v. 10). In remembering this deliverance Paul was also reminded of a crucial aspect of the believer's redemption—the resurrection. He realized that the God "who raises the dead" has not limited his work of deliverance to a future hope. The same God who delivered Paul and whom Paul trusts to deliver him from death in the resurrection, can be trusted to deliver them from future dangers (v. 10).

While Paul recognizes God alone as the effective cause behind his deliverance, he hastens to thank the many believers who prayed on his behalf. After all, it was "in answer to" those prayers that God's "gracious favor" (or "gift"; Gk. *charisma*) of deliverance was granted (v. 11). In the Bible we often find prayer having a vital role in securing God's deliverance (e.g., 2 Kings 19:14–36; Acts 12:5–11). The prayers of the righteous are indeed powerful and effective (James 5:16). Herein lies the mysterious relationship between prayer and the sovereign acts of God. Within his sovereignty God has made room for a response to the prayers of his people. Since so many have prayed for his deliverance, it is only right that Paul relates the success of their intercession so that they can join him in giving thanks to God.

2. Explanation of Paul's Recent Conduct (1:12–2:13)

2.1. Paul's Only Boast—His Integrity Among Them (1:12–14)

Paul will shortly answer the specific charges of his opponents in regard to his change of plans (vv. 15–17), but in these verses we can detect the undertones of two slanderous accusations aimed at undermining his credibility and relationship with the Corinthians. From the emphatic way he boasts of his integrity (v. 12) it seems obvious that his opponents had accused him of being less than sincere and upright in his conduct. And from verse 13 it is apparent that they charged Paul with being purposely vague and even devious in his letters. In essence they contended that there was much more to Paul than meets the eye; his true motives and agenda lay outsic what they could see, hear, and read.

Paul is unshaken by these accusations, n only because they are unfounded, but als because his conscience is clear. He has walke before the Corinthians and "in the world" wi integrity (NIV "holiness") and openness. "Si cerity" carries the idea of purity in motive (c 2:17). Moreover, Paul's conduct has n depended on "worldly [*sarkikos*, lit., fleshly wisdom" but on "God's grace." Consequentl his letters bear the same character of integrit He writes what he means, and he means wh he writes. There is no secret message or hidde meaning behind his words. Christian worke need to take heart and instruction from Paul' example. There is no better antidote for unju criticism than a clear conscience before God.

Verse 15 shows Paul's pastoral heart an wisdom. His words to the Corinthians ar filled with encouragement even whe acknowledging a deficiency in their relation ship. He expresses hope that they will come t understand fully and appreciate his tru motives and ministry among them; yet at th same time he also affirms that they hav already begun to do so. His hope looks ahea to the "day of the Lord Jesus" when they ca be as proud of him as he is of them.

2.2. Paul Defends His Change of Plans (1:15–2:4)

2.2.1. It Was Not the Result of Vacillatin (1:15–17). Paul felt confident he had th understanding, trust, and esteem of most of th Corinthians as a faithful minister of the gospe Thus, he had intended to grant them a doubl blessing by visiting them twice—both on th way to, and then coming back from, Macedo nia. This was apparently a change of earlie plans since 1 Corinthians 16:5–8 indicates h intended only one visit. As we discovered ear lier, Paul's plans were changed by disturbin news following the writing of 1 Corinthians necessitating him to make a hasty and painfu visit straight from (and back to) Ephesus. Hi change of plans provided his opponents th occasion to criticize Paul and engage in fault finding. They pointed to the frequent chang of plans as proof that Paul was weak, indeci sive, and fickle.

In verse 17 Paul does not deny that he ha a change of plans, but only that he was vacil lating in doing so. He does not operate in a worldly (lit., "according to the flesh") manner, saying "yes" one moment and "no" the next, as if his words of promise mean nothing. Paul's opponents are doing more than personal nit-picking, they are laying down a serious charge: Paul and his words cannot be trusted.

2.2.2. They Can Rely on the Sure Word of God (1:18–22). It seems probable that Paul's opponents argued that since he could be so lax in his promises, his ministry (and especially the gospel he preached) could not be depended upon. Such an accusation is painful to a person of integrity. Though short of taking an oath, Paul appeals to the character of God himself in his defense. The message he preaches is not his own but God's. Since God is faithful, his Word possesses the same fidelity as its Author. Consequently, Paul argues that his message was not a vacillating "Yes" and "No" (v. 18). He and his companions preach Jesus Christ, the Son of God, who never wavers between "yes" and "no" and is himself the definitive "yes" to all the promises of God (v. 20).

This fact explains why Paul and the Corinthians, when worshiping, say "Amen." They not only affirm the trustworthiness of God's Word fulfilled in Christ, but by their faith-filled affirmation they bring glory to God. Thus, the integrity of Paul's preaching ministry at Corinth is integrally bound up in and backed by the character of God, whose Word Paul preaches.

Paul concludes the defense of his integrity by offering a concrete illustration of God's trustworthiness. In verses 21–22 we find a sentence containing four participles, all having God as the understood subject. Paul is doing more here than listing aspects of God's saving activity accomplished in Christ; he is describing the faithful character of God, who makes good his redemptive promises. God is the One who enables Paul, together with the Corinthians, to "stand firm in Christ" and has "anointed" them. He is the same One who has "set his seal of ownership" on them and "put his Spirit in [their] hearts" as a pledge. To what actions do these participles refer and how do they portray the fidelity of God?

The first participle (*bebaion*) can be translated "confirms" or "establishes," which describes either the action of "strengthening" or "securing" something. This is the meaning chosen in the NIV text: God is the one who causes Paul and the Corinthians to stand strong in their faith in Christ (cf. Harris, 325). But the verb can also refer to a "confirming" or "guaranteeing" of something (Heb. 2:3; cf. also *bebaiosis* in Heb. 6:16). If the latter sense is adopted, Paul's words flow naturally from the defense motif. The trustworthiness of God, on which hangs Paul's own integrity, is seen first in God's *guaranteeing* or *confirming* us *in Christ*.

What divine activity this refers to is open to interpretation. It can be argued that Paul intends the three remaining participles ("anointed," "set his seal," and "put [lit., gave] his Spirit") to refer to the work of the Spirit in validating, identifying, and securing us as those belonging to Christ (cf. Fee, 1994, 290–91). Thus the phrase "*bebaion* in Christ" would refer to God's work of bringing us into a saving relationship with Christ (Fee, 1994, 291; Martin, 27).

The God who has brought us "into Christ" (*eis Christos*) has "anointed [*chrisas*] us." This obvious play on words recalls the literal meaning of "Christ" (or Messiah): "the Anointed One." Luke makes it clear in his Gospel that the identification and validation of Jesus as the Messiah is linked to his empowering by the Spirit (Luke 4:1, 14, 18). It seems that Paul is drawing on that motif and applying it to believers. Believers, who have been incorporated into Christ (the Anointed One), to some extent share the same anointing. That Paul intends his readers to identify God's anointing with the gift of the Spirit given to the church (Acts 2:38) is almost certain (cf. 1 John 2:20, 27; 3:4). The sentence structure of 2 Corinthians 1:21–22 ties the last three participles closely together: God who anointed us is the very one who "also" (or "indeed"; Gk. *kai*, which seems stronger than simply "and" here) sealed us and put the Spirit into our hearts.

As in Ephesians 1:13 and 4:30, the seal of 2 Corinthians 1:22 points to the Spirit himself as the seal. A "seal" in the Greco-Roman world was a mark of identification placed on something either by the owner or sender. As such it guaranteed the authenticity and protection of the item on which the seal rested. The Spirit is that seal for believers, marking and identifying them as God's very own possession. This Spirit-seal has also been placed in the believer's heart as the "deposit" (*arrabon*) on the believer's inheritance in Christ (cf. Eph. 1:13–14). Again the Spirit is himself that deposit (cf. 2 Cor. 5:5). The KJV translation of *arrabon* ("earnest"), though archaic, is still instructive. "Earnest money" refers to an initial payment given as pledge or guarantee of the full payment of goods or services. The Spirit is the down payment that God now sends into our hearts to guarantee the full spiritual inheritance that awaits the believer.

Thus, Paul can look ahead to "the day of redemption" (Eph. 4:30), when God will complete the work begun when he sealed the believer with the promised Holy Spirit (Eph. 1:13). That initial gift of the Spirit was but the "firstfruits" of a great end-time harvest, which for Christians will mean "the redemption of our bodies" (Rom. 8:23). This must refer to the *parousia* ("coming") of Christ, attended by the believers' resurrection, when our "natural" and "perishable" bodies will be raised as "imperishable" and "spiritual" bodies (1 Cor. 15:42, 44).

Pentecostals are sure to wonder, given the emphasis in these verses, where the baptism in the Holy Spirit might be found. We hasten to comment that Paul undoubtedly believed that the Christian life is characterized by the Spirit's indwelling presence and power. To him the experience of Spirit-baptism described in Luke-Acts is the normal experience of New Testament believers. Consequently, we should not expect Paul to think of separate categories of Christians who are and are not baptized in the Spirit (Horton, 239).

This is not to say, however, that Paul equates the work of the Spirit in regeneration with the Spirit-baptism. A literal rendering of Ephesians 1:13 reads: "In him you also, after listening to the word of truth, the gospel of your salvation—having also believed, you were sealed in him with the Holy Spirit of promise." In other words, the sealing with the Holy Spirit follows the hearing and believing of the gospel. What non-Pentecostals argue is that the context deals with salvation, not power for service (Acts 1:8)—the purpose Jesus earmarked for baptism in the Spirit (Acts 1:5). Here is where 2 Corinthians 1:21–22 is instructive, since the "anointing" of God is closely linked to the divine activity of "sealing"; and, as we saw, evidence of the Spirit's power in his ministry served to identify Jesus as the Anointed One.

It is our suggestion, then, that the baptism in the Holy Spirit is primarily embraced by the participles "anointed" and "sealed." The participles that describe God's "confirming" believers in Christ and "putting the Spirit in our hearts as a pledge" point to God's saving activity in securing our beginning in Christ and having guaranteed the fullness of our inheritance at redemption's end. They form a bracket around the two inner participles, which describe the Spirit's work in empowering believers to serve God and visibly marking them as his people, evidenced by the gifts and graces of his Spirit.

2.2.3. It Was to Avoid a Painful Confrontation (1:23–2:4). Paul now returns to his defense of not coming to the Corinthians as planned (1:15–17). Earlier (v. 18) he stopped short of a formal oath, but here he abandons all restraint and calls on God to validate the truth of what he is about to say. The beginning of verse 23 literally reads, "And I call on God as a witness to my soul." In this manner he swears before the living God, who searches the hearts and minds of human beings (Ps. 139:23; Jer. 17:10), that his delay in coming is as he says—to spare the Corinthians another harsh and painful confrontation (2 Cor. 2:1–2; see "Occasion and Purpose" in the Introduction).

No doubt the Corinthians would vividly recall here the sharp conflict between Paul and his antagonists during the "painful visit," so he avoids the offense of what could be misconstrued as a veiled threat. He does not want them to think he is the sort of person who enjoys throwing his apostolic weight around and telling them exactly how they are to practice their faith. Instead, Paul sees himself as a "fellow worker" with them (*synergos*; NIV, "we work with you") in the service of their faith, a faith he hopes will be practiced with joy and not coerced by the tyrannical exercise of authority. In fact, Paul acknowledges that such an approach is altogether unnecessary, as the Corinthians were already standing firm in the faith (v. 24).

The memory of the previous painful encounter is still fresh in Paul's mind. He does not wish to repeat that experience, primarily because he does not enjoy inflicting pain and sorrow (2:1–2) on those whom he loves (2:4). It is, in fact, absurd to make sorrowful the very ones who are supposed to be your source of joy

(2:2–3a). His delay in coming to them was in one sense self-serving: He did not want to make them sorrowful, nor did he want himself to grieve.[2] Here we witness the paternal heart of Paul. His joy derives from seeing his spiritual children (cf. 1 Cor. 4:15) joyfully and faithfully serving Christ. Discipline, such as that which accompanied the painful visit, may be necessary, but it is not something Paul relishes.

The apostle had no doubt stated as much in his letter (2:3) that followed the painful visit. This letter of tears had been written when Paul was suffering "great distress and anguish of heart" (2:4) in the emotional wake of that experience. It was not written to inflict pain, but to demonstrate the special love he had for them. For Paul, loving the Corinthians meant issuing a harsh rebuke needed to restore their faith, even if it meant the personal anguish of causing those he loved pain and distress. His example teaches us that true love will do what is best for those loved, not what is convenient or comfortable. It requires a vulnerability that involves the personal risk of rejection and criticism.

2.3. Paul Urges Forgiveness for an Offending Brother (2:5–11)

Having expressed the sorrow he experienced during his painful visit to Corinth, Paul now talks about the man who was largely responsible. Both the identity of this man and nature of the offense are left unstated. Many ancient and older commentators identify this man with the incestuous man of 1 Corinthians 5:1–5 (see Hughes, 59–65). Yet 2 Corinthians 2:5 indicates that the offense was directed specifically against Paul, whereas Paul's outrage concerning the incestuous man was not over the rejection of his apostolic authority, but over the church's incredible tolerance of such sin in their midst. What we can say with certainty is that at Corinth Paul encountered opposition. A member of the opposition party (perhaps the ringleader) offended Paul, most likely by rejecting his apostolic authority; this left him deeply distressed (cf. 2:4).

Paul had undoubtedly insisted that the offender be disciplined, which the majority in the church (2:6) came to realize was necessary. Whether they realized this while Paul was present or only after the tearful letter is uncertain. But some of the Corinthians now felt that the discipline was insufficient and were advocating a stricter form of punishment. Paul intervenes here and counsels the church to take action to restore the offending brother.

2.3.1. Paul's Gracious Attitude of Detachment (2:5). It is common for people when they are insulted or wronged to become bitter and resentful. Often they nurse their wounded pride with ill will toward their offender. In verse 5 Paul exhibits a rare attitude in response to a personal wrong. He is able to detach himself from his personal hurt long enough to see the bigger picture. He wants the Corinthians to know that the offender in his personal attack has, to some extent, injured ("caused grief . . . to") the whole church. The addition of "not to put it too severely" at the end of the verse indicates Paul does not want to exaggerate the case. His personal grief has given way to a larger concern for others—and especially for the offending brother!

2.3.2. Paul's Concern for Restoration (2:6–11). Rather than gloating over the discipline meted out on the offender by the majority (v. 6), Paul calls for its termination. The offense has been adequately dealt with, the guilty party sufficiently disciplined. His concern was that if such discipline were unduly extended, it could result in the brother being so completely overwhelmed with grief (v. 7) that he might never recover. Paul here underscores the value and goal of church discipline: In love it seeks to correct, not punish; its ultimate objective is the restoration of the offender to spiritual wholeness and the return to full participation in Christian fellowship.

Paul is thus counseling the Corinthians here to take the first step toward realizing that goal: forgiveness. Forgiveness is necessary for reconciliation to occur and for fractured relationships to be mended. He also counsels the Corinthians to "comfort" this brother (v. 7), who was no doubt suffering the disgrace and humiliation of whatever disciplinary measures he was assigned. Such comfort requires them to "reaffirm [their] love for him" in some public or demonstrative manner (v. 8). This action would serve to declare and confirm the reality of God's forgiveness granted to him through the church's acting in Christ's authority to bind and loose sins (Matt. 16:19; 18:18; John 20:23; cf. Harris, 328).

Paul had previously written his instructions regarding the discipline of the offending brother. That provided the occasion to test (v. 9) whether the Corinthians would accept and submit to his apostolic leadership. Now Paul hopes they are willing to follow his counsel to forgive and restore the offender. Just as he acts in the authority of Christ as his apostle ("in the sight of" in v. 10 describes an action taken or done with God's or Christ's approval; cf. 1 Thess. 1:3; 1 Tim. 5:21; 6:13; 2 Tim. 2:14), so Paul states that when the Corinthians forgive the man in question, he is united with them in that action and consents to their verdict.

Paul can exhort them to forgive because he himself has already forgiven the brother (v. 10). He no doubt personally felt the need to forgive, but he overlooks any personal gain and states that his forgiveness was "for your sake." This probably refers to Paul's forgiveness as restoring the unity and harmony broken during the discipline of the offending brother. Such disunity, if left unremedied by forgiveness, provides Satan an occasion to take advantage of the church and work his destructive schemes within. Paul is well acquainted with Satan's plots and ploys, and his readiness to forgive is aimed at rendering them ineffective.

2.4. Waiting for News From Titus (2:12–13)

Paul now returns to the story that explains his recent conduct and change of plans. Having sent the "tearful letter" by Titus (see Introduction), he is left to wait for news. Apparently he had made plans to meet Titus in Troas if things went well at Corinth. After sending the letter Paul traveled north to Troas. When he did not find Titus there, he went on to Macedonia. Note that this narrative is broken off after 2:14 and does not resume until 7:5–7, where Paul writes about his reunion with Titus, who brought news that Paul's letter had met with a favorable response.

The tearful letter was painful for Paul to write. Most likely it included a harsh rebuke of the Corinthians for the recent conduct he had witnessed during his "painful visit." He could not be certain how the Corinthians would receive his correction. Paul surely waited for news from Titus with a good deal of anxiety. No doubt his imagined fears seemed to materialize when Titus failed to meet him at Troas. The situation left him, in his own words, with "no peace of mind" (lit., "no rest for my spirit," v. 13). Nevertheless, when the Lord gave him opportunity to preach in Macedonia, he took it. Fear often paralyzes the fearful apart from the grace of God. Paul drew upon that grace (see v. 14) and remained occupied in the work of the Lord.

3. Digression From Travelogue: Description of Paul's Apostolic Ministry (2:14–7:4)

With 2:14 Paul begins a lengthy digression from his travelogue (2:14–7:4), in which he both describes and defends his apostolic ministry. It is unquestionably one of the most illuminating passages in Paul's letters. In it we gain invaluable insight into his understanding of himself, the gospel, and his own apostolic calling. Of particular worth is how Paul characterizes his own apostolic ministry and its accomplishments, often in stark contrast to that of his opponents. Careful examination of this and later passages shows that Paul deeply believes that the true apostle must imitate Christ—an imitation most clearly seen in his willingness to identify with the sufferings of Christ in the work of the gospel.

3.1. Paul's Grateful Confidence (2:14–17)

3.1.1. In God to Lead in Triumph (2:14–16a). In spite of the turmoil and distress Paul experienced (2:13), he was confident of a victorious outcome. In the back of his mind here is how his anxious fears were put to rest at the coming of Titus with the latter's encouraging news. He responds by expressing grateful praise to God, drawing his reader's mind to a familiar scene—the Roman triumphal procession.

This event marked a notable victory by a conquering Roman general (see Barclay, 204–5). Here Paul paints a paradox for us. Christ is the victor (cf. Col. 1:15, the only other text in which the verb *thriambeuo*, "lead in triumphal procession," occurs), who leads Paul as one of his captives in public display and testimony to the triumph of his redemption. It is not altogether uncommon for Paul to think of himself in such terms. Elsewhere he describes believers as formerly "God's enemies" (Rom. 5:10). God, having secured the victory and throne of Christ, has taken a host of captives and given them as gifts to the church (see Ps. 68:18; Eph. 4:7–8, 10).

Through the preaching of the gospel, God spreads the knowledge of himself in Christ "in every place," just as a fragrant aroma fills the air.[3] The apostles themselves are the "fragrance of Christ" that ascends to God (v. 15a, NKJV). Christ is made known through their preaching and the character of their lives and ministry (cf. chs. 10–13). The witness of Christ comes with mixed results: To "those who are being saved," it is the "fragrance of life"; to "those who are perishing," it is "the smell of death." Exactly what association Paul has in mind here is not clear. Perhaps he is echoing the Jewish notion that the law (Torah) has the dual effect of producing both life and death upon its hearers (cf. Deut. 30:15–18; see Barrett, 101–2, for a Talmudic reference). Similarly, the gospel results in life to those who believe and death to those who refuse the message of God's salvation in Christ.

3.1.2. In the Integrity of His Ministry (2:16b–17). Paul suddenly realizes the weight of the truth just uttered and the awesome responsibility that attends it. Thus he asks, "And who is equal to such a task?" (v. 16b). His mind then wanders to those who, in his judgment, are not qualified. That he has his opponents in mind when he describes those who "peddle the word of God for profit" seems certain. The Greek verb used here (*kapeleuo*) occurs only here in the New Testament. In secular Greek the noun *kapelos* was used of a street peddler who hawked his wares. Intent only on dispensing his goods for gain, these profiteers did not hesitate to misrepresent the quality and value of their wares (cf. Isa. 1:22, where *kalepos* is used of those who "adulterate" the wine with water). Paul apparently has in mind not only those who engage in the preaching of the gospel with a profit mentality, but also those who corrupt its message (see Hughes, 83). His later defense of preaching without charge (11:7–12) points to those who prized their ability to draw a living from preaching the gospel.

Paul is not condemning taking support for gospel ministry (see Rom. 15:27). What he rebukes is the attitude and practice of many philosophers and teachers in the Greek world who prided themselves on having wealthy patrons and clients. Such teachers were often people-pleasers, who were motivated by financial reward and compromised the truth for personal gain. Paul distances himself from such people. His words are not his own but God's. His motives are pure as he speaks with Christ's authority in the sight of God. At the end of verse 17 we learn something further about Paul's confidence (cf. v. 14). The self-awareness of his own integrity before God gave him great freedom and boldness to speak God's message and to confront error with truth.

3.2. The Greatness and Glory of Paul's Ministry (3:1–4:6)

The thought of his opponents (v. 17) causes Paul to further distance himself from them. To his way of thinking the difference is like night and day. Neither the character of his ministry nor the content of his preaching leaves much to be compared. Unlike them the affirmation of his ministry does not rest on the external testimony of letters but on the inward work of the Spirit in the lives of the Corinthians themselves (3:1–3). Paul takes his confidence from the fact that God in Christ has implemented a new covenant, which provides the dynamic and transforming power of the Holy Spirit (vv. 4–6).

God has made Paul a minister of this new covenant of the Spirit, which in contrast to the law gives life and comes with greater glory (vv. 6b–11). This contrast is evident in the gospel Paul preaches, but its message is resisted by those who tie their salvation to the keeping of the law. Their eyes remain unseeing until they turn to Christ and receive the life-giving liberty of the Spirit (vv. 12–18). Paul recognizes the difficulty and challenges of preaching to those blinded by the god of this world. Nevertheless, he is determined to illuminate a world of spiritual darkness by preaching the Lord Jesus Christ—God's gospel of light (4:1–6).

3.2.1. Every Believer's Becoming a Letter of Christ (3:1–3). The opening of this section alludes to the ancient practice of writing letters of commendation to introduce someone and testify to his or her good character. The early church adopted this practice to screen those who sought a teaching or prophetic ministry within a church and to provide a safeguard against charlatans (cf. *Did.* 11–13). Paul's opponents came to Corinth with such letters in hand and used them to gain credibility and audience in the church.

Paul's asks two rhetorical questions, a "no" answer being understood for each. The first anticipates his opponents' charge that in affirming his own integrity (in contrast to the gospel peddlers, 2:17), Paul is again commending himself. Actually, the charge is self-incriminating, as that is exactly what Paul thinks of their use of letters of recommendation. It is not that the apostle rejects the practice of writing letters of commendation, for from his letters we know he used and wrote them (Rom. 16:1–2; 1 Cor. 16:10–11; Col. 4:10). Even in this letter Paul commends Titus and his companions to the church (2 Cor. 8:22–24). Rather, what Paul denies in the second question is that he himself needs such letters to validate his ministry among them.

In verse 2 Paul asserts that he possesses a superior letter of commendation: the grace of Christ operating through his ministry, which has produced a spiritual transformation in human lives. The Corinthians themselves are a letter from Christ and provide all the testimony and affirmation Paul needs. He contrasts this letter to the ones carried by his opponents. It is not written externally on parchment, but internally in human hearts; it does not consist of an impersonal testimony of strangers carried in hand, but the intimate referral of a transformed life borne in the heart of the apostle; it is not limited to a few who read it, but seen and read by all who witness that transformation; and it is not written with lifeless ink, but with the living Spirit of God (vv. 2–3a).

Paul continues this last contrast with images from the Old Testament. His letter is not like the Ten Commandments, which were written on cold, lifeless tablets of stone (Ex. 31:18; 32:15–16), but is written permanently on warm, responsive hearts (Jer. 31:33; 32:38–40; Ezek. 11:19; 36:26). The superiority of Paul's letter of commendation is beyond dispute. In making that clear he not only answers his opponents' criticism, but issues a harsh rebuke of their habit of self-promotion. This response also strongly defends the genuineness of his own apostleship and indirectly casts a cloud of suspicion over that of his opponents (see Harris, 334).

3.2.2. Paul's Confidence in and Enablement by God (3:4–6a). Paul is confident "before God" (v. 4) that the kind of commendatory letter he possesses testifies to the legitimacy of his own apostleship. This confidence has been given to him by Christ, but offers Paul no illusion that he is capable of judging the effects of his ministry or that the results are due to his own personal competency. Paul answers with an emphatic "no" to that very suggestion, for God is Paul's enablement, and in him Paul finds his adequacy as an apostle. This contrasts directly with his opponents, who (as the rest of the letter makes clear) are proud and self-sufficient (10:8, 12, 15; 11:6, 10, 12, 16–18, 30; 12:1, 5–6, 9, 11).

Yet it is wrong to interpret Paul's words as denying that he had anything to contribute by way of talents and abilities to his ministry as an apostle. Anyone acquainted with his life knows all too well how he was uniquely qualified to fulfill his calling as the "apostle to the Gentiles" (Barclay, 9–31). In his denial of self-sufficiency Paul is declaring that he is utterly incapable of bringing about the spiritual transformation he has just described. He may have been naturally suited for preaching the gospel in the Greco-Roman world, but the work of regeneration is God's alone.

Paul also recognizes that the God who called him to be a minister of a new covenant (v. 6) also equipped him for the task. His call can be traced to his Damascus road encounter with the resurrected Jesus (Acts 9:3–7), when the Lord described him to Ananias as "my chosen instrument to carry my name before the Gentiles" (9:15). His enablement followed immediately when he was filled with the Holy Spirit (9:17). To be a minister of a new covenant of the Spirit required the empowering presence of the Spirit in Paul's life.

That Acts 9:17 refers to Paul's experience of the baptism in the Holy Spirit seems clear. Twice in Luke-Acts the Pentecostal outpouring of the Spirit is linked to the purpose of "empowerment" (Luke 24:49; Acts 1:8). Jesus told the disciples to wait for the coming of the Spirit, when they would be "baptized with [*en*; lit., "in"] the Holy Spirit" (Acts 1:5). Paul's experience parallels that of the disciples. Having been "filled with the Holy Spirit" (Acts 2:4; cf. 9:17) they were empowered to preach the gospel boldly (2:14–36; cf. 9:20). Note also that this phrase is used five times in Acts—twice of the initial reception of the Spirit (2:4; 9:17) and three times of subsequent empowerings (4:8, 31; 13:9). Those that identify 9:17 with Paul's experience of regeneration fail to recognize that the new covenant provision of ne Spirit is multidimensional, including works f the Spirit relating to salvation (soteriological) *and* works of service (charismatic/vocational; see Stronstad, 63–73).

Earlier when Paul contrasted Moses' tablets f stone to the new work of the Spirit on tablets f human hearts (v. 3), he anticipated the contrast between the old and new covenant, which e now explores. The fundamental difference etween the two is expressed in the parallel hrases "not of the letter but of the Spirit" v. 6). God established Israel as his people and ntered into a covenant with them at Mount Sinai (Ex. 19:1). The responsibilities to Yahweh under that covenant were expressed in a written code of laws (see Ex. 19–24; Lev. 11–27; Num. 27–30). After Israel's rebellion at Kadesh Barnea (Num. 13:1–20:13) and forty years of discipline in the desert (Deut. 1:6–4:43), a new generation renewed and ratified hat original covenant (Deut. 27–30).

The Old Testament historical books chronicle a long succession of rebellions and increasing faithlessness. They confirm the sad truth, summarized by Jeremiah, that despite the loving care, protection, and provision of God, Israel failed to obey the terms of God's covenant law (Jer. 31:32). Consequently, the prophet looked forward to a day when God would establish a "new covenant"—one fundamentally different from the old. While the old covenant made clear what God required, it provided no power or dynamic to meet those demands. The new covenant, however, contains the extraordinary promise that God will effect an internal work in the hearts of his people: "I will put my law in their minds and write it on their hearts. I will be their God, and they will be my people" (31:33). Likewise, Ezekiel looked ahead to Israel's restoration and relates a similar promise: "I will give you a new heart and put a new spirit in you; I will remove from you your heart of stone and give you a heart of flesh. And I will put my Spirit in you and move you to follow my decrees and be careful to keep my laws" (Ezek. 36:26–27).

In other words, both Jeremiah and Ezekiel relate that the impulse and motivation for obedience under the new covenant will come from within, from hearts imprinted with the law of God and moved by a personal relationship with God. Ezekiel identifies the indwelling of the Spirit as the cause for this inner transformation (cf. 11:19, 20; 18:31, 32; 37:14; 39:29; also Isa. 32:15–18; 44:3–5; 59:19–21; Joel 2:28–29). It is this distinctive characteristic of the new covenant that Paul seizes upon in contrasting the old and new covenants. Whereas the first was based on a contractual letter (Exod. 24:1–7), the second is based on the presence and power of the indwelling Spirit.

3.2.3. The Greater Glory of the New Covenant (3:6b–11). The contrast between the two covenants is further explained in terms of its opposite results or effects: "The letter kills, but the Spirit gives life." But Paul offers no explanation of this statement. To understand it we must turn to the summary of the old covenant in Deuteronomy 30, where Moses placed before Israel a choice involving two very different paths:

> See, I set before you today life and prosperity, death and destruction. For I command you today to love the Lord your God, to walk in his ways, and to keep his commands, decrees and laws; then you will live and increase, and the Lord your God will bless you in the land you are entering to possess.
>
> But if your heart turns away and you are not obedient, and if you are drawn away to bow down to other gods and worship them, I declare to you this day that you *will certainly be destroyed*. (Deut. 30:15–18, italics added)

The choice was simple, life or death: life if they expressed their love for Yahweh by obeying the law, and death if they failed to do so. But as we saw from Jeremiah, Israel broke the covenant by failing to obey the terms of that covenant (Jer. 31:34). Consequently, this prophet longed for a new covenant (v. 31), which promised to remedy the situation that resulted in Israel's failure: God would write his law on their hearts. Ezekiel, we also learned, modified this promise of heart transformation into a heart *transplant* (Ezek. 36:26), accomplished by Yahweh's putting his Spirit within the people (v. 27). He graphically depicted the Spirit as Yahweh's life-giving agent, who breathes new life into his people (37:1–14). The vision of the dry bones come to life ends with the promise, "I will put my Spirit in you and you will live" (v. 14). We now begin to understand a vital contrast between the two covenants: Without the provision of the Spirit, the old covenant led to death.

Elsewhere in his writings Paul explores how the law results in death. In Romans 7, for example, we find the same life–death, Spirit–law contrast: "But now, by dying to what once bound us, we have been released from the law so that we serve in the new way of the Spirit, and not in the old way of the written code" (Rom. 7:6). He makes it clear that the reason why believers must die to the law is because to live under it invites the domination of our sinful nature (lit., "flesh") with its "sinful passions aroused by the law" (v. 5). It is not the law, however, that is to blame (v. 7). Rather, it is sin, taking the law (which is "holy, righteous and good" [v. 12]) and using it to promote sinful acts and spiritual death, that is the culprit (vv. 8–11). Paul also had this sinful use of the law (v. 13) in mind when he wrote, "The sting of death is sin, and the power of sin is the law" (1 Cor. 15:56). Thus, the law itself cannot be faulted, but without the provision of the Spirit it is powerless against sin and can only lead to death.

By contrast, the new covenant comes with the provision of the Spirit. The Spirit is of the *living* God (2 Cor. 3:3) and is thus the *life-giving* Spirit (v. 6b). It is the operation of the Spirit in new covenant believers that makes possible the fulfillment of what the law required. The life given by the Spirit is the eternal life of God himself, given as a gift through his Son Jesus Christ (Rom. 6:23; cf. John 20:31; 1 John 5:11–12). That life is now made available to the children of God, who have been raised with Christ to "newness of life" (Rom. 6:4, NRSV) by the same Spirit that raised Jesus from the dead (8:11; see Fee, 1994, 307). Paul calls this new life "the new way [or newness] of the Spirit" (Rom. 7:6). It is precisely this operation of the Spirit under the new covenant that sets believers free from the "law of sin and death" (8:2) and enables them to meet fully the requirements of the law as they live "according to the Spirit" (8:4).

The new covenant provision of the Spirit not only earmarks the major distinction between the two covenants, but also introduces the *superiority* of the new over the old. Beginning with verse 7, Paul shows that the new covenant comes with greater glory. To do so Paul admits that both covenants possess a ministry characterized by glory. The glory effect by the ministry of the Spirit (v. 8) under th new covenant is a glory, however, that cann be compared to the former glory (v. 11). T prove his point Paul uses a well-known an self-evident form of reasoning that argues th "if something is true in a case of lesser impo tance, how much more is it true in a case o greater importance" (a Jewish form of reason ing used from the time of Hillel; cf. Mat 7:11). If the old covenant, which resulted i death (v. 7; cf. v. 6) and condemnation (v. 9 came with glory, how can the new covenan empowered by the life-giving Spirit (v. 6) an resulting in righteousness, fail to come wit abounding glory? If that former covenant wa attended with a glory destined to fade (v. 7; c v. 12), how much greater is the glory of th new covenant, which is destined to remai (v. 11; cf. v. 18; Rom. 8:16–21, 29–30; Heb 8:13; 13:20).

3.2.4. The Veil That Conceals (3:12–16) Because their hope resides in a superio covenant (implied here; cf. Heb. 8) wit greater and permanent glory, Paul and his companions are able to speak openly with grea boldness. Unlike Moses, who veiled his face in the presence of the people, they have nothing to conceal. The story in Exodus 34:29–35 describes how, after speaking with Yahweh on Mount Sinai and coming down to the people, Moses' face shone brightly with the glory of the Lord. As a result he put a veil over his face.

A problem surfaces when we compare Paul's reason for that concealment with the text of Exodus. He claims that the veil Moses put over his face was designed to prevent the children of Israel from seeing the glory fade from his face (3:13), whereas the text in Exodus suggests it was to keep the people from being overcome by fear (Ex. 34:30, 34–35). Actually, Paul does not deny the latter reason, but argues that the primary reason was to prevent the people from looking "at the end of that which was fading" (2 Cor. 3:13, pers. trans.). Paul's words suggest that he has more than Moses' face in mind.[4] The Greek phrase "was fading away" is identical to the words in verse 11 that refer to the old covenant, which, although attended with glory, was destined to pass away with the coming of the new.

The Exodus story involving Moses' veil reminds Paul of the spiritual dullness of his

›ople. Like the Israelites of old, who failed to)mprehend the transitory nature of the law f. Gal. 3:19, 23–24) in the lesson of the veil, ›ws in Paul's time still exhibited minds hard- ıed to the truth of the gospel. Paul's mis- onary journeys document how frequently he ıcountered Jews who were still looking ıtently to Moses and the law as the means of ›ceiving God's salvation. The veil that oscured their spiritual vision remained intact 'henever the law was read; only "in Christ," ıat is, only by believing in Christ, could it be fted (2 Cor. 3:14b–16).

3.2.5. The Life-Giving and Liberating pirit (3:17–18). Only when people under- tand that "Christ is the end [i.e., goal] of the ıw so that there may be righteousness for veryone who believes" (Rom. 10:4) can they xperience the liberating truth of verse 17: The Lord is the Spirit; and where the Spirit of he Lord is, there is freedom." Scholars debate vhether Paul has Christ or God the Father in nind when he says, "The Lord is the Spirit." A lausible case can be made for either, consis- ent with the context. However, Paul's words hould not be interpreted to mean that he is dentifying Christ or Yahweh of the Old Tes- ament with the Spirit. The verb "is" can mean omething like "signifies/represents" or 'stands for"; that meaning serves Paul's anal- ›gy between the Lord in Exodus 34 and the Spirit's work under the new covenant.

The Lord in Exodus is to be compared to he Spirit. When Moses went into the Tent of Meeting or "turned to the Lord," he removed his veil and had access to the presence of God and a revelation of his will. Now whenever a person turns to the Lord, the Spirit removes the veil from dulled minds to reveal the knowledge of God in Christ and to give the experience of his presence (see Fee, 1994, 311–12). In that presence, Paul contends, there is freedom, a freedom unknown to those who, without the Spirit, are bound by a covenant of letter, leading to condemnation and death (vv. 6–9).

Believers in Christ have had the veil removed and now have access to the presence of God. The Spirit who effected that unveiling is now occupied in a marvelous work of spiritual transformation. Unveiled, we are made to reflect God's glory. The process is one of being increasingly transformed into the very likeness of God's glory. That glory, we later learn, is the glory of Christ, who is the image of God (4:4; cf. Rom. 8:29; Heb. 1:3).

This work of transforming us into the image of Christ is the work of "the Lord . . . the Spirit" (v. 18). The phrase is conceptually parallel to that of verse 17a ("the Lord is the Spirit"), where Paul compares the work of unveiling by the Spirit to the revelation of the Lord to Moses. Thus, Paul concludes by emphasizing that the entire process of transformation, from the unveiling of hardened hearts leading to conversion, to the experience of spiritual freedom, and to the progressive work of glorification belongs to the ministry of the Spirit (see Hughes, 338).

3.2.6. The Gospel That Brings Light (4:1–6). In 4:1 Paul resumes the prior theme of 3:6: his appointment and commission by God as a minister of the new covenant. He asserts, despite the criticisms and accusations leveled against him, that he has no reason to lose heart. Two facts buoy his spirits. (1) He has been commissioned to preach the gospel under the new covenant with its dynamic work of the Spirit and prospect of eternal glory. (2) He gratefully realizes that this privileged charge is the result of God's mercy. Paul probably has in mind what he later related in 1 Timothy 1:12–16. Even though the apostle was a "blasphemer . . . persecutor and a violent man," even "the worst" of all sinners, yet unbelievably, Paul recalls, "I was shown mercy" (v. 13). Still more incredible is that the same merciful God considered him faithful and put him into the service of Jesus Christ (v. 12), whom he had so zealously persecuted (see Acts 9:1–15). Paul saw his commission into Christ's service to preach the gospel as the result of God's "grace" (Gal. 1:15–16).

In verses 2–5 Paul defends himself against false charges leveled against him. Note that his emphatic denials throughout the letter often echo these charges. Apparently his opponents were accusing him of various forms of deceit (12:16) and wrongdoing (7:2). From 4:2 we can detect three accusations against him: (1) that Paul had engaged in shameful and underhanded behavior or methods; (2) that he was deceitful and cunning, perhaps manipulative, in order to get his own way; and (3) that through his preaching and teaching he was distorting the gospel.

Paul issues a forceful denial to these charges. He and his companions "have renounced [such] secret and shameful ways." By contrast, their conduct has been public and open to inspection. Paul is confident that any honest observer will know the integrity of his ministry. More important, Paul's conscience is clear before the one who called him. His example should teach us that we too can best weather the storms of controversy and false accusations under the shelter of a clean conscience before God.

Another possible accusation surfaces in verse 3. "Even if our gospel is veiled" suggests that, for the sake of argument, Paul will concede his opponents' charge. They may accuse him with being vague and obscure in his teaching (which does have a certain credibility, cf. 2 Peter 3:16), perhaps even investing his words with secret meaning, veiled to all but the spiritually perceptive or astute. Paul answers that whatever veiling does exist is not the fault of his preaching but the consequence of unbelief on the part of "those who are perishing" (2 Cor. 4:3; cf. 2:15; 1 Cor. 1:18). In their case, Satan, "the god of this age" (cf. John 12:31), has blinded the minds of the unbelieving and made them imperceptive to the light of the gospel (2 Cor. 4:4). The devil's goal ("so that" is best seen as introducing a purpose clause) is to make these people incapable of comprehending and receiving the truth of the gospel, which discloses the divine glory revealed in Christ, "who is the image of God" (cf. John 1:14, 18; Col. 1:15).

We should keep in mind that the veil image here recalls those whose minds are dulled at the reading of Moses (3:14–16). It seems certain from 11:22 that some of their number were among Paul's opponents. In 4:3 Paul draws an equation: those who are perishing = those who do not believe. In 1 Corinthians 1:18 "those who are perishing" are those who regard the message of the cross as foolishness. In 2 Thessalonians 2:9–10 Paul identifies "those who are perishing" with the ones that have succumbed to the deception of Satan, "because they refused to love the truth and so be saved." His words here, then, not only describe the spiritual condition of his opponents, but implicate them in the work of Satan, whose work is to blind minds to the light of the gospel.

Returning to a familiar accusation of his opponents (cf. 3:1; 5:12), Paul denies that his preaching is about self-promotion (4:5). Perhaps this is related to the earlier charge of distorting the word of God. In any case, Paul sur marizes the substance of his preaching: "Jes Christ as Lord" (cf. Rom. 10:9). As for t false accusation, if he or his company preach anything about themselves, it was their role servants to the Corinthians because of Jesu In that role they imitated their Lord, who hur bled himself and took on the form of a serva to accomplish the task of redemption (Ph 2:5–8). In an earlier correspondence Pa expressed his pastoral concern for t Corinthians as their spiritual father (1 Co 4:15). Despite opposition to his apostlesh and numerous criticisms, Paul sought to w their submission to his authority through se vanthood and love.

The reason why Paul preached Christ in th role of a servant is given in 4:6. Paraphrasin Genesis 1:3, he draws a comparison betwee God's creative act in making light shine out c darkness and the spiritual illumination th occurred in his own heart at his conversion (c 2 Cor. 5:17). Paul preaches Christ because th Creator himself has shattered the darkness th once enshrouded his heart. Through the gosp he has embraced the knowledge of God's glor revealed in the person of Christ. Havin received the light of the gospel of Christ, Pau has become a light-bearer. He understood we his Savior's words, "Neither do people light lamp and put it under a bowl" (Matt. 5:15).

3.3. The Trials and Triumph of Apostolic Ministry (4:7–5:10)

In the previous section Paul spoke in glow ing terms of his ministry under the new covenant, with its great and glorious hope tha awaits the believer. The gospel he preached is the revelation of God's glory in the face o Christ (4:4, 6). Through it God has brought his inextinguishable light into the world (cf. John 1:4–10). Paul understood his role as a chosen vessel to bear that light to both Jew and Gentile, but he also knew the suffering his calling demanded (Acts 9:15–16). Paul now turns to reflect on the reality of those trials, God's purpose in them, and the hope that is sustained through them.

3.3.1. The Paradox of Paul's Sufferings (4:7–11). It seems that Paul was struck with the paradox he has just described. The "treasure" (v. 7) has reference to the "light of the knowledge of the glory of God in the face of ırist" (v. 6), known and experienced by Paul ıd his companions. It encompasses the total ality that belongs to the new covenant ministry of the Spirit (3:3–18). Paul is gripped by e contrast between the unfathomable worth ıd enduring value of this "gospel-treasure" ıd the unworthiness and human frailty ("jars ' clay") of those who now carry it to the orld. But he also realizes that this paradox is necessary one. God has chosen to bring the ›spel to the world through human weakness[5] › that the exceeding greatness of his power of ılvation may be seen as his work and not a ıman deed.

Verses 8–9 contain four sets of contrasts ıat illustrate both the weakness of Paul in carrying out his apostolic calling and the power of ίod to overcome that weakness and deliver im: Paul had known afflictions pressing in om all sides, but was never so hemmed in as › be crushed. He had encountered bewilderıg circumstances, but never reached the point f despair. His enemies had dogged his footteps, but never did God leave him in their lutches. They had knocked him to the ground, ut they were prevented from delivering the atal blow.

In summary, Paul describes these experinces in physical terms, identifying with (even articipating in) "the death of Jesus" (v. 10), so hat God might reveal his resurrection power. This power infuses Paul's mortal body with the ife of Jesus and has preserved him despite lifehreatening trials (vv. 10–11). These are not nly the consequences of these trials but God's ›urpose as well.

3.3.2. Paul's Confidence in Sufferings 4:12–15). Paul realizes that although his sufferings have brought him face-to-face with ›hysical death, they are the means God has ısed to bring life to the Corinthians (v. 12). The lisclosure of God's power through human weakness and the impartation of life through leath are themes that lie at the core of Paul's ınderstanding of the gospel and his own calling as an apostle. It is, after all, "the message *logos*] of the cross," with its apparent foolishness and weakness, that displays the power of God for salvation (1 Cor. 1:18).

In 1 Corinthians 1:18–2:5 Paul had already expounded the paradox of the cross. Gordon Fee (1987, 65) draws attention to the stark contrast there between *sophia* ("wisdom"), so esteemed among the Greeks, and the "message of the cross." The contrast concerns two conflicting notions of wisdom and power. The cross is the wisdom of God; but judged by the wisdom of this world, it is foolishness. God took a symbol of death and weakness and made it the channel and revelation of his saving power. In 2:1–5 Paul showed how he, as the bearer of this message, reflects the same paradox. His weakness is the instrument God chose to demonstrate the Spirit's power (v. 4), so that no one might boast before God (1:29) or credit faith to the preaching of human wisdom (v. 5). To the Corinthians, enamored with wisdom and power, Paul offered a new paradigm of both: wisdom in the folly of the cross, power in the weakness of the cross. Paul's gospel revealed the former; his sufferings and trials willingly endured for the sake of Christ demonstrated the latter.

Here in 2 Corinthians 4:12–15, Paul expresses his confidence in preaching the gospel despite the attendant suffering. Trials and sufferings are the anvil on which his faith and trust in God have been forged. Instead of silencing him, they have compelled him to proclaim boldly the gospel and testify to God's faithfulness. Like the psalmist in Psalm 116:10, whose faith in God was vindicated by his deliverance, Paul cannot help testifying to his faith. His confidence flows from knowing that the resurrection/exaltation of the Lord Jesus (cf. Acts 2:32–36; Rom. 1:4; 10:9; Eph. 2:20–22) assures the believer of a personal resurrection. Believers *in Christ* will be resurrected *with Christ* (Eph. 2:5–6; cf. 1 Thess. 4:14). Furthermore, the resurrection that brought Jesus into his Father's presence guarantees our presentation before God (and/or Christ—see 2 Cor. 11:2; Eph. 5:27; Col. 1:22) with all the saints.

Paul is thereby encouraged (cf. v. 16), and his confidence is sustained in light of what he knows about the results of his sufferings (v. 15). (1) They are benefiting others; through them the Corinthians have come to faith in the gospel. (2) The Corinthians are sharing their faith, so that God's saving grace is reaching more and more people. (3) Such expanding grace has served to multiply the praise of grateful hearts, thus promoting the glory of God.

3.3.3. Paul's Hope in Sufferings (4:16–18). Because of what Paul knows and believes (cf. above), he does not despair or "lose heart." The mention of God's glory reminds him of the hope that anchors his faith in the midst of suffering. He knows that God's goal for the believer is to be conformed to the image of his Son (Rom. 8:29), in whom is revealed the glory of God (2 Cor. 4:6). It is, after all, Christ in us that is "the hope of glory" (Col. 1:27).

But until the realization of that hope, Paul waits with the sober awareness of his own mortality. Outwardly, he says, our physical bodies are "wasting away" or "decaying." However, at the same time the hope of glory is at work. Inwardly, we are undergoing a daily spiritual renewal (v. 16b; cf. Gal. 4:19; Col. 3:10). In this Paul makes clear that the glorification of the believer is not merely a future hope, but an ongoing process in this life. Moreover, sufferings are instrumental in that process. Through "light and momentary troubles" God is producing "for" (or, perhaps better, "in") us an eternal glory that far outweighs all temporal troubles (v. 17; cf. 3:17; Rom. 8:17–18, 29–30, 37–39). This transformation occurs as we endure trials, looking forward to the eternal reality that awaits us and even now is being worked in us.

The contrast of things seen and unseen, temporal and eternal (v. 18), describes the conflicting realities that believers must hold in tension if they are not to lose heart in the midst of suffering. We, like Paul, must develop an "otherworldly" vision that keeps a steady focus not on the visible world of this temporal life, but on the unseen world of the eternal (cf. Col. 3:1). The former is changing and passing away (1 Cor. 7:31; cf. 1 John 2:17); the latter holds the permanent and unchanging reality of a world to come—a world in which the process of glorification, begun on earth through the indwelling Spirit (2 Cor. 3:18), will find its consummate end (4:17; cf. 1 John 3:2).

3.3.4. Paul's Hope in the Face of Death (5:1–10). In the midst of suffering and persecution (4:8–9) Paul found God's comfort in the hope of glory (4:17). Although facing death constantly, he did "not lose heart" (4:16), for despite the weakness and mortality of his flesh, he discovered the operation of divine life and experienced God's power to deliver (4:10–12).

Now in 5:1–10, Paul continues this twofold theme of glory through suffering and of life in the midst of death (Hughes, 346). He elaborates on the reason why (5:1 begins with *ga* lit., "for") not even the prospect of death ca shake his confidence. He is assured that wher ever his body, like a tent, becomes worn out, i torn down, and is destroyed, a new tent woul be coming.[6] That is, he knows that God ha provided another habitation.

But unlike his earthly tent, which is tempo ral, this "building from God" belongs to th heavenly realm and so is eternal. The identifi cation of the "earthly tent" as our "house" (Gk *oikia*, v. 1; NIV translates this noun as a verb "we live in") and the comparison with "an eter nal house in heaven, not built by huma hands" strongly suggest that Paul is speakin of another body suited for its eternal environ in the heavens. The apostle uses this sam earthly-heavenly contrast in 1 Corinthian 15:35–50 to describe the transformation tha will take place at the believer's resurrection Paul undoubtedly has in mind here a "spiritua body" (1 Cor. 15:44), which awaits a Christia after he or she dies and is raised or which believer receives when a mysterious transfor mation enables one to elude death and put o the imperishable and immortality (1 Cor 15:51–55; cf. 1 Thess. 4:13–17).

Paul goes on to express his intense desire for a new tent covering (vv. 2–4). Verses 2 and 4 (NASB) both begin with an emphatic "fo indeed" and insist that in our present body "we groan" (cf. the groaning mentioned in Rom 8:22–23). Adding a new metaphor, Paul indi cates that the believer, while still housed in his or her earthly tent, longs to be "clothed" with a heavenly dwelling. His words suggest tha intuitively believers know that the shedding of the old earthly tent at the time of death will no leave them "naked" (v. 3; i.e., "without bodily existence"). That is, after death there awaits for every Christian a heavenly expression of our earthly body (Fee, 1994, 325). An exchange of clothing will thus take place—the earthly for the heavenly and the temporal for the eternal. As a result, Paul asserts, "what is mortal [will] be swallowed up by life" (v. 4).

The Christian should not regard this spiritual transformation as some strange and unexpected event. God has given us advance notice and prepared us for this very end when he gave us his Spirit (5:5). The indwelling Spirit, who continually effects an inward work of glory in the believer (3:18), is a token "deposit *arrabon*; cf. comments of this word at 1:22], "guaranteeing" that our bodies are destined for a far more glorious future. Just knowing this provides Paul with an assured hope that fuels his confidence (vv. 6, 8) in the face of death. In fact, the certainty of the resurrection with its promised transformation makes the prospect of death for him a welcomed and even preferred one. Although death necessitates being separated from our earthly body, it also means being in the presence of the Lord and receiving the blessing of his communion and fellowship (cf. Phil. 1:22–23).

The parallel structure of 6 and 8 indicates that to be "at home in the body" is to be "away from the Lord," but to be "away from the body" is to be "at home with the Lord." Both these verses relate to and are summarized by verse 7: "We live [lit., walk] by faith, not by sight." Verse 6 shows that we walk "by faith" (v. 7) when we are "away from the Lord" and "at home in the body." Conversely, we walk "by sight" when, though away from the body, we are in the Lord's presence. It is more than likely that the "sight" to which Paul refers depicts the same hope of the apostle John when he wrote, "Dear friends, now we are children of God, and what we will be has not yet been made known. But we know that when he appears, we shall be like him, for we shall see him as he is" (1 John 3:2).

Since death does not terminate our communion with Christ but will usher us into his presence, believers should have as their supreme ambition to please the Lord. This is all the more important when we realize that our earthly service (while "in the body") will be judged after death at the judgment seat of Christ. This event brings a sober conclusion to Paul's teaching on the believer's hope in the resurrection: All Christians will stand before Christ's tribunal in heaven (cf. Rom. 14:12; 1 Cor. 3:12–15), whereupon the true character of their works will be exposed and judged. The New Testament teaches that believers will have to give an account of both their faithfulness and unfaithfulness, receiving rewards or suffering loss accordingly (Matt. 25:21–29; 1 Cor. 3:15; Col. 3:24–25; 2 John 8).

This entire passage teaches that the resurrection of the body creates a continuity between this life and the life to come. The common denominator is the Spirit; we have the down payment now and will have the fullness then. We possess bodily existence in both places—a natural, physical body here on earth and a spiritual one when we are at home with the Lord in heaven. But the most important element of continuity is that of relationship. Then, as now, we will still be able to love and serve the Lord. We will still seek to please him.

3.4. The Nature and Function of Apostolic Ministry (5:11–7:4)

3.4.1. The Motivation of Apostolic Ministry (5:11–16). Paul possesses two great motivations for ministry, his fear of God (v. 11) and the love of Christ (v. 14). (1) The realization that he will one day have to give account of his apostleship before the judgment seat of Christ (v. 10) is a sobering reality for Paul. It inserts the "fear of the Lord" into the equation. This fear is not a paralyzing terror, but an awe-filled reverence for the sacredness and eternal consequences of his service.

In the Old Testament the "fear of the LORD" was the attitude that characterized God's people as they sought to walk in wisdom (Prov. 1:7) and avoid evil (Job 28:28; cf. Prov. 16:6). The Israelites were required to fear the Lord if they wanted to walk in his ways, love him, and serve him with complete devotion (Deut. 10:12). In the early church living or walking in "the fear of the Lord" is linked with the work of the Spirit (Acts 9:31). Elsewhere, believers, after being exhorted to "be filled with the Spirit" (Eph. 5:18), are told to submit to one another "in the fear of Christ" (5:21, NASB). In 2 Corinthians 7:1, believers are instructed to perfect holiness in their lives out of a fear of God. It seems, then, that in Paul's thinking, fearing the Lord is an attitude of reverence that should characterize the life of the Spirit-filled church.

Such an attitude motivates Paul "to persuade" people to accept the gospel of Christ (v. 11). Unfortunately, some in Corinth were hindering that acceptance by calling into question his motives and conduct. The apostle is confident of his own integrity; all he is and does are known and open to God. But he also wants the Corinthians at large to know the truth concerning his apostleship among them. His hope is that they already recognize the rightness of his conduct and the purity of his motives.

This marble podium, called the Bema, was used by Roman officials in Corinth to announce official business. It is said Paul addressed Corinthians from this same platform.

In verse 12 Paul anticipates his critics' next move. He knows some will see in his statements about his integrity before God and human beings as another attempt at self-promotion (cf. 3:1). But his goal is not to commend himself but to provide an adequate answer to those who attack and disparage his apostleship.[7] He describes these opponents as taking pride in outward appearance. No doubt they pointed to such externals as letters of commendation (3:1), their own Jewish pedigree (11:22), or the presence of miracles (12:11–12). Their worldly esteem of appearance is later reflected in Paul's subtle put-down of their claim to have known Jesus "according to the flesh" (NASB; see comments on 5:16). In contrast, Paul would rather boast in what is only visible to the eyes of God—purity of heart and motive. He is confident that God knows all that he is and has done. Whatever service he has rendered has been in the service of God and his church at Corinth (5:13).

It is difficult to know exactly what is behind the accusation that Paul was "out of [his] mind." Perhaps some were overwhelmed at the story of his conversion and apostolic calling. Faced with the unique claims and passion of his vision-laden testimony (Acts 26:19; cf. 2 Cor. 12:1–6), these detractors, like Festus, could offer the only explanation acceptable to their worldly minds: "You are out of your mind, Paul" (Acts 26:24). Whatever other explanations of this accusation are possible (e.g., religious mania [Hughes, 191] or ecstatic experiences with visions [Barrett, 166]), clearly this was not the first time Paul was called insane. Furthermore, in his service to God Paul was sharing the same persecution and verbal abuse leveled against his Lord (Mark 3:21; cf. Matt. 10:24).

(2) In verses 14–15 Paul reveals the second great motivation of his ministry: "Christ's love." The verb used here for "compel" (*synecho*) describes the irresistible impact of Christ's love on the apostle, leaving him no option but to serve. The context makes it clear that it is Christ's love for Paul, not Paul's for Christ that compels him. However, these choices are not mutually exclusive. A more literal translation of verse 14b reads, "having considered/concluded [*krinantas*] this." This clause introduces the demonstration of Christ's love—"that one died for all"—but it also provides an explanation for why Christ's love compels Paul's devoted service. When Paul judges the magnitude of Christ's universal love of humanity, seen in his selfless death for all, he must serve; he can do nothing less than witness to him. What Christ did fills Paul with an overflowing gratitude and love (note the role of one's love for Christ as a key motivating factor for Christian service in Matt. 22:37; Mark 12:30; Luke 10:27; John 14:15, 21, 23).

Paul is firmly convinced that because Christ died "for all," all died. Two important questions arise: (1) In what sense did Christ die for all? (2) What kind of death did all experience as a result of Christ's death? (1) The first question debates whether Paul had in mind that Christ died in our place (a substitutionary death) or on our behalf (i.e., for our benefit) (on this issue, see Martin, 130–33; Hughes, 193–97). Actually, Paul may have had both thoughts in mind, for Christ's death *in our place* certainly has *benefits* that accrue on our behalf, not the least of which is our release from sin's penalty. Paul may be emphasizing that Christ's death benefits all by making it possible for all to die to sin and self (v. 15) and to live for Christ (Barrett, 168–69).

(2) However, Paul's compact formula-like wording, "one died . . . all died" (v. 14), is rem-

reminiscent of Romans 5:12, where Paul teaches that all humanity became identified with Adam, whose sin affected all (cf. also Paul's comments on the effect of the atoning death of Christ in such passages as Rom. 3:24–26; 6:1–11; 7:1–6; 8:1–4; 1 Cor. 15:3–4, 12–22; Gal. 3:13–14; Eph. 1:7; 2:11–16; 5:2, 25; Col. 1:13–14, 20–22; 2:11–15). Here, in a similar way, Paul is stating that all who accept Christ are identified with him and share in his death. Although the effects and benefits of that death are unstated, verse 15 elaborates on one: a new life of selfless service for the One who died and rose again on our behalf.

The thought of verses 14–15 sketches what Paul more fully develops in Romans 6:1–14, where he expounds on the significance of Christian baptism. Baptism testifies to the union and participation in the death and resurrection of Christ. Sharing in Christ's death not only means freedom from sin's penalty, but also from its power in our lives. Sharing in his resurrection provides entrance into a new life, free from the bondage of sin and free to serve God (6:6–11).

The mention of Christ's death and resurrection (vv. 14–15) causes Paul to think further about the saving consequences of that event and its implications for his ministry. One practical consequence in his own life is that he no longer sees things as he once did (v. 16). Unlike his critics, he cannot esteem or regard people "from a worldly point of view," one that takes great stock in outward appearance (cf. v. 12). He admits to having known Christ *kata sarka* (lit., "according to the flesh"). Though it is certainly possible, Paul is not referring to having known the earthly Jesus. Instead, what Paul seems to have in mind is a new way of knowing Christ, inaccessible to those caught up in the prestige of external and worldly association. Though left unsaid, Paul knows Jesus as Christ, the risen Lord. That knowledge comes only by the Spirit and by faith (1 Cor. 2:1–14; cf. Matt. 16:16–17).

3.4.2. The Message of Apostolic Ministry (5:17–6:2). Still thinking of Christ's death and resurrection, Paul offers a second consequence that explains why "from now on" he can no longer maintain "a worldly point of view" (v. 16). The cross and resurrection have effected a radical break with Paul's former life and brought him into vital union with Christ and into a totally new sphere of existence. Paul has become a new person with a new identity (cf. Gal. 2:20) and now belongs to another world (Denney, 210). The change is so dramatic that it can only be described as a "new creation." His entire former life—its relations, conditions, and situations—"has gone" (Gk. aorist tense, denoting an accomplished fact); in its place "has come" and now exists (the implication of the Gk. perfect tense) a new life "in Christ."

The great changes described above can only come "from God" (v. 18). However, Paul now turns to an objective result of Christ's death and resurrection: reconciliation. Reconciliation removes the enmity that stands between God and humanity because of sin and replaces it with peace (Rom. 5:10–12; Eph. 2:13–15). It is the most relational facet of God's redemption: removing alienation, restoring us to God's favor, and bringing us into his presence (Eph. 2:16–19). To accomplish this requires a remedy for the problem of sin, which God met by "not counting men's sins against them" (2 Cor. 5:19), that is, through forgiveness (cf. Rom. 3:6–8).

Paul makes it clear that far from being a passive party in this transaction, God himself is the author and initiator of reconciliation. He is the One "who reconciled us to himself" through the personal agency of his Son. The unity of divine purpose between Father and Son is such that Paul can say, "God *was in Christ* reconciling the world unto himself" (v. 19, ASV, italics added). That is, Christ was united with God the Father in this divine work of reconciliation. Furthermore, God initiated the worldwide proclamation of his reconciliation; he was the One who "gave us the ministry

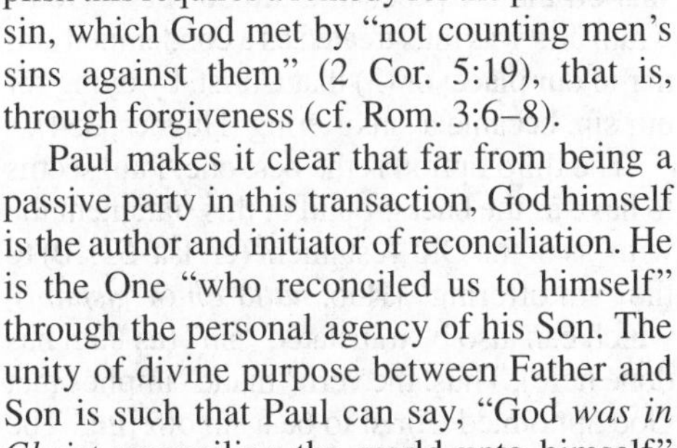

A stone baptistery at Tabgha, in Galilee, a town located at the base of the Mount of Beatitudes. In a letter to the Corinthians, Paul explains the significance of Christian baptism.

of reconciliation" (v. 18) and "committed to us the message of reconciliation" (v. 19). From provision to proclamation, God is the author, architect, and prime mover of reconciliation.

Paul now examines his apostolic calling. He sees himself as an "ambassador" commissioned and authorized by Christ to be his representative and messenger to the world. His mission is to be the voice of God, passionately calling an alienated world to be reconciled to God (v. 20). What allows God to make such a gracious offer of reconciliation and salvation (6:2) is his own provision of atonement. God has taken the sinless Christ (cf. also Rom. 8:3; Heb. 4:15; 7:26; 1 Peter 1:19; 1 John 3:5) and made him "to be sin for us." There is debate over exactly what Paul meant by this phrase. The options are: (1) that Christ became sin in his incarnation by taking on the form and likeness of fallen humanity (cf. Phil. 2:7); (2) that Christ, by bearing our sins on the cross,became the object of God's wrath and was thus treated as a condemned sinner in our place; or (3) that Christ, by dying for our sin, became a sin offering (Hughes, 354).

The third option is the best one. Paul seems to have as the background of this statement the witness of the Old Testament (cf. Isa. 53:10) to the "sin offering" (Heb. *hatta'ah* or *'asham*), which can also be translated "sin" (as Paul has done here). Thus, the verb "made" implies that God appointed Christ to be a sin offering. The vicarious (substitutionary) nature of the Old Testament sin offering (Lev. 4:4–24) created a virtual identification between that offering and the sin that required it. When the worshiper laid his hands on the animal (Lev. 4:24), it symbolized the transference of guilt from the worshiper to the sin offering and signified to the worshiper that God's judgment for sin had fallen on the offering. In exacting the death of the sin offering, God was in effect judging sin. Paul's words express this identification as well.

The purpose behind the sacrifice of the sinless Christ was "so that in him we might become the righteousness of God" (v. 21). The "righteousness of God" can refer to a righteousness that either comes from God as the source or expresses the character and nature of God. Given Paul's emphasis in this passage on what God has done in Christ, the former sense is to be preferred. Nevertheless, the righteousness of God is something that the believer "becomes." It is a righteousness found "in Christ," whom Paul elsewhere describes as having become "our righteousness" (1 Cor. 1:30). For Paul the righteousness of God in Christ included not only a right standing before God on the basis of faith (Rom. 4:9; Gal. 3:9), but also the provision to partake of the righteous character of God himself (Hughes, 355).

Paul returns to his apostolic calling and the proclamation of the good news. As Christ's ambassador and God's voice of reconciliation (5:20), Paul sees himself as a fellow worker with God (6:1). This responsibility carries with it a sense of urgency, for God is now offering salvation through him. God's impassioned appeal thus becomes Paul's own, and he urges the Corinthians "not to receive the grace of God in vain," for the "day of salvation" has dawned and the day of God's grace is before them (6:1–2, NASB, quoting Isa. 49:8).

Paul hears in his own preaching of the gospel an echo of God's promise to restore Israel after the Exile. He sees his own day as the time when God is extending his grace and is present to deliver. This is all the more reason why the Corinthians should be careful not to receive God's grace in vain. The tense of the verb "receive" commonly refers to a simple past event, which the context warrants here, presumably the conversion of the Corinthians (Martin, 166).

"In vain" can mean "empty, without effect" or "for nothing." Those dismissing outright the possibility that Paul could have in mind a fall from grace do so more out of prior doctrinal commitment than consideration of the text (e.g., Martin, 166). Another unlikely proposal is that Paul is merely exhorting humanity in general not to reject God's offer of salvation (Hodge, 154). Rather, in the words "we urge *you*," Paul clearly has the Corinthians in mind. Paul is thus addressing Christians in Corinth who had received the saving grace of God, but who were conducting themselves in a manner that denied the reality and purpose of that grace. While Christ indeed had died for all, it was not automatic that all would no longer live for themselves but for Christ (v. 15) (Barrett, 183). If such a Christian walk were automatic, Paul would hardly have reason to include so much moral and ethical instruction and issue so many exhortations and warnings in this letter (see 6:14–17; 7:1; 8:10–15; 9:6–10; 12:19–21; 13:5, 11).

3.4.3. The Sufferings of Apostolic Ministry (6:3–10). After expounding on the message of

:conciliation, exhorting the Corinthians to :ceive that word of reconciliation (5:20) and ot to render useless the grace of God, which ıey received in the gospel (6:1), Paul turns to escribe the manner of his life and ministry mong them. Actually verse 3 continues the sen-:nce begun in 6:1, which was interrupted by the ld Testament quotation in 6:2. Uninterrupted would read (lit.): "We urge you not to receive od's grace in vain . . . putting no stumbling lock in anyone's path." Paul is describing, then, ıe manner in which that appeal was given.

In exhorting others to receive God's saving race, Paul's paramount concern is never to iscredit his ministry by hindering the work of ıat grace in anyone. Always and in everything was his desire to live in a manner that spoke 'ell of himself as a servant of God. Although ıis passage details Paul's sufferings and hard-ıips, it also describes how he conducted him-:lf in that commendable manner.

Paul describes his apostolic ministry in terms f a series of nine trials and afflictions (vv. 4–5; f. also 4:8–9; 11:23–29; 12:7–10), which fall ıto three sets of three (Kruse, 132). "Troubles, ardships and distresses" describe a wide range f those difficult circumstances of life that pres-ıre us, create adversity, or box us in, threaten-ıg to crush us. "Beatings, imprisonments and ots" denote persecution Paul endured at the ands of his enemies. "Hard work, sleepless ights and hunger [or fastings]" refer to the vol-ntary hardships he endured in his apostolic 'ork. Note that the apostle is not ashamed of 'hat he has suffered for the sake of Christ. In ıct, he showcases them in this letter. This, as 'e have previously noted (see comments on :7–11), is intentional and draws attention not nly to the power of God operating through ıman weakness, but also to the common expe-ence Paul shares with his Savior.

In verse 6 Paul turns to the inner graces that ave sustained him in the midst of trials: purity" (or sincerity), "understanding" (or nowledge), "patience" (control under provo-ation), and "kindness" (goodness or generos-y). The phrase "in the Holy Spirit" suggests ıat Paul has in mind the Spirit as the source of ıese spiritual graces, several of which are par-lleled in his list of the fruit of the Spirit (Gal. :22–23). It seems more than coincidental that sincere [genuine or unfeigned] love" imme-iately follows his reference to the Spirit, even as love is the first fruit of the Spirit mentioned. "Truthful speech" follows "sincere love" in verse 7 (cf. Eph. 4:15). "In the power of God" can either indicate that God empowers Paul's testimony to the truth (cf. 1 Cor. 2:4) or that he endures hardships with God's power (vv. 4–5). Given his emphasis in this letter on God's power demonstrated through weakness (4:7; cf. 12:9; 13:4), the latter is preferred.

Paul then uses the metaphor of weapons to continue his list of inner resources (v. 7b). In preaching the gospel as Christ's ambassador, Paul has entered the arena of spiritual warfare. The "weapons of righteousness" in both hands signify that he is fully armed. But unlike worldly combat, Paul's weapons are not external but internal (cf. also Rom. 6:13; Eph. 6:11–17; 1 Thess. 5:8), consisting of the qualities of inward righteousness. Paul does battle "in the power of God," with weapons forged by walk-ing with God in the midst of trials without sur-render or compromise of his integrity. The inner strength that these weapons afford have equipped Paul to endure the changing and often paradox-ical circumstances of his apostolic calling.

Paul concludes this section by listing a series of contrasting situations (vv. 8–10) that he has encountered. He has experienced praise and shame, was bragged about and slandered, was viewed as a genuine servant of God and as a deceitful fraud, and was treated as a celebrity and ignored. But the changing circumstances, no matter how negative, did not dictate the final outcome. Paul had repeatedly faced death ("dying"), yet he lived on (cf. 4:10–11); he had been "beaten" (cf. 11:23–25), but "not killed."

None of these circumstances dictated how Paul chose to view them. His service for Christ had brought him sorrow, deprivation, and poverty, but in those circumstances he never lost sight of the divine perspective. That knowledge allowed him to rejoice in sorrow, realizing that through his poverty he brought the riches of heaven to impoverished souls. Though the world saw him as possessing noth-ing, Paul knew he possessed "every spiritual blessing" in Christ (Eph. 1:3).

3.4.4. The Intimacy and Joy of Apostolic Ministry (6:11–7:4). Paul breaks off his account of apostolic suffering with an impassioned appeal to the Corinthians for mutual openness and affection (vv. 11–13). As their "father" in the faith (cf. 1 Cor. 4:15), he longs for intimacy with his spiritual children. But he knows that true affection is freely given, and so he coaxes but does not command. Throughout his correspondence with them he has *always* (implied in the prefect tense here) spoken openly; his love and affection have never been hidden. Now he urges them to return his affection, to "open wide" their hearts toward him as he has done.

What follows is a plea for holiness (6:14–7:1) and constitutes one of Paul's most notorious digressions. In the Introduction (see "Literary Unity") we argued that contrary to some scholars' opinions, there is no good reason for questioning Paul's authorship of this passage or seeing it as an intruding fragment from an earlier letter. Earlier (6:1) Paul exhorted the Corinthians not to "receive God's grace in vain." There we concluded that Paul had in mind the possibility of living in a manner that not only contradicted the nature of their new life in Christ (5:17), but also threatened their spiritual well-being. He went on to assure them of his intention never to do anything that would cause them to stumble, recounting his life of integrity despite suffering for the sake of the gospel (6:3–10). Now after his plea for mutual affection and openness, Paul returns to his prior concern and an unresolved problem that he had earlier warned the Corinthians against—idolatry (see 1 Cor. 10:1–22).

In 1 Corinthians Paul had been direct in commanding the believers in Corinth not to be "idolaters" (1 Cor. 10:7) and to "flee from idolatry" (10:14). Here, however, Paul approaches the problem from a different angle. Perhaps, given the prominence that idolatry had in the Corinthian culture (see Murphy-O'Conner), Paul's outright condemnation and threat of judgment fell on unresponsive ears. In any event, Paul addresses the same problem here, but in relation to the Old Testament principle of holiness or "separation." His strategy of head-on confrontation, however, is unchanging: "Do not be yoked together with unbelievers."

From 1 Corinthians 5:9–10 we know that Paul is not forbidding all association with unbelievers, which would be impossible and require one, in his words, "to leave this world." Paul apparently has a particular kind of relationship in mind. "Yoked together" (v. 14) recalls Deuteronomy 22:10, which prohibited putting an ox and donkey in the same yoke when plowing. It may also carry the sense of "mismated" and refer to the prohibition in Leviticus 19:1 against the crossbreeding of animals. In eith case the Old Testament laws of this nature we instituted to teach the principle of spiritual se aration. Israel was to avoid practices and belie that would lead the people to adopt the co rupting ways of their pagan neighbors.

Consequently, what Paul seems to have i mind here is the forming of relationships th would harness a believer and unbeliever an lead to some form of spiritual compromise wi paganism, idolatry in particular. Exactly wh kind of relationships he had in mind is uncertai he was not specific. Instead he leaves us a cle principle to apply under the guidance of th Holy Spirit. Christians today would be wise t avoid entering into any relationship—persona business, marital, etc.—which forces them int situations of compromise and threatens th purity of their devotion to Christ (cf. 11:3).

To make his point, Paul goes on to ask fiv rhetorical questions, which stress how radicall unnatural and incompatible it is for believe and unbelievers to be paired in close relatio ship. Each question features a pair of opposite is patently absurd, and expects an immedia denial. For example, would one expect rig teousness (which is defined elsewhere in Pa as being consistent with the law [see Ro 7:12; 9:31; 10:5; Phil. 3:9]) to partner with law lessness? Can one force the fellowship of lig and darkness? "A believer" and "an unb liever," he says, have about as much in com mon as Christ and Belial, the prince of evil.

The final question raises the stronge objection against such unholy alliances. W hear in Paul's words the objection of the O Testament prophets to idolatry: What possib agreement can the temple of God have wit those worthless and lifeless idols fashioned b human hands (see Jer. 2; cf. Isa. 2:8)? No also the emphasis here on believers ("we" being the "temple of the living God." Paul quotation from the Old Testament echoes number of verses that declare God's speci relationship to Israel (Lev. 26:11–12; cf. E 6:7; 25:8; 29:45; 1 Kings 6:13). Yahweh presence among them demonstrated that the belonged to him as his people and that he w uniquely their God. In his quotation Paul com bines the idea of God's indwelling his peop (Ezek. 37:27) with Leviticus 26:11–12. Th accords with what he earlier wrote to th 'orinthians about being the "temple of God" ı which dwelt the Spirit of God (1 Cor. 3:16–7; cf. 1 Cor. 6:19; Eph. 2:22).

Paul's appeal is essentially an appeal to oliness. As Israel's special status demanded eparation from those things that defile or ıake a person unclean before God, so too the 'orinthians should safeguard their moral and piritual purity (v. 17) by not becoming entan-led in relationships with unbelievers. The urpose for this separation is not ritual or cer-monial, but relational—to preserve the inti-ıacy of their relationship with the Father ᵛ. 18). If the Corinthians heed Paul's counsel, ıey can be assured of continuous fellowship ᵛith God as his sons and daughters.

Such promises of relationship with the Lord re all the more reason we should avoid con-uct that leads to moral or spiritual contami-ation and jeopardizes our intimacy with the ather. In speaking of contaminating "body it., flesh] and spirit" in 7:1, Paul is not refer-ng to two categories of sin, but using ıetaphors that represent the defilement of the 'hole person—within and without (cf. 1 Cor. :34; 1 Thess. 5:23). Such purification shows everence for God and promotes the comple-on of his holiness in and among his people.

In 7:2, Paul returns to his former appeal for ıutual openness and affection (see 6:13). This me he justifies his appeal by reminding them f his faultless conduct among them. It is likely ıat the denials listed here reflect the charges f his opponents against him. However, Paul quick to reassure the Corinthians that in ıentioning these charges, he is not putting ıem in the camp of those he condemns—"I o not say this to condemn you" (v. 3). Rather, he reminds them of sentiments previously expressed (cf. 6:11); his love and commitment toward them has permanently secured them in his heart. Nothing in life, not even death itself, can sever the bonds of his love for them.

What is more, despite his present trials, Paul has reason to be encouraged. News brought by Titus (7:6) has renewed his confidence in them and provided an occasion to boast about them and rejoice.

4. Return to Travelogue: Good News From Titus (7:5–16)

4.1. Paul Comforted in Macedonia (7:5–7)

Paul now picks up the account of his travels that he discontinued at 2:13. Recalling the background of this moment, we understand why Paul says that upon entering Macedonia he was physically exhausted, anxious, and depressed (vv. 5–6). Earlier problems had caused him to make a hasty visit to Corinth in

The theater at Ephesus was one of the sights Paul would have seen on his return to the city. On Curetes Street, above, statues of prominent people lined both sides of the street. The last repairs on the street were in the fourth century.

an effort to set things right there. But the visit had only made things worse and was deeply and personally painful for him. Shortly after returning to Ephesus, still hurting from his experience, he wrote a stern and impassioned letter of rebuke to the church (2:4–5) and sent it by Titus. Traveling north toward Troas, Paul busied himself with ministry and waited anxiously for news of the Corinthians' response to his letter. His hopes of meeting Titus at Troas were met with disappointment (2:12), so he pressed on to Macedonia.

We are told nothing of the events and hardships behind Paul's words, "harassed at every turn—conflicts on the outside, fears within" (v. 5). In addition to the demands and dangers related to his ministry, he no doubt carried a inner burden of doubt, fear, and self-criticism concerning his handling of the Corinthian affair. One can only imagine what relief the arrival of Titus and the accompanying good news (v. 7) brought to Paul's spirit. Titus's arrival was nothing less than God's merciful comfort. His fears and worries turned into joy as Titus told of their genuine sorrow for sins against Paul and their affection and passionate concern for him.

4.2. The Harsh Letter and Its Effect—Reasons to Rejoice (7:8–16)

First, Paul rejoiced because the discipline he had administered brought about the desired effect—repentance. As the Corinthians' father in the faith, his goal was to restore them spiritually. Like a loving father he took up the rod of correction with some ambivalence. He took no delight in bringing them sorrow; in fact, he regretted having to do so (v. 8). But knowing that their spiritual life and well-being was at stake, he could not neglect his duty of disciplining those whom he loved.

Now, however, he rejoices (v. 9), not because he made them sorrowful, but because of the positive effect his discipline has yielded. The sorrow he had caused them was not the worldly variety that tears down and destroys through sin, but a "godly sorrow [that] brings repentance," "leaves no regret," and "leads to salvation" (v. 10).

Verse 11 expresses Paul's sheer joy over the change of heart and conduct in the Corinthian believers. In one long exclamation he erupts in joy over how earnest and sincere they are in righting past wrongs. Once they may have sided with his challengers, but now they sho a genuine sense of outrage and indignation how he was mistreated. Repentance has rekindled a reverential fear (*phobos*) and affectio for Paul (the NIV incorrectly translates *phobo* here as "alarm"). The object of their fear is le unstated. It may be a fearful respect of himsel absent at his earlier visit (see Barrett, 211), o a fear of God and his judgment of sin. Th Corinthians now long for his coming and ar ardent in their desire to punish the wrongdo ers. This entire transformation shows that the have made every effort to rectify past wrong and now stand "innocent" or blameless. The response is the fruit of true repentance, and fo this Paul rejoices.

A second reason to rejoice concerns Titu who carried the harsh letter from Paul. N doubt he accepted his mission with some fe and apprehension as to what awaited him i Corinth. Now Titus adds to the comfortin good news with a report that his misgiving had been put to rest by a warm and responsiv reception (vv. 13, 15). In fact, all the good th Paul had said about them proved to be true (v 14–15). Rather than fill Titus with details o past wrongs and prepare him for the wors Paul had amazingly "boasted" about the goo that could be found in the church. Pastors o troubled churches would do well to learn fro Paul; he refused to let the problems blind hi from seeing the positive. Titus's report vind cated Paul's faith and confidence in th Corinthians, and he could now rejoice.

5. The Macedonian Collection for the Jerusalem Saints (8:1–9:15)

For some time Paul had been involved in co lecting money for the saints of Jerusalem (c the references to Paul's concern for the poo and to this collection in Rom. 15:25–29; 1 Co 16:1–2; Gal. 2:9–10). Judea had fallen on har times as a result of a famine, which left man saints afflicted (Acts 11:28–29). Paul felt tha the Gentile churches owed a debt of gratitud to Israel and Jerusalem, the Mother Church (c Rom. 11:13–25; 15:27), for their role in bring ing them to faith in Christ. No doubt he sa in this offering a powerful symbolic gesture. not only showed that the Gentiles were spir tually indebted to the Jerusalem church, but symbolized the spiritual unity of both Jew an Gentile in the church of Jesus Christ (cf. Ep

13–18). Paul had already introduced the offer-g to the Corinthians (2 Cor. 8:6; cf. 1 Cor. 5:1–4), but it had probably stalled because of e conflicts that surfaced in the church. Now ith the good news from Titus, Paul feels con-dent he can urge them to complete it.

5.1. Paul Urges the Grace of Giving (8:1–15)

5.1.1. The Macedonian Example (8:1–5). addition to the coming of Titus, the mention f Macedonia (7:5) undoubtedly provided nother comforting memory to Paul. The fection of the Macedonian churches Philippi, Thessalonica, and Berea are men-oned in Acts) for Paul and their support of his inistry were unrivaled (cf. Phil. 1:5; 4:15–5). Eventually, Paul will make a direct appeal the Corinthians to complete the offering ey had begun (vv. 6–12), but here he hopes motivate them with an inspiring example of enerosity.

Paul's words in this section tell a story of xtraordinary sacrifice and surprising joy. The Iacedonian churches had experienced intense ersecution (cf. 1 Thess. 1:6–7; 2:14). This severe trial" had left them deeply impover-hed; yet despite their hardship and suffering, ey responded with "rich generosity" by giv-g sacrificially in this collection for the poor Cor. 8:2–3). Furthermore, the Macedonians ot only gave willingly, but also spontaneously nd with great joy. Paul was, perhaps, reluctant t first to take from those who were themselves great need, for they had to beg him for the privilege of sharing [*koinonia*] in this service the saints."

For Paul, the noble character of the Mace-onians' selfless conduct was evidence of the peration of the grace of God and its enable-ent.[8] We should note that in 1 Corinthians :4–7 *charis* is closely related to *charismata*—e gracious endowments of Christ given by e Spirit (Fee, 1994, 338). Consequently, Paul ould see the liberality of the Macedonians as e Spirit's influence and empowering to act in ccord with God's grace. The grace that nables such a generous and selfless act not nly flows out of his grace in redemption, but flects the gracious character of God himself, ho in his generosity rescued us from spiritual overty by the gift of his Son (see Rom. 5:6–; 6:23).

The Macedonian response to Paul's min-istry surpassed his expectations. It was not lim-ited to their participation in the collection. As God would have it ("in keeping with God's will," v. 5), the latter was but an extension of having first given themselves to the Lord. These Christians discerned that devotion to Christ rightly required the support of his ser-vants engaged in his work.

5.1.2. Paul's Appeal for Generous Giving (8:6–12). Paul is now ready to urge the Corinthians to complete the offering they had earlier begun. Verse 6 reveals his wisdom as a master motivator. He bases his present appeal on the praiseworthy example of the Macedon-ian churches (vv. 1–5). The Corinthians are being led either to compare themselves favor-ably with the Macedonians, or to contrast their present favorable circumstances with that of the impoverished churches (Harris, 367). In either case, Paul is encouraging the Corinthi-ans to love and good works (cf. Heb. 10:24).

Paul's encouragement does not focus on their failure to complete this "act of grace" (i.e., the offering), but on their good beginning. His words are filled with praise for them. His confident desire is that just as they have excelled in every Christian grace and endow-ment ("faith . . . speech . . . knowledge . . . earnestness and . . . love" [v. 7; cf. 1 Cor. 1:4, 7; 13:1–3]), they will also excel in completing this gracious act of giving. Wisely, Paul does not try to command compliance (v. 8), although that would have been within his apos-tolic right (see 2 Cor. 10:8, 13; cf. 1 Cor. 14:37). Rather, his tactic is to motivate them by urging them to strive to meet the Mace-donian example in demonstrating the sincerity of their love for Paul.

If the above was not reason enough to com-plete their work of benevolence, Paul has one more reason for the Corinthians to contem-plate. He has saved the most compelling rea-son for last, as he holds up the supreme example of grace—the Lord Jesus Christ (v. 9). He points to the Incarnation as the com-plete model of selfless grace that responded to the distress of others. The Lord Jesus volun-tarily surrendered his heavenly riches for our sake and took on the poverty of our humanity (cf. Phil. 2:6–8), in order that we might gain the spiritual riches of salvation in Christ (cf. Eph. 1:7, 18; 2:7; 3:8, 16; Phil. 4:19; Col.

1:27). Though some may see a contrast between the preincarnate riches of Christ and the poverty of the Macedonian church, we should point out that the acts of both Christ and the churches of Macedonia reveal divine grace (2 Cor. 8:1, 9). A case can be made for a true parallel, as it was precisely while in his state of poverty (i.e., the Incarnation) that Jesus gave himself completely as a sacrifice for our sin (Phil. 2:8).

Finally, Paul is ready to issue a direct exhortation (v. 11) to the Corinthians to complete the work they have begun. Again, however (cf. v. 8a), he assures them that he is not making demands, but only giving his advice and counsel for their own benefit (v. 10). He has no doubt regarding their desire to complete the work they had begun a year earlier. That was evident, for they were among the first to respond to the project. Now they should fulfill that desire by completing the offering according to their means. Paul adds the assurance that whatever they have to give is acceptable, provided it is given willingly (v. 12). Like the widow in the temple (Mark 12:41–44), it is not the amount of the gift that is significant to God, but the degree of sacrifice. But Paul's words also have a biting criticism for rich and indulgent Christians who seldom extend their giving beyond what is comfortable and convenient.

5.1.3. The Goal of the Appeal (8:13–15). Paul is aware that the prosperity of the Corinthian church is a spawning ground for social tensions. Apart from the work of God's grace, humanity is capable of incredible selfishness, and the Corinthians were still growing in that grace (e.g., 1 Cor. 11:18–22). He thus explains that the offering was not about helping some by depriving or afflicting others. Rather, the offering was designed to bring about a more equal distribution of resources so that those in want might have their needs met by those who had an abundance (vv. 13–14).

Paul recalls the words of Exodus 16:18 in order to illustrate this principle of equality. God himself provided this type of equality during Israel's desert journey by daily supplying manna. Each person gathered just enough for his or her daily needs so that no one had either lack or surplus. It would be wrong to interpret Paul as advocating a form of communism that eliminates personal wealth.[9] His concern is that the Corinthians voluntarily act in love, in keeping with God's grace, by responding to the di tress of fellow believers and by giving sacrif cially to meet their need.

5.2. Paul Arranges for the Integrity and Success of the Offering (8:16–9:15)

The Jerusalem offering was important Paul; thus, he sees a need to take specific ste to ensure its success. His strategy is threefol (1) In 8:16–24 he prepares the Corinthians receive those who will be responsible for co lecting the funds by praising their virtues an qualifications. (2) He praises the Corinthia themselves for their zeal and willingness participate and urges them to make good h boasts about them and to live up to his conf dence in them (9:1–5). (3) He encourages the generosity and participation by teaching the principles of giving (9:6–15).

5.2.1. Paul Sends Praiseworthy Delegat (8:16–24). Paul knew that he had enemies an critics in Corinth, who would not hesitate discredit his work by accusing him of using th offering for personal gain. Consequently, h took precautions to see to it that such fals charges would be difficult to make. Pa wisely left the task of completing the offeri at Corinth to trusted men, known and we respected by the Corinthians, but also loyal Paul. His antagonists would be hard-pressed mount a credible attack against Paul's integrit when he was not personally involved in co lecting the funds and when his associates, wh could personally vouch for him, were so highl regarded within the church.

In verses 16–17 Paul reminds the Corinth ans of Titus, who will arrive shortly to hel complete the offering. He was a logical choic to mention first since he was the one who ha just arrived in Macedonia with the good new about the positive response to Paul's discipl nary letter (7:5). Also, as we learned earli (7:13–15) and now hear again (8:16), Tit was not only well received but had develope a special bond of affection for the Corinthian He bore in his heart the "same concern (*spoude*, perhaps better trans. "earnestness" [a in 7:11; 8:7] or "passionate zeal") for them a Paul had (see 7:5–16). Titus is not only co ing to them willingly, but eagerly, havin enthusiastically accepted Paul's appeal to go Corinth. Paul saw in this the work of God, f which he gives thanks. The apostle has accomplished much in these two verses. In commending Titus, he has not only restated his own zeal for the Corinthians, but assured them that they have someone coming to them who shares a God-generated enthusiasm for them.

Beginning with verse 18 Paul introduces two unnamed brothers who accompany Titus. Presumably they are so well known that no identification is necessary. Such is surely the case with the first brother, who was "praised by all the churches for his service to the gospel" and had been appointed by the churches (v. 19) to travel with Paul to "carry the offering." "Offering" here is literally "grace" (*charis*); Paul sees the collection as an "act of grace," which emphasizes the gracious character of the divine work being done among the churches. It is being administered by Paul for the "honor" (*doxa*, lit., "glory") of the Lord himself.

This appointment of Paul's colleague also has a practical purpose. It not only shows the apostle's "eagerness to help," but also serves as a safeguard against those who might try to find fault in his administration of the offering. After all, this colleague and the brother to be mentioned (v. 22) have been sent by the churches as "representatives" (or "emissaries," v. 23) to administer the collection. Paul saw the wisdom of being accountable to others and of delegating responsibility. His concern was that God's work be done "right" (or "honorably"), first and foremost before the Lord, but also before other people (v. 21; cf. Rom. 2:24; 12:17–18; 1 Tim. 6:1; Titus 2:5).

A third delegate is introduced at verse 22 as "our brother." He does not possess the fame of the previously mentioned brother, but comes with sterling credentials of a proven ministry. Paul relates that this man has often been tested "in many ways" and found to be "zealous" (*spoudaios*, or "diligent"). He is even more likely to be so, given the "great confidence" he has for the Corinthians. Here was someone known and respected by Paul and probably by the Corinthians themselves—someone who, they could be assured, believed in them.

Paul could not have chosen better delegates to go to Corinth. In Titus he had a trusted companion and fellow worker (v. 23) who had worked among them, earned their respect, and won their hearts as well. In the two unnamed brothers, he had people personally appointed by the churches whose labor in the gospel was known to the Corinthians and who had brought glory to Christ. In closing Paul exhorts the believers in Corinth to live up to his confidence and proud expectations of them by completing the offering as a demonstration of their love before the churches. Since the broken fences of fellowship had been mended, now was time for the Corinthians to obey this call to action (v. 24). With the words "so that the churches can see it," Paul is probably underscoring the unity of all the churches in this collection.

5.2.2. Paul Commends Their Willingness to Give (9:1–5). This section continues Paul's exhortation to generosity among the Corinthians. Here we learn something about the content of his boast concerning them. We can also see more of "Paul the motivator," as he continues to encourage them to complete the benevolence offering.

Paul begins with an emphatic statement (almost a boast) of his confidence in them: He really does not need to write to them about this ministry to the Jerusalem saints because he already knows how eager and ready they are to respond to this need. In fact, he had boasted to the Macedonians that the Achaians (including the Corinthians) were ready and prepared to give a year ago. What is clear is that Paul is using one church to motivate the other. In chapter 8 he held up the Macedonians as an example for the Corinthians to follow in their selfless giving. Now we learn that the Macedonian response was due in part to motivation provided by Paul holding up the Achaians as an example: "Your enthusiasm has stirred most of them to action" (v. 2). When Paul was motivating the churches, rather than criticize one church to another, he "boasted" of one church to another. A marvelous lesson surfaces: Positive affirmation is a more potent motivator than criticism.

To ensure that his boast does not fall to the ground, Paul is sending the brothers on ahead to make final preparations (vv. 3, 5). He is trying to prevent any embarrassment to himself, and especially to them, if perhaps any Macedonians (to whom Paul had boasted) should come and find the gift still unprepared. The appeal to save face before the Macedonians is unmistakable, and Paul is not beyond applying a modicum of guilt. After all, they are merely arranging for the collection of an offering that was previously promised.

Twice Paul refers to the offering as a "generous gift" (*eulogia*, v. 5). This Greek word, usually translated "blessing," can also refer to an act or gift that blesses (e.g., Rom. 15:29; cf. Eph. 1:3). It is not to be given "grudgingly," as if given by people motivated by covetousness or greed. Furthermore, in context *eulogia* is placed over against the concept of sparcity ("sparingly") in verse 6. Thus, Paul may have chosen a word freighted with meaning to present his wish that the Corinthians eagerly prepare a generous offering to serve as a bountiful blessing to needy saints.

5.2.3. Paul Teaches Principles About Giving (9:6–15). Paul's final step in motivating the Corinthians is to teach them various scriptural principles related to giving. The first can be called the "principle of sowing and reaping," for which he employs the imagery of the harvest (v. 6; cf. Prov. 11:25; 22:8–9; Luke 6:38). The lesson is simple: The more a farmer sows, the greater the harvest. This supports the notion that *eulogia* (v. 5) is rightly translated "generous gift." In effect, Paul is saying that generosity should be cultivated in our giving.

Along with generosity God loves giving that is done cheerfully (cf. Rom. 12:8) and freely, without a grudging sense of duty or compulsion (v. 7). Paul pauses to give incentives to those who give in the above manner. (1) For one thing, "God is able to make all grace abound to you" (v. 8). In context the word "grace" here denotes God's bountiful provisions, both spiritual and material. God's abounding grace results in the Corinthians' having not only all that they need, but a surplus to participate fully in every good work, such as the collection at hand. With such participation the material blessings cross over into spiritual ones.

To illustrate this Paul quotes a portion of Psalm 112:9: "He has scattered abroad his gifts to the poor, his righteousness endures forever." It is noteworthy that Judaism had long drawn a connection between giving alms to the poor and righteousness, such that the two were virtually equivalent (Martin, 291). This notion is surely behind the words of Jesus in Matthew 6:1–2, where the "acts of righteousness" is parallel to giving to the needy. Paul is not here contradicting his own doctrine of justification by faith apart from the works of the law (see Rom. 3:24, 28; 4:1–13; 5:1; Gal. 2:16; 3:8, 11, 24; 5:4; Titus 3:7). Rather, his point is one that the psalmist makes, that practicing mercy toward the poor has the effect of augmenting or promoting the righteousness in one's own moral life. "Righteousness," in other words, is to be identified here with the righteous character of such merciful acts (see v. 10). God, the gracious supplier of seed and bread, will increase his people's store of seed so that they may continue to participate in such good deeds (v. 8) and thereby abound in a "harvest of . . . righteousness."

(2) Paul then cites another spiritual incentive. Through him and those administering the collection, the generosity of the Corinthian gift will cause many to turn grateful hearts to God in thanksgiving (vv. 11–12). By meeting the needs of God's people, they will cause a volume praise to ascend to God—grateful hearts glorifying God because they see in this generous gift proof that the Corinthians not only profess the gospel but live in obedience to its teachings. Paul could not have given us a stronger incentive for not only preaching the good news but living it as well. That is, when God's people, redeemed by his grace, mirror his mercy through acts of compassion and love, it creates a powerful and compelling message not easily resisted.

(3) Paul closes with one final incentive. The liberality of the Corinthians will cause the recipients to pray fervently and affectionately for them, with prayers inspired by the surpassing grace of God at work within them. At the mention of God's redeeming grace, Paul breaks out in praise, thanking the Lord for his indescribable gift. Since this gift is given by God himself as evidence of his abounding grace and is beyond description, Paul certainly has in mind Christ, the Son of God himself (Rom. 6:23; 8:32; 2 Cor. 8:9; cf. Eph. 1:6).

6. The Affirmation and Defense of Paul's Apostolic Ministry (10:1–13:14)

In the Introduction to this letter we argued that the change in tone that occurs at 10:1 need not be interpreted to reflect a fragment of a separate letter. Dramatic changes in tone are certainly not absent in other Pauline writings (e.g., Rom. 11:33; 1 Cor. 16:1; Gal. 3; Phil. 3:2). A shift in subject matter or to a different target audience are plausible explanations. If this let er was written over an extended period of time, t is possible that Paul received disturbing news of further trouble caused by his adversaries. These chapters were then penned in response o that situation. In exhorting and issuing a varning to the entire church, he also specifically identifies the views of his opposition (e.g., 1:4, 12–13, 15, 20–23; 13:2). This lends weight to the view that Paul writes these chapters primarily with false teachers (cf. 11:13–15) and their adherents in mind (Hodge, 228).

6.1. Paul Answers His Critics (10:1–18)

Throughout the previous nine chapters we have caught glimpses of Paul's critics and the charges they laid at his doorstep (see 1:13; cf. 1:17–20; 2:17; 3:1; 4:2–3, 5; 5:12; 7:2). However, the apostle now takes his opponents head-on in a lengthy defense of his apostolic ministry. Here we see their views and accusations against him most clearly.

6.1.1. Concerning Apostolic Authority and Presence (10:1–11). The first accusation s directed against Paul personally, who, in the eyes of his opponents, lacked the authoritative "presence" of a true apostle. To them an apostle should carry himself like an apostle by being bold and decisive and by reflecting an unwavering authority. In contrast they point out that Paul was meek and mild in their presence, but wrote bold letters when he did not have to confront them personally (v. 1). Clearly implied is that Paul lacked the personal courage and confidence to say what had to be said to their faces.

The answer Paul gives shows how wrong his critics are. What they have mistakenly interpreted as timidity was Paul's attempt to imitate the meekness and gentleness of Christ (cf. Matt. 11:29). He does not enjoy the harsh and painful confrontations of discipline (7:8), nor does he want to be seen as trying to frighten his spiritual children into submission by his letters (10:9). In fact, he begs them to respond so that it will not be necessary for him to exercise the boldness he intends to direct against some of them (v. 2). Later he explains that the present letter is being written to avoid having to be harsh when he does come. His apostolic authority has been given primarily for the purpose of "building up" the saints, not tearing them down (13:10, NRSV).

Those who equate apostolic authority with bold confrontations or heavy-handedness only show that their criteria for judging belong to the "standards of this world" (*kata sarka*, lit., "according to the flesh"). Paul repeatedly denies that his means, methods, or manner of ministry is alien to the new covenant life of the Spirit (1:17; 5:16; 10:2–3; 11:18; cf. Gal. 5:16–25). He understands that although he lives "in the world [*sarki*, lit., "flesh"]" and is thus subject to the weaknesses and limitations of mortal flesh (Fee, 1994, 341), he is waging spiritual warfare (see Eph. 6:12), where worldly human means and methods are useless. The weapons needed must instead be spiritual, drawing on God's power to tear down spiritual strongholds (vv. 3–4).

Traveling within the sophisticated intellectual world of the Greeks, Paul portrays their philosophical systems as fortresses to be demolished. Their arrogant and pretentious claims of truth are depicted as rising up in opposition to the knowledge of God revealed in Christ. Furthermore, in his preaching of the gospel Paul sees himself as bringing every worldly system of thought into subjugation to the teachings of Christ (v. 5). His words remind us that the Lordship of Christ extends over the mind as well as over the will and heart. The proud intellectual who comes to Christ must forsake dependence on reason and human understanding operating in a self-directed life apart from God.

Beginning in verse 6, Paul answers directly the accusation that he lacks apostolic boldness. He definitely has the authority to discipline and is ready to do so, but not before making every effort to bring the Corinthians to complete obedience. This process serves to weed out the truly insubordinate from those willing to submit to God. Only then will he "punish every act of disobedience." When it comes to affirming his identity and authority as Christ's apostle, Paul takes a back seat to no one (v. 7b). But he parts company with his opponents over the criteria for judging apostolic presence. He refuses to link this judgment with outward appearances, such as a confident air of authority and swiftness to administer discipline.

What Paul's enemies fail to understand is that Christ gave him the authority of an apostle to build up his church, not to tear it down (v. 8). It was not even his intention to frighten his spiritual children into submission by his letters (v. 9). Despite their scorn for his meekness and lack of public eloquence (v. 10), Paul will not be made to feel ashamed. Addressing his critics directly (v. 11), he lays down a not-so-subtle warning: When he comes, there will be no two faces to Paul. They can expect that the bold apostolic authority that they admit to reading in his letters will be transformed into deeds toward those he must discipline.[10]

6.1.2. Concerning Legitimate Boasting (10:12–18). With sarcasm Paul admits there is a kind of boldness he does not possess. It is the kind that his opponents demonstrate when they compare and align themselves with those who engage in self-promotion by bragging on themselves (v. 12). How foolish to make themselves the standard by which they measure others and then commend themselves as having achieved that standard. By declaring that he will not boast outside "proper limits" but will confine his boasting "to the field" appointed him by God, Paul is identifying his adversaries as interlopers or intruders into Corinth, a place to which God had sent him to establish his church. As the apostle to the Gentiles (Gal. 2:8; cf. Acts 9:15), Corinth was a part of the rightful sphere of Paul's ministry (2 Cor. 10:13).

If, as suggested by 11:22, these intruders are Jewish, they may have come from Jerusalem, where the church had previously and formally acknowledged Paul's apostleship to the Gentiles (Gal. 2:1–10; see Harris, 383). Paul denies that his boasting is excessive, for the Corinthians are within the proper limits of the sphere of ministry given to him by God. After all, they did first hear the gospel from Paul and his companions (v. 14). Paul further denies that he boasted and took credit for the work of others, which was evidently what his opponents were doing (vv. 15–16). However, his ambition in the work of Christ was not restricted to taking the gospel as far west as Corinth. Paul's hope was that as the Corinthians grew in faith, the sphere of his ministry among them would expand and result in his taking the gospel to regions beyond.

This, then, is the real goal and source of pride for the apostle: to take the gospel to people who had not yet heard the good news. Herein lies a legitimate cause for boasting, but it is a boast that never takes credit for another's work or regards the success of gospel ministry as one's own. Citing Jeremiah 9:24, Pau admonishes his readers to give God all th glory and credit for what is accomplished fo the Lord. Our real goal should be to pleas Christ (2 Cor. 5:9) and our true reward to gai his approval (10:18; cf. Matt. 25:21), some thing unattainable to those bent on self approval.

6.2. Paul Exposes His Critics (11:1–15)

Paul has been answering his critics, bu realizes that he must do more than defend him self. If the work of God is to be preserved, h must protect the Corinthians from those wh would endanger their faith. In this section h seeks to do this by exposing his critics, th error of their teaching, and the deceptive char acter of their ministry.

6.2.1. By Revealing His Spiritual Passio for the Corinthians (11:1–6). To answer th charges of his critics Paul had just said muc about what God did through him in the wor of the gospel. The problem was that in doin so he sounded very much like his critics i their self-commendation (10:12). Thus Pau begins the present section with a plea for th Corinthians to bear with him while he engage in the foolishness of a practice that he else where rejects (see 3:1; 5:12). He feels confi dent that they will do so, but still gives thre reasons why he feels compelled to ask for thei audience.

(1) Paul carries in his heart a godly jealous (v. 2, which begins with *gar*, "for"), whic seeks to protect the Corinthians and safeguar their spiritual purity. The image of a jealou husband is borrowed from the Old Testament where Yahweh is said to be "jealous" over hi people (e.g., Ex. 20:5; 34:14; Deut. 4:24) whom he has betrothed to himself (Hos. 2:19–20). Here Paul identifies the betrothed a Christ and himself as the father of the bride. I bringing the Corinthians the gospel, Pau became their spiritual father, but he is also thei shepherd. His love and concern did not en with overseeing their spiritual birth. Rather, i endures in his present desire to preserve th church's purity and devotion to Christ, who i their prospective husband. Paul's passion is no without a measure of anxiety, as the threat o seduction and defilement is real. There ar those in Corinth who would lead them astray

even as Satan under the guise of a serpent craftily deceived Eve in the Garden of Eden (2 Cor. 11:3).

(2) The next reason Paul desires a hearing involves the grave danger to the Corinthians if they fail to heed his counsel. Verse 4 provides the key to understanding the opponents of Paul addressed in chapters 10–13 (Martin, 334). It is doubtful that the apostle intended this verse to allude to the doctrinal content of his opponents' preaching, but the structure of the verse does suggest that he is summarizing the character and effects of their ministry. They are being led by an apparent ringleader, who comes and preaches "another Jesus," different from the one preached by Paul. It is impossible know for certain what Paul's opponents taught about Jesus. But given his repeated boasts of weakness and willingness to identify with the sufferings of Christ in this letter (e.g., 11:23–33; 12:7–10; 13:1–6), it is possible that they failed to give proper credit to the instrumentality of the cross in securing God's salvation. Even more likely is that they failed to see in Jesus' death on the cross a model of God's power perfected through weakness (13:4).

Such preaching as Paul's opponents did was equivalent to offering the Corinthians a "different Spirit"[11] and a "different gospel" from the one they had received. Keep in mind that for Paul there is only *one* Jesus, *one* Spirit, and *one* gospel. His concern is that the Corinthians are being offered a counterfeit version of Christianity, and to his dismay they are willing to "put up with it" (*anechomai*; cf. also vv. 19–20)!

(3) Finally, in a somewhat sarcastic fashion Paul alludes to the Corinthians' lack of spiritual discernment. Since they are so receptive to error, they might as well hear what *he* has to say. After all, he is not inferior to any of those considered to be "super-apostles" (v. 5), even if he lacks the rhetorical eloquence so admired by his critics (v. 6). These "super-apostles" are probably the Jerusalem "pillars" (cf. Gal. 2:9), not Paul's opponents—whom he calls "false apostles, deceitful workmen," who masquerade "as apostles of Christ" (v. 13), and agents of Satan, disguising themselves "as servants of righteousness" (vv. 14–15). But if Paul is unskilled in speech, he is certainly not lacking in knowledge, something that should be obvious to the Corinthians, who have had ample exposure to his teaching. Paul's words carry a stinging rebuke for those who, in weighing the worth of a preacher, prefer style over substance and charisma over content.

6.2.2. By Contrasting Them with His Willingness to Preach the Gospel Without Charge (11:7–12). Paul begins this section by asking a rhetorical question: "Was it a sin for me to ... [preach] the gospel of God to you free of charge?" Behind this verse lies his opponents' accusation that Paul does not conduct his affairs as a true apostle. His refusal to take wages for his preaching must have seemed strange, given his own teaching that apostles had a right to earn their living from the gospel (1 Cor. 9:6–14). Furthermore, their objection reflects the attitude of those reared in the Greek philosophical tradition, where philosophers commonly took money for their teaching. In fact, the Sophists regarded teaching that was freely given a sure sign that the teaching was worthless.

Why then did Paul expose himself to this criticism by refusing to receive support? There is strong irony in his answer, perhaps designed to shame his audience. To the proud Corinthians Paul humbled ("lowered") himself by taking up manual labor for his support. But Paul willingly did this so that they might be lifted up ("elevated") out of their sin through the preaching of the gospel. The truth is that Paul had served them by robbing other churches (v. 8); that is, he took money from those who were themselves needy and could not afford to give (e.g., the Macedonians; see v. 9; also 8:1–5; Phil. 4:15–16). Although Paul had the right to receive support from the Corinthians, he made it clear earlier that he was determined not to "hinder the gospel of Christ" by doing so (1 Cor. 9:12). Such hindrance would certainly have occurred if Paul had given his opponents any grounds for accusing him of "peddl[ing] the word of God for profit" (2 Cor. 2:17). Paul's gospel was not for hire, and he wanted no accusation that he had pinned a price tag to his ministry.

But Paul's motives for preaching without charge were not entirely defensive. In verse 9 he reminds them that his policy was aimed at not placing a burden on them, although the Corinthian church was surely prosperous enough to have borne it (Fee, 1987, 541–44). Paul was determined not to be a burden to the

Corinthians even when in need. Instead, he waited for support to come through the generosity of the Macedonian churches. Furthermore, he considered it a privilege and reward not to request support (1 Cor. 9:17–18). Whereas his opponents might want to boast in their status as "supported" apostles, Paul would boast in choosing to offer the gospel free of charge (2 Cor. 11:10).

In verse 11 Paul anticipates his opponents' twisted interpretation of his policy: The reason he refused to take support from them was due to a lack of love and affection on his part. This he emphatically denies. God knew his heart and knew that he loved the Corinthians deeply. By refusing to accept their support, he was creating a clear distinction between himself and his opponents, who, in pretending to be apostles (vv. 13–15), sought to present themselves on an equal plane with Paul and his associates. Furthermore, his no-charge policy underscored the character of grace and sacrifice in Paul's ministry. This touches the heart of the issue of what it meant to be a true apostle (see 11:22–12:13, where Paul shows that apostolic credentials have less to do with externals and more with whether one emulates the character of Christ and imitates his self-denial).

6.2.3. By Denouncing Them As Masquerading Impostors (11:13–15). At the mention of these would-be apostles, Paul suddenly turns from a defense of his policy as an apostle to unmask them and reveal their true identity. They are " false apostles" and workers of deceit, who masquerade as apostles of Christ. Even more condemning, they are agents of Satan, the master of deceit (John 8:44), who conceals the true nature of his work (cf. 1 Peter 5:8) by disguising himself as an angel of light. Is it any wonder, then, that his servants follow his example and deceptively pass themselves off as "servants of righteousness"?

The last sentence of verse 15 leaves no doubt that Paul views the work of his opponents as worthy of God's judgment. The words "what their actions deserve" literally reads "according to their works." This phrase is nearly identical to Paul's words in 2 Timothy 4:14, when he condemns the opposition of Alexander the metalworker, who did him "a great deal of harm." Because of his opposition to the gospel, Paul writes, "the Lord will repay

WORDS OF JESUS NOT FOUND IN THE GOSPELS

Passage	Description
Acts 1:4–5, 7–8	Jesus' words to his disciples shortly before his ascension
Acts 9:4–5; 22:7–8, 10, 18, 21; 26:14–18	Jesus' words to Paul at the time of his conversion
Acts 9:11–12, 15–16	Jesus' words to Ananias at the time of Paul's conversion
Acts 11:7, 9	Jesus' words to Peter in Joppa
Acts 11:16	Peter recalls Jesus' words about John the Baptist
Acts 18:9–10	Words of encouragement to Paul in Corinth
Acts 20:35	Saying of Jesus: "It is more blessed to give than to receive"
Acts 23:11	Words of encouragement to Paul imprisoned in Jerusalem
1Co 11:24–25	Record of Jesus' words about the Lord's Supper in the Upper Room
2Co 12:9	Jesus' words regarding Paul's thorn in the flesh
Rev 1:8, 11–12, 17–20	Jesus' words to John in exile on Patmos
Rev 2:1–3:22	Jesus' message to the seven churches in Asia Minor
Rev 4:1	Jesus invites John to see visions of the last things
Rev 16:15	Jesus' promise to return "like a thief"
Rev 22:7, 12–16, 20	Jesus' promise, "I am coming soon!"

him for what he has done" (cf. also Rom. 3:8; Gal. 1:8–9; Phil. 3:18–19, for references to God's judgment according to our works).

6.3. Paul Defends the Legitimacy of His Apostolic Ministry Through Foolish Boasting (11:16–12:13)

6.3.1. Paul's Right to Engage in Such Boasting (11:16–21). Paul now returns to his defense and the theme of "foolish boasting" introduced in 11:1. He apologizes for stooping to his opponents' level and boasting (v. 16). He knows it is foolish and does not follow the example of the Lord (v. 17). Nevertheless, this is necessary if Paul is to make his case before a church bent on comparing him to his rivals. Furthermore, he might as well boast, given the church's demonstrated tolerance for such worldly (lit., "fleshly") boasting (v. 18).

With words drenched in irony and dripping with sarcasm, Paul states his confidence in the Corinthians' wisdom and readiness to accept happily such foolishness (v. 19). In fact, their capacity for tolerating fools was boundless, as verse 20 describes. They put up with those who act like tyrants, seeking to enslave their subjects. Just how this slavery was imposed is not clear, but given their Jewish heritage (v. 22), Paul's opponents probably sought to deprive the believers in Corinth of their liberty in Christ by insisting that they keep the law of Moses (Hughes, 399). This for Paul was a return to spiritual bondage (cf. Rom. 6:14–15; Gal. 2:4; 4:22–31; 5:1).

The exploitation Paul charges his opponents with (v. 20) most likely refers to their greedy consumption of any material support offered. While the apostles certainly had a right to be housed and fed (1 Cor. 9:4–7), these impostors may have been eating their hosts out of house and home (Barrett, 291; cf. the later regulations in Did. 11:3–12). Paul then points out the heavy-handed authority by which they take advantage of, or even seek to overpower, the Corinthians (cf. Barrett, 291), arrogantly exalting themselves and making the believers endure shameful insults ("slaps you in the face" is a metaphor for a stunning insult; cf. Matt. 5:39).

With a closing flurry of irony Paul feigns shame at coming up "weak" by comparison. He had come to the Corinthians in the meek and gentle spirit of Christ (10:1), but they were unimpressed and seemed to prefer the arrogant authoritarianism of his rivals. Consequently, Paul decides to fight fire with fire and answer a fool according to his folly (Prov. 26:5). He assures his readers that regardless of the subject of his opponents' boast, he can boast with the best of them.

6.3.2. Paul Boasts in Natural Qualifications (11:22). Paul now begins the foolish boast mentioned in several previous verses (11:1, 6, 16; cf. 10:8). Apparently, these rivals prided themselves in regard to physical descent. The three expressions used in this verse underscore their ethnic identity as Jews. In this they had no advantage over Paul, who could make identical claims. Like them he was a "Hebrew," a full-blooded Jew (cf. Phil. 3:5). He is also an "Israelite," a member of the chosen people of God. As a descendent of Abraham, Paul obviously has his natural racial identity in view. However, he may also have in mind his spiritual heritage as a covenant son of the promise (Gal. 3:6–18).

6.3.3. Paul Boasts of Trials and Sufferings (11:23–33). With verse 23 Paul's boasting takes a sharp and unexpected turn from his nationality to his accomplishments as a "servant of Christ." But if his audience expected glowing tales of church plantings and missionary exploits, they were to be shocked and disappointed. Instead, Paul begins to catalog the sufferings and trials endured in his service of Christ (many of which are not recorded in Acts; see Hughes, 405–17; Martin, 376–83; Hodge, 271–76, for correspondences between this list and Acts).

The list is long and includes persecutions (vv. 24–25b, 32–33), life-threatening dangers (vv. 25c–26), physical hardships (v. 27), and psychological burdens borne out of a pastoral concern for the churches (v. 28). Paradoxically he boasts not in successes, but in what would normally be seen as failures (vv. 24–27), not in deeds of power, but in weakness (29–30). When God chose Paul as an apostle to the Gentiles, he promised him a cup of suffering (Acts 9:15–16). From these verses and Acts we learn that God had made good his promise. Perhaps no Christian in the history of the church was more unwavering and zealous in preaching Christ in the face of relentless persecution, hardships, and personal sufferings (Hughes, 407).

Herein lies the uniqueness of Paul's boast and its strategic genius. His rivals played to their audience's fascination with externals. To them true apostles were known by their rhetorical eloquence, authoritative manner, and charismatic presence. Miracles, signs, and wonders (12:12) were authenticating marks of apostolic ministry and consistent with this criteria. But the Corinthians were not ignorant of their duty as Christians to imitate the character of Christ (10:1), nor of the mystery of the cross, which revealed the wisdom and power of God through the seeming folly of human weakness (1 Cor. 2:1–8; 2 Cor. 4:7–11). The incomparable boast of Paul was that he was unrivaled in his imitation of Christ's sufferings in obedience to God's will (cf. Mark 8:33–34). This demanded nothing less than a dying to self (Rom. 6:6; Gal. 2:20; Col. 3:3–9; cf. Eph. 4:22–24).

The prideful self-promotion of Paul's opponents stood in stark contrast to the *cruciform life*—the path taken by Jesus on his way to the cross. By boasting of his sufferings for the sake of Christ, Paul has accommodated his opponents' love of comparison and citing of apostolic credentials. However, he has also put forward a criterion they cannot begin to meet—a life of self-denial and suffering in obedience to his apostolic calling.

6.3.4. Paul Boasts of Weakness Due to Great Revelation (12:1–10). Paul feels compelled to continue boasting even though he doubts anything can be gained from it (v. 1). He is prepared to boast of "visions and revelations" given him by the Lord.[12] Although unstated, Paul most certainly had in mind the activity of the Spirit. In an earlier correspondence, *apokalypsis* ("revelation") designated a gift of the Spirit (*charisma*) through which God communicates with his people (1 Cor. 14:6, 26, 30). Elsewhere the word refers to the personal revelation of Jesus Christ that accompanied Paul's apostolic call (Gal. 1:12; Eph. 3:3–4; cf. 2:2).

But however important such revelations were to Paul personally, he does not here regard them as proof of his apostleship. On the contrary, he only foolishly boasts of visions and revelations to expose what his opponents erroneously regard as an identifying mark of an apostle. For Paul, revelations are a private matter of personal spirituality, not some test of authentic apostleship (Fee, 1994, 348). Consequently, he reluctantly boasts of a "man he knows" rather than referring to his own experiences directly (see esp. v. 7, which demonstrates that the "visions and revelations" referred to in vv. 2–5 are his own). As for when Paul had this revelation, he writes that it was "fourteen years" prior to the writing of 2 Corinthians (ca. A.D. 56). This places the experience about A.D. 42–43, which falls within the long period Paul spent in Syria and Cilicia (Gal. 1:21; cf. 2:1) and about which Acts is virtually silent (cf. Acts 9:30; 11:25).

Paul's description of this vision-revelation is fascinating. He recounts having been "caught up to the third heaven" or "paradise." The two expressions are synonymous as Paul uses the same Greek verb (*harpazo*) with both (vv. 2, 4) to designate where the revelation took place. The word "paradise" (*paradeisos*) occurs only twice more in the New Testament (Luke 23:43; Rev. 2:7), but in neither is it associated with the "third heaven." Such an identification was made in Jewish apocalyptic literature, which was widely read among first-century Greek-speaking Jews. Interestingly, the Septuagint translated the "Garden of Eden" with the Greek word *paradeisos* (Gen. 2:15; 3:23, 24), and Revelation 2:7 promises, "To him who overcomes, I will give the right to eat from the tree of life, which is in the *paradise* of God." Access to the Tree of Life in the Garden of Eden symbolized life-giving fellowship with God, secured through faithful obedience (see Gen. 3:23–24; cf. 2:17). Thus, Christ promises the overcoming believer that he will restore what was lost through the Fall.

For Paul, then, "paradise" is a heavenly place in the presence of God where communion and communication with him take place. Strangely, this visionary experience left Paul unable to tell whether he was "in the body" or "apart from [or without] the body" (cf. Rev. 1:10). Perhaps the otherworldly splendor of what Paul heard and saw caused him to lose all awareness of his own bodily existence (Harris, 395). The loftiness of these revelations was such that even if it were permissible to speak of such things, no human words would suffice (2 Cor. 12:4).

The kind of experience Paul describes was certainly esteemed among his opponents and perhaps among the Corinthians at large. The believers in Corinth undoubtedly knew that Paul had been the recipient of "visions and revelations," since he frequently told the story of his conversion (Acts 9:3–9; 22:6–21; 26:12–18; Gal. 1:16) and even had a vision while in Corinth (Acts 18:9–10). Nevertheless, Paul is still unwilling to cater completely to their preference for self-commendation (cf. 3:1) and foolish boasting. Since he felt forced to defend the legitimacy of his apostleship, he acknowledges his revelations (v. 5a). In fact, even if Paul did boast of them, that would not be foolish since he would be speaking the truth (v. 6). Still, he does not want the Corinthians to conclude that these revelations have made him special or have given him a right to boast personally. The only circumstances that Paul feels comfortable boasting about are those that reveal his "weaknesses" (v. 5b).

Paul's mention of his weaknesses provides him with the occasion to boast of one in particular. To prevent the magnitude of these revelations from leading to self-exaltation and conceit (v. 7), a "thorn in [the] flesh" was given to him. He identifies this further as "a messenger of Satan" sent "to torment" him. Although it is impossible to determine the exact nature of Paul's thorn in the flesh, it was probably some form of physical affliction or sickness. (1) There is no compelling reason to depart from the literal sense of "in the flesh" as referring to the body. While Paul does on occasion use the phrase to refer to the carnal sinful nature (e.g., Rom. 7:5; 8:8–9), he often uses it to describe natural bodily or physical existence (see Rom. 2:28; 8:3; 2 Cor. 10:3; Gal. 2:20; 6:12; Eph. 2:11; Phil. 1:22, 24; 3:3–4; 1 Tim. 3:16). (2) Paul has already dealt with the same subject of God's power being demonstrated through physical frailty and human weakness (2 Cor. 4:7–15). The parallel between the two passages is unmistakable and strongly suggests Paul is here presenting another example of the same truth.

The text reads that a thorn "was given" to Paul, presumably by God (since Satan would certainly not try to keep Paul from pride) (v. 7). Some may object to what may appear as an unholy alliance (i.e., God's giving Paul something that he views as "a messenger of Satan"). However, we must remember that while Satan is at times presented as the instrument of discipline in the hands of God (e.g., 1 Cor. 5:5; 1 Tim. 1:20), he is limited by the sovereign purposes of God, as in the case of Job (Job 2:1–10). Despite Paul's persistent prayer for the removal of this "thorn" (2 Cor. 12:8), he came to understand that it served a positive and redemptive purpose—it kept him from a destructive pride. Furthermore, it served to magnify the grace of God operating in his life (v. 9). To call attention to his weaknesses was to glorify the One who is able to perfect his power through human weakness.

Consequently, Paul came to the point where he no longer viewed the weaknesses of his flesh as liabilities but as assets. He was content to live with them, discovering God's strength by accepting his weaknesses (v. 10). In fact, they had become his boast because the secret of God's power lay in his willing identification with weakness. Without saying as much, Paul's own situation parallels the path taken by his Savior, who through identification with human weakness enabled God's power to be revealed and released for the salvation of humanity (Phil. 2:5–11; cf. Eph. 1:19–20; Col. 1:9–12).

6.3.5. The Proof of Paul's Apostolic Ministry (12:11–13). Paul has finished his foolish boasting, which he never would have started if not forced to do so. Actually, the Corinthians are partly to blame for Paul's foolishness. They should have provided his defense by commending him to his opponents. They knew well the character of his ministry—that he was in no way inferior to those touted as "super-apostles." His words "even though I am nothing" reveal his true humility and disdain for personal comparisons bent on self-promotion. With irony dripping from his pen Paul begs their forgiveness for one deficiency. Unlike his rivals he failed to become a financial burden on them by charging for his services (v. 13).

Despite this half-comic criticism, Paul is well aware that his apostleship is under attack and with it the integrity of the gospel itself. That is why he had denounced his opponents at Corinth as "false apostles, deceitful workers," those who were "disguising themselves as apostles of Christ" (11:13, NRSV). In defense of his own apostleship he writes, "The *signs of a true apostle* were performed among you with all perseverance, *by signs and wonders and miracles* (v. 12, NASB, italics added). "Signs" (*semeia*), "wonders" (*terata*), and "miracles" (*dynameis*) are most likely different designations for the same thing. The different words point to the different effects produced. They are divine acts that validate a message, bring a sense of wonder at the divine presence, and display the mighty power of God at work (Hodge, 291–92).

Many Pentecostals and charismatics assume that the "signs of a true apostle" (NIV, "the things that mark an apostle") in the first half of the verse are the miraculous "signs, wonders and miracles" of the second half. While the word for "signs" is the same in both places, there are good reasons to conclude Paul meant something different. (1) The word *semeion* has a wider range of meanings than just "miracle" (see Matt. 26:48 [Judas's kiss]; Rom. 4:11 [circumcision]; 2 Thess. 3:17 [Paul's signature]). (2) The grammar of this verse suggests that the terms at the end of the sentence describe the *manner* in which the signs of a true apostle were performed.

To what, then, do the "signs of a true apostle" refer? In chapters 10–13 Paul has been pointing out the marks of true apostolic ministry. In addition to spiritual power to confront evil (10:3–4, 8–11; 13:2–4, 10) and divine (visionary) revelations, they include such character traits as: (1) jealous care for the churches (11:2, 28); (2) true knowledge of Jesus and his gospel (11:6); (3) selfless ministry, such as his sacrificial self-support so as not to burden the churches; (4) the absence of self-serving or heavy-handed discipline (11:20–21); (5) willingness to suffer and be afflicted for the cause of Christ (11:23–29); and (6) patient endurance of the "thorn in the flesh" (12:7–9).[13]

It should be noted that the "false apostles" (11:13) could and probably did make claims to revelations and superior knowledge of the truth (11:5–6; 12:1–7). They came disguised by Satan as "servants of righteousness" (11:15), possibly because of their demands for and showy displays of piety. They may also have come with counterfeit "signs" empowered by Satan. Nevertheless, when Paul wants to defend his claim to genuine apostleship, he does not point to miracles, but to the Christlikeness reflected in his personal conduct, character, and willingness to suffer for the sake of the gospel. These qualities, for Paul, are the marks of a true apostle. They stand in bold relief against the superficial criteria of those self-promoting impostors at Corinth.

The lesson for those who desire to see signs and wonders in the church should be obvious. Supernatural manifestations are integral to, but not the definitive mark of, New Testament apostolic ministry. Signs and wonders must be judged as to their true source or origin. One key way of judging is to discern the character of the minister (and his or her ministry) through whom these signs and wonders appear. They must be ministered in the moral and spiritual character of the Crucified One.

6.4. Paul Plans a Third Visit (12:14–13:14)

6.4.1. Paul's Intention Not to Be a Burden (12:14–18). As noted in the Introduction, Paul had made two earlier visits to Corinth by the time he wrote this letter: the founding visit (Acts 18:1–17) and the "painful visit," which necessitated the "sorrowful letter" (2 Cor. 2:1–4). Paul is now preparing to visit the believers there a third time. He wants it understood that as before (1 Cor. 9:13–18), he intends to preach without payment so as to not burden them. He is not coming for what he can get from them, but in order to provide for his spiritual children (2 Cor. 12:14b). Like a loving and benevolent parent, Paul is ready to spend everything he has, including himself, for their welfare. As a spiritual father, he knows that such intense love is only satisfying when returned. He longs for a response of love in equal measure from his children (v. 15).

In verse 16 Paul again reminds the Corinthians that he did not accept support from them, but adds what suspiciously looks like an accusation that had nonetheless been levied against him: "I caught you by trickery." Apparently, his rivals charged that although Paul personally refused support and did not burden them directly, he craftily did so indirectly through his associates. Paul is confident they know differently and can answer that accusation for themselves (v. 17, a Greek question that expects a "no" answer). All they have to do is to recall the coming of Titus and an unnamed but well-known "brother." Certainly they knew that Titus did not exploit them, and Paul and his associates conducted themselves in the exact same manner and spirit (v. 18). The integrity of their walk was a matter of public knowledge and spoke for itself; it was the only defense Paul needed.

6.4.2. Paul's Fears and Misgivings Over the Coming Visit (12:19–21). The apostle wants to avoid leaving the false impression with the Corinthians that he has been speaking in defense of himself (v. 19). This may appear as a contradiction, seeing that chapters 10–13 comprise an extended defense of Paul's apostolic ministry. However, Paul perceives a fundamental difference in defending the legitimacy of his apostleship and defending himself personally against slanderous accusations. The first undermines the integrity of his ministry and calls into question the gospel he preaches. The second merely assaults his personal reputation. The latter is of no great significance and Paul can ignore it, knowing that God knows the truth.

As people who are "in Christ" (note that Paul saw the entirety of a believer's life in union and identification with Christ; see Rom. 9:1; 1 Cor. 15:19, 31; Eph. 1:12; Phil. 1:26; 3:3), Paul and his companions have done everything "in the sight of God" and are known by him (2 Cor. 4:2; cf. 2:17; 5:11; 7:12). He has spoken not for his benefit but for theirs, not to shore up his reputation but to build up and strengthen their faith.

Verses 20–21 show the vulnerable and human side of Paul. As the prospect of his visit draws near, he carries with him a good deal of anxiety about what he will find when he arrives at Corinth. He entertains the possibility that the Corinthians will not receive the counsel of this letter, but will continue to listen to and support those false teachers (11:13–15). Were that to happen, both he and the Corinthians would have reason to complain and both would be disappointed in each other. Paul particularly fears the spiritual havoc his opponents can wreak upon the church in the form of strife, disorder, and disunity (v. 20b).

Paul then imagines the worst of his fears—that he will find sin so widespread and rampant that he is driven to mourn over the presence of sexual sins (v. 21b) that he thought were long ago repented of and abandoned by the Corinthians (see 1 Cor. 5:1–13; 6:12–20). The fact that Paul singles out sexual sins strongly suggests that such sins were being promoted by the teaching of his opponents—a form of libertinism (see Barrett, 332). Such an experience would "humble" Paul (2 Cor. 12:21a). We should understand this expression only in a permissive sense. What Paul expresses is his hope that such a painful experience as the earlier "tearful or sorrowful visit" will not again be repeated or allowed by God.

6.4.3. Paul Warns of Possible Discipline (13:1–4). Having stated his personal fears about the upcoming third visit, Paul takes on the authoritarian posture of an apostle and issues a stern warning. The Corinthians can be assured that the truth will be uncovered and revealed. To support his point he quotes a portion of Deuteronomy 19:15: "Every matter must be established by the testimony of two or three witnesses." To what Paul refers by "the two or three witnesses" is uncertain. Does he have three individuals in mind: Paul, Timothy, and Titus—all three of whom were known in Corinth and could give testimony to the truth? Does he have in mind the convening of a court with the assembled church present (see 1 Cor. 5:3–5; cf. Matt. 18:15–17)?

Most likely, in the light of verse 2, Paul sees the witnesses as his warnings. As pointed out above, he had issued a warning (probably through his first letter) against "those who sinned earlier" (cf. 12:21). He then reminds the Corinthians that he had given them another warning when he was with them "the second time" (i.e., the "sorrowful visit"). Now he repeats that warning a third time, "while absent." The Corinthians have been amply forewarned; it is now time for the apostolic pretenders and their supporters ("any of the others") to be called into account. These impostors have mocked Paul's meekness (10:1), and incredibly the Corinthians not only endured their abusive use of authority (11:20), but were impressed by it. They apparently identified this outward display of authority as proof of apostleship—proof that Christ was speaking through them. In no uncertain terms Paul tells them that if they are looking for that kind of evidence, they will find it at his impending visit, when he will not spare anyone. After all, the Christ that speaks through Paul is not weak but a mighty power among them (13:3).

But the very criterion that the false apostles and their followers insist on for apostleship betrays their ignorance of what it takes to be an apostolic servant of Christ. What is more, it reveals a tragic flaw in their faith and understanding of the gospel itself. After all, it was through the weakness of the cross that God released his resurrection power and made it available to all who will identify with Christ (v. 4). Christ voluntarily humbled himself and took on the weakness of a human existence in order to obey God's will even to the point of death on a cross (Phil. 2:8). Paul chose to follow the example of Jesus, who like a lamb led to slaughter (Isa. 53:7) did not retaliate against his oppressors, but who trusted in God to vindicate him (53:11–12). Even as Christ now lives through the power of the resurrection, Paul, though weak in the eyes of other humans, lives by the Spirit (2 Cor. 3:3, 6, 8) to serve them in the power of the resurrected Christ.

6.4.4. Paul's Plea for Self-Examination to Avoid Discipline (13:5–10). Paul does not want to discipline the Corinthians; thus, he calls them to self-examination. They know all too well that Jesus Christ lives within them (see Rom. 8:9). That being the case, surely the character of their faith should attest to that fact. Note that twice in verse 5 Paul repeats the reflexive pronoun "yourselves." Instead of scrutinizing his apostolic demeanor and demanding outward evidence of apostolic authority, the Corinthians should be examining their *own* Christian experience to see if it reveals the character and presence of Jesus Christ. While sure that they will not admit to failing that test, Paul is also confident that they will see evidence of the same genuineness of faith in him and his associates (v. 6). In recognizing as much, the Corinthians will also have to admit to the genuineness of Paul's apostleship and gospel (Harris, 403).

Paul then prays that the Corinthians will do nothing wrong (v. 7). As before (3:1; 5:12; 12:19), he denies the well-worn accusation that he is defending or commending himself. Even if he comes out looking as one who is disapproved by comparison, he is concerned that they do the right thing. His chief responsibility is never to oppose the truth, but to promote it at all times. Consequently, what does it matter if Paul and his companions are seen as "weak" (i.e., meek and nonauthoritative) when among the Corinthians, so long as they are strong in their faith? Paul's prayer goes even further in his desire to see them become fully mature (NIV, "perfection") in the faith (v. 9).

Paul concludes this section of his letter on a positive note. He hopes that the present letter will make it unnecessary for him to use his apostolic authority to discipline them when he comes (v. 10). After all, the Lord called him to build up his church, not to tear it down.

6.4.5. Paul's Closing Greeting (13:11–14). The closing greeting of this letter begins with a series of pastoral exhortations. Rather than "good-by" it seems best to translate the verb *chairete* literally as the command "rejoice," in a manner similar to how Paul uses this verb at the close of other letters (e.g., Phil. 3:1; 4:4; 1 Thess. 5:16). "Aim for perfection" (lit., "be made complete") expresses Paul's hope that the Corinthians will grow to Christian maturity (cf. 2 Cor. 13:9), perhaps by heeding the counsel and teaching given them in this and all previous correspondence (Harris, 405). "Listen to my appeal" seems a better rendering of *parakaleo* than "be comforted" (NASB) and strengthens the call to unity and harmony ("be of one mind" and "live in peace") that follows. These last two exhortations seem to be targeted at the disorder and disunity described in 12:20. If the Corinthians give heed to Paul's counsel, they will be acting in accord with "the God of love and peace,"[14] who dwells in their midst and fellowships with them.

"Greet one another with a holy kiss" reflects a common oriental custom that endures to the present. It was widely practiced in the early church (see Rom. 16:16; 1 Cor. 16:20; 1 Thess. 5:26; 1 Peter 5:14) as a symbol of unity and fellowship within the household of God. It may also have symbolized forgiveness and reconciliation as the liturgical "kiss of peace" did in the post-apostolic church (see Martin, 501). Paul sends his greetings from "all the saints," who probably include all the churches recently visited throughout Macedonia (2 Cor. 8:1; cf. 2:13; 7:5; 11:9).

The closing benediction (v. 14) presents something both typical and unique among Paul's letter closings. The concepts it contains are certainly to be found throughout his writings, but the precise form of this benediction occurs nowhere else. Although Paul does express elsewhere the work of redemption from a Trinitarian perspective (cf. Rom. 5:1–8; 1 Cor. 12:4–6; Eph. 1:3–14; 4:3–6), we find that perspective in a benediction only here. Whether the words were already in use in the church as a liturgical blessing we cannot know for certain. However, this verse agrees remarkably with and condenses Paul's understanding of God's salvation in Christ. Gordon Fee has called it "the most profound theological moment in the Pauline corpus" (Fee, 1994, 363).

The "love of God" for lost sinners is what Paul presents as the motive for providing peace (i.e., reconciliation) through Christ (Rom. 5:1, 7–8). The "grace of the Lord Jesus Christ" expresses God's love for us and is seen in Christ's death, which removes the enmity between us and God because of sin, reconciles us to him, and grants us a right standing before him (Rom. 5:9–11; 2 Cor. 5:16–6:1). The "fellowship [*koinonia*] of the Holy Spirit" speaks of our mutual participation in and appropriation of the redemptive love and grace described above. It includes the blessing and provision of the new covenant life in the Spirit (3:6–18). This involves a vital living relationship with the Spirit himself (Rom. 8:2–16; Gal. 5:16–18, 22–25) and all the gifts he graciously bestows on members within the body of Christ (1 Cor. 12:4–31; cf. Rom. 12:3–8; Eph. 4:7–11). It results in their spiritual transformation (Titus 3:5), their equipping for service within the body (1 Cor. 12), and their empowerment to be Christ's witnesses in the world (Acts 1:8). In other words, Paul's closing benediction expresses his wish that the Corinthians experience the fullness of God's redeeming love and grace through the ministrations of the Holy Spirit.

THE OLD TESTAMENT IN THE NEW

NT Text	OT Text	Subject
2Co 3:13	Ex 34:33, 35	Veil of Moses
2Co 4:6	Ge 1:3	Creation of light
2Co 4:13	Ps 116:10	Faith and speech
2Co 6:2	Isa 49:8	God's day of salvation
2Co 6:16	Lev 26:11–12; Eze 37:27	God living with us
2Co 6:16	Jer 32:38	God and his people
2Co 6:17	Eze 20:41	Separate from the world
2Co 6:17	Isa 52:11	Touch no unclean thing
2Co 6:18	2Sa 7:14	Father and son
2Co 8:15	Ex 16:18	God provides enough
2Co 9:9	Ps 112:9	Gifts for the poor
2Co 10:17	Jer 9:24	Boasting in the Lord
2Co 13:1	Dt 19:15	Two or three witnesses

NOTES

[1]For example, the Greek words for "joy /to be joyful" (*chara/charenai*), "comfort" (*paraklesis*), and "troubles/being harassed" (*thlipsis /thlibomenoi*) link 7:4 with 7:5–7. Thematically, Paul also speaks of "having confidence" in the Corinthians in 7:4 and 16. The important theme of God's comfort in the midst of trials appears not only before and after the disputed passage (1:3–11; 7:5–7, 12–13) but throughout it as well (4:7–5:8; 6:1–10; 7:4; see Carson, Moo, and Morris, 273–74).

[2]Four times in four verses (2:1–4) Paul denies that his actions were motivated by a desire or goal to make the Corinthians sorrowful. This emphatic denial suggests a charge of Paul's opponents—that Paul in his desire to exert his apostolic authority was callous and indifferent to the personal pain he was inflicting.

[3]Paul may have in mind the sweet-smelling incense carried by priests in the triumphal procession, or the smell of sacrifices that were offered at a Roman temple at the procession's end (see Harris, 332). Paul may also be likening the preaching of the apostles to Old Testament burnt offerings, which are described as "an aroma pleasing to the LORD" (Lev. 1:9, 13, 17).

[4]It is unlikely that the Greek phrase *tou katargoumenou* (masculine or neuter participle)—"that which was fading away"—refers to the "glory" (*doxa*, a feminine noun) of Moses' face. Rules of grammar would require the participle to be feminine. C. K. Barrett (119) is probably correct in suggesting that the neuter participles of vv. 10–11—"what was glorious" and "what was fading away"—refer to the old covenant.

[5]Several times in this letter Paul underscores his own human weakness. It often appears in the context of his trials and sufferings for the sake of the gospel. Nevertheless, in each instance he testifies to the power of God working in and through his ministry (see 2:14–16; 4:7–18; 6:3–13; 11:21–12:10; 13:3–4, 9–10).

[6]Note, however, that Paul did hold to the possibility that he might still be alive at the Parousia (cf. 1 Thess. 4:14–15).

[7]In 12:11 Paul states that the Corinthians had ample evidence of the character of his apostleship

and that they should have commended him. It may be that Paul is here implying that they should have been proud of him and come to his defense (Hughes, 351).

[8]The word "grace" (*charis*) is used ten times in chapters 8–9 and is variously translated. As Paul uses it, the primary emphasis is on what God has done and provided in redemption through Jesus Christ.

[9]This would be hard to support in view of Paul's admission to being on both sides of the economic fence (Phil. 4:12), and in view of the fact that elsewhere the New Testament acknowledges, without censorship, the presence of the rich (e.g., James 1:10). The issue is not whether one possesses wealth, but how one uses that wealth in the service of the Lord (Matt. 25:14–25; Acts 4:36–37) and whether its possession prohibits one from following Christ (Matt. 19:16–22; cf. Acts 5:1–11).

[10]The Greek in verse 11 is compressed and allows for the translation, "Let such a person consider this, that what kind of persons we are in word through letters, such persons (we are) in deed when present." The NIV translates the understood verb in the future ("will be"). However, if the literal rendering be allowed, Paul may simply be denying any inconsistency or hypocrisy on his part. What he is and intends when writing his letters does not change when he is with them.

[11]The NIV has "spirit," suggesting something other than the Holy Spirit, such as a disposition alien to the spirit of Christ (Martin, 336). Although this would support our earlier contention that Paul's opponents failed to take on the weakness, self-sacrifice, and humility of Christ (see Introduction), it misses the big picture of what Paul is trying to portray here. His opponents have come preaching an alien gospel. Thus, both Jesus, who provides for God's salvation, and the Holy Spirit, who brings the believer into the reality of salvation, are misrepresented (Fee, 1994, 344).

[12]Paul probably does not distinguish between "visions" and "revelations," for the vision of Christ recorded in Acts 9:3–9, 12 is called a "revelation" in Galatians 1:12 (cf. v. 16).

[13]For a thorough exegetical treatment of this issue, see Wayne Grudem, "Should Christians Expect Miracles Today," in Greig and Springer, 63–66.

[14]There is debate as to whether the phrase "God of love and peace" views God as the One who gives love and peace or as the One whose essential nature is love and peace. Both are grammatically possible and affirm biblical truth. The suggestion that Paul intends to include both meanings also has merit, since in Paul's writings God is both characterized by love (Rom. 5:8) and peace (15:33) and is the One who supplies both love (5:5) and peace (5:1; 14:17; see Barrett, 343). However, I have chosen the former sense as a way of agreeing with Paul's earlier insistence that the Corinthians test themselves to see if their Christian experience betokens the "weakness" of Jesus on the cross (vv. 4–6).

BIBLIOGRAPHY

Books: William Barclay, *The Mind of St. Paul* (1958); C. K. Barrett, *A Commentary on the Second Epistle to the Corinthians* (1973); D. A. Black and D. Dockery, *New Testament Criticism and Interpretation* (1991); F. H. Brinsmead, *Galatians—Dialogical Response to Opponents* (1982); D. A. Carson, *From Triumphalism to Maturity* (1984); D. A. Carson, D. J. Moo, and Leon Morris, *An Introduction to the New Testament* (1992); James Denney, *The Second Epistle to the Corinthians* (1894), Gordon D. Fee, *The First Epistle to the Corinthians*, NICNT (1987); idem, *God's Empowering Presence: The Holy Spirit in the Letters of Paul* (1994); G. S. Greig and K. N. Springer, eds. *The Kingdom and the Power* (1993); Donald Guthrie, *New Testament Introduction*, rev. ed. (1990); Murray Harris, "2 Corinthians," *The Expositor's Bible Commentary* (1976), 10:301–406; Charles Hodge, *An Exposition of the Second Epistle to the Corinthians* (1973, repr.); Stanley M. Horton, *What the Bible Says About the Holy Spirit* (1976); Philip Hughes, *Paul's Second Epistle to the Corinthians*, NICNT (1962); Colin Kruse, *Second Corinthians*, TNTC (1987); Ralph P. Martin, *2 Corinthians*, WBC (1986); Ronald H. Nash, *Christianity and the Hellenistic World* (1984); Alfred Plummer, *A Critical and Exegetical Commentary on the Second Epistle of Paul to the Corinthians*, ICC (1975, repr.); Roger Stronstad, *The Charismatic Theology of St. Luke* (1984).

Articles: P. W. Barnett, "Opponents of Paul," in *The Dictionary of Paul and His Letters* (1993), 644–53; Hans D. Betz, "2 Cor. 6:14–7:1: An Anti-Pauline Fragment?" *JBL* 92 (1973): 88–108; Gordon D. Fee, "II Corinthians vi.14–vii.1 and Food Offered To Idols," *NTS* 23 (1977): 140–61; J. A. Fitzmyer, "Qumran and the Interpolated Paragraph in 2 Cor. 6:14–7:1," *CBQ* 23 (1961): 271–80; R. P. Martin, "The Opponents of Paul in 2 Corinthians: An Old Issue Revisited," in *Tradition and Interpretation in the New Testament*, ed. G. F. Hawthorne and O. Betz (1987), 279–89; Jerome Murphy-O'Conner, "The Corinth That Saint Paul Saw," *BA* 47 (1984): 147–59.

GALATIANS

William Simmons

INTRODUCTION

1. The Holy Spirit and Galatians

The person and work of the Holy Spirit played a prominent role in the churches of Galatia. For example, the evangelism of Galatia was initiated by a supernatural movement of the Holy Spirit (Acts 13:2–4). The Spirit also evidenced charismatic gifts in their midst. The disciples of Pisidian Antioch, for example, are described as being filled with joy and with the Holy Spirit (13:52). The Lord enabled Paul and Barnabas to perform signs and wonders in Iconium (14:3). And Paul evidenced the gift of healing in Lystra, when a cripple was fully restored (14:8–10; 1 Cor. 12:9). Clearly the founding of the churches of Galatia and the ministry of Paul and Barnabas among these churches were the result of the work of the Holy Spirit.

The Holy Spirit also played a key role in solving the many problems in Galatia. Something had gone terribly wrong among these initial congregations of Paul. Even though the Galatians were the first to hear the law-free gospel, they were turning to legalism (Acts 13:39; Gal. 4:8–10). Paul had clearly preached justification by faith, but they were seeking to be justified by works (Gal. 2:16; 3:1, 10–11). Furthermore, it was in their very midst that Paul had explicitly proclaimed he would go to the Gentiles (Acts 13:46–48). Now some of these people were wanting to become Jews (Gal. 5:2). They had become bewitched and were in danger of casting away their salvation (3:1; 4:11,19).

In seeking to bring the Galatians back into the fold, Paul does not simply restate the gospel message, for reiterating doctrinal formulations will not undo the damage there. He must point to something more tangible, some unquestionable experience to wrest the Galatians away from the troublemakers. It is here that Paul concentrates on the experience in the Holy Spirit (Betz, 1974, 146).

For example, in Galatians Paul does not primarily associate key concepts such as "grace," "righteousness," and "adoption" with the cross and resurrection. On the contrary, these major themes are related to *the experience of the Spirit* (3:2, 5, 14; 4:6, 29; 5:5; 6:8). Moreover, negative sociological terms such as "immature," "slave," and "pedagogue" (3:24–25; 4:1–2) are contrasted with more positive terms associated with the Spirit, such as "sons," "free," and "Father" (3:19–4:7) (Lull, 1980, 118, 127–28, 131). Paul's central point is that the Galatians' reception of the Spirit serves as an undeniable proof that they are the children of God (3:1–5) (Wedderburn, 1988, 171). The experience of the Spirit and the reception of grace are virtually correlates of one another in this letter. Both create an awareness that God is truly at work in the believer.

This truth becomes particularly evident with regard to Paul's doctrine of justification by faith. In Galatians, the gift of the Spirit and justification are inseparable. For Paul notes that the Galatians' reception of the Spirit was received in the same way that Abraham received the righteousness of God (3:6; cf. also Rom. 8:1–17; 1 Cor. 6:11; 2 Cor. 3:8–9) (Dahl, 1977, 133). Solely on the basis of faith in Christ, uncircumcised Gentiles are indwelt with God's Holy Spirit, apart from works of the law. Thus, the presence of the Spirit among the Galatians is that divine endorsement that redefines the place of the law and establishes the centrality of faith.

The theological significance of the Spirit in Galatians is evident from the examples given above. That is, the manner in which the Spirit worked among the Galatians reveals the nature of God and their relationship to him. Again, Paul's argument will only carry weight if the work of the Spirit is distinct and undeniably real. The function of the "Abba cry" in 4:6–7 proves this point (Lemmer, 1992, 359). Under the charismatic influence of the Spirit, the Galatians shout, "Abba, Father!" This cry of ecstasy creates a filial consciousness that is a testimony to the reality of their place in God. It is the primary proof that says, "You belong." This must be a continuing reality in the church for it to have any force in Paul's appeal. Therefore, such activity of the Spirit is not an incidental part of the worship service. Rather, it is essential to the presence of God among the believers. It means that they have been born of the Spirit and that the Spirit empowers them to live as Christians (4:21–31; 5:16–26).

Finally, the sociological implications of the Spirit in Galatians are also important. If God demonstrates his loving solidarity with the Galatian believers by granting his Spirit by faith, how can they discriminate and entertain distinctions among themselves? Hence there is neither Jew nor Greek, slave nor free, male nor female, for they are all one in Christ Jesus (3:28) (Heine, 1987, 153). The unifying presence of the Spirit is what makes Peter's separation from the Gentiles all the more unacceptable (2:11–15) (Dunn, 1992, 116–17).

It follows that the letter to the Galatians is of special significance for Pentecostals. For in it the abiding presence of the Holy Spirit is the hallmark of Christian life and worship. The indwelling of the Spirit, with his accompanying gifts and fruit, serves as evidence that one has been fully accepted by God. It is a tangible sign that we have been justified by faith apart from the law. Thus the dynamic presence of the Spirit in the life of the believer clearly marks the end of the law and any attempt at securing righteousness through works. The Spirit creates a divine solidarity with the Father that nothing can dissolve. In other words, the supernatural activity of the Spirit is not some incidental aspect of Pentecostal worship. It is the divine sign authenticating our salvation experience. The Spirit serves as the path to mature development in Christ. It serves as the key to Christian liberty and deliverance from a slavish obedience to the law. It engenders an atmosphere of unity and mutual acceptance that prohibits discrimination and segregation in the body of Christ.

These truths will guide the rest of the study. But prior to addressing the text, we should ask ourselves some important questions. Have we permitted our works for Christ to replace the work of Christ? Has some form of legalism, regardless of how subtle, undermined the grace of God in our lives? Has a spirit of works-righteousness displaced the work of the Spirit in our service to God and humans? Finally, are we seeking a religion that we can control rather than a faith that guides? Fortunately, Paul's care for the Galatians will help us address these issues.

2. Authorship

a. Internal Evidence

There can be no doubt that Paul wrote Galatians. It is considered one of the most "Pauline" of all of the New Testament letters. Its affinity to Romans is unmistakable and has been described as a rough draft of that great letter. Nearly every line pulsates with the spirit and mind of the great apostle. As in Romans, the two great Pauline themes, justification by faith alone and life in the Spirit, form a major part of the content of Galatians. Its vocabulary consistently shows the apostle's hand. Words like "grace," "faith," "righteousness," "law," "flesh," and "Spirit" appear on every page and are used in the classic Pauline sense. We need to entertain no reservations concerning the Pauline authorship of Galatians (Bruce, 1982, 1).

b. External Evidence

What we can gather from outside the biblical text is equally supportive of Pauline authorship. The early church fathers unanimously accept Paul as the author, and the earliest canons of Scripture list Galatians with the Pauline letters (Betz, 1979, 1).

3. Occasion

Paul wrote to the Galatians because troublemakers and "agitators" had infiltrated their churches (1:7; 5:10–12). They were spreading heresy that threatened the very salvation of Paul's converts. These "false brothers" (2:4) seem to be similar to the Jewish Christian legalists found in Acts 11:1–3 and 15:1–3. Converted Pharisees claimed that in order for the Gentiles to be saved, they had to obey the law of Moses and be circumcised (15:5). In Galatia, it appears that such persons argued that Paul had only half evangelized them and that the law of Moses had to be added in order for them to be saved. So the heretics were seeking to compel the Gentiles to be circumcised (Gal. 5:1) and observe Jewish ceremonial laws, such as religious holidays and purity regulations (2:1–14; 4:10). They were trying to substitute a system of works-righteousness for the gospel of grace Paul preached. In short, they wanted to reinstate Judaism as the primary religious model for Gentile Christians. Gentiles had to become Jews to be part of God's people. For these reasons the troublemakers in Galatia are often referred to as Judaizers (cf. 2:14).

The Judaizers realized that Paul and his gospel of salvation by grace through faith were major obstacles preventing them from accomplishing their goals. So they attacked the person and authority of Paul in an effort to undermine his influence in Galatia (4:16). They stressed that he was not a disciple of the historical Jesus, as were Peter, James, and John (2:9). In fact, Paul was simply a product of these "pillar" apostles and was indebted to them for his religious knowledge and experience (1:18–19). They charged Paul with hypocrisy, preaching circumcision in some settings, but forbidding it in Galatia (5:11).

Paul fully realized the critical nature of the situation. If the Judaizing heresy succeeded, it would make Christianity a mere sect of Judaism. Its teaching struck at the core of Christianity. What the Judaizers preached was no gospel at all (1:7); and if the Galatians accepted this false teaching, they would be turning from God and fall from grace (1:7; 5:4). If they permitted themselves to be circumcised, they would place themselves under the curse of the law (3:10–11), and Christ would be of no benefit to them (5:1–2). For such reasons, Paul pronounced a twofold curse on the troublemakers and stated that they awaited the judgment of God (1:8–10; 5:10).

Paul also wrote to defend himself against the slander of his opponents. Yet he did so only because his apostolic authority was vitally connected with the law-free gospel to the Gentiles. Therefore, with regard to his calling and message, he stressed his independence from the Jerusalem apostles (1:18–2:6). Yet he also had to convince the Galatians that James, Peter, and John accepted his message and mission to the Gentiles (2:7–10). Furthermore, Paul had to expose the false motives of the Judaizers. They were not interested in the welfare of the Galatians. Instead, they wanted to gain glory for themselves and to avoid persecution (4:17; 6:13). They wanted to enslave the Galatians to the "weak and miserable principles" of this world by converting them to Judaism (4:3, 9).

4. Date and Destination

Although Galatians is unquestionably written by Paul, its destination and date are difficult to determine. Paul clearly addresses the letter "to the churches in Galatia" (1:2). In his day, however, the word "Galatia" had a twofold meaning. It could refer to the ancient kingdom of the Gauls, which encompassed the *northern* regions of Pontus, Phrygia, and Cappadocia. On the other hand, "Galatia" could also refer to the Roman province of Galatia, which

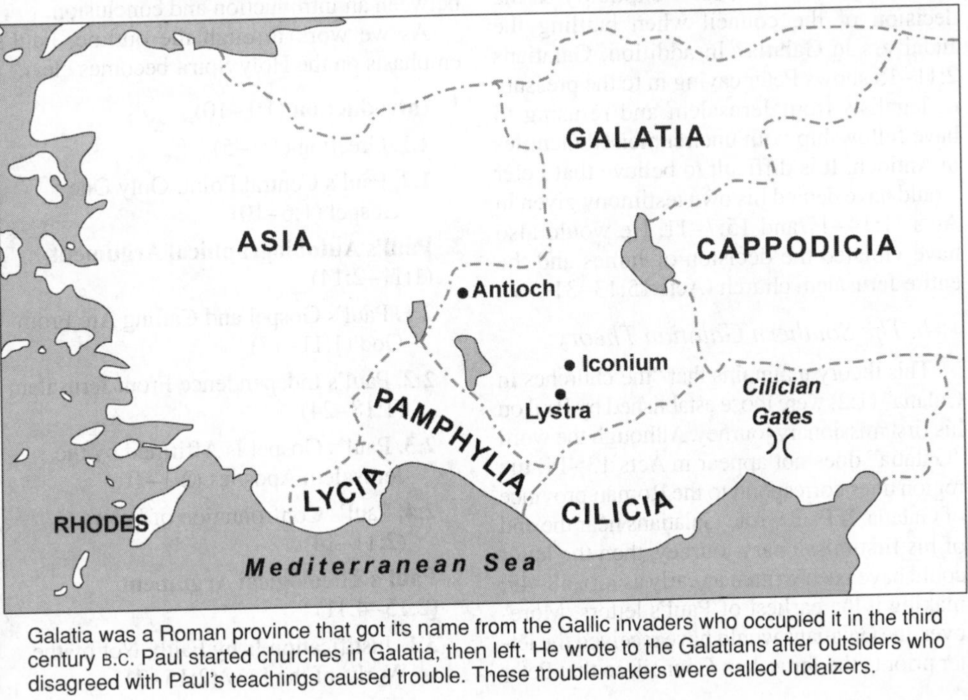

Galatia was a Roman province that got its name from the Gallic invaders who occupied it in the third century B.C. Paul started churches in Galatia, then left. He wrote to the Galatians after outsiders who disagreed with Paul's teachings caused trouble. These troublemakers were called Judaizers.

extended further to the *south*, including the cities of Antioch of Pisidia, Lystra, Derbe, and Iconium. Those who believe that Paul wrote to the northern regions hold to the "Northern Galatian Theory"; those who maintain that the Galatian churches were located in the southern region affirm the "Southern Galatian Theory." Each theory affects the dating of the letter.

a. The Northern Galatian Theory

This theory focuses on the missionary activity of Paul as recorded in Acts 16:1–6 and 18:23. Both passages explicitly mention "Galatia" and briefly summarize Paul's travels on his second and third missionary journeys. If Paul addressed this region shortly after his second missionary journey, he could not have written earlier than A.D. 51–52. If he penned Galatians near the close of his third missionary journey, he would have written in about A.D. 55–56.

This particular theory must overcome two major difficulties. Acts does not record Paul establishing any churches in this northern region. All it says is that he passed through the area and strengthened the disciples (Acts 18:23). Furthermore, this theory holds that Paul wrote Galatians after the decree of the so-called "Jerusalem Council" of Acts 15. If this is so, why did he not refer explicitly to the decision of the council when battling the Judaizers in Galatia? In addition, Galatians 2:11–15 shows Peter caving in to the pressure of legalists from Jerusalem and refusing to have fellowship with uncircumcised Gentiles in Antioch. It is difficult to believe that Peter would have denied his own testimony given in Acts 11:14–17 and 15:7–11. He would also have violated the decision of James and the entire Jerusalem church (Acts 15:13–31).

b. The Southern Galatian Theory

This theory maintains that "the churches in Galatia" (1:2) were those established by Paul on his first missionary journey. Although the word "Galatia" does not appear in Acts 13–14, the region does correspond to the Roman province of Galatia. If Paul wrote Galatians near the end of his first missionary journey, then the letter could have been written as early as A.D. 48–49, making it the earliest of Paul's letters. Moreover, the Galatians would have received the letter prior to the Jerusalem Council, so that Peter would not have had any directives from Jame and the church at Jerusalem concerning fel lowship with Gentiles. Thus his withdrawal i Antioch from table fellowship with Gentil believers becomes more comprehensible. Thi scenario also explains why Paul did not refer t the Jerusalem Council in Galatians.

Reputable scholars have built formidabl arguments in defense of both theories. Th exact destination of Galatians, and hence th precise dating, cannot be determined with cer tainty. Yet the Southern Galatian Theory seem to harmonize best with what we know fron Acts and Paul's own words in Galatians. Thi view means that the major principles of Paul' theology had already been established at a early stage in the development of the church.

OUTLINE

In spite of the trying circumstances in which Paul wrote, Galatians is a well-organized letter. It consists of the following three well-defined arguments: autobiographical, theological, and practical. The autobiographical section argues for the apostolic authority of Paul. The theological section clearly sets forth the major doctrines of the faith. The practical section calls for the application of these beliefs. These sections are sandwiched between an introduction and conclusion.

As we work through the outline, Paul's emphasis on the Holy Spirit becomes clear.

1. Introduction (1:1–10)

- **1.1.** Greeting (1:1–5)
- **1.2.** Paul's Central Point: Only One Gospel (1:6–10)

2. Paul's Autobiographical Argument (1:11–2:14)

- **2.1.** Paul's Gospel and Calling Are From God (1:11–17)
- **2.2.** Paul's Independence From Jerusalem (1:18–24)
- **2.3.** Paul's Gospel Is Affirmed by the Jerusalem Apostles (2:1–10)
- **2.4.** Paul's Confrontation of Peter (2:11–14)

3. Paul's Theological Argument (2:15–4:11)

- **3.1.** Justification Is by Faith, Not by the Works of the Law (2:15–21)

3.2. The Spirit Is Received by Faith (3:1–5)
3.3. Abraham Is Justified by Faith (3:6–9)
3.4. The Curse of the Law (3:10–12)
3.5. The Promise of the Spirit (3:13–14)
3.6. The Priority of Promise Over Law (3:15–18)
3.7. The Purpose of the Law (3:19–25)
3.8. Unity in Christ (3:26–29)
3.9. The Spirit and Adoption (4:1–7)
3.10. Renewed Warning and Rebuke (4:8–11)

4. Paul's Practical Argument (4:12–6:10)
4.1. An Appeal for Reconciliation (4:12–16)
4.2. The False Motives of the Judaizers (4:17–20)
4.3. True Sons Are Born by the Spirit (4:21–31)
4.4. Waiting in the Spirit (5:1–5)
4.5. Renewed Warning and Rebuke (5:6–12)
4.6. Living in the Spirit (5:13–26)
4.7. Sowing to Please the Spirit (6:1–10)

5. Conclusion (6:11–18)
5.1. Paul's Sign of Authenticity (6:11)
5.2. Once More: Exposing the Judaizers (6:12–15)
5.3. Final Words and Benediction (6:16–18)

COMMENTARY

1. Introduction (1:1–10)

1.1. Greeting (1:1–5)

Paul wastes no time in getting to the heart of the issue in Galatians. He uses every word of his greeting *to defend the gospel of grace*. His strategy is basically twofold. He must substantiate his apostolic authority and stress the complete sufficiency of Christ for salvation. Both issues address the problems that the Judaizers have created in Galatia. In an effort to gain a hearing there, they must discredit Paul; in order to draw the Galatians into Judaism, they must undermine the person and work of Christ.

Paul follows the conventions of Greco-Roman letter writing in this letter. That is, he identifies himself as the author, includes a greeting, and goes on to address the recipients (Hansen, 1994, 31–32). Thus, the first word of the text is "Paul." But even here, Paul may be setting forth his special call to minister to the Gentiles. For his Hebrew name, Saul, was used only prior to his first missionary journey. Beginning with Acts 13:9, the apostle is always referred to by his Greek name, Paul. It is as if Paul wants his entire identity to be associated with the Gentile world, including his personal name (Cole, 1984, 30).

The next word in the text is "apostle." The meaning of this word is derived from the religious administration rabbinic word *shaliach*, which designated someone officially "sent out" or "commissioned" to accomplish a specific task (Bruce, 1982, 72). The one so commissioned was empowered with the same authority as the one who sent him out (cf. Acts 9:1–2, where Saul obtained official documents from the high priest empowering him to persecute the Christians in Damascus). The Lord Jesus and the early church used this term to designate spiritual leadership. In its restricted sense it refers to the original twelve apostles appointed by the Lord (Matt. 10:2–4; Luke 6:13–16; Acts 1:19–26). In its broader sense, the early church used "apostles" to designate ministers sent out to preach the gospel (Acts 14:4, 14; Rom. 16:7; Gal. 1:19).

Paul clearly claims to be an apostle in the restricted sense in Galatians as in his other letters (1:1; cf. Rom. 1:1; 1 Cor. 1:1; Eph. 1:1). Also, since he was directly commissioned by the Lord, Paul is emphasizing that he and his message have been authorized by God, so that he speaks with the authority of Christ (2 Cor. 10:8). His apostleship rests on the same basis as the apostles before him. So if any in Galatia reject his apostolic authority, they will have to reject the authority of the other apostles as well, including James, Peter, and John, the so-called "pillar" apostles (Gal. 2:9).

Paul does not include an article ("the") before the word "apostle." Its absence makes "apostle" serve more as a description of Paul's character than as a title or office. Paul does not say that he has been appointed to a specific office in the church. Indeed, Peter and the rest of the apostles had appointed Matthias as an apostle to replace Judas (Acts 1:12–26), but Matthias is never heard of again. In contrast, Paul has been divinely called and is being used by God to spread the gospel to the entire Gentile world (Acts 9:1–28:31). Thus, through a supernatural work of God, Paul's entire being takes on the nature of "apostle." In other words, "apostle" is not something Paul does or an administrative post he occupies; *it is who he is*.

Consequently, Paul's apostolic authority is "not from men nor by man." These words may reflect the accusations of the Judaizers. They probably claimed that Paul was just a "Johnny come lately" with regard to the faith. He had not been a disciple of Jesus during his earthly ministry. In fact, it was well known that he had rejected the faith and violently persecuted the church, beginning with Stephen (Acts 7:58–8:3; 9:1–2). The Judaizers claimed that everything Paul knew about Jesus was learned from men like James, Peter, and John. He is *their* disciple, not a disciple of Jesus. Paul was subordinate to the original apostles, and he was making a false claim to apostolic authority. Paul was a fraud, and his message of justification by faith apart from works of the law was equally fraudulent.

These charges are why Paul emphatically states that his calling and message were "not from men nor by man." Paul's place in the kingdom did not have its origin with any man or group of men. Nor did God communicate his will for Paul through any human intermediaries. Rather, Paul's apostolic authority and mission to the Gentiles came as a divine mandate, made known to him through supernatural revelation on the Damascus road (Acts 9:1–8; 22:1–11; 26:9–20) (Kim, 1981, 82, 97–98). As the prophets of old, Paul maintains that he was divinely chosen to fulfill a crucial role in God's plan of salvation (cf. Isa. 49:1–3; Jer. 1:4–5; Gal. 1:15–16).

In stark contrast to being made an apostle by other people, Paul's authority came "by Jesus Christ and God the Father." The divinity of Jesus is strongly implied at this point: Jesus is placed on the same order as God the Father (1:12). Paul's point is that he has received a joint commission from Jesus Christ *and* God the Father. No doubt the troublemakers in Galatia made much of those who were acquainted with *Jesus* of Nazareth. For this reason Paul's inclusion of the name "Jesus" with "Christ" has significance here. "Jesus" means "Savior" and was the designated name given to our Lord at birth (Matt. 1:21, 25; Luke 1:31; 2:11). Although Paul was confronted by the exalted Christ on the Damascus road, he fully understood that the Messiah, that is, "the Anointed One," is one and the same with Jesus from Galilee. His repeated use of such phrases as "Jesus Christ" and "Christ Jesus" demonstrates that Paul refuses to allow any essential dichotomy between the earthly Jesus and the exalted Christ (Rom. 1:3; 1 Cor. 1:1; 2 Cor. 1:1; Gal. 2:16; Phil. 2:11; Col. 2:6). So those who claim to have known Jesus have no advantage over the apostle Paul. He too has met Jesus.

The resurrection of the earthly Jesus shows that he is the same person as the exalted Christ. By mentioning the resurrection, Paul simultaneously affirms a belief of conservative Judaism and presents a cardinal doctrine of the Christian faith (cf. 1 Cor. 15). The Pharisees, contrary to the Sadducees, believed that the dead would be raised in the last day (Matt. 22:23–32; Mark 12:18; Acts 23:6–10). For them, the resurrection was the pivotal event dividing this present age from the age to come. For Paul, the resurrection of Jesus by the Father has already marked the turn of the ages. Jesus is the firstfruits of the resurrection (1 Cor. 15:20–23). His cross and resurrection are the end-time events that, to a degree, bring the age to come into the present. In a corresponding way, the outpouring of the Holy Spirit grants the believer "the firstfruits of the Spirit" and ushers in the powers of the future age (Acts 2; Rom. 8:23; 1 Cor. 12:1–14:40; Gal. 5:5).

Those who have been raised with Christ and empowered by his Spirit form an end-time community, already bringing to some extent the kingdom into this world. Hence throughout his letters, and especially Romans and Galatians, Paul understands the normal Christian life to be one of extraordinary fulfillment. He exhorts believers to live the resurrected life by "walking in the Spirit" (Rom. 6:1–10; 8:1–27; Gal. 5:16–18, 25). This "realized eschatology" will remain the hallmark of the church until the glorious manifestation of the children of God and the liberation of all creation (Rom. 8:18–21). Of course, the important question is why the Galatians would be tempted to embrace the primitive and partial revelation of Judaism when they have entered into the pirit-empowered life in Christ. Why should ey be entangled in the elements of this world hen they have been liberated by the exalted hrist through the Spirit? These are the questions Paul wants them to ponder as he unfolds e gospel in this letter.

The Judaizers surely wanted to marginalize e apostle Paul, to portray him as a maverick ho had no followers, as one who was isolated n the fringe of the church. Paul counters such fforts by mentioning "all the brothers with e" (1:2). The word "brothers" probably efers to Paul's coworkers, frequently menoned in his letters (1 Cor. 1:1; 2 Cor. 1:1; Phil. :1; Col. 1:1; 1 Thess. 1:1–2; 2 Thess. 1:1; hilem. 1). Although the expression communicates a masculine meaning in contemporary rgon, it was probably understood in more eneric terms in Paul's day, for Paul also commends female coworkers in his letters (Rom. 6:1–2; Phil. 4:2–3). At any rate, the menoning of "brothers" evidences a solidarity vith Paul that stands over against the Judaizrs (Ridderbos, 1957, 41). He is not alone in is belief that God justifies by faith, apart from e works of the law.

"To the churches of Galatia" indicates that his letter was a circular letter. After it was read n one church, it would be passed on to the next ntil it reached the churches of an entire region.

The most revealing point is that Paul ncludes no thanksgiving for the saints as he oes in his other letters (cf. Rom. 1:8; 1 Cor. :4; Phil. 1:3). This terse, thankless introducion shows how tense the relationship is etween Paul and the Galatians. Nevertheless, e still addresses them as "churches." Despite neir difficulties and the threat of the Judaizers, ne Galatians are still part of the body of Christ. They have not yet committed apostasy.

Paul appears to be combining Greco-Roman and Hebrew forms of greeting in 1:3. The Greeks and Romans greeted one another vith *charein*. This meant something like 'health and well-being to you." But Paul has illed this secular greeting with Christian conent. In Pauline theology, "grace" serves as an umbrella term encompassing all the goodness of God that is preeminently seen in the person and work of Jesus Christ. "Peace" comes from he Hebrew *shalom* and designates that sense of total well-being that can only come from a ight relationship with God. Hence the source of these blessings is "from God our Father and the Lord Jesus Christ" (cf. 2 Cor. 1:2–4; 9:8). Again, the divinity of Christ is in evidence here. Just like the Father, Jesus serves as the source of divine grace and peace.

The complete sufficiency of Christ—surely the crux of the issue in Galatians—is expressed in 1:4: Jesus "gave himself for our sins." The Judaizers argued that the death of Jesus is not sufficient to save us. One must believe in Jesus *plus* circumcision (5:6; 6:15). One must believe in Christ *plus* works of the law (2:16). Paul categorically denies such a theology, if one can call it that. There is no room for self-made "righteousness," which the Old Testament itself describes as "filthy rags" (Isa. 64:6). He counters this false teaching with atonement language that probably originated with the Lord himself (cf. Mark 10:45). Jesus is the all-sufficient atonement, fulfilling all the sacrificial requirements of the Old Testament (cf. Isa. 53:5, 12; Rom. 3:25–26; 4:25). Jesus is the only source of the true righteousness and forgiveness of sins (Gal. 2:20–21; 3:1, 13; 4:4; 5:1, 11, 24; 6:12, 14).

Once again, the cross of Christ is viewed as the end-time event. The atonement of Christ does not simply forgive us of our sins, but also delivers us "from the present evil age." This age is dominated by the "god of this world" (2 Cor. 4:4; 1 Cor. 2:6; Eph. 2:2) and is condemned already (John 3:18). But the deliverance of the saints starts even now (Gal. 5:1). Because of the cross of Christ and the indwelling of the Holy Spirit, the spiritual freedom of the last day is brought into the present experience of the believer. This is "walking in the Spirit" (5:5). As Bruce so aptly states,

> The indwelling Spirit not only helps them to look forward in confidence to the life of the age to come (cf. 5:5); he enables them to enjoy it even while in the mortal body they live in the present age. Thanks to the work of the Spirit, applying to believers the redemption and victory won by Christ, the "not yet" has become for them the "already" (Bruce, 1982, 76).

Paul's words clearly point out the ethical distinction that exists between the two ages. The cross brings forth the "new creation" of the end time (6:15). New birth can never be accomplished by the law, which Paul indicates belongs to this evil age. The law is simply another example of the "basic principles" (*stoicheia*) of this world that only lead to bondage (4:3, 9). But the Spirit, the promise of Abraham, enables the believer to live the resurrected life (3:6; 4:5, 28–29; cf. Rom. 4:18–21).

Paul is careful to add that the saving work of Christ was done "according to the will of our God and Father." He makes several important points here. (1) He is claiming that God himself designed the plan of redemption in Jesus Christ. (2) He acknowledges the preeminence of the Father in the divine plan. Although he has repeatedly represented Jesus as equal with the Father, ultimately the Son submits everything to the Father (1 Cor. 15:20–28). (3) He has included the Galatians in the family of God. Again, the Judaizers were arguing that in order to be a child of God, one first had to become a child of Abraham (Gal. 3:6–9, 18; 4:22). For this reason, Paul manages to mention "the Father" in three of the first five verses of Galatians. The Spirit himself testifies in their hearts that they are the children of God (4:6–7).

Because of the grace of God in Christ, Paul closes his greeting with words of praise (1:5). In none of his other letters does he include words of praise in the greeting. Some argue that Paul inserts these words in the place where he normally expresses thanks. On the other hand, he may be protecting himself against the faultfinding scrutiny of the Judaizers. Paul knows that orthodox Jews habitually follow the divine name with the *berakhah* (traditional Jewish blessing). By including words of praise at this point, he too expresses his reverence for the Father.

1.2. Paul's Central Point: Only One Gospel (1:6–10)

Galatians is perhaps the most "human" of Paul's letters. Because of the critical situation in Galatia, he bares his soul here. His emotions and spirit pour forth on every page. In other words, in defending the gospel, Paul also reveals his personality and character.

The body of this letter opens with shock and outrage that the Galatians are "so quickly" deserting the one who called them (1:6). The words "so quickly" support an early dating of the letter as set forth in the introduction. Shortly after the founding of the Galatian churches, Judaizers had infiltrated their ran
and sought to seduce them away from Chris

The Greek word for "deserting" (*met*
tithemi) was used in classical Greek to descri
both a change of political views and deserti
one's commanding officer in battle. This latt
image characterizes the believers in Galati
Paul does not portray the Galatians as innoce
victims, being drawn away against their wil
Rather, he clearly states that they are active
deciding to abandon the one who called the
Paul points to the Judaizers as starting the tro
ble, but squarely places the blame on the Gal
tians for cooperating with their heresy. An
they are *still* cooperating, as the present tens
of the verb "deserting" shows.

Paul's indignation is not primarily due t
their rejection of him. Indeed, the crisis i
Galatia is not about allegiance to his apostoli
leadership per se (Duncan, 1966, 16–17). Aft
all, he is not the one who called them by th
grace of Christ. Only God can issue the effe
tual call to salvation (1 Cor. 1:9). No one kne
this better than the apostle himself (1:15). S
in a fundamental sense, the Galatians ar
deserting God, leaving the only true God wh
calls by grace in Christ. Thus for Paul, grace i
both the means by which God works and th
place to which they are called (Rom. 5:2; 6:14
11:6; Eph. 2:5, 8). To turn to a god who call
them to legalism and enslavement to the law i
to turn to a false god. The Galatians are in dan
ger of falling from grace. They are on the verg
of eternal perdition.

Of course, a distorted view of God in
evitably takes on doctrinal expression. In turn
ing *from* God the Galatians have turned *t*
"another gospel," though Paul quickly adds
"which is not another" (1:7, KJV). The appar
ent contradiction in Paul's statement is clari
fied by the special vocabulary he uses. Th
word for "another" in verse 6 is *heteron* an
refers to something that is qualitatively differ
ent. One would use *heteron* to describe the dif
ference between an apple and another fruit
like an orange. But the word for "another" i
verse 7 is *allon*, which refers to something tha
is quantitatively different. One would use *allo*
to describe the difference between two apples

In other words, Paul is not rejecting
gospel that is simply in another form fro
what he preached. James, Peter, and Joh
packaged their message differently from Paul

ut it was still the gospel of grace. No, Paul is ejecting a message that was essentially different in content from what he preached to the ialatians (Lightfoot, 1957, 77). The message f the Judaizers had a different content from ne gospel of grace; it is "really no gospel at ll" (NIV). That is why Paul can say that the nes (note the plural) troubling the Galatians vere trying "to pervert the gospel" into somehing else (1:7). They were consciously twisting its message, changing it into a system of vorks-righteousness. Again, the verbs "throwng" and "trying" are in the present tense, vhich indicates that the Judaizers are at work ven as Paul writes the letter.

The intensity of Paul's spirit is evidenced in :8–9. In an effort to reach the Galatians, he esorts to extreme forms of expression. He creates what might be called "a worst case scenario" and follows it up by pronouncing a louble curse on anyone preaching a false mesage in Galatia. To make sure he addresses very conceivable possibility, Paul uses what grammarians call a "denied condition" or a 'contrary-to-fact condition." In a hypothetical vay, he exhorts the Galatians to consider the ollowing possibilities. *If* the orthodox leadership of the church, which includes Paul and his colleagues, or if even an angel from heaven, should come and preach a message contrary to what was first delivered in Galatia, let such a one be condemned to hell!

The word translated "eternally condemned" in verses 8 and 9 is *anathema*. This word is used throughout the Greek translation of the Hebrew Scriptures (the LXX or Septuagint) to translate *herem*—a Hebrew word referring to someone or something that was to be destroyed by God. For example, when Israel entered the Promised Land to destroy the heathen, they viewed their mission in terms of *herem*. Anything that was to be the object of divine wrath and vengeance was *herem*. Paul's point is clear. Anyone or anything that preaches a gospel different from what was originally preached in Galatia is to be eternally condemned.

The inclusion of an "angel from heaven" may be more than a rhetorical device. An ancient Hebrew tradition held that God used angels to communicate the law to Moses on Sinai (cf. 3:19–20). The Judaizers may have referred to this tradition in an effort to win the Galatians over to the law. Therefore, Paul warns that even if one of these angels should come and preach contrary to the gospel of grace, it should be condemned to hell.

The situation in Galatia is so serious that Paul leaves no room for error or misunderstanding. He does not want the Galatians to miss this point, so he repeats it in verse 9. The introductory words "as we have already said" may refer to a previous warning Paul delivered while in Galatia. He was aware of and feared the corrupting influence of the Judaizers at an early stage in his ministry. Thus Paul pronounces a twofold curse on them, calling the unmixed wrath of God down on them.

Paul's aggressive attack on the troublemakers brings to mind one of their charges against him. The Judaizers have slandered Paul as a "man-pleaser," painting him as someone who was willing to compromise the requirements of the law to curry the favor of the Gentiles. They claimed that the reason Paul did not require the Gentiles to be circumcised or submit to the law of Moses was so that he might gain more converts for himself.

The basis for this accusation is unclear. The Judaizers may have viewed Paul's willingness to accommodate various ethnic groups for the sake of the gospel as pandering to the masses (1 Cor. 9:19–23). After all, did he not have Timothy circumcised in Lystra (Acts 16:1–3), but then refused to have Titus circumcised in Jerusalem (Gal. 2:1–5)? Is this not evidence that Paul was a hypocrite, operating on the basis of human standards rather than submitting to God?

Paul counters such charges by asking the rhetorical question, "Am I now trying to win the approval of men, or of God?" (1:10). The way in which this question is phrased calls for a negative answer. That is, considering his battle with the Judaizers and the scandalous message of the cross he preaches (5:11; 6:12; cf. 1 Cor. 1:20–25), does it appear that Paul is "trying to win the approval of men" and not God? Of course not!

The final statement in verse 10 sounds as if Paul admits he was a "man-pleaser" at one time, for he states, "If I were *still* trying to please men." But this is not the case now. Paul again employs a "contrary-to-fact condition" to get his point across: *If* he were still trying to please men (which in reality he is not), *then* he would not be a servant of Christ—but he is in fact a *doulos* ("slave") of Christ, committed to the will of his Master (Rom. 1:1).

Paul's accommodation of the various people groups represents his missionary strategy. Indeed, this was why Timothy was circumcised. Since his mother was Jewish and his father Gentile (Acts 16:1), Timothy could not effectively minister in either culture. His circumcision "normalized" him with respect to the Jewish world, giving him greater opportunities to evangelize; it had nothing to do with his salvation. The situation with Titus was different, however. Both of his parents were Gentiles (2:3). Yet the Judaizers were insisting that he be circumcised *in order to be saved*. Paul refused to yield to their pressure (2:5). In all of this, he never compromised the content of the gospel. For Jew and Gentile the only way of salvation was by grace through faith.

We can gather from this section that Paul exercised mature Christian love in dealing with the Galatians. He cared enough to confront them when they strayed from the truth of the gospel. The church today is in desperate need of this kind of love. It is a love that is not self-centered, but has a genuine interest in the welfare and spiritual development of others. It is a love that is more concerned with the spiritual quality of church members than with the numerical quantity of church membership.

2. Paul's Autobiographical Argument (1:11–2:14)

Paul's knowledge of Greek rhetoric is in evidence here. A trained public speaker would begin his address by giving an extended exhortation, which would then be followed by some type of meaningful narrative. In 1:1–10 Paul has exhorted the Galatians not to forsake the one who called them and to remain faithful to the true gospel. Those who preach a false gospel are to be condemned to hell. Beginning with verse 11, Paul relates the story of his own conversion and calling. The purpose of this autobiographical section is to further validate his gospel by relating the supernatural means by which it was communicated to him.

2.1. Paul's Gospel and Calling Are From God (1:11–17)

The opening words of verse 11, "I want you to know, brothers," probably do not mean that Paul is sharing new information with the Galatians. It is unlikely that he founded the churches of Galatia without telling them about how he received the gospel. Rather, these words are simply a literary device Paul uses to remind the Galatians of what they once knew. Their actions indicate that they have forgotten what Paul shared with them in the beginning, and he wants them to recall that the gospel he proclaimed to them did not originate with any human being. The Judaizers were probably spreading the rumor that Paul's doctrine of justification by faith, apart from works of the law, was contrived by Paul himself; his gospel was not a divine message. They portrayed Paul as an inventor of religion.

Paul counters this charge through the special use of Greek grammar. The Greek word used for "by" is *hypo*, and in this context communicates "agency" or "means." In other words, his gospel did not come to him by any human agency or means (see v. 12). He did not "receive" the gospel from any human being. Here Paul employs the language of Jewish oral tradition. The word for "receive" (*paralambano*) was used by the Jews to describe the passing on of religious tradition. Paul rejects therefore the notion that his gospel is simply a link in a long chain of religious teachings. As honorable as this might be, he was not just a custodian of sacred beliefs and creeds.

In this sense Paul was different from his Galatian converts. They received the gospel through him; he, on the other hand, received the gospel through no person, nor did anyone teach it to him. Again the mischief of the Judaizers is in evidence here. They no doubt argued that everything Paul knew about the gospel he learned from those who had a more immediate relationship to Jesus. And everyone knows that the teacher is superior to the one taught (Matt. 10:24; Luke 6:40). Paul denies dependence upon any human teacher. On the contrary, he received the gospel through divine "revelation."

With these words Paul reflects the ancient belief that truth cannot primarily be received through teaching, but through supernatural revelation (Betz, 1979, 62). He himself received the gospel through the revelation "of Jesus Christ." The meaning of the words "the revelation of Jesus Christ" is open to interpretation. Does Paul mean that Jesus Christ was *ie origin* of the revelation to him, or does he nean that Jesus Christ was *the content* of the evelation? Actually, Paul may have both ideas n mind. Galatians 1:15–16 states that it leased God to reveal his Son in Paul so that e might preach the gospel among the Gentiles. If Paul is referring to his Damascus road xperience in these verses (and it seems likely iat he is), it was the risen Christ who first confronted him for the gospel (Acts 9:1–16; 22:1–6; 26:9–18). Jesus was not only the source of ne revelation to Paul, but he also formed the ontent of the gospel.

Paul's lack of dependence on church tradi-on seems to contradict what he says elsewhere. n 1 Corinthians 11:23–26 and 15:3–8, Paul learly indicates, using typical Jewish terminology for the reception and passing on of religious tradition, that he has received the raditions of the Lord's Supper and the resur-ection from those who were in the Lord before im. He even praises the Corinthians for holding fast to the traditions that he passed on to hem (11:2). Furthermore, there are many places n Paul's writings that indicate his use of early hurch traditions (cf. Phil. 2:5–11; 1 Thess. 4:1–, 15–17; 1 Tim. 3:16; 4:8–10; 2 Tim. 2:11–13). Iow then can he claim sole dependence on ivine revelation in Gal. 1:11–12?

In answering this question we must make he distinction between the essence of the ospel message and the many stories and vents that communicate that message. No uman being communicated to Paul the core nessage that we are justified by faith apart rom works of the law. No human being taught im that both Jews and Gentiles are equal in God's sight and are accepted by him on the asis of faith in Christ. But this does not mean hat he did not learn various Christian beliefs nd practices from those who were converted efore him. Therefore, his gospel and calling ame through divine revelation, yet he espected the teachings that had been formu-ated from the very beginning of the church.

To support his claim to direct revelation, Paul ecounts his persecution of the church (1:13–4). The connection between his persecution of he church and his claim to divine revelation is ot immediately apparent. But his strategy eems twofold. He first reminds them of what hey have heard in the past. Then he uses the ery words of his enemies to further his aims.

Paul reminds the Galatians that they have heard of his "previous way of life." He does not speak of his "former faith" or "former religion." Rather, he represents Judaism as a way of approaching life. Paul does not view his former life in Judaism as praiseworthy. He never sought to hide the dark beginning he had in the church. He frequently related his persecution of the church when sharing how he came to Christ (Acts 22:1–21; 26:4–18; 1 Cor. 15:8–10). In so doing here, Paul accomplishes at least four things

(1) By stressing his deplorable conduct prior to his conversion, Paul magnifies the grace of God in his life. Only the sheer grace of God could turn such a violent killer into an obedient servant of the gospel.
(2) He demonstrates that religious zeal does not necessarily lead to godliness. In fact the opposite is often the case (Phil. 3:6).
(3) His enemies did not miss the opportunity to dredge up the dark past of the apostle Paul. They suggested that his murderous persecution of the church is simply indicative of his character. Paul was a violent man, whose words were not to be trusted. They reasoned that his "gospel" was just a product of his flawed character. By getting his past out in the open, Paul has once again cut the ground from beneath his opponents.
(4) Finally, Paul's persecution of the church demonstrates that he was not a "seeker" as far as Christianity was concerned. He was not dissatisfied with his life in Judaism and was not a willing convert to Christianity (Acts 26:9). Thus, his calling and conversion could have only come through the miraculous intervention of God.

Paul admits that he persecuted the church "intensely," beyond what one would reasonably expect. In fact, his goal was "to destroy" the church—to rid the earth of all believers (Acts 9:1–2).

In verse 14 Paul emphasizes his outstanding performance in Judaism (cf. 2 Cor. 11:22; Phil. 3:5–6). He was at the "head of the class," advancing beyond many of his contemporaries in Judaism. His total commitment is seen in his zeal for the "traditions of my fathers" (i.e., the oral teachings of the Pharisees, which they claimed originated with Moses; Matt. 15:2–6; Mark 7:5–13). Paul probably learned these traditions while studying at the feet of Gamaliel (Acts 22:3). Thus Paul was not content with keeping the 613 commands of the Old Testament, but sought to follow the innumerable religious precepts of his ancestors. Any charge that Paul was soft on circumcision because he was never really dedicated to the law is without foundation.

Paul uses the word "zealous" to describe his dedication to these ancestral traditions (cf. also Phil. 3:6). This word is derived from the Greek word *zeloo* and means "to boil." It clearly describes the white-hot intensity of Paul's commitment to Pharisaic Judaism. This special use of "zeal," however, had a long history in Jewish religious tradition. It is traceable to Judas Maccabeus and most notably associated with the "Zealots" (Bruce, 1982, 91). The latter were committed to "the sole rule of God" and did not hesitate to use violent means to further their religious and political ends. Indeed for the fervent Jew, there was no higher virtue than zeal for Yahweh. The zeal of Phinehas, for example, led him to slaughter a Hebrew man who defiled Israel by sleeping with a Midianite woman (Num. 25:6–13). A psalmist praises Phinehas for this deed and says that his murderous zeal *was counted as righteousness* before God (Ps. 106:30–31).

Could it be that Paul was modeling the zeal of Phinehas in his persecuting the church? Did he believe that his violent action against the church would be counted as righteousness before God? And did his Damascus road experience convince him that there is a zeal that is not according to knowledge (Rom. 10:2)? Regardless of how we might answer these questions, one thing is clear: Paul no longer associates the crediting of righteousness with misguided zeal. He now realizes that the faith of Abraham is that which justifies one in the sight of God (Gen. 15:6).

In verse 15 Paul relates his calling in terms reminiscent of the Old Testament prophets (Isa. 49:1–6; Jer. 1:5). His conversion was not simply one among many in the church. No, his coming to faith was an important part of God's plan for the ages. As Paul relates, it pleased God to separate him from his mother's womb for the purpose of the gospel. The phrase "set me apart from my mother's womb" (cf. NIV note) recalls the sovereign hand of God in the lives of great men of faith (Judg. 13:5; Pss 22:10; 58:3; 71:6). Therefore, even before he was born, Paul believes that God had predestined him to be the apostle to the Gentiles. Paul's point is that his calling is totally the work of God.

The word for "set apart" in 1:15 reflects the Hebrew root *parash* (from which the word "Pharisee" comes). The Pharisees prided themselves in being the "separated ones," that is, the people really consecrated to God. It is as if Paul is saying that even though he was a Pharisee (Phil. 3:5), he was never really set apart for the true work of God until he became a Christian. For Paul, God worked in two distinct phases in his life: (1) In the eternal wisdom of God he was separated for kingdom work; (2) he was called to be an apostle to the Gentiles.

Undoubtedly Paul had extraordinary insight into the special role he was to play in God's plan of salvation. Yet the most important point here is not the role itself, but how that role came about. His calling and mission was completely due to the grace of God. Furthermore he received this special role through divine revelation (1:16). The word "reveal" must be associated with the word "pleased" in 1:15. In other words, it *pleased* God *to reveal* his Son to the apostle Paul—a reference to his Damascus road experience.

There has been much debate about the meaning of the words "in me." Does the word "in" refer to location? That is, is Paul saying that he received an internal revelation of Christ in his spirit? Or should these words be rendered "to me," in which case Paul is describing an objective revelation of Christ that existed externally? Or should these words be interpreted as meaning "by me," so that Paul is the instrument or means by which Christ was revealed to others? In some sense all three interpretations are valid, but "to me" harmonizes best with other records of Paul's conversion (Acts 9:1–19; 22:6–18; 1 Cor. 9:1; 15:8). Moreover, the description of an objective external revelation coincides with the prophetic call Paul expressed in 1:15 (cf. Isa. 6:1–9; Ezek. 1:4–3:11).

The revelation of Christ had a profound transforming effect upon the mind and spirit of Paul. It meant that he had been terribly wrong in persecuting Christians and in rejecting Jesus the Messiah. But perhaps most importantly, meant that he was fundamentally wrong in ecting *that understanding of God* portrayed Jesus and the early Christians. Jesus' accepice of the outcasts and sinners in the name God and the early Christian Hellenists' ceptance of Gentiles meant that God desired lowship with the ungodly (Matt. 11:19–24; ike 7:34–50; Acts 11:19–20; Rom. 4:5).

Paul perceived that his theology was essenilly wrong "from the ground up." As noted, s was especially true with regard to the law. s zeal for the law had actually led him to pose God and his people. That which he ought would bring him righteousness and e only brought sin and death (Rom. 7:9–11). ich a profound experience naturally carried ighty consequences. Herein lies the value of erpreting "in me" as "by me." Paul realized at he had to share such an extraordinary sion of God with others and that he would be e primary instrument for actualizing this sion in the world. Hence Paul indicates that e revelation of Christ on the Damascus road is for a specific purpose—*so that* he might reach [Christ] among the Gentiles."

The theme of independence is picked up ain in verses 16b–17. Upon receiving the sion Paul did not confer immediately with ny man," and specifically did not seek counl with the Jerusalem apostles. Rather, he ent into Arabia and then on to Damascus.

Paul's account seems to conflict with ike's record in Acts, which records no trip to rabia but indicates that immediately after his nversion Paul went into Damascus. After ing baptized by Ananias and receiving his ght, he began to preach in the synagogues ere (Acts 9:8–20). Yet Paul's use of the word nmediately" in Galatians 1:16 suggests that ere was no intervening period between his nversion and his journey into Arabia.

In resolving this apparent conflict, the eaning of "Arabia" plays a crucial role. The iditional interpretation is that it refers to the nai peninsula. Those who hold this interpretion believe that immediately after his conrsion, Paul went into the Sinai desert for a riod of quiet contemplation, in order to sort it the weighty implications of his Damascus ad experience. In support it is noted that loses received the law on Mount Sinai and at Elijah too communed with God there. Paul, then, is following in the tradition of these prophets, spending three years after his conversion communing with God in the desert.

As plausible as this interpretation might seem, it is fraught with difficulties. As noted, Luke has Paul going directly to Damascus after his conversion. It is unlikely that Luke would have omitted a three-year period in Paul's life. Also, Paul has been careful in giving an accurate account of the early years of his ministry. If he did go directly to Damascus and not into the Sinai desert, his opponents would surely note this discrepancy. So more than likely the word "Arabia" is being used in a broader sense than the Sinai desert. It could also refer to the kingdom of the Nabateans, Damascus being the principal city. Note Paul's words in 2 Corinthians 11:32–33, where he states that the governor of King Aretas sought to capture him in Damascus. He evaded capture by being lowered over a wall in a basket. This means that immediately after his conversion Paul began evangelizing throughout the *kingdom* of Arabia. This interpretation preserves the harmony between Luke's account in Acts and Paul's own words in Galatians.

2.2. Paul's Independence From Jerusalem (1:18–24)

Paul's opponents claim that their authority came from Jerusalem (2:4–5, 11–14; 4:25–26). By not going there Paul demonstrates that his calling and apostleship are independent of the highest authority in the church. Even though the Judaizers have appealed to earthly authorities, Paul claims the highest recommendation, that is, God. Because he received his gospel and calling through divine revelation, he had no need "to go to school" in Jerusalem. Herein lies the purpose of the phrase, "then after three years, I went up to Jerusalem" (1:18). His absence from Jerusalem shows that Paul felt no need to inquire of the other apostles. Exactly how the three years should be reckoned, however, is open to interpretation. Is Paul speaking of three years after his return from Damascus or three years after his conversion? If reckoned from the time he returned to Damascus, it would have been more than three years since Paul had been in Jerusalem.

When Paul went to Jerusalem, he wanted to talk with Peter. Peter plays a prominent role in

Galatians and in the history of the early church. He was one of the "pillar" apostles (2:9). He had been acknowledged as the "apostle to the Jews" (2:7–8). And he was the apostle whom Paul confronted in Antioch (2:11–14). The Gospels and Acts likewise acknowledge the prominent role of Peter. It was the Lord who gave him the Aramaic name "Cephas" (the Greek being "*Petros*"), meaning a "rock" or "stone" (Matt. 16:16–19). Peter was numbered among the inner circle of the Lord (Matt. 17:1; 26:37; Mark 5:37; 9:2; Luke 8:51; 9:28). He may have been one of the first apostles to see the resurrected Lord (Luke 24:34; 1 Cor. 15:5) and appears to have been the first leader of the church in Jerusalem (Gal. 1:18; Acts 1:15). So Paul's mention of his meeting with Peter is very important.

Why did Paul meet with Peter? The word translated "to see" or "inquire" (*historeo*) originally meant to inquire into or to learn something by inquiry (cf. our word "history"). In time, however, this word meant to visit someone for the purpose of getting more acquainted. So did Paul visit Peter for the purpose of gaining information about the gospel, or did he simply want to get better acquainted with the apostle to the Jews? It is unlikely that Paul sought information about the essential message of the gospel. If he had, his entire argument about being independent from the Jerusalem apostles would have been called into question. At the same time it is difficult to believe that these two great apostles did not talk about the faith and matters concerning the church.

In other words, Paul's visit with Peter accomplished both elements. He got to know Peter better and probably gained information about certain church traditions, such as the Lord's Supper, the resurrection, and Christian baptism. But Peter did not teach him the content and meaning of the gospel, for Paul had already been preaching that for at least three years. His emphasis that he visited for only "fifteen days" supports this interpretation. He was not present long enough to have been schooled by Peter, as his opponents were claiming.

Paul's care in relating the facts can also be seen in verse 19. After stating that he saw none of the other apostles, he recalls that he did see James, the brother of the Lord. Paul's mention of James in conjunction with the other apostles raises the question: Does Paul view James a an apostle, or does he mean that he saw n other apostles but did see another significa person in the church? It seems that Paul did n restrict the meaning of "apostle" to the Twel (cf. 1 Cor. 15:5–7). So Paul probably consi ers James to be an apostle in that he had see the risen Lord. Nevertheless, the apostol authority of James is not the central issue her Paul wants the Galatians to know that h meeting with James was of no material signi icance. He mentions James because he alo with Peter is viewed as being important to th Judaizers.

The intensity of Paul's spirit is evident verse 20. He swears before the Lord that he not lying. In typical Hebrew fashion h solemnly affirms "before [the face of] Go that what he has written is the truth. The ser ousness of the oath indicates that oth accounts concerning Paul's early years in th church have been circulating and have reache the Galatians.

Paul's words in verse 21 coincide with Ac 9:26–30. In order to escape the murdero intent of the Hellenistic Jews of Jerusale Paul fled to the coasts of Tarsus via Caesar (9:30). His point is that soon after his brief vi with Peter, he distanced himself from th Jerusalem apostles. There was no time for hi to receive any extensive tutoring from them

There seems to be another discrepan between what Paul says in 1:22 and Luke record in Acts. In Galatians Paul claims th the churches of Judea did not know him "pe sonally." How could Paul have persecut Christians in Jerusalem yet remained unknow to them (Acts 8:3; 9:26–31)? It is possible th the majority of Christians who had fled fro Jerusalem as a result of the persecution Stephen had not yet returned there. Those wh escaped the persecution would not have know what Paul looked like. Also, Paul may ha simply coordinated the persecution, using ot ers to actually apprehend the believers. In th way he would not have been recognizable the church in Jerusalem. In any case, the Chri tians in Jerusalem did not know him as believer, only as a persecutor.

The news of Paul's conversion quick spread abroad in the church. The grammar verses 23–24 indicates that the churches Judea kept on hearing the same report: The o

ʼho once persecuted them was now preaching ɪe faith that he once tried to destroy. It is interːsting that the phrase "the faith" stands for "the ospel." This testifies to the centrality of faith ɪ the early church. There is no indication that ɪe churches of Judea questioned Paul's reaching of the gospel. They apparently nderstood that what he preached was the ame as what they believed. This is a powerful ɪessage directed to the Judaizers. From the ery beginning the churches of Judea accepted is preaching of "the faith" and praised God ecause of it.

Paul has built a powerful argument against is accusers. His experience in the Lord and is initial years of ministry authenticate his alling and gospel. He was not taught the ospel by other people nor was he commisioned by the leadership of the church. It was iod who called him and revealed his Son in im. Thus he had no need to consult with anyne and immediately began preaching the ospel throughout Palestine, Syria, and Cilicia. Ie had minimal contact with the church in erusalem and its leadership.

Now that Paul has established his indepenence from the mother church, he changes the ature of his argument. He is independent, but e is not a maverick. He must now go on to how that although he does not require the ffirmation of the Jerusalem apostles, he nevrtheless has been accepted by them. And erein lies the personal lesson for each of us ʼho have been called of the Lord. (1) Our tesmony has power only to the degree that it elates to the rest of the body of Christ. (2) Our ersonal vision of Christ must correspond to ɪe corporate understanding of the church. 3) Finally, our interpretation of Scripture must e in harmony with those of genuine faith and ntegrity (2 Peter 1:20). If these principles old, then our calling and ministry will be both nique and common at the same time.

2.3. Paul's Gospel Is Affirmed by the Jerusalem Apostles (2:1–10)

For the third time Paul uses the word "then" cf. 1:18, 21). He is clearly relating a chronoogical series of events, being careful not to eave out anything. He must not give his adveraries any opportunity to discredit his testiɪony. So 2:1–10 describes the next visit Paul ɪade to Jerusalem. This would have been some fourteen years after his meeting with Peter and James in 1:18–20 (see 2:1). Once again we must ask whether Paul is figuring this visit from the time of his conversion or from the time of his last visit to Jerusalem? Since he is emphasizing his infrequent contact with Jerusalem, the fourteen years may be reckoned from the time of his last visit. If this is true, then his second trip to Jerusalem took place some seventeen years after his conversion, considering that he had already spent three years in Arabia (1:17–18).

A central issue here is whether the meeting described in 2:1–10 is the so-called "Jerusalem Council" of Acts 15 or the "Famine Visit" of Acts 11:27–30? If we opt for the former, then we must assume that the "false brothers" of Galatians 2:4 are the same men who came to Antioch in Acts 15:1. These men would belong to the "sect of the Pharisees" (15:5), who explicitly demanded that the Gentiles be circumcised and obey the law of Moses. Their Judaizing campaign was overturned by the council, and James issued a written decree informing the churches of their decision (15:23–29).

However, identifying Galatians 2:1–10 with Acts 15 creates more problems than it solves.

- In Galatians Paul says he went up to Jerusalem "in response to a revelation" (2:2), while in Acts the church in Antioch sent Paul and Barnabas to Jerusalem (Acts 15:2).
- In Galatians Paul clearly states that his meeting with the Jerusalem apostles was done in private (Gal. 2:2), but the conference of Acts 15 was conducted in public.
- In Galatians Paul simply states that he presented his gospel to the apostles and that Titus was not compelled to be circumcised (Gal. 2:3). He does not say that circumcision was the main reason the meeting was called, as is so evident from the Acts account.
- Also, Galatians 2 says nothing about the specific guidelines set forth in Acts 15:20–21, 29. Conversely, remembering the poor is referred to in Galatians 2:10, but not in the Acts account.
- Finally, if Galatians 2:1–10 is the same meeting as Acts 15, why did not Paul simply refer to the written decree of James to settle the matter when dealing with the Judaizers in Galatia?

For these reasons and others that will be discussed below, I conclude that the meeting in Galatians 2:1–10 is not the Jerusalem Council of Acts 15. Rather, it is likely a meeting Paul had during the "Famine Visit" of Acts 11:27–30.

Although Paul was motivated by divine revelation, he also has his feet firmly planted on the ground. He is a shrewd strategist, who understands the motives and devices of people. For example, Paul anticipates opposition in Jerusalem and thus takes Barnabas and Titus along with him (2:1). He has chosen these delegates because they represent the scope of his ministry. With regard to the gospel, Paul is comfortable with circumcised Jewish Christians like Barnabas. But he is also able to have fellowship with uncircumcised Gentile Christians like Titus. And most importantly, both Barnabas and Titus fully affirm Paul and his gospel.

Barnabas figures prominently in the life of Paul and the early church (Acts 4:36–37). It was he who first introduced Paul to the church and accompanied him on his first missionary journey (Acts 9:27; 11:22–25; 13:1–14:28). Also the mentioning of Barnabas in Galatians 2:1, without any qualification or introduction, indicates that he was well known to the Galatians. Finally, the Judaizers would not forget to tell the Galatians that Barnabas sided with Peter in Antioch when the latter separated himself from the Gentiles (2:11–14).

Titus, being less prominent than Barnabas, was probably taken along to assist in the journey (Acts 12:25; 15:37–41). He was an important coworker of Paul (2 Cor. 2:13; 7:6). However, as an uncircumcised Gentile, Titus could serve as a "test case" for Paul's law-free mission to the Gentiles. If he was not required to be circumcised by the Jerusalem apostles, then no Gentile could be forced to be circumcised in the church.

Paul does not say that "we" went up to Jerusalem, but that *he* took Barnabas along with him. This means that Paul deliberately took the initiative to have these persons accompany him on this visit. Thus, if the Galatians had any questions about the meeting in Jerusalem, they could refer to Barnabas and Titus.

Paul says that he went up "in response to a revelation." Once again he stresses the importance of supernatural revelation in his life and ministry (1:12, 16). Paul's point is that in making this trip, he was being obedient to the revealed will of God. His submission to that will stands in stark contrast to what his enemies shared with the Galatians. They probably said that Paul had been "called on the carpet" by the Jerusalem apostles and had to answer for his ministry in Galatia. Therefore Paul states that in making the trip, he was inspired by God, not intimidated by human beings.

Paul does not share the content of the revelation, so we do not know why the Lord directed him to go to Jerusalem. Yet we can be sure that *Paul did not go to Jerusalem because he doubted the validity of his calling and message*. Although more will be said below, his motive seems to have been more pragmatic than theological. If the Jerusalem apostles failed to see what God was doing through Paul, then his efforts would have been greatly complicated. On the other hand, if they had the spiritual discernment to recognize God's grace in his life, his work among the Gentiles would have been helped.

In Jerusalem, Paul did not submit his gospel to the scrutiny of the masses. Perceiving that a public debate might yield more problems than solutions, he chose to present his gospel in a private setting (2:2). Particularly, he presented his gospel "to those who seemed to be leaders" (a phrase used twice in v. 6 and again in v. 9, where "those reputed to be pillars" are specifically identified as James, Peter, and John). To modern ears, Paul's description of the Jerusalem apostles seems negative and a bit sarcastic. Yet his goal is not to depreciate the status of James, Peter, and John. He is simply relating the estimation of these persons *from the perspective of the Jerusalem church* (Verseput, 1993, 49). Although Paul acknowledges their authority, he does not accept the inordinate veneration that the Judaizers afforded them (2:6).

Paul uses an athletic motif when expressing the concerns he had at the meeting (cf. also 1 Cor. 9:25–27; Phil. 3:12–14). The imagery is of a long-distance runner who has given everything he has to the race, only to be disqualified by some technicality. Paul feared that all of his efforts might be undermined by issues that had nothing to do with the gospel itself, such as circumcision and dietary laws.

f the leadership erred in imposing such things n the Gentiles, Paul would no doubt have ontinued his work and preached the same nessage. But his efforts would have been reatly frustrated.

In verse 3 Paul returns to the subject of Titus. His "test case" worked: Titus was not 'compelled to be circumcised." How should ve interpret "compelled"? Does it mean that ircumcision was not even mentioned at the neeting, and that is why Titus was not forced o undergo the ritual? If this was the case, then Paul could have understood the silence of ames, Peter, and John as an implicit endorsement of his law-free gospel to the Gentiles Bruce, 1982, 106ff.). Or do the words "not ompelled" mean that Titus *voluntarily* submitted to circumcision, but was not forced to lo so? Or is Paul stating that the "false brothrs" of 2:4 pressed the circumcision issue, but vere unsuccessful in getting their agenda across? Although more will be said below, the ast option seems most likely. After meeting vith James, Peter, and John, some tried to orce Titus to be circumcised, but Paul and Barnabas (note the "we" in v. 5) successfully esisted their efforts.

Who were these people who sought to have Titus circumcised? The identity of Paul's pponents in Galatians raises many questions. Are they the same persons as we read of in Acts 15:1–5? Do Paul's enemies in Galatians onsider themselves to be Christians, or are ney non-Christian Jews who, motivated by ewish nationalism and politics, seek to influnce the church in Galatia? It is even possible nat Paul's opponents are Gentiles who became roselytes to Judaism prior to accepting Christ. They may have argued that if they had to be ircumcised to be saved, so do the rest of the Galatians. In addition, one might ask whether Paul is addressing one single group or various roups with similar beliefs and intents? In ther words, do the words "some . . . throwing ou into confusion" (1:7), "false brothers" 2:4), "certain men . . . from James" (2:12), the ne "who has bewitched you" (3:1), "those eople who are zealous to win you over" 4:17–18), and "those agitators" (5:12) all efer to the same persons?

We may never know the exact identity of uch persons or groups, but Paul surely views ll of them as enemies of the gospel of grace. In 2:4 he describes them as *pseudadelphoi* (lit., "pseudo-brothers"). Thus Paul does not consider them to be Christians, although his use of the word "brothers" may indicate that the troublemakers viewed themselves as part of the church. At any rate, these false brothers were not members of the local churches in Galatia, for Paul describes them as foreign agents who have infiltrated Galatia with hostile intent.

They are involved in what may be called "spiritual espionage," for the purpose of sabotaging the joyous life in Christ experienced by the Galatians. Their manner of entry is described as *pareisaktos* (a word only used here in the Bible), that is, "secretly smuggled in." This word was used to describe the illegal smuggling of goods and the clandestine entry of spies. Moreover, these false brothers have "infiltrated our ranks to spy on [us]" (2:4). That is, they have come into the churches as if to participate in worship and to affirm the community of faith, but their real intention is to "spy on the freedom [Paul and the Gentiles] have in Christ."

"Freedom" in this context refers to the Spirit-filled life of the new age, which was totally unencumbered by the rituals and regulations so characteristic of the old order. The false brothers planned to destroy their freedom in Christ by "enslaving" the Galatians to the law and circumcision (2:4). Indeed, life in Christ and life under the law are so antithetical that Paul does not hesitate to describe the latter in terms of cruel slave labor.

Yet the plotting of the false brothers failed. Despite their best efforts, they were unable to force their Judaizing agenda on the leadership in Jerusalem. Titus was not compelled to be circumcised (2:3), for Paul and Barnabas did not succumb to their relentless pressure. They resisted the false brothers so that the freedom of the gospel might continually abide toward the Galatians (2:5).

The repetition of the phrase "those who seemed to be important" in verse 6 indicates that Paul is returning to the main argument he started in verse 2. He expands on this description of the Jerusalem apostles by adding, "whatever they were makes no difference to me." Again, it is difficult to avoid the impression that Paul is trying to disparage the role of James, Peter, and John. However, the context warrants against this impression. The Judaizers were seeking to discredit Paul by emphasizing that he was not a disciple of the historical Jesus. They viewed this as a serious shortcoming because the Jerusalem church had decided that an apostle had to have been a follower of Jesus from the days of John the Baptist until the day the Lord ascended into heaven (Acts 1:21–22). Paul himself clearly admitted that this was not his experience (Gal. 1:13). The Judaizers seized upon this open admission and claimed that Paul was no true apostle. To strengthen their power base, they stressed the historical connection that the Jerusalem apostles had with Jesus.

Paul will not allow himself to be drawn into this issue. He could have easily pointed out that James, the present leader of the church in Jerusalem and the half-brother of the Lord, was in fact not a disciple of Jesus during his ministry on earth (Matt. 13:55; Mark 3:21; 6:3; John 7:1–5). But to permit his opponents to divide him from the Jerusalem apostles would be to play right into their hands. He must demonstrate his solidarity with the leadership of the church, for he is an integral part of that leadership.

Thus Paul remains consistent in his approach. He emphasizes that he sees things from God's perspective, not from a human viewpoint. What the apostles were at one time is of no consequence to Paul, for it is of no consequence to God. The possible relationship of the Jerusalem apostles to the historical Jesus is irrelevant to Paul, for God "does not judge by external appearance" (2:6). Unlike the troublemakers in Galatia, God does not play favorites. The personal experiences of James, Peter, and John may have been impressive from a strictly human perspective, but their life before Jesus' ascension granted them no distinct advantage over the apostle Paul. *Everything is of grace*.

Nevertheless, even if one were to accept the inflated estimation of the Judaizers, "those who seemed to be important . . . added nothing to [Paul's] message." The word "added" no doubt refers to the efforts of the Judaizers to add circumcision and ceremonies of the law of Moses to the gospel of grace. In contrast to what the "false brothers" may have been telling the Galatians, the net effect of the meeting in Jerusalem was that Titus was not circumcised, the agenda of the troublemakers was rejected, and James, Peter, and John did not add any requirements to Paul's law-fre gospel to the Gentiles.

Most importantly, the leadership i Jerusalem possessed the spiritual insight tha the Judaizers so clearly lacked. The Jerusale apostles recognized that Paul had bee entrusted to preach the gospel to the unci cumcised Gentiles and that Peter had bee entrusted to preach the gospel to the circum cised (2:7). The wording of verses 7–10 i important because Paul may be relating th exact words of the meeting. His use of the Ara maic name "Cephas" in place of the Hellenize "Peter" indicates as much. Also words like "ci cumcised," "uncircumcised," "entrusted, "worked," and "poor" (cf. RSV) were probabl spoken by James, Peter, and John during th consultation in Jerusalem. Again, the mai point here is that "those who seemed to b important" agreed with Paul that ministry is divine *trust* (2:7) in which *God* works (2:8) b his *grace* (2:9) in those who have been *gifted* i a particular area (2:7–8).

We ought to note the basis for the decisio in Jerusalem. James, Peter, and John did nc arrive at their decision after much deliberatio and argumentation. They simply recognize the supernatural work of God in each of th apostles and understood that this special grac was evidenced in respective fields. It becam evident that Paul was being used to minister t the Gentiles, while Peter was gifted in ministr among the Jews. The word for "worked" in 2: is *energeo* and communicates the idea c "energy" or "dynamic activity." The leadershi in Jerusalem no doubt cited the miraculou activity of God in the lives of Peter and Pau the likes of which is recorded throughout Ac (see Acts 3:1–10; 5:1–10; 13:4–11; 14:8–10 On this basis, they could not deny what Go was doing through these two great men.

But how should we understand the phrase "the uncircumcised" and "the circumcised (RSV)? Do they indicate some kind of ethni division of labor in the ministry? Does thi mean that Paul could *only* evangelize Gentile and that Peter could *only* work among th Jews? Peter's ministry to Cornelius and hi presence in Antioch cast doubt on this inte pretation (Acts 10:1–11:18; Gal. 2:11–15 Also, Paul ministered to Jews throughout th Roman empire (Acts 13:14; 14:1; 17:2). An attempt to divide the ministry into geographi ꞔgions would have been impractical. Jews ɾere spread everywhere, and many Gentiles ved in Israel. Instead, the terms above should e understood in an inclusive rather than in an xclusive sense: Paul was primarily gifted in vangelizing Gentiles, but could also minister ɔ Jews; Peter was most effective with Jews, ut was not prohibited from winning Gentiles.

The central point of this passage is found in erse 9. Those who were viewed as practically arrying the entire church upon their shoulders *styloi* means "pillars" or "columns") gave the right hand of fellowship" to Paul and arnabas. The shaking of hands was an ancient ractice signifying acceptance and agreement. : originally demonstrated that the parties ıvolved carried no concealed weapons and ıat they desired unity and peace (the custom ontinues to this day). We could say that with ꞔgard to Paul's ministry to the Gentiles, "they ıook on it."

Paul is extremely careful not to omit any etails of the meeting. Therefore, he mentions ıe words concerning "the poor" (2:10), who robably refers to the poor saints in Jerusalem Acts 12:25; 24:17; Rom. 15:26). But even ere the Jerusalem apostles added nothing to aul. He and his coworkers were already takıg care of the poor and would continue to do ɔ (1 Cor. 16:1–4; 2 Cor. 8:1–15). In any case, ıe church's care of the poor had nothing to do ʼith how one becomes saved. The leadership ı Jerusalem added no requirements for the ɨentiles.

Paul's words in this section contain many ractical lessons for the minister today. (1) To e spiritual is not to be naive. There were ıany problems in the early church, and Paul ʼas fully aware of them. He developed strateɨes to deal with these problems and knew ʼhere to go to get them resolved. (2) Paul new when to confront and when to cooperte. He confronted the Judaizers because the ıtegrity of the gospel was at stake (2:5), but e fully cooperated with the leadership of the hurch. He acknowledged respective fields of ıinistry and was eager to advance programs or the common good (2:7–10). (3) In sumıary, Paul provides us with a model for grapling with thorny issues in the church. The ıodel is dynamic and multifaceted. It comınes flexibility with firmness and authority ith submission.

2.4. Paul's Confrontation of Peter (2:11–14)

Paul does not want the Galatians to misunderstand the points just made. He clearly welcomes the affirmation of the Jerusalem apostles. Yet he will not compromise the integrity of the gospel to remain in their good graces. It is for this reason that Paul includes his confrontation with Peter in Antioch. His willingness to confront a chief apostle proves that he will not give in to pressure when the truth of the gospel is at stake.

Exactly when this confrontation occurred is difficult to determine. The directives of the Jerusalem Council in Acts 15 may shed some light here. These directives were specifically designed to ensure table fellowship between Jews and Gentiles. Yet Peter's refusal to eat with Gentiles in Antioch contradicts the decision of the council. Therefore, his actions are difficult to understand if the events of Galatians 2:11–14 happened after the Jerusalem Council. After all, James had issued a written decree ensuring the unity of the church, a decree that had been distributed to all the churches (Acts 15:22–29). If Peter's defection occurred after these events, would Paul not have appealed to the council when confronting Peter? At any rate, the words of James would have been powerful weapons against the Judaizers. Paul could have reminded the Galatians (and Peter) that the leader of the Jerusalem church had already decided that Jews and Gentiles were equal in the sight of the Lord. Of course, it could be argued that the "men . . . from James" (2:12) went to Antioch to see if the Gentiles were following the guidelines of the council. But why would representatives from James have to be sent to Antioch when Peter was already present? Peter completely understood the decision of the council and had argued for its implementation (Acts 15:7–11).

Peter's conduct is less problematic if we conclude Paul's meeting with "James, Peter [Cephas] and John" (2:9) was actually the "Famine Visit" of Acts 11:27–30 rather than the Jerusalem Council of Acts 15. In this case Paul's confrontation with Peter may have occurred between the famine visit and the Jerusalem Council. This scenario still places the defection of Peter in Antioch after the Cornelius event of Acts 10. So Peter would have known that Jews and Gentiles were saved by grace. Nevertheless, he may have been confused about how Gentiles should relate to Jews in the church. Indeed, the Gentiles are saved by grace through faith, but does this mean that they can simply ignore the religious customs of their Jewish brothers?

Regardless of where we place the incident in Antioch, there can be no doubt that Paul strongly disagreed with Peter's actions. When Peter arrived in Antioch, Paul "opposed him to his face." (2:11). The conflict was in the open, and the Galatians could check on the accuracy of Paul's account. Paul uses strong language to get his point across. He employs the language of the law court to reveal Peter's error. In a juridical sense, Peter "was clearly in the wrong." Paul does not say that he condemned Peter, nor that God condemned him. It was Peter's own actions that condemned him before the church and the Lord.

The basis for Peter's guilt was threefold. (1) Prior to the arrival of the men from James (2:12), both Jews and Gentiles enjoyed unrestricted table fellowship. The Gentiles were not required to follow any of the dietary laws of the Old Testament. Furthermore, there is no evidence that the Jewish Christians in Antioch were observing such practices either (Hill, 1992, 134–37). Peter himself ate freely with uncircumcised Gentiles. (2) But when the men from James arrived, Peter withdrew himself from the Gentiles and associated only with the Jews. (3) Peter's poor example led others to act similarly, thus dividing the church in Antioch into Jewish and Gentile factions. He was guilty of hypocrisy and instigating division in the church (2:13).

The identity of the "men . . . from James" is uncertain. They do not seem to be the same troublemakers found in Acts 15:1–6, or at least they are not making the same demands. The Judaizers there were pressuring the Gentiles to be circumcised, and nothing is said about circumcision in Galatians 2:11–14. More than likely these men are the same as the "false brothers" mentioned in 2:4.

But why does Paul associate these agitators with James? (1) Perhaps Paul is not using the name "James" as a personal designation. "From James" may simply refer to the jurisdiction of the apostle James. If so, Paul is simply noting that the troublemakers came from James's jurisdiction, that is, from Jerusalem. (2) "James" may be shorthand for the conservative Jewish sector of the church that James represented. In this sense, the false brothers were "from James" in that they identified with the conservative Palestinian, Hebrew-speaking portion of the church (cf. Acts 6). If this is so, it must be granted that the troublemakers were more radical than James himself, for he fully accepted uncircumcised Gentiles into the church. Note that Paul never directly implicates James with the trouble at Antioch. If he had actually been at the heart of the problem, Paul would not have hesitated to blame him as well. (3) Perhaps the agitators were actually sent by James, but misrepresented his intentions once they arrived in Antioch. Since Paul clearly states that they were from James but does not implicate him in the trouble, this final option seems most probable (cf. also Acts 15:24).

What exactly did the "men . . . from James" require? Unlike Acts 15:1–6, we do not have a record of their words, so we cannot be sure of their message. Paul only describes the negative consequences of their arrival, but does not relate what they said. Presumably they felt that Peter's table fellowship with Gentiles expressed a lack of respect for Jewish dietary laws. Since Jewish nationalism was on the rise, freely associating with Gentiles in Antioch may have been disturbing to some conservative Jewish Christians (Smallwood, 1981, 123). Also, non-Christian Jews, being zealous to preserve the traditions and identity of Israel, may have pressured Christian Jews to separate themselves from Gentiles. In short, Christian Jews may have felt obliged to emulate the social and political concerns of their Jewish friends. Thus, social and political factors may have led the men from James to interpret the agreement of Galatians 2:8–10 in a literal way: Paul was permitted to associate with Gentiles, but Peter was only to have fellowship with Jews.

Regardless of the exact identity of the men from James and their message, one thing is clear: Peter feared "those who belonged to the circumcision group" (2:12). Again the identity of "the circumcision group" is problematic. Are they the Judaizers so frequently attacked by Paul in Galatians and elsewhere in the New Testament (Acts 11:2; Titus 1:10)? Or do they represent all Jewish Christians in the church? Or does the term simply stand for all non-Christian Jews?

In addressing these issues the following should be noted. "The circumcision group" cannot refer to Christian Jews in general. Paul was circumcised, but he was certainly not a part of that group. Also, Peter was circumcised and eventually became part of the problem in Antioch. Yet Paul does not identify him with "the circumcision group." Remember that prior to the arrival of the men from James, Peter and other Christian Jews ate with the Gentiles in Antioch. So the Christian Jews in Antioch were not the cause of the problem. It was "the circumcision group" who first terrorized the church there, not Peter and his fellow Jewish Christians. It is tempting to identify "the circumcision group" with "the men . . . from James." But this would be a mistake. Paul appears to have viewed the men from James as being part of the church, although "the circumcision group" are consistently addressed as non-Christians (Phil. 3:2–6).

It may well be that at this early stage in the church, such fine distinctions between various groups is not possible. The early chapters of Acts lend ample evidence that the Jewish Christian church was struggling with its identity vis-à-vis Judaism. If Acts 15 tells us anything, it tells us of this kind of struggle. For example, one sector of the Jewish church embraced a new identity in Christ that made no distinction between Jews and Gentiles. Paul and his coworkers belonged to this group. But another sector of the church accepted Jesus as the Messiah, yet was still significantly associated with historic Judaism. This group no doubt experienced considerable tension between their new-found faith in Christ and their previous life in Judaism. This kind of tension may be reflected in the ambivalent behavior of Peter and "the men . . . from James." It was this group that was particularly vulnerable to the pressure of Jewish nationalists.

Indeed, Josephus records that by A.D. 40, Jewish freedom fighters were stepping up their campaign against the Romans (*Jewish War*, 2:118; *Antiquities* 18:23). In the eyes of such militant Jews, any Israelite who associated with Gentiles, especially anyone who ate with them, was a traitor (Esler, 1987, 147). Table fellowship was viewed as collaborating with the enemy because it undermined the distinct identity of the Jews. Within this particular context, the "men . . . from James" may have judged fellowship with Gentiles to be too inflammatory to an already tense situation (Sanders, 1990, 185–86). So just as Saul the Pharisee had persecuted Jewish Christians for not requiring Gentiles to be circumcised, "the circumcision group" are now pressuring Jewish believers to separate themselves from Gentiles.

For all of these reasons Paul clearly states that Peter is guilty of "hypocrisy" (2:13). The word *hypokrisis*, borrowed from the Greek theater, literally means "to speak from beneath the mask." It describes how actors would converse with each other between scenes. Often the nature of their conversation did not match the expression of the mask they wore. So the essential meaning of "hypocrisy" denotes an inconsistency between one's internal convictions and one's external expression (Earle, 1979, 186).

With regard to Peter in Antioch, his actions were inconsistent with his theological convictions. The grammar of 2:12 supports Paul's charge of hypocrisy. The verbs "draw back" and "separate" are both in the imperfect tense, which speaks of continuous action in past time. So Peter was gradually, yet continuously separating himself from the Gentiles, with whom he had previously dined. He was fully conscious of what he was doing. In a subtle yet unmistakable way, he was saying that the Gentiles were unacceptable.

The special context of table fellowship made Peter's hypocrisy even more serious. For the Jew table fellowship meant acceptance in the name of God. That is, even a common meal was understood to have some sacramental significance. Thus Peter's refusal to eat with the Gentiles strongly implied that the Gentiles were not accepted by God. He was saying that in order for the Gentiles to be a part of the people of God, they had to Judaize—become Jews and seek their salvation by observing all the works of the law (Dunn, 1992, 101).

Peter's cowardly compromise had devastating consequences for the church in Antioch. It started a chain reaction that affected "the other Jews" (2:13). Paul notes that even Barnabas was caught up with Peter's "hypocrisy" (2:13). Now, Barnabas was the one who introduced Paul to the Gentile mission in Antioch (Acts 11:25–26). It is difficult to understand how he could have given in to such behavior. He surely knew better. Only Peter's role as the apostle to the Jews can serve as an explanation. In some way Barnabas interpreted Peter's example as setting policy, and he felt duty-bound to follow that policy.

The public nature of the confrontation is reiterated in 2:14. Paul addressed Peter "in front of them all." Paul's aggressive response to Peter is due to the serious issues at stake. He recognizes that Peter is "not acting in line with the truth of the gospel." These words can only mean that Peter's behavior violated the central principles of the faith, in that he was strongly implying that God's covenant grace was restricted to the people of Israel. Uncircumcised Gentiles were sinners and thus deserved exclusion from the commonwealth of Israel (Dunn, 1992, 102).

Paul exposes Peter's hypocrisy by asking, "You are a Jew, yet you live like a Gentile.... How is it, then, that you force Gentiles to follow Jewish customs [i.e., to Judaize]?" In other words, if Peter (a Jew by race and culture) does not live by the letter of Jewish law, why is he trying to force Gentiles to become law-observant Jews?

It is important to note the inferences that Paul makes in 2:14. He begins by moving from the particular to the universal. Peter's action as an individual has substantial implications for *all* Gentiles. Paul then affirms the essential unity of the law. To fail in one part of the law is to fail the entire law as an integrated system. In other words, Peter cannot pick and choose which laws he will observe. If he transgresses one law, then he becomes a lawbreaker. As a transgressor, he has failed the law as a whole. On the other hand, if the Gentiles are forced to submit to the dietary laws of the Torah, this means that they are obligated to keep all the precepts of the law. Although Peter may not have realized it at the time, he was forcing the Gentiles to convert to Judaism (cf. 5:3). The Gentiles at Antioch would have had to become circumcised and obey the entire law of Moses.

The contemporary implications of this passage are apparent, yet weighty. The public confrontation of two major leaders of the church is a sure sign that there is trouble in the camp. The spiritual stature and experience of the persons involved (Paul and Peter) ensures that the issues at stake are great. On the one hand, such open conflict is disturbing and possibly even discouraging to those who are new to the faith. Nevertheless, at times critical problems requir radical methods. For when the head is con fused, the body cannot function. Peter wa confused about central principles of the faitl and was indeed disrupting the body of believ ers in Antioch. He established a dangerou precedent, which would certainly destroy th unity of the church. Paul could not permit thi kind of dissension to spread beyond the wall of the church in Antioch. He had to confron Peter, and he had to do it now.

We must be careful to observe that 2:11–1 is not about power; it is about principle. Th lesson here is not really about conflict, it i about conviction. Paul had the spiritual dis cernment to understand that there were issue at stake that transcended personalities and pol itics. And he had the moral courage to act o his convictions regardless of the cost. This i the mark of true spiritual leadership. And thi is the only kind of leadership that can keep th church tuned to the perfect will of God.

3. Paul's Theological Argument (2:15–4:11)

Galatians has been described as a rough dra of Paul's letter to the Romans. Indeed man parallels can be drawn between these two let ters. Galatians 2:15–21 can serve as schematic outline for Paul's greatest letter, fo in these seven verses he sets forth the cardina doctrines of the faith so masterfully develope in Romans. It also occupies a strategic place i the structure of this letter, serving as a bridg joining Paul's argument from experience pre sented in the opening chapters with his theo logical argument found in the next section o the letter.

3.1. Justification Is by Faith, Not by the Works of the Law (2:15–21)

Paul has reasoned from his personal expe rience in the Lord, his infrequent contact wit Jerusalem, and his confrontation of Peter i Antioch. The underlying theme in each o these sections is divine revelation. Go revealed his Son to him on the Damascus roa and called him to be an apostle to the Gentile No one taught him the gospel, for he receive it directly from the Lord (1:11–12, 15–16 Similarly, it was the Lord who led him to vis those in Jerusalem who were apostles befor him (2:2). And divine revelation instilled i

Paul an unshakable confidence in the authority of the gospel. In turn this confidence granted him the boldness to confront anyone who would compromise the truth of the gospel, even the apostle Peter (2:11–14).

Beginning with 2:15, Paul moves from his biographical argument to his theological argument. These two phases are not unrelated, for he makes this transition by setting forth the theological implications of his experiences in the Lord. The transition is so subtle that it is difficult to determine where one thought ends and another begins. He simply moves from the individual privileges enjoyed by all Jews to the theological principles that apply to all people, whether Jew or Gentile.

Herein lies Paul's point. If, as traditional covenant people, Christian Jews realized that the law and circumcision have come to an end in Christ, then why are some of them trying to force "Gentile sinners" to submit to the law? The meaning of the phrase "Gentile sinners" is to be found in the words "Jews by birth" (2:15), which denotes persons who were born into the rich religious heritage of the Jews (Rom. 9:4–5). Being Jews by race, they received all the blessings of the covenant and the explicit guidelines of the law. The Gentiles enjoyed no such privileges; they were born outside of the covenant and hence did not have the law. The very circumstances of their birth constituted them as "sinners" in the eyes of the Jews (Verseput, 1993, 53).

The central theme of Galatians is clearly expressed in 2:16, where Paul emphatically states that no one is justified by observing the law, but righteousness only comes through faith in Jesus Christ. With these words he drives home his point by contrasting the effectual power of faith in Christ with the impotence of observing the law. For Paul these two are mutually exclusive. This pivotal verse, however, raises the following questions. What does Paul mean by "works of the law" (a literal translation)? Also, how are we to interpret "faith of Jesus Christ" (also a literal translation)? And what is the nature of the righteousness spoken of here?

(1) The meaning of the thrice-repeated phrase "works of the law" is intensely debated. Traditionally it has been interpreted as meaning the entire Old Testament law. For this reason the NIV renders the phrase "observing the law." Yet we must remember that Paul never depreciates the law itself. In Romans he teaches that the law is holy, just, and good (Rom. 7:12). That is, it is from God and reflects the essential character of its Creator. In Galatians Paul claims the moral content of the law is summed up in one commandment, to love one's neighbor as oneself (Gal. 5:14).

Thus, it is not entirely accurate to take "works of the law" as being the same as observing the whole law. James Dunn argues that to equate "works of the law" with the whole law falsely represents Judaism as a works-righteousness religion. Therefore, Dunn maintains, "works of the law" refers only to those aspects of the law that promoted Jewish nationalism and ethnic distinctiveness (Dunn, 1992, 116). He is no doubt correct in this assessment, especially as it relates to Galatians. The "men from James" and the "false brothers" are surely interested in promoting Jewish ethnic distinctives.

Nevertheless, one must question whether Paul is simply combating Jewish nationalism in Galatians. As will be noted below, he says that he "died to *the law,*" not that he died to "works of the law" (2:19). In 3:10 Paul seems to equate "observing the law" with "everything written in the Book of the Law." He goes on to say that no one is justified by *the law* and that *the law* is not of faith (3:11–12). Indeed, the redemptive work of Christ delivers us from the curse of *the law* (3:13). In the end Dunn is not justified in limiting the meaning of "works of the law" to those elements that promoted Jewish nationalism.

F. F. Bruce is more on target when he interprets "works of the law" as denoting a manner of observing the law. He understands the phrase to stand for a spirit of legalism that sought to win favor with God by keeping various commandments and rituals. This interpretation preserves the integrity of the law as a whole, but rejects the works-righteousness mentality of the Judaizers. Bruce's understanding also allows for Dunn's interpretation but is not restricted to it. Bruce would agree that the Judaizers possessed a spirit of works-righteousness whereby they scaled the heights of heaven by intensifying Jewish norms and practices. He also accepts that "the false brothers" observed the law in an exclusive and self-serving way, which in effect forever labeled

Gentiles as "sinners." Yet unlike Dunn, Bruce claims that first-century Judaism viewed the law as a means of justification (cf. also Cohn-Sherbok, 1983, 72). Paul emphatically rejects this understanding of the law in Galatians.

(2) Therefore, justification does not come through observing the law, but through "faith of Jesus Christ." Grammatically the phrase "faith of Jesus Christ" can refer to the kind of faith that Jesus demonstrated during his earthly ministry. In this case, Paul would be exhorting the Galatians to have the same kind of faith that Jesus had. On the other hand, the phrase can be interpreted as "faith *in* Jesus Christ." In this instance "Jesus Christ" stands for his entire redemptive work, being preeminently manifested in the cross and resurrection. Insofar as "Jesus Christ" is placed in antithesis to "works of the law" (and the law in general in 3:10–14), the latter rendering is to be preferred. One is not justified by keeping the law, but by placing one's trust in the person and work of Jesus Christ.

(3) Finally, what exactly is meant by "righteousness" or "justification" in 2:16? For example, does Paul understand justification to effect a moral change in the individual? If this be so, then when one is justified by faith, one is automatically transformed into a good person. Justification would then be equivalent to moral purification. Or is Paul using justification in a juridical or legal sense? That is, those who place their trust in Jesus are justified with respect to the requirements of the law. In this case Paul's point would be that one is placed in a right relationship to God's law.

In addressing this issue, we should note that Paul consistently associates the experience of justification with the faith of Abraham (3:6–9; Rom. 4:10–11). He teaches that Abraham believed God and it was *credited* to him as righteousness. The word for "credited" is *logizomai*, a bookkeeping term that means "to charge or credit to one's account." Thus, when Abraham placed his faith in the promises of God (Gen. 15:1–6), it was exchanged for the righteousness of God. God granted or gave to Abraham his righteousness in response to the latter's faith.

Theologically, this transferal of righteousness did not produce a moral transformation in Abraham (which falls more in the category of regeneration), nor did it empower Abraham to obey the law (which relates more to sanctification). Rather, Paul is using justification in its legal or "forensic" sense. Justification in Christ is the "not guilty" of God; through faith in Jesus the believer is placed in a right relationship to all the legal requirements of the law, is acquitted of all the penalties of the law, and hence is delivered from the curse of the law (3:13). Paul concludes 2:16 by alluding to Ps. 143:2. The law itself testifies that apart from grace, no one will be justified in the sight of God.

Paul's words in 2:17–21 have been notoriously difficult to interpret. The complexity of these verses is probably due to the fact that Paul is addressing several accusations at once. The Greek text also evidences the joining of several points and responses to charges. In other words, the substance of his thought can only be ferreted out by reconstructing the accusations that lay behind his words in 2:17.

These false charges probably resulted from a misunderstanding of Paul's doctrine of justification by faith. Paul's enemies in Galatia have undoubtedly claimed that justification by faith leads to a licentious and sinful lifestyle. Unfortunately, some misguided persons in the church served to substantiate this charge; they abused the doctrine of justification and turned their freedom in Christ into license. Such persons presumably reasoned that if where sin abounded grace increased, then they should keep on sinning to receive more grace (Rom. 5:20; 6:1–4). The Judaizers therefore charged that everyone who seeks to be justified by faith alone has abandoned the law.

In other words, to Paul's enemies, to trust in Christ was to place oneself outside the confines of the law and consequently to make oneself a sinner. Since it was Christ who was leading people away from the law, Christ is a minister of sin. Thus faith in Christ did not lead to righteousness, but actually promoted lawlessness and sin.

Paul recasts their accusations in the form of a question. The first part of it is an accurate representation of the facts, but the latter half is not. It *is* true that in the process of seeking to be justified by faith in Christ, it becomes evident that we are sinners. The matchless righteousness of Christ and the unyielding demands of the law clearly reveal our sinfulness. Nevertheless, this does not mean that

Christ is the cause of our sin. Paul responds to such absurd logic with the words *me genoito* ("Absolutely not!"). He reserves this expression to communicate his utter rejection of ideas or beliefs (cf. 3:21; 6:14; cf. also Rom. 3:4, 6, 31; 6:2, 15; 7:7, 13; 1 Cor. 6:15). Such thoughts should never come into one's head!

In verse 18 Paul once again turns the table on his opponents. Christ is not the one promoting sin but his opponents, the Judaizers. Paul uses architectural imagery to describe their ill will. They are attempting to reconstruct the dilapidated structure of the law, a structure that was demolished by the power of the gospel. He argues that anyone who seeks to rebuild that which they once destroyed is admitting that they were wrong at some point. Thus to prefer the bondage of the law over the freedom of the gospel is to place oneself in the category of "law breaker." To submit to the law rather than receive the grace of Christ means to come once again under an oppressive system that was never designed to save.

In fact, it is not Christ who is a minister of sin, but the law is what leads to sin. As Paul explained in Romans 5:20, the law entered *so that sin might increase*. To pressure Gentiles to submit to the law is to make them transgressors. Thus, the Judaizers are the ministers of sin!

Verse 19 is one of those key verses that explains the meaning of what has already been stated, yet also sets the stage for what follows. It gives further proof that Christ cannot be construed as the minister of sin, nor can those who are "in Christ" be understood in this way. For to be a transgressor requires a law to be transgressed (Rom. 5:13). But the law has come to an end for all those who are in Christ Jesus (Rom. 10:4). In that Christ has received the full penalty of the law on the cross, all those who are "in him" have also died to its condemning power. Indeed, it was the law itself that revealed sin to Paul and showed him his need of God's grace in Christ (Gal. 3:24; Rom. 7:7). In this way the law was the instrument that led him to die to the law so that he might live his life unto God (Gal. 2:19).

Paul's claim that he has been crucified with Christ is further developed in 2:20. The faith union between the believer and Christ is so close that the experiences of one is shared by the other (cf. Rom. 6; 1 Cor. 6:15–20). By faith the believer is able to participate in the cross of Christ, experience burial in baptism, and enjoy the resurrected life through the Spirit (Rom. 6:3–5; 8:23). Thus Bruce rightly concludes that the indwelling Christ is practically equivalent to the indwelling of the Holy Spirit (Gal. 3:26–29; 4:6; 5:16–25) (Bruce, 1982, 144). Paul is no longer the driving force in his life; it is Christ, who lives through him.

In stark contrast to the all-consuming, merciless demands of the law, Paul states that the Son of God loved him and sacrificed his life for the benefit of all those who believe. Again, it is Christ who takes the lash of the law for us and makes true spiritual life possible.

In 2:21 Paul may again be relating the accusations of the Judaizers. Presumably they claimed that justification by faith apart from the law was an abuse of the grace of God. Paul maintains that exactly the opposite is true. Their efforts to coerce Gentiles to come under the law evidenced their contempt for the sacrifice of Christ. Indeed, *if* the Judaizers were correct in asserting that righteousness could be gained through the law, then Christ would have died for nothing. For any attempt to earn righteousness through the law puts God's grace on the shelf and impugns the value of the cross.

The supreme value of the sacrifice of Christ comes through every word of this passage. The glory of the cross will not be eclipsed by anything that we can achieve. How foolish to seek our own righteousness, however innocent and sincere we may be in our attempts! We must forever join with the great apostle and count all as refuse so that we may win Christ (Phil. 3:7–9).

3.2. The Spirit Is Received by Faith (3:1–5)

The Judaizers have had some success in causing the Galatians to doubt their salvation. Their heresy of "Christ *plus* the law" has obscured the once clear vision of the cross. Therefore, Paul must lead the Galatians to reaffirm the fundamentals of the faith. Simply rehearsing the gospel message will not do, for they know it and have judged it to be insufficient. He must point to some undeniable spiritual experience that will lead them back to the sure grace of God.

Significantly, of all the Christian experiences that may serve this purpose (e.g., water baptism, the Lord's Supper) Paul emphasizes experience in the Holy Spirit. He goes on to argue that the miraculous activity of the Spirit, both in the churches and within the Galatians' hearts, serves as proof that they have been unconditionally accepted by God (Wedderburn, 1988, 171). It follows that the Spirit's activity must have been *visibly* and *audibly* perceived in order for Paul's argument to have any positive effect on his readers (Lemmer, 1992, 384).

Indeed, this is the same line of argument Peter used when Cornelius and his household received the Holy Spirit (Acts 10:44–48). As Bruce notes, these Gentiles received the Spirit in "Pentecost fashion" (Bruce, 1988, 217). Peter and his colleagues heard them speaking in other tongues and immediately understood that God had accepted the Gentiles *as they were*, without first becoming Jews. When opposed by "the circumcised believers" in Jerusalem, Peter pointed to visible and audible signs of the Spirit as evidence that no person is unclean in the sight of God (Acts 10:9–16, 34–35; 11:4–10). In the same way the supernatural manifestation of the Spirit serves as the undeniable truth on which Paul defends his law-free gospel to the Gentiles. The initial reception of the Spirit and his ongoing work in their midst were of an ecstatic and enthusiastic nature. As in the case of Peter, Paul was likewise able to point to these signs as proof that God was at work among them (Betz, 1979, 135).

In building his case, Paul argues from what the Galatians knew and then addresses what they did not know. They knew that the Spirit was active among them; what they did not know was that they were already the children of God without submitting to the law of Moses and circumcision (Lull, 1980, 109). Thus the outpouring of the Holy Spirit on the Gentiles, together with the granting of spiritual gifts, were clear signs that the Galatians had been justified in Christ. By helping the Galatians recall their experience in the Spirit, Paul demonstrates that reception of the Spirit and justification are inseparable from each other (Williams, 1987, 97). Receiving the Spirit is essentially equivalent to receiving the grace of God (Dunn, 1975, 202).

Most importantly, these authenticating signs of the Spirit were experienced by the Galatians *while they were uncircumcised and had absolutely no contact with the law*. If they received the fullness of the Spirit under such conditions, how can they now think that circumcision and the law will gain them anything in the sight of God?

Paul opens this chapter with four rhetorical questions, set in rapid-fire succession and designed to shock the Galatians back to reality so that they will once again comprehend the true gospel. The intensity of his argument can be seen in the phrase, "You foolish Galatians!" These words reveal Paul's emotional state, which in turn sets the tone for all that follows.

In no uncertain terms Paul asks, "Who has bewitched you?" The word for "bewitched" (*baskaino*) is used only here in the New Testament. It originally meant to cast a spell on someone by means of an "evil eye." Paul is probably using the word figuratively rather than literally (Lemmer, 1992, 373). That is, the path the Galatians were threatening to take was so strange that Paul suggests they have come under some kind of magic spell. The hypnotic words of the Judaizers have so entranced them that they have lost sight of the clear message of the gospel. Note that Paul asks *who* (singular) has done this evil work among them. It is as if he knows that a single person is orchestrating the trouble in Galatia, but fails to mention his name (cf. also 5:10).

The clouded judgment of the Galatians is even more astonishing because Paul had so clearly portrayed Christ's crucifixion before them. The word translated "portrayed" (*prographo*) literally means "to write beforehand." This word is frequently used to refer to Old Testament prophecy (Rom. 15:4; Jude 4) though here the word probably refers to the place of Paul's message rather than the time of his preaching. It can be rendered "placarded" or "boldly written before you." The crucifixion of Christ was so graphically presented to the Galatians that it was as if the cross was displayed on a billboard before their eyes.

In 3:2 Paul asks the rhetorical question "Did you receive the Spirit by observing the law, or by believing what you heard?" It is not as if Paul does not know the answer to this question. He asks so that the Galatians might reexamine their experience in the Spirit. Having properly assessed the way they received the Spirit, they will then be able to understand how they have been saved.

Once again the critical role the Spirit plays in Paul's argument is evident. He says, " would like to learn *just one thing* from you." If the Galatians can only perceive the meaning of the Holy Spirit in their lives, then the problems in Galatia are all but solved. Again, we see the antithesis of "works" and "faith." If the Galatians received the Spirit by observing the law, then the Judaizers have a case. On the other hand, if the Spirit indwelt the Galatians on the basis of faith alone, no amount of law-keeping has any value.

The expression literally translated "hearing of faith" is an interesting one. It can either describe the manner in which the Galatians received the gospel, or it can mean the content of what they heard. That is, the phrase can mean they heard "in faith," or that what they heard was "the faith." Bruce is no doubt correct that both interpretations are applicable here. The Galatians were faithful hearers of *the faith* (i.e., the gospel).

In 3:3 Paul again confronts the senseless course the Galatians are threatening to take. He asks if they are so "foolish" (unintelligent, *anoetos*) to have begun in the Spirit, yet now seek to be made complete in the flesh. The work of the Judaizers is again evident here. They have made the Galatians feel "incomplete" unless they undergo circumcision and obey the law of Moses. The word "human effort" (lit., "flesh," *sarx*) does not refer to the physical body in this instance. Rather, it refers to the fallen human nature in its unregenerate weakness (5:13, 24; Rom. 13:14; 1 Cor. 3:1–3). It refers to the self apart from the Spirit of God (Rom. 7:25; 8:3).

We should note here that Paul has contrasted Spirit with flesh whereas he usually contrasts Spirit with law. In other words, he is equating works of the law with works of the flesh. Any attempt to become complete in Christ through observing the law is a manifestation of the flesh, not of the Spirit. What Paul is really confronting is two totally different ways of living. To depend on faith is to live in the Spirit, but to rely on works of the law is to walk in the flesh.

The final question in this section is whether the Galatians have "suffered so much for nothing" (3:4). The word translated "suffered" (*pascho*) can also mean "to experience." If we take this interpretation, Paul is asking whether the Galatians have experienced so many things in the Spirit for no purpose. In other words, he is telling them that if they come under the law, they effectively negate any benefit they had received in the Spirit. On the other hand, the Galatians may have actually suffered for their faith in Christ. Paul does not explain the exact nature of their suffering, but it was probably due to the scandal of the cross (4:29; cf. Acts 14:22; 1 Cor. 1:22–23). No doubt the Judaizers had been pressuring the Galatians for some time. In the main they have successfully resisted this pressure. Yet some have recently started to give in to their demands. If the Galatians yield to the Judaizers, their experience in the Spirit becomes a thing of the past. Their suffering for the faith would be in vain.

The final words of 3:4, "if it really was for nothing," interject an element of hope in the midst of a desperate situation. Paul implies that the Galatians' experience in the Spirit may in fact not have been in vain. He is not exactly sure of their present status. Communications being what they were, the Galatians may not have yet cast away their faith. This mixture of doubt and hope is expressed again in 4:11.

The dynamic work of the Spirit among the Galatians is seen in 3:5. The verb forms are all present, thus denoting the continuous impartation of the Spirit and the working of miracles. The word for "give" or "grant" contains a directional sense; that is, the Spirit is bestowed *upon* the Galatians. Again, the imagery is reminiscent of the outpouring of the Holy Spirit at Pentecost (Acts 2:1–4). As in the beginning, the Galatians are being endued with power from on high (1:7). Note that God is the one pouring out the Spirit and working miracles, not the apostles. It is God who responds to faith, not humans.

The phrase "works miracles" is significant. "Works" (*energon*) communicates the idea of the forceful release of energy; "miracles" (*dunameis*) likewise reflects the idea of dynamic power. These types of miracles served as proof of the Galatians' salvation. They were powerful and memorable, and Paul does not miss the opportunity to appeal to their influence on the church (Lemmer, 1992, 383). The issue here is similar to that of 3:2. Did God work these miracles because they observed the law or because they responded by believing? Of course, the answer is that the Galatians experienced the miracle-working power of God on the basis of faith alone. What value, then, is observing the law? The Galatians must concede, "None, whatsoever."

In conclusion, their past and present experience of the Spirit is a divine affirmation that they cannot deny. The work of the Spirit in them means that their salvation is complete, lacking nothing. They need not add circumcision or works of the law to feel they have been totally accepted by God. The Spirit witnesses daily that they are God's children.

All of this means that Paul and his message are also from God, for it was through him and his preaching of the gospel that the Galatians came to faith and thus partook of the Spirit. Therefore, the Galatians should realize that the "religious slavery" of the Judaizers is really no option when compared with the gospel of grace (Lemmer, 1992, 386). Indeed, as Paul will show, the authenticating sign of the covenant is not circumcision and the law, but the reception of the Spirit by faith—and Abraham serves as the prime example of this spiritual truth (cf. 3:6–9).

The extraordinary value of the Holy Spirit is clearly presented in this section. His miraculous activity serves as the seal of God in the believer's life (Eph. 1:13–14). His presence means that we belong to God. The Spirit is the down payment of the Lord, guaranteeing full redemption in the future (Rom. 8:23; 2 Cor. 1:22). The inner working of the Spirit is God's witness that we are his children (Rom. 8:14–16). In this way, the Spirit dispels doubt. He grants assurance and hope. Indeed he is the promised Comforter (John 14:16–17; 15:26–27).

3.3. Abraham Is Justified by Faith (3:6–9)

Paul introduces Abraham at this juncture in his argument, primarily because his opponents, in trying to get the Galatians to submit to the law and circumcision, have no doubt emphasized the role of Abraham in Judaism. They have stressed that God made a covenant with Abraham and with all of his offspring (Gen. 15:1–6). Therefore, all covenant blessings come through Abraham and are only inherited by his descendants, the Jews. The validating sign of the covenant with Abraham is circumcision (Gen. 17:9–14)—a sign that holds true for Gentile proselytes as well (17:13).

The conclusions to this line of thinking were obvious and straightforward. In order for the Galatians to receive covenant blessing they must first become children of Abraham—that is, they must be circumcised. The troublemakers probably stressed the works that Abraham performed in obedience to God. As James states, Abraham was justified by works in offering his son Isaac (James 2:20–24). Although he understood such deeds as the fruit of genuine faith, the "men from James" did not. They cited these deeds as examples of what one must do to earn salvation. In other words, to them, Abraham was the prime example of one who was saved by works.

Even though Paul begins to discuss Abraham and justification, he has not left the subject of the Spirit. For the first word in 3:6 is *kathos*, which means "just as" or "in the same manner." In other words, the Galatians received the Spirit in the same way as Abraham received the righteousness of God (Dahl, 1977, 133). The infilling of the Spirit and being justified by faith are essentially connected. Once again the charismatic activity of the Spirit in their lives is proof that they have been justified by faith. This experience is exactly the same experience as Abraham had when he trusted God by faith (cf. 3:6, where Paul emphasized that Abraham believed God and it was credited to him as righteousness [Gen. 15:6]).

Paul clearly has a different perspective on Abraham than do the Judaizers. This difference is especially evident in Romans 4:9–25, where Paul examines the circumstances under which Abraham received the righteousness of God. He argues that Abraham was declared righteous some fourteen years *prior to* being circumcised (Rom. 4:10; cf. Gen. 17:10). And, as will be noted below in 3:17, Abraham was justified some 430 years *before* the giving of the law. So Abraham was justified by faith when he was an uncircumcised "Gentile sinner" (cf. 2:15) who had no relation at all to the law of Moses.

These facts completely redefine what it takes to be a child of Abraham (3:7). The verb for "understand" may be an indicative (i.e., a statement) or an imperative (i.e., a command). Since the Galatians plainly do not know that those who are of faith are the sons of Abraham, the imperative is preferred: Paul is commanding the Galatians to understand that one becomes a child of Abraham through faith alone. Those whose manner of living is characterized by faith are reflecting the nature of their father Abraham. So in contrast to the Judaizers, who taught that Abraham is the father of the circumcised, Paul taught that Abraham is the father of all *those who believe* (cf. Rom. 4:1–3).

In 3:8 Paul anticipates that his opponents will present his doctrine of justification as a recent development and hence not worthy to be trusted. But Paul asserts that even prior to Abraham "the Scripture foresaw" that the Gentiles would be justified by faith. In this instance "the Scripture" stands for the foreknowledge of God. Paul's point is that God always planned to justify the Gentiles by faith, and that this plan would first be revealed in Abraham. The doctrine of justification by faith alone was "announced [preached] . . . in advance" (*proevangelizomai*) to Abraham (Paul cites Gen. 12:2; 18:18 as support). Traditionally the Jews interpreted, "All peoples on earth will be blessed through you" to mean that Gentiles must come to Israel in order to receive any of God's blessings. In contrast, Paul interprets these words to mean that Abraham is the representative of all who are justified by faith, whether Jew or Gentile.

This understanding is repeated in 3:9, but with an added nuance. In 3:8 Paul stressed that Abraham is the one through whom justification by faith was first made known and that Abraham is the prime example of one so justified. Now he emphasizes the solidarity Gentile Christians have with Abraham. Since the Galatians are characterized by faith (cf. 3:7 above), they are blessed *with* Abraham, for he is also a man of faith.

Paul has turned once again the tables on his opponents. They claimed to be part of an exclusive community that originated *in* Abraham and that stood *with* him in the presence of God. Paul now teaches that the community of God is not exclusive, but inclusive. Belonging to his people has nothing to do with being a physical descendant of Abraham, but everything to do with having faith like Abraham. All those who share this faith stand with Abraham as a single community saved by grace.

In this passage, as well as throughout Galatians, Paul is combating the universal desire to domesticate God. That is, human beings have a relentless drive to pull God from on high and reduce the divine to the mundane. Every generation has demanded its own version of the "golden calf." We must have something physical, something tangible that can be manipulated and regulated. It is that "something" which grants the illusion that one can control the Uncontrollable. This is the essence of "religion," and it is frighteningly akin to magic and idolatry. That "something" falsely convinces some that they are the gatekeepers of the Almighty, granting access to a few while barring the rest. It can take many forms, even the notion that a particular race or family are by their genetic makeup the exclusive people of God.

But the true God can never be reduced to "something." God is Spirit and seeks those who worship him in Spirit and in truth (John 4:23–24). The things of God are spiritual and are spiritually discerned (1 Cor. 2:14). Thus Paul rightly understands that the sign of God's covenant could never be some surgical procedure (i.e., circumcision). In the same way, the people of God could never simply be the result of human procreation. On the contrary, in that God is Spirit, they must be born of the Spirit (John 3:3–8). They are "children of promise," for they came into being because of God's promise (Gen. 15:4–6). They were begotten by faith, saved by grace, and indwelt by the Spirit (Rom. 1:16–17; Eph. 2:8–9; 1 Cor. 6:19–20). And it is these kinds of children, and only these, who are the children of Abraham (Rom. 9:7–8).

3.4. The Curse of the Law (3:10–12)

The Judaizers have praised the law as a blessing, but Paul teaches that the law brings a curse. He does not say that the law is a curse; rather, striving for "success" in the law is doomed to failure. To fail the law is to bring judgment on oneself. Thus, in the end all those who seek to be justified by works of the law will suffer the end-time judgment of God. They are cursed. But all those who trust in Christ by faith will find themselves reckoned as "righteous."

In 3:10 Paul refers to Deuteronomy 27:26 to prove his point. The issue here is whether he has misrepresented the meaning of this verse, for it does not say that those who keep the law are under a curse, but that those who do not observe everything in the law are cursed. In other words, the verse implies that if one keeps everything contained in the law, then one will escape the curse. In a purely hypothetical sense, Paul would agree. Yet in reality he does not believe it is possible to keep the whole law (Gal. 2:16). Even if one flawlessly kept all of its rites and ceremonies, at some point one would fail the spirit of the law. In a technical sense Paul himself was perfect in the sight of the law (Phil. 3:6), yet he still sinned by coveting (Rom. 7:7). Inevitably, the outcome of anyone who seeks to keep the law is to fall short of its unyielding demands. To fail in part is to fail the whole (cf. Gal. 2:14–15).

In 3:11 Paul presents observing the law and justification by faith as mutually exclusive (cf. 2:19–21). He cites Habakkuk 2:4 in defense of the latter (cf. also Rom. 1:17). The revelation of Christ has greatly influenced how Paul interpreted this Old Testament text. The historical context of Habakkuk 2:4 was one of political persecution and oppression. The Jews were under foreign domination and were pleading to Yahweh for deliverance. The Masoretic Text (the received Hebrew Scriptures) says that the righteous Jew will be rewarded with life because of his loyalty to God. The Greek translation of the Old Testament (the Septuagint [LXX]), however, reads that the righteous Jew will live because of *my* faithfulness ("my" refers to God's faithfulness). The Qumran community and the rabbis interpreted these words to mean that all doers of the law will escape judgment because God will not forsake them in the last day. In time the element of faith became more closely associated with the individual than with God.

This is the element that Paul picks up on. Being faithful to God in Christ will lead to righteousness or justification. So, unlike the early Hebrew text, Paul is not emphasizing the ability to escape judgment because of personal righteousness. Rather, one receives the gift of righteousness by faith and hence is no longer subject to God's judgment.

In 3:12 Paul again notes that faith and works represent two different ways of living. He is not saying that one cannot revere the law while approaching God in faith. As Paul teaches elsewhere, by faith "we uphold the law" (Rom. 3:31). Rather, he insists that when it comes to being justified, faith and works are mutually exclusive. It becomes clear that by its very nature a works-righteousness mentality is antithetical to humbly accepting the grace of God in Christ.

Paul cites Leviticus 18:5 in support of this spiritual principle. Again, this Scripture does not explicitly state that it is wrong to obey the law. On the contrary, it teaches that the person who seeks to obey the law must live by *all* that the law commands. That is, it is concerned with the degree to which one performs the requirements of the law, and it is this emphasis on performance that undermines the principle of simply trusting God for salvation.

At times we do not realize the implications of a particular act or decision. A single step may lead us down a path we will regret later. This is especially true in the area of faith and ethics. A belief or moral decision is never an isolated item; it is always part of a wider world of ideas and values. A selfish thought is just a single manifestation of living in the flesh. A carnal decision is just one evidence of our love for the world and the things of the world.

So it was with the Galatians and the law. They thought that they could pick and choose what parts of the law they would observe. But the law is a unified system. To buy into one aspect of the law is to be indebted to the whole law. In the same way self-righteousness does not come in individually wrapped packages. To claim *any* righteousness apart from the righteousness of Christ is to be drawn into an entire system of legalism. Once this has happened, we have fallen from grace (Gal. 5:4), for anything that is of works is not of grace (Rom. 11:6).

3.5. The Promise of the Spirit (3:13–14)

The grace of God is the foundation of Paul's experience and teaching. Thus when speaking of the reception of the Spirit, he emphasizes what Christ has done for the believer, not what we must do for ourselves. Deliverance from sin and the condemnation of the law can only come through Jesus Christ. Therefore, as in 2:20–21, Paul speaks of Jesus' death on the cross. It is the vicarious sacrifice of Christ that does for us what we could never do for ourselves. For God did not simply dismiss the demands of the law. Rather, the unrelenting requirements of the law (cf. Ex. 21:30; Deut. 27:15–26; 30:15, 19) were completely met on the cross. By substituting his life for us Christ bore the curse of the law for all who believe.

Paul quotes Deuteronomy 21:23 to explain how Christ delivered the believer from the curse of the law: "Everyone who is hung on a tree" is cursed of God. In the ancient world criminals were commonly impaled on a stake or "tree" (Num. 25:4; Josh. 10:26–27; 2 Sam. 21:6). The Romans refined this form of execution and crucified thousands whom they deemed malefactors or enemies of the state. Consequently, in the eyes of both Jews and Gentiles, anyone who died such a shameful death was regarded as a lawbreaker and a sinner and was evidently cursed of God. Herein lies the power of the atonement. By coming "in the likeness of sinful man" (Rom. 8:3), Jesus became sin for us (2 Cor. 5:21) and endured God's wrath reserved for sinners. Therefore, the law can extract no more from us, for it took its full penalty from Jesus (Rom. 8:1–4).

In 3:14 Paul returns to the blessing of Abraham mentioned in 3:8–9. Again, the person of Abraham and the reception of the Holy Spirit are interrelated (cf. 3:5–6), for this blessing is the promise of the Holy Spirit. In other words, the fulfillment of God's promise to Abraham is the granting of countless Spirit-filled children who have been justified by faith. Thus, the purpose of Christ's atoning death was not just to remove the curse of the law; it provided the promised Spirit to the Gentiles. This blessing was possible because Christ's death destroyed the distinction between Jews and Gentiles, breaking down the middle wall of partition that divided them (Eph. 2:14–16). This empowering of the Holy Spirit can only come to those who are "in Christ Jesus." Thus, "in Christ Jesus" now serves as the defining element of the people of God.

The all-sufficiency of Christ is clearly set forth here. Receiving the Spirit is not based on our own goodness and piety. It is the work of Christ that atones for our sins and cleanses us from unrighteousness (Rom. 4:24–25), and it is the work of Christ that sanctifies us and makes us a fit dwelling for the Holy Spirit (1 Cor. 1:30). Because of his sacrifice we need only ask in faith to receive the Holy Spirit (John 14:14–16).

3.6. The Priority of Promise Over Law (3:15–18)

Throughout Galatians Paul associates words like grace, faith, revelation, and freedom with the gospel, but describes the law with words like works, bondage, and curse. In 3:15–18 he continues to contrast the gospel with observing the law, emphasizing that God's promise is far superior to the law. He uses an analogy from everyday life to help the Galatians understand this principle.

In 3:15 Paul cites the common legal practice of making a last will and testament. For the word "covenant" Paul had two choices in the Greek language: *syntheke* or *diatheke*. *Syntheke* literally means "to place together" and describes a legal agreement between two equal parties; each party had the right to negotiate the terms of the agreement until a satisfactory settlement was reached. On the other hand, *diatheke* means "to place through" and describes an agreement between two unequal parties. The terms of the agreement were completely determined by the superior member, and the receiving party could only accept or reject the agreement.

It is significant that Paul chose *diatheke* to describe the covenant between God and humanity. He has set the terms of the agreement, and we must either accept or reject these terms. The closest human analogy to such a covenant is a last will and testament. The person who makes the will determines how it will be executed. Paul again appeals to the legal categories of the day when he speaks of the will being "duly established." Once the will is legally ratified, no one can alter its terms by adding to it or taking from it. Paul's point here is that God made a covenant with Abraham based on faith. The subsequent addition of the law cannot nullify the terms of this covenant. The original agreement was based on promise, and no amount of law-keeping can change this.

The Judaizers have made much of "the seed" of Abraham. They have argued that the promises of God have been made only to "the seed" of Israel. In 3:16, however, Paul notes that with regard to inheriting the promise, the word "seed" is in the singular and not in the plural (cf. Gen. 12:7; 13:15; 17:7; 24:7). He takes this to mean that the promises of God are to be inherited by one person (a seed), not by many people (seeds). He concludes that this one seed is Christ.

Paul's argument has received some criticism because in both Greek and Hebrew the singular "seed" has a collective sense. (The same holds true in contemporary English: We speak of "bird seed," not "bird seeds.") But God made a distinction between the seed of Abraham who was Isaac and the seed of Abraham who was Ishmael (Gen. 12:7; 13:15; 17:7; 24:7). In other words, the principle of selecting *one* seed to receive the promise out of many possible seeds was already established at an early stage in Israel's history. Indeed, Paul may be alluding to Isaac as a type of the one elect seed, who is Christ.

To drive home his point, Paul explicitly cites the number of years that intervened between the covenant made with Abraham and the giving of the law on Mount Sinai. Working from the LXX rendering of Exodus 12:40, Paul reckons that after God had promised to bless Abraham, 430 years elapsed before the law was given. (The Hebrew text, factoring in the time that Abraham wandered in Canaan and the entire time that his descendants were held captive in Egypt, implies 645 years.) Regardless of the figure, Paul's point is evident: God's promise was validated at the time it was given and no legal system, especially one given centuries after the promise was ratified, can change this fact.

Previously Paul showed that faith and law are mutually exclusive (3:12). Now he insists that promise and law are also contrary to one another (3:18). If an inheritance is established and governed by law, then promise has no place in the arrangement. Yet the Scripture clearly states that God based the inheritance on promise and that it was to be received by faith. The perfect tense of "gave" points to a continued ongoing inheritance by the children of Abraham. Paul has already established that those who are like Abraham in faith are his children (3:7–9). Therefore, all who accept Christ by faith, whether Jew or Gentile, will inherit the promises of God. But how can one be sure one has received the promise of Abraham? Paul's answer is the same as before: All who have been supernaturally empowered by the Holy Spirit can be assured that they have received the promise of Abraham (3:1–5, 14).

In the midst of the uncertainty of this world, one thing stands firm: The promises of God never fail. They are as sure as his word. However, the Lord has not only spoken his word; he has also acted on it. The Word became flesh and lived among us (John 1:14). His coming authenticated his commitment to us. Indeed, he has ratified his covenant promises through that one great act, the death and resurrection of Christ (Rom. 1:4). Furthermore, God has mercifully granted his Holy Spirit as an "earnest" or "down payment" (2 Cor. 1:22; 5:5). This foretaste of the age to come grants us hope that the full realization of God's covenant is at hand. For our full redemption is nearer than when we first believed (Rom. 13:11).

3.7. The Purpose of the Law (3:19–25)

Paul has arrived at a pivotal point in his argument. He has plainly shown that the law does not bring righteousness. On the contrary it brings a curse to all those who devote themselves to it. The oppressive consequences of the law had so dominated the human experience that only the death of God's Son could break its stronghold.

Why then was the law given in the first place (3:19)? If the law proved so ineffectual in solving the sin problem, what was its purpose? Did God make a mistake in giving the law, only to realize later that salvation can only come by grace through faith?

In answering these questions, we must keep in mind that Paul has already established that grace and promise take priority over law and works (3:15–18). This priority existed in God's mind from the beginning and was not some kind of *ad hoc* response to the failure of the law. The priority of grace is precisely Paul's point in emphasizing that the promise came to Abraham 430 years before the giving of the law (3:17). Therefore, the thought that God arrived at the plan of salvation by a long process of trial and error must be rejected out of hand. He did not experiment with the law only to move on to grace and faith later.

In addressing the law's purpose Paul states that it "*was added* because of transgressions" (3:19). The verb for "added" literally means "to place in addition to." This understanding harmonizes with what he has already taught in Galatians and with what he says in Romans. The law "came in alongside of" an already existing plan of grace (Rom. 5:20).

But this addition of the law does not explain what Paul means by "because of transgressions." Was it intended to inhibit evil in the world by reducing the number of individual transgressions? Initially, this seems plausible. Yet this interpretation is diametrically opposed to what Paul says in Romans. As indicated above, he teaches there that the law was given so that sin might *increase*, not decrease (Rom. 5:20). The law brings sin to light in our lives and produces an overwhelming sense of condemnation and wrath (7:7). Far from inhibiting sin, the law actually entices one to commit that which the law forbids (7:8, 13)! And, as will be noted below, Galatians 3:22–24 supports the notion that the law was never intended to stop sin in the world.

The words "until the Seed to whom the promise referred had come" lends support to this view. The law was added after grace for the purpose of demonstrating the need for grace. Its tenure was only until the seed, that is, Christ should come (3:19) and actualize the promise in all who believe. In this way, Christ is the end of the law for all who believe (Rom. 10:4).

As a master strategist Paul once again uses the words of his enemies. The "false brothers" sought to impress the Galatians by saying that 'the law was put into effect through angels by a mediator—Moses (Ex. 19:7, 9, 21–25; Deut. 4:14; this tradition is found in the LXX's rendering of Deut. 33:2). The belief that the law was given by angels, however, can be seen in the words of Stephen (Acts 7:38, 53) and by the author of Hebrews (Heb. 2:2).

Again Paul stands the argument of his enemies on its head. The appeal to angels and Moses' role as a mediator does not enhance the authority of the law; the presence of these intermediaries only demonstrates that, unlike the gospel, the law was not directly given by God. But the promise was given directly to Abraham without mediators (Gen. 12:1–3). Moreover, God directly revealed the gospel through his only begotten Son (John 1:14; Heb. 1:1–2). This is Paul's point in 3:20. A mediator necessarily implies a plurality of persons, but God is one. He alone authored the plan of salvation and personally realized that plan in the world. Most importantly, he alone can apply that plan in accordance with the terms he established—promise, faith, and grace rather than law, works, and ceremonies.

In 3:21 Paul uses one of his favorite forms of argumentation. He anticipates the rebuttal of his opponents, presents their objections, and goes on to refute their position. By undermining his enemies in advance, he forcefully drives his point home to the Galatians. In the light of Paul's words in 3:19–20, the anticipated objection is that the law is contrary to the promises of God (3:21). Of course, if this were true, then an enormous contradiction would exist in Paul's theology. Moreover, since the law and the promises both originated from God, then God would be shown to be at odds with himself, if in fact the law was against the promises.

The very nature of Paul's question in 3:21 reflects how absurd such a notion really is. He has framed the rhetorical question, "Is the law, therefore, opposed to the promises of God?" in such a way as to imply a negative answer. That is why he responds to his own question with his classic *me genoito* (cf. 2:17 and discussion there). The thought that God's law and promises are contrary to one another is unthinkable to Paul. The real issue is that the law by nature was never intended to save. In fact, as noted previously, the unrelenting demands of the law only served to accentuate sin and the need for grace. In the midst of a fallen world the law was incapable of imparting life. If it could, then the death of Christ would have been unnecessary (2:21). It is the letter that kills, but it is the Spirit that gives life (2 Cor. 3:6). The fact that salvation only comes by faith in Christ reveals the insufficiency of the law.

The universality of sin is affirmed in 3:22. In one sense sin is the great equalizer in the theology of Paul. Apart from Christ, everyone starts on the same page, so to speak. All have sinned and fall short of the glory of God (Rom. 3:23). Every human being is hopelessly enslaved by the power of sin and thus condemned before God (Rom. 3:9; 5:17; 7:14). The word for "concluded" or "shut up" in 3:22–23 is *synkleio*, which is used to describe the enclosing of a school of fish in a net (Luke 5:6; Earle, 1979, 201). The strict demands of the law have ensnared everyone in the same net, the bondage of sin. Consequently, God's promise can never come through the law, but through faith alone.

Paul again emphasizes the epoch-making event of the cross in 3:23 (recall 3:19). The phrase "before this faith came" points to both the limited tenure of the law and the pivotal role of Christ in God's plan. Here "this faith" is essentially the same as the gospel of grace. Prior to the good news, the law had humankind under lock and key. In describing the liberating effect of the gospel, Paul returns to the idea of revelation (cf. 1:12; 2:2). Although the story of Abraham shows that salvation was always by grace through faith (3:9–20; Rom. 4:1–5), the coming of Christ graphically revealed God's plan in no uncertain terms (Gal. 3:1). With this revelation the moral accountability of the human race has increased exponentially (Acts 17:30). Indeed, Christ marked the turn of the ages. The powers of the age to come are pouring into this present age through the person and work of the Holy Spirit (2:4–47). In the light of the supreme revelation of Christ and the continuous affirmation of that revelation through the Spirit, there is no excuse to remain imprisoned by the condemning effect of the law (Gal. 2:4; 5:1, 13; cf. 2 Cor. 3:17).

Paul employs an image from contemporary Greco-Roman culture to explain further the limited role of the law. The image is that of a pedagogue or household slave who was entrusted with tutoring his master's children. Although the NIV uses the verbal expression "put in charge" to describe Paul's message in 3:24, Paul actually uses the noun *paidagogos*. This word refers to the tutorial service of a slave. The pedagogue would accompany his charge to school, carrying the child's study materials and ensuring his safe arrival. When lessons were over, the slave would escort the child home and drill his pupil on what was learned that day.

The tutors of Paul's day were often harsh taskmasters, who did not hesitate to use the cane if the student did not demonstrate discipline and proficiency. Nevertheless, his sole purpose was to instill the rudimentary lessons of life and to lead his student to a state of maturity. Once that state had been achieved, the tutor had reached his goal and was no longer necessary. Paul's main message with this illustration is that the law also had a limited purpose. Its task was elementary, its discipline harsh, and its tenure limited to the coming of Christ. Hence, those who rightly understood the purpose of the law would be guided to the saving power of Christ. Once its charges reached the level of spiritual maturity in Christ, the law fulfilled its goal and was no longer needed (Rom. 10:4).

Of course, this word picture contained a stinging indictment against the Judaizers. The extent of their spiritual immaturity was directly proportional to their submission to the law. If the Galatians accepted the agenda of the Judaizers, they would not be adding to their faith but subtracting from it. Adding the law is not a progression to a greater understanding of God, but actually a regression back to the elemental principles of morality and life.

Paul's words in 3:25 explicitly state the moral of the story: Those who live by faith "are no longer under the supervision of the law" (lit. "do not need a schoolmaster"). In no uncertain terms Paul informs the Galatians that they do not need what the Judaizers have to offer.

Paul's words in 3:19–25 should be weighed carefully in the light of our own personal beliefs and practices. Just how do we view the function of the law in our lives? Do we fully realize its limited role? Or do we view its numerous mandates and instructions as a recipe for salvation, rather than a road map to Christ? Be assured that any addition of the law to the grace of Christ does not represent spiritual progress. Rather, such an arrangement guarantees a return to a more elementary level of spiritual existence. As Paul will note in 4:9, to live at such a level is to live no differently than the pagans, who do not know God.

3.8. Unity in Christ (3:26–29)

The words "you are all sons of God" express two major themes that will be developed throughout the letter. "All" points to the inclusive nature of the gospel; "sons" reflects the spiritual maturity of those who believe in Christ. In turn these two themes reflect Paul's understanding of the dynamic unity of the church. "All," both Jews and Gentiles, have been incorporated into one body of Christ; and if "all" are in Christ, then they are God's children.

Paul uses two images to describe what happens when one becomes a member of the church. First, we have been baptized into Christ. The word *baptizo* means "to dip or plunge." In its earliest usage the word contained an element of violence or force. It was used to describe the sinking of ships or those who drowned. When relating how the Gentiles conquered Israel, Josephus writes that Jerusalem was "baptized" with a flood of Gentile oppressors. This element of violence and force is retained in Paul's understanding of baptism. In Romans 6 Paul teaches that we have been baptized *into Christ's death*. Thus water baptism symbolizes the spiritual death of "the old self" and the resurrection to newness of life in Christ (Rom. 6:6–8).

The second image Paul uses is that of being 'clothed with Christ." This image represents one being completely enveloped in the presence of Christ (Eph. 4:24; Col. 3:10). In this way the believer assumes an entirely new identity. The Galatians need not stand before God scantily clothed in the rags of their own righteousness (Isa. 64:6; Zech. 3:3–7). Because they have been justified by faith, they are now covered by the infinite righteousness of Christ (Rom. 5:17–18; 1 Cor. 1:30; Eph. 6:14).

The importance of 3:28 cannot be overemphasized, for it strikes at the heart of the difficulties in Galatia. The discord of the Judaizers is swept away by a single line. Paul forcefully states that ethnic, social, and even sexual distinctions are of no consequence in Christ. Jesus is the unifying factor that transcends these kinds of distinctions. This verse serves as a pivotal one summarizing Paul's argument, but also prepares the reader for the rest of the letter.

It is possible that the words of 3:28 were spoken at Christian baptisms (Witherington, 1981, 597). The threefold repetition (in the Greek) of "there is neither," followed by the three pairs of opposites ("Jew/Greek," "slave/free," "male/female"), supports this view. That is, Paul may be citing a well-known tradition used by the church when the Galatians were baptized (Heine, 1987, 153). If so, then his use of the tradition serves several purposes. (1) He is reminding the Galatians of a central truth they heard at a significant time in their lives, i.e., baptism. (2) He is stating that the ethnocentric agenda of the Judaizers conflicts with what is universally accepted by the church (cf. 1 Cor. 12:13; Col. 3:11). (3) He is indicating that his own understanding of the body of Christ is in complete harmony with what has been taught by the church. All of these points serve to affirm his ministry and message.

Even though the practical role of 3:28 is fairly clear (to undermine the effects of the Judaizers), the theological function of the verse is debated. Some argue that Paul is simply emphasizing how one becomes saved. However, with regard to salvation, sex and social status never had any relevance in Christianity or in Judaism. Women and slaves were saved in the same way as men and free persons. Thus, the message of 3:28 addresses more than the issue of salvation. Again the thrice-repeated "there *is* neither" may lend some insight here, in that Paul is addressing some critical event that has *now* made ethnic, social, and sexual distinctions irrelevant. This event may well refer to the universal reception of the Spirit as discussed in 3:1–5.

It is clear that the experience of charismatic gifts had significant sociological and ethical consequences for the church (Barth, 1967, 138, 141–42). Both Jews and Greeks, males and females, slaves and free, all received the Spirit by faith. Thus, the experience of the Spirit created a solidarity that dismantled previously existing barriers of all kinds. Most importantly the charismatic activity of the Spirit granted a freedom that could be enjoyed by all who were in Christ, regardless of sexual identity or station in life (1 Cor. 11:2–16; 2 Cor. 3:17). In other words, the unifying Spirit of God is completely antithetical to the spirit of the Judaizers.

The Judaizers have repeatedly appealed to Abraham as their father; as his children, they consider themselves to be the heirs of the promise. Yet in what Stephen Fowl calls an extraordinary demonstration of "interpretive power," Paul in 3:29 completely reverses the argument of his adversaries (Fowl, 1994, 79). He claims that one must first "belong to Christ" in order to be the seed of Abraham. It should be noted that his expression is conditional: *If* one belongs to Christ, *then* one is Abraham's seed. It is this kind of arrangement that establishes heirs according to the promise. Since the Judaizers do not "belong to Christ," they are not the seed of Abraham. They, not the Galatians, are the ones who will not inherit the promise of God.

Fowl rightly notes that such "interpretive power" could only be received by a community that was itself endowed of the Spirit. Paul understands the Galatians to be such a community and proceeds to relate the story of Abraham to the Galatians' reception of the Spirit.

The contemporary church has perhaps lost sight of the powerful significance of water baptism. Baptism is unquestionably a joyous Christian occasion. The spirit of celebration and the presence of gilded baptismal pools, however, may obscure the deadly seriousness of the event. Baptism represents a violent death to the world and things of the world. It means that everyone who has been baptized into Christ has been baptized into his death. Consequently, the believer is dead to this world but alive unto God in Christ (Matt. 20:22–23; Rom. 6:1–14). It also represents full incorporation into a unique community, the body of Christ. Those baptized are making an open proclamation that ethnic, social, and sexual barriers, so characteristic of a fallen world, have no place in the community of faith. Although we may have diverse backgrounds and talents, we are all equally the children of Abraham and joined by one Spirit (1 Cor. 12:1–13).

3.9. The Spirit and Adoption (4:1–7)

Paul now continues to develop the pedagogue/child analogy he began in 3:24–25. Just as the progressive development of a child frees it from its tutors (3:24–25), the maturation process of an heir frees him or her from the supervision of guardians and stewards (4:1–7). In both cases Paul uses analogies from domestic life to demonstrate the superiority of the gospel over the law. For example, in 4:1–7 words like "heir," "sons," and "adoption" reflect the freedom and maturity of the gospel, while "child," "slave," "trustees," and "guardians" stand for the bondage of the law.

Paul describes here the situation of a young heir whose father has died. The word for "child" in 4:1 is *nepios* and refers to the period of infancy through preadolescence. During this period, although the child is legally the heir of his father's estate, he has no control over it. As long as the heir is in this period of childhood, he is placed under guardians and household slaves. This arrangement remains in force until the time of his maturity (Jobes, 1993, 299).

Paul's use of "we" in verse 3 indicates that such childhood experiences are common to all, whether Jew or Greek. Even though a child is not a slave, in one sense he or she is enslaved. Children are limited to an elemental understanding of life and the world. They are restricted to an infantile perception of things and can only receive simple instructions. They are by nature temporarily shackled to the simple and immature. Paul describes this bondage as "the basic principles of the world" (cf. Col. 2:8, 20). This expression was commonly used in pagan culture to describe both the spiritual powers that were thought to guide the path of the stars and planets and the rudimentary lessons of life.

But what does this somewhat dismal portrayal of childhood have to do with the law and the gospel? Is Paul saying that being subject to the law is no different than being controlled by demonic powers? Certainly not, for as previously noted, Paul teaches that the law expresses the very character of God (Rom. 7:7, 12). More than likely "the basic principles of the world" means that the law is limited in its ability to reveal God and to bring one to God. In effect, the law can only teach the "ABCs" of life. It presents the building blocks of morality in legal form. In Rom. 2:14–15 Paul argues that through the common grace of God, the Gentiles were also subject to such basic moral principles. Nevertheless, the sense of the analogy is clear. The best the law could offer does not advance a person toward spiritual maturity.

The limited tenure of the law is set forth in 4:4. The phrase "when the time had fully come" marks the end of the period of tutelage as set forth in 3:24–25; 4:1–2. God's foreordained plan was that the law would dictate the basics of morality *until* the coming of Christ. Jesus is the focal point of world history; he is the fulcrum on which the turn of the ages depends. This phrase, however, does not primarily refer to a specific time or date in history. Rather, it means that when every component was in place and when all things were in accordance with God's plan, then God sent his Son. Similarly "sent" does not primarily communicate distance or space; rather, it speaks of commissioning an authoritative envoy. Therefore, when the world stage was just right, the Father commissioned his Son to bring salvation.

It has been argued that "born of a woman" simply refers to natural birth and has nothing to do with the virgin birth. But why would Paul explicitly state that which is natural or common? On the contrary, the words "God sent his Son" and "born of a woman" refer to the preexistence of Christ and his incarnation (John 1:14; Phil. 2:5–11). The incarnation of Christ is further qualified by the words "born under law." God-incarnate was a Jew by race and religion. He came as one of the traditional covenant people (John 1:11) and was subject to all the precepts and ordinances of the law, including circumcision (Luke 2:21, 23–24, 27).

All of this was done to fulfill God's purpose. Indeed, the initial word of 4:5 is *hina*, meaning "in order that." The incarnation of Christ within the racial and religious context of Judaism was done "in order that" God's plan might be accomplished. Jesus was completely incorporated into the warp and woof of Jewish society so that he might "redeem those under law." In his life he obeyed the law, and in his death he received the full penalty of the law. In this way he was uniquely qualified to "buy back" or "redeem" those who were enslaved by the law. The imagery here is of buying the freedom of a slave (cf. also Rom. 3:24–25).

With the words "that we might receive the full rights [lit., the adoption] of sons" Paul switches imagery. Now he is drawing on the Greco-Roman legal practice of adoption. The word for "adoption," *huiothesia*, literally means "to place as sons." In the New Testament, Paul alone uses this word to describe our incorporation into the family of God (Rom. 8:15, 23; 9:4; Gal. 4:5; Eph. 1:5). As prescribed by Roman law, even fully grown adults could be adopted into a family. Those adopted were entitled to all the rights and privileges of natural-born children, including inheritance. The meaning of the imagery is clear. Even though the Gentiles were not natural-born children of God (i.e., Jews), because of Christ, they have been fully adopted into his family and are entitled to receive the inheritance of God's covenant people.

But there must be an official witness to the adoption in order for it to be fully validated. In 4:6 Paul claims that the witness to the adoption of the Gentiles, and the Galatians in particular, is none other than the Holy Spirit. In this way Paul is able to interrelate the adoption motif, the story of Abraham, and the experience of the Holy Spirit in Galatia (cf. 3:1–5, 14). The promise to Abraham is the Spirit (3:15). All become the children of Abraham through faith (3:8–9). Those under the law have been freed from its oppressive guidance and adopted into the family of God. As children, they are heirs of the promise of Abraham (3:6–9), i.e., recipients of the Spirit. And the Spirit witnesses to their adoption into the family of God by crying, "*Abba*, Father!" (4:6).

The word *Abba* was a common Aramaic term used by children to refer to their father. It expresses familial love, describing the intimate relationship between a loving father and his child. Jesus broke with Jewish convention when he frequently referred to the Father as *Abba* (Mark 14:36). Whether Paul knew that Jesus used *Abba* cannot be determined with certainty. What is certain is that Paul understood the Spirit-inspired "*Abba* cry" as proof of the Galatians' adoption.

The word "cry" (*krazo*) refers to a loud, audible shout, frequently associated with a battle cry (Betz, 1974, 147). The supernatural movement of the Holy Spirit led the Galatians to shout forth spontaneously, "*Abba*! Father" (Dunn, 1975, 240). What further proof do uncircumcised Gentiles need that they have been fully incorporated into the family of God (Williams, 1987, 97)?

Paul summarizes his argument in 4:7, where he teaches that the destiny of a son is radically different from that of a slave. How much different is the destiny of an heir of God from one who is a slave to the law!

In closing, the concept of development and fulfillment is present in 4:1–7 as in 3:24–25. Paul is reemphasizing the point that all those who truly love God strive to be complete or mature. To remain under the law is to stay at the level of elementary instruction (recall the pedagogue of 3:24–25). Similarly, those under the law remain at a level of immaturity so that can never fully receive their inheritance. Yet those who lay hold of Christ by faith are swept into the family of God by his Spirit. They are not brought in as undeveloped children nor regarded as household slaves. They are adopted as mature sons, fully eligible to inherit the promises of God. The Spirit confirms their special status by speaking through their hearts and souls, crying, "*Abba*! Father!"

Once again, the charismatic experience of the Spirit serves as a standard that defines their place in the plan of God (3:1–5). They are not under the law, but under grace. They are not saved by works, but by faith.

3.10. Renewed Warning and Rebuke (4:8–11)

In this section, Paul expands on "the basic principles of the world" mentioned in 4:3. He clearly associates a slavish obedience to Jewish ceremonies and rituals with a pagan lifestyle.

Now that Christ has come, paganism and Jewish legalism are placed in the same category. They both represent systems that fall short of salvation.

In 4:8, Paul continues to develop two key themes of the letter, i.e., "knowledge" and "nature." Recall that in 2:15, Paul noted that he and Peter were "Jews by birth." This means that their parentage, culture, and religion were essentially different from the Gentiles. Now Paul states that in times past the Galatians were in bondage to gods who were "by nature . . . not gods."

Paul expresses here the classic Jewish argument against idolatry. Indeed, the prophets relentlessly attacked the worship of idols. Centuries earlier Isaiah sarcastically described the whole process of idol-making (Isa. 44:9–20). How could one cut timber and carve an idol to worship, and then warm oneself and cook with the remnants? Paul used a similar argument when preaching to the pagan philosophers in Athens (Acts 17:16–34). Regardless of the historical context, the point remains the same: The gods of the heathens are not divine in their essential makeup. Although there may be many so-called "gods" and "lords," there is only one true God (1 Cor. 8:4–6). The Gentiles sacrifice to demons (10:18–20); to confuse demonic powers with the one true God is the ultimate deception (Isa. 44:20; Rom. 1:18–25). Thus were the Galatians prior to Christ's coming: They were in spiritual bondage and without hope; they did not know God.

From a Jewish perspective "knowing" (4:9) has little to do with mental processes or the acquisition of facts. Rather, "to know" is to have a meaningful relationship with someone or to experience something. Thus the Scriptures speak of knowing God and also of knowing sin (Gen. 2:9, 17; Ex. 6:7; Jer. 24:7). In Galatians 4:9, Paul states that the Galatians now know God—then he quickly corrects himself. The Galatians are not the ones who have established a special relationship with God. On the contrary, God has taken the initiative in grace to incorporate them into his family. He has continued to develop that relationship through the person and work of the Holy Spirit. Considering the goodness of God, why would the Galatians want to abandon the Lord? Why would they forfeit the Spirit-empowered life for legalism?

Several critical issues arise at this point. Paul uses the word *palin* ("again") twice in 4:9. Does this mean that the Galatians are desiring to serve false gods *again*? The context of the letter does not support this. Idolatry is not an issue in Galatians. Paul's words in 4:10 lend clarity here. The Galatians are assigning special religious significance to "days and months and seasons and years." These words must certainly refer to the religious calendar of the Jews. No doubt the Judaizers have convinced the Galatians that their salvation is not complete unless they honor Jewish holy days. Of course, observing such days also involves practicing all of the ceremonies and rituals associated with each religious event. As indicated above, in the light of Christ, all such observances are essentially in the same category as pagan idolatry.

4. Paul's Practical Argument (4:12–6:10)

For Paul theology and practice are inseparable. His doctrine of salvation is thoroughly connected with his understanding of sanctification. Therefore, true justification must find expression in reconciliation (4:12–16), walking in the Spirit (5:16–26), and mutual care and concern for others (6:1–10).

4.1. An Appeal for Reconciliation (4:12–16)

The opening of 4:12 is puzzling. Paul strongly exhorts the Galatians to become like him, because he is as they are. Considering everything that Paul has written to this point, we might ask in what sense could Paul be like the Galatians? They are foolish and bewitched (3:1). They are in the process of deserting the one who called them to salvation (1:6). They desire to remain at a level of spiritual immaturity, requiring pedagogues and guardians (3:24–25; 4:1–3). We can understand that Paul would want the Galatians to become like him, for he often challenges his converts to imitate him in Christ (1 Cor. 4:6; 11:1; Phil. 3:17). But the manner in which Paul is like the Galatians is not immediately apparent. More than likely the phrase "I am as you are" is an appeal to their common experience in Christ. Paul is free, and he desires that the Galatians be free as well.

Paul's words in 4:13–16 shed additional light on these issues. He is calling the Galatians back to the relationship that they enjoyed before the arrival of the troublemakers. As will be noted below, prior to the coming of the Judaizers, Paul and the Galatians were brothers in the Lord. Their relationship was characterized by mutual love, respect, and care. But Paul's enemies had poisoned their hearts and minds toward him, portraying him as one who compromised the law of God for personal gain and power. Nevertheless, Paul wants the Galatians to know that he has not changed his affections for them. Hence he desires that they be like him, that is, really free. It is they who have changed, not the apostle Paul.

In complete contrast to the ill will of the Judaizers, the Galatians had ministered to Paul in the past, and he was grateful for their assistance. In the beginning Paul preached to them while physically ill. In some way Paul's illness provided the occasion for him to share the gospel with the Galatians ("it was *because* of an illness that I first preached the gospel to you").

The exact nature of Paul's illness cannot be determined. The phrases "weakness of the flesh" and "trial in my flesh" (4:13–14, lit. tr.) make one think of the "thorn in the flesh" mentioned in 2 Corinthians 12:7. Yet even here Paul does not share the particular nature of the "thorn." What is clear is that the illness was repulsive in some way. In spite of this, the Galatians were not put off by Paul's illness, nor did they "treat [him] with scorn"—*ekptyo*, a word that literally means "to spit out." In the ancient world spitting was thought to have supernatural power. It was one way to be delivered from a spell cast "by the evil eye" (cf. 3:1).

Paul's words about the Galatians "tearing out their eyes" may give some insight. He may have suffered from an eye infection common to the region of southern Galatia (Bruce, 1982, 209). The symptoms of this disease were unpleasant to look upon. If Paul had such an ailment, the Galatians refused to ostracize him. On the contrary, they received him as "an angel of God" (4:14). The word for "angel" (*angelos*) may simply mean "messenger." Did the Galatians then receive Paul as a messenger of God or as an angel of God? The context of Galatians indicates that more is at stake here than simply being a person bearing a message. The strong contrast between rejection and acceptance indicates that "angel" is to be preferred.

The remark that the Galatians accepted Paul "as Christ Jesus" confirms this. When Paul first met the Galatians, then, despite his troublesome eye ailment, they afforded him with the veneration due an angel. It was as if Jesus Christ had visited their community in the person of Paul.

The tremendous shift in attitude toward Paul is set forth in 4:15. The Galatians were filled with joy when Paul first arrived. Where is their affection for him now? Have the Judaizers so vilified Paul as to make him their enemy? Appealing to the language of the law court, Paul solemnly swears that this was not always the case. He recalls that if it were possible, they would have plucked out their eyes and given them to him. Although it was impossible to transplant their eyes to Paul, the imagery communicates their intense devotion.

In 4:16 Paul rhetorically asks, "Have I now become your enemy by telling you the truth?" Paul here interrelates his own character with the gospel he preached. When the Galatians received the gospel, they expressed sacrificial love for Paul. Now that they are rejecting the gospel, they apparently regard him with disdain. Herein lies the heart of the problem. The false gospel of the Judaizers has alienated them from God's grace and from all those who represent that grace. So in the end it is not the Galatians or the apostle Paul who are responsible for problems in Galatia. In this sense Paul and the Galatians are the same (4:12).

The spiritual maturity and love of Paul are clearly evident in these verses. He refuses to let his anger for the Judaizers be transferred to those whom he loves in the Lord. He chooses to focus on problems rather than on people. In this way he avoids being caught up in the "blame game," which can only further destroy relationships. He pours his energy into recalling the time when Christian love and fellowship joined him to the Galatian church. In godly fashion, he will not hold their sins against them. Rather, he seeks full reconciliation with those who desperately need to return to the fold (cf. 2 Cor. 5:20).

4.2. The False Motives of the Judaizers (4:17–20)

Godly zeal is good, but religious zeal can lead to carnal ambition and strife. As Jesus noted, the Pharisees would cross land and sea to gain one proselyte, but would not lift a finger to help their neighbor (Matt. 23:15). Such "zeal" is completely self-motivated. It has no interest in the welfare of others.

The Judaizers were driven by this kind of zeal. In their effort to prove their zeal for Judaism, they pressured the Galatians to accept the law of Moses and be circumcised. If the Judaizers could make proselytes of the Galatians, then the Galatians would become "zealous for them" and not the Lord (4:17). In other words, the Judaizers wanted to increase their power and influence by making disciples for themselves. If their plans were going to have any chance of success, they had to "alienate" the Galatians. The troublemakers realized that Paul was the major obstacle impeding their Judaizing campaign. If they could sever the relationship between the Galatians and Paul, they could alienate the Galatians from the true gospel (cf. 4:19). Paul's main point in 4:17 is that devotion to the Judaizers and devotion to God are mutually exclusive.

Paul's words in 4:18–19 recall the parable of the sower (Matt. 13:3–9; Mark 4:3–8; Luke 8:5–8). The spiritual roots of the Galatians are shallow, and to that extent they are unstable. When Paul was present, they were devoted to him and his teaching. When the Judaizers were present, they transferred their allegiance to them (4:20). Once again the problem lay with the nature and orientation of their zeal. As long as they were enamored with the ambitions of this group or that, they were hopelessly set adrift in a sea of opinions. Yet if they could wholly rely on the grace of God in Christ, they would be able to see their way through to the gospel and recognize true servants of the Lord.

The situation in Galatia is grave. The Galatians may well have lost out with the Lord; they may have already fallen from grace (cf. 4:11). Yet Paul's love for them is unchanged. He refers to them as "my dear children" (4:19) and grieves for them as a mother for a wayward child. If she could only birth him or her again and restart the life-giving process! This is Paul's desire. The whole conflict in Galatia has caused him to struggle *again* in "the pains of childbirth" so that Christ may be reformed in them.

Paul is wrestling with the prospect that the Galatians may need to be reborn in the Lord. Bruce interprets this whole passage in terms of sanctification and not salvation (Bruce, 1982, 212–13). But the central theme of the entire letter, one that appears on nearly every line, is how one can be saved. The image of being born a second time is too strong to ignore. There can be no doubt that Paul fears for their salvation.

Paul's frustration and pain are so clearly evident in 4:20. The situation is so critical that he fears his letter alone will not do the job. He places more confidence in a personal visit. Paul wishes he could look the Galatians straight in the eyes and they could hear the inflections of his voice. The power of his presence just might bring them back to their senses.

The spiritual lesson of this section is not difficult to discern. Godly zeal always focuses on the Lord and selflessly works for the benefit of others. Carnal ambition may build the empires of this world, but it can never build the kingdom of God. Those who are truly motivated by the Lord do not flinch from the pain and suffering required to birth souls into the family of God.

4.3. True Sons Are Born by the Spirit (4:21–31)

This section demonstrates how masterfully Paul integrates the various parts of his letter. In 4:21–31 he continues to contrast the law and the gospel by drawing on words and images previously employed. For example, the entire discussion expands the theme of "covenant" introduced in 3:15–18. Also the law is consistently associated with terms like bondage, slavery, and the flesh (cf. 2:4; 3:13, 19–25), but the gospel is identified with freedom, promise, and the Spirit (cf. 3:1–9, 14–18; 4:1–7). Perhaps most significant is the way Paul joins his words about giving birth to the Galatians in 4:19 with his words concerning the children of promise in 4:21–31. Again Paul's burden is to make sure that the Galatians have been born into the kingdom.

It is for this purpose that Paul directs the Galatians to evaluate their status in Christ by contrasting the promised child of Abraham (i.e., Isaac) with the child of Hagar (i.e., Ishmael). He manages to interrelate all of these concepts by presenting a unique interpretation of Hagar and Sarah. In 4:24 Paul explicitly states that he is speaking allegorically (NIV "figuratively"). The verb *allegoreo* appears only here in the New Testament (*TDNT*, 1:260).

Just why Paul chose to use an allegory at this point is open to debate. Some have argued that he has used all of the theological and rational arguments at his disposal and now turns to a less conventional means of persuading the Galatians. Yet Paul is not the kind of person to be at a loss of what to do, especially when central tenets of the faith are at stake. On the contrary, his use of allegory is in complete accord with his teaching on the Holy Spirit throughout the letter. For example, he has consistently turned to the Galatians' experience in the Holy Spirit to validate their salvation (3:1–5). Even the story of Abraham in Galatians 3–4 was thoroughly intertwined with their understanding and experience of the Spirit. This deliberate use of the Spirit as a means of unlocking the truths of Scripture can only lead to one conclusion: Those who are of the Spirit can understand the things of the Spirit (1 Cor. 2:13–14). Hence Paul is addressing the Galatians as spiritual and strongly implies that the Judaizers are not.

Herein lies the theological significance of the allegory in 4:21–31. As noted in our treatment of 3:16–19, the Judaizers had no doubt given a conventional interpretation of "the seed" of Abraham—that in order to be part of the covenant one must be a biological descendant of Abraham or be circumcised (Gen. 17:9–14). Paul refuses, however, to be bound by such an "elemental" understanding of the Scriptures (cf. 4:9–10). As Stephen Fowl notes, Paul demonstrates that he is a Spirit-empowered master of the Scriptures by giving an allegorical interpretation of Abraham. In other words, Paul shows his "interpretive power" by giving a "counter-conventional" rendering of a well-known story in the Old Testament (Fowl, 1994, 77–79). Those who are spiritual will be able to discern the superiority of Paul and his message as compared with the lackluster interpretation of the Judaizers (1 Cor. 2:15; Gal. 6:1).

The real theological genius of Paul becomes evident when we realize how he uses this allegory. The Judaizers probably told the Galatians that they were the descendants of Hagar and hence were not part of the covenant. They would have argued that one must be born of Sarah to inherit the promises of Abraham (Bundrick, 1991, 356). As usual, Paul turns this argument on its head, completely reversing the role that Hagar and Sarah played in that argument. Paul interprets the Hagar/Ishmael lineage as representatives of the present status of the Jews, while the Sarah/Isaac lineage (which traditionally represented the Jews) he makes as representative of Gentile Christians (Ebeling, 1985, 234).

The words "you who want to be under the law" (4:21) indicate that some of the Galatians have not yet submitted to the Judaizers. Also, "are you not aware of what the law says" probably echoes the taunts of the troublemakers. No doubt the Judaizers were continually chiding the Galatians for not hearing what the law said, particularly with regard to Abraham and circumcision. In defense of his position Paul also appeals to the law, but chooses to focus on the wives of Abraham and their children rather than on Abraham himself. In so doing he does not quote the Scripture verbatim but summarizes the main points of Genesis 16:15 and 21:2–3, 9.

Paul does not concentrate on the mothers per se, but begins to contrast the circumstances surrounding the births of their two sons. He notes that Ishmael was born of the slave woman, Hagar, and that Isaac was born of the free woman, Sarah (4:22). Furthermore, Ishmael was born *kata sarka* (4:23; lit., "according to the flesh"; NIV, "in the ordinary way"; cf. also 3:3). This phrase simply means that Ishmael resulted from natural procreative processes. On the contrary, Isaac was born as a result of God's promise to Abraham. Thus Sarah is no longer viewed as simply the biological parent of the Jews. She is now the mother of all those who are "born" through the promise of God, i.e., the gospel.

The mentioning of the word "promise" at the end of verse 23 naturally recalls the principle of covenant set forth in 3:15–18. Beginning with 4:24 Paul notes that there were two covenants, one given on Mount Sinai and another originating from "the Jerusalem that is above" (4:26). Paul argues that Mount Sinai stands for the giving of the law to Moses (cf. 3:17). By extending the allegory a bit further, he states that Mount Sinai and Hagar symbolically represent the same thing, bondage to the law (cf. 3:10–15). This representation is true because the slave woman, Hagar, can only beget slave children. The collective meaning of these symbols reflects the present bondage of Jerusalem. Paul's thoughts can be schematically represented by the following: Mount Sinai = the law of Moses = Hagar and her children = present Jerusalem.

Paul no doubt included Jerusalem for a number of reasons. From a spiritual perspective, all Jews, regardless of where they lived, looked to Jerusalem as the center of Judaism. On a political level, Jerusalem also served as the source of zealous nationalism that sought to preserve Israel by intensifying the observance of the law. With regard to the Galatians in particular, Jerusalem was the headquarters for the Judaizers. So in an allegorical sense, Jerusalem represents the freedom-destroying legalism that Paul is combating throughout his letter (cf. 2:4–5, 12–14). This representation of Jerusalem contains some grave implications for the Jews. Jerusalem is enslaved with all of her children (4:25). Paul's judgment means that the Jews are excluded from the covenant of grace. They are lost and are in desperate need of the gospel (Rom. 9:1–3; 10:1).

All of this is in complete contrast to "the Jerusalem that is above" (4:26). The idea of two Jerusalems, an earthly Jerusalem and a heavenly city, was well established in Jewish thought. The origin of this concept may be traced to Exodus 25:40, which says that Moses received a "pattern" for the construction of the tabernacle (Bruce, 1982, 221). The idea of "pattern" implies an ideal reality in heaven that has a corresponding physical reality on earth. This type of imagery is found throughout the New Testament, especially in the letter to the Hebrews and Revelation (Heb. 11:10, 16; 12:22; Rev. 3:12; 21:2, 9–27).

Having made this analogy, Paul goes on to teach that the Jerusalem above is free and is the mother of us all. He may be referring to such Scriptures as Psalm 87:5 and Isaiah 54:1–13. The important point is that from Paul's perspective the Jerusalem above represents the life-giving power of the gospel, but the earthly Jerusalem stands for bondage to the law.

Paul substantiates his allegorical interpretation of Hagar and Sarah by referring to Isaiah 54:1, where the prophet celebrates the release of Israel from captivity and her restoration to the Promised Land. For Isaiah this miraculous deliverance was nothing less than the granting of children to a barren woman. B God's grace she who by nature could have n children would bear more offspring than sh who was not barren. Paul's intention is obv ous. The Jews, who were to be fruitful for th Lord, have now become barren. The Gentile who by nature could not bear children for Go now give birth to many children into the king dom (Gal. 4:27).

Nevertheless, Paul is careful to anchor th whole story in the context of God's grace. Ju as the rebirth of Israel in the land (4:27) did n come from her own ability, birth into the king dom also results from the supernatural inte vention of God. Also the miraculous birth o Isaac perfectly typifies the experience of th Galatians (4:28). Note that even though Isaa has been implied all along (4:22–23), this i the first time his name appears in the allegor (4:28). Thus, Paul's point is that the Galatian have not been born "in the ordinary way" lik Ishmael (4:23). On the contrary, they are lik Isaac because they have been born as the resu of the promise of God (cf. also Rom. 4:13–25

In 4:29 Paul compares the strife that existe between Ishmael and Isaac with the troubl caused by the Judaizers in Galatians. His con cluding words, "It is the same now," estab lishes this connection. "The son born in th ordinary way" (i.e., Ishmael) persecuted "th son born by the power of the Spirit" (i.e. Isaac). The Bible does not explicitly say tha Ishmael persecuted Isaac. Ishmael did taun Isaac at the celebration of his weaning (Gen 21:9), but the rabbis consistently interprete Genesis 21:9 as reflecting the hostility Ishmae had for Isaac (Betz, 1979, 249–50). Signifi cantly, Ishmael chided Isaac at a point in hi life when he was making the transition from absolute dependence as an infant to a mor mature and independent state.

Moreover, this transition indicates tha Isaac was one step closer to claiming the inher itance of Abraham. Could this imagery relat to Paul's words concerning the immaturity o those under the law and the maturity of thos in Christ? Does the weaning of Isaac paralle the deliverance from the harsh pedagogue o the law as set forth in 3:23–25? Could it be tha the maturation of Isaac reflects the freedom o the heir from his supervisor as seen in 4:1–7 Considering the consistency of Paul's argu ment, such connections are entirely possible.

In a subtle yet significant way Paul has substituted the word "Spirit" for "promise" in 4:29. In so doing he has made those "born as a result of the promise" equivalent to those "born by the power of the Spirit." Paul is justified in making this parallel for he has previously taught that the promise of Abraham is the Spirit (3:14).

The degree to which Paul is able to integrate various theological concepts is truly extraordinary. Prior to the giving of the law Abraham was justified by faith because he believed God's promise that he would have a son. In that the Gentiles have the same faith as Abraham, they now become the children of Abraham. Hence God's promise to Abraham has been fulfilled; he has indeed become the father of many nations. The ultimate fulfillment of the promise, however, is the Spirit (3:14). So the reception of the Spirit by the Galatians (3:1–3), with the accompanying "*Abba* cry" (4:6), constitutes God's promise to Abraham in all of its fullness.

Paul brings home the solemn message of the allegory by making reference to Genesis 21:10. This Scripture declares that the son of the slave woman (Ishmael) will not partake of Abraham's inheritance with the son of the free woman (Isaac) (4:30). Again, this profound statement means that the Jews have now been excluded from covenant blessings. Yet the Galatians have not been birthed by the legalism of Judaism. They have been born again through the freedom of the gospel (4:31).

In summary, Paul's words in 4:21–31 should be especially relevant to Spirit-filled believers. It is evident that the Holy Spirit serves as the interpretive lens through which Paul views the Scriptures and the work of God in the world. Therefore, for him there can be no sterile dissecting of the revelation. There certainly can be no prostitution of the word to serve carnal ambitions and agendas. The only legitimate approach to the Scriptures is one that has been forged by the Holy Spirit (1 Peter 1:10–12). And only those who have been led by the Spirit are so empowered to plumb its depths.

Such depths penetrate to a level of understanding that leaves the elemental and superficial far behind (4:3, 9). It is a privileged journey that leads to liberty and abundant inheritance (2:4–5; 4:7). It is a journey that escapes the narrow gaze of the pedagogue and bids farewell to overbearing trustees and guardians (3:24–25; 4:1–2). It is a journey "in Christ" (2 Cor. 1:21), "by grace" (Eph. 2:5–8), and through the Holy Spirit (3:5), reserved only for those who are spiritually mature (Col. 2:10).

4.4. Waiting in the Spirit (5:1–5)

The theme of chapter 5 is clear: The believer has been called to freedom in Christ and is not to live in bondage to the law (Osiek, 1980, 59). But the grammatical construction of 5:1 is awkward. One must relate the words "to/for freedom that Christ has set us free" to the principles contained in the allegory of 4:21–31. That is, as children of the free woman (4:31) the Galatians are to live up to their family heritage. Thus, the combined message of the allegory and Paul's words in 5:1–13 mean that the initial deliverance of the Galatians was for a purpose. They were freed to live in freedom (Ebeling, 1985, 241).

Therefore, Paul follows this indicative statement with a command: "Stand firm ... and do not let yourselves be burdened again by a yoke of slavery." The word for "stand firm" (*stekete*) was a military term, which meant to hold one's position and not permit the enemy to encroach upon one's territory (Yandian, 1985, 202). So Paul's message to the Galatians is that they are to stake out their territory in Christ and not yield to the tactics of the Judaizers.

The "yoke of slavery" no doubt refers to the law. When Jewish males became "sons of the law" at their Bar Mitzvah, they were said to "take the yoke of the kingdom." Similarly, at the Jerusalem Council Peter does not want "the yoke" to be placed on the neck of the Gentiles (Acts 15:10). Although salvation is a free gift, the Galatians must be continually vigilant. The Judaizers want to bind them to the yoke of the law.

Throughout the letter Paul has used his apostolic authority to bring the Galatians back into line. The words "Mark my words! I, Paul, tell you" (5:2) is another example of this kind of authority. The critical issues at stake merit his solemn and weighty declaration. For if the Galatians undergo circumcision, then Christ will be of no benefit to them.

Scholars are divided on how one should interpret "circumcise" here. The verb can either be rendered "circumcise yourselves" or "be circumcised" (i.e., by others). Since Paul never represents the Galatians as passive victims but squarely places the blame at their feet, the former rendering is preferred. *If* the Galatians proceed to circumcise themselves, they will forfeit the atoning benefits of Christ. The *if* once again indicates that the situation is not beyond repair, but this central fact remains: The principle of circumcision and the grace of God in Christ are mutually exclusive.

The words "again I declare" (5:3) recall the imagery of the law court (2:11; 4:15). As an expert lawyer prosecuting his case, Paul clarifies the consequences of the Galatians' actions. Since he senses the need to repeat such facts over and over again, the Galatians have not fully understood the significance of accepting circumcision. As James notes, to keep one part of the law obligates one to keep the whole law (James 2:10; cf. also Gal. 3:10–11). Although Paul singles out the rite of circumcision here, we must remember that this physical act is not the real problem. As previously noted, Paul had circumcised Timothy so that he might minister more effectively to the Jews (Acts 16:3). Rather, it is the legal system represented by circumcision, along with the thought that this legalism can obtain salvation, that Paul finds unacceptable.

In his characteristic and somewhat blunt manner, Paul lays bare the issues at hand. Anyone seeking to be justified by the law has severed his or her relationship with Christ and fallen from grace (5:4). The verb translated "been alienated" (*katargeo*) was used to describe the ending of a relationship with someone or something (Ridderbos, 1957, 188). Paul uses the same word in Romans 7:1–6 to describe how a marriage comes to an end with the death of one of the partners (Bruce, 1982, 231). In that passage Paul taught that believers have become dead to the law so that they might be married to Christ. The situation in Galatia is exactly the opposite: The Galatians are seeking to be married to the law, and in so doing they are killing their relationship with Christ. Thus Paul warns that to seek to come under the law is to end all relationship with Christ. His atoning sacrifice is of no benefit to legalists.

The Greek word for "fallen away" (*ekpipto*) was frequently used to describe flowers falling away from their stems after they had withered and died. To come under the law is to be cut off from the life-giving flow of God's grace. In a spiritual sense, if the Galatians embrace the law instead of Christ, they will wither, die, and fall from the saving power of God.

In 5:5 Paul alludes to a new aspect of the Galatians that has not yet been discussed. Apparently they suffered from what might be called "religious impatience." They were unwilling to wait in the Spirit for the full realization of their salvation, craving instead tangible signs and rituals that granted a false sense of security. Their distorted vision of God led them to believe that a physical mark in the flesh was proof they were saved. Being able to perform religious ceremonies gave them a sense of forging their own salvation in the here and now.

Yet, as the writer of Hebrews argues, such practices represent carnal commandments and ordinances (Heb. 7:16; 9:10). They are deeds of the flesh, not of the Spirit. Stephen preached that it was this kind of "religious impatience" that demanded a golden calf from Aaron (Acts 7:40–43). Rather than wait on the revelation of God's word, the Hebrews demanded something physical to pin their faith on. In short, they became idolatrous and regressed to a primitive level of existence. Ironically, those who had been freed from Egypt longed to be enslaved again—and so it was with the Galatians. Christ had freed them from paganism. Why should they want to be enslaved again (Gal. 4:8–10)?

God has indeed provided signs of our salvation, but they are spiritual and are spiritually discerned (cf. 1 Cor. 2:14). Those who are spiritual realize that they are saved in the present, yet full redemption is still future (Rom. 8:22–23; 1 John 3:2). The believer's experience in the Holy Spirit perfectly reflects these principles. The outpouring of the Spirit is an end-time phenomenon marking the beginning of the last days (Acts 2:4–17). So the powers of the age to come are being presently realized in the church through the presence of the Spirit and his accompanying gifts (1 Cor. 12). Moreover, the fruit of the Spirit serves as markers clearly identifying the children of God in this age. These are the *spiritual* signs the Galatians should look to as evidence of their salvation (Gal. 3:1–5), not physical rituals and ceremonies of ages past.

The present manifestation of the Spirit also speaks of our full redemption that is yet future ı contrast to the religious impatience of the alatians, by faith we must await "*through the* ɔ*irit* the righteousness for which we hope" :5). The word Paul uses for "await" is the .me one used in Rom. 8:19, 23, 25, where it ɛscribes fallen creation awaiting its deliver-ıce and the believer awaiting the resurrection. ı fact, these two events are interrelated. For the ıd-time resurrection of the saints by the Spirit ill usher in this cosmic restoration (8:21). In e meantime, the Holy Spirit infuses the life ' the redeemed with hope and purpose (8:24–)). We are saved by hope (8:24), and it is the ɔirit who grants us the patience to live out that ɔpe until the coming of Christ (Gal. 5:5).

Practically speaking, "religious impa-ence" is the downfall of many dedicated hristians. They seek tangible signs of their ılvation rather than seeing with the eye of ith. Such signs might include impressive ıilding programs or increased church mem-ɛrship. Yet to the degree that we rest our des-ıy on the things of this world, to that same ɛgree we cut ourselves off from the grace of hrist. We should not be surprised that the alm of grace is essentially invisible. It must ɛcessarily be so, for as Paul states, "He is the ıage of the *invisible* God, the firstborn over l creation" (Col. 1:15). We must wait in the ɔirit for our redemption, which is nearer than hen we first believed (Rom. 13:11). For these asons Paul states, "So we fix our eyes not on hat is seen, but on what is unseen. For what seen is temporary, but what is unseen is eter-ıl" (2 Cor. 4:18).

4.5. Renewed Warning and Rebuke (5:6–12)

One would think that Paul has said enough prod the Galatians back to the fold. But he kes no chances and thus launches into ıother stint of warning and rebuke in 5:6–12.

Paul begins by saying that "in Christ Jesus ɛither circumcision nor uncircumcision" ɛcomplishes anything for the kingdom. The ord for "accomplish" (*ischyo*) refers to the herent power residing in a person or thing. ıul repeats this message throughout his let-ɛrs (3:28; cf. 1 Cor. 7:19; Col. 3:11). Such out-ard signs may have meaning on a purely ıman level, but they are irrelevant to God. ıey may serve as social indicators, labeling ıe as a Jew or Gentile, but have no place in the church. What really matters to God is faith working through love. The word for "working" (*energeo*; cf. our word "energy") communicates the operation and application of power. It is not the outward signs of religiosity that matter, but the realization of inward faith through love.

Paul frequently employs sporting imagery in his letters (1 Cor. 9:24–26; Phil. 2:16; 1 Tim. 4:7; 6:12; 2 Tim. 4:7). His knowledge of athletics may reflect his familiarity with the Olympic games and perhaps also with the Isthmian games held near Corinth, but his interest goes beyond entertainment. The games serve as metaphors for one's spiritual progress or the lack thereof. Note Galatians 2:2, where Paul used the race motif to express doubts about his work among the Galatians. In 5:7 Paul acknowledges that they were running well. He is no doubt referring to the time soon after he had preached the gospel to them. The word for "running" is in the imperfect tense, indicating that the Galatians had continued on the right path for some time.

Yet someone had "cut in on" them, so that they were no longer obeying the truth. In this context, the word *enekopsen* refers to a foul in sports—one runner tripping up another one and so preventing him from finishing the race (Bruce, 1982, 234). The singular interrogative pronoun "who" as well as Paul's mention of "the one who troubles you" in 5:10 may point to a single "ringleader" of the Judaizers. Nevertheless, Paul's full attention is devoted to the restoration of the Galatians. He does not waste time nor energy in pursuing the troublemakers, though he does note their tactics: They are trying to persuade the Galatians not to obey the truth.

Although 5:8 is brief, it serves to integrate major portions of the letter. "That kind of persuasion" naturally refers to Paul's warning in 5:7. That this persuasion "does not come from the one who calls you" recalls 1:6–7, where Paul was astonished that the Galatians have so quickly abandoned "the one who called [them]" for a qualitatively different gospel. In these verses as well as in 5:8, the "one who calls" is God. Also, the "persuasion" in 5:8 is evidently the false gospel of 1:6–7. The cunning of the Judaizers is revealed here as well. They have been telling the Galatians that they do not need to abandon Jesus; they just need to add the law.

Bruce notes that since this persuasion does not come from God, then it must come from Satan. He refers to 1 Thessalonians 2:18, where Paul claims that Satan had hindered him and his coworkers from visiting the Thessalonians. The word for "hindered" is the same word translated "kept . . . from" in 5:7. Whether the Judaizers realize it or not, they are being used by Satan to lead the Galatians astray (Bruce, 1982, 234).

Although the words, "A little yeast works through the whole batch of dough" (5:9) contain a scriptural principle, Paul is not quoting from Scripture. Rather, this saying represents a common proverb of the day, somewhat analogous to our expression, "One rotten apple spoils the whole barrel." In the Scriptures yeast usually symbolizes sin and moral corruption (Matt. 16:6–11; Mark 8:15; see Osiek, 1980, 63). Hence the Jews were to rid their households of all yeast and to eat unleavened bread at the first Passover (Ex. 12:14–20; Deut. 16:3–8). The putrefying effect of a small amount of yeast permits it to corrupt a large portion of dough (1 Cor. 5:6–8). In other words, even a minute quantity of the Judaizing heresy can pollute the churches in Galatia.

In that Paul questions the spiritual status of the Galatians (4:11, 19–20), his words in 5:10 seem out of place. How is he persuaded in the Lord that the Galatians will take no other view? It may be that Paul is using his own skills of persuasion. When faced with an unpleasant situation or a particularly obstinate person, Paul often expresses confidence that the right thing will be done. For example, when addressing the potentially explosive situation in Philemon, Paul feels confident that Philemon will do more than he asks (Philem. 21). Similarly, Paul affirms his confidence in the Corinthians even though they have been delinquent in gathering a collection for the poor saints in Jerusalem (2 Cor. 8:1–24; esp. vv. 22, 24).

Therefore, in 5:10, Paul persuades the Galatians to accept the gospel by stating that he is confident they will do this very thing; he has no such confidence in the troublemakers. The use of the singular in "the one who is throwing you into confusion" relates to the singular "who" in 5:7 (see above). Is Paul speaking generically here or does he have in mind an arch-Judaizer? The final words of 5:10 seems to indicate the latter. Paul suspects that son person is orchestrating the troubles in Galati but fails to name him specifically. But he do not need to know his exact identity. Gc knows who he is and his destiny is seale Those who preach a false gospel are *anathem* under the judgment of God (1:8–9).

In an effort to sabotage Paul's influence Galatia, the Judaizers claimed that he st preached circumcision. If that is true, then w does he forbid the Galatians to be circumcise Their goal was to portray Paul as a hypocri There is no scriptural evidence to support th slander. Acts clearly teaches that Paul preach justification by faith immediately after his co version (Acts 9:20). Perhaps the Judaizers mi understood or deliberately misrepresent Paul's actions in 1 Corinthians 9:20 and Ac 16:3. Paul was willing to accommodate t cultural distinctives of all people so that might win them to Christ. Yet his respect f their customs and practices did not alter h message of justification by faith. The circur cision of Timothy fell in this category. Sin he was of mixed parentage, he was unable minister effectively to either Jew or Genti By circumcising Timothy Paul "normalize him with respect to the Jewish world. Thus f Paul circumcision occasionally was a part his missionary strategy, but played no role his doctrine of salvation.

In refuting the Judaizers Paul asks t rhetorical question, "Brothers, if I am st preaching circumcision, why am I still bei persecuted?" (5:11). The "stumbling bloc and "foolishness" of the cross (1 Cor. 1:18–2 had made Paul the object of ridicule and pe secution (Acts 9:23; 13:45; 14:19; 16:22–2 17:32; 19:28–31; 21:30–36). His point is th he is *still* (the word occurs twice in 5:11) bei persecuted. This can only mean that he h refused to promote traditional Judaism as way of salvation and is thus suffering for th In any case, the preaching of circumcisi would remove the "stumbling block" of t cross. It is this disturbing and, on one lev confusing message of the cross that clears t way for a new vision of God in Christ (1 C 1:20–25). Therefore Paul will not forfeit th discomforting aspect of the gospel for sor Jewish religious practice.

Paul's utter disgust with the Judaizers pou forth in 5:12. If the agitators in Galatia belie hat a little cutting wins favor with God (i.e., he circumcision of the foreskin), then Paul vishes they would be totally committed to it ınd castrate themselves! Paul may be referring ıere to the cult of Cybele, which practiced cas-ration of its priests. The sect originated in 'hrygia, and the Galatians would have been ıware of its bizarre practices. Since this self-nutilation was often carried out in a mad renzy, Paul's description of the Judaizers as 'agitators" is not without significance. The 'zeal" of the troublemakers (4:17–18) and the esulting agitation it has caused in Galatia are ssentially the same as that evidenced in pagan arbarism.

Paul's approach to conflict resolution ppears foreign to the church today. In dealing vith the Galatians, he sounds harsh and at imes uses crude imagery. It is especially mportant to point this out in an age when the ighest virtue is not offending anyone. When roblems arise, we are taught to seek a "win-vin" solution. That is, at the end of the day veryone should walk away from the negoti-ting table with something in hand. Some hings, however, are nonnegotiable. If all par-ies walk away with something, everyone ends p with nothing. Paul's methods and language nay appear harsh and insensitive, but they are ctually evidence of his deep concern for the Galatians. When it comes to the eternal destiny f souls, sometimes love means war.

4.6. Living in the Spirit (5:13–26)

Freedom is the hallmark of life in the Spirit. Note what Paul wrote to the Corinthians, 'Now the Lord is the Spirit, and where the 'pirit of the Lord is, there is freedom" (2 Cor. :17). There is freedom from sin and from the elf-defeating consequences of sin (Rom. 8:2). Even the creation is anxiously awaiting to hare in the glorious freedom of the children of God (8:21). But the work of the Judaizers has hreatened the freedom of the Galatians. They ame to "spy on" their freedom in Christ (Gal. :4); Paul exhorts the Galatians to stand firm n that freedom (5:1).

He had expressed dismay at how quickly he Galatians deserted the one who *called* them 1:6); the theme of "calling" again surfaces in :13 (cf. also 5:8). Here Paul explains the ntent or purpose of God's call: The Galatians ave been called to live a life of freedom. But some believers had presumably misinterpreted their freedom in Christ. They reasoned that if we are saved by grace, then we can keep on sinning, and God will supply more grace (Rom. 6:1–4). Others were deliberately abus-ing their freedom in Christ to cover up their sinful lifestyles (cf. 1 Peter 2:16). And still oth-ers saw no need for practical Christian living. If we are saved by grace apart from works of the law, why do good deeds at all (cf. James 2:14–26)?

Yet to be free from the law does not mean one can live lawlessly. Liberty must not be construed as license. For these reasons Paul commands that the Galatians not use their free-dom "to indulge the sinful nature" (5:13). The word for "indulge" (*aphorme*) is actually a noun, not a verb. It means a starting point or a base of operation. The Galatians must not use their freedom in Christ as a launch pad for "the sinful nature" (lit., "the flesh," *sarx*).

What is the flesh? It is that aspect of human nature that continually leads to sin. It is com-pletely egocentric, hostile to the Spirit, and has no concern for one's neighbor (Rom. 7:18; 8:8–13; 2 Cor. 7:1; Gal. 5:16–17; see Fee, 1994, 204). Herein lies the crux of the issue of Galatians 5:13. What should guide the Christ-ian life now that we have been freed from the harsh disciplinarian of the law (cf. 3:24–25)? Paul's response to this question is paradoxical. He claims that Christian freedom is a type of slavery. For the law of the Spirit of life (Rom. 8:2) "enslaves" one to serve his or her neigh-bor in love (Gal. 5:13). Thus divine love empowered by the Holy Spirit is the only rule or law the Galatians have to follow (5:14–23).

Another paradox is set forth in 5:14. *If* the Galatians submit to the law of love, they will in fact fulfill the law. For Paul notes that the entire law is summed up in the one command, "Love your neighbor as yourself" (Lev. 19:18; cf. also Rom. 13:9). Even though Paul makes no ref-erence to Jesus, his words closely parallel what Jesus said (Matt. 22:36–40; Mark 12:28–31; Luke 10:25–28); both view Leviticus 19:18 as the summation of the law (Ridderbos, 1957, 201). But Paul's version differs from that of Jesus in that he does not include the command to love the Lord with one's whole heart. Since Paul is addressing Christians, he probably took love for God for granted (Osiek, 1980, 67). That is, he and the Galatians understood that love for God served as the basis for loving one's neighbor. The bottom line is that, just as in Romans 3:24–25, the law testifies to something greater than itself. The fulfillment of the law is not legalism, but is the expression of God's love for others. No ritual or legal ceremony can produce this love; it is an aspect of the fruit of the Spirit (Gal. 5:22).

Because of the Judaizers, the entire climate in Galatia was characterized by "the flesh." The flesh is thoroughly egocentric, disobedient to God, and antithetical to the Spirit (Rom. 7:18; 8:8–13; 2 Cor. 7:1). It has no inclination to love one's neighbor as described above (Gal. 5:14). Although the saving work of God has dealt a mortal blow to the flesh (Rom. 6:1–6), a believer can still be in the flesh (1 Cor. 3:1–3). Indeed Galatians 5:15 indicates that some of the Galatians were living in the flesh. "Biting" and "devouring" portray the savagery of a dog fight that ends in the destruction of all involved. Hence, Paul warns that if they continue to attack one another viciously, they should take heed that they not totally "destroy" each other.

Nevertheless, how can the Galatians escape the carnal strife so graphically set forth in 5:15? How can they guard against being entangled in the carnal commandments of the law? How can they protect themselves against the carnal motives of the Judaizers? Paul's answer to all of these questions is that they must "live [lit., walk] by the Spirit" (5:16). Paul uses the word "walk" metaphorically to describe one's entire way of living (Eph. 2:10; 5:2, 8; Col. 2:6; 1 Thess. 2:12; 4:1). In other words, he commands the Galatians to allow the Holy Spirit to control every aspect of their lives.

If the guiding principle of their lives is the Holy Spirit, the Galatians will not fulfill "the desires of the sinful nature" (5:16). This is true because the leading of the Holy Spirit is diametrically opposed to the impulse of the sinful nature, and vice versa (5:17). The phrase "so that you do not do what you want" is open to interpretation. It can mean that when the Galatians want to walk after the sinful nature, the Spirit opposes that desire. Yet it can also mean that when they want to be led by the Spirit, the sinful nature undermines their intentions as well. Since the Galatians are filled with the Spirit (3:2), Paul is probably noting that the sinful nature is preventing them from serving God as they wish.

This interpretation coincides with Paul's treatment of the flesh (sinful nature) and the Spirit in Romans 6:1–8:27. The Galatians are not to offer their members as instruments of unrighteousness, but to present themselves to God as instruments of righteousness (6:13–14, 19). The renewed mind may actually desire to do the will of God, but the sinful nature prevents the realization of that will. Those in the flesh find themselves doing what they hate. An increased knowledge of the law only serves to multiply transgressions (7:14–25; see Fung 1988, 252). Deliverance from this vicious cycle can only come through the power of the Spirit (8:1–4, 9).

Paul's words in Galatians 5:18 summarize his entire burden for the Galatians. The life of faith is qualitatively different from life in the flesh. Similarly, as Paul has been arguing, the Christian life is essentially different from life under the law. Therefore in his mind, life in the flesh and life under the law are practical equivalents. They both produce the same results.

The sinful nature (flesh) and the law are powerful and powerless at the same time. They are powerful in that they work hand in hand to bring forth sin but also to condemn sin (5:19; Rom. 5:20; 7:8–11). On the other hand, they are powerless because neither the sinful nature nor the law can bring forth salvation. On the contrary, the partnership of the sinful nature and the law produces spiritual frustration and a sense of guilt and condemnation. Life in the flesh and life under the law are both subject to the *stoicheia*, the "basic principles" of life (4:3, 9). To be under the law is to be subject to a harsh pedagogue (3:24). Thus those who are led by the flesh and are subject to the law will continue to experience moral failure and an awful dread of the judgment.

None of this applies to those who are led by the Holy Spirit, because the nature and function of the Spirit are opposite that of the law and the sinful nature. The contrast between the freedom and power of the Spirit, and the negative effects of the law and the sinful nature can be seen in the following examples. The Spirit does not minister oppression and bondage, but liberty and power. The Spirit anoints to set captives free and to adopt the faithful into the glorious liberty of the children of God (Luke 4:18; Rom. 8:15–16, 21; 2 Cor. 3:17). In contrast to the impotence of the law

THE FRUIT OF THE SPIRIT

The aspects of the fruit of the Spirit advocated by Paul in Galatians 5:22–23 occur not only here but also elsewhere in the Scriptures. Most of the attributes are those by which God himself lives.

Aspect	GK Number	Definition	Attribute of God	Attribute for Christians
love	G26	sacrificial, unmerited deeds to help a needy person	Ex 34:6; Jn 3:16; Ro 5:8; 1Jn 4:8, 16	Jn 13:34–35; Ro 12:9–10; 1Pe 1:22; 1Jn 4:7, 11–12, 21
joy	G5915	an inner happiness not dependent on outward circumstances	Ps 104:31; Isa 62:5; Lk 15:7, 10	Dt 12:7, 12, 18; Ps 64:10; Isa 25:9; Php 4:4; 1Pe 1:8
peace	G1645	harmony in all relationships	Isa 9:6–7; Eze 34:25; Jn 14:27; Heb 13:20	Isa 26:3; Ro 5:1; 12:18; Ro 14:17; Eph 2:14–17
patience	G3429	putting up with others, even when one is severely tried	Ro 9:22; 1Ti 1:16; 1Pe 3:20; 2Pe 3:9, 15	Eph 4:2; Col 1:11; Heb 6:12; Jas 5:7–8, 10
kindness	G5983	doing thoughtful deeds for others	Ro 2:4; 11:22; Eph 2:7; Tit 3:4	1Co 13:4; Eph 4:32; Col 3:12
goodness	G20	showing generosity to others	Ne 9:25, 35; Ps 31:19; Mk 10:18	Ro 15:14; Eph 5:9; 2Th 1:11
faithfulness	G4411	trustworthiness and reliability	Ps 33:4; 1Co 1:9;10:13; Heb 10:23; 1Jn 1:9	Lk 16:10–12; 2Th 1:4; 2Ti 4:7; Tit 2:10
gentleness	G4559	meekness and humility	Zec 9:9; Mt 11:29	Isa 66:2; Mt 5:5; Eph 4:2; Col 3:12
self-control	G1602	victory over sinful desires		Pr 16:32; Tit 1:8; 2:12; 1Pe 5:8–9; 2Pe 1:6

the Spirit empowers us to actualize the kingdom on earth (Acts 2:4; 1 Cor. 2:4; 12:1–31; 14:1–40). Although the law was made weak through the sinful nature, the Spirit mortifies the deeds of that nature (Rom. 8:3, 13). The law accentuates our weaknesses (7:8–10), but the Spirit administers strength in place of our weaknesses (8:26). Therefore, the Spirit-filled believer is not under the law and consequently not bound by the sinful nature (Gal. 5:18).

The Judaizers have not only undermined sound doctrine in Galatia, but they have also destroyed the spiritual atmosphere of the churches (5:15). Their entire agenda was based on the sinful nature, not on the Spirit (4:8–10, 17). For these reasons Paul begins to contrast the works of the sinful nature with the fruit of the Spirit in 5:19–23. Such lists of virtues and vices are found throughout the New Testament (Rom. 1:24–31; 1 Cor. 5:9–13; 6:9–11; 2 Cor. 12:20–21; 1 Thess. 4:3–6). They were also common in the ancient world, especially among the Stoic philosophers (Ridderbos, 1957, 205). Paul recognizes that even the Gentiles can discern right from wrong. In this sense they become a law unto themselves (Rom. 2:26–27).

With regard to the works of the sinful nature Paul states that they "are obvious" (5:19). He means that the character of these acts is beyond question. All but the most depraved recognize that such behavior is vile, hateful, and destructive (Gench, 1992, 294).

The first set of vices addresses sexual immorality. This word (*porneia*) refers to sexual impropriety of all kinds. "Impurity" (*akatharsia*) literally means "uncleanness." Paul never uses this word to refer to ritual or ceremonial impurity (Mark 7:1–5, 14; Acts 10:14, 28). On the contrary, for Paul "uncleanness" always has an ethical or moral content, usually relating to sexual perversion (Rom. 1:24; 6:19; Eph. 4:19). *Aselgeia* ("debauchery") refers to uninhibited lust that has absolutely no regard for God, self, nor others (Bruce, 1982, 247).

In 5:20 Paul addresses idolatry and the occult. "Idolatry" is a work of the sinful nature because an idol is basically a self-projection. It is the act of creating "god" in humanity's own image (Ex. 20:4; Lev. 26:1). Idolatry is the fleshly desire to control the supernatural to gratify the lusts of the sinful nature. This is why "coveting" is equivalent to idolatry (Col. 3:5). "Witchcraft" (*pharmakeia*; cf. our word "pharmacy") does not denote evil in itself, but drugs were used in witchcraft and in some occult practices during idol worship.

"Hatred, discord, jealousy, fits of rage" are all manifestations of the sinful nature in social relationships. The word for "hatred" is actually in the plural, indicating the continuous expression of a hostile spirit. "Discord" (sometimes translated "strife") is derived from the Greek goddess Eris; she was the god who inspired wars (Bruce, 1982, 248). "Jealousy" (*zelos*), literally meaning "zeal," can be a virtue if touched by the Spirit (2 Cor. 11:2). But when fueled by the sinful nature, it degenerates into a begrudging jealousy that loathes the success of others. "Fits of rage" describes that unbridled anger that indiscriminately kills and maims any so unfortunate to be in its path.

"Selfish ambition" describes one who has a mercenary spirit (Bruce, 1982, 249). The net effect of the flesh is that it causes "dissensions" in the body of Christ (1 Cor. 1:11–12). "Factions" comes from *haireseis* (cf. our "heresy"), a word that originally contained no evil connotations and referred to different types of religious and political parties. Josephus used this word to describe religious sects such as the Pharisees, Sadducees, and Nazarenes. In time, however, the word came to describe false teachers and their doctrines.

Unlike "zeal," the word for "envy" (*phthonos*) always has an evil meaning. It refers to a mean-spirited attitude that resents the good fortune of others. The word is actually in the plural and indicates a continuous jealousy in a variety of circumstances. The last two vices ("drunkenness" and "orgies") reflect on the hedonistic lifestyle so prevalent in pagan culture (5:21). Paul concludes his list of vices with "and the like." He is able to make such a generality because of what he said previously in 5:19. The nature of the flesh is easily discerned.

At this point Paul expresses the crux of the issue: Anyone who continues to practice the works of the flesh will not inherit the kingdom of God. Therefore, the works of the sinful nature are antithetical to the principles of the kingdom. Paul had preached this to the Galatians "before" when he was with them (Acts 14:22). The carnal campaign of the Judaizers has led him to reemphasize these points again

Paul goes on to contrast "the fruit of the Spirit" with the works of the sinful nature. Just as the sinful nature manifests itself in different ways, the fruit of the Spirit has a variety of expressions. "Fruit" (*karpos*) is in the singular and shows the essential unity of the fruit of the Spirit. In other words, the Spirit-filled believer must demonstrate *all* the characteristics of the Spirit, not this virtue or that one.

In that the whole law is fulfilled in love (5:14), *agape* appears first in the list. This is the Spirit-empowered love of God that unerringly seeks the welfare of others (1 Cor. 13). In this sense "love" is the source of all the graces of the Spirit (Eadie, 1977, 422ff.).

"Joy" (*chara*) has nothing to do with that fleeting, lighthearted emotion so common to the world. Rather, it is that deep-seated knowledge that we are saved in the present, yet our full redemption lies in the future (1 John 3:2). The powers of the age to come are continually transforming us into the image of Christ (Rom. 8:29). Therefore, regardless of our personal circumstances the believer experiences a joyous confidence that our destiny is in God.

This experience of joy leads to "peace" (*eirene*). "Peace" does not refer to some fragile truce between hostile parties. God's peace is not dependent on the changing landscape of a fallen world. Rather, Paul is speaking of peace with God and the peace that comes from God (Rom. 5:1; 15:13, 33). It is that divine peace that transcends all human understanding, yet gives full knowledge that all is well with my soul (Phil. 4:7). In short, Paul speaks of God's peace that is born of righteousness and grants joy in the Holy Spirit. Unlike the works of the sinful nature, this is the kingdom of God (Rom. 14:17).

"Patience" (*makrothumia*) speaks of that resilience of spirit that refuses to attack when provoked or despitefully used (cf. Eph. 4:2). Paul uses this word to describe how God patiently bore with vessels of wrath (Rom. 9:22). Its meaning is similar to "long-suffering" (*hypomone*), literally translated "to hold out under a heavy load." Even when subjected to continued pressure, the Spirit-filled believer does not resort to "fits of rage" (see Gal. 5:20).

"Kindness" (*chrestotes*) is that sensitivity to the mental, spiritual, and emotional framework of others a quality that can discern the "load limit" of an individual (Ps. 103:14).

"Goodness" (*agathosyne*) is that steadfast commitment to the benefit of others. This is the true spirit of the law when it is unencumbered by sin and the flesh. It reflects the character of its Maker and thus is holy, just, and *good* (Rom. 7:12). Similarly, the Spirit-filled believer fulfills the law by evidencing the goodness of God (Rom. 3:21).

Since Paul is addressing those who have already been filled with the Spirit, *pistis* (usually translated "faith") means "faithfulness." It denotes the opposite of cynicism.

"Gentleness" (*prautes*, translated "meekness" in the KJV) is the opposite of that arrogant attitude so often confused with self-confidence. Gentleness is the opposite of a rash, headstrong spirit that frequently runs roughshod over the feelings of others.

"Self-control" (*egkrateia*) is related to the word *kratos*, which refers to God's mighty power. It is a type of spiritual power that subjugates all fleshly impulses (1 Cor. 9:27).

The words "against such things there is no law" summarizes Paul's thoughts concerning the fruit of the Spirit (5:23). The Spirit and the law are two totally different categories. The law cannot mandate the fruit of the Spirit, nor can it facilitate the practical application of them. The barrenness of the law has nothing to say to the fruitfulness of the Spirit.

Paul's emphasis on sanctification continues in 5:24: "Those who belong to Christ Jesus have crucified the sinful nature with its passions and desires." The word "crucified" points to a single crisis experience in the past. Thus for the believer crucifixion with Christ represents the definitive break with the flesh. This concept was introduced in 2:20, where Paul states, "I have been crucified with Christ and I no longer live, but Christ lives in me." Similarly, Paul teaches that "our old self" has been crucified with Christ, so that the believer is no longer to serve sin (Rom. 6:6). As will be noted below, Paul boasts in the cross of Christ, through whom the world is crucified to him and he to the world (Gal. 6:14).

Paul's message is clear. Spirit-filled believers have made a clean break with sin, the world, and the flesh. But questions remain. In what sense have we been crucified? How does this crucifixion take place? And what role do we play in the experience of crucifixion? In answer, note that our crucifixion is always related to the cross of Christ. We have not crucified ourselves, but in a passive sense we have been crucified "in Christ." Thus Christ's death on the cross serves as the sole foundation for all other crucifixions in the body of Christ. By faith we are able to participate in the death, burial, and resurrection of Christ (Rom. 6:1–6). In short, from God's perspective Christ's experiences have become our experiences.

Nevertheless we as believers do have an active role in crucifying the flesh (5:24) . The Ephesians are commanded to put off the old self and to put on the new self (Eph. 4:22–24). The Romans are exhorted to stop offering their members as instruments of unrighteousness (Rom. 6:13). They must not live according to the sinful nature, but according to the Spirit (8:1, 4). The Corinthians are challenged to cleanse themselves of all contamination of the body and spirit (2 Cor. 7:1). Even though Christ is our holiness (1 Cor. 1:30), believers are commanded to realize holiness in everyday living (Rom. 12:1; 1 Cor. 3:16–17; 6:19–20).

Paul's mandate for holy living is not a new legalism. On the contrary, true holiness can only be wrought by the Spirit of holiness (Rom. 1:4). Hence in Galatians 5:25, Paul exhorts, "Since we live by the Spirit, let us keep in step with the Spirit." This verse is better translated, "If in fact we are living by the Spirit, then we ought also to walk by the Spirit." Holiness is a lifestyle that is completely governed by the dictates of God's Spirit (5:16, 18; Parsons, 1988, 120). The word translated "keep in step" (*stoichomen*) is derived from *stoichos*, meaning a "row" or a "line." So those who submit to the Spirit literally have their steps ordered by the Spirit (Ps. 37:23; 1 Pet. 2:21).

Narcissism has no place in the Spirit-filled life (5:26). Any self-promotion distorts the body of Christ and casts the sincere contribution of others in a poor light (1 Cor. 12). In turn this "false image" incites others to carnal ambition and petty jealousy. The failure of one tends to implicate all (1 Cor. 5:6; Gal. 5:9).

As Pentecostals we have done a good job of emphasizing the gifts of the Spirit. The importance of the fruit of the Spirit deserves more attention. The Corinthians were anxious to experience the charismatic power of the Holy Spirit, yet were filled with carnal ambition and strife (1 Cor. 3:1–3). Scripture insists that believers will be known by their fruit, not their gifts (Matt. 7:17–19; 12:33; Luke 6:43–44).

4.7. Sowing to Please the Spirit (6:1–10)

Paul continues to develop the theme of the Spirit in chapter 6. Specifically, he describes how those who are led by the Spirit should relate to others in the church. "[Those] who are spiritual" (6:1) must evidence the fruit of the Spirit in all of life. They must always have a redemptive or restorative function in the body of Christ.

The grammar of 6:1 suggests that Paul is not addressing a specific problem in Galatia. Rather, he creates a hypothetical situation for the purpose of instruction. The Galatians must know how to respond to a person overtaken by sin. The verb *prolambano* (translated "caught" in the NIV) does not point to a conscious or deliberate transgression. For whatever reason the person has fallen into the trap of sin (Fung 1988, 285). Under such circumstances that person is to be restored "gently" (lit., "in a spirit of gentleness"; cf. 5:23). "Restore" (*katartizo*) underscores the need for gentleness; this word was often used to describe the setting of broken bones and joints (Lightfoot 1981, 215).

"But watch yourself, or you also may be tempted" is a warning for those doing the restoring. They must zero in on their weaknesses like trained marksmen and never let them out of their sights (Guthrie, 1973, 142). If they do not, they too may fall prey to the deceitfulness of sin (Rom. 7:8–11).

This type of spiritual mentoring is to characterize the entire community. In 6:2 Paul exhorts the Galatians to "carry each other's burdens." The word "burden" (*baros*) is primarily associated with "pressure" or "weight." Unlike "transgression" in 6:1, it does not imply any wrongdoing; it simply refers to the pressures and trials we all face in this fallen world. Each member of the body of Christ is to be sensitive to the hardships that others may be experiencing (1 Cor. 12:26). In this way the believer obeys the command, "Love your neighbor as yourself" and thus fulfills "the law of Christ" (cf. Gal. 5:14; Matt. 5:43; 19:19; 22:39; Luke 10:27; James 2:8). However "the law of Christ" does not constitute a new legalism for the Christian. Here "law" refers to th principle of love that is to undergird and guide all aspects of the church.

The principle of self-examination in 6:1 is addressed again in 6:3–4. To think too highly of oneself is to deceive oneself. This kind of illusion will inevitably have serious consequences. Thus the mature believer must walk circumspectly lest he or she also fails the grace of God (Rom. 11:21; 1 Cor. 10:12). Arrogance and conceit (Gal. 5:19) have no place in the church. The surest safeguard against these sins is not a general inquisition but personal introspection. Each believer is to "test" his or her own work. This word (*dokimazo*) relates to the testing of metal coins through a refiner's fire (Guthrie, 1973, 144). Similarly the Spirit-filled believer is to constantly expose his or her ministry to the refining fire of the Lord (1 Cor. 3:13–15; James 1:2–4; 1 Pet. 1:7). These "self-tests" are a matter of spiritual accountability, the results of which will show in what one can legitimately rejoice.

This kind of self-appraisal is necessary, for in the final analysis "each one should carry his [or her] own load" (6:5). Initially this verse seems to conflict with 6:2, yet Paul uses a different word for "burden" here—*phortion*, which refers to a heavy pack or load that is deliberately taken up (Burton, 1956, 334). Unlike the uninvited daily "pressures" of 6:2, this verse refers to those tasks and obligations that we each choose to bear. Each believer is personally responsible for following through on such obligations and must bear up under such pressures of everyday life (Kuck, 1994, 289–97).

Paul introduces a new subject in 6:6–10. Just as the natural realm is governed by certain "laws," the life of faith is also subject to "spiritual laws." Paul explains here the principle of reciprocity—"A man reaps what he sows" (6:7)—and continues this agricultural motif through 6:10.

In 6:6 Paul teaches that one who has been instructed in God's Word should "share all good things with his instructor." In short, Christian teachers are entitled to material support from their pupils in the same way that pastors are eligible for support from their congregations (1 Cor. 9:3–12).

Paul sternly warns the Galatians, "Do not be deceived: God cannot be mocked" (6:7). One may convince oneself that he or she is walking in the Spirit, but may actually be living in the flesh. God cannot be deceived in this way (Stagg, 1991, 247). The Spirit accurately discerns the thoughts and intents of the heart (Rom. 8:26–27; Heb. 4:12–13). The nature of our thoughts, words, and deeds yields consequences consistent with their nature: "A man reaps what he sows."

Paul further develops this farming analogy by speaking of two crops. If one sows seeds of a sinful nature, one will reap a harvest of destruction (like the works of the sinful nature in 5:19–21). This fruit has nothing to do with the kingdom. On the contrary, if one sows seeds of a spiritual nature, then one will reap a harvest of the Spirit (6:8). This fruit is the fruit of the Spirit (5:22–23) and leads to eternal life.

But good crops do not happen automatically. Intense cultivation and care are needed throughout the growing process. So believers must not become fatigued in doing the hard work of the kingdom. They must patiently await God's reward (James 5:7–8).

The words in 6:10, "Therefore, as we have opportunity," may be better translated, "Now, therefore, as we have time." These final words strike an end-time note. The Lord of the harvest is coming, and believers must seize every opportunity to do good (Luke 10:2–16; Eph. 5:16; Col. 4:5). But good deeds are not to be done indiscriminately. The "family" of God is to take priority (Acts 2:44–45; 4:32–37). Then those who are outside the household of God can receive the surplus of blessings granted to the church.

The primary message of this section is that every believer is accountable to others, to oneself, and to God. We cannot turn our backs on those who have been overtaken by sin, nor can we ignore our own weaknesses without inviting moral disaster. Finally, we cannot escape being accountable to the moral laws of God. They are as consistent as the laws of nature. To violate them is to suffer spiritual barrenness; to obey them is to reap a harvest of eternal life.

5. Conclusion (6:11–18)

The intensity of Paul's spirit is present throughout Galatians. The closing of the letter is no exception. In 6:11–18 Paul gives his personal sign of authenticity, recaps the essence of the Judaizing problem, mentions the personal conflict he has with the troublemakers, and pronounces a blessing upon the Galatians.

5.1. Paul's Sign of Authenticity (6:11)

The literature of the early church contains many *pseudepigrapha* ("false writings"), which sought to supply information not included in the Scriptures (such as more on the childhood of Jesus) or to spread false doctrine. Often the names of great spiritual leaders were forged on these writings to increase their credibility. Apparently someone may have used Paul's name to write a false letter to the Thessalonians (2 Thess. 2:2). Even though Paul often used an amanuensis (male secretary) to write his letters, he personally signed them (George, 1994, 430). As he wrote in 2 Thessalonians 3:17, "I, Paul, write this greeting in my own hand, which is the distinguishing mark in all my letters. This is how I write."

Galatians 6:11 indicates that Paul fears the Judaizers might forge his name on a letter in order to spread their false doctrine, so Paul adds his personal signature to this letter. The words "See what large letters I use" may point to his failing eyesight. That is, his personal greeting was in a larger script than that used by his scribe.

5.2. Once More: Exposing the Judaizers (6:12–15)

Even when closing his letter, Paul does not miss the opportunity to attack the Judaizers, exposing one last time the false motives, superficiality, and self-interest of these troublemakers.

Paul contrasts the works of the sinful nature with that of the Spirit here again. The Judaizers want "to make a good impression" outwardly (6:12). That is, they are concerned with an external mark in the flesh that has nothing to do with the Holy Spirit. Their methods are equally unsavory, for they are not acting in love. On the contrary, they are trying "to compel" the Galatians into being circumcised. Their motives are self-serving and have nothing to do with the spiritual welfare of the Galatians. They hope to avoid the persecution of the cross, that is, the kind of persecution Paul experienced throughout his ministry (5:11). They know that to preach the sole sufficiency of the cross will automatically call into question the status of the law. Any devaluation of the law will invite persecution from their countrymen (Weima, 1993, 99).

In 6:13 Paul reveals the hypocrisy of the Judaizers. Their motives are similar to that of Peter in Antioch (2:11–15); they are trying to force the Gentiles to obey the law even though they have failed that perfect standard themselves (3:10–12; James 2:10). They have no real concern for the Galatians; they are only trying to make trophies of the flesh in order to demonstrate their devotion to Judaism (Cousar, 1982, 152). In so doing they break the law, for they are driven by carnal pride, which the law condemns (Pss. 40:4; 101:5; Isa. 13:11).

Paul's foundation for boasting is completely antithetical to that of the Judaizers. Far from avoiding the scandal of the cross and the persecution that it brings, he revels in its wisdom and power (5:11; 1 Cor. 1:18–25, 31; 2 Cor. 13:4). It is the determining factor in all that he preaches and does (Gal. 3:1; 1 Cor. 2:2). In fact, the cross brings about an entirely new set of ideals that have nothing to do with the things of this world. The carnal boasting of the Judaizers only reveals how indebted they are to the values of this world.

Paul's total identification with the cross draws him into the experience of Christ so that he too is crucified (2:20). In effect, the world and everything that it stands for has been crucified to Paul, and Paul has been crucified to the world (5:24; 6:14). The tense of the verb "crucified" reflects a definitive action in the past that has continuing results into the present. Therefore, Paul is saying that he has been crucified with Christ in the past, but the effects of that crucifixion define his existence in the present. As far as the world is concerned, Paul and all those who are in Christ are dead men (Rom. 6:2, 8; 2 Cor. 5:14).

This death to the world also includes death to legalism and all meaningless rituals (2:19; Col. 2:20). Thus Paul states, "Neither circumcision nor uncircumcision means anything; what counts is a new creation" (6:15). This verse essentially summarizes the entire letter. No physical procedure (removal of the foreskin) or lack thereof has any spiritual significance (Rom. 2:25–26; 1 Cor. 7:19). What matters is a spiritual transformation that affects every aspect of one's life and person (Rom. 8; 12). There must be a circumcision of the heart, which can only be done by the Spirit of God (Rom. 2:29; Phil. 3:3; Col. 2:11). Only then does God's law become inscribed on tablets of human hearts and not on tablets of stone (Jer. 31:33; 2 Cor. 3:3).

In the final analysis the only thing that mat-
:rs to God is being born of the Spirit, that is, eing a "new creation" (2 Cor. 5:17; cf. Eph. :24). Those who have been born of the Spirit re the children of promise (Rom. 4:16; Gal. :6–9; 4:28–29). They have been empowered to valk in the Spirit, evidencing his fruit and gifts a their lives and ministries (Acts 1:8; 1 Cor. 2:1–31; Gal. 3:5, 22–23). It is they, not the udaizers, whom the Spirit affirms as the chil-ren of God and through whom the Spirit cries, *Abba*! Father!" (Gal. 4:6–7; cf. Rom. 8:15–17).

5.3. Final Words and Benediction (6:16–18)

The last three verses of Galatians contain 'aul's benediction. But even here the intensity f his spirit is evident. Between the words of lessing in verses 16 and 18, he fires off one ast salvo at his opponents.

A blessing of peace and mercy is common nough in Jewish prayers; similar words are ound at the close of each of Paul's letters Rom. 16:20; 1 Cor. 16:23–24; 2 Cor. 13:14; tc.). There is some dispute concerning the hrase "the Israel of God" (6:16). Should it be nderstood in an exclusive sense—that is, that nly those who follow the one rule (the prior-ty of the new creation) are the true Israel of God? If so, Paul is equating the church with srael. Or should the blessing be understood in n inclusive sense—that is, anyone who fol-ows this one rule is to receive mercy and eace, *even the Israel of God*?

This latter interpretation seems to agree vith the spirit and theology of Paul. His is a 'theology of inclusion" that ignores social and acial distinctions (3:28). Yes, even Israel will eceive mercy and peace if she accepts that one nust be born again by the Spirit (John 3:3–8). According to Paul this blessing will undoubt-edly come to Israel, though only a "remnant" vill be saved (Rom. 11:1–6).

Unlike the Judaizers, who sought to show heir devotion through the flesh of others (cf. :13), Paul points to his own battered body as roof of his commitment to Christ (6:17). The vord for "marks" is *stigmata*, a word used to efer to a brand or tattoo that identified a slave s belonging to a particular master. Hence the marks" probably refer to scars that Paul eceived when he was stoned and flogged Acts 14:19–20, 16:23; 2 Cor. 11:23–29).

THE OLD TESTAMENT IN THE NEW

NT Text	OT Text	Subject
Gal 3:6	Ge 15:6	Faith of Abraham
Gal 3:8	Ge 12:3; 18:18	Gospel to Abraham
Gal 3:10	Dt 27:26	Curse of the law
Gal 3:11	Hab 2:4	The righteous live by faith
Gal 3:12	Lev 18:5	Living by the law
Gal 3:13	Dt 21:23	Curse of the cross
Gal 3:16	Ge 13:15; 24:7	Offspring of Abraham
Gal 4:27	Isa 54:1	Joy of the barren woman
Gal 4:30	Ge 21:10	Expulsion of Ishmael
Gal 5:14	Lev 19:18	Love your neighbor as yourself

Paul's final greeting comes in 6:18. Although fairly typical of greetings in his other letters, there is one striking difference: He does not give any personal greetings (contrast esp. Rom. 16:1–16). This may reflect the strained relationship between Paul and the Galatians. On the other hand, the last word of the text, apart from the "Amen," is "brothers." Therefore, in spite of all the troubles and confusion in Galatia, Paul still considers them his "brothers."

BIBLIOGRAPHY

M. Barth, "The Kerygma of Galatians." *Interp* 21 (1967): 131–46; H. D. Betz, *A Commentary on Paul's Letter to the Churches of Galatia* (1979); idem, *Spirit, Freedom, and Law: Paul's Message to the Galatian Churches*, SEA 39 (1974); F. F. Bruce, *The Book of Acts*, NICNT (1988); idem, *The Epistle to the Galatians: A Commentary on the Greek Text* (1982); D. R. Bundrick, "*Ta stoicheia tou kosmou* (Gal. 4:3)," *JETS* 34 (1991): 353–64; E. D. Burton, *A Critical and Exegetical Commentary on the Galatians*, ICC (1956); D. Cohn-Sherbok, "Some Reflections on James Dunn's 'The Incident at Antioch (Gal 2:11–18),' " *JSNT* 18 (1983): 68–74; R. A. Cole, *The Epistle of Paul to the Galatians* (1984); C. B. Cousar, *A Bible Commentary for Teaching and Preaching Galatians*, Interpretation (1982); N. Dahl, *Studies in Paul* (1977); G. S.

Duncan, *The Epistle of Paul to the Galatians* (1966); J. D. G. Dunn, *Jesus and the Spirit: A Study of the Religious and Charismatic Experience of Jesus and the First Christians as Reflected in the New Testament* (1975); idem, "The Incident at Antioch (Gal. 2:11–18)," *JSNT* 18 (1983): 3–57; idem, "Yet Once More—'The Works of the Law': A Response," *JSNT* 46 (1992): 99–117; J. Eadie, *Commentary on the Epistle of Paul to the Galatians: Based on the Greek Text*, 1977; R. E. Earle, *Word Meanings in the New Testament* (vol. 4; 1979); G. Ebeling, *The Truth of the Gospel: An Exposition of Galatians* (1985); F. Esler, *Community and Gospel in Luke-Acts: The Social and Political Motivations of Lukan Theology* (1987); G. D. Fee, "Freedom and the Life of Obedience: Gal. 5:1–18," *RevExp* 91 (1994): 201–17; S. E. Fowl, "Who Can Read Abraham's Story? Allegory and Interpretative Power in Galatians," *JSNT* 55 (1994): 77–95; R. Y. K. Fung, *The Epistle to the Galatians* (1988); F. T. Gench, "Galatians 5:1, 13–25," *Interp* 46 (1992): 290–95; T. George, *Galatians,* NAC (1994); D. Guthrie, *Galatians* (1973); G. W. Hansen, *Galatians* (1994); S. Heine, *Women and Early Christianity: A Reappraisal* (trans. John Bowden, 1987); C. C. Hill, *Hellenists and Hebrews: Reappraising Division Within the Earliest Church* (1992); K. H. Jobes, "Jerusalem, Our Mother: *Metalepsis* and Intertextuality in Galatians 4:21-31," *WTJ* 55 (1993): 299–320; S. Kim, *The Origin of Paul's Gospel* (1981); D. W. Kuck, "Each Will Bea His Own Burden: Paul's Creative Use of an Apoc-alyptic Motif," *NTS* 40 (1994): 289–97: H. R. Lemmer, "Mnemonic Reference to the Spirit as a Persuasive Tool (Galatians 3:1–6 Within the Argument, 3:1–4:11)," *Neot* (1992): 359–88; J. B. Lightfoot, *St. Paul's Epistle to the Galatians* (1957, [rev.] 1981); D. J. Lull, *The Spirit in Galatia: Paul's Interpretation of PNEUMA as Divine Power*, SBLDS 49 (1980); C. Osiek, *Galatians* (1980); M. Parsons "Being Precedes Act: Indicative and Imperative in Paul's Writing," *EvQ* (April 1988): 99–127; H. N Ridderbos, *The Epistle of Paul to the Churches of Galatia* (1957); E. P. Sanders, *Jewish Law From Jesus to the Mishnah* (1990); M. E. Smallwood, *The Jews Under Roman Rule: From Pompey to Diocletian: A Study in Political Relations,* SJLA 20 (1981); F. Stagg, "Galatians 6:7–10," *RevExp* 8£ (1991): 247–51; D. J. Verseput, "Paul's Gentile Mission and the Jewish Christian Community: A Study of the Narrative in Galatians 1 and 2," *NTS* 39 (1993): 36–58; A. J. M. Wedderburn, "Paul and Jesus: Similarity and Continuity," *NTS* 34 (1988): 161–82; J. A. D. Weima, "Gal. 6:11–18: A Hermeneutical Key to the Galatian Letter," *CTJ* 28 (1993): 90–107; S. K. Williams, "Justification and the Spirit in Galatians," *JSNT* 29 (1987): 91–100; Ben Witherington III, "Rite and Rights for Women—Galatians 3:28," *NTS* 27 (1981): 593-604; R. Yandian, *The Spirit-Controlled Life* (1985).

EPHESIANS

J. Wesley Adams
with Donald C. Stamps (posthumously)

NTRODUCTION

. A Majestic Letter

phesians is a majestic letter that stands as one f the mountain peaks of biblical revelation— a class with Romans, the Fourth Gospel, nd Hebrews. Writers have referred to it as the Switzerland of the New Testament," "the)ueen of the Epistles" (Barclay), and "the rown of St. Paul's writings" (Robinson). John 'alvin considered it his favorite letter. 'oleridge, the great poet, viewed Ephesians as the divinest composition of man." Nowhere the Spirit of revelation more evident than this letter. Charles Hodge rightly observes: The epistle reveals itself as the work of the loly Ghost as clearly as the stars declare their aker to be God" (Hodge, xv).

Ephesians, as the capstone of Paul's reveatory understanding of God's eternal purposes in Christ for the church, has a character ll its own among Paul's letters. There is a onspicuous absence of theological controersy (as is found in Galatians and Romans) nd of pastoral problems (as in the Thessaonian and Corinthian letters). Instead "it is a astorally warm letter and spiritually sensitive its advice, peaceable [and deeply reflective] tone and readily overflowing into [prayer nd] joyful worship" (Turner, 1222). It is reathtaking in its eternal comprehensiveness, et marvelously concise in its presentation.

Regrettably in the modern era, as I have oted elsewhere (Adams, 4–6), New Testaient scholars have sometimes focused more ttently on critical issues about the origin of phesians and the authenticity of Paul's uthorship than on his profound message for ie church. But wherever the revelation of od's glorious plan of redemption in Christ esus is regarded as primary in importance, nd wherever the practical implications of life *in Christ*" for the believer and the church are mphasized, Ephesians continues to be a uch loved, much read, and much preached ook. It addresses such directly relevant issues r the church in renewal and such prophetially important issues for bringing the church to maturity—i.e., "the whole measure of the fullness of Christ" (4:13)—that it may prove to be the premier New Testament letter for the end-time church.

2. Authorship

As in all his letters, Paul identifies himself clearly at the outset of Ephesians: "Paul, an apostle of Christ Jesus" (1:1). In characteristic fashion he also ascribes his apostolic authority to "the will of God" (1:1; cf. 2 Cor. 1:1; Gal. 1:1; Col. 1:1). As in his undisputed letters, Paul's name later reappears in Ephesians: "I, Paul, the prisoner of Christ Jesus for the sake of you Gentiles" (3:1; cf. 2 Cor. 10:1; Gal. 5:2; Col. 1:23; 1 Thess. 2:18). Frequently Paul uses the first person singular, and he requests his readers to pray that he may fearlessly declare the gospel as an ambassador in chains (6:19–20). Paul commends Tychicus as the letter's carrier and his personal representative to bring news to the readers on Paul's behalf (6:21–22).

In spite of this evidence, controversy has surrounded its authorship in modern times. This issue was first disputed in 1792 by Evanson, who could not reconcile the letter's title with its content. In the 1820s some German scholars disputed Paul's authorship on other grounds. Since then, many New Testament scholars have disputed its authenticity (notable contemporaries are R. Schnackenburg, C. L. Mitton, and A. T. Lincoln), based on supposedly non-Pauline vocabulary and style and post-Pauline theological and ecclesiological concepts (for thorough summaries of the issues raised about authorship and answers given in response, see Guthrie, 490–508; Foulkes, 19–49; Caird, 11–29).

While Andrew Lincoln (lxxiii) argues that non-Pauline authorship does not detract from the letter's validity in the New Testament canon or from the authority of its message, T. K. Abbott (xvii-xviii, xxiv) carefully pointed out years before that authenticity is a weighty issue. For someone other than Paul (or his designated amanuensis) to have written Ephesians, given the explicit claims to be written by Paul and the various references to his personal circumstances as author, would require a forgery with intent to deceive the readers as to its true origin.

F. F. Bruce (1961, 12) focuses on another authorial problem that confronts scholars who accept the pseudonymous thesis. He remarks that Ephesians is such a remarkable testimony of inspiration and assimilation of Pauline revelation that if not written by Paul himself, then it would have had to be written by his equal or his superior spiritually and intellectually. Bruce adds that we have no knowledge of a second Paul of such stature in early Christianity. Along the same line Henry J. Cadbury, emeritus professor of Harvard Divinity School, addressed the same problem of pseudonymity in the form of a question: "Which is more likely—that an imitator of Paul in the first century composed a writing ninety or ninety-five percent in accordance with Paul's style or that Paul himself wrote a letter diverging five or ten percent from his usual style?" (quoted by Brown, 378). The present writer fully accepts the clear witness of authorship in the inspired text of Ephesians and believes that all alleged discrepancies can be explained adequately based on Paul's circumstances when writing the letter and on its unique content and purpose.

3. Date and Place of Writing

Ephesians expressly states it was written by Paul while a "prisoner of Christ Jesus for the sake of you Gentiles" (3:1), "as a prisoner for the Lord" (4:1), and as "an ambassador in chains" (6:20). Paul testifies in 2 Corinthians 11:23 that he had been imprisoned many times (c. A.D. 55/56), more than any other apostle. Later, Acts records two outstanding imprisonments of Paul: two years at Caesarea (24:1–26:32) and two years at Rome. (28:16–31). Paul's Pastoral Letters (the order of writing being 1 Timothy, Titus, 2 Timothy) record Paul's missionary activity after his first Roman imprisonment and ending with a second one in Rome. In addition to these three notable prison experiences, some propose that a fourth major one occurred at Ephesus.

Some writers have sought to make a case for Paul writing Ephesians while a prisoner at Caesarea or even during an unrecorded imprisonment at Ephesus. But the view that Paul wrote Ephesians during his first Roman imprisonment (A.D. 60–62 or 61–63) referre to in Acts 28 holds the field among New Testament scholars and is most probable. During this time he wrote Philemon, Colossians, Ephesians, and perhaps Philippians. The bes judgment is that Ephesians was written shortl after Colossians (and Philemon) c. A.D. 62 with all three letters carried simultaneously b Tychicus to their destination (cf. Eph. 6:21-22; Col. 4:7).

4. The Recipients

Unlike other letters by Paul, the identity of th original recipients of this letter is uncertain The salutation "to the saints in Ephesus" (1:1 would appear to settle the issue except for tw considerations. (1) The words "in Ephesus" d not appear in the text of the earliest and bes Greek manuscripts, indicating that it was mos likely not in the original.[1] (2) There are no personal references to the readers or mention o anyone by name, as is characteristic in Paul' letters to churches he founded or where he wa well known. That he was well known at Ephesus is clear from Acts 19, having spent nearl three years there in a powerful, Spirit-anointe ministry (cf. 20:31).

For these and other reasons it is commonl believed that Paul wrote Ephesians for a wide readership than just Ephesus. Initially it ma have served as a circular letter for numerou churches in the large and well-populate Roman province of Asia, where Ephesus wa located. Originally each church may hav inserted its own name in 1:1, testifying to th relevance of its profound message for all tru churches of Jesus Christ. Eventually the lette came to be identified with the mother churc in Ephesus, the capital and foremost metropolis of the province.

5. Occasion for the Letter

Acts and Paul's Prison Letters contain historical data that can be pieced together concerning the occasion for writing Ephesians. Whil under house arrest in Rome awaiting his tria before Caesar, Paul was permitted to receiv a steady stream of visitors (Acts 28:16–31 Among these were church representatives suc as Epaphras (from Colosse) and Tychicus (native of Ephesus). These men may have bee converted under Paul's ministry when "all th

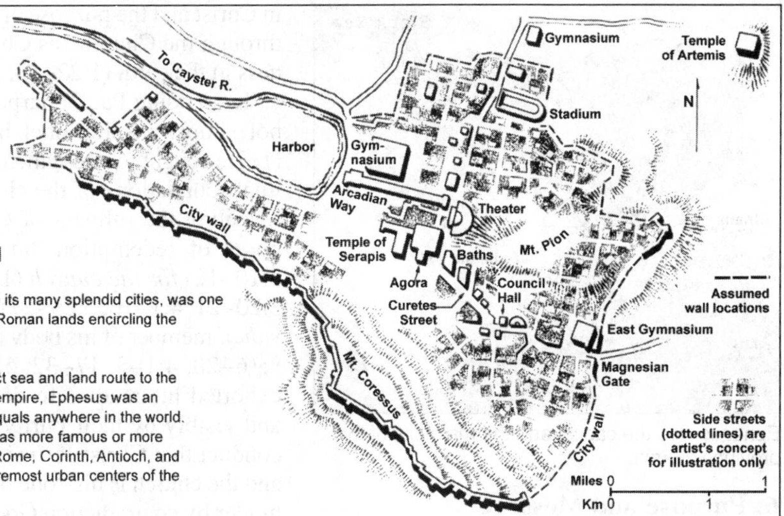

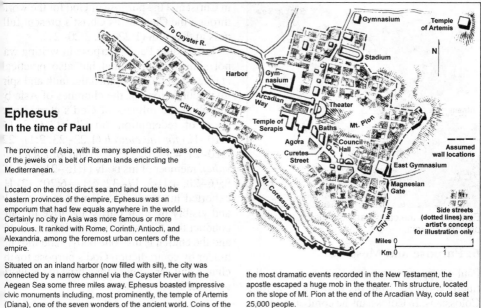

Ephesus
In the time of Paul

The province of Asia, with its many splendid cities, was one of the jewels on a belt of Roman lands encircling the Mediterranean.

Located on the most direct sea and land route to the eastern provinces of the empire, Ephesus was an emporium that had few equals anywhere in the world. Certainly no city in Asia was more famous or more populous. It ranked with Rome, Corinth, Antioch, and Alexandria, among the foremost urban centers of the empire.

Situated on an inland harbor (now filled with silt), the city was connected by a narrow channel via the Cayster River with the Aegean Sea some three miles away. Ephesus boasted impressive civic monuments including, most prominently, the temple of Artemis (Diana), one of the seven wonders of the ancient world. Coins of the city proudly displayed the slogan *Neokoros*, "temple-warden."

Paul preached to large crowds in the city. The silversmiths complained that he had influenced large numbers of people in Ephesus and in practically the whole province of Asia (Ac 19:26). In the most dramatic events recorded in the New Testament, the apostle escaped a huge mob in the theater. This structure, located on the slope of Mt. Pion at the end of the Arcadian Way, could seat 25,000 people.

Other places doubtless familiar to the apostle were the Commerical Agora, the Magnesian Gate, the Town Hall or "Council House," and the Street of the Curetes. The location of the lecture hall of Tyrannus, where Paul taught, is unknown.

ews and Greeks who lived *in the province of* *sia* heard the word of the Lord. God did such] extraordinary miracles through Paul that] the name of the Lord Jesus was held in igh honor.... In this way the word of the Lord pread widely and grew in power" (19:10–11, 7c, 20).

Paul's comments about Epaphras suggest e evangelized the Lycus Valley during Paul's phesian ministry and helped found churches n Colosse, Hierapolis, and Laodicea. Epahras visited Paul at Rome to bring a report bout these churches (see Col. 1:7; 4:12; 'hilem. 23). He apparently brought news of alse teaching at Colosse, which prompted 'aul to write Colossians.

Meanwhile, a runaway slave from Colosse amed Onesimus came into contact with Paul t Rome and was converted. After discipling im, Paul decided to return him to his Christan master, Philemon, at Colosse for pardon. 'aul took this occasion to write a cover letter ddressed to Philemon, carried by Tychicus, nd a letter to the entire church at Colosse. 'ychicus and Onesimus first sailed to Ephesus, efore going on by foot through the Lycus Valy to Colosse.

Before Tychicus and Onesimus departed, Paul wrote yet a third letter, Ephesians, which he intended as a more general letter to be circulated by Tychicus at Ephesus and other churches in the province of Asia. Ephesians may well be "the letter from Laodicea" mentioned in Colossians 4:16. This setting can account for most of the unusual features of Ephesians and most satisfactorily explains the remarkable resemblance and close affinity that exist between it and Colossians (cf. Eph. 6:20; Col. 4:7).

The literary similarities between Colossians and Ephesians are so close they are sometimes referred to as the "twin letters." One writer has counted as many as forty coincidences of thought and language between them. Yet these are "so intimately woven into the fabric of each epistle that it is impossible to believe they are due to any attempt at imitation or forgery" (W. Martin, 1015). These *similarities* can reasonably be accounted for if Paul wrote them both about the same time. The *differences* owe to his shift of focus to the subject of the church in Ephesians and away from the controversy over heretical teaching as in Colossians.

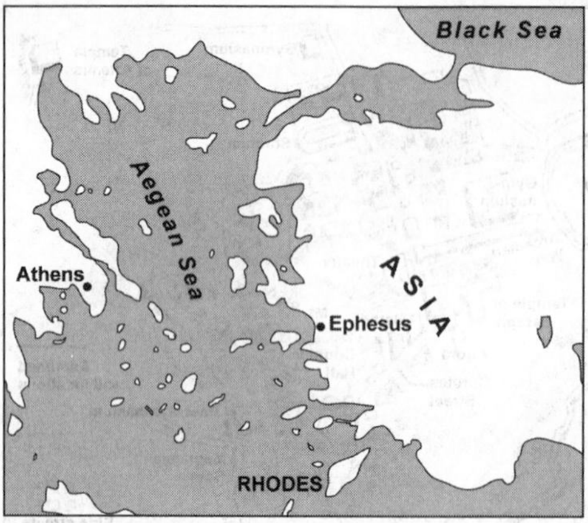

Ephesus was the capital and the main city of the province of Asia.

6. Purpose and Message

Paul's purpose in writing Ephesians was distinctly different from his purpose in writing Colossians. In Colossians he combats and corrects a false teaching involving Jewish and pagan elements that tended to deny the Lordship of Christ in the universe and the completeness of his redemptive work in history. Paul responds to this heresy by developing the theme of Christ's person and work in relation to the whole cosmos, including those principalities and powers given prominence in the heresy. As F. F. Bruce remarks (1984, 231), "Ephesians carries on the same train of thought by considering the implications of this for the church as the body of Christ."

In Ephesians Paul writes about God's eternal purposes in Christ to create from among Jews and Gentiles a new humanity through the cross (2:11–18) and a new community as Christ's body in the earth (1:22–23; 2:19–22; 3:6). In this way God chose to proclaim and model the gospel of reconciliation to the world, even to make known his manifold wisdom "to the rulers and authorities in the heavenly realms" (3:10).

Though Paul was confined to his rented apartment in Rome as a prisoner, he soared like an eagle into the heavenlies of revelation. He was now free to pen what J. Armitage Robinson (10) calls "one supreme exposition, noncontroversial, positive, fundamental, of the great doctrine of his life—that doctrine into which he had been advancing year by year under the discipline of his unique circumstances—the doctrine of the unity of mankind in Christ and the purpose of God for the worl through the Church" as Christ's present ful ness in the earth (1:22–23; 3:20–21).

In so doing Paul's purpose in writing wa not simply inspirational but also practica (1) He sought to strengthen the faith and spi itual foundations of the churches of Asia b revealing the fullness of God's eternal pu poses of redemption "in Christ" (1:3–1 3:10–12) *for the church* (1:22–23; 2:11–2 3:20–21; 4:1–16; 5:25–27) and *for each ind vidual* member of his body (1:15–21; 2:1–1 3:16–20; 4:1–3, 17–32; 5:1—6:20). (2) H exhorted his readers to demonstrate plainl and visibly by their purity and love in dail conduct that Christ Jesus is their "one Lord and the church is his "one body," and thus n hinder by contradiction God's purpose for th church and her witness for Christ to the worl (4:1–6:20).

7. The Ministry of the Holy Spirit in Ephesians

Whereas the foremost themes in Ephesians a Christ, the church, and God's eternal plan c redemption, it is the Holy Spirit and his role i relation to the believer and the church as God' empowering presence that makes us the peopl of God and the body of Christ in the earth. Con cerning the prominence of the Holy Spirit i Ephesians, Gordon Fee comments (732) "There is hardly an aspect of Christian life i which the Spirit does not take the leading rol and there is hardly an aspect of the Spirit's rol that is not touched on in this letter."

In 1:13 the Holy Spirit is called (lit.) "th Spirit of promise," whose prominent ne covenant presence is a sign that the last day have come (Joel 2:28–32; Acts 2:16–21 Jesus promises to baptize his disciples with (c in) the Holy Spirit (Acts 1:5), as John the Bap tist had predicted (Mark 1:8; John 1:33), an he refers to the Spirit in this context as the on whom the Father had promised (Luke 24:4 Acts 1:4). Peter at Pentecost testifies that Jesu having been exalted to God's right hand, "ha received from the Father the promised Hol Spirit" and has poured out what his audienc now sees and hears (Acts 2:33). Thus the bap tism in the Spirit is directly connected to "th Spirit of promise" as both an individual an corporate experience, important to believer becoming the "one body" of Christ.

In Ephesians the Holy Spirit is further described as the mark or seal of God's ownership (1:13), the first installment of the believer's inheritance in Christ (1:14), "the Spirit of wisdom and revelation" (1:17), the one who enables the believer to come into intimacy with the Father (2:18), the one by whom God dwells in the church (2:22), the revealer of the mystery of Christ (3:4–5), and the one who strengthens believers in their inner being (3:16). In the church believers are to preserve "the unity of the Spirit through the bond of peace" (4:3); "there is one body and one Spirit" (4:4). The Holy Spirit is grieved by sin in the lives of believers (4:30). They are admonished to go on being "filled with the Spirit" (5:18), to be equipped for spiritual warfare with "the sword of the Spirit, which is the word of God" (6:17), and to "pray in the Spirit on all occasions" (6:18).

STRUCTURE AND OUTLINE

In the simplest possible terms there are two basic themes in the New Testament: (1) how we are redeemed by God—i.e., by grace through faith; and (2) how we, as the redeemed of the Lord, are to live—i.e., the ethical imperatives of grace. Comprehensively, all other themes may be subsumed under one of these two broad categories—theological or ethical.

Ephesians falls naturally into these two distinct categories, as the following outline of the letter indicates. Chapters 1–3 contain glorious theological declarations about the redemption God has provided in Christ; chapters 4–6 consist largely of practical instruction about the demands that God's redemption in Christ makes on our lives individually and corporately as the body of Christ. This does not mean that Paul places theology in one pigeonhole and ethics in another. The two are inseparable parts of one whole and are often intermingled in the same paragraph. Nevertheless, for purposes of presentation and organization Paul tends to set forth one, then the other, in his plea for the total Christian life.

Part I: Glorious Theological Declarations About Redemption (chaps. 1–3)

1. Salutation (1:1–2)

2. The Preeminence of Christ Jesus in Redemption (1:3–14)

- **2.1.** Christ's Preeminence in the Father's Eternal Plan (1:3–6)
  - **2.1.1.** The Father's Blessings in Christ (1:3)
  - **2.1.2.** The Father's Election in Christ (1:4)
  - **2.1.3.** The Father's Predestination for Adoption in Christ (1:5–6)
- **2.2.** Christ's Preeminence in the Realization of Redemption (1:7–12)
  - **2.2.1.** Redemption Through His Blood (1:7–8)
  - **2.2.2.** Redemption Under One Head (1:9–12)
- **2.3.** Christ's Preeminence in the Holy Spirit's Role (1:13–14)
  - **2.3.1.** The Spirit As Our Seal of Faith in Christ (1:13)
  - **2.3.2.** The Spirit As the First Installment of Our Inheritance in Christ (1:14)

3. Apostolic Prayer for the Believers' Spiritual Enlightenment (1:15–23)

- **3.1.** The Context of Paul's Apostolic Prayer (1:15–17a)
- **3.2.** The Focus of Paul's Apostolic Prayer (1:17b–19)
- **3.3.** Christ's Exaltation, Lordship, and Headship As the Measure of God's Available Power (1:20–23)

4. The Results of Redemption in Christ Jesus (2:1–3:13)

- **4.1.** Christ Saves Sinners From Their Hopeless Predicament (2:1–10)
  - **4.1.1.** Humanity's Desperate Plight Without Christ (2:1–3)
  - **4.1.2.** Salvation by Grace Through Faith in Christ (2:4–10)
- **4.2.** Christ Reconciles Mutually Hostile People Groups to God and One Another As a New Humanity (2:11–18)
  - **4.2.1.** The Gentile Exclusion From God and the Covenant People (2:11–12)
  - **4.2.2.** The Gentile Inclusion in the One New Humanity in Christ (2:13–18)
- **4.3.** Christ Unites Separate People Together As One New Community (2:19–22)

COMMENTARY

Part I: Glorious Theological Declarations About Redemption (chaps. 1–3)

In chapters 1–3 Paul writes about the glorious redemption God has planned and provided in Christ for the believer and the church. After his salutation, he begins with a magnificent hymn of redemption (1:3–14), which offers praise to God the Father for choosing and predestining us in Christ for adoption as his sons (1:3–6), for redeeming us through Christ's blood (1:7–12), and for giving the Holy Spirit as our seal and the first installment of our inheritance (1:13–14). Paul stresses that in redemption, always by grace through faith in Christ Jesus, God is reconciling us to himself (2:1–10), is breaking down dividing walls between us and others who are being saved (2:11–15), and is uniting Jews and Gentiles together as one new humanity and one new community, the church (2:16–22). God's wisdom and purpose in redemption is manifold as he moves "to bring all things in heaven and on earth together under one head, even Christ" (1:10).

Twice in these chapters Paul breaks forth into profound apostolic prayers, first for our spiritual enlightenment concerning these things (1:16–23), and second for the spiritual fulfillment of them in our lives (3:14–21).

1. Salutation (1:1–2)

Paul begins his letters to churches with a salutation in which he identifies himself as an apostolic writer and addresses his readers in the form of a Christian greeting. This salutation has two additional distinguishing features: (1) It is the briefest salutation in all Paul's letters, and (2) the identity of the addressees is somewhat uncertain. As noted in the introduction, the words "in Ephesus" (1:1) do not appear in many of the most ancient and reliable Greek manuscripts, indicating they were probably not in the original. The grammatical construction in these same manuscripts suggests that the earliest copies of Ephesians had in mind a plurality of place names.

The letter has a universal quality about it, as one might expect if it were originally targeted for several churches as a circular letter. Since Ephesus was the mother church and chief city of the province and was located at the front end of the letter's circulation, it is easy to see how this letter eventually came to be identified in the title and salutation with Ephesus.

The salutation contains three important statements. (1) Paul identifies himself as "an apostle of Christ Jesus by the will of God" (1:1). Herein lies his authority for writing. The New Testament word "apostle" first applied to the twelve disciples as Christ's commissioned leaders for his church. It soon came to be an official designation for a wider number of church leaders in the first century, such as James (the Lord's brother), Paul, Barnabas, and perhaps others. The word "apostle" itself means a messenger who is commissioned to represent someone and who goes in the authority of the one who does the commissioning.

Paul received his call and commission directly from "Christ Jesus." He belonged to Christ and represented him. Thus when Paul speaks or writes, he does so as an authorized spokesman for Christ, as he makes clear in all his letters. Paul's message is Christ's own message, and Paul conveys it by the revelation and authority of Christ. Some people today read a passage or verse in one of Paul's letters that conflicts with their own cherished ideas and they respond: "That is just Paul's opinion or idea; I don't agree with Paul." Since Paul writes as "an apostle of Christ Jesus," however, those who disagree with him disagree also with Christ, whom he represented as a commissioned spokesman.

Paul adds that he is an apostle "by the will of God." He did not attain to apostleship by aspiration, by usurpation, or by nomination from a church committee. Rather, this intensely nationalistic Jewish rabbi and bitter persecutor of the church became an apostle of Christ Jesus by "the activity of God's sovereign will" (Hendriksen, 70).

(2) The letter is addressed "to the saints ... the faithful in Christ Jesus" (1:1b). The word "saints" (*hagioi*), a common New Testament word for believers, literally means "holy ones," those set apart and consecrated to be God's own possession. In the New Testament true believers are called "saints," not "sinners"; the latter are those who are under the law of sin and death (Rom. 8:2) and whose lives are characterized by sinful practice (1 John 3:8) and bondage to the sinful nature. Saints, on the

other hand, are those who through Christ Jesus experience the law of the Spirit of life (Rom. 8:2) and whose lives are characterized by righteousness (Rom. 6:13, 16, 19–20, 22). They are not sinless (1 John 1:8; 2:1–2), but their prevailing characteristic is righteousness (3:7).

Paul further characterizes the saints as "the faithful in Christ Jesus." The word "faithful" (*pistoi*) literally means "faithful ones." It refers to those who have placed their wholehearted trust in Jesus as Savior and Lord and who are constant in their devotion to him. They keep the faith, are constant in faith, and persevere in faith in the Lord Jesus.

(3) Paul conveys his normal Christian greeting to the readers in verse 2: "Grace and peace to you from God our Father and the Lord Jesus Christ." "Grace" (*charis*), adapted from *charein* (the Greek greeting), is a distinctive Christian word, and "peace" is the characteristic Hebrew form of greeting. Grace is God's gracious and loving initiative to redeem us back for himself through the saving action of his Son. "Peace" is the firstfruit of God's saving grace in our lives. Derived from the Hebrew *shalom*, it conveys a fullness and wholeness of God's gift of life, a well-being that covers spirit, soul, and body and that flows from our being reconciled to God and living in communion with him as our Creator and Redeemer. Both "grace and peace" come as gifts from God and the Lord Jesus Christ as "joint authors" (R. Martin, 133).

2. The Preeminence of Christ Jesus in Redemption (1:3–14)

These twelve verses form a single, complex, unbroken sentence of 202 words in the Greek text. To appreciate fully its length, disregard the division of 1:3–14 into sentences and paragraphs in our English versions and view it as a series of connected phrases and subordinate clauses. Then take a deep breath and try to read it through in one breath. It truly is breathtaking. It is like a Niagara Falls of inspiration and revelation. Each successive phrase flows out of the preceding one and gives birth to the following one until it has reached its grand conclusion.

Ephesians 1:3–14 is one of the most profound passages in the Bible and perhaps the most magnificent single sentence in all literature. The passage is a theological hymn of praise for God's glorious redemption, presented in three stanzas of varying length and each stanza ending with the repeated refrain "to the praise of his glorious grace" (1:6) or "to the praise of his glory" (1:12, 14).

There is a Trinitarian character about these stately verses. Each stanza highlights the contribution that each member of the Godhead makes in planning or carrying out redemption. The Father chose to redeem a people for himself (1:3–6), the Son at the cost of his sacrificial death is also the Redeemer and the one in whom the church is chosen (1:7–12), and the Holy Spirit applies the work and living presence of Christ to the church and to human experience (1:13–14). The scope of redemption is revealed as being from eternity before creation (1:4) to its future complete realization at Christ's second advent (1:14).

In God's plan Christ is the "centerpiece" of redemption—of the Father's plan in eternity, of the outworking of redemption in history, and of the Holy Spirit's ministry. The phrase "in Christ" ("in him," etc.) occurs repeatedly and permeates the entire passage. The focus of praise is everywhere on what God has done for us "in Christ." This phrase is the key one of this passage, of this letter, of Paul's own experience, of the church, and of the Christian life. R. C. H. Lenski (350) remarks: "Christ is the golden string on which all the pearls of this doxology are strung. He is the central diamond around which all diamonds are set as rays. 'The Beloved One' ['the One he loves,' NIV] is the divine designation made prominent." In 1:3–14 glory flashes upon glory until Paul has piled up in one sentence the vast and almost indescribable riches of redemption that God has provided as our inheritance in Christ Jesus.

2.1. Christ's Preeminence in the Father's Eternal Plan (1:3–6)

Redemption has its inception in the heart of God the Father and centers in God the Son. Because of the Father's purpose Paul begins this hymn with an outburst of praise "to the God and Father of our Lord Jesus Christ" (v. 3a). Notice the verbs in verses 3–5 all focus on the Father's action: he "has blessed us" (v. 3), "he chose us" (v. 4), and "he predestined us" (v. 5).

2.1.1. The Father's Blessings in Christ (1:3). This verse contains three variations of the Greek word for "blessed" or "blessing."

1) The first word, "praise," is the word *ulogetos*, often translated "blessed." Here the object of our blessing or praise is God, who is preeminently and intrinsically worthy of it in his character and redeeming love. (2) God is the One "who has blessed [*eulogesas*] us" (i.e., bestowed blessings on us). (3) He has done so by giving us "every spiritual blessing [*eulogia*] in Christ." Thus Paul defines and summarizes the goal of redemption: *Blessed* be God and *blessed* are we with every spiritual *blessing*. The goal of God's redeeming love is to bring about a world filled with blessing. Satan's goal is to steal, kill, and destroy; God's goal is that we might have the blessings of full life "in Christ" (cf. John 10:10).

Christ is the centerpiece. All spiritual blessings from God the Father come to us "in Christ," in his person and work. Expressions such as "in Christ," "in him," "in the Lord," "in whom," etc., occur 160 times in Paul's letters—36 times in Ephesians and 10 times in 1:1–13 (1:1, 3, 4, 6, 7, 9, 10, 12, 13). Experiential union with Christ constitutes the heart of Paul's faith. "In Christ" refers to the sphere in which we as believers live, move, and have our being. Life "in Christ" is the opposite of our former unregenerate life "in Adam," which was characterized by disobedience, slavery to the sinful nature, condemnation, and death. Our new existence is characterized by salvation, sonship, grace, walking by the Spirit, righteousness, and eternal life.

The "spiritual" blessings "in the heavenly realms" are to be distinguished from material blessings, also bestowed by God. Material blessings are emphasized in the Old Testament (e.g., Deut. 28:1–14), whereas spiritual blessings are emphasized in the New Testament. Noteworthy in Ephesians 1:3 are the three occurrences of the Greek preposition *en* ("in"): God has blessed us "*in* every spiritual blessing *in* the heavenlies *in* Christ" (lit. trans.). J. B. Lightfoot (312) summarizes the force of this: "We are united to God **in** Christ; so united we dwell **in** heavenly places; so dwelling we are blessed **in** all spiritual blessings."

Clearly spiritual blessings come from being united to and abiding in Christ. The blessings Paul has in mind are referred to in the extended passage: We are chosen to be holy and blameless (1:4), predestined to be adopted as sons (1:5), redeemed through the blood of Christ (1:7), taken into the counsels of his will through the scope of redemption (1:8–10), appointed to live for the praise of his glory (1:11–12), given the message of truth (1:13a), and sealed with the Holy Spirit of promise (1:13–14).

The phrase "in the heavenly realms" (1:3b) is unique to this letter (also in 1:20; 2:6; 3:10; 6:12)—a phrase that refers to the spiritual realm. In 1:20–22 it refers to the realm where the risen Christ is seated as Lord over every authority. In 2:6 it refers to the sphere where spiritually alive believers enjoy union and fellowship with Christ. In 3:10 it refers to the realm of spiritual rulers and authorities, to whom "the manifold wisdom of God" is made known through the church. Finally, in 6:12 it refers to the realm of spiritual warfare, where believers wrestle against the forces of darkness and evil. "The heavenly realms" is not so much a contrast between a celestial location and an earthly one as it is between the spiritual sphere of existence and the material dimension of life. In 1:3, 20, and 2:6 it especially expresses something of the awe and glory of the believer's spiritual union with Christ in the realm of his Lordship.

2.1.2. The Father's Election in Christ (1:4). Verse 4 traces God's activity in verse 3 back to its ultimate source in order to explain *how* it was being carried out—by means of God's elective choice: "He chose us." From the word translated "chose" (*eklego*) the word "election" is derived. "God has blessed us with every spiritual blessing by means of his elective choice" (Summers, 11).

There is an element of mystery in the biblical doctrine of election that has baffled the greatest minds of the church for centuries. Those who confidently dogmatize and systematize it as a packaged theology have not understood Paul's heart or mind on this subject. Paul's intent in this verse is to magnify God's initiative as the God of infinite love in giving us as his finite creation every spiritual blessing through the redemptive work of his Son.

Verse 4 presents four important truths about the teaching of election. (1) Election is *Christocentric*; that is, election is always centered in Christ: "He chose us *in him*" (1:4a). Christ himself is "the Chosen One of God *par excellence*" (Bruce, 1984, 254). Christ is called the Son who has been chosen (Luke 9:35) and the

Messiah who is God's Elect One (23:35; John 1:34); God introduces his Servant in Isaiah 42:1 as "my elect one." As such Christ is the foundation of our election. Only in union with him do we participate as elect ones. Spiritual life is necessarily relational (John 15:1–8); no one is among the elect apart from a living faith-union with Christ. It is all "in him" from beginning to end. No individual is chosen or rejected in eternity by absolute decree in violation of his or her will. We become one of the elect when, by faith, Christ's redemptive death on the cross becomes the basis for our "forgiveness of sins, in accordance with the riches of God's grace" (1:7).

(2) Election in Christ is essentially *corporate*; that is, God chose *a people* in Christ ("us," the church). It was true already of Israel in the Old Testament that her election was essentially corporate and applied to individual Israelites only as they were genuinely identified with God and the covenant community (cf. Ezek. 18:5–32). Likewise in Ephesians, the elect are identified corporately: "the church, which is his body" (1:22–23; cf. 2:16), "God's people and members of God's household" (2:19), "members together of one body, and sharers together in the promise in Christ Jesus" (3:6), "I am talking about Christ and the church" (5:32). Election is thus a corporate issue for the church and embraces individual persons only as they are identified with Christ and his body in the earth, the new covenant community.

(3) Election involves an *eternal plan* by God. This plan was formed before the creation of the world (v. 4b), before time began, in eternity, when God alone existed. "In that pre-creation eternity . . . [God the Father] formed a purpose in his mind" (Stott, 36). He determined that all persons who would believe in his Son (people who did not yet exist) would become his own "sons" through the redeeming work of Christ (which had not yet taken place). Our salvation in Christ is not an afterthought on God's part. He did not wait for the calamity of sin to plan for salvation. God created us in love and in his image, thus with the power of free will. Free will affords the possibility of rebellion, as in the case of Satan's fall. Thus God acted before the fact with an eternal plan. Salvation in the Son is the fulfillment of God's glorious plan and purpose from eternity. Through the incarnation of Christ election is fulfilled and realized in history.

(4) Finally, election has as its purpose the *holiness* of God's people—that they might "be holy and blameless in his sight" (v. 4c). Paul repeatedly emphasizes this paramount purpose in Ephesians (2:21; 4:1–3, 13–32; 5:1–21; cf. also 1 Peter 1:2, 14–16). Fulfillment of this purpose *for the corporate body* of Christ is certain, as Ephesians 5:27 makes clear: Christ will "present her to himself as a radiant church . . . holy and blameless." Fulfillment of this purpose *for individuals* in the church is conditional on their personal faith in Christ Jesus and their remaining faithful to him. In a parallel passage (Col. 1:22–23) Paul makes this equally clear: Christ will "present you holy in his sight without blemish . . . *if* you continue in your faith, established and firm, not moved from the hope held out in the gospel." When biblically understood and proclaimed, Paul's teaching of election should lead believers to righteousness, not to sin.

The phrase "in love" at the end of verse 4 has perplexed translators. Did Paul intend it to be included with the thought of verse 4 or to go forward to the thought of verse 5? If the former (as in the KJV, NKJV, NRSV), then it further defines the goal of election, namely, "to be holy and blameless in love," or holy and blameless, coupled with love (Bruce, 1984, 256). If "in love" belongs to what follows (as in the RSV, NASB, NIV), then it emphasizes the motive of God in predestination: "In love he predestined us to be adopted as his sons" (1:5). Certainly the latter emphasis is in keeping with the general tenor of the passage. The former emphasis, however, finds support in Paul's habit of placing *en agape* ("in love") *after* the clause it qualifies (e.g. Eph. 4:2, 15, 16; 5:2; Col. 2:2; 1 Thess. 5:13). Thus the reader may want to include it with the message of both verse 4 and verse 5, since it logically and theologically fits both places.

2.1.3. The Father's Predestination for Adoption in Christ (1:5–6). Verse 5 continues Paul's revelation about the preeminence of Christ in the Father's plan of redemption. God has predestined us to adoption through Christ. Along with our blessing and election in Christ, these three elements relate to the Father's eternal purpose of redemption and cannot be separated.

The verb "predestine" (*proorizo*) occurs six times in the New Testament, once in Acts 4:28) and the others in Paul's letters (Rom. 8:29, 30; 1 Cor. 2:7; Eph 1:5, 11). The verb means "to decide beforehand" and applies to God's purposes comprehended in election. Election is God's choosing "in Christ" a people for himself, and predestination concerns what God has planned beforehand to do with those who are chosen. Thus the issue of predestination is not God's deciding beforehand who will and will not be saved, but his deciding beforehand what he plans the elect in Christ to be or become. God predestined that the elect (i.e., those who are being saved in Christ) should be: conformed to the likeness of his Son (Rom. 8:29), called (8:30), justified (8:30), glorified (8:30), holy and blameless (Eph 1:4), adopted as his sons (1:5), redeemed (1:7), for the praise of his glory (1:11–12), recipients of the Holy Spirit (1:13), recipients of an inheritance (1:14), and created to do good works (2:10).

To illustrate Paul's teaching about election and predestination, consider the analogy of a great ship (i.e., the church, the body of Christ) on its way to heaven. The ship is chosen by God to be his very own vessel. Christ is the Captain and Pilot of the ship. All people are invited to be part of this elect ship and its Captain, but only those individuals are permitted to board the ship who place their faith and trust in Christ Jesus. As long as they remain on the ship, in fellowship with the ship's Captain, they are among the elect. If anyone chooses to abandon the ship and its Captain, that person ceases to be part of the elect. Election is always a matter of fellowship with the Captain and staying on board his ship. Predestination tells us about the ship's direction and destination, and what God has decided beforehand for those remaining on it.

God has clearly decided beforehand that his elect will "be adopted as his sons through Jesus Christ." Adoption into God's family flows from the loving, good pleasure of God's will and desire to have many sons and daughters in his family (by adoption), all sharing the likeness of his only Son (by nature) (cf. Rom. 8:29; Heb. 2:10). Only Paul among the New Testament writers uses the word "adoption," and he does so five times (Rom. 8:15, 23; 9:4; Gal. 4:5; Eph. 1:5). In some of these references Paul seems to draw a parallel between God's act of adoption and current Roman legal practice. Sonship by adoption has both a present and future dimension to it and is perhaps the most comprehensive concept that Paul uses in relation to our restoration in redemption. F. F. Bruce (1961, 29) comments about the comprehensiveness of adoption:

> This "adoption" is more than our relationship to God as his children which is ours by the new birth; it embraces all the privileges and responsibilities which belong to those whom God has acknowledged as His freeborn, full-grown sons. It is a status which we receive in Christ our Redeemer, through faith (Gal. 3:36; 4:5); which we appropriate in practice through obedience to the Spirit's guidance (Rom. 8:14f.; Gal. 4:6f.); which will be given full and universal recognition at the Second Advent of Christ, for the day when the Son of God is revealed will also be the day of the revealing of the *sons* of God (Rom. 8:19). And when that day dawns, Paul assures us all creation will share in its joy.

Because adoptive sonship is the result of God's gracious will, put into effect through Christ, it will redound "to the praise of God's glorious grace" (1:6). Concerning this clause Max Turner (1226) aptly remarks: "And because we are already united with Christ through the Spirit, that grace, including sonship, can be said to be already freely bestowed on us; providing this is qualified by the assertion, 'in the One he loves' (i.e., Christ; cf. Mark 1:11; 9:7; Col. 1:13)."

2.2. Christ's Preeminence in the Realization of Redemption (1:7–12)

This second stanza in Paul's theological hymn offers praise that through the life and death of the beloved Son, God the Father has revealed his glorious grace (1:6–8; cf. John 1:14, 17) and actualized his purpose to redeem a people for himself (Eph. 1:7; cf. 1 Peter 1:18–21; 2:9–10). God's provision of redemption in Christ covers the full range of human need—forgiveness, deliverance, reconciliation, peace, love, new life, wisdom, understanding, community, acceptance, order, security, hope, and victory in the conflict with Satan and his forces.

2.2.1. Redemption Through His Blood (1:7–8). The word "redemption" (*apolytrosis*) occurs three times in Ephesians (1:7, 14; 4:30). In classical Greek it meant "to set free for a ransom . . . and is used of prisoners of war, slaves, and criminals condemned to death" (*TDNT*, 4:351–52). Most likely Israel's redemption from Egypt served as the prototype for Paul's use of this word, where it meant emancipation from slavery and oppressive bondage, and restoration to true liberty as God's people. For spiritual Israel (the church) redemption includes emancipation from the guilt, penalty, and power of sin (John 8:34; Rom. 7:14; 1 Cor. 7:23; Gal. 3:13), and restoration to true liberty as the children of God (John 8:36; Gal. 5:1) (Hendriksen, 83).

Paul uses *apolytrosis* in the sense of deliverance with a price—in this case it was costly, the "blood" of Christ (a direct reference to Jesus' sacrificial death on the cross as the innocent Lamb without blemish). "His blood" recalls the Passover lamb in Egypt, whose blood was applied to each Hebrew home in order that death and God's judgment might pass over them and that the blood might give them freedom from slavery.

"Redemption through his blood" obtains for us "the forgiveness of [our] sins" (1:7b). "Forgiveness" (*aphesis*) is derived from the verb *aphiemi*, meaning "to send away." Psalm 103:12 is the perfect commentary on forgiveness: "As far as the east is from the west, so far has he removed our transgressions from us." God forgives our sins through faith in Christ, not because he views our sins lightly, but because the atoning death of his Son was in our place and on our behalf. His forgiveness is in no way stingily measured; rather, it is given "in accordance with the riches of God's grace" (Eph. 1:7c)—a characteristic expression of Paul (cf. Rom. 2:4; 9:23; 11:33; 2 Cor. 8:9; Col. 1:27; 2:2). Grace is infinitely more valuable and precious than any tangible wealth. Six times in Ephesians Paul writes about the riches of God's grace, mercy, and glory (1:18; 2:4, 7; 3:8, 16).

Verse 8 carries the thought further: God "lavished on us" his grace of forgiveness. This expresses God's overwhelming generosity in giving. He does not withhold and give the bare necessity; he gives abundantly. The lavish character of grace is further accompanied by "all wisdom and understanding" (1:8b; cf. Isa. 11:2). Note Paul's prayer in Colossians 1:9, that we may be filled with "all spiritual wisdom and understanding." As gifts bestowed by God, "wisdom and understanding" are not attributable to native intelligence or human attainments in learning. However, they may be *increasingly appropriated* through prayer and attention to God's Word and Spirit. Robinson (30) distinguishes between "wisdom" and "understanding": "Wisdom" sees the heart of a matter and knows it as it really is; "understanding" relates to discernment or prudence in right conduct, that is, an "understanding that leads to right action."

2.2.2. Redemption Under One Head (1:9–12). Paul now introduces us to another feature of the Father's loving action toward us in redemption: "He made known to us the mystery of his will" (1:9). Like the features in 1:3–8, the focus is on the Father's action and what he has done on our behalf "in the One he loves" (1:6), Christ Jesus, who is the supreme object of his love (cf. Mark 1:11; 9:7; Col. 1:13).

The word "mystery" (*mysterion*) is a recurring one in Ephesians (3:3, 4, 6, 9; 5:32; 6:19). Paul uses this word to refer to something in the purpose of God that *formerly* was hidden or kept a secret, "something undiscoverable by human reason" (W. G. M. Martin) and "too magnificent to be fully grasped" (Max Turner). *But now* this secret has been brought into the open (cf. Rom. 16:25–26). In the Jewish intertestamental apocalyptic literature and in the Qumran writings "mystery" was used for God's secret plan that would be revealed at the end of history. Paul, on the other hand, emphasizes that the unlocking of the mystery has already occurred in the revelation of Christ, so that we need not wait for the events that conclude this age in order to know the strategy of God's will (*TDNT*, 4:819–22).

Sometimes Paul uses *mysterion* to refer to the entire scope and sphere of God's redemptive purpose in Christ (Rom. 16:25; 1 Cor. 2:7; Eph. 1:9–10; 6:19; Col. 1:26; 1 Tim. 3:9, 16); at other times he refers to a particular aspect of God's purpose, such as the inclusion of the Gentiles in the plan of redemption (Rom. 11:25; Eph. 3:3–9), the instant physical-to-spiritual transformation of the bodies of living believers at Christ's Second Advent (1 Cor. 15:52), and the holy union between Christ and the church as his body (Eph. 5:32).

To the natural mind unenlightened by God's revelation in Christ and the Scriptures, the purposes of God in human history remain a mystery; life ultimately does not make sense. For people "darkened in their understanding and separated from the life of God" (Eph. 4:18), life is (as Shakespeare had Macbeth describe it) "a tale told by an idiot, full of sound and fury, signifying nothing" (*Macbeth*, Act V, Scene V).

Nor is religion the answer. Generally speaking, religion is people trying to find and be right with God through their own efforts. Redemption, on the other hand, is entirely by God's initiative. He has chosen to reveal himself and his ultimate purpose for his creation to those who receive the revelation of his Son. As 1:9 indicates, God's benevolent redemptive action in the incarnation of Christ was by God's own free determination and in accordance with the riches of his grace. Stated another way, redemption was not the result of any external pressure, but was the outworking of God's own "gracious purpose" in Christ (Westcott, 20).

God has purposed to complete redemption "when the times will have reached their fulfillment" (1:10). The Greek word for "times" is *kairos*, a word that has to do with epochs or the great eras of life. Markus Barth (1:128) states that the phrase "the fullness of times" (lit. trans., 1:10a) carries "the idea of consecutive periods of history which are to be crowned and completed by an era surpassing all previous periods." As Paul notes elsewhere, God sent his Son into the world "when the time had fully come" (Gal. 4:4). Likewise, when the time is again full or ripe, God will complete his plan of redemption by sending his Son a second time.

The goal or crown of God's redeeming purpose in Christ is "to bring [unite] all things in heaven and on earth together under one head, even Christ." The "all things" include both heavenly and earthly creation. The purpose of God was set in motion when, through Christ, "all things were made" (John 1:3). Not only did Christ create "all things ... things in heaven and on earth," but also "all things were created ... *for him*" (Col. 1:16). Paul adds that in Christ, the head of the church, God has begun his master plan to restore the universe to himself (Col. 1:18–20). In Romans Paul also touches this theme when he says all creation because of sin has been subjected to discord and suffering, but will in the day of redemption's consummation "be liberated from its bondage to decay and brought into the glorious freedom of the children of God" (Rom. 8:21).

The broken unity and disharmony of creation because of Adam's transgression will in the end be restored and harmonized through Christ. Thus Christ Jesus is not merely the Messiah of Israel, nor is the designation "Savior of the world" large enough for him. "In the fullness of the times" Christ will be "the Savior of the universe," and all discord will cease. The unity and harmony for which God's creation in heaven and on earth longs will then become a reality under the headship of the Lord Jesus Christ. "Already Christ is head of his body, the church, but one day 'all things' will acknowledge his headship" (Stott, 42).

This glorious prospect of redemption for the entire universe has caused some theologians to conclude that the Bible teaches "universalism," the notion that everyone and everything will ultimately be saved. They speculate that at some point *in eternity* all the impenitent will be brought to penitence, and that even Satan and the whole demonic realm will be reconciled to God, so that literally "*all things*" created will be redeemed and gathered together under the rule of one head, even Christ. Paul, however, speaks of "*all things*" being brought together under the headship of Christ, not at some distant point in eternity, after the lake of fire has accomplished a temporal task of achieving universal penitence (as some universalists believe), but rather *at the Second Advent of Christ* ("the fullness of the times"), when the Antichrist and false prophets, Satan and his angels, and all the unrighteous and unrepentant will be cast into the lake of fire to suffer separation from God "forever and ever" (Rev. 20:10, 15; 21:8).

Who or what, then, are the "all things in heaven and on earth" that will be united under Christ's headship on the day of final redemption? John Stott (44) eloquently answers that question as follows:

> Certainly they include [all] the Christian living and Christian dead [including the Old Testament redeemed], the church on earth and the church in heaven. That is, those who are "in Christ" now (verse 1), and who "in Christ" have received blessing (verse 3), election (verse 4),

adoption (verse 5), grace (verse 6), and redemption or forgiveness (verse 7), will one day be perfectly united "in him" (verse 10). No doubt the angels will be included too (cf. 3:10, 15). But "all things" (*ta panta*) normally means the universe, which Christ created and sustains. So Paul seems to be referring again to that cosmic renewal, that regeneration of the universe, that liberation of the groaning creation, of which he has already written in Romans. God's plan is that "all things" which were created through Christ and for Christ, and which hold together in Christ, will finally be united under Christ by being subjected to his headship. For the New Testament declares him to be "the heir of all things." So [the] NEB translated verse 10, "that the universe might be brought into a unity in Christ," and J. B. Lightfoot writes of "the entire harmony of the universe, which shall no longer contain alien and discordant elements, but of which all the parts shall find their centre and bond of union in Christ." In the fullness of time, God's two creations, his whole universe and his whole church, will be unified under the cosmic Christ who is the supreme head of both.

However, though Paul soars into the heavenlies of revelation here in 1:10 to obtain a glimpse of cosmic reconciliation in the future, the reconciliation he *emphasizes* throughout Ephesians is that of divided people groups (such as Jews and Gentiles) being reconciled together through the cross (e.g., 2:16), in order to produce the one body of Christ, the church, "as the first stage in the unification of a divided universe" (Bruce, 1984, 261).

The NIV begins 1:11 with the words, "In him we were ... chosen." The verb "chosen" carries the meaning "we have been chosen as God's portion" (Robinson, 146) or as God's own inheritance (cf. 1:18). Among all the nations in Old Testament times, God viewed Israel as his chosen portion or possession (Deut. 32:8–9). Likewise, under the new covenant those who are in Christ are the new Israel of God, God's "chosen people, a royal priesthood, a holy nation, a people belonging to God.... Once you were not a people, but now you are the people of God" (1 Peter 2:9–10; cf. Ex. 19:6). Both Paul and Peter ascribe to the church, including believing Gentiles, the very words that described the special privilege of Israel under the old covenant.

Paul goes on to state three important truths about the church as God's inheritance. (1) The inheritance of God was not an accident of history; it was predestined by God according to his plan (1:11b). (2) What God plans is sure of fulfillment as he "works out everything in conformity with the purpose of his will" (1:11c). The emphasis on predestination here (and in 1:5) does not nullify "real human choice and responsibility, as the appeals of the rest of the letter make clear, but assures us of God's overarching sovereign power and directing purpose at work in the believer" (Turner, 1226). (3) God chose the church as his portion "in order that we ... might be for the praise of his glory" (1:12). This refrain at the end of the second stanza of Paul's praise-hymn (cf. also 1:6, 14) emphasizes that the purpose and highest achievement of God's redeemed people is "the praise of his glory." Not just our verbal worship but the very testimony of our lives before an unbelieving world should declare such praise (cf. 2:1–10, 19–22; 3:9–21; 4:1–6:20).

"We" in 1:12 is specifically described as those "who were the first to hope in Christ." Most commentators believe this expression denotes Jewish Christians, while the "and you also were included in Christ" (1:13a) denotes Gentile believers who came to be joined to God's portion also. Other commentators believe that just as "we" throughout 1:3–11 clearly refers to all believers (not just Jewish ones), so it is in 1:12. But the most natural understanding is that Paul here joins together *as one people* both himself as representing Jewish believers (1:12) and his readers as representing Gentile believers (1:13; cf. 3:1; 4:17). Thus he introduces for the first time an important theme of Ephesians, namely, that both Jews and Gentiles have been reconciled in Christ as "members together of one body, and sharers together in the promise in Christ Jesus" (3:6; cf. 2:11–22).

2.3. Christ's Preeminence in the Holy Spirit's Role (1:13–14)

Verse 13 is the beginning of a twofold transition. (1) It marks the start of the third and final stanza of Paul's praise-hymn, where he changes his focus from the work of Christ in providing redemption *for the believer* to the work of the Holy Spirit *in the believer* on Christ's behalf. Jesus promised his twelve disciples before his death that when the Holy Spirit came as the Paraclete and the Spirit of truth (John 14–16), he would come as the executor of Christ's estate (esp. 16:14–15). Paul assures true believers that they are "marked in him [Christ] with a seal, the promised Holy Spirit" (Eph. 1:13c).

(2) Paul also moves from attention on the Jews "who were the first to hope in Christ" (1:12a) to the Gentiles and their relationship to the gospel (1:13a). The way in which the Gentiles "were included in Christ" and their redemption are the same as for the Jews. Significant here are the three verbs used by Paul to describe the progressive steps by which they are "included in Christ": hearing, believing, and sealing. (a) They "*heard* the word of truth, the gospel of your salvation" (1:13b). The Gentiles, existing in their hopeless state of transgressions and sins (2:1), living in darkness and depravity (4:17–19), and being objects of God's just wrath (5:5–6, 8), heard the good news of God's salvation in Christ that Paul and other evangelists proclaimed as a grace gift to be received by faith (2:1–10). This proclamation was accompanied by the Holy Spirit's work of convicting the Gentiles "of guilt in regard to sin, righteousness and judgment" (John 16:8). (b) They "*believed*" (1:13c). Having heard the truth empowered by the Holy Spirit, the Gentiles put their faith (1:13b) in the Lord Jesus Christ so as to be saved by God's grace (2:5, 8). (c) The Gentiles "were *sealed* with the promised Holy Spirit" (1:13c, lit. trans.).

2.3.1. The Spirit As Our Seal of Faith in Christ (1:13). This is the first reference in Ephesians to the Holy Spirit's role in redemption. Hereafter there will hardly be any aspect of his role in the Christian life that Paul does not touch on. The believer is marked or sealed in Christ with the seal of "the promised Holy Spirit." There are two issues here: the "seal" and the "promised" Holy Spirit.

(1) The seal in ancient times was a mark of ownership or personal possession. By bestowing the Holy Spirit as a seal, God marks us in Christ as those who are authentically his (cf. 2 Cor. 1:22). In New Testament times warm wax was applied to letters, contracts, and official papers, and the signer then pressed his identification into it. Bruce (1984, 265) states

The Theater in Ephesus was the site of the riot described in Acts 19:23–41. Paul had been preaching against the goddess Artemis. A silversmith, fearing a loss of business in images of Artemis, called together other craftsmen to stop Paul. Angered, the men shouted "Great is Artemis of the Ephesians!" They seized Paul's traveling companions and rushed to the theater. There the city clerk appealed to the crowd, saying any charges could be handled in the courts, then dismissed the crowd.

that "by giving believers the Spirit, God 'seals' or stamps them as his own possession." Therefore, we have evidence that we are God's adopted children and that our redemption is real when the Holy Spirit indwells us as the life-giving Spirit of Christ (Rom. 8:9), bears witness that God is our Father (8:15), and produces in us the fruit of a right relationship to him (Gal. 5:22–23).

(2) The designation "promised" gift of the Spirit, as in Acts 2, relates principally to the promise of Joel 2:28–29 as interpreted and applied by Peter, the book of Acts, and the rest of the New Testament. Paul's applications in Ephesians include the Holy Spirit's coming to impart "wisdom and revelation" so that we may know God better and be enlightened about the implications of our life "in Christ" (1:17–20), to strengthen us in our inner being and reveal the love of Christ (3:16–19), to produce unity among God's people as the first step toward cosmic unity (4:2–4), to inspire godly living (4:30) and Spirit-filled worship (5:18–20), and to make prayer truly effective (6:18–20).

2.3.2. The Spirit As the First Installment of Our Inheritance in Christ (1:14). The aforementioned role of "the promised Holy Spirit" marks believers as authentically God's people. "These activities of the Spirit foreshadow in type and quality what he will do more fully in the new creation [i.e., the age to come], and so the Spirit with whom God marks us with his stamp of ownership is also appropriately called the ['deposit,'] 'pledge,' 'guarantee,' even 'first installment' of our inheritance (cf. Rom. 8:23; 2 Cor. 1:22; 5:5)" (Turner, 1227). The word "deposit" (*arrabon*) is of Semitic origin and was used in commercial transactions. It denoted a pledge wherein a buyer handed over something of value to a seller as a deposit or earnest payment to secure the transaction until the purchase price was paid in full. The Holy Spirit is the "deposit" that guarantees the future inheritance "of those who are God's possession" (1:14b). In this age the Holy Spirit is given by the Father to us who believe as his earnest payment of what we will receive in greater fullness in the day of final redemption (cf. 4:30).

In 1:1–14 the word "inheritance" is used in two different ways: to describe (1) that which is God's portion or inheritance in his redeemed people (1:11; cf. v. 18), and (2) the everlasting portion God has reserved for "the faithful in Christ Jesus" (1:1, 14). The fullness of redemption and our inheritance as God's people—of which the presence of the Spirit in the church and in the believer is presently God's "deposit" (NIV), "pledge" (NASB, NRSV), "guarantee" (NJKV), or "earnest" (KJV)—awaits the full revelation of Christ and the sons of God at his second coming (Rom. 8:23). On that day of final redemption, all who were chosen and adopted as sons and daughters in Christ, who were redeemed through his blood, and who were marked with the seal of the promised Holy Spirit, will truly be "to the praise of his glory" (1:14c).

This third chorus of the hymn's doxology recalls the unfulfilled destiny to which Israel was called, namely, "to be my people for my renown and praise and honor. But they have not listened" (Jer. 13:11). This destiny will be realized fully when Christ presents to himself "a radiant church, without stain or wrinkle or any other blemish, but holy and blameless" (Eph. 5:27), having been cleansed "by the washing with water through the word" (5:26).

3. Apostolic Prayer for the Believers' Spiritual Enlightenment (1:15–23)

3.1. The Context of Paul's Apostolic Prayer (1:15–17a)

The relationship between 1:3–14 and 1:15–23 is important to note. The former is a profound *hymn of praise* for God's redemptive blessings in Christ; the latter is Paul's *prayer of intercession* for the spiritual eyes of believers to be opened to know experientially the fullness of these blessings. Thus Paul couples together praise and prayer, worship and intercession, as two necessary parts of truly knowing God.

Some believers focus on praise but are complacent about prayer. They love to worship God and affirm that all spiritual blessings are already theirs, but they show little spiritual hunger to know him better or to intercede for a greater revelation of God's purpose and power for the church. Other believers pray diligently for more spiritual blessings, but seem oblivious that God has already blessed them in the heavenly realms with every spiritual blessing in Christ. Paul, by personal example in this letter, resists such polarization and combines praise and prayer together. He deeply praises

God that in Christ all spiritual blessings are already ours, but he also earnestly prays that the Spirit of wisdom and revelation may enable believers and empower them to know the fullness of what is theirs in Christ.

What caused Paul to move from praise to God to prayer for his readers? "For this reason" relates to some report he had heard about them. Whereas 1:3–14 was written in more contemplative terms, he now becomes more personal and relational with his readers: "Ever since I heard about your faith and your love for all the saints, I have not stopped giving thanks for you, remembering you in my prayers" (1:15–16a). As news of their faith and love reached Paul at a distance, he was filled with joy and thanksgiving. Paul often interlocks faith and love in the equation of Christian living (cf. Gal. 5:6).

Foulkes (59) notes two characteristic features of Paul's prayer life that occur in verse 16. (1) It is persistent: "I have not stopped giving thanks for you, remembering you in my prayers." Paul practiced what he preached when he exhorted his new converts at Thessalonica to "pray continually" (1 Thess. 5:17; cf. Rom. 12:12; Eph. 6:18; Col. 4:2). (2) It is accompanied by thanksgiving (cf. Eph. 5:20). Elsewhere in his letters, Paul taught that gratitude should be "the unfailing accompaniment of intercession" (Phil. 4:6; Col. 3:15–17; 4:2; 1 Thess. 5:18). Phillips paraphrases Paul: "I thank God continually for you and I never give up praying for you."

"Remembering you" in this context means "asking on your behalf"; the literal rendering ("making mention of you") suggests that in his intercession Paul actually brought his readers by name before God. Clearly the object of his prayer in 1:17 is that of a serious request, not an issue of recollection. When one considers the burden that Paul carried in his heart for all the churches, in some cases for converts he had never met, one can only exclaim with Bruce (1961, 38): "What an intercessor he must have been."

The foundation of Paul's unshakable faith and confidence in prayer is "the God of our Lord Jesus Christ, the glorious Father" (1:17a). The first phrase refers to Paul's assurance that "God is for us. . . . He who did not spare his own Son, but gave him up for us all—how will he not also along with him, graciously give us all things?" (Rom. 8:31–32). The second phrase (lit., "the Father of glory") refers to the perfection of God's Fatherhood (cf. Eph. 3:15). If we as imperfect earthly fathers know how to give good gifts to our children, says Jesus, "how much more will your Father in heaven give the Holy Spirit to those who ask him" (Luke 11:13). Paul proceeds to pray that his readers may be fully endowed with the Holy Spirit's ministry of revelation.

3.2. The Focus of Paul's Apostolic Prayer (1:17b–19)

The essence of Paul's apostolic prayer is embodied in the twice-repeated phrase "that you may know" (1:17, 18). Know what? Know God better and know his ways. Although Paul's prayers elsewhere often range more widely than this, they typically include the heart of this petition: that you "may have power . . . to grasp . . . and to know" (3:18–19a); "asking God to fill you with the knowledge of his will through all spiritual wisdom and understanding" (Col. 1:9); that you "may abound more and more in knowledge and depth of insight" (Phil. 1:9).

The knowledge for which Paul so diligently prays is not intellectual knowledge "about God," but the most vital of all knowledge and the highest form of all understanding: to know God himself and understand his ways. But how can a finite human being know and comprehend the infinite? The most brilliant minds cannot know or understand God. It is impossible without the factors involved in Paul's twofold request: (1) that God "may give you the Spirit of wisdom and revelation" (1:17), and (2) "that the eyes of your heart may be enlightened" (1:18).

"Spirit" (*pneuma*) has no definite article in verse 17 in the Greek. Robinson (39) notes: "With the article ['the'] very generally the word indicates the personal Holy Spirit; while without it, some special manifestation or bestowal of the Holy Spirit is signified." Thus "spirit" is not capitalized in most translations (KJV, NKJV, NASB, RSV, NRSV). However, as F. F. Bruce (1984, 269) states, "a spirit of wisdom and revelation can be imparted only through him who is the personal Spirit of wisdom and revelation." Thus the NIV translation is more in keeping with the intent of Paul and the prophecy of Isaiah, "The Spirit of the Lord will rest on him—the Spirit of wisdom and of understanding, the Spirit of counsel and of power, the Spirit of knowledge and of the fear of the Lord" (Isa. 11:2).

Paul is asking in effect that the same ministry of the Holy Spirit that rested on Jesus will come upon the believer, imparting "wisdom and revelation." The Holy Spirit plays the key role in the fulfillment of Paul's Ephesians prayer, for he is the object of the verb "give" and will enable believers to know God and his Son "better." Note the prayer is not for sinners to know God *initially* (in salvation), but for saints to know God *intimately* (in revelation).

And who have come to a place in their spiritual pilgrimage where they do not need to know God better? Paul's converts had not. Even Paul, in spite of all his many revelations of Christ (Acts 22:14, 17–21; 23:11; Gal. 1:12), never came to that point in his own life. Twenty-five years or more after his initial revelation of, and life-changing encounter with, the risen Christ on the Damascus road, he longed for more: "I want *to know* Christ and the power of his resurrection and the fellowship of sharing in his sufferings, *becoming like him* . . ." (Phil. 3:10).

"Wisdom" (*sophia*, 1:17) is not related to human ingenuity or cleverness, but is a gift of God. It is God-given insight into the true nature of things. Paul contrasts it with being worldly wise (1 Cor. 1:19–20). Christ is "the wisdom of God" (1:24, 30); as we partake of him by the Spirit, we become spiritually wise. "Men who know many things are all around us; men of spiritual wisdom are so rare that they are worth far more than their weight in gold" (Bruce, 1961, 39). "Revelation" (*apokalypsis*) is God's disclosure of himself or some spiritual reality to us by the Holy Spirit. Paul describes this activity of the Spirit in 1 Corinthians 2:10–11:

> But God has revealed it to us by his Spirit.
>
> The Spirit searches all things, even the deep things of God. For who among men knows the thoughts of a man except the man's spirit within him? In the same way no one knows the thoughts of God except the Spirit of God.

The purpose of God in giving wisdom and revelation is to "know him better." There are two Greek words for knowledge: *gnosis*, which refers to abstract knowledge or objective facts about God; and *epignosis*, which refers to knowing God himself, experientially and intimately. Paul uses the latter one here. "If theology, knowledge *about* God, is impossible without divine revelation, how much more so is that acquaintance with God Himself, that *epignosis*, of which the apostle speaks here!" (Bruce, 1961, 39).

The second factor in Paul's twofold request is "that the eyes of your heart may be enlightened" (v. 18). The "heart" here is a partial synonym for one's mind, emotions, and will, even "the spirit of the mind." Our inward vision has need of being illuminated by the Holy Spirit with spiritual understanding if we are to know God's ways and eternal purpose.

Paul mentions three specific areas in his apostolic prayer where spiritual enlightenment is needed. (1) He prays for enlightenment concerning "the hope to which he has called you" (1:18b). This hope and calling has a past, present, and future dimension to it and centers in Christ, "the hope of glory." The calling has its beginning in God's initiative in election, adoption, redemption, and the gift of the Holy Spirit (1:3–14). The present dimension of the hope and calling includes God's call to be conformed to the image of his Son (Rom. 8:29), "to be holy and blameless in his sight" (Eph. 1:4), to be joined together with other members of his body in peace, to live in harmonious fellowship and unity (2:11–18; 4:2–3), "to live a life worthy of the calling" (4:1), and to share in his sufferings and in his glory (Rom. 8:17; Phil. 1:29). The future completion of the hope will be in our participation in the resurrection glory of Christ Jesus when we behold him face to face, are transformed perfectly into his image, and are glorified with him forever. In this letter Paul describes this completion of the hope in corporate terms (Eph. 5:27).

(2) Paul prays that we may know "the riches of his glorious inheritance in the saints" (1:18c). Does this refer to our inheritance or God's? Is it the inheritance that God *gives to* the saints in the age to come (as in 1:14)? Or is it the inheritance that God himself *receives in* the saints (as alluded to in 1:11)? Some interpreters believe the former, but the preposition "in" and the context of Ephesians generally point to the latter. The saints constitute God's inheritance. In the Old Testament Israel

was God's portion; in the New Testament Christ and his body (comprised of both Jews and Gentiles) is the totality of God's inheritance. It is in this inheritance that "he will display to the universe the untold riches of his glory [cf. 3:10; also 1:20–23; 3:21]. We can scarcely realize what it must mean to God to see His purpose complete, to see creatures of His hand, sinners redeemed by His grace, reflecting His own glory" (Bruce, 1961, 40). Surely our spiritual eyes need to be enlightened to understand the inestimable value that God places on the redeemed people of Christ as his own inheritance.

(3) Paul prays that we may know by revelation and in experience God's "incomparably great power for us who believe" (1:19a). "Incomparably" (*hyperballon*, a word used in the New Testament only by Paul; cf. 2:7; 3:19) reflects his almost frustrated desire to express in words the inexpressible greatness of God's power. Because of his exceedingly great power and the limitations of human language, we cannot receive the full revelation of what Paul seeks to convey about God's power unless the Holy Spirit enlightens the eyes of our heart.

In 1:19 Paul presses the limitations of human language to convey something of the magnitude of God's power: "that power is like the working of his mighty strength." He uses four key words to describe God's power. (1) "Power" (*dynamis*) is the Greek word from which English words "dynamic" and "dynamo" are derived; this indicates something of the thrust of this word. *Dynamis* is a reservoir of potential God-power that, when directed toward believers, is like the "working" of God's mighty strength. (2) "Working" (*energeia*) is the term from which is derived our word "energy"; it denotes "energizing" power in operation. (3) The word "mighty" (*kratos*) denotes "power as force, mastery, power as shown in action" (Salmond, 276), power that overcomes resistance (as in Christ's miracles). (4) "Strength" (*ischys*) refers to "inherent power," as the power in the arm of a strong man, power that is available when needed. Paul piles synonym upon synonym to indicate the fullness of God's power and how infinitely real is his power made available to "us who believe." The remainder of Paul's prayer directly relates to this realm of God's "incomparably great power."

3.3. Christ's Exaltation, Lordship, and Headship As the Measure of God's Available Power (1:20–23)

In 1:20–23 Paul refers to three realities in Christ that further demonstrate the magnitude of God's great power: Christ's resurrection-ascension (1:20), Christ's enthronement as Lord "far above all rule and authority, power and dominion" (1:21), and Christ's appointment as "head over everything for the church" (1:22–23).

(1) God demonstrated his dynamic power and mighty energy "when he *raised him* [Jesus] from the dead *and seated him* at his right hand in the heavenly realms" (1:20). When the New Testament wishes to emphasize the fullness of God's love for us, it points to Christ's death (e.g., Rom. 5:8). But when it wishes to demonstrate the reality of God's power, it points to Christ's resurrection. Not only does that event provide believers with the hope of resurrection life in the future (1 Cor. 15:20, 23), but also in Christ believers now experience through faith the power of God who raises them from spiritual death to "newness of life" (cf. Eph. 2:4–5). Furthermore, as Christ was raised and then seated at God's right hand in a place of honor and authority, God's power has also "raised us up with Christ and seated us with him in the heavenly realms in Christ Jesus" (2:6). Thus "Christ's resurrection and ascension express the measure of the Father's power [and authority] made available to us" (Foulkes, 63).

(2) God the Father also demonstrated his power in where he raised Christ *to*—the throne, the place of highest honor and authority, "far above all rule and authority, power and dominion and every title" (1:21). In God's administration of the universe there are different levels of authority, human and angelic. Whatever forms of authority and governing powers there are in the universe, by God's power Christ has been *enthroned as Lord* in the heavenly realms, far above them all, "not only in the present age but also in the one to come" (1:21).

Christ's exaltation echoes the messianic promise of Psalm 110:1, "The LORD says to my Lord: 'Sit at my right hand until I make your enemies a footstool for your feet.'" Reference to phrases in Psalm 110:1 clearly occur here: God's "right hand," Christ ascending to "sit" there, and God placing "all things under his feet" (1:22, which corresponds to "a footstool for your feet"). Thus the demonic "rulers," "authorities," and "spiritual forces of evil" against which Paul later summons believers to stand (6:10–12) are "under [Christ's] feet" (1:22) and ours if we are "seated with him in the heavenly realms" (2:6). Although Satan and his demonic host have not yet conceded Christ's victory, his exaltation as Lord is evidence that he reigns in absolute supremacy. Though we do not yet see everything in subjection to him, we do see Jesus "crowned with glory and honor" (Heb. 2:8–9). His authority and Lordship will be fully manifest in the future (Ps. 8:6; 1 Cor. 15:25–27; Heb. 2:6–8).

(3) The third realm in which God's power is demonstrated as being available for his people is in *Christ's headship* (1:22–23). Christ has been appointed "head over everything," that is, the supreme head over creation, the final manifestation of which awaits the future (cf. 1:10). He is presently head "for the church, which is his body." This concept of the church as "the body of Christ" is unique to Paul's letters among New Testament writings. This revelation began for Paul on the Damascus road encounter with the risen Christ: "I am Jesus, whom you are persecuting" (Acts 9:5). Paul was persecuting the church, but to persecute the church was to persecute Jesus in that the body and the head are inseparably joined together as one.

Here Paul speaks not just of the church as Christ's body (Eph. 1:23; 4:4; cf. also 1 Cor. 6:15; 12:12–21; Rom. 12:4–5), but also of Christ as the church's head (implied in 1:10; explicit in 1:22–23; 4:15–16; 5:23; also Col. 1:18). "The organic relation between head and body suggests the vital union between Christ and the church, sharers of a common life, which is his own risen life communicated to his people. The church is here the complete or universal church—manifested visibly . . . in local congregations" (Bruce, 1984, 275).

The universal church, Christ's body consisting of all true believers, is "the fullness of him who fills everything in every way" (1:23). It is not readily apparent what Paul had in mind with this startling statement. The problem centers in the words "the fullness [*pleroma*] of him who fills." Grammatically, several possibilities are legitimate.[2] Does *pleroma* refer to the church or to Christ? And who is it that "fills everything"?

In a sense the church is the full complement of Christ, just as the body is the necessary complement of the head in the constitution of a complete person. The church, his body, is the full complement of Christ who, as deity, "fills everything"—i.e., the entire universe. And Christ himself is also the "fullness"; according to Colossians 2:9 the "fullness" (*pleroma*) of deity resides in him. Here, however, the fullness of Christ resides in the church. As the *pleroma* of deity resides in Christ in bodily form, so the *pleroma* of Christ resides in the church as his body. Thus the church is "a partaker of all that He owns and is, for the purpose of continuing His work" (Hanson, 126).

4. The Results of Redemption in Christ Jesus (2:1–3:13)

Paul expressed adoration and praise in 1:3–14 for God's master plan of redemption as formulated by the Father in eternity, made possible by the Son in history, and applied by the Holy Spirit in the lives of believers. He then prayed in 1:15–23 for believers to know God better and to have their spiritual eyes enlightened to understand more fully God's saving power in Christ at work in their lives and the church. Now in chapter 2 Paul begins to unveil further actual results of redemption and the power of God's saving grace in Christ for Jew and Gentile alike.

4.1. Christ Saves Sinners From Their Hopeless Predicament (2:1–10)

Like 1:3–14 and 1:15–23, 2:1–10 constitutes a single sentence in the Greek text. Paul begins by describing the former sinful state of the Gentiles (2:1–2) and the plight of all humanity, including the Jews (2:3) in their unredeemed past. He then contrasts sharply God's saving grace in Christ Jesus and the new redeemed life that believers have been given in Christ (2:4–10).

4.1.1. Humanity's Desperate Plight Without Christ (2:1–3). Paul mentions five tragic facts that characterize human beings without Christ. (1) Their life is characterized by spiritual death (2:1). Spiritual death is a state of separation from God created by "transgressions and sins." "As for you" (2:1) refers to Paul's Gentile readers, whereas "all of us" (2:3) includes Paul himself and all Jews.

The Greek in 2:1 begins with a present participial phrase, "you being dead," and joins vith a similar phrase in 2:5, "we being dead," n anticipation of the main subject and verb hat occurs in verses 4–5, "God . . . made us live." The present tense of "being dead" xpresses a continuous state of existence efore being made alive with Christ. Existence part from Christ is a life that belongs to the ealm of sin and death. Note carefully that Paul s not saying that humanity without Christ will ne day die, but that they are dead already even while they are physically alive (cf. 1 Tim. 5:6). t is an existence void of spiritual and eternal ife, a realm dominated by spirits of death and he ever-present prospect of eternal death (cf. Rev. 20:14–15).

The words "transgressions and sins" (2:1) lescribe the sphere of death for the sinner. 'Transgressions" (*paraptomata*) refers to tumbling into sin, which is universally true of ll humanity as descendants of Adam. "Sins" *hamartiai*) is a more common New Testament vord for sin and relates to "sin as a habit" or 'sin as a power." According to Eadie (119), '*paraptomata*, under the image of 'falling,' nay carry an allusion to the desires of the flesh . . while *hamartiai*, under the image of 'missng the mark,' may designate more the desires f the mind, sins of thought and idea, of purose and inclination." It is out of this morass f sin and death that God initiates redemption s a work of his grace.

(2) Those without Christ follow "the ways f this world" (2:2). This phrase refers to the vays, character, and influence of unregenerate umanity during this present evil age (cf. Gal. :4; 1 John 2:15–17). If we do not conform to Christ, we conform to the world by going long with the prevailing character of our genration and the direction of the tide of sin round us.

(3) Unregenerate humanity is under the lomain of "the ruler of the kingdom of the air" 2:2b). This is an obvious reference to Satan, vho by usurpation rules as the god of this age. n 2 Corinthians 4:4 Paul states that Satan as 'the god of this age has blinded the minds of nbelievers, so that they cannot see the light of he gospel." Sinners are entangled and blinded. Ephesians 6:12 refers to a network of evil spirts with authority under the control of Satan as heir ruler; their sphere is described as "in the eavenly realms" (i.e., the spiritual realm), the quivalent of "the kingdom of the air." Satan's sphere of operation is limited, in contrast to the universal rule of God.

Even though the sphere of Satan's kingdom or authority is limited and temporal, it is nevertheless real and powerful. Verse 2 further describes him as "the spirit who is now at work in those who are disobedient" (lit., "sons [h*uioi*] of disobedience"). Either we are related to God and energized by his power (1:20), or we are related to Satan's kingdom and "energized" by him ("at work" translates the Greek word *energeo*, lit., "energizing"). Stated another way, if God is not our Father and we his sons and daughters by adoption, then Satan is our spiritual father and we are his children of rebellion. Satan energizes people for evil purposes because "disobedience, conscious resistance to the will of God, lays men open to the working of Satan and his hosts" (Westcott, 30).

(4) People without Christ (Jew and Gentile alike) have a propensity for "gratifying the cravings of our sinful nature" (2:3). Paul confesses, including himself, that humanity unaffected by God's grace in Christ is inclined to indulge the lusts and desires "of our sinful nature [Gk. *sarx*, flesh]" in one form or another. Paul admits elsewhere that the form of his own preconversion indulgence was "every kind of covetous desire" (Rom. 7:8). *Sarx* denotes human nature that universally has been corrupted by sin; "its desires and thoughts" (2:3) inevitably produce, if unchecked, sins like "the acts of the sinful nature" (Gal. 5:19–20; cf. 1 John 2:16).

(5) All persons without Christ are "by nature children of wrath" (2:3d, NASB). This state of things exists because through Adam "sin came into the world" (Rom. 5:12), and all Adam's descendants (Jews and Gentiles alike) subsequently inherited the sinful nature with its propensity toward sin and became transgressors (3:9–10, 23). It is primarily this latter fact that Paul is addressing here. He refers to God's wrath not because we came under it at birth as descendants of Adam, but because we have "all sinned" (5:12). Thus in Ephesians 2:3 "children of wrath" is an expression that parallels the thought of transgressors (2:1) and "sons of disobedience" (2:2) (cf. Robinson, 49–51).

That "religious" Jews were as much under the sentence of sin's judgment and God's wrath as pagan Gentiles is the main point of Paul's presentation in Romans 1–3. Such is the universal devastation of sin and the hopeless condition of the human race to which Christ has come as Redeemer. In the prophetic words of Isaiah, "See, darkness covers the earth and thick darkness is over the peoples" (Isa. 60:2). But into this situation "the light has come" (60:1, 3).

4.1.2. Salvation by Grace Through Faith in Christ (2:4–10). The loving, redeeming action of God in this section stands in strongest possible contrast to the desperate plight of sinful humanity under God's wrath in 2:1–3. In breathtaking and sweeping terms, Paul contrasts what his readers were "at one time" (2:3) without Christ and what they now are in Christ; what "all of us" (2:3a) are "by nature" (2:3d) and what we are "by grace" (2:5, 8); the reason for God's wrath (2:3) and the initiative of God's love (2:4); the spiritual reality that we "were dead" (2:1) but God "made us alive with Christ" (2:5); the fact that we were hopelessly bogged in the muck of sin as Satan's slaves (2:2–3), but God "raised us up with Christ and seated us with him" (2:6) in a position of honor and power. These contrasts will bring glory to God "in the coming ages" (2:7).

Verse 4 reveals the great value God places on sinful humanity. Even while we were dead in our transgressions and sins, God loved us. He looked down on us in our deadness (dead people cannot rise); because he is "rich in mercy" (2:4; cf. Ex. 34:6; Ps. 103:8; Jonah 4:2; Mic. 7:18) and because of the "muchness" (*pollen*) of his love (2:4), he "made us alive with Christ" (2:5). The Greek adjective *pollen* means "much," not "great"; it refers to the infinite abundance of God's love, not its size (cf. 3:17–19). Thus Paul boldly asserts in verses 5 and 8 that "it is by grace you have been saved." No person can possibly, by self-effort, human merit, or good works, hope to escape the death of sin (2:1); the entrapment of the world, the devil, and the flesh (2:2–3); or the wrath of God (2:3). Instead, we are rescued by God's initiative, who in the wealth of his mercy and the abundance of his love has chosen to justify us "freely by his grace through the redemption that came by Christ Jesus" (Rom. 3:24).

In 2:4–7 three verbs form the compound predicate of this long sentence: "made alive" (2:5), "raised up" (2:6), and "seated" (2:6). The subject of these verbs is God; their action describes what he has *already* done; the direct object of all three verbs is the plural pronoun "us." Here Paul links our salvation directly to what God has done in Christ historically. The three verbs mentioned above refer to the three successive historical events in Jesus' life after his death on the cross: resurrection, ascension, and being seated at the Father's right hand. These salvation events are at the center of the gospel.

Paul adds the prefix *syn* (meaning "together with") to each of the three verbs, thus linking us to Christ in these events. Thus, because of God's grace, we participate *with Christ* in these moments of his triumph over death and all evil. That we who were dead in sin and by nature children of God's wrath should be made alive *with Christ*, raised up *with Christ*, and seated *with Christ* in the heavenly realms is surely an unimaginable demonstration of God's mercy, love, and grace. Salvation here, as in chapter 1, is in union with Christ Jesus. God has blessed us as his redeemed people in Christ (1:3) and "seated us with him in the heavenly realms" (2:6). As John Stott (81) notes, "if we are seated with Christ in the heavenlies, there can be no doubt what we are sitting on: thrones."

This is not mere mysticism. "Temporally indeed, we live on earth so long as we remain in this body; but, 'in Christ Jesus' we are seated with Christ where he is" (Bruce, 1961, 50). This language about the spiritual realm testifies to "a living experience, that Christ has given us on the one hand a new life (with a sensitive awareness of the reality of God, and a love for him and for his people) and on the other a new victory (with evil increasingly under our feet)" (Stott, 81). We were dead, but now we have been made alive in Christ; we were under the dark domain of Satan's rule, but now we have been raised with Christ in triumph over sin and death; we were slaves in captivity, but now we have been enthroned with Christ in the heavenlies. In Christ the future inheritance has already begun in the present as a glorious reality and assurance, made possible by the indwelling Holy Spirit (1:13–14).

What moved God to provide so great a salvation for sinners? Paul uses four words (in this order in the Greek): God's "mercy" (2:4), "love" (2:4), "grace" (2:5, 8), and "kindness" (2:7). Paul reaches the heights of revelatory nderstanding when he adds that God has edeemed us in Christ "in order that in the oming ages he might show the incomparable iches of his grace" (2:7) to all the universe hroughout all eternity. In raising Christ from he dead and exalting him at his right hand, iod the Father has demonstrated "the incomarable [*hyperballon*] greatness of his power" 1:19–20); in raising us from spiritual death to hare Christ's place of exaltation in the heavnlies, God displays "the incomparable *hyperballon*] riches of his grace" (2:7), and he vill continue to do so throughout all the ages f eternity.

In 2:8–10, one of the great evangelical ummaries of the New Testament, Paul xpresses the heart of his "grace" message: ᵋedemption through union with Christ eleases us from a life of sin and death and nables us to partake of Christ's resurrection fe, which is God's grace precisely because it erives totally from him—his initiative, his iercy, his love, his kindness, his intervention. 'here are three foundational words of the ospel—"saved," "grace," and "faith."

(1) *Salvation* (Gk. *soteria*) means "delivernce" and is a comprehensive word involving iore than justification or forgiveness. Paul ses it here to include deliverance from the eath of sin (2:1), the ways of the world (2:2), ie dominion of Satan (2:2), and the wrath of iod (2:3). Positively, it includes "the totality f our new life in Christ, together with whom 'e have been made alive, exalted, and seated the heavenly realm" (2:4–7); (Stott, 83). The Iew Testament teaches that salvation has three tages in its completeness: the *past*, which is rounded in the finished work of Christ's death n the cross; the *present* reality for those who re united by faith to Christ Jesus and are ıdwelt by the Holy Spirit; and the *future* tage, which will occur at the second coming *arousia*) of Christ, including the resurrection f our body.

(2) *Grace* (*charis*) is God's merciful and ving initiative to provide for us and offer to s salvation in Christ as a free gift. Bruce 961, 51) makes this astute observation about race here: "If the raising of Christ from death) sit at His [the Father's] own right hand is the ıpreme demonstration of *God's power* [1:19–1], the raising of the people of Christ from piritual death to share Christ's place of exaltation is the supreme demonstration of *His grace*" (italics mine).

(3) *Faith* (*pistis*) is our response to God's grace and a response made possible by grace, through which we receive God's free gift of salvation in Christ. Faith is firmly believing and humbly trusting in Christ as one's Redeemer and Deliverer. True faith includes the fruit of repentance and issues forth in a life of obedience to Christ Jesus as Lord.

Paul further emphasizes that we are saved by God's grace through faith in Christ by adding two denials and two affirmations:

Denial 1: "And this not of you" (lit. trans.) (2:8c)
Affirmation 1: "It is the gift of God" (2:8d)
Denial 2: This is "not by works, so that no one can boast" (2:9)
Affirmation 2: "We are God's workmanship" (2:10a).

Some believe the "this" of the first denial refers to faith—i.e., that even the faith by which we are saved is a gift of God (e.g., Augustine, C. Hodge, E. K. Simpson). This interpretation may be theologically true, but that is not Paul's point here. "This" (Gk. *touto*) is neuter, whereas "faith" is a feminine noun. Thus the antecedent of "this" is not "faith"; rather, the whole event and experience of being saved by grace through faith is not our doing, but God's free gift to us. Stott (83) paraphrases Paul's thought as follows: "[Salvation] is neither your achievement ('not your own doing') nor a reward of any of your deeds of religion or philanthropy ('not because of works'). Since, therefore, there is no room for human merit, there is no room for human boasting either."

The essence of legalistic religion is the belief that salvation is by works, that is, the result of something a person does. It is impossible to be saved any other way than by God's grace because all the unsaved are spiritually dead (2:1), under Satan's dominion (2:2), enslaved to sin (2:3), and under God's wrath (2:3). In order for people to be saved God must take the initiative to act on behalf of the sinner, which he has done in Christ (2:4–5). Because of what he has done, not what we do, believers are made alive spiritually in Christ (2:5; Col. 1:13), delivered from the power of Satan and sin (Eph. 2:5–6; Col. 1:13), made a new creation (Eph. 2:10; 2 Cor. 5:17), and receive the Holy Spirit (Eph. 1:13–14; cf. John 20:22).

No amount of self-effort or religious devotion can accomplish the above. Rather, "it is by grace you have been saved through faith—and this not from yourselves, it is the gift of God" (2:8). The activity of God's grace centers in his Son—his death, resurrection, and enthronement in heaven as Lord. As to the demonstration of his grace, first comes the call to repentance and faith (Acts 2:38). With this call the Holy Spirit enables a person to respond to the grace of God through faith. Those who respond in faith to the Lord Jesus Christ are made alive with Christ (2:5) and therein are regenerated or born again by the Spirit (John 3:3–8). They are raised and seated with Christ in the heavenly realms and continue to receive grace because of their union with him at the place of power, enabling them to resist sin and live according to the Spirit (Rom. 8:13–14). Believers then serve God and "do good works" (Eph. 2:10; cf. 2 Cor. 9:8) because of God's grace that works in them (1 Cor. 15:10). God's grace operates in the people of Christ both "to will and to act according to his good purpose" (Phil. 2:13). From beginning to end, then, salvation is by the grace of God operating in the believer through faith.

Verse 10 emphasizes what we are *in Christ*, in contrast to what we were *in sin* (2:1–3). We are now "God's workmanship" (*poiema*), "His work of art, His masterpiece" (Bruce, 1961, 52). *Poiema* occurs elsewhere only in Romans 1:20, where it refers to "what has been made" by God in original creation. Here it refers to the new creation in Christ (cf. 2 Cor. 5:17); we are "created [*ktisthentes*] in Christ Jesus" for good works. Both of these Greek words are related to creation. "Salvation is creation, re-creation, new creation" (Stott, 84)—that which God alone can do. We can never be saved *by* "good works," just as we cannot re-create ourselves. But we are saved *for* "good works" and even "created" in Christ for that purpose. The only hope for dead people is resurrection, and Christ Jesus is "the resurrection and the life" (John 11:25). He is also the Creator: "All things were created by him and for him" (Col. 1:16). Both the activity of resurrection and creation point to the indispensability of God's initiative and God's grace.

But salvation *sola gratia, sola fide* (by grace alone, by faith alone) can be misrepresented (cf. Rom. 6:1). We misunderstand Paul if righteous living is forgotten and grace becomes an excuse for sinning on the mistaken assumption that if Christians carelessly sin their lapses only give God's grace more opportunity for display. Paul's response to this interpretation of grace was, "By no means!" "Perish the thought!" (Rom. 6:2). F. F. Bruce remarks: "Those who continue to 'walk' in the trespasses and sins which characterize the unregenerate state show that they are not God's workmanship, whatever professions they may make" (1961, 52).

Hence Paul in Ephesians 2:10 refers to good works as indispensable to salvation—"not as its ground or means, however, but as it [necessary] consequence and evidence" (Stott 84–85). Titus 2:14 is the best commentary Christ "gave himself for us to redeem us from all wickedness and to purify for himself a people that are his very own, eager to do wha is good." Just as in Christ we are predestine for adoption (1:4), so in Christ we are predestined to do good works.

Ephesians 2:1–10 in the Greek text end with the phrase "that we should walk in them" (NASB; NIV, "to do"). This paragraph began with us "walking" (*peripateo*) in the death o transgressions and sins (2:1–2) and ends with us "walking" (*peripateo*) in good works tha God planned in advance for all who ar redeemed in Christ. Thus the strong contras between life without Christ and life in Chris is complete. It is the contrast between tw ways of living (in sin or by grace) and betwee two masters (Satan and God). Stott (85) adds "What could possibly have effected such change? Just this: a new creation by the grac and power of God. The key expressions of th paragraph are surely *but God* (verse 4) and *b grace* (verses 5, 8)."

4.2. Christ Reconciles Mutually Hostile People Groups to God and One Another As a New Humanity (2:11–18)

Ephesians 2 divides into two halves: Th first half (2:1–10) reveals that out of the wealt of God's grace he is saving individual sinne through Christ and fashioning them as hi grace trophies and workmanship; the secon half (2:11–22) further reveals the nature of God's saving grace and activity in corporate terms, namely, how Gentiles and Jews (two mutually hostile people groups) who receive God's gracious salvation in Christ are being fashioned together into the one body of Christ as God's masterpiece of redemption. In so doing God is creating in and through Christ a "new humanity" (2:11–18) and a "new community" (2:19–22).

4.2.1. The Gentile Exclusion From God and the Covenant People (2:11–12). Verses 11–12 begin much like 2:1-2, by revealing the desperate plight of the Gentile or pagan world outside of Christ. In 2:1–2 they are portrayed as "dead in transgressions and sins"; in 2:11–12 they are described as alienated from God and his covenant people Israel. Whereas the key word in 2:1–2 is "dead," the key word in 2:11–12 is "alienated" (*apallotrioo*; NIV, "excluded"). The Greek verb means "to estrange, exclude, alienate." It occurs only three times in the New Testament, twice in Ephesians and once in a parallel passage in Colossians.

The alienation caused by sin is twofold: alienation from God our Creator (4:18; cf. Col. 1:20–21), and alienation from our fellow human beings (Eph. 2:12). Alienation from God along with its replacement of vertical reconciliation in Christ is found in 2:1–10; alienation from other people and its counterpart of horizontal reconciliation through the work of the cross is emphasized in 2:11–22.

Paul reminds his Gentile readers in verse 11 of their pre-gospel disadvantaged status. Genesis 1–2 reveals the fundamental unity of the human race in the beginning. After the Fall (Gen. 3) and the great Flood (Gen. 6–8), separation occurred as humanity divided into different ethnic groups (Gen. 11). From among the nations, God chose Abraham and his Hebrew descendants to be his covenant people (Gen. 12–50). Circumcision of the Jewish males became the external sign to remind them of their covenant identity and responsibilities.

But God's purpose in choosing Israel to be a light to the Gentiles eventually was lost in ethnic segregation and exclusivism. In Paul's day the Jews arrogantly despised the pagan Gentiles as dogs and viewed them contemptuously as the "uncircumcised." Paul does not endorse this derogatory label, but simply notes its current use as a way of introducing the great socioreligious chasm that existed between Jews and Gentiles before it was abolished in Christ.

Paul goes on in verse 12 to remind the Gentiles that before Christ they had experienced a tragic fivefold deprivation. (1) They "were separate from Christ" and all the blessings of God in him (cf. 1:3; 2:6). As unregenerate Gentiles they had no promise of the coming Messiah, no one to give light to their darkness or hope for their future

(2) They were "excluded from citizenship [*politeia*] in Israel" by reason of their birth. *Politeia* is derived from *polites* ("citizen"), which in turn comes from *polis* ("city, city-state"). Excluded from citizenship *in Israel* meant Gentiles were outsiders politically/religiously of Israel as the community of God's revelation. Stated another way, they were alienated from the covenant people who were a living theocracy and knew the one true God.

(3) Gentiles were "foreigners to the covenants of promise," that is, cut off from all the spiritual history and promises of messianic salvation that the covenants with Abraham, Moses, and David contained. As Paul notes in Romans, the Jews "had been entrusted with the very oracles of God" (Rom. 3:2, NASB). Their spiritual privileges were many: "Theirs is the adoption as sons; theirs the divine glory, the covenants, the receiving of the law, the temple worship and the promises. Theirs are the patriarchs, and from them is traced the human ancestry of Christ, who is God over all, forever praised" (9:4–5). The Gentiles had been excluded from this river of God's revelation and redemption.

(4) and (5) The last two deprivations are stated bluntly: "without hope and without God in the world." In a fallen world with all its sin, suffering, and death, humankind needs an infinite hope, which faith in Christ alone can give. Otherwise, life is dark, troubled, and hopeless. The Gentiles were without the hope of Israel and without the revelation of the God of Israel. The Gentiles were not without "gods" (they had many), but their gods proved empty and cruel. They were without a true knowledge of God, such as had been revealed to Israel.

4.2.2. The Gentile Inclusion in the One New Humanity in Christ (2:13–18). Paul goes on to describe how redemption makes all people one in Christ. Verse 13 begins with two important phrases: "but now," which stands in contrast to "formerly" (v. 11) and "at that time" (v. 12); and, "in Christ Jesus," which stands in contrast to "separate from Christ" (v. 12). These two expressions emphasize how the Gentiles' situation has dramatically changed from being "far away" to being now "brought near." This new nearness to God is both "in Christ Jesus" and "through the blood of Christ." The latter refers to the historical event of Jesus' death on the cross; the former involves the believer's conversion and present union with Christ. The next five verses explain what has been accomplished by Christ's redemptive death on the cross.

Verses 14–18 reveal the heart of Paul's message of reconciliation and how God has begun his eternal plan of cosmic (though not universal) reconciliation (1:10). The key word in this passage is *peace*; it occurs four times (vv. 14, 15, 17 [2x]).

Verse 14 begins with an emphatic declaration: "For he [Christ] himself is our peace." Christ and only Christ has provided the solution to the problem of the alienation from God and from other people that plagues the human race. He is the Reconciler of people to God and the Reconciler of people to people. Thus the gospel is the message of reconciliation (2 Cor. 5:17–21). Here in Ephesians Paul proclaims Christ Jesus himself, because of his redemptive blood (2:14), as "our peace" in a twofold sense: (1) He reconciles us as sinners to God through the cross (v. 16), and (2) he reconciles mutually hostile people groups (such as Jews and Gentiles) to one another and "has made the two one" (v. 14b; also vv. 15, 16, 17, 18).

Reconciliation is the central issue of this passage. Nothing but the gospel can genuinely offer us peace with God (Rom. 5:1), "and nothing but the gospel can remove the barriers which divide mankind into hostile groups in our own age" (Bruce, 1961, 54). Peace between Jew and Gentile required destroying "the barrier, the dividing wall of hostility" (v. 14c). No color bar, ethnic conflict, class distinction, or political division was more absolute than the barrier between Jew and Gentile in the first century A.D. Bruce adds (ibid.): "The greatest triumph of the gospel in the apostolic age was that it overcame this long-standing estrangement and enabled Jew and Gentile to become truly one in Christ."

When Paul wrote these words in Ephesians "the dividing wall" was still a prominent feature of the Jewish temple in Jerusalem. Sto (91–92) graphically describes its foreboding prominence:

> The temple building itself was constructed on an elevated platform. Round it was the Court of the Priests. East of this was the Court of Israel, and further east the court of the women. These three courts—for the priests, the lay men and the lay women of Israel respectively—were all on the same elevation as the temple itself. From this level one descended five steps to a walled platform, and then on the other side of the wall fourteen more steps to another wall, beyond which was the outer court or Court of the Gentiles. This was a spacious court running right round the temple and its inner courts. From any part of it the Gentiles could look up and view the temple, but were not allowed to approach it. They were cut off from it by the surrounding wall, which was a one-and-a-half meter stone barricade, on which were displayed at intervals warning notices in Greek and Latin. They read, in effect, not "Trespassers will be prosecuted" but "Trespassers will be executed."

Paul himself was nearly killed only three c four years earlier by an angry Jewish mob a Jerusalem who believed a rumor that he ha taken a Gentile from Ephesus, name Trophimus, with him into the temple (Act 21:27–32). At the moment he wrote this lette he was literally a prisoner "for the sake of yo Gentiles" (Eph. 3:1). Though the dividing wa and temple stood until the Romans destroye Jerusalem in A.D. 70, Paul declared boldly th Christ had destroyed that wall already in prin ciple when he died on the cross (c. A.D. 30 "The [symbol] still stood; but the thing [it] sig nified was broken down" (Robinson, 60 Through Christ both Jew and Gentile alik now "have access to the Father [in heaven' temple] by one Spirit" (2:18).

Peace and oneness between Jew and Genti also required "abolishing in his flesh [i.e., i Jesus' physical death on the cross] the law wit its commandments and regulations" (2:15; c Col. 1:22; 2:11–12). What Paul refers to here a

Herod's Temple

The temple built in Jerusalem by King Herod was the third temple built on the hill called Mt. Moriah. King Herod, an Idumaean, built the extravagant temple as a way to win favor with the Jews. Construction of the temple was begun in 19 B.C. and not finished until A.D. 64.

Herod had the surface of the hill leveled. He then built a strong retaining wall around the perimeter of the hill with massive smooth-faced stone blocks laid without any mortar. Still visible today are the southeast corner and a section of the Western Wall, also called the Wailing Wall. This "platform," covering an area about 450 meters from north to south and 300 meters from east to west, is called the Temple Mount.

The temple that had been built by the Babylonian exiles was torn down, replaced by Herod's temple.

The temple and its courts were built on a raised platform. Herod's temple had columns of white marble, with gates of silver and gold. A curtain separated the Holy Place in the temple from the Most Holy Place.

A columned portico ringed the entire Temple Mount. The section at the south end had four rows of columns. The other porticoes had two rows. At the northwest corner of the Temple Mount stood Antonia Fortress. Although Gentiles could enter the courtyard surrounding the temple, signs were posted barring them from the three central courts, which were restricted for use by the priests, the Jewish men, and Jewish women. The penalty was death.

The temple and the walls surrounding it were destroyed by the Romans in A.D. 70.

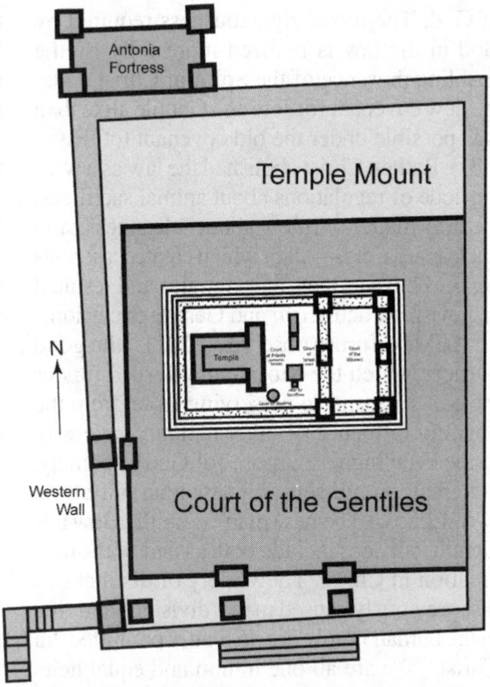

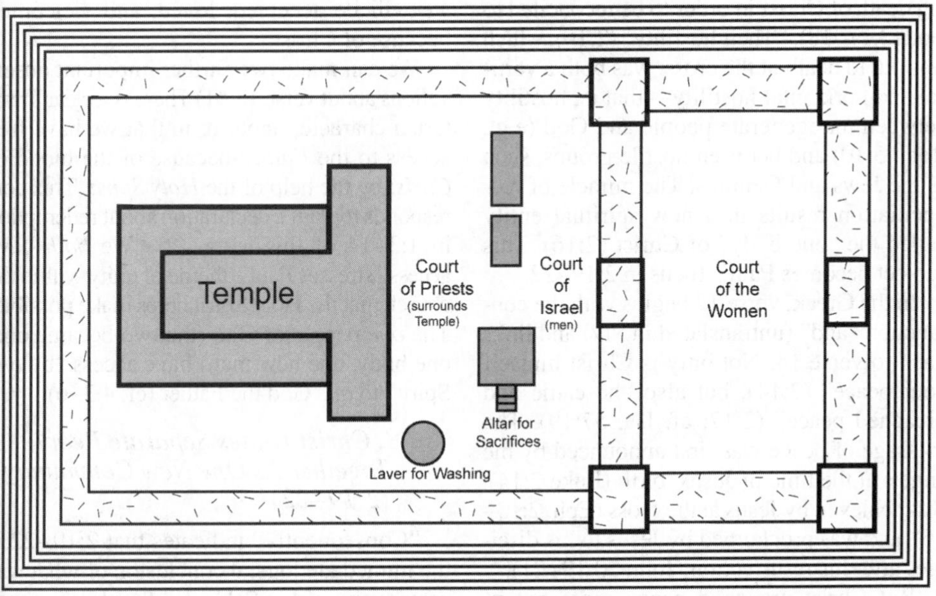

being abolished in Christ's death is not the law as a revelation of the moral character and will of God. The moral righteousness required by God in the law is realized more fully by the enabling presence of the Spirit of Christ under the new covenant for Jew and Gentile alike than was possible under the old covenant (cf. Rom. 3:31). Rather, Christ abolished the law as a written code of regulations about animal sacrifices, dietary matters, rules about cleanness and uncleanness, etc.—all of which created a serious barrier between Jews and Gentiles and resulted in Jewish particularism and Gentile exclusion.

As Max Turner observes (1231), "the good purpose which the Mosaic law served [under the old covenant] in preserving Israel from the ungodly influence of other nations, gave way to the even higher purpose [of God]," namely, "to create in himself one new man out of the two" (2:15). "The new man" is neither Jew nor Gentile but does include both as part of the new creation in Christ. The variety of distinctions that previously caused major divisions and rifts in the human family are no longer permitted "in Christ." We are all one in him and equal heirs of the grace of God (cf. Gal. 3:28–29).

Peace and oneness between Jew and Gentile required that both be reconciled "to God through the cross" (2:16). This presupposes that Jews as well as Gentiles were sinners alienated from God (2:3) and needed the atoning death of Christ in order to be reconciled to God (2:17–18). "Their hostility" (2:16), which was put to death at the cross, was both a vertical and horizontal hostility—that is, hostility between unregenerate people and God (e.g., Rom. 5:10) and between hostile groups, such as the Jews and Gentiles. The miracle of reconciliation results in a new spiritual entity called the "one body" of Christ (2:16). This subject becomes Paul's focus in 2:19–22.

In the Greek, verse 17 begins with the conjunction "and" (untranslated in NIV) and links back to verse 14. Not only is Christ himself "our peace" (2:14), but also "he came and preached peace" (2:17; cf. Isa. 57:19). The message of peace was first announced by the angels at the time of Jesus' birth (Luke 2:14), was achieved by Jesus at the cross (Eph. 2:13–16), and was proclaimed by Jesus to his disciples after his resurrection (John 20:19–21).

But Christ preached peace more extensively—peace "to you who were far away" (i.e., the Gentiles, who were without hope an separated from God, 2:12–13) and peace "t those who were near" (i.e., the Jews, who ha "the covenants of the promise," 2:12)– through the preaching of the gospel by Pete Paul, and other first-century evangelist Notice that the Gentiles were unable to com to Christ; he had to go to them through hi messengers. Moreover, the Jews had to hav the gospel preached to them as well. An whenever the message of peace and reconci iation (only made possible through the cros is proclaimed in the world today, "it is Chri who proclaims it through us" (Stott, 103).

Subsequent to Jesus' death and resurrectio "through him we both [Jew and Gentile believ ers] have access to the Father by one Spirit (2:18). The word "access" (*prosagoge*) ca mean "introduction," in the sense that throug Christ by the Spirit we are introduced to Go as Father. But more likely this word calls t mind a royal court scene in an ancient Middl Eastern kingdom, where an official called *prosagogeus* facilitated admission into th presence of the king. The Holy Spirit facilitate access to and an intimate fellowship with th Father that the "redemption through [Christ's blood" (1:7) makes possible. This meanin parallels 3:12 and the teaching in Hebrew 10:19–22. We have the right to approach wit confidence our heavenly Father, knowing th we will be accepted, loved, and welcome because of Christ.

We can make two further important obse vations about verse 18. (1) There is a clear Trin tarian character about it, in that we have fre access to the *Father* because of the blood c *Christ* by the help of the *Holy Spirit*. This co responds to Paul's declaration about redemptio in 1:3–14 of this letter. (2) "We *both* hav access" stresses Paul's theme of unity within th church that the Holy Spirit helps make possibl The *one* people of God (the two became on one body, one new man) have access "by *on* Spirit" to *one* God the Father (cf. 4:3–6).

4.3. Christ Unites Separate People Together As One New Community (2:19–22)

"Consequently" indicates that 2:19–22 i the immediate logical conclusion of what wa previously said in 2:11–18. In a larger sens it is the fruit of all Paul has written thus far i

Ephesians about redemption in Christ. The goal that the Father planned and Christ accomplished in his death-resurrection-ascension was to create through redemption something entirely new—something that would result "in the praise of his glory" (1:6, 12, 14) and reveal in the coming ages "the incomparable riches of his grace" (2:7). That something new was a people redeemed by God's grace as "God's workmanship" (2:10), to become a new creation and a new humanity.

In Christ, God remade or re-created a portion of the old humanity (Jews and Gentiles), and by overcoming the powers of division "made the two one" (2:14), thus creating "in himself one new man out of the two" (2:15); "in this one body" (2:16) he reconciled "both of them to God [and to one another] through the cross" (2:16). An important goal of redemption was thus to unite divided people into one new community (2:19). Paul uses three analogies to describe the corporate nature of redemption (citizenship, a family, and a building), each of which emphasizes that the place of Christian Gentiles in the new community is not at all inferior to that of Christian Jews.

4.3.1. The Analogy of Citizenship (2:19a). "You are no longer foreigners and aliens [as was previously true before faith in Christ, cf. 2:11–13], but fellow citizens with God's people." If the church is viewed as God's kingdom or a "holy nation" (1 Peter 2:9), the Gentile believers are full citizens, not resident aliens. They have received in Christ all the rights and privileges from which they were previously excluded (2:12). The word "foreigners" (*xenoi*) refers to short-term visitors to a country; "aliens" (*paroikoi*) refers to resident aliens who have officially settled in a foreign country but have no intrinsic rights. Such was the status of Gentiles under the old covenant who converted to the Jewish faith. But now because of Christ, Gentile converts have full citizenship and all the rights pertaining thereto. They are "fellow citizens" with those "who were the first to hope in Christ" (1:12), having heard the word, believed in Christ, and been sealed with the Holy Spirit (1:13). Thus they are full and equal heirs with Jewish believers of the grace of God and the inheritance that God has for his redeemed people (1:14).

4.3.2. The Analogy of a Family (2:19b). Using the analogy of the church as God's family, Paul assures his Gentile readers that they are full "members of God's household." They are not second-class citizens or household servants; they have the full privileges that sons and daughters enjoy, and all the rights of the Father's blessing and inheritance in Christ (cf. 1:13–14). One Father makes Jews and Gentiles in the church brothers and sisters, members together of one family. This analogy suggests an intimate and loving relationship with God and one another.

4.3.3. The Analogy of a Building (2:20–22). "Essentially the church is a community of people. Nevertheless, it may be likened in a number of respects to a building, and especially to the temple" (Stott, 106). The phrase "built on the foundation" is the transition to this analogy of the church as a building in process of construction. In 2:20–22 Paul reassures the Gentiles that they are an integral part of the church that God is building.

Four aspects of the building under construction are emphasized. (1) The first is *the foundation* (2:20). Nothing is more basic to a sound superstructure than a solid foundation. In Jesus' parable of the two builders at the conclusion of his Sermon on the Mount, he emphasized the importance of a solid foundation. Ultimately only the house built on the solid foundation of rock stands. That foundation in Jesus' parable was himself and his words (Matt. 7:24–27).

What is the rock on which the church is built? Paul assures the Gentiles they are "built on the foundation of the apostles and prophets" (2:20). This phrase can be viewed three different ways: (a) The foundation consists of the apostles and prophets themselves; (b) the foundation refers to that on which the apostles and prophets were themselves built (i.e., Christ); or (c) the foundation refers to that which was laid by the apostles and prophets. The answer to this issue depends in part on the identity of the "prophets" mentioned here. Lenski (452–53) claims that they are the Old Testament prophets. He argues that because there is only one definite article with "apostles and prophets," Paul sees the two categories as one class. The Old Testament prophets and New Testament apostles shared the common responsibility of being the primary vessels of divine revelation as recorded in Scripture under the two covenants. In this view, "the foundation" on which the church is built is the Christocentric and authoritative testimony of the apostles and prophets as found in the Old and the New Testaments.

It is unlikely, however, that this view represents Paul's intent, because (a) the word order is "the apostles and prophets," not "prophets and apostles"; and (b) in the two other occurrences in Ephesians where apostles and prophets are mentioned together (3:5; 4:11), the reference is clearly to Christian prophets as church leaders. The New Testament apostles and prophets constituted the foundational ministries in the church, not only in 2:20 and 3:5, but also in 1 Corinthians 12:28; "And in the church God has appointed first of all apostles, second prophets . . . ." Paul states clearly in Ephesians 3:5–6 that the mystery of Christ, veiled to previous generations, "has now been revealed by the Spirit to *God's holy apostles and prophets*. This mystery is that through the gospel the Gentiles are heirs together with Israel, members together of one body, and sharers together in the promise in Christ Jesus." This crucial revelation was first revealed to "the holy apostles and prophets" in the first century.

The church is thus "built" on the original infallible revelation of Christ to the first apostles and prophets. It should be added, however, that godly and visionary leaders, people full of the Word and of "the Spirit of wisdom and revelation" (1:17), continue to be needed to lead the church "until we all reach unity in the faith and in the knowledge of the Son of God and become mature, attaining to the whole measure of the fullness of Christ" (4:13).

(2) The church God is building has a "*chief cornerstone*," which is "Christ Jesus himself" (2:20b). What is the significance of the cornerstone? The word here and in 1 Peter 2:6 is drawn from Isaiah 28:16, "See I lay a stone in Zion, a tested stone, a precious cornerstone for a sure foundation. . . ." The cornerstone, "itself part of and essential to the foundation" (Stott, 107), serves to hold the whole structure together (2:21a). From it the rest of the foundation is laid outward along the line of future walls; and with it as a fixed reference point the walls rise in a straight line, with the outer angle of the cornerstone assuring that other angles are true.

The cornerstone occupied the preeminent place in the whole structure. In ancient times the royal name was often inscribed on it. The church as the temple of God is being built out and up from the revelation of Christ given through and elaborated on by the foundational ministries of apostles and prophets.

(3) A third aspect of the building is *the individual stones* that collectively comprise "the whole building" that, in Christ, "is joined together and rises to become a holy temple in the Lord" (2:21). First Peter 2:5 expresses the same thought: "You, also, like living stones, are being built into a spiritual house." "The whole building" refers to the church universal rather than each local congregation (Bruce, 1984, 307). The phrase "is joined together" (2:21) describes "the complicated process of masonry by which stones are fitted together" (Wood, 42). In the Greek "is being joined together" and "rises" (lit., "grows," reminding us that the church is a living organism) are both present tense; this tense indicates a continuous process of building and growth (cf. 2:22, "are being built together").

The participle "to become" is passive and points to God's role in making each part fit into the whole. "You too" (2:22a) refers to the inclusion of the Gentile believers in the "holy temple in the Lord" (2:21b). The Greek word for "temple" here is not *hieron*, which is used for the entire temple precinct, but *naos*, which refers to the inner sanctuary that includes the Holy Place and Most Holy Place (Robinson, 71).

(4) Paul concludes with the purpose for which the building is being built, already hinted at in his use of *naos*, namely, "a *dwelling in which God lives* by his Spirit" (2:22). The tabernacle and temple under the old covenant were the dwelling place for the God of Israel. In the New Testament Paul has previously called individual believers "the temple of God" in whom the Holy Spirit dwells (1 Cor. 3:16). But now in a much fuller sense Paul refers to believers collectively, Jew and Gentile alike, as the temple and dwelling place of God in the earth (2:22).

God is not waiting, however, until the church is a finished building to come to live in it; he is indwelling it each step of the process. Note that in 2:22 we have another of the many indirect Trinitarian references in Ephesians: The church is being built together *in Christ* as a dwelling place *for God* (the Father) to live *by his Spirit*.

The remnants of the columns that lined Curetes Street in Ephesus give an indication of the grandeur of the city, which was on a major trade route. At left another view shows the length of Harbor Street leading into the city. Paul returned to Ephesus at the end of his second missionary trip.

4.4. Paul and the Church As the Revelatory Media of God's Manifold Wisdom in Redemption (3:1–13)

Chapter 3 opens with Paul's anticipating his prayer for the full realization of Christ in the church and in the believer. His opening phrase, "For this reason," repeated in 3:14, refers back to God's gracious plan of redemption that includes the Gentiles (especially 2:13–22, where redeemed Gentiles are coequal members with the Jews in the one body of Christ). But between the occurrence of this phrase in verses 1 and 14, Paul digresses in an inspired excursion to expand briefly on the central theme of Ephesians—i.e., the bringing together of all things under one head, even Christ (1:9–10)—and on his own God-appointed role as apostle to the Gentiles.

After this brief but important digression, Paul utters his second major prayer in this letter, an apostolic prayer for the believers' spiritual fulfillment (3:14–21) so that God may be glorified in the church (Christ's body) as he is in Christ Jesus.

4.4.1. Paul As a Sovereign Vessel (3:1–9). Paul, about to begin his second apostolic prayer, suddenly pauses. Perhaps, having reached "a resting-place in his thoughts . . . he remembers where he is and why he is here" (Robinson, 74). As he reflects on his present circumstances as a prisoner of Christ for the sake of the Gentiles, he deliberately elaborates further on the mystery of the gospel in respect to the Gentiles. Paul was a prisoner in Rome of the Roman emperor Nero, but he speaks of himself rather as "the prisoner of Christ Jesus." He refuses to think of himself as a victim of injustice, either at the hands of the Jews or the Romans.

Believing in the Lordship of Christ over his life, he declares he is Christ's prisoner (cf. 4:1; 6:20) "for the sake of you Gentiles." The statement is a plain fact, the historical circumstances of which are recorded in Acts 21:17–22:21. Paul's encounter with hostile Jews in Jerusalem, which nearly cost him his life and resulted in four subsequent years of imprisonment at Caesarea and Rome, "arose directly out of his Gentile ministry" (Bruce, 1984, 309–10). In the middle of a sentence, therefore, it occurs to Paul that he must explain an aspect of God's mystery before his Gentile readers will be fully prepared to say "amen" to his prayer for them.

Verses 2–6 address Paul's mandate from Jesus Christ himself to serve the Gentiles (cf. Acts 22:14, 21; 26:15–18; Gal. 1:15–16; 2:7–9). He begins by reminding his readers of "the administration of God's grace that was given to me for you" (3:2). The grace to which Paul refers here is not "saving grace" (as in 2:5, 8) but the revelatory message and divine commissioning that was involved in his going to the Gentiles (cf. 3:7–8). "Grace implies 'givenness' and Paul underlines this factor" (Wood, 45) in that it was given to him for their benefit.

The Greek word for "administration" (*oikonomia*) literally means "steward of the house" or chief custodian. Paul was the chief steward in God's first-century house for administrating God's grace to the Gentiles (cf. 1 Cor. 9:17; Col. 1:25). He was commissioned by Christ to make known to the Gentiles the gospel, along with the implications of this message for Gentile inclusion into the church as full members of the body based on grace, not law.

Paul's administration of God's grace for the Gentiles involved both wisdom and revelation (v. 3): *wisdom* to build correctly God's church (1 Cor. 3:10), and revelation about "the mystery" (*mysterion*) of the gospel (3:3, 4, 6, 9; on this word, see comments on 1:9). Paul mentions five things about "the mystery" here. (1) The mystery was "made known . . . by revelation" (3:3; cf. v. 5). Elsewhere Paul emphasized the revelatory nature of his calling, commissioning, and message (e.g., 1 Cor. 15:8; Gal. 1:12, 15–16). He did not conceive this radical plan of the gospel as a matter of his own initiative; he did not formulate a new doctrine through his own insight. Rather, the mystery came to him directly from God. Furthermore, the administration of God's grace was given to him in order to "make plain to everyone the administration of this mystery, which for ages past was kept hidden in God, who created all things" (3:9). That is, not only was the mystery "made known" to Paul by revelation, but also it was his responsibility to make it known to others.

(2) Paul identifies the heart of the mystery as "the mystery of Christ" (3:4) in that he is both its source and substance (Hendriksen, 153). Christ himself is called "the mystery of God" (Col. 2:2; cf. 1:26–27) because in him "the unseen God is fully revealed; 'the mystery of Christ' may best be understood as the mystery which consists in Christ . . . [and] which is disclosed in him" (Bruce, 1984, 313). The gospel Paul preached was "by revelation from Jesus Christ" (Gal. 1:12)—that the Gentiles could be saved by grace through faith in Christ apart from observing the ordinances of the Jewish law (cf. Gal. 2:15–21; 3:10–14, 17–25). Precisely because it was a law-free gospel in the above sense,

> it was as applicable to Gentiles as to Jews (the law being the barrier that had formerly kept them apart). The incorporation of Gentiles [on an equal basis] along with the Jews in the new people of God . . . was implicit in that gospel. This incorporation is the aspect of the "mystery of Christ" which is now emphasized. (Bruce, 1984, 313)

(3) That God intended the blessing of Abraham and the promise of messianic salvation through the Jewish theocracy to include the Gentiles was *not* previously hidden (v. 5). It was clearly revealed in the Old Testament books of the Law, the Prophets, and the Writings (e.g., Gen. 12:1–3; Deut. 32:43; Ps 18:49; 117:1; Isa. 11:10). What had been hidden in previous generations and unforeseen even by the Old Testament prophets was this God's plan of redemption in Christ (the Mes

siah) involved destroying the old line of demarcation that separated Jews and Gentiles (2:14–15). The old covenant, national Jewish theocracy, was to be replaced by a new spiritual race (Christians) and a new international community (the church) in which both Jews and Gentiles would be admitted on an equal basis in Christ with no distinction.

This eternal plan of the Father (1:4) to create in Christ "one new man out of the two" (2:15) by bringing together Jew and Gentile as "one body" (2:16), previously unknown "in other generations" (3:5), "was kept hidden in God" (3:9) as "the mystery of Christ" (3:4). It was the revelation of this mystery that Paul was commissioned by Christ to make known to the Gentiles.

(4) Furthermore, it was this mystery that "has now been revealed by the Spirit to God's holy apostles and prophets" (3:5) as the foundation upon which the church is built (2:20–22).

(5) Paul goes on to elaborate on this mystery in verse 6 by using a triad of compound words, each of which has the Greek prefix *syn* (meaning "together with"). The Gentiles are not saved by a salvation designed just for them as outcasts (as with Gentile proselytes to Judaism). Rather, they are "*heirs together with*" the Jews of the blessings pledged to Abraham and his descendants—"heirs of God and coheirs with Christ" (Rom. 8:17).

The Gentiles are also "*members together*" with the Jews of the one body of Christ. The Greek word used here (*synsoma*) does not occur in classical Greek writings and only here in the New Testament. Paul, in other words, coins a new word to emphasize that Gentiles have equal rights with Jews as members of Christ's body.

Finally, the Gentiles are "*sharers together*" with the Jews in all the historic covenants of promise that were given to Israel and are now fulfilled in Christ. Jew and Gentile share equally the life and salvation that is in Christ Jesus through the gospel (cf. Gal. 3:6–29). As Paul noted elsewhere, "There is neither Jew nor Greek, slave nor free, male nor female, for you are all one in Christ Jesus. If you belong to Christ, then you are Abraham's seed, and heirs according to the promise" (Gal. 3:28–29).

Paul declares that he was called to be a servant of "this gospel" (3:7) and "this grace" (3:8). When Paul speaks of "this gospel," he refers to the revelation of Jesus Christ and to all that he was commissioned to proclaim in Christ; "this grace" was his specific mission to make known "the unsearchable riches of Christ" (3:8) to the Gentiles.

Paul goes on to explain that he became a "servant" (*diakonos*) or a "minister" (NASB, NKJV) of this gospel "by the gift of God's grace . . . through the working of his [God's] power" (3:7). Paul did not decide to be a minister of the gospel as a vocational choice. His vocational choice was to be a Jewish rabbi. Instead, God took the initiative, apprehended him on the Damascus road, chose to reveal his Son to him, and drafted him into service as an apostle to the Gentiles—all this as a gift of grace.

Nor was Paul's subsequent ministry merely the efficient use of his natural abilities. Rather, it was the direct result of God's power working through him. The words Paul uses here for "working" (*energeia*) and "power" (*dynamis*) are the same as those used in 1:19–20 to describe God's power in raising Christ from the dead. "And rightly so; it was this resurrection-power working in Paul that enabled him to accomplish what he did in bringing God's gracious purpose to fruition among the Gentiles" (Bruce, 1961, 63).

Lest Paul seem to think of himself too highly because of his calling as a sovereignly chosen vessel, he confesses sincerely that he is "*less than the least* of all God's people" (3:8). He creates a unique expression to portray the reality of his situation. This double diminutive is not a statement of exaggerated humility. It expresses his sensitive awareness that as a Christ-hater and violent persecutor of the church, he was the least worthy of all ministers of the gospel (cf. 1 Cor. 15:9–10; 1 Tim. 1:12–17).

Recall, however, that earlier in this letter (1:1) Paul spoke of his authority as that of an apostle—because of God's amazing grace, God's own choice and commissioning, and God's incomparably great power at work in him "to preach to the Gentiles" (3:8). The word "preach" (*euangelizo*) means "to announce good news," the good news of "the unsearchable riches of Christ" (3:8). Some of these riches Paul has disclosed in the first two chapters of Ephesians.

The word "unsearchable" (*anexichniastos*) means literally "not capable of being tracked out." In the Septuagint version of Job, this word is used in connection with God's creation and providential dealings, matters that go beyond our limited understanding. Paul used the word in Romans 11:33 when referring to God's dealings with the Jews and Gentiles in salvation history. Translators have struggled to find an English equivalent for this word of inexpressible abundance. Encompassed in Paul's mandate to preach to the Gentiles the "unsearchable" (NIV, NKJV), "unfathomable" (NASB), "boundless" (NRSV), "incalculable" (J.B. Phillips), "untraceable" (Emphasized NT), and "infinite" (Jerusalem Bible) riches of Christ is the responsibility "to make plain to everyone the administration of this mystery" (3:9). Paul writes Ephesians 1–3, in part, with this very purpose in his mind and heart.

4.4.2. The Church As a Corporate Vessel (3:10–13). Paul's revelation of "the mystery" of the gospel as disclosed in Ephesians continues to broaden: from eternity past, where it was conceived in the Father's heart (1:4; 3:11), to the incarnation of Christ as the basis for its realization in history (1:7; 3:11; cf. John 1:14), to its unveiling revelation to Paul and other apostles and prophets as human vessels of understanding (3:3, 5), to the public demonstration of the mystery in a new redeemed humanity (2:1–10), to a new comprehensive community of the redeemed (the church) as God's family and Christ's body on the earth (2:11–22; 3:6).

In 3:10 Paul takes it yet another step forward: God intends "now, through the church," to make known his "manifold wisdom to the rulers and authorities in the heavenly realms." "Now" indicates a new fullness of time and purpose in God's plan (Westcott, 48). "Manifold" means many-colored or multivaried. This word was used to describe the variety of colors in flowers, embroidered cloth, and beautiful tapestries. God's "manifold wisdom" is displayed in creation, in his Son as wisdom incarnate, and now in the church. Certainly God's wisdom as seen in creation and embodied in Christ "is a many-splendored thing, iridescent with constantly unfolding beauties" (Wood, 48).

But what about the church? Surely in God's eternal purpose the church is not meant to be a drab, homogeneous organization or a conglomerate of fragmented ecclesiastical institutions. Rather, the "one body" of Christ, as a display of God's "manifold wisdom," is mea[nt] to be like a beautiful tapestry in its diversit[y] (multiethnic, multicultural) and in its harmon[y] (one Spirit, one hope, one Lord, one faith, on[e] baptism, one God and Father of all; cf. 4:4–6[)]. There is no other community in the world lik[e] the true church of Jesus Christ.

As Paul became a conduit of revelation t[o] the Gentiles concerning "the unsearchabl[e] riches of Christ" (3:8), so the church is to be [a] conduit of revelation in the heavenly realm[s] concerning "the manifold wisdom of God[''] (3:10). The revelation to heavenly rulers an[d] authorities is not a redemptive proclamation o[f] God's grace in Christ, but a redemptive displa[y] of God's wisdom through the church.

Who are these "rulers and authorities"[?] Some have suggested they "represent" politi[-] cal, social, economic, religious, and cultura[l] structures that God hopes to change in th[e] world through the church (Caird, 66–67[;] Barth, 1:365). Most evangelical and Pente[-] costal scholars, however, concur that they refe[r] to "the heavenly realms." The rulers an[d] authorities may refer to good angels (cf. Col[.] 1:16), who long to know the wisdom of God i[n] redemption (1 Peter 1:12). Or they may refe[r] to demonic rulers (cf. Eph. 6:12–18; cf. Dan[.] 9:2–23; 10:12–13; 2 Cor. 10:4–5), who hav[e] long opposed God's "eternal purpose" i[n] Christ (Eph. 3:11). Or, as seems most likely[,] they may encompass both God's angels an[d] Satan's forces, who witness as spectators th[e] vindication of God's wisdom as demonstrate[d] in the cross (1 Cor. 1:23–24, 30; Col. 2:15) an[d] as manifested through the church.

In the outworking of God's eternal purpos[e] in Christ, the church has a central plac[e] because of her union with Christ the head. Th[e] joining together of redeemed Jews and Gen[-] tiles as a united people in one body is an inte[-] gral part and central issue in God's eterna[l] purpose. In Jesus' final prayer before the cros[s] in John 17, he prayed that his disciples and th[e] church would be "brought to complete unity[''] (17:23) in love as a visual witness of the lov[e] and oneness that exists between the Father an[d] the Son (17:20–26).

In order for this to be a reality, God's peopl[e] must in union with Christ be able to approac[h] the Father "by the Spirit" (Eph. 2:18) wit[h] "freedom and confidence" (3:12). In Chris[t] there is no longer "the dividing wall" (2:14

that under the old covenant kept Gentiles at a distance from God and separated them from the Jews; nor is there any longer the veil that kept all worshipers separated from God's presence in the Most Holy Place. The "freedom" to which Paul refers in 3:12 is the same freedom in Hebrews where believers are encouraged to "approach the throne of grace with confidence" (Heb. 4:16) and with "confidence to enter the Most Holy Place by the blood of Jesus" (10:19).

Paul concludes this section (begun in 3:2) by referring again to his sufferings for the Gentiles (v. 13; cf. v. 1). This time, however, he exhorts them not to be discouraged by his imprisonment as their champion and couples together the themes of "sufferings" and "glory" (prevalent throughout the New Testament).

Paul's perspective of his sufferings is clearly stated in a parallel passage in Colossians:

> Now I rejoice in what was suffered for you [Gentiles], and I fill up in my flesh what is still lacking in regard to Christ's afflictions, for the sake of his body, which is the church. I have become its servant by the commission God gave me to present to you the word of God in its fullness. (Col. 1:24–25)

Paul knew his sufferings for Christ were storing up for him "an eternal weight of glory" (2 Cor. 4:17) and were preparing him to share in Christ's glory (Rom. 8:17). He also knew that this glory "would be shared by those on whose behalf the present affliction was endured" (Bruce, 1984, 323).

5. Apostolic Prayer for the Believers' Spiritual Fulfillment (3:14–21)

In chapter 1 Paul's inspired hymn of praise for God's glorious plan of redemption in Christ (1:3–14) is followed by earnest intercession for the saints to know their God better by revelatory experience and understanding (1:17–23). In chapters 2–3 Paul's inspired exposition about God's powerful grace in redemption for the individual sinner (2:1–10) and the corporate body of Christ (2:11–3:13) is followed by earnest intercession for the spiritual fulfillment in fullness of all that God has planned for his people. Concerning this pattern where revelation is followed by intercession, John Stott (132) makes the observation: "As Jesus watered with prayer the good seeds of instruction he had sown in the Upper Room [John 13–17], so Paul follows up his teaching with earnest prayer. . . ."

5.1. Paul's Earnest Entreaty (3:14–19)

Paul's prayer begins with the phrase "for this reason" (3:14), which first occurred in 3:1 and which points back to the revelation of God's mercy and grace that included the Gentiles through faith in Christ into the "one body" on an equal basis (2:13–22; 3:2–13). Thus he resumes the prayer he almost began but postponed in 3:1.

"I kneel" (3:14) literally means "I bend my knees." The normal posture for Jews when praying was standing with arms outstretched toward heaven (cf. Matt. 6:5; Luke 18:11, 18). Paul's bending his knees was not even an upright kneeling position, but rather one of prostration, with the head touching the ground (depicting "humility, solemnity, and adoration" [Hendriksen, 166]). Barclay (150) adds: "Paul's prayer for the church is so intense that he prostrates himself before God in an agony of entreaty."

"Before" the Father represents a face-to-face access made possible because of Christ's redemptive blood and by the Holy Spirit (2:18; 3:12). Though Paul approaches God as "Father," it conveys not just family intimacy but also honor, respect, and reverence. As Max Turner (1235) reminds us, "in the east the father is the ruler over the family, the one to whom all questions of importance are related, and to whom the children (however old they may be) are expected to defer in obedience."

This sense of God's patriarchal role is heightened by the additional phrase "from whom his whole family [*pasa patria*] in heaven and on earth derives its name." There are three possible translations of the phrase *pasa patria*: "every family" (RSV, NEB, NASB, NRSV), "whole family" (KJV, NKJV, NIV), or "all fatherhood" (JBP, NIV margin, F. F. Bruce). The first rendering may be understood to refer to the angelic family in heaven and the redeemed families on earth (both Jew and Gentile) that make up the one family of God. The second rendering retains Paul's emphasis throughout Ephesians on the redeemed as one family and on the unity of believers as a new humanity and one body of Christ. According to this view the words "in heaven and on earth" refer to the church triumphant in heaven and the church militant on earth. The third rendering emphasizes a play on words between *pater* ("Father," 3:14) and *patria* ("fatherhood," 3:15). Bruce (1961, 67), an advocate of this view, translates and interprets Paul's words as follows:

> "I bow my knees to the Father after whom all fatherhood takes its name." That is to say, every species of fatherhood in the universe is derived from the original archetypal Fatherhood of God: His is the only underived Fatherhood. And the more nearly any fatherhood, natural or spiritual, approaches in character to God's perfect Fatherhood, the more truly does it manifest fatherhood as God intended it to be.

Paul's prayer that follows is made up of three major petitions (3:16–17a; 3:17b–19a; 3:19b). Each petition involves a Greek *hina* clause of purpose, which literally translated is "in order that" (3:16, 18, 19b). These *hina* clauses mark the three issues more distinctly in Greek than in English.

(1) The first petition (3:16–17a) focuses on a two-pronged request that flows from the abundant wealth of God's glory (NASB, NKJV, NRSV) or perhaps from the abundance of God's glorious wealth (NIV). Since God is infinite and eternal, so is the measurement of his generosity when responding to prayers. Paul asks (a) for God's empowering presence through the Holy Spirit to "strengthen" (same word in 1:19) believers in their "inner being" (3:16), and (b) for Christ's indwelling presence to reside in the "hearts" of believers through faith (3:17a).

For interpreters with a dichotomous understanding of human personhood (inner and outer person), the "inner being" and "heart" are synonymous metaphors for one's "true and enduring self" (Bruce, 1961, 67), which daily may be renewed even as the outer person is wasting away (2 Cor. 4:16). Likewise, the Holy Spirit and the Spirit of Christ are viewed as interchangeable terms (cf. Rom. 8:9–11). "To have Christ dwelling in us and to have the Spirit dwelling in us are the same thing. Indeed, it is precisely by the Spirit that Christ dwells in our hearts" (Stott, 135).

Those who view human personhood as a trichotomy (spirit, soul, and body; cf. 1 Thess. 5:23; Heb. 4:12) see Paul's intentions as more distinctly defined. He prays that believers may be strengthened and renewed by the Spirit in their "inner being" (human spirit) so that Christ may reside as Lord in their "hearts" (i.e., "soul," involving mind, emotions, and will) through faith. According to this interpretation Christ resides actively as Lord of the heart or seat of the believer's selfhood and volitional activity as we are strengthened by God's empowering Spirit in our innermost being. The aorist tense of the verb "dwell" (3:17a) carries the sense of "take up his abode" or "take up residence" as Lord "through [a life of] faith." Bruce adds that "the initial act of faith, by which the believer is united to Christ, is followed by the life of faith, in which that union is maintained" (1984, 327). H. C. G. Moule expands on the implications:

> The word [Paul] selected (*katoikein*) ... is a word made expressly to denote residence as against lodging, the abode of a master within his own home as against the turning aside for a night of the wayfarer who will be gone tomorrow.... [It is] the residence always in the heart of its Master and Lord, who where he dwells must rule; who enters not to cheer and soothe alone but before all things else to reign. (Quoted by Stott, 136).

We should note again the Trinitarian content of Paul's thought in 3:14–17a. He prays to *the Father* (v. 14) that he will strengthen believers through *the Spirit* so that *Christ* may reside in their hearts as Lord.

(2) The next major petition (3:17b–19a) is for believers to be empowered to grasp the love of Christ. Believers in whose hearts Christ resides as Lord are "rooted and established in love" (3:17b). "Being rooted" in love is like a tree or plant with deep roots in the soil; "being founded" on love is like a building with strong foundations laid on solid rock. Both metaphors, as Stott points out (136), "emphasize depth as opposed to superficiality." They denote a growing and established relationship in Christ that will bear fruit and that is lasting. Moreover, the two metaphors are participles in the Greek perfect tense and thus denote an established relationship in Christ—not meaning a static sense

but involving growth with him. The metaphors thus convey a deep, solid relationship, one that issues forth in fruit and life.

Having asked the Father by the empowering presence of his Spirit to strengthen believers so that Christ may reside as Lord in their lives, and having noted their roots and foundation in God's love, Paul now prays for the empowering Spirit to give his Gentile readers, "together with all the saints" (in keeping with his theme of unity), a revelatory grasp of the four-dimensional love of Christ. "To grasp" means "to hold as one's own" its reality by personal knowing. "To grasp this revelation in its totality is not the achievement of a moment" (Bruce, 1984, 328), as Paul himself testifies in Philippians 3:12–16. It was his own lifelong ambition; now he expresses this earnest desire for all believers.

To know the breadth and length and height and depth of Christ's love is to know something "that surpasses knowledge" (3:19a). The Greek text is not entirely clear as to what the four-dimensional language used here refers and, therefore, has been a subject of great debate.[3] Some interpreters emphasize that this language is merely poetic hyperbole for the all-encompassing love of Christ; therefore, the four dimensions are not to be ascribed individual or separate significance. However, there is biblical precedence for using such four-dimensional language with individual (not just accumulative) significance. Note Zophar's discourse about the mysteries of God's wisdom in Job 11:8–9:

> They are higher than the heavens—
> what can you do?
> They are deeper than the depths of the grave [Sheol]—what can you know?
> Their measure is longer than the earth
> and wider than the sea.

One interpreter also finds a parallel in Romans 8:37–39: "Whether you go forward or backward, up to the heights or down to the depths, nothing will separate us from the love of Christ" (Mitton, 134).

In the context of Ephesians, where the mystery of Christ's love for the Gentiles is immeasurable and surpasses knowledge, Paul is stressing that

> it is wide enough to reach the whole world and beyond (1:9, 10, 20). It is long enough to stretch from eternity to eternity (1:4–6, 18; 3:9). It is high enough to raise both Gentiles and Jews to heavenly places in Christ Jesus (1:13; 2:6). It is deep enough to rescue people from sin's degradation and even from the grip of Satan himself (2:1–5; 6:11, 12). The love of Christ is the love he has for the church as a united body (5:25, 29, 30) and for those who trusts him as individuals (3:17). (Wood, 52)

To know Christ's love experientially "is to know Christ himself, in ever widening experience, and to have his outgoing and self-denying love reproduced in oneself" (Bruce, 1984, 329). That Paul is referring to an experiential knowledge of Christ's love is apparent in 3:19a, where he exclaims that it "surpasses knowledge." Moreover, regardless of how much we know of Christ's love, there is always more to know because it is infinite and inexhaustible.

(3) Like the other two, Paul's last major petition (3:19b) is introduced by "that" (*hina*, lit., "in order that"). This petition is the climax of progression in his apostolic prayer: that Christ may dwell in our hearts as Lord (3:17) in order that we may grasp the four-dimensional love of Christ (3:18) in order that we "may be filled to the measure of all the fullness of God."

The subject of "fullness" (*pleroma*) occurs in both Colossians and Ephesians. In Colossians the focus is on the fullness of Christ Jesus as the incarnation of God (Col. 1:19; 2:9) and the source of our fullness (Col. 2:10). In Ephesians the focus is on the fullness of the church as the body of Christ (1:23; 4:13) and the believer's part in that fullness (3:19; 5:18). The preposition "to" (Gk. *eis*) in the phrase "filled *to* the measure" suggests that believers are to be progressively filled to the measure of God's fullness, just as the church is to progressively "grow up into [Christ]" (4:15) until we attain "the whole measure of the fullness of Christ" (4:13).

But can the finite ever reach the fullness of the infinite? Can humanity become God? Obviously this kind of thinking misses the point Paul is making. The fullness that God intends for individual believers and for the church is the fullness of Christ, in whom *alone* dwells all the fullness of God in bodily form. Thus Paul adds in Colossians 2:10, "You have been given fullness in Christ." By knowing Christ through faith as the indwelling Lord and by grasping through progressive revelation the love of Christ, we in the end can be integrated into "all the fullness of God" in Christ. Surely apostolic intercession cannot reach farther than this.

5.2. Paul's Glorious Doxology (3:20–21)

This doxology is not only the conclusion of Paul's prayer, but also the climax of the first half of Ephesians and a transition to the second half. It may be regarded as the summit of the entire letter, with chapters 1–3 ascending to a "spiritual peak" in the doxology and with chapters 4–6 descending to focus on important practical aspects of redemption for the church and individual believers. The doxology again reminds Paul's readers of the incomparable greatness of God's power and rich grace at work in them (1:19–2:7)—"not to encourage selfish requests, but to promote confident hope in his new creation, and petitions that correspond with God's intent for the church in the present age" (Turner, 1236).

Lest his readers think that he has asked for too much in his intercession, Paul declares that God is capable of doing "immeasurably more than all we ask" (v. 20). As Bruce (1984, 330) notes, "it is impossible to ask God for too much. His capacity for giving far exceeds his people's capacity for asking—or even imagining." Paul writes "immeasurably more" (*hyperekperissou*), another one of his created hyper-superlatives, which occurs only here and in 1 Thessalonians 3:10; 5:13. *Hyper* is the equivalent of the Latin "super," *ek* means "out of," and *perissos* means "more than sufficient, over and above, abundant" (Abbott, 357). Thus *hyperekperissou* expresses the superabundance of God's ability to answer prayer over and beyond our noblest aspirations.

Paul makes five forceful affirmations about God's ability to answer prayer. (1) He is *able* to do what we ask, because as God he has the power to answer. (2) He is able to do what we *ask*, because we have free access to him as our Father through Christ by one Spirit. (3) He is able to do *all* we ask or imagine, because he knows our thoughts and is infinitely wise as to when and how to answer. (4) He is able to do *more than* all we ask or imagine, because his plans are larger than ours. (5) He is able to do *immeasurably* more than all we ask or imagine, because as God he gives according to the superabounding riches of his grace.

God's infinite ability to answer prayer beyond our limited ability to ask is "according to his power [*dynamis*] that is at work within us" (3:20b). In 1:19–21 Paul has described this *dynamis* as the power that raised Christ Jesus from the dead and enthroned him as Lord over all things in the heavenly realms, and which also raised us from spiritual death and seated us with him in the heavenly realms. It is no lesser power than this that works within us individually (who are indwelt by his empowering presence) and within us corporately (who are God's dwelling place by his Spirit). Notice that the Christian life about which Paul prays encompasses both the transcendence of God, who is *above us* as our heavenly Father (3:14–15), and the immanence of God, who works powerfully and gloriously *within us* as his redeemed people (3:20–21).

As Paul concludes his inspired prayer on his knees before the Father (v. 21), he suddenly bursts forth in a mighty acclamation: "to him the glory" (lit. trans.). As the power comes from God (3:20), the glory must go to him (3:21). His glory is the sum of all his attributes. It is most perfectly seen "in the church and in Christ Jesus." "God is to be glorified in the church because the church, comprising Jews and Gentiles, is his masterpiece of grace" (Bruce, 1984, 331).

God has chosen through the church to make known his wisdom to the spiritual rulers and authorities in the heavenly realms. Though "the heavens declare the glory of God," even greater glory is shown by his handiwork of grace and reconciliation in the church. Moreover, because the church consists of those who are united in Christ as members of his body and in whom Christ dwells as Lord, God's glory "in the church" cannot be separated from God's glory "in Christ Jesus" (Bruce, 1984, 331). As Foulkes aptly states (107): "The glory of God is most gloriously seen in the grace of His uniting His [redeemed] sinful creatures to His eternal, sinless Son."

The finely woven knot of redemption that binds together Christ's church in relationship is to be "for the praise of his glory" (1:6, 12, 14) "throughout all generations [in history], for ever and ever [in eternity]! Amen [i.e., 'so let it be']" (3:21). On this mountain peak of inspiration and revelation the first half of the letter ends. Paul is now ready to address some practical matters that are necessary if the manifestation of God's glory is to be seen in the saints.

Part II: Practical Instruction for the Church and the Believer (chaps. 4–6)

In chapters 1–3 of Ephesians, Paul has written about God's eternal purpose of redemption in Christ and its outworking in history. He has described how God is creating a new humanity and a new community (the church) on earth. In chapters 4–6, Paul addresses the practical outworking of salvation in the everyday living of God's redeemed people, both on a personal level and in the body of Christ. He especially touches on issues that involve the church's unity as the "one body" and the church's purity as God's holy temple and Christ's holy bride.

Paul has instructed and prayed for his readers in the first half of the letter; now he turns to exhorting them. Instruction, intercession, and exhortation are his "formidable trio" (Stott, 146) in Ephesians. Stated another way, Paul turns from the "mind-stretching theology" (ibid.) in chapters 1–3 concerning what God already has done in Christ (i.e., the indicative) to focusing on what believers are to be and do as a consequence (i.e., the imperative; thirty-five directives occur on how the redeemed ought to live). This division, however, must not be viewed as comprised only of imperatives, as theology continues to be interwoven with the practical exhortations.

Verse 1 introduces not just the issues addressed in chapter 4, but also the whole second division of the letter. It begins with an exhortation: "I urge you [beseech you (KJV, NKJV); beg you (NRSV)] to live a life worthy of the calling you have received." The verb "to live" in the Greek is "to walk" *(peripateo)*, which occurs eight times in Ephesians (five times in chaps. 4–5). As a metaphor it refers to behavior or conduct. Believers are to "to walk worthy" (4:1), "no longer walk as the Gentiles do" (4:17), "walk in love" (5:2), "walk as children of light" (5:8), and "walk carefully and wisely" (5:15) (all lit. trans.). The verb denotes the changed manner of living that should characterize believers, because of their new life in Christ, in *all* relationships—private, public, and domestic.

The verb "walk" also contains the idea of progress forward, moving ahead toward the goal of full maturity in Christ. In 4:1 believers are exhorted to walk or "live a life worthy of the calling." "Worthy" (*axios*) means literally "bringing up the other beam of the scales" (*TDNT*, 1:379). Thus Paul is declaring there must be a balance between the faith believers profess and the faith they practice. Their "calling" comprises God's initiative and intention at their conversion (cf. Phil. 3:14); "to walk worthy" is their responsibility in daily living (cf. Phil. 1:27). Those who share in common the divine call are "the called-out ones" (*ekklesia*, the church).

6. Implementing God's Purpose for the Church (4:1–16)

In this passage Paul calls believers to be true to their destiny and calling as the body of Christ. By definition the body is a unity and entails oneness (4:2–6). But the church also has multiplicity and diversity as an integral part of its unity; "to each one" Christ has apportioned grace and gifts as parts of the whole (4:7). Furthermore, he has given leadership gifts to help the church grow together and move forward toward true spiritual maturity and the church's measure of the fullness of Christ (4:8–16).

6.1. Preserve the Unity of the Spirit (4:1–6)

The New Testament has two classic passages on the subject of Christian unity: Ephesians 4:1–16 and John 17. In John 17 Jesus petitions the Father concerning his initiative and role in making the church one. In Ephesians 4 Paul exhorts believers concerning their responsibility to cherish and guard carefully the unity of the Spirit God has given and to pursue diligently the full measure of what God intends. The responsibility of believers is both individual and corporate.

6.1.1. Individual Responsibility (4:1–2). The first way we as believers walk worthy of our calling is to relate properly to one another as members of the body of Christ—with complete humility, gentleness, patience, mutual forbearance, and love. "Completely humble" (v. 2) is a compound word meaning "'lowliness of

MINISTRY GIFTS OF THE HOLY SPIRIT

Gift	Definition	General References	Specific Examples
Apostle (Specific)	Those specifically commissioned by the resurrected Lord to establish the church and the original message of the gospel	Ac 4:33–37; 5:12, 18–42; 6:6; 8:14, 18; 9:27; 11:1; 15:1–6, 22–23; 16:4; 1Co 9:5; 12:28–29; Gal 1:17; Eph 2:20; 4:11; Jude 17	12 apostles: Mt 10:2; Mk 3:14; Lk 6:13; Ac 1:15–26; Rev 21:14 Paul: Ro 1:1; 11:13; 1Co 1:1; 9:1–2; 15:9–10; 2Co 1:1; Gal 1:1; 1Ti 2:7 Peter: 1Pe 1:1; 2Pe 1:1
Apostle (General)	Any messenger commissioned as a missionary or for other special responsibilities	Ac 13:1–3; 1Co 12:28–29; Eph 4:11	Barnabas: Ac 14:4, 14 Andronicus and Junias: Ro 16:7 Titus and others: 2Co 8:23 Epaphroditus: Php 2:25 James, Jesus' brother: Gal 1:19
Prophet	Those who spoke under the inspiration of the Holy Spirit, bringing a message from God to the church, and whose main motivation and concern were with the spiritual life and purity of the church	Ro 12:6; 1Co 12:10; 14:1–33; Eph 4:11; 1Th 5:20–21; 1Ti 1:18; 1Pe 4:11; 1Jn 4:1–3	Peter: Ac 2:14–40; 3:12–26; Ac 4:8–12; 10:34–44 Paul: Ac 13:1, 16–41 Various people: Ac 13:1 Judas and Silas: Ac 15:32 John: Rev 1:1, 3; 10:8–11; 11:18
Evangelist	Those gifted by God to proclaim the gospel to the unsaved	Eph 4:11	Philip: Ac 8:5–8, 26–40; 21:8 Paul: Ac 26:16–18
Pastor (Elder or Overseer)	Those chosen and gifted to oversee the church and care for its spiritual needs	Ac 14:23; 15:1–6, 22–23; 16:4; 20:17–38; Ro 12:8; Eph 4:11–12; Php 1:1; 1Ti 3:1–7; 5:17–20; Tit 1:5–9; Heb 13:17; 1Pe 5:1–5	Timothy: 1Ti 1:1–4; 4:12–16; 2Ti 1:1–6; 4:2, 5 Titus: Tit 1:4–5 Peter: 1Pe 5:1 John: 1Jn 2:1, 12–14 Gaius: 3Jn 1–7
Deacon	Those chosen and gifted to render practical assistance to members of the church	Ac 6:1–6; Ro 12:7; Php 1:1; 1Ti 3:8–13; 1Pe 4:11	Seven deacons: Ac 6:5 Phoebe: Ro 16:1–2

MINISTRY GIFTS OF THE HOLY SPIRIT (cont.)

Gift	Definition	General References	Specific Examples
Teacher	Those gifted to clarify and explain God's Word in order to build up the church	Ro 12:7; Eph 4:11–12; Col 3:16; 1Ti 3:2; 5:17; 2Ti 2:2–3	Paul: Ac 15:35; Ac 20:20; 28:31; Ro 12:19–21; 13:8–10; 1Co 4:17; 1Ti 1:5; 4:16; 2Ti 1:11 Barnabas: Ac 15:35 Apollos: Ac 18:25–28 Timothy: 1Co 4:17; 1Ti 1:3–5; 4:11–13; 6:2; 2Ti 4:2 Titus: Tit 2:1–3, 9–10
Helper	Those gifted for a variety of helpful deeds	1Co 12:28	Paul: Ac 20:35 Lydia: Ac 16:14–15 Gaius: 3Jn 5–8
Administrator	Those gifted to guide and oversee the various activities of the church	Ro 12:8; 1Co 14:3; 1Th 5:11, 14–22; Heb 10:24–25	Barnabas: Ac 11:23–24; 14:22 Paul: Ac 14:22; 16:40 20:1; Ro 8:26–39; Ro 12:1–2; 2Co 6:14–7:1; Gal 5:16–26 Judas and Silas: Ac 15:32; 16:40 Timothy: 1Th 3:2; 2Ti 4:2 Titus: Tit 2:6, 13 Peter: 1Pe 5:1–2 John: 1Jn 2:15–17; 3:1–3
Giver	Those gifted to give freely of their resources to the needs of God's people	Ac 2:44–45; 4:34–35; 11:29–30; 1Co 16:1–4; 2Co 8–9; Eph 4:28; 1Ti 6:17–19; Heb 13:16; 1Jn 3:16–18	Barnabas: Ac 4:36–37 Christians in Macedonia: Ro 15:26–27; 2Co 8:1–5 Christians in Achaia: Ro 15:26–27; 2Co 9:2
Comforter	Those gifted to give comfort by acts of mercy to people in distress	Ro 12:8; 2Co 1:3–7	Paul: 2Co 1:4 Hebrew Christians: Heb 10:34 Various Christians: Col 4:10–11 Dorcas: Ac 9:36–39

mind,' the humble recognition of the worth and value of other people, the humble mind which was in Christ and led him to empty himself and become a servant" (Stott, 148). Behind all discord lies pride; behind all harmony and unity lies humility. It is essential to unity and peace in the church as Christ's body.

"Gentle" may also be translated "meek." Meekness is not weakness but bridled strength. The Greek word calls to mind the picture of a strong and high-spirited thoroughbred horse that when broken yields to the controlling hand of his master. As a Christian virtue it depicts strength that is gentle and under control, one who is "master of himself and servant of others" (Stott, 149). As in the Greek-speaking world of Paul's day, so in our day "humility" and "gentleness" are generally repugnant qualities in the secular world. But they both reflect the character of Jesus and are essential to harmony in the church.

"Patience" and "bearing with one another" are essential virtues for tolerating the failures, weaknesses, and irritations of one another, in the absence of which no community of people can live together in peace.

"Love" (*agape*) is the last quality mentioned and encompasses the preceding four; it is, in fact, "the crown and sum of all [Christian] virtues" (Stott, 149). Because love seeks the well-being of others and the good of the body of Christ, Paul commends it as the virtue that "binds them all together in perfect unity" (Col. 3:14). In essence, Paul is urging believers to cultivate the fruit of the Spirit in their lives (cf. Gal. 5:22–23), especially those aspects that apply to preserving the unity of the Spirit in the body of Christ. The absence of the five qualities in 4:2 will jeopardize that unity.

6.1.2. Corporate Responsibility (4:3–6). Verse 3 states two important issues about unity and church fellowship. (1) Believers are not responsible to achieve unity as if it were a human product; rather, it already exists as an impartation of the Spirit to the church. As the Spirit who indwells the heart of every believer is "one Spirit," so his presence makes all in whom he dwells to be *one people* in Christ. Though great differences divide us—cultural, ethnic, gender, age, social standing, education, temperament, geography—if we are all indwelt by the one Spirit of Christ, we are one and belong to the same church. This "unity of the Spirit" is a supernatural gift of God.

(2) But, Paul adds, there is human responsibility that goes with this gift of the Spirit. We are to "make every effort" to keep, cherish, and guard it. Markus Barth (2:428) calls attention to the note of urgency in Paul's use of the Greek verb *spoudazo* here. It excludes all passivity or wait-and-see attitudes. With resolute determination and diligence believers must take the initiative to preserve the unity of the Spirit. "The bond of peace" describes God's peace working as a chain that binds God's people together and preserves their unity or oneness.

The Holy Spirit's gift of unity to the church is further defined in 4:4–6 in seven creed-like statements clustered around the three Persons of the Trinity: "one Spirit" (v. 4), "one Lord" (v. 5), and "one God and Father" (v. 6). The repetition of the word "one" occurs seven times in these verses and underscores the theme of unity.

In this first triad of "ones," there is "one body," the church, made up of all the redeemed. Anyone who has been redeemed through faith in Christ belongs to this body. We and that person are one because there is only "one Spirit" to whom we all owe our animating life and spiritual existence. "Just as the human body has the animating spirit to give it life, so this one body has the animating Holy Spirit to give it life" (Summers, 76).

The Holy Spirit as the energizing, life-giving, life-sustaining power of the one body imparts to the church "one hope" (i.e., "the hope of the gospel" with its saving message, Col. 1:23) and moves the church toward the goal of "the hope of glory" (Col. 1:27), which looks to the consummation of all redemption in the future coming of Christ. The Holy Spirit is the deposit and guarantee of this hope (1:13–14).

The second triad speaks of "one Lord" (v. 5), as over against the polytheism of the pagan world, which new converts renounced (cf. 1 Cor. 8:6; 12:3, 5). This Lord is the Lord Jesus Christ, who is the head of his one body, the church. "No one can serve two masters" (Matt. 6:24); Christ Jesus himself is the holy focus of the "one faith" by which all people (Jew and Gentile alike) are saved and reconciled to God.

Believers give public testimony to their one faith in one Lord through "one baptism"—the baptism "into the name of the Lord Jesus" (Acts 8:16; 19:5; cf. 1 Cor. 1:13–15). Early Christian baptism involved immersion in water as a picture of the believer's identification with Christ in his death, burial, and resurrection (Rom. 6:3–5) and marked the occasion for incorporating new believers into Christ's body. The baptism in or with the Spirit regularly followed water baptism (Acts 2:38; 8:14–17; 19:5–6; though at least once even preceded it, 10:44–48) and was more directly related to being empowered by the Holy Spirit for witness and ministry.

Is the "one baptism" here water baptism or Spirit baptism? Bruce (1984, 337) maintains it is Christian baptism (especially in water but also closely associated with the gift of the Spirit; cf. Acts 2:38). Wood (56) makes a helpful observation: "Falling as it does in the second triad (related to Christ) and not in the first (related to the Spirit), [this reference in 4:5] appears to indicate water baptism and not primarily the baptism with the Spirit."

The last person in this Trinitarian passage is "the one God and Father of all, who is over all and through all and in all." God is Father of all the redeemed in Christ. Paul is not thinking here of God's universal fatherhood of all humanity as Creator. Rather, there is a specific context: All the redeemed in Christ are members of one body, are submitted to one Lord, and by virtue of a saving relationship to the Son have God as their adoptive Father. "One" God emphasizes the monotheistic unity of God as in the Old Testament (cf. Deut. 6:6), but Paul adds the New Testament confession "and Father."

The triple designation in connection with the Father is unlike those that occurred with the one Spirit and the one Lord, and it is not easy to interpret. The three prepositional phrases may refer to God's transcendence ("over all"), his immanence ("through all"), and the indwelling presence of his Spirit in believers ("in all"). Ralph Martin (154) suggests that it contains a Trinitarian allusion to the *one God* "who is known in His self-revelation as Father 'above all,' Son 'through all' (the use of the preposition here answers to the same idea of mediation in 2:18), and Spirit who is 'in all' the family of God."

Finally, one may wonder at the reverse order in which the members of the Trinity are mentioned here: "one Spirit . . . one Lord . . . one God and Father." The reason relates to the overall theme of the passage, namely, "the unity of the Spirit" in the body of Christ. The unity that Paul addresses relates both to local congregations and the church universal. Ray Summers (79–80) eloquently concludes:

> One stands in reverent awe as he looks at this idea of oneness—one body, one Spirit, one hope, one Lord, one faith, one baptism, one Father. How very much there is here to bind all believers together in . . . oneness! At the same time one stands with head bowed in shameful confession of the failure of the Lord's people to carry out Paul's exhortation, "Be speedy to guard over carefully the oneness which the Spirit produces."

6.2. Grow Toward the Mature Fullness of the Body of Christ (4:7–16)

Whereas Paul in 4:1–6 focused on the church's unity as one body, in this section he turns his attention to the issue of the one body growing up to full maturity.

6.2.1. Christ's Provision of Grace Gifts (4:7). There is a striking shift of focus that occurs in verse 7. In 4:6 Paul emphasized the oneness of God's family by stating that God is Father of us *all*. Now, however, he changes the focus: "*To each one of us* grace has been given." Paul thus moves from the theme of the oneness of unity to the thought of diversity within unity. The "grace" spoken of here is not the saving grace of 2:8, but a grace for ministry according to our allotted individual portion of Christ's gift. No one person in the body of Christ possesses Christ's gift or anointing in its entirety, but Christ has apportioned a share to each member of the body. Though Paul does not use the word *charismata* ("grace gifts") as he does in Romans 12:6 and 1 Corinthians 12:4 (cf. 1 Peter 4:10–11), he clearly has in mind those very gifts with which the members of Christ's body are endowed (cf. Rom. 12:7–8; 1 Cor. 12:8–10).

6.2.2. Christ's Position As the Gift-Giver (4:8–10). Christ gives grace gifts as the ascended and exalted Lord Jesus (cf. Acts 2:33–36). Since he is the one who baptizes his people with the Holy Spirit, it follows that he is the one giving the gifts of the Spirit to his body. In verse 8 Paul illustrates his thought by referring to an event pictured in Psalm 68:18, where the theocratic king ascends his throne and receives a host of captives ("prisoners of war") as evidence of his victory, along with the plunder or spoils of war, which he distributes among his men. Paul describes the conquering Christ here as ascending to his throne with captives (in the sense of Col. 2:15) and as giving grace gifts to his people for carrying out the ministry of his kingdom.

Paul follows this up by an addendum (in parentheses) that Christ's ascension also involved a descent "to the lower, earthly regions" (4:9; lit., "to the lower parts of the earth"). This unusual expression has provoked a variety of interpretations, of which the following four are the main ones. (1) As in John's Gospel, Jesus' ascent from earth back to heaven (e.g. John 13:1, 3; 14:2–4) was preceded by his descent from heaven to earth (1:1–2, 14). Thus the expression "the lower parts of the earth" simply means "earth below" (Bruce, 1984, 343) and refers to Christ's descent in the Incarnation and his humiliation of the cross. (2) "The lower parts of the earth" refers to the grave. Jesus not only descended from heaven to earth, but also as part of his atoning death for sin was placed inside the earth itself, from which he was raised. (3) "The lower parts of the earth" refers to Hades or the region of departed spirits beyond the grave. (4) G. B. Caird (73–74) has proposed an entirely new interpretation. Because the context concerns Christ's giving gifts to the church after his ascension, he believes the descent mentioned after the ascension in verse 9 refers to Christ's returning to earth by the Spirit at Pentecost, laden with gifts for his church. Thus the sequence is ascension first, then followed by descension at Pentecost to distribute gifts.[4]

Caird's view is not impossible, but verse 10 makes it unlikely in that Christ is described as ascending "to fill the whole universe" rather than redescending from it to bring gifts. Though some of the ancient church fathers adopted the third view, the vast majority of biblical scholars since the Reformation have held the first view, which parallels Paul's thought in the *kenosis* passage (Phil. 2:6–9) and fits well the overall context of Ephesians.

6.2.3. Christ's Purpose in Giving the Fivefold Ministry Leaders (4:11–13). In his place of exaltation as Lord and Christ (Acts 2:36), Jesus sits enthroned over the whole universe (Eph. 1:10, 20–23). "It was he [*autos*, emphatic pronoun] who gave some to be apostles ... prophets ... evangelists ... pastors and teachers" as gifted leaders for his church (4:10). Paul makes a distinction here (and elsewhere) between those *grace gifts* given by the Spirit to individual believers (4:7–8; cf. 1 Cor. 12:4–11) and these five categories of *gifted persons* given by the Lord himself "to proclaim the word and lead" (Lincoln, 249) his church universally (Eph. 4:11; cf. 1 Cor. 12:28).

Briefly stated, "apostles" (lit., "sent ones") refers to those individuals specifically called, commissioned, and given authority by the Lord Jesus Christ himself to be his representatives in proclaiming the gospel and establishing the church (cf. 2:20; 3:5). The New Testament "prophets" were those individuals uniquely gifted in receiving and mediating direct revelation from God. In Ephesians the prophets are mentioned three times alongside the apostles (2:20; 3:5; 4:11). The "evangelists" in New Testament times were those individuals (like Philip in Acts 8) especially anointed to preach the good news of Christ and his kingdom to cities and individuals so as to awaken faith. "Pastors" denotes those God-called individuals whose spiritual gifts caused them to devote themselves to shepherd and care for the flock of God. "Teachers" were those individuals especially gifted to expound the Word of God with effectiveness and power. (For an expanded discussion on each of the above five ministries, see the excellent article by Donald Stamps, "The Ministry Gifts of the Church" [in *The NIV Full Life Study Bible*, 1830–32].)

Two topics of special interest arise in connection with verse 11. (1) As to sentence structure (especially clear in the Greek), apostles, prophets, and evangelists are each mentioned separately (preceded by the definite article), while pastors and teachers are linked together. K. H. Rengstorf maintains that in Paul's thinking these two are so interrelated as to be inseparable in a responsible local church ministry (*TDNT*, 2:158). Those who shepherd also teach, and those who teach also shepherd. Lincoln (250), on the other hand, argues that the omission of the definite article before teachers does not necessarily mean that pastors and teachers were always coupled together in one person. He states: "It is more likely that they were overlapping functions, but that while almost all pastors were also teachers, not all teachers were also pastors."

That teachers formed a separate category of ministry in the early church seems clear in 1 Corinthians 12:28, where God is said to have appointed for his church "first apostles, second prophets, third teachers." A helpful New Testament distinction to keep in mind is the difference between "the teaching role" that generally characterized all the ministries as proclaimers of the Word and "teachers," a term that specifically refers to one of the five leadership callings and anointings that Christ gave to his church.[5]

(2) What is the contemporary relevance of apostles and prophets? It has been almost universally assumed by commentators that apostles and prophets were unique ministries in the first century that have subsequently become extinct and have been replaced by the apostolic and prophetic word of the New Testament canon. It has also been assumed that evangelists, pastors, and teachers continue to be necessary church leaders in every generation. This widespread assumption has been examined and found wanting by Jack Deere in his stimulating book, *Surprised by the Power of the Spirit* (241–51). Just as God has restored an experiential understanding of baptism in the Holy Spirit and the charismatic gifts to the church worldwide in the twentieth century, is it beyond the realm of possibility that God would also restore the ministry of apostles and prophets, not for laying again the church's one foundation or for writing Scripture (since the canon is closed), but for bringing his church to full maturity (Paul's main emphasis in 4:11–13)? Deere explores sound biblical and theological reasons for reexamining this possibility with an open mind.

In verses 12–13 Paul states both the purpose and duration of the fivefold ministry in the context of bringing the church to maturity. As to *purpose*, he describes the church as a living organism (the body of Christ) that is to grow up to its God-intended stature. Previously he referred to the church as a new humanity that God is creating (i.e., the "one new man," 2:15). Stott (170) describes the progression of Paul's thought: "To the oneness and the newness of this new 'man' he now adds matureness. The *one new man* is to attain *mature manhood*, which will be nothing less than *the measure of the stature of the fullness of Christ*, the fullness which Christ himself possesses and bestows." The fact that 4:11–16 is a single sentence in Greek underscores the purpose and role of the fivefold ministry leaders in helping Christ's body grow up to its mature fullness.

By their ministry of the Word (revealing, declaring, and teaching the gospel) and according to their unique gifts, the apostles, prophets, evangelists, pastors, and teachers "prepare God's people for works of service, so that the body of Christ may be built up." This verse expresses three coordinate purposes: to equip the saints, to serve the church's needs, and to build up the body. Interpreters generally understand the function of the fivefold leaders to be embodied in the first clause—i.e., the job of preparing or equipping God's people—while the saints are then prepared to do the works of service and to build up the church.[6]

That the equipped saints are to become ministers in the broad New Testament sense of all members of the body functioning according to their gifts for the common good (Rom. 12:4–8; 1 Cor. 12:4–31) is an obvious application. In the context of this passage, however, it appears that the ministry of the fivefold leaders is also still in view throughout verse 12 by virtue of their being saints and leaders (cf. 1 Cor. 12:28) so that they equip the saints, serve the church's needs, and help build up the body of Christ. On the other hand, a clergy-dominated ministry that excludes lay ministry is itself contrary to what Paul teaches in 4:7, 16, where all members of the body actively participate in the building up of the body of Christ.

The conjunction "until" (4:13) conveys the *duration* for which Christ has given the fivefold ministry. Jack Deere (248) notes: "If taken literally this would mean that the church will have apostles [and prophets] present until it reaches the maturity described in verse 13. . . . At present it is difficult to view the church as having reached the level of maturity described in verse 13."

The ultimate purpose for which Christ gave the fivefold ministry leaders to the church was to bring the body of Christ to its mature fullness, which is defined in three ways (4:13): (1) that all believers may reach not simply faith in Christ, but "unity in the faith"; (2) that they may not simply know about Christ, but have "the knowledge [*epignosis*, full knowledge] of the Son of God"; and (3) that they may attain not simply Christ, but "the whole measure of the fullness of Christ." Only then will we "become mature" (lit., "become a perfect or full-grown person").

Three additional matters in verse 13 are noteworthy. (1) The phrase "until we *all*" clearly refers to the whole church corporately, not simply to all of us individually. (2) Whereas Paul exhorted believers earlier to guard carefully "the unity of the Spirit" (4:3), here he states that "unity in the faith" is a goal to be attained (Wood, 59). This realization of unity will occur because the church comes to a full experiential knowledge of Christ as the Son of God. (3) Paul describes the full maturity of the church as literally "the measure of the stature of the fullness of Christ." The corporate body of Christ is to reach the full stature of the personal Christ (her head).

Luke points to this goal in the book of Acts. In Acts 1:1 he states that his first book (the Gospel of Luke) records "all that Jesus *began* to do and teach." Acts (Luke's second volume) in effect records all that Jesus *continued* to do and proclaim after his ascension through the church by the power of the Holy Spirit. That the Holy Spirit reproduces the life and ministry of Jesus through the church is one of the foremost theological keynotes of Acts. The same gospel that Jesus proclaimed, the church is to proclaim. The same miracles Jesus performed, the church is to perform. The same power of the Spirit by which Jesus ministered, the church is to minister.

Paul has used the word "fullness" (*pleroma*) already in 1:23 in relation to the church. The church is to grow up according to the standard measurement of Christ's fullness in all aspects of life and ministry. Bruce (1961, 88) writes, "When the goal is ultimately reached, and the body of Christ has grown up sufficiently to match the Head Himself, then will be seen that full-grown Man which is Christ together with His members." Though this union will not be complete until the time when the church is glorified together with Christ, that future hope should act as a powerful incentive now to the church's growth to full maturity.

6.2.4. Christ's Plan for Church Growth (4:14–16). Verses 14–16 are still part of the single Greek sentence that began in 4:11. By beginning verse 14 as a new paragraph with the word "then" (Gk. *hina*; lit., "in order that"), the NIV blurs somewhat the exact relationship to the preceding line of thought. The ascended Christ gave the fivefold ministry to the church for the purpose of leading it forward to its future destiny of full-grown maturity. He gave them "in order that" we might not be trapped "in the immaturity of infancy (prey to every pressure) but begin to grow up towards the anticipated maturity, that is, into the very likeness of Christ" (Turner, 1239).

Paul first points out that as the church grows out of spiritual infancy, it leaves behind a corresponding instability (v. 14). To remain spiritual infants (cf. 1 Peter 2:2, where infants refers to new converts) after sufficient time has passed (1 Cor. 3:1–2; Heb. 5:13) is to be spiritually unstable and vulnerable to deception. "Infants are defenseless, unable to protect themselves; in the spiritual life they are an easy prey for false teachers and others who would like to lead them astray from the true path" (Bruce, 1984, 351).

Paul paints a graphic word picture of the instability of immature believers. They are like little boats in a stormy sea, totally vulnerable to the danger of the wind and waves. They are helplessly "tossed back and forth by the waves, and blown here and there by every wind of teaching." Whatever new gust of teaching happens to be blowing most strongly at the time, they are swept along with it. They are easily taken in "by the cunning and craftiness" of false teachers "in their deceitful scheming." Immature believers, without a foundation in the apostolic gospel (2:20), are gullible. "Their opinions tend to be those of the last preacher they heard or the last book they read, and they fall an easy prey to each new theological fad" (Stott, 170). Such immaturity becomes increasingly dangerous as false christs, prophets, and teachers multiply in "the last days" (cf. Matt. 24:4–14, 23–25).

In strong contrast to the instability of spiritual immaturity and the duplicity of false doctrine are the bedrock certainty and integrity of the gospel (4:15). The apostolic gospel is characterized by both *truth* and *love*. "Speaking the truth in love" means "living the truth in love"

(Westcott, 64), not just using one's voice. It includes truth morally expressed in character and action. "Those who blindly follow the ways of error, come to spiritual disaster; those who accept the truth become men of truth themselves" (Bruce, 1961, 88–89).

Truth, according to New Testament revelation, is always inseparably bound together with love. There is no such thing as "all truth and no love," any more than there can be "all love and no truth." The balance is important, as Stott notes (172): "Truth becomes hard if it is not softened by love; love becomes soft if it is not strengthened by truth." When the truth of the gospel is held in love, presented in love, and contended for in a spirit of love, the body of Christ "will in all things grow up into him who is the Head, that is, Christ." In the steady progression from infancy to being full-grown, the church becomes more and more conformed to its Head, Christ himself.

All growth in the body of Christ is ultimately in relationship to the Head (4:15–16). But healthy relationships among members of the body are also essential to a healthy, growing, loving body. Two compound participles prefixed by *syn* ("with" or "together") describe how "the whole body" and each interrelated part of the whole are integrated together. The first was used in 2:21 of the church as a temple that is "joined together" (NIV) or "fitted together" (NASB). The second verb, translated "held together" (NIV) or "knit together" (NKJV, NRSV), relates to the role of the "supporting ligament[s]." Salmond (337) gives a helpful summary of Paul's thought in this verse:

> The body is fitly framed and knit together by means of the joints [ligaments], every one of them in its own place and function, as the points of connection between member and member and the points of communication between the different parts and the supply which comes from the head.

R. Martin (158–59) believes the supporting ligaments refer back to 4:11 and thus equates it with Christ's gift of the fivefold ministry.

> By this chain reaction of Christ—his ministers—his people the whole body is edified as *love* becomes the "atmosphere" in which this process of mutual encouragement and responsibility is exercised, with each part of the church playing the role appointed for it. Christ the head imparts His risen life and bestows by the Spirit His gifts of ministries. His ministers fulfill their mission by equipping the saints (v. 12) and being the ligaments of the church's cohesion to Christ and one another. Christ's people make the contribution ... needful for Christ's design to be realized for the body's upbuilding and growth into him.

7. Outworking Christ's Life in Believers (4:17–5:21)

Paul's message to the Gentiles in Ephesians 1–3 focuses on God's plan of redemption that comes as a gift through faith in Christ and not as a result of merit or self-effort. In chapters 4–6 he stresses that the message of grace carries with it ethical and moral consequences, which he variously refers to as "the fruit of the light" (5:9), "the fruit of righteousness" (Phil. 1:11; cf. Heb 12:11), and "the fruit of the Spirit" (Gal. 5:22–23). Here (as in Gal. 5–6) Paul emphasizes that his gospel of grace not only frees us from Jewish legalism, but also frees us from the former life of sin and the acts of the sinful nature. Thus, Paul began the second half of the letter by exhorting his Gentile readers "to walk worthy" (4:1; see comments) of their calling in Christ.

In the section now before us (4:17–5:21) Paul picks up the metaphor "walk" (*peripateo*) and further applies it to essential Christian living. He uses this word negatively in 4:17 (twice)—"no longer walk as the rest of the Gentiles walk" (NKJV)—and then positively three times—walk in love (5:2), walk in light (5:8), and walk in wisdom (5:15). Paul also picks up the "then–now" contrast of 2:1–22—i.e., what the Gentiles were and how they lived before conversion in contrast to their entirely new way of life in Christ following conversion.

This "before and after" contrast sometimes overlaps but is described broadly in four ways: living in deception versus living according to "the truth that is in Jesus" (4:21; i.e., 4:17–19, 21–25, 28); living a sinful lifestyle versus being a new humanity created in God's likeness of righteousness and holiness (4:20–5:7); walking in the moral and spiritual darkness of the surrounding world versus living as children of the light (5:8–14); and finally, living according to the world's folly versus living according to God's wisdom ways (5:15–21).

7.1. *Cease Living According to the Old Self (Sinful Nature) (4:17–19)*

Paul insists that his Gentile readers "no longer live as the [unregenerate] Gentiles do" (4:17) in their pagan lifestyle. Most notable here is Paul's emphasis on their thinking. Unsaved Gentiles are characterized by futile thinking, darkened intellects, and spiritual ignorance. In contrast to the darkness and ignorance of pagan unbelievers, believers have been taught "the truth that is in Jesus" (4:21); in contrast to their futile thinking, the minds of believers have been "made new" (4:23).

Unregenerate people who live according to their sinful nature are characterized by "futility" in their "thinking" (NIV) or "minds" (NASB; NKJV; NRSV). Though "futility" is sometimes associated with idolatry in the New Testament, "the primary reference here is to 'good-for-nothing notions' (NEB) underlying irresponsible behavior" (Wood, 61). Futile thinking, a darkened intellect (though sometimes brilliant in IQ or learning), and spiritual ignorance begin with the deliberate rejection of moral light and God's known truth (cf. Rom. 1:18–23).

The steps mentioned here in the downward spiral of depraved living are as follows. First comes "the hardening of their hearts" (4:18c), which results in a deep-seated "ignorance" (4:18b). Next depraved Gentiles are "darkened in their understanding [intellect, NASB] and separated from the life of God" (4:18a). Finally, they lose all moral "sensitivity" (4:19a) and give "themselves over to sensuality so as to indulge in every kind of impurity, with a continual lust for more" (4:19). Nothing ever satisfies their foul and perverse desires. Stott summarizes Paul's words (177): "Hardness of heart leads first to darkness of mind, then to deadness of soul under the judgment of God, and finally to recklessness of life. Having lost all sensitivity, people lose all self-control. It is exactly the sequence which Paul elaborates in Romans 1[:18–32]."

7.2. *Commence Living According to the New Self in Christ (4:20–24)*

Paul now contrasts the Gentiles' sinful "old self" with its former way of life (4:22) and their "new self" that in Christ is created spiritually and morally to be like God "in true righteousness and holiness" (4:24). Whereas unregenerate Gentiles are characterized by hardness, darkness, and a reckless lifestyle (4:17–19), Gentile believers have "come to know [lit., learned] Christ" (4:20). Consequently, their hearts are no longer darkened and their lives are no longer characterized by alienation, impurity, and sensuality.

This dramatic change occurred in connection with their having "learned Christ" (NASB, NKJV, NRSV), "heard of him," and been "taught in him" (4:20–21). (1) The expression "learned [*emathete*] Christ" means to be discipled (*mathetes*) to Christ as Lord and to his standard of moral purity. (2) The next expression (lit., "you heard him") means that the Gentile converts had heard the voice of Christ through the preaching of the gospel (the preposition "of" is not in the Greek text). (3) They had been "taught in him" as the sphere of their life. Stott (179) notes that "when Jesus Christ is at once the subject, the object, and the environment of the moral instruction being given, we may have confidence that it is truly Christian."

Verse 21 adds "the truth that is in Jesus." Paul does not usually refer to Christ simply by his historical name. That he does so here strongly affirms that the Christ of faith is the Jesus of history, who is the embodiment of truth (John 14:6).

Fundamental to what the Gentile converts had learned and been taught in Christ (many of them by Paul himself in person several years before) were two truths. (1) A believer at conversion has "put off [the] old self, which is being corrupted by its deceitful desires" (v. 22). This change occurs through a faith identification with Christ in his death, burial, and resurrection, as testified to in the waters of baptism (cf. Rom. 6:2–7; Col. 3:9–10). The "old self" is not to be made better or improved. It is to die and be buried in order that a whole new life can emerge. In God's order death precedes life, crucifixion precedes resurrection.

(2) The believer at conversion has "put on the new self, [which is] created to be like God in true righteousness and holiness" (v. 24). The putting off of our corrupt and degenerating sinful nature is like the removal of a filthy garment that is good for nothing but destruction. The putting on of our new nature in Christ (resurrection life) is like being clothed with a brand new garment. Paul calls what we were before and after conversion as (lit.) "the old man" and "the new man"—the former being

decrepit, deformed, and tending to corruption," the latter being like "a new man, fresh, beautiful, vigorous" (Stott, 181). The old was dominated by unholy lusts; the new is created according to "righteousness and holiness."

This is the way Paul's Gentile readers had "learned Christ" and been "taught in him." The line of demarcation between the old life in sin and the new life in Christ was to be clear and decisive. A process, however, is also involved (indicated by the present tense in "put off" and "put on"), which Paul describes as being "made new in the attitude [*pneuma,* spirit[7]] of your minds" (v. 23). Renewing the mind is a work of the Holy Spirit, whereby our former futile thinking and darkened intellects are changed so that we come to be filled with Christ's way of thinking. A daily and continuous "inward renewal of our outlook is involved in being a Christian" (Stott, 182). Because believers are a new creation in Christ, we "must no longer live as the [unregenerate] Gentiles do" (4:17), which Paul enlarges upon in what follows.

7.3. Live Righteously As a New Creation (4:25–32)

Having contrasted the old self under the influence of the sinful nature and the new self that is created in God's likeness, Paul now describes the practical outworking of the new person in Christ in terms of righteous living. "Therefore" (4:25) is the bridge "between principle and practice" (Wood, 64). In looking at Paul's five practical examples of righteous living, notice they all share two common features: They concern our relationships with other people, and each one involves negative prohibition that is balanced by positive command.

7.3.1. Put Away Lying and Speak Truthfully (4:25). To do away with "falsehood" and to "speak truthfully" is in keeping with who we are in Christ, since "the truth . . . is in Jesus" (4:21). Believers must renounce "the lie" of Satan (cf. Rom. 1:25) and all the lesser lies of the old self, and must conform their speaking to "the truth" of Christ. This command means first that we are to speak truthfully with our neighbors, whom we are commanded by God to love. Even more so, we must relate truthfully and in a trustworthy manner with "all members of [Christ's] one body" as the household of faith. Otherwise, trust is impossible and true community relationships break down.

"Deceitful scheming" (4:14) and "falsehood" are works of the enemy to undermine the unity of the Spirit in Christ's body and, therefore, must not be permitted in the church fellowship. As Stott remarks (185): "fellowship is built on trust, and trust is built on truth. So falsehood undermines fellowship, while truth strengthens it." This verse does not endorse untactful bluntness in our speaking, for such speaking can also be detrimental to community relationships.

7.3.2. Do Not Sin Through Anger (4:26–27). Many translations put this in the form of a command—"Be angry but do not sin" (NKJV, NASB, NRSV)—as if Paul is encouraging righteous anger. This misses the point of his thought in this context. Contextually, it is in effect a warning about sinful anger (cf. 4:31). Paul's thought is: "If you become angry, beware! You are at sin's door!" Turner adds (1240): "If in the West anger is regarded as a sign of manliness, Jewish tradition was more aware of its divisive, demonic, and corrupting power. . . . Anger and the related sins of vs. 29 and 31, are the epitome of socially destructive and alienating sins, and so characteristic of the old creation."

Thus Paul places three restrictions on anger, each of which calls attention to its potential danger. (1) "Do not sin" (4:26a) indicates that anger easily leads to sinning in areas such as egotistical pride, malice, vengeance, rage, violence, and even murder (cf. Matt. 5:21–22). (2) "Do not let the sun go down while you are angry" (4:26b) suggests that if accounts are not settled quickly, anger will lead to bitterness and broken relationships. (3) "Do not give the devil a foothold" (4:27) indirectly warns that anger can easily open a door of opportunity to the devil and give him a place of operation. J. A. Bengel's comment sums up this passage well: "Anger is neither commanded, nor quite prohibited; but this is commanded, not to permit sin to enter into anger: it [anger] is like poison, which is sometimes used as medicine, but must be managed with utmost caution" (quoted by Earle, 317). The greatest antidote to the poison of indulged anger is self-initiated forgiveness (4:32).

7.3.3. Forsake Stealing and Work Diligently (4:28). One of the most elementary ethical principles is the command not to steal (Ex. 20:15; Mark 10:19; Rom. 13:9). Paul mentions

COMPARISON OF EPHESIANS AND COLOSSIANS

Paul wrote both Ephesians and Colossians about the same time, from prison in Rome. There are an amazing number of similarities in content between these two books.

Theme	Ephesians	Colossians
Paul's greeting	Eph 1:1–2	Col 1:1–2
Holy and without blemish in God's sight	Eph 1:4; 5:27	Col 1:22
Redemption through Christ's blood	Eph 1:7	Col 1:14, 20
Wisdom, knowledge, and understanding from God	Eph 1:8, 17	Col 1:9–10
Knowledge of God's will	Eph 1:9	Col 1:9
All things (re)created through Christ	Eph 1:10	Col 1:16
Paul heard about faith and gave thanks	Eph 1:15–16	Col 1:3–4
Paul's continual prayer for Ephesians/Colossians	Eph 1:16	Col 1:9
The believer's hope	Eph 1:18	Col 1:5, 27
An inheritance for the saints	Eph 1:18	Col 3:24
Strengthened by God's power	Eph 1:19; 3:16; 6:10	Col 1:11
Christ's power over rule, authority, and dominion	Eph 1:21	Col 1:13, 16; 2:10, 15
Christ as the Head of his body, the church	Eph 1:22; 4:15–16	Col 1:18, 24
Christ as God's fullness	Eph 1:23; 3:19	Col 1:19; 2:9
Christ fills all things	Eph 1:23	Col 3:11
Apart from Christ people are dead in sin	Eph 2:13	Col 2:13; 3:7
God made us alive in Christ and in his resurrection	Eph 2:5–6	Col 2:12–13
Reconciliation through Christ's blood	Eph 2:13	Col 1:20
Christians called to peace	Eph 2:14–15	Col 3:15
Christ abolished the law and its regulations	Eph 2:14–15	Col 2:14
Being built up in Christ	Eph 2:20–22	Col 2:7
Paul's call by God's grace to reveal God's mystery	Eph 3:2–4	Col 1:25–27; 2:2
God's grace at work in Paul	Eph 3:7, 20	Col 1:29
God's mystery hidden for centuries	Eph 3:9	Col 1:26
Rooted in Christ and his love	Eph 3:17	Col 2:7
Humility, gentleness, patience, and love	Eph 4:20, 31; 5:1	Col 3:12–14
Encouragement to unity	Eph 4:3	Col 3:14
Becoming mature/perfect in Christ	Eph 4:13	Col 1:28
Obtaining fullness in Christ	Eph 4:13	Col 2:10
Growth in Christ	Eph 4:16	Col 2:19
Apart from Christ, alienation from God	Eph 4:18	Col 1:21
Impurity and lust in unbelievers	Eph 4:19	Col 3:5
Putting off the old self and putting on the new	Eph 4:22–24	Col 3:9–10
Putting off falsehood and lies and speaking the truth	Eph 4:25	Col 3:9
Putting away filthy language	Eph 4:29; 5:4	Col 3:8
Speaking in order to help others	Eph 4:29	Col 4:6
Getting rid of anger, malice, and slander	Eph 4:30	Col 3:8
Being forgiving	Eph 4:31	Col 3:13
Believers should allow no one to deceive them	Eph 5:6	Col 2:4, 8
God's coming wrath	Eph 5:6	Col 3:6
Doing what pleases the Lord	Eph 5:10	Col 3:20
Walking carefully and making the most of every opportunity	Eph 5:15	Col 4:5

COMPARISON OF EPHESIANS AND COLOSSIANS (cont.)

Theme	Ephesians	Colossians
Singing psalms, hymns, and spiritual songs	Eph 5:19	Col 3:16
Giving thanks to God the Father	Eph 5:20	Col 3:17
Instructions for wives	Eph 5:22	Col 3:18
Instructions for husbands	Eph 5:25	Col 3:19
Instructions for children	Eph 6:1	Col 3:20
Instructions for fathers	Eph 6:4	Col 3:21
Instructions for slaves	Eph 6:5–8	Col 3:22–25
Instructions for masters	Eph 6:9–10	Col 4:1
Praying and keeping watch	Eph 6:18	Col 4:2
Praying for Paul, the missionary	Eph 6:19–20	Col 4:3–4
Tychicus as Paul's messenger	Eph 6:21–22	Col 4:7–8
Closing benediction	Eph 6:24	Col 4:18

hieves among those transgressors who cannot "inherit the kingdom of God" (1 Cor. 6:10). When a thief is converted through faith in Christ, that person must not only give up stealing but also learn to work diligently, "doing something useful" or beneficial (cf. 4:29), so as to be able "to share with those in need." True believers engage in honest labor and do not cheat their employers or employees, share rather than hoard, and demonstrate a generous rather than a greedy spirit.

In conversion putting off the "old" unregenerate lifestyle that takes advantage of others for one's own benefit (4:22) means putting on the "new" regenerate life in Christ, where we give generously and joyfully to supply what is needed in the lives of others (cf. 2 Cor. 8:14). The change in outward conduct is preceded by a change in heart. Only Christ "can transform a burglar into a benefactor" (Stott, 188).

7.3.4. Discontinue Unwholesome Talk and Speak Edifying Words (4:29–30). Paul turns from the way we use our hands to the way we use our mouths. Unwholesome, unedifying, or ungodly speech should not proceed from the mouth of one who confesses Christ Jesus as Lord. "Unwholesome talk" includes any kind of conversation that is detrimental or harmful to other people. Proverbs states that a discerning person "uses words with restraint" (Prov. 17:27), but "a fool's mouth is his undoing" (18:7). The way we speak is a solemn responsibility because (1) "the power of life and death" is in the tongue (18:21), and (2) we will have to give account on the Day of Judgment for every careless word we speak (Matt. 12:36).

Therefore, Paul urges all believers to speak "only what is helpful for building others up" (4:29). Whereas unsanctified talk tends to tear others down or inflict death, edifying words "benefit [lit., give grace to] those who listen." Similarly in Colossians 4:6 Paul exhorts believers: "Let your conversation be always full of grace, seasoned with salt, so that you may know how to answer everyone." Paul's point is inescapable: If we are a new creation in Christ, we must develop a whole new standard of conversation (Stott, 188).

Verse 30 is a solemn interruption. At the beginning of chapter 4, Paul urged believers to live in a manner worthy of their holy calling in Christ (4:1) and to preserve "the unity of the Spirit" (4:3) as the one body of Christ. Because the sins Paul has been describing since 4:25 are unworthy of our calling in Christ and destroy relationships and unity in the body of Christ, to continue in them will "grieve the Holy Spirit of God." Paul seems to use the full ascription "the Holy Spirit of God" deliberately (Fee, 714). In doing so he refers to a similar sin of Israel in Isaiah 63:10 and to the specific character of the Holy Spirit as "that Spirit who is characterized by holiness and who is God himself at work in believers" (Lincoln, 307).

Barth (2:550) sees expressed here an underlying possibility that those who grieve the Holy Spirit by continuing in their sin risk forfeiting future redemption. Note the emphasis in 4:30

on the role of the Holy Spirit as God's seal of authentication, whereby we are marked "for the day of [final] redemption" (cf. 1:13–14). It should also be soberly observed, however, that grieving the Holy Spirit may (in light of other New Testament passages) progressively lead to a hardening of heart (Heb. 3:8, 13–14), a resisting of the Holy Spirit (Acts 7:51), a putting out of the Spirit's fire (1 Thess. 5:19), and even insulting the Spirit of grace (Heb. 10:29) and blasphemy against him (Matt. 12:31). The eternal consequences of the latter is especially clear in Scripture. To avoid the first steps in the hardening process, we as believers in the fear of the Lord should turn away from all sin that grieves the Holy Spirit of God.

7.3.5. Get Rid of Malice and Be Forgiving (4:31–32). Paul concludes the fivefold cluster of negatives (sinful attitudes and behavior) and positives begun in 4:25. The negatives point to a way of living that believers must "put off" as a new humanity in Christ (4:22), while the positive admonitions involve the changed heart and behavioral pattern that characterize believers who have "put on" the new nature (4:24). The six unholy attitudes and actions mentioned in 4:31 stem from the root of "malice." R. Martin (162) refers to malice as "the parent of the unhappy brood of earlier terms." Malice is an "active ill will" (Webster) toward other people, a poisonous source from which derives "all bitterness, rage and anger, brawling and slander." Bruce (1984, 364) suggests that malice is the inner source from which all previously mentioned unworthy speech (4:29) derives.

"Bitterness" (cf. Col. 3:19) denotes that "irritable state of mind that keeps a man in perpetual animosity—that inclines him to harsh and uncharitable opinions of men and things—that makes him sour . . . [and] brings a scowl over his face, and infuses venom into the words of his tongue" (Eadie, 357). Robinson (194) defines this as "a resentful spirit which refuses to be reconciled." "Rage and anger" involve emotional outbursts and seething emotional resentment against another person. "Brawling" refers to all kinds of outbursts of "contentious shouting" (Bruce, 1984, 364). "Slander" is abusive speech that seeks to defame and destroy the reputation of another.

The converse of the reprehensible conduct in 4:31, from which believers must be free, is the loving behavior characterized by a kind, compassionate, and forgiving spirit (4:32). "Be" is literally "become." Paul recognized that his readers have not yet attained maturity in these areas of Christian graces. To become "kind" is to learn to exercise thoughtful consideration toward others. To become "compassionate" (*eusplanchnoi*) means to become "tenderhearted." This rare word expresses "the deepest concern and feeling for our fellowman in need" (Summers, 105). It is a quality that Jesus demonstrated when he saw the shepherdless multitudes or an individual in desperate need. Compassion too is part of our being conformed to Christ.

"Forgiving" (*charizomenoi*) comes from the word *charis* ("grace"). Thus to forgive each other is to show grace to one another—i.e., to forgive freely and graciously, not grudgingly. Paul strengthens the grace aspect in forgiving by adding that one's forgiveness of others is to be "just as in Christ God forgave you." Just as God's forgiveness flows from his grace, so our forgiveness of others is to flow freely from grace.

Finally, Paul expresses the close association of Christ and the Father in our forgiveness (cf. 4:32 with Col. 3:13). As Bruce states (1984, 365), "in the whole work of redemption the Father and the Son act as one." It is "in Christ" that the Father has given us "redemption through his blood, the forgiveness of sins, in accordance with the riches of God's grace" (1:7). There is a sense in which we too "in Christ" forgive others according to the riches of God's grace toward us.

7.4. Live Holy As Children of Light (5:1–14)

Beginning with 4:17 Paul shifted his focus to the practical outworking of Christ's life in the believer, first in terms of the personal transformation from living according to the sinful nature to living in harmony with Christ's life within (4:17–24). Then he applied the dynamics of this new life to appropriate Christian behavior within the church fellowship in both negative and positive terms (4:25–32). Now Paul appeals to believers to live out their calling as children of light in relation to the world around them (5:1–14). His readers—whom he calls "dearly loved children" (5:1), "God's holy people" (5:3), and "children of light"

5:8)—are to reflect the life of their heavenly Father and in so doing "to be both a challenge :o contemporary society and a rebuke of it" (R. Martin, 162). For this to happen, there must be a clear contrast between believers and the world. Paul describes that contrast here in erms of love and light.

7.4.1. Walk in Love (5:1–7). Living as God's children and God's holy people involves walking in love. For the third time Paul uses he word *peripateo* (trans. "live" in 5:2; see comments on 4:1; 4:17–5:21) when discussing he conduct of the Ephesian believers (cf. also 5:8, 15). To "live a life of love" (5:2) involves being "imitators of God" (5:1). Imitating God s the logical consequence of our knowing him as Father. Just as children will imitate a loving earthly father, so believers are to imitate heir loving heavenly Father. Paul says in Romans 5:8, "But God demonstrates his own ove for us in this: While we were still sinners Christ died for us."

Paul has already prayed that we be "rooted and established in love" (3:17). Now he exhorts us to "live a life of love, just as Christ oved us and gave himself up for us" (5:2). The Greek word for love here is *agape* (God-like ove), which loves with a pure giving of the elf for the well-being of the one to whom love s shown. *Agape* is not based on merit. Christ demonstrated this pure, unmerited love for us when he gave his life in death on the cross as a "fragrant offering and sacrifice." "Fragrant" ecalls the odor of Old Testament sacrifices hat ascended to heaven and pleased God. Jesus' death as the sacrifice for sin was pleasing to the Father because it was on behalf of our salvation.

Paul turns from the self-sacrifice of Christ o the very opposite, the self-indulgence of the sinner (5:3–4), from *agape* love to its perversion, lust; he mentions three manifestations of elf-indulgence and love's perversion. "Sexual immorality" and "impurity" comprehensively over every kind of heterosexual (premarital nd extramarital) and homosexual sin possible, ll of which defile the conscience and destroy ove. "Greed" describes the inner desire of the heart for that which is not rightfully one's own. t can also refer to sin in the sexual realm, such s coveting another man's wife or someone else's body for selfish gratification (Ex. 20:17; f. 1 Thess. 4:6).

These three sins are not even to be mentioned or talked about among "God's holy people," "so completely are they to be banished from the Christian community" (Stott, 192). This was a high standard in the province of Asia, where sexual orgies were regularly practiced in connection with the worship of the Greek goddess Artemis of the Ephesians (cf. Acts 19:23).

In verse 4 Paul contrasts sexual vulgarity in speech with godly thanksgiving, possibly "as alternative pagan and Christian attitudes to sex" (Stott, 192). The parallel passage in Colossians, however, suggests Paul has a broader contrast in mind. The conversational contrast in this case is between worldly minded people, who have sex constantly in their thought and speech, and God's holy people, who "let the peace of Christ rule" their hearts (including thought and speech) with thanksgiving (Col. 3:15–17).

Verse 5 contains a solemn warning and pronouncement: No one who gives himself or herself to practice the aforementioned sexual sins

The fertility goddess Artemis was worshiped in Ephesus.

"has any inheritance in the kingdom of Christ and of God," no matter what profession he or she makes about being a Christian. Bruce (1961, 103) discredits a common rationalization about this verse that misrepresents the point Paul is making: "The idea that Paul means that such people may be true Christians even so, but that their behaviour will debar them from any part or lot in a future millennial reign of Christ, is totally unwarranted by the context and by New Testament teaching in general."

Paul goes on to state that a "greedy person . . . is an idolater" because his or her affection is set on earthly things rather than on things above, so that some earthly object of desire has "the central place which God alone should have in the human heart" (Bruce, 1961, 104). Paul knew that his message of freedom from the law and exhortation to love could easily be used to excuse sexual sin. Thus he adds: "Let no one deceive you" (5:6) into believing that some immoral, impure, or greedy persons do have an inheritance in the kingdom of Christ. Such assurance and false security involve deception and "empty words." Upon such people "God's wrath comes." The danger of forfeiting our inheritance in God's kingdom is a real one for "those who are disobedient," that is, those who know God's moral law and willfully disobey it. "Therefore do not be partners with them" (5:7), lest you share in their doom.

7.4.2. Walk in Light (5:8–14). In 2 Corinthians 6:14 Paul asks, "What fellowship can light have with darkness?" The obvious answer is "none!" In Colossians Paul reminds believers that God the Father has rescued us from the domain of darkness and placed us in the kingdom of his Son, which is "the kingdom of light" (Col. 1:12–13). Here in Ephesians 5:8 Paul declares to his readers: "You were once darkness, but now you are light in the Lord." To be "in Christ" who is "the light of the world" (John 8:12) means to be light also.

The contrast between darkness and light in 5:8–14 is similar to that found elsewhere in the New Testament. "Darkness" represents ignorance, sin, moral failure and ruin, deception, spiritual death, and the whole realm of Satan; "light" represents truth, righteousness, moral purity, spiritual life, and the whole realm of Christ. Believers were formerly not only *in* darkness (i.e., in the environment of darkness and under its influence), but they were also themselves darkness. Now because of the[ir] faith union with Christ, they are light. "'The[ir] lives and not just their environment' had bee[n] changed from darkness to light" (Stott, 199[?]). Thus Paul adds: Walk or "live as children [of] light"—i.e., let your conduct conform to you[r] new identity. The fact that we are "light in th[e] Lord" indicates that there is residing in us hi[s] grace and power for holy living.

Paul parenthetically explains that "the fru[it] of the light," the manner of life produced in th[e] believer, is characterized by "goodness, righ[t]eousness and truth" (5:9). The deeds of dark[]ness are the opposite of this fruit: evi[l], wickedness, and falsehood. The thought i[n] 5:10 expands the last statement in 5:8: Chil[]dren of light "find out [*dokimazo*] what please[s] the Lord" (cf. Rom. 12:2). *Dokimazo* means t[o] test, discern, and approve the genuineness [of] all that pleases God.

The contrast between "the fruitless deeds [of] darkness" (5:11) and "the fruit of the light[" (5:9) is similar to that between "the acts of th[e] sinful nature" and "the fruit of the Spirit" i[n] Galatians 5:19, 22. The "acts of the sinfu[l] nature" or the "deeds of darkness" cannot b[e] described as "fruit" because they do not hav[e] the seed of life in them but are sterile and issu[e] in death. Light invariably exposes the tru[e] character of the deeds of darkness (5:11). Evil[]doers thus hate the light for fear of bein[g] exposed (John 3:20). But only as exposur[e] occurs will there be conviction by the Hol[y] Spirit and the possibility of salvation (16:8).

Verse 12 suggests that the very mention [of] the shameful vices of the disobedient should b[e] offensive to God's people, who are morally sen[]sitive. The power of light, however, is not onl[y] that it exposes and "makes everything visible[" (5:14), but it also transforms whatever it illu[]mines into light. Verse 14b is perhaps from a[n] early Christian baptismal hymn that draws o[n] several Old Testament passages (cf. Isa. 26:19; 52:1–2; 60:1–2). It reveals that "conversion i[s] nothing less than awakening out of sleep, ris[]ing from the dead and being brought out [of] darkness into the light of Christ" (Stott, 201).

7.5. Live Wisely As Spirit-Filled People (5:15–21)

For the fifth time since 4:1 Paul uses th[e] word "walk" (*peripateo*), translated "live[" (see comments on 4:1; 4:17–5:21). Pau[l] xhorts believers to "be very careful" to live /isely as God's Spirit-filled people (5:15). Careful" contains the meaning of exactness r accuracy, "which is the outcome of carefulness" (Vine, 1:25). Paul then does a play on /ords: Live not as *asophoi* ("unwise") but as *ophoi* ("wise"). He goes on to mention three ractical ways for living wisely.

7.5.1. Make the Most of Every Opportunity (5:16). In a parallel passage in Colossians :5, Paul urges believers to behave wisely in elation to unbelievers and to make the most of very opportunity for witnessing to them. Here is focus is on making the most of every opportunity in relation to life generally, "because the ays are evil." Wise people seize every fleeting pportunity to do good; once it has passed, it ; gone forever. Someone once advertised: LOST, yesterday, somewhere between sunrise nd sunset, two golden hours, each set with ixty diamond minutes. No reward offered, for ey are gone for ever" (quoted by Stott, 202). sure sign of wisdom is making the best use f our time in the midst of frivolous and evil ays. Failure to do so is a sign of folly.

7.5.2. Understand the Will of the Lord 5:17). Whereas wisely making the best use of pportunities has to do with diligence, understanding the Lord's will has to do with discernment. Wisdom for daily living resides in God's will. In seeking to discern that will, we must always distinguish between his general vill and his particular will. The former is ound in Scripture—e.g., it is not his will that ny should perish but that all should come to epentance and a saving knowledge of Christ 2 Peter 3:9). His particular will for one's life omes through scriptural principles, community counsel or wisdom, prayer, and direction evealed by the Holy Spirit.

> Trust in the LORD with all your heart
> and lean not on your own
> understanding;
> in all your ways acknowledge him
> and he will make your paths straight.
> (Prov. 3:5–6)

When our whole life relates to God's will in its general and particular dimensions, then we are iving carefully and wisely.

7.5.3. Be Filled With the Spirit (5:18–21). The verb structure of this passage, consisting f two imperatives (5:18) followed by four participles (5:19–21), reveals that these four verses comprise one unit of thought. The four participles modify the primary imperative in 5:18 ("be filled"), describing four consequences of being filled with the Spirit: singing (5:19a), being joyful (5:19b), giving thanks (5:20), and submitting to one another (5:21).

This whole section (4:17–5:21) contains sets of contrasts, beginning with the "before" and "after" contrast of converted Gentiles who have come to know Christ. A contrast occurs again in 5:18: drunkenness versus spiritual fullness. Drunkenness is a deed of darkness and a work of the sinful nature (it is not a disease), which "best accounts for its appearance here" (Fee, 720; cf. Lincoln, 345–46).

The tenses of the two imperatives in 5:18 indicate a "never do so" in reference to indulging in intoxicating wine and an "always do so" in reference to being filled with the Spirit. Gordon Fee (721–22) notes that the actual expression of the second imperative is unusual. "Paul says not, 'be full of the Spirit' [genitive], as though one were full of Spirit in the same way that another is full of wine, but 'be filled by the Spirit,' with the emphasis on being filled to the full by the Spirit's presence" (or with "the fulness which the Spirit gives" [Masson in Martin, 166]).

The precise form of the verb "be filled" (*plerousthe*) is significant for four reasons. (1) It is an *imperative* and is thus a command. Being filled with the Spirit is not an optional or tentative suggestion, as if we are at liberty to take it or leave it. It carries an urgent weight of importance. (2) It is *plural* and thus applies to the body of Christ collectively. God's people collectively are to "be so 'full of God' by his Spirit that our worship and our homes give full evidence of the Spirit's presence: by song, praise, and thanksgiving that simultaneously praise and adore God and teach the community" (Fee, 722). (3) It is *passive* and thus could be translated, "Let the Spirit fill you" (NEB). There should be such an openness and obedience to the Holy Spirit that nothing hinders him from filling us. (4) It is a *present tense* and thus carries the idea of an ongoing action. As our physical bodies need the constant renewal that sleep brings, so the body of Christ needs the constant renewal that the Spirit makes possible.

Paul then mentions four consequences that occur when we as the body of Christ are filled and renewed by the Holy Spirit's empowering presence (vv. 19–21). (1) There is *singing* of all kinds (5:19), which "functions both to instruct the believing community and to praise and adore God" (Fee, 722). A Spirit-filled people are filled with singing of three kinds. "Psalms" refers to the Old Testament book of Psalms, which was the songbook both of Judaism and the early church. It represents the singing of Scripture generally. "Hymns" refer to early Christian compositions, some lines of which are preserved in the New Testament. Early Christian hymns were typically confessions of faith concerning the person of God and the truth of the gospel. "Spiritual songs" were more spontaneous expressions of the life of the Spirit within the believer and the community (e.g., a prophetic song, such as 1 Sam. 2:1–11; Luke 1:46–55, 68–79). F. F. Bruce (1961, 111) suggests that spiritual songs were likely "unpremeditated words sung 'in the Spirit,' voicing praise and holy aspirations." Toward the end of the second century, Tertullian describes the Christian love feast as a time when "each is invited to sing to God in the presence of the others from what he knows of the holy scripture or from his own heart" (*Apology*, 39).

(2) Another consequence of being a Spirit-filled people is an overflowing joy expressed through "singing and psalming with the heart to the Lord" (5:19b, lit. trans.). This corresponds to Paul's personal testimony in 1 Corinthians 14:15: "I will sing with my spirit, but I will also sing with my mind." This singing with the heart or with one's spirit is the personal dimension of the believer's life and joy in the Spirit and is thus directed solely "to the Lord."

(3) A third expression of being Spirit-filled is "always giving thanks to God the Father for everything" (5:20). A grumbling and complaining attitude is incompatible with the Holy Spirit. The Holy Spirit teaches us that God makes all things work together for good in our lives (Rom. 8:28) and thereby enables us to be thankful wholeheartedly at all times. "In the name of our Lord Jesus Christ" reminds us of the centrality of Christ in our faith and of the Trinity: We, being filled with the *Spirit*, give thanks to the *Father* in the name of the *Lord Jesus Christ*.

(4) The final consequence of being Spirit-filled is the grace of mutual respect and submission in the body of Christ (5:21). It is unbecoming for believers to be self-assertive, to manipulate and control others, or to insist on getting their own way. Believers are instead called to humble themselves and to "submit to one another out of reverence for Christ" (5:21). Even leaders among God's people, whom fellow members of the body of Christ are instructed to honor and obey with loving respect (1 Cor. 16:16; 1 Thess. 5:12–13; Heb. 13:17), earn such recognition by being servants, not lords (Luke 22:24–27; 1 Peter 5:3).

Likewise, as a spiritual principle, submission, humility, gentleness, and patience must be shown mutually to one another in the Christian family. The wife must submit (i.e., yield in love) to the husband's responsibility of leadership in the family. The husband must submit to the needs of the wife in an attitude of love and self-giving. Children must submit to the authority of the parents in obedience, and parents must submit to the needs of their children and bring them up in the instruction of the Lord. Mutual submission and reverence for Christ makes possible peace in the church and the Christian home. Paul addresses these issues in more specific detail in 5:22–6:9.

8. Applying Christ's Lordship to Household Relationships (5:22–6:9)

God intends that a saving relationship to Christ and submission to him as Lord will affect positively every relationship and every area of the Christian community and of our individual lives. Since God has established the family as the most basic unit of society, it is not surprising that Paul emphasizes that being properly related to Christ shapes the way husbands and wives, parents and children, and even masters and household slaves relate to one another.

A few preliminary observations about 5:22–6:9 will help illuminate the passage. (1) The definite article in Greek precedes the categories of people being addressed:—i.e., "the wives" (5:22), "the husbands" (5:25), "the children" (6:1), "the fathers" (6:4), "the slaves" (6:5), and "the masters" (6:9). This construction is called the generic use of the definite article. "In such usage the article binds all of the individuals into one class" (Summers, 120). Paul is thus addressing comprehensively all Christian wives, husbands, children, parents, slaves, and masters.

(2) The verbs that go with these collective nouns are present imperatives; that is, they are commands that point to something that should be true of our conduct on a continuous basis. For example, "the husbands" are to "love" and "keep loving" their wives (5:25). Translators and interpreters agree that the verb "submit" in 5:21 (a participle) was intended by Paul to serve as the verb in 5:22. In Greek a participle sometimes carries the force of an imperative (command). What is only implicit in verse 22 and suggested in verse 24 is commanded explicitly in the parallel passage in Colossians 3:18. Elsewhere in 5:22–6:9 an imperative is consistently used, Hence, Ephesians 5:21 is best viewed as a transitional verse to this whole passage.

(3) Social or cultural considerations also help us understand Paul's construction of the passage and his emphases. For example, first-century Greek, Latin, and rabbinic teachers of ethics addressed themselves only to the free male members of society. The gospel, however, lifted women, children, and slaves to places of honor and responsibility in the church and its social order. Moreover, women, children, and slaves not only experienced freedom and respect in the church; they were expected to conduct themselves responsibly in their new standing and in a way that brought honor to their Lord. Thus Paul's order of address is wives first, then husbands; children first, then fathers; slaves first, then masters. This revolutionary elevating of the oppressed to a place of honor and responsibility also explains why Paul devotes three verses of instruction to children (6:1–3) but only one to fathers (6:4), and four verses to slaves (6:5–8) but only one to masters (6:9).

(4) The whole passage has recurring references to "the Lord." The conduct required of each collective category of people "step by step is totally dependent upon the reality and validity of Christ's work and his presence" (Barth, 2:758).

8.1. Wives and Husbands (5:22–33)

This passage is the longest statement in the New Testament on the relationship of husbands and wives (cf. Col. 3:18–19; 1 Peter 3:1–7). In 1 Peter 3, Peter says more to wives about submitting to their husbands; here in Ephesians Paul directs more attention to the husband's responsibility to love his wife as Christ loves the church. Concerning the subject of "submission" in 5:22–6:9, F. F. Bruce writes (1984, 383):

> While the household code is introduced by a plea for mutual submissiveness [v. 21], the submissiveness enjoined in the code itself is not mutual. As in the parallel code in Col. 3:18–4:1, wives are directed to be subject to their husbands, children to be obedient to their parents, and slaves to their masters, but the submissiveness is not reciprocated: husbands are told to love their wives, parents to bring up their children wisely, and masters to treat their slaves considerately. As for the section dealing with wives and husbands, its distinctive feature in Ephesians is that the relationship between husband and wife is treated as analogical to that between Christ and the church.

After exhorting mutual submission in the body of Christ (5:21), Paul addresses the specific issue of wives (5:22–24) and husbands (5:25–31). He admonishes wives to submit to their husbands as their head, even as the church submits to Christ as her head. Then he directs husbands to love their wives, even as Christ loved the church. Paul carefully compares the husband-wife relationship to the Christ-church relationship (note the frequent use of the comparative "as" and "just as" in 5:22, 23, 24, 25). Then Paul expands the analogy and focuses almost entirely on Christ and the church (5:26–27). After further instruction, he in 5:31 quotes Genesis 2:24 about oneness in marriage, in 5:32 makes a final reference to Christ and the church, and in 5:33 summarizes the entire passage: The husband "must love his wife," and "the wife must respect her husband."

8.1.1. Wives, Submit to Your Husbands (5:22–24). How does the submission required of all in 5:21 relate to the submission of wives suggested in 5:22 and stated clearly in 5:24? Verse 21 states a comprehensive principle before Paul addresses the specific roles of husbands and wives, parents and children, and masters and slaves. Thus Paul reminds all Christians, men and women, of the call to submit to one another before reminding wives of their particular responsibility to submit to their husbands because of God's order and role differences in marriage.

The verb "submit to" (*hypotasso*) reappears in 5:24, where Paul says that "wives should submit to their husbands in everything" as the church submits to Christ. The church's submission to Christ involves being loyal, faithful, devoted, pure, and loving. This issue of submission represents the essence of Paul's teaching to wives since it is the entire focus of his charge in Colossians 3:18, "Wives, submit to your husbands, as is fitting in the Lord." Every New Testament passage on this subject uses the same verb *hypotasso* (Eph 5:22, 24; Col. 3:18; Titus 2:4–5; 1 Peter 3:1). Paul uses the middle voice in Greek to emphasize the voluntary nature of wives' submission. *Hypotasso* denotes "submission in the sense of voluntarily yielding in love" (BAGD, 848). Yielding to others rather that asserting oneself should characterize the people of God generally (cf. Phil. 2:3–8).

In verses 22–24 Paul defines the nature of the wives' submission in four ways: "to your [own, *idiois*] husband (5:22; *idiois* is in the Greek but left untranslated in the NIV); "as to the Lord" (cf. Col. 3:18, "as is fitting in the Lord"); "for the husband is the head of the wife"; and "as the church submits to Christ" (5:24).

Paul explains in 5:23 why the wives are to submit to their own husbands: "For the husband is the head [*kephale*] of the wife." Some interpret "head" to mean "source," denoting origin rather than authority. In this context, however, Paul defines what he means by "head" when he adds: "The husband is the head of the wife as Christ is the head of the church" (5:23). It should be evident that Christ is head of the church because he is God's appointed authority over it, and thus the church is to submit to him in everything (5:24). The two concepts of submission and headship mutually explain one another: "The church submits to Christ's authority because He is the head or authority over it" (cf. 1:22; 4:15) (Knight, 169).

Paul's general comments in 1 Corinthians 11:3 about men and women are instructive concerning the issue of divine order in the husband-wife relationship: "Now I want you to realize that the head of every man is Christ, and the head of the woman is man, and the head of Christ is God." The following issues are raised by Paul in 1 Corinthians 11:3, 8–9 and Ephesians 5:22–33: (1) Paul is clear that in Christ a perfect spiritual equality exists among men/husbands and women/wives as heirs of God's grace; yet it is an equality involving order and subordination with respect to authority. As God is the head of Christ, Christ is the head of man, and man the head of woman. The word "head" expresses both authority and divine order (cf. Judg. 10:18; 1 Cor. 3:23; 11:8, 10; 15:28; Eph. 1:21–22; 5:23–24; Col. 1:18; 2:10).

(2) Paul thus bases the husband's headship not on cultural considerations but on God's purpose and order in creation (1 Cor. 11:8–9) and on the parallel analogy of Christ's headship of the church (Eph. 5:23).

(3) Subordination is not demeaning because it does not imply inferiority or suppression. Just as Christ is not inferior or second-class because the Father is his head, so a wife is not a second-class person because her husband is her head (5:23; cf. 1 Cor. 11:3).

(4) Furthermore, in God's kingdom leadership never implies being "greater." Servanthood and obedience are the keys to greatness in the kingdom (Matt. 20:25–28; Phil. 2:5–9).

(5) How does the husband's headship in the marriage relationship relate to Paul's statement in Galatians 3:28, where he asserts the radical social nature of the gospel by stating that in Christ "there is neither Jew nor Greek, slave nor free, male nor female, for you are all one in Christ Jesus"? Here Paul declares that the gospel removes all ethnic, racial, nationalistic, social, economic, and sexual barriers in Christ and in the church. All in Christ are equal heirs of "the gracious gift of life" (1 Peter 3:7), the promised Spirit (Gal. 3:14; 4:6), and renewal in God's image (Col. 3:10–11). Within the context of spiritual equality, however, men remain men, and women remain women (Gen. 1:27). Their God-assigned roles in marriage and society remain unchanged (1 Peter 3:1–4).

8.1.2. Husbands, Love Your Wives (5:25–33). God's intention that wives submit to their husbands as the church submits to Christ requires an active grace. In verse 25 Paul confronts the husband with a much more difficult charge, one that requires an even greater supernatural enablement: "Husbands, love your wives, *just as* Christ loved the church and gave himself up for her." Notice that Paul does not tress the husband's "authority over his wife ›ut his love for her" (Stott, 231). The hus›and's headship or authority is not that of a lomineering man who makes all decisions and equires submission by his wife. Rather, Paul :arefully safeguards the dignity and well-being ›f a wife by defining her husband's authority n terms of the power and depth of his selfacrificing love for her.

Moreover, Paul uses the present tense of the mperative to emphasize that the husband's elf-sacrificing love for his wife is to be coninuous and unceasing. Paul's term for love is *gapao*, which is more than the spasmodic xpression of romantic love that comes from hysical attraction or desire. It even goes eyond the dimension of friendship love and nduring affection. The kind of love the husand must have for his wife is an unselfish ove that actively seeks the highest good and vell-being of the wife. It is the love of comnitment that remains steadfast through every ircumstance or adversity. It is love that is nwavering in the emotional ebb and flow of ife. That is the only kind of love that will nable a marriage to hold together "as long as 'ou both shall live."

The pattern for the husband's love for his vife is that of Christ's love for the church. Paul lescribes this love in four ways. (1) It is *a selfacrificing love* (5:25), the love Christ xpressed on the cross. No higher standard of ove is conceivable. C. S. Lewis (in *The Four .oves*, 1960, 148) states that a Christ-like sort ›f love

> is not most fully embodied in the husband we should all wish to be but in him whose marriage is most like a crucifixion; whose wife receives most and gives least, is most unworthy of him, is—in her own mere nature—least lovable.... [This love is] seen not in the joys of any man's marriage but in its sorrows, in the sickness and sufferings of a good wife or the faults of a bad one, in his unwavering (never paraded) care or his inexhaustible forgiveness: forgiveness, not acquiescence.

(2) The husband's Christ-like love is *a anctifying love* (5:26–27). Paul uses five 'erbs to describe the unfolding dimensions of 'hrist's love for his bride, the church. He "*loved* her" (5:25b), "*gave himself up* for her" (5:25c), "to *make* her *holy*" (5:26a), "*cleansing* her" (5:26b), "and *to present* her to himself as a radiant church, *without stain or wrinkle*" (5:27). Christ's self-sacrificing love for the church has a sanctifying and beautifying effect on her. Likewise, when the husband loves his wife "as Christ loved the church," that love will sanctify and beautify his bride. Note that Christ makes the church holy by "cleansing her by the washing with water" (not baptismal regeneration, but the washing of regeneration in Titus 3:5, to which water baptism testifies) "through the word" (either the confession of faith or the Spirit-quickened word of God that releases faith).

(3) The husband's Christ-like love is *a providing love* (5:28–30). Paul refocuses on the husband's love for his wife and mentions two things about it as a providing love. (a) Husbands are to love their wives "as their own bodies" (5:28a). As the church is the "body" of Christ on earth, so the wife is an "extension" of her husband. Together husband and wife are two complementary parts of one personality. Thus, when the husband lovingly cares for his wife, he "loves himself" (5:28b). (b) When a husband thinks of his wife as part of himself, he will provide and care for her properly "just as Christ does the church" (5:29). "Feeds" and "cares for" (lit., "nourishes" and "cherishes") refer to practical and tangible provision and affection.

(4) The husband's Christ-like love is *a secure love* (5:31–32), a holy union and bonding that is for life. Paul in 5:31 refers to Genesis 2:24 as the basis for this point (as does Jesus, cf. Matt. 19:5–6). That the husband and wife in marriage "become one flesh" is part of the "mystery" of marriage (Eph. 5:31b–32a). Their lives are so closely joined together that they can be spoken of as one. In this oneness the wife can submit to her husband, and the husband can love and cherish his wife so as to give up his own interest for her well-being. Thus Paul sees the "profound mystery" of the Christ-church relationship prefigured in the marriage bond. Throughout 5:22–33 Paul has interpreted the marriage relationship in the light of the Christ-church union. In so doing, he has thereby transformed the concept of marriage into the highest marriage ideal that the world knows.

Verse 33 summarizes the mutual responsibilities of the husband and wife to each other. The wife's responsibility is restated in terms of "respect" (lit., "fear"). It is fear, however, "in the sense of awe or reverence that is appropriate respect for the husband" (Summers, 127).

8.2. Children and Parents (6:1–4)

8.2.1. Children, Obey Your Parents (6:1–3). The saving power of Christ and the enabling presence of the Holy Spirit make possible harmonious relationships in a family. Paul now discusses the Christian parent-child relationship. Whereas the breakdown of marriage relationships and disobedience by children toward parents are signs of a disintegrating society, godly and harmonious family relationships are themselves a salt and light testimony of Christ in society.

Paul, writing to the corporate body of Christ, commands children to "obey [their] parents" (6:1). The present imperative of the verb "obey" speaks of obedience as a continuous or habitual conduct. Then Paul gives four motives for doing so. (1) "Obey your parents *in the Lord*." This phrase may be interpreted one of two ways: (a) It defines the limits of obedience as being to Christian parents; thus viewed, "in the Lord" modifies "parents" (Bruce, 1961, 121). (b) Others view the expression as qualifying the verb "obey." If this is the proper understanding, "in the Lord" simply shows the spirit in which the obedience is to be yielded: Christian obedience "as to the Lord" (Abbott, 176; Lincoln, 402).

(2) Children should obey parents because "this is right" (cf. the parallel passage in Col. 3:20, "This is well-pleasing to the Lord"). The sense here is that this is righteous. "Right" (*dikaion*) uses the same root word as "righteousness" (*dikaiosyne*). Stott (238–39) argues that obedience to parental authority is a "natural law" or "general revelation" that is right and true in all cultures through the centuries.

(3) Children should obey parents because it is a "commandment" of God (6:2)—the one to "honor your father and mother" (cf. Ex. 20:12; Deut. 5:16). Again, the verb "honor" is a present imperative (*tima*) and conveys the necessity of a continuous honoring of one's parents (Summers, 129). Salmond states (375): "Obedience is the duty; honor is the disposition [from] which the obedience is born." Honor relates to respect for one's parents and is different from total agreement.

(4) Paul's final motive for obeying parents is because believers are given a promise by God for doing so: "that it may go well with you and that you may enjoy long life on the earth" (6:2–3). Bruce (1961, 121) notes that this is the fifth commandment in the Decalogue, but the first and only one with an attached promise. And it is "first" not just in relation to the Decalogue but also the whole pentateuchal law. Proper respect for parents demonstrates a principle of right living that carries within itself the rewards of well-being and the continuance of life.

8.2.2. Fathers, Do Not Exasperate Your Children (6:4). As the wives' responsibility of submission is followed by the husbands' responsibility to love (5:22–33), so here children's obligation to obey is followed by parents' responsibility to their children. Fathers are addressed because of their governmental role as leaders or heads of the family (the mothers' responsibility is subsumed under theirs).

The fathers' responsibility is stated in terms of a negative and a positive command. (1) Negatively, fathers must "not exasperate [their] children" (6:4). Earthly fathers are crucial in forming their children's concept of the heavenly Father. They should remember that right relationships with their children are more important than right performance by the children. The father must avoid irritating, inciting resentment, or disheartening his children by imposing unreasonable expectations, harsh or unfair treatment, severe discipline, and so forth. This does not imply that the father is to have a "hands off" policy toward his children. It simply means he must conduct himself so as to not predispose his child to disobedience or rebellion.

(2) Paul gives fathers a positive command: "Bring them up." The father is responsible for taking the initiative in the home for training and instructing the children concerning the Lord. To "bring up" means to nourish tenderly or to give careful and loving care. This task is further described in a twofold way. (a) "Training" (*paideia*) means upbringing and instruction "chiefly as it is attained by discipline and correction" (BAGD, 608). It thus relates to character development. (b) "Instruction" (*nouthesia*) relates to issues involved with the path of righteousness.

Paul's prepositional phrase at the end of verse 4, "of the Lord," can be interpreted one of two ways: In the Greek ablative case, it means "concerning the Lord"; in the genitive case, it indicates "the Lord is the guiding standard or source." Both possibilities are true. Because children are "a heritage from the LORD" (Ps. 127:3), "training" and "instruction" are supremely important responsibilities of fathers (and mothers). Even though the training by fathers and the conduct of children are often less than perfect, where the father-child relationship is godly and right, the outcome will generally be right and wholesome (cf. Prov. 22:6).

8.3. Slaves and Masters (6:5–9)

8.3.1. Slaves, Obey Your Earthly Masters (6:5–8). Since, like wives and children, slaves were elevated by the gospel to a place of honor and respect in the church, Paul addresses them first with four verses concerning the responsibility that goes with their new standing. The fact that Paul addresses slaves at all indicates that they were accepted and respected members of the church, who could honor their heavenly Master by the way they served their earthly masters. In each of the four verses addressed to the slaves, Jesus Christ is the focus and master motive for their service: "just as you would obey Christ" (6:6), "like slaves of Christ" (6:6), "as if you were serving the Lord, not men" (6:7), and "because . . . the Lord will reward everyone for whatever good he does" (6:8).

One may ask, "Why did not the New Testament explicitly condemn slavery as wrong instead of adjusting the relationships of believers within it?" The early church was politically powerless in the first-century Roman world. If it had attacked the Roman institution of slavery directly and sought to emancipate slaves on a general scale, it would have confirmed "the suspicion of many people in authority that the gospel aimed at the subversion of society. It was better to state the principles of the gospel clearly, and leave them to have their own effect in due course on this iniquitous institution" (Bruce, 1961, 125). The gospel of Christ, however, did give slaves spiritual freedom and personal dignity. It also set in motion principles that helped remove the harshness of Roman slavery and eventually led to its banishment in the Christian community (cf. Paul's letter to Philemon).

Paul instructs Christian slaves along two lines. (1) He admonishes them to "obey [their] earthly masters" (6:5). Spiritual freedom was not to lead them to rebel against their masters. On the contrary, as a believer the slave should render an even greater obedience and faithfulness now "because the honour of Christ and the gospel was bound up with the quality of his service" (Bruce, 1961, 123). Paul exhorts slaves to obey their masters (a) "with respect and fear" (lit., "fear and trembling"), lest their conduct bring reproach to the name of Christ; (b) "with sincerity of heart"—i.e., "without secondary or ulterior purpose" (Summers, 132), such as "to win their favor when their eye is on you"; and (c) "doing the will of God from your heart" (lit., "with all your soul," the opposite of reluctance or listlessness).

(2) Paul admonishes Christian slaves to serve their earthly masters (a) "wholeheartedly" (6:7; lit., "with good will"), which suggests a ready willingness that "does not wait to be compelled" (Robinson, 211), and (b) as if they "were serving the Lord, not men." The reason for such service is "that the Lord will reward" them (6:8). The "Well done" pronounced by Christ at the judgment (cf. Matt. 25:21, 23) is far more important than temporal benefits or the lack thereof. Thus the Christian slave can serve cheerfully even an unreasonable master, knowing that his or her reward will come from Christ.

8.3.2. Masters, Treat Your Slaves Fairly (6:9). Paul admonishes masters to "treat [their] slaves in the same way"—i.e., with respect and according to the Golden Rule. They are to give their slaves every courtesy that they themselves hope to receive. Paul forbids Christian masters to use threats or any form of harshness in order to secure obedient service, such as was common among Roman masters.

The phrase "both their Master and yours" indicates that Paul is addressing the Christian master-slave relationship (just as he was with Philemon and Onesimus). "There is no favoritism with" their heavenly Master; God views masters and slaves on an equal basis and shows no partiality. "Favoritism" (NIV) or "partiality" (KJV, NASB, NRSV) is a compound word consisting of two words meaning "face" and "to receive." The Lord in heaven does not receive or view a person based on facial appearance, external circumstances, or status in life; rather, he receives a person according to his or her response to his grace and the inner condition of the heart. To treat a fellow human in less than a just and righteous way is to answer to him who shows no partiality.

Are these words relevant for today? Though the master-slave relationship is not exactly parallel to our employer-employee relationship, nevertheless the principles Paul gives in 6:5–9 apply to Christian employees and employers. Note how Paul reverses the emphasis in contemporary management-labor disputes where "each side concentrates on securing its own rights, and on inducing the other side to do its duty. . . . [Paul] urges each side to concentrate on its responsibilities, not its rights" (Stott, 258–59). The application of this emphasis is the best approach to a solution of mutual problems at any level of life.

9. Standing Empowered and Equipped in the Spiritual Battle (6:10–20)

It is common for New Testament writers to end their letters with an appeal based on the central message of the letter. This is what Paul does in 6:10–20; in other words, these verses must be understood in the context of the whole of Ephesians. This passage is not a diversion or an appendix for persons who have "a special interest in demons and spiritual warfare" (Turner, 1242). Rather, it relates to God's plan of redemption and the cosmic reconciliation that is the goal of Christ's death-resurrection-exaltation.

These verses relate to the manner in which we were extracted by God's saving grace in Christ from sin and death and the clutches of Satan. It relates to how we must now live as redeemed Gentiles and Jews, wives and husbands, children and parents, slaves and masters, given the fact that in this world we live in a war zone that is under attack and being challenged by God's malicious enemy—Satan and his network of evil spirit powers. "Thus Paul has chosen to recast his message in the form of a battle address" (Turner, 1242) in which the whole church is viewed corporately as being "in a battle whose ultimate antagonists are God and the devil" (Lincoln, 442).

The New Testament frequently uses military language to describe the reality of spiritual warfare that accompanies both the cosmic spiritual battle between God and Satan (vertical warfare) and the earthly conflict between believers and the evil spirits of this dark age (horizontal warfare). Paul instructs his readers to "be strong in the Lord and in his mighty power (6:10), to "put on the full armor of God" in order to "stand against the devil's schemes" (6:11), and "to resist [lit. Gk.] when the day of evil comes" (6:13). He insists that our battle is not a flesh-and-blood struggle but one against the enemy spirits, which he describes in four categories: "rulers," "authorities," "powers of this dark world," and "spiritual forces of evil in the heavenly realms" (6:12). Likewise, our weapons are not fleshly or earthly but spiritual (2 Cor. 10:4). Thus Paul states that our equipment for this battle is the full armor of God (6:14–18).

This language is an abrupt change from the domestic setting of 5:22–6:9. We might wish we could live out our lives in peaceful tranquillity, but the fact is that God's enemy is also ours, and he is militant. "Moreover, there will be no cessation of hostilities, not even a temporary truce or cease-fire, until the end of life or of history when the peace of heaven is attained" (Stott, 262).

Verse 10 begins with the word "finally." This word does not denote that Paul is coming to the ending of his letter; rather, it means "from now on, henceforth" and thus points to "the remaining time." Paul is therefore emphasizing that "the whole of the interim period between the Lord's two comings is to be characterized by conflict. The peace that God has made through Christ's cross is to be experienced only in the midst of relentless struggle against evil. And for this the strength of the Lord and the armour of God are indispensable" (Stott, 262–63).

The spiritual war we are in has a unique feature. We do not chase the enemy or make swift moves of attack against him (thus the Roman soldier's key attack weapons, the twin javelins, are missing from Paul's list). Instead, we "take [our] stand" against the enemy (6:11), "stand [our] ground" (6:13), and "stand firm, then" (6:14). We are to hold a strong position, "the crown of the hill . . . and the enemy must weary itself in constant uphill attack" (Turner, 1243). The strong position Paul has in mind is that we are seated with Christ in the heavenly realms (1:20; 2:6), where Christ sits far above all rulers and authorities and powers (1:21), with "all things under his feet" (1:22). The believer's victory has been secured by Christ himself through his death on the cross, and we are to stand in that victory.

At the cross Jesus waged the crucial battle against Satan, "having disarmed the [evil] powers and authorities [and] made a public spectacle of them" (Col. 2:15; cf. Matt. 12:29; Luke 10:18; John 12:31; 19:30). Thus D-Day occurred at Jesus' death and resurrection, at which time God planted his flag on the earth in the form of the cross. The enemy was dealt a fatal blow and the outcome has been assured, but the war is not over. The victory is "already but not yet." The complete victory, V-Day, is yet to come when Christ returns. In the meantime, it is a "day of evil," and we are to stand on the ground won by Jesus Christ.

As good soldiers of Christ, we are to endure hardship (2 Tim. 2:3), suffer for the gospel (Matt. 5:10–12; Rom. 8:17; 2 Cor. 11:23; 2 Tim. 1:8), fight the good fight of the faith (1 Tim. 6:12; 2 Tim. 4:7), wage war (2 Cor. 10:3), persevere (Eph. 6:18), be more than conquerors (Rom. 8:37), be victorious (1 Cor. 15:57), triumph (2 Cor. 2:14), defend the gospel (Phil. 1:16), contend for the faith (Phil. 1:27; Jude 3), not be frightened by opponents (Phil. 1:28), put on the full armor of God (Eph. 6:11, 13), stand firm (v. 14), destroy Satan's strongholds of deception with the truth (2 Cor. 10:4), take captive every thought (2 Cor. 10:5), and be powerful in battle (Heb. 11:34).

9.1. Our Ally—God (6:10–11a)

"The Lord" our God is an omnipotent ally. Though our enemy is a formidable foe, he is neither omnipotent, omnipresent, nor omniscient. Only God is an infinite being; Satan is finite. However, he is a real and powerful enemy, who roars like a lion, seeking people to devour (1 Peter 5:8). If we attempt combat with him in our own strength and resources, we will be overcome. Paul exhorts us to find our strength "in the Lord and in his mighty power" (cf. 1:19–20; 3:16–21).

The verb "be strong" is a present passive imperative, meaning "to be strengthened" or "be empowered." A more literal rendering of 6:10 is, "Be empowered in the Lord and in the might of his strength" (cf. 3:16). In this war it is both foolish and dangerous to attempt to be strong in a self-reliant way. Rather than being self-sufficient, Paul exhorts believers to be supernaturally empowered with the might and strength of the Lord (cf. Ps. 18:1, 31–32, 39).

A second imperative occurs in 6:11a: "Put on the full armor of God." For believers to prevail in the face of the devil's attacks, they not only need God's power but also his armor. The armor is God's not just in the sense that he provides it, but also it is the armor that the Messiah (Isa. 11:4–5) and Yahweh himself wears (59:17). Paul's wording makes clear that God supplies the armor, but we are responsible to put it on. We are not "born again" with it on. We must dress and live in the armor, and never disarm under an illusion that the hostilities have subsided or ceased.

9.2. Our Enemy—Satan and His Forces (6:11b–12)

Paul admonishes believers to take a stand "against the devil's schemes." In war a proper assessment of the enemy is crucial. To underestimate our spiritual enemy may cause us to neglect God's power and armor as the necessary provisions for spiritual warfare. "Schemes" refers to the devil's cunning methods that he uses against believers and the church. Some of his strategies are temptation, accusation, intimidation, deception, and division. Already mentioned (4:27) is Satan's plan "to exploit strained relations and angry feelings between believers so as to damage their personal or corporate welfare and witness" (Bruce, 1984, 404). Paul also exhorts believers not to be ignorant of the devil's schemes lest he have an advantage over them (2 Cor. 2:11). Here believers must be spiritually empowered and equipped so that they can "stand against" those schemes.

Verse 12 clearly reveals that our real enemies in life are not humans, but evil spirits that are subject to the devil (cf. 2:2; 6:11). The word "struggle" denotes hand-to-hand encounter or face-to-face combat; it was used for a wrestling match (cf. KJV, NKJV). Whereas "flesh and blood" wrestling was a common sport in Ephesus and the province of Asia, the church is engaged in "a spiritual power encounter" of cosmic dimensions, which makes God's armor and weapons necessary.

Three features characterize the demonic spirits that are arrayed against the church:

They are powerful (with differing rank and influence), evil (hating the light and dwelling in the dark places of sin and falsehood), and cunning (deceitful and plotting schemers) (see Stott, 263–66). This host of evil spirit powers are apparently fallen angelic beings (cf. Jude 6; Rev. 12:4) under the command of Satan (cf. John 12:31; 14:30; 16:11; Rev. 12:7) as the god of this age (2 Cor. 4:4; 1 John 5:19). Along with Satan they energize the ungodly (Eph. 2:2), oppose God's will and people (Dan. 10:12–13; Matt. 13:38–39), and seek to attack believers in this age (cf. 1 Peter 5:8; also Job 1–2). They constitute a great multitude (Rev. 12:4, 7) and are assigned different positions of rank and authority in the kingdom of darkness (Eph. 6:12).

Paul mentions four ranks among the hosts of Satan that rule over darkness and oppose all believers and the church. (1) "Rulers" (*archai*) are evil spirit powers that hold "dominions entrusted to them" (Thayer). Delling writes (*TDNT*, 1:479): "*Arche* always signifies 'primacy,' whether in time: 'beginning' . . . , or in rank: 'power,' 'dominion,' 'office.'" Perhaps here they are regional rulers in the demonic ranks, such as "the [spirit] prince of Persia" and "the [spirit] prince of Greece" in Daniel 10:12–13, 20. (2) "Authorities" (*exousiai*) may refer to those evil powers who are given authority by Satan to preside over evil structures in the world. (3) "Powers" (*kosmokratoroi*) literally means "world rulers," who alongside Satan rule over the present world order organized in rebellion against God. (4) "Spiritual forces of evil" either comprehensively embraces all the evil spirit powers (Lincoln, 444) or refers to the vast hosts of lower-ranking demons that serve the wicked purposes of Satan in general destruction and keeping people in bondage.

Paul uses the expression "in the heavenly realms" five times in Ephesians. It always has to do with the unseen spiritual sphere in contrast to the material dimension of life that is visible (see comments on 1:3). The New Testament suggests six stages in the unfolding drama of Satan and his demonic hosts: "their original creation, their subsequent fall, their decisive conquest by Christ, their learning through the church [3:10], their continued hostility, and their final destruction" (Stott, 273).

9.3. Our Weaponry—The Full Armor of God (6:13–20)

9.3.1. The Armor (6:13–17). In 6:13 Paul repeats the exhortation previously given in 6:11 ("Therefore put on the full armor of God")—this time in view of 6:12, the hosts of Satan that are involved in the spiritual war. A different word for "put on" (*analabete*) is used here, however, than in 6:11, where *endysasthe* (meaning "be clothed in") occurs. *Analabete* means "take up" in resolute fashion so that even under the most severe attack, the believer may resist the enemy and "stand" his or her ground.

Three times Paul exhorts believers to "stand" (6:11, 13, 14). By this he means that the believer and the church are to remain steadfast and unmovable, standing when the spiritual battle is intense and holding ground when the conflict is nearing its end, being "neither dislodged nor felled, but standing victorious at one's post" (Salmond, 3:385). Note that different aspects of standing are emphasized in the overall passage (6:10–20). We are to "stand firm" (6:14a) in Christ's victory and strength (6:10), against the devil's schemes (6:11), with our armor securely in place (6:11a, 13a), and in prayer (6:18–20).

To resist the enemy "when the evil day comes" refers to those times when the enemy's assault is fiercest against us. The "already but not yet" tension of the last days operates during the entire period between the first and second comings of Christ, though it is most evident during those times that "most share the terrible quality of 'the [final] evil day'" (Turner, 1243).

In 6:14–17 Paul lists the various pieces of armor worn by a Roman soldier and then applies them spiritually (cf. Isa. 11:4–5; 59:17). Note that his metaphors are not used rigidly (e.g., in 1 Thess. 5:8 the breastplate is faith and love, whereas here it is righteousness). Note also that Paul mentions alertness in prayer (6:18) as necessary in order to be fully prepared for spiritual warfare.

Verse 14 introduces two important items: truth and righteousness. Truth is likened to the soldier's belt around the waist and righteousness to a breastplate. The belt was a leather apron that secured the soldier's tunic when fighting, helped protect the body, and held the sword in place when not fighting. The "breastplate" provided protection from the neck to the upper part of the thighs (i.e., the body's entire trunk and vital organs).

Turner (1243) notes that here truth and righteousness (though often interpreted as references to the gospel and its offer of righteousness by faith), as in Isaiah 11:5; 59:17, "denote quality of character, and they stand alongside 'holiness' at 4:24–25 and 'goodness' at 5:8–9. Paul is saying that the church's basic equipment in the spiritual battle is integrity [character] and righteous living [conduct], and they are effective because these qualities bear the stamp of Jesus and the new creation he brings (4:17–24)."

Certainly it is true that any righteousness we have is given as a free gift of God through faith in Christ (Rom. 3:21–22; 4:13). But it is also true (see Eph. 4:22–24; 5:9; 6:14) that righteousness refers to uprightness in character and conduct. In spiritual warfare we must be girded about by truth in speech and behavior (living in truth) and protected by moral righteousness or integrity. Duplicity or lack of integrity will expose one directly to the enemy.

Verse 15 is sometimes interpreted to mean a readiness of the feet "to proclaim the gospel of peace" (NRSV). Paul's point, however, involves a preparation of our feet for standing firmly in battle, not for spreading the gospel. He is emphasizing the importance of firm footing when fighting the enemy. The Roman soldier wore nobnailed sandals with cleat-like studs underneath so that no matter how slippery the ground, he could stand firm-footed in hand-to-hand combat.

The NIV rightly translates this verse that our feet are "fitted with the readiness that comes from the gospel of peace." It is not readiness to proclaim the gospel (though that is important) but readiness in battle, "to stand unmoved against the foe" (Foulkes, 175), that is produced in us by the peace of God through the gospel. It is "the peace of God, which transcends all understanding [that] will guard" our hearts and minds in Christ Jesus (Phil. 4:7) when Satan attacks, thus giving us confidence to stand our ground and not retreat in fear or despair.

The word for "shield" (v. 16) is related to the Greek word for door. Thus the shield Paul has in mind is not the small, round one but the large, rectangular shield (2 1/2' wide by 4' long), made of alternating layers of wood, bronze, and oxhide. In battle it could be used side by side with others to form a wall of protection in front or a roof overhead. The leather was soaked in water before battle so that flaming arrows dipped in pitch would be extinguished or fall harmlessly to the ground.

"Faith" is the shield that provides the believer protection from "all the flaming arrows of the evil one." Those "flaming arrows" include temptation, accusations, persecution, slander, heresy, and other attempts to defeat the believer and divide the church. All such arrows are to be countered with faith. According to Turner (1244), faith in Ephesians

> is the radical openness to God that allows Christ's full indwelling, and brings a deeper grasp of his unfathomable love (cf. 3:17). "*Take up the shield of faith*" thus suggests a deliberate and positive holding on to the God revealed in the gospel; firm and resolute dependence on the Lord which quenches the fiery attempts of the enemy to harm and to spread panic.

The last two pieces of armor that a Roman soldier takes up are the helmet and the sword (v. 17). The helmet was designed to protect the head in battle. The believer's mind is a major battleground in spiritual warfare. Our deliverance from and victory over the evil spirits of darkness intricately involve the battleground of our thought life. Whether "the helmet of salvation" refers to the assurance of salvation that we have now in our union with Christ (forgiven, seated with him in the heavenly realms, delivered from Satan's bondage, and adopted into God's family) or to the hope (confidence) of final salvation (cf. 1 Thess. 5:8) at the second coming of Christ (including the eternal banishment of sin, death, and Satan as our enemies), "there is no doubt that God's saving power is our only [sure] defense [for the mind] against the enemy of our souls" (Stott, 282).

Regarding the sword, the Spirit is not himself the sword; it is "the word of God." There are four distinguishing characteristics about this sword. (1) It is "the sword *of the Spirit*" in that it originates from him; he imparts and empowers the revelation of both the written and spoken word of God.

(2) The sword is the only piece of equipment not solely for defensive purposes. Without it we have no way to repel the devil when attacked.

(3) The word for "sword" (*machaira*) denotes a short sword or dagger (12–14 inches) that a soldier used to repel the enemy in hand-to-hand combat, not the long-handled sword to slay the enemy (*rhomphaia*).

(4) The Greek term translated "word" is not *logos* (biblical revelation generally or Christ himself) but *rhema* (a specific word of Scripture or an individual utterance given in the heart by the Holy Spirit). It corresponds to the declaration in Revelation 12:11: "They overcame him [Satan] by the blood of the Lamb [i.e., Jesus' decisive victory at the cross] and by the *word* of their testimony" [i.e., the confession of their mouth].[8] It was the threefold use of "the word of God" by Jesus at his temptation in the wilderness that enabled him to repel Satan (cf. Matt. 4:4, 7, 10). Through using God's word and the testimony of our mouths, we have the sword or dagger to repel any and all attacks of Satan and his hosts.

9.3.2. Alertness Through Prayer (6:18–20). Paul concludes this passage by exhorting the fighting saint and the church to be prayer warriors. Scholars have discussed whether Paul intended prayer to be the seventh weapon in spiritual warfare. But prayer is not just another weapon; it is part of the conflict itself. To fail to pray is tantamount to surrender to the enemy.

Grammatically, the two participles in 6:18, "praying" and "keeping alert," are connected with the verb "stand firm then" of 6:14a. Being spiritually equipped with God's armor for battle combined with an alertness in prayer is the combination Paul seeks (Turner, 1244). To "pray in the Spirit" means to be led and empowered by the Holy Spirit in prayer. Most likely Paul uses this phrase here (as in 1 Cor. 14:14–15) to include praying in tongues. As Fee (731) writes:

> What Paul says about this kind of praying in 1 Cor. 14:1–5 and 14–19 demonstrates that he engaged in it regularly, and that he urged the believers in Corinth to do so as well. The same is most likely true of Rom. 8:26–27 (q.v.). If this more specific "praying in the Spirit" is in view, then one must also be prepared to enlarge one's understanding of the nature of such praying . . . [as] a way of engaging the enemy in the ongoing conflict.

A feeble prayer life and occasional "grocery list" petitions are surely not effective in spiritual war. We need to lean more heavily on praying in and by the Spirit in personal and corporate prayer and intercession.

Paul has a "two-directional focus" for persevering prayer on the part of believers. (1) He exhorts individual believers and the church to pray on behalf of other saints involved in spiritual warfare. In verse 18 "all" occurs four times in the Greek (the third time is rendered "always" in the NIV)—pray "on *all* occasions" (both regularly and constantly), "with *all* kinds of prayers and requests" (indicating thoroughness and intensity), "persevering at *all* times" (demonstrating persistence and alertness), "for all the saints" (because of Satan's attacks against the church).

(2) In verses 19–20 Paul admonishes believers to pray for him that as a prisoner of Christ he may at every opportunity "fearlessly make known the mystery of the gospel" as "an ambassador in chains" (cf. 3:1; 4:1; Acts 28:16, 20; Phil. 1:7, 13–14, 16; Col. 4:3, 18; Philem. 1, 9–10, 13). Thus Paul's final exhortation in this letter has to do with evangelism. Prayer is not only for the purpose of enabling believers to stand in battle, but also for the advancement of the gospel of Christ.

10. Conclusion (6:21–24)

10.1. Commendation of Tychicus (6:21–22)

Verses 21–22 and Colossians 4:7–8 are virtually word for word identical, indicating that both letters were written by Paul at about the same time and carried simultaneously to their destinations by Tychicus. Paul commends Tychicus as a "dear brother and faithful servant in the Lord" (cf. Col. 4:7, "a faithful minister and fellow servant"). He is mentioned by name elsewhere in Acts 20:4; 2 Timothy 4:12; and Titus 3:12. Paul uses Tychicus not only to deliver the letter, but also to inform the readers in greater detail upon his arrival about "how [Paul was] and what [he 'as] doing," in order to "encourage" them (cf. ph. 3:13). The absence of Paul's customary st of greetings to leading individuals in the hurch (cf. Col. 4:10–17) supports the view at Ephesians was originally a circular letter or more churches than just the one in Ephesus see the introduction).

10.2. Benediction (6:23–24)

Paul concludes this majestic letter with an postolic blessing that centers around the grace and peace" with which he began the etter (1:2). Here, however, he mentions them in reverse order and less closely tied ogether" (Bruce, 1984, 414). Paul's pro-ouncement of "peace" (6:23) is not simply he Hebrew greeting of well-being, but the eace that comes through the reconciliation of he cross "to the brothers" (i.e., the peace of Christ that forges a bond among believers in is church; cf. 2:14; 4:3). Coupled with peace" is "love with faith" (i.e., love accom-panied by faith; cf. 1:15; also Gal. 5:6, where 'faith expresses itself through love")—all hree of which are "from God the Father and he Lord Jesus Christ" (6:23).

"Grace" (6:24) is the final word of bene-diction, even as it was the first word of salu-ation (cf. 1:2). Paul pronounces grace "to all who love our Lord Jesus Christ." The letter's ast phrase, "undying love," means literally ove that is "incorruptible" or "immortal." Love for Jesus that has been poured into our hearts by the Holy Spirit (Rom. 5:5) is "free from every element liable to corruption" Salmond, 3:394) and is thus "undying love."

THE OLD TESTAMENT IN THE NEW

NT Text	OT Text	Subject
Eph 1:22	Ps 8:6	Everything subject to Christ
Eph 4:8	Ps 68:18	Ascension and gifts
Eph 4:25	Zec 8:16	Speaking the truth
Eph 4:26	Ps 4:4	Anger and sin
Eph 5:31	Ge 2:24	Institution of marriage
Eph 6:2–3	Ex 20:12; Dt 5:16	Fifth commandment

NOTES

[1]"In Ephesus" does not appear in the Chester Beatty papyrus, p^{46} (earliest extant manuscript of Paul's letters), nor in the old and reliable Sinaiticus and Vaticanus manuscripts. It is also omitted in Marcion, Tertullian, and Origen. It does occur in commentaries from John Chrysostom onwards and in the Alexandrinus manuscript, indicating the designation is ancient, if not original.

[2]Commentators vary considerably in their interpretations of this verse; for quality sources that discuss the various possibilities, see Delling, "*pleroma*," *TDNT*, 6:304–6; F. F. Bruce, 1984, 275–77; Stott, 61–66.

[3]For a summary of the many and diverse interpretations, see Barth, 1:395–97.

[4]Ralph P. Martin expresses sympathy with this view in *The Broadman Bible Commentary*, 156.

[5]For a thorough examination of the pervasiveness of "the teaching role" in biblical times under both covenants, see my unpublished Ph.D. dissertation: John Wesley Adams, "The Teaching Role in the New Testament: Its Nature and Scope As a Function of the Developing Church," Baylor University, 1976.

[6]Gordon Fee notes that this interpretative approach is based on the different prepositions used in verse 12: the first phrase begins with *pros*, which states the purpose of the fivefold ministry leaders, although the second and third are *eis* phrases, which indicate the goal is the ministry of the saints in building up the body (Fee, 706, n. 155; similarly Robinson, Westcott, Barth, Mitton, Stott, Bruce). T. David Gordon, New Testament professor at Gordon-Conwell Theological Seminary (69–78), argues that to interpret 4:12 as limiting the fivefold ministry function only to "equipping" saints for service is a mishandling of this text (similarly Eadie, Abbott, Lincoln, Turner).

[7]Although most scholars and translations regard *pneuma* in 4:23 as referring to the human spirit, Gordon Fee finds this problematic and devotes more than two pages to showing cause for believing Paul is speaking of the Holy Spirit and his work (Fee, 710–12). Regardless of how one translates *pneuma* (human spirit or Holy Spirit), renewing the mind is a work of the Holy Spirit.

[8]It is noteworthy that *logos* as used in Revelation 12:11 refers to the believer's loyal witness for Christ even unto death, rather than to the *logos* of Scripture.

BIBLIOGRAPHY

T. K. Abbott, *A Critical and Exegetical Commentary on the Epistles to the Ephesians and to the Colossians*, ICC (1897); J. Wesley Adams, "Ephesians: A Preacher's Treasury of Truth," *The*

Preacher's Magazine 54 (June–August 1979): 4–6; William Barclay, *The Letters to Galatians and Ephesians* (1976); Markus Barth, *Ephesians*, AB, 2 vols. (1974); Raymond B. Brown, "Ephesians Among the Letters of Paul," *RevExp* 60 (Fall 1963): 372–79; F. F. Bruce, *The Epistle to the Ephesians* (1961); idem, *The Epistles to Colossians, Philemon, and Ephesians*, NICNT (1984); G. B. Caird, *Paul's Letters From Prison*, New Clarendon Bible (1976); Jack Deere, *Surprised by the Power of the Spirit* (1993); G. S. Duncan, *St. Paul's Ephesian Ministry* (1929); John Eadie, *Commentary on the Epistle to the Ephesians* (n.d.); Ralph Earle, *Word Meanings in the New Testament* (1986); Gordon D. Fee, *God's Empowering Presence: The Holy Spirit in the Letters of Paul* (1994); Francis Foulkes, *The Epistle of Paul to the Ephesians*, TNTC (1963); T. David Gordon, "Equipping Ministry in Ephesians 4?" *JETS* 37 (March 1994): 69–78; Donald Guthrie, *New Testament Introduction*, 3d ed. (1990); Stig Hanson, *The Unity of the Church in the New Testament: Colossians and Ephesians* (1946); William Hendriksen, *The Epistle to the Ephesians* (1967); Charles Hodge, *A Commentary on the Epistle to the Ephesians* (1950); Lewis Johnson, "The Pauline Letters From Caesarea," *ExpTim* 68 (1956–57): 24–26; George W. Knight, "Husbands and Wives As Ana logues of Christ and the Church," *Recovering Bib lical Manhood and Womanhood*, ch. 8 (1991); R. C H. Lenski, *The Interpretation of St. Paul's Epistle to the Galatians, Ephesians and Philippians* (1937 J. B. Lightfoot, *Notes on the Epistles of St. Pau* (1957); Andrew T. Lincoln, *Ephesians*, WB (1990); Ralph P. Martin, "Ephesians," *Broadma Bible Commentary*, vol. 11 (1972); W. G. M. Mar tin, "The Epistle to the Ephesians," *New Bible Com mentary* (1954); C. Leslie Mitton, *Ephesian* (1976); J. Armitage Robinson, *St. Paul's Epistle t the Ephesians* (1914; 1979); S. D. F. Salmond, "Th Epistle of Paul to the Ephesians," *The Expositor Greek Testament*, vol. 3 (1903; 1976); E. K. Simp son and F. F. Bruce, *The Epistles of Paul to the Eph esians and the Colossians*, NICNT (1957); Donal C. Stamps and J. Wesley Adams, *The Full Life Stud Bible* (1991); John R. W. Stott, *The Message of Eph esians* (1979); Ray Summers, *Ephesians: Patter for Christian Living* (1960); Max Turner, "Eph esians," *New Bible Commentary* (1994); W. E. Vine *An Expository Dictionary of the New Testament*, vols. (1940); B. F. Westcott, *St. Paul's Epistle to th Ephesians* (1906; 1978); A. Skevington Woo "Ephesians," *EBC*, vol. 11 (1978).

PHILIPPIANS

David Demchuk

INTRODUCTION

The first exposure of the city of Philippi to the gospel is recorded in Acts 16:6–40. On his second missionary journey, the apostle Paul, acutely aware of the leading of the Holy Spirit in his journey through Asia Minor, landed in the port city of Troas. There he received a vision of a man from Macedonia calling his companions and himself to "come over to Macedonia and help us" (16:9). Paul concluded that God was calling them to go in that direction and proceeded from Troas to Macedonia.

After landing at the port city of Neapolis, Paul traveled ten miles to Philippi, "a Roman colony and the leading city of that district of Macedonia" (16:12). There Paul proclaimed the gospel faithfully. One of his most notable converts was a seller of purple fabric, Lydia of Thyatira (16:14ff.). She immediately welcomed the apostle and his party into her home, which no doubt became the core of the first house church in that city.

At some point during his initial stay in Philippi Paul was in the center of a significant controversy concerning the deliverance of a young girl from an evil spirit, which had enabled her to foretell the future. The owners of this slave girl dragged Paul and his companion, Silas, before the magistrates of the city, and the two evangelists were beaten and thrown into prison (16:19–24). This imprisonment set the stage for a spectacular earthquake while Paul and Silas were worshiping God there at midnight. This earthquake led to the conversion of both the Philippian jailer and his family (16:30–34).

Paul's first recorded appeal to his rights as a Roman citizen occurred the morning after his imprisonment. The magistrates gave the jailer orders to release Paul and Silas, no doubt expecting them to go their way without further incident. Paul refused, however, bringing his citizenship to the attention of his captors. The magistrates, concerned over the reprisals that would ensue from the unjust punishment of a Roman citizen, sought to appease the men and begged them to leave the city. After returning to Lydia's home and taking time to encourage the fledgling church there, they complied with the magistrates' request and left the city.

The city of Philippi had been founded in 360 B.C. by Philip of Macedon. It was built on the village of Krenides in Thrace and served

Philippi
In the time of Paul

The Roman colony of Philippi (*Colonia Augusta Julia Philippensis*) was an important city in Macedonia, located on the main highway leading from the eastern provinces to Rome. This road, the Via Egnatia, bisected the city's forum and was the chief cause of the city's prosperity and political importance. Ten miles to the south, on the coast, was Neapolis, the place where Paul landed after sailing from Troas in response to the Macedonian vision.

As a prominent city of the gold-producing region of Macedonia, Philippi had a proud history. Named originally after Philip II, the father of Alexander the Great, the city was later honored with the name of Julius Caesar and Augustus. Many Italian settlers from the legions swelled the ranks of citizens and made Philippi vigorous and polyglot. It grew from a small settlement to a city of dignity and privilege. Among its highest honors was the *ius Italicum*, by which it enjoyed rights legally equivalent to those of Italian cities.

Ruins of the theater, the acropolis, the forum, the baths, and the western commemorative arch mentioned as the "gate" of the city in Acts 16:13 have been found. A little farther beyond the arch at

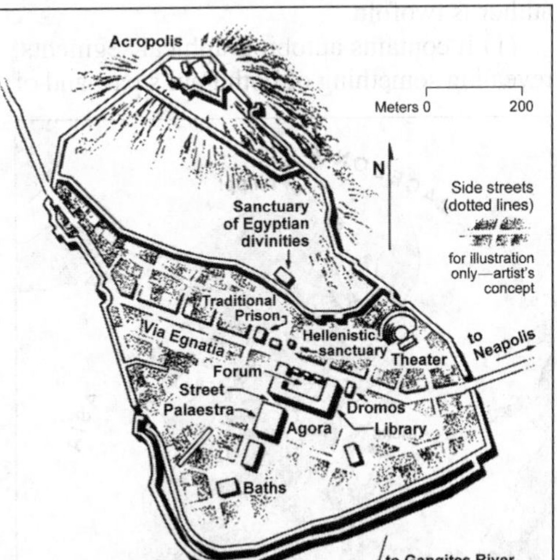

the Gangites River is the place where Paul addressed some God-fearing women and where Lydia was converted.

as a significant military center. When Rome conquered the area some two hundred years later, Philippi became a chief city in Macedonia—one of the four Roman districts of what is today known as Greece. There the famous battle between the armies of Brutus and Cassius and those of Octavian and Mark Antony took place (c. 42 B.C.). Octavian's victory led to the establishment of the Roman empire, and he is remembered by the name under which he ruled that empire—Augustus.

Philippi flourished as a colonial city in the Roman empire; it is the only Roman city referred to as a "colony" in the New Testament (Acts 16:12). Many veterans from Roman wars, particularly the later conflict between Antony and Octavian, settled there, having received an allotment of land for their service to Rome. The city took pride in its status as a Roman colony, enjoying tax-exempt privileges. It promoted Latin as its official language and modeled many of its institutions (e.g., civic government) after those of Rome. The magistrates that Paul and his companions first encountered in Acts 16 bore the honorary title "praetors." The Philippian sense of pride is evident in Acts 16:21, where several citizens refer to themselves as "Romans."

1. Author

There is no dispute that Philippians is a Pauline letter—a fact documented by Paul's own introduction (see comment on 1:1). The significance of this letter in our understanding of the author is twofold.

(1) It contains autobiographical segments, revealing something of both Paul's past and of his present understanding of what was going on in his life. In an aggressive polemic launched against the Judaizing false teachers who were impacting the church at Philippi, Paul opens the door on his own past (Phil. 3:5ff.). Although he was a Roman citizen (born in the Greek culture of Tarsus), his pedigree in Judaism was impeccable. He was not a Hellenist, but a Hebrew-speaking Jew (3:5—"a Hebrew of Hebrews"). From his birth in God's covenant community, his education as a Pharisee, and his strict adherence to the law, Paul was without blemish. However, it was his experience of having Christ "take hold" of him (3:12) that dramatically changed the course of his life. Paul's Damascus Road conversion (Acts 9:1–31) caused him to see the futility of trying to achieve salvation through keeping the law. He now saw all of his accomplishments as refuse in light of his relationship with Christ. The zeal with which he had pursued his previous course of life was now focused on his service for Christ (3:13). He had an acute sense of God's calling and direction, and his life was subordinated to his task of preaching the gospel (1:19–20).

Paul went to Philippi because of a vision of a man from Macedonia who said, "Come ... and help us."

(2) Philippians also provides a glimpse into the heart of this great apostle. From its outset it reveals the deep bond between Paul and the church. Although the Philippians were an example of his work as an apostle (about whom he would boast on the day of Christ, see 2:16), they were also his close friends. They were sharers in his ministry, brothers and sisters whom he longed for with the affection of Christ (1:8). Paul had a keen sense of responsibility for these believers, so much so that he conceded that he would survive his imprisonment for their benefit (1:25). Paul's sense of responsibility extended beyond the church to his coworkers. He expressed his relationship to Timothy in warm, familial terms (2:19), and admitted that concern over the health of Epaphroditus caused him a great deal of personal anxiety (2:28).

2. Date and Origin

One of the enigmatic issues facing the student of Philippians is the date and place of the book's origin. Four possible locations from which Philippians was written have been advocated. The traditional view has been the city of Rome, but Caesarea, Corinth, and Ephesus have also been discussed as possibilities. The overwhelming evidence points to either Rome or Caesarea, but adopting either of these two options is not without its problems.

Rome is the traditional source for the letter's origin. The primary external evidence for this comes from the second-century Marcionite Prologue, which sets the book in the time of Paul's Roman imprisonment. The letter is described there as Paul's words of praise to the church, carried by Epaphroditus.

As we begin to assess which option is most viable, internal evidence makes a number of points clear in regards to the letter's origin. Beginning in 1:7, Paul writes that this letter is being written from prison. The imprisonment is serious, for the apostle implies that his death may be imminent (2:17). In fact, he is struggling with his desire to be with Christ or to remain with the Philippians so that he may strengthen them (1:20–24).

Paul's imprisonment is with a palace guard or *praetorium*, assumed to be the elite corps of guards located in Rome (note also the reference to "Caesar's household," 4:22). The letter notes a number of trips to and from the city in which Paul was imprisoned (2:19, 24-25). The Philippians were undoubtedly alerted to Paul's imprisonment by a messenger bearing the unfortunate news. This prompted the Philippians to send Epaphroditus to assist Paul at his place of incarceration (2:25). A messenger from Paul then alerted the Philippians to the seriousness of Epaphroditus's illness. In response to the Philippians' concerns, Paul promised to send Timothy (2:19) and Epaphroditus (2:25) to them in yet another journey.

The primary thrust of arguments for either Corinth or Ephesus as the place of the letter's writing is the time it would have taken to make the journeys between Paul and his recipients if Rome were the place of writing—between 7–8 weeks each. This suggests that Paul's two-year Roman imprisonment is somewhat doubtful as the provenance of this letter. However, only two journeys for certain were made during the apostle's imprisonment: Epaphroditus's trip to bring relief to Paul (2:25), and the obvious return journey to Philippi by the messenger bearing news of Epaphroditus's condition (2:26). Another journey (bearing news to the Philippians of Paul's imminent imprisonment) could well have been made while Paul was en route to Rome. Moreover, were one to choose Ephesus or Corinth as the place of writing, there is no clear indication that Paul underwent the type of imprisonment there that is alluded to in Philippians.

Acts records three imprisonments for Paul: one in Philippi (Acts 16:23ff.), one in Caesarea (chs. 21–23), and one in Rome (28:30). Both Caesarea and Rome fit the internal data reasonably well. They both had *praetoria*—Rome's, of course, was the famous guard known by that name, while in Caesarea Luke notes that Paul was imprisoned in Herod's *praetorium* (23:25). The term "Caesar's household" can refer to the actual cadre of individuals serving the emperor in Rome or to the imperial civil service, located in major cities throughout the empire. Paul's reference to his defense of the gospel (Phil. 1:8) could allude to one of his meetings before Festus (Acts 21–23). However, Paul's sense of his imminent death and his feeling that his task was complete (1:16–17) do not echo the confident appeal to Caesar that he made in Caesarea, but seem more appropriate to the Roman imprisonment.

Paul's letter to the Philippians, then, is likely to have been written during the final segment of Paul's ministry, while he was imprisoned either in Caesarea or Rome. Although it is difficult to determine with absolute certainty, evidence weighs in favor of the traditional view of Rome. This would put the date of authorship between A.D. 60–62.

3. Genre

Of all of the Pauline letters, Philippians is the most warm and relational. It is obvious from even a cursory reading that Paul cares deeply for the Philippian church, and the mutuality of that feeling is reflected in their tangible expressions of care for him. The letter has resulted from the Philippians' generous response to Paul's needs as well as from his concern for their welfare.

There is some question as to whether Philippians is one letter or a composite of two. This problem comes about as a result of a proposed dual conclusion to the letter (3:1; 4:4). Note too the comment of Polycarp, who refers to Paul's "letters" in his *Letter to the Philippians* (see O'Brien, 12). Some scholars, therefore, see the letter as it is found today as the product of an editor, who combined at least two of Paul's letters.

Although this may seem a plausible explanation for the particular ending of the book, other factors need to be taken into consideration. It is not inconceivable that Paul, in writing such a personal letter, may have pursued a particular train of thought after 3:1—in much the same way that a person may abruptly change subjects in a personal conversation. After a diversion, then, he returns to his concluding comments (4:4). Furthermore, if an editor had in fact performed a "cut and paste" operation on Philippians, he did a rather poor job of it. One would expect such an individual to refine a letter, eliminating precisely those aspects that make it seem repetitive or cumbersome. Finally, there are no fragments of two separate letters in existence today. All existing manuscript evidence shows the book in much the same form as it appears today.

4. Themes

a. Joy

The overwhelming occurrence of the "joy" word group in the letter has led to Philippians being known as "The Epistle of Joy." The noun "joy" (*chara*) occurs five times (1:4, 25; 2:2, 29; 4:1), while the verb "rejoice" (*chairo*) occurs nine times (1:18 [2x]; 2:17, 18, 28; 3:1; 4:4 [2x], 10) and *synchairo* ("rejoice with") twice (2:17, 18). *Kauchema*, an etymologically unrelated word that denotes a joy-filled boast or glory, occurs twice in the letter (1:26; 2:16).

Joy governs Paul's outlook from the beginning of the letter to its conclusion. The apostle responds with joy to the successful proclamation of the gospel, regardless of the personal cost to himself (1:18), illustrating that joy is rooted in more than just one's circumstances. In fact, at one point in the letter he calls the Philippians to rejoice with him in their mutual sacrifice for the gospel of Christ (2:17). Both the prayers of the Philippians and the Holy Spirit's continued presence in his life (pointing to his vindication) gave Paul great joy (1:19). He further notes that his joy will be made complete by their unity (2:2).

In 1:25, joy is characteristic of the believer who exhibits a growing faith. In 4:4 Paul exhorts his hearers to "rejoice in the Lord." As their joy is rooted in a relationship with Christ, believers will be able to replace their anxiety with a confident trust in God. This is evidenced by their presenting needs to God in prayers and receiving God's peace (4:2–6). Paul's own life illustrates this. Even though he is in prison and unsure about the outcome of his trial, he is concerned that the believers rejoice with him "in the Lord" (3:1).

b. Servanthood

Another significant theme of this highly personal letter is that of servanthood. Philippians 2:5–11 paints a picture of Jesus, the Servant-Savior, that finds its Old Testament roots in Isaiah 53. Our Lord did not retain his rightful claims he had being God. Rather, he relinquished those claims and took on the additional nature of a servant, becoming God in flesh, humankind's Redeemer. His death on the cross was his supreme act of humility. The consequence of this attitude of servanthood was God's exaltation of Jesus, giving him a name above every name.

This theme surfaces throughout the letter. Already in 1:1, Paul refers to himself and Timothy as "servants" of Jesus. This reference stands in contrast to Paul's characteristic introduction of himself as apostle. Paul goes on to reflect the true nature of a servant in his deep concern for the church at Philippi (cf. 1:17)—a concern so great that Paul is willing to remain alive for their sakes (1:24). He extends this selfless attitude regarding those who preach the gospel with the intent of adding to Paul's suffering. Regardless of their motive, Paul asserts that he is content as long as Christ is being preached. The apostle's reflection on the value of his own achievements (3:7ff.) as well as his commitment to being content in every situation (cf. 4:11) reflects in his own life the image of Christ as servant.

Timothy and Epaphroditus are also examples of servanthood. Paul commends Timothy to the church both for his genuine interest in them (2:20) and for his commitment to serve Paul in the work of the gospel (2:22). Epaphroditus had been sent to serve Paul in Rome, ministering to the practical needs of the apostle. In so doing, this man risked his life for the sake of the gospel (2:30). In the middle of his own needs, he was deeply concerned that others would be anxious for his welfare (2:26)!

The recipients of this letter are also challenged to model this kind of servanthood. They are to be one in spirit and purpose, reflecting the attitude of Christ towards one another

2:1–2, 15). They are also called to emulate Paul's lifestyle (3:17). Paul's concern for the Philippians in this regard is so acute that he names two church leaders and calls for them to "agree with each other in the Lord" (4:2). In the same passage, he also asks another leader, whom he refers to as "loyal yokefellow," to ensure that this attitude is in fact mirrored in the lives of the church leaders at Philippi (4:3).

c. The Character of God

Paul says a number of things about the character of God in this letter. From the beginning, he portrays God in a warm, personal manner. God is first and foremost "our Father" (1:2), and the Philippians are his children (2:15). To reinforce this perspective, Paul refers to God as "my God" (1:3). God is the source of all grace (1:7), the One who is active in the sanctification of the believers at Philippi (1:6; 2:13) and is the guarantor of their ultimate salvation (1:28). Paul is keenly aware that God alone judges the motives and attitudes of the heart and calls on him to testify of Paul's love for these believers (1:8).

The true character of God is revealed through his sending of Jesus to be the Savior (2:5–11). God's vindication of Jesus through his resurrection and ascension reveals both his justice and sovereignty in bringing the plan of salvation to completion. The proclamation of this salvation—the gospel—is for Paul the proclamation of the very word of God (1:14). The message states that salvation is to be received through the imputation of God's righteousness, not through keeping the law. It is founded on the work of Christ and is based on faith (3:9).

It is because of this work of Christ that believers, who were once alienated from God, can now know him as "the God of peace" (4:9) and as the God who provides for the needs of his people (1:19), encouraging them to bring all their requests to him through every form of prayer (4:7). He actively directs the lives of believers (1:15) and breaks through the natural course of events to bring supernatural healing—showing precisely that kind of mercy on Epaphroditus by healing him from a near-fatal illness (2:27).

Paul is also aware of the responsibility believers have to fulfill the responsibilities demanded by this relationship with God. The Christian's worship is in the sphere of "the Spirit" (3:3). Furthermore, Paul is an example of one who wrestled with God's plans for his future (1:14–26), ultimately committing himself to God's sovereign purpose (1:27). Paul's concern was to finish well (3:12–14) and to have his friends in Philippi do the same, so that he would have just cause for boasting "on the day of Christ" (2:16).

Paul continually encourages the believers in Philippi to be of the same mind (cf. 2:2, 14; 4:2ff.). This attitude reflects God's desire for unity among his people (cf. Ps. 133), wholeheartedly devoted to serving him. The Philippians must maintain unity, working out their corporate salvation with reverence and awe (2:13). As with the nation of Israel, they must also reflect God's character and announce the good news of salvation to a world still alienated from him (2:14–16).

d. Conflict and Suffering

This letter addresses three areas of conflict or suffering that impacted the church at Philippi. (1) The first was external and concerned the church's relationship with the pagan culture and world surrounding it. That the Philippian church was experiencing pressure from the culture of a city that prided itself in its close ties to Rome should not be surprising. Paul and his companions experienced persecution at the inception of their ministry there (cf. Acts 16). His response to this type of suffering was to call his hearers to live as heavenly citizens in a culture where Roman citizenship meant everything (1:27; 3:20). Their call was to stand firm in their faith, unfrightened by opposition (1:28). In response to the pressure and persecution exerted by a pagan society, the church was called to live "without fault in a crooked and depraved generation" (2:15). Where the citizens of Philippi bowed their knees to lord Caesar, believers are reminded that all worship is due Christ, the true Lord, before whom all nations will ultimately bow (2:11).

(2) The Philippians were also experiencing a conflict with false teaching penetrating the church (or, at the very least, they were warned of its eventuality). The particular issue that Paul squared off against was the teaching of the Judaizers (cf. esp. Paul's letter to the Galatians). The proponents of this teaching advocated that

the Gentile believers had to adopt the Jewish system of keeping the law in order to be justified. The particular issue around which the conflict centered was the insistence that male Gentile converts undergo circumcision—a rite that symbolized membership in God's covenant community (Gen. 17:10).

Paul spares no mercy in countering this teaching. Unlike his response to persecution from outside the community, he calls the Philippians to recognize the futility of trying to attain righteousness by their own works. He repudiates these efforts, referring to them as "rubbish" (3:7). The apostle refers to these false teachers as "dogs," "mutilators of the flesh," and evildoers (3:2)—strong invectives, designed to offend their pride. In light of this false teaching, he again calls the Philippians to follow his example of pressing on to know Christ with all diligence (3:12–13).

(3) The final arena in which this church so loved by Paul was experiencing conflict was within their community. Two key church leaders in Philippi—Euodia and Syntyche (4:2)—appear to have had a significant disagreement. Paul's exhortation to these two factious sisters lacks the vehemence of his polemic against the Judaizers. He appeals to them to be like-minded; in fact, this appeal occurs throughout the letter, coupled with a call to cease complaining and arguing (2:14). Presumably this problem was widespread within the church. Paul's corrective here also includes a response to follow his own example as he responds to other believers with whom he has conflicts (cf. 1:12–18). Most important, their responsibility was to reflect the nature of Christ in their dealings with one another (see above).

OUTLINE

1. **Greeting** (1:1–2)
2. **Introductory Words of Appreciation and Prayer for the Philippians** (1:3–11)
   - **2.1.** Thanksgiving (1:3–6)
   - **2.2.** Note of Appreciation (1:7–8)
   - **2.3.** Prayer for the Philippians (1:9–11)
3. **Paul's Description of His Current Situation** (1:12–30)
   - **3.1.** Paul's Perspective on His Imprisonment (1:12–14)
   - **3.2.** The Importance of Proclaiming the Gospel (1:15–18a)
   - **3.3.** Paul's Understanding of His Imprisonment (1:18b–26)
   - **3.4.** Exhortation to the Philippians in Light of Paul's Suffering (1:27–30)
4. **Refocusing One's Behavior in Light of Christ's Example** (2:1–18)
   - **4.1.** Behavior in Light of Christian Experience (2:1–4)
   - **4.2.** Behavior in Light of Christ's Example (2:5–11)
   - **4.3.** Exhortations in Light of Christ's Example and the Christian's Experience (2:12–18)
5. **The Ministry of Paul's Associates** (2:19–30)
   - **5.1.** Timothy (2:19–24)
   - **5.2.** Epaphroditus (2:25–30)
6. **Warning Against Straying From the Gospel** (3:1–4:1)
   - **6.1.** Warning (3:1–4a)
   - **6.2.** Paul's Credentials (3:4b–6)
   - **6.3.** Paul's Overarching Purpose (3:7–14)
   - **6.4.** Perspective of False Teaching (3:15–16)
   - **6.5.** Concluding Comments in Light of the Prevalence of False Teaching (3:17–4:1)
7. **Concluding Exhortations** (4:2–9)
   - **7.1.** Personal (4:2–3)
   - **7.2.** Corporate (4:4–9)
8. **Paul's Gratitude for the Philippians' Gift** (4:10–20)
   - **8.1.** Commitment to Contentment (4:10–13)
   - **8.2.** Thanksgiving and Doxology (4:14–20)
9. **Paul's Farewell** (4:21–23)

COMMENTARY

1. Greeting (1:1–2)

This letter begins with a form not uncommon in personal letters written in the Greco-Roman world. Most letters in the ancient world began with an identification of the sender. In this leter, two senders are identified—"Paul and Timothy." Then Paul, in typical fashion, names he recipients: the entire body of believers in Philippi and their leaders. Finally the letter's opening contains a salutation, which is characteristically Pauline: "grace and peace."

It is important to note that Paul opens this letter in a manner different from most of his other letters. In general, Paul begins each letter with an apostolic designation or, as in Romans and Titus, with an identification of himself as both "servant" and "apostle" (though in 1 and 2 Thessalonians and Philemon he uses neither of these words). In Philippians, however, Paul simply refers to himself as "servant." This introduction sets the stage for a predominant theme in the letter: the need for the church at Philippi to mirror the servanthood of Christ.

The apostle's use of the word "servant," coupled with the absence of an assertion of apostolic authority in the letter, gives us the first of many glimpses at the cordial relationship that existed between Paul and this church. In his recent commentary Gordon Fee makes a significant contribution to our understanding of Philippians by noting that this letter is an example of a genre known as a friendship letter. Some of the characteristics of such a letter include: a greeting, a prayer, a discussion of issues pertaining to the sender's life, questions to the recipients, information about mutual friends, exchanges of greetings, and a closing wish for health (see Fee, 3). The use of the word "servant" also signals the absence of any serious polemic in Philippi, hence making an appeal to apostolic office unnecessary.

Paul also mentions Timothy in his introduction. This convention is only evident in Paul's early letters to the Thessalonians, where Paul identifies himself, Silas, and Timothy in a brief, nondescript introduction. Presumably Timothy served Paul in the capacity of an amanuensis (i.e., a secretary writing down Paul's words); in fact, some speculate that Timothy actually coauthored the book of Colossians with Paul. As Philippians continues, it becomes obvious that Timothy has moved beyond the role of mentoree to the apostle. When it comes to the work of the gospel, he is an equal with Paul—a co-servant, as it were.

Timothy was one of Paul's traveling companions, having initially joined the apostle in his second missionary journey (Acts 16:1ff.). This native of Lystra assisted Paul in Corinth (2 Cor. 1:19) as well as in Ephesus, where he eventually became overseer of the church (1 Tim. 1:3). Timothy also traveled with Paul to Jerusalem with the collection (Acts 20:4ff.) and later was with the apostle (now a prisoner) in Rome (cf. Phil. 1:1; Col. 1:1).

Philippians is addressed to all the Christians in Philippi. The emphasis of *all* should not be overlooked, given the existence of some leadership rivalry addressed by Paul later in the letter (4:2–3). The believers are referred to as "the saints" (*hagioi*), a favorite Pauline word, which is borrowed from the Old Testament image of Israel as God's chosen people. The nation had been "set apart" to serve God and reflect his holy character to the surrounding nations (Lev. 11:44–45). In a parallel manner, the Christians at Philippi were God's chosen people. Their standing (further defined by the phrase "in Christ Jesus") is due to the fact that they have been chosen by God and that the vicarious atonement of Jesus Christ has been applied to their lives. They now experience a restored relationship to God through Jesus Christ.

Paul then identifies a subgroup of the saints: "the overseers and deacons." The leadership roles identified and defined in the Pastoral Letters appear to be a part of the church structure at this time. In classical Greek, "overseers" (*episkopoi*) were those who gave supervision or protection; they later came to denote officials of the state. In the New Testament, the term came to be roughly synonymous with elder (*presbyteros*), one who presided over a congregation, no doubt exercising the spiritual gifts of governance and leadership (cf. Rom. 12:4–6). These individuals were appointed by the apostles (cf. Titus 1:5) and subsequently functioned as apostolic designates, in the same way as a vice-regal officer represented royalty in a colony where a king exercised his jurisdiction.

"Deacons" (*diakonoi*), a separate leadership group, have their precedent in church life drawn from the commissioning of the Seven in Acts 6. These individuals functioned as servants in the community, occupying themselves with many of the practical and benevolent tasks that the church was called to perform. It should be noted that both terms occur in the plural, an indication that leadership in the early church was not exercised by single individuals, but by a group equipped by the Holy Spirit for leadership.

This section concludes with Paul's characteristic greeting: "Grace and peace." The word "grace" (*charis*) denotes the entirety of God's saving activity in Jesus Christ, centering in his gift of salvation to those who place their faith in Christ. "Peace" is the typical Hebrew greeting (*shalom*), which carries with it a meaning far deeper than the cessation of conflict. It reflects a wish for well-being for the entire person. "Peace" points to "'harmony,' 'tranquility,' 'wholeness,' 'well-being,' 'salvation' of the total person, reconciliation of that person to God—peace at the deepest level" (Hawthorne, 11). The word order suggests that peace with God comes only as a result of having first experienced the grace of God (cf. Rom. 8:1).

2. Introductory Words of Appreciation and Prayer for the Philippians (1:3–11)

The depth of Paul's relationship with the church at Philippi becomes readily apparent in this section of the letter. This introduction follows a format similar to many of Paul's letters (see Rom. 1:8ff.; Eph. 1:3ff.; 1 Thess. 1:2ff.). Although examples of letters from the Greco-Roman world of this time period contain similar words of appreciation for their recipients, Paul builds on this form and carries it a step forward, making it an occasion for prayer on behalf of his hearers.

2.1. Thanksgiving (1:3–6)

Paul begins with an expression of thanks to God. "My God" highlights the warm tone of this letter and openness of the apostle's relationship with the Lord. The reason for this expression of thankfulness soon becomes apparent: his relationship with the church in Philippi. At every remembrance of them his heart rises to God in gratitude.

The phrase "every time I remember you" (v. 3) presents some grammatical difficulties. Should it be translated as in the NIV, or (as some suggest) "in your every remembrance of me" (i.e., referring to the Philippians' gifts for Paul rather than his prayer on their behalf)? The context of the passage (with Paul making further reference to his prayers in v. 4) points to the correctness of the NIV interpretation, and the apostle's use of the word "remembrance" in other contexts normally points to his prayers for others (cf. Rom. 1:9; 2 Tim. 1:3; Philem. 4).

Verse 4 highlights the nature of Paul's remembrance. The word for "prayer" here is not the one Paul usually uses (*proseuche*), but *deesis*, which refers to intercession rooted in a realization of another's need (see Hawthorne, 17). It is significant that later on Paul asserts with confidence that "my God will meet all your needs according to his glorious riches" (4:19). He is positive that God will hear and answer his prayers on their behalf.

Paul's prayers for the Philippians are offered in an attitude of "joy." This is the first occurrence of a term that, as noted in the introduction, is a significant theme of the letter. Paul's prayers reflect a joy that is rooted in his relationship with the risen Christ, but it is also manifested on account of his relationship with the church at Philippi.

This relationship has grown steadily from the time of Paul's earliest contact with the Philippians (Acts 16). "From the first day" the church had manifested an attitude of "partnership" in Paul's ministry in the proclamation of the gospel. This partnership (*koinonia*) was one of the concomitant evidences of the Spirit's outpouring on the day of Pentecost, where believers held all things in common in order to exercise care for the members of the fledgling church (Acts 2:44ff.). It will become clear that the most tangible thing in Paul's mind is the Philippians' acts of assistance while he was imprisoned (Phil. 4:10). Both this letter and Acts reveal that such *koinonia* was the norm in Paul's relationship with the church at Philippi.

The culmination of Paul's fond remembrance of the Philippians' partnership with him is his confident pronouncement of verse 6: God will bring the salvation he has begun in the lives of his hearers to full and final culmination at the return of Christ. Their specific "good work" of kindness caused Paul to reflect on the supreme work that it mirrored—God's gracious provision of salvation in Christ. This work has God as its author and will continue until "the day of Christ Jesus." This phrase is rooted in the Old Testament concept of the Day of the Lord (cf. Isa. 2:12; Ezek. 13:13; Zeph. 1:7, 14). But whereas the Old Testament motif predominantly depicted a dreaded future judgment for sin, the picture behind Paul's use of the phrase is one filled with hope and anticipation for the believers; it represents the culmination of their salvation.

2.2. Note of Appreciation (1:7–8)

Following his eloquent expression of thanksgiving, Paul's greeting takes on almost a defensive tone. It appears as if he is anticipating the Philippians' response to his gracious words to be one of surprise or even self-deprecation (cf. vv. 5–6). Thus, Paul asserts that his comments to them are perfectly warranted—it is "right" or just (*dikaios*). It would mirror the Philippians' response to him if the situation were reversed. It is justified because Paul's feelings for these believers are deeply felt. The word *phroneo* ("feel, think") is a distinctively Pauline term, occurring ten times in this letter (1:7; 2:2[2x], 5; 3:15[2x],19; 4:2,10[2x]). This word group indicates both an underlying mental attitude and the resultant behavior that follows (cf. O'Brien, 67)

Paul elaborates his feelings for his recipients: He has all of them "in my heart." The words Paul uses could also be translated to make the Philippians the subject of the phrase: "since you have me in your heart." But recent commentators have accepted the traditional rendering of the phrase as preferred (see Fee, 90; O'Brien, 68). The word "heart," both in Greek and Hebrew thought, pointed to the seat of a person's will and emotions; it refers to the depth of care that Paul had for these Christians. The key phrase that illuminates Paul's gratitude is the fact that the Philippians participated jointly (*synkoinonos*) in God's grace with him. For Paul, grace ultimately points to God's provision of salvation through Jesus Christ. The specific example of this "larger" grace is the Philippians' assistance of him while he was imprisoned in Rome.

The nature of Paul's life in Rome is described in the phrase immediately preceding (v. 7): "whether I am in chains or defending and confirming the gospel." The reality of Paul's imprisonment was that he did in fact find himself in chains, both in transit to Rome (Acts 27) and in his current place of confinement. This imprisonment allowed opportunity for Paul to give a reasoned defense of the gospel. In so doing, he presented himself as a legal witness, furnishing a guarantee as to its veracity (cf. 28:23).

In verse 8, Paul calls on God to serve as his witness (cf. also Rom. 1:9; 2 Cor. 1:23) in regard to his love for the church at Philippi. The purity of his inner motives in ministering to the church are known only to God and attested by him. This sentiment is further described as a longing that reflects the very "affection of Christ Jesus." The word for "affection" (*splanchna*; lit., bowels, intestines) refers to the organs of the human body that were thought to be the location of the will, the emotions, and the personality of a person. This term is used in the Synoptics for the compassion of Jesus (cf. Matt. 14:14; 20:34; Mark 6:34; 9:22) and for a person's response to those in need (Luke 10:33)—a response that reflects the compassion of God. Paul's compassion for the Philippians comes from a source beyond himself—from Christ.

2.3. Prayer for the Philippians (1:9–11)

Paul concludes his greeting with a prayer for the Philippians. The abridged content of the prayer is simply this: that their "love" (*agape*) may grow and grow so that it may develop in a greater and more profound way. The significance of this simple request should not be overlooked in light of the fact that love is the primary means by which God deals with humankind. His love motivated the sending of his Son, Jesus, to provide our salvation (Rom. 5:8). God's very nature is love (1 John 4:8). This love, Paul notes, will abide forever (1 Cor. 13:13).

Paul prays for something to occur concurrently with the Philippians' growth in love: growth in Christian "knowledge and depth of insight." "Knowledge" refers to an awareness of God's will as revealed through the gospel; "depth of insight" refers to the practical application of that truth—a moral discrimination or wisdom. In other words, Paul is concerned that the Philippians' love will truly reflect the gospel and be practical in its outworking.

As a result of this increase in love, knowledge, and insight, the Philippians will be able to "discern" those things that are "best" or most appropriate for fulfilling their calling as Christians. In current terms, we might say "that God [will] help you to focus your energies on those things which are truly important" (cf. Fee, 101). Christian love is not blind but discriminating.

Furthermore, the infusion of God's love and wisdom will keep them "pure and blameless until the day of Christ" (see also 2 Tim. 1:12). The keeping power of this love is seen in its preservation from impurity and blame (v. 10b). "Pure" points to a garment that could be held up to inspection by sunlight; "blameless" refers to that which does not cause one to stumble. The two words point to the inward integrity and outward conduct of Paul's hearers (cf. Hawthorne, 28). One impacts the individual, one the entire community.

Verse 11 denotes the positive consequence of Paul's prayer in the lives of his hearers: They will be filled with "the fruit of righteousness" (also called "the fruit of the Spirit" in Gal. 5:22). This fruit "comes through Jesus Christ" and reflects his very nature. The result will be that God receives "glory and praise."

3. Paul's Description of His Current Situation (1:12–30)

Paul's letter continues to follow the common pattern of letters of his day. After the greeting, letters moved into a detailed description of the sender's particular circumstances.

In this section, Paul uses his own suffering in a paradigmatic fashion, to model for the Philippians a Christian's response to persecution. It falls neatly into four segments, in which Paul gives his perspective on his current imprisonment (1:12–14), underscores the primary importance of the gospel's proclamation (1:15–18a), reflects on what he feels will be the outcome of his current imprisonment (1:18b–26), and concludes with an exhortation to the church in light of his own experience (1:27–30). This last section serves as a bridge to the central portrayal of Christ as an example to follow (2:1–11).

3.1. Paul's Perspective on His Imprisonment (1:12–14)

Paul begins this section by addressing his hearers with a favorite term for fellow Christians, "brothers" (and sisters, no doubt), as he draws their attention to his understanding of God's purpose for his imprisonment. Paul did not respond to imprisonment with fear, anger, or even denial. In a situation that at first glance might appear to thwart God's best purpose for the apostle's ministry, Paul manifests a confident assurance in the sovereignty of God. Regardless of what he or anyone else felt about the situation, Paul is positive that this imprisonment has really served to advance the gospel (1:12). The word Paul uses to describe the successful proclamation of the gospel ("advance") has its origin in the Greek navigational world picturing a ship making headway or driving something forward by means of blows (Balz and Schneider, 3:157). Paul understands God's ability to work what would appear to be the most problematic of circumstances for his own will (cf. Rom. 8:28).

The gospel is advanced in two areas (vv. 13–14): through Paul's own sphere of influence, and through those believers who have taken courage from Paul's experience in chains. (1) Paul was able to make it clear that he was in chains because of his faith in Christ. His imprisonment in Rome took the form of house arrest, with the apostle under the supervision of various members of Caesar's elite guard. Paul was allowed to receive guests (Acts 28:23) and to carry on his public ministry even though he was in chains and under guard (28:16ff.). While imprisoned, the apostle was required to assume responsibility for his living expenses (28:30).

During this time, then, it can be reasonably assumed that Paul regularly shared details of his story with the many visitors he received. The effect of this continual proclamation of the gospel was similar to the ripple of waves seen when a rock is thrown into a pond. Ever-widening circles of influence moved beyond Paul to his friends, his guards, their friends and families, until the story influenced the entire palace administration.

The phrase "for Christ" (*en Christo*; lit., "in Christ") is worthy of note (v. 13). The preposition is not the one that gives the sense of "on behalf of" (*hyper*); rather, the apostle uses the preposition "in" (*en*). In other words, even in prison, Paul is deeply conscious of the fact that he is united with Christ. Part of the cost of his being in Christ happened to be his being in prison, but imprisonment and its attendant perils did nothing to change Paul's relationship with the risen Savior. His current situation was simply another opportunity to live out his commitment to serve the One who was the supreme example of servanthood.

(2) Paul's imprisonment also served to illustrate the words of Jesus, "Unless a kernel

f wheat . . . dies, it remains only a single seed. But if it dies, it produces many seeds" (John 12:24). As a result of what had happened to Paul, a majority of the brothers in the Lord began proclaiming "the word of God," the Christian message in its entirety (cf. Hawthorne, 35).

Their proclamation of the gospel was a feat of bold undertaking. More than ever before, these believers fearlessly dared to proclaim the good news. The Holy Spirit used the crisis of Paul's imprisonment to further empower his followers in their preaching. This is not unlike what occurred immediately following Pentecost in Jerusalem (Acts 3:23–31). The encouragement "the brothers" received was more than a polite "pat on the back"; it was a confident assurance or persuasion. A profound paradox illustrated throughout church history is that as God's people are oppressed or persecuted, their boldness in sharing their faith increases, and the church grows and is strengthened.

3.2. The Importance of Proclaiming the Gospel (1:15–18a)

Paul notes that the preaching of the gospel since his imprisonment has fallen along two lines. Some were proclaiming the good news because of their love of Paul and their commitment to the message, but others were doing so out of motives marred by personal ambition and an apparent dislike for Paul. Regardless of the situation or motivation behind this proclamation of the gospel, however, Paul rejoices because Christ is being preached.

The language of verse 15 sets up a contrast. On the one hand, there were those who proclaimed Christ out of envy and rivalry. The word "envy" points to an emotion, an internal attitude of the heart, while "rivalry" refers to open factions and quarreling—the overt fruit of the inner attitude of envy. On the other hand, others were proclaiming Christ out of goodwill (*eudokia*, see 2:13). This word most often refers to God's good pleasure (e.g., Eph. 1:9), but it can also refer to a person's good wishes or disposition (Balz and Schneider, 2:75).

In other words, some individuals were preaching the gospel out of pure motives, others out of impure motives. The activity of preaching (*kerysso*) described the public proclamation of the gospel; this verb denoted the function of a herald. It was complemented by another popular word for preaching, *euangelizomai* ("to proclaim the good news"), which focused more on the content of the message preached rather than the activity of preaching.

Verses 16–17 further elaborate on the two groups referred to in verse 15. Those proclaiming out of goodwill were motivated by love; they had a clear understanding that Paul's imprisonment was for "the defense [*apologia*] of the gospel." *Apologia* was a technical term pointing to the presentation of a judicial defense, which later came to include both a legal and philosophical defense of the faith. Note that the word describing Paul's confinement ("put") can carry the sense of an assignment or a destiny. Paul uses this word to reflect his own understanding that he is in prison according to God's specific plan and purpose.

The other group was proclaiming the gospel out of "selfish ambition" (v. 17). This word was considered somewhat pejorative; the nobility often used it to denote those who worked for a daily wage and were motivated by personal survival; they, by contrast, were free to donate their skills and resources to whatever cause they deemed worthy of their noble effort (cf. Fee, 212). Paul allowed that these preachers with tainted motives were, however, still proclaiming the gospel, despite their animosity towards him. Paul uses yet another word (*katangello*) for the proclamation of the gospel here.

Who were those preaching the gospel with wrong motives? Were they Paul's ongoing opponents, the Judaizers, for whom the keeping of Jewish ceremonial law was indispensable for salvation? These are the ones whom Paul angrily refers to as "dogs" and "mutilators of the flesh" (3:2). But none of Paul's imprecations against the Judaizers is echoed here. He refers to both groups mentioned as "brothers," indicating that they are all fellow believers (v. 14). It is obvious that even in the early church there were evidences of interpersonal conflict and those who had insincere motives.

3.3. Paul's Understanding of His Imprisonment (1:18b–26)

Paul moves on to supply the answer for a question he may be hearing the Philippians echo: "What is going to happen to you, Paul?" He asserts that he will maintain a posture of joy despite his circumstances. Because of the Philippians' prayers and the activity of the Spirit in his life, he knows he will be delivered. His deliverance will take the form of either a release from prison or death. The former option is merely a foretaste or temporary reprieve of the latter, when God's full and final purposes for Paul's life will be realized.

Paul's opening words echo his confidence: "I will continue to rejoice." Clearly his joy is not contingent on his circumstances; rather, it is rooted in the success of the gospel. As the gospel is proclaimed (regardless of motive), Paul's calling as an apostle and vision for the spread of the good news throughout the Gentile world is being fulfilled, and he can thus rejoice.

In verse 19, the apostle expresses confidence that the situation he finds himself in will ultimately result in "my deliverance" (*soteria*; lit., "salvation"). This phrase echoes Job 13:16, where Job asserts his trust in God that his trial will ultimately result in his deliverance (with the sense of vindication). As with Job, the salvation Paul anticipates is no doubt eschatological in nature and will ultimately vindicate the gospel. However, the context of Paul's words cannot be overlooked, and it appears as if Paul is also anticipating some form of deliverance from his current imprisonment (cf. vv. 25–26).

Paul further asserts that this confidence has come from two sources (v. 19): the prayers of the Philippians and the "help given by the Spirit" (lit., "help of the Spirit"). The word "help" (*epichoregia*) denoted a husband's provision for his wife. It later came to refer to the lavish patronage of a wealthy benefactor in outfitting a choir for a festival or a religious occasion. We should also note that Paul is not referring to a supply merely given *by* the Holy Spirit but rather a supply that *is* the Holy Spirit himself. In other words, he has experienced an overwhelming presence of the Holy Spirit in the middle of his current difficulty, and with that presence he may have even received some revelatory insight regarding the outcome of his imprisonment.

The Holy Spirit is "the Spirit of Christ Jesus." Paul draws a close identity between the Holy Spirit and the risen Christ. In 2 Corinthians 3:17–18, Paul identified the risen Christ and the Spirit in terms of experience—that is to say, the experience of the Spirit is the experience of the risen Christ. In 1 Corinthians 15:45, Paul reinforces that the ministry of th[e] risen Christ is accomplished through th[e] agency of the Spirit. Ontologically, the two ar[e] separate persons, but in terms of the believer'[s] experience, they are closely related. For exam[-]ple, both the Spirit and the risen Christ are spo[-]ken of as interceding for believers (Rom. 8:26[,] 34). Paul speaks of the love that both Chris[t] and the Spirit bestow (8:35; 15:30). Believer[s] are children of God by the Spirit and childre[n] of God in Christ (8:14–15). Sanctificatio[n] occurs in Jesus (1 Cor. 1:2) and in the Spiri[t] (Rom. 15:16). In short, all the blessing[s] bestowed by Christ are conveyed by the Spirit.

Verse 20 begins Paul's own wrestling wit[h] the situations he faced. His overarching senti[-]ment, his "hope-filled eager anticipation" (O'Brien, 113), is that regardless of the out[-]come, Christ will be exalted in his body. Hi[s] concern in this regard is that he will not b[e] ashamed; that is, in the presence of God, h[e] will be vindicated (the idea of vindication fro[m] shame is common in the Psalms; cf. Ps. 35:26–27). Also, he wishes Christ to be openly an[d] courageously glorified through his trial. Not[e] the continually shifting focus of Paul's though[t] here—future vindication, yet open and courageous proclamation in the present.

This shifting of perspective continues in verse 21: To continue to live is Christ. That is to say, for the apostle, his walk with Christ and his ministry were inextricably linked with life itself. Death was gain or profit simply because it was the realization of everything for which he had lived his life. Continuing with this thought in verse 22, the apostle reflects on a continued life in the flesh, that is, with the frailty of physical life. His ongoing physical existence would be nothing more and nothing less than total devotion to Christ. All he does will be fruitful labor, as its focus will be on those things that are eternal. Almost as though he is anticipating a question about his preferred alternative, he responds that he cannot tell, deferring that issue to God, who holds the destiny of all life in his hands. Paul's future is not his choice, nor is it the choice of the Roman empire, as powerful as it may be. Paul's destiny is in God's hands alone.

Even though Paul's ultimate destiny is in God's hands, vacillating between the two time horizons—the present and the future—created a tension within Paul. The word "torn" (v. 23) ictures the interaction of two opposing forces. ts figurative sense points to a preoccupation, lmost to the point of distress, of choosing etween two alternatives. The first has a future rientation: to die or to depart this life. Paul's hoice of words in describing death as a departure" pictures striking a camp or weigh-ng anchor to return home. Death for Paul was ot a plunge into an abyss, but a journey home, o where he would be united with Jesus Christ. 'he apostle leaves no doubt that his death vould yield an immediate audience in the resence of Christ, which was "better by far" or him than to go on living.

The apostle realized, however, that there vas more to consider in the situation than his wn interests. Again, the compelling picture of Christ's servanthood (see the introduction and omments on 2:5–11) motivated Paul to think of others. Of the two alternatives Paul envi-ioned, it is most beneficial for the Philippians or "more necessary") that Paul remain alive 1:24). Fully persuaded of their need for him, Paul seems confident that he will remain alive nd continue with them (see Fee, 152). In other vords, Paul envisions at least some short-term elief from his imprisonment. The purpose of is returning to them is to see the Philippians dvance ("progress") and rejoice in their faith.

As a result of his return, Paul knows the Philippians will boast (*kauchema*, trans. "joy" n NIV in v. 26) in Christ. The *kauchema* word group, occurring some sixty times in the New Testament, is used fifty-five times in Paul's writings alone. In its negative sense, it refers to prideful gloating; but in its positive sense, it denotes a joyful response of confidence, resulting from putting one's faith and trust in God. The word here does not point to empty actions of a pompous fool but finds its roots in the person and work of Jesus Christ alone.

3.4. Exhortation to the Philippians in Light of Paul's Suffering (1:27–30)

In what appears to be a sobering submission of his will to the overarching plan of God in his current situation, Paul balances his confident assertion of verses 24–26 with a word of caution. Regardless of what his future holds, the Philippian church has its own responsibility to live out the truths of the gospel. The challenge to "conduct [them]selves" (v. 27; lit., "live as citizens") in a manner worthy of the gospel is significant since these believers were residents of a colony of the Roman empire (see the introduction). The citizens of Philippi tried to emulate the people of Rome in the way they conducted their lives. Paul thus uses this term to remind the Christians in that city that they were citizens of a heavenly empire, which had more bearing on their lives than their fleeting relationship with Rome (cf. also 3:20).

Paul challenges the Philippians to live in a manner worthy of the gospel whether he is present with them or not. He goes on to define that lifestyle: They should be united, standing firm in one Spirit (v. 27; one of the results of the outpouring of the Holy Spirit on the believers in Jerusalem was unity, cf. Acts 2:42ff.). Only the word of the Holy Spirit can bring and maintain the unity required for the church to move forward. Such unity will enable believers to fight together for an issue much larger than their petty interpersonal conflicts—that is, the message of the gospel (the word "faith" here points to the content of the message about Jesus). The word "contend" (*synathleo*) was used in the context of both war and athletic events. A current analogy might be seen in the phrase "work as a team."

Another facet of the Philippians' "stand[ing] firm" should be their refusal to be intimidated by those who opposed the gospel (v. 28). This verse contains the first reference in this letter to the Philippians' suffering. Paul does not define the nature of their suffering. But if the experience of the apostle and his companions on their first trip to Philippi is any indication, opposition from this devoutly loyal Roman city would have continued to impact the church. The influence of the empire, with its emperor cult, would have been felt in Philippi.

The attitude of the opponents of these believers in rejecting the gospel will result in God's judgment (v. 28)—the ultimate consequence of rejecting Christ and his messengers. Paul knew this only too well when he realized on the Damascus Road that by persecuting the church, he was persecuting Christ (Acts 9:5). Conversely, the persecution stands as an indicator that the believers in Philippi will experience ultimate salvation because of their confident faith in Christ. For Paul the concept of salvation contained three aspects: past (justification), present (sanctification), and future (glorification). Here he is pointing believers to their future salvation.

These ruins at Philippi are from the Agora, the marketplace, that dates back to the Roman era when the city was an important military center. Note the carving of a soldier.

Moreover, the Philippians have been graciously given the privilege not only to believe, but also to experience suffering for the sake of Christ (v. 29). This echoes the words of Jesus as he warned his disciples that his servants will not be greater than their master, but they too will be called on to suffer for him (John 15:20). Here Paul makes clear that being a partner in the gospel entails sharing in the suffering. In verse 30, he brings the paradigmatic function of this section to completion: The Philippians saw and heard how Paul responded to suffering for the sake of the gospel (see Acts 16), and this would in turn enable them to process their own experience.

4. Refocusing One's Behavior in Light of Christ's Example (2:1–18)

Paul moves from a discussion of his imprisonment and how it has served as a paradigm for the Philippians' response to *external* suffering to a focus on their lives as they relate to *internal* affairs of the church. It appears from comments throughout the letter (e.g., 4:1–3) that there were some minor problems within the life of the congregation, the "epicenter" of which lay in and around the leadership (esp. Euodia and Syntyche, cf. 4:2). Paul begins remedial action directed towards the congregation at large; later he addresses specific situations. He challenges the believers in Philippi to live in unity in light of their Christian experience (2:1–4). He then sets Christ before them as the supreme example of humility and servanthood (2:5–11). Finally, he gives some practical admonitions for them in their relationships with one another, calling them to live devoted lives whether he is with them or not (2:12-18).

4.1. Behavior in Light of Christian Experience (2:1–4)

Verses 1–4 comprise a single sentence in the Greek text, which makes any English rendering a little awkward. The simple flow of the exhortation is this: "Since you all share a comıon Christian experience [v. 1], make my joy omplete [v. 2a] by sharing an attitude and festyle similar with that common experience vv. 2b–4]."

These exhortations or conditions (v. 1) hould be seen as an appeal to a common real-ty they share as a result of being Christians. 'he idea of "if you have . . ." may better be xpressed as "since you have. . . ." Paul is not etting out an exhortation that is contingent on ertain realities being true in their lives. Rather, e is challenging them under the assumption hat such conditions do in fact exist. This com-non experience consisted of: encouragement rom being one in Christ, comfort from God's ove, fellowship of the Spirit, and tenderness nd compassion.

(1) The phrase "encouragement [*paraklesis*] rom being united with Christ" points to all the lessings that the Philippians have received as result of their salvation experience. Paul's hought can be interpreted as referring back to he common consolation they have received rom Christ as they went through various trials pointing back to 1:15ff.). More likely, how-ver, the phrase carries the sense of being equiv-lent to "salvation," experienced in the sphere f Christ (cf. O'Brien, 171). It should be noted hat the term Paul normally uses to point to the lessings of salvation is not *paraklesis*, but *haris* (grace). The phrase "in Christ" occurs ome 150 times in Paul; it is virtually absent rom the rest of the New Testament. It points o believers' position as a result of their expe-ience of salvation through faith in Jesus Christ.

(2) The next condition to which Paul refers s "comfort from [God's] love" (lit., "comfort f love"). The word "comfort" (*paramythion*) ictures much the same thing as *paraklesis* loes, possibly with a sense of "incentive." Love, of course, is the word *agape*, which lenotes the manner of love God the Father howed the world both by sending his Son to ring the gift of salvation (John 3:16) and by alling Christians the "children of God" 1 John 3:1). The inclusion of God, Christ, and he Spirit in this sentence parallels Paul's hought in his benediction of 1 Corinthians 13:14, which enumerates the three persons of he Trinity and the characteristic terms by which they relate to believers.

(3) The third expression, "fellowship *koinonia*] with the Spirit" is another important aspect of the believer's experience. *Koinonia* among Christians was a characteristic of the early church (Acts 2:42ff.), which owed its inception to the acts of the Holy Spirit. Note that this fellowship is not only one that the Holy Spirit brings, but also a fellowship that consists in their participation in the Holy Spirit himself. The working of the Spirit in their midst, with his gifts, manifestations, and power, is what makes up their fellowship with him.

(4) The final condition, "tenderness and compassion," is difficult. The word the NIV translates "tenderness" (*splanchna*; see comments on 1:8) refers to emotions coming deep from within one's being. Elsewhere in Paul's letters, "compassion" (*oiktirmos*) refers to God's mercy (Rom. 12:1; 2 Cor. 1:3). Is the focus of this word on the Philippians' love for each other (cf. Col. 3:12) or on God's compassion for them? In this passage, God has in fact birthed in their hearts tenderness and compassion, a work whose focus no doubt points outward, to their solidarity and commitment to one another.

In light of these realities, Paul challenges his hearers to "make [his] joy complete." The idea behind making something complete is bringing it to fulfillment or to its ultimate goal. In Philippians, Paul notes that he experienced joy in suffering, joy in being remembered in his time of need by the Philippians, and joy in the gospel's being preached. For him, the crowning joy is that the church, the redeemed community, will live out the reality of the gospel.

After appealing to the Philippians' shared salvation experience, Paul challenges them to mirror a number of qualities in their lives (vv. 2b–4), all of which hinge on or expand the first one: "being like-minded" (v. 2b). This expression points to much more than sharing common thoughts or opinions; it denotes one's total thought and emotive processes, which are ultimately reflected in one's lifestyle. For Paul, there was no disparity between a person's thoughts and ensuing lifestyle—they were bound up as one.

A characteristic of like-mindedness is that the believers should have "the same love" for one another. Paul urges the Philippians to love one another because they have all received the same love from God (2:1). Being "one in spirit and purpose" literally translates, "singleness of soul, having your minds set on one thing." This phrase emphasizes the importance of purity of motives and goals. Recall how Paul has already acknowledged those who are preaching the gospel out of mixed motives (cf. 1:15ff.).

In verse 3, Paul challenges the Philippians to move toward a lifestyle that will not mirror the characteristics of his opponents. "Selfish ambition" was one of the motives he identified in those who preached the gospel hoping to add to his suffering (1:17). Coupled with this, "vain conceit" (*kenodoxia*) was also to be avoided. This word literally means "empty glory," denoting no doubt an attempt to take for oneself the glory meant for God. Such an attitude ultimately reflects one's attitude towards others. Note how in Paul's description of Christ in 2:5–11, he identifies him as one who empties himself (*kenoo*) and later receives glory (*doxa*) from God, having chosen the path of obedience and servanthood.

The remedy for selfish ambition is adopting humility in one's outlook (v. 3b). (This no doubt triggered the lengthy Christ hymn that follows.) In the Greco-Roman world, an attitude of humility was despised, seen as a characteristic of an individual of low birth or of a slave. This would not be a stance easily adopted by citizens of a city proud of their Roman citizenship, such as the people of Philippi. In its biblical sense, humility is the only appropriate posture to take toward God. Only as an individual humbles himself or herself will God lift that person up, whereas those who are filled with pride will be brought low by God. An attitude of humility makes one take a realistic view of oneself and truly value the role and the importance of others (cf. Rom. 12:3ff.). Paul has no room for a false humility that bows and scrapes for the sake of personal gain.

Paul's final exhortation in this section (v. 4) deals with the Philippians' goals. The idea contained within the word "look" (*skopeo*) suggests looking towards something or looking with a goal in mind. The Philippians are not just to look out for those things that concern and interest them; they are to set their focus "also [on] the interests of others." Again note the balance here in Paul: The desired focus is not on others' affairs to the exclusion of oneself, but a true sharing or *koinonia*—a focus on others as well as oneself. This attitude of being mindful of others' needs has both a forward and backward focus in terms of its placement in the letter. It looks back to Paul's example of puttin the Philippians' needs first (choosing to remai with them, 1:25), and looks forward to Christ example of not feeling that the prerogatives c deity were "something to be grasped" and ut lized for his own purposes (2:6).

4.2. Behavior in Light of Christ's Example (2:5–11)

These verses are pivotal in this letter. The focus primarily on the attitude of Christ as a example for the Philippians to emulate. A such, they address the ongoing problem c infighting alluded to in the letter. Scholars hav questioned whether 2:5–11 is a surviving frag ment of an early Christian hymn. The prevai ing view has been that these verses are an earl hymn about Christ, written with a didactic c kerygmatic purpose in mind. Opinions var among scholars, however, when it comes to th literary analysis of the hymn.

Although the idea of the passage as bein a surviving vestige of apostolic worship i appealing, that view does present some diffi culties. (1) The entire hymn does not fit neatl into the procrustean bed scholars have mad for it. For example, it has been argued that th last phrase of verse 8 ("even death on a cross" disrupts the flow of the passage. Consequently many have argued that it is an addition by Paul (2) Viewing the "hymn" as an early Christia kerygmatic or didactic tool does not do justic to the context of which it is part. It is clear fron the progress of Paul's argument that his pur pose for including it (or writing it) is not pri marily to present an eloquent Christolog (though it is that), but to remind the Philippi ans of the supreme example of humility Almost in anticipation of their revulsion at th thought of something so "culturally incorrect as humility, he shows the purpose for Christ' humbling himself was to fulfill God's will God ultimately vindicated Christ by exaltin him, and the entire process that verses 6–1 chronicles was for the glory of God the Fathe (v. 11). (3) Note also that it is not beyond th ability of Paul, under the inspiration of th Spirit, to construct literature of the nature see here (cf. 1 Cor. 13).

Paul begins by noting Christ's frame o mind and his ensuing lifestyle, which th Philippians are encouraged to pursue. (Th phrase "Your attitude should be the same a

. . ." translates a form of *phroneo*; see comment on 1:7.) The phrase "Your [plural] attitude" points to the fact that this attitude should permeate the fabric of their Christian community.

The inclusion of the words "as that of Christ Jesus" is literally "of Christ Jesus." There is some uncertainty as to the interpretation of this phrase. Are the Philippians called to have the same attitude toward one another as they manifest towards Christ (supplying the sense "which *you have* in Christ Jesus")? Or are the Philippians called to manifest the same attitude that Jesus manifested (supplying the sense "which *was* in Christ Jesus")? Given the context and the purpose of the passage, the second option seems more appropriate, so that Paul is challenging the Philippians to mirror what they have seen in Christ (cf. Fee, 200ff.: O'Brien, 210ff.).

In contemplating the attitude of Jesus Christ, Paul launches into one of the most complete Christological passages of the New Testament. According to him, Jesus was first and foremost a divine being. "In very nature" and form he was God (v. 6). The word the NIV translates "nature" is *morphe*, which, in extrabiblical use, denotes an outward manifestation that corresponds to an inward nature. Ascertaining the precise meaning of the term here is difficult, partly because verses 6–7 are the only occurrences of this word in the New Testament (aside from a later reading in Mark 16:12). Hawthorne appropriately suggests that Christ was "the essential nature and character of God" (84). The verb "being" is not the usual verb "to be." Rather, Paul uses *hyparcho*, which means "to exist" and suggests that Christ existed from eternity.

The concept of *morphe* is further developed in the latter part of verse 6, where Paul asserts that Jesus had "equality with God" (lit., "the being equal with God"). The term "equality," then, is not used in an adjectival sense, but in an adverbial one—that is to say, "Jesus, equally being God." This deity was something Jesus refused to recognize as his inalienable right. He laid aside the rights (not his deity) and did not champion them.

The word "grasp" (*harpagmos*) has been defined as to seize or snatch something, often in a violent way. There has been considerable debate as to its precise meaning. Two predominant views have emerged. (1) *Harpagmos* should be translated in such a way as to denote that Jesus did not possess deity and viewed it as a status that could be snatched or stolen. (2) Jesus was in fact God, but he did not view that status as something that he had to cling to at all costs. Equality with God was not something to be grasped in a greedy manner and used for his own gain. Rather, Jesus poured himself out for others.

Although lexically either interpretation can stand, the latter one fits the context better (for further discussion, cf. Silva, 117–18; O'Brien, 215–16). Jesus, whose very nature was God, did not think that that status had to be tenaciously retained for some personal advantage. Again, note the impact these words would have had on Paul's hearers, who prided themselves in their Roman citizenship with all its attendant rights and privileges. Instead of amassing and exercising his privileges, Jesus gave until he was empty. The solution to the Philippians' unity problems was in their adoption of this mindset of Jesus.

The question of which meaning of *harpagmos* should be applied is further illuminated in verse 7. Jesus "made himself nothing"—a function that presupposes he was deity. This phrase has stood at the center of some controversies and even heresies concerning the person of Jesus Christ. What exactly did Paul mean when he said Christ "made himself nothing"? Did he empty himself of "all but love," as Charles Wesley penned in his popular hymn "Amazing Love"? How does Jesus' emptying affect our understanding of his incarnation?

As with the rest of this section, part of the answer lies in the following phrase (v. 7b): Jesus emptied himself by his assuming the nature of a servant. The mystery of the Incarnation begins to unfold—Jesus, the second member of the Trinity, does not lay aside his deity. God cannot divorce himself from his very nature. Rather, Jesus' emptying must be seen in the fact that he as God poured himself into the mold of a servant. This is further implied by Paul's use of the word "taking." The "nature" (cf. the use of the word *morphe* again) Christ chose to assume was that of a slave. He did not simply appear as a slave; he was very much a slave. Here we have one who was "in very nature God" taking on an additional "very nature," that "of a servant." This summarizes the twofold nature of the Incarnation: Christ was at once fully God, yet fully human.

The question has been raised as to whether Paul is alluding here to Isaiah 52–53 (the familiar "Suffering Servant of Yahweh" passage). Although this parallel is not without grounds elsewhere in Scripture, the words used here and in the LXX make the connection somewhat obtuse. In the LXX, the servant of Yahweh is rendered *pais kyriou*. In Philippians, however, Paul uses the common word for slave (*doulos*) to describe Jesus. This picture of common slavery would have been seen as the ultimate form of humiliation in the eyes of Paul's hearers—God becoming a common slave, with no rights or privileges.

The emptying is further defined in the latter part of verse 7: Jesus Christ was made "in human likeness." The verb translated "being made" (*ginomai*) contrasts with the word *hyparcho* in verse 6, in that it implies a coming into being or a becoming. The word "likeness" (*homoioma*) is an ambiguous one, for it can have the sense of being an exact duplicate, an identity, or an equivalent. The word is perhaps deliberately ambiguous, allowing for Jesus to be similar to human beings, yet not identical to them in every respect. That is, Jesus was at once like a human being, yet as God he was also without sin. Note, however, that the main thrust of the word is not ontological, but the reinforcement of the fact that the One who was God now became man.

Verse 8 pictures the life and ministry of Jesus in microcosm. In Fee's terms, Jesus "was seen to have been a man" (215). Even though he was God, he appeared no different from any other human being. As a man, he further humbled himself by becoming obedient to the point of death on a cross. To be humbled from the point of being God to being a human person would have been enough. But Paul reinforces the reality that Jesus became even more abased than that. He was born in relative insignificance, and he died a cruel death on a cross.

With the picture of Christ's humiliation complete, the mood changes significantly. The two particles *dio kai* ("therefore") at the beginning of verse 9 mark the transition to Paul's discussion of the consequences of Jesus' humility. The subject of this latter part of the hymn changes as well. Whereas the focus of verses 5–8 was on Jesus, the subject of verses 9–11 is God the Father, Jesus being the object of his activity. Again bear in mind that the focus of this entire section was to convince the Philippians of the importance of maintaining the attitude of Christ in their relationships with one another.

The steps of Jesus' abasement were met with one act of God whereby he "exalted [Jesus] to the highest place." Paul clearly has Jesus' resurrection and ascension in mind—God's act of vindication for the Savior. According to Jewish understanding, anyone who was hanged on a tree came under the curse of God (cf. Gal. 3:13); according to Paul, however, Jesus' death on the cruel cross was not cursed, but received God's favor. The word for "exalt" is a compound word consisting of the preposition "above" (*hyper*) combined with "exalt" (*hypsoo*; Jesus used the same word in John 12:32, "I, when I am *lifted up* from the earth, will draw all men to myself"). Paul's intent here is to indicate that insofar as Christ stooped so low, he has been exalted so high that he has the glorious rank of equality with God.

A concomitant action to God's exaltation of Christ is God's gift of a name. In biblical times a name served not only a means of recognizing an individual, but it also revealed something of his or her character. In Jesus' case, the name he received was not just any name, but "the name that is above every name" (v. 9b). In Jewish tradition God's revealed name (Yahweh) was never spoken by anyone. As a result a number of periphrastic expressions were employed to refer to God: the Holy One, the Majesty on High, the Name, etc. The phrase "the name that is above every name" is a clear allusion to that practice; in verse 11 the name is noted—"Lord" (*kyrios*, the LXX word used for Yahweh). The word that describes God's giving of this Name to Christ is *charizomai*—an act of giving that centers in God's grace (*charis*). The grace of God—the sum of all the blessings that come as a result of this death and exaltation—comes to us only because God first "graced" Jesus with his exalted name and position.

The consequence of God's exaltation of Christ is seen in verse 10: All creation will worship him. The NIV phrase "at the name of Jesus" seems to imply the worship of the name of "Jesus." The name "Jesus" is in the genitive case in the text and is better understood as the name that belongs to Jesus. That name is the ery name of God—"Lord" (*kyrios*, v. 11). 'he picture here is one of complete submission nd obeisance. Since the normal posture for rayer was standing, the bowing of the knee ıdicates deep submission and respect. This icture is also future-oriented, for not every nee has yet bowed to the Lordship of 'hrist—this is part of the "already/not yet" ension in Paul. But this submission will some-ay be universal; note the expression "in eaven and on earth and under the earth."

The predominant cosmology of Paul's day ictured a three-tiered universe, consisting of eaven (the abode of God and his angels), arth (the abode of humanity), and the lower ealms (the abode of malevolent spirits). The oint of Paul's phrase in verse 10 is not to sin-le out specific aspects of Christ's rulership, ut rather to note the totality of it. Paul realizes ıat there were those not bowing to Christ, but owing to another lord—Caesar. A day will ome, however, when their knees will bow to 'hrist. Verse 11 contains the parallel phrase—every tongue [will] confess that Jesus Christ ; Lord." The idea of a confession (*exomolo-eo*) entails a public declaration and is most ften seen in the LXX in the context of giving iod praise.

These two phrases ("every knee should ow . . . every tongue confess") come from Isa-ah 45:23. The context of this passage is God's romise to an exiled nation that Jerusalem will ne day be inhabited by his children Israel, and oth Israel and her enemies will give God the lory he is due.

The statement "Jesus is Lord" occurs hroughout Paul's letters (e.g., Rom. 10:9), but his is the only instance where the earthly name Jesus," along with the messianic designation Christ" ("the Anointed One"), are used in con-unction with the title "Lord." Later in the life f the church, a particular heresy—Docetism—rose, claiming that the earthly Jesus died on the ross and was buried, but that the true spark of ivinity in him was liberated. In Paul's teach-ng no distinction can be made between the ncarnate Jesus and the heavenly Lord.

Although the particular confession "Jesus 'hrist is Lord" brings glory to God the Father, his section encompasses a far greater scope. 'he entire picture Paul paints here of Christ—rom his preexistence, through to his incarna-ion, to his exaltation—brings glory to God. God's ultimate purpose was to reconcile humankind to himself; and in what Paul calls (lit.) "the fullness of time" (cf. Gal. 4:4), Christ came to fulfill God's purpose in history.

4.3. Exhortations in Light of Christ's Example and the Christian's Experience (2:12–18)

In light of Christ's example, Paul goes on to encourage the Philippians to deal with the issues that face them as a church. He calls on them to manifest the same obedience that has been characteristic of their initial response to the gospel (Acts 16:1ff.). He also challenges them to obedience regardless of whether he is present with them. Their calling is to obey not just because he is around, but because obedience is a fitting response to God.

The task to which the Philippian believers are to turn their attention is to continue building their community, striving to put aside petty squabbling and to become united in Christ. Paul refers to this task as working out their salvation (v. 12b). Considerable confusion has surrounded verses 12–13. Is Paul teaching that his hearers must supplement their faith with personal works as a necessary requirement for salvation? Does verse 12 contradict verse 13?

Some of the confusion may be clarified when we recognize that both the pronoun "your" and the verb "work out" are plural. In other words, Paul is not suggesting that an individual's justification before God requires some kind of supplemental labor to make it effective. Moreover, it should be noted that the word "salvation" (*soteria*) in Paul carried with it three distinct senses. There is a past dimension to salvation: justification—when an individual is declared righteous because of one's faith in Christ and is moved from being under the dominion of sin to a position of reconciliation with God. There is a future dimension to salvation: glorification—when God's full purposes in reconciliation are fulfilled at the second coming of Christ. But there is also a present dimension to salvation: sanctification—the process by which an individual grows and conforms more and more to the image of Christ.

This process of sanctification is what Paul is referring to in these verses. There is no need to posit that the word "salvation" has a weakened meaning in this verse. For Paul salvation meant being a part of a community of believers—a body, which has as its mandate growth in Christ (Eph. 4:15–16). Part of the growth process occurred in the context of struggle and conflict. The believer's sanctification not only occurs individually, but is borne out in community. It is to be fleshed out in "fear and trembling"—that is, in what the wisdom writers label "the fear of the Lord" (Ps. 111:10; Prov. 2:5), an awe-filled lifestyle of reverence and obedience.

That the Triune God is the ultimate sanctifier is plain in Paul. In various passages he affirms that the Father (1 Thess. 5:23), the Son (1 Cor. 1:2), and the Holy Spirit (Rom. 15:16) all act in this capacity. He now reinforces that fact for the Philippians (Phil. 2:13). Their partnership in community is with one another, but it is also with God, for it is he who empowers them. His role as the One working in them means that his power actually produces tangible results in them—both the ability to act according to his will and the willingness and desire to do it.

The specifics of how believers are to work out this salvation are laid out in verse 14. This corrective also provides some insight into the nature of the problem plaguing the church in Philippi. They are to "do everything without complaining or arguing." The word for "complaining" (*gongysmos*) is onomatopoetic, picturing the dull, nondescript babbling of birds. "Arguing" (*dialogismos*) refers to reasoned debate, not unlike that which occurs in a courtroom. Much of what has occupied Paul in this letter has to do with interpersonal conflict and arguing. He would no doubt concur with James that the tongue is in fact the most unruly member of the body (cf. James 1:26ff.). It was precisely this kind of behavior that caused Israel to be judged by God through their desert wanderings (Num. 11:1; 14:1ff.).

Verses 15–16 are a part of the same sentence as verse 14 and point to the goal or result of stopping the arguing and complaining (or positively, give the ultimate result of the working out of one's salvation with fear and trembling). It is apparent from the first clause that Israel's grumbling in the desert was on Paul's mind. In stopping their own grumbling, the Philippians would become blameless (*amemptoi*, without reproach or fault—a word used by Paul to describe his strict adherence to the law as a Pharisee; cf. 3:6). They also would be pur or sincere (*akeraioi*, unmixed, or in the case o metals, unalloyed). They would be unlik Israel, who because of their grumbling and dis obedience were "no longer his children, but warped and crooked generation" (Deut. 32:5 cf. Matt. 17:17; Acts 2:40). By dealing with th problem of internal strife, the Philippians, a members of God's redeemed community, th new Israel, had the potential of becomin faultless, something Israel could never clain before God.

As God's chosen people, the Philippia believers are to shine as God's beacon in th world (cf. Isa. 49:6). The Old Testament view light as a metaphor for God's law (Ps 119:105). For the psalmist, God was both ligh and salvation (27:1). The coming of the Mes siah was the coming of light to dissipate dark ness (Isa. 9:2; Matt. 4:16; John 1:4–5). Jesu called his disciples "the light of the world (Matt. 5:14). It is, however, Daniel's end-tim vision of the wise who "shine like the brigh ness of the heavens," who "lead many to righ teousness," that informs Paul's message her (Dan. 12:3).

Believers are light precisely because thei role is to proclaim and model the gospe (v. 16a). Here "hold out" naturally flows fron verse 15b. As the Philippians stand firm an are uncompromising in their proclamation c the good news, they will become lights in culture opposed to the message. The gospe here is called "the word of life" because it i the message of eternal life.

In the latter part of verse 16, Paul shifts hi focus to himself. His citation from Daniel 12: may have served to remind the apostle of hi role in the eschatological plan of God. He ma also have in mind his own vindication befor God as he endeavored to model the servant hood of Christ. For Paul, "the day of Christ (see also 1:10) closely parallels the Old Tes tament concept of "day of the LORD" and is time of hope and of accountability. As he tell the Philippians, he did not want to face that da having "run . . . for nothing."

Paul's close relationship with the church i conveyed in this verse. The believers in Philip were his ground for boasting before God— boast that reflected the attitude of a father, jus tifiably proud of his children's noble accom plishments. Their faithfulness to the gospe assured him that the fruit of his labor would continue long after he was gone. His ministry had produced enduring fruit. Paul saw his own fulfillment of God's calling in his life in two metaphors: (1) He was an athlete, one who ran with a single purpose and a determination to finish well; (2) he was also a laborer, one who worked to the point of exhaustion, yet who was always cognizant that the work had to continue, so that his efforts would not be in vain.

Paul's thoughts turn briefly back to himself in verse 17. The language of this verse is taken from sacrificial imagery of the Old Testament. It is unlikely that the apostle has a foreboding of his martyrdom here. After all, he was confident that his current imprisonment would not end in death (1:25). Rather, he is reflecting on his own ministry and that of the Philippians as they seek to make the gospel known in their community. Paul refers to his own experience in prison as being a "drink offering" (cf. Num. 15:1–13). The Philippians' own struggle as a church to work out their salvation is what Paul means by the words "sacrifice" and "service coming from your faith." If, as Paul puts it, their obedience is like a sacrifice to God, his current struggles in prison are like a libation or drink offering that accompanies the sacrifice. The appropriate response to both of those situations is to "rejoice" together (v. 18).

5. The Ministry of Paul's Associates (2:19–30)

Verse 19 begins a new major section of Philippians as Paul turns his focus away from himself and the Philippians to two key associates with him in Rome, Timothy and Epaphroditus. The former was Paul's traveling companion and "son" in the faith; the latter, a special envoy from the church at Philippi sent to minister to both the temporal and spiritual needs of Paul during his Roman imprisonment. This section contains the travel plans for Timothy and Epaphroditus to return to Philippi. Paul's mention of the plans includes a commendation of both men, and in fact he portrays them as examples of true Christian servants, who look "not only to [their] own interests, but also to the interests of others" (2:4).

5.1. Timothy (2:19–24)

Paul begins this section with what appears to be a lack of confidence. However, his hope is not the mood of cautious optimism, but rather an assertion of his submission to Christ. He hopes that it is the will of Christ for Timothy to return to Philippi soon. The particular issue is the timing of Timothy's trip to Philippi, not the certainty of it (see also v. 23). The adverb "soon" can have the meaning of "immediately" or "quickly" or, in this case, "as soon as possible."

Although the time of Timothy's trip to Philippi is uncertain, its nature and duration are not. Paul is sending Timothy with the express purpose of bringing back a report about the affairs of the church—the trip is a fact-finding mission. As one who has taken a genuine interest in the affairs of others (2:4), Timothy will believe the best in regard to the Philippians. Paul is confident that when he hears Timothy's report, he will be greatly encouraged (cf. "cheered" in v. 19). The duration of Timothy's stay in Philippi will not be long, for Paul is anticipating news back from Timothy prior to his own departure, which he trusts would be "soon" (cf. v. 24).

The high esteem in which Paul holds Timothy is reflected in verse 20. There is no one else who shares a kindred spirit with him ("like him" is *isapsychos*; lit., "equal-souled"). They have a similar outlook and vision when it comes to the Philippians. This is evident in the fact that Timothy takes a genuine interest in their affairs. His concern (*merimnao*; cf. 4:6, where this word means "worry") for them is more than a passing one; it is deep and abiding.

In verse 21, Paul contrasts the attitude of Timothy with that of others in his company in Rome. The apostle is not commenting on the condition of every Christian in Rome, but probably has in mind the same group he refers to in 1:15, who preached the gospel out of impure motives (O'Brien, 321). It was their attitude that disqualified them. Their motives were selfish and did not further the gospel. Only Timothy (and Epaphroditus, of course) were either able or willing to undertake the journey.

After that note of regret, Paul returns optimistically to Timothy (v. 22). He appeals to the Philippians' own experience to demonstrate that Timothy has in fact "proved himself." This proof implies that Timothy's character was weighed and assessed (no doubt through shared experiences) and had withstood the test.

Timothy "served with" Paul for the sake of the gospel. Paul here uses a word related to *doulos*—the very character Jesus assumed in his incarnation. In other words, Timothy modeled for the Philippians the very lifestyle Paul advocated they assume. Timothy's commitment is not only to Christ and to the gospel, but also to Paul. He has labored "as a son" with Paul. In his letters to him, Paul addressed Timothy as "my true son in the faith" (1 Tim. 1:2) and "my dear son" (2 Tim. 1:2).

In light of Timothy's concern for the church, his attitude, and his proven faithfulness, Paul anticipates sending the young man to Philippi soon. His one caveat is the outcome of his own current situation as a prisoner under house arrest. The phrase the NIV renders "as soon as I see how things go with me" is a challenge to translate. Some commentators (e.g., Silva, Hawthorne) see Paul as implying that he will send Timothy only after Paul no longer has need for his assistance in Rome. An interpretation of this nature would have Paul asserting his own needs over those of the Philippians. But this attitude flies in the face of Paul's exhortation in 2:4 to be concerned about "the interests of others." Rather, the picture here is of someone looking into the distance trying to see something; it is comparable to the English idiom "when I see my way clear" or "when the dust settles."

The reason that Paul's hope in sending Timothy is more than just fanciful speculation becomes clear in verse 24. Paul is "confident in the Lord" that he himself will come to them soon. In the current situation, his ability to travel to Philippi was more severely hindered than Timothy's. Because Paul was persuaded he would soon leave prison, his hope for Timothy's travel plans should be seen as a fait accompli in the Lord.

5.2. Epaphroditus (2:25–30)

Epaphroditus is mentioned only in the book of Philippians. It is clear that Paul esteemed this man highly. He was a special envoy from Philippi sent to assist Paul while in prison. His primary role was to bring a monetary gift to help Paul defray the expenses of living under house arrest. Epaphroditus no doubt delivered the latest news to Paul from Philippi, and his presence with Paul and Timothy was of tremendous encouragement.

Paul feels strongly that he must send Epaphroditus back to Philippi (as the messenger who carried this very letter to the church there). He expresses his appreciation for Epaphroditus, whom he sees as a "brother, fellow worker [cf. Euodia and Syntyche, 4:2] and fellow soldier." This last metaphor, used occasionally by Paul to picture the advance of the gospel (cf. Eph. 6:10–17; 1 Tim. 2:3–4), was probably born out of Paul's frequent imprisonments and out of his daily interaction with the members of the Praetorian guard watching him.

Paul's glowing words for Epaphroditus are not directed just toward him, but toward the entire church at Philippi since he was their "messenger" (lit., "apostle"—the original word speaks of an envoy or an ambassador of the congregation—one sent as a duly deputized representative of another, as seen in the Hebrew word *shaliach*). As such, he performed all the duties for Paul they would have done themselves had Paul been present in Philippi. In regard to Paul, Epaphroditus was a *leitourgos*—one who rendered a sacrificial service by "tak[ing] care of my needs."

Paul explains the reason for Epaphroditus's return. As a trusted representative of the church at Philippi, he no doubt left behind a community for which he cared and which cared for him. He longed again to be reunited with these friends (a sentiment Paul often expresses). A second reason for Epaphroditus's return to Philippi is the anxiety he felt when the Philippians had learned of his illness. One of the harsh realities of the world in which Paul and his companions lived was that illness often ended in death. Epaphroditus was justifiably concerned that when they heard that he was ill they might conclude that he had died. He desired to alleviate their anxieties by coming to them in person, very much alive.

In verse 27 Paul informs the Philippians that their worst fears in regards to this beloved apostle were almost realized. But God spared the life of Epaphroditus, showing mercy on Paul as well. Although Paul recognized death to be far better because of the blessedness of going to be with Christ (1:23), he would still have felt intense sorrow at losing a companion and coworker in the gospel. This sorrow would further magnify the sorrow Paul was already experiencing as a prisoner in Rome. The bond created among believers through their shared ıion with Christ is profound. Death creates orrow in that it severs that bond of one with the her, albeit only temporarily until that day hen all will be together in the presence of God.

As a result of Epaphroditus's concerns and r the sake of the Philippians, Paul is eager send him home (v. 28). As a result, he envi-ons that the Philippians will again rejoice. At e same time, knowing about Epaphroditus's lief and their renewed joy will relieve some f Paul's own sorrows and anxieties.

Given the mutual concern and care Epa-hroditus and the Philippians had for one ıother, Paul's exhortation in verse 29 to "wel-ome" their messenger seems almost unnec-ssary. There is no doubt that the church will ceive Epaphroditus back into their fold with xuberant rejoicing. Paul's exhortation thus kes on the mood of a commendation, as if to y: "Welcome and esteem him well, for he erved well!"

The "honor" Paul calls the church at hilippi to give Epaphroditus is due to the xemplary service this man had rendered to the ord, Paul, and the church at Philippi. In per-rming the work of Christ Epaphroditus ecame so ill it almost cost him his life. As if at were not enough, Paul reminds the Philip-ians that the risks Epaphroditus took were not ıst to fulfill his own calling, but were so that e might be able to help them fulfill their duty Paul, which they had not been able to com-lete because of their absence.

. Warning Against Straying From the Gospel (3:1–4:1)

hilippians 3:1 begins a new section of this let-r, in which Paul focuses on the possibility of ıe church in Philippi succumbing to false aching. This is the third area of difficulty aul has addressed in the letter (the first two re his imprisonment and the persecution of ıe Philippians). Although there was no evi-ence that the church in Philippi had strayed om the faith, Paul's missionary experience old him that it would only be a matter of time efore the believers there would encounter a hallenge from the enemies of the gospel. long with his exhortation, Paul describes his ast credentials in Judaism and his present ommitment to Christ. This section contains hat might best be called Paul's "mission tatement."

The NIV translation of *to loipon* as "finally" (v. 1) gives the impression that Paul is concluding his letter at this point. Yet he is only about three-fifths of the way through the actual letter. Even if he had intended to end the letter here, something else presumably caught his attention and led him to continue it. This seemingly awkward transition has given rise to the theory that Philippians is really a combination of at least two letters (see the introduction). It is not unusual, however, for Paul to use this phrase to refer to other, miscellaneous matters (1 Thess. 4:1) or to mean "furthermore," pointing the way to further discussion.

6.1. Warning (3:1–4a)

Paul's command for the Philippians to "rejoice in the Lord" is one of Paul's key themes throughout the letter and provides a transitional link between his previous discussion and what is to follow. Those who see this as Paul's conclusion would tend to translate "rejoice" as "farewell" (e.g., NEB). The rationale behind this particular translation of *chairete* is its use as a common greeting in secular letters of the era. However, such a reading marks an unwarranted superfluous departure from Paul's habitual use of the term in the letter. The apostle is moving into an area on which he has previously instructed the Philippians, but does so undaunted ("no trouble"). The reason for this forthrightness is that he wants to prevent them from being tripped up.

The issue Paul is referring to is the work of the Judaizers, false teachers whom he encountered frequently throughout his ministry. These individuals were Jewish Christians who felt that the only way Gentile believers could be a part of the community of faith was to observe the ceremonial law, including the ritual of circumcision. The first indication in the history of the church where the relationship between Jews and Gentiles became a major problem was the first church council in Jerusalem (Acts 15). After deliberating the role of the Jewish law in light of the Gentiles, the church determined that there were four requirements they would encourage the Gentile church to observe: abstaining from food offered to idols, avoiding blood, avoiding eating meat from animals that had been strangled, and refraining from sexually immoral practices.

Unfortunately, this decision did not resolve the issue. In at least two of his letters to young churches (to churches in Galatia and Corinth), Paul countered the proselytizing practices of these individuals. He referred to them as "false apostles, deceitful workmen" (2 Cor. 11:13) and accused them of preaching a false gospel (Gal. 1:8–9). At one point in his concern for the church and his frustration over the activities of the Judaizers, he found himself wishing that they would do permanent injury to themselves (Gal. 5:12).

In verse 2 of our present passage, Paul calls for his listeners to be on the lookout for these false teachers. His description of them is highly unflattering, and the terms in the original text form an alliterative triad so that they will not easily be forgotten by his audience. He refers to them as "dogs" (*kynas*), a disparaging term. In light of the fact that Jews regularly referred to Gentiles as dogs (Mark 7:27), the expression was even more poignant as Paul turned it back on the Judaizers. These Judaizers were not the only Jews who thought they were doing the Lord's work—Paul had himself earlier persecuted the church, thinking he was fulfilling his duty as a Pharisee, only to find out he was doing evil. He reminds them that they are not performing righteous acts in compelling Gentiles to observe the Jewish ceremonial law in order to be saved—they are, in fact, "men who do evil" (*kakous ergatas*). In delivering his final blow, Paul says that the very act (circumcision) that they feel gives them special status before God is nothing more than a horrible mutilation of the flesh (*katatomen*).

In verse 3 Paul notes that it is not those who have received the external mark of circumcision who are the people of God, but those who have undergone an inner transformation, an inner circumcision. Circumcision had been instituted by God as a sign of Israel's participation in the covenant (Gen. 17:9ff.). It became meaningless as the Israelites, though circumcised, persisted in breaking that very covenant. In light of their spiritual condition, the prophets looked for a day when Israel would carry within their beings the sign of the covenant—a condition described as being circumcised in their hearts (Jer. 4:4; Ezek. 44:7).

Paul insists that true believers, not the Judaizing party, are in fact "the circumcision." He uses three phrases to define them. (1) They
were those "who worship by the Spirit
God." The word the NIV translates "worshi
(*latreuo*) is used in the LXX and in the book
Hebrews to refer to the service of priests in t
temple (cf. Ex. 23:25; Deut. 6:12; Heb. 8:
10:2). The word is also used in Romans 12:
where Paul urges his hearers to offer their bo
ies to God sacrificially as a "spiritual act
worship." Paul goes on to encourage th
Roman Christians to allow their minds to b
renewed and their lives to be empowered b
the Spirit, exercising their gifts to serve on
another (12:2–8). Worshiping by the Spir
entails submitting oneself to God and living
life of obedience and faith (cf. Phil. 2:12ff.).

(2) The Philippian believers are to take prid
not in any physical signs of membership, b
rather in Christ and his work. They are to plac
no confidence in the rules and rituals valued b
those under the law. The Christian's boa
should never be in being blameless with respe
to the demands of the law (cf. 3:4). The true ci
cumcision are those who place their faith i
Christ alone, and their grounds for boasting a
in him. As the exalted Lord over the cosmo
he was the One who rightly deserved such glor

(3) "The [true] circumcision" are those "wh
put no confidence in the flesh." For Paul, th
idea of "flesh" (*sarx*) often meant the natur
venue of human existence (Rom. 9:3; 1 Co
10:18), but he frequently uses the word in a the
ological sense to refer to the condition c
humanity in rebellion against God. The ultima
consequence of being dominated by the flesh i
death (Rom. 8:6). The calling of the Christia
is to crucify the flesh and its acts and liv
according to the Spirit (Gal. 5:16ff.). Thus, *sar*
carries a sharp double meaning in Paul. (a)
is an outright renunciation that any observanc
of ceremonial law, such as circumcision, ca
gain one's salvation. (b) In light of Paul'
broader use of the term *sarx*, he exposes th
actions of the Judaizers for what they reall
are—deeds performed in rebellion against Go

As far as Paul is concerned, the devotio
of the Judaizers is in keeping the law, the
glory is in their achievements, and their con
fidence is in an outward ritual. In case there i
a thought in anyone's mind that Paul has ove
stated his case, he goes on in the next sectio
to point out that he knows what he is talkin
about: Before he became a Christian, he ha
embraced their convictions and lifestyle.

6.2. Paul's Credentials (3:4b–6)

Paul now explains why he is so convinced hat requiring the Gentiles to follow the Jewsh laws to receive salvation must be rejected. Iis credentials in Judaism were such that even he Judaizers would envy them, but he turned is back on them in order to follow Christ.

Paul enumerates the qualifications that nade him a Jew of the highest order (vv. 5–6).)f the seven qualifications listed, the first four vere his because of birth, while the last three vere due to his personal achievements as a levout Pharisee. (1) If circumcision is of alue, then Paul can boast of that credential. Ie was not circumcised as a proselyte, but in trict conformity to the law, on the eighth day fter his birth (cf. Lev. 12:3).

(2) Paul had been born a member of the eople of Israel, God's chosen nation. Even hough he was born in Tarsus, a Gentile city, his amily tree could be traced back to Israel. He vas a pure Israelite and as such inherited all the rivileges of being a member of the covenant ommunity. In the time of Paul, in order for one o hold civic office in Israel, one had to prove nembership in "pure Israel" (Jeremias, 273).

(3) Paul was a member of the tribe of Benamin. Benjamin, by tradition, was the only ne of Jacob's sons born in the Promised Land. 'his tribe occupied the territory that included erusalem and the temple (which represented he presence of Yahweh in the midst of his eople). Benjamin was the tribe from which srael's first king, Saul, came (for whom Paul vas named). At the time of Ezra, the tribes of udah and Benjamin formed the nucleus of the estored nation of Israel, and the tribe of Benamin carried a favored social status.

(4) The phrase "Hebrew of Hebrews" oints to two further facts about Paul's life. a) He was born not to proselytes, but to parnts who could trace their lineage through the ages of Israel's history. (b) Paul was not aised in a manner strongly influenced by Helenism (those who had undoubtedly absorbed ome of the Gentile customs of that culture). Vhile Paul was fluent in Greek, he also spoke Iebrew and Aramaic. And although born in 'arsus, Paul was educated in Jerusalem, at the eet of the prominent rabbi Gamaliel.

(5) In his observance of the law, Paul was a Pharisee." This sect of Judaism traced its istory to the time of the Maccabean Revolt in the second century B.C. and prided itself in its strict separation from the world. Pharisees devoted themselves to the Mosaic Law and the oral traditions of the rabbis. They dedicated themselves to achieving righteousness by carefully observing the law. Their motivation for adherence to the law (both written and oral) was their hope of being raised from the dead.

(6) As a Pharisee, Paul was so zealous that he actively sought out members of the fledgling church in order to destroy it. Fervent commitment to God's law motivated every action of the devout Pharisee. Many Pharisees believed that the Messiah would come once the world was in submission to that law. It is entirely possible, therefore, that Paul's persecution of the church was driven by a desire to see the Messiah come. In this regard Paul's theology was changed through his encounter with the risen Christ on the road to Damascus, where he was confronted by the very Messiah whom he thought he was serving (see Acts 9:1ff.).

The word Paul uses to describe the community of Christians here is *ekklesia*—those who have been called out. This word's meaning comes from the LXX rendering of the Hebrew term *qahal*, a word often used to describe Israel's gathering in formal assembly—usually for an occasion of worship, a feast, a celebration, or a covenant ratification (e.g., Lev. 23; Deut. 4:10; 29:1; Josh. 8:35). Paul uses the word to describe the redeemed community—those who are of the new Israel, who have placed their faith and trust in Jesus Christ. *Ekklesia* refers to both individual house churches (cf. Rom. 16:23) and the church universal (cf. Eph. 1:22; Col. 1:18).

(7) Paul notes that he was "faultless" when it came to observing the strict rituals and regulations of the law. In another area of rabbinic teaching it was thought the Messiah would come when Israel fully learned to keep the Sabbath; this may have been a motivating factor in his former lifestyle. Paul's understanding of "righteousness" here is limited by the word "legalistic." This is the type of righteousness that he goes on to contrast with the true righteousness that comes through faith in Christ (3:9).

6.3. Paul's Overarching Purpose (3:7–14)

Despite his impressive credentials in Pharisaism, Paul asserts that these credentials pale in significance when it comes to pursuing his true purpose—gaining righteousness in Christ. This section begins what might be seen as Paul's theological understanding of his Damascus Road experience in comparison with his career as a rabbi in Pharisaism.

In verse 7, Paul borrows language from the commercial world. All the qualifications he has enumerated—his heritage, his accomplishments considered by the Pharisaic world to be credits (gain) to his account—were not reasons for God to accept him. In fact, they were just the opposite; they were nothing. Paul considered them to be of no value whatsoever because of Christ. The NIV translation "for the sake of Christ" may imply that Paul had made a decision to count his past in Judaism as nothing in comparison to the work he was now undertaking on Christ's behalf. Nothing could be further from the truth! It was because of the revelation of Christ on the road to Damascus that Paul was left with no choice but to recognize that the course he was pursuing in Judaism was dead wrong. It was the "because-of-Christ" experience that was the great turning point in Paul's thinking.

Verse 8 reinforces and clarifies this point. Paul changes tenses here, moving from an understanding in light of a past experience to a settled conviction in the present, and he considers his achievements in Judaism to be "loss." Everything is loss when compared to the one important thing in his life—his relationship with Christ. In keeping with metaphors from the world of commerce, Paul deems this relationship to be of "surpassing" value.

Paul defines that relationship further in the next phrase of verse 8. It is not based on obedience to the law, whether oral or codified. Rather, it is based on knowledge of the exalted Lord—Jesus Christ. "Knowing Christ Jesus my Lord" is not a written or formalized body of knowledge. The term *gnosis* points to the act of knowing rather than the content of knowledge. Paul's relationship with Christ did not come as he studied about him (as it did in regard to the law) but occurred in a face-to-face confrontation with Christ on the road to Damascus.

On the basis of that experience with Christ, Paul lost all the things he once valued as the means of achieving favor with God. The sense behind the word "loss" should not be construed in a deprived sense; that is to say, Paul is not sharing this with his hearers to elici sympathy because he has lost something truly valuable. Instead, it has only been since he has come to know Christ that he has found something really valuable. As a matter of fact, that which was lost to him he considered to be common waste. The NIV translates the Greek word used here with the euphemistic term "rubbish," but the sense of the word denotes filth or excrement. That human attempts at attaining righteousness should be thought of in such terms should not have come as a surprise to the Pharisee—the prophet Isaiah had made this plain centuries before (cf. Isa. 64:6). Yet Pharisees persisted in their efforts to attain God's favor through their actions.

The last phrase of verse 8 highlights Paul's purpose in considering everything to be rubbish: in order "that [he] may gain Christ." Gaining Christ means being "found in him" (v. 9). The phrase "in Christ" or "in him" occurs frequently by Paul's writings to denote a number of ideas, two of which are predominant. (1) It describes agency—that is, what God has done in or through Christ (Rom. 3:24). (2) It describes the location, realm, or sphere in which believers live in light of their appropriation of Christ's saving work (1 Cor. 12:5). The phrase used in this latter sense is related to the body of Christ—a metaphor for the church seen elsewhere in Paul (Rom. 12:3ff.; 1 Cor. 12:4ff.). This metaphor denotes the corporate relationship the church has both with the Lord and with one another.

Paul contrasts the righteousness he had endeavored to attain as a Pharisee with the righteousness he has attained through Jesus. The wording of verse 9 in the NIV may leave the impression that Paul is holding out two options as to the manner in which he will be found in Christ—with a righteousness that comes from the law or a righteousness that comes from God. In reality, however, Paul knows he will not be in Christ if he persists in trying to attain righteousness by keeping the law. He will *only* be found in Christ with the righteousness imputed to him through faith in Christ.

The undesirable righteousness, which falls far short of God's standard, is that which comes through observing the law. The concept of "law" in the Old Testament referred to ceremonial regulations (pertaining to the worship of God and the sacrificial system), the civi code (focusing on helping Israelites live as God's people in harmony with one another and their neighbors), and the moral law (e.g., the Ten Commandments, on which other laws were built). An entire tradition of oral law, designed to prevent the pious Israelite from breaking the Mosaic Law, had developed and was codified. This oral code added countless regulations. It had been Paul's goal as a Pharisee to follow all those laws; as a result of keeping them, he hoped to be deemed righteous. This righteousness was Paul's "own" righteousness, since it was brought about by his own effort.

The righteousness to be favored is one that comes by faith. The truly righteous person, then, is one whose life is characterized by faith in Christ and whose life is based on that relationship (cf. Rom. 1:17). We are justified only through accepting the vicarious work of Christ on our behalf. Paul further clarifies this righteousness in the concluding phrase of verse 9: It has God as its source and faith as the grounds on which it is appropriated (Acts 3:16).

In verse 10, Paul concludes his thoughts. He begins by restating his goal (cf. "gaining Christ" in v. 8), which is to "know Christ." The knowledge comes first in knowing "the power of [Christ's] resurrection." "Power" (*dynamis*) points to the miraculous power of God and is often associated in Paul's letters with the work of the Holy Spirit (1 Cor. 2:4; 1 Thess. 1:5). This life-giving power was manifested by God in raising Jesus from the dead. The agent of this power was the Holy Spirit (cf. Rom. 8:11; 1 Cor. 12:6). This was the power the disciples experienced when the Holy Spirit descended on them at Pentecost (cf. Acts 2:1ff.). This was also the power Paul experienced both on the road to Damascus and when Ananias laid his hand on him (9:5–19).

Paul knows that the third person of the Trinity is the agent who brings the benefits of Christ's vicarious death into people's lives. The Spirit acts in the initiation of salvation, bringing individuals into Christ's body (1 Cor. 12:13; cf. also 6:11; Titus 3:5). The Spirit then sanctifies believers (both individually and corporately), reproducing the character of the exalted Lord in their lives (cf. Gal. 5:22). The Spirit also empowers Spirit-filled believers for ministry (cf. Acts 1:8; Rom. 12:1–8; 1 Cor. 12; Eph. 4:1–16). Moreover, in experiencing the Holy Spirit, Paul also experiences Jesus (cf. 1 Cor. 15:45; 2 Cor. 3:17–18; also Phil. 1:9). Thus, in reality, experiencing the power of Jesus' resurrection is for Paul experiencing the presence of Jesus himself.

Paul's experience of knowing Christ came not only through the empowering of the Holy Spirit. As the young church in Jerusalem became aware, that experience went "hand in glove" with experiencing suffering. After Paul was filled with the power of the Spirit and miraculously healed of blindness, God warned him how much he would have to suffer for his Name (9:16). In his diatribe against his opponents in 2 Corinthians, Paul enumerates the history of his suffering (2 Cor. 11:23–29). For Paul, sharing in Christ's sufferings was a prerequisite for sharing in his glory to come. In fact, the believer's present sufferings are insignificant in light of the glory to be revealed (Rom. 8:17–18).

Jesus prepared his disciples for the reality of facing persecution just as he had (John 15:20). The early disciples counted it a badge of honor to be worthy to suffer for the name of Christ (Acts 5:41). Participating in Christ's sufferings had the effect of "becoming like him [lit., conformed to him] in his death" (Phil. 3:10). (1) Note that the tense of the verb "conform" indicates activity that is currently occurring. In other words, Paul is referring to his ongoing sufferings, in which he is continually made like Christ in his death. His future, physical death is merely the ultimate conclusion that will conform him to Christ's death. (2) The Greek word for "conform" is related to the word *morphe* ("nature") in 2:6–7; it points to Christ's act of humbling himself to bring redemption to humankind. For Paul, suffering continually brought him back to this picture.

Paul concludes this section (v. 11) by giving the goal of knowing Christ—both the power of his resurrection and the fellowship of his suffering (in which Paul reflected the attitude of Christ in 2:6–11). It was the goal of the zealous Pharisee to attain to the resurrection from the dead. All of Paul's effort in keeping the law prior to his conversion was focused on the hope of resurrection. The irony of his comments here is that it is not law-keeping that brings this hope, but rather knowing Christ. Resurrection was the culmination of Paul's salvation. The tentativeness expressed here ("and so, somehow, to attain") should not be construed as indicating Paul's lack of assurance of the resurrection, but rather its occasion.

Verses 12–14 present Paul's outworking of his desire to know Christ. In these verses are allusions that contrast his former life under Judaism with his ongoing relationship with Christ. He was born with all the credentials of a "pure" Jew, but he readily admits he had not obtained all of his goals in terms of knowing Christ. Neither had he reached a point of complete maturity or fulfillment (cf. 1 Cor. 14:20). This stands in contrast to the blameless performance of the law to which he has already referred. Instead of zealously persecuting (*dioko*) the church (v. 6), he presses on (*dioko*) to attain the goal for which he was grasped by Christ in his conversion.

In verses 13–14 Paul uses the image of a race as he further considers his life. He (Paul's comment is emphatic here—lit., "not even I myself") does not consider that he has achieved this goal of complete maturity. This emphasis was another broadside at the Judaizers—considering his impressive credentials in Judaism, not even he considered himself to have attained his goal as a Christian. Paul's focus is concentrated on one thing: putting the glorious achievements (the rubbish) behind him and pressing forward to the ultimate prize. The sense of the Greek pictures a runner in the final stages of a race, refusing to take a backward look to ascertain where his nearest opponent is. Rather, his eyes and energies are focused towards the finish line. He runs with the goal fixed clearly in his vision and for a reason fixed clearly in his mind—to win the prize. This "prize," to which God has called him, is salvation in Christ. This was an upward, heavenly call, whose final goal is glorification.

6.4. Perspective of False Teaching (3:15–16)

Verses 15–16 link the Judaizing problem discussed by Paul in verses 1–14 with the general tenor of his concern for the infighting occurring in the church. Given the close proximity of these verses to Paul's arguments about the believers' responsibility to know/experience Christ and receive his righteousness, there is no indication that Paul is shifting gears here. His use of the *phroneo* word group provides a clear link to his discussion in 2:1–4 (see comments there). In light of the connec tion established in this passage, it is not unre alistic to postulate that some of the conflict the Philippians were having among themselve pertained to the Judaizing issue.

In verse 15, Paul encourages those "who ar mature" to reflect the perspective he shared i verses 11–14. In what appears to be a chang of attitude, Paul, who did not feel he ha attained perfection (*teleioo*), is now numberin himself among the mature (*teleioi*). Again, a in 2:2ff., *phroneo* refers not only to one' thought process, but to the emotions, attitudes and ensuing lifestyle that proceed from them.

In the event that some believers think dif ferently, God will reveal it to them. The wor "reveal" (*apokalypto*) carries somewhat of technical sense in Paul. He often uses it in con nection with his own conversion. The gospel Paul argues, came to him "by revelation" (Gal 1:12). More specifically, it was a revelation o Jesus Christ, given to Paul by God (1:16). Th content of this revelation was that "Jesus i Lord"—a cardinal truth reflected in Philippi ans 2:6–11. The term *revelation* often refers t an unveiling of something that was previousl concealed but has now been revealed becaus of a gracious act of God. For Paul, therefore revelation meant more than just an unveiling It was specifically the act of God's unveilin his redemptive purposes in Christ, the Messiah

The thrust of the last clause of verse 1 takes on an entirely different sense in light o this issue at hand. The current reading in th NIV suggests that Paul is willing to tolerate dif ferent opinions, as though Paul is saying: "I you want to hold a different view, go ahead; am sure God will sort things out for you." Thi paraphrase, however, does not in any wa reflect Paul's stand on the issue of righ teousness that comes by faith versus righ teousness gained through keeping the law Verses 1–14 clearly reflect that this issue wa a "hill" Paul was prepared to die on. It was piv otal to the gospel. In fact, verse 15 brings ou a truth about the nature of the gospel for th Philippians to consider. The phrase "God wil make clear to you" points to the fact that thi gospel is truth that believers do not have apar from revelation. That is, it is "made clear" t the individual heart by the Holy Spirit.

Paul's concluding exhortation in this sec tion (v. 16) is that the Philippians should ensur hat their lifestyle reflects their standing in :hrist. The word translated "attained" denotes oming up to a certain level or standard, while live up to" is a word borrowed from the mil-:ary world. It originally meant to be arranged 1 a line with the precision characteristic of the .oman army, and thus came to denote the naintaining of a straight course.

6.5. *Concluding Comments in Light of the Prevalence of False Teaching (3:17–4:1)*

Up to this point in chapter 3, Paul's focus as been on the threat presented to the church rom the Judaizing teachers, whose goal was) add the regulations of Jewish law to the ientiles who had professed faith in Christ. The resent section should be seen as a broadening f the focus, in which Paul challenges his lis-:ners to stand firm against all manner of false :aching, primarily through imitating Paul and thers who follow his example. He notes the eneral characteristics of false teachers (vv. 8–19), and then moves into an eschatological oxology (which has significant parallels to 1e picture of Christ portrayed in 2:6–11). He oncludes this section with a personal appeal 1at the Philippians stand firm. This appeal :veals the close relationship that this apostle ad with the church at Philippi.

Verse 17 provides the transition from the revious section into a wider application of the uth Paul has already shared. He defines liv[ing] up to what we have already attained" v. 16) in practical terms. The hilippians are called to do that y being imitators of Paul. The vord *mimetes* denotes copying an xample and is strengthened by 1e preposition *sym* (giving the :nse of "together")—hence the IV rendering, "join with others in ɔllowing my example." This is ot an unusual request for Paul to 1ake of his listeners (cf. 1 Cor. :16; 2 Thess. 3:7). They are to ote those who walk according to 1e example of Paul and live their ves with that model in view. The hessalonian believers are :ferred to in this same sense Thess. 1:7), as is Timothy Tim. 4:12) and Paul himself (2 Thess. 3:9). Paul mentions the lifestyle of these positive role models in contrast to those who "live as enemies of the cross of Christ" (cf. Phil. 3:18).

In verses 18–19, Paul shifts his focus to false teachers. It is difficult to ascertain whom Paul is targeting here. Various groups, including the Judaizers, Jews, Gnostic libertines, and itinerant teachers, have been proposed as possibilities (cf. Fee, 363ff.). Such speculating may be unnecessary, as Paul appears to be characterizing general qualities of people who live as enemies of the cross of Christ. The issues are not new to the Philippians, for apparently Paul has addressed the issues with them on earlier occasions (cf. 3:1). The point to note in verse 18 is the impact this situation has on Paul. His concerns for the integrity of the gospel message and for the fledgling church are so intense that the prospect of false teaching brings him to the point of tears.

These false teachers have as their ultimate destiny eternal "destruction." The idea behind the word "destiny" (*telos*) can also contain the sense of goal or purpose. The false teachers have as their purpose the destruction of the gospel, but their ultimate destiny will be eternal destruction. "Their god is their stomach"—a phrase that points to the fact that they worship the flesh (unbridled sensuality). Paul categorizes the deeds of the flesh in a passage such as Galatians 5:19ff, and notes there that living according to the flesh is diametrically opposed to the gospel.

One of the stone remnants found in the ruins of Philippi is this carving that includes a Christian cross.

Paul further characterizes false teachers as those whose "glory is in their shame." Some commentators see this phrase and the one that precedes it as a dual reference to the Judaizers' preoccupation with dietary laws and circumcision (with "shame" referring to circumcision). This interpretation is tentative; we should rather see this expression as pointing to the fact that in general, false teachers are so skewed that they actually find their glory in those things that bring them shame (cf. Rom. 1:18ff.). Their mindset is "earthly," which contrasts with the heavenly (or "above things"; cf. Col. 3:1) focus of believers. Earthly things are those that are transitory and will pass away, in contrast to the heavenly things, which are eternal. An earthly orientation is also an orientation to the sphere of sin and, consequently, can be seen as a parallel to "flesh."

In verses 20–21, Paul jumps to a description of those whose mindset is not earthly. In contrast to the false teachers, the Philippians' mindset is heavenly because their "citizenship is in heaven." Here we see another allusion to their Roman citizenship, in which they took so much pride (cf. 1:27). The Philippians were well aware of the privileges they had. When Paul established the church in Philippi, he had claimed his own rights as a Roman citizen (Acts 16:37). Here he asserts that the only citizenship that really matters is the heavenly one.

Paul then mentions the church's eager expectation of Christ's promised return. "Eagerly await" refers to the anticipation of creation and humankind for Christ's return, bringing with him the final consummation of salvation (Rom. 8:19ff.; 1Cor. 1:7; Gal. 5:5). Paul expected that Christ could return at any moment. He was positive towards the prospect of entering into Christ's presence, either through the Savior's return or through his own death.

When he returns, the Savior will effect the final transformation, bringing salvation to its climax. Paul's introduction of the word "Savior" (*soter*) here is noteworthy, since he uses it elsewhere only in Ephesians 5:23 and in the Pastoral Letters. The word points to the believer's final salvation and serves to remind the Philippians that their hope is in Christ, not in Caesar, who was proclaimed savior of the Roman empire.

The transformation that Paul anticipates here is one in which our bodies, still in a humbled state, will be ultimately redeemed. Christ, who had humbled himself in the Incarnatio (2:6–8), was glorified through his bodily resurrection and ascension (2:9–11); believers ar now anticipating his return. In light of Christ' vicarious death on the cross, believers are justified, yet we still have to deal with the sir frailty, and limitations of a physical body in fallen world. The great culmination of redemption, however, is not freedom from that body as many in the Greco-Roman world wer anticipating. At the consummation of salvatio the body itself will be redeemed. This nev body will have the same form (*symmorphon* as Christ's resurrection body—eternal an hence imperishable. This is accomplishe through the outworking of divine "power, through which Christ brings everything int subjection to himself (cf. 2:10).

Verses 20–21 are a wonderful parallel t 2:6–11. Paul repeats some key concepts tha surface there. The one who took on the form c a slave (*morphe*, 2:7) will cause the believer' body to conform (*symmorphe*, 3:21) to his glc rious (*doxa*, 2:11; 3:21) body. Jesus, wh through his incarnation came to have a huma likeness (*schema*, 2:7), will, through the out working of God's power, transforr (*metaschematizo*, 3:21) the believer. The moti of universal obeisance to Christ (2:10) is fu ther reflected in Christ's subjection of a things (3:21). Moreover, Paul uses the identi cal title for Christ: *kyrios Iesous Christos,* "th Lord Jesus Christ" (cf. 2:11; 3:20).

Paul concludes this exhortation in 4:1 wit a call for the Philippians to stand firm both i the true gospel and in its ensuing lifestyle, a a soldier would hold a position in battle (cf 1:27). This exhortation denotes the stron desire of the apostle for his close friends. The are at first, "brothers [and sisters]," member of the family of God, the body of Christ. A such they are greatly loved by Paul and deepl missed by him. They are the source of his "jo [*chara*] and crown" (*stephanos*—a victor garland, received by winners of athleti events). In a sense, the Philippians will be pa of Paul's eschatological reward (cf. 2:16), bu are also presently his joy and the reward for hi labors among them.

7. Concluding Exhortations (4:2–9)

In this section, Paul moves toward some prac tical applications of the truths he has deve

›ed throughout the book. He begins with a ord of admonition to two sisters in the church ho were embroiled in some type of distract- g controversy. He then moves on to a few eneral exhortations to the church that carry any of the same themes and key words seen arlier.

7.1. Personal (4:2–3)

Paul's admonition in these two verses marks unusual occurrence in his writing. It is not nusual for the apostle to face off against prob- ms, objectionable practices, or false teaching ithin his churches (e.g., 1 Cor. 1:10ff.; 5:1; 1ff.; Gal. 3:1). However, this is one of the few ccasions where he actually names the people volved (cf. 1 Tim. 1:20). For the most part, aul prefers to keep those involved in contro- ersy cloaked in anonymity. The fact that he entions these individuals here reflects on the riousness of the situation at hand, his close lationship with the Philippians, and his high egard with which he held the two sisters to hom he makes this heartfelt appeal (cf. Fee, 89ff.). He obviously regards these women and e rest of the congregation as mature enough deal with the issue publicly.

Paul offers an earnest entreaty to two omen in the congregation at Philippi, Euodia nd Syntyche (possibly deaconesses in that hurch). Women had played a predominant ole in the founding of that Macedonian church see Acts 16:14). There is no reason to believe at Paul is addressing ongoing problems etween the Jewish and Gentile factions of that ongregation using these two names as pseu- onyms, as some have argued. The use of these wo names is well attested in other literature cf. Hawthorne, 179).

Paul addresses each of the women sepa- ately, possibly to show his impartiality in the ituation. The word by which he makes his ntreaty is *parakaleo*, a word that denotes an arnest plea—often to individuals who are ubordinates to the one making the plea (cf. ee, 391; O'Brien, 478). He encourages them display unity in their thinking and atti- udes—that they think (*phroneo*, cf. 2:1–4) the ame thing. That they are to do this "in the ord" reflects the fact that this issue had little do with petty squabbles but rather focused n an issue surrounding the outworking of the ospel message within the church.

Paul's appeal is further reinforced by his comments in verse 3, where he appeals to a third party, "loyal yokefellow" (*gnesie syzyge*), to assist in mediating in this dispute. There has been much speculation as to the identity of this individual—with identities ranging from Paul's wife to Epaphroditus, Luke, Timothy, or even an individual named "Syzygus." Hawthorne has speculated that the term has a broad reference to the entire church at Philippi (Hawthorne, 180). There simply is not enough evidence to indicate whether any of these options is likely. It is sufficient to say that both the Philippians and Paul would have known the individual, who was likely an associate of Paul. This latter assumption is reflected in Paul's use of the more formal word "ask" (*erotao*) rather than the harsher "plead" (*parakaleo*).

The reason for Paul's appeal becomes apparent in verse 3. These women, along with Clement and other coworkers, have contended along with Paul, as if they were in a gladiatorial combat (*synathleo* cf. 1:27), all for the sake of the gospel. Now at a time when there are strained relationships, Paul urges this "loyal yokefellow" to partner together with these two ladies to bring a solution (*syllambano*). It is significant that the terms "fellow workers," "contended," and "help" are all compounded with the preposition meaning "with" (*syn*), emphasizing the vital role of the Christian community and teamwork in Paul's thinking.

That these two women should agree is not unusual, given that they should be focused on the same goal—their names written in the "book of life." This latter term is alluded to in the Old Testament (Ex. 32:32; Ps. 139:16; Dan. 12:1) and in later Judaism (1QM 12:3). In that the citizens of Philippi had their citizenship formally entered into registers of that city, it is poignant that Paul refers to a citizenship register of infinitely more significance here.

7.2. Corporate (4:4–9)

Paul moves from addressing a specific situation (4:2–3) to a series of staccato-like imperatives addressed to the entire church. This style of exhortation is seen elsewhere in Paul (cf. 1 Thess. 5:23ff.), and, given the fact that the majority of the original recipients would have been hearing the letter read, these exhortations are presented in a form easily remembered. They are based on foundational themes of the letter and are a practical application of those themes in the life of the Philippian church.

The exhortation of 4:4 echoes a key theme that has surfaced throughout this letter (cf. 3:1; 4:1). It takes the form of both a parting "farewell" and a command for joy (Hawthorne, 181). The apostle encourages the Philippians to "keep on rejoicing" (the significance of the present imperative). As well as being continuous, this joy is to be independent of the many circumstances that impact them. It is not a joy that surfaces only when situations are advantageous, but is to be manifested on all occasions ("always"). Almost in response to an anticipated query, "But what about . . . ?" Paul reiterates his words: "I will say it again: Rejoice!" Their response to whatever situations come their way is to be the same—joy.

The Philippians should have no trouble modeling this exhortation. It was Paul's own response when he met opposition to the gospel on his arrival in Philippi. When he and Silas were unjustly and illegally beaten and jailed by the Philippian magistrates, they responded by singing with joy in the confines of that prison (Acts 16:25). For Paul, joy was a key characteristic of the kingdom of God (Rom. 14:17) and also a fruit of the indwelling Holy Spirit (Gal. 5:22). The Philippians should rejoice as they concerned themselves with the situations that had impacted Paul and Epaphroditus. It was to be their response in the face of opposition (1:28). The reason why this could be their deeply settled response to these many adverse circumstances was that it was rooted in One who does not change and who is sovereign over all human affairs. Their rejoicing was to be "in the Lord"; he was both the source of this joy and the object of it.

Paul's next exhortation has to do with the outworking of the Philippians' walk with the Lord. Their "gentleness" (*epieikes*) is to be evident to all people, Christian and non-Christian alike (v. 5). This word denotes a sense of reasonableness and occurs in secular writings to illustrate the idea of equitable justice, exercised according to the spirit, not necessarily the letter, of the law. In the Philippian context, it undoubtedly points to their need to exhibit humility and patience in the midst of misunderstanding and maltreatment—in the same way that Christ suffered (cf. 2:1–11).

The phrase that governs this response of the Philippians is found in the latter part of verse 5: "The Lord is near." The word "near" can have either a spatial or a temporal sense; most likely both senses can be drawn out of it here. The Lord's nearness in a spatial sense points to his continued presence with them and should serve as a motivation to godly behavior. His nearness in a temporal sense brings renewed encouragement and hope for the Philippians' ultimate salvation, and with that vindication from their current suffering.

Paul's exhortation in verse 6 follows logically on the assurance of verse 5b. Because the Lord is near, the Philippians should "not be anxious about anything." It is evident throughout this letter that they were experiencing a measure of anxiety (see comment on v. 4). The wording of this exhortation carries the sense that they are to stop worrying about anything (given the use of the Greek present imperative). Paul wants them to experience freedom from the crippling burden of anxiety—a freedom about which Jesus himself spoke (cf. Matt. 6:25–34).

In addition to the prohibition about anxiety, Paul also encourages a positive response. Believers are to commit everything to God in prayer. To emphasize this point, he uses three words for prayer: prayer (*proseuche*), petition (*deesis*), and the offering of requests (*aitemata*). The point Paul is making here is not to offer various options of contrasting styles of prayer. Rather, he is emphasizing the pervasive role of prayer in the life of the believer. Paul cannot envision a life lived without prayer.

The idea contained in the word "present" (*gnorizo*) is accurately reflected in the KJV translation of the latter part of verse 6 ("let your requests be made known"). The word denotes an openness and freedom in prayer whereby one exposes deep needs to God, partnering together with him. The word in no way implies that God is not aware of our requests before we ask them. It should also be noted that the milieu in which these requests are presented to God is one of thanksgiving (cf. Eph. 5:18–20; Col. 4:2; 1 Thess. 5:18).

The consequence of living an anxiety-free life of prayer is found in verse 7: "The peace of God" will fill the believer. This is the only use of the expression "peace of God" in the New Testament, and a number of commentators interpret this peace as the very peace experienced in the presence of God. It is a peace that is "the serenity where God lives" (O'Brien, 496). The outworking of this peace is best illustrated in the Hebrew word *shalom*—wholeness and total well-being (which only God can bestow; cf. Eph. 2:14; 2 Thess. 3:16).

This peace moves beyond a finite understanding of human beings; our plans, reasoning, and thought processes cannot replicate this divine peace. The role of this peace is to "guard" the entirety of the believer's inner being, from the center of emotions and feelings (the heart) through to the reasoned thought processes of the mind. The word "guard" would have evoked for Paul's hearers the image of a Roman garrison protecting a city such as Philippi (cf. 2 Cor. 11:32; Gal. 3:23). The peace of God brings protection from the attacks of the evil one to those who are "in Christ." Note how the apostle emphasizes the tremendous sphere of protection the believer has in relationship with Christ.

Paul concludes this series of exhortations by giving a general list of virtues that are to govern the Philippians' lives; he also notes some specific items that he wishes them to put into practice. The main verb of verses 8-9 is "think" (*logizomai*), a favorite word of the apostle. It is used here in the sense of focusing one's attention on something, with a view to having it ultimately govern one's behavior (Fee, 415). The expression "keep this in the forefront of your mind" may convey the sense of this important verb. Both verbs in the sentence ("think" and "put . . . into practice") carry the sense of continuous actions. In other words, Paul is advocating an ongoing lifestyle. The sense behind "put . . . into practice" is one of modeling or imitating behavior (cf. 3:17).

Many of the words Paul uses in verse 8 are common on virtue lists of both Stoicism and Jewish wisdom writings. What is clear is that Paul is referring to a general set of high values (hence his use of "whatever"), which reflects the best of their culture's ethical teachings. These teachings represent, albeit in an incomplete way, realities that the Philippians should reflect in their lives as believers. These virtues can only be truly fulfilled through the gospel.

(1) Paul's list of virtues begins with truth. To the Hebrew mind, truth would have been seen as that which stood over against falsehood, where the Greek (Platonic) mindset would have seen truth as that which stood over against what is apparent or fleeting. (2) The things that are "noble" are those worthy of respect, things that are transcendent or morally upright (used of deacons in 1 Tim. 3:8). (3) Those things that are "right" fulfill God's standards of justice and also represent the fulfilling of one's moral obligations to God and to fellow citizens. (4) Purity denotes those things that are ethically or religiously pure. In Old Testament worship, sacrifices were pure in that they were unblemished or untainted with evil. The word is also used to refer to chastity or moral purity (1 Tim. 5:22; Titus 2:5). (5) The next virtue, loveliness, occurs nowhere else in the New Testament. In its secular use, it refers to anything found admirable or worthy of love (cf. Fee, 418). (6) The final virtue in Paul's list is that which is "admirable"—of good reputation or free from offense.

Paul then sums up this list using two words. These virtues, and many like them, are "excellent" and "praiseworthy." The excellence to which Paul refers (*arete*) is common in Stoic thought and refers to moral excellence—everything that is good in human beings. The term is used only here in Paul and three times in Peter's letters (cf. 1 Peter 2:9; 2 Peter 1:3, 5). Those things that are praiseworthy (*epainos*) meet with widespread public approbation.

In verse 9, Paul moves from general virtues that should occupy the Philippians' thoughts to more specific issues. The pronoun shift in the original is missed in the NIV. "Whatever" (v. 9) is probably more appropriately rendered "those things that" (cf. Hawthorne, 189). The Philippians are called to put into practice the formal teaching they have "learned" from Paul. They are to do the same with the traditional teachings of the gospel they have "received" from him ("receive" is often used in Paul in a technical sense, referring to the handing down of traditional Christian teachings from the apostles; cf. 1 Cor. 11:23; 15:1, 3).

Moreover, Paul calls the Philippians to imitate his life—both those things they have heard about him and those things they have had an opportunity to observe firsthand. For Paul, there was to be no dissonance between belief and lifestyle. Here he rephrases his call that the church think "Christianly," a theme that resurfaces throughout the letter (recall Paul's use of *phroneo*). The outcome of all this is that "the God of peace will be with [them]" (cf. v. 7)—a wish Paul often expresses for his hearers (cf. Rom. 15:33; 16:20; 2 Cor. 13:11; 1 Thess. 5:23).

8. Paul's Gratitude for the Philippians' Gift (4:10–20)

This section of the letter is Paul's word of thanks (even though the word is not mentioned in the section!) for the gift sent to him by the Philippian church. This gift was delivered to him by Epaphroditus (2:25–30). The gift has been alluded to earlier in the letter (1:3, 5; 2:25), and is part of the Macedonians' ongoing commitment of support for Paul (cf. 4:16). Some have questioned whether this was a separate letter, later appended to the main letter by an editor. Given the fact that this note of thanks was a significant reason for Paul's writing, it is most appropriate to see this acknowledgment at this emphatic position in the letter. As the majority of the church heard this letter read, these words would have resonated in their hearing as their final and lasting remembrance of the letter. In this concluding acknowledgment of their support for him, Paul reflects both a sense of independence (vv. 10–13) and interdependence (vv. 14–19) in his relationship with the Philippians.

8.1. Commitment to Contentment (4:10–13)

Paul begins by expressing his joy at the Philippians' renewed concern for him. The particular event that triggered this outburst of joy was the coming of Epaphroditus with the gift from the church. Paul's joyful response (appropriately translated "rejoice"; cf. Fee, 428) communicates his thankfulness. The magnitude of his gratefulness is heightened by the word "greatly" (placed in an emphatic position in the sentence). Their rejoicing was "in the Lord," an expression linked with joy throughout the letter (cf. 3:1; 4:4).

The phrase "you have renewed your concern for me" connotes various things. The word "renewed" pictures the rejuvenation of a tree or plant in the spring, after a dormant season. Paul is not expressing that the Philippians' concern for him somehow lapsed as he was forgotten by them. He is implying that although they always cared for him, their care has now finally produced fruit—a tangible outworking in the gift sent to him. "Concern" translates a common word in the letter (*phroneo*; cf. 1:7; 2:2, 5). In his choice of words Paul speaks not only about being aware of someone's needs, but he also implies a practical application of that thought. In their giving they were in fact modeling towards him the thinking he has been trying to get them to exercise towards one another. This is further reinforced in the latter part of verse 10, where Paul acknowledges that the Philippians were indeed concerned for him, but were prevented from expressing this concern by a lack of opportunity (cf. O'Brien, 519).

This note of appreciation does not arise out of a sense of relief. The apostle is not saying "At last you've come through for me—I was getting desperate!" Paul underscores in verses 11–14 his freedom from the tyranny of need. His joy does not come from having his needs met, but that the Philippians' concern is rooted in the Lord. Paul's relationship with God has led to a sense of contentment that transcends his immediate circumstance. Stoic philosophers used the word "contentment" (*autarkes*) to denote the desirable character of a person that enabled one to live in a self-sufficient manner. This individual would live a life removed from the influence of external circumstances and pressures. For Paul, this contentment did not consist of self-sufficiency, but rather in dependency on God. It was God's power in him that enabled him to live above his present circumstances. This contentment was "learned," not in a theoretical way, but in the experiences through which God had led Paul up to this point in his life.

Paul expands on this contentment in verse 12. He has experienced both need and abundance. (The word for "need" here is the same one that pointed to Christ's humbling in 2:8, but given this context, it probably refers to economic deprivation.) He then employs two sets of contrasting verbs to show the extremes through which he has experienced this contentment: when he was well fed and when he went hungry, and when he was in times of abundance and when he had to go without. Through all these scenarios, he discovered the secret of contentment.

In a triumphal conclusion, verse 13 reveals the ultimate source of Paul's contentment: "I can do everything through him who gives me strength." This verse's context has often been violated and its truth pressed into the service of capricious whims. Clearly the apostle is referring to the wide range of his own experiences (v. 12). The significance of verse 13 is found in the fact that Paul's ability to cope with life's adversities did not come through self-sufficiency (as the Stoics taught), but through Christ-sufficiency. This strengthening was a part of Paul's ongoing Christian experience and was rooted in his being united with Christ.

8.2. Thanksgiving and Doxology (4:14–20)

Paul now reiterates his mutual interdependence with the Christians at Philippi. He recounts their sharing in his ministry from the time of their first encounter up to the most recent gift delivered by Epaphroditus.

Paul begins with a note of appreciation (v. 14). In case his hearers draw the conclusion from the previous verses that Paul is not thankful for their gift, he emphasizes, "It was good of you to share in my troubles." The phrase "it was good" is as close as Paul comes to actually saying "thank you" in this part of the letter (cf. Hawthorne, 202). He saw the Philippians' gift as more than just a token duty; it signified that the church really did have him in their hearts (cf. 1:7). They were partners, sharing in his difficulties. The word "troubles" is used here in the typically Pauline sense, pointing to hardship, persecution, or suffering. The Philippians truly lived out their faith as members of the body of Christ, where when one member suffers, all suffer (1 Cor. 12:26).

In verses 15–16, Paul joyfully recounts the Philippians' support extended towards him. He calls to mind the early days, when the gospel was first proclaimed in Philippi (Acts 16:4ff.). As the apostle moved through Macedonia to Achaia on his second missionary journey, the only church that supported his endeavors was the church at Philippi. In language borrowed from the world of commerce, he saw their partnership as a matter of "giving and receiving" (words roughly equivalent to the concepts of debiting and crediting). Paul "gave" the gospel to the Philippians while "receiving" their support. In fact, verse 16 notes that they sent assistance more than once to Paul even before he left Macedonia, while he was still in the neighboring city of Thessalonica (cf. Acts 17:1–9). The Philippians, in turn, "gave" of their material and moral support to Paul, having received and acted on the message of good news that they had heard.

In verse 17, Paul reiterates the purity of his motives in his expression of thanks to the believers in Philippi. He is not looking for "more of the same" or giving thanks to somehow lay groundwork for future favors. His motivation is for their benefit. His description of their reward for partnering with him is expressed in financial terms: Their partnership in the gospel will yield interest or dividends (lit., "fruit"), which will in turn accrue "to [their] account."

Continuing with the analogy of the world of banking, Paul notes in verse 18 that he has been paid in full (the expression denotes a receipt drawn up for payment in full in discharge of a bill; cf. Martin, 1976, 167). In fact, his account is overflowing because of the recent gift brought by Epaphroditus. He then switches metaphors and proceeds to describe their gifts to him in language of his Old Testament heritage. Their gifts are a "fragrant offering [cf. Ex. 29:18; Lev. 1:9], an acceptable sacrifice [cf. Rom. 12:1]," phrases denoting the quality required of sacrifices to be pleasing to God and acceptable to him (Paul uses similar language in Eph. 5:2, in describing Christ's sacrifice on the cross).

Paul responds to the magnitude of the Philippians' gift by confidently assuring them that God will reward them for their participation. The warmth of this response is seen first in his use of the personal reference, "my God" (cf. 1:3). Given the fact that they have faithfully met his needs, God will in turn meet their needs. His provision for them will be in a manner "according to his glorious riches," an expression that denotes both the source of their provisions and the abundant way in which they are given to the Philippians (cf. O'Brien, 547).

The word "glorious" (lit., "in glory") presents a number of interpretive options. It can point to the fact that God's blessing on the Philippian believers will be reserved for a future age—that is, when they get to heaven. It can carry an adjectival sense and serve to define "riches" (cf. NIV, "glorious riches"). It can be used in an adverbial sense and define the verb "meet" ("gloriously meet all your needs"). Fee advocates that the expression is best understood in a locative sense, referring to the "ineffable and eternal glory in which God dwells" (Fee, 453). This supply is available to the Philippians through Christ, the one for whom Paul counted "everything a loss" (3:8). Paul concludes this confident assertion with a doxology that ascribes eternal praise to God for his wonderful provision for them (4:20).

9. Paul's Farewell (4:21–23)

Whereas secular letters often concluded with a wish for good luck or good health, extended by the author to the recipient, Paul typically concluded his letters by offering words of greeting (e.g., Rom. 6:3ff.; 1 Cor. 16:19ff.; 1 Thess. 5:26ff.). Philippians reflects this style as the apostle wraps up this letter with some final greetings. This final section of the letter may well have been a note that Paul himself actually penned, after his scribe concluded the more formal part of the letter. This section is addressed to a number of individuals within the church—possibly the leaders referred to in 1:1 (hence the use of the plural imperative "greet").

In verse 21, Paul is not merely giving a blanket greeting to the church at Philippi, in the sense that a person today may request that someone "say hi to everyone for me." In keeping with his warm and cordial relationship with the Philippians, he is asking that each and every believer in the congregation have a greeting conveyed to them. Note how its inclusiveness reflects Paul's emphasis on unity in the letter. "In Christ Jesus" refers to the standing each of the saints enjoys and does not reflect on the nature of the greeting Paul is requesting.

Paul further expands his personal greeting to include all the saints in Rome, especially those in Caesar's household. Although it is doubtful that these individuals were anything more than soldiers, slaves, and civil servants in the service of the empire, their significance should not be minimized. In a milieu such as Philippi, where those who proclaimed Christ as Lord were being marginalized by those who worshiped Caesar, it would have been encouraging to know that Christians were actually in the employ of the emperor.

Paul's final words of benediction echo his opening words. His hearers are reminded of the "grace" extended to them because of the vicarious work done for them by their now exalted Lord (2:6–11). The entire focus of the letter has been Christ, and now Paul prays that his grace will extend into the hearts and lives of each of the Philippian believers as they press on "toward the goal" (3:14). Amen!

BIBLIOGRAPHY

H. Balz and G. Schneider, *Exegetical Dictionary of the New Testament*, 3 vols. (1994); F. F. Bruce, *Paul, Apostle of the Heart Set Free* (1978); M. Dunham, *Galatians, Ephesians, Philippians, Colossians, Philemon*, Communicator's Commentary (1982); G. Fee, *Paul's Letter to the Philippians*, NICNT (1995); G. F. Hawthorne, *Philippians*, WBC (1991); J. Jeremias, *Jerusalem in the Time of Jesus* (1969); H. Kent Jr., "Philippians," in *EBC*, vol. 11 (1978); S. Kim, *The Origin of Paul's Gospel* (1982); J. B. Lightfoot, *Philippians*, Crossway Classic Commentaries (1994); R. Martin, *Carmen Christi: Philippians 2:5–11 in Recent Interpretation and in the Setting of Early Christian Worship* (1983); idem, *Philippians*, NCBC (1976); H. C. G. Moule, *Philippians*, Cambridge Greek New Testament (1897); T. O'Brien, *Commentary on Philippians*, NIGTC (1991); M. Silva, *Philippians*, Baker's Exegetical Commentary on the New Testament (1992); F. Thielman, *NIV Application Commentary: Philippians* (1995).

COLOSSIANS

Sven K. Soderlund

INTRODUCTION

The letter to the Colossians is normally classified as one of Paul's four Prison Letters (along with Ephesians, Philippians, and Philemon). Of these it shares the closest affinity with Ephesians, but has elements in common with Philemon as well since both were sent to the same city. The letter was written in response to a theological/Christological crisis threatening the church in Colosse, of which Paul had been informed by his co-worker Epaphras. In the process of refuting the false teachings concerning Christ, Paul takes the opportunity to instruct the Colossians on a wide range of issues, from prayer to the details of practical living.

1. Authorship, Date, and Provenance

The letter opens (1:1) and closes (4:18) with a clear affirmation of Pauline authorship (in 1:1 Paul includes his associate Timothy in the greeting). Yet in the last century this assertion of Paul as the author has increasingly been challenged, so that today many scholars prefer to classify the letter as "Deutero-Pauline," meaning that it was written in a later period, probably by a disciple of Paul. The main lines of evidence in the argument have to do with matters of vocabulary and style, theological differences between Colossians and other letters of Paul, and its relationship to Ephesians. Thus, for instance, some studies focus on tabulations of vocabulary and syntactical constructions deemed uncharacteristic of Paul (e.g., the number of words unique to this letter, the frequency of certain grammatical constructions in comparison with other letters, and the relative length and complexity of sentence structure; see Mark Kiley, *Colossians As Pseudepigraphy* [1986]).

As for theological themes, scholars point out that this letter omits discussion of familiar Pauline topics (e.g., justification, law, righteousness, and salvation) and introduces new concepts not broached elsewhere (e.g., the "cosmic Christ"). Others argue that the close relationship of Colossians to Ephesians implies that neither letter is authentic, on the grounds that it is unlikely for the same person to produce two such similar works.

Yet not all scholars are persuaded by these arguments against Pauline authorship. When set in a larger context, many of the so-called unique features of Colossians—grammatical, stylistic, and theological—fall within the range of Pauline expression when due allowance is made for a new situation, a new readership, a new phase in the apostle's own life, and possibly the greater degree of freedom permitted to the secretarial assistant (might it even have been Timothy? cf. 1:1b; see the discussion in O'Brien, 1982, xli–xlix; also Carson, Moo, and Morris, 1992, 331–34). Furthermore, note that all arguments advanced against Pauline authorship are internal and circumstantial. As to *external* testimony, the church fathers consistently accepted Pauline authorship. While this is not the place to engage in a detailed discussion of this large and complex debate, it is the place to state the perspective from which the following commentary is written, namely, an acceptance of and confidence in the explicit statements of 1:1 and 4:18, which affirm Paul the apostle as author.

The issues of date and place of composition are closely tied together. The fact that it is one of the Prison Letters (cf. the reference to Paul's "chains" in 4:3, 18 as well as the mention of Aristarchus as a "fellow prisoner" in 4:10) limits the range of possibilities for date and location of composition. On the basis of our knowledge from the book of Acts, Paul was in prison on three occasions: in Philippi (Acts 16:16–40), Caesarea (chs. 24–26), and Rome (28:30–31). Realistically, only Caesarea and Rome are serious contenders (Paul had only an overnight stay in the jail in Philippi). Although some scholars have argued for Caesarea as the place of composition, the traditional site is that of Rome.

In this century, Ephesus has also been proposed as the site of Paul's residence at the time of writing. The argument for this is the proximity of Colosse to Ephesus and the consideration that the slave Onesimus (cf. 4:9; Philem. 10), whom Paul met in prison and led to faith, would more likely have fled from his home in Colosse to a neighboring city like Ephesus rather than to faraway Rome. A weakness in this argument is the absence of any concrete knowledge of an Ephesian imprisonment, though Paul does write in 2 Corinthians 11:23 of having been in prison frequently, possibly including Ephesus.

In the end, Rome remains the site with least difficulties, especially when considered together with the most probable place of composition for Ephesians and Philippians. On this reasoning, then, the letter would have been written from Rome, sometime between the years A.D. 60 and 62, probably earlier rather than later in that period—that is, during that phase of Paul's Roman imprisonment reflected in Acts 28:30–31, when he was able to stay in his rented quarters receiving guests, preaching and teaching (and presumably writing!) about the kingdom of God and the Lord Jesus Christ.

2. Readership and Occasion for Writing

The letter was sent to "the holy and faithful brothers in Christ at Colosse" (see comments on 1:2), that is, to the congregation of believers in the city of Colosse. At the time of writing, Colosse was a city of modest size in the south-central region (Lycus Valley) of the Roman province of Asia (modern western Turkey), approximately ninety miles inland from the Greek coastal cities of Ephesus and Miletus on the Aegean Sea. Although it had known more prosperous times in previous centuries, Colosse increasingly lost ground to its neighboring cities of Laodicea and Hierapolis (cf. 2:1; 4:13) since a major north-south/east-west road junction had been moved west from Colosse to Laodicea. Perhaps it was the smallest of the several cities to which Paul wrote letters, though the size of the city and the congregation has nothing to do with the importance of the letter and its teaching for us.

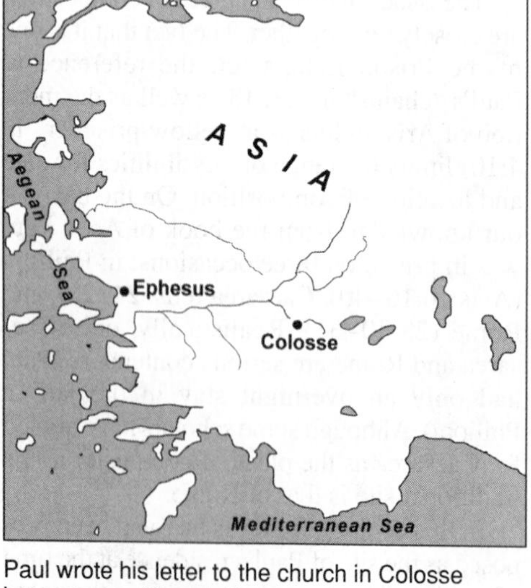

Paul wrote his letter to the church in Colosse between A.D. 60 and 62.

The church in Colosse had been planted by Epaphras, a native of Colosse and one of Paul's coworkers (see the comments on 1:7; 4:12–13), probably during the time of Paul's three-year ministry in Ephesus. Initially it had fared well (see Paul's prayer of thanksgiving, 1:3–8), but with the passing of time problems arose. These had to do with a number of theological issues, especially with new teachings from outsiders regarding the person of Christ. In comparison with the original apostolic proclamation, these teachings seriously undervalued Christ's person and work and consequently led to several sub-Christian practices of both a mystical and legalistic nature.

Although the exact content of the so-called "Colossian heresy" is not as clearly spelled out as we might have wished (see the suggestions in the commentaries; e.g., Barth and Blanke, 1994, 21–40; Bruce, 1984, 17–26; O'Brien, 1982, xxx–xxxviii), the issue was important enough for Paul to compose a major refutation and send it to the church in Colosse even before the presumed return of their representative, Epaphras. This "refutation"—in reality, a marvelous affirmation about the person and work of Christ—constitutes the heart of the letter (principally 1:15–3:4). The central section is preceded by Paul's typical opening prayers of thanksgiving and intercession (1:3–14), and followed by a series of edifying exhortations regarding true Christian living (3:5–4:6), all brought to a close in the final greetings (4:7–18).

3. Text and Canon

The text of Colossians was transmitted as part of the larger Pauline corpus and as such reflects the same kind of textual problems we find throughout the other letters and indeed throughout the New Testament. However, apart from a few uncertain readings, the textual difficulties are not of an extensive or serious nature, so that with confidence it can be said that "there is no reason to doubt that we have the text of the letter substantially as Paul wrote it" (Carson, Moo, and Morris, 1992, 337).

The same thing can be said with regard to the adoption of the letter into the canon. From the middle of the second century it was being read as Scripture in the church and quoted authoritatively by authors such as Justin Martyr, Irenaeus, Clement of Alexandria, and Tertullian. Also before the end of the second century it was included in the canonical lists of Marcion and the Muratorian Canon and formed part of the ancient Syriac and Old Latin translations of the New Testament. In short, there can be no doubt about its right to inclusion in the Christian canon as authoritative Scripture.

OUTLINE

1. **Introductory Greetings** (1:1–2)
   - **1.1.** Authors (1:1)
   - **1.2.** Recipients (1:2a)
   - **1.3.** Greetings (1:2b)
2. **Paul's Prayer** (1:3–14)
   - **2.1.** Prayer of Thanksgiving (1:3–8)
     - **2.1.1.** Thanksgiving Directed to God (1:3)
     - **2.1.2.** Thanksgiving Motivated By the Colossians' Faith and Love (1:4–8)
       - **2.1.2.1.** Colossians' Faith and Love Inspired By the Hope Stored Up for Them (1:4–5a)
       - **2.1.2.2.** Colossians' Hope Communicated in the Preaching of the Gospel (1:5b–8)
   - **2.2.** Prayer of Intercession (1:9–14)
     - **2.2.1.** Initial Request: That the Colossians Be Filled With the Knowledge of God's Will (1:9)
     - **2.2.2.** Ultimate Goal: That the Colossians Live a Life Worthy of the Lord and Please Him in Everything (1:10–14)
       - **2.2.2.1.** Means of Achieving This Goal (1:10b–12a)
       - **2.2.2.2.** Transition to a New Theme: The Father Has Secured the Believers' Redemption Through His Son (1:12b–14)
3. **Christ's Supremacy** (1:15–23)
   - **3.1.** Christ's Supremacy in Creation (1:15–17)
   - **3.2.** Christ's Supremacy in Redemption (1:18–20)
   - **3.3.** Christ's Redemptive Work Applied to the Colossians (1:21–23)
     - **3.3.1.** The Reality, Means, and Purpose of the Colossians' Reconciliation (1:21–22)
     - **3.3.2.** Exhortation to Remain Firm in the Faith (1:23)
4. **Paul's Ministry** (1:24–2:5)
   - **4.1.** Nature of Paul's Ministry: To Be a "Servant" of the Church (1:25; cf. 1:23)
   - **4.2.** Mandate of Paul's Ministry: To Announce the "Word of God in Its Fullness" (1:25; cf. 1:28a)
   - **4.3.** Message of Paul's Ministry: "Christ in You, the Hope of Glory" (1:26–27; cf. 2:3)
   - **4.4.** Goal of Paul's Ministry: To "Present Everyone Perfect in Christ" (1:28b; cf. 2:2–3)
   - **4.5.** Costs of Paul's Ministry: Labor, Struggle, and Suffering (1:29–2:1; cf. 1:24)
   - **4.6.** Resources of Paul's Ministry: Christ's "Energy" Powerfully At Work in Him (1:29b)
   - **4.7.** Rewards of Paul's Ministry: To See the Firmness of the Believers' Faith (2:4–5)
5. **Warnings Against False Doctrines and Legalistic Practices** (2:6–3:4)
   - **5.1.** Exhortations to Perseverance and Description of False Teachings (2:6–8)
   - **5.2.** Exposition of the Doctrine of Christ (2:9–15)
     - **5.2.1.** Christ's Person (2:9–10)
     - **5.2.2.** Christ's Work (2:11–15)
   - **5.3.** Specific Warnings Against Legalism (2:16–19)

COMMENTARY

1. Introductory Greetings (1:1–2)

Paul begins his letter to the Colossians—as, indeed, he does all his letters—with the standard Greco-Roman letter formula: "X to Y, greetings." This formula remained fixed for centuries in the correspondence literature of antiquity, both Hebrew and Greek. Yet, while Paul adopted the standard convention, he did not hesitate to modify and adapt it. In fact, in comparison with the tedious monotony of the introductory formulas of hundreds of letters that have survived from antiquity, Paul's introductions are positively creative. Each of the introductions to his thirteen letters is essentially the same in structure, but also different in length and content. Thus the introduction to Colossians has certain similarities and certain differences in comparison with the other letters.

1.1. Authors (1:1)

First introduced are the "authors," Paul and Timothy, though to what extent Timothy was actually involved in the composition of the letter is a moot question. Paul has a lovely habit of associating his coworkers in the introductory greetings of various letters (regarding Timothy see 2 Cor. 1:1; Phil. 1:1; 1 Thess. 1:1; 2 Thess. 1:1; Philem. 1) and of employing the first person plural "we" rather than the singular "I" in large sections of his letters (e.g. Col. 1:3–14). Yet this may mean nothing more than that these trusted coworkers were with him at the time of writing, supporting and encouraging the apostle in his various missionary tasks, including his writing ministry. Certainly there is no doubt that Paul was the principal author of this letter.

The descriptions of Paul and Timothy in this letter are identical to those found in 2 Corinthians 1:1. In both cases Paul introduces himself as "apostle of Christ Jesus by the will of God," and Timothy as "our brother." Paul's appeal to his apostleship "by the will of God" is probably intended to establish his credentials as the authorized teacher of doctrine, a point certainly relevant to this letter, given the significant doctrinal issues at stake in Colosse. His reference to Timothy as "*our* brother" is the NIV rendering of what is otherwise literally translated "*the* brother," the article in the Greek text perhaps pointing to the special sense in which Timothy was "brother" to Paul (that is, as "fellow worker," cf. Rom. 16:21).

1.2. Recipients (1:2a)

The intended readers of the letter were "the holy and faithful brothers in Christ [Jesus] at Colosse" (v. 2a). However, there is an ambiguity in the Greek text surrounding the translation of the words *hagiois kai pistois adelphois*, rendered in the NIV by the adjectival phrase "holy and faithful brothers." Each of the words needs to be looked at. Instead of reading *hagiois* as an adjective and translating "holy . . . brothers," *hagiois* may be read as a noun and translated simply as "saints" (KJV, JB) or, on the basis of OT associations (cf. Ex. 19:6; Lev. 11:44; 19:2, etc.) as "God's people" (GNB, REB). This is, in fact, how *hagioi* is used in Ephesians 1:1 and Philippians 1:1, and that may well have been the way Paul intended it in Colossians 1:2 as well (in 1:4, 12, 26, *hagioi* functions as a noun; in 1:22; 3:12 as an adjective).

Assuming the noun use of *hagioi* in 1:2, *pistois* ("faithful") then modifies *adelphois* ("brothers") by itself, and the phrase can be translated either as "faithful brothers" (describing the "faithful" character of the Colossians), or, as in the NIV margin, "believing brothers" (identifying the Colossian "brothers" positionally as believers). But since it would be a redundancy for Paul to say "*believing* brothers" (are there any other kind?), we assume the intended meaning of *pistois* in this context is "faithful"—possibly a commendation of those Colossians who had remained faithful in the face of the new teachings that were disrupting their church (see below on 1:23; 2:5–7).

Finally, there is the matter of the translation of the word *adelphoi* by the gender-specific word "brothers." Although *adelphoi* is the word that Paul regularly uses in his letters to refer to the company of believers, it is clear that by this term he does not mean only male believers (note that "the brothers in Laodicea" in 4:15 include Nympha, a woman). The term *adelphoi*, as Paul uses it is, in fact, not gender-specific. By it he means to include the *adelphai* ("sisters") as well. For this reason it is permissible and strongly desirable to translate the word by the English compound expression, "brothers and sisters" (cf. NRSV). Putting it all together, the opening phrase of verse 2 might well be translated, "To the saints [or, To God's holy people] and faithful brothers and sisters. . . ."

These "saints" and "faithful brothers and sisters" are now identified as living at one and the same time in two places: they are both "in Christ" and "in [or "at," NIV] Colosse." As believers they experience a special communion with Christ since they are in him and he in them (cf. Col. 1:27–28; also Gal. 2:20–21). Yet this spiritual sphere of existence does not remove the Colossians from involvement in their own city and culture. On the contrary, the challenge for them is to be in the world but not of the world (as in Jesus' prayer for his disciples, cf. John 17:14–18). Their responsibility was to bear witness to the truth of the gospel in Colosse, all the while cultivating their own life of devotion and piety "in Christ."

1.3. Greetings (1:2b)

The introduction closes with the standard invocation of the "grace and peace" formula. Yet for Paul it was more than just a formula. It was his sincere desire that the Colossians share in all the blessings of the new and old covenants that were available to them. "Grace" (*charis*) was the word especially associated with the blessings of the new era. John expressed it in the phrase, "The law was given through Moses; grace and truth came through Jesus Christ" (John 1:17). Nevertheless, it was Paul who, more than any other writer of the New Testament (96 out of 156 occurrences in the New Testament), made it a key word of his theology. By it he sought to signify all the blessings of divine favor that were now freely available to the community of God's people.

"Peace" was a word with deep roots in the Old Testament. Although Paul wrote in Greek and used the Greek word *eirene*, he no doubt had in mind the broader and richer concept of "peace" contained in the Hebrew word *shalom*. What he wished for the Colossians was the experience of full harmony and creativity at the deepest levels, the kind of well-being that can only come from knowing and serving God. No doubt in making this invocation he had in mind the ancient Aaronic blessing, "The LORD turn his face toward you and give you *shalom/eirene*" (Num. 6:26). The source of these blessings, both in Old and New Testament times, was "God our Father."

Such is the brief introduction of the letter to the Colossians. That Paul can pour so much significant vocabulary and theological content into an introductory correspondence formula worn thin by time is a witness to the work of the creative Spirit within him and a constant reminder of the challenge for us to transform even the routine and ordinary things of life into the extraordinary by the touch of that same Spirit.

2. Paul's Prayer (1:3–14)

In typical Pauline fashion, the introductory greetings are followed by an apostolic prayer report (cf. also Rom. 1:8–10; Eph. 1:15–19a; Phil. 1:3–11; 2 Thess. 1:3–4, 11–12; Philem. 4–7), consisting of a thanksgiving section and an intercessory section (vv. 3–8 and vv. 9–14). The twofold nature of this prayer—obvious enough through even a simple reading of verses 3–14—is confirmed by the specific prayer vocabulary Paul uses at the beginning of each paragraph (v. 3 and v. 9). In both of these verses, he employs both the general term for prayer (*proseuchomai:* "when we *pray,*" v. 3; "we have not stopped *praying* for you," v. 9), as well as a specific word for prayer that is going to dominate the paragraph—namely, thanksgiving in verse 3 ("We always *thank* God"), and petition or intercession in verse 9 ("*asking* God to fill you"). Additional links between the two paragraphs are the emphasis on the constancy of Paul's thanksgiving and intercession ("We *always* thank God," v. 3; "*we have not stopped* praying for you," v. 9) and the repetition of the phrase "bearing fruit" and "growing" (v. 6 and v. 10).

It is important to observe the sequence of Paul's introductory prayers in this and other letters: thanksgiving first, followed by petition and intercession. Paul undoubtedly intended the clarity and frequency of this pattern to serve as a model for the prayer life of his recently established congregations—and, by extension, for all those who follow.

2.1. Prayer of Thanksgiving (1:3–8)

This paragraph, which in the Greek consists of one long sentence, expresses first to whom the prayer is directed (v. 3) and then the motivation for the thanksgiving (vv. 4–8).

2.1.1. Thanksgiving Directed to God (1:3). As the blessings of "grace and peace" come *from* "God our Father" (v. 2), so now the prayer of thanksgiving is directed *to* "God, the Father." This pattern of addressing prayer—whether thanksgiving or otherwise—to God the Father (rather than another person of the Trinity; though cf. 1 Tim. 1:12) is well established in Paul's writings and elsewhere (cf. Matt. 6:9; Luke 11:2; Rom. 1:8; 1 Cor. 1:4; 2 Cor. 1:3; Eph. 1:3; Phil. 1:3; 1 Thess. 1:2; 2 Thess. 1:3; 2 Tim. 1:3; Philem. 4), where, in each case, prayer is addressed to God as "Father," identified as such explicitly in the text or implicitly in the context. Believers who wish to follow biblical models of prayer will take note accordingly.

In the case of Colossians 1:3 (as well as in the doxological introductions of 2 Cor. 1:3 and Eph. 1:3), the thanksgiving and praise items are directed not just to "God, the Father," but to "God, the Father of our Lord Jesus Christ." To be sure, he is "*our* Father" (v. 2), but in a special way he is the Father of the "Lord Jesus Christ" (cf. Rom. 15:6; 2 Cor. 1:3; 11:31; Eph. 1:3). While the precise nature of this special relationship between the Father and the Lord Jesus is not further defined here, the fact of it is nevertheless strongly affirmed by Paul's manner of expression. It is to this "Father," then, the Father both of us and of the Lord Jesus Christ, that prayers of thanksgiving are to be addressed.

2.1.2. Thanksgiving Motivated By the Colossians' Faith and Love (1:4–8). In verses 4–8, which consist of a series of cascading clauses, one dependent on the other (without sentence breaks, as is done in most of the modern translations, including NIV), Paul first cites his primary reason for giving thanks (note the importance of thanksgiving in this book; see 1:12; 2:7; 3:15, 17; 4:2) and follows it up with words of explanation and elaboration.

The principal motivation for thanksgiving is the Colossians' faith and love—their faith "in Christ Jesus" and their love "for all the saints" (v. 4)—both, no doubt, communicated to Paul by Epaphras. These vertical and horizontal relationships intersect in the life of the Colossian believers, their love flowing out of their faith. Reflection on the Colossians' faith and love leads Paul to consider the different steps by which they came to participate in these Christian graces.

2.1.2.1. Colossians' Faith and Love Inspired by the Hope Stored Up for Them (1:4-5a). The faith and love that inspire the thanksgiving prayer have a specific cause: namely, the "hope[1] that is stored up for you [i.e., the Colossians] in heaven" (v. 5a). "Hope" in this context must be understood not as a subjective longing on the part of the Colossians, but rather as an objective certainty—what Paul later in the prayer refers to as the "inheritance" that the saints in the kingdom of light will attain (v. 12). With such a "hope" awaiting them, the Colossians are eager to express their faith in Christ Jesus and their love for God's people.

2.1.2.2. Colossians' Hope Communicated in the Preaching of the Gospel (1:5b–8). But how did the Colossians learn about this "hope" stored up for them in heaven? They heard about it "in the word of truth," namely, in the preaching of "the gospel" (v. 5b). Mention of the word "gospel" at the end of verse 5 prompts Paul to reflect further on this important subject. It is a gospel that is bearing fruit and growing throughout the world as well as mong the Colossians, primarily because it is gospel that communicates "God's grace in all s truth" (v. 6). Specifically, the Colossians earned about this gospel from Epaphras, aul's "dear fellow servant" and their "faithful inister" (v. 7). Epaphras was a member of the olossian community of believers (4:12; see omment there), and he had reported to Paul ne good news about their "love in the pirit"—nicely paraphrased in the REB as "the ve the Spirit has awakened in you" (v. 8).

This is the first of only two occurrences of ne word "Spirit" (*pneuma*) in Colossians (the ther is in 2:5). The adjective *pneumatikos* "spiritual," "of the Spirit") occurs in 1:9 and :16e. Paul's primary concern in this letter is o refute false teachings having to do with *hristology* rather than *pneumatology*; hence, e concentrates on Christ rather than the Spirit. Nonetheless, it is important to observe how in he opening paragraph of this letter Paul indirectly affirms a full-blown Trinitarian position s the background for all his other comments n the Godhead (see G. Fee, 1994, 636–57, for thorough discussion of Paul's use of "S/spirit" terminology in Colossians).

2.2. Prayer of Intercession (1:9–14)

The opening phrase of verse 9, "For this eason," links the intercessory part of the prayer with the preceding thanksgiving. Motivated by the good report concerning the Colossians' faith and love, Paul now turns to pray for hem in a number of specific ways. It is clear hat for Paul, good progress in the lives of his converts and daughter churches was no cause for slackened intercession. In fact, according o the evidence that we have, Paul engaged in intercession as much for confirmation and stability in the faith as for crisis situations.

2.2.1. Initial Request: That the Colossians Be Filled With the Knowledge of God's Will (1:9). Paul begins his intercessory prayer by asking God that the Colossian believers be filled with "the knowledge of his will." Paul knew from experience the importance of knowing and doing God's will. After all, he had been appointed an apostle "by the will of God" (Col. 1:1) and regularly sought God's will in all his affairs (cf. Rom. 1:10; 15:32). Hence he was genuinely concerned that believers in his churches learn to do the same (cf. Rom. 12:2; Eph. 5:17; 6:6).

Paul goes on to make two further observations with respect to the knowledge of this divine will (1:9): It is available in full measure ("asking God *to fill* you with the knowledge of his will"), and it has its source in the Spirit ("through all *spiritual* wisdom and understanding"). That "spiritual" means "of the Spirit" seems obvious for at least four reasons: (1) The word *pneumatikos* ("spiritual") is related to *pneuma* ("Spirit") in the same way as *kyriakos* ("Lord's"; cf. 1 Cor. 11:20) is related to *kyrios* ("Lord"); (2) where Paul uses this word elsewhere, he relates it to the Spirit (e.g., 1 Cor. 2:13; 12:1); (3) the wording of Colossians 1:9 is similar to Ephesians 1:17 ("the Spirit of wisdom and revelation"); and (4) Pauline theology generally is Spirit-oriented. Thus, the phrase that in the NIV is rendered "through all *spiritual* wisdom and understanding" should instead be translated "by means of all *the Spirit's* wisdom and understanding/ insight" (G. Fee, 1994, 648–57; see also comments on Col. 3:16).

2.2.2. Ultimate Goal: That the Colossians Live a Life Worthy of the Lord and Please Him in Everything (1:10–14). The knowledge of God's will is fundamental to the Christian life, but it is not an end in itself. Rather, it has as its ultimate goal godly *living:* "that you may live a life [lit., "walk"] worthy of the Lord and may please him in every way" (v. 10a), a sentiment echoed in other Pauline contexts (with the same verb "walk" in Eph. 4:1; 1 Thess. 2:12; with the verb *politeuomai* ["live as citizens"] in Phil. 1:27).

2.2.2.1. Means of Achieving This Goal (1:10–12a). How, then, can the Colossians live such a life and please the Lord "in every way"? Verses 10b–12a give the answer in a series of four parallel participial clauses, all dependent on the preceding phrase, "live a life worthy of the Lord and . . . please him in every way": "bearing fruit in every good work," "growing in the knowledge of God," "being strengthened with all power . . . [for] endurance and patience," and "joyfully giving thanks to the Father."

This is practical living at its best. It was a prayer that Paul could pray for the Colossians on the basis of his knowledge of Christian ideals generally, as well as on the basis of his knowledge of the situation in Colosse specifically. But independent of the original situation that gave it birth, the prayer remains a powerful model of intercessory prayer on behalf of friends, family, acquaintances, groups, and churches. It embodies the highest biblical ideals for which we are to strive: fruitfulness, growth in the knowledge of God, strength for endurance, and joyful thanksgiving.

2.2.2.2. Transition to a New Theme: The Father Has Secured the Believers' Redemption Through His Son (1: 12b–14). Mention of the word "Father" at the beginning of verse 12 triggers a new series of associations. Paul prays that the Colossians will "joyfully [give] thanks to the Father"—that is, the Father whom he has previously qualified as "our Father" (v. 2) and "the Father of our Lord Jesus Christ" (v. 3).

But what has the Father done for which we are to give thanks? In an important transitional passage (vv. 12b–14), intended (so it seems) gently to introduce the readers/hearers of the letter to its central Christological theme (vv. 15–20), Paul highlights two critical actions of the Father: He "has qualified you [i.e., the Colossians] to share in . . . the kingdom of light" (v. 12b) and he "has rescued us [note the change from "you" to "us"] from the dominion of darkness and brought us into the kingdom of the Son he loves" (v. 13). And how did the Father accomplish this salvific work? He did it through the Son, "in whom we have redemption, the forgiveness of sins" (v. 14)—a soteriological statement of highest importance, which will be developed at greater length in the next couple of chapters.

Little by little, therefore, the prayer of intercession modulates into a passage of great intensity and theological concentration. Obviously the prayer itself, including the transitional segment, has been constructed with much care and forethought. In fact, the "forethought" element in both the prayer proper (vv. 3–12a) and the bridging portion (vv. 12b–14) is evident in the several ways in which the passage anticipates not only the Christological hymn of 1:15–20, but also other important aspects of the entire letter. This construction becomes clear by the way significant vocabulary is repeated both in the prayer and in the body of the letter. For example:

- "to fill" in 1:9 and 1:25; 2:10; 4:17
- "fullness" in 1:19 and 2:9
- "knowledge" in 1:9–10 and 2:2–3; 3:10
- "wisdom" in 1:9 and 1:28; 2:3, 23; 3:16; 4:5
- "understanding" in 1:9 and 2:2
- "strengthened with all power" in 1:11 and "his energy, which so powerfully works in me" in 1:29
- the great redemption affirmations of 1:13–14 ("he has rescued us"; "in whom [i.e., the Son] we have redemption, the forgiveness of sins"), to which theme the letter shortly returns in 1:20–22; 2:13–14

The repetition of these words and phrase functions as part of the glue that holds togethe the different parts of the letter. They also pre pare the reader for what is immediately ahea (Paul does something similar in Phil. 1:3–11 2 Thess. 1:3–10).

3. Christ's Supremacy (1:15–23)

In agreement with the section heading foun in the NIV at 1:15 ("The Supremacy of Christ") the outline adopted here likewise assumes tha a major new division begins at this point in th letter. Such an assumption is indeed reasonabl and defensible, since—as almost all ar agreed—verse 15 begins the great Chris Hymn, with its remarkable combination o Christological content and poetic form. However, it must be recognized that in the Greek sentence structure of verses 14–15 no shar division exists, as is implied in the NIV's new sentence and paragraph commencing at vers 15. On the contrary, verse 15 begins with a relative pronoun and verb, which, if translated literally, would read simply, "who is . . ." (cf. KJV, RV, ASV); in other words, Paul is simply continuing the long sentence begun in verse 9.

The practical lesson to observe from this is that in the mind of Paul there was no sharp division between prayer and theology. On the contrary, in his letters theology is born in and flows out of prayer and often returns to prayer;[2] in fact, it is sometimes difficult to determine where one leaves off and the other begins. Certainly there is no conflict or tension between them. Devotion and doctrine, spirituality and theology, piety and profundity go hand in hand. This was the perspective of the primitive church; it is a perspective that the modern church desperately needs, too.

Having introduced "the Son" in 1:14 as the one "in whom we have redemption, the forgiveness of sins," Paul now proceeds to cite a creedal formula that highlights Christ's role in the principal events of the biblical drama, namely, in the work of creation and redemption. This strong affirmation of Christ's person and work is then applied to the experience of the Christian believers in Colosse. The basic outline of the section, therefore, looks as follows:

Christ's supremacy in creation (1:15–17)
Christ's supremacy in redemption (1:18–20)
Christ's redemptive work applied to the Colossians (1:21–23).

Although this schema seems to present a three-point outline, in reality what we have are two major parts: the Christ Hymn itself (vv. 15–20), with two subdivisions (vv. 15–17, vv. 18–20), and the application paragraph (vv. 21–23).

As for the Christ Hymn, considerable debate exists regarding the background, function, and form of this "hymn." Was it written by Paul, or did it exist already as a confessional statement in the apostolic church, one that Paul simply has integrated into his letter? Assuming that it did exist as an independent creedal affirmation in the apostolic church, how far did the original hymn extend? Did it extend all the way to the end of verse 20, or—as some believe—only to the end of verse 18a? These questions, as interesting and important as they are in their own right, cannot be pursued in detail here (see Martin, 1978, 61–66; O'Brien, 1982, 32–42). Whether Paul wrote it or whether it was something he adopted (and adapted) from the church of his day are matters of relative indifference as far as its message is concerned. Either way, the sentiments expressed here enjoy his apostolic imprimatur. If the original hymn ended with verse 18a, we assume Paul extended it so that the complete Christological confession now concludes with verse 20.

Of more immediate relevance is the weighty and challenging content of this creed or hymn. The key word in the title outline of this section ("supremacy") is rooted directly in the text of verse 18: "that in everything he might have the supremacy." The Greek word translated "supremacy" comes from the verb *proteuo*, meaning "be first, have first place," so that verse 18 might well be translated, "that he might come to have first place in everything" (BAGD, 725). This position of "first place," "supremacy," or "preeminence" (KJV) is the point toward which the whole hymn moves. As already noted, the two critical spheres in which Christ's supremacy is demonstrated are those of creation and redemption.

3.1. Christ's Supremacy in Creation (1:15–17)

With respect to Christ's role in creation, Paul makes the following points in these verses:

- Christ is "the image of the invisible God" (v. 15a)
- Christ is "the firstborn over all creation" (v. 15b)
- Christ is the creator of all things (v. 16a)
- Christ is the goal of all creation (v. 16b)
- Christ is antecedent to creation (v. 17a)
- Christ upholds all of creation (v. 17b)

The hymn begins with a magnificent declaration of Christ's supremacy in creation: "He is the image of the invisible God, the firstborn over all creation." The two key words here are "image" and "firstborn," both vital to an understanding of Christ's nature and status. The underlying Greek word for "image" is *eikon*, which signifies the "likeness" of a person, whether in the form of a picture or statue (cf. Jesus' reference to the "image" of Caesar on the Roman coin in Matt. 22:20 and parallels; Paul's condemnation of the "images made to look like mortal man and birds and animals and reptiles" in Rom. 1:23; and the eight references to the beast and his "image" in Rev. 13:14). The degree of likeness of the image to its original naturally varied, but in classical usage the word *eikon* could communicate the concept not just of "resemblance" but of actual participation in the reality to which the image pointed. Probably this is the way in which Paul's use of the word is to be taken here (cf. also the significant parallel in 2 Cor. 4:4).

In Colossians 1:15 the reference to the "image of God" is expanded to read "the image of the *invisible* God." That God is "invisible" is the uniform teaching of Scripture (see, e.g., John 1:18; 4:24; 1 Tim. 1:17; 6:16; 1 John 4:12). Paul makes clear that Christ is the perfect and dynamic visible representation of the "invisible God" because he participates in the Godhead itself. This manner of expression is simply Paul's way of affirming the fundamental truth about Christ's identity with God, a truth reiterated elsewhere in the New Testament in different words (cf. John 1:18; 12:45; 14:9; Heb. 1:3). If we inquire into the theological background of Paul's use of the "image" metaphor, it is no doubt to be found in the Genesis account of the creation of man and woman "in the image of God" (Gen. 1:26–27), as well as in the personified "Wisdom" motif of Proverbs (cf. Prov. 8:22–31) and perpetuated in Hellenistic-Jewish writings, such as the Wisdom of Solomon (cf. Wisd. Sol. 7:26).

The word "firstborn" is an equally weighty and significant word in this context. The English compound word is a literal translation of the Greek *prototokos*, which in biblical Greek is used both literally and metaphorically. In its literal use it is found in Luke 2:7 with reference to Mary, who "gave birth to her firstborn, a son" (see also the literal use in Heb. 11:28). Basing themselves on the literal meaning of this word, the Arians of the early fourth century contended that Christ was a created being, hence not fully God. This was a tragic failure of interpretation and of the function of language. Everything else in the letter cries out against such a literal application of the word. Rather, *prototokos* should be read here in its figurative sense as "privileged one" or "exalted one," a meaning it derives from its association with the special privileges of the firstborn.

This is unquestionably the meaning "firstborn" bears in the Greek version of Psalm 89:27, a most important passage for interpreting the word in the Colossian Christ Hymn. In Psalm 89 God makes the promise to David, "I will also appoint him my firstborn, the most exalted of the kings of the earth." In this verse, the phrase "the most exalted of the kings of the earth" is in synonymous parallelism (which means that the second element in a verse defines or elaborates on the first) with "firstborn" and hence defines it. As is well known, Psalm 89 is one of the great "messianic" psalms and exercised enormous influence both in the Jewish and Christian communities. It spoke of God's eternal covenant with David and his line of successors (cf. vv. 35–37), implying thereby the eventual coming of a new David, the Messiah.

It was along these lines that Paul surely understood and used the word *prototokos* in the Colossian Christ Hymn. Rather than a statement about Christ's humanity and "createdness," therefore, it is an affirmation about his exaltation and deity. As "firstborn" in this figurative sense, then, Christ is also Lord "over all creation" (correctly translated in the NIV, in preference to the more literal "*of* all creation," RSV/NRSV)—that is, supreme owner and master of creation.

The question arises, however, about how Christ can be spoken of in this exalted way. Verses 16 and 17 give the answer. The reason (note the Greek causal conjunction, *hoti*, translated "For" in the NIV) is that Christ was both the agent and purpose of creation ("all things were created by him and for him," v. 16), as well as being antecedent to ("He is before all things," v. 17a) and the sustainer of creation ("in him all things hold together," v. 17b)—strong affirmations indeed of Christ's preexistence (cf. John 1:1–3) and of his unifying, upholding role in creation (cf. Heb. 1:3).

In reading these lines of the Christ Hymn, it is hard to miss the emphasis that falls on the phrase "all things," repeated four times. The repetition is obviously intended to insist on Christ's total involvement in and lordship over all creation. So as not to leave any doubt about the exhaustive nature of this involvement, the hymn pauses in the middle of verse 16 to explain what is meant by the phrase "all things": It includes "things in heaven and on earth, visible and invisible, whether thrones or powers or rulers or authorities." This phrase constitutes a truly remarkable declaration. Christ is creator not only of the "visible" things on "earth," but also of the "invisible" things in "heaven." What is more, the "invisible" things include the spiritual beings called "thrones," "powers," "rulers," and "authorities," even the "powers and authorities" who had put themselves in opposition to his rule and who were later to be vanquished on the cross (2:15)!

With such a transcendental role in creation, little wonder that many have referred to Christ as the "cosmic Christ" and the teaching contained in these verses as "cosmic Christology." It is one of the high moments in biblical theology, with echoes elsewhere in the New Testament in such passages as John 1:3 and Hebrews 1:2–3.

Finally, we must not miss the implicit teaching of this part of the Christ Hymn. Since creation is a prerogative of deity (cf. Matt. 19:4; Mark 13:19; Eph. 3:9; 1 Tim. 4:3; Heb. 2:10; Rev. 4:11; 10:6), Christ's role in creation is a tacit but unequivocal declaration of his own deity.

3.2. Christ's Supremacy in Redemption (1:18–20)

This cosmic role in creation is now matched by Christ's role in redemption (vv. 18–20). Again Paul makes six points:

- Christ is "the head of the body, the church" (v. 18a)
- Christ is "the beginning" (v. 18b)
- Christ is "the firstborn from among the dead" (v. 18c)
- Christ is supreme in everything (v. 18d)
- Christ is the one in whom the "fullness" of God dwells (v. 19)
- Christ is the one through whom God has reconciled all things to himself (v. 20)

It is obvious that in this part of the Christ Hymn, the focus of Christ's role has changed significantly from that of the first half. Instead of the sphere of his activity being creation, it is now the church, of which he is the "head" (v. 18a; cf. Eph. 1:22). Instead of his being the agent of creation, he is now the agent of reconciliation (v. 20). Yet there are also deliberate parallels built into the two parts of the hymn. As Christ existed "before all things," so now he is "the beginning" of the entire redemptive process (v. 18b). As he was the "firstborn over all creation," so now he is the "firstborn from among the dead," that is, the first to be resurrected with a spiritual body (v. 18c). As he created and sustained "all things," so now "all things" are reconciled to God through him (v. 20a). As "all things" created through Christ were said to include "things in heaven and on earth," so now in the reconciliation of "all things" it makes no difference whether they are "things on earth or things in heaven" (v. 20b).

Such comparisons and contrasts are part of the impressive poetic quality of this magnificent piece. The climax, however, is reached in the last phrase of verse 18, the phrase that in many ways sums up the thrust of the entire hymn by declaring that the purpose of Christ's role in creation and redemption was "that in everything he might have supremacy" (v. 18d).

As with Christ's supremacy over creation, the listener/reader is anxious to know by what right Christ attains to this "supremacy" in redemption. How does he merit such a position of transcendental rank and priority? Verses 19–20 give the answer: It is because (note again the causal *hoti*, translated "For" in the NIV, as in v. 16) "God was pleased to have all his fullness dwell in him" (v. 19), and "through him [i.e., Christ] to reconcile to himself all things . . . by making peace through his blood, shed on the cross" (v. 20).

These are statements of enormous import when it comes to assessing Paul's understanding of Christ's person and work. That God's "fullness" dwelt in Christ is the strongest possible way of declaring Christ's participation in the deity. That God made "peace through his blood, shed on the cross" is the clearest possible way of affirming Christ as the agent of redemption. In short, the reasons for Christ's supremacy "in everything" are both ontological (who Christ is) and soteriological (what he has done). Both themes will be elaborated in 2:9–15.

It is reasonable to ask what is involved in the reconciliation of "all things" (compare the discussion above on the fourfold mention of the creation of "all things"). Possibly this is an allusion to the scriptural theme that not only redeemed humanity will participate in the benefits of Christ's death, but also the entire creation, for God has promised that it, too, will be restored and re-created following the disastrous effects of the Fall (cf. Gen. 3:17; Isa. 65:17; 66:22; Rom. 8:20–23; Rev. 21:1–5). But does the phrase "all things" include even more? A teaching known as "universalism" holds that not only "all *things*" but also all *people* of whatever sort and from whatever background will also be one day totally reconciled to God. Such a teaching flies in the face of the insistent thrust of Scripture—not least of all of Paul—of the ultimate judgment on the wicked.

It is remarkable how the brief verses of this Christ Hymn have managed to place Christ in the center of the whole drama of biblical revelation, the two principal themes of which are the doctrines of creation and redemption. Small wonder, therefore, that in everything he should be acknowledged as absolutely supreme!

3.3. Christ's Redemptive Work Applied to the Colossians (1:21–23)

The Christ Hymn is magnificent in its declaration of who Christ is and what he has done. But what relevance does this have for the believers in Colosse? Is it anything more than a theoretical statement about ontology and soteriology? Absolutely! It is a statement with profound implications for how the Colossians are to live their lives, including how they are to view their past, present, and future. Consequently, in the application paragraph of verses 21–23 Paul elaborates on some of these implications.

The language describing Christ's redemptive work in verses 20, 22 is that of "reconciliation" (different forms of the verb "to reconcile," *apokatallasso*, are used), rather than that of "redemption" (*apolytrosis*, a noun), as in verse 14. However, the difference is not critical since "redemption" and "reconciliation" simply emphasize different aspects of the same salvific process. In the first part of this section Paul highlights three truths about the Colossians' reconciliation to God—its reality, means, and purpose (vv. 21–22); this is followed by a strong exhortation to the Colossians to remain firm in the faith (v. 23a). The paragraph concludes with a transitional sentence (v. 23b), which introduces the new material of the following section.

3.3.1. The Reality, Means, and Purpose of the Colossians' Reconciliation (1:21–22). Paul begins this application section by reminding the Colossians of what their condition was like prior to their Christian experience and by contrasting that situation with the reality of their present "reconciled" condition. It is a classic statement of the "before . . . after" or "once . . . but now" formula (cf. the same pattern in Eph. 2:1–3 and 2:4–9; 2:11–12 and 2:13). The Colossians' former condition (v. 21) was one of being "alienated from God" and "enemies" of God—a state of estrangement and hostility that resulted entirely from their "evil behavior." But how different is their state "now"! God has reconciled them to himself (v. 22a), creating an entirely new reality for them in which, by implication, they are no longer his enemies but his friends.

It was God's intent "to reconcile to himself all things" (v. 20), and in that comprehensive reconciliation the Colossian believers can be assured of their inclusion. The means by which God accomplished this reconciliation was "by Christ's physical body through death" (v. 22b)—a different way of saying what Paul expressed earlier in the phrase "through [Christ's] blood shed on the cross" (v. 20), as well as an anticipation of yet another formulation of the same important soteriological theme in 2:13–14.

The purpose of this reconciliation is here expressed in a combination of cultic and judicial language. It encompasses a threefold objective, namely, that God would bring the Colossian believers into his presence "holy [*hagios*]," "without blemish [*amomos*]," and "free from accusation [*anenkletos*]" (v. 22c). These terms describe both present and future realities of believers. Earlier in the letter the Colossians have already been referred to as being "holy" (1:2), a truth reinforced again in 3:12. In his letter to the Philippians, Paul challenges the believers there to live "without fault [*amomos*] in a crooked and depraved generation" (Phil. 2:15); similarly deacons are expected to have "nothing against them" (*anenkletos*; 1 Tim. 3:10; Titus 1:6). Yet in the context of Colossians 1:22, it may well be that the phrase "in his sight" refers more to the eschatological reality of full perfection in God's presence at the end of time (cf. 1 Cor. 1:8, "so that you will be blameless [*anenkletos*] on the day of our Lord Jesus Christ," referring to the Parousia). In any event, we should observe that the purpose of God's work of reconciliation is similar to the purposes of election as expressed in Ephesians 1:4: "He chose us in him . . . to be holy [*hagios*] and blameless [*amomos*] in his sight."

3.3.2. Exhortation to Remain Firm in the Faith (1:23). God has done his part; now it corresponds to the Colossians to do theirs. They will appear before God "holy . . . without blemish and free from accusation" only if they continue in the faith, "established and firm, not moved from the hope held out in the gospel" (v. 23). The two words "established" and "firm" have to do with the laying of foundations of buildings, reflected in the GNB rendering of the exhortation, namely, that believers should "continue faithful on a firm and sure foundation." If they are "grounded and settled" (KJV) in this way, they will, of course, not be 'moved from the hope held out in the gospel," he same "hope" that was stored up for them in ıeaven and of which they had heard in the ›reaching of the gospel (1:5).

Just as the mention of the hope of the gospel n 1:5 inspired Paul to think about the way the Colossians had heard about it and the way it vas growing "all over the world" (1:6), so now ıe refers to it as the gospel "that you heard and hat has been proclaimed to every creature ınder heaven" (v. 23b), the latter phrase not o be taken absolutely literally but alluding ather to Paul's policy of planting the gospel in every major center of the civilized world, from vhere it could spread out into the surrounding listricts.

The gospel had indeed come to the Colossians and was being proclaimed all over the vorld. This was wonderful, but it did not hap›en by itself. The question is, Who was esponsible for carrying the message? In the ase of the Colossians, it was Epaphras, Paul's 'fellow servant" (*syndoulos*) and Christ's 'faithful minister" (*diakonos*) (1:7), who had ›rought the message to them. In a special way, ıowever, it was Paul himself who had become . "servant" (*diakonos*) of the gospel (1:23). This responsibility weighed heavily on him. At his stage of his life particularly, he was led to eflect on the privileges and responsibilities of the ministry he had been given (cf. Eph. 3:1–13). So now, the mention of the "gospel"—a word dear to Paul's heart—leads him to rehearse for the Colossians various important aspects of that ministry, lest they think this was somehow a light matter or an easy task. In effect, therefore, the last part of verse 23 serves as the transitional phrase and point of departure for the next main section of the letter.

4. Paul's Ministry (1:24–2:5)

In 1:15–23 Paul has begun the great assignment confronting him in this letter, that of explaining the doctrine of Christ to the Colossians—a subject he picks up again in 2:6–3:4. In the meantime he inserts a personal reflection on his own involvement in the Christian ministry.

He does this for at least two reasons. (1) On the one hand, we must remember that Paul at the time of writing was in prison, probably in Rome. At this particular moment, his life does not appear to be in danger; nonetheless, he finds himself in Rome much later and under very different circumstances from those originally envisaged. His goal on leaving the Aegean region at the end of his third missionary journey had been to make only a brief visit to Jerusalem before proceeding directly to Rome and beyond there to Spain (cf. Rom.

The Great Forum was the main marketplace of Rome when Paul was held there as a prisoner. Paul's letter to the Colossians is one of the four Prison Letters he wrote. The paved street is the Via Sacra, one of the most beautiful roads in the Roman Empire. The road got its name because of all the sacred buildings and processions.

15:23–29). How differently things had turned out! Paul was arrested in Jerusalem, imprisoned in Caesarea for two years, shipwrecked on a Mediterranean island, and finally detained in Rome for two more years as a prisoner in "chains" while awaiting trial before Caesar (cf. Acts 28:30; Col. 4:10, 18).

Paul was seldom one to complain, yet time was no longer on his side. In his own estimation he was already an "old man" (Philem. 9), and the prospects of release and future ministry were at best uncertain. In circumstances such as these, caught in the midst of opposing and potentially hostile forces, it is natural for a person to reflect on his or her life's calling, its joys and sorrows, its privileges and responsibilities, and its rewards and costs. This is what Paul does, both in this letter and in the sister letter to the Ephesians (Eph. 3:2–13). It is an understandable and legitimate exercise. We can be thankful that Paul left us these personal reflections, for they help us understand the nature and ideals of his ministry much better.

(2) There is another reason why Paul was motivated temporarily to change his topic and write something more personal. This reason has to do with his sense of dramatic propriety—that is, what is rhetorically most effective. Paul is no doubt conscious of the serious and concentrated nature of the theological teaching that he is imparting to the Colossians. The Christ Hymn with which he began the body proper of the letter (1:15–20) is a superb Christological statement, profound and rich like few passages in any of his letters. Yet he was also aware that, in order for this teaching to be fully comprehended and its implications fully realized, it would be necessary to elaborate on the condensed and poetic expression of this Christological confession in a more extended and explanatory form (see 2:6–3:4). Thus, 1:24–2:5 serves as a respite from the intensity of theological reflection demanded of listeners and readers up to this point.

Writers and playwrights from time immemorial have used this technique of dramatic interlude. Certainly the Greek playwrights were no strangers to such dramatic technique. So with Paul, for not only was he a profound theologian, he was also a highly skilled writer and communicator. He knew when it was prudent to change topics in order to keep his readers' and listeners' attention at maximum pitch. A personal interlude serves his purposes well. Th change of topic does not mean that the mate ial contained in the "personal interlude" is an less inspired than any other portion of the lette It is only an "interlude" in the dramatic/struc tural sense. On the contrary, these verses com municate important insights not only into Paul own ministry but also into the character c Christian service generally.

In the commentary below, Paul's reflectior on this subject will be reviewed thematicall The seven themes broached by the apostle i these verses are those of the nature, mandate message, goals, costs, resources, and reward of his ministry.

4.1. Nature of Paul's Ministry: To Be a "Servant" of the Church (1:25; cf. 1:23)

At the end of verse 23 and at the beginnin of verse 25, Paul uses an identical expressior *egenomen ego* [+ *Paulos*, v. 23] *diakonos*, th is, "I [Paul] have become a servant." In the fo mer instance, he says he had become a serva of the "gospel"; in the latter, of the "church. In both cases the emphasis falls on the wo *diakonos* ("servant").

In its New Testament usages, the wo *diakonos* is variously translated "servant, "minister," or "deacon." Related words ar *diakonia* ("service," "ministry") and *diakone* ("to serve," "to minister"). This family c words originally had to do with table servic (see Luke 10:40; 17:8; 22:27; Acts 6:2). Even tually in Christian circles *diakonos* took on specialized meaning of the office of "deacon in the church (cf. 1 Tim. 3:8–13). Howeve when Paul uses the word with reference t himself (Col. 1:23, 25; Eph. 3:7) and hi coworkers (Epaphras in Col. 1:7; Tychicus i Eph. 6:21 and Col. 4:7; Timothy in 1 Tim. 4:6 he probably intended to say more about th *nature* of his ministry than about its officia status. In other words, his use of *diakonos* pa allels his application of the word *doulo* ("slave," "servant") to himself and his fellov workers (cf. Rom. 1:1; Gal. 1:10; Phil. 1:1 Titus 1:1).

By his use of these terms Paul was sayin that his life as "servant" of the gospel an "slave" of Jesus Christ was one of sacrificia self-giving. It should be noted that in thi respect both his attitude and vocabulary reflec he example and teaching of Jesus (cf. Mark 10:43–45, where the words *doulos*, *diakonos*, and *diakoneo* all occur in close proximity).

4.2. *Mandate of Paul's Ministry: To Announce the "Word of God in Its Fullness" (1:25; cf. 1:28a)*

By what right can Paul speak of having become a "servant" of the gospel and the church? According to his own testimony, such a designation was validated by the mandate or "commission" (*oikonomia*) God had given him. The word *oikonomia* comes from two common Greek words, *oikos* ("house") and *nomos* ("law"), and has to do, therefore, with the "law" or management of a household. An *oikonomos* was hence the manager or administrator of a household or business (cf. Luke 12:42; 16:1, 3), and his assignment was the administration (*oikonomia*) of the business in question (cf. Luke 16:2–4). The older translation of this word in Luke was "stewardship" (KJV), which still communicates the sense of responsibility and accountability associated with the word.

Paul has been given a certain "commission" or "stewardship" from God, and he was obliged to fulfill the tasks associated with this responsibility (cf. Eph. 3:2). The primary duty with which he associates his "commission" is that of communicating "the word of God in its fullness" (lit., "to fulfill the word of God," KJV). Communicating the word of God in this way involves at least three functions: proclaiming, admonishing, and teaching (1:28a).

The verb "to proclaim" (*katangello*) is one of the strong announcement verbs employed in the account of Paul's missionary activity (cf. Acts 13:5, 38; 15:36; 16:17, 21; 17:3, 13, 23; 1 Cor. 2:1). "To admonish" (*noutheteo*, lit., "to bring to mind") and "to teach" (*didasko*) are two closely related activities (as is shown by their juxtaposition again in Col. 3:16, only in reverse order), connected with the work of discipleship (for *noutheteo* see Acts 20:31; 1 Cor. 4:14; 1 Thess. 5:12, 14; 2 Thess. 3:15; for *didasko* see 1 Cor. 4:17; Col. 2:7; 2 Thess. 2:15).

It is interesting to note that according to Acts, when Paul gave his farewell address to the Ephesian elders in Miletus (Acts 20:18–35), he associated these same three activities of proclamation, teaching, and admonition with his ministry in Ephesus.[3] Apparently this kind of three-pronged approach to ministry was a settled pattern with him, one that he undoubtedly meant to hand on to his understudies and newly planted churches.

4.3. *Message of Paul's Ministry: "Christ in You, the Hope of Glory" (1:26–27; cf. 2:3)*

The commission given to Paul was "to present . . . the word of God in its fullness" (1:25). But what was the message announced in this "word of God"? In verses 26–27 Paul tells us. The sum and substance of it is wrapped up in the last phrase of these two verses: It is "Christ in you, the hope of glory"—one of Paul's best-known Christological utterances, simple in its formulation, yet profound in its implications. Its rich content merits some elaboration.

Not surprisingly, the heart of Paul's message was "Christ." It was, after all, Christ who had radically changed his life. Prior to his encounter with Christ on the road to Damascus, Paul had been a zealous believer in God and in the religion of his ancestors. But as a result of that encounter, he realized that his previous perspective on life and religion had been inadequate and misguided. Now he understood that the one he had been persecuting was in fact his Savior! Henceforth, he intended to give himself to preaching only Christ and him crucified (1 Cor. 2:2). So complete was his identification with Christ that he felt he only lived as Christ lived in him (Gal. 2:20). Everything else in life he counted as "loss" and "rubbish" compared to the "surpassing greatness of knowing Christ Jesus" his Lord (Phil. 3:8). Unquestionably, therefore, the center of Paul's life and theology was Christ, the one "in whom are hidden all the treasures of wisdom and knowledge" (Col. 2:3).

But the relationship Paul enjoyed with Christ was not intended for him alone. On the contrary, the Christ he preached was "Christ *in you*"—the "you" referring to the "saints" (that is, believers), to whom God had "chosen to make known . . . the glorious riches of this mystery." And what was this glorious "mystery" that had been "kept hidden for ages and generations, but is now disclosed to the saints"? It was that Christ, as the "hope of glory," was also made "known among the Gentiles"—a point made even more clear in Ephesians 3:2–6.

That the Gentiles would one day participate in the benefits of God's redemption had been revealed to the prophets in ages past (cf. Isa. 49:6); but that this radical extension of God's mercy would be accomplished through a crucified Messiah was only now made plain. And the person principally charged with communicating this revelation was Paul himself, the "apostle to the Gentiles" par excellence (Acts 22:21; 26:17–18; Gal. 1:15–16; Eph. 3:1). Therefore, when Paul writes of the "mystery" being "Christ in you," although ultimately *all* the "saints" (that is, both Jews and Gentiles) are included, in the context of Colossians 1:26–27 it seems likely that he is thinking here especially of the believing Gentiles, those who made up the majority, if not the entirety, of the church in Colosse.

That Christ was "in *you*" Gentiles was a bold declaration to any Jews who happened to be listening. That Christ was resident "*in* you" was a revolutionary concept for all, Jews and Gentiles alike. The phrase makes plain that the Messiah was not only someone who lived, died, and rose again at a particular time and place in history, but was also someone who now lived "in" the community of believers. At a personal level, this was a truth to which Paul elsewhere bore testimony when he boldly declared that "Christ lives in me" (Gal. 2:20). Radical as all of this may have seemed, it was in fact only the converse and logical counterpart to Paul's so-called "mystical theology," by which he declared believers to be "in Christ." Christ in them, they in him—these were revolutionary concepts, but no more so than Jesus' own words, "Remain in me and I will remain in you" (John 15:4). If Paul was unaware of those precise words of Jesus, he certainly was aware of the truth contained in them—another evidence of Paul's theology being deeply rooted in Jesus' own teaching.

This leads to the last phrase by which Paul describes the Christ whom he proclaims, namely, as "the hope of glory." It is a nice-sounding phrase, but what does it mean? One possibility is to understand "of glory" as a descriptive or qualitative genitive and simply translate the phrase "glorious hope" (Barclay, 1975). There would certainly be no falsehood in that interpretation, yet Paul's intention goes deeper. He has already referred to the Colossians' "hope" twice in the letter: "the hope that is stored up for you in heaven" (v. 5), and "the hope held out in the gospel" (v. 23). This "hope" is an objective and assured reality, probably equivalent—as already noted—to the "inheritance of the saints in the kingdom of light" (v. 12).

As for the word "glory," it has strong associations with the presence and power of God (e.g., the "Shekinah" glory of God in the Old Testament). Following this line of interpretation, to speak of Christ as "the hope of glory" is to speak of him as the believers' guarantee of participating in "the glory of God" (GNB; cf. Col. 3:4, "When Christ, who is your life appears, then you also will appear with him in glory"; see also Rom. 5:2; 8:17). Had the Colossians been reconciled to God through Christ? Did they have Christ in them? They could then be assured of sharing in future "glory" with him. This was a message well worth preaching!

4.4. Goal of Paul's Ministry: To "Present Everyone Perfect in Christ" (1:28b; cf. 2:2–3)

Paul preaches, teaches, and admonishes (v. 28a) in order to "present everyone perfect in Christ" (v. 28b)—that is a high calling indeed. It seems on the surface like a hyperbolic expression ("everyone perfect"!), yet there is no reason to think that Paul meant otherwise than what his words communicate. Nonetheless, a couple of points of clarification may be useful.

We must be especially careful to clarify the meaning of the word translated "perfect" (*teleios*). This word basically means "complete," but according to the particular context in which it is found, it can carry the nuance of either "perfect" or "mature." If Paul in 1:28 is thinking about the quality of spirituality that can be attained on earth, the preferred translation here would be "mature" (cf. RSV/NRSV, NEB/REB, GNB; also in NIV at 1 Cor. 2:6; 14:20; Eph. 4:13; Phil. 3:15; Col. 4:12). The ideals of that kind of discipleship are probably best expressed in Paul's intercessory prayer of Colossians 1:9–12a (see above), along with other qualities of the Christian life and character as described in 1:23; 2:5–7; 3:1–4:1; cf. also Epaphras's prayer in 4:12. There is no doubt that Paul and his coworkers earnestly sought to cultivate these qualities in the lives of their converts and newly founded congregations.

Yet there is reason to question whether that was the meaning intended by Paul in 1:28 as the ultimate goal of his ministry. A comparison with 1:22 suggests that in both these verses, Paul has in mind an eschatological rather than a temporal context. In 1:22 Paul writes that the purpose of God's work of reconciliation was "to present" (*paristemi*, the same verb as is used in 1:28) the believers "holy in his sight, without blemish and free from accusation." As argued above, the context envisaged by the phrase in 1:22 is probably the last day, when God will bring the believers before him fully sanctified (cf. also 1 Cor. 1:8; 2 Cor. 4:14; 1 Thess. 3:13; 5:23). If (as seems likely) this is also the setting of 1:28, Paul then views his ministry as preparing believers for their ultimate presentation before God "perfect in Christ." The NIV has correctly caught Paul's nuance in 1:28 by translating *teleios* with "perfect" rather than "mature."

But when speaking of ministry goals, Paul has in mind not only ultimate "perfection"; he is also deeply concerned about practical living here and now (as already seen, cf. 1:10–12a). In 2:2–3 some of these more immediate goals of his ministry come to the fore. The reason for his hard labors, he says, is that believers everywhere "may be encouraged in heart and united in love, so that they may have the full riches of complete understanding, in order that they may know the mystery of God, namely, Christ." The sentence speaks of four experiences that Paul wishes to see realized in the life of his converts: encouragement of heart, unity in love, full assurance (cf. BAGD, 670, under *plerophoria*) through understanding, and a more profound knowledge of the "mystery of God," who is Christ. It is hard to think of a more noble set of goals for any kind of Christian pastoral ministry.

4.5. Costs of Paul's Ministry: Labor, Struggle, and Suffering (1:29–2:1; cf. 1:24)

The goals of Paul's ministry, both short-term and long-term, are certainly noble. Yet the fulfillment of these goals does not come without effort or cost. Paul makes this plain in this section. If he wishes to present "everyone perfect in Christ," it means that he must also "labor" (*kopiao,* 1:29) and "struggle" (*agonizomai*, 1:29; cf. *agon*, 2:1). These are strong words, which describe the considerable cost involved in Paul's ministry.

The verb *kopiao* is often associated with hard physical labor, as in the hard work of fishing all night (Luke 5:5) or that of the "hardworking farmer" who should be the first to receive a share of the crops (2 Tim. 2:6). In Paul's case he made it a practice of supporting his ministry by working with his hands as a tentmaker, which involved strenuous and tiring effort both night and day (cf. Acts 20:34–35; 1 Cor. 4:12; 1 Thess. 2:9). The fact that Paul applied the same verb to the exercise of his spiritual ministry (cf. Gal. 4:11; Phil. 2:16) means that the task of church planting and church oversight was for him an equally demanding and tiring process.

The verb *agonizomai* was originally associated with engagement in an athletic or military contest (cf. 1 Cor. 9:25; 1 Tim. 6:12; 2 Tim. 4:7). From there it came to be used figuratively of any struggle, including the spiritual struggle of "wrestling [*agonizomenos*] in prayer" (Col. 4:12). Whether in the military or in athletics, to engage in this kind of "struggle" necessitated the exercise of self-discipline and sacrifice (cf. 1 Cor. 9:24–27). In the same way, the noun *agon* (Col. 2:1) is used elsewhere for fighting "the good fight [*agon*] of faith" (1 Tim. 6:12; 2 Tim. 4:7), as well as for the persecution and opposition that Paul encountered in such places as Philippi and Thessalonica (cf. Phil. 1:30; 1 Thess. 2:2). In Colossians 2:1 the addition of the qualifier "how much" (*helikon*) emphasizes the intensity of the struggle Paul experienced on behalf of the believers, even those whom he had not met personally.

So real was the "cost factor" in Paul's life that it was actually the theme with which he began the entire personal review of his ministry commencing in verse 24, where he wrote of the "sufferings" (*pathemata*) he had endured for the believers in Colosse. This is the same word used in 2 Timothy 3:11, where Paul writes of the "persecutions and *sufferings*" he had sustained on his first missionary journey in Antioch, Iconium, and Lystra (cf. Acts 13:13–14:20); it is also the word used when writing to the Philippians about his own ambition to share in the "sufferings" of Christ (Phil. 3:10).

All of this is understandable enough, at least from a grammatical and philological point of view, even though the reason why suffering of such intensity should be necessary—particularly in the life of such a self-giving servant—may remain a mystery. But what is even more difficult to understand is the continuation of the sentence in verse 24: "and I fill up in my flesh what is still lacking in regard to Christ's afflictions." These words have given rise to various interpretations, primarily because they appear to suggest that there may be something lacking in Christ's redemptive work that had to be supplemented by the apostle. Since such a proposition flies in the face of the rest of Colossians, which emphasizes the completeness of Christ's work on the cross (see esp. 1:19–22; 2:9–15), there must be another way of understanding these words.

One such way interprets Paul's words in Colossians 1:24 in the light of the Philippian passage referred to above—that is, simply as another way in which Paul could give strong expression to his total sense of identification with Christ, both his "power" as well as his "sufferings" (Phil. 3:10; see also Rom. 6:1–6; 2 Cor. 4:10). Another way of understanding Paul's words is to relate them to the rabbinic concept of the "woes" or "birth pangs" of the Messiah, which the nation would have to suffer at the coming of the Messiah as a prelude to his future glory. It may be that even Romans 8:22 alludes to the same theme. Certainly Paul could not have conceived of himself as adding anything to Christ's completed work. What he did affirm was the necessity of being willing to suffer with and for Christ in the cause of the ministry, that is, "for the sake of his body, which is the church" (1:24). Perhaps Paul was aware of Jesus' words, "If they persecuted me, they will persecute you also" (John 15:20). Of one thing we can be sure: Paul knew that suffering was part of the call to discipleship and ministry (cf. Acts 9:16; 14:22; 1 Thess. 3:4).

4.6. Resources of Paul's Ministry: Christ's "Energy" Powerfully at Work in Him (1:29b)

Paul's commitment to ministry entailed labor, struggle, and suffering. Yet he was not left to his own resources in this assignment. The Greek text has three words that emphasize the nature of the divine enabling at his disposal to help him overcome: the noun *energeia*, the participle *energoumene* (from the verb *ener geo*), and the noun *dynamis*.

The semantic connection between th Greek *energeia* and the English "energy" i obvious. In the New Testament *energeia* i used exclusively by Paul and always with ref erence to divine beings. Its basic meaning i "working, operation, action," but Paul uses i especially to emphasize the power inherent i that "working." Thus, for instance, when h uses it again with reference to the *energeia* o God that raised Christ from the dead (Col 2:12), the NIV translates *energeia* appropriatel by "power." The cognate verb *energeo* (agai used primarily by Paul; cf. also Matt. 14:2 Mark 6:14; James 5:16) means to "work, be a work, operate, be effective." The nou *dynamis* is the standard word for "power" o "strength." A literal translation of 1:29 helps t put it all together: "I labor," says Paul, "strug gling according to his energy [or 'power'] tha is at work in me in power [or 'powerfully']."

Undoubtedly it was this "energy" of Chris powerfully at work in him that gave Paul th strength to carry on in the face of many hard ships. In giving testimony to his dependenc on this divine enabling, he was merely puttin into practice what he had earlier prayed for o behalf of the Colossians. In 1:11 he prayed tha they would be "strengthened with all powe [*dynamis*] according to his glorious might" i order to display "great endurance an patience." It was a *dynamis* that Paul man times had had to depend on (he refers to i again in Eph. 3:7). And as it was available t him, so it was available to the Colossians an to all other believers and Christian worker who would follow (cf. Eph. 1:19–20).

4.7. Rewards of Paul's Ministry: To See the Firmness of the Believers' Faith (2:4–5)

If there are resources for effective ministry there will also be genuine rewards. This resul was certainly Paul's experience. In fact, s great was his ability to take delight in his min istry—in spite of all its challenges and diffi culties—that he both begins and closes thi section of personal "interlude" with the wor "rejoice" (*chairo*, 1:24 and 2:5). And what wa it that gave him such joy in the exercise of hi ministry? Essentially it was seeing the "order liness" (*taxis*; cf. the use of this word in 1 Co

:40) and "firmness" (*stereoma*) of the lievers' faith (2:5), especially in the face of e serious challenges to the orthodoxy of their ith in Christ, the kind of challenges to which alludes in 2:4 and to which he will return 2:6–3:4.

In 1:23 Paul had written of the importance the Colossians continuing in their "faith, tablished and firm, not moved from the hope ld out in the gospel." In 2:6–7 he will insist ain on the importance of continuing to "live [Christ], rooted and built up in him." His eat fear was that his converts would lapse to unbelief or various forms of legalism, so at his own ministry among them would have en in vain (cf. Gal. 2:2; 4:11; Phil. 2:16; Thess. 3:5). When Paul learned from Epaaras that the Colossians were standing firm in e faith, this was cause for great rejoicing and anksgiving (cf. 1:3–8).

Now he is writing to them, though absent om them "in body" yet present with them "by e Spirit" (pers. trans.). This latter phrase is ually translated as in the NIV, "I am present ith you in spirit" (that is, with lowercase "s" "spirit"), with the connotation that although aul is absent from the readers, they are onetheless *in his thoughts*. However, Gordon e has effectively argued that the reference re to *pneuma* ("S/spirit") is not anthropologal but pneumatological. That is, although he physically absent, Paul considers himself uly present with the believers by the Spirit as ey gather in the presence and power of the pirit for the reading of the letter (cf. 1 Cor. 5:3; e Fee, 1994, 121–27, 645–46). Therefore, he lights "to see how orderly [they] are and how rm [their] faith in Christ is" (Col. 2:5).

To see that his intense labor for the Lord d resulted in such orderly conduct and firmss of faith in the lives his converts, for Paul at was reward enough. Many can testify to similar sense of deep satisfaction when being ld of the steadfastness of those to whom they ave ministered. Such reports are the antidote any sense of self-pity or complaint in the ce of the equally real struggles and sufferings the ministry. Paul knew both sides, but it is couraging to think that he was able to begin d end this brief review of his ministry on the ositive note of rejoicing. It would be a marelous thing if all who have followed in his eps could do the same.

5. Warnings Against False Doctrines and Legalistic Practices (2:6–3:4)

Little by little Paul has been warming up to his theme. Following the customary greetings and prayer of thanksgiving and intercession (1:1–14), Paul plants the central thesis of his letter: Christ is supreme in creation and redemption. As we have seen, this declaration of Christ's supremacy is contained in a passage of concentrated theological substance and superb poetic quality (1:15–20). Then follows a brief paragraph applying the benefits of Christ's work to the life of the Colossian believers (1:21–23), which in turn yields to a longer section of Paul's reflections on his ministry for the church (1:24–2:5).

The apostle is now ready to resume the exposition of the doctrine of Christ and to apply this in specific ways to the situation facing the Colossians. The nature of this situation, which is fraught with danger for the Colossian church, has already been alluded to in 2:4 and is significantly elaborated in 2:8. In between are verses 6–7, which function as part of the transition point to the new section (cf. the similar function of 1:12b–14, above), while verses 9–15 constitute the heart of the theological exposition of what was initially affirmed in the Christ Hymn (1:15–20). This concentrated theological reflection is followed by a series of warnings against various expressions of legalism and mysticism promoted by the false teachers (2:16–19). The entire section concludes with a couple of contrasting paragraphs on what it means to have died and risen with Christ (2:20–3:4).

5.1. Exhortations to Perseverance and Description of False Teachings (2:6–8)

In truth, it is difficult to find a fixed point of division where Paul's account of his ministry experience leaves off and the new teaching section commences. This ambiguity—amply illustrated in the commentaries—reminds us of the earlier shift in subject matter from the intercessory prayer to the Christ Hymn in chapter 1 (where verses 12b–14 functioned as a transition passage). Similarly, verses 6–7/8 act here as the linking passage between Paul's personal testimony and his Christological exposition.

The transition point is marked at the beginning of verse 6 by the connecting phrase, "So then," a phrase that looks back to the preceding material and anticipates the introduction of a new topic. The "backward look" is reinforced in the continuation of the sentence: "just as you received Christ Jesus as Lord, continue to live in him, rooted and built up in him, strengthened in the faith as you were taught, and overflowing with thankfulness" (vv. 6–7). Here Paul alludes to almost every paragraph written up to this point.

The phrase "just as you received Christ" naturally reminds us of the Colossians' "faith in Christ Jesus," the faith they demonstrated when the gospel first came to them (1:4–7). The reference to Christ Jesus as "Lord" is another way of speaking of his supremacy (1:15–20). The exhortation to "live in him ... strengthened in the faith" harks back to 1:23 ("if you continue in your faith, established and firm"), as well as to 2:5 ("I ... delight to see how orderly you are and how firm your faith in Christ is"). Finally, the clause "as you were taught" recalls the statement in 1:7, that "you learned it [i.e., the gospel] from Epaphras," while the concluding phrase "overflowing with thankfulness" naturally ties in with Paul's own thanksgiving prayer of 1:3–8 and his intercessory prayer in 1:12a that they should be "joyfully giving thanks to the Father."

As becomes obvious from the above review, one of Paul's primary concerns in the letter is the steadfastness of the Colossians' faith (1:9–12a, 23; 2:5, 6–7). Admittedly, this may have been an understandable preoccupation of the apostle for any of his churches; yet the persistent exhortations to steadfastness in this letter must be seen against the particular problem confronting the church in Colosse, namely, the presence of false teachings and false teachers threatening the stability of the Colossian faith community. This situation was alluded to in 2:4 and is now explicitly elaborated in 2:8. Together, these two verses give a clear indication of the nature of the teachings in question.

In brief, the false teachings are said to be but "fine-sounding arguments" (v. 4) and to consist of "hollow and deceptive philosophy, which depends on human tradition and the basic principles of this world rather than on Christ" (v. 8). In these words the falseness, emptiness, and deceitfulness of the new teachings are fully exposed. Their fundamental flaw was that they were based on "human traditio (as opposed to divine revelation) and on "tl basic principles of the world" (*ta stoicheia tc kosmou*), rather than on the doctrine of Chri

Precisely what is meant by the phrase *stoicheia tou kosmou* has been much debate Paul previously used the phrase in Galatia 4:3 (also *stoicheia* by itself in Gal. 4:9), whe the NIV translates the phrase in the same wa as in Colossians, "the basic principles of tl world." But it has been strongly urged by son scholars (cf. the discussion in O'Brien's con mentary, 1982, 129–32; Arnold, 1996, 162 94) that both in Galatians and Colossians tl phrase is more sinister than that, referring n so much to mere "principles" as to "spirits" "forces" (cf. the translation "elemental spiri of the universe" in the NRSV and REB). Th meaning would tie in with Paul's frequent all sions in this letter to the "powers and author ties" (cf. 1:16; 2:10, 15).

If this line of reasoning is correct, we ca understand even more fully the urgency i Paul's warnings. Not only are the teaching based on "human tradition"; they are als demonic. Little wonder that Paul soberl warns the Colossians not to be deceived b such doctrines (v. 4) or to be taken "captive by them (v. 8)—a word that suggests carryin someone away from the truth into the slave of error (cf. BAGD, 776, under *sylagogeo*).

5.2. Exposition of the Doctrine of Christ (2:9–15)

All the teachings described in verses 4 an 8 are said to be "not according to Christ" (li eral translation of the phrase *ou kata Christo* with which v. 8 concludes). If these represe the negative or false teachings concernin Christ promoted by the errorists, Paul now pr pares to present the positive or true teachin concerning Christ. This he now does explicit and deliberately in verses 9–15. In the proce he informs us about other features of the pe nicious doctrine "not according to Christ."

Admittedly, this information is commun cated indirectly and inferentially. That is to sa we assume that Paul's method of refutatio was to state the positive side of what th Colossian errorists were denying, leaving us reconstruct the background situation. Th method of interpretation is called "mirror rea ing," a method fraught with danger if presse

THE COLOSSIAN HERESY

Most scholars see in the letter to the Colossians evidence of a heretical group that was pressuring true believers there to adopt their teachings. Paul labels these teachings as "hollow and deceptive philosophy," based on "human traditions" (Col 2:8). Judging from the content of this letter, the following appear to be the main tenets of the heretics and Paul's rebuttal to them.

Teaching of heresy	Paul's answer	Relevant texts
Emphasis on worship of angels, called "thrones," "rulers," "powers," and "authorities"	Christ created these powers and he rules over them; believers are delivered from their power	Col. 1:13, 15–17; 2:9–10, 15, 18–19
Angels are intermediaries between God and human beings	Christ is the only mediator we need	1:13–23; 2:6, 9–10
Endorsed submission to the "basic principles of the world"	Christ rules over them, and Christians have died to them in Christ	2:8, 20
Endorsed circumcision	Believers undergo a form of circumcision in the death of Christ, experienced through baptism	2:11–13
Endorsed special religious days and legalistic food rules	Do not listen to such rules; believers have died to them and their power is canceled	2:14, 16–17, 20–23
Emphasis on a special, secret knowledge	God fills all believers with his wisdom, knowledge, and understanding	1:9–10, 28; 2:2–4, 22

oo hard or dogmatically. However, if used udiciously it can help us reconstruct with clarty the situation Paul was addressing. But it eeds to be said that, regardless of the degree of accuracy in our modern reconstructions of he "Colossian heresy" by means of such "miror reading," the truth of Paul's doctrine of Christ remains unaffected.

We should note further that when we speak of the "doctrine of Christ" being expounded in hese verses, it is a doctrine set forth not in isoation but always in relation to its impact on Christian believers. For this reason, the subject of various verbs and participles in this section s actually the second person plural "you," tated or implied. At other times the subject of he main verb is identified as or understood to e "God," but always God acting in or through Christ. The principal point, however, is that egardless of who happens to be the subject of a particular verb or participle, the focus emains consistently on Christ, who he is and what he has done (or what has been done through him). This is confirmed by the frequent use in these verses of the little phrase "in him" (or variants, "in whom," "with him"), all referring to Christ (sometimes explicitly identified by the name "Christ" in the NIV, even though the Greek has the pronoun "him" or "whom"; cf. vv. 9 and 10). The nature of his person is expounded in verses 9–10; the nature of his work, in verses 11–15.

5.2.1. Christ's Person (2:9–10). Paul warns the Colossians in verse 8 not to let anyone take them captive by "hollow and deceptive philosophy," the kind of teaching that "depends on human tradition and the basic principles of this world rather than on Christ." The reason they must not succumb in this way is then given: It is "because [*hoti*; NIV 'For'] in Christ all the fullness of the Deity lives in bodily form" (v. 9). On the basis of this juxtaposition of warnings (v. 8) and reasons for the warnings (v. 9), we can only assume that the

Colossian false teachers were in fact denying the truth about the person of Christ affirmed in verse 9, namely, Christ's "Deity." Presumably they were saying that Christ possessed something less than God's "fullness," in flat contradiction to the Christ Hymn's assertion that "God was pleased to have *all* his fullness dwell in him" (1:19).

In 2:9, an explanatory repetition of 1:19, the key words are "fullness," "Deity," and "bodily form." Each word is important and rich in its own way. The noun "fullness" (*pleroma*) comes from the verb "to fill" (*pleroo*), used previously in 1:9 ("asking God *to fill* you with the knowledge of his will") and in 1:25 ("to make the word of God *fully known*," NRSV), and will be used again in 2:10 ("*you have been given fullness* in Christ") and finally at 4:17 (in the admonition to Archippus, "See to it that you *complete* ['*fulfill*,' KJV/RSV] the work you have received"). Both verb and noun occur regularly in Paul's writings, but nowhere else in such concentration.

Why does Paul use these words so frequently in this letter? The answer may have something to do with the emergence of an incipient form of Christian Gnosticism,[4] in which a technical term for the totality of "aeons" said to constitute the spiritual world from which Christ presumably came. If the Colossian errorists represented an early form of this divergent teaching, they would have maintained that Christ was part of the spiritual *pleroma* but not independent of it, hence not fully equal with God. Such a form of teaching, or anything similar to it, Paul rejected out of hand. This becomes abundantly clear in his choice of words that qualify *pleroma* in the rest of the verse.

It is not just "fullness" that is associated with Christ, but "*all*" God's fullness—probably a deliberate redundancy on Paul's part, in order to emphasize the completeness of Christ's identification with God. That this is his intention is reinforced in the subsequent phrase in verse 9, when Paul refers to "all the fullness *of the Deity*" that dwells in Christ, an exceedingly critical and weighty expression, no doubt implied in 1:19 but now made explicit. The word "deity" (*theotes*) occurs in the New Testament only here but is used elsewhere in Greek literature. It is similar to the noun "divinity" (*theiotes*, cf. Rom. 1:20) but stronger than the latter since *theotes* derives directly from *theos* ("*God*"), while *theiotes* derives from the adjective *theios* ("divine," cf. Acts 17:29; 2 Peter 1:3–4).

Simply put, Paul has used the strongest possible language to refer to the absolute deity of Christ: "all the fullness of the Deity" lives in him continually (the verb "lives" is in the present continuous tense). Furthermore, it lives in him "in bodily form" (*somatikos*), a Greek adverb that in this context can be translated "in reality" or "in actuality" (cf. the use of *soma*, "body," in 2:17 with the meaning of "reality"), but which with equal justification can be rendered as in the NIV ("in bodily form") and taken as a primary reference to Christ's incarnation (cf. John 1:14). It is hard to imagine a more definitive declaration of Christ's divine nature. In Paul's exposition of the doctrine of Christ, this understanding of his deity is the nonnegotiable starting point.

An important application of this great truth follows. If God's "fullness" lives in Christ, as it surely does, then, since the believers are incorporated into Christ, they also have "been given fullness [lit., 'have been made full'] in Christ" (v. 10a; cf. Eph. 3:19, where Paul prays that the Ephesian believers will be "filled to the measure of all the fullness of God"). At this point Paul does not elaborate on the content of the fullness they have been given, though earlier in the letter, employing the same verb, he prayed for God "to fill [them] with the knowledge of his will through all spiritual wisdom and understanding" (1:9; cf. similar prayer wishes in Rom. 15:13; Phil. 1:11; 4:19). If, as seems possible, the false teachers claimed that spiritual "fullness" could be achieved only by the addition of other forms of worship and/or legal regulations (see below), Paul is affirming in no uncertain terms that the believer's salvation is complete in Christ, not requiring the intervention of any other intermediaries or adherence to any form of legalism. They were already and truly "complete" in Christ!

But how can the believers in Colosse be sure that their salvation is complete in Christ? The answer lies in who Christ is and in what he has done. In verse 15 Paul will declare how Christ "disarmed the powers and authorities"—those spiritual beings that apparently were such a fascination to the Colossian errorists; here, in verse 10b, Paul anticipates the result of that vicorious struggle by declaring Christ's status as "head" over every such "power and authority." Just as Christ was earlier pronounced to be "head" of the church—that is, both its source and supreme authority (1:18)—so now he is affirmed to be the source (cf. 1:16) and ruling authority over all spiritual beings, whether benign or hostile. This position of authority is not surprising for One in whom "all the fullness of the Deity lives," but this truth needed to be emphasized in a community where the validity of such a claim was in all likelihood being challenged.

In short, Paul's point in verses 9–10 is that Christ as the embodiment of "all the fullness of the Deity" and Christ as "the head over every power and authority" were ample assurances to the Colossians of their own "fullness in Christ." And if these truths functioned as assurances of the completeness of their salvation, they ought to do so in no less measure for all subsequent believers, whether "Greek or Jew ... barbarian, Scythian, slave or free," for truly "Christ is all, and is in all" (3:11), to the praise of God's glorious name!

5.2.2. Christ's Work (2:11–15). In the next verses the focus shifts from who Christ is to what he has done. But what he has done, he has done not for himself but rather for the benefit of the community of faith—in this particular case, the community of faith in Colosse. For this reason the benefactors of Christ's work often seem to be in the foreground as the subject (or object, as the case may be) of the verbal constructions in verses 11–14; but remember again that the intention throughout is to explain what they have received *as a result of Christ's work on their behalf* (or, in verses 13–14, as a result of God's work through Christ). The benefits are several: They have been "circumcised" in Christ (v. 11), buried and raised with him (v. 12), made alive with him (v. 13a), forgiven (v. 13b), declared innocent of the accusations contained in the written code (v. 14), and liberated from hostile spiritual forces (v. 15).

The list begins with a reference to the benefit of having been "circumcised" in Christ. This might appear a strange place for Paul to start, since the rite of circumcision was such a controversial topic in the early church. Moreover, Paul himself was the one who had led the charge against any attempt to impose the Jewish rite of circumcision on Gentile converts. Yet it is clear that what Paul means with this word here is quite different from submission to a literal, physical circumcision. Instead, he is talking in this context about a circumcision "not ... done by the hands of men," but rather one "done by Christ."

The passage relates most closely to Romans 2:28–29, where Paul explains that circumcision is not something "merely outward and physical." On the contrary, true circumcision is "circumcision of the heart, by the Spirit, not by the written code" (a perspective already present in the Old Testament, cf. Deut. 10:16; 30:6; Jer. 4:4; Ezek. 44:7). The only difference here from Romans is that on this occasion, the circumcision is said to be done not "by the Spirit" but "by Christ"[5] and involves "the putting off of the sinful nature," thus anticipating the later discussion of what God's chosen people must put to death (Col. 3:5–11) in their lives.

The fact that Paul begins the list of benefits flowing from Christ's work with this reference to the circumcision "not ... done by the hands of men" suggests that the Colossian troublemakers were in fact promoting the opposite, namely, a circumcision literally done "by the hands of men." Together with references in verse 16 to the keeping of religious festivals, New Moon celebrations, and Sabbath days, this further suggests that the problematic teachings in Colosse had a strong Jewish influence.

Not only have the believers in Colosse been circumcised "with the circumcision done by Christ" (v. 11), but they have also "been buried with him in baptism and raised with him through [their] faith in the power of God" (v. 12). Paul again borrows a metaphor from his letter to the Romans. In Romans 6:3–4 Paul asks rhetorically, "Don't you know that all of us who were baptized into Christ Jesus were baptized into his death?" He then continues, "We were therefore buried with him through baptism into death in order that, just as Christ was raised from the dead ... we too may live a new life." To make the point doubly clear he adds, "If we have been united with him ... in his death, we will certainly also be united with him in his resurrection" (6:5).

In other words, what was true for the Romans was true for the Colossians and is true for all who "have been united" with Christ; for all such people, their baptism is a powerful symbol of their having been buried and raised with Christ. It is another of the enormous benefits of the redemptive work of Christ. So powerful was this image of the death and resurrection of Christ as a model for the Christian life that it continues to dominate a great deal of the ensuing discussion to 3:4.

Certainly the theme of death/life is there in the very next verse: "When you were dead in your sins . . . God made you alive with Christ" (2:13). That this continues the death and life theme is obvious, even if the phrase "dead in your *sins*" describes a different state from "buried with him in *baptism*" (v. 12). In reality, the statement in verse 13 is another of the great Pauline "before-after" passages, which has a certain similarity in structure to 1:21–22, though in fact it finds its closest parallel in Ephesians 2:5 (God "made us alive with Christ even when were dead in transgressions").

But not only is the "death-life" theme present in Colossians 2:13; the "uncircumcision-circumcision" theme is there as well, for the full sentence reads, "When you were dead in your sins *and in the uncircumcision of your sinful nature*, God made you alive with Christ." This sentence, of course, reminds us of verse 11 and the believers' spiritual circumcision "in the putting off of the sinful nature" by a circumcision not done by human hands but by Christ. In effect, therefore, verse 13 is a kind of restatement of verses 11–12, only in reverse order.

In all of this, however, the main point of what Paul is saying must not be lost. It is contained in the principal clause of the sentence, namely, "God made you alive with Christ." The introductory subordinate clause answers the question "*when*" God made them alive—that is, "When you were dead in your sins." The subsequent subordinate clauses in verses 13b–14 answer the question *how* God made them alive with Christ, each similarly introduced by a participial construction, namely, "having forgiven" (v. 13) and "having canceled" (v. 14).

In the NIV, verse 13b begins a new sentence, "He forgave us all our sins. . . ." While this may be a defensible concession to modern English style in its preference for shorter sentences, it unfortunately obscures the dependence of both this and the following clauses on the previous main verb, God "made you alive." To better reflect this dependence, therefore, one could translate more literally, "having forgiven us all our sins," in parallel with the phrase at the beginning of verse 14, "having canceled the written code." It is possible to communicate the precise nature of this relationship by translating the Greek participle in yet another way, namely, with an English subordinate clause, thus: "God made you alive *when* [or '*because*'] he forgave us all our sins. . ." (cf. the NRSV, which attempts to reflect the participial subordination). The point is that, while it was God who "made [the believers] alive" (v. 13a), the resultant new life was dependent on the forgiveness accomplished through Christ on the cross (cf. Eph. 4:32).

The need for forgiveness implies that a wrong was committed—here referred to as "our sins" (*paraptomata*) or, better, "our trespasses" (so KJV, RSV, NRSV). Another interesting observation on this phrase is the change of pronoun from the second person plural ("you," referring to the Colossians) to the inclusive first person plural ("us") at verse 13b (cf. the same change at 1:13). Because of this change and the sudden appearance of new vocabulary in verses 13b–15, some commentators have seen in this section the remnant of another public confession that Paul incorporated into his exposition. This suggestion, however, has gained less favor than the recognition of a church creed lying behind 1:15–18a/20.

Verse 14 introduces the second action of God in Christ highlighted by Paul. In addition to forgivennesss, he has also "canceled the written code . . . that was against us." Verse 13 had used the metaphor of "death" to describe the desperate plight of unbelievers. Verse 14 employs another strong metaphor to depict the situation of pre-Christians, namely, the metaphor of a "written code" drawn up against them. In the Greek, the word for this "written code" is *cheirographon*, meaning simply a "handwritten document" but with the special sense of a handwritten document acknowledging indebtedness—in fact, an "IOU."

Paul explains two things about this certificate of indebtedness. (1) It was accompanied with certain "regulations." What these "regulations" were we are not told, but most probably they had to do with the demands of the Mosaic Law, which could, in any case, never be met. (2) Thus, the "written code" stood hopelessly "against us" and "opposed to us"—another instance of Pauline redundancy to reinforce the seriousness of the human condition. The plight was indeed serious and would have been absolutely desperate but for the intervention of God, who "having canceled" it, "took it away, nailing it to the cross."

Paul's words slip by quickly but evoke powerful images and are of transcendental importance. The solution to the human condition is again seen to be God's redemptive work in Christ on the cross, a work described in the bold image of God's nailing the accusing document to the cross and then declaring it null and void. The net effect of this strong language for the Colossians is once more to assure them that their salvation was complete in Christ (cf. 2:10). Least of all was there any need for the kind of legalistic practices promoted by the troublemakers in Colosse (as detailed in 2:16–23). Adherence to such practices would simply signal a return to their pre-Christian days, when they lived under the shadow of the cursed "written code, with its regulations," that stood against them but that had now been done away with on the cross.

Having had their trespasses forgiven and the bond of indebtedness canceled, believers are truly "made ... alive with Christ" (v. 13). One might have thought that this statement was the climax of Paul's argument and that all had now been said. The believers' salvation was, after all, complete, and their life in Christ assured. But there remains something important for Paul to say. Not only have believers been forgiven and the cursed bond canceled; the effects of Christ's death on the cross surpass even so great a result. In addition to all the foregoing, his death also had drastic implications for that order of spiritual beings previously referred to in 1:16 and 2:10 as "thrones," "powers," "rulers," and "authorities." In 2:15 Paul lays hold of a battle image to describe how the hostile "powers and authorities" among them have been "disarmed" and how God "made a public spectacle of them, triumphing over them by the cross." As in the previous verses, this, too, is potent language.

The subject matter is definitely the "powers and authorities." This subject has fascinated many students of Paul's letters; it was obviously an important part of his theology, especially prominent in the Colossian-Ephesian correspondence. One of the dilemmas associated with the interpretation of these "powers and authorities" is the way they are referred to in both positive and negative ways. For instance, in the Colossian Christ Hymn they are presented as objects of Christ's creation, part of the "things ... visible and invisible" that were created "by him and for him" (1:16). Similarly in 2:10 Christ is said to be the "head over every power and authority." Yet at 2:15 they are obviously enemies with hostile intent.

Although some scholars have sought to demythologize these powers and interpret them as human or societal ills, a natural reading of the text suggests that many of them were, in fact, "spiritual forces of evil in the heavenly realms" (Eph. 6:12). Thus, the connection between Colossians 2:14 and 15 suggests that these powers were the ones who held the document of accusation against unbelievers and that it was from them that it had to be wrested. This, then, is where God intervened in Christ. He "disarmed" the powers and "made a public spectacle of them, triumphing over them."

The word "disarmed" is found only in this letter in the New Testament (here and at 3:9). The meaning of the Greek verb used at this point is literally "to take off" or "strip off" clothes (cf. the translation at 3:9, "you have taken off your old self"). Similarly, a related noun occurs at 2:11, in the context of "putting off" the sinful nature. If this is the meaning intended at 2:15 (given the Greek "middle" form of the verb), then the passage speaks of God (or Christ) stripping himself of the hostile powers that had wrapped themselves around him like a cloak (cf. GNB, "Christ freed himself from the power of the spiritual rulers and authorities"). However, if the middle form of the verb is understood here as a true "deponent" (i.e., middle in form but active in meaning), then the appropriate translation would be "disarmed" (cf. NIV, NRSV, REB), or in expanded form, "He stripped the principalities and powers of their armour" (F. F. Bruce, *The Letters of Paul: An Expanded Paraphrase,* 1965).

This latter meaning fits well with the subsequent verbs, "he made a public spectacle of them, triumphing over them." The scene is that of a triumphal procession, in which the victors led their captives through the city streets of the home city, exposing them to scorn and humiliation—precisely as Paul put it, making a "public spectacle of them." This is what has happened to the celestial enemy powers at Christ's crucifixion: They were stripped, humiliated, and fully conquered. And if we ask how God stripped and conquered the "powers" so effectively, the answer is as potent as it is short: it was done "by the cross;" In other words, Jesus' death defeated the powers; the document of indebtedness was wrested from them and nailed to the cross as a sign of its total nullification.

The idea, therefore, that the Colossians—or anyone else—should either fear or honor such defeated foes is absurd. They have been conquered, and believers have been set free. This triumph is the glorious message of God's deliverance through Christ on the cross—a fitting climax to Paul's grand exposition of the person and work of Christ, in which he is presented as fully God and as the competent agent of the work of redemption.

In the above exposition of verses 13b–15, the subject of the verbs and participles has been assumed to be God, as is implied in the NIV and other translations. It should be noted, however, that there is an ambiguity in the Greek text about who is the subject of the verbal constructions in these verses. "God" is undoubtedly the subject of the verbs in verse 13. But beginning with the participle "having canceled" in verse 14, it is possible that Christ is the one who canceled the written code against us and who disarmed the evil powers. But we do not need to worry about trying to resolve this ambiguity. We know God was acting in Christ; by the same token Christ did not act independently of God. The mystery of the Trinity lies at the root of the ambiguity.

5.3. Specific Warnings Against Legalism (2:16–19)

Beginning with verse 16, we are clearly in a new section—one that returns to the warnings of 2:4, 8. The connecting particle "therefore" (*oun*) links the new passage with the preceding one, which, as we have seen, expounds the doctrine of Christ. At first sight it may appear strange that such legalistic practices as those mentioned in 2:16–23 have anything to do with Paul's exposition of the person and work of Christ. Yet that is precisely what he maintains, and with good reason.

The exposition of verses 9–15 above has proceeded on the premise that Paul is addressing a real-life situation in Colosse, whereby certain teachers were promoting doctrines not according to Christ (v. 8). We have been able to form an idea of what these doctrines were by the process of mirror reading. In the errorists' view, apparently, Christ was not fully God nor was his work sufficient to make believers "complete." The "powers and authorities" were forces alive and well—so they may have argued—who still needed to be placated. The purpose of Paul's exposition in verses 9–15 was to refute such heresies vigorously and definitively. This he does, carrying the argument to a resounding conclusion in the uncompromising affirmation of the victory of Christ on the cross and the decisive defeat and humiliation of the powers.

This sounds like the climax of the argument, and in one sense it is, but it is not the *end* of the argument. For not only did the teachers represent a false doctrine concerning the person of Christ, they also promoted a series of false practices that flowed directly from their sub-Christian view of Christ. It is to the refutation of these practices that the apostle now turns. In our exposition of these verses it will be useful to remember that while many of the specific practices highlighted in this passage no longer relate to us, the principle that bad theology leads to bad practice remains as true as ever.

5.3.1. Regarding Food Laws and Holy Days (2:16–17). The first set of concerns that Paul addresses has to do with the imposition of food laws ("what you eat or drink") and the observance of holy days ("a religious festival, a New Moon celebration or a Sabbath day"). He encourages the Colossians not to let anyone "judge" them with respect to these things. That is, they are not to allow others "to pass judgment" on them or "to take them to task" for exercising their freedom in Christ. The reason such regulations have no relevance is that they are but a "shadow" of the "reality" (*soma*; lit., "body") found in Christ.

The background to the kind of legalistic practices referred to in verse 16 has been much debated. Was it Jewish, pagan, or some kind of combination of both (for extended discussion on the possibilities, see O'Brien, 1982, xxx–xxxviii)? Given the nature of the regulations nentioned, it is difficult to imagine that there vas no Jewish influence in these practices. Aost likely the teaching represented a form of ewish-pagan syncretism, such as was not inknown in Phrygia, the ethnic region in vhich Colosse was situated.

Whatever the background, note how the prohibition passage follows hard on the announcement of the defeat of the hostile powers in verse 15. This connection has led to the peculation that the observance of the food estrictions and calendar regulations was in ome way linked to the false teachers' interest n those spiritual powers. If this was so, it vould have given Paul all the more reason to mphasize the defeat of the powers and the utility of legalistic practices tied to them in ny way. Indirectly, Paul is affirming yet again he believers' completeness in Christ. Nothing nore was needed to make their salvation ecure—least of all, such shadowy representations of spiritual reality as the legalistic adherence to a set of food laws and observance of particular holy days as necessary for one's salvation. To submit to such practices would be to come under a form of slavery again, the kind of slavery from which they had been delivered in the defeat of the "powers."

5.3.2. Regarding False Humility and the 'Worship of Angels" (2:18–19). We come now to the second major prohibition: "Do not et anyone ... disqualify you for the prize." The verb translated "disqualify ... for the prize" is a rare word that occurs in the New Testament only here. It has no expressed object, so that at its most basic level, Paul is simply saying, 'Do not let anyone disqualify you" (NRSV). But 'disqualify" from what? The NIV (along with many commentators) assumes an unexpressed object: "the prize." This assumption may be legitimate since the noun form of the same word group means "prize" (cf. 1 Cor. 9:24; Phil. 3:14). The prize in question would presumably mean their freedom in Christ or even Christ himself.

Others, however, understand the verb in question as synonymous with "to condemn," arguing that this makes a better contextual parallel with "judge" in verse 16 (cf. GNB, "Do not allow yourselves to be condemned by anyone"). In either case, the point is that the Colossians must not let themselves be pressured or defrauded by false teachers, who would put them under bondage to a new set of legal requirements.

But what kind of people are putting such pressure on the Colossian believers? Although difficult to interpret in detail, verses 18–19 tell us a great deal about their character and form of worship. Verse 18 declares the wrong they do, while verse 19 describes the good they fail to do. Writing about them in the third person singular (cf. NIV, "anyone"), Paul first describes them as people who delight "in false humility" (or, perhaps, as those who insist "on self-abasement"; NRSV). The word "humility" (*tapeinophrosyne*) occurs in 3:12 in a positive sense as one of the Christian virtues that believers are to "put on." But the context in 2:18 is obviously a negative one, hence the NIV translation "*false* humility." Since *tapeinophrosyne* occurs in some contexts as a technical term for fasting and is used again in 2:23 in immediate association with "harsh treatment of the body," it is just possible that the idea of "self-abasement" (NRSV) or "self-mortification" (REB) attaches itself to the word even in verse 18.

In addition to delighting in such show of humility, the heretics also indulge in "the worship of angels." Assuming that this is the correct translation (rather than "the worship [of God] by angels"; cf. O'Brien, 1982, 143), Paul is alluding to a cult of angelic worship, not attested within Judaism as such, but not inconceivable in the mix of religious movements represented in that part of Asia Minor. Nor is it surprising, perhaps, that at the beginning of the twenty-first century, with the wide range of new religious practices emerging all around, our era should also include a widespread interest in "angelic" beings. While angels are obviously part of the created order and play a role as God's messengers, any interest in such beings that leads to worshiping them is unquestionably a perversion. So it was in Paul's day, and so it is in ours.

Not content with promoting the worship of angels, Paul continues that "such a person goes into great detail [*embateuo*] about what he has seen, and his unspiritual mind puffs him up with idle notions" (v. 18b). At least that is one possible translation of a difficult phrase. The word *embateuo* means literally to "set foot upon" (hence the RSV and NASB translate "*taking his stand* on visions"). But basing itself on a related meaning of the word, namely, to "enter into" a place or possession, hence figuratively to "investigate" a subject closely, the NIV translates idiomatically, "goes into great detail." With the discovery that the word was also used as a technical term in the initiation rites of the mystery religions, some commentators have proposed the translation "the things which he has seen at his initiation" (F. F. Bruce, 1984, 117).

What is certain is that the reference is to some kind of spiritual experience (probably elitist) pursued by devotees of the new teaching, an experience that led their "unspiritual mind" being idly "puffed . . . up." What becomes clear, then, is that the kind of spirituality practiced by the propagandists in Colosse was a perverse mixture of false humility and spiritual pride—a thoroughgoing distortion of true spirituality as described later in 3:12–17.

What led these propagandists to pursue the kind of legalistic practices and mystical experiences described thus far? In verse 19 Paul explains that it was because they had "lost connection with the Head," or perhaps they had even outrightly repudiated the Head (see Harris, 1991, 123)—the "Head," of course, referring to Christ (cf. 1:18; 2:10). Although the Greek is not clear enough for us to determine whether Paul is implying that the errorists in question had at one time belonged to the "Head," what is certain is that they did not do so now. The proof of this was their adherence to false teachings and false practices. Had they been truly connected to Christ as head of the church, they would not have sought alternate teachings or practices. Instead, they would have realized that Christ was all-sufficient in his person and in his law of freedom.

The rest of verse 19 explains why it is so important to be connected properly to the "Head." It is from him that "the whole body, supported and held together by its ligaments and sinews, grows as God causes it to grow." Earlier Paul made use of the "head-body" metaphor to describe the relationship between Christ and the church (1:18, 24; see also Eph. 1:22–23; 4:15–16; 5:23). Here he makes it clear that the head is the source of the body's unity and growth. United to him and totally dependent on him, the body grows as God ordains. By the same token, those not united to the head are in effect cut off not only from it but also from the support system of the "body," that is, the church.

Tragically, such was the predicament of the false teachers. Teachings that seriously misrepresented the person of Christ along with legalistic practices that undermined his sufficiency had led to this state of affairs. With good reason, therefore, Paul has repeatedly urged the Colossian believers to be faithful (cf. 1:11, 23; 2:5–6) and not let anyone rob them of their prize (2:18) by succumbing to a philosophy not according to Christ (2:8), with its aberrant legalism (2:16–17) and unhealthy mysticism (2:18–19). Paul has employed strong words and strong warnings, yet no stronger than the situation demanded, for what was at stake was nothing less than the central core of the faith—the person and work of Christ (2:9–15). In the history of the church, challenges to the high Christology of the New Testament documents have always been met with vigorous response from the believing community. So it has always been, and so it must always be, if the church has any regard for its health and future—nay, its very existence.

5.4. Consequences of Having Died and Risen With Christ (2:20–3:4)

The force of Paul's arguments in 2:6–19 could not have failed to impress the Colossians. Yet the issue was so critical and the temptation to succumb so real (see below) that Paul was anxious to reinforce his point once more, this time not from the perspective of the "head-body" metaphor (v. 19), but from that of the "death-resurrection" theme (see 2:12–13), now applied in a thoroughly practical way to the Colossians' confrontation with the local errorists. In verses 20–23 Paul reviews the implications of having died with Christ; in 3:1–4, he deals with the implications of having risen with Christ.

Although some commentators and translations (including the NIV) begin a major new section at 3:1 (cf. the NIV subtitle at this point, "Rules for Holy Living"), it is preferable to view 2:20–23 and 3:1–4 as belonging together, treating opposite aspects of the same issue. That they do, in fact, belong together is clear from the way each of them commences with the parallel phrases, "Since you died with Christ" (2:20), and, "Since, then, you have been raised with Christ" (3:1). The section on ethical conduct begins properly, therefore, at 3:5, though it would not be wrong to see this whole section (2:20–3:4) as transitional between the core of Paul's refutation of error (2:6–19) and the applied section on ethical living commencing with 3:5.

5.4.1. Those Who Have Died With Christ Should Not Submit to "Human Commands and Teachings" (2:20–23). Paul introduces this subsection with a rhetorical question (the only one in the entire letter): "Since you died with Christ to the basic principles of this world, why, as though you still belonged to it, do you submit to its rules: 'Do not handle! Do not taste! Do not touch!'?" This question is revealing in at least four important ways. (1) It makes clear that there was no doubt in the apostle's mind that the Colossian believers had in fact "died with Christ." Even though grammatically the question is introduced by a conditional clause (lit., "If you died with Christ"), it is the kind of conditional clause in Greek that assumes the reality of the proposition in view, the sense being, "If, as is the case, you died with Christ," hence legitimately translated by the NIV (and other versions), "*Since* you died with Christ."

(2) If we take seriously the present continuous tense of the verb *dogmatizesthe* ("do you submit?" = "are you submitting?")—as we must—it then suggests that the Colossian believers (or at least some of them) were in danger of actually succumbing to the new form of legalism. This danger is probably why Epaphras had gone to Rome to seek Paul's counsel in the first place. It was a serious and critical situation.

(3) The rhetorical question also reveals Paul's understanding of the connection that existed between "the basic principles of this world" and the legalistic practices promoted by the false teachers. The sentence makes clear that such regulations as "Do not handle! Do not taste! Do not touch!" are directly linked to the operation of those "basic principles." If, as argued on 2:8, "the basic principles of this world" (*ta stoicheia tou kosmou*) should be interpreted as the "elemental spirits of the universe"—that is, the hostile "powers and authorities"—then we can appreciate even better the critical nature of the situation. Paul is dealing with not just a controversy over a few dietary regulations and holy days; rather, he is facing a case of submitting to a new form of servitude to those spiritual forces.

(4) If we have correctly read the passage—and much points in this direction—it also explains something of Paul's exasperation, hinted at in the form of the question. Paul's firm conviction—already communicated in this and other letters, and no doubt previously taught by Epaphras—was that the Colossians, together with all believers, had been "buried with [Christ] in baptism" (2:12; cf. Rom. 6:4). This burial with Christ implied having died to the *stoicheia tou kosmou* (2:20), those spiritual "powers and authorities" that had been vanquished on the cross and therefore should have held no dread or power for believers in Christ. Unfortunately, they still held a fascination for the heretical teachers. By yielding to sub-Christian regulations, the Colossians were risking coming under the sway of these forces again. How could they possibly contemplate such a regression? It was intolerable! This is the force of Paul's question and the basis for his deep concern.

In verses 22–23 Paul identifies three severe deficiencies in the prohibitions that make them utterly unacceptable as models for Christian rules of conduct. (1) They have to do with things "destined to perish with use." That is to say, their sphere of application is only the earthly and temporal, the things that will perish without any eternal significance.

(2) They are based exclusively on "human commands and teachings"—essentially a restatement of 2:8, where the "philosophy" of the heretics was said to be based on "human tradition." In that earlier passage the teaching of the heretics was also described as "hollow and deceptive," fatally flawed because it was not based on Christian revelation. The same could have been said about the specific dietary and holy day regulations detailed in 2:16–18. Without a revelatory base, they stood condemned as futile human fabrications.

(3) Such regulations, while they may have an "appearance of wisdom," in reality are totally useless when it comes to "restraining sensual indulgence." What gives them the "appearance of wisdom" is the pseudo-religious character of "their self-imposed worship, their false humility, and their harsh treatment of the body" (the last one no doubt referring to various forms of asceticism). But such artificial and forced expressions of piety, even though impressive to some, are meaningless

when it comes to the exercise of true spirituality. In short, everything about the new form of teaching and religious practice by which the Colossians were being wooed was false. Paul was aghast at the thought that any in the Colossian community should submit to the imposition of such worldly "rules." By no means could such prohibitions and regulations commend themselves to people who had "died with Christ" (v. 20).

5.4.2. Those Who Have Been Raised With Christ Should Seek the Things That Are Above (3:1–4). Paul quickly turns to the other side of the Christian experience. Not only have Colossians died with Christ, they have also been raised with Christ. This fact likewise has far-reaching implications for the way they should act, think, and live. Just as 2:20–23 reminded the Colossians of Paul's earlier reference in 2:12 to "having been buried with [Christ]," so now the reference to having been "raised with Christ" reminds them of the parallel phrase, also in 2:12, of "[having been] raised with [Christ] through your faith in the power of God," as well as the phrase in 2:13, "God made you alive with Christ." By the same token, just as having "died with Christ" meant being dead to the influence of the "basic principles of this world" (see comments on v. 20), so now having been "raised with Christ" means being alive to those things that are "above," that is, setting one's affections and mind not on earthly, temporal things but on those that are heavenly and eternal, the sphere "where Christ is seated at the right hand of God."

The reason the Colossians are to seek the things above is that they have been raised with Christ (3:1–2). Verses 3–4 give two reasons why they must set their hearts and minds on the eternal realm (note the conjunction "For" at the beginning of v. 3), which involve both a realized and a future eschatological perspective. (1) The former is clearly expressed in verse 3, "For you died, and your life is now hidden with Christ in God." Essentially this is the corollary statement to verse 1a, "Since, then, you have been raised with Christ." Having been raised with Christ of necessity implies having died with him (cf. 2:12, 20), and there is a sense in which that death with Christ is a continuing experience (note the adverb "now"), where the believer's life keeps on being "hidden with Christ in God." This teaching is what is meant by "realized eschatology". The benefits of Christ's death and resurrection are a present, ongoing reality in the life of the believing community; Christ is truly their "life" (v. 4).

(2) But there is also a future dimension to this eschatology, as the rest of verse 4 makes clear. A day is coming when Christ will appear and then the Colossian believers, who are now "hidden with Christ," will also "appear with him in glory." In light of that glorious appearing of Christ and the believers with him, this was all the more reason for the Colossian believers to cultivate the heavenly perspective and to avoid at all costs the earthbound fixation of the legalistic troublemakers in Colosse.

So ends Paul's Christological exhortation and vigorous refutation of the "Colossian error." So ends also the central doctrinal core of the letter. This is not to say that there is no more doctrine in the rest of the letter or that there has been no practical application up to this point. On the contrary, we have observed several such "practical" exhortations. Nevertheless, the fact remains that there is now a major shift of emphasis from doctrine to praxis. The shift is clearly marked in the concentration of imperative verbs following 3:4, not entirely absent previously but never to the same degree as 3:5–4:6. As in Paul's other letters, the indicative becomes the basis for the imperative; that is to say, what God has done in Christ and who the believers are in him becomes the basis for how they are expected to live.

6. New Life in Christ (3:5–4:6)

In the development of the doctrinal section of this letter (1:15–3:4), Paul has set forth a high Christology, which gave the lie to human-based and demonically inspired teachings not rooted in Christ (2:8) that were troubling the church in Colosse. This positive presentation of the doctrine of Christ (1:15–20; 2:9–15) also necessitated a vigorous refutation of the legalistic and erroneous practices promoted by the false teachers (2:16–3:4). Throughout this development, Paul has sought to apply the teaching directly to the situation in the Colossian church; in the process he made use of different metaphors to illustrate and clarify his meaning, chief among which has been the metaphor of death and resurrection (cf. 2:12–13; 2:20–3:4).

In turning now to the intentionally more practical part of the letter, characterized by a series of specific commands and concrete advice, it is interesting to note that the death/resurrection theme sets the stage for the development of this section as well. Gradually the subject matter transposes itself into the theme of "putting off" and "putting on" (3:9–11), but in reality this is just another way of speaking of death to the world and life in Christ. In short, the entire section of 3:5–4:6 describes the life of believers who have been "raised with Christ" (3:1) and who are now called on to live out this new life in Christ. This new life implies certain principles of conduct, both negatively (what not to do) and positively (what to do). The section is not intended, however, to be a legalistic straitjacket of "do's" and "dont's," but rather an exhortation to the kind of behavior that flows from the believer's participation in the resurrection life of Christ.

The latter point is worth emphasizing in the light of the number of imperatives found in this section. Verbal imperatives and prohibitions, explicit and implicit, direct and indirect, are found in 3:5 ("put to death"), 3:8 ("rid yourselves"; lit., "put off"), 3:9 ("do not lie to each other"), 3:12 ("clothe yourselves"), 3:13 ("bear with each other and forgive"), 3:14 ("put on love"), 3:15a ("let the peace of Christ rule"), 3:15b ("be thankful"), 3:16 ("let the word of Christ dwell in you"), 3:17 ("do all in the name of the Lord Jesus"), 3:18 ("submit"), 3:19 ("love"), 3:20 ("obey"), 3:21 ("do not embitter"), 3:23 ("work"), 4:1 ("provide"), 4:2 ("devote yourselves to prayer"), 4:3 ("pray for us"), and 4:5 ("be wise in the way you act toward outsiders").

Clearly, the imperative is the dominant verbal form in this section, whereas in the previous sections the "indicative"—the form of the verb employed to make a statement—was the norm. This pattern of movement from doctrinal indicative to ethical imperative is by no means unique to this letter; other clear examples are the letter to the Romans and the letter to the Ephesians. In fact, to varying degrees, this pattern underlies all of Paul's letters and embodies a fundamental principle of the Christian life: The "ought" (i.e., the ethical demands of the Christian life) flows out of the "is" (i.e., the reality of what God has done in Christ). It is because of *who* believers are in Christ that they are called on to live in holiness, integrity, and generosity.

The active pursuit of these virtues does not, of course, secure one's salvation. That was done in Christ and by Christ, as previously explained by Paul (esp. in 2:13–15). Yet believers are not without responsibility in how they live. They must seek to live in accord with the great work of redemption accomplished for them. Thus this section of the letter serves as a reminder of the mysterious intermingling of divine initiative and human responsibility to which Paul's letters and, indeed, the whole of Scripture bear witness. In the face of such mystery, believers are expected to respond both in wonder and in obedience. Without participation in the life of Christ, the list of ethical responses embodied in the imperatives seems onerous; by the same token, a genuine experience of the resurrection life of Christ can make them seem joyful.

In highlighting the ethical imperatives associated with life in Christ, Paul focuses initially on the contrast between the actions of the "old self" (lit., "old man," 3:9) and the "new self" (3:10), terminology employed again in Ephesians 4:22, 24—though use of these phrases in both Colossians and Ephesians was already anticipated in Paul's earlier letter to the Romans (cf. Rom. 6:4, 6). In Colossians, the deeds of the "old self" are said to be those of the "earthly nature" (lit., "the members that are on the earth," 3:5), whereas the deeds of the "new self" are those that are motivated by a mind fixed on "things above" (3:1–2). These contrasts dominate the two paragraphs 3:5–11 and 3:12–17.

The practical portion of the letter then continues with an important set of instructions for household relationships (3:18–4:1) and closes with a final set of exhortations regarding prayer and witness (4:2–6). The challenge for the Colossians—as for all of us—was to make the theology of the indicative/imperative paradigm real and operative in their lives and human relationships.

6.1. Putting Off the Old Self (3:5–11)

The section begins with another strong connective, "therefore" (*oun*, cf. 2:6, 16; 3:1), linking the immediately preceding paragraphs with the new material. Since the Colossian believers had both died and been raised with

Christ, they were urged to renounce all forms of legalism and to seek the things that are above; that was essentially the message of 2:20–23 and 3:1–4 respectively. Now the implications of the resurrection life with Christ are taken a step further: The Colossians are exhorted to "put to death" (3:5) the things that belong to their "earthly nature" and to "rid [them]selves" (3:8) of a variety of negative character traits. Paul adjoins a list of five things—not intended to be exhaustive but representative—that they are to "put to death" and five things (ultimately six, since in v. 9 a separate sentence is added) that they are to get rid of. Each list, in turn, is followed by a statement giving specific reasons (vv. 6, 10–11) why such behavior is inappropriate (cf. similar lists in Rom. 1:29–32; 1 Cor. 5:9–11; 6:9–10; Gal. 5:19–21; Eph. 5:3–4).

The things that the Colossians—and by extension, all believers—are to "put to death" are "sexual immorality, impurity, lust, evil desires and greed" (3:5). The list is dominated by sexual sins but terminates with the addition of "greed" as another of the sins that belong to the "earthly nature." Such juxtaposition of sexual sins and greed may seem surprising, but is not unique in the Scriptures (cf. Mark 7:22; Rom. 1:29; Eph. 4:19; 5:3, 5) and is therefore a sober reminder of the subtle connection between sins of the flesh and of the heart. Greed, whether expressed in sexual or material possessiveness, is a form of "idolatry" (also stressed in Eph. 5:5), which always incurs "the wrath of God." It certainly did in biblical times and still does today.

To this first list of vices Paul adds a second list of things the Colossians are encouraged to "put away" or "put off" (cf. NIV, "rid yourselves of"). The vices mentioned are "anger, rage, malice, slander, and filthy language" (v. 8). The sexual overtone is still there in the mention of "filthy language"; otherwise the list highlights expressions of anger and malice directed against others. To these five vices is added a special warning against telling lies to one another (v. 9). Such damaging attitudes and wrongful treatment of other people is totally unbecoming those who have "taken off [their] old self" and "put on the new self" (vv. 9–10a).

This new self is in the process of "being renewed in knowledge in the image of its Creator" (v. 10b), and in that renewal there is to be no abuse or distinction of persons since all, whether "Greek or Jew, circumcised or uncircumcised, barbarian, Scythian, slave or free" (v. 11a), are equally created in God's image and are worthy of dignity, honor, and respect. In this new order of things, characterized by mutual love and respect, the unifying force is Christ, who "is all, and is in all" (v. 11b). In short order, therefore, Paul has shown how Christ, the principal agent of creation and redemption, is also the basis for all ethical behavior.

6.2. Putting on the New Self (3:12–17)

If there are vices to put to death (v. 5), to get rid of (v. 8), and to take off (v. 9), there are also virtues to put on, positive qualities befitting those who are "God's chosen people, holy and dearly loved" (v. 12a). This contrast between "putting off" and "putting on" was already introduced in verses 9–10, but is now expanded in verses 12–17 (esp. vv. 12–14; vv 15–17 constitute a related but independent subunit). The verb *endyomai* (used in both v. 10 and v. 12) literally means to "clothe oneself," "to wear"—hence the NIV translation at verse 12, "clothe yourselves."

The qualities with which believers are to clothe themselves are again five in number: "compassion, kindness, humility, gentleness and patience" (v. 12b)—qualities, it has been noted, that in other contexts are associated with God or Jesus (for "compassion," cf. Luke 6:36; Rom. 12:1; 2 Cor. 1:3; James 5:11; for "kindness," cf. Rom. 11:22; Titus 3:4; for "humility," cf. Matt. 11:29; Phil. 2:8; for "gentleness," cf. Matt. 11:29; 21:5; 2 Cor. 10:1; for "patience," cf. Rom. 2:4; 9:22; 1 Peter 3:20; 2 Peter 3:15). Because they are "divine" qualities, several of them are also listed as part of the fruit of the Spirit (Gal. 5:22–23; those also mentioned in Col. 3:12 are "kindness," "gentleness," and "patience"). In essence, they are those Christian graces especially necessary in relationships to "reduce or eliminate friction: ready sympathy, a generous spirit, a humble disposition, willingness to make concessions, patience, forbearance" (Moule, 1957, 123). How enriching is congregational life when those virtues are present; how impoverished when they are absent!

To the five virtues that the Colossians are exhorted to "put on," Paul now adds three ore—forbearance, forgiveness, and love (vv. 3–14)—though this time expressed in xtended participial constructions rather than a list of single words. The exhortations to rbearance and forgiveness (v. 13) are repeated identical form in Ephesians 4:2 ("bearing ith one another") and 4:32 ("forgiving each ther"), both times in conjunction with virtues imilar to those mentioned in Colossians 3:12. he subject was obviously much on Paul's aind and of first importance for the well-being f his fledgling congregations.

But of greatest importance was the exercise f "love," the supreme virtue that binds all the thers together "in perfect unity" (v. 14). This mphasis relates to what Paul had expressed arlier in the letter about one of the chief goals f his ministry, namely, that believers would e "united in love" (2:2). In the case of the olossians he had reason to be glad, for Epahras had recently reported to Paul about their love in the Spirit" (1:8). The Greek noun nderlying the translation "love" in these conexts is, of course, *agape*—a word that, though ittle used in pre-Christian times, became a uintessential Christian word to express that orm of high regard and deep appreciation that hristians are to show one another, all based n the *agape* love of God in Christ toward umankind (cf. esp. 1 John 4:7–21).

In verses 15–17 the clothing metaphor rops into the background, but the concern emains the Colossians' participation in Chrisian graces. Two such graces dominate this aragraph, namely, that believers experience oth "the peace of Christ" (v. 15) and "the vord of Christ" (v. 16). The phrase "the peace of Christ" is no doubt to be interpreted as the eace that Christ gives, the peace that he is minently qualified to give (cf. John 14:27) ince "he himself is our peace" (Eph. 2:14). aul's desire is that this peace "rule" (*brabeuo*, it., "act as arbitrator") in our hearts and thus romote unity among those who are part of the one body." The pursuit of such peace and nity is not an option, but something to which he believers have been "called" as part of their Christian witness. In addition, they are called o thankfulness, one of the Christian virtues specially emphasized in this letter, as previously noted (see comments on 1:3).

In verse 16, the Colossians are urged to allow "the word of Christ" to dwell in them richly. This "word of Christ" may mean "the word spoken by Christ" (subjective genitive) or "the teaching about Christ" (objective genitive). The two are neither identical nor mutually exclusive alternatives. Paul's much more common phrase is "the word of *God*" (once "the message [word] of the *Lord*," 2 Thess. 3:1), but in the letter to the Colossians, with its special emphasis on the person and work of Christ, it is perhaps not surprising that he should think of the divine word as "the word of *Christ*."

There are two areas where this "word" should be particularly applied, namely, in the Colossians' exercise of their teaching and singing ministries. As the "word of Christ" is allowed to penetrate their teaching, the latter will be done "with all wisdom"; as the same "word" inspires their "psalms, hymns and spiritual [better, 'Spiritual' or 'Spirit-inspired'; cf. Fee, 1994, 653–54] songs" addressed to God, believers will be filled "with gratitude . . . to God." One senses here that the needs of the primitive church were not much different from those of the contemporary church. A healthy and vibrant church will allow "the word of Christ" to characterize all its teaching and worship life—a critical reminder at a time when some church communities find it tempting to experiment with substitutes for an encounter with the living "word of Christ."

The section closes with a ringing appeal to the Colossians to do everything, whether in word or deed, "in the name of the Lord Jesus" (v. 17). To do something "in the name" of someone is to do it as that person's representative. Thus, the believers in Colosse are urged to speak and act in a way that commends them as representatives of Christ. Moreover, they are to do it while "giving thanks to God the Father" through Christ—yet another link in the chain of references to "thanksgiving" running through this letter, but especially noteworthy as the common denominator to 3:15–17. As the exhortation to let the "peace of Christ" rule in their hearts ends with the phrase "and be thankful," so the appeal for the "word of Christ" to dwell richly in them closes with the exhortation to sing "with gratitude" to God. Thus the three themes, "the peace of Christ," "the word of Christ," and thanksgiving to God in everything round out Paul's heartfelt desires for the Christian community in Colosse.

6.3. Living in Positive Social Relationships (3:18–4:1)

At this point the apostle inserts a passage designed to illustrate how the new life in Christ works itself out in the dynamics of household relationships. The passage is by no means unique to this letter; similar *Haustafeln* ("tables of household rules") are found elsewhere in the New Testament as well as in secular writings (e.g., Eph. 5:21–6:9; 1 Tim. 2:8–15; 6:1–10; Titus 2:1–10; 1 Peter 2:17–3:9).[6] The passage in Colossians is, however, generally considered to be the earliest Christian example, along with Ephesians, of this genre.

The section consists of three pairs of exho
tations directed, in turn, to wives and husband
children and parents, slaves and masters—pr
gression is from more to less intimate forms
relationships. Comparison and contrast wi
other examples of household rules in Greek ar
Jewish literature highlights two distinctives
the Christian version of this genre: the reci
rocal responsibility of each of the parties in th
specified pairs, and the repeated emphasis th
mutual obligations are to be exercised "in th
Lord" (cf. 3:18, 20, 22, 24; 4:1).

This means, first, that in a Christian settin
it is not just husbands, parents, and maste

SONGS IN THE NEW TESTAMENT

Paul encourages believers to sing "songs, hymns and spiritual songs" (Eph 5:19; Col 3:16). The OT, of course, has an entire book of songs (the Psalms). But the NT also contains songs that God's creatures sing in praise of their Maker and Redeemer. This chart lists these songs; those about which scholars are uncertain are listed in italics.

Songs in the Gospels	
The song of Mary	Lk 1:46–55
The song of Zechariah	Lk 1:68–79
The song of the angels at the birth of Jesus	Lk 2:14
The song of Simeon	Lk 2:29–31
The song of the crowds on Palm Sunday	Mt 21:9; Mk 11:9–10; Lk 19:31; Jn 12:13
Songs in NT Letters	
Doxology to God	Ro 11:33–36
Hymn of love	1Co 13
Wake-up song	Eph 5:14
Hymn to the human and divine Jesus	Php 2:6–11
Hymn to Jesus as supreme Lord	Col 1:15–20
Hymn on the life of Jesus	1Ti 3:16
Songs in Revelation	
Song of the four living creatures	Rev 4:8
Songs of the twenty-four elders	Rev 4:11; 11:17–18
Song of the four living creatures and the twenty-four elders	Rev 5:9–10
Songs of the many angels	Rev 5:12–13; 7:12
Songs of the great multitude of saints	Rev 7:10; 19:1–3
Songs of the loud voice(s) in heaven	Rev 11:15; 12:10–12; 19:5
Songs of the seven angels (including the song of Moses and the song of the Lamb)	Rev 15:3–4, 6–8

who are regarded as free agents and assumed to enjoy authority or privilege; second, it means that family and social relationships are essentially religious in character in that they are all to be exercised under the Lordship of Christ. Both points are reinforced in the Ephesian version of the household rules, where the whole section is introduced by the general command, "Submit to one another out of reverence for Christ" (Eph. 5:21).

Although wives, children, and slaves are exhorted to submit to (v. 18) or obey (vv. 20, 22) their husbands, parents, and masters respectively, the latter in turn have the responsibility to love their wives (v. 19), encourage their children (v. 21), and deal equitably with their slaves (4:1). The neat parallelism of the three pairs of exhortations is broken by the lengthy charge to slaves, a phenomenon perhaps best explained by the circumstances surrounding the return to Colosse of the runaway slave Onesimus (see 4:8 below, and the letter to Philemon).

The fact that all of these relationships are to be exercised "in the Lord" does not mean that there is no element of cultural relativity present in these commands. For instance, it cannot be assumed that Paul's exhortation to slaves implies his approval of the institution of slavery. Paul is not writing a social or political tract but giving instructions on how Christian witness is to be lived out in a particular cultural context. In a similar way, the broader theological principle about equality of all persons, laid out in 3:11—that in the new community of faith "there is no Greek or Jew, circumcised or uncircumcised, barbarian, Scythian, slave or free, but Christ is all, and is in all" (cf. the similar statement in Gal. 3:28, that in Christ "there is neither Jew nor Greek, slave nor free, male nor female")—no doubt has practical implications for the relationship between husbands and wives. It is interesting to observe, however, that the authority of parents over children remains constant in Scripture, though the admonition for parents not to abuse their authority is strongly emphasized in Colossians 3:21 as well as in Ephesians 6:4.

6.4. Cultivating the Disciplines of Prayer and Witness (4:2–6)

Just before his closing greetings, Paul has a final set of instructions for the Colossians touching on their prayer life and their witness to "outsiders." Just as he began the letter with a prayer of thanksgiving and intercession (cf. 1:3–8, 9–14), so now he encourages the Colossians to engage in the same ministries. "Devote yourselves to prayer," he says (4:2), echoing not only the language of prayer from the introduction to the letter (cf. 1:3, 9), but also his earlier exhortation in Romans 12:12 ("Be . . . faithful in prayer"), perhaps in conscious imitation of the first disciples and apostles (cf. Acts 1:14; 2:42; 6:4). Common to each of these passages is the use of the verb *proskartereo* in association with prayer, a strong verb meaning "to adhere to, persist in, persevere in." As the Colossians devote themselves to prayer, they are urged to be "watchful and thankful" (for "watchful," see 1 Cor. 16:13; for "thankful," cf. Paul's preoccupation with this theme in this letter [see comments on Col. 1:3; 3:16–17]).

In verses 3–4 Paul continues with the theme of prayer, but now asks the Colossians to pray *for him* in the same way that he had begun the letter praying *for them* (cf. similar requests in Rom. 15:30–32; 2 Cor. 1:11; Eph. 6:19; Phil. 1:19; 1 Thess. 5:25; 2 Thess. 3:1–2; Philem. 22). His request is threefold. (1) He asks the Colossians to pray for an "open . . . door" of opportunity in sharing the word. The image of an "open door" was well known in Hellenistic literature. Paul had used it twice previously in relation to his missionary work. In 1 Corinthians 16:9, he affirmed that an open door of ministry was available to him in Ephesus in spite of many opponents. Leaving Ephesus, he acknowledged another open door of ministry opportunity for him in Troas, but he had been unable to take advantage of it because of his anxious spirit (2 Cor. 2:12–13). Now, although in "chains" (Col. 4:18), he hopes that God will open for him another "door" of service.

(2) Paul asks the Colossians to pray that he may have the appropriate message to announce, namely, "the mystery of Christ," the essence of which, as he explained in 1:26–27, was "Christ in you [Gentiles], the hope of glory."

(3) Paul invites prayer support so that he will be able to announce this message "clearly." Such a threefold prayer request for positive ministry opportunities, relevant content, and

clear delivery is one we would do well to imitate when praying both for our own ministries and for all who serve the cause of Christ.

In verses 5–6 Paul shifts his attention from the Colossians' prayer activity to their witness in relation to "outsiders." His concern has to do with their behavior (v. 5) and their speech (v. 6). He asks them first to be "wise" in how they behave, making "the most of every opportunity" (lit., "redeeming the time"; see also Eph. 5:16). In short, they must be prudent and resourceful in their actions. As for their speech, it is to be "full of grace" and "seasoned with salt," with the goal of having an appropriate answer for everyone.

Taken together, Paul's exhortations on prayer and witness show him to be a deeply spiritual and immensely practical person. This model of passion and practicality in ministry must have made a deep impression on his emerging congregations, as it should on us.

7. Final Greetings and Instructions (4:7–18)

Paul closes all his letters with words of greeting and miscellaneous instructions for the intended recipients, though curiously the two congregations not known to him by face (those in Rome and Colosse) receive the most detailed greetings and closing instructions. In the present letter we can identify four subdivisions in this final section: Paul's commendation of his messengers (vv. 7–9), greetings from his coworkers (vv. 10–14), closing instructions to the Colossians (v. 15–17), and his own handwritten greeting (v. 18).

7.1. Paul's Commendation of His Messengers (4:7–9)

This passage commending Tychicus and Onesimus as the bearers of the letter and as Paul's personal representatives is repeated in almost identical form in Ephesians 6:21–22 (another witness to the close relationship between these two letters). In addition to accrediting the two messengers, the passage is an example of the "apostolic disclosure" formula found in some of Paul's letters, whereby the apostle wants his readers to be informed of his personal circumstances (cf. Rom. 1:13; 2 Cor. 1:8; Eph. 6:21; also, Phil. 1:12; Col. 2:1). On this occasion the letter carriers themselves will communicate "all the news" concerning Paul (v. 7) and "everything that is happening" with respect to his imprisonment and future plans (v. 9).

It is a lovely thing to observe how warmly Paul commends his personal messengers. Tychicus he calls "a dear brother, a faithful minister and fellow servant in the Lord." From Acts 20:4 we know that Tychicus was from the province of Asia, probably a convert during Paul's ministry in Ephesus, later appointed by the churches of Asia (along with Trophimus) as their representative in accompanying Paul to Jerusalem with the offering for the Jewish believers in that city. Clearly he was a brother of trust and confidence. In the Pastoral Letters we hear of him still functioning as Paul's emissary (2 Tim. 4:12; Titus 3:12).

Onesimus was the runaway slave for whom Paul had to intercede so that his master, Philemon, would take him back and forgive the renegade's crime. Yet, in spite of Onesimus's past history, Paul applies similar terms of endearment to him as he does to his own coworker by calling the now converted runaway a "faithful and dear brother" (v. 9). For Paul, social standing evidently meant little when it came to evaluating a person's ultimate worth and character.

7.2. Paul's Conveyance of Greetings from His Coworkers (4:10–14)

Paul then relays greetings to the Colossians from six of his coworkers present with him, three of whom are Jews (Aristarchus, John Mark, and Jesus, called Justus, vv. 10–11) and three of whom are Gentiles (Epaphras, Luke, and Demas, vv. 12–14). Of the first two we know a considerable amount, but of "Jesus, called Justus" we have only the mention of his name on this one occasion. Aristarchus was from Thessalonica, possibly a convert from Paul's ministry there on his second missionary journey (Acts 17:1–9) and one of Paul's companions during his ministry in Ephesus (19:29). Along with Tychicus and others, he accompanied Paul to Jerusalem (20:4) and later journeyed with him to Rome (27:2), where he appears to have stayed with the apostle as his "fellow prisoner."

John Mark accompanied Paul and Barnabas on the first missionary journey, whose departure for home eventually occasioned the bitter split between the two (Acts 13:13; 15:36–41).

Generally associated more with the ministry of Peter, it is interesting to see him now in company with Paul, and especially to hear Paul's warm words of approval: "If he comes to you, welcome him" (with which may be compared his words of commendation of the same Mark in 2 Tim. 4:11). Even if these are the only three Jews among Paul's fellow workers in Rome, he is nevertheless thankful for them, for they had "proved a comfort" to him in the midst of his many discomforts and uncertainties (v. 11).

Of the three Gentiles with him, Paul gives special attention to Epaphras (vv. 12–13). This is understandable, given the fact that this man was the evangelist-pastor who had recently come from the Lycus Valley to Rome to consult with Paul regarding pastoral concerns in his home area. Earlier in the letter Paul identified Epaphras as his "dear fellow servant " and "faithful minister of Christ on our behalf" (see comments on 1:7). Here the apostle adds further comments about his background and present activity. Epaphras is "one of you," he says, meaning that Colosse was his home city. More important, he is a "servant [*doulos*] of Christ Jesus" (v. 12), who is "working hard" not only for the Colossians but also for those at Laodicea and Hierapolis, neighboring cities in the Lycus Valley (v. 13). The way he is working hard is by "wrestling in prayer" for the Colossians that they "may stand firm in all the will of God, mature and fully assured" (v. 12).

What is noteworthy about this description of Epaphras is the way it reflects Paul's own ministry, even to the point of repeating some of the same language from earlier parts of the letter. As Paul had begun with a prayer of thanksgiving and intercession (1:3–14) and had exhorted the Colossians to engage in the same ministry (4:3), so now he cites the example of Epaphras as someone who was effectively modeling this ministry of prayer, both in form and content. He was "wrestling [*agonizomenos*] in prayer," says Paul, thus employing the very word he had used to describe his own ministry in 1:29 (there translated "struggling"; cf. the use of the noun *agon* in 2:1, again translated "struggling" in the NIV). The content of Epaphras's prayer—that the Colossians would "stand firm in all the *will* of God, *mature* [*teleioi*] and fully assured"—echoes the kinds of fruit Paul himself worked for in his ministry (cf. 1:9, "asking God to fill you with the knowledge of his *will*," and 1:28, "that we may present everyone *perfect* [*teleion*] in Christ"). In other words, the disciple had learned well from his mentor and was now modeling the kind of prayer activity that Paul wanted to see reproduced in the life of the Colossian congregation.

Also conveying greetings were Paul's "dear friend Luke, the doctor" and Demas. The latter, although mentioned again in Philemon 24, later deserted Paul "because he loved this world" (2 Tim. 4:10). Luke, however, was a friend true from beginning to end. Assuming Luke to be the companion of Paul who joined the missionary party in the so-called "we" sections of Acts, he had first linked up with Paul and his companions in Troas (Acts 16:10) and then stayed on in Philippi, perhaps as one of the leaders in that beloved congregation. Several years later he again joined Paul on the apostle's last journey to Jerusalem (along with Tychicus and Aristarchus and others; cf. 20:4–6), and, like Aristarchus, finally accompanied Paul the prisoner on the long journey to Rome (27:1–2). With reason Paul could call Luke his "dear friend" (NIV; lit., "beloved," *agapetos*), one of the terms of endearment he reserved for his close associates (see vv. 7 and 9 above with reference to Tychicus and Onesimus).

7.3. Paul's Closing Instructions to the Colossians (4:15–17)

The final instructions bear further witness to the close relationship between the neighboring churches in the Lycus Valley, in this case between the church in Colosse and that in Laodicea (cf. Epaphras's concern in v. 13 for the churches in Laodicea *and* Hierapolis). Paul asks the Colossians to greet the "brothers" (and sisters; see comment on 1:2) in the church in Laodicea, as well as to exchange letters (regrettably, his letter to the Laodiceans has been lost; not so, however, with John's letter to the same group of believers a generation later, cf. Rev. 3:14–22). The fact that he wanted the Laodiceans to read his letter to the Colossians suggests that the problems confronted in this letter were not unique to the church in Colosse but probably affected all the churches in the Lycus Valley.

Next Paul has a special greeting for two individuals: Nympha, along with "the church [that meets] in her house," and Archippus.

The city of Colosse became less important than its neighbors, Laodicea and Hierapolis, which became prosperous. Laodicea was one of the seven churches in Revelation, where it was described as "lukewarm—neither hot nor cold—I am about to spit you out of my mouth."

Whether Nympha and her house church was part of or in addition to the "brothers [and sisters]" referred to in the first phrase is not clear from the grammar of the sentence. What is clear, however, is that Paul wished by this means to recognize Nympha in a special way, perhaps to commend her for her leadership. For Archippus (who may have been part of Philemon's household, cf. Philem. 2) he has a more sober message: "See to it that you complete the work you have received in the Lord." The circumstances behind the exhortation are lost to us. What is not lost, however, is Paul's concern for the loyalty and commitment of this coworker, no less than his commendation of those who were progressing well.

7.4. Paul's Handwritten Greeting (4:18)

Having finished dictating the letter, Paul now closes it with a handwritten note, his personal signature as it were (cf. 1 Cor. 16:21; Gal. 6:11; 2 Thess. 3:17; Philem. 19). This way of closing his letters was probably Paul's custom even in those letters where there is no explicit mention of a personal note (cf. the study by H. Gamble Jr., *The Textual History of the Letter to the Romans*, 1977, 76–80). On this occasion he asks the Colossians to "remember his chains," meaning that they should pray for him in his imprisonment, even as he had asked them earlier to pray for a door of opportunity to proclaim the message "for which I am in chains" (4:3).

Paul's closing benediction, "Grace be with you," brings the letter back full cycle to where it began in 1:2 with the invocation, "Grace and peace to you from God our Father." This is appropriate enough, for of all the divine blessings, grace was the one that had made its greatest impact on Paul and the one he most yearned for his converts to experience. May we all experience the same!

NOTES

[1]It is, of course, noteworthy that Colossians 1:3–5 contains another example of the famous triad of "faith, hope and love" (1 Cor. 13:13), though not with coordinated elements as in the 1 Corinthians passage (in the Colossian passage the faith and love "spring from" the believer's hope), nor in the same order (faith, love, hope in Colossians). Other passages in Paul's writings where these three elements are found in close association with one another are Romans 5:1–5; Galatians 5:5–6; Ephesians 4:2–5 and 1 Thessalonians 1:3; 5:8.

[2]Another prime example of this phenomenon is the parallel letter to the Ephesians, where prayer and theology alternate between one another, especially in chapters 1–3, but also in the applied section of chapters 4–6.

[3]"You know that I have not hesitated to preach [*anangello*—a near synonym of *katangello*] anything that would be helpful to you but have taught [*didasko*] you publicly and from house to house" (Acts 20:20); "I have not hesitated to proclaim [*anangello*] to you the whole will of God" (20:27); "For three years I never stopped warning [*noutheteo*] each of you night and day with tears" (20:31).

[4]Gnosticism was originally an oriental form of religion that promoted the necessity of a special kind of *gnosis* ("knowledge") for the redemption of the soul. Eventually this religious teaching with its views on angelic intermediaries, body/spirit dualism, and ascetic/libertine practices affected large areas of the Christian church. The "Colossian heresy" has often been assumed to consist of a particular mixture of incipient Gnosticism and Judaistic borrowings.

[5]In this context it is best to understand the Greek genitive construction *tou Christou* (lit., "of Christ," cf. KJV, RSV/NRSV, NASB) as a "subjective genitive," i.e., referring to the circumcision effected "by Christ" (as in the NIV; cf. GNB)—probably an allusion to his atoning death. Others have explained the

genitive as "objective," i.e., the circumcision that was done on Christ; or as a "possessive" genitive, "Christ's circumcision," with the implication that Christian circumcision of the heart "is Christ's way of circumcision" (NEB/REB, cf. JB).

[6]The employment of this genre of literature in the New Testament (since the time of Luther known as "*Haustafeln*") has been the object of several special studies; see John E. Crouch, *The Origin and Intention of the Colossian Haustafel*, 1972; George E. Cannon, *The Use of Traditional Materials in Colossians*, 1983 (esp. "Traditional Parenetic Materials: The Household Code," 95–132).

BIBLIOGRAPHY

Clinton E. Arnold, *The Colossian Syncretism: The Interface Between Christianity and False Belief at Colosse* (1996); William Barclay, *The Letters to the Philippians, Colossians, and Thessalonians* (1975); Markus Barth and Helmut Blanke, *Colossians*, AB (1994); F. F. Bruce, *The Epistles to the Colossians, to Philemon and to the Ephesians*, NICNT (1984); D. A. Carson, Douglas J. Moo, and Leon Morris, *An Introduction to the New Testament* (1992), 331–42; James D. G. Dunn, *The Epistles to the Colossians and to Philemon: A Commentary on the Greek Text*, NIGTC (1996); Gordon D. Fee, *God's Empowering Presence: The Holy Spirit in the Letters of Paul* (1994); Murray Harris, *Colossians and Philemon*, EGGNT (1991); J. B. Lightfoot, *St. Paul's Epistles to the Colossians and to Philemon* (1875; repr., 1987); Eduard Lohse, *Colossians and Philemon*, trans. William R. Poehlmann and Robert J. Karris, Hermeneia (1971); Ralph P. Martin, *Colossians and Philemon*, NCB (1978); C. F. D. Moule, *The Epistles of Paul to the Colossians and to Philemon*, CGTC (1957); Peter T. O'Brien, *Colossians, Philemon*, WBC (1982); N. T. Wright, *Colossians and Philemon*, TNTC (1986).

1 AND 2 THESSALONIANS

Brian Glubish

INTRODUCTION TO 1 THESSALONIANS

No substantial reason exists for doubting the opening words of 1 Thessalonians 1:1—this letter is most certainly the work of the apostle Paul. What we have before us is likely the first of his contributions to the New Testament, which we can date approximately at A.D. 50 or 51.[1] Paul is writing either from his brief stay at Athens (1 Thess. 3:1; cf. Acts 17:16–34), or more likely from his next and prolonged missionary venture in Corinth (Acts 18:1–18).

It is a fledgling group of believers in Thessalonica that is to receive this urgent letter. Macedonia's flourishing capital city of Thessalonica, a harbor on the Aegean Sea, was located on the major east-west thoroughfare of the Roman Empire—the Via Egnatia. Its relatively large population of around 200,000 included a Jewish constituency large enough to support the Jewish synagogue that was to be Paul's initial preaching point in the city.

Paul's ministry at Thessalonica is indebted to divine orchestration. It was to be much more than a mere whistle-stop on a busy ministry itinerary. Before addressing the precise occasion for the letter, a survey of events leading up to Paul's visit will be instructive.

When his life was interrupted by the Lord on the road to Damascus, Paul did an about-face that was to rock Judaism and the sect known as the Way. Not only was he now following the leader of those he once so vehemently persecuted, he would be instrumental in the breaking down of the barrier between Jew and Gentile through his uncompromising mission as apostle to the Gentiles.

With one successful missionary journey completed and reported on back at Antioch, Paul became eager to press on to new territory. Two factors must be noted here. (1) After much dispute and concern, the anti-Gentile sentiment felt by some Jewish Christians was to have had been laid to rest by the council at Jerusalem (Acts 15:1–29). Pillars such as Peter, Barnabas, and James spoke to the issue and concluded that Gentiles were to be full partners in the faith. God had made it abundantly clear through the pouring out of the Holy Spirit, which included the important evidence of glossolalia, that those outside the house of Israel need not jump through any hoops of Judaism. Faith alone justifies! With such a fundamental issue settled, Paul must have been overjoyed; his gospel would not be altered; he was free to continue preaching the marvelous grace of Jesus for all. He must get on the road!

(2) The other factor to note is a negative one. The dynamic tandem of Paul and Barnabas was torn apart by "sharp disagreement" (Acts 15:36–41). They went their separate ways, apparently for now, unreconciled. With his new partner Silas, Paul visited Derbe and Lystra, where he enlisted Timothy as part of the ministry team. Eventually Paul hoped to evangelize Asia but was "kept by the Holy Spirit" from doing so (16:6). As he attempted to move up into Bithynia, "the Spirit of Jesus would not allow them to" (16:7). We can only speculate on why Paul was not completely in tune with God's itinerary. Is it perhaps in part because his sensitivity to the specific leading of the Spirit was somewhat dulled by his breakup with Barnabas? Did Paul himself have further lessons to learn regarding the ways in which

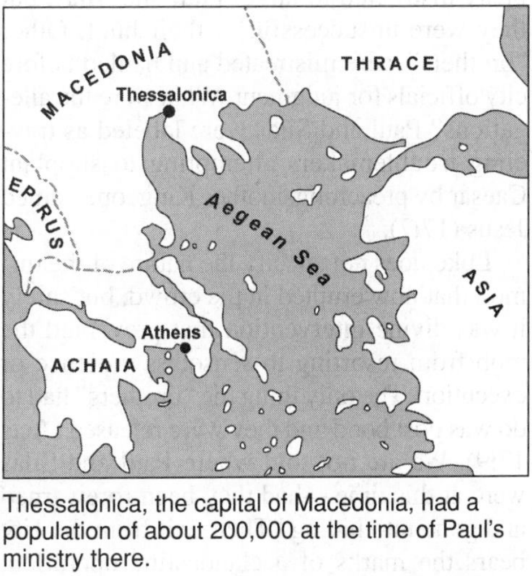

Thessalonica, the capital of Macedonia, had a population of about 200,000 at the time of Paul's ministry there.

the Spirit moved? Whatever the case, it took a vision in Troas to get the team on track (16:9–10) and into Macedonia, where a dramatic sequence of events resulted in the planting of churches in Philippi and Thessalonica.

Initial success greeted Paul in Philippi. Converts were made and a home church established, but the tide turned as Paul and Silas were flogged and jailed. Despite the miraculous prison release and the conversion of the jailer, the team was asked to leave town (Acts 16:39–40). Paul would later write to the Thessalonians a reminder of the suffering and insult received there (1 Thess. 2:2). The next significant ministry occurred in Thessalonica (Acts 17:1–9); Luke's record dovetails with the reconstruction of events we can piece together from the internal evidence of the Thessalonian correspondence.

Paul's strategy was to begin his evangelism among the Jews, which was convenient, for they were a ready-made group located in the synagogue. Luke records that Paul was able for three Sabbaths to testify to the gospel, proving from their Scriptures that Jesus was the Messiah (Acts 17:2–3). His ministry bore fruit—some Jews believed, though the majority of converts were Gentiles. Along with the success, storm clouds quickly formed on the horizon, the winds of persecution howled. At the instigation of "jealous" Jews a mob gathered, consisting of "bad characters from the marketplace" (17:5; note the KJV's dramatic rendering: "certain lewd fellows of the baser sort"). This mob was bent on violence, obviously instructed to target Paul and Silas, but they were unsuccessful in their hunt. Other "brothers" were mistreated and hauled before city officials for judgment. What were the allegations? Paul and Silas were labeled as traveling troublemakers attempting to supplant Caesar by preaching another King, one named Jesus (17:7).

Luke does not specify the nature of the turmoil that now erupted in the crowd, but surely it was divine intervention that prevented the mob from resorting to senseless violence or execution. The only thing the "brothers" had to do was post bond and they were released (Acts 17:9). We are not told where Paul and Silas were at this time—had they been forewarned and gone into hiding? Their exit from the city bears the marks of a clandestine operation. Under cover of night they were shuttled off to Berea (17:10). Here Paul's ministry was also cut short by persecution; he next preached in Athens, then established himself an eighteen-month ministry in Corinth (18:1, 11). There he was rejoined by Silas and Timothy (18:5), no doubt getting a much-coveted report of the situation in Thessalonica. This report spawns Paul's first letter to the Thessalonians.

Paul is a tenacious defender of the gospel. He is a strong leader, a resilient preacher fueled by his personal revelation of Jesus Christ. He is intolerant of opponents; he can be quite severe in his response to them. But there beats within Paul the soft heart of a pastor. His spiritual children are of the utmost concern to him; he has not forgotten them despite the miles between them. First Thessalonians stands as a tribute to Paul's tender, consuming pastoral care for converts. He had not wanted to leave the new church in Thessalonica. Such a brief stay did not appear to be long enough to establish a body of believers that could function independently even under the best of circumstances. But to lose their spiritual father and to experience persecution at such an early stage in their development was a test of faith; not even Paul was confident they would survive unscathed. He must do something to remedy the situation.

In the letter the tension builds as Paul reveals how worried he has been over the spiritual welfare of the new Christians in Thessalonica. He has been in agony for some time, intensely longing to see them (1 Thess. 2:17). Finally, "when we could stand it no longer" (3:1), he sent Timothy to minister in the emergency and to report back to Paul in Corinth. Timothy has now just returned, Paul's stomach has been in knots of anxiety, and there is a huge sigh of relief in his words: "For now we really live, since you are standing firm in the Lord" (3:8).

There is more to Timothy's report than that the church is thriving. He reports on three other issues. (1) Paul is forced to defend his ministry and motives (1:5; 2:1–10; 3:5–10) in response to allegations that he has abandoned the new converts and that he did not care about them enough to return once the initial winds of persecution faded (2:17–18). (2) There is misunderstanding regarding eschatology, that is, the unfolding of events of the Lord's return (4:13–5:11). (3) There are issues of conduct for which the believers need correction and exhortation (4:1–11; 5:12–22). Paul tackles these issues with typical passion and transparency.

OUTLINE OF 1 THESSALONIANS

1. **Salutation** (1:1)
2. **Paul's Thanksgiving** (1:2–10)
   - **2.1.** Thanksgiving Directed to God (1:2)
   - **2.2.** Thanksgiving Due to Thessalonian Response (1:3–10)
     - **2.2.1.** Response of Faith, Love, and Hope (1:3)
     - **2.2.2.** Response of Deep Conviction (1:4–5)
     - **2.2.3.** Response of Imitation, Modeling (1:6–8)
     - **2.2.4.** Response of Serving and Waiting (1:9–10)
3. **Paul's Defense, Part 1: A Summary of Ministry in Thessalonica** (2:1–16)
   - **3.1.** A Successful and Bold Effort (2:1–2)
   - **3.2.** A Sincere and Loving Effort (2:3–12)
   - **3.3.** An Authoritative but Resisted Effort (2:13–16)
4. **Paul's Defense, Part 2: Desire for the Thessalonians** (2:17–3:13)
   - **4.1.** A Heart Torn and Desperate (2:17–18)
   - **4.2.** A Heart Fond and Consumed (2:19–20)
   - **4.3.** A Heart Wracked With Anxiety (3:1–5)
   - **4.4.** A Heart Relieved (3:6–8)
   - **4.5.** A Heart of Prayer (3:9–13)
5. **Paul's Directions for the Thessalonians** (4:1–5:22)
   - **5.1.** Regarding Previous Instruction (4:1–12)
     - **5.1.1.** Grow in Obedience and Purity (4:1–8)
     - **5.1.2.** Grow in Brotherly Love, Stewardship, and Respect (4:9–12)
   - **5.2.** Regarding the Return of the Lord (4:13–5:11)
     - **5.2.1.** Retain Hope for the Dead in Christ (4:13–14)
     - **5.2.2.** Realize the Sequence of Events (4:15–18)
     - **5.2.3.** Ready Yourself for the Return (5:1–11)
   - **5.3.** Regarding Conduct in the Christian Community (5:12–22)
     - **5.3.1.** Respect Authority (5:12–13)
     - **5.3.2.** Remedy Needs (5:14–15)
     - **5.3.3.** Rejoice, Pray, and Recognize the Spirit's Leading (5:16–22)
6. **Conclusion** (5:23–28)
   - **6.1.** Paul's Prayer Wish (5:23–24)
   - **6.2.** Paul's Requests and Benediction (5:25–28)

COMMENTARY ON 1 THESSALONIANS

1. Salutation (1:1)

In typical Pauline fashion and following contemporary letter-writing convention, the apostle opens by identifying the writers. The names of Silas and Timothy are included, but the extent to which they were involved in the formation of the letter is uncertain. Though the letter's composition is not a paragraph-by-paragraph team effort, it is based in part on Timothy's report of the Thessalonian situation (3:6), and perhaps Silas is Paul's scribe taking dictation (cf. also 1 Peter 5:12). Because the three were close partners in the recent ministry in Thessalonica, Paul is most comfortable referring to the other two using the personal pronouns "we" and "us" consistently (e.g., 1:2; 2:2; 3:1; 4:1, 13; 5:1, 12). Silas and Timothy share in Paul's concern over the matters addressed by the letter.

The address of the letter is the next component, and here Paul locates the church not only geographically (in Thessalonica), but most importantly, he identifies the spiritual sphere of its existence: "in God the Father and the Lord Jesus Christ." The preposition "in" (*en*) takes on splendid Christian meaning when used in phrases such as "in God" and "in Christ." Paul delights in the mystical union we have as children of God; it is in him that we live and move and have our being (Acts 17:28). Our present security and our future hope lie in Christ (Eph. 1:3–13; 1 Thess. 4:14; 2 Thess. 1:12). We live in the presence of Christ; he is not remote from his church. The abundant life can be enjoyed because of the power and intimacy of being in Christ. Not only is Paul in Christ, but Christ lives in him (Gal. 2:20). "Christ is the redeemed man's new environment" (Stewart, 157).[2]

Paul then employs a brief but theologically loaded greeting that is no mere hello! It reflects a prayer wish that "grace" (God's divine favor that effectively works to sustain and empower the believer) and "peace" (the well-being of the whole person) would be their portion. Compare the formula in the closing benediction of 5:28: "The grace of our Lord Jesus Christ be with you."

2. Paul's Thanksgiving (1:2–10)

Let Paul not be accused of exploiting the letter convention of a thanksgiving section for any insincere purposes of disarming or winning over his audience. He is a man whose life is marked by gratitude for what God has done both in him and through him in the winning of converts. Making disciples is his *raison d'être*. New believers are proof of his apostolic calling (1:6), they are his children (2:7, 11), and they are his crown of glory and joy (2:19–20). Here we get a glimpse into an aspect of Paul's prayer life: The giving of thanks was a way of life for him.

2.1. Thanksgiving Directed to God (1:2)

Paul recognizes the work of God that brought the Thessalonians to faith. The apostle is the instrument, but it is a gracious God who is willing to use Paul and to entrust him with so noble a task (2:4). Paul will not think too highly of himself (Rom. 12:3) for he knows full well that it is God who begins and finishes the good work (1 Cor. 3:5–7; Phil. 1:6; 2:13). Thus his frequent prayers are characterized by the giving of thanks and intercession for their well-being (1 Thess. 3:10; 5:23–24; 2 Thess. 2:16–17).

2.2. Thanksgiving Due to Thessalonian Response (1:3–10)

2.2.1. Response of Faith, Love, and Hope (1:3). The triad of Christian virtues—faith, love, and hope—structures not only the thanksgiving at hand, but also in loose fashion the entire letter.[3] The first response Paul mentions literally translates "the work of faith." Such a rendition could be cause fo alarm since it appears to fly in the face of justification by faith alone. Is Paul referring to the work that saved us, as if our faith is a work o some sort? The NIV translates more idiomatically, representing well Paul's point: He i thankful for their "work [*ergon*] produced b faith." Bruce (21) says the "reality of saving faith is attested by its practical effect, 'the work of faith.'" On the one hand, the truth stand that states that our attempts to be justified ar no more than filthy rags (Isa. 64:6); we cannot be saved by works (Eph. 2:8–9). On th other hand, we are known by our fruit, we ar to imitate Christ, we are to let our light shin (which the Thessalonian Christians did s well; 1 Thess. 1:7–8), and we are to put off the "old self with its practices" and "put on the new self" (Col. 3:9–10).

The faith of the Thessalonians was not by any means dead (cf. James 2:18; 1 John 3:9-10), as it resulted in work of the highest sort These believers had passed a clear test of genuine conversion; they exhibited a new disposition that overshadowed any shortcomings in conduct or doctrine that Paul must address. We can identify their work to include the following: They became imitators of Paul (1 Thess 1:6), they became models of transforming faith (1:7), they were truly serving God (1:9), and they were persevering in the faith despit severe opposition (1:6; 2:14–15; 3:3–8).

The next item in the thanksgiving triad i "labor [*kopos*] prompted by love." Again, th NIV makes clear the sense of the literal phrase "labor of love" (cf. 2 Thess. 1:3). It is not a onetime act to which Paul refers, but labor in a collective and ongoing sense. The distinction between the "work produced by faith" and "labor prompted by love" may be, as Bruce says, "more rhetorical than substantial" (12) Others, however, prefer to see the word *ergon* to emphasize the actual exertion put out by the Thessalonians into their works of faith (cf. Thess. 1:11; 2:17; Morris, 51; Hendriksen, 4 n. 35). The motivation for this exertion is *agape* ("love")—the self-sacrificing, unconditional and initiating love demonstrated by God. The Thessalonians' imitation of their Lord (1:6) wa demonstrated by their love for God, for one another (4:9–10),[4] and for Paul's team (3:6) The ability to love one another has its source in God, for God is love (1 John 4:7, 16).

The third item on Paul's list is their ɜndurance inspired by hope" (lit., "the ndurance/steadfastness of hope"). Ample vidence exists for characterizing these elievers as steadfast. Their new life began nder adversity, yet they received the good ɜws with joy (1:6). They suffered the loss of ieir spiritual father, yet their growth was not :unted. Through all the negative circum-:ances they stood firm (3:8). They had been ıught by Paul that trials are the destiny of elievers (3:3–4); it remained to be seen how ell they had learned until they had been ·sted in the arena of conflict. Paul marvels at ıe quality of character these believers pos-ɜssed. They are inspired by their hope in 'hrist, by the benefits of being members of 'od's kingdom and sharers in his glory (2:12), nd ultimately by the hope of joining Jesus in ıeir eternal inheritance (1:10; 4:17–18; 5:10–1; 2 Thess. 3:5).

Concerning suffering, there is a tension in cripture that must be respected or we will go om one extreme to the other. Although God as promised strength, provision, and protec-on (e.g., Ps. 37:25; 91:1–16), and inasmuch s the power of prayer is highly endorsed Matt. 7:7–8; John 15:7; 1 Thess. 5:17; James :15–16; etc.), Christians are not exempt from ıffering. Believers are forewarned that they ill suffer (John 15:20; Acts 14:21–22; Thess. 3:4). The record of Scripture clearly epicts the saints suffering (Acts 5:40; 7:59; :1; 12:2; Heb. 11:35–38). Mistreatment, rison, torture, and death are not necessarily 'arded off by claiming promises of protection. ı alarming numbers Christians around the 'orld are presently being martyred, abused, nd denied basic human rights.[5] For many eople being a Christian means taking up a ross of persecution. Rather than seeing such elievers as those whose faith was not able to ppropriate God's promise of care, we should iew them as precious saints of whom the 'orld is not worthy (Heb. 11:38).

If God's children were meant to be pro-·cted at all times from all harm, then the ·aching of Scripture to be prepared, not to be ıarmed or surprised at suffering (James 1:2, 2; 1 Peter 4:12–16) but to endure, would ɜcome meaningless at worst, or at best, plan 3" for those whose weak faith could not gen-·ate protection. Our attitude to persecution is not to be a moaning, passive resignation, but a resolute spirit of courage, perseverance, and even rejoicing (Acts 5:41; James 1:2; 1 Peter 4:13). The Scripture teaches us to adopt the eternal perspective (Rom. 8:18; 2 Cor. 4:16–18). The Thessalonian believers were able to endure and stand firm because of the hope their eternal perspective provided. For that resolve Paul was most grateful.

2.2.2. Response of Deep Conviction (1:4–5). Paul continues his thanksgiving by addressing the readers as "brothers" (which he does twenty-one times in 1 and 2 Thessalonians), indicating that not only are they loved by God, they are deeply loved by the apostle (2:8). To counter allegations to the contrary, he will later deal with the issue of the sincerity of his love (2:7–3:13). For now, though, he affirms the reality of their being objects of God's love. He confidently declares that they have been chosen by God (2 Thess. 2:13–14). The Old Testament provides the framework for understanding the concept of election. God chose Abraham and his descendants "in order to make himself known to the rest of mankind" (Bruce, 13). Israel, God's chosen people, was called to enjoy God's favor and to be a light to the nations, revealing God's merciful salvation to the Gentiles (Isa. 42:6–7; 49:6). Now the Thessalonians have been chosen, and their reputation shows they are fulfilling their calling to be a light to the nations (1:8).

The concept of God's sovereignty can be a theological minefield one must traverse in order to harmonize notions of election/calling and free will (for a summary of Paul's teaching on election, see Hendriksen, 49–50). Paul worships God as he writes on this topic: "For he chose us in him before the creation of the world" (Eph. 1:4); he is not concerned with debating all the implications of how and when God chooses or whether his calling can be resisted. His purpose is to remind the believers of truth in order to evoke assurance and a sense of splendid privilege. It is God who has chosen these believers in Thessalonica; he reached out in love to seemingly unworthy candidates (1 Thess. 1:9; cf. Rom. 5:8). They responded to God's reaching love with deep conviction—they are now the church, the called-out ones.

What evidence does Paul have that they have been genuinely converted? They heard the gospel, witnessed the power of the Holy Spirit, and in their deep conviction were transformed.

Gordon Fee argues for the likelihood that Paul's "Spirit-empowered word was regularly accompanied by Spirit-empowered miracles as well . . . [which] the Thessalonians undoubtedly experienced" (Fee, 45; see also Wanamaker, 79). One of Paul's marks of apostleship is the powerful accompaniment of signs and wonders (Rom. 15:18–19; 2 Cor. 12:12; cf. Gal. 3:5). Thus the proof to be offered of their calling is their experience of power that convinced them of the truth.

2.2.3. Response of Imitation, Modeling (1:6–8). Related to that proof is their transformation, which is described in terms of being imitators. The truth of the gospel was not only heard with powerful anointing, but was also witnessed in the missionaries' lives among them. The new believers responded to what they heard, and they put their faith into shoe leather by imitating what they saw. Shortly Paul will say more about how he and his friends lived among them (2:1–12), but for the moment he expresses gratitude for their imitation, which we can identify in three respects. (1) Like Paul they endured severe suffering directly attributable to their conversion.

(2) They "welcomed the message with the joy given by the Holy Spirit." Paul's conversion story, his subsequent dedication to evangelizing, and his teaching on the Holy Spirit indicate how he welcomed the message. In Paul's life and teaching "joy is one of the certain hallmarks of genuine spirituality" (Fee, 47). The amazing work of the Spirit is to strengthen us with joy in circumstances that would normally rob us of it (Neh. 8:10).

The joy Paul talks about is not an attitude secured only after the trial is over, but it is ours to possess, so that in the very midst of adversity we can "consider it pure joy" (James 1:2; cf. John 16:22, 33; Phil. 1:29; 3:10). This joy is the gift of the Holy Spirit, and realizing this gift can set the troubled believer's mind at ease. Morris (60) says the transformation of suffering from a vehicle of despair to one of joy "does not come about by autosuggestion, or any other human device." Joy is, after all, a fruit of the Holy Spirit (Gal. 5:22). Paul testifies to the Corinthians of the constant barrage of conflicts he faced as he ministered through Macedonia, but God's comfort provided joy so that he could report, "in all our troubles my joy knows no bounds" (2 Cor. 7:4).

(3) The final point of imitation is their sha ing with others the message that had resulte in their affliction in the first place (1:8). Th church may have to go underground, but eve then it does not remain silent and hidden; continues to be the light. According to Act persecution is not a setback paralyzing th church's mission. On the contrary, boldne characterizes the believers as they continu fulfilling the Great Commission. Paul swell with fatherly pride as his thanksgiving com mends them for how they model the faith, n in secret, but in full sight! The verb Pa chooses in verse 8 ("rang out") is foun nowhere else in the New Testament. The wor graphically conveys the powerful sound of trumpet blast or "the rolling of thunder" (Mo ris, 61 n. 29). The news of their faith h become widespread and has no doubt been source of inspiration to other believers whe ever the story is told.

2.2.4. Response of Serving and Waitin (1:9–10). In verse 9 Paul refers to believe ("they") he has encountered who already ha heard of the Thessalonian success story. H hears from these secondary sources goo reports of how the Thessalonian believe received Paul—they had surely reciprocate the love demonstrated by the apostle. Mo important to him is the complete turnabout i their lives. These believers now serve "the liv ing and true God," though recently they ha been steeped in paganism. From pagans t saints, such is the transforming power of th gospel, and Paul exults in the results. Th Thessalonians have severed all inappropria ties to their former way of life and are no dedicated to the God who has chosen the Such a severance came at a price greater tha "the distress and anguish of heart experience by persons who broke with their past as the received the gospel" (Malherbe, 48).

The context of the letter shows that th Thessalonians endured much more than inwa struggles that are common with such a radic change in lifestyle (2:14). Regardless of th cost, the break has been made; there can be n straddling of fences when it comes to th gospel. Paganism in its various forms could b tolerant of other gods, at times syncretistic; b the recognition of the true God and his revel tion in Jesus Christ exposed the vanity of the "no gods" (Isa. 44:6–20) and the impossibi y of syncretism. God demands wholehearted ervice, as illustrated in the struggle of the Jews o purify their devotion to Yahweh and to tear own the high places (2 Chron. 20:33; 21:11; 8:24–25; Ps. 78:55–59). The Thessalonians till need to grow in their faith and service, but hey are heading with single-mindedness and ood speed in the right direction.

Paul concludes this thanksgiving by moving rom the concept of serving to that of waiting. Christians actively serve God and live out their aith in the community of believers and before watching world. Meanwhile, in so doing, the eliever is ever-conscious of the return of Jesus the Parousia). Christians wait for this great moment, but it is not waiting in the sense of etiring or ceasing all activities that accompany ngoing existence and celebration of life on arth, although some did have that misconception (4:11–12; 5:14; 2 Thess. 3:10–12).

In the earlier letters of Paul the eschatological tone is one of expectation for an imminent eturn. It was as if the church expected the curain of eternity to be pulled back at any moment—certainly within their lifetime 1 Thess. 2:19; 4:13–5:11; 2 Thess. 1:6–7; cf. Cor. 15:51–52). As the years of ministry olled by, even Paul, who anticipated witnessing the Parousia in his lifetime, realized that eath would likely be his usher into the presence of Jesus (2 Tim. 4:6–8).

Nearly two thousand years later, how is the vaiting of the church to be described? How can oday's saints be expected to greet eagerly each ew day as perhaps the Day? By and large, Christians are not quitting jobs to wait and vatch (in the meantime sponging off the rest of he church for food and shelter). Rather, we are aced with an opposite response to the idle elievers in Thessalonica. The tendency in our ffluent societies is to be so consumed by our ole within society that the prospect of Jesus' eturn is too remote to motivate us daily to eager xpectation. Here we need to be found imitating the early church, which worked hard to proide for the temporal needs of the community f faith, ever-conscious of the high calling of tewardship of resources and talents. They were church that also waited with bated breath for he sight of their Savior and the fulfillment of heir salvation. The nonoccurrence of the Parouia does not nullify the fact that Jesus will return. et our affections be fixed on things above so that with the air of expectancy we can say, "Amen. Come, Lord Jesus" (Rev. 22:20).

The flipside to this matter is that enough cases exist of predicting Christ's return to caution us even as we approach the conclusion of another millennium. It is only natural that endtime fervor will increase as the year 2000 approaches. More and more preaching and popular Christian literature will focus on the possibility. This focus, in balance, can serve the church well if it helps us to be more fervent in our witness, in our love for Christ and one another, in restoring the attitude that we have a higher calling. One hopes that the church will avoid any damaging end-time hysteria, and especially major disappointment, should the year 2000 or 2001 pass and lead us into continued witness on this earth to the glorious grace of Jesus Christ.

When Jesus does come back, he comes to rescue! The believer is not to be frightened; there is no condemnation to fear (Rom. 8:1; 1 John 4:18). Jesus returns to deliver believers from "the coming wrath." There will be a time when God will once and for all judge the sinfulness of humankind (1 Thess. 5:9; see also Rom. 2:5; 5:9). What is this wrath? James Stewart (219) contends that the concept of wrath is difficult to grasp fully, for our anthropomorphisms fall short as we try to understand God's infinite character through the grid of our own feelings and character. He claims that wrath "is the totality of the divine reaction to sin . . . not God's outraged dignity retaliating." In provocative summation Stewart writes (221): "God's wrath is God's grace. It is His grace smitten with dreadful sorrow. It is His love in agony. It is the passion of His heart going forth to redeem."

Thus, justice is equally part of God's ways as is his mercy. The wages of sin must be paid (Rom. 6:23), and those who reject the payment made by Jesus Christ will be held accountable. Paul is eternally grateful that the Thessalonians will be among those rescued!

3. Paul's Defense, Part 1: A Summary of Ministry in Thessalonica (2:1–16)

In chapter 1 Paul has celebrated the remarkable faith of the Thessalonian Christians. At great risk, and for some at great cost, they remained faithful to Christ and thereby achieved a commendable reputation. Paul was proud of his spiritual children and thankful to God for them. Now he shifts the focus to himself as a defense against allegations of insincerity and deliberate deceit.

Who was taking potshots at the apostle? According to Thomas (249), identifying Paul's opponents "is a puzzle difficult to piece together." One may not get all the pieces together, but surely part of the puzzle includes the very ones who stirred up the trouble that necessitated Paul's escape from Thessalonica: jealous Jews. They considered Paul's message to be an affront to Judaism—which is not surprising, since Paul himself acknowledges that the preaching of Christ crucified is "a stumbling block to Jews" (1 Cor. 1:23). Moreover, they were jealous of the success of his mission as many God-fearing Greeks were won over to Christ. Whatever the local Jewish perception was of the equality of these God-fearers, they were considered as part of the fold of the synagogue (and financial contributors!). When the controversy in Thessalonica culminated in the mob's actions, these God-fearers would have been forced to sever ties—the new Christian church was not welcome at the synagogue. Nevertheless, their exit would have been felt keenly. A good strategy would be to try to win them back, and the best way to rattle confidence in the message was to undermine the messenger.

Malherbe (48; see also Fee, 41) proposes another piece that might fit into the puzzle. The Thessalonians had a past from which to break; thus converted pagans would have had associates and relatives who could not understand their conversion or be positive about it. In those days it was not uncommon for popular preachers of philosophy or religion (and there was a veritable smorgasbord of beliefs to offer) to sell their message on the streets or wherever they could get a listening ear. Some were sincere, but as in our day, others were outright charlatans. It requires no stretch to imagine Paul being accused by jealous Jews and cynical pagans alike of being a lunatic or a huckster (Wanamaker, 94).

3.1. A Successful and Bold Effort (2:1–2)

Paul commences his defense with an opening statement describing in general terms his estimation of his ministry in Thessalonica: it "was not a failure [*kenos*, empty, vain]." Pau uses this same word three times in 1 Corinthi ans 15 as he shows how crucial the doctrin of the resurrection is, otherwise "our preach ing is useless [*kenos*] and so is your faith (1 Cor. 15:14). In verse 58 he encourages dili gent labor for the Lord because of the strength giving hope of the resurrection of al believers—such "labor . . . is not in vai [*kenos*]." The third reference is related to vers 58; though it occurs back in verse 10, we le it until now to emphasize Paul's longing to ful fill God's calling for him: "His grace to m was not without effect [*kenos*]."

Wherever Paul ministered, whatever he di it was all to be assessed by the gauge of stew ardship: Have I worked hard for Jesus? Hav I been faithful? Have I discharged my duties As an obedient slave to Christ, he worked wit all his heart (Col. 3:23). Converts were the fru of his ministry, which proved that he "did nc run or labor for nothing [*kenos*]" (Phil. 2:16 Paul is confident in the success of his visit i Thessalonica, but he admits later that for a agonizing spell he was worried that the Chris tians there may have given up and his "effor might have been useless [*kenos*]" (1 Thes 3:5). Timothy's positive report to Paul cause the sun of optimism to shine brightly.

The success of Paul's evangelism in Thes salonica is brought into bolder relief when see against the backdrop of his suffering. H reminds the readers here of the disgracefu treatment he endured before coming to thei city. We do a disservice to Paul and thereby ro ourselves of greater insight if we listen with th ear of nonchalance to Paul's testimonies o hardships. His overwhelming catalogue c hardships (see 2 Cor. 11:23–29) raises th question: At what point would I have give up? The lashing Paul and Silas took in Philip was a severe physical price to pay. Add to th Paul's experience of insult (1 Thess. 2:2; KJ translates "shamefully entreated"), and w "see something of the deep hurt that Paul ha experienced in the indignities which had bee heaped on him" (Morris, 69). Paul had bee bold and brave to preach in Thessalonica, bu after trouble there and then in Berea, and afte a discouraging and disappointing stint i Athens, his entry into Corinth was anythin but bold: "I came to you in weakness and fea and with much trembling" (1 Cor. 2:3).

The pain and insult he carried from Philippi were offset by God's provision of help to continue with the mission. The phrase "with the help of our God" renders a Greek expression that has the nuance of giving courage or boldness. That was certainly the type of help God provided (see Acts 4:29; 9:27, where the same root word is used). This notion of provision alludes back to 1:5, where Paul speaks of the Holy Spirit's role in the arrival of him and his company and in his presentation of the gospel. He was able to worship God with song in the immediate aftermath of the Philippian adversity (Acts 16:25); he will continue to worship God with obedience to his calling in Thessalonica. Obedience was risky; he was daring to face this "strong opposition," but with the confidence God gave him he was bold to do so.

3.2. A Sincere and Loving Effort (2:3–12)

After implying that adequate proof of his sincerity was his willingness to endanger his well-being for their sake, Paul moves to address specific allegations. As is frequently the case in his letters, when Paul addresses an issue, he does so because it has been occasioned by one thing or another. We do not stretch the text when we assume that Paul defends his message and motives because he is being slandered at those very points that he brings out. Thus, in verse 3 he lays it all on the table—he will not be found guilty of "error," "impure motives," or trickery. He will not be lumped in with the hucksters of the day.

(1) Paul dismisses the notion that his preaching was in "error" (*plane*). This word can be translated "deceit" (cf. KJV), but the context suggests the connotation of "mistake," since deliberate deceit is covered by the last word of the three in Paul's list. The Jews who were discrediting Paul were apparently arguing that, regardless of Paul's sincerity, his message was false, especially regarding his identification of Jesus as the Messiah.

(2) The next allegation does not focus on his message but on his motives, which are said to be mixed or "impure." Thus the dispute here is with Paul's integrity. The word *akatharsia* ("impure motives") can also be translated "uncleanness" (cf. KJV), giving the connotation of sexual impurity.[6] Barclay (189) argues that since Christians were suspected of sexual immorality because of their "love feasts," it is possible that Paul was likewise suspected. Moreover, pagan religions had rituals that involved prostitution, and presumably the uninformed and ill-motivated assumed that this new sect called Christianity practiced the same.

(3) The final point Paul refutes is that he was in some way deceitful. The Greek word *dolos* can conjure up the fishing imagery of "bait." If that is the intent here, Paul is being portrayed as someone trying to lure or catch the unsuspecting (see Morris, Williams), hence the NIV's "trying to trick you" is an appropriate idiom (see the similar accusation in 2 Cor. 12:16). Some years later, in a bit of a reversal, Paul will warn Timothy of the wicked and deceitful, who will "worm their way into homes and gain control over weak-willed women" (2 Tim. 3:6).

The same threads of accusation can be traced through to our century as evangelists and television ministers have often been questioned and ridiculed. Sadly, sincere public ministries and charlatans alike have been painted with the same broad brush by skeptics. Whether ignited by someone's preaching error, nonsense, or outdated religion, by seeking power or an empire, or by bilking the gullible out of money, the fuel for the fires of accusation has remained essentially the same. Hence we must heed the charge to live pure and upright lives in order to avoid bringing reproach to the name of Christ (Titus 1:6–9; 1 Peter 3:13–17; 4:14–19).

Using the adversative conjunction "but" in 2:4 (which the NIV translates "on the contrary" to emphasize the change in direction), Paul moves to a positive defense by speaking of the cornerstone of his ministry. God has approved him and therefore entrusted him to preach the gospel. The word "approved" (*dokimazo*) is based on the idea of testing that has been passed successfully. God has done the testing; he knows the deep recesses of Paul's heart, where any sinful motives would be nurtured (1 Sam. 16:7; Ps. 94:11; 139:23–24; Prov. 21:2). Paul's motives were frequently tested: Every beating or imprisonment, all adversity was a test asking the question, "Paul, are you in this for yourself or for God?" Paul confidently appeals in this verse to the results of God's testing: Since he has been approved, he has now been "entrusted with the gospel." Paul is ever-conscious of remaining a faithful steward (1 Cor. 4:2).

We saw earlier Paul's concern that his efforts would never be in vain (2:1), and in order to ensure that his labors in Thessalonica not fail, he must answer his opponents. These enemies have conducted their own tests, which, according to them, have proved he was a scoundrel. But they had not brought all the evidence into the mix when they drew the sorts of conclusions Paul denies in verses 4–6. For one thing, he was not a man-pleaser, a fact indicated by his avoidance of using flattery to win people over. To do so would, of course, amount to deceit. His audience was well aware of this fact; thus Paul can remind them "you know [this to be true]" (v. 5).

Paul's next point ("nor did we put on a mask to cover up greed") is essentially a continuation of the defense against the allegation of insincerity, specifically regarding personal gain.[7] The word "mask" attempts to capture the literal meaning of the Greek word *prophasis*, something that looks good or attractive but is deceitful. Therefore, it is proper to refer to a mask or "cloak" (KJV) used to cover up something, in this case to veil the wrong motive of greed. Previously the apostle reminded them of what they knew of his impeachable character; he can also invoke God as a "witness" in his defense, an invocation a man of integrity need never fear.

All believers have been given a sacred trust from God; we are all Christ's ambassadors, who are to deliver faithfully to our society the message of God's offer of reconciliation to sinful humankind (2 Cor. 5:18–20). We are salt and light (Matt. 5:13–15); we are fishers of men and women (4:19); we gratefully accept the privilege and responsibility of the Great Commission (28:19–20) as we are enabled by the power of the Holy Spirit (Acts 1:8). May Paul's words strike the proper chord in our lives: "as though God were making his appeal through us" (2 Cor. 5:20).

With God as his witness, Paul clears the table totally of any charges of wrongdoing and personal gain. In verse 6 his denial that he sought any praise relates directly to his earlier dismissal that he was a man-pleaser (v. 4). Paul's motives are right; his self-esteem is healthy and is fed by the joy and deep conviction the Holy Spirit provides. It does not matter what people think, be it thoughts of vilification or praise. It is God's giving of praise or glory that matters, as is demonstrated in his refusal to take pride in all his accomplishments—all that matters is that he will in the end gain Christ (Phil. 3:8).

In verse 6b Paul presents further proof that he has not been gallivanting around for selfish reasons. He speaks of his office as apostle and implies that the position is worthy of much respect. Meanwhile, he provides a splendid example of meekness for authority figures. Although he later writes, "The elders who direct the affairs of the church are worthy of double honor, especially those whose work is preaching and teaching" (1 Tim. 5:17; cf. 1 Cor. 9:14), he does not personally press for his own rights to that honor.

The expression "we could have been a burden to you" is one that suggests the authority or weight an apostle could impose, but this prerogative is counterbalanced by Paul's shift of roles from authoritative apostle to "gentle ... mother" (v. 7). No image portrays a more universal and timeless example of tenderness than does a mother's love for her children (cf. Matt. 23:37). Thus, as Bruce (33) says about Paul's team, "more impressive than their disclaimer of unworthy motives and actions is the assertion of their loving care for their converts." These assertions are substantiated, for six times in chapter 2 Paul reminds them of their personal knowledge of what he claims (vv. 1, 2, 5, 9, 10, 11). God is witness, but so are the Thessalonians, who have seen the extent of Paul's sincere commitment.

In verse 8 Paul employs three phrases to elaborate on his gentle maternal care for them: "We loved you so much," "we were delighted to share," and "you had become so dear." Paul has been like a tireless, dependable mother who is driven by love to care for her child's every need. At times the demands are draining; they do not cease once night falls, but the mother is there to nurse and care. Similarly Paul worked "night and day" (v. 9) in order to nurture the Thessalonians in the gospel. He reiterates the measures he took to avoid imposing any burdens on them to care for him—it is foolish to demand that a young child should have to pay or take care of its mother! In another context of defense for his ministry, again using the metaphor of parental care, Paul writes, "I will very gladly spend for you everything I have and expend myself as well" (2 Cor. 12:15).

Such is the character of Paul's ministry. He is highly concerned that nothing detract from his effectiveness, including being branded as lazy or as a parasite. The degree of this concern is illustrated when several years later Paul would meet with the Ephesian elders and relate that his ministry was free of any covetousness and that he himself worked hard with his own hands (probably plying his trade as a tentmaker; see Acts 18:3) to supply the needs of his ministry team (20:33–34).

We can contrast Paul's attitude with that of the apostles when they chose seven deacons because they did not want "to neglect the ministry of the word of God in order to wait on tables" (Acts 6:2–4). However, so we do not conclude that Paul is more noble in this matter than the other apostles, we should note that the precise nature of their daily (and nightly) occupation is not detailed by Luke. He does not record this incident to promote full-time leadership with pay, but to show the division of ministry's labor in the early church. Of church leaders, Paul can say that they are worthy of their hire (1 Tim. 5:18), but he chose to help himself as much as possible. Yet, even in Thessalonica he received support, for which he was most grateful (Phil. 4:16). Perhaps Paul's upbringing has much to do with working with his hands, for it was expected even of rabbis to have a trade: "There were no paid teachers in Palestine" (Morris, 80).

The story of Paul's self-sacrificing model of leadership rings out across the centuries and should be heard clearly by all who are called to leadership positions, paid or otherwise. It is only to be expected that ministry demands will be hard and exacting. Those who sincerely care for people and honor God's call will be found imitating Paul's dedication.

Verse 10 leads us to a further example of the sincere and loving effort expended for the Thessalonians. In broad, bold terms Paul declares that both God and they are witnesses of the impeccable nature of his work among them. Marshall (73) explains that the double invocation is significant in that the readers had observed what by all appearances had to have been sincerity, but God is made witness to verify that the missionaries are not "guilty of a subtle deception practiced upon the human witnesses."

Paul makes three claims that might strike our ears as arrogant, but in light of the context of allegations to the contrary, these claims must be made. Christians may, out of false humility or perhaps awareness of personal shortcoming, decline to refer to themselves as "holy, righteous and blameless." Paul never claimed to be perfect, of course; like all believers he had to grow in Christ (Phil. 3:12). But in regard to ministry and motivation he could pronounce himself innocent of any wrongdoing. The best interests of others were his priority. He was merely the humble instrument of delivering God's message of grace to them.

Continuing his defense, Paul switches to the paternal aspect of parental care (vv. 11–12). He never sought to exercise the authority of an apostle for special treatment, nor was he a power monger. The authority he did exercise was that of a father who has his children's welfare in mind. The main fatherly function he points to is that of training "a child in the way he should go" (Prov. 22:6), that is, "to live lives worthy of God" (1 Thess. 2:12). Wanamaker (106) says "the father in the ancient world was normally responsible for the moral instruction and behavior of his offspring."

Paul then employs another list of three items to explain how he performed this function of father (notice this chapter's other sets of three in vv. 3, 5–6, 10, and 19). (1) He was an encourager (*parakaleo*; same root word translated "appeal" in 2:3), seeking to motivate his children (cf. the same word in Rom. 12:1; 1 Cor. 4:16; 2 Cor. 2:8; 6:1; Eph. 4:1; Philem. 9–10). His method of presenting positive motivation to elicit proper conduct is instructive. He was one who took heed to the words, "Fathers, do not exasperate your children; instead, bring them up in the training and instruction of the Lord" (Eph. 6:4; cf. Col. 3:21).

(2) The next item in Paul's list is translated "comforting" (*paramytheomai*); in this context it evokes the sight of a father whose child may be down or frightened by the challenges that growing up brings. The father is sensitive and recognizes the child's need to receive warm consolation or some upbeat cheerleading. The spiritual childhood of the Thessalonians was beset by hardships, but their father comforts

them (e.g., his reminder that trials are the destiny of the believer, 3:3).

(3) The final word in the list is "urging" (*martyromai*), which suggests the authority a father can exert. There are times when a child needs to hear in unequivocal words that certain actions are required or forbidden within the family.

As one discharges the duties of encouraging, comforting, and urging, the goal is to see children walking "worthy of God" (cf. Eph. 4:1; Phil. 1:27; 2 Thess. 1:5). What is a worthy life? We can be sure that Paul does not mean "worthy" in the sense of earning salvation or of doing things that will make God love the believer more than he already does. Christians have become new creatures in Christ (2 Cor. 5:17); they have taken off their "old self with its practices" (Col. 3:9). Now they are ready to live lives of obedience and imitation of Christ with the empowering of the Holy Spirit to grow in proper conduct (Gal. 5:16; 1 Thess. 4:7–8; Titus 2:11–12). A child in God's family has answered the call to submit to God's standard for a lifestyle characterized by holiness and love.

God has called the believer to participate in "his kingdom and glory." This kingdom has already been inaugurated. Jesus preached the good news of the kingdom (Luke 4:43), and he sent his disciples to do the same (Mark 16:15; Luke 9:2). Luke records the early church's preaching of "the good news of the kingdom of God," which was part and parcel of preaching "the name of Jesus Christ" (Acts 8:12; cf. 19:8; 28:23). But the kingdom is presently not operating in all of its potential (Heb. 2:8; Rev. 11:15). That fullness will be reached when Jesus returns (2 Thess. 1:7). The great hope of the saint is to share in God's glory, where there will be no interference from the kingdom of darkness. Paul refers to the hope of this inheritance of glory as a comforting stimulus for saints to persevere (Rom. 8:17–18; 2 Cor. 4:16–18). Any cost we must pay will be worth it all when we finally see Christ (Heb. 12:1–2).

3.3. An Authoritative but Resisted Effort (2:13–16)

As he concludes his recap of the mission at Thessalonica, Paul picks up the thread of thanksgiving again. Three features echo the letter's opening thanksgiving section. (1) We again see Paul's disposition of gratitude—h continually thanks God (1:4). (2) The secon similarity can be mapped as follows:

"our gospel came to you"	"with power" (1:5)
"you accepted it"	"which is at work in you" (2:13)

The gospel came to the Thessalonians, an they received it. Its power worked mightily i transforming them, likely with the demonstra tion of signs and wonders (see comments a 1:4). (3) The final repeated theme is that o imitation, especially in regard to one' response to suffering (1:6).

The Thessalonians received the truth tha Paul authoritatively preached, but it was no his word, it was God's. There is a verbal sim ilarity between Paul's phrase "which you hear from us" (*akoes par hemon*) and the wordin of Isaiah 53:1 in the LXX: "Who has believe our message?" (*akoe hemon*). We cannot b certain if Paul is intentionally drawing fro the Isaiah passage (Bruce, 44, thinks so despite his knowledge and quotation of the LX in his letters. But such an allusion does fit we with Paul's point, for in answer to Isaiah' question, "Who has believed our message? Paul can say, "You Thessalonians did!"

The phrase "you accepted it not as the wor of men" (v. 13) is surely a gibe against th cynic's judgment that the missionaries we spinning tales to gull the simple (2:3). Paul offe proof that what he preached was God's wor when he says it "is at work in you who believe.

One of the amazing ways in which th gospel's power worked in the believers in The salonica was in their response to suffering They learned quickly about the cost of disc pleship, but they learned well, and in so doin became part of the fellowship of sufferin (Phil. 3:10). Paul links the Thessalonians wi the believers who were in the first churches o Judea. This common ground of suffering pro motes Christian unity across barriers of rac and geography, for regardless of one's societ all suffer for the common cause of Christ. Rea izing solidarity in suffering with other sain becomes a source of comfort and strength.

In verses 14–16 Paul elaborates on th theme of suffering as he identifies the sourc of their troubles ("your own countrymen") an compares what they have been experiencing the persecution of the Judean churches. These verses have been a source of embarrassment over the years as many have felt that Paul is promoting bigotry—the Jews are to blame for the suffering of Christians. Others have gone even further by seizing this section as ammunition for a racial supremacy propaganda—the Jews are Christ-killers! In retaliation against the Jews, pogroms and inquisitions have occurred that have smeared church history with innocent blood.

Paul would be horrified to see such twisting of his words. We must keep in mind his main point, which is not to harangue the Jewish race, but to point out to his readers that they should not be surprised at persecution from the hands of their own countrymen—even though it was some of the local Jews who instigated it in Thessalonica (Acts 17:5). Perhaps we can hear Paul saying, "If Judaism, which worshiped the one true God, could allow God's own prophets to be killed, and if they who anticipated the Messiah's arrival could be so blind as to let their own Messiah be crucified, then how much less should you be surprised at the antagonism of pagan countrymen, who are not God's chosen people?"

Paul is not enjoining hatred for his own people, any more than Jesus did. Our Lord encouraged his followers by pronouncing a blessing on those who would be persecuted (Matt. 5:11–12). He rebuked the hypocritical Jewish leadership in the harshest of terms as he told them they were no different from their ancestors, who shed the blood of the prophets (23:29–36). Peter's Pentecost sermon accuses in general terms the "men of Israel" for killing Jesus "with the help of wicked men" (Acts 2:22–23). As Luke records it in his next sermon, Peter points the prophet's finger at the Sanhedrin (4:10). Stephen's address to the Sanhedrin concludes with shocking invective: "You are just like your fathers: You always resist the Holy Spirit! Was there ever a prophet your fathers did not persecute? They even killed those who predicted the coming of the Righteous One. And now you have betrayed and murdered him" (Acts 7:51–52). We would not accuse the Old Testament prophets of anti-Semitism in their condemnation of rebellious, hard hearts, nor would we so label Jesus, Peter, or Stephen.

Paul is in the prophetic line as he states the truth about what his fellow Jews did. He loves his people. His usual practice is to preach to his own people first (Acts 9:20; Rom. 1:16). In passionate longing for them he writes, "For I could wish that I myself were cursed and cut off from Christ for the sake of my brothers, those of my own race" (Rom. 9:3). The similarity to the following lament of Jesus is striking: "O Jerusalem, Jerusalem, you who kill the prophets and stone those sent to you, how often I have longed to gather your children together, as a hen gathers her chicks under her wings, but you were not willing" (Matt. 23:37). Let us be cautious and not ignore Paul's point or blow it out of proportion. He is not promoting an attitude of racial hatred or revenge.

The apostle deals with Jewish antagonism toward the gospel because he has experienced firsthand the painful frustration that opposition brings. Curiously, he does not even hint at his own pre-Christian role in being part of that line of persecutors, whereas elsewhere it is very much a part of his testimony (Bruce, 46; see Acts 22:4–5; 26:9–11; Gal. 1:13; Phil. 3:6). Those who vehemently resisted his efforts to lead Gentiles into the kingdom of God incurred Paul's anger.

Verse 16 contains a stark picture of doom as Paul describes how the sins of his persecutors are continually being "heap[ed] up" (he uses an intense word here). "The wrath of God" is their lot. The use of the aorist tense, which yields the translation "the wrath . . . has come upon them at last," has resulted in the theory that verses 15–16 are a later, non-Pauline interpolation. The rationale is that this wrath refers to God's judgment at the fall of Jerusalem in A.D. 70. Such insistence on syntax is unnecessary, for as Morris (92) reminds us, "the use of this tense does not refer to the imminence of the punishment. It refers to its certainty."

4. Paul's Defense, Part 2: Desire for the Thessalonians (2:17–3:13)

At 2:17 Paul makes the transition from defending his actions while in Thessalonica to defending his actions—or alleged nonaction—once he had left the city (Fee, 41). He must explain why he left the church to fend for itself. In order to do so, he will emphasize the anguish he experienced over the whole situation and speak of his all-consuming desire for their welfare.

In a letter to the Thessalonians, Paul explains why he had to leave the city, that he was "torn away." Hostility was growing among the Jews against the Christians. White Tower, a landmark on the harbor, was built long after Paul had left the city.

4.1. A Heart Torn and Desperate (2:17–18)

One can hear Paul's detractors sabotaging his reputation: "If these missionaries were so sincere and concerned for you, if their message is such powerful truth, why would they abandon you at a time when you needed them the most? Surely it proves they are frauds when they run scared, concerned to save their own skin without any thought for those they left behind! If they truly cared for you, why would they not come back?" Paul immediately gets to the heart of the matter as he defends their exit from and failure to return to Thessalonica.

Once again addressing them fondly as "brothers," Paul relates his story in graphic terms: "We were torn away." He assures them that he, Silas, and Timothy had not wanted to leave, but the hostile circumstances forced them out. Paul's choice of words for "torn away" (*aporphanizo*) is most fitting in light of the recent discussion of his maternal and paternal disposition to them (2:6–12). The root word *orphanizo* means "to make an orphan," and used here in the passive voice can be translated "bereaved." Paul has experienced something akin to what parents suffer when they lose a child—his heart has been torn and is in much turmoil. Was all his fathering to be for naught? Any parents who have experienced the initial panic when they discover their young child has wandered off out of their sight in a crowded mall or park can relate well to Paul's feeling. It may have been only for a few moments, but in that short span of time the parents wonder if they will ever see their child again, if there has been foul play, and they perhaps berate themselves: "How did we let this happen?"

Paul emphasizes that out-of-sight did not mean out-of-mind, for while they were separated physically, his thoughts were very much consumed with them. He continues with the vivid language to express how he felt during this period. The word translated "intense longing" (*epithumia*) may seem to be an unusual choice by Paul, for its most frequent connotation in the New Testament is "lust" (e.g., see 4:5, where it is rendered "passionate lust").[8] But by employing such a startling word normally left to his vice lists, Paul emphasizes how strongly he felt about his converts. Being torn away did not result in diminished concern; rather, it magnified the extent of his passion for them.

So it was with "fierce passion" (Morris, 94) he "made every effort to see [them]." Here the terminology indicates anything but a shallow expression of intention to see the Thessalonians at some nebulous future time. Paul's testimony is clear as he describes this intense effort as (lit.) "an abundant one" (*perissoteros*). Also the type of effort he made (*spoudazo*) was an eager effort, one that had to be hastened. He was not going to give in to defeat, but without delay he himself tried desperately "again and again" to come back to them.

Unfortunately lost to us is the precise nature of the barriers Paul could not overcome, but the bottom line was that "Satan stopped us." We do not know if the apostle, in an attempt to return, was discovered and physically prevented, or if Satan's stirring up of trouble endangered him so that the ongoing threat quashed every intention. The latter is more likely. Paul may have reasoned that laying low for a brief period would see the threat ebb, only o find the danger was still great. He decided o move on with his mission, but the Thessaonians were still on his mind.

4.2. A Heart Fond and Consumed (2:19–20)

With great pride Paul avers his fondness for he believers from whom he was torn away. Despite frustrated attempts to see them again, is heart does not become distracted by subequent travels and other converts. Somehow Paul manages to maintain strong ties with hose he has won to Christ, even though his tinerant ministry separates them by many niles. The Thessalonians would be tremenlously encouraged to read how highly Paul steemed them. With another triad (see comnents at 2:12) the apostle asks the rhetorical question, "What is our hope, our joy, or the crown in which we will glory?" Paul's hope is hat the fruit of his labor will remain and grow strong (2:1). His spiritual children bring him oy, for he sees them maturing and reaching heir potential in Christ. Perhaps Paul is echong the wisdom tradition: "A wise son brings oy to his father" (Prov. 10:1; also, 15:20; 23:24). How are the Thessalonians wise sons? They stand firm in the truth regardless of the voices calling them to go astray.

The third member of this triad may also have roots in the wisdom tradition: "Children's children are a crown to the aged" (Prov. 17:6). Although the Wisdom Literature was wellknown to one trained as a rabbi, as Paul was, the arena of sports also furnished him with the imagery of the "crown." He writes of the athlete who disciplines himself "to get a crown that will not last; but we do it to get a crown that will last forever" (1 Cor. 9:25). The victorious athletes of ancient days received wreaths or crowns of olive, laurel, or parsley leaves as their prize (Williams, 55), but such prizes were subject to deterioration. Not so with Paul's crowns—his converts were living trophies of grace (cf. Phil. 4:1). The proud victor in a race can admire his wreath as a symbol of his fine achievement, but as time marches on the athlete eventually loses the skill and fortitude that distinguished him. The treasured wreath can be at once a source of joy and a faint voice of mockery, reminding the owner that there can be no further success. But for Paul, as long as he has breath, there are more victories to be won (Phil. 1:22); meanwhile, he can always glory in his converts.

Concerning the notion of taking glory in the Thessalonians (*kauchesis* in 2:19; lit., "object of boasting" or "a boast"), Bruce points to an apparent contradiction and presents a resolution. This same Paul later writes, "May I never boast except in the cross of our Lord Jesus Christ" (Gal. 6:14). Yet Paul does not violate his own code here, for certainly those who were led to bow at the foot of the cross are legitimate objects of glorying or boasting. "Christ crucified was demonstrated afresh by their faith to be the power and wisdom of God" (Bruce, 58).

The fullest expression of glory will be enjoyed at the return of Jesus Christ. It is here in verse 19 that the word *parousia* first occurs in the New Testament, chronologically speaking. (Back in 1:10 this return was implied; Paul uses the word seven times in the Thessalonian correspondence: 2:19; 3:13; 4:15; 5:23; 2 Thess. 2:1, 8–9.) *Parousia* literally means "presence" or "arrival" and, as Wanamaker says (125), it became a "technical term for the coming of Jesus as sovereign Lord." He also identifies the connection between the Parousia of Jesus and the Old Testament concepts of the Day of the Lord (Isa. 2:10–12; Amos 5:17–18), "the day of salvation when God would come to rule over Israel (Isa. 52:6–10)." As Paul looks to the Lord's return, he is mindful of the reason he is called by God to share the good news of Jesus Christ—he does not want to be found empty-handed or to report a buried talent when his master comes back (Matt. 25:25).

Paul answers his rhetorical question of verse 19 with succinct affirmation: "Indeed, you are our glory and joy." No matter what others may say to the contrary, Paul's heart is fond of, and consumed by, his converts in Thessalonica.

The dynamic of relationship between the spiritual parent (and mentor) and the convert is still a source of gratitude and joy in today's church. We will continue to owe one another the debt of love (Rom. 13:8), and we have the joyous obligation to preach the gospel to all (1:14–15). We, too, passionately seek to share Christ so that our calling is not in vain, but will result in the victor's crown when Jesus returns.

Related to this matter is the issue of church leadership. Those who shepherd the flock or are involved in some aspect of leadership will serve their charge well if they see their people—through thick and thin—through the eyes of gratitude for what God's power has accomplished. Such a perspective will give strength to the leader and will in turn be strength to the follower. An aloof attitude or leadership that does not cultivate the warmth of a Christian family is destined for the frustration of impeded growth and lack of effectiveness. A healthy, reproducing church with strong bonds of love is a testimony to the world and a tribute to the Lord Jesus Christ.

4.3. A Heart Wracked With Anxiety (3:1–5)

This next component of Paul's defense is marked by the apostle's double admission of overwhelming anxiety: "When we/I could stand it no longer" (vv. 1, 5). Try as he might, his attempts to get back to Thessalonica were hindered, and Paul was at the end of his rope. In this urgent situation his missionary team sought for a remedy and devised the plan to send Timothy back to Thessalonica. We are not told of their rationale, nor do we know how it was that Timothy could return unhindered and Paul could not. Bruce (64) suggests that being part Greek would allow Timothy to slip back unnoticed, whereas Paul's distinctive Jewish appearance would give him away. Whatever the case, God allowed the safe and profitable return of Timothy as Paul's representative. What makes this particular tack such a strong defense is that it was clearly Paul who was pushing for the visit because his heart was wracked with anxiety. Contrary to what his accusers might say, Paul cared deeply for the Thessalonians.

Not to get lost in the drama is Paul's confidence in Timothy for such a vital and formidable task. According to Luke's account, it was early in the second missionary journey that Paul enlisted Timothy (Acts 16:1–2). His age is not mentioned, although he is commonly thought to have been a young adult. Keep in mind that Paul and Barnabas had recently split up over allowing another young man, John Mark, to assist them. Therefore, Paul had reason to be wary of the reliability of younger disciples. Obviously Paul did not on principle let age disqualify anyone, for he was impressed with what he saw in Timothy and with what was said about him. We do not know how much time elapsed between Paul's meeting with Timothy and the present crisis in Thessalonica, but we do know of Paul's trust. He speaks well of Timothy as his "brother" and endorses him highly as "God's fellow worker" (3:2).

Timothy was sent to do more than evaluate the faith of the Thessalonians; he was to minister strength and encouragement in what Paul expected to be a devastated church. In verse 3 Paul makes explicit his fear. He has thus far defended his ministry at Thessalonica and his reasons for not personally returning to nurture them despite his extreme concern for them. Now he bares his heart entirely—he was afraid they might be "unsettled" (*saino*) in their faith because of their trials.

Saino literally refers to the wagging of a dog's tail and thereby takes on the figurative meaning of being agitated or shaken. Bruce (62) rejects the relevance of the imagery of tail wagging and prefers the translation "to perturb mentally," a connotation based on an extrabiblical papyrus. Outright rejection of the relevance of the original meaning is not necessary, for the literal logically gives rise to the figurative. Paul's point is clear: He is distressed over the spiritual well-being of the Thessalonians and is wondering how well they have learned what he taught them in person regarding the certainty of experiencing trials (v. 4; for a sampling of what must have been the essence of this teaching on suffering, see comments on 1:3). It is one thing to be told about the role suffering plays in the Christian's walk of faith; it is entirely another thing to be convinced, within the adversity, that persevering is the only viable option—one that can even be cause for rejoicing.

Paul's preaching was up front regarding the cost of discipleship. He knew that honesty, at the risk of scaring away potential converts, was vital for the establishment of any church. All those who hear the good news of forgiveness of sin and the promise of eternal life must also hear that there is a price to be paid. They must then answer the question, "Am I willing to follow Jesus?" The Christian is fundamentally at odds with the kingdom of this world, and the resultant conflict manifests itself in various ways, depending on the society in which one is placed. Whether the price is loss of respectability, rejection, or verbal or physical abuse, the Christian's eternal perspective gives hope, and the Holy Spirit empowers one to be faithful.

This hope and empowerment are aspects of God's grace, which is without doubt sufficient for any trial. This grace denies adversity its natural result of despondency and yields an attitude of joy, based on the knowledge that God is in control and that in some small way, the footsteps of Jesus are being followed (Acts 5:41; James 1:2–4; 1 Peter 2:21; 4:12–14).

Thus the Thessalonians were not surprised by the adversity, because they had been prepared by Paul, even though their training had been cut short by persecution itself. Paul's reiteration that he could stand the suspense no longer (v. 5) builds on the earlier admission that he is anxious that trials would unsettle them (v. 3). He now identifies the source of their trials: "the tempter" (cf. also Matt. 4:3), that is, the devil. There are only two references to the devil in this first letter (cf. "Satan" in 1 Thess. 2:18), and in 2 Thessalonians Paul mentions him by name only once ("Satan" in 2 Thess. 2:9), despite his lengthy explanation of the agenda of the man of lawlessness. Paul has no doubt that the human adversaries are in some way stimulated by the devil. Christians are resisting more than flesh and blood (Eph. 6:12), and he is doing what he can to outfit them with the armor of God so they can stand firm and emerge victorious.

The temptation with which Satan is baiting the Thessalonians is to avoid adversity by turning from their faith in Christ. Paul apparently fears the worst, that some of his children will succumb. As Bruce suggests (64), Paul's words to the Corinthians concerning the possibility of escaping temptation through God's help (1 Cor. 10:13) "was illustrated by the experience of his Thessalonian friends." This suggestion merits consideration, especially when one considers the context of 1 Corinthians 10, where Paul is discussing how the people of promise, the Israelites, gave in to the temptation to ignore their commitment to God and who, when they did so through idolatry and grumbling, were destroyed (10:5–10). Israel's failure serves as a lesson for Christians to stand firm and resist all temptations to imitate wayward Israel. Whether Paul taught the Thessalonians of Israel's example is not as certain as the fact that they recognized the danger and found God's provision of escape—they stood firm, and Paul's efforts were not useless!

On the whole, New Testament teaching about the devil's schemes and about spiritual warfare is not as extensive as we would like. For example, James can simply say, "Resist the devil, and he will flee from you" (James 4:7), but we would prefer to see a detailed treatment of methods of resistance. Where Scripture is somewhat spare in such details, we should exercise caution in our speculations about the devil and his methods.

We must not, however, underestimate or dismiss the reality of the devil's existence and his desire to hinder or destroy the work of God. Perhaps Paul would write more extensively in these matters if he were writing to an audience that was skeptical about the powers of darkness and therefore untrained in how to battle Satan. We can assume that Paul personally taught the Thessalonians the basics of what they needed to know. In the Scripture we have ample warning and instruction in the fundamentals of spiritual warfare. Aided by the Scripture and submitting to the gifts and power of the Holy Spirit, we can resist the devil most effectively.

4.4. A Heart Relieved (3:6–8)

Paul nears the end of his defense against allegations that he abandoned the Thessalonians by moving from the lively description of his anxiety to the resolving of this agony. Even though we saw earlier that the believers had made great progress and stood so firm that they achieved a fine reputation (1:7–8), Paul's lengthy defense is so constructed that for us as readers, the tension still mounts within the letter until he gives the news of Timothy's report. Significant in Paul's wording in verse 6 is his use of the word *euangelizo*, which in the New Testament is reserved for denoting the preaching of the gospel—evangelizing. Paul is not averse to using this term as he does because, in preparing for the worst, he is absolutely delighted with Timothy's splendid good news about how the Good News has taken deep root.

Timothy reports that the "faith and love" of the Thessalonians is healthy. The tandem "faith and love" harks back to the initial thanksgiving of 1:3, the content of which is indebted to Timothy's news. Paul is thrilled to hear that the Thessalonians have persevered and also have maintained their warmth for the apostle despite the accusations of his opponents. The relationship between father and children has not deteriorated, and Paul is relieved to hear that they have not given up on him. They long to see him as he does them (2:17).

In 3:7 Paul continues with transparent discussion of his feelings as he admits to them how much of an encouragement their faith was to him at a time when distress and persecution gnawed at his own soul. As is often the case, those who aim to encourage others are often themselves recipients of encouragement because of the resolve and faith of the afflicted. Timothy was sent as an agent of comfort and strength to the Thessalonians; he came back as a Thessalonian ambassador to minister comfort and strength to Paul. The words "distress" and "persecution" do not require separate attention since the combination is a stylistic device to emphasize the extreme nature of the adversity ("distressing persecution"). The apostle also employs the same pair of words in his catalogue of hardships (cf. 2 Cor. 6:4).

Along with the expressions of thanksgiving, verse 8 stands prominent as a high point in the letter: "For now we really live." This exclamation reveals a huge sigh of relief, which the mounting tension demanded. "Paul's concern for his converts and sense of oneness with them breathes through all his correspondence" (Bruce, 67). The Thessalonians are his joy and crown (2:19–20); they are the fruit and very fulfillment of his calling. In all the adversity, in his attempts to return to Thessalonica, and finally in the nervous waiting for word from Timothy, normal life had stopped for Paul. But now the good news results in jubilant relief; he is no longer handicapped by the heavy burden of uncertainty.

We ought not to forget that Paul later exhorts the Philippians: "Do not be anxious about anything, but in everything, by prayer and petition, with thanksgiving, present your requests to God" (Phil. 4:6). This exhortation rings true and rises above mere platitude, for Paul is not exempt from the highs and lows of human existence. He, too, has his own anxieties to control and to present to God. He does not shrug off his anxiety too easily.

4.5. A Heart of Prayer (3:9–13)

Verses 9–10 constitute one long interrogative sentence in the Greek, but the NIV has clarified and captured Paul's intent by making verse 9 the rhetorical question and verse 10 a partial response to that question. The apostle radiates the gratitude of a proud father's heart as he asks, "How can we thank God enough for you . . . for all the joy we have?" All the former anxiety of the unknown status of these converts bursts forth in characteristic thanksgiving. The apostle never takes for granted the marvelous keeping power of God. We saw earlier his natural disposition to thanksgiving (1:2; 2:13), and once again we see the tremendous joy Paul received from his converts (2:19–20).

As the Thessalonians were to later read this document, surely they received strength and resolve from Paul's affirmation. If there were any serious doubts about the apostle's sincerity, the record of his efforts and the proclamation of his love and joy would dispel all questions. Leaders who take stock of their feelings toward those in their care and find this type of joy with its resultant intercession have ready confirmation of God's calling and a sign of encouragement to keep on. When such passion for people is missing, it is cause for alarm. How can leaders effectively shepherd when they are indifferent to the sheep? Paul's leadership model continues to be inspiring and instructive.

Verse 10 answers, in part, just how Paul has been demonstrating his appreciation to God for them. That is, his gratitude leads him to pray. His prayers are characterized by their frequency ("night and day") and their intensity ("most earnestly"). The latter is indicated by Paul's typical fondness for using compound words for emphasis (Bruce, 68), such as here the adverb *hyperekperissou* (lit., "exceedingly abundantly"). His point is clear; that is, his desire for the Thessalonians' well-being is so great that he cannot exaggerate how intensely he intercedes for them. The manner of his prayer is impressive, and the content of these prayers is what we would expect from a loving father torn away from his children. He longs to see them face-to-face and "supply what is lacking in [their] faith."

The verb "supply" (*katartizo*) is used elsewhere in the New Testament of restoring or mending (e.g., the repairing of nets, Mark 1:19), but in this context with the concept of "what is lacking," the notion of supplying or equipping is most accurate. Paul wants to help the believers in Thessalonica to continue to excel in their faith. There are some areas that need attention nd as a loving father he has not washed his ands of the responsibility to nurture them.

It may be surprising that, on the one hand, aul can so enthusiastically sing their praises, et, on the other hand, refer to a lack in these eople. But in no way do we sense disappointment or the anger of impatience on his art. The apostle has a healthy grasp of the ruth that Christians need time to mature, for ven spiritual growth is a natural process. A iscerning spiritual father can make llowances for the conduct of children who are rowing up in the faith. It is heavy-handed to nsist on a level of holiness or conduct charcteristic of the mature Christian. A natural ather does not expect his two-year-old to act ike and assume the responsibilities of a eenager. Converts are to be instructed, growth s to be expected, and at times firm admonition r correction is necessary where growth is eing resisted. Such is the task of strengthenng converts in the faith (3:2; 2 Thess. 2:17).

In verses 11–13 Paul lists three additional rayer wishes that focus on God's direct nvolvement in the answering of the petitions. 1) Paul's initial prayer wish of verse 11 is baseally the same request of verse 10, where he rays to see them again. But if that visit is to appen, God must "clear the way." The wordng of this request reflects that it is born out of he frustration of repeated unsuccessful attempts o return (2:18). Satan marshaled a resistance hat foiled Paul's plans, but this man of God elieves in the power of prayer to meet and vercome the hindrance. Nothing can separate he believer from God's love, and the apostle is etermined that Satan will not keep the Thesalonians from Paul's love, for with God's help e and they will be more than conquerors in this ituation (cf. Rom. 8:37; 1 John 4:4).

(2) Paul prays that God will continue to nake their love "increase and overflow for ach other and for everyone else" (v. 12). The hessalonians have already been applauded or their "labor prompted by love" (1:3) and or their love of Paul (3:6), but a key componient of maturing is the increase of genuine aith expressing itself in love (Gal. 5:6b). As aul admits here, his love continues to grow as vell. They can further imitate him in this egard (1 Thess. 1:6).

(3) Paul's final wish is for the overall spiriual well-being of the believers in Thessalonica, that they will be strong, "blameless and holy" (v. 13). They have already proven to be strong through what they have endured, and with God's help they will "remain firm and unmoved whatever the future may hold" (Morris, 113; cf. 2 Thess. 3:3). The two words "blameless and holy" are to be understood as a unit, together expressing "blameless in holiness" (Bruce, 72; cf. 1 Thess. 5:23). Paul will soon move to his directions regarding issues of sanctification, and thus this wish provides a tidy transition into chapters 4–5. But before he moves on to this topic, he preludes another topic of upcoming discussion, the return of the Lord.

The believer is to live in holiness awaiting Christ's return "with all his holy ones." Paul does not discuss who these holy ones are. In the New Testament the word used here (*hagioi*) refers to the redeemed, the saints of God, but there is some question whether it should be restricted to them. In 2 Thessalonians 1:7 Paul writes about what will happen "when the Lord Jesus is revealed from heaven in blazing fire with his powerful angels."

The Old Testament concept of the Lord's coming with judgment provides the conceptual framework for the identification of these holy ones (Bruce, 73–74; Morris, 114), and it is this framework that promotes the understanding that angels are to be included in the word *hagioi*, if not the only referent. For example, Zechariah writes, "Then the LORD my God will come, and all the holy ones with him" (Zech. 14:5). This is traditionally understood as speaking of the angels that are part of the Lord's entourage. This understanding is supported by the gospel tradition, when Jesus speaks of the Son of Man as coming "in his Father's glory with the holy angels" to judge (Mark 8:38) or to separate the sheep from the goats (Matt. 25:31–33; cf. Jude 14–15; 1 Enoch 1:9).

If Paul is alluding to Zechariah, and if 2 Thessalonians 1:7 is a direct parallel to 1 Thessalonians 3:13, then there is a strong case for claiming that the "holy ones" are angels. The context of 3:13 fits into the judgment picture, for Paul's prayer is that the Thessalonians may be found blameless when the Lord returns with his angels to judge humankind. Morris, however, argues (115) that since *saints* is a New Testament term reserved for believers, it is likely that "both angels and departed saints will be associated with the Lord when He returns." Bruce (74) suggests the relevance here of the prophecy of Revelation 14:1–14 regarding the appearance of Jesus on Mount Zion with 144,000 of the redeemed; thus, the case can be made that Paul has in mind the glorious retinue of angels and departed saints alike.

The bottom line is that meditation on this spectacular future event is a powerful stimulus to persevere in faith and right living. Whether it is angels or saints or both that accompany Jesus, the focal point is the separation of the sheep and goats. The Judgment Day is coming, and we must live holy lives in anticipation of welcoming our Savior, not in fear of condemnation.

Thus Paul's lengthy defense concludes. He has vindicated his conduct and message while among them and defended his subsequent departure and delay to return to them. Despite what his detractors have alleged, his desire for the Thessalonians is abundantly sincere. The believers in Thessalonica possess his heart.

5. Paul's Directions for the Thessalonians (4:1–5:22)

Now that Paul has completed the defense of his ministry while in Thessalonica and firmly established the case for his deep love for them, he makes the transition to a final section of directions regarding behavior and doctrine. The various points Paul addresses are not random, off-the-cuff musings about what the church might need to hear. Timothy's report brought back good news (3:6), but we can safely assume that the content of chapters 4–5 represents other news regarding need for growth and correction. With the gentle but firm authority of a loving, patient parent Paul now deals "with his own children, encouraging, comforting and urging" them to live worthy lives (2:11–12) and to "supply what is lacking in [their] faith" (3:10). For the time being he cannot fulfill this role in person, but he is confident that the power of God will use this letter as an effective substitute for a visit. The Thessalonians may be model Christians, but they are not perfect—they still need some tuning up.

5.1. Regarding Previous Instruction (4:1–12)

Paul's technique for eliciting worthy conduct is noteworthy. Before he deals with specific matters he takes a moment to affirm th direction in which the Thessalonians are head ing. In general terms he reminds them of th previous instruction he personally gave o how to please God (cf. 2 Thess. 2:15), and h commends them because they are indee pleasing God (1 Thess. 4:1; note the contras with others who displease God and resist th gospel in 2:15). The apostle has thus estab lished a nonthreatening posture that will facil itate his exhortation.

5.1.1. Grow in Obedience and Purit (4:1–8). The apostle understands huma nature and the value of a pat on the back. H will not exasperate his children by condemn ing their lack of maturity; he believes they wil respond to the positive approach of exhorta tion. There is a vast difference between lack o maturity and lack of progress in maturity. O other occasions, of course, Paul adopts a dif ferent method. For example, he speaks harshl to the Corinthians, who should have know better and progressed further in their faith; h has to treat them like "mere infants in Christ' (1 Cor. 3:1–3) and threatens that he may hav to employ the "whip" (4:21; see other exam ples of strict rebuke in 6:5; 11:17; 2 Cor. 2:1–4; 13:2, 10).

Pastoral ministry is difficult today, for in a congregation one will have a broad spectrun of believers, ranging from the veterans witl decades of Christian experience to those who are rookies in the faith. What complicates mat ters further is that some veterans resist matu rity and need to be treated like mere infants A pastor's challenge in any sermon or teaching venue is to keep in mind the various levels o need, for if he or she employs the whip, some who are not deserving of it may feel the sting Yet if he or she patiently coddles the newly converted, slack, long-time members may sense no need to mature and use their spiritua gifts to assist the work of the ministry (Eph 4:12–14).

As we noted earlier regarding 2:19–20, it is imperative for leaders to be passionate fo those entrusted to their care. It is this passior and the reliance on God's wisdom that wil enable the leader to navigate through all the quirks and challenges presented by the saints Those who are called by God, for howeve small a task, can trust that the Holy Spirit wil anoint their sincere efforts of love (1:4).

Paul praises the Thessalonians for their God-pleasing lifestyle and urges these model Christians to continue to grow. A Christian lifestyle that is stuck in the rut of contented mediocrity is remedied by growth (cf. "more and more"). Paul pursues excellence of service to Christ in his own life and the lives of all saints. Anything less than loving God with all one's heart and strength is substandard, especially considering the grace available to Christians. This pursuit is demonstrated in the six times Paul uses variations of the terms *perisseuo* and *perissos,* which indicate abundance or excellence (2:17, "every effort"; 3:10, "most earnestly"; 3:12, "overflow"; 4:1, 10, "more and more"; 5:13, "highest"). This call to excellence is not new for the Thessalonians, for Paul had instructed them on such matters when he was in Thessalonica (4:2), and they have proven to be obedient. Likewise, our lives are to abound with Christlike living.

Apparently a refresher course in some matters of previous instruction is necessary. Thus, Paul addresses the need for sexual purity. He begins this address with the overarching premise on which conduct is based: "It is God's will that you should be sanctified [*hagiosmos*]" (v. 3). Considering their recent pagan backgrounds, it is not surprising that some believers need to be told in strong terms that sexual immorality (*porneia*) is contrary to God's code of holiness. As Morris says of this society (121), "continence was regarded as an unreasonable demand on a man." Satiating one's sexual appetite outside the marriage relationship was deemed by some to be no more aberrant than would be eating when hungry (1 Cor. 6:13). Regardless of how commonplace such behavior was in society, the new Christians were to be a counterculture that obeyed God's will, not the will of the masses.

Accordingly, all Christians are to live a life of sanctification or holiness. We have been set apart or consecrated to live as God desires, and while we are not yet in a state of total sanctification (i.e., perfectly holy in all aspects of life), we are in process whereby "more and more" our conduct conforms to God's will. The gospel assures us that we have been made holy by the sacrifice of Jesus (Heb. 10:10); we are justified or proclaimed forgiven and are free from all charges against us (Col. 2:13–14). We are part of the "radiant church, without stain or wrinkle or any other blemish, but holy and blameless" (Eph. 5:27). God sees the perfect righteousness of Jesus as our righteousness (2 Cor. 5:21), and we can therefore be his children, free of all condemnation.

Since this is so, our conduct is to be pleasing to God, not in hopes of earning his love or in unhealthy fear that too many demerits will incur his wrath. Children must be instructed how to conduct themselves as God desires. Obedience is the mark of discipleship, and while all that matters is "faith expressing itself through love" (Gal. 5:6), we still need instruction in what it means to "keep in step with the Spirit" (Gal. 5:25). Paul has no fear of being labeled a legalist for commanding conformity in specific matters of conduct. His letters are replete with detailed conduct requirements, which are given with the understanding that we should truly desire to "live lives worthy of God" (1 Thess. 2:12; cf. Eph. 4:1; 2 Thess. 1:5).

Paul enjoins self-control as an important weapon against immorality, and it is part of God's will that the Thessalonians learn how this virtue applies to all aspects of life (v. 4). The word translated "to control" (*ktaomai*) is not the same one found in Paul's fruit of the Spirit (*enkrateia;* Gal. 5:23), but the context here makes the terms virtually synonymous. Controlling oneself is not the mere assertion of human willpower, for the Holy Spirit is the source of the power needed (see Fee, 444, on the cooperative effort between the Christian and the Spirit in producing spiritual fruit).

Certainly holiness and self-control apply to much more than sexuality, but this is the particular application that the Thessalonians need to hear. The Christian must control "his own body" or "vessel" (KJV; Gk. *skeuos*). He uses this word in 2 Corinthians 4:7, where our bodies are referred to as "jars of clay" ("earthen vessels," KJV). The imagery of a vessel is useful for understanding Paul's teaching on holiness, for the Holy Spirit resides in and works through the saint (2 Tim. 2:20–21). Paul elsewhere expresses the same concept with different words: "Your body [*soma*] is a temple of the Holy Spirit, who is in you" (1 Cor. 6:19). His subsequent charge to the Corinthians—"you were bought at a price. Therefore honor God with your body" (6:20)—neatly parallels his point to the Thessalonians that a Christian should "control his own body in a way that is holy and honorable" (1 Thess. 4:4). Both passages have contexts regarding the impropriety of sexual immorality and the Christian's response of fleeing all such practices.

The word "holy" is the same Greek word (*hagiasmos*) translated "sanctified" in verse 3; it indicates that we are set apart by God for sacred use. Therefore, we should conduct ourselves in a manner appropriate to or consistent with something set apart. Paul uses the word "honorable" (*time*) in connection with the vessel metaphor here and in Romans 9:21 concerning the potter's right to make "some pottery for noble purposes [*time*] and some for common use [*atimia*]." Unlike the ignoble or dishonorable objects of wrath, we are objects of love and grace, chosen by God for privileged use; we are those through whom God makes his gospel appeal (2 Cor. 5:20).

In verse 5 Paul descriptively contrasts the Thessalonian believers with those who live "in passionate lust." These converts were familiar with the lifestyle of the heathen; for some it was not so long ago that they were rescued from that way of life (1:9; cf. 1 Cor. 6:11). As well, although they were not subject to the type of constant media barrage faced by our modern society, which normalizes much that is contrary to holiness, they too lived within their society and knew the pressure of being different. The heathen live as they do because, as Paul says, they do not know God (Rom. 1:18–27). This lack of knowledge does not excuse them from judgment; they are indeed children of disobedience (Eph. 2:2; 5:6; Col. 3:6). It is by such a contrast that Paul reinforces the strong conviction that they, since they do know God, are no longer to act in such matters as pagans do (1 Thess. 5:6–8).

Paul's next statement is stern: "No one should wrong his brother or take advantage of him" (v. 6). It is clear that the context is still the issue of sexual immorality. The KJV somewhat ambiguously renders the phrase "in any matter," but the NIV more properly specifies "in this matter," thus maintaining the necessary link with the previous discussion. The imperative is plain: The pagans may strive to satisfy their sexual appetites regardless of repercussions, but God's children, who have been called to a higher standard, should control themselves and remain within God's boundaries for sexual expression.

As if that is not reason enough to conform, Paul reminds his readers of the deplorable impact sexual wantonness will have on the family of believers. Just as each part of the family can edify the whole through godly, loving service, so too a member who refuses to obey weakens the whole. It is tragic enough for a believer to persist in sexually immoral behavior, but how much worse if the license results in illicit relationships with others within the family of God? Sinful sexual relationships are never a mere matter of two consenting adults—there are victims who are being cheated out of what God intended marriage to be, and there is a holy Father whose will is being disregarded. Nor should we disregard the reproach with which outside observers will view the church when its members are not conforming to God's prescription for holiness.

The vehemence with which Paul deals with this matter of sexual misconduct suggests strongly that he is dealing with a problem within the church at Thessalonica. Paul does not say the church is characterized by this sin as if the problem were rampant; on the contrary, as we saw earlier, the church is characterized by its deep commitment to the Christian faith. Nevertheless, there were likely incidents of impropriety, and the church must be urged in no uncertain terms to shore up its boundaries and be united in its pursuit of holiness. Paul's warning of verses 6–8 is harsh, but it must be so because the nature and danger of sexual immorality warrants the strictest of admonitions—God "will punish" the disobedient.

Paul's warning harks back to the oral teaching he previously gave to them. The wording of verse 6b is emphatic: "as we have already told you and warned you." We can safely assume that Paul's ministry team had enough time with the new converts to teach not only the rudiments of salvation, but also the basics of Christian ethics and the consequences of deviancy. One who professes faith in Christ but is flippant about the call to holy living is making a shallow profession and runs the risk of God's judgment. Marshall (112) rightly argues that God's judgment is not a mean-spirited getting even with anyone who heats up God's anger to the boiling point. Rather, "God takes the side of the victims of crime and wickedness and secures justice for them, and . . . he acts as the upholder of the moral order against those who think that they can break it with impunity."

Paul reiterates in verse 7 his declaration of verse 3. The purpose of God's call is not to live impure lives; therefore, a Christian does not persist in, rationalize away, or relabel misconduct so that it appears right in his or her own eyes. Even if individuals refuse to repent, they must be made to know that God does not approve, nor does he ignore—there will be a reckoning. For the third time in verses 3–7 Paul uses the word *hagiasmos* ("holy life"; cf. also in vv. 3 and 4), thus emphasizing an aspect of stewardship that is part of our call. We are not only stewards of the gospel message (2:4), we are stewards of our bodies and our relationships with one another. God requires faithfulness of his stewards (cf. 1 Cor. 4:2).

The apostle concludes his warning with the bottom line to disobedience (v. 8). It is not only that one disobeys a pastor or some other authority figure. Disobedience is rejection of God (Ps. 51:4; John 12:48; 15:20). It is this reality that ought to shock one out of indulgent complacency into eager conformity. Paul is ever confident that his gospel and his instruction are God's. There is no waffling, no seeking of compromise or shifting of boundaries all in the spirit of tolerance. Therefore, to accuse Paul of being inconsiderate of societal norms or of being old-fashioned and narrow-minded is to so accuse God.

Paul affixes to this warning what appears at first blush to be an incidental comment about the God they risk rejecting: It is he "who gives you his Holy Spirit." Two lines of thought should be recognized here. (1) As to character, God is Spirit (John 4:24) and he is holy (Lev. 21:8b; 1 Peter 1:16; Rev. 4:8); hence he prescribes holy conduct. (2) Paul believes that in Christ the new covenant spoken of by the prophets has been enacted. The benefits of this covenant include the gift of a powerful ally within all participants: "I will put my Spirit in you and move you to follow my decrees and be careful to keep my laws" (Ezek. 36:27; cf. 37:14; Jer. 31:31–34).

Paul uses the present participle here (lit., "giving"), and although some have done so, it is unsound to conclude this giving refers only to what happens at conversion, when the new believer is indwelt by the Holy Spirit. The Christian is to keep on being filled with the Holy Spirit (Eph. 5:18, where the verb also implies continual action). "Thus the Spirit is understood as the constant divine companion, by whose power one lives out holiness, i.e., a truly Christian ethic" (Fee, 53; see also Marshall, 114). Therefore to reject instruction for holy living (whether in outright disdain, through apathy or carelessness, or in disregard for consequences) is to reject the power of the Holy Spirit, which God makes available to conform to his calling.

We have a divine call to holiness; we also have divine empowerment to be holy—what a glorious arrangement by our gracious God! Even within Paul's warning is implicit the positive stimulus of God's loving grace. God makes it entirely possible for his children to grow in obedience and purity.

5.1.2. Grow in Brotherly Love, Stewardship, and Respect (4:9–12). Paul now makes the shift from the specific directions regarding sexual purity to the general call to exercise and grow in "brotherly love" (*philadelphia*, from the verb *phileo*, "to love, have affection"). Some interpreters have made too much of the distinction between *agapao* and *phileo* by claiming that the former is the superior type of love God demonstrates, while the latter is an inferior love above which Christians can rise. Originally *philadelphia* was used of the love between blood brothers and sisters, then was fittingly borrowed by the Christian community of brothers and sisters in Christ (BAGD, 858). Paul's direction to grow in their expressions of this brotherly love is not a concession to some inability to demonstrate anything more than affection, for, in fact, Paul also uses the word *agapao* in the same verse.

The apostle's point is that the Christian community is to be characterized by the loyalty and deep care that imitates God's level of commitment to them (John 13:34–35). The extent of squabbling or division that existed in the Thessalonian church was not on a grand scale. Some, most likely a small minority, were threatening harmony through being lazy (1 Thess. 4:11–12; 5:14; 2 Thess. 3:10) and being busybodies (2 Thess. 3:11). But by and large the church was characterized by love. Paul knows the dynamics of relationships and that unless careful attention is paid to maintaining harmony, the church can be one small step away from strife. He therefore urges the saints to press on vigorously in the direction they have already been heading.

Paul says he has no need to write to the Thessalonians about the matters of brotherly love, and he is thus confident he can keep his discussion to a minimum. A brief reminder is all they need at this stage, for they have already been well instructed by him (4:1–2), and above all, they have been "taught by God." This concept of being taught in this manner relates to the fulfillment of prophecy and the benefits of the promised new covenant. In verse 8 (see comments) Paul has already mentioned the gift of the Holy Spirit, which helps us pursue holiness.

Concerning the new covenant, Jeremiah records that the Lord says, "I will put my law in their minds and write it on their hearts" (Jer. 31:33). Similarly Isaiah writes, "All your sons will be taught by the LORD" (Isa. 54:13), and Jesus affirms the application of these prophecies to the new covenant: "'They will all be taught by God.' Everyone who listens to the Father and learns from him comes to me" (John 6:45). Paul recognizes his role in this new age: He is the agent of God's instruction—as God anoints him, God's people will hear God's teaching. The apostle can rest assured that as long as he is a faithful steward (1 Thess. 2:4), God will nurture and complete the work begun in the converts (Phil. 1:6).

Paul's skill as a tactful leader is demonstrated especially in verse 10. In no sense is the impression given that the converts are not good enough; there is no tone of harshness or impatience. Rather, he joyfully affirms their progress—the Thessalonians' ample display of love is witnessed throughout Macedonia (1:7–8). Marshall (115) believes that this love would have included hospitality for Christians traveling through Thessalonica, "since in the ancient world it was difficult for travelers to get decent accommodation except from their friends ... hospitality was a much-commended virtue in the early Church" (cf. 3 John 5).

Another aspect of the Thessalonians' love is generosity. Paul uses them (and the Macedonians in general) as an example to motivate the Corinthians to be likewise generous with finances. He boasts about them: "Out of the most severe trial, their overflowing joy and their extreme poverty welled up in rich generosity.... Entirely on their own, they urgently pleaded with us for the privilege of sharing in this service to the saints" (2 Cor. 8:2–4). Their giving was an eloquent testimony of their faith and love.

Paul not only affirms their progress in demonstrating love, he also urges them "to do so more and more." He again uses the verb *perisseuo* ("to abound"; see comments at 4:1), and the picture we should see is not one of frenetic striving toward an unreachable goal. All too often some Christians feel woefully incompetent and guilty, never good enough despite their efforts, as if attainment of perfection is the only achievement that matters in God's sight. What does matter is that through the help of our ally, the Holy Spirit, we can abound in love; that is, our lives must be characterized by the increasing tendency to love (2 Peter 1:8) over against the retreat to self-centeredness. Paul is concerned that saints might become wrongfully satisfied with their lifestyles and thereby risk the danger of slackness—a malaise that can creep up undetected. Positive words of exhortation are Paul's effective stimuli to growth.

All believers constitute one great family—the "household of faith" (Gal. 6:10 KJV; cf. Eph. 2:19). This family, which transcends all racial, social, and economic barriers, is to be a sanctuary from the world, free from anything that divides or destroys. Ideally family members do not exploit each other. They ought not to fear that other believers will wrong or cheat them (1 Thess. 4:6; cf. 1 Cor. 6:7–8), and they can expect to be encouraged and helped in time of need (Gal. 6:2; Col. 3:16). The Christian family is a generous network of peace and harmony (Rom. 12:16–18). The ideal is set before us; however, the reality is that the church does wrestle with cases of sibling rivalry. But to such conflicts the family does not surrender. Spiritual siblings need to mature and let the solidarity of the Cross, the model of Christ, and the example of saints past and present inspire progress toward the ideal.

Stewardship and respect are Paul's next subjects (vv. 11–12). As he tackles the issue of stewardship Paul speaks of another trait of Christians—"ambition." Halfheartedness is foreign to one raised to love God with all his or her being. Paul's own ambition escorted him to a place of prominence in Judaism (Gal. 1:14). But when Jesus turned his life around, is ambition was raised to a new level by the verwhelming grace extended to him despite is feelings of extreme unworthiness (1 Cor. 5:8–10).

The imperative of verse 11, "make it your mbition," is rich etymologically. The word *hilotimeomai* is a compound word joining *hilos* ("love, fondness") and *time* ("honor, alue, distinction") and speaks of loving the onor or value of a certain course of action. As n the previous verse we see Paul's drive for xcellence. The first of three goals that Paul ays the Thessalonians should pursue is "to ead a quiet life." This is not a goal one would eadily connect with ambition, for one might e more prone to associate visible success in ife and prominent achievement with the esults of such drive. Yet when consideration s given to what Paul means by "quiet" and to he context of his directive, the wisdom ecomes more apparent. Paul does not mean ilence or soft-spokenness, but the stillness or uietness of life that is not rude or attention-seeking. It does not draw attention for the wrong reasons.

Unfortunately some of the Thessalonian converts were in need of this reminder. Paul's method here is interesting, for he does not single out the offenders at this point—he addresses he church as a whole. Later he will specifically address the violators (5:14). Perhaps his point is o ensure initially that others in the church will be deterred from following suit.

The next two goals the Thessalonians are to pursue is the minding of one's own business and working hard. These two goals go hand in glove, for when one has too much idle time, it is all too easy to become a busybody (cf. 2 Thess. 3:11). God has appointed that wherever possible we as human beings should work for the basic needs of life. In the Christian family, those who cannot work for whatever reasons come under the care of those who do work. This care is brotherly love at its best—no one is allowed to grow hungry or cold so long as resources are available. A Christian is a faithful steward, who works hard at what God has provided and who keeps an eye out for family needs. Paul himself emphasized how hard he personally worked to supply his needs so as not to be a burden on any (1 Thess. 2:9; 2 Thess. 3:8). The economics of this Christian community will be unduly strained if some members refuse to do their part, and Paul has learned that such is the case in Thessalonica.

There are two plausible reasons for the abuse of the system. (1) As in any group of people, there can easily be a few who are not as motivated to work, especially when there is a system of which they can take advantage. Laziness is industrious at finding the path of least resistance. (2) It is commonly thought that some in Thessalonica were so convinced of the imminent return of Jesus that their employment was "watching and waiting." "Undue eschatological excitement had induced a restless tendency in some of the Thessalonian Christians and made them disinclined to attend to their ordinary business" (Bruce, 91). The latter is the more likely explanation, especially since Paul will pick up the eschatological theme shortly.

Why were some disposed to such a radical approach while others were sensible enough to conform to Paul's former instructions? We cannot say. Nor do we know how getting so caught up with the Second Coming affected the rest of the church beyond that it taxed the generosity of the saints. If there were those who so sincerely believed the Parousia was imminent that they quit working in order to be ready, we can assume they must have viewed with some disdain those who were "unspiritual" and continued to work. Family harmony was endangered. Paul's direction is to the point: Get to work! There is no reason to believe that minding the daily responsibilities of life is unspiritual. Paul later wrote to the Colossians, "Set your hearts on things above" (Col. 3:1) without needing to clarify that some things on earth need attention too. Common sense can be trusted to strike the right balance, and Paul with his brief direction on this matter hopes the idle ones will pay attention.

Paul gives two important reasons in verse 12 for adhering to his words. (1) He wants the daily life of the Thessalonians to "win the respect of outsiders." These believers were models by which other Christians were inspired, but outsiders (unbelievers) are observing them as well. The impact of their conversion on society will be felt, as indicated by the uproar in the community when Paul was there. Paul may be concerned that the Christians do their best not to instigate any further persecution or ridicule through idleness and refusal to mind their own business. He believes it is possible to make a positive impression on a watching world through diligent attention to one's contribution to society even in the mundane activities of labor. Respect is often hard to earn, and the Christian community as a whole can suffer reproach through the deviancy of a few.

(2) Paul also wants to prevent unnecessary dependence on the charity of other Christians. There were surely some who legitimately needed Christian charity, and it would be selfish and unjust to siphon off the help for these worthy beneficiaries to lazy Christians. For the latter to return to supporting themselves will also win back the respect of their fellow Christians.

5.2. Regarding the Return of the Lord (4:13–5:11)

Most of the remainder of the letter is devoted to guidance concerning the Parousia. The bulk of all Paul's teaching on the return of Christ is found in his correspondence with the Thessalonians and the Corinthians (1 Cor. 15:12–58; 2 Cor. 4:13–5:5). There are a number of other references in the Pauline corpus, but they are brief—generally only mentionin the Parousia—and do not discuss the attenda circumstances. Even Paul's letter to th Romans, which more than any other docume outlines his doctrine, has little detail of th nature of the saints' eternal existence. We da not conclude that Paul was disinterested i these matters. Perhaps the oral tradition wa prevalent enough not to warrant any adde epistolary treatment. Nevertheless, the churc at Thessalonica is in need of clarification o these end-time matters. As he clarifies thing Paul's concern is not to establish a time fram for the Parousia but to remedy anxiety and t prepare his readers to be ready for it.

5.2.1. Retain Hope for the Dead in Chris (4:13–14). Verse 13 demonstrates that th church in Thessalonica was experiencing som unsettling confusion about what would happe to those who died before Jesus returns. Pau has to alleviate the anxiety, which arose in on faction of the church and became a going con cern for the community at large. The uncertai genesis of this confusion spawns speculatio that ranges from the belief that Paul taught th Thessalonians little or nothing o this subject, to the theory tha Gnostics had infiltrated the youn church and were teaching tha there was to be no Parousia.

Paul waited in Athens while Timothy returned to Thessalonica to check on the new Christians there. This ancient theater in Athens has been restored and is in use today.

What we do know is that Pau had instructed the believers i Thessalonica concerning end time events. For example, the must wait for the coming o Jesus, when they will be deliv ered from God's wrath (1:10 3:13); they also know somethin of the nature of God's kingdo (2:12). Although speculation is risky exegetical tool, it is one that when used cautiously, can yield measure of insight into implications of a text.

Paul's teaching likely include the issues of the resurrection o the dead in Christ and the future unfolding of God's eternal kingdom. Lüdemann (212) suggests that Paul used the formula "we do not want you to be ignorant" only to introduce new material for his readers. Therefore, he "had no previously dealt with the fate of Christians who died." We do not dispute Lüdemann's assertion regarding the formula's introduction of new material. However, this scholar is too broad in his identification of the new material Paul presents. It is overly restrictive to argue that Paul believed so intensely in the imminency of the Parousia that initially he neither personally considered nor taught regarding the pre-Parousia deaths of Christians. After all, the recent experience of persecution surely exposed the risk Christians faced.

Whether Paul was aware of the actual tradition or not, Jesus taught his disciples of this risk: "They will put some of you to death" (Luke 21:16). Thus the early church could not be surprised that some believers would die before the advent of Jesus. Also, Paul would not have forgotten witnessing the death of Stephen (Acts 8:1). As a Pharisee, even in his preconversion days Paul believed in the resurrection of the faithful (23:6–8). No major change of this point of theology was necessary once he understood that Jesus had conquered death and removed its sting (1 Cor. 15:54–57; 2 Tim. 1:10). Any new material Paul was adding of which he did not want the Thessalonians to be ignorant is not about the general hope of the resurrection of the dead in Christ. Rather, believers had to be taught that saints who died will still fully take part in all the events of the Parousia along with the remaining saints. The reason Paul never taught these details before is because when he was with them, the confusion had not yet arisen.

Timothy's report of the Thessalonians' confusion alerted Paul to address this issue with further instruction. We can reconstruct the essence of their inquiry as follows: "Paul, we believe that Jesus is returning soon, just as you taught us. But what about those among us who have died? We know they are in paradise, but will they miss out on the privilege of participating in this glorious event?" In his response Paul employs the common euphemism "those who fall asleep" for those who have died (cf. Deut. 31:16; Dan. 12:2; 1 Cor. 11:30; 15:51), although he is not averse to using the term *dead* (*nekros*), as we see in verse 16.

The Thessalonian inquiry is probably not a hypothetical one; rather, because of either persecution or natural causes some have already died. Paul's instruction is consoling; there is no need for ultimate grief, because hope burns brightly. It was hope in God that strengthened Paul during his distress over being separated from the Thessalonians (2:19), and he is confident that when we grasp the reality of hope in God, we will receive strength to meet any circumstances. Unbelievers have reason to grieve, for despite whatever belief they may have about the immortality of the soul, the truth is they die without Christ. Therefore, any hope they have is in vain. As Christians, we mourn our losses because we deeply miss our loved ones, but we receive comfort from the knowledge that those who died in Christ are now enjoying the presence of Christ (Luke 23:43; Phil. 1:23) and one day will see a splendid reunion in eternity (4:17).

We can speak confidently in terms of death being a "passing on" from one stage of existence to a more glorious and eternal one. Jesus, through his own death and resurrection, destroyed death (2 Tim. 1:10). Since it no longer has mastery over him (Rom. 6:9–10), it has no power over us, for we are in Christ. Certainly we may die before the Parousia, but death will not separate us from enjoying God's eternal love (8:38–39). Death is not the morbid end of existence; it is indeed a graduation or promotion to being more alive than the confines of earthly existence could ever have allowed.

In verse 14, with a creedal "we believe" Paul affirms the basis for our hope. The implications are clear and comforting: If Jesus died and rose again (and he did!), then we have every reason to believe "God will bring with Jesus those who have fallen asleep in him." His resurrection is the strong guarantee or firstfruits that all who belong to him will also rise (Rom. 8:11; 1 Cor. 15:20, 23; 2 Cor. 4:14).

5.2.2. Realize the Sequence of Events (4:15–18). While the Thessalonians had some prior knowledge of the resurrection of the dead in Christ, they were not sure how this resurrection would fit into the events of the Parousia. Paul now explains briefly what will transpire by appealing to "the Lord's own word." It is possible that Paul is familiar with traditional teaching on these matters, some details of which are not included in the Gospel accounts (John 21:25), or it may refer to "a prophetic utterance in Jesus' name" (Bruce, 98). Matthew 24:30–31 preserves some elements attending the Parousia that are echoed by Paul. This reference to the Lord's own word is intended to authorize or confirm the validity of what Paul is about to outline. Let no detractor accuse him of inventing stories of false hope in order to build up a following. The apostle is a steward of the truth, and he will faithfully execute his duties as accurately as he can (cf. 1 Thess. 2:4).

Verse 15 reveals the Thessalonians' precise concern that those who have fallen asleep will be disadvantaged when Jesus returns. The concern appears not to be that the deceased will miss out on eternal life, but that they will be denied participating in the grand celebration of the Parousia. Paul's response is unequivocal—those who are alive "will certainly not precede those who have fallen asleep." No Christian will be omitted from these events; in fact, as Paul explains, the deceased will have a slight advantage—they will rise first.

The Lord's return for his saints will begin in regal fashion as depicted in the three accompaniments listed in verse 16. (1) There will be a "loud command" *(keleusma)*. This is a specialized word, used in military situations as a battle cry or authoritative order (Morris, 143). Some see this as God's command to his Son to return for the believers, but more likely the image Paul presents is that of an announcement or call to the saints to meet their Lord. We see a close parallel with the tradition Paul may have known in the following words of Jesus: "Do not be amazed at this, for a time is coming when all who are in their graves will hear his voice and come out—those who have done good will rise to live" (John 5:28–29; see also 11:43, on the calling of Lazarus from the tomb).

(2) Next is "the voice of the archangel." What will this messenger say? Some have understood the voice and the loud command to be the same. Paul provides no name for this angel, although "Jewish tradition knew of seven archangels" (Bruce, 100; for their names see 1 Enoch 20:1–7; Jude 9). As heralds of God, an angel announced to the shepherds the birth of Jesus and a host of them praised God on that majestic occasion (Luke 2:9–14). It is most fitting for the return of the King of kings that a herald will once again announce tidings of great joy.

(3) "The trumpet call of God" is also part of the majestic splendor of the Parousia. This detail coincides with Paul's description of the last trumpet, which will sound as "the dead will be raised imperishable, and we will be changed" (1 Cor. 15:52). Jesus taught that the coming of the Son of Man will be attended by the sending of his angels "with a loud trumpet call" (Matt. 24:31). According to Revelation 11:15 a trumpet blast will precede the cosmic announcement that "the kingdom of the world has become the kingdom of our Lord and of his Christ."

Once these three accompaniments have occurred, "the dead in Christ will rise first." Paul emphasizes that the departed saints will not only be part of the event, they will rise *first*, that is, be resurrected in their glorified or imperishable bodies before those who are still living will be changed (1 Cor. 15:51) and gathered to meet the Lord. Departed loved ones will not miss out, nor have they been underprivileged by death.

A mistaken connotation of the euphemism "fallen asleep" has persuaded some to believe that there is an intermediate state of soul sleep that one enters at death and is then awakened out of by these events of the Parousia. But Scripture makes it clear that there is conscious existence immediately after death. Writing to the Philippians Paul is convinced as he faces an uncertain future that he is really in a win-win situation. If he should be released from prison, he will be thrilled to continue his ministry; but if he should be executed, he also gains, for he will finally be with Christ (Phil. 1:20–23).[9]

Once the dead in Christ have been transformed for their participation, those "who are still alive . . . will be caught up together with them in the clouds to meet the Lord in the air" (v. 17). The word translated "caught up" (*harpazo*) is rendered in the Latin by the verb *rapere*, hence the popular term *rapture*. Of the thirteen times *harpazo* is used in the New Testament, this is the only time it is used in conjunction with the Parousia (e.g., see Acts 8:39; 2 Cor. 12:2, 4). The apostle does not use the term in his other extended treatment of Parousia events in 1 Corinthians 15:50–58, nor does he use it in 2 Corinthians 4:14, when he writes that the saints will together be raised and presented to Christ.

Paul's reference to meeting in the clouds is reminiscent of the biblical imagery of God's presence in clouds at other momentous events, such as the transfiguration of Jesus (Matt. 17:5) and his ascension (Acts 1:9). Jesus also uses the imagery when speaking of the Son of Man's appearance in the sky (Matt. 24:30; cf. Dan. 7:13). Exodus reports how a pillar of cloud facilitated Israel's departure from Egypt (Ex. 13:21; 14:19–20) and how God came to Moses "in a dense cloud" prior to the giving of the Ten Commandments (19:9; cf. also 19:16, where the thick cloud of God's presence is accompanied by "a very loud trumpet blast"). Later God's glorious presence in the form of a cloud descended on the Tent of Meeting, and its resting or lifting off the tabernacle signaled when he desired Israel to rest or resume traveling (40:34–38).

This joyous meeting with Jesus is the awaited "blessed hope" of all believers of all generations (Titus 2:13). In using the word "meet" Paul may be evoking the imagery of an official welcome delegation that is sent out to greet a visiting dignitary "and escort him back on the final stage of his journey" (Bruce, 102; cf. Matt. 25:6; Acts 28:15). Unlike the Lord's prior coming at the Incarnation and his brief time with the disciples, this meeting will be an everlasting one. There will be no tragedy to sever our uniting with him; there will be no further events in the agenda of God's kingdom that will again necessitate his departure.

Thus as Paul suggests in verse 18, there is abundant encouragement to be found in the prospect of our ever being with the Lord. The Thessalonians, who were distraught over the fate of lost loved ones and perhaps over the prospect of their own deaths, were surely relieved by the clarification of the sequence of events at the Parousia.

As we study 4:13–18 it is important to remember Paul's purpose. He is trying to remedy as expeditiously as possible the problem of misunderstanding among the Thessalonians regarding the participation of deceased Christians in the great reunion with Christ at his return. We approach the text with a curiosity foreign to the original readers, a curiosity that has been piqued by an interim of almost two thousand years and by popular modern eschatological theories. We wonder about the exact location of Jesus' Parousia—will it be in the air space over Jerusalem? Will the whole world be able to hear the voice of the archangel and the trumpet blast, or is it only for the ears of Christians? Will unbelievers witness the rapture of Christians, or will it be an instantaneous disappearance?

These and a host of other questions are not answered by Paul. It is natural for us to be curious and to search the Scriptures for answers; but where none are given, we must be sure to bow in submission to God, who has revealed what is necessary for us to know and who has concealed much of what we long to know. What we need to learn from this passage is that the day is certainly coming when Jesus will return for the redeemed. It will be a glorious event, in which all Christians will fully and equally participate—an event that inaugurates the consummation of all the ages. We, along with all brothers and sisters in the church universal, will one day be united with our Lord—forever!

5.2.3. Ready Yourself for the Return (5:1–11). Paul continues with his discussion of the Parousia, but he moves from comforting to exhorting the Thessalonians to appropriate conduct in the light of the advent of Jesus. The key for Christians is to be alert or watchful and therefore self-controlled, demonstrating a holy lifestyle of expectation for the imminent return of Christ.

Paul writes that he does not need to tell the believers in Thessalonica anything more than what they already know (v. 1), but he does begin with a cautionary recapitulation of traditional teaching concerning when the Day of the Lord will occur. His use of the phrase "times and dates" has led some to distinguish between the two words. Morris (150) comments that here the noun "times" (*chronos*) refers to the progression of time, while "dates" (*kairos*) indicates "the nature of events that will characterize the end time." It may be, however, that the two words are synonymous and that Paul is employing a stock phrase that simply but emphatically refers to the time of the end.

Jesus uses the same phrase ("times or dates") in his final words to his disciples when they inquired if he was at that time going to restore fully the kingdom to Israel (Acts 1:6–7). His response was that the precise chronology was God's business, not theirs. Their business was to be witnesses of Christ and his coming kingdom (1:8). That is not to say that Christians are to ignore the general signs Jesus does provide (e.g., Matt. 24). Paul's point is similar: One is to be consumed with a life of ready service in the light of the certainty of Jesus' return, and not be consumed with unhealthy fixation on pinpointing a specific date.

Verse 2 explains why Paul does not need to write in any great detail on the subject: They already "know very well" what general facts can be known. To spur his readers to readiness he then outlines the content of the previous teaching they received from him concerning "the day of the Lord."

Before commenting on Paul's outline, a brief explanation of the concept "day of the Lord" is in order. The Old Testament portrays God as bringing to an end the oppression and wickedness of the world. Judgment will come and the world will be punished (Isa. 13:9–11; Amos 5:18–20; Zeph. 1:14–2:3); all nations will receive the treatment they deserve (Obad. 15). For those who are righteous this terrible day of wrath need not be feared, for it is also a day of deliverance (Joel 2:28–3:1; Obad. 16–21). Wanamaker (179) observes that the phrase was naturally assimilated by Christians because of the word "Lord," which they rightly identified with Jesus. It is this assimilation that allowed for a variety of synonymous phrases, such as "the day of Christ Jesus" (Phil. 1:6) or "the day of the Lord Jesus" (2 Cor. 1:14; see also Bruce, 109).

To press home his exhortation to readiness, Paul reports some of the oral tradition that circulated regarding Jesus' teaching on the end times. The Gospels in their present form had not yet been written at the time of this letter (this particular oral teaching would later be recorded in Matt. 24; Mark 13; Luke 21:5–36). The first illustration Paul borrows from this tradition is that of "a thief in the night" (1 Thess. 5:2; cf. Matt. 24:43–44). The resident whose dwelling was robbed went to bed assuming that that night would be like any other night; it would be uneventful, giving way to another day of life as usual. That is what made the thief so effective—he was unexpected. Vigilance is the answer to thwart the robber, and by analogy, watchfulness marks the Christian's lifestyle (cf. the parable of the ten virgins; Matt. 25:1–13).

The apostle borrows his second example from the Old Testament prophetic tradition, which addresses the deceitful preaching of a people-pleasing message of "peace . . . when there is no peace" (Jer. 6:13–14; Ezek. 13:8–16). Paul shows that people make the wrong assumption that "peace and safety" will be their portion indefinitely, when all along the repercussions of ungodly living are building and will soon catch up with them.

Paul underscores his declaration that sudden "destruction" is the sure outcome by using another metaphor common to Old and New Testaments, that of labor pains. In this case Paul uses the illustration not to demonstrate that after much pain something beautiful will be born (as in Rom. 8:22–23). Instead, he shows the inescapable result of a sinful life—as surely as a pregnant woman will suddenly experience the contractions and give birth, so too the sinful life will come to full term.

Paul's example is similar to the process James describes: "Then, after desire has conceived, it gives birth to sin; and sin, when it is full-grown, gives birth to death" (James 1:15). There is no escape; no one is exempt from reaping the consequences of rebellion against God. Being merciful, God does not mete out his judgment immediately; rather, he allows for the one route of escape through Jesus Christ. God's long-suffering sadly goes unrecognized and sinners feel invincible; they have not been punished yet, therefore they wrongly conclude there will never be any punishment. But God's word is sure, and despite appearances of getting away with a sinful life, a day of reckoning looms (1 Thess. 1:10; 2:16; 2 Thess. 1:6–10; 2 Peter 2:3–13).

On such a note Paul contrasts the Thessalonians: "But you, brothers, are not in darkness" (v. 4). Unlike the unsuspecting unbelievers, Christians are fully aware that the day of judgment will come; but it is not a day to dread, because they are prepared by virtue of being in Christ. In verses 4–7 Paul utilizes the common metaphors of darkness to represent evil (Isa. 59:9; Matt. 6:23; Rom. 13:12; Eph. 5:11; 1 John 2:11) and light to represent purity or righteousness (2 Cor. 6:14; Eph. 5:8–10; 1 Peter 2:9; 1 John 1:5). Christians can be called "sons of the light and sons of the day" (1 Thess. 5:5) because they have turned from rebellion to serve God (1:9) and have accepted the lavish gift of the righteousness of Jesus (1 Cor. 1:30; 2 Cor. 5:21).

Consequently, since Christians are not children of darkness, they must not act like those who are asleep" (v. 6). Paul is comfortable vith piling up his metaphors as he writes more vith a sense of urgency than with attention to olished rhetoric. He then weaves in the conept of sleeping, not as a euphemism for death as he did in 4:13), but as the antithesis of alertess. The contrast continues: The unbeliever is nsuspecting of judgment, lulled to sleep in gnorance and disinterest regarding his or her uture fate. But the vigilant Christian is neither lack nor self-indulgent in matters of darkness.

To stress the point further, Paul uses a "trusm" (Wanamaker, 184) or a proverb in verse 7. he usage will cause confusion if the saying is ressed to be a contrast between good people, vho behave themselves by sleeping at night, nd those who carouse when they should be leeping. Paul has just used the term *sleeping* n a negative fashion in verse 6, and it is likely hat he intends that connotation to govern his se of the saying. In other words, sinners are sleep rather than alert, and they indulge in runkenness rather than in exercising selfontrol. That is not to say that all sinners are runks, but the concept of drunkenness is nerely representative of any form of godlessess and self-indulgence.

In verse 8 Paul repeats his call to self-conrol. As in verse 6, he uses the word *nepho,* vhich literally means "sober" and hence fits he context of contrast with drunkenness beter than the Greek word translated "selfcontrol" in Paul's list of the fruit of the Spirit (*enkrateia*; Gal. 5:23). In the figurative sense believers resist being intoxicated by the allurements of the world. They set their minds on things above (Col. 3:1–2) and seek the priority of service in God's kingdom (Matt. 6:33).

The apostle then gives a blueprint for this exercise of self-control: The Thessalonians are encouraged to develop the three cardinal virtues of faith, love, and hope (1 Thess. 1:3). Reminiscent of his more extensive description of the armor of God in Ephesians 6:13–18, the apostle describes these three virtues in terms of two pieces of armor with which the Christian must be equipped. As protection against spiritual slumber and self-indulgence, we are to put on the breastplate of "faith and love" and the helmet of "the hope of salvation" (1 Thess. 5:8).

Paul writes to the Romans in similar fashion, encouraging them to avoid slumber and to be prepared for the coming day by putting aside the deeds of darkness and putting on the armor of light (Rom. 13:11–14). The lesson is clear: The Thessalonians must continue to stand firm in the faith and in demonstrating love (1 Thess. 1:8; 3:8, 12; 4:1, 9–10) until Jesus returns. They must not be detoured into slackness by the pressures of persecution or by the delay of the Parousia. They are to keep in the forefront of their minds the hope of ultimate salvation, for someday they will see Jesus face to face. Then it will indeed be worth it all.

Paul concludes his exhortation to readiness with the reminder that God did not appoint believers "to suffer wrath" (v. 9). As children of God, condemnation is not our lot (Rom. 8:1). God chose us (1 Thess. 1:4) and Jesus rescued us (1:10); therefore our salvation has been secured. Then, for the first time in the letter Paul explicitly mentions the means by which rescue has been made possible: "He died for us" (5:10). Jesus is our substitute in that he took our place of condemnation and paid the wages for our sin (Rom. 6:23; 2 Cor. 5:21; Gal. 3:13; 1 Peter 1:18–21; cf. Isa. 53:6). This verse neatly picks up the issue that initiated the discussion—it does not matter whether a Christian has died or remains alive, for every believer will be taken to be with Jesus to live forever with him.

The Thessalonians are to use this blessed hope as an abundant source of encouragement to continue being models of the Christian faith (v. 11). Within the body of Christ, when one becomes disheartened or weary, it is the privilege and responsibility of others to build him or her up. This call to mutual encouragement and edification implies another aspect of watchfulness—looking out for one another's needs so that no one suffers needlessly, or at least alone.

What was a most powerful source of inspiration for saints of old must remain so. Jesus is coming back for his church. Let us not be nonplused about the Parousia, for "our salvation is nearer now than when we first believed" (Rom. 13:11). Through worship and ministry of God's Word the faithful should ever remind themselves of this glorious hope. The fact that Jesus has not yet returned need not dishearten us; nor should we be discouraged by those who mock our persistent belief in that which seems so farfetched to them. We know that all things proceed according to our forbearing God's schedule (2 Peter 3:3–9). Let us therefore maintain a sharp eternal perspective as we fulfill our call in the present edition of the Lord's church.

5.3. Regarding Conduct in the Christian Community (5:12–22)

Paul rounds off his letter with further directions regarding a wide spectrum of conduct that results from living in the light, which is thus an elaboration of the Thessalonians' faith, love, and hope (v. 8). As for specific issues dealt with, some came to Paul's attention through Timothy's report and others are of the variety that are applicable in any church setting (Marshall, 145). Therefore not all the imperatives are necessarily custom fit for the unique needs of the Thessalonian church; many are equally relevant for today.

5.3.1. Respect Authority (5:12–13). When one considers that Paul likely had not much more than three weeks to establish the church in Thessalonica (Acts 17:2) and that he had not been in communication with the believers there until Timothy was sent, the question naturally arises regarding for whom it is that Paul encourages respect. Did Paul have enough time to choose and train leaders? Were these leaders as new to the faith as the rest of the Christian community?

Luke records that during Paul's first missionary journey he appointed elders "in each church and, with prayer and fasting, committed them to the Lord" (Acts 14:23). Morris (164–65) sees this custom as evidence that elders, albeit inexperienced ones, had been chosen by the missionary team. Perhaps some naturally rose to prominence based on their willingness and ability to serve as spiritual leaders, and what Paul is then asking is that the church "recognize as their leaders precisely those people who functioned in such a way as to toil for them, to protect and care for them" (Wanamaker, 193; see 1 Cor. 16:15–16 for such an example).

The word translated "respect" is literally "know," but the context indicates that more than mere recognition is necessary. Full recognition of who these leaders are and what they mean to the church will result in respect for their important function. It may be that Timothy brought back news of some opposition to the leadership.[10] Paul presents a strong threefold defense of their present leaders in order to restore or maintain proper respect for them. This defense parallels his own self-defense in chapters 2–3, as will be demonstrated. The grammar of verse 12 rules against seeing the three characteristics of leadership listed therein as being three different ministry gifts (unlike the listing of different gifts in Rom. 12:6–8).

(1) The Thessalonians' respect for authority will be healthy when they are aware of how hard leaders must work. They have no easy task, for the burden of the church's welfare has been put on their shoulders by God. Paul had to defend his ministry against allegations of insincerity, and he did so in part by reminding his readers of how hard he toiled for their benefit because of his love for them (2:8–9).

(2) The next point presents some translation variations. Paul's choice of the word *proïstamenoi* may indeed be a reference to the office of leadership (Morris, 166), hence the NIV's "those ... who are over you." Not to be ignored, however, is that the word also has connotations of protecting and caring, and it is those functions that demonstrate who the leaders are (see Bruce, 117, who translates, "[those who] care for you in the Lord"). This care and protection are paralleled in Paul's self-description as a gentle mother (2:7) and in his intense desire to protect them by supplying what is lacking in their faith (3:10).

(3) Also needed is admonishment. At times Christians need more than encouragement; they need stronger words of correction or reprimand. Faults or weaknesses must be exposed and remedied, and warnings of dangers or errors must be given. This endeavor requires wisdom and a measure of diplomacy, for it is not entirely a pleasant one. At times it is most unwelcome by the recipients, but it is part of the task of urging Christians to live worthy lives. Paul's own exercise of admonishing is implied in his function as their spiritual father (2:11–12) and in the warning to live holy lives if they wish to avoid rejecting God (4:7). We also see Paul's explicit admonishment later in 5:14, where the same word translated "admonish" here in verse 12 is rendered "warn." Thus, just as the Thessalonians respected and loved Paul in his performance of these three functions, so too should they respect and love their present leaders.

All this hard work, which involves caring and admonishing, is ample reason for holding leaders "in the highest regard in love" (v. 13). This respect is earned, and on the leader's part, is not sought after, lest the danger arise of becoming people-pleasers and of expecting praise from the wrong source (2:4–6). Paul stresses the level of regard they should show with his use of the superlative "highest" (*hyperekperissou*; see comments on 3:10).

The responsibility of spiritual leadership is enormous. While individual believers must take charge of their personal growth and exercise of faith, leaders are to facilitate growth at the individual and corporate levels. They need wisdom and strength from God to nurture a community of believers who are at differing levels of Christian maturity, to promote unity within the body, and to guide the church to fulfill its role in the Great Commission. The call to leadership of any sort is not to be taken lightly either by the one called or by the ones led. Diligent work and a caring heart are indeed worthy of the highest respect. As leaders fulfill their responsibility and as the believers respond positively to them, the saints are well on the road to adhering to Paul's next imperative, namely, to "live in peace with each other" (v. 13b; cf. Rom. 12:18).

5.3.2. Remedy Needs (5:14–15). The Thessalonian church is a marvelous example of the power of God's grace to initiate conversions and to maintain new believers in the faith. Paul is thankful for God's marvelous work in them (1:3; 2:13; 2 Thess. 1:3), and he commends them for their extraordinary testimony (1 Thess. 1:7–8). Nevertheless, even with all the positive things to be said about the Thessalonian believers, some things need to be remedied. Paul has no ax to grind—his directions are sincerely intended to encourage and edify the body. There are those who need to be spurred on to work, and idleness is denounced (see comments on 4:11).

Paul is also aware that some are "timid" (v. 14b); perhaps from relationships established while in Thessalonica, he may have specific people in mind. Those who are timid or fainthearted are not to be despised for being as they are. Perhaps Paul is referring to any of the converts who, in the face of the adversity at Thessalonica, have not been able to handle the stress with the same courage as others (Morris, 169). This very concern is displayed earlier where Paul voices his worry that some might be unsettled by the trials they faced (3:3–5). For such ones the remedy is sympathetic consolation and words of cheer, which remind the fainthearted of the grand eternal scope of things—in the end, the compensation of being with Jesus is more than adequate.

The church is also obligated to "help the weak" (v. 14c). The distinction between those identified as timid and those as weak is that the latter are either those who are "economically needy" (Wanamaker, 198) or those who are weak in the faith as they battle temptations and struggle to do God's will (Marshall, 151). These Christians need help in the form of those who will support and stand by them through thick and thin, for it would be devastating to them if those who are stronger gave up on them. Such people genuinely need much care and attention; here again we see the need for the hard work involved in building up the body of Christ.

From these specific targets of the idle, timid, and weak, Paul casts out a broader net: "Be patient with everyone" (v. 14d). All believers have needs that require the energy of others and foibles that need to be tolerated as we grow together in Christ. As experience so often testifies, patience can be that hardest toil of all, but it is a great catalyst for the mutual edification process. Bearing the burdens of one another is the privilege of being in the family of God (4:9–10; cf. Gal. 6:1–2). As Wanamaker so aptly says (198), Paul likely sought through these directions "to give the whole community a sense of pastoral responsibility." Such responsibility is surely the apostle's thrust as he expects it to be normative that all God's people are equipped "for works of service, so that the body of Christ may be built up" (Eph. 4:12).

Paul formulates his next injunction with both negative and positive stipulations (v. 15). He prohibits the repaying of evil for evil (cf. Rom. 12:17). Such refusal to lash out in revenge against any person who might inflict harm or abuse is a natural outworking of the patience Paul speaks of in the previous verse. Patience is not only a ministry to help brothers and sisters in Christ and to promote unity within the body. It is the high road Christians are to take when confronted with any degree of antagonism the world presents. It is all too inviting to resort to "an eye for an eye" when we have been wronged, but we must be on guard against this tendency. The avoidance of revenge is remarkable enough, but add to that the positive stipulation to practice kindness instead, and the task seems daunting indeed (cf. Rom. 12:14, 21). Jesus himself taught this twofold response of restraint and love when he required turning the other cheek, going the extra mile, and loving one's enemies by praying for them (Matt. 5:38–47).

As readers of the text it is one thing to applaud such a noble ethic, but it is entirely another matter to put ourselves into the situation of these Thessalonian believers and attempt to feel what they felt as they faced persecution. How would we respond to intense ridicule and physical abuse? How difficult would it be to suffer indignity silently, let alone seek the welfare of our antagonists? Perhaps the initiative to conform to this ethic will be strengthened as we remember that we too were once enemies of a God who was patient and merciful, and who demonstrated love rather than vengeance. Those presently our enemies may one day become brothers and sisters in Christ. The task may initially appear to be daunting, but behind all of Paul's ethical teaching lies the assurance that the Holy Spirit is our strength and that God's grace is sufficient to enable us for all of life's challenges.

5.3.3. Rejoice, Pray, and Recognize the Spirit's Leading (5:16–22). In short order Paul serves up a flurry of eight brief imperatives. The first three (vv. 16–18) pertain to inner attitudes that the Christian is to cultivate; the last five (vv. 19–22) address the role of prophecy within the church.

(1) The list begins with "be joyful always" (v. 16). Such an expectation may seem unusual in light of the adverse circumstances of Paul's audience, but the Scriptures uniformly present encouragement to rejoice along with the rationale for the attitude. Jesus taught his disciples that they could rejoice despite persecution (Matt. 5:10–12); Luke records how in fact the disciples did rejoice after being beaten by the Sanhedrin authorities (Acts 5:41; 16:25), and the New Testament letters are consistent in their witness to be joyful in suffering (Rom. 5:3; Col. 1:24; Heb. 10:33–34; James 1:2; 1 Peter 1:6).

Scripture gives three powerfully uplifting reasons why the Christian can maintain this joyful attitude. (a) A sense of worth and privilege comes with suffering for such a noble cause—it is for the sake of Jesus. The shame and pain of torment are offset by the remarkable realization that Christians are blessed to identify with Jesus, who suffered for them (Acts 21:13; Rom. 8:17; Phil. 3:10; 2 Thess. 1:5; 1 Peter 4:13).

(b) Saints have discovered great solace in maintaining the eternal perspective that clearly sees the temporary against the backdrop of a glorious eternal inheritance (Rom. 8:18; 2 Cor. 4:14–18; 1 Thess. 5:10–11; Heb. 10:35–36).

(c) Joy is a fruit of the Spirit; that is, it is a function of the Holy Spirit to empower the Christian to rejoice (Gal. 5:22). A natural result of being filled with the Spirit is the attitude of joy that prevails regardless of contrary circumstances that would dishearten and destroy a Christian's faith if not for the sufficient grace of God. Paul applauds the Thessalonians for their initial embracing of the gospel "with the joy given by the Holy Spirit" despite persecution (1 Thess. 1:6; see Acts 13:52, where Luke shows a correlation between joy and the Holy Spirit).

It is the challenge for the believers of today to throw off any tendency to linger in despair and to gain a thorough and convincing knowledge of our eternal destiny. The saints who have so ably demonstrated how it can be done are worthy of imitation. The dynamic indwelling of the Holy Spirit ensures that no believer needs to be denied of the liberating fruit of joy.

(2) Paul next commands his readers to "pray continually" (v. 17). He has testified how he has prayed for them (1:3; 3:10; 2 Thess. 1:11); thus, he himself modeled the critical role of a believer praying. The notion of unceasing prayer is not that the Christian converses only with God at all times. Rather, we must be mindful of the need and ability we have to fellowship with God through petition, thanksgiving, and praise; therefore, we must persevere in prayer (Bruce, 124; cf. Rom. 12:12). A continuous predilection to prayer cultivates the awareness of God's presence in both the mundane and the spiritual and makes all of life sacred and joyful.

(3) The third attitude Paul enjoins is that of giving "thanks in all circumstances" (v. 18). As with prayer, Paul practices what he preaches

(1:2; 2:13; 3:9; 2 Thess. 1:3; 2:13). The principle of being grateful, as with rejoicing, is not to be restricted to the positive issues of life that so easily evoke thankfulness (note the qualifier "all"). A distinction must be made between being thankful *for* everything (even for the evil that happens to us) and being thankful *in* everything (good or bad). Paul demonstrates the latter as he testifies how he can maintain an even-keeled level of contentment regardless of his circumstances—Christ gives him the strength to be content (Phil. 4:11–13).

The apostle is absolutely convinced that his life is in God's strong hand of control. He can therefore be thankful even within suffering because he knows that God is working all things out for good and that nothing will nullify his inheritance in Christ (Rom. 8:28, 38–39). What he knows to be true for his own situation, he knows to be so for God's children in Thessalonica. They have much for which to be thankful, not the least of which is that they have been rescued from God's wrath (1 Thess. 1:10; cf. 2 Cor. 9:15) and will one day join their Savior for eternity (1 Thess. 4:17). In the meantime they are to be strengthened by gratitude as they live out their lives in the sufficient and glorious strength God provides through the Holy Spirit (3:13; 4:8).

The last half of verse 18 ("for this is God's will for you in Christ Jesus") is best understood when the antecedent of "this" is seen not as one's circumstances but one's attitudes. In other words, God wants the Christian to have a thankful heart, and Paul likely has in mind that all three attitudes are God's will: One is to be joyful, prayerful, and thankful.

(4) The next five imperatives may initially appear to be unrelated general commands, but closer attention to their substance shows them to be connected to the ministry of prophecy. Paul begins with the general warning, "Do not put out the Spirit's fire" (v. 19). The verb Paul uses means literally "extinguish" (*sbennymi*), and this pertains to the putting out of a fire or flame (Mark 9:44; Eph. 6:16)—hence the NIV's clarifying addition of the word "fire." This is a most appropriate verb in this context since fire at times symbolizes the Holy Spirit (Matt. 3:11; Acts 2:3; 2 Tim. 1:6).

(5) Paul's concern here is that the Thessalonians might extinguish the work of the Holy Spirit by treating the gift of prophecy with contempt (v. 20), that is, ruling prophecy out as a legitimate and necessary phenomenon for the welfare of the Christian community. The gift of prophecy should be understood not so much as that which only predicts, but as "spontaneous, Spirit-inspired, intelligible messages, orally delivered in the gathered assembly, intended for the edification or encouragement of the people" (Fee, 170; cf. Joel 2:28; 1 Cor. 12:10; 14:1–4).

Why Paul feels a need to caution against despising such a gift is unclear. One reason may be that there are feelings of contempt toward prophecy because of false prophecies regarding the Parousia. In his second letter Paul will address the disquiet caused by a false prophecy, report, or letter (2 Thess. 2:2). If the expectation of an imminent Parousia results in some Christians feeling justified in being idle, it is not an unreasonable leap to consider that perhaps these people in their spiritual fervor are prophesying regarding dates. Or perhaps there are attempts by these idle ones to exploit prophecy to justify their idleness and to pit themselves against those who continue to occupy themselves in part with the daily responsibilities of life. Certainly the potential for abuse is great. Much harm and confusion result from prophetic words that contradict the more sure word of the prophecy of Scripture (2 Peter 1:19–20), or that are simply so bizarre or shallow that it is difficult to take them seriously. But abuse never rules out the value of the genuine gift.

(6) Paul's next three imperatives are the measures to be taken to foster a more healthy exercise of this spiritual gift. First priority is the testing or evaluating of any prophecy (v. 21). In some circles of today's church there is a reticence to meet all spiritual utterances with common-sense critique, as if such an approach itself is unspiritual. Discernment is also a spiritual gift, but some Christians are threatened or embittered if they are corrected and told their prophecy is out of line. A healthy community of believers is not necessarily one that is free of any inappropriate exercise of the spiritual gifts. Rather, it is one that can address what is out of line with a balanced respect that does not shatter the would-be prophet (who may well have the gift but just needs some guidance in its operation) or discount outright any and every manifestation of the gift.

(7) As Paul goes on to say, once prophecy has been tested, the church is to hold on to the good (v. 21b) and (8) to discount evil, disruptive, and damaging prophecies (v. 22).

Although Paul's warning here deals specifically with the spiritual gift of prophecy, the general principle holds true where in any fashion we, by our traditions or fondness for personal and corporate comfort zones, squeeze out or restrict the moving of the Holy Spirit. Paul's desire that Christians live by the Spirit and keep in step with the Spirit (Gal. 5:25) is the positive counterpart to the imperative against putting out the Spirit's fire. The church is to discern not just what is valid prophecy, but also how the Spirit moves in hearts and directs through all the various gifts and demonstrations of the fruit of the Spirit (Gal. 5:22–23). To fail to keep in step is to allow the body to be robbed of the dynamic God has made available.

Arrogance and pride restrict the flow of God's empowering grace. By contrast, it is to a humble, surrendered church that God will pour out his grace (1 Peter 5:5). Let us not presume to know exactly how the Spirit aims to move in our corporate and personal worship settings, nor how much or how little time the Spirit might take to create a fresh renewal of the awareness of God's presence and design for his children. May the church be ever hungry for, aware of, and receptive to the multifaceted moving of the Holy Spirit.

6. Conclusion (5:23–28)

Paul ends his letter in typical fashion, employing the conventional elements of prayer wish, further greetings, and benediction. He weaves into his conclusion brief summary remarks that reprise a few of the key issues he addressed in the body of the letter.

6.1. Paul's Prayer Wish (5:23–24)

Early in his letter Paul told the Thessalonians how he remembered them in prayer and in his giving of thanks. He now closes with a prayer wish or request for their spiritual well-being (see the similar use of prayer requests in 3:11–13). Paul is emphatic as he recognizes that "God himself" is the source of peace for these believers in all the adversity and anxiety that assail them (1:1; Phil. 4:7) and for the challenges of maintaining family harmony (1 Thess. 5:13).

The apostle then expresses his desire that God will "sanctify [his readers] through and through" (v. 23). In his directives regarding conduct Paul earlier wrote that sanctification was God's will for them and that they were to take an active role in pursuing a holy life (4:3–4, 7). Through the work of the Holy Spirit God provides the ability we need to conform to his will (see comments on 4:8).

Related to the hope for the whole or complete sanctification of the believers is Paul's desire that their "whole spirit, soul and body be kept blameless at the coming of our Lord Jesus Christ." This desire recalls his words of 3:13, although there instead of using the tripartite formula, he refers to the heart as the center of the sanctification process. Any apparent inconsistency in Paul's choice of terms is removed when one realizes that the heart is seen as the essence of a person's being—thus one part stands for the whole.

This is the only time Paul uses this threefold formula of spirit, soul, and body, and in light of the context of a prayer wish, we should exercise caution in how much formal theology can be inferred. Paul is emphasizing how sanctification applies to the whole of a person's being as is indicated by the Greek words translated "through and through" and "whole." As Bruce says (130), "it is precarious to try to construct a tripartite doctrine of human nature" from such a context. Marshall (162) tentatively suggests that "it may be possible to think of spirit as the higher aspect of human personality, and the soul as the centre of will and emotion."

Paul does not use the noun "body" (*soma*) elsewhere in this letter, although he does refer to the body metaphorically (see *skeuos*, 4:4). All other uses of the word "spirit" (*pneuma*) in the letter refer to the Holy Spirit (1:5, 6; 4:8; 5:19), and "soul" (*psyche*) is used only at 2:8, where Paul speaks of how the missionary team was willing to share their "lives." Despite not using these three individual words in a way that allows precise differentiation, Paul emphasizes how the process of sanctification encompasses the whole person (2:12) and urges believers to "live lives worthy of God" (cf. 4:7, 12). This threefold formula is likely a product of Paul's upbringing in Judaism, which infused him with the passion to love God with all his heart, soul, and strength (Deut. 6:5; Mark 12:30).

The marvelous potential of the gospel is that t is the power of God to transform the entire eing to make the Christian whole. The child of God is liberated to lead a new life—the old has een superseded (Rom. 1:16; 6:4; 2 Cor. 5:17; f. Isa. 1:18). We are not left on our own to sanctify ourselves, but as Paul says in 1 Thessaloians 5:24, if God calls (cf. 1:4; 4:7), he can be rusted to make it possible to be ready to meet esus without any fear of rejection (Phil. 1:6).

6.2. Paul's Requests and Benediction (5:25–28)

It is not unusual for Paul to request prayer for imself or his companions (Rom. 15:30–32; Cor. 1:11; Eph. 6:19–20; 2 Thess. 3:1). This s no shallow request; he knows the power of rayer and the value of enlisting fellow believrs in this aspect of a ministry partnership. There s an honor that comes with being asked to pray or someone, because it signals that a trust has een placed in you. Paul has prayed much for hese believers, and he continues to do so; but e is not above admitting his need to have othrs uphold him. Whether it be through prayer, inancial help, or volunteer aid, Paul is ever rateful for support. The request for prayer formed a bond of mutual intercession" (Wanaaker, 207) with the Thessalonian Christians.

Consistent with this notion of promoting olidarity with the believers is Paul's request hat they, on his behalf, "greet all the brothers vith a holy kiss" (v. 26; cf. Rom. 16:16; 1 Cor. 6:20; 2 Cor. 13:12). Culture dictates customs n these incidental practices; therefore, we vould be remiss if we were to accuse a church f being unbiblical that does not practice the oly kiss. The giving of a warm Christian reeting is what Paul is asking of them. This ractice of giving such greetings is easily ansferable into whatever the norms of one's ociety are for such expression—be it a firm andshake or a brotherly/sisterly hug.

Paul's last request is that the letter be read to ll the church (v. 27; cf. Col. 4:16). The importance of the letter being shared with all believrs is seen in Paul's "charge" or adjuring them o read it. Up to this point he has been content o use simple imperatives in his letter, but here e gives a solemn command to ensure that his vish be fulfilled. All the Thessalonian believrs are to be privy to the document; the whole hurch has been targeted for the instruction and encouragement found therein. Public reading would help to prevent any misinterpretation that might occur if a few attempted to summarize what they think Paul wanted others to know. It will also serve to further the bond of unity that the apostle wishes to promote.

The letter closes with the benediction that "the grace of our Lord Jesus Christ be with [them]" (v. 28; cf. Rom. 16:20; 2 Thess. 3:18). Although the formula is simply stated, it is nonetheless profound in its implications. Paul believes that grace is necessary and is sufficiently available for all Christians to live as God desires. He opened his letter with a similar pronouncement (1 Thess. 1:1) and now brings closure to its ministry with his recognition of the power of the grace provided through the Lord Jesus Christ.

INTRODUCTION TO 2 THESSALONIANS

Paul's second letter to the Thessalonians is in many respects similar to the first one sent after Timothy returned from his visit to investigate how the fledgling persecuted church was doing. Paul, Silas, and Timothy had to flee shortly after planting the church. After a period of great concern for their welfare and after frustrated attempts to return, Timothy managed to revisit the converts and minister strength and encouragement to them (1 Thess. 3:2). He reported to Paul about their persevering faith, the need for some direction regarding matters of conduct, and the importance of correcting some theological misunderstandings regarding the return of Christ (Parousia). In lieu of a personal visit, the first letter was designed to supply what was lacking in their faith (3:10).

However, through some source unknown to us, Paul soon gets wind of persistent problems; hence the similarity between the two letters. He writes again, encouraging them to endure persecution without worrying that God has abandoned them, and he reminds them of their hope of being part of God's kingdom (2 Thess. 1:4–12). Next, we can infer from Paul's own words that someone has upset the community of believers with some alarming teaching regarding the Day of the Lord. Not only is the teaching disruptive, it has been wrongly attributed to Paul (2:1–3). Paul's authentic teaching, either during his initial visit or in his first letter, has

While in Athens, Paul was brought before the Areopagus, the supreme council of the city, to explain his teachings. The council met on this rocky hill northwest of the Acropolis. The name Areopagus originally was the name of the hill but became the name of the council, even after it moved to a different site. Paul's speech, in Acts 17:22–31, can be read from the plaque on the stone structure at the bottom of the hill.

been misunderstood, disregarded, or twisted. He therefore needs to restore proper understanding.

Finally, some Thessalonian converts have disregarded Paul's directives about work habits in the first letter to such an extent that his sanctions are severe, intending to shame the deviants into conformity (3:6, 14–15). The major violation is a persisting in idleness, which is taxing the welfare of the church body.

The two letters were most likely written within the brief span of a few weeks or months. Thus Paul likely writes 2 Thessalonians around A.D. 51 while he is still ministering in Corinth.

OUTLINE OF 2 THESSALONIANS

1. **Salutation** (1:1–2)
2. **Paul's Thanksgiving** (1:3)
3. **Encouragement in Times of Persecution** (1:4–12)
   - **3.1.** Paul's Boast (1:4)
   - **3.2.** Evidence of Being Worthy (1:5)
   - **3.3.** Full Compensation Will Come (1:6–10)
   - **3.4.** Paul's Prayer (1:11–12)
4. **Correction Regarding the Day of the Lord** (2:1–3:5)
   - **4.1.** Discounting False News (2:1–2)
   - **4.2.** The Man of Lawlessness (2:3–8)
   - **4.3.** Mass Deception (2:9–12)
   - **4.4.** Security of the Saints (2:13–3:5)
5. **Directions Regarding Restoring the Idle** (3:6–15)
6. **Concluding Remarks** (3:16–18)

COMMENTARY ON 2 THESSALONIANS

1. Salutation (1:1–2)

Paul opens in his customary manner as he fo lows the basic letter-writing convention of h day (see comments on 1 Thess. 1:1). There a only two differences between the salutatior f the two letters. In verse 1 Paul refers to God s "our Father," whereas the pronoun "our" is ot used in 1 Thessalonians 1:1. Also, the pening greeting pronouncing "grace and eace" has in addition the source of blessing, vhich is "God the Father and the Lord Jesus Christ" (v. 2).

Any variance between the two salutations an simply be attributed to Paul's writing flex-bility; he is under no compulsion to adhere to strict formula. Thus no ramifications should e drawn from the differences, as if Paul is ttempting to make some theological point in e present letter over against the first one. lthough this pronouncement of grace and eace is standard for Paul's letters, it is in no ise a cliché. He knows how critical grace and eace are to the lifeblood of the community of elievers.

. Paul's Thanksgiving (1:3)

aul's declaration of thanksgiving is made omewhat more forceful by the use of "we ught always to" and "and rightly so." These wo elements, which are not part of the first let-er's thanksgiving section, indicate Paul's con-nued delight in the Thessalonians as trophies f God's grace. Previously Paul had expressed ratitude for their faith, love, and hope 1 Thess. 1:3); here he is pleased that their faith as not only held fast, but has been "growing nore and more." As well, Paul states that their ove has been increasing; it has not leveled ff.[11] Paul's concern about what was lacking in eir faith (3:10) has been partly assuaged, for is earlier challenge to love more and more 3:12; 4:10) has been met successfully. Little vonder that Paul is insistent about how thank-ul he, Silas, and Timothy ought to be for God's mighty work in Thessalonica.

. Encouragement in Times of Persecution (1:4–12)

The passing of the months between Paul's time n Thessalonica and the writing of this second ocument has not brought an end to the per-ecution. Nor has Jesus returned yet to rescue em from their hardships. Paul's first letter ontained words of encouragement, but he nderstands the need to sustain their morale vith further grounds for maintaining a positive utlook. He therefore commends them for eir perseverance, reminds them of God's perspective and his compensation, and assures them of his continuing prayerful interest in their well-being.

3.1. Paul's Boast (1:4)

In the previous letter Paul applauded the Thessalonians for their amazing testimony that had become so well known that he had no "need to say anything about it" (1 Thess. 1:8). Now he admits like a proud father that he and his partners have been boasting about the Thessalonians' remarkable endurance in the face of extreme adversity. This boasting matches the third part of the thanksgiving in the first letter ("endurance inspired by hope," 1:3).[12]

To hear about how their spiritual father has been bragging on their accomplishments would strengthen any flagging spirits. They realize that they have run the race brilliantly thus far; now is not the time to cower or quit. The power of a positive word fitly spoken (Prov. 25:11) can invigorate saints to press on in the face of difficulty. James warns about the destructive power of the tongue (James 3:3–12), but the tongue's powerful ability to inspire and bless should not be underestimated. Paul is at ease in complimenting the believers because he knows how much it means to be so encouraged. Blessed is the church that sincerely practices this use of the tongue.

3.2. Evidence of Being Worthy (1:5)

Endeavoring to encourage the saints further, Paul assures the Thessalonians that the experience of persecution is not a sign that God has forsaken them or is punishing them, or that such circumstances are beyond God's control. Paul shifts the perspective with a brief theology of suffering to show that although suffering is a harsh lot, it is part of the Christian's destiny (cf. 1 Thess. 3:3). There is some question whether the "evidence" Paul speaks of is the endurance of the believers, their experience of persecution, or a combination of both (cf. 2 Thess. 1:3). The NIV seeks to clarify with its rendering "all this is evidence," so that "all this" (words added in the NIV) includes both the persecution and the steadfast response to it.

Jesus apprised the disciples that persecution would come (John 15:20), and the early church not only passed on the same teaching (Acts 14:22) but experienced the fulfillment of Jesus' words. The New Testament letters uniformly present persecution not as some rare occurrence but as the norm in a world hostile to the kingdom of light (see comments on 1 Thess. 1:3; 3:3). Persecution for Jesus' sake is therefore an indicator of the rightness of God's judging of believers as worthy candidates for his kingdom.

The perseverance of the Thessalonians is likewise solid evidence that they are God's children (1 Thess. 3:3; cf. Rom. 5:1–4; Heb. 10:36). Ill winds are blowing forcefully on these Christians, but they are stalwart. Thus they demonstrate how well they understand the concept that it is exceedingly better to forfeit one's comfort and if necessary one's life, so as not to endanger one's soul (Mark 8:34–37).

3.3. Full Compensation Will Come (1:6–10)

To know that injustice of any sort will one day be corrected is a great boost to one's sense of well-being. God desires that justice should roll on like a river (Amos 5:24). His children can be sure that wickedness will not escape judgment, nor will righteousness go unrewarded.

Paul affirms both sides of God's justice. He first points to the negative side—those who trouble the Thessalonians will not get away with it (v. 6). This action of God should not be seen as a gleeful getting even with a pack of soulless brutes, although the simplicity of expression in verse 6 could lend itself to such a picture (also vv. 8–9; 2 Peter 2:12–17; Jude 10–13). Perhaps such biblical expressions are akin to the imprecatory psalms, which call for painful judgment on one's oppressors (e.g., Ps. 3; 58; 59) not because one is thirsty for blood but because one longs so passionately for God's justice to rescue his people from the wicked. The wages of sin will be paid by the persecutors—unless, of course, like for one named Saul, repentance should happen their way (Bruce, 154).

The positive side of God's justice is that his children will be rescued from all turmoil and adversity and be lavishly compensated for every tear (v. 7). Paul simply writes that they will be repaid with "relief" or rest (*anesis*). From the perspective of eternity Paul elsewhere describes his own troubles as "light and momentary" (2 Cor. 4:17), even though he admits how conflicts on the outside and fears within have prevented the experience of "rest" (*anesis*, 7:5).[13] The Christian life is fortified by meditation on eternal reward—there is indeed an eternal glor that outweighs all tribulations of life. Morri (201) rightly states that such meditation "is legitimate activity of the saints who are passin through trials." Jesus himself endorses the con templation of blessings in the afterlife when h encourages his disciples to rejoice and be gla even in tribulation because of the great rewar that heaven will be (Matt. 5:12).

By using the phrase "and to us as well (v. 7) Paul identifies with the Thessalonian he is not writing theoretical platitudes from th safety of an ivory tower. Paul took to heart th advice he delivered to the churches, for he wa well acquainted with the cost of followin Christ. Well-doing was not always applaude the resistance and fierce antagonism he face took a toll, but Paul never gave in. Th prospect of reaping in due season and of on day meeting his Lord made any price we worth paying (Rom. 8:18).

While immediate compensation for the righ teous and retribution for the wicked would b appealing, Paul makes no guarantee that an ultimate settling of accounts will occur until th Day of the Lord. The apostle describes that da in terms of a revelation (*apokalypsis*) of "th Lord Jesus . . . from heaven." Paul is not uniqu in encouraging his churches by appealing that magnificent day when Jesus is gloriousl revealed. In order to help his audience fin strength to endure their painful trials Pete writes, "But rejoice that you participate in th sufferings of Christ, so that you may be ove joyed when his glory is revealed" (1 Peter 4:1 see also 1:5; 5:1). The time is coming when th truth about Jesus Christ that has been reveale to believers by the Holy Spirit (Matt. 16:1 1 Cor. 2:10) will be recognized by all. Trag cally, the revelation of truth will then incrim nate the ungodly rather than be the source their salvation.

The Old Testament prophets expected th the Day of the Lord would be not only deliv erance for the righteous, but also final judg ment against the ungodly (Mal. 4:1–2; se comments on 1 Thess. 5:2). Employing hi fondness for triads (see comments on 1 Thes 2:10) Paul describes the attendant circum stances of this revelation in imagery evocativ of absolute authority. (1) At the head of his li is that Jesus will be revealed "from heaven. He will come from the seat of ultimate autho ity and majesty, the very sphere of God's habitation, the throne room of the kingdom of God (Acts 7:56; Heb. 1:3–4; 8:1; 12:2; Rev. 3:21). Jesus will return to establish finally the subjection of all that God has ordained for his Son (Heb. 2:7–8). At his incarnation he came without resistance as a lamb to be sacrificed; one day he will return as the Lion of Judah, whose authority cannot be resisted.

(2) The next aspect of the revelation is that it will be "in blazing fire." Fire can be symbolic of the Holy Spirit (1 Thess. 5:19), of God (Deut. 4:24), more specifically of God's judgment (Isa. 66:15–16; Jer. 21:12; 2 Peter 3:10, 12), and of the punishment of the wicked (Matt. 7:19; 25:41; Rev. 20:15). What follows in verses 8–9 makes clear the picture of God's judgment and the ensuing punishment of unbelievers.

(3) Paul's imagery of the splendor and of the omnipotent advent of Christ is rounded off with a third detail: Jesus is to be accompanied "with his powerful angels" (see comments on 1 Thess. 3:13).

The payback Paul spoke of earlier in verse 6 is detailed in verses 8–9 with the explanation of who deserves punishment and of what that punishment consists. The grammar here allows for the possibility of two categories of people whom God will punish: "those who do not know God" and those who "do not obey the gospel of our Lord Jesus." The former group could be identified as Gentiles, who Paul says have some knowledge of God but have refused to submit to him (Rom. 1:21–32; cf. Ps. 79:6), and the latter group would be the Jews who displease God (1 Thess. 2:14–16). However, it is not clear that Paul intends to distinguish two groups; both are described elsewhere in Scripture in terms of lacking knowledge and being disobedient (Hos. 5:4; Rom. 11:31–32). Paul may simply be using synonymous parallelism, with which he was so familiar because of his expertise in the Old Testament literature. Thus "those who do not know God are more precisely defined as 'those who disobey the gospel'" (Bruce, 151).

The punishment of these people will be "everlasting destruction" and exclusion "from the presence of the Lord" (v. 9). The terrible finality of their fate is clear—there will be no opportunity for a change of heart once judgment has come down. Some wish to ameliorate the calamitous scope of this punishment by theorizing that the disobedient will be annihilated from all existence. But as Wanamaker says (229), "there is no evidence in Paul (or the rest of the NT for that matter) for a concept of a final annihilation of the godless."

For Paul what makes their fate most tragic is that the ungodly will be shut out from enjoying the majestic and glorious presence of the Lord. It is the endurance-inspiring hope of all believers to bask someday in the splendor of God, once and for all free from the torment of one's old nature and able to behold the Savior face-to-face (v. 10). Our attempts to comprehend what it will be like fall far short of that reality, despite all the superlatives we might employ. Suffice it to say that we will be enraptured in such worship as we have never known. That is our destiny; but it is not the destiny of those without Christ, for they will be "shut out from the presence of the Lord." Rather than the appearance of Jesus being an event at which to marvel, it will mark the final judgment of condemnation. The ensuing response of the wicked is soberly conveyed in Jesus' description: "There will be weeping and gnashing of teeth" (Matt. 13:42).

Thus, while meditations on our future hope of glory inspire courage and endurance to run the race well (cf. Heb. 12:1–2), we must also be motivated to fulfill the Great Commission to the best of our Spirit-empowered ability. We must be faithful stewards redeeming the time, working to do our part in the harvesting of souls for the kingdom of God. Paul looked forward with great longing to be with Jesus, but he was also driven to share the good news of rescue from this eternal destruction. He spent his life with abandon in order to persuade all he met to bow their knees in submission to the Lordship of Christ. Paul had warned that the fire of the Spirit not be put out in the corporate worship settings (1 Thess. 5:19); we must avoid quenching the fire of the Holy Spirit, who empowers us to first and foremost be witnesses to all (Acts 1:8). The perishing must be rescued from the very fate we have escaped.

Paul has alleviated the distress of the innocently suffering Thessalonians with his review of the glorious eternal reward awaiting those who persevere. In addition he describes the terrible fate awaiting the wicked. He provides no timetable for the dispensing of rewards and punishments, except to say that full compensation will come on "the day" (v. 10). This word is the abbreviated form of the familiar eschatological concept of the "Day of the Lord" (see comments on 1 Thess. 5:2).

The apostle does not restrict himself to using any one formula, abbreviated or otherwise, when referring to these end-time events. He moves fluidly, interchanging the terms *coming* (*parousia*; 1 Thess. 2:19; 3:13; 4:15; 5:23; 2 Thess. 2:1, 8), *revealing* or *revelation* (*apokalypsis*; 1 Cor. 1:7; 2 Thess. 1:7), *appearing* (*phaneroo*; Col. 3:4) and *appearance* (*epiphaneia*; 2 Thess. 2:8; 1 Tim. 6:14; 2 Tim. 4:1, 8; Titus 2:13). It is because he previously had taught the converts the basics of what will transpire and what he knew of how the pieces fit together that he does not need to do anything more than remind and briefly clarify. We can assume the readers could make the proper connections for full understanding with the information they had received.

We would certainly enjoy a more systematic elaboration of the teaching. We must, however, cautiously make do with what we have and assume that God has given enough information in his Word for us to maintain a proper balance between serving him and awaiting his return. We know that the Day of the Lord will consist of a series of events, such as the rapture of the saints and the judgment of the wicked. It is concerning these events that various theories are presented to make the most sense of how exactly these events will transpire. One theory held by many Christians is that the coming of Jesus for his saints (1 Thess. 4:17; 2 Thess. 2:1) is the same as his coming with the saints (1 Thess. 3:13), when he comes to execute judgment on the nations.

Another popular theory suggests that there is an interval of time between the Rapture and the return of Christ to judge. This position further yields two possible interpretations on the length of this interval. One is that seven years will pass (Daniel's seventieth week; Dan. 9:24–27), which will include the Great Tribulation, when the Antichrist will be revealed and unleash an unparalleled reign of terror that will be cut short by his defeat at Armageddon upon the return of Jesus with his saints (Rev. 16:16; 17:14). The other interpretation is that the Antichrist will seize control of the world, reigning relatively peaceably for three-and-a-half years, but before things take a turn for the worst the Rapture occurs. Then after the next three-and-a-half years of tyranny Jesus returns to earth. Both these positions subscribe to the belief that when he returns with the saints, he will establish his millennial rule (Rev. 20:4–15), after which the judgment of all the wicked will be conducted.

It appears, then, that the Day of the Lord is to be seen not as a literal twenty-four-hour period. Rather, it can refer either to the whole scope of events God has ordained to transpire or to any one of its components. It is this fluidity of terminology, along with the difficulty of interpreting Revelation and some of the other prophetic literature, that results in differing views among Christians. Surely we have learned that one's personal understanding of the unfolding of end-time events is not the basis for being considered an equal brother or sister in Christ (for more detailed study of these and other interpretations, see R. Ludwigson, *A Survey of Bible Prophecy* [1973] and S. Horton, ed., *Systematic Theology: A Pentecostal Perspective* [1994]).

In verse 10b Paul reminds the Thessalonian Christians of their certain participation in the everlasting and glorious presence of Jesus at his return. They will be included in the great host of saints because "[they] believed" the gospel to which Paul had testified when with them. The expression "our testimony" is more than mere mental assent to a set of facts. As usual for Paul it implies faith in Christ, repentance and serving the living God (1 Thess. 1:9).

3.4. Paul's Prayer (1:11–12)

Regarding the Thessalonians Paul has much for which to be thankful (1:3–4), but the race set before them has not yet been completed. The apostle therefore continues to pray with fervor that all those who began the race will run it honorably so that "our God may count you worthy of his calling" (1:11; see also 1:5; Eph. 4:1; 1 Thess. 1:4; 2:12; 3:13–4:1). It is all too easy to misunderstand the issue of what constitutes the worthiness to which Paul refers. He is definitely not speaking about earning our salvation through works that attempt to convince God of our candidacy for worthiness. Such a concept nullifies the need for the sacrificial death of Jesus as the payment for the sin that had disqualified us from attain-ng worthy status. In ourselves we all fall short of God's perfect standard, but in Christ we are declared worthy.

Yet, for however much he defends the truth that works do not make the Christian righteous, Paul recognizes that there are works to be done; there is holiness to grow in; there is conduct that is appropriate for the child of God. Bruce writes (157): "If their Lord is to be glorified in them at his Advent, he must be glorified in their present way of life." To one degree or another all of the apostle's letters address the responsibilities of the Christian to pursue virtue and to represent Jesus with a blameless lifestyle (Phil. 2:15; 1 Thess. 3:13; 5:23). The entire Scriptures testify to the principle of fruit-bearing as evidence of genuine conversion (e.g., Matt. 3:8; 7:17; John 15:16; Rom. 7:4).

Paul thus longs for the Thessalonians to persevere constantly in the faith by enduring trials and eschewing evil, finally being deemed worthy of their calling. It is to this end that he intercedes for them. Little need be said about how Christian leaders can adopt this and other Pauline prayers as models of prayer for the saints under their care. One dare not assume the position of leadership if one does not assume the posture of habitual prayer.

While the responsibility of living the worthy life may be great, Paul reminds us that God's power is available to "fulfill every good purpose of yours and every act prompted by your faith" (v. 11; see comments at 1 Thess. 1:3 on the expression "work of faith"). Paul has in view here the power that God makes available to us through the Holy Spirit (on this provision of power to live the Christian life, see comments on 1 Thess. 4:8). As Christians we can be much encouraged that God's great work in us did not diminish after our conversion; how much more will his power that brought us from death to life continue to enable us to walk in his ways!

In verse 12 Paul bares his heart, for underlying his prayers for the Thessalonians is his intense desire that the "Lord Jesus may be glorified in you, and you in him." It is truly an amazing thought that he who has been glorified by God himself (John 17:1–5) can be glorified even further by those he came to save. The successful work of the cross is magnified by each person who is born again. Another New Testament writer describes how Jesus was able to endure the cross because of the joy set before him (Heb. 12:2). Surely that joy consisted not only of the knowledge of his future exaltation, but also of knowing that there would be countless souls over many generations who would turn to him for salvation. There is rejoicing in heaven over one sinner who repents (Luke 15:7, 10), and glory continues to come to Jesus with the conversion of each soul (John 17:10). As each Christian lives a life worthy of his or her calling, that person also brings glory to God (John 15:8).

Saints also enjoy a measure of glory now as they experience in part the benefits of being the dearly loved children of God (John 17:22; 1 John 3:1). The day is coming when the experience will be total, and complete glorification will be achieved at the appearance of the Lord (Rom. 8:23; 1 Cor. 15:42–44). Paul's prayer reminds the readers of the bigger picture of future reward. Oftentimes circumstances tend to blur one's vision and erode resolve, but this reminder serves to stimulate perseverance and fidelity to the calling. There will one day be a great reversal as persecution gives way to glory and sorrow and hardship turn to joy and delight. As Paul often does, he states that this final turnabout is due entirely to "the grace of our God and the Lord Jesus Christ."

4. Correction Regarding the Day of the Lord (2:1–3:5)

After encouraging the Thessalonians through his expression of gratitude for them, through the description of their future reward, and through his prayer for their ultimate glorification, Paul turns to his main purpose. He must correct a serious misunderstanding about the Parousia. Despite the eschatology he taught in person and later in his first letter, some false teaching has been introduced. Perhaps it is a mistaken interpretation of his earlier instruction that has unsettled the Thessalonian believers. He must first rebut the teaching or wrong interpretation, then clarify the truth about the Day of the Lord.

4.1. Discounting False News (2:1–2)

According to the Greek text Paul begins his discussion with the phrase "we ask you, brothers." He uses the verb *erotao* (also in 1 Thess. 5:12), which can essentially mean the same as *parakaleo* ("to urge," see 2 Thess. 3:12; also

Rom. 12:1). In his preamble to his request the apostle states that his concern is about "the coming [*parousia*] of our Lord" and the ensuing gathering of the saints (*episynagoge*; cf. Mark 13:26–27; 1 Thess. 4:14–17).

In verse 2 Paul gets to the heart of the matter as he urges the Thessalonians not to panic that they have somehow missed the coming of the Day of the Lord. Paul is asking them to be sure to toe the line on his previous teaching, as is seen in the two parts of his graphic request. (1) They are "not to become easily unsettled." Paul uses the verb *saleuo* ("to shake, agitate") and identifies the mind (*noos*) as that which one ought not allow to be agitated. Bruce's translation here is lively and catches the thrust of Paul's point (161): "We beg you not to be quickly shaken out of your wits." (2) The verb "alarmed" (*throeo*) adds to the overall picture of a group of Christians sorely terrified by some wrong teaching.

Paul does not identify precisely the origin of this false news in his listing of three possible sources. (1) The NIV translates the first as "by some prophecy" (lit., "by a spirit," i.e., a spirit-inspired utterance). Here is a case where Paul's directions to discern the validity of prophecies needed to be followed (1 Thess. 5:21–22; see comments). In a community of believers enduring persecution and one that has been taught to be prepared for the Lord's return, it would not be unexpected to have some spiritually charged individuals giving words of prophecy pertaining to their plight.

Bruce gives two possibilities for understanding what Paul means here (163): "The prophecy might be a false prophecy or it might be a genuine prophecy misunderstood." Conceivably one or more Christians may have prophesied that the Day of the Lord had begun. Meanwhile the saints had not been rescued from persecution, and Jesus had not been seen gathering them to be with him. Had they missed out? Little wonder that panic could set in with those who were convinced by this type of news.

(2) Another possible source Paul lists is that of a "report" (lit., "through a word"). Assuming this term is distinguishable from a prophetic word, it is likely that Paul has in mind something orally taught or preached.

(3) The final possible origin of the misinformation is a "letter supposed to have come from" Paul or his colleagues. Some commentators prefer to see this as a reference to his first letter (so Marshall, 187), and certainly the Greek grammar here does not rule out that it could be a genuine letter (Bruce, 164). Someone may have misinterpreted something the apostle said or wrote; but if that was what he meant, he could have stated so more explicitly (note how he handles a misunderstanding of a previous letter in 1 Cor. 5:9–11). Also, his emphasis on the genuineness of this letter (3:17) seems to be a reaction to someone wrongly using Paul's authority (Bruce, 164).

4.2. The Man of Lawlessness (2:3–8)

Whether false teachers are upsetting the Thessalonians (as in Gal. 1:7–9; Phil. 3:2) or sincere Christians are mistaken in matters concerning the future is not specified by Paul. What is crucial to him is that the Christians must not be deceived by any teaching contrary to what he has told them before or to what he will explain further (2 Thess. 3:14). Paul uses an intense form of the verb "deceive" (i.e., "utterly deceive"). Like a caring spiritual parent, Paul is protective of the welfare of his converts (1 Thess. 2:7–12). Deceit must be excised immediately before its damage becomes irreparable.

Paul's remedy is to allude to and elaborate on his previous teaching. He begins by stating in no uncertain terms that the "day [of the Lord] will not come until the rebellion occurs and the man of lawlessness is revealed." We must recognize that simple references to "the rebellion" and to "the man of lawlessness" would immediately be grasped by the Thessalonian readers since they had prior teaching (2:5) as a framework for understanding. It would have been satisfying for our curiosity if Paul had explicitly detailed how verses 3–8 fit into the material concerning the Rapture discussed in 1 Thessalonians 4:15–17. However, since we are not privy to this additional and fuller teaching, our conjectures must proceed cautiously, employing the evidence of other relevant Scriptures.

The two signs that Paul says must happen first are not necessarily mutually exclusive; it is "probable that one complex event is in mind" (Marshall, 188). The term *rebellion* (*apostasia*) denotes a falling away or apostasy, and for Paul to label it simply as "the rebellion" lends credence to the notion that it is a technical term given to an expected falling away of unprecedented proportions. In his lengthy discussion of the signs pointing to the end of the age Jesus says, "At that time many will turn away from the faith and will betray and hate each other" (Matt. 24:10). Some years later, Paul, writing to Timothy, lists a number of fruits of rebellion or godlessness that will mark the last days (2 Tim. 3:1–5).

According to Bruce (167), this rebellion Paul speaks of is likely "a general abandonment of the basis of civil order . . . a large-scale revolt against public order." Perhaps that may be part of the general construct, for we must recognize how heavily Paul seems to be borrowing at several points from the tradition recorded in Matthew 24.[14] There Jesus specifies a falling away from the faith (Matt. 24:15), but he does compare the social atmosphere at the time of his coming to that of Noah's day prior to the Flood (24:37–39)—it was a time of great wickedness, violence, and corruption (Gen. 6:5, 11–12). This is clearly a picture of the lack of civil order.

Along with the turning against God comes the revealing of "the man of lawlessness." Although Paul does not use the term *Antichrist* here, it is clear that he is the one whom John calls "antichrist" (1 John 2:18) and "the beast" (Rev. 19:19–20; see Bruce's helpful excursus on the Antichrist, 179–88). Some have suggested that Paul's willingness to use the verb *apokalypto* (the same root is used in 1:7 regarding Jesus) is proof of the supernatural preexistence of this figure, as if he were Satan incarnate. No doubt there is a supernatural source behind his ability to deceive, to perform miracles, and to set himself up to be worshiped. But to be the agent of Satan is a far cry from being Satan born in the flesh. Before Paul describes the program of this archenemy of God, he wants to make abundantly clear the encouraging news that this opponent is "doomed to destruction" (KJV: "son of perdition"; cf. John 17:12).

In verse 4 Paul aligns himself with the prophecy of Daniel, who had the vision of one who would "speak against the Most High and oppress his saints" (Dan. 7:25) and who would cause the "rebellion that causes desolation" in the temple of God (8:13). The precursor of this end-time figure was Antiochus Epiphanes IV, who desecrated the Most Holy Place and later, in 167 B.C., set up a pagan altar right in the Jewish temple. Yet Jesus in his Olivet Discourse makes it clear that there will still be a fulfillment of Daniel's prophecy (Matt. 24:15), and Paul adheres to that tradition when he writes how this archenemy will set "himself up in God's temple, proclaiming himself to be God."

Thus, Paul identifies the Antichrist's underlying motive in his determined rise to prominence—he aims to usurp God. Paul does not attempt to identify who this person is or from where he will come. He does not specify if he expected one of the Roman emperors to be the Antichrist, although in their day the seat of the emperor provided the most likely scenario for such a character. What is important to the apostle, and therefore for modern readers as well, is that this man is absolutely evil and has a deluded agenda to be worshiped in the place of God.

Verse 5 appears to be a "gentle criticism" (Marshall, 192) of the readers who ought to remember the details Paul is reviewing. It is precisely because he "used to tell" them these things that he need only write in general terms that would trigger their recollection of his more extensive teaching. Unfortunately, we are without the benefit of this prior instruction, but the broad strokes yield for us a big picture that can still be recognized; it is one that moves us to be prepared to stand firm until we ourselves meet the Lord.

In verse 6 Paul claims that his readers already "know what is holding [the man of lawlessness] back." When he was with them, the apostle had explained why this man had not yet been able to make his appearance—it is not "the proper time." From that phrase we can infer that God is the One who sets the limits to this final show of opposition; it is his timetable that the Antichrist must keep. So while Paul speaks of a coming period of terrible opposition, Christians can take heart in knowing that, despite appearances to the contrary, God is in total control.

The apostle then acknowledges that "the secret power of lawlessness is already at work" (v. 7). The sense in which this power is secret is that wickedness in its fullness has not yet had a chance to reign as supremely or as openly as Satan would want. It has not been revealed to humankind the havoc that unchecked evil can wreak. But the measure of evil that presently does exist should be an ample deterrent for Christians to stand firm and to seek aggressively the rescue of others—this world desperately needs the salt and light Christians can bring. Sin is an active principle, opposing vigorously the kingdom of God and enslaving many. Paul's thought that lawlessness is already at work is similar to John's declaration that in this hour the coming Antichrist has already been preceded by many antichrists (1 John 2:18).

If this power is already at work, when will the Antichrist himself be revealed? As we can expect, Paul is not going to answer by pointing to a calendar, but he does point to God's private agenda. Paul picks up the thread he introduced in verse 6 regarding something that is restraining or holding back the Antichrist until God decides to remove the present restrictions on evil. There he referred to this withholding in impersonal terms ("what is withholding him"), while in verse 7 he refers to "the one who now holds it back," implying that a person is the agent of the restraint.

Again, Paul's readers know specifically what he means, whereas we must grapple in the dusk of speculation. Out of this groping have arisen numerous theories as to the identification of this force (v. 6) and person (v. 7) of restraint. Some scholars argue that Paul is speaking cryptically of the relative peace and order of the Roman empire and emperor so as not to incite further political sanction (Acts 17:6–9) against the Christians in case the letter was to get into the wrong hands. Others suggest that Paul is referring to the work of the Holy Spirit, for the Greek noun for "spirit" (*pneuma*) can take either a neuter or masculine pronoun (see Marshall's discussion of seven theories and his evaluations, 196–200). Regardless of which theory we hold, the bottom line is that God is ultimately in control; he is the one who establishes the times and seasons, and when he so decides that restraint will be removed.

Paul has effectively established that God is the architect of the last days. He then states, for the third time, that this "lawless one will be revealed" (v. 8; also in vv. 3, 6). All three uses of the verb "reveal" (*apokalypto*) are in the passive voice, thus emphasizing that the Antichrist cannot overrule God's timetable and enter the stage prematurely. The first two uses of this verb occur in the context of God' schedule for when he can be revealed; the thir addresses the fate awaiting the Antichrist onc he is revealed: He will be overthrown an destroyed.

The imagery in the phrase "overthrow wit the breath of his mouth" is reminiscent of Isa iah's words, "with the breath of his lips he wi slay the wicked" (Isa. 11:4), and of John' vision, "out of his mouth comes a sharp swor with which to strike down the nations" (Rev 19:15). Obviously the imagery is not intende to be taken literally; there will not be a litera sword coming from the Lord's mouth, nor wi his breath in a mighty blast of exhalatio destroy his enemies. Rather, the word of judg ment from his mouth will seal the fate of hi enemies.

When the writer of Hebrews speaks of th word of God being powerful and sharper tha a two-edged sword (Heb. 4:12), it is in the con text of warning and promise—to ignore th warning seals one's fate of being barred fro entering God's eternal rest (4:1–3). God' word or pronouncement is irresistible; it can not be appealed, ignored, or compromised. Al who are children of lawlessness will be con demned for opposing God through their dis obedience. Satan and all who are in hi employ, regardless of their brief surge o power, wickedness, and deception, can merel oppose God—they will never conquer. Thei rebellion will be soundly quelled by Almight God; the Antichrist and Satan himself will on day be removed (Rev. 20:10), and th redeemed of the Lord will forever experienc the glory of God and the fellowship of thei Lord and Savior.

4.3. Mass Deception (2:9–12)

Before that new day dawns, "the lawles one" will do what he can to oppose God. I verse 9 Paul speaks of this Antichrist's comin with the Greek noun *parousia,* which has s generally been used to refer to Christ's adven that the technical term *Parousia* has bee coined to speak of Jesus' return. Paul's will ingness to use terms like *revealing* and *comin* here appear to be a parallel to or a "parody o Christ's Parousia" (Bruce, 173). Perhaps he i attempting to portray the Antichrist as "Satan' messiah, an infernal caricature of the true mes siah" (Moffatt, 49). If so, then the apostle's ref erence to the incredible works Satan empowers this person to do ("miracles, signs and wonders") may be a triad borrowed from traditional material regarding the ministry of Jesus (Acts 2:22). At the very least Paul may simply be reworking the warning of Jesus about false Christs who "will appear and perform great signs and miracles" (Matt. 24:24).

The Antichrist is going to be effective in convincing many to follow and worship him (vv. 4, 10). A key to his persuasion is the ability to perform miracles; many will be attracted to these supernatural manifestations, which Paul calls "counterfeit" (*pseudos*; lit., "false"). These miracles are counterfeit not because they are staged or fake. Scripture gives every indication that they are genuinely supernatural (Matt. 24:24; Rev. 13:12–14; 19:20). They are counterfeit because they are not trustworthy signs that the agent is divine—they are false claims to deity.

Unfortunately, as Paul states in verse 10, many people will be deceived. The wicked intent of Satan, represented by the phrase "every sort of evil," is masked by the facade of wonder. In their astonishment at these signs people will yield to the leadership of the evil miracle worker. Paul's wording here is notable, for he modifies those who will be deceived as "those who are perishing." In other words, those who are duped are merely being carried further along the path on which they have chosen to travel: the path of disobedience. Their "unbelief has made them gullible" (Bruce, 173).

When Jesus speaks of false Christs performing miracles, he says the intent is "to deceive even the elect"; but his next words, "if that were possible" (Matt. 24:24), are testimony to the keeping power of God on behalf of his children. Paul does not debate whether God's elect can be deceived at that time; instead, he emphasizes that all who are deceived and take the path of destruction do so willingly. They have made a prior choice to reject the truth of God. As Jesus said, "Men loved darkness instead of light" (John 3:19). It is because of their refusal to serve God that he "sends them a powerful delusion" (2 Thess. 2:11) by which they will believe "the lie" (cf. Rom. 1:25). The word "lie" (*pseudos*) is the same word as that used in verse 9, where it denoted the powerful but counterfeit workings of the evil one. Thus "the lie" that so many will accept as truth is that the Antichrist is worthy of their allegiance; he will be seen as a messiah.

A difficult concept for modern readers to grasp is that God is active in this regression into delusion ("God sends them a powerful delusion," v. 11), as if he is encouraging rather than discouraging it. Old Testament passages pose similar problems for us. For example, God hardens Pharaoh's heart, thus delaying Israel's exodus from Egypt (Ex. 7:3; 10:16–20); the Lord approves the use of a lying spirit to lure Ahab into a fatal battle (1 Kings 22:20–22). God's ways are certainly inscrutable at times, and so we must be careful how we interpret the ancient mindset that understood God to be actively involved in control of good *and* evil—so much so that the writers could, without fear of blasphemy, write about how God allowed Satan to have restricted freedom to torment (Job 1:12; 2:6) and how God could bring a deep sleep over disobedient Israel so they would not grasp the truth (Isa. 29:10).

Elsewhere Paul speaks of God's giving over of sinful humanity to their desires (Rom. 1:26, 28), a notion one might wrongly construe as a mean-spirited and vindictive act on his part. However, to accuse God of wrongdoing is a sign of misunderstanding just how much he has done to turn humankind to his ways. God does not force people down a path they do not want to take, nor does he idly watch as people choose the path of error. God is most actively intervening to demonstrate his love to sinners (Rom. 5:8); he sets up all manner of detours of grace, which are designed to reroute the sinner to avoid destruction (2:4; 2 Peter 3:15–16).

But we also know that God honors the gift of free will; tragically, it is a gift many choose to abuse. Any "hardening of heart" or sending of delusion is an act of rightful judgment (Ps. 51:4; Rom. 2:2). C. S. Lewis, in his attempt to reconcile the concepts of hell and the mercy of God, says that the condemned will "enjoy forever the horrible freedom they have demanded, and are therefore self-enslaved" (*The Problem of Pain,* 115–16). We dare not dispute God's justice—the wages of sin is still death (Rom. 6:23; 9:19–20). A holy God can be trusted to make absolutely fair judgments.

Sadly, as Paul puts it in his conclusion about this work of the Antichrist, the wicked do not only reject the truth. In what seems like a perverse answer to God's outpouring of love, the wicked "have delighted in wickedness" (v. 12). Writing to the Romans the apostle elaborates on humankind's descent into depravity, insofar as the truth of God is exchanged for a lie. There is no shame demonstrated by those living in decadence, and incredibly, approval is given to those who practice unbridled freedom (Rom. 1:25–32). Condemnation is their lot.

Paul's discussion regarding the man of lawlessness is sobering. He has been deliberately cautious in explaining how this epitome of evil will operate; he takes pains to offset any reference to this man and his treacherous work by alluding frequently to God's control of the whole scenario and by assuring his readers of the ultimate fate of the Antichrist and all who serve him. In so doing, the apostle not only clarifies the eschatology for the Thessalonians, he also as their pastor consoles his readers. They can take heart, for the Day of the Lord is yet to come; and when it does, the relatively brief but astonishingly wicked career of the Antichrist will fail to usurp God and will result in his eternal destruction. The Thessalonian Christians can thus still comfort one another with the truth that they will be with the Lord forever (1 Thess. 4:17–18).

Today's Christians can also take heart from Paul's words. We humbly confess the difficulty in piecing together the precise details of chronology and in understanding apocalyptic literature. What is to be taken symbolically and what is to be taken literally? Paul wishes the Thessalonians to live in the blessed hope of the Parousia of Jesus. Two millennia have obscured some of what the Thessalonians knew, but the expectation of Christ's return is still one of the key and thrilling tenets of our faith. This hope gives strength to serve, resolve to persevere, incentive to lead worthy lives, and passion to evangelize. We join with Paul in his heart's cry, *Marana tha!* ("Come, O Lord!"; 1 Cor. 16:22).

One final point arises here; it is a side issue but nonetheless one to be noted. Paul's teaching provides us with a check regarding being wise about the power of lawlessness that is at work in our world. Satan is diligently active in blinding eyes from the glorious truth of the gospel (2 Cor. 4:4). He aims to destroy the work of God (John 10:10; 1 Peter 5:8). In his first letter Paul charged the Thessalonians t test everything (1 Thess. 5:21). The devil' work is often subtle, and we require the discernment of the Holy Spirit to enable us to recognize his schemes.

The apostle outlines how many will b deceived by the miracles energized by Satan Today with the resurgence of interest in th supernatural world Christians must be wary o automatically attributing credibility to anyon who demonstrates miraculous signs. If Sata can masquerade as an angel of light (2 Co 11:14), Christians ought to be vigilant and pra fervently for discernment. The test of fruit bearing can take time to conduct (Matt. 7:20) but the church is obligated to do so in order t hold to the good and "avoid every kind of evil" (1 Thess. 5:22). The following solemn word of Jesus compel us to rely heavily on the powe of the Holy Spirit: "Many will say to me o that day, 'Lord, Lord, did we not prophesy i your name, and in your name drive out demon and perform many miracles?' Then I will te them plainly, 'I never knew you. Away fron me, you evildoers!'" (Matt. 7:22–23).

4.4. Security of the Saints (2:13–3:5)

Paul has just dealt with some serious matters; he now continues with one of the thread of that discussion—the thread of eternal destiny. He has discussed the fate of the wicke and appears eager now to offset that discussio with a more positive emphasis on the glory o being a child of God. It is odd for the apostl to shift to a thanksgiving section at this poin in the letter. Ancient letter format usuall included the thanksgiving section as part of th introduction. What makes it even odder is tha the first part of verse 13 is practically identica to 1:3. Why does Paul repeat himself?

Marshall (205) suspects that this thanksgiving section "is meant to be an antidote to th feelings of uncertainty aroused by the suggestion that the Last Day had already come." T that we can add that perhaps in light of th heavy-handed discussion of the destructio awaiting the wicked, Paul naturally bursts int expressing gratitude because these converts i Thessalonica will be exempt from such a destiny. Paul was a soul-winner who cared deepl for people to be rescued from the comin wrath (1 Thess. 1:10). He can rejoice that on day righteousness will flourish and evil will b

• more, but he takes no delight in the knowl-ge that so many people will face condem-.tion. Therefore, he works relentlessly to angelize.

As a result, Paul expresses his happy oblig-ion to thank God always for the turnabout in e Thessalonian believers. He addresses them ith a more tender personal tone than in 1:3 as calls them "brothers loved by the Lord." It ay be that recalling what they have been ved from compels him to think so fondly of em here. He speaks of God's act of choosing em (see comments on 1 Thess. 1:4; 4:7; 24) "from the beginning," thus denoting the nfidence Christians can have that God's ernal purposes will bear fruit—his master an is unfolding.

The agency through which the salvation of lievers is brought is twofold. (1) Paul points the "sanctifying work of the Spirit" (see mments on 1 Thess. 4:3–4, 7). It is possible at the Greek word *pneuma* denotes the man spirit here, thus yielding the translation hrough the sanctification of [your] spirit." ut that is not the referent here. The NIV has operly rendered Paul's concept of the role of e Holy Spirit in sanctification. (2) While the ork of the Holy Spirit is essential, so too is e response of the person called—one must lieve "the truth" (see comments on 1:10; cf. e contrast in 2:10–11 to those who reject the uth and believe the lie).

In verse 14 Paul builds on the schema of od's choosing the Thessalonians. He uses the rb *kaleo* here ("called"; 1 Thess. 2:12; 4:7; 24), a verb that goes hand in hand with the act choosing. The distinction is that God *chose* em from the beginning, whereas the *calling* fers to "the initial summons to faith" (Mar-all, 208). The means by which God sum-oned the Thessalonians was the preaching of ul's ministry team. The apostle recognizes e critical role Christians must play in faith-lly sharing the good news. Christians must be ithful stewards (1 Thess. 2:4) because, as Paul powerfully reasons, the lost cannot call on e Lord to be saved unless someone is sent to each so they can have opportunity to hear and lieve (Rom. 10:13–15).

Salvation implies two things: a being saved om something—God's "coming wrath" Thess. 1:10; cf. 5:9)—and a being saved to mething—sharing or obtaining "the glory of our Lord Jesus Christ" (2 Thess. 2:14; cf. 1:10; also 1 Thess. 2:12; 4:17; 5:9–10). As Christians we can rejoice in God's merciful love that has reached out to us and brought us into his marvelous kingdom of light (1 Peter 2:9), where we now experience lavish blessings of grace and provision. We presently enjoy close fellowship with our Lord Jesus, but the day is coming when we will fully share in his glory as we see him face to face (cf. 1 John 3:2). Such glorious hope enables us to meet life's challenges with resolve and helps us abide by Paul's instructions to stand firm and hold onto the truth (2 Thess. 2:15).

The imperative "stand firm" is a typical component of Paul's exhortations (1 Thess. 3:8; cf. Phil. 1:27; 4:1), expressing great passion for his converts. He longs to see them fight the good fight of faith; he can bear no casualties without his heart being wrenched. There are many snares along the Christian path—temptations to indulge the flesh, to allow inappropriate attitudes to flourish unchecked, and to cave in to the pressures of adversity and persecution. Paul is neither paranoid nor pessimistic; he is a realist who prescribes preventative measures to promote the welfare of his spiritual children. Paul gives the Thessalonians one of the most integral strategies for standing firm: "hold to the teachings we passed on to you." The noun translated "teachings" is *paradosis,* which literally means "a handing over, hence tradition" (cf. Rom. 6:17).

For some Christians in evangelical circles the idea of tradition is a negative one, smacking of lifeless formalism and dead orthodoxy. The fact that Paul uses the term so positively should force one to reconsider being narrow-minded. One has only to read carefully the tradition recorded in Paul's letters to see how vibrantly he presents the exciting truth of the gospel. It is not uncommon for him to wander off into praise in mid-thought as he weaves his tapestry of tradition (2 Cor. 9:15; Eph. 1:14; Phil. 1:11).

The tradition Paul speaks of is that which has been "passed on" (lit., "taught") to the Thessalonians either "by word of mouth or by letter." This refers to the teaching given during his initial ministry visit, to the previous letter, and perhaps also to the content of this second letter. The Thessalonians were quick to receive Paul's gospel and subsequent teaching (1 Thess. 2:13;

4:1, 6; 5:2; 2 Thess. 1:10; 2:5). Without a standard body of Christian doctrine and ethics Christianity would have been doomed to the fate of syncretism. The gospel would have been diluted with pagan additives until what was left is no gospel at all (Gal. 1:6–7). With no New Testament yet written, the peril of heresy was constant, and a firm appeal to tradition was necessary. As seen earlier in 2 Thessalonians 2:2, the threat of false teaching was present and needed the remedy of a return to apostolic instruction.

We face the dilemma of ascertaining what is genuine biblical tradition and what is denominational preference regarding certain matters of belief and conduct. History shows how easily encrustation can occur as church practices evolve and become tantamount to inspired Scripture. Battle lines are then drawn between sincere Christian groups. Whenever one group's sacred cows are not revered by another group, it is profitable for both parties to reassess both Scripture and doctrine and make sure that the errors of legalism on the one hand and compromise on the other are avoided. As realists we understand that honest attempts to ignore minor differences have fallen short. Even among groups claiming to be Spirit-filled these efforts fall short—minor differences have proved to be much more than minor.

Denominations will always be with us until the Parousia! Those who baptize by immersion will be suspicious of those who sprinkle. Those who speak in tongues will look askance at those who do not. Those who do not allow women to be ordained ministers will rankle those who do. The list goes on! Perhaps as we admit that these differences will continue, we can then thank God sincerely that those who differ are not our real enemies. They are brothers and sisters in Christ. Therefore, perhaps we need to focus on the happy obligation of Paul's thanksgiving: "We ought always to thank God" for each other (2:13).

Verses 16–17 constitute the prayer wish so typically a feature of ancient letter writing. We might expect it to be placed in the concluding remarks, but Paul is flexible. As in the first letter, he injects a prayer wish both in the body of his letter and at the conclusion (1 Thess. 3:11–13; 5:23; 2 Thess. 3:16). Such a deviation from standard letter-writing convention suggests that Paul is earnest as he rises above trite, cliché practices. The warmth of his prayer most evident as he exults in the divine love a grace that "gave us eternal encouragement a good hope." Both of these gifts are apropos f the Thessalonians since encouragement w help them persevere through persecution a hope will maintain their eternal perspective future glory.

Paul then specifies his wish for the The salonians that this lavish grace will continue "encourage" and "strengthen" them (v. 17; c 3:3; also 1 Thess. 3:8). One of the ways t Lord encourages believers is through the fe lowship of the saints, who are to spur o another on (1 Thess. 5:11). It is incumbent every member of the body of Christ to do wh he or she can to comfort, console, and supp other members of the family of God. The ra has not yet been completed, and until it i God's grace is a daily staple for survival a success. Wanamaker (271) comments on ho Paul shows his concern for "the inward state his converts" (encouraged hearts) and for the "outward behavior." Every word and deed is be worthy of their calling (1 Thess. 2:12 God's strength is needed for this life of hol ness (3:13), and the Thessalonians can b secure in knowing that God will meet the every need (2 Thess. 2:17).

Although a chapter break has been intro duced at this point, the transition is not to completely new discussion. The material 3:1–5 still contains elements pertaining to th security of the saints as they persevere Christ. Paul does move from his prayer wis for his readers to requesting prayer for himse and his colleagues. He also did this in his fir letter (see comments on 5:25) but only in th most general of fashions. Here, however, h specifies two related petitions.

(1) The first request reveals much abo Paul's passion—his ultimate concern is for th kingdom of God. When Paul dreams, he do not envision personal profit or acclaim; h dreams of winning more people to the faith. H therefore asks that the gospel "may sprea rapidly and be honored." The Greek word f "spread rapidly" (*trecho*) literally means " run." Paul is comfortable with using spor imagery (1 Tim. 6:12; 2 Tim. 2:5; 4:7), but he it may be that he is borrowing the metaphor the psalmist: "He sends his command to th earth; his word runs swiftly" (Ps. 147:15).

Paul's point is clear: He longs for the rapid dvance of the gospel, that it may "speed on" Bruce, 197). All hindrances to effective evan-elism must be torn down through prayer, and Paul enlists the Thessalonians to participate the future effectiveness of his ministry. He lso compliments them, for he sees them as the leal harvest—they received the message with onor immediately and became models of faith roughout the land (1 Thess. 1:7–8). If only l preaching points would yield the same fine sults!

(2) Paul's other request is for the personal fety of his ministry team, "that we may be elivered from wicked and evil men" (v. 2). aul never had the luxury of trouble-free min-try. From the outset one of his valuable min-try abilities was that of fleeing from or nduring persecution. From his first endeavors Damascus, where he had to escape in a bas-et (Acts 9:25; 2 Cor. 11:32–33), to his trip to hessalonica (Acts 17:5–10), and later on his nal trip to Jerusalem, Paul was a marked man. he credentials he lists in his catalogue of suf-rings are impressive (2 Cor. 11:23–28).

Note therefore that this second request does ot betray an aversion to hardship; he is not oking for an easy road of personal comfort. is concern is that the gospel will not be owed down by the work of evil men who ppose Paul. As he demonstrates time and gain, he is willing to take his licks so long as e gospel can be promoted (Phil. 1:12–14). he comment "for not everyone has faith" is explanatory comment on why there can be is opposition; it comes from those who are ostile to the truth of the gospel (see comments n 1 Thess. 2:14–16).

After stating his two requests, Paul makes grand statement of affirmation: "The Lord is ithful" (v. 3; cf. 1 Thess. 5:24). This state-ent of trust is a fine bridge between his belief at the Lord will answer the Thessalonians' ayer for him, and his shift back to his con-ern for them that the Lord "will strengthen nd protect you from the evil one." Paul's ayer has just been that they will be strength-ned (2:17), and he now demonstrates his faith at the Lord will indeed grace them with rength. Next he mentions the issue of pro-ction "from the evil one," assuring them that od will protect his children from encounter-g more than they can handle. God's daily supply of grace is sufficient for each believer to meet life's challenges; meanwhile, behind the scenes, God's grace is also working to shield us from insurmountable trials.

The expression "from the evil one" can also be translated simply "from evil" (see KJV). The same Greek expression is used in the Lord's Prayer (Matt. 6:13), where the NIV also translates "from the evil one." Our recitations of the Lord's Prayer may be more used to the simpler rendering "from evil," but there is not much difference in the two possible translations. Both amount to the same thing, for we recognize that behind evil is the father of evil; to be protected from the evil one is to be shielded from his destructive schemes.

In verse 4 the apostle explicitly states, "We have confidence in the Lord." The object of his trust is the obedience of the Thessalonians. In 2:15 he charged them to hold to the teachings that included not only theological truths (e.g., regarding the Parousia) but also ethical imperatives. For his readers this statement functions as affirmation and encouragement to continue in obedience to the truth they have received and are now receiving in this letter.

Verse 5 constitutes another prayer wish that is similar to the previous one (2:16–17) and is born naturally out of his pastoral concern for their spiritual welfare. He invokes the Lord to "direct [their] hearts." The verb "to direct" (*kateuthyno*) or "to make straight" is used in its simple form (*euthyno*) in the Gospel account of John the Baptist's calling to "make straight the way for the Lord" (John 1:23). The Lord will direct our paths, for as the good shepherd (John 10:11) he can be trusted to lead and protect (Ps. 23:1–3).

Paul lists two locations into which the Thessalonians' hearts need direction. The first is the sphere of "God's love." Paul is referring to the whole gamut of that love, which chose and called them, which provided redemption in the sacrifice of his Son, and which has prepared a splendid future inheritance for his children. Paul prays elsewhere that believers will comprehend something of the unfathomable dimensions of divine love (Eph. 3:18–19), and he portrays the security this love provides: Nothing can separate the Christian from this love (Rom. 8:38–39).

The second location into which the Thessalonians' hearts need direction is that of

"Christ's perseverance." The KJV translates the phrase "into the patient waiting for Christ," which is a grammatical possibility. As Bruce says (202), such a rendering "chimes in happily with the emphasis on the Parousia which characterizes these two letters," but the immediate context of being strengthened and protected weighs the balance in favor of the NIV translation.

The Thessalonian converts have been assailed by persecution from without and alarm from within regarding confusion over the Day of the Lord. Paul has described how there will be mass deception in the last days, which will result in the unfortunate destruction of so many people. But like a father, he speaks words of assurance and strength to convince his children that their future is secure in Christ. The Lord will provide direction and protection for them until that day when they see Jesus. The Lord can be trusted to do the same for us. May we be inspired to study to know more deeply God's rich love for us, and may we avoid losing heart as we look to and imitate Jesus' example of perseverance (Heb. 12:2–3; 1 Peter 2:21–24). May the Lord so direct our hearts.

5. Directions Regarding Restoring the Idle (3:6–15)

Paul reserves the remainder of the body of the letter to address the persisting problem of idleness. We do not know how many needed correction on this matter; it was likely a small minority, but that is all it takes to bring turmoil and disharmony into a church. (For discussion of why some were refusing to work and of the potential problems raised, see comments on 1 Thess. 4:11; 5:14.) Lack of conformity to Paul's briefer admonition in the first letter necessitates a more lengthy treatment. He had hoped that the gentle nudge in the previous letter would be sufficient; such was not the case.

Therefore the apostle seems somewhat more testy and is forthright in his efforts to turn up the heat of apostolic authority. There are three points to consider in verse 6 that attest to this flexing of authority. (1) Paul invokes "the name of the Lord Jesus Christ." As an apostle Paul has been commissioned to minister in the name of Jesus and to speak in that name. He is generally reluctant to push his weight around, but when challenged, as in this case by blatant disregard for his initi[al] warning, he will appeal to his calling as a[n] apostle (cf. 2 Cor. 12:11; 13:2). To invok[e] Christ's name "is one of the most powerf[ul] forms of theological coercion available [to] Paul" (Wanamaker, 281). This strategy is n[ot] unlike his rebuke of the Corinthian devian[ts] by showing how shameful it was that as mem[-]bers of Christ and as temples of the Hol[y] Spirit they were engaging in sexual immora[l]ity (1 Cor. 6:15–20). Jesus is being dragge[d] into the arena of misconduct, and it is Jesu[s,] not Paul, who is ultimately being disobeye[d] (1 Thess. 4:8).

(2) The next sign of Paul's authority is h[is] choice of the verb "we command" (*parangell[o,]* also used in vv. 10 ["gave ... rule"], 12). It con[-]notes a greater tone of formality and obligatio[n] than does the verb *parakaleo*, often translate[d] "urge." The hammer of office has come dow[n] and it had better not be ignored any further.

(3) A third point meant to get the offende[r] to sit up and take notice is Paul's sanction [to] "keep away from every brother who is idle an[d] does not live according to [his earlier] teach[-]ing" (cf. Rom. 16:17–18; see further com[-]ments at 2 Thess. 3:14). The combined weig[ht] of these three points at the outset of his instru[c]tion is great indeed. Violators beware! Pa[ul] previously used the term *teaching* (*paradosi[s]*) in 2:15, and he refers to a specific example [of] such teaching in 3:10.

Paul's command becomes even more forc[e]ful in that he can demonstrate his own confo[r]mity to it. He preaches what he himse[lf] practices and can therefore boldly repeat wh[at] they have already been told: "Follow o[ur] example" (cf. 1 Thess. 1:6). Lest they have fo[r]gotten Paul's example in these matters, h[e] spells it out for them. He can categorical[ly] deny that he and his fellow missionaries we[re] in any sense idle during their time in Thess[a]lonica (2 Thess. 3:7). No one can accuse the[m] of being charlatans aiming at a life of ease (se[e] comments on 1 Thess. 2:3–6). Paul goes on [to] point out his standard practice to pay for h[is] own room and board (2 Thess. 3:8); he do[es] not look for handouts.

To add more clout to that point Pa[ul] emphatically details the extreme lengths [to] which he went in order to avoid damaging the[ir] evangelistic efforts (v. 8). They labored an[d] toiled (*kopos* and *mochthos*, two words th[at] peak of hard effort), putting in long hours 'night and day"). Paul made this point with hese same two words in his previous letter 1 Thess. 2:9). There he emphasized how apos-les could rightfully ask for support to free hem up for exercising their ministry full time no doubt a night-and-day occupation as well, f present-day ministry demands are any gauge). He infers in this present letter that they lo have a "right to such help" (2 Thess. 3:9), ut they have denied it.

This was a costly denial of rights, for when ne considers how urgently Paul considered he winning of souls to Christ, one wonders why he accepted the distraction of needing to arn support. Could not those long hours be etter invested in the work of evangelism? We ee here Paul's ability to be content in any sit-ation (Phil. 4:11–12). He does not consider imself too important to get his hands dirty, as f he were God's only ambassador who should ot be tied up in trivial matters such as work. There are times in his ministry career where he lid accept support (Phil. 4:14–18), but he will ot get into the rut of expectation. Paul's notives are pure, and his practice allows him he claim of being a worthy model to follow 2 Thess. 3:7).

Paul then reminds his readers of what may ave been a proverb original to him: "If a man will not work, he shall not eat" (v. 10). The say-ng is blunt and effective, as is his next state-nent about the slothful: "They are not busy; hey are busybodies" (v. 11). The NIV captures he sarcastic wordplay of the original language (*ergazomenous* ... *periergazomenous*). Those with too much idle time on their hands have the unfortunate tendency of exerting energy into inappropriate pursuits, one of which is med-dling in other people's business (1 Thess. 4:11).

Paul does not need to specify the nature of this occupation of busybody; the Thessaloni-ans are well aware of the problems caused. Human nature remains the same, still provid-ing ample testimony that gossip, rumormon-gering, complaining, and being critical are among the fruit of the idle life. Add to that the possible cloak of hyperspirituality these errant Thessalonians may have sported—a claim to be the ones who are "truly" waiting for the return of Jesus (see comments on 1 Thess. 5:20)—and we can see how disturbing these people can be.

Although Paul has said to "keep away" from the unruly people (v. 6), he does not give up on them; restoration is still his hope. Thus, verse 12 reads like Paul's aside to them, attempting to convince them to toe the line. He is emphatic in his address to "such people" as he employs a tandem of verbs, "we command and urge." As we have seen (v. 6), the verb "to command" connotes authority. The second verb, "to urge" (*parakaleo*), is perhaps a soft-ening of the first (Morris, 256) and reveals Paul's pastoral heart. He does not want to abandon these people to their unruly ways, because he is their spiritual father—he too must exercise appropriate patience.

Included with his plea is an additional invo-cation of Jesus' name (v. 12; cf. v. 6). It may well be that we have here a prophetic word within this letter, specifically meant for this group. The matter, in other words, is more than one of obedience to Paul's wishes. The apostle views himself as a spokesman for Jesus—the very one for whom the idle are waiting. First he deals with the symptoms, the remedy for which is to settle down and lead a quiet life (cf. 1 Tim. 2:2; 1 Peter 3:4). Busybodies can be trans-formed into peaceable, caring Christians. Paul urges them to cooperate with what the Spirit surely longs to do. Then Paul addresses the root problem, which is idleness. The remedy for that is to get to work and support themselves.

The apostle then takes a brief break from his focus on the deviants and gives a general instruction to the rest of the church: "Never tire of doing what is right" (v. 13; cf. 1 Thess. 5:15). His concern is likely that others may join the idle pack. It may be that those who legitimately need care and support because they are unable to work are being labeled as lazy—Paul's own teaching against the idle could be stretched too far so as to include them. "The hard-working members of the church may have been tempted to give up being charitable because they felt advantage was being taken of them by the idle" (Mar-shall, 226). But verse 13 is so abrupt and gen-eral in scope that one wonders how the Thessalonians would have taken Paul's words in any other way than that others were not to join the ranks of the indolent.

Paul then brings the focus back on the sanc-tion he imposed (v. 6), though now he elabo-rates (vv. 14–15). He apparently feels his letter's appeal alone may not immediately resolve the issue, so he tells the others to "take special note of" anyone who disobeys his instructions and to shun such a person. This shunning does not seem as harsh a treatment as the action he orders of the Corinthian believers regarding the immoral brother ("hand this man over to Satan," 1 Cor. 5:5). We can be sure he is not speaking of a complete excommunication with no hope of return upon repentance.

We are not given precise details of how such treatment is to be applied. The dissociation is meant to shame the culprits into taking stock and realizing how serious the offense has become, and thereby to conform themselves to the apostolic teaching. Paul's pastoral heart, ever hopeful of reconciliation, is wonderfully demonstrated as he pleads for the church not to regard the offender as an enemy but to "warn him as a brother" (v. 15). Marshall (228) states that "one of the problems of exercising discipline is the temptation to allow personal feeling to affect the application." A deplorable tendency in dealing with the unrepentant is to allow hostility to fester to such a point that intense hatred is felt and displayed, or tragically where the offender is considered as dead—no longer seen as part of the family.

The church has been put in a doubly difficult position of having to balance the taking of the tough measure of dissociation with maintaining strong brotherly love for the unruly. The wisdom and power of the Holy Spirit must be called on to obey this teaching of verse 15. As long as there are people who refuse to comply with biblical teaching on truly Christian conduct, leadership must consider at what point and how Paul's instruction should be implemented. Tough love may be a cliché to some, but it describes well the need at times for bolder displays of love than constant coddling. The church must believe that with such extreme measures of discipline, the Holy Spirit can effect the necessary change in the heart of the wayward.

6. Concluding Remarks (3:16–18)

As he did with his first letter, Paul closes with a prayer wish, a final greeting, and a benediction. The prayer wish is the third one of this brief letter (2:16–17; 3:5), which indicates Paul's natural predilection to pray constantly (1:11; cf. 1 Thess. 1:3). It is typical to desire "peace" for one's readers, but it is an especially fitting wish for the Thessalonians. Paul's concept of peace is all-encompassing, for it refers to the spiritual well-being of his converts. While he may prefer that the Thessalonians not have to face adversity, he knows that Christians are destined for trials (1 Thess. 3:3–4). Absence of adversity is not the criterion for possession of peace; recognizing that God is in control of one's life and realizing that the Holy Spirit is the administrator of the grace of peace are the criteria.

The Thessalonians have faced persecution and ostracism since they turned from their old way of life. Some have also been intensely troubled by misconceptions of how the Day of the Lord would transpire. Also, the peace of the Christian community has been threatened from within by busybodies, whose preference to be idle is taxing the harmony of the church. Paul's prayer wish for peace "at all times and in every way" is most appropriate for their needs.

His next statement, "the Lord be with all of you," brings to mind the great truth that while there is the blessed hope of one day being with the Lord forever (2:1; cf. John 14:1–2; 1 Thess. 5:17–18; Titus 2:13), there is the other great truth that we can enjoy his presence now and thereby receive peace for life's journey.

In verses 17–18 Paul himself takes up the pen to write the closing words of greeting and benediction. In light of the false report he spoke of in 2:2, it is possible that Paul does so as a guarantee of authenticity. Paul presumably dictated his letters (Rom. 16:22; see also comments on 1 Thess. 1:1), but at times he added a personal touch by penning the last words (1 Cor. 16:21; Gal. 6:11; Col. 4:18). He did not close his first letter to the Thessalonians with this sort of explicit statement, though he may have written the concluding remarks nonetheless. As he says here, to write in his own hand "is the distinguishing mark in all my letters."

This statement makes us wonder how many other letters Paul has written to other churches by this time. The letters to the Thessalonians are likely the earliest documents of the New Testament (although some suppose Galatians to be), so we conclude that not everything Paul wrote was preserved by God as inspired Scripture. Nevertheless, our curiosity is piqued by he speculation of what we may have learned from such letters.

The closing words are identical to those of his first letter (see comments on 1 Thess. 5:28) with the exception of the additional word "all." We need to draw no special conclusions about that minor difference. Paul believes that God's grace through the Lord Jesus Christ is sufficient for believers to enable them to stand firm and to walk worthy. Therefore, his last words vault above shallow formality as he pronounces the benediction on his dearly loved converts at Thessalonica.

NOTES

[1]Kümmel presents two benchmarks for dating the work: (1) The inscription at Delphi of a letter of Emperor Claudius provides evidence that Gallio governed the province of Achaia from A.D. 51–52 (Acts 18:2, 12); and (2) concerning the expulsion of the Jews from Rome in 49 he writes, "with some probability the chronology of Paul can therefore be worked out, backward and forward from this fixed point" (253). Thus the estimation of A.D. 50–51 is likely. Some argue that the letter to the Galatians was written around A.D. 49, thus coming before 1 Thessalonians, but that dating is by no means certain.

[2]Stewart's book resonates with delight in exploring the meaning and implications of the phrase "in Christ." "To be 'in Christ,' to have Christ within, to realise your creed not as something you have to bear but something by which you are borne, this is Christianity. It is more: it is release and liberty, life with an endless song at its heart" (169).

[3]Paul addresses their great work of faith in 1:4–3:5, their labor of love in 3:6–4:11, and patience of hope in 4:13–5:11. The pattern is repeated in the final chapter: Work of faith is in 5:11, labor of love in 5:12–22, and patience of hope in 5:23–24. The categories are not mutually exclusive, the seams are loose, and Paul's intention with these categories is difficult to ascertain. Nevertheless, scholars are alert to Paul's thanksgiving sections being somewhat programmatic for the body of his letters (e.g., Wanamaker, 73; Fee, 42).

[4]In 4:9–10 Paul uses without any necessary appeal to separate nuances, two words for love: the first is a compound word employing *philia* (*philadelphia*, "brotherly love"); the second is *agape*.

[5]See *Christianity Today*, July 15, 1996, for informative, sobering coverage of persecution in the contemporary church.

[6]So Bruce, Morris, Thomas, and others. Wanamaker (95) feels both issues of integrity and immorality are included.

[7]In Phil. 1:15–18 Paul addresses his own attitude toward those who preach Christ out of wrong motives!

[8]The term is used thirty-eight times in the New Testament, and only two other uses have positive connotations: Luke 22:15, regarding Jesus' desire to eat the Passover with his disciples, and Phil. 1:23, regarding Paul's desire to depart and be with Christ.

[9]Jesus comforts the thief on the cross: "Today you will be with me in paradise" (Luke 23:43). In no wise persuasive are the attempts to change the meaning of the consolation Jesus offered him by construing the sense as "Now [today] I am saying to you, you will be with me in paradise [at some point in the future]." Such a rendering is redundant and strained. Nor can the pessimistic musing "the dead know nothing" (Eccl. 9:5) be used with any force in this matter. Also, one ought to be cautious in employing the parable of the rich man and Lazarus (Luke 16:19–31) as a theological primer. The main thrust of the parable is not to expound on specifics about the afterlife. If it were there are difficulties, for example, can those who die in their unrighteous state literally see and call out to Abraham? Jesus' point here was to warn against hard hearts and unbelief.

[10]Morris ponders the probability that resistance mounted because "inexperienced leaders exercised their authority in a rather tactless fashion" (164–65).

[11]Some scholars, notably Wanamaker (37–45) have suggested that 2 Thessalonians was actually the first letter written. But the increased growth in faith and love for which Paul gives thanks here fits best into the argument in favor of the canonical sequence of these two letters; that is, since the first letter there has been an increased development in Christian virtues.

[12]Verse 4 can rightfully be seen as part of the thanksgiving section, for its content springs out of Paul's thanksgiving to God; that is, it is as if Paul is saying, "I thank God that your faith and love are such that we can boast about your endurance." But in order to emphasize the transition verse 4 makes into the longer discussion of persecution and retribution I have chosen in the outline to restrict the thanksgiving proper to verse 3.

[13]A family of terms also translated with the concept of *rest* is derived from the root verb *pauo* ("to stop, cease, rest"). Jesus promises to give rest (*anapauo*) to those who come to him (Matt. 11:28; in v. 29 is the noun *anapausin*). In the letter to the Hebrews is the prominent theme of entering the rest (*katapausin*) that God has promised (Heb. 4:1, 3, 10). The noun Paul uses here is synonymous with that of the above passages.

[14]Following are other parallels between Paul's correspondence to the Thessalonians and Matthew 24 that demonstrate how Paul has been influenced by traditional Synoptic material:

Matthew 24	*1 and 2 Thessalonians*
24:8: re. birth pains	1 Thess. 5:3 (the metaphor is used differently)
24:9: persecution and death	1 Thess. 3:3–4
24:10: turning away	2 Thess. 2:3
24:11: false prophets	2 Thess. 2:2 (perhaps 1 Thess. 5:19–22)
24:11: deception	2 Thess. 2:10–11
24:12: increase of wickedness	2 Thess. 2:12: "delighted in wickedness"
24:13: stand firm	2 Thess. 2:15
24:15: abomination of desolation	2 Thess. 2:4
24:24: false Christs and signs and wonders	2 Thess. 2:9
24:30–31: re. details of the Return	1 Thess. 4:16–17; 2 Thess. 1:7; 2:1
24:42, 44: "keep watch"	1 Thess. 5:6: "be alert"
24:43: re. thief	1 Thess. 5:4
24:51: re. punishment	2 Thess. 1:8–9

BIBLIOGRAPHY

W. Barclay, *The Letters to the Philippians Colossians and Thessalonians*, DSB (1975); F. F Bruce, *1 and 2 Thessalonians*, WBC (1982); G. D Fee, *God's Empowering Presence: The Holy Spirit in the Letters of Paul* (1994); W. Hendriksen, *Exposition of I and II Thessalonians* (1979); R. Jewett *The Thessalonian Correspondence: Pauline Rhetoric and Millenarian Piety* (1986); G. Krodel "2 Thessalonians," *The Deutero-Pauline Letters* Proclamation Commentaries (1993); W. G. Kümmel, *Introduction to the New Testament*, trans. H. C Kee (1975); G. Lüdemann, *Paul, Apostle to the Gentiles: Studies in Chronology*, trans. F. S. Jones (1984); A. J. Malherbe, *Paul and the Thessalonians* (1987); I. H. Marshall, *1 and 2 Thessalonians* NCBC (1983); J. Moffatt, *The First and Second Epistles to the Thessalonians*, *EGT* (1978 repr.); L Morris, *The First and Second Epistles to the Thessalonians*, TNTC (1979); J. Plevnik, "The Taking Up of the Faithful and the Resurrection of the Dead in 1 Thessalonians 4:13–18," *CBQ* 46 (1984): 274–83; J. S. Stewart, *A Man in Christ* (1975 repr.); R. L. Thomas, "1, 2 Thessalonians" *EBC*, vol. 11 (1978), 229-337; C. A. Wanamaker, *The Epistles to the Thessalonians*, NIGTC (1990); R. A. Ward, *Commentary on 1 & 2 Thessalonians* (1973); D. J. Williams, *1 and 2 Thessalonians*, NIBC (1992).

THE PASTORALS

Deborah Menken Gill

INTRODUCTION

1. General Introduction to the Pastorals

First Timothy, 2 Timothy, and Titus make up the Pastoral Letters, so-called (since the eighteenth century) because each contains advice and encouragement to younger pastors about life and ministry. Yet more than private letters, their tone is that of official documents with normative instructions about combating heresy, developing church organization, and encouraging pastoral care of particular groups. They seem to repeat earlier oral instructions given to Timothy and Titus and also offer endorsement of their ministries to their communities. Because of their similar content and since the three claim the same author, they appear to have been written around the same time and raise similar questions among scholars. We can therefore investigate matters of introduction to all three letters at the same time.

a. Authorship of the Pastorals

Authorship is the most significant issue of the Pastorals. In fact, modern higher-critical scholars contest the authorship of these letters more severely than any others attributed to Paul. Although present-day critics consider their spuriousness an established fact of scholarship, it was not until the nineteenth century that the first attacks on their authenticity were made. Since then, two alternatives to Pauline authorship have been proposed: pseudonymity (i.e., pious forgery) and fragment theory (i.e., that an admirer of Paul incorporated authentic Pauline portions into these letters written in an era after Paul's lifetime).

Alternative Theories. *Pseudonymity* was known in the ancient world, but among Jews and Christians the practice was less common in some genres than in others (on this issue, see Carson, Moo, and Morris, 1992, 367–71). For example, though pseudonymous apocalypses are prevalent among the Apocrypha of the Old Testament, it is rare to find a pseudonymous letter (and the only two that can be described as such [the Letter of Jeremiah and the Letter of Aristeas] are not true correspondences in form). The New Testament Apocrypha demonstrates that Christians produced pseudonymous Gospels and Acts; yet falsely attributed letters are few, and all date from the fourth to thirteenth centuries (none are from anywhere near New Testament times). It would have been easier to detect a false claim to authorship in an intimate, personal letter than in other genres. There is no evidence that the church ever accepted a pseudonymous letter.

Although it was a phenomenon commonly accepted outside orthodox Christianity, the church did not take pseudonymity lightly. Paul warned against forgeries in his name (2 Thess. 2:2; 3:17), and the early church expelled an elder from office for writing pseudonymously (Tertullian, *On Baptism*, 17). It did not matter that the content was edifying and orthodox or that the author wrote out of love for Paul; the church refused to accept spurious letters.

The literary character of the Pastorals argues against pseudonymity. Absent from the Pastorals are the kind of legendary touches that appear in early Christian pseudonymous writings (e.g., the apocryphal Acts of Paul or Acts of Andrew). The personal reminiscences in the Pastorals bear the stamp of historical peculiarity. It is doubtful that a person who warns strongly against deceivers (1 Tim. 4:1; 2 Tim. 3:13; Titus 1:10) and firmly asserts, "I am telling the truth, I am not lying" (1 Tim. 2:7), would freely put Paul's name to letters he had not composed.

Ancient evidence affirms the church's acceptance, since the second century, of the Pastoral Letters as genuinely Pauline. Polycarp quotes them, and the writings of Ignatius contain frequent allusions. They are included in the Muratorian Canon and affirmed by Athenagoras, Irenaeus, and Tertullian. Any hint of pseudonymity casts serious doubts on an ancient document's canonicity. If there had been an ancient inkling of forgery, it is not likely that the early church would have held so strongly to the tradition of Pauline authorship.

As for the *fragment theory*, scholars are divided on what sections they suppose to be authentic portions, but the most commonly claimed fragments are: 2 Timothy 1:16–18; 3:10–11; 4:1–2a, 5b–22; and Titus 3:12–15. It is unlikely, however, that such personal fragments would be preserved over more theological ones. It is also unlikely that an admirer of Paul, years after his death, would identify him as "a persecutor and a violent man" (1 Tim. 1:13) and "the worst of sinners" (1:16). And why would a forger concentrate the fragments in one letter and then write three letters so similar when the content could have been contained in one? All these considerations point to the improbability of either pseudonymous composition or forgery from fragments.

Evidence for Authenticity. Why have scholars challenged Pauline authorship and what evidence do they summon in its favor? It is on the basis of New Testament chronology and because of the style of writing and nature of contents of the Pastorals, which differ from other letters of Paul, that the authenticity of the Pastorals has been so seriously contested among contemporary Bible scholars. The following considerations are important.

(1) It is argued that if the Acts of the Apostles is taken as a biography of Paul's Christian life, then there is no place for the Pastorals. Acts, however, makes no claim that the end of the book corresponds with the end of Paul's life. Though Acts closes with Paul's imprisonment in Rome, the circumstances of his imprisonment are not severe—he is not awaiting immediate death (cf. Acts 28:16, 23, 30; Phil. 1:12–14). Festus thought Paul "had done nothing deserving of death" (Acts 25:25) and Agrippa found no case against him (26:32). Paul's writings from that imprisonment (the Prison Letters) reflect his expectation of release and further ministry (Phil. 1:19, 25–26; 2:24; Philem. 22). It is not only possible, but probable, that Paul was released from his first Roman imprisonment and experienced additional ministry, including his correspondence to Timothy and Titus.

(2) Literary differences between the Pastorals and Paul's other writings have been used as an argument against authenticity. P. N. Harrison has presented some impressive statistics on vocabulary (cf. Harrison, 1921, 20ff.; Wikenhauser, 1958, 446; Carson, Moo, and Morris, 1992, 360–61). Of the 848 words (excluding 54 proper names) in the vocabulary of these letters, 306 are *hapax legomena* of Paul (words that do not appear in his other ten letters), 175 of which do not occur elsewhere in the New Testament. It should be noted, however, that Romans has a similar proportion of *hapax legomena* (261 out of 993, excluding proper names).

(3) Other stylistic features of the Pastorals have been presented as evidence against genuineness. Certain words and expressions characteristic of Paul are not found in the Pastorals, and those characteristic of the Pastorals are not found elsewhere in Paul. The syntax of the Pastorals is more smooth and direct than other Pauline writings. And the average word length of the Pastorals' vocabulary is longer than the word length in the other letters of Paul. Particles, prepositions, and pronouns are often omitted in the Pastorals. Yet irregularities of style can be and are often attributable to a difference in circumstances (such as subject matter, addressee, environment, age, experience, and the passing of time) or to the use of an amanuensis (a scribe who took down a letter via dictation). There is no denying the peculiar vocabulary and style of the Pastorals, yet such characteristics do not disprove authenticity.

(4) Some scholars consider the contents of the Pastorals indicative of an era after the life of Paul. They contend that the emphases on orthodoxy and the preservation of tradition are concerns from a later period of history, when the church was becoming institutionalized. Tradition and orthodoxy, however, are also the weapons used in combating heresy, and attacking heresy is a primary purpose of these letters.

(5) Organization of the church, so highly developed as to include offices and instructions in governance (as described in the Pastorals) is cited as another anachronism to authenticity. Yet widows are also mentioned in Acts 6:1; 9:39, 41 and 1 Corinthians 7:8. Offices of overseer and deacon are mentioned together in Philippians 1:1, and in Acts 20:17–36 Paul addresses the Ephesian elders. Other leaders of communities are mentioned in Paul's earlier letters (e.g., 1 Cor. 16:15–16; 1 Thess. 5:12–13). Granted, the Pastorals address ecclesiastical organization, but it is evident from the directness of the instructions given that such structure is still in its early stages.

(6) Finally, some scholars argue that the heresies attacked in these letters are from a post-Pauline period. But even though Gnosti-

ism did not fully develop until the second century, incipient Gnosticism and gnosticizing tendencies existed earlier. The false teachers (1 Tim. 1:3–11; 4:1–10; 6:3–5, 20–21; 2 Tim. 2:14, 23; 3:1–9, 13; 4:3–4; Titus 1:14–15) and dualistic ideas (1 Tim. 4:3; 2 Tim. 2:18) can be attributed to gnosticizing Judaism and gnosticizing elements infiltrating the church.

Summary. Thus, the arguments against Pauline authenticity of the Pastorals on the basis of their contents do not prove these letters postdate Paul. By demonstrating the improbability of alternative theories of authorship and examining the challenges against authenticity, most conservative Protestant scholars take the text as trustworthy—note how each of the three letters, in its very first verse, presents Paul as the author—and accept the genuineness of Pauline authorship of the Pastoral Letters.

b. Overview of the Theology of the Pastorals

Since these three letters contain advice from an older apostle to young pastors, their content is practical in nature. Together they comprise a sort of handbook for church leaders. They contain qualifications for church leaders (bishops/overseers [1 Tim. 3:1–7; Titus 1:5–9] and deacons [1 Tim. 3:8–13]); advice on pastoring various members of the church (men and women, young and old [1 Tim. 5:1–2], widows [5:3–16], elders [6:1–2b], and the wealthy [6:17–19]); general advice on spiritual leadership (leading by example [6:11–16] and exhorting strength instead of timidity [2 Tim. 1:3–2:7]); and instructions on public prayer (1 Tim. 2:1–8).

The primary theological focus, from a doctrinal standpoint, in the Pastorals is orthodoxy: sound teaching (2 Tim. 2:8–4:8), suppressing false teachers (Titus 1:10–16), and teaching good conduct (2:1–3:8a). The false teaching Paul is at pains to refute seems to be an early form of Gnosticism. Gnosticism distorted Jewish ideas and opposed Christian ideas as well. Its dualistic philosophy taught that material things are evil; only spirit could be good. Thus, some Gnostics believed that the Hebrew God (Yahweh) was considered evil, having created this material world. "Gnosticism turned upside-down the Genesis account of the Creation and Fall, making the snake a hero who leads Adam and Eve away from God's deception, and presenting Eve as the source of life and enlightenment" (Kroeger, Evans, and Storkey, 1995, 439). Understanding this Gnostic background makes it clear that the function of 1 Timothy 2:11–15 is not to limit theologically women's leadership in the church, but to refute false doctrine taught by the Gnostics in Ephesus and to reaffirm orthodoxy in its place. As Gundry writes (1994, 416):

> The doctrinal basis for these instructions [both practical and confessional] is God's grace, which brings salvation, leads to godly living, and offers the "blessed hope" of Jesus' return (Titus 2:11–14). The experiential basis for these instructions is regeneration by the Holy Spirit (Titus 3:3–7).

The way in which Paul affirms true doctrine also offers us theological insights into first-century worship. Note what Hanson (1982, 15) writes:

> His great aim is not to introduce new teaching, but to persuade his readers to stand by the old.... Scholars have come to the conclusion that most of the author's references to doctrine are really quotations, quotations from early Christian hymns, as in 1 Timothy 3:16; 2 Timothy 2:11–13; or from very early creeds, as in 1 Timothy 2:5–6; or perhaps from a prayer used in the Eucharist, as in 1 Timothy 1:17; or even a baptismal service, as probably in Titus 3:4–7.

By quoting preexisting worship fragments, Paul gives us theological glimpses into the early church at worship.

2. First Timothy

a. Recipient and Destination

Both 1 and 2 Timothy are addressed to Timothy while he is in ministry in Ephesus, having been commissioned by Paul (1 Tim. 1:3). Though these letters contain greetings, prayers, endorsements, and counsel that Timothy is to share with his congregation, for the most part they are personal and intimate, private letters of guidance to Timothy from his mentor, Paul.

Timothy was Paul's missionary associate, coworker, and trusted emissary over an extended period of time. Paul calls him "our brother" (2 Cor. 1:1; 1 Thess. 3:2; Philem. 1), "fellow worker" (Rom. 16:21; 1 Thess. 3:2), "my son whom I love, who is faithful in the Lord" (1 Cor. 4:17; cf. 1 Tim. 1:2), and "apostle of Christ" (1 Thess. 2:6). He was a native of Lystra in Lycaonia (Asia Minor). His father was a Gentile (pagan) and his mother a Jewish Christian named Eunice (Acts 16:1; 2 Tim. 1:5), who was probably converted during Paul's first mission in that city (Acts 14:6–23).

Already a Christian and well-spoken of by the believers in the area (Acts 16:1–2), Timothy, as a young man, was chosen by Paul to accompany him on the second missionary journey (Acts 16:3). Paul had him circumcised, making him fully acceptable to the Jews—thus a more effective coworker. From then on, Timothy was a regular companion of the apostle (Acts 17:14–15; 18:5; 19:22; 20:4; 2 Cor. 1:1, 19; Phil. 1:1; 1 Thess. 1:1; 2 Thess. 1:1). He accompanied Paul and Silas through Asia Minor, to Troas, then over into Macedonia, and down to Athens in Achaia. From Athens, Paul sent Timothy to Thessalonica on important business: to encourage the Thessalonians, to assess their situation, to explain Paul's longing to see them and the reason why he could not visit them at that time, and to bring back the official report to the apostle (1 Thess. 3:2–3, 5–6).

On Paul's third missionary journey Timothy was similarly commissioned, traveling from Ephesus through Macedonia to Corinth with other weighty responsibilities: to carry Paul's letter (1 Corinthians), to serve as an apostolic reminder, and to resolve a disturbing situation (Acts 19:22–23; 1 Cor. 4:17; 16:10; Phil. 2:19, 23). At the close of the third missionary journey, when Paul left Corinth for Jerusalem with the collection from the Christian communities, Timothy accompanied him (Acts 20:4) and stayed with him during his first Roman imprisonment (Phil. 1:1; Col. 1:1; Philem. 1).

The Pastorals portray Timothy as youthful and inexperienced, easily intimidated, and requiring instruction and encouragement. J. Gillman (1992, 6:559) points out how Paul's instructions in 1 Corinthians 16:10–11 reveal the apostle's apprehension over Timothy's reception in Corinth:

> "See that you put him at ease among you," as if Timothy was nervous and easily intimidated; "let no one despise him," as if he had been rejected previously by them or as if the sentiment against Paul would overflow toward Timothy; "send him on his way in peace," as if he had left without their support earlier.

One might wonder whether Paul had doubts about Timothy's effectiveness as a leader. Yet, judging from his entrusting Timothy with such important missions, we see the confidence the apostle had in his understudy.

As Paul's companion and coworker, Timothy is named as joint-sender of six of Paul's letters: (in chronological order) 1 and 2 Thessalonians, 2 Corinthians, Colossians, Philemon, and Philippians. The high regard Paul had for the person and service of Timothy is seen in Philippians 2:20–23, and the significance of the relationship between Timothy and the apostle is seen in his being the recipient of two pastoral letters. Timothy, "his son," is one of the people the apostle wanted by his side at the end of his life (2 Tim. 4:9, 13, 21). If Timothy did join Paul in Rome and became imprisoned at that time, such would explain the comment in Hebrews 13:23 that Timothy had just been released from prison.

In 1 Timothy 1:3 Paul implies that he intended Timothy to return to and remain in Ephesus. Later tradition, preserved by Eusebius (*Ecclesiastical History*, 3.4), asserts that Timothy became the first bishop of Ephesus. This city, on the western coast of Asia Minor (modern Turkey), was the fourth largest city in the Roman empire. In about 1000 B.C. Ionian Greeks conquered the area. Ephesus became a world-class city and had a reputation for intellectual snobbery, oriental culture and tradition, and a predominance of goddess religion. By the mid-third century B.C., Jews settled in the area around Ephesus, and by the first century A.D., the Jewish population may have numbered seventy-five thousand. Archaeological evidence attests, however, that the Jews in Asia Minor syncretized the religion of Yahweh with paganism, using magic and distorting narratives from Genesis (Kroeger and Kroeger, 1992, 47–55).

Paul introduced Ephesus to Christianity briefly on his second missionary journey and left Priscilla and Aquila there to continue his ministry (Acts 18:18–21). This couple took aside the great Alexandrian preacher Apollos and gave him more accurate and adequate teaching about esus. (Thus, here in the church of Ephesus is a woman whose teaching of a man and leadership in the church the apostle Paul himself commissioned and commended [cf. Rom. 16:3–4]. This background insight will shed light on the meaning of 1 Timothy 2:11–15.)

When Paul returned to Ephesus on his third missionary journey (Acts 18:23; 19:1–20:36), he ministered the baptism in the name of Jesus and the baptism in the Holy Spirit to a group of disciples in Ephesus who had been uninformed regarding these matters. Paul preached boldly in the synagogue for three months and then lectured daily for two years in the hall of Tyrannus. Scripture records "that all the Jews and Greeks who lived in the province of Asia heard the word of the Lord" (Acts 19:10). Such extraordinary healings and demon expulsions took place through the apostle that seven sons of Sceva (Jewish exorcists) attempted to use the name of Jesus in their incantations, with unfortunate results (19:11–16). The overwhelming success of the power encounter between Christ and evil resulted in an enormous bonfire of books of magic, burned by those who had practiced sorcery but who now believed in Christ (19:17–20).

The wave of community transformation affected the whole economy of Ephesus. When the business of the silversmiths (who made souvenirs of the temple of the goddess Artemis/Diana) suffered, they incited the entire city to riot (Acts 19:23–41). After the uproar, Paul set sail for Macedonia and Achaia and later returned to Miletus to bid a tearful farewell to the Ephesian elders before returning to Jerusalem (20:13–37). In that address he warned the elders of the church that deviant doctrine would be a threat in Ephesus. To counteract such opposition to orthodoxy, which did arise, Paul wrote the Pastoral Letters.

b. Provenance, Purpose, and Date

Although the text does not mention explicitly the place of origin of 1 Timothy, it is generally assumed from 1:3 ("As I urged you when I went to Macedonia, stay there in Ephesus") that Paul was still in Macedonia, reiterating earlier instructions. First Timothy and Titus have a similar aim and purpose; they are essentially books of church order. Paul left Timothy in Ephesus to counteract false teachers and to lead the church. First Timothy has a less specific occasion than does Titus; it seems the apostle felt Timothy's need not only of specific instructions on organizing the church, but also of personal encouragement and challenge.

Dating the letter depends on authorship and New Testament chronology. Those who see the letter as pseudonymous place it somewhere after the turn of the second century. J. A. T. Robinson takes Paul's departure from Ephesus to Macedonia in 1 Timothy 1:3 to be equivalent to his departure to Macedonia mentioned in Acts 20:1, after the riot in Ephesus; he dates the letter A.D. 55, when Timothy was very young (Robinson, 1976, 82–88). This seems far too early to most scholars.

From the time Timothy joined Paul on the second missionary journey, he was usually present with the apostle on his travels. Most who accept the letter as genuinely Pauline see no date prior to the third missionary journey to which the letter can be assigned. And since the errors attacked in 1 Timothy had not yet arisen on the third missionary journey (Acts 20:29), the letter is clearly subsequent to that mission. Moreover, the organization Paul exhorts Timothy to establish in Ephesus indicates that the church was past its early years of existence.

Locating the writing of the letter between Roman imprisonments would date it in the A.D. 60s, probably the early 60s. The chronology of Paul's life is not certain, but it is generally held that he was in Rome (the first time) around A.D. 59–61. Allowing a couple of years for his imprisonment (Acts 28:30) puts his release at about 61 or 62. We do not know whether Paul went to Spain, as he had desired before his imprisonment (Rom. 15:28). It is traditionally held that Paul was martyred under Nero (who died in 68). Although Eusebius dates Paul's death at 67, most others date it during the height of the Neronian persecution (ca. 64–65). Therefore, placing the letter after both Paul's release from prison and his subsequent visit to Ephesus and before his final imprisonment in Rome, it can be dated around A.D. 61–63.

3. Second Timothy: Provenance, Purpose, and Date

Though the recipient and destination of 2 Timothy are the same as of 1 Timothy (see "Introduction to 1 Timothy: Recipient and Destination"), the circumstances surrounding the author are drastically different. The second letter to Timothy is written by Paul from Rome, fettered as a prisoner and expecting execution soon (2 Tim. 1:8, 16–17; 2:9; 4:6). He is lonely and summons Timothy to join him quickly, before winter when navigation ceases (4:9–13, 20–21a); yet he seems uncertain that he will ever see him again.

The letter consists of warnings against false teachings and exhortations to steadfastness and courage. Its form is a literary testament, in which Paul looks back on his finished course and forward to his crown. Less concerned with ecclesiastical arrangements in this letter, the apostle focuses on his young successor and the task committed to him.

This letter cannot be dated during Paul's first Roman imprisonment. The first Roman imprisonment was mild, whereas the second was severe (cf. Acts 28:30–31 with 2 Tim. 2:9). In the first imprisonment Timothy and Mark were with Paul; in the second he entreats them to join him (cf. Col. 1:1; 4:10; Philem. 24 with 2 Tim. 4:9, 11). Trophimus had accompanied the apostle to Jerusalem when Paul was arrested and sent to Rome the first time, but was left sick in Miletus prior to Paul's second imprisonment (cf. Acts 21:29 with 2 Tim. 4:20). If 2 Timothy were written during the first imprisonment, Paul's cloak and books would have been at Carpus's house for about five years (cf. 2 Tim. 4:13 with Acts 20:5–6).

Those who take the Pastorals as pseudonymous date 2 Timothy after the turn of the second century. Those who consider this letter authentic, however, place it during Paul's final imprisonment in Rome. It seems that subsequent to his writing of 1 Timothy, Paul traveled to Asia Minor (Troas and Miletus) one final time, but now he is in prison again. His situation has become severe and his martyrdom is imminent. Though the New Testament order of the Pastorals places Titus last, 2 Timothy is Paul's final letter—his testament to his beloved son. If Eusebius, who dates Paul's martyrdom at A.D. 67, is correct, then the date of this letter would be 66 or 67. If Paul's martyrdom occurred at the height of the Neronian persecution, his last letter would have been written around 64–65.

4. Titus

a. Recipient and Destination

This letter is addressed to Titus while he is in ministry on the island of Crete, having been commissioned by Paul as pastor there (Titus 1:5). Like Timothy, Titus was also a chosen traveling companion, fellow worker, and trusted emissary of the apostle.

Though Titus is never mentioned in Acts, Galatians 2:1–15 indicates he was a Gentile Christian from the church in Antioch, who was chosen to travel with Paul and Barnabas to Jerusalem. At that time the apostle successfully resisted demands that Titus be circumcised (2:3). This journey was either the visit to deliver the famine funds (Acts 11:27–30) or the visit to the Jerusalem Council (15:2–29). The latter seems more likely, since the Council had convened to settle the circumcision issue, and Paul's purpose there was to present to the Jerusalem leaders his gospel mission to the Gentiles. Thus Titus, a "test case" of the Gentiles, became a prototype for the Gentiles. Although uncircumcised, he was a powerful witness to salvation from God and reception by the church.

Near the end of Paul's third missionary journey, after word reached him in Ephesus that some of the Corinthians had turned against him, the apostle commissioned Titus to mediate the difficult situation. Trusted coworker of Paul with proven pastoral skill, Titus carried Paul's so-called "sorrowful letter" (2 Cor. 7:6–7, 13–16) from Ephesus to Corinth. His mission was so successful that he restored the Corinthian church, which had almost been lost to Paul, and fostered the matter of the collection of the famine relief fund (for the poor saints in Jerusalem). Shortly afterwards, Paul sent Titus as his forerunner back to Corinth again, this time from Macedonia (where the two had rendezvoused), to complete the collection and to carry 2 Corinthians (2 Cor. 8:6, 16–20; 12:18).

Thus, Titus can be described as a dearly loved helper in whom Paul had confidence and trust. Not only did the apostle entrust him with delicate and difficult duties, but he merited Paul's confidence—he was successful on these challenging assignments. Once, when Titus missed a prearranged rendezvous, Paul was deeply concerned for his partner (cf. 2 Cor. 2:13, "I still had no peace of mind, because I did not find my brother Titus there"; 7:5–6, "[I was] harassed at every turn—conflicts on the outside, fears within" [until the reunion with Titus occurred]).

Outside Paul's letter to Titus (and Galatians nd the Corinthian correspondence, already iscussed), the only other New Testament refrence to this man is 2 Timothy 4:10, which ientions a journey of Titus from Rome, where e had been with Paul, to Dalmatia.

The most likely time for the Cretan church have been planted seems to be following 'aul's first Roman imprisonment. The only ther New Testament record of Paul's being on 'rete is a brief stop at the harbor at Fair Iavens (Acts 27:7–8) while a prisoner en oute to Rome (ca. A.D. 60). The evangelistic vork with Titus could not have taken place uring this short visit, and it is unlikely they vorked together there earlier. Titus 1:5 indiates that Paul had ministered with Titus in Crete for some time and then left Titus there to ontinue the organization of the community nd to carry out the work of ministry.

b. *Provenance, Purpose, and Date*

Paul writes from Nicopolis in Macedonia Titus 3:12), where he plans to spend the winer. Paul's purposes for the letter are: to reiterte earlier instructions on completing the work n Crete he and Titus had begun (1:5), to sumnon Titus to join him as soon as Artemas or Tychicus relieve him (3:12), and to assist Zenas and Apollos on their journey (3:13). The etter is similar in form and content to 1 Timthy; it is essentially a letter on church order.

Those who see the Pastorals as pseudonymous date Titus sometime in the second cenury. J. A. T. Robinson (1976, 81–82) attempts o place it on Paul's journey to Jerusalem in A.D. 57. This is problematic, however, since Acts puts Paul neither in Crete nor Nicopolis. Therefore, placing the letter after both Paul's release from prison and his subsequent visit to Crete and before his final imprisonment in Rome, Titus was probably written around 61–63 (i.e., around the time of 1 Timothy).

OUTLINE OF 1 TIMOTHY

1. Introduction (1:1–20)
- **1.1.** Salutation (1:1–2)
- **1.2.** Purpose of Letter: Hold the Fort of Faith in Ephesus (1:3–20)
  - **1.2.1.** Timothy's Task: Fighting False Doctrine (1:3–11)
    - **1.2.1.1.** Timothy's Commission Reiterated (1:3–4)
    - **1.2.1.2.** Author's Objective Identified: Love (1:5)
    - **1.2.1.3.** Error Into Which Some Have Wandered: False Use of the Law (1:6–7)
    - **1.2.1.4.** Corrective: Proper Use of the Law (1:8–11)
  - **1.2.2.** Paul's Testimony: The Lord's Grace Unto Paul (1:12–17)
    - **1.2.2.1.** Appointed Apostle in Spite of His Past (1:12–13a)
    - **1.2.2.2.** Shown Mercy in Spite of Ignorance and Unbelief (1:13b–14)
    - **1.2.2.3.** Saved in Spite of His Sin (1:15)
    - **1.2.2.4.** Displayed As a Showpiece of God's Patience (1:16)
    - **1.2.2.5.** Doxology (1:17)
  - **1.2.3.** Encouragement to Fight (1:18–20)

2. Setting the Church in Order: General Principles for Grounding the Troubled Church in Ephesus (2:1–3:13)
- **2.1.** On Prayer for Peace (2:1–8)
  - **2.1.1.** Exhortation to Pray for Peace (2:1–2)
  - **2.1.2.** Grounds and Fulfillment of Exhortation (2:3–7)
    - **2.1.2.1.** God's Will: Salvation and Enlightenment (2:3–4)
    - **2.1.2.2.** Christ's Role: Sacrifice and Witness (2:5–6)
    - **2.1.2.3.** Paul's Call: A Preacher and Apostle (2:7)
  - **2.1.3.** Desire for Men to Pray (2:8)
- **2.2.** On Women's Dress and Lifestyle (2:9–15)
  - **2.2.1.** Preference for Their Spiritual Adornment (2:9–10)
  - **2.2.2.** Command That They Be Taught (2:11)
  - **2.2.3.** Command That They Be Silent (2:12)
  - **2.2.4.** Creation Order Reiterated (2:13)
  - **2.2.5.** Fall Into Sin Explained (2:14)
  - **2.2.6.** Hope for Their Salvation Announced (2:15)
- **2.3.** On Overseers (3:1–7)
  - **2.3.1.** Leadership Aspirations Affirmed (3:1)

COMMENTARY ON 1 TIMOTHY

1. Introduction (1:1–20)

1.1. Salutation (1:1–2)

Letters in the Greco-Roman period typically began with terse salutations: writer's name, addressee's name, and a greeting; for example, "Paul, to Timothy, greetings." Paul's early letters had brief salutations (1 Thess. 1:1a; 2 Thess. 1:1), but in his subsequent letters the epistolary salutations became elaborated. By the time of the Pastoral Letters, Paul expands on all three parts of the salutation.

Paul identifies himself by name and title: "Paul, an apostle of Christ Jesus." (Although Paul frequently uses the order "Jesus Christ," "Christ Jesus" is the regular order in the Pastorals.) In letters in which Paul needs to stress his authority, he calls himself an apostle (1 Corinthians, 2 Corinthians, Galatians, Ephesians, and Colossians). In more personal letters he refers to himself as a "servant" (Philippians and Romans) or "prisoner" (Philemon). Although Timothy is a close personal friend, Paul stresses apostleship for the sake of the opponents in Ephesus, who are meant to overhear the reading of this letter.

Paul emphasizes his apostleship by adding "by the command of God." His usual description is "by the will of God." The Greek word for "command" here was used for royal commands that had to be obeyed. In order to strengthen the commands Timothy will issue in the apostle's name, Paul implies that Timothy, too, is under command, divine command.

Note the epithets used for the sources of Paul's commission: "God our Savior" and "Christ Jesus our hope." God inaugurates the plan of salvation and Christ Jesus will bring redemption to its consummation on the last day. The identification of God as Savior has a rich history. The phrase is Jewish (Deut. 32:15; Ps. 24:5; 65:5), and Jesus' name in Hebrew means "the Lord saves." In the pagan mystery religions of Paul's day, the gods, who supposedly gave life and saving knowledge, were called "saviors." Greco-Roman state religion applied the term to Zeus, Apollos, and Asclepius. Most important was the use of the term for the Roman emperor: savior of the state by upholding order and good government. In deliberate rivalry to emperor worship, Paul identifies God as Savior, emphasizing "our."

Although Timothy's father was a Gentile, his mother was a Jewess. According to the law of matrilineal descent, Timothy could be considered a Jew. Yet according to some Jewish teaching, Timothy's birth would be illegitimate. No doubt these considerations motivated Paul's having him circumcised (Acts 16:3). Scholars have suggested that Timothy's father was already deceased at the time of his circumcision. Had he been alive, he probably would not have allowed it. In his father's place Paul became a surrogate: authenticating Timothy's Jewishness through circumcision, recognizing his qualifications as the true descendant of Abraham through faith in Christ (cf. Gal. 3:26–29), and adopting Timothy as his own son. Paul now declares Timothy's legitimacy as the apostle's own son in the faith.

Paul's typical epistolary greeting is "grace and peace." Already in his earliest letters, Paul transformed the common Greek *chairein* ("Greetings!") into a Christian greeting, *charis* ("Grace [to you]!"). He added to it the Hebrew greeting, *shalom* ("Peace!"). But only in the letters to Timothy does Paul embellish the greeting to "Grace, mercy and peace." Perhaps, in light of the difficulties Timothy is having in Ephesus, the apostle wishes him God's mercy as well as grace and peace.

1.2. Purpose of Letter: Hold the Fort of Faith in Ephesus (1:3–20)

1.2.1. Timothy's Task: Fighting False Doctrine (1:3–11).

1.2.1.1. Timothy's Commission Reiterated (1:3–4). Paul launches into the letter proper by reminding Timothy of his task. "As" enforces the reminder and introduces an *anacoluthon* (a sentence that does not follow grammatically). The words omitted here are supplied in brackets: "As I urged you [in person, so now I urge you in writing]. . . ." When Paul went on his way to Macedonia, he urged Timothy to remain in Ephesus in order to silence false teachers. Perhaps because of Timothy's reluctance, Paul had to *urge* him. Ephesus was one of the most important cities in Asia Minor, both geographically and culturally. Timothy's timidity may have caused him to shrink from such a task.

Paul seeks to enhance Timothy's authority by showing him to be one under the authority of the apostle. The root of the verb translated "command" in 1:3b is different from the root of the noun translated "command" in 1:1. The verb here is a military term, meaning "to impress upon, pass on commands from one to another, give strict orders (authoritatively)."

The apostle's opponents are those who (lit.) "teach other/different [doctrine]." Though they desire to be "teachers of the law" (v. 7), they are no more than "teachers of novelties," that is, of things alien to the true gospel. Paul's polemic against the heresy is not sufficient to identify with certainty the doctrine he is opposing. The teachers are broadly described as those who are devoted "to myths and endless genealogies." Myths and genealogies are linked not only here, but also in Hellenism (Greek culture), Hellenistic Judaism (Judaism influenced by Greek culture), and Gnosticism (a mystery religion in which salvation was supposedly secured by knowing secrets such as myths and genealogies).

"Myths" (*mythos*) could include fables, legendary stories, or fiction, that is, spurious doctrine in contrast to gospel truth. This word was often used pejoratively, thus denoting false and foolish stories. Judaism of the period found delight in the composition of mythical histories based on the Old Testament (see, e.g., the Book of Jubilees). Myths were also integral to teachings of the Gnostics, who had, for example, alternative versions of the creation account.

There was keen interest in tracing one's lineage through the family tree in postexilic Judaism, especially among Jews who survived the Babylonian exile. For example, the ability to validate one's ancestry was required to authenticate those who could serve in the second temple under Ezra and Nehemiah (Neh. 7:64–65). "Genealogies" played a part in controversies between Jews and Jewish Christians. The strongest connection of myths and genealogies is in Gnosticism. Gnosticizing interpretations of Old Testament genealogies were understood mythically, and mythical speculations on the enumerations of principalities and aeons were central to Gnostic theology. The apostle calls these genealogies "endless," that is, interminable or unrestrained.

The teachers preoccupied with such concerns brought no wholesome result. They did not promote "God's work" (lit., "the stewardship of God"). Devotion to such issues does not help carry out the stewardship entrusted by God. Instead, they "promote controversies" (i.e., speculations, lit., "out-of-the-way researches"). The word is used contemptuously as an antonym of edification.

1.2.1.2. Author's Objective Identified: Love (1:5). Paul contrasts the purpose, end, or goal of his instruction (preaching) with the results of activities of the false teachers. Paul's aim is love that "comes from a pure heart and a good conscience and a sincere faith." The prevalence of triadic expressions in the Pastorals shows an inclination toward edifying language. Active love, the charitable treatment of others, has the following prerequisites: purity in the totality of moral affections, sensitive self-judgment, and faith that is literally, "unhypocritical" (i.e., without hypocrisy or pretense), but rather sincere and consistently results in love for God and others.

1.2.1.3. Error Into Which Some Have Wandered: False Use of the Law (1:6–7). It is characteristic in early Christian polemics to identify opponents with the Greek word *tis/tines* [plural], translated "certain" (1:3) or "some" (1:6, 19). "Some" have missed the mark of love and the virtuous sources from which it issues (a pure heart, a good conscience, and a sincere faith). They have failed to take aim and thus swerved off the right path, turning aside to foolish talk, idle chatter, or empty arguments. In the style of the Pastorals' polemic, there is a constant attack on the opponents, but little identification of them. The verb "turned to" (*ektrepo*) was sometimes used as a medical term meaning "to be dislocated." The aberrant teachings of these false teachers are a painful presence in the body of Christ.

Although the heretics aspire to be teachers of the law, they are wholly unqualified, being both unintelligent and ignorant. "Teachers of the law" was a technical term from Judaism (cf. Luke 5:17; Acts 5:34). These opponents of the apostle seek official recognition and status by their exacting exegesis and legalistic demands. Although they continue to make confident assertions, insist they are right, or give their opinion in a firm, dogmatic tone, they are continually (such is the emphasis of the present tense here) unable to comprehend.

1.2.1.4. Corrective: Proper Use of the Law (1:8–11). Paul explains that the law's benefit is proportionate to its proper, legitimate use, that is, its use that is agreeable to its design: the restraint of evildoing. Provided we treat it as law, the law is an excellent thing (cf. Rom. 7:12, 16). It works well when we respect it; but if we break it, it condemns us. Paul introduces this statement as an acknowledged principle with the phrase "we know."

The law was not instituted for the sake of the righteous—it has little relevance for them—but for the unrighteous. Paul then lists fourteen different kinds of unrighteous people (grouped into four double categories: "lawbreakers and rebels," "the ungodly and sinful," "the unholy and irreligious," and "those who kill fathers or mothers"; and six single categories: "murderers," "adulterers," "perverts," "slave traders," "liars," and "perjurers"), and then includes all other kinds of sinners in "whatever else is contrary to the sound [wholesome, healthy] doctrine." His order is first to refer to persons guilty of offenses against God, and then to those committing crimes against others. Beginning with the fourth in Paul's sequence, the list coincides roughly with the Decalogue. In the ancient world, virtue and vice lists (cataloguing kinds of sinful and saintly behavior) were common (cf. Rom. 1:31). It was customary to cite the most serious and unusual crimes in such lists. The catalogue included here appears to be a Christian adaptation of a Hellenistic-Jewish list.

More specifically, the people for whom the law was instituted are: (1) the lawless; (2) those who are insubordinate, unruly, independent, undisciplined, and rebellious; (3) nonworshipers of God, that is, those who are impious, irreverent; (4) the sinful; (5) those to whom nothing is holy, for whom there is no inner purity; (6) the profane, that is, those who behave irreverently and contemptuously towards the things of God; (7) those who kill their fathers (patricide; lit., "father-strikers," those who strike their fathers down in death or disrespect); (8) those who kill their mothers (matricide); (9) murderers; (10) adulterers and fornicators, that is, those who practice sexual immorality; (11) perverts, such as sodomites, homosexuals (lit., "[males] who practice intercourse with males" [cf. 1 Cor. 6:9]); (12) slave traders (lit., "ones who catch a man by the foot," including all who exploit other men or women for their own selfish ends; (13) liars; and (14) perjurers, those who lie "against [their own] oath" of honesty.

Paul concludes by describing the true source of sound doctrine: "the glorious gospel of the blessed God, which he entrusted to me." The first phrase describes the content and character of the gospel; the second, its source; and the final, Paul's relationship to it.

1.2.2. Paul's Testimony: The Lord's Grace Unto Paul (1:12–17).

1.2.2.1. Appointed Apostle in Spite of His Past (1:12–13a). Paul is thankful to Christ Jesus for granting him strength, for considering him faithful, and for appointing him to ministry. The gracious enablement is as appreciated as the divine calling, the empowerment as necessary as the commission. Though Paul is conscientious in his labors, he is convinced of the effectiveness of the grace of Christ (see 1 Cor. 10:15). He uses the aorist tense in "has given ... strength," recalling a particular time when he became aware of this increasing strengthening (perhaps 2 Cor. 12:7–10). Having been deemed trustworthy, Paul was appointed to service as an apostle.

As in 1 Corinthians 15:9–10 and Galatians 1:13–17, Paul contrasts his pre-Christian life with his present Christian life. He lists his former identities as being a blasphemer (one who slanders God), a persecutor (who pursues persons as a hunter), and a violent, sadistic man (Gk. *hybristes*).

> The word [*hybristes*] indicates one who in pride and insolence deliberately and contemptuously mistreats and wrongs and hurts another person just for hurting sake and to deliberately humiliate the person. It speaks of treatment which is calculated publicly to insult and openly to humiliate the person who suffers it. The word is used in Romans 1:30 to describe a man of arrogant insolence, and pictures one of the characteristic sins of the pagan world. (Rienecker, 1980, 617)

1.2.2.2. Shown Mercy in Spite of Ignorance and Unbelief (1:13b–14). Paul avails himself of the Jewish distinction between conscious and unconscious sins (Lev. 22:14; Num. 15:22–31). He does not claim that his acting out of ignorance and unbelief makes him any less guilty, but mentions such in explaining the possibility of his pardon. But "the grace of our Lord" knows no bounds; it increases to overflowing and was "super-abundant" on Paul. Grace, by its nature, is wholly undeserved; grace, in its measure, is nothing but lavish. The unmerited kindness and divine enablement abounded exceedingly on the apostle, and faith and love were its effects.

1.2.2.3. Saved in Spite of His Sin (1:15). Paul introduces the next statement as "a trustworthy saying that deserves full acceptance," and by concluding it with a personal application, he makes it his own testimony. Its introductory formula, "here [this] is a trustworthy saying," appears five times in the Pastorals (1 Tim. 1:15; 3:1; 4:9; 2 Tim. 2:11; Titus 3:8), yet nowhere else in the New Testament. Each time it introduces a preexisting Christian catechetical or liturgical saying (e.g., a fragment of a hymn [2 Tim. 2:11–13], a faith formula [1 Tim. 1:15], or an aphorism or proverb [beginning in 4:8]), and affirms its truth (Kelly, 1963, 54). This statement itself, "Christ Jesus came into the world to save sinners," was an early Christian confession. According to this saying, the purpose of Christ's coming was to save, rescue, and deliver sinners (cf. 1 John 3:8b).

Paul then identifies himself, not as having been, but as *being* the worst of sinners (cf. 1 Cor. 15:9; Eph. 3:8). Although Paul is convinced that grace has delivered him from the penalties of the sins of his past, he is humbled by his memory and consciousness of sin in the present, and in this sense he still recognizes himself as a sinner.

1.2.2.4. Displayed As a Showpiece of God's Patience (1:16). Paul's salvation is for the purpose of displaying the unlimited patience of Christ Jesus to other candidates of faith. The verb for "display" is an intensified form of "show," as if laying the index finger on an object. Patience here is *makrothymia* (etymologically, God's "distance [from his] wrath"; i.e., the outworking of his anger), that is, his long-suffering or forbearance. As an example to others, Paul is a prototype of grace. He is a missionary paradigm: unique as an apostle, yet typical as a convert from whom the worst of sinners can take hope.

1.2.2.5. Doxology (1:17). As in other instances in the Pastorals (1 Tim. 2:5–6; 5:21; 6:13–16; 2 Tim. 1:9–10; 2:8; 4:1), Paul seems to quote liturgical material. This time he soars into a doxology, a confession of praise to God, in which four characteristics are attributed to God: (1) eternity, everlastingness; (2) immortality, incorruptibility, that is, immunity from decay; (3) invisibility, inability to be seen; and (4) singularity, the only God ever to exist. Recognition of these divine qualities prompts eternal ascription of honor and glory to God.

1.2.3 Encouragement to Fight (1:18–20). Paul's testimony in 1:18–19a leads him to remind Timothy of the command given in 1:3–4. As further support for the charge and encouragement to his young friend, Paul this time reminds Timothy of "the prophecies" once made about him. The apostle hopes that, inspired by them, Timothy will "fight the good fight" and will cling to faith and a good conscience.

Paul then cites two examples of faithlessness. The two apostates (Hymenaeus and Alexander) are infamous fathers of heresy (probably the same as those mentioned in 2 Tim. 2:17; perhaps 4:14). It is not clear exactly what these two men rejected, turned their backs on, or repudiated. The Greek identifies it by a feminine singular relative pronoun (translated "these" in NIV), the antecedent of which could be any of the following: the command, instruction, charge; the fight, military expedition, campaign, warfare; the faith; or a good conscience. The result of the apostasy of these men, however, is clear: they "have shipwrecked their faith." This image is vivid to Paul, who at the time of the Pastorals had suffered four shipwrecks. On each occasion he had lost everything but his life.

Paul's response was severe: He "handed [them] over to Satan" to teach them a lesson (cf. 1 Cor. 5:5). Satan is a torturous tutor; the verb "hand over" is more closely associated with punishment than with instruction. They must learn to stop slandering God, which in this case probably refers either to their false teaching or their opposition to the gospel message.

2. Setting the Church in Order: General Principles for Grounding the Troubled Church in Ephesus (2:1–3:13)

2.1. On Prayer for Peace (2:1–8)

2.1.1. Exhortation to Pray for Peace (2:1–2). Paul's instructions on prayer are first on his agenda and foremost in importance. He urges or exhorts that four kinds of prayer be offered for all people. (1) "Request" (*deesis*), that is, petition or intercession, derives from the verb that means to have the good fortune "to have an audience with the king" so as to present a petition. The word was regularly used for a petition to a superior. (2) "Prayer" (*proseuche*) is the common word for prayer. (3) "Intercession" (*enteuxis*), another word for petition or intercession, comes from a verb that means "to appeal to." (4) "Thanksgiving" (*eucharistia*) is the word from which Eucharist, the liturgical title for the Lord's Supper, derives.

The apostle makes special mention of prayer for governing authorities and explains its purposes or results. The word for "being in authority" here etymologically indicates to "have [a position] over." It could include all those in prominence or superiors. The description of the effectiveness of these prayers includes four expressions for the kinds of lives prayer will cause us to lead: (1) "peaceful," quiet, tranquil, or undisturbed; (2) "quiet" or still; (3) "in all godliness" or religious devotion, that is, having the right attitude toward God

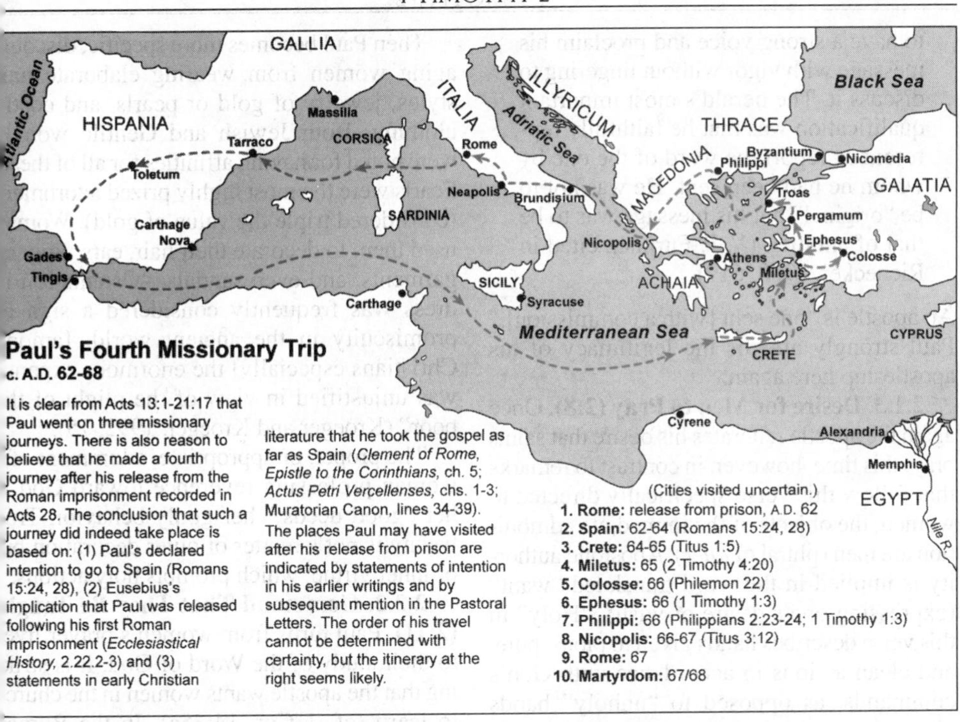

Paul's Fourth Missionary Trip
c. A.D. 62-68

It is clear from Acts 13:1-21:17 that Paul went on three missionary journeys. There is also reason to believe that he made a fourth journey after his release from the Roman imprisonment recorded in Acts 28. The conclusion that such a journey did indeed take place is based on: (1) Paul's declared intention to go to Spain (Romans 15:24, 28), (2) Eusebius's implication that Paul was released following his first Roman imprisonment (*Ecclesiastical History*, 2.22.2-3) and (3) statements in early Christian literature that he took the gospel as far as Spain (*Clement of Rome, Epistle to the Corinthians*, ch. 5; *Actus Petri Vercellenses*, chs. 1-3; Muratorian Canon, lines 34-39). The places Paul may have visited after his release from prison are indicated by statements of intention in his earlier writings and by subsequent mention in the Pastoral Letters. The order of his travel cannot be determined with certainty, but the itinerary at the right seems likely.

lerived from possessing a true knowledge of Jod; and (4) "[in all] holiness," gravity, seriousness, or dignity, that is, the moral earnestness that affects one's outward demeanor and nward intention.

2.1.2. Grounds and Fulfillment of Exhortation (2:3–7).

2.1.2.1. God's Will: Salvation and Enlightenment (2:3–4). Paul explains that the idea of universal prayer for all is both good (not just *agathos*, "right, practically and morally good," but *kalos*, "beautiful, and aesthetically good—pleasing in human eyes") (Lock, 1973, 22–23) and pleasing in God's eyes.

The will of God our Savior is that all people "be saved and . . . come to a knowledge of the truth." Although the Greek text has words that differentiate "man [male person]" (*aner*) from "human being [generic person]" (*anthropos*), the NIV text does not distinguish these words in translation. At times this may leave the wrong impression with modern readers, who no longer read "man/men" as generic. A careful commentary or a consultation of the original text will make this point clear to the reader.

2.1.2.2. Christ's Role: Sacrifice and Witness (2:5–6). Paul seems to be quoting here again. The original text of 2:5–6 has been recognized as poetry and is indented as such in the Greek New Testament. These verses were probably an early Christian hymn of five lines:

> For there is one God
> and one mediator between God and
> humankind [*anthropon*]
> Christ Jesus, himself human [*anthropos*],
> who gave himself as a ransom for all
> ["men" is not present in the Greek
> text],
> the testimony given at the proper time.

This hymn affirms the singularity and unity of God as held by Jews, then adds the Christian revelation of Christ as the mediator or go-between. Such mediation was made possible by the Incarnation and culminated in the crucifixion of Christ, when his life was offered as the price paid for release of a slave. All this occurred in the time ordained by God.

2.1.2.3. Paul's Call: A Preacher and Apostle (2:7). Paul's commission is to share this testimony among the Gentiles as a "herald," "apostle," and "teacher."

The herald was someone who had important news to bring. He often announced an athletic event or religious festival, or functioned as a political messenger, the bringer of some news or command from the king's court. He was

> to have a strong voice and proclaim his message with vigor without lingering to discuss it. The herald's most important qualification was that he faithfully represent or report the word of the one by whom he had been sent. He was not to be "original" but his message was to be that of another. (V. P. Furnish, cited in Rienecker, 1980, 619)

An apostle is "one sent [with a commission]." Paul strongly affirms the legitimacy of his apostleship here again.

2.1.3. Desire for Men to Pray (2:8). Once again the apostle reiterates his desire that saints pray; this time, however, in contrast to remarks that follow this verse specifically directed to women, the objects of the immediate admonition are men (plural of *aner*). Apostolic authority is implied in the word translated "want" (expressing one's desire or wish). "Holy" in this verse describes hands given to pious, pure, and clean actions in accordance with God's commands, as opposed to "unholy" hands given over to wrath and quarrelsomeness.

> The most general attitude for prayer in antiquity, for pagans, Jews, and Christians alike, was to stand with hands outstretched and uplifted, the palms turned upwards. The frescoes of *orantes* in, e.g., the Roman catacombs, provide vivid illustration from the life of the early Church. (Kelly, 1963, 66)

2.2. On Women's Dress and Lifestyle (2:9–15)

2.2.1. Preference for Their Spiritual Adornment (2:9–10). A literal translation of the Greek text begins this verse with "likewise also the women"—apparently indicating that women are to pray in the same manner men are commanded to pray, but are at the same time advised to be careful concerning their personal appearance. The apostle's desire is that their clothing (or demeanor, deportment) be modest (i.e., well arranged, well ordered, moderate) "with decency and propriety." These latter two terms carry a sexual nuance and denote feminine reserve and moral repugnance to doing what is dishonorable. They refer to perfect self-mastery of the interior appetites, to inner self-government that puts reins on all passions and desires.

Then Paul becomes more specific, discouraging women from wearing elaborate hai styles, jewelry of gold or pearls, and costl clothing. Both Jewish and Gentile wome were noted for having affinities for all of these Pearls were the most highly prized adornmen (considered triple the value of gold). Wome used them to decorate their hair, ears, fingers garments, and even sandals. "Ostentation i dress was frequently considered a sign o promiscuity in the ancient world, [amon Christians especially] the enormous expens was unjustified in view of the plight of th poor" (Kroeger and Kroeger, 1992, 75).

The proper, or appropriate, adornment of woman professing reverence toward God i her "good deeds," her godly behavior. Tru beauty is not a matter of outer decoration bu of inner virtue, which prompts holy actions.

2.2.2. Command That They Be Taugh (2:11). Paul turns from women's prayer live to their study of the Word of God. It is strik ing that the apostle wants women in the churc to learn (cf. 1 Cor. 14:35a). In the Roma period, outside of the aristocracy, mos women, whether Jewish or Gentile, wer deprived an education. The situation was n better in the religious world: Gentile wome were not allowed to participate in the officia Greek and Roman state religion, and Jewis women were discouraged from studying th Torah and not counted in the synagogue quo rum. Yet Paul mandates a different standard i Christianity: "A woman should learn" (lit., "le a woman be discipled [*manthano*] or taught.

The Old Testament advocates silenc before the Lord (Ps. 46:10; Isa. 41:1; Hab 2:20; Zech. 2:13). Such an attitude is espe cially conducive to learning. Even rabbinica scholars were required to learn in silence which was understood as a wall around wis dom. Three times the Septuagint (the Gree translation of the Old Testament) adds "sub mission" to the "silence" enjoined by th Hebrew Old Testament (Ps. 37:7; 62:1, 5 Silence and submission were considered to b states of ultimate receptivity.

From the deportment Paul required o female students or disciples (quietness and fu submission, see vv. 11b, 12b), we are reminde again of the problematic situation in Ephesus The false teachers had made special inroad among women—likely because these wome ad *not* been taught the truth by the church. 'herefore, Paul desired to equip these women /ith truth so that they could stand against rror. His command in 2:11 that women learn ; the corrective against the foolish workers of Timothy 3:6–7, who are "always learning ut never able to acknowledge the truth."

2.2.3. Command That They Be Silent 2:12). The next sentence has been interpreted y many to be the apostle's unequivocal denun-iation of women's leadership, his absolute rohibition against ever putting a woman in a osition of authority over a man. Such an inter-retation has been perplexing to Full Gospel 'hristians, who recognize the Holy Spirit's quipping for Christian leadership without egard for gender as was promised by Joel 2:28–32) and fulfilled on the Day of Pentecost Acts 2:17–21). How can the two biblical state-nents (the promise [and its fulfillment] and the rohibition) be reconciled?

Admittedly, this passage poses special chal-enges to interpreters.[1] (1) The verb *authenteo* NIV, "have authority over") is not clear. And ince this word occurs only once in the entire Iew Testament and not at all in the Septuagint, /e must go outside Scripture to discern its neaning.

(2) The word order is unusual; a literal ranslation reads: "To teach, on the contrary, to woman I do not grant permission, nor to *uthentein* a man but to be in silence."

(3) The grammatical challenge is to moothly render a text with two negative par-icles (*ouk* and *oude*) and three infinitives *didaskein, authentein,* and *einai*).

(4) The verses following the injunction in :12 raise additional questions: (a) Why the eference to order in creation? (b) Why the xplication on deception and transgression? (c) Vhy the connection between salvation and hildbearing?

(5) Most significantly, the traditional inter-retation (i.e., prohibiting women's leadership) nakes Paul's words here contradict his prac-ce of affirming women's Christian leadership lsewhere.

The verse begins with the word *didaskein,* to teach." The Pastorals place great empha-is on teaching because only accurate teaching an combat the false doctrine raging in Eph-sus. It is clear that women were somehow nvolved in the false teaching (1 Tim. 4:7; 5:11–13; 2 Tim. 3:6–7; Titus 1:11). Yet Paul does not forbid women's leadership altogether. Elsewhere in the Pastorals he takes a positive view concerning women's teaching (see 2 Tim. 1:5; 3:14–15; 4:19; cf. Acts 18:26b). Outside the Pastorals the New Testament contains numerous affirmations in the letters of Paul about women in ministry (Rom. 16:1–2, 3–5, 6, 7, 12; Phil. 4:3).

Note also that it was the apostle Paul him-self who, in his absence, had left Priscilla and Aquila to pastor the first believers in this very city of Ephesus (Acts 18:19). Priscilla's joint-teaching with her husband of the eloquent Alexandrian (male) preacher Apollos was well known (Acts 18:26). Paul had highest com-mendation for this woman teacher and Eph-esian church leader, who was still alive and much appreciated at the time of writing the Pastorals (Rom. 16:3–4; 2 Tim. 4:19). Histor-ical context, therefore, makes it clear that the apostle did not forbid women's teaching (as some have interpreted this text), but forbade their teaching of false doctrine, just as 1 Tim-othy 1:3–4 and Titus 1:9–14 forbid false teaching of other heretics. (The verses that fol-low [i.e., 1 Tim. 2:13–15] reveal the nature of the heretical teaching Paul forbade.)

The greatest challenge to interpreting 1 Timothy 2:12 concerns the meaning of the second infinitive, the rare verb *authenteo* (infinitive form *authentein*). Although the meaning "to have authority over" has been tra-ditionally accepted for use in this context, such a translation is seriously contested today by conservative scholars who have conducted extensive research on the uses of the word out-side the New Testament. The range of mean-ings of *authenteo* include the following: (1) to begin something or be responsible for a con-dition or action; (2) to rule or dominate; (3) to usurp power or rights from another; (4) to claim ownership, sovereignty, or authorship (Kroeger and Kroeger, 1992, 84).

The Kroegers offer two alternative transla-tions that take into account the verse's unusual word order, its grammatical challenges, its his-torical context, and the recent lexical research into this word. (1) "I do not allow a woman to teach nor to represent herself as originator of man" (ibid., 103). (2) "I do not allow a woman to teach that she is the originator of man" (ibid., 191–92). Such a teaching (that Eve was created first and that she originated Adam) was one of the Gnostic versions of creation. In this verse, Paul is prohibiting women's teaching of such heresy.

Since such an interpretation takes 1 Timothy 2:12 not as prohibition against all women's teaching and authority in ministry, it is consistent with Paul's other affirmations of women's leadership. Note also how clear this interpretation is in the context of the verses that follow.

2.2.4. Creation Order Reiterated (2:13). After Paul prohibits the teaching of this aspect of Gnostic heresy, he states the orthodox view regarding the chronology of creation. He emphasizes the Genesis account and asserts definitively: "For Adam was formed first, then Eve."

2.2.5. Fall Into Sin Explained (2:14). Another Gnostic myth taught that the temptation of the serpent did not result in sin but in enlightenment, and that it was Eve, in the sharing of the fruit, who brought the light to Adam. To correct that heresy, Paul is obliged to explain the Fall, Eve's deception, and the first transgression.

2.2.6. Hope for Their Salvation Announced (2:15). The apostle concludes the matter by promising salvation for women—in spite of childbearing—if they continue in faith, love, and holiness with sobriety. Gnostic myths contained an elaborate teaching on the dissemination, to each of their descendants at birth, of particles of divine light from the first couple, who were endowed with these particles at creation. Every subsequent generation distributes their particles of light among their progeny. After death, when a Gnostic individual attempts to make the heavenly journey off this material planet, he or she is prohibited from leaving earth until all his or her light particles are recollected. If, by having children, a Gnostic's particles of light have been passed on to others, she is trapped on earth until the death of every generation of her descendants, when all her particles of light may be regathered.

In Gnostic teaching, in other words, the bearing of children virtually made eternal salvation impossible. Presumably that is why the false teachers in Ephesus were forbidding marriage (4:3). "Some Gnostic texts condemned childbearing, and others implied that it was impossible to gain eternal life as a woman" (Kroeger, Evans, and Storkey, 1995, 442). Thus, Paul corrects that erroneous teaching, as well, by promising salvation—in spite of bearing children—if these women lead lives c Christian holiness.

The proper interpretation of this passag puts an end to the false allegation that the tra ditional welcoming of the ministry and lead ership of women in Full Gospel, Pentecosta and charismatic church circles (and the con temporary acceptance of women ministers i mainline denominations) is in violation o Scripture. Just as Peter on the Day of Penteco promised that in these last days God's Spir would equip women as well as men for min istry (Acts 2:16–18), and just as Paul recog nized that in Christ sexual distinctions ar irrelevant (Gal. 3:28), so also this passage doe not prohibit women's teaching men or the exercise of spiritual leadership. Instead, it con fronts a specific local problem in Ephesu silences its false teachers, and corrects the false teachings.

2.3. On Overseers (3:1–7)

2.3.1. Leadership Aspirations Affirme (3:1). The apostle turns his attention to specifi leadership positions in the church by quotin another apparently well-known adage. Alread by this time the early church had a collectio of sayings (*logia*) that stated in short, memo rable fashion nuggets of truth commonly hel by believers. These sayings existed before th time of the composition of the Pastorals, an in recognition of their general acceptance we introduced with a quotation formula such a we see here: "Here is a trustworthy saying (see comments on 1:15).

This Christian saying affirms a believer aspiration to serve the church in a leadershi or oversight position. Any such believer, ma or female (the word *tis* is inclusive of both ge ders), desires to do a good work, a noble tas The apostle in quoting this *logion* commen the office of overseer to anyone who meets th qualifications that follow (vv. 2–7).

The responsibilities of overseer, superi tendent, or bishop (*episkopes*) are far fro clear in this early period. The title seems to b equivalent to the role of elder or presbyt (*presbyteros*) (5:17; Titus 1:5), yet little i known of their precise functions. The roles o the offices of the church were fluid and flex ble in the New Testament era. Not until th early patristic period were they standardize and regulated.

2.3.2. Leadership Qualifications Estab-shed (3:2–7). Paul begins his discussion of equirements for candidates for church leader-hip with a serial list of twelve unadorned ualifications (vv. 2–3), followed by three equirements each accompanied by a rationale vv. 4–7). It is important to note that the entire st is framed by what is called an *inclusio*, a terary bracketing device around a particular ubject. The first requirement (v. 2a) is that an verseer "be above reproach"; the last require-ent (v. 7) is that the overseer "have a good eputation with outsiders." The entire subject, erefore—qualifications for church leaders— bracketed by the importance of being above eproach.

This is not a list of spiritual requirements— one of the items is specifically Christian. Nor it a job description of duties of overseers. ather, the items reflect the highest ideals of ellenistic moral philosophy. The list suggests at the behavior of false teachers was bring-ig the gospel into disrepute. "Therefore Paul concerned not only that elders have Christ-n virtues (these are assumed) but that they eflect the highest ideals of the culture as well" Fee, 1988, 78–79). Lists of qualifications ere commonplace in antiquity among reeks, Romans, and Jews. The standard of eaders being "above reproach" was widely eld in the ancient world. "Paul, recognizing e challenges Christianity faced right at the utset from the world's prejudice, was deter-ined to outdo the world's standards of moral-y and not to let scandal stain the church's eputation" (Keener, 1991, 87).

(1) The first and foremost qualification, en, is that overseers have sterling character, at is, that they be unimpeachable. It should ever be possible to (lit.) "catch an overseer ut" of the bounds of integrity.

(2) The next qualification—that an overseer e "the husband of one wife" (there is no "but" i the Greek as translated in the NIV)—is easy) translate but difficult to interpret. Three cir-les of issues are involved: (a) Is the apostle ondemning divorce, polygamy, concubinage, r something else? (b) Is the apostle requiring verseers to be married as opposed to never iarried? (c) Is the apostle requiring that over-eers be male as opposed to female?

(a) The first circle of issues in the interpre-tion of the qualification that an overseer be "the husband of one wife" is: What, in the first century, did "husband of one wife" mean? The traditional interpretation takes the phrase to mean "the husband of only one wife *during his lifetime*," sometimes adding the qualifier "*unless she dies*." Such a rendering of the qualification permits persons remarried after the death of a spouse the opportunity to serve in church leadership, but prohibits those remarried after divorce from leadership candidacy. Full Gospel believers maintain a high view of the permanence of marriage and want their leaders to be exemplary of the same. They also maintain a high view of God's grace and want their practices to demonstrate grace in action. Consequently, the struggles over this text have been so great that charismatic congregations have split and Pentecostal denominations have divided over the interpretation and application of this requirement for church leaders.

The issue becomes especially complicated when the candidate for church leadership falls into one of the following categories: if one's divorce and remarriage took place prior to conversion, or if the believer was the "innocent party" in a divorce (i.e., if the marriage was terminated on biblical grounds). Jesus permitted divorce if the other partner was unfaithful (Matt. 5:31–32), and Paul permitted divorce if the other partner deserted (1 Cor. 7:15). Even more complicated is the issue if an ecclesiastical annulment has taken place (for which there is no New Testament Scripture to cite).

Some churches acknowledge that adultery and desertion are biblical grounds for divorce, but in no case permit remarriage. Their support is (i) that neither in Mark 10:11–12 nor in Luke 16:18 is Jesus' statement on divorce qualified with an "exception" clause (cf. Matt. 5:31–32)—that is, that every remarriage constitutes adultery; and (ii) that Paul subordinates his exception to the divorce decree of Christ as Paul's own charge and not the Lord's (cf. 1 Cor. 7:10–16). (Paul seems to be unaware of Christ's making any exception.) Other churches permit remarriage in the case of persons who experienced divorce on biblical grounds. Their logic is that the purpose of ancient divorce was as a legal sanction for remarriage.

The context of our modern world and the rapid rise of divorce (both outside and inside the church) call us to wrestle with this text. Perhaps the context of the ancient world and its family and social structure can shed light on the issue. What did "the husband of one wife" mean to the original readers of 1 Timothy, to first-century Jews, and to pagans? What specific reproach in that cultural context did the apostle Paul want candidates for Christian leadership to be unstained by? Was it divorce, polygamy, concubinage, or something else?

Divorce was commonplace in the first century among pagans. Judaism also permitted divorce on many grounds, making it easy for a husband to divorce his wife (see Matt. 19:3, where the Pharisees ask Jesus if divorce can take place "for any and every reason," and 19:10, where even Jesus' own disciples are shocked at the severity of his reply). Keener states: "It is next to impossible that [Paul] is addressing the remarriage of divorced men, because no one in antiquity, whether Jewish or Greco-Roman, would have looked down on the remarriage of *men*" ([Keener's emphasis], Keener, 1991, 100).

Polygamy was against Roman law, though officially legal in Palestinian Judaism. Nevertheless, even among Jews monogamy was the norm. Since polygamy was practiced neither by Jews outside of Palestine nor by local Greeks in Asia Minor, it seems unlikely that Paul is writing a proscription against polygamy for church leaders in Ephesus.

Though concubinage was not the usual practice, it was not unknown in the first-century Greco-Roman world. Soldiers, who could not officially marry until their term of military service had been fulfilled (a period lasting twenty years), are known to have taken concubines. While 1 Timothy 3:2 could be prohibiting concubinage, it was probably not common enough in Ephesus to merit prohibition here.

The purpose of the qualifications for church leaders is to guard the reputation of those in ministry from the reproach of those *outside* the church. If divorce was socially acceptable at the time of the writing of the New Testament, if polygamy was not practiced in Ephesus, and if concubinage was uncommon, from what behavior considered scandalous in the social setting of the first century is the apostle Paul excluding candidates for church office? Are there any further insights in the text?

The term "husband of one wife" found in the qualifications for overseer in both 1 Timothy 3:2 and Titus 1:6 as well as in the qualifications for deacon in 1 Timothy 3:12 has its counterpart in the term "wife of one husband" (NIV footnote) found in the qualifications for widows meriting financial support by the church in 1 Timothy 5. The structure of Paul's qualifications for older widows (5:3–16) is remarkably similar to Paul's qualifications for older men/male elders (5:17–25). It seems these widows had a place of ministry and honor, a paid office of prayer (cf. vv. 5, 9–16).

The Latin word *univira* and the Greek word *monandros*, both meaning "[wife] of one husband" (lit., "one-man [woman]"), are terms attributed not only to godly widows, but found as funerary inscriptions of virtuous Roman wives being honored by the husbands who survived them. The term "single-husband" wives speaks of women who fulfilled the "one husband ideal" of antiquity: (a) they married only once and (b) were absolutely faithful to their one and only husband all their lives. "The *functional* stress of the term is on the wife's faithfulness as a good wife through the duration of the marriage. . . . [She] was faithful to her husband, never taking interest in another man during their marriage" ([Keener's emphasis], Keener, 1991, 95). In fact, the NIV renders the "wife of one husband" in 1 Timothy 5:9 as a widow who "has been faithful to her husband." Since antiquity held no "one-wife ideal" for men, when the term is used in the masculine, a "one-woman [man]" (i.e., "[the husband] of one wife"), it is thought to refer to a faithful and loyal spouse, never taking interest in another woman during their marriage.

> [Marriage] to one partner in a lifetime is never applied as a qualification for leaders in the ancient world; it is not even a frequent praise of men (who in that culture filled most of the leadership roles), being reserved most often for women. The ideal of marital fidelity, however, is often required of leaders. . . . [Having one's] household in order was a frequent ancient standard for leadership. (ibid., 95)

> What *was* ridiculed in this culture was successive divorce, bigamy (including marriage to a concubine on the side), and marital infidelity. ([Keener's emphasis], ibid., 100–101)

A candidate for church leadership living a morally loose life would scandalize the reputation of the church (as was the case in Corinth, 1 Cor. 5). Note too how the prophet Nathan grieved because King David's sexual immorality gave the enemies of the Lord a cause for which to blaspheme (2 Sam. 12:14).

If Keener is correct, this qualification for overseers (and deacons and widows) means *marital fidelity*, so that the apostle's real focus is on the sexual morality of candidates for church leadership. Such an interpretation suggests that Paul might sanction the leadership of some who had been victimized by divorce while disqualifying from leadership believers who had ever been sexually unfaithful to their spouse (thus, perhaps, prohibiting the restoration to ministry of leaders who had fallen morally, since they proved themselves to not be "one-woman men"). If the NIV translation of the female counterpart of the term is applied consistently, then this qualification for overseers (3:2; Titus 1:6) and for deacons (1 Tim. 3:12) would be rendered "faithful to their spouses."

In sum, the interpretation and application of the criterion for an overseer that he be "husband of one wife" is a difficult issue for several significant reasons:

- God has a very high regard for the permanence of marriage (cf. Mal. 2:16; Matt. 19:6b; Mark 10:9).
- There remains a lack of consensus on the meaning of the expression translated "husband of one wife."
- There is the importance of exercising a sensitive nature in dealing as Christ would with the lives of persons involved in unfortunate marital situations.

Polygamy and concubinage do not seem to be at the crux of this issue behind Paul's instructions here; but whether it is remarriage after divorce or marital unfaithfulness that disqualifies an elder from office is still debated. Every denomination and fellowship and every independent congregation must prayerfully settle the matter for themselves. In such cases of theological or practical uncertainty, our Lord charged the church with the authority to make binding decisions; and even though individual congregations and fellowships may arrive at different conclusions, Christ has committed himself to honor those decisions made by his representatives (Matt. 16:19; 18:18–19). Our attitude must be as our Lord's—to respect the judgments of other believers on disputable matters though they may differ from our own. (Compare the apostle's advice regarding differences of convictions on another important first-century moral issue, eating meat sacrificed to idols [Rom. 14:1–23; 1 Cor. 8:1–13].)

(b) The second circle of issues in the interpretation of the qualification that an overseer be "the husband of one wife" is whether the apostle is requiring church leaders (overseers in 3:2 [cf. Titus 1:6]; deacons in 1 Tim. 3:12; widows in 5:9) to be married as opposed to never married.

In the specific local context of first-century Ephesus and Crete, it is possible that Paul is specifying marriage as preferable for church leaders. The marriages of these local leaders would be a testimony that they had rejected the false teaching that forbade marriage, an attitude the apostle is combating in the Pastoral Letters (see 4:3). The presence of such a heresy in the historical context of this letter might also contribute to Paul's encouragement that younger widows remarry and to his specification that only "one-husband" wives (i.e., widows, not simply older women) be put on the role of the church's paid staff. "It may be that those in positions of honor in this church needed to have been married before in order to stand as an example against the rhetoric of false teachers who rejected marriage" (Keener, 1991, 92).

Yet this qualification, even if that is the meaning here, was not a universal requirement for church leaders, but an example of representatives of Christ being above reproach to those outside the church in the specific cultural situation of Ephesus. Marriage was certainly not a normative qualification for Christian leadership. Timothy was probably unmarried, Barnabas had no wife (1 Cor. 9:1–5), Paul himself was single (1 Cor. 7:7–8), and our Lord never married. Even if Paul were suggesting that overseers and deacons in Ephesus (and Crete) be married, such a qualification would not be binding on Christian leaders in other situations.

(c) The final circle of issues in the interpretation of the qualification that an overseer be "the husband of one wife" is this: Is the apostle requiring that overseers be male as opposed to female? Again, in this specific setting it is possible that Paul may be specifying unique requirements to counteract local problems. Where the false teachers have had special success among ignorant women (Keener, 1992, 111–12), the apostle may be suggesting overseers be male. Yet, though such a hypothesis is possible, it is not probable—most of the false teachers themselves seem to have been male.

When Paul broached the subject of overseers, he did not specify the gender of overseers but used the generic word "anyone/whoever." The NIV makes use of the masculine pronoun ten times in the list of qualifications simply because there is no generic third-person singular pronoun in the English language. It would be clearer to translate the list as qualifications for overseers (plural), so that the gender-neutral pronoun of the third-person plural, "they," could be used. The original Greek, however (even in the singular), is inclusive of both genders. The apostle could have easily been male-specific, as he was in 1 Timothy 2:8, but he chose to be gender-inclusive with regard to overseers.

Since Paul commended the spiritual oversight of female Christian leaders such as Phoebe (described literally as "minister of the church in Cenchrea," Rom. 16:1–2) and Junia (a female apostle, noteworthy among apostles, Rom. 16:7), and commissioned Priscilla and Aquila to oversee the infant congregation in Ephesus (Acts 18:19), it is not likely that he considered maleness a requirement for ministry in either Ephesus or anywhere else.

The next three qualifications in verse 2 are similar: (3) temperance or sobriety; (4) self-control or sensibility; (5) and respectability or good behavior. Temperance is often used in regard to alcoholic beverages, but since verse 3 specifically addresses "not given to drunkenness," it is more likely that the term here is used in the wider, metaphorical sense, that is, "free from every form of excess, passion, or rashness." Thus, the minister is to be clearheaded, sober-minded, vigilant. The latter two qualifications occur together in ethical lists of secular writings as high ideals of behavior required for various occupations. They speak of internal character and external deportment—the well-ordered private life from which flows the well-ordered fulfillment of all duties.

(6) It is necessary that an overseer be "hos pitable" (v. 2), another Greek virtue. Hospital ity is a duty of all believers individually (5:1(and of the whole church collectively (Rom 12:13; 1 Peter 4:9; 3 John 5), but finds its high est expression in overseers who are describe in early Christian writings as trees shelterin sheep and singled out for special praise for thi role (1 Clem. 1:2, 10–11). A special blessin is attached to this ministry (Heb. 13:2).

Hospitality in the New Testament is mor than entertaining one's friends, relatives, an neighbors or having dinner guests once week. It refers to opening one's home to thos who are unknown or different from ourselve The adjective "hospitable" literally mean "loving strangers." It refers to caring for th needy in the congregation and community an to opening one's home to traveling minister especially strangers.

The early church could not have survive without the practice of this virtue.

> When someone traveled in antiquity, it was most natural to find someone of the traveler's own country or trade, who would gladly provide accommodations for the night. Inns charged unfairly high prices and usually doubled as brothels, so travelers often carried letters of recommendation so they would be received by friends of their patrons in other cities.
>
> This would be especially true of Jewish travelers, loath to stay in a brothel if other alternatives were available. Synagogues and school-houses could be used for this purpose, but it was best to stay in a host's home. It appears that it was proper for the host to insist that the guest stay, allowing the guest to leave only if the guest insisted. Paul had often profited from this custom in his own travels.
>
> Although the virtue of this kind of hospitality should be practiced in all cultures, it probably appears in *Paul's* list because it was a sign of great respectability in that culture. ([Keener's emphasis], Keener, 1991, 97)

(7) It is necessary that an overseer be "abl to teach" (v. 2). Teaching is considered a spi itual gift in the New Testament (cf. Rom. 12: 1 Cor. 12:28–29; Eph. 4:11). Overseers are t be identified with the group of elders withi

the congregation who are occupied with preaching and teaching (1 Tim. 5:17). Titus 1:9 specifies three qualifications of spiritual teachers: an understanding of truth consistent with apostolic tradition, an ability to impart it clearly to others, and an ability to refute the errors of those who pervert it. The requirement that spiritual leaders have a teaching aptitude is consistent with the prohibition of novices being authorized to teach (v. 6).

(8) The overseer must not have a problem with alcohol (v. 3; lit., not be "overfond of wine"). Fee (1988, 81) asks whether this crieria suggests that the false teachers were given to drunkenness.

> Perhaps not, in light of their asceticism noted in 4:3. But they may have been ascetic about certain foods and overindulgent about wine. In any case, drunkenness was one of the common vices of antiquity; and few pagan authors speak out against it—only against other "sins" that might go along with it (violence, public scolding of servants, etc.). The overseer is not necessarily to be a total abstainer (5:23), but neither is he to be given to drunkenness (cf. 3:8; Titus 1:7); this is uniformly condemned in Scripture.

The next three qualifications seem to go together and most likely reflect the false teachers' behavior. The false teachers as described in 6:3–5 and 2 Timothy 2:22–26 (cf. Titus 3:9) were given to strife and quarrels. Thus, the true elder must (9) not be a "violent," pugnacious person, a "striker"—one who is inclined to fighting, belligerent, and contentious; (10) but "gentle" and considerate—even in correcting opponents (2 Tim. 2:23–25); and (11) "not quarrelsome."

(12) The list continues with the requirement that the overseer "not [be] a lover of money" (v. 3). First Timothy 6:5–10 explains that greed is one of the "deadly sins" of the false teachers, the cause of their ultimate ruin. A warning against avarice is included in every list of qualifications for leadership in the New Testament (3:8; Titus 1:7; cf. Acts 20:33; see comments on 1 Tim. 6:5–10; 2 Tim. 3:6–7).

In the final three concerns (the leaders' family lives, their maturity in the faith, and their reputation with outsiders) Paul offers the rationale for each requirement. These three also seem to be issues for the false teachers.

(13) The most detailed requirement in the list of qualifications of bishops concerns their control over children. This virtue was frequently extolled in antiquity and was often presented as a prerequisite for leading others. Since New Testament congregations met in homes and were based on the household framework (including family members, slaves, and servants), the stability of the home was important to the maintenance of a strong church. Since this was a standard requirement for respectable leaders, it was a necessary characteristic for Christian leaders to be "above reproach" (v. 2) in this area as well.

> But control over the household was also more easily implemented in that period than it is today. One could not be honorable in Greco-Roman society who did not honor and obey one's parents; this held true in Judaism as well. The father also held a traditional role of authority in Roman society; even though the power of life and death was rarely exercised over adult children, the continuing right of the father to decide whether infant children should be raised or discarded marked his position of power in the home. His paternal authority legally extended even to grandchildren and great-grandchildren, if he lived that long.
>
> Although parental love for children was the expected norm, discipline, often harsh discipline (including flogging), was stressed in the children's education. Although Paul sides with the minority who disapproved of severe discipline (Eph. 6:4), the culture as a whole was much more oriented toward filial obedience and parental authority than ours is today. (Keener, 1991, 98)

Overseers must "manage" their families well (*proïstemi*, a verb without a suggestion of sternness), keeping their children in submission with all respect. The rationale for this requirement is that learning to manage one's household prepares a person to manage God's household well. The word *proïstemi*, used of elders in 5:17 ("direct") and in 1 Thessalonians 5:12 ("are over"), implies the exercise of guidance and caring concern. The kind of respect commanded by the overseer is "the perfect blend of dignity and courtesy, independence and humility" (Rienecker, 1980, 623).

> The force of the phrase "with proper respect" probably means not so much that [children] will "obey" with "respect" but that they will be known for both their obedience and their generally good behavior. . . . There is a fine line between demanding obedience and gaining it. The church leader, who must indeed exhort people to obedience, does not thereby "rule" God's family. He "takes care of it" in such a way that its "children" will be known for their obedience and good behavior. (Fee, 1988, 82–83)

(14) Overseers must not be novices in the faith. The rationale? Elevating new believers too soon could tempt them to become proud. Since this is exactly what is said of the false teachers in 6:4 (cf. 2 Tim. 3:4), it appears that some of them may have been recent converts, whose "sins . . . are obvious" (1 Tim. 5:24). The words translated "not . . . a recent convert" are a metaphor literally meaning "not a newly planted person" (Fee, 1988, 83), probably referring to one recently baptized (cf. 1 Cor. 3:6, where Paul uses the verb for making converts). Thus candidates are to be carefully evaluated before appointment to leadership (cf. 1 Tim. 5:22).

At the time of Paul's writing this letter, Timothy's congregation in Ephesus is over ten years old, with sufficient seasoned leaders to choose from. This requirement is absent, however, from the list of criteria for leaders in the younger congregation on Crete in Paul's letter to Titus.

(15) An overseer must have "a good reputation" among those outside the church, so as to avoid disgrace. This whole list concerns observable behavior as a witness to the community of outsiders. As Fee (1988, 83) explains:

> the emphasis seems to be that a bad reputation with the pagan world will cause the *episkopos* to "fall into disgrace," or be slandered, and thus the church with him; and that would be to "fall . . . into the devil's trap." It is a "trap" set by the "devil" when the behavior of the church's leaders is such that outsiders will be disinclined to hear the gospel.

The scandals of certain Christian leaders c our time have disgraced the whole church an deepened America's disinclination towards th gospel. Many times the church is much mor forgiving of ministers' failures than the world i It is before "outsiders," however, that the repu tation of ministry leadership is to be sterling.

2.4. On Deacons (3:8–13)

2.4.1. Generic Qualifications for All Dea cons (3:8–10). In the same vein as he did wit overseers or bishops, the apostle discusses th qualifications (though not duties) for thos who serve the church as deacons or minister Though they function as helpers of the churc rather than its overseers, their moral and spi itual requirements are similar; thus, the apos tle introduces their qualifications wit "likewise."

Who or what were the deacons? Althoug it is common practice to consider thos selected to wait on tables in Acts (6:1–6; 21:8 as prototypes of the role, those men are nc called deacons.

> In fact they are clearly ministers of the Word among Greek-speaking Jews, who eventually accrue the title "the Seven" (Acts 21:8), which distinguishes them in a way similar to "the Twelve." Thus we are left with the almost certain reality that *episkopoi* [overseers] and *diakonoi* [deacons] are distinguishable functions in the church, but without knowing what they were. (Fee, 1988, 86)

Fee considers it likely that both "overseers and "deacons" come under the larger categor of "elders" (Fee, 1988, 78). Both were leader of the church. The word *diakonos* is, in fac Paul's favorite term to describe his own and hi coworkers' ministries (e.g., Rom. 16:1; 1 Co 3:5; 2 Cor. 3:6; Col. 1:23; 4:7). The word i used of Timothy in 4:6. Though the NIV doe not maintain a distinction, in English version *diakonos* is usually translated "deacons" whe it appears in the New Testament in the plura and "minister" when it appears in the singular As is true of other New Testament titles, ther seems to be a fluctuation in emphasis betwee the office and function.

Just as assistants (NIV, "those able to help" help administrators (NIV "those with gifts c administration") (1 Cor. 12:28), it seems tha

QUALIFICATIONS FOR ELDERS/OVERSEERS AND DEACONS

Qualification	Office	Scripture References
Self-controlled	Elder	1Ti 3:2; Tit 1:8
Hospitable	Elder	1Ti 3:2; Tit 1:8
Able to teach	Elder	1Ti 3:2; 5:17; Tit 1:9
Not violent but gentle	Elder	1Ti 3:3; Tit 1:7
Not quarrelsome	Elder	1Ti 3:3
Not a lover of money	Elder	1Ti 3:3
Not a recent convert	Elder	1Ti 3:6
Has a good reputation with outsiders	Elder	1Ti 3:7
Not overbearing	Elder	Tit 1:7
Not quick-tempered	Elder	Tit 1:7
Loves what is good	Elder	Tit 1:8
Upright, holy	Elder	Tit 1:8
Disciplined	Elder	Tit 1:8
Above reproach (blameless)	Elder / Deacon	1Ti 3:2, 9; Tit 1:6
Husband of one wife	Elder / Deacon	1Ti 3:2, 12; Tit 1:6
Temperate	Elder / Deacon	1Ti 3:2, 8; Tit 1:7
Respectable	Elder / Deacon	1Ti 3:2, 8
Not given to drunkenness	Elder / Deacon	1Ti 3:3, 8; Tit 1:7
Manages his own family well	Elder / Deacon	1Ti 3:4, 12
Sees that his children obey him	Elder / Deacon	1Ti 3:4–5, 12; Tit 1:6
Does not pursue dishonest gain	Elder / Deacon	1Ti 3:8 Tit 1:7
Keeps hold of the deep truths	Elder / Deacon	1Ti 3:9 Tit 1:9
Sincere	Deacon	1Ti 3:8
Tested	Deacon	1Ti 3:10

the New Testament ministry of deacons is to assist the overseers/bishops. Their subordinate role is evidenced by the absence of mention of any responsibility for teaching or hospitality and by the fact that their preliminary scrutiny appears even more rigorous than that of overseers (Kelly, 1963, 81). Several of the qualifications for deacons seem to suggest guidelines for people involved in house-to-house work (see qualifications [2] and [8] below) and in the oversight of the church relief funds (see qualifications [4] and [10] below).

By adding a masculine qualifier to verse 8 that is *not* present in the Greek[3] (thus rendering the verse, "Deacons likewise are to be *men* worthy of respect [emphasis added] . . ."), many English translations and paraphrases (e.g., NIV, NASB, Phillips, Living Bible, NEB, and Jerusalem Bible) leave the impression that deacons must be male. The KJV, TEV, RSV, NRSV, and the NIV Inclusive Language Edition are true to the original text in *not* making these verses masculine exclusive. In fact, the qualifications for deacons come in three sections clearly seen in the NIV paragraphing: generic qualifications for all deacons, both male and female (vv. 8–10); specific qualifications for female deacons (v. 11); and specific qualifications for male deacons (v. 12). Deacons can be male or female.

There are six generic qualifications for all deacons. (1) They must be "worthy of respect," dignified, serious, stately. The Greek word is a derivative of the word used in verse 4 for the behavior of overseers' children, "with proper respect." Similar to the *inclusio* bracketing overseers' qualifications with the requirement of "being above reproach," "worthy of respect" is a "cover" term, encapsulating all the criteria that follow.

The next three qualifications are prohibitions in the original language. (2) Deacons should not be duplicitous (lit., "double-tongued"), but fully trustworthy in what they say (NIV, "sincere"). The word may refer to gossip (saying one thing to one person and something different to another) or to hypocrisy (saying one thing while thinking or doing another). (3) As is true of overseers (v. 3), deacons are not to "indulge in much wine." (4) Also like overseers (v. 3), deacons are not to pursue "dishonest gain." The deacons' responsibilities over the congregation's monetary affairs could expose them to many financial temptations.

(5) Most of all, deacons must be people of conviction. The "deep truths [lit., mystery] of the faith" that deacons are required to "keep hold of" are equivalent to truths of the objective body of Christian teaching that transcends human reason, accessible only by divine revelation. "Paul is insisting on the intimate relation between sound belief and a conscience free from stain and self-reproach; without the latter, the former must be sterile" (Kelly, 1963, 82). The consciences of deacons must be void of offense.

(6) The final generic qualification for all deacons is that they must be first evaluated, and if found blameless, then they may serve. Just what kind of evaluation, examination, or probation was required is uncertain, but the idea of selecting persons approved after examination is also found in 1 Corinthians 16:3 and 2 Corinthians 13:5. The phrase "if there is nothing against them" is a synonym for the being "above reproach" required of bishops (v. 2), translated "blameless" in the first of elders' qualifications in Titus 1:6. The sentence in Greek begins with *kai* ("also"), perhaps implying that like bishops and elders, deacons must also be scrutinized before appointment.

2.4.2. Specific Qualifications for Female Deacons (3:11). Verse 11 is rendered in the NIV as qualifications for deacons' wives. Yet such an interpretation obscures the other legitimate translations of the Greek text, which reads literally, "In the same way, *women* are to be worthy of respect, not malicious talkers but temperate and trustworthy in everything [emphasis added]." Who are these women?

There are three options. Since the Greek word used here (*gynaikas*, plural of *gyne*) can be translated either as "women" or "wives," the text can be understood as listing qualifications (a) for all Christian women in general (b) for the wives of deacons, or (c) for female deacons. Judging from context, option (a) seems unlikely. Since this verse falls in the center of a section concerning deacons, these "women" must have something to do with the office of deacon.

Option (b) has been the traditional interpretation, based on the assumption that women are not permitted to serve in offices of ministry in the church. That assumption remained largely unchallenged up to the rise of the early fundamentalist/evangelical movement[4] and the birth of Pentecostalism,[5] both of which welcomed women into the ministry. More recently, contemporary discoveries concerning the early church have provided the support from history for the ministry of women that these more modern movements have supported in practice. We now have literary evidence that women served as deacons[6] and inscriptional evidence documenting by name and title the ministry of women in the various offices of the early church, including that of deacon.[7]

In light of the evidence for female deacons in the early church, scholarly consensus is shifting in favor of a translation that exposes the ambiguity of the Greek and the possibility of the three interpretations (see NRSV). Option (c) is appearing more and more frequently in Bible footnotes (cf. NRSV) or even in the text (REB) and in commentaries.

Thus, both historically and theologically, option (c), "women [deacons]," is a legitimate translation. Grammatically speaking, option (b), "[deacons'] wives," is not a good translation. Since, *gynaikas* can mean either "women" or "wives," one of the ways original writers clarified for readers their usage of the term was to put a possessive noun, pronoun, or article (which can function as a possessive pronoun) in front of the noun. For example, "*deacons'* women," "*their* women," or "*the* women [of the deacons]" would be translated "*their* [*deacons'*] wives." The noun *gynaikas,* however, has no article or modifier in verse 11; thus, the verse is speaking not about wives of deacons, but women deacons.

There are several additional points in favor of seeing this verse as qualifications for female deacons. (1) The Greek word *hosautos* ("in the same way, likewise" (cf. v. 8) "indicates a new paragraph in a sequence of rules for a different roup of officials" (Barrett, 1963, 61), that is, emale deacons. (2) The virtues required of hese women are the kind expected of ministers, not of their spouses. (3) Since the New Testament had no special word for female deacons, the apostle presumably had to write, "likewise women [deacons]," where "women" functions as an adjective, thus "female deacons" (ibid.). (4) No special requirements are mentioned for the wives of bishops who occupy an even more influential position than deacons (Guthrie, 1990, 85). "For these reasons he translation 'women deacons' is likely to be he correct one" (Kelly, 1963, 83).

The NIV offers a footnote, suggesting the translation "deaconesses." To readers of the English Bible, such a translation is a lexical refinement of option (c), "women deacons," yet t too is unacceptable. The term *deaconess* is anachronistic; that office was a later development (which limited female deacons' ministry primarily to women). This order began during a less charismatic, more institutionalized period of church history and was specifically designed to reduce the roles that ministering women had been fulfilling up to that time.

It seems clear, therefore, that the words of 1 Timothy 3:11 are intended for female deacons. While these qualifications are addressed specifically to them, they are similar to the generic qualifications for all deacons. There is no indication in the text that the roles of female deacons differ from those of male deacons.

(7) They must be "worthy of respect" (cf. v. 8, qualification [1]). (8) They must not be "malicious talkers" (cf. v. 8, qualification [2]). This word in Greek (*diabolos*; lit., "accusers, slanderers") is the same word as that translated in the New Testament as "devil" (the notorious accuser; cf. Zech. 3:1–2; this is the meaning of the Heb. word *hassatan*, "Satan"). Though their pastoral functions may provide frequent opportunities to such temptation, female deacons should not use their tongues to slander the members of the congregation they serve. (9) Temperance, too, is a requirement reiterated for women deacons (cf. v. 2, qualification [3] of overseers; v. 8, qualification [3] of deacons). (10) Finally, female deacons must be "trustworthy in everything" (cf. v. 8, qualification [4]).

2.4.3. Specific Qualifications for Male Deacons (3:12). Fee suggests that after emphasizing qualifications specific to female deacons, Paul adds two qualifications specific to male deacons almost as an afterthought (Fee, 1988, 89). As with overseers, a deacon should also be the husband of one wife (cf. v. 2) and a good manager of his own family (cf. v. 4). Because of the first-century social structure, these two qualifications are addressed to male but not to female deacons.

2.4.4. Commendations for Worthy Deacons (3:13). Deacons, both male and female, who "deaconize" well—that is, who serve or minister effectively—acquire for themselves a double reward. Gaining "an excellent standing" (*bathmos*) can refer to their influence and reputation in the church or before God. This word literally means a "step" or "grade," similar to our modern use of these terms relative to levels on a professional rank or business pay scale. It has been suggested that *bathmos* may refer to an ecclesiastical promotion, from the office of deacon to that of bishop/elder (Barrett, 1963, 63). It seems as if Paul is using this word in reference to deacons' standing in the believing community (as opposed to before God), because the second facet of their reward has to do with their confidence in the faith.

The Greek word for "assurance" refers to boldness or openness toward others (2 Cor. 3:12; Phil. 1:20; Philem. 8) or God (Eph. 3:12; Heb. 10:19, 35). Confidence before God is probably what is intended here since Paul specifies that the assurance is "in their faith in Christ Jesus." Thus, the double reward is a good reputation with people and a confidence before God.

> These two commendations, of course, are precisely what the false teachers lack. Their "diseased teaching" (cf. 1:19), which includes improper behavior and a soiled reputation, has also caused them to abandon genuine faith in Christ (1:5). (Fee, 1988, 90)

3. Setting Timothy Straight: Specific Counsel for Establishing Young Timothy in Leadership (3:14–6:10)

3.1. Defending the Faith (3:14–4:5)

3.1.1. Right Conduct in the Church (3:14–16). The letter now moves from its first to its second major section. At the point of transition the apostle reiterates his statement of purpose. He began the letter with a charge to Timothy to stay on in Ephesus to oppose false teachers (1:3), then he gave specific advice regarding establishing the church (2:1–3:13). Now he repeats his purpose, punctuating it with an early Christian hymn.

Paul anticipates a rendezvous with Timothy in the near future, but in case there is a delay, he lays out specific counsel for Timothy's leadership in the church. Just as overseers and deacons are to manage their own and God's house well (cf. 3:4, 12), Timothy is charged with the same responsibility. It is expedient that the congregation knows how to behave, for God's people are the church, "the pillar and foundation of the truth." The church's sacred trust is truth; if truth is compromised, the church itself is at stake. The false teachers have already abandoned truth (cf. 6:5; 2 Tim. 2:18; 3:8; 4:4). It is crucial that Timothy not only silence the teachers of error (1 Tim. 1:3–11), but that he also set the church back on its right foundation.

Paul mixes his metaphors from church as family (cf. "God's household") to church as temple (cf. "pillar and foundation"). The Greek has two words for "temple." *Hieron* is the whole temple complex, the place where people congregate for worship; *naos* is the inner sanctuary (e.g., the Most Holy Place), the place where God dwells. Pagan Greek temples were often small shrines, a foundation and a few pillars to house an idol. Paul's image of the church as God's *naos* is not that God joins with us, the congregation, at our meeting place of worship, but that the church (the body of believers) is the sanctuary in which God is pleased to dwell (cf. 1 Cor. 3:16–17; 2 Cor. 6:16; Eph. 2:21).

> With these two images, family and temple, Paul expresses the two urgencies of this letter: his concern over proper behavior among believers vis-à-vis the false teachers, and the church as the people entrusted to uphold and proclaim the truth of the gospel. (Fee, 1988, 92)

The mention of "truth" in verse 15 stimulates the apostle into an exclamation: "Beyond all question, the mystery of godliness is great." "The adverb rendered 'beyond all question' (Gk. *homologoumenos*) means 'by common consent,' and expresses the unanimous conviction of Christians" (Kelly, 1963, 88). What follows is a recitation of the "mystery" (i.e. revealed truth) of "godliness" (the content o basis of Christianity, i.e., our faith). "One o the most interesting features of the Pastorals i the frequent quotation of extracts from con temporary worship. It gives us a much riche notion of what worship was like in this early period than we would otherwise have gained" (Hanson, 1982, 45).

All scholars agree that what follows was a early Christian hymn, but the analysis of the poetic structure of the six lines, the meaning o several lines, and the meaning of the hymn a a whole have caused considerable debate. In the original language each line has two mem bers: a verb (in the aorist [past tense] passive followed by a prepositional phrase. The sub ject of each verb is Christ (understood). Mod ern English versions reflect the possibilities o poetic structure. The JB views each line as a separate stanza. The GNB and RSV identify two stanzas of three lines each (of various pat terns). The NIV sets the hymn in three stanza of two lines each. A modern English para phrase of the hymn by Lock (1973, 42 expresses one interpretation of its poeti nuances:

> In flesh unveiled to mortals' sight,
> Kept righteous by the Spirit's might,
> While angels watched him from
> the sky:
> His heralds sped from shore to shore,
> And men believed, the wide world o'er,
> When he in glory passed on high.

As Fee (1988, 92–95) explains: "In view o so many difficulties and disagreements, one offers an interpretation with some reserva tion." Here is a summary of his interpretation The significance of lines 1, 4, and 5 seem mos clearly interpreted as a gospel hymn, that is, a song expressing the story of salvation through Jesus. If so, we may have a hymn of two stan zas of three lines each, on the humiliation and exaltation of Christ. The first stanza expresse the story of Christ's earthly ministry, climax ing in triumph; the second stanza explains the message of Christ as proclaimed by the church concluding in glory.

Line 1 is characteristic of New Testamen hymns. "He appeared in a body" is universally recognized as an affirmation of the Incarna tion (cf. John 1:14; Rom. 1:3; Phil. 2:7–8

'his room of the Qumran community near the Dead Sea has ·een identified as the scriptorium, where scribes recorded infor- ıation on scrolls. The Dead Sea Scrolls, which included a copy of saiah that was older than any previously known copy, were found ı pottery jars in a nearby cave in 1947.

Books were written on scrolls in Bible times. The beginning of this scroll, a reproduction, is shown below. Hebrew is read from right to left. In 2 Timothy 4:12 Paul asks Timothy to bring him his "scrolls, especially the parchments."

vith implications of preexistence (cf. John :1; Phil. 2:6).

"[He] was vindicated by the Spirit" may efer to Christ's resurrection. Since in the 3reek "spirit" (*pneuma*) has no article, it is ınclear whether this line refers to the Holy Spirit or to Christ's own spirit during his incar- ıation. The phrase could mean the Holy Spirit ɔroved Christ true through miracles and the esurrection, or that Christ's character was val- dated by the way he ruled his own spirit.

"[He] was seen by angels" could refer to the vorship in heaven of the ascended Christ. In 3reek, *angelos* means both angel or messenger. The line could mean that Christ's earthly life vas witnessed by heavenly beings (as we see hroughout the Gospels), or that Christ's life vas witnessed by the messengers (i.e., the wit- ıesses) of the gospel. As Fee (1988, 94) explains, if line 2 refers to Christ's resurrection ınd line 3 to his ascension, "then the first three ines sing Christ's incarnation, resurrection, and glorification and form a stanza about Christ ıimself, as he is seen 'from glory to glory.'"

Lines 4 and 5 ("[he] was preached among he nations [Gentiles]" and "was believed on n the world") are generally recognized as eferring to the period of early apostolic his- ory when the good news spread throughout he known world. Line 6 ("[he] was taken up in glory") is the glorious climax. As Christ's triumph in his mortal condition reached its zenith in eternal glory in his heavenly station, so too Timothy, if he is triumphant in his task at hand, will find a glorious reward in heaven.

3.1.2. False Teaching Exposed (4:1–5).

3.1.2.1. End-Time Apostasy Anticipated (4:1–2). Much of the rest of 1 Timothy is devoted to advice to Timothy regarding conduct of his ministry. The apostle's counsel is set against a backdrop of the false teaching and wicked practices of the heretics in Ephesus. Paul elaborates on the charge expressed in chapter 1, first examining the errors of the false teachers (4:1–5; cf. 1:3–11, 19–20), then instructing Timothy on his role in Ephesus (4:6–16; cf. 1:18–19).

> First, he says that their emergence should have come as no surprise—the Spirit clearly forewarned about them; second, he indicates that the true source of their teaching is demonic; and third, he gives some specifics of their errors and the reasons why they are errors. (Fee, 1988, 97)

This paragraph is joined to the hymn that precedes it with the mild adversative conjunction *de*. Though the NIV does not translate it, the idea conveyed is "*However*, the Spirit clearly says that in the later times some will abandon the faith [i.e., the truth]." The Holy Spirit, through the gift of prophecy, indicated the appearance of such apostasy in advance of its occurrence. Paul sees the "later times" as the present situation in Ephesus. The church recognized the coming of the Holy Spirit as the beginning of the end times (Acts 2:16–17).

> Paul himself believed, and belonged to a tradition that believed, that the End would be accompanied by a time of intense evil (cf. 2 Thess. 2:3–12), including a "falling away" of some of the people of God (see 2 Tim. 3:1; cf. Matt. 24:12; Jude 17–18; 2 Pet. 3:3–7). Thus the present scene was clear evidence for Paul of living in the later times (the time of the End). (Fee, 1988, 98)

Paul brands the error as demonic and the activity of his opponents as inspired by Satan (Dibelius and Conzelmann, 1972, 64).

"Such teachings come through hypocritical liars" (v. 2), that is, through people who are outwardly false (whose abstinence [v. 3] is a pretense) and who are stating as fact things that are not true. Their "consciences have been seared as with a hot iron." The verb in this clause may indicate that this searing has obliterated the ability to discern truth from falsehood, or it may indicate that they have been branded as one of Satan's own.

3.1.2.2. Strict Asceticism Ameliorated (4:3–5). Two of these false teachings are now listed: prohibition of marriage and abstinence from certain foods. Though these prohibitions may relate to the charge that the false teachers "want to be teachers of the law" (1:7), how do they relate to the allegation that the false teachings were "myths and endless genealogies" (1:4) and that they taught that "the resurrection has already taken place" (2 Tim. 2:18)?

> These people may have been those who insisted that the new age had already been introduced by Christ and they failed to distinguish the pres[ent] times of refreshing, which the resurrection of Jesus had initiated, from the consummation to be inaugurated by the yet fut[ure] resurrection. (Rienecker, 1980, 625)
>
> In Corinth this kind of view about the End was apparently linked to Hellenistic dualism, which believed matter to be corrupt, or evil, and only spirit to be good. Just as some Corinthians denied a future bodily resurrection (1 Cor. 15:12, 35), and some at least took a dim view of sex (7:1–7) and marriage (7:25–38), it is altogether likely that something very much like that is being given out as "Law" in Ephesus. Hence the road to purity was marked off for them through abstaining from marriage (to be like the angels after the resurrection [Matt. 22:30]?) and from "certain foods." (Fee, 1988, 99)

These tendencies are characteristic of Gnosticism.

Paul does not respond to the marriage issue but he does challenge their food taboos. Though he typically addresses the matter of eating or not eating certain foods with some ambivalence—one may or may not partake as one wishes (cf. Rom. 14:1–23; 1 Cor. 10:23–33; Col. 2:16, 21)—"when one goes beyond mere 'judging' to demanding abstinence for religious or theological reasons, as in Colossians 2, Paul comes out fighting" (Fee, 1988, 100).

Paul's reasons for refusing food abstinence are twofold: "For everything God created is good," and "nothing is to be rejected if it is received with thanksgiving . . . it is consecrated by the word of God and prayer." The first argument attacks directly the notion of dualism, in that everything God created is good (Gen. 1) and should not be rejected (for reasons of ritual uncleanness [Rom. 14:14]). The second argument is evidence that the early Christians (as did the Jews) offered thanksgiving with their meals; such prayers sanctify food as appropriate for eating.

3.2. Learning to Lead (4:6–16)

3.2.1. Principles of Leadership (4:6–9). At this point, Paul addresses Timothy personally. The tone of this section is almost wholly constructive—there are no denunciations or refutations here. Instead, the apostle encourages his young friend to excel as a leader in a difficult situation by resisting error and living as a model. His counsel to Timothy is fitting advice to any minister of the gospel called to serve in similar situations.

Timothy is to "point these things out to the brothers." The verb "point out" denotes no hin of authoritarianism. The idea is gentle, neither to "order" nor "instruct," but to "suggest." The Greek word translated "brothers" (or in older translations "brethren") bears the inclusive sense of "brothers and sisters." The church is a family in which we are all siblings. The goal is for Timothy to "be a good minister of Christ Jesus." The word for "minister" here is *diakonos* again (see comments on 3:8). Timothy is to be a servant among siblings, not a lord over subjects. His life as a minister is to evidence his being "brought up in the truths of the faith and of the good teaching that [he has] followed." He is to nourish and sustain himself on the gospel and sound doctrine. "The metaphor is that of feeding with the idea of reading and inwardly digesting and the present participle suggests a continual process" (Rienecker, 1980, 626).

In sharp contrast to "truths of the faith" and "good teaching" stand "godless myths" and "old wives' tales" (v. 7; cf. 1:4). These myths are to be strongly refused and rejected; they are suitable only for "superstitious old women." These last three words in English translate one word in Greek, a sarcastic epithet used by the philosophers implying absolute gullibility. Not only were women in Ephesus believing these myths, they were teaching them. Thus Timothy is obliged to silence such teachers and correct their error (see comments on 2:11–15).

In verses 7b–8 Paul enjoins Timothy to vigorously "train [himself] to be godly."

> The comparison between the Christian life and athletic exercise or sport is, of course, a favorite with Paul (cf. esp. 1 Cor. 9:24–27).... [There] is a genuinely Christian self-discipline which Timothy ought to practice. It consists ... in general self-control, continuous devotion to the gospel tradition, and perhaps most of all (as 4:10 suggests), accepting cheerfully the cross of suffering which all Christians must expect. (Kelly, 1963, 99)

As Paul reflects on such training, he quotes what sounds like a common proverb: "Physical training is of some value, but godliness has value for all things."

> Paul will allow that "physical training" (*gymnasia*) "is of some value," a value, however, that is limited strictly to this age. But he says that only to set up his real concern. *Eusebeia* (godliness) is where the real value lies. Indeed, it "has value for all things" (better, "in every way"), because it holds promise for life, "both the present life and the life to come." ... Here is a clear reference to Paul's understanding of Christian existence as basically eschatological. "Life," which means "eternal life" (see 1:16), has already begun. The "life" of the future is therefore both a "present" reality and a hope of "life to come." (Fee, 1988, 104)

The phrase in verse 9, "this is a trustworthy saying," appears for the third of five times in the Pastorals (see comment on 1:15). It is debated whether this statement here refers forward to verse 10a or 10b or backward to all of verse 8 or perhaps only to verse 8b. Since "godliness has value for all things" has the ring of a saying and is, in fact, what Paul goes on to elaborate here, that element of verse 8 seems to be what he is endorsing as the "trustworthy saying."

3.2.2. Models of Leadership (4:10–12). The parenthetical comment in verse 10 ("and for this we labor and strive") refers to verse 8b, the goal of Christian "training"—godliness and its resulting rewards. Paul continues here the athletic metaphor begun in verse 7 with the verb "strive" and uses another verb ("labor") associated with the teaching ministry of elders (*kopiao*, trans. "work" in 5:17). The reason Paul and Timothy are in this spiritual contest is "because" (a better translation here than "that") they "have put [their] hope in the living God," whose help can be counted on both in this life and in the life to come. He is the living hope, for he "is the Savior [see comment on 2:4–6] of all [people], and especially of those who believe." The apostle is aware that the church represents only a fraction of humanity, yet salvation is available to all.

In verse 11 Paul issues a charge repeated throughout the Pastorals, that Timothy is to "command and teach these things" (see 5:7; 6:2b; 2 Tim. 2:2, 14; Titus 2:15). He has used the first verb in 1:3, 5, 18; it can also be translated "charge" or "instruct." The things Timothy is to "teach" may refer to 4:8–10, or perhaps everything from 2:1 on (cf. 4:6).

The apostle then goes on to encourage the young pastor: "Don't let anyone look down on you because you are young." This exhortation may expose a hidden agenda for Paul's writing this letter. This statement cuts two ways. It is meant to bolster the confidence of a younger (probably a thirty- to forty-year-old), perhaps timid, man. But it is also meant to be read by the congregation as an apostolic endorsement. Fee (1988, 107) states succinctly: "Not only are they 'not' to 'look down on' him 'because' he is 'young,' but they are to 'look up' to him . . . [as] 'an example for the believers.'" The role of Christian leaders as models is pervasive throughout Paul's writings (1 Cor. 4:6; 11:1; Phil. 3:17; 1 Thess. 1:6; 2 Thess. 3:7, 9; cf. 2 Tim. 1:13).

Paul mentions five spheres of modeling. (1) "Speech" refers to daily conversation; Timothy should not be argumentative (cf. Col. 3:8; 4:5–6). (2) "In life" or lifestyle refers to behavior or conduct, which should be marked by propriety and grace. (3) "In love," (4) "in faith" (fidelity), and (5) "in purity" (chastity, innocence, and integrity) speak of three interior qualities that influence exterior deportment.

3.2.3. Practicalities of Leadership (4:13–16). From Timothy's personal life, Paul turns to his public ministry. In the apostle's absence, his young assistant is to "[continually] devote [himself] to the public reading of Scripture, to preaching and to teaching" (v. 13). The first task probably refers to selecting and preparing the passages to be read from the Old Testament; the second, to his exposition and application of Scripture; and the third, to the teaching of Christian doctrine. These are the parts of public worship in which Timothy provides leadership. From other passages we know these were not the only parts of a New Testament worship service. Also included were prayer (2:1–7; cf. 1 Cor. 11:2–6), singing (1 Cor. 14:26; Col. 3:16; cf. 1 Tim. 3:16), charismatic utterances (1 Cor. 11:2–16; 12–14; 1 Thess. 5:19–22), and the Lord's Supper (1 Cor. 11:17–34).

The next charge Paul gives, "Do not neglect your gift [*charisma*]" (v. 14; lit., "do not neglect the in-you gift"), speaks of a gracious endowment or spiritual gift enabling Timothy to carry out his ministry in the community of believers. "The due execution of these tasks depends not upon Timothy's native ability but upon a divine gift, or spiritual endowment which has been given him" (Barrett, 1963, 70). The Holy Spirit is the one who has equipped Timothy for his ministry of preacher/teacher/pastor in Ephesus; he must learn to rely on this source and not his own efforts; and he must not leave that gift unused. It is a great temptation to try to do the work of the Spirit in the arm of the flesh. This warning is for all of us. Just as Paul prays for the Colossians (Col. 1:9–11), we too must be filled with the knowledge of God's will and with the power of God's Spirit to do his will in his way.

Timothy's spiritual gift "was given" to him through a "prophetic message" and was accompanied by (the Greek *meta* is better translated "with" or "by" than "when") the laying on of the hands of elders. The NIV leaves an anachronistic impression that when Timothy was ordained (a rite not yet standardized), the Holy Spirit responded to the laying on of hands by imparting, at that moment, the spiritual gift he would need to fulfill the position into which he was installed. The most probable analogy for what is referred to here is found in Acts 13:1–3, where the Spirit speaks (v. 2), apparently through the prophets (v. 1), in response to which the prophets and teachers lay on hands in some form of consecration. In any case, the evidence there and elsewhere (2 Tim. 1:6–7) indicates that the Spirit is the crucial element; the laying on of hands, though not insignificant, is the human response to the Spirit's prior activity (Fee, 1988, 108).

As a summary statement (vv. 15–16), Paul begins by urging Timothy to "be diligent in these matters; give yourself wholly to them." The first verb is frequently an agricultural term for "cultivating"; with the second verb Paul picks up the athletic metaphor from verses 7–10 again (Fee, 1988, 109). The goal of such practice and devotion is "that everyone may see your progress." Fee suggests, based on evidence from 2 Timothy 2:16 and 3:9, "progress" may have been a slogan of the false teachers, an elitist appeal (through their speculative nonsense) to "advance" into "deeper truths." "If so, then this is a bold counter statement to their kind of 'progress.' . . . By Timothy's being a faithful minister of the word of the gospel, the people will be able to see the real thing" (ibid.).

Verse 16 offers three more admonitions as explanation of "these matters" mentioned in verse 15. By "watch your life [closely]," Paul emphasizes Timothy's crucial role as a model. By "[watch your] doctrine closely," the apostle emphasizes Timothy's role as a teacher. By "persevere in them," he adds one last time his apostolic emphasis that this is how the young pastor "will save both [himself] and [his] hearers." Barrett (1963, 73) explains that

> the author did not mean that the ministry itself, however devoted, was actually the saving agent. God only saves; yet his salvation may take effect through faithful preaching and teaching, and this is a truth no minister dare forget.

3.3. Relating to Others in the Church (5:1–16)

3.3.1. Treatment of Old and Young (5:1–2). As a transition to the apostle's advice regarding Timothy's relationships with specific categories of people in the congregation, Paul deals first with issues related to Timothy's youthfulness. In 4:12 the apostle exhorted: "Don't let anyone look down on you because you are young." Now he cautions (v. 1), "Do not rebuke an older man harshly, but exhort him as if he were your father." We can paraphrase, "Never be harsh with a senior." Paul not only instills confidence in the young pastor, but also demands courtesy towards his flock. "In God's household (note the 'family' theme in each case) there is an appropriate way for the leader to treat people—exactly as one does in one's own family (assuming a cultural ideal of great deference and respect in the home)" (Fee, 1988, 92–112).

Similarly, Paul advises, "treat younger men as brothers, older women as mothers, and younger women as sisters." It appears that relationships with younger women were an area of special concern in the Ephesian congregation (cf. 5:11; 2 Tim. 3:6–7), because the apostle specifies that "absolute purity" is required with them.

3.3.2. Treatment of Widows (5:3–16).

3.3.2.1. Honor for Qualifying Widows (5:3). The next two major sections (on widows and elders) bring into focus some of Timothy's major problems in the church. The apparent concern with widows is the relationship of younger widows with the false teachers. Presumably these younger widows can be identified with the "weak-willed women, who are loaded down with sins and are swayed by all kinds of evil desires" (2 Tim. 3:6–7). Such would account for the strength of emphasis and the inordinate length of this passage compared to other issues addressed in this letter. Therefore, the apostle urges that only "genuine widows" be accorded the honor of being enrolled on the church's official "widow roster" (cf. vv. 9, 11) and thus be granted not only recognition of their ministry, but also support of their financial needs.

This is the earliest passage in Christian history regarding a special class or order of widows who served the church and were supported by it. From it we learn that not every widow could qualify as a "widow" in the technical sense, and that those who did had special rights and specific duties. At this period in history the term *widow* was used to designate both any woman who had been widowed and the office of "widows of the congregation." Such fluidity in the use of the term demonstrates that the office was not yet rigidly standardized (cf. similar comments on ch. 3 regarding offices of overseer/bishop, deacon, and elder). By the subapostolic period, however, widows were a significant part of the ministry staffs in local congregations. By that time, according to Kroeger, Evans, and Storkey (1995, 447),

> widows were regarded as persons having special opportunities for Christian service. They were widely used in the ministry of the early church and given special seats of honor in front of the congregation. A large church, such as Hagia Sophia in Constantinople, might have hundreds of widows on its staff. They visited homes, brought food for the hungry, cared for the sick, comforted the bereaved, prayed for all who made their requests known, assisted in Christian instruction and baptism, and counselled those in need. So powerful were they in prayer that early Christian literature sometimes calls widows "the altar of God."

The first concern addressed by the apostle is that "real" widows get the help they deserve. "Give proper recognition to those widows who are really in need" (v. 3) is literally, "Honor widows who are truly widows." The kind of honor to be granted to widows and elders is financial remuneration in verse 17 and respect in 6:1. Thus, the "recognition" exhorted by Paul is not only esteem for their ministries but also care for their needs.

> A recurring theme in both Old and New Testaments is the care of widows (Deut. 10:18; Job 22:9; 24:3; 31:16; Ps. 94:6; Is. 1:23; 10:2; Mark 12:40; James 1:18 [*sic*; should be 1:27]). God pronounces a curse against those who withhold justice from widows (Deut. 27:19) while those who care for them are promised God's blessing (Jer. 7:5–7). "You shall not abuse any widow," warns Exodus 22:22, for God is the defender of widows (Deut. 10:17; Pss. 68:5; 146:9). Malachi 3:5 declares that those who defraud laborers of their wages and oppress widows do not fear the Lord Almighty. God repeatedly commanded that his people should relieve the affliction of widows.
>
> There is also an emphasis on letting widows help themselves. The tithe of the produce every third year was designated for the widow, the fatherless, the stranger and the Levite (Deut. 26:12; 27:19)....
>
> An individual who leaves a widow in destitution has denied the faith and is worse than an infidel (1 Tim. 5:4, 8). 1 Timothy arranged for widows in financial need to be compensated in return for their labors in the church (5:3–16); and Paul was of the opinion that a laborer was worthy of her hire (5:18). (Kroeger, Evans and Storkey, 1995, 446–47)

In the modern Western world, though some widows are financially destitute, other widows are comfortably cared for by their deceased husband's insurance and annuities. How can we apply the intent of this biblical requirement to our modern situation? Among those women suffering financial hardships today, those who are often most vulnerable to mistreatment and exploitation are the divorcees. Today's church is challenged also to assist financially the women and families of divorce "who are really in need," who love the Lord, and who serve the church.

3.3.2.2. Qualifications of Widows (5:4–10). The first *disqualification* for being considered a widow of the church is having "children or grandchildren" (v. 4). A priority in the "practice" of the "religion" of these descendants is to provide for their widowed mothers and grandmothers. It is primarily not the church's but children's responsibility to support widows. Again, we see the emphasis on Christian behavior in God's household (both of the community and biological family; cf. 3:4–5, 12, 15). Such "repaying their parents and grandparents" for the care they themselves received "is pleasing to God" (cf. the fifth commandment, Ex. 20:12).

To qualify as a genuine widow (the adverb "really" is repeated in vv. 3, 5, 16), however, requires more than financial destitution. True, she must be "all alone" and "in need" (vv. 3, 5, 16), that is, with no family to support her. But a genuine widow must also be godly and given to prayer. Thus, three characteristics of a "true widow" are given: aloneness, need, and godliness. Tying into what was said in verses 3–4, the "real widow" has been "left all alone" with neither husband nor children to support her. Yet a genuine widow does not despair; instead, she "puts her hope in God and continues night and day to pray and ask God for help." Note how similar this description is to that of the female prophet Anna in Luke 2:36–38, who was also a widow.

In contrast to the piety of the genuine widow is the "widow who lives for pleasure" (v. 6). Instead of being a trusting, prayerful woman, this woman's self-indulgence results in her being "dead even while she lives." This kind of widow matches the description of the younger widows of verses 11–13. Paul adds the instruction of verse 7 to those he has already given Timothy in order that "widows," like overseers/bishops (3:2) and deacons (3:8), might be above reproach. "All members of the church should be free of reproach, but it is particularly important that this should be true of those who hold public position within it, and draw their support from it" (Barrett, 1963, 75).

The responsibility to provide for one's relatives (v. 4) is revisited in verse 8 with even greater force. Anyone who disregards this obligation to care for the needs of one's family is guilty of having "denied the faith." For in failing to show love, that person is "nothing" (1 Cor. 13:2). According to James, the faith of such a person will not result in salvation

James 2:14). In illustrating that "faith by itself, if it is not accompanied by action, is dead" (2:17), he describes the scenario of a believer who knows of brother or sister in need and does nothing tangible about it (2:15–16). The apostle Paul describes such behavior here as that of an "unbeliever" (1 Tim. 5:8; lit., "one who disbelieves"). "Indeed, he is 'worse than an unbeliever,' not so much because many heathen and Jews did care for their parents as because, having accepted the privileges of Christian discipleship, he has refused its obligations" (Barrett, 1963, 75).

In verses 9–10, Paul gives several further qualifications for enrollment of widows (cf. vv. 4–5). The verb for "be put on the list" (*katalego*) is a technical term that "makes it absolutely clear that there was a definite order of widows" (Kelly, 1963, 115). Tertullian (in *Ad uxorem* 1.7) also translated the term ecclesiastically as "to accept into the clergy" (Dibelius and Conzelmann, 1972, 75). The requirements of the roster for genuine widows seems well developed for such an early period. It is likely that the apostle followed the Jewish model and perhaps that of the Jerusalem apostles (cf. Acts 6:1).

(1) A true widow had to be "sixty [years]." This was an advanced age in antiquity. It was thought to be "old age" when sexual passions had waned and remarriage was out of the question. Such an age requirement would greatly reduce the number of the church's ministering widows who might be led astray into the kind of behavior that would compromise their office of ministry.

(2) That a widow must have been "the wife of one husband" (NIV, "faithful to her husband") corresponds with the qualifications for offices of overseer (3:2), deacon (3:12), and elder (Titus 1:6; see comments on 1 Tim. 3:2, 12). The expression was frequently used to eulogize women who married only once, but it was also used for those who had been faithful to their spouse in marriage. Although there is pagan evidence of disqualification from religious service of women who had been married more than once, the church father Theodore of Mopsuestia considered this qualification to be "chastity with her husband, no matter whether she has had only one, or whether she was married a second time" (Dibelius and Conzelmann, 1972, 65).

(3) That a widow must have a good reputation corresponds with the qualifications for offices of overseer (3:2, 7), deacon (3:10), and elder (Titus 1:6; see comments on 1 Tim. 3:2, 7, 10). The list of conditions for a widow's enrollment resembles a job description in the past tense. "Members of the widows' order had practical duties to perform in the community; so the best testimonial a newcomer could produce was to point to zeal and efficiency in carrying out these tasks voluntarily" (Kelly, 1963, 116). The widow's testimony of good deeds is described with four specific items and a generalizing conclusion.

(a) She must have brought up "children"—a cultural and biblical ideal of womanhood. "[But] it is absurd to suppose . . . that Paul is excluding childless candidates. . . . One of the big problems facing the early church was the care of orphans (cf. Hermas, *Mand.* vii.10; *Apost. Cost.* III, iii.2; etc.); it seems likely that the official widows were given charge of these" (Kelly, 1963, 116). (b) She must have a reputation for "hospitality," just as was required of the overseer (3:2) and all other Christians (Rom. 12:13). "The widows had their part to play, alongside overseers in the reception and entertainment of itinerant evangelists, preachers, messengers, and ordinary Christians travelling to and fro which formed a prominent feature in the daily life of the early Church" (ibid., 117). (c) She must have "wash[ed] the feet of the saints." It is unclear whether this statement is meant literally or figuratively. There is a lack of knowledge of local customs. Either way, this aspect of her reputation is indicative of humble servanthood. (d) She must have "help[ed] those in trouble." The specifics of this requirement, too, are unclear, but it reflects a generous and serving spirit. (e) She must have "devot[ed] herself to all kinds of good deeds." To sum up, her good reputation must precede her to the office of widow in the church.

3.3.2.3. On Younger Widows (5:11–15). Paul then cites further disqualifications for the office of widow. (1) Age is one factor. Younger widows must be disqualified from consideration for service and remuneration as widows of the church. The verb *katastreniao* (NIV, "sensual desires overcome their dedication"; lit., "wax wanton against"), which appears only here in the New Testament, gives the reason. It "suggests the metaphor of a young oxen trying to escape the yoke. The younger widows would not wish to be tied to church duties if further opportunity came for marriage" (Guthrie, 1990, 103).

Such a scenario (remarriage) invokes judgment upon these young widows, since their wantonness is considered to be against Christ and a violation of "their first pledge." Scholars have offered three suggestions for "their first pledge." (a) The commitment to her first husband is broken by a widow's remarriage, thus abandoning the ideal of being married only once (cf. v. 9). (b) Remarriage of a widow in the church is an abandonment of Christ himself, tantamount to going after Satan (v.15). (c) Remarriage is the breaking of a widow's pledge to perpetual widowhood, like a vow of celibacy in joining the order. "It is implied that a woman when enrolled as a widow gave an undertaking—as it were, to Christ himself—not to marry, but to engage herself wholly to the church" (cf. 1 Cor. 7:34) (Barrett, 1963, 76). "The vow of celibacy was regarded as a sort of marriage with Christ. In much later times the woman who entered a religious order was called a 'spouse of Christ'" (Hanson, 1982, 60).

(2) "The second reason for not counting the younger widows among true widows is that in their present singleness they are *not* doing what they should be doing (prayer, v. 5, and the good works of vv. 9–10), and *are* doing things they should not" (Fee, 1988, 122). Instead of being gainfully employed with the care of a husband and children in their own home, "they get into the habit of being idle and going about from house to house" (v. 13). "One wonders whether the problem here is simply that of wasting their own time, and that of others as well, or whether perhaps it involves a disrupting of the various worshiping communities" (ibid.).

Among the kinds of service required of widows of the church is house-to-house ministry. The apostle fears that a great temptation for younger widows, while making those rounds, is to turn times of testimony and confidential counsel into gadabout gossip sessions. Instead of constructive activities of visitation, expected of mature ministering widows, the younger widows might become involved in destructive idleness and talebearing. Their sins of the tongue mentioned here correspond to those of the false teachers (see 1:6–7; 4:7; 6:3–4; 6:20). Note also the relationship of this section with the requirement that deacons not be double-tongued (3:8) and that female deacons not be slanderers (3:11; see comments on 3:8, 11).

> Paul is drawing a vivid picture of the mischief-making tittle-tattle to which he thinks that women still young enough to be in the social swim will be especially prone—although the church's fuller experience has shown that neither older women nor male office-bearers are necessarily exempt from the same temptation. (Kelly, 1963, 118)

Instead of idleness and gossiping, the apostle urges three activities for younger widows and expects one positive result (vv. 14–15). They are "to marry, to have children, to manage their homes," thus giving the "enemy no opportunity for slander." According to Paul's way of thinking (cf. 1 Cor. 7:25–40), remarriage is not the theoretical ideal, but the sensible course for women who are alone and in their prime, especially with a history (in Ephesus) of incontinence. Kelly (1963, 77) reflects that "the wife and mother holds an office at least as honorable and fruitful as that of the enrolled pensioner and servant of the church."

Fee explains that the apostle's counsel that younger widows remarry does not contradict verses 11–12, which seem to criticize remarriage and disqualify younger widows on the basis of their tendency toward remarriage. "In verses 11–13, Paul was giving reasons why they should not be counted among the real widows—basically because they fail to meet the qualifications given in verses 9–10. Now he advises what young widows should do, since they are rejected as being 'true widows'" (Fee, 1988, 92–123).

The emphatic statement that "some have in fact already turned away to follow Satan" (v. 15) demonstrates that verses 11–13 are not merely hypothetical concerns of the apostle; rather, the problem is in existence now and the urgency is critical. The verb "turned away" is recurrent of both the false teachers and those they have influenced.

3.3.2.4. Encouragement of Individuals' Support of Widows (5:16). What was stated generically (irrespective of gender) in verse 8

"If anyone does not provide for [one's] relatives"; cf. v. 4) is now specified for the female Christian. "If any woman who is a believer has widows ['in her family' is not in the Greek], she should help them."[8] Why this injunction is addressed specifically to women believers providing for widows is unclear to us; we are uncertain of the background. Perhaps Paul knew of wealthy women in Ephesus, similar to Lydia in Philippi (Acts 16:14–15) or Chloe in Corinth (1 Cor. 1:11), who had already taken women into their households. The apostle encourages them to continue caring for them, that the church be not burdened. Such would leave the resources of the church available to care for others.

> The reason why Paul does not impose the same obligation on a Christian man of similar position should be obvious. If such a man were unmarried or a widower, it would be most unsuitable for him to take over responsibility for a group of widows; whereas if he were married, the responsibility in all its practical aspects would naturally devolve upon his wife. (Kelly, 1963, 121)

3.4. Working With Leaders in the Church (5:17–25)

3.4.1. Double Honor for Hard-Working Elders (5:17–18). Fee suggests that the word "elders" in verse 17 probably includes "all who direct the affairs of the church," that is, the overseers of 3:1–7 (cf. Acts 20:17, 28; Titus 1:5–7) and the deacons of 1 Timothy 3:8–13. "The choice of the term itself (see also Acts 14:23; 15:4) undoubtedly reflects the church's Jewish heritage; elders were already a permanent feature of the synagogue" (Fee, 1988, 128).

The first aspect of the ministry of elders is that of managing or directing "the affairs of the church." Paul used the verb *proïstemi* in 3:4, 12 for managing and caring for one's own family. The verb literally means "to stand first, rule, administrate, govern, superintend." The substantive participle form derived from this verb, which is the descriptive title of a person in that position, is the earliest term used by the apostle for church leaders (see Rom. 12:8; 1 Thess. 5:12; cf. a related word used for Phoebe's ministry lauded in Rom. 16:2). By the time of Justin Martyr (ca. A.D. 150, *First Apology* 1.67), a noun in the singular denotes the one leader of a congregation. Commendation is due those elders who fulfill such ministry *well*.

The second aspect of an elder's service is the "work . . . [of] preaching and teaching." The verb used here (*kopiao*) is one of Paul's favorites for those in gospel work; he uses it of his own and Timothy's ministries (4:10) as well as for that of others (e.g., 1 Cor. 15:10; 16:16; 1 Thess. 5:12; cf. also Rom. 16 throughout). It means to work until one is exhausted. It is a clear indication of apostolic values that this verb was used with reference to the teaching aspect of an elder's work and not the administrating. Paul is commending ministers for investing themselves most wisely for their greatest ministerial effectiveness. He does not say, "Wear yourself out with administration and try to preach well." Instead he says, "Administrate well, but really labor in your ministry of the Word."

Double honor is due elders who lead well and work hard in the ministry of the Word. Based on the verse that follows, we know that "honor" includes, at least, financial remuneration. The emphasis of the apostle, however, is probably not that elders who preach should get twice the salary of those who do not or that elders merit twice as much as widows. Rather, just as was true for ministering widows above, these elders merit a twofold honor: respect and remuneration. Paul reiterates a theme he emphasized elsewhere: Those who minister the Word to a congregation should be supported by it (1 Cor. 9:7–14; cf. 2 Cor. 11:8–9; 1 Thess. 2:7).

In verse 18, in good rabbinical style, Paul quotes Moses as primary scriptural support (Deut. 25:4) and Jesus as expert authority (Luke 10:7;[9] cf. Matt. 10:10) for the practice he had just commended to the Ephesian congregation.

The apostle did not present a detailed job description for elders; this was not his point. His concern was to reward those who did their work well; but since not all elders in Ephesus were doing so, he now turns to address that problem.

3.4.2. Handling Grievances Against Elders (5:19–21). Since no one is exposed to as much complaint and backbiting as the minister who serves faithfully, elders deserve more than just financial protection. They deserve the trust of the congregation unless charges are substantiated by multiple witnesses. In other words, ministers should be accorded the same innocent-until-proven-guilty treatment as is to be granted to anyone (2 Cor. 13:1; cf. Deut. 19:15; John 8:17; Heb. 10:28). Calvin said such a practice "is a necessary remedy against the malice of men; for none are more liable to slanders and calumnies than godly teachers" (quoted in Barrett, 1963, 80).

But if the charges can be substantiated, the elder's sins must not be hushed up but exposed publicly (v. 20). This public example will be a strong warning not only to other elders, but also to the congregation at large. The apostle's entreaty comes on strong in verse 21 as

> he urges Timothy to observe these rules without prejudging the issue, doing nothing out of favoritism.... He invokes God and Christ Jesus and the elect angels because the final judgment will be in their hands; Timothy must exercise his judicial functions as their representative, and also as one who will himself be judged by them. (Kelly, 1963, 127)

Note that the role of angels in the final judgment is seen also in Matthew 25:31; Mark 8:38; Luke 9:26; Revelation 14:10.

3.4.3. Hasty Ordinations Prohibited (5:22–25). Liability for the misconduct of elders is shared by those who ordain them. Therefore, Timothy must use careful consideration before appointing church officials. The Christian leaders who are called on to judge and punish must live above reproach themselves.

The advice in verse 23 seems out of place, interrupting the connection between verses 22 and 24. Some have conjectured it to be a misplaced saying or a gloss that was mistakenly included in the text, even though there is no manuscript support for either hypothesis. It is more likely that Paul's comments on personal purity and not partaking "in the sins of others" (v. 22) jogged the apostle's memory concerning the issue of total abstinence promoted by the false teachers (4:3) and now practiced by the young pastor, Timothy.

The present tense prohibition in verse 23 (lit., "do not be drinking") does not forbid a practice from beginning; it demands the cessation of a practice already in process. Paul is advising Timothy to "stop drinking only water" (NIV) or to "drink water no longer." All other uses of this verb in antiquity referred to drinking *only* water, that is, abstaining from wine. Timothy had presumably gotten entangled in the false teachers' view of purity, and it was causing him physical problems. Wine has been known as a remedy against dyspeptic complaints, as a tonic, and as remedy for the effects of impure water. The apostle's comments reflect the widespread use of wine in antiquity for medicinal purposes.

What about the issue of total abstinence from alcohol in our modern world? Abstinence is a significant holiness issue among many Pentecostals today. Yet the practice of drinking wine with meals, though not drunkenness, is culturally accepted among many charismatics and Pentecostals in certain countries. The rationale for total abstinence is commendable. One will neither become drunk nor become a drunkard if he totally abstains from alcohol. One will never cause a former alcoholic to stumble back into sin by her example if she totally abstains from alcohol. It is better to be safe than sorry!

Having loving tolerance for those with differing opinions in debatable matters is also virtuous—especially in light of the fact that Scripture, both Old and New Testaments, tolerates the drinking of alcoholic beverages and, in fact, *commends* its use (in moderation) for certain maladies. There is no question that the apostle Paul was encouraging Timothy to terminate his abstinence from alcohol and start taking a little wine. Full Gospel people, regardless of their view on the issue, would do well to take the position of the Reformers: "In essentials unity, in nonessentials liberty, and in all things charity."

In verses 24–25 the apostle returns to the issue of evaluating the character of prospective elders.

> There are people, he points out, whose sins are immediately obvious, running ahead of them to judgment—a graphic way of saying that even the most inexperienced and undiscerning chief pastor has no excuse for not noticing them.... There are others, however, whose sins trail behind them, i.e., will only be brought to light when they appear before the all-seeing Judge. The existence of such people underlines the necessity for extreme care in selecting ministers. (Kelly, 1963, 129)

Paul is not one to end on a negative note; consequently he states the aphorism of verse 24 in the affirmative: "Good deeds are obvious, and even those that are not cannot be hidden" (v. 25). The moral for Timothy is not to reject candidates who at first do not seem to possess the qualities demanded, because good works cannot be concealed and will eventually come to light. In other words, truly worthy people eventually surface. Cream always rises to the top!

3.5. Exhorting Believing Slaves (6:1–2a)

Slaves are the final demographic category addressed by Paul in this letter. That the early church was made up of both many slaves and many slave owners may come as a surprise to the modern reader, but it is important to remember three things concerning the historical and theological context. (1) The institution of slavery was deeply enmeshed in Greco-Roman culture. Though slavery was at the bottom of the social chain, it was considerably different from what was practiced in American history. Fee explains that it was rarely racially motivated, and though manumission was a common practice, in many cases slavery was preferred to freedom because of the security and good position it sometimes offered. (2) Since Christians were expecting the return of Christ imminently, the church invested its energies more in evangelism rather than in social reform. (3) Since the true freedom and servitude of believers are based on their relationship to Christ, their social position in this world was not considered as important as their relationship to Christ (Kelly, 1963, 130).

In spite of the New Testament's apparent tolerance of slavery in the culture and the awareness of its presence in the church, that is not the end of the story. Though Paul addresses both Christian slaves and Christian masters (cf. Eph. 6:5–9; Col. 3:22–4:1) and Christian slaves were owned by cruel and unreasonable masters (Titus 2:9–10; 1 Peter 2:18–20), the Christian attitude toward slavery is best summed up by Paul in his letter to Philemon. Arguing for manumission, he asserts that Onesimus is to be regarded "no longer as a slave, but better than a slave, as a dear brother" (Philem. 16). The early church did in fact practice what it preached. That very slave, Onesimus, was set free and eventually, so it seems, became the bishop of Ephesus, and by A.D. 220 Callistus, a former slave, had risen to be bishop of Rome. Perhaps these verses (1 Tim. 6:1–2a) are another evidence of slaves ministering as leaders in the church.

3.5.1. Honor Masters for the Sake of Christ (6:1). Barrett suggests that the first Greek words in the verse—literally, "Such of the above as those who are under the yoke of slavery"—refer "not to slaves in general (though it would not be inapplicable to any slave) but particularly to elders who are slaves" (Barrett, 1963, 82). The admonition to deem one's master "worthy of full respect" is given with a decisively missionary motive. If Christian slaves are rebellious, "God's name and [the] teaching [of the church]" fall into disrepute. Here again, as was evident earlier with Paul's instructions to bishops and deacons, how the church is viewed by outsiders is essential to how we conduct our Christian lives (cf. 2:2; 3:7; 5:14).

3.5.2. Honor Believing Masters Still More (6:2a). The admonition to respect masters is all the more fitting in the case of believing masters. Just as Paul admonished Philemon that Onesimus was more than a slave—he was a brother (Philem. 16)—so now he says the same of believing masters. They are more than masters, they are brothers. Christian slaves must, therefore, not neglect their obligations simply because believing masters' discipline may be less taxing, since it is tempered by love. Instead, they should serve such masters even better, knowing that the benefit will go to one of the beloved believers.

3.6. Fighting False Teachers and the Love of Money (6:2b–10)

3.6.1. Teaching of Orthodoxy Commanded (6:2b). As the apostle moves into his final miscellaneous injunctions, he urges Timothy that "these are the things you are to teach and urge on them." Though "these ... things" could refer to what immediately precedes this verse (advice concerning slaves), it more probably refers to what follows (injunctions concerning false teachers—the reason for this whole letter and the apostle's instructions since 2:1).

3.6.2. Teachers of Heresy Described (6:3–5). In a final indictment of false teachers, Paul contrasts the things that Timothy should teach with the erroneous doctrines of the heretics. The verb he uses here for teaching false doctrine (the same as in 1:3) means "to teach another doctrine," that is, a false or heretical one. The teachings of these men do not agree with the sound or healthy instruction that is godly.

The syntax of verses 3–5 is a conditional sentence assumed to be true. In other words, even though the statement begins with the conditional particle "if," the grammar Paul uses reveals that he knows he is expressing the way things actually are. He characterizes the false teacher in two ways. (1) "He is conceited and understands nothing" (v. 4). The NEB calls him a "pompous ignoramus." Those who think they are wise (and are thus bloated with self-importance) but who understand nothing is a recurrent motif in Pauline writings (cf. 1:7; cf. 1 Cor. 1:18–4:21; 8:1–3; 2 Cor. 10–12; Col. 2; Titus 1:15–16). (2) The false teacher also "has an unhealthy interest in controversies and quarrels about words." Instead of an interest in sound or healthy doctrine (cf. v. 3), they have a "morbid craving" (BAGD, 543) for controversy.

Paul then describes two devastating effects of this false teaching: detriment to the community of Christ and spiritual sickness of the teachers themselves. Heresy, arguments, and word-wars produce envy or jealously, the deadly sin of people taking sides against one another (Rom. 1:29; Gal. 5:21). "Envy" often causes outbursts of strife or quarreling (also in the lists of Rom. 1:29; Gal. 5:20). "Strife" in turn produces "malicious talk" and "evil suspicions." In a nutshell, there is constant friction. In the name of knowledge and wisdom, these false teachers have produced error and destruction.

Not only does the church suffer, but the teachers themselves experience terminal spiritual sickness. They have become people "of corrupt mind"—their thinking has become decayed to the state of complete rottenness. And they have "been robbed of the truth." In trying to make money off the gospel, they have become impoverished (or have impoverished themselves) from truth. It was their greed all along that led these false teachers down the path of error.

3.6.3. Temptations of Money Exposed (6:6–10). In immediate contrast to the last words of verse 5, Paul turns the phrases. The false teachers think that "godliness is a means to financial gain," but the real gain is godliness that does not seek material gain. "Contentment" (v. 6), as used by the philosophers means "satisfaction, self-sufficiency, independence"; but as Paul uses it (cf. Phil. 4:11), he turns the tables on the Stoics and declares that true contentment is *Christ*-sufficiency, not *self*-sufficiency (Fee, 1988, 143).

In verses 7–8 Paul gives two reasons why "godliness with contentment is great gain" (v. 6). (1) Since material gain is temporal, greed is irrational. Paul's words echo those of Job 1:21, "Naked I came from my mother's womb, and naked I will depart." (2) Sufficiency surpassed is still sufficiency, so that the pursuit of wealth is futile. A superabundance of "enough" meets no more needs than enough does. It is virtuous to be content, that is, satisfied with enough.

In verse 9 Paul returns to the avarice of false teachers and of all "who want to get rich." Fee (1988, 144–45) describes the results of greed as a downward spiral. The greedy "fall into temptation." As anyone who has ever fished knows, the enticement (i.e., the bait, the temptation) leads to "a trap." The trap is the "foolish and harmful desires that plunge [us] into ruin and destruction." The original language is vivid here: These desires are like a personal monster that drags to the bottom, submerges, and drowns its victims. The words for "ruin" and "destruction" suggest an irretrievable loss (Guthrie, 1990, 113).

Paul concludes the matter (v. 10) by quoting a Greek proverb and citing personal testimony. "For the love of money is a root of all kinds of evil." Fee (1988, 145) clarifies, "This text neither says, as it is often misquoted, that *money* is the root of all evil nor intends to say that every known evil has avarice as its *root*.... Greed is a trap full of many hurtful desires that lead to all kinds of sin." The sad reality is that "some people"—in Paul's context, the wayward elders of the Ephesian congregation—"eager for money, have wandered from the faith." Having abandoned the faith for error, they have impaled themselves with many pangs.

4. Conclusion: Final Charges and Benediction (6:11–21)

In his final charges to Timothy, the apostle leaves his young pastor friend with four imperatives, a solemn charge, and a final doxology.

4.1. Keep the Faith (6:11–12a)

4.1.1. Flee From Materialism (6:11). Paul instills confidence as he identifies Timothy as a "man of God," an Old Testament term for one of God's servants or agents. The apostle admonishes him to "flee from all this" (i.e., the doctrines and practices of the false teachers) and to "pursue" a virtuous life. "Righteousness" is right conduct; "godliness," right relationships with God and others; "faith," adherence to the truth; "love," charity toward all; "endurance," tenacious patience through trying situations; and "gentleness," a meek, tender spirit.

4.1.2. Fight for Faith (6:12a). Paul then turns to the concept of fighting and holding fast. "The good fight of the faith" is actually an athletic (and not military) metaphor, encouraging him to (lit.) "keep contending in the contest of faith."

4.2. Maintain Obedience (6:12b–15a)

The concept of "tak[ing] hold of the eternal life" continues the athletic metaphor. The young contender is to focus on the prize and continue the contest to its triumphant conclusion when he takes hold of the reward of the course to which he was called. Paul reminds Timothy of his confession of faith, most likely made at his baptism, in front of many witnesses. In light of the past, present, and future, the apostle encourages the maintenance of obedience.

The apostle's solemn charge to Timothy, given in the sight of God (who is able to preserve life) and in the sight of Jesus Christ (who made the greatest confession of all), is to "keep this command [i.e., to persevere in faith and in ministry] without spot or blame." His perseverance is to continue "until the appearing of our Lord Jesus Christ." The Second Coming is described as being certain ("which God will bring about") and as resting in God's sovereignty ("in his own time").

4.3. Blessed Be God (6:15b–16)

The thought of Christ's return and God's sovereignty sparks a majestic doxology. Kelly (1963, 146) suggests this doxology, with Old Testament and Jewish overtones, is "a gem from the devotional treasury of the Hellenistic synagogue which converts had naturalized in the Christian Church." The God who will bring about Christ's appearing in his own time is described in majestic splendor with five epithets, followed by a doxology. Every imaginable lexical means is incorporated to stress the uniqueness and sovereignty of God.

(1) He is "God, the blessed and only Ruler." The use of "only" emphasizes God's sovereignty.

(2) He is "the King of kings and Lord of lords." This phrase in Greek differs from the construction used in Revelation 17:14 and 19:16. "The difference emphasizes the fact that God is actually the governor of all earthly princes" (Barrett, 1963, 87). He is the King of the ones who reign as kings, and the Lord of those who exercise lordship.

(3) He is the one "who alone is immortal." His existence is without end and is not subject to the power of death.

(4) He is the one "who lives in unapproachable light." The splendor of his absolute holiness makes his dwelling place unapproachable.

(5) He is the one "whom no one has seen or can see." He is invisible, not because his dwelling place is obscure, but because it is too bright for mortal eyes.

Doxology: "To him be honor and might forever. Amen." A doxology is an articulation of praise to God. Since there is no verb in this sentence, it can be read either as a statement (i.e., "Honor and might is [due] to him forever") or as an imperative or exhortation (i.e., "[Let] honor and might be [due] to him forever"). The "Amen," an expression of agreement meaning "Let it be" or "Make it so," is more likely the latter. This doxology commands that honor (respect, recognition, value, or worth) and absolute dominion be ascribed to God eternally.

4.4. Instruct the Wealthy (6:17–19)

The apostle has already addressed those who want to become rich; now he finishes the letter with advice to those who are already wealthy.

4.4.1. To Focus on God (6:17). Paul begins by giving Timothy two negative commands for "those who are rich in this present world." (1) They must not be arrogant, that is, to think of themselves as exalted or lofty. (2) They must not put their hope in wealth but in God. Riches are uncertain, but God is faithful. He is the One who provides. And his manner is to provide *all* things, to do so *richly*, and not just to meet our bare necessities but to provide for us in a manner that brings us enjoyment and pleasure.

4.4.2. To Cultivate Generosity (6:18–19). Then Paul follows the prohibitions with positive commands. "Command them to do good, to be rich in good deeds, and to be generous and willing to share." Goodness and generosity, demonstrated both actively and passively, should characterize the righteous rich. As Jesus said, such goodness and generosity are investments in eternity (Luke 12:33; 18:22; cf. Matt. 6:19–21), for the rich thereby "lay up treasure for themselves" and establish "a firm foundation for the coming age." In so cultivating Christian generosity, the rich will grasp "the life that is truly life."

4.5. Guard the Deposit (6:20–21a)

The apostle's final charge to Timothy is to "guard" or keep safe that which has been entrusted into the young pastor's care. Scholars have debated what that deposit sacredly entrusted to Timothy is: the sound teaching of the gospel, his spiritual endowment for ministry, or the task of resisting false teachers and keeping his own life pure. By comparison with 2 Timothy 1:12 (see comment) and 1:14, it seems best to understand "the deposit" as the truth of the gospel. One final time, the apostle urges Timothy to "turn away from godless chatter and the opposing ideas of what is falsely called knowledge" (see also 1:6; 4:7; cf. 2 Tim. 2:23). Sadly, Paul reiterates the loss of some professing believers to the faith through this error.

4.6. Closing (6:21b)

"Finally, with an abruptness that has within it its own pathos, Paul signs off with his typical benediction: 'Grace be with you'" (Fee, 1988, 162). It is a brief but sincere prayer that God's grace might be with not only Timothy but also those under his care (the word "you" is plural). The situation is critical, the closing is brief, but the divine aid is available and sufficient to enable success to Paul's successor.

THE OLD TESTAMENT IN THE NEW

NT Text	OT Text	Subject
1Tim 5:18	Dt 25:4	Not muzzling an ox

OUTLINE OF 2 TIMOTHY

1. **Introduction** (1:1–18)
   - **1.1.** Salutation/Greeting (1:1–2)
   - **1.2.** Warm Reminiscences (1:3–7)
     - **1.2.1.** Recalling Timothy's Tears, Paul Remembers Him in Prayer (1:3–4)
     - **1.2.2.** Remembering Timothy's Godly Heritage, Paul Reminds Him to Rekindle His Gift (1:5–7)
   - **1.3.** Opening Encouragement (1:8–14)
     - **1.3.1.** Join the Suffering (1:8–12)
     - **1.3.2.** Two Further Imperatives (1:13–14)
   - **1.4.** Recent News (1:15–18)
     - **1.4.1.** The Asians Abandoned Paul (1:15)
     - **1.4.2.** Onesiphorus's Household Refreshed Him (1:16–18)
2. **Personal Exhortations to Paul's Successor** (2:1–13)
   - **2.1.** Be Strong by Grace (2:1)
   - **2.2.** Pass the Torch to the Faithful (2:2)
   - **2.3.** Endure As These Examples (2:3–6)
     - **2.3.1.** Suffer As a Soldier—Don't Get Entangled! (2:3–4)
     - **2.3.2.** Compete As an Athlete—According to the Rules! (2:5)
     - **2.3.3.** Work Hard As a Farmer and Share of the Crops (2:6)
   - **2.4.** Reflect for a Moment (2:7)
   - **2.5.** Basis for the Appeal (2:8–13)
     - **2.5.1.** Remember Jesus Christ: The Superlative Example (2:8–9)
     - **2.5.2.** Consider Paul's Rationale: The Salvation of Others (2:10)
     - **2.5.3.** Meditate on This Statement: A Hymn of Endurance (2:11–13)
3. **Leadership Exhortations to Paul's Successor** (2:14–26)
   - **3.1.** Keep Your Doctrine Straight! (2:14–18, cf. v. 23)
     - **3.1.1.** Teach Them Not to Wrangle Over Words (2:14)
     - **3.1.2.** Train Yourself to Be Accurate With the Word (2:15)
     - **3.1.3.** Steer Clear of Empty Words (2:16–18)
   - **3.2.** Live a Holy Life! (2:19–22)
     - **3.2.1.** The Seal of God (2:19)

3.2.2. A Vessel of Honor (2:20–21)
3.2.3. A Pursuer of Virtue (2:22)
3.3. (Parenthesis: Reject Foolish Speculations! [2:23; cf. vv. 14–18])
3.4. Lead Like a Humble Servant! (2:24–26)
3.4.1. Characteristics of the Lord's Servant (2:24)
3.4.2. Corrections by the Lord's Servant (2:25–26)
4. Warning Against Eschatological Wickedness and Heresy (3:1–17)
4.1. End-Time Wickedness (3:1–9)
4.1.1. Difficult Days Are Coming (3:1)
4.1.2. The Kinds of People to Avoid (3:2–5)
4.1.3. The Kinds of Things They Do (3:6–7)
4.1.4. Two Infamous Examples (3:8)
4.1.5. The End of Such People (3:9)
4.2. Encouragement in Spite of Obstacles (3:10–17)
4.2.1. Timothy Has a Record of Faithfulness (3:10–11)
4.2.2. Persecution Is to Be Expected (3:12)
4.2.3. Degeneration Will Increase (3:13)
4.2.4. Perseverance Is a Necessity (3:14–15)
4.2.5. Scripture Is Sufficient (3:16–17)
5. Solemn Charges Concerning Ministry (4:1–8)
5.1. On the Ministry of the Word (4:1–4)
5.1.1. Preach for All You're Worth! (4:1–2)
5.1.2. You Won't Always Have the Opportunity (4:3–4)
5.2. On Ministry in General (4:5–8)
5.2.1. Prove Yourself Fully (4:5)
5.2.2. I Won't Be Around Much Longer (4:6–8)
6. Conclusion: Closing Considerations (4:9–22)
6.1. Personal Remarks (4:9–13)
6.1.1. Come Quickly! (4:9–11a)
6.1.2. Bring Mark With You (4:11b)
6.1.3. I Commissioned Tychicus (4:12)
6.1.4. Bring Three Things (4:13)
6.2. Parting Warning: Watch Out for Alexander (4:14–15)
6.2.1. The Coppersmith Really Hurt Me (4:14)
6.2.2. Don't Let Him Hurt You! (4:15)
6.3. Testimony Through Trials (4:16–18)
6.3.1. I Was Deserted by All (4:16)
6.3.2. But God Was There (4:17)
6.3.3. He Will Be There (4:18)
6.4. Final Farewell (4:19–22)
6.4.1. Greet These Three (4:19)
6.4.2. News on Two Brothers (4:20)
6.4.3. Come Before Winter! (4:21a)
6.4.4. These Four (and More) Greet You (4:21b)
6.4.5. Closing (4:22)

COMMENTARY ON 2 TIMOTHY

1. Introduction (1:1–18)

1.1. Salutation/Greeting (1:1–2)

Similar to 1 Timothy, the second letter of Paul to Timothy opens with a brief salutation of the customary pattern. It may seem surprising that Paul is still stressing his apostleship to his beloved son in the faith. Why would he do so? Since this letter is more personal than his first one to Timothy, Paul's reason for this apostolic emphasis may simply be habit, or it may reflect an urgent appeal for loyalty. Paul's apostleship is described as "by the will of God," not by Paul's own volition; it is "according to the promise of life," which is the object and intention of the appointment; and that life is "in Christ Jesus," who is the source and sphere of true living.

The way Paul addresses the recipient is almost identical to 1 Timothy (see comments on 1 Tim. 1:2), except that "my dear son" replaces "my true son in the faith." As an intimate correspondence between an apostle and his understudy, there is no need in this letter to legitimate Timothy's position before the congregation; instead, Paul simply expresses the close ties they share. Timothy has always been a "beloved son" to Paul (see 1 Cor. 4:17).

1.2. Warm Reminiscences (1:3–7)

Paul's opening prayer of thanksgiving, reminding Timothy of his past loyalty, faith, and godly heritage, sets the tone for his plea for perseverance and continued loyalty.

1.2.1. Recalling Timothy's Tears, Paul Remembers Him in Prayer (1:3–4). Paul identifies himself as a sincere worshiper and servant of the God of his ancestors. His Christ is in clear continuity with the God of the Old Testament; his Christianity is the ultimate fulfillment of Judaism. Such a religious heritage he also shares with Timothy. The verb "serve" indicates Paul's carrying out of the religious duties of ministry; its present tense indicates that such serving has been a continual, unbroken habit of life (Rienecker, 1980, 637). Paul is thankful to God as he, at every occasion of prayer, both "night and day," mentions Timothy in his petitions.

It is the memory of Timothy's tears that stirs in Paul the longing to see his young friend again, in order that at their next visit their present sorrow might be replaced with joy. No doubt the elder apostle is recalling the pathos of their last parting. We see a hint of Paul's loneliness during his final vigil as he wishes for Timothy's companionship, even though the work in Ephesus is yet unfinished.

1.2.2. Remembering Timothy's Godly Heritage, Paul Reminds Him to Rekindle His Gift (1:5–7). Another memory warms the apostle's heart: Timothy's "sincere faith" (1:5). The adjective means "genuine" (lit., "unhypocritical"); the noun "faith" (*pistis*) could refer to his trust in God, but more likely indicates Timothy's "faithfulness." Genuine faithfulness, steadfastness in one's faith, prompted Paul's thanksgiving on more than one occasion (cf. Rom. 1:8; Col. 1:4; 1 Thess. 1:3; 3:6–7; 2 Thess. 1:3; Philem. 5).

In an effort to encourage Timothy's continued loyalty (to Christ, to Paul, and to his ministry), the apostle reminds the young pastor of his religious heritage. Just as Paul has continued faithful in his service to the God of his forebears (v. 3), so too Timothy's steadfastness in the face of suffering has a continuity with the faith/faithfulness of his foremothers.

> A multigenerational transmission of a rich spiritual heritage was given to Timothy from his godly mother and grandmother.... 2 Tim. 3:14–15 indicate that very early in infancy Timothy was instructed in the Holy Scriptures.... It is likely that Timothy was a product of a "mixed marriage" in that his father was a Greek and his mother was a Jewess. It appears that Timothy's father was not a believer since his faith is not mentioned. 1 Cor. 7:14 speaks of the unbelieving husband being sanctified through his believing wife so that the children can be partakers of this new life in Christ.
>
> How fortunate and blessed are children born into families where God's Word is passed to succeeding generations (Ps. 78:1–7). Many early church fathers such as Augustine, John Chrysostom, Gregory Nanzianzen, Basil, and Gregory of Nyssa celebrated the godly influence of their mothers....
>
> Recent research relative to childrearing emphasizes the interactive, developmental nature of the mother-child relationship—i.e., the reciprocal effect of the mother on the child, as well as the child on the mother. (Kroeger, Evans, and Storkey, 1995, 451–52, sidebar)

The apostle culminates his summary of Timothy's godly heritage with a hearty affirmation for the young man's faith, which "I am persuaded [says Paul], now lives in you also." "This confidence in Timothy's genuine faith becomes the springboard for the appeal that follows (1:6–2:13)" (Fee, 1988, 223). Such confidence in that godly heritage and genuine faith is the basis of Paul's reminder to "fan into flame" his spiritual gift (v. 6). This colorful verb refers

> to [stirring] up smoldering embers into a living flame, to keep at white heat. The word means either "to kindle afresh" or "to keep at full flame." Paul's statement does not necessarily contain a censure since fire in the ancient world was never kept at a continual blaze but rather kept alive through glowing coals which were then rekindled to a flame by a bellows whenever the situation demanded flame. (Rienecker, 1980, 638)

The apostle is saying to his timid friend, "Now is the time—the situation demands—that you make full use of your grace-gift from God." In 1 Timothy 4:14 we learned of Timothy's spiritual gift and in 1:18 and 4:14 of the prophecies about him; now we learn that the hands laid on him were not only those of the elders (in 4:14), but included the apostle's as well. Paul focuses on his own personal part in uthenticating Timothy's ministry in an effort ɔ bolster his youthful insecurity (cf. 1 Cor. 6:10–11; 1 Tim. 4:12).

Regarding verse 7, Fee argues (1988, 226) ıat the "spirit," not "of timidity," but of power, of love and of self-discipline" is not n inner attitude but the Holy Spirit himself.

> That Paul is referring not to some "spirit" (or attitude) that "God" has given "us" (him and Timothy, but ultimately all other believers who must equally persevere in the face of hardship), but to the *Holy Spirit* of God is made certain by several items: (a) the explanatory "for" that begins this sentence gives it the closest possible tie to verse 6; (b) the close relationship between *charisma* ("gift," v. 6) and the Spirit (v. 7) is thoroughly Pauline . . .; (c) the words "power" and "love" are especially attributed to the Spirit in Paul; and (d) there are close ties between this verse and 1 Timothy 4:14, where the "gifting" of Timothy is specifically singled out as the work of the Spirit.

urthermore, in the other "not . . . but" statenents of contrasting spirits (Rom. 8:15; 1 Cor. :12), the "but" clause clearly indicates the Ioly Spirit. "Thus, Paul's intent goes somehing like this: 'For when "God gave us" his Spirit," it was "not timidity" that we received, but power, love, and self-discipline"'" (ibid., 27). In the face of present hardships, it is God's Spirit that conquers cowardice, conributes clear thinking (especially in the face of alse teachers), provides us power, and loads s with love.

1.3. Opening Encouragement (1:8–14)

1.3.1. Join the Suffering (1:8–12). In light of the Spirit's enduement, the apostle urges Timothy with two imperatives: to "not be shamed," but to "join with me in suffering for he gospel" (v. 8). Paul first urges Timothy to hare willingly the stigma and disgrace of Christ, the crucified Messiah, and of Paul, his mprisoned ambassador. That is, Timothy must ot avoid humiliation based on the testimony of Christ or on his association with the apostle.

Moreover, Timothy must embrace suffering. Paul's unashamed testimony of Christ had frequently provoked suffering for the gospel (cf. Rom. 8:17; 2 Cor. 4:7–15; Phil. 1:12, 29; Col. 1:24; 1 Thess. 1:6; 2:14; 3:4). But suffering is not only Paul's present situation (2 Tim. 2:9); it is also the destiny demanded of Timothy (3:12). The verb translated "join . . . in suffering" means "to take one's share of evil treatment;" the aorist imperative indicates "that the action is to be done immediately" (Rienecker, 1980, 638). The enablement to undergo this suffering will come "by the power of God."

The mention of God launches Paul into a creedlike confession of the gospel (vv. 9–10), just as he does in Titus 2:11–14 and 3:4–7. This hymnic statement is particularly appropriate to Timothy's present situation of needing encouragement to rekindle his gift, to resign his cowardice, and to take his part in suffering for Christ. Although verses 8–11 are all one sentence in Greek, editors of the Greek text present verses 9–10 in poetic lines as follows (lit. trans.):

> [It is God] who has saved us
> and called us to [or with] a holy calling,
> not according to our works
> but according to his own purpose and grace,
> which was given to us in Christ Jesus
> before time immemorial,
> but has now been revealed
> through the appearance of our Savior, Christ Jesus,
> who, on the one hand, destroyed death
> and, on the other hand, brought to light life and immortality through the gospel.

Paul's point to Timothy is clear: "Be steadfast; rekindle your gift; take part in the suffering; for we are already among those who have overcome death through Christ" (Fee, 1988, 230).

Before Paul terminates the sentence, he restates his role in the proclamation of the gospel (v. 11). With regard to this gospel, Paul was appointed "a herald," "an apostle," and "a teacher." This verse echoes 1 Timothy 2:7, but Paul's emphasis here is not on appointment to minister *to the Gentiles,* but to minister *the gospel.* The emphasis of the three roles is not on Paul's authority as an apostle, but on the gospel itself and his relationship to it (Fee, 1988, 231).

Paul's roles with regard to the gospel are precisely the reason for his present plight (v. 12). Again he serves as a model for Timothy, because "[Paul is] not ashamed," for his deposit is secure in the hands of God.

The same noun (*paratheke*) used in 1 Timothy 6:20, translated there as "what has been entrusted to your care" (lit., "the deposit"), appears here in 2 Timothy 1:12 with the first person singular possessive pronoun, "my deposit" or "what he has entrusted to me" (or perhaps "what I have entrusted to him"); it appears again in verse 14, "the good deposit that was entrusted to you" ("to you" is not in the Greek). These are the only three occurrences of *paratheke* in the New Testament; in all three cases it functions as the object of the verb "guard, protect, keep safe." In 1 Timothy 6:20 and 2 Timothy 1:14 *Timothy* is to "guard the . . . deposit," while in 2 Timothy 1:12 *God* is doing the guarding.

What is "the deposit"? Is it something entrusted to God or something God entrusts to us (in this case, Paul and Timothy)? Though scholars have offered several suggestions regarding the referent of *paratheke* (Paul's soul, his confident trust, the divine gift for ministry, etc.), Barrett (1963, 97) explains that if we take "the deposit" to mean "the truth of the gospel committed to Paul to preach," this interpretation

> has the great advantage of giving to the word "deposit" the same meaning in all three passages, here and at 1 Tim. 6:20 and 2 Tim. 1:14. God himself takes ultimate responsibility for the gospel he entrusts to his preachers; hence "the word of God is not shut up" (2 Tim. 2:9). On no other ground would the world of preaching be for a moment endurable; whatever the failures and sufferings of a preacher, God himself watches over his word to perform it. His care continues up to "that great day"—of judgment and consummation; cf. 1:18; 4:8.

1.3.2. Two Further Imperatives (1:13–14). The apostle issues two more imperatives to Timothy, but these are less concerned with the pastor's personal issues (of youth and timidity) and more concerned with the continuing threat of the false teachers. (1) As he has stressed throughout the Pastoral Letters, Paul urges Timothy to "keep as the pattern of sound teaching" (see comments on 1 Tim. 1:10), which "you heard from me" (cf. 2 Tim. 2:2; 3:10; also 1 Tim. 4:6); and as you do so, Timothy, be a model of "faith and love in Christ Jesus."

(2) The other imperative, paralleling verse 12, is Paul's charge that Timothy "guard the good deposit that was entrusted [to him]" (see comments on v. 12). The sound teaching of the gospel entrusted by God to Paul, and now by Paul to Timothy, will someday be entrusted to other faithful persons, who will be able to teach it to others also (2:2). Timothy must protect the message he has received against any doctrinal contamination by the false teachers.

But Timothy does not stand alone in this task, for he is to "guard it with the help of the Holy Spirit." Again Paul affirms the young pastor's spirituality by saying, in essence, "God's precious Holy Spirit lives in both of us (cf. vv. 6–7). The same One who helped me [Paul] guard the divine treasure will be faithful to grant victory to you [Timothy]."

1.4. Recent News (1:15–18)

The apostle now shares a report of examples of both disloyalty and loyalty. Though this section appears to be a digression, it is not without purpose. In light of the appeal that Timothy "guard" that which was "entrusted to" him, the apostle remembers both many who did not keep the trust and one man who was exemplary in sharing Paul's suffering.

1.4.1. The Asians Abandoned Paul (1:15). Paul addresses a situation of which Timothy is too painfully aware: "Everyone in the province of Asia has deserted me." Since the city of Ephesus was in Asia, Timothy has been living through this defection. The details of what, when, and where these defections took place, though they are clear to Timothy ("you know"), are not clear to us. Perhaps everyone from Asia who had come to Paul in Rome (except Onesiphorus) had deserted him and returned home again. Or perhaps, and more likely, the defections in Asia had been so staggering (Kelly [1963, 169] identifies the apostle's description as "the exaggeration [of] depression") that friends from whom he would have expected loyalty, "including Phygelus and Hermogenes," had deserted him, too. Though we are not certain what this desertion involved, it seems that in abandoning Paul (perhaps at the news of his arrest), the apostle considers them

) have deserted Christ. The verb used in this erse is the same one used for spiritual defecon (see 4:4; Titus 1:14); a different verb is sed of personal desertions (see 2 Tim. 4:10).

1.4.2. Onesiphorus's Household Re-eshed Him (1:16–18). Onesiphorus is the ositive example, the model to Timothy. Paul's prayer" that "the Lord show mercy to the ousehold of Onesiphorus" indicates that Oneiphorus is not with his household at this time.

> The fact that Paul should begin his reminder about Onesiphorus in this way, by asking for *present* mercy for his household, and that at the end (v. 18a) he should ask for *future* mercy (on that Day) for Onesiphorus himself, suggests very strongly that Onesiphorus had died in the meantime. If so, it could only have increased Paul's present pain and loneliness. (Fee, 1988, 236)

Fee offers further insight on this fine fellow. ı a culture where imprisonment often involved elf-sustenance, Onesiphorus "often refreshed Paul]," no doubt bringing food and cheer to the postle. Far from being concerned over embarassment, this man took the risk of regularly isiting a state criminal condemned to death; he was not ashamed of [Paul's] chains." It seems ıat the apostle was not in a public prison and nding him took considerable effort; thus, when Paul was in Rome, Onesiphorus searched hard for [him] until he found [him]." he point of the illustration from recent events ; clear: "Don't be ashamed of the gospel or of ıe," Paul says. "Many have, but not Oneiphorus. Be like him!" (Fee, 1988, 236–37).

. Personal Exhortations to Paul's Successor (2:1–13)

2.1. Be Strong by Grace (2:1)

Paul now moves into an extended section of ersonal charges to Timothy. The nuances of ıe conjunction "then" are manifold, signaling ıat the exhortations that follow (1) are in conast to the defectors, (2) are in keeping with the xample of Onesiphorus, (c) resume the impertives of verses 8–14, and (d) continue the ncouragement that Timothy, through the nablement of the Spirit, does have the ability) succeed. Paul charges Timothy: "You then, ıy son, be strong in the grace that is in Christ esus." "Be strong" is actually a present tense passive imperative, that Timothy is to *keep on being strengthened* by God. "Grace" either has a locative sense, expressing the realm or sphere in which Timothy is to be strong, or an instrumental sense, expressing the means by which Timothy is enabled to be strong. In either case, the source of this grace is "Christ Jesus."

2.2. Pass the Torch to the Faithful (2:2)

The first task Timothy is to be strengthened for is to "entrust" (the verb related to the noun "deposit," see comments on 1:12) to "reliable [people]" (not limited to "men") "the things you have heard me say." Since Paul is urging Timothy, even though his work is not yet finished in Ephesus, to leave that city and join him in Rome, the young pastor must entrust the things he has heard Paul say to people who are trustworthy, and as such, "qualified to teach others." The preposition *dia* (NIV, "in the presence of") is better translated "*through* many witnesses," meaning that the things Paul taught have been *attested by* (and not simply mediated by) many others, from whom Timothy had also learned them (cf. 3:14).

2.3. Endure As These Examples (2:3–6)

2.3.1. Suffer As a Soldier—Don't Get Entangled! (2:3–4). The more significant reason Timothy needs to be strengthened is so that he (as Onesiphorus did) might share in the suffering. "Endure hardship with us" (the same verb as in 1:8) means "to suffer evil together, to endure affliction together, to take one's share of rough treatment."

The first model of endurance is that of a soldier, "a good soldier of Christ Jesus." Paul frequently resorts to military imagery (cf. 2 Cor. 10:3–5; Eph. 6:10–17; Philem. 2), especially in the context of struggling with opponents of the gospel (cf. 1 Tim. 1:18). "By the very nature of his occupation, the 'soldier' will often be called on to take his part in suffering" (Fee, 1988, 241).

Two more analogies unfold from the soldier metaphor: "No one serving as a soldier gets involved in civilian affairs," and "he wants to please his commanding officer." Without over-exegeting the imagery, the simple elements of the comparisons of Timothy's life to a soldier's are wholehearted devotion to the task and undivided loyalty to the commander. The "commanding officer" is, literally translated, the "one who enlisted him," whose duties were to see that his soldiers were well equipped and provided with food and shelter.

2.3.2. Compete As an Athlete—According to the Rules! (2:5). The second model of endurance is the athlete, who must "compete according to the rules," that is, lawfully. It is not clear what "rules" Timothy must adhere to, but they may refer either to rules of the contest (an athlete "was not allowed to lighten his struggle by bypassing the rules" [Rienecker, 1980, 640]) or to rules of training ("the Games required a ten-month period of strict discipline" [Fee, 1988, 242]). In either case, the athlete's course toward "the victor's crown" included suffering.

2.3.3. Work Hard As a Farmer and Share of the Crops (2:6). The third model of endurance is the "hardworking farmer." The farmer, too, will find a reward for his suffering.

2.4. Reflect for a Moment (2:7)

The apostle is certain that insight into these analogies will follow reflection on them. The compounding of the three metaphors for endurance has placed equal emphasis on "sharing in suffering" and "winning a prize." Barrett summarizes the meaning of the three analogies: "Beyond warfare is victory, beyond athletic effort a prize, and beyond agricultural labour a crop. In the same way, Timothy's share of hardship will be followed by reward" (Barrett, 1963, 102).

2.5. Basis for the Appeal (2:8–13)

This paragraph brings to a conclusion Paul's long appeal (begun in 1:6–14 and picked up again in 2:1) for Timothy to remain loyal, even to the point of suffering. Now the apostle provides the theological basis for the appeal. More important than the reward is the gospel, which Paul summarizes in this section.

2.5.1. Remember Jesus Christ: The Superlative Example (2:8–9). In a letter filled with reminiscences, the focus of attention is to be on Christ's example. In his remembering Jesus Christ, Timothy is to focus on two realities: that Jesus was "raised from the dead" and that he was "descended from David." Though emphasis on the resurrection is characteristically Pauline (cf. Rom. 1:4; 10:9), the descent from David is not (though cf. Rom. 1:3). As an apostle to the Gentiles, tracing tru messianic ancestry was less significant a issue to Paul's target audience than it was t Jews. But for Timothy, with his Jewish her itage, these two realities provided an appro priate summary of the gospel. "'Born o David's line' suggests the fulfillment o Israelite history and hope in a real human per son, and 'risen from the dead' the eschatolog ical irruption into this world (the world o David, and of Jesus of Nazareth) of the super natural and divine" (Barrett, 1963, 103).

For preaching this message the apostle i "suffering even to the point of being chaine like a criminal." The word for "criminal" is strong one, a technical term reserved for bu glars, murderers, traitors, and so on. The onl other time it is used in the New Testament is fo the brigands who were crucified alongside Jesu (Luke 23:32–33, 39). "Its use here suggests th conditions of the Neronian pogrom rather tha the relatively mild imprisonment of Acts 28 (Kelly, 1963, 177). But though his messenger i bound, Christ's gospel is not! The perfect tens emphasizes that it "has not been and is not no bound." As in Philippians 1:12–18, Paul' imprisonment did not hinder but provided fres opportunities for the sharing of the good new

2.5.2. Consider Paul's Rationale: Th Salvation of Others (2:10). It is "for the sak of the elect" that Paul "endures everything (i.e., persists patiently under all this burden The "elect" (God's chosen people) is a Chri tian application to New Testament believers c an Old Testament term for the people of Go (cf. Titus 1:1; 2:14). "Far too much ink ha been spilled on the theological implications c this term, whether it refers to the 'elect' wh are already saved or to the 'elect' but not y saved. Such theologizing quite misses Paul point" (Fee, 1988, 247).

Somehow Paul is convinced that what he going through will help the cause of the elect salvation, but just how is not made clear. Som have made almost magical conjectures concer ing the connection between Christ's suffering the messengers' sufferings, and the salvation c others (cf. 2 Cor. 1:6; Col. 1:24). The point, hov ever, is not *Paul's suffering for the gospel,* b *the gospel for which he suffers* that brings sa vation (Fee, 1988, 248). The salvation of th elect "with eternal glory" causes any tempor trials to pale by comparison (cf. Rom. 8:18).

2.5.3. Meditate on This Statement: A Hymn of Endurance (2:11–13). Paul concludes this major section of personal exhortations to his successor with another "trustworthy saying" (see comments on 1 Tim. 1:15). The parallelisms of idea and rhythmic character of the lines suggest that this passage was taken from a preexisting liturgical hymn already known to Timothy and the church in Ephesus (note the indentation in the NIV). The theology and terminology of the hymn is so Pauline that it very likely originated in one of his congregations if it was not composed by the apostle himself. The last line, "for he cannot disown himself," seems to be where Paul breaks from the hymn. His motive in quoting this hymn is to impress the connection between suffering with Christ and sharing his glory.

Though Paul's quotation of the hymn applies its truth to suffering persecution and martyrdom, its original liturgical use probably reflects a baptism service. The connection between the images of death to sin and self and resurrection to new life with believers' baptism is common (cf. Rom. 6:2–23; Col. 2:11–12; 3:3). Chrysostom, in his commentary on the passage, brings the context of baptism and martyrdom together as he exhorts, "if our death with Christ was real and complete . . . we shall be ready to share his literal death" (quoted by Lock, 1973, 96).

But as Kelly writes (1963, 180), "the Christian's death with Christ in baptism is only a first instalment. It is his vocation, being mystically united with the Crucified, to embrace a life of trial and hardships." That is, we must also "endure with him." Such is the prerequisite to "reign with him" (cf. 1 Cor. 15:24–25; Rev. 1:6; 3:21; 5:10; 20:4).

The hymn in its original language passes through a chronological progression with its tenses. From past tense ("dying" in baptism) through present tense ("enduring" contemporary sufferings), the hymn moves now into the future possibility of "disowning" Christ. "If we disown him" (a conditional sentence followed by a future verb) "suggests a remote possibility rather than a certainty" (Harris, Horton, and Seaver, 1989, 8:449). Repudiation of Christ results in his repudiation of us on the Day of Judgment (cf. Matt. 10:32–33; Luke 12:9). This second half of 2 Timothy 2:12 is the opposite of the first. Presupposing the context of suffering, it is a clear warning to Timothy and "the elect" against apostasy during persecution. The Asians of 1:15 have already defected; thus, they are clearly no longer a part of Christ's church.

This line of the hymn may point to the Gnostic identity of the false teachers. Because of their dualistic doctrine, dichotomizing the body from the spirit, a Gnostic could deny Christ with the mouth and continue to confess him with the spirit.[10] There is little evidence of Gnostic martyrs; they could publicly recant and then claim it did not count. The apostle asserts in this hymn of the orthodox: "What we say does count!—Christ will disown those who disown him."

Though the grace of God does not extend to apostasy, it does cover faithlessness. "If we are faithless, he will remain faithful." "Faithless" (*aspisteo*) does not mean without faith (i.e., "unbelieving or disbelieving") but without faithfulness. Fee (1988, 251) explains:

> This can mean either that God will override our infidelity with his grace (as most commentators) or that his overall faithfulness to his gracious gift of eschatological salvation for his people is not negated by the faithlessness of some. This latter seems more in keeping with Paul and the immediate context. Some have proved faithless, but God's saving faithfulness has not been diminished thereby.

Barrett (1963, 104) explains, "The only ground of security is not man's faithfulness but God's, that is, God's faithfulness to his word, to his promises, and to himself." The eschatological hope is rooted in the character of God.

3. Leadership Exhortations to Paul's Successor (2:14–26)

The rest of chapter 2 is a major section of exhortations to Timothy as a leader. From doctrine and holiness to humility, the apostle covers a gamut of leadership issues.

3.1. Keep Your Doctrine Straight! (2:14–18, cf. v. 23)

Leaving his personal reminiscences (for Timothy, his tears, and his sincere faith [1:3–5]) and the exhortations of things for Timothy to remember (his gift and the gospel [1:6; 2:8]), the apostle turns now to the things Timothy must "keep reminding [his parishioners] of."

3.1.1. Teach Them Not to Wrangle Over Words (2:14). "Before God," the highest authority one can appeal to, "warn them . . . against quarreling about words." This has been the chief characteristic of the false teachers (see comments on 1 Tim. 2:8; 6:4–5; cf. Titus 3:9). The congregation is to be warned not to get involved in such disputes over words carried on by the false teachers. It accomplishes no good (cf. Titus 3:8); on the contrary, it "ruins those who listen."

3.1.2. Train Yourself to Be Accurate With the Word (2:15). Timothy's own teaching must be in sharp contrast to that of the false teachers. The apostle urges him to be diligent, to do his utmost, or to "take all pains to present [himself] before God as one who can stand His test—as a real worker, as one who will never be put to shame for bad or scamped work, but as teaching rightly the one message of the truth" (Lock, 1973, 97). "Correctly handl[ing]"—or as the KJV has it, "rightly dividing"—"the word of truth" appears only here in the New Testament. This colorful verb literally means "to cut straight, impart the word of truth without deviation" (Zerwick and Grosvenor, 1979, 641). It has multiple analogies: "a plow driving a straight furrow" (Chrysostom), a road-maker driving his road straight, a priest properly preparing a sacrifice, and "a mason squaring and cutting a stone to fit it into its proper place" (a definition based on Prov. 3:6; 11:5). The word was frequently used in liturgies to describe the duties of the bishop and to denote orthodoxy ("straight or right teaching") (Lock, 1973, 98–99; Rienecker, 1980, 642).

3.1.3. Steer Clear of Empty Words (2:16–18). The apostle now issues a clear warning to Timothy (cf. 1 Tim. 6:20). The verb in the imperative, "avoid godless chatter," literally means to "to shift or go around so as to avoid or shun"; the direct object means "profane, empty talk." The content of the false teachers' message is without purpose.

As to results, false teaching will produce "more and more" ungodliness and "spread like gangrene." Not only does it hurt the teachers, but all those who listen are infected by its poison. This empty talk spreads like a flock of cattle "grazing" in a pasture, a verb used for a spreading sore. The noun was the ancient Greek medical term for gangrene, cancer, or a spreading ulcer.

> It is a disease by which any part of the body suffering from inflammation becomes so corrupted that unless a remedy be seasonably applied, the evil continually spreads, attacks other parts, and at last eats away at the bones. The metaphor illustrates insidiousness and nothing could more suitably describe the manner of advancement of most false teachings, whether ancient or modern. (Rienecker, 1980, 642)

Two examples of false teachers are "Hymenaeus and Philetus, who have wandered away from the truth" (see 1 Tim. 1:6; 6:21). No doubt the same Hymenaeus whom Paul had "handed over to Satan" in 1 Timothy 1:20 is still at work "destroy[ing] the faith of some."

These two men are teaching "that the resurrection has already taken place." This overrealized eschatology, that the resurrection is experienced in our spiritual dying and rising with Christ in baptism, was a false teaching Paul encountered repeatedly (1 Cor. 4:8; 15:12; 2 Thess. 2:2), a doctrine that fit in well with the dualism of Gnosticism. In making one's resurrection a spiritual, that is, a nonliteral phenomenon, these false teachers were attempting to overturn the keystone of the faith, and indeed had already overturned the faith of some. "For Paul, denial of our (future bodily) resurrection is to deny the faith itself, in that it is to deny our past (Christ's own resurrection, on which all else is predicated) and our present as well" (Fee, 1988, 257). The entire chapter of 1 Corinthians 15 is devoted to defeating the false doctrine that denied the literal, physical resurrection of Christ and his saints. Note the profound theological and spiritual implications of the heresy spread by Hymenaeus and Philetus in 1 Corinthians 15:13–14, 16–17:

> If there is no resurrection of the dead, then not even Christ has been raised. And if Christ has not been raised, our preaching is useless and so is your faith. . . . For if the dead are not raised, then Christ has not been raised either. And if Christ has not been raised, your faith is futile; you are still in your sins.

3.2. Live a Holy Life! (2:19–22)

3.2.1. The Seal of God (2:19). Not one to end on a negative note, the apostle, just as in e hymn in 2:13, culminates this section also ith a comment on the faithfulness of God. Jsing a strong adversative conjunction "nevertheless," Paul is convinced that, in spite of pponents and defections, "God's solid founation stands firm." God's good work in Ephsus cannot be thwarted by false teachers. It as withstood the opposition and continues to tand secure.

The seal of the Lord, his mark of ownerhip, bears a double inscription concerning a ight relationship and a righteous life. "The ord knows those who are his"—the confience of God's people is not that we know im, but that he knows us. "Everyone who onfesses the name of the Lord must turn away rom wickedness"—a commitment to Christ vill be evidenced by a clean break from sin nd wickedness.

3.2.2. A Vessel of Honor (2:20–21). Paul's ext analogy rests on the variety of articles in n ancient house of the more well-to-do. There re expensive articles, like those "of gold and ilver"; but there are also inexpensive ones, ike those "of wood and clay." Some serve noble," honorable purposes, such as enteraining guests at public meals; some serve ignoble," humble, ordinary purposes, such as ontaining waste to be eliminated. The netaphor is a common one, both in antiquity nd in the Old (Jer. 18:1–11) and New Testanents (Rom. 9:19–24), but the apostle's appliation in this context is new.

The word "therefore," which begins verse 1 (not translated in the NIV), ties the applicaion of the analogy to verse 19, that "everyone vho confesses the name of the Lord must turn way from wickedness." "If a [person] leanses [oneself] from the latter"—the realm f the ignoble, that is, false teachings—such person "will be an instrument for noble puroses." Only those articles with noble, honorble, righteous purposes count. It is not the alue of the vessels or the material from which hey are made, but the contents of the containrs that matter. Therefore, in order to be "useul to the Master and prepared to do any good vork," one is "made holy," that is, set apart for acred purposes, by separating oneself from vil teachings and practices.

3.2.3. A Pursuer of Virtue (2:22). Paul alls Timothy to "flee the evil desires of youth" nd to "pursue" Christian qualities. These evil desires, Fee contends (1988, 263), are not sensual passions but the kinds of things that entice headstrong young people: "novelties, foolish discussions, and arguments that all too often lead to quarrels." Lock adds to the list "impatience, love of disputation, self-assertion as well as self-indulgence" (Lock, 1973, 101). Instead of engaging in these, the pastimes of the false teachers, Timothy is to be a pursuer of virtue. The first three virtues in the list ("righteousness, faith, love") Paul used in his similar imperative of 1 Timothy 6:11 (see comments). Timothy must also "pursue . . . peace, along with those who call on the Lord out of a pure heart." "Brotherly concord should flourish among Christian people (cf. Rom. 12:18)" (Kelly, 1963, 189).

(3.3. Parenthesis: Reject Foolish Speculations! [2:23; cf. vv. 14–18])

Paul interrupts his own flow of thought to come back to address those "stupid arguments." Fee (1988, 264) helps us to trace the connection of his thoughts.

> Precisely because Timothy is to "pursue peace," he must "not have anything to do with" (same verb as in 1 Tim. 4:7) "foolish" (cf. Titus 3:9, a strong pejorative) "and stupid" (*apaideutos*, "uninstructed, ill-informed") "arguments" (see disc. on 1 Tim. 6:4; Titus 3:9). . . .
>
> Timothy, therefore, is to "pursue peace" (v. 22), which means to reject "foolish" debates, based on lack of instruction, because such debates only "produce" (lit., "give birth to") "quarrels" (*machai;* cf. Titus 3:9; cf. also "word battles," *logomachiai,* 1 Tim. 6:4; 2 Tim. 2:14)—one of the serious sins of the false teachers (see esp. disc. on 1 Tim. 6:4–5).

3.4. Lead Like a Humble Servant! (2:24–26)

3.4.1. Characteristics of the Lord's Servant (2:24). The last leadership issue touched on by the apostle Paul is attitude. Unlike the false teachers, "the Lord's servant must not quarrel." The title used here ("the Lord's servant") is probably influenced by Isaiah's images of the Messiah (Isa. 42:1–3; 53). The verb "quarrel" (*machomai*) "was generally used of armed combatants, or those who engage in hand-to-hand struggle. It was then used of those who engage in a war of words, i.e., 'to quarrel, to wrangle, to dispute'" (Rienecker, 1980, 643). If the Lord's servant, Christ, did not fight, neither should his servant, Timothy, and neither should you or I.

"Instead, [the Lord's servant] must be kind to everyone, able to teach, not resentful." Instead of quarreling, those in ministry must stand against error, but with a different disposition. As has been said, "If we do as the enemy does, we have become as the enemy is." Kindness is an attitude in sharp contrast to the false teachers, yet such is how Timothy must treat even them (v. 25; cf. "speaking the truth in love" in Eph. 4:15). He must have the ability to teach (cf. 1 Tim. 3:2). He must not be resentful, but tolerant, patient, ready to put up with evil. "The word denotes an attitude of patient forbearance toward those who are in opposition" (Rienecker, 1980, 643).

3.4.2. Corrections by the Lord's Servant (2:25–26). "Those who oppose [Timothy] he must gently instruct." What a lesson for all servants of the Lord! How often ministers attack those who oppose them and send them farther away from repentance. This gentle, submissive attitude is the noun *praütes* ("meekness"). "It denotes the humble and gentle attitude which expresses itself in particular in a patient submissiveness to offense, free from malice and desire for revenge (cf. 2 Cor. 10:1)" (Rienecker, 1980, 643). This gentle manner of the teacher itself is to be the instrument that God's hands use to grant the opponents a change of heart—to "grant them repentance leading them to a knowledge of the truth."

Such gentle instruction will also bring those influenced by the false teachers "to their senses and [enable them to] escape from the trap of the devil, who has taken them captive to do his will." Seeing the opponents as deceived, trapped, and captive to the devil makes it easier to instruct them in gentleness. *Ananepho* ("come to [one's] senses") is a verb meaning "to sober up, return to sobriety." "The metaphor implies some previous duping by evil influences as in the case of intoxication; the devil's method is 'to numb the conscience, confuse the senses and paralyze the will'" (Rienecker, 1980, 643–44). With such an understanding of the dilemma of the errorist God's servant can be sympathetic, recognizin[g] the deluded state of the opponents so that th[e] approach in teaching can be a clear attention t[o] the truth without an attack on the person.

The emphasis of instruction is clear[ly] redemptive. "Paul wants Timothy to model [a] kind of teaching that will not simply refut[e] error (Titus 1:9; 2:15) and save his hearer[s] (1 Tim. 4:16) but that will also be used by Go[d] to rescue those who have already been entan[-]gled in the false teaching" (Fee, 1988, 266).

4. Warning Against Eschatological Wickedness and Heresy (3:1–17)

4.1. End-Time Wickedness (3:1–9)

4.1.1. Difficult Days Are Coming (3:1[...] Abruptly the apostle now turns his attentio[n] to end-time wickedness and the disasters [o]f doctrinal error. This discussion is a major shi[ft] in the letter away from personal instructions t[o] Timothy to a focus on the false teachers. It i[s] the apostle's final attack on heresy before hi[s] closing personal encouragement to Timothy.

Though the Pastoral Letters repeatedl[y] address the issue of false teachers, in this con[-]text Paul sets the conflict in theological pe[r]spective—the presence of false teachers as a[n] indication of the end times. The New Testamen[t] uses the expression "last days" to refer to th[e] coming of Christ, the advent of the New Ag[e], the Christian era (cf. Acts 2:16–21; Heb. 1:2[)]. In other words, the end times have alread[y] arrived and we are now living in that era.

The point Paul wants Timothy to "mark[»] (i.e., understand, recognize, realize) is tha[t] "there will be terrible times in the last days.[»] The verb "be" in this sentence is not the sim[-]ple copulative, but one that indicates some[-]thing that is at hand or imminent. Fee (1988[,] 269) points out the connection between the en[d] times and trouble as a motif common in Jew[-]ish apocalyptic of the Old Testament (Dan[.] 12:1), in intertestamental literature (1 Enoc[h] 80:2–8; 100:1–3; Assumption of Moses 8:1; [2] Baruch 25–27; 48:32–36; 70:2–8), in th[e] words of Jesus (Mark 13:3–23), and in th[e] writings of the early church (1 Cor. 7:26[;] 2 Peter 3:3; 1 John 2:18; Jude 17–18). Thes[e] end times are described as "terrible," not sim[-]ply because they will be difficult or dangerous[,] but because of the evil associated with them.

4.1.2. The Kinds of People to Avoid (3:2–). In spite of Paul's use of the future tense in he previous verse, his catalogue of vices that ollows reflects the prevailing problems of agan society, proving that Timothy was lready experiencing these ills. We have lready seen a vice list in 1 Timothy 1:9–10 cf. Rom. 1:29–31; 1 Cor. 6:9–10), one with clear design to it; this list of eighteen charcteristics, however, seems to lack an organiational pattern.

(1) The list begins by describing these people s "lovers of themselves" (v. 2). Selfishness tops he list of end-time wickedness. (2) Materialism omes in second place; people will be "lovers f money" and the things it can buy them. (3) Arrogance is the third vice. The word "boastful" efers to "one who brags and boasts about his ccomplishments and in his boasting he overasses the limits of truth and stresses the fact to nagnify himself in his attempt to impress" (Rieecker, 1980, 644). (4) The "proud" person (i.e., rrogant or haughty) is "one who shows himself bove his fellow" (ibid.). (5) The "abusive" are hose who use their speech to slander others. The Greek term furnishes the root of the Engsh word "blasphemous." (6) Those "disobeient to their parents" are the rebellious. (7) They are "ungrateful" or unthankful and (8) unholy" or irreligious (cf. 1 Tim. 1:9).

(9) Those "without love" (v. 3) are those without love for family or kin, callously evoid of the love between parents, that is, evoid of natural affection. Seneca cites the ractice of exposing unwanted babies as an llustration of such heartless inhumanity and ack of natural affection (Brown, 1976, 2:542). 10) The "unforgiving" are those whose hosility will admit no truce, those who refuse recnciliation, the implacable. (11) The slanderous" are those whose (lit.) "diabolical" words set people at variance with one another. They promote quarrels in hope that they may ain from them (Lock, 1973, 106). (12) Those without self-control" lack power and self-discipline in regard to anything from conversation o appetite; they are intemperate. (13) The brutal" are like wild beasts—untamed and ncivilized. (14) The people "not lovers of the good" are unresponsive to goodness; they hate good and have no qualms regarding virtue.

(15) The "treacherous" (v. 4) are traitors nd betrayers. "The word was used of one who betrays his country or one who is a traitor to his oath or one who abandons another in danger" (Rienecker, 1980, 644). (16) The "rash" are reckless. This adjective comes from the verb meaning "to fall forward or ahead"; that is, by being hasty in speech or action, these people "stop at nothing to gain [their] ends" (Kelly, 1963, 194). (17) The "conceited" have (lit.) "become filled, or filled themselves, with smoke" or have "become puffed up, or puffed themselves up." Both images, like the Hebrew image of mist, smoke, or vapor, signify vanity, emptiness, inauthenticity (see also 1 Tim. 3:6; 6:4). (18) In the list of eighteen kinds of wicked people, there have been numerous instances of misdirected love. This final example is the worst case—people who are "lovers of pleasure rather than lovers of God." These hedonists keep up the "appearance of piety" (cf. 1 Tim. 2:2; Titus 1:16) while denying its power. Paul has returned the focus of his remarks directly on the false teachers.

> They liked the visible expressions, the ascetic practices and the endless discussions of religious trivia, thinking themselves to be *obviously righteous* because they were *obviously religious*. But they thereby "denied" the essential "power" of the Christian *eusebeia* [godliness], since they engaged in so many of the "irreligious" attitudes and practices that characterized the pagan world. (Fee, 1988, 270–71, emphasis added)

The apostle Paul has one explicit imperative to Timothy in regard to these kinds of people: "Have nothing to do with them."

4.1.3. The Kinds of Things They Do (3:6–7). In verse 6 the apostle once again exposes the practices of the religious charlatans. Fee (1988, 271) points out that though Timothy and his congregation learned nothing new about the false teachers through Paul's scathing rebuke of them here, the modern reader is enlightened by this censure. Some of the kinds of religious quackery the false teachers were engaged in related to women. This information serves as the background to Paul's teaching in 1 Timothy 2:9–15; 3:11; 4:7; 5:3–16.

Paul links the practices of the false teachers that follow with the vice list that precedes with these words: that these "are the kind who worm their way into homes and gain control over weak-willed women." The Greek verb descriptive of the way they get into the homes ("worm") implies insidious methods: They creep in or sneak in under false pretenses. "Gain control" is the verb for taking prisoners at spear point; its metaphorical use implies taking captive by misleading or deceiving. Such was the method of the false teachers (cf. v. 13; also 1 Tim. 4:1–2).

The women who fall prey to these teachers are described pejoratively with the diminutive, (lit.) "little women," meaning "silly, foolish, or idle" women; it is a word of contempt. These women are described further as "loaded down with sins" and "swayed by all kinds of evil desires." These women's sins are heaped or piled up to the point of overwhelming them; the perfect tense implies a continual state or condition. They are also being driven by a variety of impulses or lusts. This may suggest a sexual involvement of the false teachers with these women, but it does not need to be confined to such a meaning.

These women are described finally as: "always learning but never able to acknowledge the truth" (v. 7). Kelly (1963, 196) interprets this and the preceding two phrases as follows:

> Women, and of course men too, are most ready to embrace the gospel, in its authentic but also, alas, its perverted form, when they are most conscious of the squalor and futility of their lives.... [They are] avidly, and perhaps morbidly, curious about religion and prepared to fall for any novel theory put before them, but, since they lack serious purpose and are simply attracted by novelty as such, they prove "incapable of reaching a knowledge of the truth."

4.1.4. Two Infamous Examples (3:8). Timothy's opponents of truth in Ephesus are likened to two of Pharaoh's sorcerers who opposed the truth and Moses. Though their names are not mentioned in Exodus 7:11; 9:11, documents of later Judaism elaborated on the Moses legend and named two of the magicians as Jannes and Jambres. Though we cannot be certain that the Ephesian false teachers were involved in sorcery, Plummer points out "the connexion between heresy and superstition is a very real and a very close one" (quoted in Guthrie, 1990, 158). This fact is as true i modern times as it was in ancient times. Th contemporary New Age Movement is clearl a combination of heresy and superstitio These men are further described as "men c depraved minds," who have "rejected" th faith. "They have lost the power to reason . . they cannot pass the tests of faith" (Barret 1963, 112).

4.1.5. The End of Such People (3:9). Th success of these teachers will be short-live their folly will be exposed. Guthrie (1990, 16 explains, "Imposture is always tracked dow in the end."

4.2. Encouragement in Spite of Obstacles (3:10–17)

4.2.1. Timothy Has a Record of Faithfulness (3:10–11). Paul's encouragement to Timothy is another appeal to loyalty and enduranc based on his godly heritage and faithful history. Turning away from discussing the fals teachers, Paul contrasts his appeal to Timoth with the words: "You, however, know all abou [lit., have closely followed]...." Next the apostle rehearses his own virtues (in contrast to th vices of false teachers listed in 3:2–5) tha Timothy had observed and imitated in thei mentoring relationship together. (1) Paul' "teaching" heads the list. The instruction of th apostle is orthodox. (2) His "way of life" o conduct is holy. (3) His "purpose" or resolve i single-minded and steadfast. (4) His "faith" i God, (5) his "patience" with others, (6) hi "love" for all, and (7) his "endurance" in trying situations are exemplary in every way.

In particular, Timothy is to remembe Paul's (8) "persecutions" and (9) "sufferings, such as the "kinds of things [that] happened t [him] in Antioch [cf. Acts 13:50], Iconium [c 14:2–6] and Lystra [cf. Acts 14:19–20]," Timothy's own hometown. "Yet the Lord rescue me from all of them," reminds Paul. Fee (198 277) paraphrases the purpose of Paul' rehearsal:

> Look, you were there in Lystra when I was stoned. You recall that such sufferings were visible to you from the time you began your Christian walk. So don't bail out now in the midst of this present—and coming—distress.... So take heart, pilgrim, because you, too ... are due your share of the sufferings.

4.2.2. Persecution Is to Be Expected (3:12). Persecution is a principle of Christian living. This is a gnomic or universal truth.

4.2.3. Degeneration Will Increase (3:13). The Greek is almost ironical here: "Evil men and impostors will *get better and better* at *becoming worse and worse*, deceiving others while being deceived themselves."

4.2.4. Perseverance Is a Necessity (3:14–15). Timothy is charged to "continue in what you have learned and become convinced of," that is, the truth of the gospel. The veracity of Timothy's doctrine rests on the integrity of his teachers (both the apostle and Timothy's mother and grandmother) and his lifelong knowledge of the Scriptures. Such knowledge mixed with faith in Christ Jesus produces "salvation."

4.2.5. Scripture Is Sufficient (3:16–17). Inspiration is a principle of the Word, rendering it totally useful to Timothy in his ministry. Since Scripture in its totality is "God-breathed" (i.e., of divine origin), it is useful in all aspects of ministry. Paul enumerates four such aspects: "teaching" (gospel instruction), "rebuking" (exposing error), "correcting" (redirecting wrong behaviors), and "training in righteousness" (nurturing believers in holiness). The result (or purpose?) of the effective application of Scripture is that the godly person [the Greek is gender-inclusive here] will be able to meet all the demands of Christian life and ministry.

5. Solemn Charges Concerning Ministry (4:1–8)

5.1. On the Ministry of the Word (4:1–4)

5.1.1. Preach for All You're Worth! (4:1–2). As Paul nears the conclusion of his final letter, he addresses his younger colleague with sober personal exhortations "in the presence of God and of Christ Jesus." As with oaths and charges in the Old Testament, the names listed are cited as witnesses. This is especially clear in light of the description of Christ Jesus as the one "who will judge the living and the dead." As an everlasting witness, he is qualified to judge those who will be alive at the time of his coming as well as those who have already died.

In light of Christ's "appearing" and the coming of "his kingdom," Timothy is charged to "preach the word," that is, to announce or be a herald of the truth. This solemn charge to the young pastor is modified with four additional commands. (1) Keep at it, stand by your post of duty (i.e., your preaching), whether or not it is convenient to you or your hearers. (2) Correct "with such effectual feeling . . . as to bring one, if not always to a confession, yet at least to a conviction, of sin" (Trench, 1953, 13). (3) "Rebuke" or sharply censure those who are in error. (4) "Encourage" (i.e., beg, urge, advocate, admonish) them all. These commands and instructions are all to be carried out "with great patience"—a temperament characterized by a long fuse, putting up with people who are slow to respond to correction and instruction.

5.1.2. You Won't Always Have the Opportunity (4:3–4). Though Timothy is already experiencing the "terrible times" of "the last days" (3:1), the apostle warns him that evil will increase with the approach of the end. The days will come, and had indeed already

The Colosseum in Rome, showing the rooms below the arena floor where slaves trained as gladiators; prisoners and animals waited until it was time for them to go into the arena and fight in a deadly sport considered entertainment by the Romans.

arrived, when people will not tolerate the wholesome teaching of orthodoxy but "will amass teachers to suit their own desires, i.e., who will tell them either things they want to hear or things calculated to excite their fancy or whet their curiosity, irrespective in both cases of their truth" (Kelly, 1963, 206–7). They will deliberately turn away from the truth to lies and "myths" (cf. comments on 1 Tim. 1:4).

5.2. On Ministry in General (4:5–8)

5.2.1. Prove Yourself Fully (4:5). The apostle now gives four commands to Timothy in contrast to the work of the false teachers. (1) Be alert that *you* are not deceived! That is, stay "in a vigilant, wakeful considerate frame of mind taking good heed to what is proceeding around and pursuing its course with calm and steady aim" (Rienecker, 1980, 648). (2) "Endure hardship" (cf. 1:8; 2:3). (3) "Do the work of an evangelist" (i.e., keep preaching the message). (4) Carry out your ministry responsibilities to the full.

5.2.2. I Won't Be Around Much Longer (4:6–8). This letter now takes on a darkened tone as the apostle informs Timothy that he anticipates the end of his own life imminently. After addressing the problem of the false teachers and offering encouragement to his young successor, Paul opens the window into his own suffering with the emphatic first-person pronoun. It is as if he wrote, "but as for *me*." He describes his anticipated end with five vivid word pictures. (1) He pictures his impending martyrdom as if his life blood is a libation at the point of being poured out on the altar of sacrifice.

(2) He describes his departure from this life as if he were a ship lifting anchor as it leaves the shore or as a soldier who strikes his tent before a march. "What might seem the end to Timothy appears to the apostle as a glorious new era when he will be released from all his present restrictions" (Guthrie, 1990, 169).

The next three word pictures (v. 7) are built on three verbs in the perfect tense, thus indicating culmination or completion, giving a sense of finality. (3) Paul concludes that his contest or struggle, either athletic or military in symbolism, has been fought well.

(4) He comments that he has completed his course, using the athletic metaphor of a foot race. His concern was not in winning but in finishing and in doing his best.

(5) He has "kept the faith." This phrase i pregnant with metaphorical possibilitie Scholars suggest it refers to "the athlete' promise to keep the rules" (Easton), "the mil itary man's oath of fidelity" (Calvin), "metaphor of a steward" (Guthrie), or "a busi ness formula for keeping an engagement (Deissmann) (all cited in Guthrie, 1990, 169-70). At any rate the apostle has remained faith ful and true.

In verse 8 Paul returns one more time to th athletic metaphor, this time with an eschato logical twist. The laurel wreath (the victor' crown) is safely reserved in heaven for him Scholars differ on what this "crown of righ teousness" is. Fee (1988, 290) explains tha some refer it to "the prize awarded for a righ teous life" (Bernard, Barrett, and Kelly) Pfitzner contends that it "consists of the gift o righteousness, which only the Judge, as H who alone is [righteous], can give." Fee (ibid. concludes that final righteousness is granted t believers, "not necessarily as an award for thei achievement" but because they have alread received the righteousness of Christ.

The crown of righteousness is not unique t Paul; one is also being prepared by God fo Timothy (if he will remain faithful) and fo every believer who "has longed for his appear ing." All those who have given up their per sonal desires in order to promote th manifestation of Christ have a crown of righ teousness reserved in heaven for them.

6. Conclusion: Closing Considerations (4:9–22)

These closing verses form the climax of th letter, the apostle's private words to an intimat friend. As the great apostle makes his fina preparations for the end of his life, it is clea that he is suffering loneliness.

6.1. Personal Remarks (4:9–13)

6.1.1. Come Quickly! (4:9–11a). His firs request is that Timothy do his best to come t him quickly in Rome. Though Paul's death i imminent, he hopes that delays in the Roma judicial system will permit sufficient trave time for Timothy to make the trip and shar fellowship with the apostle one last time.

Paul then explains why he is alone. Dema has deserted him, having chosen to love thi present world over loving Christ's appearing

The apostle shares our Savior's experience of feeling forsaken. Crescens and Titus have also left, most likely in ministry, to Galatia (in Asia Minor, modern-day Turkey) and Dalmatia (ancient Illyricum, modern-day Yugoslavia), respectively. Luke is the only one of his coworkers present with Paul.

6.1.2. Bring Mark With You (4:11b). When Timothy comes, he is asked to bring along Mark (John Mark). On Paul's first missionary journey, Mark, a relative of Barnabas, had deserted the mission (Acts 13:13). Though Barnabas was willing to forgive Mark and give him a second chance on their second missionary journey, Paul was not. The contention between Paul and Barnabas was so great that the ministry team split up and went in different directions (Acts 15:36–41). In the intervening years, however, Mark had done some growing and the apostle had done some mellowing. They became coworkers together again (Col. 4:10; Philem. 24). Now toward the end of Paul's life, he urges Timothy to go and "get Mark [implying he was not in Ephesus] and bring him with you, because he is helpful to me in my ministry." The Lord had brought about a beautiful healing and reconciliation that restored a positive partnership of mutual edification and ministry effectiveness for Christ.

6.1.3. I Commissioned Tychicus (4:12). Guthrie explains that the frequent references in Paul's writings to Tychicus illustrate what a reliable associate he was. He was the letter carrier of both Colossians and Ephesians, and perhaps the epistolary aorist verb in this verse indicates that Paul is sending this letter to Timothy by Tychicus as well. Most likely Paul is sending Tychicus to Ephesus with the commission to carry on the ministry in Ephesus for Timothy during his absence while visiting Paul in Rome (cf. Titus 3:12) (Guthrie, 1990, 173).

6.1.4. Bring Three Things (4:13). Paul's threefold request to Timothy offers insight into his present conditions and personal interests. It seems as if the apostle was arrested in Miletus (cf. v. 20), en route from Nicopolis through Corinth, or in Troas itself, where he left his cloak with Carpus. It was a large, heavy, sleeveless woolen garment in a circular shape with a hole in the middle for the head. It provided protection from the rain and cold, especially when traveling (Rienecker, 1980, 649). This warm cape would be a blessing as winter approached and might indicate that Paul's dungeon was cold. The apostle expected Timothy to follow the same route from Ephesus to Rome that he had followed, asking him to pick up Paul's cloak on the way.

Paul also asks for his "scrolls, especially the parchments." The first word refers to papyrus rolls, the second to parchment codexes (books formed of sheets or leaves attached at the spine). The former were inexpensive, made of a reed and used for general purposes; the latter were expensive, made of animal skins, very durable, and reserved for important documents. The "scrolls" could have been Paul's personal collection of scriptural books or maybe even his stock of papyrus to continue his correspondence with the churches. The "parchments" could have been Paul's legal papers, such as his certificate of Roman citizenship, Old Testament writings, or pre-New Testament writings of the words and works of Jesus Christ. In Paul's aloneness and discomfort he apparently planned to draw strength by meditating on God's Word and perhaps even to continue to dispense strength to others through his writing.

6.2. Parting Warning: Watch Out for Alexander (4:14–15)

6.2.1. The Coppersmith Really Hurt Me (4:14). Fee (1988, 296) suggests that it was Alexander who had Paul arrested. His doing of great harm could be translated "showed forth many evil things against me" (Guthrie, 1990, 175); the verb is often used in the legal sense for the work of an informant (Fee, 1988, 296).

6.2.2. Don't Let Him Hurt You! (4:15). Alexander's strong opposition to "our message" may refer to his withstanding the gospel Paul preached or to his being a witness for the prosecution at Paul's trial. Timothy is counseled to be on his guard against Alexander.

Who was this Alexander the metalworker? He may be a person about whom we have no biblical record, the Jew who tried to quiet the riot in Ephesus (Acts 19:33–34), or the one who, along with Hymenaeus, had been excommunicated by Paul (1 Tim. 1:19–20). (The last two could refer to the same person.) Perhaps Alexander sought revenge on Paul. He may have had a personal vendetta that caused the imprisonment and martyrdom of the apostle. But "the apostle curbs his natural resentment by citing the words of Psalm 62:12" (Guthrie, 1990, 174), namely, that "the Lord will repay him for what he has done" (2 Tim. 4:14).

6.3. Testimony Through Trials (4:16–18)

6.3.1. I Was Deserted by All (4:16). Perhaps it was the thought of the cloak Paul had left in Troas that reminded him of his arrest, which reminded him of Alexander, which in turn now reminds him of his first defense (probably the Roman *prima actio*, similar to a grand jury hearing or a preliminary hearing before the emperor or a magistrate; see Fee, 1988, 296). Although at that trial Paul stood all alone, he offers forgiveness to all whom he felt abandoned him.

6.3.2. But God Was There (4:17). In contrast to all who had deserted him, "the Lord stood at [his] side." The presence of Christ brought the apostle strength and safety. As in Acts 24:1–20 (cf. 26:1–32) Paul took full advantage of his trial to give a testimony for Christ, so that the "message [was] fully proclaimed and all the Gentiles [were able to] hear it." The "lion's mouth" from which Paul was delivered has been variously interpreted as Satan, Nero, or death itself. The latter option is strengthened by Psalm 22, whose contents seem to be alluded to in this literary context (cf. Ps. 22:1, 4–5, 21).

6.3.3. He Will Be There (4:18). The recent deliverance (vv. 16–17) reminds Paul of God's faithfulness to always "save him to/for" Christ's heavenly kingdom. Fee (1988, 298) summarizes:

> Once again the focus of the letter is on eschatology, in the form of one of Paul's triumphant certainties: What God has already accomplished in Christ, he will see through to final consummation; the salvation he has begun he will indeed complete.

And that truth calls for words of glory to God in another doxology: "To him be glory for ever and ever. Amen." In spite of the dire realities of his present situation, the apostle lifts his gaze to the One who is greater! God is his glory and the lifter of his head.

6.4. Final Farewell (4:19–22)

6.4.1. Greet These Three (4:19). Paul sends greetings to several prominent members of Timothy's congregation. Priscilla (Gk. *Priska*) and Aquila were the first pastors of the church in Ephesus, which Paul is presently grooming Timothy to lead. *Priska* is a woman's name from the patrician class (the privileged class of Roman citizens, the ruling class whose designation derives from the Roman word for senator). Romans often shortened names in the middle; for example, Silas (the name of the coworker on Paul's second missionary journey [Acts 15:40]) is short for Silvanus (the name of Paul's amanuensis) who took dictation for the letters to the Thessalonians (cf. 1 Thess. 1:1; 2 Thess. 1:1).

Prisc[ill]a and Aquila are the couple from Rome that originally met Paul on his second missionary journey in Corinth, where the three of them lived together and worked together in tentmaking and in ministry for a year and six months (Acts 18:1–11). When Paul left Corinth, they accompanied him to Ephesus. He left them there as the first pastors of the infant congregation (vv. 18–19). There this couple took aside Apollos, the great Alexandrian evangelist, and expounded to him the things of God more accurately (vv. 24–28).

Four out of the six times that this couple is mentioned by Paul (in his letters) or by Luke (in Acts), the wife's name is listed first (highly unusual in the first century). From the biblical account of their ministry and the high education enjoyed by women of the patrician class, scholars have concluded that Priscilla had the more prominent or public role in ministry than her husband. It is important to note that Priscilla's spiritual leadership was never disparaged by Paul or Luke—both she and Aquila were well loved and respected in their gospel work. Churches met in their home both in Ephesus and in Rome (Rom. 16:3–5; 1 Cor. 16:19).

There are many couples in Pentecostal and charismatic circles who partner together in ministry; some play equal roles in leadership, sometimes the husband takes the lead, and sometimes the wife takes the lead. Priscilla and Aquila are models not only of couples partnering together in ministry, but also models of the fact that in making full use of God-given gifts in ministry, it is as *positive* a thing for a woman to be in leadership over a man as for a man to be in leadership over a woman.

The greeting to "the *household* of Onesiphorus" (without including a specific greeting to him) suggests that he had already died (see comments on 1:16–18). Reference to his household may refer to his extended family of relatives and/or slaves or to a church that met in his house.

6.4.2. News on Two Brothers (4:20). Paul fills in the details concerning two more coworkers. Erastus stayed on in Corinth; Trophimus remained in Miletus because of sickness. There was a city official from Corinth whose name was Erastus (Rom. 16:23) and a helper of Paul by the same name (Acts 19:22); more likely Paul is referring to the latter person.

6.4.3. Come Before Winter! (4:21a). Paul urges Timothy's haste, not only because he would need his cloak for winter, but also because shipping was closed from November to March.

6.4.4. These Four (and More) Greet You (4:21b). Paul sends greetings to Timothy and the church in Ephesus from some of his friends in Rome. Eubulus, Pudens, Linus, and Claudia are four Latin names, indicating that the local congregation contained Roman believers and, most likely, Roman leaders. It is noteworthy that the fourth name is a woman's name. All the brothers and sisters from Rome are included in Paul's greetings to Timothy and the Ephesians.

6.4.5. Closing (4:22). Paul's final farewell is a two-part closing: a blessing to Timothy personally and "grace" for all. The last extant words ever penned by the apostle Paul are a prayer that God's grace will be with all his people.

OUTLINE OF TITUS

1. **Introduction: Greeting** (1:1–4)
2. **Appointing Church Leaders** (1:5–2:1)
   - **2.1.** Commission to Appoint Elders (1:5)
   - **2.2.** Qualifications for Overseers (1:6–9)
   - **2.3.** The Need for Elders (1:10–2:1)
     - **2.3.1.** General Principle (1:10–11)
     - **2.3.2.** Specific Example (1:12)
     - **2.3.3.** Example Affirmed (1:13a)
     - **2.3.4.** Example Applied (1:13b–14)
     - **2.3.5.** Example Explained (1:15–16)
     - **2.3.6.** The Call for Sound Doctrine (2:1)
3. **Advising Church Members** (2:2–3:11)
   - **3.1.** Specific Advice (2:2–14)
     - **3.1.1.** Advice for Older Men (2:2)
     - **3.1.2.** Advice for Older Women (2:3–5)
     - **3.1.3.** Advice for Youth (2:6–8)
     - **3.1.4.** Advice for Servants (2:9–10)
     - **3.1.5.** The Enablement Available [to Keep the Advice] (2:11–14)
   - **3.2.** Encouragement to Exhort (2:15)
     - **3.2.1.** Recap of Command (2:15a)
     - **3.2.2.** Reaffirmation of Titus's Authority (2:15b)
   - **3.3.** The Advice Applied (3:1–8)
     - **3.3.1.** Practical Examples (3:1–2)
     - **3.3.2.** Personal Testimony (3:3–8)
   - **3.4.** Two Prohibitions (3:9–11)
     - **3.4.1.** Refuse Worthless Wrangling (3:9)
     - **3.4.2.** Reject Divisive People (3:10–11)
4. **Conclusion** (3:12–15)
   - **4.1.** Final Instructions (3:12–14)
     - **4.1.1.** Request for Titus's Company (3:12)
     - **4.1.2.** Admonition for Titus's Assistance (3:13)
     - **4.1.3.** Exhortation on Church's Behavior (3:14)
   - **4.2.** Closing (3:15)
     - **4.2.1.** Greetings (3:15a–b)
     - **4.2.2.** Benediction (3:15c)

COMMENTARY ON TITUS

1. Introduction: Greeting (1:1–4)

In his letter to Titus, Paul describes his duties as an apostle in greater detail than in the other two Pastoral Letters (1 and 2 Timothy). He calls himself "a servant [slave] of God" and "an apostle of Jesus Christ." The designation "servant of God" is Paul's favorite self-designation (cf. 1 Cor. 4:1–2). Paul ordinarily begins his letters with the single description of himself as a slave of Jesus Christ (cf. Rom. 1:1; Phil. 1:1). But if the situation surrounding the correspondence is one of urgency requiring apostolic authority, he adds "an apostle of Jesus Christ." Paul's calling himself first a "servant" and secondly an "apostle" suggests that Titus's situation was not as urgent as Timothy's (cf. comments on 1 Tim. 1:1).

In this letter Paul expands the description of his apostleship in terms of its purpose. He was chosen "for the faith of God's elect . . . [with a view to their coming to] the knowledge of the truth that leads to godliness." In the Pastoral Letters "truth" is synonymous with the gospel and "godliness" is its true aim (see comments on 1 Tim. 2:2; 3:16 concerning godliness). The ultimate goal of Paul's apostleship is for "the hope of eternal life." Dibelius and Conzelmann (1972, 131) summarize:

> Thus the Christian religion for which the "apostle" works in ministry is characterized by means of three expressions: as the faith of those who have been chosen, and the "recognition of truth," and finally as "hope," in a way analogous to that of 2 Tim. 1:1.

This hope is secure because of two facts. (1) It was "promised before the beginning of time" by "God, who does not lie"; and (2) in his own good time God has manifested his Word through the means of preaching. In other words, God's promise can be trusted because "the promise formed part of God's eternal purpose ratified before the created order existed," and because God "has demonstrated the truth of his promise by actually revealing his purpose on the plane of history.... God's word cannot be manifested in the void; it has been given concrete expression in the preaching with which [Paul himself] (the pronoun is deliberately emphatic) [has] been entrusted" (Kelly, 1963, 227–28).

After his eloquent and involved introduction, Paul reaches his recipient, Titus, whom he calls "my true son [lit., child] in our common faith" (v. 4; cf. 1 Tim. 1:2). The apostle considers Titus one of his own spiritual offspring, a convert and disciple of his. Though Acts makes no mention of Titus, he is clearly a trusted member of the apostle's entourage (2 Cor. 2:13; 8:23; 12:18; Gal. 2:3; see also "Introduction to Titus: Recipient and Destination"). The greeting "grace and peace," though different from the letters to Timothy, conforms to other Pauline letters; but "from God the Father and Christ Jesus our Savior" is a unique variation on the typical turn of the phrase in the Pastoral Letters, "God our Savior" (cf. 1 Tim. 1:1; 2:3; 4:10; Titus 1:3; 2:10; 3:4).

2. Appointing Church Leaders (1:5–2:1)

2.1. Commission to Appoint Elders (1:5)

In this verse, Paul indicates the reason why he left Titus in Crete. It seems that the mission to Crete was recent enough and the churches young enough that Titus was charged with setting right "what was left unfinished," that is, to "appoint elders in every town." Paul had already given orders to Titus concerning these appointments, and this letter is a written reiteration of earlier oral instructions.

2.2. Qualifications for Overseers (1:6–9)

The qualifications in verse 6, as stated in the original language, are conditions or indirect questions regarding candidates being considered for office. The Greek translates literally: "If anyone is without indictment, has one spouse, whose children have faith and are not open to the charge of being wasteful of money or being unruly—this one is then able to be considered for being appointed as an elder" (see comments on 1 Tim. 3:2–7 regarding leadership qualifications of overseers, especially the discussion concerning "husband of ... one wife").

Paul seems to be using the word "elder/presbyter" (*presbyteros,* v. 5) and "overseer/bishop" (*episkopos*, v. 7) interchangeably (see comment on 1 Tim. 5:17). At this early period in church history, offices were fluid and indistinct.

Paul calls overseers of the church "stewards of God" (NIV, those "entrusted with God's work"). Stewards (people charged with administrating the affairs of a household) were well known to the first-century audience. Since such people were responsible to the owner for the care of his or her house, they had to be blameless (see comments on the *inclusio* of 1 Tim. 3:2–7). Note also that overseers are not simply responsible to the church as its employees, they are responsible to God as his servants, caring for the things of God.

Paul lists five vices that disqualify candidates from this office. Overseers must not be (1) "overbearing" (self-willed), (2) "quick-tempered" (inclined to anger), (3) "given to drunkenness" (see comments on 1 Tim. 3:3), (4) "violent" (quick to solve a problem with violence), or (5) given to "pursuing dishonest gain."

Paul then itemizes six qualities required of Christian overseers. They must be (1) "hospitable" (lit., "lovers of strangers"), (2) "[lovers of] what is good" (either lovers of good things or good people), (3) "self-controlled," (4) "upright" (righteous), (5) "holy" (devout), and (6) "disciplined" (in com-lete control of one's self, possessing complete elf-mastery, which controls all passionate npulses and keeps the will loyal to God) (Rieecker, 1980, 652).

Overseers are charged with the responsibil-.y to "hold firmly to the trustworthy message s it has been taught" (v. 9). The verb "to hold rmly" has the dual connotation of holding out gainst something hostile and making "steadast application" (Rienecker, 1980, 652). The easons for this instruction are equivalent to ne tasks Paul enjoined Timothy (cf. 2 Tim. :2) and Titus (cf. Titus 1:13) to do: to encourge the faithful and to confute the opponents.

> The church leader, for that is surely what elders are, must be able to "encourage" (better, "exhort"; cf. 1 Tim. 4:13; 5:1; 6:2) "others by sound doctrine" (see discussion on 1 Tim. 1:10). He [or she] must also be able to "refute" (or "convict"; cf. 1 Tim. 5:20; 2 Tim. 3:16; 4:2) "those who oppose it." (Fee, 1988, 175)

2.3. The Need for Elders (1:10–2:1)

2.3.1. General Principle 1:10–11). The preceding aragraph mandates high tandards for Christian leadrship, and this paragraph ells us why. Elders play a ritical role in the life of the hurch by "silenc[ing]" the pponents of truth (v. 11). The Greek is vivid here—pponents must be "muzled." Who are these oppoents of truth? Other church nembers who are "rebelious" (v. 10). These "many ebellious people" come in wo types: (1) the passive, 'mere talkers"—whose vorthless words (no matter ıow impressive) have no olid content of truth, and (2) he active, "deceivers"—vhose aim is to delude the nind. Regardless of their nethod, the purpose of both inds of Titus's opponents is he same: "dishonest gain" (cf. 1 Tim. 6:5). These false teachers are religious mercenaries—winning converts for the purpose of making money. Some of these opponents have Jewish roots: "those of the circumcision group."

What a job description for Christian leaders—"shutting up people!" How does a leader silence the rebellious? Imagine that every Christian leader holds two buckets in his or her hands: a bucket of gasoline in one and a bucket of water in the other. When an insubordinate and rebellious member of the church tries to upset things in the group, the leader has the choice to use the bucket of gasoline to add fuel to the fire or to take the bucket of water and extinguish the source of the conflict before it spreads. The church needs more leaders who can "silence" the rebellious.

The conquest of these rebellious people in Crete is remarkable—they have ruined, upset, or overturned "whole households." Rebellion

Ruins of the great palace in the ancient city of Cnossus on the island of Crete. The city, seat of the legendary King Minos, was at its peak from c. 2000–1400 B.C. At left are the Horns of Consecration. Paul warned Titus about rebellious people on Crete.

turns things upside down; it puts folks topsy-turvy. It confuses people to the point that they do not know which way is up. In an era of house churches, entire segments of the Cretan congregation had been led astray by such people.

This chapter underscores the need for trustworthy leadership both in Titus's day and in our own. House churches, cells, and small groups must have leaders who are blameless models (vv. 6–7a), virtuous people-lovers (vv. 7b–8), biblically orthodox (v. 9), and loyal to the vision of the church, and certainly not rebellious and insubordinate (vv. 10–11). They must be able to "silence" the rebellious (v. 11), "encourage" the faithful, and "refute" the opponents (v. 9), "rebuk[ing] them sharply" (v. 13). These items make an excellent checklist for assessing Christian leaders and a syllabus for training them.

2.3.2. Specific Example (1:12). Paul quotes Epimenides of Cnossus in Crete, a religious teacher and wonder-worker, who lived ca. 305–240 B.C. Kelly (1963, 235–36) explains:

> Epimenides, it seems, stigmatized the Cretans as "always liars" because they claimed to have the tomb of Zeus on their island. This was a flagrant imposture, for Zeus was the chief of the gods and, in the view of his devotees, very much alive. The saying, however, became a popular slogan, a jibe giving expression to the shocking reputation for mendacity which the Cretans had in the ancient world. So prevalent was this that the verb "to Cretize" (Gr. *kretizein*) was a slang word for lying or cheating. . . .
>
> No deep innuendoes need be read out of "pernicious beasts, idle bellies." . . . Paul regards the line as expressing, with rough and ready accuracy, the untruthfulness, boorishness, and greed of the dissident group in Crete.

The quote in verse 12 is interesting in that it hits on the same three points Paul addressed in verses 10–11. "Liars" are the same as "mere talkers and deceivers" (v. 10b); "evil brutes" are similar to "rebellious people" (v. 10a); and "lazy gluttons" are in it "for the sake of dishonest gain" (v. 11) (see Fee, 1988, 179). With the support of "one of their own prophets," Paul's charge and command now have a newfound strength.

2.3.3. Example Affirmed (1:13a). "This tes-timony is true" refers back to the quotation from Epimenides. Having used the Cretans' own her as a measure against them, Paul calls a judgmen on them. Enter the task of the overseer.

2.3.4. Example Applied (1:13b–14) "Rebuke them sharply" (not with a ligh rebuke, but with a straight-to-the-heart, shar rebuke), so that "they will be sound in th faith," that is, healthy in doctrine (not disease and infectious). Paul identifies two source that the false teachers draw on for their claims They are "Jewish myths" (see comment o 1 Tim. 1:4) and "commands of those wh reject the truth." The specific names of th issues that today's church leaders face may dif fer, but the general sources are the same unproved theories and extrabiblical legalism The elders of today will find their job no les difficult and no less necessary than those con cerning whom Paul wrote.

2.3.5. Example Explained (1:15–16). Th elder has been instructed and the enemies an error identified; now for the ontological ratio nale. Paul explains that "to the pure, all thing are pure." This is not a claim concerning th nature of a Christian's environment, but a clain concerning the outlook of the saints. Since thos who are pure, innocent, and faithful are looking for the same, that is what they see. By contrast the eye that is always looking for evil will b sure to find it. Compare Jesus' comments i Matthew 6:22–23 (par. Luke 11:34–36).

The characteristics of the impure person ar further explained (vv. 15b–16). The impure ma appear as sheep, professing to know God, bu "their minds and consciences are corrupted." Their claims are empty because their works ar evil and everything in their life denies Christ Since these people are "detestable" and "disobedient" to God himself, they are unqualifie for any good thing. Two ramifications of the las clause of verse 16 are that the impure are unfi for church leadership, and their participation i ministry is not to be regarded as a good thing.

2.3.6. The Call for Sound Doctrine (2:1). In light of the conflict with the rebellious people (1:10–14), Titus is urged to speak the truth (lit., "speak what is consonant with healthy teaching"). In this way, he will no only model how to silence the impure, but wil also mentor followers into becoming pure leaders for the future.

3. Advising Church Members (2:2–3:11)

3.1. Specific Advice (2:2–14)

3.1.1. Advice for Older Men (2:2). The apostle now launches into an extended section of instructions to various groups of believers regarding their character and conduct. The language is so nonspecific and the section so similar to ancient extrabiblical discussions regarding virtuous behavior that it seems as if Paul is not so much addressing actual problems extant in the Cretan congregations but, "in a general way [is calling] for good works and a lifestyle on the part of Christians that 'will make the teaching about God our Savior attractive' (v. 10)" (Fee, 1988, 184). Verses 2–10 are a spiritual safeguard—a medicine or remedy that prevents disease.

Paul first commands four virtues for "the older men." The Greek word for "older men" (*presbytes*)—and for "older women" (*presbytis*) in 2:3; cf. also *presbytera* ("older women") in 1 Timothy 5:2—is related to the Greek word in Titus 1:5 for "elders" (*presbyteros*). All are derived from the lexical root *presbys*, "old." "In the Jewish and Christian spheres it is often hard to distinguish between the designation of age and the title of office" (Bromiley, 1985, 931). All of above words can also be translated "elder [whether male or female]." In the Pastoral Letters Paul uses the word "elders" inclusively, that is, for both kinds of church leaders ("overseers/ bishops" and "deacons/helpers/ministers/servants") and for both genders (male and female).

Paul's specific instructions are that the older men should be (1) "temperate" or sober (cf. 1 Tim. 3:2, 11); (2) "worthy of respect" or of good character (cf. 1 Tim. 3:8); (3) "self-controlled" (cf. 1 Tim. 3:2; Titus 1:8; 2:5–6); and (4) "sound" or wholesome and healthy in the three cardinal virtues: "'faith' toward God, 'love' toward all, 'endurance' to the End. Although nothing like the latter is explicitly said of the following groups, it may be assumed that such is expected of all" (Fee, 1988, 186).

3.1.2. Advice for Older Women (2:3–5). Similarly, "the older women" (*presbytis*, see comments on 2:2; this word was used by Philo for women past sixty in *On the Special Laws* 2.33) are to be "reverent in the way they live." Fee (1988, 186) explains:

> The word translated "reverent," *hieroprepeis,* often means simply "holy" (e.g., 4 Macc. 9:25; 11:20), but it could also carry the more specialized sense of "acting like a priestess," resulting from its use to describe the conduct of a priest. Since it is an unusual word (occurring only here in the Gk. Bible), it may well be that Paul intends this broader connotation. In demeanor they are to be what would be fitting for temple service.

Their behavior must be "not . . . be slander[ous]" (lit., "diabolical"). Though the first-century culture often admired heavy drinkers, Paul adds that the older women must not be "addicted to much wine" (cf. 1 Tim. 3:8, 11). Their lifestyle should be characterized by "teach[ing] what is good"—that is, mentoring morality and vivifying the virtues—so that they may "train the younger women" (lit., "bring them to their senses, wise them up [in their wifely responsibilities]") in seven attributes. (1) "Husband-loving" and (2) "child-loving" are two adjectives found frequently in ancient pagan praise of good wives. The older women should also demonstrate to the younger women how to be (3) "self-controlled" (cf. v. 2), (4) morally "pure" or chaste (cf. 1 Tim. 5:22), (5) skilled in homemaking or domestic duties, (6) "kind" or benevolent, and (7) "subject to their husbands" (see comment on v. 9). The purpose of right living is for the sake of the gospel and how it will be viewed by unbelievers. Throughout the Pastoral Letters Paul frequently makes this point (see comments on *inclusio* at 1 Tim. 3:2–7).

3.1.3. Advice for Youth (2:6–8). Paul is emphatic in instructing Titus to exhort the younger men (and women, for the adjective is inclusive of all youth) also to be "self-controlled." This is the same requirement given to older women in verse 2 and to younger women in verse 5 (the verb "train" in v. 4 is also a part of this word group; see comment).

In a manner reminiscent of 1 Timothy 4:12, Paul exhorts Titus to "set [the younger people] an example [in everything] by doing what is good" in his own personal life. His teaching must be characterized (1) by "integrity," untainted by impurity of motive, partiality toward certain people, or doctrinal error (in contrast to the rebels of 1:10–16); (2) by "seriousness" (cf. 1 Tim. 3:4), which inspires respect; and (3) by "soundness of speech [cf. Titus 1:9, 13; 2:1–2; also 1 Tim. 1:10] that cannot be condemned," since it is above reproach and contradiction. "If Titus' 'teaching' is pure in motive, demeanor, and content, his opponents 'may be ashamed,'" since they will find no cause for accusation in either Titus or Paul (Fee, 1988, 189).

3.1.4. Advice for Servants (2:9–10). Slaves are instructed "to be subject to their [own] masters in everything." The voice of the verb in verse 9 (with reference to slaves), in verse 5 (with reference to younger women), and in 3:1 (with reference to all believers) is better translated in the middle (i.e., with a reflexive idea) than in the passive. Thus, instead of slaves, women, and believers being urged to "be subject," the idea is that of their own volition they are to "subject themselves."

The Christian attitude required of slaves is exemplified in the instructions that they "try to please [their masters]," that is, that they be pleasant and obliging and not "talk back to them" in an argumentative manner. Christian slaves are also "not to steal from [their masters]." "Since slaves were often entrusted with buying goods and also often had a degree of private ownership," pilfering or misappropriating funds was a common temptation for them (Fee, 1988, 190). Paul wants the slaves' demonstration of trustworthiness to be a witness to others (cf. v. 5). Their godly lifestyle should be like a jeweler's best setting to exhibit, in the manner most flattering, God's gem—the glorious gospel (Rienecker, 1980, 654).

3.1.5. The Enablement Available [to Keep the Advice] (2:11–14). This paragraph (along with 3:4–7) is the theological core of the letter. It is the theological basis (the "indicative," describing what God has done for us) for the instructions (the "imperative," describing what God expects of us) in 1:10–2:10. Paul begins with an explanatory "for," tying together what must be taught to the various groups in verses 2–10 with the reason why (vv. 11–14). "For the grace of God that brings salvation *has appeared* to all [people] [emphasis added]." "The essential meaning of the [verb in italics] is to appear suddenly upon a scene and is used particularly of divine interposition, especially to aid, and of the dawning of light upon darkness" (Rienecker, 1980, 654). The aorist tense indicates a once-and-for-all-time act of God's grace, "the glorious appearing of our great God and Savior, Jesus Christ" (v. 13; cf. 2 Tim. 1:10).

The grace of God "teaches us" ethically in two directions (v. 12): (1) negatively, to renounce, repudiate, or disown "ungodliness and worldly passions" or desires; and (2) positively, "to live self-controlled [see comments on vv. 2, 5, 6], upright [cf. 1 Tim. 6: 11] and godly lives." God's grace teaches us to live in a holy manner in this present age while we await our perfect holiness at the second coming of Christ (v. 13; cf. Gal. 5:5; Col. 1:5; 2 Tim. 4:8). The purpose of Christ's sacrificial death is to rescue us "from all wickedness" and to cleanse us as a people set apart for himself, "eager to do what is good" (v. 14).

3.2. Encouragement to Exhort (2:15)

3.2.1. Recap of Command (2:15a). Having laid the theological foundation, the apostle returns in a general way to tell Titus that the foregoing are the instructions he is to teach.

3.2.2. Reaffirmation of Titus's Authority (2:15b). The three verbs in verse 15 are durative imperatives. Titus is to *keep on* addressing these issues, *continually* encouraging the faithful and *persistently* reprimanding the wayward. He must make use of "all [the] authority" of one under divine command, for such is the commission of a Christian minister.

In contrast to Paul's admonition to Timothy, Paul makes no mention of Titus's youth when he counsels, "Do not let anyone despise you" (cf. 1 Tim. 4:12). The two verbs translated "despise" in these verses of the NIV, though built on the same stem, vary in the force of their contrasting prepositional prefixes. The verb Paul used with regard to Timothy is "look *down* on, despise, disparage, or underrate"; the verb Paul used in Titus's case is "to look *around,* overlook, dismiss, or disregard" (Bromiley, 1985, 421). Ancient writers used the former verb to designate "contempt properly speaking," and the latter verb to "designate contempt for another joined with an inflated notion of one's own importance" (Quinn, 1990, 178). Perhaps Titus was older than Timothy, but the disregard from others (e.g., the "many rebellious people" of 1:10–14) was still a real possibility. In spite of insolence from his opponents, Titus is to speak with full authority.

3.3. The Advice Applied (3:1–8)

3.3.1. Practical Examples (3:1–2). Paul instructs Titus to "remind the people" of five duties, attitudes, and virtues. The verb "remind" implies they should already recognize these things as implications of the gospel (Fee, 1988, 200–201). Civil obedience tops the list: submission "to rulers and authorities" (see comment on 2:9) and general "obedience." Fee (ibid., 201) explains that in a day "when the state was still a benefactor of Christians," a positive attitude towards rulers and authority existed (cf. Rom. 13:1–8). "These imperatives raise all kinds of questions for today's Christians."

Civic duty follows: Christians should "be ready to do whatever is good." That is, they "should be among the foremost in showing public spirit" (Scott, quoted in Fee, 1988, 201). Moreover, believers are "to slander no one," "to be peaceable" (lit., to be unquarrelsome; cf. 1 Tim. 3:3), "[to be] considerate," and "to show true humility toward all."

3.3.2. Personal Testimony (3:3–8). After giving practical examples for applying his advice (vv. 1–2), Paul continues by explaining the rationale of his appeal (v. 3). His first support is personal testimony. "At one time we too were" the same as the unbelievers (probably including the false teachers) now are: "foolish, disobedient, deceived and enslaved by all kinds of passions and pleasures. We lived in malice and envy, being hated and hating one another."

Paul then describes God's gracious response to the human condition in a highly condensed creedal formulation of the doctrine of salvation. In verse 8 he asserts that this statement is trustworthy (see comment on 1 Tim. 1:15). This creed can, therefore, be relied upon as orthodox (cf. the salvation hymn in 2 Tim. 1:9–10 and the affirmation formula in 1 Tim 1:15).

The "kindness" mentioned in verse 4 is that aspect of God's goodness that is generous, patient, and merciful. It is God's ability to ignore our failings and minister to us. His "love" is, literally, philanthropy—God's compassion for humanity exhibited in Christ's appearance (cf. 2:11) among sinful people, enlightening the world with the good news of a loving and forgiving Father.

Paul states strongly that salvation is not a result of "righteous things we had done," but that we were rescued from the penalty we merited by God's "mercy." While justice is getting what we deserve, *mercy* is *not getting* what we deserve. Two aspects of salvation are described: (1) the "washing of rebirth"—that is, our cleansing from sin at the moment of our regeneration, symbolized by water baptism; and (2) the "renewal by the Holy Spirit"—that is, the continual process of becoming new in Christ as we cooperate with the counsel of the Holy Spirit (cf. Rom. 12:2; Gal. 3:3). This Holy Spirit has been given in abundant measure by our Savior Jesus Christ, who "poured [the Spirit] out on us generously . . . so that, having been justified by his grace, we might become heirs having the hope of eternal life." Justice is getting what we deserve; mercy is not getting what we deserve; and *grace* is *getting* what we do *not* deserve.

In the last part of verse 8 Paul expresses his desire that Titus "continually insist upon, speak confidently about, or to make a point of" Paul's previous statements (Rienecker, 1980, 656). The purpose of this is that the believers might be careful to continually devote themselves to doing what is good. For, as Fee (1988, 208) explains, "doing what is good benefits everyone, not only by affecting them positively, but also by attracting them to the truth of the gospel."

3.4. Two Prohibitions (3:9–11)

3.4.1. Refuse Worthless Wrangling (3:9). Paul commands Titus to continually avoid three things in verse 9. The verb translated "avoid" means "to stay out of the path or vicinity of" these things, "to stand aside, to step around, to turn away or shun" (Rienecker, 1980, 657). The three items are: (1) "foolish controversies"—that is, inquiries, speculations, investigations, discussions, and debates; (2) "genealogies" (see comment on 1 Tim. 1:4); and (3) "arguments and quarrels about the [Mosaic] law." "Arguments" are primarily in the realm of heated discussion (such as political or domestic strife, discord, quarrel, wrangling, and disputation), while "quarrels" most likely involve threats of and actual violence (Liddell, 1968, 1085).

Why should one avoid such things as these? Because, they are "unprofitable and useless." That is, they are futile and bring no reward; the time spent on them will never be redeemed.

3.4.2. Reject Divisive People (3:10–11). The second prohibition that Paul makes is against factious people, those who cause division through disagreements. "Warn [them] once, and then . . . a second time"; that is, try to help them correct their wrong by warning or counseling with them. Such foes are only to get two chances and then they are to be shunned.

> The reason the "divisive person" is to be rejected is precisely that, in his divisiveness, "such a man" demonstrates that he "is warped and sinful; he is self-condemned." In persisting in divisive behavior, the false teacher "has become perverted" or "turned aside and is continuing in his sinning," thus "being self-condemned." That is, by his very persistence in his sinful behavior he has condemned himself, thus putting himself on the outside, hence is to be rejected by Titus and the church. (Fee, 1988, 212)

4. Conclusion (3:12–15)

4.1. Final Instructions (3:12–14)

4.1.1. Request for Titus's Company (3:12). At the end of the letter Paul makes two personal requests. First, he asks Titus to join him in Nicopolis. Paul is traveling through Macedonia and plans to remain for a time in Nicopolis, where it is warmer. He intends to send either Artemas or Tychicus to minister in Crete in the absence of Titus during his visit with Paul. Tychichus "from the province of Asia" (Acts 20:4) had accompanied Paul in delivering funds for the poor in Jerusalem. He served Paul during his Roman imprisonment and carried the letters of the apostle to the churches of Ephesus and Colosse (Eph. 6:21–22; Col. 4:7–8). Paul calls him "the dear brother and faithful servant in the Lord" (Eph. 6:21).

4.1.2. Admonition for Titus's Assistance (3:13). The second request is that Titus help Zenas and Apollos. Zenas's title indicates he was a Jewish lawyer rather than a Roman lawyer. He was apparently Apollos's traveling companion on his missionary journeys. Paul's care for Apollos shows their good relationship.

4.1.3. Exhortation on Church's Behavior (3:14). "To devote themselves to doing what is good" means that Christians must not be lazy. Gospel workers should not only teach what is good, but also do what is good. If so, they will not only be able to meet their material needs, but will leave eternal fruit.

4.2. Closing (3:15)

4.2.1. Greetings (3:15a–b). In Paul's othe letters he always mentions the names of th people who are with him. In this letter, how ever, he simply writes, "Everyone with m sends you greetings," and "Greet those wh love us in the faith." This is most likel because Titus knows all the people who ar with Paul in Nicopolis.

4.2.2. Benediction (3:15c). In the closin sentence Paul prays, "Grace be with you all." The blessing of the Father and the Son tha Paul pronounced on Titus at the opening of thi letter he bestows at the close of this letter o all the believers in Crete.

NOTES ON THE PASTORAL LETTERS

[1]The entire book by Richard and Catherine Clark Kroeger, *I Suffer Not a Woman*, is devoted to this passage. It contains much historical and cultural background and grammatical insights—the fruit of ten years of lexical research on the word *authentec* (trans. by NIV as "have authority over"). My comments draw from the Kroegers' work.

[2]The one notable exception, which constitutes a bias in translation, is Romans 16:1. Since the minister (*diakonos*) in this text, Phoebe, is female, translators have been hesitant to acknowledge the status that the apostle Paul ascribed to her. In that text the NIV translates the office title as a "servant," while offering a footnote that suggests the translation "deaconess." Such is inaccurate since the translation "deaconess" is anachronistic (from another time period). See also comments on 1 Timothy 3:11.

[3]None of the ancient manuscripts specifies that these are qualifications for male officers. There is no manuscript evidence to believe that this was even an issue to the early church. Such masculine exclusivity in relation to deacons is a convention of the English translations, not of the original language text. The word *diakonos* can be either masculine or feminine, depending on the Greek article, which in this case is missing.

[4]Believing the second coming of Christ was near and desiring to enlist every willing vessel in the work of the harvest, early fundamentalism in America (1880–1930) strongly supported women's ministry. Janette Hassey documents this advocacy as well as the reasons for its decline in later fundamentalist circles in *No Time for Silence: Evangelical Women in Public Ministry Around the Turn of the Century* (1986). Another book documents women's vast contributions as missionaries in the nineteenth and early twentieth centuries: R. Pierce Beaver, *American Protestant Women in World Mis-*

ion: A History of the First Feminist Movement in North America (1968; first published as *All Loves Excelling*; 1980, rev. ed.).

[5]Recognizing the outpouring of the Holy Spirit as the fulfillment of Acts 2, when both "sons and daughters will prophecy [preach]," women in Pentecostal circles have been recognized as called and gifted by God for ministry ever since the beginning of its early twentieth-century revival. The Assemblies of God, for example, has a rich history of stalwart handmaidens of the Lord, having ordained women to the gospel ministry from its inception. African-American Pentecostalism not only has a glowing history of women ministers, but some of the greatest female preachers alive today are among its ranks. Although some charismatics have taken a reactionary stance against the mainline denominations' ordination of women, the new Pentecostals (e.g., the Word Movement and the Third Wave) embrace ministering women.

[6]In fact, the Distinctive Diakonate in London, England, is entirely devoted to researching and restoring the New Testament office of deacon to the contemporary church. Their discoveries have fueled an effort to return women to this office. See also the note on deacons referring to Philippians 1:1 in Kroeger, Evans, and Storkey, 1995, 407.

[7]Recent evidence documenting women's extensive participation in ministry in the early church as well as lexical and background studies challenged traditional interpretations of several New Testament passages and have called the church to rethink its traditional teaching regarding women's roles in ministry. For example, Australian scholar Greg Horsely's extensive studies of papyri of ancient church documents and ancient inscriptions (including tombstone epitaphs) have recovered the names of and evidence for five female elders, one official female teacher, and nine female deacons of the early church. A summary of these sources appears in "Early Evidence of Women Officers in the Church," *Priscilla Papers* 1/4 (Fall, 1987): 3–4.

[8]So surprising was this switch to a female subject of the sentence that some copyists altered the text (supposing they were correcting it) to make it inclusive of both genders.

[9]"It should be noted that in the only other instance where Paul actually cites the words of Jesus (1 Cor. 11:24–25), he also cites a version he shares with Luke, in contrast to Mark and Matthew. This should surprise us none, given Paul's apparent closeness to Luke" (Fee, 1988, 129).

[10]Gnosticizing tendencies may be the theological background for the necessity of Paul's explanation in 1 Corinthians 12:3 that calling Jesus accursed does not square with the claim to be a Spirit-filled believer.

[11]This qualification is stated in the masculine in this context, though the concept of having one spouse is used with regard to both male and female church leaders; cf. comments on "the husband of one wife" at 1 Tim. 3:2, 12 and "the wife of one husband" at 5:9.

BIBLIOGRAPHY ON THE PASTORAL LETTERS

Commentaries. C. K. Barrett, *The Pastoral Letters in the New English Bible* (1963); M. Dibelius and H. Conzelmann, *The Pastoral Letters*, Hermeneia (1972); G. D. Fee, *First and Second Timothy, Titus* NIBC (1988); D. Guthrie, *The Pastoral Letters*, TNTC (1991); A. T. Hanson, *The Pastoral Letters*, NCBC (1982); R. W. Harris, S. M. Horton, and G. G. Seaver, *The Complete Biblical Library, Volume 8: Study Bible, Galatians–Philemon* (1989); J. N. D. Kelly, *A Commentary on the Pastoral Letters* (1963); W. Lock, *A Critical and Exegetical Commentary on the Pastoral Letters*, ICC (1973); J. D. Quinn, *The Letter to Titus*, AB (1990).

Other Works. G. W. Bromiley, *Theological Dictionary of the New Testament: Abridged in One Volume* (1985); Colin Brown et al., *The New International Dictionary of New Testament Theology*, 3 volumes (1976); D. A. Carson, D. Moo, and L. Morris, *An Introduction to the New Testament* (1992); J. Gillman, "Timothy," "Timothy and Titus, Letters to," and "Titus," in *Anchor Bible Dictionary*, vol. 6 (1992); R. H. Gundry, *A Survey of the New Testament*, 3d ed. (1994); D. Guthrie, *New Testament Introduction*, rev. ed. (1990); P. N. Harrison, *The Problem of the Pastoral Letters* (1921); C. S. Keener, *. . . And Marries Another: Divorce and Remarriage in the Teaching of the New Testament* (1991); idem, *Paul, Women, and Wives: Marriage and Women's Ministry in the Letters of Paul* (1992); C. C. Kroeger, M. Evans, and E. Storkey, *Study Bible for Women: The New Testament (NRSV)* (1995); R. C. Kroeger and C. C. Kroeger, *I Suffer Not a Woman: Rethinking 1 Timothy 2:11–15 in Light of Ancient Evidence* (1992); W. G. Kümmel, *Introduction to the New Testament*, 17th ed. (1973); R. S. Liddell, R. Scott, and H. S. Jones, *A Greek-English Lexicon*, 2d ed. (1968); F. Rienecker, *A Linguistic Key to the Greek New Testament*, ed. Cleon L. Rogers Jr. (1980); J. A. T. Robinson, *Redating the New Testament* (1976); R. C. Trench, *Synonyms of the New Testament* (1953); A. Wikenhauser, *New Testament Introduction*, trans. J. Cunningham (1958); M. Zerwick and M. Grosvenor, *A Grammatical Analysis of the Greek New Testament* (1979).

PHILEMON

Sven K. Soderlund

INTRODUCTION

The letter to Philemon is by far the shortest of Paul's letters preserved in our canon; hence it is found at the end of the Pauline collection (by and large the Pauline letters have been arranged in terms of length). However, its importance should not be measured by its length or position—as sometimes appears to be the case, judged by the infrequency with which it is read, preached, and studied in the contemporary church. The letter, in fact, has a powerful message that must be known and heeded. This message has to do not so much with theology—though theology is present—as it does with praxis, the application of Christian truth to life. Here the application is the much-needed skill of conflict resolution, the neutralization of social distinctions in the Christian community, and the eventual undermining of the institution of slavery.

1. Authorship, Date, and Provenance

Along with Romans, 1 and 2 Corinthians, Galatians, Philippians, and 1 Thessalonians, this is one of those letters concerning which there is virtually no doubt in the scholarly community about its Pauline authorship. It claims to be written by Paul (v. 1) and has all the marks of his style, and its existence in the canon can be explained only on the basis of its authenticity. The debated questions have to do more with *where* and *when* it was written.

An important consideration in answering these questions is its relationship to the letter to the Colossians, since a number of observations point to the fact that these two letters were written at the same time and from the same place. Note that both letters were obviously written during one of Paul's imprisonments (Philem. 1, 9, 10, 13, 23; cf. Col. 4:3, 10, 18). Moreover, with one exception, the people who send greetings at the beginning and end of both letters are the same: Timothy (Col. 1:1; Philem. 1); Epaphras, Mark, Aristarchus, Demas, and Luke (Col. 4:10–14; Philem. 23–24); only "Jesus called Justus" of Colossians 4:11 is not mentioned in Philemon. Furthermore, one of the leaders in the Colossian church, Archippus, is addressed in both letters (Col. 4:17; Philem. 1). Most important, however, is the fact that Onesimus, the runaway slave being sent back to Philemon (cf. Philem. 12), is identified in Colossians 4:7–9 as a native of Colosse and is returning there in company with Tychicus. Given these correspondences, it is clear that whatever is determined about the date and provenance of Colossians must apply equally to the letter to Philemon—and vice versa (cf. discussion of the authorship of Colossians in the introduction to Colossians).

The actual location of Paul's imprisonment is less certain since there is no explicit reference in either letter as to their place of composition. According to earliest tradition, Rome was the city of origin of all the so-called Prison Letters (Ephesians, Philippians, Colossians, and Philemon); yet in the case of Colossians/ Philemon some scholars have proposed Ephesus as the place of composition on the grounds that this city would have been much more accessible to a runaway slave from Colosse (Colosse was only some ninety miles inland from Ephesus). The problem with this suggestion is that there is no mention anywhere, neither in Acts nor in Paul's letters, of an Ephesian imprisonment for Paul. Furthermore, it could be argued that the remoteness and relative anonymity of the larger metropolis of Rome is a likely reason why Onesimus would have fled there.

A Roman provenance would also be more consistent with Luke's presence with Paul at the time of composition (Philem. 24; Col. 4:14); we have no indication that Luke ever was with Paul in Ephesus. In the absence of compelling evidence to the contrary, therefore, this commentary proceeds on the assumption that the letter to Philemon was written from Rome during the early phase of Paul's imprisonment there, between the years A.D. 60–62.

2. Background and Message

The reconstructed "story line" of the letter is simple enough. A well-to-do Christian brother, Philemon, who is also a friend of Paul and

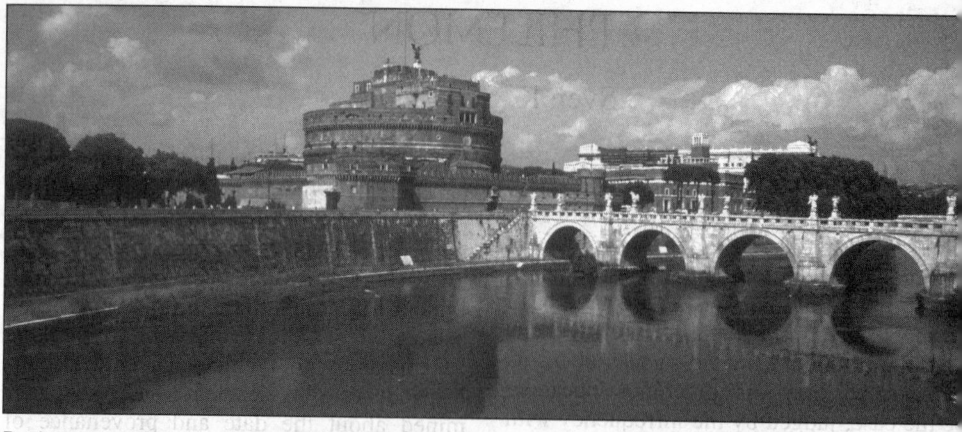

Paul's letter to Philemon, a leader of a house church in Colosse, was most likely written while the apostle was imprisoned in Rome. The Tiber River flows through Rome. The mausoleum shown here was built by Hadrian about A.D. 120, after Paul's death.

leader of a house church in Colosse, owns a slave, Onesimus. Onesimus has run away from his master to Rome, probably robbing Philemon of some of his money or property in the process (cf. Philem. 18). In Rome, through an unknown sequence of events, Onesimus encounters Paul and becomes a believer. While still in Rome, Onesimus becomes a great help to Paul during his imprisonment.

After some time, however, Paul decides to send Onesimus back to his rightful owner. The appropriate occasion for this was provided by the visit to Rome of the Colossian evangelist, Epaphras, whose task it was to share with Paul some concerns about the church situation in Colosse (see the introduction to Colossians). In response to this news, Paul writes a letter to the believers in Colosse to be delivered by his emissary, Tychicus, who could now also serve as the ideal companion for Onesimus on his journey back to Colosse (cf. Col. 4:7–9). But since the unexpected arrival of Onesimus in Colosse could prove awkward for all concerned, Paul also composes this letter of recommendation on behalf of the culpable, but now converted, runaway slave.[1]

The simplicity of this story line, however, should not dull us to the literary qualities of the letter or to the impact of its message. As will be observed in the commentary, the letter to Philemon is a masterpiece in the use of diplomatic technique and rhetorical devices. Technically, the letter may be categorized as a "letter of recommendation," one of the epistolary types well known from antiquity (see Chan-Hie Kim, *Form and Structure of the Familiar Greek Letter of Recommendation* SBLDS [1972], esp. 123–28; cf. also Rom 16:1–2; 1 Cor. 16:15–16, 17–18; Phil. 2:29-30; 4:2–3; 1 Thess. 5:12–13a). In this example, Paul uses all the literary conventions appropriate to that category, though with his own creative touch.

But the letter is more than just a specimen of diplomatic and persuasive writing. It also communicates Christian truth and example on various fronts. Among other things it demonstrates the powerful impact of the gospel in the conversion of a runaway slave and his rehabilitation as a useful Christian servant. It shows Paul as an indefatigable witness even in the midst of restricted prison conditions, reaching out not only to "Caesar's household" (cf. Phil. 4:22) but also to a lowly slave and criminal. It testifies to the insignificance of hierarchy in the Christian community in its application of similar terms of endearment to both master and slave, thus planting the seed for the eventual abolition of slavery.

Most directly, perhaps, it shows how the message of reconciliation is to be worked out among Christian brothers and sisters by the exercise of forgiveness and love, and how the larger community (cf. vv. 1–2, 23–24) can play the role of conscience in the resolution of conflict and the restoration of fellowship. In a society like ours, where people are urged to insist on their own rights, to take matters quickly to court, or to demand liberal compensation—even among Christians—the message of this letter seems not only relevant but urgent. In a sense, the letter can be read as a particular application of Paul's exhortation given to the entire Colossian community: "Bear with each other and forgive whatever grievances you may have against one another. Forgive as the Lord forgave you" (Col. 3:13). As such, the letter comes down to us across the centuries with the challenge, "Go and do likewise" (cf. Luke 10:37).

OUTLINE

1. **Introductory Greetings** (vv. 1–3)
   - **1.1.** Author (v. 1a)
   - **1.2.** Recipients (vv. 1b–2)
   - **1.3.** Greetings (v. 3)
2. **Prayer** (vv. 4–7)
   - **2.1.** Prayer of Thanksgiving (vv. 4–5, 7)
   - **2.2.** Prayer of Intercession (v. 6)
3. **Appeal on Behalf of Onesimus** (vv. 8–22)
   - **3.1.** Basis of the Appeal (vv. 8–9)
   - **3.2.** Subject of the Appeal (vv. 10–16)
   - **3.3.** Goal of the Appeal (vv. 17–22)
4. **Final Greetings and Grace** (vv. 23–25)

COMMENTARY

1. Introductory Greetings (vv. 1–3)

Although the shortest and most personal of Paul's letters, the introductory greeting formula is the same as in all his other letters ("X to Y, greetings"), a formula used not only by Paul but by most letter writers of antiquity. Nonetheless, within the stereotyped structure of the formula, there was also room for flexibility and creativity—a flexibility fully exploited by Paul. Of special interest here are the similarities and differences that this greeting formula has in comparison with that of the letter to the Colossians, the letter to which this document is most closely related.

1.1. Author (v. 1a)

The opening phrase of the letter is identical to that of Colossians with the exception that where Colossians describes Paul as "an apostle of Christ Jesus by the will of God," the letter to Philemon simply identifies him as "a prisoner of Christ Jesus." This change of title from "apostle" to "prisoner" is significant, however, for whereas the letter to the Colossians is also one of Paul's "prison" letters (cf. Col. 4:3, 10, 18), his status as prisoner is much more emphasized in the brief letter to Philemon. Not only does the letter begin with the reference to Paul's being a prisoner, but the phrase is repeated in verse 9. In verses 10 and 13 there is a reference to Paul's "chains," and in verse 23 Paul mentions Epaphras as his "fellow prisoner in Christ."

It seems clear that at this point in his career Paul was very conscious of his status as a prisoner. But we should observe of *whom* he says that he is a prisoner: not of the Romans or of Caesar—which would have been technically correct if he had said so—but "of Christ Jesus." We recall that Paul on various occasions calls himself "a slave [*doulos*] of Christ Jesus" (Rom 1:1; Phil. 1:1; Titus 1:1; cf. Gal. 1:10), but in what sense was he also "a *prisoner* of Christ Jesus"? Probably this phrase can best be explained by reference to Ephesians 3:1, where Paul describes himself as "the prisoner of Christ Jesus *for the sake of you Gentiles*" (cf. Eph. 4:1). The reason he was in prison was directly related to his ministry as an apostle of Christ to the Gentiles; the Romans were only the intermediaries. Ultimately his life and destiny resided in the hands of the Lord Jesus. Wherever he was, therefore—even in prison—he was the Lord's.

But Paul was not alone. In addition to those mentioned in the final greetings (vv. 23–24, Epaphras, Mark, Aristarchus, Demas, and Luke) as being present with Paul, there was also Timothy, his loyal friend and understudy. That Timothy stands apart from the rest of Paul's coworkers is highlighted by the way he is associated with Paul in the introductory greetings of several of his letters (cf. 2 Cor. 1:1; Phil. 1:1; Col. 1:1; 1 Thess. 1:1; 2 Thess. 1:1). Especially noteworthy, however, is the fact that even in this the most personal of Paul's letters, Timothy is still introduced alongside Paul. The relationship between the apostle and his young associate was apparently so close that even under these delicate circumstances, Paul did not hesitate to have Timothy's name joined to his own in the greeting. It is another reminder that, in truth, Paul had "no one else like [Timothy]" (Phil. 2:20).

Probably both Timothy and Paul had become acquainted with Philemon during the time of their ministry in Ephesus (Acts 19).

1.2. Recipients (vv. 1b–2)

Three people are mentioned by name in the greeting—Philemon, Apphia, and Archippus. However, as becomes obvious later on, only one of these is intended as the principal recipient, namely, Philemon, the person referred to in the subsequent verses by the singular pronoun "you/your." In the meantime, each of the persons addressed in the greeting is in turn introduced by a descriptive phrase: Philemon as Paul's "dear friend [cf. Col. 1:7; 4:7, 9, 14] and fellow worker"; Apphia as Paul's "sister" (cf. Rom. 16:1) in the Lord; and Archippus as his "fellow soldier" (cf. Phil. 2:25).

Whether these three formed part of the same household as husband, wife, and son is impossible to know for certain, though the suggestion certainly seems attractive. It also fits with the way that "the church that meets in your home" is greeted in the last phrase of the verse, implying the existence of a host family (Philemon, Apphia, and Archippus) and a house church,[2] all forming part of a community of believers in Colosse. Along with Timothy and the other coworkers mentioned in the greetings of verses 23–24, Philemon's household and house church all become part of the cloud of witnesses observing with heartfelt concern the drama unfolding between Paul, Onesimus, and Philemon.

1.3. Greetings (v. 3)

The greeting or salutation formula ("Grace to you and peace from God our Father and the Lord Jesus Christ") is identical to that found in most of Paul's letters (cf. Rom. 1:7; 1 Cor. 1:3; 2 Cor. 1:2; Gal. 1:3; Eph. 1:2; Phil. 1:2; 2 Thess. 1:2). Although it had evidently become a formalized expression, it was no less sincere for its frequent repetition. The phrase sought to invoke all the blessings associated with the old and new covenants on the community of faith gathered in Colosse.

"Peace" recalls the Aaronic blessing of Numbers 6:26, while "grace" became Paul's choice word for expressing the extension of God's loving favor to his people through Christ (see comments on Col. 1:2). Paul always wanted the best for his converts, individually and corporately. The blessings he had experienced in his encounter with God through Christ he unhesitatingly coveted for them as well. In this way, even within the fairly predictable structure of an epistolary opening, Paul models pastoral care and unstinting love.

2. Prayer (vv. 4–7)

In keeping with his usual convention, Paul follows up his introductory greeting with a prayer of thanksgiving and intercession. What is different about this letter is its focus on one individual—Philemon—rather than on a congregation (cf. also 2 Tim. 1:3), along with its brevity (strictly speaking only three verses, with a fourth [v. 7] loosely attached). The paragraph moves through the following stages: verse 4 introduces the themes of thanksgiving and intercession; verses 5–6 respectively give the content of the thanksgiving and the intercession; verse 7 returns indirectly to the theme of thanksgiving by acknowledging the significance of Philemon's love for Paul and the Colossian congregation.

2.1. Prayer of Thanksgiving (vv. 4–5, 7)

The personal aspect of this letter becomes immediately apparent at the beginning of the prayer, since all the pronouns and verbs are in the singular: "*I* always thank *my* God as *I* remember *you* [sing. in Greek]," with which may be compared the parallel prayer in Colossians 1:3, where all corresponding pronouns and verbs are in the plural: "*We* always thank God, the Father of *our* Lord Jesus Christ, when *we* pray for *you* [plural in Greek]." However, the *motive* for Paul's thanksgiving in the personal letter is identical to that expressed in the congregational letter, both being prompted by the disciples' "faith in the Lord Jesus" and their "love for all the saints" (Philem. 5; cf. Col. 1:4; on this see O'Brien, 1982, 278–79).

What is especially emphasized in this letter, however, is Philemon's "love for the saints," a subject elaborated in verse 7, where Paul commends Philemon for having "refreshed the hearts of the saints." The word translated "hearts" (*splanchna*) literally means "inward parts," but was often used figuratively to refer to the feelings of affection or compassion (cf. Col. 3:12) or to the seat of those emotions. We are not told in what specific ways Philemon had demonstrated compassion, though comparison with other passages where the verb "refresh" is found (e.g., 1 Cor. 16:18; 2 Cor. 7:13; Philem. 20; cf. Matt. 11:28) suggests that it had to do with a ministry of encouragement. As a consequence, this expression of Philemon's "love" (vv. 5, 7) for the Colossians had given Paul himself "great joy and encouragement," not least because he was about to appeal to Philemon for a further demonstration of that same generosity of spirit (v. 20).

2.2. *Prayer of Intercession (v. 6)*

Whereas verses 5 and 7 give the reasons for Paul's thanksgiving, verse 6 contains the content of his petition on behalf of Philemon. Unfortunately the precise nature of the petition is not as easy to determine as we would wish, the Greek syntax of this part of the sentence being unusually complicated. Literally, the sentence may be translated as in the NASB: "that the fellowship of your faith may become effective through the knowledge of every good thing which is in you for Christ's sake."

But what does it mean? The greatest ambiguity surrounds the phrase "the fellowship [*koinonia*] of your faith"; that ambiguity arises because of the uncertainty of what meaning is to be applied to the word *koinonia*. The common meaning of *koinonia* is usually "fellowship" or "sharing," but according to context the latter meaning can have different nuances—e.g., "sharing" in the sense of a "contribution" (cf. Rom. 15:26), "partnership" (cf. Phil. 1:5), "fellowship of sharing in" (cf. Phil. 3:10), or "sharing verbally," i.e., "communicating."

The NIV translation of verse 6 ("I pray that you may be active in sharing your faith") has understood the phrase in question as referring to Philemon's communicating his faith verbally, "sharing" it presumably with both believers and unbelievers. Although this is a possible interpretation, it has the danger of limiting our understanding of Philemon's role to that of verbal communication. Given his ministry in the community as the well-to-do host of the house church (v. 2) and as Paul's anticipated host and probable benefactor (v. 22), the suggestion lies near at hand to think of Philemon's "sharing" as extending to his material resources as well. More likely, therefore, we should understand Paul's words as a reference to Philemon's "generosity which springs from [his] faith" (O'Brien, 1982, 280).

But even if the intended nuance of the phrase "the fellowship of your faith" remains uncertain, there is little doubt about the ultimate goal of Paul's prayer for Philemon. It is that the exercise of his faith will lead him into a "full understanding of every good thing we have in Christ" (v. 6b), that is, into an ever-growing awareness of all the resources available in Christ. The implication of this is clear: Whereas an inactive faith leads to stagnation, an active faith leads to spiritual growth—surely a principle of universal application.

3. Appeal on Behalf of Onesimus (vv. 8–22)

In the greeting (vv. 1–3) and prayer report (vv. 4–7) Paul has skillfully been preparing Philemon for the primary purpose of the letter, namely, his appeal on behalf of the runaway slave, Onesimus. The appeal itself constitutes the "body" of the letter (vv. 8–22), and this, too, is developed with great skill and sensitivity.

From the beginning of the letter, Paul has in mind a specific request toward which the whole letter moves, namely, the request that Philemon should welcome Onesimus as he would welcome Paul himself (v. 17). To get there, however, Paul has to proceed slowly and diplomatically. Commencing at verse 8, therefore, Paul engages the topic stage by stage, focusing in turn on the basis of the appeal (Philemon's "love" and Paul's circumstances, vv. 8–9), the subject of the appeal (Onesimus, the converted slave, vv. 10–16), and the goal of the appeal (Philemon's acceptance of the runaway slave, vv. 17–22).

What drives the letter is the interaction between the members of this trio of Christian brothers: Paul the advocate, Onesimus the runaway slave, and Philemon the offended slave owner. Each one knows the other two, but the three have never met together. In the background is the congregation in Colosse, no doubt observing the unfolding crisis in Philemon's household with a mixture of sympathetic but apprehensive interest.

3.1. *Basis of the Appeal (vv. 8–9)*

Given Paul's apostolic authority, he realized that he "could be bold and order [Philemon] to do what [he] ought to do" (v. 8). Yet he prefers a different strategy—a strategy of "appeal" (cf. the use of the verb *parakaleo* in vv. 9–10). The basis of the appeal is twofold: Philemon's "love" and Paul's circumstances. As for Philemon's generous "love for all the saints" in Colosse, Paul had already been informed about this, probably from Epaphras (v. 5). Moreover, Paul himself had received "great joy and encouragement" from the demonstration of that "love" (v. 7). Now on the basis of that same "love" (v. 9a)—this is the point of "therefore" at the beginning of verse 8—he determines to appeal to Philemon for a further demonstration of it as regards Onesimus.

But Paul does not content himself with an appeal to Philemon's love; he reinforces his petition by appealing also to his own circumstances as "an old man and now also a prisoner of Christ Jesus" (v. 9b). Not only should Philemon accede to Paul's request "on the basis of love," but also for *Paul's* own sake, that is, in consideration of his age and condition (v. 9b). By this time Paul would be in his sixties and with adequate reason could call himself "an old man"[3] relative to the life expectancy of the times. Not only was he old, but he was also a prisoner for the sake of the gospel. These considerations, Paul hopes, will carry additional weight with his friend in assessing the merits of the request.

3.2. Subject of the Appeal (vv. 10–16)

Up to this point in the letter—more than a third complete!—there has as yet been no mention of Paul's specific reason for writing, much less the mention of the person's name for whom Paul is interceding. But in verse 10 it all comes out into the open with sustained rhetorical force (in the Greek text, the mention of the name "Onesimus" appears only at the end of a long clause, intentionally, no doubt, in order to maximize rhetorical suspense; cf. the literal rendering of v. 10 in the NASB, "I appeal to you for my child . . . Onesimus").

Having mentioned him, however, Paul is now free to say several things about him. This he does in the subsequent verses in a series of three parallel clauses at the beginning of verses 10, 12, and 13 respectively, which may be literally rendered "whom I have begotten in my chains" (v. 10), "whom I have sent to you" (v. 12), and "whom I wished to keep with me" (v. 13).

The phrase "whom I have begotten in my chains" (cf. NIV, "who became my son while I was in chains") is undoubtedly a reference to Paul's involvement in leading Onesimus to faith in Jesus Christ. We are not told anythin about the circumstances that brought the age apostle and the young runaway togethe though one can imagine that there is an inte esting tale attached to it. As a result of his cor version, Onesimus became Paul's "son" (c Timothy in 1 Cor. 4:17; 1 Tim. 1:2, 18; 2 Tin 1:2; 2:1, and Titus in Titus 1:4), and Pau became Onesimus's "spiritual father" (GNB).

This positive introduction of the "father son" relationship between Paul and Onesimu is immediately tempered, however, by refe ence to the negative aspect of the previou relationship between Philemon and Onesimu namely, the recognition that despite the mean ing of Onesimus's name as "profitable" o "useful," the runaway had in fact become quit "useless" to his owner (v. 11). Paul hastens t add, however—still employing skillful word play—that after the time of Onesimus's con version, the latter had again become "useful," both to Philemon and to himself.

In the second and third parallel clause mentioned above ("whom I have sent to you," v. 12; "whom I wished to keep with me," v. 13), Paul continues the positive note struck in verse 10. Not only is Onesimus his "son" he has even become his "very heart" (v. 12; cf comments on v. 7). Not surprisingly, therefore Paul would like to have kept Onesimus with him in prison as a companion and helper in Philemon's stead (v. 13). But Paul will not presume to do anything without his friend's consent, lest any favor on Philemon's part seem "forced" rather than "spontaneous" (v. 14). Consequently, Paul has decided to send Onesimus back to his rightful owner (v. 12), though not without the secret wish, perhaps, that Philemon will eventually send Onesimus back to serve Paul again (see comments on v. 21).

All along Paul has been leading up to the specific request he intends to make of Philemon. But just before he makes the point explicit (v. 17), he offers his friend one further reflection on the significance of Onesimus's flight. Perhaps there was a transcendent reason for it all, says Paul, namely, to bring Onesimus to faith, with the positive result that Philemon "might have him back for good—no longer as a slave, but better than a slave, as a dear brother" (vv. 15–16).

This realization, of course, raises profound questions about the outworking of God's puroses through human failure and transgression in this case, the theft and flight of Onesimus), uestions that Paul does not stop to probe furner at this point. Instead, his strategy is simly to encourage Philemon to consider the ositive outcome of Onesimus's negative ction, that through all that has happened)nesimus has become a "dear brother," both as a man" and "in the Lord." This status of dear brother" was certainly true of Onesimus n his relationship to Paul and "even more"—o at least Paul hopes—in his relationship to 'hilemon.

3.3. Goal of the Appeal (vv. 17–22)

The moment has finally arrived when Paul s ready to articulate his request directly to his riend. Stripped of all the rhetorical preamble vv. 1–16) as well as the shorter—but no less ouching—postlude (vv. 18–21), it all comes lown to one small phrase: "Welcome [Onesmus] as you would welcome me" (v. 17). But he brevity of the phrase should not deceive us. t is as weighty as it is brief. "Welcome him," 'aul exhorts, just as "you would welcome ne"—not grudgingly or reluctantly, but varmly, generously, openly. In effect, Paul is isking Philemon to receive back his renegade lave with the same degree of warmth and ffection with which he would receive the ipostle himself, the one to whom Philemon owes his very life (v. 19).

The implication of Paul's request is that in he community of faith to which Philemon belongs and of which Onesimus is now also a part, social distinctions and past grievances should count for nothing. This amounts to a specific application of the principle laid down in the congregational letter to the Colossians, to the effect that in Christ there is no "slave or free" (Col. 3:11). Forgiveness and equality of treatment are what should characterize relationships in the new community, not social class or schemes for getting even. Such a message is as radical—and as challenging—now as it was then.

The formulation of the request does not stand alone, however; it is both preceded (v. 17a) and followed (v. 18) by conditional clauses, each of which in its own way is calculated to lend weight to the simple but direct request of verse 17b. The specific request in question is actually the "answering" part to the introductory conditional clause "if you consider me a partner [*koinonos*, a word applied to Titus in 2 Cor. 8:23]" (v. 17a)—a deliberate choice of words that affirms something positive about the relationship between Paul and Philemon that the latter would certainly not wish to deny. Now Paul hopes that Philemon will not deny him the specific favor he is asking.

This leads to verse 18, which contains the second conditional sentence: "If he [Onesimus] has done you any wrong or owes you anything, charge it to me." By this offer of restitution, the apostle removes any financial objection that Philemon might have had for receiving the slave back. In fact, Paul takes the matter so seriously that he does something quite out of the ordinary: He stops dictating, takes the secretary's quill, and writes with deep emotion: "I, Paul, am writing this with my own hand. I will pay it back." Paul often writes the final greeting of a letter in his own hand (cf. 1 Cor. 16:21; Gal. 6:11; Col. 4:18; 2 Thess. 3:17), but only in this letter does he break into the middle of the dictation to write, in effect, a personal "IOU"! Then, as if with an afterthought—but what a powerful afterthought!—the apostle adds, "not to mention that you owe me your very self" (v. 19).

We have no way of knowing how Philemon owed his own self to Paul; presumably he is talking of Philemon's conversion and all the positive benefits that flowed from it. But the details are irrelevant; the point is that Philemon and Onesimus stood on common ground, in that both had found life through the ministry of Paul. The implication is that the least they could do now was to be reconciled to each other.

Paul closes the body of the letter with a final appeal to Philemon for his cooperation and obedience (vv. 20–21), along with a personal request for hospitality (v. 22). The appeal for cooperation and obedience harks back to vocabulary employed earlier in the letter and so helps to reinforce the points made previously. Paul begins the windup by addressing Philemon as "brother," the same term used by the apostle in verse 7 (cf. also "dear friend" in v. 1b).

Paul's earnest request that he may have some "benefit" from Philemon reminds us of Paul's earlier word play on the name "Onesimus" (cf. vv. 10–11): The Greek verb employed in verse 20a, *oninemi* (lit., "that I may be profited"), comes from the same root as *onesimos* ("beneficial, profitable"). The exhortation to "refresh my heart" (v. 20b) uses the same vocabulary as the phrase in verse 7, "you, brother, have *refreshed the hearts* of the saints."

The reference in verse 21 to Philemon's "obedience" sounds strange, given Paul's earlier disavowal of any use of his apostolic authority (vv. 8–9). The point, however, is that if Paul had truly wished to assert his authority over Philemon, he would not have made the effort to write such a carefully crafted letter of persuasion. Therefore, the existence of the letter is itself a testimony to the strategy of "appeal" rather than of "command." At the same time, there is never any doubt in the reader's mind—nor in Paul's!—about the expected response. In fact, Paul is "confident" that Philemon will do "even more" than what he has been asked to do.

What does this "more" refer to? Comparison with verses 13–14 has suggested to many interpreters the probability that Paul is really looking for the eventual return of Onesimus to himself as his helper, but this time with Philemon's "consent" and blessing (v. 14). Whether this ever materialized we simply do not know. It may be, in fact, that the course of events took a very different turn. Even as Paul was alluding to the return of Onesimus as his helper, he was also anticipating his own release and eventual return to the Aegean area. Although he had not previously visited Colosse (cf. Col. 2:1), this time he hoped to make a personal visit—hence the request, "Prepare a guest room for me, because I hope to be restored to you in answer to your prayers" (v. 22).

Whether Paul ever realized his dream of visiting Colosse, or whether Onesimus ever returned to Rome to serve the apostle again, we cannot know. But one thing we do know and can affirm with confidence is that the letter to Philemon, in spite of its brevity, stands as a powerful testimony to the apostle's vitality, diplomacy, literary craftsmanship, and—especially—his love "in the Lord" for individuals regardless of social rank.

4. Final Greetings and Grace (vv. 23–25)

With one exception, the names of those who sent greetings to Philemon's household (vv. 23–24) are identical with those who in Colossians 4:10–14 sent greetings to the church in Coloss[e] (the exception is "Jesus called Justus" in Co[l.] 4:11). This otherwise exact correspondence o[f] names is one of the strong reasons for assumin[g] that Philemon's place of residence was in fac[t] Colosse (along with the clear indications tha[t] both Onesimus and Epaphras were Colossians; cf. Col. 4:9,12).

Though the names are the same in both letters, the order is different. In Philemon the person mentioned first is Epaphras, the evangelis[t] from whom the Colossians had first heard the gospel (cf. Col. 1:7), but who was now a "fellow prisoner" with Paul (the same term i[s] applied to Aristarchus in Col. 4:10). The others who send greetings to Philemon are Mark, Aristarchus, Demas, and Luke (cf. a differen[t] order in Col. 4:10–14). Perhaps this variety in sequence of names signifies that among Paul's "fellow workers"—the same term applied to Philemon in verse 1—there was no fixed orde[r] of rank. Especially noteworthy here is the mention of Demas—the one who was later to desert Paul (cf. 2 Tim. 4:10)—*before* the mention of Luke (reversed in Col. 4:14).

Does the mention of these names sugges[t] that all of Paul's coworkers were aware of the contents of the letter? Probably, yes. It is har[d] to think that they would have been ignorant o[f] the dynamics surrounding the return of Onesimus to Colosse. The matter was most likely a public one—more public than Philemon might have wished. It reminds us—as surely i[t] must have reminded Philemon—that the eyes of the world, so to speak, are on us to see how we resolve conflicts among Christians. It reminds us too that conflict resolution among brothers and sisters, often thought to be private, more often has broader ramifications.

In different ways, we are all called to respond with love and generosity to conflict situations in which we have been directly involved as well as to those situations where we are bystanders to others' troubles. Paul's coworkers had no doubt learned to be silent and prayerful bystanders, thus making a positive rather than a negative contribution to the resolution of the tension between the alienated parties, Philemon and Onesimus. If this is a right interpretation of the role of the brothers mentioned in verses 23–24, they serve as wonderful models for us.

The letter closes (v. 25) with the invocation f Paul's famous "grace" formula, directed this me towards an individual ("your [sing.] pirit") rather than towards a congregation. Vhether one or many, the same grace was— nd remains—available to all.

NOTES

[1]Similar letters of intercession for runaway laves have survived from antiquity, the most amous one being that of Pliny, *Epistles*, 9.21 (see ohse [1971], 196–97, n. 2).

[2]For other references to "house churches" in the postolic era, see Rom. 16:5, 23; 1 Cor. 16:19; Col. :15. For a discussion of this phenomenon and furner bibliography, see Robert Banks, *Paul's Idea of ommunity*, rev. ed. (1994), 26–36, 203–4.

[3]Many recent commentators and translations uggest that the Greek word *presbytes* (translated old man" in the NIV and elsewhere) should rather e translated "ambassador" (cf. O'Brien [1982], Iarris [1991], Bruce [1984], REB, NRSV marg.). The rgument is that although the normal spelling for old man" was *presbytes*—as in all our manuscripts f verse 9—and the standard spelling for "ambasador" was *presbeutes,* in manuscripts from antiqity the two forms are often interchanged; indeed, here are specific cases in Greek literature where *resbytes* means "ambassador." This line of interretation would agree with Paul's juxtaposition of ambassador" and "prison" (lit., "chains") elsewhere (cf. Eph. 6:20). Furthermore, it would have the advantage of avoiding any suggestion that Paul is appealing to Philemon on the basis of self-pity, which would seem out of character for Paul, who normally thought of his sufferings and imprisonment for Christ as an honor. But the argument is not conclusive. In either case, what remains true is that Paul's appeal in this verse is based on his *own situation* rather than on that of Philemon or even of Onesimus.

[4]The play on the Greek words is *achreston* ("useless") / *euchreston* ("useful"). Both *onesimus* and *euchrestos* mean "useful." There may be a further play on words involving the title *christos,* thus: *achrestos* ("useless") = *a-christos* ("without Christ"); *euchrestos ("useful") = eu-christos* ("good Christian")!

BIBLIOGRAPHY

Commentaries on Philemon have most frequently been combined with those on the letter to the Colossians. Some independent studies on Philemon have been published, however.

F. F. Bruce, *The Epistles to the Colossians, to Philemon and to the Ephesians,* NICNT (1984); Murray Harris, *Colossians and Philemon*, EGGNT (1991); John Knox, *Philemon Among the Letters of Paul: A New View of Its Place and Importance*, rev. ed. (1959); Eduard Lohse, *Colossians and Philemon,* trans. William R. Poehlmann and Robert J. Karris, Hermeneia (1971); Peter T. O'Brien, *Colossians, Philemon*, WBC (1982); Norman R. Petersen, *Rediscovering Paul: Philemon and the Sociology of Paul's Narrative World* (1985).

HEBREWS

J. Wesley Adams

NTRODUCTION

. A Mysterious Gold Mine

ebrews is unlike any other book in the New estament. It ranks first in eloquence and arning and is distinctive in its content, liter-y form, manner of referring to the Old Tes-ment and unique Christological emphasis; et it is the most enigmatic book in the New estament. It has been called "the riddle of the ew Testament" because of uncertainty con-rning who wrote it, to whom it was written, what locality, and at what point in the first ntury A.D. Thus, the book presents unique fficulties for the interpreter. Seeking answers the riddle, however, can itself be enlight-ning and bring greater understanding. For is reason it is profitable to explore the mys-ry that surrounds Hebrews in order to dis-over its enduring message and relevance.

At first reading, Hebrews appears difficult understand or apply to life today. Its com-lex argument is clothed in Old Testament oncepts and allusions drawn from Israel's iesthood and sacrificial system. One of the ain tasks of the commentator is thus to make ear the intricately developed argument and explain the significance of its background. dded to the problem of unfamiliar language d concepts are the warning passages, which n easily be misunderstood and misapplied if ot interpreted in the context of the entire ook. For believers who want to dig deeply, owever, the book of Hebrews offers a rich old mine of wisdom and revelation of God e Father and Jesus the Son. The book emonstrates that effective pastoral encour-gement and warning should be grounded in ood exposition and biblical theology.

. Literary Form

a. Unique and Unconventional

Concerning its unique, unconventional form, rigen observed: "It begins like a treatise, pro-eeds like a sermon, and concludes like a letter." stead of beginning with a salutation, the first aragraph of Hebrews is like the opening words f a formal theological treatise (1:1–4). Then the book proceeds more like a sermon than a conventional New Testament letter, alternating between a carefully constructed argument (based on Old Testament exposition) and earnest exhortation. One writer suggests that Hebrews was "a written sermon somehow prevented from being delivered orally and therefore dispatched with a note to the intended hearers to be read aloud by one of them" (Bartlet and Grobel, 1965, 11:291; cf. Lane, 1991, 1:lxx–lxxiv). The book concludes like a letter (13:18–19, 22–25).

b. Distinctive style

The author's rich vocabulary and polished oratorical style approaches classical Greek style more nearly than any other New Testament writer (except perhaps Luke 1:1–4). In addition to demonstrating the skill of an orator, the author also reveals the carefulness of a scholar as he presents his argument. Every word in every clause plays its full part in conveying with precision the meaning intended. The original language of Hebrews was clearly Greek, not Hebrew. The author's argument is based on the meaning and force of Greek words that could not have occurred had he written in Hebrew.

3. The Original Recipients

a. Author's Personal Knowledge of the Recipients

Hebrews was written to a select group of believers in a specific locality. The author knew the recipients as well as their needs and the dangers they faced. He believed many of them ought to be teachers themselves (5:12). He requested their prayers (13:18), looked forward to visiting them in the future (13:19, 23), and sent news about their mutual friend Timothy (13:23). He recalled "earlier days" when his friends had endured persecution (10:32), generously given to other believers (6:10), joyfully faced the trial of having their property confiscated because of their faith in Christ (10:34), and stood by others in their sufferings (10:33). He knew about their present attitude toward their leaders (13:7, 17) and sent them all greetings (13:24). The author clearly had a relationship with these people.

b. Jews or Gentiles, or Both?

The readers are nowhere identified explicitly in the book itself. The title in all early Greek manuscripts is simply "To [the] Hebrews." Though this title is probably not original, it does go back at least to the second century and is the regular designation for the book thereafter. There is no evidence that it ever circulated under any other name. This title represents the belief of the church at an early date that the original readers were Jewish Christians—almost certainly converted Hellenistic Jews in the Roman world, not Palestinian Jews (see W. Manson, 1951, ch. 1). For example, the Old Testament with which the readers and author were familiar was the Greek version of the Scriptures, not the Hebrew. Also, "their knowledge of the ancient sacrificial ritual of Israel was derived from the reading of the Old Testament and not from firsthand contact with the temple service in Jerusalem" (Bruce, 1990, 9).

Some recent interpreters have argued that Hebrews was not written to Jews at all, but to Gentile believers who were in danger of returning to paganism and thus turning "away from the living God" (3:12). They argue that if Jewish believers lapsed into Judaism, they would not thereby be renouncing "the living God" since they would continue to worship the God of Israel. This reasoning is faulty, however, for Hebrews teaches that the old covenant is now obsolete (8:13); God under the new covenant speaks and relates to his people by his Son (1:1–3). To turn away from Jesus, the Son of God, is to depart from faith in the living God, who became incarnate and was fully revealed in his Son (1:3).

A few interpreters have suggested the recipients were a mixed congregation and that the title is purely symbolic. But the vast majority of interpreters and the cumulative weight of evidence suggests that the believers addressed in this book were a small community of Hellenistic Jews in the Roman world.

c. Evidence of the Readers' Jewishness

When the author of Hebrews warns his readers about the danger of falling away from their faith in God, he illustrates his point by referring to the Israelites, who had experienced God's grace and mercy at the Exodus but then fell away in unbelief and perished in the wilderness (3:7–19). "What was possible f
Israelites then was equally possible f
Israelites now" (Bruce, 1990, 6). The "foun
dation" in 6:1–3 also indicates the Jewis
background of the readers. The reference t
Jesus' death as providing "a ransom to set the
free from the sins committed under the fir
covenant" (9:15) directly points to Jewish co
verts. The emphasis that the old covenant ha
been superseded and made obsolete by the ne
covenant and Jesus' death (e.g., 8:1–10:18
would be pointless if the readers were not pre
disposed to live under the old covenant.

Throughout Hebrews, the author appeals t
the authority of the Old Testament Scripture
with a confidence that his readers wi
acknowledge it, even if their loyalty to th
gospel is wearing thin. This likelihood woul
be true especially of Jews who recognized th
authority of the Old Testament before becon
ing Christians and who would continue to d
so even if they denied Christ and returned t
Judaism. Gentile converts from paganism
however, adopted the Old Testament only a
part of the Christian faith. If they gave up fait
in Christ, the Old Testament would go as wel

Moreover, throughout Hebrews the author'
argument is based on Jewish premises, such a
the belief that the tabernacle, sacrifices, an
Levitical priesthood were instituted by God f
the Jews under the old covenant. Hebrews pe
sistently refers to the Jewish ways of worshi
and manifests a conspicuous absence of refe
ence to pagan ways, such as we read in Paul'
letters to Gentiles or to mixed congregation
We may safely conclude, therefore, th
Hebrews was written to Jewish believers wh
were wavering in their faith in Jesus and co
sidering returning to the security of Judaism.

d. Location of the Recipients

One cannot be absolutely certain about th
recipients' location since it is undesignated i
the book itself. There are, however, some issue
of probability. (1) As suggested above, th
recipients were probably Jews of the dispersio
rather than Jews in Palestine, though som
older scholars such as Westcott (1889 198
and more recently Buchanan (1972) have sug
gested Jerusalem as the destination. Jews of th
dispersion resided in almost every importa
city of the Mediterranean world. Some of thos
that have been identified as the possible orig

al destination of Hebrews are: Colosse, Eph-sus, Galatia, Cyprus, Corinth, Syria, Antioch of Syria, Berea, Alexandria, and Rome.

(2) Current New Testament scholarship views Rome as the most probable destination for Hebrews (e.g., Guthrie, Attridge, Bruce, Lane, Ellingworth, Peterson). The phrase "those from Italy send you their greetings" (13:24) is the strongest clue about locality. Though it is not impossible that this phrase means people living "in Italy" send their greetings to believers outside Italy, the most natural meaning of "from Italy" is that Italian believers living away from their homeland send greetings to their fellow countrymen somewhere in Italy. "Within this area, the most important church, and therefore the most likely destination, was Rome" (Ellingworth, 1993, 29).

Several other factors support this conclusion. (a) Earliest evidence of Hebrews being known and used is at Rome, where Clement of Rome cites from it extensively in a pastoral letter to the church in Corinth about A.D. 95. (b) The allusions to the recipients' generosity (6:10–11; 10:33–34) agrees well with the known history of the church community in Rome from other sources (cf. Ignatius, *Romans*, salutation). (c) The reference to "foods" (Heb. 13:9) suggests a situation like that in Romans 14. (d) The description of early sufferings endured by the recipients (10:32–34) corresponds to the experience of Roman Jewish Christians during "the Claudian edict of expulsion in A.D. 49" (Lane, 1991, 1:lviii). (e) Timothy, whom the author mentions as having relational ties to the readers (13:23), was well known to Christians at Rome (cf. Col. 1:1; Philem. 1). (f) The unusual designation of "leaders" among the recipients as *hegoumenoi* (13:7, 17, 24) "is found outside the New Testament in early Christian sources associated with Rome (e.g., 1 Clem. 21:6; Herm., *Vis*. 2.2.6; 3.9.7)" (Lane, 1991, 1:lviii).

Although it cannot be proven, there are more reasons for connecting Hebrews with Rome than any other location. The hypothesis that Hebrews was originally sent to a house church within the larger church community in Rome, predominantly comprised of Jews ("Hebrews") with strong conservative ties to Judaism, "gives a concreteness to Hebrews that other hypotheses lack, and it affords a plausible framework for the document" (Lane, 1991, 1:lviii).

4. Authorship

The author of Hebrews is not identified, either in the ancient title or in the book itself, nor does the writer refer to any circumstances that might reveal his identity or his readers with certainty (perhaps because of life-threatening persecution on both ends). The KJV title, "The Epistle of Paul the Apostle to the Hebrews," was prefixed by editors in later centuries and has no textual authority. The ancient title in Greek manuscripts simply reads: "To [the] Hebrews." Authorship of Hebrews has been a mystery at least since the early second century.

Sections of the old Roman wall still can be found in the city. The book of Hebrews was written to a specific group of believers by someone who knew them well. There are good reasons to believe that this group was part of the church in Rome.

Undoubtedly, the author's identity and personal greetings were communicated verbally by the person who delivered Hebrews to its original destination—information lost to subsequent generations.

a. The Testimony of History

Among the early church fathers there is no clear or uniform testimony concerning the authorship of this book. The first trace of its use is by Clement of Rome toward the end of the first century, possibly before the death of John the apostle. Although Clement freely cites from Hebrews, he never mentions the author by name. Even though he writes to a church founded by Paul (Corinth), he never attributes it to the apostle. A period of silence about Hebrews follows in Christian literature, during which time authentic knowledge about the origin of the book seems to disappear.

The first known discussion of its authorship occurs at a Christian school in Alexandria (Egypt), where a teacher named Pantaenus (c. A.D. 185) suggests that Hebrews was written by Paul (though we are not told on what grounds he based his opinion). Clement of Alexandria, a disciple of and successor to Pantaenus, saw an obvious difference between Paul's style of writing and that of Hebrews. He conjectured, therefore, that Paul originally wrote Hebrews in Hebrew, and it was afterwards translated into Greek by Luke for the Greeks.

Origen (A.D. 185–254), the successor of Clement of Alexandria, mentions that a variety of opinions about the authorship of Hebrews existed and states his own perplexity on the subject: "God only knows." Thus during his day the question of authorship apparently was an open one, on which everyone was free to state his own opinion. With the passing of the scholarly Origen, there was a decline of interest in such matters, and the Alexandrian church subsequently came to hold Pauline authorship as a matter free from doubt. Based on the Alexandrian tradition, "the authority of Hebrews as a work of Paul established itself in the third century over all the eastern Churches" (W. Manson, 1951, 2).

In the western half of the Mediterranean world, the opposite was true. The churches until after the middle of the fourth century were "decidedly against the Pauline authorship [of Hebrews]" (Schaff, 1950, 1:819). This is especially significant in that the earliest traces of Hebrews are found in the Roman church (cf. above). Contemporary with Pantaenus's and Clement's opinions at Alexandria about Paul's authorship is the unhesitating testimony of Tertullian in North Africa (c. A.D. 190) that Barnabas was the author of Hebrews. The majority of the Western churches, however, held that authorship of Hebrews was anonymous until the unsubstantiated claims of Pauline authorship gradually spread to the West during the latter part of the fourth century.

Even after Hebrews was officially canonized at the Council of Carthage in A.D. 419 and placed among Paul's letters, church scholars like Jerome and Augustine expressed reservations about its having been written by Paul. When both men finally conformed to the prevailing view, it secured for Pauline authorship an unchallenged position until the Reformation. In summary, the testimony of history from the first to fifth centuries is indecisive and adds nothing substantial toward a solution of the anonymity of Hebrews.

During the revival of biblical studies at the time of the Protestant Reformation, the question of who wrote Hebrews reemerged, and divergent views again were expressed. Erasmus suggested Clement of Rome; Luther believed Apollos was the author; and Calvin was inclined to believe that Luke wrote it. Biblical scholars since that time have considered almost every possible solution to the mystery of authorship.

b. The Testimony of Internal Evidence

Profile of the author. A personality profile of the author can be derived from a careful study of Hebrews itself. The author was a man of exceptional learning, who possessed a masterful command of the Greek language. His literary skill and oratorical abilities point to a writer of rare eloquence in the first century. Moreover, his vocabulary, figures of speech, and manner of argument all indicate he was permeated with the literary and theological methods of a Jewish man of Alexandrian training or influence. For example, his method of introducing and using Old Testament material is like that of Philo, the famous Alexandrian Jewish philosopher-teacher. He uses phrases and images common among other Alexandrian writers. The entire spirit and atmosphere of Hebrews speaks of Alexandrian influence.

The evidence of Hebrews itself also reveals, with the highest degree of probability, that the author was a Hellenistic Jew by birth, not a Palestinian—

> thoroughly at home in the Greek Scripture (less so, if at all, in the Hebrew); familiar with the Alexandrian Jewish theology (less so, if at all, with the rabbinical learning of Palestine); a pupil of the [original] apostles ... an independent disciple and co-worker of Paul; a friend of Timothy; [and not least] ... an inspired man of apostolic insight, power and authority, and hence worthy of a position in the [New Testament] canon as "the great unknown." (Schaff, 1950, 1:822)

Paul's authorship. Many conservative Bible scholars today believe Paul's authorship is unlikely, since the author's oratorical and polished writing style, Alexandrian background, exclusive use of the Septuagint, manner of introducing Old Testament quotations, method of argument and teaching, and reluctance to identify himself in the letter are all distinctly non-Pauline. Furthermore, although Paul vehemently insisted that the gospel he preached was given to him by firsthand revelation from Christ (cf. Gal. 1:11–12) and always regarded his apostleship to be on the same level as the original twelve (e.g. 1 Cor. 15:7–8; Gal. 2:6–9), the author of Hebrews places himself among the second-generation Christians to whom the gospel was confirmed by eyewitnesses of Jesus' ministry (2:3). New Testament interpreters generally agree that the cumulative evidence and author's statement in 2:3 weigh decisively against Paul's authorship of Hebrews.

c. The Testimony of Plausibility

If not Paul, who then may have written Hebrews? Scholars have looked at a variety of possibilities, and the merits of each have been weighed: Luke, Clement, and Barnabas since ancient times, and Apollos since the Reformation; in modern times proposals include Priscilla and Aquila, Silas, Peter, Philip, Epaphras, Aristion, and Jude. From these names the following have emerged as the most likely candidates: Barnabas (first mentioned by Tertullian, c. A.D. 190), Luke (first suggested by Clement of Alexandria, c. A.D. 195–200), Priscilla and Aquila (Harnack, in 1900), and Apollos (the choice of Luther and many contemporary scholars).

Barnabas. In favor of Barnabas is: (1) He is named early in church history as the author; (2) he was a native of Cyprus, and Cypriots were known for their excellence in Greek; (3) he was a Levite, a fact that would contribute to a thorough knowledge of the Old Testament priestly and sacrificial system that Hebrews carefully reinterprets as being fulfilled in Christ; and (4) Barnabas is called in Acts 4:36 the "Son of Encouragement" (NASB, NIV) or exhortation. Since the author of Hebrews calls his book "my word of exhortation" (13:22), some have seen this as a hint of Barnabas's authorship.

Evidence against Barnabas's authorship of Hebrews is: (1) He, like Paul, was not among the second-generation believers, as is the author of Hebrews (2:3; cf. Acts 4:36–37); and (2) there is no evidence that Barnabas had been influenced by Jewish-Alexandrian training, as is characteristic of the author.

In favor of Luke is: (1) He qualifies for the author's description in 2:3 as having received the gospel from eyewitnesses of the Lord; (2) he was capable of writing excellent Greek prose, as is evident in the preface to his Gospel; and (3) he was an educated man with certain affinities in style with Hebrews.

Evidence against Luke's authorship is: (1) He was a Gentile rather than a Jew; (2) Luke's style of writing in Luke-Acts is not oratorical as is the style of Hebrews; moreover, the similarity of Luke's vocabulary and manner of expression with that of Hebrews is no greater than the similarity between 1 Peter and Paul's letters; and (3) there is no indication of Luke having been influenced by Alexandria.

Priscilla. Adolf von Harnack has proposed that Priscilla, with the assistance of her husband, wrote Hebrews. In favor of Priscilla plus Aquila is the following evidence: (1) They were Jewish believers and fulfill the qualification of highly cultured teachers; (2) they belonged to the Pauline circle as did the author, and were associated with Timothy in Corinth for eighteen months as well as at Ephesus; (3) they belonged to one of the household churches in Rome to whom Hebrews may well have been originally addressed; and (4) Harnack's strong point is "the enigma of anonymity," that a woman author adequately accounts for the suppression of the author's name. It was a man's world, and there would be every reason for keeping quiet that a woman had written an authoritative letter. Priscilla and her husband were cultured Hellenistic Jews. A woman who could instruct Apollos in the faith (Acts 18:26) was a gifted teacher.

Against a predominantly feminine authorship by Priscilla are the following observations by Dods (n.d., 4:224):

> (1) A single authorship is unquestionably demanded by certain expressions in the Epistle [11:32; 13:19, 22, 23, etc.].... It is not possible to construe these singulars as referring to more than one writer; but it is quite possible to construe the plurals of the Epistle as referring to the single writer or to the writer uniting himself with his readers. (2) That this one writer should have been Priscilla is certainly improbable, both on account of Paul's prohibition [see 1 Tim. 2:12] which so good a friend as Priscilla would observe, and because the writer seems to have been one of the *hegoumenoi* [those who preside, govern, rule, lead the way; i.e., chief officials or leaders in early Christianity] which Priscilla could not have been. (3) The impression made by the Epistle is that it proceeds from a masculine mind.... [Decisive is the use of a masculine participle in 11:32]. (4) In addition to these points is the important consideration that Priscilla and Aquila were Roman in background rather than Alexandrian.

Apollos. Many New Testament scholars in recent centuries believe the eloquent Apollos is the most likely person to have written Hebrews. Acts 18:24–28 gives the following profile of Apollos:

> Now a certain Jew named Apollos, an Alexandrian by birth, an eloquent man, came to Ephesus; and he was mighty in the Scriptures. This man had been instructed in the way of the Lord; and being fervent in spirit, he was speaking and teaching accurately the things concerning Jesus, being acquainted only with the baptism of John; and he began to speak out boldly in the synagogue. But when Priscilla and Aquila heard him, they took him aside and explained to him the way of God more accurately. And when he wanted to go across to Achaia, the brethren encouraged him and wrote to the disciples to welcome him; and when he had arrived, he helped greatly those who had believed through grace; for he powerfully refuted the Jews in public, demonstrating by the Scriptures that Jesus was the Christ. (NASB)

This description fits well what we know abo the author of Hebrews: He was a Jew, a nativ of Alexandria, and a man of rare eloquenc (which would account for its literary form) an mighty in the Old Testament Scriptures; h was fervent in spirit, well instructed in the wa of the Lord, and persuasive in convincing th Jews that Jesus was the Christ. As Lange pu it: "If a writer should attempt to put into one c two brief sentences all the qualifications whic would be demanded for the authorship of th Epistle to the Hebrews, he would need only t write the sentences contained in Acts xviii. 24 etc." (Moll, n.d., 22:10).

Objections raised against Apollos are (1) His name is conspicuously absent i ancient times. At first this consideration look weighty, but when we consider the conflictin and superficial nature of the authorship dis cussion in ancient times, it loses most of it force. "Where the positive testimony is of s little value, the negative testimony of silenc cannot be allowed any great weight" (ibid 22:10). (2) There is no evidence that Apollo was a writer. But neither is there evidence tha Mark or Jude were writers other than their sin gle contribution to the New Testamen (3) There is no record of him having any con nection with Rome, the likely destination o Hebrews. This objection, however, is nc entirely substantial either. Aquila and Priscilla who took a personal interest in Apollos an were responsible for teaching him the way o the Lord more perfectly, were from Rome, an a congregation met in their home in that cit (Rom. 16:3–5). Apollos was a man wh moved about freely, not residing in one local ity for any great length of time. It is therefor not at all improbable that he visited Rome an was perhaps intimately acquainted with th Jewish-Christian congregation that met in th home of Aquila and Priscilla. He was also a close acquaintance of both Paul and Timothy.

In conclusion, among those in the New Testament who might have written Hebrews, Apollos is the one most fitted by education, life circumstances, gifts, background, and experience to have authored such a book. A. M. Hunter remarks that if Apollos did not write Hebrews, then it must have been "his twin brother" (1975, 64).[1] Regardless of who wrote Hebrews, this much is certain: The author wrote with an apostolic fullness of the Spirit and with apostolic insight, revelation, and authority. The ultimate acceptance of Hebrews as New Testament Scripture in spite of uncertainty about its authorship "testifies to the intrinsic power of the epistle itself" (Guthrie, 1983, 19).

[...]. Date

When was Hebrews written? A first-century date is required by three facts: (1) the extensive use of it by Clement of Rome (c. A.D. 95); (2) the testimony of the author that he and his readers had heard the gospel from those who had been eyewitnesses of Jesus' ministry (2:3); and (3) the reference to Timothy's release in 13:23, assuming this Timothy was Paul's coworker (as seems likely).

But when in the first century was Hebrews written? The absence of any reference to the end of the Jewish sacrificial system (which occurred with the destruction of Jerusalem) suggests a date before A.D. 70, since the author writes as if this is still a current issue for his readers. His sustained argument that Christ has superseded and fulfilled the old covenant provisions of priesthood and sacrifices, thus making them obsolete, suggests that the temple ministry had not yet ceased. After all, a convincing climax for his argument would have been to point to the fact that they had already ceased. When the author quotes Jeremiah's prophecy about the establishment of a "new covenant," he emphasizes that the "new" has made the "old" obsolete. Then he adds: "And what is obsolete and aging will soon disappear" (8:13). This sounds like a prophetic statement immediately preceding A.D. 70.

Numerous passages in Hebrews are more forceful if the historical context is near or during the Roman war of A.D. 66–70 and the siege against Jerusalem, "when there was a compelling call to loyal Jews to cast in their lot with those fighting against Rome" (Morris, 1981, 8). Bruce dates Hebrews just before the outbreak of Neronian persecution (c. A.D. 65), when the imminence of persecution in Rome was apparent. He does so because the phrase in 12:4—"in your struggle against sin, you have not yet resisted to the point of shedding your blood"—suggests to him a time before Nero's violent persecution (1990, 21). If this statement is understood as synonymous with martyrdom, however, then Hebrews may have been written as late as A.D. 69. The mention of Timothy but not Paul (13:23) may indicate a time frame after Paul's martyrdom (A.D. 67) but before Jerusalem's destruction (c. A.D. 70). A date, therefore, between A.D. 67–69 seems to fit best all known circumstances.

6. Purpose and Message

The author refers to his work as "my word of exhortation" (13:22), which he writes as a "pastoral response to a community in crisis" (Lane, 1991, 1:xcix). The crisis involved primarily Jewish Christians who (1) were encountering the pressures and discouragement of another season of persecution, and (2) were in danger of forfeiting their faith in Christ to return to their former old covenant faith. The author writes to deepen the conviction level of their faith, to exhort them to hold on to their confession of him until the end, to challenge them to go on to spiritual maturity, and to warn them of the consequences of unbelief or abandoning faith in Christ.

The message involves both exhortation and exposition. The author's primary purpose is exhortation: "to arouse, urge, encourage, and exhort those addressed to maintain their Christian confession [as converted Jews] and to dissuade them from a course of action that the writer believed would be catastrophic" (Lane, 1991, 1:c). The main focus of his *exposition* of Old Testament Scripture is Jesus—the Son of God and the high priest of our confession—and his unique, once-for-all-time sacrifice for sin. Its primary purpose is to set forth the death of Jesus as the fulfillment of the old covenant provisions of redemption that now makes the Jewish sacrificial system obsolete, to reveal the majesty of Jesus as the fulfillment of Old Testament messianic prophecy, and to show the present relevance of Jesus as the believer's high priest and mediator in heaven.

The primary purpose of the author's *exhortation* in Hebrews is to motivate the Jewish readers to steadfast loyalty to Christ with a persevering tenacity of faith. The exposition provides the ground for faith; the exhortation calls for the demonstration of faith. The latter takes precedence over the former in expressing the author's purpose in writing. The persuasiveness of the exhortation is due to the convincing exposition of Scripture as the voice of God. The purpose of Hebrews, therefore, is

> to strengthen, encourage, and exhort the tired and weary members of a house church [probably in Rome] to respond with courage and vitality to the prospect of renewed suffering in view of the gifts and resources God has lavished upon them. The writer's intention is to address the sagging faith of men and women within the group and to remind them of their responsibility to live actively in response to God's absolute claim upon their lives through the gospel. (Lane, 1991, 1:c)

An appreciation of this dynamic interrelatedness between exposition and exhortation in Hebrews will help us understand more fully the overall message of the book.

7. The Enduring Relevance of Hebrews

Hebrews continues to speak to the church today and makes a profound contribution to our overall understanding of the gospel and spiritual heritage in Christ. The following are five examples. (1) Hebrews models a holy respect for the Old Testament Scriptures as the divinely inspired and authoritative word of God. The author consistently introduces Old Testament Scripture as God speaking, revealing his "conviction that the ultimate source of the biblical text is God" (Lane, 1991, 1:cxvii). In its extensive use of the Old Testament, Hebrews provides rich insight into early Christian interpretation of Old Testament typology, history, worship, and prophecy in view of their fulfillment in Christ. It reveals a profound continuity between the old and new covenants that centers in God's revelation of Christ through the Holy Spirit. Although the old covenant is regarded in Hebrews as now obsolete because of the new, the Old Testament Scripture clearly is not. A careful study of Hebrews will enlarg our appreciation and understanding of the Ol Testament as part of the Christian's Bible.

(2) The entire book of Hebrews is Christc centric. It provides a clear and distinctive wi ness as to who Jesus is, including more tha twenty different names and titles for him. *Lor* occurs twice; *Jesus*, his human name, is use eight times; *Christ* is his most frequent name When a definite article occurs before the nam Christ, the name generally refers to his messi ahship. Combinations also appear—e.g., *Lor Jesus*, *Jesus Christ*, and *Jesus the Son of Goc* Most distinctive, however, are the names *So* (1:2, 5, 8; 3:6; 5:5, 8; 7:28), *Son of God* (6:6; 7: 10:29), and especially *priest* (5:6; 7:3, 11, 17 21; 8:4; 10:21) and *high priest* (2:17; 3:1; 4:14 15; 5:10; 6:20; 7:26; 8:1; 9:11). Other titles fc Christ that are soteriological are *mediator of new covenant* (8:6; 9:15; 12:24), *source of eter nal salvation* (5:9), *author of salvation* (2:10 *forerunner* (6:20, NASB), *apostle and high pries whom we confess* (3:1), *great Shepherd of th sheep* (13:20), and *firstborn* (1:6).

Hebrews emphasizes Christ's deity and pre existence, his humanity, and his exaltation a the Son and heavenly mediator. Under the ol covenant God's revelation was partial and pro gressive and his provisions of redemption tem porary, but the author of Hebrews forcefull declares that God's revelation and redemptio in his Son is complete and full. Nothing ca ever be added to his redemptive work. Th message of Hebrews is essential today as th church encounters religions and cults that pro claim something other than the all-sufficienc of Christ's atoning death for our salvation.

(3) It is especially timely for any individua church, or generation encountering a sever trial and testing of their faith. Hebrews give a thoroughly Christ-centered and eternal pe spective on life and assures believers that i Christ they are receiving a kingdom that can not be shaken. It powerfully exhorts believer to be faithful and steadfast in the face of seri ous adversity. Its challenge to persevere i faith and hope is unsurpassed in Scripture Hebrews 11, the most significant chapter in th Bible on faith, pays tribute to a gallery of Ol Testament heroes of faith who lived accordin to the reality of things invisible and eternal i the most trying circumstances. In this respec Hebrews (along with 1 Peter and Revelation

s a book for the suffering church and believers who live in the end time.

(4) It exhorts the readers to go on to full maturity in Christ, with sober warnings about the consequences of abandoning the Christian faith. Hebrews warns clearly about the dangers of apostasy more than any other New Testament writing. It does so, however, in a context of confident trust that the readers will persevere in faith and remain loyal to Christ.

(5) Hebrews is an excellent model for witnessing to non-Christian Jews about Jesus Christ and his fulfillment of the Old Testament. Moreover, it offers encouragement to contemporary Jewish Christians to remain steadfast in their faith and loyal commitment to Jesus Christ. Hebrews is thus an important New Testament book for the church today.

3. Structure

The author describes the book as a "word of exhortation" (13:22). In 1:1–10:18 he presents his case: As God's Son, Jesus is the full and complete revelation of God about redemption. The argument is based on Old Testament exposition and is interspersed with exhortations and warnings. The argument is that Christ is superior to the prophets (1:1–4), angels (1:5–2:18), Moses (3:1–6), and Joshua (4:1–11) in his revelation of God, and greater than the Levitical priesthood in his ministry of mediation and sacrifice for sin (4:14–10:18). The exposition serves exhortation, as the latter is the author's immediate purpose for writing.

In 10:19–13:17 the author largely exhorts his readers to steadfast faith, hope, and holiness, but with an interspersing of Old Testament exposition and warnings. Throughout the book the author alternates between exhortation and exposition, warning and encouragement in order to help a small community of Jewish believers to avoid a spiritual disaster.

For this reason the warning passages are not digressions nor parentheses in the author's thought and purpose. Rather, the intertwining of exposition and practical exhortation form an integral part of the book's structure. When we consider that Hebrews was something like a written sermon "intended to be read to a congregation, the force of these warning passages becomes even more obvious" (Marshall, 1969, 139). I. H. Marshall (1969, 137–57) identifies five warning passages (2:1–4; 3:7–4:13; 5:11–6:20; 10:19–39; 12:12–13:19). W. Lane (1991, 1:ci) also finds five warnings but identifies them slightly differently (2:1–4; 3:7–19; 5:11–6:12; 10:19–39; 12:14–29). I have subdivided two of the longer passages where the hortatory warnings are essentially two instead of one and thus find a total of seven (see "Outline"). As Marshall points out (1969, 137), the warnings "appear to teach the possibility of backsliding and apostasy in the Christian life." Though these passages present apostasy as a "real" possibility, the author's goal is to inspire in his readers a persevering faith and confident trust in Christ.

OUTLINE

Part One: The Argument: Christ and His Provision of Redemption Is Superior to Judaism (1:1–10:18)

1. Christ's Supremacy As the Full Revelation of God (1:1–4:13)

- **1.1.** Superior to the Prophets (1:1–4)
- **1.2.** Superior to the Angels (1:5–14; 2:5–18)
  - **1.2.1.** Superior to the Angels in His Nature (1:5–14)
  - **First Hortatory Warning: The Peril of Spiritual Drifting** (2:1–4)
  - **1.2.2.** Superior to the Angels in His Redemptive Mission (2:5–18)
- **1.3.** Superior to Moses (3:1–6)
  - **1.3.1.** Superior to Moses in Relation to His Task (3:1–4)
  - **1.3.2.** Superior to Moses in Rank and Authority (3:5–6)
  - **Second Hortatory Warning: The Snare of Unbelief** (3:7–19)
- **1.4.** Superior to Joshua (4:1–13)
  - **1.4.1.** Superior to Joshua in the Rest Provided (4:1–5)
  - **1.4.2.** Exhortation to Enter His Rest (4:6–13)

2. Christ's Supremacy As the One Mediator Between God and Humankind (4:14–10:18)

- **2.1.** Superior to Aaron and the Levitical Order in His Qualifications to Be High Priest (4:14–7:28)
  - **2.1.1.** Superior to Aaron and the Levitical Order in His Ability to Understand and Help Humanity (4:14–16)

2.1.2. Superior to Aaron and the Levitical Order in His Divine Appointment and Godly Life (5:1–10)

Third Hortatory Warning: The Danger of Remaining Spiritually Immature (5:11–6:3)

Fourth Hortatory Warning: The Fearful Possibility of Irretrievable Apostasy (6:4–20)

2.1.3. Superior to Aaron and the Levitical Order in His Likeness to Melchizedek (7:1–10)

2.1.4. Superior to Aaron and the Levitical Order in His Abiding Permanence (7:11–25)

2.1.5. Superior to Aaron and the Levitical Order in His Perfection As the Son (7:26–28)

2.2. Superior to Aaron and the Levitical Order in His Ministry As High Priest (8:1–10:18)

2.2.1. Superior to Aaron and the Levitical Order Because His Ministry Is Located in a Better Sanctuary (8:1–5)

2.2.2. Superior to Aaron and the Levitical Order Because His Ministry Is Based on a Better Covenant (8:6–13)

2.2.3. Superior to Aaron and the Levitical Order Because His Ministry Is Performed Through a Better Priestly Service (9:1–22)

2.2.4. Superior to Aaron and the Levitical Order Because His Ministry Is Fulfilled by a Better Sacrifice (9:23–10:18)

Part Two: The Application: Exhortation to Steadfastness (10:19–13:17)

3. The Challenge to Remain Steadfast in Faith (10:19–11:40)

3.1. Faith and New Covenant Worshipers (10:19–25)

Fifth Hortatory Warning: The Seriousness of Deliberate Sin and Its Consequences (10:26–31)

3.2. The Righteous Must Live By Faith (10:32–39)

3.2.1. Past Victory (10:32–34)

3.2.2. Present Challenge (10:35–39)

3.3. Essential Characteristics of Faith (11:1–3)

3.4. Examples of Faith From the Old Testament (11:4–38)

3.4.1. Faith During the Antediluvian Period (11:4–7)

3.4.2. Faith From the Patriarchal Period (11:8–22)

3.4.3. Faith During the Exodus Era (11:23–29)

3.4.4. Faith During the Conquest (11:30–31)

3.4.5. Faith From the Time of the Judges, the Davidic Kingdom, and Beyond (11:32–38)

3.5. Faith and the Fulfillment of the Promise (11:39–40)

4. The Call to Persevere As Sons (12:1–13)

4.1. The Incentive of Their Forefathers' Example (12:1)

4.2. The Incentive of Christ's Example (12:2–3)

4.3. The Incentive of Their Father-Son Relationship to God (12:4–11)

4.3.1. The Lord's Discipline Is Part of the Father's Love (12:4–6a)

4.3.2. The Lord's Discipline Relates to Sonship and Training (12:6b–8)

4.3.3. The Proper Attitude Toward the Lord's Discipline Is Submission (12:9)

4.3.4. The Goal of the Lord's Discipline Involves Sanctification and Character (12:10–11)

4.4. Community Commitment to Finish the Race (12:12–13)

5. The Ongoing Commitment to Live Holy Lives Under the Covenant of Grace (12:14–13:17)

5.1. The Priority of Holiness (12:14–29)

5.1.1. Practical Holiness of Life Is a Foundational Issue (12:14)

Sixth Hortatory Warning: The Danger of Falling Short of God's Grace (12:15–17)

5.1.2. Incentives for Holy Living Under the New Covenant (12:18–24)

Seventh Hortatory Warning: The Folly of Refusing God and His Kingdom (12:25–29)

5.2. The Practice of Holiness (13:1–17)

5.2.1. Demonstrate Practical Love (13:1–3)

5.2.2. Maintain Marital Fidelity and Sexual Purity (13:4)

5.2.3. Stay Free of Material Lust and Greed (13:5–6)

5.2.4. Hold to the Sound Teaching of the Gospel (13:7–12)

5.2.5. Joyfully Bear the Reproach of Christ (13:13–16)

5.2.6. Properly Respect Your Spiritual Leaders (13:17)

6. Conclusion (13:18–25)

6.1. Final Request (13:18–19)

6.2. Final Benediction (13:20–21)

6.3. Final Exhortation (13:22–23)

6.4. Final Greetings and Blessing (13:24–25)

COMMENTARY

Part One: The Argument: Christ and His Provision of Redemption Is Superior to Judaism (1:1–10:18)

In Hebrews 1:1–10:18, the author establishes first that Jesus, as God's messianic Son (1:5; Ps. 2:7), is the full and complete revelation of God to the Jewish people. He shows respect for the Old Testament revelation and mentions that the Jews ("our forefathers," Heb. 1:1) were singled out in many ways to receive God's special revelation of himself. Nonetheless, Old Testament revelation was partial and temporary; now a new epoch ("these last days," 1:2) has dawned with the appearance of God's Son; he is the ultimate and complete revelation of God in history. Hebrews goes on to contrast various aspects of the partial and incomplete Old Testament revelation (involving the prophets, angelic messengers, Moses, Joshua, etc.) with God's Son (1:1–4:13), and thereby indicates the supremacy and finality of God's revelation in Christ.

Moreover, Jesus is vastly superior as God's eternal high priest (Heb. 5:6; 7:17–18; Ps. 110:4) to the whole Old Testament Levitical order of ministry and worship, which was a temporary provision that anticipated future fulfillment in God's Son (4:14–10:18). The key word of Hebrews is "better" (used thirteen times). Since Jesus is superior to the angels and all Old Testament mediators, he offers a better rest, covenant, hope, priesthood, sacrifice for sin, promises, and approach to God. Even when comparative terms are absent in Hebrews, the author's argument takes the form of a comparison (e.g., 2:2–4; 3:3–6a; 5:4–10; 10:26–29; 12:25).

1. Christ's Supremacy As the Full Revelation of God (1:1–4:13)

1.1. Superior to the Prophets (1:1–4)

These four magnificent verses form a single, powerful sentence in Greek and introduce the entire book of Hebrews. They contain a capsule summary of almost everything that the author will expound on concerning the supremacy of Jesus as the Son of God in his dual role of Revealer and Redeemer.

Had God remained silent and not spoken, the human race would have perished in the darkness of sin and ignorance. Fortunately for us, God chose to speak by progressively revealing himself, first in Old Testament times and finally in his Son. Hebrews eloquently opens with an elaborate and carefully constructed sentence that begins with a participial phrase (1:1), main clause (1:2a), and two subordinate clauses (1:2b) with God as the subject, followed by two subordinate clauses and further participial phrases with the Son as the subject (1:3–4) (Ellingworth, 1993, 89). The eloquent alliteration and assonance in verse 1 is impossible to reproduce fully in English. The initial words—*polymeros* and *polytropos*—are two alliterative adverbs with the prefix "*poly*," meaning "many." These two words literally mean "in many parts and in many ways."

Weymouth's translation expresses well the meaning of verse 1: "God, who of old spoke to our forefathers in many fragments and by various methods through the prophets." God's revelation of himself in Old Testament times came "in many fragments" because it was progressively given bit by bit to first one prophet and then another; it was also spoken to and through the prophets, using a wide variety of methods.

> He spoke to Moses in the burning bush (Exod. 3:2ff.), to Elijah in a still, small voice (I Kings 19:12ff.), to Isaiah in a vision in the Temple (Isa. 6:1ff.), to

> Hosea in his family circumstances (Hos. 1:2), and to Amos in a basket of summer fruit (Amos 8:1). God ... convey[ed] his message through visions and dreams, through angels, through Urim and Thummim, through symbols, natural events, ecstasy, a pillar of fire, smoke, or other means. (Morris, 1981, 12)

Yet all of this "did not add up to the fullness of what God had to say" (Bruce, 1990, 46). God's revelatory word was incomplete until God revealed himself fully in his Son.

The author of Hebrews draws two important contrasts in his opening statement. (1) "In the past" (*palai*, lit., "of old," not simply "formerly") (1:1a) is contrasted with "in these last days" (1:2a). God's revelation of himself has deep roots in the days of old, the time of "our forefathers," which is synonymous with the Old Testament era. "These last days" refers to the time of the Messiah, when the Lord brought "great salvation" to his people (cf. 2:3). The New Testament reveals that the "last days" were inaugurated with the incarnation of Christ and will be consummated at his second coming. Thus the phrase "these last [*eschatou*, from which we get *eschatological*] days" means that with Jesus the messianic age has begun and God is speaking climactically, definitively, and finally in his Son. "Any further speaking about what remains to happen in the future is but the elaboration of what has already begun" (Hagner, 1983, 2).

(2) "Through the prophets" (1:1) is contrasted with "by his Son" (1:2). There is both continuity and discontinuity in Jesus with God's earlier Old Testament revelation. There is *continuity* in that the same God who spoke through the Old Testament prophets has also spoken "by his Son." The former revelation was a preparation for the latter revelation, and the latter was the fulfillment of the former. "God's word spoken in his Son is continuous with, and not alien to, what has preceded" (Hagner, 1983, 1). But there is also *discontinuity* in Jesus with the Old Testament prophets because of his nature as the Son. The Greek includes neither the definite article nor a possessive pronoun with the word "Son." This does not mean, however, that Jesus was simply one son among many. Rather, it stresses that God's ultimate revelation came through "one who is Son" (Westcott, 1889/1980, 7). It is the Son's Sonship, his unique nature as Son that is stressed here.

That the author speaks of Jesus as the incomparable and unique Son is made immediately clear in the various revelations about him in 1:2b–3. The prophets were simply God's servants, but for his ultimate revelation to humankind, God chose his Son (cf. Mark 12:1–12). The prophets were Spirit-anointed individuals of the Word; Jesus is the Anointed One and the Word incarnate. The prophets were Yahweh's messengers; Jesus is the message. The prophets bore God's revelation "in part" (cf. 1 Cor. 13:9); Jesus embodies God's revelatory grace and truth in full measure (cf. John 1:14). And herein resides the essence of the message of Hebrews: God has spoken in his Son at the end of the age in a full and complete way so that there must be no turning away from him.

The Christ-revelation is superior to the Old Testament revelation not just because it came last or at the end of an era, but because of the "transcendent character of the person, the rank, the status, and the authority of Him through whom and in whom it comes" (W. Manson, 1951, 89). The author uses seven glorious phrases to describe the true nature of Jesus as the Son of God (1:2b–4), revealing him as the highest revelation that God can give. These phrases constitute one of the most comprehensive Christological statements in the New Testament.

(1) God has appointed him as "heir of all things" (1:2b). This fulfills the messianic promise in Psalm 2:8. Heirship is related to Sonship; since he is the only Son, he is the sole heir of all creation, which exists because of him as the agent of creation and for him as the heir of creation. Two special observations are important theologically. (a) "Appointed [*etheken*] heir" does not mean there was a time when he was not heir; *etheken* (a Greek aorist) must be viewed as timeless. "It is the present reality of the appointment that the writer is concerned about, and not about when it was made.... There was never a time when the Son was not the heir" (Guthrie, 1983, 64–65). (b) The concept of "heir" does not suggest the death of the Father for it to be activated. "The term [heir] points to lawful possession but without indicating in what way that possession is secured" (Morris, 1981, 13).

(2) The Son was God's agent "through whom he made the universe" (1:2c). The phrase "the universe" literally means "the ages" and refers to "the whole created universe of space and time" (Bruce, 1990, 47). This corresponds to other New Testament declarations that the eternal Son was the active agent in creation: "Through him all things were made; without him nothing was made that has been made" (John 1:3); "for by him all things were created: things in heaven and on earth . . . all things were created by him and for him" (Col. 1:16). God created everything outside himself through the Son and for the Son. Thus, the Son has the place of preeminence in the beginning (in creation) and at the end (in inheritance).

(3) "The Son is the radiance of God's glory" (Heb. 1:3a). The Greek word *apaugasma* (only here in the New Testament), if used passively, means "reflection" (RSV, NRSV)—a shining forth of a brightness from without. Here, however, it is used in the active meaning of "radiance" (NIV, NASB)—an outshining because of brightness within—as is confirmed by most of the early church fathers (*TDNT*, 1:508).

Apaugasma was a Hellenistic word used by Philo and the author of an intertestamental book called Wisdom of Solomon. They use it of the sun and its rays as an analogy of how the transcendent God could manifest himself in the world. In the New Testament, Jesus, God's Son, is "the light of the world" (John 9:5) and as such is the radiance of God's glory, just as the ray is the light of the sun (cf. John 1:4–5, 9). In similar language, Paul assures us that God has "made his light shine in our hearts to give us the light of the knowledge of the glory of God in the face of Christ" (2 Cor. 4:6). To radiate God's glory in this way "presupposes that the Son shares the same essence as the Father, not just his likeness" (Guthrie, 1983, 66).

(4) This is made clear in the next phrase of our author: The Son is "the exact representation of [God's] being" (Heb. 1:3b). *Charakter*, the Greek word for "exact representation" (used only here in the New Testament), refers to the impression or mark that an engraving stamp left on a wax seal or coin. The correspondence between the engraved impression and engraving stamp is exact. Likewise, the Son, who radiates God's glory, does so because he shares God's nature.

The word *hypostasis* ("being") refers to the essence, the underlying reality, the very nature of a thing or a person. In other words, the Son is of one essence with the Father. Thus Jesus could say, "Anyone who has seen me has seen the Father" (John 14:9). He is the exact "image of God" (2 Cor. 4:4), "the [visible] image of the invisible God" (Col. 1:15), and "the fullness of the Deity . . . in bodily form" (2:9). Whatever God is in his character, nature, or essence, Jesus is the "exact representation." Therefore, God's revelation of himself is no longer fragmentary and incomplete as in Old Testament times; in the person of Jesus the revelation of the Father is full and complete.

(5) As the Son was in the beginning the active agent in creation, so in the present he is the one "sustaining all things by his powerful word" (Heb. 1:3a). Philosophers through the ages have been prone to ask questions like: "What is the underlying reality in the universe?" "What is the dynamic that sustains all that exists and causes our solar system to continue in an orderly pattern?" Paul's answer was that in Christ "all things hold together" (Col. 1:17). Likewise, the author of Hebrews declares that the Son sustains "all things," and then adds "by his powerful word." Morris notes: "Nothing is excluded from the scope of the Son's sustaining activity. The author pictures the Son as in the first instance active in creation and then as continuing his interest in the world he loves and bearing it onwards toward the fulfillment of the divine plan. And this he does 'by his powerful word'" (1981, 14). The "word" (*rhema*) is regarded as being active and powerful. It was the creative power of his word that called the universe into existence; as a complement "all things" created are sustained by the awesome power of his word and carried along forward to the final goal.

(6) The eternal Son—who in the divine ordering of the universe is its Creator, Sustainer, and End—"became flesh and made his dwelling among us" (John 1:14) for the purpose of providing "purification for sins" (Heb. 1:3d). An answer to the problem of sin has been the agelong quest of all religions (Guthrie, 1983, 67). The fact that the Son of God came to deal decisively with the sin problem is an issue that powerfully grips our author and becomes a major focus of this sermon. "Purification" (*katharismos*) means cleansing

or removal of sin along with its defiling effect. This purification or cleansing was provided for in Jesus' death as the "once-for-all-time" sacrifice for sin.

The verb "provided" is in the aorist tense and points to past action that is complete. The term for "sin" (*hamartia*) occurs twenty-five times in Hebrews, a total exceeded only by the forty-eight times in Romans. Hebrews makes clear that the old covenant sacrifices, which had to be repeated continually, were inadequate to deal with the problem of *hamartia*. Only the blood of Jesus could purge our sins. Thus Jesus' "purification for sins" rightly belongs with the six other phrases that describe his uniqueness as Son in relationship to God.

(7) The final great declaration about the Son is that after the event of purification was completed, "he sat down at the right hand of the Majesty in heaven" (1:3e). The exaltation of the Son as he sits enthroned at the Father's right hand, the place of honor and authority, involves a threefold testimony: (a) His work of purification for sin is finished and complete; (b) the Son is indeed the promised Messiah (Ps. 110:1; this messianic Psalm also establishes the nature of his priestly role, as Hebrews later emphasizes); and (c) his present activity in heaven includes his ministry as mediator between God and humankind (Heb. 7:23–25), whereby he provides free access to God's presence and grace (4:14–16). All three truths are elaborated in Hebrews.

These seven brief power-packed phrases reveal that God's complete revelation in his Son comes not just in what he says, but in who he is. He is the perfect embodiment of the three main Old Testament offices: As *the prophet* (cf. Acts 3:22–23), he speaks God's ultimate word; as our *high priest*, he provides the perfect mediation and cleansing for sin; and as the *messianic king*, he reigns with God at his right hand.

Verse 4 is transitional, concluding the thought in 1:3e about Jesus being superior to the prophets because of his ascension to God's right hand and introducing what follows about his being superior to the angels. Two things seem surprising when we first read this verse, namely, that the Son "became" superior to the angels and that he "inherited" a name superior to theirs. The Son as described in 1:2–3 is clearly *eternally* superior to the angels in both his person and his name. In what sense then did he "become" superior and "inherit" a better name? The answer relates to his human role of humiliation and to his subsequent exaltation (mentioned in 1:3).

Philippians 2:6–11 is the best commentary to explain the content and relationship of Hebrews 1:3d-e and 1:4. The eternal Son "being in very nature God" (Phil. 2:6) and therefore superior to the angels, voluntarily emptied himself of the glory and prerogatives that were rightfully his from eternity, took the very nature of a human being and a servant and was "obedient to death—even death on a cross" (2:7–8), in order to provide "purification for sins" (Heb. 1:3). Afterwards, however "God exalted him to the highest place" (Phil 2:9a), where "he sat down at the right hand of the Majesty in heaven" (Heb. 1:3). At that time, the incarnate Son, Jesus, "became" much superior to the angels in heaven.

Moreover, God gave the incarnate Son "the name that is above every name, that at the name of Jesus every knee should bow, in heaven [including angels] and on earth and under the earth, and every tongue confess that Jesus Christ is Lord, to the glory of God the Father" (Phil. 2:9b–11). In summary, the content of Hebrews 1:4 connects directly with the declaration made at the end of 1:3 about the Son's ascension to the Father's right hand. As a result of his ascension, he is given a unique status and an honored name that clearly marks him as superior to the angels.

1.2. Superior to the Angels (1:5–14; 2:5–18)

Angels were highly esteemed by the Jews (and Christians) because they lived in closest proximity to God and participated as heavenly messengers in revealing God's purposes to his people. Angels had even played an important role in the giving of the Old Testament covenant (2:2; cf. Deut. 33:2; Acts 7:53; Gal. 3:19). Perhaps the Jewish believers to whom Hebrews was originally addressed had a deficient understanding of the Incarnation and tended to esteem angels on a par with Jesus himself. Or perhaps the logic of some of the readers was along this line: Humanity has been created a little lower than the angels; Jesus was a man; therefore, Jesus is lower than the angels. Thus, Hebrews everywhere emphasizes an exalted view of Christ as deity, even while at the same time placing great importance on the real humanity of Jesus. Here our author elaborates about Jesus' superiority to the angels in his nature (Heb. 1:5–14) and in his redemptive mission (2:5–18). Between these two discourses lies his first hortatory warning (2:1–4).

1.2.1. Superior to the Angels in His Nature (1:5–14). Our author makes clear assertions about the supremacy of the Son over angels by appealing to seven Old Testament passages as scriptural authority and confirming evidence. Among the passages cited (five are from the Psalms), some were viewed as messianic in Jewish writings; others were understood to be messianic by the church in view of what God "has spoken . . . by his Son" (1:2a).

Our author cites these seven Old Testament passages as having prophetic significance in at least three ways: (1) God himself is presently speaking from the passages (i.e., Scripture is viewed as the voice of God); (2) what was partially fulfilled in an Old Testament historical context is now interpreted according to its fuller long-range prophetic meaning in connection with the Messiah (Old Testament prophecy often had this feature of an immediate and long-range fulfillment); and (3) passages that during Old Testament times were understood as describing Yahweh are prophetically applied to his Son (cf. the author's contrast of partial Old Testament revelation with the full and complete revelation in Christ [1:1–2a]).

The fact that the author makes his point about the Son's superiority to the angels by simply quoting (without interpretation) the Old Testament passages as accumulative evidence may indicate that these were all commonly regarded as messianic prophecies in the early church. Note that the original apostles initially got their Christocentric interpretation of the Old Testament from their risen Lord himself (cf. Luke 24:25–27, 32, 45–49; Acts 1:2–3). Added to this was the Spirit-given understanding of the Old Testament that came as a consequence of the post-Pentecost fullness of the Spirit of revelation (particularly to the apostles and writers of New Testament Scripture). Therefore, the Old Testament passages cited in Hebrews 1 were not arbitrarily chosen "proof texts" by the author; they have been drawn from a rich treasury of Old Testament messianic Scripture.

(1) The first quotation (1:5) is from Psalm 2:7: "You are my Son; today I have begotten you" (lit. trans.; cf. KJV, NASB, NKJV, NRSV). Though the angels were sometimes collectively called "the sons of God," none of them was ever singled out and given the status "Son of God." The Jews came to realize that Psalm 2

THE "GREATER THANS" IN HEBREWS

One of the author's main points in Hebrews is that Jesus is greater than all those things associated with the Jewish religion and way of life. Sometimes he actually uses the word "greater than"; sometimes he does not. But in all cases the theme is clear.

Theme	Passage in Hebrews
Jesus is greater than the prophets	1:1–3
Jesus is greater than the angels	1:4–14; 2:5
Jesus is greater than Moses	3:1–6
Jesus is greater than Joshua	4:6–11
Jesus is greater than the high priest	5:1–10; 7:26–8:2
Jesus is greater than the Levitical priests	6:20–7:25
Jesus as the high priest after Melchizedek is greater than Abraham	7:1–10
Jesus' ministry is greater than the tabernacle ministry	8:3–6; 9:1–28
Jesus' new covenant is greater than the old covenant	8:7–13
Jesus' sacrifice is greater than OT sacrifices	10:1–14
Experiencing Jesus is greater than the experience on Mount Sinai	12:18–24

had only an imperfect or partial application to David and that it "would be most fully realized in the Messiah of David's line who would rise up in the time of fulfillment" (Bruce, 1990, 53). When the Father spoke from heaven at Jesus' baptism (Mark 1:11 and parallels) and later at his transfiguration (Mark 9:7 and parallels), he incorporated the Psalm 2:7 phrase: "You are my Son." Clearly the early church understood Psalm 2 to be a messianic prophecy that was fulfilled in Jesus (see Acts 13:33).

"Today" may refer to Jesus' incarnation, resurrection, or enthronement at the Father's right hand. The author of Hebrews is more concerned about "the significance of the begetting in terms of the Son's status ... than to tie it down to a specific occasion" (Guthrie, 1983, 73).

(2) The next quotation (2 Sam. 7:14) also emphasizes the Father-Son relationship and "marks the Messiah as distinct from the creator-creature relationship between God and the angels" (ibid., 73). The words had an immediate, partial fulfillment in Solomon as David's son who was chosen to build the first temple. But its long-range prophetic significance was not fulfilled until David's greater Son, Jesus the messianic Son of David, came.

The many references in the Gospels to Jesus as the "Son of David" clearly identify him with the Davidic covenant given in 2 Samuel 7 and as the Davidic Messiah. The New Testament witness is that salvation has come in God's Son, "who as to his human nature was a descendant of David, and who through the Spirit of holiness was declared with power to be the Son of God by his resurrection from the dead" (Rom. 1:3–4)—making him infinitely greater than the angels. Evidence from the Dead Sea Scrolls indicates that some non-Christian Jewish groups in the first century also interpreted 2 Samuel 7:14 as messianic.

(3) The third quotation is from Deuteronomy 32:43 in the Septuagint (though Ps. 97:7 bears a close resemblance): "Let all God's angels worship him." The time frame for this worship by angels is described in the words that precede the quote: "when God brings his firstborn into the world." Clearly the "firstborn" refers to the Son of the previous verses. He is the "firstborn" not because he was a created being, but because he is the heir of all things as the sovereign Lord over all creation (cf. Col. 1:15). "Firstborn" refers to being "first in position," "supreme." In Psalm 89:27 "firstborn" is used of David's position as king—although he was not the firstborn son of Jesse—because he was "first in position" as ruler. The eternal son is "first in position" as the supreme ruler of all creation.

The point at which God's firstborn comes into the world must refer to the Incarnation when Jesus Christ was born in Bethlehem and the angels of God worshiped him (Luke 2:1–20). Our author considered this conclusive evidence that the angels themselves regarded Jesus—although human born—to be superior as the Son of God. Note that the original context of the third quotation (Deut. 32:43; Ps 97:7) involved the worship of Yahweh. In its long-range prophetic fulfillment, Hebrews 1:6 identifies the Son clearly as the object of worship and thus as one with Yahweh of the Old Testament. This identification is yet more evidence of the Son's deity and superiority to the angels.

(4) The fourth quotation, from Psalm 104:4 (in the LXX)—"He makes his angels winds, his servants flames of fire"—further emphasizes the point of the Son's supremacy by showing that the function of angels (glorious as it is) is inferior to his (1:8–9). The Jewish Targum describes angels as God's messengers who carry out his bidding as swiftly as the wind and as mightily as flaming fire (see Morris, 1981, 19). The description of angels as "winds" and "flames of fire" does reveal, however, that their function is transitory. They serve as heavenly messengers dispatched from God's throne, whereas the Son rules with the Father at the throne "for ever and ever" (1:8).

(5) The next quotation (from Psalm 45:6–7) is introduced as referring prophetically to the Son, who is introduced as God ("Your throne, O God," Heb. 1:8), thus underscoring further the deity of the Son. "God" is best understood in the vocative case here and again in the phrase "God, your God, has set you above your companions" (1:9). Most likely Psalm 45 was composed to be sung at the royal wedding of an Israelite king. The Davidic king as God's theocratic representative was on occasion referred to hyperbolically as *Elohim*, "God" (see *FLSB* note on Ps. 82:6). The ultimate fulfillment, however, can only be in the messianic king, *the* Son of David, who sits enthroned at the Father's right hand. "What

was symbolically true of the ancient Hebrew monarch only by virtue of his office, the writer of Hebrews sees to be wholly true of Christ by virtue of His nature" (Hawthorne, 1986, 1507).

The Son's place as supreme ruler is indicated by references to his everlasting "throne," "scepter," "kingdom," standard of "righteousness," and "anointing" above all others. As part of his nature as the Son, he "loved righteousness and hated wickedness" (*anomia*; lit., "lawlessness") more perfectly than anyone else. He did not just "love righteousness" or just "hate wickedness"; that he demonstrated both with equal intensity is stated as the basis for his great anointing as "the Anointed One" (Heb. "Messiah"; Gk. "Christ"). Those described as the Son's "companions" are probably the "many sons" of Hebrews 2:10, whom the "first-in-position" Son is not ashamed to call "brothers" (2:11). "Their joy is great because of their companionship with him, but his is greater still" (Bruce, 1990, 61).

(6) The sixth quotation, from Psalm 102:25–27 (in the LXX), is the longest of the seven. The words quoted applied originally to Yahweh in the Old Testament; here they find their fulfillment in the Son and call attention to his eternality and supremacy over creation (cf. Heb. 1:2). The psalmist, who in his affliction prays to Yahweh, is oppressed by his own brevity of life and the perishable nature of the material heavens and earth. He praises Yahweh, however, as constituting "the permanence and security that he so painfully lacks" (Hagner, 1983, 14). The author of Hebrews considers these words as prophetically applicable to the Son in view of his part in creation (cf. 1:10 with 1:2). Though the material universe seems substantial and permanent, it will eventually wear out like a suit of clothes (1:11) and then "be changed" (1:12a). But the Son stands in bold contrast to the transitory character of the created order: "They will perish, but you remain" (1:11a); "they will all wear out. . . . But you remain the same, and your years will never end" (1:11b–12c). The Son is extolled as God—unchanging and eternal.

(7) The final quotation is from Psalm 110:1, to which our author alluded earlier (1:3) when speaking about the Son's enthronement at the Father's right hand in heaven. The following significant observations are noteworthy about this verse and psalm. (a) Psalm 110 was regarded as messianic by both first-century Judaism and the early church. It is doubly important for our author, who sees in it not only a prophetic declaration that the Messiah will be a king like David, but also he will be a priest like Melchizedek (cf. Ps. 110:4 with Heb. 5:6–10; 7:1–28).

(b) The revelation that the Son was enthroned (as in Ps. 110:1) was the ultimate contrast between him and the angels. At no time did God ever say to an angel: "Sit at my right hand until I make your enemies a footstool for your feet" (Heb. 1:13). In 1:3 and 10:12–13, the Son's enthronement and victory come after and are linked to his once-for-all-time sacrifice for sin.

(c) In Scripture the angels are depicted as bowing or standing before God as worshipers and servants (cf. Dan. 7:10; Luke 1:19; Rev. 8:2); that the Son is described as being seated at the Father's side in honor and authority is indisputable evidence of his superiority to the angels.

(d) The fact that the Son presently reigns with the Father at the throne, though strangely his enemies are not yet "a footstool" under his feet, speaks of "the already-but-not-yet" tension in the message of the gospel. Although decisive victory has occurred *already* in Jesus' death-resurrection-ascension, there is also a future fulfillment of that victory that is *not yet* realized and awaits his second coming (cf. Heb. 9:28). God will render all Christ's enemies utterly powerless in that one final completion of his victory (cf. Rev. 19:11–21).

Our author, having made his point about the Son's superiority, does not wish to belittle the function of God's angels (Heb. 1:14). They worship God in heaven (Isa. 6:1–4; Rev. 5:11–12; 7:11–12), do his will (Ps. 103:20), behold his face (Matt. 18:10), are superior to humans (Heb. 2:6–7), and inhabit heaven (Mark 13:32; Gal. 1:8). Their primary activity in relation to earth, however, is their participation in Christ's redemptive mission (see Matt. 1:20–24; 2:13; 28:2; Luke 1–2; Acts 1:10; Rev. 14:6–7) and their service to "those who will inherit salvation" (Heb. 1:14).

In this capacity angels rejoice over one sinner who repents (Luke 15:10), serve on behalf of God's people (Dan. 3:25; 6:22; Matt. 18:10; Heb. 1:14), observe the life of the Christian congregation (1 Cor. 11:10; Eph. 3:10; 1 Tim.

5:21), bring messages from God (Zech. 1:14–17; Acts 10:1–8; 27:23–24), bring answers to prayer (Dan. 9:21–23; Acts 10:4), appear in dreams to believers (Matt. 1:20; 2:13, 19), sometimes help interpret prophetic dreams and visions (Dan. 7:15–16), strengthen God's people in trials (Matt. 4:11; Luke 22:43), protect saints who fear God and hate evil (Ps. 34:7; 91:11; Dan. 6:22; Acts 12:7–10), punish those who are God's enemies (2 Kings 19:35; Acts 12:23; Rev. 14:17–16:21), fight against the demonic (Rev. 12:7–9), and carry the saved to heaven (Luke 16:22) (*FLSB*, 340).

In summary, our author's seven Old Testament quotations confirm that the Son is the Messiah, the object of angelic worship, sovereign Lord over creation, and enthroned in heaven (after providing salvation by his sacrifice for sin, Heb. 1:3). Behind 1:14 is the understanding that the Son is the Savior (cf. 2:9–10); the angels are "ministering spirits," commissioned by God to serve those who are to inherit his salvation. In the remainder of Hebrews, the author will describe the role of Jesus on our behalf in providing salvation and the role of persevering faith on our part in relation to him.

First Hortatory Warning: The Peril of Spiritual Drifting (2:1–4)

This is the first of seven passages in Hebrews (see Outline) where the author combines urgent exhortation and solemn warning in order to move his readers to a place of renewed confidence, hope, and persevering faith in Christ. These seven warnings are not digressions, but relate directly to the author's main purpose. The close connection between this paragraph and the exposition in 1:5–14 demonstrates that scriptural exposition for our author was not an end in itself but rooted out of his concern for his readers and their perilous situation.

The author's rich vocabulary and gifts as an orator are evident again. The Greek construction of 2:1–4 consists of two sentences: a direct statement (2:1), followed by a long explanatory sentence (2:2–4), which includes a rhetorical question ("how shall we escape") with a condition ("if we ignore [or neglect] such a great salvation") (2:3a).

The word "therefore" (2:1) connects this paragraph to the Son's incomparable splendor and supremacy in chapter 1. Because the Son is superior to the prophets and the angels, what God "has spoken to us by his Son" (1:2), if neglected, makes one that much more culpable: "We must pay more careful attention, therefore, to what we have heard" lest we "drift away."

The expression "what we have heard" refers to God's revelation in his Son about salvation (cf. 2:3a). Here the danger of drifting away is due not to a rebellious refusal to heed the gospel, but to a carelessness about the commitment to Christ that it requires. The verb *prosecho* (lit., "to give heed") means not only "pay attention" with the mind to what one hears, but also "to act upon what one perceives" (Morris, 1981, 21). This verb is analogous to *katecho* in 3:6, 14; 10:23, where the readers are admonished to "*hold fast* to their confession of faith, without which the goal of salvation cannot be reached" (Lane, 1991, 37).

The Greek word translated "drift away" (*pararreo*) has nautical overtones, as when a ship drifts past a harbor to shipwreck. The picture thus conveyed in 2:1 is that of Christians who are "in peril of being carried downstream past a fixed landing place and so failing to gain its security" (Bruce, 1990, 66). The result of drifting from Christ is a worse end than that experienced by those who disobeyed the law of Moses under the old covenant (vv. 2–3; cf. 10:28). As Bruce notes, "our author is warning Christian readers, who have heard and accepted the gospel, that if they yield to the temptation to abandon their profession, their plight is hopeless" (1990, 66).

"The message spoken by angels" (2:2) refers to the law given at Sinai. Here we begin to see the primary reason why the Son's superiority to the angels was emphasized in 1:5–14. The author makes an a fortiori argument (i.e., arguing from a lesser, well-accepted truth to a greater truth, for which there is even stronger evidence) from angels to the Son, from law to gospel (cf. 7:21–22; 9:13–14; 10:28–29). The angels were of instrumental importance in the lesser matter of the law; the Son is of supreme importance in the greater matter of the gospel (Hagner, 1983, 21). If the law accompanied by angels was honored, how much more should we respect God's word that came in his Son! If "every violation and disobedience" of the law had inescapable consequences, how can we hope to escape the consequences of ignoring the gospel of Christ? Our author writes "to awaken the conscience to the grave consequences of neglecting" God's message in his Son (Guthrie, 1983, 80).

The answer to the rhetorical question in verse 3—"How shall we escape if we ignore such a great salvation?"—is obvious: No escape is possible. In Hebrews "salvation" (*soteria*) was promised by the Old Testament prophets (1:1), is fulfilled by Jesus in the present time (2:3, 10; 5:9), and will be consummated in his future coming (cf. 1:14; 6:9; 9:28; see *TDNT*, 7:989–1012). Some link the word "escape" with deliverance from the bondage of Satan, the power of sin, and the penalty of death. Although it is certainly true that life without Christ is one of continuing slavery to Satan, sin, and death, the emphasis here and elsewhere in Hebrews is on the inescapable, terrible, and eternal consequences for apostasy (cf. 6:4–6; 10:26–31). The first steps in that catastrophic direction occur when Christians drift away from Christ (2:1) and ignore God's glorious salvation in his Son (2:3a).

The author identifies his readers as fellow believers by using the pronoun "we" in 2:1, 3a and "us" in 2:3. As I. Howard Marshall points out, the warning addresses "people who have heard the gospel and responded to it. At no point in the Epistle is it warrantable to assume that the readers originally addressed by the author are not Christians" (1969, 139). By using the preacher's "we," our author not only identifies the readers as believers, but also includes himself and all other believers in the same warning (cf. 3:6, 14; 10:26–27; 12:25).

The author goes on in 2:3b–4 to enumerate three levels of witness to the great salvation about which Hebrews speaks (cf. Luke 1:1–4). (1) It was announced "by the Lord" himself (2:3b) in his ministry and in his death-resurrection-ascension. Jesus embodied the messianic salvation promised by the prophets and was himself the message that he proclaimed (cf. Mark 1:14–15; Luke 4:18–21). The description here of Jesus as "the Lord" links him with God's name in the Old Testament and thus as the divine Son (1:2–3).

(2) The Lord's message "was confirmed to us by those who heard him" (2:3c)—that is, by eyewitnesses of Jesus' ministry and resurrection, especially the twelve apostles, and by Paul, to whom the Lord himself appeared (cf. 1 Cor. 9:1; 15:8). Two matters are particularly significant in this statement. (a) Our author "is aware of the passage of time, which separates the period of Jesus from his own day" (Lane, 1991, 39). He and his readers ("us") received the gospel not from the Lord himself, but from "those who [had] heard him." Most scholars consider this fact alone as conclusive against Paul being the author of this letter (see Introduction). (b) Jesus' message "was confirmed" by reliable eyewitnesses of Jesus' life-death-resurrection, firsthand witnesses who authenticated the truthfulness of the message and guaranteed its accuracy (cf. Luke 1:2, 4; Acts 1:21–22).

(3) "God also testified" to the validity of the gospel "by signs, wonders and various miracles, and gifts of the Holy Spirit" (2:4). The same signs, wonders, and miracles that occurred during Jesus' earthly ministry (Acts 2:22) continued to happen in the early church from Pentecost onward, as Acts and the New Testament letters testify (Acts 2:43; 4:30; 5:12; 6:8; 14:3; 15:12; 19:11–12; 28:8–9; Rom. 15:19; 2 Cor. 12:12). Not just apostles but also deacons like Stephen and Philip had signs, wonders, and miracles accompany their witness of Christ and proclamation of the gospel (Acts 6:8; 8:6–8). Paul declares that when he preached the gospel at Thessalonica, he did so "not simply with words, but also with power, with the Holy Spirit and with deep conviction" (1 Thess. 1:5).

That this was an expected standard in the early church is evident throughout the New Testament (e.g. ,Mark 16:20; John 14:12–14; 1 Cor. 2:4–5; Gal. 3:5). The charismatic gifts of the Holy Spirit were especially prevalent in the early church as an important aspect of the continuing activity of the Spirit in the body of Christ (Acts 2:4; 10:44–46; 19:6; Rom. 1:11; 1 Cor. 12:4, 7–11; 14:1–5, 26–31; 1 Thess. 5:19–21; 1 Peter 4:10).

The author expresses a high regard for the Holy Spirit's presence and ministry here and elsewhere in Hebrews (cf. Heb. 3:7; 6:4; 9:8, 14; 10:15, 29). He calls attention to both diversity ("distributed") and sovereignty ("according to his will," 2:4) in the function of the Spirit's gifts, an emphasis expressed also by Paul (1 Cor. 12:4, 11). For both writers, the gifts of the Holy Spirit are a sign of present messianic salvation and the reality of Christ as exalted Lord of the church (cf. Acts 2:33, 36; 1 Cor. 12:3; Eph. 4:7–10). Note that supernatural manifestations were sufficiently widespread in the early church that our author could confidently appeal to them as evidence that authenticates the gospel. Bruce observes that such an appeal could not have been made here or by other New Testament writers if the readers had not seen, experienced, or heard of such things (1990, 69).

1.2.2. Superior to the Angels in His Redemptive Mission (2:5–18). This section continues the thought begun in 1:5–14 about the Son's superiority to the angels, but from a different perspective. In chapter 1 the emphasis was on the nature of the Son as deity; here the focus is on his humanity and suffering as necessary components of his redemptive mission. Angels, on the one hand, are servants; their humanward mission as "ministering spirits" is "to serve those who will inherit salvation" (1:14). The Son, on the other hand, is the Savior; his humanward mission as "the author of their salvation" (2:10) is "to save completely those who come to God through him" (7:25). But as Savior, the Son's redemptive mission involved both humiliation and glory. Herein lay a stumbling block for Jewish minds. Angels are superior to human beings, and Jesus was a human being. How then could Jesus who suffered and died truly be superior to the angels?

In addressing this issue, the author of Hebrews makes several points. He first reminds his readers that God has not "subjected the world to come" to angels (2:5). The phrase "world to come" recalls Israel's prophetic hope of a "new heavens and a new earth" (e.g., Isa. 65:17–25), when "the earth will be full of the knowledge of the Lord as the waters cover the sea" (11:9). This time of redemptive fulfillment would be the work of the Davidic Messiah (11:1–10), as a shoot that springs up "from the stump of Jesse" (11:1) or "the Root of Jesse" (11:10). Synonyms in the book of Hebrews for "the world to come" are the promised "rest" of God (Heb. 4:1–11), the heavenly "city with foundations, whose architect and builder is God" (11:10), "a better country—a heavenly one" (11:16), "the heavenly Jerusalem" (12:22), and "the city that is to come" (13:14).

Hebrews indicates, however, that this future promise and reality has begun already with the commencement of "these last days" (1:2) and the enthronement of the Christ at the right hand of God (1:13). By faith "its benefits are being experienced in advance by believers (e.g., 2:4; 6:4–6; 12:22–24) as they await the return of Jesus to bring them into the full enjoyment of the salvation he has already won for them (e.g., 9:28; 10:36–39)" (Peterson, 1994, 1327). This tension between the already (realized eschatology) and the not yet (future eschatology) in Hebrews is summed up in 2:8b: "God left nothing that is not subject to him [Christ]. Yet at present we do not see everything subject to him."

God never subjected the world to come to angels because he appointed his Son to be the "heir of all things" (1:2), a fact that our author sees prophetically anticipated in Psalm 8, from which he now quotes verses 4–6 (in the Septuagint) (Heb. 2:6–8a). The original context of Psalm 8 extols the glory of God in creation (vv. 1–3) and in humans, whom God gave dominion over the rest of creation (vv. 5–8; cf. Gen. 1:26–31; 3:14–19). Because of Satan, sin, and death, however, humankind has been unable to exercise dominion as God originally intended. Thus Psalm 8 is fulfilled perfectly only in one man, Jesus Christ. Since perfect dominion is promised to the Messiah in Psalm 110:1 (our author's favorite psalm), he finds his clue there "to the ultimate meaning and application of Ps. 8:4–6" (Peterson, 1994, 1327). What was true of the first Adam in original creation is now more fully true of Jesus Christ as the last Adam and "head of the new creation and ruler of the world to come" (Bruce, 1990, 72).

The prophetic application of Psalm 8 to Jesus was facilitated by the expression "the son of man" (Heb. 2:6), the title that Jesus himself preferred during his earthly ministry. As Hagner notes, "once the mind turns to Jesus in verse 6, the temporal sequence of incarnation and exaltation can readily be perceived in verse 7" (1983, 25). The statement in 2:8a, "and put everything under his feet," corresponds closely to the messianic passage in Psalm 110:1 (quoted by our author in Heb. 1:13). "Everything" includes his enemies (1:13), and the whole of creation (cf. Eph. 1:22) must ultimately be brought to subjection to the Son.

As the perfect man, Jesus became the true representative of the human race and the ultinate fulfillment of Psalm 8. Only he could fulfill "the declared purpose of the Creator when he brought the human race into being" (Bruce, 1990, 74). But in so doing, he had to identify fully with the human condition, including human suffering (cf. Heb. 4:15–16; 5:8), in order to "blaze the trail of salvation for mankind and to act effectively as his people's high priest in the presence of God. This means that he is not only the one in whom the sovereignty destined for humanity is realized, but also the one who, because of human sin, must realize that sovereignty by way of suffering and death" (Bruce, 1990, 74). Therefore the Son, who has already been introduced as superior to the angels, had to be made "a little lower than the angels" (2:7a) before he could be "crowned ... with glory and honor" (2:7b) as Lord over all things.

In verses 8b–9 our author interprets the words just quoted from Psalm 8. The masculine pronoun "him" in Hebrews 2:8b refers first to humanity and ultimately to Christ (as is true of the entire psalm). But foremost in our author's mind is the prophetic application to Jesus, as 2:9 makes clear. Although God has put all things under the dominion of the Son of Man, Jesus, "yet at present we do not see everything subject to him" (2:8b). What we presently see is Satan, sin, and death as ever-present realities in our fallen world. "But we [also] see Jesus, who was made a little lower than the angels [his incarnation], now crowned with glory and honor [his exaltation] because he suffered death" (2:9; cf. Phil. 2:8–11). Jesus' death and exaltation provide present assurance for believers that all things are already "under his feet" (Heb. 2:8a); his second coming will consummate what was accomplished at the cross (cf. Col. 2:15; 2 Thess. 1:5–10). Note that the name "Jesus" occurs here for the first of thirteen times in Hebrews. It is our author's favorite designation for the Savior and emphasizes his humanity.

Finally in his comments on Psalm 8, our author adds that "by the grace of God [Jesus] ... taste[d] death for everyone" (Heb. 2:9c). Three important truths are succinctly embodied here. (1) Jesus' death on the cross to accomplish salvation was an act of God's grace. (2) His death was on behalf of (*hyper*) every sinner; that his death was a substitutionary atonement for our sin is a clear teaching of Hebrews (cf. 5:1; 7:27). (3) His death was not a "limited atonement"—that is, for a few select people, as some claim—but he provisionally tasted death "for everyone." His death avails for all who by faith submit to him as Lord and Christ (cf. Rom. 10:9–13).

Verse 10 begins in Greek with the words "it was fitting." For Jesus, an innocent man, to be condemned by his nation's leaders, abandoned by his disciples, executed as a criminal by imperial Rome, forsaken by God, and finally left to die in despicable weakness, pain, and disgrace—how could this be fitting or right? To the unenlightened observer in the first century, it was not at all evident how this was anything other than the curse of God or misfortune. To the Jews of that day, "the idea of a suffering Messiah was abhorrent and the Christian claim that it was fitting must be viewed against this background. . . . Whatever the reason for the cross, there is no doubt that it is most revealing of the nature of God. It is in this sense that it was fitting" (Guthrie, 1983, 88).

The description of God as the One "for whom and through whom everything exists" reveals two essential truths: (1) that Jesus' suffering was not an accident of history but rather the purpose of God from the creation of the world (cf. Rev. 13:8), and (2) that God himself initiated the sufferings of Jesus in order to perfect him as "the author of . . . salvation." Only in this way could God accomplish his purpose of "bringing many sons to glory." Jesus had to become human like us (though he was the Son of God from eternity) in order that we could become sons like him (through redemption). Note that God's purpose is to have "many sons," not just a few. To bring them "to glory" points "to the splendour of ultimate salvation" (Montefiore, 1964, 60).

Jesus is "the author of their salvation." The word *archegos* ("author") has two related meanings: (1) leader, ruler, prince, and (2) originator, founder, author. Translators have variously rendered this word as "captain" (KJV, NKJV), "pioneer" (RSV, NRSV), "leader" (Moffatt, Williams, NEB), and "author" (ASV, NASB, NIV). Bruce suggests the essential idea is that of "pathfinder" or "trailblazer"; thus, Jesus "blazed the trail of salvation along which alone God's 'many sons' could be brought to glory" (1990, 80). The word occurs again in 12:2 (also in Acts 3:15; 5:31) in connection with Jesus.

The verb to "make perfect" (*teleioo*) occurs here for the first time in Hebrews and appears frequently throughout the letter (5:9; 7:19, 28; 9:9; 10:1, 14; 11:40; 12:23; other forms of the root are in 5:14; 6:1; 7:11; 9:11; 12:2). The meaning of this prominent word in Hebrews is different when applied to Jesus than when applied to believers. Jesus was already morally and spiritually perfect. The perfect Son became the perfect Savior "through suffering." Here, as elsewhere in the New Testament, the sufferings of Christ and our salvation "are inextricably bound up together" (Guthrie, 1983, 89). His perfect obedience and substitutionary death qualified him to be the perfect representative of humanity and to bear the penalty of sin on our behalf.

Verse 11 reiterates the full identity of God's Son with those he came to redeem. "The one who makes men holy" is Jesus (cf. 9:13; 10:10, 14, 29; 13:12), who, by virtue of sharing a common humanity with us, made possible our sanctification by the sacrifice of his life in obedience to God's will (10:10; cf. Phil. 2:8). "Those who are made holy" are those who are redeemed by his blood from sin's guilt and power (Heb. 13:12; cf. Rom. 6) and who are thereby set apart as the special people of God (cf. 1 Peter 2:9–10). As Bruce eloquently comments: "Sanctification is glory begun, and glory is sanctification completed" (1990, 81).

The focus here, however, is not on the act of sanctification but on the fact that both the sanctifier and the sanctified "are of the same family." There is no word in the Greek that corresponds to "family"; it simply says they are "of one." This phrase can be interpreted one of two ways: (1) Both Jesus and the redeemed have their origin from the same Father, or (2) both have their human descent from Adam. The latter, which is more likely in this context, emphasizes again that Jesus shares our humanity. For this reason "Jesus is not ashamed to call them brothers." Notice that God's holy people, redeemed by Jesus through his suffering, are variously called "sons" (2:10), "brothers" (2:11–12), "children" (2:13), and "Abraham's descendants" (2:16).

The close relationship between Jesus and the redeemed is supported by three Old Testament quotations in 2:12–13. The first comes from Psalm 22, the opening words of which Jesus quoted from the cross: "My God, my God, why have you forsaken me?" (Matt. 27:46; Mark 15:34). Other portions of this psalm strikingly parallel the description of Jesus' crucifixion in the Gospels. This psalm was widely recognized by the early church as messianic and as a prophetic preview of Jesus' own experience. Thus our author quotes Psalm 22:22 (from the Septuagint) as if Jesus were speaking them: "I will declare your name to my brothers." In referring to the "congregation" (*ekklesia*) of the redeemed as "my brothers," the full identification of Jesus with humanity is again stressed.

The next quotation (from Isa. 8:17, Septuagint), "I will put my trust in him" (Heb. 2:13a), indicates that Jesus, who is identified here with Isaiah's experience and thus with humanity, placed his trust in God's faithfulness in carrying out his earthly mission, just as all men and women of God must trust him in the dark or difficult days of life.

The third quote is from Isaiah 8:18: "Here am I, and the children God has given me" (Heb. 2:13b). These words originally referred to Isaiah and his children, who were linked with himself in the service of God. Isaiah's identification with his children prophetically points to "the close link between Christ and his people" (Guthrie, 1983, 91). This is the only place in the New Testament where new covenant believers are referred to as the "children" of Christ (cf. "children of God," 1 John 2:28–3:10). The focus here, however, as in Hebrews 2:11–12 ("my brothers"), is once again on the real humanity that Jesus shares in common with those he came to save. This thought introduces the remaining verses of chapter 2.

In 2:14–15, the author addresses more directly the issue of why the preexistent Son (1:2) became a flesh and blood human being. Because "the children have flesh and blood, he too shared in their humanity" (2:14a) in order to get at their real problem—Satan, sin, and death. Westcott comments about the two verbs, "have" and "shared": The first refers to "the common nature shared among men as long as the race lasts"; the second "expresses the unique fact of the incarnation as a voluntary acceptance of humanity" (1889/1980, 53).

The close association between sin and death (cf. Rom. 5:12; 6:23) explains why the power of death is destroyed by Jesus' once-for-all sacifice for sin. Such liberation from sin and death required a "blood and flesh" (actual order in the Greek text) incarnation. By becoming truly human, the eternal Christ made himself vulnerable to death. And here is the great paradox: "By his death" Jesus destroys the devil, "who holds the power of death" (Heb. 2:14b), and sets free "those who all their lives were held in slavery by their fear of death" (2:15). Later our author makes clear how Jesus' death accomplished the release of believers "from the guilt of their sin and their consciences from the dread of its consequences" (Hawthorne, 1986, 1510; cf. 9:14; 10:11–22). In the first century the fear of death was real and prevalent. But the good news of the gospel was that Christ came to deliver "men and women from this fear (Rev. 1:18). They are saved with a sure hope of life eternal, a life whose best lies beyond the grave" (Morris, 1981, 29).

Concerning the destruction of the devil and the power of death, we must distinguish between what Christ has already accomplished in his life-death-resurrection and that which awaits consummation at his return. The devil was defeated through Jesus' ministry (Matt. 12:28–29; Luke 10:17–18) and at the cross (John 19:30; Col. 2:15), but his final destruction awaits our Lord's second coming (Rev. 20:10). Similarly, Jesus has broken "the power of death" through his own death-resurrection, but its actual banishment in human experience awaits his second coming (cf. Heb. 9:28; cf. 1 Cor. 15:51–55). Nevertheless, by faith we now participate in Christ's victory over the devil and the power of death as a foretaste of their future complete destruction.

The extended comparison between the Son and the angels comes to an end in 2:16–18. Because the Son's mission in his incarnation was to help "Abraham's descendants" (2:16) and not angels, he became like Abraham's descendants "in every way" (2:17). Our author may deliberately refer to the descendants of Abraham as part of his appeal to Hebrews. Nevertheless, it appropriately refers also to all new covenant believers, who are the heirs of what was promised to Abraham (6:15, 17; Gal. 3:29).

The Son became like Abraham's descendants for a threefold purpose: (1) to be their "merciful and faithful high priest" (2:17b); (2) to "make atonement for the sins of the people" (2:17c); and (3) to intercede for and give help to "those who are being tempted" (2:18). The term "high priest" is applied to Jesus only in Hebrews among all New Testament books. Our author develops this as one of his major themes (beginning in ch. 5). Hebrews 2:17 is the first hint that Jesus himself fulfilled the Old Testament role of high priest on the annual Day of Atonement (cf. Lev. 16), when by blood sacrifice the high priest made atonement for the people's sins (cf. 7:27; 9:11–12, 24–26; 10:14). As high priest, Jesus was both "merciful and faithful."

The verb "make atonement" (*hilaskomai*) means "to propitiate" or "wipe out" the people's sins, which alienate God; this process makes possible reconciliation with God. Moreover, "it is God himself who provides the propitiation (cf. Rom. 3:25) out of his deep love for mankind (Rom. 5:8)" (Guthrie, 1983, 95). In order to be an effective high priest, the Son had to identify with those whom he represents in the area of temptation and trial, a point stated more fully in Hebrews 4:15–16 and that relates directly to the difficulties of the readers.

1.3. Superior to Moses (3:1–6)

The adverb "therefore" (3:1a) links all that has been said in 1:1–2:18 with what the author is about to introduce. The opening verses of Hebrews established that the Son is the full and ultimate revelation of God and thus superior to the Old Testament prophets and their revelation (1:1–4). Next, in a lengthy discussion, the Son of God was shown to be superior to the angels, even in his humiliation as a human being (1:5–14; 2:5–18). Now our author turns his attention to Moses and reveals how Jesus is superior to him whom the Jews regarded as the greatest of men.

Moses was the mediator through whom Israel was given the law, the covenant, the tabernacle worship, national identity, and ultimately Judaism. Lane notes that "it is difficult to exaggerate the importance of Moses in Judaism and the veneration with which he was regarded" in the first century (1991, 74). The comparison in Hebrews of Jesus and Moses was especially relevant for the Jewish Christians being addressed, who were being tempted to drift back into Judaism. Our author accepts Moses' greatness but reveals that Jesus' greatness and glory far surpasses that of

Moses (cf. 2 Cor. 3:7–18). The comparison between the Mosaic era (with its sacrifices, priesthood, and promises) and Jesus as the mediator of the new covenant is one that continues throughout this book (esp. 4:15–10:31; 12:18–24; Lane, 1991, 73).

Before introducing the comparison between Moses and Jesus, the author addresses his readers directly as "holy brothers, who share in the heavenly calling" (3:1). "Holy" and "brothers" are two common designations for believers in the New Testament; here they are joined together as if to stress the genuineness of their faith. They are "holy" because they have been redeemed by the blood of Christ and set apart by God for himself. They are "brothers" (generic use; includes male and female believers) because their elder brother, Jesus, has made them members of God's family. As such they "share in the heavenly calling." "Share" is literally "sharers" (*metochoi*), a word that also occurs in 3:14 and in 6:4; in each instance this noun refers to those who have responded to God's call to salvation in Christ (Lane, 1991, 74; Attridge, 1989, 106).

"The heavenly calling" (only occurrence in the New Testament) refers both to God's initiative and to believers' participation in the spiritual realm, which stands in contrast to the earthly sphere (cf. the use of "heavenly" in 6:4; 8:5; 9:23; 11:16; 12:22). The designation "holy brothers" especially underscores "the dignity with which God has invested them [as sharers in 'the heavenly calling'], a dignity which it would be insulting to God for them to treat lightly" (Bruce, 1990, 91). Thus the author exhorts his readers: "Fix your thoughts on [i.e., consider carefully and attentively] Jesus, the apostle and high priest whom we confess."

Under the old covenant the role of "apostle" was first held by Moses, while the office of "high priest" was first filled by Aaron. The former was "a sent one" from God to represent him among the people; the latter served as a representative of the people in the presence of God. Jesus, the object of the believer's faith and confession under the new covenant, is both "the apostle and high priest"; he combines both the apostolic role of Moses and the priestly function of Aaron in his redemptive mission.

Our author makes the comparison with Moses immediately in 3:2–6; later he makes the comparison with Aaron in considerable detail under the title of "high priest" (4:14–10:18). Lane notes also that "whenever 'high priest' occurs in Hebrews, the Day of Atonement stands in the background" (1991, 75). The title "apostle" for Jesus appears only here in the New Testament, though the idea that the Father "sent" him is a prominent theme in John's Gospel. Hebrews is unique in the New Testament in developing the theme of "high priest" in relation to Jesus. In the Greek the human name "Jesus" occurs at the very end of 3:1, indicating that it is as "the Son of Man" that he accomplishes his work as apostle and high priest (Morris, 1981, 31).

1.3.1. Superior to Moses in Relation to His Task (3:1–4). Both Jesus and Moses were "faithful" to God and did what he appointed them to do. The statement that "Moses was faithful in all God's house" alludes to Numbers 12:7 (in the LXX), though this theme is not developed until verse 5. The emphasis here is that Jesus was faithful, with the reference to Moses being subordinate (almost parenthetical). The "house" (Heb. 3:2) in which Moses served faithfully was not the tabernacle but God's household, or the people of God as the community of faith. It is significant that the author of Hebrews does not speak of a house of Moses and a house of Jesus (i.e., Israel and the church). Rather, both Moses and Jesus were faithful in the one house of God. Thus continuity exists between Moses and Jesus at two points: (1) They were both faithful, and (2) they both related to the same house, though in different ways. The one house points to the continuity between the old and new covenants in the progressive revelation of God.

Having shown continuity between Jesus and Moses in 3:2, our author asserts in 3:3–4 the superiority of Jesus to Moses. He is "worthy of greater honor [*doxa*, glory] than Moses" because he is the builder of God's house, whereas Moses was simply part of the house itself. There was no way for Moses, honored as he was, to be anything other than a human being and a member of God's people. But Jesus is much more than a man (cf. 1:1–3). As God's Son, he is the builder and founder of the church (cf. Matt. 16:16, 18). "The builder of a house has greater honor [*time*] than the house itself" (Heb. 3:3b). *Doxa* and *time* are closely related in meaning here (cf. 2:7, 9) and are thus both translated "honor" by NIV.

Verse 4 widens the argument begun in verse 3a and further explains the analogy stated in verse 3b by using a literary structure called chiasm:

A Jesus is worthy of more glory than Moses
B as the house-builder receives more honor than the house;
B' for every house is built by someone,
A' but God is the builder of everything.
(cf. Lane, 1991, 77)

Three pairs of comparison occur—Jesus/Moses; builder/house; God/universe. The main point is that "Jesus is worthy of more glory than Moses, in the same measure as God has more honor than the universe he created" (Lane, 1991, 77). Theologically, it is also true that the Son is one with the Father, who makes all things, and that God through his Son made the universe (1:2) and builds his own house, the community of faith (3:3b–4; see Bruce, 1990, 93). Expanding the initial analogy to include the universe reveals the fuller significance of the glory and honor of Jesus as Son (Attridge, 1989, 110).

1.3.2. Superior to Moses in Rank and Authority (3:5–6). Our author throughout the passage intends to show continuity between Moses and Jesus; but the superiority of Jesus to Moses is also clearly asserted and reaches its climax with scriptural support in these verses. Again, both men are presented as faithful in relation to God's house. Moses, however, was faithful as a servant *in* God's house, whereas Jesus was faithful as the Son who presided *over* God's house. As Lane notes, the argument concerning Jesus' superiority rests "on the distinction between *therapon*, 'servant,' and *huios*, 'son,' and between the prepositions *en* ('in the house') and *epi* ('over the house')" (1991, 78).

Verse 5 alludes strongly to Numbers 12:7 (Septuagint) but with a new application. In Numbers, Moses is placed on a higher level than other prophets as a servant of God who communicated with him face to face; in Hebrews, he is placed in a subordinate role to Jesus the Son. Rather than using *doulos*, the common Greek word for a household servant, the author uses *therapon*, which describes "a free man offering personal service to a superior" (Ellingworth, 1993, 207). This word usually occurred in relation to the priesthood but is used here in connection with Moses' prophetic role. The prophetic testimony of Moses (Heb. 3:5b) pointed to a time in the future when there would be a fuller revelation and the ultimate representative from God (cf. Deut. 18:15–19); the author of Hebrews writes that this is now fulfilled "in these last days" (Heb. 1:2) in the person of God's own Son.

In verse 6, the author insists that both the Son's status and authority were greater than that of Moses. Whereas Moses was faithful as a servant (honorable though he be), "Christ is faithful as a son." The title "Christ" occurs here for the first time. Although the NRSV has "Christ . . . was faithful" (past tense), the NIV, as most translations, uses the present tense as the more "unmarked tense" to encompass the constant faithfulness of Christ in relationship with his believing people.

The preposition "over [*epi*] God's house" expresses more than just the superiority of Christ's role to that of Moses; it conveys his Lordship over God's people and the truth in Hebrews that God has put all things under his feet (Ps. 110:1/Heb. 1:13; Ps. 8:6/Heb. 2:8; see Ellingworth, 1993, 210). Jesus is invested with greater glory and authority than Moses because God has appointed him to rule as the exalted Son and the royal priest (Ps. 110; cf. 1 Sam. 2:35; 1 Chron. 17:14) over his house.

"And we are his house" (Heb. 3:6b) makes clear that the metaphorical term "house" in this passage refers to God's redeemed people, "the household of the faith" (NASB, Gal. 6:10; cf. Eph. 2:19; 1 Tim. 3:15; 1 Peter 2:5; 4:17) as a community of believers. God's house ultimately encompasses the believing people of God in the Old Testament and all those under the new covenant. The house is the same for them and us. As Hawthorne notes (1986, 1511), "this passage argues strongly for a continuity between ancient Israel and the new 'Israel of God' (cf. Gal. 6:16)."

The author of Hebrews adds a conditional element: We are God's house only "if we hold on to our courage and . . . hope" (3:6c), that is, remain firm in what we confess and hope in Christ. As one of the major hortatory emphases of Hebrews, this element marks "the beginning of a sustained effort to persuade the hearers to remain loyal to Christ in the presence of pressures that would encourage them to abandon their confession" (Lane, 1991, 80; also Attridge, 1989, 111). Bruce adds: "The apparent postponement of their hope, and various kinds of pressures brought to bear upon them, all combined to threaten the steadfastness of their faith. Hence our author, in deep concern, urges upon them that they have everything to gain by standing fast, and everything to lose by slipping back" (1990, 94–95).

Hebrews views the possibility of remaining steadfast in faith or abandoning faith as a real choice facing the readers; the author illustrates the consequences of the latter by referring to the destruction of the rebellious Hebrews in the desert after their glorious deliverance from Egypt (the next section, 3:7–19).

Second Hortatory Warning: The Snare of Unbelief (3:7–19)

The final statement in 3:6 serves as a transition to the solemn warning and exhortation in 3:7–19. As a comparison was drawn between Moses and Jesus in 3:1–6, so now a parallel is drawn between (1) the response of unbelief and disobedience by the Hebrews who were redeemed out of Egypt under Moses' leadership (3:7–11), and (2) the possibility of the same response by the Hebrews who were redeemed by Christ under the new covenant provisions of salvation (3:12–19).

Moses had been faithful to the end (3:2, 5), but most of those who left Egypt with him were unfaithful. They all shared by faith in the first great Passover deliverance but afterward because of unbelief hardened their hearts against God and perished in the desert (cf. Num. 13:26–14:38). Likewise, Christ, who is far superior to Moses, is also faithful (Heb. 3:2, 6), but the author of Hebrews was deeply concerned that the community of Hebrew Christians he is addressing, who had experienced the deliverance of the cross, were now in danger of hardening their hearts and of perishing because of unbelief concerning the promise of God. This section reveals the progressive nature of unbelief: (1) The seed of unbelief is sown and allowed to sprout; (2) unbelief leads to hardness of heart; (3) hardness leads to disobedience and rebellion; and (4) rebellion leads to apostasy and forfeiting forever God's promised rest.

The powerful warning and exhortation in this section begins with a quotation from Psalm 95:7–11 (Heb. 3:7–11) and follows with the author's application for his readers (3:12–19). The application is framed by the repetition of the verb *blepo* ("see to it," 3:12; "so we see," 3:19) and the noun *apisti* ("unbelieving," 3:12; "unbelief," 3:19). Lan observes: "The warning against unbelief in v 12 and 19 provides a literary and theologica frame for the admonition to maintain the basi position of faith, which is centrally placed i v. 14" (1991, 83).

The comparison of Israel in the desert wit the church today reveals the legitimacy c typology in relation to God's redemptiv action in the Exodus and his promise o Canaan to Israel. Whereas allegory may arbi trarily find hidden or symbolic meaning in story or event,

> typology acknowledges the factuality of the past event and presupposes a genuine correspondence between the saving and judging activity of God in the past and the present. It is based not on superficial resemblances but on the consistency of the divine action within the frame of reference established by revelation. (Lane, 1991, 90–91)

Paul writes to the Corinthians, for example that Israel's grumbling and disobedience an subsequent destruction in the desert serve a examples and warnings "for us, on whom th fulfillment of the ages has come" (1 Cor 10:11). Similarly, Jude (v. 5) refers to the deser generation—whom the Lord redeemed out o Egypt to be his people but whom he late destroyed because of their unbelief—as a lesson for his readers. Likewise, our author warn his readers "against giving up their faith an hope" (Bruce, 1990, 97). The warning o Hebrews 3:7–19 is that "those who have experienced the redemption of the cross may fin themselves in a similar situation" (Hagner 1983, 43) to the desert generation who perished, if they harden their hearts in unbelie and turn back from Christ to their former wa of life. The passage represents a serious exhortation to persevering discipleship and unwavering faith.

"As the Holy Spirit says" (3:7) introduce the quotation from Psalm 95 and reveals tw important convictions held by the author o Hebrews: (1) The Old Testament Scriptures ar God's revelatory word given by the Holy Spiri (thus not human-bound); and (2) the Holy Spirit still speaks to the church today throug them (thus not time-bound).

Psalm 95 itself divides into two parts: The first is a call to worship God from the heart (95:1–7a), and the second is a warning not to harden one's heart against God as did Israel at Kadesh (95:7b–11; cf. Num. 13–14). At the threshold of obtaining what God had promised, Israel at Kadesh forgot God's past redemption and rebelled in unbelief at God's promise. The psalmist warns his generation not to emulate their hardness. Hearing God's "voice" today, as then, has the potential of hardening one's heart if we do not respond in faith. In the Bible, "heart" (*kardia*) metaphorically refers to one's whole inner being—mind, emotions, and will—with an emphasis on one's cognitive and volitional powers. To harden one's heart is to disregard God's voice and to act according to one's own desires or fears.

Psalm 95:8 reveals that this hardening by Israel first occurred at Meribah and Massah, when there was no water; they grumbled at Moses and tested the Lord in their unbelief (Ex. 17:1–7). The Septuagint translates "Meribah" and "Massah" by their descriptive meaning, "rebellion" and "testing." Because of their hardened hearts, the Israelites did not discern God's purpose or appreciate his provisions for them in their desert journey. Thus they "tested and tried [God] . . . for forty years" (Heb. 3:9). Hagner notes that this reference to forty years may have had special significance for our author and his readers insofar as it had been about forty years (assuming that Hebrews was written shortly before A.D. 70) since Jesus died as the Passover Lamb and accomplished the new covenant exodus from the slavery of sin (1983, 45).

Verse 10 indicates that God's anger was not provoked by a single incident of the Israelites but by their persistent refusal to trust him: "They have not known my [God's] ways" because the condition of their hearts was hard and unbelieving. Psalm 103:7 states that Israel saw God's mighty acts, but Moses knew God's ways. Moses knew God's ways because his heart was sensitive and trusting, having been dealt with by God in his own personal desert before the Exodus. He emerged from the brokenness and loneliness of his desert as a humble, meek, believing, and God-fearing man. On the other hand, Israel's hardness of heart and rebellion at Kadesh was "the culmination of a series of episodes in which Israel provoked the Lord through their bitter complaint, disobedience, and unbelief" (Lane, 1991, 90), in spite of having witnessed God's mighty acts and deliverance in the Exodus.

As the climax of it all, God "declared on oath . . . 'They shall never enter my rest'" (Heb. 3:11). These words are paralleled in Numbers 14:30, "Not one of you will enter the land." The finality of God's judgment "must be seen as a just . . . recompense for Israel's tragic defiance" (ibid., 96). The word "rest" (*katapausis*), however, refers not primarily to the Promised Land, but to an appointed place of spiritual rest where there is no more striving or fear, only contentment and peace in the presence of God. In an often quoted interpretation, Rabbi Aquiba understood Psalm 95 (and Num. 14:35) to mean that the Hebrews who perished in the desert would have no part in the age to come (*b. Sanhedrin* 110b).

In Hebrews 3:12, the author applies the Psalm 95 warning to his fellow believers. That his readers are genuine Christians is again indicated by the word "brothers" (cf. 3:1).[2] He is concerned that none of them be lost: "Be careful," he exhorts, "that none of you has a sinful, unbelieving heart that turns away [*apostenai*, lit., departs] from the living God" (pers. trans.). Like the Hebrews mentioned in Psalm 95:7–11, God's people under the new covenant "sometimes turn away from God in apostasy. . . . This may be provoked by suffering or persecution or by the pressures of temptation, but the root cause is always unbelief" (Peterson, 1994, 1330).

Apostasy refers to abandoning what one has previously believed, in this case, a disowning of Jesus as the Son of God and a departing from the fellowship of believers. Our author calls it a turning "away from the living God." For these Hebrew Christians to break with the church and return to their previous place in Judaism is viewed as "outright apostasy, a complete break with God . . . a form of the irretrievable sin—the sin against light" (Bruce, 1990, 100; cf. 6:4–6). As with the desert generation, apostasy is not so much a decision of the moment as it is the culmination of a process of hardening the heart (3:8, 13, 15) in unbelief (3:12, 19; cf. 4:2), resulting in the end in rebellion against God (3:8, 15, 16), disobedience (3:18; cf. 4:6), and finally turning away from God (3:12; cf. 3:10).

An important safeguard against apostasy is a loving, nurturing community of true believers, who "encourage one another daily" in the Lord (3:13). Isolation from other believers particularly makes one vulnerable to the world's wisdom and lies, to the many temptations of the devil, and to "sin's deceitfulness." To yield to these pressures results in "a reduced sensitivity of conscience, which makes it more difficult to recognize the right path on a subsequent occasion" (Bruce, 1990, 101). "Today" carries with it both a note of urgency and an inherent warning that windows of opportunity do not last forever. The mistaken belief that returning to Judaism was a better choice than suffering reproach with Christ (cf. 12:4–5; 13:12–13) was part of "sin's deceitfulness" for them.

Believers are sharers (*metochoi*, plural) "in Christ" (3:14, NIV), "partakers of Christ" (NASB, NKJV), "partners of Christ" (NRSV). As Christ came to share our humanity, so "in Christ" we share his life, grace (4:16), salvation (2:10), kingdom (12:28), suffering (13:12–13), and glory (2:10). To begin well is commendable, but we must "hold firmly till the end the confidence we had at first" (3:14b). As Bruce states, "it is only those who stay the course and finish the race that have any hope of gaining the prize" (1990, 101; cf. 12:1–3). We must persevere until Jesus comes the second time (cf. 9:28) or until we go to him through death (cf. 2 Cor. 5:8).

"Confidence" in this context suggests "the assurance an owner of property may have because he possesses the title-deeds.... So long as we exercise faith, we have the assurance that our share cannot be taken from us, any more than another can claim ownership of our property if he does not possess the deeds" (Guthrie, 1983, 108). The converse is, if we cease holding on by faith and revert to a state of unbelief and rebellion, we forfeit the deed by default. In Hebrews 3:15 the opening two lines of Psalm 95:7b–8a are repeated (cf. Heb. 3:7–8; 4:7).

The implications of Psalm 95:7–11 for Christian readers are further pressed by a series of five compelling rhetorical questions (Heb. 3:16–18). The fact and consequences of rebellion (3:16a), willful sin (3:17b), disobedience (3:18b), and unbelief (3:19) are specifically mentioned. The first question, "Who were they who heard and rebelled?" (3:16a), concerns the issue of identity. The answer comes in another question, "Were they not all those Moses led out of Egypt?" (3:16b), that is, the very people "who had experienced God's redeeming power" (Bruce, 1990, 102) in the Exodus. The sheer mass of the rebellion is emphasized by the word "all" (that only two men out of an entire nation were exceptions supports the comprehensiveness of "all").

The third question, "And with whom was he angry for forty years?" (3:17a), calls attention to the lengthy duration of the provocation. The answer comes in the form of another rhetorical question, "Was it not with those who sinned, whose bodies fell in the desert?" (3:17b); the defiant conduct of the Israelites at Kadesh was especially "sinful" and resulted in the penalty of death as a just judgment (cf. Rom. 6:23). The fifth question points to their disobedience, "And to whom did God swear that they would never enter his rest if not to those who disobeyed?" (3:18). Though the Israelites had made a covenant to obey God and "had every encouragement to persevere in faith during their journey to the promised land . . . they [nevertheless] disqualified themselves from entering his rest because they persistently *disobeyed* him" (Peterson, 1994, 1330).

Verse 19 states that at the heart of the Israelites' disobedience and sinfulness was "unbelief," which excluded them from entering the reality and fulfillment of God's promise. God's oath in 3:18 (cf. 3:11) was final and irrevocable: "They [will] never enter his rest." Three observations are noteworthy: (1) God's promised rest was never confined just to the land of Canaan. God's rest "transcends all earthly prefigurations" (Hagner, 1983, 47), as becomes clear in 4:1–13; "rest" refers primarily to the goal of redemption.

(2) The desert generation had experienced the redeeming grace and power of God. Their "tragic failure ... to attain the goal of their redemption calls attention to a pattern of response to God's voice that must not be emulated" (Lane, 1991, 89), namely, the hardening of heart that leads to rebellion and disobedience.

(3) The unbelief that led God irrevocably to exclude that generation from his rest introduces the warning that repentance and recovery are impossible after a certain point of apostasy, a theme developed more fully later

in Hebrews (cf. 6:4–8; 10:26–31; 12:16–17). The overwhelming implication of this passage is that *unbelief* will ultimately expose new covenant believers "to the same precarious situation as Israel at Kadesh" (Lane, 1991, 89).

1.4. Superior to Joshua (4:1–13)

Whereas Moses led the Israelites out of Egypt, it was Joshua who led them into the land of promise and rest. But even Joshua could not secure for the Israelites the true rest of God. Our author exhorts his readers to enter into the superior rest that God has promised and that the New Testament Joshua, Jesus Christ, makes possible. The word "rest" (*katapausis*), which first occurs in 3:11 and is repeated in 3:18, permeates 4:1–11. The noun occurs six times (4:1, 3 [twice], 5, 10, 11), and the cognate verb (*katapauo*) three times (4:4, 8, 10). Hebrews 4 is the foremost chapter in the Bible on God's promised rest for his people.

In interpreting this passage, we must keep in mind that our author speaks of three kinds of rest: (1) the Canaan-rest, into which Joshua led the second generation of Israelites (implied in 4:8), (2) God's own rest following creation (4:4), and (3) the spiritual rest into which believers are to enter by faith. The latter is spoken of repeatedly: "the promise of entering his rest" (4:1), "we who have believed enter that rest" (4:3a), "they shall never enter my rest" (4:3c, 5), "some will enter that rest" (4:6), "there remains . . . a Sabbath-rest for the people of God" (4:9), "anyone who enters God's rest" (4:10), and "make every effort to enter that rest" (4:11).

There are also three important preliminary observations to make about the character of the rest God promises his people. (1) The rest in Canaan is a type or symbol of the spiritual rest God promises his people in Christ. (2) This spiritual rest is prefigured in the Sabbath-rest of God. (3) This spiritual rest—like other aspects of the kingdom of God—involves both present reality and future hope for the people of faith. Whereas 3:12–19 emphasizes the past experience of the desert generation who were excluded from God's rest because of unbelief, 4:1–11 focuses on the present opportunity facing new covenant believers of entering into God's rest by faith.

1.4.1. Superior to Joshua in the Rest Provided (4:1–5). "The spiritual counterpart of the earthly Canaan" (Bruce, 1990, 105) is the promise of entering God's rest. Because this promise continues to be the present goal of God's people, our author urges his readers not to fall short of it. "Let us be careful that" (lit., "let us fear lest") are the first words in verse 1 and are emphatic. A proper fear of God and of the consequences of unbelief and apostasy (3:12, 18–19) is a recurring note in Hebrews (cf. 10:27, 31).

The author's pastoral concern is again evident: "that none of you be found to have fallen short of it" (cf. 3:12–13; 4:11). Entering God's rest does not occur automatically after conversion to Christ, just as Israel did not automatically enter Canaan after their redemption from Egypt. The readers, as Bruce notes, "will do well to fear the possibility of missing it, just as the generation of Israelites which died in the wilderness missed the earthly Canaan, although that was the goal which they had before them when they set out from Egypt" (1990, 105).

The word "promise" (*epangelia*) occurs fourteen times in Hebrews, more often than in any other book in the New Testament (cf. ten times in Galatians). The author's basic argument is that entry into the land of Canaan did not constitute the fulfillment of the promise (though it is a type or symbol of the promised rest; cf. 4:8–9). The promises God gave under the old covenant, he fulfills under the new for those who have faith to inherit them.

The conjunction "for" links verse 2 directly to the concern expressed in verse 1. The Israelites in the desert had "the gospel [lit., good news] preached" to them in their deliverance from Egypt and their covenant with God at Sinai, accompanied by supernatural signs and miracles. They did not enter into God's rest, however, though the invitation was given, because "those who heard did not combine it with faith." The New Testament Hebrew Christians had the good news of Jesus preached to them in the deliverance of the cross and the new covenant in his blood, with God confirming its reality with "signs, wonders and various miracles, and gifts of the Holy Spirit" (2:4). "The promise of entering his rest still stands" (4:1) for new covenant believers, but that promise must be appropriated by faith if the desert life with its struggles and fears is to be exchanged for God's rest. Only faith can secure the promise.

Is God's rest into which believers are invited to enter something for the present or future? Certainly God's rest in its fullest sense awaits the age to come, but there is also a present sense of entering by faith, as verse 3 indicates: "We who have believed [past tense] enter [present tense] that rest" (cf. the present tense emphasis in 4:1, 10, 11). Faith makes possible realities in the present that are future, unseen, or heavenly (cf. 11:1).

In 4:3–5, two important facts are emphasized: (1) God's rest is a present, completed reality (4:3c–4), and (2) the Israelites were not permitted to enter God's rest (4:3b, 5b) because of their unbelief and disobedience (3:19; 4:6). Note that our author quotes from Genesis 2:2 in Hebrews 4:4 and refers to Psalm 95:11 (twice) in Hebrews 4:3, 5. His concern for his readers is that they enter into God's rest now *by faith* and not miss it forever, as did the desert generation. Unbelief closes one's heart to God and makes his promise of no effect.

What is God's rest? It is based on the completion of his work in creation (4:3c, 4), of which the Sabbath is an enduring testimony. Our participation in his rest is based on the finished work of Christ on the cross; his being "seated" (which includes the thought of rest) at the Father's right hand is the enduring testimony. That God rested does not mean he is thereafter in a state of idleness, but only that there is nothing to add to what he had done. He rested from creating because "his work [of creating] has been finished since the creation of the world" (4:3c).

Peace and settledness occur when the creature finds rest in the Creator. Entering the rest of God by faith is a personal experience of the human spirit and soul. It involves coming out of the desert of struggle and weariness of the soul and entering into the spiritual rest and strength of the Creator himself. We enter God's rest by believing his Word, trusting in him instead of ourselves, and refusing to be distraught by our circumstances. By repentance and faith, quietness and trust (cf. Isa. 30:15), we are invited to rest in the sufficiency of the all-sufficient One.

1.4.2. Exhortation to Enter His Rest (4:6–13). Verse 6 summarizes the preceding argument: (1) The invitation to enter God's rest "still remains," and those who have faith "will enter"; and (2) the desert generation was excluded irrevocably "because of their dis obedience." God's promises to his people ar often conditional. If one generation does nc fulfill the condition, then the promise passe on to another generation. Our author focuse on only two generations: the Exodus genera tion and his own. The former generation for feited the promise because of unbelief an disobedience; he is concerned that some of hi readers not repeat the failure of their ancestors

God's promise of rest must be appropriate by faith. If we do not take hold of God's promis by faith, we will not obtain what he promises and he will extend his offer to others. Referenc to the "disobedience" of the desert generatio restates the point made in 3:16–18 and 4:2. Jus as unbelief and disobedience are closely con nected in 3:19 and 4:6, and as faith (*pistis* involves faithfulness, even so believing an obeying are joined together as the necessar conditions for inheriting what God promises.

Whereas the focus of 4:3, 5 is on Psaln 95:11, the emphasis in Hebrews 4:6–7 is o Psalm 95:7b–8a, namely, the urgency o "today" in entering God's rest. The eschato logical "last days" foreseen by the prophet began when God spoke to us through the incar nation of his Son (Heb. 1:1–2). This segmen of history is the "certain day" (4:7) that Goc set for fulfilling the promise of entering hi rest. Thus the exhortation, "Today, if you hea his voice, do not harden your hearts," has spe cial meaning for the readers of Hebrews unde the new covenant. On the one hand, it is ar urgent appeal not to harden one's heart in view of what God is speaking in his Son; on the other hand, it announces that the time has come for the fulfillment of God's promise tc bring his people into his rest. It is a crucial time of opportunity, and to harden one's heart "today" would be disastrous.

It is clear from Psalm 95 and Hebrews 4 that the promise of entering God's rest was not fulfilled when Joshua led the next generation of Israelites into Canaan. The temporal rest in the settlement of Canaan was "only a type or symbol [at best] of the complete rest that God intended for his people" (Lane, 1991, 101). In Greek (and Hebrew), "Joshua" and "Jesus" are the same name. Thus, a natural parallel is set up between the Old Testament "Jesus," who led his generation into the earthly Canaan, and Jesus, the Son of God, who leads new covenant believers into their spiritual inheritance (4:8). While this parallel was a theme in early Christian typology, the author of Hebrews focuses on "the contrast between the temporal 'rest' which Israel entered under Joshua and the true [spiritual] rest which is still reserved for the people of God" (Bruce, 1990, 109).

Verse 9 sums up the argument: "There remains, then, a Sabbath-rest for the people of God." The real parallel to the rest provided by Jesus Christ is not Joshua's rest but God's rest, here spoken of as "Sabbath-rest" (*sabbatismos*). "God's rest" (4:10) is linked with the original Sabbath, when God finished his work of creation and rested on the seventh day. "Anyone who enters God's rest also rests from his own work, just as God did from his" (4:10). The earthly Sabbath is a weekly reminder of God's rest. Isaiah 58:13 indicates that the Sabbath-rest represented a desisting from one's own way and a delighting in the Lord.

The spiritual reality of God's rest in the present tense involves the yielding of our wills to God so that we no longer do as we please but joyfully live according to his will; we cease from our "own work" and let him work in us according to his good pleasure. On the one hand, the rest of faith is a place of peace and assurance that comes when one is entirely free from unbelief and all the insecurity that accompanies unbelief; on the other hand, entering into God's rest also involves a ceasing from the struggles of self (self-centeredness, self-effort, etc.), a resting from the strivings of a works-oriented life by surrendering oneself fully to God, resulting in peace, well-being, and security in him.

That our author has in mind the experience of a present spiritual rest for his readers and not just a future end-time rest, is evident in the exhortation given in verse 11: "Make every effort [*spoudazo*] to enter that rest." *Spoudazo* means "be diligent" (NASB, NKJV), "earnestly strive" (Alford), "exert ourselves" (Berkeley). To enter God's rest requires diligence, not passivity; wholehearted pursuit, not indifference; an active faith expressed in obedience, not the unbelief and disobedience of the Old Testament Israelites. As Guthrie comments, "the writer clearly thinks that there is a grave danger of history repeating itself" (1983, 116).

To avoid another spiritual tragedy, the author exhorts believers to enter the rest about which Jesus spoke: "Take my yoke upon you and learn from me, for I am gentle and humble in heart, and you will find rest for your souls" (Matt. 11:29). It was through meekness and humility of heart that Jesus found his rest in the Father, and Jesus invites believers to share in God's rest. It involves freedom from the struggles of the self-life with its toil, anxiety, weariness, and fear, and provides a place of peace wherein we "enjoy with God the satisfaction and perfection of his work in creating and redeeming us" (Peterson, 1994, 1331). Those who enter that rest will not "fall [away] by following their [the desert generation's] example of disobedience."

The conjunction "for" (v. 12) connects verses 12–13 directly with the exhortation in verse 11. We may enter into God's rest by submitting to the surgery of God's word. "The word of God" is anything that God speaks, whether in the Scripture, in his Son (1:2), in the preaching of the gospel, or by the voice of the Holy Spirit. Here it especially refers to Psalm 95:7–11 and our author's exhortation in chapters 3–4. Unlike human words, God's word is all-knowing and all-pervasive and embodies the very character of God himself. It is living, active, piercing, and discerning. Furthermore, it possesses the power to achieve God's purpose in sending it forth (cf. Isa. 55:11) and always demands a response. It blesses those who receive it in faith and judges those who disregard it (Bruce, 1990, 111).

God's word is like a sharp sword (see Isa. 49:2; Rev. 19:15), the sword of the Spirit (Eph. 6:17); here it is described as "sharper than any double-edged sword" (Heb. 4:12; cf. Rev. 1:16). The image conveyed is not so much one of judgment as that of a razor-sharp surgeon's knife that wounds, cuts, and pierces in order to heal us. God's word penetrates so thoroughly our inner being that it discerns and defines the obscure dividing-line between "soul [*psyche*] and spirit [*pneuma*]" (4:12). Concerning the differences between "spirit" and "soul," Guthrie comments (1983, 119; cf. Spicq, 1952, 1:52–54):

> The New Testament use of *pneuma* for the human spirit focuses on the spiritual aspect of man, *i.e.*, his life in relation to God, whereas *psyche* refers to man's life irrespective of his spiritual experience, *i.e.*, his life in relation to himself, his

[own] emotions and thought [and choices]. There is a strong antithesis between the two in the theology of Paul.

Though many interpreters believe that Paul's distinction between soul and spirit is not present in this passage, there is no good reason to discount it. God's word awakens and strengthens his life in our spirit and exposes our soulishness, where it conflicts with the life of God within us. The activity of God's word is further described: "It judges [*kritikos*; quick to discern, ASV] the thoughts and attitudes of the heart" (4:12).

Hebrews speaks often about the "heart." Negatively, the heart may be "hardened" (3:8, 15; 4:7), go "astray" (3:10), and be "sinful, unbelieving" (3:12). Positively, because of God's dealings and our response of faith, we may have God's law written on our hearts (8:10; 10:16); our hearts are sprinkled with Christ's blood (10:22) and strengthened by grace (13:9). By willingly submitting to God's piercing word, our hearts may be softened and changed so that we may truly enter into God's rest.

The alternative to letting God's word judge our hearts now is to harden them against it, in which case that word will condemn us in the end, as it did the desert generation. The image in 4:13 of being "uncovered" and "laid bare" expresses vividly the truth that none of us can successfully hide from or deceive our Creator and Judge, "to whom we must give [final] account" (cf. Eccl. 12:14; Rom. 14:12; 1 Cor. 4:5; 2 Cor. 5:10). Hebrews 4:12–13 reminds us of the seriousness of our choices when responding to God and his word.

2. Christ's Supremacy As the One Mediator Between God and Humankind (4:14–10:18)

"High priest" is a key word in Hebrews. Already Christ has been introduced as having "provided purification for sins" (1:3) and as being "a merciful and faithful high priest" (2:17). The exhortation in 4:14 links back to 3:1—"Fix your thoughts on Jesus, the apostle and *high priest* whom we confess." The author will now begin a full-scale argument about Jesus as our "great high priest" (4:14), vastly superior to Aaron and the whole Levitical order of priestly mediation (which Jesus both fulfills and makes obsolete), and as a priest forever "in the order of Melchizedek" (5:6; 7:17–18; Ps. 110:4). As our high priest, Jesus ha offered the perfect once-for-all-time atonin sacrifice for our sins, sympathizes with ou weaknesses, and represents us before th Father at heaven's Most Holy Place, the thron of grace (4:14–10:18). In his eternal role o high priest, he is the foundation for a perse vering and steadfast faith.

2.1. Superior to Aaron and the Levitical Order in His Qualifications to Be High Priest (4:14–7:28)

2.1.1. Superior to Aaron and the Leviti cal Order in His Ability to Understand an Help Humanity (4:14–16). We can enter int God's rest and remain steadfast in faith "sinc we have a great high priest" who can "help us (4:16). In the Old Testament the high pries was generally referred to as "great priest. Here the fuller expression "great high priest contributes to the overall comparison of Jesu as even greater than Aaron and his successors

His greatness is immediately evident b two facts. (1) He "has gone through the heav ens" into the holy presence of God at th throne room on our behalf, just as the Old Tes tament high priest passed through the veil int the Most Holy Place on behalf of the people o the Day of Atonement. Subsequently, Jesu was "exalted above the heavens" (7:26; cf Eph. 4:10) and now sits enthroned (implied i 4:16, "throne of grace") as "both Lord an Christ" (Acts 2:33, 36). There he continues hi heavenly ministry of priestly mediation an intercession.

(2) Our high priest is "Jesus the Son o God." His earthly name "Jesus" speaks of hi humanity and his ministry as our Savior fro sin (cf. Matt. 1:21); his title "Son of God" speaks of his deity and power as high priest t bring us into fellowship with God. He is both immanent (with us) and transcendent (abov us), both sympathetic and powerful. "There fore . . . let us hold firmly to the faith we pro fess." Knowledge of the greatness and glory o Jesus as our high priest is a key to entering int God's rest and the life of steadfast faith.

An important qualification of a high pries is that he be sympathetic, gentle, and patien with those who go astray through ignorance unintentional sin, or weakness (4:15; 5:2). Ou author anticipates the possible objection tha esus' sheer greatness as God's Son, enthroned n heaven at the Father's side, might imply he s aloof and unable to share in our troubles or ympathize with our weaknesses. To counter uch reasoning, the writer makes three asserions to the contrary. (1) Our high priest is able 'to sympathize with our weaknesses." "Symathize" (*sympatheo*, lit., "suffer along with") loes not refer to psychological sympathy "feel sorry for") but to an existential compasion wherein our high priest suffers along with s in our weaknesses and brings active help Lane, 1991, 108, 114). "Weaknesses" refers o any area of vulnerability inherent in frail umanity.

(2) Our high priest was "tempted in every vay, just as we are." His temptations were not taged or fake; they were as genuine as ours. In every way" does not mean he went through every temptation that collectively we have, but hat he was tempted in the same three basic vays we are all tempted: the desire of the flesh, he desire of the eyes, and the pride of life (cf. Gen. 3:6; Luke 4:3, 6–7, 9–11; 1 John 2:15–6). Jesus' temptations especially revolved round avoiding his mission as the Suffering Servant. In Hebrews the temptation of the eaders also involves the avoidance of suffering for Christ. In this sense he experienced the ull range of temptation.

(3) Jesus was nevertheless "without sin." This fact does not mean that he was incapable of sin but that he was sinless because of concious decisions in the midst of real temptaion. Temptation itself is not sinful; yielding s the point of sinfulness. Jesus alone knows he full intensity of temptation because he lone did not yield. Thus we have a high priest n whom is joined *perfect sinlessness* and *perect sympathy*, fully enabling him to "deal gently with" us (5:2).

Therefore, says our author, "let us ... pproach the throne of grace with confidence" 4:16). Under the law of Moses the only person who was permitted to "approach" the tabernale mercy seat in the Most Holy Place was the igh priest, and that was restricted to once a ear on the Day of Atonement. Jesus' accomlished work of atonement at the cross and his osition as high priest at the heavenly mercy seat ("throne of grace") have obtained for new ovenant believers "what Israel never enjoyed, amely, immediate access to God and the freedom to draw near to him continually (7:19, 25; 9:8–12, 14; 10:1, 22)" (Lane, 1991, 115).

There are three important features in verse 16. (1) Our approach to God through Christ is to be characterized by a holy "confidence" or boldness that is free from fear. It is the confidence of approaching God as "our Father" because of the blood of Christ. (2) Our approach must be to "the throne of grace." Coming to God's throne and into his royal presence would "be overawing were it not that its main characteristic is grace, *i.e.*, the place where God's free favour is dispersed" (Guthrie, 1983, 124). We draw near the throne of grace through prayer in Jesus' name. Andrew Murray states, "The measure of our nearness of access to God is the index of our knowledge of Jesus" (n.d., 171). (3) At the throne we receive a threefold assistance in our hour of trial or temptation: "mercy," "grace," and timely "help" from God. "Mercy" relates to God's pardon and love made possible by the sacrifice of his Son; "grace" involves a God-given desire and power in our inner being, enabling us to be victorious in temptation and the trials of life; and God's grace, available "to help us in our time of need," is an appropriate and timely help.

2.1.2. Superior to Aaron and the Levitical Order in His Divine Appointment and Godly Life (5:1–10). The connection of this passage with the preceding three verses is especially made clear in Greek by the opening conjunction *gar* ("for"; omitted in the NIV). The author now focuses on the qualities that should characterize "every high priest" in the Aaronic priesthood from God's point of view. These qualities are briefly summarized under (1) horizontal requirements that relate to those he represents (5:1–3), and (2) a vertical requirement in relation to God (5:4). Then he shows how Christ fulfilled these requirements in superior fashion (5:5–10).

(1) The first horizontal requirement for the priest was that he be "selected from among men" (5:1), not from among angels or celestial beings. He must be subject to the same human weaknesses, pressures, and trials of life as other human beings, because he "is appointed to represent" the covenant people before God with "gifts and sacrifices for sins." What is primarily in view here is the high priest's ministry on the Day of Atonement, when he offered sacrifices for sin for himself and the people (cf.

5:3). That Christ fulfilled this high priestly ministry is emphasized in Hebrews 9–10.

For the high priest to fulfill his ministry in a worthy manner, he not only had to give attention to the precise performance of his priestly ministry, but also demonstrate an inward forbearance and compassion that enabled him "to deal gently with those who are ignorant and are going astray" (5:2). The two participles used here share one definite article, which suggests that one category of people is intended—namely, all "those who err through ignorance" (Zerwick, *Biblical Greek*, quoted in Lane, 1991, 108).

The Mosaic Law did not make provision of atonement for defiant and deliberate transgressors. Those who sinned defiantly were to be excluded from the people of God and from his provision of atonement (Num. 15:30–31). But the high priest could sympathize and have compassion on those who erred through ignorance, because he himself was subject to the same weaknesses. For this reason, the high priest had "to offer sacrifices for his own sins, as well as for the sins of the people" (5:3).

On this point, of course, Jesus was dissimilar to Aaron and the Levitical order; although he was tempted in every way as we are, he "was without sin" (4:15). This is one of the foremost distinguishing features of Jesus as our high priest. Because he was "'holy, free from guile and defilement,' [he] had no need to offer a preliminary sacrifice for himself. It is by enduring the common weaknesses and temptations of the human lot, not by yielding to them, that he has established his power not only to sympathize with his people but to bring them help, deliverance, and victory" (Bruce, 1990, 121). Jesus' key similarity to Aaron lay in his making atonement for the sins of the people, though his sacrifice for sin was infinitely superior to that of the Aaronic priests (see chs. 9–10).

(2) The second requirement for the Levitical high priest was vertical: "He must be called by God" (5:4). The role of high priest was so important that no man had the right to take "this honor upon himself." Only God has the prerogative and power to establish a man as high priest. God's appointment of Aaron (Ps. 105:26) set the pattern for all his heirs and successors (Ex. 28:1–3; Num. 23–26, esp. 25:10–13). The Bible records that those who did attempt to take the honor of performing high priestly duties came under God's judgment—as in the cases of Korah (Num. 16), Saul (1 Sam. 13:8–14), and Uzziah (2 Chron. 26:16–21). Others, not of Aaronic descent who in times of national crisis did fulfill the intercessory and mediatorial ministry like that of the Aaronic priests, did so by the direct call and appointment of God—as in the case of Samuel (1 Sam. 7:3–17).

The general requirements for the office and ministry of high priest, as represented by Aaron and his descendants (5:1–4), are specifically applied to Jesus Christ in 5:5–10, but in reverse order. (1) Christ qualifies to be high priest because "just as Aaron was, so Christ also" (5:4c–5a) was appointed by God and "did not take upon himself the glory of becoming a high priest" (5:5). There is a similar pattern of comparison and contrast here between Aaron and Jesus as there was between Moses and Jesus in chapter 3. Moses and Jesus were alike in their faithfulness to God, who appointed them (3:1–2); but then the discontinuity between them is emphasized, and Jesus is seen as clearly superior to Moses in their essential differences (see 3:3–6a).

Likewise, Aaron and Jesus were alike in that God himself appointed them to the office of high priest, rather than their elevating themselves to that position. But the writer then shows, implicitly, the discontinuity between Jesus and Aaron and the superiority of the former by linking two messianic psalms with Christ: Psalm 2:7 identifies him as the Davidic Messiah (invested with royal power and authority as the Son), and Psalm 110:4 identifies him as the priestly Messiah after the likeness of Melchizedek.

In some Jewish circles two Messiahs were expected, one a king and the other a priest. Perhaps the original recipients of Hebrews held this twofold messianic hope. Bruce adds: "But here they are assured that Jesus, who was acclaimed by God as the Davidic Messiah in Ps. 2:7, was also acclaimed by God as high priest in Ps. 110:4. Christians acknowledge no two Messiahs, but one, and that one is both king and priest" (1990, 123–24). Note that Christ's sonship is also asserted in Psalm 2:7. Jesus as the Son of God was the predominant emphasis in Hebrews 1:1–4:13; now Jesus as the "priest" or "high priest" is the primary focus in 4:14–10:18.

Psalm 110:4 states, "You are a priest forever" 5:6). "Forever" is another feature of Christ's uperiority. Aaron and all his priestly successors ad their day and then passed from the scene. Christ as priest abides forever and has no need f a successor. Insofar as Melchizedek (cf. Gen. 4:18) was both king and priest and without ecorded successors, Jesus is a priest after his ikeness. The translation "in the order of Melchizedek" (5:6c) is misleading in that "there vas no succession of priests from Melchizedek nd thus no 'order.' Jesus, however, was a priest f this kind—not like Aaron and his successors" Morris, 1981, 49). A fuller application of Psalm 10:4 and Melchizedek's kind of priesthood to esus occurs in Hebrews 7.

(2) Hebrews 5:7–10 discusses in far greater letail a second reason Jesus qualifies to be igh priest—because of his humanity, in vhich he experienced (as the divine Son) both esting and suffering. The contrast here etween Jesus' sufferings and his present xalted state as high priest has remarkable parllel in 1:3d: "After he had provided purification for sins, he sat down at the right hand of he Majesty in heaven." Hebrews 5:7–8 ssures us that Jesus participated fully in the uman experience of suffering (cf. 2:14–18) nd is therefore capable of fully sympathizing vith us in our trials and testings (cf. 4:15; 5:2).

Jesus entered so fully into the condition of uman suffering that it drew from him prayers and petitions with loud cries and ears" (5:7). These descriptive words are nparalleled anywhere in the New Testament n terms of their intensity. Since "prayers and etitions" are plural, our author may have nown of several incidents in Jesus' life when e prayed with such intensity. For us who are estricted to the New Testament, the words ound like Jesus' agony in the garden of Gethemane, when his prayers were so intense that e sweat drops of blood (cf. Matt. 26:31–46; uke 22:41–44). Jesus, who wept at Lazarus's rave in the face of human suffering and grief, vas capable of the strong emotions, suggested y the words "loud cries and tears." Guthrie omments: "Our high priest was not so far bove us that tears were beyond him" (1983, 29). He truly did identify completely with our uman plight of suffering.

Jesus' intense prayers were addressed "to he one who could save him from death" (5:7). Moreover, "he was heard" by the Father, but the answer came not in the avoidance of the experience of death. Rather, Jesus was heard in that he received God's grace to undergo his appointed suffering and was then delivered out of death through resurrection. Sometimes our fervent prayers seem to go unanswered, but are later answered in unexpected and fuller ways.

Verse 7 adds that Jesus was heard "because of his reverent submission." The Greek noun *eulabeia* can mean "fear," "piety," or "reverent awe." Some scholars believe that all these meanings are valid here (*TDNT*, 2:751–54). Thus we find in recent versions "because of His godly fear" (NKJV), "because of His piety" (NASB), and "because of his reverent submission" (NIV; NRSV). In Jesus' intense prayers there was both personal piety and reverent submission to the Father's redemptive will.

"Although he was a son" (v. 8) means "Son [of God] though he was" (cf. 1:2–5; 4:14); the writer goes on to state that Jesus "learned obedience from what he suffered" (5:8). Jesus, as the incarnate Son of God, had to learn in his humanity (as is true of all sons, cf. 12:7–11) "what it means to obey God when encircled by human sufferings and temptations. If His sufferings and temptations were genuine ... then His obedience could have been won [i.e., realized] only through suffering" (Hawthorne, 1986, 1514).

Moreover, Jesus was "made perfect" (5:9) through his suffering in that he became the perfect Savior and high priest because his sufferings and temptations were completed without sin. Thus our author effectively connects Jesus' saving work with his ministry of high priest. Being God's eternal Son and fully human (God's incarnate Son) qualified him in every way to be "the source of eternal salvation for all who obey him" (5:9) and to be the perfect high priest after the likeness of Melchizedek (5:10).

The salvation Jesus makes possible is "eternal," not just because "it extends beyond time but because it is true, heavenly, and not human-made" (Lane, 1991, 122; cf. 9:23–24). Such a salvation is "for all who obey him" (5:9). Jesus is the obedient one; true faith and union with him will be evidenced by the fruit of obedience in us (cf. John 8:31; Rom. 1:5; 16:26; James 2:17–26), which enables him to transform us into his likeness and thereby to prepare us for union with him in eternal glory. As Murray states, "obedience to God's will on earth is the way to the glory of God's will in heaven" (n.d., 189).

Finally, it is noteworthy that three phrases in Hebrews 5:9–10 are introductory to the exposition that follows in 7:1–10:18. That Jesus was a high priest like Melchizedek (5:10) is fully disclosed in 7:1–28; that Jesus was "made perfect" (5:9) in relation to our redemption is fully set forth in 8:1–9:28; and that Jesus is the "source of eternal salvation" (5:9) is fully explained in 10:1–18. In the meantime, the author inserts hortatory warnings in 5:11–6:20 in order to stir his readers out of their state of spiritual vacillation so they can receive the "solid food" (5:12) that follows in 7:1–10:18 (cf. Lane, 1991, 125–28).

Third Hortatory Warning: The Danger of Remaining Spiritually Immature (5:11–6:3)

Our author has already introduced the superior qualifications of Christ to be our high priest (4:14–5:10). But before proceeding to explore the profound meaning of that priesthood (7:1–10:18), he chides his readers about their spiritual dullness and exhorts them to move on to spiritual maturity (5:11–6:3). He warns them that there is serious peril in being dull of hearing and acting like spiritual infants when they should be going on to maturity in the Lord. If they persist in spiritual regression, they may experience irretrievable apostasy in the end (6:4–20).

These two hortatory warnings, as with the previous ones (2:1–4; 3:7–19), reveal unmistakably that the author is pastorally addressing real believers whose spiritual condition is well known to him. After an intense warning (6:4–8), however, the author informs his readers (whom he calls "dear friends," NIV; "beloved," NASB, NKJV) that he confidently expects "better things in your case—things that accompany salvation" (6:9).

The author has "much [more] to say about" (5:11) the subject of Christ's priesthood (begun in 4:14), including, of course, Melchizedek as a prefigurement of Christ (5:10). But further discussion of that priesthood "is hard to explain"—not because of the author's limitations or because it is a difficult subject, but "because [his readers] are slow to learn." The expression "are slow" might suggest that they were naturally slow learners. However, the Greek verb suggests they have not always been so; rather, they have "become slow."

"Slow to learn" in Greek is literally "dull of hearing" or "sluggish in hearing" (cf. the previous emphasis about the importance of attentive hearing in 2:1; 3:7–8, 15; 4:2, 7). The believers have abandoned the zeal that characterized their earlier Christian life (cf. 10:32-34) and have become "dull of hearing" (NASB, NKJV) and sluggish in understanding (5:12). They have been believers long enough that they themselves by now should be teachers of the gospel; instead, "you need someone to teach you the elementary truths of God's word all over again."

The book's larger context suggests that their dullness of hearing and spiritual regression to an infantile stage was a recent development in order to sidestep confrontation with fellow non-Christian Jews or to avoid further persecution because of their identity with Christ. "The elementary truths [lit., oracles] of God's word" most likely refers to a Christocentric understanding of the Old Testament. Their dullness of hearing concerning these "Christ truths" is a dangerous condition for Jews who have been called to radical obedience to Jesus (5:9). It implies "an unwillingness to probe the deeper implications of Christian commitment and to respond with faith and obedience (cf. 2:1–4; 4:1–2). If this apathetic attitude was not checked, it would lead to spiritual inertia and the erosion of faith and hope" (Lane, 1991, 136).

The contrast between "milk" and "solid food" in 5:12 is the difference between spiritual infancy and spiritual adulthood or maturity (5:13–14), not the Pauline contrast between worldly and spiritual (1 Cor. 3:1–4). In this context "solid food" refers to the author's subject about the high priesthood of Christ as the vastly superior fulfillment of what the Aaronic priesthood was a mere type or shadow.

Verses 13–14 contain a fivefold contrast between spiritual infants and the spiritually mature. (1) Spiritual infants need constantly to be taught (5:12); the mature are able to teach others (5:12)—not in the sense of formal teaching (i.e., a teaching charisma) but in their eagerness to share their faith and knowledge of Christ with others.

(2) Spiritual infants live on a diet of "milk"—that is, the ABCs of God's revelation—which these Christians require repeatedly "all over again" (5:12, 13a); the mature live on a diet of "solid food" (5:14).

(3) Spiritual infants are inexperienced or infantile in their understanding of "teaching about righteousness" (5:13); by implication the mature are experienced in that word. It is not clear whether "righteousness" here refers to the righteousness of God that is revealed in Christ and freely made available to all who believe, or whether it refers to the right conduct that mature believers are to demonstrate as the fruit of God's righteousness in them. In either case, the full "teaching about righteousness" should embody both these elements.

(4) Spiritual infants lack discernment concerning good and evil, what honors God and what dishonors him; the mature, however, have their spiritual faculties trained by constant practice to distinguish good and evil (5:14: cf. NASB, NKJV, NRSV). Bruce remarks that spiritually mature people "have built up in the course of experience a principle or standard of righteousness by which they can pass discriminating judgment on moral situations as they arise" (1990, 136).

(5) Spiritual infants know only "the elementary teachings about Christ" (6:1–3); by implication the mature are those who have pressed on to more advanced revelation about Christ, such as his high priestly ministry (6:1; cf. 5:11).

Since 6:1–3 continues 5:11–14, the opening words come as a surprise: "Therefore let us leave the elementary teachings about Christ and go on to maturity." We might have expected the author (like Paul) to accommodate himself to his readers' supposed need of "milk" (5:12c; cf. 1 Cor. 3:2). Instead, he exhorts them to pursue the mature path. Why "therefore"? "Probably because their particular condition of immaturity is such that only an appreciation of what is involved in Christ's high priesthood will cure it" (Bruce 1990, 138). Lane, on the other hand, believes "therefore" indicates the author used irony in 5:13–14 in order to shame his readers for acting like infants rather than like mature adults. "Therefore," because of the shamefulness, they should act like the spiritual adults they are in reality, and move on to maturity (1991, 139).

"The elementary teachings about Christ" form a basic foundation that the readers are to leave behind, not in the sense of abandoning it but of going on to build an adequate superstructure. The foundation has been properly laid in their lives and need not be laid again and again (6:1c). "Maturity" in this context involves active response to and application of the gospel of Christ (5:14; 6:1) by diligently pursuing the full realization of their hope (6:11), and by demonstrating unwavering faith and steadfast endurance (6:12).

The summary list of "elementary teachings" that follows is not exclusively Christian, for "practically every item could have its place in a fairly orthodox Jewish community" (Bruce, 1990, 139). The list falls into three groups of two each: personal response to God ("repentance" [from deeds that lead to death] and "faith," 6:1); outward ordinances ("instruction about baptisms" [perhaps Jewish ceremonial cleansings initially; water and Spirit baptisms under the new covenant] and "the laying on of hands" [for anointing or impartation], 6:2); and truths about the future ("the resurrection of the dead" and "eternal judgment," 6:2).

Insofar as these elementary truths were already part of Old Testament teaching, the Jewish readers had this general foundation when they accepted the fuller revelation of their meaning in Christ. Because of the Jewishness of this foundation, however, it was possible under the pressure of persecution to give up gradually the more distinctively Christian features of these truths without feeling they had abandoned the basics. It is at the point of this subtle danger of reverting back to Judaism without the appearance of "falling away" from God that the author challenges them to go on to maturity in Christ (6:1–3) and confronts them with the most solemn warning yet in his letter (6:4–8). The conditional statement in 6:3 suggests that some readers may not be able to advance because by their own decision they can "place themselves beyond the range of God's permission" (Hawthorne, 1986, 1515).

Fourth Hortatory Warning: The Fearful Possibility of Irretrievable Apostasy (6:4–20)

Some interpreters combine 5:11–6:20 as one hortatory unit. Nevertheless, there are good reasons for dividing the passage into two separate (though related) warnings. Whereas 5:11–6:3 focuses on the danger of spiritual sluggishness and spiritual regression with an exhortation to press on to maturity, the second warning focuses on the dreadful possibility of irretrievable apostasy if such regression continues unchecked (6:4–8). The author then encourages and challenges his readers to progress forward in hope and persevering faith (6:9–20).

Hebrews 6:4–6 constitute one long, complex sentence in Greek, which solemnly warns about the possibility of falling away (apostasy) from the Christian faith and the impossibility of being restored once such a condition has occurred. The sentence begins with the declaration "it is impossible," followed by five aorist participles in parallel construction describing who are being discussed (6:4–6a), followed by an infinitive stating the impossibility of repentance for apostates (6:6a), and concluding with two present participial phrases stating why apostates cannot be restored (6:6b).[3]

The word "impossible" (*adynatos*) occurs four times in Hebrews. In 6:18 it is "impossible" for God to lie; in 10:4 it is "impossible" for the blood of animals to remove sins; in 11:6 it is "impossible" to please God without faith; and here (6:4) it is "impossible" for apostates to be restored through repentance. In each instance the impossibility is stated absolutely.

Who are the subjects of this impossibility? The vast majority of New Testament scholars believe that verses 4–5 describe genuinely converted Christians—persons who are exhorted throughout Hebrews to persevere in their faith, not individuals who must be persuaded to become true Christians (see endnote 2). John Calvin (consistent with his theological presuppositions) and many of his followers believe that the persons here described were never among the elect. I. Howard Marshall is representative of modern biblical scholarship when he states: "A study of the descriptions provided here in a series of four [Greek aorist] participles suggests conclusively that genuine Christian experience is being described" (1969, 142).

(1) "Those who have once been enlightened" (6:4a) signifies not simply that those being referred to had received Christian instruction but that there had occurred "a decisive entrance of the light of the gospel into their lives" (Peterson, 1994, 1335), which resulted in the renewal of the mind and Christian experience.

(2) That they had "tasted the heavenly gift" (6:4b) refers to their having received the gift of Christ himself, along with all the spiritual blessings he graciously bestows. "Tasting" indicates more than just a knowledge of Christ; it suggests "experiencing something in a manner that is real and personal (not merely 'sipping')" (Peterson, 1994, 1335). The Calvinistic distinction between "tasting" and "eating" is unjustified here. The verb "to taste" speaks of experiencing the flavor or reality of what is eaten, not the amount of what is eaten.

(3) That the subjects also had "shared in the Holy Spirit" (6:4c)—lit., "having become sharers/partakers of the Holy Spirit"—clearly refers to a Christian experience in Hebrews (cf. John 20:22). The author uses the word "sharers" (*metochoi*) three times in Hebrews as one of his technical terms for those who have responded to God's call to salvation (Lane, 1991, 74; Schmidt, *TDNT*, 3:487–93). Thus true believers are "[sharers] in the heavenly calling" (3:1), "[sharers] in Christ" (3:14), and "[sharers] in the Holy Spirit" (6:4c). Bruce adds: "Whether it is possible for one who has been in any real sense a partaker of the Holy Spirit to commit apostasy has been questioned; but our author has no doubt that it is possible . . . to 'outrage the Spirit of grace' (10:29)" (1990, 146).

(4) Those being described "have tasted the goodness of the word of God and the powers of the coming age" (6:5). Notice that what is tasted is not God's Word itself but its goodness. This distinction is important, since it is possible to read God's Word "sincerely but without relish" (Guthrie, 1983, 143). The only way to experience the *goodness* of God's Word, however, is by the Holy Spirit. He is also the one who enables believers to experience the powers of the future age through "signs, wonders and various miracles, and gifts of the Holy Spirit" (2:4), and to partake now as a foretaste of the blessings of future salvation (9:11).

Thus, in these four descriptive aorist participles listed one after the other (6:4–5), the author intentionally presents the weight of accumulative evidence that the persons described had witnessed "the fact that God's alvation and presence [in Christ were] the nquestionable reality of their lives" (Lane, 991, 142).

"If they fall away, [it is impossible, 6:4a] ͻ be brought back to repentance" (6:6a). lthough the believers in 6:4–5 are described s having experienced a spiritual awakening, aving become partakers of Christ and the ndwelling of the Holy Spirit, and having nown God's goodness through his Word and ower, our author now presents their falling way from the faith as a real possibility. The hrase "if they fall away" (NIV; also NKJV) is ot a conditional clause in the Greek (there is o "if" in Greek). Rather, the phrase is an orist participle (as in verses 4–5) and should e translated in the past tense—lit., "having allen away" (cf. ASV, NASB, NEB, NRSV, Villiams). Thus, our author warns that for iose persons who calculatingly and volition- lly commit apostasy after having been shar- rs of Christ and the Holy Spirit, it is npossible for them "to be brought back to epentance."

Then our author adds two more participles his time present, durative ones) to describe recisely what their lapse from faith means and hy it is impossible to restore them to repen- ance. (1) The impossibility exists because they are crucifying the Son of God all over gain" (6:6b). The impossibility of repentance ere involves more than grief for past sin; it ncludes a change of mind or attitude toward hrist, such as occurred initially at Christian onversion. The seriousness of apostasy esides in the fact that "it is not the result of a uick decision in a weak moment, but of a radual hardening process within the mind hich has crystallized now into a 'constant ttitude of hostility towards Christ'" Hawthorne, 1986, 1516). This fact is con- eyed here by the present tense participle. The nguage of crucifying Jesus again identifies postasy with the cynicism, unbelief, and mal- e that originally led to his crucifixion.

(2) "Subjecting him to public disgrace" 5:6c) suggests shameful repudiation and con- empt for Christ and "an attitude of unremit- ng hostility" (Guthrie, 1983,144). That both articiples describing the significance of apos- sy are present tenses indicates "the action of postasy involves a continuous and obdurate ance toward Christ . . . [which] removes them from the only sphere where true repentance and reconciliation with God are possible" (Attridge, 1989, 172)—that is, in Christ himself. Thus their falling away or apostasy is irretrievable.

F. F. Bruce properly observes (1990, 147–49) that 6:4–6 has been both "unduly minimized" and "unduly exaggerated." It has been *unduly minimized* by those who argue in one form or another that the persons described in 6:4–5 were never fully regenerated Christians (e.g., Grudem, 1995, 133–82), or that this was only a hypothetical case being presented by the author and not something that can actually happen in experience (e.g., Hewitt, 1960, 110–11). The passage also has been *unduly exaggerated* by those who teach that once a person has been converted and baptized into Christ and his body, and then lapses back to his or her former sinful life, there can be no future pardon or restoration to Christian fellowship (e.g., Tertullian on post-baptismal sin). This interpretation applies the passage out of context and makes no distinction between "backsliding" and "apostasy."

The meaning of 6:4–6 may thus be summarized: (1) To "fall away" (v. 6) refers not to sin generally but to apostasy specifically, and involves a disowning of faith in Christ *after* having experienced his grace and salvation (often to embrace something else, such as Judaism, Buddhism, atheism, etc.). Anyone who repudiates "the salvation procured by Christ will find none anywhere else" (Bruce, 1990, 149). (2) The two present participles in verse 6 suggest enduring action that makes repentance impossible. Scripture and experience alike indicate that it is possible for volitional human beings to make decisions and arrive at a state of heart and life where they are no longer capable of responding to God in true repentance. (3) The passage is a warning, not a statement of fact. Neither the community addressed nor any of its members have yet abandoned their faith in Christ (6:9), though apostasy is a real danger for them. (4) The author's ultimate purpose is evident in 6:9–20 (as throughout Hebrews)—that is, to encourage his readers to remain steadfast in faith and to inherit the promises in Christ.

Verses 7–8 illustrate how the outcome of God's grace in the lives of Christians is not always the same, using the metaphor of two kinds of land (cf. Mark 4:3–20 and parallels). Those who persevere in faith are like cultivated land that, after receiving rain (God's grace), produces a useful crop (6:7). Those who abandon faith in Christ are like land that, after receiving rain (God's grace), "produces thorns and thistles . . . and is in danger of being cursed" (6:8). The mention of "blessing" (6:7) and "curse" (6:8) points to a covenant context. "The promise of blessing is attached to obedience, but the curse sanction is invoked in opposition to apostasy and disobedience (cf. Deut 11:26–28)" (Lane, 1991, 143).

Having given words of rebuke (Heb. 5:11–6:3) and severe warning (6:4–8), the author goes on to reassure his readers of his confidence in them and warm affection for them. "We are confident" (6:9) stands at the beginning of the Greek sentence and sounds a note of certainty based on (1) his relationship to them ("dear friends," NIV; lit., "beloved"), (2) his knowledge of their genuine "love" for God and deeds of service to his people (6:10), and (3) God's justice (6:10). The "better things" (6:9) are in contrast to the apostasy and the curse mentioned in 6:6, 8. The author is confident that his readers will be like the land in 6:7, which produces good fruit and receives God's blessing—"things that accompany salvation" (6:9).

These believers have in the past stood their ground in the face of suffering, were publicly exposed to insult and persecution, stood by others who were being so treated, sympathized with prisoners, and joyfully accepted the confiscation of their property because of their fai (10:32–34). And they "continue to hel (6:10) God's people in the present. In the ways they have demonstrated the genuinene of their Christian profession. What they ha done will not go unnoticed by a just God (c Matt. 5:11–12).

"We want each of you to show this san diligence to the very end" (6:11). The auth expresses a strong desire that each individu in the congregation will persevere in dilige faith (lit., "keep on showing diligence") un the return of Christ, when "the fullness of t hope" (lit. trans. of v. 11c) will be fully rea ized (cf. 9:28). The role of "hope" as a mo vation for persevering in love and faith is important element in Hebrews and the ear church. Biblically, hope is confidence based God's Word or promises. In these vers "love" (v. 10), "faith" (v. 12) and "hope" (v. 1 appear together, as often they do elsewhere the New Testament (Rom. 5:2–5; 1 Cor. 13:1 Gal. 5:5–6; Col. 1:4–5; 1 Thess. 1:3; 5:8; He 10:22–24; 1 Peter 1:21–22).

Verse 12 begins with a Greek *hina* clause purpose: (lit.) "in order that you do not becon lazy" (i.e., "sluggish," "dull," or "lethargic NIV "slow" in 5:11). Instead, the readers are "imitate those who through faith and patien inherit what has been promised" (6:12). Tl author previously warned his readers in 5:1 6:3 that sluggishness, "if not checked, wi develop into an inability to make any progre at all" (Guthrie, 1983, 149), which in turn ca lead to apostasy (6:4–6). Ther fore, such laziness must be dil gently avoided. The exhortatic to imitate earlier saints who their faith inherited promises illustrated by the life of Abraha in 6:13–15 and anticipates t illustrations in Hebrews 11, t great "faith" chapter. "Fait enables the believer to be stea fast until what was promised obtained; "patience" suggests quality of being undismayed difficulties" (Morris, 1981, 58).

In order to further combat t influence of non-Christian Jew along with the readers' prese inclination to drift in the directic of their arguments (2:1–3), t

This lush vineyard in Judea, with Tel Gezer in the background, illustrates the message of Hebrews 6:7–8. Christians who persevere in the faith are compared with farmland that receives plenty of rain and produces an abundant crop.

uthor now emphasizes two biblical facts: (1) the nduring validity of God's promise to Abraham ıade more sure by a divine oath, and (2) the upreme example of Abraham (mentioned ten mes in Hebrews) as a person who believed ;od's promise and faithfully persevered in hope) the end in spite of adverse circumstances that ave his faith no encouragement.

Foundational to all God's covenant promses and redeeming activity was God's promise) Abraham (Gen. 12:1–3), repeated on umerous occasions and in different forms in)ld Testament history (e.g., Gen. 15:1–21; 6:2–4; 28:13–15; Ex. 3:6–10). But on one articular occasion, after Abraham had nearly acrificed Isaac in obedience to God's test, ;od made the truthfulness of his promise mphatic with an oath (Gen. 22:16, "I swear y myself, declares the LORD"). Hebrews :13–14 indicates that this oath further encourged Abraham to wait "patiently," after which e "received what was promised" (6:15).

Westcott (1889/1980, 158) notes that God's se of an oath suggested further delay before the ılfillment of the promise. If God's intention /as to fulfill his promise immediately, there /ould have been no need for an oath. Abraam's patient waiting is seen in his willingness to await God's time for the fulfillment of the romise" (Morris, 1981, 59). In Abraham's lifeme God began fulfilling his promise (after wenty-five years waiting for Isaac, Gen. 21:5; ixty more years waiting for his grandchildren, 5:26), but the ultimate fulfillment came only ı the Lord Jesus Christ (cf. Gal. 3:16). Thus the eaders are exhorted to imitate Abraham's faith nd patience in waiting for the fulfillment of ;od's promises to them (cf. 6:12; 11:8–19).

The significance of God's oath is emphaized in 6:16–18. In human agreements "the ath confirms what is said and puts an end to ll argument" (6:16). The word "confirms" *bebaiosis*) is a technical word for legal guarntee and points to the binding confirmation of n oath. God himself swore by himself in a egally binding oath to Abraham in order "to ıake the unchanging nature of his purpose ery clear"—not just to Abraham, but "to the eirs [plural] of what was promised" (6:17). The heirs" refer to the spiritual descendants f Abraham (cf. Gal. 3:7, 26–29), especially to we . . . us" (6:18c) who are new covenant elievers in Christ (cf. ch. 8).

God underscores "the unchanging [and irrevocable] nature of his purpose" (6:17) by giving "two unchangeable things in which it is impossible for God to lie" (6:18)—namely, the promise to Abraham and the oath that accompanied it. This God did in order to provide the greatest possible incentive for his people to believe and trust him. The exceptionally strong double affirmation in verses 17–18 counters any Jewish argument that faith in Christ involves a change or departure from, rather than the fulfillment of, the promises on which the Old Testament saints based their faith. "We who have fled" (6:18c) refers specifically to new covenant believers who have fled the unbelief of the world with its hostility to God, in order "to take hold of the hope offered to us" (6:18c) in Christ.

Having emphasized that the believer's hope resides not in wishful thinking but in God's unchanging purpose and trustworthy promise supported by his oath, our author goes on to state that "we have this hope as an anchor for the soul" (6:19). "Hope," like a ship's anchor, counteracts the tendency to "drift away" (2:1) by stabilizing "the soul" in every circumstance. "Firm" means that Christ-centered hope "is undisturbed by outward influences," and "secure" means that "it is firm in its inherent character" (Westcott, 1889/1980, 163). Moreover, by our hope "we are moored to an immoveable object . . . [that is] the throne of God himself" (Bruce, 1990, 155) in "the inner sanctuary behind the curtain" (6:19b).

This language of the Old Testament tabernacle and temple refers to heaven's Most Holy Place, where God is enthroned in all his glory and "where Jesus, who went before us, has entered" (6:20a). "On our behalf" reintroduces Jesus' high priestly ministry of mediation and intercession. His going before us as a forerunner (*prodromos*) indicates that we will follow.

Peterson (1994, 1336) insightfully summarizes the meaning of the imagery in 6:19–20 and the larger passage:

> Our destiny [in Christ] is to live for ever in God's holy and glorious presence. We can literally go where Jesus has gone. Thus the heavenly sanctuary is another way of describing "the world to come" (2:5), the "Sabbath-rest for the people of God" (4:9), and "the heavenly country" or "city" (11:16; 12:22–24;

13:14), which has been the ultimate hope of the people of God throughout the ages. This hoped-for goal has been achieved and opened up for us by our Savior. Jesus as our "*hope*" has entered the sanctuary and remains there "*as an anchor for the soul, firm and secure*."

So the antidote to spiritual apathy and apostasy is the renewal of hope. Hope is the motivation for faithfulness and love. The basis for our hope is the promise of God, confirmed with an oath. Since the saving promises of God have already been fulfilled for us in the death and heavenly exaltation of the Lord Jesus Christ, this gives us every encouragement to believe that those who trust in Jesus will share with him in the promised eternal inheritance.

In the final statement of 6:20, the author returns to another prophetic promise (Ps. 110:4), also accompanied by the divine oath, that finds fulfillment in Jesus, who "has become a high priest forever, in the order of Melchizedek." This theme is developed in chapter 7.

2.1.3. Superior to Aaron and the Levitical Order in His Likeness to Melchizedek (7:1–10). Chapter 7 expounds on the priesthood of Christ as prophesied in Psalm 110:4, a Christological theme found only in Hebrews in the New Testament. The message of this verse, namely, that God makes an oath to establish his Son as a priest forever after the likeness of Melchizedek, burns like fire in the author's spirit. In view of this, he focuses on the subject of Melchizedek as a type or prefigurement of Christ's unique priesthood, a fact previously alluded to (5:6, 10; 6:20). His main purpose is to reveal further how Jesus as our high priest (4:14–16) is superior to Aaron and the Levitical priesthood. In 7:1–10 he identifies the Melchizedek of prophecy in Psalm 110:4 with the Melchizedek of history in Genesis 14:17–20. In Hebrews 7:11–28 he expounds on the prophetic significance of Psalm 110:4 more directly in relation to Christ.

The author of Hebrews deeply respects the biblical text as he refers to the historical background of Melchizedek in Genesis. Using Genesis 14:17–20, he addresses two major questions: (1) Who was Melchizedek (7:1–3)? and, (2) what significance can be derived from his encounter with Abraham (7:4–10)?

Melchizedek bore two important title (7:1). (1) He was "king of Salem," the city tha later became Jerusalem (cf. Ps. 76:2). "Salem' (related to the Heb. *shalom*) means "peace" thus he was "the king of peace" (a title tha anticipates the Messiah; e.g., Isa. 9:6–7) (2) Melchizedek also is introduced as "pries of God Most High," that is, the God of Abra ham. Although Melchizedek was a non Israelite and thus outside the mainstream o redemptive history, he nevertheless knew Go by revelation and was designated by God a priest. Because of his priesthood, he "blessed Abraham as he was "returning from the defea of the [four] kings," and he received fron Abraham "a tenth of everything" (7:2a), tha is, of the spoils from the battle. (This issue i addressed in more detail in 7:4–10.) Psalm 11 prophesied that God's Messiah-Son, lik Melchizedek, would be both king (110:1–3, 5- 7) and priest (110:4).

Verses 2b–3 further elaborate on the sig nificance of Melchizedek. His name is a com pound noun, comprised of two Hebrew words *melek*, which means "king," and *tsedek*, whic means "righteousness." Thus, his name liter ally means "king of righteousness." Verse explains that "king of Salem" means "king c peace." This combining of righteousness an peace (cf. Ps. 85:10) further anticipates the dis tinctive ministry of the Messiah.

"Without father or mother" does not sug gest Melchizedek was without parents or wa of heavenly origin. Rather, it is synonymou with "without genealogy" and simply mean he has no recorded ancestry, as was required i the Levitical priesthood. In the historical se ting of Genesis, the Scripture is silent abou Melchizedek's priestly descent: "Nothing i said of his parentage, nothing is said of hi ancestry or progeny, nothing is said of hi birth, nothing is said of his death" (Bruc 1990, 160). Moreover, nothing is said abou him being replaced by a successor; he remain in his place in history as a living priest (cf. 7:8

In all this, by way of silence, Melchizede prefigures Christ, who was without beginnin of days or ending of life and has no successo Hawthorne makes a significant observatio "The writer of Hebrews does not identif Melchizedek with Christ, but says that h resembles '*the Son of God*' (v. 3). Melchizede thus was the facsimile of which Christ is th ɜality" (1986, 1518). Thus the notion of eter-ality—"a priest forever" (7:3)—is only pre-ıgured in Melchizedek but is realized in ˈhrist.

In 7:4–10 the author continues to speak of ⁄Ielchizedek's greatness. His priesthood is the istorical precedent for another kind of priest-ood besides that of Aaron, "a superior priest-ood based on a character apart from line of escent and ordained by God apart from law" Lane, 1991, 171). "Just think how great he ʼas" (7:4)! Abraham, "the patriarch" of the Iebrew people, "gave him a tenth of the plun-er" (7:4) and received his priestly blessing 7:6). In these two ways, Abraham—"who had ıe promises" (7:6)—doubly acknowledged ıat he was "the lesser" and Melchizedek "the reater" (7:7).

Likewise, Melchizedek was greater than the evitical priests, whom he preceded and super-eded in time, insofar as he was the superior of ıbraham, the ancestor of the priests (7:5–6, 9–0). When Abraham paid a tithe to ⁄Ielchizedek, so did Levi, who "was still in the ody of his ancestor" (7:10). Since ⁄Ielchizedek is greater than Abraham, his riesthood is therefore greater than the Levit-ɜal priesthood. All of this points to the supe-iority of Christ's priesthood; for since Christ s greater than Melchizedek as the reality is reater than the prefigurement, so Christ is uperior to Abraham, Levi, and all his descen-ants. Therefore, Christ is "the ultimate dis-lacement of the Levitical priesthood" (Lane, 991, 171).

2.1.4. Superior to Aaron and the Leviti-al Order in His Abiding Permanence 7:11–25). In 7:11–25 the history of Genesis 4:17–20 is left behind, and the author turns is attention to the prophecy of Psalm 110:4. ʼirtually all the phrases in this prophecy are pplied to Christ's priesthood: "like ⁄Ielchizedek" (Heb. 7:11–14), "forever" 7:15–19, 23–25), "the Lord has sworn and ʼill not change his mind" (7:20–22). The uthor's exposition of Psalm 110:4 is not only ˈhristological but intensely practical. He hows how God, who gave the Levitical priest-ood, continues to act decisively in the present ı his appointment of Christ as eternal priest—ar superior to Aaron and the Levitical priests. even important aspects about the superiority f Jesus' priesthood are mentioned in this passage, all of which point to the abiding permanence of his high priestly ministry.

(1) The rhetorical question at the outset of 7:11 is deduced from the prophetic statement in Psalm 110:4 and suggests that the Levitical priesthood must be judged inadequate since the messianic priest was predicted to be "in the order of Melchizedek, not in the order of Aaron." The inadequacy of the Levitical priesthood was twofold: (a) It was incapable of securing the "perfection" (*teleiosis*) of the people (7:11); that is, it could not enable them to draw near to God on a continual basis. Approaching God through Jesus as high priest "is now stronger and surer and more complete than in the Old Testament and later Judaism" (*TDNT*, 2:331).

(b) Furthermore, Aaron's order of priesthood "was neither designed nor competent to inaugurate the age of fulfillment" (Bruce, 1990, 165; cf. 7:18–19). The Levitical system was designed as a shadow anticipating the substance; the substance attains perfection and ushers in the age of fulfillment. Verse 12 adds that the change in priesthood prophesied in Psalm 110:4 necessarily involved also "a change [setting aside] of the [Mosaic] law." Whereas the author's main perspective concerning the law and the gospel is one of continuity involving preparation and fulfillment, here he acknowledges an important discontinuity between the old and the new. As Bruce remarks: "In principle Paul and our author are agreed that the law was a temporary dispensation of God, valid only until Christ came to inaugurate the age of perfection" (1990, 167).

(2) Jesus "belonged to a different tribe," that is, the royal tribe of Judah rather than the priestly tribe of Levi (vv. 13–14). In the Old Testament era, no one but the descendants of Aaron "ever served [on a regular basis] at the altar" of burnt offering in the Jewish tabernacle/temple. "For it is clear" (7:14) that Jesus' priesthood ("our Lord") was not dependent on physical descent from Aaron as prescribed in the Mosaic law. The Greek word translated "descended" (*anatello*; 7:14) is used in the Septuagint for the rising of a star or the sprouting of a branch in contexts that were regarded as Old Testament messianic prophecies (e.g., Num. 24:17; Jer. 23:5). There is thus a double hint of Jesus' being both the royal Messiah and the priestly Messiah, as in Psalm 110.

(3) In 7:15–17 the author intensifies the comparison between Jesus as priest and the Aaronic priests by prefacing his remarks now as being "even more clear" (v. 15a; cf. v. 14a). In verses 13–14 he stated that the promised priest like Melchizedek did not possess the Levitical qualification of proper ancestral descent; in 15–17 he declares that the new priest "has become and remains" (the sense of the Greek perfect tense) a priest "on the basis of the power of an indestructible life" (7:16).

The expression "indestructible life" strikingly defines the prophetic meaning of "forever" in Psalm 110:4 and refers to the eternal existence of Jesus, the new priest, from the perspective of his resurrection. Lane (1991, 184) notes that the word "indestructible" is

> carefully chosen . . . [and] well suited to acknowledge that although Jesus' human life had been exposed to *katalusis*, "destruction," through crucifixion, his life was not destroyed by the death suffered on the cross. The phrase *dunamin zoes akatalutou* ["power of an indestructible life"] describes the new quality of life with which Jesus was endowed by virtue of his resurrection and exaltation to the heavenly world, where he was formally installed in his office as high priest.

Thus Jesus fulfills the Psalm 110:4 prophecy by virtue of his resurrected life, which does not and cannot end (7:17).

(4) Verses 18–19 emphasize that the Levitical system with all its regulations "is set aside" (lit., "annulled") by the coming of Christ as the messianic priest (in fulfillment of Psalm 110:4) because the former regulation "was weak and useless" (7:18). The author's point is that while the Levitical law served its purpose before the age of fulfillment, it had to go because it was imperfect and useless in bringing God's people into God's presence.

Whereas a former regulation is annulled, "a better hope is introduced [in Christ], by which we draw near to God" (7:19). Whereas the Levitical system kept people at a distance from God, Christ as the new covenant priest has opened up a way of free access to God. The word "better," a favorite word of our author (used thirteen times), characteristically refers to the superior provision of redemption introduced and made possible by Christ, such as better rest, a better hope, a better covenant, better sacrifice, better promises, and so fort The thought of drawing "near to God" has bo a present (4:16) and future (6:18–20) aspect it. Here the emphasis is on the certainty access made possible by Christ's effective an permanent priesthood.

(5) Jesus' priesthood is further described superior to the Levitical priesthood in that h has the security of God's oath behind it, whi the order of Aaron does not (vv. 20–22). Psal 110:4 is quoted again, but this time beginnin with an earlier phrase: "The Lord has swor and will not change his mind." The oath pr vides assurance from God that the new pries hood of Christ is a permanent one and thus w continue forever. The verb "he became" (He 7:21a) is unusual (the periphrastic perfe tense) and itself may suggest a continuin state. The divine oath provides full assuran that Christ's priesthood is final, etern unchangeable, and therefore "the guarantee c a better [see 7:19] covenant" (7:22).

The word "covenant" (*diatheke*) is anoth important term in Hebrews, occurring no le than seventeen times (compared to no mor than three times in any other New Testame book). Here priesthood and covenant are boun up together. Since Jesus is vastly superior to th Levitical priests, his covenant is better tha theirs. It is the "new covenant" predicted b Jeremiah (Jer. 31:31–34), the subject of chap ter 8, and a key term in the argument that fo lows in Hebrews 8:1–10:18. The "better hope is linked to the "better covenant."

(6) Verses 23–25 focus on the temporal an eternal contrasts between the two priesthood Whereas "death prevented" the Levitic priests "from continuing in office" (7:23 "Jesus lives forever" as the resurrected an ascended Lord, and therefore "he has a pe manent priesthood" (7:24). In 7:16 the auth had declared that Jesus was "a priest forever, based on "the power of an indestructible life. Now he emphasizes the abiding permanen of his priestly ministry in contrast to the Levit ical priests, whose ministry was continual interrupted by death.

According to Josephus, there were eighty three high priests who lived and died fro Aaron to the destruction of the second templ in A.D. 70 (*Antiquities* 20.227). The high pries ood of Jesus, on the other hand, is "permaent." The word used here (*aparabatos*) means inviolable" and thus "unchangeable." Jesus 'ill never have to hand his priestly ministry ver to someone else, because it is absolute, ternal, and unchangeable.

The word "therefore" at the beginning of erse 25 points to the logical and practical conequences of Jesus' being "a priest forever" in ılfillment of Psalm 110:4. He is able to do what o Levitical priest was ever capable of doing, amely, "to save completely those who come to iod through him" (7:25). Peterson observes ıat the theme of "approaching," "drawing ear," or "coming" to God is prominent in Iebrews (cf. 4:16; 7:19; 10:1, 22; 11:6; 12:18, 2). He adds that this theme "expresses the idea f a relationship with God. The Old Testament riesthood and sacrificial system only imperectly provided for such a relationship, but Jesus is able to save completely' those who relate to iod through him" (1994, 1338).

(7) Finally, because Jesus' high priestly ninistry is a permanent one, "he always lives o intercede" (7:25b) for God's people. The irect result of his intercession is twofold: (a) Ve can confidently approach God's throne as place of grace, not judgment, and thereby eceive his mercy, grace, and help to sustain us n every test and temptation of life (4:14–16). b) Jesus secures for us, as our interceding riest, all that is necessary for complete salvaion as we "come to God through him." The erb "come" indicates that those who respond y faith in constantly coming to God through Christ are the ones he is able to save. The interession of Christ is made in his supreme place n heaven as the one who died for our sins and vas raised for our justification, not in "a coninuous liturgical action in heaven for our benfit" (Morris, 1981, 71).

2.1.5. Superior to Aaron and the Levitical Order in His Perfection As the Son 7:26–28). The author now explicitly states the nability of Aaron and the Levitical priests to ttain the goal of perfection and the full realzation of perfection that is attained by Jesus as he Son. He emphasizes the Son's perfection in erms of his character, sacrifice, and heavenly ninistry.

Verse 26 begins with the important conunction *gar* ("for," omitted in NIV), which ooks back to Jesus' continuing heavenly intercession (7:25) and ahead to his perfect suitability for this role (7:26–28). As our high priest forever, Jesus "meets our needs" (lit., "is fitting for us"). This expression here and in 2:10 refers to his perfection in his priestly role.

Five qualities that are perfectly seen in Jesus Christ are mentioned in 7:26. (1) He is "holy" (*hosios*). Two Greek words for "holy" occur in the New Testament: *hagios*, which points to the quality of being set apart for God; and *hosios*, which emphasizes the character issue of purity and fidelity (without moral defection). (2) "Blameless" means "innocence" in the sense of being without guile and untouched by evil. (3) "Pure" means "undefiled" and thus fully qualified to fulfill the role of high priest in the presence of God. (4) Moreover, unlike the Aaronic priests, Jesus is "set apart from sinners." (5) Finally, he is "exalted above the heavens." Bruce aptly comments about the latter two features: "Although he came to earth 'in the likeness of sinful flesh,' lived among sinners, received sinners, ate with sinners, was known as the friend of sinners, yet he is set apart from sinners, 'in a different class from sinful men,' and is now exalted above all the heavens to share the throne of God" (1990, 176). The personal holiness, sinlessness, and sphere of Christ's high priestly ministry all speak of his perfection as the Son and thus of his superiority to the Aaronic order of priests.

The author goes on to describe Jesus' primary achievement as the perfect high priest, namely, his once-for-all-time sacrifice for sin (v. 27): "He does not need to offer sacrifices day after day, first for his own sins and then for the sins of the people," as did "the other high priests." This is true for two reasons: (1) because he himself was sinless, and (2) because his unique offering of himself for sin terminated the whole system of Levitical sacrifices (both the daily sacrifices and the annual Day of Atonement). As the spiritually and morally perfect high priest (v. 26), Jesus was able to offer the perfect and definitive sacrifice (v. 27). That his sacrifice for sins was "once for all" (*ephapax*) signifies that it was both complete and permanently valid, with no need of repetition. The decisive character of the work of Christ is a hallmark of Hebrews. Although explicitly introduced here for the first time, it waits for further development in chapters 9–10 (see 9:12, 26, 28; 10:10).

The author's appreciation for forceful antithesis is well demonstrated in verse 28 as he underscores and summarizes the profound differences between Christ and the Levitical priests in a concluding threefold contrast. (1) The first antithesis is between "the law" and "the oath," both of which are said to "appoint" (though God himself ultimately constituted both law and oath); the former appointed the Levitical priests, while the latter "appointed the Son." Because the law was temporary and the priests whom it appointed were ineffective in attaining God's goal of redemption for his people, God made an oath "to establish a radically different priesthood to supersede the Levitical institution" (Lane, 1991, 195). The idea of superseding is indicated by the phrase "which came after the law."

(2) The second antithesis is between the Old Testament high priests as "men" and the New Testament priest as "the Son." The divine oath concerning the New Testament priest as prophesied in Psalm 110:4 and the divine Son as foreseen in the messianic Psalm 2:7 are both fulfilled in Jesus Christ and thus are legitimately combined together.

(3) The final antithesis is between the former priests who were "weak" and the new priest who "has been made perfect forever." The Levitical high priests were "weak" because they were subject to the earthly limitations, frailties, and mortality, common to sinful humanity. The Son, however, "has been made perfect forever" through suffering (2:10; 5:8–9), so that his high priestly mediation may continue uninterrupted forever in the heavenly sanctuary. Thus, the high priesthood of the Son "is absolutely efficacious and eternally suited to meet his people's need" (Bruce, 1990, 179). He is incomparably perfect.

2.2. *Superior to Aaron and the Levitical Order in His Ministry As High Priest (8:1—10:18)*

So far the author of Hebrews has described the greatness and superiority of Jesus as our high priest. He now turns to look at the crowning part of his argument: the greatness of Jesus' *ministry* as high priest and how he carries out his duties. The next two and one-half chapters reveal that his ministry is unspeakably superior to the former priesthood because it is (1) located in a better (heavenly) sanctuary (8:1–5), (2) based on a better (new) covena (8:6–13), (3) performed through a better (ete nal) service (9:1–22), and (4) fulfilled by a be ter (perfect) sacrifice (9:23–10:18).

2.2.1. Superior to Aaron and the Leviti cal Order Because His Ministry Is Locate in a Better Sanctuary (8:1–5). The authc begins with two important statements that sur up the main "point" of what he has been say ing concerning Jesus as the Christian's hig priest (8:1–2). (1) The first statement stresse that Jesus' position in heaven is one c supreme honor and authority: He is seated "a the right hand of the throne of the Majesty i heaven" (cf. 1:3 and Psalm 110:1, which spea of the exaltation of the Son). "The posture c sitting points to a completed work" (Morris 1981, 74). The expression "throne of th Majesty in heaven" is a reverent way o describing God as the ruler of heaven an earth. Christ thus shares in the Father's rule.

(2) Christ "serves in the sanctuary, the tru tabernacle set up by the Lord" (v. 2). The heav enly throne room is thus also the celestial Mos Holy Place or "the true tabernacle," wher Christ serves as our high priest. The earthl tabernacle constructed by Moses at God's com mand (cf. 8:5) "corresponds to a heavenly real ity, and it is in the heavenly reality that Christ' ministry is exercised" (Morris, 1981, 75). Thi is a crucial point in the author's argument fo the superiority of Jesus' priesthood to that of th Levitical order. "True tabernacle" is in contras not to what is false but to what is simply a shadow of the true reality. Bruce notes tha heaven's "sanctuary" and "tabernacle" belon "to the same order of being as the saint's ever lasting rest of chs. 3 and 4, the better countr and well-founded city of 11:10, 16, the unshak able kingdom of 12:28" (1990, 182).

If Jesus ministers as high priest in the tru tabernacle, what is the nature of his ministry Logically, where there are priests, there ar sacrifices to be offered. The author made th point already in 5:1, which he now repeats i 8:3: "Every high priest is appointed to offe both gifts and sacrifices ['for sins' in 5:1]." "Gifts and sacrifices" (cf. Lev. 21:6; Heb. 5:1 9:9) refer to the variety of sacrifices that th Levitical priests offered to God on behalf o the people as prescribed by the law of Moses Jesus as high priest, therefore, must also "hav something to offer" for the removal of sin

Iere the author does not state what that some-ing is, though it is clear in 7:27 that "he ffered himself," a subject to be developed ore fully later (9:14).

In 8:4 the contrast between the two orders f priesthood is mentioned again. Whereas the w regulated the earthly ministry of the Levit-cal priests, Jesus' priesthood is emphatically ot of this earth. "On earth Jesus was a layman .. [and] performed no priestly functions in any arthly sanctuary" (Morris, 1981, 75). But his riesthood is categorically superior to the arthly in that it is exercised elsewhere in the ue sanctuary of the heavenly realm.

The service of the Levitical priests on earth "at a sanctuary" that at best is only "a copy nd shadow of what is in heaven" (8:5). lthough the earthly sanctuary was instituted y God, it was incomplete and imperfect. The vords "copy and shadow" both point to a reater reality in heaven behind what is seen n earth. Guthrie comments (1983, 175):

> A copy of a great master-work of art is not the real thing but gives some idea of what the original is like. The resemblance is incomplete and not until the original is seen is the full glory recognized. Similarly a shadow cannot in fact exist unless there is an object to cast it. There is some correspondence, but the shadow is inevitably a distorted and somewhat featureless picture of the real. The writer's purpose is not to reduce the glory of the shadow, but to enhance the glory of the substance.[4]

The author's mind goes back to Exodus 5:40, where God revealed to Moses how to uild the earthly tabernacle: "See to it that you nake everything according to the pattern hown you on the mountain" (Heb. 8:5c; cf. cts 7:44). The term "pattern" (*typos*), from vhich we get the word "type," indicates that Aoses was shown something objectively visble, not just given verbal instruction (Lane, 991, 207). The pattern "may have been a nodel for which the verbal directions served s a commentary; it may have been the heavnly dwelling-place of God which Moses was ermitted to see" (Bruce, 1990, 184). Thus, the arthly tabernacle was an imperfect but real epresentation of the greater heavenly reality; f so, how much greater is the high priestly ministry of Jesus in heaven than the ministry of Aaron's descendants on earth.

Concerning Old Testament typology, five important elements characterize Old Testament types (Broomall, 1960, 534). (1) They are thoroughly rooted in Old Testament history and not mythical (e.g., Melchizedek is a historical figure). They occur in some part of Hebrew history and find their full embodiment or antitype in New Testament history.

(2) Old Testament types are prophetic in purpose, pointing to a future fulfillment at the time of the Messiah. Thus Melchizedek, a contemporary of Abraham and king of Salem (Gen. 14:18–20), prophetically points to the Lord Jesus Christ, who alone is the priest forever.

(3) Old Testament types are designed by God himself as an integral part of redemptive history. In other words, they are not an afterthought read back into the Old Testament in retrospect. Rather, they were designed by God from the outset of redemptive history to prefigure something else at a later stage of redemptive history.

(4) Old Testament types are Christocentric. They all point to Jesus Christ in one way or another, anticipating various facets of his ministry—a point that Hebrews makes repeatedly.

(5) Old Testament types are edificatory, that is, they have spiritual meaning for God's people under both covenants (old and new). The Old Testament believers were edified by the tabernacle worship, sacrifices, and priestly ministry. How much more are New Testament believers edified under the ministry of Jesus, who fulfills all the Old Testament types. The former were the shadow, the reality resides in Jesus Christ.

2.2.2. Superior to Aaron and the Levitical Order Because His Ministry Is Based On a Better Covenant (8:6–13). In chapter 8 "the ministry Jesus has received" (8:6) is superior to the Aaronic priesthood because he is the minister of the sanctuary in heaven (8:1–5) and because he is the mediator of the new covenant on earth (8:6–13).

Three comparatives occur in 8:6. (1) "Superior" (*diaphoroteros*) is a word used in Hebrews for the supremacy of Christ (a) as the Son of God and thus the full revelation of God (e.g., 1:4), and (b) as the one mediator (high priest) between God and humankind (8:6). As such Jesus has incomparably greater honor, power, and authority than the Aaronic priests.

(2) The second comparative, also translated "superior" in the NIV, is a different Greek word, *kreitton* (lit., "better"), and refers to Jesus as being the "mediator of a better covenant" (KJV, NKJV, NASB, NRSV). In Hebrews "mediator" is always associated with the new covenant (8:6; 9:15; 12:24; cf. 7:22), since "the new covenant required a new mediator" (Lane, 1991, 208). A mediator is an arbitrator or go-between, whose assignment is to keep two parties in fellowship with one another (in this case, God and humans) according to the terms of the covenant.

(3) The new covenant is better than the old because "it is founded on better [*kreitton* again] promises." Those "better promises" are recorded in the long quotation from Jeremiah that follows in 8:8–12.

Because something was "wrong with that first covenant," a second or better covenant was necessary (8:7). By "first covenant" is meant the Sinai covenant, not the chronologically earlier covenants God made with Noah or Abraham. The essential fault with that "first covenant" was "the people" (8:8a, i.e., the Israelites), who "did not remain faithful to my covenant . . . declares the Lord" (8:9).

The word "covenant" (*diatheke*) occurs at least seventeen times in Hebrews and is crucial in the author's argument for the supremacy of Christ. God chose to redeem and enter into relationship with Abraham's promised descendants by means of a covenant. The covenant was established not on a coequal basis but with God himself as the sole initiator, laying down the terms under which his covenant relationship with Israel would exist. The Israelites became his covenant people (corporately) at Mount Sinai and pledged loyal and steadfast love to him (Ex. 19:3–8).

This covenant was imperfect, however, in that it was primarily an external relationship rather than one from the heart. Both the law and tabernacle worship were external to the people. When the people failed in their relationship to God under the old covenant, God promised through Jeremiah that he would "make a new covenant" with his people, at which time the law and worship would be internalized as heart reality, based on knowing him and giving his people free access to him.

Hebrews strongly argues that the first covenant was imperfect and incomplete, a temporary provision by God until the time for the perfect was to come (cf. 8:6–7). The "new covenant" was not an afterthought in God's mind that became necessary simply because the first covenant was not working. Rather, the new covenant was necessary from the beginning and was always in God's heart and plan of redemption.

How do we know that God always intended a new covenant? (1) He prophetically revealed his plan for a new covenant to the Old Testament prophets centuries before it became a historical reality (8:8–12; cf. Jer. 31:31–34; Ezek. 37:26–28). (2) God never intended the first covenant to be permanent since his plan from the beginning centered in his Son even before the creation of the world (Eph. 1:4). That the first covenant was temporary and anticipated the superior covenant from the beginning is apparent from all the types and shadows built by God into the old covenant that prefigured Christ by design. (3) Christ, not the old covenant provisions, is the fulfillment of the original Abrahamic covenant (Gal. 3:14, 16, 29) and all the Old Testament types and shadows (Heb. 4:1–10:18; cf. Luke 22:7–8, 14–22).

The new covenant foretold by Jeremiah stands in contrast to the failure of the old one. The root problem of the first covenant, after God had taken Israel "by the hand to lead them out of Egypt" (stressing God's initiative), was the covenant people "did not remain faithful to my covenant" (Heb. 8:9; lit., "they did not continue in my covenant"). Instead, they went after other gods, as the Old Testament prophets emphasize. The new covenant, therefore, promised to establish a new relationship with the covenant people of Christ, with three characteristics. (1) It would be inward: "I will put my laws in their minds and write them on their hearts" (8:10). God's holiness and righteousness have been imparted and internalized in believers by the indwelling Holy Spirit, so that there is a new heart and an inner desire to be God's holy people.

(2) The new covenant would be personal: "They will all know me, from the least of them to the greatest" (8:11). Knowing God is not just a community experience but a matter of direct personal knowing of God by each individual member of the covenant community. "The true Christian community is intended to be a group in which all are on an equal footing through a common and personal experi-

nce of the Lord" (Guthrie, 1983, 177). lebrews sees this promise fulfilled in the irect approach to God that Christ as our high riest makes possible (4:16; 7:25; 10:19–22; f. 12:22–24).

(3) The new covenant would thoroughly eal with sin: "I will forgive their wickedness nd will remember their sins no more" (8:12). Believers will know fully the reality of God's orgiveness of their sins through a cleansed onscience (cf. 9:14). Whereas the blood of ulls and goats could only cover over sin, the lood of Christ enables sin to be blotted out so hat God remembers it no more.

The author concludes by focusing on the mplications of the key word "new" in Jeremiah's prophecy (8:13). God, who had established the first covenant in anticipation of the ew, has now fulfilled and antiquated the old y establishing the new. "By calling this ovenant 'new,' he [God] has made the first ne obsolete." Formerly God had spoken hrough the law and the Old Testament rophets, but now he speaks through his Son, who is here to stay. Since all that was associated with the first covenant "will soon disappear," it is futile to contemplate returning to t. God takes away the first covenant in order o establish the second (10:9). Historically, the emple with its old covenant sacrifices and riesthood did disappear in A.D. 70, shortly fter the writing of this book, when Jerusalem was destroyed by the Romans.

2.2.3. Superior to Aaron and the Levitical Order Because His Ministry Is Performed Through a Better Priestly Service 9:1–22). In some ways 9:1–10:18 is the heart of the author's argument. In considerable detail e contrasts the old covenant priestly service the earthly) and the new covenant priestly ministry of Christ (the heavenly) in order to complete his argument that the old was simply foreshadowing of and a preparation for the ew, and that the new fulfills, surpasses, and eplaces the old. Consequently, his readers annot turn back in nostalgia to the old without disastrous results (cf. 10:19–31).

In the present section, the author reveals his appreciation for the glories of the past (9:1–10) but also points his readers to the far surpassing glory of Christ's priestly ministry (9:11–22). By repeating at the beginning of 9:1 the catchword from 8:1–13, "the first covenant," the author skillfully enhances the continuity of what preceded with what follows as he shifts from one aspect of his theme to another (Lane, 1991, 217).

Thematically, in chapter 8 Jesus is seated in heaven as (1) the minister of the sanctuary in heaven (8:1–5), and (2) the mediator of the new covenant on earth (8:6–13). In chapter 9 the inadequacy of the old order is especially seen in relation to the medium of blood. Only the power of Christ's blood can open the sanctuary in heaven and inaugurate the new covenant on earth. The word "blood" does not appear in Hebrews until chapter 9, where it occurs twelve times. In contrast to the limited usefulness of the blood of goats and bulls under the old covenant (9:6–10, 12–13, 18–22), the blood of Christ opens the Most Holy Place in heaven and effectively cleanses our consciences so that we are able to enter (9:12–14). By the blood of Christ the new covenant is established and put into effect (9:15–22).

In 9:1, the author introduces two important subjects related to the priestly ministry under "the first covenant": (1) "regulations for worship," and (2) the "earthly sanctuary" (or "tabernacle," 9:2a), which he discusses in reverse order in 9:2–5 and 9:6–10. The tabernacle is called "earthly" or "worldly" (*kosmikon*) because it was made with human hands (cf. 8:2; 9:11, 24) and denotes the sphere of its activity, in contrast to the heavenly sphere not made with human hands, where Jesus Christ now ministers (cf. 8:5–6; 9:11–12).

The author stresses that the Old Testament tabernacle (as constructed by Moses in the desert) was divided into two compartments: "the Holy Place" (9:2) and "the Most Holy Place" (9:3). These two compartments (NIV "rooms") of the one tabernacle are distinguished by the numerical terms "first" and "second." Each room contained furniture with symbolic meaning as instructed by God, and the veil that separated the two rooms also had deep meaning.

In verse 2 three furnishings are mentioned in the Holy Place. (1) "The lampstand" was seven-branched and held seven oil lamps (Ex. 25:31–40; 37:17–24). The oil lamps were fed with olive oil (itself rich in biblical symbolism). The lamp wicks were trimmed and lighted each evening, burned continuously through the night, and then were extinguished

The Tabernacle Fulfilled in Jesus

According to the writer to the Hebrews, the Old Testament tabernacle was a shadow pointing to the real thing, Jesus Christ (8:6; 9:23; 10:1). This chart depicts how the various parts of the tabernacle are fulfilled in Jesus Christ.

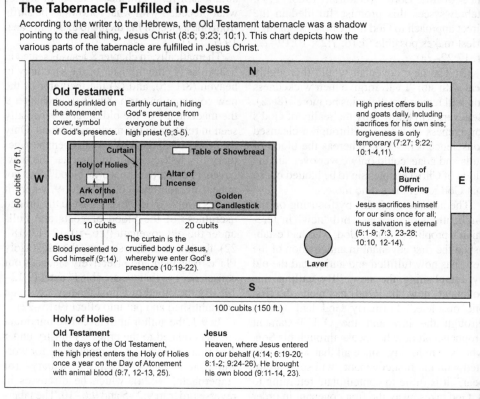

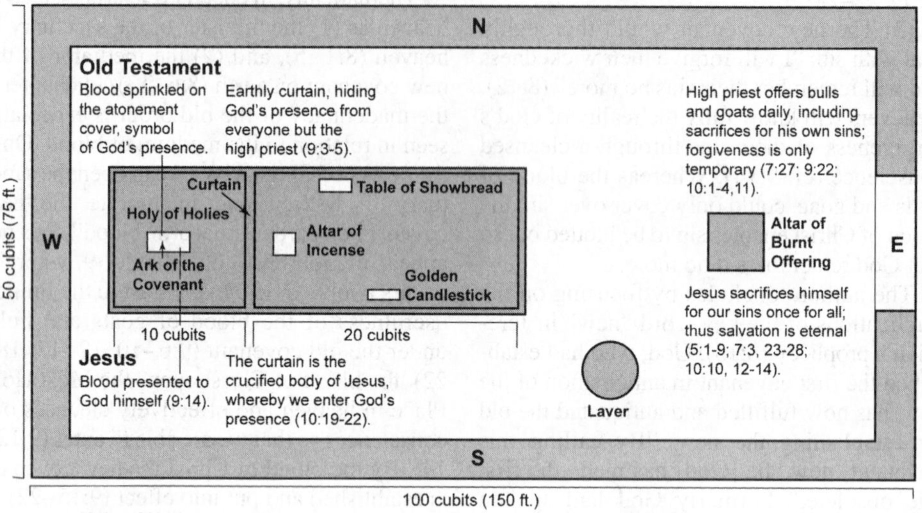

Holy of Holies

Old Testament
In the days of the Old Testament, the high priest enters the Holy of Holies once a year on the Day of Atonement with animal blood (9:7, 12-13, 25).

Jesus
Heaven, where Jesus entered on our behalf (4:14; 6:19-20; 8:1-2; 9:24-26). He brought his own blood (9:11-14, 23).

each morning. God served as Israel's light in a dark world. Prophetically, the lampstand pointed to Jesus, who declared: "I am the light of the world" (John 8:12).

(2) The Holy Place also contained "the table" and (3) "the consecrated bread." Twelve cakes of unleavened bread (one for each of the twelve tribes), arranged in two rows of six each, were displayed on a table thirty-six inches long, eighteen inches wide, and thirty inches high. They were eaten each Sabbath by the priests and replaced with fresh bread. The bread represented Israel's complete dependence on God for their daily bread. Prophetically, the bread points to Jesus, who declared: "I am the bread of life" (John 6:48).

After designating the location of the Most Holy Place (9:3), the author in verses 4–5 describes two furnishings associated with it: "the golden altar of incense" and "the gold-covered ark of the covenant." The identification of the altar of incense with the Most Holy Place is surprising since the Old Testament places it immediately before the veil in the Holy Place, where it was in daily use (cf. Ex. 30:6–8). The most likely explanation for this seeming dis crepancy is that the author had in mind its asso ciation in terms of significance rather than it location of place. Hawthorne (1986, 1521 explains this distinction as follows:

> It must be noted that the writer says there is a tent "called the Most Holy Place, which had the golden altar of incense" (3–4). He does not say "in which is the golden altar" as he did in describing the position of the furniture mentioned above in v. 2. The substitution of "having" for "in which" "itself points clearly to something different from mere position." It was probably intended to mean that the altar properly belonged to the holy of holies [in function]. "The ark and the altar of incense typified the two innermost conceptions of the heavenly sanctuary, the manifestation of God and the spiritual worship of man. And thus they are placed in significant connection in the Pentateuch: Ex. 30:6; 40:5; cf. Lev. 4:7; 16:12,18."

Montefiore concurs: "Our author does not ctually commit himself to the view that the ltar of incense is situated in the sanctuary: he ıerely says that it belonged to the sanctuary" 1964, 145). Its significance is clear: The priests vere to place a censer of fire on the altar and urn incense on it every morning and evening. ragrant smoke filled the Holy Place and pentrated into the Most Holy Place (God's presnce). The incense smoke represented the erpetual prayers of God's people ascending to God on his throne (cf. Rev. 8:3–5).

The "ark of the covenant" was the most mportant part of the Most Holy Place (Ex. 5:10–22; 26:33; 40:21). It was a rectangular chest (3 3/4 feet long, 2 1/4 feet wide, 2 1/4 eet high), made of acacia wood and overlaid vith pure gold inside and outside. The lid of he ark was called "the atonement cover" or 'mercy seat" (ASV). Here the atoning blood vas sprinkled by the high priest on the annual Day of Atonement. Two gold cherubs were arved as one piece with the ark's top, one at ach end facing each other with their wings pread forward. "The cherubim of the Glory, vershadowing the atonement cover" (9:5), epresent the heavenly scene, where cherubim hover at the throne of God. There Jesus serves as the Christian's high priest, ministering as nediator and intercessor at the throne of grace on our behalf (cf. 4:14, 16; 7:24–25; also Rom. 8:34).

The threefold description of the ark's conents—"the gold jar of manna, Aaron's staff hat had budded, and the stone tablets of the covenant" (9:4)—is mentioned here only in he Bible as all being inside the ark. There are two contrasting views about the contents' significance. (1) They were part of the positive testimony of the covenant: the manna as a reminder of God's provision in the desert, Aaron's staff as a reminder of God's mighty acts, and the two stone tablets of the Ten Commandments as a reminder of God's standard of holiness for his people (cf. *FLSB*, Heb. 9:4 note). (2) The contents were symbols of Israel's rebellion (cf. Chrysostom: "the tables of the covenant because he broke the former ones, and the manna because they murmured . . . and the rod of Aaron which budded because they rebelled") and were placed between God and the people's sin at the place of atonement (Hawthorne, 1986, 1521).

The author ends abruptly his brief discussion of the tabernacle and its furnishings with the declaration that "we cannot discuss these things in detail now" (9:5b). Why not? Because these furnishings (though full of prophetic symbolism) are secondary to his main argument. Bruce notes that the author "leaves us with the impression that he could have enlarged at some length on their symbolism had he chosen to do so" (1990, 205). Instead, he keeps to his primary focus when describing the tabernacle in 9:2–5, which is the distinction and independent significance of its two compartments (Lane, 1991, 217).

Herein lies an important theological underpinning of Hebrews. The Levitical priests could enter the Holy Place to minister, but a veil separated them from direct access to God's holy presence as represented by the Most Holy Place. God as holy and Israel as sinful could not dwell together.

> The tabernacle thus expressed the union of two apparently conflicting truths. God called man to come and worship and serve Him, and yet he might not come too near: the veil kept him at a distance. . . . The entrance of the high priest once a year for a few moments was a faint foreshadowing that the time would come when access to the Holiest would be given. In the fullness of time, righteousness and love would be revealed in their perfect harmony in Him, in whom those types and shadows find their fulfillment. (Murray, n.d., 285)

The distinction between the tabernacle's two compartments is further described in 9:6–7 in terms of the regulations for priestly service there. The covenant people under the old covenant could approach God only through priestly representatives. The priests on behalf of the people "entered regularly into the outer room [the Holy Place] to carry on their ministry." This included daily trimming and lighting of the lamps (Ex. 27:21), weekly replacement of the bread of consecration (Lev. 24:5–9), and twice daily burning of incense on the incense altar (Ex. 30:7–8).

"But only the high priest entered the inner room [the Most Holy Place], and that only once a year," on the Day of Atonement. Entrance into the Most Holy Place was "never without blood, which he offered for himself and for the sins the people had committed in ignorance" (cf. Lev. 16). Because of humanity's sinfulness, we can never approach God's holy presence "without blood." Atoning blood as the medium by which we have access to God is repeatedly stated from this point on in Hebrews (9:12, 13, 14, 18, 20, 21, 22; 10:4, 19, 29; cf. 11:28; 12:24; 13:11, 12, 20). Lane observes that "this fact underscores the importance of the reference to Christ's blood in the ensuing argument" (1991, 223).

The use of the word "offered" (*prosphero*) in verse 7 in reference to the high priest's application of blood in the Most Holy Place is especially significant and without parallel elsewhere in Scripture. This annual event "finds its eschatological fulfillment in Christ's death (*prosphora*, 'offering'; 10:10, 14). The creative use of unusual terminology to describe the atonement ritual in v.7 is indicative that the writer's interpretation of the Levitical rite is controlled by the Christ-event" (Young, 1980–81, 207–10).

The author next states that the Holy Spirit was revealing through the pattern of tabernacle worship that there was no direct access to God. "As long as the first tabernacle was still standing," the congregation of God's people had no direct access "into the Most Holy Place" of God's presence (v. 8). The "first tabernacle" may refer either to the "first room"/tent—that is, the Holy Place (Lane, 1991, 224; Peterson, 1994, 1340)—or to the entire sanctuary of the "first" covenant, involving both the Holy Place and the Most Holy Place (Bruce, 1990, 208). The former view holds the "first room" symbolically represents the "first covenant"; the latter interpretation sees the whole tabernacle serving that purpose (the more likely view).

The whole tabernacle thus serves as "an illustration for the present time" of the person and finished work of Christ, whose blood alone can "clear the conscience of the worshiper" (9:9). A clear conscience was something that Old Testament "gifts and sacrifices" alone could not provide. Hebrews teaches that the real barrier to free access to God is inward, not outward; spiritual, not material. The barrier exists in the conscience. Only when one's conscience is cleansed is a person "free to approach God without reservation and offer him acceptable service and worship. And th sacrificial blood of bulls and goats is useless i this regard" (Bruce, 1990, 209).

The Old Testament ordinances of Levitic worship involved such things as "food an drink and various ceremonial washings (9:10). These external, temporary provisior were valid only "until the time of the ne order." Christ fulfills what is anticipated an foreshadowed in the old covenant. His comin was thus a complete amendment or reforma tion of Israel's religious structure. As Bruc notes, "the old covenant was now to give wa to the new, the shadow to the substance, th outward and earthly copy to the inward an heavenly reality" (1990, 211).

Verses 11–12 form one long sentence i Greek, as do verses 13–14. These four verse form the core of our author's argument. Thi paragraph contrasts the definitive nature c Jesus' priestly service with the priestly servic under the old order (9:1–10). Under the ol covenant, the forms and regulations governin priestly service were obligatory "until the tim of the new order" (9:10). Now that Chris (*Christos*, "anointed one," Messiah) has com as high priest, "the good things" that are t come with the new order "are already here (9:11).[5] Guthrie aptly notes that "whereas th old [order] was a foreshadowing of bette things to come, the new [order] rests on a already accomplished fact" (1983, 185) Because Christ has appeared, "the shadow have given way to the perfect and abiding real ity" (Bruce, 1990, 212).

Among the "good things" that we hav already begun to experience in messiani redemption with the rending of the veil Hebrews emphasizes especially two. (1) W now have the perfect high priest who intercede and serves on our behalf in the heavenly sanc tuary, of which the Aaronic priests and th earthly tabernacle were only a foreshadowin (4:14–16; 7:23–26; 8:1–2, 5; 9:11–14). (2) Th blood of Christ provides decisive inner cleans ing from sin, provides full access into the Mos Holy Place of God's presence, and enables believers to worship and serve God in his pres ence with a clear conscience (9:12–14).

(1) Christ serves "as high priest of the gooc things that are already here" by virtue of his having fulfilled perfectly the high priestly role symbolized on the annual Day of Atonement

he high priest, with the offering of sacrificial ood, passed through the outer room into the lost Holy Place. There "the blood of goats and lves" (9:12) was sprinkled on the atonement over as an intercession for the people. Like-ise, Jesus, after sacrificing himself on the cross d in keeping with the reality of what the Day f Atonement foreshadowed, "went through the reater and more perfect tabernacle that is not an-made, that is to say, not a part of this cre-ion" (9:11) and "entered the Most Holy Place nce for all by his own blood" (9:12).

The superior and perfect tabernacle through hich Jesus passed refers to the heavenly sanc-uary ("not man-made"), especially the outer ortion (corresponding to the Holy Place), on is way to the heavenly presence of God at the rone (corresponding to the Most Holy Place). esus entered the immediate presence of God ot by virtue of the blood of animal sacrifices ut by virtue of "his own blood." His blood stifies to the reality of his incarnation, his bedience unto death, the efficacy of his sac-fice on the cross, and his life laid down and oured out for our eternal redemption. His lood justifies all who believe in him (Rom. :24–25), cleanses the human heart and con-cience from the guilt and defilement of sin Heb. 9:14), sanctifies God's people (13:12; cf. John 1:7), and opens the way for the blood-ashed redeemed to come directly to God for race and mercy (Heb. 4:14–16), worship, and ervice (9:12, 14).

(2) The words "he entered the Most Holy lace once for all" (9:12) convey a marked inality about what Christ has done and stand n contrast to the repetitive function of the aronic priesthood, who entered the earthly ounterpart year by year. But Christ's redemp-ive action is definitively complete and there-ore excludes all necessity or possibility of epetition. Lane (1991, 239) notes that in this ontext the author sees Jesus' death, ascension, nd entrance into the heavenly Most Holy lace as constituting a unity, with the stress alling on his arrival there "in order to con-ummate the work of salvation in the presence of God" (9:24–26).

Stated another way, Christ's once-for-all acrifice on the cross requires no repetition 7:27; 10:10), and his once-for-all exalta-ion/entrance into the heavenly presence of God forever validates the "eternal redemption" (9:12) obtained at the cross. The word "redemption" here means "release" from the judgment and guilt produced by sin, a release made possible at great cost to the Redeemer. "Eternal redemption" relates to its "once for all" provision and to its standing offer of forgiveness, wherein God remembers our sins no more (cf. Jer. 31:34).

Verses 13–14 continue the contrast between the old order and the new. The old order provided for an outward cleansing in two ways: (a) "the blood of goats and bulls" (cf. Lev. 16:15–16) as a sin offering, and (b) "the ashes of a heifer sprinkled on those who are ceremonially unclean" (Num. 19:1–22), such as when touching a dead body. The burnt heifer ashes were mixed with water and sprinkled on those who were defiled so that they were not cut off from covenant relationship. The limited and external efficacy of these old order provisions prepares the way for the "how much more" argument about the sacrifice of Christ under the new order (9:14). Bruce comments that the earlier Old Testament sacrifices "were but token sacrifices; the sacrifice of Christ was a real self-offering accomplished on the moral and spiritual plane" (1990, 217).

Our author makes four important statements in verse 14 that indicate why "the blood of Christ" is efficacious. (a) It was "through the eternal Spirit" that Christ offered himself to God. The meaning of the phrase "eternal Spirit" is not entirely clear in Greek. When spelled with a capital "S," it is understood as referring to the Holy Spirit (as in the NIV and most translations). Most likely this phrase means that as Jesus depended on the power of the Holy Spirit in every facet of his life and ministry to accomplish the will of the Father, so he offered himself through the power of the Holy Spirit in his substitutionary death (cf. Isa. 42:1). The Spirit and the blood go together in redemption (1 John 5:8).

(b) Jesus "offered himself unblemished to God." Whereas the Old Testament animal sacrifices were required to be without physical defect, the author affirms that Jesus' life of perfect obedience to the Father that culminated in his death on the cross represented a morally and spiritually unblemished sacrifice for sin. His self-sacrifice was both perfect and complete, and his blood was inexpressibly precious to God and efficacious for sin.

(c) The fact that Jesus was morally and spiritually perfect means that his blood is divinely empowered for cleansing "our consciences from acts that lead to death." Cleansing our conscience is in contrast to the old covenant's outward cleansing (9:13). Bruce notes that "it is an inward and spiritual purification that is required if heart-communion with God is to be enjoyed" (1990, 218). As sensibility to physical pain pervades the whole body, so the defilement of conscience pervades our whole spiritual being. When the conscience is cleansed, our whole spiritual nature is cleansed.

Under the old covenant, defilement could come from contact with a dead body; the defilement mentioned in relation to conscience that requires cleansing is "from dead works" (lit. trans.) or "from acts that lead to death" (NIV). "Dead works" generally have a religious connotation and refer to acts related to law-righteousness or deeds done in order to gain merit with God. When the efforts of self prove invalid or the defilement of legalism occurs, the conscience may need to be cleansed from the awareness of failure or self-righteousness. But the NIV rendering that points to defilement from sinful acts and attitudes that pollute the conscience with guilt and lead to spiritual death is more likely the thought here.

(d) When our consciences are cleansed from spiritual defilement and pollution, we are emancipated spiritually "so that we may serve the living God." The blood of Christ not only makes possible inner and spiritual cleansing, but also opens to us the Most Holy Place of God's living presence so that we may serve him as a holy priesthood (cf. 1 Peter 2:5, 9) and as perfected worshipers "in spirit and truth" (John 4:23). This is why we were created in the image of God, and this is the goal of all redemption; but the blood of the old covenant was never able to attain this end. Now that the new order has come (9:10–11), the Most Holy Place has been opened to us by virtue of the blood of Christ and our consciences cleansed by the same blood, so that we may be wholly separated as priests to serve him, both now and for all eternity.

A parallel development between chapters 8 and 9 is reflected in 9:15a. In 8:1–6, Jesus serves as high priest on our behalf in the heavenly sanctuary; in 8:7–12, he is the mediator of the better covenant that brought the blessing of Jeremiah 31:31–34 to God's people on earth. In 9:11–14, Jesus by his own blood opened the heavenly Most Holy Place for the redeemed to enter; in 9:15–22, he is the mediator of the new covenant, with the emphasis now being on his death and its necessity for the ratification of the new covenant. "For this reason" (9:15a) points to a strong causal relationship between 9:11–14 and the result stated in 9:15. "Because Jesus freely offered his life in obedience to God, he became the priestly mediator of a new covenant" (Lane, 1991, 241).

Three important consequences are stated in 9:15b–17 as resulting from Christ's death as the mediator of the new covenant. (1) Because of his death, "those who are called may receive the promised eternal inheritance." "Those who are called" refers to believers generally (including Old Testament saints who have died) and reminds us of God's initiative in extending the heavenly calling (cf. 3:1). The promise of an inheritance under the old covenant was mostly on the earthly level, such as the land of Canaan; the covenant inaugurated by Christ holds forth the promise of an "eternal inheritance." In Hebrews this is, as Peterson (1994, 1341–42) states, the

> equivalent of "the world to come" (2:5), the "Sabbath-rest for the people of God" (4:9), "the heavenly Jerusalem" (12:22) and other such descriptions of our destiny as Christians. Jesus has opened the way to his inheritance for us by dealing with the sin that keeps us from drawing near to God.

The Christian's inheritance encompasses all the new covenant blessings of eternal salvation (1:14; 3:1; 5:9; 10:36).

(2) Christ died "as a ransom to set them free from the sins committed under the first covenant" (9:15c). The word "ransom" refers to "the price paid to set free a slave or prisoner or a person under sentence of death" (Morris, 1981, 88). Only Jesus' death as a covenant sacrifice possesses the power to set free those captive to sin. Its power is retroactive in its effect and thus valid for all who trusted God for the forgiveness of sins under the first covenant. Moreover, Jesus tasted death "for everyone" (2:9). Since he is the representative man (the second Adam), his redemptive death is the representative death. Thus he is able to save all who "come to God through him" (7:25).

(3) The death of Christ as the mediator of the new covenant assured that "the last will and testament" of that covenant was put into effect, thus making the new covenant terms active and unalterable (9:16–17). The mention of an "eternal inheritance" in verse 15 leads the author to utilize the dual meaning of the Greek word *diatheke*, which can be translated as either "covenant" or "will." Normally in Hebrews the word means "covenant." But in this passage, the author switches to the second meaning of *diatheke*—"a last will and testament." The reason for this decision is that he now emphasizes the death of "the one who made" the *diatheke* (9:16), with the added comment that it "is in force only when somebody has died" (9:17).

A few commentators (e.g., Westcott, Hawthorne, and most recently Lane) have argued that *diatheke* means "covenant" here, as elsewhere in Hebrews. According to this view, the death in 9:16 refers to the animals slain when ratifying a covenant. The natural reading of 9:17, however, requires the literal, not symbolic death of the one who makes the *diatheke*. This is not true of a "covenant," but it is true of a "will" (NIV). Using the legal language of Roman law, a person's "last will and testament" does not become effective until "the death of the one who made it." Hagner notes that "the uniqueness of Christ and his work is such that while it is expressed in categories of both covenant and will, it transcends the ordinary stipulations of both" (1983, 126). The uniqueness of Christ is seen in that he is both testator and executor of the will, both surety and mediator.

The author then returns to his expositional argument, namely, what happened when the first covenant was established: "[It] was not put into effect without blood" (9:18). The next three verses illustrate this fact in some detail by underscoring the close connection between the Mosaic Law and the sealing of the covenant by the sprinkling of blood. Moses did two things. (1) He "proclaimed every commandment of the law to all the people" (9:19a). That is, he carefully explained the terms of the covenant, so that all the people understood that covenant membership meant they must obey God's laws. (2) Moses emphasized the importance of the blood in relation to the covenant, as our author shows by referring to Exodus 24:1–8 (perhaps alluding also to Lev. 8:15, 19; 14:4–6; Num. 19:18–19). Moses took half the blood of the animals sacrificed and put it in basins; the other half he threw on the altar.

The blood in the basins, mixed with water, was then sprinkled—by using "scarlet wool and branches of hyssop"—on "the scroll and all the people" (9:19). Then the writer adds: "This is the blood of the covenant" (9:20), whereby the covenant relationship and covenant obedience to God were sealed. Lane rightly observes that central to the author's argument is the fact that "there is an intimate relationship between covenant and sacrificial blood" (1991, 244). Still other details of Old Testament sprinkling of blood are alluded to in 9:21 to indicate further the comprehensive importance of blood in the establishing of the covenant between God and Israel.

The author then concludes: "The law requires that nearly everything be cleansed with blood" (9:22a)—almost everything, but not absolutely everything. A few rare exceptions are mentioned in the Old Testament, such as cleansing by water, incense, fire (e.g., Lev. 5:11–13; Num. 16:46; 31:22–23, 50). But the fundamental premise stands: "Without the shedding of blood there is no forgiveness" (9:22b).

This is the third declaration in chapter 9 that emphasizes the crucial importance of sacrificial blood: There is no access to God "without blood" (9:7); there is no inauguration of the first covenant "without blood" (9:18); and there is no forgiveness "without . . . blood" (9:22). Thus the writer stresses the importance and efficacy of covenant blood in this chapter. Blood provides access (9:7); blood cleanses the conscience (9:14); blood establishes the covenants (9:18); blood sanctifies the people (9:19); blood cleanses all vessels of worship (9:21); blood cleanses almost everything under the law (9:22a); and blood makes possible the forgiveness of sins (9:22b) (cf. Lane, 1991, 246). The meaning of forgiveness, however, and the reality to which the blood of the first covenant pointed were never fully realized until Christ came (9:11) and shed his own blood in order to cleanse our consciences and forgive our sins.

2.2.4. Superior to Aaron and the Levitical Order Because His Ministry Is Fulfilled by a Better Sacrifice (9:23–10:18). The word "then" in 9:23 (*oun*, "therefore") connects what is forthcoming with what was stated in 9:19–22 (esp. 9:22b). The necessity for animal sacrifices and the application of blood to the Old Testament tabernacle, its vessels, and its worshipers point to the necessity for a perfect sacrifice and the greater application of blood to the heavenly reality, of which the earthly order was but a faint foreshadowing. The Mosaic system was simply "the copies of the heavenly" originals. But "better sacrifices" than those provided under the old order are needed if "the heavenly things themselves" are to be purified.

Two problems arise at this point. (1) Why the plural "better sacrifices"? The plural occurs "because of the generic contrast with the sacrifices of the old covenant" (Hagner, 1983, 128). But when our author applies the principle to its new covenant fulfillment, he speaks plainly and emphatically of only one such superior sacrifice—namely, Jesus' once-for-all sacrifice of himself (cf. 9:26b, 28a).

(2) The second problem concerns "heavenly things themselves" needing purification. Lane believes 9:23 "clearly implies that the heavenly sanctuary had also become defiled by the sin of the people" (1991, 247). Peterson responds that heaven itself cannot be defiled by human sin, "otherwise God would have had to leave it" (1994, 1342). Bruce suggests that the redeemed are God's true tabernacle under the new covenant, and they are the ones who need spiritual cleansing by the blood of Christ (1990, 228–29).

Although what Bruce says is theologically true, the difficulty with this interpretation is that "the heavenly things themselves" is a strange way to refer to God's people on earth (Morris, 1981, 91). Furthermore, verse 24 reminds us that the context of chapter 9 concerns the contrast between the earthly and the heavenly, that is, the Levitical priestly ministry in the earthly man-made sanctuary and "heaven itself," where Jesus as our high priest enters "through the greater and more perfect tabernacle that is not man-made" (9:11) into the Most Holy Place of God's presence. This clearly continues to be the context for 9:23. As the infectious defilement of sin reaches beyond the individual to taint society and the earthly tabernacle of worship, perhaps it somehow extends in some sense to the heavenly realm as well (Lane, 1991, 247).

Certainly it seems clear in 9:23 that the perfect and complete sacrifice of Christ on the cross did purify the heavenly realm from spiritual defilement of some kind, most likely "defilement" that resulted from the rebellion of Satan and his angels in heaven (cf. Col. 1:20, 2:15). Just as the pervasive effect of Satan's rebellion in heaven reaches to the earth, so the smoke of the earth's wickedness rises back to heaven (cf. Rev. 14:10–11a; 19:1–3). Also the sinful plight of the earth is reflected in the heavenly realm in relation to the intercessory prayers of heaven's saints for salvation and justice in the earth (cf. Rev. 8:1–5; 15:5–8). Concerning these things, "we see but a poor reflection as in a mirror" (1 Cor. 13:12).

"For" in 9:24 further ties the purifying of "the heavenly things themselves" (9:23) to Jesus' ascension and entry into "heaven itself, now to appear for us in God's presence." The author amplifies the contrast introduced in 9:11, based on the Day of Atonement imagery. Jesus as our high priest did not enter the earthly, "man-made sanctuary that was only a copy of the true one" (9:24), but rather the heavenly, "more perfect tabernacle that is not man-made" (9:11). The Greek word for "copy" in 9:24 is *antitypa* (antitype), which is used here in contrast to "the true one" (i.e., original one); more commonly "antitype" means the reality to which a "type" points (cf. 1 Peter 3:21).

The author then further elaborates on what was introduced in 9:12. On the one hand, the Levitical "high priest enters" the tabernacle's "Most Holy Place every year with blood that is not his own" (9:25)—that is, with "the blood of goats and calves" (9:12). On the other hand, Christ's entry into heaven's Most Holy Place is decisive, not something to be done "again and again" (9:25), as under the first covenant. His entry involves "his own blood" (9:12), which represents the finished and perfect "sacrifice of himself" (9:26) for "eternal redemption" (9:12). Because Jesus' act of atonement is eternally efficacious, it need not be repeated. Indeed, it is impossible to do so since it would require suffering death "many times" (9:26a), whereas everyone (including Christ) "is destined to die once" (9:27).

Verse 26 then states five truths about Christ and his death. (1) "He has appeared" (9:26) refers to his incarnation and affirms that his death was a historical, flesh-and-blood reality. (2) His incarnation and death was a once-for-all event. (3) It occurred "at the end of the ages" (lit., "at the consummation of the ages"), that is, at the time of messianic fulfillment (also called "these last days," 1:2). (4) The purpose of his death was "to do away with sin" (cf. 1 John 3:5). In the Old Testament the blood of animal sacrifices could only cover sin, not remove it. But Jesus' atoning death makes possible the annulling of sin's power and the removal of sin's defilement. (5) His death involved the voluntary "sacrifice of himself" as the Son of God (cf. 1:3), a superior and efficacious sacrifice that was impossible under the Levitical order.

In the last two verses of chapter 9, the author points out a parallel between the universal experience of humankind and that of Jesus Christ. In both instances the experience of physical death is a divine appointment. Contrary to the belief of reincarnation, after death comes eternal judgment for everyone (9:27). After Christ's death, as the perfect sacrifice "to take away the sins of many" (9:28), comes eternal salvation for those who believe. "Many" here does not mean that Jesus died for the sins of many, but not for all; rather, "'all' may be expressed by 'many' when the largeness of the 'all' is being stressed" (Hawthorne, 1986, 1524). Earlier it was explicitly stated that Christ died "for everyone" (2:9). The language of "many" echoes the Servant of the Lord in Isaiah 53:12 ("he bore the sin of many").

Christ, who dealt decisively with sin by the sacrifice of himself at his first coming, "will appear a second time" (9:28b) for a different purpose—"to bring [final] salvation to those who are waiting for him." This reappearing recalls the experience of the Levitical high priest on the Day of Atonement. After he had gone into the Most Holy Place with blood to make atonement for the people's sins, the Israelites would wait apprehensively while he was out of sight and then rejoice greatly when he reappeared. Likewise Christians, knowing that their high priest and mediator has entered the heavenly Most Holy Place of God's presence, are waiting with earnest anticipation for his reappearing with all the blessings of their full salvation and eternal inheritance (cf. Rom. 8:19, 23, 25; 1 Cor. 1:7; Phil. 3:20).

In chapter 10 the author comes to the conclusion of his long, sustained argument (4:14–10:18) concerning the superiority of Christ's high priestly ministry to that of the Levitical order under the old covenant. He forcefully restates the superior character of Christ's sacrifice for sin (1) by succinctly summarizing the inadequacies of the old covenant sacrifices for approaching God (10:1–4), and (2) by further showing from Old Testament Scripture that Christ is the complete and all-sufficient sacrifice for sin (10:5–10). As both the perfect mediator and the perfect sacrifice, Christ makes possible the experience of the full realization of the prophetic, new covenant promise of Jeremiah 31:33–34 (Heb. 10:11–18).

"The law" of Moses (10:1) with its sacrificial system was severely limited because (1) it contained "only a shadow" (*skia*) and "not the realities (*eikon*) themselves," and (2) it could not "make perfect" those who desired to approach God as worshipers. The contrast between *skia* and *eikon* (lit., "image" that casts the shadow) is the contrast between the old and new covenants, the law and the gospel, Mosaic animal sacrifices and the once-for-all-time sacrifice of Christ. A shadow is an incomplete revelation of its object, "the barest outline of the reality" (Guthrie, 1983, 207). Once the actual form or reality is seen, the shadow becomes irrelevant.

The law served as "a past witness to a future reality" (Lane, 1991, 259) when it foreshadowed "the good things that are coming" (10:1). Those "good things" (future from the Old Testament perspective) have now come (9:11) in the high priestly ministry and sacrificial death of Christ.

An evidence of the inadequacy and incompleteness of the Old Testament sacrifices was that they had to be "repeated endlessly year after year." Although sacrifices were offered by the Levitical priests on a daily basis and on the annual Day of Atonement for the sins of the people, they could "never . . . make perfect those who draw near to worship." The perfection of God's people related to the decisive cleansing of their consciences from the defilement of sin so that they might wholeheartedly enter into God's holy presence as worshipers. If the Old Testament sacrifices had achieved this goal (10:2), "would they not have stopped being offered?" If God's Old Testament people had experienced a decisive once-for-all cleansing of the conscience, they would have had unhindered access to God and "would no longer have felt guilty for their sins." Such was not the case, however, since it required the finality of Christ's atoning death to provide God's people with a once-for-all cleansing from sin and free access to God as worshipers.

The solemn entrance of the Levitical high priest into the Most Holy Place on the Day of Atonement, with sacrificial blood in hand to sprinkle on the atonement cover, was a twofold testimony. (1) It was "an annual reminder" (10:3) (a) that the reality of the people's sins constituted a barrier to unhindered access to and fellowship with their holy God; and (b) that sin brought the judgment of death and that a penalty of death, represented by the animal sacrifices, had to be paid for their sins.

(2) The annual Day of Atonement ritual testified that sin's barrier continued to exist year after year "because it is impossible for the blood of bulls and goats to take away sins" (10:4). The blood of animal sacrifices could only temporarily "cover" sin, not remove it. Only Christ's blood could take sins away (9:28). God required the Old Testament sacrifices as an object lesson to teach Israel that a sufficient sacrifice was needed to pay the penalty of sin, cleanse the conscience from sin's defilement, and provide worshipers with unhindered access to God.

In the paragraph that follows (10:5–10), the author argues that the ineffective Levitical sacrifices have been replaced by the complete and all-sufficient sacrifice of Christ (the Messiah) for sin. In 10:5–7 our author appeals to Psalm 40:6–8 (in the Septuagint) as prophetic support for his argument. Portions of this psalm may have been understood to be messianic (cf. Bruce, 1990, 239), with the preexistent Christ himself speaking in Psalm 40:6–8. In our author's exposition of the passage (10:8–10), he appropriately applies Psalm 40:6–8 to Christ and his work, since "Christ is the goal of the Old Testament Scriptures" (Hagner, 1983, 136).

The Psalm 40 quotation begins with a statement of God's dissatisfaction with the conventional sacrifices and offerings when unaccompanied by a corresponding desire to obey him (cf. 1 Sam. 15:22; Ps. 50:8–10; 51:16–17; Isa. 1:10–13; 66:2–4; Jer. 7:21–24; Hos. 6:6; Amos 5:21–27). In addition to agreeing with this Old Testament prophetic theme, the preexistent Christ predicts his incarnation ("but a body you prepared for me") and states his intention as the incarnate Servant-Son ("I have come to do your will, O God"). The reference to "the scroll" (Heb. 10:7a) is probably to the Torah (the five books of Moses).

In our author's exposition of Psalm 40:6–8 in Hebrews 10:8–10, he emphasizes two issues. (1) He underscores God's displeasure with the formality of Old Testament sacrifices and his doing away with them in the sacrifice of his Son. The four terms used here for sacrifices (10:8) comprehensively cover the different types of Levitical sacrifices as required by the law: (a) "Sacrifices" refer to two types of animal sacrifices: "the fellowship [peace] offering" (Lev. 3), which demonstrated Israel's fellowship with God, and "the guilt offering" (Lev. 5), which was required when the property rights of another were violated, intentionally or unintentionally; (b) "offerings" refer to "the grain offerings" (Lev. 2), which symbolized dedication to God of the fruit of one's labor and represented thanksgiving to him; (c) "burnt offerings" (Lev. 1) involved burning an animal totally as a sign of the dedication of oneself to God; and (d) "sin offerings" (Lev. 4), were animal sacrifices given to atone for unintentional sins or sins of ignorance.

(2) In contrast to the Levitical sacrifices, our author emphasizes the volitional and voluntary nature of Christ's obedience: "Here I am . . . I have come to do your will" (10:9a). Through his perfect obedience, Christ "sets aside the first [i.e., the Levitical order] to establish the second [i.e., the new covenant based on his blood]." Christ's perfect obedience to the will of God is explicitly seen in "the sacrifice of the body of Jesus Christ once for all" (10:10b). This expression emphasizes the completeness and finality of Christ's bodily sacrifice for sin.

God's people are thereby sanctified ("made holy," 10:10a) by his sacrifice because it has provided a decisive cleansing from sin and its defilement, which in turn enables us to have unhindered access to God and henceforth to "offer him acceptable worship" (Bruce, 1990, 243). Our sanctified worship and consecrated service to God are now possible because of Christ's "whole-hearted obedience . . . perfectly expressed" (Peterson, 1994, 1343) in his complete and all-sufficient sacrifice of himself for sin for all time (thus a sacrifice without need of repetition).

It matters intensely that Christ's obedience was perfect and full when he sacrificed his body in death on the cross. The whole Levitical system of sacrifices has now been abolished by the realization of the true desire of God for loyal obedience to his will. Moreover, it matters greatly that his sacrifice for sin was "once" for all people of all times. This contrasts sharply with the repetitious nature of the Levitical sacrifices. Morris notes that "there is no other religion in which one great happening brings salvation through the centuries and through the world. This is the distinctive doctrine of Christianity" (1981, 100).

In 10:11–12, the author contrasts Jesus and the Levitical priests one final time from yet another angle. The new point of contrast centers around their present posture as priests. "Day after day" every priestly descendant of Aaron "stands" while performing his priestly duties. The posture of *standing* indicates that the work of the Levitical priest continues because his sacred duties are always unfinished. "Again and again he offers the same [animal] sacrifices." This repetition is necessary because animal sacrifices "can never take away sins."

Jesus, on the other hand, is in a *sitting* position (10:12). His posture speaks of rest, not work, and signifies that his sacrificial work is "a finished work and an accepted sacrifice" (Bruce, 1990, 245). His priestly sacrifice is timelessly efficacious—"offered for all time." And his atoning sacrifice is efficaciously complete: "one sacrifice for [all] sin." Bruce adds that "the worth of his sacrifice and the dignity of his person are further indicated in that he has taken his seat not merely in the presence of God but at 'God's right hand'" (1990, 246)—the place of highest honor. Through faith in Jesus Christ and because of his perfect sacrifice and present mediation, "we may approach God with freedom and confidence" (Eph. 3:12), in order to worship (Heb. 10:19–25), "receive mercy and find grace" (4:16), and serve him with a glad heart (Deut. 28:47).

In verse 13 the author again cites Psalm 110, one of his main Old Testament texts, where the Messiah's kingly role (110:1) and priestly function (110:4) are united together. The time that "he waits for his enemies to be made his footstool" corresponds to the time between the enthronement of Christ and his final triumph over his enemies, that is, the present era between Christ's ascension and second coming. The delay in subjugating his enemies represents a prolongation of the day of grace and is therefore a token of God's mercy and longsuffering (Hughes, 1977, 402).

The evident fruit of the efficacy of Christ's finished work on the cross and his subsequent enthronement at God's right hand is that "he has made perfect forever those who are being made holy" (10:14). This was something the Levitical priests and sacrifices could never do. "Made perfect forever" refers to the completed action of Christ's eternally efficacious, sacrificial death, whereby he takes imperfect people and makes them fit for God's fellowship forever. "Those who are being made holy" is a present participle and emphasizes the progressive sanctifying work of Christ by the Spirit in the lives of his people during this present age.

Our author finds Scriptural support for these conclusions in the "new covenant" prophecy of Jeremiah (Heb. 10:15–17). He again demonstrates a profound respect for the authority of the Old Testament Scriptures as the Word of God and for the ministry of the Holy Spirit, who inspired the Scriptures to be written (cf. 2 Peter 1:20–21). The phrase "the Holy Spirit also testifies to us about this" (10:15) uses a present tense verb to indicate the Holy Spirit is speaking to us now through the prophetic revelation of the prophets.

In 10:16–17 the author's abbreviated quote from Jeremiah 31:33–34 supports his preceding discussion in two ways. (1) The Holy Spirit had predicted through the prophet Jeremiah that the "new covenant" era would mark the perfection and sanctification of God's people (cf. Heb. 10:10, 14). This occurred because of Jesus' redemptive sacrifice for sin and the ministry of the Holy Spirit, whereby God's laws are internalized in the renewed hearts and minds of God's people, together with an impartation of "the will and power to carry them out" (Bruce, 1990, 248). (2) Jeremiah's promise of a time when God would decisively forgive "their sins and lawless acts" and would "remember [them] no more" has occurred precisely because Jesus "offered for all time one sacrifice for sins" (10:12).

Since Jeremiah's prophecy has been fulfilled by Jesus Christ and the new covenant is now a reality, only one conclusion about the

Levitical system of sacrifices is possible. "Where these [sins and lawless acts] have been forgiven, there is no longer any sacrifice for sin." The former animal sacrifices are obsolete. What they sought to convey is now perfectly fulfilled in Christ (Guthrie, 1983, 209). God's people now have freedom to worship and serve him with a clear conscience and the personal assurance that their past sins have been "eternally blotted out from God's record, never to be brought up in evidence against them" (Bruce, 1990, 248).

Part Two: The Application: Exhortation to Steadfastness (10:19–13:17)

3. The Challenge to Remain Steadfast in Faith (10:19–11:40)

The author of Hebrews, a man mighty in the Scriptures, has concluded his carefully reasoned argument (1:1–10:18). He has argued that God's plan of salvation has moved beyond the old covenant—with its types and shadows, its temporary and incomplete provisions of access to God—to the new covenant provisions of salvation, which center in God's Son, Jesus Christ, by whom all believers now have open access into the Most Holy Place of God's presence. Chapter by chapter he has shown how the Christ-revelation is vastly superior to the Old Testament revelation in that Jesus Christ embodies the spiritual realities of which the old covenant was only a shadow.

His conclusion is clear: Christ is the ultimate and final plan of God for our salvation. The author now turns from his carefully reasoned and sustained argument to a profound and earnest application of its positive truth to the lives of his readers. There must be no retreat in the Christian life. Instead, believers must remain steadfast in faith, in perseverance, and in holiness in order to inherit the promises of God.

Unbelief was the deadly sin that caused the Israelites to turn back at Kadesh Barnea and to perish in the desert (ch. 3). Faith would have been their way into the Promised Land. Faith is also the entryway into Christ and all the spiritual promises embodied in him. To retreat or turn back from him in unbelief will result in their perishing, just as their forefathers did in the desert. Thus, Hebrews urgently exhorts the new covenant Israelites to enter into their privileges in Christ and to remain steadfast in faith unto the end, like their forefathers in chapter 11.

3.1. *Faith and the New Covenant Worshipers (10:19–25)*

These verses summarize (in one long sentence in Greek) the author's argument since 7:1 about Jesus' role as our high priest, his efficacious blood of the new covenant, and his opening up of the heavenly sanctuary to new covenant worshipers. In view of all that Christ has accomplished on our behalf, we have two comprehensive blessings as new covenant worshipers (10:19–21). Based on these blessings (cf. "since" at the beginning of verses 19 and 21) the author gives three earnest exhortations to believers (10:22–25).

(1) The first comprehensive blessing is "confidence [*parresia*] to enter the Most Holy Place by the blood of Jesus" (10:19). *Parresia* is an important word in Hebrews, occurring four times (3:6; 4:16; 10:19, 35; 10:35). Sometimes it means bedrock belief or bold assurance; here it conveys the idea of bold freedom because of authorization to enter "the Most Holy Place" of God's presence.

The old covenant manifested a foreboding fear connected with the presence of God. Aaron's sons Nadab and Abihu died while offering unauthorized fire and incense before the Lord (Lev. 10:1–2). It was a fearful moment when the high priest entered through the veil of the tabernacle into the Most Holy Place on the Day of Atonement. It was customary for him not to linger there lest the people be terrified (Morris, 1981, 103). But new covenant believers, as a holy priesthood (1 Peter 2:5), are authorized to enter the Most Holy Place of God's presence *boldly* by virtue of the blood of Jesus.

This authorized freedom of entrance is described as "a new and living way" (10:20). It is *new* in contrast to the old covenant way (with the animal sacrifices), both with respect to the finality of Christ's sacrifice of himself and its efficacious effect. It is also *living* because it is forever linked with the risen Lord Jesus himself, whose life endures on our behalf. The idea of the "way" in Hebrews, previously introduced in 9:8, speaks of our access to God through Christ.

This new and living way into God's presence is "through the curtain, that is, his body" (10:20; lit., "his flesh"). In the earthly tabernacle the high priest entered the Most Holy Place through a curtain or veil. In the Synopic Gospels the curtain in the temple was torn n two at Jesus' death, symbolizing that the way was now open through the barrier that separated God's people from his presence. Similarly here in Hebrews, our author is declaring "that every barrier to the presence of God has forever been torn down through the blood and flesh (cf. 2:14 for this same order) of Jesus" (Hawthorne, 1986, 1525). This means that in Jesus' sacrificial death, "God himself is unveiled to us and the way of access to him is thrown wide open" for those who trust in him (Bruce, 1990, 251).

(2) The second comprehensive blessing we have as new covenant worshipers is "a great priest over the house of God." The expression "great priest" is "the literal rendering of the most common Hebrew title for the high priest" as the superlative priest (Bruce, 1990, 253; cf. 4:14). Jesus, the foremost superlative priest, serves as high priest over God's house, which is the community of believers. This verse has its parallel in 3:6a: "Christ is faithful as a son over God's house." The clause that follows in 3:6b identifies God's house as believers, who maintain their confidence and hope in him. Jesus' *servanthood* is seen in his dying in order to make a way to God for us (10:19–20); his *lordship* is seen in his ruling over all who come to God through him (10:21). As Morris notes, "once again we have the highest Christology combined with the recognition that Jesus rendered lowly service" (1981, 104).

The two comprehensive blessings are followed by three exhortations that point out the response of new covenant worshipers: "Let us draw near" (10:22); "let us hold unswervingly" (10:23); and "let us consider how" (10:24). Each of these are present tense verbs in Greek and are tied in action to the triad of Christian virtues: faith (10:22), hope (10:23), and love (10:24–25).

(1) "Let us [continue to] draw near to God with a sincere heart in full assurance of faith" (10:22). It is in continually drawing near to God that

> the Father's face is seen and His love tasted. Here His holiness is revealed and the soul made partaker of it. Here the sacrifice of love and worship and adoration, the incense of prayer and supplication, is offered in power. . . . Here the soul, in God's presence, grows into more complete oneness with Christ, and more entire conformity to His likeness. Here in union with Christ, in His unceasing intercession, we are emboldened to take our place as intercessors, who can have power with God and prevail. Here the soul mounts up as on eagle's wings . . . strength is renewed, and the blessing and power and love are imparted with which [we as] God's [new covenant] priests can go out to bless a dying world. Here each day we may experience the fresh anointing [of God's Spirit and presence]. (Murray, n.d., 355–56)

The author cites four conditions for drawing near to God (10:22). (a) We are to do so "with a sincere heart"—that is, with a genuine, pure heart free from pretense. Spiritually the "heart" represents the whole of our inner life. We must be right inwardly when approaching God by virtue of what Christ has done for us.

(b) We are also to draw near to God "in full assurance of faith"—that is, without doubt or misgiving that free access to God is open to us through Christ as our sacrifice and high priest. Guthrie notes that the preposition "*in*" suggests that "this faith-assurance is the sphere or environment in which approach is to be made" (1983, 213). Our author of Hebrews adds that anyone who draws near to God "must believe that he exists and that he rewards those who earnestly seek him" (11:6).

(c) Another condition for drawing near to God is "having our hearts sprinkled to cleanse us from a guilty conscience." The language of sprinkling is derived from the Old Testament law and involved the external application of animal blood to the worshiper (e.g., Ex. 24:8; 29:21). In Hebrews it refers to the inward cleansing of the heart by Christ's blood, which frees the conscience from guilt and enables the new covenant worshiper to approach God sincerely.

(d) The fourth condition is "having our bodies washed with pure water." Almost all commentators see this as a reference to the waters of Christian baptism, which under the new covenant replaces all previous cleansing rites. The two clauses—"sprinkling" our hearts and "washing" our bodies—are an example of rhetorical parallelism and point to the inward and outward aspects of Christian conversion.

(2) The second exhortation is: "Let us hold unswervingly to the hope we profess" (10:23).

Our author returns to his concern for the readers, who are in danger of turning away from their faith and confession of hope in Christ (cf. 2:1–3; 3:12–14; 4:1; 6:4–6; 10:26–31). "Unswervingly" literally means "swerving neither to one side or the other" and thus means to be "firm," "stable," "steadfast" (Lane, 1991, 289). For the readers to "hold unswervingly" to their "hope" in Christ as converted Jews included remaining steadfast in their faith that he is their sacrifice for sin and their high priest before God. "Hope," however, is more comprehensive than "faith," for it includes specific promises of God about the future (Guthrie, 1983, 214). The strongest possible incentive for holding unswervingly to hope is God's trustworthy character: "He who promised is faithful." As Bruce aptly observes, "our hope is based on the unfailing promise of God; why should we not cherish it confidently and confess it boldly" (1990, 256).

(3) The third exhortation is: "Let us consider how we may spur one another on toward love and good deeds" (10:24). This verse focuses on "love" (10:24–25), which completes the triad with faith (10:22) and hope (10:23). Christians must mutually encourage and "spur one another" ("incite," "provoke") to practical expressions of love. The objective of this action is the increase and deepening of "love and good deeds" among believers. Love must have "a practical outcome" (Guthrie, 1983, 215) and "a tangible expression" (Lane, 1991, 289).

The twofold "let us" in verse 25 are not additional exhortations, though they appear so in the NIV. Rather, they are present tense participial phrases—lit., "not giving up meeting together" and "encouraging one another"—that supplement and support the exhortation of 10:24. That is, the readers cannot spur one another on to practical expressions of love if they cease actively coming together in the corporate meetings for the purpose of mutual encouragement.

Why were some readers "in the habit of" being absent from the local assembly? Was it because of apathy or indifference? Or was it due to fear of persecution if seen by outsiders? Or were some growing weary of waiting for the return of Christ? Whatever the reason[s], the writer of Hebrews regarded the neglect or desertion of corporate worship/fellowship "as utterly serious" (Lane, 1991, 290). Believers can and must show love (*agape*) for one another through active participation in corporate fellowship and by encouraging one another.

Believers need each other, especially in view of their trying circumstances and as they "see the Day approaching" (10:25). "The Day" that is drawing near is a day of reckoning. There are three main interpretations as to its meaning. (a) The Roman siege against Jerusalem may have begun already when Hebrews was written. Thus the day of the destruction of the city and the temple as prophesied by Jesus may have been an imminent

Persecution was part of life as a Christian at the time Hebrews was written. Many Christians hid in their underground burial grounds, called catacombs, the walls of which they painted with stories from the past. Here Samson is depicted with the jawbone of a donkey, as in Judges 15. Peter and Paul were buried in the catacombs of Rome.

event and a sober sign for all Jews (Christian and otherwise) regarding the dissolution of the old order. (b) It may refer to the Day of Judgment, when "each of us will give an account of himself to God" (Rom. 14:12). (c) It may refer primarily to the nearness of Christ's return and to the accountability that it represents. This would provide further incentive for being an active participant in the life of the church.

However long may be the period between the first coming of Christ and his return, the time of his return is always near (Rev. 1:3). Bruce comments that "each successive Christian generation is called upon to live as the generation of the end-time," for whom Christ may return soon (1990, 259). Since we as true believers already experience "the powers of the coming age" (6:5) and have received "a kingdom that cannot be shaken" (12:28), there is a present reality in our worship and end-time hope. Therefore, let us hold unswervingly to that hope in loyalty to Christ and his people.

Fifth Hortatory Warning: The Seriousness of Deliberate Sin and Its Consequences (10:26–31)

This severe warning is parallel, both in form and function, to the 6:4–8 warning about the nature of apostasy and its irreversible consequences.[6] From 7:1–10:18 the mediatorial work of Christ as our high priest has been emphasized. Because of the power of his blood to blot out our transgressions and to cleanse our consciences from sin's defilement, we are admonished as new covenant worshipers to approach God's throne as a place of grace, mercy, and help in time of need. To desert God's provision of corporate grace in Christian gatherings (10:25), however, can lead to spurning his provision of personal grace in relation to Christ, which then opens the way to deliberate sin and eternal loss. In this event "the Day approaching" (10:25) will mean serious judgment (10:27) instead of glorious salvation (cf. 9:28). This solemn thought of judgment becomes the occasion for the severe warning that follows.

The author's words "if we deliberately keep on sinning" (10:26) are clearly addressed to his readers and himself as Christians (cf. 2:1). In the Greek the position of the word "deliberately" as first in the sentence emphasizes the willful and calculating nature of the sin. What is being referred to here is not a single deliberate transgression after Christian conversion. Rather, the verb "*sinning*" is the present participle of continuous action. Thus the NIV correctly translates it as "deliberately keep on sinning," involving intentional persistence.

This intentionality of the persistent sinning indicates a rejection of Christ and contempt for the Holy Spirit (10:29), which necessarily removes one from the sphere of grace. The Old Testament law made provision for unintentional sinful behavior but not for defiant sin. The person guilty of defiant sin was to be "cut off" from the covenant people because he or she was in effect blaspheming or despising the Lord (Num. 15:30–31). Thus, the sin in Hebrews 10 does not involve being ensnared or overtaken in a transgression (cf. Gal. 6:1); rather, it involves deliberately and defiantly sinning so as to despise the Lord (10:29).

As in 6:4–8, the specific sin our author has in mind is calculated rejection of Christ (i.e., apostasy). Also as in 6:4–8, the vast majority of New Testament scholars believe that the warning in 10:26–31 is directed to persons who were genuinely converted Christians but were beginning to vacillate in their faith in Christ (see endnote 2). They are referred to here as true Christian believers in four ways. (1) They "have received the knowledge [*epignosin*] of the truth" (10:26b). Whereas *gnosis* means "knowledge" as in intellectual knowledge, *epignosis* suggests a full, certain, and experiential knowledge, as in authentic Christian experience. "The truth" is the Christian revelation as embodied in Christ, that is, "saving truth" (Lane, 1991, 292).

(2) They have been "sanctified" (i.e., set apart as holy) by "the blood of the covenant" (10:29). In Hebrews these expressions mean that the readers had been cleansed by the blood of Jesus and had entered into the Most Holy Place of God's presence through Jesus as their high priest.

(3) In earlier days, the readers "had received the light" (10:32), as in "the light of the gospel of the glory of Christ" (2 Cor. 4:4). As spiritually enlightened Jewish believers, they had "stood [their] ground" when persecuted for their faith in Christ (10:32–33).

(4) Finally, they are among those who have demonstrated "confidence" in Christ; now they need to persevere in faith as "those who believe and are saved" (10:35–36, 39).

If a person receives "the [experiential] knowledge of the truth" in Christ and then rejects him, that person "give[s] up the only way of salvation" (Bruce, 1990, 261). A premier message of Hebrews is that Christ's all-sufficient sacrifice for sin is the only answer to the sin problem. To repudiate Christ and his sacrifice means that "no sacrifice for sin is left" (10:26c). In other words, there is no other way of forgiveness or acceptance with God. "To abandon that once-for-all sacrifice for sin is to abandon all hope of salvation" (Peterson, 1994, 1345).

What does remain is "a fearful expectation of judgment" (10:27a). God's inescapable judgment is further described as a "raging fire that will consume [his] enemies" (10:27b; cf. Isa. 26:11). As Korah and his followers were consumed by God's fiery judgment under the old covenant (Num. 16:35; 26:10), so apostates will face the fiery and irrevocable judgment of God under the new covenant. "Their fate is the same as those who never turned to Christ or who actively opposed the gospel" (Peterson, 1994, 1345). This serious inevitability of judgment for the apostate is forcefully underscored in Hebrews 10:28. Any Israelite who rejected or defied the law of Moses under the old covenant was put to death "without mercy" if sufficient witnesses were found. How much more severe punishment must await the apostate who rejects or defies God's provision of grace under the new covenant!

Verse 29 contains three descriptive indictments of the apostate, each of which reveals the gravity of the sin about which the readers are being warned. (1) The apostate by his or her decision and action has in effect "trampled the Son of God under foot." This vivid language conveys contemptuous denial or repudiation of Christ's true nature and identity.

(2) Such a persons by their own action have also "treated as an unholy thing the blood of the covenant that sanctified" them. Christ's atoning blood brings the believer into a sanctified or holy covenant relationship with God (cf. 10:10; 13:12). To abandon that relationship is in effect the equivalent of treating Christ's blood as "unholy" (*koinon*, lit., "common"). Thus, instead of believing by faith that the blood of Christ is God's sacred means of our salvation, it is regarded as no different than the blood of any other person (i.e., not efficacious) and thus commonplace.

(3) The person who turns away from Christ has also "insulted the Spirit of grace." Hebrews largely focuses on the person and work of Christ and does not develop a theology of the Holy Spirit. Nevertheless, the Holy Spirit is viewed as a person (not an impersonal influence), who speaks and imparts to believers the full benefits of God's grace and the work of Christ (cf. 2:4; 3:7; 6:4; 9:8, 14; 10:15). As believers, we may grieve the Holy Spirit when we ignore his presence, voice, or leading (Rom. 8:5–17; Gal. 5:16–25; 6:7–9). We may also resist the Holy Spirit (Acts 7:51) and put out his flame within us (1 Thess. 5:19). Most serious of all, one may insult the Holy Spirit.

Bruce observes that the author of Hebrews "is not given to wild exaggeration and when he uses language like this, he chooses his words with his customary care" (1990, 261). Defiance of the Mosaic law resulted in the death penalty for an Israelite under the old covenant (10:28). "How much more severely do you think a man deserves to be punished" when he has trampled under foot the Son of God, repudiated the holy purpose of his blood, and who thereby insulted the Holy Spirit's work of grace? This "denotes contempt of the most flagrant kind" (Moffatt, 1924, 151) and is probably synonymous with what Jesus called blasphemy against the Holy Spirit, "an eternal sin" (Mark 3:29).

The severity and inevitability of the punishment awaiting apostate Christians is indicated by two quotations from Deuteronomy 32. (1) God promises, "It is mine to avenge; I will repay" (Heb. 10:30a; see Deut. 32:35). God himself takes personal responsibility for judging and dispensing vengeance on his adversaries. (2) Again, "the Lord will judge his people" (Heb. 10:30b; Deut. 32:36). In doing so he will vindicate the righteous and punish the apostate. Anyone contemplating apostasy should remember: "It is a dreadful thing to fall into the hands of the living God" (Heb. 10:31). The word "dreadful," translated "fearful" in 10:27, means "frightening" or "terrifying." It is terrifying because God is living—awesome in majesty and holiness—and a "consuming fire" (12:29; cf. Isa. 33:14), which will destroy all his enemies.

Does the teaching of 10:26–31 exclude the possibility of repentance and forgiveness for the willful apostate? I. Howard Marshall notes that Martin Luther believed that this question is not addressed in the passage. Marshall adds, however, that "the general tenor of the passage, coupled with the [explicit] teaching of ch. 6, suggests that the impossibility of return may be in the author's mind. In any case, the passage is again a hypothetical one, in the sense that it refers to a danger threatening the readers and not a sin into which they had actually fallen" (1969, 149). This passage is hypothetical only in the sense that it has not yet happened to the readers; the possibility of apostasy itself is not hypothetical but real in Hebrews.

3.2. The Righteous Must Live By Faith (10:32–39)

The author's declaration in 10:38, "but my righteous one will live by faith" (quoted from Hab. 2:4), is the hallmark of this section. For the righteous there is no alternative to a life of faith. "Faith" means a steadfast trust in God, even though God is invisible and the visible world is full of trouble and hardship. Faith also carries the nuance of faithfulness and loyalty to the Lord Jesus Christ, even when identity with him means sharing his reproach and suffering. This passage both emphasizes what is required of faith and prepares the reader for the descriptive examples of faith in 11:1–40.

3.2.1. Past Victory (10:32–34). As the severe warning in 6:4–8 was followed by encouraging words in 6:9–12, so the warning in 10:26–31 is followed by encouragement and exhortation in 10:32–36 (for a comparison of the degree of parallelism between the two chapters, see Lane's chart, 1991, 296–97). Here the author encourages his readers to "remember those earlier days" when they were first enlightened, during the time of their first love (cf. 6:4, 10). At that stage in their Christian life, they had "stood [their] ground in a great contest in the face of suffering." The word "contest" (*athlesis*, from which derives the English word "athletic") originally referred to the intense competition in a sports arena. Here it is used metaphorically for the intense persecution and suffering the readers had endured steadfastly in faith.

The believers' past display of firm commitment to Christ in the face of suffering is recalled in order "to strengthen their Christian resolve for the present" (Lane, 1991, 297). Although we cannot date this earlier experience of persecution precisely, it does correspond to the experience of Roman Jewish Christians during Claudius's edict of expulsion begun in A.D. 49. This persecution was directed against the Jewish people generally, but included Jewish Christians, as is evident with Aquila and Priscilla (Acts 18:2; see Bruce, 1990, 268–70).

Verses 33–34 give details about the suffering these believers previously endured. The literary structure of the two verses is in the form of a chiasm, which reveals two separate categories of suffering (cf. Lane, 1991, 299):

A "Sometimes you were publicly exposed to insult and persecution" (10:33a);
  B "at other times you stood side by side with those who were so treated" (10:33b).
  B' "You sympathized with those in prison" (10:34a)
A' "and joyfully accepted the confiscation of your property" (10:34b).

The "A" category represents active and direct persecution against the readers, involving public ridicule (10:33a) and seizure of property (10:34b). The "B" category represents empathetic solidarity with other believers in their persecution (10:33b) and imprisonment (10:34b).

The expression "publicly exposed" (10:33a) is vivid, conveying being exposed to ridicule and shame as a public spectacle. Their humiliating public ordeal is described with two key words. (1) "Insult" indicates verbal ridicule and abuse. It also occurs in 11:26, where it describes the ridicule and reproach that Moses endured because of his rejection of his royal position in Egypt for the sake of Christ, and in 13:13, where it describes what awaits those who go outside the camp with Christ. It is closely associated with the reproach endured by Christ himself (cf. Rom. 15:3). (2) "Persecution" may be translated "affliction" (cf. Col. 1:24) and indicates that acts of violence also occurred along with the verbal abuse (Lane, 1991, 299).

In addition to their own persecution, they "stood side by side" (10:33b) with others in their suffering. The Greek word used here describes the strong camaraderie that exists in a close-knit Christian community. Suffering together for Christ "is fellowship on the deepest level"

(Guthrie, 1983, 222). Such camaraderie included sympathizing "with those in prison" (10:34a)—presumably those imprisoned because of their faith in Christ. In ancient times prisoners were dependent on friends and relatives for their food and supplies. Those without outside assistance were often left to die from starvation and exposure. Displaying genuine compassion for religious prisoners, however, was dangerous as it could draw persecution toward oneself and one's family. Yet the readers had forthrightly shown such compassion.

In the past the readers had also "joyfully accepted the confiscation" (10:34b) of their property. That they could rejoice in such sufferings with Christ (cf. Luke 6:22–23) in the past demonstrated precisely the faith to which our author now calls them in the present and of which he speaks in chapter 11. Their faith in earlier days had enabled them to joyfully let go of temporal "possessions," because they knew they had "better ... possessions" that were eternal (10:34c). "Better" is a key word in Hebrews (occurring thirteen times) and expresses "the superior quality of the reality Christians possess through Christ" (Lane, 1991, 300).

Although the world through persecution had inflicted insult, injury, and imprisonment on believers and had plundered their earthly possessions, the believers knew it could not separate their hearts from Christ and their heavenly treasures. They had demonstrated true faith that counts every sacrifice a joy and every loss a gain, and that knows God will turn all Christian suffering into an eternal weight of glory.

3.2.2. Present Challenge (10:35–39). Whereas the readers had demonstrated faith, hope, and love in "earlier days," they were now in danger of growing weary and losing heart (cf. 12:3), even to the point of giving up their faith in Christ. Thus the author exhorts and challenges them: "Do not throw away your confidence; it will be richly rewarded. You need to persevere so that when you have done the will of God, you will receive what he has promised." Earlier in this chapter, the word "confidence" (*parresia*) referred to the believer's bold freedom to enter openly into the Most Holy Place of God's presence because of the blood of Christ (e.g., 10:19; cf. 4:16). Elsewhere it carries the sense of bedrock belief and bold confession of Christ (e.g., 3:6). "Confidence" as used here includes both meanings. Without "confidence" the believer lacks the necessary courage and strength to persevere in faith in disheartening circumstances; he or she also lacks the ability to access the throne of grace in prayer and thereby to press into the full privileges of God's fellowship and grace.

The rich reward (cf. 10:35b) corresponds to the "better and lasting possessions" in 10:34c and to the blessing of full salvation God has promised to those who wait for Christ (cf. 9:28; 10:23, 25; cf. Lane, 1991, 302). As long as salvation involves future promise, believers "need to persevere" (10:36a) in order to do God's will and "receive what he has promised" (10:36c). The word "need" indicates "something absolutely necessary, not merely desirable" (Morris, 1981, 111). Without persevering resolve, patient endurance, and the daily renewal of faith, we cannot inherit what God has promised. Murray observes: "Between the faith that accepts a promise, and the experience that fully inherits or receives it, there often lie years of discipline and training needed to fit and perfect you for the inward possession of what God has to give" (n.d., 415). The intervening years of waiting for the fulfillment of what God promises require persevering faith and faithfulness. Doing the will of God (the obedience of faith) is the way to receive the promise of God (the reward of faith).

In 10:37–38 the author cites from Old Testament Scripture as further evidence of the believers' need for perseverance. The time of waiting for the promised return of Christ is not yet over. How long must we wait? In view of the brevity of this life and the endless duration of eternity, our waiting is not long. "For in just a very little while [echoing the thought of Isa 26:20], 'He who is coming will come and will not delay'" beyond the appointed time (see Hab. 2:3). For the people of faith, the Lord's coming is always near. God's people trust him by living not only by faith in the unseen present but also in hope of the anticipated future at which time God promises to intervene in history on behalf of the righteous. During the interval between promise and fulfillment, "my righteous one will live by faith" (Heb. 10:38a cf. Hab. 2:4).

Paul quotes this same statement from Habakkuk 2:4 in Romans 1:17 and Galatians

3:11 to stress how a person becomes righteous, namely, by faith. The author of Hebrews, however, quotes this Old Testament text in keeping with its contextual prophetic emphasis, namely, those who are righteous must go on living by faith. The one who perseveres in faith will receive the fulfillment of what God promises (10:36). But God adds: "If [anyone] shrinks back, I will not be pleased with him" (Heb. 10:38b).

Steadfast faith or shrinking back in unbelief are presented as opposite responses in Hebrews. On the one hand, the shrinking back response will result in death and destruction, as it did for the Israelites in the desert (3:12–19). On the other hand, the response of steadfast faith and loyal commitment to Jesus Christ will lead to life and the inheritance of what God has promised (6:12; 10:36). Stated another way, those who persevere in faith will gain their life, while those who shrink back will lose it and prove themselves as reprobates (Bruce, 1990, 274).

In 10:39 the author again identifies himself with his readers by rejecting the choice and destiny of shrinking back and by affirming for them the response of steadfast faith. "But we are not of those who shrink back and are destroyed [as apostates], but of those who believe and are saved" (10:39). Inspiring Old Testament heroes of faith from among their forefathers, men and women who dared to believe and were saved, form the subject of the chapter that follows.

3.3. Essential Characteristics of Faith (11:1–3)

Chapter 11 is a carefully constructed treatment of the topic of faith. This topic is formally introduced by the quotation from Habakkuk 2:4 at the end of chapter 10: "My righteous one will live by faith" (10:38). The faith emphasis in Habakkuk and in Hebrews is on the faith by which the righteous live their lives, not on the faith by which we are justified or declared righteous (as in Romans and Galatians). Faith in Hebrews is closely connected with steadfast endurance and with inheriting the promises of God (cf. 6:12). It enables the whole course of the believer's life to be regulated by the promises of God (i.e., the future) and by spiritual realities that are presently invisible—in spite of adversity or discouraging circumstances. Faith is trust in God "that enables the believer to press on steadfastly whatever the future holds for him [or her]" (Morris, 1981, 112).

The word "faith" (*pistis*) occurs more often in Hebrews than in any other New Testament book—twenty-four times in chapter 11 alone. It is the activity of faith, however, rather than faith as a body of beliefs, that is emphasized. The activity of faith involves the following characteristics. By faith:

- "we . . . are saved" (10:39)
- we have hope based on God's promises (11:1a)
- we are certain of invisible spiritual realities (11:1b)
- we receive God's commendation or approval (11:2)
- we understand that God by his word created the material universe (11:3)
- we worship God (11:4)
- we leave behind an enduring testimony (11:4)
- we believe and seek God by pursuing him and his promises (11:6)
- we please God (11:5–6)
- we fear God rather than people (11:7, 27)
- we are different from our evil generation and perishing world (11:7)
- we obey God and adventure into the unknown of God's full will for our lives (11:8–9)
- we are sustained and drawn by a heavenly vision (11:10)
- we regard God as faithful (11:11)
- we inherit God's promises (11:11–12; cf. 6:12)
- we are willing to welcome his promises at a distance if necessary (11:13)
- we live as pilgrims and strangers on earth (11:13)
- we are looking for a better/heavenly country (11:14–16)
- we do not return to the country we have left, that is, the world (11:15)
- we pass God's hard tests (11:17–19)
- we believe God is greater than death (11:19)
- we confidently bless the next generation of believers (11:20–21)
- we foresee the future visitation of God (11:22)

- we have revelation and fearless courage (11:23)
- we forego present pleasures for the sake of future reward (11:24–26)
- we see him who is invisible (11:27)
- we depart from Egypt (i.e., the corrupt world system) and embrace God's miraculous provisions (11:27–29)
- we are delivered from the destroyer because we know by revelation the significance of the blood of the Lamb (11:28)
- we conquer a city by the revealed purpose and power of God (11:30)
- we cooperate with what God is saying and doing (11:31; cf. 4:2)
- we do mighty exploits as God's people and receive God's miraculous deliverances (11:32–35a)
- we willingly suffer for righteousness' sake (11:35b–38)
- we successfully run the race with endurance (12:1–3).

Because of a living faith in God, all these things are either true or possible, as illustrated in the lives of Old Testament saints.

But what precisely is faith? Some regard verse 1 as the Bible's only attempted definition of faith. What is given here, however, is not a formal definition but two essential elements of faith—elements illustrated in the lives of those listed in this chapter. The two elements correspond to the two halves of verse 1.[7]

(1) "Faith is being sure [*hypostasis*] of what we hope for." The key word, *hypostasis*, can be understood in an objective or subjective sense. *Hypostasis* literally means "that which stands under." (a) Objectively understood, it means "substance," the "essence" of a matter, "objective reality." This understanding is represented by the KJV/NKJV ("faith is the substance of things hoped for"), NEB (" faith gives substance to our hopes"), NJB ("faith can guarantee the blessings that we hoped for"), and by such interpreters as Spicq (1952, 2:337–38), Attridge (1989, 305–10), Lane (1991, 325–26, 328–29), Ellingworth (1993, 564–65), and Koester (*TDNT*, 8:586). According to its objective significance, faith enables us to take hold of and possess the reality of what God has promised before that promise is realized. Hope looks always to the future, but faith lays hold of its reality now. Through the operation of faith God "calls into being that which does not exist" (Rom. 4:17b, NASB). Accordingly, "things which in themselves have no existence as yet [in the physical realm] become real and substantial by the exercise of faith" (Bruce, 1990, 277).

(b) Subjectively understood, *hypostasis* means "assurance" (NASB, NRSV), "confident assurance" (Weymouth, NAB), "being sure" (NIV) of those things hoped for, based on God's promise. Faith and hope are closely related. "Hope" in the Bible has its foundation not in wishful thinking, but in that which God has promised. Faith confidently expects what is promised, in contrast to presumption, which expects what it wants. Thus the NIV emphasizes "faith as an expression of our confidence in God's promises ['what we hope for']" (Peterson, 1994, 1346).

In actuality, faith is *hypostasis* both in its objective and subjective meaning. Faith takes hold of (in the present) the reality of what God has promised (hope) and is sure that it will come to pass in the future (cf. Mark 11:24). The difference between faith and presumption is this: Faith is our response to God's revelatory word and initiative; presumption expects God to respond to our word and initiative.

(2) Faith is being "certain [*elenchos*] of what we do not see" (11:1b). Whereas "what we hope for" relates to that which is promised (11:1a), "what we do not see" relates to that which is invisible (11:1b). *Elenchos* is the key word concerning faith and things invisible. Like *hypostasis*, *elenchos* can be understood in an objective or subjective sense. (a) Objectively understood, it means "bring to the light," "test," "evidence," "proof." This understanding is represented by the KJV/NKJV ("the evidence of things not seen"), Williams ("the proof of the reality of the things we cannot see"), and NJB ("prove the existence of realities that are unseen"). As there are two kinds of knowledge, sensory and revelatory, so also there are two kinds of sight: physical and spiritual. The natural eye sees what is visible (physical sight), while the eye of the heart through the operation of faith sees what is invisible (spiritual sight). Thus, faith is able to grasp the evidence of spiritual reality that is invisible to the physical eye. In the words of a twentieth-century woman of faith, "faith is like radar that sees through the fog to the reality of

things at a distance that the human eye cannot see" (Corrie ten Boom).

(b) Subjectively understood, *elenchos* means "the conviction" (NASB, NRSV) or certainty (NIV) of things unseen. Faith that grasps or takes hold of spiritual realities produces a confident conviction or certainty about "invisible realities [not just the unseen future promise] such as the existence of God, his faithfulness to his word and his control over our world and its affairs" (Peterson, 1994, 1346).

In summary, the objective understanding of faith in 11:1 includes the reality of subjective assurance (all based on God's grace and the revelation/promise of his Word) as the fountainhead of a life of faith. It is the activity and obedience of faith that is primarily illustrated in chapter 11. Faith like that of Noah, Abraham, and Moses takes hold of future realities in the present, recognizes the reality of things invisible, and governs all of life by these realities. In a similar way, Paul says that we—as a people of faith—"fix our eyes not on what is seen, but on what is unseen. For what is seen is temporary, but what is unseen is eternal" (2 Cor. 4:18). As long as we live this side of eternity, "we live by faith, not by sight" (2 Cor. 5:7).

Hebrews 11:1 provides not so much a precise definition of faith as it gives a description of what authentic faith does and sees. It affirms that God provides substance and evidence in the practice of faith, enabling us confidently to believe that what he promises (i.e., hope that looks to future fulfillment) will eventually come to pass, and that what is invisible (the spiritual realm) is in fact true reality (though it lies beyond the natural field of comprehension).

It was because of this kind of faith that "the ancients were commended" (11:2). "The ancients" is (lit.) "the elders," not in a technical sense but with the meaning "ancestors" (i.e., Old Testament saints). The verb "were commended" (*martyreo*) is used seven times in Hebrews, each in reference to the witness of the Scriptures (7:8, 17; 10:15; 11:2, 4, 5, 39). Thus, 11:2 means that the ancestors, on account of their faith, received "the approving testimony of Scripture, and consequently of God himself, who speaks by his Spirit through the written word" (Trites, quoted in Lane, 1991, 330). By testifying to their faith as recorded in Scripture, God preserved them as "witnesses" (12:1; *martyr*) "of true faith for us" (Peterson, 1994, 1346). These witnesses are listed (11:4–32) in historical sequence from Abel to David, Samuel, and the prophets, in outline of salvation history as it advanced forward to Jesus, faith's "author and perfecter" (12:2).

Before proceeding to the testimony about the ancestors' faith (beginning in Gen. 4 with Abel), the author illustrates (in v. 3) the principle (in v. 1) that faith grasps the evidence of things not seen (from the Gen. 1 account of creation). As Peterson notes, "the writer begins where Genesis begins, because faith in God as the Creator of everything that exists is fundamental to the Bible's view of reality" (1994, 1347). "By faith we understand that the universe was formed at God's command." Peterson comments: "If God is in control of nature and history, past and present, every generation of believers can trust his promises about the future, no matter what it costs them" (1994, 1347).

"By faith" (*pistei*) is placed at the beginning of the sentence for emphasis, as it is eighteen times in this chapter, with a cumulative impact intended. The emphasis here is that "by faith we understand." There are two kinds of knowledge: *sensory knowledge*, that is, knowledge obtained through the five physical senses; and *revelatory knowledge*, that is, knowledge about God and the spiritual realm conveyed from God's Spirit to our spirit and understood by faith. In the God-realm we do not understand by the natural mind but by revelation and faith. Thus the natural mind cannot understand things given by God (cf. 1 Cor. 2:12), including creation; only a "renewed mind" can comprehend such things.

Concerning the relationship between faith and understanding, Augustine perceptively wrote: "Understanding is the reward of faith. Therefore, seek not to understand that you may believe, but believe that you may understand" (*In Evangelium Johannis tractatus*, 29.6). Revelation and faith necessarily precede understanding that the universe "was formed by God's command" (*rhemati*, God's spoken word), as revealed in the "God said[s]" of Genesis 1:3, 6, 9, 14, 20, 24, 26. Thus, the testimony of God's written Word is intrinsic to a faith that understands "that what is seen was not made out of what was visible."

The unregenerate person may believe that the material earth and universe evolved out of existing gases and formless matter, but faith understands otherwise. "Faith discerns," as Peterson notes, "that the universe of space and time has an invisible source [i.e., the will of God and the power of God's spoken word] and that it continues to be dependent on God's command [i.e., sustained and held together by God; cf. Col. 1:17]" (1994, 1347). Bruce (1990, 279) holds that the author of Hebrews was affirming in 11:3 the doctrine of *creatio ex nihilo* ("creation out of nothing"; for a discussion of this issue, see Hughes, 1977, 443–52). We may add that the "new creation" (2 Cor. 5:17) of the believer, brought about by Christ, is similar to original creation in that (1) both involve a creative miracle of God made possible by the power of his word, and (2) our understanding of the miracle in each instance is by faith, based on God's revelation in Scripture.

3.4. Examples of Faith From the Old Testament (11:4–38)

The author proceeds to describe the dynamic power of faith at work in people's lives in various ways during the centuries preceding the first coming of Christ. Their testimony of faith is meant to inspire steadfast faith in us who live in the centuries preceding the second coming of Christ. The list moves systematically from Genesis through Joshua (11:4–31), with special attention being given to Abraham and Sarah (11:8–19), and Moses (11:23–28). This section concludes with a brief summary of the triumphs of faith in the midst of great obstacles and trials, stretching from the judges to the Maccabean era of the second century B.C. (11:32–38).

3.4.1. Faith During the Antediluvian Period (11:4–7). The author selects three men of God for special mention from creation to the great Flood: Abel, Enoch, and Noah. Their lives illustrate various aspects of faith demonstrated during this period.

Abel (11:4). Three things are mentioned about the faith of Abel. (1) He is commended as a worshiper of God. Why did God show regard for Abel's worship while rejecting Cain's? Some believe the quality of Abel's sacrifice was better; others believe the quantity of Abel's offering was greater; still others believe it was because Abel offered a blood sacrifice and Cain a grain offering. These suggestions all miss the point. Scripture only tells us that "Abel offered God a better sacrifice than Cain did" because Abel's sacrifice was the worshipful expression of his life of faith. It represented the yielding up of himself to God; he held nothing in reserve. It represented a wholehearted devotion to the Lord, not simply a religious ritual. By faith he entered into the spiritual and inner reality of the sacrifice to the invisible God.

(2) He is "commended as a righteous man." Cain was not righteous; God told him that his offering would be acceptable only if he did what was right (Gen. 4:3–7; cf. Prov. 15:8). Cain's life was spiritually and morally deficient, as his subsequent murder of his brother revealed. God rejected Cain's worship because his heart was not right. Abel, on the other hand, demonstrates the close association between righteousness and faith in 10:38. His worship gave God pleasure because he lived and acted by faith as a righteous man.

(3) He was commended for his testimony. Abel died as the first prophetic martyr in history (cf. Luke 11:50–51); his enduring testimony to successive generations continues to speak of the life of faith that pleases God as a faithful and wholehearted worshiper of God.

Enoch (11:5). Whereas in Abel faith speaks through a martyr, in Enoch faith finds enduring testimony through a man who never died but "was taken from this life . . . because God had taken him away." The verb *metatithemi*, which occurs twice in this verse, means "transferred" or "translated" from one realm to another. The translation of Enoch directly from this world to the next (without dying) places him in the same unique category as Elijah the prophet. The expression "could not be found" conveys the notion that his disappearance was true "despite a thorough search" (BAG, 1957, 325).

What is most important to our author, however, is not his miraculous translation but his having pleased God as a man of faith. The Hebrew text of Genesis states twice that Enoch "walked with God," speaking of his close and intimate fellowship with God. Here (as in the Septuagint) it says that "he . . . pleased God," indicating that his life of spiritual intimacy with God was especially pleasing to him. It is also indicative that Enoch's life of intimacy with God was characterized by faith, since "without faith it is impossible to please God" (11:6).

In 11:6, the author applies the standard of faith operating in Enoch to all his readers part from faith neither Enoch nor any of us an please God. This verse does not say that ithout faith it is difficult to know and please iod, but rather that it is "impossible ... ecause anyone who comes [*proserchomai*; cf. :25; 10:22] to him" as a worshiper (cf. 10:1) ıust demonstrate the two elements of faith escribed in 11:1. (1) We "must believe that he xists." Faith involves what is not directly pparent to the physical senses (Hagner, 1983, 67), that is, "what we do not see" (11:1b). ruce (1990, 286–87) writes with penetrating ısight at this point:

> Belief in the invisible spiritual order involves, first and foremost, belief in him who is "King of ages, immortal, invisible, the only God" (1 Tim. 1:17); and belief in God carries with it necessarily belief in his word. It is not belief in the existence of *a* God that is meant, but belief in the existence of *the* God who once declared his will to the fathers through the prophets and in these last days has spoken in his Son.

(2) We must believe "that he rewards those ho earnestly seek him." Faith involves elieving and trusting God according to his Vord and promises, resulting in a confidence bout "what we hope for" (11:1a). Faith nables us to believe that God's word is true,) desire and seek him earnestly (even if oth- rs do not; cf. Ps. 53:2), and to keep our hearts pen to him as we wait humbly with perse- erance for the reward of our faith. Faith nables us to believe in the goodness of God's haracter when the circumstances of our lives re harsh and adverse. The more secure and ıtimate our relationship to God, the stronger ill be our faith in him. Faith operates out of lationship, not in a vacuum. Thus, faith seeks od's face and fellowship, as did Enoch, even ı a generation that is exceedingly corrupt (cf. ude 14–15). And what is the reward for those ho diligently seek God? As with Enoch, it is e joy of finding him, knowing him, pleasing im, and enjoying him forever.

Noah (11:7). The example of Noah espe- ially illustrates the willingness of faith to elieve what God has said and to risk one's putation and future on its coming to pass. By faith Noah" believed God's warning about things not yet seen." When God told Noah about future events, he asked him to do something never before done in order to save his family from unprecedented judgment by the Flood (cf. Gen. 6:13–22).

In this context the author mentions four accomplishments of Noah's faith. (1) Noah believed God's message and, accordingly, "in holy fear built an ark." "Holy fear" here represents (a) "reverent submission" to God (cf. 5:7, where Jesus' response to the Father is so described), and (b) holy awe concerning God's word of coming judgment. Noah's response of obedient faith and holy fear is demonstrated in building the ark.

(2) The next two accomplishments of Noah's faith have a corporate dimension to them, the first of which relates to salvation. Noah's faith was effective not only on his own behalf, but also on behalf of his family. By faith Noah believed and acted on God's warning to him. In doing so his faith grasped the reality of God's word, became the proof of "things not yet seen," and thereby saved his family.

(3) On the other hand, because of his faith Noah also "condemned the world." He is described in 2 Peter 2:5 as a preacher of righteousness, who confronted his generation with God's message (cf. Gen. 6:9; Ezek. 14:14, 20). Paul refers to his own life and testimony as "the aroma of Christ among [both] those who are being saved and those who are perishing. To the one we are the smell of death; to the other, the fragrance of life" (2 Cor. 2:15–16). Similarly, for those who were being saved, Noah's faith was salvation and life; but for those who were perishing, his faith was condemnation and death. When the flood waters came, they were the means by which the remnant realized its saving destination (cf. 1 Peter 3:20–21). But the same waters were the condemnation of the world's unbelief and the means of their destruction. Again, as in 11:6, Noah's action dramatizes the two elements of faith in 11:1. Although no one had ever heard of a flood, and though Noah was scorned by his contemporaries for holding such a belief, nevertheless he (a) was sure that what God had promised would come to pass (11:1a), and (b) was certain of things not yet seen (11:1b).

(4) The last accomplishment of Noah's faith was that he "became [an] heir of the righteousness that comes by faith." Noah is the

first man explicitly called righteous in the Old Testament. He responded to God with "a full measure of faith" (Lane, 1991, 340) in believing what God said and then acting on it. "Heir" without the definite article is more accurately translated "an heir," which suggests "that others who respond to God with the faith that Noah demonstrated will share with him in the righteousness God bestows upon persons of faith" (Lane, 1991, 341). In Hebrews Jesus, the Son of God, is the "appointed heir of all things" (1:2), and we who steadfastly believe in him are described as the heirs of salvation (1:14), of the promises of God (6:12, 17; cf. 9:15), and of the righteousness that comes by faith (11:6).

3.4.2. Faith From the Patriarchal Period (11:8–22). The Old Testament patriarchal period stretches from Abraham to Joseph. Abraham is the center of attention; only one verse each is given to Isaac (v. 20), Jacob (v. 21), and Joseph (v. 22). This is understandable since Abraham, the man of faith par excellence in the Old Testament, plays a central role in the beginning of Hebrew history and the outworking of God's salvation plan. He is mentioned more extensively in the New Testament than any other Old Testament figure (e.g., John 8:31–58; Acts 7:2–8, 16–17; Rom. 4:1–24; Gal. 3:6–18, 29; Heb. 6:12–15; 7:1–10; 11:8–19).

Here in Hebrews 11 three major episodes of Abraham's life are mentioned to illustrate three important facets of his journey of faith. (1) In obeying God's call to depart from Ur of Chaldea for an undesignated land of promis Abraham demonstrated *faith for the unsee future* (11:8–10). (2) During his long years c waiting for the promised son and descendan in humanly impossible circumstances, Abra ham demonstrated *faith for the impossibl promise* (11:11–12). (3) When God requeste him to sacrifice Isaac (his only son c promise), Abraham demonstrated *faith for th severe trial or test* (11:17–19). In addition t these ways in which faith is powerfully illus trated, a parenthesis in 11:13–16 calls attentio to a common thread of faith that runs throug Abraham's life and that of the other patriarch

(1) Abraham demonstrated *faith for th unseen future*. "By faith Abraham, whe called" by God to leave Ur of Chaldea for promised "place . . . obeyed and went, eve though he did not know where he was going (11:8; cf. Gen. 12:1–3; 15:7; Acts 7:2–3). Th call of God is always accompanied by th promise of God, and true faith in the promis is always joined to obedience to the call (Mu ray, n.d., 438). The focus of this verse is on th correlation between Abraham's faith and h prompt response of obedience to the call. Th verb "when called" (present participle) ind cates that he obeyed by faith even as he wa being called, that is, while the call "was sti sounding in his ears" (Morris, 1981, 118).

Abraham's call involved (a) leaving th security of the known and the familiar, and (l pursuing the promise and inheritance of Go in spite of the unknown and the unseen (c 11:1). This verse is "a classical statement of th

Nomadic Bedouins live in tents in the desert, just as Abraham did after God told him to leave his home i Ur and travel more than a thousand miles to the "land of Canaan."

ɔbedience of faith" (Morris, 1981, 118), for Abraham went forward by faith, not sight. He knew God was calling him to go forward, but he did not know where it would lead. "To leave the certainties one knows and go out into what is quite unknown—relying on nothing other than the Word of God—is the essence of faith" (ibid.). This is what the author of Hebrews wants his readers to emulate: a life of steadfast faith, wherein we give ourselves fully to God himself, to God's call to a pilgrim life of following him faithfully, and to God's promise nvolving a future but yet unfulfilled hope—all in joyful obedience.

Abraham's faith emphatically involved more than his initial act of obedience in leaving the secure comforts of the influential city of Ur. It also involved migrating to "the promised land" and living there in tents "like a stranger in a foreign country" (11:9). Lane notes that "the sharp contrast between '*the promised land*' and '*a foreign country*' serves to throw into bold relief the writer's portrayal of the unsettled life of Abraham" (1991, 350). His new situation in Canaan required as much faith as did his leaving Ur. Wherever Abraham pitched his tent, he incurred the stigma of a stranger and a nomadic wanderer. This required "renewed faith and a fresh commitment of obedience" (Lane, 1991, 350) day by day. That Abraham "lived in tents, as did Isaac and Jacob," vividly testifies to their shared status as nomadic aliens residing in a foreign country and to their mutual pilgrimage of faith as "heirs . . . of the same promise." By faith they were sure of the promise and certain of that which they did not yet see (11:1).

The ultimate promise of which the patriarchs were all fellow heirs, however, was not earthly Canaan but the transcendent city of God (11:10). Abraham knew by revelation that the earthly land of promise was not the ultimate destination of his pilgrimage of faith. When he received God's call to leave the city of Ur, Abraham also received a vision of God himself (Acts 7:2), which may have included a vision of "the city with foundations, whose architect and builder is God." If so, from that point on "he was looking forward to the city [of God]" as his goal.

The verb "was looking forward" (lit., "he expected") is intensive in force and carries the sense "he expected with an absolute confidence" (Spicq, 1952, 2:347). The imperfect tense emphasizes "continuous expectation" (Lane, 1991, 344). His forward-looking faith had substance and evidence, and thus assurance and confidence, which led him steadfastly to endure the stigma and inconveniences of living in tents as an alien resident in a foreign country.

The description of the city as having "foundations," in contrast to Abraham's nomadic existence of living in tents, speaks of a promise that is "well-based" and secure. The city's foundations are indeed eternal, seeing that its "architect" (i.e., "designer") and "builder" (i.e., "creator") is God himself. Although a few interpreters have sought to make a case that this city of God refers to the earthly Jerusalem, which Abraham foresaw as part of his descendants' inheritance (cf. Buchanan, 1972, 188–89), the author of Hebrews undoubtedly had the heavenly Jerusalem in mind (see 11:16; 12:22; 13:14; cf. Rev. 21:2). For Abraham the promise related to the future and was presently unseen; yet because of faith, its reality was a present motivating factor in his life and tenuous circumstances. The heavenly vision sustained him on his earthly journey because he was living by faith, not by sight.

(2) Abraham demonstrated *faith for the impossible promise*, that is, that he would father "descendants as numerous as the stars in the sky and as countless as the sand on the seashore" (11:12). It was humanly impossible for Abraham to have children for two reasons: (a) His wife, Sarah, had throughout her life been barren (11:11) and was now past the childbearing years (cf. Gen. 15:1–6; 17:15–22; 18:9–15). As she approached ninety years of age, long "past the age of childbearing" (Gen. 18:11), Sarah laughed incredulously at the prophecy that she would have a son within a year: "After I am worn out and my master is old [impotent], will I now have this pleasure? [i.e., sexual pleasure and the honor of having a son]" (Gen. 18:12). As Lane observes, "the sharing of physical intimacy had apparently ceased for the couple and menopause had occurred long ago" (1991, 354).

(b) Abraham's own body had ceased to function sexually. The latter is especially indicated by the phrase "as good as dead" (Heb. 11:12), meaning he had lost his physical ability to father a child (cf. Rom. 4:19). Only by a miracle could they even resume sexual relations. "By faith Abraham . . . was enabled to become a father [*eis katabolen spermatos*, lit., to deposit the sperm] because he considered him faithful who had made the promise" (11:11). By faith Abraham believed God was trustworthy and, therefore, would be faithful to his promise. As Peterson observes, "the ground of his confidence was the word of God and he trusted that God would be faithful to his word" (1994, 1347). The innumerable and uncountable descendants in verse 12 are a testimony to and the fruit of Abraham's faith.

Abraham is the subject of verse 11 in the NIV translation (also TEV, NRSV), rather than Sarah being the subject as in some translations (e.g. KJV/NKJV, NASB, NEB). Two weighty considerations decisively support the NIV. (a) The phrase *eis katabolen spermatos* in verse 11 is a fixed Hellenistic idiom for the male function in procreation, not the female ability to conceive. (b) The subject of verse 12 stands in close relationship to verse 11, since the pronoun "one" (*enos*; "man" is not in the Greek text) and the qualifying participle "as good as dead" are both masculine in gender (Lane, 1991, 344) and have as their antecedent the subject of verse 11. Accordingly, Abraham remains the continuous subject of 11:8–12. The phrase "Sarah herself was barren" (11:11) is best taken, as Bruce notes, "as a circumstantial clause" (1990, 296; also Attridge, 1989, 325; Lane, 1991, 344; Ellingworth, 1993, 588) that provides additional evidence of the impossible nature (humanly speaking) of God's promise.

An aside. In 11:13–16 the author, in good literary fashion, pauses to summarize what he has been saying about the true nature of faith as first described in 11:1. The identity of "all these people" is initially unspecified, but the latter part of the verse identifies them as those who openly confessed (by the manner in which they lived) that "they were aliens and strangers on earth" (cf. 1 Peter 2:11, where "aliens and strangers" is a designation for the Jewish Christians of the Dispersion; cf. 1:1). This description, along with the words of Hebrews 11:14–16, identify the people as Abraham and Sarah, along with Isaac and Jacob (cf. 11:9, 11).

Although God had promised these people a place (11:8), they remained pilgrims "in the promised land" (11:9), because their forward-looking faith was waiting for the greater promise of a heavenly city (11:10) and country (11:16). "The objective character of the promise" (Lane, 1991, 356), because of their faith, was substantial reality to them (11:1). They were still living in accordance with the operating principle of faith "when they died," even though they did not receive the ultimate fulfillment of "the things promised [things that awaited the coming of Christ; cf. 11:39–40]; they only saw them [through eyes of faith] and welcomed them [as things hoped for] from a distance." Even though the promises were deferred in time, their fulfillment was nevertheless certain and, therefore could be joyfully welcomed from a tempora[l] distance. This vividly illustrates the statemen[t] about faith in 11:1.

The opening phrase in verse 14 shifts to the present tense: "people who say such things show." The author wants the confession of 11:13c to be the testimony and experience of his readers. They are able to live as "aliens and strangers" (11:13c) in this world because "they are looking for [desiring, longing for] a country of their own." Their foremost longing is no[t] materialistic or nationalistic (i.e., this worldly); instead, it is for a spiritual homeland of thei[r] own, identical with "the city" with eterna[l] foundations in 11:10 and the "better country— a heavenly one" in 11:16. Bruce writes tha[t] "their 'pilgrim's progress' through this world had as its goal a home elsewhere. Canaan wa[s] no more their home as they sought the country of their hearts' desire than the wildernes[s] was the home of their descendants in Moses' day who journeyed from Egypt to Canaan" (1990, 298–99).

If the patriarch's longing for a country ha[d] been for the land of their forefathers i[n] Mesopotamia, their unsettled, nomadic livin[g] in Canaan would have given them reason t[o] return (11:15). "If their hearts had been in th[e] country they had left" (NEB), they could hav[e] turned back. But their faith in God and hi[s] promises excluded that possibility an[d] annulled that natural desire for their forme[r] "homeland." When Abraham sought to obtai[n] a bride for his son Isaac, he wanted her to b[e] from his former homeland. But neither he no[r] Isaac returned there. Instead, Abraham dispatched his servant to make the journey, instructing him: "Make sure that you do no[t] take my son back there" (Gen. 24:6). Similarly even though Jacob did return there when fleeing from the wrath of Esau and likewise obtained a wife there (two, in fact), he regarded Canaan his "place" (Heb. 11:8), not Mesopotamia. Moreover, he heard God say: "Go back to the land of your fathers" (Gen. 31:3). It was in Canaan, not Mesopotamia, where Sarah and Abraham, Isaac, Jacob, and Joseph all chose to be buried.

All these people wholeheartedly believed God's word of promise. Had they been earthly-minded with their hearts focused on materialistic things, they would have turned back to Mesopotamia. But faith is the opposite of shrinking back (cf. 10:38). The patriarchs' steadfast faith in pressing forward "stands in sharp contrast to the generation that wandered in the wilderness and failed to enter God's rest (4:6), but who instead desired to return to Egypt" (Hagner, 1983, 177). The patriarchs "singlemindedly . . . walked the path of faith" (Morris, 1981, 121) and set their hearts on pilgrimage (cf. Ps. 84:5–7).

"Instead" (11:16) of regulating their lives by natural desires of human reason, such as returning to the more tranquil "good life" of Mesopotamia, the lives of the patriarchs were regulated by faith and the vision of a "better" country. The word "better" (used thirteen times in Hebrews) usually describes the superiority of those promises fulfilled in Christ to those confined to the old covenant. Here it is used synonymously with "heavenly," that is, the transcendent, everlasting, well-founded city and country of God, which awaits those who place their faith, trust, and confidence in him (cf. 12:22; 1 Cor. 2:9; Rev. 21:1–22:6). As pilgrims of faith the patriarchs fixed their eyes, as must we, "not on what is seen, but on what is unseen. For what is seen is temporary, but what is unseen is eternal" (2 Cor. 4:18).

In the context of God's prophecy against the house of Eli, God declares: "Those who honor me I will honor, but those who despise me will be disdained" (1 Sam. 2:30). The patriarchs honored God by their steadfast faith, and he honored them by unashamedly calling himself "their God" (11:16b)—"the God of Abraham, the God of Isaac and the God of Jacob" (Ex. 3:6, 15, 16; etc.). Bruce observes: "What higher honor than this could be paid to any mortal? These three patriarchs were not faultless, but God is not ashamed to be called their God, because they took him at his word." Bruce adds that although Jacob's conduct was in some ways the least exemplary of the three, "God is called the God of Jacob, much more frequently in the Bible than he is called the God of Abraham or Isaac. For all his shortcomings, Jacob had a true sense of spiritual values which sprang from his faith in God" (1990, 300).

When referring to God's designation of himself as the God of the patriarchs from Exodus 3:6, Jesus adds: "He is not the God of the dead, but of the living" (Matt. 22:32). Jesus' words, like those in the present passage, point to the fact that the patriarchs (along with other men and women of faith who lived before Christ) will share "in the same inheritance of glory as is promised to believers in Christ of New Testament times" (Bruce, 1990, 301), "for he has prepared a city for them" (Heb. 11:16c). The city of God is specifically prepared for righteous people, like the patriarchs who lived by faith (10:38) as "aliens and strangers on earth" (cf. 11:8–10, 13), looking beyond present circumstances to the future as promised by God.

(3) Having concluded his parenthetical comments about the common thread of faith in the patriarchs (11:13–16), the author returns to the supreme example of Abraham's faith (1:17–19). The recurring expression "by faith" (*pistei*) introduces the third major demonstration of Abraham's faith, *faith for the severe trial or test*, when Abraham was called to sacrifice his son Isaac (cf. also James 2:21–23). "God tested" Abraham (Heb. 11:17a) at the point of his most cherished values in life.

The test was a fierce challenge of Abraham's faith in at least three areas. (a) It tested Abraham's faith concerning God himself and their relationship. Could or should God be trusted when giving such a command? Can God's character be trusted when human circumstances do not make sense? Abraham's conclusion was "Yes, God is trustworthy." He chose to trust God from the heart rather than restrict his response to the head (cf. Prov. 3:5–6). He chose to believe that God's love is unchanging and that God's wisdom is infinitely greater than Abraham's own limited understanding. Only when we have settled the issue of God's trustworthiness can we believe that God's will is *always* good, reasonable, and perfect (cf. Rom. 12:2).

(b) God's request also tested Abraham's faith in relation to his natural affection and love for his "one and only" (*monogenes*) son (11:17b). The Greek word *monogenes* means literally "one of a kind" or "unique." Isaac, the "miracle son" of Abraham and Sarah in their old age, had a special place of affection in their hearts and a unique place in salvation history. He was the "only" son of Sarah and Abraham, the "only" son of promise, and therefore truly "unique and irreplaceable" (Bruce, 1990, 303).

(c) God's request tested Abraham's indomitable faith in the promise of God about an innumerable and uncountable posterity through Isaac (cf. 11:12; Gen. 15:2–6). How could God's promise that "through Isaac . . . your offspring will be reckoned" (Heb. 11:18) be reconciled with God's command to sacrifice him? Apart from faith they seemed hopelessly contradictory, with the latter canceling out the former. But Abraham believed that God would work out his purpose and fulfill his promise even if he could not explain how. This was faith in the fire, faith being refined like gold and being made complete (cf. James 2:22; 1 Peter 1:7). The testing of faith makes possible a maturity of faith; an untested faith cannot fully be a mature faith.

There is a discernible progression in Abraham's faith on his journey to maturity. When Abraham by faith obeyed God's call to leave Ur of Chaldea, he surrendered his past. When he had to wait year after year (twenty-five altogether) "in hope against hope" (Rom. 4:18, NASB) for a humanly impossible son, he surrendered his present. But when he was asked by God to sacrifice his son of promise, he had to surrender his future as well. The faith that is most complete "is able to surrender God's promises back to him for their fulfillment according to his will" (*FLSB*, note on 11:13).

By faith Abraham accepted what he could not understand, based on God's integrity and the reliability of his word. The measure of Abraham's surrender of his future is indicated by the two occurrences of the verb *prosphero* in verse 17, translated as "offered" (11:17a) and "about to sacrifice" (11:17b). "Offered" is the perfect tense of *prosphero*, indicating completed action. It conveys, as Morris notes, "that as far as Abraham was concerned the sacrifice was complete. In will and purpose he did offer his son. He held nothing back" (1981, 122). The second occurrence of *prosphero* is in the imperfect tense indicating the action was interrupted in proces and therefore not consummated because God intervened in time to spare Isaac's life. When we fully surrender future treasures to God, he often gives them back in unexpected ways. Peter reminds Christians that at the end of the journey after tested faith has been proven "genuine," it will "result in praise, glory and honor when Jesus Christ is revealed" (1 Peter 1:7).

The conflict between Abraham's unshakable confidence in the integrity of God and his word on the one hand, and his faithful obedience to God's command to sacrifice Isaac on the other hand, found resolution in his heart by placing his full confidence in God's power to raise his son from the dead (11:19). "Abraham reasoned [i.e., counted as true] that God could raise the dead" (11:19a). For Abraham God's power to raise the dead was revelation and faith. Thus when arriving at Mount Moriah where the sacrifice of Isaac was to occur, Abraham instructed his servants to stay behind with the donkey and added: "I and the boy [will] go over there. We will worship and then we will come back to you" (Gen. 22:5). Abraham fully expected to sacrifice Isaac as God had commanded and then to come back with Isaac raised from the dead, since the fulfillment of God's promises depended on Isaac's survival.

God's integrity and God's power were the source of Abraham's assurance and certainty. The author of Hebrews adds that Abraham's faith was vindicated by receiving "figuratively speaking [*en parabole*] . . . Isaac back from death" (11:19b). *Parabole* means "parable". Lane (as others) believes that *en parabole* here means "in a foreshadowing" (1991, 362–63). This incident with Isaac was a veiled "foreshadowing" or a prefiguring of Jesus' sacrifice and resurrection as God's one and only Son. Bruce adds (1990, 304–5) that it was mos likely this incident that Jesus had in mind when he said: "Your father Abraham rejoiced at the thought of seeing my day; he saw it and was glad" (John 8:56).

Isaac, Jacob, and Joseph were recipients of the same covenant as Abraham. Moreover they demonstrated, like Abraham, "the visionary perspective of faith" (Lane, 1991, 364) that enabled them to see beyond the limits of their own lives to those things promised by God but as yet unseen (11:1). When the dying patriarchs blessed their sons (and grandsons), they revealed their steadfast, forward-looking faith in God and in the future fulfillment of his promises. Lane observes that "although they all died without having experienced the fulfillment of the promises, they 'saw' their realization with the eyes of faith and saluted them from a distance" (1991, 364).

Isaac. "By faith Isaac blessed Jacob and Esau in regard to their future" (11:20). Three things are noteworthy here. (1) The act of blessing Jacob was directly tied to the covenant promises given by God to Abraham. When Isaac imparted the blessing to Jacob, the promises concerning the future that had been passed to Isaac from Abraham were then activated in Jacob. In this fashion Abraham's spiritual heritage was passed down to the fourth and fifth generations.

(2) The order of blessing was Jacob first, then Esau. This was contrary to Isaac's own natural preference for his firstborn son. Nevertheless, by faith Isaac pronounced the blessings promised to Abraham upon Jacob, the younger son, as God's own choice. Isaac did give a blessing to Esau as well regarding the future, though not those tied to Abraham's line of promise.

(3) Isaac's blessing "in regard to their future" was not about an unknown future but about a future "as yet unseen" (Lane, 1991, 364).

Jacob. "By faith Jacob, when he was dying," expressed faith concerning the future (similar to that of Isaac) as he "blessed each of Joseph's sons" (11:21). Like Isaac, Jacob blessed Ephraim and Manasseh in the reverse order of their birth; but unlike Isaac, Jacob deliberately bestowed the greater blessing on the younger son as he discerned that he was God's choice (cf. Gen. 48:8–20). He believed that God's promises would be carried out according to God's purpose and timing. Jacob, worshiping God "as he leaned on the top of his staff" in his old age, broken but not bitter, blessing his sons and grandsons, is itself a picture of faith and submission to God's ways. Lane adds: "Jacob's final act of worship, leaning upon the top of his staff, was characteristic for one who lived his life as a stranger and sojourner" (1991, 365).

Joseph. There were many incidents and moments in Joseph's life that could have been selected to illustrate his faith. But again our author chose an incident "when his end was near" that revealed "the same firm faith in the fulfilment of God's promises" (Bruce, 1990, 306) and the certainty of "things to come" that had characterized his forefathers. "By faith Joseph . . . spoke about the [future] exodus of the Israelites from Egypt" (11:22)—a promise God had spoken to Abraham before the birth of his promised son and many years before his descendants went to Egypt during a time of famine (Gen. 15:12–16). Joseph had to believe that his descendants would one day depart from Egypt and return to the Promised Land.

Even though Joseph had lived all of his adult life in Egypt and had risen to a position of great prominence and honor, nevertheless—"with the foresight that faith confers" (Lane, 1991, 366) and with bold confidence about events "as yet unseen"—he "gave instructions" (cf. Gen. 50:24–25) that his bones be buried, not in Egypt, but in Canaan, the land of God's promises to Abraham, Isaac, and Jacob. Joseph's faith proved to be justified, as Israel's departure from Egypt became perhaps the most significant event in all of salvation history before the coming of Christ. When the Exodus did occur centuries later, Joseph's coffin and embalmed body were carried from Egypt (Ex. 13:19) as he had requested in faith. When the Israelites settled in Canaan after the Exodus and Conquest, his mortal remains were buried at Shechem (Josh. 24:32).

3.4.3. Faith During the Exodus Era (11:23–29). The third segment of Old Testament history mentioned in this chapter is that of Moses and the Exodus. Moses as a man of faith is highly honored in both Judaism and Christianity. As Morris points out, however, a fundamental difference of perspective about Moses' place in history occurs between the two. "Whereas the Jews tended to put Moses in the higher place and see Abraham as one who kept the law before Moses, the Christians, with their emphasis on faith, preferred to put Abraham in the more exalted place and see Moses as one who followed in the steps of Abraham's faith" (1981, 125). Thus, it is not surprising that Hebrews 11 devotes twelve verses to Abraham as an example of faith and half that number to Moses. Neither is it surprising, however, that the faith of Moses is more extensively discussed than that of Isaac, Jacob, and Joseph combined.

Verse 23 reveals that Moses' faith actually began with his courageous parents. Moses' life was spared as an infant because of the faith of his parents, who "hid him for three months after he was born," in defiance of Pharaoh's edict to kill all Hebrew male babies at birth (cf. Ex. 1:22). At the cost of great personal risk, his parents trusted God for a deliverance.

The author cites two explanations for the act of faith by Moses' parents. (1) They hid him "because they saw he was no ordinary [*asteion*] child" (11:23b). *Asteios* literally means "beautiful" or "strikingly attractive." Stephen (Acts 7:20) states that the infant Moses was "fair [*asteios*] in the sight of God." These two passages indicate that Moses, even as an infant, had about him some kind of discernible elective favor relating to God's as yet unseen purposes for Israel. Because Moses' parents had some inkling that he was a son of destiny, they risked their own lives to preserve his life and God's vocational purpose for him (Lane, 1991, 370). According to Josephus, God-given revelation about this was communicated to Moses' father, Amram, in a night vision (*Antiquities*, 2.210–16).

(2) Moses' parents "were not afraid of the king's edict" (11:23c). Had their defiance of Pharaoh's decree been discovered, the penalty would have been severe under a despotic ruler. Nevertheless, instead of fearing Pharaoh, they trusted God with their lives (cf. Ex. 1:17–21). Their faith in God's power to accomplish his sovereign purposes gave them fearless courage to act righteously over against the king's edict. Moses' parents are a noble example of the capacity of faith to overcome fear.

When Moses "had grown up," he too demonstrated faith by his own moral choices (11:24–25). For him, as for us, right choices involve both negative and positive decisions. Negatively, he "refused to be known as the son of Pharaoh's daughter" (11:24b). The tense of the verb "refused" indicates a specific act of choice (Guthrie, 1983, 239). This was not the decision of a rebellious adolescent or a decision made impulsively that Moses would later regret. He understood fully what he was doing. Undoubtedly, Israel's future leader had pondered deeply about the oppressive policy of Pharaoh against the Hebrew people and believed strongly it was morally wrong. He understood that his privileged position and power in Egyptian aristocracy as the adopted son of Pharaoh's daughter was at stake. As an act of faith and good conscience, Moses decisively gave it all up to be identified with his own oppressed people. By the world's standards this decision was "an act of folly" (Bruce, 1990, 310). But as Stephen indicates in Acts 7:25, Moses' faith included a firm conviction that God was calling him to rescue his people.

Moses not only made a difficult negative decision, he also made a difficult positive choice. He faced two alternatives: "mistreat[ment] . . . with the people of God" or the enjoyable (though transient) "pleasures of sin" (Heb. 11:25). By faith he chose the former rather than the latter. The expression "mistreated along with" suggests being closely linked together in suffering, "a solidarity in suffering" (Guthrie, 1983, 239). The luxurious comforts and security of living in the royal courts were sinful for Moses to enjoy when his own people were being mistreated as oppressed slaves by that same royalty. For Moses to have continued in his privileged aristocratic position as a royal heir after having "seen the path of duty clear before him, would have been sin—the crowning sin of apostasy against which the recipients of this letter needed so insistently to be warned" (Bruce, 1990, 310–11). Moses weighed the issues carefully and then made a choice, out of faith, to do what he knew to be right.

Unlike Esau, who traded long-range good for present momentary pleasure, Moses traded momentary pleasure for future long-range good (11:26). Moses was able to make such a choice for two reasons. (1) He was a man with spiritual values: "He regarded disgrace for the sake of Christ" as a greater value than all the material wealth of Egypt. The identification of Moses' suffering with that of Christ is not arbitrarily reading back into history the New Testament perspective. There are several possible ways to understand this. (a) The stigma or reproach that came by identifying with the suffering of God's people is the same reproach that Christ later received and was thus an identification with Christ (DeAngelo, quoted in Lane 1991, 373). (b) The eternal Christ in some way identified with the suffering people of God in Old Testament times; thus, when Moses suffered, he did so with Christ (Morris, 1981, 126). (c) Moses chose to suffer the reproach that nec-

›ssarily accompanies "the anointed one"—that s, any anointed envoy of God (Hawthorne, 986, 1528). (d) In view of the types and shad-›ws of Hebrews, Moses' willingness to suffer or the sake of advancing God's redemptive ›lan was also for the sake of Christ in that all edemptive suffering flowed toward Christ, vho is its ultimate fulfillment and embodiment. n any case, the main point here is clear: Faith's values triumph over worldly materialism.

(2) Moses was a man of prophetic vision: 'He was looking ahead to his [as yet unseen] eward." He confidently believed that God xists and rewards "those who earnestly seek im" (11:6). Whether the reward that Moses vas anticipating was God's mighty deliverance of the Hebrews from Egypt or was an eternal, ranscendent reward later to be bestowed by God himself, Moses by faith was "sure of what he] hoped for and certain of what" he did not ee (11:1). He looked *away from* the present emporal, material, and sensual pleasures of Egypt and looked *to* the enduring, as yet unseen, piritual reward of God. The believers addressed n Hebrews could identify with Moses' experi-ence of suffering and his hard choices because hey too had experienced similar suffering for he sake of Christ and were presently facing ome hard choices that would require a forward-ooking faith, like that of Moses.

Because of faith Moses "left Egypt, not earing the king's anger" (11:27). Moses left Egypt on two occasions—when fleeing to Midian after slaying an Egyptian oppressor Ex. 2:11–15), and when leading the Israelites out at the Exodus. The majority of contempo-ary interpreters believe the reference here is o the former departure (e.g. Bruce, 1990, 312; Attridge, 1989, 342; Lane, 1991, 374; Elling-worth, 1993, 615). Some interpreters, how-ever, believe the Exodus departure is referred o here (e.g., Westcott, 1889/1980, 373; Mon-efiore, 1964, 204; Spicq, 1952, 2:359; Hagner, 1983, 183). Most likely the sequence in verses 27–29 is chronological: Moses left Egypt and went to the Midian desert (11:27); when he eturned, he kept the first Passover (11:28); afterward, he led the Exodus of Israel from Egypt through the Red Sea (11:29).

But 11:27 states that Moses did not fear the king's anger, whereas Exodus 2:14–15 notes hat Moses was afraid after killing the Egypt-an and thus fled to Midian. Bruce (1990, 313) believes there is no contradiction, however, since Moses' fear was about his violent action becoming public knowledge and was not immediately connected in Exodus 2:14 to his flight:

> He was afraid, admittedly, but that was not why he left Egypt; his leaving Egypt was an act of faith. "By faith he left Egypt, and not because he feared the king's anger" (NEB). By his impulsive act of violence he had burned his boats as far as the court of Egypt was concerned; but he might have raised a slave's revolt there and then. By faith, however, he did nothing of the kind; "he had the insight to see that God's hour had not yet struck, and therefore he resolutely turned his back on the course he had begun to tread, and retraced his steps till he entered on the harder way. For it was harder to live for his people than it was to die for them" (Peake).

Moses did not fear Pharaoh's anger "because he saw him who is invisible" (11:27). Perhaps Moses had a prophetic dream or vision in which he saw God and was reassured and directed what to do next (cf. Matt. 1:20–21; 2:13–14). More likely, however, seeing "him who is invisible" refers to Moses' "life-long vision of God," wherein lay the secret of his faith and perseverance (Bruce, 1990, 314). Lane notes a key to understanding the latter part of verse 27, namely, that the verbal expression used there is a fixed Hellenistic idiom meaning "he kept seeing continually" (1991, 375). The emphasis here falls not on perseverance but on continually seeing the invisible God (BAGD, 405). The reality of the unseen is the foremost issue of faith in Hebrews 11, as is evident in the following list:

Verse 1—"what we hope for . . . what we do not see"
Verse 3—"what is seen was not made out of what was visible"
Verse 6—"that [God] exists and that he rewards"
Verse 7—"things not yet seen"
Verse 8—"did not know where he was going"
Verse 10—"looking forward to the city with foundations"
Verse 13—"saw [things promised] and welcomed them from a distance"

Verse 14—"looking for a country"
Verse 16—"longing for a better country"
Verse 22—"Joseph . . . spoke about the exodus of the Israelites from Egypt"
Verse 26—"looking ahead to his reward"
Verse 27—"saw him who is invisible"

In addition to these explicit references, the heroes of faith throughout the chapter acted as they did because of their confident assurance and full conviction about the unseen reality of God and his promises (Hagner, 1983, 169).

It was also "by faith" that Moses "kept [instituted] the Passover" (11:28), with careful attention to all the detailed instruction given at God's command (cf. Ex. 11:1–12:28). Special mention is made here of "the sprinkling of blood." The blood of the paschal lamb was applied to the top and sides of the door frame of each house by using a sprig of hyssop (Ex. 12:22). Wherever the blood of the lamb was sprinkled, the destroyer angel would pass over the house and "not touch the firstborn of Israel." By faith Moses and the Israelites (following his example) complied with God's directive, thus sparing their firstborn children and livestock from the plague of death that ravaged the Egyptian households (cf. Ex. 11:4–5; 12:12, 27, 29–30).

Finally, it was Moses' faith that inspired God's people so that they "passed through the Red Sea as on dry land" (Heb. 11:29). They acted "by faith" specifically in reference to God's command to Moses to move forward (Ex. 14:15). As in our salvation, the deliverance that had been provided by God for the Israelites had to be appropriated by them through the response of faith. That is, the faith of Moses and the people made possible the impossible crossing of the sea as on a dry river bed. The Egyptians, having no faith, attempted to follow the Israelites in crossing, and "they were drowned." Their fate reveals that the faith of Moses and the Israelites had substance and reality to it. It also reveals that God is awesome in power and mighty to deliver those who demonstrate the response of faith in him. The Exodus events—the central redemptive action of God in the Old Testament—were appropriated "by faith."

3.4.4. Faith During the Conquest (11:30–31). The author in chapter 3 mentioned the unbelief and faithlessness of the desert generation. Not surprisingly, therefore, there is no mention of them in this chapter after the mirac ulous Red Sea crossing. The testimonies o faith are resumed with the entrance into th Promised Land and the fall of Jericho.

Surprising is the omission in 11:30 o Joshua's name as a hero of faith, although h is mentioned by name in 4:8 and his fait implied in 4:2. Certainly it was Joshua's fait at Jericho, like Moses' faith at the Red Sea, tha made possible the corporate triumph of faith Joshua believed and implemented God' instruction given him by the angelic comman der of the Lord's army (Josh. 5:14). But the fa of Jericho involved the people's faith also Lane aptly states: "Faith in this instance con sisted in the readiness to act in accordance wit God's mandate. It was expressed by Joshua the priests, and the company of fighting men' (1991, 378), as well as by the people generall who "marched around [Jericho's walls] fo seven days."

Only faith could see the city being con quered in this fashion. In the natural, as Bruc observes, "nothing could seem more foolis than for grown men to march around a stron fortress for seven days on end, led by seve priests blowing rams' horns. Who ever hear of a fortress being captured that way?" (1990 317). Nevertheless, on the seventh day, whe Joshua and the Israelites circled the city seve times and the rams' horns sounded, the people as instructed, "gave a loud shout [and] the wal collapsed [as a direct act of God]; so every man charged straight in, and they took the city' (Josh. 6:20). Is this kind of faith still relevan today? Bruce answers: "It is by this same fait that other Jerichoes [i.e., strongholds], bot large and small, can still be overthrown' (1990, 317). It is "by faith" that we engage i spiritual warfare to conquer stronghold (2 Cor. 10:4), advance God's kingdom, an possess what God has promised.

Because of her faith, Rahab the prostitut and her family were spared during the destruc tion of Jericho (11:31; cf. Josh. 6:23). Excep for Sarah (Heb. 11:11), Rahab is the only woman mentioned by name in the Hebrews 1 list of faith champions. Her faith is reveale in her welcoming and hiding the two spies sen by Joshua to Jericho in advance of the con quest. It is also evident in her confession, " know that the LORD has given this land to you' (Josh. 2:9)—a faith based on hearing an believing the report of Israel's miraculous exodus from Egypt and Israel's victories east of the Jordan preceding Jericho (2:10–13). "By faith" she believed that Israel's God was the God of heaven and earth (2:11).

Furthermore, Rahab demonstrated her faith (cf. James 2:25) by risking "present peril for the sake of future preservation" (Lane, 1991, 379; cf. Josh. 2:12–16). Thus, when Jericho was conquered and its inhabitants destroyed, Rahab "was not killed with those who were disobedient" (i.e., the unbelievers of the city). "Disobedience" and "unbelief" are synonymous in Hebrews (cf. Heb. 3:18–19; 4:6). That Rahab was spared—a woman, a Gentile, a secular prostitute and open sinner—is a classic Old Testament example of a person who, because God is rich in mercy and abounding in grace, is saved by grace through faith (cf. Eph. 2:3–9).

3.4.5. Faith From the Time of the Judges, the Davidic Kingdom, and Beyond (11:32–38). To this point the author has expounded on select Old Testament examples of faith from Abel to the Conquest (11:4–31). Conquering the Promised Land, however, marked only the beginning of great testimonies of faith in Israel's subsequent history. Knowing that time and space will not permit him to continue writing in such detail (11:32a), he proceeds to give a random sampling of six Old Testament names in rapid succession (11:32). Then he concludes the narrative with a general summary of the faith exploits of judges, kings, prophets, exiles, and martyrs (11:33–38), who "are etched deeply in the annals of Israel's history" (Hawthorne, 1986, 1528).

Four of the six names listed in verse 32 as examples of faith are from the time of the judges: Gideon (Judg. 6:11–8:32), Barak (Judg. 4:6–5:31), Samson (Judg. 13:2–16:31), and Jephthah (Judg. 11:1–12:7). A couple of facts are noteworthy about these men. (1) For no apparent reason the first two and the last two men are named in the reverse order of their Old Testament appearance (as the above references indicate). (2) Although the Old Testament reveals that all four men demonstrated deficiencies of one kind or another, they all demonstrated faith in their keen awareness of the reality of the invisible God and in battling against overwhelming odds on his behalf. It is not perfectionism (i.e., faultlessness) but faith that God approves.

The last two persons named in 11:32, David (1 Sam. 16–2 Sam. 24) and Samuel (1 Sam. 1–15), are not surprising. David's great exploits as a youth (slaying a lion, a bear, and Goliath) and as Israel's second and greatest king securely place him in faith's hall of champions. Likewise, Samuel served God and Israel valiantly from his youth to old age as a man of faith, intercessor, and faithful prophet. Lane aptly remarks that Samuel's "long life was distinguished by the integrity and intensity of an active faith" (1991, 385). However, they too are surprisingly mentioned in the reverse order of their Old Testament appearance. The purpose of this reversal may have been to connect Samuel more closely with "the prophets" at the end of verse 32, since he was the formal beginning of the long line of "prophetic succession" in subsequent Old Testament history (cf. Acts 3:24; Bruce, 1990, 320).

The mere mention of "the prophets" (which would include not only those who wrote Old Testament prophetic books but also nonwriting prophets, such as Elijah and Elisha) was sufficient "to evoke a clear impression of men who were exemplars of faith to their own generation. Faith informed both their word and their actions" (Lane, 1991, 385).

In 11:33 the characteristic phrase "by faith" now changes to "through faith" (*dia pisteos*), as the author shifts from describing the faith of specific individuals to a summary recital of faith achievements by the old covenant saints generally. The short descriptive clauses that follow in these two and one-half verses, are arranged in three clusters of three. (1) The first cluster describes faith as making possible great achievements on behalf of the theocratic nation. In combat with Israel's enemies (i.e., hostile neighboring nations), mere men like Joshua, the judges, and David through faith "conquered kingdoms." Also in leading God's covenant people and in opposing evil, such men "administered justice." Their rule and administration was representative of God's rule, which is founded on "righteousness and justice" (Ps. 97:2) and carried out in wisdom and personal integrity. Through faith they also "gained what was promised" by God on specific occasions, as with Gideon (Judg. 6:12–16; 7:7), Barak (4:6–7, 14), and Samson (13:5). This phrase may also refer to obtaining further promises concerning the future, as with David (2 Sam. 7:8–16).

(2) The second cluster of three describes those who through faith experienced remarkable deliverance from certain death (Heb. 11:33–34b). The testimony of faith that "the mouths of lions" were shut surely refers to Daniel's experience of deliverance in the lions' den, where his diligent and uncompromising prayer life and devotion to God were vindicated (Dan. 6).

The allusion to Daniel's experience brought to mind the remarkable deliverance of Daniel's three friends—Shadrach, Meshach, and Abednego—who through faith saw "the fury of the flames" quenched on their behalf and emerged from the fiery furnace unharmed after they refused to bow and worship Nebuchadnezzar's towering golden image (Dan. 3). The essence of their faith, however, is found not in their deliverance from the flames but in their willingness to die for their God. Their faith shone like a brilliant diamond as they trustingly placed their lives in the hands of God: "If we are thrown into the blazing furnace, the God we serve is able to save us from it, and he will rescue us from your hand, O king. But even if he does not, we want you to know, O king, that we will not serve your gods or worship the image of gold you have set up" (Dan. 3:17–18). It was this kind of tough faith that "quenched . . . the flames."

Finally the statement that some "escaped the edge of the sword" describes the experiences of Elijah (1 Kings 19:2–18), Elisha (2 Kings 6:31–7:2), Jeremiah (Jer. 36:19, 26), and other men and women of faith who were spared death by the sword. (Note, however, that 11:37 reminds us that other men and women of equally valid faith "were put to death by the sword.")

(3) The third cluster describes those who through faith tapped the strength and supernatural power of God (11:34c–35a). Through faith there were those "whose weakness was turned to strength." The Greek literally says these individuals "were empowered from weakness," indicating that the source of their new strength was God's power (cf. 2 Cor. 12:9–10; Phil. 4:12–13). It is repeatedly said of the judges that the Spirit of the Lord came upon them in power, whereby the enemy was overthrown and God's kingdom established or advanced (e.g., Judg. 3:10; 6:34; 11:29; 14:6, 19; 15:14). Only through faith and the power of the Holy Spirit can our weakness be turned into strength. This is the testimony of Hannah (1 Sam. 2:4), Samson (Judg. 16:17–21, 25–30), and numerous saints under both covenants.

Whenever the weakness of the judges and Israelites became the occasion, through faith, for the demonstration of God's power, they "became powerful in battle and routed foreign armies." Virtually the same language can be used to describe the Maccabean triumph over Antiochus IV Epiphanes and his Seleucid troops in later Jewish history (Lane, 1991, 387). Like Jonathan, they knew that "nothing can hinder the LORD from saving, whether by many or by few" (1 Sam. 14:6). Like Jehoshaphat, they believed the battle was not theirs but God's (2 Chron. 20:15), so that one person could chase a thousand and two put ten thousand to flight (cf. Deut. 32:30; Josh. 23:9–10).

Finally, because of faith "women received back their dead, raised to life again." For the original recipients of Hebrews, such mighty works would bring to mind the Zarephath widow (1 Kings 17:17–24), the Shunammite woman (2 Kings 4:18–37), the widow at Nain (Luke 7:11–15), the sisters of Lazarus (John 11:3, 43–44), and perhaps others.

"Others" in 11:35b stands out in bold contrast—not necessarily to the six individuals and "the prophets" mentioned in 11:32, but to all those who have experienced victories like those described in the preceding verses. "Others" refers to godly men and women who, instead of being delivered, were subjected to severe hardship, persecution, and even violent death because of their steadfast faith in God. True faith not only enables great exploits for God to be realized (11:33–35a), but also brings believers into great conflict with the world. Genuine faith does not immunize believers from suffering persecution, hardship, ridicule, or death. On the contrary, faith sanctifies suffering. And suffering tests, proves, and matures faith. It is not the outcome of suffering but the outcome of faith that matters.

Some through faith are delivered from the sword (11:34), while others because of faith are "put to death by the sword" (11:37). The outcome of faith in both instances is triumph: in this life for the former, in the life to come for the latter, with great reward. Thus, a theology of faith must include both a theology of suf fering and a theology of the power of God, which is the coupling together of the theology of the cross and the theology of the resurrection/Pentecost.

Some saints "were tortured"—that is, they were cruelly subjected to intense and unrelieved suffering by their persecutors. The "torture" indicated here was that in which a person was stretched on a frame and beaten until dead (Bruce, 1990, 325). Some totalitarian political systems today still use derisive torture to control and manipulate people. Nevertheless, when offered freedom if they would renounce their faith, saints of old "refused to be released, so that they might gain a better resurrection" (11:35b). "Better resurrection" stands in contrast to the resurrection referred to in the first half of verse 35; the difference is between resuscitation to mortal life and resurrection to eternal life (Hagner, 1983, 190).

When the original recipients of Hebrews read verse 36—"some faced jeers and flogging, while still others were chained and put in prison"—they would recall how some among their own group had suffered these things for their faith (cf. 10:32–34). It would also reassure them that they were not the first to walk this path (Bruce, 1990, 327). Other faithful Israelites "were stoned" (e.g., Zechariah, 2 Chron. 24:21; cf. Matt. 23:37). Still others "were sawn in two" (11:37) with a wood-cutting saw, the means of torture inflicted on the prophet Isaiah by the wicked king Manasseh (according to ancient Jewish tradition).

Some through faith "escaped the edge of the sword" (11:34), but others through faith "were put to death by the sword" (a common occurrence in ancient times; cf. 1 Kings 19:10). In the New Testament the apostle James, the brother of John, was "put to death with the sword" (Acts 12:2); but when Herod planned to do the same to Peter, God delivered him. Why by faith one dies and by faith another lives is part of the mystery of God and spiritual warfare.

Although being a person of steadfast faith does not always entail violent opposition, it often does mean being "destitute, persecuted and mistreated." This language of destitution, along with that of people who "wandered in deserts and mountains, and in caves and holes in the ground" (11:38), is especially descriptive, as Bruce notes,

> of those godly Jews who fled from the persecution under Antiochus Epiphanes [a type of the end-time Antichrist]. . . . When they were besieged in their hiding places they refused to break the law by offering resistance or leaving their caves on the sabbath day, but died "in their innocence" to the number of a thousand persons. . . . They were outlawed as people who were unfit for civilized society; the truth was that civilized society was unfit for them. (1990, 329)

The profound conclusion of Hebrews concerning all the despised and ill-treated men and women of faith is that "the world was not worthy of them" (11:38a).

3.5. Faith and the Fulfillment of the Promise (11:39–40)

The author concludes this magnificent chapter by reminding new covenant believers that we are part of the same triumphal procession of faith, which is incomplete apart from us. All those whose faith is recounted in this chapter "were . . . commended for their faith" by God, "yet none of them received what had been promised [lit., the promise]" (11:39). They had received the fulfillment to specific promises (plural) as in 11:11, 33, but they had not received the fulfillment of the promise (singular).

This definitive promise involves God's "better" plan (11:40a), which he has unveiled in his Son (1:1–2). In the language of Hebrews, this better plan embraces the "better" hope, rest, promises, covenant, sacrifices, high priest, country, possessions, and resurrection—all of which form the promised inheritance of the covenant people of faith. "Yet none of them [i.e., the old covenant saints] received what had been promised" (11:39b) because it awaited the coming of Christ and the new covenant people. Thus "only together with us would they be made perfect" (11:40)—that is, be made complete in every way through the fulfillment of what God had promised in his Son, of which we too are partakers.

In the time gap between God's promise and fulfillment, faith is the spiritual dynamic that causes God's people to press forward toward the "things hoped for" in God's promise. Thus, faith is the bridge between promise and fulfillment. In the interim between promise and fulfillment, faith must be tough in the hard times, resilient in trying circumstances, obedient to God and his Word at all times, and able (like love) to endure all things, while moving toward the goal embodied in what God has promised. Faith does not shrink back or give up when discouraged. It is always daring, adventurous, and willing to risk all for the sake of the things promised but not yet seen. The complete fulfillment of "the promise" awaits the second coming of Christ and the consummation of this age.

4. The Call to Persevere As Sons (12:1–13)

The link between faith and endurance in chapter 11 becomes the platform for the call to perseverance in 12:1–13. Two phrases in 11:40 signal the return to personal application for the original readers and for us: "something better for us" and "only together with us." Having described the spiritual history and triumphs of past saints made possible because of their faith and endurance, the author again focuses on challenging his readers to be steadfast in faith and perseverance so as to endure through trials (cf. 12:1–3, 7 with 10:32, 36). He develops three major incentives that should inspire his readers to persevere as believers in the Lord.

4.1. The Incentive of Their Forefathers' Example (12:1)

Paul frequently uses the imagery of an athletic contest to describe the discipline, focus, and dedication needed to live the Christian life (e.g., 1 Cor. 9:24–27; Gal. 2:2; 5:7; Phil. 2:16; 3:13–14; 1 Tim. 6:12; 2 Tim. 4:7–8a). The author of Hebrews also refers to the Christian life as "the race marked out for us" (12:1c). He identifies with his readers as one of those running the race ("we," "us").

Verse 1 states three things about the race. (1) There is a vast host of inspiring witnesses surrounding us (12:1a). The word "cloud" is used metaphorically for a host of "witnesses," which refer back to the large number of named and unnamed champions of faith in chapter 11. But in what sense are they witnesses? Are they watching in heaven (as spectators in a stadium) and cheering the present generation of Christian runners as they progress toward the goal? Or are they witnesses in the sense of examples to the present generation about the possibilities of faith and endurance because of having successfully run the race themselves before them? F. F. Bruce believes the author intends the latter (Bruce, 1964, 333). Likewise, J. Moffat states that it is "what we see in them, not what they see in us, that is the writer's main point" (1924, 193). Leon Morris, however, believes both ideas may be present. He remarks: "Perhaps we should think of something like a relay race where those who have finished their course and handed in their baton are watching and encouraging their successors" (1981, 133).

(2) We are to run the race to win (12:1b). The point here, however, is not that only one person can win the race but that an athlete does certain things in order to complete successfully the race. The runner lays aside everything that hinders running and avoids anything that might disqualify him from winning. The distinction between "everything that hinders" and "the sin that so easily entangles" is noteworthy. "Hinders" means any kind of weights, an encumbrance that may not be sin but that hinders running the race to win. Athletes shed any unnecessary body weight and carry no baggage in a race. In like manner, Christians must avoid distractions and all hindrances in order to realize the full will of God.

"The sin that so easily entangles" us is unbelief (the antithesis of faith) and related sins as discussed in Hebrews, such as spiritual drifting, dullness, prolonged immaturity, and deliberate sinning. These things may tangle the feet and trip a person up so that he or she falls, drops out of the race, and misses the prize, "which is God's gracious gift of eternal life to all who complete the race" (Peterson, 1994, 1329).

(3) We are to run the race "with perseverance" (12:1c). When the Christian life is compared to a race, it is not like a sprint or hundred-yard dash, but like a marathon or cross country race. It requires determination and perseverance over the long course. It is not difficult to run fast for a short distance, but to run a steady and persistent race for the long distance requires endurance. The heroes of faith ran with perseverance, and so must we.

4.2. The Incentive of Christ's Example (12:2–3)

Jesus' earthly life is the supreme example of and incentive for persevering faith. As a runner fixes his gaze on the goal, so we are to "fix our eyes on Jesus" (12:2a) as our fixed point of reference. If we fix our eyes on problems, people, or circumstances, we stumble or sink, as did Peter, who took his eyes off Jesus by looking at the wind and waves when walking on the water and began sinking (Matt. 14:28–31). By fixing our eyes on Jesus, we are anchored in faith and are progressively transformed into his likeness (cf. 2 Cor. 3:18; 4:16–18; Phil. 3:12–13).

But Jesus is not only "the object of faith's vision" (Hawthorne, 1986, 1529), he is also its "author and perfecter" (12:2b). "Author" (*archegos*) can also be translated "pioneer" or "leader." As "author" Jesus is the source and initiator of true faith, having opened the way to God through his death on the cross. As the "pioneer" or "leader" of faith, he is out front in the race, leading the way. He is also faith's "perfecter" (*teleiotes*), in that he brings faith to its perfect goal. As the Son of God, he "has realized faith to the full from start to finish [and] . . . has fulfilled God's promises for all who believe" (Peterson, 1994, 1349). The word "perfecter" suggests that "all that faith hopes for finds its consummation in Him" (Hawthorne, 1986, 1529). Thus, "author and perfecter" span the whole spectrum of Jesus' activities in relation to our faith.

In connection with Jesus' role as "leader" in faith, he models for us purposeful endurance (12:2c–3). At Gethsemane Jesus committed himself to endure the suffering of the cross, which included being "despised and rejected by men" (Isa. 53:3), and being stricken, smitten, and afflicted by God as a punishment for our transgressions and iniquities (53:4–5). Crucifixion itself was a grim form of capital punishment, the most despicable and degrading form of death in the Roman world, reserved for slaves and non-Roman criminals of the lowest depths. Jesus had to have unshakable faith in the character of the Father as he faced the cross. Bruce says of Jesus' ordeal of suffering: "It was sheer faith in God, unsupported by any visible or tangible evidence, that carried him through the taunting, the scourging, the crucifying, and the more bitter agony of rejection, desertion, and dereliction" (1990, 338).

Jesus was able to scorn the suffering of the cross and the shame attached to it because he "endured the cross" purposefully, that is, "for the joy set before him" (12:2c). Even the night before his crucifixion, when Jesus prayed his high priestly prayer, he asked the Father that his disciples might be filled with his joy (John 17:13). Jesus saw beyond the cross to the inexpressible joy of salvation's wondrous plan being finished (cf. 19:30). When he died as the sacrifice for sin and even as he now lives as high priest, having "sat down at the right hand of the throne of God" (Heb. 12:2c; cf. Ps. 110:1), it was and is not for himself that he endured the cross. Rather, it was for all those who would believe in him and thereby be filled with his joy and glory (John 17:20, 22).

His joyful purpose as he went to the cross was to bring many sons to glory (Heb. 2:10). In like manner we are to regard our sufferings (which are far less than Christ's) "as a small price to pay for the prize to be secured at the end of the race set before [us]" (Hawthorne, 1986, 1529). The readers are exhorted to "consider" the example of Jesus, who endured "opposition from sinful men" (12:3a)—the same situation the readers were facing—so that they might not "grow weary and lose heart" (12:3b). The message of Christ's example is: Persevere in the face of all manner of trials, persecution, and suffering for righteousness' sake.

4.3. The Incentive of Their Father-Son Relationship to God (12:4–11)

Throughout Hebrews the author calls his readers to new resolve and faithfulness in the midst of their trials and adversity. Although they have already endured intense persecution (involving insults, imprisonment, and seizure of their property, 10:32–34), in their "struggle against sin" they have "not yet resisted to the point of shedding . . . [their] blood" (12:4). As a house church within the larger church community (cf. 13:17, 24), they have so far not experienced a bloody persecution. Their "struggle against sin" refers, most likely, to the sin of their oppressors, who are seeking to pressure them into abandoning their faith. To resist "to the point of shedding your blood" means to the point of being killed or martyred by oppressors.

In other words, thus far none of his readers have had to die for their faith. But the persecution was wearing them down and causing them to lose perspective. Yet their trial of suffering paled in comparison with that endured by valiant heroes of faith who preceded them (esp. 11:35b–38; 12:1), and by Jesus himself, who submitted to the cross (12:2–3). Verse 4 in effect "shames" the readers a bit for "a weakening of resolve and a failure of nerve" (Lane, 1991, 417) and challenges them to be firm in their faith and loyalty to Christ, regardless of the cost.

4.3.1. The Lord's Discipline Is Part of the Father's Love (12:4–6a). Experiencing hostility and suffering unjustly can disturb faith and provoke questions about God's love. The author addresses this issue in 12:5–11 by showing how God takes adversity and the harsh experiences of life and lovingly uses them as educative discipline to train us as his children in faith and develop in us the character of sonship (cf. Ps. 119:67, 71).

Lane notes that "the stylistically rhetorical character" of 12:5 favors taking the opening phrase as a question: "Have you forgotten that word of encouragement that addresses you as sons?" This question, he adds, "represents a firm, but gentle, rebuke. The members of the house church appear to have forgotten completely the biblical concept of disciplinary or educative suffering" (1991, 420). Thus in 12:5b–6 the author refers to Proverbs 3:11–12, in which the discipline of the Lord and sonship are coupled together; he quotes it as God's personal word to those who enjoy sonship under the new covenant through faith in Jesus Christ.

The Greek word for "discipline" (*paideia*) is rich in meaning and derives from the parent-child relationship in ancient times. It not only carries the nuances of rebuke and correction, but also involves the positive teaching, training, and guiding instruction of a loving parent in order to bring a son or daughter to mature adulthood. "The Lord disciplines those he loves" (12:6a) because, as a loving Father, he desires good for his children. We are to endure our trials as an expression of his loving discipline.

Verse 5b describes two possible, though opposite, wrong responses to the Lord's discipline in the midst of our adverse circumstances. (1) We may respond insensitively by "mak[ing] light of" it, that is, by shrugging it off and not taking it seriously. This response often involves disregarding the Lord's discipline or despising it. (2) We may also respond oversensitively and "lose heart when he rebukes" us. This response often involves resentment; it is the response of a child who is inclined to withdraw or give up whenever any correction is applied by the parent, no matter how lovingly purposeful it may be. Contrary to these two wrong responses we—as God's beloved sons and daughters—should regard the Lord's discipline as evidence of his responsible love, grace, and commitment to us as our Father.

4.3.2. The Lord's Discipline Relates to Sonship and Training (12:6b–8). All children must be disciplined; thus, the Lord's discipline and sonship necessarily go together. "He punishes [*mastigoo*, a different word from *paideia*; lit., 'scourges' or 'chastises' for correction] everyone he accepts as a son" (12:6b). Punishment here suggests discipline, not judgment. It relates more to our future than our past, more to what we are to become than to past failure or bad behavior. God's discipline can be corrective, but it especially involves training and character issues. Therefore, we are to "endure hardship as discipline" (12:7a) since God is treating us as his children. Just as a responsible earthly father would not neglect disciplining a son or daughter whom he loves (12:7b), so it is with God and his children. Even Jesus, as God's only begotten Son and the appointed heir of all things, "learned obedience from what he suffered" (5:8).

Discipline is the bridge between faith and obedience. The Father's discipline is purposeful in that it trains us in obedience and character as his sons and daughters through our experiences of suffering, which are themselves demonstrations of the genuineness of our sonship and his love. Not being disciplined by the Father is evidence that the undisciplined person is an "illegitimate" child (12:8), without the family honor and privileges of a true child and left more or less on his or her own. Such persons are usually filled with self-hatred and are characterized by low self-esteem because they were not valued enough to be disciplined. Thus the experience of disciplinary suffering is evidence that the Father is assuming full responsibility for our training as "true sons" (12:8). The Lord's discipline is thus both purposeful and necessary.

4.3.3. The Proper Attitude Toward the Lord's Discipline Is Submission (12:9). A father who fails to discipline his child is deficient in his parental responsibility. Likewise, a child not properly disciplined in the early years loses out on his sonship. In a permissive age when the authority of parents to discipline is eroding, there is an accompanying loss of an essential element of sonship. Consequently, in such an environment "sons" find it difficult to understand or submit to the discipline of the Lord. On the other hand, when our "human fathers" appropriately disciplined us as sons and daughters, "we respected them for it." Why? In part we intuitively knew that they had rightful authority to do so, but even more their loving discipline conveyed that we were worthwhile or valuable and would be the better for it.

The author then argues from the lesser to the greater, from the human to the spiritual plane: "How much more should we submit to the Father of our spirits and live!" The expression "the Father of our spirits" is unique in the New Testament (cf. Num. 16:22; 27:16). The present context, however, makes its meaning clear. Bruce's comment is incisive: "As 'the father of our flesh' [NIV, human fathers] are our physical [or earthly] fathers, so 'the Father of our spirits' is our spiritual (or heavenly) Father" (1990, 344).

The attitude of volitional (if not joyful) submission to our heavenly Father's discipline is essential. Otherwise, his discipline does not profit us, we are not trained by it, and its purpose is accordingly missed. Lane observes that "God's right to discipline ... proceeds from the highest authority" (1991, 424). But if we have not learned to respect the authority and discipline of our earthly parents, we will likely find it difficult to trust and submit to God's authority and discipline. Lane adds: "The much greater degree of respect owed to God as Father makes submission to the imposition of divine discipline all the more necessary than was true in the case of ordinary paternal discipline" (ibid.).

As "the fear of the Lord is the beginning of wisdom" (cf. Prov. 9:10), so submission to the Lord's discipline in godly fear leads to wisdom and a full life (cf. 3:7–8, 11–18). Only a fool will resist God and spurn his discipline, since such response leads to death instead of life. Insofar as Satan seeks to exploit every experience of adversity for his purposes, we are advised to resist him in every trial even as we submit to God (James 4:6–8).

4.3.4. The Goal of the Lord's Discipline Involves Sanctification and Character (12:10–11). There is an important qualitative difference between the discipline of an earthly father and that of our heavenly Father. The former may be done imperfectly, unjustly, or even out of anger because of human imperfection. Moreover, its duration is "for a little while as they thought best" (12:10a), that is, during childhood. In contrast, "God disciplines us" perfectly and righteously out of his infinite wisdom and loving concern for our *eternal* well-being. He never neglects it or overdoes it, but administers it consistently "for our good" over the whole course of our life. The goal of his discipline is clear: "that we may share in his holiness" (12:10b).

God's "holiness" (*hagiotetos*) is "the essential attribute of God's character, which Christians are to share" (Lane, 1991, 425; cf. Procksch, *TDNT,* 1:114). The stress here is not on human endeavor (as in 12:14), but on God's initiative to bestow his life and character on us as a gift through the process of his discipline. The Father's discipline, properly received, has the "salutary effect of maturing Christians [in faith and character] as men and women of God" (Lane, 1991, 425) by conforming them to the likeness of Christ (cf. Rom. 8:18, 28–29). Although the varied discipline of the Lord seems "painful" (12:11a) while it is being administered, yet in the end "it produces a harvest of righteousness [i.e., sanctification or a godly life and character; cf. 1 Peter 4:1–2] and peace for those who have been trained by it" (Heb. 12:11b).

Those who have been "trained" by the Lord's discipline are those who have accepted it in the right spirit by volitionally submitting to God and his purpose in it. This submission is not simply accepting a few instances of his discipline with poise, but "it is the habit of life that is meant" (Morris, 1987, 138). The verb "train" (*gymnazo*; cf. the English word "gymnasium") is frequently connected with athletic training. It thus points back to the theme in 12:1 of running a long-distance race with endurance and resolve to reach the finish line triumphantly.

Paul refers to the same principle when he told believers at Thessalonica that the persecutions and trials they were enduring were both evidence of God's righteous judgment that would come on their persecutors and the means by which they themselves would "be counted worthy of the kingdom of God" (2 Thess. 1:4–7). Bruce adds that "the person who accepts discipline at the hand of God as something designed by his heavenly Father for his good, will cease to feel resentful and rebellious" (1990, 346). Instead the believer will come to a place where his or her soul is at peace and rest. Life will be more teachable, more righteous, and more responsive to the will of God. God's discipline, which makes possible our sharing in his peace and holy character, ultimately prepares us to enjoy him forever.

4.4. Community Commitment to Finish the Race (12:12–13)

The two concluding verses to 12:1–13 contain a two-pronged exhortation. (1) Individual members in the church community, who have "feeble arms" and "weak knees," are to "strengthen" themselves in view of God's loving discipline, good purpose, and available grace. "They are urged to put things right and get moving" (Morris, 1981, 139). It is not too late for them to participate as trained athletes in the race and to persevere with new resolve. (2) The church community as a whole must stay on God's chosen path and provide compassionate help for the weakest members among them (12:13).

Two Old Testament Scriptures seem to be the inspiration behind this two-pronged exhortation (1) The reference to Isaiah 35:3–4a is meant for those who were previously referred to as weary and in danger of losing heart (Heb. 12:3, 5):

> Strengthen the feeble hands,
> steady the knees that give way;
> say to those with fearful hearts,
> "Be strong, do not fear."

Fear and despair are exhausting; the author exhorts these kinds of believers to throw off those negative and wearisome weights.

(2) The exhortation in 12:13 from Proverbs 4:26 to "make level [lit., straight] paths for your feet" is an admonition to follow God's path without deviating to the right or left. Detours and uneven ground are especially dangerous for the spiritually "lame," whose legs can be easily dislocated and thereby become spiritual casualties. The community must stay on the straight path so that "the lame" can be "healed." In other words, right decisions by the strong will benefit the weak, and they can all complete the race together, rather than some falling to the wayside.

5. The Ongoing Commitment to Live Holy Lives Under the Covenant of Grace (12:14–13:17)

The believer's life of faith under the new covenant of grace, as a result of God's full revelation in his Son and of Jesus' sacrificial death, is accompanied by both greater privileges and greater responsibilities. We are not simply to persevere in faith and receive what God has promised through his Word, but also to "share in his holiness" (12:10) and live a life that is holy unto the Lord (12:14). In receiving Christ we receive "a kingdom that cannot be shaken" (12:28a); through his mediation we can encounter and "worship God acceptably with reverence and awe" (12:28b). These privileges are greater than the ones under the old covenant, though they also carry greater obligations in love, purity, and spiritual vision and values (13:1–16). Christians are called to imitate the faith of their former spiritual leaders (13:7), to submit obediently to the spiritual authority of their present leaders (13:17), and thereby "to live honorably in every way" (13:18).

5.1. The Priority of Holiness (12:14–29)

As holiness belongs to the essence of God and is his highest glory, so it is to characterize God's people. We were chosen in Christ to be holy (Eph. 1:4), and God disciplines us as his children so "that we may share in his holiness" (12:10). His nature becomes our nature; his life, our life; his values, our values. He was pure and undefiled by sin; his purity is to become our purity. Lane observes that "in Hebrews 'pure' and 'holy' are interchangeable terms because those who have been made holy are those for whom Christ has made purification.... Christians have within their reach the holiness that is indispensable for seeing God" (1991, 451).

5.1.1. Practical Holiness of Life Is a Foundational Issue (12:14). Holiness "is not an optional extra in the Christian life but something which belongs to its essence. It is the pure in heart, and none but they, who shall see God (Matt. 5:8). Here [Heb. 12:14], as in v. 10, practical holiness of life is meant" (Bruce, 1990, 348). Thus 12:14 begins by exhorting believers to earnestly pursue peace and holiness as a way of life. "Make every effort" (*dioko*) conveys diligence in the pursuit of peace and holiness, not a self-striving that produces dead works and self-righteousness.

Many interpreters understand the pursuit of "peace" in 12:14 to refer to peace with everyone (as in NIV). The Greek preposition in this verse, however, is *meta* with the genitive, which carries the sense of "along with" (cf. 11:9; 13:23). Thus "all men" especially means along with "all the other believers" (cf. 13:24; Lane, 1991, 438), who are also being admonished to pursue Christ's peace in community. As a direct object of the verb *dioko*, peace is viewed as an objective reality tied to Christ and his redemptive death on the cross, which makes possible harmony and solidarity in Christian community (cf. Col. 1:20).

Similarly, "holiness" is essential to Christian community (cf. 12:15). Sin divides and defiles the body of Christ, just as cancer does a human body. To pursue holiness suggests a process of sanctification in which our life and manner of living are set apart for God as holy and God-honoring. Approaching and lingering in the Most Holy Place of God's presence is the place where we are transformed into his likeness. In union and fellowship with God himself in the Most Holy Place resides the power of "peace" and "holiness." Andrew Murray rightly observes: "He who does not know what it is to enter in and tarry and worship in the Holiest, to separate himself from the world and its fellowship, to hold communion with the Holy One, will seek in vain by his prayers or efforts to become holy" (n.d., 499).

Verse 14 concludes that "without holiness no one will see the Lord." To "see" the Lord and "know" him intimately are closely related. To see the Lord "is the highest and most glorious blessing mortals can enjoy, but the beatific vision is reserved for those who are holy in heart and life" (Bruce, 1990, 349). Things that are unholy effectively block seeing and knowing God and in the end keep the person from inheriting the kingdom of God (cf. 1 Cor. 6:9–10).

Sixth Hortatory Warning: The Danger of Falling Short of God's Grace (12:15–17)

Believers must be vigilantly watchful over the spiritual well-being of each member of the church. The verb translated "see to it" (*episkopeo*; 12:15a) conveys the idea of spiritual oversight and is related to the function of "overseers" or elders. This verb is a present active participle with the force of an imperative and carries the sense of "watching continually." Three subordinate clauses of warning follow this verb, each one introduced by the words "that no one" (*me tis*): Watch continually—

> "that no one misses the grace of God" (12:15a)
> "that no bitter root grows up . . ." (12:15b)
> "that no one is sexually immoral or . . . godless" (12:16a).

This appeal to spiritual watchfulness is a call to the church as a whole.

The exhortation "see to it that no one misses the grace of God" (12:15a) is a key statement. Remaining steadfast in faith (10:19–11:40), enduring discipline as children (12:1–13), and pursuing peace and holiness (12:14) are all related to the grace of God, as is everything involving our salvation. If entrance into the Christian life is by the grace of God, even so the continuance and completion of it is by the grace of God. The dreadful possibility of missing God's grace is not because his grace is inaccessible, but because some may choose not to avail themselves of it. For this reason it is possible for a person (though once a believer) not to reach the goal that is attainable only by his grace operating through faith (cf. 3:12; Bruce, 1990, 349).

Marshall makes several observations concerning this warning passage (1969, 149–51). (1) It is possible for a believer to draw back from the grace of God (12:15a; cf. 2 Cor. 6:1; Gal. 5:4). The context of the warning here, as elsewhere in Hebrews (e.g., Heb. 2:1–4; 6:4–8; 10:26–31), indicates that a true believer is meant.

(2) Where the grace of God is missed, bitterness will take root and potentially defile other members in the church (12:15b). The deadly sins of unbelief and a poisonous root of bitterness function like a fatally contagious disease that can "defile many" in the community.

(3) No one should be "sexually immoral [*pornos*; lit., fornicator] or . . . godless like Esau." Esau was a sensual man rather than a spiritual man—entirely earthly-minded rather than heavenly-minded—who traded away "his inheritance rights as the oldest son" (12:16b) for the momentary gratification of his physical senses.

He represents those who would make the unthinkable exchange of long-range spiritual inheritance (i.e., things hoped for but not yet seen, 11:1) for present tangible and visible benefits, momentary though they be. Afterwards, when Esau realized the foolishness of his choice, he wanted to inherit his blessing but could not since "he was rejected" by God (12:17a).

Attridge notes that the comment on Esau "conveys the sharpest warning" of this passage (1989, 369). Though some have understood verse 17b to mean that Esau could not change Isaac's mind, the more likely sense is that of rejection by God—that is, repentance was not granted by God. "God did not give Esau the opportunity of changing his mind and gaining what he had forfeited. The author intends his readers to apply this story to themselves and their salvation. Just as Esau was rejected by God, so can they be rejected if they spurn their spiritual birthright" (Marshall, 1969, 150). Bruce concurs that this example of Esau "is a reinforcement of the warning given at an earlier stage in the argument, that after apostasy no second repentance is possible" (1990, 352).

Esau's "tears" represent regret for having lost his birthright, not repentance for having despised and shown contempt for God's gift of a birthright and for the covenant by which it was secured. This is all immediately applicable to the readers of this book, for Esau represents "apostate persons who are ready to turn their backs on God and the divine promises, in reckless disregard of the blessings secured by the sacrificial death of Jesus" (Lane, 1991, 455). In other words, a person may miss the grace of God and the spiritual inheritance of eternal life that he or she might have received. In such cases "God may not permit . . . an opportunity of repentance. Not all sinners go this far; but an apostate may well find that he has stretched the mercy of God to its limit, so that he cannot return" (Marshall, 1969, 150–51).

5.1.2. Incentives for Holy Living Under the New Covenant (12:18–24). Our author characteristically follows his severe warning with words of encouragement. He reminds the readers of their glorious privileges under the covenant of grace, which make their response of steadfast faith and loyal commitment all the more meaningful and necessary. This passage paints a picture of profound contrast between the covenant of law given at Mount Sinai and the covenant of grace represented by the heavenly Mount Zion. It serves to underscore why believers must diligently pursue the peace and holiness found in Christ and carefully guard against apostasy in their midst. The bold contrast between the sevenfold description of fear and terror at God's holiness manifested at Mount Sinai and the sevenfold description of festive joy in God's presence at Mount Zion (12:22–24) is striking indeed.

The contrast between 12:18–21 and 12:22–24 is introduced by the verb *proserchomai*, "to come to" (v. 18, repeated in v. 22). This verb is used in Hebrews exclusively in reference to approaching God (cf. 4:16; 7:25; 10:1, 22; 11:6; see Lane, 1991, 460). In 12:18 it introduces the *unapproachability* of God's holiness at Mount Sinai and the separation that existed between God and Israel. In 12:22 the verb introduces the *approachability* of God in his awesome holiness at Mount Zion as a result of Jesus' ministry as mediator and his efficacious blood. Sinai and Zion thus serve as rich prophetic metaphors that point to the qualitative differences in one's relationship to God under the old and new covenants, under law and grace.

The seven descriptive words or phrases in 12:18–20a for the law-giving event at Mount Sinai are as follows. (1) "A mountain that can be touched" describes Sinai as something visible and tangible. Although the word "mountain" is omitted here in many manuscripts, it is mentioned in verse 20 and is to be understood here. The word "Sinai" appears nowhere in the passage; yet the phenomena described clearly point to the Sinai event (cf. Ex. 19:16–22; 20:18–21; Deut. 4:11–12; 5:22–27).

The manifestation of God's presence and holiness in the next four descriptive terms in 12:18b—(2) "burning with fire," (3) "darkness," (4) "gloom," and (5) "storm"—depict a scene that would strike terror to any heart. (6) Reference to "a trumpet blast" (12:19a) at Mount Sinai is repeatedly mentioned in the Old Testament accounts (e.g. Ex. 19:16, 19; 20:18). It represents the angelic declaration of God's presence (as with the regal introduction of a king) and calls attention to the authoritative character of God's commands that are then spoken.

(7) The final descriptive phrase is that of "a voice speaking words" (12:19). This audible voice of God at Sinai so terrified the people,

The chapel on Mt. Sinai (below) was built in 1934 on the spot where tradition says Moses received the Ten Commandments from God. The stones used are from a sixth-century chapel. St. Catherine's Monastery (left), with its origins in the fourth century, is located in the valley where the Israelites waited for Moses to return.

they "begged that no further word be spoken to them, because they could not bear what was commanded" (12:19b–20a). God's voice "evoked fear rather than understanding" (Lane, 1991, 462) because of his holiness and humanity's distance, a separation that could be fully bridged only in the incarnation of Christ and his atoning death. Sinai was so charged with the holiness of God that for human beings or beasts to touch it meant certain death (12:20b). Not only was the sight terrifying to the people, but even Moses himself, who was in close relationship with God, was "trembling with fear" (12:21).

The whole description in 12:18–21 emphasizes not only the unapproachability of God under the old covenant, but also the dreadful possibility of drawing back so as to miss the grace of God (12:15), consequently to be rejected by him (12:17), and to "fall into the hands of the living God" (10:31) in judgment. "For our 'God is a consuming fire'" (12:29), apart from the mediatorial work of Jesus Christ and his efficacious blood (12:24).

Christians, however, are privileged to live their lives, not according to the fearful revelation that is represented at Sinai, but according to the joyful revelation of Christ and his covenant of grace. The festive atmosphere of Mount Zion (12:22–24), contrasted to the preceding solemn atmosphere of Mount Sinai, emphasizes the superior privileges of Christians in worship and access into God's holy presence under the new covenant. Each of the seven descriptive images of Mount Zion stands in sharp contrast to the seven terrifying features at Mount Sinai.

(1) You have not come to an earthly mountain that burns with fire and is enveloped in darkness, gloom, and storm, "but you have come to Mount Zion, to the heavenly Jerusalem, the city of the living God" (12:22a). These three phrases are synonymous in that they describe (though in different terminology) the same reality. "Mount Zion," the hill in Jerusalem on which Solomon's temple was built, became a symbol of the place of true worship of God. Whereas the earthly Zion was the place of worship and meeting for the tribes of the old Israel, the heavenly Zion is the meeting place for the new Israel (Bruce, 1990, 356). The heavenly Mount Zion is where the Lamb stands with the 144,000 in Revelation 14:1.

The "heavenly Jerusalem" is a foreshadowing of "the new Jerusalem" as the home of the redeemed of all ages at the end of history (cf. Rev. 21:1–22:6). By faith believers take hold of this spiritual reality yet future as if it were already present. This city is the objective city to which Abraham and all pilgrims of faith are looking forward. Its foundations are solid and eternal, for its "architect and builder is God" (Heb. 11:10). It is the home "of the living God" and his people, who by faith are redeemed by the blood of Christ (cf. 11:8, 16; 13:12–14).

(2) At the heavenly Mount Zion believers join a vast host of angels who surround God, as at Mount Sinai; but at Zion, unlike Sinai, it is a festive gathering. The dense multitude of angels is described as "thousands upon thousands of angels" (12:22b) in a great worship assembly, joyfully celebrating "the victory achieved by Christ" (Lane, 1991, 467).

(3) Gathered with the angels in worship is "the church of the firstborn" (12:23). Westcott notes that one striking feature here is that angels and the redeemed people of God are "no longer separated as at Sinai, by signs of great terror, but united in one vast assembly" (1889/1980, 413). The designation "firstborn" has been variously interpreted as referring to angels, Old Testament saints, the first Christians, Christians who have died, and to Christian martyrs. The most probable meaning, however, is that the firstborn ones are those who are reborn through Christ and thus refer to new covenant believers generally.

In 1:6 the incarnation of the Son, Jesus Christ, is referred to as the "firstborn" (cf. Rom. 8:29; Col. 1:15; Rev. 1:5). It is "through their union with him who is the Firstborn *par excellence* that all the people of Christ are the 'firstborn' children of God" (Bruce, 1990, 359). Their birthright has not been foolishly exchanged for momentary gratification or the temporal things of this world, as Esau had done. The additional phrase, "whose names are written in heaven," is clearly a reference to the redeemed of the Lord, not to angels (cf. Luke 10:20; Phil. 4:3; Rev. 21:27). Some interpreters consider firstborn a comprehensive term for all "faithful men and women of both the old and new covenants who will comprise 'the first-born citizens of heaven' (NEB)" (Lane, 1991, 469).

(4) Among the seven images that describe the heavenly reality to which Christians have come, the center phrase is: "to God, the judge of all men" (12:23b). The revelation of God as judge of all humanity encompasses both the old and new covenants. Through Christ as mediator, however, Christians—unlike the Israelites at Sinai—are able to approach the very presence of God, even in his solemn role as judge, without the fear of condemnation. Nevertheless, the mention of God as judge serves as a strong incentive for those still trying to live holy lives while on earth, knowing that nothing is hidden from his sight (cf. 4:13). Since we know that "the Lord will judge his people" (10:30), apart from an enduring confidence in Christ and his blood made possible through faith and perseverance, it is "a dreadful thing to fall into the hands of the living God" (10:31). Thus, we should not disregard the Lord (cf. 12:25).

(5) Part of God's role as judge is properly to reward and vindicate the righteous for their suffering for his sake. Thus at Mount Zion we also join "the spirits of righteous men made perfect" (12:23c). The word "spirits" is variously used in Hebrews. God is described as "the Father of our spirits" (12:9), and angels are "ministering spirits" (1:14). Morris believes the phrase in question here simply conveys the spiritual nature of the heavenly city, where the righteous now live. More likely, however, it refers to the deceased righteous of the pre-Christian eras (e.g., ch. 11), who have already been "made perfect" because of the retroactive sacrifice of Christ and his present mediatorial ministry on their behalf (Bruce, 1990, 360). Lane holds that "righteous men" embraces all faithful believers in heaven from both old and new covenants "who have been 'perfected' on the basis of Jesus' sacrifice" (1991, 471; also Attridge, 1989, 376). The righteous are possibly referred to as "spirits" because they do not yet have resurrection bodies.

(6) All believers by faith have come "to Jesus the mediator of a new covenant," who is the reason for the festive assembly on Mount Zion. Herein is a foremost theme of Hebrews, namely, the high priestly ministry of Jesus on behalf of true believers. In pointing to Jesus as mediator of the new and more effective covenant, the author "provides the balancing contrast to Moses, mediator of the old covenant, terrified and trembling in the presence of God (v. 21)" at Mount Sinai (Lane, 1991, 472). This sums up the message of

Hebrews: How much "better" and surpassingly superior is the new covenant when compared with the old, and Jesus when compared with Moses. To turn back to the old when the new has arrived is not only folly, but also apostasy and judgment (cf. 12:25, 29).

(7) Finally, the cost and testimony of the new covenant, "the sprinkled blood" (12:24b) of Jesus, also accounts for the joy and freedom of access into God's holy presence that believers have on Mount Zion. It "speaks a better word than the blood of Abel" (12:24b). Whereas Abel's blood cries out for justice and vengeance, Jesus' blood satisfies God's justice and speaks of forgiveness of sins and the cleansing of the conscience (cf. 10:12, 22). Jesus' blood accomplishes what Abel's blood, righteous though he was, could not achieve. Only the blood of Jesus can bring us to the glorious and joyful destination of the heavenly Jerusalem, the city of God.

Seventh Hortatory Warning: The Folly of Refusing God and His Kingdom (12:25–29)

The author now finishes comparing the old covenant revelation of God at Sinai (12:18–21) and the new covenant revelation at Mount Zion (12:22–24) by giving this one final warning based on the aforementioned comparison. The urgency of the warning is conveyed through a prophetic anticipation of the great end-time shaking that will shake everything that can be shaken and will remove all that fails to stand. Only what is associated with God's kingdom (and his Son) will remain. If it was fearful to transgress under the old covenant and the punishment then was inescapable, how much more serious it is to ignore deliberately God's grace and the fuller revelation of his Son under the new covenant. To refuse God's mercy that precedes his judgment is to make oneself culpable before the judge, "for our 'God is a consuming fire'" (12:29). This final warning is counterbalanced, as Hagner points out, by an emphasis "on the ultimate security of those who remain faithful" (1983, 215).

The "hook-word" between the preceding paragraph (12:18–24) and this warning (12:25–29) is the word "speaks" (12:24, 25). The privileged status of Christians as children of God carries with it "a qualitatively greater responsibility . . . to listen attentively to the voice of God. Those who deliberately ignore the eschatological revelation of God through his Son and who [thereby] show contempt for the blessing of the new covenant cannot possibly escape judgment" (Lane, 1991, 474–75).

"See to it that you do not refuse him who speaks"—the speaker being God himself, as at Mount Sinai. The Israelites in the desert did not escape God's judgment when they disregarded his voice to them. "In these last days he has spoken to us by his Son" (1:2), and we must "pay more careful attention" to what God has spoken through his Son (2:1–4). Now that warning is brought full circle: "If they [i.e., the Israelites of old] did not escape when they refused him who warned them on earth, how much less will we, if we turn away from him who warns us from heaven?" By arguing from the lesser to the greater (cf. 2:2–3; 10:28–29), the truth is again pressed home: To disobey the gospel of Christ "incurs judgment more certain and terrible even than that incurred by disobedience to the law [cf. 3:16–18]" (Bruce, 1990, 363).

The spirit of the warning here is the same as that thrice stated before: "Today, if you hear his voice, do not harden your hearts as you [Israelites] did in the rebellion" (3:7–8, 15; 4:7). The present tense of the participle in 12:25a (lit., "him who is speaking") indicates that the danger is real and pressing. The readers' refusal to listen is not yet an accomplished fact (as argued by Westcott, 1889/1980, 419), but it is a real possibility that threatens the house church being addressed (Lane, 1991, 478).

At Mount Sinai, God's "voice shook the earth, but now he has promised," in Haggai 2:6, to "once more" shake the entire universe (Heb. 12:26). The words "once more" convey a shaking that has a sense of finality about it, that is, the shaking at the consummation of history (cf. Mark 13:31; 2 Peter 3:7). The fulfillment of this end-time shaking is clearly associated here with God's wrath and judgment, as in Isaiah 13:13. Again, the underlying warning is that those who reject the new covenant revelation of Christ will receive an even more severe judgment in the end than do those who refused the old covenant revelation.

The writer again refers to "the words 'once more'" (12:27) and interprets them as pointing to the greater shaking wherein occurs "the removing of what can be shaken . . . so that what cannot be shaken may remain." Those who are subject to God's wrathful judgment are shaken and removed; those who share by faith in God's unshakable kingdom (12:28) as steadfast partakers of Christ (3:14) are unshaken and remain. The word "removing" means the removal of something from one location to another; the word "remain" means "to endure," "to be lasting." Lane (1991, 483) explains the full meaning of the author's application of this descriptive language as follows:

> The event [of God's final shaking] will result in the decisive removal from the community of those who have disregarded God's speaking and rejected his solemn warning (v. 25). They will experience not only the loss of their birthrights (cf. vv. 16–17) and the blessing of the new covenant reviewed in the vision of vv. 22–24 but also the invoking of the curse sanctions of the covenant (cf. v. 25b). Among that which "remains" are those who share in the unshakableness of the Judge who is God of all (v. 27b). Their fidelity to the new covenant is the ground of the assurance that they will enjoy an eternal salvation, receiving as their legacy an unshakable kingdom (v. 28a).

Thus the final shaking will expose the heart and willingness or unwillingness of each person to submit to him who has spoken from heaven in his Son.

Believers who share in Christ have good reason to be thankful, since "we are receiving a kingdom that cannot be shaken" (12:28). This material, created order is transitory and perishable. Everything that can be shaken will be, but eternal realities will never pass away. The kingdom of God, unlike the kingdoms of this world, is an everlasting kingdom (Luke 1:33; cf. Dan. 2:44–45; 4:3; 7:14, 18). The Word of God also is unshakable; though heaven and earth pass away, what God has spoken will not pass away but endure forever (cf. Mark 13:31). Jesus Christ himself remains "the same yesterday and today and forever" (Heb. 13:8). The inheritance of the saints "can never perish, spoil or fade," because it is kept secure in heaven for those who persevere in faith until the end (1 Peter 1:4; cf. Heb. 3:14).

The appropriate response to receiving God's unshakable kingdom and his unchangeable grace is worshipful service given willingly and lavishly to him, based on a thankful heart that is captured by the holy wonder and awe of God himself. The word "worship" (v. 28, *latreuo*) is the word used for "service" to the Lord of various kinds. It is used earlier in Hebrews to describe the service of the Levitical priests (e.g., 8:5; 9:9; 10:2; cf. also 13:10). Here it is used spiritually for the entire life of devotion of the Christian, accompanied by "reverence and awe" before the "consuming fire" (12:29) of his holiness and righteousness.

The closing declaration, "for our 'God is a consuming fire,'" picks up the description of God's manifestation at Mount Sinai (12:18). The burning fire and darkness of Sinai foreshadow the reality that will be seen when the judgment of God in his holiness breaks forth on those who reject his Son. "His holiness is a fire, which, by the eternal law of His nature must consume all that is evil. [Likewise] His love is a fire, which must burn up and destroy all that hinders or refuses the triumph of love" (Murray, n.d., 515). Thus, the awesome fire of God can be encountered either as the fire of judgment or as the refiner's purifying fire. Whether it meets us as an enemy or a friend depends on how we are related to his Son.

5.2. The Practice of Holiness (13:1–17)

In 12:14 the author declared that holy living is a priority in the Christian life. We who have been redeemed and sanctified by the blood of Christ (13:12) are called to demonstrate purity (God's holiness in us; cf. 12:10) through the outworking of a distinctively Christian lifestyle that involves social, ethical, and moral choices, such as are described in 13:1–17. The very concept of acceptable worship in 12:28 involves revelation of the refiner's fire (12:29) and the implementation of holy living in reverence to God and service to others (see comments on 12:28–29). True worship, therefore, is directly related to the kind of holy living as presented in 13:1–17. Both 12:14 and 12:28 are connecting links between the preceding section (12:14–29) and the one now before us.

A main characteristic of 13:1–17 is the present imperative (cf. 13:1, 2, 3, 7, 9, 17; cf. also 13:18, where prayer is requested), a literary form called paraenesis. This terse style of dmonition uses imperatives as crisp commands in concise form, reminiscent of the literary style of the New Testament book of ames. Hence, no single topic receives extensive treatment in these verses. The purpose of he advice is not to teach but to jog the memory nd focus the attention on the God-honoring ifestyle that is to characterize all Christians.

Consistent with this purpose, the rapid series f pungent exhortations in 13:1–17 addresses he will of believers to live holy lives and not ose their resolve or focus: "Keep on loving ach other as brothers" (13:1); "do not forget to ntertain strangers" (13:2); "remember those in rison . . . and those who are mistreated" (13:3); marriage should be honored" (13:4); "keep our lives free from the love of money and be ontent with what you have" (13:5); "remember your [past] leaders . . . imitate their faith" 13:7); "do not be carried away by all kinds of trange teachings" (13:9); "we have an altar" 13:10); "let us, then, go to him outside the amp" (13:13); "let us continually offer to God sacrifice of praise" (13:15); "do not forget to lo good and to share with others" (13:16); obey your leaders and submit to their authority" (13:17). For an insightful study of the literary form, structure, symmetry, and artistry of his section, see Lane, 1991, 495–509.

5.2.1. Demonstrate Practical Love (13:1–3). To show love to other believers is an essential aspect of what it means to pursue the holiness, without which "no one will see the Lord" 12:14). This is a common New Testament eaching, as indicated in John's statement: "For nyone who does not love his brother, whom e has seen, cannot love God, whom he has not een. And he has given us this command: Whoever loves God must also love his rother" (1 John 4:20–21; cf. John 13:34; Rom. 12:10; 1 Thess. 4:9; 1 Peter 1:22; 2 Peter :7; 1 John 2:9–10; 3:11, 14–18). It is thus ppropriate that the revelation of God's holiness in Hebrews 12:28–29 should be followed y the admonition, "Keep on loving each other s brothers" (13:1). This emphasis in the early hurch derives from the teaching of Jesus himelf, who summed up the Old Testament law in he twofold command to love God and one's eighbor as oneself (Matt. 22:37–40; Mark 2:29–31; cf. Rom. 13:9–10). Thus, love is the ll-important Christian virtue, greater even han faith and hope (1 Cor. 13).

The brotherly love referred to in 13:1 is the word *philadelphia*. It expresses the quality of love, often referred to in Hebrews, that binds believers together as brothers and sisters in the family of God (cf. 2:11–12, 17; 3:1, 12; 10:24; 13:22–23). Such love for one another had already characterized the lives of the original readers (10:32–34). If their faith was beginning to waver, it would lead to a corresponding weakening of the bond of love that had united them together.

The practice of holiness is seen not only in the expression of practical love to fellow believers in one's own church community, but also in extending hospitality to "strangers" (13:2). The early church for the most part met in homes. The house churches provided a natural setting for showing hospitality to traveling Christians; hospitality in turn "served to expand the network of interdependence that unites the family of God" (Lane, 1991, 511). Lane adds that traveling preachers and teachers of the gospel and refugees from persecution actually "relied upon a network of Christian homes for shelter and provisions" (1991, 512). The Didache, an important second-century Christian document, states: "Let anyone who comes in the name of the Lord be received. . . . If he comes as a traveler, help him as much as you can" (12:1–2).

There are clear New Testament references to this kind of hospitality in Paul's travel plans and that of his companions (e.g., Rom. 15:28–29; 16:1–2; 1 Cor. 16:10–11; Phil. 2:24, 29; Philem. 22) and of the church's practice generally (2 John 5–11; cf. Rom. 12:13; 1 Peter 4:9–10). The phrase, "by so doing some people have entertained angels without knowing it," alludes to Abraham's encounter with three mysterious visitors to whom he showed hospitality and who predicted the birth of Isaac within a year's time (Gen. 18:1–21). This reference is intended to inspire among believers a willing disposition to extend hospitality to Christian strangers and travelers, with the expectation that the guests as God's messengers (*angeloi*) may in turn enrich the lives of the host family (cf. Bruce, 1990, 371; Lane, 1991, 512–13).

The admonition to show compassion for prisoners and the mistreated further demonstrates that Christian love was an important aspect of holy living. "Remember those in prison" especially refers to fellow believers who have been imprisoned as an act of persecution for their faith. In ancient times prisoners suffered severe deprivation unless they were supplied food, clothes, blankets, and so forth by family or friends during their confinement. Prisoners out of sight could quickly be forgotten; thus the admonition to "remember" them.

Sometimes people feared being identified with such people lest they be subjected to the same treatment. But the readers are admonished to remember them "as if you were their fellow prisoners," that is, in the same circumstances and one with them. The readers had courageously demonstrated this kind of solidarity with and practical love for imprisoned believers in the past (see comments on 10:32–34) and are now urged to continue doing so in the present. The reference to "those . . . mistreated" (13:3b) includes the larger number of brothers and sisters in Christ who, though not imprisoned, are experiencing persecution and abuse because of their faith (cf. 11:25, 36–38). To support these fellow believers is not only an act of love but also itself a confession of faith.

5.2.2. Maintain Marital Fidelity and Sexual Purity (13:4). To respect marriage, its sacred vows, and its physical intimacy is another aspect of the holy living to which God calls his people. Such respect carries with it implications concerning sexual purity for both those who are married and single. "The marriage bed" is a euphemism for sexual intimacy and intercourse between a husband and wife. Contrary to the sexually promiscuous lifestyle of the world, God's high standard for human sexuality is purity and fidelity. Sexual union and intimacy are reserved for the marriage relationship, which God regards as honorable and pure. Intrusion of a third person sexually into the marriage relationship defiles it and receives condemnation from God. Likewise, sexual intimacy and intercourse before marriage or outside of the marriage covenant are viewed by God as a transgression of forbidden boundaries.

"God will judge the adulterer and all the sexually immoral." "Adulterers" denotes married individuals of either sex who engage in sexual activity outside the marriage relationship. It necessarily involves unfaithfulness to the marriage covenant and a betrayal of one's marriage spouse. Adultery often involves th breaking of two marriage covenants and th betrayal of two separate marriage spouses (double tragedy). The word for "the sexuall immoral" (*pornoi*) is literally "fornicators. Fornication covers a wide range of sexua activity outside of marriage, including hetero sexual intimacy by unmarried individuals homosexual intercourse, lesbian relationships use of a prostitute, and other degrading pas sions. Those who defile marriage by adulter or transgress forbidden boundaries throug fornication can be certain of God's judgmen "For because of such things God's wrat comes on those who are disobedient" (Eph 5:6; cf. 1 Cor. 6:9–10; Col. 3:5–6; 1 Thess 4:3–6). Paul's words in 1 Thessalonians 4: closely correspond to the exhortation here "For God did not call us to be impure, but t live a holy life."

5.2.3. Stay Free of Material Lust an Greed (13:5–6). Illicit sexual desire and th love of money often share in common the cor sinful desire called "covetousness" (cf. Ex 20:17). They are frequently linked together i the New Testament (e.g., 1 Cor. 5:10–11; Ep 4:19; 5:3–5; 1 Thess. 4:3–6). Covetous desire cause a person to pursue his or her own self centered aims, whether sexual or financia without regard for the spiritual well-being o others (Morris, 1981, 147). Another commo motivation for both sins is love of pleasure The second-century writer Lucian wrote: "Th love of pleasure brings in adultery and the lov of money" (*Nigrinus* 16).

Concerning money and possessions, Jesu warned that we "cannot serve both God an Money" (Matt. 6:24; Luke 16:13), and that rea life consists not in the abundance of posses sions (Luke 12:15). Similarly, Paul in his let ters often associates greed and idolatr together (e.g. 1 Cor. 5:11; Eph. 5:5; Col. 3:5 indicating that there is a demonic dimension t material lust and greed as well as a betrayal o trust in God.

In order to pursue holiness and live hol lives before the Lord, Hebrews thus admon ishes us: "Keep your lives free from the love o money and be content with what you have (13:5a). In a similar vein Paul wrote to Timo thy that "godliness with contentment is grea gain" and that we should be content with food clothing, and the basic provisions of life, know ng that "people who want to get rich fall into temptation and a trap and into many foolish and harmful desires that plunge men into ruin and destruction. For the love of money is a root of all kinds of evil. Some people, eager for money, have wandered from the faith and pierced themselves with many griefs" (1 Tim. 6:6–10).

The keys to being free from the love of money are: (1) being content with what we have, which requires dealing ruthlessly with the issue of greed and covetousness; and (2) having confidence that God will be our source of provision (cf. Matt. 6:25–33), which is the issue of faith. The author rightly emphasizes that contentment is determined not by how much money one has, but by how much trust one has in God and his unfailing presence (Heb. 13:5b) as our helper in life (13:6a). God's assurance, "Never will I leave you; never will I forsake you" (13:5b), is a composite revelation of his faithfulness from the Old Testament (e.g., Deut. 31:6, 8; Josh. 1:5).

The believer's response to God's assurance is a quote from Psalm 118:6–7 and contains a threefold trust and confidence. (1) "The Lord is my helper" (13:6a), that is, we are to trust God as our helper in every experience of holy living and in every ordeal of testing or persecution. (2) Because of God's enabling presence and grace, the believer can confidently say, "I will not be afraid" (13:6b). Fear and faith are opposites. Fear enables Satan to work against us; faith enables God to work for us. The believer is to be free from the love of money and from the fear of deprivation or death through faith in God as a trustworthy helper in every time of need. (3) The rhetorical question, "What can man do to me?" (13:6c), is in fact a bold confession of trust in God as "my helper." The trusting believer can boldly declare with Paul: "If God is for us, who can be against us? . . . Who shall separate us from the love of Christ? Shall trouble or hardship or persecution or famine or nakedness or danger or sword? . . . No, in all these things we are more than conquerors through him who loved us" (Rom. 8:31, 35, 37).

5.2.4. Hold to the Sound Teaching of the Gospel (13:7–12). The next three verses should be viewed as one unit of thought, with 13:8 being the bridge between 13:7 and 13:9. Jesus Christ is the unchanging focus of the gospel message (13:8) that was preached faithfully and authoritatively by their original leaders (13:7), and that must remain the standard of truth by which all manner of teachings are judged (13:9) (cf. Lane, 1991, 528–29).

"Remember [present tense stresses continuation, i.e., keep on remembering] your leaders, who spoke [past tense, i.e., former leaders] the word of God to you" (13:7). Three times in this chapter the writer mentions the readers' spiritual leaders (13:7, 17, 24). Each time he uses *hegoumenoi*, a word that refers to men of authority in a leading position (e.g., political, military, or church leaders). In 13:17 the readers are to obey their leaders, and in 13:24 the author sends his greetings to all the leaders; in both of these verses current leaders are being designated. In 13:7, however, it is their former leaders who must be remembered.

Two important facts about these former leaders are recalled. (1) They proclaimed "the word of God" (13:7a); that is, they were men of spiritual authority by virtue of their being centered in God's Word. Most likely the house church being addressed in Hebrews was founded as a result of their preaching and teaching ministry. If so, these founding fathers are referred to previously in 2:3–4 as anointed men who themselves had heard the Lord and subsequently became preachers, and whose ministry was attested by God with "signs, wonders and various miracles, and gifts of the Holy Spirit" (2:4). It appears that these "former leaders are now deceased [and] . . . their preaching belongs to the community's past" (Lane, 1991, 527).

(2) They were men of "faith" (13:7b), whose quality of faith and exemplary "way of life" placed them alongside the heroes of faith under the old covenant (see 11:4–38). Their life and faithfulness to Christ were so exemplary that the author now exhorts the readers, "Imitate their faith." As Bruce observes, there is more power in the testimony of a person whom we have known or seen than can be conveyed through merely reading or hearing the account of another (1990, 375). The admonition to "consider the outcome" of their lives also points to their being deceased; now the totality of their life can be seen along with their final triumph of faith in going to be with the Lord.

Because these former leaders are no longer with them and because their loss was most likely keenly felt, the subsequent changes in leadership may have resulted in unsettling changes generally for the congregation. Nevertheless, "Jesus Christ"—whom their leaders faithfully preached and who remains the object of their faith—"is the same yesterday and today and forever" (13:8). No matter what the readers face today or what lies ahead for them in their tomorrow, Christ will be "the same." He shares the same unchangeableness as God himself (cf. Ps. 102:27; Isa. 48:12). Though all else changes around us, Jesus does not change. He is the same tomorrow as he was yesterday and will be forever. Bruce (1990, 375) explains clearly in the context of Hebrews the past, present, and future as applied to Jesus:

> *Yesterday* Jesus "offered up entreaties and supplications, with loud cries and tears, to the one who was able to save him from death" (Heb. 5:7); *today* he represents his people in the presence of God, a high priest who has a fellow-feeling with them in their weakness, because he "endured trial in all respects like" themselves, "while remaining free from sin" (4:15); *for ever* he lives, this same Jesus, "to intercede for them" (7:25). His help, his grace, his power, his guidance are permanently at his people's disposal; why then should they lose heart? Others serve their generation by the will of God and pass on; "but this one, because he continues 'for ever,' has a priesthood which is untransferable" (7:24). He never needs to be replaced, and nothing can be added to his perfect work.

The author exhorts his readers to continue having an unchanging faith in the unchanging Christ as the believer's high priest forever (a capsule summary of the message of the entire book). As our faith takes hold of this truth and rests in him as "the same" forever, our faith "will participate in His unchangeableness" (Murray, n.d., 526).

In contrast to the enduring testimony of God's Word (13:7) and the stability and unchangeableness of Christ (13:8) are the diverse and "strange teachings" of another message being circulated among these Jewish Christians. The situation here has some parallels to Paul's problem in Galatia, where his converts were being drawn away from "the grace of Christ" to "a different gospel," which was causing them to lapse from grace and be ensnared in the bondage of the Old Testament law (cf. Gal. 1:6–9; 5:1–6). The warning "do not be carried away" points to a similar danger in these teachings that were foreign to the gospel of Christ preached by their founding fathers (13:7–8).

The references to "ceremonial foods" (13:9), an altar and eating (13:10), and the Old Testament ritual of the high priest (13:11) all point to an old covenant Jewish context for the competing teaching. Its "strangeness" consisted in its alien character when compared with the gospel of Christ (Guthrie, 1983, 272), not that it was foreign to the Jewish mindset (as with Gnosticism). These Jewish Christians must not entertain teachings about old covenant food rituals, feasts, or sacrificial meals as a means of spiritual nourishment for them.

As followers of Christ, "our hearts [are] to be strengthened by [his] grace, not by ceremonial foods." Throughout Hebrews the author has emphasized that all the forms, foods, rituals, and priestly ministry of the old covenant have been fulfilled (and therefore made obsolete) in Christ (cf. 9:10). Furthermore, rather than foods facilitating the strengthening of one spiritually, when placed in a "religious" setting they instead "divert the heart from the grace mediated through the word of God" (Lane 1991, 531) and through faith in Christ. Thus we are to have our hearts strengthened "by grace" alone, grace that comes from the throne of grace, not "by ceremonial foods." "For the kingdom of God is not a matter of eating and drinking, but of righteousness, peace and joy in the Holy Spirit" (Rom. 14:17).

Although the laws of nutrition tell us that what we eat has something to do with health and our overall physical well-being, food has nothing to do whatever with our spiritual well-being. Bruce rightly notes that "voluntary fasting [i.e. abstaining from food], in the spirit of our Lord's instruction in Matt. 6:16–18 ... [can be spiritually edifying]; but that is not the subject here" (1990, 377).

The phrase "we have an altar" in 13:1 marks the author's return to his theme in the central chapters of Hebrews, namely, that the Levitical priesthood, sacrifices, and Old Testament sanctuary find their fulfillment in the death and enduring ministry of Jesus Christ. Christ is the believer's high priest before the ltar, the believer's sacrifice for sin on the altar, nd the believer's altar. Our altar is both Christ nd the cross, and the Levitical priests and worhipers do not share in the benefits of what is rovided there. "'Eating from the altar' is a figrative expression for participating in the sacifice" (Lane, 1991, 539) and partaking of the acrificial meal that sometimes followed. The hrase "have no right to eat" refers not to the ord's Supper but figuratively to the eternal ustenance of the sacrifice of Christ that must e appropriated by faith in Christ himself.

In Hebrews the expression "high priest" sually signals a reference to some aspect of he Day of Atonement ritual (Lev. 16; e.g., Ieb. 5:3; 7:27; 8:1–3; 9:7, 11–12, 24–26). The two distinguishing features of the "sin ffering" on the Day of Atonement are referred o in 13:11–12. "The blood" of the sacrifice vas carried "into the Most Holy Place," and 'the bodies" of the sacrifice were "burned outide the camp"—both of which foreshadowed Christ's sacrifice as a sin offering on the cross our Day of Atonement). (1) Jesus' blood was prinkled in heaven's Most Holy Place, by vhich forgiveness of sin and access to God ave been obtained (9:12) and where his blood ontinues to be the power of our entrance and ellowship there (10:19–20). Thus comes the all in Hebrews: "Let us . . . go to him" (cf. 4:16; cf. 10:22).

(2) Jesus' body, however, was made to sufer "outside the city gate" in order to "make the eople holy through his own blood" (13:12). Thus, Jesus' death on the cross outside the city valls of Jerusalem corresponds to the burning of the sacrificial body outside the camp of srael on the Day of Atonement. The clear purose of his death was to sanctify his people so hat they would be presentable to God and ould share in his glory. "Outside the camp" nd "outside the city gate" not only represented the fulfillment of the Day of Atonement itual in Jesus' death on Golgotha, but also onvey that Jesus' death involved the shame of a criminal's execution and exclusion from the acred precincts of Jerusalem. The practical mplication of the enormous rejection and hame bound up in this imagery is made clear n the exhortation that follows.

5.2.5. Joyfully Bear the Reproach of Christ (13:13–16). The key admonition in hese four verses is: "Let us, then, go to him outside the camp" (13:13a). The expression "outside the camp/city gate" occurs three times in three verses (13:11, 12, 13) and is the central thought in this passage. Here it conveys a twofold meaning. (1) The readers must break decisively all their emotional and religious ties with Judaism (see Hughes, 1977, 580–82; Lane, 1991, 545–46; Peterson, 1994, 1352). When Jesus was led outside Jerusalem's walls to be crucified, it was "a token of his rejection by all that Jerusalem represented. . . . In this context the 'camp' stands for the established fellowship and ordinances of Judaism" (Bruce, 1990, 381). To sever ties to Judaism was a hard but necessary thing for these Jewish Christians, who were feeling "the pull of their Jewish heritage at a time when they were growing weary with . . . sustaining their commitment to Jesus in a hostile society" (Lane, 1991, 346). "Outside the camp" can equally apply to any religious institution that compromises one's loyal devotion to Christ Jesus or the Word of God.

(2) A more general summons to discipleship is also intended, as the phrase "bearing the disgrace he bore" (13:13b) indicates. To go to Jesus "outside the camp" is parallel to the call to discipleship that he gave, which involves denying ourselves, taking up our cross, and following him (Matt. 10:38; 16:24; Mark 8:34; Luke 14:27). Being identified with Christ crucified in the first century was a stigma and scandalous humiliation for the Jews and foolishness to wisdom-seeking Gentiles, as Paul pointed out (1 Cor. 1:23). Bearing the same kind of shame, rejection, and reproach that Jesus himself experienced is an integral part of being discipled. Thus, remaining "inside the camp" involves any situation where we compromise following Jesus for the sake of retaining respectability or acceptance among people where our relationship means something; going "outside the camp" is paying the price of rejection and disgrace.

The author mentions three ways in Hebrews 13:14–16 by which we can joyfully bear the reproach of Christ. (1) We must keep our eternal destination and heavenly reward in view at all times (13:14). We can decisively leave the earthly securities of an earthly city if "we are looking for the city that is to come," that is, the "enduring" one. Abraham left the affluent city of Ur to follow God by faith and was able to endure as a pilgrim in this world because "he was looking forward to the city with [enduring] foundations, whose architect and builder is God" (11:10; also 11:16). Likewise, Moses left Egypt to follow God by faith and suffered "disgrace for the sake of Christ ... because he was looking ahead to his reward ... [and] because he saw him who is invisible" (11:26–27).

Such faith and unwavering focus on the heavenly goal with its permanence and stability are necessary if we are to follow Jesus "outside the camp" and bear the reproach he bore. After all, our true citizenship and allegiance are in the kingdom of God, not in the religious and political institutions of this world. As Bruce states, "every earthly institution belongs to 'the things that are shaken' (12:27); in none of them can the human heart find permanent rest" (1990, 382). The more we follow Jesus, bearing his reproach, the more we will find access through him to enter into his glory.

(2) Another way by which we can joyfully bear Jesus' reproach is "through [him ... to] continually offer to God a sacrifice of praise" (13:15a). The blood of Christ that sanctifies us and separates us unto God for his service will cause us to go outside the camp on earth (discipleship) and bring us into the Most Holy Place in heaven (worship). Discipleship is the main issue in 13:13–14; worship from the heart is the central issue in 13:15–16. In fellowship with Jesus and as a participant by faith in the benefits of his once-for-all sacrifice, we are called to worship God with the "sacrifice of praise," that is, a sacrifice consisting of gratitude and thanksgiving to God.

The language of sacrifice, so prominent in Hebrews, finds one last expression here and in 13:16. Whereas Jesus' sacrifice for sin was a once-for-all sacrifice, as a counterpart to the whole system of sacrifices under the old covenant is the Christian's continuous "sacrifice of praise" for Jesus' sacrifice on the cross and the manifold grace of God that comes to us through him. The Christian's praise is specifically to be offered up to God "through Jesus," our high priest, and not through any other priest (Jewish or otherwise).

The "sacrifice of praise" is also called "the fruit of lips that confess his name" (13:15b; cf. Hos. 14:2). Speech is one of our most wonderful endowments from God. Our lips belong to him when we are redeemed by Christ, and they are to be used in continual praise and confession of his name. Confessing his name openly and publicly for his sake, for our sake and for the sake of those who hear us "is an indispensable element of a vigorous Christian life" (Murray, n.d., 534). There can be no continual joyful life if we do not continually give him the fruit of our lips.

(3) Finally, we must "do good and ... share with others [*koinonia*]" (13:16). The former expression refers to acts of kindness that show concern for the well-being of others. *Koinonia* refers to the shared life and spiritual camaraderie of believers joined together by Christ in the community of faith. When we leave "the camp" and the earthly securities it represents, we are not on our own with Jesus. We instead become members of another community, that of his disenfranchised followers on earth, who bear the reproach of the glorious Son. These people comprise a warm fellowship, unlike the impersonal society from which we must depart. *Koinonia* here includes the action of tangibly giving to and/or receiving from fellow believers financial help "as a sign of shared partnership." Without these kinds of practical demonstrations of love among Christians, "praise of God lacks integrity" (Lane, 1991, 552).

Our "sacrifice of praise" and deeds of loving devotion are the kinds of sacrifices with which "God is pleased." Since Christ's atoning sacrifice is decisively in the past, the response of our lives in worshipful praise and works of love "are the only appropriate sacrifices remaining [cf. Rom. 12:1; James 1:27; 1 Peter 2:5] to the redeemed community" (Lane, 1991, 553).

5.2.6. Properly Respect Your Spiritual Leaders (13:17). Proper respect for spiritual leaders includes obedience and submission. Whereas 13:7 points back to the former leaders of this congregation, this verse refers to current leaders. Obeying them and submitting to their authority are in the best interest and spiritual welfare of the readers (cf. 1 Cor 16:16; 1 Thess. 5:12). Disobedience and insubordination can only make them more vulnerable to strange teachings from other sources and to their own inclination to abandon their Christian faith by returning to Judaism.

The word for "leaders" (*hegoumenoi*; cf comments on 13:7) refers to leading men in the church community, whose spiritual authority derives from a twofold source. (1) Foremost it derives from "the word of God" (cf. 13:7), which they are called and gifted by God to proclaim. There is no suggestion here of a hierarchical structure or of ecclesiastical authority that derives from a church office. The authority of their leaders is spiritual in nature and derives more directly from God than from office or title. (2) Their authority is also pastoral and derives from their diligence as faithful overseers: "They keep watch over you [*psychon*, lit., your souls; cf. 10:39] as men who must give an account" to God. The purveyors of strange teaching do not do this.

The verb "keep watch" (*agrypneo*) means to "keep oneself awake, be awake" (BAGD, 14). It pictures spiritual leaders who with constant vigilance stay awake nights in their concern for the spiritual well-being of those entrusted to their care (cf. Luke 21:36; Eph. 6:18; the cognate noun refers to "sleepless nights" in 2 Cor. 11:27–28). Leaders are expected to do the work of ministry joyfully. The alternative is that disobedient and unsubmissive sheep will make the leaders' job "a burden," which the author says "would be of no advantage to you."

This sober remark indicates that the spiritual well-being of a congregation is affected by the response of members to their spiritual leaders. In other words, "the tensions that exist between the community and their leaders must be resolved" (Lane, 1991, 556). Bruce speculates that these leaders may have been those "in the wider city church from whose fellowship and jurisdiction the group addressed in the epistle was tempted to withdraw" (1990, 385).

6. Conclusion (13:18–25)

6.1. Final Request (13:18–19)

The author's final request underscores the importance of prayer. "Pray for us" (present imperative) carries the sense of "keep on praying for us." That this request occurs without a literary transition from verse 17 indicates that the author was somehow included as one of the "leaders." The very nature of the book itself suggests that he had a position of authority and had responsibility for the people to whom he writes.

The main question of interpretation in this prayer request concerns the nature of the plural in "pray for us" (13:18a). Is it an authorial plural, by which the author refers to himself alone (so Bruce, 1990, 386; Attridge, 1989, 402; Peterson, 1994, 1353), or is it a genuine plural, which includes a group of unnamed leaders along with himself (so Westcott, 1889/1980, 446; Guthrie, 1983, 277; Lane, 1991, 556; Ellingworth, 1993, 724–25)? If the latter, does the plural refer to fellow leaders like himself and Timothy, who are itinerant, or does it include the present community leaders in 13:17?

Lane believes the rest of 13:18 is clearly apologetic. The request "pray for us, [for, *gar*, omitted by the NIV] we are sure we have a clear conscience and desire to live honorably in every way," is an unusual reason for requesting prayer. It must suggest some kind of defense. If so, the author may be defending the integrity (of motives and conduct) of himself and their present leaders, "whose counsel and guidance the community appears to have resented" (1991, 556). Perhaps the attack that the defense implies was by the false teachers in 13:9 or by some members of the congregation who were influenced by them.[8] Possibly the author has written by invitation of the present leaders to address the problem and here joins himself with them in requesting prayer that all issues be resolved cleanly.

The first-person singular, "I particularly urge you to pray so that I may be restored to you soon" (13:19), conveys the author's own personal request. The desire to "be restored . . . soon" suggests that his present physical separation is involuntary and points to a previous personal relationship with and presence among them. This further indicates that Hebrews was not originally an anonymous homily but was written because of a close relationship with the readers.

6.2. Final Benediction (13:20–21)

This is one of the most eloquently formed, theologically packed, and comprehensively written benedictions in the New Testament. As the climactic ending of the book, it has a corresponding balance to the exalted Christological introduction in 1:1–3. The eight main points of the benediction concisely express some of the main themes of the book. (1) "May the God of peace" (13:20a) identifies God as the source and giver of peace on both a personal and corporate level. Since the congregation was spiritually unsettled and experiencing turmoil, this pronouncement of God's peace over them is especially appropriate (cf. Rom.

15:33; 16:20; 2 Cor. 13:11; Phil. 4:9; 1 Thess. 5:23; 2 Thess. 3:16).

(2) It was "through the blood of the eternal covenant" (13:20b) that God (3) "brought back from the dead our Lord Jesus" (13:20c). This linking together of Jesus' blood and resurrection expresses an important truth in Hebrews: "Jesus died on the cross as a covenant sacrifice and . . . entered into the heavenly sanctuary and there sprinkled his own blood, prior to the resurrection. The resurrection of Jesus occurred by virtue of the sprinkling of the blood in the heavenly sanctuary and the establishment of the new covenant" (Lane, 1991, 563).

The new covenant is "eternal" because it is based on a better sacrifice and is superior to the old in that it endures forever. It will never become obsolete or need replacing, as did the old covenant. It might seem surprising that this is the only explicit reference to Jesus' resurrection in Hebrews. Elsewhere the emphasis is on Jesus' exaltation at God's right hand (cf. the prominence of Psalm 110:1, 4) in the author's exposition of Jesus' high priestly ministry. Now, however, the author declares that an important part of establishing the eternal covenant was bringing back from the realm of the dead our Lord Jesus as a supernatural demonstration of God's mighty power and the necessary precedent for his enduring mediatorial ministry as our priest forever.

(4) The description of Jesus as "that great Shepherd of the sheep" (13:20d) is rooted deeply in the New Testament revelation of him (e.g., John 10:1–18; 1 Peter 2:25; 5:4; cf. Mark 6:34; 14:27; Matt. 9:36; 18:12–14; 25:32; 26:31; Luke 15:3–7). The adjective "great" emphasizes one final time "the incomparable superiority of Jesus, the mediator of the new covenant, to Moses, the mediator of the old covenant" (Lane, 1991, 562). Moses is described in the Old Testament as "the shepherd of the sheep" whom God "led out" of Egypt; Jesus is "the great Shepherd of the sheep" whom God "led out" of the realm of death. Jesus alone qualifies to serve as the mediator of the eternal covenant (ibid.).

(5) The author's petition in the benediction is that the new covenant people might be equipped by God "with everything good for doing his will" (13:21a). These are the charismatic (grace) gifts of God, whereby we are equipped for godly action (cf. 1 Peter 4:10–11). "It is God who strengthens the heart with grace (13:9), who fills and supports the heart with charismatic gifts (2:4; 6:4–5; 13:9), so that it neither wavers nor suffers deficiency but possesses the capacity to do the will of God" (Lane, 1991, 564).

(6) In this way God "may work in us what is pleasing to him" (13:21b). This is in keeping with Paul's statement that "it is God who works in you to will and to act according to his good purpose" (Phil. 2:13).

(7) "Through Jesus Christ" (Heb. 13:21c) reminds us one last time of the mediatorial ministry of Christ on our behalf. We approach God and offer acceptable worship to him through Christ. Whatever is pleasing to God (cf. 13:15–16) "will be accomplished 'through Jesus Christ' as the mediator of the grace and power of God within the new covenant community" (Lane, 1991, 565).

(8) To whom do we ascribe "glory for ever and ever" (13:21d)? To God, the subject of the benediction, or to Jesus Christ, the immediate antecedent of the doxology? Perhaps the author was not making a precise distinction here, but generally speaking it is to God the Father through Christ the Son that glory is ascribed (cf. 13:15).

6.3. Final Exhortation (13:22–23)

The author describes his entire book as "my word of exhortation" (13:22). Lane suggests that this phrase was an "idiomatic designation" for a homily or edifying discourse in the first century, as Acts 13:15 and other sources indicate. It customarily referred to the exposition and application of the Scripture that was read aloud to an assembled congregation (1991, 568). This is a good description of Hebrews as a whole, though it was written instead of spoken because of the circumstances of the author (Heb. 13:19, 23).

Gently and affectionately—"Brothers, I urge you"—the author entreats his readers to bear with the homily that he has written briefly. (The NIV word "letter" is not in the Greek.) Bruce notes that the book might be viewed as a long letter but not as a long homily, since it could be read aloud to the congregation in an hour (1990, 389). Even if it is regarded as a letter, it is not as long as Romans or 1 Corinthians.

The designation of Timothy as "our brother" (13:23) is one of many clues that Paul ɨd not write Hebrews, since he typically ›ferred to Timothy as "my son." Timothy is lmost certainly the same person as associated ·ith Paul (Bruce, 1990, 390). Apparently he ad recently been released from prison, and the ıthor expects that the two of them will travel ›gether to visit the readers in the near future. imothy is the only person mentioned by name ı the whole book. The author's brief mention f a planned visit indicates that his personal reference was to speak directly with them in erson, not to substitute his presence with ›mething written.

6.4. Final Greetings and Blessing (13:24–25)

The last two verses have the most letter-ke characteristics in the book. They contain ıree different kinds of greetings. Note that the ord for "greet" (*aspazomai*) was an intimate term in that culture and conveyed the idea of a warm embrace (Windisch, *TDNT*, 1:496–502). (1) In the first person the author sends his personal greetings to all the current leaders and to "all God's people" (13:24a)—probably referring to fellow believers "of other house churches than their own in the city-wide fellowship to which they belonged" (Bruce, 1990, 391).

(2) Grammatically, the greetings of "those from Italy" (13:24b) can be from Italians residing outside of Italy or those from within Italy. The one other parallel to "from Italy" in the New Testament, however, clearly means "from" while residing "outside" Italy (Acts 18:2). If the author is writing to a Jewish-Christian house church in Rome (see Introduction), then Italian believers (perhaps from various parts of Italy) now residing outside Italy at the same location as the author send

THE OLD TESTAMENT IN THE NEW

NT Text	OT Text	Subject
Heb 1:5	Ps 2:7	You are my Son
Heb 1:5	2Sa 7:14; 1 Ch 17:13	Father and Son
Heb 1:6	Dt 32:43	Rejoice, O nations
Heb 1:7	Ps 104:4	Angels and winds
Heb 1:8	Ps 45:6–7	God's eternal throne
Heb 1:10–12	Ps 102:25–27	The unchangeable God
Heb 1:13	Ps 110:1	At God's right hand
Heb 2:6–8	Ps 8:4–6	Lower than the angels
Heb 2:12	Ps 22:22	Declaring God's name
Heb 2:13	Isa 8:17	Trust in God
Heb 2:13	Isa 8:18	God's children
Heb 3:2, 5	Nu 12:7	Faithful Moses
Heb 3:7–11, 15	Ps 95:7–11	No rest for the wicked
Heb 4:3, 5, 7	Ps 95:7–11	No rest for the wicked
Heb 4:4	Ge 2:2	God rested the seventh day
Heb 5:5	Ps 2:7	You are my Son
Heb 5:6	Ps 110:4	Melchizedek
Heb 6:14	Ge 22:17	God's oath to Abraham
Heb 7:17, 21	Ps 110:4	Melchizedek
Heb 8:5	Ex 25:40	Pattern of the tabernacle
Heb 8:8–12	Jer 31:31–34	The new covenant
Heb 9:20	Ex 24:8	The blood of the covenant
Heb 10:5–9	Ps 40:6–8	Offerings and obedience
Heb 10:16–17	Jer 31:33–34	The new covenant
Heb 10:28	Dt 17:6	Two or three witnesses
Heb 10:30	Dt 32:35	God avenges sins
Heb 10:30	Dt 32:36; Ps 135:14	God judges his people
Heb 10:37–38	Hab 2:3–4	Persevere in faith
Heb 11:18	Ge 21:12	God's choice of Isaac
Heb 12:5–6	Pr 3:11–12	Love and discipline
Heb 12:13	Pr 4:26	Level paths for your feet
Heb 12:15	Dt 29:18	No root of bitterness
Heb 12:20	Ex 19:12–13	Not touching the mountain
Heb 12:21	Dt 9:19	Moses' fear
Heb 12:26	Hag 2:6	One more shaking
Heb 12:29	Dt 4:24	God is a consuming fire
Heb 13:5	Dt 31:6	Faithfulness of God
Heb 13:6	Ps 118:6–7	The Lord is my helper

their greetings to fellow believers in their homeland. If the author were writing "from Rome" or some other Italian city, it would be more natural to include greetings from that particular locality rather than "from Italy" generally.

(3) The third greeting, in the form of a common New Testament Christian blessing—"Grace be with you all" (13:25)—often brought closure to worship in the early church or to a New Testament letter. It represents more than formal closure, however. Saints in biblical times knew that the pronouncement of blessing "activates" the power of God to bestow grace and spiritual blessing (Lane, 1991, 571). It is with this in mind that the author concludes his homily and lays down his quill.

NOTES

[1]Interpreters who support Apollos as the likely author include Alford, 1859, 4:58–62; Bartlet, 1913, 548–51; Howard, 1951, 80–91; Lenski, 1966, 21–24; T. W. Manson, 1962, 254–58; Moll, n.d., 22:9–10; Montefiore, 1964, 9–15; Spicq, 1952, 1:207–19. Some who cautiously commend Apollos as the most likely candidate include Ellingworth, 1993, 21; Guthrie, 1990, 679–80; Robertson, 1932, 5:329; Zahn, 1909, 2:356.

[2]The argument by some interpreters that not all the readers were genuine Christians—that is, that some were only interested but uncommitted Jewish inquirers, and that it was these among the group who are addressed in the warning passages and who were in danger of drifting away from "the possibility of" salvation in Christ—has neither textual nor contextual support in Hebrews. Throughout Hebrews our author addresses his readers as genuine Christians, not as those whom he hopes to persuade to become genuine Christians. Those whom he warns he exhorts as fellow believers: "Hold on to our courage and . . . hope" (3:6); beware that none of you "turns away from the living God" (3:12); "we have come to share in Christ if we hold firmly till the end the confidence we had at first" (3:14); "let us hold firmly to the faith we profess" (4:14); "let us leave the elementary teachings about Christ and go on to maturity" (6:1); "let us hold unswervingly to the hope we profess" (10:23); "if we deliberately keep on sinning after we have received the knowledge of the truth, no sacrifice for sins is left, but only a fearful expectation of judgment" (10:26–27a); "a man deserves to be punished . . . who has treated as an unholy thing the blood of the covenant that sanctified him" (10:29); "you need to persevere so that when you have done the will of God, you will receive what he has promised" (10:36); "consider him who endured such opposition from sinful men, so that you will not grow weary and los[e] heart" (12:3).

[3]Hebrews 6:4–6 is a problem passage f[or] Calvinists and Arminians alike. Calvinists dislik[e] the possibility of true believers falling away, an[d] Arminians dislike the impossibility of apostate[s] being restored. For a sketch of the many differe[nt] ways this passage has been interpreted by scholar[s] see Solari, 1970, 1–7; Eaton, 1995, 208–12.

[4]It is commonly assumed that the Platonic con[-]cept of heavenly "ideas" as the archetypes of a[ll] earthly things lies behind the author's use of "cop[y] and shadow." Lane points out, however, that th[e] author's contrast as developed in 8:1–5 is antithe[t-]ical to the serene, unhistorical, and philosophica[l] metaphysics of Plato. The contrast here is betwee[n] a historical situation in the past (the Levitical orde[r]) and one that has superseded it in time (Christ's exa[l-]tation), and is thus an eschatological distinctio[n] rather than a philosophical one. For an insightf[ul] treatment of this issue, see Lane, 1991, 207–8).

[5]Disagreement exists among ancient Greek man[-]uscripts about how the verb in 9:11a was originall[y] written. Early manuscript evidence goes both way[s], as do modern translations: (1) The future idea i[n] "that are to come" (KJV, NASB, NKJV) is supported b[y] the greatest number of manuscript witnesses; (2) th[e] present idea in "that have come/are already here["] (NEB, NIV, RSV, NRSV), is supported by the oldest an[d] greatest diversity of manuscript types. This readin[g] is also favored for style and context reasons. Mo[st] biblical scholars on Hebrews concur with Lane th[at] the focus on contrast by the author in the immed[i-]ate context (9:10–11) is decisive for settling the var[i-]ant reading in favor of the NIV rendering (1991, 236[).]

[6]For a discussion and development of the strik[-]ing parallelism between 6:4–12 and 10:26–36, se[e] Lane, 1991, 291, 296–97. For a summary of the his[-]tory of the interpretation of the 10:26–31 warnin[g] passage, see Grässer, 1963, 192–98.

[7]Some scholars (e.g., Ellingworth, 1993, 56[0]; Lane, 1991, 328–30) view the two halves of 11:1—"what we hope for" and "what we do not see"—a[s] virtually synonymous in referring to future realitie[s]. The supporting evidence of chapter 11, howeve[r], points to two distinct (though related) realms requi[r-]ing the activity of faith: things hoped for/the futur[e] (11:1a) and things invisible (11:1b) (e.g., Attridg[e], 1989, 310–11; Bruce, 1990, 277; Peterson, 199[4], 1346). "'Things invisible' are not simply the equiv[-]alent of 'things hoped for.' Things invisible o[r] unseen are not only future, but also present, or rathe[r] eternal, realities, such as God, 'the unseen one' (11:27); God's existence and providence (11:6[);] God's fidelity (11:11); and God's power (11:19)" (Attridge, 1989, 311).

[8]Ellingworth (1993, 724) mentions this as [a] possibility, but readily acknowledges it as simpl[e] speculation.

BIBLIOGRAPHY

Henry Alford, *The Greek Testament*, vol. 4 1859); H. W. Attridge, *A Commentary on the Epis-le to the Hebrews*, Hermeneia (1989); William Bar-clay, *The Letter to the Hebrews* (1957); James Vernon Bartlet and W. Kendrick Grobel, "The Epis-le to the Hebrews," *Encyclopaedia Britannica*, vol. 11 (1965); James Vernon Bartlet, "The Riddle of he Epistle to the Hebrews," *Expositor* 8 (1913): 548–51; idem, "The Epistle to the Hebrews Once More," *ExpTim* 34 (1922–23): 58–61; Wick Broomall, "Type, Typology," *Baker's Dictionary of Theology* (1960); F. F. Bruce, *The Epistle to the Hebrews*, NICNT (1964/1990); George Wesley Buchanan, *To the Hebrews*, AB (1972); Marcus Dods, "Hebrews," *EGT*, vol. 4 (n.d., 1976 reprint); Ralph Earle, *Word Meanings in the New Testament* 1986); Michael A. Eaton, *A Theology of Encour-agement* (1995); Paul Ellingworth, *Commentary on Hebrews*, NIGTC (1993); E. Grässer, *Der Glanbe in Hebaebrief* (1963); Wayne Grudem, "Perseverance of the Saints: A Case Study From Hebrews 6:4–6 and Other Warning Passages in Hebrews," *The Grace of God, The Bondage of the Will* (1995); Don-ald Guthrie, *New Testament Introduction* (1990); idem, *The Letter to the Hebrews*, TNTC (1983); Donald A. Hagner, *Hebrews*, Good News Com-mentary (1983); Gerald F. Hawthorne, "Hebrews," *The International Bible Commentary* (1986); Thomas Hewitt, *The Epistle to the Hebrews*, TNTC 1960); W. F. Howard, "The Epistle to the Hebrews," *Interpretation* 5 (1951); Philip E. Hughes, *A Com-mentary on the Epistle to the Hebrews* (1977); A. M. Hunter, *The New Testament for Today* (1975); William L. Lane, *Hebrews*, 2 vols., WBC (1991); G. H. Lang, *The Epistle to the Hebrews* (1951); R. C. H. Lenski, *The Interpretation of the Epistle to the Hebrews and the Epistle of James* (1966); T. W. Manson, *Studies in the Gospels and Epistles* (1962); William Manson, *The Epistle to the Hebrews* (1951); I. Howard Marshall, *Kept By the Power of God: A Study of Perseverance and Falling Away* (1969); James Moffatt, *A Critical and Exegetical Commentary on the Epistle to the Hebrews*, ICC (1924); Carl Bernhard Moll, "The Epistle to the Hebrews," *Lange's Commentary on the Holy Scriptures* (n.d., 1960 reprint); Hugh Montefiore, *The Epistle to the Hebrews*, Black's/Harper's New Testament Commentary (1964); Leon Morris, "Hebrews," *EBC*, vol. 12 (1981); Andrew Murray, *The Holiest of All* (n.d.); David G. Peterson, "Hebrews," *New Bible Commentary (21st Century Edition)* (1994); A. T. Robertson, *Word Pictures in the New Testament*, vol. 5 (1932); Theodore H. Robinson, *The Epistle to the Hebrews*, The Moffatt New Testament Commentary (1933/1964); Philip Schaff, *History of the Christian Church*, vol. 1 (1950); E. F. Scott, *The Epistle to the Hebrews* (1922); J. K. Solari, "The Problem of Metanoia in the Epistle to the Hebrews," Ph.D. diss. (1970); C. Spicq, *L'Ep"tre aux Hebreux*, 2 vols. (1952); A. M. Stibbs, "The Epistle to the Hebrews," *New Bible Commentary* (1970 rev. ed.); Charles A. Trentham, "Hebrews," *The Broadman Bible Commentary*, vol. 12 (1972); B. F. Westcott, *The Epistle to the Hebrews* (1889/1980); R. McL. Wilson, *Hebrews*, New Century Bible (1987); N. J. Young, "The Gospel According to Hebrews 9," *NTS* (1980–81); Theodore Zahn, *Introduction to the New Testament*, vol. 2 (1909).

JAMES

Timothy B. Cargal

INTRODUCTION

Questions about the authorship and historical setting of the letter of James have been widely debated, not only in modern times but also among the early church fathers. One thing is certain: This book was among the last to be accepted by the church into the recognized canon of the Scriptures. The most important reasons for its delay were concerns about the letter's authorship and its gradual recognition and use by the church generally. These facts need to be considered when seeking answers to questions about who wrote the book, when it was written, for whom, and why.

1. Author

The author of this book identifies himself in his opening greeting (1:1) as "James," or in Greek *Iakobos*, a transliteration of the Hebrew name familiar from the Old Testament as "Jacob." Since "Jacob"/"James" was a common Jewish name in the first century (there are five or more different men named "James" in the New Testament itself), the question naturally arises as to the precise identity of the "James" who wrote this book. Unfortunately, the author does not give us any clues regarding his personal biography other than including himself among the "teachers" (3:1) of the church.

The traditional identification of the author since the period of the church fathers is that this James was the brother of Jesus (Mark 6:3; Gal. 1:19) and an early leader of the church in Jerusalem (Acts 15:13; 21:18; Gal. 2:9), who became known as "James the Just." Three arguments generally offered to support this identification may be considered here. (1) James does not seek to identify himself by the use of a patronymic (a name indicating one's father or ancestor, such as "son of Zebedee" or "son of Alphaeus" [Matt. 10:2, 3]) or any specific title (such as "apostle"). This decision suggests that the author was well known and perhaps that he was not one of the original disciples, both of which were true of James the Just. (2) It is often suggested that only someone with the prominence and influence of James the Just could have written in the authoritative tone found in this letter (containing more than fifty imperative verbs within its 108 verses). (3) The theology and language of the letter with its Jewish-Christian characteristics are consistent with what is known about James the Just from Acts and Galatians.

Although these arguments do support the possibility that the letter was written by James the Just, they are far from conclusive. One can never draw firm conclusions from what someone fails to say that might have been expected (so-called "arguments from silence"), such as in this case, the absence of titles or other personal references. Whether the earliest Christian readers of this letter actually recognized it as authoritative teaching by one of the "pillars" of the church (Gal. 2:9) is at least questionable since it was among the last books to be accepted by the church into the canon of Scriptures, in part because of doubts about whether it was written by an apostle. Finally, similarities of language or thought between this letter and statements in Acts attributed to James the Just are too limited to be of much help. Nevertheless, many Catholic and conservative commentators maintain that James the Just is the probable author of this letter.

Most critical scholars, however, have held that the letter is pseudonymous, written by someone else who uses James the Just's name to give added authority to his work. Some of the arguments offered for this position are no longer as persuasive as they once might have been. For example, it was argued that James the Just would have lacked both the fluency in Greek and the literary ability to write this letter, which is generally considered among the best literary Greek within the New Testament. But recent findings regarding the ability of the Jewish population of Palestine to speak Greek and the possibility that James might have been assisted by a secretary have rendered this argument inconclusive at best. A major weakness with this view is that most ancient pseudonymous writings go to great lengths to link explicitly the work to the person whose name is used. As we have already seen, such references to the traditions about James the Just are entirely lacking in this letter.

The weakening of arguments in favor of pseudonymity, however, does not directly support the traditional view of authorship. The chief problem with the position that James the Just wrote this letter remains, namely, its date (see the fuller discussion below). The presence within the letter of some features that seem to predate James's death along with other indications of a period later than his death have led two evangelical commentators (P. Davids and R. Martin) to conclude that although the letter contains materials that originated in the preaching of James, the letter as it appears in the New Testament was written by one of his disciples sometime after he was executed by the high priest Ananus II in A.D. 62 (see Josephus, *Antiquities* 20.9.1 [197–203]).

However, a third possibility remains, namely, that the author was indeed named "James" but is otherwise unknown to us from early Christian tradition. This proposal would explain why there are no explicit attempts to connect the author with traditions about James the Just and would permit a time of writing after his martyrdom. If the author was not an early apostle or widely known in the church, it would also help explain the delay in acknowledging its canonicity because of doubts about its apostolic origin.

Ultimately, however, James did not base his authority to write this letter on his personal identity, but rather on his status as "a servant of God and of the Lord Jesus Christ" (1:1). That credential was the basis for his claim to authority both with his original audience and with modern Christian believers (see commentary).

2. Date and Place of Writing

The letter of James has been variously dated as the earliest of the New Testament writings, as among the latest, and as somewhere in between. Obviously those who identify the author as James the Just must date the letter before A.D. 62 (see above). Many of these scholars place the book prior to the "Jerusalem Council" (Acts 15) and so date it in the mid-40s. Others are persuaded that the discussion of faith and deeds in 2:14–26 presupposes Paul's teaching about justification by faith and so date the letter to the late 50s.

There are indeed striking parallels between the discussions of the relationship of "faith" and "deeds" (Greek, *ergon*) to salvation in 2:14–26 and Romans 3:21–4:25, including common examples (Abraham, James 2:21–23; Rom. 4:1–22), shared proof-texts (James 2:23; Rom. 4:3, 22 all cite Gen. 15:6), and similar phrasing (compare "a person is justified by works and not faith alone" [James 2:24, lit.] and "faith without works is dead" [2:26, lit.] with "a person is justified by faith without works of the law" [Rom. 3:28, lit.]). If there is even indirect influence between Paul and James at this point, then the letter's date is related to whether Paul is responding to James (this letter is early), James is responding to Paul (a date after the mid-first century), or the debate is not directly between Paul and James (suggesting a late first-century date).

This third possibility describes the general consensus among current scholarship, namely that James is responding to a misunderstood or misapplied conception of Paul's teaching. Paul taught that proper Christian deeds would be a product of the life of faith and salvation (Phil. 2:12–13), although such works contributed nothing to a person's justification (Rom. 3:28; cf. Eph. 2:8–9). Certain "libertarian" groups that came after Paul took his teaching to an extreme. They held that as long as one had faith in Christ (that is, believed the correct things about his deity and work in bringing about forgiveness), it did not matter whether one's acts were good or evil. Paul had himself anticipated this abuse and flatly rejected it (Rom. 6:1–2). It is against this same misunderstanding of the gospel that James argues when he states "deeds" are the evidence of one's faith (James 2:18). Thus, James's disagreement is not with Paul, but with those who have either misunderstood or abused Paul's teachings.

If this reconstruction of the historical context of the discussion in James 2:14–26 is correct, it suggests a date for writing this letter later than the mid-first century. Time must be allowed not only for the circulation of Paul's ideas and letters, but also for the development and circulation of the misapplication that James then sought to counter. Thus, this letter was probably written in the last quarter of the first century by a James other than James the Just (see "Author"). Such a date is in keeping with the absence of quotations from this letter ɒy the church fathers prior to the late second ːentury and its late acceptance into the New Testament canon.

The letter of James provides no obvious ndications of its place of origin. Many commentators who hold to the traditional view of uthorship by James the Just have argued that number of the images and figures of speech n the letter suggest a Palestinian provenance. Among the most commonly cited examples re sirocco winds (1:11), fire of Gehenna (NIV 'hell," 3:6), saline springs (3:11), and "the utumn [early] and spring [latter] rains" (5:7). The value of these images for indicating actual xperiences of the author, however, is underut by their presence in earlier literary sources.

Other hints of a Palestinian origin may be ound in the relationship of the letter to other arly Christian traditions. There are similaries between the ethical teachings in this letter nd the so-called "Q" sayings of Jesus preerved in the gospels of Matthew and Luke, nd most scholars hold that "Q" originated in 'alestine. Also, the fact that the earliest quoations from the letter of James and that the nost consistent support and use of it are found n the writings of Origen and other Alexanrian and Palestinian fathers of the late-second hrough fourth centuries may indicate that the etter first circulated in that region. Given the bsence of any indications that the letter orignated outside Palestine, a Palestinian proveance seems the most plausible.

3. Recipients

This letter is addressed to "the twelve tribes cattered among the nations" (lit., "in the disersion/Diaspora"; 1:1). The reference is learly symbolic since the tribal structure of srael had ceased having any literal twelvefold spect from at least the time of the Assyrian onquest of the northern kingdom in 722 B.C. The question then becomes how far does ames extend the metaphorical element of his lesignation for his readers?

The most "literal" interpretation of the saluation is that copies of the letter were sent to ews ("the twelve tribes") who were living outide Palestine ("scattered among the nations"; f. John 7:35). However, since the letter is bviously not an evangelistic tract intended to onvert Jews to Christianity, this understandng may be quickly set aside. The recipients are presented as already having faith in Jesus Christ (2:1), and thus the language about "the twelve tribes" is usually understood as symbolic of the belief that Christians are now the people of God, a new or spiritual Israel.

How literally should the description of being "scattered" be understood? We know that some early Christians thought of themselves as the chosen people of God who had been "dispersed" or "scattered" throughout an evil world and longed to return to their spiritual home with God (1 Peter 1:1; cf. Phil. 3:20; Heb. 11:13; 13:14). Although James is concerned about the distinctions between what is "earthly" and what "comes down from heaven" (3:15), he does not specifically develop this image of Christians as spiritual aliens in an evil world. Consequently, some interpreters who hold the traditional view of authorship have suggested that the letter was sent from Jerusalem to Christians who had been scattered from there by persecution (cf. Acts 8:1; 11:19–20). But again, the history of the letter's acceptance into the canon does not support the conclusion that it was widely disseminated from the beginning.

This commentary will take the position that James did refer to his readers as a "Diaspora" in a metaphorical sense, but that he developed the metaphor in a way that is particular to this letter. James believed that his readers had become "scattered" by "wander[ing] from the truth" (5:19). Just what that "truth" was from which they had wandered and how James hoped to turn them back from this error (5:20) will be discussed below (see "Purpose"). But since James had such particular knowledge and concerns about the recipients, it is probable that the letter was directed to a single congregation with which he had a personal relationship.

The evidence already discussed regarding the letter's date and origin suggests that this congregation was located somewhere in the general region of Palestine. Because of the variety of issues discussed in this short letter—including matters related to rich, poor, and merchant classes (2:1–9, 15–16; 4:13–15; 5:1–6)—the church seems to have spanned a broad range of society, at least in its contacts if not also in its membership. There may also have been some tensions within the congregation over matters of social status and authority (3:1–2; 4:1, 11–12).

4. Purpose

The letter of James has long been recognized as an example of religious paraenesis, that is, ethical instruction rooted in religious beliefs and values. Such literature seeks not only to influence and direct the behavior of its readers, but further to ground their actions in a particular understanding of the world and their place within it. How do these general purposes of this type of literature relate to the specific case of the letter of James?

James's ultimate objective is to change the behavior of his readers, both by denouncing evil actions (called "sins of commission" by later theologians) and by identifying even the failure to do the good things that one might have done as a sin (4:17, later called "sins of omission"). He identifies the root problem with their behavior as being related to "wisdom" (especially 3:13–18). He contrasts wisdom that "is earthly, unspiritual, of the devil" and that leads to evil activity with "the wisdom that comes from heaven," which leads to behavior reminiscent of what Paul calls the "fruit of the Spirit" (compare 3:17–18 with Gal. 5:22–23). If believers are to succeed in living in a way that pleases God both by what they avoid and what they do, they must have this heavenly rather than earthly wisdom.

James tells his readers that the only way to receive this wisdom is as a gift from God (1:5). Their problem is that they have hesitated to ask God for this gift, apparently because they believe that God might send trials into their lives as a way of testing them and teaching them wisdom (see comments on 1:2–4). James reminds them that "every good and perfect gift" comes from God (1:17), and that God is not the source of temptations in their lives (1:13–14). By focusing on God's goodness, they can have the faith to ask for the wisdom they need and to trust that God will generously give them wisdom "without finding fault" (1:5). Those who "doubt" that God gives only good gifts are "double-minded," both trusting God to provide the wisdom they need and fearing that God uses trials and temptations (1:13 and comments) as the means for instructing them in this wisdom. Such 'double-minded doubters' will not receive anything from God and will remain unable to live a life that is consistently pleasing to God (1:6–8).

Thus, James's foundational purpose in writing is to bring back his readers, who have "wander[ed] from the truth" (5:19) that God is the giver of "every good and perfect gift . . . who does not change like shifting shadows" (1:17). In this way they will have the faith to ask God for the gift of wisdom they need to turn "from the error of [their] way," both in terms of missed opportunities to perform God's will and sinful actions (1:27), and so "cover over a multitude of sins" (5:20). Proper trust in God's goodness is for James the prerequisite to behavior that both pleases God and shows his love and goodness to others.

OUTLINE

As with many New Testament letters, the general flow of James is from a more theological discussion to a more pragmatic treatment of practical matters facing the readers. It is the opening theological discussion that provides the context and basis for the exhortations that follow. Although James does follow this basic structure, the fact that even his theological opening is so practical in its concerns has sometimes made the pattern more difficult to discern. Nevertheless, we have already seen something of how these theological and practical concerns relate to the purpose of the letter; it remains to isolate these concerns within the structure of the letter itself.

Following the conventional epistolary introduction, James develops his letter in four basic movements. The first unit (1:2–21) develops his broader concerns about his readers' beliefs concerning the nature of the relationship between God and Christian believers. He encourages them to trust God for the wisdom they need rather than trying to learn it through their responses to the hardships of life. In the second unit (1:22–2:26), James begins to focus his diagnosis of their problem. He shows them how their actions reveal that they do in fact still lack wisdom (cf. 1:5) and emphasizes again that any form of belief that does not result in actions consistent with God's will cannot provide spiritual life (2:14, 26). In the third (3:1–4:10) and fourth (4:11–5:20) units he deals with the readers' responsibilities for their own actions and for the spiritual lives of others, respectively.

This understanding of the movement of the letter is represented in the following outline:

COMMENTARY

1. Salutation (1:1)

For discussion of the identity of James and the recipients of this letter, see the "Introduction." James identifies himself simply as a "servant" or "slave" (Greek, *doulos*) of God and of the "Lord" Jesus. This imagery of "slave"/"lord" does two things as he opens his letter: It establishes his authority with his readers and introduces what will be a major underlying theme of the letter.

The assertion that James's self-designation as a "servant" establishes his authority may strike many modern readers as somewhat strange, since in more recent slave economies the status of slave certainly did not bestow authority on a person. However, within Greco-Roman culture slaves could achieve a measure of authority and social status if their master used them as personal representatives. In such cases, the slave received ancillary social status commensurate with the status of the master and could exercise the master's authority. Thus, to be the "servant of God and of the Lord Jesus Christ" was to hold a position of honor and considerable authority within a Christian community.

Nevertheless, even within that culture slaves lost their independence to the will and desires of their masters. It is this fact that hints at one of James's major themes, namely, that a Christian's actions are to be determined by the will of God. This theme is stated most explicitly in 4:13–15, but it underlies all of his discussions of wisdom, the word, and deeds.

Rather than following their own "evil desire," which will "give birth to sin" and ultimately to "death" (1:14–15), they should "listen to the word" to learn what God's will is and then "do what it says" (1:22). By describing himself as a "servant of God," James indicates he has accepted God's will as his own.

2. Trials, Wisdom, and the Word (1:2–21)

As noted in the introduction ("Outline"), James begins his letter by diagnosing what he understands to be the problems with his readers' beliefs about their relationship with God. They believed that God used "trials" as a means of instructing and correcting them so as to make them "mature and complete, not lacking anything" (1:4) and ultimately earning them "the crown of life" (1:12). James suggests, however, that "trials" serve a different purpose in the Christian life. Rather than being opportunities for *self*-improvement, trials serve to reveal our need for and dependence on God and drive us to ask God for the things we need. He assures his readers that God indeed "gives generously to all without finding fault" (1:5). Trials do not teach Christians wisdom; rather, trials convince us to forsake our self-reliance and to "humbly accept the word planted in [us by God], which can save" us (1:21).

2.1. Reasons for Rejoicing in Trials (1:2–12)

2.1.1. The Purpose of Trials (1:2–4). James begins his letter by discussing the relationship between the trials of current life and the Christian faith. The NIV follows the consensus among translators in interpreting the opening phrase as an exhortation for the readers to respond to trials with joy because the testing of their faith ultimately serves a positive purpose by increasing their endurance and maturity. However, the Greek verb translated "consider" could be an indicative rather than an imperative; that is, James may be commenting on their usual response to such trials ("You consider it pure joy . . .") rather than encouraging them to respond in a new way ("Consider it pure joy . . ."). Usually Greek verbs have different forms and spellings in the indicative and imperative moods, but in the case of this verb *(hegeomai)* the forms are the same. Which sense, then, did James intend?

Most translators and commentators hav preferred interpreting the verb as an exhorta tion because there are so many imperativ verbs within this letter (the exact numbe varies among interpreters between about 5 and 59 in 108 verses). However, a person reac ing or hearing this letter for the first tim would not have known what was coming Since in verse 3 James emphasizes the knowl edge that the readers' already have ("becaus you know that . . ."), the indicative mood gain support from the immediate context. It is fur ther supported by the fact that James include among their knowledge the idea that onc "perseverance" has completed its work the will "not lack anything" (v. 4). At the sam time he asserts that "if any of you lacks wis dom," it must be received as a gift from Go (1:5; see below on 1:5–8).

Thus, James begins his letter by describin his readers' beliefs about trials and the testin of their faith and their responses to them. The believed that the difficult experiences of lif provide opportunities for spiritual growth an development, an idea expressed in other place in Scripture as well (cf. Rom. 5:3–5; 1 Pete 1:6–7). It is for this reason that they were abl to respond with "pure joy" when they encoun tered such circumstances. Nevertheless, Jame seems to have some concerns that his reader are not fully carrying through with thi process, since verse 4 can also be translated "But perseverance must finish its work if yo are going to be perfect and complete, lackin nothing."

In what follows it will become clearer tha James does not share all their beliefs about th testing of faith, particularly regarding the ori gins of these trials (see esp. 1:14–15), or tha perseverance in the face of such trials is all tha is required to reach spiritual maturity (v. 5). I is important to notice, however, that Jame does not tell them that their joyful response i itself out of place. The assurance that w belong to God and that we are protected b God's care (Rom. 8:31–39) is a source of jo and peace in the trials of this life (cf. Matt 5:11–12; Phil. 4:4–7). Their problem was tha they had put too much reliance on their ow abilities to learn God's wisdom through endur ing the hardships of life.

These opening verses of the letter thus serv as a warning against spiritual pride. Spiritua

JAMES AND THE SAYINGS OF JESUS

James shows a remarkable familiarity with the words spoken by Jesus in the Gospels, especially in the Sermon on the Mount (Mt 5–7). This chart depicts the many parallels between James and Jesus that scholars have noted both parallels in words and in themes.

Theme	James	Gospels
Joy in persecution	1:2	Mt 5:11–12; Lk 6:22–23
A person's goal of being perfect and mature	1:4	Mt 5:48
Asking and receiving from God	1:5	Mt 7:7; Lk 11:19
Asking in faith and not doubting	1:6	Mt 21:21–22; Mk 11:22–24
Reversal of proud and humble	1:9–10; 4:6, 10	Mt 23:12; Lk 14:11; Lk 18:14
Sun scorching plants and they wither	1:11	Mt 13:6; Mk 4:7
Blessings for perseverance under trial	1:12	Mt 5:11–12
God as the giver of gifts	1:17	Mt 7:11; Lk 11:13
Not only listen to, but do the Word of God	1:22; 2:14, 17	Mt 7:21–27; Lk 6:46–49
Compassion for those who are needy and hurting	1:27; 2:15	Mt 25:34–36
The poor to inherit the kingdom	2:5	Mt 5:3; Lk 6:20
Love your neighbor as yourself	2:8	Mt 22:39; Mk 12:31
Not breaking the least commandment	2:10	Mt 5:19
Judgment on those who show no mercy	2:13	Mt 18:23–34; 25:41–46
Through obedience becoming friends of God	2:23	Jn 15:13–15
Teachers judged more strictly	3:1	Mk 9:38, 40; Lk 20:45, 47
We are judged by what we say	3:2	Mt 12:37
What corrupts is what comes out of our mouths	3:6	Mt 15:11, 18; Mk 7:15, 20; Lk 6:45
Same source cannot produce good and evil	3:11–12	Mt 7:16–18; Lk 6:43–44
Peacemakers blessed by God	3:18	Mt 5:9
A (spiritually) adulterous people	4:4	Mt 12:39; Mk 8:38
Friendship with the world means enmity with God (or vice versa)	4:4	Jn 15:18–21
Laughter to be turned into mourning	4:6	Lk 6:25
Not judging others	4:11–12; 5:9	Mt 7:1–2
God can both save and destroy	4:12	Mt 10:28
Foolishness of planning the future apart from God	4:13–14	Lk 12:18–20
Punishment for those who know God's will but refuse to do it	4:17	Lk 12:47
Woe to the rich	5:1	Lk 6:24
Wealth removed by moth and corrosion	5:2–3	Mt 6:19–20
Self-indulgence with no concern for the poor	5:5	Lk 16:19–20, 25
Returning Judge is at the door	5:9	Mt 24:33; Mk 13:39
Persecution of prophets	5:10	Mt 5:10–12
Do not swear oaths	5:12	Mt 5:33–37
Restoring an erring brother sister	5:19–29	Mt 18:15

growth and maturity cannot be achieved through one's own efforts. No matter how joyful or patient a person's response is to the hardships of life, spiritual maturity and completeness ("not lacking anything") cannot be obtained through human determination and perseverance. As James will emphasize in the following verses, spiritual wisdom can only be obtained as a gift from God. Since it is a gift, then there can be no grounds for pride or boasting (compare Eph. 2:8–9). If there is any hidden blessing in the experience of trials, it is not that they provide opportunities for personal or spiritual *self*-improvement. Trials can bring joy because they remind us of our need for God and motivate us to rely on his strength rather than our own (compare 2 Cor. 12:7–10).

2.1.2. Asking for the Gift of Wisdom (1:5–8). James believed that the only way to gain true, spiritual wisdom was as a gift from God (v. 5). Since it is a "wisdom that comes from heaven" (3:17), it must originate with God; any wisdom that originates in ourselves can ultimately only be "earthly, unspiritual," and may even be "of the devil" (3:15). He agrees with his readers that "perseverance" during "the testing of your faith" does provide benefits such as "maturity" (1:3–4), but such cannot make up for a lack of heavenly wisdom.

What is at issue in these verses, then, is a long-standing question of emphasis within the Israelite and early Jewish wisdom traditions. Some of the sages stressed the idea that God uses hardships in this life as a means of correction and discipline for the people of God (Job 5:17; cf. James 5:11), especially with the expectation that one result of this discipline will be learning wisdom. It was perhaps because James's readers likewise emphasized this aspect of the earlier tradition that they had been able to "face trials" with "pure joy" (1:2–4 and comments).

James, however, stresses a different strand of the wisdom tradition. He aligns himself with those sages who emphasized the hardships of life are not the "school of hard knocks" in which one learns wisdom, but rather are occasions that cause believers to recognize their complete dependence on God and which drive them to ask God for the wisdom that can only be obtained as a divine gift. The chief example of this emphasis in the Scriptures is Solomon, who, faced with the responsibility of ruling over the chosen people, asked God for the gift of wisdom (1 Kings 3:7–9; cf. Prov. 2:6; Wisd. Sol. 8:21; 9:6; Sirach 1:1). This divine gift was sometimes even referred to as "the spirit of wisdom" (Wisd. Sol. 7:7) and was associated with the coming of God's "holy spirit from on high" (Wisd. Sol. 9:17, NRSV), though James himself does not develop this specific notion of "wisdom" as a spiritual gift.

James emphasized that God "gives [wisdom] generously to all without finding fault," so long as they ask "with faith" (*en pistei*; James uses a prepositional phrase, not a verbal construction, as the NIV's "must believe" suggests) rather than "doubt." But what does "faith" mean in this context? Many interpreters have concluded that "faith" for James is a matter of believing certain correct things about God, having a "proper theology" (cf. 2:18–19). This understanding at first seems to be supported by the contrast he makes with "doubt," that is, an intellectual uncertainty. The problem with this understanding in verse 6 is that James here relates "doubt" not to uncertainty, but to "double-mindedness" and "instability" (v. 8).

James has developed the image of "a double-minded [*dipsychos*] man" from the Jewish concept of a "divided heart" or "two inclinations." The issue here is not being torn by two contradictory ideas or beliefs, but being torn by two desires—a desire for or inclination toward what is good and a competing desire for or inclination toward what is evil. One implication for making requests from God that can be drawn from this idea is that what one asks for must be consistent with good desire rather than evil (see 4:3 and comments).

James develops another implication here in verses 5–8. When he states that one must ask for wisdom without "doubt," he means that one must make the request without reservation. Thus, the contrast with "faith" focuses on the usual meaning of that word in the common Greek of the first century, namely, "trust." When one asks God for "wisdom," one must wholeheartedly trust (lit., "ask with faith") that God will "give generously to all without finding fault," and not both trust and distrust God from a divided heart ("not doubt").

But what is it that causes "doubt" in the sense of distrust? Precisely the idea that God may respond to the request for "wisdom" not with a "good and perfect gift" (1:17) but by "finding fault" and sending "trials of many kinds" (1:2), so that one may learn "wisdom" (cf. 1:13 and comments). Those who think they must gain "wisdom" by their own efforts in the struggles of life cannot receive wisdom simply as God's gift (v. 7), and so will remain "unstable" (v. 8).

What James has not yet done is to fill out what he means by the word "wisdom" itself. As will become clearer as the letter continues, he understands "wisdom" in practical terms. It is an understanding of the will of God that informs and directs all of one's actions in life (4:13–15). Indeed, James will identify wisdom with the "word of truth" by which God "chose to give us birth" (1:18). It is a "word planted in you, which can save you" by conforming the will of the divided human heart to God's will (1:21 and comments). Since the gift of wisdom is so closely tied to the new "birth" from God and to salvation, it is not surprising that James begins his letter by emphasizing the only means by which one can obtain this "wisdom that comes from heaven" (3:17).

2.1.3. Taking Pride in the "Crown of Life" (1:9–12). Another tradition derived from Israelite and early Jewish wisdom reflection that plays an important role in the letter of James is the so-called "piety of the poor." This tradition emphasized that God has a special concern for the poor (1:27; 2:16 and comments) and will intervene at the end of time to judge the rich for their exploitative social and economic practices (5:1–9). James uses the effects of the hot, dry sirocco winds upon young vegetation to paint a vivid image of this impending judgment (v. 11).

It is because "God opposes the proud but gives grace to the humble" (4:6, citing Prov. 3:34) that James can offer the advice in 1:9–10 that so blatantly contradicts the normal reactions of human society and conventional wisdom. Thus, while "the brother in humble circumstances" can "take pride in his high position" (v. 9) that God will ultimately provide (v. 12), the rich, who now boast about their wealth and power (cf. 4:13–16), can only "take pride" in an ironic sense since the basis of their boasts and pride "will pass away" (v. 10; for another possible reason why the rich can "take pride in his low position," see comments on 5:1–9).

Another aspect of the "piety of the poor" was its acceptance of the strand of the wisdom tradition that saw the trials of this life as a means of divine instruction. Since we have seen that James's readers held that view (though James himself had some reservations about it; see comments on 1:5–8), it is reasonable to conclude that they tended to identify themselves with the "brother in humble circumstances."

The irony is, as later sections of the letter will show, that the readers were quite status conscious and did not always avail themselves of opportunities to demonstrate God's concern for those in need (2:14–17). They already "take pride in [their] high position," perhaps considering themselves morally superior to the "rich" even while identifying themselves with the trappings of status and power (see 2:1–13 and comments). They even think about their own salvation by using an image of social status, "the crown of life." This crown is the *stephanos*, the laurel leaf crown that was awarded for victory in athletic contests or was worn as a badge of social honor, as distinct from the *diadema*, the crown of royalty (Rev. 19:12). Thus, even as James affirms God's judgment on those who boast in their self-reliance and gain riches by exploiting others, he in a subtle way draws attention to and expresses concern about his readers' desires for wealth and questions the depth of their allegiance with the poor.

These verses, in other words, serve both to affirm that the glorious blessings prepared for those who faithfully love God are not to be compared with the hardships of this life (v. 12; cf. Rom. 8:18, 31–39) and to warn against a devotion to God based solely upon the hope for material reward in the future. Actions that arise ultimately from a person's desire to fulfill his or her personal pleasure will eventually lead to materialism and away from God, even if that personal pleasure is "spiritualized" as a "heavenly reward." People can only find true spiritual peace when they are motivated by a desire to please God that arises from genuine love for God and not love for the spiritual and physical blessings that God can provide. As Augustine said, "Our hearts are restless, O God, until they rest in you" (*Confessions*, 1.1.1).

2.2. The Origins of Spiritual Death and Life (1:13–21)

2.2.1. The Internal Origin of Temptation (1:13–16). Within this paragraph, James directly confronts his readers' belief that God uses trials to teach wisdom, although this is not always clear in English translation. The Greek verb *peirazo*, translated by English "tempt" in these verses of the NIV, is the cognate of the noun *peirasmos*, translated "trials" in 1:2, 12. In fact, because of these earlier uses of the noun it is most likely that first-time readers of the letter would have understood the Greek as: "When tested, no one should say, 'God is testing me.'" It is only James's later statement that "desire . . . gives birth to sin" (v.15) that would seem to require the narrower meaning of "tempt" here in verse 13. At a minimum we can say that when one states, "God is tempting me," these "temptations" are considered to be specific instances of the "trials" that serve to "test" their "faith" and instruct them in "wisdom."

James counters this view by emphatically asserting that "God cannot be tempted by evil, nor does he tempt anyone" (v. 13). God does not tempt or test people to instruct them in wisdom (as some of the sages taught); rather, "God . . . gives generously to all without finding fault" (1:5 and comments).

But James does not go to an opposite extreme and locate the origin of all temptations and trials with Satan; rather, he places the primary responsibility on our own "evil desire" (v. 14; cf. 4:1). To the extent that believers try to locate the source of all their temptations in any external source, whether God or Satan, it distracts them from their real problem—themselves. The only way a person can avoid the instability of "double-mindedness" (1:8) is for this internal "evil desire" to be replaced by transforming a person's nature (see 1:21 and comments) so that his or her will is established by God's desire. The attempt to locate all our problems outside of ourselves is nothing less than deception (v. 16).

For James, the will or desire is the ultimate source of every action. He develops this idea through the imagery of conception and birth: "After desire has conceived, it gives birth to sin; and sin, when it is full-grown, gives birth to death" (v. 15). The fact that human desires ultimately lead to death is itself proof that such temptations do not originate with God and that their character and consequences are fundamentally evil. God's will or desire, in the sense of the capacity to will certain things, is fundamentally different than the divided human will: "For God cannot be tempted by evil" (v. 13). Christians can "believe and not doubt" (1:6), that is, have complete trust in God, because God's will can only be good, never evil. James further emphasizes this point in the next paragraph by explicitly contrasting the sequence of human "evil desire . . . sin . . . death" with the results born of God's desire.

2.2.2. Birth Through the Word (1:17–18). By stressing that "every good and perfect gift is from above" (v. 17), James emphasizes two points crucial to his argument in this opening chapter. (1) He makes it clear that a "perfect gift" such as wisdom, required to make a person "mature" (1:4; "mature" in 1:4 and "perfect" in 1:17 translate the same Greek word, *teleios*), cannot be received through human effort, but can only come from God. (2) In stating that "every" such gift has its origins in God, James also affirms his conviction that *only* good gifts come from God. That God is "the Father of the heavenly lights, who does not change like shifting shadows," probably alludes to astronomical phenomena such as solar or lunar eclipses or the phases of the moon. Since God's will does not vacillate or pass through phases of giving good gifts and bad gifts (cf. Luke 11:11–13), a person can trust that every gift from God will be good and will not result in either temptation or trial (1:13 and comments).

God's will differs from the human will not only in its perfect goodness but also in its effect. Whereas the human will, because of its inclination toward evil arising from our sinful nature, leads to actions that ultimately result in death, God's will leads ultimately to life. James, in fact, contrasts these different effects by directly paralleling the three-stage processes that begin in the human and divine wills.

With regard to the human process, "after desire has conceived, it gives birth to sin; and sin . . . gives birth to death" (1:15). With respect to the divine will, on the other hand, God "chose to give us birth through the word of truth, that we might be a kind of firstfruits" (v. 18). In each instance one's will through an intermediate action (either human "sin" or God's "word of truth") has clear and definite consequences ("death" and "birth" respectively). James will hint at the specifics of the way in which God uses the "word of truth" (i.e., God's gift of "wisdom," 1:5) to "give us birth" in 1:21. This striking contrast between actions that arise from the human will and actions that arise from the "word of truth" is a major feature of the remainder of the letter.

Because so much more heat than light has been shed on the issue of gender specific names and metaphors for God in recent years, it is important to pause for a moment and consider the images James uses here in verses 17–18. He begins by referring to God as "the Father of the heavenly lights," using the mas-

:uline parental imagery that has become the ısual Christian name for the first person of the Trinity, God "the Father." James then effortessly shifts to feminine parental imagery for God when he speaks of God's choice "to give ıs birth," using a Greek word (*apokueo*) typi:ally used to refer to the process of a woman's abor and delivery (cf. 1:15). Thus, James's anguage in these verses pictures God netaphorically as both father and mother.

The point to be drawn from this is not that God's nature is some kind of androgynous mixure of male and female, but that both the mas:uline and feminine images for God in Scripture (and there are many of both) are netaphors that describe the person of God in ways that humans can understand. Gender dis:inction tends to be fundamental to our concept of "person," at least in Western cultures. Consider the debate about whether the Holy Spirit may be referred to as "it" in English; most reject this because the neuter pronoun has a strong "impersonal" nuance, and the Spirit is definitely a person. But neither "maleness" nor "femaleness" is a property of God, and Scripture reminds us that God transcends these qualities of human existence by using both masculine and feminine images to reveal God to us.

2.2.3. Saved by the Implanted Word (1:19–21). Like when reading a mystery novel, things often appear clearer and more significant when we read the conclusion first. This strategy is particularly helpful in making sense of this paragraph of James's letter since the final clause is both the capstone and key to what precedes it. James admonishes his readers to "humbly accept the word planted in you, which can save you" (v. 21; lit., "save your souls").

This exhortation sums up many of the themes raised by James to this point in his letter. (1) Note that it is the "word ... which can save" a person's "soul" or "life" (Greek, *psyche*), recalling that it was "through the word of truth" that God "chose to give us birth" (1:18). James hints at how the word accomplishes this by describing it as the word "planted in you." The Greek word for this "implanting" (*emphytos*) is related to the word for "nature" (*physis*); thus, it is the "implanting" of the word into a person that transforms his or her nature (cf. Jer. 31:33). The divided human will (1:8) is inclined not only toward good things but also to toward "evil desire" and "sin." It can only escape "death" (1:14–15) if its nature is transformed by God's "word" as the "wisdom" that conforms our will to God's will (cf. Rom. 12:2).

(2) The fact that one must "humbly accept" this word underscores yet again that it must be received as a gift (1:5) rather than learned through personal endurance of "trials" (1:2 and comments) or other accomplishments about which one might "take pride" (1:10). Those who humbly accept the word recognize that their "high position" is a gift given by God (1:9). As Mozart and others have dedicated their works: *soli Deo gloria*, "to God alone be the glory."

This emphasis on the necessity to internalize God's word adds additional meaning to James's exhortation that "everyone should be quick to listen, slow to speak and slow to become angry" (v. 19). He is not simply repeating the conventional wisdom of "mind your manners," but also more specifically encouraging Christians to be "quick to listen" to God's word. We need to be reminded to be "slow to speak," not only because our words can sometimes be hurtful to other people, but also because we sometimes speak rashly and incorrectly about God (e.g., "God is tempting me," 1:13).

James's admonition to be "slow to become angry" once again contrasts the result of human desire, "man's anger," with God's will, "the righteous life that God desires" (v. 20). Only by having our divided nature unified by a will to do God's word implanted in us can we "get rid of all moral filth and the evil that is so prevalent" (v. 21) not only externally in the world in which we live, but also internally within our own "evil desire" that "gives birth to sin and ... death" (1:15).

3. Faithfully Doing the Word (1:22–2:26)

Having to this point shown why his readers need to be transformed by internalizing God's word, in the next major division of his letter James turns his attention to the consequences that should be evident in their lives. He connects such terms as "word," "law," and "deeds" to make the point that one's deeds should be an expression of the changes God has made within the person (cf. Luke 6:45). This unit reaches its climax in 2:26, "As the body without the spirit is dead, so faith without deeds is dead." Although some interpreters (including such a notable theologian as Martin Luther) have been concerned that James's argument could lead to a Christian legalism where salvation is obtained by deeds rather than through faith in Jesus Christ, this danger is lessened when the whole pattern of his beliefs is kept in view.

James is concerned that Christians have a living faith, by which he means two things. (1) It must be a faith that can "save" the person (2:14), that is, a faith capable of bringing spiritual life rather than death. Since James has already emphasized that the "word" of God is what generates spiritual life (1:18, 21), saving faith is clearly tied to the wisdom that must be received from God as a gift (1:5). Thus, faith is not itself a deed or a work; it is not a mental exercise such as has been characterized as the ability to "believe ten impossible things before breakfast." Faith is the willingness to have complete trust in God for what one needs spiritually and in every other aspect of life.

(2) Christians must have a living faith in the sense that they live it out in their daily actions. Professing trust or belief in God, James insists, is not enough. Faith must be demonstrated by what one desires and does (2:18), because these things arise from the word—God's will—that has been implanted in them (1:21). Thus, even though James relates this "word" to "the perfect law" (1:22–25), he is not advocating a legalistic salvation. One does not build one's own faith and earn God's gifts by doing things that are pleasing to God. Rather, one can only do God's will once that will has been implanted within a person who trusts God to give it as a "good and perfect gift" (1:17), instead of trying to learn wisdom by her or his own efforts.

3.1. Acting Consistently With the Word (1:22–2:13)

3.1.1. Living What One Hears (1:22–25). To genuinely "accept the word planted in you" (1:21), you must "do what it says" (lit., "be a doer of [the] word," v. 22). James insists that those who "merely listen to the word" (lit., who are "only hearers") have deceived themselves. Although they have accepted the word in one ear, he suggests that it has simply gone out the other if it does not produce a lasting effect in the hearers. His simile for this experience is that of a person who studies himse[lf] in a mirror, and yet he "immediately forge[ts] what he looks like" once he steps away from [it] (v. 24). When everything appears in place an[d] no further preparation is anticipated, we forg[et] what we have seen in the mirror because ou[r] appearance does not generally change how w[e] live our lives.

James continues the visual imagery by hi[s] description of the person who sees himself i[n] the "perfect law" (v. 25). Rather than "go[ing] away and immediately forget[ting]" what h[e] has seen, he "continues" to act in accordanc[e] with that law. This person is not a "forgetfu[l] hearer" (lit. trans.), but a "doer of the work" (li[t]. trans.). By returning to the earlier auditor[y] imagery ("hearer"), James is able to establis[h] clearly the link between "doers of the word" (v. 22) and "doers of the work" (v. 25). Thus, th[e] work or "deeds" (Greek, *ergon*) that James wi[ll] discuss in chapter 2 are a person's response t[o] the word given by God. Though a person "wi[ll] be blessed in what he does" in response to th[e] word, the initial blessing of the gift of the wor[d] itself is not earned by what one does.

One other aspect of James's imagery i[n] these verses warrants special comment. H[e] describes the word as "the perfect law tha[t] gives freedom." We do not normally conceiv[e] of "law" as something that grants the freedom to act, but rather as something that prohibits o[r] restricts certain actions. Too often this attitud[e] about "law" colors our perceptions of God'[s] will as well. Our first instinct is to think abou[t] the sins we must avoid and to characterize ou[r] standards of piety first and foremost by wha[t] we do not do (as my mother has ofte[n] described her own Pentecostal upbringing as an adolescent, "We don't drink, or smoke, o[r] date those who do"). James, however, challenges us to see God's law as something "tha[t] gives freedom."

But freedom from what? In part, freedom from our own "evil desire" that entices and deceives us into actions that lead to both difficulties in this life and ultimately spiritual death (1:14–15). If we are to be free to be what God has created us to be, then we must be internally transformed by God's word/law so that our desires are united in and with God's will (cf. Jer. 31:33; Rom. 8:2).

3.1.2 Pure and Faultless Religion (1:26–27). Echoing his earlier admonition to be "slow to speak" (1:19) and anticipating more extended discussions of human speech that come later (3:2–12; 4:11–16), James here indicates that a sign of whether one's religious piety is acceptable to God is the ability to "keep a tight rein on [the] tongue."

James does include within this admonition a prohibition against malicious or vulgar speech, but the two examples of improper speech that immediately follow this statement within the letter illustrate other abuses of human language that need to be reined in by Christians. (1) Believers must be sure that their speech and actions are consistent with one another. James illustrates this problem by reminding his readers that they have dishonored the very people with whom they believe God is especially concerned by using their language to show favoritism within the community of faith, destroying the unity that is God's will (2:1–5). (2) Human speech can be used as a sign of religious piety and concern even as it serves as a pretext for not undertaking action that God would desire (2:15–16 and comments). Thus, believers should only speak those things that they are willing to put into action; they must "practice what they preach" and not fall into empty religious platitudes. A person who does not control his language in these ways "deceives himself and his religion is worthless" (v. 26).

Even in the area of speech, James emphasizes the need to remember that there are not only sins of commission (i.e., evil actions and associating with impure things—"keep oneself from being polluted by the world"), but also sins of omission (i.e., failure to do those things that God desires be done in his name—"to look after orphans and widows in their distress," v. 27; cf. Matt. 25:37–40). A "pure and faultless" religion in God's eyes is as much a matter of what one does as what one does not do. In part because of its roots in the Holiness revival movements and in part because of its rejection of the "social gospel movement" of the early twentieth century, Pentecostalism has been quick to emphasize personal holiness and slow to speak about social responsibility. James reminds us that it is not a matter of "either . . . or," but of "both . . . and."

3.1.3. An Example of Inconsistency (2:1–9). James now provides a specific example of what it means to be one who does what the word says rather than being one who merely listens to it (see 1:22). The problem is "favoritism" (v. 1), or, to apply his description more directly to modern categories, the discriminatory practice of "classism." That he should choose this particular sin (v. 9) is telling because his readers had utilized the traditional wisdom of the "piety of the poor" to identify themselves as those who, despite their "humble circumstances, ought to take pride in [their] high position" (1:9) because "God [has] chosen those who are poor in the eyes of the world to be rich in faith and to inherit the kingdom" (v. 5). Although they sought to claim for themselves God's special concern for the poor, their own actions revealed that they themselves identified with the rich and powerful and discriminated against the poor.

There has been considerable debate among interpreters regarding the precise purpose of the "meeting" (v. 2) that provides the setting for his example. Ultimately, however, James is not concerned with whether the church has gathered to worship or to address some business or disciplinary action; his concern is with the blatant favoritism shown to the wealthy and the disrespect for the poor (cf. v. 6). Whereas the man "wearing a gold ring and fine clothes" is told, "Here's a good seat for you," the "poor man in shabby clothes" is told, "You stand there," or "Sit on the floor by my feet" (vv. 2–3). Thus, the rich are directed to sit *"here"* among the readers while the poor are segregated in order to "stand *there*" away from the readers, or at least to defer to the readers' superior status by sitting "on the floor" at their feet. By this blatant act of favoritism James is able to subtly expose his readers' true allegiance with the rich and powerful.

James is determined to show that such discrimination is incompatible with genuine "faith" (v. 1 lit. translates, "Do not have the faith of our glorious Lord Jesus Christ with favoritism"), so he offers three arguments against such behavior. These arguments can be reordered to show their relative importance within James's theology. (1) Christians should not give special treatment to the wealthy because they have proven themselves unworthy of such honor. They have exploited and legally harassed Christians, even slandering them for their religious commitment (vv. 6–7; cf. 5:4–6). Those who demonstrate such behavior deserve judgment rather than honor (1:10–11; 5:1–3).

(2) More importantly, Christians should not show any form of favoritism, for "the royal law found in Scripture" commands us, "Love your neighbor as yourself" (v. 8, citing Lev. 19:18).

(3) The ultimate reason for not discriminating against the poor is that "God [has] chosen those who are poor"; it is God's will that they be honored rather than "insulted" (v. 6). Indeed, the argument given by the citation from Leviticus is just a specific example of God's will that they have heard in the word and that they are to do.

Thus, James again emphasizes that we must have our own "evil thoughts" (v. 4) and desires replaced by the wisdom of God's will if we are to avoid sin (see 1:14–15 and comments). "The royal law found in Scripture" (v. 8) is "the perfect law that gives freedom" (1:25) to do what we know God desires, once it has been "planted in" us (1:21). Showing "favoritism" for the wealthy (vv. 1–4) rather than "look[ing] after orphans and widows in their distress" is not the "pure and faultless" religion that is acceptable to "God our Father" (1:27).

Unfortunately, discrimination and prejudice arising from social and economic differences are still all too familiar in our churches. In some respects, it is even more pernicious than the blatant, legally sanctioned and imposed racism of America's past. Many Christians will readily accept members of other racial and ethnic groups so long as they are of their own or higher economic status, but they are suspicious and unaccepting of anyone from the poverty of the inner city. Who is more likely to receive special and favorable attention in our churches, the well-to-do, who can contribute to our ministries and projects, or a homeless person off the streets?

James, in other words, speaks across the centuries to label our "classism" as sin and to remind us that God still chooses "those who are poor in the eyes of the world." If our wills have been conformed to God's will, then we also will choose them and love them as ourselves. But such love requires actions, not just religious platitudes (see 2:15–17).

3.1.4. The Need for Consistency (2:10–13). James now interjects a brief summary comment on the need for consistency in one's words and deeds (see esp. v. 12) before moving on to his second example of failure in this regard among his readers (see comments on 1:22–2:26). Many interpreters have taken James's assertion that "whoever keeps the whole law and yet stumbles at just one point is guilty of breaking all of it" (v. 10), and his announcement that we will "be judged by the law that gives freedom" (v.12), as evidence of the legalistic tendency of his theology. However, this impression arises at least in part because modern, Western cultures have a different understanding of "the law" than what James has in mind.

For modern readers in Western democracies, "the law" is conceived primarily as a formal collection of individual statutes that generally serve to restrict activities. Although we expect in constitutional democracies that these statutes will be consistent with the social contract established within the particular constitution of the government, no one expects that even that foundational document is completely unified in its intent and formulation; the United States' constitution was almost immediately amended by the Bill of Rights. Thus, it strikes us as fundamentally unjust to assert that simply because someone has committed a minor offense they should have the book thrown at them; a parking violation does not make one also guilty of vehicular homicide.

Most Jews in the first century, however, had a much different understanding of "the law." They viewed particularly their religious law as a unified whole, which defined their approach to all of life. In fact it can be argued that the Hebrew word usually translated into English as "law" (*torah*) in most instances is better rendered "instruction." The law taught them how to live "the good life" pleasing to themselves, to other people, and to God. Since the law was a unified whole, ultimately you could no more break only a part of it than you can "just break the stem" of a crystal goblet; the reservoir of the goblet may be intact, but it is still the whole goblet that is broken because it is useless.

Indeed, the Greek phrase in verse 11 translated by the NIV as, "For he who said" (*ho eipon*), is ambiguous. It can mean either, "For the law has said," or, "For the one who (i.e., God) has said." This ambiguity is not a problem for James since in his mind there is no real difference, for the "law" was the expression of the unified will of God for all of life. For that reason it is a "law that gives freedom" rather than a law that restricts freedom (see 1:25 and comments).

The choice of the two particular citations from the Ten Commandments (the prohibitions against adultery and murder, v. 11) are especially interesting within the context of this whole letter. James seems to imply by his phrasing that although his readers may not have committed adultery (though he does later refer to them as "you adulterous people," 4:4; see comments), there is a sense in which they have committed murder. Some commentators have suggested that James is recalling Jesus' teaching that extended the prohibition against 'murder" to apply to all forms of anger directed at persons (Matt. 5:21–22). But James makes much more direct allegations of murder later in his letter (see James 4:2; 5:6). Perhaps he intends to suggest that their failure "to look after orphans and widows" (1:27) or to meet the physical needs of others within the church (2:15–16) has resulted in deaths that may be considered murder. Thus, although they have kept themselves pure by avoiding the sin of adultery, their "sins of omission" have resulted in "murder" (see comments on 1:26–27); thus, they have "become lawbreakers."

Genuine consistency of words and deeds (to "speak and act," v. 12), then, entails not only avoiding the sins one preaches against, but also demonstrating the love and grace of God about which one preaches. James's emphasis on "keep[ing] the whole law" (v. 10) does not result in legalism because "the stress is not on the observance of a sum total of minutiae, but on the maintenance of a complete integrity of word and deed" (Laws, 1980, 116) with regard to God's will that has been "planted in you" (1:21).

James draws this summary to a close with one final rebuttal to allegations of legalism: "mercy." God, who is the "one Lawgiver and Judge" (4:12), will judge with mercy those who have internalized the divine will and acted with mercy toward others, for "mercy triumphs over judgment!" (2:13).

3.2. A Faith That Lives and Makes Alive (2:14–26)

3.2.1. Deeds Are the Evidence of Faith (2:14–19). James now offers his second example of the need for consistency between words and deeds, and in the process makes the argument for the inseparability of "faith" and the "deeds" that should necessarily arise from such consistency. He opens this section with two rhetorical questions (v. 14). "What good is it [or, What is the benefit], my brothers, if a man claims to have faith but has no deeds?" It becomes clear that James has in view two particular "benefits" that should arise from "faith." The first is presented in his second rhetorical question: "Can such faith save him?" Faith should be able to provide the benefit of salvation to the one who possesses it; if it cannot, then that faith is in some sense defective (but not a false faith, as we shall see below). But faith should also have a second benefit: It should benefit others by showing God's goodness to them (vv. 15–16).

This twofold concern for the "good" that "faith" should accomplish is an important reminder for our individualistic culture. Faith is not just about saving our individual souls from eternal judgment, but about building communities that demonstrate God's love both among believers themselves and in the world in which they live.

Many have heard in James's phrase, "If a man *claims* to have faith," the insinuation that this "claimed faith" is not "real faith." The particular details of his example in verses 15–16 show, however, that the faith must be genuine because it has produced one result that James has earlier said that faith will have in a believer's life. When confronted by a destitute and hungry member of the Christian community, another member of the church ("one of you") responds by saying, "Go in peace, be warmed and be filled" (NASB). This apparently formulaic response actually reveals that this person knows what God's will requires in this situation. Jews in the first century often used passive voice verbs to avoid having to name God explicitly as the subject performing the actions, lest they inadvertently "misuse the name of the LORD [their] God" (Ex. 20:7). Thus, we may paraphrase this blessing as, "Go in God's peace; may God warm you and provide you with all the food you need." Since those who would offer this blessing know God's will, their "faith" must be a genuine trust in God that has led them to ask for and to receive the gift of wisdom that is an understanding of God's will (1:5–8 and comments).

Nevertheless, James can ask them "what good" has been accomplished by their knowledge of God's will if they do not act to meet what they know to be God's desire for the believer in need. If in fact our desire has become the same as God's desire (see comments on 1:19–21), then how can we do "nothing about his physical needs" (v. 16)? James is not denouncing the pronouncement of God's blessing on the "poor in the eyes of the world" whom God has chosen (2:5), only the failure to become servants of God's mercy, justice, and love (cf. Matt. 23:23; Luke 11:42). A faith only spoken about ("*claims* to have faith," v. 14) and "not accompanied by action, is dead" (v. 17), producing neither physical benefit for others nor the benefit of salvation for oneself.

The objection that James anticipates to his argument is difficult to interpret since early Greek manuscripts lack any punctuation such as periods, commas, or quotation marks that would help us figure out where the objection (what "someone will say," v. 18) ends and James's response begins. The NIV rendering of the objection, "You have faith; I have deeds," has James's rhetorical dialogue partner essentially concede the argument. However, the sense is probably to be understood as less specific than "you" (James) and "I" (the one making the objection), and more general in its reference: "Here is one who claims to have faith and another who points to his deeds" (NEB). The point of the objection is that "faith" and "deeds" are separable.

Another way to translate the Greek that makes it clearer in terms of James's theology that faith and deeds are inseparable is as follows: "But someone will say, 'Do you have faith?' And I will respond, 'I have works.'" The objection thus is that James's emphasis on deeds might imply that faith itself is of little or no importance. James responds that if his deeds are consistent with God's will rather than with his own "evil desire," then they are proof that he has faith—i.e., trust in God to provide the wisdom he needs (see again comments on 1:13–16, 19–21). Conversely, if one does not have deeds consistent with God's will ("Show me your faith without deeds"), then his or her faith is possibly still mingled with doubt (see 1:5–8 and comments).

James's conception of "faith" primarily as a matter of trust in God's goodness is central to understanding his argument from the unity of God. The NIV translation of verse 19, "You believe that there is one God" (*heis theos estin*) follows one group of Greek manuscripts of the letter that takes the statement as an intellectual assent to monotheism. One may paraphrase it as, "You believe that there is one, and only one God." But others of the oldest and best manuscripts read, "You believe that God is one" (*heis estin ho theos*), a statement in keeping with first-century Jewish beliefs about the unity of God.

This second reading seems more likely to be original because it is more compatible with James's emphasis on the consistency and unchangeableness of God (see 1:17–18 and comments). Whereas human beings have a nature that is divided between good and evil desires, "God is one" in the divine will and purpose. It is the demons' certainty in the unchangeableness of God's desires and decrees that causes them to "shudder" in the face of certain eschatological judgment. What they believe determines their actions, even if it does not lead to submission to God's will. One's faith—what one truly believes as opposed to what one professes to believe—is inseparably linked to one's actions.

3.2.2. Saved by a Faith That Works (2:20–26). The invective James uses for addressing his dialogue partner (first introduced in 2:18) is unquestionably harsh—"You foolish man" (v. 20). The Greek word (*kenos*) literally means "empty" but carries several nuances. Most scholars point to its use to disparage a person's intellectual ability and relate it to the Aramaic term of contempt, *raqa* ("fool;" see Matt. 5:22), a word with connotations of moral as well as intellectual weakness. Although the idea of intellectual deficiency is supported by the immediate context ("do you want *evidence*"), the broader discussion here in chapter 2 of claims unsubstantiated by actions may point to the meaning "foolish boasting" found in some other Greek literature. Finally, it may be that James wants to suggest that claims to faith unsubstantiated by deeds can only be "empty words"; the dialogue partner is "empty" in the sense of lacking any "deeds" with which to demonstrate his faith (2:18). This final nuance is supported by the pun within James's question: "Faith without deeds (*ergon*) is useless (*arge*, i.e., *a* + *ergon*, deedless)."

Two questions need to be answered about James's use of the Abraham and Rahab illustrations as "evidence": What "deeds" did they perform for which they were "considered righteous" (vv. 21, 25), and what does James mean when he says they were "considered righteous"?

(1) In response to the first question, several interpreters have sought to restrict "deeds" to acts of mercy or Christian charity, some going so far as to suggest that James is not in fact concerned with "faith" and "deeds," but only with expounding his earlier statement, "Mercy triumphs over judgment" (2:13). While it is certainly true that acts of mercy are a major concern for James (reaching back to the definition of "pure religion" in 1:27), it is indeed strange that if he had wished to limit "deeds" to acts of Christian charity, he would have chosen to emphasize Abraham's deed of "offering his son Isaac upon the altar" (v. 21; see Gen. 22:1–18). Why not parallel Rahab's hospitality to "the spies" (Greek *angelos* in James 2:25; see Josh. 2) with Abraham's hospitality to "the angels" (Greek *angelos* in Gen. 19:1) on their way to Sodom (cf. the story in Gen. 18)?

If we reexamine the story of the "binding of Isaac" in Genesis 22:1–19 and the ways it was traditionally developed in Judaism and early Christianity, several features suggest reasons why James may have chosen this specific incident to expand the definition of "deeds" beyond acts of mercy. As both Genesis and the Jewish traditions regarding the "ten trials of Abraham" make clear, the call to "offer" Isaac was a "test" (cf. Gen. 22:1); this would seem to confirm James's readers' belief that God can be the source of testing (see 1:13 and comments). James may, however, have wanted to emphasize another part of the Abraham tradition by making this incident the "fulfillment" of the quotation from Genesis 15:6, "Abraham believed God." James believed that faith was related to knowledge about God's goodness and trust that God will only give "good things" to those who ask in faith (James 1:5, 17–18). He may be suggesting that what made it possible for Abraham to accept God's will regarding the offering of Isaac was his belief that God would raise Isaac from the dead if he were sacrificed (see Heb. 11:17–19).

Another feature of this story that warrants attention is the final pronouncement by "the angel of the LORD" in Genesis 22:16–18: "Because you have done this and have not withheld your son, your only son, I will surely bless you . . . because you have obeyed me" (lit., "heard my voice"). Abraham was blessed because he had "done" what he "heard" from the Lord's "voice," just as James had earlier asserted that the one who is a "doer of the work" of the "word planted in" him (1:21) rather than a "forgetful hearer" will be "blessed in what he does" (1:25). "Deeds" are not restricted to acts of mercy, but include all acts of obedience to God's will. It is in this sense that Abraham's "faith and his actions were working together, and his faith was made complete by what he did" (v. 22); had Abraham not believed God to be good, his will could not have been established to offer his son as he had heard from the voice of the Lord.

To emphasize faith and deeds as inseparable, James recounts the story of Abraham's near-sacrifice of his only son, Isaac, on Mt. Gerizim in obedience to God's command. Mt. Gerizim is seen here in the background. The Great Stone Pillar in the middle of the photo was part of the temple-fortress at Shechem.

(2) Returning to the question of what James means when he says Abraham was "considered righteous for what he did" (v. 21), the logical place to begin is with the use of the noun "righteousness" in verse 23. While there is no indication that James understood the statement "it was credited to him as righteousness" as a forensic act of justification (as is found in Paul's interpretation of Gen. 15:6; see Rom. 4:1–3, 9–13, 23–25), James's rhetorical questions in 2:14 make it clear that to be "considered righteous for what he did" is to be "saved." James is not merely arguing that a "faith working with deeds" is more "righteous" before or more pleasing to God; he is arguing that only "faith and . . . actions . . . working together" can "save." What is at stake is salvation and justification in an eschatological sense.

James completes his appeal to the evidence of Abraham in verse 24 by contrasting the proper belief that "a person is justified by what he does" with the improper belief that "faith alone" justifies a person. But it must be emphasized that the point stressed by this contrast is *not* that "deeds alone" justify a person (which would be a kind of legalism), but that "faith alone" (i.e., in the absence of a response in one's life) cannot justify. Thus, in James's theology the presence of "deeds" is evidence both of the prior reception of "wisdom" that establishes the will to act and of "faith," which is the prerequisite to receiving "wisdom" as a "gift" from God (1:5–8 and comments).

In similar fashion, James's allusion to the Rahab story underscores his conviction that it is knowledge of God's goodness that leads to trust in him and ultimately to acts that accomplish the divine will. According to Joshua 2:1–21, Rahab herself explained that the reason for her faith in God was the reports she had heard of the Israelites' miraculous deliverance from Egypt. Her actions in concealing the spies directly resulted in the saving of her life and the lives of her family when Jericho was destroyed. Her "faith" led to "deeds" that saved her from death.

Abraham and Rahab were common examples within the Jewish tradition of the importance of showing hospitality to strangers. It is probable, therefore, that James's readers would have made this connection even in the absence of any explicit mention of Abraham's hospitality (see above). Thus, James's two examples together serve to illustrate, explicitly and implicitly, his two interests in this section of the letter: That faith necessarily leads to deeds is the explicit point of the Abraham example and the implicit point of the Rahab allusion, and that hospitality as an expression of God's concern for the poor (see James 2:14–16) is explicitly stated with regard to Rahab and implicitly illustrated by Abraham. James's argument here "concerns at the general level the translation of faith into appropriate deeds but . . . at the particular level concerns the way in which the poor are treated within the community" (Johnson, 1995, 249).

James sums up his theology in the simile that concludes the chapter: "As the body without the spirit is dead, so faith without deeds is dead" (v. 26). The certain result of removing "deeds" from "faith," just as removing the spirit from the body, is death.

4. Preparing Oneself for Judgment (3:1–4:10)

Having set the theological context for his ethical admonitions, James now shifts his focus even more specifically to practical issues that face his readers. These changes in behavior are urgent, for believers are to be judged by the "one Lawgiver and Judge" (4:12) in the near future (see 5:9), and some "will be judged more strictly" than others (3:1). The certainty of this impending judgment before God carried with it responsibilities both for oneself and for others.

James uses this segment of his letter to encourage his readers to look first within themselves to be sure they are prepared individually for judgment before focusing on preparing others (cf. Matt. 7:1–5). He warns them against too quickly presuming to be teachers (3:1) and states emphatically that no teacher has the authority to judge others (4:11–12). This desire to exercise authority over others (as opposed to assuming responsibility for their spiritual care; see 5:13–20) is symptomatic of the core problem that faces his readers—both then and now. All evil actions arise "from your desires that battle within you" (4:2; see also 1:14–15 and comments), and those desires manifest themselves in the coveting of social status (3:1), "envy and selfish ambition" (3:16), and pride (4:6). The only solution to this problem is to "humble yourselves before the Lord" (4:10; cf. 1:21). Throughout this section, James continues to emphasize the connection between a person's speech and all his or her actions (3:2).

4.1. Human and Heavenly Wisdom (3:1–18)

4.1.1. The Beneficial Power of Speech (3:1–5a). Although James is concerned about possible abuse of the teaching office by those who lack spiritual maturity, he does believe that human speech plays an important role in determining and controlling all conduct. He begins, then, by separating himself somewhat from the readers, not because he is worthy of special honor but because he is subject to greater scrutiny ("we who teach will be judged more strictly," v. 1). He then draws his readers back into his discussion ("We *all* stumble," v. 2), again not to elevate them so much as to make clear that "teachers" do not have superior status or moral perfection within the church (teachers also "stumble").

These rhetorical moves are important because the teaching office was highly esteemed within the early church, and the presumption of "many" within the congregation to which he is writing to be teachers is yet another evidence of their preoccupation with and longing for status and power (see 1:9, 12; 2:1–4 and comments). Those who can withstand the stricter judgment that awaits teachers are those whose speech and actions are consistent; they not only are "never at fault" in what they say, but also are "able to keep [their] whole body in check" (v. 2).

James uses two metaphors to describe the ability of the tongue "to keep [the] whole body in check"—the bit in the horse's mouth and the ship's rudder. In both instances, some small part in relation to the whole is able to control the direction and actions of the whole. But the relationship of the tongue to the body is not truly analogous to that of bits and rudders; it does not *directly* control a person's actions. Because of the imperfect fit of the analogy, some commentators have suggested that James is extending his discussion of the role of teachers within the church. It is the teacher's "tongue" that controls the whole "body" of the church.

But James's chief concern in this portion of his letter (see comments on 3:1–4:10) is with the attitudes of individual believers, not with the corporate life of the church (an issue he addresses in 5:13–20). Thus, he probably intends his metaphors to be understood in a more general sense. He may be illustrating the idea from Jesus' teachings that "out of the overflow of the heart the mouth speaks" (Matt. 12:34; cf. James 3:10, where the divided human desire issues both "praise and cursing"). The "tongue," itself a metaphor for human speech, clearly indicates the nature of the internal desires that ultimately guide and determine all of a person's actions. James draws attention to this fundamental issue of the human will by explicitly saying that bits are used "to make [horses] *obey us*" (v. 3), and that the rudder steers the ship "wherever the pilot *wants to go*" (v. 4).

To this point James has emphasized the positive aspects of human speech. If it "is never at fault" in expressing acceptance and conformity to God's will as one's own, then it is "able to keep [the] whole body in check" and so steer one away from the "many ways" in which "we all stumble" (v. 2). But he now hints that too often the "tongue" does not serve this noble purpose. Although "the tongue is a small part of the body, . . . it makes great boasts" (v. 5). Boasting can be "evil" (4:16) if it indicates self-reliance and self-achievement rather than being an expression of confidence in and praise for what God has done in the person (see 1:9–10 and comments). James shifts his attention to such improper uses of human speech in the following verses.

4.1.2. The Destructive Power of Speech (3:5b–12). James's harsh denunciation of the destructive power of human speech almost seems to argue against his preceding statements about its ability to be a "check" on a person's behavior. This tension is seen most clearly in contrasting his statement in verse 8 that "no man can tame the tongue" with his earlier description of "a perfect man" as one who "is never at fault in what he says" (3:2). But James does not intend for his language to be taken too literally or the flow of his thought to be pressed for strict logical consistency. Rather, James is using the poetic language "of hyperbole, with an understood exhortation to strive to do precisely what is said to be impossible" (Laws, 1980, 154); he calls on us to become mature (Greek, *teleios,* translated "perfect" in NIV) by taming our tongues and so controlling all our behavior.

James's letter has more the rhetorical flavor and flourish of a sermon than the disciplined and nuanced language of a theological essay. Thus, despite the strongly negative images ("set on fire by hell," v. 6), he does not believe that human speech is an unmitigated evil. Rather, it too often manifests the continuing divided desires within a person (capable of both "praise and cursing," v. 10) and for that reason is a particularly pernicious and "restless evil" (v. 8).

Continuing his contrast of the tremendous effects of the small and seemingly insignificant "tongue" (see 3:3–4), James now likens human speech to a spark that can ignite a wildfire. The usual English translation "forest" (Greek, *hyle*) may call to mind the wrong image for modern Europeans and Americans, who usually associate that word with old-growth hardwood forestation. In Palestine and much of the eastern Mediterranean basin, the typical forestation patterns suggest more an image of "brushwood" or "undergrowth," and so we would do better to imagine a rapidly spreading brush fire.

The image of "fire" was conventionally used in Greek ethical teaching to symbolize one's passions and desire. The earlier images of the charioteer and helmsman (3:3–4) were traditional figures for the dominance of reason. By joining these three traditional images, James emphasizes not only the extremely destructive impact of uncontrolled speech but also prepares for a return to his theme that "evil desire" (1:13–15) is the ultimate source of his readers' problems (4:1–10).

The reason that human speech is so destructive both to the individual ("It corrupts the whole person") and to those in the community (it "sets the whole course of his life on fire," v. 6) and so uniquely difficult to control (vv. 7–8) is because its evil is "restless" (Greek, *akatastatos,* the same word translated "unstable" in 1:8). As a manifestation of the divided desires toward good and evil of the "double-minded" person, people around us cannot know what to expect from our speech. Will "we praise our Lord and Father," or will "we curse men, who have been made in God's likeness" (v. 9)? Thus, it destroys us personally by continuing the division inside ourselves. It poisons (v. 8) community by making people afraid to trust and open themselves to us because they do not know whether they will receive nurture and support (5:13–20) or will be burned by "cursing" and judgment (4:11–12; cf. 1:5–8 and comments).

If "no man can tame the tongue" (v. 8), is there then no way to quench this fire? James suggests the solution by his images in verses 11–12. Since incompatible things cannot come from the same source ("Can both fresh water and salt water flow from the same spring?") and something cannot produce what is different from its own nature ("Can a fig tree bear olives, or a grapevine bear figs?"), the solution is for the source within the person to be unified in a proper nature. That is, not only must the human will be unified rather than divided, but it must be unified according to its proper nature.

That proper nature is determined by the fact that we "have been made in God's likeness" (v. 9), and so our will should properly be like God's will. James has already shown that the human will can only be conformed to God's will by "humbly accept[ing] the word planted in you" by God (1:21; see comments). Thus, while "no man can tame the tongue" in his own strength (cf. 1:5–8 and comments), it can be checked (3:2) if God has unified the desires to which it gives expression.

4.1.3. Actions Reveal the Origins of Wisdom (3:13–18). This chapter began with James's warning against presuming to be teachers, and he may be furthering that idea in verses 13–14. The proper way to demonstrate that one is "wise and understanding" is not by simply standing before others and speaking one's knowledge, but "by [one's] good life, by deeds done in the humility that comes from wisdom." True spiritual wisdom can only be demonstrated by a consistency of word and deeds that not only expresses what God's will is but acts to accomplish God's will in the world (2:14–16 and comments). If one's motivation for being a teacher is "bitter envy and selfish ambition," it shows rather that one's internal desires ("in your hearts") are still divided and that one has not yet accepted "wisdom" as a gift from God (1:21 and comments). To "boast about" wisdom as if it were one's own accomplishment is self-deception (to "deny the truth," v. 14; cf. 1:10–11).

For James, the only real wisdom is "the wisdom that comes from heaven" (v. 17); but before turning to it, he first exposes the true nature of the so-called "wisdom" (note how the NIV places the word inside quotation marks in v. 15) that finds expression in "bitter envy and selfish ambition." He uses three adjectives to describe this non-wisdom. (1) It is "earthly"; James makes explicit that it does not originate with "the Father of the heavenly lights" and so cannot be a "good and perfect gift" (1:17).

(2) It is "unspiritual" (Greek, *psychikos*). The word suggests not that so-called "wisdom" is opposed to spiritual things per se, but rather that it originates in the human "soul" (Greek, *psyche*) rather than with God's Spirit (cf. John's linkage of the Spirit and being "born from above," John 3:5–8; see NIV text note on 3:3).

(3) This false "wisdom" is ultimately "of the devil" (Greek, *daimoniodes,* lit. "demonic"). By this word James does not mean that it is "of the devil" in the sense of originating with the devil, but that it is "demonic" in quality. This so-called "wisdom" has its true nature exposed by the fact that it results in "disorder and every evil practice" (v. 16). Rather than being genuine "wisdom," it is simply the same "evil desire" that "gives birth to sin" (1:14–15), about which James earlier warned his readers.

The picture James paints of what is considered "wisdom" by most people is indeed troubling, but we need to be careful not to push his language too far. He does not mean to suggest that there is nothing good within humanity (recall his reminder that we "have been made in God's likeness," 3:9). The problem with "earthly, unspiritual" wisdom is that it arises from the human soul. As such, it shares the divided desires of the "double-minded." It is capable of good ("we praise our Lord and Father," 3:9), but most often leads to "every evil practice." When our "wisdom" is typified by "humility" (v. 13) that recognizes its ultimate source is in God (1:5, 21) and not in ourselves (as a result of our "selfish ambition," vv. 14, 16), then the good desire within us from being created in God's likeness unites with God's will in a "good life" (v. 13).

It is to the qualities that typify that "good life" that James turns in verses 17–18. The list of characteristics or virtues that James provides here is similar to Paul's description of the "fruit of the Spirit" (Gal. 5:22–23; cf. James 3:17). Both Paul and James emphasize that these characteristics should be the natural consequence of a life that has been renewed by God.

What is of particular interest in James's list is how many of the terms directly express actions rather than simple qualities. Those who have the "wisdom" from the "word planted in you" (1:21) are not only "peace-loving," but are themselves "peacemakers." They are "considerate" of others rather than seeking their own "selfish ambition." They are "submissive" to God's will rather than being "dragged away and enticed" by their own "evil desire" (see 1:14). Their actions are "full of mercy" (cf. 2:12–13). They are "impartial and sincere" rather than being those who "show favoritism" (2:1, 9). The result of living in accord with "the wisdom that comes from heaven" is "a harvest of righteousness" (cf. 2:21–23).

4.2. Divine Judgment and Acceptance (4:1–10)

4.2.1. Actions of Evil Desire (4:1–4). In keeping with his insistence that it is a person's internal desires that determine actions (1:13–15 and comments), James now argues that the problems faced by the community as a whole ("fights and quarrels among you") likewise "come from your desires that battle within you" (4:1). As long as there is no "peace" (3:17) within individual believers, there can be no peace within the community.

The somewhat staccato quality of James's short phrases in verses 2–3 and the absence of punctuation conventions in the Greek combine to make it difficult to present the relationship between his ideas in English translation. Perhaps the best balance between the style and the ideas is achieved by translating the verses as two couplets, where the first line of each couplet presents the internal attitudes that give rise to the action presented in the second line.

> You desire but do not have,
> so you kill.
> You are envious and unable to obtain,
> so you quarrel and fight. (pers. trans.)

These "fights and quarrels" within the individual that lead to "quarrels and fights" within the community would be prevented if people would simply ask God for the things they need, particularly the "wisdom"/"word" that would conform their desires to God's will. For even when they do ask, their divided and evil motives (manifested here by the desire to "spend what you get on your own pleasures") assure that they will not "receive anything from the Lord" (1:7; see comments on 1:5–8).

There is a strong tendency among commentators to interpret James's charge that "you kill" (4:2) as a figure of speech rather than an accusation of actual murder. According to these commentators, James is following Jesus' lead in referring to hatred as murder (see Matt. 5:21–22). But there may be a way in which James believes the allegation is appropriate in a more literal sense. If a failure "to look after orphans and widows" (1:27) and other indigent members of the community (2:15–16) has resulted in unnecessary deaths, then the evil desire to "spend what you get on your own pleasures" (4:3) may well be a kind of murder (see comments on 2:11; 5:6). We must ask ourselves whether our own desire to "spiritualize" as hatred James's accusation that "you kill" masks guilt concerning a failure to use the things God has given us for the benefit of those in need. It is much easier to appease our consciences that we do not hate anyone so strongly as to wish they were dead than to confront what our own checkbooks reveal about whether our wills have been truly conformed to God's will for the poor (2:5–7, 15–16 and comments).

James's designation of his audience as "you adulterous people" (v. 4) probably arises both from his earlier association of the commandments against murder and adultery (2:11) as well as the common association of "pleasures" (4:3) with sexual desire. But it also recalls two powerful images from the Old Testament. One is the description of the "way of an adulteress," who "eats" (a euphemism for sexual relations) but then says, "I've done nothing wrong" (Prov. 30:20). Her declaration fits with the impunity and matter-of-fact attitude with which James accuses his own readers of committing sins.

The other image is the prophetic tradition that viewed Israel as God's unfaithful wife (Jer. 3:20; Ezek. 16; Hos. 2:2–5; 3:1). Just as Israel had sought to form covenants not only with the God of Abraham but also with Baal, Asherah, and other Canaanite deities, so James's readers have sought both "friendship with the world" and with God. But as surely as adultery destroys the relationship of spouses within a marriage, so the dual desire for good and evil—friendship with God and with the world—ultimately makes one "an enemy of God."

4.2.2. Submitting to God (4:5–10). James's appeal to "Scripture" in verse 5 presents a problem for interpreters since what follows in the remainder of that verse is not a direct quotation from any book in either the Old or New Testament. Some commentators have suggested that James was citing a Jewish or early Christian book that has not survived, and still others that he was making only a broad allusion to the biblical theme of God's jealousy for the chosen people. The difficulty, however, is not limited to the ambiguity of the reference, but also includes uncertainty regarding the very idea expressed by the last half of the verse.

This uncertainty concerns the grammatical function of the word "spirit" within the verse. If it is the subject of the clause, then the verse may be translated as, "the spirit he [God] caused to live in us envies intensely" (so NIV). In this reading the clause reiterates once again James's concern that people can be "double-minded," having their desires split between things that are good (it is "the spirit that God caused to live in us") and things that are evil (nevertheless it "envies intensely," being motivated by "envy and selfish ambition," 3:16).

Alternatively, the word "spirit" in verse 5 could be the object of the verb in this clause, resulting in the translation, "God jealously longs for the spirit that he made to live in us" (NIV note). This rendering provides the basis for the interpretation that the appeal to "Scripture" is to the broad theme of God's jealousy for the chosen people. Most Greek nouns have distinct forms for subject and object usage, but this is not the case with grammatically neuter nouns (such as "spirit," *pneuma*). Only context can resolve such grammatical ambiguity, and the context is itself part of the difficulty in this instance.

Returning to the particular issue of James's appeal to "Scripture," it should be noted that there is an easily identifiable biblical quotation from Prov. 3:34 in verse 6, preceded by the introduction formula, "That is why Scripture says." The simplest solution, then, is that James appeals not to two different scripture passages (one in v. 5, another in v. 6), but rather wice introduces his appeal to Proverbs 3:34. 'hus, verses 5–6 contain two sentences—a hetorical question ("Or do you think Scripture ays without no reason?"), followed by a tatement giving a "reason" why God "gives ɪs more grace." Just such a reason is provided ›y taking "spirit" as the object of the second entence of verse 5: "God longs jealously for he spirit that he made to live in us and gives ɪs more grace." The proverb is the proof text, nen, that the Scripture's promise of "grace" s not "without reason." It is because God longs jealously" for the chosen people that ames can call them an "adulterous people" for lesiring "friendship with the world" (v. 4).

The promise in the proverb that God "gives ,race to the humble" also provides the basis or James's call to "submit yourselves . . . to iod" (v. 7) and to "humble yourselves before he Lord, and he will lift you up" (v. 10; cf. :9–10). Between these parallel exhortations, ames offers practical advice on how one can ive out this attitude of humility before God. Vhereas we should "resist the devil" (4:8) by ejecting the self-interest characteristic of the o-called "wisdom" that is "earthly, unspiri-ual, of the devil" (3:15–16), we must "come ear to God" with complete trust that he "will ome near to us" (v. 8) and "give generously" 1:5) the "wisdom that comes from heaven" 3:17; cf. 1:17). That gift of wisdom will purify [the] hearts" (see comments on 1:21) f the "double-minded" by conforming their vill and their actions ("wash your hands") to iod's will (4:8).

The "laughter" and "joy" that come from friendship with the world" must be replaced vith the grief, mourning, and gloom of realiz-ıg that one has "become an enemy of God" (vv. , 9). Such an attitude of genuine humility and epentance—both turning away from evil and ırning to God—is the only way to prepare one-elf for the "one Lawgiver and Judge" (4:12).

. Preparing One's Neighbor for Judgment (4:11–5:20)

Iaving called his readers individually to repent y admonishing them to "humble yourselves efore the Lord" (4:10), James concludes his etter by encouraging them to follow his exam-le by calling other sinners to repentance 5:19–20). His pastoral concern extends to ıose clearly within the Christian community ("My brothers, if one of you should wander from the truth," 5:19), those whose standing within the church is somewhat more question-able (the merchants in 4:13–16), and even those who "have condemned and murdered innocent men" (5:6).

Christians cannot accomplish this prophetic task, however, by speaking against and judg-ing those who need to repent (4:11–12). Rather, they must remind them of God's good-ness and provision through communal prayer, praise, and confession (5:13–16) so as to restore genuine faith and trust in God by removing "doubt" from these "double-minded" persons (see 1:5–8 and comments). It is this service to the Lord (1:1) that James has himself sought to accomplish on his read-ers' behalf through the writing of this letter.

5.1. Judgments on Those Who Forget God (4:11–5:9)

5.1.1. Judging or Submitting to the Law? (4:11–12). James begins the transition from his call to believers to prepare themselves for the coming judgment by calling them to ful-fill their responsibility to others who will face judgment. He accomplishes this rhetorical move by resuming the warning about judg-ment from 3:1 that he will focus upon in 5:1–9 and by giving admonitions regarding the proper attitude one should have toward others.

James is unmistakably strong in his denun-ciation of how believers sometimes treat one another ("do not slander one another," v. 11). This tendency to speak to one another in judg-mental and condemnatory ways, perhaps with-out true justification ("slander"), is certainly one of the reasons he warns against presump-tuously assuming the responsibilities of a teacher (3:1). The proper role of the teacher is to restore "a sinner from the error of his way" (5:20), not to condemn him (cf. Matt. 7:1–5).

James isolates two problems that arise when people claim for themselves the prerog-ative of judgment that rightly belongs to God, the "one Lawgiver and Judge" (v. 12). (1) By condemning others we ultimately condemn the law itself. Perhaps James believes this to be the case because in condemning people we con-demn those "who have been made in God's likeness" (3:9), and thus we implicitly con-demn God himself (cf. Rom. 14:1–8, esp. vv. 4, 8). (2) Those who judge others ultimately stand in judgment over the law rather than submit themselves to it ("When you judge the law, you are not keeping it," James 4:11); that is, inevitably the standard of behavior becomes the will of the human judge rather than the will of God (see 4:13–17). Rather than focusing on others' failures to observe God's law, we should concentrate on submitting ourselves to God (4:7) and his law.

One pitfall of stressing the truth that God is the "one Lawgiver and Judge" is that it can prompt people to serve God out of fear of punishment rather than as an act of love and devotion. The realization that God is "the one who is able to save and destroy" (v.12) can summon both gratitude ("save") and fear ("destroy") within a person. How does James relate this fact to his conviction that God is the source of "every good and perfect gift" and only of good things (1:17 and comments)? Would not "doubt" and double-mindedness (see 1:6–8 and comments) result from not knowing whether one would receive salvation or destruction from God?

In response to the first question, James would note that whether destruction is a bad or a good thing depends upon one's perspective. Obviously God's judgment has negative consequences for those who are destroyed (compare the demons who shudder in their certain knowledge of the judgment that awaits them, 2:19). Yet James believes such punishment is not only consistent with God's justice but good in itself. That is, it is a good thing for God to destroy those whose "evil desire" has given birth to sin and death (1:14–15). Moreover, God's judgment saves those to whom God has given birth (1:18, 21) and rewards them with the emblem of the only status that matters—"the crown of life" (1:12; see also 1:9; 4:10).

To the second question James would respond that there is no reason for any individual to have uncertainty or "doubt" about her or his fate in God's judgment (again, even demons know enough about God to be certain in this regard). The only ones who will "doubt" will be those who struggle on their own to learn God's will in the hardships of life (1:2–4) and who remain torn between their desire to do good and an "evil desire" that tempts and entices them (1:13–15). Conversely, those who trust in God's goodness and have accepted "wisdom" as God's generous gift (1:5), received by "the word planted in [them]" (1:21), know that their will has been con formed to God's will. What, then, is there t fear (cf. Ps. 27:1; Rom. 8:31–39)? Those wh genuinely believe in God's goodness will trus God and entrust themselves to God's mercy for "mercy triumphs over judgment" (2:13).

5.1.2. Planning According to God's Wi (4:13–17). God's will has been a constant sub theme throughout this letter; now it rises to th surface. James chooses to treat this theme b warning against pretentious boasting (v. 16 about one's ability to control one's life (cf 1:2–4 and comments). Judging from the activ ities in which the recipients of these admoni tions plan to engage, they are members of th merchant class (they travel from city to city t "carry on business and make money," v. 13) but as his summary statement in verse 1 makes clear, the attitudes that James enjoins o the merchants are for everyone.

Although James does not believe that boast ing is intrinsically evil (see 1:9, where he use the same Greek word, *kauchaomai*), he doe believe that there are problems with the par ticular boasts of the merchants ("All *suc* boasting is evil," 4:16; cf. 1:10–11). It shoul also be pointed out that the problem is not wit making plans for the future per se, as Jame makes clear when he states that "you ought t say, 'If it is the Lord's will, we will live an do this or that'" (v. 15). Future plans becom evil boasting when they are made without con sideration for the divine will, and Jame emphasizes two particular issues in this regard

(1) The first problem with such planning i that it ignores the fact that human life is depen dent on God ("If the Lord wills, we will liv . . ."). James emphasizes this differenc between human and divine existence by hi reminder concerning the limits of huma knowledge ("you do not even know what wi happen tomorrow") and his metaphor o human life as a fleeting "mist" (v. 14). Sinc God is the one controlling events, all huma plans are ultimately contingent upon his wil we cannot do anything that God chooses t prevent.

(2) More importantly, however, God's wi should provide the *content* of our future plans Our plans should not simply be contingent o God's assent ("if the Lord wills"), but should b determined by *what* God wills. Thus, the prob

›m with the merchants' boasts is that their plans re ultimately expressions of their own desires nd materialism ("we will … carry on business nd make money," v. 13; cf. 1:14–15; 4:3).

James's concern in emphasizing these two roblematic aspects of the merchants' boastful lans has been well summarized by Douglas Ioo: "What James encourages is not the conant verbalization of the formula *If the Lord ills*, which can easily become a glib and ıeaningless recitation, but a sincere appreciaon for God's control of affairs and for his speific will for us" (1985, 157).

James underscores his admonition to the ıerchants and extends it to all believers in erse 17: "Anyone, then, who knows the good e ought to do and doesn't do it, sins." This tatement recalls his earlier admonitions callıg on Christians to do God's word and not ıerely hear it (1:22–25) and to demonstrate ıeir "faith" by their "deeds" (2:14–26) and ıeir wisdom by their "good life" (3:13). These sins of omission," like the "sins of commision" in 1:15, result from a failure "to do" the ıings that one "knows" God wants done in the vorld. The implicit warning here is that "sins f omission" can easily become "sins of comıission," as he makes clear in the opening erses of chapter 5 by his denunciation of the ppression of the poor by the rich.

5.1.3. Misery in the Day of Slaughter 5:1–9). James's harsh warning to the rich who ppress others (v. 4) in an attempt satisfy their wn desire for "luxury and self-indulgence" v. 5) seems justified, given the disastrous ffects of their actions ("You have condemned nd murdered innocent men," v. 6). Yet, when onsidered against his earlier admonition not o "judge" or "slander" others (4:11–12), the tridency of the attack may seem too extreme consider, "Their corrosion will … eat your lesh like fire," v. 3).

One might assert that there is no inconsisency since James's warning against judging thers specifically referred to one "who speaks gainst his brother or judges him" (4:11); cerainly the actions of the rich described here reclude their being considered members of he church. Are we then to assume that one tandard of conduct applies toward those who hare our faith, but another to those who do ıot? Apparently not, since James renews this dmonition at the conclusion of this paragraph: "Don't grumble against each other, brothers, or you will be judged" (v. 9). How, then, are these two passages to be related?

The first thing to realize is that James is drawing these images from the traditional indictments against the rich found in the writings of Israel's prophets and in the "piety of the poor" (see comments on 1:9–12). That is not to say, however, that these images do not express the genuine plight of poor independent farmers who were oppressed by wealthy agriculturists. The shear volume of the produce raised on their huge estates permitted them to exercise considerable control over the markets where crops were sold. They were also able to exploit the day laborers because so much of the arable land was under their control, limiting the possibilities of finding work.

Since it is reasonable to assume that these "rich" agriculturists were not among James's original audience, he apparently includes these indictments from the "piety of the poor" tradition for two reasons: (1) to assure his readers that their "cries … have reached the ears of the Lord Almighty" (v. 4), and (2) to encourage them to "be patient" until God intervenes to restore justice to the world (vv. 7–8). But why should they have to "be patient"? Why does God not intervene immediately to "destroy" (4:12) those who oppress others? Why is God *still* "standing at the door" (5:9)?

The answer to those questions is tied to the response James hopes that "the misery that is coming" will evoke from the rich, namely, that they will "weep and wail" (v. 1). This verse marks the second time that James has admonished some one to "wail." In 4:9 James had called the readers to repentance by saying, "Grieve, mourn and wail." Interestingly, the verb "grieve" (*talaiporeo*) in that earlier verse is cognate to the noun "misery" (*talaiporia*, 5:1). There is also a connection with the earlier description of the rich in 1:10–11; the image of the passing beauty of the flower there is clearly paralleled by James's description of the decay of material possessions here in 5:2–3.

James's call for the rich to "weep and wail" is not, then, some sadistic jeer rejoicing in the future destruction of evil oppressors. Rather, his hope is that when "misery" does come into their lives, they will recognize their dependence upon God and repent for their past sins. If they will do this, then the "low position"

(1:10) brought about by their "misery" will lead them to "humble [themselves] before the Lord, and he will lift [them] up" (4:10; cf. 1:9).

James provides one further indication that he intends this warning to the rich to be a call to repentance rather than a celebration of their demise, although his terse Greek style makes it somewhat more difficult to notice. Verse 6 reads literally, "You have condemned, you have murdered the righteous; he does not oppose you." The NIV translators have correctly identified James's use of the singular noun "the righteous" as collective; it is not a particular individual who has suffered at the hands of the rich, but "innocent men." However, James provides no explicit subject for the singular verb "oppose" in the final clause. Is it "the righteous" as a group who do not oppose the rich, or is there some particular individual?

James uses the verb "oppose" (Greek, *antitasso*) only one other time; "God opposes the proud but gives grace to the humble" (4:6). If "God" is the implied subject of the verb here in 5:6, James certainly does not mean to say, "God does not oppose you." However, by punctuating the clause as a question rather than a statement (recall that the earliest Greek manuscripts have no punctuation marks), the translation would be, "Does not God oppose you?" The particular Greek negative used (*ou*) indicates James expects an affirmative answer to the rhetorical question; certainly God opposes those whose arrogance and self-indulgence leads them to condemn and murder others. But if you will "humble yourselves before the Lord" (4:10), James reminds both the rich and us, God "gives grace to the humble" (4:6).

Genuine repentance, of course, will result in a change of actions, for part of humbling oneself before God is accepting God's will as one's own (1:21 and comments). One particular change that will occur in the repentant rich will be a new desire regarding their "hoarded wealth" (5:3). Their practice of amassing personal fortune by failing to pay their workers (v. 4) is the basis for James's particular charge that they have "murdered innocent men" (v. 6), because "to take away a neighbor's living is to commit murder; to deprive an employee of wages is to shed blood" (Sirach 34:26–27, NRSV).

The images of the corrosion of precious metals and moth-eaten garments likewise indicate not only that they will "pass away like wild flower" (1:10), but also that they hav been withheld from their proper use. As Pet Davids has remarked, the fact that "the ga ments which are food for moths and the mone which is tarnishing are not being used by the owner [when] they could have been used by th poor . . . points to their being withheld from th service for which God intended them" (198 176). If the rich accept God's will as their ow they will use their possessions to meet th needs of others (2:15–16) rather than living "i luxury and self-indulgence" (5:5; cf. 4:3).

Thus, James calls us to "be patient . . . unt the Lord's coming" (v. 7) because God's dela provides further opportunities for repentanc (cf. 2 Peter 3:9). As spiritual farmers, we are t wait for the ground to produce "its valuabl crop" of souls through the storms of "th autumn and spring rains." The "misery that i coming upon" the rich (James 5:1) is to serv the same purpose in the lives of unbeliever that "trials" serve in the life of believers (1:2 4). They are reminders that we cannot achiev spiritual maturity either through material suc cess (cf. Luke 12:16–21) or our own determi nation. They call both poor and rich to humilit before God and simple acceptance of the grac and gifts God will provide (James 1:5; 4:6).

The promise that "the Lord's coming i near" (v. 8) is encouragement to those wh have accepted God's will as their own and warning to those who have "hoarded wealth i the last days" (v. 3) so that they can live "i luxury and self-indulgence" (v. 5). Rather tha "grumbling against each other" (v. 9) becaus of the injustice of "man's inhumanity to man, James encourages us to work for their redemp tion. The time is short; "the Judge is standin at the door!"

5.2. The Responsibilities of Prophets (5:10–20)

5.2.1. The Perseverance of Job (5:10–11 These verses mark the transition from James' instructions about our responsibility, in th light of God's judgment, for those who are ou side the community of the church to ou responsibility for those within it. He makes th transition by offering two examples for believ ers to follow: "the prophets who spoke in th name of the Lord" (v. 10), and Job's faithfu ness during hardship (v. 11). The particula point James emphasizes from both examples is that "we consider blessed those who have persevered." It was these men's knowledge about God, that "the Lord is full of compassion and mercy," that gave Job "perseverance" and the prophets "patience in the face of suffering."

Believers need to follow Job's example of "perseverance" by not "wander[ing] from the truth" (5:19) that God is the unvarying source of all good things (1:17). They need to follow the prophets' example by speaking "in the name of the Lord," that is, using their speech to show the Lord's "compassion and mercy" (v. 11), in order to bring back those who wander from this truth either by sinful actions or by blaming God for their struggles (1:13). Those who do these things will be blessed with eternal life and forgiveness of sins (5:20).

James's examples, however, do not only look to the past. He reminds us that we "have seen what the Lord finally brought about" (v. 11) in the story of Job (see especially God's gracious restoration of the possessions he lost, Job 42). James's exact phrase is "the end of the Lord" (Greek, *to telos kyriou*), and the word "end" was frequently used in the sense of "the conclusion of the matter." But James also probably has in mind the end that the Lord *will* finally bring about "in the last days" (5:3). It is the knowledge that "the Lord's coming is near" (5:8) that both strengthens our perseverance and gives urgency to our prophetic task.

5.2.2. Responsibilities of Faith Within the Community (5:12–18). James introduces this segment of his letter with the words "Above all" (v. 12). He does not mean by this interjection that the prohibition of oaths that immediately follows is the single most important injunction of his letter. Rather, the expression was a standard formula used to mark the approaching close of a letter, and it serves to emphasize the importance of the conclusion as a whole. James sets the responsibility that Christians have for one another squarely within the context of their relationship with God. Because their responsibilities to deal honestly, to pray, and to rejoice with other believers are only particular examples of their responsibility in their relationship with God, these exhortations "above all" are important.

This context of communal responsibility as an obligation to God gives an added meaning to James's reference to Jesus' prohibition of oaths (see Matt. 5:34–37). James is not worried with what specific words may or may not be used in oaths (or whether taking an oath is wrong in itself), but with the necessity that Christians relate to one another with undeniable truthfulness. Our relationship with God connects to this prohibition in several ways. We should not call upon God ("swear . . . by heaven," a common euphemism for referring to God) to guarantee our apparently questionable truthfulness. Any blatant dishonesty that enlists God as an accomplice makes one "an enemy of God" (James 4:4) and will result in one being "condemned" (5:12).

Perhaps James is particularly concerned about oaths because some of his readers have been swearing to voice their displeasure with the hardships of their present lives, particularly the exploitation of the weakest members of society by the most powerful (cf. 5:1–6). Consequently, James moves from prohibiting inappropriate speech ("oaths") to providing examples of appropriate speech within the Christian community. The proper response to "trouble" is prayer, and to happiness is "songs of praise" (v. 13). In these ways believers demonstrate that they recognize their complete dependence upon God in times of both suffering and joy.

For James, both prayer and praise exhibit "a disposition of trustful submitting to God's good will (see 1:2–9), . . . and the efficacy of prayer is connected with [the] willingness to submit to the divine plan and to await God's intervention" (Martin, 1988, 200–201). James's specific remarks about prayers for healing and confession fit within this same context and demonstrate that even prayers for the most personal aspects of life appropriately belong in the communal life of the church.

These instructions regarding prayer for the sick and anointing with oil have particular significance for Pentecostal and charismatic Christians. Not only do the "elders" of the church have a responsibility to pray for others (v. 14), but all Christians have the responsibility to "pray for each other so that you may be healed" (v. 16). This responsibility cannot be delegated to only those who may have the spiritual gift of healing.

The specific role of the "elders" as those who are to "anoint . . . with oil" suggests that

James believed this act had a special religious significance. Although oil was widely used for medicinal purposes in the Greco-Roman world (cf. Luke 10:32–33), the New Testament references to anointing with oil in conjunction with prayer for the sick (only here and Mark 6:13) do not hint that the act was intended to be medically therapeutic. James probably intends the anointing with oil to be a religiously symbolic act rather than merely a physical focal point for one's faith. Just as the priests in ancient Israel anointed people and things with oil to set them apart to God (e.g., Ex. 40:9–15; cf. the metaphorical use of "anointing" in Luke 4:18–19; 2 Cor. 1:21–22), the anointing of the sick may symbolize their being set apart for God's special care.

Two aspects of James's instructions regarding prayer for the sick have become potential pitfalls in Pentecostal doctrines of divine healing. (1) By relating healing and forgiveness ("the prayer offered in faith will make the sick person well [Greek *sozo*, translated elsewhere in the letter as "save"] . . . [and] if he has sinned, he will be forgiven," v. 15), James echoes the traditional view that connected sin and sickness (John 9:1–2). But James does not intend to offer an explanation for the origin of illness. In his three previous uses of *sozo* (1:21; 2:14; 4:12), the word has consistently had the sense of the salvation of the person with an eye toward our complete redemption at the end of time (so also in 5:20). Thus, James emphasizes that we should be concerned with both the physical and spiritual well-being of the person. Certainly some injury and illness is the natural consequence of sinful acts, but James does not teach that every disease results from sin (cf. John 9:3).

(2) The second pitfall relates to James's confident assertion about the "[powerful and effective] prayer of a righteous man" (v. 16) and his illustration of this point by Elijah (vv. 17–18). If "Elijah was a man just like us," then why were his prayers answered in so spectacular a fashion though our prayers for healing sometimes go unanswered? Some have sought to affix blame for such unanswered prayers by impugning the "righteousness" either of the sick person or of those who pray on her or his behalf. James's assertion is not about affixing blame, however, but about his trust in God's goodness. Just as God answered Elijah's prayers and so enabled him to fulfill his prophetic mission, so God will answer the prayers of believers as they perform their mission in behalf of others.

To the degree that James offers any explanation as to why some prayers for healing do not result in physical restoration, it is that the elders are "to pray over . . . and anoint him with oil in the name of the Lord" (v. 14). The invocation of "the name of the Lord" is both an appeal to the power and authority of God and a recognition that our desires—even in prayer—must be conformed to God's will (cf. 4:3 and comments). Perhaps James would also challenge our opinion that so many prayers for the sick go *un*answered. Recall that he wrote that "the prayer offered in faith will save [*sozo*] the sick person; the Lord will raise him up" (v. 15). Physical life is not the only life, or even the most important life, there is (see 5:20). God's goodness in raising us to eternal, spiritual life is an answer to "the prayer of faith" that completely trusts in God's goodness to make us whole in the fullest sense.

5.2.3. Covering a Multitude of Sins (5:19–20). James concludes his letter by encouraging us to do for others what he has done through writing to the people of God "scattered among the nations" (1:1). If we should see someone "wander from the truth," it is God's will that we "should bring him back" (v. 19), because "God jealously longs for the spirit that he made to live in us" (4:5, NIV note) when he "chose to give us birth through the word of truth" (1:18). In this way we too become "servant[s] of God and of the Lord Jesus Christ" (1:1).

The "truth" from which some "wander" is James's conviction that God is the source of "every good and perfect gift" (1:17) and of nothing bad or evil. For James, this theological "error" (v. 20) has profound ethical consequences. Those who believe that God may be a source of bad things in their lives (1:13) will "doubt" God's willingness to give them the wisdom that they lack as a generous gift (1:5–8). Their failed efforts to teach themselves wisdom in the struggles of life will mean that they remain "double-minded," wanting to please God but also having an "evil desire" that tempts them to "sin" (1:14–15). Such people cannot be brought back to God through condemning words (4:11–12), but only by being gain convinced of God's goodness so that ney will trust God and "humbly accept the vord [he] planted in" them (1:21; cf. 4:7–10).

James closes his letter with a wonderful romise to those who fulfill this responsibil-ty for the spiritual lives of others: "He who urns a sinner from the error of his way will ave his soul from death, and will cover a mul-itude of sins" (v. 20, NASB). There is some mbiguity in this promise regarding the ntecedent of the pronoun "his" that modifies he word "soul." Is it the soul of the one "who urns a sinner" or the soul of the sinner himself hat is saved from death? The NIV resolves this mbiguity in favor of the sinner's soul when t translates "his soul" simply as "him." But it s also possible that the antecedent is "whoever urns a sinner"; by performing this work one ot only "will save his [or her own] soul from leath," but will also "cover [the] multitude of ins" that have been committed by both these nembers of the community. Both of these neanings are possible because James believes hat it is by performing such "deeds," deeds hat are consistent with God's will, that Chris-ians are "blessed" (1:22–25) and that their faith" is able to save them from spiritual death 2:14, 26).

THE OLD TESTAMENT IN THE NEW

NT Text	OT Text	Subject
Jas 2:8	Lev 19:18	Love your neighbor as yourself
Jas 2:11	Ex 20:14; Dt 5:18	Seventh commandment
Jas 2:11	Ex 20:13; Dt 5:17	Sixth commandment
Jas 2:23	Ge 15:6	Faith in Abraham
Jas 4:6	Pr 3:34	Grace for the humble

BIBLIOGRAPHY

T. B. Cargal, *Restoring the Diaspora: Discursive Structure and Purpose in the Epistle of James* (1993); P. H. Davids, *The Epistle of James*, NIGTC (1982); M. Dibelius, *James*, Hermeneia (1975); L. T. Johnson, *The Letter of James: A New Translation with Introduction and Commentary*, AB (1995); S. Laws, *A Commentary on the Epistle of James*, HNTC (1980); R. P. Martin, *James*, WBC (1988); D. J. Moo, *James*, TNTC (1985); P. Perkins, *First and Second Peter, James, and Jude*, Interpretation (1995).

1 AND 2 PETER

Roger Stronstad

NTRODUCTION 'O 1 PETER

'irst Peter is classified as one of the catholic r general letters, assigned this classification ecause unlike Paul's letters, which were writ-:n to an individual or to Christians in a sin-le location (e.g., Corinth or Rome), Peter ddressed his letter to Christians in several rovinces: Pontus, Galatia, Cappadocia, Asia, nd Bithynia. Five factors are important to the ackground of the exposition of this general :tter: (1) authorship, (2) date and place of vriting, (3) recipients, (4) occasion and/or urpose, and (5) overall structure.

. Authorship

'he writers of the New Testament did not have specific biographical interest in any of the postles and heroes of the New Testament, uch as many readers have today. Neverthe-:ss, they have reported enough incidental nformation to enable us to construct a com-osite picture of Peter.

a. Peter in the Gospels

When Peter first appears on the pages of ne New Testament, he and his brother ndrew were fishing partners of James and ohn, sons of Zebedee (Luke 5:10). Peter was narried and lived at Capernaum (4:38–39), nough formerly he had lived at Bethsaida 'ohn 1:44). He is known in the New Testa-nent by three names: Simon/Simeon (son of ohn), Cephas, and Peter, the Greek translation f the Aramaic name Cephas (1:42).

Along with James and John, Peter formed an nner circle of Jesus' disciples. Typically, he is ne first named of the three. These three disci-les accompanied Jesus when he restored life) the daughter of Jairus, the synagogue official Capernaum (Mark 5:37). They also appeared lone with Jesus on the so-called Mount of 'ransfiguration (9:2). In part, Peter's select osition was due to his spiritual sensitivity, and is no surprise that the public ministry of Jesus vas crowned by Peter's confession, "You are ne Christ" (8:29). Because Peter recognized that Jesus is the Christ, that is, the Messiah, he became the rock on which Jesus would build his church (Matt. 16:17). This is fulfilled in Acts 1–12, which reports Peter's Spirit-filled leadership in the primitive church.

Peter was an impetuous and mercurial person. For example, on impulse he walked on water after Jesus invited him to do so (Matt. 14:29). Later, when Judas betrayed Jesus, he wielded his sword in a misguided attempt to defend his Master (John 18:10). But in spite of his faith and courage, he denied Jesus (Mark 14:66–72), as Jesus had, in fact, warned him (14:30).

b. Peter in the Acts of the Apostles

The book of Acts portrays Peter as the dominant apostle in the primitive church (Acts 1–12). He initiated the choosing of the twelfth apostle (1:15–26). He preached to the massed Pentecost pilgrims on the day of Pentecost (2:14–36), and, along with the other apostles, taught (2:42) and performed many wonders and miraculous signs (2:43), such as the healing of the crippled beggar (3:1–10). Twice he witnessed before the Sanhedrin (4:8–12; 5:29–30). Besides giving leadership to the charismatic community in Jerusalem (1:2–6:7), Peter subsequently ministered outside of that city—first, with John in Samaria (8:14–25), and then throughout some of the cities of western Judea (Lydda, Joppa, and Caesarea; 9:32–11:18). An angel delivered him out of the hands of King Herod, the executioner of James (12:1–18). He last appears in Acts defending Paul's and Barnabas's mission to the Gentiles (15:6–11).

The apostle Peter of Acts is a charismatic prophet. Along with the other 120 disciples on the day of Pentecost, he was baptized with the Holy Spirit (1:5), empowered by the Spirit (1:8), and filled with the Spirit (2:4). In the language of Joel, Peter had the Spirit of prophecy poured out on him (2:17–21). As a result, like Jesus before him (Luke 24:19), Peter was a prophet mighty in works and word. Indeed, all of his words of witness, not only in Jerusalem but also in Samaria and western Judea, were inspired by the Spirit

(2:14; 4:8, 31; etc.), and all of his works of witness, whether in Jerusalem or Samaria or western Judea, were empowered by the Spirit. For numerous reasons Peter's reputation as a "pillar" apostle was well earned (Gal. 2:9).

In many ways it was Peter, rather than Paul, who was Luke's great hero of the early church. In geographic terms Peter ministered in Jerusalem (Acts 1–6), then in Samaria (Acts 8), and finally in western Judea (Acts 9–11). In ethnic terms he ministered to Jews (Acts 1–6), Samaritans (Acts 8), and Gentiles (Acts 10–11). It is little wonder, then, that in Luke's narrative strategy Peter's ministry is the pattern and standard against which Paul's ministry is portrayed. For example, if Paul was filled with the Holy Spirit three times (9:17; 13:9, 52), so was Peter before him (2:4; 4:8, 31). If Paul was called to be the apostle to the Gentiles (9:15), Peter had already established the precedent for ministry to the Gentiles by going to the house of the Gentile Cornelius (10:1–11:18; 15:6–11). Paul's ministry would be itinerant and peripatetic (13:1–28:31), as was Peter's earlier (9:32–11:18).

Luke reports numerous additional parallels between Peter and Paul, including the following: (1) both Peter and Paul heal cripples (3:1–10; 9:32–35; 14:8–13); (2) both heal the sick by external instrumentality (e.g., Peter's shadow [5:5], and Paul's aprons and handkerchiefs [19:12]); (3) Peter and Paul are agents to bestow the gift of the Holy Spirit (8:15–17; 19:1–7); (4) both curse magicians (8:18–24; 13:6–12); (5) both raise the dead (9:40; 20:10); and (6) not only Peter, but also Paul is put on trial before the Sanhedrin (4:1–22; 22:30–23:10). Clearly, though Paul's ministry in Acts extends farther than does Peter's, Peter's ministry establishes both the ethnic and charismatic precedents for Paul.

c. Peter and Rome

While Acts is silent about Peter's final years of ministry, he evidently visited Rome, perhaps as early as the reign of Claudius (A.D. 41–54). The church historian Eusebius (ca. A.D. 265–339) records the tradition that after Simon the Sorcerer went to Rome in the reign of Claudius, God guided Peter to that same city, "as against a gigantic pest on life" (*Ecclesiastical History*, 2.14). If this tradition has any historical base, Peter might have fled to Rome after his miraculous deliverance from the persecution against the apostles by Herod (Ac 12:1, 19). It is likely that Peter also visited t church at Corinth during this time (1 Cor. 1:1 9:5; *Ecclesiastical History,* 2.25.7–8).

Peter was also in Rome during the reign Nero (A.D. 54–68), Claudius's successor. Eusbius records the testimony of Clement, whi links Peter and Mark together in the authorsh of Mark's Gospel. Those who had hea Peter's proclamation of the Gospel exhort Mark, a long-time companion of Peter, make a record of what had been said. Peter, was reported, neither forbade nor encourag Mark to do this (*Ecclesiastical Histor* 6.14.6–7). This tradition is significant, n only because it associated both Peter and Ma with Rome, but also because it gave apostol authority to a Gospel that was written by som one who was not himself an apostle.

Eusebius also preserves the tradition th Peter was executed in Rome during Nero persecution of the Christian community ther Nero had Paul beheaded and, at about the san time, had Peter crucified. Both were buried the same cemetery and were considered joi founders of the church in Rome (*Ecclesias cal History,* 2.25.5–8). A fanciful account Peter's martyrdom is preserved in the apo ryphal *Acts of Peter* (E. Hennecke, *New Te tament Apocrypha*, 2:314–22).

This bust shows a youthful Nero, the emperor of the Roman Empire from A.D. 54 to 68. Nero, who persecuted Christians in Rome, had Peter killed in A.D. 64 About the same time he also had Paul beheaded.

2. Date and Place of Writing

According to the available evidence 1 Peter was written in Rome. Note the letter's closing greeting: "She who is in Babylon . . . sends you her greetings" (1 Peter 5:13). That Peter's reference to Babylon is a cryptic reference to Rome, rather than a literal reference to either the Mesopotamian or to the Egyptian cities of that name, is supported by two considerations: (1) John also identifies the city of Rome as *Babylon* in his Apocalypse (Rev. 17–18), and (2) Colossians identifies Mark with Paul during the latter's Roman imprisonment (Col. 4:10), and it is improbable that the combination of Paul and Mark and Mark and Peter are in two different cities.

Several factors yield a date for the letter in the early 60s. (1) It was written before Peter's martyrdom at the hands of Nero in A.D. 64. (2) It was written after the church had been widely established throughout Pontus, Galatia, Cappadocia, Asia, and Bithynia (1 Peter 1:1). Luke reports that the province of Asia (i.e., cities such as Ephesus, Colosse, and Laodicea [Col. 4:16]) was evangelized during Paul's lengthy stay at Ephesus (Acts 19:10; A.D. 53–56). Thus, Peter could not have written his letter before A.D. 56. Thus a date between A.D. 56 and 64, and likely closer to the latter, is most probable. The varying traditions reported by Eusebius fully support these observations about when and where Peter wrote this letter (*Ecclesiastical History*, 2.15.2; 3.3.2).

3. Recipients

We can infer much about the recipients of Peter's letter from the content of the letter. Peter's audience is made up of Christian communities scattered widely over five of the Roman provinces of what is now western and central Turkey (1 Peter 1:1). His audience, therefore, includes both Jewish Christians and Christians from a variety of Gentile people groups.

Evidence that Jewish Christians are among the recipients includes the following: (1) Peter appropriates and applies to his audience the term *diaspora* (1:1), a technical term used to describe the nation of Israel scattered among the Gentile nations (John 7:35; 2 Macc. 1:27); (2) he appeals to fulfilled Old Testament prophecy (1:16 et al.); and (3) he appropriates metaphors from the Old Testament, such as the temple and stone metaphors (2:4–10), to describe his audience. All of these features are best explained by a Jewish Christian component as among his recipients.

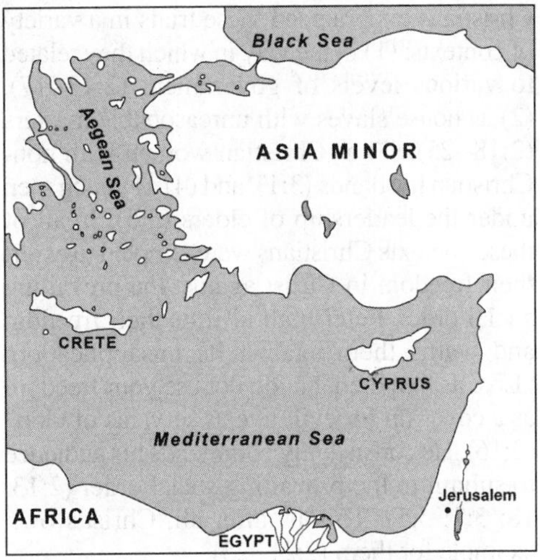

Peter's guidance in 1 Peter is directed at both Jewish and Gentile Christians in Asia Minor, an area that now includes western and central Turkey.

Although Peter's audience includes a significant number of Jewish Christians, his readers are mainly Gentile Christians. This element is indicated by Peter's observation, "For you have spent enough time in the past doing what pagans choose to do—living in debauchery, lust, drunkenness, orgies, carousing and detestable idolatry" (1 Peter 4:3). It is further reinforced by the author's appeal to Hosea to describe his audience: "Once you were not a people, but now you are the people of God; once you had not received mercy, but now you have received mercy" (2:10).

In addition, Peter's audience includes household slaves and women whose husbands are not yet Christian (2:18; 3:1). It is a multigenerational audience, including both the aged and the young (5:1–5). As is to be expected from the relatively late date of this letter (the early 60s) as well as from its destination outside of Palestine, no one in his audience has had any firsthand experience with the earthly Jesus (1:8). Finally, it is an audience that is afflicted by various trials (1:6).

4. Occasion and/or Purpose

Peter wrote his letter because the Christians scattered throughout western and central Turkey were distressed by various trials (1 Peter 1:6).

Christians experienced these trials in a variety of contexts: (1) in the way in which they related to various levels of government (2:13–17), (2) as house slaves with unreasonable masters (2:18–25), (3) as Christian women with non-Christian husbands (3:1), and (4) as young men under the leadership of elders (5:5). In all of these contexts Christians were tempted to assert their freedom in Christ against the prevailing social order. Peter both affirms their freedom and warns them against its misapplication: "Live as free men, but do not use your freedom as a cover-up for evil; live as servants of God" (2:16). He consistently commands his audience to submit to the prevailing social order (2:13, 18; 3:1; 5:5). This is, after all, Christ's own example for them (2:21–25).

Peter not only wrote because his audience was, in general, beset by various trials, but he also wrote specifically because some of them were suffering from "the painful trial" (1 Peter 4:12), that is, overt persecution. They were being "insulted because of the name of Christ" (4:14) and were suffering "as . . . Christian[s]" (4:16). This kind of suffering was divine chastisement (4:17) and was according to God's will (4:19). Again, Christ is the example of suffering according to God's will (3:17–22). Both the various trials and the painful trial, Peter affirms, were instruments of refinement by testing (2:7; 4:12). Consequently, in the midst of such testing, God's people were not to retaliate (3:9) but were to keep a good conscience (2:19; 3:16) and rejoice (1:8; 4:13).

Living in a sometimes unsympathetic, harsh culture, disadvantaged under the prevailing social or power structures, and reviled because they identified with Christ and were being pressured to conform to the sinful lifestyle of their peers, many believers in Peter's far-flung audience either had lapsed or were in danger of lapsing in holy living. On the one hand, they had to rid themselves of malice, deceit, hypocrisy, envy, and slander (2:1); that is, they had to abstain from sinful desires (2:11). On the other hand, they had to continue to leave the sins of their pagan past: "debauchery, lust, drunkenness, orgies, carousing and detestable idolatry" (4:3). Finally, they were not to suffer as "a murderer or thief or any other kind of criminal, or even as a meddler" (4:15).

To live the requisite life of holiness, the Christians who made up Peter's audience had to be prepared for action and be self-controlled (1:13), not conform to their evil desires (1:14), obey the divine imperative "Be holy" (1:16), and function as a holy priesthood and holy nation (2:5, 9). The life of holiness was possible for these beleaguered Christians because they had been chosen "through the sanctifying work of the Spirit" (1:2) and because the holiness of God was the foundation for the holiness of his own people (1:16).

The reader who turns from the Acts of the Apostles to 1 Peter may be surprised to observe how infrequently Peter, the leading charismatic apostle of Acts, writes about the Holy Spirit. In fact, he writes about the Spirit directly just four times and indirectly but one time. He refers to the Spirit for the first time in the Trinitarian formula of the salutation: "chosen according to the foreknowledge of God the Father, through the sanctifying work of the Spirit, for obedience to Jesus Christ" (1:2). He next writes about "the Spirit of Christ," who is the Spirit of prophecy speaking through the prophets (1:10–11). In the same context, he observes that the gospel has been preached to his dispersed audience "by the Holy Spirit sent from heaven," that is, by the same Spirit of prophecy who had spoken about Christ through the prophets (1:12).

In the one indirect reference to the Holy Spirit, Peter alludes to the Spirit when, in the barest of summaries, he writes about "the gift" or charisma (of the Spirit) that each Christian has received from among the various gifts of speaking and service (4:10–11). Finally, Peter writes about "the Spirit of glory and of God," who rests upon his long-suffering audience (4:14). In this context the Spirit brings blessing to those who participate in the sufferings of Christ; that is, the glory of the resurrection is the ultimate reward for those who suffer.

The importance of a biblical subject or doctrine is not always to be determined by the frequency of its references, however. For example, as the doctrine of the virgin birth demonstrates, a few references may convey an important teaching. And so it is with Peter's few references to the Holy Spirit. Lying behind these five references is a wealth and range of apostolic, early Christian teaching about the Spirit and the Trinity; the role of the Spirit in sanctification, in prophecy, and in evangelism; the charismata (i.e., the gifts of the Spirit for ffective Christian service); and eschatological divine approbation through the resurrection. In these references Peter alludes to a rich and widespread legacy of teaching about the Holy Spirit and the experience of the Spirit that his audience has received.

. Overall Structure

First Peter is a letter, and in its overall structure it conforms to the typical structure of letters in New Testament times. This structure includes the following basic components: (1) salutation (1:1–2), (2) the body of the letter (1:3–5:11), and (3) the concluding comments and greetings (5:12–14). The body of the letter focuses on three successive themes: holiness (1:3–2:10), submission and suffering (2:11–4:19), and (3) pastoral oversight (5:1–11). Peter's model for holiness is God the Father (1:15–16), his model for submission and suffering is Christ (2:21–25; 3:17–22), and his model for pastoral oversight is Peter himself (5:1).

OUTLINE OF 1 PETER

. **Salutation** (1:1–2)

. **Living Like God: Holiness** (1:3–2:10)

- **2.1.** A Living Hope (1:3–12)
  - **2.1.1.** Cultivate a Future Orientation (1:3–5)
  - **2.1.2.** Rejoice in Present Trials (1:6–9)
  - **2.1.3.** Adopt the Attitude of the Prophets (1:10–12)
- **2.2.** A Call to Holy Living (1:13–2:3)
  - **2.2.1.** Adopt Christian Attitudes (1:13–16)
  - **2.2.2.** The Motivation for Holy Living (1:17–21)
  - **2.2.3.** The Social Dimension of Holy Living (1:22–25)
  - **2.2.4.** Negative and Positive Dimensions of Holy Living (2:1–3)
- **2.3.** God's Holy People: A Temple and a Nation (2:4–10)
  - **2.3.1.** The Stone or Temple Metaphor (2:4–8)
  - **2.3.2.** The New Nation (2:9–10)

. **Living Like Christ: Submission and Suffering** (2:11–4:19)

- **3.1.** Submit for the Lord's Sake (2:11–3:12)
  - **3.1.1.** Introductory Exhortation (2:11–12)
  - **3.1.2.** Submit to Government (2:13–17)
  - **3.1.3.** Slaves, Submit to Masters (2:18–25)
  - **3.1.4.** Wives, Submit to Husbands (3:1–7)
  - **3.1.5.** Summary Exhortation (3:8–12)
- **3.2.** Suffer for the Lord's Sake (3:13–4:19)
  - **3.2.1.** Suffer for the Sake of Righteousness (3:13–17)
  - **3.2.2.** Christ: The Model for Suffering (3:18–22)
  - **3.2.3.** The Ethical Imperative (4:1–6)
  - **3.2.4.** A Series of Practical Imperatives (4:7–11)
  - **3.2.5.** Suffer As a Christian (4:12–19)

4. Living Like Peter: Pastoral Oversight (5:1–11)

- **4.1.** Shepherd the Flock of God (5:1–4)
- **4.2.** A Series of Practical Imperatives (5:5–11)

5. Concluding Comments and Greetings (5:12–14)

COMMENTARY ON 1 PETER

1. Salutation (1:1–2)

Peter begins his letter with the pattern or formula that was common to letters in the world of New Testament times: sender to addressee, greeting.

The sender identifies himself as "Peter." The short biographical essay in the introduction to this commentary on 1 Peter summarizes what is known about Peter in both the New Testament literature and early church tradition. Peter cites himself as "an apostle of Jesus Christ." In qualifying himself as an apostle, he is expressing a twofold consciousness: (1) that he is under the authority of Jesus, and (2) that he is the authoritative representative of Jesus to his audience.

Peter addresses his letter "to God's elect, strangers in the world." The word translated as "strangers" simply means, "staying for awhile in a strange place" (BAGD, 625). This word is used to describe both Abraham (Gen. 23:4; Heb. 11:13) and Christians (1 Peter 1:1; 2:11).

Peter's audience is "scattered throughout" the Roman provinces of "Pontus, Galatia, Cappadocia, Asia, and Bithynia"—the region of modern day western and central Turkey. Little is known about the evangelization of these provinces. Converted Pentecost pilgrims may have first carried the gospel to Cappadocia, Pontus, and Asia (Acts 2:9–11). Somewhat later, Paul and his companions evangelized Galatia and Asia (Acts 13–14; 19; Col. 1:7). Finally, Paul reports to the Romans, "so from Jerusalem all the way around to Illyricum, I have fully proclaimed the gospel of Christ" (Rom. 15:19). From this report it is evident that the gospel had been strategically spread throughout the eastern part of the empire several years before Peter writes his letter to the churches scattered throughout these Roman provinces.

The word "scattered" (*diaspora*) was a technical term that describes the nation of Israel scattered among the Gentile nations (John 7:35; cf. 2 Macc. 1:27). It was also used "of Christians who live in dispersion in the world, far from their heavenly home" (BAGD, 188; see James 1:1; 1 Peter 1:1). Peter's address reminds his audience that, like Abraham, they have neither permanent residence nor citizenship on this earth, and that, like Israel, they are dispersed among godless and often hostile peoples.

Peter's audience, the scattered aliens, are also "chosen" (1:2). This word describes "those whom God has chosen from the generality of mankind and drawn to himself" (BAGD, 242). In describing his audience this way, Peter extends to them the words of Jesus to his disciples, "You did not choose me, but I chose you" (John 15:16). In the apostolic church this term quickly became a technical term for God's people (Rom. 8:33; Col. 3:12; 2 Tim. 2:10; Titus 1:1).

These Christians have been chosen "according to the foreknowledge of God the Father." Here Peter affirms a widespread New Testament perspective: God has taken the initiative in choosing human beings for salvation—an initiative that springs from his foreknowledge ("to foreknow," Rom. 8:29; cf. 1 Peter 1:20; "foreknowledge," Acts 2:23; 1 Peter 1:2). God's foreknowledge is a reminder that, in contrast to the temporal limitations afflicting humankind, he is outside of time, and therefore he can both know ar choose in advance of events in time.

Peter's audience, moreover, has been ch sen by "the sanctifying work of the Spirit." is the Spirit who effects the sanctification holiness of God's chosen exiles. Because h is the divine agent of sanctification, the Spi of God is most commonly called the Ho Spirit in the New Testament. This sanctifyin work introduces the dominant theme of th opening section of his letter—the theme holiness (1 Peter 1:3–2:10).

Finally, Peter's audience has been chose "for obedience to Jesus Christ and sprinklin by his blood." In entering a saving relationshi with God, his chosen receive many benefi and privileges; they also receive new oblig tions, foremost of which is to obey their Sa ior, Jesus Christ. This obligation is appropriat for Christians have been sprinkled with h blood. That is, they have been saved redeemed through the sacrificial death Jesus. This indebtedness to Jesus for salvatio is the most powerful of all motivations for liv ing in obedience to Jesus.

As Peter here addresses his audience, h reminds them that salvation is the cooperativ effort of the triune God. The Father's role to choose or elect people to salvation, th Spirit's role to sanctify or transform their live and Jesus' role to take the penalty of their sir upon himself in his self-sacrifice.

Peter greets his audience with "Grace an peace be yours in abundance." In the Greek speaking world of New Testament times, th customary greeting was *chairein* (lit "rejoice"), a word similar to the word trans lated "grace" (*charis*), which became the cus tomary Christian greeting. Similarly, in th Hebrew world, the customary greeting wa "peace" (*shalom*). In New Testament letter these greetings are customarily united (e.g Rom. 1:7; 1 Cor. 1:3; 2 Peter 1:2). This reflec the fact that the gospel is for both Greek c Gentile and Jew; that is, for all humanit Moreover, the apostles do not simply utiliz these terms for their conventional meaning, bu rather infuse them with theological signifi cance. Thus, these greetings summarize c encapsulate the gospel: Grace signifies th work of God in salvation, and peace describe the blessing that comes to those who receiv this salvation (Rom. 5:1).

. Living Like God: Holiness (1:3–2:10)

ter instructs his readers by giving them three odels to pattern their lives after. God is the st model—for holiness (1:3–2:10); Christ is e model for submission and suffering (2:11–19), and the apostle is the model for leader- ip among God's people (5:1–11).

2.1. A Living Hope (1:3–12)

Peter is addressing an audience of exiles ho are dispersed among godless peoples :1). Moreover, his audience is beset by vari- s trials (1:6). These include the struggle or arfare against the downward pull of the flesh :1, 11; 4:1–4), unjust suffering (2:18–20), d suffering as a Christian (4:16) or persecu- on (4:12). As the antidote for Christians in ese circumstances, Peter first of all gives his aders a twofold orientation: (1) They have en born again to a living hope and are there- re to cultivate a future and eternal perspective :3–5), and (2) they are to rejoice both in pre- nt trials (1:6) and in Jesus himself (1:8).

2.1.1. Cultivate a Future Orientation :3–5). Peter introduces this future orienta- on as part of his blessing addressed to "the od and Father of our Lord Jesus Christ!" This troductory blessing first speaks of God's otive toward humanity, "his great mercy." od's purpose was to "[give] us new birth." he word translated "new birth" is used exclu- vely by Peter in his first letter (1:3, 23). Nev- theless, the origin of born-again terminology no doubt derived directly from the teaching f Jesus to Nicodemus (John 3:3–9). This is it one of several New Testament words that escribe entry into the Christian life. Other ords include "justified" (the language of the w court), "redeemed" (the language of the ave market), and "propitiated" (the language f the sacrificial system). This born-again nagery is appropriate for entry into the Chris- an life and is further developed in 2:1–3.

Our new birth initiates "hope." Unlike con- mporary English connotations of this word, ch as wishful thinking, the New Testament onnotations are positive and dynamic. Hope ay be defined as the present certainty of iture prospects. This hope that Peter writes bout is a "living" hope, "through the resur- ction of Jesus Christ from the dead"—a eme that dominates Peter's preaching in the book of Acts (2:22–36; 3:14–15; 4:10; etc.). It is hope because Christ's resurrection guarantees the future resurrection of the Christian (Rom. 8:23–25; 1 Cor. 15:12–58).

Writing of both hope and resurrection turns Peter's thoughts to "an inheritance that can never perish, spoil or fade—kept in heaven for you" (1:4). Inheritance, which theologically speaking is the language of eternity, is the goal of the new birth. Its greatness is that this inheritance is imperishable, in contrast to silver and gold (1:7, 18). It is also undefiled or pure, in contrast to the works of the human nature (2:1). Moreover, this inheritance is also unfading, in contrast to the fragile character of humankind (1:24; cf. Isa. 40:6–7). Such an inheritance is reserved in heaven, that is, in God's presence, for the believer.

This hope in the resurrection and subsequent inheritance would truly be wishful thinking were it not for the fact that God's people "are shielded by God's power" (1:5). God's promises are guaranteed by his intrinsic veracity and witnessed to by his faithfulness in history. However, Peter also assures his readers that God has the power to perform what he has promised. Although power is the divine guarantee of this inheritance, "faith" is the human response necessary to appropriate God's provision. This faith needs to endure "until the coming of the salvation that is ready to be revealed in the last time." Thus, both God's power and the Christian's faith are directed toward the final consummation of God's saving provision.

Peter's challenge to his readers at the outset of his letter to cultivate a heavenward and future orientation puts the present, with its trials and tribulations, in a proper perspective. It also reminds us that salvation has three temporal dimensions. In the past, when he or she was born again, the Christian was saved from the penalty of sin. This entry into the Christian life has initiated an ongoing process of growth or sanctification. This is salvation from the power or downward pull of sin. The past and present dimensions of salvation lead to the future, when God's people will be finally saved from the very presence of sin.

2.1.2. Rejoice in Present Trials (1:6–9). Having oriented his readers to a heavenly and future perspective, Peter now balances his instruction with a lesson on the Christian response to the difficult circumstances of life.

Contrary to human nature, Christians can have joy in a time of trial and tribulation, to the extent that they rejoice in Jesus Christ.

"In this you greatly rejoice." "This" refers specifically to Peter's previous statement on final salvation (1:5), and more generally to everything he has written about the living hope and inheritance of the Christian (1:3–4). The rejoicing of believers transcends the circumstances of their lives, who have "suffered grief in all kinds of trials." Peter's word for "trial" (*peirasmos*) is better translated as "testing." The verbal form of the word is used to describe the testing of Jesus in the desert (Mark 1:13). The noun is used in a similar context by James (James 1:2), and Peter will use it later in this letter to describe fiery trials (1 Peter 4:12). Peter qualifies these testings in two ways: They are "for a little while" and "of all kinds." In his discussion, he sets up a contrast between final salvation and present trials, and between rejoicing (which is the response of the human spirit) and distress (which is the natural psychological response).

Peter reminds his audience that the many trials or testings they experience are so that their faith "may be proved genuine" (1:7); that is, the trials are the means of testing the faith of God's people in order to show whether or not it is genuine. Peter views this proving of faith to be "of greater worth than gold, which perishes." Implicit in this comparison is the fact that proven faith is an experience greater than any human treasure, such as gold. Such proving of faith is precious, "even though refined by fire." It is a treasure because it not only proves faith, but because it also refines and purifies faith. This refining process is already being experienced by the audience Peter is addressing (4:12).

Proven faith will "result in praise, glory and honor when Jesus Christ is revealed" (1:7). This clause is ambiguous—perhaps deliberately so. It means either that praise, glory, and honor will be given to those of tested faith, or that those of tested faith will in the last days glorify Christ. We do not have to choose between either of these meanings, for both are true.

Having written of the revelation of Jesus Christ Peter recalls that his readers "have not seen him" (1:8). While Peter's readers have not had the same privilege of personal association with Jesus that he has had, they "love [*agapao*] him." As Peter writes of their love, he may be recalling how he who had been a disciple ha denied Jesus in his hour of trial (Mark 14:66 72), and later could only confess to a filial rath than an *agape* quality of love (John 21:16–18

By the way of contrast, Peter's readers a characterized by the *agape* quality of lov Even though they "do not see him now," the not only love him, but they also "believe i him." Jesus is the object of both their love an their belief, which is being put to the test. Th Christ-centered love and faith enable thes Christians to be "filled with an inexpressib and glorious joy." In their experience, Jesu has made the difference between present di tress (1:6) and the incredible joy (1:8) that tra scends every trial of life.

This precious experience of proven an purified faith results in "receiving the goal c your faith, the salvation of your souls" (1:9 This is the consummation of the savin process to be revealed in the last time (1:5 "when Jesus Christ is revealed" (1:7).

2.1.3. Adopt the Attitude of the Prophe (1:10–12). For their future orientation in regar to their salvation, Peter points to the exampl and the encouragement of the prophets.

First of all, the prophets prophesied "co cerning this salvation." Peter is not denyin that the prophets ministered to their own ge eration. He is, however, convinced that the prophesied of the same salvation that hi Christian audience looks forward to (1:3–9 This salvation can also be termed "grace, which points to the undeserved character c salvation and echoes the theological signifi cance of the greeting, "Grace and peace b yours in abundance" (1:2). Moreover, Pet observes that the prophets did not understan the future dimension of the salvation of whic they prophesied: They "searched intently an with the greatest care."

The subject of their inquiry was twofol focusing on "the time and circumstances t which the Spirit of Christ in them was poin ing" (1:11). The Spirit of prophecy was als the Spirit of Christ, for he spoke of the comin "Christ" (Greek equivalent for the Hebre term *Messiah* or "Anointed One"). In speakin about Christ through the prophets, the Spir "predicted the sufferings of Christ"—a them that will become dominant later in the lette (2:21–25) and is rooted in the Old Testame prophets (Isa. 53:9). The Spirit of Christ als predicted "the glories that would follow." This relates to the praise, glory, and honor at the revelation of Jesus Christ (1:7), and to the present experience of inexpressible and glorious joy (1:8). This Christological or messianic pattern of present suffering/future glory is equally true for the Christian (5:10). The Spirit, who spoke through the prophets as the Spirit of Christ, is to Christians the "Spirit of glory and of God," who rests on them (4:14).

While the prophets did not fully understand the future, "it was revealed to them that they were not serving themselves, but you" (1:12). Therefore, their ministry was in part to Israel and in part to the church. Not only did the prophets predict the future by the inspiration of the Spirit of Christ, but the apostles, heirs, and successors to the prophets, have also "preached the gospel to you by the Holy Spirit sent from heaven." Though it is true that the prophets did not fully understand the messianic age of salvation they predicted, it is also true that even angels share their same ignorance.

Just as the prophets did not understand the future dimension of God's program of salvation, so Peter's audience, beset by various trials, will not fully understand how God is working out his program of salvation for their lives. Moreover, in Peter's appeal to the experience of the prophets, we observe a definite apostolic consciousness of the progressive unfolding of revelation. The apostolic community knows more of God's plans and purposes than the prophets of Israel, because they live this side of the cross.

2.2. A Call to Holy Living (1:13–2:3)

Though like the prophets Peter's audience might not fully understand the future, in the present they are to live a life of holiness—a lifestyle modeled after the character of God himself. At this point in his letter, Peter reverses his argument. In 1:3–9, he placed a future orientation before his readers, who are beset by trials. Now he focuses on the need for holiness in the face of trial—that is, on the need to reflect and demonstrate God's holy character in the crucible of the trials of life. First he commands his audience to adopt Christian attitudes (1:13–16). Next he presents the death of Christ as the motivation for holiness (1:17–21). He then describes the social dimensions of holiness (1:22–25). Finally, he discusses negative and positive aspects of holiness (2:1–3).

2.2.1. Adopt Christian Attitudes (1:13–16). For Peter, it is imperative that his audience live a holy life. To this end he commands them to adopt new attitudes (1:13–14) and to model the holy character of God in their conduct (1:15–16).

Peter instructs his audience to "prepare your minds for action." This language is rooted in the culture of the Old Testament (Ex. 12:11; 1 Kings 18:46) and suggests dressing for action. As Peter uses this metaphor, it points to attitudes rather than to dress, for he literally writes of the "loins of your mind." This metaphor reminds his readers that the doctrine of salvation has moral or ethical implications, and these begin with a change of attitudes. The Christian who adopts these new attitudes will "be self-controlled"; that is, he or she will be "well-balanced, self-controlled ... self-possessed under all circumstances" (BAGD, 538).

Peter next commands his readers to "set your hope fully on the grace to be given you when Jesus Christ is revealed." This hope is the complement of self-control. It balances the present experience of testing and proving (1:6–7) with the prospect of future grace. Earlier Peter's greeting reminded his audience that grace is a present blessing (1:2). But grace will also be brought to them at the consummation of the ages, at the revelation of Jesus Christ. This future grace is the imperishable, undefiled, and unfading inheritance that God's people will receive. As is true for initial salvation (being born again, 1:3), so for final salvation (inheritance, 1:4) God's people ever relate to him on the basis of divine grace, not reward.

To the extent that Peter's audience follows his command to prepare their minds for action, they will become "obedient children" (1:14). Indeed, God has chosen them to obey Jesus Christ (1:2). This obedience is a family obligation, for those whom God has chosen are his children because they have been born again (1:3, 23). To this family Peter writes, "Do not conform to the evil desires you had when you lived in ignorance." The new birth and the obligation to obey God means that his children cannot be conformed to the former lusts of sinful desires, which had dominated their lives while they were still ignorant of God's holy calling and were unaffected by the sanctifying power of the Holy Spirit (1:2).

Obedience has both a negative and a positive dimension. God's children are not to be conformed to their former evil desires; rather, they are to "be holy" themselves in all they do (1:15). This is because "he who called you is holy." That is, God is the model for the behavior or conduct of his children. Clearly, God's children must reflect the family characteristic of holiness—a characteristic in vivid contrast to their former lifestyle (1:14; 2:1; 4:3). In contemporary terminology, this relationship between the Father and the conduct of his children is "role modeling."

This obligation to holiness involves obedience to Scripture, for it is written: "Be holy, because I am holy" (1:16). Peter quotes here from Leviticus 11:44—a quotation that has a twofold significance. (1) It points out that God's people under the new covenant have the same standard of holiness as did God's people under the old covenant. That is, although there may be a real difference in the expression of holiness—predominantly cultic terms for Israel and moral terms for the church—the obligation to holiness has not changed. Of course, this obligation to holiness could not change, for God, the model for holiness, does not change. (2) Peter's appeal to Leviticus 11:44 points to the conviction that the church is heir and successor to Israel (see 2:9).

Insofar as salvation is a matter of grace and the one who called them to salvation is holy, it is imperative that Peter's audience be holy. However, in order that they might conform to this command, they must adopt attitudes and conduct in keeping with their holy model. Negatively, they are not to persist in their former evil desires or sinful conduct (1:14); positively, they are to be self-controlled in conduct (1:13). They are to take on the identity of being holy (1:15–16). To the extent that God's people heed this command to holy living, they will adopt new attitudes towards sin (2:1–3), the state (2:13–17), slavery (2:18–25). and marriage (3:1–7).

2.2.2. The Motivation For Holy Living (1:17–21). Peter not only commands his audience to conform their conduct to the divine model (1:13–16), he also seeks to motivate them to living a life of holiness (1:17–21). He uses two means in this goal: the fear of the God, who holds them accountable for their conduct (1:17), and the cost of their redemption (1:18–21).

(1) Peter reminds his audience that God the Father "judges each man's work impartially" (1:17). To speak of God as judge is a reminder of both his moral standard and his moral purpose for his children. God's judgment is impartial because it is based on reality—that is, on each person's work or conduct. Knowing that the Father has a moral purpose for his children, Peter instructs his audience to adopt a lifelong reverence: "Live your lives as strangers here in reverent fear." God's children are ultimately accountable to their Father for their present conduct.

(2) Though reverent fear is a legitimate and powerful motivation for holy living, Peter moves to an even more powerful motivating factor: the price of salvation, which is not only the present experience but also the future hope of Peter's audience (1:3–9). Concerning this salvation, Peter reminds his audience that they have been "redeemed" (1:18). "Redeem" has the general meaning "set free . . . rescue," and the specific meaning "set free by paying a ransom" (BAGD, 482). The apostolic use of this term is no doubt rooted in the consciousness that Jesus expressed concerning the nature of his own ministry. He instructed his disciples to model their ministry after his: "For even the Son of Man did not come to be served, but to serve, and to give his life as a ransom for many" (Mark 10:45).

This redemption terminology, moreover, is rooted in God's great act of redeeming or freeing Israel from its Egyptian bondage (Ex. 6:6; 15:3); therefore, it emphasizes that what God has done in the remote past for Israel, he is doing in the present for a new people of God, the church. When writing of the cost of redemption, Peter contrasts a hypothetical price with the actual price. His audience has not been redeemed "with perishable things such as silver or gold" (cf. 1:7 for similar terminology in regard to the precious value of the testing of faith), but with "the precious blood" of Jesus.

In describing the redemption price as blood, Peter uses sacrificial terminology. Echoing the description of the Passover service, this sacrifice is "a lamb without blemish or defect" (cf. Ex. 12:4–5). Generally this terminology describes the physical perfection of the Passover lamb; but as used by Peter, it describes the moral perfection of Christ, who is the precious redeeming sacrifice. This contrast between perishable gold and precious blood informs Peter's readers that the death of

›sus is a treasure of inestimable worth. This rice, paid by Christ for our salvation, should ıotivate us to model our conduct after the holy haracter of God.

Moreover, the redemption found in the eath of Christ was not an emergency plan ;od devised to make the best of a situation that ad gotten out of hand, for Christ "was chosen efore the creation of the world" (1:20). God ıtended to offer his son as a sacrifice of ›demption before creation and the entry of sin ıto the world. This eternal redemptive pur-ose underlies God's choice according to his oreknowledge (1:2).

Christ initiated the fulfillment of God's ternal redemptive purpose when he "was evealed in these last times." This language eflects the two-age perspective of Judaism—he former days/the last days or this age/the ge to come. From the perspective of Peter and he other apostles, Jesus has inaugurated the ast days (Acts 2:17; Heb. 1:1–2). Peter then ›bserves that Christ appeared "for your sake." Christ's death was not for any fault of his own, ›ut was for our benefit. That is, because Christ lied, we have been redeemed.

Christ's appearance in these last times has ›nabled Peter's audience to "believe in God" 1:21). The God who is the object of their faith ›r belief is qualified as the one "who raised Jesus] from the dead and glorified him." Here Peter writes of the resurrection, through which God declares his acceptance or approval of Christ as the Passover sacrifice (cf. Rom. 1:4), and of the inevitable complemen-ary aspect of glorification or exal-ation (cf. Acts 2:32–33). In light of the divine resurrection-exalta-ion of Jesus, the "faith and hope" of Peter's audience "are in God."

2.2.3. The Social Dimension of Holy Living (1:22–25). Holy living, modeled after divine holi-ness and motivated by Christ's sacrificial death, is not something merely individual and private; it is also expressed in interpersonal relationships. Peter observes of his audience: "You have purified yourselves by obeying the truth" (1:22). That is, Peter's readers are actually living the obedience and holiness that he earlier exhorted them to live (1:14–15). Moreover, they must express a heartfelt or "sincere love for your brothers." In other words, this social dimension to holiness involves expressing God's love to the members of his family in an active way. Peter brings these dimensions together in his second letter, when he writes of the crowning virtues, namely, brotherly kindness and love (2 Peter 1:7).

Having written of the social and family dimension of holy living, Peter recalls that his audience has entered this relationship through having been "born again" (1 Peter 1:23). Returning to terminology by now familiar to them, he describes this birth as "not of perishable seed, but of imperishable" (cf. 1:4–7, 18–19). Peter is using the language of human procreation to describe eternal and spiritual realities, for the imperishable seed is "the living and enduring word of God." For Peter the word of God is not something that deteriorates, but is as enduring and permanent as God himself.

Having made his contrast between perishable and imperishable seed, Peter recalls an appropriate Scripture to emphasize and reinforce this contrast (1:24–25). He quotes:

> All men are like grass,
> and all their glory is like the flowers
> of the field;
> the grass withers and the flowers fall,
> but the word of the Lord stands forever.

This text from Isaiah 40:6–8 (also alluded to in James 1:10–11) compares human frailty to

These flowers are in full bloom in the Sinai desert after a rain, but like all flowers they will wither and die. Peter contrasts the short duration of flowers with the permanence of God's word. "Grass withers and the flowers fall, but the word of the Lord stands forever."

the grass of the field. It also gives a vivid contrast between such frailty and the eternal character of God's word. It was this "word that was preached" to his audience (1:25; cf. 1:12).

Peter's exposition of the doctrinal basis for the living hope that his audience is experiencing (1:3–12), and his subsequent command to practice holy living after the divine model (1:13–25), teach that right doctrine and right conduct (ethics) are both inseparable and mutually interdependent. Right doctrine without right practice is hypocrisy, and right practice without right doctrine is legalism. James too reminds us that the two together are pure and faultless religion (James 1:27).

2.2.4. Negative and Positive Dimensions of Holy Living (2:1–3). Having discussed both the doctrinal and ethical dimensions of salvation, Peter now applies this twofold truth to his audience. "Therefore," he writes—that is, in light of both God's provision of salvation and the complementary obligation to holy living—his readers are to "rid yourselves of all malice and all deceit, hypocrisy, envy, and slander of every kind." This catalogue of sins briefly lists some of the lusts that had formerly characterized their attitudes and conduct (1:14; 2:11; 4:13). Though they are classified in different ways, Peter's catalogue of sins is similar to other such lists in the New Testament. Jesus called them sins that come from the heart (Mark 7:21–23); James called them earthly, natural, and demonic wisdom (James 3:14–15); and Paul classified them as "the acts of the sinful nature" (Gal. 5:19–21) or the "old self" (Col. 3:9).

In addition to putting aside sin, Peter's audience must, "like newborn babies, crave pure spiritual milk" (2:2). This terminology develops the language of 1:23, where Peter has described his audience as "born again ... through the living and enduring word of God." Believers must adopt the insatiable and often voracious appetite of newborn babies and feed on the spiritual milk of the word. Such feeding will result in their "grow[ing] up in your salvation." That is, though Peter's audience are babies in respect to their appetite, they are to be growing to adulthood in their conduct and spiritual maturity.

As an encouragement to his readers to feed on God's word for their spiritual growth, Peter reminds them of their past experience: "now that you have tasted that the Lord is goo
(2:3). Peter has used several words to describ
God's goodness or kindness, such as grac
peace, and salvation. However, God's kindne
is most clearly evident in the fact that accor
ing to his great mercy, he has caused them t
be born again (1:3). Having already tasted c
God's kindness, his children may be confide
that they will not be disappointed in feeding c
his preached word.

2.3. God's Holy People: A Temple and a Nation (2:4–10)

In 1:3–2:3, Peter has employed the famil
metaphor to describe his audience. God is the
father (1:3, 17); they have been born agai
(1:3, 23) and feed on his word (2:2). Moreove
they are obedient children (1:14), have man
brothers (1:22), and in their holy living refle
the family characteristics (1:15–16). In th
present section (2:4–10), Peter describes hi
audience with new imagery: They are both
temple and a nation. Peter here adopts termi
nology from the Old Testament and applies i
spiritually to God's family of New Testamen
times.

**2.3.1. The Stone or Temple Metapho
(2:4–8).** Before applying this imagery to hi
audience, Peter first applies it to Jesus. I
responding to God's call, his readers hav
"come to him, the living Stone." Such
description of Jesus sounds strange to moder
ears. However, written by one who earlier ha
his own name changed by Jesus from Simon t
Cephas (Aramaic) = Peter (Greek) = Roc
(English, John 1:42), and who had heard Jesu
speak of himself in Old Testament terms as
rejected stone (Mark 12:10–12; cf. Ps
118:22), this metaphor was both appropriat
and meaningful. Peter qualifies this stone as
"living," not only making it clear that he is
writing metaphorically and spiritually, but perhaps also alluding to the resurrection of Jesus
from the dead (1:3, 19–21). He develops thi
allusion to the death and resurrection of Jesus
in describing him as "rejected by men," on the
one hand, "but chosen by God and precious to
him," on the other hand.

Not only is Jesus a living stone, but Peter's readers are also "like living stones," a description that points to their close identification with him. Peter continues to describe his readers by using a cluster of Old Testament images. They

The people in the foreground are dwarfed by the huge stones used in the time of Herod to build the Western Wall of the Temple Mount. This section is near Barclay's Gate. Peter calls Jesus "the living stone."

are "being built into a spiritual house to be a holy priesthood, offering spiritual sacrifices" (2:5). In using this terminology from the Old Testament, Peter affirms that God's people in New Testament times are the spiritual heirs and successors to Israel.

God's true temple is no longer Herod's magnificent temple, whose wonderful stones and wonderful buildings were so admired by the disciples (Mark 13:1), but it is the chosen exiles who are scattered throughout the world (1:1). Moreover, the true priesthood is no longer restricted to the tribe of Levi, but it is now all God's people, sanctified or made holy by the Spirit (1:3). After Jesus' death (1:19), the true sacrifice is no longer bulls, goats, or sheep, but it is now the spiritual worship of all God's people. This has been made possible "through Jesus Christ."

Jesus' achievement in creating the successor to the sacrificial system of Old Testament times—a spiritual house, priesthood, and sacrifice—is not a new innovation, but fulfills God's long-range plan announced in the Scriptures. Peter demonstrates this thesis with a string of three quotations (Isa. 28:16; Ps. 118:22; and Isa. 8:14). He could earlier assert that Jesus was chosen and precious (1 Peter 2:4), for in the language of the Old Testament he is "a chosen and precious cornerstone" (cf. Isa. 28:16). As the living fulfillment of this Scripture, Jesus is the key to the superstructure of the spiritual house made up of many living stones (2:5).

Peter observes that Jesus is not only precious in the sight of God, but also precious to those "who believe" (2:7a; cf. Isa. 28:16b). However, as the Scripture announces, he is also a dividing or separating factor. This division takes place in the human response to Jesus. That is, because Jesus is of precious value to those who believe, to those who disbelieve he is "the stone the builders rejected" (1 Peter 2:7b; cf. Ps. 118:22).

Furthermore, to those who reject Jesus, he becomes, in the language of Scripture, "a stone that causes men to stumble and a rock that makes them fall" (1 Peter 2:8; cf. Isa. 8:14). Israel has stumbled over Jesus "because they disobey the message." Here, as elsewhere in the New Testament, unbelief (2:7) and disobedience (2:8) are closely associated (cf. Heb. 3:18–19). This disobedience is to "the message," which for Peter is the twofold apostolic proclamation that Jesus is the Christ and that salvation is found in him (1:11–12, 23–25).

Having just described the human responsibility to respond to Jesus Christ, Peter now shifts his emphasis to God's sovereignty, observing that such disobedience "is also what they were destined for" (2:8b). That is, it is part of God's sovereign purpose for Israel. This truth is one of those many biblical paradoxes, such as the divine/human nature of Jesus, which can be neither harmonized nor negated. According to Peter, Israel must bear full responsibility for their rejection of Jesus, although at the same time this rejection is in keeping with God's sovereign purpose.

2.3.2. The New Nation (2:9–10). In contrast to present Israel, who through unbelief and disobedience rejected their Messiah, through faith in Christ Peter's audience has become a new nation—"a chosen people, a royal priesthood, a holy nation, a people belonging to God." This new status as a theocratic nation is what God had originally purposed for Israel in the Mosaic covenant (Ex. 19:5–6). As Peter applies this text to God's family of New Testament times, he once again affirms that the messianic community is heir and successor to Israel.

Moreover, in constituting this people to be a new nation, God intends for them to "declare the praises of him who called you out of darkness into his wonderful light." Both in word and deed God's new nation must proclaim his mercy (1:3), his holiness (1:16), his saving purposes in Christ (1:12, 25), and (in Exodus typology) his call to nationhood. That is, just as God had earlier called Israel out of Egypt (Hos. 11:1), so he has now called his new nation out of spiritual darkness into the marvelous light of his salvation or redemption.

Peter justifies his claim that God has created a new nation to be heir and successor to Israel by appealing to Hosea. Both Hosea's marriage and the names of his children become a parable of the broken covenantal relationship between Israel and God. Quoting from Hosea, Peter applies the significance of the names of Hosea's second and third children to his audience, for once they were "not a people," but now they are "the people of God"; once the "had not received mercy," but now they "hav received mercy" (2:10; cf. Hos. 1:6, 9; 2:23 Even though in Hosea the text announces th ultimate restoration of Israel, for both Peter an Paul (Rom. 9:25) this text announces the salvation of the Gentiles, who along with Jewis Christians have become the new people of Go

Not only does Peter's audience, who hav been sanctified by the Holy Spirit (1:3), mode the Father's divine holiness at the individua level (1:16), but in fulfillment of the Old Testament temple and nation imagery, they als model his holiness at the community level— as both a holy priesthood (2:5) and a hol nation (2:9).

3. Living Like Christ: Submission and Suffering (2:11–4:19)

Peter opened his letter with a doctrinal exposition of salvation (1:3–12), followed by a exhortation to his audience to express their salvation in ethical or moral conduct (1:13–2:3) He concluded by describing his audience a heir and successor to Israel (2:4–10). Fundamental to these opening words is Peter's observation that God is holy and that his people both individually and as the messianic community, are to model their conduct after the divine attribute of holiness.

In this next section (2:11–4:19), Pete emphasizes how Christ is the model for submission and suffering. He returns to the general subject of the many necessary tests that are the Father's means of proving the faith of his people (1:6–7) and applies the model of Chris to the conduct of his audience as they face specific areas of testing. To summarize the apostle's teaching, just as holiness is the family trait of the Father, so submission and suffering are the family characteristics of the Son; such qualities ought to shape Christ-like living in God's people.

3.1. Submit for the Lord's Sake (2:11–3:12)

As one of the Twelve, Peter had witnessed how Jesus voluntarily submitted to death on the cross (2:21–24). He had also heard him teach that discipleship requires submission rather than retaliation (Matt. 5:38–42). After a brief introduction (2:11–12), Peter applies this theme of Christian submission to three specific elationships: (1) to the government by everyone (2:13–17); (2) to masters by slaves (2:18–25); and (3) to husbands by wives (3:1–7). The following chart illustrates the close relationship between Peter's teaching and Paul's on his subject.

Citizens/ government	1 Peter 2:13–17	Rom. 13:1–7
Slaves/masters	1 Peter 2:18–25	Eph. 6:5–9; Col. 3:22–4:1
Wives/husbands	1 Peter 3:1–7	Eph. 5:22–33; Col. 3:18–19

3.1.1. Introductory Exhortation (2:11–12). For the first time in his letter, Peter addresses his audience as "Dear friends," reminding them of his pastoral concern and of God's love toward them. He also reminds them that they are "aliens and strangers"; that is, they are citizens of a divine rather than an earthly kingdom (1:1; 2:9). With that in mind, Peter exhorts them "to abstain from sinful desires." These lusts or desires are fleshly since they are expressed through the flesh. He earlier defined them as "evil desires" (1:14), in contrast to holy living (1:15–16); they include such sins as malice, deceit, and hypocrisy (2:1). Using terminology similar to Paul's description of his struggle against indwelling sin (Rom. 7:23) and of the opposition between flesh and Spirit (Gal. 5:17), Peter observes that these lusts wage "war against [the] soul."

In contrast to falling captive to hostile and destructive desires, Peter's readers are to "live . . . good lives among the pagans." His concern is that they maintain a good reputation, which reflects his earlier exhortation to holy living (1:13–2:3); it also anticipates the central theme of this section of the letter—the need for believers to live in submission. Presumably Peter has heard that the pagans were accusing some of his readers "of doing wrong." In context, this not only reflects participation in fleshly lusts, but also probably refers to antigovernment activity (2:16), wrongdoing as slaves (2:20), and/or disrespect on the parts of wives toward their unbelieving husbands (3:2).

In contrast to causing slander as evildoers, the "good deeds" publicly practiced by Peter's audience should cause those who see them to "glorify God on the day he visits us"—that is, on the day when Jesus Christ is revealed (1:7, 13). Abstinence from sin (2:11) or, positively, excellent behavior and good deeds (2:12) will result in the salvation of Gentiles, who will in turn join Peter's readers to glorify God when Jesus reveals himself at the end of the age.

3.1.2. Submit to Government (2:13–17). For Judaism of the first century, submission to foreign government was a volatile issue, which ultimately exploded in the Jewish revolt of A.D. 66–73. As his public ministry reached its climax in Jerusalem, Jesus' critics tested him on this issue, asking, "Is it right to pay taxes to Caesar or not?" (Mark 12:14). Holding a denarius for them to look at, Jesus asked, "Whose portrait is this? And whose inscription?" (12:16). Having forced his opponents to admit that it was Caesar's, Jesus taught, "Give to Caesar what is Caesar's and to God what is God's" (12:17). In other words, because the coin has Caesar's portrait, it belongs to him; therefore, it is proper to pay taxes (cf. Rom. 13:6–7).

Human beings, however, have been created in the image of God, and therefore they owe ultimate allegiance to God, not to Caesar or any human government. Similarly, Peter's audience, who are foreigners and strangers (1:1; 2:11), citizens of a divine kingdom (2:9), and who confess Jesus, not Caesar, as Lord (2:13), are faced with the issue of their attitude and conduct toward government. Echoing the teaching of Jesus, Peter now instructs them on their relationship to human government.

The apostle begins with the command: "Submit yourselves . . . to every authority instituted among men." The motive in submission is not simply civic responsibility, but it is "for the Lord's sake"—so that Christianity will not be slandered and a reproach be put on Christ. In general, it is necessary to submit to every human institution; specifically, it means that Peter's audience must submit "to the king, as the supreme authority."

Such submission is not only to be given to the king, but also to his representatives; that is, "to governors, who are sent by him." According to Peter, government is responsible to maintain the moral condition of society. Human institutions, whether in the person of the king or his representative, govern in order "to punish those who do wrong and to commend those who do right." Peter recognizes that there are reciprocal obligations in human society. Citizens are obligated to submit to government, and governments are obligated to preserve law and order for the peace, protection, and security of their subjects.

Since all citizens must submit to government, God's people must submit in particular because "it is God's will." This perspective contrasts to that of intertestamental Judaism, where zeal for the law periodically sparked anarchy and rebellion. From Peter's perspective, his readers are disobeying God's will if they do not submit to the government. Moreover, such submission has the beneficial effect in that it "should silence the ignorant talk of foolish men." In other words, submission is not only according to God's will, but it also removes an occasion for the ignorant—that is, the Gentile world—to slander God's people.

Though Peter's readers are expected to submit to government, and many of them are slaves (2:18ff.), they are to "live as free men." Nevertheless, Peter cautions, "do not use your freedom as a cover-up for evil." Therefore, while freedom is not incompatible with submission, it is incompatible with anarchy or lawlessness. Freedom is paradoxical. Believers are not only to act as free human beings, but they are also to act "as servants of God." Peter uses the normal word for "servant" here, to emphasize both God's ownership and their reciprocal obligation to submit to his will (2:15).

In verse 17 Peter uses a fourfold command to summarize his initial command that his audience submit to every authority instituted: "Show proper respect to everyone: Love the brotherhood of believers, fear God, honor the king." The order of these imperatives is from general to particular—all people, God's family, and finally, God himself and the king (his representative in human government). God's people, therefore, have universal responsibilities, but they are not equal. God's family of the created order and the king are to be honored. More particularly, the Christian family is to be loved (see comments on 1:22–23). Finally, God is to be feared—that is, reverenced and worshiped—for he manifests grace, mercy, and kindness (1:2–3; 2:3).

Human government has its legitimate sphere of God-given authority, and Christians are obligated to submit to it. It is striking that Peter, writing during the reign of the Emperor Nero, still sees the state as a divinely ordained institution for the preservation of good and the punishment of evil. However, there came a point in Peter's experience when Nero usurped divine prerogatives, and Peter, along with many other Christians, resolutely put God's authority before Caesar's and went to their death, as martyrs.

3.1.3. Slaves, Submit to Masters (2:18–25). Christianity bestowed not only religious equality, but also racial, social, and sexual equality on its members (Gal. 3:19–21). As a result, it met with a ready response among the disenfranchised elements of Roman society, and most churches had a high percentage of adherents from this level of society (1 Cor. 1:26–29). Consequently, in writing to his audience, Peter had to address the attitude and conduct that the Christian slave needed to adopt toward his or her master.

Addressing those who had the greatest right to pursue freedom (2:16), Peter writes: "Slaves, submit yourselves to your masters with all respect." He does not use the ordinary word for "slave," which is translated "servants" (2:16), but rather the word that is best translated "house slave." However, while he addresses a particular class of slaves, his teaching applies to all slaves: They must submit to their masters. Peter uses *despotes* for "master" (a word that has entered the English language as "despot," though in Greek it did not always have the English connotation of tyrant).

The submissive attitude that the servant is to adopt is that of respect or, more literally, fear. Even though Peter has just used this word to describe their attitude toward God (2:17), in the slave-master relationship it has the lesser connotation of simple respect. Reflecting the radical character of Christianity, this respect is to be rendered "not only to those who are good and considerate"—a relatively easy challenge—"but also to those who are harsh." Peter's description of these masters has a variety of connotations, including those who are "crooked, unscrupulous and dishonest" (BAGD, 756). In his estimation, whether the master is considerate or harsh, as a Christian the slave must render both submission and respect to the master.

The submission of a Christian slave to his master "is commendable" (lit., "grace"; cf. 1:3). As in 1:7, Peter's language may be deliberately ambiguous, for no master, no matter how harsh, would disapprove of submission and respect; but more importantly, God approves of such conduct. In 2:13 Peter had commanded that his audience submit to government for the Lord's sake. Here he introduces another dimension in motivating the slave to submit: "because he is conscious of God." Knowing that submission finds favor in God's sight, a slave can only maintain a good conscience in God's sight through submission. For many slaves in Peter's audience, this desire to maintain a good conscience before God will undoubtedly require that each one "bears up under the pain of unjust suffering."

Peter is under no illusion that the conduct of every Christian slave in his audience is exemplary and realizes that for some their suffering is deserved. Thus, he asks rhetorically, "How is it to your credit if you receive a beating for doing wrong and endure it?" Clearly, there is no credit for enduring deserved punishment. But the opposite is also true. Thus, Peter encourages the slaves in his audience: "If you suffer for doing good and you endure it, this is commendable before God." In this promise of divine approval for unjust suffering, Peter repeats the substance of the previous verse, that suffering unjustly for the sake of conscience finds favor with God.

In his salutation Peter observed that his readers in general had been chosen or called to obey Jesus Christ. Now in addressing the Christian slaves in his audience, Peter observes, "to this you were called," namely, to endure patiently suffering for doing right. Knowing that this may be difficult to accept, he immediately continues with the reminder that "Christ suffered for you." Not only was Jesus' suffering redemptive—on their behalf—but it was also exemplary, "leaving you an example, that you should follow in his steps." The unjust suffering that the slaves in his audience experience, is, therefore, the reciprocal obligation to the prior suffering of Jesus. Because he suffered on their behalf, as they follow his example, they may have to suffer unjustly for the sake of conscience toward God.

Though Jesus is an example of suffering for the slaves in his audience, his suffering was also unique, for "he committed no sin, and no deceit was found in his mouth" (cf. Isa. 53:9). Peter's quotation from Isaiah, therefore, reminds his audience that though their conduct is relatively righteous and their suffering is relatively undeserved, Jesus' conduct was absolutely righteous and his suffering absolutely undeserved.

The absolute injustice in Jesus' suffering was dramatically evident in his response to his tormentors and executioners. As an eyewitness to the death of Jesus, Peter recalls that "when they hurled their insults at him, he did not retaliate; when he suffered, he made no threats." This response both confirms his sinlessness and reinforces the undeserved character of his suffering. Jesus could adopt an attitude of nonretaliation because "he entrusted himself to him who judges justly." In writing about Jesus' submission to unjust suffering, Peter emphasizes both the trustworthiness of God and his exclusive role of his being the just Judge, who will ultimately vindicate those who suffer unjustly.

When he introduced the example of the suffering of Jesus, Peter reminded his audience that Jesus had suffered "for you"—that is, on their behalf or for their benefit (2:21). Now he reminds them that in his suffering Jesus was their substitute, for having entrusted himself to God, "he himself bore our sins in his body on the tree." The Jews judged him worthy of death on the charge of blasphemy (Mark 14:64); the Romans crucified him on the charge of sedition, for his supposed claim to be the king of the Jews (15:26); but Jesus' disciples, including Peter's audience, experienced his death as a substitutionary sacrifice for sin.

Jesus' death for sin produces a twofold result in those who appropriate its saving significance: negatively, "so that we might die to sins," and positively, that we might "live for righteousness." In other words, this dying to sin and living to righteousness results in holy living (1:15–16). Alluding to the mission of the suffering servant in Isaiah, Peter applies the benefits of Jesus' death to his audience by writing, "by his wounds you have been healed" (cf. Isa. 53:5). Though this terminology is often used to defend the doctrine of divine (physical) healing, in the context of Peter's argument it applies to the spiritual healing made possible when Jesus bore our sins in his body on the cross.

Continuing to draw his inspiration from the suffering servant text in Isaiah, Peter describes the past condition of his audience: "For you were like sheep going astray" (cf. Isa. 53:6). This common pastoral metaphor was given great relevance by Jesus in his parable of the shepherd and the lost sheep (Luke 15:3–7) in order to justify his characteristic fellowship with sinners (15:1–2). Though in the past his readers were like wayward sheep, now "you have returned to the Shepherd and Overseer of your souls." In describing Jesus as shepherd, Peter is no doubt also recalling our Lord's emphatic claim, "I am the good shepherd" (John 10:14)—a claim that evokes both the divine shepherd imagery (Ps. 23:1; Isa. 40:11) and the royal shepherd imagery (Jer. 3:15; 23:4) of the Old Testament.

As their spiritual shepherd, Jesus is also their spiritual "overseer," a term often translated "bishop," but which also has the general meaning "guardian." Peter's confidence in Jesus' pastoral oversight of his congregation is no doubt buttressed by his own earlier testing (Luke 22:31–32), denial (John 18:15–27), and subsequent restoration as an undershepherd (21:15–17).

Peter's teaching that slaves submit to their often harsh masters is liable to prove offensive to many modern readers of his letter. He not only fails to champion human rights or advocate social reforms, but he actually supports the status quo in Roman society. Nevertheless, though his teaching may not conform to current attitudes on human rights, it can be neither glossed over nor rejected for being simply culturally conditioned.

In fact, although Peter's instructions to slaves may be socially conservative, they are spiritually radical and revolutionary. He advocates that God's people voluntarily surrender even their most basic human rights in order to promote their Christian witness and to maintain their good conscience before God. This teaching also makes it clear that Christianity can be lived irrespective of whatever adverse social conditions prevail over God's people. As the apostle directs the slaves in his audience to model their lives after Christ, he teaches them that to submit to unjust suffering is the most Christlike response they can give to their circumstances.

3.1.4. Wives, Submit to Husbands (3:1–7). Continuing his teaching on the theme of submission, Peter addresses the wives in his audience: "In the same way be submissive to your husbands." That is, in the same way as Christians generally are to submit to government (2:13–17) and Christian slaves are to submit to their masters (2:18–25), Christian wives are to submit to their husbands. Such submission is more than an occasional duty, for Peter's language points to a present or habitual response.

Moreover, wifely submission is particularly important, for it is probable that more, rather than fewer, women in Peter's audience had husbands who did "not believe the word." This condition stands in contrast to the divine call to obey Christ (1:2, 22) and is equivalent in meaning to the words "unbeliever," "unsaved person," or "non-Christian." Therefore, Peter observes that the submission of a Christian wife to her husband can have an evangelistic purpose: "so that . . . they may be won over without words by the behavior of their wives." As he addresses these wives in his audience, Peter develops a play on words. While their husbands are disobedient to the word or gospel (1:12, 23–25), these women are to witness without a word; that is, in silence. In Peter's estimation, good behavior or wifely submission is most effective in winning the disobedient to obedience to Christ.

This silent word of witness becomes effective when husbands "see the purity and reverence of your lives." Wifely behavior is a matter of both attitude and conduct; it is to be both morally chaste or pure and respectful. Here Peter applies characteristics that are to be true for all Christians, especially wives. That is, just as all Christians are to be holy (1:15–16), so wives are to be chaste. Furthermore, just as all Christians are to fear or reverence God (2:17) and slaves are to respect their masters (2:18), so wives are to respect (lit., "fear") their husbands. Such wholesome and submissive behavior is both the obligation of a Christian wife toward her husband and is an effective means of evangelizing or winning an unbelieving husband to Christ.

Having discussed wifely virtues such as submission, chastity, and respect, Peter goes on to instruct the wives in his audience concerning their beauty, which "should not come from outward adornment" (i.e., through "braided hair and the wearing of gold jewelry and fine clothes"). Peter does not prohibit external adornment; but he knows that holiness is a matter of attitudes and conduct (1:13–2:3) and that it can never be a matter of external austerity. Rather, as the next verse shows, he contrasts two kinds of beauty—one that is merely decoration (3:3) and one that is an inward quality (3:4).

The beauty of Christian wives "should be at of your inner self." This inner beauty is, in ct, "the unfading beauty of a gentle and quiet irit." Gentility or meekness and quietness or anquillity not only complement the qualities ' submission, chastity, and respect, but like e believer's inheritance (1:4) and the seed of iritual birth (1:23), they are imperishable. ecause such beauty is unfading, it also con- asts to the superficial and transient character ' external adornment. Moreover, the enduring eauty of character will both prove to be most tractive to the husband and will be "of great orth in God's sight."

Just as Peter earlier directed the slaves in his idience to Christ as an example of submis- on to unjust suffering (2:21–25), so here he irects the wives in his audience to the women f Israel as examples of the adornment of ifely submission. Using some of his most aracteristic terminology, these examples ere "holy [cf. 2:5, 9] women . . . who put eir hope [cf. 1:3, 21] in God." As examples, ey "used to make themselves beautiful. They ere submissive to their own husbands." In is dual context of adornment and submission) their own husbands, wives of both Old Tes- ment and New Testament times are to be dis- nguishable in character and conduct.

Having appealed to the general example of e holy women of Old Testament times, Peter ow appeals to the specific example of Sarah, who obeyed Abraham." Her obedience is evi- ent in the manner of her address, who, calling im "her master," gave to Abraham both the ubmission and the respect that Christian vives are to show to their husbands (3:1–2). n the same way that men and women of faith ecome the children of Abraham (Gal. 3:7), so vomen who respectfully obey or submit to heir husbands "are her daughters if you do vhat is right" (lit., "good"). To do good to their usbands empowers Christian women to "not give way to fear." Therefore, as Peter describes t, wifely submission is neither servile nor fear- ul; it is one dimension of holy living.

Having written of the duties of wives oward their husbands, Peter now instructs the usbands in his audience about their respon- ibilities toward their wives (3:7). "In the same vay be considerate as you live with your vives." He introduces the duties of husbands oward their wives by the term "in the same way" (cf. 3:1). This term compels husbands to realize that just as they can rightly expect submission from their wives, they also have an equal and reciprocal duty towards their wives. Primarily, husbands are to treat their wives with consideration or understanding, an understanding that develops from the knowledge of wives both as women and as individuals. In particular, considerate husbands will recognize that the wife is "the weaker partner." In describing women in this way, Peter simply makes a commonplace observation—women are generally physically weaker than men.

Though husbands are to recognize that their wives are physically weaker and treat them accordingly, they must also recognize that their wives are spiritually their equals. Hence, husbands are to "treat them . . . as heirs with you of the gracious gift of life." That is, husbands are to regard their wives as the recipients of God's grace, a grace that is in every way equal to his grace toward them. The result will be "that nothing will hinder your prayers." In other words, Peter teaches that husbands who fail to regard their wives as fellow heirs of God's grace will themselves forfeit God's grace; he will refuse to hear their prayers.

As is true for Peter's instruction to slaves, so his instruction to wives is easy to misunderstand and misrepresent. Therefore, in the first place, we are to observe that Peter does not teach that *women* are to submit to *men*; rather, he simply teaches that *wives* are to submit to *husbands*. Moreover, he does not define submission in terms of servility, but in terms of chastity and respect. Finally, husbands have equal and reciprocal duties toward their wives. Clearly, Peter's teaching elevates and ennobles the status of women in marriage and emphasizes that the marriage relationship has mutual responsibilities for both husbands and wives.

3.1.5. Summary Exhortation (3:8–12). Peter has presented Christ as the model for submission and has illustrated its application to Christian conduct through the specific examples of citizens, slaves, and wives (2:13–3:7). Now he applies this teaching to Christian conduct in general.

Peter begins his exhortation with the word "finally," indicating that he is about to summarize the implications of submission to Christian conduct in general. Cataloguing several virtues, using terminology that is virtually unique to this letter, he exhorts his readers to "live in harmony with one another," that is, to be "like-minded, united in spirit" (BAGD, 569). This exhortation to harmony is an obvious contrast to the real or potential strife between citizens and government, slaves and masters, and wives and husbands where the Christian has not submitted, for the Lord's sake, to those who exercise authority.

More generally, however, Peter exhorts all God's people to live in harmony in every relationship. He then adds to his catalogue, exhorting his audience to "be sympathetic," using a word that is used elsewhere of both Jesus and his disciples, which means "sympathize with, have or show sympathy with" (BAGD, 778; cf. Heb. 4:15; 10:34).

Echoing his earlier teaching on the family relationship of God's people (1:3, 22–23), the apostle exhorts his audience to "love as brothers." This brotherly love will be promoted when God's people respond to the exhortation to be "compassionate"—that is, to be "tenderhearted" (BAGD, 326; note Eph. 4:32). This lifestyle is possible only insofar as God's people surrender their rights and become "humble."

At this point in Peter's exposition the emphasis shifts from attitudes to overt action and from relationships within the family of God to relationships toward the world. To those who receive ill treatment he exhorts, "Do not repay evil with evil or insult with insult." This exhortation is especially pertinent for citizens, slaves, and wives who might be suffering unjustly from governments, masters, and husbands, respectively, in their abuse of authority. Rather than reciprocating evil for evil, Peter exhorts his audience to repay evil and insult "with blessing." As Jesus had taught the disciples, "Blessed are you when people insult you . . . and falsely say all kinds of evil against you" (Matt. 5:11).

Peter here shifts the emphasis of blessing from the suffering Christian to the persecutor. Here is conduct that exemplifies Christlike submission, for Peter has already observed that "when they hurled their insults at him, he did not retaliate" (2:23). God's elect must not only submit to unjust suffering, but they also must bless their antagonists. Such conduct is necessary, Peter writes, in order "that you may inherit a blessing."

To explain his exhortation and perhaps als[o] to undergird his apostolic authority with bibl[i]cal authority, Peter appeals to Psalm 34:12–1[6]:

> Whoever would love life
> and see good days
> must keep his tongue from evil
> and his lips from deceitful speech.
> He must turn from evil and do good;
> he must seek peace and pursue it.
> For the eyes of the Lord are on the righteous,
> and his ears are attentive to their prayer,
> but the face of the Lord is against those who do evil.

Peter's appeal to this wisdom psalm reflects [a] common understanding of the Old Testamen[t] within apostolic Christianity. Scripture wa[s] seen as authoritative not only for doctrine (c[f.] 1 Peter 1:24) but also for attitudes and conduc[t] (cf. also 1:16, which quotes Lev. 11:44). Psalm 34, therefore, has direct relevance for Peter'[s] exhortation. It explains his teaching that Go[d] obligates himself to bless those who bless thei[r] antagonists.

This divine blessing, moreover, is not limite[d] to the future revelation of Jesus (1:4–5), but i[s] a present inheritance of the righteous (i.e., thos[e] who do good). The main point of Peter's quotation of Psalm 34 has both positive and negative dimensions. Positively, it teaches that th[e] one who blesses instead of reviles can expect [a] blessing from the Lord, "for the eyes of the Lor[d] are on the righteous and his ears are attentiv[e] to their prayer." Negatively, it teaches that th[e] one who returns evil for evil can only expect th[e] Lord's displeasure or judgement, for "the fac[e] of the Lord is against those who do evil."

3.2. *Suffer for the Lord's Sake (3:13–4:19)*

In this section Peter develops the centra[l] subject of the previous section, though h[e] shifts the emphasis. In the life situation of th[e] Christian slave, Christ was the model for submission to suffering (2:18–25). Here th[e] emphasis is on suffering unencumbered by th[e] call to submission. Furthermore, it is no[t] restricted to the predicament of Christian slaves, but is predicated as the potential experience of all of God's people. Therefore, Peter's teaching on suffering continues directly from the concluding paragraph of the preceding section (3:8–12), with the expressions "doing good" (3:10, 13) and "blessing" (3:9, 14) linking the two sections together. Peter not only opens this section on the subject of suffering (3:13–17), but concludes it on the same subject (4:12–19). These two paragraphs bracket an appeal to the example or model of Christ's suffering (3:18–22), a subsequent command to right living (4:1–6), and a series of practical commands (4:7–11).

3.2.1. Suffer for the Sake of Righteousness (3:13–17). At this point in his letter Peter addresses a question that was both millennia-long (e.g., Job) and was also faced by his audience: Why do the righteous suffer? He finds the answer to this paradoxical predicament in the (perhaps) inscrutable will of God (3:17)—an answer he buttresses by an appeal to the redemptive suffering of Christ (3:18; cf. 2:21–25).

Challenging his audience with a rhetorical question, Peter asks, "Who is going to harm you if you are eager to do good?" He assumes his audience, which is to model itself after Christ, will be eager or enthusiastic for good deeds, even to the extent of returning a blessing for evil (3:9). Although those who do not model themselves after Christ may, in contrast, often return evil for evil (3:9), Peter expects that even they will not return harm or evil for good when they find it eagerly promoted and practiced, by God's people.

Implying a future, less probable condition by his sentence structure, Peter continues, "But even if you should suffer for what is right." That is, some among his audience, who are not yet suffering, may, like those slaves he has addressed earlier (2:18–20), suffer in the future. This conditional exception to his rhetorical question (3:13) makes suffering for the sake of righteousness parallel to receiving harm or evil for doing good. It also echoes his earlier teaching that citizens are to submit to government "for the Lord's sake" (2:13), and that slaves are to submit to unjust suffering "for the sake of conscience" (2:19, lit. trans.).

To those who will suffer for doing right or good, Peter announces that they "are blessed." This announcement summarizes his earlier promise of blessing given to those who return blessing for evil (3:9), who do good (3:11), and who are righteous (3:12). Furthermore, Peter reinforces his promise of blessing with an encouragement from the prophets: "Do not fear what they fear; do not be frightened" (cf. Isa. 8:12). This assurance of divine blessing is to liberate the Christian who suffers from the attitudinal bondage of fear and agitation.

Addressing his audience with an imperative, Peter continues, "But in your hearts set apart Christ as Lord." Though he has earlier instructed his audience to submit to legitimate human authority (e.g., government, masters, husbands), he now commands his audience to make Christ's cosmic lordship experientially real in their own attitudes and conduct—they are to do nothing less than "consecrate, treat as holy, reverence" (BAGD, 8–9) Christ as Lord. This lordship is to be in their hearts; that is, it is both internal and spiritual. Thus, for Peter, not only blessing, but the lordship of Christ is the antidote for fear and agitation.

When Christ is truly Lord, his people will "always be prepared to give an answer." Rather than giving a personal answer or defense for their good and righteous conduct, believers are to defend their faith "to everyone who asks." God's suffering people are to "give the reason for the hope that you have." This hope is living, based on the resurrection (1:3); it is an imperishable, undefiled, and unfading inheritance (1:4); and it is guaranteed by divine protecting power (1:5). Both blessing and the lordship of Christ are the antidote for fear and agitation, but hope undergirds the sufferer and gives him or her endurance.

Peter then suggests that the attitude of the defender is as important as his or her answer. The ever-ready defense is to be given "with gentleness [a word that denotes 'humility, courtesy, considerateness, meekness'; BAGD, 699] and respect [lit., fear]." Making a deliberate play on words, those who have made Christ as Lord in their hearts are not to fear their antagonists, but like Christian wives who fear/respect their unbelieving husbands (3:6), they are to answer their questioners with fear/respect.

In addition to defending their faith with gentleness and respect, Peter's audience must keep "a clear conscience." From Peter's perspective, a good conscience arises by the removal of sin and is symbolized in baptism (3:21); it motivates God's people to suffer unjust treatment (2:19) and is to be maintained even if people "speak maliciously against your good behavior in Christ." Not only was Jesus, who committed no sin, insulted, but in a similar manner those who slander the conduct of Peter's readers also speak against them in a derogatory manner.

In other words, Peter reminds his audience that in their suffering they are simply receiving the same verbal and physical abuse as their Savior. The purpose of maintaining a good conscience, of knowing that one has done right in spite of slander, is so that those who speak maliciously "may be ashamed of their slander." Therefore, good behavior not only maintains a good conscience before God, but it will both "silence the ignorant talk of foolish men" (2:15) and put them to shame, exposing their accusations for what they truly are—slander.

Concluding his teaching on suffering with a general application of his earlier instructions to slaves (2:18–20), Peter writes that "it is better ... to suffer for doing good than for doing evil." Peter has observed two causes of suffering: for doing what is right (2:19; 4:16) and for doing what is wrong (2:20; 4:15). If the Christian is to suffer, it is better that it be for the former reason than for the latter.

Moreover, addressing those who may have entertained the false expectation that divine blessing (3:9, 14) ought to secure freedom from suffering, Peter inserts the conditional qualification, "if it is God's will." As in 3:14, the grammatical construction of this clause indicates a future, less-probable condition. Suffering is part of God's will for his people (note 4:19), yet Peter does not know whether such suffering will be the plight of everyone. Thus, he announces that it may be a possibility, but it is not a certainty for each of them. In writing of God's will, Peter is emphatic, and his statement may be translated, "if the will of God should so will." That God might will his people to suffer unjustly for doing what is right is not a theological dilemma for Peter, for God willed that his Son should so suffer (2:21–24; 3:18; 4:13). Thus, like holiness and submission, suffering is simply one of the family traits of God's people.

Peter makes three points about Christian suffering. (1) It should be undeserved—for the sake of righteousness (3:14), for good behavior (3:16), and for doing what is right (3:17). (2) God's blessing comes to those who suffer undeservedly (3:14). (3) Suffering is within the bounds of God's will for his people (3:17). Clearly, these Petrine perspectives on suffering are incompatible with the self-indulgent attitude toward suffering that is prevalent among so many Christians in an affluent and largely untested contemporary church in North America.

3.2.2. Christ: The Model for Suffering (3:18–22). The following chart illustrates that the structure of Peter's teaching on suffering parallels his earlier instruction to slaves (2:18–25).

The problem of undeserved suffering	2:18–20	3:13–17
Christ: the model sufferer	2:21–25	3:18–22

Though the context has shifted from submission to suffering, here, as in the earlier passage, Peter introduces the example of the sufferings of Christ for the same twofold purpose. (1) By appealing to the example of Christ, Peter removes the sufferings of his audience from a purely personal plight and places them in a redemptive and Christological context. (2) On the other hand, he wants to encourage and fortify those in his audience who either are suffering, or who will suffer, undeservedly. Moreover, as he discusses it, the redemptive death of Christ is not simply an event, but it is a process that includes his death (3:18), his ministry in the Spirit (3:18b–19), and his exaltation (3:22).

Having just written of suffering for doing what is right according to God's will (3:17), Peter now naturally turns again to the example of Christ's death. This death is an example for Peter's audience, but it is also unique, "for Christ died for sins once for all." That is, in contrast to the (many?) sufferings faced by Peter's audience, Christ died once for all (note Heb. 9:12, 28; 10:10). Moreover, in writing that Christ died for sins, Peter affirms that the sins of humanity, and not some fault of Christ's own, caused his death. Indeed, his death was the death of the "righteous"—the uniquely and absolutely righteous one—as a substitute "for the unrighteous"—on behalf of sinners (cf. Rom. 5:6–8).

The purpose of Christ's unique, substitutionary death was "to bring you to God." He died to present those who have been "sprinkled by his blood" (1:2) to God. Christ's death was unique in character and purpose, but it gains its fullest significance in that having been "put to death in the body," he was "made alive by the Spirit." Peter contrasts Christ's death, a past experience with present redemptive results, and his being made alive, his subsequent unchangeable state. He also contrasts the body (the realm of his death) and the Spirit (the realm of his life).

Before attempting to interpret this and the following verses, two observations need to be made. (1) It is perhaps fitting to apply Peter's observation about Paul's letters here. Paul, he observes, wrote to you "some things that are hard to understand" (2 Peter 3:16). The difficulty of this passage means that any interpretation given to it is necessarily tentative. (2) As the following chart indicates, both 2 Peter and Jude contain a parallel passage that helps to illuminate this text.

Spirits/angels in bonds	1 Peter 3:19	2 Peter 2:4; Jude 6
The rescue of Noah	1 Peter 3:20	2 Peter 2:5

Following his death, Jesus, having been made alive by the Spirit, "went and preached." The verb "preach" means "announce, make known" (BAGD, 431). Jesus, therefore, made an announcement "to the spirits in prison." The word "spirits" is used in the New Testament for "angels," whether they are good or evil (Luke 10:20; Heb. 1:14). That it refers to fallen angels in this verse is supported by the qualification that they are now "in prison," and by the parallel passages in 2 Peter and Jude, which use the word "angels" rather than "spirits." Therefore, Peter implies, Jesus, by virtue of his death, went to imprisoned angels and announced his victory over death and the consequences of that triumph, namely, that their own judgment is sealed.

Those spirits now in prison had "disobeyed long ago"; indeed, this disobedience was the cause of their imprisonment. In both letters this judgment on angels turns Peter's thoughts to the judgment on the world in the time of Noah. However, Peter observes that that judgment was delayed "when God waited patiently in the days of Noah." Concerning delayed judgment, Peter writes, "[the Lord] is patient with you, not wanting anyone to perish, but everyone to come to repentance" (2 Peter 3:9; cf. Rom. 2:4). God's patience extended "while the ark was being built" (1 Peter 3:20); that is, while Noah built the ark, God waited for people to repent and thus avert his judgment. However, only "a few people, eight in all, were saved through water." In spite of an opportunity to repent while the ark was being built, out of all people only Noah and his household were saved (2 Peter 2:5; cf. Gen. 6:19; 7:7). Thus, the flood waters were the means of judgment on the world and were at the same time the means of the salvation of Noah's family.

Peter applies the example of Noah's salvation from the flood waters to his readers, writing that "this water symbolizes baptism that now saves you also." The adjective that is translated "symbolizes" also comes into the English language as the word "antitype." Thus, "the saving of Noah from the flood is a type, or 'foreshadowing,' and baptism corresponds to it" (BAGD, 76). The significance of baptism is not to be found in ritual cleansing—"not the removal of dirt from the body"—but it is to be found in "the pledge of a good conscience toward God." As Peter's Pentecost preaching informs us, this good conscience is nothing less than the forgiveness of sins (Acts 2:38). Though Jesus died for sins, this good conscience or forgiveness of sins is sealed "by the resurrection of Jesus Christ." Therefore, in providing salvation from sin, the resurrection of Jesus is the necessary complement to his death.

God's people stand before him with a good conscience, not only through the resurrection of Jesus, but also because of his exaltation, for he is "at God's right hand" (cf. Acts 2:32–35). Historically, the ascension of Jesus, which was witnessed by Peter and the other apostles (1 Peter 1:9–11), ended his earthly ministry. Having "gone into heaven," he enjoys the honor and authority that were denied him on earth. God raised him to this position of authority—"with angels, authorities and powers in submission to him" (cf. Eph. 1:20–22; Col. 1:16; 2:15). Therefore, Jesus' death had a cosmic dimension, for God subjected hostile spiritual powers to him.

Implicit in the juxtaposition of these two paragraphs (3:13–17; 3:18–22), Christ's death is an example of suffering for those whom God may will to suffer for doing what is right. Moreover, Christ's death is the pathway to vindication (resurrection, 3:21) and honor (exaltation, 3:22), just as his readers' unjust suffering is the pathway to blessing (3:14). In addition, the rescue of Noah is a symbol or type of Christian baptism; as for Noah and his household, so for the Christian, water is the means of salvation. However, in contrast to Noah's rescue from judgment, baptism signifies the inner reality of forgiveness. Therefore, Christ's death and resurrection is a pattern for God's people, and the ritual of baptism signifies that pattern (4:1–2; cf. Rom. 6:3–5). On the other hand, Noah's rescue through the flood waters is also a type of salvation of God's people, and baptism symbolizes that salvation.

3.2.3. The Ethical Imperative (4:1–6). Peter now develops the ethical or moral implications of Christ's death and resurrection for the conduct of God's people. (1) He commands his audience to die to sin and live for the will of God (4:1–2). (2) He reinforces his command with a contrast, not only between their former and present conduct, but also between pagan and Christian conduct (4:3–6).

Peter now summarizes his appeal to Christ's death in 3:18–22, addressing his readers with, "Therefore, since Christ suffered in his body." Echoing his earlier emphasis on the physical dimension of Christ's redemptive suffering (2:24), the expression "suffered in his body" is equivalent to "died for sins" (4:1; cf. 3:18). Using a word that often had military connotations, Peter next commands his audience to "arm yourselves also with the same attitude." It is necessary for his audience to make themselves ready or to equip themselves with the same purpose (lit., insight, thought) as Christ had, whose name they bear (4:14), "because he who has suffered in his body is done with sin." Therefore, just as Christ suffered in his body, dying for sin, so Peter's audience is to suffer also in the body; that is, suffer for doing what is right and for the sake of righteousness (2:20; 3:14), putting an end to the practice of sin in their lives.

Peter expects his readers to adopt Christ's attitude to sin and suffering so as to live. This attitude for life extends to death—throughout "the rest of his earthly life." As Peter describes it, this Christian lifestyle has both negative and positive dimensions. Negatively, the Christian does not live "for evil human desires." Peter has already described this sinful nature to his audience as "the evil desires you had when you lived in ignorance" (1:14), and gave as examples of these former lusts, malice, deceit, hypocrisy, jealousy, and slander (2:1). In the following verse he will describe this conduct as "doing what pagans choose to do" (4:3).

In contrast to this prohibited conduct, positively, his audience is to live "for the will of God." In Peter's perspective, God's will is the same for the Christian as it was earlier for Israel, and it is found in the imperative, "so be holy in all you do, for it is written, 'Be holy, because I am holy'" (1:15b–16). Clearly, to live for the will of God, his people must model both the suffering of Christ and the holiness of God in their conduct.

Displaying good rhetorical ability, Peter links verse 3 to the previous verse, not only logically but also linguistically: "For you have spent enough time in the past doing what pagans choose to do." In verses 2–3 he implicitly contrasts time that extends into the future and time that is past. These two time periods, moreover, are characterized by two contrasting lifestyles. For his audience, living for the will of God characterizes the present-future time, whereas living according to the desire of the pagans has characterized past time. In making the Christian-pagan contrast, Peter applies to the church, which is the spiritual heir to Israel (2:9–10), the twofold Jew-Gentile division of humanity. As Gentiles, his audience had been "living in debauchery, lust, drunkenness, orgies, carousing and detestable idolatries." This list of pagan sins supplements Peter's earlier list of sins (2:1), which in his perspective are incompatible with holy living.

Christian conduct is radically different from pagan conduct, for in all of this, "they think it strange that you do not plunge with them into the same flood of dissipation." Those whose conduct is dominated by the sins that Peter has just listed are surprised that others refuse to plunge with them "into the same stream of debauchery" (BAGD, 793). Because Peter's readers refuse to join with the pagans in their sin, "they heap abuse on you," in the sense that they "injure the reputation of, revile, defame" (BAGD, 142) God's people. However, although Peter is concerned that his audience should maintain a good reputation in the world, it is not to be at the cost of sinful conduct.

The pagans may malign Peter's audience for its holy living, but, in turn, "they will have to give account to him who is ready to judge the living and the dead." Here, for the third me in this letter, Peter writes about God in his ıpacity as judge. Earlier, he wrote that God npartially judges according to each one's ork and that he judges righteously (1:17; 23); now he writes that God also judges the ving and the dead. This phrase reminds eter's audience that all humanity is accountble before God. By implication, this accountbility results in the condemnation of the ıgans who malign God's people—those who ten suffer for the sake of righteousness.

At this point, Peter turns from the condemıtion of the pagan world to the vindication of od's people. This vindication is good news, or this is the reason the gospel was preached ven to those who are now dead." The purpose the good news that formerly had been proaimed to some who are now dead is twofold: o that they might be judged according to men regard to the body," and so that they may ive according to God in regard to the spirit." 'ith a continuing emphasis on the "body," hristians, who have suffered in the body (4:1) ıd who also live for the rest of the time in the ody for the will of God (4:2), are also judged the body. This judgment is not in regards to n, but it is in regards to their humanity, for hristians are judged as human beings. That is, ven though they have been chosen, sanctified, orn again (1:1–3), and redeemed (1:18), they main in the flesh and will die.

However, in spite of physical death, they e alive in spirit (cf. Rom. 8:10–11). Thus, as eter describes it, the experience of God's eople, though it is not identical to Christ's, osely parallels his death and vindication: oth suffer in the flesh (4:1), and both die :18a; 4:6a), but in spite of death, both live spirit (3:18b; 4:6c).

In sum, Christ's substitutionary death for n has implications for Christian conduct or hics. Negatively, believers are to put an end sin; positively, they are to live for the will of od. To the degree that God's people obey this nperative, their conduct will differ from both eir former conduct and from the conduct of e non-Christian world. Ironically, to live for od's will invites the slander of those whose ves are dominated by sin. However, all eople are accountable to the divine judgment. inners come under his condemnation, hereas God's people receive his commendaon or vindication.

3.2.4. A Series of Practical Imperatives (4:7–11). In the progression of his letter, Peter moves from the ethical imperative (4:1–6) to a series of practical instructions (4:7–11). This practical instruction is of two kinds: (1) that which relates to attitudes and conduct in interpersonal relationships (4:7–9), and (2) that which relates to attitudes and conduct in the exercise of the gifts of grace (4:10–11). The conjunction of these two dimensions shows the intimate and interdependent connection between areas of service that many of God's people tend to divide into independent and isolated categories. As the following chart demonstrates, Peter's teaching on these subjects closely parallels Paul's, though it is briefer and reverses the Pauline order.

Practical instruction/love		
1 Peter 4:7–9	Rom. 12:9–21	1 Cor. 13:1–13
The exercise of gifts		
1 Peter 4:10–11	Rom. 12:6–8	1 Cor. 12:1–31

The common substratum of teaching between the two apostles, on this and many other subjects, does not detract from the competence, integrity, or authority of either.

Failing to keep to the overall theme of this section (suffering), Peter goes off at a word. He has just reminded his audience that God is the judge of all humankind, and his thoughts turn to the final consummation of all things. Thus, he writes, "the end of all things is near." The Greek word translated "near" also means "goal." From Peter's perspective, history has a specific end and goal: the final judgment on all humanity (4:5) and the final salvation of God's people at the revelation of Jesus Christ (1:9). This end has drawn near. Although later Christianity has often interpreted this term to be a time reference, for Peter and apostolic Christianity in general, it refers to an event without specific reference to the length of the lapse of time. In other words, the public ministry and subsequent death of Jesus for sins (2:24; 3:18) has made possible the complementary revelation of Jesus for judgment in the last time.

This knowledge that Christ has brought the end near ought to influence present attitudes and conduct. "Therefore," Peter commands, "be clearminded." Peter does not want his audience to be dismayed by the prospect of the end of the world or to be caught up in eschatological or apocalyptic fervor; rather, he desires that they be "reasonable, sensible, serious, keep [their] head" (BAGD, 802). Not only does he command his audience to be clearminded, but he also commands be "self-controlled so that you can pray."

Repeating the substance of an earlier appeal that his audience "love one another deeply, from the heart" (1:22), Peter now urges, "above all, love each other deeply." He teaches them that in the light of approaching judgment, clearmindedness and self-control are important, but love is most important. In intensity, love is to be deep or earnest; in application, love is for one another or the entire family of God's people.

Love is vital "because love covers over a multitude of sins." In biblical teaching, love does not excuse sin; instead, it brings the sinner to repentance. James writes, "Remember this: Whoever turns a sinner from the error of his way will save him from death and cover over a multitude of sins" (James 5:20; cf. Prov. 10:12). Similarly, in the context of Peter's teaching, to cover a multitude of sins with love restores the sinner and averts impending judgment (1 Peter 4:5). Furthermore, this ministry of restoration solemnizes Peter's command to be self-controlled for the purpose of prayer (4:7). Love combines with prayer to effect the restoration of the sinner.

Peter goes on to command his readers to "offer hospitality to one another without grumbling." He may regard hospitality to be a specific example of the exercise of love, for throughout the New Testament hospitality is closely associated with love (Rom. 12:9, 13; Heb. 13:1–2). Even though hospitality is a prominent virtue in apostolic Christianity, it is not to be dispensed indiscriminately: Those who do not adhere to apostolic Christianity are not to receive it (2 John 10–11), but those who do adhere are to be given hospitality (3 John 5–8). Peter teaches that in the exercise of love, the attitude in which hospitality is administered is as important as hospitality itself. It is to be given without grumbling, murmuring, or complaint.

The prospect of the approaching end of all things also has implications for the exercise of gifts in Christian service. Peter writes that "each one should use whatever special gift he has received" (4:10). This word "gift" translates the Greek word *charisma,* which Paul commonly uses when he writes of the "gift (*charismata*) of the Spirit (Rom. 12:6; 1 Co 12:4–9, 28–31). In common with Paul's teac ing, Peter teaches his audience that each o has received a gift (1 Cor. 12:7). Moreover, t word "gift" reminds his readers that ministry service is apart from human merit; indeed, it through the manifold grace (*charis*) of God.

As everyone has received a gift, they are " serve others." Here Peter reminds his audien that the gifts are for service and that just as th are to love one another (4:8) and be hospitab to one another (4:9), they are to serve o another. The gifts, then, are not for person or private benefit, but are for the benefit of t Christian community. Moreover, his reade are to exercise their gifts by "faithfully admi istering God's grace in its various forms," as "good administrators of God's varied grac (BAGD, 560). Just as some of his readers a house slaves (2:18), everyone in his audien is a "(house)-steward, manager" (BAG 560). As stewards in God's household, th administer the manifold, or varied, grace God, a grace that is as diversified as the nu ber of God's people.

Having emphasized the principles that eve Christian has a gift and that each one is to ser others faithfully with the gift he or she h received, Peter focuses on two representati gifts to illustrate this principle: the ministry the word and administrative service. (1) Wr ing of the ministry of the word, the apos encourages his audience: "If anyone speaks, should do it as one speaking the very words God." In writing of this speech gift, Peter do not clarify whether this gift is either the exp sition of the word of God in the sense of Scri ture (Acts 7:38; Rom. 3:2; possibly Heb. 5:1 or the speech gifts, such as the word of wisdo the word of knowledge, prophecy, vario kinds of tongues, and the interpretation tongues (1 Cor. 12:8–10). He simply emph sizes that all those who have received such gift need to realize that they proclaim a divi rather than a human message.

(2) In Peter's perspective, administrati service complements this ministry of the wo (Acts 6:1–6). "If anyone serves," Peter conti ues, one is not to serve in one's own streng but "he should do it with the strength God pr vides." The purpose of serving by the streng of God is "so that in all things God may

praised through Jesus Christ," who is the agent through whom God is glorified. There is an implicit contrast in Peter's teaching: Whereas service performed in human strength may fail, service rendered by divine power brings glory to God. Having written that God is to be glorified by the service of his people, Peter concludes with a doxology: "To him be the glory and the power for ever and ever. Amen."

The approaching consummation of all things has implications for the present conduct of God's people. Because the end is near, we must be clearminded, self-controlled, deeply loving, and hospitable. Moreover, in the exercise of our diverse gifts, we as God's people are responsible to be good stewards or faithful servants. Concerning the gifts themselves, Peter teaches: (1) God has given each and every one of his people a gift; (2) these gifts are for serving others and not for any personal gain or self-aggrandizement; (3) these gifts are graces, given apart from all human ability, achievement, or merit; and (4) because they come from God and are for the service of others, they are to be used to glorify God and not to enhance the status and prestige of those who exercise the gifts.

3.2.5. Suffer As a Christian (4:12–19). For the third time in his letter Peter addresses the problem of suffering (4:12–19). Just as he had earlier shifted the emphasis from suffering as the present plight of the slaves in his audience to suffering as the potential plight of all God's people (2:18–25; 3:13–17), so here he shifts the emphasis from the general subject of suffering to suffering as a means of the testing of God's people (3:13–17; 4:12–19). Peter's teaching in this section not only echoes his earlier teaching on suffering, but it also closely parallels his earlier teaching on the testing of God's people (1:6–9). Consequently, his teaching on suffering as a means of testing also has close affinities with the teaching of both Paul and James on the subject of testing (Rom. 5:3–5; James 1:2–4).

In 2:11, Peter addressed his readers as "dear friends." No doubt because of the painful nature of his subject, he concludes his teaching on suffering by once again addressing them in the same manner. Having thus assured his audience of both his pastoral concern and of God's love toward them, he commands, "Do not be surprised at the painful trial you are suffering."

Some interpreters assume that Peter's language refers to the outbreak of the Neronian persecution against Christians in A.D. 64. Blaming the Christians in Rome for the outbreak of the great fire that devastated the city, Nero executed some by covering them with pitch and then setting them on fire to give light to his garden. However, Peter's reference to a painful or fiery ordeal more naturally reflects his earlier teaching concerning the testing of faith by fire (1:6–7). Since God tests people in order to prove their faith, it is not "as though something strange were happening to you." In a play on words, Peter's readers should not be surprised at the fiery ordeal, for testing is not something strange or surprising. Implicit in his perspective is the idea that rather than being surprised by testing, God's people ought to expect it.

In contrast to reacting in surprise to their test, Peter's audience ought to "rejoice." Though on the human level they may find this trial distressing (1:6), on the spiritual level his readers are to rejoice to the degree that they "participate in the sufferings of Christ." For God's people the various trials they experience are a means of testing. Much more than this, however, they identify his people with the shame and ignominy of Christ's suffering and death. It is in this identification with Christ that Peter perceives a future purpose in present joy: "so that you may be overjoyed when his glory is revealed." Just as there is a dramatic contrast between the shame and ignominy of Christ's suffering and his glorification, so there is an implicit contrast between the present suffering of his readers and their future glory. In the day that they share in the glory of Christ, they will rejoice with exultation (cf. 1:6, 8). Therefore, from Peter's perspective, the present plight of suffering is the painful prelude to final overwhelming joy.

In the present, however, Peter's readers do not share Christ's glory but his sufferings, "if you are insulted because of the name of Christ." The word Peter uses here for "insult" means "reproach, revile, heap insults upon" (BAGD, 570) and is a synonym for the insults that were heaped on Christ at the cross (2:23). Earlier in his teaching, Peter instructed slaves to submit to unjust suffering for the sake of conscience (2:19) and all God's people to expect to suffer for the sake of righteousness

(3:14). Here, they are to suffer for (lit., in) the name of Christ.

Echoing Jesus' promise of blessing to those disciples who will be insulted on his account (Matt. 5:11), Peter assures his audience that "you are blessed" (cf. 3:14). His readers are blessed, not through any personal gain or benefit that they might receive through suffering, but because "the Spirit of glory and of God rests on you." Earlier, Peter named the Spirit as the Spirit of sanctification (1:2), the Spirit of Christ (1:11), and the Holy Spirit (1:12). Now he calls him "the Spirit of glory," because the Spirit is the agent of glorification (cf. Rom. 1:4; Phil. 3:3). In Old Testament terms, he is also "the Spirit of God," who rested on the elders of Israel (Num. 11:25–26), Elisha (2 Kings 2:15), and the forthcoming Davidic branch (Isa. 11:2). In contrast to Old Testament times, however, the Spirit of God now rests on all his people.

Inevitably, Peter's readers are to share the sufferings of Christ; but "if you suffer," Peter explains to his readers, "it should not be as a murderer or thief or any other kind of criminal, or even as a meddler." Whereas Peter has assured his readers that they are blessed if they are insulted for the name of Christ, suffering in itself is not meritorious and may be the result of conduct that is incompatible with Christian conduct.

Peter has already challenged the slaves in his audience with the question, "But how is it to your credit if you receive a beating for doing wrong and endure it?" (2:20). Now he gives four sins that God's people are admonished to avoid: murder, theft, evildoing, criminal behavior or meddling. The meaning of the word "meddler" has not yet been determined with certainty, but in context it may mean either "concealer of stolen goods; spy, informer or one who meddles in things that do not concern him" (BAGD, 40). This catalogue of wrongdoing, in an order of decreasing seriousness, simply represents a cross section of wrong actions that are inconsistent with doing good (3:13–14) and, therefore, constitute the wrong grounds for suffering.

For Peter's readers, the alternative to suffering as a wrongdoer is to "suffer as a Christian." Peter here uses a rare New Testament name for God's people. In the only other occurrences of this word in the New Testament, Luke records that the disciples were first called Christians at Antioch (Acts 11:26) and that Agrippa mocked Paul for trying to make him a Christian (Acts 26:28). Classical authors of the first and second century, such as Lucian, Tacitus, Suetonius, Pliny the Younger, and Trajan, used this word negatively to describe the followers of Christ (BAGD, 886). It is evident, therefore, that the name Christian was used by outsiders, often with a pejorative rather than complimentary meaning.

It is in this sense that Peter observes that his readers suffer as Christians. In context, to suffer as a Christian is equivalent to being "insulted because of the name of Christ" (4:14). If anyone in his audience should suffer for being identified with Christ, Peter exhorts such a one not to "be ashamed." The name Christian may be a term of abuse; but rather than feeling ashamed, like Christ who despised the shame of the cross (Heb. 12:2), "praise God that you bear that name." That is, Christians must praise or glorify God when they suffer because the Spirit of glory and of God rests on them (4:14; cf. 1:8), and also because tested faith results in praise, glory, and honor when Jesus Christ is revealed (1:7).

Having exhorted his readers to rejoice in suffering as Christians, Peter now reminds them that "it is time for judgment to begin with the family of God." God must even judge his own family or household, should they do wrong (2:20; 4:15). Since God judges the wrongdoing of Christians, Peter asks his audience the rhetorical question, "If it begins with us, what will the outcome be for those who do not obey the gospel of God?" Christians have been chosen to obey Jesus Christ (1:2). Yet, in spite of having been judged as people, they live in the spirit, even though they will die physically (4:6). In contrast, those who refuse to obey the gospel preached to them (1:12) will be judged far more severely than divine chastisement on his people. By implication, they will not only die physically, but they will also remain spiritually dead.

Peter quotes from Proverbs to reinforce his warning about divine judgment: "If it is hard for the righteous to be saved, what will become of the ungodly and the sinner?" (cf. Prov. 11:31). This rhetorical question is appropriate for Peter's teaching because it also contrasts the salvation of the righteous and the condemnation of the sinner.

Concluding his teaching on suffering, Peter addresses "those who suffer according to God's will." Since to suffer as a Christian contradicts most people's expectations concerning divine blessing, for the second time in this letter Peter explicitly teaches that God wills the suffering of his people (cf. 3:17). Those who suffer according to God's will "should commit themselves to their faithful Creator and continue to do good." That is, they are to model their response to suffering after the pattern of Christ, who "entrusted himself to him who judges justly" (2:23). Whereas Christ entrusted himself to God as judge for vindication, Christians entrust themselves to God as creator for care and protection. Thus, those who do good (3:17) entrust themselves to the One who, both in creation and redemption, will faithfully do good to them.

Peter's teaching on suffering is one of the biblical answers to the question: Why do the righteous suffer? His answer to this question is that God wills that his people should suffer (4:19), for at least two reasons: (1) because undeserved suffering tests their faith (4:12), and (2) because undeserved suffering identifies them with the undeserved redemptive sufferings of his Son (4:13). Moreover, God blesses those who share the sufferings of Christ (4:14). However, since wrongdoing violates his holy character, he judges those who suffer for doing evil (4:15, 17–18). Finally, since God wills both to test his people and to identify them with his Son through undeserved suffering, they are not to be surprised should they suffer (4:12); they are to rejoice (4:13), to glorify God (4:16), and to entrust themselves to him with the confidence that he will do right by them (4:19).

4. Living Like Peter: Pastoral Oversight (5:1–11)

Addressing "strangers" (1:2) who have been dispersed among godless and often hostile people, Peter opened his letter with an imperative to holy living based on the model of God the Father (1:3–2:10). Because many of his readers may suffer unjustly at the hands of unsympathetic and often abusive government officials, masters, or husbands, in the dominant central section of his letter Peter commands them to submit to authority and to suffer undeservedly after the model of Christ (2:11–4:13). In this concluding section of his letter, Peter addresses the elders who are responsible to shepherd the flock of God (5:1–4). Writing as a fellow elder, Peter is their model for leadership over God's people (5:1–11). He concludes his teaching with a series of commands that are applicable not only to elders but also to all of God's people (5:5–11).

4.1. Shepherd the Flock of God (5:1–4)

Peter directs his teaching primarily to the duties and motives of elders (5:1–4). His emphases are distinctly his own, but his teaching may be compared to Paul's instruction to elders and bishops (Acts 10:17; 20:17–35; 28:31; 1 Tim. 3:1–7; 5:17–20; Tit. 1:5–9) and deacons (1 Tim. 3:8–10).

In the light of his preceding teaching on holiness, submission, and suffering, and also in light of the fact that it is "time for judgment to begin with the family of God" (4:17), Peter now appeals to the elders in his audience. The word translated "elder" commonly means "old man" (1 Tim. 5:1). However, in both Jewish and Greek custom, it became a technical term to designate civic and religious officials (Num. 11:25–30; Matt. 16:21; 26:3; 27:41). Similarly, apostolic Christianity adopted this term, which has entered the English language as the word "presbyter," a term used for some of the church's leadership roles (Acts 14:23; 15:2; 20:17, 28).

Peter's appeal to the elders is "as a fellow elder"; that is, he appeals on the basis that he is an elder himself and that he, therefore, exercises similar leadership responsibilities. Though it is more implicit than explicit, as their fellow elder he is the model for their own leadership over God's people. Peter also feels he has the right to exhort them because he is a "witness of Christ's sufferings." As a witness of Christ's ministry, death, and resurrection, he is qualified to be an apostle (Acts 1:21–22); as such, he exercises apostolic authority (1:1). Finally, Peter is "one who also will share in the glory to be revealed." This appeal, based on the suffering-glorification pattern of Christ's ministry (1:11), identifies Peter with the elders' own suffering and future glorification (cf. 1:7–8; 4:13).

Using pastoral language, Peter commands the elders to "be shepherd's of God's flock that is under your care." This pastoral imagery is rooted in the description of the Lord as the shepherd of his people (Ps. 23:1) and also echoes Jesus' claim to be the good shepherd (John 10:11; note 1 Peter 2:25; 5:4). Moreover, this command echoes Jesus' command to Peter to "feed my lambs/sheep" (John 21:15–17) and is similar to Paul's charge to the elders at Ephesus to "be shepherds of the church of God" (Acts 20:28). In other words, based on the pastoral care of God, Jesus, and the apostles, elders are undershepherds, exercising pastoral care over God's people.

Peter now introduces three motivations, each with a negative and positive dimension, to guide the leaders in their pastoral ministry. (1) Elders are to shepherd God's people "not because you must, but because you are willing, as God wants you to be." In other words, God desires that elders serve not out of a sense of duty or obligation, but willingly.

(2) Elders are not to be "greedy for money, but eager to serve." The word translated as "greedy for money" is better translated as "in fondness for dishonest gain" (BAGD, 25; note 1 Tim. 3:8; Titus 1:7). Rather than exploiting their office for economic advantage, elders are to serve "willingly, readily, freely" (BAGD, 706).

(3) Elders are to serve God's people, "not lording it over those entrusted to you, but being examples to the flock." Here Peter echoes the teaching of Jesus, who observed that the "rulers of the Gentiles lord it over them" (Mark 10:42). In contrast to this Gentile model of leadership, the disciples are to become servants and are to follow the Christological model, "for even the Son of Man did not come to be served, but to serve, and to give his life as a ransom for many" (10:45). Similarly, just as Christ is the model for the service of the disciples, so elders are "examples" (lit., "types") for the flock. That is, elders most closely conform to Christ's example, not when they lord it over his people, but when they themselves lead by example.

While elders must surrender both gain and authority to shepherd the flock of God (5:2c–3), Peter reminds them that there is a day of reward for them "when the Chief Shepherd appears." Peter is the only writer in the New Testament to give Jesus the title "Chief Shepherd" (note 2:25). This title is appropriate because Jesus earlier applied the shepherd imagery to his own ministry (John 10:11–18).

In 1:20 Peter observed that Jesus had appeared in these last times for believers and that they can look forward to "an inheritance that can never perish, spoil or fade" (1:4); now he writes that when the Chief Shepherd appears at the end of the age, "you will receive the crown of glory that will never fade away." This crown is like the wreath awarded to the winner of an athletic contest (1 Cor. 9:25). Whereas Christ received a crown of thorns as the human reward for his ministry (Mark 15:17), the elders will receive the unfading crown of glory as the divine reward for their pastoral ministry, if they conform themselves to the standard of Peter's teaching (5:2–3).

Peter's instructions to the elders contain several lessons that are applicable to every Christian who exercises any form of pastoral leadership over God's people. (1) From Peter's perspective the attitudes that underlie one's ministry are, if anything, more important than the ministry itself. That is, although it is imperative that Christian leaders shepherd the flock, they are not to be motivated by a sense of duty; instead, they are to serve voluntarily and willingly. (2) Even though Christian leaders are to be supported by those to whom they minister (Matt. 10:9–10; 1 Cor. 9:1–18; 1 Tim. 5:17–18), they are not to use their office for financial gain, but they are to serve eagerly and freely. (3) In the exercise of spiritual oversight over God's people, Christian leaders are not to be authoritarian; rather, they are to lead by example. (4) Christian leaders are to serve with a future and heavenly expectation.

In spite of the fact leaders may receive little reward in this life, if they adopt these attitudes, they will receive an unfading crown of glory in the life to come. In other words, all Christian leaders are to adopt the attitudes of Christ and the apostles toward their ministry.

4.2. A Series of Practical Imperatives (5:5–11)

Peter concludes his letter proper with a series of practical imperatives. First, he addresses the young men in his audience (5:5a), and then his entire audience (5:5b–10). He ends with a doxology addressed to the God of all grace (5:11). For the most part, these imperatives closely parallel similar teaching in the letters of both Paul and James.

Having commanded the elders in his audi-nce to shepherd the flock of God, Peter now ommands "young men, in the same way [to] e submissive to those who are older." That is, ust as elders are responsible to shepherd the oung men, so the young men have the recip-ocal responsibility to submit to their elders. In his context, Peter probably gives the word elder" a double meaning, referring not only to hurch leaders but also to old men in general. 'his obligation to submit to their elders asso-iates young men with Christian citizens, laves, and wives, who have likewise been xhorted to submit to those who exercise legit-mate authority over them (2:13–3:7).

Passing on from the duty of young men owards elders, Peter commands his entire audi-nce to "clothe yourselves with humility toward ne another." This imperative repeats his earlier xhortation that all of God's people become umble (3:8). Similarly, using the same Greek vord for humility, Paul exhorted the Philippi-ns, "but in humility consider others better than ourselves" (Phil. 2:3). God's people clothe hemselves with humility when they adopt a roper attitude both toward themselves and oward others in the Christian community.

Peter reinforces his imperative by remind-ng his audience that Scripture teaches that God opposes the proud but gives grace to the umble" (1 Peter 5:5; cf. Prov. 3:34; James :6). In light of this principle, Peter commands is readers to "humble yourselves, therefore, nder God's mighty hand." In common with ther New Testament writers, Peter observes hat there is a divine purpose in humility—so that he may lift you up in due time." In other vords, just as suffering is the prelude to glo-ification (1:11), so humility is the prelude to xaltation.

This humiliation-exaltation pattern is based n the example of Christ, who humbled him-elf and was subsequently highly exalted by God (cf. Phil. 2:8–9). James also applied this Christological pattern to his audience, com-nanding them to "humble yourselves before he Lord, and he will lift you up" (James 4:10). 'his pattern has a twofold dimension: On the ne hand, God's people are to humble them-elves in the present; on the other hand, God vill exalt his people at the appropriate time.

Addressing those who are being tested by arious trials (1:6; 4:12), such as suffering for good behavior (2:20; 3:13–17) and for being a Christian (4:14–16), Peter urges them to "cast all your anxiety on him." Jesus taught his disciples to adopt an anxiety-free attitude, using the verb "be anxious/worry" six times in just ten verses (Matt. 6:25–34). Similarly, Paul commanded the Christians at Philippi to "not be anxious about anything" (Phil. 4:6). All of this teaching reflects the perspective of the psalmist who wrote, "Cast your cares on the LORD and he will sustain you" (Ps. 55:22). Therefore, while circumstances may arouse their anxiety, Peter's readers are to take every anxiety and cast it on God, much in the same way that the disciples, "threw [lit., cast] their cloaks on the colt" that Jesus was about to mount (Luke 19:35).

Peter assures his anxiety-ridden audience that they can cast all their cares and worries on God "because he cares for you." Thus, he reminds his audience that in spite of appearances to the contrary, God does truly care about them in their present predicament. This is a great sustaining and undergirding comfort for God's people in their time of trial, testing, and suffering.

For the third time in his letter Peter writes of self-control, tersely commanding, "Be self-controlled" (note 1:13; 4:7). Complementing this imperative, Peter next commands his readers to be "alert." Jesus had commanded his disciples to be alert or watchful three times (Matt. 24:42; 25:13; 26:41). Now, in a different context, Peter passes that same imperative on to his audience.

Sobriety and watchfulness are necessary because "your enemy the devil prowls around like a roaring lion." By definition, "the devil" is "the slanderer" (BAGD, 182). He is also the "opponent in a lawsuit . . . since he appears in court as an accuser" (cf. Rom. 8:33), or is "the enemy, opponent in general" (BAGD, 74). Peter, therefore, both warns his audience that there is someone who slanderously accuses them, and identifies this enemy of their souls. Emphasizing the ferocity of such an enemy, Peter writes that he prowls about like a roaring lion, "looking for someone to devour." Though like an animal of prey he desires to devour or swallow up God's people, he cannot harm them since they are protected by God's power (1:5). Because God cares for his people (5:7), he has, as it were, extracted the fangs and clipped the claws of their enemy.

Having warned his audience about their enemy, Peter now commands, "Resist him." This word has a meaning to "set oneself against, oppose, resist, withstand" (BAGD, 67). To his similar command James adds, "and he will flee from you" (James 4:7b). Peter, however, describes *how* his audience can resist him—"standing firm in the faith." They are to remain steadfast in the faith "because you know that your brothers throughout the world are undergoing the same kind of sufferings." In other words, Peter's readers must realize that their various trials are not unique; rather, they are common to the Christian brotherhood. This is because they are foreigners and strangers in a hostile and sinful world.

Though Peter knows that their suffering is according to God's will (3:17; 4:19), he seems to imply that some of this suffering that tests his people is mediated through the devil (cf. Job 1–2). Therefore, they will resist the devil to the extent that they remain firm in the faith and not succumb to the pressure of persecution.

The single, most dominant theme in this letter is that of suffering. Peter has taught that for the present those who suffer are to commit themselves to God (4:19). Having earlier reminded his readers that their trials are for a little while (1:6), he now concludes his teaching with the encouragement: "And the God of all grace, who called you to his eternal glory in Christ, after you have suffered for a little while, will himself restore you and make you strong, firm and steadfast." Here Peter contrasts suffering that lasts for a little while and glory that is eternal.

Echoing in part the wording of his salutation (1:1–2), Peter reminds his readers that they have been called because of God's all-encompassing grace and are called in Christ because of his redemptive sacrifice (1:18–19; 2:24; 3:18). Moreover, if suffering is a means of testing and also a prelude to glorification, then it is also the first stage by which God will restore, or "put into proper condition" (BAGD, 417), that process of salvation that was initiated with Christ's death and is appropriated by faith. Finally, using three words with overlapping meanings, God will also make his suffering people strong, firm, and steadfast. Peter here matches the preceding command to steadfastness (5:8–9) with the overwhelmingly emphatic guarantee of divine preservation.

Having guaranteed that God perfects, confirms, strengthens, and establishes his people, Peter concludes with a doxology: "To him be the power for ever and ever. Amen." In common with other doxologies, this one ascribes eternal power, rule, and sovereignty to God (cf. 1 Tim 6:16; 1 Peter 4:11; Jude 25; Rev. 1:6; 5:13).

In this concluding paragraph of his letter Peter again focuses on some aspects of the human and divine dimensions of salvation. It is imperative for God's people to humble themselves, cast all their anxieties on him, be self-controlled, be alert, and resist the devil. In turn, God obligates himself to exalt those whom humble themselves, to care for his people, and to perfect, confirm, strengthen, and establish his people.

THE OLD TESTAMENT IN THE NEW

NT Text	OT Text	Subject
1Pe 1:16	Lev 11:44–45	Holiness commanded
1Pe 1:24–25	Isa 40:6–8	Eternity of the word
1Pe 2:6	Isa 28:16	Trust in the cornerstone
1Pe 2:7	Ps 118:22–23	Rejected cornerstone
1Pe 2:8	Isa 8:14	A stone on which people stumble
1Pe 2:9	Isa 43:21	Declaring God's praise
1Pe 2:10	Hos 1:6, 9	Not God's people
1Pe 2:10	Hos 2:23	Now God's people
1Pe 2:22	Isa 53:9	Sinless servant
1Pe 2:24	Isa 53:4	Taking out infirmities
1Pe 2:25	Isa 53:6	Like sheep gone astray
1Pe 3:10–12	Ps 34:12–16	Turn from evil
1Pe 3:14–15	Isa 8:12–13	Do not fear
1Pe 4:8	Pr 10:12	Love covers sin
1Pe 4:18	Pr 11:31	Receiving due reward
1Pe 5:5	Pr 3:34	Grace for the humble

5. Concluding Comments and Greetings (5:12–14)

Because of the relatively low level of literacy as well as the difficulty in obtaining writing materials, letters in New Testament times were generally dictated to a professional scribe and signed off by the sender. New Testament letters often give evidence of being composed in this way. For example, Tertius was Paul's scribe when he wrote his letter to the Christians in Rome (Rom. 16:22). Even when the scribe is not named, Paul customarily indicates at what point he personally signed off (1 Cor. 16:21; Gal. 6:11; Col. 4:18; 2 Thess. 3:17). Similarly, Peter has used a scribe to write this letter to the Christians in the Roman provinces of Asia Minor.

"I have written to you briefly," he informs his audience, "with the help of Silas." Without doubt, Peter's scribe is to be identified with the prophet Silas (Acts 15:32), who not only carried the decision of the Jerusalem Council to Antioch (Acts 15:22–32), but also accompanied Paul on his second missionary journey (Acts 15:40–18:5). As to the two forms of his name, either he had both a Semitic and a Latin name like Paul, "or *Silvanus* is the Latin form of the same name that is Grecized as *Silas*" (BAGD, 750). With the words "whom I regard as a faithful brother," Peter commends Silas to his readers. Peter's use of Silas, a former companion of Paul, as his scribe accounts for many of the similarities between the letters of these two apostles.

Peter has written this brief letter to his audience for the purpose of "encouraging you and testifying that this is the true grace of God." In other words, he has written to encourage or exhort his audience to Christian conduct and to inform or witness to them about the nature of their salvation. For Peter, there is only one appropriate response to God's saving grace, and it is imperative that his audience "stand fast in it."

Joining Peter, "she who is in Babylon ... sends you her greetings." Since the Greek word for church is feminine, the feminine article that is here translated "she" most likely refers to a church rather than to an individual. Babylon is probably a cryptic reference to Rome (cf. Rev. 16:19–18:24). This church is united with Peter's audience by divine election, having been "chosen together with you" (note 1:1).

Not only does the church at Rome send greetings, but "so does my son Mark." Mark is to be identified as Barnabas's cousin, John Mark (Acts 13:13; 15:36–38), who was with Paul during his imprisonment in Rome (Col. 4:10; Philem. 24). Early church tradition links Peter and Mark in Rome (Eusebius, *EH*, 6.14.6–7). Mark is Peter's son in the same way that Timothy is Paul's "true son in the faith" (1 Tim. 1:2). Thus, Peter wrote this letter to the Christians of Asia Minor from Rome shortly before his martyrdom at the hands of Emperor Nero (ca. A.D. 64–65).

In closing, Peter commands his readers to "greet one another with a kiss of love." This salutation is identical with the holy kiss of Paul's letters (cf. Rom. 16:16; 1 Cor. 16:20; 2 Cor. 13:12; 1 Thess. 5:26). Finally, echoing his initial greeting (1 Peter 1:2), Peter invokes a blessing on his audience: "Peace to all of you who are in Christ."

INTRODUCTION TO 2 PETER

Early in the history of the church 2 Peter was classified as a "disputed book" (Eusebius, *Ecclesiastical History*, 3.1.1). Though it was eventually received as canonical, the book has continued to generate considerable controversy. For example, Petrine authorship is questioned, with many scholars identifying it as a pseudonymous or pseudepigraphic document. It is also debated whether this book is a first-century or a second-century work. The relationship between 2 Peter and 1 Peter on the one hand, and between 2 Peter and Jude on the other hand, is also disputed. For such a short letter the introductory issues for 2 Peter are almost as complex as such issues are for the study of the Gospels. As a result, this letter still defies scholarly consensus.

1. Authorship

If there is something approaching a consensus about 2 Peter, it is that Peter is not the author of the letter that bears his name; rather, it belongs to the category of pseudepigrapha, and (perhaps) the actual author was a companion or disciple of Peter writing in his name—hence, writing in his authority. This position is based on a variety of observations, such as (1) claimed differences in style between 1 and

2 Peter, (2) differences in subject matter, (3) literary dependence on Jude, (4) use of the language of the mystery religions and Gnosticism, and (5) the milieu of the early Catholicism of the second century.

But the significance of these arguments is often wildly exaggerated by their proponents. Based on the available data there is nothing compelling about the theory of pseudonymous authorship and nothing that precludes Petrine authorship. (1) Though it is often arbitrarily rejected as an explanation for the difference in style between 1 and 2 Peter, the use of a different amanuensis for each letter is a sufficient explanation just as it is for the differences in style between many of the Pauline letters.

(2) As to subject matter, the occasions of 1 and 2 Peter differ; nevertheless, Peter's teaching about godliness in his second letter (1:3–11) is substantially the same as his teaching about holiness in his first letter (1 Peter 1:3–2:10).

(3) Peter's literary dependence on Jude, if it can be convincingly demonstrated, no more disproves Petrine authorship than Matthew's or Luke's dependence on Mark disproves the authorship of the Gospels that bear their names.

(4) The language of religious mystery, and more so of Gnosticism, is neither new nor late (i.e., second century). It is current in the world of New Testament times. Instead, it is the theology of these religious movements that is new. And where Peter appears to use the language that is to be found in these religious movements, he is using the language of the false teachers against themselves.

(5) Contrary to what is often asserted, 2 Peter simply does not have the distinctive characteristics of early Catholicism, namely, the increasing institutionalization of the church, the crystallization of the "faith" into set forms, and the fading anticipation of an imminent Parousia.

There is one decisive factor *in favor of* Peter's authorship for this letter: the central argument of the letter is a warning about false teachers, with an implied polemic against these same false teachers. Though seldom recognized, this is fatal to the pseudonymous authorship theory, especially the view that espouses a date after Peter's death. The letter clearly implies contact between the false teachers and Peter's audience. That is, the threat is actual and not theoretical. But no one in Peter's audience would get a hearing with the false teachers by appealing to this letter, in whole or in part, if it were pseudonymous. The false teachers would simply repudiate it by saying: "We all know Peter died in Rome in the reign of Nero. Therefore, this letter was not written by Peter. Thus, it has no authority. In this letter you have no basis for rejecting us or our teaching."

Doubtless, Christians in the 80s or later would have to admit that this newly received letter could not have been written by Peter, and, therefore, utterly lacked apostolic authority. In light of the situation—the presence and threat of false teachers—the theory that the letter is pseudonymous is self-defeating and self-refuting.

The introduction that follows, therefore, will proceed on the assumption of Petrine authorship—that the sender is actually Peter. For a brief summary about Peter see the section "Authorship" in the Introduction to the commentary on 1 Peter.

2. Date and Place of Writing

A number of factors help to establish the approximate date and the location for the writing of 2 Peter. On the assumption that Peter wrote this letter, obviously it was written before his martyrdom under Nero (c. A.D. 64). Further, Peter knows about the letters that Paul had written to the churches, and he is now writing to the same churches (3:15–16, to churches in cities such as Ephesus, Colosse, Laodicea [Col. 2:1; 4:16]). Therefore, Peter wrote this second letter after Paul's release from Roman imprisonment (A.D. 62) and sent it to the same audience (3:1) as he did 1 Peter, itself written in the early 60s. When Peter writes this letter, he expects that his death is imminent (1:14). This evidence indicates that Peter wrote this letter from Rome, shortly before his martyrdom in about A.D. 64.

3. Recipients

Peter addresses this letter "to those who through the righteousness of our God and Savior Jesus Christ have received a faith as precious as ours" (1:1b). If there were no other data in this letter about its destination, we would take it to be addressed to all believers. But toward the end of this letter the author identifies the letter as the second one he has written to them (3:1). This means the following: (1) He is writing this letter to the five provinces n northwest Asia Minor (1 Peter 1:1); (2) he s writing to a mixed audience of both Jewish and Gentile Christians; and (3) though these people have not seen the Lord (1 Peter 1:8), they have had the gospel preached to them by Spirit-empowered (1 Peter 1:12) apostles (2 Peter 3:2), which certainly includes Paul and Barnabas (Acts 16:6–7; 19:1–10; Rom. 15:19) and may include the Lord's brothers, Peter himself (1 Cor. 9:5), and others.

Peter's recipients are a mixed audience, including slaves, women with unbelieving husbands, young and old men (1 Peter 2:13; 3:1; 5:5), and false teachers (2 Peter 2:1). The latent pagan libertinism of 1 Peter (1:14; 2:11; 4:3–4) has become the platform of the false teachers (2 Peter 2:1–22).

4. Occasion and Purpose

Peter writes this letter because his death is approaching (1:14). Jesus had forewarned him about his martyrdom prior to his ascension (1:14b; cf. John 21:19). Peter views his death as (lit.) "putting aside a tent" (2 Peter 1:13–14a), and, in the language of Jesus' transfiguration experience, a "departure" (1:15; Gk. *exodus*; cf. the same word as that used in Luke 9:31).

Peter also writes his letter because, just as false prophets were among the Israelites, false teachers have come among his audience. They are threatening to lead the church into a denial of "the sovereign Lord who bought them" (2:1). This denial is a moral denial, in that they "carouse in broad daylight" (2:13); it is to return to the pagan libertinism they had put in the past (cf. 1 Peter 4:3). This moral denial of Christ finds encouragement and comfort in a second denial, that of the second coming, the Parousia, of Christ (2 Peter 3:4–5), and in the complementary denial of divine judgment.

From the context of Peter's letter it is apparent that the false teachers about whom Peter is writing are *false prophets*. This is evident along several lines. His "testament" is that of an eye-witness to the Transfiguration and in the tradition of the prophets (1:16–21). Furthermore, he compares the false teachers who are among Peter's audience to the false prophets among the Israelites (2:1). In addition, teaching is one of the primary functions of the Christian prophet. Jesus is the model for the role of the prophet as teacher. After he received the Holy Spirit at his baptism (Luke 3:21–22) and immediately before he identified himself as the Spirit-anointed prophet (4:16–30), Luke reports that Jesus began teaching (4:15). Similarly, on the day of Pentecost the disciples become Spirit-baptized, Spirit-empowered, and Spirit-filled prophets (Acts 1:5, 8; 2:4, 16–21).

Thus, Peter, a prophet since Pentecost, now writes this letter as a true prophet, who is attacking the false prophets or teachers among his audience. This confrontation is not an isolated event in the world of the New Testament. For example, about twenty years earlier Paul, a true, Spirit-filled prophet (Acts 13:1–9), confronted and cursed a Jewish false prophet named Bar-Jesus (13:4–12).

Peter faces his twofold predicament—his imminent death and the crisis of the false teachers—by giving instruction (1:3–11), a remembrance or testament (1:12–21), an exposé and denunciation of the false teachers (2:1–3:7), and an exhortation (3:14–18). This "testament" aspect is the only unique element (subgenre) in the letter, but it may be compared to two "testaments" of Paul (Acts 20:18–35; 2 Timothy). All three of these testaments are in a long tradition reaching back through the intertestamental period (e.g., Testaments of the Twelve Patriarchs) to Joshua (Josh. 23–24) and Moses (Deut. 31).

OUTLINE OF 2 PETER

1. **Remember Your Calling** (1:1–15)
   - **1.1.** Salutation (1:1–2)
   - **1.2.** Reminder of Divine Supply (1:3–4)
   - **1.3.** Reminder of Human Responsibility (1:5–11)
   - **1.4.** Personal Reminder of Peter (1:12–15)
2. **Remember Your Warnings** (1:16–2:22)
   - **2.1.** Peter Remembers His Past Experience (1:16–18)
   - **2.2.** Reminder of Prophetic Authenticity (1:19–21)
   - **2.3.** Warning Reminder of False Teachers (2:1–3a)
     - **2.3.1.** Warning Against Their Destructive Heresies (2:1)
     - **2.3.2.** Outcome and Methodology (2:2–3a)

- **2.4.** Warning Reminder of Inevitable Judgment (2:3b–9)
  - **2.4.1.** Warning Reminder From Historical Precedent (2:3b–6)
    - **2.4.1.1.** Celestial Judgment (2:3b–4)
    - **2.4.1.2.** Terrestrial Judgment (2:5)
    - **2.4.1.3.** Civic Judgment (2:6)
  - **2.4.2.** Deliverance of the Righteous (2:7–9)
- **2.5.** Warning Reminder of Their Character (2:10–22)
  - **2.5.1.** Morally Bankrupt (2:10)
  - **2.5.2.** Contrast to Angels (2:11)
  - **2.5.3.** Actions of Those Lacking in True Knowledge (2:12–19)
  - **2.5.4.** Warning Reminder of Turning Away From Truth (2:20–22)

3. Remember Your Future Hope (3:1–18)

- **3.1.** Purpose of the Letter (3:1–2)
- **3.2.** Reminder of the Future Hope (3:3–10)
  - **3.2.1.** Reminder That Scoffers Are Inevitable (3:3–4)
  - **3.2.2.** Reminder of God's Past Faithfulness (3:5–6)
  - **3.2.3.** Reminder of God's Future Faithfulness (3:7–10)
- **3.3.** Reminder of Christian Conduct (3:11–14)
  - **3.3.1.** Conduct in View of the Lord's Return (3:11–12)
  - **3.3.2.** Reminder of the Lord's Promise (3:13)
  - **3.3.3.** Reminder to Be Diligent, Spotless, and Blameless (3:14)
- **3.4.** Reminder of Apostolic Harmony (3:15–16)
  - **3.4.1.** Reminder of Paul's Letters (3:15)
  - **3.4.2.** Nature of Paul's Letters (3:16)
- **3.5.** Reminder to Be on Guard (3:17–18a)
- **3.6.** Doxology (3:18b)

COMMENTARY ON 2 PETER

1. Remember Your Calling (1:1–15)

1.1. Salutation (1:1–2)

The letter opens with the standard formula for letters in the first century: sender, recipient, blessing (cf. Acts 15:23; 1 Peter 1:1). The full name of the apostle as used here ("Simon Peter") is found both in Matthew 16:16 and Luke 5:8. Some commentators argue that both names are used since Peter is addressing a Jewish-Gentile audience. Others hold wrongly that it is designed to give weight to an anonymous writer using Peter's authority.

The twofold title of Peter is significant. "Servant" no doubt follows Peter's command to "live as free men ... live as servants of God" (1 Peter 2:16b). Whereas Peter uses only the title "apostle" in his former letter, the addition of "servant" clearly sets up a contrast to the false teachers whom he labels as "slaves of depravity" (2 Peter 2:19). "Apostle" carries the weight of authority in issues of doctrine and ethics. Later in the letter, Peter will refer to the "command given by our Lord and Savior through your apostles" (3:2). Since this second letter deals with issues of immorality and license, he relies on his apostolic authority in issuing his indictment. Moreover, there is the sense of deep humility married to great authority where these two terms are linked together. In this way, Peter reflects the Lord Jesus.

The recipients are most likely the same as those of 1 Peter (cf. 2 Peter 3:1), that is, "God's elect, strangers in the world, scattered throughout Pontus, Galatia, Cappadocia, Asia and Bithynia" (1 Peter 1:1). Thus, Peter's audience are those residents of the provinces of central and northeastern Asia Minor (modern-day Turkey). This also helps explain how Peter and his audience are familiar with Paul's writings (2 Peter 3:15), such as the letter to the Galatians.

The following phrase, "those who ... have received a faith as precious as ours" (1:1), means that the precious faith is the same for all people. Peter assures his audience that they have the same faith as the apostle himself. He captures this truth in 1 Peter 1:8, "though you have not seen him, you love him." This equality comes directly from "the righteousness of our God." This phrase carries the connotation of agency. It does not necessarily mean that "righteousness" here refers to the soteriological aspect of conversion, but following Peter's usage of the same word throughout 2 Peter it carries the meaning of ethical righteousness (1:1–2; 2:5, 7, 8, 21; 3:13). Indeed, the idea here follows what Peter has just asseverated about the same precious faith, that the agency of ethical righteousness is impartial.

Peter's salutation in verse 2 is the typical alutation found throughout New Testament etters. It carries both Greek (*charis*, "grace") nd Hebrew (*shalom*, "peace") greetings. What nakes this salutation unique is that nowhere lse in the New Testament is the agency of knowledge" used in conveying the greeting. Clearly this aspect was added for the polemical ature of the letter against those who did not ave the true knowledge. In other words, Peter as already established one of the main themes: xperiential knowledge of God and Christ.

1.2. Reminder of Divine Supply (1:3–4)

In 1:3 Peter gives his audience the key to the oly living that he wrote about in 1 Peter 3:2–0. Note the balance between the divine agent nd the human agent: (1) "his divine power" and his own glory and goodness," and (2) "our nowledge of him." As in 1:2 and throughout the est of this letter, *knowledge* is a key term for Peter. It is a *relational* word, referring to those who have an intimate, relational knowledge of God. It is never bare fact, but experienced reality. God's divine power, glory, and goodness and ur knowledge of him have "given us everything we need for life and godliness." Peter's concern ere is twofold: soteriological (cf. 1 Peter 1:5) nd ethical. This will set the tone for the rest of he letter. Those professing to be Christians in hapter 2 disprove it by their *ethics*; godliness annot be divorced from Christian living.

The call of God comes to everyone. Peter eveals the agency of this call—namely, God's glory and goodness." Therefore, our experiential knowledge of God, which we receive hrough "his divine power," has supplied us with everything we need both soteriologically nd ethically. Peter views the call of God in erms of his divine plan, "the God of all grace, who called you to his eternal glory in Christ" 1 Peter 5:10b).

The "these" in 1:4 refers directly to the preceding verse, that is, to God's power, glory, and goodness. The reference here, however, is not to life and godliness but to the promises. This will contrast later on to the seductive promises of 2:19. Here the promises are both "great and precious." Peter used these two adjectives in his first letter when he described a faith "of greater worth than gold" (1 Peter 1:7) and mentioned "the precious blood of Christ" (1:19).

These precious promises have a twofold result: (1) participation in the divine nature—that is, we will be holy, reflecting the character of God; and (2) escape from "the corruption in the world." This parallels 1 Peter 1:14 and is contrasted to the false teachers, who have not escaped "the corruption of the world" (2 Peter 2:20). This corruption is "caused by evil desires" (1:4), which Peter has previously told them, "Do not conform to the evil desires you had when you lived in ignorance" (1 Peter 1:14). Thus, for Peter, salvation indicates a change in desire and behavior.

1.3. Reminder of Human Responsibility (1:5–11)

In this section on human responsibility, Peter takes great care to make a list that corresponds to the holiness section of his previous letter. Observe that there are eight qualities in his list, several of which compare to Paul's list of "the fruit of the Spirit" (Gal. 5:22–23). One notable difference is that whereas Paul begins with love, Peter ends with love. The qualities listed here are all qualities that characterized the life of Christ. Thus Peter is using the person who served as a model for his life. Note as well that almost every one of these qualities has its negative counterpart with the false teachers of chapter 2. The chart below demonstrates how six of the eight qualities finds a corresponding place in 1 Peter.

Quality	Greek	1 Peter	2 Peter	Galatians
Faith	*pistis*	1:5, 7, 9, 21	1:5	
Goodness	*arete*	2:9	1:5	5:22
Knowledge	*gnosis*	3:7	1:5	
Self-control	*enkrateia*	1:13; 4:7; 5:8	1:6	5:23
Perseverance	*hypomone*		1:6	5:22
Godliness	*eusebeia*		1:6; 3:11	
Kindness	*philadelphia*	1:22	1:7	5:22
Love	*agape*	4:8; 5:14	1:7	5:22

Peter begins his list with "faith." Faith is the essential and fundamental principle in a relationship with God (1 Peter 1:5, 7, 9, 21). Biblical faith incorporates two invariable elements into its quality: (1) Faith is a firm conviction, basing itself on the revelation of God. It is that unquestioning allegiance to God manifesting itself in an unshakable resolve that what God has said, he is able and willing to accomplish. (2) More than just a conviction, faith is demonstrated in the action it produces. Peter, by using this word, unites the concept of faith and works in that a firm saving conviction of God's Word produces personal conduct in an ethical and moral manner. This is in complete accordance with Peter's soteriology, encompassing right living with belief in God.

"Goodness" naturally follows on the heels of faith for this term is not some ethereal quality; rather, it is faith in action. It denotes a righteousness that comes by faith—put into action. As with all the other qualities listed here, goodness is dynamic. It is belief in God put into action by kindness bestowed on others. Here we begin to recognize how faith brings us into line with the character of God. Paul uses this term in contrast to "sternness" in Romans 11:22.

"Knowledge" for Peter is never the mere accumulation of facts. It is, like goodness, a dynamic quality rather than a static one. It is a term of *relationship*. Insofar as one knows God and is known by him, the stronger and deeper the relationship grows. In fact, knowledge is a key concept for Peter's notion of ethical conduct. This knowledge is not merely an intellectual exercise but a work of the Holy Spirit. Thus, what begins with faith and is outworked by goodness, is now governed by knowledge of God.

"Self-control" follows knowledge in Peter's chain of dynamic qualities. This quality is more than mere temperance, although that is part of self-control. It acts as a safeguard against the abuse of knowledge. Those, for example, who would flaunt the Christian liberties, even to the point of license (as do the false teachers), have the knowledge but not the self-control to disabuse themselves from their deeds. This quality is under the auspices of the Holy Spirit (Gal. 5:22–23).

"Perseverance" is not a new concept for Peter's audience (1 Peter 2:20). Literally meaning to "abide under," this quality looks back to the faith that began the chain. Indeed faith and perseverance cannot be divorced Perseverance for the Christian may have it outworking passively—as in trials and tribulations (Luke 21:19)—or actively—as in persisting (Luke 8:15; Rom. 2:7; Heb. 12:1). Peter perhaps places perseverance at this point for only after enduring self-control does the mind and body discipline itself to holiness and right living. Again, each quality, each character trait builds on the other in a dynamic and exponential way.

"Godliness" is that quality that distinguishes all forms of religion from Christianity. It is a devout attitude or piety that characterizes one's humble attitude toward God. But it is more than just looking pious—it manifests itself in the acts of God. In other words, godly people act with the same charity, the same mercy, the same generosity with which God acts.

"Brotherly kindness" is set up in contrast and complement to the next quality, love. Such kindness in Peter's chain is that of affection—the dear and kind feelings one has toward one's friend. It is the culmination of human love for another human being. It is bound by a loyalty and a forbearance to the eccentricities of another.

"Love," on the other hand, is completely supernatural. Peter uses both "brotherly kindness" and "love" to distinguish between that which one can naturally evoke and that which the Spirit enables. Love—that *agape* quality—was to be the discriminating quality among all of the disciples to demonstrate to the world that they were indeed Christians (cf. John 13:34–35). Peter wisely places it as the culmination of his list of qualities. Indeed these were the two words that personally caused him much distress when he talked with Christ after the resurrection (cf. John 21:15–17). For the contemporary Christian, love is imparted supernaturally by the Spirit as a fruit (Gal. 5:22). Thus, Peter has outlined a dynamic and distinguishing list of those qualities that should reflect the Christian's life.

In verse 8 Peter identifies the above list as "qualities." These are trademarks or identity markers of the believer. To these qualities of identification, he now adds the phrase "in increasing measure." This is significant because holiness, godliness, love, goodness, faith, and so on, are not static. They are not a one-time display but ongoing, ever-increasing qualities. In other words, the list is dynamic.

The result of the growth in these qualities is twofold: (1) It keeps a believer from being ineffective, and (2) it keeps a believer from being unproductive in the knowledge of the Lord. Ineffective Christianity may often be worse than no Christianity at all. It is to the ineffective, lukewarm Christian, after all, that Jesus declared he would spit them out of his mouth (Rev. 3:16). Tepid Christianity can be clearly avoided by possessing the qualities of verses 5–7 in *increasing* measure. Being unproductive in the knowledge of the Lord brings with it a sense of accountability. To gain information continually and rarely or never put it into practice is a dangerous habit for a Christian.

If static qualities lead to ineffective and unproductive lives, lack of possession receives an even greater censure: being nearsighted, blind, and forgetful (v. 9). Here is the danger of nominal Christianity, of that insipid way of life that begins and ends at the doorway of a church. The Christian life is to be dynamic and forward-moving. Indeed, Christian growth is a theme of the entire New Testament. Nearsightedness and blindness are not merely two distinct traits, but rather a downward journey. Such people do not see the big picture in any of their actions and thus often lead others astray. That these people are saved is not in question by the phrase "that he has been cleansed from his past sins." It is the forgetfulness or spiritual amnesia that is the root of the problem.

In light of the warning of insipid Christianity, Peter then exhorts his readers to greater zeal (v. 10). He encourages them to make their "calling and election sure." This is entirely consistent with what Peter has already written. Christianity is a call to holiness (1 Peter 1:15) and an assurance of election (1:1). The apostle also gives his audience the way to make their calling and election sure: "if you do these things." There are no esoteric actions or requirements in the Scripture. Here Peter has clearly and succinctly told them how to live.

Peter goes on in verse 11 to cite one of the most thrilling aspects of Christianity, the believer's hope for the future. Note that he does not discuss reward or living accommodations; rather, he draws from the parable of stewardship in the kingdom (Matt. 25:14–30). The believer "will receive a rich welcome" from the Lord "into the eternal kingdom." This welcome is in itself a reward. Peter's reference to the "kingdom" naturally comes from the teaching of Christ. The fact that it is an "eternal" kingdom is a reference from prophecy (Dan. 7:27).

This whole introductory section has been marked by soteriology, ethics, and eschatology. In a nutshell, Peter has given his readers everything they needed to know about living a holy life. He now proceeds to give them a testament.

1.4. Personal Reminder of Peter (1:12–15)

The personal reminder, or testament section, of this letter is not unique to the Scriptures. Note what Luke records in Acts 20:18–35 and what Paul writes as a testament in 2 Timothy (especially ch. 4). This is fully consistent with a thematic outline of this commentary. This second letter has rightly been termed *a reminder to stimulate Peter's readers to wholesome thinking*. In fact, the entire letter is designed around remembrance: (1) remembrance of past experience, (2) remembrance of the present warning, and (3) remembrance of a future hope.

In verse 12 Peter tells his readers that he "will . . . remind [them] of these things." "These things" refer to verses 1–11. This concept of reminder is not one that is wholly welcomed in our society. We crave something new all the time and hold the idea that the pastor should only say something once and never speak of anything negative; this attitude is the furthest thing from Peter's mind. "Always remind" is done out of love and as a safeguard for his readers, for humans easily forget. The historical narrative of the Old Testament is replete with the recurring phrase "and they forgot. . . ." For Peter the reminder comes even though he realizes that his audience knows what he is talking about and that they are firmly established in the truth.

Peter's desire to remind and refresh his readers' memory is fueled by the knowledge that his own time on earth will soon be up (vv. 13–14). This adds an element of urgency to his letter. The revelation of his imminent death comes from the Lord himself. Whether Peter is referring to Jesus' words in John 21:18 or to an unrecorded vision or dream is unclear.

What is clear, however, is that Peter knows for certain that his death is near.

The heart of Peter shines in verse 15. He has taken to heart the Lord's commands to feed and tend his sheep (John 21:15–16). Regardless of whether Peter is here referring to his written letters or to the transference of leadership to another person, thus entrusting his readers' care to some overseer, he is putting forth every effort to make sure that they never forget the things he has said. The apostle's words here recall Moses' reminder to the Israelites (Deut. 31–33) and Joshua's to the same body of people (Josh. 23–24). More important, Jesus told his disciples: "But the Counselor, the Holy Spirit, whom the Father will send in my name, will teach you all things and *will remind you* of everything I have said to you" (John 14:26, italics added).

2. Remember Your Warnings (1:16–2:22)

This part of Peter's testament begins the warning reminder of the letter. Indeed, his warning is based on past experience and future threat.

2.1. Peter Remembers His Past Experience (1:16–18)

Peter begins this section by assuring his readers that he and the apostles did not follow anything cleverly invented (v. 16). In this way he distinguishes between the true and the false. What they have been taught is based on eyewitness account. His reference to the power and coming of the Lord is related to the transfiguration story in Mark 9:1–8. Luke, however, records the precise fact that "they saw his glory" (Luke 9:32b). If truth is established on the witness of two or three people, certainly Peter, James, and John qualified.

Peter witnessed Christ's majesty with his eyes in that he saw the glory of Jesus (along with Moses and Elijah), and with his ears in that he heard a voice from heaven that affirmed Jesus' sonship and his pleasing stand before the Father (vv. 17–18). Furthermore, although Peter does not record it in his letter, the Gospel writers record, "Listen to him." This is the basis for Peter's earlier statement that he did not listen to "cleverly invented stories" (v. 16). Peter calls the Mount of Transfiguration a "sacred" mountain. This adjective (*hagios*, "holy") is a recurring one in his letters. Peter writes of a "holy priesthood" (1 Peter 2:5), "holy nation" (2:9), a "sacred command" (2 Peter 2:21), and "the holy prophets" (3:2).

2.2. Reminder of Prophetic Authenticity (1:19–21)

Peter now begins to set up his contrast between true and false prophets. He gives a stern command to his readers that they should pay attention to the word of the prophets. He can say this since he has the authoritative backing of Scripture itself. The inspired psalmist called God's "word . . . a lamp to [his] feet and a light for [his] path" (Ps. 119:105). In a similar vein, Peter speaks of the prophetic word as "a light shining in a dark place" (2 Peter 1:19).

Peter gives a time span for this light: "until the day dawns and the morning star arises in your hearts." It is possible that "the morning star" here refers to Balaam's fourth oracle in Numbers 24:17a: "I see him, but not now; I behold him, but not near. A star will come out of Jacob; a scepter will rise out of Israel." It is also a self-proclaimed title of Christ in Revelation 22:16. Peter is possibly using the example of a false prophet as a representation of the dark place and the morning star as prophetic of Christ. Whatever this verse means, its focus is on paying attention to the prophetic word.

Peter ascribes the origin of prophecy to the Holy Spirit (vv. 20–21). This theme is fundamental to the doctrine of the inspiration of Scripture and is evident throughout the Old and New Testaments. Peter himself is conscious of the Spirit's role in prophetic inspiration, for the Spirit guided the Old Testament prophets as they wrote about the Messiah (1 Peter 1:11). Furthermore, Luke records that "the Scripture had to be fulfilled which the Holy Spirit spoke long ago through the mouth of David" (Acts 1:16; cf. 2:30). Thus, Peter demonstrates that prophecy never came about by a prophet's own interpretation, nor did it ever originate in the human will. Again, this contrasts to the "cleverly invented stories" (2 Peter 1:16) and will stand in contrast to the false prophets of chapter 2.

2.3. Warning Reminder of False Teachers (2:1–3a)

2.3.1. Warning Against Their Destructive Heresies (2:1). Peter begins his section on the false teachers with "but there were also false prophets among the people." Perhaps this is a reference to Balaam, whom he will specifically cite later (2:15–16), for he has already cited a phrase from his oracle in Numbers (see comment on 1:19). Peter warns that in a similar manner, false teachers will "secretly introduce destructive heresies" to the church. This is the challenge to the New Testament church. Heresy begins with specious arguments and reading into Scripture, basing doctrines and beliefs on the silence of Scripture rather than on an explicit word.

The crux of Peter's message is a warning against those who morally deny the Lordship of Christ. It contrasts the divine voice speaking in the Transfiguration, where Peter heard the command to listen to God's Son. These false teachers are not listening and thereby morally deny Christ's sovereign ownership of their lives. Such a denial will reap swift destruction. The theme of "who bought them" is important to Peter's soteriology (1 Peter 1:18–19).

2.3.2. Outcome and Methodology (2:2–3a). The presence of false teachers is not a new phenomenon. It seems tragically predictable that with the introduction of heresy, "many will follow" them. What is even more tragic is that often the lie captures good-hearted people, and they themselves "bring the way of truth into disrepute" because of the example they are to others.

The motive of the heresy is "greed"—financial gain (2:3). One merely needs to examine the word-faith theologies of North American sects to see the relevancy and urgency of Peter's warning. False teachers exploit Christians with clever stories that they have made up (1:16), a pattern in direct opposition to the truth to which Peter and the other apostles have witnessed.

Peter then sets up his argument from history. In light of the deeds of these false teachers, he asserts that the judgment on all such people is not dormant. He goes on to demonstrate this by referring to judgment on all strata of creation: celestial, terrestrial, and civic.

2.4. Warning Reminder of Inevitable Judgment (2:3b–9)

2.4.1. Warning Reminder From Historical Precedent (2:3b–6).

2.4.1.1. Celestial Judgment (2:3b–4). Peter first appeals to the celestial judgment of the angels who sinned. Jude goes into greater detail, describing that these angels did not keep their position of authority but abandoned it (with the implication of sexual activity; see Jude 6–7 and comments). Peter is using a "light and heavy" argument: If God did not spare the angels who challenged him but sent them to hell, how much more will he judge those who deny the Lordship of Christ.

2.4.1.2. Terrestrial Judgment (2:5). Not only did God judge celestial sin, but he also judged the antediluvian world. One begins to notice the impartiality of God's dealings and judgments on sin and wickedness. A significant difference from the celestial judgment is that Noah, a preacher of righteousness, along with seven of his family, were preserved. This incident is probably cited for a twofold purpose: (1) Human beings significantly differ from angels, and Peter finds it impossible to write about a remnant (an important concept here) with respect to the angels; and (2) just as Noah endured and was righteous in an unrighteous world, so too the audience that Peter addresses can endure amid the false teachers.

2.4.1.3. Civic Judgment (2:6). The "if" clause focuses the audience's attention once again on the "light and heavy" argument: If God judged the angels who sinned by casting them into hell, if God judged the ancient world by a destroying flood, if God condemned the cities of the plain by burning them to ashes, how much more likely is it that the false teachers will also receive a judgment! Here for the first time in this triad Peter actually calls the threefold judgment "an example." There is no partiality in God's judgments; this is what will happen to the ungodly.

2.4.2. Deliverance of the Righteous (2:7–9). Just as the Lord delivered Noah and his family because of righteousness, so too the Lord rescued Lot, a righteous man, from the destruction of Sodom and Gomorrah. This is a most puzzling passage. When one reads the Genesis account, the reader is not left with the idea that Lot is "righteous" (same word as is used for Noah in v. 5). In fact, one would think the complete opposite. Peter, however, sheds a different light on the Lot story. He uses two key words to characterize Lot's disposition: "distressed" and "tormented."

Peter is concerned here about his readers; that is where the sense comes in figuring out this passage. He insists that Lot was righteous but distressed by the filthy lives of lawless men; in fact, Lot "was tormented in his righteous soul" every day by what he saw and heard. So too the righteous souls of those to whom Peter is writing may soon come under such trials. The good news is that just as the Lord knew how to save Lot, in a similar manner he will rescue the godly from trials. In fact, Peter balances it out by saying that God "knows how to rescue godly men from trials and to hold the unrighteous for the day of judgment." Peter is here establishing the righteousness and justice of God (see also 1 Peter 2:23). This passage will become more encouraging as the dark days of false teachers and heresies grow stronger.

2.5. Warning Reminder of Their Character (2:10–22)

2.5.1. Morally Bankrupt (2:10). Having established a historical precedent for judgment on the false teachers, Peter now expounds upon their character. One of their first and obvious character traits is that by following "the corrupt desire of the sinful nature ... [they] despise authority." Every church, every religious institution, every Christian family is aware of this sad truth: Many problems originate with despising authority. Whether it be an unteachable spirit or a resistance to correction, it begins with a conflict of authority. Naturally, if people despise authority, the chief and telltale sign of this fact is boldness and arrogance (v. 10b). They have no awe or reverential fear of things greater than themselves or of divine things.

2.5.2. Contrast to Angels (2:11). In contrast to these "bold and arrogant . . . men," angels, whom Peter says are "stronger and more powerful," do not dare to bring accusations against such celestial beings in the presence of the Lord. One needs only to think of televangelists, who stomp on the head of the devil or argue in front of the camera with demons, to realize that this happens today. Novels in which the protagonist can actually insult a demon and get away with it fill the shelves of Christian bookstores. Peter's words bring his audience into proper perspective. In fact, held against the celestial hierarchy, the pride of the false teachers is painfully obvious.

2.5.3. Actions of Those Lacking in True Knowledge (2:12–19). In verse 12 Peter shows the folly of the ways of the false teachers. These men have no concept of what they are doing, and therefore their actions are blasphemous. In fact, their actions are no longer human but animalistic—"brute beasts." Because of this tendency, destruction is inevitable: "They will be paid back" (v. 13). Over and over Peter takes great pains to remind his readers and warn the false teachers that a pay-back time is coming. In the light of the threefold judgments already cited, these men will receive recompense for their evil actions.

Peter turns from animal imagery to medical imagery when he calls the false teachers "blots and blemishes" (v. 13). In fact, they are stains upon righteous living. They "carouse in broad daylight" (i.e., in full view) and do so in the company of believers. How this is possible is that they have *secretly* introduced heresies (2:1). No false teacher wears a sign indicating his theological and ethical position. But slowly, speciously, insidiously, the false teachers creep in and stain the fellowship of true believers.

In verse 14 Peter tells us five characteristics of these false teachers. (1) They have "eyes full of adultery." John calls this "the lust of [one's] eyes" (1 John 2:16). These men look for sin in everything they see. (2) Their sin is constant. Rather than always doing good, these men constantly sin. (3) They "seduce the unstable." Peter will later on describe the unstable man as one who distorts and twists Scripture (2 Peter 3:16). The choice of the verb "seduce" is significant. These men sound orthodox but gradually shift their teachings into the realm of heresy. (4) These false teachers are "experts in greed." This goes back to what Peter earlier highlighted as their motive (2:3). Greed is the chief and besetting sin for false teachers. (5) They are "an accursed brood." This is one of the most damning phrases in all of Scripture. To be accursed is to be separated from God (cf. Rom. 9:3).

In verse 15 Peter uses the example of Balaam, a false prophet, to show the modus operandi of the contemporary false teachers. The reference to love of "wages" gives the idea of greed-motivated action. Peter demonstrates how these false teachers leave the straight way

MAJOR ARCHAEOLOGICAL FINDS RELATING TO THE NEW TESTAMENT

Site or Artifact	Location	Scripture
ISRAEL		
Herod's Temple	Jerusalem	Luke 1:9
Herod's Winter Palace	Jericho	Matthew 2:4
Herodium	Near Bethlehem	Matthew 2:19
Masada	Southwest of Dead Sea	cf. Luke 21:20
Early Synagogue	Capernaum	Mark 1:21
Pool of Siloam	Jerusalem	John 9:7
Pool of Bethesda	Jerusalem	John 5:2
Pilate Inscription	Caesarea	Luke 3:1
Inscription: Stone Sign at Temple Barring Gentiles	Jerusalem	Acts 21:27–29
Skeletal Remains of Crucified Man	Jerusalem	Luke 23:33
Peter's House	Capernaum	Matthew 8:14
Jacob's Well	Nablus	John 4:5–6
ASIA MINOR		
Derbe Inscription	Kerti Hüyük	Acts 14:20
Sergius Paulus Inscription	Antioch in Pisidia	Acts 13:6–7
Zeus Altar (Satan's Throne?)	Pergamum	Revelation 2:13
Fourth-Century B.C. Walls	Assos	Acts 20:13–14
Artemis Temple and Altar	Ephesus	Acts 19:27–28
Ephesian Theater	Ephesus	Acts 19:29
Silversmith Shops	Ephesus	Acts 19:24
Statues of Artemis	Ephesus	Acts 19:35
GREECE		
Erastus Inscription	Corinth	Romans 16:23
Synagogue Inscription	Corinth	Acts 18:4
Meat Market Inscription	Corinth	1 Corinthians 10:25
Cult Dining Rooms	Corinth	1 Corinthians 8:10
Court (Bema)	Corinth	Acts 18:12
Marketplace (Bema)	Philippi	Acts 16:19
Starting Gate for Races	Isthmia	1 Corinthians 9:24, 26
Gallio Inscription	Delphi	Acts 18:12
Egnatian Way	Kavalia (Neapolis), Philippi, Apollonia, Thessalonica	cf. Acts 16:11–12; 17:1
Politarch Inscription	Thessalonica	Acts 17:6
ITALY		
Tomb of Augustus	Rome	Luke 2:1
Mamertime Prison	Rome	2 Timothy 1:16–17; 2:9; 4:6–8
Appian Way	Puteoli to Rome	Acts 28:13–16
Golden House of Nero	Rome	cf. Acts 25:10; 1 Peter 2:13

in order to follow Balaam (cf. also Jude 11; Rev. 2:14). The sin of Balaam was a grievous one, not unlike the sin of the false teachers—syncretism. In Numbers 25, this syncretism involved the union of the worship of Yahweh with the worship of Baal. Because syncretism makes the worship of false gods look like the worship of the Lord, it is so seductive, so deceptive, so secret. That is how the false teachers can "carouse in broad daylight" (2 Peter 2:13). Syncretism also explains how these false teachers can be part of the love feasts of the church—it lulls other believers into complacency. Thus, following the way of Balaam means to introduce heresies that deny the Lordship of Christ while still maintaining a veneer of orthodoxy. This has to be one of the most pernicious and seductive evils of the contemporary church.

Balaam was judged for his "wrongdoing" by a rebuke from the Lord (v. 16). Peter is here emphasizing again that judgment against wrongdoing is inescapable. There is an irony in his phrase "a beast without speech," for he previously likened the false teachers to brute beasts.

The two metaphors of "springs without water" and "mists driven by a storm" (v. 17) give the idea of unreliability and instability. These false teachers are untrustworthy and unstable. In fact, they are like Balaam, unreliable in his office as a prophet and unstable in his madness to go and curse Israel for profit. The end result, as for the fallen angels and all followers of sin, is "blackest darkness." The accusation of "empty, boastful words" (v. 18) is the outworking of the metaphor of springs without water. These people will promise anything in order to gain one's trust.

Furthermore, the methodology of the false teachers is utterly heinous. They appeal to "the lustful desires of sinful human nature"—desires in complete contrast to the qualities that believers should have in an ever-growing degree and from which they have just escaped (cf. 1:8–9). Tragically, those who fall victim are the ones who are just escaping from a depraved life. Too often the church has failed in its mentoring and teaching roles and has left new converts open and susceptible to the seduction of the false teachers.

The ultimate irony is that these empty promisers "promise ... freedom, while they themselves are slaves of depravity," that is, in the very grip of bondage themselves (v. 19). The proverb Peter uses is apt: These men are mastered by greed and lust and therefore are its slaves. It is significant that Peter calls himself a slave, but a slave of Christ (1:1).

The following chart summarizes fifteen actions of the false teachers and thirteen character traits. Indeed, as Peter lucidly points out, whatever has mastered a person, that person is a slave to it.

2.5.4. Warning Reminder of Turning Away From Truth (2:20–22). There are two main viewpoints that commentators take on these verses. On the one hand, some say that Peter is referring to the false teachers as people who have never truly been saved, because the dog and the pig are only doing what it is in their nature to do; hence the new, Christlike nature was never part of their conversion experience. Others, on the other hand, believe that this is both a warning and a reality to those who are saved: a *warning* to take heed and grow in the qualities of Christ listed in chapter 1, and a *reality* in that if a saved person becomes entangled again in the world and is overcome by it, judgment is inevitable.

The second of these options has more credibility attached to it. If words have meaning, then the phrases "escaped the corruption of the world by knowing our Lord and Savior Jesus Christ" and "known the way of righteousness" must refer to a conversion experience. Throughout Peter's letter, the term *know* carries with it the experiential and intimate knowledge that only comes from experience (see comments on 1:2). It is absurd to think that these accolades could apply to an unregenerate person, who was never saved in the first place.

3. Remember Your Future Hope (3:1–18)

3.1. Purpose of the Letter (3:1–2)

In 3:1 Peter indicates that this is his second letter. He also cites here the reason for both letters: reminders. They are designed to remind the people to think in a wholesome manner. This is interesting for such a purpose is uncommon in contemporary society. Many homilies and sermons are now geared toward self-esteem and focused entirely on one's psyche. Peter, in contrast, writes his letter to "stimulate his audience] to wholesome thinking" through reminders. He has fulfilled his goal in that he has reminded them of their past experience and of a present danger, warning them to know the difference between true prophecy and false teaching. He now goes on to remind them of their future hope.

Peter's admonition in verse 2 is to the authority of the Old Testament and of the teachings and commands of the Lord communicated through the apostles. In other words, "the holy prophets" represent the Old Testament and the "apostles" represent the New Testament. Again, Peter uses the word "recall" to fit his purpose of a reminder letter. He distinguishes the false prophets from the Old Testament writers by calling the latter "*holy* prophets."

3.2. Reminder of the Future Hope (3:3–10)

3.2.1. Reminder That Scoffers Are Inevitable (3:3–4). Peter warns his readers that scoffers will come, and they should not be surprised when it happens. They will come "in the last days." For Peter, and indeed for sacred history, the last days are made manifest at Pentecost with the pouring out of the Holy Spirit. Peter was fully aware of this in his sermon delivered on Pentecost, which began with a quotation from Joel: "In the last days . . . I will pour out my Spirit on all people" (Acts 2:17). Thus, for nearly two thousand years the church has been in the last days, and for the same amount of time scoffers have come. The source of the scoffing is "their own evil desires."

The basis of the scoffing is the apparent lack of fulfillment of Jesus' promise of a return. This is similar to the doubt about God's word that the serpent put in the mind of Eve. These scoffers cause us to question Christ's second coming. They appeal to the time continuum as the proof for their mocking: "Everything goes on as it has since the beginning of creation." What is at stake here is the reliability of God and the trustworthiness of prophecy (i.e., Scripture). Peter sagaciously warns his

CHARACTERISTICS OF FALSE TEACHERS IN 2 PETER

Verse	Deed	Character Traits	End Result
Verse 1	introduce destructive heresies; deny the sovereign Lord		swift destruction
Verse 2	shameful ways; bring the way of truth into disrepute		
Verse 3	exploit with made-up stories	greed	condemnation and destruction imminent
Verse 10a–b	despise authority	bold; arrogant	
Verses 10c–12	slander; blaspheme	no fear in slandering; like brute beasts; creatures of instinct	will perish
Verse 13	carouse; revel in pleasure	blots; blemishes	will be paid back with harm
Verse 14	ceaseless sin; seducers	eyes full of adultery; experts in greed	accursed brood
Verse 15	left the straight way		
Verse 17		springs without water; mists driven by storm	blackest darkness reserved for them
Verse 18	mouth empty, boastful words; entice people		
Verse 19		slaves of depravity	
Verse 20			worse off now than at the beginning

audience against such specious arguments since he knows that it is a human peccadillo to doubt the faithfulness of God and his Word. Note from the following chart how Peter is aware, through experience, of the pattern of last days, both as to promise and to scoffers.

Last days	2 Peter 3:3	Acts 2:17
Promise	2 Peter 3:4	Acts 1:4
Scoffers	2 Peter 3:3	Acts 2:13

3.2.2. Reminder of God's Past Faithfulness (3:5–6). Peter now sets up his second argument from historical precedent. (The first one was in regards to inevitable judgment; see 2:3b–9.) God's Word has always been reliable. Peter shows that creation itself was formed from God's Word (cf. John 1:1–4). This is one indisputable area that the mockers have deliberately forgotten. If, by his Word, God created the world, then he will faithfully keep his promise of return.

Both the act of creation by God's Word to show his faithfulness to his promise and the act of judgment on the world by his Word to show his faithfulness to his promise are irrefutably upheld. Indeed, God's creation, God's judgment by the Flood, and God's saving of Noah are all based on his trustworthiness to fulfilling his promises.

3.2.3. Reminder of God's Future Faithfulness (3:7–10). Having established the basis of God's faithfulness in keeping his Word, Peter now turns from the past to the present and future. The same Word has reserved "the present heavens and earth" for the judgment of "fire" (v. 7). This judgment will also result in the destruction "of ungodly men." In other words, just as God has been faithful in his acts of creation and preservation, so too he will be faithful in his acts of judgment on a sinful world. All this stands in contrast to the mocking of the scoffers, who want to know where the promise of God's coming is.

God's chronometer is different from ours. With a play on words, Peter does not want his readers to forget this one thing, which the scoffers have forgotten: "With the Lord a day is like a thousand years, and a thousand years are like a day" (v. 8). In case believers are discouraged or depressed regarding the coming of the Lord, or the scoffing of the mockers has caused them to doubt God's faithfulness, the Lord's timing is vastly different from human time. It is to a life of faith that we are called not to a life of proof and fact. With this truth established, it makes little difference to the believer if the Lord returns tomorrow or if he returns in the next millennium, for to the Christian, God *will* return according to his promise.

In verse 9 Peter points out that the motivation behind the Lord's timing is one of mercy. In fact, he insists that the Lord's patience is based on mercy. This is in contrast to the idea some may have that God is "slow in keeping his promise." That apparent slackness is intended to lead to the salvation of many souls. In a letter where an entire chapter is devoted to judgment and punishment, the heart of God is still merciful and patient.

Whether Peter consciously knew he was writing prophetically or not, he again testifies that the promise of Scripture is that "the day of the Lord will come" (v. 10). This is crucial and of paramount importance. The last decades of this century have noted a sharp decline in the study of eschatology. This is a costly loss to the church, for the return of the Lord is sure and imminent. Perhaps too, one's ethical behavior is proportional to one's belief in the second coming of Christ.

Peter goes on to emphasize the manner in which the Second Coming will take place: "like a thief." This expression speaks of suddenness and surprise. No doubt Peter remembered the Lord's words himself in the Olivet Discourse where he promised to return like a thief in the night (Matt. 24:43). The message is clear: Be on the alert. The day of the Lord will take by surprise only those unprepared; those who are looking for his coming will be ready.

Peter then gives a glimpse into the twofold judgment of the earth. (1) The heavens and the elements will disappear in a destructive, judgmental fire, and (2) everything "will be laid bare" on the earth. That is, everything will come under the scrutinizing eye of the Lord. What people have done in secret will then be proclaimed from the rooftops.

3.3. Reminder of Christian Conduct (3:11–14)

3.3.1. Conduct in View of the Lord's Return (3:11–12). In verse 11 the theme of holiness comes up again. This time it is in light of the transitory nature of material things.

Peter's question is rhetorical: If everything will be destroyed and all things on earth will be laid bare for inspection, what kind of persons ought we to be? Even though the question is rhetorical, Peter answers the question: "holy and godly."

As already implied, those who are godly and holy will indeed be looking forward to the coming of Christ (v. 12). In fact, they will "speed its coming." They will not be taken unaware; in fact, they will be able to recognize it. It is the ungodly and the unholy who will have no idea that destruction is about to take place. Once again, Peter reiterates the mode of destruction: fire. This stands in contrast to the first mode of terrestrial judgment: water. Both elements have destructive and sterilizing abilities.

3.3.2. Reminder of the Lord's Promise (3:13). Even though the present order will be destroyed by fire, that is not where the focus of the Christian's mind is to be. Peter goes back to the surety of God's promise. Believers ought to look forward to a new order, one characterized by "righteousness." It is this quality that characterized Noah and Lot (2:5–9). *Righteousness*, for Peter, is the term for living ethically and morally in an immoral world (see comments on 1:1). He does not know of a salvation apart from righteous living.

3.3.3. Reminder to Be Diligent, Spotless, and Blameless (3:14). If the chief character trait of the newly created order is righteousness, Peter urges us to "make every effort to be found spotless, blameless and at peace with [the Lord]." Once again, the apostle is calling his readers to take on the divine nature. Whereas the false teachers are "blots and blemishes" at the love feasts (2:13), his dear friends are to be spotless, just as Jesus was "without blemish or defect" (1 Peter 1:19). There is an obvious impression of human responsibility flowing throughout Peter's letter. While God is the One who makes precious promises, and while we receive his divine power and calling, human responsibility is added to the divine element. Ethical and moral living is not an instantaneous acquisition after conversion, it is a daily consistent lifestyle.

3.4. Reminder of Apostolic Harmony (3:15–16)

3.4.1. Reminder of Paul's Letters (3:15). This verse refers back to God's chronology in 3:8–9. Note also the reference to "bear in mind." This is wholly consistent with the "remembrance" letter that Peter is writing (see comments on 3:1–2). Peter now writes about Paul. He knows about Paul's letters to the churches of northwest Asia Minor. Perhaps he has read them, or perhaps someone has reported the content of the letters to him. Possibly, although it is speculation, while in Rome Peter and Paul spoke to each other about their writings. It is also possible that Peter learned the contents of Paul's letters from Luke, Silas, or Mark.

3.4.2. Nature of Paul's Letters (3:16). Peter shows that Paul has written the same prophetic truth that he himself writes. In fact, their letters say essentially the same things. There is one notable difference: Peter acknowledges that Paul writes "some things that are hard to understand." The caution he makes is that "ignorant and unstable people distort" these letters. Earlier Peter called those who are easily seduced by the false teachers "unstable" (2:14). He then elevates the writings of Paul's letters to that of "the other Scriptures." Perhaps Peter knew that what Paul wrote was inspired by the Spirit since Paul was filled with the Spirit in Acts 9.

We can guess with some degree of certainty the issue Paul wrote about that was distorted. Peter's entire letter relates to ethical and moral living. Indeed, he has written in both 1 and 2 Peter for God's people to be holy, that is, to take on the character of Jesus. Presumably Paul's writings on liberty and Christian freedom were taken to the extreme, so that these unprincipled teachers were promoting licentiousness.

3.5. Reminder to Be on Guard (3:17–18a)

For a second time Peter addresses the recipients as "dear friends" (cf. 3:1). He affirms that they already know what he has written and are

THE OLD TESTAMENT IN THE NEW

NT Text	OT Text	Subject
2Pe 2:22	Pr 26:11	Dog returns to vomit
2Pe 3:13	Isa 65:17	New heavens and new earth

probably even modeling his principles in their lives. He warns them to "be on [their] guard" in order not to be swayed away from truth by these modern-day Balaams. Here again the argument for the possibility of Christians falling away is strengthened by Peter's warning "and fall from your secure position."

Verses 17–18a give Peter's final contrast between the righteous and the unrighteous. The chart delineates between the two types of people.

3.6. Doxology (3:18b)

All theology should lead to doxology. Peter's letter ends on a note of exhortation and praise. As the people "grow in the grace and knowledge of our Lord and Savior Jesus Christ," their lives and worship will be praise to him.

CONTRAST OF CHARACTER IN 2 PETER

Righteous	Unrighteous
Faithful (1:5)	Scoffer (3:3)
Good (1:5)	
Knowledgeable (1:5)	Ignorant (3:16)
Self-controlled (1:6)	Unstable (3:16)
Persevering (1:6)	Nearsighted, blind (1:9)
Kind (1:7)	Greedy (2:3)
Loving (1:7)	Seducer (2:14)
Holy (3:11)	Depraved (2:19)
Godly (3:11)	Ungodly (2:6)
Blameless (3:14)	Lawless (3:17)
	Despise authority (2:10)
	Arrogant, bold (2:10)
	Carouser (2:13)

1–3 JOHN

Robert Berg

NTRODUCTION

he books that follow 2 Peter in the New Tes-ment are called 1, 2, and 3 John or the Johan-ine letters. However, many scholars contend at the so-called first Johannine letter is nei-her Johannine nor a letter. We will address ich claims in this introductory section. This ommentary presents an analysis of the histor-cal background to each of these books of the Jew Testament as an aid to interpretation. uch a discussion is especially important in elation to these letters. Indeed, 1 John contains tatements that are easily misunderstood apart om the perspective gained from a study of the ircumstances that led to its being written. For his reason, the consideration of these writings nder the heading of "general" or "catholic" etters is not particularly appropriate; 1, 2, and John are addressed to specific recipients fac-ng specific issues. Time invested in a survey f introductory material for the Johannine let-ers will be richly rewarded when specific pas-ages are being considered.

. Author

Much controversy has surrounded this issue. irst John is anonymous; 2 and 3 John are vritten by an individual calling himself "the lder." The association with John, the son of Zebedee, is rooted in early church tradition. By the end of the second century, 1 John and, o a lesser extent, 2 John were being cited as uthoritative by the church fathers; by the hird century, 3 John was also being consid-ered in this manner.

The first specific claim that the Gospel of ohn and 1 John were written by the same per-on was made by Dionysius of Alexandria in he third century. For many years there was loubt about common authorship of the Gospel nd all three letters because 2 and 3 John were uthored by "the elder," seemingly to be dis-inguished from the apostle associated with the Gospel and 1 John. Second and 3 John even-ually were attributed to the apostle as well, who was thought to have called himself "the elder" out of modesty. Such reticence can be seen as analogous to the manner in which John, presuming he is the author, is believed to have referred to himself in the Gospel as the "disciple whom Jesus loved."

The evidence in the texts themselves has been used to argue both for and against common authorship of the Gospel and the letters. The case against common authorship rests on various observations. (1) Scholars claim that the letters reflect a much later time. Though the Gospel arose out of a period of separation from the Jewish synagogue, the letters reflect a time when the Christian community being addressed faced an entirely new crisis; the break from Judaism was in the past, and now the conflict was between segments of the Christian group.

(2) The thought and language of the letters, particularly 1 John, is different from that of the Gospel. So, for example, terms in the Gospel for Jesus himself (e.g., "Word," "life") in the letters refer to the teaching or tradition of the church. It is not unusual to read in commentaries the judgment that 1 John is a decidedly inferior work to the Gospel in creativity and style.

(3) It is inconceivable to some that an apostle such as John would not cite his name and its inherent authority in the struggle against the false prophets.

None of these arguments is compelling. The perceived differences in thought and expression can arguably be accounted for by the change in purpose, format, and circumstances. And we simply cannot be so certain that an apostle would not, for whatever reason, refer to himself as "the elder." In any case, common authorship of all these books by John, the son of Zebedee, ultimately is not crucial in terms of interpretation and certainly not in terms of inspiration and authority. There is no reason why an associate of John could not be responsible for the writing of 1 John (or be "the elder"), just as such a person was apparently responsible for the testimony of John 21:24. The "we" of that verse suggests that the "disciple whom Jesus loved," whether or not we can with assurance identify him with John the apostle, was the authoritative witness for a group of believers.

The remarkable similarities between the Gospel and 1 John, evident from the first verses of each, indicate that though common authorship cannot be proved, a common tradition and outlook cannot be questioned. With such qualifications in mind, then, this commentary on 1 John will use the name "John" as the most convenient way to refer to the writer.

2. Date and Place of Writing

It makes best sense of the texts to propose that the letters were written after the Gospel. (The occasion for the letters will be examined further below.) If the Gospel is dated about A.D. 90, as is common, the letters would presumably be dated some years later, possibly in the later 90s. If the Gospel is earlier, we can adjust the date of the letters accordingly.

There is no internal indication of the place of writing. Based on early tradition, the best case can be made for Ephesus, a city in Asia Minor, where, according to a famous anecdote attributed by Irenaeus to Polycarp, a younger associate of John, John apparently lived and worked. In the story, the apostle ran out of a public bath in Ephesus, crying that Cerinthus, the "enemy of the truth," was inside (*Against Heresies*, 3.3.4). Christian sources in the second century also identify John the apostle with the John who wrote the book of Revelation, which is addressed to a number of churches in Asia Minor, including Ephesus. In any case, knowledge of the specific location of the writer and his readers is not critical to interpretation of the books.

3. Recipients

The believers reflected in John 21:24, who "know that his [the author's] testimony is true," and in the Gospel of John itself demonstrate that the witness of the disciple whom Jesus loved was preserved and propagated. These believers had experienced a wrenching separation from the synagogue (John 16:1–4) and comprised one side of a debate with representatives of Pharisaic Judaism. The hostile confrontations that Jesus has with the Jewish leaders in this Gospel would have been seen as prototypical of their own experience (15:20–21). There is nothing in the letters that suggests continuous confrontation with the synagogue, but this ordeal would certainly have left i mark on them.

Modern scholars often refer to these belie ers as "the Johannine community." This ter is meant to describe Christian believers wh have certain traditions and practices that di tinguish them from other Christian groups. I other words, just as the members of church that were founded by Paul may be referred t as a part of "Pauline Christianity," so the existed at the same time believers whose fai can be discerned in what is called the "Johan nine writings." This "community" would mo likely have been an association of a number c congregations or house churches.

Second and 3 John suggest that some c these local groups may be geographicall removed from one another. The fact th 1 John is written suggests that these believe are not all in the same location; presumably th author is resident with one segment and write to address other segments who share like fait (see 2 John 1, 13). Both 2 and 3 John indicat a certain distance between the elder and th recipients of his letters (2 John 12; 3 John 1 14). These two shorter letters also portray a si uation in which "brothers" travel from on community locale to another (2 John 10–1 3 John 5–10). Their cohesion appears to rest i their commitment to a common Christian tra dition, which is to some degree supervised b those who have transmitted the traditio (1 John 1:1–4). The "elder" of 2 and 3 Joh probably can be identified with these people i authority. In an urban area such as Ephesus Gentiles presumably make up part of the com munity, though there is little in the letters t argue this one way or another.

The recipients are believers who have bee born of God and received the Spirit (3:1–3, 21 24; 4:13–15; 5:1–5, 13). The writer addresse them in affectionate terms, such as "dear chil dren" and "dear friends" (lit., "beloved"). Sec ond John is addressed to "the chosen lady an her children," probably meaning a church an its members; this reading is supported by th concluding greeting from "your chosen sister, the local congregation of Johannine believer with whom the elder, at least at that time, i residing. Third John is addressed to an indi vidual, Gaius, evidently a member of anothe of these local communities. What is especiall interesting is the only reference in the letter

THE GOSPEL OF JOHN AND THE FIRST LETTER OF JOHN

There is a remarkable similarity of language and theme between the gospel of John and the first letter of John. The following chart outlines where these parallels are.

Theme	1 John	Gospel of John
Word was from the beginning and became flesh, and we saw it	1Jn 1:1; 2:14	Jn 1:1–2, 14
We could touch the "Word of life"	1Jn 1:1	Jn 20:27, 29
The Word was "the life"	1Jn 1:2; 5:20	Jn 1:4; 11:25; 14:6
The Word was "with the Father"	1Jn 1:2	Jn 1:1, 18
We must testify to the Word	1Jn 1:2	Jn 15:27
Complete joy available through Christ	1Jn 1:4	Jn 3:29; 16:24; 17:13
Light from God dispels darkness	1Jn 1:5–7	Jn 1:4–5; 3:19–21
Life through the blood of God's Son	1Jn 1:7	Jn 6:53–56
The Word has no place in unbelievers	1Jn 1:10	Jn 5:38
Jesus as the atoning sacrifice for the sin of the world	1Jn 2:2; 3:5; 4:10	Jn 1:29; 3:16–17; 11:51
Loving God involves obeying his commands	1Jn 2:3, 5; 3:22; 5:2–3	Jn 14:15, 21; 15:10
Jesus as our example	1Jn 2:6	Jn 13:15
Jesus' command to love one another	1Jn 2:7; 3:11, 23; 4:7, 11	Jn 13:34; 15:12, 17
Jesus as the true shining light	1Jn 2:8	Jn 1:9; 8:12; 9:5
Walking in darkness and stumbling	1Jn 2:11	Jn 11:9–10; 12:35
Word of God living in us	1Jn 2:14	Jn 5:38
Those who do not have the love of God in them	1Jn 2:15	Jn 5:42
Knowledge gained through the Holy Spirit	1Jn 2:20, 27	Jn 14:16
Knowing the truth	1Jn 2:21	Jn 8:32
Knowing the Father involves knowing the Son	1Jn 2:23	Jn 8:19; 14:7
Remaining in the Father and the Son	1Jn 2:24, 27; 3:24	Jn 15:4
God's love that makes us his children	1Jn 3:1–2	Jn 1:12; 3:16
Those who do not know God	1Jn 3:1	Jn 15:21; 16:3
The Son of God is sinless	1Jn 3:5	Jn 8:46
The devil has been sinning from the beginning	1Jn 3:8	Jn 8:44
Being born of God	1Jn 3:9; 4:7; 5:1, 4, 18	Jn 1:13; 3:3, 6
Hatred from the world	1Jn 3:13	Jn 15:18–19; 17:14
Crossing from death to life	1Jn 3:14	Jn 5:24
Jesus laid down his life for us	1Jn 3:16	Jn 10:11
Laying down our lives for others	1Jn 3:16	Jn 15:13
Truth is found in the Son of God	1Jn 3:19	Jn 14:6; 18:37
God knows all things	1Jn 3:21	Jn 21:17
Receiving from God what we ask	1Jn 3:22; 5:14–15	Jn 14:13–14; 15:7, 16; 16:23
The command to believe in God's Son	1Jn 3:23	Jn 6:29
Jesus has come in the flesh	1Jn 4:2	Jn 1:14
Overcoming the world	1Jn 4:4; 5:4–5	Jn 16:33
The world loves those of the world	1Jn 4:5	Jn 15:19
Those who are not from God do not listen to him	1Jn 4:6	Jn 8:47
The Spirit of truth	1Jn 4:6; 5:6	Jn 14:17; 15:26; 16:13
God sent his one and only Son so we can live	1Jn 4:9, 14; 5:11–12	Jn 1:18; 3:16–17, 36; 20:31
No one has seen God	1Jn 4:12, 20	Jn 1:18
Jesus is the Savior of the world	1Jn 4:14	Jn 3:17; 4:42; 12:47
We are in God and God is in us	1Jn 4:16	Jn 15:4–5; 17:21
Jesus and the water and the blood	1Jn 5:6–8	Jn 19:34–35
Human testimony and divine testimony	1Jn 5:9–10	Jn 5:32–37; 8:14–17
How to know we have eternal life	1Jn 5:13	Jn 20:30–31
Believing on the name of God's Son	1Jn 5:13	Jn 1:12
Satan as the prince of this world	1Jn 5:19	Jn 12:31; 14:30
Knowing the true God	1Jn 5:20	Jn 17:3
Jesus as true God	1Jn 5:20	Jn 1:1; 20:28

to any church organization. Diotrephes appears to be a leader of a church near where Gaius lives, but he has in a number of ways rejected the authority of the elder.

4. Occasion and Purpose

A reconstruction of the immediate historical background to the Johannine letters suggests that the community has gone through a "church split." Unfortunately, many modern Christians have had first- or second-hand experience with the rancor that accompanies such situations. If one has experienced or observed how former friends can become bitter enemies, how both factions can claim to be in the right and "demonize" the other, and how church members not committed to either faction are courted by the competing claims of the two sides, one can begin to get a sense for the dynamics behind the argument of 1 John. Some people had left the community (1 John 2:19). Their departure would have been bad enough, given the author's passionate commitment to love each other. But three factors made things much worse: Those who left (1) espoused a grossly unacceptable view of Jesus Christ, (2) demonstrated a disdain for the demand for behavior in keeping with Christian discipleship, and (3) attempted to proselytize the members of the faithful community, represented by the writer.

(1) The first factor is the denial of the Incarnation, the historical reality of God becoming human, of Jesus Christ "come in the flesh" (1 John 2:22–23; 4:1–3; 5:5; 2 John 7). Given the emphasis in 1 John, we may conclude that the crucial point of contention was the salvific nature of Jesus' death (1 John 1:7; 2:2; 4:10; 5:6). We do not know exactly what these opponents believed. Many have suggested an identification with the beliefs of Cerinthus, from whom John fled in the public bath story. Central to the views attributed to Cerinthus is that he maintained the spiritual Christ descended on the righteous man Jesus after his baptism, but eventually departed from him, so that Jesus suffered and died alone (Irenaeus, *Against Heresies*, 1.26.1). It often has been argued that 1 John 5:6 was directed against just such a teaching.

Others have associated the ideas of the opponents with docetism. Docetism (from the Greek word *dokeo*, to seem) held that Jesus was not really human; he just "seemed" to be. Ignatius, writing to a church in Asia Minor just decades later than these letters, warns against those who "do not confess that he was clothed in flesh" (*Letter to the Smyrnaeans*, 5:2).

This first issue, then, is one of "Christology," a term that refers to how a person or group thinks about Jesus Christ. The Christology of the opponents may be said to be deficient because they apparently rejected crucial elements of the Christian confession of the deity and humanity of Jesus.

(2) The second factor that made the departure of these opponents worse is that they showed little interest in exhibiting the sort of behavior that was called for in a child of God. John repeatedly indicts them for lack of love for the brothers (1 John 2:9–11; 3:11–24; 4:7–21). But it is difficult to know precisely what this means. Possibly those who left were only concerned about their own members and thus showed love only for those "on their side." John perhaps interpreted this as a failure to love the brothers, since "the brothers" for him were the members of *his* group. In addition, 1:6, 8, 10 probably reflect the position taken by the secessionists that they were not involved in sinful activity and thus not guilty of sin.

This attitude was alarming to John not only because it repudiated God's word, but also because it might be embraced by members of his own community (1 John 1:5–2:2). There is no indication in the letters that those who left were guilty of any flagrant sin; we would expect to find such sin denounced specifically. But the very concept of being in a sinless state had to be rejected harshly because it struck at the very foundation of the faith and one's standing with God: the atoning death of Jesus Christ.

(3) In addition to the Christological error and the deficiency in conduct, the third factor was probably most responsible for John's writing this letter. The antichrists not only deceived themselves (1 John 1:8) but were actively seeking to deceive the members of the community associated with the writer (2:26; 5:1). And they were apparently having some success in gaining numbers; that "the world listens to them" (4:5) suggests their numbers were growing. The real crisis here was the danger that members of John's group might also join them. The very existence of 1 John, with its

urgent appeals to "remain" in what they had been taught and its clearly defined tests to be administered regarding belief and behavior, proves that the situation was serious. Johannine believers were not to receive these false prophets into their homes nor even to give them a greeting (2 John 10–11).

There is an additional consideration of this issue that is of particular interest to Pentecostals. As some scholars have argued, the understanding and experience of the Spirit seem to have played a key role in the events leading up to the crisis reflected in the letters. The Gospel of John provides much evidence that the Johannine community gave considerable attention to the Holy Spirit. The Spirit effected their birth from above (John 3:3–8) and their acceptable worship of God (4:24), indwelt them as the source of living water (4:14; 7:37–39), taught them all things (14:26), and led them into all truth (16:13). Jesus even said that his followers would be better off when he left them because only then would the *parakletos* come (16:7).

In contrast to such a high profile for the Spirit in the Gospel, teaching on the Holy Spirit in 1 John is noticeably muted. Why does the writer not appeal to the Spirit as a rebuttal to the claims of the opponents? In fact, the writer does appeal three times to the Spirit, and in each case the role of the Spirit is simply to bear witness to a correct understanding of Jesus Christ (1 John 3:24–4:6; 4:13–15; 5:6–8). The section beginning with 3:24 has special interest. How do we know that God lives in us? By the Spirit he gave us. But then we are immediately confronted with a further question: How do you know that this Spirit (or spirit!) you have is from God (4:1)? What we find in the section that follows (4:1–6) is an attempt to submit matters of the Spirit to verifiable standards in adherence with the faith preserved by the witnesses reflected in the prologue. The presence of God's Spirit is tested by whether a person confesses that Jesus Christ has come in the flesh. A second test for the presence of the "Spirit of truth" is whether the person listens to (i.e., gives heed to or obeys) the writer and his fellow witnesses (4:6).

Other factors suggest that the opponents were claiming the presence of the Spirit. It is significant that the Spirit references are all concentrated in those sections of the book (see below) in which John responds to the false Christology. This is the case even though the Christological sections make up a much smaller percentage of 1 John than do the moral sections. In the first of these sections (2:18–27), there are two references to the *chrisma*, or anointing; these are unique in the New Testament, and almost certainly this word is a way of referring to the Holy Spirit. The emphatic "you" in 2:20 indicates that the opponents may have been asserting that it was *their* group that had the anointing (note also the related statement in v. 27). If the choice made by the NIV later in verse 20 is correct in translating "and all of you know the truth," this might also reflect a response to the claim of the other side that *they* were the ones who knew the truth.

The reference in 1 John 3:24 to the Spirit is strictly not in a Christological section according to our outline, but may as well be, since it functions as the transition to the next verses with their focus on matters of spirit. In this section it is most clear that the opponents, the false prophets who have "gone out" (4:1; identical to the antichrists who "went out" in 2:18–19), had "spirit" of some sort; no doubt these opponents claimed that it was *they* who had God's Spirit. It is plausible that the opponents emphasized the role of the *parakletos*, the distinctive Johannine term for the Holy Spirit found in the Gospel of John (John 14:16, 26; 15:26; 16:7), and the writer of 1 John for this reason not only avoids this identification but assigns the title to Jesus himself (1 John 2:2).

If the secessionists negated the physical reality of Jesus—or at least the importance of the physical death of Jesus—such a view could have been encouraged by a focus on the work of the Spirit. They may have concluded that since the Spirit indwells everyone born of God and gives direct access to God, the figure of Jesus is not essential in the continuing scheme of things; life is linked with the Spirit rather than with Jesus. This view in turn would have contributed to their perception that forgiveness of sins based on the atoning death of Jesus was not a matter of concern for them (1 John 1:5–2:2). Such a view might explain the language of 2 John 7–9, which also refers to the secessionists as antichrists and deceivers who "went out." The readers are then warned that the one who "goes ahead" and does not remain in the teaching of Jesus does not have

God. If the opponents have in essence "moved on" from Jesus to the Spirit as the focal point of their experience, this language is understandable. Should this be a fair representation of what was happening, it serves as a warning that those who give a more central place to their experience of the Spirit than they do to their commitment to the Jesus who gave his life for them are in danger of losing all contact with the God they claim to serve.

In sum, then, the purpose of 1 and 2 John is to demonstrate the errors of the opponents in the areas of Christology and practical conduct, to assure the members of the community that they *are* in right relationship with God through his Son, and to exhort them to renewed love for one another in the face of a church split and the threat that the opponents posed.

Third John gives little indication that the issues in 1 and 2 John are in view. The elder, apparently a figure of spiritual authority, writes to Gaius, a member of the community in another location. Perhaps the Demetrius mentioned in 3 John 12 carried the letter. Gaius is commended because of his hospitality to "brothers" associated with the elder. Diotrephes is denounced because he rejects the authority of the elder, speaks maliciously about him, and uses his position to deny any reception by the local church of these "brothers." The letter thus serves to commend Gaius and to exhort him to further faithful service.

5. Structure

Discerning a clear structure in 1 John is difficult. Some have even despaired of finding any coherent development of thought. One scholar, with only part of his tongue in cheek, has written: "Indeed 1 John makes almost as good sense when read backward, sentence by sentence" (Parker, 1956, 303). What we find are two or three themes that are repeated throughout, often with minor variations in presentation. Thus we would not suggest that the author of 1 John had any particular outline in mind when he wrote. But the format given below is useful in that it portrays the flow of the argument and the points of emphasis.

The outline presented here for 1 John is an adaptation of the three sections proposed originally by T. Haering a century ago and accepted in some form by various commentators since. Two notes bear mentioning. (1) Though there are only two or three main themes, the language used to present these themes varies considerably. Metaphors are enlisted and interwoven to make (basically) the same point. The metaphors themselves, though vivid, are expendable enough that they do not lend themselves well to use for an overall structure. For example, light and darkness seem to be major concepts early in the letter; each is used six times between 1:5 and 2:11. But then the metaphor is dropped completely and neither light nor darkness is mentioned again. Other metaphors serve the purpose.

(2) There are transitional phrases or verses between one section and another that could be placed with what precedes or follows, or even divided between the two. For example, the latter part of 3:24, which we have included in the section 2:28–3:24, is an introduction to 4:1–6; the address in 4:1 best divides the sections, but conceptually, the preceding sentence fits well with what follows. Another example is 5:1. This seems best placed in the Christological section 5:1–12, but the reference to the "child" clearly serves as a link to the moral section in 4:7–21. For the author, the Christological and moral are integrally related, and the outline should not be taken to undermine that unity.

John's primary concerns, then, are Christological (proper belief in Jesus Christ) and moral (proper conduct by the believer). In his massive commentary, Raymond Brown has proposed that 1 John be divided into two parts, the first governed by the "message" in 1:5 that God is light and the second by the "message" in 3:11 that God is love (Brown, 1982, 116–29). This division is attractive, but sections of the book simply do not fit into such an outline; 2:7–11, for example, make better sense in the second part of the letter, and 4:1–6 certainly are out of place. In any case, however, a twofold emphasis is prevalent. First John stresses the observance of divine commands, and in 3:23 we find a precise identification of the command: Believe in Jesus Christ and love one another (Christology and conduct). There are two instances in which a person "makes [God] out to be a liar" (1:10): when a person claims not to have sinned (conduct; 1:10) and when a person does not believe in the Son of God (Christology; 5:10).

First John does not have the formal elements of a letter. It has thus been called a tract or a treatise. But it is clear that although it is not a letter formally, it has been written for a particular group. The frequent insertions of personal addresses, such as "dear children," also give the writing the feel of a letter, though the prologue and the conclusion tend to do just the opposite.

Second and 3 John follow the standard letter format of the time. Each cites the sender of the letter, the recipient(s), and a blessing or wish; these elements are considered part of the salutation. The body of the letter follows, which, in keeping with custom, briefly conveys the pertinent information of the letter. There then follows a closing, usually including another greeting. The twofold message discussed above for 1 John is also the content of the body of 2 John, conduct (vv. 4–6) and Christology (7–11), and may be reflected in the "truth and love" of verse 3. Third John refers to a number of individuals and makes a few different points; its outline is less focused than that of 2 John.

OUTLINE OF 1 JOHN

1. **Prologue** (1:1–4)
2. **The Message** (1:5–2:27)
    - **2.1.** Behavior of the Christian (1:5–2:17)
        - **2.1.1.** The Message: God Is Light (1:5)
        - **2.1.2.** Three False Claims Regarding Sin Are Refuted (1:6–2:2)
        - **2.1.3.** Knowing God Means Obeying God's Word (2:3–6)
        - **2.1.4.** The Love Commandment (2:7–11)
        - **2.1.5.** Exhortation of the Community (2:12–14)
        - **2.1.6.** Love of the World as the Antithesis to Love of God (2:15–17)
    - **2.2.** Belief in the Christ (2:18–27)
        - **2.2.1.** The Antichrists Who Have Gone Out Into the World (2:18–19)
        - **2.2.2.** Remaining in the Teaching of the Anointing About Jesus (2:20–27)
3. **The Message Again** (2:28–4:6)
    - **3.1.** Behavior of the Christian (2:28–3:24)
        - **3.1.1.** The Hope of the Children of God (2:28–3:3)
        - **3.1.2.** A Mark of the Children of God: Not Continuing in Sin (3:4–10)
        - **3.1.3.** Another Mark of the Children of God: Loving Fellow Believers (3:11–24)
    - **3.2.** Belief in the Christ (4:1–6)
        - **3.2.1.** Belief in Jesus as a Test of Who Is From God (4:1–3)
        - **3.2.2.** Affirmation That the Readers Are From God (4:4–6)
4. **The Message Yet Again** (4:7–5:12)
    - **4.1.** Behavior of the Christian (4:7–21)
        - **4.1.1.** The Example of Love: God's Gift of His Son (4:7–10)
        - **4.1.2.** The Example of Love: Followed by God's Children (4:11–21)
            - **4.1.2.1.** God's Love Made Complete in Our Love for One Another (4:11–16)
            - **4.1.2.2.** God's Love Made Complete in Our Confidence on the Day of Judgment (4:17–18)
            - **4.1.2.3.** Love for Fellow Believers Must Accompany Love for God (4:19–21)
    - **4.2.** Belief in the Christ (5:1–12)
        - **4.2.1.** By Believing in Jesus We Obey God's Commands (5:1–5)
        - **4.2.2.** By Believing in Jesus We Accept God's Testimony About His Son (5:6–12)
5. **Concluding Remarks** (5:13–21)
    - **5.1.** The Assurance of Eternal Life and Our Approach to God (5:13–15)
    - **5.2.** The Sin That Leads to Death (5:16–17)
    - **5.3.** The Children of God Kept From the Evil One and in the True God (5:18–20)
    - **5.4.** Final Warning (5:21)

COMMENTARY ON 1 JOHN

1. Prologue (1:1–4)

The first four verses of 1 John are called a prologue (lit., what comes before the main body of the work), a section often more formal than what follows. A prologue can present key elements of the book as a whole, somewhat as a preacher may tell his congregation what he is going to tell them before he tells them. The prologue of 1 John attempts this much less fully than does its more famous counterpart in the Gospel of John (John 1:1–18), and it is inevitable that an evaluation of the present verses consider that other prologue. Just as there are remarkable similarities in vocabulary, style, and thought between the Gospel of John and 1 John, so there are striking parallels in the two prologues. They use similar words: "Word," "life," "see," "testimony," "Father." Both testify to the appearance among humanity of the source of divine life, Jesus Christ, who has come from and made known God the Father. Above all, the opening words of 1 John ("That which was from the beginning") immediately bring to mind John 1:1: "In the beginning. . . ."

Having said this, it is important to caution against a presumption that the words in 1 John are used in the same way as they are in the Gospel of John. Indeed, we will find that some words common to both are *not* used with the same meaning. In accordance with the basic rule of interpretation, our decisions about the meaning of words in 1 John will be guided primarily by the context. Unfortunately, there will be numerous passages where the context leaves us puzzled; at these points, especially, other Johannine usage will be valuable.

The grammar of these verses is less than clear in the Greek. "Proclaim," the main verb of the series of relative clauses in verse 1, does not appear until verse 3. The flow of thought is also undermined by the interruption in verse 2 of this series of clauses by an elaboration of the "life" mentioned at the end of verse 1. In an effort to alleviate the difficult Greek construction, the NIV has inserted in verse 1 a dash, followed by "this we proclaim. . . ." The KJV, as it often does, retains the original awkwardness; verse 2 is parenthetical and the main verb is not expressed until verse 3. Compared to that of the Gospel of John, then, this prologue seems much less polished, and this makes it harder to follow and to interpret with confidence. But our concern in studying 1 John is not to collect examples for a Greek grammar text. The way in which the phrases are penned and the urgency of the "interruption" of verse 2 are important guides for evaluating what is central to the presentation of John.

The book begins with four clauses introduced by relative pronouns, translated in the NIV by "that which." The very first words refer to that which "was from the beginning." The opening words of the Gospel of John, "in the beginning," clearly allude to the same phrase of Genesis 1:1. The prologue of the Gospel intends with the phrase to assert the preexistence of the Word, later identified as Jesus, God's Son. The Son existed with God the Father before anything was created. It is possible, then, that "beginning" in 1 John 1:1 should be understood in this way. The reference, then, would be to God's Son, who was with God "in" (and has been "from") the beginning.

Two considerations, however, make us cautious about too readily drawing this conclusion. (1) Although "from the beginning" can refer to this precreation existence of the Son (it *may* mean this in 2:13–14), the five other, less ambiguous uses of this phrase in this letter refer to some other "beginning." In four of these five, "from the beginning" refers to the origins of the believing community addressed in 1 John (2:7; 2:24 [2x]; 3:8; 3:11). (2) All of the relative pronouns in verse 1 (and those of v. 3 as well) are neuter in gender. The significance of the neuter gender is that there is no apparent antecedent for these pronouns; that is, though in Greek a pronoun must agree in gender with the word to which it refers, there is no word anywhere in the prologue that is a neuter. Thus the NIV has translated each of these "that which" rather than "he who," which is what we would expect were the writer concerned to emphasize the personality of whatever or whoever was from the beginning. It is not impossible that a person can be referred to with such neuter pronouns, but it would be unusual.

We are confronted in the very first phrase, then, with a tension that recurs in the first three verses. Clearly Jesus Christ, the Son of God, is in mind by the author's allusion to the "beginning" as recorded in John 1:1. The reference to touching by hands in 1 John 1:1 can hardly be a reference to anything but the genuine humanity of the Son of God who, according to John 1:1, 14, was eternally with God and then at a point in time "became flesh." Yet John seems to be concerned not only with Jesus' preexistence, but also with the foundational role of the earthly ministry of this Jesus and the conservation of accurate teaching about him. The second phrase, "which we have heard," could e understood in the sense that Jesus was heard y his followers. At the same time, the mean- ıg appears to encompass the *message about* esus. The usage in 2:24 reflects a critical emand of the readers: "See that what you ave heard from the beginning remains in ou." This conjunction of the verb for hearing nd "what you heard from the beginning" explicitly repeated in the second half of 2:24, ut not reflected in the NIV) is a close parallel 1:1. This "beginning" would be a reference the reliable message having its origins in esus himself and to its faithful preservation in e witnesses represented by John.

Before proceeding, the question must be sked: Who are the "we" referred to in this pro- gue? The reader might ask the same question f the famous statement of John 1:14: "We ave seen his glory. . . ." The Gospel of John as addressed to those who had not had the rivilege of physically seeing Jesus (see John 0:29), and so the "we" may well refer to eye- itnesses. However, both John and 1 John ften use "see" spiritually; in this sense, all elievers have "seen" the glory of God in esus. John frequently includes his readers hen he refers to "we," "us," and "our." Note ow he writes that "*we* have one who speaks the Father in *our* defense" (1 John 2:1), or *we* ought to lay down *our* lives for *our* broth- rs" (3:16).

But it is just as evident that "we" is *not* iclusive in this prologue, for "you" is distin- uished from "we" (1 John 1:2–3). Here the we" seems to refer to John and others like him ho bear a mediating role between Jesus and e readers. It is these individuals who have eard, seen, and touched, and hence bear wit- ess and proclaim to the readers. These refer- nces to sensory contact with the origins of the aith serve not only to affirm the perceptible eality of Jesus. It is important to understand at they also serve the writer as a basis of uthority. Since this letter is addressed to a ommunity that believes that it needs no acher (2:27), John's authority is rooted in the erifiable fact that he is an eyewitness to the earer of life. The prologue, then, verifies the rigin and content of the community's teach- ıg, Jesus Christ. The prologue also verifies e means by which that teaching was pro- laimed and continues to be proclaimed to the ommunity—John and his fellow witnesses.

The third phrase, "[that] which we have seen with our eyes," further serves this dual emphasis. As noted above, "seeing" in the Johannine literature can refer to a spiritual rather than a physical perception, though this is less common in 1 John than in the Gospel of John. Here, the reference to "with our eyes," especially in light of the phrases that follow, is best understood in a literal way. This is what might be called a mutual guarantee: The reality of the physical ministry of Jesus is attested by the witnesses, and the authority of the witnesses, in turn, is attested by their direct contact with Jesus.

The next two phrases elaborate the same point. The verb translated "looked at" seems to be a stylistic variation on "seeing." The specification of what "our hands have touched" provides the strongest physical claim in the whole series. It is an additional element in the validation of the reliability of the writer. On the other hand, it may well be a polemical response to those who have left the community and who deny that "Jesus Christ has come in the flesh" (1 John 4:3; 2 John 7). Jesus had a real human body that his associates actually touched.

The phrase "concerning the Word of life" in Greek follows immediately after the verb "touch," though it certainly is to be related to all the clauses in some way. The NIV has drafted the verb "we proclaim" from verse 3 to do double duty here in verse 1. John, however, does not get around to a main verb until verse 3, primarily because the reference to "life" leads him into an elaboration that breaks the flow of thought. In any case, what John has experienced and that to which he bears witness concern "the Word of life."

The NIV translators have capitalized "Word" and in doing so have done some interpreting for the reader; whether they have served the reader well in this case is debatable. Remember that the original copies of the New Testament were written in all capital letters. The Greek word used here, *logos,* can mean many things depending on the context. In the five other passages in 1 John in which *logos* is used, the NIV translates with either "word" or "message." Why then "Word" in 1:1? As you may have guessed, it is because of John 1:1: "In the beginning was the Word (*logos*). . . ."

We have already noted a relationship between the prologue of the Gospel of John and of 1 John; many think that the one in 1 John is a conscious adaptation from the one in the Gospel. The use of *logos* as a reference to the Son of God is limited to the Gospel's prologue; this might support the proposal of *logos* being used this way in the prologue of 1 John, even though it is not used in this sense anywhere else in the book. If the reference is, then, to Jesus, the Word, the genitive construction that follows, "of life," is an "appositive genitive"; that is, "life" is another term for, or serves as a specification of, "Word." The message is thus about the Word (Jesus Christ), who is life (cf. John 14:6).

This understanding makes perfect sense, particularly given the model of the prologue in the Gospel of John. There the Word was with God in the beginning and became flesh; that is, the divine Son became a human being. In this prologue in 1 John, the Word, who was "with" (v. 2; Greek *pros*, as in John 1:1) God and who was from the beginning, "appeared to us" in a manner that allowed him to be heard, seen, and touched; that is, the divine Son became a human being.

But there are also reasons why *logos* perhaps does *not* refer to the divine Word, but rather to the revelation or message that originated in Jesus. (1) If the writer meant to identify *logos* with the person of Jesus Christ, one would expect that the pronouns of verse 1 would be masculine, to agree with *logos*. If, however, *logos* means revelation or message, the neuters are more easily explained. (2) As mentioned above, *logos* denotes in all other instances in 1 John a "word" or "message" (1:10; 2:5, 7, 14; 3:18). Particularly striking is the reappearance of "*logos*," "heard," and "from the beginning" in 2:7, which identifies the "old [command], which you have had since the beginning" with the "message [*logos*] you have heard." A focus on the original message of the gospel aligns well with a main theme in the book, as we will see. (3) It seems odd, if *logos* were a reference to Jesus, the divine Word, that John would interrupt his flow of thought to elaborate not on the Word, but on the qualifying term, "life." As noted by most commentators, the emphasis in verse 2 is not on the *logos*, but on the life associated with it. It is not the Word that appeared, but "the life." If, however, *logos* does refer to the gospel message, "of life" then it describes the nature of the message (cf. the Johannine "bread of life") o the content of it ("the message about life").

In other words, there is tension between reference to Jesus, the Word, who was in/fron the beginning absolutely, and the gospel message, which was from the beginning of th believing Johannine community. But thi should not surprise anyone familiar with th Gospel of John. There we find an analogou fluidity in the use of terminology. Perhap most relevant for our consideration is the fac that Jesus himself can be identified as "the life" (14:6), and yet his "words" can also be identified as "life" (6:63). As we proceed throug 1 John, it will become clear that the person o Jesus is central to the purpose of the book. A the same time, it is evident that the repeate emphasis of the writer is that the readers hol to a particular teaching *about* Jesus, a teachin that is preserved and proclaimed by the wit nesses referred to in the prologue.

When the writer gets to the "*logos* of life, he interrupts his series of relative clauses t focus on this "life." This word in both th Gospel of John and 1 John is equivalent t "eternal life" (cf. John 5:39–40; 6:53–54 10:10, 28; 1 John 5:11). Its importance i Johannine thought cannot be overestimated John 20:31 states that the purpose for the writ ing of the Gospel is that its readers may believ that Jesus is the Christ, the Son of God, an by believing, may have life in his name. An the purpose of 1 John, according to 5:13, is tha its readers, who believe in the name of the So of God, may know that they have eternal life "Life" is that divine principle or quality o existence that characterizes the Father and th Son (John 5:26), was embodied on the earth i Jesus Christ (14:6), and was made availabl through Jesus (3:16; 6:33). Those who believ in Jesus "have" this life (e.g., 3:36; 5:24; 6:47 in them.

The New Testament, rooted in the teachin of Jesus himself, asserts that blessings that th Jews anticipated in the future had been brougl into the "now" (Luke 11:20; Rom. 8:23; Heb 8:7–13). This emphasis on the present expe rience of the blessings of the kingdom of Go is most developed in the Johannine writing When Martha affirmed that she believe Lazarus would "rise again in the resurrectio at the last day," Jesus declared, "I am the res urrection and the life" (John 11:24–25

'owhere can we find a more dramatic state-
ient of the principle: In Jesus, God has inau-
urated the coming age and its blessings.

That this "life" is described as "eternal" ıdicates much more than that it is everlasting r unending. Death, to be sure, has been vanıished; those who believe in him who is the ːsurrection and the life "will never die" (John 1:26). But we are dealing with something ıore than animated existence. "I tell you the uth, whoever hears my word and believes im who sent me has eternal life and will not e condemned; he has crossed over from death ı life" (5:24). "Death," then, is also a principle or quality of existence; it characterizes all 'ho, though alive physically, do not have ife." To describe this life as "eternal," then, simply another way of associating it with iod. "Now this is eternal life: that they may now you, the only true God, and Jesus Christ, 'hom you have sent" (17:3). Actually, orthoox Christianity traditionally has maintained ıat *all* humans will "spend eternity" in reward r in punishment. In the Johannine tradition, ːternal" life is life characterized by a certain uality, not by a certain duration. It seems lear, then, that the reference to "eternal life" ı 1 John 1:2 is only a variation, though posbly for emphasis, on the "life" at the beginning of the verse.

It is asserted twice in verse 2 that the (eteral) life "appeared." The verb used here speaks f a making known, a showing of someone or ımething for what it/he/she is. It is used in John to refer to the first (3:5, 8) or the second 2:28; 3:2) coming of Christ. At the end of 1:2, 'e read that the eternal life appeared "to us," ːcalling the earlier "the life appeared; we have ːen it [using the same verb form as in the third hrase of v. 1] and testify to it. . . ." The word anslated "testify" is a favorite of the writer, sed predominantly in situations of conflict or ifference of viewpoint. The scene portrayed a courtroom, in which a witness is called pon to testify solemnly. Of particular interst are those instances in which the testifying based on a "seeing"; the witness declares 'hat he has seen and hence knows to be true. mong these testimonies are words attributed ı Jesus himself (in the third person): "He tesfies to what he has seen and heard, but no one ccepts his testimony"(John 3:32). In John :11, where the "we" sounds like the early believers speaking with Jesus, John declares: "We speak of what we know, and we testify to what we have seen." The authority of the witness of the community is also integrally linked to what John has seen with his eyes: "The man who saw it has given testimony, and his testimony is true. He knows that he tells the truth, and he testifies so that you also may believe" (19:35; cf. 1 John 4:14). So, here in the prologue, we find again a testimony based on a seeing.

There is a natural progression in verse 2. Divine life appeared in the person of Jesus Christ. This life was seen by those who were with Christ. Those who saw this life now (present tense) testify to this experience; they testify to what they know. And, in a second present tense verb, those who saw and testify also "proclaim" what they know to be true. The author considers what we call 1 John to be a proclamation—a proclamation "to you," the readers, whose spiritual status was in doubt because of the influence of the false teachers.

This letter is a proclamation of the eternal life "which was with the Father and has appeared to us." This language can scarcely be taken to refer to anything but the Son of God in truly human form. The repetition of the identical form of the verb "appear" in this verse catches our attention. Here, it can safely be concluded, is an important point: The visible, audible, and tangible Jesus was the manifestation of God's bringing life. And, for the Johannine community, God is best known as Father. Certainly other segments of the early church thought of God as Father and would have used this address (Matt. 6:9; Luke 11:2; Gal. 4:1–6). The Gospel of John is noteworthy, however, in the distinctive use of the simple terms "Son" and "Father" with reference to Jesus and God. First John develops this metaphor found in the Gospel (see John 8:42) of God as Father and pushes it to otherwise unknown limits (see below on 1 John 3:9).

John's brief detour from the avenue of relative clauses onto the "circle of life" ends with verse 2, and we are back on the avenue. In Greek, the first words after "appeared to us" at the end of verse 2 are: "What we have seen [the *third* time this exact same verb form has been used] and what we have heard [the same verb form as in v. 1] we proclaim to you." This sort of syntax is what one might expect more from a transcript of oral comments than from a carefully designed written prologue. In any case, the repetition of verbal forms describing seeing and hearing reinforces the emphasis on the physical reality of Jesus that we already have noted.

The NIV does not reflect the degree to which a distinction is made in Greek between "we" and "you." As noted above, the "we" reflects John and the fellow witnesses whom he represents, and the "you" denotes the recipients—believers and members of the community, who are in danger of falling prey to the deceits of the opponents. It is the former group that has had intimate contact with the life; the latter group receives the proclamation of these witnesses. The witnesses have fellowship "with the Father and with his Son, Jesus Christ." Although this is the first specific use of Jesus' name, he has been at the center of this prologue "from the beginning." According to both the Gospel of John and 1 John, being in relationship with God necessarily entails acceptance of Jesus as his Son (John 3:36; 5:23; 10:30; 1 John 2:23; 5:12).

The book is written so that the recipients "may have fellowship" with the writer and the other witnesses. The word "fellowship" (Greek *koinonia*) can refer to the sharing of most anything; it is related to the word for "common," so that implicit in the word is having something in common with another person. The two ways that the term is most used in the New Testament are found in this verse. (1) John desires for the readers to "have fellowship with us." In this sense, fellowship is the sharing of faith in Jesus Christ and the commitment to one another called for by this faith. (2) This fellowship, however, is also with God the Father and his Son, Jesus Christ. There is ample basis in the Gospel of John to conclude that the Johannine believers had been nurtured in a community that stressed what might be called a "mutual indwelling" of God and the believer: The believer is in Jesus or the Father (John 15:4–5; 17:21), and the Father or Jesus is in the believer (14:20, 23; 15:5; 17:26). True divine fellowship is thus with the Father and the Son.

The word *koinonia* is not used in the Gospel of John, and it is possible that this may have been a term of the opponents; as we will see below, their claim to have *koinonia* with God is rejected (1 John 1:6), and the writer's cour terclaim (1:7) is enlightening regarding th issues involved. Though "our" fellowshi could be inclusive of the readers, it is mor likely, given the consistent use of "we" in th prologue for the witnesses, that it is not. Th opponents claim to have fellowship with Go but they are mistaken; their deficient view c Jesus Christ means that they have fellowshi with neither the Father nor the Son. Joh exhorts his readers to attend to his messag because *koinonia* with God is only possib with adherence to the "word of life," which h not the opponents, proclaims.

In the midst of the sorrow of the disciple at their last meal with Jesus, Jesus promised hi own joy (John 15:11; see also 17:13). That jo would replace the grief that they would suff when Jesus was killed (16:20–24) and is ofte termed a "fullness of joy," a benefit granted th person who is in relationship with the one wh overcomes the world (16:33). Though th reading "your joy" has much manuscript sup port and makes perfect sense, the best readin seems to be "our joy" (as in 2 John 12). In th case, the witness states that his joy is incom plete unless his spiritual children are in ger uine fellowship with God and his Son (c 2 John 4; 3 John 3). In other words, "we wri this" so that the recipients continue in this tru fellowship; according to 1 John 5:13, the rea ers do believe in Jesus and do have eternal lif But the writer is greatly concerned because th fellowship is in danger.

In sum, the prologue to 1 John serves (1) affirm the genuine humanity of Jesu Christ, the Son of God; (2) assert the autho ity and reliability of the witnesses represente by John; and (3) call the readers, in a prelim nary way, to remain in fellowship with Go and his Son and with those who bear witnes to the appearance of the divine life in huma experience. Although the prologue does n introduce all the important themes of the wor it gives us a preview of major aspects of th argument of 1 John.

2. The Message (1:5–2:27)

2.1. Behavior of the Christian (1:5–2:17)

2.1.1. The Message: God Is Light (1:5 By all accounts, the declaration of verse 5 is crucial one. It has even been suggested that th

; virtually a thesis statement for the whole ook. Its importance is indicated by its initial osition following the prologue, the use of key erbal ideas from the prologue ("hear" and proclaim/declare"), and the centrality of conept that "God is light" to much of the arguient of the book.

Johannine writing is notable for such stateients about God: for example, "God is spirit" John 4:24); "God is love" (1 John 4:8, 16). ıvolved in the claim that God is "light" is both ie manner in which God deals with humany and his very nature. "Light" is a common iblical image for the revelation of God or the alvation made available by him (Pss. 27:1; 19:105, 130; Prov. 6:23; Isa. 60:19–20). It lso describes the holiness, purity, and ıtegrity of the Lord (Ps. 104:2; 1 Tim. 6:16). 'he verses that follow indicate John's concern) establish at the outset that God's character ; of a certain type and that this character equires certain behavior in those who are his nd rules out other sorts of behavior.

The phrase following "God is light" is mphatic: "In him there is no darkness at all." key point of the prologue is also maintained. 'his message was heard "from him," certainly reference to Jesus, and in this writing is being eclared to the readers; again, faithful witesses testify to what they know to be true.

A trait of the Johannine writings should be oted at this point. Light was a common ietaphor in the ancient world in reference to ie divine. But the New Testament was written t a time in history when there were many iovements that perceived of the world and/or uman existence "dualistically"; that is, they iought that reality was best understood in rms of two opposite powers or principles, ıch as "light" and "darkness." These two ɔrces, whether gods or internal human tenencies, were in continual conflict, the outome of which was in doubt, since neither had decisive advantage.

Both the Gospel and the letters of John xhibit a dualistic way of thinking and writing. here are a variety of stark contrasts portrayed: ght versus darkness; truth versus falsehood or eceit; life versus death; from above versus om below. The metaphor of light and darkess enters early into the Gospel of John and John; in both, this conflict is portrayed in the fth verse of the first chapter, though in contrast to the ancient world, the resolution of this conflict was never in doubt. We must recognize that the terminology is fluid. In the Gospel, Jesus is "the light of the world" (8:12), meaning primarily that he came from God to bring divine life by delivering people from darkness (8:13; see also 1:4–9). In 1 John, "God is light." Although numerous passages suggest that the writer of 1 John often felt no compulsion to distinguish clearly between the Father and the Son, the switch to God as light rather than Jesus is probably motivated by the circumstances (see below). And the fact that though God is light (1 John 1:5), he can be said to be "in the light" (v. 7) also demonstrates the flexibility of language.

Students of the Johannine writings have sought insight into this dualistic world of thought and expression by comparing it with the writings of other groups. For many years, scholars have proposed a connection with what is known as "gnostic" thought. The term *Gnosticism* comes from the Greek *gnosis*, meaning knowledge. A gnostic was one who believed that one's salvation was based on the acquisition of some secret knowledge rather than on the historical event of the death of Jesus. Fully developed Gnosticism, later than the New Testament, typically involved elaborate myths, numerous levels of divine beings, and the association of the physical with evil.

Much research has occurred over the past few decades on recently unearthed writings that portray what might be called a "gnostic Christianity." First John cannot with any justification be labeled "gnostic," though it is possible that those it warns against had gnostic tendencies. The writer does use terminology that was popular among Gnostics; for example, "knowing" is a characteristic Johannine term (John 8:32; 14:7; 17:3; 1 John 2:3–5, 13–14; 4:16). But, like *logos* in the prologue of the Gospel, this terminology is used to proclaim the decidedly ungnostic truth that God appeared in material human form and died a real death that provides salvation for those who believe.

The past few decades have also brought to the attention of the world what have been called the Dead Sea Scrolls. One portion of these scrolls consists of copies of the Hebrew Scriptures, significant because they predate by centuries any previous copies of these writings and thus are telling witnesses to the accuracy of the transmission of the text. A large number of other scrolls consist of writings of a Jewish sect active during the time of Jesus. Lively debate continues on the connection between the scrolls and the supposed community that lived in Qumran, near the caves where the scrolls were found. What is important for our study is that these writings exhibit language and, in some cases, thought similar to the Johannine writings.

Some segments describe the conflict between the sons of the light and the sons of darkness, and one portion (*Manual of Discipline* 3:15–26) is particularly remarkable in the way that it speaks of the spirit of truth and the spirit of deceit (cf. 1 John 4:6). Here we find much more of a case for comparison with 1 John. The group reflected in the scrolls shares many features with the first Christians. They were Jewish in background, were committed to the faithful observance of the commands of God and to the authority of a revered witness (the "Teacher of Righteousness"), and expected the soon coming of God to the earth. And also like the early church, they perceived themselves to be a holy remnant amidst a sea of unbelief and unrighteousness. The parallels between these groups is striking. A belief in Jesus Christ as the Son of God, of course, is what most distinguished the community of John from the Qumran sect. As we will see, that was a major component of what distinguished it from those whom 1 John warns against.

2.1.2. Three False Claims Regarding Sin Are Refuted (1:6–2:2). In 1 John, the terminology of light and darkness is not utilized to relate stories about the origins of the universe (as with the Gnostics) or to map out the sides in the final battle between good and evil (as at Qumran). Rather, this language serves in 1 John to drive home a moral point: *No one can claim to be in relationship with the God who is light who does not live in a way that is in keeping with the character of that God.*

The three "if we claim . . ." statements in verses 6, 8, and 10 are probably John's characterization of the position taken by those against whom he is writing. In each case, he follows the claim of the opponents with a repudiation of it and then, in 1:7, 9 and 2:1–2, he completes each unit with an "if . . ." phrase of his own that affirms a correct position. That John proceeds immediately after the prologue to address this issue suggests (1) that the question of "sin" and the connection between one's behavior and one's relation with God was a pressing one, (2) that the theological assertion in 1:5 set the stage for the argument to be made in these following verses, and (3) that the wording of the first rejected claim in verse 6 motivated the writer to refer to authentic fellowship in the prologue itself (1:3–4).

In other words, 1:6, 8, and 10 contain claims that are roughly parallel, though there appears to be an intensification as the reader proceeds through this trio. The "we" of the prologue, which referred to the witnesses over against the "you" of the readers, has been left behind in verse 5. Now the "we" is inclusive of the readers and is used, consciously at times, to contrast the true followers of God with the "they" of the opponents (2:19; 4:5–6). From now on, John uses the more familiar "I" to refer to himself. This, in conjunction with the frequency of terms of endearment, such as "my dear children," shifts the focus from a group of unique witnesses to the joint faith and experience of all in the believing community.

The opponents apparently "claim to have fellowship with [God]." But this is impossible, John claims, because God is light (v. 5) and is in the light (v. 7); there is not a speck of darkness in him (v. 5). Recall that in this framework the two realms (light–darkness; truth–falsehood; life–death) are mutually exclusive; one is either in one realm or the other. To have any association with God, then, one must "walk in the light." "Walk" is a common metaphor for "live" and is seen in both Old and New Testaments (Ps. 1:1; Rom. 8:1). If anyone walks in the darkness, then, this reality belies the claim to have fellowship with God; such a person does not live by the truth.

John often uses the family of words associated with the terms for "lie" and "deceit" to characterize his opponents (1:8; 2:4, 22, 26; 3:7; 4:1, 6, 20; 2 John 7); these are various ways of referring to the antithesis of the truth. "Truth" in the Gospel of John denotes that which corresponds with God's character of absolute reliability and authenticity and with reality as God has made it known (John 17:17, "Your word is truth"). Because Jesus is God revealed in human form, he is "full of grace and truth" (1:14) and can be understood as the personification of truth (14:6). The "Spirit of truth" (14:17) is so-called because the Spirit leads to truth (16:13), which ultimately means that the Spirit is a witness to Jesus, the truth (14:26; 15:26; 16:14).

This letter uniformly uses the word "truth" not in a personal sense of Jesus, but as a designation of what corresponds to reality as revealed by God in Jesus, a usage common in the Gospel as well (e.g., John 5:33; 8:40, 44–46). When a person lives in the darkness and yet claims to have fellowship with the God who is light, he lies and does not live by the truth; if such a one is not a liar, then God is (1 John 1:10; 5:10). Jesus said, "Whoever follows me will never walk in darkness, but will have the light of life" (John 8:12). The behavior of the opponents is proof that they are removed from light, truth, and life. The word translated "live by" in the NIV at the end of verse 6 is from a Greek word meaning "do." Though "doing the truth" or "doing righteousness" (1 John 3:10) is in keeping with Hebrew style (e.g., Mic. 6:8), in this letter the repeated use of this "doing" verb accentuates the emphasis on practical action in contrast to easily made verbal claims (1 John 3:18).

Having disproved the first claim of his opponents, John exhorts his readers to proper behavior based on correct teaching. If we live in accordance with and are enlightened by God's revelation of himself, we have fellowship with . . . one another! This is a bit of a surprise. We would have expected the denial that the opponents have fellowship with God to be followed up with a claim that the faithful community *does* have fellowship with God (cf. 1:3). Instead, the writer says that we have fellowship with one another. Fellowship with other believers is an essential element of living in the light; it previews the basic theme of brotherly love found throughout the book.

The second result of living in the light is that "the blood of Jesus . . . purifies us from all sin." The terminology of purification of sins is rooted in the sacrificial system of the first covenant (Lev. 14:19; 16:30), but is unique in the New Testament here, though the idea certainly is not. We can say that the coming of Christ and the writing of Scripture are the basic elements of God's solution to the situation caused by human sin. One significant aspect of 1 John is its focus on the atoning death of Jesus (1 John 2:2; 4:10); in the Gospel of John this concept is relatively undeveloped, while the Incarnation itself is central. It makes good sense to suggest that this attention to the death of Jesus resulted from the beliefs and claims of the opponents, which are being answered in this section of the book. Sin (which John later identifies as lawlessness [3:4] and wrongdoing [5:17]) comes into the discussion because of the second and third claims of the opponents to be cited in 1:8 and 10. What is established in verses 6–7 is that fellowship with God and other believers and the purification of sins that makes such fellowship possible is available only to those who live in the light.

We must *not* conclude that believers need to achieve a certain level of righteous behavior before God will purify them of sins. It is vital that we understand these words in the context in which they were written. The light is the realm of God revealed in Jesus Christ. The opponents have removed themselves from this realm by denying the saving work of Jesus and the lifestyle to which he has called his followers. By so doing, they are in darkness, apart from God and from the cleansing of sins provided in his Son.

The second claim attributed to the opponents in 1:8 is more puzzling. The results of this claim parallel the results noted in verse 6: We deceive ourselves (we lie), and the truth is not in us (we do not live by the truth). What is startling is the claim "to be without sin." Did John's opponents actually make such a claim? What might it mean? Two things bear noting. (1) Such a claim is not so preposterous given the Johannine tradition with which the opponents had been associated prior to their leaving the community. It is conceivable that the identification of sin with failure to believe in Jesus in the Gospel of John (16:9) may have led to a perception, however wrong, that as long as one believed, there was no sin. (2) Before we write off the opponents as weird theological extremists, we should notice that the writer of 1 John himself makes a similar claim for his own community in 3:9 and 5:18. If 1 John can make the claim, the opponents could easily have done so as well.

One approach to this apparent contradiction between John's claim and the opponents' claim is to notice the difference in terminology. In verse 8, the actual wording of the claim of the opponents is that they "[are] without sin." In the Gospel of John this phrase appears to carry the connotation of being guilty of sin (John 9:41; 15:22, 24; 19:11). Absence of guilt would require no forgiveness or cleansing. The language of the claim in verse 10 seems even bolder: "We have not sinned." Some scholars hold that a "principle" of sin is in view in verse 8 and particular acts of sin in verse 10. If indeed the opponents adhered to the tradition seen in the Gospel of John, they may have concluded that since they had been born of God, they had committed no sin. Such a claim, of course, could only be rooted in a prior acceptance of the principle that sin was no longer a possibility for the one born of God. The effect of the claims of verses 8 and 10, then, would rule out the need for confession and forgiveness since there was neither sin nor guilt.

To claim that one never sins is self-deception (1:8). After all, God's Word gives ample witness to the pervasiveness of sin (as Paul argues in Rom. 3). To deny what God has said proves that his Word is not in us and that, in essence, we believe him to be a liar (1:10). But if we acknowledge that we do sin and if we confess these sins, God, in accordance with his faithful and righteous character, will forgive these sins and purify us from all unrighteousness (1:9).

The wording of 5:17 suggests that sin and unrighteousness are hardly distinguishable, as does the reference to purification of sin in 1:7 and of unrighteousness in 1:9. The latter term, *adikia,* is perhaps introduced as a contrast to the characterization of both God (1:9) and of Jesus (2:1) as *dikaios*, righteous. When we confess that we behave at times in an unrighteous manner, Jesus, who is righteous, speaks in our behalf to the Father, who himself is righteous and faithful to forgive us. If we refuse to acknowledge such in our lives, however, no forgiveness and purification are possible.

Addressing his "dear children" with a personal, pastoral "I," the author states that he is writing so that they "will not sin." But his response to the third of the false claims is that "if anybody does sin," there is provision for it. It may be that the reason why there is a switch from the first person plural of the other claims and counterclaims to the indefinite "anybody" is that the latter sounds more discrete and somewhat less accepting of sin when it occurs. But given the denial that anyone can even claim to be without sin, the sense might be, "When anybody sins. . . ."

Jesus is called "the Righteous One," which may be an early Christian title for him (Acts 3:14; 22:14). This trait is important not just because it qualifies him to be an appropriate sacrifice for sins (1 John 2:2), but also because it establishes him as the example of behavior for all those who believe in him (2:6; 4:4–5). John also calls Jesus a *parakletos* (NIV, "one who speaks . . . in our defense") in the presence of (*pros*, as in John 1:1 and 1 John 1:2) the Father. This word is found only in the Johannine writings, and in the other instances, all in the Gospel of John (14:16–17, 26; 15:26; 16:7), it refers to the Holy Spirit. English equivalents are inadequate because of the variety of functions attributed to this *parakletos*: comforter, teacher, witness to Jesus, one who convicts the world, and guide. It is surprising, given this distinctive term for the Spirit in the Johannine tradition, to find it used with reference to Jesus. Perhaps the opponents had overemphasized the role of the Spirit, and our author desires to put the focus back on Jesus.

To call Jesus a *parakletos* was not, of course, a totally new innovation, for Jesus promised the coming of "another" *parakletos* (John 14:16); Jesus himself was the model *parakletos*. As an advocate, he speaks in our defense before the Father, the judge. The concept of representing or interceding for us before the Father can be found elsewhere in the New Testament (Rom. 8:34; Heb. 7:25). But we must disavow the idea that Jesus has to cajole an otherwise unsympathetic God into reluctantly letting us off. The judge is God the Father, who loved and sent his Son (John 3:16; 1 John 4:9–10), who has given birth to children (John 1:12–13; 1 John 3:9; 5:4), and who is faithful to forgive and cleanse us (1 John 1:9).

Furthermore, Jesus is "the atoning sacrifice" for our sins and for the sins of the whole world. The Greek word used here, found in the New Testament only here and in 4:10, appears in nonbiblical texts with the connotation of "propitiation," that is, the appeasing of an angry deity by means of certain acts. Ancient cultures offer many examples of the sacrifice of a life, animal or human, to gain the favor of a god. But because there is no mention of the wrath of God here and because God himself provides the means, many scholars prefer the term *expiation*, the removal of the guilt or offense of sin.

The biblical use of the word group, not surprisingly, is most concentrated in Exodus, Leviticus, and Numbers, which describe the requirements of the sacrificial system of the covenant initiated at Sinai. A word closely related to the one used in 1 John 2:2 occurs in Romans 3:25, where Jesus is called a "sacrifice of atonement" (NIV), dealing with sins in a just manner through his blood. The same key elements are found here: an atoning sacrifice, for sins, through Jesus' blood, and God's justice/righteousness. Whether or not one chooses to emphasize the wrath of God against sin, it is clear in 1 John that the death of Jesus is the basis on which all can have their sins forgiven and come into the light of relationship with God; lacking this, all are in the darkness of alienation from God. Though John does not use the term "reconciliation," this is what he is talking about. Paul likewise teaches that those who were once separated from God and were his enemies have been brought into a peaceful relationship with him through the blood of Jesus (Eph. 2:1–18; Col. 1:20–22).

2.1.3. Knowing God Means Obeying God's Word (2:3–6). As indicated above, the argument of 1 John is linked to the threat of a group that had left the church and was now attempting to gain converts. The three claims of these opponents in 1:6, 8, 10 were refuted by appeal to the nature of God, who is light and who has provided a means by which sins can be forgiven. The next section (2:3–11) also contains three claims that most likely come from these opponents. Rather than the "if we claim" language of the previous section, 2:4, 6, 9 all begin with "the one who says." (The NIV does not indicate the identical form in these verses, translating "the man who says" in v. 4, "whoever claims" in v. 6, and "anyone who claims" in v. 9.) The thrust of 2:3–11 focuses on the rebuttal of these three claims. Although the attention to sin that predominated 1:5–2:2 is left behind, the concern in 2:3–11 continues to center on the practical behavior of believers. They keep God's commands and love fellow believers. By 2:11, the writer has returned to the metaphor of light and darkness; once again, a person lives in one or the other.

The first issue raised in 2:3–11 is the matter of "knowing" God. What does it mean to "know" God? Is such knowledge verifiable either to the individual or to others? It is important to be aware that "knowing" in biblical language most commonly involves more than the intellect; when I say I know the state capitals or I know who the president of France is, I am not using the word in the typical sense found in Scripture. Biblical "knowing" involves an active experience with and of a person or thing. When Genesis 4:1, for example, tells us that "Adam knew Eve his wife" (KJV), this means that he had sexual relations with her. "Knowing" is thus a particularly apt term for the intimacy shared between husband and wife; the depth of this bond is depicted in the language of "one flesh," physical and spiritual.

Human beings have been created with a deep longing to "know" the God who gave them life. This kind of knowledge involves the intellect, of course, because being made in the image of God includes the intellect. But it goes far beyond knowing things *about* God. It is not fulfilling to the human spirit merely to recite a statement that God is love; we hunger for an experience of the God whose love infinitely exceeds even the purest form of love we can find anywhere else. It is also God's desire that people know him, that they be in relationship with him. And it is a noteworthy promise that when God makes a new covenant with his people, "they will all know [him]" (Jer. 31:34). According to the Gospel of John, the Son shares mutual knowledge with God the Father (John 10:15), and he made it possible for his followers to "know" the Father as well (14:7). Indeed, eternal life may be described as knowing God and his Son, Jesus Christ (17:3). This sort of knowledge is what distinguishes the people of God (17:25–26).

Apparently the opponents John addresses were making the claim to know God (2:4), and John feels he must disprove this claim. But how can such a claim be denied? Is not a person's relationship with God something that I cannot judge "or [I] too will be judged" (Matt. 7:1)? Yet Matthew records Jesus later in the same chapter giving guidelines for discerning prophets: "By their fruit you will recognize [lit., know] them" (7:16). John applies this teaching to the crisis at hand. He uses the same term for his opponents in 1 John 4:1 as Jesus used in Matthew 7:15: "false prophets." As Jesus warned of false prophets who would "deceive" (24:24), so John warns against those who "deceive" (1 John 2:26; NIV uses "lead ... astray") and who are characterized by the spirit of "deceit" (4:6; NIV "falsehood").

The foundation of the case against the opponents is, to use Jesus' metaphor, their "bad fruit." As John writes here, they do not "obey his commands" (1 John 2:3). Obedience to God's revealed will is a repeated theme in both the Old and New Testaments. The books of Moses are replete with instructions to God's people to obey the divine commands; this was an essential part of their covenant relationship with the Lord. The Johannine tradition reiterates this truth in Jesus' words to his disciples: "If anyone loves me, he will obey my teaching, [and my Father and I will] make our home with him" (John 14:23); the love and indwelling are impossible apart from the obedience. Thus the writer can boldly state that the claim of the opponents is a lie. Note how 2:4 is remarkably similar to 1:6:

1:6	**2:4**
If we claim to have fellowship with him	The man who says, "I know him"
yet walk in the darkness	but does not do what he commands
we lie	is a liar
and do not live by the truth.	and the truth is not in him.

In each case we find a claim of the opponents, a brief notation of their actual behavior, a blunt rejection of the claim as false, and the removal of the opponents from the sphere of truth, that is, from God himself. This pattern illustrates the threat to which 1 John is a response and the strategy the author uses to counteract it—show the discrepancy between the claims of the opponents and their behavior or teaching. John hopes that his conclusion in each case is evident to his readers.

Yet it is clear that some of the people being addressed are confused about whom to believe and where they themselves stand. Those "who are trying to lead you astray" (2:26) claim that *they* are the ones who have knowledge of God. Could they be right? Could we be wrong? John sets as one of his primary goals to relieve this uncertainty and to assure his readers that *they* (or sometimes *we*), not the opponents, are in truth, in the light, in God. The frequency of the phrase "in/by this we know" (2:3, 5; 3:16, 19, 24; 4:2, 13; 5:2) and similar phrases (3:10; 4:9, 10, 17) demonstrates that 1 John is written at least in part to establish criteria by which its readers may *know* that they have eternal life (5:13). If they are assured of this, they will withstand the deceptive teaching of the opponents.

The two criteria—proper belief in Jesus Christ and proper behavior—in one sense can be applied universally, and in another must be understood as being particular to the situation. True Christians will always believe in Jesus as God's Son and as the means by which sins are forgiven, and will live in keeping with the nature of God and his revealed will. However, the "test" for proper belief in 1 John was in specific response to the false teaching of the opponents—did Jesus come in the flesh? A group today might pass this "test" about the meaning of the Incarnation, but fail on some other count.

John assures his readers that "we know that we have come to know him" (2:3). How? This assurance is rooted in the fact that a believer obeys God's commands. In such a person, "God's love is truly made complete" (v. 5). This statement does not mean there is something deficient about the divine love, just as the statement that Jesus was made "perfect through suffering "(Heb. 2:10) implies no failure on his part. In each case, what has no defect in itself is brought to completion in that it comes to serve the purposes of God to the fullest extent. A hammer, for example, may be without defect, but it is only "brought to completion" when it is used to drive a nail, its ultimate purpose. The love of God, then, is not complete until it is acted out in the lives of believers.

It is difficult to decide the precise meaning of this "love *of God*" (2:5; NIV "God's love"). These "of" phrases, called genitives, can be ambiguous. We know that the "love of money" means that money is what is loved. And we know that the "love of a mother" means the love that a mother has for her child. But what about the "love of God"? Does this refer to God's love for us, our love for God, or one of a number of other grammatically possible senses? Each of these genitive forms has to be evaluated in its own context. The meaning here seems to be the love that originates in God and is now an experienced reality for believers through Jesus Christ. Many people who know no Greek have heard of *agape* as the God-kind of love. This word, which comes into its own in the New Testament, is nearly defined in 4:10–11, where the *love* of God is identified with the *act* of God in sending his Son as the solution for our sins. Though one might argue, based on John 3:16, that God's love is what motivates the act, John here is above all else concerned to identify God's love with practical behavior. Love is active. Jesus showed us what *agape* is, and believers should follow his example (1 John 3:16).

John also assures his readers that "we are in him" (2:5). Again we find an affirmation from John based on a response to a claim of the opponents. Verse 6 contains the second of the three claims in 2:3–11 attributed to them: They claim "to live in him." This phrase is barely distinguishable from the claim to "know him" in verse 4. What we confront for the first time in verse 6 is the use of the verb *meno* (lit., "remain"). This popular Johannine word is what the KJV translates as "abide" in the famous vine and branches passage (John 15). There Jesus' followers are exhorted to "remain" (NIV) in the vine, Jesus. If a believer remains in Jesus, Jesus will remain in him or her (15:4). But it is the keeping of his commands that is the prerequisite for remaining in Jesus and his love (15:10), as well as for the indwelling of the believer by the Father and the Son (14:23).

This mutual indwelling of the believer with the Father and/or the Son becomes a major theme in 1 John, and it should not be surprising that John develops especially the requirement for obeying divine commands. The readers must "remain" in the teaching and keep the commands they have heard from the beginning in order to "remain" in God (2:24; 3:24). When it comes down to it, the "commands" that must be obeyed to assure divine indwelling are the two that are basic to the whole book: Believe properly in Jesus and love fellow believers (3:23–24; 4:15–16). The word "remain" assumes greater relevance since the readers are being exhorted not to leave and join the false prophets, but to remain in the truth revealed in Jesus and witnessed by John.

The one who claims to "live in him" must live as Jesus did. There are some aspects of Jesus' ministry that are unique and unrepeatable. No one else can be an atoning sacrifice for the sins of the world, for example. But the writers of the New Testament often appeal to Jesus as a model of behavior and attitude for his followers (1 Cor. 11:1; Phil. 2:3–11; Heb. 12:2–3; 1 Peter 2:20–25). This practice no doubt has its origins in the instruction of Jesus himself (John 13:2–17). The context of 1 John 2:6 indicates that John primarily has in mind the divine love that Jesus demonstrated (vv. 5, 7–11) in his daily life as well as in his death. The other two 1 John passages in which the word translated "must" in v. 6 appears (3:16; 4:11) emphasize the same theme: Believers ought to love one another as Jesus loved us.

2.1.4. The Love Commandment (2:7–11). The readers are addressed as "dear friends" (*agapetoi*, a word based on *agape*, mentioned in v. 5). This is a term of affection, and it seems particularly appropriate here since the topic is the love that characterizes Christian lifestyle. These are people who live in the realm of God's love.

A comparison with 2 John 5–6 demonstrates that this "old command" is the one to "love one another." At his last meal with his disciples, Jesus gave them what he called a "new command"; the newness apparently is linked to the manner in which Jesus himself had loved his disciples (John 13:34). Thus John does not write the believers a "new command," but one that they have had since the beginning of their Christian lives. He therefore emphasizes in his attack against the false prophets that his message is rooted in Jesus; as 1 John 2:6 noted, the one who claims to "live in him" must follow the example of Jesus. This "old command," then, is no different from the "word" that they have heard; it originated with Jesus, and *agape* is fulfilled when one obeys "his word" (v. 5).

"Yet I *am* writing you a new command," John continues (v. 8). To say that it is new when he has just denied that it is new is not a contradiction. It originated with Jesus and thus is not new. Yet it *is* new in that its truth "is seen in him and you" (v. 8). What is crucial here is the "and [in] you" part. The meaning of "[true] . . . in you" in verse 8 is nearly that of "truly" of v. 5 and the "in truth" of 3:18: The love of

God by nature is something that must be lived out. The "newness" of the command is thus tied to the manner in which the readers have actualized the divine love taught and modeled by Jesus; they are willing, in stark contrast to the opponents, to lay down their lives for their fellow believers (John 15:12–13; 1 John 3:16).

Because true believers are putting into deeds the principle of love, the darkness is passing away and the true light is already shining. Here we have a return to the darkness and light metaphor of 1:5–7. There it was established that light is the realm of God and darkness the antithesis of all that God represents. The language here is so similar to John 1:9 that it is probable that 1 John is adapting from it. In the Gospel, Jesus is "the true light that gives light to every man"; yet the darkness remains as the condition in which many exist because they choose not to come to the light. The "sons of light" (John 12:36) can expect no better reception than that granted the light himself (3:19–21; 15:20–21).

It is unlikely, then, that John means by the darkness "passing" that conditions for the gospel will gradually improve as the light of the truth gradually eliminates all traces of hostility to God. The latter statement of verse 8 is based on the former: The truth of the new command is seen "in him and you"; that is, the light shines and the darkness passes *in the lives of believers*. It is the one who follows Jesus who no longer walks in darkness (John 8:12; 12:46). In contrast, the opponents are "in the darkness" even now (1 John 2:9); they are in the realm of the world, under the control of the evil one (5:19). The realms of light and darkness will continue until Christ returns, and so it is safe to say that Jesus' words to his disciples about trouble in this world (John 16:33) will remain true until then. But so is the pronouncement of that same verse, that he who is the light has overcome the world. We need no longer be under the sway of darkness.

In 2:4, 6 we found characterizations of the opponents in the form of "the one who says." In verse 9 we meet the third of these forms. As with the first two, the claim has been set up in the previous verse by a true affirmation: The light is shining. Yet, writes John, the one who claims to be in the light (or be "in him," or "know him," or "have fellowship with him") and hates his brother is in darkness.

We must consider what is meant by "hate" and "brother." When someone says, "I hate you," we take it to mean that this person holds an active hostility toward you; it is not understood to mean that you are a somewhat less desirable person than, say, Bill. In the Bible, however, to "hate" can have a quite different sense. When Malachi 1:2–3 records God as saying, "I have loved Jacob, but Esau I have hated," we should not take his hate in the sense of activity hostility. This is rather the language of vibrant contrast. God does not hate as the person did in the example above; it simply means that Esau was not the son chosen to continue the line to the Messiah. When Jesus says that we should "hate" our lives in this world, he means only that we should "not love" or put the highest priority on earthly life, for we will then "lose" it (John 12:25). So here John draws a contrast with someone who has *agape* love for fellow believers (1 John 2:10; so also in 3:14–15). Not having *agape* can mean careless neglect rather than active hostility.

Who, then, is the "brother" who is being "hated," and how might this hatred be displayed? The language of brotherhood is based on the language of fatherhood; that is, fellow believers are brothers and sisters because God is our Father. In Johannine terminology, only Jesus is God's Son, but believers who have been "born of God" (3:9; 5:1, 4, 18) are God's children (3:1–2). Hatred toward brothers, then, must refer to some attitude or behavior toward believers. Did the opponents go around abusing Christians? How could their numbers be growing and how might they be attractive to some of John's community if the behavior of the opponents was so abusive? It may not have been abusive at all. Indeed, the issue may come down to a matter of who defines who a "brother" is. From John's perspective, the "brothers" are the members of his community. Note that in 2:19 John makes it clear that these false prophets were not, and never had been, part of the believing community; the split simply brought this to light. It may be that the opponents did not even consider the members of the group represented by John as "brothers," just as John excludes *them* from the believing community.

In any case, "hatred" of the brothers appears to be a lack of active concern for the material needs of other believers (3:17–18).

When a person sees a real need and does not act to meet it, this can only be called hatred. Whether such a disinterest in practical needs was caused by a particular theological tendency is unknown to us. The interest of these opponents in personal spiritual experience could have led to a deficiency in concern for the good of the community; we know that something like this happened in Corinth (1 Cor. 12–14). What we can be sure of is that the readers must be aware of such behavior on the part of the opponents; otherwise, John's appeal to it as a proof of their error would be futile.

Active concern for fellow believers, then, is a practical test by which one can discern whether a person is of God or not. The one who demonstrates love is "in the light" (v. 10), regardless of verbal claims made by others. In such a person exists nothing that will cause him or her to stumble. This is in contrast to people who "are in the darkness and walk around in the darkness"; such people do not know where they are going (and so are bound to stumble with some regularity) because the darkness has blinded their eyes (cf. John 11:9–10). As portrayed by the story in John 9, spiritual blindness is far more serious than physical blindness. The only way to the light is to admit blindness (9:39–41) and to be willing to have one's life illuminated by the piercing light of God (3:19–21). To claim to be in the light (1 John 2:9) or to be in fellowship with the God who is light (1:5–6) while failing to admit sin or to love one's brothers is to consign oneself to the darkness.

2.1.5. Exhortation of the Community (2:12–14). A glance at the text of the NIV tells us that 2:12–14 is distinctive in 1 John; these verses have a style with some of the qualities of poetry. Six times we find "I write to you," followed by alternating addressees and then by a clause beginning with "because." Repetition in general and of certain phrases in particular justify the printing of the section in this way. The effect John desires is the affirmation and exhortation of his readers.

There are four different Greek terms used in addressing the readers: two similar words translated "dear children" (vv. 12, 13c), "fathers" (vv. 13a, 14a), and "young men" (vv. 13b, 14b). A variety of proposals have been made concerning how many different groups are involved. The best solution is to understand "dear children" as referring to the whole community of believers. This approach is supported by the fact that both of these terms, *teknia* (cf. 2:28; 3:7, 18; 4:4; 5:21) and *paidia* (cf. 2:18), are used outside of this stylized section to refer to all readers, although the other two are not. "Fathers" probably refers to those believers who are relatively older and more mature in the faith, and "young men" to those relatively younger.

The NIV translation throughout the section of "because" suggests that what is written is based on or a result of the fact of what is cited in the explanatory clause. It should be stated that the word translated "because" (*hoti*) could just as properly be translated "that"; in other words, each such clause might be not explanatory (e.g., in v. 14, "because you are strong") but declarative ("that you are strong"). Either way, the section is meant to encourage believers in the face of uncertainty. A father might encourage his son who is engaged in an activity about which he feels some insecurity by saying, "I am proud because you're doing such a good job!" Some of the recipients of 1 John, like this son, are not so sure about how well things are going. John, like the father, is aware of the uncertainty and wants to exhort them to greater confidence and performance. This section fits well into the purpose of this letter as a whole.

What is said to the "dear children," then, affirms about all the believers of John's community that their sins have been forgiven on account of Jesus' name and that they have known the Father—both statements pronounced earlier (1:9–2:3). In biblical thought, one's "name" is much more than a series of letters with a certain sound; it stands for one's very identity. To "believe in [Jesus'] name" (John 1:12; 1 John 3:23; 5:13) is to believe in who he really is; it is comparable to believing in him (John 3:18). For something to be done "in Jesus' name" means that it is done with the authority of Jesus by those who have submitted themselves to his Lordship (John 14:13–14; 20:31; Acts 2:38; 1 Cor. 5:4). To come or be sent or accomplish things "in his [God's] name" (John 5:43; 10:25; 12:13) is to act as a representative of and with the authority of God. Jesus came "in the name" of the Father, and he in turn sends out his disciples in his name. Forgiveness of sins, then, is based on the atoning work of Jesus (2:2) and his commissioning of his followers to proclaim that message (John 20:21–23). It is not unimportant to note that the knowledge of God and the forgiveness of sins, as other blessings granted believers, are linked in the prophetic expectation of the latter days (Jer. 31:34).

The "fathers" are twice described as those who have known him who is from the beginning, presumably to commend their long-term commitment in the face of the opponents' desertion. Whether the "him" refers to Jesus or to the Father is debatable, but the opening of the prologue suggests that Jesus is in mind.

The "young men" have overcome the evil one (mentioned twice); they are strong, and the word of God lives in them. It is not surprising to find strength associated with youth, but it is only on the basis of the work of Christ and the indwelling word of God that they have overcome the evil one (John 16:33; Rev. 12:11). In this case, those overcome are the opponents (1 John 4:4) and the world with which they are associated (5:4–5). The word translated "the evil one" can be rendered simply "evil," as it is usually rendered in the Lord's Prayer (Matt. 6:13) and in Jesus' own prayer in John 17:15. But the NIV is probably correct in interpreting it as a personal reference (1 John 3:12; 5:18–19); in Johannine language, the devil (3:8, 10) is a murderer (John 8:44), and 1 John 3:11–15 links "the evil one" with one who is a "murderer." Human beings are either children of God or children of the devil, and their acts reveal the distinction (3:9–10). God animates believers; the devil animates and controls the world (4:4; 5:18).

2.1.6. Love of the World as the Antithesis to Love of God (2:15–17). "The world" (*kosmos*) can have different connotations, depending on how it is used. This fact is nowhere more evident than in the Johannine writings. In the Gospel of John, the world may be a global sphere, equivalent to the earth (cf. John 21:25). It was so loved by God that he sent his Son into the world to bring life (3:16), and it was (and is) the desire of Jesus that the world may believe (17:21, 23). It was the scene of Jesus' redemptive ministry (1:9; 9:5) and of the continued ministry of his followers (17:15, 18). Yet "the world" can also refer to that which is contrary to God (8:23; 17:14, 16), a realm whose ruler is the devil (12:31; 14:30; 16:11). In 1 John, *kosmos* can also be used without negative connotations. Jesus is the Savior of the world and the atoning sacrifice for the world's sins (1 John 2:2; 4:14). It is the place where we live (4:17), and its goods are to be shared with others (3:17). But often "world" in 1 John means that which is in contrast to God. It is under the sway of the evil one (5:19) and is where the antichrist has appeared (4:3). It is the realm into which the false prophets have defected (4:1, 5).

Since, according to 3:13, it is the world that hates believers (because it hated Jesus, cf. John 15:18–19), it might be surprising to read the warning that we should not love the world or anything in the world. Is this not like saying to the person in the light, "Don't love the darkness"? Or might it be that "world" has a different connotation here? Love for the world is the antithesis to the love of the Father, that is, the *agape* that is one of the distinguishing features of the true believer (1 John 2:15). What exactly is meant by love for the world will have to be informed by what is said about "everything in the world" in verse 16.

The love of God is incompatible with love for the world because what is in the world, first of all, are the "cravings of sinful man." This may not be the best way to translate what the text literally says: "the desires of the *sarx*." This Greek word does not in the Johannine writings have the negative sense that it has in Romans 8, for example, where the meaning clearly is the sinful nature. In the Gospel of John *sarx* is what the Word became (John 1:14; see also 6:51–56); the only other use of the word in 1 John is to insist that Jesus Christ came in it (1 John 4:2). In the Gospel, the word more commonly refers to the natural, physical realm; it is unable to attain to the divine world of the spirit (John 3:6), but it is not its archenemy either (1:13; 6:63; 8:15). So the "desires of the *sarx*" might better be rendered "physical desires."

In the next phrase, the NIV renders the same Greek word "desires" as "lust," which is centered in the eyes. But in line with the previous phrase, this is better understood to refer to what is visually appealing; the eyes, like the *sarx*, do not operate in the spiritual realm. Physical eyes are meant for seeing visible things; thus they function as God intended. But the problem arises when the physical, what is tangible and visible, becomes the primary focus of human life. The "boasting of what he has and does" clarifies the first two phrases and describes many modern people, for whom the accumulation of material possessions assumes the highest priority.

John's attack, then, is not against gross sinful activity, such as sexual immorality, which some extract from the use of *sarx* and "lust." Actually, there is nothing in all of the Johannine letters that even hints at flagrant sinful behavior in the opponents; given the critical situation, we would have expected John to have used such ammunition had it been available. The reason "the world" listens to the opponents is that they "speak from the viewpoint of the world" (1 John 4:5). They do not provoke hostility from the world because that results only when the light of God's message exposes its evil deeds (John 7:7; cf. 1 John 3:12).

The opponents of John may have been like certain opponents of Paul, who appealed to the visible and impressive (2 Cor. 10–11). In response, Paul insisted that Christians must fix their eyes (spiritual) not on the visible, which is only temporary, but on the unseen, which is eternal (2 Cor. 4:18). This is remarkably similar to the language of the concluding verse of the section: Everything associated with the world "passes away"; the one who does the will of God lives forever. The allure of what is material is great. But only a fool lays up treasure on earth, soon to be lost, rather than treasure in heaven, which will never be lost (Matt. 6:19–21).

2.2. Belief in the Christ (2:18–27)

2.2.1. The Antichrists Who Have Gone Out Into the World (2:18–19). Verse 18 contains one of only two uses of the phrase "last hour" in the New Testament. It may be John's intensified form of a phrase often found in the Gospel of John, "last day." The early Christians were convinced they were living "in the last days" (Acts 2:16–17; Heb. 1:2). The New Testament often speaks about the return of Christ and the conditions that would prevail just prior to this event. One anticipated development was the appearance of false prophets and "false christs" and, in some texts, an individual who would represent the epitome of rebellion and would lead the final opposition against God (2 Thess. 2:1–12; Rev. 13). Only in 1 and 2 John is this person called the "antichrist" (2:18, 22; 4:3; 2 John 7); the readers know such a figure is coming.

This individual is not important in himself, but only as a representative of the opponents, who hold a false view of Christ (see v. 22). Believers know that it is the "last hour" "because many antichrists have come." More precisely, John means to say that the false prophets advocate a teaching about Christ that is a manifestation of the spirit of antichrist (4:3).

As discussed in the introduction, this verse portrays a church split, and verses 18–27 reflect the harsh language usually associated with such a division. A segment of the community has left, and their departure proves that they never really belonged to the believing church; otherwise they would not have left. The book's emphasis on the revealing nature of one's deeds is seen again; the actions of the deserters show them for what they always were (cf. 1 Cor. 11:19). What they have failed to do is "remain"; once again, the verb *meno* is crucial, whether it be in God, in the word they received, or in the community of faith.

2.2.2. Remaining in the Teaching of the Anointing About Jesus (2:20–27). The "you" in verse 20 is emphatic and might be so indicated by italics: "But *you* have an anointing from the Holy One." The title "Holy One" may refer to the Father, who is holy (John 17:11), but more likely is to Jesus, whom Simon Peter confessed as "the Holy One of God" (6:69).

Pentecostals identify this "anointing" (*chrisma*) with a special enabling of a person, such as a preacher, by the Holy Spirit. It is only in 1 John 2:20, 27 that we find this term in the New Testament. This *chrisma* is best understood in relation to the verb *chrio*, to anoint. In the Old Testament, individuals were anointed for service to God and his people, and a literal pouring of oil became identified with the bestowing by God of the Holy Spirit (1 Sam. 16:13; Isa. 61:1). Luke's Gospel in particular narrates Jesus' reception of the Spirit at his baptism (Luke 3:22), his subsequent guidance by the Spirit (4:1), and his self-conscious fulfillment of the "anointing" passage of Isaiah 61 (Luke 4:18–21). It seems apt, then, that believers are said to have a *chrisma*, an anointing, from the *christos*, the Anointed One himself.

But the anointing is not associated here with fiery preaching. Since they have an anointing, "all of you know the truth." As suggested by a footnote in the NIV, there are important early copies of this verse that read, "and you know all things," which would not be unlike the statement in verse 27 that the anointing teaches them "about all things." But the text in the NIV makes good sense in line with the emphatic "you" earlier in the verse. It is the members of the faithful community, *not* the false prophets, who have the anointing (despite their claims). And in contrast to the possible claims of certain opponents that they are the ones who "know," the writer insists that *all* true believers know (and thus do not need self-proclaimed enlightened people to teach them, v. 27). The "anointing," then, is the indwelling Spirit, who, in fulfillment of the promise of Jesus (John 14:26; 16:13), directs believers to true understanding.

The writer goes on to assure his readers that he is convinced that they *do* know the truth. Just as darkness has no part in light, "no lie comes from the truth." The "liar" in the Gospel of John is the devil; there is "no truth in him" (John 8:44). In 1 John, the "liar" depicts the opponents, who fail the two key tests of Christology and morality (1 John 2:4, 22; 4:20); they are the children of the father of all lies (3:10; cf. John 8:44).

The opponents are brothers of those "children of the devil" who rejected Jesus as the Christ during his earthly ministry (John 8:41–47). In a manifestation of the end-time antichrist, they deny that Jesus is the Christ—thus denying not only the Son, but the Father who sent him and who is revealed completely in the Son (John 1:18; 10:30; 14:9). We do not know how exactly the opponents denied that Jesus is the Christ. It seems clear that they were not Jews who rejected the Christian claim that Jesus is the Messiah foretold in the Jewish Scriptures; that sort of opponent was the antagonist in the Gospel of John, but the struggle with the synagogue is not in evidence in the letters. Their view in some sense involved the denial that Jesus Christ had "come in the flesh" (1 John 4:2).

Judging from what 1 John emphasizes in response, it appears that the crucial issue was the genuine and atoning death of Jesus for the sins of all (2:2; 4:10). Christian faith requires the affirmation that Jesus of Nazareth, a true, physical human being (1:1–2), was the divine Christ, the Son who was from the beginning with God (1:2; 4:15). Many Jews in the Gospel of John claimed to have God as their Father (John 8:41), but rejected Jesus as being from God. The Gospel insisted that rejection of the Son was the equivalent of rejection of God the Father (3:36; 5:23; 8:47; 15:23). So here (and in 2 John 9), one's status with God is dependent on one's reaction to the Son. The terminology of "having" the Father (1 John 2:23) is unique in the New Testament. We must avoid any thought, of course, of having some sort of hold on the Almighty God. Rather, this is the Johannine language of indwelling; not only is the believer indwelt by the Spirit (John 14:17; 1 John 3:24) and the Son (John 17:23, 26), but by God the Father as well (John 14:23; 1 John 3:24; 4:12).

The Greek construction of 2:24 is like that in 2:27, and the NIV's "as for you" used in verse 27 could begin this sentence as well. The description of the opponents in verses 22–23 is sandwiched between contrasting affirmations about the believing community in verses 20–21 ("you have an anointing," and "you know the truth") and in verses 24–25. The distinction, however, is dependent on their guarding against the influence of those who deny the Son.

The importance of the verb *meno* for this writing is evident in verse 24 (on *meno*, see notes on 2:6); though the NIV does not make this clear, this word is used three times in verse 24, and "what you have heard from the beginning" is spelled out twice. The true message about Jesus Christ, which they have heard since the beginning of their spiritual lives (cf. 2:7), must be maintained. Although this "remaining" can be viewed as a present reality (2:14), the emphasis here is on an active holding firm to what may be lost. The urgency of this call for vigilance is seen by (1) the solemn denial of association with God to those who reject the message cited in the verses 23–24; (2) the verbal command rendered "See that . . ."; and (3) the conditional phrasing, "If [you remain]. . . ." Only when proper belief is maintained will one remain in the Son and, as a result, in the Father.

This dwelling in the Son and in the Father is the essence of "eternal life" (see notes on 1:2). The assurance of those who have a proper belief in Jesus as the Son so that they have this life is a primary purpose of the writing of 1 John (5:11–13).

This interpretation is confirmed in verses 26–27. The things being written concern those "who are trying to lead you astray." These people, of course, are those who deny that Jesus is the Son, who have left the community, and who have been termed "antichrists." The appeal to "remain" is relevant particularly in this context; John is anxious to warn his spiritual children against the toxic influence of these opponents (cf. 3:7). But he constructs his next sentence, as he did in verse 24, to make the contrast most evident. There are deceivers out there, but "*as for you*, the anointing you received from him [God, although 'him' may refer to Jesus] remains in you" (on anointing, see notes on v. 20).

As in verses 20–21, the anointing of the Spirit is linked with instruction; recipients of the anointing know the truth (v. 20) and do not need anyone to teach them. It is noteworthy that the only use in the letters of John of the verb "to teach" are the three instances in this verse. In light of verse 27, we best understand this statement not as a repudiation of all Christian teachers, but of the particular teaching of the opponents. You do not need to listen to *them*. While some might object that John is acting as a teacher himself, he would more readily identify himself as a faithful witness of Christ (see notes on 1:1). Such witnesses hand on the teaching of Christ (cf. 1 Cor. 15:3–4), in contrast to those who claim to be more "advanced" teachers (2 John 7–10).

The anointing of the true believers, which 1 John in each case identifies with its divine bestower ("from the Holy One" in v. 20; "from him" and "his" in v. 27), teaches them "about all things." This reminds one of Jesus' promise in John 14:26 that the Spirit will teach his followers "all things." In both cases, the provision is for divine guidance in whatever circumstances or need believers find themselves. As 14:26 makes explicit, this instruction will always be in accord with Jesus' own teaching. This is precisely what disqualifies the teaching of the opponents. Their message (in a sense, their so-called "anointing") is a lie—a word uniformly associated with the opponents (1:8; 2:21). The believers' anointing is true—in accord with the truth of God in Christ.

3. The Message Again (2:28–4:6)

3.1. Behavior of the Christian (2:28–3:24)

3.1.1. The Hope of the Children of God (2:28–3:3). The basic issues have been raised and addressed. False teachers, who fail to teach correctly about Jesus Christ and to demonstrate love for other believers, pose a threat to the faith of the recipients of 1 John. These first readers are exhorted to continue in the teaching and practice rooted in the faithful witnesses to Jesus himself. The section beginning in 2:28 is a variation on these themes. The call to "remain in him" (NIV "remain/continue in him") that concluded the previous section is repeated in the first verse of this new section; obviously, this is a crucial concern for John.

As noted in the discussion of 2:18, the coming of the false teachers heralds the arrival of the "last hour"; specifically, it is the last hour before "he appears." Though it is true that the emphasis in the Johannine writings is on the present possession of life, this does not preclude the expectation seen elsewhere in the New Testament of a cataclysmic return of Christ. John 6, for example, speaks of the resurrection of the last day (vv. 39–40, 54). In 1 John 2:28, the desire to be confident and unashamed at the coming (*parousia*) of Christ is cited as an incentive to continue in Christ. Such confidence before God at the point of the judgment of all who are unprepared (Matt. 24–25; 2 Thess. 2:8–12) is only possible when a person has truly believed in the Son (John 3:18, 36; 5:28–29). Only in this way can one be found "blameless and holy in the presence of our God and Father" at the *parousia* of our Lord (1 Thess. 3:13). The Son of God appeared to bring life and take away sin (1 John 1:2; 3:5, 8). He *will* appear a second time, and the result for the believer will be an even deeper relationship with God (3:2; cf. John 14:1–3).

First John 2:29 is another reminder in this letter that confidence at his coming can be based solely on right belief and practice now. Since Jesus is righteous, those who have been born of him do what is righteous (2:6). Those, like John's opponents, who do not believe and behave in a righteous manner are thus not born of him and face judgment at the *parousia*.

The word order in 3:1 emphasizes, as does the NIV, the great love that the Father has lavished on us. We are "called children of God!

And that is what we are." All who believe in the Son are "born of God" (John 1:12–13) and "have the Father" (1 John 2:23). The verb tense indicates that this love was given and continues to be given to us. The unbelieving world is unable to perceive this family because our origins and life are of a divine rather than of a human nature (John 1:13). Thus they did not know God the Father (17:25) or the Son (1:10).

It is difficult to know whether the "him" at the end of 3:1 refers primarily to God or to Jesus, especially since knowledge of one entails knowledge of the other (cf. John 8:19; 16:3). In any case, unbelievers recognize neither God nor his children. Jesus had told his disciples that they could expect no different treatment or reception than he himself had received (15:18–16:4). We do well to remember that the opponents and their claims and apparent success (1 John 4:4–6) are never far from the discussion. The dual affirmation in both 3:1–2 that we are "children of God" makes best sense when we recall that the recipients of 1 John appear to be in doubt concerning precisely this matter. Could the opponents be right? This letter insists that *we* who continue in the Son and in true belief and practice are God's children and will face God with confidence at Christ's coming.

Not even we know what we "will be." What believers *do* know, however, is that when Christ appears, we will be "like him" because we "shall see him as he is." In a sense, the "seeing" of the Son during his first appearing was transformational (1:1–3), and so the "seeing" of the Son at his second appearing will also be transformational. We will be changed (1 Cor. 15:51–52), and we will comprise the harvest of which Jesus was the firstfruits (1 Cor. 15:20). The process of "progressive glorification" (2 Cor. 3:18) will in a moment be perfected, for we will behold the Son in all his glory; then the seeing will be "face to face"(1 Cor. 13:12).

The words of 1 John 3:3 function much as did 2:29. Since the coming Son is pure, those who have "this hope" will purify themselves; this expectation calls for appropriate behavior. Again implicit is the claim that the opponents have no such hope. "Hope" in the New Testament is the assurance or certainty of something yet future. The certainty of Christ's return, then, is another motivation to continue in him and to live a holy life.

3.1.2. A Mark of the Children of God: Not Continuing in Sin (3:4–10). The reference to "the law" in verse 4 is unique in 1 John. In fact, the word "law" is not used, but rather a word meaning "lawlessness." Sin is identified here as doing what is lawless. Since the debates about the Mosaic law have been left behind in the Gospel of John, and since "the law" itself is never referred to, it seems likely that lawlessness here means an attitude of general rebellion toward the requirements of God.

The verses that follow return overtly to the opponents and their behavior. They defy the essential commands of God: to believe in the Son and to love other believers (3:23). John's critical point is that the lives of believers will not be characterized by sin. Jesus' (first) appearance was to take away our sins, though he himself was without sin (cf. John 8:46; Heb. 4:15). Once again, John appeals to the example of Jesus. Those who claim to live (lit., "remain") in him should live as he did (1 John 2:6, 29; 3:3); "no one who lives in him keeps on sinning."

The NIV properly translates the present tense verb as "keeps on sinning" rather than "sins," though each is grammatically acceptable. Similarly, the next phrase, which literally means, "No one who sins," is well rendered, "No one who continues to sin." John is not making a claim for absolute sinlessness in the believer. The claim of verse 5 is unique to Jesus; only "in him is no sin." Indeed, the writer has earlier rejected the possibility of anyone claiming to be without sin or to have not sinned. He is not now contradicting his own position. The conflict with the opponents again serves as a key. Sin is an attitude of rebellion against God's commands, which in 1 John are belief in the Son and love for the brothers. Even a Mosaic command such as the prohibition of murder is in 3:11–15 referred specifically to the (opponents') failure to show love for other believers. Thus, the writer can conclude that no one who continues to sin (that is, the opponents) has either seen him or known him.

This language of not "seeing" or "knowing" God is reminiscent of references to unbelieving Jews who characterize the "world" in the Gospel of John (5:37; 8:19; 14:17;16:3). In this letter, the opponents come to be identified with the world (1 John 4:1–6; 5:1–5). Whether it be Jews who claim to know God but reject Jesus, or false teachers who claim to know God and fail to believe in Jesus Christ who has come in the flesh, the point is the same: One cannot be in relationship with God without acceptance of and belief in the Son, Jesus Christ.

The reference in 3:7 to those leading others astray is similar to that mentioned in 2:26; 1 John was written in large measure to guard the readers from the opponents who sought to deceive the faithful. The thought of verses 7–10 is similar to that reflected in Jesus' debate with his opponents in John 8:31–47. In that passage, Jesus argued that one's behavior, and in particular, one's response to him, indicates one's spiritual lineage. The unbelieving Jews claimed that Abraham was their father. Jesus acknowledged that they were physical descendants of Abraham, but denied that they were his *children*. Children, from this perspective, have the characteristics of their father. The Jews' rejection of Jesus, and hence of God, proved that they were not the spiritual children of believing Abraham. Rather, they were the spiritual children of the devil.

The parallels between the language of Jesus in John 8 and that of 1 John 3 are striking. In each, a demonstration of the ancestry of "children" is made based on reception or rejection of God's message, and the devil is associated with sin, murder, and being in rebellion against God "from the beginning." In 1 John 3, since Jesus is righteous, so those who believe in him (children of God) do what is righteous. In contrast, those who do what is sinful are of the devil. The devil is the prototype of the person who is "lawless" (v. 4) and in rebellion against God; it is what we find the devil doing from the beginning of the biblical record in Genesis 3–4. The Son of God, however, came "to destroy the devil's work," and thus he stands as the prototype of all those who stand against the devil's rebellion against God.

At this point, 1 John repeats the claim that such an attitude is impossible in the believer (v. 6) and illustrates the point by intensifying the metaphor of being "born of God" from 2:29. Verse 9 is in an abcba (chiastic) pattern:

a No one who is *born of God*
b will *continue to sin*,
c. because *God's seed remains in him*;
b' he *cannot go on sinning*,
a' because he has been *born of God*.

The middle line graphically identifies the basis for both "a" and "b": "God's seed [*sperma*] remains in him." Thus the believer, in this metaphor, carries the genetic material of the Father. The aphorism "like father, like son" is taken here to new lengths.

This line of argument has been followed in the interest of driving home the point of verse 10. We can *know* who is on the side of God and who is on the side of the devil. Two criteria are involved, in this verse stated in a negative fashion: "Anyone who does not do what is right" or "does not love [other believers]" is not a child of God. These correspond with the two bases for the argument of the whole book: proper belief and behavior. Verse 10, then, is another way of stating what is claimed in 3:23 and 5:1–2.

Doing "what is right" is best interpreted not in terms of observing certain rules or abstaining from certain activities but in terms of the contrast in verses 7–8 between doing what is sinful (rebelling against God's commands) and accepting God's commands. As we noted on verse 6, this contrast is not a claim to sinless perfection in the believer. Rather, these criteria served the original readers as tests by which to gauge the validity of the opponents' claims to speak for God. They sinned in that they rejected God's call to believe in Jesus as the Son of God and denied the mandate to demonstrate loving concern for the community of believers.

Though it is not our business to judge other people, it is our responsibility to evaluate the teaching and behavior of those who claim to be Christians. This responsibility is especially the case with those who are in positions of authority and leadership. God will determine the eternal destiny of each person. The Christian is called upon to determine whether a particular teacher ought to be heeded and supported. If we neglect to do this and end up receiving the message of a false teacher, as we will see in 2 John 11, we "share in his wicked work."

3.1.3. Another Mark of the Children of God: Loving Fellow Believers (3:11–24). The next paragraph renews the concern demonstrated in 2:7–11, that no one can claim to be a believer and not show love for others. Such a person "hates" others (2:9, 11), and an observer can with confidence conclude that such a person is living apart from the light of God.

The love principle is called a "command" in 2:7. But it is so fundamental to John and his readers that it can, along with teaching about the nature of God (1:5), be termed "the message"—a message, as in 2:7, that they have heard from the beginning of their Christian lives in the community. This command is rooted in the directive recorded in John 13:34. At his last meal with the disciples, Jesus stated that their demonstration of love for one another would serve as evidence to all that they were his disciples. Similarly, 1 John claims that love for fellow believers serves as evidence of being children of God. This standard can be used to evaluate others (1 John 2:7–11; 3:10, 14–23; 4:7–8, 19–21) or oneself (3:14, 19–20).

The writer cites the negative example of Cain, possibly for two reasons. (1) The Cain incident illustrates the key point in this section: Outward actions reveal one's inward nature. Cain belonged to the evil one, the devil—so called also in 2:13–14 and 5:18–19. In keeping with the logic of "like father, like son" seen in verses 7–11, Cain's actions revealed what was within: evil and sin, rebellion against God's commands. By contrast, his brother's actions were "righteous"; within himself Abel was like the righteous God (cf. v. 7). Deeds necessarily demonstrate nature. This is how Jesus Christ showed us what love is like; he laid down his life for us (v. 16). Thus, words about Christian love are insufficient. In the case of the opponents, such words are belied by actions (2:9; 3:15; 4:20). True believers, then, must love "with actions and in truth" (v. 18). This is how believers know that they have passed from death to life (v. 14).

(2) John incorporates the Cain story in order to dramatize the evil of the opponents. We earlier saw how the opponents were described as "hating" other believers (see notes on 2:9). Aided by the Cain story, the author now presses the case: "Anyone who hates his brother is a murderer, and you know that no murderer has eternal life in him" (v. 15). The opponents are identified with Cain; their actions demonstrate that, like Cain—and like the original prototype, the devil himself—they are evil and in rebellion against God. Further, John writes that his readers should not be surprised if "the world hates you." Jesus told his disciples to expect no better treatment than he himself had received; the world would hate them just as it had hated him, because they, like him, do not "belong to the world" (John 15:18–16:4). The placement of this statement identifies the opponents with the world. "*We* have passed from death to life, because we love our brothers" (v. 14). *They* show by their lack of such love that they belong to the world, which "is under the control of the evil one" (5:19), and so they remain "in death" (v. 14).

Once again, Jesus is cited as a model for Christian behavior. His sacrificial death is the essence of what love means. For all Christians, of course, Jesus' death is more than a mere example for behavior. It is the ground on which any experience of life and love is possible. In Paul's language, all of us were dead in sin and objects of God's wrath until God, by means of the atoning death of Jesus Christ, made us alive (Eph. 2:1–5). John states that it is because God "is love" and has bestowed love on us that we are found to be the children of God (1 John 3:1; see also 4:8–10, 19). So, while Jesus' death is more than an example of behavior, it is that as well.

The expression that is used in verse 16, "to lay down one's life," is a distinct Johannine expression. It is used a number of times in John's Gospel to refer to Jesus' sacrificial death (John 10:11, 15, 17). John 15:12–13 is particularly important, where Jesus says: "My command is this: Love each other as I have loved you. Greater love has no one than this, that he lay down his life for his friends." John makes essentially the same point here: Jesus provides the perfect model of love. Those who follow him must have the same attitude and behave in the same way (cf. Paul's words in Phil. 2:3–11). We have known (experienced) love through Jesus Christ; now we must act upon that love with others.

Verse 17 suggests, however, that what is in mind is something rather short of the sacrifice of one's physical life. The wording used here once again indicates that the opponents are in view. How can one indwelt by God's love and having material possessions possibly see a needy brother and not have pity on him? "To not have pity" as used here means more than merely failing to feel sorry for someone. The Greek expression is literally "to close one's inward parts [*splanchna*]" (an expression unique in the Johannine writings). Elsewhere in the New Testament, *splanchna* refers to what we might call one's "heart" (Philem. 7, 12, 20), or the seat of affection (2 Cor. 6:12), or compassion (Col. 3:12). God himself is said to have a merciful *splanchna* (Luke 1:78). Those born of God, who are animated by the love of God, will demonstrate such an attitude in their behavior. They will open their hearts to meet the needs of others.

Divine love must, then, be seen "with actions and in truth." The phrase "in truth" probably means more than simply "truly" or "genuinely." (On "truth" see notes on 1:6.) Uniformly in the Johannine writings "in (the) truth" means "in keeping with God's revelation in Jesus," or, more simply, "in Jesus Christ" (John 4:23–24; 16:13; 17:17, 19; 2 John 1, 3–4). So "with actions and in truth" may have the sense of "with actions deriving from the truth." (This sense clarifies the first pair in this verse also: words that derive from the tongue.) First John 3:19 supports this interpretation, since it goes on to restate the principle of verse 14, that it is by this love demonstrated that we know that we "belong to the truth." The same divine love that motivated Jesus, who is the truth, to lay down his life for us (v. 16) motivates all those who belong to him to act sacrificially in love.

The wording of verses 19–21 is somewhat obscure, but the NIV most likely conveys the sense intended. The phrase that begins verse 19 signals another instance of the writer's concern to assure his readers of their right standing with God. Both main verbs in this verse ("know" and "set at rest") are in the future tense, but probably are best understood in the present with the "whenever" of verse 20. Because the indwelling truth is demonstrated in the behavior of believers, we can know that we belong to the truth, and we can set our hearts at rest in God's presence (now) whenever our hearts condemn us.

The word translated "condemn" is used in the New Testament only in verses 20–21 and in Galatians 2:11, where Paul describes Peter as being "in the wrong" (NIV). In biblical thinking, the heart is viewed as the center of mental and psychological processes. The citation from Isaiah 53:1 in John 12:40 illustrates how "understanding" is related to one's heart. Jesus' comfort of the disciples in John 14:25–27 also illustrates how they can have peace; their "hearts" should not be troubled because the Spirit would bring to mind what Jesus had said to them. As in John 14:1, 27, "heart" is singular, suggesting that the community of believers is in view. Being "condemned by one's heart" may then be roughly similar to being "stricken by one's conscience."

There is no question about whether this experience of "condemnation" will ever happen. It will. The thought is similar to that in 1 John 2:1–2. According to those verses, this letter was written so that the readers might not sin; but whenever anyone does sin, we have an advocate *pros* (toward) the Father in Jesus Christ. Likewise, the standing of the believer before (*pros*) God (3:21; cf. v. 19) is assured. If the hearts of believers say that we have failed God, we can "set our hearts at rest." This fact is true for two reasons. Looking back to verses 18–19, the truth of God's abiding in believers produces actions that verify one's faith. Moreover, according to verse 20, God, who knows everything, is greater than our hearts. This is a balancing principle to the test of actions and so provides a welcome measure of grace. Deeds are essential, especially in the circumstances surrounding this letter, when false teachers were denying their importance. Yet it is vital to know that God knows our hearts even when our deeds may not measure up to the example set by Jesus.

A Greek play on words, lost in our English translation, reinforces this insight. The word for "know" (*ginosko)* at the end of verse 20 is the base word for and rhymes with the word for "condemn" (*kataginosko*) earlier in the verse. That is, God's knowledge (*ginosko)* supersedes our hearts' condemnation (*kataginosko*). The God who knows everything knows those who are his better than they know themselves. Ultimately, this letter was written to assure its readers that if they believe in the name of the Son of God, they have eternal life (cf. 5:13).

While believers will on occasion experience such a sense of "condemnation," the normal state of affairs is that our hearts make no such accusation. And we have a confidence before God that in 1 John is associated either with an assurance at the second coming (2:28; 4:17) or, as here, with our approach to God in prayer. We can come to God with confidence and receive whatever we ask because we obey his commands and do what pleases him.

Prayer is answered and petitions granted because, as 5:14 puts it, we ask "according to his will." Asking selfishly and for superfluous things seems not to be in view at all. When we are conscientiously abiding by God's revealed will, our prayers will be in keeping with the divine will. The command we must obey and the idea of doing "what pleases" God are to believe in Jesus as the Son and to love one another (v. 23). We have seen how central these two matters are in 1 John. When we believe what God has told us to believe and when we live in the manner in which he has told us to live, we will receive from God all that we may need and request.

"Those who obey [God's] commands live [lit., remain] in him," and God lives in them (v. 24). This language recalls that of the farewell discourse of Jesus in John 14–16. Believers dwell in him and he in them (John 14:23), especially in the sense of "remaining" (15:4–7). This intimate relationship is tied to the believer's keeping of his commands (14:15, 21; 15:10) and results in petitions being granted (14:13–14; 15:7, 16; 16:23–24).

Finally, in yet another example of the "this is how we know" motif in 1 John, believers are also assured that God remains in them "by the Spirit that he gave us." This too is parallel to the farewell discourse, for it is in John 14–16 that Jesus promised the coming of the Spirit to indwell the believer (14:16–17) and to bear witness to Jesus (14:26; 15:26; 16:13–15). This reference to the Spirit serves a dual function for the writer. It provides an additional basis of assurance to the faithful readers, since the Spirit is granted only to believers (John 7:37–39; 14:16–17). In addition, the reference to the Spirit serves as a point of transition into the next section of the book, where "spirit" becomes a central theme.

3.2. Belief in the Christ (4:1–6)

3.2.1. Belief in Jesus as a Test of Who Is From God (4:1–3). In the outline that has been proposed, this section develops crucial matters of belief that distinguish true believers from the opponents, which were first discussed in 2:18–27. There the group that departed is identified as antichrists because they "deny that Jesus is the Christ" (2:22). In this passage the denounced teaching is described more specifically. The readers are warned that they should not "believe every spirit, but test the spirits to see whether they are from God." The following verses refer to spirits that do or do not acknowledge Jesus Christ. Though the New Testament can describe an evil spirit who inhabits a human body and who interacts with Jesus (Mark 5:1–20), it is unlikely that John has in mind such demonic entities in this passage. In fact, there are fundamentally only two spirits under consideration. One is of God (v. 2), while the other is of the antichrist (v. 3); one is the Spirit of truth, while the other is the spirit of falsehood (v. 6). These correspond, of course, to the two groups in conflict.

Several things in this passage indicate that it is more about the opponents than about "spirits" per se. (1) The readers are told to test the spirits "because many false prophets have gone out [*exerchomai*] into the world." There can be no doubt that this is another reference to the opponents, whom John already said have gone out (*exerchomai*) from the community (2:19; see also 2 John 7) and who are uniformly associated with the root word for false or lie (1 John 1:6; 2:4, 21–22; 4:20; in a different sense: 1:10; 5:10). (2) Elsewhere in the Johannine letters, "acknowledging" is done by people (2:23; 4:15), and, decisively, the parallel in 2 John 7 secures this reading. (3) It is only a stylistic variation to call the opponents "antichrists" (1 John 2:18; see 2 John 7) or those who exhibit the "spirit of the antichrist" (1 John 4:3). (4) The language of verses 4–6 contrasts "you" (true believers) with "them" (the opponents).

The terminology of "spirit," then, is a means by which John characterizes the conflicting groups. The opponents are characterized by a spirit that does not acknowledge Jesus. True believers are characterized by a spirit, or possibly by *the* Spirit, that does acknowledge Jesus. Although the word for "test" is unique here in Johannine writing, it is often used in the New Testament in a positive manner, to refer to a process of critical evaluation (e.g., Luke 14:19; Rom. 12:2; 2 Cor. 13:5). The closest parallel to 1 John 4:1 is Paul's command in 1 Thess. 5:21 to "test everything." In its immediate context, this probably refers to the evaluation of prophetic utterances in the congregation. Careful evaluation is precisely what 1 John 4:1–6 encourages. In fact, the writer repeatedly has provided the tests by

BIBLICAL EVIDENCE FOR THE TRINITY

According to the Bible, there is only one God (Dt 6:4; Isa 45:21; 1Ti 2:5; Jas 2:19). But this one God has revealed himself in three persons: the Father, the Son, and the Holy Spirit. The word used to express this doctrine is "Trinity"—"tri-unity," "three-in-oneness." While this word is not used in the Bible, it adequately expresses biblical teaching. There is little difficulty acknowledging the Father as God. Regarding the deity of Jesus the Son, see the chart on "Passages Indicating the Deity of Christ." As to the Holy Spirit being specifically called God, see Luke 1:32, 35 and Acts 5:3–4.

Hints in the OT of the Trinity	
God speaks of himself as "us" rather than "me"	Ge 1:26–27; 3:22; 11:7; Isa 6:8
God promises to send someone who is God	Isa 7:14; 9:6
The "angel of the Lord" speaks as if he is the Lord	Ge 16:10; 22:15–17; Ex 3:6; 23:20–23; Jdg 6:14
The Trinity in the NT	
Father, Son, and Holy Spirit have one name	Mt 28:19
Father, Son, and Holy Spirit were present at Jesus' baptism	Mt 3:16–17; Lk 3:21–22
The Spirit is sent by the Father through the Son	Jn 15:26
The Spirit testifies that we are God's children and co-heirs with Christ	Ro 8:16–17; Gal 4:4–6
One Spirit, one Lord Jesus, and one God	1Co 12:4–6
A blessing from Father, Son, and Holy Spirit	2Co 13:14
Chosen by the Father, sprinkled with Jesus' blood, and sanctified by the Spirit	1Pe 1:2
The Spirit testifies that Jesus came from the Father	1Jn 4:2
Other places in the NT where Father, Son, and Holy Spirit appear together	Ro 5:5–6; 1Th 1:2–5; 2Th 2:13; Tit 3:4–6; Jude 20–21
Holiness is ascribed to Father, Son, and Holy Spirit	Jn 17:11; Ro 1:4; 1Co 1:30
Eternity is ascribed to Father, Son, and Holy Spirit	1Ti 1:17; Heb 1:2–3, 8; 9:14
Father, Son, and Holy Spirit each know everything	Mt 6:8, 32; Jn 2:24–25; 1Co 2:10–11
Father, Son, and Holy Spirit are each all-powerful	Ps 135:5–7; Mt 28:18; Ro 15:13, 17; 1Co 15:24–27
Father, Son, and Holy Spirit are each everywhere present	Ps 139:7–10; Jer 23:24; Mt 28:20
Father, Son, and Holy Spirit all involved in creation	Ge 1:1–2; Ps 104:30; Jn 1:3
Father, Son, and Holy Spirit all involved in giving spiritual life	Eze 37:14; Jn 10:10; Eph 2:4–5
Father, Son, and Holy Spirit all involved in miracles	1Ki 18:38; Mt 4:23–24; Ro 15:19
Father, Son, and Holy Spirit all involved in teaching	Ps 71:17; Isa 48:17; Jn 13:13; 14:26
Father, Son, and Holy Spirit all experience grief because of sin	Ge 6:6; Lk 19:41–44

which the believer can determine whether an individual belongs to God or not.

It is not surprising, then, to find in verse 2 yet another example of the "this is how you can [know]" formula. The Spirit of God is known by the acknowledgment that "Jesus Christ has come in the flesh." As we noted in the introductory section on the occasion and purpose of 1 John, this seems to respond to a view of the opponents that denied the historical reality of God's becoming human (2:22–23; 5:5; 2 John 7). Furthermore, the way in which this letter stresses the saving nature of Jesus' death (1 John 1:7; 2:2; 4:10; 5:6) suggests that the opponents minimized or even rejected this fundamental Christian tenet. It is speculation to attempt greater precision on the details of a teaching that brought about this insistence on Jesus Christ's being a genuine human being. What can be said is that Christians believe that the Jesus who died on the cross was both fully God and fully human. Had he not been fully God, he could not have been the perfect sacrifice necessary for the cleansing of sin. Had he not been fully human, he could not have been *our* perfect sacrifice, one like us in every way yet without sin (Heb. 2:17; 4:15).

End time events are occurring. The readers had been instructed in the past that an individual would arise in the last days who would lead a rebellion against God (see notes on 2:18), but it is only in 1 and 2 John that this figure is called the "antichrist." It is remarkable, however, that in the only place in which the term is used, nothing is said about the antichrist other than that he "is coming" (1 John 2:18; 4:3). What *is* important is that the appearance of false prophets, who exhibit the spirit of rebellion against God and his commands, signals the coming of the last days (2:18; cf. Mark 13:22). Jesus had predicted that his followers would be hated (Matt. 24:9; cf. 1 John 3:13), that many would turn from the faith (Matt. 24:10; cf. 1 John 2:19) and hate each other (Matt. 24:10) rather than loving each other (1 John 3:11), and that many false prophets would arise and deceive many people (Matt. 24:11; cf. 1 John 4:1; 2:26; 3:7). Even had they known the Pauline instruction to the Ephesian elders that some from their own group would abandon the faith (Acts 20:30), it must have been traumatic to see former associates become enemies of Christ—antichrists!

3.2.2. Affirmation That the Readers Are From God (4:4–6). Given the fact that the false teachers are continuing to lure those who have not broken away (2:26), it is crucial that the writer establish distance between them and the readers. The faithful must see that alignment with the opponents is not a possibility. Thus the polemic is sharp. They are liars. They are deceivers. They are in darkness. They are murderers. They are of the devil. They are antichrists.

But throughout this section (as earlier) the writer addresses his readers with terms of affection: "dear children" (2:28; 3:7, 18; 4:4), "brothers" (3:13), and "dear friends" (lit., "beloved": 3:2, 21; 4:1). And along with the contrast between the "spirits" that characterize the two sides, the writer uses a simple preposition to focus on the origin and nature of each. The seven places in 4:1–6 where the NIV reads "from" are all translations of the Greek word *ek*, which means "out of" or "from." The NIV has attempted to render the variation of sense expressed by John, for example, in 2:19: "They went out from [*ek*] us, but they did not really belong to [lit., were not *ek*] us." To be *ek* someone or something means that that someone or something is the origin or nature of your being. Believers are *ek* the truth (2:21; 3:19) in that they live in accordance with the truth. The opponents are *ek* the devil (3:8) in that they act in accordance with the devil. For the same reason, Cain is said to be *ek* the evil one (3:12).

The predominance of this word in 4:1–6 indicates that in this key passage the writer is using this device to buttress his case. While the opponents are not *ek* God (vv. 3, 6) but are *ek* the world (v. 5), the readers and the faithful witnesses are *ek* God (vv. 2, 4, 6). This is the basis for the test of verse 1: Is a spirit *ek* God or not? The standard having been set (vv. 2–3), the opponents will fail and the true believers will pass this test.

Verses 4–6 function primarily as assurance. In language depicting struggle, John declares that his readers have "overcome them" (i.e., the opponents). The latter are *ek* the world and speak *ek* the world, and therefore the world listens to them (v. 5). Apparently the opponents are having success in gaining adherents, or at least an audience. But their success should not be a surprise, the writer argues. Since the opponents have forsaken Jesus' teaching, the world no longer hates them but accepts them (cf. John 15:18–25); their going out into the world, therefore, involves the abandonment of what distinguished them from the world.

In the face of this reception by the world of the opponents, John reminds his readers of Jesus' proclamation: "In this world you will have trouble. But take heart! I have overcome the world" (John 16:33). They have similarly overcome the worldly opponents because the "one who is in you is greater than the one who is in the world" (1 John 4:4). Although many texts speak of Jesus as residing in the believer, the references in the immediate context make it more likely that John has God primarily in view here (see 3:24). God is greater than the devil, who has control over "the world" (5:19).

The thought expressed here is analogous to that of 3:19–20. In both passages, God's sufficiency supersedes the believers' perception of insufficiency. Whether it be a condemning heart or the worldly success of the opponents, God is "greater." According to verse 6, "we are from [*ek*] God"; and though the unbelieving world listens to the false prophets, those who know God "listen to us." We thus have yet another criterion by which standing with God can be tested and how one can recognize the Spirit of truth as opposed to the spirit of falsehood. The "we" of verse 6 is a return to the "we" of the prologue: The writer speaks here as a faithful witness of Jesus. Those who continue in his authoritative teaching are characterized by God's Spirit; those who do not are characterized by a spirit of deceit.

The section we have entitled "The Message Again" thus repeats with greater elaboration the two key tests by which the readers may "know that they have eternal life" (5:20): love for fellow believers and belief in the divine Christ having become fully human.

4. The Message Yet Again (4:7–5:12)

4.1. Behavior of the Christian (4:7–21)

4.1.1. The Example of Love: God's Gift of His Son (4:7–10). The writer returns one final time to the theme of Christian love for one another. The call of 4:7 is a reiteration of a command of Jesus handed on from the start of this community (3:11). Why should we love one another? Because "love comes from [*ek*] God," and "everyone who loves has been born of [*ek*] God and knows God." Because God is love (v. 8), those who are born of God, his children, exhibit this same familial characteristic (note 3:10). Knowing God—another way of describing a relationship with God—has already been linked with keeping his commands; claims to know God without obeying him (2:4) and abandoning of sin (3:6) can be discounted.

The pattern of verses 7–11 is directly parallel to that of 3:11, 16–17: (1) the call to love one another (4:7–8), (2) the definition and demonstration of divine love in the sacrifice of Jesus Christ (4:9–10), and (3) the call to love in a manner in keeping with (2) (4:11). The second section is more elaborate and actually consists of two parallel statements—similar to what is called synthetic parallelism in Hebrew poetry, in which a second statement (v. 10) makes roughly the same point as the first (v. 9), but with variation and elaboration. Both statements are introduced with a "this is," which sets up the basis by which the divine love has been made known. Verse 9 declares, in language reminiscent of John 3:16, that God sent his one and only (*monogenes*) Son that we might live through him. Although, as verse 12 avers, no one has ever seen God, John 1:14, 18 claim that this unseen God has been uniquely "seen" in the *monogenes*.

What is important in verse 9 is that (a) God's love was for us, so that we might live; and (b) it was shown through God's sacrificially sending his one and only Son into the world. Verse 10 restates, then, this same point: (a) God's love was for us, to provide an atoning sacrifice for our sins; and (b) it was shown through God's sending his Son as this sacrifice (see notes on 2:2). The elaboration of this second verse includes the statement that God loved us initially; we did not love him. Christian love for others, following the model of Jesus, is not affected by the attitude of the other.

4.1.2. The Example of Love: Followed by God's Children (4:11–21).

4.1.2.1. God's Love Made Complete in Our Love for One Another (4:11–16). Although verse 11 can be understood as the completion of verses 7–11, it also serves to begin a new section, suggested by the address, "Dear friends," which focuses on the necessity of the example of God's love being followed by believers. While John 1 claims that the unseen God has been revealed in Jesus Christ, 1 John 4:12 proposes that when believers love one another, God lives in us and is revealed in us; in such a loving community, God's love "is made complete." This expression refers to the fulfillment of a task or principle in action (cf. John 4:34; 5:36; 17:4; 19:28; 1 John 2:5; 4:17–18). God, who is love, is revealed when those who have been born of him live out this "inborn" parental nature. Moreover, God has given us the ultimate example to follow when he sent his one and only Son that we might live.

It may seem that the writer is lapsing into redundancy. And it is true that the remainder of chapter 4 treads familiar territory: verse 13 reiterates 3:24, while verse 15 is a variation of 2:23, and the latter part of verse 16 restates verses 7–8. But there are new developments and interesting elaborations of established points. In verse 14, the writer switches from the inclusive "we" (all believers have been given the Spirit, v. 13) to the "we" of the faithful eyewitnesses of Jesus and custodians of Jesus' teaching. This group has seen (1:1; cf. John 1:14) and now bears witness (1:2) that the Father has sent his Son to be the "Savior of the world." This phrase, found in Johannine writing only here and in John 4:42, is noteworthy in that it depicts the unbelieving world as the object of God's saving work. To be sure, this truth is affirmed in texts such as John 3:16 and 1 John 2:2. But since "the world" bears such a negative connotation in the Johannine writings (see notes on 2:15), such references are a necessary reminder to some scholars who have claimed that the world is virtually written off in Johannine thought.

The writer does devote considerable attention to distinguishing between the children of God and the children of the devil. But God sent Jesus to be the means by which individuals become children of God, in order to "destroy the devil's work" (3:8). Only disbelief and disobedience confine a person to the realm of the world. To all who believe in Jesus God gives the right to become his children (cf. John 1:12). If *anyone* acknowledges that Jesus is the Son of God, God lives in that person and he or she in God (1 John 3:15). We can rely on the love of God, who is greater than whatever might be a hindrance to our assurance of faith (3:20; 4:4). Again we find the dual emphasis of the book: Whereas verse 15 roots mutual indwelling in faith, verse 16 bases it on living in love. As noted above, love is "made complete" only when it is actively demonstrated in the way urged throughout this letter.

4.1.2.2. God's Love Made Complete in Our Confidence on the Day of Judgment (4:17–18). It has often been observed that Johannine thought focuses on the present reality of what are commonly held to be future events, such as judgment and resurrection (John 3:17; 5:24–25; 11:24–25). But this does not mean that John has eliminated future expectation. There will be a resurrection on the last day and a judgment day (5:28–29; 6:39–40, 44). We must therefore guard our behavior, so that we can have confidence on that day of judgment (1 John 2:28). We can have this confidence because in our earthly lives (cf. "in this world," v. 17), "we are like him" who will himself be the judge (cf. 2:28; John 5:27).

The "him" in 1 John 4:17 probably refers to Jesus. The Greek word is *ekeinos*, a demonstrative pronoun that as a rule John uses to refer to Jesus (2:6; 3:3, 5, 7, 16; 4:17). In a sense believers are like Christ now (3:3, 7); this likeness will be made complete when they see him as he is (3:2). Paul contrasts bondage to fear with the freedom of God's children to approach God by calling "Abba, Father" (Rom. 8:15). In a similar way, 1 John states that fear is incompatible with "perfect love," because fear is related to the expectation of punishment.

The references to "perfect love" and to the fearful person who "is not made perfect in love" must be read in light of the meaning of "made complete" in verses 12 and 17. The one who is made complete (v. 17) is the one who lives in love (v. 16), and God's love is made complete in us if we love one another (v. 12). "Perfect love" appears, then, to be love made complete, love that is acted out. We are "like him" in this life to the extent our lives are characterized by sacrificial love, just as Jesus' life was (3:16). When our lives evidence Christian love, we know we have passed from death to life (3:14), we know we belong to the truth (3:19), we know that we have been born of God (4:7), and we live in God and he in us (4:12, 16).

4.1.2.3. Love for Fellow Believers Must Accompany Love for God (4:19–21). This final section in the book devoted to the love of fellow believers returns again in verse 19 to the fact that our love for others is based on God's prior love for us (v. 10). The focus is not on divine grace toward undeserving sinners, as it is in Romans 5:6. Rather, the point is once again the necessity of practical Christian love in keeping with both the nature and the example of God.

The form of verse 20 is directly parallel to that of 1:6 and 2:4: (a) + (b) = (c), where (a) is a claim to be in relationship with God, (b) is a behavior that is conflict with the claim in (a), and (c) is an assertion that the claim of (a) is a lie or that the person making the claim is a liar. Without doubt one who shows no love for fellow believers who are right in front of him should not be believed when that person claims to love God. Claims to love an unseen

God are easily made. The real test of being a child of God is to love believers in need. This is the command of God: Love for God must be accompanied by love for fellow believers.

4.2. Belief in the Christ (5:1–12)

4.2.1. By Believing in Jesus We Obey God's Commands (5:1–5). The first few verses of this final section on proper belief serve as a transition from the previous passage. In the latter part of verse 1 we find yet another variation on the theme of brotherly love in 4:7–21. Literally, this verse says that everyone who loves the "one who begot" also loves the "one begotten" by him. The translation of the NIV, though it does not reflect the fact that both terms are forms of the same Greek word, conveys the sense. It presumes the validity of the point made earlier that children bear the nature of and reflect the character of the parent.

Once again John insists that those who accept proper teaching about Jesus (see notes on 4:1–3) are "born of God" (cf. 2:29; 3:9; 5:4, 18—the perfect tense indicates that they "are" born of God because at a point in the past they "were" born of God); they can even be said to have "God's seed" within them (3:9). This fact leads, not surprisingly, to another test of authenticity: "This is how we know that we love the children of God: by loving God and carrying out his commands." (The phrase "this is how we know" is found in 2:3, 5; 3:16, 19, 24; 4:2, 6, 13; in addition, "we know" or "you know" occur in 2:18, 29; 3:2, 5, 14, 15; 4:2, 16; 5:13, 15, 18, 19, 20.) This may be the first of John's "tests" that actually *is* surprising, because it is the exact reverse of what he has been emphasizing throughout the letter. Repeatedly up to now, love for others has been validating love for God (see esp. 4:20). Now we have love for God validating love for others!

Scholars have proposed a variety of explanations for what seems to be the circularity of the reasoning. We suggest that in 5:1–5, the writer in this final "variation on a theme" emphasizes the ultimate criterion, which is more basic even than the criterion of love for the brothers. This most fundamental element is the belief in Jesus as the Son of God. This is so because one is a child of God as a result of such belief (v. 1). Love for fellow believers, though it is a crucial *evidence* of being God's child, cannot be the *basis* for being God's child, because of the uncertainties involved. Have I loved my brother *enough*? Can I be sure exactly *who* qualifies as being a brother?

What John does as he moves toward the conclusion of the book is revert to the most fundamental principle: belief in Jesus. Everything in verses 1–5 is framed by the references to believing in Jesus at the beginning of verse 1 and the end of verse 5. And the requirement of love ultimately must be viewed in light of belief. This is accomplished in a series of steps.

Step 1 (v. 2): How do we know that we are loving God's children in the proper way? We know this, most basically, by the fact that we love God and keep his commands.

Step 2 (v. 3): What is love for God? It is to obey his commands. Reading verse 2 in light of verse 3, then, we see that love for God is identified with keeping/obeying God's commands. But what exactly are the commands to be obeyed that can be identified with loving God? We already have seen that in 1 John "his commands" can be reduced to belief in Jesus and love for others (3:22–23). The flow of thought clearly indicates that it is the former that the writer has in mind.

Step 3 (vv. 3–4): "His commands" are not burdensome because everyone born of God has victory over the world (see John 16:33).

Step 4a (v. 4): Our victory is our faith.

Step 4b (v. 5): Who has this victory? Only the one who believes that Jesus is the Son of God. The essence of obedience to God's commands is to believe in God's Son (cf. John 6:28–29). This paragraph serves to put the love command in perspective. Love for fellow believers was absent in the opponents, and this shortcoming proved that they were not God's children. Love serves as evidence. But only belief in Jesus as the Son of God is the ultimate basis for one's standing with God (see the notes on 5:13).

4.2.2. By Believing in Jesus We Accept God's Testimony About His Son (5:6–12). The opponents also claim to know God and to be his children. But, according to 2:22, they deny "that Jesus is the Christ." Their view involves in some sense a denial of the genuine humanity of Jesus or at least the significance of Jesus' physical death (the "in the flesh" of 4:2–3). The affirmation of 5:6 is undoubtedly a response to this deficient view of Jesus.

But it is much more difficult to say with any certainty how this formulation is best understood. In this context, John insists that Jesus Christ came "not . . . by water only," but "by water and blood" (v. 6). Many interpreters have taken this as a reference to the sacraments of baptism and the Lord's Supper. This makes little sense, though, in the context of a debate over the nature of Jesus Christ. Another suggestion is that the water and blood refer to the fluids that flowed from Jesus' side (see John 19:34); this would be a way, then, of denoting Jesus' death in particular. A problem with this reading is that "came by" seems awkward. The two terms are best understood as referring to events in the earthly life of the Word made flesh (John 1:1, 14; 1 John 1:1–2). "Water" probably speaks of Jesus' baptism by John and "blood" signifies his death.

We must acknowledge, however, that we can only be tentative in this explanation as to why John insists that Jesus did not come "by water only," but "by water and blood." It was suggested early in church history that this language relates to the teaching of the opponents, adopted from Cerinthus (see the Introduction for comments on Cerinthus). Presumably they denied a clear identification of the divine Christ, the Son of God, with the human Jesus. They may have admitted that the Spirit of God came upon Jesus at his baptism, given the tradition from the Gospel of John (John 1:32–34). But they would have denied, in this reconstruction, the presence of the Son of God when the human Jesus died on the cross.

In other words, in the terminology of the opponents, the divine presumably "came [on Jesus] in [*en*] water." John insists, however, that since Jesus was the eternal Word, he was the Christ, the Son of God throughout his time on earth, *including his death on the cross*; adapting their language, John stresses that Jesus came "in [*en*] water and in [*en*] blood." Taken together with the pointed references to Jesus' death as an "atoning sacrifice" (2:2; 4:10), this reference suggests that it is the saving significance of the genuinely human Son of God that the writer most desires to affirm in the face of the false teachers.

The Spirit of God testifies to this truth because the "Spirit is the truth." In the Johannine tradition, more than in any other New Testament tradition, the role of the Holy Spirit is to bear witness or to testify to Jesus (John 14:26; 15:26; 16:13–15). Because his primary role is to focus on Jesus, who is the truth (14:6), he is called the Spirit of truth (14:17; 16:13; 1 John 4:6). The Spirit is brought into the discussion at this point because of the allusion to Jesus' baptism. In association with the tradition concerning that baptism, the Baptist testified that he saw the Spirit coming and remaining on Jesus (John 1:32–34). If the opponents were claiming that the Spirit rested on Jesus temporarily, John may be seeking to rebut their case by reiterating the Spirit's role as witness to the true identity of Jesus and by using one of his favorite words, "remain," to stress the permanence of the Spirit's presence. Also, the opponents apparently claimed the anointing of the Spirit for themselves. But as 3:24–4:6 makes quite clear, the Spirit of God *cannot* be associated with anything less than a full confession of Jesus as the Son of God.

Then follows a remarkable torrent of uses of the word group based on the Greek root *martyr*: *martyreo* ("testify") in verses 6, 7, 9, and 10, and *martyria* ("a witness") in verses 9 (3x), 10 (2x), and 11. The only other two times when this word group is used in 1 John is also in connection with the truth that Jesus Christ is the Son of God (1:2; 4:14). John seems to have reserved this terminology for the most important purpose he has in writing this book: bearing solemn testimony to the person of Jesus, the divine Son. The Spirit, the water of his baptism, and the blood of the cross are united ("one") in their witness to Jesus; each points to the truth of the writer's proclamation about Jesus. (On the additional words of v. 7 in the KJV referring to the Father, the Word, and the Holy Ghost, see Brown, pp. 775–87.)

The Gospel of John had set a precedent for the "witness" motif. For example, in a short section of John 5, the following are said to "bear witness" to Jesus: Jesus himself (John 5:31), God (5:32, 37), John the Baptist (5:33), Jesus' works (5:36), and the Scriptures (5:39). God's testimony is greater than a human being's testimony, and we accept it (1) because t is the testimony of God and thus utterly reliable, and (2) because it is testimony about God's Son and so is infinitely more important than the common matters about which people give testimony.

Inherent in this reasoning is the principle that if a truth of lesser import is established, so much the more is the truth of a greater import established. If we accept human testimony about matters of minor import, surely we must accept God's testimony about matters of spiritual life and death. This divine testimony is in the heart of the person who believes in the Son of God. Verse 10 presents the reader with three uses of the verb "to believe" and three uses of the word group "witness." The one who does not believe God has made him out to be a liar (see 1:10) because he has not believed the "testimony that God has given" about his Son. This is the testimony: God has given to believers eternal life, which, in Johannine terminology, refers to the quality of existence that derives from fellowship with God (see notes on 1:2). And this life is (only) in his Son. Simply put: The person who has the Son has life, but the one who does not have the Son does not have life. To "have" the Son, of course, means to believe in Jesus Christ in accord with God's revelation of him. All else hinges on this truth.

5. Concluding Remarks (5:13–21)

5.1. The Assurance of Eternal Life and Our Approach to God (5:13–15)

The statement of purpose in 5:13 supports our contention that in 5:1–12 the writer has brought the argument to its most fundamental level. Throughout the book there is evidence that 1 John was written to provide the readers the criteria by which they might know that they were children of God and that they therefore had eternal life.

It is crucial to observe that this assurance was not based on their having love for fellow believers or on not sinning. Eternal life was rooted in believing in the name of the Son of God. This connection is virtually the same one made in the statement of purpose in John 20:31—that the reader might believe that Jesus is the Christ, the Son of God, and thereby might have life in his name ("the name" is a stylistic way of referring to all that Jesus is, so that believing in the Son in 1 John 5:10 is no different from believing in his name in 5:13). Note also that though love for fellow believers is one of the two central themes of this book, this concern is absent from both the prologue and the conclusion. The writer began in the prologue with what is most important: the faithful proclamation of the truth that God has provided divine life, and this life is in his incarnate Son, Jesus Christ (1:1–2). The final section returns to this same important theme: proper belief in Jesus as the Son of God for eternal life.

This belief in Jesus is the basis of the love for fellow believers commanded by God and for the absence of sin called for in 1 John. It also is the basis of the confidence with which we can approach God with our requests. In 3:21–22, this confidence in prayer was tied to the fact that we do the things that please him; verse 23 specified these things as belief in Jesus and love for fellow believers. In 5:14, "this" confidence is narrowed to the belief iterated in verse 13. When believers are "in" God and God is "in" them (cf. 2:24; 3:6, 24; 4:4, 12, 13, 15, 16; 5:20), they know that whatever they ask "according to his will" will be granted.

The Gospel of John and 1 John contribute key insights into Christian prayer. Does God grant "anything" that we request? Jesus, in John 14:14, tells his disciples: "You may ask me for anything in my name, and I will do it." Some might take this to be an unlimited promise that whatever is asked will be granted, so long as "in Jesus' name" is tacked on at the end of the prayer. But "in my name" involves much more than mouthing a few words. To do something "in the name" of someone is to act not only with the authority of the other, but in accord with that person's character and will. Thus, Jesus was sent by the Father, with the authority of the Father, and acted in accord with the Father's character and will: "in my Father's name" (John 5:43; 10:25). The effectiveness of believers' prayer is also tied to the purpose for what is requested: that the Father may be glorified (14:13). Subsequent references in the Gospel indicate that petitions will be granted so that the believers will be fruitful (15:16) and their joy be made complete (16:24). This letter adds that we receive what we ask because we obey God's commands and do what pleases him (1 John 3:22), and, in this text, when we ask "according to his will."

The overall picture of Christian prayer, then, is that when the child of God is living in accord with the known will of God and makes a request aimed at glorifying God and at being fruitful in God's work, God will do what is asked. The wrong motives that lead to selfish prayer (James 4:3) can be avoided if we hold fast to his teaching: "If you remain in me and my words remain in you, ask whatever you wish, and it will be given you" (John 14:7).

5.2. The Sin That Leads to Death (5:16–17)

The practice of prayer remains the subject in verse 16, where the reader is exhorted to pray for a fellow believer in a particular circumstance. What exactly John has in mind in verses 16–17, however, is questionable. Prayer should be made for a fellow believer who commits a sin "that does not lead to death." This sin is contrasted starkly with "a sin that leads to death." The writer makes clear that he is not directing that prayer be made in that case.

Some have read in these phrases the basis for the distinction between "mortal" (serious enough to lead to death) and "venial" (minor) sins. Others hold that this refers to intentional and unintentional sins, the latter being forgivable and the former not (Num. 15:22–30). But it is more advisable to interpret these otherwise unknown terms in the context of the conflict with the opponents that lies behind the entire book. "Death" is the arena in which those people live who have not been born of God. "Anyone who does not love remains in death" (1 John 3:14). This passage, among many others in 1 John, is directed at the false teachers. The latter part of 5:12 could well be restated: He who does not have the Son of God is in death. So John is stating that although all wrongdoing is sin (v. 17), some sin does not result in a loss of spiritual life in Christ. But there is a sin that does result in death: the denial that Jesus Christ is the Son of God.

The urgency of the threat has led John to emphasize the need to pray for a "brother" in the believing community. Similarly, the Johannine writings focus on the need to love other believers (John 13:14; 15:12, 17; 1 John 3:11, 23; 2 John 5). But just as this concern does not negate a different command to love our enemies (Matt. 5:44), 1 John 5:16-17 does not imply that we should refrain from praying for unbelievers. God sent his Son so that those in the unbelieving world might be saved from their sins (2:2; 4:14).

5.3. The Children of God Kept From the Evil One and in the True God (5:18–20)

Verse 18 repeats 3:9 and then adds that the "one who was born of God [i.e., Jesus] keeps him safe," and the evil one (i.e., the devil, cf. 3:7–12) cannot touch him. We know that we, as children of God, are kept safe from and even have overcome the evil one (2:13–14), because the Son of God came to destroy his works (3:8). Yet unbelievers, who comprise the world, do the devil's work (3:7–12) and are under his control (5:19; lit., the world "lies in" the evil one).

The reference to Jesus as the "one who was born of God" is unique. It is also a bit surprising since the language of being born of God uniformly has been used in describing believers. There is a significant alteration in verb tense, however. The believer "has been born" of God—this tense (the perfect tense) emphasizes a present status (now we are the children of God [3:2]) based on a birth in the past. The reference to Jesus Christ as "the one who was born of God" is in what is called the aorist tense, which denotes that at a specific time in the past the Son of God was born into human existence (John 1:1, 14; Luke 1:32; 1 John 1:1–2). In Johannine terminology the distinction is maintained: Jesus is the Son, we are children; Jesus "was born of God," we "have been born of God." By his unique birth, then, the Son has come and given us understanding that we may know him who is true.

Though "him who is true" (v. 20) could easily be Jesus, with whom the adjective "true" is often associated in the Gospel of John (John 1:9; 6:32; 8:16; 15:1), the wording of the following phrase indicates that it refers to God, who is true (7:28; 17:3). The coming of Jesus has allowed us to know God (1:14, 18; 17:3, 6, 26).

The next sentence in verse 20 states literally: "And we are in him who is true in his Son Jesus Christ." The NIV has added the word "even," thereby acknowledging that the "in" can be taken in more than one way. It can simply mean that we are "in" both God and his Son. But a survey of Johannine writing suggests that "in" has the sense of "through" here: Through our belief in the Son we are also "in" God the Father. Being in God is only possible when one is in the Son (John 3:36; 1 John 5:12). He is the true God, and he "is" eternal life. That is, eternal life is to know the only true God and Jesus Christ, whom God sent (John 17:3).

Note once again the repetition of "we know" (the beginning words of verses 18, 19, and 20). To the last, John is intent on assuring his readers of their being God's children. In contrast to the opponents who, with the rest of the world, are "in" the evil one, those who are "in" Jesus Christ the Son of God are "in" God.

5.4. Final Warning (5:21)

First John does not follow a formal letter form. Yet 5:21 reads like a concluding statement. What is interesting is that in this last sentence we find a word unique in the Gospel and letters of John. The word "idol" regularly in the New Testament refers to images associated with pagan worship and forbidden in the Mosaic law (Ex. 20:4). (There are ten other places where this word is used in the New Testament, and it always refers to pagan images [see, e.g., 1 Cor. 8:4, 7].) It might be concluded, then, that such consistent usage requires that meaning here—that the writer is warning against worship of pagan images.

The telling argument against this understanding, however, is that it has nothing to do with anything else John has written in this letter. It is difficult to believe that he would with such tenacity focus on two key points throughout the entire work (belief in the Son and love for fellow believers) and then conclude with a reference to something totally disconnected from these concerns. It seems better, then, to understand the reference to "idols" figuratively. An idol, in a wider sense, can be anything that is made the object of devotion or attention and that displaces ultimate devotion to the one true God. John has just reiterated that we have come to know this God and that this knowledge is possible only through his Son, Jesus Christ. An idol, then, is anything that prevents the true worship (John 4:23–24) required by God. The rejection of God's own testimony about his Son is thus idolatry.

This is what the false teachers represent. By their failure to accept what God has said, they state that God is a liar (1 John 5:10). They have subordinated God and his word to reason, to experience, or to whatever might be the basis for their denial of the Son. This is idolatry. So, in line with the whole of 1 John, John's parting comment about the opponents is: Stay away from them!

OUTLINE OF 2 JOHN

1. **Salutation** (vv. 1–3)
2. **Walking in Love** (vv. 4–6)
3. **Remaining in the Teaching of Christ** (vv. 7–11)
4. **Final Greeting** (vv. 12–13)

COMMENTARY ON 2 JOHN

1. Salutation (vv. 1–3)

Unlike 1 John, 2 John follows the standard letter format. The first three verses comprise what is called the salutation. This includes (1) the sender, (2) the recipient(s), and (3) a blessing. (1) The sender identifies himself as "the elder." For a brief consideration of the authorship of 2 John, consult the introduction to these letters. "The elder" here may simply denote an older man (see, e.g., Acts 2:17). Or it may refer to an official either in the Jewish community (often linked in the Gospels with the chief priests) or in the early Christian church; the reference in Acts 14:23, for example, seems not to require a certain minimal age. We are well aware of the importance of such individuals both from Acts, where they are linked to the apostles (Acts 15) and from Paul's writings (1 Tim. 5:17; Titus 1:5).

What we can conclude with some assurance is that "the elder" knows and is known by the readers, and that he addresses the readers as someone having authority. He expects his readers to follow his instructions regarding what they should believe and how they should behave (vv. 7–11). Perhaps the elder has the responsibility of overseeing a number of congregations that are associated to some degree; the "lady" and the "sister" of verses 1 and 13 are best understood as figurative references to churches. If the tradition is correct in identifying the elder as the apostle John, 2 John may have been written from Ephesus to a congregation some distance away that he may have visited from time to time (v. 12). Third John 13–14 is parallel to verse 12. Its recipient,

Gaius, may be a member of another congregation in this association.

(2) The "chosen lady" is best understood, then, as one of these congregations, and "her children" is a way of referring to the believers in that church. In Johannine language, we are children of God, of course, but in a secondary sense, the elder can refer to believers as "my children" (3 John 4). In addition, the sense of "belonging to" something can be described in terms of being a child or a son (John 12:36; 1 Thess. 5:5, 8).

The word "chosen" is the same one translated "elect" in the NIV in such verses as Mark 13:20, 22; Titus 1:1; and 1 Peter 1:1. These texts, along with others, indicate that this term was commonly used as a synonym for believers. The verbal form is often used as well to emphasize that believers have been chosen or selected. Note, for example, in the Gospel of John: "You did not choose me, but I chose you" (John 15:16; cf. also 6:70; 13:18). The manifest importance of personal responsibility seen in this letter does not negate the truth that the church consists of those who are the elect of God (see also v. 13). This tension is parallel to that found in the Gospel of John, where "whoever believes" (e.g., 3:16–21) must be balanced with the language of God's sovereign choosing (e.g., 10:25–29).

As in 1 John 3:18 (see notes there), the phrase "in truth" means more than "truly"; it is roughly the equivalent of Paul's "in Christ." The elder writes that his love for these believers is shared by "all who know the truth," that is, by true believers. Further, the wording of verse 2 suggests that this love exists "because of the truth." It is the truth that is found only in Jesus Christ that provides the basis for the love shared among his followers. This truth "lives [again, as in 1 John, the word is 'remain' or 'abide'] in" believers, and it, like the Spirit of truth who guides into all truth (John 16:13), "will be with us forever" (cf. 14:16).

(3) The greeting of verse 3 combines the same three elements of Christian experience as do 1 Timothy 1:2 and 2 Timothy 1:2. This similarity and the fact that these words are fairly rare in Johannine books suggests that the elder is using standard language for a greeting. "Grace" is the favor God demonstrates toward us when we can offer nothing to merit such favor (John 1:14, 17; Rom. 3:24; Eph. 2:8). "Mercy" speaks of the compassion that God displays in saving us (Luke 1:50, 54; Titus 3:5). "Peace" is the state of well-being denoted by the Hebrew *shalom*. It is rooted in right standing with God (Rom. 5:1) and extends to our relations with others (Eph. 2:14–18). The Gospel of John records Jesus promising his followers a peace that defies the trouble of the world (John 14:27; 16:33).

As is common in the salutation of New Testament letters, God the Father and Jesus, his

The Basilica of Augustus at Ephesus was built in the first century A.D., after the time when the apostle John served as pastor of the church there.

on, are the source of these blessings. The fact ıat verse 3 concludes with "in truth and love" ; significant for two reasons. (a) This is the ɔurth time in John's salutation that "truth" is ited. This indicates that what is true is as cruial to the purpose of 2 John as it was in 1 John :f. vv. 7–11). (b) "Truth and love" reflect the mphasis on proper belief in Jesus Christ :ruth) and proper conduct toward others ove), evident also in 1 John (see notes bove). This twofold emphasis neatly serves to ivide the bulk of 2 John: love in verses 4–6, uth in verses 7–11.

. Walking in Love (vv. 4–6)

he focus on truth continues into verse 4. The lder rejoices because he has found certain ıembers of this church "walking in the truth." he connotation of truth in the Johannine writıgs and the parallel in verses 7–11 to the cris in 1 John suggest that "walking in the truth" another variation on the theme of remaining the faithful teaching about Jesus Christ in the ıce of the false teaching of the antichrists, who alk in darkness (1 John 1:6; 2:11). It probably an be concluded that since "some" of the comunity are walking in the truth, others are not. hese others may be sharing in the wicked ork of the opponents (2 John 11).

The language of the Father commanding ɜnd of v. 4) is comparable to 1 John 3:23, here the Father's command is summarized y believing in the Son (truth) and loving one nother. Thus, it is not surprising that in verse the church ("dear lady") is called to love one nother; this is one of the most characteristic ıemes in the Johannine books (John 13:34–5; 15:12, 17; 1 John 3:11; 4:7, 11). Similarly, ıe statement that this command is not new but ne known from the beginning of the Christın community is also found in 1 John 2:7.

The flow of thought from verse 5 to verse 6 uplicates that found in 1 John 5:3: The love ıat God requires can be equated with keeping is commands. Jesus told his disciples that ıey would remain in his love and be his iends if they kept his commands (John 15:10, 4). In 1 John especially, practical love shown others is a test by which true children of God an be distinguished from the children of the evil (1 John 3:10–15). Since believers are ıdwelt by God, who is love, they will display ıe divine love that acts sacrificially for others (4:7–21). The New Testament can describe love as a "fruit of the Spirit" (Gal. 5:22), suggesting that love will develop naturally from the indwelling Spirit.

Yet the Johannine tradition confronts us also with the important truth that love is not essentially a feeling or even an attitude. Love is sacrificial conduct. This is love: God sent his Son for us (1 John 4:9). This is how we know what love is: Jesus Christ laid down his life for us (3:16). As a result, this is love in our lives: to act sacrificially on behalf of fellow believers (3:16; 4:11, 19–21). This obligation is the daily, continual call on the believer—to walk in love.

3. Remaining in the Teaching of Christ (vv. 7–11)

As discussed in the introduction to the Johannine letters, the "deceivers" who are causing the trouble that has led to the writing of 2 John, may be identified with the opponents in 1 John (where they are called "false prophets" [4:1] and "antichrists" [2:18]). The root word behind the term "deceivers" is uniformly applied to the opponents in the first letter. They deceive themselves when they claim to be without sin (1 John 1:8). They are characterized by a spirit of deceit, in contrast to the Spirit of truth (4:6). They are actively seeking to win the allegiance of members of the faithful community by deceit (2:26; 3:7). This was the crisis that was calling forth the writing of both 1 and 2 John.

The language of "many" who have "gone out into the world" is paralleled in 1 John 4:1; 2:19 supplements this by stating that it was "from us" that they "went out." These deceivers, then, had been members of the Johannine community. Their primary description is that they "do not acknowledge Jesus Christ as coming in the flesh." The parallel to 1 John 4:2–3 is unmistakable, though the verb tense for "come" is different here (a present tense) from that in 1 John 4:2 (a perfect tense). Some scholars have argued that this change indicates a difference in meaning, possibly that the 2 John "coming" refers to the presence of Christ in the elements of the Lord's Supper. But we regularly find variations of terminology in Johannine writing for stylistic rather than substantive reasons. Thus, it seems preferable to take 1 John 4:2 and 2 John 7 as referring to the same thing—Jesus Christ came in the flesh.

In some Pauline passages, "flesh" refers to what is in conflict with the Spirit and is by definition evil (Rom. 8:1–17). It does not carry that connotation here, however. Rather, "flesh" speaks of humanity. The Word, who is God, became flesh, that is, became a human being, and lived among us (John 1:1, 14). We are ignorant of the precise details of the teaching of the deceivers. But as discussed in the introduction, it seems to involve a denial of the real humanity of the Son of God or at least a denial of the essential significance of his humanity for his saving work on the cross. This best explains the emphasis in 1 John on the "atoning sacrifice for our sins" (1 John 2:2; 4:10) since this terminology was not used in the Gospel of John.

We do not know when or how some of those involved in this Christian community came to "deny" (1 John 2:22–23) Jesus as the Christ, the Son of God. But their abandonment of the truth has served to reveal their true nature and the fact that they never really belonged to the Christian fellowship (2:19).

The elder at this point is concerned not with the opponents per se, but with his readers and the possibility of their being won over by these deceivers and antichrists. Therefore he calls on them to "watch out" (v. 8). What they have worked for may be lost. We are reminded of the instruction of Jesus to "work for" food that endures to eternal life, food given by the Son of Man. That passage demonstrates that what may seem to be an overly narrow focus on believing in Jesus in 1 and 2 John is founded in the tradition of the Lord himself. When asked what was the "work" God requires, Jesus replied with a prototypical narrowing: "The work of God is this: to believe in the one he has sent" (John 6:29). What believers have worked for is a full reward from God. They hope for the return of Christ, for they will not be judged but will be like their Lord (1 John 2:28; 3:2; 4:17). The readers must be on guard lest this standing be lost.

The wording of verse 9 is intriguing. The "teaching of Christ" could mean either Christ's own teaching handed down through faithful witnesses or teaching about Christ. It is true that the repetition of Jesus' command to love one another (John 13:34; 15:12) in the letters (1 John 3:11; 2 John 5) indicates that the actual teaching given by Jesus was preserved in this community. Indeed, the prologue of 1 Joh declares that the faithful witnesses have passe on to the readers what "we have heard." Yet given the thrust of verse 7, the second possibility seems more likely. The concern of th elder at this point is not the faithful transmission of instruction from Jesus, but correc teaching about him, specifically affirming hi humanity. The believer must continue (lit "remain") in this teaching.

In a section similarly concerned with th dangerous beliefs about Christ held by th opponents, John exhorts his readers to "se that what you have heard from the beginnin remains in you" (1 John 2:24). Note tha "remaining" is not a passive concept. It is concerted act of will and action by which fals teaching is resisted and truth is proclaimed Unless one forcibly maintains a certain path another may divert one's direction and "lea astray" (NIV of 1 John 2:26; 3:7). The possibility of turning to what is false become greater as we fail to renew our commitment t what is true. The person who continues in thi true teaching, however, has the Father and th Son. The Johannine tradition makes the poin that one cannot "have" God without acceptin the Son; to accept one is to accept both, and t reject one is to reject both (John 5:23; 12:44 15:23; 1 John 2:23).

Since, therefore, remaining in the teachin of Christ means to believe in Jesus in the wa commanded by God, it means "having" th Father and the Son. This phrase is equivalen to being "in" God (1 John 2:24; 4:15) or having life (5:12). The Christian's fellowship i with the Father and with his Son, Jesus Chris (1:3). The opponents have failed to continue i this teaching. Instead, they have "run ahead (2 John 9). In the introduction to these letter we suggested that the opponents may hav believed that their experience of the Spir enabled them to advance beyond the traditional teaching handed down from Jesu through his disciples. They may have centere their attention on the Spirit rather than Jesus because the Spirit teaches all things (Joh 14:26) and guides into all truth (16:13). In an case, to fail to hold firm to the teaching c Christ is to be separated from God.

The dynamics of the situation is illuminate somewhat by verses 10–11. The elder i removed from the recipients by some distanc le is aware that "some" of the congregation re walking in the truth (v. 4). This fact sug-ests that some are not doing so. False rophets have left the believing community, spousing a view of Christ that, if assumed, vill result in spiritual death. How, then, does he elder instruct his readers to proceed in these ense circumstances? *He requires total sepa-ation from them.* Anyone who comes to ohn's readers not bringing this teaching of Christ should not be received into their houses.

This reference in verse 10 may have the ense of not taking in someone for lodging. But the sense may be closer to the command ot to allow one of these false teachers to be velcomed at a house-church gathering. This atter sense may be suggested by the absence f the "your" in the Greek before "house" and y the obvious concern here with teaching. Teaching most naturally occurs at a scheduled neeting of the believers in a house church. Since the teaching of the opponents is spiritual oison, it is essential that they not be allowed ny opportunity to administer it. They are to be efused entrance to such a gathering. They hould not even be "welcomed."

The word "welcome" was the common reeting used at personal meetings (see Matt. 6:49; 28:9) and in the greeting of letters (James :1). The prohibition, then, may be stronger than imply a refusal to welcome such a person into he home or house church. It may even extend o the refusal to speak a greeting on the street. Should this be the intention, it would resemble he practice of exclusion from the synagogue John 9:23; 12:42; 16:2), in which the person ut out was treated socially as one who did not xist. Paul's directions for treatment of one who rofesses Christianity and yet lives in an mmoral manner (1 Cor. 5:11) reflect a similar pproach. The recipients are to have nothing to lo with such a person, for to welcome him into house or possibly even to speak a greeting to im is to "share in his wicked work."

The fact that his work is "wicked" identifies t with the devil, who is called "the wicked [evil] ne" in 1 John 3:12; 5:18–19. Scripture links the ast days with the appearance of false prophets nd false christs to deceive many (Matt. 24:5, 1, 23–24; 1 John 2:18). Furthermore, the ppearance of a figure commonly identified as he antichrist is specifically associated with leception in the last days (2 Thess. 2:1–12; Rev. 13; cf. 2 John 7). This is no different from being one of the "antichrists" (1 John 2:18) or having the "spirit of the antichrist" (4:3). John therefore requires a refusal to grant any aid or encour-agement whatsoever.

4. Final Greeting (vv. 12–13)

The feeling expressed by the elder is one with which most of us are familiar. Writing is a mar-velous means of communication. But there are times when we sense the limitations of the form. The elder has much to share with these believers. So he hopes to visit them and speak face to face. The Greek uses an idiom, which literally reads to speak "mouth to mouth." The equivalent of "meet face to face" or "have a heart-to-heart talk," the expression is used in the Old Testament, including one instance describing how God communicated with Moses (Num. 12:8). It is the intimacy of per-sonal dialogue that the elder anticipates. The love he holds (see 2 John 1) for his readers, seen most clearly in the letter through his con-cern for their spiritual welfare, can in that way be best expressed. In the intimacy of personal fellowship, the seemingly harsh words of verses 10–11 will be tempered by the "grace, mercy and peace" (v. 3) of God seen in the elder.

No doubt the elder is concerned about those not included in the "some" who were walking in the truth (v. 4). A personal visit, he hopes, will not only solidify the faith of some, but also, possibly, call to account those whose walk may be in danger. We know from 3 John that the elder was rebuffed by an individual of some authority and that the elder's fellow believers were refused hospitality. The elder himself may have wondered at his own recep-tion. But his attitude in the letter is positive. He hopes to fellowship with them so that "our joy may be complete" (2 John 12).

This language of this hope is probably rooted in the promise of Jesus to his disciples that "your joy may be complete" (John 15:11; 16:24). Such joy was contingent on believers "remaining" in the Son, as the Gospel passages make clear. One thing that is in danger from the influence of the false teachers, then, is the joy of Christian life in God. First John, with its warnings against the deceivers, was written "to make our joy complete" (1 John 1:4). And when the elder finds some of the members of the community maintaining their belief in the Son and their commitment to his commands, he receives "great joy" (2 John 4; cf. 3 John 4). Jesus had promised his disciples his "peace," unlike that of the world (John 14:27); his peace would sustain them through times of trial. In a similar way, Jesus tied his joy "in" his followers to his sharing his words with them (John 17:13). The elder makes the same appeal. The joy of the Son will be completed in the believers only if they remain firmly in the "teaching of Christ" (v. 9).

The notes on verse 1 suggested that the "chosen lady" was a figurative way of referring to a church, and "her children" were the members of this church. Similarly, then, "the children of your chosen sister" likely refers to the members of the congregation where the elder lives. The manner in which he concludes the letter serves not only to send final greetings, but also to remind his readers of their participation in the community of faith that extends to the congregation from which he writes. These are the ones who know the truth (v. 1), who love them because they share the indwelling divine truth (v. 2). They, with the elder, stand with the recipients in their commitment to walking in the commands of the Lord.

OUTLINE OF 3 JOHN

1. **Salutation** (vv. 1–2)
2. **Gaius Commended** (vv. 3–8)
   - **2.1.** Gaius Commended for Faithfulness (vv. 3–4)
   - **2.2.** Gaius Commended for Hospitality (vv. 5–8)
3. **Diotrephes Denounced** (vv. 9–10)
4. **Exhortation to Good** (vv. 11–12)
   - **4.1.** Imitation of the Good (v. 11)
   - **4.2.** Demetrius as an Example (v. 12)
5. **Final Words and Greeting** (vv. 13–14)

COMMENTARY ON 3 JOHN

1. Salutation (vv. 1–2)

This letter gives every indication of having been penned by "the elder" who was responsible for 2 John (see notes on 2 John 1). Like 2 John, this work conforms to the standard letter form of the time. In contrast to 2 John, however, the recipient is an individual (Gaius) rather than a congregation. We are aware of a Gaius who was a companion of Paul (Acts 19:29; Rom. 16:23), but we are no doubt dealing with a different person here. He is called a "dear friend" (so also in 3 John 2, 5, 11). This address is the singular form of the word used a number of times in 1 John as an address to the believers (e.g., 1 John 2:7; 4:1). It is based on the root word for "love" (*agape*) and so is rendered "beloved" in the KJV. The elder elaborates on his affection for Gaius in that he loves (*agapao*) him in the truth (cf. 2 John 1). "In the truth," as was noted on 2 John 1, amounts to a Johannine version of "in Christ," who is the truth and in whom alone is found the truth.

Third John lacks the "greeting" per se, as it is found in 2 John 3 and in most New Testament letters. On the other hand, 3 John does include what is unique in the New Testament but familiar in secular letters of the period: a "health wish." First-century letters often included after the greeting a "prayer" or "wish" for the health and well-being of the addressee. John expresses a desire that Gaius may be prospering and in good health as his soul is prospering. The subsequent verses testify to the welfare of Gaius's spiritual life. He demonstrates faithfulness to the truth, steadfastness in walking in the truth, and love and hospitality, all of which speak of the genuineness of his spiritual experience.

The "soul" can have many connotations in the New Testament. The prevalent usage in the Johannine literature is in the context of the idea of "laying down one's life [soul]," as in 1 John 3:16. But the sense here appears to be closer to the sense of the "inner person," as when Jesus said that his "soul" was troubled (John 12:27). The elder's prayer is that Gaius might have physical health and well-being commensurate with his spiritual person. Since this concern is a common element in a letter of the first century, it is inappropriate to claim that this verse teaches that God intends all believers to live in material prosperity. One can find hardly anything in the Johannine tradition to support such an idea. Indeed, Jesus told his disciples that they could expect nothing better than he himself had experienced: They would be hated, put out of the synagogues, and killed for their faith (John 15:18–16:4). The sight of a believer lacking material possessions should not lead to teaching in faith-building techniques, but to meeting of his or her needs by sacrificial giv-ıg (1 John 3:17–18).

. Gaius Commended (vv. 3–8)

2.1. *Gaius Commended for Faithfulness (vv. 3–4)*

Some believers have delivered a good ›port regarding Gaius. We cannot be certain ʻho these "brothers" (a common designation ›r Christians in John 20:17; 21:23; and in the ›hannine letters) are or what has caused them › travel from the region in which Gaius lives › that of the elder. It is possible, though, that ıey may be identified with the brothers men-oned in verse 5 and/or verse 10. One scenario as these believers being sent by the elder to ıe church over which Diotrephes (verse 9) has ıfluence, subsequently finding hospitality om Gaius, and returning to the elder to report n what has happened. In any case, they testify › the faithfulness of Gaius and to his persis-›nce (the present tense of the verb) in Chris-an conduct.

The language of verse 3 is similar to that ›und in 2 John 4: the elder has received "great ›y" because of reports of those who are walking in the truth." We have seen that both and 2 John were written primarily to prevent ıeir readers from straying from the teaching f Christ that constitutes the truth (2 John 9). ı the midst of the influence of the false teach-rs, the elder no doubt feels great relief along ʻith great joy when he hears that some, at ›ast, are maintaining the faith (1 John 2:18–7; 4:1–6; 2 John 4, 7–8).

Unlike 1 and 2 John, however, 3 John pro-ides no indication of a conflict over Christol-gy. Diotrephes may be in doctrinal error, but ıe elder does not state that this is the case. As ıe letter itself will show, the issue is one of ehavior, and so "walking in the truth" (v. 4) ı this case may refer predominantly to love ›r the brothers. First John gives ample evi-ence of the Johannine association of love with ving in the truth (1 John 2:3–11; 3:16–19). ›hn thinks of those like Gaius as his children, ı the same way that he considers those to ʻhom he writes 1 John as his children (1 John :1). They are his spiritual dependents, if you ʻill. This relationship explains the manner in ʻhich he both gives directives (2 John 10–11) nd expresses displeasure when his instruc-tions are not followed (3 John 9–11). Both physical and spiritual parents can relate to the sentiment expressed by the elder in verse 4.

2.2. *Gaius Commended for Hospitality (vv. 5–8)*

The present tense of "you are faithful" again suggests that this is Gaius's continuing practice. He has served his brothers in Christ, though they may be strangers to him. In light of verse 10, "the brothers" are those who are in some way associated with the elder, at least some of whom are unknown to Gaius. In contrast to Diotrephes, Gaius has welcomed these broth-ers, and they have reported of Gaius's love before the church where the elder is situated.

This section serves not only as a commen-dation for past behavior, however. The elder goes on to exhort Gaius to similar conduct in the future when such brothers may return to him. They should be helped on their way with whatever material assistance they may need (cf. 1 Cor. 16:6, 11). The phrase "worthy of God" conveys the point so often made in 1 John: Those who claim to belong to God must act in a manner that reflects the nature and, in particular, the sacrificial love of God (1 John 1:5–6; 3:16–20; 4:7–21). Anything less than loving hospitality to traveling Chris-tian brothers would not "be worthy" of the God who is love (4:8, 16). John thus encourages continued hospitality, though the reader might infer from 3 John 9–10 that such conduct may cause Gaius trouble with Diotrephes. Others who have sought to be hospitable to these brothers have been put out of the church.

These brothers went out on their mission "for the sake of the Name." The absence of any word or phrase qualifying "the Name" (as in 1 John 3:23; 5:13) is unusual; one might expect at least a modifying "his" (2:12; cf. John 1:12, 20:31). This verse, then, provides one of the first examples of a usage that became common in early Christian literature. Jesus had come in the name of his Father (John 5:43; 10:25), meaning that he ministered as a representative of and with the authority of God. To say that Jesus made known the Father's name (17:6) is to say that Jesus made known the Father. In a similar way, Jesus grants the authority of his name to his disciples (14:13–14; 16:23–24), and believers in the book of Acts are baptized in his name. Particularly relevant for this usage is Jesus' prediction in John 15:21 of the rejection and persecution to be suffered by his followers: "They will treat you this way because of my name." Those who faithfully proclaim the message of Jesus will endure affliction from the ungodly simply because they bear "the Name" (Acts 5:41; 1 Peter 4:16–18).

These brothers receive no help from the pagans and even worse, active hostility from some who would have been expected to render assistance (vv. 9–10). Such brothers deserve hospitality. Those who grant it are those who "work together for the truth" of Jesus Christ, in contrast to those who share in the evil work of those who oppose the truth. Although a clear indication of a doctrinal battle over a correct belief in Jesus is lacking in 3 John, the distinction between those who represent the truth and those who do not is just as manifest.

3. Diotrephes Denounced (vv. 9–10)

The elder has written to "the church," presumably a reference to a congregation near where Gaius lives. Such a letter may have taken the form and tone of 2 John, also written by the elder. It gives the impression that the elder has some authority over the congregation addressed; he expects his prohibition of hospitality to false teachers in 2 John 7–11 to be followed. But the letter in this case has not been honored, because of the influence of an individual named Diotrephes, one "who loves to be first [among them]." He "will have nothing to do with us"; in other words, he rejects John's authority. The "among them" (not reflected in the NIV of v. 9) suggests that Gaius is not a part of the group or even the congregation involved. The manner in which verse 10 seems to inform Gaius of the actions of Diotrephes also suggests that Gaius is somewhat removed from the events described.

In any case, Diotrephes, whatever his position in this church, is thwarting the purposes of the elder. He does this by gossiping maliciously about him and those with whom he is associated, by refusing to welcome the brothers, and by stopping those who do wish to show these brothers hospitality and excluding them from the church. In other words, in a congregation some distance from the elder, an individual has gained enough power to oppose openly the authority the elder represents. He speaks "evil words" (lit. trans.) about the elder and those with him—words that have influ
enced the allegiance of at least some.

Rather sarcastically, the elder continues b
stating that, "not satisfied with that,
Diotrephes has gone further, even refusing t
accept "the brothers" who are associated wit
the elder. In fact, he is able to "put out" of th
church those who seek to offer them hospital
ity. This indicates that more than hostile word
are being spoken; those exhibiting rebelliou
conduct have gained control of the congrega
tion. The elder writes that if he comes, he wi
bring to the attention of all the actions c
Diotrephes. He assumes, of course, or at lea
hopes, that though "the brothers" who repre
sent him have been rejected, the elder himsel
will be received by the church.

4. Exhortation to Good (vv. 11–12)

4.1. Imitation of the Good (v. 11)

It is natural to imitate those whom we hold i
high regard. Children love to do things just a
their parents do them. In a similar manner, Pa
urged his spiritual children to imitate him (1 Co
4:16; 11:1; 1 Thess. 1:6; 2 Thess. 3:7–9), an
1 John emphasizes the necessity of followin
the example of Jesus (2:6; 3:16), which can b
said to be imitating God himself (Eph. 5:1
Though the neuter gender is used ("*what* is evil
and "*what* is good"), 2 John 11 makes clear th
John has the example of people in mind.

The person who does what is good is "fro
God" (on the sense of *ek*, translated "from" c
"of," see notes on 1 John 4:1–6), but the pe
son "who does what is evil has not seen God.
This statement is the sort of criterion for eval
uating true belief so prevalent in 1 John (e.g
3:7–10). The reader immediately thinks c
Diotrephes as one who "does what is evil."
can be concluded that he is not in right rela
tionship with God; unrighteous conduct belie
one's claim to have seen God (1 John 3:6).

4.2. Demetrius as an Example (v. 12)

Though Diotrephes may be a negativ
example, a man named Demetrius is cited a
one who does what is good and is thus worth
of emulation. The reason why he is introduce
at this point probably is that the elder is com
mending him to Gaius for future consideratio
In addition to citing the unanimous witnes
regarding him from every corner, the elder hin

self adds his testimony. He even adds a rather solemn statement of the reliability of his word (similar language is found to underscore the truth of the witness to Jesus' death in John 19:35). What this suggests is that Demetrius is unknown personally to Gaius, though Gaius may have heard the name before. He is not only a foil to Diotrephes in the elder's instruction, but may well be one who will soon be needing hospitality. It is possible that Demetrius has traveled with the letter, and 3 John 12 is a type of recommendation to Gaius.

The elder, therefore, makes it clear: Gaius's commendable hospitality (vv. 5–8) as a demonstration of his "walking in the truth" (v. 4) must be carried on. "The truth itself," as it were, testifies to Demetrius as one of the brothers whose work "for the truth" (v. 8) mandates hospitality. To imitate the inhospitality of Diotrephes would be to ally with what is evil over against what is from God (v. 11).

5. Final Words and Greeting (vv. 13–14)

The language in these two verses is remarkably akin to that of 2 John 12. The elder has much more to say, but he wants to wait to deal with those things until he can do so face to face (lit., as in 2 John, "mouth to mouth"). In our day of telephone and electronic mail, by which we can get immediate reaction, we have a hard time relating to the time it took to get a response. Paul's anxiety over the new converts in Thessalonica reached the point where he could not "stand it any longer" (1 Thess. 3:1, 5). His best option was to await the return of Timothy, his delegate, with news of their circumstances. The elder no doubt experienced many days of concern over the spiritual state of the distant churches in his charge.

One difference of verse 14 from 2 John 12 is that the elder adds the word "soon." This word regularly means "at once" or "immediately" in the New Testament and possibly reflects a greater urgency than in 2 John. Diotrephes is such a challenge to the authority of the elder and to the message he represents that a personal visit is needed right away. Since Gaius seems to be in the same general area, the elder hopes to see him in the near future. This possibility in itself provides an additional incentive to Gaius to maintain his high standards of behavior (cf. Philem. 22).

A peace greeting is common at either the beginning (2 John 3; often in Paul) or the ending (Gal. 5:16; Eph. 6:23; 1 Peter 5:14) of New Testament letters. Such a greeting finds its roots in the Hebrew *shalom* and/or the usage by Jesus himself (John 20:19, 21, 26). Especially in the Johannine tradition, this "peace" is one bestowed only by the Son (14:27; 16:33). "The friends" (either a term for believers or those who know Gaius) send their greetings as well. Finally, Gaius is instructed to greet "the friends ... by name." This may mean that the elder knows some believers there or simply that he desires the faithful to be greeted. The only other instance in the New Testament of the phrase translated "by name" is in John 10:3, which emphasizes the individual attention given by the shepherd to each sheep.

The elder, in his role as spiritual father, takes seriously his responsibility to guard the sheep entrusted to him. His letter and his intended visit give evidence that the threat posed by Diotrephes is a major concern to him. Gaius's personal contact with some of the elder's spiritual children is one way in which the elder strives to keep them walking in the truth (3 John 3–4).

BIBLIOGRAPHY

R. E. Brown, *The Letters of John*, AB (1982), 30; G. Burge, *The Anointed Community: The Holy Spirit in the Johannine Tradition* (1987); J. H. Charlesworth, ed., *John and Qumran* (1972); E. E. Ellis, *The World of St. John* (1984); T. F. Johnson, *1, 2 and 3 John*, NIBC (1993); E. Malatesta, *Interiority and Covenant*, Analecta Biblica 69 (1978); I. H. Marshall, *The Epistles of John*, NICNT (1978); P. Parker, "Two Editions of John," *JBL* 75 (1956): 303–14; S. S. Smalley, *1, 2, 3 John*, WBC (1984).

JUDE

Roger Stronstad

INTRODUCTION

1. Authorship

Jesus was the firstborn son of Mary and Joseph (Luke 2:7). By the time he begins his ministry, the family had grown to include four younger brothers and an unspecified number of sisters. Mark identifies the four brothers of Jesus as "James, Joseph, Judas and Simon" (Mark 6:3), presumably listing them in order from the eldest to the youngest. In his list of Jesus' brothers Matthew reverses the order of the two youngest brothers (Matthew 13:55). The author of the letter that bears the name of Judas identifies himself as, "Jude [lit., Judas], a servant of Jesus Christ and a brother of James." Of the several Judes in the New Testament this one can only be Jude, one of the four younger brothers of Jesus.

In the early days of Jesus' public ministry his extended family did not accept him as the Messiah. One day, after a large crowd had gathered around Jesus, they came to take charge of him, explaining, "He is out of his mind" (Mark 3:21). Though this extended family may not have agreed with the judgment of the other members of the family, shortly after this Jesus' mother and his brothers also came to take him away (Mark 3:31–32). Later his brothers, not believing in him, taunted him about going up to Jerusalem at the Feast of Tabernacles to do miracles there and show himself to the world (John 7:1–5).

But prior to the day of Pentecost following the Passover during which Jesus was crucified, the picture has changed; in addition to the apostles, "Mary the mother of Jesus and his … brothers" are numbered among the 120 believers who are constantly in prayer (Acts 1:14). Later, when writing to the church in Corinth, Paul gives the explanation for the transition from the unbelief of the brothers (John 7:5) to their belief (Acts 1:14). When writing about the resurrection appearances of Jesus he reports: "Then he appeared to James" (1 Cor. 15:7). The New Testament is tantalizingly silent about whether or not Jesus also appeared to Jude and the other brothers. Regardless of whether Jesus did appear to them, the reality of his resurrection transformed Jude and his brothers into believers.

In time, James became a prominent leader in the church in Jerusalem (cf. Acts 15:12–21; Gal. 1:19; 2:9). In contrast, neither Jude nor his other two brothers, Joseph and Simon, are identified outside the Gospels. Nevertheless, like the other apostles and like Peter, Jude and his brothers traveled about with the Gospel (1 Cor. 9:5). It is in this context of a widespread ministry that Jude writes in his letter. Eusebius reports the tradition, which he found in Hegesippus, that the emperor Domitian (A.D. 81–96) ordered the execution of Jude's grandsons because they were descendants of David (Eusebius, *Ecc. Hist.*, 3.19.1).

2. Date and Place of Writing

In his salutation Jude gives no clues about either the date or the place of writing. Some infer a late, even postapostolic date for the letter from two of Jude's statements: (1) He writes about "the faith that was once for all entrusted to the saints" (v. 3), and (2) he calls upon his audience to "remember what the apostles of our Lord Jesus Christ foretold" (v. 17). But these statements do not necessarily imply a late date. The faith which was entrusted to the saints is the message of the gospel given to the disciples from the beginning and through them to their converts. Further, the apostolic prophecy about scoffers in the last days (vv. 17–18) implies neither that the apostles are dead nor that some future age has dawned, for they taught that with the outpouring of the Holy Spirit on Pentecost, the last days have already dawned (Acts 2:17).

The problem of immorality in the church, which is the issue Jude deals with in his letter, was not a late-developing problem. It arose as early as the time when Paul wrote to the churches of Galatia and Rome and continued to be a problem toward the end of the first century (Rev. 3:4). Based on these observations we can conclude that Jude must have written his letter during his active ministry. If 2 Peter borrows from Jude, then Jude must have written this letter some time earlier than Peter's martyrdom in Rome during the reign of Nero.

Jude also gives no direct information about either the place of writing or the destination of the letter. But his letter belongs to the milieu of Judaism. Most naturally, but by no means certainly, this locates the place of writing somewhere in Palestine. But we know from Paul's letter to the Corinthians that Jude (and the other brothers of Jesus) traveled throughout the Roman Empire (1 Cor. 9:5). Therefore, this letter may have been written from any one of those parts of the empire consistent with the Jewish atmosphere that Jude's letter breathes. Since there is a literary relationship between Jude and 2 Peter, its origin may be Rome itself, with its large mixed Jewish/Jewish-Christian community.

3. Recipients

Jude addresses his letter "to those who have been called, who are loved by God the Father and kept by Jesus Christ" (v. 1). These called, beloved, and kept Christians are a community, or communities, of Jewish Christians. The recipients may be living in Palestine itself or in some part of the world of the Diaspora, where Jews had accepted Jesus as their Christ or Messiah. The Jewish-Christian milieu of the letter is evident from the fact that it is steeped in the Old Testament, and it valued the pseudepigraphical writings.

Like the charismatic community that was established in Jerusalem beginning on the day of Pentecost (Acts 2:1–6:7), Jude's recipients are also a charismatic community. The apostles who spoke to them are prophets (Jude 17–18). In contrast, the false teachers in their midst, "do not have the Spirit" (v. 19). Through this accusation against the false teachers Jude implies that the apostles do have the Spirit; that is, that they are the true prophets. Further, without explanation, Jude instructs his audience to "pray in the Holy Spirit" (v. 20). He does not explain what he means by this instruction because he knows that this is part of the charismatic life of the community he now addresses.

4. Occasion and Purpose

Between the time Jude first contemplated writing to his audience and the time he actually writes, he learns about, "certain men ... [who] have secretly slipped in among you" (v. 4). Jude identifies these men as "dreamers" (v. 8), a word for charismatic prophets (Acts 2:17; cf., Joel 2:28). Toward the end of his letter Jude also observes that they "do not have the Spirit" (v. 19). These men, then, are probably itinerant (false) prophets who have come among the recipients of Jude's letter. Whatever claims they make in order to validate their ministry, it is evident that they are false prophets by the observations that they "change the grace of our God into a license for immorality and deny Jesus Christ our only Sovereign and Lord" (v. 4b). Thus, like the false teachers/prophets of 2 Peter, they advocate a moral libertinism, which is nothing less than a moral denial of Jesus.

In this context Jude writes with a threefold purpose. (1) On the one hand, his audience is to contend for the faith that was once for all delivered to them (v. 3) by the true prophets, the apostles (v. 17). On the other hand, they are to reject the "new" dream-revelation of the false prophets. (2) Jude also calls his audience to persevere in their Christian walk (vv. 17–21). (3) Finally, he calls his audience to preserve others in mercy (vv. 22–23).

OUTLINE

1. Address (vv. 1–2)

2. Warning Charge With Examples (vv. 3–16)

- **2.1.** Reason for the Charge—Infiltration of Ungodly Men (vv. 3–4)
- **2.2.** Reminder of Past Judgments (vv. 5–7)
  - **2.2.1.** Destruction of Those Who Did Not Believe (v. 5)
  - **2.2.2.** Celestial Judgment (v. 6)
  - **2.2.3.** Civic Judgment (v. 7)
- **2.3.** First Set of Character Traits (vv. 8–10)
  - **2.3.1.** Contrast to Angelic Submission to Authority (v. 9)
  - **2.3.2.** Trademark: Rebellion (v. 10)
  - **2.4.** Old Testament Prototypes (v. 11)
- **2.5.** Second Set of Character Traits (vv. 12–13)
  - **2.5.1.** First Metaphor—Broken Promises (v. 12)
  - **2.5.2.** Second Metaphor—Instability (v. 13)
- **2.6.** Surety of Judgment (vv. 14–16)

3. Call to Persevere (vv. 17–23)

3.1. Awareness of Present Situation (vv. 17–19)

3.2. Exhortations to Persevere (vv. 20–21)

3.3. Evangelize With Mercy (vv. 22–23)

4. Doxology (vv. 24–25)

COMMENTARY

1. Address (vv. 1–2)

Jude begins his letter with the standard formula for letters in the first century: sender, recipient, blessing (cf. Acts 15:23; 1 Peter 1:1). Jude identifies himself as a "servant of Jesus Christ" rather than as his brother. Some commentators believe this signifies humility on his part, while others think that Jude wishes to convey the truth that his birth relation to Christ as half brother in no way gave him preeminence or status. In fact, however, he is adopting a term that Peter, John, and Paul all use to identify themselves.

The threefold identification of the recipients is significant in respect to the rest of the letter. Jude addresses them as: (1) "those who have been called," (2) those "who are loved by God the Father," and (3) those who are "kept by Jesus Christ." The call of God goes out to all humanity (1 Peter 2:9). Jude is referring here to a call to salvation, not a specific call to ministry. He begins with this qualifier to distinguish his readers from those who deny the Lordship of Christ by their licentious actions. The reality of being loved by God is the basis for their calling. It is not grounded in anything they have done; rather, the love and mercy of God establishes their call. Later he will admonish them to "keep yourselves in God's love" (v. 21). Finally, Jude's audience receives the divine protection of Christ, the assurance of salvation; the ultimate security for the believer is that the Lord himself is keeping watch (cf. Ps. 121:7; 1 Peter 1:5).

Jude follows his address with a salutation, which is really a benediction: "Mercy, peace and love be yours in abundance." It is different from both Paul's characteristic benediction, "grace and peace to you" (e.g., Phil. 1:2; Col. 1:2), and Peter's, "grace and peace be yours" (1 Peter 1:2; 2 Peter 1:2). Jude begins his blessing with the word "mercy." The mercy of God, so great and unfathomable, pardons us from sin. This is a significant term for the author, for it appears three times at the close of this short letter. By beginning and ending his letter in this manner, Jude wants his audience to recognize and administer mercy from first to last. Even the darker passages speaking on judgment need to be read through the lens of mercy.

"Peace" in the New Testament is much more than merely an absence of war. It is a settled condition of relationship. Whereas all were at enmity with (i.e., opposed to) God prior to conversion, believers are now in a relationship of peace (i.e., well-being) with him. The word order here is paramount: Mercy precedes peace in the conversion of the sinner.

"Love" completes the threefold salutation. This is linked to the identity marker of verse 1, "who are loved by God the Father." Love characterizes the relationship of God to the believer and the abundant living that the believer is to experience.

Peace and love, along with mercy, are pronounced "in abundance" upon the recipients. The Christian's life demonstrates the goodness of God through these three qualities. Indeed, William of Langland in *Piers Plowman* wrote: "But all the wickedness in the world that man might work or think is no more to the mercy of God than a live coal in the sea."

2. Warning Charge With Examples (vv. 3–16)

2.1. Reason for the Charge—Infiltration of Ungodly Men (vv. 3–4)

Jude identifies the recipients of his letter as "dear friends." This is significant, for the tone of the letter takes on a severity that is rare in the New Testament letters. Jude makes his audience aware of a letter he planned to write to them, but was interrupted because of the urgency of the present situation. Thus, the letter "about the salvation we share" never made it into the canon, whereas the more urgent letter that Jude felt he had to send did. The present circumstances warranted a powerful and succinct warning letter. As the letter progresses the reader begins to understand Jude's need for urgency.

Jude exhorts his readers to "contend for the faith." No doubt this is the same salvation that he has just referred to. He qualifies this faith by the phrase, "that was once for all entrusted to the saints." This qualifier is of great importance. It emphasises two major elements of the Christian faith: (1) There is no new revelation in terms of canon (i.e., once for all); and (2) this faith has been entrusted to believers.

In verse 4, Jude clearly establishes the motivation behind this letter: "For certain men . . . have secretly slipped in." The charge is severe and unreserved. The covert entrance of these heretics into the fellowship of believers does not diminish the truth of who they are. Clearly, their condemnation has from long past been established. These men are accounted "godless," for they "change the grace of our God into a license for immorality." It is precisely the fact that they promote licentiousness that concomitantly makes them "deny Jesus Christ" as Lord. In this way they are similar to the false teachers of 2 Peter (see comments on that letter).

In contrast to the false teachers mentioned in 2 Peter, however, Jude has two notable differences. (1) Whereas Peter notes these men to be "false teachers" from the beginning, Jude merely uses the qualifier "certain men." (2) Peter's second letter is a warning against those who *would* enter into fellowship with the true faith (2 Peter 2:1). But here in Jude the infiltration has already begun. This fact accounts for the urgency and the direct language of Jude's letter.

2.2. Reminder of Past Judgments (vv. 5–7)

2.2.1. Destruction of Those Who Did Not Believe (v. 5). Jude now proceeds to prove from historical precedent that God does not allow the present kind of immorality and subversion to continue. Like Peter in 2 Peter, he reminds his readers of what they already know from their teaching (i.e., the faith once for all delivered to them). In light of God's great salvation of Israel from the bondage of Egypt, the reader must keep in mind that such deliverance is no guarantee of eternal security. In fact, the very people who were delivered (i.e., redeemed) by God's power from the slavery in Egypt were destroyed in the desert for their unbelief. Clearly, Jude is using this example to warn his audience that even if certain people have professed faith in Christ, if the continued lifestyle of faith is not present, the reality of judgment is imminent. This forms the first proof from Scripture.

2.2.2. Celestial Judgment (v. 6). Jude now turns as his second proof from the salvation history of the Jews to the celestial judgment on disobedient angels. Like 2 Peter, Jude refers to 1 Enoch and portions of the Old Testament to strengthen his examples. Perhaps Jude's use of the judgment on angels was to demonstrate the impartiality of God's righteous acts. Indeed, if God does not spare angels, who have been created a little higher than the human race, what chance do people have if they persist in sin and disbelief?

The issue, however, is deeper. Jude delves into the motive. These angels "abandoned their own home"; that is, they "did not keep their positions of authority." This is important, for this proof from historical precedent demonstrates a judgment on account of rebellion. The rebellious angels Jude has in mind were not content to remain in the order or domain for which God ordained them. This concept will be further developed when Jude specifically refers to the dispute between Michael and Satan (v. 9). These angels are reserved in darkness, awaiting the judgment of the last day. Note that the method of restraining the angels is "with everlasting chains for judgment." Jude wants to show his audience the seriousness of the sin of rebellion and licentiousness.

2.2.3. Civic Judgment (v. 7). Jude links this third proof from Scripture to the judgment on angels by the phrase, "in a similar way." The connection has two possible explanations. (1) The connection may be one of *cause*. That is, just as "Sodom and Gomorrah and the surrounding towns" were punished for their perversion and immorality, so too the angels were held in chains. If this explanation is correct, the sin of the angels may be that of sexual union with human women (cf. Gen. 6:1–4). This explanation has some merit, though increasing scholarship on Genesis seems to read "sons of God" in Genesis 6 not as angelic beings but as the pedigree of Seth.

(2) The connection between the rebellious angels and Sodom and Gomorrah is perhaps better linked by the fact that both are given as *examples* of punishment for sin and unbelief, with the specific violation of sexual purity cited in the case of the cities of the plain. The link for all three examples is that each one deals with disobedience and lack of faith. Moreover, each one deals with the inevitable judgment that occurs as a result of sin, with three different sins being listed: disobedience,

rebellion, and sexual immorality. Note from the following chart the examples from historical precedent, the judgment, and the reason for the judgment:

Example	Judgment	Reason
Deliverance from Egypt	Destroyed those who did not believe	Unbelief
Angels	Darkness/kept in chains	Rebellion
Sodom and Gomorrah	Eternal fire	Sexual immorality/ perversion

With these three examples Jude now begins to show alarming similarities to the contemporary problem his readers are facing.

2.3. First Set of Character Traits (vv. 8–10)

2.3.1. Contrast to Angelic Submission to Authority (vv. 8–9). The key to understanding verses 8–10 is bound up in the phrase "in the very same way." This earmarks Jude's purpose for the three illustrations he has just cited. He now turns from "certain men" to "these dreamers" (i.e., self-proclaimed prophets; see Introduction, "Occasion and Purpose"). These men have three dominant character traits: lust ("pollute their own bodies"), rebellion ("reject authority"), and irreverence ("slander celestial beings"). Note from the following chart how these three character traits parallel those of the warning examples of judgment.

Reason (historical)	Accusation (contemporary)
Unbelief	Reject authority
Rebellion	Slander celestial beings
Sexual immorality/ perversion	Pollute their own bodies

For many, these character traits are all too familiar in North American church circles. One merely needs to watch some of the antics of those televangelists who stomp on the head of the devil or pretend to joust with him in front of the camera to be shocked at how close we come to paralleling Jude's description of those who morally deny Christ's Lordship.

To show the extreme to which these men have gone, Jude cites that even the top-ranking angel never entered into an irreverent dispute with the devil (v. 9). Jude's reference to the dispute between Michael and the devil over the body of Moses comes from the apocryphal book Assumption of Moses (cf. Testament of Moses). But this is not the full weight of the illustration. Jude's use of this text is to demonstrate that not even an archangel is autonomous. This is in contradistinction to those angels who acted autonomously when they "did not keep their positions of authority but abandoned their own home" (v. 6). Both examples are given to illustrate actions that are by nature autonomous from the established order of God. To relate it to the present, Jude provides a stark contrast—these men, who speak abusively against what they do not understand, are the complete antithesis to dependence on God, whom they profess to serve.

2.3.2. Trademark: Rebellion (v. 10). Like 2 Peter, Jude refers to these men as "unreasoning animals." A trademark of ungodly men is their despising of authority, that is, acting autonomously. Every church, every religious institution, indeed, every family is painfully aware of this sad truth: Problems originate with the despising of authority. In fact, after constant abuse these men are no longer human, but bestial—creatures of instinct.

2.4. Old Testament Prototypes (v. 11)

Jude again uses a threefold example of how these sinful men have acted. In the first triad (vv. 5–7) he established the irrevocable fact of judgment on sin. In the present triad, Jude exposes the nature of their sin. Note from the following chart how skillfully Jude has woven his argument from historical precedent. Each triad of examples builds on the previous. He begins with a New Testament malediction, "Woe to them." Indeed, just as the Lord pronounced judgment on the unbelieving scribes and Pharisees, Jude pronounces the same curse on these evil men. It is here that Jude lines up with Peter's evaluation of these men as "false teachers." Hence, the severity of the judgment is even more serious. He explains their actions by proof from Scripture:

Reason (historical)	Accusation (contemporary)	Examples
Unbelief	Reject authority	Cain
Rebellion	Slander celestial beings	Korah
Sexual immorality/ perversion	Pollute their own bodies	Balaam

(1) "They have taken the way of Cain." Cain was the first murderer (Gen. 4:1–9). More than

that, he was envious and eschewed any accountability for his brother, thereby rejecting the natural law of God against murder. According to the record of Hebrews 11:4, Cain serves as an example of a man without faith. For the false teachers to take the way of Cain implies spiritual murder. It implies that they do not believe themselves accountable for their brother's actions. Indeed, there is no love in these men at all.

(2) "They have rushed for profit into Balaam's error." Like 2 Peter, Jude uses Balaam's sin as an example of what these men are like. Balaam was a false prophet and a paradigm of the false teacher, which shows the modus operandi of the contemporary dreamers/false prophets. The explicit reference to "profit" here in Jude and to "wages" in 2 Peter 2:15 (cf. also Rev. 2:14) gives the idea of greed-motivated actions.

The sin of Balaam was a grievous one, not unlike that of these men—syncretism. That is what makes it so seductive, and that is why they have crept in unnoticed. Blatant heresy would have been immediately detected. But these men have secretly crept into the fellowship and seductively spread their licentious syncretism, offering a Christianity that is, in fact, no Christianity at all. The reference to Balaam comes from Numbers 25, where he led the children of Israel into syncretism (i.e., the union of the worship of Yahweh with the worship of Baal). The entryway into the syncretism was "sexual immorality" between the men of Israel and the Moabite women (Num. 25:1). Thus, by rushing for profit into Balaam's error the false teachers have introduced a moral denial of Christ's Lordship while still maintaining a veneer of orthodoxy.

(3) "They have been destroyed in Korah's rebellion." Here is the crux of the proof from Scripture of the sinful actions of these men. Korah's name is synonymous with rebellion against appointed and anointed leadership (Num. 16:1ff.). This character trait ties in with second triad of illustrations. Just as Korah wanted autonomy from the divinely appointed leader of the Israelites, so too these men slander celestial beings who do not act autonomously.

2.5. Second Set of Character Traits (vv. 12–13)

Jude then proceeds to characterize the false teachers again, this time using more intense and severe language. Rather than feeding the flock of God with truth, these men, in their greed, feed themselves (cf. Ezek. 34:2). Like 2 Peter, Jude uses medical imagery for these men: "blemishes at your love feasts" (v. 12). That is, they are stains upon those living righteously. The deepest sense of *koinonia* ("fellowship") is the common meal among believers, the love feast. Jude points out that these men are partakers of this feast without one shred of conscience to convict them. They are only in it for themselves, feeding only themselves.

2.5.1. First Metaphor—Broken Promises (v. 12). Jude then brings a chain of connected metaphors. This first couplet contains metaphors of unfulfilled promise. Both clouds and autumn trees are metaphorically used to convey promise. The farmer looks to the clouds hoping for rain; the orchard grower looks to his trees in autumn expecting fruit. However, these clouds are without rain and these trees are without fruit. In fact, the trees are uprooted—thus dead twice—first of all dead in that they have not provided the fruit they were meant to grow; then, being uprooted, dead from the root. It is a picture of unfulfilled promise, so too these men are full of vain and empty promises.

2.5.2. Second Metaphor—Instability (v. 13). The second couplet contains metaphors of instability. Wild waves of the sea are unstable for sailors. Likewise, a sailor plotting his course by wandering stars is sure to get lost out at sea. Thus, these men are unstable; true believers cannot put then trust or faith in them, for like wandering stars, they will be led astray.

2.6. Surety of Judgment (vv. 14–16)

Jude concludes this section on the character traits of the false teachers by showing the inevitability of judgment. It is interesting that he uses Enoch as his model, for unlike the angels that fell from their first estate, Enoch, who was translated to God because of his faith, prophesies about the return of the Lord with his angels in judgment. Jude is here quoting from the apocryphal book of 1 Enoch. The purpose for the quote is obvious: The Lord is coming to judge the ungodly.

In verse 16, Jude offers one final set of character traits of the ungodly before returning to his Christian audience. The main picture one gets of these men is that they are malcontents.

Always grumbling and complaining, they are never happy. The source of their faultfinding is "their own evil desires." With great pride they brag about themselves while flattering others for gain. Once again, it is all too horrifying to realize that people such as these are present in church circles today.

3. Call to Persevere (vv. 17–23)

3.1. Awareness of Present Situation (vv. 17–19)

Jude now brings the letter full circle. Once again, he focuses on the readers as his "dear friends." Like Peter in 2 Peter, he calls on them to "remember what the apostles of our Lord Jesus Christ" foretold. Indeed, these subversive men should not have taken the Christians unaware, for their presence in the church had been predicted by the apostles (see esp. 2 Tim. 4:1; 2 Peter 3:3). Sadly, their presence is a mark of "the last times." It is significant that Jude contrasts these men to the Christians by remarking that they "do not have the Spirit."

3.2. Exhortations to Persevere (vv. 20–21)

Jude contrasts his exhortations to his friends with the exposure of the ungodly men:

Christian community	**False teachers**
Build yourselves up in your most holy faith	The men who divide you
Pray in the Holy Spirit	Do not have the Spirit
Keep yourselves in God's love	Worldly minded

This "most holy faith" is the same faith with which Jude begins his letter when he exhorts his readers to "contend for the faith that was once for all entrusted to the saints." Then he adds, "Pray in the Holy Spirit." Certainly this echoes Paul's concept of praying in the Spirit (Eph. 6:19). Jude is not explicit on whether this is *glossolalia* or prayer prompted by the Spirit in one's native tongue. Nevertheless, the agency of the Holy Spirit is explicit. Jude proceeds to give two further commands: "Keep yourselves in God's love," and "wait for the mercy of our Lord Jesus Christ." Note here again the predominant theme of mercy and love (see comments on v. 2). Note also Jude's Trinitarian formula:

God the Father: abide in God's love
Jesus Christ: wait patiently for Christ's return
Holy Spirit: pray in the Spirit as the effective agent

3.3. Evangelize With Mercy (vv. 22–23)

Not only are the true believers to wait for the mercy of the Lord, but they are to exercise mercy on others. The Christian is to greet the doubter, the skeptic, with mercy. Perhaps Jude remembers the Lord's merciful response to Thomas's doubt. In any case, he calls for the Christian to be merciful on those who are doubting. Some, however, are not just doubting, they are already in the fire. Undoubtedly Jude's reference to fire here is pejorative. Yet his ultimate goal is to "save them" from such eternal damnation.

In verses 22–23 "mercy" is again cited as the tool to winning or saving these people. Jude alludes to Zechariah 3:1–7, where Joshua's garments have been stained. Here we have the biblical witness for the oft-quoted phrase: "Love the sinner; hate the sin." We are to mix this mercy "with fear"—fear of our own vulnerability and of our own proclivities toward sin. It is only by mercy that others see the grace of God.

4. Doxology (vv. 24–25)

Jude ends his letter with a note of hope and assurance. The doxology shows how the Christian can be assured of his or her salvation—it is God who keeps us from falling. Indeed, God is to be praised for his ability to keep us from falling and to present us before his glorious presence without fault and with great joy. With this knowledge, we ascribe to God our Savior "glory, majesty, power and authority." In this light, may we continue to serve him until he returns.

THE OLD TESTAMENT IN THE NEW

NT Text	OT Text	Subject
Jude 9	Zec 3:2	Rebuking Satan

REVELATION

Timothy P. Jenney

INTRODUCTION

1. Plan of This Commentary

This volume's typical format has been a running commentary on each paragraph in every book in the New Testament. The commentary on Revelation follows that same format, with one important addition. Major articles on important figures, places, and themes are scattered throughout the regular commentary. Each of these articles draws together all the material in Revelation on its respective topic, giving the reader instant access to the broad scope of this subject. This seemed to be the best way to handle Revelation's complex and interwoven themes without weighing the commentary down with endless and needless repetition.

The running commentary is numbered sequentially (1.1., 1.2., 1.3., etc.), just as in the other books in this volume. Each article appears at the verse in Revelation containing the most important appearance of its subject. When the subject appears at other places in Revelation, cross-references direct the reader to the appropriate article. An alphabetical index of all of the articles can be found at the very end of this commentary.

2. Author

The author of the book of Revelation identifies himself simply as "John" (1:4), with no title other than "your brother and companion" (v. 9). The earliest church fathers believed it was written by John the apostle, but in the third century Dionysius of Alexandria challenged this assumption. He compared the Gospel of John and Revelation and found the contrasts in theology, vocabulary, and grammar too great to be able to believe that they were authored by the same person.

One wonders why Dionysius rejected the apostle John as the author of Revelation rather than the Gospel. After all, Revelation identifies its author as John, while the fourth Gospel makes no such claim. One possibility is that the Gentile church was becoming increasingly anti-Semitic. Dionysius himself made no secret of his own distaste for the millenarianism in Revelation (which gives Israel and the Jews a special place in prophecy).

Most modern scholars follow Dionysius, rejecting John the apostle as the author of Revelation. Before World War II one might argue that this was due to the anti-Semitic attitudes of the German scholars who dominated New Testament studies. This is no longer true. More recently, scholars have been reluctant to admit Jesus' message had *any* eschatological component, let alone an apocalyptic or millenarian one (H. Koester, 14, recently took New Testament scholars to task for precisely this attitude).

These attitudes might account for a certain scholarly predisposition against Johannine authorship of Revelation, but what of the specific objections first raised by Dionysius? He is correct about the differences in language and grammar. The two works are very distinct. Many of the differences are due to the differences between a gospel and an apocalypse, while others are because Revelation draws heavily on various Old Testament apocalyptic passages for its vocabulary and imagery. It is also not hard to imagine that John's proficiency in Greek and his writing style may have changed significantly, especially since thirty or so years perhaps elapsed between the writing of the two works. Other scholars speculate that John may have used a skilled amanuensis when he wrote the Gospel, or even that his disciples wrote it to commemorate their teacher after his death, whereas he was alone on Patmos when he wrote Revelation.

The argument that the two books have a different theology is more significant, especially since this argument centers on eschatology. Many people have observed that the Fourth Gospel contains no apocalyptic eschatology (unlike the Synoptics) and none of Jesus' extensive teachings on his return (e.g., Matt. 24–25; Mark 13; Luke 17). Instead, it emphasizes how to live the Christian life on earth.

In our opinion, this is also the message of Revelation: how to live like a Christian and how to die like one. Its apocalyptic language and imagery are only the vehicle, not the message. Its message is prophetic, and very little of it was actually futuristic. John reminds his audience that God shares in their suffering and promises to deliver them soon. In the meantime, they are to strive to be "faithful witnesses" and to worship the real King of kings and Lord of lords.

The Gospel and the book of Revelation not only have the same message, but also the same eschatological *center*. That center is the vision of Zechariah 14, one of the liturgical readings for the Feast of Tabernacles (note the commentary on the Gospel of John by B. Aker in this *Full Life Bible Commentary*, which relates the central portion of that Gospel to the Feast of Tabernacles). Only the Fourth Gospel records Jesus' words at Tabernacles, "If anyone is thirsty, let him come to me and drink. Whoever believes in me, as the Scripture has said, streams of living water will flow from within him" (John 7:37–38).

The closest parallel in the Old Testament for this Scripture reference is Zechariah 14:8, part of one of the liturgical readings for the Feast of Tabernacles. It says, "On that day living water will flow out from Jerusalem" (considered to be the navel of the earth). The Gospel interprets the living water of Zechariah 14:8 as the promised outpouring of the Holy Spirit (John 7:38–39; cf. 4:14; 20:22). The Gospel goes on to portray the crucifixion as a merger of Passover and Tabernacles: Jesus' body was the Passover sacrifice (John 1:36; 19:36; cf. Ex 12:46); the blood and water that flowed from his side were the libations ("drink offerings") for Tabernacles (John 19:37; cf. Zech. 12:10).

Revelation has a similar dependency on Zechariah 14, so much so that it can be characterized as an expansion of it. Both begin with a proclamation of the Day of the Lord (Zech. 14:1; Rev. 1:10) and end with a vision of a new Jerusalem in which everyone and everything are holy (Zech. 14:20–21; Rev. 21). Both predict plagues as God's judgment on the unbelievers (Zech. 14:12–15; Rev. 6:1–17; 8:6–9:21; 16), including drought (Zech. 14:18; Rev. 11:6). Both portray the coming of the Lord with his heavenly hosts (Zech. 14:5; Rev. 19:11–16) and the great battle that follows (Zech. 14:2; Rev. 19:17–21). Both feature a river of living water (Zech. 14:8; Rev. 4:6; 22:1–2, 17) and worship of God as king of the earth (Zech. 14:9, 16–17; Rev. 11:17–19).

In conclusion, we accept Revelation's own claim that it was authored by John. While it could have been any Christian author named John in the first century, the earliest church

Early church fathers believed that the apostle John, not another John, wrote the book of Revelation while on the island of Patmos, banished there because of his faith by Emperor Domitian.

fathers believed it was the apostle who bore that name. We find no substantial reason to reject their claim. Though the Fourth Gospel does not bear John's name, its overall message and eschatological center agree with Revelation. There is no legitimate reason why the two could not have been written by the same person, even though they do differ in language, vocabulary, and genre. Those who feel that the differences outweigh the similarities would do better to reject John the apostle as the Gospel's author rather than as the author of Revelation.

3. Liturgical Setting

Even casual readers of Revelation cannot miss its high liturgy and extensive descriptions of worship. Unfortunately, most Christians today are not familiar with Jewish liturgy or the Feast of Tabernacles, a familiarity that Revelation's author could take for granted among his audience. Consequently, we miss the source from which Revelation drew its images: the first-century celebration of the Feast of Tabernacles. The liturgical texts for this feast came from the Old Testament, though many of its first-century practices were "additions"—expressions of popular piety not prescribed in the Mosaic Law.

The link between the Feast of Tabernacles and apocalyptic eschatology neither began nor ended with Revelation. Zechariah 14, written long before the first century, bears witness to the antiquity of the tradition. It persisted among Jews long after Revelation was written. Jerome, commenting on Zechariah 14:6 in the late fourth century A.D., mentions that the Jews still interpreted Tabernacles "as a figure of things to come in the millennium" (see Danièlou, 1964a, 6). Even today, the Jewish liturgy for Tabernacles mingles prayers for the resurrection of the dead with its petitions for rain.

This means that the genius of Revelation's author was *not* his use of Tabernacles to teach eschatology. The link between the two was well established. His genius was the way in which he used the feast to help his first audience interpret their own situation. He put their plight in perspective, helping them see their place in God's great plan of the ages.

The very popularity of Tabernacles and its eschatology in the first century has made it more difficult for modern Christians to understand Revelation. The Christian church gradually moved away from its Jewish roots, eventually developing a distaste for the Jews that rapidly grew into active anti-Semitism. Knowledge of Tabernacles and its eschatological message was lost, and with it a clear understanding of Revelation's message. In his day John could assume his audience was familiar with all the various rituals, Scripture, and themes of the feast; now the church scarcely knows about Tabernacles, let alone its liturgy.

The church seems to have reached a turning point in recent years, however. Ecumenism and open dialogue have enabled biblical scholars to share resources. Younger Jewish and Christian scholars have even begun to work together to recover their common first-century heritage. Contemporary messianic Judaism, while divisive at times, has also made it more acceptable to be both Jewish and Christian. These Jews have accepted Jesus as their Messiah but retained their distinctive culture, modifying their liturgy only where the gospel message demands it. Consequently, they are especially open to interpretations of the New Testament that use Judaism.

This commentary has benefited enormously from these scholars and this new openness. This is the first commentary to use Tabernacles as a backdrop for the entire book of Revelation in many, many years.[1] There are, however, a number of other commentators who have identified portions of Revelation as taken from the liturgy of Tabernacles. These portions include Revelation 7 (most recently by J. A. Draper and H. Ulfgard) and Revelation 21–22 (e.g., P. Burrows).

What made Tabernacles such an ideal vehicle to carry the message of Revelation? The Feast of Tabernacles (or Feast of Booths) was the most popular feast of the Israelite agricultural year (see Josephus, *Ant.* 4.4.1; 15.3.3). It celebrated the end of the harvest season and especially the harvest of grapes, the last crop of the year. Its popularity and antiquity is evidenced by its many different titles: the "festival to the LORD" (Lev. 23:39, 41), the "Feast of Ingathering" (Ex. 23:16; 34:22), the "appointed feast" (Lam. 2:6–7; Hos. 12:9), or even simply "the festival" (1 Kings 8:2, 65; 12:32). Contemporary Jews often refer to it by its Hebrew name, rendered in English as *Sukkot(h)* (or *Succoth*).

The ancient popularity of Tabernacles extended beyond Palestine. Among Jews in the eastern Diaspora, it was the premier occasion for pilgrimages to Jerusalem (Harrison, 535), the time at which they would present their tithes at the temple (Cicero, *Pro Flacco* 28.68; cf. Deut. 14:22–27; 16:14). The feast was also popular among the Christians of Asia Minor. Many of them were doubtless pilgrims to the Jerusalem festival and, perhaps, familiar with its celebration in the synagogues of the Diaspora as well (see next sec., "Audience").

Tabernacles was a vintage feast. As such, it had much in common with other vintage feasts of the region. It was a time of celebration. Now that the crops had been harvested, the people gathered at Jerusalem to rest (Lev. 23:39; Num. 29:12, 35), rejoice (Lev. 23:40; Deut. 14:26; 16:14–15), and feast. In fact, Deuteronomy says that the people were to consume a tithe of their annual crops, including wine, during this single week (Deut. 14:22–26; 16:16–17; cf. 2 Chron. 31:5–6)! The celebrants erected temporary shelters from tree branches (the "tabernacles" ["tents"] or "booths" for which the feast was named), in which they ate and slept (Lev. 23:40; Neh. 8:14–17). These booths reminded them of the temporary shelters their ancestors used during the time of their wandering in the desert (Lev. 23:42–43).

Tabernacles also had some distinctly Jewish features. The seven-day feast began and ended with a single Sabbath. It followed two other Jewish celebrations, New Year (Rosh Hashannah) and the Day of Atonement (Yom Kippur; see Lev. 23:23–32; Num. 29:1–11). In turn, it was followed immediately by Simchat Torah, the celebration of the giving of the law at Sinai (sometimes called the eighth day of Tabernacles; see Lev. 23:36, 39; Num. 29:35; 2 Chron. 7:9; Neh. 8:18). The priests sacrificed seventy bulls for the sins of the various Gentile nations and a final one for God's covenant people, the Israelites (Num. 29:13–38). In addition, Moses had commanded the priests to read God's law in its entirety every seventh year during this feast (Deut. 31:9–13; cf. Neh. 8).

The Feast of Tabernacles is the likely setting for a number of Old Testament stories. These include the Benjamite kidnapping of the women of Shiloh (Judg. 21:15–24), Hannah's prayer for a child and the birth of Samuel (1 Sam. 1:1–2:11), the dedication of Solomon's temple (1 Kings 8:1, 65–66; 2 Chron. 6:3; 7:8–10), and the postexilic dedication of the rebuilt altar (Neh. 8:1–18; cf. Ezra 3:1–4; 1 Esdras 5:51). The feast was also certainly the occasion at which many of the Old Testament prophets delivered their messages to the crowds (e.g., Isa. 4; 30:29; Jer. 31:12–14; Amos 9:11; Hag. 2:1; Zech. 9:9; 14:16–19).

As Tabernacles grew in popularity, its celebration acquired a number of features not required by the law. The Jewish Mishnah lists the lighting of giant menorahs in the temple courtyard, all night dancing to flutes by torch light, dawn processions ending with libations of water and wine at the bronze altar, prayers for rain and the resurrection of the dead, the priests marching around the altar, and the people carrying fruit and waving palm branches (*Moed. Sukkah*). The libations were especially popular. One high priest, Alexander Janneus, refused to offer them properly (100 B.C.). The ensuing riot resulted in six thousand deaths (Josephus, *Ant.* 13.372–73; m. *Sukk.* 4.9).

The first-century liturgy of the Feast of Tabernacles also gives us some idea of the themes associated with it. It included a daily reading of the Great Hallel (Ps. 113–18), most of the passages of the Torah that gave instructions for the feast (Ex. 23:14–19; 34:22–24; Lev. 23:33–36, 39–43; Num. 29:12–38; Deut. 16:16–17; 31:9–13), and other passages linked by time or circumstance. The latter included the story of Solomon's dedication of the temple (1 Kings 8:2ff.), prophecies of the coming Day of the Lord (Ezek. 38:18ff.; Zech. 14:1ff.; Mal. 3:1–5), admonitions on tithing (Mal. 3:10ff.), and a comparison of a man blessed by God with a well-watered tree (Jer. 17:7ff.).

The Feast of Tabernacles became the focus for Jewish hopes for national independence and a Davidic Messiah. Judas Maccabeus used it as a model for the first Hanukkah, at which he rededicated the Jerusalem altar in 164 B.C. (1 Macc. 4:54–59; 2 Macc. 1:1ff.). His brother Jonathan chose to be vested as high priest during the Feast of Tabernacles in 152 B.C. (1 Macc. 10:21). Their brother Simon expelled the last foreign troops from Jerusalem in 141 B.C. The crowds hailed his victory by waving palm branches and singing psalms and hymns of praise (1 Macc. 13:51; cf. 14:4–15)—all liturgical elements taken from Tabernacles. A century later (35 B.C.), the Jews spontaneously proclaimed Aristobulus (a descendant of

Simon) as king during Tabernacles, despite the fact that Herod the Great was already the king! Herod had the young man executed (Josephus, *Ant.* 15.3.1–3).

These events help us understand Jesus' triumphal entrance. Though it was the time of the Passover, the people of Jerusalem greeted Jesus with elements from the Feast of Tabernacles (Matt. 21:1–11; Mark 11:1–11; Luke 19:28–38; John 2:12–16). They did so because of their longing for Jewish independence, just as their ancestors had done for the Maccabees and their successors. The cutting and waving of palm branches, the quotation from the Great Hallel (Ps. 118:25–26), and even the title "Son of David" (Matt. 21:9) were all closely tied to the Feast. Nor did the link between Tabernacles and Jewish independence end with Jesus' death. The leaders of both Jewish revolts against Rome (A.D. 66–70 and 132–135) minted coins in Jerusalem with symbols and slogans from the Feast (see Ulfgard).

Thus, the Feast of Tabernacles was an excellent choice for the setting of Revelation. The immediate problem its audience faced was emperor worship (Rev. 13:4–8, 11–17; 20:4). Tabernacles, with its historic link to the reign of the Davidic Messiah, was an appropriate liturgical response. It was an apologetic in ritual form to the incorrect and improper worship of the Roman emperor. Revelation declares that worship should only be directed to the *real* "KING OF KINGS AND LORD OF LORDS" (19:16), not the pretender on the throne of Rome.

4. Audience

There is no reason to doubt Revelation's own claim that its message was directed to the seven churches of Asia Minor: Ephesus, Smyrna, Pergamum, Thyatira, Sardis, Philadelphia, and Laodicea (1:11). Its use of Jewish liturgy and the Feast of Tabernacles is additional confirmation of its destination. The churches of Asia Minor were more Jewish than was typical and their Jewishness lasted much longer. As late as the fourth century, Chrysostom lamented that many Asiatic Christians still celebrated the Feast of Tabernacles with the Jews of the region (*Adv. Jud.* 1.1.5). Likewise, Eusebius observed that these churches had historically held to an older, more Jewish tradition concerning the timing of the Passover (*Eccl. Hist.* 5.23–24).

The Asiatic Christians' eschatology was particularly Jewish and related to the Feast of Tabernacles. Danièlou brings together the evidence in his *The Theology of Jewish Christianity.* According to Irenaeus, the elders received the teaching from the apostle John, who had received it from Jesus (*Haer.* 5.33.3). Moreover Papias, one of John's disciples, was one of the elders who had received this unwritten tradition (ibid., 5.33.3–34; cf. Eusebius, *Eccl. Hist.* 3.39.11–12; cf. Danièlou, 1964b, 380–85). Methodius of Olympus (third century A.D.), another Asiatic Christian, also related his eschatology to Tabernacles (*Conv.* 9.5). Revelation's message and its use of imagery from the Feast of Tabernacles fit this region perfectly.

5. Date and Occasion

The book of Revelation provides no specific date for its composition, though it does give us a clue. Revelation 17:9–10 says: "The seven heads are seven hills on which the woman sits. They are also seven kings. Five have fallen, one is, the other has not yet come." The simplest interpretation of this puzzle is that this verse refers to seven Roman emperors, five of whom have already died. The Roman emperors, in order, were Augustus (27 B.C.–A.D. 14), Tiberius (A.D. 14–37), Gaius (37–41), Claudius (41–54), and Nero (54–68). This suggests that the book can be dated sometime shortly after Nero's death.

Modern scholars have been reluctant to accept this interpretation, though that has been slowly changing. Donald Guthrie, in his 1970 *New Testament Introduction*, cited three schools of thought. The majority of scholars at that time dated Revelation to the last several years of the reign of Domitian (A.D. 90–95), others to the period immediately after Nero's assassination (A.D. 68–70), and still others to the reign of Vespasian (A.D. 70–80; see Guthrie, 949–61). Twenty years later, E. S. Fiorenza wrote that this older majority was being increasingly challenged in favor of a Neronian date (Fiorenza, 1989, 415). Now, a decade later, the trend has continued, fed in part by our greater understanding of conditions in the Roman provinces of the East.

The Neronian date (A.D. 68–70) does seem to be the best choice. Roman history says that Nero was the first emperor to persecute Christians (Suetonius, *The Twelve Caesars* 6.16–38;

Tacitus, *The Annals of Tacitus* 15.38–43). Likewise, he seems to be the best choice for the beast who is past (Rev. 17:8, 11; see "The Beast From the Sea" at 13:1). His name is also the best solution for the enigmatic number of the name of the beast, 666 (13:17–18). Finally, as already indicated, the book itself seems to support this date.

In the light of the above evidence, we would date the composition of Revelation to late A.D. 68 or early 69, during the seven-month reign of Galba.[2] This was after the fire of Rome in A.D. 64 and Nero's subsequent persecution of Christians (including the traditional deaths of Peter and Paul). It was also written after Nero's return from Greece and his subsequent assassination. The city of Rome was then in a turmoil; Galba had, at least temporarily, secured the throne. Vespasian, in the midst of laying siege to Jerusalem, had to abandon his plans in order to contest that succession. His departure briefly took the pressure off Jerusalem—an apparently miraculous deliverance for that city in accordance with Zechariah 14. This was the same year that Jerusalem minted coins with symbols of the Feast of Tabernacles on one side and an allusion to Zechariah 14:20 on the other (see Ulfgard). Finally, an impostor had appeared in Asia Minor at this time, claiming to be Nero, and had frightened the people greatly (Tacitus, *The Histories* 2.8, see "The Beast From the Sea" at 13:1). This, in our opinion, is exactly the kind of environment of turmoil and conflict that the Apocalypse demands.

These events need to be understood in light of the larger conflict between two competing eschatologies, Roman and Christian, each with their own rituals. Christians had an "unrealized eschatology." They looked forward to the return of Jesus Christ and the inauguration of his millennial reign, a hope they nurtured in their annual celebrations of the Feast of Tabernacles.

The Roman empire promulgated a "realized eschatology." Koester (11) writes: "From the time of Caesar to the false Neroes of the time of Domitian, the Roman world was dominated by prophetic eschatology. It was an eschatology that was political, revolutionary, and saturated with the sense of doom and the expectation of paradise." It proclaimed the new age was present. Caesar Augustus, the first emperor of Rome, had already inaugurated it. Apollo was its god; Augustus was its savior, the victorious "Son of God." The new age was universal—it would include all nations; therefore each Caesar could style himself the "king of kings and lord of lords." The official religion of this new age was the imperial cult and the worship of the Roman emperor.

Roman emperor worship can be demonstrated from the time of Julius Caesar on, but proving *forced* worship of the emperor whether in an outlying province or Rome itself, is another matter. This is especially true for forced worship of the emperor where refusal carried a penalty of death. Note, however, that the Roman emperor always seemed most "divine" to those at a great distance from Rome, in contrast to those acquainted with the politics and intrigues of the capital city. Consider, too, that Egypt and Babylon had worshiped "divine rulers" for hundreds of years. In other words, worship of the emperor was not a *Roman* innovation, but a Near Eastern import that moved to Rome by way of the Hellenistic conduit. One should expect it would have appeared earlier and stronger the further east one moved from Rome.

This conflict placed Christians in the eastern Roman province of Asia under enormous pressure. In fact, says Koester (9–10), "every movement of liberation would naturally [have] confront[ed] the state-sponsored realized eschatology of the Caesars." Christians worshiped a man who had been put to death by Rome for claiming to be the Son of God. Jesus was a "victim of the established authorian political order." Christians further claimed his return would establish the (real) new age and usher in his kingdom. Jesus, not Rome, would rule over the nations of the earth. Obviously, any Christian who refused to worship the emperor would be seen as treasonous, seditious, and revolutionary.

The author of Revelation takes an uncompromising position against the worship of anyone but God (13:4–8, 11–17; 20:4)—it is idolatry (2:14, 20; 9:20; 21:8; 22:15), nothing less. Christians must worship the *real* God and his Messiah, the *real* "KING OF KINGS AND LORD OF LORDS" (19:16). Prayer and worship are not trivial acts, but the second most valuable things Christians can offer God (see "The Prayers of the Saints" at 5:8; "Worship in Revelation" at 5:11). Only martyrdom is a more precious offering

14:13; 20:5–6: see "Overcomers" at 2:7; "Testify, Testimony, Witness" at 6:9). The numerous songs of praise in Revelation reinforce this message (5:9–14; 7:10, 12, 15–17; 11:15–18, etc.).

It is apparent from the book of Revelation that some persecution has already taken place. More will come shortly. Revelation was written in the calm between these two storms. The book's seven letters confirm this.

The book only cites *one* person as a martyr in all the seven letters to the churches of Asia Minor. A man named Antipas was slain at Pergamum (2:13); even then, the text reads as if the event lay some years in the past. However, official persecution looms on the horizon. Thus, John cautions Smyrna that "the devil will put [lit., is about to throw] some of you in prison" (2:10), and he exhorts them to "be faithful, even to the point of death" (2:10). He also encourages the members of each church to be *willing* to be martyred (see "Overcomers" at 2:7).

Revelation does not describe these opponents of God and his people either as a homogeneous group or as equally culpable. The book is specific about each group and its "crimes." Careful analysis can isolate and identify the following seven individuals or groups that have opposed, are opposing. or will soon oppose the church:

(1) Satan himself
(2) Rome and its inhabitants
(3) a Roman emperor
(4) a priest of the imperial cult in Asia Minor, probably at Pergamum
(5) certain adversarial Jews in Asia Minor
(6) certain compromising groups of Christians
(7) those who worship the beast and/or his image

Articles about each group appear in the main body of this commentary.

6. Genre

The book of Revelation belongs to the general category of apocalyptic literature. The term *apocalyptic literature*, however, has fallen into disfavor among scholars because of its ambiguity. The word itself is based on Greek word meaning "revelation" (*apokalypsis*). An *apocalypse* is a revelation received through a vision, a dream, a heavenly journey, or (in some cases) an angelic messenger. In keeping with this, the book of Revelation is an *apocalypse*, containing a series of visions (Rev. 9:17; 13:1; 21:2; 22:8), a heavenly journey (4:1), and an angelic messenger (1:12ff.; 10:1, 8–9; 17:3, 7, 15; 22:8, 16). Revelation also contains *apocalyptic eschatology*, as do a number of other biblical passages (e.g., Isa. 24–27; 55–66; Ezek. 37–48; Dan. 7–12; Joel; Zech. 14; Matt. 24; Mark 13), but the term is both too controversial and too complicated to define in a phrase or two.

Until recently, the field of apocalyptic eschatology was a scholarly battlefield. There was disagreement about virtually everything surrounding it, including its features, origins, and functions. The list of features varied widely from scholar to scholar, as did their analyses of which features were primary and which secondary—even the lists of which works should be identified as apocalyptic.

Others based their analysis on the origin of apocalyptic. The majority view was that it was late and the result of the failure of prophecy. The minority was divided among two other views: Gerhard von Rad's position that apocalyptic evolved from wisdom literature (and was therefore late), and F. M. Cross and Paul Hanson's position that apocalyptic was most directly related to Near Eastern stories of creation (and was therefore early).

The field seemed permanently divided until Hanson proposed a sociological solution. He argued that apocalyptic eschatology should be identified by its *function*, not its features. He defined the genre (1979, 28) as

> a system of thought produced by visionary movements; [it] builds upon a specific eschatological perspective in generating a symbolic universe opposed to that of the dominant society. This symbolic universe serves to establish the identity of the visionary community in relation to rival groups and to the deity, and to resolve contradictions between religious hopes and the experience of alienation ... by according ultimate meaning solely to the cosmic realm, from which imminent deliverance is awaited.

How does this aid our study of Revelation? Apocalyptic eschatology seems to appear in times of great societal stress. When calamity strikes or two radically different cultures collide, the greatest casualty is not the destruction of property or the loss of individual lives—it is the destruction of a societal worldview. These shared values are what enable the members of a given society to work collectively and intuitively toward common goals, even when individual members of the society may have their own particular (even adversarial) agendas. Apocalyptic eschatology is an attempt to restore or maintain this worldview in the light (or darkness!) of a rapidly changing world. In fact, apocalyptic eschatology tries to bring order out of chaos—just like the creation stories of old.

Apocalyptic appeals to individuals who feel threatened by the rapid changes around them, by a world that apparently no longer has any absolutes. It simplifies this chaos of multiple shades of ethical and moral grays by imposing a black and white matrix over it. The apocalyptic world has no grays, no neutral parties, no spectators. Its primary characteristic, long identified but still often misunderstood, is dualism: Everything in history, everything in creation, every person and everything in life, is either good or evil; there is no middle ground.

This phenomenon also helps explain why apocalyptic eschatology often includes lists similar to that found in wisdom literature. These lists may contain signs—the signs of the various seasons, the orderly movement of stars, or the names and assignments of the heavenly angels. Whatever they contain, their basic function is to provide a sense of both *order* and *stability*. They demonstrate that God has everything under control, giving hope to the reader by broadening his or her perspective. This helps the reader reintegrate into society and function in the real world.

This is not to say that apocalyptic affirms chaos, for it does not. Chaos is but a temporary condition, one more opportunity for God to reveal his glory. He will do this, soon, through inversion. Inversion usually means that God will reverse the position of things: Mountains will fall; valleys will rise; the poor will be rich; the rich will become poor; the oppressed will be the victors; their persecutors will be punished; where injustice reigns, God will establish justice; where there is war, there will be peace; the first shall be last and the last first. Occasionally, inversion means that it is the audience's perspectives that need to be reversed: They thought they would be rulers, forgetting they must serve first; they thought they would live forever, not realizing that life lay beyond the grave; they thought they would be victorious, not realizing the greatest victory would be achieved through personal martyrdom. Revelation teaches inversion of both kinds.

Finally, apocalyptic eschatology addresses those who feel impotent. It does not call for revolution, but revelation. It does not trivialize the readers' pain by suggesting they transcend the earthly plane, nor does it call them to transform the society around them. Instead, they should transfigure their perception and focus their attention on the only thing left within their control: their own actions. God or his chosen representative (e.g., the Messiah) will take care of everything else.

To summarize, the primary features of apocalyptic eschatology are dualism, inversion, the reestablishment of order and the defeat of chaos by God and/or his personal representative, and an appeal to readers to readjust their perceptions and to remain faithful to their beliefs, in spite of what is happening around them. Every other feature is secondary.

7. Message and Purpose

Books of the Bible are communications from God. As such, we ought to approach their study with humility. God has specific things he wants to teach us and specific ways in which he wants us to change our attitudes, our feelings, and/or our behavior. Nowhere are these basic principles more important than in the study of Revelation.

People want to know something about the future, Christians no less than others. Unfortunately, many Christians have tried to force answers from Revelation it was never designed to give. It was written to teach us how to live for God in the present, not to provide raw material for idle speculation about the future. We will learn far more if we let this book shape our agenda, rather than forcing it to submit to ours.

Most apocalyptic and prophetic writings contain historical reviews. This is also true of Revelation. This historical prologue serves to remind readers that God has been active throughout history. It places the current situation in context as well as encourages its readers to trust God. After all, they have reason for hope: The all-powerful God has already demonstrated the ability to deliver his people and his willingness to act on their behalf.

Prophetic and apocalyptic writings are alike another way. Both tend to focus on the present (i.e., the situation of the first recipients). Much of Revelation addresses the needs of its rst audience, interpreting their situation, ssessing their behavior, and prescribing hanges in their actions. The seven letters to e churches of Asia Minor are an excellent xample. The monumental events happening round those churches had distracted them om their divinely appointed tasks. The letters nstruct each church to return to those tasks, refocus on the one thing that was under their ontrol: their behavior.

The smallest portion of prophetic and apoclyptic writings is often the future. This is nderstandable. The writing has to strike a delcate balance: to describe enough of future lessings to encourage the obedient, enough of uture punishment to discourage disobedience, ut not so much as to distract readers by encourging undue speculation about the future.

Revelation's depiction of the future is a triking example of minimalism. Its details of ewards and punishments are extensive and mposing, but they provide only a rather cursory sketch of future events. In fact, John's ision of the future has little that is unique. Most of it can be found in the various prophets f the Old Testament, especially Isaiah, Ezekiel, and Zechariah. Perhaps the book's greatest contribution to eschatology is the way t gathers these scattered references together nd synthesizes them into a coherent whole.

So, what does Revelation have to teach us? ts message can be reduced to seven simple hemes, all of which should affect the way we ive in the present:

(1) God is in control, not Satan.
(2) Watch for the coming of the Lamb, not the beast.
(3) Fight all your battles with spiritual weapons, not the weapons of this world.
(4) When in doubt, worship! It is the most powerful expression of faith possible.
(5) You are being harvested, and everything that is harvested dies. Have courage!
(6) The bride is almost ready for her wedding to the Son.
(7) The wedding preparations are complete, the festivities of harvest's end have begun, no other signs remain. Listen ... the last trumpet is about to sound.

The general purpose of Revelation, like that of every biblical book, is to encourage us to live more godly lives. That purpose can be reduced to seven specific commands, each of which begins with a W. The alliteration should make these commands easy to memorize:

(1) Wake up (3:2).
(2) Worry not about future trials (2:10).
(3) Wait patiently for God's deliverance (3:10; 6:11).
(4) Watch for the coming of the Lamb (1:7).
(5) Witness, even when it means martyrdom (6:9; 11:7; 12:11).
(6) Work for the kingdom of God (2:2, 19, 23; 14:13; 19:8).
(7) Worship God and God alone (14:7, 11; 15:4; 19:10; 22:8).

8. Organization

a. The Literary Elements

The structure of Revelation is exceedingly complicated. Its author wove four major literary forms together in a single work: (1) letters and epistolary material, (2) descriptions of ritual objects and performances, (3) an allegorical narrative, and (4) the narrator's various interjections.

(1) **Epistolary.** The first kind of literature is *epistolary*. This includes the seven letters to the seven churches of Asia Minor (2:1–3:22). Letters (epistles) by definition are occasional literature: They address specific situations contemporary with the writer and reader(s), without the chronological confusion so often present in apocalyptic eschatology. The material in Revelation's seven letters is critical for reconstructing the occasion and the date of the book. In addition, Revelation has an epistolary introduction (1:1–9) and conclusion (22:6–21).

(2) **Ritual descriptions.** The second kind of literature in Revelation is the most common. It is also what gives the book its distinctive character. This feature is the various descriptions of rituals and their interpretations. This material includes the visions of Jesus Christ standing among the seven lamps of the menorah (1:12–20), the worship around the heavenly throne (chs. 4–5), the opening of the seven seals (5:1–6:17; 8:1–5), the celebration of the resurrected multitude (7:1–17; 14:1–5; 19:1–9), the sounding of the seven trumpets (8:6–9:21; 11:15–19), and the pouring of the seven libations of wrath (15:1–21).

All these rituals were used by Christians and Jews in their celebrations of the Feast of Tabernacles during the first century. In the author's vision, each of the historical events (past, present, and future) finds its proper place in the liturgy of Tabernacles. The presentation of these events is determined by the ritual sequence of the feast, not by their chronology in history.

(3) **Allegorical narrative.** The third type of literature in Revelation can best be described as a single, extended, allegorical narrative that has been broken into two parts: the activities of the dragon and his two "beasts" (12:1–13:18) and God's judgment of them (17:1–20:15). The way in which Revelation's author wove this allegory into the various descriptions of rituals aids us in interpreting the book and helps us identify the date of its composition.

(4) **Narrator's interjections.** The fourth kind of literature is the least frequent in this book. It is the author's own interjections, scattered throughout the book (e.g., 2:7a, 11a, 17a; 9:12; 11:14; 14:12; perhaps also 9:20–21). These interrupt the various scenes and emphasize certain points. Thus, they serve as literary exclamation points.

b. The Structure

The structure of Revelation is complex. It has dual introductions (Rev. 1:1–8) and conclusions (22:6–21); each has apocalyptic and epistolary subsections. The body of Revelation (1:10–22:5) is a series of visions, the first of which includes a letter for each of the seven churches of Asia Minor (2:1–3:22). Immediately following the letters, John journeys into heaven. There he sees God's throne and records his vision of it (ch. 4), just as Isaiah (Isa. 6) and Ezekiel (Ezek. 1) did before him.

The throne vision moves easily into a record of the rituals of worship that surround it. The heart of Revelation is its descriptions of these three separate rituals: the opening of the seven-sealed Torah scroll (5:1–6:17; 8:1–5), the blowing of seven trumpets (8:6–9:21; 11:15–19), and the pouring of seven liquid sacrifices, called libations (15:1–16:14, 16–21). Each seven-fold ritual is interrupted once, between the sixth and seventh of the series. The worship of 144,000 Jews and a multitude of Gentiles interrupts the breaking of the seven seals (Rev. 7); the author's call to prophesy (ch. 10) and his description of the two witnesses (11:1–13) interrupt the series of seve trumpet soundings. The seven libations a interrupted by an exhortation: "Behold, I com like a thief! Blessed is he who stays awake an keeps his clothes with him, so that he may n go naked and be shamefully exposed" (16:15

These interruptions make outlining Revela tion difficult, but they do help us understand th relationship between the three ritual series. Th rituals can be interpreted as consecutive (thre different sets of judgments, each set followin the other in chronological order), congruer (three different descriptions of the same divin judgments, all of which happen during a singl time period), or some even more complicate arrangement (e.g., series that overlap, serie within series, etc.). The position of this com mentary is that the interruptions suggest that th three sevenfold series are congruent; they cove the same period of time, but from different per spectives. There are at least five other parallel among the series that confirm this reading:

(1) Each ritual has seven elements. The num ber seven often represents completeness here it signifies God's total judgment on al of his creation throughout human history
(2) The first quartet of each series lacks detail The reason is that each quartet is a genera description of God's judgment up to th present crisis, either during the histori past (seals) or on his entire creation (trum pets and bowls). The second two quartet even follow the same sequence: earth, sal water, fresh water, and astral bodies.
(3) The descriptions for the fifth and sixth judgments are the most detailed of any within each series. This is the classic method by which an apocalyptic write positioned himself within his writings: He gave the most attention to the recent past the present, and the near future. This makes sense, as his readers were most concerned with the events that affected them
(4) The seventh and final repetition is always worship, whether silence and the burning of incense (8:1–5) or acclamation and applause (11:15–19; 16:17–18).
(5) Each series ends in the same manner—with a description of thunder, lightning, and an earthquake.

The following chart, "The Structure of Revelation 6:1–16:21," represents these same parallels graphically.

Num.		Seals	Trumpets		[Two Extended Fables]		Bowls	
1	HISTORIC PAST	WHITE horse, its rider has a bow and is given a crown; he goes out to conquer (6:1–2)	EARTH	Hail, fire, and blood fall upon the earth; 1/3 of the earth and its vegetation is burned (v. 7)	THE IMMEDIATE PAST AND THE PRESENT CONFLICT	The conflict between Christ and the Dragon [Satan], is described using elaborate apocalyptic imagery. The Dragon is angry at the Church because he has been defeated in heaven and knows he has but a short time on the earth (12:1–8)	EARTH	Poured on earth; those who worship the Beast break out with sores (16:1–2)
2		BRIGHT RED horse, its rider is given a sword and permitted to take peace from the earth (vv. 3–4)	SALT WATER	Fire falls into the sea; 1/3 of the sea, its creatures, and its ships perish (v. 8)			SALT WATER	Poured on sea; it becomes like blood and everything in it dies (v. 3)
3		BLACK horse, its rider has a balance and brings famine, but he may not harm the oil and the wine (vv. 5–6)	FRESH WATER	A star falls into the fresh waters; 1/3 become fatally bitter to drink (vv. 10–11)			FRESH WATER	Poured on fresh waters; they become blood; the angel and the “altar” declare it just (vv. 4–7)
4		PALE horse, its rider is named Death and Hades follows him; they are given power to kill 1/4 of the earth (vv. 7–8)	ASTRAL BODIES	1/3 of astral bodies, day and night are darkened; an eagle cries “Woe” 3x (vv. 12–13)		The Beast from the Sea appears; men worship it; it conquers the saints— <u>a call for the saints to endure</u> (13:1–10)	ASTRAL BODIES	Poured on sun; it becomes hotter and scorches men, but they do not repent (vv. 8–9)
5	OCCASION OF BOOK	Martyred souls under the altar ask God “HOW LONG WILL PRESENT PERSECUTION LAST?” They are told “a little longer” (vv. 9–11)	NON-CHRISTIANS	FIRST WOE: Locusts from the abyss torment unrepentant men for 5 months; their king is named “Destroyer” (9:1–12)			NON-CHRISTIANS	Poured on throne of the Beast; its kingdom is darkened and men curse God (vv. 10–11)
6	PRESENT AGE ENDS	TRADITIONAL SIGNS OF THE END OF THE AGE: sun blackened, moon turned to blood, stars fall from sky, etc. Inhabitants of earth cry out that THE GREAT DAY OF WRATH HAS COME (vv. 12–17)	EASTERN POWERS	SECOND WOE: Four angels bound at the Euphrates are released to kill 1/3 of mankind; the remainder still do not repent (9:13–21)		The Beast from the Earth appears; it wages war by economic means against those who will not worship the Beast's image; its number is 666 (vv. 11–18)	EASTERN POWERS	Poured on Euphrates River; its water dries up to prepare the way for the “kings of the east;” the Beast, the False Prophet and the Dragon assemble for battle (vv. 12–14, [16])
[Break] Major Sukkoth Allusions		**144,000** plus great mixed crowd of martyrs, **DRESSED IN WHITE ROBES AND HOLDING PALM BRANCHES,** stand before the throne of God and worship (7:1–17)	An angel announces that there will be no more delay; the author of Revelation called to prophesy; the **TWO OLIVE TREES AND LAMPSTANDS** appear (10:1–14)		**144,000** [no mixed crowd] worship the Lamb (14:1–5); three angelic judgements (vv. 6–11) <u>A call for the saints to endure</u> (vv. 12–13); **TWO ANGELIC HARVESTS** (vv. 14–20)		“Lo, I am coming like a thief! Blessed is he who is awake, keeping his garments that he may not go naked and be seen exposed!” (v. 15)	
7	NEW AGE BEGINS	Silence in HEAVEN for one-half hour; seven angels with trumpets are introduced; LIGHTNING, THUNDER, QUAKES (8:1–5)	NEW AGE BEGINS	God assumes reign over earth; heavenly temple opens; elders worship; LIGHTNING, THUNDER, QUAKES (11:15–19)	[nothing]		NEW AGE BEGINS	Poured into the air; a voice says, “It is done!” LIGHTNING, THUNDER, QUAKES, HAIL (vv. 17–21)

Once the rituals are concluded, only about five chapters remain of the body of Revelation. They detail God's future punishment of his enemies (18:1–20:15) and his allies' eternal rewards (21:1–22:5).

OUTLINE

1. **The Introduction** (1:1–8)
   - **1.1.** The Apocalyptic Introduction (1:1–3)
     - **1.1.1.** The Divine Source and Angelic Mediator (1:1a)
     - **1.1.2.** The Human Intermediary (1:1b–2)
     - **1.1.3.** The (Soon-to-Be) Blessed Recipients (1:3)
   - **1.2.** The Epistolary Introduction (1:4–7)
     - **1.2.1.** The Author (1:4a)
     - **1.2.2.** The Audience (1:4b)
     - **1.2.3.** The Greeting (1:4c–5a)
       - **1.2.3.1.** The Eternal God (1:4c)
       - **1.2.3.2.** The Holy Spirit (1:4d)
       - **1.2.3.3.** Jesus Christ (1:5a)
     - **1.2.4.** The Liturgical Prayer (1:5b–6)
     - **1.2.5.** The Liturgical Prophecy (1:7)
     - **1.2.6.** The Liturgical Exhortation (1:8)
2. **The Visions** (1:9–22:5)
   - **2.1.** The Occasion (1:9–11)
   - **2.2.** The First Vision: The Christ Standing in the Menorah (1:12–3:22)
     - **2.2.1.** Jesus' Appearance (1:12–16)
     - **2.2.2.** Jesus' Instructions (1:17–20)
     - **2.2.3.** Jesus' Message: The Letters to the Seven Churches (2:1–3:22)
       - **2.2.3.1.** To Ephesus (2:1–7)
       - **2.2.3.2.** To Smyrna (2:8–11)
       - **2.2.3.3.** To Pergamum (2:12–17)
       - **2.2.3.4.** To Thyatira (2:18–29)
       - **2.2.3.5.** To Sardis (3:1–6)
       - **2.2.3.6.** To Philadelphia (3:7–13)
       - **2.2.3.7.** To Laodicea (3:14–22)
   - **2.3.** The Second Vision: The Christ at the Throne of God (4:1–13:18)
     - **2.3.1.** The Prophet's Invitation to (Fore)see (4:1)
     - **2.3.2.** The Heavenly Throne Room (4:2–11)
     - **2.3.3.** The First Ritual: The Opening of the Seven Seals (5:1–6:17; 8:1–5)
       - **2.3.3.1.** The Call for a Worthy Reader (5:1–5)
       - **2.3.3.2.** The Appearance of the Lamb (5:6–14)
       - **2.3.3.3.** The Opening of the Scroll (6:1–17; 8:1–5)
         - **2.3.3.3.1.** The First Four Seals: The Historic Past (6:1–8)
         - **2.3.3.3.2.** The Fifth Seal: The Immediate Past (6:9–11)
         - **2.3.3.3.3.** The Sixth Seal: The Immediate Future (6:12–17)

A. First Interlude: The People of God (7:1–17)
- **A.1.** The Sealing of God's Servants (7:1–3)
- **A.2.** The Worship of God's Servants (7:4–17)
  - **A.2.1.** The 144,000 (7:4–8)
  - **A.2.2.** The Gentile Multitude (7:9–10)
  - **A.2.3.** The Angels, Elders, and Creatures (7:11–12)
  - **A.2.4.** The Identification of God's Servants (7:13–17)

- **2.3.3.3.4.** The Seventh Seal: The Immediate Future (8:1–5)
- **2.3.4.** The Second Ritual: The Seven Trumpet Blasts (8:6–9:21; 11:15–19)
  - **2.3.4.1.** The First Four Trumpet Blasts (8:6–12)
  - Narrator's Interjection: An Eagle Cries "Woe" (8:13)
  - **2.3.4.2.** The Fifth Trumpet Blast: An Army of Locusts (9:1–11)
  - Narrator's Interjection: The First "Woe" Is Past (9:12)
  - **2.3.4.3.** The Sixth Trumpet Blast: 200,000,000 Cavalry (9:13–21)

B. Second Interlude: The Prophets of God (10:1–11:13)
- **B.1.** The Author's Call to Prophesy (10:1–11)
  - **B.1.1.** The Mighty Angel's Appearance (10:1–4)
  - **B.1.2.** The Angel's Proclamation (10:5–7)
  - **B.1.3.** The Angel's Prophecy (10:8–11)

B.2. The Two Witnesses' Ministry (11:1–13)
B.2.1. Their Description (11:1–6)
B.2.2. Their Deaths (11:7–10)
B.2.3. Their Resurrection (11:11–13)
Narrator's Interjection: The Second "Woe" Is Past (11:14)

2.3.4.4. The Seventh Trumpet Blast: God's Enthronement (11:15–19)
2.3.4.4.1. The Hymns of God's Enthronement (11:15–18)
2.3.4.4.2. The Site of God's Enthronement (11:19)

C. An Allegorical Narrative (12:1–13:18)
C.1. The Dragon's Previous Failures (12:1–16)
C.1.1. The Dragon Fails to Kill a Newborn Infant (12:1–6)
C.1.2. The Dragon Fails to Defeat the Archangel Michael (12:7–12)
C.1.2.1. The War in Heaven (12:7–9)
C.1.2.2. The Song of Triumph (12:10–12)
C.1.3. The Dragon Fails to Kill the Infant's Mother (12:13–16)
C.2. The Dragon's Current Campaign (12:17–13:18)
C.2.1. The Dragon's Latest Prey (12:17–13:1)
C.2.2. The Dragon's Newest Allies (13:2–18)
C.2.2.1. A Beast From the Sea (13:2–8)
Narrator's Interjection: "He Who Has an Ear . . ." (13:9–10)
C.2.2.2. A Beast From the Land (13:11–17)
Narrator's Interjection: "The Number of the Beast . . ." (13:18)

2.4. The Third Vision: The Christ on Mount Zion (14:1–16:21)
2.4.1. His 144,000 Companions (14:1–5)
2.4.2. The Three Angelic Proclamations (14:6–11)
2.4.2.1. Fear God and Worship Him (14:6–7)
2.4.2.2. Babylon Has Fallen (14:8)
2.4.2.3. Those Who Worship the Beast Will Be Punished (14:9–11)
Narrator's Interjection: The Saints Must Endure (14:12)
2.4.3. The Divine Proclamation: Blessed Are the Martyrs (14:13)
2.4.4. The Harvest of the Earth (14:14–20)
2.4.4.1. Wheat Harvest (14:14–16)
2.4.4.2. Grape Harvest (14:17–20)
2.4.5. The Third Ritual: The Pouring of Seven Libations (15:1–16:21)
2.4.5.1. The Worship of the Martyrs (15:1–4)
2.4.5.2. The Angels Receive the Bowls (15:5–16:1)
2.4.5.3. First Four Libations (16:2–9)
2.4.5.4. Fifth Libation (16:10–11)
2.4.5.5. Sixth Libation (16:12–14)
2.3.3.3.3. The Sixth Seal: The Immediate Future (6:12–17)
D. Third Interlude: "See, I Am Coming Like a Thief" (16:15)
2.4.5.5. Sixth Libation (continued) (16:16)
2.4.5.6. Seventh Libation (16:17–21)

C.3. The Allegorical Narrative (continued) (17:1–20:15)
C.3.1. The Prostitute Who Rides the (Land) Beast (17:1–6)
C.3.2. The Interpretation of the Allegory (17:7–18)
C.3.2.1. The Beast (17: 7–8)
C.3.2.2. The Seven Hills (17:9–11)
C.3.2.3. The Ten Horns (17:12–14)
C.3.2.4. The Great Prostitute (17:15–18)
C.3.3. The Future Judgment of the Dragon and His Allies (18:1–20:15)
C.3.3.1. Of the Great Prostitute, Babylon, the City of Rome (18:1–19:10)
C.3.3.1.1. The Proclamation of Her Sins (18:1–3)

C.3.3.1.2. An Exhortation to Abandon Her to Her Fate (18:4–8)
C.3.3.1.3. A Description of the Mourning (18:9–19)
C.3.3.1.3.1. Of Her Lovers (18:9–10)
C.3.3.1.3.2. Of Her Suppliers (18:11–17a)
C.3.3.1.3.3. Of Their Shippers (18:17b–19)
Narrator's Interjection: "Rejoice!" (18:20)
C.3.3.1.4. The Proclamation of Her Fate (18:21-24)
C.3.3.1.5. A Description of the Celebration: The Greatest Hallel Ever (19:1–9)
C.3.3.1.5.1. Praise to God for His Judgment (19:1–5)
C.3.3.1.5.2. Praise to God for His Blessing (19:6–9)
C.3.3.1.6. A Warning to Worship God Alone (19:10)
C.3.3.2. Of the Beasts and Their Armies (Armageddon) (19:11–21)
C.3.3.2.1. The White Horse Rider (19:11–16)
C.3.3.2.2. The Invitation to the Foul Banquet (19:17–18)
C.3.3.2.3. The Fate of the Beasts and Their Armies (19:19–21)
C.3.3.3. Of the Dragon and His Army (20:1–10)
C.3.3.3.1. The Dragon Bound for One Thousand years (20:1–3)
C.3.3.3.2. The Martyrs Reign With Christ (20:4–6)
C.3.3.3.3. The Dragon Released for His Destruction (20:7–10)
C.3.3.4. Of the Unrighteous Dead (20:11–15)

2.5. The Fourth Vision: The Bride of Christ, the New Jerusalem (21:1–22:5)
2.5.1. Her Setting: New Heavens and a New Earth (21:1)
2.5.2. Her Presentation (21:2)
2.5.3. Her Husband's Proclamations (21:3–8)
2.5.3.1. "We Will Live Happily Ever After" (21:3–4)
2.5.3.2. "I Am Making All Things New" (21:5–6a)
2.5.3.3. "I Have Rewarded the Faithful" (21:6b–7)
2.5.3.4. "I Have Punished the Rebellious" (21:8)
2.5.4. Her Portrait (21:9–27)
2.5.5. Her Home: A New Paradise on Earth (22:1–5)

3. The Conclusion (22:6–21)
3.1. The Apocalyptic Conclusion (22:6–17)
3.1.1. The Angelic Mediator (and Fourth Blessing) (22:6–7)
3.1.2. The Human Intermediary (22:8–11)
3.1.3. The Doxology (22:12–13)
3.1.4. The Fifth Blessing (22:14–15)
3.1.5. The Divine Source (22:16)
3.1.6. The Open Invitation (22:17)
3.2. The Epistolary Conclusion (22:18–21)
3.2.1. The Final Exhortation (22:18–19)
3.2.2. The Liturgical Benediction (22:20)
3.2.3. The Apostolic Final Greeting (22:21)

COMMENTARY

Revelation is a combination of a letter (a circular letter to several different churches) and an apocalypse. It has two introductions and two conclusions: one each for the apocalypse and one for the letter.

1. The Introduction (1:1–8)

1.1. The Apocalyptic Introduction (1:1–3)

The first introduction in Revelation is apocalyptic. It is broken into three separate sections: the source of the vision, the intermediaries (both angelic and human), and intended audience.

1.1.1. The Divine Source and Angelic Mediator (1:1a). The Greek word here translated "revelation" (v. 1) should read "apocalypse." An apocalypse is a kind of literature that records visions, dreams, or heavenly journeys (Acts 2:17; 9:10; 10:3). John uses this word at the beginning of the book to let his readers know what type of work this is. Since apocalypses usually reveal things, the word "revelation" is also appropriate. The best choice is probably to translate this word by the phrase "revelation by a vision."

The next phrase, "of Jesus Christ," is ambiguous. It can mean either "revelation about Christ" or "revelation that comes from Christ." While both are certainly true, the qualifying phrase "which God gave him" (v. 1) seems to emphasize the second point: Jesus Christ is the source of this revelation (or "apocalypse"). He has more authority to speak about God the Father and heavenly things than any other being, including Moses (John 1:17–18; cf. Ex. 33:1–34:1). Thus, we can trust this revelation.

The issue of authority is important. The ability to speak with authority about spiritual matters comes from a close personal relationship with God, not from the size of someone's ministry, the weight of one's academic degrees, or one's ability to sway a crowd (cf. John 3:10–12). Many different apocalypses circulated in the early church, each of which claimed to be written by some important Old Testament person: Enoch, Ezra, Abraham, Baruch, and so forth. Why? Anyone who wrote in one of their names automatically added credibility to his writings. Many writers did exactly that, never admitting the words were actually their own. Today we call these books pseudonymous (lit., "falsely named").

1.1.2. The Human Intermediary (1:1b–2). Revelation is different from other apocalypses, which is one reason why it is in our Bible. John does not hide his identity. He is a good witness, as he reminds his audience (1:2). God chose him to attest to the first coming of Jesus, the Word of God (John 1:1ff.; 1 John 1:1–4). He alone, of all the twelve disciples, saw the crucifixion (John 19:25–27), Jesus' ultimate "testimony" (Rev. 1:3; see "Testify, Testimony, Witness" at 6:9). Though his own role here is only that of a scribe, he nevertheless takes personal responsibility for his writing.

1.1.3. The (Soon-to-be) Blessed Recipients (1:3). Revelation skips the identity of its first readers here, deferring it until verse 4. Instead, we have the first blessing of the book, pronounced on the messenger who reads it, the ones who hear it, and especially those who obey it.

One can already see some cultural differences from our day. There is but one copy of this apocalypse at the outset. A single messenger will carry it from John to the seven churches in Asia Minor (v. 4), reading it in each congregation in turn. The first audiences will hear it being read, not read it for themselves. Only later will copies be made for each Christian church. Even then, it will be more than a thousand years before enough copies exist for every believer to own one. This is precious cargo indeed.

1.2. The Epistolary Introduction (1:4–7)

The second introduction in Revelation is that of a letter. Like modern letters, ancient ones had certain elements that usually appeared in a specific order: author, audience, greeting, and prayer. Revelation follows that general format.

1.2.1. The Author (1:4a). The author simply identifies himself as John. The very fact he identifies himself so simply indicates he expects the churches to recognize him easily (for further information on his identity, see "Author" in the introductory section of this commentary).

1.2.2. The Audience (1:4b). Revelation is addressed to seven specific ancient churches. The Romans called Asia Minor the "province of Asia"; all seven of the churches were located there. The book's original audiences were the people of those churches, not contemporary Christians. We have to be humble enough to admit that we are only "eavesdropping" on God's message to them. God continues to speak through Revelation to Christians today, but we must honestly consider what this book said to its original audience first. Only after we have done that can we ask what God says to us through it.

This point is especially important in interpreting Revelation. Christians have abused this book more than any other in the Bible. Each year brings some new "insight," each more sensational than the last. The previous year's interpretation (often by the same writer) is often forgotten in the midst of the wave of promotion for the latest publication. The instability of these kinds of books should warn us that they are the result of human efforts, not God's guidance. We should not let ourselves be shaken by them (Eph. 4:14).

Since God is eternal and unchanging (James 1:16–17), we should expect the same to be true of his Word (Matt. 5:18). His message to his church is faithful and dependable, not erratic or unstable. When we consider what this book said to its original audience, it steadies our interpretation, making it more balanced. Too often we twist Revelation, forcing it to answer questions about each new daily headline—even if the book has nothing to say about it. We must learn to care more about what God wants to say than what we want to hear—they are often very different! This attitude of submission pleases God and tunes our ears to his voice.

1.2.3. The Greeting (1:4c–5a). John's greeting begins with the traditional "grace and peace," familiar to any reader of the letters of Peter or Paul (e.g., 1 Cor. 1:3; 1 Thess. 1:1; 1 Peter 1:2). Since the letters in the Bible are inspired by God, the greetings usually include the names of each member of the Godhead. Their titles are modified in the light of the audience's plight. The title in Revelation emphasizes the Father's eternality, the Spirit's omnipresence, and the martyrdom of Jesus, the Son of God—all of which foreshadow the main message of the book. The readers will have to remember them if they are to endure through the upcoming trials.

Revelation is from . . .

1.2.3.1. The Eternal God (1:4c). God the Father is the one "who is, and who was, and who is to come" (v. 4; cf. v. 8). This is one of the most misquoted verses in the Bible. The order is not chronological, as one might expect (i.e., "was, is, and is to come"). It deliberately places the present before both the past and the future, emphasizing that God the Father is the God "who is."

This title does two things. (1) It reminds us of God's covenant name in the Old Testament. He revealed himself there as Yahweh (or Jehovah). That name means "I AM" in Hebrew (Ex. 3:14). (2) His title foreshadows the real impotence of the "beast" (Rev. 17), which these early Christians found so threatening. Revelation describes this beast as "once was, now is not, and will come" (17:8, 11). These Christians thereby recognized that this beast was not an eternal, unchanging God, nor would he ever be a match for Yahweh, the God "who is."

1.2.3.2. The Holy Spirit (1:4d). The Spirit is described as the "seven spirits" or, better, the "sevenfold Spirit" in front of God's throne. He is later described as "seven lamps" (4:5). This image surely comes from a Jewish menorah, a seven-pronged lampstand with seven flames. Its position in front of the throne reminds one of the interior of the tabernacle or temple. There the menorah burned continually in front of the ark of the covenant, God's throne in the Old Testament (Ex. 25:37; 37:23). It reminded the Israelites that God never slept or took a day off. He was always "on duty" and able to defend his people (Ps. 121; cf. 1 Kings 18:27). In the same way, the flame that appeared on each believer on that first Pentecost after the resurrection was a visible symbol of the Spirit's presence (Acts 2).

It is surely no coincidence that there are seven flames—one for each of the seven churches mentioned in Revelation. The point is that the presence of the Spirit continues to burn among them (1 Cor. 3:16; 6:19). God has not forgotten them, nor is he removed from their suffering. John's vision of Christ walking among the lampstands (Rev. 1:12–13) will reinforce this message.

1.2.3.3. Jesus Christ (1:5a). Jesus has the most unusual set of titles. We would have expected "Messiah" or "Son of God," but the titles listed here remind us of his earthly life. Jesus was "the faithful witness"; he testified about God faithfully, even to the point of giving up his life. He was "the firstborn from the dead"; God raised him on the third day. Thus he is now "the ruler of the kings of the earth" (v. 5); he reigns supreme in heaven.

If we want to appreciate these titles, we have to remember that the first followers of Jesus were called followers of "the Way" (Acts 9:2; 19:9, 23; 24:14, 22; cf. John 14:4–6). The titles here describe "the Way" to eternal life in chronological order. First, we must live faithfully, testifying about God even if it means death. Then we will experience resurrection and glorification. This is the path all followers of Jesus must walk.

Unfortunately, many members of these early churches tried to take a shortcut. They wanted to skip the part about a life of faithful endurance, even death, and go immediately to the glorification stage. This change in their theology had been influenced by their booming conomy: Asia Minor was experiencing nprecedented regional prosperity. They had een seduced by triumphalism (cf. 1 Cor. :8ff.), a theology somewhat akin to the conemporary doctrine of "Kingdom Now." Some f them may even have believed they would ever personally experience death (cf. 1 Thess. :13–18). Convinced that Jesus would return mmediately and establish his kingdom, they vere caught unaware when fierce persecution ame from Rome.

The first step is the one those early believrs did not want to take: death. "Faithful maryr" is a much better translation of the Greek hrase than "faithful witness." It not only neans death to self ("self-denial"), but physial death for the sake of the gospel ("martyrlom"; see "Testify, Testimony, Witness" at :9). This translation also helps us to undertand better why they would want to avoid leath and go right to being "ruler[s] of the ings of the earth" (1:5). Martyrdom is usually ainful. Who would not want to escape maryrdom if it could be avoided?

Revelation is a call to Christian martyrdom. Vith all its fantastic images, its most important nessage says exactly what Jesus did while he vas still on earth: "Take up [your] cross and ollow me" (Matt. 16:24; cf. Luke 9:23). Paul ad to remind the Philippians of this truth too, vith an early hymn recorded for us in Philipians 2:6–11:

> Your attitude should be the same as
> that of Christ Jesus:
>
> Who, being in very nature God,
> did not consider equality with God
> something to be grasped,
> but made himself nothing,
> taking the very nature of a servant,
> being made in human likeness.
> And being found in appearance as a man,
> he humbled himself
> and became obedient to death—
> even death on a cross!
> Therefore God exalted him to the
> highest place
> and gave him the name that is above
> every name,
> that at the name of Jesus every knee
> should bow,
> in heaven and on earth and under
> the earth,
> and every tongue confess that Jesus Christ
> is Lord,
> to the glory of God the Father.
>
> Therefore, my dear friends, as you have always obeyed—not only in my presence, but now much more in my absence—continue to work out your salvation with fear and trembling, for it is God who works in you to will and to act according to his good purpose.

The cross of Christ has continued to challenge Christians down through the ages. Contemporary American Christians often forget that suffering was the present reality for most Christians in the biblical times, just as it is today. We would do well to remember that it is our own experience that is atypical. Let us never be seduced by the wealth surrounding us or those who connive for power and glory. We must humble ourselves and be obedient to God. The first step of "the Way" of Christ is still humility and self-denial. It is often accompanied by suffering, sometimes even by martyrdom. Power and glory, being a "ruler of the kings of the earth," will come after our death and resurrection (Matt. 20:21–23; 2 Tim. 2:12)—just as it did for Jesus.

The great devotional writers of recent times knew this and wove it into their allegories of Christian life. Reading their writings will help remind us of this great truth (see, e.g., Hannah Haurnard's *Hinds' Feet in High Places*, or John Bunyan's *Pilgrim's Progress*). It will also help us to develop a healthy theology, one immune from changes in our economy.

1.2.4. The Liturgical Prayer (1:5b–6). At this point in a normal letter, we would expect a prayer. Considering the persecution of the seven churches, they probably expected to find a prayer for deliverance, the defeat of the enemies of the church, and the immediate return of Jesus Christ. John asked for none of these, tacitly implying that everything was as it should be.

Instead of asking for an easier situation, John prays that God will be glorified through it. His prayer also encourages the churches to be obedient. He reminds them of the past: Jesus loved them so much he sacrificed his life for them. He also reminds them of the future: They will be an eternal kingdom and a priesthood for God, if they obey. This ancient promise to Israel (Ex. 19:6) had been recently extended to include the church (1 Peter 2:5, 9; cf. Rev. 5:10).

The prayer here is more formal, more liturgical, than that of the other letters in the New Testament. This fits with the descriptions of the solemn "high church" rituals that will appear later in the book. John ends the prayer with the traditional "Amen," though here it may also be a wordplay on one of the titles of Jesus (see "The Amen" at 3:14).

1.2.5. The Liturgical Prophecy (1:7). In a usual letter of the New Testament, the body directly followed the prayer. Here John includes two more liturgical elements: a prophecy (v. 7) and an exhortation (v. 8). These may well have represented elements in the order of service of these seven ancient churches. They too set the atmosphere for the book's upcoming rituals.

The prophecy of Jesus' coming is a blend of two Old Testament prophecies. One concerns the Son of Man's coming with the clouds (Dan. 7:13; cf. Matt. 26:64; Mark 13:26; Luke 21:27; Acts 1:9–11; 1 Thess. 4:17), the other predicts that people will mourn when they see the one they have pierced (Zech. 12:10; cf. John 19:34).

Revelation proclaims that Jesus is "coming with the clouds" (v. 7). The association of God with clouds is ancient. A rainbow in the clouds is a reminder of the Noahic covenant (Gen. 9:13–16). God also displayed his presence among the Israelites in the desert by a cloud during the day (Ex. 13:21; see "The *Shekinah* Canopy" at 7:15). The Old Testament describes God as "rid[ing] on the clouds" (Ps. 68:4; cf. 104:3), clouds that are even more noticeable when he comes to judge on the Day of the Lord (Ezek. 30:3; Dan. 7:13; Joel 2:2; Zeph. 1:15). Similarly, Jesus will return "with the clouds" on the Day of the Lord.

John's use of "with the clouds" rather than "in the clouds" is unusual (only the Hebrew text of Dan. 7:13 has this expression). The prophecy may refer to the thunderclouds that preceded the fall rains in Israel. The high priests prayed for those rains, as they did for the resurrection of the dead, at the daily dawn drink offerings each year during the Feast of Tabernacles (John 7).

1.2.6. The Liturgical Exhortation (1:8). The last liturgical element in the introduction is an exhortation. It emphasizes God's ete nality, his presence, and his power. "Alpha" the first letter in the Greek alphabet, "Omeg the last. "The Alpha and the Omega" (1: 21:6; 22:13) is another way of saying that Gc is "the First and the Last" (1:17; 22:13; cf. Is 44:6; 48:12) or "the Beginning and the En (Rev. 21:6; 22:13; cf. Heb. 7:3). Both of the latter phrases appear in the prophecies of Is iah, where they describe God's uniqueness ar his foreknowledge (see Isa. 44:6–8; 46:10):

> "This is what the LORD says—
> Israel's King and Redeemer, the LORD
> Almighty:
> I am the first and I am the last;
> apart from me there is no God.
> Who then is like me? Let him proclaim i
> Let him declare and lay out before me
> what has happened since I established m
> ancient people,
> and what is yet to come—
> yes, let him foretell what will come.
> Do not tremble, do not be afraid.
> Did I not proclaim this and foretell it
> long ago?
> You are my witnesses. Is there any God
> besides me?
> No, there is no other Rock; I know
> not one."
> I make known the end from the beginnin
> from ancient times, what is still
> to come.
> I say: My purpose will stand,
> and I will do all that I please.

The titles remind the reader of Revelatio that God has had everything planned, down the smallest detail, for a long, long time. Th Alpha and the Omega here refer to the Fathe not the Son, as one can see by comparing th phrase in verse 8, "who is, and who was, ar who is to come," with its twin in verse 4. Th two phrases balance and enclose this epistola introduction.

2. The Visions (1:9–22:5)

The bulk of Revelation is a record of John visions of heavenly rituals. After briefly sketc ing the occasion (1:9–11), John will have fo of these visions (or perhaps one vision with fo scenes). The first three are all of Christ: (1) i the menorah (1:12–3:22), (2) at the throne God (4:1–13:18), and (3) on Mount Zion (14:1

6:21). The fourth vision is of Christ's bride, the hurch (21:1–22:5). The vision describes the ›ride and her surroundings in great detail, but .ot the ritual itself, her wedding.

2.1. The Occasion (1:9–11)

Like the seven churches, John was also xperiencing persecution for his faith. He was ›n the isle of Patmos "because of the word of ;od and the testimony of Jesus" (v. 9). Like hem, he would have to exercise "patient ndurance" until the return of Jesus Christ. In ›ther words, both the prophet and his audience hared a similar situation, just as they shared similar faith in God.

John was among those who were baptized n the Holy Spirit on the day of Pentecost (Acts). Now he is "in the Spirit" once again. The rumpet blast (see "Trumpet" at 8:2) alerts him hat God is about to speak. God then gives him vision. Visions, like dreams, are character- stic of the end times (Joel 2:28–31; cf. Acts :16–21). Proverbs 29:18 says, "Where there is no vision, the people perish" (KJV), or "Where there is no revelation, the people cast off restraint" (NIV). The seven churches (and John) needed this vision in order to be patient and persevere.

Those who seek to understand Revelation must remember that most of the book is a record of a vision. It records what John *saw,* even more than what he heard. This perspective is important. The way objects appear and individuals act in a vision is often more important than what is said. Otherwise, God would have simply communicated what he wanted to say with words rather than with pictures.

Contemporary interpretations of the book of Revelation can be classified into three general categories, based on what kinds of actions believers are supposed to take: transforming, transcending, or transfiguring. (1) Some see the book as a call to arms, revolt, and revolution. They intend to "transform" society. This appeals to those who believe themselves to be powerful and capable of taking effective

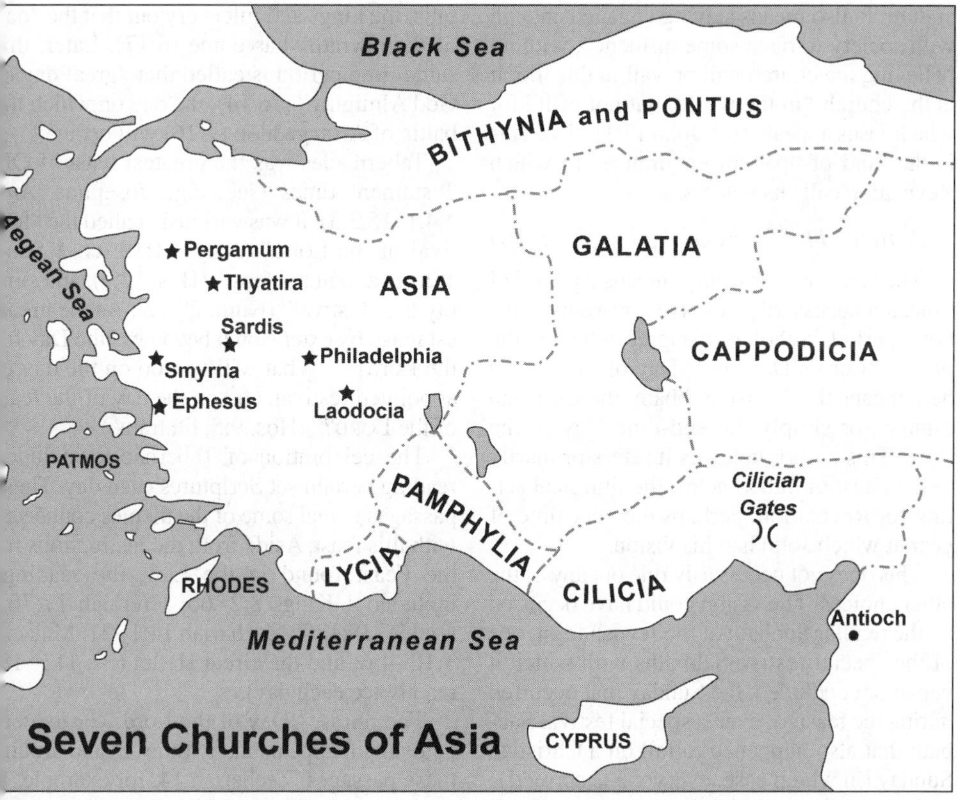

ohn wrote Revelation to the seven churches in the province of Asia. After leaving the island of Patmos, e spent his last years in Ephesus.

action. Zealots, militia members, and "Kingdom Now" adherents fall into this category.

(2) Others claim that the correct response is "transcending." This could be a sort of "Christianized" form of transcendental meditation: denying the reality of the flesh in order to rise above pain, suffering, and persecution. One simply ignores reality or disengages from the world at large. This is close to what the evangelical church in the United States did in the first half of the twentieth century. Withdrawing from the larger society, it erected its own counterculture, a sort of Christian ghetto, with its own culture, music, stores, schools, and colleges. It decided simply to wait for Jesus to return and left the world to its fate. The modern fundamentalist Christian communes are simply a more extreme version of this response.

(3) The most difficult response is "transfiguration." Transfiguration in this sense means reinterpreting one's situation. We neither deny it nor hope to change it. Transfiguration means recognizing that suffering is painful but necessary for Christian maturation. One must simply endure. It also means staying engaged enough with society to have some influence, without believing the church will prevail in this life. It is the church "in the world, but not of it" for which Jesus appealed (cf. John 17:11–14). This is the kind of "patient endurance" to which Revelation calls its readers.

Article: The "Day of the Lord" (1:10)

The Hebrew word "day" means a period of time, not necessarily a twelve- or twenty-four-hour period. Scholars disagree whether the phrase "Lord's Day" (or "Day of the Lord") here means the Jewish Sabbath, the Christian Sunday, or simply the end-time Day of the Lord. This author believes it refers primarily to the Feast of Tabernacles, the liturgical setting for Revelation, perhaps the very time of year at which John had his vision.

This does not necessarily rule out any of the other choices. The vision could have occurred on the regular Sabbath of the Jewish feast, one of the special festive Sabbaths with which it began or concluded, the Sunday that occurred during the feast, or even a special festival Sabbath that also happened to fall on a Christian Sunday (in which case, everyone is correct!).

It would be critical for interpretation if John's vision was connected with the Feast of Tabernacles. Revelation is filled wi hymns, rituals, quotations and allusions Scripture, and religious objects and symbol If these images were drawn from the Feast Tabernacles, our chances of understandi them are much better. The more we lea about this feast, especially as it was practic in John's day, the better we will understa Revelation.

The proofs for a Tabernacles background Revelation are extensive but complicate Rather than lumping them all together, I wi be weaving them throughout this commentar That way the observations will appear whe they will be most immediately useful. A overview and a survey of the Bible schola who have recognized the Tabernacles settin appears in the introduction to this commenta (see "Liturgical Setting").

This passage contains an important clue the Tabernacles background. John uses a ancient title for the Feast, the "Day of th Lord" (v. 10). In addition, the author uses tw synonyms later in the book. When judgme falls, the kings and rulers cry out that the "da of their wrath" has come (6:17). Later, th same time period is called that "great day God Almighty" (16:14), the day on which th battle of Armageddon (v. 16) will occur.

Tabernacles was the greatest feast of Ol Testament times (see, e.g., Josephus, *An* 4.4.1; 15.3.3). It was variously called the "fe tival of the LORD" (Judg. 21:19; cf. 1 Sa 1:20), "appointed feast" (Hos. 12:9), and sir ply the "festival" (Num. 29:12). As the grea est feast, by extension it becomes "the Day [the Lord]": "What will you do on the day appointed festival, and on the day of the fea of the LORD?" (Hos. 9:5, lit. trans.).

The celebration of Tabernacles include reading certain set Scriptures each day. Thes passages reveal some of the themes connecte with this feast. Aside from the instructions f the Feast found in the Law, the reading included 1 Kings 8:2–66, Jeremiah 17:7ff Ezekiel 38:18ff., Zechariah 14:1–21; Malac 3:10–4:6; and the Great Hallel (Ps. 113–1 read twice each day).

The phrase "Day of the Lord," or its ne equivalent, appears many times in and aroun these passages. Zechariah 14, for example, a miniature Revelation. It begins with the "da of the LORD" (Zech. 14:1; cf. Rev. 1:10) an nds with a holy city where the nations come › worship God at the Feast of Tabernacles Zech. 14:16–21; cf. Rev. 21–22). Malachi peaks of "the day of his coming" (Mal. 3:2), the day when I [the LORD] act" (v. 17, see NIV ote), and the "great and dreadful day of the ORD" (4:5). The prophet Ezekiel foresees the ay of his coming (Ezek. 39:8), while Jere-iah warns of the "day of disaster" (Jer. 7:16–17). The psalmist reminds the people at this is "the day the LORD has made" (Ps. 18:24). Other references from these Scrip-ures include "that day" (Ezek. 38:18–19; 9:11; Zech. 14:4, 6, 8–9, 13, 20–21) and "the ay" (Ezek. 39:8; Mal. 4:1, 3; cf. "the day I rought my people Israel out of Egypt" Kings 8:16]).

Many modern scholars have recognized at the prophetic concept of a future "Day of e Lord" evolved from the liturgy of the Feast f Tabernacles (Gray, 4–5, 14; Cross, 111). aniélou goes even further. In his *Primitive hristian Symbols,* he says that Revelation ontains the first "Christian eschatological ymbolism of Tabernacles" (6).

The liturgy of Tabernacles also explains the ook's use of other passages. It is filled with uotes and allusions to the major passages in e Old Testament that describe the Day of the ord (Isa. 2:12; 13:6, 9; 22:5; 34:8; Ezek. 7:10; 3:5; 30:3; Joel 1:15; 2:1, 11, 31; 3:14; Amos :18–20; Obad. 15; Zeph. 1:7–8, 14–18). umerous passages in Revelation contain sim-ar descriptions of the sun, moon, and stars eing shaken (or darkened) and the earth quak-ng (Rev. 6:12–14; 8:5, 7–12; 9:2; 11:13, 19; 2:4; 16:8–11, 18–21; 20:11), events particu-arly related to this "day" in prophetic literature.

In some ways, we are the opposite of the rst readers of Revelation. They knew a great eal about the Feast of Tabernacles and about eir own situation; the book of Revelation was ew to them. We, by contrast, are familiar with evelation but often ignorant of both the strug-les of the first-century church and the Feast f Tabernacles.

If we could look at Revelation from their oint of view, we would immediately recog-ize its connection with Tabernacles. No one ho celebrated that feast in the first century .D. could have missed the connection. The hrase "Day of the Lord" appeared far too fre-uently in the liturgy of the feast. This is the reason the author of Revelation uses it in his opening bid for their attention: "On the Lord's Day I was in the Spirit" (Rev. 1:10).

2.2. The First Vision: The Christ Standing in the Menorah (1:12–3:22)

2.2.1. Jesus' Appearance (1:12–16). The sight of Jesus standing among the lampstands should be an encouragement to every Chris-tian. The seven lampstands are symbolic of the seven suffering churches (v. 20). Jesus is not far away; he is right there with them (Matt. 18:20; John 14:18). These lampstands are each part of the menorah that stands before the throne of God (4:5).

Thus, it is not just Jesus who is nearby, but the Father (Heb. 13:5). He did not desert the Israelites when they refused to enter the Promised Land. He remained in the tabernacle, in the center of the Israelite encampment, dur-ing those long forty years of wandering through the desert. On a later occasion, he sent his people into exile for their sins. Yet even there he did not abandon them. He equipped his throne with wheels so he could go into exile with them (Ezek. 1). In fact, the real throne of God is always among the praises of his people (Ps. 22:3; John 4:21–24), wherever they happen to be and whatever they happen to be going through.

God does not take pleasure in our suffering. He does not allow us to suffer because he hates us, is trying to punish us, or simply enjoys our pain. Rather, he suffers right along with us (Jer. 4:18; 31:20). Suffering matures us and tempers us. It tests the quality of our commitment and our obedience to God. Our character is not shown when obeying God is easy or pleasant. It is revealed when we continue to obey, even when the going gets rough. Even Jesus learned something about the relationship between obe-dience and suffering while he was on earth (Heb. 5:8; cf. 12:1–11). If Jesus could not escape the lessons of suffering, can we hon-estly hope to avoid them? Sorrow and suffer-ing, as Hannah Haurnard has explained, are the constant companions of those who hope to scale the heights with "hinds' feet."

The bleakness of suffering in this life is bal-anced by a firm picture of the glory in the world to come. It is just as Paul wrote in Romans 8:17–18:

> Now if we are children, then we are heirs—heirs of God and co-heirs with Christ, if indeed we share in his sufferings in order that we may also share in his glory.
>
> I consider that our present sufferings are not worth comparing with the glory that will be revealed in us.

Our suffering in this life can be compared to that of a woman in labor. While she awaits the arrival of her newborn, labor is painful and intense. But as soon as she sees her child, the memory of the pain pales into insignificance. What is two or three hours of labor (or twenty-four or forty-eight), compared to the joy a child will bring his or her parents for the next forty or fifty years? So it is with the children of God, as Paul continues (Rom. 8:22–24a):

> We know that the whole creation has been groaning as in the pains of childbirth right up to the present time. Not only so, but we ourselves, who have the firstfruits of the Spirit, groan inwardly as we wait eagerly for our adoption as sons, the redemption of our bodies. For in this hope we were saved.

The appearance of Christ in all his glory reminds us of what awaits those who follow him. We will finally see the One whom we have loved from afar for so many years. We will live with him forever. Were that not enough, we will be just "like him" (1 John 3:2). The picture of Jesus in Revelation 1:11–16 is a far cry from his appearance on the cross (Isa. 53). Here he radiates with life and vitality (cf. Ezek. 8:2). He is powerful and kingly. He is divine. Here is the "ruler of the kings of the earth" (Rev. 1:5). Could this be the same Jesus who was the "Lamb, who was slain" (Rev. 5:6, 9, 12; 13:8)?

There is a dramatic incongruity between Christ's appearance here and his appearance on earth. They are at the opposite ends of the spectrum. The same is true of the church. We do not presently appear as we really are. We have to choose which "reality" we are going to believe. We have to decide whether to follow "the Way" of Jesus.

2.2.2. Jesus' Instructions (1:17–20). What a shock it must have been for John to see Jesus in all his glory! How could this be the same person with whom he walked around Palestine? Even after his resurrection, Jesus nev appeared to his disciples in his full roy regalia. Only his transfiguration on the mou tain comes close. Even that shook Peter, as th Synoptic Gospels indicate (Matt. 17:1– Mark 9:2–8).

John was a wise man to fall to his feet whe he saw Jesus. "The fear of the LORD is th beginning of wisdom" (Ps. 111:10). Only thos who do not know God do not fear him. Wh then does Jesus tell John not to be afraid? It because John has been washed in the blood the Lamb.

This entire incident is reminiscent of Isaia 43. The chapter is too long to cite here, but speaks of fear, (v. 1), witnesses (v. 10), salva tion (v. 11), redemption (v. 14), and the pun ishment of Babylon (v. 14). It begins in similar manner: "Fear not, for I have redeeme you; I have summoned you by name; you ar mine" (v. 1). It is further tied to this passage b the concept of Jesus' eternality (cf. "the Fir and the Last," Rev. 1:17) (Isa. 43:10–11):

> "You are my witnesses," declares
> the LORD,
> "and my servant whom I have chosen,
> so that you may know and believe me
> and understand that I am he.
> Before me no god was formed,
> nor will there be one after me.
> I, even I, am the LORD,
> and apart from me there is no savior."

Jesus places his hand on John (v. 17) an reassures him by reminding him of his deat and his resurrection (John had witnessed both His title is now "the Living One" (v. 18).

Article: The Keys (1:18)

Jesus also tells John that he holds "the key of death and Hades." The word "Hades should not be confused with hell or the lake c fire (20:14). It means "the grave" and is equiv alent to the Hebrew *sheol*. The resurrection c the righteous dead is one of the great promise to those who follow Jesus. He and he alon holds the keys to it (see "Resurrection of th Righteous" at 20:4).

There are two related rabbinic traditions th may help us to understand the keys. One trad tion says they are the keys to the early and th latter rain, another claims they unlock child birth and the resurrection of the dead. Both lin the keys to the Messiah and the Feast of Tabernacles (b. *Ta'anith* 2a-b; *Midr. Rabba Genesis* 13:6; t. *Suk.* 3:10B). Each morning during the feast, the high priest prayed for the fall (latter) rain and the resurrection of the dead.

An interesting archaeological discovery, now located at the Metropolitan Museum of Art in New York City, bears witness to this connection. It is a six-sided blown-glass bottle embossed on each side with symbols associated with the Feast of Tabernacles. Archaeologists discovered a fragment of an identical bottle during the excavation of old Jerusalem. Engle has suggested that these bottles were manufactured in great numbers and sold to pilgrims during Tabernacles.[3]

The symbols on the bottle include two keys, a pitcher, a reed flute, a cluster of grapes, and a two-handled cup or bowl. Engle surmises that the pitcher icon symbolizes the gold pitcher used in the water libation ceremony. The two-handled chalice represents a container, either of liquid for the libations or of oil for the menorahs erected in the temple court for the Feast. The reed pipe was blown around the altar each day but the Sabbath. The reference to the grape harvest is clear in the cluster of grapes. This author believes the bottle itself, with its vines, branches, braids, and upper vent, resembles one of the booths in which pilgrims lived during the Feast (cf. Lev. 23:42–43; Neh. 8:14–17).

This type of six-sided blown-glass bottle was sold to pilgrims during the Feast of Tabernacles. The symbols on the bottle sides include two keys, a pitcher, a reed flute, a cluster of grapes, and a two-handled cup or bowl. The Metropolitan Museum of Art, gift of Henry G. Marquand, 1881 (81.10.224). Used by permission.

Article: John's Task (1:19)

Many modern readers make the mistake of thinking that everything in Revelation is in the future or at least was in the future for John and his first-century churches. Nothing could be further from the truth. Jesus specifically told John that he was to write about his past, his present, and his future (v. 19).

This is actually normal for apocalyptic and prophecy, since both are derived from the shape of the covenant. The covenant form, first identified by George E. Mendenhall, is as follows: identification of parties, historical prologue, stipulations (commandments), provisions for public reading and deposit, witnesses to the covenant, and blessings and cursings (benefits for keeping the covenant and penalties for breaking it).[4]

The historical prologue is a brief summary of the relationship of the parties up to that point (their past). The commandments of the law are instructions for daily living (their present). The blessings or cursings (their future) were incentives for acting correctly, assuming they wanted to be blessed in the future. A single prophecy or prophetic oracle often has the same shape. It reviews the past, critiques the people's present actions, then warns or promises them about the future. In fact, it would not be an exaggeration to say that predictions of the future exist primarily to motivate people to live correctly in the present!

Many different apocalypses from the time period of Revelation follow the same pattern as the covenant or prophetic oracle: the past, the present, and the future. This literary device helps readers to remember that God is in control. He has had everything planned for a long, long time.

This realization is profoundly important for the interpretation of Revelation. Not only does this book describe events that are in our past, but events that were part of the author's past! Revelation 12 is an excellent example: It details Jesus' birth and ascension.

There is a simple, three-part formula for the interpretation of apocalyptic and prophecy:

(1) What was past for the author is past for us.
(2) What was present for the author is past for us.
(3) What was future for the author could be our past (fulfilled prophecy), our present (prophecy now being fulfilled), or still in our future (unfulfilled prophecy).

Obviously, this makes dating the author's vision critical. Fortunately, writers of apocalyptic usually leave two kinds of clues for their readers. (1) They will place themselves in their writing in order to establish their own historical position in the story. (2) Descriptions of their present tend to be much more detailed than those of either their past or their future. This is because their primary concern, like that of the prophets, continues to be how people should act in the present. John does both of these in Revelation, as we will see.

Even with these tips, the future part of the prophecy remains the hardest to interpret. Its fulfillment did not occur before the time when the Bible was completed, so we cannot go to the Bible to find out if it has been fulfilled since then. We can know for sure only by studying church history, reading the daily paper, and seeking God with an open heart and mind. Even then, the Bible cautions us against an unhealthy obsession with idle speculations (1 Tim. 1:3–4; Titus 3:9). In our study of Revelation, we should never become so caught up with the future that we fail to live for God in the present.

2.2.3. Jesus' Message: The Letters to the Seven Churches (2:1–3:22). No part of Revelation has suffered more abuse in interpretation than the seven letters to the churches of Asia (Minor). Some have argued that each church represents a period of time in the "age" of the church, others that each represents a stage in the life of any individual church or denomination, still others that each stands for a stage in the life of an individual Christian.

The simplest view, and the one we advocate, is that these were real letters to real churches in Asia Minor. The letters are not arranged from best (Ephesus) to worst (Laodicea), nor from worst to best. They are arranged geographically—from the port of Ephesus, counterclockwise along the major roads of Asia Minor, back to Ephesus. In addition, each letter contains some allusion to local events or culture of the time. Undoubtedly this reassured the congregations that John (and Jesus, who dictates the letters) understood their situations (see comments on 1:12–3:22). Finally, the letters are pastoral in tone—messages from a loving God, through a godly bishop, to the congregations under his oversight.

These churches really existed—and really struggled—just as the letters describe. Other schemes of interpretation are unnecessary and can damage Revelation's message. These schemes often trivialize, or even ignore, the very real suffering of these churches in the hope of making Revelation more relevant to modern readers (we are sympathetic to the motivation, but object to the method).

How should we interpret these seven letters? Exactly the same way we interpret Galatians, Thessalonians, or any other letter in the New Testament. Consider the following. Jesus' titles, one of which opens each of the seven letters, are not confined to just one city or time period; he holds the same titles today, everywhere. The blessings on those who overcome, which conclude each letter, also belong to all overcomers, everywhere. They are not restricted to the "spiritual champions" of the first century. Moreover, when God says he hates immorality (2:20) or idolatry (2:14), one can be sure he still feels the same about those who do such things.

Church by church, these letters describe the historical situation at the time Revelation was written. Careful reading of them will help us understand the rest of the book—and the reason why God gave John this great vision to encourage them.

Each of the seven letters of Revelation has some things in common with the others. They all have the same five elements, and in the same order: specific addressee, author, body of the letter (which is split into two sections, affirmation and exhortation), narrative interjection, and closing blessing. (1) Each letter is addressed to the human leader (the "angel" or "messenger") of the local congregation. Real angelic beings, one would assume, would not have needed a letter from John to inform them of God's will!

(2) The author of each letter is Jesus Christ. The titles by which he describes himself are different for each church. In each case, the title is the one most relevant to the needs of the church. The titles help sharpen the message for those who first heard the text of Revelation; contemporary readers of Revelation will find that these same titles yield important clues about the church's situation.

(3) The body of each letter, though short, assesses each congregation's condition. Generally, the first section is positive; the second, an exhortation (often in the context of a criticism). There are three exceptions: Sardis, the fifth church, receives no compliments, while Smyrna (the second) and Philadelphia (the sixth) are not criticized. Laodicea, the seventh and final church, is often characterized as the worst of the seven churches. Yet it receives a compliment, though only a "lukewarm" one.

(4) The narrative interjection, "he who has an ear, let him hear what the Spirit says to the churches" (a common liturgical exhortation?), is the same in each letter.

(5) The blessings are all different, but they do share certain features. (a) They are not universal but conditional; only the "overcomers" in each congregation will receive these future rewards (see "Overcomers" at 2:7). (b) The blessings appear to have been selected with an eye to the local culture of each congregation. In other words, understanding them requires a knowledge of both Revelation's biblical sources and the church's historical and cultural context. The best work on the latter is Colin J. Hemer's *The Letters to the Seven Churches of Asia in Their Local Setting,* on which the following analyses draw heavily.

2.2.3.1. To Ephesus (2:1–7). The first letter of Revelation is directed to the congregation that met in the port of Ephesus (cf. Acts 18:18–19:41). The home of Priscilla and Aquila (18:27), this city was likely the place where the messenger who delivered the book of Revelation arrived. Paul and Apollos had both had a hand in establishing the church there. Paul's ministry in particular was accompanied by what Luke labels "extraordinary miracles" (19:11). The Christian community also experienced extraordinary opposition there, led by the silversmiths' guild, whose members crafted the profitable images of Artemis (19:23–40; cf. 2 Tim. 4:14–17). Paul left the city shortly after the riot instigated by this group.

This letter describes Jesus as someone who "walks among" his churches and "holds" their pastors in his right hand (2:1b; cf. 1:12, 20). Thus, he is both present and sustaining. The image ties this first letter to the vision of the previous chapter (1:12ff.), perhaps also in a positive way to the important precious metals industry in Ephesus (Acts 19:23–40).

Jesus commends the Ephesian church for taking a firm stance against false apostles

(vv. 2, 6). Apollos's early misunderstanding of Christian baptism (Acts 18:25–26; 19:1–3) foreshadowed the problem Ephesus would have with false teachers and their teachings (Rev. 2:2; cf. Eph. 4:21; 1 Tim. 1:3; 2 Tim. 3:1–9; 4:3–4). Paul specifically mentions three different false doctrines in his various letters: forbidding some to marry (1 Tim. 4:3), commanding abstention from certain foods (4:3), and teaching that bodily resurrection had already taken place (2 Tim. 2:18). Apparently, the church had resisted these teachings and those of the Nicolaitans (Rev. 2:6; see "The Nicolaitans, the Balaamites, and the Jezebelites" at 2:6).

Unfortunately, the church did not do as well in the areas of its behavior or its passion for Christ (vv. 4–5). Their first several years were characterized by miracles and great growth (Acts 19:11–20), but they have since "fallen" from that level (Rev. 2:5). They still make sacrifices for the kingdom and work diligently (v. 3), but their ardor has cooled (v. 4). The church is doomed—unless they repent and return to the deeds that once helped make them great (v. 5).

This letter points out that correct doctrine is not enough to make a church strong, not even when accompanied by hard work. Nor does a glorious past guarantee a bright future. Great churches spring from a great passion for Jesus Christ (e.g., Ps. 42:1; Luke 24:32). In such a climate, the gospel is proclaimed (Acts 19:10), the sick healed, and demons exorcized (v. 12). Sins are confessed (v. 18) and evil vanquished (v. 19). In short, the kingdom of God manifests itself in power.

Article: The Nicolaitans, the Balaamites, and the Jezebelites (2:6)

The early church, like the church of today, had both internal and external problems. In Pergamum, the opponents of true Christianity are described as followers of Balaam and/or the Nicolaitans, who eat food offered to idols and commit immorality (2:14–15). In Thyatira the prophetess Jezebel is teaching her followers to do the same things (vv. 20–22), which our author calls "Satan's . . . deep secrets" (v. 24). Because of their similar actions, it seems best to group these people together, whether or not they were part of the same formal sect.

The basic problem is probably idol worship or some close equivalent. Ritual feasting in front of an idol and sexual intercourse with a cult prostitute were both common practices in many religions throughout the Roman empire. This may even be a reference to some of the practices of the emperor cult to which we have referred earlier. Again, there is not enough evidence to speak definitively, but enough to set forward a tentative hypothesis.

Still, this author believes that there is a strong possibility that some Christians in Pergamum and Thyatira and some Jews in Philadelphia and Smyrna are *already* participating in emperor worship at the writing of this book. If our suspicion is correct, then the frightening exhortations against those who worship the emperor or his image in the book (14:9–11; 16:2; 20:4) assume a much different light. They are not meant to keep people away from emperor worship, but to scare them out of it!

The interjection "He who has an ear . . ." is common to all seven letters (2:7, 11, 17, 29; 3:6, 13, 22), as well as appearing once later in the book (13:9). In the first three letters, the narrator's interjection appears before the blessing, but the order is switched in the last four letters. The frequency with which a similar expression appears elsewhere in Scripture (Matt. 11:15; 13:9, 43; Mark 4:9, 23; Luke 8:8; 14:35) suggests it may have been part of the liturgy of the earliest Christians.

The condemnation that "they have ears, but cannot hear" was a familiar critique of idols (e.g., see Ps. 115:1–6; 135:17). People who worship idols eventually become just like their "god": Though they have ears, they too become unable to "hear" the voice of God (Deut. 29:4; Isa. 6:10; Jer. 6:10; Ezek. 12:2). This characterization is gradually extended to everyone who refuses to obey God (Matt. 13:15; Mark 8:18; Rom. 11:8).

The blessing for the Ephesians who overcome, the conquerors, is eternal life. Specifically, the Ephesians will be granted the right to eat the fruit of the tree of life (see "Tree of Life" at 2:7).

Article: Overcomers (2:7)

The Greek word *nikao* appears seventeen times in Revelation. It is an important key for unlocking the message of this book. Unfortunately, its meaning and importance are obscured by the many different ways in which the NIV translates it. It appears not only as "overcome" (17:14), "overcomes" (2:7, 11, 17, 26; 3:5, 12, 21; 21:7), and "overcame" (12:11), but also as "triumph[ed]" (5:5), "bent on conquest" (6:2), "overpower" (11:7), "conquer" (13:7), "be[en] victorious" (15:2), and "conqueror" (6:2).

The Greek verb simply means "to overcome," but its meaning in Revelation is more complex and dependent on the context. The book describes not only a war between two opposing sides, but a war of two opposing strategies. The dragon's strategy is to "overcome" through the familiar weapons of earthly war: political power, military might, assassination, and intrigue (6:2; cf. 11:7; 13:7; 19:19; 20:7–9; chs. 12–13). The Lamb's strategy, by contrast—already demonstrated by his life and death (5:5; cf. John 16:33)—is unusual: to "overcome" through speaking the truth and sacrificing his own life (Rev. 11:7; 12:11; 15:2; 17:14).

Thus, the meaning of "overcoming" itself undergoes an apocalyptic inversion in Revelation. Followers of the Lamb are instructed to "testify" to the truth of Jesus Christ, up to and including becoming willing martyrs for the faith (12:11; 14:13; 20:6; see "Testify, Testimony, Witness" at 6:9). Those who do witness in this manner, and especially those who die (6:9–11), are the "overcomers" who will receive God's special blessings (2:7, 11, 17, 26; 3:5, 12, 21; 21:7). Spiritually, this makes perfect sense. After all, death is a Christian's ultimate defeat of the world and all its temptations. Someone once said that everyone lives and dies—the only difference is the manner of their living and their dying. Revelation's message is that Christians should determine to live and die and live again for the glory of God.

Some might imagine that all is fine and well for individual Christians, but still wonder about the effect of such a strategy on the conflict as a whole. How can one defeat an enemy by dying? Consider the game of checkers as an analogy. Pieces that reach the end of their journey, the eighth rank, are not eliminated from the game. Instead, they are "crowned." Immediately they become more powerful, being able to move in several additional directions.

So it is with martyrs. Having reached the end of their earthly journey (the death of the body), they are not retired from action. Like the pieces in checkers, they too are "crowned" (Rev. 2:10) and become more powerful (Mark 8:35; John 12:24). No longer tempted by the world, its weapons cannot even touch them. They have traded fleshly bodies for indestructible, glorified ones (1 Cor. 15; Rev. 19:14; 20:4). They can never be killed again!

Article: Tree of Life (2:7)

The right to eat from the tree of life is the specific blessing promised in this first letter to those who overcome (2:7). In fact, all God's people will enjoy this privilege (22:14). The tree of life once stood in the Garden of Eden (Gen. 2:9). That tree will line the banks of the river of life in the future Paradise of God (Rev. 22:2, 14, 19). Its fruit, available throughout the year, conveys eternal life to those who eat of it (Gen. 3:22, 24; Rev. 22:2); its leaves provide healing (Rev. 22:2). Elsewhere it appears as a symbol of hope, healing, and eternal life (Prov. 3:18; 11:30; 13:12; 15:4). Little else is known of it, though one can surmise that it flourishes only where there is an abundant supply of "living water." Hemer (42, 44–50) suggests that the Ephesians probably compared this tree with the vast groves of the temple of Artemis in their city.

Revelation, like the Gospel of John, reimages Jesus' cross as the tree of life (John 19:34–37), which stands in the midst of a river of living water (Ezek. 47:12; Zech. 14:8–10 [both liturgical readings for Tabernacles]; Rev. 22:2). His piercing was the fulfillment of prophecy (John 19:34, 37; cf. Zech. 12:10) that produced "a fountain . . . [for] the house of David and the inhabitants of Jerusalem, to cleanse them from sin and impurity" (Zech. 13:1; see "Living Water [or Water of Life]" at 7:17). The same image appears in Revelation where the river of life is described as flowing "from the throne of God and of the Lamb" (Rev. 22:1; cf. Jer. 2:13; 17:13); Jesus' throne is, of course, related directly to the cross, where he was "lifted up" (John 3:14; 8:28; 12:32; cf. Isa. 52:13–15) and "glorified" (John 7:39; 11:4; 12:16, 23; 13:31–32) for all to see.

Just as Jesus' body was the ultimate Passover Lamb (John 1:29, 36; 19:33, 36; cf. Ex. 12:46; Num. 9:12), so the blood and water that flowed from his side was the ultimate Tabernacles libation (John 19:34; cf. 7:37–39; see "Libations" at 15:1). The high priest offered the libations with prayers for the fall ("latter") rains and the resurrection of the dead. The death of Jesus brought both resurrection (John 11:24–25; see "The Resurrection of the Dead" at 20:4) and the "rain" (Isa. 45:8; Hos. 6:3; Joel 2:23–32)—or river—of the Holy Spirit (John 7:39; 20:22; Acts 2).

2.2.3.2. To Smyrna (2:8–11). Unlike Ephesus, the church of Smyrna is not mentioned in any other book in the New Testament. This is somewhat odd, for ancient Smyrna was famous for its beauty (Hemer, 59–60). In antiquity its name was connected with the Greek word for myrrh, and the city itself with the sufferings with which myrrh was associated. Certainly Christians would have linked myrrh with the suffering of the Christ (Matt. 2:11; Mark 15:23; John 19:39; cf. Rev. 18:13). Thus Revelation speaks of the "afflictions" of the city (Rev. 2:9).

The letter's description of Jesus emphasizes his martyrdom and subsequent resurrection (2:8b), paraphrasing his proclamation from the first chapter (1:17–18). This would have been especially meaningful to the Christians who will soon face their own persecution and martyrdom (v. 10). Focusing on Jesus' success and their own eternal future will make it easier to endure their own earthy trials, however painful they may be in the interim (Heb. 12:2–3).

This letter has no criticism of the congregation at Smyrna, one of only two churches so honored in Revelation (see also Philadelphia, 3:7–13). Jesus commends them for their spirituality in the face of slander (see "The Synagogues of Satan" at 2:9) and poverty. He warns them that the persecution will increase for a period of time, but encourages them not to be afraid and to remain faithful (v. 10). Satan is ultimately behind all such plots, but God permits it only so that their faith can be tested (cf. James 1:2–4, 12; 1 Peter 4:12–19). Ultimately, they will win the "crown of life" (Rev. 2:10), in which Hemer (59–60) sees an allusion to the magnificent architecture that "crowned" Smyrna. This "crown," however, is the laurel wreath. It was (and remains) a symbol of victory, as at the Olympic games. In Jewish society, it was part of the festive attire for Tabernacles (see "Crowns, Wreaths, and Diadems" at 4:10).

In many ways the church at Smyrna is the opposite of the congregation at Laodicea. Though poor in material terms, these Christians have great spiritual wealth (Rev. 2:9). Laodicea's material possessions, by contrast, have blinded them to their spiritual poverty (3:14–17). Those who teach that spirituality brings wealth often forget to mention that wealth frequently causes spiritual downfall (Matt. 6:24; Luke 16:13; 1 Tim. 6:10). Scripture teaches that wealth can lead to haughtiness and self-dependence rather than to dependence on God (Matt. 19:23; Luke 6:24; 1 Tim. 6:9–18; Heb. 13:5).

How can we escape this trap? It is simple. We should give (excess) money away as soon as we earn it (Matt. 19:21), investing it in the kingdom of God (Acts 4:34–35; 1 Tim. 6:18). Let our faith be in God's ability to provide daily (Matt. 6:11; Luke 11:3), not in our ability to save ever-increasing amounts (Ps. 73; Luke 12:13–34).

Article: The Synagogues of Satan (2:9)

The phrase "synagogue of Satan" (2:9; 3:9) is puzzling. The book of Revelation is not generally anti-Semitic. To the contrary, it paints an inclusive picture of the kingdom of God as containing both Jews and Gentiles. The twenty-four elders around the throne (4:4, 10; 11:16; 19:4) probably represent the twelve elders of the church and twelve elders of Israel (see "The Twenty-Four Elders" at 4:10). The architecture of the new Jerusalem is also ethnically sensitive. It has twelve gates inscribed with the names of the tribes of Israel (21:12) and twelve foundations inscribed with the names of the twelve apostles of the Lamb (v. 14). Both Jews and Gentiles worship God in heaven (7:1–17). In fact, the 144,000 Jews are singled out for special privileges: They will be the Lamb's constant companions (14:1–5).

Why then does the book use such harsh language to describe the synagogues of Smyrna and Philadelphia? We cannot be sure. We do know that Roman legal action against Christians in the early years was often initiated by Jews. If the specific problem here is the worship of the Roman emperor, the Christians undoubtedly expect support from the Jewish quarter for their refusal. Is it possible that the Jews of these two cities have found some legal technicality that allows them to conscientiously participate, weakening the Christians' own case for refusal?

Notice that these groups of Jews are accused only of slandering (2:9) and lying (3:9) about the churches. This is especially significant when one considers the descriptions of the 144,000 righteous Jews: "No lie was found in their mouths" (14:5), and they "did not defile themselves with women" (v. 4). They are the opposite of the Jews of Smyrna and Philadelphia in one way; does that also imply that the members of these synagogues did participate in sexual immorality? Did this "defiling" occur in some ritualistic context, perhaps even the worship of the Roman emperor? There simply is not enough evidence to judge.

We can be sure of one thing: God does not discriminate on the basis of race, gender, or ethnicity (Joel 2:28, 32; Acts 2:17–18, 21; Gal. 3:28). The author of Revelation does not condemn the Jews at Smyrna and Philadelphia simply for being Jews, but for their immoral actions. In fact, the two synagogues seem to have been exceptions, for none of the other five letters mention any such problem.

On "he who has an ear . . ." see comments on 2:7. The blessing on those in Smyrna who conquer (see "Overcomers" at 2:7) is simply eternal life, though the phrasing is unusual. Calling eternal punishment the "second death" (see "The Second Death," below) sharply contrasts it with the physical death of the body. It challenges us to shift our perspective, to place more value on the life of the soul than on the life of the body. Most people devote far too much attention to the health of their bodies and far too little to the health of their souls. This is why physicians typically earn more than pastors, even though their work is similar: Physicians help people avoid (or at least postpone) the death of the body (the *first* death); pastors work to help people escape the eternal punishment of the soul (the *second* death).

Article: The Second Death (2:11)

The "second death" (2:11; 20:6, 14; 21:8; cf. Heb. 9:27) is eternal punishment in the lake of fire (Rev. 20:14; 21:8; cf. Matt. 5:22; 18:8–9; Jude 23). Originally prepared as a punishment for Satan and his angels (Matt. 25:41), the lake of fire will also be the eternal home of those who chose to follow them. Thus, the "wages of sin is death" (Rom. 6:23; cf. Gen. 2:17; 3:3). The story of the rich man and Lazarus gives us a vivid glimpse of its torments (Luke 16:19–31). Other passages in the New Testament provide additional details. It is a place of darkness (2 Peter 2:17; Jude 6, 13), where people will weep and gnash their teeth (Matt. 8:12; 22:13; 25:30).

2.2.3.3. To Pergamum (2:12–17). The church at Pergamum literally existed in the shadow of the imperial cult. The city was an important political and religious center in Asia Minor in the first century A.D. The coins of the era show the Roman emperor being crowned as the province's ruler in the Pergamum temple (Hemer, 83). The city was also the site of one of the first temples to a Roman emperor, Caesar Augustus (founded in 29 B.C.). Hemer (84) notes that the temple "served a precedent for the cult in other provinces." Here also is the site where Antipas, the only Christian martyr mentioned by name in Revelation, is slain (Rev. 2:13).

Pergamum's political and religious importance is probably enough by itself to explain Revelation's enigmatic description of the city as the place "where Satan has his throne" (v. 13). Yet scholars suggest three other possibilities that may have reinforced the image: (1) The city's acropolis had a "throne-like" appearance when seen from the direction of Smyrna; (2) the city's altar to Zeus Soter looked like a throne and was decorated with a frieze that showed a woman fighting a serpent (early Christians may well have interpreted it as the church's struggle against Satan); and (3) the Pergamum Asklepios cult also celebrated its god as "Soter" (*soter* is the Greek word for "Savior") and identified it with a serpent (Hemer, 84–85).

Jesus is here described as the wielder of a "sharp, double-edged sword" (2:12), the image linking yet another letter with the vision of the first chapter (1:16). Since this sword comes from Jesus' mouth (19:15), it should probably be identified with the Word of God (Heb. 4:12). Still, note that Jesus *slays* the ungodly with it when he returns (Rev. 19:15, 21; cf. Ps. 149); he does not try to convert them.

The letter goes on to commend the church at Pergamum for being faithful in spite of their exposed position. Nevertheless, some members of the congregation are continuing to participate in idolatrous and immoral activities (see "The Nicolaitans, the Balaamites, and the Jezebelites" at 2:6). They must repent (2:16). Otherwise, the one with the "sharp, double-edged sword" will also fight against them (vv. 12, 16).

On "he who has an ear . . ." see comments on 2:7. Those in Pergamum who conquer (see "Overcomers" at 2:7) will be given the right to eat from "the hidden manna." This reference is first to the manna God provided his people in the desert (Ex. 16; Num. 11:7–9; Deut. 8:3, 16), some of which Aaron placed in a jar that was then kept in the ark of the covenant (Ex. 16:33–34; Heb. 9:4). The miracles of manna and water came to symbolize God's provision for his people in the desert (Neh. 9:20; Ps. 78:15–25). Some Jews reasoned that if the Messiah was someone "like [Moses]" (Deut. 18:15), he would also give them manna to eat (John 6; cf. 2 Bar. 29:4–7)—the "bread of angels" (Ps. 78:25) to accompany "the best of meats and the finest of wines" (Isa. 25:6).

The promise of a "new name" (2:17) alludes to prophecies of Isaiah, where God promises that Jerusalem will have a "new name" (Isa. 62:2) and will be adorned like a bride for her wedding (61:10), and that he will rejoice over her "as a bridegroom rejoices over his bride" (62:5). In short, this is a promise that the overcomers at Pergamum will be counted among the people of God (see "The New Jerusalem" at Rev. 21:10).

The reference to "a white stone" is more puzzling. Hemer (96ff.) lists some suggestions. Among the more plausible are that it was a token of admission to an event or membership in a privileged group, one of the jewels that (according to rabbinic tradition) fell from heaven with the manna, or a judicial vote for acquittal (and thus a proclamation of innocence or righteousness). While these are all attractive options, the book of Revelation does not provide us with enough evidence to select any of these with certainty.

2.2.3.4. To Thyatira (2:18–29). Thirty-eight miles to the east and north of Pergamum lay Thyatira, an important industrial and commercial center for the region of Lydia. It was a growing city at the time of Revelation's composition, with its most prosperous days yet to come (Hemer, 107). It was also home to a large number of trade guilds, including those who worked with various metals. The name of the city appears only one other time in the New Testament as the home city of Lydia, a Christian and seller of purple cloth in Philippi (Acts 16:14).

The description of Jesus, with his fiery eyes and feet of glowing bronze (2:18), has long been understood as a reference to Thyatira's thriving metals industry. A similar description appears two other times in Revelation (1:14–15; 19:12; cf. Dan. 7:9). This striking image is reminiscent of the fourth man, the "son of the gods," who stood in the fire with Shadrach, Meshach, and Abednego (Dan. 3:25). Those three men, the reader will remember, refused to bow down to a statue of another emperor with delusions of divinity—and God delivered them.

The letter commends the church in the areas of its attitudes, actions, and ardent passion for Christ (2:19), but rebukes it for its tolerance of false teaching (see "The Nicolaitans, the Balaamites, and the Jezebelites" at 2:6). The letter directs specific attention to a woman named Jezebel (2:20)—probably not her real name, but an allusion to the Jezebel who promoted the worship of Baal in ancient Israel and died an ignominious death (1 Kings 16:31; 18:4; 2 Kings 9:30–37). This Jezebel, prophesies Jesus, will trade her bed of adultery for a "bed of suffering," along with all her lovers (Rev. 2:22). Apparently, she has enticed others into sharing her lusts by labeling her teachings "deep secrets" (v. 24). The phrase implies some connection with Gnosticism and the mystery religions prevalent in the Hellenistic world. Her coming judgment will demonstrate that God still knows a person's innermost thoughts and desires (v. 23; cf. 1 Chron. 28:9; Ps. 7:9; 139:23) and rewards her or him accordingly (Ps. 4:1–4; Jer. 17:10).

The blessing for the conquerors in Thyatira (see "Overcomers" at 2:7) contains the additional requirement that they must have done "[God's] will to the end" (v. 26). This emphasis on actions strengthens the probable connection between Gnosticism and Jezebel's "deep secrets" (v. 24). Some varieties of Gnosticism taught the salvation of the soul but not the resurrection of the body. Reasoning that the body was inherently evil, they went on to suggest that what the body did was therefore irrelevant—opening the door to all sorts of immoral behavior. This doctrine would have appealed to Jezebel and her followers, providing an excuse for their immorality.

The blessing for those who choose to do God's will is that they will rule the nations with Christ (Rev. 2:27; 5:10; 20:6; 22:5; cf. 2 Tim.

2:12); they will be coheirs (Rom. 8:17; Gal. 3:29). Jesus is the one who rules with an iron scepter (Rev. 2:27; 12:5; 19:15; cf. Ps. 2:9; see "The Son of David" at 5:5).

The reference to the gift of "the morning star" is less clear. It definitely refers to receiving Christ, for Jesus calls himself the "bright Morning Star" elsewhere in Revelation and connects it with his messiahship (Rev. 22:16; cf. Num. 24:17). What is not clear is this phrase's meaning in the larger cultural context. It appears often enough (Isa. 14:12; Matt. 2:2–9; 2 Peter 1:19) that it ought to be recoverable, but more work needs to be done on this concept. On "he who has an ear . . ." see comments on 2:7.

2.2.3.5. To Sardis (3:1–6). The city of Sardis had a long and glorious past. Still an important commercial center in New Testament times, its best days were behind it. The wealth of the city was derived, in part, from gold deposits in the region (Hemer, 131). It was also known for its production of richly dyed fabrics and clothing (146). The city was destroyed by a catastrophic earthquake in A.D. 17 (which also affected Philadelphia), but was quickly rebuilt, in part because of a generous gift from Tiberius (Hemer, 134).

As in the letter to Ephesus, Jesus is here described as the one who holds "the seven stars" (i.e., the pastors, 3:1; cf. 2:1). The addition of the "seven spirits of God" is unique among the seven letters, though the same phrase is scattered throughout Revelation (1:4; 3:1; 4:5; 5:6; see comments on 1:4).

It is understandable that the church's location in such a wealthy and illustrious city would only enhance its reputation (3:1). Unfortunately, the reality is somewhat different. The letter calls the church to "Wake up!" (v. 2). All is not yet lost, but their work is still unfinished and their spiritual vitality is virtually extinguished. The problem here is not doctrinal; there is no mention of false teachers or false teachings. Rather, the problem is obedience (v. 3). They know the truth but have apparently been lulled into complacency by the comfort and prosperity around them. Only a few members of this congregation have white robes, which symbolize righteous deeds (v. 4; see "White Robes" at 7:9).

Just as a person's wealth can be stolen in a single night or a city be suddenly destroyed by an unexpected earthquake, so the Lord's coming will be sudden and unexpected: "like a thief" in the night (3:3; 16:15; cf. Matt. 24:43; Luke 12:39–40; 1 Thess. 5:2; 2 Peter 3:10). While wealth can insulate a person from many of the daily crises that afflict the poor, it provides no protection against the coming of the Lord (Rev. 6:15–16).

The conquerors of Sardis (see "Overcomers" at 2:7), those "who have not soiled their clothes" (3:4), will receive two blessings. (1) They "will . . . be dressed in white" robes in the world to come (v. 5). Symbolic of the "righteous acts" of the saints (19:8), this color is also appropriate for the celebration of a feast day or a wedding (see "White Robes" at 7:9). (2) Their names will never be removed from the list of God's people (3:5; see "Book of Life," below). On "he who has an ear . . ." see comments on 2:7.

Article: Book of Life (3:5)

Revelation repeatedly mentions "the book of life" (3:5; 13:8; 17:8; 20:12, 15; 21:27; cf. Ex. 32:32; Ps. 69:28; Phil. 4:3). It is a book that lists the names of all those who are righteous. The unrighteous are variously said to have not been written in it (Rev. 13:8) or, more commonly, been blotted out from it (Ex. 32:32; Rev. 3:5). To the church at Sardis, Jesus promises that he will not blot out from the book of life the name of anyone "who overcomes" (3:5; see "Overcomers" at 2:7). Those whose names are inscribed in the book will not marvel at the beast or worship him—contrasting those believers with the "inhabitants of the earth" (13:8; 17:8). Furthermore, the names of these individuals are known to God in advance, for they have been inscribed "from the creation of the world" (13:8, NIV note; cf. 17:8).

This "book of life" records those who will escape the "lake of fire" (20:15), based on deeds that have been recorded in still other books (20:12–13). Those whose names are enrolled practice neither "shameful or deceitful" deeds; they are clean, so they have the right to enter the new Jerusalem (21:27).

The phrase "book of life" or its near equivalent appears a number of times in the Old Testament, especially in passages related to the celebration of the Feast of Tabernacles (Ex. 32:32–33; Isa. 4:3; Mal. 3:16; cf. Dan. 12:1; 1 Enoch 104:1; 4 Ezra 2:40; 6:20). Since this feast was also the occasion of many marriages, perhaps this was the time at which some official roster of Israelites was updated. Unfortunately, we have no details that enable us to identify this practice further.

Revelation's threat of removal from the book of life (3:5; 13:8–9; 17:8) recalls the first appearance of this phrase in Exodus 32:32–33, and it is for the same reason. In that passage, God says of those Israelites who worshiped the golden calf that he would blot their names out of his book. Revelation makes the same claim of those who worship the beast. Both have the same sin, inappropriate worship; both have the same context, the Feast of Tabernacles.

2.2.3.6. To Philadelphia (3:7–13). Thirty miles east-southeast of Sardis lay Philadelphia (Hemer, 153). The name of the city (meaning "brotherly love") commemorated the loyalty of the two brothers that founded it (155). The city sat at the conjunction of three major trade routes, two of which led into Phrygia (154). Thus it served important military and commercial interests. Its soil was extremely fertile and suitable for grape vines, being enriched by various volcanic deposits (155).

The earthquake of A.D. 17 that destroyed Sardis also wreaked devastation in Philadelphia. The latter was troubled by smaller tremors for years afterward, to the extent that many of the town's inhabitants moved permanently outside of the city's walls (Hemer, 156–57).

Jesus is introduced here as the rightful heir of David: He "holds the key of David" (3:7; cf. 1:18; see "The Son of David" at 5:5). This is an allusion to Isaiah 22:22, as is the description of this key: "What he opens no one can shut, and what he shuts no one can open" (Rev. 3:7). No doubt this is a great encouragement to a weaker church (3:8) that feels harassed by a local Jewish synagogue (v. 9; see "The Synagogues of Satan" at 2:9). No doubt the sharp conflict between the church and the synagogue, both offspring of the same mother religion and thus siblings, is an embarrassment in the community that has prided itself as the city of "brotherly love."

The letter to the church at Philadelphia commends the believers for their deeds (3:8) and their patience endurance (v. 10), in spite of their weakness (v. 8). In addition to enduring the same economic trials as the rest of the city's population, the church has the added burden of attacks from the local Jewish synagogue (v. 9). Their faithfulness in those times will soon be rewarded: God will grant them special protection in the time of tribulation that he will send on the earth's inhabitants (v. 10; see "Inhabitants of the Earth" at 6:10).

In particular, Jesus promises to force these "Jews . . . [who] are liars" (v. 9; see "Sin Lists in Revelation" at 9:20) to admit the love that he (and his Father) have for the church (see "The Mystery of God" at 10:7). The use of the word "acknowledge" places an interesting spin on some Old Testament passages (e.g., Ps 79:6; Isa. 61:9), especially one of Isaiah's prophetic oracles: "But you are our Father, though Abraham does not know us or Israel acknowledge us; you, O LORD, are our Father, our Redeemer from of old is your name" (Isa. 63:16).

The body of the letter concludes with a promise that Jesus will return soon (3:11) and with an exhortation to "hold on" in the meantime. The "crown" (v. 11) that they are to protect is yet another reference to the Feast of Tabernacles (see "Crowns, Wreaths, and Diadems" at 4:10). The wreaths of vines and leaves, worn during this festival, would have special importance to a people whose economy is largely dependent on the productivity of its vines.

The blessings for conquerors in Philadelphia (see "Overcomers" at 2:7) all pledge stability—a precious promise to people who live with the daily insecurity of earthquakes, tremors, and cracking walls and buildings. They will be "pillars" in God's temple (3:12)—those in Solomon's temple were of cast bronze, over twenty-six feet high and seventeen feet around (1 Kings 7:15, 21). They will never have to leave the safety of walls again (Rev. 3:12). They will bear God's name (v. 12; 14:1; 22:4; alternately his "seal," 7:2; 9:4; see comments on 7:1–3; see also "The Mark of the Beast" at 14:9). They will also bear the name of a brand-new, heavenly city—their earthly city having recently been made uninhabitable—the New Jerusalem (v. 12; see "The New Jerusalem" at 21:10). Like the conquerors of Pergamum, they too will have new names (3:12; cf. 2:17). On "he who has an ear . . ." see comments on 2:7.

2.2.3.7. To Laodicea (3:14–22). The seventh and final letter is addressed to the church at Laodicea, a city that was situated astride the intersection of two major routes: the first from Ephesus to Syria and the second from Pergamum and Sardis to the southern coast (Hemer, 180). The city derived its considerable wealth from the combination of trade, banking, manufacturing, and the production of fine, glossy black wool and eye-salve (181–82, 196–99). It, and its sister cities Colosse and Hierapolis (Col. 4:12–16), lay in the river valley formed by the Lycus, a tributary of the Meander. The valley's volcanic character accounts for the famous hot springs of the area, as it does for the region's susceptibility to earthquakes. The area suffered a devastating earthquake in A.D. 60, just nine years before Revelation's composition. The wealth of the city was such that they refused imperial aid and rebuilt the city at their own expense (Hemer, 191–95).

At the writing of the letter to the Colossians, Paul had not yet visited Laodicea (Col. 2:1), though he refers to a letter of his that the church there had in its possession (4:16). He also takes time to pass along greetings from Epaphras, a native of the region who had worked hard on behalf of the three churches of the Lycus valley (v. 12).

The depiction of Jesus in Revelation 3:14 is the most majestic of the seven: He is "the Amen, the faithful and true witness, the ruler of God's creation" (3:14). The middle title is in keeping with the general theme of Revelation: Jesus is the one who has triumphed through martyrdom (cf. 1:5; 2:13; 19:11; see "Testify, Testimony, Witness" at 6:9).

Jesus' other two titles, "Amen" and "ruler of God's creation," appear to be linked. The argument is rather technical. Proverbs 8 personifies Wisdom as God's first work and his assistant in the creation (Prov. 8:22–31; cf. "let us make man in our image," Gen. 1:26). Proverbs calls Wisdom God's "craftsman" (Heb. *'amon*, Prov. 8:30); *Bereshith Rabbah* 1.1 renders the word God's "truth" (Heb. *'amen*) (Burch, 23–27; Hemer, 185). The link between "Amen" and creation also appears in the prophecies of Isaiah, where we are promised that the "God of truth" (Heb. *'elohe 'amen,* Isa. 65:16) "will create new heavens and a new earth" (v. 17). Whatever the case, Revelation is not alone in asserting Jesus' presence at creation (see Col. 1:15–16; Heb. 1:2, 10; cf. John 1:4–9 with Gen. 1:3) or his dominion over it (Matt. 28:18; Col. 1:16–18; Heb. 2:8).

Perhaps more than any other letter, the letter to Laodicea is laced with references to the city's local culture. Unlike their famous supply of hot and cold water, the deeds of the Laodiceans are merely "lukewarm" (3:16). Some of these waters were saturated with minerals and consequently unpalatable. In a similar manner, Jesus finds their mediocre faith

The seventh and final letter is to Laodicea, a wealthy city located on two major trade routes. The people there are warned that their wealth has blinded them to the fact that their faith is only "lukewarm." The area is still famous for its hot springs.

indigestible. Their material wealth has blinded them to their spiritual poverty (v. 17). Thus, the letter counsels them to buy some heavenly "[eye] salve" to correct the condition (v. 18). That same spiritual blindness has caused them to mistake their expensive black garments with fashionable attire for heaven; they do not realize they are naked, lacking the white robes required of all God's people (v. 18; 7:13–14; cf. Matt. 22:11–14; see "White Robes" at 7:9).

Finally, the letter's portrayal of Jesus petitioning at their door is touching, reminiscent of his statement that he had no place to rest on earth: "Foxes have holes and birds of the air have nests, but the Son of Man has no place to lay his head" (Matt. 8:20; Luke 9:58). His humility (Matt. 11:29) is a sharp contrast with Laodicea's various earthly rulers (Hemer, 202–7). The Laodiceans have to decide which model of leadership to follow.

However wealthy the Laodicean church may have been, none of its members can claim the right to a throne. It is this very thing that Jesus promises to those who conquer as he conquered (v. 21; see "Overcomers" at 2:7). Therein lies the rub. If the heavenly throne can be purchased with wealth or influence, the Laodiceans will be well-positioned. As it was, this throne can only be won through suffering and martyrdom (3:19; 5:5–10; 20:6; 22:5; cf. Acts 3:18; 5:41; Rom. 8:17–18; Phil. 3:10–11; Heb. 2:9–10; 1 Peter 4:12–13)—a life far from the Laodicean norm. Still, this is the "way" of Jesus and the path that those who want to follow him must walk (John 14:4–6; Acts 9:2; see comments on Rev. 1:5a). On "he who has an ear . . ." see comments on 2:7.

2.3. The Second Vision: The Christ at the Throne of God (4:1–13:18)

2.3.1. The Prophet's Invitation to (Fore)see (4:1). One of the distinctive features of an apocalypse is the manner in which God reveals information to his messenger. While prophecy passes on the words of God, apocalypses are truly audiovisual; they involve seeing as well as hearing. Thus an apocalypse may describe a vision, a dream, or (as in this case) a heavenly journey.

John's vision of heaven began with Jesus' invitation to "come up here" (v. 1; see also "Trumpet" at 8:2). Traditionally, a heavenly journey is the most authoritative kind of apocalypse. The reason is that the closer one comes to God, the source of all wisdom and knowledge, the greater the accuracy with which one can speak. This is at the heart of both Gabriel's (Luke 1:19) and Paul's (2 Cor. 12:1–5; cf. Gal. 1:11ff.) claims to be able to speak authoritatively. The more contemporary expression of hearing something "straight from the horse's mouth" carries a similar idea: Accurate information comes from those closest to the source.

2.3.2. The Heavenly Throne Room (4:2–11). John begins by describing God's heavenly court. Even casual readers of the Old Testament would have recognized this as the heavenly reality on which the desert tabernacle and the Jerusalem temple (and ultimately, Jewish synagogues) were based. Moses built the earthly tabernacle according to the "pattern" God showed him of the heavenly one (Ex. 25:9, 40; Num. 8:4; Acts 7:44). Unfortunately, Moses could only construct an earthly "copy" or "shadow" of that heavenly one (Heb. 8:5). Made by imperfect human beings of earthly materials, it did not endure even as long as the pyramids of Egypt.

Though the earthly tabernacle and temple are now long gone, the heavenly one remains. It is eternal. The Lord himself erected it (Heb. 8:2), and God reigns in it (Rev. 4:2). This is the sanctuary at which Jesus serves as our great high priest (Heb. 8:1–2). This is also the sanctuary John saw. By his description, we know he is standing in front of and facing the heavenly equivalent of the Most Holy Place.

Article: The Throne of God (4:2)

The first thing John saw in heaven was God's throne (v. 2; cf. similar visions at Isa. 6; Ezek. 1; Dan. 7). Though he does not describe the throne itself, we do have a description of the earthly "copy," the ark of the covenant (2 Sam. 6:2; 1 Chron. 13:6; Ps. 99:1). The ark was a wooden chest overlaid with gold, topped by a lid of pure gold, the "atonement cover." The chest was probably constructed of wood for practical rather than theological reasons. A solid gold chest of this size would have been almost impossible to move. The wood not only made it lighter, but made it strong enough so that the hollow interior could be used for storing valuables.

The ark-throne had no backrest but was provided with a canopy. A cherub sat on either side of the top, facing the center, its wings spread up and over the cover to form a canopy (Ex. 25:10–22). The ark had four legs, with a golden ring attached to the base of each. Wooden rods were inserted through these rings so that the ark could be carried into battle (Josh. 6:6ff.; 1 Sam. 4) and during festival processions (2 Sam. 6; 1 Kings 8; 2 Chron. 35:3). The remainder of the time the ark rested in the Most Holy Place, separated from the Holy Place by a thick veil of purple, blue, and scarlet, with cherubim woven into the design (Ex. 26:31–32).

Ancient thrones were often surrounded by and ornamented with images that reminded the supplicant of the source and extent of the king's power. This is true of God's throne in Revelation. God's power is not derived from his command of great armies, though he is the Lord of hosts (Ps. 48:8; Isa. 6:3; Zech. 14:16–17). Nor is his power derived from control of some trade route, agricultural product, or mineral monopoly.

W. F. Albright once wrote that Israel's vision of Yahweh in general may "owe certain features to the two most majestic spectacles vouchsafed to humankind: a subtropical thunderstorm and a volcanic eruption."[5] This is a picturesque way of describing God's control of the universe at the most fundamental level: earth, fire, and water. These elements are the source of the symbols that surround his throne, the symbols of his divine power.

Earth. Revelation emphasizes God's control of earth in two ways. (1) It reminds us that God created the earth (Rev. 3:14; 4:11; 10:6; 17:8; cf. Gen. 1:1; Ps. 24:1). The implicit threat is clear: The God who created the world also has the power to destroy it (see comments on 21:1). (2) Even inanimate rock and dirt recognize their true master (Luke 19:40). The earth quakes in God's presence, especially when he is angry (Rev. 6:12; 8:5; 11:13; 16:18; cf. Judg. 5:5; 2 Sam. 22:8; Ps. 18:7; Nah. 1:5). Earthquakes have awesome destructive power; in apocalyptic literature, they are a perfect physical parallel to the upheaval in the spiritual realm.

Fire. God also controls fire, a category that includes light, lightning, even rainbows (light forms a rainbow when it is refracted into its separate component colors by water, usually rain). A 360-degree rainbow, like that which surrounds God's throne (Rev. 4:3), is called a "glory." Like earthquakes, fire and lightning have tremendous destructive power when they rage out of control. When controlled, however, fire can provide warmth on cool evenings, heat for food, or light from torches or lamps. God rules fire and decides whether to dispense it as a blessing or a curse.

Isaiah, Daniel, Ezekiel, and Revelation all describe God and his throne as surrounded by fire (Rev. 1:14; 2:18; 8:5; 10:1; 11:5; 14:18; 15:2; 18:8; 20:9, 14; 21:8) and/or its various other forms: lightning (Rev. 4:5; 8:5; 11:19; 16:18; cf. Ex. 19:16; Job 36:32; 37:15; Ps. 97:4; Ezek. 1:4, 13–14; Dan. 10:6), light (Rev. 8:12; 21:23; 22:5), or rainbows (Rev. 4:3; cf. 10:1; Gen. 9:13; Ezek. 1:28). In addition, seven lamps, which "are the seven spirits of God," burn in front of the throne (Rev. 4:5; cf. 1:12–13; 2:1). Finally, the heavenly temple is "filled with smoke from the glory of God and from his power" (Rev. 15:8; cf. Ex. 13:20–22; 14:19–20; 1 Kings 8:10–11; Isa. 6:4).

Water. Water is the last of the three elements that God controls, whether the water is in the clouds (Rev. 1:7; cf. Ps. 135:7; Jer. 10:13), the heavens (rain) (Rev. 11:6; cf. Lev. 26:4; Deut. 11:11, 14; Zech. 14:17–18; Matt. 5:45), the earth (fountains) (Gen. 2:5–6), the rivers, or the sea. This also includes water in its destructive forms, such as floods (Gen. 7:7; cf. Ps. 29:10) or hail (Ex. 9:18; Ps. 105:32; Rev. 11:19; 16:21).

The river of water in front of the throne (Rev. 4:6) recalls the water that flowed from the rock in the desert (Ex. 17:5–7; Num. 20:8–13; 21:17–20) and Ezekiel's prophecy of the new temple (Ezek. 47). The "sea of glass" (Rev. 4:6; 15:2; cf. 21:11; 22:1) is identical to the river of the "water of life" (21:6; 22:1, 17). The fact that it flows from the throne is another way of indicating that God is the *source* of this life-giving water. The same kind of images appear when the heavenly multitude rejoices over the destruction of Babylon: "Then I heard what sounded like a great multitude, like the roar of rushing waters and like loud peals of thunder" (19:6; see also "The Celestial River [or Crystal Sea]" at 22:1; "Living Water [or Water of Life]" at 7:17).

Summation. King David brought all these powerful symbols together when he described the nature of God's vengeance (see 2 Sam. 22:8–16 and Ps. 2:10–12):

The earth trembled and quaked,
the foundations of the heavens shook;
they trembled because he was angry.
Smoke rose from his nostrils;
consuming fire came from his mouth,
burning coals blazed out of it.
He parted the heavens and came down;
dark clouds were under his feet.
He mounted the cherubim and flew;
he soared on the wings of the wind.
He made darkness his canopy around
him—
the dark rain clouds of the sky.
Out of the brightness of his presence
bolts of lightning blazed forth.
The LORD thundered from heaven;
the voice of the Most High resounded.
He shot arrows and scattered the enemies,
bolts of lightning and routed them.
The valleys of the sea were exposed
and the foundations of the earth
laid bare
at the rebuke of the LORD,
at the blast of breath from his nostrils.
Therefore, you kings, be wise;
be warned, you rulers of the earth.
Serve the LORD with fear
and rejoice with trembling.
Kiss the Son, lest he be angry
and you be destroyed in your way,
for his wrath can flare up in a moment.
Blessed are all who take refuge in him.

Article: The Four Living Creatures (4:6–9)

Surrounding God's throne are four living creatures (v. 6). They are cherubim (Ezek. 1:13; 10:15, 20), sometimes also called seraphim (lit., "burning ones"; see Isa. 6:2). There are four descriptions of these living creatures in the Bible (Isa. 6; Ezek. 1, 10; Rev. 4). The details vary from vision to vision, though the descriptions can be easily reconciled.

Each cherub is roughly human-shaped and glows like fire (Ezek. 1:5, 13). It has straight legs. Its feet are hooved like a calf's, only made of burnished bronze (Ezek. 1:7). Each has four faces: that of a human being, a lion, an eagle, and an ox (Ezek. 1:10; 10:14; Rev. 4:7). Each cherub is rotated with respect to its companions, so that a lion, an eagle, a human being, and an ox always face each of the four cardinal directions (John here describes only the faces he sees, omitting those on the other sides of each cherub). The creatures always move straight ahead, never turning (Ezek. 10:11).

Ezekiel describes the cherubim as having four wings, two for flying and two with which to cover their bodies. Each wing has a hand underneath it (Ezek. 1:8; 10:8, 21). Isaiah and John agree regarding the cherubim's use of their four wings but mention two other wings, with which each cherub covers its face (probably the face directed toward God's throne; Isa. 6:2; cf. Rev. 4:8). The wings, like the rest of their bodies, are covered with eyes (Ezek. 10:12; Rev. 4:6).

Outside of references to God's throne or temple, the cherubim seldom appear. Genesis describes how God placed a cherub as a guard at the entrance into Eden. David sings of God's riding the cherubim to his deliverance (2 Sam. 22:11; Ps. 18:10). Ezekiel speaks of a former "guardian cherub" who had been driven from God's presence for his pride (Ezek. 28:14–16); many people believe Satan (Lucifer) is this fallen cherub.

Article: The Triagion (Holy, Holy, Holy) (4:8)

The four living creatures have only one song, an eternal paean of praise, but they sing it without ceasing: "Holy, holy, holy." It has been sung in heaven since the beginning of the world. Isaiah heard it long ago (Isa. 6:3); now when John visits heaven, the four living creatures are still singing.

It is not that God is so egotistical that he had to create syncophants to sit around and sing his praises. If he were, he would have made these creatures weak and dependent. Yet one gets the impression that God made these four creatures as powerful and fierce as possible. Despite this, they sit so close to God's throne that they are overwhelmed by his presence. Basking eternally in his glory, they can do nothing but worship.

What is it about God that overwhelms them? It is his holiness, not his wisdom, power, or glory. The holiness of his presence is so powerful that it kills those who enter it unclean (Ex. 28:35, 43; 30:20–21; cf. the Day of Atonement [Lev. 16] and the man who touched the ark and died [1 Chron. 13:9–10]). Perhaps C. S. Lewis put it best when he said that our mortal bodies are too weak to withstand but a fraction of God's presence. Were we to experience more, we would be unmade. The bodies of the saints are not glorified so that we will not experience pain, but so that we may be strengthened as we stand in God's presence.

Article: The Twenty-Four Elders (4:10)

Next to the four living creatures, the closest worshipers to God's throne are the twenty-four elders. Twenty-four elders (Rev. 4:4, 10; 5:5–6, 11; 14:3) is twice the number one might expect, since twelve often represents completeness in apocalyptic literature. Though nowhere stated, these elders are probably twelve Jews (Ps. 122:4; cf. Matt. 19:28; Luke 22:30) and twelve Gentiles, each ruling over his respective groups. The author of Revelation goes to great lengths to make room in heaven for both groups, while representing them as one people of God (see comments on 7:1-17).

These elders are dressed in white robes (see "White Robes" at 7:9) and wear golden crowns, which they lay at God's feet (4:4, 10). They have special privileges, such as being the closest humans to God's throne and having thrones of their own on which to sit (4:4). They lead in worship (5:14; 7:11; 11:16; 19:4) with harps and golden bowls of incense (5:8).

Article: Crowns, Wreaths, and Diadems (4:10)

The twenty-four elders wear "crowns of gold," which they lay before the throne in worship (4:4, 10). Actually, most of the "crowns" (*stephanos*) in Revelation are wreaths, like the laurel wreaths worn by ancient victorious Olympic athletes (1 Cor. 9:25; 2 Tim. 2:5). This is the kind of "crown" Jesus wore on the cross: a plaited wreath of thorns (Matt. 27:29; Mark 15:17; John 19:2, 5; cf. Heb. 2:7, 9). Unfortunately, the NIV only translates this Greek word "wreaths" at Acts 14:13, using "crowns" everywhere else in the New Testament. We usually think of crowns in connection with ruling, while wreaths carry the idea of winners in a contest. It is the latter sense that is emphasized here.

Many of the first-century celebrants at the Feast of Tabernacles attired themselves with wreaths in addition to their white festival garments (see "White Robes" at 7:9). The laurel wreath was an established tradition at this feast (Isa. 28:1–5; Lam. 5:16; Zech. 9:16). It was such a common practice that noncanonical Jewish and Roman writers both take note of it (e.g., Jub. 16:30; 4 Ezra 2:42–48; 2 Baruch 15:8; Ps. Sol. 2:20–21; Tacitus, *Hist.* 5.5).

Jesus promises all faithful believers a wreath of victory in the life to come (cf. Rev. 2:11; 3:11)—made of gold, not plants, so that it will never fade. This wreath is variously called a "crown of righteousness" (2 Tim. 4:8), a "crown of life" (Rev. 2:10; James 1:12), or a "crown of glory" (1 Peter 5:4). Similar wreaths adorn the white horse rider who conquers (Rev. 6:2), the majestic woman of chapter 12 (12:1), and the angel of the harvest (14:14). Curiously, the plague of locusts wear something that appears similar (9:7).

The second kind of crown in Revelation is the kind commonly associated with kings and queens. It is called a "diadem" (*diadema*). Only three individuals wear these crowns in Revelation: the dragon (12:3), the beast from the sea (13:1), and Jesus (19:12).

Historically, we know that the emperors of Rome claimed the title "king of kings and lord of lords" for themselves, accepting worship and divine honors. Nero even styled himself "ruler of the inhabitants of the earth." Their pride and pretension are only equaled by Satan himself, who sought to raise his throne above the Almighty God (Rev. 12:3–5; cf. Ezek. 28:1–20). This is why Christian worship of the Roman emperors was such a heinous sin (see "Worship of the Beast" at 13:4). The first hymn in Revelation (4:11) recites just the first of many reasons why worship should only be directed to God, not the beast: He is the Creator, the source of life for everyone (see "Worship in Revelation" at 5:11).

There is only one person in the universe who carries the titles "King of kings and Lord of lords" by divine right: Jesus Christ (19:2; cf. 17:14; Phil. 2:9; 1 Tim. 6:15). Revelation is the story of his annihilation of these human usurpers—and the reestablishment of correct worship.

2.3.3. The First Ritual: The Opening of the Seven Seals (5:1–6:17; 8:1–5). This is the first of three rituals in Revelation. In each case, the ritual dictates what happens on earth and when. Thus, the book answers the questions, "Is God aware of what is happening on earth?"

and "Is he capable of responding to it?" God is not only aware of what is happening on earth, he controls it. In fact, events on earth are shaped and triggered by the worship around the throne. Now there is a powerful theology of worship!

Article: The Ritual Structure of Revelation (5:1)

The organization of the inner part of Revelation (chs. 5–16) is unusual. The book does not organize events geographically, chronologically (i.e., historically), or even alphabetically. It organizes them liturgically. This is in keeping with its great message: Worship orders, regulates, and controls the universe.

At the center of the book are three great sevenfold rituals: the opening of the seven-sealed Torah scroll (5:1–6:17; 8:1–5), the blowing of seven trumpets (probably made from ram's horns) (8:6–9:21; 11:14–19), and the pouring of seven liquid sacrifices, called libations (15:1–16:14, 16–21). The descriptions of each of these rituals pause after the sixth and before the seventh, or final, one of the series. A description of God's people and of their worship in heaven (ch. 7) forms the first pause, the one between the sixth and the seventh seals. The second pause, the one after the sixth trumpet blast and before the seventh, tells the story of the author's call to prophesy and the fate of the two witnesses (10:1–11:13). The final pause, the shortest, is a single verse: "Behold, I come like a thief! Blessed is he who stays awake and keeps his clothes with him, so that he may not go naked and be shamefully exposed" (16:15). The pauses, like contemporary commercial breaks in the televising of Olympic contests, help build the audience's excitement and increase their anticipation of the conclusion of each series.

The first ritual is the opening of the scroll that has writing on both sides. The ritual is broken into three parts, each one with a description, an action, and a response. The three parts are (1) the call for a worthy reader (5:1–5), (2) the appearance of the Lamb (5:6–14), and (3) the actual opening of the scroll (6:1–17; 8:1–5).

2.3.3.1. The Call for a Worthy Reader (5:1–5). In a typical apocalyptic vision, scrolls contain secret knowledge that the visionary will pass on to his audience—often predictions of future events. The focus of these apocalypses is the contents of the scroll. This is not the case in Revelation. In fact, the book never records the reading of this scroll, simply the breaking of the seven seals that secure its contents.

Revelation's focus is not on the content of the scroll but on the character of its reader: Jesus. He is the only one in the entire realm who is worthy (5:3–5; cf. Isa. 29:10–18). What qualifies Jesus to open the scroll? It is not his divinity, eternality, omniscience, omnipresence, or other characteristics of divinity. This scion of David is worthy to open the scroll because he has "overcome" (NIV "triumphed") in a totally unexpected fashion. He laid down his life for the people he loved (5:9, 12; see "Overcomers" at 2:7 and "The Slain Lamb" at 5:6).

Article: The Son of David (5:5)

Again and again, Revelation stresses that Jesus is the promised descendant of David, whose throne and kingdom will never end (2 Sam. 7:12–13; cf. Isa. 16:5; Ezek. 34:23–25; Hos. 3:5). He is the Christ (i.e., the Messiah) (Rev. 1:1, 5; 11:15; 12:10; 20:4, 6; cf. 1 Sam. 2:10; Ps. 18:50). He is the "Root of David" (Rev. 5:5; cf. 22:16; Isa. 11:10; 53:2) and his offspring (Rev. 22:16; cf. Matt. 21:9, 15; 22:43–45; Luke 1:32). He is the "Lion of the tribe of Judah" (Rev. 5:5; cf. Gen. 49:9; Mic. 5:8). Jesus holds the key of David (Rev. 3:7; cf. Isa. 22:22) and the iron scepter of Judah (Rev. 2:27; 12:5; 19:15; cf. Gen. 49:10; Num. 24:17; Ps. 2:9; 45:6; 60:7; 110:2; Heb. 1:8).

2.3.3.2. The Appearance of the Lamb (5:6–14). The Lamb's appearance prompts those around the throne to break out in a fresh paean of worship (5:8–14). He looks "as if [he] had been slain" (v. 6) for a good reason: He was. His sacrifice enabled him to cleanse his people from their sins (v. 9; cf. 7:9–14; see "The Gentile Multitude" at 7:9). They will inherit the earth (Matt. 5:5) and reign on it (Rev. 5:10).

Article: The Slain Lamb (5:6)

There is a sharp contrast between the different images of Jesus in verses 5 and 6. While the description of Jesus as the Lion occurs only once (v. 5, but cf. 10:3), Revelation refers to Jesus as the Lamb thirty-one times (5:6, 8, 12, 13; 6:1, 3, 5, 7, 16; 7:9, 10, 14, 17; 12:11; 13:8; 14:1, 4[2x], 10; 15:3; 17:14[2x]; 19:7, 9; 21:9,

4, 22, 23, 27; 21:1, 3). Not only is he portrayed as a lamb, but one that has been slain (5:12; 13:8) and one whose blood has been shed (7:14; 12:11).

Revelation's earliest audience could not have expected this image. Symbols of messiahs in apocalyptic literature are generally strong and forceful. The Messiah is often portrayed as a great military leader, sometimes with miraculous or even divine powers of destruction. When animal images are used, as in the book of Enoch, the Messiah is represented by the largest of the domestic animals—a bull (Enoch 85ff.). By all rights, the lion image should be more common than the lamb.

After all, consider that Jesus' opponent is the beast. How could a lamb possibly defeat a beast? The beast is a carnivore, the lamb an herbivore. The beast is a predator, the lamb its natural prey. Could a lamb savage the beast with its sharp claws? It has none. Perhaps a lamb could rip out the beast's throat with its fangs? Sorry, lambs have no fangs. Could a lamb crush a beast with its superior weight? No, lambs are small animals, light in weight. Why, a lamb is not even fleet enough of foot to run away from a predator! In fact, lambs have no natural defenses at all, no weapons of war. When a lamb and a beast come into conflict, the lamb invariably dies. The Lamb Jesus defeated the beast just as his followers must: He died.

Revelation tells how the dragon was/will be defeated: "They overcame him by the blood of the Lamb and by the word of their testimony; they did not love their lives so much as to shrink from death" (Rev. 12:11); and again, "In her was found the blood of prophets and of the saints, and of all who have been killed [lit. slain] on the earth" (18:24). This is why the triumphant Lamb appears here "looking as if it had been slain" (5:6).

The war against the beast and his minions will not be fought with physical weapons or troops, but with spiritual ones. The chief weapon in the Christian arsenal is martyrdom. It totally frustrates the beast because it places us beyond his grasp. Jesus modeled this for his followers on the cross. He also said, "Take up [your] cross and follow me" (Matt. 16:24). Power, glory, and acclaim lie beyond the grave.

Article: The Prayers of the Saints (5:8)

In the aftermath of the first destruction of Jerusalem, Jews who wanted to worship God could not offer animal sacrifices according to the Mosaic Law. There was no consecrated altar. In time, they came to agree on three equivalents, which have been called the three great works of Judaism: prayer (the sacrifice of time), fasting (the sacrifice of body weight), and the giving of alms (the sacrifice of wealth). Note Jesus' teaching on these three works in Matthew 6:1ff.

Several times in Revelation, the prayers of the saints are likened to the incense that burned before the Most Holy Place (5:8; 8:3–4). This was a special blend of valuable spices, mixed in exact proportions. The Israelites were to use it only for God and in this specific place. The penalty for its improper use was excommunication of the offender from God's people (Ex. 30:34–38).

The same principles apply to the prayers of Christians. Prayer is an act of worship. As such, it may only be offered to God. He values it highly and considers it the same as the incense of old. Prayers may not be directed to the Roman emperor, to his image, or to any other being—whatever others may consider their civic duty to be. This is "worship of the beast" (see "Worship of the Beast" at 13:4). Violation of this principle will result in exactly the same penalty God once imposed on the Israelites: The offender will be excommunicated forever (14:9–11; cf. 20:4).

Article: Worship in Revelation (5:11)

The great theme of Revelation is worship. It is a book of worship on worship. Sadly, few people seem to recognize this. Their interest in Revelation is limited to calculating the exact date of Jesus' return (even though he himself said he did not know that date, see Matt. 24:36; Mark 13:32), the identity of the beast, and the meaning of various current events. Since Revelation was not written to address these questions, it is no wonder that these people go away frustrated, their predictions changing as often as the headlines of the daily news. Meanwhile, these same people skip over Revelation's incredible paeans of praise, skim through its rich adoration of God and the Lamb, and skew what is left in favor of their own predilections.

Those who are obsessed with the end of time do not need another chart or time line, but a revelation of God that will enable them to worship whatever happens. Our security as Christians comes from knowing the one who is in charge, not what will happen or when each event will occur. Worship strengthens our relationship with God and enables us to see things from his perspective.

By any standard, Revelation's focus is worship. The word "worship" (Gk. *proskyneo*) appears only sixty times in the entire New Testament. Over one-third of those times are in a single book: Revelation (3:9; 4:10; 5:14; 7:11; 9:20; 11:1, 16; 13:4[2x], 8, 12, 15; 14:7; 15:4; 16:2; 19:4, 10[x2], 20; 20:4; 22:8–9). The word "Hallelujah" (Heb. for "Praise the Lord!") appears only four times in the New Testament, all of them in Revelation (19:1, 3–4, 6). Four of six New Testament references to incense (5:8; 8:3–4; 18:13) and the only two references to "censer" are in this book (8:3, 5). As if this were not enough, Revelation contains more hymns than the entire rest of the New Testament put together. A quick thumbing through the New Testament will confirm this. Look for lines of poetry. The NIV indents and offsets poetry lines (e.g., 5:9–10), so that they can be easily recognized.

Scholars today generally agree that most of these pieces of poetry are hymns from the early church. Hymns in Revelation appear at 1:7; 4:8, 11; 5:9–10, 12, 13; 7:10, 12, 15–17; 11:15, 17–18; 12:10–12; 15:3–4; 16:5–7; 18:2–8, 10, 16, 19–24; 19:1–8. These hymns include the song of Moses and of the Lamb (15:3) as well as several "new songs" (5:9; 14:3). Often the singing is accompanied by the music of harps (5:8; 14:2; 15:2). Many of the lyrics in Revelation continue to be used in contemporary worship songs: different rhythms and tempos, different instruments and tunes, but the same unchanging adoration directed to an eternal God.

Why does Revelation spend so much time on worship? The crisis facing the seven churches of Asia Minor was a liturgical one: Who deserves to be worshiped and why? (see "Worship of the Beast" at 13:4 for an extensive description of the problem). Since the problem was liturgical, the solution had to be also. Thus, Revelation not only condemns false worship (13:4, 8, 12, 15; 14:9, 11; 16:2; 19:10, 20; 20:4; 22:9), it models correct worship. A study c worship in Revelation reveals that correct wo ship has three essential elements: (1) corre focus, (2) correct content, and (3) correct origi

(1) Correct focus: The only correct focus c worship is God and the Lamb (4:10; 5:1 7:11; 11:15–16; 12:10; 14:7; 19:4; cf. 21:2 22:3). No angel is worthy (19:10; 22:9), le alone some mere (and sinful!) human being Worship of any "beast" is a sure ticket to ete nal damnation (14:9–11; cf. Rom. 1:18–32).

(2) Correct content: The content of worshi is important. It must convey truth. Even whil Jesus was on earth, he said that those who wis to worship God must worship him in spirit an truth (John 4:23–24). In Revelation, hymn specifically praise God the Father for both hi character and his works: his holiness (4:8), hi work of creation (4:11), his justice (16:5–7) his judgment of the prostitute (19:2), hi revenge of his servants (19:2), as well as othe unspecified righteous acts and great deed (15:3–5). Jesus receives worship for his deat and for cleansing a multitude so that they coul serve God (5:9–12). Both the Father and Jesu are worshiped together for their joint partici pation in the plan of salvation (7:10) and thei rightful reign over the earth (11:15–18; 19:6) This is not to say that worship should be lim ited to these exact themes, but that it should always be biblically and theologically correct.

(3) Correct origin: The most biblically and theologically correct worship is meaningless to God if it is only lip service (Isa. 29:13; Jer. 7:1–16; Amos 5:21–24). True worshipers of God in Revelation include the four living creatures (see "The Four Living Creatures" at 4:6–9), the twenty-four elders (see "The Twenty-Four Elders" at 4:10), the angelic host (5:11; 7:11), the 144,000 (see "144,000 Jews" at 7:4), and the "great multitude" of Gentiles (see "The Gentile Multitude" at 7:9). Ultimately, however, "every creature in heaven and on earth and under the earth and on the sea, and all that is in them" will bow before God's authority (5:13; cf. Isa. 45:23; Rom. 14:11; Phil. 2:10).

Human beings who choose to worship God in Revelation all have certain characteristics. They "have washed their robes . . . in the blood of the Lamb" (7:14; cf. 22:14), some having shed their own blood in order that the enemy might be defeated (12:11). Whether Jew (7:4) or Gentile (7:9), they have "obey[ed] God's ommandments and h[e]ld to the testimony of esus" (12:17). They are pure and blameless 14:4; 21:27), having righteous deeds of their wn (19:8). They have "overcome" the world see "Overcomers" at 2:7), so they appear "as bride beautifully dressed for her husband" 21:2) (see "The Bride of Christ" at 21:9).

These believers perfectly model the ancient neaning of worship. The Bible never limits vorship to singing, but includes any action lone for God. God's people have a certain harnony between their expressions of praise and heir daily lives. Their choices and chants miror one another perfectly. There is no dissoance between their actions and their words. Both are orchestrated by the Holy Spirit (Rom. :5–9; cf. John 5:19; 12:49, 50; 14:9–11).

2.3.3.3. The Opening of the Scroll (6:1–17; 8:1–5). The description of the breaking of he scroll's seven seals has a certain rhythm—ike a countdown. In regular order, the breakng of each seal initiates another event on earth. Each seal reinforces the fact that God is n charge.

2.3.3.3.1. The First Four Seals: The Historic Past (6:1–8). The four horsemen of the first four seals, in our opinion, represent the conflict-filled historic past of the first audience and thus our own). Horses were instruments of war in biblical times. These represent the 'wars and rumors of wars" (Matt. 24:6; Mark 13:7; cf. Luke 21:9) that have characterized all of human history. They dole out conquest (Rev. 6:2), war (v. 4), famine (v. 6), and plagues and wild beasts (v. 8).

The lack of detail in each scene is deliberate. It means these scenes can be applied to any war or human tragedy (e.g., Ezek. 14:13–22). It also guarantees that these seals will not distract the audience's attention from the author's real focus: the fifth and sixth seals.

2.3.3.3.2. The Fifth Seal: The Immediate Past (6:9–11). The description of the fifth seal is strikingly different from the first four. It is significantly longer than any of the seals that preceded it—an indication of its importance. It also has no horses, further separating it from the four previous seals. Rather than global or international problems, it addresses the personal problem posed by Christian martyrdom: "When will God avenge us?"

In our opinion, the fifth seal describes the occasion of this book. Christians have been killed for their faith; their position "under the altar" implies a sacrificial death. They, and the other members of their churches, want to know how long they will have to wait for God's vengeance on their murderers.

The content and sequence of these five seals is strikingly similar to Jesus' teaching on the end times at Matthew 24:6–9:

> [Seals 1–4] You will hear of wars and rumors of wars, but see to it that you are not alarmed. Such things must happen, but the end is still to come. Nation will rise against nation, and kingdom against kingdom. There will be famines and earthquakes in various places. All these are the beginning of birth pains.
>
> [Seal 5] Then you will be handed over to be persecuted and put to death, and you will be hated by all nations because of me.

God's answer to the question, "How long?" must have been unexpected and disappointing to the first audience. Though they will have to wait only "a little longer," still more Christians will be martyred. In fact, God's judgment of the earth will be set into motion when the total number of martyrs reaches a preset figure (see also "White Robes" at 7:9).

Article: Testify, Testimony, Witness (6:9)

One of the major themes in Revelation is its call to Christian martyrdom. It teaches that true believers will have to give up their lives in order to be faithful to Jesus. The Greek root *martyr* is at the heart of this teaching. Originally, the verb derived from this root meant simply "to bear witness, testify," but it eventually came to mean "to be a martyr." Revelation marks an important transition for this word; in it "testify" means "testifying to the extent of giving one's life," that is, "martyrdom." Both Jesus and the early church placed a high value on martyrdom (Mark 8:34; 1 Cor. 13:1).

The various forms of this root word are translated into English as "testify," "testimony," and "witness" (the latter rather than the more awkward "testifier"). The highest example of this great personal sacrifice is Jesus, as evidenced by his own crucifixion. In Revelation, Jesus is the "faithful witness" (Rev. 1:5; cf. 3:14) who still "testifies" (22:20), as does his apocalypse (22:16). His death is the means by which he has "overcome" the world (5:1–9; see "Overcomers" at 2:7). Antipas, a martyr at Pergamum, is the only other person called a "faithful witness" (2:13).

There have been other Christian martyrs, as evidenced by the "souls under the altar" whose blood cries out to God for vengeance (6:9–10; cf. 16:7; Gen. 4:10); there will be more to come (Rev. 6:11). The two "witnesses" also will be (or have been) martyred (11:3, 7). While martyrdom is a grim topic, Christian martyrs will nevertheless ensure victory over the forces of evil (12:11) and have special rewards in the world to come (20:4–6). In fact, even the timing of Christ's return seems to be controlled by the number of Christians martyred (6:11).

Revelation lays the blame for these murders squarely at the feet of the Roman empire. This is clearly shown at a number of places: (1) the reference to beheading, the ancient penalty for treason committed by a Roman citizen (20:4); (2) the great prostitute (the city of Rome) holds a cup filled with the blood of these Christian martyrs (17:4–6); and (3) an otherwise inexplicable reference to Rome as the city where the decision to kill Jesus was really made (11:8).

Article: Inhabitants of the Earth (6:10)

The phrase "the inhabitants of the earth" appears seven times in Revelation (6:10; 8:13; 11:10; 13:8, 14; 17:2, 8). It refers to those who are at home on the earth; it is always morally negative. These people have martyred Christians (6:10) and rejoiced over their deaths (11:10). The beast will deceive them (13:14; 17:2, 8), and they will worship him (17:8). Therefore God will judge them (6:10; 8:13).

These "inhabitants of the earth" are the opposite of Christians, who are only "aliens and strangers" on earth (Heb. 11:13; cf. 1 Peter 1:1, 17; 2:11) but at the same time "citizens [of heaven]" (Eph. 2:19; cf. Phil. 3:20). Their home is with God (Rev. 7:15; 12:12; 13:6; 21:3).

Nero minted coins with his own image. Inscribed on them was his title "Ruler of the inhabitants of the earth." In using this phrase to describe the opponents of God, Revelation clearly sets the stage for Christian civil disobedience. When the laws of humanity and the laws of God are in conflict, Christians must obey the higher authority. In doing so, they demonstrate to which realm their heart really belongs.

2.3.3.3.3. The Sixth Seal: The Immediate Future (6:12–17). The longest description of any seal in Revelation is that of the sixth. Generally, interpreters of apocalyptic consider the longest and most detailed account to represent the original audience's present—their immediate concern. We agree that this is the case here. Furthermore, this is also *our* present. Like the seven churches of Asia Minor, we await the Lamb's decision to break the final seal.

Besides the fact that the description of the sixth seal is the longest, there are several other good reasons to consider it to be the historic present. (1) The rhythmic breaking of the seals pauses at the sixth and is interrupted by chapter 7. There God tells the angels to make sure that all of his people have been identified before the earth is judged (the judgment prefigured at 6:12). This task of identifying God's people is the proclamation of the gospel to the whole world, the task with which the church has been occupied these past two thousand years. Thus, the long pause between the sixth and seventh seals has allowed millions more to ask God for forgiveness. This will ensure that God will receive worship for all eternity from people "from every nation, tribe, people and language" (7:9) as well as from a full remnant of Israel (v. 4). Surely, this goal is worth a brief pause!

(2) A review of the last two millennia of human history will demonstrate that God's Judgment Day has not yet arrived. Jesus taught clearly that such an event would be unmistakable (Matt. 24:27–31). Up to now there has been no universal recognition of it, no widespread flight into the mountains and hills, and no sweeping plea for clemency.

(3) The astral signs mentioned have not occurred, or at least not all together. Matthew's description of Jesus' crucifixion mentions the sun's turning dark (27:45) and a violent earthquake (v. 51), but he says nothing about either the moon's turning red or the stars' falling from the sky. There have been other eclipses since then and the smoke of various wars has turned both the sun and moon dark. Still, these have not been accompanied by stars (comets?) falling from the sky or the sky rolling up "like a scroll."

Therefore, we place the original audience f Revelation (and contemporary readers) at ie beginning of the sixth seal, before the astral gns, in the interlude detailed in the following iapter. Because so much described in the xth seal is still to come, I have titled it "The nmediate Future" rather than "The Present."

Article: Signs in the Heavens (6:12)

The sixth seal contains the astral signs, long oretold by the prophets, that herald the arrival f God's Day of Judgment. These include the ın and moon turning dark (Rev. 6:12; 8:12; f. Isa. 13:10; 24:23; Ezek. 32:7; Joel 2:10; :15; Matt. 24:29; Mark 13:24) or, alternately, ed (Joel 2:31; Acts 2:20), and the stars falling rom the sky and the heavens rolling up like a croll (Isa. 34:4; cf. Matt. 24:29; Mark 13:25). 'his inversion of the natural order in the heavns reflects the chaos in the earthly realm.

The Jewish Tosephta *Sukkah* 2:6 on the 'east of Tabernacles contains a poignant xplanation of some of these signs:

A. When the lights are in eclipse, it is a bad omen for the whole world.

B. It is to be compared to a mortal king who built a palace and finished it and arranged a banquet, and then brought in guests. He got mad at them and said to the servant, "Take away the light from them," so all of them turned out to be sitting in the dark.

C. R. Meir did say, "When the lights of heaven are in eclipse, it is a bad omen for Israel, for they are used to blows.

D. "It is to be compared to a teacher who came into the school house and said, 'Bring me the strap.' Now who gets worried? The one who is used to being strapped!"

E. When the sun is in eclipse, it is a bad omen for the nations of the world.

F. [When] the moon is in eclipse, it is a bad omen for Israel,

G. since the gentiles reckon their calendar by the sun, and Israel by the moon.

H. When it is in eclipse in the east, it is a bad omen for those who live in the east.

I. When it is in eclipse in the west, it is a bad omen for those who live in the west.

J. When it is in eclipse in-between, it is a bad omen for the whole world.

K. When it is like sack-cloth, it is a sign that punishment by pestilence and famine is coming into the world.

Article: "Who Will Stand?" (6:17)

Those who have profited under the reign of evil are those who will be most threatened by its deposition. Deceived into thinking that the present situation will last forever, these people have amassed all kinds of earthly power: political (kings and princes), military (generals), and economic (the rich and mighty). When the King appears, these pawns will have their first glimpse of real power. He will expose their pettiness and impotence for what it really is. In fear they will lead the general flight into the remotest regions. Having long worshiped gods of mineral and stone, they will cry out to the mountains and rocks to shield them from God's judgment. They will cry in vain, and the mountains and rocks will refuse to respond. These inanimate objects will show greater sense than any of the earthly kings. They will recognize their Creator and tremble that his justice is at hand (Hos. 10:8; cf. Ps. 114; Ezek. 38:20; Amos 4:13; Mic. 1:4; 6:1).

"Who can stand" the Day of the Lamb's wrath? The next chapter reveals the answer. Only one group will escape, only one group will be able to stand: God's people, Jews (7:4–8) and Gentiles alike (7:9–17), will stand with the angels (7:1), worshiping around the throne.

Notice that the solution to surviving the coming tribulation is not fleeing or relocating to some remote location, buying firearms, or storing rations. The only way to escape that coming destruction is to wash our robes and make "them white in the blood of the Lamb" (7:14).

A. The First Interlude: The People of God (7:1–17)

A.1. The Sealing of God's Servants (7:1–3)

The scene of the heavenly multitude in Revelation 7 creates a pause or interlude between the opening of the sixth and the seventh seal. This interlude serves several purposes. (1) It is the literary equivalent of an inset in a drawing. The inset contains a magnified view of one of the main drawing's smaller parts, showing more intricate details than the regular view allows. In the same way, this chapter contains an expanded view of the small space between the breaking of the sixth seal and the astral signs—the original audience's historic present.

(2) This interlude heightens the tension of the book by postponing the conclusion—in the same way as a good mystery draws out the final chapter before the plot is exposed. To this point, everything has been proceeding apace. Now everything is in place. In fact, the angels have to restrain the destructive forces lest they erupt too soon (7:1). Why has the series not ended? Why the pause? This heightened tension parallels the desperate tension the original audience must have felt as they waited for the return of Jesus Christ.

(3) Finally, the details in this scene help explain why the return of Jesus Christ has been delayed longer than our audience expected. God is not slow or uncaring. He has waited because he is "not wanting anyone to perish" (2 Peter 3:9). The final blow will not fall until "we" have sealed all the servants of God (Rev. 7:3). The "we," without any other clear antecedent, must refer to the church and her Great Commission (Matt. 28:18–20).

A.2. The Worship of God's Servants (7:4–17)

A.2.1. The 144,000 (7:4–8). John now sees in his vision 144,000 Jews, 12,000 from each tribe, who form part of "the servants of our God" (7:3).

Article: 144,000 Jews (7:4)

The 144,000 people in Revelation are ethnic Jews. The author underscores their ethnicity by identifying each of them as members of one of the twelve tribes of Israel (7:5–8). Their appearance here testifies to the faithfulness of God and the certainty of his promises.

In the Old Testament, God promised to preserve a "remnant" (a small fraction) of Israel from destruction (Isa. 28:5; 37:31; Jer. 23:3; 50:20; cf. Rom. 11:1–5), despite their sins. Not only would he save them from destruction, but he promised them a new covenant (Jer. 31:31–33) and a new relationship with him (Hos. 2:14–23; cf. Rev. 21:3). His promise included the ten tribes of the north (Isa. 11:16; Jer. 3:11–12, 18; 23:8) as well as the two southern tribes. (The popular myth of the ten lost tribes of Israel is just that—a myth; God never did lose them.)

These Jews are not here just because of their ethnic qualification, but because of their character. The book says they have been sealed with "his name and his Father's name" (14:1; cf. 7:3), so they have acknowledged both God the Father and Jesus the Messiah; they have been "redeemed" (14:3). They have also avoided the sins of many of their fellow Jews, since they neither lied about the Christians (14:5; cf. 3:9) nor became involved in sexual immorality (14:4; cf. 2:14, 20; 9:21; 17:2; 21:8; 22:15). Their reward is to be the Lamb's constant companions (14:4) and to have a song of worship only they can sing (14:3).

The number 144,000 (Rev. 7:4; 14:1, 3) is not a limit on the number of Jews allowed in heaven, but the opposite. It attests to the magnanimity of God. If he had preserved but a single member from each tribe, it would have been enough to fulfill his ancient promise. This enormous number is one thousand times a full remnant (twelve people) from *each* of the twelve tribes!

A.2.2. The Gentile Multitude (7:9–10). The number of Gentiles among God's people clearly eclipses the small number of Jews. One wonders how the earliest Jewish followers of Jesus reacted to the huge numbers of Gentiles who also wanted to follow him as Messiah.

Article: The Gentile Multitude (7:9)

Despite the astonishment of the circumcised believers that the Holy Spirit had been poured out "even on the Gentiles" (Acts 10:45), the Old Testament contains many passages that describe a time when the Gentiles will come to worship the one true God (Ps. 22:27–28; 86:9; Jer. 3:17; Ezek. 38:23; Mic. 4:2; Zech. 2:11; 8:22–23; 14:16; Mal. 1:11). The best known is probably Isaiah 45:20–23 (Rom. 14:11; Phil. 2:10):

> Gather together and come;
> assemble, you fugitives from
> the nations. . . .
> Turn to me and be saved,
> all you ends of the earth;
> for I am God, and there is no other.
> By myself I have sworn,
> my mouth has uttered in all integrity
> a word that will not be revoked:
> Before me every knee will bow;
> by me every tongue will swear.

The countless Gentiles in this heavenly multitude (7:9) are the living fulfillment of these prophecies; the "other tongues" of Pentecost (Acts 2:4, 11) foreshadowed their diversity (Rev. 5:9). God's new covenant in Jesus Christ offered forgiveness to whoever wanted to come (Acts 2:38–39; cf. Mark 8:34), regardless of nationality, ethnicity, wealth, or social status (Acts 10:34; Gal. 3:28). They came. The size of this multitude testifies to the success the gospel mission would have among the Gentiles.

God has declared these Gentiles righteous because of their faith in his promises, just as he did for Abraham (Gen. 15:6; cf. Rom. 3:21–24). Thus, Abraham has become a "blessing" and the "father" of many nations (Gen. 17:4; Rom. 4:7–8). The early church council of Acts 11 was correct: "God has granted even the Gentiles repentance unto life" (Acts 11:18).

Article: White Robes (7:9)

The phrase "white robes [clothes]" appears only sixteen times in the New Testament, nine of which are in Revelation. God's people in Revelation wear white robes (7:9, 13–14; cf. 16:15; 22:14). Jesus promises the church at Sardis and Laodicea that the faithful will be clothed in white clothes (3:4–5, 18). Those who, by their martyrdom, have already demonstrated their faithfulness are given white robes at the fifth seal (6:11). Similarly, the twenty-four elders in heaven wear white robes (4:4). The host that follows the rider of the white horse to war are garbed in white (19:14), as is the bride of Christ (19:8). The seven other New Testament references are all associated with the transfiguration of Christ (Matt. 17:2; Mark 9:3; Luke 9:29), his resurrection (Matt. 28:3; Mark 16:5; John 20:12), or his ascension (Acts 1:10).

The prophetic images of the shining faces and shining white garments of the resurrected righteous (Rev. 7:9; cf. Matt. 17:2; Luke 9:29; 1 Enoch 38:4; 62:15–16; 104:2; 2 Baruch 51:3, 10; 4 Ezra 7:97, 124) appear to have been drawn from the crowds at the Feast of Tabernacles. Perhaps the Tabernacles crowds dressed in white in anticipation of their inclusion in the resurrection of the righteous.

Apparently, many Tabernacles celebrants anointed themselves with fragrant-smelling oils and wore white linen (cf. 2 Sam. 6:14; Isa. 61:2–3). These could not have been everyday garments, for they would have soiled easily in the fields and on the dusty streets of the ancient cities. They were special garments for days when no work was required—feast days. Thus white garments eventually came to represent both "no work" and "no dirt" and were associated with purity and festive or even nuptial rejoicing. The same crowds wore laurel wreaths (crowns) and carried palm branches, both of which also appear in Revelation (see "Crowns, Wreaths, and Diadems" at 4:10 and "Palm Branches," below).

Article: Palm Branches (7:9)

The most commonly recognized Tabernacles allusion in Revelation is the appearance of palm branches in chapter 7. The 144,000 and the great mixed multitude dressed in white robes at 7:9 are waving palm branches (cf. Lev. 23:40; Neh. 8:15; 4 Ezra 2:45–46; Jub. 16:30–31; m. *Suk.* 3:1–4:7). Palms were carried by the Tabernacles celebrants throughout the festivities of the seven-day feast. They were shaken during the daily reading of the Great Hallel (Ps. 115–118), at the beginning and end of Psalm 118, "Give thanks to the LORD, for he is good; his love endures forever" (Ps. 118:1, 29), and at "O LORD, save us; O LORD, grant us success" (v. 25).

History records two times when Jewish crowds spontaneously cheered victors with palm branches, even when it was not the Feast of Tabernacles. The first was Simon Maccabeus's conquest of the Acra, the old Seleucid fortress, in Jerusalem in 141 B.C. The people celebrated that victory by waving palm branches and singing psalms and hymns of praise (1 Macc. 13:51; cf. 14:4–15). The second time was during Jesus' triumphal entry into Jerusalem (Matt. 21:1–11; Mark 11:1–11; Luke 19:28–38; John 12:12–16), when people cut branches (of the palm tree, cf. John 12:13), waved them, and shouted phrases from the Hallel (Ps. 118:25–26).

The multitude in Revelation waves palms to celebrate a victory, not to draw God's attention to their plea for salvation. They cry out, "Salvation belongs to our God, who sits on the throne, and to the Lamb" (Rev. 7:10), not "O LORD, save us" (Ps. 118:25).

A.2.3. The Angels, Elders, and Creatures (7:11–12). The family portrait would not be complete without the rest of God's servants: the angels, the elders, and the four living creatures

(v. 11). Without regard to the differences in their ages, experiences, numbers, or natures, they worship God together around his throne (v. 12). Doubtless, their song is in perfect harmony.

A.2.4. The Identification of God's Servants (7:13–17). These five verses provide an excellent example of one of the most important principles in biblical interpretation. When interpreting obscure passages, check to see if the interpretation is given before inventing one's own. Verses 14–15 here give the interpretation of the great multitude. One of the elders explains to John that these people belong to God (v. 15). They have repented of their sins and been forgiven (v. 14). They have endured great persecution (v. 14) and will now receive great rewards (vv. 15–17). These Jews and Gentiles are the sum total of God's people, not a mere portion (see "The Great Tribulation," below).

Article: The Great Tribulation (7:14)

It is a mistake to read the phrase "the great tribulation" (7:14) as if it refers only to a specific period of time (e.g., seven years or even three and one-half years), rather than the intense persecution Christians have endured throughout history. The Greek word here translated "tribulation" (*thlipsis*, v. 14) appears four other times in Revelation. The first describes the historic "suffering" that John and his churches were enduring when he wrote Revelation (1:9). The second and third both refer to the "afflictions" the church of Smyrna experienced at that time (2:9–10). The fourth is a threat: God will cause those who follow the prophetess Jezebel in Thyatira to "suffer intensely" (lit., "with great suffering") unless they repent (2:22).

The phrase "great tribulation" is no more specific. It appears four times in the New Testament, including Revelation 7:14. Stephen used it to describe the "great suffering" that a famine caused Jacob and his family in Canaan (Acts 7:11). Jesus used the phrase when he cautioned his disciples that a time of "great distress" (Matt. 24:21) would come on the church, followed immediately by the heavenly signs of Revelation's sixth seal (Matt. 24:29; cf. Rev. 6:12–14). The phrase's final appearance, already mentioned, is God's threat to make certain Christians in Thyatira "suffer intensely" unless they changed their ways (Rev. 2:22).

Thus, the "great tribulation" is not a future period of time, somehow separate from the "age of the church," but the church's experience throughout history. It does not refer to what God will do to the world, but what the world has done to the church—and the reason why God is so angry.

If this is true, then Revelation 7 does not describe some small portion of God's people, rescued at the last moment from a beleaguered world. All of God's people are here, their character strengthened by the persecution Satan had hoped would undo them. James knew this when he wrote in James 1:2–4:

> Consider it pure joy, my brothers, whenever you face trials of many kinds, because you know that the testing of your faith develops perseverance. Perseverance must finish its work so that you may be mature and complete, not lacking anything.

Article: Blessings of the World to Come (7:15)

What will be the eternal reward for those who have served God on earth? They will continue to serve God, and he will grant them everything they need for eternal life and happiness. They (we!) will have plenty of food and drink (v. 16). Never again will we ever be homeless (v. 15), feel sorrow (v. 17), or be separated from our Savior (v. 15). God will make sure we have shade from the heat of the sun (a peculiarly Near Eastern blessing) (v. 16; see "The *Shekinah* Canopy," below). In fact, the blessings of 7:15–17 read like Psalm 23 with a twist: The Lamb will shepherd the people, not a person shepherd the lambs (v. 17)! Truly, "we are his people, the sheep of his pasture" (Ps. 100:3).

Article: The Shekinah Canopy (7:15)

One of God's more interesting promises in Revelation is that he will "spread his tent" over his people (7:15). This promise is to do more than provide shelter; it also includes an offer of eternal fellowship.

The ancient Israelite understanding of the *Shekinah* (God's "glory," his "visible presence") is at the heart of this promise. When God brought the Israelites out of Egypt, he guided them with a cloud during the day and a pillar of fire at night (Ex. 13:21). The cloud was not only visible by day, but shielded the Israelites from the intense desert sun; the pillar of fire provided both light to see and heat to drive away the evening chill. The *Shekinah* was visible over the tabernacle whenever they camped (Ex. 40:38; Num. 9:15–16). Later, the Israelites looked back to their desert travels fondly as the time when they were closest to God (Jer. 2:2; Hos. 13:4–6). Though they lived in tents, it was the time when God literally lived among them (Ex. 29:45–46). As a reminder of their experience, they lived in booths at the Feast of Tabernacles (Lev. 23:42–43).

Isaiah prophesied that sometime in the future God would once again live with his people (Isa. 4:5–6):

> Then the LORD will create over all of Mount Zion and over those who assemble there a cloud of smoke by day and a glow of flaming fire by night; over all the glory will be a canopy. It will be a shelter and shade from the heat of the day, and a refuge and hiding place from the storm and rain.

The Hebrew word for "canopy" in this passage (*chuppah*) is used of a wedding canopy. Thus, the fellowship that God promises us with him is pictured in terms of the most intimate of human relationships.

At his victorious enthronement, the Lamb will marry his bride, the church, the new Jerusalem. She will be pure (Rev. 21:27; cf. v. 8). Her wedding to the Messiah will be celebrated by a great banquet (19:7; cf. Matt. 22:1–14) and even greater joy (Rev. 19:7–9; see "The Bride of Christ" at 21:9).

Article: Living Water (or Water of Life) (7:17)

Living water is water that flows, whether from a river, a spring, or a fountain. The Hebrew concept of "living" simply means that it moves by itself, but it is appropriate here in several different ways. (1) Moving water is more highly oxygenated. It can support a higher population of aquatic life per cubic inch than still water. More fish means more food for the people that populate its shores. (2) Moving water is healthier than stagnant water. Movement at the water's surface allows better exchange of waste and gases. Thus it forms a poor environment for the anaerobic bacteria that cause disease and death. (3) Finally, and according to the Mosaic code, "living water" is the only kind of water that cannot be contaminated, no matter how much uncleanness it removes (Lev. 11:32–36). It has that power because it is constantly being renewed from a hidden source.

"Living water" is a powerful image of the healthy, holy life that flows from a proper relationship with the living God (Rev. 7:17; cf. Isa. 49:9–10). It is his gift to us (Isa. 55:1ff.; cf. Rev. 21:6; 22:17). He is the source, whether pictured as a spring, a river, or a fountain (Ps. 36:7–9; 46:3; Isa. 44:3; Jer. 2:13; 17:13; Ezek. 47; cf. John 4:10–11; 7:38). The living water flows from his house (Ezek. 47:1; Joel 3:18; Zech. 14:8) and from his throne (Rev. 22:1; cf. John 7:38; 19:34–37[?]). Once unstopped, this water will be sufficient to cleanse the earth (Isa. 35:5–10; Zech. 14:20–21; cf. Gen. 7:11ff.). Then once again the glory of the Lord will fill the earth (Ps. 57; 108:5; Isa. 6:3) and everyone will know the Lord (Isa. 11:9; Hab. 2:14; Zech. 14:9) (see "The Celestial River (or Crystal Sea)" at 22:1).

2.3.3.3.4. The Seventh Seal: The Immediate Future (8:1–5). The seventh seal completes the first ritual series. It includes an interval of silence (8:1) and an incense offering (vv. 3–5). It also introduces the seven angels with trumpets (see "Trumpet" at 8:2), who will call forth the next seven plagues (8:6ff.).

In ancient Israel, the incense altar stood inside of the tabernacle and temple, directly in front of the ark of the covenant (Ex. 30:1–6; Heb. 9:4). Only one kind of incense could be offered on the altar; its formula required a precise blend of precious spices and the finest olive oil. God forbade its use for any other purpose: It was holy or consecrated to the Lord (Ex. 30:31–38). Here in Revelation, the incense is offered to God and mingled with the equally consecrated prayers of the saints (Rev. 8:3–4; see "The Prayers of the Saints" at 5:8).

David prayed in Psalm 141:1–2:

> O LORD, I call to you; come quickly
> to me.
> Hear my voice when I call to you.
> May my prayer be set before you
> like incense;
> may the lifting up of my hands be like
> the evening sacrifice.

Like David, the saints of Asia Minor also have called out to God (Rev. 6:9). The present scene points out that God has heard their cry. He has often rendered judgment against sin by fire (Gen. 19:28; Num. 11; 16; Deut. 29:23; 2 Kings 1:10, 12), and we can trust him to do it again (Rev. 8:5, 7; 9:18; 11:5; 16:8; 18:8; 19:20; 20:9, 15; 21:8; cf. 2 Peter 3:10–12). God hears the prayers of his servants (James 5:16).

This scene ends, as do the other groups of seven rituals, with thunder, lightning, and earthquakes (8:5; 11:19; 16:18). These are the elemental symbols of God's power (4:5; see "The Throne of God" at 4:2). Their appearance in the seventh seal, seventh trumpet, and seventh bowl encourages us to interpret the three ritual series as congruent rather than consecutive (see "The Ritual Structure of Revelation" at 5:1).

Article: Trumpet (8:2)

Trumpets are found throughout the book of Revelation (1:10; 4:1; 8:2–13; 9:1, 13; 10:7; 11:15). Made from a ram's horn (Josh. 6:4), the Jewish trumpet was called a *shophar* (Ex. 19:16–20). It had no valves and therefore was not a melodic instrument, but its loud, piercing sound made it perfect for ordering troops during battle (Judg. 3:27; 6:34; 7:18–22; 2 Sam. 18:16; Jer. 4:19–21; 42:14; 1 Cor. 14:8). Since that was its primary function, people throughout biblical times would have associated the instrument with war.

The other occasions on which trumpets were used should be understood as extensions of its use in war. The Israelites sounded trumpets at the Day of Atonement, the various feasts of the Lord, including the Feast of Tabernacles (Lev. 25:9; Ps. 81:3; Joel 2:15; see "The Dawn Procession of Tabernacles" at 11:19), and the enthronement of the Israelite king (1 Kings 1:34).

The many trumpets in Revelation can be explained by the book's extensive depictions of war, its symbolic use of the Feast of Tabernacles, and its description of the enthronement of God and his Messiah. All three of these themes merge in the trumpet blast that heralds the second coming of Jesus (Joel 2:1; Zech. 9:9–14; Matt. 24:31; 1 Cor. 15:52; 1 Thess. 4:16; Rev. 11:15).

2.3.4. The Second Ritual: The Seven Trumpet Blasts (8:6–9:21; 11:15–19).

2.3.4.1. The First Four Trumpet Blasts (8:6–12). The first four seals described God's judgment throughout all of human history (6:1–8); now the first four trumpet blasts (8:6–12) reveal God's judgment on all of creation. The two quartets are alike in another way: Both are deliberately sparse, thus more universally applicable (see sec. 2.3.3.3.1 [Rev. 6:1–8]).

Later in Revelation, an angel will describe God as the one who created "the heavens, the earth, the sea and the springs of water" (14:7). The division of God's creation into these four parts reveals a cosmology common to most of the ancient Near East. In addition, the use of polar opposites to describe the whole is a typical Semitism (e.g., the expression "from Dan to Beersheba" in 2 Sam. 17:11 is an expression for "the entire land of Israel," or "the tree of the knowledge of good and evil" in Gen. 2:9, 17 for "the tree of all knowledge"). Thus, the angel is simply saying here that God created everything. In a similar manner, the first four trumpet blasts reveal God's judgment on everything—all of his creation.

After the Flood, God promised that he would never again destroy the earth by water (Gen. 9:11–15), so this judgment is by fire (Gen. 19:24; Deut. 32:22; 2 Kings 1:10; Luke 3:17; Heb. 10:27; 2 Peter 3:7). Each domain of creation responds differently to the heavenly fire. (1) When the first trumpet sounds, the green grass reacts normally by burning (Rev. 8:7).

(2) The sea's response is more unexpected: It turns to blood (v. 8). This response is similar to the plagues of Egypt (Ex. 7:20)—also judgments for oppressing God's people.

(3) Fresh waters become bitter when touched by fire at the third trumpet blast (v. 11), an apocalyptic reversal of the miracle God worked for his people in the desert. There he turned bitter waters sweet by using a piece of wood (Ex. 15:23–25), whereas here he turns fresh waters bitter with a star named Wormwood (Rev. 8:11).

(4) Finally, God darkens the light of the sun, moon, and stars by one-third at the fourth trumpet blast (Rev. 8:12; cf. Joel 2:31; 3:15; Amos 8:9). This is not a total reversal of his creation of these heavenly bodies (Gen. 1), but it certainly indicates their end is near (cf. Gen. 1:16). This too is reminiscent of the plagues of Egypt, this time of the plague of darkness that covered the land for three days (Ex. 10:21–23).

This second sequence of seven underscores od's control of all things. He is in charge and is been for a long time. He does not react to ises, but anticipates them. Worship, once ;ain, controls the physical creation.

Narrator's Interjection: An Eagle Cries Woe" (8:13). When Americans hear the word agle," they automatically think of the ation's symbol, the bald eagle. The bird rep- sents freedom, majesty, bravery, and the auty of an unspoiled wilderness. This is tally different from its meaning in biblical mes. The Bible makes little distinction etween various kinds of raptors: eagles, vul- res, kites, sea gulls, and so forth. All of these rds were considered unclean (Lev. 11:13–20; eut. 14:12) because they ate carrion, includ- g the flesh of human beings (see "The Two reat Eschatological Feasts" at Rev. 19:7–9, 7–21). Thus, these birds came to symbolize ath and desolation (Deut. 28:49; Jer. 49:22; am. 4:19; Hos. 8:1). In fact, the Greek word anslated "Woe!" (Rev. 8:13) is pronounced *ai*. It is the sound the birds make as they cir- e above the battlefield dead.

The eagle in this passage cries "*Ouai*" three mes. Each cry represents one of the follow- g three trumpet blasts: the fifth, an army of custs (or army as numerous as a cloud of custs, 9:1–12); the sixth, an army of two mil- on cavalry from the east (9:13–21; 11:14); id the seventh, the proclamation that "the ingdom of the world has become the king- om of our Lord and of his Christ, and he will ign for ever and ever" (11:15).

2.3.4.2. The Fifth Trumpet Blast: An rmy of Locusts (9:1–11). The fifth trumpet mounces the arrival of a great army of ocusts." This army does not devour green lants (v. 3), but afflicts the inhabitants of the orld with scorpion-like stings for five onths. Though their sting is not fatal, those ho are stung wish they would die (vv. 4–5).

Sometimes the author characterizes this my as human, describing human faces and air (vv. 7–8), sharp teeth (v. 8), iron armament . 9), and battle sounds like those made by orses and chariots (v. 9). At other times, he escribes them as insects, with wings (v. 9), ils, and stingers (v. 10). Based on the infor- ation given herein, it is difficult to decide hether this army is a literal plague of locusts an army so big it looks like a plague of locusts (i.e., a metaphor; personally, I lean toward interpreting it as a human army, such as the long-haired Parthians). God has used both people and insects in the past to carry out his plans, so both are equally possible.

Several times in the Bible God used insects to achieve his will. He sent a plague of locusts to Egypt when the pharaoh refused to release the Israelites. They devoured all of the foliage in the land (Ex. 10:4–20). Similarly, God promised to use hornets to drive out the inhabitants of Canaan to prepare the way for the Israelites to settle the region (Deut. 7:17–21; cf. Isa. 7:18). But God has also used armies. He punished Jerusalem by sending Nebuchadnezzar's army to destroy it (Jer. 25:9; 27:6–8). The prophets often described large armies, such as Nebuchadnezzar's, in terms usually reserved for natural disasters: a plague of locusts (Judg. 6:5), a roaring sea (Jer. 6:23), or a storm cloud (Ezek. 38:9, 16). The most interesting passage for students of Revelation is the language of God's prophecy to destroy Babylon (Jer. 51:14, 27–29):

> The LORD Almighty has sworn by himself:
> I will surely fill you with men, as with a swarm of locusts,
> and they will shout in triumph over you....
> Lift up a banner in the land!
> Blow the trumpet among the nations!
> Prepare the nations for battle against her;
> summon against her these kingdoms:
> Ararat, Minni and Ashkenaz.
> Appoint a commander against her;
> send up horses like a swarm of locusts.
> Prepare the nations for battle against her—
> the kings of the Medes,
> their governors and all their officials,
> and all the countries they rule.
> The land trembles and writhes,
> for the LORD's purposes against Babylon stand—
> to lay waste the land of Babylon
> so that no one will live there.

We may not know exactly what kind of plague the fifth trumpet announces, but we can be sure of one thing: The God who avenged the people of the Mosaic covenant with such vigor will certainly do no less for those who belong to Jesus.

Article: The Abyss (9:1)

The word “abyss” (Gk. *abyssos*) and its equivalent “the deep” (Heb. *t^{e}hom*) do not appear often in the Bible. It is part of the language of creation (Gen. 1:2) and the Flood (7:11). It evokes images of the ocean deeps, the primordial depths, the grave, and the underworld (Job 36:16; Ezek. 31:15; Jonah 2:5). It is a dark place, located outside of the physical world and normally accessible only through death.

“Abyss” appears eight times in Revelation (Rev. 9:1, 2[2x], 11; 11:7; 17:8; 20:1, 3), occurring only one other place in the New Testament (Luke 8:31). The army of locusts comes from there (Rev. 9:1–2), as does the (sea) beast (11:7; 17:8). The angel in charge of the pit is named Apollyon (a Gk. word meaning “Destruction,” 9:11). Here is where Satan will be chained for one thousand years (20:1–3). The Abyss is therefore different from the lake of fire, which most people call “hell,” the place of eternal torment for Satan, his demons, and those who follow them (20:14–15).

Those people or things who are associated with the Abyss carry with them the smell of death and sometimes even the odor of evil. The contemporary expression the “pit of hell” conveys the same sort of meaning as “Abyss,” though it is a bit more negative. Like the Abyss, the “pit of hell” can be both literal (the actual place where someone is confined) and figurative (their actions indicate this is really the place where they belong).

Narrator’s Interjection: The First “Woe” Is Past (9:12). The narrator’s interjection here keeps us from getting lost in the details of the fifth plague, reminding us that two more “woes” are yet to come.

2.3.4.3. The Sixth Trumpet Blast: 200,000,000 Cavalry (9:13–21). The sixth trumpet blast is accompanied by a voice from the horns of the golden altar (v. 13). This golden altar is the altar of incense (Ex. 40:5; Heb. 9:4), on which the prayers of the saints were offered earlier (Rev. 8:3). Its mention here seems to indicate that this plague came in answer to the prayers of the saints. A similar link can be found between the third plague of the bowls (16:4–7) and the appeal of the martyred saints under the brazen altar (6:9–11). God knew in advance of their prayers, so he had already set the time when these angels would be released (9:15).

This sixth plague of trumpets (9:13–21 appears identical with the sixth plague c bowls (16:12–16). The four angels of th Euphrates River (9:15) have been holding bac the four winds of the earth (7:1). These wind once released, will disperse and evaporate th water in the Euphrates so that troops can cros it (9:16; 16:12; cf. Isa. 11:15). This will set th stage for the battle of Armageddon (Re 16:16), a great slaughter in which one-third c all human beings will die (9:15; 19:17–21; se “The Two Great Eschatological Feasts” a 19:7–9, 17–21).

The “nation from the north” (e.g., Jer. 25:9 46:2–10; Ezek. 26:7) is not Russia, but th countries on the eastern side of the Euphrate The phrase is literally true. These troops had t go up and around the desert in order to invad Palestine, thus they always came int Jerusalem from the north. The Assyrian an Babylonian empires lay on the other side of th river in biblical times (where Iran and Iraq ar now located).

Like the plagues of the sixth seal (6:12–17 and the sixth bowl (16:12–16), this plague als lies in the future. It was in the future when Joh prophesied it in the first century; it remain unfulfilled today. We should not, then, be to troubled that the details cannot be identifie with any great precision. No doubt those wh survive this great future battle will find Reve lation’s description more than adequate.

Article: Sin Lists in Revelation (9:20

The final two verses of chapter 9 conclud the list of six plagues with a “sin list” (9:20 21). “Sin lists,” found also at 21:8 and 22:1 provide us with insights into the specific prob lems in Asia Minor the book addresses: The deal primarily with behavior, not with doctrin or attitudes. When we compare the three list as in the following chart, we see that the boo condemns seven different kinds of behavio murder, sexual immorality, vileness, the prac tice of magic arts, idolatry, lying, and thef Two further sins have to do with attitude cowardice and unbelief; both of these are ofte revealed by how a person behaves when unde great stress.

It is no great surprise that the Bible list these activities as sins. The surprise is that th three lists all limit themselves to the same kind of sins and omit the more common one

THREE "SIN LISTS" OF REVELATION

Rev. 9:20–21	Rev. 21:8	Rev. 22:15	Gal. 5:19–21
	cowardly unbelieving (faithless) vile		impurity and debauchery
murders	murderers	murderers	
sexual immorality	the sexually immoral	the sexually immoral	immorality and orgies
magic arts	those who practice magic arts	those who practice magic arts	witchcraft
worship demons and idols	idolaters	idolaters	idolatry
	all liars	everyone who loves and practices falsehood	
thefts			
			[missing in Rev.] hatred, discord, jealousy, fits of rage, selfish ambition, dissentions, factions and envy, drunkenness

hatred, dissension, envy, rage, and so forth (e.g., Gal. 5:19–21). The reason is that the lists target the specific sins that Revelation addresses: the activities of the seven different individuals or groups who oppose God: (1) Satan (the serpent or dragon), (2) a Roman emperor (the "sea" beast), (3) the leader of the imperial cult in Asia Minor (the false prophet or "land" beast), (4) the city of Rome and its inhabitants (the great prostitute or Babylon), (5) certain antagonistic Jews (found especially in Smyrna and Philadelphia), (6) certain Christians who have compromised their faith, and (7) those who worship the beast (the inhabitants of the earth). It is not that the Apocalypse intends to limit divine judgment to these groups and their sins, but rather focuses on them.

Thus "cowardly," "faithless," and "idolatrous" probably refer to those who had been worshiping the beast, especially those who claimed to be Christians (13:8, 12; 14:11). "Liars" refers to certain slanderous Jews (2:9; 3:9; cf. 14:5), perhaps those who initiated legal action against Christians in the Roman courts. While doubtless there were many in the ancient world who were "immoral" or "fornicators," the author of Revelation is especially concerned about Christians (2:14, 21–22) or Jews (14:4) who were immoral. This was probably reinforced by the fact that the illicit sex often involved temple prostitutes and was thus linked to idolatry. It is no coincidence that the lists also mention idolatry. "Murderers" certainly refers to those who killed Christian martyrs (past, present, or future; 6:9; 11:7; 13:15). "Magic arts" and "thefts" are less clear. The former may refer to the magical signs performed by the false prophet (13:16–17; cf. 2 Thess. 2:9), while the latter may indicate those who took advantage of the inability of those without the mark of the beast to buy or sell (13:15; 19:20).

Why would a loving God inflict these kind of plagues on people? God longs for all sinners to repent (2 Peter 3:9), for he knows that the wages of sin is death (Gen. 2:17; Rom. 6:23). Yet these people have rejected God's generous offer of mercy and forgiveness (John 1:9; 3:16). What can he do? Perhaps a demonstration of his power and wrath will convince them to change their minds. Alas, the plagues reveal these people's stubborn wickedness. Not only do they not repent (Rev. 9:20), but they curse God in their anger (16:9, 11). God will have n choice but to bar them from ever entering hi holy city (21:15). They will spend eternity i the lake of fire instead (21:8).

B. Second Interlude: The Prophets of God (10:1–11:13)

The first interlude in Revelation gave the audience an explanation for the delay in Jesus return (some of God's servants had yet to b sealed, 7:1–3) and a reason for hope (hov diverse and numerous God's servants woul be, once all were sealed, 7:4–10). It also se this interpretation of the original audience' present in a historical framework. They wer in the sixth of the seven seals, awaiting onl the astral signs that would herald the Day o Judgment (6:12) and the breaking of the sev enth seal (8:1).

The second interlude (10:1–11:13) onc again appears between the sixth in a series an the seventh. Like the first (ch. 7), the secon covers the original audience's historical pre sent. It includes John's own prophetic ca (10:1–11:3) and the ministries of the tw greatest figures in early Gentile Christianity Peter and Paul (11:4–13). It will also introduc the dragon's servant, the (sea) beast (11:7) Simultaneously, it will minimize the beast' importance by contrasting him with th divinely empowered servants of the Most Hig God: John, Peter, and Paul.

B.1. The Author's Call to Prophesy (10:1–11)

B.1.1. The Mighty Angel's Appearanc (10:1–4). Who delivered this prophecy (i.e. the book of Revelation) to John? The choice seem to be Jesus or a very high angel (10:1–4; cf. Dan. 12:6–7). This author leans towar the latter choice. First, this being is calle "*another* mighty angel" (10:1), a clear reference to the first "mighty angel" in Revelation the one who cried out for someone worthy t open the scroll (5:2). The Lamb also appear in this earlier scene and is clearly a differen character than the angel. With Revelation' stress on the uniqueness of the Lamb, it seem unlikely that it would introduce him elsewher as simply "another mighty angel," that is, on of several.

Moreover, the conclusion to this apocalyps states three separate times that an angel gav is revelation to John. The first time the angel identified as the angel sent by "the Lord, the od of the spirits of the prophets" (22:6). The st time, Jesus personally identifies him as "my igel" (22:16). In between John falls down to orship this same angel, but the angel refuses, ying, "Do not do it! I am a fellow servant with ou and with your brothers the prophets and of l who keep the words of this book. Worship od!" (22:9). Clearly, this is not Jesus.

Why then does this angel appear to have so any divine features? In Jewish literature, the gher an angel ranks, the closer he stands to od's throne and the more attributes of divinity possesses. This angel is high indeed. He is bed with a cloud and has a rainbow above his ad, both elements that surround God's throne :3–5). His face shines like that ofJesus, as do s legs (10:1; cf. 1:13–16). He speaks with the ar of a lion (10:3), like Jesus, the Lion of dah (5:5). In fact, in the light of the last feare, which seems to be unique to Jesus, perhaps e could go so far as to identify this angel as sus' personal messenger (22:16).

B.1.2. The Angel's Proclamation (10:5–). The angel's message has two parts, both lemnized and secured by his oath before the reator (vv. 5–6). The first part is that there ill be no more delay (v. 6), the second that the nystery of God" is about to be accomplished.

Article: The Mystery of God (10:7)

What is the "mystery of God" (10:7) and hen will it be completed? Paul spoke of it veral times (Col. 1:27; 2:2; 4:3), describing in detail when he wrote the church of Ephus (one of the seven churches to which Revation is addressed). He said, "This mystery that through the gospel the Gentiles are heirs gether with Israel, members together of one ody, and sharers together in the promise in hrist Jesus" (Eph. 3:6).

This interpretation of "mystery" as the ospel is confirmed by a close reading of the reek text. The word "announced" (Rev. 10:7) ere is a poor translation. A better choice ould have been "proclaimed the good news" Gk. *euangelizomai*). The clear reference is to e gospel message, just as it is at 14:6, where e same word appears.

God revealed this gospel, at least in part, to is prophets (Isa. 40:9; 52:7; 60:6; 61:1; Joel 32; Nah. 1:15), though the only time it is specifically called a "mystery" is in the book of Daniel (Dan. 2:18–19, 27, 30, 47). There Nebuchadnezzar has a vision of a great idol that is smashed by a "rock cut out of a mountain, but not by human hands" (2:45). God further reveals that through it he will "set up a kingdom that will never be destroyed, nor will it be left to another people. It will crush all those kingdoms and bring them to an end, but it will itself endure forever" (v. 44).

When will this mystery be fulfilled? A proper understanding of the timing is critical. It will be in the days after the angel has already blown the sixth trumpet blast, just prior to the seventh and final blast (Rev. 10:7). In other words, the mystery of God will be accomplished in the time period represented by the sixth trumpet blast. The seventh trumpet simply announces its completion.

In short, the message of this angel is much like that of the angel in Revelation 7. God is not delaying; he is wrapping up the greatest plan of all the ages. He is sealing the last of his servants (7:1–3) and establishing a kingdom that will endure forever (10:7). Very little remains to be done before history finally ends in eternity.

B.1.3. The Angel's Prophecy (10:8–11). It is obvious that John understands his call to be like that of Ezekiel. He is called to prophesy (Rev. 10:11; cf. Ezek. 2:1–5) and given a scroll to eat (Rev. 10:8–9; cf. Ezek. 3:1), which tastes like honey (Rev. 10:9; cf. Ezek. 3:3). Like Ezekiel, he will write a book that begins with a revelation of God's throne (Rev. 4; cf. Ezek. 1) and end with a description of the new Jerusalem (Rev. 21–22; cf. Ezek. 40–48). Ezekiel, however, was called to prophesy to Israel (Ezek. 3:1), while John prophesies to (and about) "many people, nations, languages and kings" (Rev. 10:11).

B.2. The Two Witnesses' Ministry (11:1–13)

B.2.1. Their Description (11:1–6). The book of Ezekiel contains an extensive description of a future temple, complete with exact measurements of its dimensions (Ezek. 40:1ff.). John's original audience probably expected something similar here. John even receives a measuring rod (Rev. 11:1), but he never uses it. In fact, the only measurements in the book are those of the new Jerusalem (Rev. 21:16–17), which fall near the end of this book and are measured with a different rod (21:15; cf. 11:1). John's vision does not duplicate Ezekiel's, but complements it. Ezekiel prophesied about buildings, John prophesies about the worshipers that will use them (11:1; cf. chs. 7, 21–22).

The angel directs John's focus to the outer court that will be given to the Gentiles "for 42 months" (see "1,260 Days, 42 Months, or 3 1/2 Years" at 12:6). There he sees two menorahs (seven-pronged lampstands; see Ex. 25:31–36; cf. Zech. 4:1–14). On most occasions, it would be unusual to find lampstands in the outer court. The descriptions of the tabernacle and temple all place a single menorah in the Holy Place (Ex. 26:35; Num. 8:2–4; 2 Chron. 4:20; Heb. 9:2), not two outside the building and in the outer court. The only time menorahs appeared in the outer court was during the Feast of Tabernacles. Revelation links these menorahs to this Feast by their fire (here, the power to destroy, v. 5), their ability to withhold rain, and their power to send plagues on the earth (v. 6; cf. also 15:1; 16:1–21). These are all found in Zechariah 14 (esp. vv. 12–19), which describes an eschatological celebration of Tabernacles and was one of the traditional readings for the Feast of Tabernacles in the first century A.D.

Article: The Two Lampstands (11:4)

The Jewish Mishnah gives us the most complete description of the menorahs of the Feast of Tabernacles and how they were used each evening. It also admits they were an "amendment" (an additional feature or practice not prescribed by the Mosaic Law). Thus, those familiar with the Bible but not the other Jewish literature of the period generally do not recognize the festival context.

The Mishnah (*Suk.* 5:1–4a) says:

> At the close of the first Festival-day of the Feast they went down to the Court of Women where they had made a great amendment. There were golden candlesticks there with four golden bowls on the top of them and four ladders to each candlestick, and four youths of the priestly stock and in their hands jars of oil holding a hundred and twenty *logs* which they poured into all the bowls.
>
> They made the wicks from the worn out drawers and girdles of the priests and with them they set the candlesticks alight, and there was not a courtyard in Jerusalem that did not reflect the light of the . . . [menorahs].
>
> Men of piety and good works [*hasidim*] used to dance before them with burning torches in their hands, singing songs and praises. And countless Levites [played] on harps, lyres, cymbals and trumpets and instruments of music, on the fifteen steps leading down from the Court of the Israelites to the Court of Women, corresponding to the Fifteen Songs of Ascents in the Psalms; upon them the Levites used to stand with instruments of music and make melody.

The Jewish Tosephta adds several detai
First, it says that Rabbi Simeon b. Gamali
(the apostle Paul's mentor, cf. Acts 22:3; c
5:34) often joined the torch dancers; he cou
juggle eight torches without dropping a sing
one (t. *Suk.* 4:4). Then it gives the words to t
most commonly sung songs (t. *Suk.* 4:2–9):

> The people: *"Happy is he who has not sinned, but all who have sinned he will forgive."*
>
> The wonder workers: *"Fortunate is my youth, which did not bring my old age into shame."*
>
> The penitents: *"Fortunate are you, O years of my old age, for you will atone for the years of my youth."*
>
> The Levites: *"A Psalm of Ascents. Come bless the Lord, all you servants of the Lord, who stand by night in the house of the Lord"* (Ps. 134:1) and *"Lift up your hands to the holy place and bless the Lord"* (Ps. 134:2).
>
> The departing crowd: *"May the Lord bless you from Zion, he who made heaven and earth"* (Ps. 134:3).

Revelation's festival setting is identical, b
the emotions associated with it are differen
There is no dancing around these menoral
and no singing. In fact, there is no forgivenes
for the scene is one of judgment. The onl
rejoicing occurs among those who celebra
when the two prophets are killed (Rev. 11:10
It is short-lived, however, for the prophets wi
be resurrected, the earth will quake, a portic
of the city will be destroyed, and the remai
ing population will then be "terrified ar
[give] glory to the God of heaven" (vv. 11–13

Article: The Two Witnesses (11:6)

Who are these two witnesses? Since John loes not identify them, a number of theories ave been advanced. Some argue that they are noch and Elijah, because Scripture records he death of neither (Gen. 5:24; 2 Kings 2:11) nd "man is destined to die once" (Heb. 9:27). Therefore, they must come back to earth to die. Others look to Jesus' transfiguration for a clue Matt. 17:3; Mark 9:4; Luke 9:30), identifying hese two witnesses as Moses and Elijah, representatives of the Law and the Prophets. Besides, they argue, the circumstances of Moses' death were unusual (Deut. 34:5; Jude), and the prophets said Elijah would come gain (Mal. 4:5; cf. Matt. 17:10–12; Mark :11–13).

This author believes the best candidates for hese two witnesses are Peter and Paul, the two postles of Gentile Christianity. When Luke writes his story of Christianity's expansion nto the Gentile world, he divides his book into biographies of these two men: Peter (Acts 1– , 10–12) and Paul (Acts 9, 13–28). The Gentiles first heard the gospel from Peter (Acts 10; 5:7), while Paul was considered the apostle o the Gentiles (Gal. 2:7–9; cf. Acts 13:46; 5:12; 18:6; 21:19; Eph. 3:1). Paul founded nany of the churches in Asia Minor, including everal of those to which Revelation was pecifically addressed (Ephesus [Acts 18:19; 9:1] and Thyatira [Acts 16:14]); he had also vritten the church at Laodicea (Col. 2:1; 4:13, 5). Peter became associated with the church t Rome, the capital of the Roman empire. According to church tradition, Nero put both nen to death in A.D. 65 (see "The Beast From he Sea" at 13:1).

B.2.2. Their Deaths (11:7–10). The (sea) east is only able to slay the two witnesses (or prophets," 11:10) once they have finished heir divinely assigned task (11:7). Not content nerely with their deaths, the inhabitants of the ity make them a public spectacle by refusing hem burial (v. 9). They even celebrate by ending gifts to one another (v. 10). If the two vitnesses are indeed Peter and Paul, no other ecord of these details has survived. However, hese kind of indecencies were typical of Rome in this period (see "The Two Witnesses" t 11:6).

The city in which the two witnesses died vas Rome. Revelation repeatedly calls this city the "great city" (11:8; 16:19; 17:18; 18:10, 16, 18, 21). The book also uses a number of metaphors to describe Rome, most of them drawn from the Old Testament. Like Sodom (Rev. 11:8; cf. Gen. 19), Rome was immoral and inhospitable to outsiders. Like the pharaoh of Egypt who "did not know about Joseph" (Ex. 1:8; cf. Rev. 11:8), Rome's emperor oppressed and enslaved the people of God. Like Nebuchadnezzar's "Babylon" (cf. Jer. 50–51; Rev. 11:9), Rome was a vast city with an incredible diversity of people, which ruled over the nations of the earth (see "Babylon the Great" at 17:5). It was also the city that killed Jesus (11:8). After all, a Roman emperor appointed Pontius Pilate to his position. That same emperor was responsible for setting the policies of the empire, policies that led to the death of Jesus Christ. Thus, the decision to crucify Jesus was really made in Rome, not Jerusalem.

B.2.3. Their Resurrection (11:11–13). The story of the two witnesses ends with an inversion of apocalyptic proportions. The two dead are resurrected (vv. 11–12), while many of those who were alive are killed (v. 13). Part of the city that stood collapses to the ground in a cloud of dirt (v. 13), while the witnesses who have fallen are raised up in the clouds of heaven (v. 12). Those who celebrated (v. 10) are now terrified (v. 13). Those who rejoiced in the silencing of God's two witnesses (v. 10) now use their own lips to acknowledge the God of heaven (v. 13).

In a real way, this conclusion foreshadows the end of every Christian's life. The scales of justice will balance in the world to come. The poor will be rich, the hungry filled, those who wept will laugh (Luke 6:20–21). The weak will be strong (Ezek. 34:16), the blind see, and those who were captives freed (Isa. 61:1–4). Hannah knew this and celebrated it in her song of praise (1 Sam. 2:12–10), just as Mary did in her Magnificat (Luke 1:46–55). We must remember this if we are to endure to the end.

Narrator's Interjection: The Second "Woe" Is Past (11:14).

2.3.4.4. The Seventh Trumpet Blast: God's Enthronement (11:15–19). The seventh trumpet is the only one that has not yet sounded. It is the one for which God's people have long waited. It will be as Paul said (1 Cor. 15:51–52; cf. Isa. 27:13; Matt. 24:31; 1 Thess. 4:16):

> Listen, I tell you a mystery: We will not all sleep, but we will all be changed—in a flash, in the twinkling of an eye, at the last trumpet. For the trumpet will sound, the dead will be raised imperishable, and we will be changed.

The sounding of a trumpet called ancient armies to war. This last trumpet blast will call the dead in Christ to join the heavenly host at the battle of Armageddon (Rev. 16:15–17; 19:14; see also Joel 2:1–11; Zech. 9:15 [cf. Matt. 24:27; Luke 17:24]; Matt. 24:31). There the Messiah will "destroy those who destroy the earth" (Rev. 11:18) and begin his thousand-year reign on the earth (11:15; 20:1–6; cf. Zech. 14). Jesus' followers will receive their rewards at that time (Rev. 11:18; cf. 20:1–6), including an invitation to the wedding supper of the Lamb (19:9; cf. Isa. 25:6).

2.3.4.4.1. The Hymns of God's Enthronement (11:15–18). God's most recent triumph has provided a new opportunity for reaffirming his rule (11:17–18). These hymns blur and blend the rule of God and his Messiah (11:15; cf. 7:15–17; 12:10; 22:1, 3) in the same way as the ancient Israelites must have combined the enthronement of Yahweh and their king (Isa. 6:1–3; cf. Rev. 4:8). Specifically, God has fulfilled the promise of Psalm 2. He has given the nations to the Son as his inheritance (2:8; cf. Ps. 110); his reign will be eternal (Rev. 19:6).

Article: The Enthronement of God and His Messiah (11:15)

The latter part of Revelation 11 contains an enthronement ceremony, or at least enough of one that the book's first audience would have recognized it. The ceremony does not mark the beginning of God's reign; it is a reaffirmation of its continuity. God has always ruled over all creation, including planet Earth. His rule may be challenged here from time to time, but it was/is never threatened.

This point is more easily understood by looking at the ancient enthronement ceremony in the Israelite Feast of Tabernacles. Long before David captured Jerusalem, the Israelites knew that Yahweh was their king (Num. 23:2; Deut. 17:14; 1 Sam. 8:7). Each year they were to gather together at Tabernacles to celebrate his deliverance of them (Lev. 23:33–44, esp. v. 43). Every seventh year they were to recite his laws in their entirety at that same feas (Deut. 31:9–13).

The Israelites believed God's action formed a fundamental and unchanging patterr They found it again and again—in the storie of creation, the Flood, their own exodus fron Egypt, and the conquest of Palestine (as well a some Near Eastern myths). In essence, the pat tern was that God had claimed them as his ow people, so he could be counted on to delive them from tribulation. Their responsibility wa to celebrate his kingship, his victory, and hi choice to dwell among them in his sanctuar (e.g., Ex. 15; Deut. 33; Ps. 68; 113–118).

During the monarchy, the Israelites held a annual celebration of the reign of their king du ing the Feast of Tabernacles. This "ritua enthronement" marked either the investiture o a new king or the reaffirmation of the reign o the current one, whichever the current politica situation demanded. It also celebrated Yahweh' kingship and reinforced his relationship with hi earthly king (Ps. 68; 95; 145; cf. 1 Kings 8:14 20). God's selection, both of David and the cit of Jerusalem, was an important theme in the ri ual. Many of the psalms in our Bible were prob ably written for and performed at the event (e.g Ps. 2; 45; 68; 72; 110).[6]

When the monarchy ended, the Israelite retained their belief in a godly Messiah wh would come to deliver them from their tribu lation (Jer. 33:17–22; Ezek. 34:23–24; 37:24 25; Zech. 12:7–10). They also continued t associate his arrival with the Feast of Tabe nacles (Zech. 14). This is the reason wh Jonathan's investiture as high priest took plac during Tabernacles (1 Macc. 10:21) and wh the crowd chose to proclaim Aristobulus I king during another Tabernacles celebratio (Josephus, *Ant.* 15.3.3). It is also the reason th crowd used symbols and Scriptures from th Feast of Tabernacles to greet Jesus of Nazare at his "triumphal entry" (Matt. 21:1–11; Mar 11:7–11; John 12:12–15).

Revelation applies the ancient pattern cel brated at Tabernacles to the Christians' situ tion in Asia Minor. The book spells out God judgment on the rebellious nations, his deli erance of his people, the subsequent coronatic and wedding of the Davidic Messiah, and th reaffirmation of God's reign. Since God ha claimed these Christians as his people, he cou be counted on to deliver them from tribul ion—just as he had the Israelites of old. Like the Israelites, these believers' chief responsibility was to celebrate God's kingship, victory, and dwelling among them—in worship.

2.3.4.4.2. The Site of God's Enthronement (11:19). The dramatic conclusion to the series of seven trumpet blasts is the sight of the ark of the covenant. It appears in the heavenly temple in the Most Holy Place (11:19; cf. Heb. 8:2–5). The ark is God's throne, the place where his presence rests (see "The Throne of God" at 4:2). The Most Holy Place is his throne room. This is where the ark would have been placed after the enthronement procession, in the years when the priests still carried it at the head of their processions (2 Chron. 35:3; cf. Ex. 37:5; Deut. 10:8; Josh. 3:8; 6:4–6).

The symbols of God's presence (lightning, thunder, etc.) appear here (11:19; cf. 4:5). Revelation also uses these symbols as a literary device. By ending each series of seven with similar symbols (8:1–5; 11:19; 16:17–21), it encourages us to interpret them as congruent. Each series covers human history (items 1–6 in each series) and concludes with a vision of the worship of the eternal God (item 7). The message is clear: The current conflict, indeed all of human history, will culminate in a great outpouring of worship to God.

Article: The Dawn Procession of Tabernacles (11:19)

Here Revelation has yet another parallel to one of the ceremonies of the Feast of Tabernacles, namely, the dawn procession. The origin of this procession is likely the ancient annual reenthronement of the Israelite king. By the time of the New Testament, Israel had been without a Davidic king for six hundred years. Still, that hope was nurtured by the dawn procession each morning of the Feast of Tabernacles.

Once again, the Jewish Mishnah provides us with a description of this ceremony, one neither prescribed by the Mosaic Law nor described in full by the writers of the Old Testament. The Mishnah says (m. *Suk*. 5:4b–5a):

> Two priests stood at the upper gate which leads down from the Court of the Israelites to the Court of Women, with two trumpets in their hands. At cockcrow they blew a sustained, a quavering and another sustained blast. When they reached the tenth step they again blew a sustained, a quavering and another sustained blast. They went on until they reached the gate that leads out to the east. When they reached the gate that leads out to the east, they turned their faces toward the west and said, "Our fathers when they were in this place turned *with their backs toward the Temple of the Lord and their faces toward the east, and they worshipped the sun toward the east;* but as for us, our eyes are turned toward the Lord." R. Judah says: They used to repeat the words "We are the Lord's and our eyes are turned to the Lord." They never blew less than twenty-one blasts [i.e., seven times repeating the series, "a sustained, a quavering, and another sustained blast"] in the Temple [in a day]. (emphasis added)

Notice the number of parallels in Revelation's description of the seven trumpets. (1) The horn used at Tabernacles is the same as in Revelation: the *shophar*. It was made from the horn of a ram. (2) The number of trumpet blasts are identical: seven (8:2–9:21; 11:15–19). This is the same as the minimum number of soundings for Tabernacles (m. *Suk*. 5:5a). (3) The two menorahs appear in the outer court

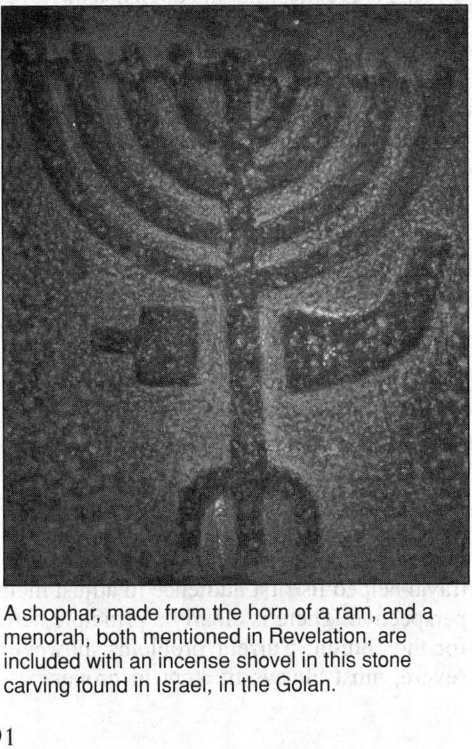

A shophar, made from the horn of a ram, and a menorah, both mentioned in Revelation, are included with an incense shovel in this stone carving found in Israel, in the Golan.

in Revelation and at the Feast of Tabernacles (see "The Two Lampstands" at 11:4). (4) Both Revelation and the Mishnah tie their descriptions of menorahs of the feast to the dawn procession. (5) Finally, the author's own perspective in Revelation moves as if he himself were in the dawn procession.

This last parallel requires a more detailed explanation. The seven angels first appear before God's throne and near the incense altar (8:2–5). It is reasonable to assume the first trumpet blast was in the same location. There is no discernible movement during the next five trumpet blasts, but by the sixth trumpet John is in the outer court (11:1–2). Here he sees the two menorahs (vv. 3ff.). The final trumpet in Revelation sounds immediately before John sees the ark of the covenant in the heavenly temple (v. 19).

Now, the ark of the covenant could only be seen from outside of the temple if one were *east of the temple and facing west*. This is *exactly* the position and the viewpoint with which the Levites ended each dawn procession: at the eastern gate and facing west (m. *Suk*. 4b). It is this point in the ceremony where they disavowed their forefathers' worship of other gods and pledged themselves once again to Yahweh.

This is exactly what the audience of Revelation must do: They must disavow the worship of other "gods" and pledge themselves once again to Yahweh and Jesus the Messiah. After all, they are about to be put to the test. Six trumpets have already sounded. They must decide which way to turn by the seventh, and final, trumpet blast.

C. An Allegorical Narrative (12:1–13:18)

C.1. The Dragon's Previous Failures (12:1–16)

By this point in the book, Revelation has already identified its historic present twice and set it in an historical framework (Rev. 7; 11–12). The beast has also appeared in the same historical framework, but briefly and only as a minor character (11:7–10). Since he really was only a minor character, Revelation's portrayal helped its first audience to adjust their perspective. There is clearly a principle here for the church: Current problems, however severe, must always be kept in proper perspective. The only "proper perspective" is God's great plan for us.

Chapter 13 deals with the two beasts that wreaked so much havoc among the churches of Asia Minor. Chapter 12 provides background information essential for evaluating them—the history of the dragon's failures. Not only does it identify the real power behind the beast's throne (Satan), but it characterizes Satan as a habitual failure. The beast's reign is only the latest of Satan's attempts to thwart God's plan. It is doomed to fail—just as all other attempts already have.

C.1.1. The Dragon Fails to Kill a Newborn Infant (12:1–6). The first of the dragon's past exploits mentioned here is his failed attempt to slay Jesus as a newborn infant (12:4–5). The reference to an "iron scepter" proves that the infant is to be identified as Jesus. Psalm 2 prophesies that the Messiah will rule over the nations with an "iron scepter" (Ps 2:9; cf. Heb. 1:5). Elsewhere, Revelation refers to Jesus using this same phrase (Rev. 2:27; 19:15; see also "The Son of David" at 5:5).

Jesus actually escaped Satan at least twice. The dragon's first assassination attempt used Herod (another vicious ruler with Roman authority) to try to kill him when he was a newborn infant (Rev. 12:4–5; cf. Matt. 2:1–18). Satan's plans were thwarted when God sent an angel to warn Joseph to flee to Egypt with the child (Matt. 2:13). Then, having triumphed over Satan on the cross (a Roman instrument of capital punishment, Rev. 11:8), Jesus escaped the dragon's grasp again when he rose from the grave and ascended into heaven (12:5).

Of course, Jesus died on the cross prior to his resurrection and ascension, a point that would not have been lost on the first readers of Revelation (1:5; 5:6). So too they may have to die in order to defeat the dragon (12:11).

Article: The Heavenly Woman (12:1)

The heavenly woman of Revelation 12 cannot be identified with certainty; there is simply not enough evidence. What we do have is two concrete facts: (1) She gave "birth" to Christ (v. 5), and (2) she fled into the desert sometime afterward (v. 6).

Biblical scholars are divided among three different theories. (1) The woman represents Israel. A woman of Israel (Mary) gives birth to Jesus; we also know that Jews, the descendants of Israel, did flee into the desert prior to the fall of Jerusalem in A.D. 70. (2) The woman represents the church. Mary believed in Jesus and followed him, so she was part of the church. In fact, some argue she was the first member of the church. Thus, one could say the church gave birth to Jesus. There were also members of the church who fled into the desert prior to Jerusalem's destruction. (3) This woman represents Mary herself. While there is no independent tradition of Mary fleeing into the desert, it is certainly possible she did; John would have known for sure (John 19:26–27).

In any case, we must not allow the question of the woman's identity to distract us from the real point of the story. The escape of the woman's son is the first in a list of the dragon's defeats in Revelation 12.

Article: The Dragon (12:3)

The dragon of Revelation is specifically identified as "that ancient serpent called the devil or Satan" (12:9; cf. 20:2). He is pictured as red, with seven heads, ten horns, and seven crowns (12:3), and having a frog-like evil spirit coming from his mouth (16:13).

Though obviously a powerful figure, the dragon is successful at only one thing: He sweeps a third of the stars from heaven with his tail (12:4). The rest of his life is a dismal failure. He tries to destroy the Messiah at birth, but fails (v. 4). He is defeated by Michael and his angels in heaven (v. 7) and is banished to earth with his followers (v. 9). Next, he tries to destroy the woman of chapter 12, but fails yet again (vv. 13–16). Finally, enraged, he attempts to wage war against the rest of the children of God (v. 17); he will not be successful at that attempt either!

In order to battle God's people, the dragon enlists the services of two other beasts—one from the sea (13:1–2) and the other from the earth (13:11). Together, their lies will enable them to gather the kings of the earth and their armies to battle the forces of heaven. The Messiah and his heavenly host will defeat them soundly (19:20–21). The dragon will be bound in chains for a thousand years (20:2), then released briefly so he can deceive the nations into waging yet another futile war (20:7–9). He will lose that conflict as well (v. 9). Finally, he will be cast into the lake of fire, where he will remain forever, in eternal pain and torment (v. 10).

The binding of the dragon deserves some reflection. God does not have to do it personally; he does not even have to get up from his throne. Nor does the Messiah have to bind Satan personally. The task is not even difficult enough to require the services of an archangel. It takes only a single angel from heaven, who is so unimportant as to not even be named, to enchain Satan and cast him into the Abyss (20:1–3).

Though a frightening figure to those on earth, the dragon is no threat to heaven. He is portrayed like a mad dog for whom his master still has some small, temporary use.

Article: 1,260 Days, 42 Months or 3 1/2 Years (12:6)

There are three numbers that appear in Revelation, all of which express the same period of time: 1,260 days (11:3; 12:6), 42 months (11:2; 13:5), and 3 1/2 years ("a time, times and half a time" in 12:14; cf. Dan. 7:25; 12:7). A number of things take place during this same period. Gentiles trample on the city of Jerusalem (Rev. 11:2), the beast blasphemes (13:5), the two witnesses prophesy (11:3), and God protects the woman in the desert (12:6, 14).

The question is how literally to take these numbers. Jewish apocalyptic literature often uses patterns or paradigms to interpret history, patterns that can then be applied to future events. Invoking a key phrase from one of them invokes the memory of the pattern for the reader. Revelation is filled with examples, such as calling Rome "Babylon" or "Sodom." (A similar phenomenon today might be the way a sensually dressed woman is called a "Jezebel" or a powerful Christian leader a "Peter" or "Paul.")

The only other book in which these numerical phrases appear in the Bible is in Daniel. There they appear twice. (1) The first reference is in a description of how God's kingdom will defeat the fourth human kingdom, generally identified as Rome (Dan. 7:23–27):

> The fourth beast is a fourth kingdom that will appear on earth. It will be different from all the other kingdoms and will devour the whole earth, trampling it down and crushing it. The ten horns are ten kings who will come from this kingdom. After them another king will arise, different from the earlier ones; he will

> subdue three kings. *He will speak against the Most High and oppress his saints and try to change the set times and the laws. The saints will be handed over to him* for *a time, times and half a time.*
>
> But the court will sit, and *his power will be taken away and completely destroyed forever. Then the sovereignty, power and greatness of the kingdoms under the whole heaven will be handed over to the saints, the people of the Most High. His kingdom will be an everlasting kingdom, and all rulers will worship and obey him.* (emphasis added)

(2) The other reference is in a passage usually identified as describing Antiochus Epiphanes IV, the Seleucid ruler who desecrated the Jerusalem altar (i.e., the "abomination that causes desolation," Dan. 11:31). When Daniel asks how long it will take for "these . . . things" to happen, the angelic figure replies, "It will be for a time, times and half a time. When the power of the holy people has been finally broken, all these things will be completed" (12:6–7).

This second passage from Daniel is too long to quote in its entirety, but the section most relevant to Revelation says the following (Dan. 11:29–12:3):

> [The king of the North] will turn back and vent his fury against the holy covenant. He will return and show favor to those who forsake the holy covenant.
>
> His armed forces will rise up to desecrate the temple fortress and will abolish the daily sacrifice. Then they will set up *the abomination that causes desolation.* With flattery he will corrupt those who have violated the covenant, *but the people who know their God will firmly resist him.*
>
> Those who are wise will instruct many, though for a time they will fall by the sword or be burned or captured or plundered. When they fall, they will receive a little help, and many who are not sincere will join them. *Some of the wise will stumble, so that they may be refined, purified and made spotless until the time of the end,* for *it will still come at the appointed time.*
>
> The king will do as he pleases. He will exalt and magnify himself above every god and will say unheard-of things against the God of gods. He will be successful until the time of wrath is completed, for what has been determined must take place. . . . He will pitch his royal tents between the seas at the beautiful holy mountain. Yet he will come to his end, and no one will help him.
>
> At that time Michael, the great prince who protects your people, will arise. There will be a time of distress such as has not happened from the beginning of nations until then. *But at that time your people—everyone whose name is found written in the book—will be delivered. Multitudes who sleep in the dust of the earth will awake: some to everlasting life, others to shame and everlasting contempt. Those who are wise will shine like the brightness of the heavens, and those who lead many to righteousness, like the stars for ever and ever.* (emphasis added)

If the first passage refers to Rome and the second to Antiochus IV, then they obviously do not refer to the same event. Most historians do recognize two separate "abomination[s] of desolation," one at the time of Antiochus (165/164 B.C.) and one by Rome, during the destruction of Jerusalem in A.D. 70 (Matt. 24:15; Mark 13:14).

If this is true, then John was invoking one of the paradigms we mentioned earlier. He did this in order to help his audience understand the nature of their conflict, to reinterpret it. They needed to remember that this was not the first time God used an evil ruler to advance his divine purpose. These evil rulers never last long, nor will their backer (Rev. 12:12); but while they are here God will use them. Like the saints of old, the readers of Revelation are being refined like gold (Dan. 11:35). Once resurrected, their reward will be great. God's kingdom, unlike that of these earthly rulers, will last forever (Dan. 7:27; 12:1–3). Thus, believers must be faithful, even unto death.

C.1.2. The Dragon Fails to Defeat the Archangel Michael (12:7–12).

C.1.2.1. The War in Heaven (12:7–9). The second of the dragon's failures is his attempt to usurp God's throne. Satan apparently never ets very far, for Revelation does not portray im battling the Lord God Almighty or even the Messiah. He and his angels are not even strong nough to defeat Michael and his angels (vv. 7–). Defeated, Satan and his forces are thrown ut of heaven and onto the earth (vv. 9–13; note sp. vv. 10–11):

For the accuser of our brothers,
who accuses them before our God day
and night,
has been hurled down.
They overcame him
by the blood of the Lamb
and by the word of their testimony;
they did not love their lives so much
as to shrink from death.

C.1.2.2. The Song of Triumph (12:10–2). The triumphant heavenly song bridges the ragon's defeat in heaven with his anticipated efeat on earth. It refers to Satan as the accuser of our brothers" (12:10), perhaps a eference to the source of Job's troubles (Job :6–12). The same phrase foreshadows Satan's ast target: Jesus Christ's "brothers [and sis- ers]" (Rev. 12:10; cf. v. 17). The song also cel- brates the manner in which they (we) will efeat him: by the blood of the Lamb and the 'word of their testimony" (lit., "report of their nartyrdom"; see "Testify, Testimony, Witness" t 6:9 and "The Slain Lamb" at 5:6).

Martyrdom is the ultimate weapon in our var against Satan. It was how Jesus defeated im. Those who follow Jesus must also "take p [their] cross" if they are to triumph over Satan (Matt. 10:38; 16:24; Mark 8:34; Luke):23). Complete victory lies only beyond the rave (1 Cor. 15:54–57).

C.1.3. The Dragon Fails to Kill the Infant's Mother (12:13–16). The dragon's hird failure is his attempt to catch the heav- enly woman (12:1, 13). God gives her the vings of an eagle (cf. Ex. 19:4; Isa. 40:31; Ezek. 17:1–7) so she can fly to her sanctuary n the desert (the passive voice, "[she] was given" [v. 14], is a typically Jewish way of expressing a divine action). The language here is that of the Exodus (Ex. 19:4), but whether this refers to the actual Exodus or one of God's later rescues of his people modeled on the Exo- dus (e.g., Ezek. 17:1) is unclear. Similarly, the description of a river swallowed by the earth (Rev. 12:16) may be a poetic way of referring to the crossing of the Red Sea, though the language is certainly unusual if that is the case.

Since this episode follows the story of the birth of the Messiah (12:5), this commentator is inclined to look for a historical event that does so. It seems likely that this event is the flight of either Jews or Christians from the besieged Jerusalem prior to A.D. 70. If so, the reference to the earth swallowing a river so the people can make their escape remains a mystery.

C.2. The Dragon's Current Campaign (12:17–13:18)

The dragon's most recent attack, at least at the time Revelation was written, is directed at the woman's other children (v. 17). This is the occasion of the book—the specific problem that prompts the writing of Revelation. Frustrated, thrice defeated but still ravenous, the dragon turns its attention to the only other prey on earth: the children of God.

C.2.1. The Dragon's Latest Prey (12:17–13:1). The dragon's latest quarries are the woman's other offspring (12:17). They are the rest of God's children, the brothers and sisters of Jesus Christ (cf. Matt. 12:46; 28:10; John 20:17: Rom. 8:29; Heb. 2:11–12, 17). The phrase "children of God" is a favorite of John (John 1:12–13; 11:52; 1 John 3:2, 10; 4:4; 5:2, 19), though it also appears occasionally in Paul's writings (Rom. 8:14–17; Phil. 2:15).

The members of the seven churches of Asia Minor were certainly among these children. They were, and we are, the only target remaining for an earthbound dragon who lacks the power of flight (12:9). As surely as he once attacked the Christians of Asia Minor, he will not ignore us (cf. 2 Cor. 2:11; 11:14; 1 Peter 5:8). We must be diligent and on guard (Eph. 6:10–18; 1 John 4:4).

Article: The Beast From the Sea (13:1)

The chief antagonist in Revelation, the greatest of the dragon's minions, is the "beast coming out of the sea." Revelation describes it as carnivorous, a predator (13:1–3). As such, according to Jewish law, it was unclean (Lev. 11:1, 10, 27). It was also unnatural, for it had bits and parts from a number of different animals (a lion, a bear, and a leopard). Moreover, its strangeness is emphasized by the fact that it came from the sea (Rev. 13:1; cf. Dan. 7:3), but was obviously not designed for such an environment. It had no fins, scales, gills, or tentacles.

The beast of Revelation cannot be identified with any of the four beasts of Daniel 7. It has no bird's or eagle's wings, no ribs in its mouth, or no fearsome iron teeth (Dan. 7:4–7); it has seven heads, not four (Rev. 13:1; cf. Dan. 7:6). Besides, each one of the beasts in Daniel represented a kingdom (Dan. 7:17, 23); the present beast represents a specific ruler (Rev. 13:18; 17:8–11). John does, however, use features from all four of Daniel's beasts in his description of this latest horror. This beast from the sea has a lion's mouth (like Daniel's first beast), a bear's feet (like the second beast), a leopard's body (like the third beast), and ten horns (like the fourth beast; see Rev. 13:1–3; cf. Dan. 7:4–7). The real perversion of Revelation's world is shown by this inversion of divine order. God made Adam ruler over all the animals of the earth (Gen. 1:28); now the beasts are ruling the people (Rev. 13; 17; cf. Dan. 7).

Revelation identifies the beast from the sea as a "king" (17:11). Furthermore, he is someone who "once was, now is not, and will yet come" (v. 8; cf. v. 11). In other words, he had ruled in the past, was not ruling at the time of Revelation's composition, and was expected to return to the throne at some future time. The dragon gave him that throne (13:2). He wears crowns (13:1) and is attired in scarlet (17:3), a regal color. Moreover, since he reigns over "the great city that rules over the kings of the earth" (17:18), which has seven hills (v. 9), is inhabited by multitudes from various "nations and languages" (v. 15), and is clearly visible from the sea (Rev. 18), he must be a *Roman* emperor. This fits with the author's description of him as coming from the sea (13:1), since a Roman emperor would likely travel to Asia Minor by boat.

The problem is *which* Roman emperor the beast represents. Fortunately, Revelation's extensive descriptions, in and of themselves, are enough to identify the correct emperor. The candidates, all Roman emperors through the end of the first century A.D., are these:

Augustus (Octavian)	27 B.C.–A.D. 14
Tiberius	A.D. 14–37
Gaius	A.D. 37–41
Claudius	A.D. 41–54
Nero	A.D. 54–68
Galba	A.D. 68
Otho	A.D. 69
Vitellius	A.D. 69
Vespasian	A.D. 69–79
Titus	A.D. 79–81
Domitian	A.D. 81–96
Nerva	A.D. 96–98
Trajan	A.D. 98–117

The number of candidates can be narrowed even further. The angelic interpretation of the beast from the sea is that he is one of seven kings (17:10). This "animal of an emperor," since he is characterized three times as "once was, and now is not" (17:8–11), must be one of the *five* emperors who have already ruled at the time Revelation was written (v. 10; this is a crucial point for dating the composition of Revelation). This reduces the number of candidates to Augustus, Tiberius, Gaius, Claudius, and Nero.

It is this author's opinion that the original beast from the sea was Nero, the fifth Roman emperor. It is a matter of historic fact that he was the first to persecute Christians, an act of which the Roman historian Suetonius approves in *The Twelve Caesars* 6.16. Another Roman historian, Tacitus, describes this persecution in great detail in *The Annals of Tacitus* 15.44:

> But no human aid, no largess from the Emperor, no supplications to heaven, did anything to ease the impression that the fire [of Rome] had been deliberately started. Nero looked around for a scapegoat, and inflicted the most fiendish tortures on a group of persons already hated by the people for their crimes. This was the sect known as Christians. Their founder, one Christus, had been put to death by the procurator Pontius Pilate in the reign of Tiberius. This checked the abomination for a while, but it broke out again and spread, not merely through Judaea, where it originated, but even to Rome itself, the great reservoir and collective ground for every kind of depravity and filth. Those who confessed to being Christians were at once arrested, but on their testimony a great crowd of people were convicted, not so much on the charge of arson, but of hatred of the entire human race. They were put to death amid every kind of mockery. Dressed in the skins of wild beasts, they

were torn to pieces by dogs, or were crucified, or burned to death: when night came, they served as human torches to provide lights. . . . These Christians were guilty, and well deserved their fate, but a sort of compassion for them arose, because they were being destroyed to glut the cruelty of a single man and for no public end.

As should be apparent from this passage, Nero did not persecute Christians specifically for their faith, but for a crime of which he himself was accused: that of setting fire to Rome (Suetonius, *The Twelve Caesars* 6.38; Tacitus, *Annals* 15.38–43; cf. Rev. 17:16).

This fits Revelation's depiction of the beast from the sea at a number of points. (1) Revelation does *not* describe this emperor as slaughtering Christians for refusing to worship his image, a point often missed by casual readers of the book. Rather, the second beast (the "land beast") is responsible for those sorts of death (13:15). Revelation does say the beast from the sea killed the "two witnesses" (11:7; see "The Two Witnesses" at 11:6), but notice that the text does not state that their deaths were a result of their testimony, simply that the beast was not permitted to slay them until "they have finished their testimony" (11:7). The beast *is* repeatedly accused of blasphemy against God (13:1, 5–6; 17:3) and of receiving his authority directly from Satan (13:2, 4). This could easily have been the Christian assessment of Nero.

(2) In addition to his persecution of Christians, Nero is an excellent candidate for "the beast" because his sexual practices can only be described as "beastly." None of the Roman emperors were chaste, but Nero descended to new depths—depths particularly appalling to Jews and Christians. Even the Roman historians of the period seem disgusted by his actions. Tacitus, for example, records his incestuous relationship with his mother, Agrippina (*Annals* 14.2), and his public homosexuality (15.37). He sums up his opinion of one particular night of revelry by saying that "Nero tried every pleasure, licensed and unlicensed. It seemed that there were no further depths of degradation for him to plumb" (15.37; cf. 14.14–15).

Suetonius records Nero's rape of the vestal virgin Rubria and his castration of and subsequent marriage to Sporus (*The Twelve Caesars* 6.27–28). The historian also reports that Nero went so far as to invent new kinds of depravity: "Nero practiced every kind of obscenity, and at last invented a novel game: he was released from a den dressed in the skins of wild animals, and attacked the private parts of men and women who stood bound to stakes" (6.29). Surely, of the five Roman emperors from among whom we have to choose, Nero best fits the description of Revelation. In all senses of the word, he was a *beast*.

(3) The historical record of Nero's physical appearance matches Revelation's description. Suetonius described Nero as being of average height, with a "pustulous" (marked by raised spots of another color that were infected with pus) and "malodorous" body. His belly was "protuberant," his neck "squat," and his legs "spindly." Moreover, his eyes were blue and his hair "light blond." The latter he wore long and "kinked," like a chariot driver's (*The Twelve Caesars* 6.51). His beard was also an unusual color for that place and time: bronze.

Now, the physical description of the beast in Revelation is given in three similes. On the surface, they are descriptions with which any Roman emperor would be pleased: three aggressive, predatory beasts—a leopard, a bear, and a lion (Rev. 13:2). This *could* mean that this emperor had the speed and agility of a leopard, the stability of a bear, and the ferocity of a lion. But it could also mean that his body was spotted like a leopard and his mouth surrounded by a golden mane, like a lion's. (The further reference to bear's feet continues to elude this author. There are certain fungi that can infect a person's toenails, making them resemble claws. These fungi are regularly found in unsanitary conditions, like those in which Nero reveled. If, however, Nero had such a condition, no historical reference to it has survived apart from Rev. 13:2.)

Where would the author of Revelation get such personal details on the habits of Nero? What was not public knowledge about this emperor (and there appears to have been little that was not) could easily have come from people like those whom Paul mentioned at Philippians 4:22: "All the saints greet you, *especially those of Caesar's household*" (NASB, emphasis added).

(4) We have the enigmatic "number" of the name of the beast: 666 (13:18). Scholars have

long known that this sum can be attained by transliterating the Greek version of Nero's name and title ("Nero, Caesar") into Hebrew letters, then adding their numerical value. An ancient textual variant provides an odd sort of confirmation. The uncial manuscript labeled C (Codex Ephraemi Rescriptus) has the number 616 instead of 666. This sum is the result of converting Nero Caesar to Hebrew letters from Latin, then adding the numeric value of the letters (see Guthrie, 959–60).

(5) Finally, history informs us of the belief that after Nero died of a mortal wound, he would return to life (cf. Rev. 13:3, 12, 14). Such a belief was widespread in ancient times, though not until well after the period we would assign to the composition of the book. Thus, it is usually used as an argument for dating Revelation during the reign of Domitian or later.

There is a better possibility, however—that Revelation was not written as a result of this belief, but because of a real event. That event was that someone appeared soon after Nero's death and claimed to be the emperor himself! Tacitus, covering events between March and April of A.D. 69 in his *Histories* 2.8, writes about a certain person that came to his attention:

> About that time Achaia and Asia Minor were terrified by a false report that Nero was at hand. Various rumours were current about his death; and so there were many who pretended and believed that he was still alive. . . . The pretender in this case was a slave from Pontus, or, according to some accounts, a freedman from Italy, a skilful harp-player and singer, accomplishments, which, when added to a resemblance in the face, gave very deceptive plausibility to his pretensions. After attaching to himself some deserters, needy vagrants whom he bribed with great offers, he put out to sea. Driven by the stress of weather to the island of Cynthus, he induced certain soldiers, who were on their way from the East, to join him, and ordered others, who refused, to be executed. He also robbed the traders and armed all the most able-bodied of the slaves. The centurion Sisenna, who was the bearer of the clasped right hands, the usual emblems of friendship, from the armies of Syria to the Prætorians, was assailed by him with various artifices, till he left the island secretly, and, fearing actual violence, made his escape with all haste. Thence the alarm spread far and wide, and many roused themselves at the well-known name [Nero], eager for a change, and detesting the present state of things. The report was daily gaining credit when an accident put an end to it.

Could this be the actual person whom the members of these seven churches feared was the beast who would return? Notice that Tacitus mentions that the people of Achaia and Asia Minor were especially afraid. Furthermore, this person could have easily appeared in Asia Minor while Galba (the sixth emperor = "one is," Rev. 17:10) was still emperor, only coming to the attention of Tacitus sometime after Sisenna had escaped with this knowledge. With Vespasian on his way back from Jerusalem, he would appear to be the next in line for the throne ("the seventh" = "the other has not yet come; when he does come, he must remain for a little while," v. 10). Perhaps Revelation's original audience thought of this false Nero as the "eighth," which "belongs to the seven" (v. 11). He "is not, and yet will come" (v. 8) because he was thought to be Nero alive, but had not yet retaken his throne.

At any rate, Revelation predicts that this "animal of an emperor" will return after the fall of the seventh Roman emperor (17:10–11). Then he and "ten kings who have not yet received a kingdom," but will "receive authority as kings" for one hour, will conspire together (the action is represented as future, see 17:12–13). They will make war on the saints and kill them (17:14), just as the beast did in his first appearance (13:7). In his future return, this beast will also destroy Rome by fire (17:16–18), just as Nero tried to do in the past (see "The Beast That Is to Come" at 19:19; see also "Inhabitants of the Earth" at 6:10; "The Slain Lamb" at 5:6; "1,260 Days, 42 Months, or 3 1/2 Years" at 12:6; "The Mark of the Beast" at 14:9).

C.2.2. The Dragon's Newest Allies (13:2–18). There is a bit of comic relief in this chapter for those who have eyes to see it. History proves the dragon is so weak that he cannot slay a newborn infant (12:1–6). He is so slow he cannot catch a woman who has just delivered a baby (12:13–16). He is such a poor ɜader that he and his army are defeated by a ingle archangel and the angelic troops at his ommand (12:7–12). What, therefore, are the hances that the dragon will be able to pull off victory with only a pair of beasts?

C.2.2.1. A Beast From the Sea (13:2–8). here are two beasts in Revelation, not one. he first beast, the "beast from the sea" (13:1–0), is the one usually identified as "the beast" r "the Antichrist." John describes him as having two separate periods of activity on earth 17:8–11). The first was already past at the ime Revelation was written (see "The Beast rom the Sea," below). The second was still in he future for Revelation's original audience, ust as it is for us today (see "The Beast That s to Come" at 19:19).

Article: Worship of the Beast (13:4)

What does Revelation mean when it refers o the "worship [of] the beast" (13:8, 12, 15; 4:11) or its image (13:15; 14:11)? Paul nstructs every Christian to "submit himself to he governing authorities, for there is no uthority except that which God has established" (Rom. 13:1; cf. Titus 3:1). He also says hat prayers should be made for everyone, ncluding "kings and all those in authority" 1 Tim. 2:1–2).

The question is what form these prayers nay have taken. We know that Jews offered ncense and sacrifices at the Jerusalem temple o Yahweh on behalf of the Roman emperor, at east until the beginning of the First Jewish Revolt. Other religious groups in the same period undoubtedly did much the same before their own gods at their temples.

S. R. F. Price offers a convincing analysis of the Roman imperial cult in Asia Minor. Its origins, at least in Asia Minor, lay in the Hellenistic ruler cults, which began in that area in the fourth century B.C. At the start, various Hellenistic cities established ruler cults in gratitude for certain political favors. These usually simply honored the rulers as heroes, though Alexander the Great received divine honors during his lifetime. Yet over time, Price maintains (21–26), "as the figures to be honoured grew more important, a switch was made from heroic to divine honours. The greatest honours [were reserved] for the greatest people." After several centuries of conflict, the triumph of Christianity ultimately ended the imperial cult.

The precise point at which Christianity conflicted with the imperial cult was its transition from awarding heroic honors to offering divine honors to the emperor. The former was an offering of incense (5:8; 8:3–4) or a sacrifice to a particular god in honor of the emperor. The latter was an offering directly to the emperor or his statue. Christians seemed to feel the former was a legitimate way of fulfilling Paul's instructions, whereas the latter, at least according to Revelation, was idolatry (9:20; 21:8; 22:15).

Price recites an interesting example that points out the difference between heroic and divine honors. Philo of Alexandria traveled with a Jewish embassy to the emperor Gaius (A.D. 37–41). When they arrived, the emperor accused the Jews of failing to recognize his divinity. An opposing delegation joined in the attack, accusing them of not offering sacrifices to Gaius. The Jews responded that they had done so, on three separate occasions. Gaius's response is illuminating: "All right," Gaius replied, "that's as may be, you have sacrificed, but to another, even if it was on my behalf. What good is that if you have not sacrificed to me?" (Philo, *Legat.* 357; see Price, 209).

Obviously, the Jewish delegation was willing to offer sacrifices to Yahweh on behalf of Gaius. Just as obviously, they were not comfortable offering sacrifices directly to the emperor, and both Gaius and the opposing delegation knew it.

In the light of the evidence, it seems reasonable to identify the worship of the beast in Revelation as awarding divine honors to the Roman emperor. This same issue would be a source of conflict between the Christians and Rome through the end of the third century. When Christianity became the official religion of the Roman empire, it quickly ended the imperial cult.

Narrator's Interjection: "He Who Has an Ear . . ." (13:9–10). John interrupts his narration at this point to emphasize its importance. The phrase "he who has an ear . . ." (2:7; 11, 17, 29; 3:6, 13, 22) reminds his audience of the rewards promised in the seven letters to all those who "overcome" (see "Overcomers" at 2:7). Then he paraphrases the prophet Jeremiah (13:10; cf. Jer. 15:2; 43:11). God has given the beast power over the saints for a little while (Rev. 13:7). Some of them will be killed, some enslaved (v. 10). They must be "faithful," in the sense both of trusting God and of being dependable themselves.

C.2.2.2. A Beast From the Land (13:11–17). The dragon's other minion in his latest campaign is also a beast. This second beast is from the land, not the sea (13:11; cf. v. 1). Like the first beast, he also seems to have two periods of activity: one past (13:11–18) and one yet to come (16:13–16; 19:17–21).

Article: The Beast From the Land (13:11)

The second beast of Revelation is labeled the "beast coming out of the earth." He commits the most heinous crimes in the book (14:11–17). The most likely candidates for this "land" beast are the political head of the province of Asia and/or the priest of the official religious cult at Pergamum: the Asiarch.

John's description of this beast is unique, drawing on nothing in Daniel or any of the other prophets. This beast has "two horns like a lamb" (a young ram?) but speaks "like a dragon" (v. 11). His relationship to the dragon is obvious: He opposes the people of God. Similarly, the number and relative size of his horns seems clear: He is less powerful than the Roman emperor. It is the animal that our author has chosen to communicate this last point that is most puzzling: He has horns "like a lamb"—a symbol otherwise reserved in the book for Christ. At the very least, this beast is deceptive, like a wolf in sheep's clothing; he is elsewhere identified as the "false prophet" (16:13; 19:20; 20:10). At most, our author may be implying that this beast had some former connection with Christianity. (This latter possibility should be considered *extremely* speculative, since there is no other evidence that supports it.)

The people who worship the (sea) beast do so for several reasons. Perhaps the false report of Nero's miraculous recovery (Rev. 13:3, 12, 14) convinced some of his divinity. Others may have believed in the false Nero about whom Tacitus wrote (see "The Beast From the Sea" at 13:1). In either case, the Asiarch takes full advantage of the situation. He sets up an image of the emperor, managing to make it look and sound as though it spoke. He does other signs, such as making it appear as if fire has fallen from heaven (v. 13). Ultimately, he convinces some and coerces others to worship the emperor's statue (v. 12). He kills those who refuse (v. 15) and marks those who submit so they can receive special benefits (v. 16; see "The Mark of the Beast" at 14:9).

When the (sea) beast returns, he will be accompanied by a "false prophet." With the dragon and the beast, he will conspire to do battle with the Almighty God in the future (16:13–16). Then they and their army will be defeated by the coming Messiah (19:17–21; see "The Beast That Is to Come" at 19:19).

Narrator's Interjection: "The Number of the Beast . . ." (13:18). On the number of the beast see "The Beast From the Sea" at 13:1, esp. the fourth reason for identifying him as Nero.

2.4. The Third Vision: The Christ on Mount Zion (14:1–16:21)

The third vision of Christ places him on Mount Zion (Ps. 2:6; 110:2; 125:1; Isa. 24:23), the site of the Jerusalem temple. Isaiah prophesied that this is where those who proclaimed the gospel message would see the Lord (Isa. 52:7–8):

> How beautiful on the mountains
> are the feet of those who bring
> good news,
> who proclaim peace,
> who bring good tidings,
> who proclaim salvation,
> who say to Zion,
> "Your God reigns!"
> Listen! Your watchmen lift up their
> voices;
> together they shout for joy.
> When the LORD returns to Zion,
> they will see it with their own eyes.

This is the same setting where, in chapter 15, the righteous multitude will sing the song of Moses (15:3–4). Thus, both Jews (the 144,000) and Gentiles (the multitude) worship God at this place and at this time. The descriptions of their worship are separated only by five short proclamations (14:6–13) and the depiction of the harvest of the earth (14:14–20).

2.4.1. His 144,000 Companions (14:1–5). The 144,000 are with the Lamb here, as they will be throughout eternity (14:4). The song they sing belongs only to them (v. 3; see "144,000 Jews" at 7:4). In worshiping God with a "new ong," they fulfill the prophecy of Isaiah (Isa. 2:10) and the admonitions of the psalmist (Ps. 3:3; 40:3; 96:1; 98:1; 144:9; 149:1).

The text characterizes these 144,000 Jews s truthful and sexually pure (14:4–5). The fact hat they are not liars (v. 5) means these Jews vere not among those who slandered the Christian churches in Asia (2:9; 3:9). The comment about sexual purity is more puzzling, specially since the Greek text uses a word that neans "virgins." This cannot be interpreted as exism, for nowhere else in the New Testament s intercourse, even within marriage, equated with "defiling" oneself with a woman (cf. 4:4). In addition, Revelation does not mention celibacy as a virtue elsewhere. The best nterpretation is probably that this is a reference to abstaining from idolatry (including the vorship of the beast) and the cult prostitution hat often accompanied it. This would be one nore way in which these Jews were different rom those in the synagogues of Smyrna and Philadelphia (2:9; 3:9).

2.4.2. The Three Angelic Proclamations 14:6–11). Five short sayings bridge the vision f the 144,000 and the harvest of the earth, noving the reader from a vision of future glory the 144,000) to the means by which similar lory is attained (being "harvested").

The first three of the five sayings are all ngelic proclamations (14:6–11). They are folowed by an interjection from Revelation's arrator (v. 12) and a divine proclamation v. 13). The three angelic proclamations all oncern judgment and in a way that emphaizes the martyrs' deaths. The first angel nnounces that the "hour of [God's] judgment as come" (v. 7). The second prefigures Babyon's destruction (v. 8). The third angel escribes the impending punishment of all hose who worship the beast (vv. 10–11).

2.4.2.1. Fear God and Worship Him 14:6–7). The first proclamation is a command o fear God and worship him. He is worthy of he worship because he is the Creator (v. 7) of he very earth that these people value so highly v. 6). The division of creation into four arts—"the heavens, the earth, the sea and the prings of water"—foreshadows the judgments of the first four trumpets and the first our bowls. A trumpet and a bowl affect each f these four parts, and in the same order (8:7–2; 16:2–9).

2.4.2.2. Babylon Has Fallen (14:8). The second proclamation predicts the destruction of Rome, the "Babylon" of Revelation (Rev. 18). The past tense, "fallen," is a typical Semitic way of describing a future event as being so certain that it can be considered as already completed. Babylon's sin, making the nations imbibe her "maddening wine" (v. 8), is described this way in order to tie it to the harvest of grapes that follows (14:17–20).

2.4.2.3. Those Who Worship the Beast Will Be Punished (14:9–11). The third proclamation is a warning to those who worship the beast rather than God. Like the second announcement (v. 8), the vocabulary here is linked to the upcoming harvest of grapes (14:17–20). Sinners will drink of "the wine of God's fury" (v. 10; cf. "the great winepress of God's wrath," v. 19). They will drink it from "the cup of his wrath" (v. 10; cf. 16:1, 19).

Article: The Mark of the Beast (14:9)

Aside from the identification of the beast, nothing in Revelation has generated more controversy than the "mark of the beast" (13:17; 14:9, 11; 16:2; 19:20; 20:4). We can say several things for sure. This mark identifies those who worship the beast (14:9, 11; 19:20; 20:4), much in the same way that God's seal identifies his servants (7:2–8; 9:4). The mark, either the name of the beast or his number, 666 (13:17–18), is placed on the worshiper's forehead or hand (14:9). In some circumstances, this mark allowed people to buy or sell (13:17).

Beyond these few facts, Revelation tells us nothing, though some so-called "prophecy teachers" have advanced wild speculations. Some have argued that the beast's marks (paw prints?) are or will be tattoos, brands, bar codes, or subdermal computer chips. Generally these theories are advanced as part of some larger, suspected worldwide conspiracy. The truth is we simply do not know. Such speculation only preys on people's fears and insecurities, distracting them from the real focus of Revelation: the return of the Lamb. Those who worship God have nothing else to fear, for "the one who is in you is greater than the one who is in the world" (1 John 4:4), and "do not be afraid of those who kill [only] the body" (Matt. 10:28; cf. Luke 12:4).

This author is of the opinion that the mark of the beast was real and something used by the imperial cult in Asia Minor during the first century. Though history has left no record of what that mark was, we ought to limit our speculations to those technologies available during Nero's lifetime. Better yet, we should worship God and strive for his "seal" of approval (Rev. 7:2–8; 9:4; cf. John 6:27).

Narrator's Interjection: The Saints Must Endure (14:12). The years that were to follow the writing of Revelation would be a challenge for God's children, the brothers and sisters of Jesus (14:12; cf. 12:17). The church would have to endure suffering and death for its faith (14:13), not once, but periodically and for hundreds of years. John counsels us to have patience and endure these trials (v. 12). The phrase "patient endurance" appears three times in Revelation, each associated with suffering and martyrdom for Christ (1:9; 13:10; 14:12).

Suffering is an essential experience for those who long to be conformed into the image of Christ (Rom. 8:28–39). It produces character (Heb. 12:11). If Jesus himself learned obedience by what he suffered (5:8), we will too. Besides, it is a privilege to suffer for the sake of the gospel and an even greater privilege to be a martyr. Peter and Paul, the "two witnesses" of Revelation 10, were both aware of this kingdom principle (Rom. 8:17, 18; Phil. 1:29; 3:10; 1 Peter 4:12–13; 5:11).

Consider what today's women are willing to endure for the sake of physical beauty. They watch what and how much they eat. They exercise regularly. They rise early to bathe and brush their hair, enduring the pain of teasing out the night's tangles. They shave and pluck, color and shade—all just to adorn their physical bodies. Some are even willing to endure (and pay for!) extensive dental work and plastic surgery to improve their natural beauty. If these women are willing to endure so much for so long to achieve physical beauty, how much more should the church be willing to suffer for spiritual beauty? We must be patient and endure, so that we will be ready for our bridegroom when he comes. We want to be beautiful for him on the day of our wedding.

2.4.3. The Divine Proclamation: Blessed Are the Martyrs (14:13). The divine proclamation of 14:13 makes the message of verse 12 even more explicit. God is not casual about our suffering for him, nor does he treat the death of his saints lightly. The Great Hallel (cf. 19:1–8) says: "Precious in the sight of the LORD is the death of his saints" (Ps. 116:15). Martyrdom, the greatest personal sacrifice, has the additional benefit of allowing us to enter his "rest" (Rev. 14:13; cf. Heb. 4:10–11) all the sooner (see also "Testify, Testimony, Witness" at 6:9; "Overcomers" at 2:7). The labor from which the Israelites rested at the Feast of Tabernacles was that of harvest. The labor from which these martyrs rest (14:13) is also that of harvest—only they are the harvested, not the harvesters. The next passage (14:14–20) will describe that harvest.

2.4.4. The Harvest of the Earth (14:14–20). Harvest was a familiar concept in agricultural Palestine (cf. the "land of milk and honey," Ex. 3:8; Jer. 32:22; Ezek. 20:6, 15; see "The Celestial River [or Crystal Sea]" at 22:1). The lessons of harvest were proverbial: diligent, faithful labor resulted in blessing and bounty; sloth produced little of value (Prov. 6:6–11; 10:5; 12:24; 14:23; 20:4; 24:27). It is understandable, then, that the Israelite prophets had long used harvest images to illustrate God's future judgment in other areas of life (Isa. 17:5–6; 24:13; Jer. 12:13; Hos. 6:11; Joel 3:13). Jesus also used the image (e.g., Matt. 9:37–38; 13:30, 39; 21:33–41; cf. Isa. 5:1–7[!]), as did Paul (Rom. 1:13; 1 Cor. 9:10; Gal. 6:9), James (James 3:18; 5:4), and the author of Hebrews (Heb. 12:11).

The person who was "seated on the cloud" is Jesus Christ (14:14). The phrase "like a son of man" is meant to remind the readers of Daniel 7:13–14. His crown (Gk. *stephanos*) is not the expected diadem (Gk. *diadema*, e.g. Rev. 19:12), but a wreath—the Gospels' word for Jesus' crown of thorns (Matt. 27:29; Mark 15:17; John 19:2, 5; see "Crowns, Wreaths and Diadems" at 4:10). The word underscores the scene as one of martyrdom, as does its larger context.

The author describes two angelic harvests: one of grain (14:15–16) and the other of grapes (vv. 18–19). He emphasizes the latter of these two (vv. 19–20; 15:7; 16–17), which leads one to wonder why he mentions the other harvest at all. It may well indicate that this is the end of the entire agricultural year (the *final* harvest), much as Deuteronomy instructs the Israelites to celebrate the Feast of Tabernacles for "seven days after you have gathered the produce of your threshing floor and your winepress" (Deut. 16:13).

2.4.4.1. Wheat Harvest (14:14–16). The fundamental question in the interpretation of the two harvests is what (or who) is being harvested. Harvest includes both gathering crops and collecting weeds to be burned. In fact, it is only at harvest that some species can be easily distinguished (Matt. 13:30). In other words, are these sinners or saints that are being harvested?

There is no way to tell in this first harvest; the author does not give us enough details to decide. The second harvest, the harvest of grapes, is a different story. There he provides graphic detail that the angel is harvesting Christians. They are the grapes that are harvested; theirs is the blood that stains the horses' bridles (v. 20). The Christians of Asia Minor (and, I dare say, many of the Christians in America) had forgotten one of harvest's most important lessons: Everything that is harvested—grain, vegetables, fruit—dies. So it is with the saints: Harvest means dying. In this case, the great volume of blood indicates the severity of their persecution—the number of them that will die (v. 20; cf. 6:9–11).

The harvest will be bountiful (Matt. 13:3–9, 18–23). It is a painful and bloody business now, but soon they (and we) will have rest (Rev. 14:13). The harvest will be over, the celebration will begin. For now, Christians must look beyond the temporary pain to the eternal joy that follows (Heb. 12:2; cf. Lev. 23:40). Like the Lamb (Rev. 5:5–6, 9, 12; 12:11), they must overcome (2:26; see "Overcomers" at 2:7).

2.4.4.2. Grape Harvest (14:17–20). The latter part of Revelation revolves around the wine of this eschatological grape harvest in the same way as the Feast of Tabernacles revolved around the wine from its grapes.

(1) Notice that the book gives more space to the grape harvest than the previous harvest. (2) The book does not bother to mention the crop in the first harvest, but identifies the second as grapes (v. 18). (3) This harvest and subsequent pressing of its grapes will introduce the seven libations of wine (15:1–16:21); the other harvest has no such continuing presence in the book. (4) Wine, the chief product of grapes, is an important symbol in Revelation. Because of the manner in which it is produced (by killing and crushing the grapes), its red color, and the fact that it is a fluid, it often represents blood. Jesus used it as a symbol of his own blood when he established the Christian Eucharist (Matt. 26:27–29). Wine reminded the seven churches in Asia of Jesus' sacrifice as they prepared to face their own severe (and possibly fatal) persecution. The "great prostitute" is drunk on this wine, the blood of the saints of God (17:2, 6; 18:3, 24).

God has set the timing of this harvest. It has not been rushed because of war or postponed until the battle is over. These grapes are harvested because they are ripe (v. 18). The amount of wine they produce is proof of that: It overflows the winepress, located outside the city, where Jesus also died (v. 20; cf. Heb. 13:12–13), and floods the surrounding region (v. 20).

There is a certain natural human resistance to the notion of personal martyrdom, which is even greater among those who, feeling persecuted, turn to Revelation for comfort. Perhaps this explains why so many groups have unconsciously transformed Revelation's call to come and die into a license to kill. Certainly the book's violence attracts the violent: An amazing number of serial murderers, cults, paramilitary organizations, survivalists, and the like have coopted Revelation's message for their own use. Each of these persons or groups imagine themselves to be the agent of God's wrath on the earth. They will right the wrongs, by force if necessary, finally balancing the scales of justice. They are too proud to bow to the inevitable, too impatient to wait for God's judgment on the world, and too angry to do much besides hate.

Paul, one of the Christians murdered by Nero, wrote extensively about God's wrath in Romans. Yes, there are people who deserve God's wrath (Rom. 2:5–8). We did too, before we repented and asked God for mercy (5:9). Regardless of how much we have been wronged by those who will not repent, God has the greater claim. He commands us not to take revenge but to yield to his judgment (12:19). He is patient, but we can trust him to finish what he started (9:22, 28). In fact, one can already see some of the consequences of his anger (1:18). In the meantime, do not return evil for evil. Obey the law. Submit to the rulers God has set in place (13:1–8). Wait.

Article: The Winepress of God's Wrath (14:19)

The phrase "winepress of God's wrath" (cf. Isa. 63:2–3; Lam. 1:15; Joel 3:9–17) has led some to conclude the blood is that of the persecutors rather than the persecuted. After all, they reason, why would God be angry with his own people?

Their confusion is understandable. The Greek phrase is ambiguous and difficult to translate into English. In essence, it does not say the winepress belongs to God (though it certainly may), nor is it possible that the winepress is somehow owned by God's wrath (only individuals own things, not emotions). The question is whether the winepress is the *reason* God is angry (i.e., the crime) or the *result* of his anger (i.e., the judgment).[7] The context, especially the proclamation "Blessed are the dead who die in the Lord" (v. 13), clearly indicates the winepress is the *reason* God is angry. It represents the slaughter (martyrdom) of his own children.

Martyrdom is part of God's plan; the descriptions of angels doing the harvesting affirms this fact (vv. 14–19). Still, these murderers are without excuse. They have slaughtered his children, not out of obedience but out of hatred toward God. As punishment, he will shortly force them to drink the very blood they have spilled (16:6).

2.4.5. The Third Ritual: The Pouring of Seven Libations (15:1–16:21). The third and final ritual in Revelation is the pouring of seven bowls of blood upon the earth. These seven libations each initiate a different plague on the inhabitants of the earth, especially on those who have chosen to follow the beast. The plagues will bring an end to God's judgment, his eschatological "wrath" (15:1; cf. 6:16; Rom. 1:18; 2:5).

Article: Libations (15:1)

The word "libation" is unfamiliar to many readers of the New Testament, as is the equivalent phrase "drink offering." Both are found in the Mosaic Law. That law prescribed a number of different kinds of sacrifices (the meat of various animals), grain offerings (several different kinds of flour or roasted kernels), and libations (offerings of fluids, such as wine, water, blood, etc.). Christians are probably most acquainted with the Old Testament sacrifice for sin, the "whole burnt offering," because of its relationship to Jesus' sacrifice for sin on the cross (Lev. 4; cf. Rom. 8:3; also Lev. 16; cf. Heb. 9:7–10:13). We also recognize John's portrayal of Jesus as the ideal Passover Lamb (John 19:33, 36; cf. Ex. 12:46; Ps. 34:20), but miss his equally important representation of Jesus as the ultimate libation for the Feast of Tabernacles (John 19:34, 37; cf. 7:38; Ezek. 47; Zech. 12:10; 14:8, 16; Rev. 1:7).

There are many kinds of libations or drink offerings in the Old Testament. The daily offerings at the tabernacle and temple always included a libation. Each morning and evening the priests would prepare God a "meal." It consisted of roasted meat (a lamb), baked flat bread (an unleavened bread made from grain mixed with oil and a pinch of salt), and a beverage (usually wine; see Num. 28:3–7; cf. Lev. 2:13). The beverage of this meal was called a "drink offering" or libation (Ex. 37:16; Num. 28:10; Hos. 9:4). The priests also poured out the blood from sin offerings as a libation on the base of the brazen altar (Lev. 4:25, 30, 34; cf. Rev. 6:9). David sacrificed water to God from the Bethlehem well that his men obtained at the risk of their lives (2 Sam. 23:15–16). Elijah offered twelve large jars of water to God as a sacrifice when he confronted the prophets of Baal at Mount Carmel. His action would have virtually guaranteed his death if God had failed to answer. Why? Israel was in its third year of drought, so that twelve large jars of water would have been extremely precious—the difference between life and death for an entire family (1 Kings 18:32–35; see also "The Water and Wine Libations at Tabernacles" at Rev. 16:1).

Libations were thus a familiar kind of offering to both Jews and Gentiles of the first century. Revelation transforms this familiar act of worship into an act of judgment. The blood of Cain once cried out to God for vengeance (Gen. 4:10). In the future the blood of thousands, even millions, of Christian martyrs will call on God to avenge their deaths (Rev. 15:5). Their blood, poured on the earth, will bear witness against the enemies of God, even as it will serve as a catalyst for the seven plagues that will avenge them.

2.4.5.1. The Worship of the Martyrs (15:1–4). Those who have "overcome" the beast ("been victorious," 15:2 NIV; see "Overcomers" at 2:7; "Testify, Testimony, Witness" at 6:9) worship God by singing and playing harps in chapter 15. The "beast" Nero also enjoyed playing the lyre. Suetonius says he played the

Fall of Ilium in its entirety while Rome burned in A.D. 64 (*The Twelve Caesars* 6.38). Now the martyrs play harps (5:8; 14:2; 15:2) while God judges the beast and his kingdom—a complete reversal of apocalyptic proportions!

Article: The Song of Moses (15:3)

The martyrs will sing "the song of Moses . . . and the song of the Lamb." The words for the song of the Lamb are supplied (vv. 3–4), but the author apparently expects us to remember the song of Moses from the Old Testament. The question is, "Which of Moses' songs does he mean?"

The one most familiar to contemporary Christians today is probably the song of the horse and rider, popularized in a contemporary chorus. It celebrates God's defeat of the Egyptian army during the Exodus (Ex. 15:1–21). It praises God for his salvation (15:2), his prowess as a warrior (v. 3), his uniqueness (v. 11), his strength (v. 13), and his promise to lead Israel to the Promised Land (vv. 13, 17). While these things are important, they are not specifically related to either martyrdom or Revelation's other themes.

There is, however, another song of Moses in the Pentateuch (cf. Deut. 31:22, 30; 32:44). It is a much better choice, though not as familiar to most Christians. It is found at Deuteronomy 32:1–43, immediately after the law that Moses also wrote (31:9). That law and (one would suppose) the song that went with it were to be recited in their entirety every seven years at the Feast of Tabernacles (31:10–13). God gave the song to Moses that it might be a witness to his people when many terrible troubles would come upon them because of their idolatry (Deut. 31:16, 20).

The song contrasts God's faithfulness with his people's tendency for perversity (Deut. 32:1–18). It predicts that he will have to make Israel jealous by choosing a people "who are not a people" or "nation" (i.e., the Gentiles; see v. 21; cf. Ps. 2:8). Ultimately, God will deliver them so that their adversaries will not be able to claim victory or ignore God's hand in the matter (Deut. 32:26–27). This will not happen until his people's "strength is gone and no one is left, slave or free" (v. 36).

Tabernacles imagery appears in the song's description of God's enemies, as it does in Revelation. Their "vine" comes from Sodom and Gomorrah (Deut. 32:32; cf. Rev. 11:8). Their "grapes are filled with poison and their clusters with bitterness" (Deut. 32:32). Their "wine" (cf. Rev. 14:8, 10; 16:19; 17:2; 18:3) is like "the venom of serpents" (Deut. 32:33; cf. Rev. 12:9, 15; 20:2).

The song goes into exquisite detail about God's future wrath. It will kindle a fire that "burns to the realm of death below. It will devour the earth and its harvests and set afire the foundations of the mountains" (Deut. 32:22; cf. Rev. 16:8; 17:16; 18:8; 19:12; 20:9, 14–15). God will send calamities, famines, and plagues on the earth (Deut. 32:23–25; cf. Rev. 15:1, 6, 8, etc.). He will take vengeance on his adversaries with a "flashing sword" (Deut. 32:41; cf. Rev. 1:16; 2:12, 16; 19:15, 21) and "arrows drunk with blood" (Deut. 32:42).

Perhaps the most fascinating thing about this song is that the Samaritans based most of their eschatology on a single passage in it. Deuteronomy 32:34–35 says: "Have I not kept this in reserve and sealed it in my vaults? It is mine to avenge; I will repay. In due time their foot will slip; their day of disaster is near and their doom rushes upon them." The Samaritan version of verse 43 reads: "Have I not kept this in reserve and sealed it in my vaults against the Day of Vengeance and Reward?" Revelation describes this "Day" in great detail (Rev. 6:17; 16:14), as well as God's various punishments and rewards (e.g., 7:15–17; 20:12–15).

Finally, the song of Moses affirms God's ability to heal the wounded and raise the dead (Deut. 32:39; cf. Rev. 20:5, 12–13). It promises that God will avenge "the blood of his servants" (Deut. 32:43; cf. Rev. 19:2), looking forward to a time when those servants will include both Gentiles and Israelites ("Rejoice, O nations [the Gentiles], with his people [the Israelites] . . ." (Deut. 32:43). This perfectly matches Revelation's representation of God's people as including both Jews ("144,000," see Rev. 7:3–8) and Gentiles (the "great multitude," 7:9).

Article: The Song of the Lamb (15:3)

Revelation does give the words to "the song of the Lamb," but leaves us to figure out the reason for the song's title for ourselves. The lyrics make no mention of Jesus or his death. There is also no record of Jesus' singing any specific in the Gospel records (though cf. Mark

14:26). Why then call it "the song of the Lamb" (15:3)?

The song at 15:3–4 seems to be loosely based on Psalm 86. Both affirm that God's deeds are "great and . . . marvelous" (Ps. 86:10; cf. Rev. 15:3) and prophesy that "all the nations . . . will come and worship before you, O Lord" (Ps. 86:9; cf. Rev. 15:4).

Yet Psalm 86 contains other lyrics that can really be sung truthfully by only one of David's descendants, the Messiah. Thus, it can be called the Lamb's song. Perhaps the song in Revelation is meant to evoke memory of Psalm 86, which has the complete text of the song. Psalm 86 refers to Jesus' cry to God in his day of trouble (Ps. 86:5–6). It testifies that God heard him and saved him, delivering him from the grave (86:13, 16; cf. Heb. 5:7). It also promises that his enemies will see him and be put to shame (Ps. 86:17; cf. Zech. 12:10; Rev. 1:7). Finally, the miracle of Jesus' conception in the virgin Mary through the Spirit challenges us to reconsider our interpretation of another of its lines. Only Jesus really fits the psalmist's description of himself as God's "servant" and "the son of [his] maidservant" (Ps. 86:16; cf. Luke 1:48).

2.4.5.2. The Angels Receive the Bowls (15:5–16:1). The seven angels of Revelation 15 each receive a golden bowl, reminiscent of the golden pitcher from which the priest offered a libation of water each morning of the Feast of Tabernacles. However, these bowls are not filled with water but with the blood of Christian martyrs. Their blood, poured out on the earth, will cause the most severe plagues of all.

The text never specifically says the bowls are filled with martyrs' blood, but one can easily deduce it from several different clues. (1) The appearance of these bowls immediately after the grape harvest (14:17–20) implies that their contents are related to it. (2) The text says the bowls are filled with "the wrath of God" (15:7), a clear reference back to the "winepress of God's wrath" (14:19). This is especially revealing because the "grapes" that are pressed therein produce blood, not wine (14:20). (3) Then there is the association of the bowls with the temple, "the tabernacle of the Testimony" (15:5). "Tabernacle of the Testimony" is another way of translating "Tent (or Booth) of Martyrdom" (see "The Tabernacle of the Testimony" at 15:5).

However, the contents of the bowls ar most clearly revealed by the consequences c the libations. The second bowl, emptied out o the sea, causes it to become "blood like that c a dead man" (16:3). Likewise the third bow emptied upon the fresh waters, turns them int blood (v. 4). An angel and the martyred soul under the altar praise God for these plague relating them to the blood of martyrs (16:5–7

The seven libations (chs. 15–16) thus com plete the image of the harvest/slaughter at th end of time (14:17–20). These "huma grapes" are pressed in the great "winepress c the fury of the wrath of God" (19:15)—the "juice" is "blood" (14:20). This blood is sym bolized by "wine" throughout much of th book or, through metonymy, by the cup (c 14:8; 18:3, 6) or "bowls" (15:7; 16:1ff.) use to contain it.

What can we say of the eco-theology c Revelation? Those who persecute God's se vants are responsible for the earth's conditio Though they claim to be the earth's inhabitan (8:13; 11:10[2x]; 13:14; 17:2, 8), in fact the are its destroyers (11:18). The plagues ar God's judgment on those who persecute hi servants and his children (Deut. 32:43). Thes inhabitants refuse to acknowledge God as Cre ator or his claim to own the land and its prc duce (Rev. 14:7; cf. 16:8, 11), but their action betray their knowledge of him. Why els would they persecute his prophets, torment hi servants, and slay his Son but to claim the eart for themselves (Isa. 5:1–7; Matt. 21:33–41)

Article: The Tabernacle of the Testimony (15:5)

"The tabernacle of the Testimony" is one c the alternate names for the Israelite tabernacl (Ex. 38:21; Num. 1:50, 53). Revelation's us of the title is particularly appropriate her because of its association with Christian ma tyrdom. The only person to use this phrase i the New Testament was Stephen, the firs Christian martyr (Acts 7:44). Thus, the phras recalls his death, reminding Revelation's reac ers that martyrdom has been part of Christiar ity from the beginning.

In addition, the title ought to be translate "the tabernacle of martyrdom." The very wor "testimony" means martyrdom, as we hav seen elsewhere in Revelation (see "Testify Testimony, Witness" at 6:9). The name of th building ties the preceding scene (the harvest of grapes, 14:18–20) to the ritual that will follow (the pouring out of the libations of martyrs' blood, 15:6–16:21).

2.4.5.2. The Angels Receive the Bowls (continued) (15:5–16:1). Revelation 16 opens with the command to pour the contents of the bowls on the earth. These libations are similar to the wine libations of the Feast of Tabernacles in many ways. Both Revelation and the Feast of Tabernacles have the same number of libations: seven. They both occur after the grape harvest (Deut. 16:13; Rev. 14) and use the new wine. Both call for judgment on those who do not worship God, making specific reference to the plagues of Egypt (Zech. 14:12–19; Rev. 16:1ff.).

Article: The Water and Wine Libations at Tabernacles (16:1)

The daily libations of water and wine were some of the high points of the Feast of Tabernacles (see "Libations" at 15:1). On each of the seven days of the feast, the priest filled a golden pitcher from the pool of Siloam. Leading a procession back to the temple, others blew the trumpets at the Water Gate. Then the priest proceeded up the ramp to the altar, where two silver-colored bowls had been set. He poured the two libations simultaneously into the bowls, the eastern one for the wine and the western one for the water. Each bowl had a different-sized hole in it so that the wine and the water would empty together. The fluids flowed into the bowls, down to the base of the altar, and were eventually washed into the Kidron Valley (m. *Suk.* 4).

During the libations, the priest prayed for the blessing of rain on Israel (1 Kings 8:35–36; 2 Chron. 6:26–27; t. *Suk.* 3:18E; Ps.-Philo 13.7), for a curse on those nations that were not celebrating the feast (Zech. 14:17–18; cf. t. *Suk.* 3:18G), and for the resurrection of the dead (t. *Suk.* 3:15C). Many scholars believe this was the point at which Jesus interrupted the festival on one occasion, saying, "If anyone is thirsty, let him come to me and drink. Whoever believes in me, as the Scripture has said, streams of living water will flow from within him" (John 7:37–38).

The Jewish Tosephta elaborates on the relationship between the libation, rain, and the resurrection of the dead. It ties the ritual to Ezekiel 47:1–10 (the stream that flows from the new temple), Zechariah 14:8 (the river of living water that wells up from Jerusalem at the coming of the Lord), and Zechariah 13:1 (the fountain that will appear for cleansing the house of David and the people of Jerusalem). The conclusion is "that all the waters created at Creation are destined to go forth from the mouth of this little flask" (t. *Suk.* 3:3C–3:10A).

The discussion continues, linking the water libation of Tabernacles to the rock that followed the Israelites in the desert, providing them with water wherever they went (t. *Suk.* 3:11A-D; cf. Num. 20:1–13; Deut. 2:7). It further links this rock to the song that begins, "Spring up, O well . . ." (Num. 21:17–18). The inexhaustible nature of the water is shown by the next several verses (vv. 19–20), which list the regions through which the Israelites traveled and concludes, "where the top of Pisgah overlooks the wasteland" (v. 20). The rabbis' interpretation is that this rock watered the entire desert (t. *Suk.* 3:12B) and that enough was left over to form mighty streams, as indicated by Psalm 78:20 and 105:41. The tractate proceeds to describe the libations of water and wine (t. *Suk.* 3:14) and says the water flowed into "the pit" and from thence to the abyss (where, it was assumed, the dead waited for their resurrection; t. *Suk.* 3:15A–F).

In Revelation, the bowls are not filled with either wine or water, but with the blood of martyrs. Babylon has become drunk with the "the maddening wine of her adulteries," which she has encouraged "all the nations" to drink (14:8; 18:3). The "golden cup" from which she drinks, characterized as "filled with abominable things and the filth of her adulteries" (17:4), is actually filled with the blood of martyred Christians (17:6; 18:24; cf. Zech. 12:2). Thus, the "maddening wine" is the "blood of those who bore testimony to Jesus," obtained by abominations and perversion (Rev. 17:6).

Since she and the nations have become "drunk with the blood of the saints" (17:6), God's judgment is appropriate: He will *force* them to drink blood. Thus the moon turns to blood (6:12) to foreshadow their punishment. One third of the earth, when touched by fire and hail, mixed with blood, burns at the sound of the first trumpet (8:7); the second trumpet causes one third of the sea to turn to blood (v. 8). It is thus also fitting that the two witnesses have the power to turn water into blood (11:6). The greatest outpouring of wrath is the seven bowls of blood (ch. 16).

Even though the bowls of blood have been poured out on the earth, the judgment on it is still not finished. Another voice from heaven asks God to "mix her a double portion from her own cup" (18:6). It is not until the city has been utterly destroyed and burned with fire that the heavenly host is satisfied (18:1–19).

Then the author delivers this aside: "Rejoice over her, O heaven! Rejoice, saints and apostles and prophets! God has judged her for the way she treated you" (18:20). The heavenly multitude concurs: "Hallelujah! Salvation and glory and power belong to our God, for true and just are his judgments. He has condemned the great prostitute who corrupted the earth by her adulteries. He has avenged on her the blood of his servants" (19:1–2; cf. 6:10).

2.4.5.3. First Four Libations (16:2–9). The first four libations are organized and sequenced exactly like the first four trumpet blasts. The angels pour the libations on the earth, the sea, the fresh water, and the heavens, each in turn. As in the ritual of the trumpets, these four domains represent the entirety of God's creation. Here, however, the focus is on the people who live in and use those four domains.

The plagues fall on the inhabitants of the earth, that is, those who refuse to worship God. This represents the fulfillment of the prayers of countless priests officiating at the libations of Tabernacles and one of the prophecies of Zechariah. Zechariah foresaw that just such a series of plagues would come on those who refused to worship "the King, the LORD Almighty" at the Feast of Tabernacles, singling Egypt out for special mention (Zech. 14:12, 17–19).

Six of the seven plagues in this chapter of Revelation are also tied to the plagues in Egypt. The first libation, poured upon the ground, produces sores on the worshipers of the beast (16:2); this is reminiscent of the plague of dust that caused boils in Egypt (Ex. 9:8–12).

The second and third libations turn the sea and fresh waters to blood (Rev. 16:3–4), just as the waters of the Nile became blood (Ex. 7:14–21).

The fourth libation, poured on the sun, causes it to burn seven times hotter (Rev. 16:8). This is the only plague of the seven that is unrelated to the plagues on Egypt. It seems to be drawn from a Tabernacles passage in the prophecies of Isaiah (Isa. 30:26–29).

This quartet of punishments is different from the first quartets of seals and trumpets in two ways. (1) This series of punishments is particularly appropriate. An angel makes the point, briefly interrupting the quartet between the third and the fourth libations (Rev. 16:5–6). The inhabitants of the earth lusted for the blood of God's people (v. 6; cf. 17:6), so God has given them blood to drink. This is quid pro quo justice at its highest level (6:11; cf. Deut. 32:35, 43; Rom. 12:19; Heb. 10:30). The voice of (the martyrs under) the altar (v. 7) reminds us that God promised to avenge their deaths (6:9–11). He is now in the process of fulfilling that promise.

(2) Another way in which this quartet is different from the other seals and trumpets reveals just how hard the hearts of the inhabitants of the earth have grown. One must remember that God made a promise at the Feast of Tabernacles that marked the dedication of Solomon's temple. He forewarned Israel that he would send plagues from time to time, but promised to stop them if and when people prayed (2 Chron. 7:13–14):

> When I shut up the heavens so that there is no rain, or command locusts to devour the land or send a plague among my people, if my people, who are called by my name, will humble themselves and pray and seek my face and turn from their wicked ways, then will I hear from heaven and will forgive their sin and will heal their land.

These four plagues have been horrible. The pharaoh of the Exodus experienced far less and he relented, however temporarily, but these people do not even flinch. Rather, they refuse to repent and persist in their sin. Where we would expect a cry for mercy, they spew out curses (16:9). Their actions leave God no recourse but to continue the next three plagues

2.4.5.4. Fifth Libation (16:10–11). The fifth libation causes darkness in the beast's kingdom, just as God covered another oppressive kingdom with darkness (Ex. 10:21–29) The people still refuse to repent (Rev. 16:11; cf. Ex. 10:24–29) and continue to curse the living God (Rev. 16:11).

2.4.5.5. Sixth Libation (16:12–14). Twice already we have seen that the sixth ritual in a series of seven represents the current situation of Revelation's original audience. So it is here. The sixth libation prepares the way for "the kings from the East" (v. 12). The drying of the Euphrates does not occur in Exodus, though the drying up of the Red Sea does (Ex. 14:21ff.). However, Exodus does describe a plague of frogs that covered the land (Ex. 8:1–6). Revelation has fewer frogs (only three), but they travel further—over the whole world. These are the three frog-like evil spirits in the mouths of the beast, the false prophet, and the dragon (Rev. 16:13; cf. Ex. 8:2–15). They will convince the armies of the earth to gather to wage war against God at Armageddon (Rev. 16:14).

D. Third Interlude: "See, I Am Coming Like a Thief" (16:15)

The third interlude identifies the position of the author and his original audience most precisely. It splits the sixth libation into two parts (16:12–14 and 16), calling the church to watch for the coming of the Lamb (v. 15). This places the moment of Revelation's composition after the beginning of the sixth in each series. Thus, the historic present was the 6[th seal], 6[th trumpet] and 6[th bowl], or 666 (Rev. 13:18).

At least some of the language here may be drawn from the Exodus of God's people: They too were expected to stay awake through the darkness, keep their clothes with them, and be ready to leave the land of their oppressors (Ex. 12:11). In both instances, the Passover lamb had already been slain (John 1:29; 19:36; cf. Ex. 12:6, 46).

2.4.5.5. Sixth Libation (continued) (16:16). The battle of Armageddon derives its name, no doubt, from its staging area at "the mountain of Megiddo" (Heb. *har m^e giddo*), the important pass some fifty-five miles north of Jerusalem and the site of many ancient battles. It was here that King Josiah died, slain by the Egyptian army under Pharaoh Neco (for more information on the future battle of Armageddon, see Rev. 19:11–21).

2.4.5.6. Seventh Libation (16:17–21). The seventh and final libation causes a great thunderstorm and the greatest earthquake ever upon the earth. This combination of natural disasters includes massive hail, thunder, and lightning, a more intense version of yet one more of the ancient plagues of Egypt (16:17–21; cf. Ex. 9:18–35). The calamity destroys the cities of the Gentiles and splits Rome ("Babylon") into three parts (Rev. 16:19). Even this level of destruction does not convince God's enemies to repent; they continue their stream of curses (16:21).

C.3. The Allegorical Narrative (continued) (17:1–20:15)

C.3.1. The Prostitute Who Rides the (Land) Beast (17:1–6). In many ways, this chapter provides the key to interpreting Revelation's message. The angel not only shows John the prostitute's punishment, but provides the interpretation (the "mystery," vv. 5, 7) of the prostitute, her beastly mount, its seven heads, and its ten horns.

John's extensive description of "the punishment of the great prostitute" (17:1; cf. v. 16; 18:1–24) is meant to encourage his readers, not to entertain them. The number of details is meant to be reassuring, much in the same way that all of Ezekiel's specific measurements of the new temple add to its believability (Ezek. 40:1ff.).

Article: The Great Prostitute (17:1)

In biblical times prostitutes were not only immoral, but idolatrous as well. They often served in the temples of the various gods (Gen. 38:21–22; Ex. 34:15–16; Deut. 23:17–18). This is the reason why Scripture links adultery and idolatry so often (Lev. 17:7; Deut. 31:16; Jer. 2:20). It also helps to explain why the Israelites were so tempted by idol worship.

In addition, in wisdom literature the prostitute represents a life of sinful dissipation and sloth (Prov. 7); the path of righteousness is represented by a young, virginal woman named Wisdom (Prov. 4–8). The contrast in these two lifestyles was particularly appropriate for the young men whose course of study was the proverbs. In Revelation, these same two figures are used for people who have led these two kinds of lifestyles: the idolatrous inhabitants of the earth (see "Inhabitants of the Earth" at 6:10), drunk and immoral, are "the great prostitute," while those who have "overcome the world" by following Jesus Christ (see "Overcomers" at 2:7) are the pure, chaste, virgin bride (see "The Bride of Christ" at 21:9).

By any earthly standard, the prostitute in Revelation is an imposing figure. She is "great" (vv. 1, 5, 18), which is probably better translated "large" or even "voluptuous." This is no street tramp, but a "high-class hooker," a "royal prostitute," as indicated by her royal purple and scarlet attire and her expensive jewelry (v. 4). Her trade has made her so wealthy she can even afford to drink from a gold cup (v. 4). She is at the peak of her profession.

Rome's very existence must have challenged the worldview of these early Christians. It was hard not to envy her wealth and easy lifestyle (Ps. 73:1–12). Perhaps they even thought, like the psalmist, "Surely in vain have I kept my heart pure; in vain have I washed my hands in innocence" (v. 13). No one who judges by the standards of this world could have guessed how transitory this woman's success will be. The psalmist described it well (vv. 18–20):

> Surely you place them on slippery
> ground;
> you cast them down to ruin.
> How suddenly are they destroyed,
> completely swept away by terrors!
> As a dream when one awakes,
> so when you arise, O Lord,
> you will despise them as fantasies.

This prostitute's fall will be equally sudden—it will come "in one day" (Rev. 18:8), "in one hour" (v. 19). The author of Revelation describes her punishment with a certain dark humor. The kings of the earth once gave her costly gifts of clothing and jewels, soon they will take them back. She chose to make her livelihood from being naked, soon she will have no choice but to go without clothes. Royalty once paid huge sums so that they could have a "taste" of the flesh she nourished with such great care; now they will roast it with fire and devour her. She thought she could use a ferocious beast to carry her where she wanted to go, when it was actually only bringing her along for lunch. She will be utterly alone, ruined and desolate (v. 6). Her end would have been very different if she had only tried her best to please the King of heaven (12:17; 19:16) rather than the rulers of the earth (17:2).

Article: Babylon the Great (17:5)

The second figure that represents the "inhabitants of the earth" (see "Inhabitants of the Earth" at 6:10) is the city of Babylon (14:8; 16:19; 17:5; 18:2, 10, 21), also called the "great city" (11:8; 16:19; 17:18; 18:10, 16, 18, 19, 21) and "figuratively called Sodom and Egypt" (11:8). Her opposite is the new Jerusalem (3:12; 21:2). Neither are cities per se—the new Jerusalem represents the people of God (see "The New Jerusalem" at 21:10); Babylon represents the inhabitants of the world, epitomized by the residents of the greatest city of the time: Rome. The first letter of Peter also calls Rome "Babylon" (1 Peter 5:13).

Rome is the only city that meets all the criteria in Revelation for the "great city." It was the capital of the Roman empire, which ruled "over the kings of the earth" (17:18). It sat on "seven hills" (v. 9). The city mentioned in Revelation can hardly be literal Babylon, for that city was not located on "many waters" (v. 1), nor would ships at sea be able to see the smoke of its destruction (18:11–20). Rome was at least near enough to the sea for that to be a possibility. As for the phrase "many waters," it describes both Rome's dominance of the sea in this period and her dependence on imports—unable to feed her own people, she had to import enough grain by sea to satisfy the hunger of its citizens.

Each of the names of various cities assigned to Rome by Revelation evokes a story from the Old Testament, assisting the reader in fitting Rome into the pattern of God's actions throughout history (see "1,260 Days, 42 Months, or 3 1/2 Years" at 12:6). The name "Babylon" links this vision with that of Zechariah 5:5–11. Rome had also threatened to destroy the city of Jerusalem and its temple (John 11:47–51), just as Babylon did in 586 B.C. Rome's (and particularly Nero's) immorality also eminently qualified the city to be characterized as the new "Sodom" (11:8), that Old Testament city that was destroyed by the fire of God for her immorality and wickedness (Gen. 19). Her persecution of the saints made her the new "Egypt" (11:8), out of which "I called my son" (Matt. 2:15; cf. Hos. 11:1; note also Rev. 18:4–5).

The puzzling point in the author's description is the assertion that Rome is "where also their Lord was crucified" (11:8). As a matter of historic fact, Jesus of Nazareth was crucified just outside of Jerusalem, not Rome. Yet Pontius Pilate, the overnor appointed by Rome, ordered the crucifixion. Since his authority came from Rome and his actions fit with the policies established by Rome, was not Rome herself responsible for Jesus' death? This interpretation allows the author to draw parallels between the martyrdom of the two witnesses in Rome in A.D. 65 with the martyrdom of Jesus three decades earlier.

Revelation describes Rome as extremely immoral (18:3, 9) and wealthy (18:11–17), but does not accuse her of murder. She only rejoiced when the two witnesses died (her inhabitants sent gifts to one another) and did not permit their bodies to be decently buried (11:9–10). As for the deaths of other martyrs, she is guilty only by association. The images show her "drinking" the blood of martyrs, not slaying them (cf. 17:4, 6; 18:24).

These sins still deserve God's judgment. Like Babylon before her (Jer. 50; 52), Rome will pay for her crimes. The description of the fall of Rome, this latest "Babylon," is the most detailed in Revelation; chapter 18 speaks of nothing else. The image of her burning is particularly intense and frequent (17:16; 18:8–9, 18; 19:3); it was probably taken from the great burning of Rome in A.D. 64 and expanded. In addition, Rome's inhabitants will be ravaged by plagues, pestilence, mourning, and famine (18:8). The great city, located on seven hills, will be suddenly and violently cast down (18:21).

C.3.2. The Interpretation of the Allegory (17:7–18). Here lies the greatest tip for interpretation in all of Revelation: Look for an explanation in the book before inventing one yourself (v. 7).

C.3.2.1. The Beast (17:7–8). The scarlet beast (17:3), which serves as the prostitute's mount, is the same as the (sea) beast (13:1) and the beast that comes "up out of the Abyss" (17:8; cf. 11:7). This beast, with its "seven heads," "ten horns," and "blasphemous names" (17:3; cf. 13:1, 5), was probably the Roman emperor Nero (see "The Beast From the Sea" at 13:1). He, or more probably someone like him, will lead the nations against the hosts of heaven in the future battle of Armageddon (17:14; see "The Beast That Is to Come" at 19:19). His followers will include all those whose treasure is in this world (Matt. 6:19–21), the "inhabitants of the earth" (17:8, see "Inhabitants of the Earth" at 6:10), those whose names "have not been written in the book of life" (17:8, see "Book of Life" at 3:5).

C.3.2.2. The Seven Hills (17:9–11). The beast's seven heads represent two different facts: one geographic, the other historic. The first identifies the woman as the city of Rome; the seven heads are the famous seven hills on which Rome was built (v. 9; cf. v. 18). The heads also represent seven different kings (i.e., "Roman emperors," 17:9–11; see "The Beast From the Sea" at 13:1). These details are important, for they allow us to understand Revelation in its historical setting, aiding us in interpreting its message with accuracy.

C.3.2.3. The Ten Horns (17:12–14). The interpretation of the (sea) beast's ten horns (17:12; cf. Dan. 7:7, 20, 24) rests largely on the interpretation of the beast himself. They serve under the beast and during his reign (Rev. 17:12). These may well be historic "client kings" who lived during Nero's time (the majority opinion among scholars), but as of the time of Revelation's writing (ca. A.D. 69) they had "not yet received a kingdom" (v. 12). The angel also says that these ten kings will aid the beast in his war against the Messiah (v. 14). If the war the angel had in mind was Armageddon (v. 14; cf. 16:16), then these kings may well serve the beast who is yet to come (17:8, 11; see "The Beast That Is to Come" at 19:19) rather than Nero, "the beast ... [who] once was" (17:8, 11; see "The Beast From the Sea" at 13:1). No doubt the future will tell us for sure.

C.3.2.4. The Great Prostitute (17:15–18). The prostitute (v. 15, see "The Great Prostitute" at 17:1) sits "on many waters" (17:1; cf. v. 15). Here these waters are compared to the diverse peoples over which Rome ruled (v. 15). The angel describes them in such a way as to contrast them with the great multitude of Gentiles (v. 15; cf. 7:9; 19:1, 6). In fact, this is the only time Revelation uses the word "multitude" (Gk. *ochlos*) to describe anything other than the people of God. This multitude will suffer all of the plagues of the next chapter.

C.3.3. The Future Judgment of the Dragon and His Allies (18:1–20:15). The third and final section of Revelation's great allegorical narrative is the future judgment of the enemies of God. These enemies include the city of Rome (the great prostitute), the evil civil ruler and false prophet who are yet to come (the two beasts), Satan (the dragon), and all those "inhabitants of the earth" who have chosen to follow them (the unrighteous dead).

Revelation does not encourage us to rejoice in the punishment of others, but in the establishment of God's justice on the earth. We must remember that we too deserve punishment (Rom. 3:23; cf. 2 Peter 1:9), but have accepted God's gracious offer of forgiveness (Rom. 6:23; 1 John 2:12). Since these people in this section of Revelation have rejected God's offer of mercy, they will experience his wrath (John 3:36; Rom. 1:18).

C.3.3.1. Of the Great Prostitute, Babylon, the City of Rome (18:1–19:10).

C.3.3.1.1. The Proclamation of Her Sins (18:1–3). The first of God's enemies to be punished will be the city of Rome (see "The Great Prostitute" at 17:1 and "Babylon the Great" at 17:5). The angelic proclamation in verses 2–3 reiterates her sins. She has harbored everything evil and unclean. She has committed adultery with all the nations of the earth and their kings. Finally, she has reveled in her ostentatious lifestyle. Though not mentioned until later (18:13, 24; cf. 17:6), she has also been responsible for the deaths of many prophets and saints.

C.3.3.1.2. An Exhortation to Abandon Her to Her Fate (18:4–8). Rome's punishment will be twice the value of her crimes (v. 6). She will pay for her luxurious living and her boasting with grief and torture (v. 7). God will bring plagues on her in a single day: death, mourning, famine, and a consuming fire (vv. 7–8). Nevertheless, there are innocent people in the city of Rome, or at least people who belong to God (v. 4). This message encourages them to flee the city so that they will share neither in her sins nor in her punishment (v. 4).

This is (or should be) an uncomfortable passage for most American Christians. Our nation is the "Rome" of the twentieth century. There is no evil or uncleanness in the world that has not also made its home here, often under the pretext of "free speech" or "separation of church and state." Our standard of living is far, far higher than most of the rest of the world. We rarely think of the wealth that we have, compared to other nations. When we do, we often boast that it is because of our hard work, or worse yet, our greater spirituality. That same arrogant self-righteousness encourages us to be casual about sexual immorality and other sins, even in the church. If God is just, he will have to punish America just as he did Rome.

What should Christians in America do? Certainly we should intercede for our country and its leaders (1 Tim. 2:1–2). Perhaps our country will yet turn back to God and he will spare it (Jonah 3:5–10). We should also strive to keep ourselves and our churches free from sin, if we are to be salt and light (Matt. 5:13–16). We must not share in the sins of our culture, no matter how acceptable they are to the general population.

If all else fails, we must be prepared to leave before God's judgment falls. There is a clear pattern of this in Scripture. God sent two angels to warn Lot and his family to flee Sodom and Gomorrah before its destruction (Gen. 19:12–13). Jesus warned his followers to flee Jerusalem when they saw the "abomination that causes desolation" (Matt. 24:15; Mark 13:14). Here in Revelation, God warns his people to flee from Rome (Rev. 18:4). We must be prepared to do likewise when God speaks, taking nothing with us.

C.3.3.1.3. A Description of the Mourning (18:9–19). One can tell a great deal about a person by observing who mourns at his or her passing and why (e.g., Dorcas, Acts 9:36–41). No one mourns for Rome in Revelation, only for the things they will no longer get from her.

C.3.3.1.3.1. Of Her Lovers (18:9–10). The kings of the earth will miss committing adultery with her and sharing in her wealth (v. 9). Yet their longing for these things will not be strong enough to overcome their fear at her destruction. They "will stand far off" and not lift a finger to help her (v. 10).

C.3.3.1.3.2. Of Her Suppliers (18:11–17a). Others profited from their association with Rome, like those who made fortunes supplying her with slaves and luxury goods (vv. 12–13). They too will mourn, not for the city's destruction but for the loss of a valued customer (v. 11). It shakes them to see such wealth destroyed so quickly (vv. 16–17), for it exposes their own vulnerability to destruction. Obviously, great riches will not be enough to insulate someone from God's consuming fire. Like the kings, these merchants "will stand far off" and not lift a finger to help her (v. 15).

C.3.3.1.3.3. Of Their Shippers (18:17b–19). Those who made their livelihood from shipping to Rome will also mourn, for they will now have to find new jobs. This port of call will have become unprofitable. They too will make no effort to assist Rome or lessen her suffering. Like the others, they "will stand far off" and watch (v. 17b). For all of her apparent popularity, Rome will die alone.

Narrator's Interjection: "Rejoice!" (18:20). There is a saying that "the wheels of justice grind slowly, but they grind fine." God has postponed judging Rome for many years, not willing that any should perish (2 Peter 3:9). It must have been, and continues to be, hard for Christians to wait. Yet ultimately God will balance the scales of justice. He will punish those who have mistreated his servants (Rev. 18:20, 24; cf. Matt. 21:33–41).

C.3.3.1.4. The Proclamation of Her Fate (18:21–24). Jesus once said that it would be better for a person to be drowned in the sea by having a millstone placed around his neck than to offend even one of the "little ones" who believed in him (Matt. 18:6; Mark 9:42; Luke 17:2). Rome did far, far worse—and to many more believers. Thus, her destruction will be swift, violent, and irrecoverable, just like a millstone dropped into the sea (v. 21).

The words of this angel's proclamation stress the similarities between God's judgment of Babylon in the past and his future judgment of Rome. In some cases, the words are taken directly from Jeremiah's prophecies against Babylon. In others, the images are expansions of those same prophecies. The closest parallel to Revelation 18:21–23 is Jeremiah 25:8–12:

> Therefore the LORD Almighty says this: "Because you have not listened to my words, I will summon all the peoples of the north and my servant Nebuchadnezzar king of Babylon," declares the LORD, "and I will bring them against this land and its inhabitants and against all the surrounding nations. I will completely destroy them and make them an object of horror and scorn, and an everlasting ruin. I will banish from them the sounds of joy and gladness, the voices of bride and bridegroom, the sound of millstones and the light of the lamp. This whole country will become a desolate wasteland, and these nations will serve the king of Babylon seventy years.
>
> "But when the seventy years are fulfilled, I will punish the king of Babylon and his nation, the land of the Babylonians, for their guilt," declares the LORD, "and will make it desolate forever."

Revelation has consistently labeled Rome as "Babylon," reminding its readers of the parallels between the two. Both cities were the capitals of the greatest empires of their day. The rulers of each persecuted God's people: Babylon oppressed the old Jerusalem; Rome tormented the Jerusalem of its day. God permitted both to do so, for a season. God then judged Babylon harshly and vowed it would be desolate forever (Jer. 25:12; 50–51). Rome too will not escape judgment forever; God will judge her too.

C.3.3.1.5. A Description of the Celebration: The Greatest Hallel Ever (19:1–9). The destruction of Rome prompts the saints to offer God one of the most enthusiastic worship services in all of Scripture. This worship service is based on a series of psalms that Jews call the "Great Hallel" (Ps. 113–118). The title is derived from the word "Hallelujah," a Hebrew expression that means "Praise the LORD." The phrase appears five times in the psalms of the Great Hallel (113:1, 9; 117:2; 115:18; 116:19), similar to the four times it appears in Revelation (Rev. 19:1, 3, 4, 6). This similarity is even more surprising when one realizes that the expression does not appear elsewhere in the New Testament. Though this is the most detailed allusion to the Great Hallel in Revelation, the book contains six other citations from it elsewhere (Rev. 9:20; cf. Ps. 115:4–7; Rev. 11:18; cf. Ps. 115:13; Rev. 19:7; cf. Ps. 118:24; Rev. 20:11; cf. Ps. 114:3; Rev. 22:14; cf. Ps. 118:19).

Like the waving of palm branches (Rev. 7:9; cf. Ps. 118:27), the daily recitation of the Great Hallel was a distinctive feature of the celebration of the Feast of Tabernacles. "Hallelujah" (Ps. 113:1, 9; 115:18; 116:19; 117:2; see NIV notes) and "his love endures forever" (118:1–4, 29; cf. 117:2) both appear frequently in these psalms. The psalmist exhorts the servants of God to worship him for his love (115:1), his faithfulness (115:1), and his blessings on them (115:12–15). He recalls God's deliverance of his people from Egypt (114:1–7) and provision of water from a rock (v. 8). He has personally been rescued by God (116:1–9; 118:5–16), so he encourages others to have confidence that God will save them also (115:9–10). After all, he writes, Yahweh is powerful, far superior to the idols of the nations (115:4–7). The earth trembles in his presence (114:3–7). He is Lord over all the nations (113:4; 117:1), but is also compassionate enough to lift up the downtrodden (113:7–9). Therefore, all God's servants should give him thanks (118:17–29).

The saints in Revelation could have selected the Great Hallel for these themes alone, but there is one more reason for choosing it: Psalm 118 was an important psalm in Jesus' ministry. Our Lord applied one of its verses, "the stone the builders rejected has become the capstone" (118:22), to himself (Matt. 21:42; Mark 12:10; Luke 20:17). So did his followers (1 Peter 2:7; cf. Acts 4:11). The crowds greeted Jesus with another of its verses, "Blessed is he who comes in the name of the LORD" (Ps. 118:26), at his triumphal entry (Matt. 21:9; Mark 11:9; John 12:13). Jesus said they would not see him again until they repeated it (Matt. 23:39; Luke 13:35).

C.3.3.1.5.1. Praise to God for His Judgment (19:1–5). The saints shout "Hallelujah" to God for two specific things in this chapter: his judgment of the prostitute's sin (vv. 1–5) and his blessing on his chosen bride (vv. 6–9). The prostitute's sins were so great and many that she literally "corrupted the earth" (v. 2). She slaughtered God's servants (v. 2; cf. 11:7–10). Now God has avenged their deaths, just as he promised (19:2; cf. 6:9–11). God chose to avenge them by fire (19:3; cf. 17:16). It was an appropriate punishment because Nero, one of Rome's emperors, slaughtered Christians by falsely accusing them of his own act of arson (see "The Beast From the Sea" at 13:1). God's fiery destruction of Rome in the future will nicely balance the scales of justice (Ps. 79:10).

C.3.3.1.5.2. Praise to God for His Blessing (19:6–9). The second reason the saints shout "Hallelujah" in Revelation 19 is that God has blessed his bride, the church (v. 7). He redeemed her, clothed her in finery and jewelry, and claimed her as his own (see "The Bride of Christ" at 21:9). The bride has waited for her husband to return for a long time. Now, at last, the time for her wedding has arrived (19:7). She is ready. She is attired in white garments (v. 8, see "White Robes" at 7:9), symbolic of the righteous deeds she did in the midst of a corrupt world (19:9, 14; cf. 3:4, 18; 4:4; 7:14). Now she will dine at her own wedding banquet (19:9).

Article: The Two Great Eschatological Feasts (19:7–9, 17–21)

Contrary to popular belief, there will be two great banquets at the end of time (19:7–9, 17–21), not one. Every living creature will be at one of them. Human beings have a choice: They can either be a diner or a dinner, a guest or an entrée. This is another example of Revelation's dark humor.

The living God will be the host at both banquets. He has already drawn up the guest lists and set the menu at each. He has set the dress code: Those who want to attend the wedding banquet must wear formal white robes (19:8; cf. 7:9–14; 22:14; also Matt. 22:11–14). Those attending the other feast may wear whatever they wish, including nothing at all (3:17; 16:15; 17:16). God has also set the date for both banquets; it is a closely held secret. No one else knows, not the angels, not even the Son (Matt. 24:36; Mark 13:32), and certainly not the dragon.

The two banquets will be radically different. The "book of life" contains the complete guest list for the wedding supper (cf. Ex. 32:33; Ps. 69:28; Dan. 12:1; see "Book of Life" at 3:5). The list of attendees will read like a "Who's Who" of the saints. Abraham will be there, with his son Isaac and his grandson Jacob; David will be there, so will Noah and Seth. Moses and Enoch, Peter and Paul, will join Matthew the former tax collector, Naaman the former leper, and Rahab the ex-harlot. Priscilla the deaconess, Deborah the judge, and the prophetesses Huldah and Anna will join Tabitha the seamstress, Hannah mother of Samuel, and Mary mother of Jesus. Whether poor or rich, slave or free, male or female, the guests at this banquet will be all who love God and have been washed by the Lamb.

The cuisine for the wedding banquet will be served by angels. They will also take care of the cleanup afterwards. The meal will be "a feast of rich food for all peoples, a banquet of aged wine—the best of meats and the finest of wines" (Isa. 25:6). Jesus specifically mentioned entrées of roast oxen and fat calves (Matt. 22:4); the rabbis believed the meal would include the meat of Leviathan (Isa. 27:1) and Behemoth (Job 40:15)—a kind of heavenly "surf and turf." Certainly there will be plenty of fresh water (Rev. 22:1) and fresh

INTERPRETATIONS OF REVELATION

	1–3	4–19	20–22
Preterist	Historic churches	Symbolic of contemporary conditions	Symbolic of heaven and victory
Idealist	Historic churches	Symbolic of conflict of good and evil	Victory of good
Historicist	Historic churches	Symbolic of events of history: fall of Rome, Mohammedanism, papacy, Reformation	Final judgment, millennium (?), eternal state
Futurist	Historic churches and/or seven stages of church history	Future tribulation; concentrated judgments on apostate church and on Antichrist; coming of Christ	Millennial kingdom; judgment of wicked dead; eternal state

THEOLOGICAL PERSPECTIVES ON REVELATION

	1–3	4–19	20–22
Postmillennial	Historic churches	Generally historicist	Victory of Christianity over the world
Amillennial	Historic churches	Generally historicist	Coming of Christ; judgment; eternal state
Premillennial	Historic churches representative of historical stages	Generally futurist	Literal millennial reign; judgment of great white throne; New Jerusalem
Apocalyptic	Historic churches	Generally preterist	Symbolic of heaven and victory

fruit (22:2). Finally, like Moses (cf. Deut. 18:15), Jesus will provide heavenly manna for all of his followers (Rev. 2:17; cf. Ps. 78:24; John 6:31ff.).

The guests at the second banquet will be the unclean birds and beasts: vultures, ravens and gulls, weasels, rats and lizards, hyenas, wild dogs, and jackals (Lev. 11:13–30; cf. Ezek. 39:4). Being unclean themselves, they will not be particularly picky about the food. That is good, for these unclean animals will be dining on unclean people—the flesh of kings and generals, small and great (Rev. 19:18; cf. Ezek. 39:18). Some will be pimps and prostitutes, others will be those who consider themselves "good, moral people" who need no forgiveness. Some will even be ministers and church members who have succumbed to the sins of pride and self-righteousness. Only those who have washed their garments in the blood of the Lamb will stand on the day of his wrath (Rev. 6:17; cf. 7:9).

Those who fall on that day will be food for raptors, carnivores, and all sorts of scavengers. There will be no need for cleanup afterward, for the animals will strip the flesh from their bones and the sun will bleach the bones white. The birds and beasts will dine well (19:21; cf. Ezek. 39:17–20). Though grim, this is another example of quid pro quo justice. This is how the world treated God's people (Ps. 79:1–4), now God will avenge them (v. 10). O, what terrible things the world has stored up for itself on the Day of Judgment!

C.3.3.1.6. A Warning to Worship God Alone (19:10). John is so overwhelmed by this vision that he falls down to worship the angel (19:10; cf. 22:9). Though his actions are understandable, the angel rebukes him severely and immediately. Worship should be addressed to God and God alone. It should never be given to human beings or to angels, and certainly not to some ravenous beast or image of one (13:8, 12, 15; 14:11, see "Worship of the Beast" at 13:4).

C.3.3.2. Of the Beasts and Their Armies (Armageddon) (19:11–21). The amount of space a book allots to each issue tells us something about its relative importance. Revelation spends little time on topics like Armageddon, the Millennium, and Gog and Magog, despite their popularity among some contemporary Christian groups. It is not that these things are unimportant; they are just irrelevant to the immediate trials of the church.

Consider the Revelation's treatment of the battle of Armageddon. It takes only eleven verses, a measure of its relatively low importance. Of these eleven verses, five describe the leader of the heavenly hosts: Jesus Christ (vv. 11–13, 15–16). Four describe his punishment of the beasts and their followers (vv. 17–18, 20–21). The book allots only a single verse to describe the heavenly host (v. 14) and another for the beasts and their armies (v. 19). There is no description at all of the battle.

What should we learn from this analysis? (1) Teaching on end times should use similar proportions, if it is really to be biblical. We should watch for the coming of the Lamb, not the beast. Jesus Christ should be at the center of our attention, just as he is in this book. (2) Teaching on the end times should always be laced with warnings of the wages of sin—death (Rev. 19:17–21; 20:11–15; cf. Rom. 3:23). Subjects like Armageddon are rarely worth more than a footnote. After all, the "battle" will be so lopsided that it is apparently not worth describing. In fact, Revelation describes it as more of a slaughter than a battle. Recall how the dragon and his demons lost to Michael and his angels in Revelation 11. Thus, what kind of chance will this beast and his human army have against the Son of God and all his heavenly hosts?

C.3.3.2.1. The White Horse Rider (19:11–16). The one who rides on the white horse is Jesus. It can be no one else. He is "faithful" (v. 11; cf. 1:5; 3:14) and "true" (v. 11; cf. 3:7, 14; 6:10; also John 14:16; 1 John 5:20). He will judge and wage war justly (Rev. 19:11; cf. Ps. 9:8; 72:2; Isa. 11:4; Acts 17:31). His eyes are a "blazing fire" (Rev. 19:12; cf. 1:14; 2:18). He is crowned with many crowns, for his name is "KING OF KINGS AND LORD OF LORDS" (19:16; cf. 1:5; 3:14; 17:14). He will rule the nations with an iron scepter (Rev. 19:15; cf. 2:27; 12:5; Ps. 2:9). His robe is covered with blood (Rev. 19:13), for he treads the winepress of God's wrath (Rev. 19:15; cf. 14:19; Isa. 63:1–6). A sword comes from his mouth (Rev. 19:15, 21; cf. 1:16; 2:16; Isa. 49). He is the Word of God (Rev. 19:13; cf. John 1:1, 14).

Obviously, Jesus' second coming will be very different from his first coming into Jerusalem. Then he came "gentle and riding on a donkey, on a colt, the foal of a donkey" (Matt. 21:4; cf. John 12:15; cf. Zech. 9:9). His mount, a donkey, was a sign of peace, of domestic tranquillity. His choice of mount for the second coming will be a horse, an instrument of war. That is exactly why he is coming a second time: to establish justice by force.

Perhaps the best way to think of our planet is as a tiny, rebellious, backwater province in a great empire. The Emperor has announced the impending wedding of his Son. He wants everyone to join in the celebration, so he has made an extraordinary offer. Any rebel, no matter how serious his or her crimes, can receive clemency. All he or she must do is appear before the throne, ask forgiveness, and swear allegiance to his Son. While the offer is generous, it is also limited. It will expire on some future, but unknown, date. Those who have not sworn allegiance by then will be wiped out, down to every last man, woman, and child. Once the empire is at peace, the wedding of his Son will take place. He and his bride can then relax, knowing that they will rule a kingdom that is finally at peace.

Article: The Armies of Heaven (19:14)

Who are the heavenly soldiers following the rider on the white horse (19:14, 19)? Are they God's angels, the resurrected righteous, or members of both groups? The problem arises because the phrase "holy ones" (Isa. 13:1–6; Zech. 14:5; 1 Thess. 3:13; Jude 1:14) applies equally well to both God's angels and his people. The literal meaning of the word translated "saints" (*hagioi*) in the New Testament is "holy ones." It is only because of our culture that the word is translated "saints" when the context clearly indicates Christians.

Jesus did say that he would return with his holy angels (Matt. 25:31; Mark 8:38; Luke 9:26), so we can be sure they will be there. He did not tell us whether his heavenly army would also include the resurrected righteous. I suspect we will not know for sure until that day.

C.3.3.2.2. The Invitation to the Foul Banquet (19:17–18). This is the second of the two banquets mentioned in Revelation (also at 19:21). It is the one we definitely do not want to attend (see "The Two Great Eschatological Feasts" at Rev. 19:7–9, 17–21).

C.3.3.2.3. The Fate of the Beasts and Their Armies (19:19–21). When the time finally arrives, Jesus and his heavenly host will defeat the beasts and their armies swiftly. The two leaders will be thrown into the lake of fire immediately (19:20; cf. Num. 16:30–33). Their followers will be slaughtered, with their bodies left for the birds and beasts (Rev. 19:21).

Article: The Beast That Is to Come (19:19)

How can the beast from the sea be Nero (see "The Beast From the Sea" at 13:1) and still be alive at the second coming of Jesus Christ? Revelation prophesies that this "animal of an emperor" will return sometime in the future (cf. 17:10–11). Then, he will conspire to give ten kings royal power for a single hour (17:12–13). They will make war on the saints and kill them (17:14), just as Nero once did (13:7). This "new" beast will also destroy Rome by fire (17:16–18), just as Nero tried to do in the past.

The figure of this beast that is to come has probably caused more unprofitable speculation among Christians than any other character in the Bible. Not a year goes by without another book identifying some other contemporary figure as this beast: Adolf Hitler, Mussolini, Henry Kissinger, Mikael Gorbachev, Saddam Hussein—the list is apparently endless. Yet devout Christians continue to purchase such books, making this kind of fruitless speculation highly profitable. O, that we were so eager to learn about the Lamb!

What do we know for sure? To begin with, the Lamb must appear prior to the beast. If it were the other way around (the beast appearing prior to the Lamb), Satan would be a fool to send out a beast. He could postpone his punishment forever by simply doing nothing. He would be in control, not God. This is clearly false. Those who are watching for the beast and not the Lamb are likely to get a nasty surprise.

Yet if no one knows when Jesus will return except the Father (Matt. 24:36; Mark 13:32), Satan must also be clueless. Then God alone controls the timing. Satan will have to react to events as they unfold. He probably has planned things so that, when the trumpet sounds, he can put his "beast" into play.

It seems unlikely that the devil has the power to resurrect Nero from the dead. He probably has selected someone "in the spirit and power of Nero" to step into that leadership role. Since he does not know when Jesus will return, he has probably had a long succession of candidates over the last two thousand years. Someday, when Jesus does appear, the person who is Satan's candidate at that time will actually step into the role. It will be a brief period of glory ("for one hour," Rev. 17:12–13), followed by a long, long period of punishment.

C.3.3.3. Of the Dragon and His Army (20:1–10).

C.3.3.3.1. The Dragon Bound for One Thousand Years (20:1–3). The "Millennium" is the name given to the thousand-year period when Jesus will rule on the earth from the city of Jerusalem (Rev. 20:4; cf. Jer. 3:17; Zech. 14:9). The Millennium follows the resurrection of the righteous (Rev. 20:4–5) and the battle of Armageddon (19:17–21); it precedes the battle of Gog and Magog (20:7–10) and the subsequent destruction and re-creation of the heavens and the earth (21:1–2).

Many of the prophecies in the Old Testament about Israel will be fulfilled during the Millennium. Satan will be bound and rendered incapable of tempting or deceiving humankind (Rev. 20:2–3; see "The Abyss" at 9:1). Thus, the Millennium will be a time of peace (Isa. 11:5–9), even among animals (65:25). People will live longer lives (65:20). The temple will be rebuilt (Ezek. 40–48). Jerusalem itself will be holy (Zech. 14:20–21), the goal of pilgrims from all the nations who will come to worship the Lord (14:16–19).

Though incredibly important to Israel, the promise of the Millennium was not as relevant to the struggles of the seven churches of Asia. Consequently, Revelation devotes little space to it. Within that limited space, the book's focus is on the things that would have been important to them: the promise of the resurrection and the subsequent privileges of the righteous (20:4–6). Those things were (and continue to be) as important to Christians as the restoration of Jerusalem was to the earlier Israelites. Many Old Testament prophecies provide additional details about the Millennium (e.g., Isa. 11–12; 25–27; Jer. 33:15–22; Ezek. 36–37; 40–48; Mic. 4; Zech. 8; 14:9–21).

C.3.3.3.2. The Martyrs Reign With Christ (20:4–6). The martyrs, who once were tormented by the rulers of the earth, will now rule the earth themselves (vv. 4–5). They will administrate God's kingdom under the authority of Jesus Christ (v. 6). With their white robes, shining faces, and indestructible bodies (v. 6; cf. 1 Cor. 15:53–54), they will probably seem alien to their subjects. Nevertheless, those glorified bodies will be marvelous transformations of bodies that were once broken, torn, and abused for the cause of Christ. These saints will surely testify that "by his wounds we are healed" (Isa. 53:5).

Article: The Resurrection of the Righteous (20:4)

The resurrection of the righteous is yet another of Revelation's themes that is related to the Feast of Tabernacles. Each day during the Feast the priest poured water and wine on the bronze altar, while praying for God to send adequate rain the following year and to resurrect the dead. In Revelation, the promise of resurrection serves as an encouragement to the righteous (20:4–6; cf. 2:7, 10–11, 26; 3:5; 11:11; see also Rom. 8:11), while it and the judgment that follows it also serve as a threat to the enemies of God (Rev. 20:11–15). Revelation always pictures the state of the resurrected believers in glowing terms (7:1–17; 14:1–5; 15:2–3; 19:1–9; 20:4–6; 21:1–22:6, 14). On the other hand, the unrighteous dead are raised only to be consigned to eternal punishment (20:11–15; 21:8; 22:15), the "second death" (2:11; 20:6).

Who will take part in the first resurrection (20:5)? Revelation describes those raised here as "those who had been beheaded" (v. 4). Beheading was the punishment for treason by a citizen in the Roman empire. A strictly literal interpretation would limit the first resurrection only to those who were martyred by being beheaded (thus omitting those killed by the sword, wild beasts, crucifixion, etc.). Others argue that the phrase is a figure of speech, a metonymy, in which reference to one part indicates the whole (e.g., "ten head of cattle" usually indicates ten whole cows, not just their heads). If the phrase is a metonymy, it can mean either "all martyrs" or "everyone who gave their lives to God," whether martyred or not. Today's scholars generally understand this phrase in the latter sense, martyrs simply representing the ideal and highest example of the righteous dead. The "rest of the dead" (v. 5) will be judged as the unrighteous.

What of the righteous still alive when the Lord returns? Revelation does not deal with that issue, probably because its chief concern is to prepare Christians for martyrdom. Many believe the righteous who are still alive when Jesus returns will rise into the air to meet him. A description of this event, often called the "Rapture," appears in 1 Thessalonians 4:16–17:

> For the Lord himself will come down from heaven, with a loud command, with the voice of the archangel and with the trumpet call of God, and the dead in Christ will rise first. After that, we who are still alive and are left will be caught up together with them in the clouds to meet the Lord in the air. And so we will be with the Lord forever.

Unfortunately, Revelation does not clearly position this event within its prophecies. Cerınly the righteous will have to be resurrected fore they can reign with Christ for a thound years (Rev. 20:4–6). That is why many nservative Christians (those who generally ke the Bible literally) believe that the Rapre will be "premillennial."

Beyond this general agreement, there is rce debate, especially among those known dispensationalists. These people believe that e "Age of the Church" and the "Millennium" ill be separated by a seven-year period called e "Tribulation" (sometimes referred to as)aniel's missing week"). Their problem is en more difficult because Revelation does ot refer to any kind of seven-year period.

The debate continues nevertheless. Some e an allusion to the Rapture when a voice om heaven tells John to "come up here" ev. 4:1). These people believe the Rapture ill occur before the Tribulation. Others lieve that the Rapture will occur halfway rough the Tribulation. They point to a simir passage, where the same heavenly voice ys "come up here" to the two witnesses 1:12). Exegetically, if this phrase refers to the apture, there ought to be two raptures, not ie. But neither group believes this. They do ree, however, that the Rapture and the second coming of Jesus Christ are two different ents.

Still others believe that the Rapture will cur at the same time as Jesus' second comg. The dead will be resurrected and the livg transformed, and both will rise into the air escort Jesus back to earth. Some of these ople believe in a separate, seven-year Tribution. This author finds this position curious, nce Jesus could not then come "like a thief in e night" (1 Thess. 5:2) or "at an hour when u do not expect him" (Matt. 24:42–44; Luke 2:40–42).

The problem is eliminated, however, if the ibulation is not a separate seven-year period nondispensational view). If the "time of tribution" is the same as God's "purification of the urch" (see "The Great Tribulation" at 7:14), en Revelation fits nicely with the rest of the ew Testament. Jesus' coming can be imminent id unexpected and still bring the Tribulation to end. The Second Coming now includes the apture, coming immediately before the battle f Armageddon and the Millennium. This view, ometimes called "atribulationalism" or "imminent post-tribulationalism," is the one held by this author.

Finally, there are those who take a more humorous and lighthearted approach, calling themselves "pan-tribulationalists." These people, weary of the entire debate, believe that Jesus will return whenever he decides to and everything else will "pan out" all right. They have a point. Being doctrinally "right" is less important than having godly attitudes and priorities. When this kind of endless debate distracts us from the things that God has clearly called us to do, causing serious divisions within the body of Christ, it becomes sin. When the resurrection of the righteous and the rapture of the saints finally occurs, we will all agree that it happened (hindsight is always 20/20). In the meantime, let us live so that we will be ready whenever Jesus returns.

C.3.3.3.3. The Dragon Released for His Destruction (20:7–10). The Millennium will end with a battle, the last one on earth ever (v. 8). The battle is often misnamed "Gog and Magog" (v. 8). Actually, "Gog" was a person, the chief prince of Meshach and Tubal (Ezek. 38:1–3); "Magog" was the name of the nation. "Gog and Magog" came to mean the leaders and nations from the furthest "corners of the earth" (Rev. 20:8). Nevertheless, people persist in misapplying the title.

God will release Satan for a brief period (20:7). Though his cause will be hopeless, he will still try to deceive the nations and lead them in a battle against the Almighty God (v. 8). They will gather at Jerusalem, intending to destroy the seat of God's kingdom. They will fail miserably; God will send fire from heaven down on them (v. 9; Ezek. 38:17–23). He will order Satan thrown into the lake of fire. There the dragon will join the beast and the false prophet in their eternal punishment (Rev. 20:10).

C.3.3.4. Of the Unrighteous Dead (20:11–15). After the final battle, God will judge the dead (v. 12). Angels have kept track of their deeds, writing them down in books in heaven. These will be opened and their contents read (v. 12). God will punish those whose names are missing from "the book of life" (see "Book of Life" at 3:5). They will never enter the new Jerusalem with its "tree of life" and the river of "the water of life" (22:1–2). They will be tormented with fire forever (20:14–15).

John writes specifically so that we will not mistake God's intentions. Although "Sheol" and "Hades" can both mean either the grave or the underworld, the phrase "lake of fire" (20:14–15; cf. 21:8) is unmistakable. John did not want us to think that God will simply leave the unrighteous to live as shades in the underworld or consign them back to the grave. They will be punished, cast into the same fiery torment as the dragon, the beast, and the false prophet (vv. 14–15). The fire will contain their uncleanness, keeping it from ever again corrupting God's creation.

It is hard for many of us to imagine a loving God inflicting such terrible torment. Perhaps it would be easier to accept if we kept in mind that the rewards he has promised are equally unimaginable. Curiously, one never hears anyone complain that heaven will be too nice or the saints will be treated too well. While extreme, the punishment and the blessing balance each other.

Perhaps we simply do not recognize our true potential. It is enormous, for either good or evil. God has incredibly high standards. We will either be gold refined by the fire (1 Peter 1:7; Rev. 3:18) or slag cast into the scrap heap. We will be children of God, coheirs of the universe with Christ (John 1:12; Gal. 3:28–29; 2 Tim. 2:12; Rev. 5:10), or dogs left forever outside the city gates (Rev. 22:15). We will either live in a city with an endless supply of living water (22:1–5) or die a thousand deaths in the smoldering garbage heap outside the city walls (cf. Matt. 5:22, 29–30; 23:33; Mark 9:43–47). God allows us to chose our fate; what can be fairer than that?

2.5. The Fourth Vision: The Bride of Christ, the New Jerusalem (21:1–22:5)

John's fourth vision is a revelation of the bride of Christ, the church, in all her glory. This picture of the church as a perfect bride in the future is comforting, a wonderful balance to the first vision of the seven beleaguered churches of Asia Minor (Rev. 1:12–20; cf. chs. 2–3). It gives hope and the assurance of being pleasing to Christ when he does appear. At the same time, it affirms the necessity of the trials and tribulations that perfect her—those described in the intervening chapters.

2.5.1. Her Setting: New Heavens and a New Earth (21:1). The Jewish Feast of Tabernacles was followed by a one day celebration called *Simchat Torah*. This festival celebrated the giving of the law at Sinai. It was the day on which the Jews began the annual cycle of Torah readings, starting with Genesis 1 and the creation story.

In the same way, the harvest themes of the Feast of Tabernacles (and Rev. 14:14ff.) give way to the story of God's re-creation in the final chapters of this book. In the first creation (Gen. 1), God created the environment first and the human population last; in the re-creation, he starts with the human population and ends by transforming our environment (see "The Bride of Christ" at 21:9 and "New Jerusalem" at 21:10).

God promised long ago, through his prophets, that he would do many new things (Isa. 42:9). He would give his people a new covenant to replace the one they had broken (Jer. 31:31). He would give each person a new name (Isa. 62:2; cf. Rev. 2:17; 3:12), a new heart, and a new spirit (Ezek. 36:26). God also promised to create new heavens and a new earth (Isa. 66:22; cf. 2 Peter 3:13) in which these "new people" could dwell. In that place, he promised, "the mountains will drip new wine and the hills will flow with milk; all the ravines of Judah will run with water. A fountain will flow out of the LORD's house..." (Joel 3:18). In thanksgiving, God's people will sing new songs of praise (Ps. 33:3; cf. Rev. 5:9; 14:3).

In the Jewish thought of the New Testament period, the arrival of the Messiah marked the beginning of the new age. When Jesus came to earth, he presented a new teaching (Mark 1:27), which he likened to new wine being placed into new wineskins (Matt. 9:17). His death brought about the new covenant of which the prophets spoke (Luke 22:20; Heb. 8:13; cf. Jer. 31:31).

Those who have accepted God's generous offer of salvation through Jesus since then have already experienced new birth (1 Peter 1:3). Now we are to live a new life (Rom. 6:4), in the new way of the Spirit (Rom. 7:6), because we are new creations of God (2 Cor. 5:17; cf. Col. 3:10). Our attitudes should reflect this newness (Eph. 4:23), in anticipation of the new order (Heb. 9:10; cf. Rev. 21:4) God will establish.

The final act of God's re-creation is the creation of new heavens and a new earth. Prior to that, the old heavens and earth will be destroyed by fire (2 Peter 3:7–13; cf. Isa. 65:17), after which God will replace them with new ones (Rev. 21:1; cf. Isa. 66:22). "Heavens" is plural because the Israelites thought of it as divided it into sections, though there was no clear agreement on the number of those sections.

The Hebrew word for "heavens," *shamayim,* is a dual, which implies two sections. These sections were (1) the air in which the birds fly (Gen. 1:20) and (2) the still higher realm where God dwells (Ezek. 1:26; 10:1). An expanse (KJV "firmament") separated the sections, providing a place for the sun, moon, and stars (e.g., Gen. 1:6). The apostle Paul apparently included the expanse in his numbering when he spoke of traveling to the "third heaven" (2 Cor. 2:12). However, there were some ancient writers who did believe in more sections. As an example, the intertestamental work Ascension of Isaiah describes heaven as having seven different levels (Asc. Isa. 7:21, 22; 8:7)!

However many "heavens" or "sections of heavens" there actually are, God will recreate them all. We have not yet seen them, nor the new earth that God has promised. Yet we know he is faithful. We can trust him to bring the new physical world into being at just the right time. After all, our Lord has kept all his other promises. In the meantime, our thoughts, emotions, and actions demonstrate whether we belong to the new world that is coming into being or to the old one that is passing away.

2.5.2. Her Presentation (21:2). Weddings revolve around the bride. When she appears, whatever else may be going on stops and every eye shifts to her. After all, this is her special day. This happens in Revelation too. Here God himself presents the bride and declares that she and her husband will "live happily ever after" (cf. vv. 2–4).

At the heart of the bride's joy is her renewed fellowship with God. In the beginning, God walked with Adam and Eve in the cool of the evening (Gen. 3:8), but their sin ended that casual companionship with God. God has missed it. Now once again, God will live (lit., "pitch his tabernacle") among his people (Rev. 21:3; cf. Ex. 29:45; Ezek. 37:27; Hos. 2:14–23; Zech. 8:3).

2.5.3. Her Husband's Proclamations (21:3–8).

2.5.3.1. "We Will Live Happily Ever After" (21:3–4). In a contemporary wedding, we would say that these two verses form the part where the husband and bride pledge to live happily ever after. The divine husband and his perfected bride will live together (v. 3) in perfect joy for eternity (v. 4). There will be no more tears or other expressions of pain (see "Blessings of the World to Come" at 7:15).

2.5.3.2. "I Am Making All Things New" (21:5–6a). The present tense of the verb "to be" used here is important in verse 5. It is not that God will, some day in the future, make everything new. Rather, he has already begun to do this. His reminder that "these words are trustworthy and true" (v. 5; cf. Matt. 5:18; 24:35; Mark 13:31; Luke 16:17; 21:33) is meant to give us hope in what we will be: "He who began a good work in [us] will carry it on to completion until the day of Christ Jesus" (Phil. 1:6; cf. 1 John 3:2–3; see comments on Rev. 1:8).

2.5.3.3. "I Have Rewarded the Faithful" (21:6b–7). We human beings have tremendous potential. If we follow God, our reward is greater than we can possibly imagine. In the same way, those who rebel against God face a punishment too horrible to comprehend. There is no middle ground: We become either God's children, rulers over all creation, or his rejects, fit for nothing except to be cast into the universe's smoldering garbage heap. The choice is ours.

The only requirement to begin a relationship with God is a thirst for spiritual things (Rev. 21:6; cf. Ps. 42:1; Isa. 12:3; 55:1; Matt. 5:6; John 4:14; 7:38). Those who follow God throughout their lives will "overcome the world" (see "Overcomers" at 2:7). His reward for these people is to adopt them as his own children and heirs (Rev. 21:7; cf. John 1:12–13; Rom. 8:16–17; Gal. 3:26–29).

2.5.3.4. "I Have Punished the Rebellious" (21:8). Just as God's children bear witness to their spiritual nature by displaying the fruit of the Spirit (Gal. 5:22–23), so those who rebel against him demonstrate their nature by their fleshly works (5:19–21). The specific sins listed in Revelation relate to the activities of the church's opponents detailed herein (see "Sin Lists in Revelation" at 9:20). Thus, for example, "cowardly" surely means denying Jesus Christ. It does not mean that those who have ever been afraid of anything at all (e.g., the dark, a loud noise, an unfamiliar situation) will be sentenced to eternal punishment.

2.5.4. Her Portrait (21:9–27). In the rest of chapter 21, John sees a detailed vision of the new Jerusalem, the bride of Christ.

Article: The Bride of Christ (21:9)

The bride of Christ (19:7; 21:2, 9; 22:17) is the church (John 3:29; Eph. 5:22–32). The image of a people bonded to God by a covenant of marriage is old. God speaks of Israel as his bride/wife numerous times in the Old Testament. The longest examples are the Song of Songs and Ezekiel 16, but the concept appears elsewhere frequently (Isa. 49:18; 54:6; 61:10; 62:5; Jer. 2:2, 32; Hos. 2:16).

Where is the bride of Christ described in Revelation? Why does the angel promise to show her and then go into great detail about a city? It is because the new Jerusalem is not the place where the bride of Christ will live, but a symbol of the bride herself.

This kind of symbolism is not new in Revelation. We have already met "the great prostitute" (17:1–4), who is also called the city of Babylon (v. 5). She represents the "inhabitants of the earth" (see "Inhabitants of the Earth" at 6:10) in general and the people of Rome specifically (see "The Great Prostitute" at 17:1). The pure, virginal bride of Christ, the new Jerusalem, is her complete opposite. She represents the covenant people of God.

It was the custom in some Near Eastern cultures for women to come to their weddings with their dowry displayed on their person. Wealthy women would weave gold and silver coins, pearls, and precious stones into their bridal garments. An extremely wealthy woman might be so covered with valuable metals and jewels that she looked more like a mobile city than a human being (Ps. 45:9–15).

The bride of Christ will have this kind of wealth at her wedding. The great prostitute was wealthy, but her wealth was earned through the blood of the saints (17:6). Our wealth will also have been purchased with blood. The difference is that the blood will be our own, given freely.

God values those things we have earned for him by our efforts, our sweat, blood, and tears. They are like gold, silver, and precious stones (1 Cor. 3:11–16; cf. Rev. 20:13) or crowns of glory (1 Thess. 2:19; Rev. 4:10). However, the most precious gift we can offer is our own martyrdom (Rev. 14:13). The Great Hallel, sung for millennia at the Feast of Tabernacles, affirms that "precious in the sight of the LORD is the death of his saints" (Ps. 116:15). Let us not appear before our Lord empty-handed on that day!

Notice that the city includes all God's people: (1) the Jews, who kept the Old Testament covenant, members of "the twelve tribes of Israel" (21:12), and (2) members of all the nations who accepted the covenant of Jesus Christ in the New Testament, those whose faith was passed down from "the twelve apostles of the Lamb" (v. 14). Each has its place and each contributes something to the beauty of their shared city.

This portrait of the bride of Christ is a wonderful contrast to Jesus' earlier mixed review of the seven churches of Asia Minor (Rev. 2–3). The portrait affirms both our hope that we will be pure (Eph. 5:22–32; 1 John 3:2–3; cf. Rev. 7:14) and the necessity of tribulation. Tribulation and trials refine and purify our faith (James 1:2; 1 Peter 1:6–7; Rev. 3:18), so that our heavenly bridegroom will be proud of his bride. Those who labor in the church in the meantime must keep these two pictures of her in balance: We are not what we were, nor yet what we will be.

Article: The New Jerusalem (21:10)

(1) Its Architecture. Ancient cities were plain, if not downright dirty. They had walls of rock, placed on top of bedrock or mounds of tamped earth. The gates were made of thick wood, buttressed by iron bars. The roads were dirt, only paved with stone in exceptional cases. The better buildings were of stone, lesser ones of sun-baked brick. Lacking septic systems and regular garbage removal, most cities were riddled with diseases and bad odors.

The new Jerusalem will be totally different. Her description here emphasizes her purity and perfection. The city's boundaries form a perfect cube, just like the Most Holy Place in the Jerusalem temple. Her dimensions are all multiples of twelve, a number associated with completeness as far back as the twelve tribes of Israel. The city will have semiprecious stones instead of dirt for its foundations, jasper instead of rocks for its walls, and buildings of gold, not wood or stone.

The gold, from which the city and its great street are made, is so pure it is "like transparent glass" (v. 21). Highly refined gold will take a finish that is so smooth one can see one's own reflection in it, as in a mirror. This gold is even purer. It is so free of imperfections that it can be beaten until it is virtually transparent.

The twelve foundations [courses?] of the city's walls are made from precious stones. Unfortunately, ancient gemology was too imprecise to identify these exact stones with any degree of certainty. We can be sure that they are all precious or semiprecious and chosen for their beauty. Their variety and number are reminiscent of the stones in the breastplate of Israel's high priest (Ex. 28:20; 39:13) and the glittering coverings worn by the "king of Tyre" (Ezek. 28:11ff.) prior to his deposition. The twelve gates, each one a single giant pearl, complete the picture of a fabulously wealthy, eternally pure, city of light—a perfect bride for a groom that is absolutely divine (Rev. 21:2).

Revelation's description of the new Jerusalem is most similar to that of Isaiah 60. The Old Testament prophet mentioned the city's extensive use of precious metals and materials (60:5–9, 17), eternal light from the Lord (vv. 1–2, 20)—not from the sun, moon, or stars (vv. 19, 20)—gates that will never be shut (v. 11), the righteousness of every inhabitant (v. 21), and foreign kings and nations coming to the city to worship (vv. 11–14).

(2) Its Illumination. The new Jerusalem needs no elaborate system of torches or lamps to drive away the dark. There will never be any night again (Rev. 21:25). It does not even need the light of the sun, moon, or stars any more than God needed them when he created light at creation (Gen. 1:3; cf. John 1:4–8). The new Jerusalem is lit from within by the presence of God and the Lamb (Rev. 21:23; cf. Ex. 13:21; Ps. 43:3; 118:27; Isa. 9:1–2; 60; Zech. 14:6). According to Isaiah, the brilliance of their light will attract both kings and nations (Isa. 60:3).

Some might wonder whether this light is physical or spiritual, but that question has no meaning in this place. It only bears witness to our earthly origin, where the two have been separate ever since the Fall. In the new Jerusalem, the physical and the spiritual will be one domain, not two—forever!

(3) Its Population. Ultimately, a city's purity is dependent on its inhabitants. The new Jerusalem's population will be radically different from the population of old Jerusalem just prior to its destruction in 586 B.C. At that time, God told Jeremiah, "Go up and down the streets of Jerusalem, look around and consider, search through her squares. If you can find but one person who deals honestly and seeks the truth, I will forgive this city" (Jer. 5:1). The clear implication was that Jerusalem was ten times as wicked as Sodom and Gomorrah on the eve of their destruction (Gen. 18:32).

The inhabitants of the new Jerusalem will all be pure (Rev. 21:27; cf. vv. 7–8; see "Sin Lists in Revelation" at 9:20). They will have been cleansed by God, washed in the blood of the Lamb (see "Book of Life" at 3:5). They will bring to fulfillment the prophecies long held dear by Israel (Isa. 4:2–6; 52:1ff.; Mic. 4:1–7; Zech. 13:1; 14:8, 21).

(4) Its Water Supply. Jerusalem's walls and strategic location made it a formidable fortress city in the ancient world. Its one weakness was its water supply, which had to come from outside its walls. David used this water conduit when he originally conquered the city (2 Sam. 5:6–9). Later, King Hezekiah built an elaborate tunnel system to secure the water supply and improve the city's defensibility (2 Kings 20:20). Tourists in Jerusalem can still see the remains of that tunnel today. The new Jerusalem, however, will need no such system, nor will it have any such weakness. It will have an inexhaustible supply of living water from a celestial river (see "The Celestial River [or Crystal Sea]" at 22:1).

(5) Its Ruler. Long ago [Jeru-]salem (Heb., "city of peace") was ruled by a priestly king. His name was Melchizedek (Heb. "king of righteousness"), who was also the high priest of *El Elyon* (Heb. "God Most High"). This seems to have been God's ideal, for King David penned a psalm, looking forward to a time when that would be true again (Ps. 110; cf. Luke 20:41–44).

Jesus Christ is the fulfillment of that prophecy (2 Sam. 7; Ps. 132; Ezek. 34:23; 37:24; Hos. 3:5; Zech. 12:7–8; Heb. 6:20–7:24; Rev. 3:7; 5:5). He is the Lion of Judah (Rev. 5:5), the promised descendant of David (22:16). He holds David's keys (3:7), and his reign, like his priesthood, will be eternal (2 Sam. 7:13; Heb. 7:17–24). He is the Root (2 Kings 19:30; Isa. 11:1, 10; 37:31; 53:2) and Branch (Isa. 4:2; 11:1; Jer. 23:5) of the house of David (see also "The Son of David" at Rev.

5:5). "His name will be on their foreheads" (22:4; see comments on 7:1–3).

2.5.5. Her Home: A New Paradise on Earth (22:1–5). What would a new earth be without a Garden of Eden? According to Revelation, the new Jerusalem (the bride of Christ) will live in Paradise. Here God will replant the "tree of life" (Rev. 22:14, 19), from which those who "overcome" will be able to partake (2:7; 21:6–7; cf. 22:17). The water that flows from God's throne is the source of the "living water," which Zechariah says will "flow out from Jerusalem, half to the eastern sea and half to the western sea" (Zech. 14:8). These waters will appear when "the Mount of Olives will be split in two from east to west, forming a great valley, with half of the mountain moving north and half moving south" (14:4). Together with the Kidron Valley, this new valley will form four river channels that will intersect at Jerusalem.

The last time four rivers intersected on earth was in Eden, where a river flowed out of Eden to water the garden, and there it divided and became four rivers. The name of the first river was Pishon; it flowed around the whole land of Havilah, where there was gold. The gold of that land was good; bedellium and onyx stone were there as well. The name of the second river was Gihon; it flowed around the whole land of Cush. The name of the third river was Tigris, which flowed east of Assyria. The fourth river was the Euphrates (Gen. 2:10–13).

Article: The Celestial River (or Crystal Sea) (22:1)

The celestial river is the fulfillment of the promise of abundant, clean water that flows throughout the Old Testament prophets. Their dream mingles elements of Eden, of God's provision of water in the desert, and of the Promised Land. The land of Palestine was ideal for Israel's farmers and shepherds. It was a land of milk (green grass for sheep and cattle) and honey (flowers for bees; Ex. 3:8; Jer. 32:22; Ezek. 20:6, 15). The only element it lacked was water. Without any large, deep lakes, the farmers of Palestine had to depend on God to grant enough rain each year for their crops (Zech. 10:1). Similarly, the priests and people needed clean water for the regular ceremonial cleansings that allowed them to enter God's presence (Lev. 14).

The prophetic vision was of enough water to ensure the fertility of the crops, the health of the farmers, and the holiness of the penitent. Their prophecies looked forward to the return of paradise, Eden (Gen. 1–2; cf. Isa. 51:3; Ezek. 36:35), with its multiple rivers (Gen. 2:10–14; cf. Ezek. 47; Zech. 14:8). Then humans lived in perfect harmony with the earth (Gen. 1:29–30; 2:9) and its animals (Gen. 1:26; 2:19–20; cf. Isa. 11:6–8; 65:25). They had fellowship with God (Gen. 3:8). God looked down and approved, calling it "good" (Gen. 1:31). Someday, the prophets promised, life would be that way again. Paradise would return and the curse on the earth would be lifted (Rev. 22:3).

The people of Israel had tasted a little of that paradise during their desert experience. The prophets reminded her of God's provision of water in the desert (Num. 20:8–11; 21:16–18; Ps. 105:41; 114:8; 1 Cor. 10:1–4). During these wanderings, God cared for Israel like a husband caring for his bride (Jer. 31:32; Hos. 2:15–20). He sheltered them with his Presence (Ex. 33:14), and they lacked nothing (Deut. 29:5).

This river in Revelation 22 flows from the Lord's house and his throne (Rev. 4:6; 15:2; 22:1; cf. Isa. 35:7–8; Ezek. 47; Joel 3:18; Zech. 13:1; 14:8); it nurtures the great trees that line its banks—a sign of its consistency. Each of these trees is the "tree of life" (see "Tree of Life" at 2:7); they provide food for the hungry and healing for the diseased (Rev. 22:2; cf. Ezek. 47:7, 12), signs of the river's potency. The book of Ezekiel gives more detail. The river becomes deeper and broader as it flows out from God's throne, until it becomes a mighty torrent that no one can master (47:1–5). Wherever the river flows, it brings life. It supports an incredible number of fish (47:9) and fishermen (v. 10; see also "Living Water [or Water of Life]" at 7:17).

3. The Conclusion (22:6–21)

Revelation concludes as it began, with both apocalyptic and epistolary conclusions. The first of these, the apocalyptic, is divided into six sections: the angelic mediator (vv. 6–7), the human intermediary (vv. 8–11), a doxology (vv. 12–13), a fifth blessing (vv. 14–15), the divine source (v. 16), and the open invitation to the wedding of the bridegroom and the bride (v. 17).

3.1. Apocalyptic Conclusion (22:6–17)

3.1.1. The Angelic Mediator (and Fourth lessing) (22:6–7). The angel's preface nphasizes the continuity between the visions f Revelation and God's revelations to the rophets of old. A simple scan of the many ross-references to the prophetic books in this ommentary bears witness to this. Revelation ontains little information that was new to its rst readers; it does confirm the things prophsied by Isaiah, Daniel, Ezekiel, Zechariah, nd others. Revelation's uniqueness lies in its nusual presentation and the fact that all the aterial appears in a single book.

The fourth blessing is given to those who keep [i.e., obey] the words of the prophecy in is book," not to those who only read them 2:7; cf. 1:3). This is in keeping with Revetion's emphasis on the fact that saving faith sults in correct actions. Such a call to obeience is made easier in the light of Jesus' soon turn.

How should we live in the light of Revelaon? What should we do? Not one passage in evelation suggests believers should prepare r tribulation by hoarding C rations, potable ater, firearms, or ammunition, by building emote fortress retreats, or by taking paramilary training. Strangely, those who do such ings often appeal to Revelation for support. ne can only surmise that these groups believe evelation's prophecies of future trials and ibulation, but lack faith that God will preerve them. This is sad, for the book specifially records God's promise to "keep [the hurch] from the hour of trial that is going to ome upon the whole world to test those who ve on the earth" (3:10; cf. 9:4).

Instead, this apocalypse calls for believers live their lives by the "seven Ws:"

- wake up (3:2)
- worry not about future trials (2:10)
- wait patiently for God's deliverance (3:10; 6:11)
- watch for the coming of the Lamb (1:7)
- witness, even if it means martyrdom (6:9; 11:7; 12:11)
- work for the kingdom of God (2:2, 19, 23; 14:13; 19:8)
- worship God and only God (14:7, 11; 15:4; 19:10; 22:8).

3.1.2. The Human Intermediary (22:8–11). Once again, John is an eyewitness to great events (22:8; cf. John 1:14; 19:25–27; 1 John 1:1–3). He is so overwhelmed by his vision that he falls down to worship, forgetting that his companion is only an angel. Fortunately, the angel stops him, reminding him that only God is worthy of worship.

This scene served as one final reminder to its first readers not to worship the Roman emperor (or any human being). Even the lowest angel is higher than the highest mortal, but not even the highest angel deserves worship. Fortunately, this angel was also much wiser than Nero or the many others who have proclaimed themselves to be gods since him. Our God is a "jealous God," who insists that his people worship him exclusively (Ex. 34:14).

The angel goes on to instruct John not to seal his book so that it cannot be read, in direct contrast to Daniel's instructions (Dan. 12:4, 9). The reason for the change in instructions is that "the time is near" (Rev. 22:10; cf. vv. 7, 12). The words of the book will not convince those who are determined to do evil, any more than Jeremiah was able to convince the people of his day. Revelation is meant to encourage those who live holy lives not to grow weary and give up (Rev. 2:3; cf. Gal. 6:9; Heb. 12:3). John must be content with that.

3.1.3. The Doxology (22:12–13). As the book nears its completion, it returns to a more formal, liturgical style. The saying "I am the Alpha and the Omega" at 21:6 and 22:13 balances its appearance at 1:8, forming a pleasing symmetry. Not only is Revelation a book about the importance of correct worship, its very shape leads its readers/hearers to a worship experience (see comments on 1:8).

3.1.4. The Fifth Blessing (22:14–15). The fifth blessing of Revelation is for those who wash their robes. Once again, the blessing is the result of the actions of the believers (22:12, 14), not just their intellectual agreement or righteous feelings. Jesus purchased our salvation on the cross; it is his blood that makes us and our robes whiter than snow (7:14; cf. Ps. 51:7). Nevertheless, we have a part to play in our own salvation. We must accept the gospel message, repent of our sins, and follow Jesus' commands (Acts 2:37–41).

Those who fail to do so remain unclean. They will die in their sins. They will remain eternally outside the new Jerusalem like wild "dogs" (22:15), unclean scavengers that pick through the garbage outside the city gates (the Jews had little use for dogs, which they considered ceremonially unclean; see "Sin Lists in Revelation" at 9:20).

3.1.5. The Divine Source (22:16). The book again affirms that its source is divine (22:16; cf. 1:1). Jesus delivered the information to an angel with instructions to carry it to John. John must now write down and disseminate the material to the church. The fact that we have Revelation in our Bibles today means he successfully completed his task. Now, if we will only take heed to its message!

Jesus recites some of his titles here to remind us of his authority (see "The Son of David" at 5:5, "The New Jerusalem: Its Ruler" at 21:10, and "The Morning Star" at 2:28). These titles should also remind us that God h labored for thousands of years to bring the things to pass. He will not quit at this late dat

3.1.6. The Open Invitation (22:17). In letter that describes a marriage ceremony, w might well expect an invitation to attend t festivities. Revelation contains such an inv tation, but it is not an invitation to simp attend but to participate. This bride is not individual but a community, and the comm nity still has room for anyone who wants belong.

God spoke through Isaiah long ago (Is 55:1–3):

> Come, all you who are thirsty,
> come to the waters;
> and you who have no money,
> come, buy and eat!

THE OLD TESTAMENT IN THE NEW

NT Text	OT Text	Subject
Rev 1:7	Zec 12:10	Looking on one period
Rev 1:13	Da 7:13	Coming Son of Man
Rev 1:13–15	Da 10:5–6	Vision of a man
Rev 1:15	Eze 43:2	Voice of rushing waters
Rev 2:27	Ps 2:9	Ruling the nations
Rev 4:6–8	Eze 1:4–10	Four living creatures
Rev 4:8	Isa 6:3	Holy, holy, holy
Rev 5:6	Zec 4:10	Seven eyes of God
Rev 6:2–8	Zec 6:1–6	Four different-colored horses
Rev 6:8	Eze 14:21	Four dreadful judgments
Rev 7:3	Eze 9:4	A mark on the forehead
Rev 7:16	Isa 49:10	Eternal blessings
Rev 7:17	Isa 25:8	God wipes away tears
Rev 10:4	Da 12:4	Sealed words
Rev 10:9–10	Eze 3:1–3	Eating a scroll
Rev 11:1	Eze 40:3	Measuring the temple
Rev 11:4	Zec 4:1–2	Lampstand and olive trees
Rev 11:15	Da 7:27	An everlasting kingdom
Rev 12:14	Da 7:25; 12:7	Three times and a half
Rev 13:1–2	Da 7:3–7	Beasts from the sea
Rev 13:6	Da 11:36	Blaspheming God
Rev 13:7	Da 7:21	War against the saints
Rev 14:14	Da 7:13	Coming Son of Man
Rev 17:12	Da 7:24	Ten horns as ten kings
Rev 18:13–19	Eze 27:27–32	Destruction of a sinful city
Rev 19:15	Ps 2:9	Ruling the nations
Rev 19:17–21	Eze 39:17–20	Food for the birds
Rev 20:8–9	Eze 38:1–39; 16	Gog and Magog
Rev 20:12	Da 7:10	Court books being opened
Rev 21:4	Isa 25:8	God wipes away tears
Rev 21:7	1Ch 17:13	Father and son
Rev 21:10	Eze 40; 1–2	Vision of new Jerusalem
Rev 21:12–13	Eze 48:30–35	Twelve gates of the city
Rev 22:1–2	Eze 47:1, 12	Flowing waters and fruit trees

Come, buy wine and milk
 without money and without cost. . . .
Give ear and come to me;
 hear me, that your soul may live.
I will make an everlasting covenant
 with you,
 my faithful love promised to David.

God has extended this invitation for salvation to everyone, regardless of age, gender, race, or social class (Acts 2:16–21). The sole requirement is that the recipient be thirsty (Rev. 21:6; 22:17; cf. Isa. 44:3; John 4:13–14; 7:38; see "Living Water [or Water of Life]" at 7:17).

3.2. The Epistolary Conclusion (22:18–21)

The second and final conclusion to Revelation is epistolary. It has three short sections: an exhortation (vv. 18–19), a liturgical benediction (v. 20), and an apostolic final greeting (v. 21).

3.2.1. The Final Exhortation (22:18–19). Though we have herein spoken of the "first readers" for simplicity's sake, in fact Revelation's first audience "heard" the book as the messenger from John read it to each of the seven congregations in turn. Only later was the book copied for various churches and individuals to read.

Many of the other known apocalyptic works evolved over many years, as writer after writer added to them. These verses in Revelation contain a stern warning that this book is complete as it stands. Those who seek to supplement it or edit it face plagues (22:18; cf. 9:18, 20; 15:1; 16:9; 18:4, 8) and the loss of life eternal (22:2, 14, 19; cf. 2:7).

3.2.2. The Liturgical Benediction (22:20). The liturgical benediction is antiphonal. Jesus, the "testifier" (i.e., martyr; see "Testify, Testimony, Witness" at 6:9) stands in the position of the congregational leader and reaffirms that he is coming soon. John, representing the congregation of the saints, responds positively: "Amen. Come Lord Jesus."

3.2.3. The Apostolic Final Greeting (22:21). The pastoral benediction that concludes Revelation seems especially appropriate. We are God's people because we have accepted his mercy and grace. We will need more of it in order to endure patiently until Jesus returns. So be it (Amen).

NOTES

[1]The only other one of which I am aware is V. Burch's *Anthropology in the Apocalypse*, published in 1939. Unfortunately, he did not develop his thesis with enough attention to detail to garner much support.

[2]Thus we concur with C. C. Torrey, 58ff. More recently, others have agreed with Torrey. They include A. A. Bell, "The Date of John's Apocalypse: The Evidence of Some Roman Historians Reconsidered," *NTS* 25 (1979): 93–102; J. A. T. Robinson, *Redating the New Testament* (1976).

[3]"Amphorisk of the Second Temple Period." *Palestinian Exploration Quarterly* 109 (1977): 117–22.

[4]See Mendenhall's *Law and Covenant in Israel and the Ancient Near East* (1955 reprint).

[5]See his *From the Stone Age to Christianity* (1940), 263.

[6]Patrick D. Miller, "Israelite Religion," in *The Hebrew Bible and Its Modern Interpreters* (1985), 221–22.

[7]The grammatical issue, which falls outside a commentary of this type, is whether this should be read as an objective or a subjective genitive. Most scholars agree that the decision has to be made based on the context.

BIBLIOGRAPHY

The reader who wishes to read further on any of the subjects in this introduction should consult the following bibliography. There are literally thousands of books on Revelation; sorting the wheat from the chaff is a daunting task, even for the specialist. This bibliography includes important books and a few critical journal articles, all of which are written in English. They represent a wide range of opinions, but all are scholarly and worthy of consideration.

Unfortunately, such works tend to be written at a relatively high level (scholars writing to other scholars), and none of them spends much time drawing practical applications. Devotional commentaries on Revelation, sadly, are virtually nonexistent. This author prayerfully hopes that this commentary will help to fill that gap.

Apocalyptic Literature

R. P. Carroll, *When Prophecy Failed: Cognitive Dissonance in the Prophetic Traditions of the Old Testament* (1979); J. H. Charlesworth, ed., *Apocalyptic Literature and Testaments*, 2 vols. (1983, 1985); A. Y. Collins, ed., *Early Christian Apocalypticism: Genre and Social Setting*, Semeia 36 (1986); P. D. Hanson, "Apocalyptic Literature," in *The New Testament and Its Modern Interpreters*

(1989), 465–88; idem, *The Dawn of Apocalyptic* (rev. ed., 1979); idem, "Apocalypticism," *IDBSup*, 29–34; E. Hellholm, ed., *Apocalypticism in the Mediterranean World and the Near East* (1979); E. Hennecke and W. Schneemelcher, eds. *New Testament Apocrypha*, 2 vols. (1963, 1965); R. McL. Wilson, "New Testament Apocrypha," in *The New Testament and Its Modern Interpreters* (1989).

Feast of Tabernacles

P. Burrows, "The Feast of Sukkoth in Rabbinic and Related Literature" (Ph.D. diss., 1974); J. Danièlou, *Primitive Christian Symbols* (1964a); J. Gray, *The Biblical Doctrine of the Reign of God* (1979); W. Harrelson, "The Celebration of the Feast of Booths According to Zech. xiv.16–21," in *Religions in Antiquity* (1968), 88–96; R. P. K. Harrison, "Booths, Feast of," *ISBE* (1979) 1:535; W. A. Heidel, *The Day of Yahweh* (1929); T. P. Jenney, "Tabernacles, Feast of," in *Eerdmans Bible Dictionary* (forthcoming); idem, "The Harvest of the Earth: The Feast of Sukkoth in the Book of Revelation" (Ph.D. diss., 1993); I. Mandelbaum, "Yerushalmi Sukkah (Notes and Translation)," in *In the Margins of the Yerushalmi* (1983), 7–15; P. D. Miller, "Israelite Religion," in *The Hebrew Bible and Its Modern Interpreters* (1985), 201–37; J. C. de Moor, *New Year With Canaanites and Israelites*, 2 vols. (1972); S. Mowinckel, *He That Cometh* (1954); J. Neusner, ed., *Sukkah*, vol. 17 of *The Talmud of the Land of Israel: A Preliminary Translation and Explanation* (1988); idem, ed., *The Tosephta Translated From the Hebrew. Second Division: Moed: The Order of Appointed Times* (1981); J. J. M. Roberts, "The Ancient Near Eastern Environment," in *The Hebrew Bible and Its Modern Interpreters* (1985), 75–121; A. J. Wensinck, *Arabic New-Year and the Feast of Tabernacles* (1917); G. Widengren, "Israelite-Jewish Religion," in *Religions of the Past* (1969), 222–317.

Revelation: Introductory Issues and Commentaries

D. E. Aune, *The Cultic Setting of Realized Eschatology in Early Christianity*, NovTSup 28 (1972); idem, *The Book of Revelation*, WBC (1998); J. W. Bowman, *The Drama of the Book of Revelation* (1955); V. Burch, *Anthropology and the Apocalypse* (1939; repr., 1977); R. H. Charles, *A Critical and Exegetical Commentary on the Revelation of St. John*, ICC, 2 vols. (1920); A. Y. Collins, *Crisis and Catharsis: The Power of the Apocalypse* (1984); F. M. Cross, *Canaanite Myth and Hebrew Epic* (1973); J. Danièlou, *The Theology of Jewish Christianity* (1964b); J. A. Draper, "The Heavenly Feast of Tabernacles: Revelation 7.1–17," *JSNT* 19 (1983): 133–47; E. S. Fiorenza, *Book of Revelation: Justice and Judgment* (1985); idem, "Revelation," in *The New Testament and Its Modern Interprete*[illegible] (1989), 407–28; idem, "Revelation, Book of," *IDB Sup*, 744–46; idem, *Revelation: Vision of a Ju*[illegible] *World* (1991); D. Guthrie, *New Testament Intro duction*, 3d ed. (1970); C. J. Hemer, *The Letters* [illegible] *the Seven Churches of Asia in Their Local Settin*[illegible] JSNTSup 11 (1986); H. Koester, "Jesus the Victim," *JBL* 111 (1992): 3–15; G. E. Ladd, *A Commentar*[illegible] *on the Revelation of John* (1972); R. H. Mounce, *The Book of Revelation*, NICNT (1977); S. R. F. Price, *Rituals and Power: The Roman Imperial Cu*[illegible] *in Asia Minor* (1984); J. A. T. Robinson, *Redatin*[illegible] *the New Testament* (1976); M. H. Shepherd Jr., *Th*[illegible] *Paschal Liturgy and the Apocalypse* (1960); L. L. Thompson, *The Book of Revelation: Apocalyps*[illegible] *and Empire* (1989); C. C. Torrey, *The Apocalyps*[illegible] *of John* (1959); H. Ulfgard, *Feast and Future: Revelation 7:9–17 and the Feast of Tabernacles* (1989

INDEX

The following index provides a quick overview of where the various articles that discuss different elements of the book of Revelation can be found.

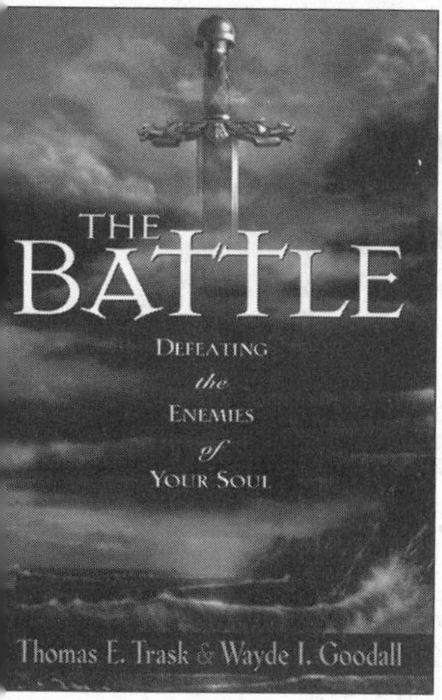

The Battle

Defeating the Enemies of Your Soul

Thomas E. Trask & Wayde I. Goodall

This book explains the true nature of our spiritual enemies and how to combat them.

Softcover 0-310-21456-4
Audio pages 0-310-21619-2

The Blessing

Experiencing the Power of the Holy Spirit Today

Thomas E. Trask & Wayde I. Goodall

This book encourages every believer to have a eeper, fuller, richer experience in the Spirit in their ves.

ftcover 0-310-22128-5

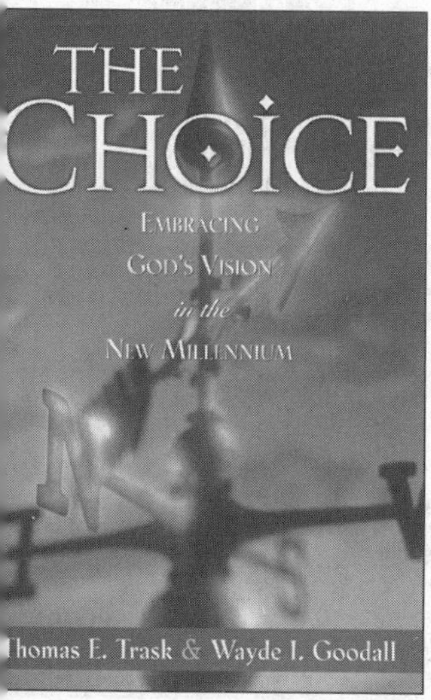

The Choice

Embracing God's Vision in the New Millenium

Thomas E. Trask & Wayde I. Goodall

This book urges believers to realize that everyone is responsible to reach the lost and everyone can have power to do all that God has asked them to do.

Softcover 0-310-22784-4

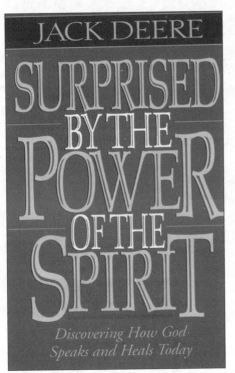

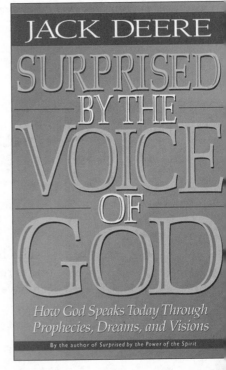

The Full Life Study Bible also includes these unique features specifically designed for Spirit-filled Christians:

THEMEFINDERS: 12 symbols located in the margin indicating verses that address specific themes such as: Baptized in/Filled with the Holy Spirit, Gifts of the Spirit, and Healing.

STUDY NOTES: Bring a practical focus for deeper understanding.

ARTICLES: 77 articles that address a wide variety of topics of doctrinal and practical importance.

CHARTS: 5 charts uniquely designed for this Bible, such as Old Testament Prophecies Fulfilled in Christ.

NIV Version

Hardcover	ISBN 0-310-91693-3 ISBN 0-310-91694-1 Indexed
Black Bonded Leather	ISBN 0-310-91699-2 ISBN 0-310-91700-X Indexed
Black Top Grain Leather	ISBN 0-310-91717-4
Burgundy Bonded Leather	ISBN 0-310-91695-X ISBN 0-310-91696-8 Indexed
Navy Bonded Leather	ISBN 0-310-91697-6 ISBN 0-310- 91698-4 Indexed

KJV Version

Hardcover	ISBN 0-310-91705-0 ISBN 0-310-91706-9 Indexed
Black Bonded Leather	ISBN 0-310-91711-5
Black Top Grain Leather	ISBN 0-310-91715-8
Burgundy Bonded Leather	ISBN 0-310- 91707-7
Navy Bonded Leather	ISBN 0-310-91709-3

ZondervanPublishingHouse
Grand Rapids, Michigan 49530
http://www.zondervan.com

A Division of HarperCollins*Publishers*

We want to hear from you. Please send your comments about this book to us in care of the address below. Thank you.

ZondervanPublishingHouse
Grand Rapids, Michigan 49530
http://www.zondervan.com